Leslie Halliwell was born in London. He buys most of the feature films and series screened by the ITV network and goes twice a year to Hollywood in search of them; he has been an enthusiast for the medium since childhood. He has managed several Rank Organization and specialist cinemas and is a member of two National Film Archive committees.

Mr Halliwell spent several years as a film reviewer for *Picturegoer* and *Sight and Sound* and has contributed to other national publications, including *The Spectator* and *Films and Filming*. He has also had two plays professionally staged. He was the man behind Granada's long-running *Cinema* series, and still advises on its junior version, *Clapperboard*.

HALLIWELL'S FILMGOER'S COMPANION

6TH EDITION

PALADIN

GRANADA PUBLISHING

London Toronto Sydney New York

Published by Granada Publishing Limited
in Paladin Books 1979

ISBN 0 586 08363 4

Sixth edition first published by Hart-Davis, MacGibbon Ltd 1977
Copyright © Leslie Halliwell 1965, 1967, 1970, 1974, 1976. 1977

Granada Publishing Limited
Frogmore, St Albans, Herts AL2 2NF
and
3 Upper James Street, London W1R 4BP
866 United Nations Plaza, New York, NY 10017, USA
117 York Street, Sydney, NSW 2000, Australia
100 Skyway Avenue, Rexdale, Ontario, M9W 3A6 Canada
PO Box 84165, Greenside, 2034 Johannesburg, South Africa
CML Centre, Queen & Wyndham, Auckland 1, New Zealand

Made and printed in Great Britain by
Richard Clay (The Chaucer Press) Ltd
Bungay, Suffolk

Granada ®
Granada Publishing ®

Contents

Foreword to the First Edition (1965) by Alfred Hitchcock

Thirty or forty years ago, when the idea of the cinema as an art form was new, people started to write highbrow treatises about it. Unfortunately, few of the books seemed to have much connection with what one saw at the local picture house. Even earlier began the still-continuing deluge of fan magazines and annuals, full of exotic photographs but short on solid information. We film-makers had our own reference books, but these were often incomprehensible to the layman and gave him more undigested facts than he needed. Nobody wrote for the sensible middlebrow picturegoer who was keenly interested in the craft of the cinema without wanting to make a religion of it.

The volume you hold in your hand aims to the first comprehensive reference book in English for that numerous but neglected audience. I feel sure it will be welcome, for audiences are taking an increasingly serious interest in their films these days – even in the flippant ones.

A concise guide to film matters past and present is obviously a good thing to have on a handy shelf, especially when the best of the old films are constantly cropping up on TV. I hope it will prove possible to bring out revised and corrected editions on a regular basis. Not that many glaring errors will be discovered: the author has done his homework rather better than the villains in my films, who always seem to get found out sooner or later.

Speaking personally, I don't know whether it is more flattering or disturbing to find oneself pinned down like a butterfly in a book which recounts all the macabre details of one's career. But being a stickler for detail, myself, I must, and do, submit; and I wish the enterprise well.

Alfred Hitchcock

Foreword to the Sixth Edition by Herbert Wilcox

When this edition of *The Filmgoer's Companion* is being read, I shall be entering my 60th year in the British film industry. Not all Glorious Years, by any means – that would have been monotonous – but with many successes and happily fewer flops to record. Throughout I have endeavoured, like the author of this book, to preserve an unswerving affection for films, and for everything involved in their production.

Being blessed with a photographic mind and a memory to match, plus a wife who is obsessive about accurate reporting, I have been appalled that so many young and inexperienced writers are indifferent to (or ignorant of) the facts of film history. My blood pressure rises whenever I read an inaccuracy, especially as the facts are invariably more interesting than the printed fiction.

Without hesitation I commend to all serious film lovers this sixth edition of a book written by a scholar of film history. I cannot fault it myself and doubt whether you will. It is to be read for reference or at leisure, to be believed and to be enjoyed.

N.B. Sadly, Herbert Wilcox died while this edition was being prepared.

Introduction to the First Edition

This book is for people who like movies. Especially it's for those who enjoyed the golden ages of the thirties and forties, now revisiting us on television, when the big studios of Hollywood turned out highly efficient and varied entertainment without being too pretentious about it. Nowadays, independent producers aim higher, which sometimes only means that they have further to fall; and most films are half as long again as they should be. But the good ones keep turning up, and Jeanne Moreau and Elvis Presley and Peter O'Toole have fans just as enthusiastic as those of Bette Davis and George Formby and Rudolph Valentino.

Everyone who watches films, whether on TV or the big screens, frequently thinks of something he'd like to check: a star's age, a director's name, what else that funny little fellow with the moustache has been in. To find out the answer to this sort of question it's sometimes been necessary to consult upwards of a dozen fairly inaccessible volumes. This book aims to bring all the available sources together while at the same time excluding inessential or dated information. A fully comprehensive work on these lines would be almost the size of the *Encyclopaedia Britannica*; but this 'potted' one should satisfy most requirements.

The arrangement is completely alphabetical, and you won't find an index at the end because the whole book is one vast index. Most of the entries refer to actors, including not only stars but several hundred familiar names from the supporting cast, people whose valiant service has seldom been recorded. Then there are directors, producers, musicians, writers and photographers – the principal ones at least. The more important the person, the longer the entry, that's a rough general rule: routine contributors get a couple of lines, Edward G. Robinson spreads over half a page. All told, however, you'll find very few of your favourites missing: if they've stuck in your memory, they're probably here. As to the list of credits, the aim has been to give the first important picture, the most recent, and a sampling of the more significant titles in between: the peak period is usually when the dates are most closely crowded. Stage work has not normally been detailed, nor has TV.

There are also notes on well-known film series, on films which have been frequently remade, on films with similar titles; on technical terms, on organizations, on general subjects like censorship and screen ratios. Finally you will find several hundred entries on individual films which seem in one way or another important, influential, or simply excellent of their kind. Unavoidably, many readers will disagree with the selection and/or the assessments: that must remain their privilege until a second edition, if called for, comes out, amended and improved according to comment received. (Bouquets, suggestions, corrections and threatening letters should be addressed c/o the publisher.)

The emphasis is firmly on Britain and Hollywood: the book is aimed at the general filmgoer, not at the egghead student of film culture who shuns commercial entertainments in favour of middle-European or Oriental masterpieces which never get further than the National Film Theatre or a very few art houses. However, references to important foreign films and personalities are fairly numerous, and even admitting its selectiveness in this field the book still ranges more widely than anything else published in English.

No one has been omitted simply because he is dead: the entries have been selected from the whole history of the cinema. But the silent period is covered in less details than the talkies, and probably few readers will quarrel with that.

This is a collection of facts rather than opinions; if a few of the latter *have* crept in, they are usually the ones most generally held.

London, July 1965   L.H.

Introduction to the Fourth Edition

Although the author's attitudes and intentions remain the same, the size and scope of this book have altered somewhat since it made its first appearance seven years ago. The second edition was nearly twice as big as the first, while for the third each entry was carefully revised and another twenty per cent of material added. Now we have an even longer fourth edition. Almost nothing has been deleted, but the material has been sifted once again, rearranged to some extent, considerably re-written and augmented, and reset in a different format.

The reader will probably find that the great improvement lies in the much larger number of complete filmographies, identified by a '□' symbol at the beginning of the list. Although most important persons are now documented in this way, a 'complete' entry should not necessarily be taken as a sign of eminence or as the author's seal of approval: some people simply made very few films, or had compact typical careers which are worth detailing as instances of what goes on in the film business: the gradual climb, the good cameo role, the star period, the two or three 'dogs' in a row, the gradual decline, the cheap horror burlesque. On the other hand, filmographies cannot be completed for several major directors and stars because not all of their earlier films can be traced. 'Incomplete' entries still aim to indicate the beginning and end dates of a career, with the dates coming closest together over the most prolific and significant period.

With some diffidence, I have tried this time to offer a further service to younger readers who may not be too well acquainted with their subjects of study. This is to indicate, by printing in italics, the subject's most significant films. I am obviously unable to indicate my reasons for such choices, most of which will be self-evident though others will undoubtedly cause dissension. The reader may interpret 'significant' as meaning commercially, artistically, critically, or simply as indicating a film in which the subject gave a good typical account of himself. My aim has been to form, out of a mass of titles, the backbone of a career. Obviously I have not seen every film ever made, so I may have ignored many titles which should have been italicized. *Mea culpa*: the aim was to be helpful.

I have continued to seek, digest and present information about producers, small part actors, silent stars, cinematographers, art directors, composers, original authors, screenwriters, and indeed anyone who has had a creative role to play in the history of the cinema. Trade matters are virtually ignored. There are more paragraphs on general topics and definitions, and on themes and subjects which movies have frequently employed, from Ancient Egypt to Devil's Island and from bathtubs to zombies. These light-hearted mini-essays seem to have given nostalgic readers a lot of fun; a list of them is offered at the end of the book. There are notes too on literary figures whose work has been adapted for films; on historical personages who have been frequently depicted; on national cinematic trends; on famous production companies; and on technical processes.

More films have been listed under their own titles, and I now give a list of these too at the end of the book. They are not all masterworks: I have included many because they were very typical of their time, others because they were popular enough to warrant several remakes, still others because although their titles are frequently bandied about as high art I suspect that few readers can say without prompting what they are all about. The information given is just sufficient to 'place' a film and to give the student a key for further research.

Cross-referencing is kept to such a minimum that it hardly exists; if it were done thoroughly, the book would double its size again and take so long to come out that it would be of historical interest only. Once you are used to the method, there must be several ways of finding the information you need.

Since almost every performer and director now works in TV as well as films, I have deleted all such comments as 'much on TV'. Most TV production is too ephemeral to be worth recording even if one had the space to note it, but I have tried to show all TV *film* series (which will be more available than tape to the student of the future) in which the subject played a continuing part. I have also taken note in the main lists of that new form, the TV movie, which fills a 90-minute or two-hour slot and after several years of trial and error is beginning to produce interesting features of a nostalgic kind.

Short films are not normally accounted for; they deserve a book to themselves.

In this age of co-production it is becoming more and more difficult to label a film as belonging to any particular country. Besides, air travel takes talent to any corner of the world at the drop of a hat. I have accordingly delected most of the 'US' and 'GB' tags except in the case of careers which hit their peak long ago. I have tried to improve the dating of films, which (as many correspondents kindly pointed out) did tend to vary in some cases from entry to entry. I can only continue to plead the impossibility of cross-checking every entry in so long a book. I aim to give the year when the film was completed and first publicly shown, and most important films are well 'dated' in my memory; but sometimes, when release is held up for months over a year's end or when an American film is shown first in Britain, it is difficult to be sure what year to quote, and the guiding decision may vary according to the source consulted. In the case of TV series, the date '67' normally means that the show began in September of that year, but the season would run over into the following March or April. In the fifties such series ran for 39 episodes, but cost has dwindled them to a maximum of 24, and many are cut off at 13, with 'mid-season' replacements coming in in January for a short run.

Corrections, in anticipation of a fifth edition in 1976 if the author can stay the course, will continue to be welcome. May I point out, however, that I have several good sources to keep me up to date with new British and American productions and with any deaths after 1972.

During the last few years there has been a deluge of new books on the film. As one might expect, ten per cent are informative and provocative, the rest are quickly remaindered and forgotten. In particular there have been a number of encyclopaedias on the subject, at least two of them very learned, well-researched and sumptuously produced. In such circumstances I wondered whether another edition of the *Companion* would be welcome. I have been assured that it is becau it covers, however briefly, a much greater range of subject matter than any other book, and because it is fun to read. If this is so, I have succeeded better than I expected in providing a one-volume 'Enquire Within Upon the Cinema', and in communicating the enjoyment that movies used to give me. No more, I have to add. I am still slightly too young to be a fuddy-duddy, but I find few films of the seventies to my taste, their explicitness being no substitute for the imagination and skill which were poured into the studio product of Hollywood's Golden Age. My work as a film buyer for television now takes me to Hollywood twice a year. It is the dullest place in the world, the empty studios with their depleted backlots retaining no trace of the glory that shone around Ernst Lubitsch, James Whale and Preston Sturges. Luckily the films live on, in one form or another; before my next edition comes out you may be able to buy a pocket cassette of *The Maltese Falcon* and play it back on your television set. By then, indeed, the movie industry as we know it may have run itself into the ground in its pursuit of new sensations at higher prices. Certainly the innocence and optimism of the old movies will never be regained, but it was a great time while it lasted.

London, September 1974   L.H.

Introduction to the Sixth Edition

Just in case anyone wonders what became of the fifth edition, that title was given by the publishers to a paperback revision of the fourth. We apologize to anyone aiming to collect a complete set!

This edition follows soon after the publication of my *Film Guide*, a kind of companion to the *Companion* which lists and describes eight thousand films, giving full credits. Nevertheless, the individual film entries in the *Companion* have been retained, as they are intended to underline trends or to be especially significant in cinema history.

As this edition also contains over a thousand new entries as well as many hundreds which have been considerably revised or made complete, it is at least ten per cent longer than last time. Its intentions and methods, however, remain the same, so the introduction to the fourth edition has been reprinted.

Once again, I am grateful to the hundreds of people who have offered advice and corrections. Any letter which arrived after the deadline will be held for the next edition. The address likely to find me most quickly is as follows: 90 Granada TV, 36 Golden Square, London W1.

In selecting the illustrations, I have again tried to cover as wide a range as possible, giving special prominence to supporting actors who, for so many years, were the backbone of the business.

London, December 1976   L.H.

Explanatory Notes

Personal Dates   The birth year of an actor or actress is often obscured beyond the powers of a crystal ball. I have chosen the earliest date as most likely to be accurate, though one can still be foxed by people like Groucho Marx, who recently admitted that in their youth the Brothers all took five years off their ages.

Doubtful dates are prefaced by 'c.' (circa).

Film Dates   See Introduction to the Fourth Edition.

Film Titles   I have given the title by which the film is known in its country of origin. Alternative titles are no longer listed, but see the appendix on title changes, which should cover most of them. (It is a formalized version of the essay on title changes in the first edition.) Foreign language titles are usually translated when the original is not widely known: i.e. I use *Les Enfants du Paradis* rather than *Children of Paradise*, but *Wild Strawberries* rather than *Smultronstallet*.

Abbreviations   These have been tidied up to some extent. The main ones now used are:

a	actor	oa	original author
d	director	w	screenwriter
p	producer	ph	cinematographer

The symbol '&' means that the function abbreviated is in addition to that normally expected of the subject. For instance, in an actor's list, '& pd' means that he also produced and directed.

Incomplete lists normally end with 'etc', which means that there may be up to as many films again as have been listed, or 'many others', which means that the list has only scratched the surface.

AA   indicates the winning of Hollywood's Academy Award. BFA indicates the winning of the British Film Academy award, sometimes known as 'Stella' and now presented by the Society of Film and Television Arts.

Most significant films   An innovation: I have tried to show, in italics, the subject's most significant films (first important role, best performance, new kind of characterization, most commercially successful film, etc). See Introduction to the Fourth Edition, and not that this applies to filmographies only; in the mini-essays all titles are italicized.

Nationalities   I still aim to indicate hereditary origins rather than place of birth or adopted citizenship. The fact that Joan Fontaine was born in Tokyo does not make her Japanese, and although she has lived many years in America her whole persona remains essentially British.

Complete filmographies   These are indicated by the symbol '□' See Introduction to the Fourth Edition.

Alphabetical order   This is adhered to on normal dictionary lines, but fictional characters are listed under the complete name (Sherlock Holmes under S). Von Stroheim comes under V, Laura La Plante under L, Cecil B. de Mille under D. Mc and Mac are treated as one, although the spelling is of course kept distinct.

Acknowledgements

My grateful thanks are due once again to the staff of the British Film Institute, to the authors of innumerable works of film research, and to the hundreds of fans who have sent corrections and additions. I regret that this latter category is too numerous to list here, but I hope I have thanked them all by letter. I have certainly tried.

This edition is dedicated to some of the more reprehensible characters we've met in a lifetime's filmgoing:

BALLIN MUNDSON
JOEL CAIRO
CASPER GUTMAN
JONATHAN BREWSTER
WALDO LYDECKER
ALEXANDER HOLLENIUS
JACK FAVELL
TONY CAMONTE
NORMAN BATES
LOUIS MAZZINI
SIR HUMPHREY PENGALLAN
CESARE BANDELLO
THE MARQUIS OF ROHAN
SAUL FEMM
ROCKY SULLIVAN
LOUIS RENAULT
SIDNEY KIDD
PHILIP VANDAMM
GILES CONOVER
CHEVALIER DEL GARDO
HEINRICH STUBEL

and PROFESSOR MORIARTY in all his guises . . .

A

Aan (India 1952). Released internationally in abbreviated form as *Savage Princess*, this historical romantic adventure, directed by Mehboob, was the first Indian film to reach world mass markets.

Abbott, Bud (1895–1974) (William Abbott). American comedian, the brusque and slightly shifty 'straight man' half of Abbott and Costello, cross-talking vaudevillians of long standing who became Universal's top stars of the early forties. Bud, seldom seen without his hat, was the bully who left the dirty work for his partner, never believed his tall but true stories of crooks and monsters, and usually avoided the pie in the face.
□ *One Night in the Tropics* (their only supporting roles) 39. *Buck Privates* 40. In The Navy 41. *Hold That Ghost* 41. Keep 'Em Flying 41. Ride 'Em Cowboy 41. Rio Rita 42. Pardon My Sarong 42. Who Done It? 42. It Aint Hay 43. Hit the Ice 43. Lost In A Harem 44. *In Society* 44. Here Come the Co-Eds 45. *The Naughty Nineties* (featuring their famous *Who's On First* routine) 45. Abbott and Costello in Hollywood 45. The Little Giant (a doomed attempt to work separately within the same film) 46. The Time of Their Lives (with pathos, another failure) 46. Buck Privates Come Home 47. The Wistful Widow of Wagon Gap 47. The Noose Hangs High 48. *Abbott and Costello Meet Frankenstein* 48. Mexican Hayride 48. Africa Screams 49. Abbott and Costello Meet The Killer 49. Abbott and Costello in the Foreign Legion 50. Abbott and Costello Meet the Invisible Man 51. Comin' Round the Mountain 51. Jack and the Beanstalk 52. Abbott and Costello Lost in Alaska 52. Abbott and Costello Meet Captain Kidd 52. Abbott and Costello Go to Mars 53. *Abbott and Costello Meet Dr Jekyll and Mr Hyde* 53. Abbott and Costello Meet the Keystone Kops 55. Abbott and Costello Meet the Mummy 55. Dance with Me Henry 56.

After a TV series (1953) using up all their old routines, the team split and Abbott retired. See *Costello, Lou*.

Abbott, George (1887–). American playwright and producer of lively commercial properties. He sporadically invaded Hollywood to supervise their filming, and stayed briefly to perform other services.
Autobiography 1963: *Mister Abbott.*
AS ORIGINAL AUTHOR: Four Walls 28. Coquette 28. *Broadway* 29 (and 42). *Three Men On A Horse* 36. On Your Toes 39. The Boys from Syracuse 40. *The Pajama Game* (& co-d) 57. *Damn Yankees* (& co-d) 58, etc.
AS PRODUCER: *Boy Meets Girl* 38. Room Service 38. The Primrose Path 40. *The Pajama Game* 57. *Damn Yankees* 58, etc.
AS DIRECTOR: Why Bring That Up? 29. The Sea God 30. Stolen Heaven 31. Secrets of a Secretary 31. My Sin 31. Too Many Girls 40, etc.

Abbott, John (1905–). British-born character actor with staring eyes, specializing in eccentric parts; in Hollywood from 1941.
Mademoiselle Docteur 38. The Return of the Scarlet Pimpernel 38. The Saint in London 40. The Shanghai Gesture 41. Mrs Miniver 42. They Got Me Covered 42. Jane Eyre 43. Secret Motive (lead) 43. The Vampire's Ghost 45. Deception 46. *The Woman in White* 48 (a memorable performance, as the grotesque invalid Frederick Fairlie). The Merry Widow 52. Public Pigeon Number One 57. Gigi 58. Who's Minding the Store 63. Gambit 66, others.

Abbott, Philip (1923–). American 'second lead' of the fifties. *Bachelor Party* 57. *Sweet Bird of Youth* 62. The Spiral Road 62. Those Calloways 65, etc.
TV series: *The F.B.I.* 65–73.

Abel, Alfred (1880–1937). German character actor of weighty personality.
Dr Mabuse 21. The Phantom 22. Metropolis 26. Gold 28. Congress Dances 31, etc.

Abel, Walter (1898–). American character actor with stage experience. Made his Hollywood debut as D'Artagnan, but later settled enjoyably into variations on a single performance of harassment and nervousness, whether as father, friend of the family or professional man.
□ *The Three Musketeers* 36. The Lady Consents

36. Two in the Dark 36. The Witness Chair 36. Fury 36. We Went to College 36. Second Wife 36. Portia on Trial 37. Wise Girl 37. Law of the Underworld 38. Racket Busters 38. Men with Wings 38. King of the Turf 39. Miracle on Main Street 40. Dance Girl Dance 40. *Arise My Love* (which provided him with a key line: 'I'm not happy. I'm not happy at all') 40. Michael Shayne Private Detective 40. Who Killed Aunt Maggie 40. *Hold Back the Dawn* 41. Skylark 41. Glamour Boy 41. *Beyond The Blue Horizon* 42. *Star Spangled Rhythm* 42. *Holiday Inn* 42. Wake Island 42. So Proudly We Hail 43. Fired Wife 43. *Mr Skeffington* 44. An American Romance 44. *The Affairs of Susan* 45. Duffy's Tavern 45. *Kiss and Tell* 45. The Kid From Brooklyn 46. 13 Rue Madeleine 46. *Dream Girl* 48. That Lady in Ermine 48. So This Is Love 53. Night People 54. The Indian Fighter 55. The Steel Jungle 56. *Bernardine* 57. Raintree County 57. Handle With Care 58. *Mirage* 65. Quick Let's Get Married 66. The Man without a Country (TV) 74.

Abie's Irish Rose. Anne Nichols' long-running Broadway comedy of 1927, about a Catholic girl marrying into a Jewish family, has twice been filmed: by Victor Fleming in 1929 and by Edward Sutherland in 1946. The theme has frequently been borrowed, most recently in the 1972 TV series *Bridget Loves Bernie*.

abortion, unmentionable on the screen for many years save in continental dramas like *Carnet De Bal* 37, and officially ostracized exploitation pictures like *Amok* 38, was first permitted as a Hollywood plot point in *Detective Story* 51. Six years later, *Blue Denim* concerned an abortion that was prevented; and the later abortion scenes in *The Best of Everything* 59, *Sweet Bird of Youth* 62, *The Interns* 62, and *Love with the Proper Stranger* 64 scarcely displayed an obsession with the subject. Meanwhile however the British gave it full rein in *Saturday Night and Sunday Morning* 60, *The L-Shaped Room* 62, *Alfie* 66, and *Up the Junction* 68; by which time it had certainly lost its shock value. By 1969 Hollywood felt confident enough to use it as the plot point of a commercial thriller, *Daddy's Gone A-Hunting*, and in 1972 it became the specific subject of *To Find A Man*.

abstract film. One in which the images are not representational but fall into visually interesting or significant patterns: e.g. Disney's *Fantasia*, Norman McLaren's hand-drawn sound films, etc.

Academy Awards. Merit prizes given annually since 1927 by the American Academy of Motion Picture Arts and Sciences. The award is in the form of a statuette known in the trade—for reasons variously explained—as Oscar. In this volume an Academy Award is noted by the letters AA after the film title or recipient.
Book 1968 by Paul Michael, *The Academy Awards*

Academy Frame. The standard film frame in a ratio of 4 to 3, more usually referred to as 1.33 to 1.

Academy Leader. Regulation length of film attached to the front of a reel about to be projected, bearing a 'countdown' and various standard images to facilitate focusing.

Accattone (Italy 1961). Written and directed by Pier Paulo Pasolini. This slum drama about the doom of a young crook seemed to mark the re-birth of Italian neo-realism, but the trend was not picked up.

accelerated motion. An effect obtained by running the camera more slowly than usual: when the resulting film is projected at normal speed, the movements seem faster because they occupy fewer frames than would normally be the case. The opposite of *slow motion* (qv).

Accent on Youth, a successful Broadway play by Samson Raphaelson, about a lazy playwright spurred to new success by his young secretary, has been filmed three times. In 1935 Herbert Marshall and Sylvia Sidney were directed by Wesley Ruggles. In 1950 it turned up as *Mr Music*, with Bing Crosby and Nancy Olson directed by Richard Haydn; and in 1959 it emerged again as *But Not For Me*, with Clark Gable and Carroll Baker, directed by George Seaton.

Ace In The Hole (US 1951). Produced, directed and co-written by Billy Wilder, this bleak melodrama remains one of Hollywood's bitterest attacks on the heartless commercialism of the gutter press. Based on the Floyd Collins case of the twenties, it stars Kirk Douglas as a hard-boiled reporter who deliberately delays rescue operations on a man trapped in a cave so that his story will make national headlines. Photographed by Charles Lang.

acetate. Another word for safety base, which replaced nitrate stock in the fifties and is much slower to burn.

Achard, Marcel (1899–1974). French writer.

The Merry Widow 34. Mayerling 36. Alibi (oa) 37. The Strange Monsieur Victor 38. Untel Père et Fils 40. Monsieur la Souris 43. Jean de la Lune (d only) 49. The Paris Waltz (d only) 50. Madame De 52. La Garçonne 57. A Woman like Satan 59. A Shot in the Dark (oa) 64.

Ackermann, Bettye (1928–). American general purpose actress.
Face of Fire 59. Companions in Nightmare (TV) 68. Rascal 69. M*A*S*H. 70. etc.
TV series: *Ben Casey* 60–64. Bracken's World 69.

Ackland, Joss (1928–). British actor of larger-than-life personality; much on TV.
Crescendo 69. The House that Dripped Blood 70. Villain 71. England Made Me 72. Penny Gold 73. The Black Windmill 74, etc.

Ackland, Rodney (1908–). British writer, sporadically in films from 1930.
Autobiography 1954: *The Celluloid Mistress*.
Bank Holiday 38. 49th Parallel 41. Thursday's Child (& d) 43. Queen of Spades 48, etc.

Acord, Art (1890–1931). American star of silent westerns: A Man Afraid of his Wardrobe 15. In the Days of Buffalo Bill 21. The Oregon Trail 23, etc. Sound ended his career.

Acosta, Rodolfo (1920–1974). Cold-eyed Mexican-American character actor, a frequent western villain or henchman.
The Fugitive 48. One Way Street 50. Yankee Buccaneer 52. Hondo 54. Bandido 56. The Tijuana Story (leading role) 57. Flaming Star 60. How the West Was Won 62. Rio Conchos 64. Return of the Seven 66. Flap 70. The Great White Hope 70, many others.
TV series: High Chaparral 67.

Aquanetta (1920–) (Burnu Davenport). Exotic American leading lady of easterns and horrors in the early forties.
Arabian Nights 42. Jungle Captive 43. Jungle Woman 44. Dead Man's Eyes 44. Tarzan and the Leopard Woman 46, etc.

Acres, Birt (1854–1918). British cinematograph pioneer, later projector manufacturer.

action still. A photograph of a scene as it actually appears in the film as opposed to one specially posed for publicity purposes. Sometimes called a frame blow-up. In TV, an 'action stills' programme has come to mean one consisting of still photographs given a semblance of life by camera movement.

actors have seldom been the subject of biopics. Anna Neagle appeared as Peg Woffington, with Cedric Hardwicke as David Garrick, in *Peg of Old Drury* 35, and Garrick was played by Brian Aherne in *The Great Garrick* 37. Miriam Hopkins was Mrs Leslie Carter in *Lady with Red Hair* 41, Charlie Ruggles (of all people) played Otis Skinner in *Our Hearts Were Young and Gay* 44, Richard Burton was Edwin Booth in *Prince of Players* 54, and Kim Novak was *Jeanne Eagels* 56. The sixties brought Julie Andrews and Daniel Massey as Gertie Lawrence and Noel Coward in *Star!* Of the idols of its own creation, Hollywood has so far given us biographies of Valentino, Jean Harlow, Lon Chaney, Diana and John Barrymore, Lillian Roth, Buster Keaton, Pearl White, W. C. Fields and Gable and Lombard.

actor-directors were rare twenty years ago but are becoming increasingly common. Those who have dared to direct themselves include Woody Allen, Alan Arkin, Sergei Bondartchuk, Marlon Brando, Mel Brooks, Richard Burton, Richard Carlson, John Cassavetes, Charles Chaplin (always), John Clements, Jean Cocteau, William Conrad, Noel Coward, Jules Dassin, John Derek, Clint Eastwood, Pierre Etaix, Jose Ferrer, Mel Ferrer, Albert Finney, Peter Fonda, Al Freeman Jnr, Hugo Haas, Laurence Harvey, David Hemmings, Paul Henreid, Charlton Heston, Dennis Hopper, Leslie Howard, Robert Hossein, Robert Hutton, Buster Keaton, Gene Kelly, Burt Lancaster, Stan Laurel, Jerry Lewis, Peter Lorre, Ida Lupino, Burgess Meredith, Ray Milland, George Montgomery, Robert Montgomery, Anthony Newley, Paul Newman, Edmond O'Brien, Dennis O'Keefe, Laurence Olivier, Nigel Patrick, Carl Reiner, Ralph Richardson, Peter Sellers, Frank Sinatra, Mark Stevens, Jacques Tati, Peter Ustinov, Erich von Stroheim, Tom Walls, John Wayne, Orson Welles, Cornel Wilde.
Many of these gave up after one attempt, and might well have had more sustained directorial careers if, like the following, they had stuck to directing other actors: Richard Attenborough, Lionel Barrymore, James Cagney, Ricardo Cortez, Helmut Dantine, Richard Haydn, Lionel Jeffries, Alf Kjellin, Charles Laughton, Jack Lemmon, Ida Lupino, Roddy McDowall, Karl Malden, Walter Matthau, Elaine May, John Mills, Jack Nicholson, Dick Powell, Anthony Quinn, Cliff Robertson, Mickey Rooney, Don Taylor, Marshall Thompson, Mai Zetterling.
On the whole, however, perhaps the lesson of the lists is that actors should stick to acting.

The Actors' Studio. Lee Strasberg's drama school in New York was well publicized during the fifties as the source of 'method' acting, which was practised by Marlon Brando among others. It corresponded closely with the Stanislavsky system: actors underwent curious mental exercises to assimilate themselves into their characters. Now seems to have been more fashionable than influential.

Acuff, Eddie (1902–1956). American supporting comedian.
Shipmates Forever 35. The Petrified Forest 36. The Boys from Syracuse 40. Hellzapoppin 41. Guadalcanal Diary 43. It Happened Tomorrow 44. The Flying Serpent 46. Blondie's Big Moment 47, scores of others.

Adair, Jean (1872–1953). American stage actress best remembered by film fans as one of the sweetly murderous aunts in *Arsenic and Old Lace* 44. Very occasional other movies include: Advice to the Lovelorn 34. Something in the Wind 46. Living in a Big Way 47.

Adam, Alfred (1909–). French character actor, usually of weak or villainous roles.
La Kermesse Héroique 35. Carnet de Bal 37. Boule de Suif 45. La Ferme du Pendu 48. The Witches of Salem 56. Maigret Sets a Trap 61, etc.

Adam, Ken (1921–). British art director, in films from 1947.
Queen of Spades 48. Around the World in Eighty Days 56. The Trials of Oscar Wilde 60. *Dr Strangelove* 63. Goldfinger 64. The Ipcress File 65. Thunderball 65. Funeral in Berlin 66. *You Only Live Twice* 67. Chitty Chitty Bang Bang 68. Goodbye Mr Chips 69. The Owl and the Pussycat 70. Sleuth 72. Live and Let Die 73. Barry Lyndon 75. The Seven Per Cent Solution 76, etc.

Adam, Ronald (1896–). British character actor specializing in well-bred but stuffy professional men.
The Drum 38. Escape to Danger 43. Green for Danger 46. Bonnie Prince Charlie 48. Angels One Five 51. Private's Progress 55. Reach for the Sky 56. Cleopatra 62. The Tomb of Ligeia 64. Who Killed the Cat? 66, many others.

Adams, Beverly (1945–). Canadian-born leading lady in Hollywood films.
Winter a GoGo 63. The New Interns 64. *The Silencers* 66. Birds Do It 66. Murderers' Row 66. The Torture Garden (GB) 67. The Ambushers 67, etc.

Adams, Casey (1917–). See under *Max Showalter* (his real name, which he has recently used).

Adams, Dorothy (c. 1915–). American character actress, usually of timorous or sullen ladies.
Broadway Musketeers 38. The Flame of New Orleans 41. Laura 44. The Best Years of Our Lives 46. The Foxes of Harrow 48. Carrie 52. Three for Jamie Dawn 56. The Big Country 58. From the Terrace 60, etc.

Adams, Edie (1929–) (Elizabeth Edith Enke). Pert American singer-comedienne, widow of Ernie Kovacs.
□ *The Apartment* 60. Lover Come Back 62. Call Me Bwana 63. It's a Mad Mad Mad Mad World 63. Under the Yum Yum Tree 63. *Love with the Proper Stranger* 64. The Best Man 64. Made in Paris 66. The Oscar 66. *The Honey Pot* 67.

Adams, Gerald Drayson (c. 1904–). Canadian screenwriter, former literary agent.
Dead Reckoning 47. The Big Steal 49. The Golden Horde 51. Flaming Feather 54. The Black Sleep 56. Kissing Cousins 64. Harum Scarum 65, many others.

Adams, Jill (1931–). British leading lady, former model, who made a number of films in the fifties.
The Young Lovers 54. Doctor at Sea 55. Private's Progress 55. The Green Man 56. Brothers in Law 57. Carry On Constable 60, etc.

Adams, Julie (formerly Julia) (1926–). (Betty May Adams). American leading lady in Hollywood from 1947.
Hollywood Story 51. Bright Victory 51. Bend of the River 52. Mississippi Gambler 53. The Creature from the Black Lagoon 54. One Desire 55. Away All Boats 56. Slaughter on Tenth Avenue 57. Raymie 60. Tickle Me 65. Valley of Mystery 67. The Last Movie 71. McQ 72. The McCullochs 75. Killer Force 76, etc.
TV series: The Jimmy Stewart Show 71.

Adams, Nick (1931–1968) (Nicholas Adamschock). American leading man who usually played neurotic or aggressive types; never quite made the big time.
Somebody Love Me (debut) 52. Mister Roberts 55. No Time for Sergeants 58. Pillow Talk 59. Hell is for Heroes 62. The Hook 63. Twilight of Honor 63. Monster of Terror (GB) 66. Young Dillinger 66. Frankenstein Conquers the World (Jap.) 66. Fever Heat 67, etc.
TV series: The Rebel 58–60.

Adam's Rib. 1. US 1923: Cecil B. de Mille marital drama with flashbacks to Genesis. 2. US 1949: brittle sex comedy with Spencer Tracy and Katharine Hepburn as married lawyers on opposite sides of a case. Written by Ruth Gordon and Garson Kanin, with neat direction by George Cukor, it introduced in supporting roles four striking newcomers: David Wayne, Jean Hagen, Tom Ewell and Judy Holliday.

Adams, Robert (1906–). West Indian Negro actor, former teacher, prominent in British films of the forties.
Sanders of the River (debut) 35. King Solomon's Mines 37. Caesar and Cleopatra 45. Men of Two Worlds (leading role) 47, etc.

Adams, Tom (1938–). Burly British leading man.
Licensed to Kill 65. Where the Bullets Fly 66. The Fighting Prince of Donegal 66. Fathom 67. Subterfuge 69. The Fast Kill 72.
TV series: Spy Trap.

Addams, Dawn (1930–). Smart and glamorous British leading lady in international films. Films mainly unremarkable.
Night into Morning 51. Plymouth Adventure 52. The Robe 53. The Moon Is Blue 53. Khyber Patrol 54. A King in New York 57. The Silent Enemy 58. The Two Faces of Dr Jekyll 60. The Black Tulip 64. Ballad in Blue 65. Where the Bullets Fly 66. Vampire Lovers 70. Sappho 70, etc.

Addinsell, Richard (1904–). British composer.
The Amateur Gentleman 36. Fire over England 37. Goodbye Mr Chips 39. Gaslight 40. *Dangerous Moonlight* (including 'Warsaw Concerto') 40. Love on the Dole 41. Blithe Spirit 45. Scrooge 51. Beau Brummell 54. The Prince and the Showgirl 57. The Admirable Crichton 57. The Waltz of the Toreadors 62, etc.

Addison, John (1920–). British composer, in films from 1948.
The Guinea Pig 49. Seven Days to Noon 50. The Man Between 53. Private's Progress 55. *Reach for the Sky* 56. Lucky Jim 57. I Was Monty's Double 58. Look Back in Anger 59. The Entertainer 60. A Taste of Honey 61. The Loneliness of the Long Distance Runner 62. *Tom Jones* (AA) 63. Guns at Batasi 64. Moll Flanders 65. Torn Curtain 66. A Fine Madness 66. The Honey Pot 67. Smashing Time 67. Country Dance 70. Mr Forbush and the Penguins 71. Sleuth 72. Dead Cert 74, etc.

addresses which have formed film titles include *13 West Street, 13 Rue Madeleine, 13 East Street, 13 Demon Street* (TV), *Ten North Frederick, 10 Rillington Place, 15 Maiden Lane, 26 Acacia Avenue, 99 River Street* and *711 Ocean Drive.* Then there were *42nd Street, 52nd Street* and *The House on 92nd Street,* not to mention Flamingo Road, Stallion Road, Madison Avenue, Rue de l'Estrapade, Montparnasse, 19, Quai des Orfèvres, Piccadilly, Bond Street, St Martin's Lane, etc. Nor should one forget Anna Neagle's London series: *Piccadilly Incident, The Courtneys of Curzon Street, Spring in Park Lane, I Live in Grosvenor Square* and *Maytime in Mayfair:* A clever scheme for disposing of an enemy was worked out in *Address Unknown.*

Addy, Wesley (1912–). Thin American character actor, usually of humourless or sinister appearance.
The First Legion 51. My Six Convicts 52. Kiss Me Deadly 55. The Big Knife 55. Timetable 57. The Garment Jungle 58. Ten Seconds to Hell 59. Whatever happened to Baby Jane 62. *Seconds* 66. Mister Buddwing 66. The Grissom Gang 71, many others.

Adler, Buddy (1908–1960) (Maurice Adler). American producer, with Columbia from 1948, Fox from 1954 (head of studio from 1956). *The Dark Past* 48. No Sad Songs for Me 50. Salome 53. *From Here to Eternity* (AA) 53. Violent Saturday 55. *Love is a Many Splendored Thing* 55. The Left Hand of God 55. Bus Stop 56. Anastasia 56. A Hatful of Rain 57. South Pacific 58. *The Inn of the Sixth Happiness* 58, etc.

Adler, Jay (c. 1907–). American character actor, brother of Luther Adler; usually plays hoboes, small-time gangsters, etc.
No Time to Marry 38. My Six Convicts 52. 99 River Street 54. The Big Combo 55. Sweet Smell of Success 57. The Brothers Karamazov 58. Seven Guns to Mesa 60. The Family Jewels 65, many others.

Adler, Larry (1914–). American harmonica virtuoso whose chief contribution to films is the score of *Genevieve* 53; also composed for *King and Country* 63. *High Wind in Jamaica* 64; and appeared in *St Martin's Lane* 38. *Music for Millions* 44.

Adler, Luther (1903–). Heavy-featured American character actor, member of well-known theatrical family (brother Jay, sister Stella).

Lancer Spy 37. Cornered 45. Saigon 48. *Wake of the Red Witch* 48. House of Strangers 49. D.O.A. 50. M 51. Rommel, Desert Fox 51. *The Magic Face* (as Hitler) 51. Hoodlum Empire 52. The Tall Texan 53. The Miami Story 54. The Girl in the Red Velvet Swing 55. Hot Blood 56. The Last Angry Man 59. Cast a Giant Shadow 66. The Brotherhood 68. Crazy Joe 73. Live A Little, Steal A Lot 75, etc.

Adler, Stella (1895–). American stage actress, sister of Luther and Jay Adler.
Love on Toast 38. Shadow of the Thin Man 41. My Girl Tisa 48.

The Admirable Crichton. Barrie's comedy, about master and man reversing roles after being shipwrecked on a desert island, has long fascinated film-makers. (Goldwyn is said to have lost interest after discovering that it was not what it sounded, a naval drama.) De Mille filmed it in 1919 as *Male and Female*, with Thomas Meighan and Gloria Swanson; a musical version, *We're Not Dressing*, turned up in 1934 with Bing Crosby and Carole Lombard; a further variation, *Our Girl Friday*, was filmed by Noel Langley in 1953 starring Kenneth More and Joan Collins; and in 1957 Kenneth More and Diane Cilento appeared in a more or less straight version of the play, under its original title, directed by Lewis Gilbert. More has since appeared on the stage in a musical adaptation, *Our Man Crichton*.

Adolfi, John (1888–1933). American director associated with George Arliss.
Fancy Baggage 29. Show of Shows 29. Sinners' Holiday 30. The Millionaire 31. Alexander Hamilton 32. The Man Who Played God 32. A Successful Calamity 33. The Working Man 33. Voltaire 33, etc.

Adorée, Renée (1898–1933) (Jeanne de la Fonté). French star of American silent films; early circus experience.
Monte Cristo 22. Man and Maid 22. *The Big Parade* 25. Tin Gods 26. Flaming Forest 27. On Ze Boulevard 27. Mr Wu 27. The Cossacks 28. The Pagan 29. Call of the Flesh 30, etc.

Adrian (1903–1959) (Gilbert Adrian). American costume designer credited with the definitive images of Garbo, Harlow and Shearer. Married Janet Gaynor.

Adrian, Iris (1913–) (I. A. Hostetter). American character actress, former Ziegfeld Follies dancer, familiar from the early thirties as wisecracking or tawdry blonde.

Paramount on Parade 30. Rumba 35. Our Relations 37. Professional Bride 41. The G-String Murders 42. Spotlight Scandals 44. I'm from Arkansas 45. Road to Alcatraz 46. The Paleface 48. G.I. Jane 51. Highway Dragnet 54. The Buccaneer 59. That Darn Cat 65. The Odd Couple 68. Scandalous John 71, many others.

Adrian, Max (1902–1973). British stage actor, ranging from Shakespeare to high camp revue and a successful one-man show of the works of Bernard Shaw.
The Primrose Path 30. Why Pick on Me? 38. Macushla 40. *Kipps* 41. *The Young Mr Pitt* 42. Penn of Pennsylvania 42. Henry V 44. Pool of London 50. *Pickwick Papers* 52. Dr Terror's House of Horrors 65. *The Deadly Affair* 67. Julius Caesar 70. *The Music Lovers* 70. The Devils 71. *The Boy Friend* 71, etc.

advertising appears seldom as a background to movies, but when it does, satire is usually in the air, as in *Christmas in July, The Hucksters, Mr Blandings Builds His Dream House, It Should Happen To You, Lover Come Back, Good Neighbour Sam,* and *How to Succeed in Business without Really Trying.* It was played fairly straight in *Madison Avenue* and *The Narrowing Circle.*

Aerograd (USSR 1935). An influential propaganda piece, written and directed by Dovzhenko in the guise of a melodrama about interference by Japanese spies in the building of a Siberian airport.

aeroplanes: see *airplanes*

The Affairs of Anatol (US 1921). A famous comedy of manners from Cecil B. de Mille's early period. Starring Wallace Reid and Gloria Swanson, it was adapted from a Schnitzler play about a newly married man who spends too much time sorting out other people's affairs instead of his own.

The African Queen (GB 1951). Immensely popular film version of C. S. Forester's yarn about a hard-bitten skipper and a prim spinster who become heroes—and lovers— during a perilous escape down an African river in 1915. Directed by John Huston from James Agee's script, with rich performances from Humphrey Bogart (AA) and Katharine Hepburn. Sam Spiegel was one of the first producers to submit Hollywood stars to the rigours of real African locations; and under the circumstances Jack Cardiff's photography is a remarkable achievement.

Agar, John (1921–). American leading man, once married to Shirley Temple; mainly in low-budgeters.
Fort Apache 48. The Brain from Planet Arous 48. Sands of Iwo Jima 49. The Magic Carpet 52. The Golden Mistress 53. Bait 54. Joe Butterfly 56. Daughter of Dr Jekyll 57. Journey to the Seventh Planet 61. Of Love and Desire 63. Cavalry Command 65. Waco 66. The St Valentine's Day Massacre 67. The Curse of the Swamp Creature 67. The Undefeated 69. Big Jake 71, etc.

L' Age d'Or (France 1930). A surrealist film by Luis Buñuel and Salvador Dali, denigrating mankind and modern society in a succession of more or less unrelated sequences. Widely banned for alleged sacrilege and indecency, it now seems obscurely dull rather than sensational.

Agee, James (1909–1955). One of America's most respected film critics, he also wrote novels and screenplays (e.g. *The African Queen* 51). A posthumous collection of his reviews was published under the title 'Agee on Film', and the screenplays followed. His novel *A Death in the Family* was filmed in 1963 as *All the Way Home*.

Agfacolor. German multilayer colour process, widely used in Europe and basically the same as Russian Sovcolor and American Anscocolor (which became Metrocolor). Noted for softness and often lack of sharpness.

Agostini, Philippe (1910–). French cinematographer. Carnet de Bal (co-ph) 37. Les Anges du Pêche 43. Les Dames du Bois de Boulogne 44. Les Portes de la Nuit 46. Pattes Blanches 48. Le Plaisir (co-ph) 51. Rififi 55, etc. Directed Le Dialogue des Carmélites 59. La Soupe aux Poulets 60, etc.

Agutter, Jenny (1952–). British actress who came to leading roles as a teenager.
East of Sudan 64. Star! 68. *I Start Counting* 70. *The Railway Children* 70. Walkabout 71. The Snow Goose (TV) 71. A War of Children (TV) 72. Logan's Run 76, etc.

Ah, Wilderness! Eugene O'Neill's gentle comedy of growing up in a small American town was produced on Broadway in 1933. In 1935 it was filmed by Clarence Brown, with Eric Linden, Lionel Barrymore, Wallace Beery and Mickey Rooney. In 1947 Rouben Mamoulian remade it as a semi-musical, *Summer Holiday*; in the same roles were Mickey Rooney, Walter Huston, Frank Morgan and Jackie Jenkins.

Ahern, Lloyd (   ). American cinematographer. The Klansman 74.

Aherne, Brian (1902–). Gentle-mannered British leading man of stage and screen; resident from 1933 in Hollywood and New York, where he became the American ideal of the charming Englishman.
Autobiography 1969: *A Proper Job.*
☐ The Eleventh Commandment 24. King of the Castle 25. The Squire of Long Hadley 26. *Shooting Stars* 28. *Underground* 29. The W Plan 32. *I Was A Spy* 33. *Song Of Songs* 33. What Every Woman Knows 34. The Fountain 34. *The Constant Nymph* 34. Sylvia Scarlett 35. I Live My Life 35. *Beloved Enemy* 36. *The Great Garrick* 37. Merrily We Live 38. Captain Fury 39. *Juarez* (as Emperor Maximilian) 39. *The Lady In Question* 40. Hired Wife 40. *My Son My Son* 40. The Man who Lost Himself 41. Skylark 41. Smilin' Through 41. My Sister Eileen 42. Forever and a Day 43. A Night to Remember 43. First Comes Courage 43. What a Woman! 43. The Locket 46. Smart Woman 48. Angel on the Amazon 48. *I Confess* 53. Titanic 53. Prince Valiant 54. A Bullet is Waiting 54. *The Swan* (first comic character role) 56. The Best of Everything 59. Susan Slade 61. *Lancelot and Guinevere* (as King Arthur) 63. Rosie 67.

Aherne, Patrick (1901–1970). Irish light actor, brother of Brian Aherne; in America from 1936.
A Daughter in Revolt 25. Huntingtower 27. The Game Chicken 31. Trouble Ahead 36. Green Dolphin Street 47. The Paradine Case 48. Bwana Devil 52. The Court Jester 56, etc.

Ahn, Philip (1911–). American actor of Korean parentage, seen in Hollywood films as an assortment of Asiatic types.
The General Died at Dawn 36. Thank You Mr Moto 38. Charlie Chan in Honolulu 38. They Got Me Covered 42. China Sky 45. Rogues' Regiment 48. I Was an American Spy 51. Love is a Many Splendored Thing 55. Never So Few 59. Diamond Head 63. Thoroughly Modern Millie 67, many others.

Aidman, Charles (1929–). American character actor, mostly on TV.
The Hour of the Gun 67. Countdown 67. Kotch 72. Dirty Little Billy 72, etc.

Aimée, Anouk (1932–) (Françoise Sorya). French leading lady, originally known simply as 'Anouk'.
Les Amants de Vérone 48. The Golden

Salamander 49. Pot Bouille 56. La Tête contre les Murs 58. La Dolce Vita 59. *Lola* 62. Eight and a Half 63. *A Man and a Woman* 66. La Fuga 66. Un Soir Un Train 68. The Appointment 69. The Model Shop (US) 69. Justine 69, many others.

Ainley, Henry (1879–1945). British stage actor in occasional films.
Sweet Lavender 23. Quinneys 25. She Stoops to Conquer 25. The Manxman 27. The Good Companions 32. The First Mrs Fraser 32. As You Like It 36, etc.

Ainley, Richard (1910–1967). British-born actor, son of Henry Ainley.
As You Like It 36. The Frog 37. A Stolen Life 39. Lady with Red Hair 40. The Smiling Ghost 41. White Cargo 42. Above Suspicion 43. Passage to Hong Kong 49, etc.

air balloons, of the spherical type with a hanging basket, have provided picturesque climaxes in films as diverse as *Trottie True*, *The Wizard of Oz* and *Charlie Bubbles*, while the initial part of the journey in *Around the World in Eighty Days* was accomplished in a splendidly ornate example of the species, and a dramatically styled version was used in *Five Weeks in a Balloon*. Balloons were popular for comic gags in silent films, notably Buster Keaton's *Balloonatic*. The most charming adaptation of the idea was in *The Red Balloon*, at the end of which a group of toy balloons carried the boy hero off into the sky; and the director of that film next made *Stowaway in the Sky*, which was about an air balloon over France. Balloons also featured in *Those Magnificent Men in Their Flying Machines, Mysterious Island, The Great Bank Robbery, Chitty Chitty Bang Bang, The Great Race*.
Barrage balloons, a familiar sight in the Britain of World War II, seldom featured in films apart from the Crazy Gang's *Gasbags*; but zeppelins or dirigibles were featured in *Dirigible* itself, *Hell's Angels, Madame Satan, The Assassination Bureau, The Red Tent, Zeppelin*, and of course in *The Hindenberg*.

airplanes, one of the most exciting inventions of the twentieth century, have naturally been a popular source of cinematic thrills. Films about aviation itself began with the newsreel shots of attempts by early birdmen, some of them with tragic results: these have been well preserved in a Robert Youngson one-reeler of the early fifties, *This Mechanical Age*. In the twenties began the long series of spectacular aerial dramas: *Wings, Hell's Angels, Dawn Patrol, Lucky Devils, Devil*

Dogs of the Air, F.P.1, Wings of the Navy, Men with Wings, Test Pilot, Only Angels Have Wings. British films on aviation were rare, exceptions being the exciting *Q Planes* and Korda's ill-fated documentary *Conquest of the Air*; but 1939 brought a need to show the nation's strength, and this was done superbly in such films as *The Lion Has Wings, Squadron Leader X, Target for Tonight, The First of the Few, Coastal Command, Flying Fortress, Journey Together* and *The Way to the Stars*. When America entered the war we were deluged with aerial melodramas, mostly with high-sounding titles and propagandist content: *Eagle Squadron, International Squadron, I Wanted Wings, Winged Victory, A Wing and a Prayer, The Wild Blue Yonder, Bombardier, God Is My Co-Pilot, Flying Tigers, Captains of the Clouds, Dive Bomber, Air Force, Flight Command, Thirty Seconds over Tokyo*, and many others. Even Disney weighed in with the instructional *Victory Through Air Power*.

During the forties began the still-continuing stream of biographies of aviation pioneers and air aces: *They Flew Alone* (Amy Johnson), *Gallant Journey* (John Montgomery), *Flight for Freedom* (Amelia Earhart), *Captain Eddie* (Eddie Rickenbacker), *The McConnell Story, Reach for the Sky* (Douglas Bader), *The Dam Busters* (Dr Barnes Wallis and Guy Gibson), *The Spirit of St Louis* (Lindbergh), *The One That Got Away* (Franz von Werra), *Wings of the Eagle* (Spig Wead), *Von Richthofen and Brown*, etc. Fictional additions to this cycle include *Ace Eli and Rodger of the Skies* and *The Great Waldo Pepper*.

Post-war air dramas from Hollywood showed a considerable increase in thoughtfulness. The responsibility of power was examined in *Command Decision, Twelve O'Clock High, The Beginning or the End, Strategic Air Command* and others, while the future of aviation was the subject of such films as *On the Threshold of Space, Towards the Unknown* and *X-15*. But there has also been room for spectaculars like *Lafayette Escadrille, Bombers B-52, The Longest Day* and *The Blue Max*, for such romantic dramas as *Blaze of Noon, Chain Lightning, Tarnished Angels* and *The Bridges at Toko-Ri*, and even for the more routine melodramatics of *Sky Commando, Battle Taxi, 633 Squadron, Sky Tiger, Jet Pilot, Flight from Ashiya* and *The Flight of the Phoenix*. Britain too has turned out routine recruiting thrillers like *The Red Beret* and *High Flight*, with a nod to civil aviation in *Out of the Clouds*; against these can be set the earnest probing of *The Sound Barrier* and *The Man in the Sky*, the affectionate nostalgia of *Angels One Five* and *Conflict of*

Wings. Airport and its all-star sequels are in a category of their own, that of aerial multi-drama, inspired by *The High and the Mighty, Jet Over the Atlantic* and *Jetstorm* and continuing into the seventies with *Skyjacked.*

In films where aviation itself is not the main subject, planes can be used for a wide variety of dramatic purposes. In *Triumph of the Will* Hitler's arrival at Nuremberg was made to seem godlike by clever photography of his plane descending through the clouds. A very different effect was given in *The Best Years of Our Lives* which began with three war veterans being given a lift home in the nose of a bomber; and the same film, in the scene when Dana Andrews walks through a scrapyard full of the planes he has so recently been flying in the war, produced a ruefully moving sense of waste and futility. Godlike again was Raymond Massey's fleet of futuristic planes in *Things to Come*; and impeccable trick photography gave memorable punch to a musical, *Flying Down to Rio*, in which chorus girls apparently performed on the wings of planes in mid-air.

Any list of the most spectacular plane sequences should include Cary Grant being chased through the cornfield in *North by Northwest*; Claudette Colbert and Ray Milland escaping from Spain in *Arise My Love*; *King Kong* being cornered on the Empire State Building; the plane crashing into the sea in *Foreign Correspondent*; the climax of *Murphy's War*, and, of course, the climactic sequences of films already mentioned such as *Hell's Angels, The Blue Max, The Sound Barrier* and *Dawn Patrol.* Comedy flying sequences can be equally thrilling, as shown by George Formby in *It's in the Air*, Abbott and Costello in *Keep 'Em Flying*, the Marx Brothers in *A Night in Casablanca*, Laurel and Hardy in *The Flying Deuces*, Duggie Wakefield in *Spy for a Day*, Ben Blue and Mickey Rooney in *It's a Mad Mad Mad Mad World*, Jimmy Edwards in *Nearly a Nasty Accident*, Pat Boone in *Never Put It In Writing*, W. C. Fields in *Never Give a Sucker an Even Break*, Spencer Tracy in *State of the Union*, Jack Lemmon in *The Great Race*, Fred MacMurray (flying a Model T) in *The Absent-minded Professor*, James Stewart in *You Gotta Stay Happy*, and practically the whole cast of *Those Magnificent Men in Their Flying Machines*. Air hostesses were featured in *Come Fly With Me* and *Boeing-Boeing.*

Plane crashes have been the dramatic starting point of many films including *Lost Horizon, Five Came Back, Back from Eternity, Fate Is the Hunter, The Night My Number Came Up, Broken Journey, SOS Pacific, The Flight of the Phoenix, Sands of the Kalahari, Survive!, Hey*

I'm Alive (TV) and *Family Flight* (TV). The *fear* that a plane will crash has also been a potent source of screen melodrama, especially in such films as *No Highway, The High and the Mighty, Julie, Zero Hour, Jet Storm, Jet over the Atlantic* and *Skyjacked*, which focus on the emotional reactions of passengers. The proximity of planes to heaven has been useful in fantasies like *Here Comes Mr Jordan, A Guy Named Joe, A Matter of Life and Death* and *The Flight That Disappeared*. Finally, plane-building was used as a symbol of power in *The Carpetbaggers*; and symbols of a more fearsome kind are the atomic bombers which figured so largely in *Dr Strangelove* and *Fail Safe.*

See also: *documentaries; helicopters.*

airships were historically shortlived, and being expensive to reconstruct appeared in few films and never very good ones. Some of the atmosphere can however be gained from *Madame Satan, Hell's Angels, The Assassination Bureau, Zeppelin* and *The Hindenberg.*

Aked, Muriel (1887–1955). British character actress usually seen as comedy spinster or gossip.
A Sister to Assist 'Er 31 and 38. The Mayor's Nest 32. *Rome Express* 32. Friday the Thirteenth 33. Cottage to Let 41. Two Thousand Women 44. The Wicked Lady 45. *The Happiest Days of Your Life* 50. The Story of Gilbert and Sullivan 53, etc.

Akins, Claude (1918–). American character actor often seen as surly western villain.
From Here to Eternity 53. The Caine Mutiny 54. The Sea Chase 55. Johnny Concho 56. The Defiant Ones 58. Porgy and Bess 59. *Inherit the Wind* 60. How the West Was Won 62. The Killers 64. Ride Beyond Vengeance 66. Return of the Seven 66. Waterhole Three 67. The Devil's Brigade 68. Flap 70. The Temper Tramp 73. Battle for the Planet of the Apes 73, etc.
TV series as star: *Movin' On* 74–75.

Akins, Zoe (1886–1958). American playwright whose *The Greeks Had a Word for It* was filmed as *Gold Diggers* (qv); *The Old Maid* was later filmed with Bette Davis. Screenplays include: Eve's Secret 25. Morning Glory 32. Camille 37. Desire Me 47.

The Alamo, originally a cottonwood tree, gave its name to a Franciscan mission in San Antonio, where in 1836 180 Americans were overpowered and slaughtered by 4,000 Mexicans. As those who died included such legendary figures as Jim

Bowie and Davy Crockett, the siege of the Alamo has figured in many a film, notably *Man of Conquest* 39. *The Last Command* 55 and *The Alamo* 60; while in *San Antonio* 45, Errol Flynn and Paul Kelly had a non-historic fight in the mission ruins.

Albee, Edward (1928–). American playwright whose only significant contribution to cinema was *Who's Afraid of Virginia Woolf?* 66. *A Delicate Balance* however was filmed in 1973.

Alberghetti, Anna Maria (1936–). Italian-American operatic singer who came to films as a teenager and has made occasional appearances. Here Comes the Groom 51. The Stars Are Singing 53. The Medium 54. The Last Command 55. Ten Thousand Bedrooms 57. Cinderfella 60, etc.

Alberni, Luis (1887–1962). Spanish-American character actor who played countless small film roles.
Sant Fe Trail 30. Svengali 31. The Kid from Spain 32. Topaze 33. Roberta 35. Anthony Adverse 36. The Housekeeper's Daughter 39. Lady Hamilton 42. Captain Carey USA 49. What Price Glory 52, etc.

Albers, Hans (1892–1960). Leading German actor with broad experience.
Rasputin 29. The Blue Angel 30. Drei Tage Liebe 31. FP 1 32. Gold 33. Peer Gynt 35. Casanova 36. Baron Munchausen 43. The White Hell of Pitz Palu 53, etc.

Albert, Eddie (1908–) (Eddie Albert Heimberger). American character actor with radio and stage experience: for nearly forty years he has been playing honest Joes, nice guys and best friends, seldom winning the girl but allowing himself an occasional meaty role out of character.
☐ *Brother Rat* 38. On Your Toes 39. *Four Wives* 39. Brother Rat and a Baby 40. An Angel from Texas 40. My Love Came Back 40. A Dispatch from Reuters 40. Four Mothers 41. The Wagons Roll at Night 41. Out of the Fog 41. Thieves Fall Out 41. The Great Mr Nobody 41. Treat 'Em Rough 42. Eagle Squadron 42. Ladies' Day 43. Lady Bodyguard 43. Bombardier 43. Strange Voyage 45. Rendezvous with Annie 46. The Perfect Marriage 46. *Smash Up* 47. Time out of Mind 47. Hit Parade of 1947 47. The Dude Goes West 48. You Gotta Stay Happy 48. The Fuller Brush Girl 50. Meet Me After the Show 51. You're in the Navy Now 51. Actors and Sin 52. *Carrie* 52. *Roman Holiday* 53. The Girl Rush

55. *Oklahoma!* 55. *I'll Cry Tomorrow* 55. *Attack!* (his most serious role) 56. *The Teahouse of the August Moon* 56. The Sun Also Rises 57. The Joker is Wild 57. The Gun Runners 58. *The Roots of Heaven* 58. *Orders to Kill* (GB) 58. Beloved Infidel 59. The Young Doctors 61. The Two Little Bears 61. Madison Avenue 62. The Longest Day 62. Who's Got the Action? 62. The Party's Over (GB) 63. Miracle of the White Stallions 65. Captain Newman MD 63. Seven Women 65. McQ 72. The Take 72. The Heartbreak Kid 72. The Longest Yard 74. Escape to Witch Mountain 75. The Devil's Rain 75.
TV series: *Green Acres* 65–70. *Switch* 75–76.

Albert, Edward (1951–). American actor, son of Eddie Albert.
Butterflies are Free 73. Forty Carats 74.

Albertson, Frank (1909–1964). American light leading man, later character actor, in films since 1922 when he began as extra and prop boy.
Prep and Pep 28. Just Imagine 31. A Connecticut Yankee 31. Dangerous Crossroad 33. Alice Adams 35. Fury 36. The Plainsman 37. *Room Service* 38. *Bachelor Mother* 39. The Man from Headquarters 40. Man Made Monster 41. Mystery Broadcast 43. Arson Squad 45. The Hucksters 47. The Last Hurrah 58. Bye Bye Birdie 63, many others.

Albertson, Jack (1910–). American character actor who started as a straight man in burlesque.
Miracle on 34th Street 47. Top Banana 54. The Harder They Fall 56. Man of a Thousand Faces 57. The Shaggy Dog 59. Period of Adjustment 62. A Tiger Walks 64. How to Murder Your Wife 65. *The Subject was Roses* (AA) 68. Justine 69. Rabbit Run 70. Willy Wonka and the Chocolate Factory 71. The Poseidon Adventure 72. Pick Up on 101 72, etc.
TV series: Dr Simon Locke 71. *Chico and the Man* 74–.

Albertson, Mabel (1901–). American character comedienne, typically cast as nosey neighbour or wise and witty grandma.
Mutiny on the Blackhawk 39. She's Back on Broadway 53. Ransom 56. Forever Darling 56. *The Long Hot Summer* 58. *Home Before Dark* 58. *The Gazebo* 60. Period of Adjustment 62. *Barefoot in the Park* 67, etc.
TV series: *The Tom Ewell Show* 63.

Albicocco, Jean-Gabriel (1938–). French director of pictorial romances.
The Wanderer 69. Le Petit Matin 71, etc.

Albright, Hardie (1903–) (Hardy Albrecht). Scottish-German Hollywood leading man of the early thirties.
Young Sinners 31. So Big 32. Song of Songs 33. The Scarlet Letter 34. Ladies Love Danger 35. Granny Get Your Gun 40. Pride of the Yankees 42. Angel on My Shoulder 46. Ski Patrol 51, etc.

Albright, Lola (1925–). Stylish, tough-talking American leading lady; roles for her Stanwyck-like personality were hard to find.
Champion 49. The Good Humour Man 50. Arctic Flight 52. The Tender Trap 56. The Monolith Monsters 57. Seven Guns to Mesa 60. *A Cold Wind in August* 61. Kid Galahad 62. The Love Cage 65. Lord Love a Duck 66. The Way West 67. Where Were You When the Lights Went Out? 68. The Impossible Years 68, etc.
TV series: *Peter Gunn* 58–61.

alcoholics have been familiar screen figures since movies began: Jack Norton and Arthur Housman made a living playing little else, and other comic inebriates include James Stewart in *Harvey*, William Powell in *The Thin Man* and its successors, Wallace Beery in *Ah Wilderness* (followed by Frank Morgan in *Summer Holiday*), Dean Martin in *Rio Bravo* (followed by Robert Mitchum in *El Dorado*) and Jackie Gleason in *Papa's Delicate Condition*.
More serious studies of alcoholism include Fredric March (followed by James Mason) in *A Star is Born*, Bing Crosby in *The Country Girl*, James Cagney and Gig Young in *Come Fill The Cup*, Spencer Tracy in *The People Against O'Hara*, Michael Redgrave in *Time Without Pity*, Claude Rains in *The White Tower*, Ingrid Bergman in *Under Capricorn*, Chester Morris in *Blind Spot*, Ray Milland in *The Lost Weekend* and *Night into Morning*, Jack Lemmon and Lee Remick in *Days of Wine and Roses*, Julie London in *The Great Man*, Van Johnson in *The Bottom of the Bottle*, Henry Fonda in *The Fugitive*, Lars Hanson in *The Atonement of Gosta Berling*, Susan Hayward in *Smash Up* and *I'll Cry Tomorrow*, Burt Lancaster in *Come Back Little Sheba*, Thomas Mitchell (followed by Bing Crosby) in *Stagecoach*, David Farrar in *The Small Back Room*, Bette Davis in *Dangerous*, Jason Robards in *Long Day's Journey Into Night*, Gregory Peck in *Beloved Infidel*, Donald O'Connor in *The Buster Keaton Story*, George Murphy in *Show Business*, Charles Laughton (followed by Robert Newton) in *Vessel of Wrath/The Beachcomber*, James Dunn in *A Tree Grows in Brooklyn*, Joan Fontaine in *Something to Live For*, Myrna Loy in *From the Terrace*, Maurice Ronet in *Le Feu Follet*, Kenneth More in *Dark Of The Sun*, Frank Sinatra in *The Joker is Wild*, Claire Bloom in *Red Sky At Morning*, Chester Morris in *Blind Spot*, and Dick Van Dyke in *The Morning After* (TV).
See also *drunk scenes*.

Alcott,   John   (   ).   British cinematographer.
A Clockwork Orange 71. Barry Lyndon (AA) 75, etc.

Alcott, Louisa M. (1832–1888). American novelist whose cosy family tales *Little Women* (qv) and *Little Men* have been frequently plundered by movie-makers.

Alda, Alan (1936–). American leading man, son of Robert Alda.
Gone Are the Days 63. The Extraordinary Seaman 68. Paper Lion 68. The Moonshine War 70. The Mephisto Waltz 71. To Kill A Clown 72. The Glass House (TV) 72. The Caryl Chessman Story (TV) 77.
TV series: *M*A*S*H* 72–.

Alda, Robert (1914–) (Alphonso d'Abruzzo). American actor with radio and stage experience.
Rhapsody in Blue (as George Gershwin) 45. Cloak and Dagger 46. The Beast with Five Fingers 47. Nora Prentiss 47. April Showers 48. Tarzan and the Slave Girl 50. Two Gals and a Guy 51. Beautiful But Dangerous (Italian) 55. Imitation of Life 59. Cleopatra's Daughter 63. The Girl Who Knew Too Much 68, etc.

Alderton, John (1940–). British light leading man, popular on TV in long-running series *Emergency Ward Ten* (from 1958) and *Please Sir* (from 1968).
The System 64. Duffy 68. Hannibal Brooks 69. *Please Sir* 71. Zardoz 74. It Shouldn't Happen to a Vet 76.

Aldo, G. R. (1902–1953) (Aldo Graziati). Italian cinematographer.
Miracle in Milan 50. Othello 52. Umberto D 52. Senso 53, etc.

Aldon, Mari (1930–). American leading lady of the fifties; former ballet dancer.
Distant Drums 51. This Woman Is Dangerous 52. The Barefoot Contessa 54. Summertime 55, etc.

Aldrich, Robert (1918–). American director who declined from gritty realism to inflated melodrama. His own producer from 1962.
☐ Big Leaguer 53. World for Ransom 5 *Apache* 54. *Vera Cruz* 54. *Kiss Me Deadly* (&

55. The Big Knife (& p) 55. Autumn Leaves 56. *Attack!* (& p) 57. Ten Seconds to Hell 59. The Angry Hills 59. The Last Sunset 60. Sodom and Gomorrah (co-d) 63. *Whatever Happened to Baby Jane?* 62. Four For Texas 63. Hush Hush Sweet Charlotte 64. The Flight of the Phoenix 65. *The Dirty Dozen* 66. The Killing of Sister George 68. The Legend of Lylah Clare 69. Too Late the Hero 69. The Grissom Gang 71. Ulzana's Raid 72. Emperor of the North Pole 73. The Longest Yard 75. Hustle 76. Twilights Last Gleaming 77.

Alekan, Henri (1909–). French cinematographer.
Mademoiselle Docteur 37. Bataille du Rail 44. La Belle et la Bête 46. Les Maudits 47. Une Si Jolie Petite Plage 48. Anna Karenina 48. Juliette ou la Clef des Songes 50. Austerlitz 60. Topkapi 64. Lady L 65. Triple Cross 66. Mayerling 68. Red Sun 71, etc.

Alexander, Ben (1911–1969). American boy actor of silent days; later character man.
Each Pearl a Tear 14. Hearts of the World 18. Penrod and Sam 23. *All Quiet on the Western Front* 30. Stage Mother 34. Born to Gamble 36. Convicts' Code 39. Man in the Shadow 57, etc.
TV series: *Dragnet* 52–59. The Felony Squad 66–69.

Alexander, Jane (1939–). American stage actress in occasional films.
□ The Great White Hope 70. A Gunfight 71. Welcome Home Johnny Bristol (TV) 71. The New Centurions 72. *All the President's Men* 76. *Eleanor and Franklin* (TV) (as Eleanor Roosevelt) 76, etc.

Alexander, John (1897–). Portly American stage actor with amiable personality.
The Petrified Forest 36. Flowing Gold 41. A Tree Grows in Brooklyn 44. *Arsenic and Old Lace* (as Uncle Teddy) 44. Mr Skeffington 45. The Jolson Story 46. Summer Holiday 48. Fancy Pants (as Theodore Roosevelt) 50. The Marrying Kind 52. The Man in the Net 59. One Foot in Hell 60, etc.

Alexander, Katherine (1901–). American actress specializing in sympathetic second leads.
The Barretts of Wimpole Street 34. The Painted Veil 34. The Dark Angel 36. Double Wedding 37. The Great Man Votes 39. The Hunchback of Notre Dame 39. The Vanishing Virginian 42. The Human Comedy 42. Kiss and Tell 45. John Loves Mary 49, etc.

Alexander, Ross (1907–1937). Budding American leading man of the early thirties.
The Wiser Sex 32. Flirtation Walk 34. Shipmates Forever 35. A Midsummer Night's Dream 35. Captain Blood 35. Boulder Dam 36. China Clipper 36. Ready Willing and Able 37, etc.

Alexander, Terence (1923–). British light leading man, often in ineffectual roles.
The Woman with No Name 51. The Gentle Gunman 52. The Runaway Bus 54. Portrait of Alison 55. The One That Got Away 57. Danger Within 59. The League of Gentlemen 60. The Fast Lady 62. The Long Duel 67. Waterloo 70. Vault of Horror 73, many others.

Alexander The Great (356–323 BC). A mighty warrior who became king of Macedonia at the age of twenty and quickly overran most of the Mediterranean before he died of a fever at the age of 33. He was played by Richard Burton in Robert Rossen's rather stolid 1956 biopic.

Alexander Nevsky (USSR 1938). Sergei Eisenstein's pulsating historic spectacle has Nicolai Cherkassov as the impassive medieval warrior who conquered barbarian hordes in a battle on the ice (photographed in summer heat by Edouard Tisse) at Nijni-Novgorod (actually shot at Lake Peipus). The splendid action sequences use music by Prokoviev in place of natural sound.

Alexandrov, Grigori (1903–) (G. Mormenko). Distinguished Russian director, former assistant to Eisenstein.
Internationale 32. *Jazz Comedy* 34. *Circus* 36. *Volga-Volga* 38. Spring 47. Glinka 52. Lenin in Poland 61.

Alexieff, Alexandre (1901–). Franco-Russian animator who devised a method of illuminating pins stuck through a screen at various levels to produce a picture. Chief examples are *A Night on a Bare Mountain* 34, and the titles for *The Trial* 64.

Alfie (GB 1966). Bill Naughton's amusing play about a cockney Lothario, while filmed rather flatly by Lewis Gilbert, with muddy colour and no subtlety, will presumably be remembered as another stage in the cinema's progress towards complete freedom in choice of subject matter: its crude attitude to sex, expressed in raw dialogue, kept box offices busy and gave the world a new view of the British at play. Michael Caine played the long title role with relish, and even made it sympathetic.

Algar, James (1914–). American writer-

director of Disney's *True Life Adventures* and associated productions.
The Living Desert 53. *The Vanishing Prairie* 54. The African Lion 55. White Wilderness 58. Jungle Cat 60. The Legend of Lobo 63. *The Incredible Journey* 63, etc.

Algiers (US 1938). The film in which Charles Boyer did *not* say 'Come with me to the Casbah'. (The line was a Hollywood legend.) The film itself, though highly successful, was a spineless remake of Julien Duvivier's *Pepe Le Moko* 36, which had Jean Gabin, in a script by Ashelbé and Henri Jeanson, as a doom-laden but romantic criminal exile who finally sacrifices himself for a woman. Tony Martin later starred in *Casbah* 48, a further Hollywood remake in semi-musical form.

Algren, Nelson (1909–). American novelist who writes of life's seamy side. Books include *The Man with the Golden Arm* and *A Walk on the Wild Side*.

Alias Nick Beal (The Contact Man) (US 1948). A pleasingly successful modern version of *Faust*, with Thomas Mitchell as an honest politician almost corrupted by smooth, suave, diabolic Ray Milland. Effectively studio-set, with the magical moments under-stated and a general feeling of shape and style. Directed by John Farrow, photographed by Lionel Lindon, from Jonathan Latimer's script.

Ali Baba. The Arabian Nights story, of a poor camel-driver who outwits forty thieves by trailing them to their magic cave which opens to a password, has been a favourite with film-makers. Edison made a version in 1902, William Fox in 1919. In 1944 Jon Hall starred in *Ali Baba and the Forty Thieves*, while in 1952 Tony Curtis was *Son of Ali Baba*. (The 1944 film was remade, with much use of footage from the original, in 1964 as *Sword of Ali Baba*, starring Peter Mann.) Meanwhile in 1954 Fernandel appeared in a French comedy version under Jacques Becker's direction. Eddie Cantor dreamed he was Ali Baba in *Ali Baba Goes to Town* 37, and the character has appeared in many other Arabian Nights films. A superior spelling was adopted for *The Adventures of Hajji Baba* 56 in which John Derek played the role.

Alice in Wonderland. This Victorian nonsense classic was written by Lewis Carroll (C. L. Dodgson) and published in 1865. Most film versions—and there were several silent ones—have included material from *Through the Looking Glass*, published in 1871. Since sound there have been two American productions using actors (in 1931 with little-known players and in 1933 with Charlotte Henry and an all-star Paramount cast); a 1950 French version with Carol Marsh and Bunin's puppets; a rather stiff and unimaginative Disney cartoon of 1951; and a stolid British live-action version of 1972.

Alison, Dorothy (1925–). Australian actress resident in Britain.
Mandy 52. Turn the Key Softly 53. The Maggie 54. Reach for the Sky 56. The Long Arm 56. The Scamp 57. Life in Emergency Ward Ten 59. Georgy Girl 66. Pretty Polly 68. See No Evil 71. The Amazing Mr Blunden 72.

All About Eve (US 1950). Writer-director Joseph L. Mankiewicz dipped his pen in venom when he wrote this story of the rise to fame of an unscrupulous actress, and won an Academy Award on both counts. Bette Davis blazed as the displaced idol, George Sanders as a waspish critic also won an Academy Award as best supporting actor, and Marilyn Monroe had a brief bit as a dumb blonde. Anne Baxter was Eve.

Allan, Elizabeth (1908–). British leading lady with stage experience; adept at delicate or aristocratic heroines.
Alibi 31. Black Coffee 31. Michael and Mary 32. Nine Till Six 32. The Lodger 33. Java Head 34. David Copperfield (US) 34. Mark of the Vampire (US) 35. A Tale of Two Cities (US) 36. Camille (US) 36. Michael Strogoff (US) 37. Inquest 38. Saloon Bar 40. The Great Mr Handel 42. Went the Day Well 42. He Stoops to Conquer 44. No Highway 51. The Heart of the Matter 54. The Brain Machine 55. Grip of the Strangler 58, etc.

Alland, William (1916–). American actor, originally with Orson Welles' Mercury Theatre: played the enquiring reporter in *Citzen Kane* 41. Later became staff producer for Universal-International: *It Came from Outer Space* 53. *This Island Earth* 56. *The Lady Takes a Flyer* 58. *The Rare Breed* 65, etc. Independently produced and directed *Look in Any Window* 61.

Allbritton, Louise (1920–). American leading lady of the forties, mainly in light comedy. Recently inactive.
Not a Ladies Man (debut) 42. Who Done It? 42. A Date with an Angel 42. Son of Dracula 43. Her Primitive Man 44. Men in Her Diary 45. San Diego I Love You 45. Tangier 46. The Egg and I 47. Walk a Crooked Mile 48. Sitting Pretty 48. The Great Manhunt 50. Felicia (Puerto Rico) 64, etc.

Allégret, Marc (1900–). French director of superior commercial films.
Mam'zelle Nitouche 31. Fanny 32. Lac Aux Dames 34. Les Beaux Yeux 35. Gribouille 37. Orage 38. Entrée des Artistes 38. L'Arlésienne 42. Petrus 46. Blanche Fury (GB) 47. Maria Chapdelaine 50. Blackmailed (GB) 51. Futures Vedettes 55. Lady Chatterley's Lover 55. En Effeuillant La Marguerite 56. Un Drôle de Dimanche 58. L'Abominable Homme des Douanes 63, etc.

Allégret, Yves (1907–). French director, brother of Marc Allégret.
Les Deux Timides 41. *Dédée* 47. *Une Si Jolie Petite Plage* 48. Manèges 49. Les Orgueilleux 53. Oasis 54. Germinal 63, etc.

Allen, Adrianne (1907–). British light actress, mostly on stage. Mother of Daniel Massey, ex-wife of Raymond.
Loose Ends 31. Black Coffee 31. The Morals of Marcus 35. The October Man 47. Vote for Huggett 49. The Final Test 53. Meet Mr Malcolm 54, etc.

Allen, Barbara Jo (c. 1904–1974) (also known as *Vera Vague*). American comedy actress, well known on radio with Bob Hope.
Village Barn Dance 40. Ice Capades 41. Mrs Wiggs of the Cabbage Patch 42. In Rosie's Room 44. Snafu 45. Square Dance Katy 50. The Opposite Sex 56, etc.

Allen, Chesney (1893–). British light comedian, for many years teamed with Bud Flanagan and the Crazy Gang, from whose more violent antics he stood somewhat aloof.
A Fire Has Been Arranged 34. Underneath the Arches 37. Alf's Button Afloat 38. Gasbags 40. We'll Smile Again 42. Dreaming 44. Here Comes the Sun 45, etc.

Allen, Corey (1934–). American supporting actor specializing in depraved adolescents.
The Mad Magician 54. Night of the Hunter 55. Rebel without a Cause 55. The Shadow on the Window 57. Party Girl 58. Private Property (lead) 60. Sweet Bird of Youth 62. The Chapman Report 62, etc.

Allen, Elizabeth (1934–) (Elizabeth Gillease). American leading lady with stage experience.
From the Terrace 60. Diamond Head 63. Donovan's Reef 63. Cheyenne Autumn 64. Star Spangled Girl 71. The Carey Treatment 72, etc.

Allen, Fred (1894–1956) (John F. Sullivan).

Baggy-eyed American radio comedian: very occasional films.
Autobiography 1954, *Treadmill to Oblivion*.
□ Thanks a Million 35. Love Thy Neighbour 41. It's in the Bag 45. We're Not Married 52. Full House 53.

Allen, Gracie (1902/06–1964). American comedienne who projected a scatterbrained image for thirty years on radio, TV and films, usually with her husband George Burns. Occasional film appearances include: College Humor 33. We're Not Dressing 34. College Holiday 36. A Damsel in Distress 38. The Gracie Allen Murder Case 39. Mr and Mrs North 42. Two Girls and a Sailor 44, etc.

Allen, Irving (1905–). Polish-American producer. Hollywood experience from 1929; films include: Avalanche (d) 47. Sixteen Fathoms Deep (d) 50. New Mexico (p) 51. Slaughter Trail (d, p) 51. In Britain from early fifties as co-founder of Warwick Films (Cockleshell Heroes, Zarak, etc.). More recently: The Trials of Oscar Wilde 60. The Hellions 61. The Long Ships 64. Genghis Khan 65. The Silencers 66. The Ambushers 67. Hammerhead 68. Cromwell 70, etc.
TV series: Matt Helm 75.

Allen, Irwin (1916–). American writer-producer who began with semi-instructional entertainments and then switched to fantasy.
The Sea Around Us 50. The Animal World 56. The Story of Mankind (& d) 57. The Big Circus 59. The Lost World (& d) 61. A Voyage to the Bottom of the Sea (& d) 62. Five Weeks in a Balloon (& d) 63. The Poseidon Adventure 72. The Towering Inferno (& co-d) 74. The Time Travelers (TV) 76, etc.
TV series in similar vein: Voyage to the Bottom of the Sea, Lost in Space, Time Tunnel, Land of the Giants, The Swiss Family Robinson, etc.

Allen, Lewis (1905–). British director in Hollywood; his career started well but spluttered out.
□ Our Hearts were Young and Gay 44. *The Uninvited* 44. The Unseen 45. Those Endearing Young Charms 46. The Perfect Marriage 46. The Imperfect Lady 46. Desert Fury 47. So Evil My Love 48. Sealed Verdict 48. Chicago Deadline 49. Valentino 51. Appointment with Danger 51. At Sword's Point 52. Suddenly 54. A Bullet For Joey 55. Illegal 56. Another Time Another Place 58. Whirlpool (GB) 59. Decision at Midnight (MRA film) 63.

Allen, Lewis M. (1922–). American

producer with theatrical experience.
The Connection 60. The Balcony 63. Lord of the Flies 64. Fahrenheit 451 66.

Allen, Patrick (1927–). Lantern-jawed British leading man who after playing assorted villains and heroes in routine films established himself as TV's *Crane*.
1984 55. High Tide at Noon 57. The Long Haul 57–8. Dunkirk 58. Tread Softly Stranger 58. I Was Monty's Double 58. Never Take Sweets from a Stranger 60. The Traitors 62. Captain Clegg 62. The Night of the Generals 66. Night of the Big Heat 67. When Dinosaurs Ruled the Earth 69. Puppet On a Chain 71. Diamonds on Wheels 73. Persecution 74, etc.

Allen, Rex (1922–). American singing cowboy, popular on radio, in vaudeville and in second features.
Arizona Cowboy 50. Under Mexicali Stars 50. The Old Overland Trail 53. The Phantom Stallion 53, etc.

Allen, Steve (1921–). American radio and TV personality, in occasional films.
□ Down Memory Lane 49. I'll Get By 51. *The Benny Goodman Story* (title role) 55. College Confidential 59. The Big Circus 59. Warning Shot 66. The Comic 70.

Allen, Woody (1935–) (Allen Stewart Konigsberg). Bespectacled American night club comedian and light playwright who has made several chaotic film appearances but internationally remains an acquired taste.
□ What's New Pussycat (& w) 65. *Casino Royale* (& co-w) 67. What's Up Tiger Lily? (& w) 67. Take the Money and Run (& w) 69. Dont Drink the Water (w only) 69. *Bananas* (& co-w) 71. Everything You Always Wanted to Know About Sex (& wp) 72. *Play It Again Sam* (& w) 72. Sleeper 73. Love and Death 76. The Front 76.

Allgeier, Sepp (1890–1968). German cinematographer. Best-known films include: *Diary of a Lost Girl* 29. *The White Hell of Pitz Palu* 29. *William Tell* 33.

Allgood, Sara (1883–1950). Irish character actress, long with the Abbey Theatre and from 1940 in Hollywood.
□ *Blackmail* 29. *Juno and the Paycock* 30. The Bride of the Lake 34. The Passing of the Third Floor Back 35. Riders to the Sea 35. It's Love Again 36. *Storm in a Teacup* 37. Kathleen 38. On the Night of the Fire 39. *That Hamilton Woman* 41. *How Green was My Valley* 41. Dr Jekyll and Mr Hyde 41. Lydia 41. The War

Against Mrs Hadley 42. Roxie Hart 42. This Above All 42. It Happened in Flatbush 42. Life Begins at 8.30 42. City without Men 43. Jane Eyre 44. *The Lodger* 44. *Between Two Worlds* 44. The Keys of the Kingdom 44. The Strange Affair of Uncle Harry 45. Cluny Brown 46. Kitty 46. The Spiral Staircase 46. Mother Wore Tights 47. The Fabulous Dorseys 47. Ivy 47. Mourning Becomes Electra 47. My Wild Irish Rose 47. One Touch of Venus 48. The Man from Texas 48. The Girl from Manhattan 48. The Accused 48. Challenge to Lassie 49. Sierra 50. Cheaper by the Dozen 50.

Allied Artists Corporation. An American production company, more recently involved in TV, which flourished throughout the thirties and forties as a purveyor of routine crime and comedy second features. Its policy was to put out the poorer product under the banner of its subsidiary, *Monogram Pictures Corporation*; 'quality' AA produce was little in evidence until the fifties, when films like *Love in the Afternoon*, *The Friendly Persuasion* and *Al Capone* came from this stable. Meanwhile the Monogram films, boasting such attractions as Frankie Darro, the East Side Kids, the Bowery Boys, Bela Lugosi and Charlie Chan, had their faithful following, and in France attracted highbrow cinéastes to such an extent that Jean-Luc Godard dedicated his film *À Bout de Souffle* to Monogram.

Allio, René (1924–). Thoughtful French director with sparse output.
□ *The Shameless Old Lady* 65. L'Une et l'Autre 67. Pierre et Paul 68. Les Camisards 70. Rude Journee pour la Reine 74.

Allister, Claud (1891–1970) (Claud Palmer). British character actor associated with monocled silly-ass roles.
Bulldog Drummond (US) 29. The Private Life of Henry VIII 32. The Private Life of Don Juan 34. Dracula's Daughter (US) 36. Captain Fury (US) 39. Charley's Aunt (US) 41. Kiss the Bride Goodbye 44. Gaiety George 46. Quartet 48. Kiss Me Kate (US) 53, etc.

All Quiet on the Western Front (US 1930). Erich Maria Remarque's book, showing World War I from the point of view of the German soldier, was turned into a landmark of cinema history by director Lewis Milestone, cinematographer Arthur Edeson and composer David Brockman. Lew Ayres, Louis Wolheim and Slim Summerville headed the cast. AA best picture, best director.

all-star films. The phrase usually denotes giant musicals of the kind which started in the early days of talkies, when each studio put on an extravaganza displaying the talents of all its contract artistes, often to little effect. Titles included *Movietone Follies, Paramount on Parade, The Hollywood Revue of 1929* (MGM), *Show of Shows* (Warner), *King of Jazz* (Universal) and *Elstree Calling.* The practice was revived during World War II: *Star Spangled Rhythm* (Paramount), *Thank Your Lucky Stars* (Warner), *Follow the Boys* (Universal), *Hollywood Canteen* (Warner) and *Stage Door Canteen* helped to cheer up the armed forces. Paramount continued into the later forties with *Variety Girl* and *Duffy's Tavern,* and Warner came up with *It's a Great Feeling* and *Starlift. Carnegie Hall* applied the technique to classical music.

Meanwhile dramatic films had found the value of an occasional all-star cast. *Grand Hotel, If I Had a Million, Dinner at Eight* in the early thirties were followed ten years later by *Tales of Manhattan, Forever and a Day* and *Flesh and Fantasy,* while the adoption of particular authors later in the forties produced all-star episodic films such as Somerset Maugham's *Quartet* and O'Henry's *Full House.* In the fifties and sixties, an occasional giant-screen epic would pack itself with stars: *Around the World in Eighty Days, How the West Was Won* and *The Greatest Story Ever Told* were perhaps the most significant of these.

All That Money Can Buy (US 1941). From Stephen Vincent Benet's story 'The Devil and Daniel Webster', this delightfully American film put the Faust legend into a nineteenth-century farming setting peopled by real historical characters. Edward Arnold as lawyer Webster and James Craig as the young farmer were both outshone by Walter Huston as Mr Scratch, the amiable devil. Bernard Herrman's vibrant music (AA) perfectly counter-pointed William Dieterle's zestful direction and production. The film has also, at various times, been known as *The Devil and Daniel Webster* and *Daniel and the Devil.*

All The King's Men (US 1949). A notable film version, written and directed by Robert Rossen, of Robert Penn Warren's exposé of American state politics, paralleling the career of the corrupt Huey Long of Louisiana. AA best picture; Broderick Crawford best actor; Mercedes McCambridge best supporting actress. John Ireland was also excellent as the jaundiced narrator.

Allwyn, Astrid (1909–). Swedish-American leading lady of minor movies in the thirties.
Reputation 32. Only Yesterday 33. Follow the Fleet 36. Dimples 37. Love Affair 39. Mr Smith Goes to Washington 39. Unexpected Uncle 41. No Hands on the Clock 41. Hit Parade of 1943, etc.

Allyson, June (1917–) (Ella Geisman). Husky-voiced American leading lady who could play a tomboy or a tease, and was equally ready with a smile or a tear. Started in 1937 two-reelers, then spent five years as a Broadway chorus dancer before making her Hollywood feature debut. Her cute sexiness kept her popular for fifteen years. Married to Dick Powell 1945–63.
□ Best Foot Forward 43. Girl Crazy 43. Thousands Cheer 43. Meet the People 44. *Two Girls and a Sailor* 44. *Music For Millions* 44. Her Highness and the Bellboy 45. The Sailor Takes a Wife 45. Two Sisters from Boston 45. Till the Clouds Roll By 46. The Secret Heart 46. High Barbaree 47. Good News 47. The Bride Goes Wild 48. The Three Musketeers 48. Words and Music (singing 'Thou Swell') 48. *Little Women* (as Jo) 49. The Stratton Story 49. The Reformer and the Redhead 50. Right Cross 50. Too Young to Kiss 51. The Girl in White 52. Battle Circus 53. Remains to be Seen 53. *The Glenn Miller Story* 54. Executive Suite 54. Woman's World 54. Strategic Air Command 55. *The Shrike* (her most dramatic role) 55. The McConnell Story 56. The Opposite Sex 56. You Can't Run Away from It 56. Interlude 57. My Man Godfrey 57. Stranger in My Arms 59. They Only Kill Their Masters 72. See the Man Run (TV) 72.
TV series: *The June Allyson Show* 59–61.

Almond, Paul (1931–). Canadian director, from TV.
□ Isabel 68. Act of the Heart 70.

Aloma of the South Seas. This sentimental romance was a silent success in 1927, with Gilda Gray and Percy Marmont. In 1941 Paramount remade it in colour, with Dorothy Lamour, Jon Hall, and lots of crocodiles and volcanoes.

Alonzo, John A. ( ). Mexican-American cinematographer.
Bloody Mama 70. *Vanishing Point* 71. Sounder 72. Lady Sings The Blues 72. Hit! 73. The Naked Ape 73. Conrack 74. Chinatown 74. Once Is Not Enough 75. The Fortune 75. *Farewell My Lovely* 75.

Alperson, Edward L. (1896–1969). American

independent producer, mainly of hokum pictures; former film salesman.
Black Beauty 47. Dakota Lil 50. Invaders from Mars 53. New Faces 54. The Magnificent Matador 56. I Mobster 59. September Storm 60, many others.

Altman, Robert (1922–). American director who had a big commercial success with M*A*S*H but subsequently demonstrated an unsympathetically experimental approach.
□ The Delinquents (& wp) 55. The James Dean Story (co-d & p) 57. Nightmare in Chicago 64. Countdown 68. That Cold Day in the Park 68. *M*A*S*H* 70. Brewster McCloud 71. McCabe and Mrs Miller 71. Images 72. The Long Goodbye 72. Thieves Like Us 73. California Split 74. *Nashville* 75. Buffalo Bill and the Indians 76.

Alton, John (1901–). Hungarian-born cinematographer in Hollywood from 1924. Won Academy Award for *An American in Paris* 51. Others: Atlantic City 44. Father of the Bride 50. The People Against O'Hara 51. The Big Combo 55. The Teahouse of the August Moon 56. The Brothers Karamazov 58. Elmer Gantry 60.

Alton, Robert (1903–1957) (Robert Alton Hart). American director, mainly of musical sequences: Strike Me Pink 36. Showboat 51. There's No Business Like Show Business 55, many others. Directed features: Merton of the Movies 47. Pagan Love Song 50.

Alvarado, Don (1900–1967) (José Paige). American 'latin lover' of the twenties: later appeared in character roles.
The Loves of Carmen 26. Drums of Love 27. The Battle of the Sexes 28. The Bridge of San Luis Rey 29. Rio Rita 29. Morning Glory 33. The Devil is a Woman 35. The Big Steal 49, etc.

Alwyn, William (1905–). Prolific British composer who progressed from documentary scoring to fictional narrative.
Fires were Started 42. World of Plenty 43. The Way Ahead 44. *The True Glory* 45. *Odd Man Out* 46. *The Fallen Idol* 48. *The Card* 52. Manuela 57. The Running Man 63, etc.

Amateau, Rod (1923–). American radio writer who in the early fifties briefly became a film director and then turned his attention to half-hour comedy TV films, of which he has since made many hundreds.
The Rebel 51. Monsoon 52. Pussycat Pussycat I Love You 70. The Statue 70. Where Does It Hurt (& co-p, co-w) 72, etc.

The Amateur Gentleman. Jeffrey Farnol's Regency novel, of an inn-keeper's son who becomes involved with highwaymen and London society, was a popular subject for British movies. In 1920 Maurice Elvey directed Langhorne Burton; 1926 saw Sidney Olcott directing Richard Barthelmess in a Hollywood version; and in 1936 Douglas Fairbanks Jnr was the star of a sound version directed by Thornton Freeland.

Amato, Giuseppe (1899–1964) (Giuseppe Vasaturo). Italian producer.
Four Steps in the Clouds (& w) 42. Open City 45. Shoe Shine 46. Bicycle Thieves 49. Umberto D 52. Don Camillo 52. La Dolce Vita 59, many others.

Ambler, Eric (1909–). Popular British novelist (works filmed include *The Mask of Dimitrios, Journey Into Fear, Background to Danger, Hotel Reserve, The Light of Day*). Also screenwriter: The Way Ahead 44. The October Man 47. The Magic Box 51. The Card 52. The Cruel Sea 54. A Night to Remember 57. The Wreck of the Mary Deare 59, etc.

Ambler, Joss (1900–1959). British character actor, often seen as heavy father or police inspector.
The Citadel 38. The Black Sheep of Whitehall 41. The Agitator 44. The Long Arm 56, many others.

Ameche, Don (1908–) (Dominic Felix Amici). American leading man with stage and radio experience. A pleasant light hero of mainly trivial films, he returned to Broadway in the sixties and became popular on TV as a circus ringmaster.
□ Sins of Man 36. *Ramona* 36. Ladies in Love 36. One in a Million 37. Love is News 37. Fifty Roads to Town 37. You Can't Have Everything 37. Love Under Fire 37. *In Old Chicago* 38. Happy Landing 38. Josette 38. *Alexander's Ragtime Band* 38. Gateway 38. *The Three Musketeers* (musical version; as D'Artagnan) 39. *Midnight* 39. *The Story of Alexander Graham Bell* (which started a long-standing joke about Ameche inventing the telephone) 39. Hollywood Cavalcade 39. *Swanee River* (as Stephen Foster) 39. Lillian Russell 40. *Four Sons* 40. Down Argentine Way 40. *That Night in Rio* (dual role) 41. Moon Over Miami 41. Kiss the Boys Goodbye 41. The Feminine Touch 41. Confirm or Deny 41. The Magnificent Dope 42. Girl Trouble 43. *Heaven Can Wait* (under Lubitsch, his best acting performance) 43. *Happy Land* 43. Something to Shout About 43.

Wing and a Prayer 44. Greenwich Village 44. It's In the Bag 45. Guest Wife 45. So Goes My Love 46. That's My Man 47. Sleep My Love 48. Slightly French 49. Phantom Caravan 54. Fire One 55. A Fever in the Blood 61. Rings Around the World 66. Picture Mommy Dead 66. Suppose They Gave a War and Nobody Came 70. The Boatniks 70.

America, America (US 1964). A long and painstaking account, directed by Elia Kazan from his own autobiographical book, of the struggles of a poor Turk to emigrate to America. Splendidly photographed by Haskell Wexler, with a stalwart central performance from Stathis Giallelis; but needlessly uncommercial.

American Film Institute. Government sponsored body rather belatedly founded in 1967. Based in Washington, its comprehensive catalogue will provide full detail on every American film ever made.

American Graffiti (US 1974). Unexpectedly successful at the box office, this youth comedy-drama set in the early sixties started a profitable run of nostalgia culminating in the TV series *Happy Days*. Directed by George Lucas.

American International Pictures. Independent production company founded in the early fifties by Samuel Z. Arkoff and James H. Nicholson (both qv). After a profitable splurge of Z pictures churned out mainly by Roger Corman the company began to set its sights on the big time.

An American in Paris (US 1951). One of Hollywood's most pleasing musicals, a five-time Academy Award winner, Splendid MGM production values, sympathetic direction by Vincente Minnelli, Gershwin tunes and careful colour photography helped to give the excitement to which the performances of Gene Kelly, Oscar Levant and Nina Foch contributed. The final musical sequence remains unexcelled as a film ballet. AA best picture, best cinematography (Alfred Gilks, John Alton), best costume design, best scoring, best screenplay (Alan Jay Lerner).

American Madness (US 1932). One of the most notable early sound dramas on a social theme, in this case the American pursuit of the dollar, with Walter Huston as an honest banker driven to desperation by the corruption around him. Written by Robert Riskin and directed by Frank Capra; after its box-office failure they subsequently expressed their social comment

and popular sentimental feeling in comedy vein.

An American Tragedy. Theodore Dreiser (qv) published his downbeat novel in 1925, about an ambitious but callow youth who is forced by the social system and his own weakness into murdering his sweetheart. Josef von Sternberg's 1931 film version though not entirely to his own liking, was a more vigorous and cinematic treatment than George Stevens' portentous 1951 remake, *A Place in the Sun*. The stars of the first version were Phillips Holmes, Sylvia Sidney and Frances Dee; of the second, Montgomery Clift, Shelley Winters and Elizabeth Taylor.

Ames, Adrienne (1909–1947). American light leading lady of the thirties.
Girls About Town 31. Husband's Holiday 32. A Bedtime Story 33. You're Telling Me 34. Woman Wanted 35. City Girl 38. Panama Patrol 39, etc.

Ames, Leon (1903–) (Leon Waycoff). American character actor, a specialist in harassed or kindly fathers and suave professional men.
Films include: *Murders in the Rue Morgue* 32. Parachute Jumper 33. The Count of Monte Cristo 34. Reckless 35. Stowaway 36. Charlie Chan on Broadway 37. Mysterious Mr Moto 38. Code of the Streets 39. Ellery Queen and the Murder Ring 41. Crime Doctor 43. *Meet Me In St Louis* 44. Thirty Seconds over Tokyo 44. Son of Lassie 45. Weekend at the Waldorf 45. Yolanda and the Thief 45. Song of the Thin Man 47. A Date with Judy 48. *Little Women* 49. Battleground 49. Crisis 50. *On Moonlight Bay* 51. Let's Do It Again 53. Peyton Place 57. *From the Terrace* 60. The Absent-minded Professor 61. The Monkey's Uncle 65. On a Clear Day You Can See Forever 70. Hammersmith is Out 72, many others.
TV series: *Life With Father* 54. *Father of the Bride* 61. *Mister Ed* 63–66.

Ames, Ramsay (1924–). American leading lady of the early forties.
Ali Baba and the Forty Thieves 44. The Mummy's Tomb 44. Calling Dr Death 44. A Wave, a WAC and a Marine 44, etc.

Amfitheatrof, Daniele (1901–). Russian composer and arranger, in Hollywood from 1938.
I'll Be Seeing You 43. Letter from An Unknown Woman 48. The Lost Moment 48. Rommel, Desert Fox 51. The Naked Jungle 54. The Trial 55. Heller in Pink Tights 60. Major Dundee 65, many others.

Amis, Kingsley (1922–). British light novelist. Films of his books include Lucky Jim 57. Only Two Can Play (That Uncertain Feeling) 62. Take a Girl Like You 67.

amnesia has been a favourite theme of the movies, and the line 'Who am I?' long since became immortal. Heroes and heroines who have suffered memorably from the affliction include Ronald Colman in *Random Harvest*, John Hodiak in *Somewhere in the Night*, Greta Garbo in *As You Desire Me*, George Peppard in *The Third Day*, Cornell Borchers in *Istanbul*, Gregory Peck in *Spellbound* and *Mirage*, Phyllis Calvert in *The Woman With No Name*, Genevieve Page in *The Private Life of Sherlock Holmes*, Jennifer Jones in *Love Letters*, Laird Cregar in *Hangover Square*, William Powell in *I Love You Again* and *Crossroads*, Joan Fontaine in *The Witches* and James Garner in *Mister Buddwing*. In *While I Live* Carol Raye was the archetypal film amnesiac, emerging out of the mist complete with theme tune. In *Portrait of Jennie* Jennifer Jones played a ghost who forgot she was dead, and the same might be said of the passengers in *Outward Bound* (remade as *Between Two Worlds*) and *Thunder Rock*. The prize for audacity was won by the scriptwriters of *The Mummy's Curse*, with its dainty modern maiden who managed to forget that she was really a 3000-year-old mummy! Perhaps the cutest twist of all was suffered by Dan Duryea in *Black Angel* and Boris Karloff in *Grip of the Strangler*: having spent the film's running time tracking down a murderer, each discovered himself to be the culprit.
See *psychology*.

Amyes, Julian (1917–). British director who became a TV executive.
A Hill in Korea 56. Miracle in Soho 56, etc.

anachronisms are fun to spot, but the ones involving language are easy to defend: ancient Romans may not have used modern slang phrases such as 'nuts to you', but nor did they speak in English anyway. Rarely indeed do the studios let through such gaffes as the extra who wore a wrist watch in *The Viking Queen*, or the TV aerials in 'Victorian' London in *The Wrong Box*. Mistakes we did enjoy include the use of dynamite in *Tap Roots*, which was set in 1860 (dynamite was not invented until 1867); the British Railways signs in *Cockleshell Heroes*, set during World War II (British Railways was formed in 1954); the death of Laird Cregar by Tower Bridge in *The Lodger*, set several years before Tower Bridge was built; and the modern lounge suits sported by Colin Clive in James Whale's Frankenstein films, otherwise apparently set in nineteenth-century Europe. See: *Boo-boos*.

anamorphic lens. One which, in a camera, 'squeezes' a wide picture on to standard film; in a projector, 'unsqueezes' the image to fill wide screen; e.g. CinemaScope, Panavision, other similar processes.

Anastasia (GB 1956). An interesting Hollywood investigation into a puzzle of recent history, namely the fate of the Czar's daughter alleged to have been executed during the Russian revolution. Written by Arthur Laurents from a TV play by Marcelle Maurette, and directed by Anatole Litvak, it marked Ingrid Bergman's (AA) return to the Hollywood screen after her European 'exile'. In a somewhat less fictionalized version of the story, *Is Anna Anderson Anastasia?* (Germany 1956), Lilli Palmer played the enigmatic claimant.

Anchors Aweigh (US 1945). Musical with Gene Kelly and Frank Sinatra as sailors on leave. Remarkable only as a forerunner of *On the Town* and for Kelly's delightful dance with a cartoon mouse.

ancient Egypt has not been a popular stopping place for movie-makers. Several films based on the Bible (qv), notably *The Ten Commandments*, have stayed awhile, and there were detailed reconstructions in *The Egyptian, Land of the Pharaohs*, and *Kawalerowicz's Pharaoh*. Otherwise it has been most frequently seen in flashbacks in *The Mummy* (qv) and its sequels.

Anders, Glenn (1889–*). American stage actor who has made occasional film appearances, usually sinister.
Laughter 30. By Your Leave 35. Nothing but the Truth 41. The Lady from Shanghai 48. M 51. Behave Yourself 51, etc.

Anders, Luana (c. 1940–). American leading lady of minor movies of the sixties.
Life Begins at Seventeen 58. The Pit and the Pendulum 61. The Young Racers, 63. Dementia 13 63. B. J. Presents 71. When the Legends Die 72. Shampoo 75, etc.

Anders, Merry (c. 1932–). American light leading lady.
Les Misérables 52. Phffft 54. The Dalton Girls 57. Violent Road 58. The Hypnotic Eye 60. 20,000 Eyes 61. House of the Damned 63. Tickle Me 65. Legacy of Blood 71, etc.
TV series: *How to Marry a Millionaire* 58.

Andersen, Hans Christian (1805–1875). Danish writer of fairy tales, impersonated by Danny Kaye in Goldwyn's 1952 biopic. Many of his tales were filmed by Disney as *Silly Symphonies*, and one of them was the basis of *The Red Shoes* 48.

Anderson, Daphne (1922–1977) (Daphne Scrutton). British light actress chiefly associated with the stage.
Trottie True 49. The Beggar's Opera 52. Hobson's Choice 54. A Kid for Two Farthings 55. The Prince and the Showgirl 57. Snowball 60. Captain Clegg 62, etc.

Anderson, Eddie 'Rochester' (1905–1977). Black comedian long associated with Jack Benny on radio and TV. His gravel voice and rolling eyes were familiar in the thirties and forties, but his amiable stereotype became unpopular in a race-conscious age. As he said in a 1970 TV appearance, when invited to resume his old role of butler, 'Massah Benny, we don' do dat no mo'...'
What Price Hollywood 30. Three Men on a Horse 35. *Green Pastures* 36. Jezebel 38. *You Can't Take It With You* 38. *Gone With the Wind* 39. Topper Returns 41. Tales of Manhattan 42. The Meanest Man in the World 42. *Cabin In The Sky* (leading role) 43. Broadway Rhythm 44. The Show-Off 46. It's a Mad Mad Mad Mad World 63, many others.
TV series: *The Jack Benny Show* 53–65.

Anderson, G. M. (**'Broncho Billy'**) (1882–1971) (Max Aronson). American silent actor, an unsuccessful vaudeville performer who drifted into films in *The Great Train Robbery* 03. Later co-founded the Essanay company and made nearly four hundred one-reel Westerns starring himself. Retired in 1920; reappeared in 1967 in *The Bounty Killer*. Special Academy Award 1957 'for his contribution to the development of motion pictures'.

Anderson, Gerry (1929–). British puppeteer who via his Century 21 productions made TV series such as *Four Feather Falls, Supercar, Fireball XL5, Captain Scarlet, Joe 90, Thunderbirds*. Less successfully he moved into gimmicky live-action with *UFO* and *Space 1999*, and into feature films with *Journey to the Far Side of the Sun*.

Anderson, James (1921–1969). American general purpose supporting actor.
Sergeant York 41. The Great Sinner 49. Donovan's Brain 53. I Married a Monster from Outer Space 57. The Ballad of Cable Hogue 70, many others.

Anderson, Jean (1908–). British stage and screen actress often cast as sympathetic nurse, tired mother, or spinster aunt.
The Mark of Cain 47. Elizabeth of Ladymead 49. White Corridors 51. The Franchise Affair 51. A Town Like Alice 56. Heart of a Child 57. Robbery under Arms 57. Solomon and Sheba 59. Half a Sixpence 67. The Night Digger 71, many others.

Anderson, Dame Judith (1898–) (Frances Margaret Anderson). Distinguished Australian actress, long in US. Stage and TV proved her best outlets: her film roles were splendidly frosty but only occasionally memorable.
□ Blood Money 33. Forty Little Mothers 40. *Rebecca* (her best role, as Mrs Danvers) 40. Lady Scarface 41. All Through the Night 42. Kings Row 42. Edge of Darkness 43. *Laura* 44. And Then there Were None 45. The Diary of a Chambermaid 45. *The Spectre of the Rose* 46. The Strange Love of Martha Ivers 47. The Red House 47. Pursued 47. Tycoon 47. *The Furies* 50. Salome 53. The Ten Commandments 56. *Cat On A Hot Tin Roof* 58. Cinderfella 60. Don't Bother to Knock 61. A Man Called Horse 70.

Anderson, Lindsay (1923–). British film director and critic.
O Dreamland 53. Thursday's Children 54. Every Day Except Christmas 57. *This Sporting Life* 63. The White Bus 67. *If* 68. O Lucky Man 72. In Celebration 74, etc.

Anderson, Mary (1920–). American supporting actress.
Gone With The Wind 39. Cheers for Miss Bishop 41. Lifeboat 43. *The Song of Bernadette* 44. Wilson 44. To Each His Own 46. Underworld Story 50. I The Jury 53. Dangerous Crossing 53, etc.

Anderson, Max (1914–1959). British documentary director, with the GPO Film Unit from 1936, later Crown Film Unit. Best known for *The Harvest Shall Come* 41. *Daybreak in Udi* 48.

Anderson, Maxwell (1888–1959). American middlebrow playwright, many of whose plays were filmed.
What Price Glory 27 & 52 *All Quiet on the Western Front* (orig sp) 30. Mary of Scotland 36. Winterset 37. Elizabeth and Essex (Elizabeth the Queen) 39. Key Largo 48. Joan of Arc (Joan of Lorraine) 48. The Wrong Man (orig sp) 56. The Bad Seed 56.

Anderson, Michael (1920–). British director who graduated to the international scene.
□ Waterfront 50. Hell Is Sold Out 51. Night Was Our Friend 52. Will Any Gentleman? 53. House of the Arrow 54. *The Dam Busters* 55. *1984* 55. *Around the World in Eighty Days* 56. Yangtse Incident 56. Chase a Crooked Shadow 57. Shake Hands with the Devil 59. The Wreck of the Mary Deare 59. All the Fine Young Cannibals 60. The Naked Edge 61. Flight from Ashiya 62. Wild and Wonderful 63. Operation Crossbow 65. *The Quiller Memorandum* 66. *The Shoes of the Fisherman* 68. Pope Joan 72. Doc Savage 75. Conduct Unbecoming 75. Logan's Run 76.

Anderson, Michael Jnr (1943–). British juvenile lead, former child actor, son of director Michael Anderson.
The Moonraker 57. The Sundowners 60. In Search of the Castaways 61. Play it Cool 62. The Greatest Story Ever Told 65. Major Dundee 65. The Sons of Katie Elder 65. The Glory Guys 65. WUSA 69. The Last Movie 71, etc.
TV series: The Monroes 66.

Anderson, Richard (1926–). Thoughtful-looking American supporting actor.
Twelve O'Clock High 50. The People Against O'Hara 51. The Story of Three Loves. 53. Escape from Fort Bravo 54. Forbidden Planet 56. *Paths of Glory* 57. *The Long Hot Summer* 58. Compulson 59. Seven Days in May 64. *Seconds* 66. Macho Callahan 70. Doctors' Wives 71. The Honkers 72, etc.
TV series: Six Million Dollar Man 73– , Bionic Woman 76– .

Anderson, Rona (1926–). Scottish actress whose film career has been desultory.
Sleeping Car to Trieste 48. Poets' Pub 49. Home to Danger 51. Black Thirteen 54. The Flaw 55. Stock Car 55. Man with a Gun 58. Devils of Darkness 65. *The Prime of Miss Jean Brodie* 69, etc.

Anderson, Warner (1911–1976). American stage and screen actor: many solid supporting performances.
Destination Tokyo 44. Bad Bascomb 46. Command Decision 48. Destination Moon 50. The Caine Mutiny 54. Drum Beat 54. The Blackboard Jungle 55. Armored Command 61. Rio Conchos 64, etc.
TV series: The Doctor 52. The Line-Up 54–55. Peyton Place 64–69.

Andersson, Bibi (1935–). Swedish actress who has ventured into international films.
Smiles of a Summer Night 55. *The Seventh Seal* 56. *Wild Strawberries* 57. The Face 58. So Close to Life 60. The Devil's Eye 61. Square of Violence 63. Now About These Women 64. My Sister My Love 66. Duel at Diablo 66. A Question of Rape. 67. The Story of a Woman 69. *The Kremlin Letter* 69. A Passion 70. The Touch 71, etc.

Andersson, Harriet (1932–). Swedish actress, a member of Ingmar Bergman's company.
Summer with Monika 52. Sawdust and Tinsel 53. A Lesson in Love 54. Smiles of a Summer Night 55. Through a Glass Darkly 62. To Love 64. Now About These Women 64. The Deadly Affair (GB) 66. Cries and Whispers 72, etc.

Andes, Keith (1920–). American light actor, usually in secondary roles.
The Farmer's Daughter 47. Clash by Night 52. Blackbeard the Pirate 52. Back from Eternity 56. The Girl Most Likely 58. Tora! Tora! Tora! 70, etc. TV series: Glynis 63.

Andress, Ursula (1936–). Swiss-born glamour star, in international films.
The Loves of Casanova (It.) 54. *Dr No* 62. Four for Texas 63. Fun in Acapulco 64. *She* 64. Nightmare in the Sun 64. *What's New Pussycat?* 65. Up to his Ears 65. The Tenth Victim 65. Once Before I Die 66. The Blue Max 66. Casino Royale 67. The Southern Star 69. Perfect Friday 70. Red Sun 71. Five Against Capricorn 72, etc.

Andrews, Anthony (1948–). British leading actor who graduated through TV.
QB VII (TV) 74. A War of Children (TV) 74. Take Me High 74. Percy's Progress 75. Operation Daybreak 76.

Andrews, Dana (1909–) (Carver Daniel Andrews). American leading man who showed promise in a wide variety of forties roles, but whose somewhat hard and immobile features limited him in middle age.
□ The Westerner 40. Lucky Cisco Kid 40. Sailor's Lady 40. Kit Carson 40. Tobacco Road 41. Belle Starr 41. Swamp Water 41. Ball of Fire 41. Berlin Correspondent 42. Crash Dive 43. The Ox Bow Incident 43. North Star 43. The Purple Heart 44. Wing and a Prayer 44. Up in Arms 44. *Laura* 44. State Fair 45. Fallen Angel 45. *A Walk in the Sun* 45. Canyon Passage 46. *The Best Years of Our Lives* 46. *Boomerang* 47. Night Song 47. Daisy Kenyon 47. The Iron Curtain 48. Deep Waters 48. No Minor Vices 48. Britannia Mews 48. Sword in the Desert 49. *My Foolish Heart* 50. Where the Sidewalk Ends 50. Edge of Doom 50. The Frogmen 50. Sealed

Cargo 51. I Want You 51. Assignment Paris 52. Elephant Walk 53. Duel in the Jungle 54. Three Hours to Kill 54. Smoke Signal 55. Strange Lady in Town 55. Comanche 56. While the City Sleeps 56. Beyond a Reasonable Doubt 56. Night of the Demon 57. Spring Reunion 57. Zero Hour 57. The Fearmakers 58. Enchanted Island 58. The Crowded Sky 60. Madison Avenue 62. Crack in the World 65. The Satan Bug 65. In Harms Way 65. Brainstorm 65. Town Tamer 65. The Loved One 65. Battle of the Bulge 65. Johnny Reno 66. Spy in your Eye 66. Hot Rods to Hell 67. The Frozen Dead 67. Cobra 67. Ten Million-Dollar Grab 68. Innocent Bystanders 72. Airport 75 75. TV series: Bright Promise (daily soap opera) 71.

Andrews, Edward (1915–). Beaming, bespectacled American character actor who can effortlessly become hearty, hen-pecked or sinister.
The Phenix City Story 56. The Unguarded Moment 56. The Tattered Dress 57. *Tea and Sympathy* 57. The Fiend Who Walked the West 58. *Elmer Gantry* (as Babbitt) 60. Advise and Consent 61. Kisses for My President 64. *Youngblood Hawke* 64. Send Me No Flowers 64. *The Glass Bottom Boat* 66. Birds Do It 66. Tora! Tora! Tora! 60. Avanti 72. Charley and the Angel 72, etc.

Andrews, Harry (1911–). Tough-looking British stage and screen actor. Often plays sergeant-majors or other no-nonsense characters.
The Red Beret (debut) 52. *A Hill in Korea* 56. Alexander the Great 56. Moby Dick 56. Saint Joan 57. *Ice Cold in Alex* 58. The Devil's Disciple 59. Solomon and Sheba 59. Circle of Deception 60. The Best of Enemies 62. Lisa 62. 55 Days at Peking 62. The Informers 63. The System 64. *The Hill* 65. Sands of the Kalahari 65. Modesty Blaise 66. *The Deadly Affair* 66. The Jokers 67. Danger Route 67. The Charge of the Light Brigade 68. The Night They Raided Minsky's (US) 68. The Seagull 68. A Nice Girl Like Me 69. The Battle of Britain 69. Country Dance 70. Entertaining Mr Sloane 70. Wuthering Heights 70. Burke and Hare 71. Nicholas and Alexandra 71. I Want What I Want 71. The Ruling Class 72. Man of La Mancha 72. Theatre of Blood 73. The Mackintosh Man 74. Man at the Top 74. The Bluebird 76, etc.

Andrews, Julie (1934–) (Julia Wells). British star of Hollywood films. A singing stage performer from childhood who became the original stage Eliza of *My Fair Lady* but failed to get the film role. She zoomed to international

stardom the same year but her refreshingly old-fashioned image seemed to pall rather quickly.
☐ *Mary Poppins* (AA) 64. *The Americanization of Emily* 64. *The Sound of Music* 65. Torn Curtain 66. Hawaii 66. *Thoroughly Modern Millie* 67. Star! 68. Darling Lili 69. The Tamarind Seed 74.

Andrews, Lois (1924–1968). American light leading lady.
Dixie Dugan 43. Roger Touhy Gangster 44. The Desert Hawk 50. Meet Me After the Show 51, etc.

Andrews, Tige (c. 1923–) (Tiger Androwaous). Lebanese-American supporting actor, usually an amiable tough.
Mr Roberts 55. The Wings of Eagles 57. Imitation General 58. China Doll 58. A Private Affair 59, etc.
TV series: *The Detectives, The Mod Squad.*

The Andrews Sisters: Patty (1918–), Maxine (1916–) and Laverne (1913–67). American close harmony singing group, popular in light musicals of the forties.
☐ Argentine Nights 40. In The Navy 41. Buck Privates 41. Hold That Ghost 41. Give Out Sisters 42. Private Buckaroo 42. What's Cookin'? 42. Always a Bridesmaid 43. How's About It? 43. Follow the Boys 44. Hollywood Canteen 44. Moonlight and Cactus 44. Swingtime Johnny 44. Her Lucky Night 45. Make Mine Music (voices) 46. Road to Rio 47. Melody Time (voices) 48.

Andriot, Lucien (1897–). French-American cinematographer long in Hollywood.
Two Lives 15. Oh Boy 19. Why Trust Your Husband 21. Hell's Hole 23. Gigolo 26. White Gold 27. The Valiant 28. Hallelujah I'm a Bum 33. Anne of Green Gables 34. The Gay Desperado 36. The Lady in Question 40. The Hairy Ape 44. The Southerner 45. And Then There Were None 45. Dishonoured Lady 47, many others; recently working in TV.

Angel, Danny (Daniel M.) (1911–). British producer, in films from 1945.
Mr Drake's Duck 50. Albert R.N. 53. The Sea Shall Not Have Them 54. Reach for the Sky 56. Carve Her Name With Pride 57. The Sheriff of Fractured Jaw 58. West Eleven 63, etc.

Angel, Heather (1909–). British-born leading lady of the thirties; in Hollywood from 1933.
City of Song 30. Berkeley Square 33. The Informer 35. The Mystery of Edwin Drood 35.

Last of the Mohicans 36. Army Girl 38. Pride and Prejudice 40. Time to Kill 42. Lifeboat 43. In the Meantime, Darling 44. The Saxon Charm 48. The Premature Burial 62, etc.

Angeli, Pier (1932–1971) (Anna Maria Pierangeli). Sensitive-looking Italian actress who after some stage and film experience at home moved to Hollywood but found only occasional worthy roles.
Teresa 51. The Devil Makes Three 52. The Flame and the Flesh 53. The Silver Chalice 55. Port Afrique 56. Somebody Up There Likes Me 57. The Vintage 57. Merry Andrew 58. *The Angry Silence* 59. Sodom and Gomorrah 62. Battle of the Bulge 65. Adio! Alexandra 69. One Foot in Hell 70, etc.

angels made appearances in many silent films: *Intolerance, The Four Horsemen of the Apocalypse, The Sorrows of Satan,* and the many versions of *Uncle Tom's Cabin* and *Faust* were among them. Since sound they have remained a favourite Hollywood device, but have naturally tended to lose their wings and become more whimsical, less awesome and often of somewhat ambiguous reality, to be explained away in the last reel as a result of the hero's bump on the head. The last completely serious angels were probably those in the all-Negro *Green Pastures* 37; since then they have been played by Claude Rains in *Here Comes Mr Jordan,* Jeanette MacDonald in *I Married an Angel,* Kenneth Spencer (and others) in *Cabin in the Sky,* Jack Benny (and others) in *The Horn Blows at Midnight,* Clifton Webb and Edmund Gwenn in *For Heaven's Sake,* Henry Travers in *It's a Wonderful Life,* Leon Ames in *Yolanda and the Thief,* Kathleen Byron and a great many extras in *A Matter of Life and Death,* Robert Cummings in *Heaven Only Knows,* Cary Grant in *The Bishop's Wife,* several actors in *Angels in the Outfield,* James Mason in *Forever Darling,* Diane Cilento in *The Angel Who Pawned Her Harp,* John Philip Law in *Barbarella,* and Harry Belafonte in *The Angel Levine.*
Used in a figurative sense, the word 'angel' has continued to be a favourite title component: I'm No Angel, Angel, The Dark Angel, Angels with Dirty Faces, Angels Wash Their Faces, Angel and the Badman, Angel Face, Angel Baby, Angels in Disguise, The Angel Wore Red, Angels One Five, Angels in Exile, etc.
See also: *fantasy.*

Angels with Dirty Faces (US 1938). A typical example of the period when Hollywood's gangster melodramas had to point a moral: the character played by James Cagney pretended to be a coward on his way to the electric chair so that he would not become an object of hero-worship for the Dead End Kids. As so often, Pat O'Brien was an Irish priest. Despite good direction by Michael Curtiz, there was precious little fun to be had from this type of social melodrama; the genre quickly declined and the Dead End Kids turned into comedians (in a so-called sequel, The Angels Wash Their Faces).

Angelus, Muriel (1909–) (M. A. Findlay). British leading lady of the thirties who had a brief Hollywood career before retiring in 1940.
The Ringer 30. Hindle Wakes 31. The Light that Failed 39. The Great McGinty 40. The Way of All Flesh 40, etc.

Anger, Kenneth (1929–). American independent film-maker who grew up in Hollywood and also wrote *Hollywood Babylon,* a scurrilous exposé of the private lives of its stars. His films are mainly short, inscrutable and Freudian.
Fireworks 47. Eaux d'Artifice 53. Inauguration of the Pleasure Dome 54. Scorpio Rising 64. Kustom Kar Kommandos 65. Invocation of my Demon Brother 69, etc.

Angers, Avril (1922–). British character comedienne whose film appearances have been infrequent.
Skimpy in the Navy 50. Lucky Mascot 51. The Green Man 56. Devils of Darkness 65. The Family Way 66. Two a Penny 68, etc.

Anhalt, Edward (1914–). American middlebrow scriptwriter. With his wife Edna Anhalt (1914–).
Bulldog Drummond Strikes Back 48. Panic in the Streets 50. The Sniper 52. Not as a Stranger 54. The Pride and the Passion 56. The Young Lions 58, etc.
Alone: A Girl Named Tamiko 63. Becket 64. Hour of the Gun 67. The Boston Strangler 68. The Mad Woman of Chaillot 69. Jeremiah Johnson (co-w) 72, etc.

Animal Farm (GB 1954). Britain's first full-length cartoon, a major achievement of the Halas and Batchelor Studios, but on the whole too conventionally animated to bring out the full satiric flavour of George Orwell's fable.

animals, as Walt Disney knew, are a sure way to success at the box office, with dogs well established as number one providers. Dog stars of the movies have included Rin Tin Tin, Strongheart (his closest rival), Ben (Mack Sennett's comedy dog), Pete (of 'Our Gang'),

Asta (of the 'Thin Man' series), Daisy (so popular in the 'Blondie' films that he starred in his own movies), and of course the immortal Lassie. Less publicized canines have successfully taken on dramatic roles in such films as *The Voice of Bugle Ann, Oliver Twist, Umberto D, Greyfriars Bobby, Owd Bob, Old Yeller, Savage Sam, The Ugly Dachshund* and *The Spy with a Cold Nose*; while Dick Powell was reincarnated as a very handsome Alsatian in *You Never Can Tell*. Rhubarb has been the only 'starred' cat, though felines have played important roles in *The Cat and the Canary, The Cat Creeps, Cat Girl, Shadow of the Cat, Breakfast at Tiffany's, The Incredible Journey, A Walk on the Wild Side, The Three Lives of Thomasina, That Darn Cat, The Torture Garden* (with its diabolical pussy), *The Wrong Box, The Goldwyn Follies* (in which the Ritz Brothers were memorably assisted by hundreds of cats to sing 'Hey Pussy Pussy'), *The Bluebird* (in which a sleek black feline was humanized very satisfyingly into Gale Sondergaard), *The Tomb of Ligeia, Eye of the Cat*, and several versions of *The Black Cat*. Other animals to achieve something like stardom have included Balthasar the donkey, Flipper the dolphin, Gentle Ben the bear, Cheta the chimp (in the Tarzan films), Slicker the seal (in *Spawn of the North*), the chimp in *The Barefoot Executive*, Clarence the Cross-eyed Lion (not to mention Fluffy), the *Zebra in the Kitchen*, and a great many horses including Rex (*King of the Wild Horses*), Tarzan (with Ken Maynard), Fritz (with William S. Hart), Tony (with Tom Mix), Silver (with Buck Jones), Champion (with Gene Autry) and Trigger (with Roy Rogers). *Born Free* and its sequels made stars of lions; *Ring of Bright Water* did the same for an otter, and *Benji* for a little dog. *Doctor Dolittle* starred a host of animals from pigs to giraffes; but perhaps one shouldn't count the anthropoids in *Planet of the Apes*.

animation. The filming of static drawings, puppets or other objects in sequence so that they give an illusion of movement. Sometimes called 'stop-frame animation' because only one frame of film is exposed at a time.

Leading figures in the history of animation include Winsor McKay (qv) who in 1909 introduced Gertie the Dinosaur, Emile Cohl (qv), Len Lye (qv), Max Fleischer (qv), Walt Disney, the UPA Group (qv), Norman McLaren (qv), William Hanna and Joe Barbera (qv), Halas and Batchelor (qv) and Ralph Bakshi (qv).

Best books on the subject are *The Technique of Film Animation* by John Halas and Roger Manvell; *The Art of Walt Disney* by Christopher Finch; *The Animated Film* by Ralph Stephenson.

Anka, Paul (1941–). American pop singer, subject of the documentary *Lonely* 62. Acted in *The Longest Day* 62 and composed the theme song.

Ankers, Evelyn (1918–). British leading lady who did not so much act as react. She also looked decorative, and after going to Hollywood in 1940 she appeared as the well-bred heroine of innumerable co-features. Married Richard Denning.
The Villiers Diamond 33. Rembrandt 36. Knight without Armour 37. Over the Moon 39. Hold that Ghost 41. Bachelor Daddy 41. *The Wolf Man* 41. The Ghost of Frankenstein 42. The Great Impersonation 42. The Mad Ghoul 43. Hers to Hold 43. His Butler's Sister 43. Ladies Courageous 44. Weird Woman 44. The Frozen Ghost 45. The French Key 46. The Lone Wolf In London 47. The Texan Meets Calamity Jane 50. No Greater Love 60, etc.

Ankrum, Morris (1896–1964). American stage actor seen in innumerable films as lawyer, judge or Western villain.
Light of the Western Stars 40. Tales of Manhattan 42. The Harvey Girls 45. Joan of Arc 48. Rocketship XM 50. My Favourite Spy 51. Son of Ali Baba 52. Apache 54. Earth Versus the Flying Saucers 56. Badman's Country 59. The Most Dangerous Man Alive 61, many others.

Anna and the King of Siam. Anna Leonowens' autobiography of her experiences as governess at an eastern court seemed in 1946 a strange choice for a Hollywood film, especially when Rex Harrison was cast as the King and Linda Darnell as his leading mistress. But Irene Dunne kept the strange mixture palatable, and John Cromwell's direction was smooth. The plot was immediately adapted by Rodgers and Hammerstein as a musical, filmed with great success in 1956 as *The King and I*. Walter Lang directed Deborah Kerr and Yul Brynner in the leading roles. In 1972 Brynner reprised in a TV series, *Anna and the King*.

Annabella (1909–) (Suzanne Charpentier). French leading lady of the thirties, in international films; once married to Tyrone Power.
Napoleon 26. Le Million 32. Le Quatorze Juillet 33. Under the Red Robe 36. Dinner at the Ritz 37. Wings of the Morning 37. Suez 38. Hôtel du Nord 38. Bridal Suite 39. Bomber's Moon 42. Tonight We Raid Calais 43. 13 Rue Madeleine 46. Don Juan (sp) 50, etc.

Anna Christie (US 1930). Early talkie version of Eugene O'Neill's waterfront play, advertised by the famous slogan, 'Garbo Talks!' Previously filmed in 1923 with Blanche Sweet.

Anna Karenina. Tolstoy's novel has been filmed many times, twice with Garbo (as *Love* in 1927, and again in 1935). The latter version, directed by Clarence Brown with Basil Rathbone as Karenin, was not eclipsed by Alexander Korda's 1948 British remake with Vivien Leigh and Ralph Richardson, though Julien Duvivier's direction achieved some pretty effects.

Annakin, Ken (1914–). British director of very variable output. Formerly a journalist.
□ Holiday Camp 46. Here Come the Huggetts 47. Miranda 48. Quartet (part) 48. Vote for Huggett 49. Trio (part) 50. The Huggetts Abroad 51. Hotel Sahara 51. Robin Hood 52. The Planter's Wife 52. The Seekers 53. The Sword and the Rose 53. Value for Money 55. Three Men in a Boat 56. Loser Take All 56. Across the Bridge 57. Nor the Moon by Night 59. *The Swiss Family Robinson* 60. Third Man on the Mountain 61. *Very Important Person* 61. The Longest Day 62. The Hellions 62. *The Fast Lady* 63. *Those Magnificent Men in Their Flying Machines* 64. Battle of the Bulge 65. The Biggest Bundle of them All 66. The Long Duel 67, Monte Carlo or Bust 69. Call of the Wild 72. White Fang 74. Paper Tiger 75.

Anna Lucasta. Philip Yordan's melodramatic play was originally (1944) set among Negroes, but on Broadway they became Polish immigrants, and it was this version which was first screened, in 1949, with Paulette Goddard as the bad girl of the family who comes back to help in a domestic crisis. In 1959 the Negro version was finally filmed with Eartha Kitt and Sammy Davis Jnr. Yordan wrote both screenplays.

Anne of Green Gables. L. M. Montgomery's popular novel for girls about an orphan teenager who comes to live with crusty relations and finally charms them into her way of thinking, was a great screen success for Mary Miles Minter in 1919. In 1934 Anne Shirley appeared in a sound remake, and followed it up in 1941 with a sequel, *Anne of Windy Poplars*.

Annis, Francesca (1944–). British leading lady, former juvenile player.
The Cat Gang 58. Cleopatra 62. The Eyes of Annie Jones 63. Flipper and the Pirates (US) 64. The Pleasure Girls 65. Run with the Wind 66. The Walking Stick 69. Macbeth 71, etc.

Ann-Margret (1941–) (Ann Margaret Olson). Swedish-American sex symbol and formidable cabaret performer; a hard worker who gradually became a good actress.
□ Pocketful of Miracles 61. State Fair 62. *Bye Bye Birdie* 62. Viva Las Vegas 64. Kitten with a Whip 64. Bus Riley's Back in Town 65. The Pleasure Seekers 65. Once a Thief 65. *The Cincinnati Kid* 65. Made in Paris 66. The Swinger 66. Stagecoach 66. Murderers' Row 66. The Tiger and the Pussycat 67. Mr Kinky 68. C.C. and Co. 70. *Carnal Knowledge* 71. R.P.M. 71. The Train Robbers 73. The Outside Man 73. Tommy 75.

Anouilh, Jean (1910–). Skilful and versatile French playwright who has frequently worked in the cinema.
Monsieur Vincent 47. Caroline Chérie 50. A Night with Caroline 52. Le Chevalier de la Nuit 53. The Waltz of the Toreadors 62. Becket 64, etc.

A Nous La Liberté (France 1931). A classic satirical comedy written and directed by René Clair, set in a factory and demonstrating the increasing mechanization of life. Photography by Georges Perinal, design by Lazare Meerson, music by Georges Auric; featuring Raymond Cordy and Henri Marchand. Chaplin's *Modern Times*, five years later, borrowed several of its ideas.

Ansara, Michael (1922–). American actor with stage experience, specializing in Indian roles.
Action in Arabia 44. Only the Valiant 51. The Robe 53. Sign of the Pagan 54. Diane 55. The Lone Ranger 58. The Comancheros 62. And Now Miguel 66. Guns of the Magnificent Seven 69. Stand Up and be Counted 72. The Bears and I 74, etc.
TV series: Broken Arrow 56–8. Law of the Plainsman 59.

Anscocolor. American process derived from Agfacolor (qv).

Anspach, Susan (1939–). American stage actress in occasional films.
□ The Landlord 70. Five Easy Pieces 70. Play It Again Sam 72. Blume in Love 72. Nashville 75.

Anstey, Edgar (1907–). British documentary producer (Housing Problems 35. Enough to Eat 36, etc.) who has for many years been chief films officer for British Transport.

Anstey, F. (1856–1934) (Thomas Anstey

Guthrie). British humorous novelist.
Works filmed: *Vice Versa* 48. The Brass Bottle
64.

Answer Print. The first complete combined
print supplied by the laboratory, usually with no
very careful attempt to grade colour or contrast.

Antheil, George (1900–1959). American
composer.
The Plainsman 37. The Buccaneer 38. Angels
over Broadway 40. Specter of the Rose 46.
Knock on any Door 49. The Fighting
Kentuckian 49. In a Lonely Place 50. The Sniper
51. Actors and Sin 52. The Juggler 53. Not as a
Stranger 55. The Pride and the Passion 57, etc.

Anthony, Joseph (1912–) (J. A. Deuster).
American director from stage and TV; former
small part actor and dancer.
The Rainmaker 56. The Matchmaker 58. Career
59. All in a Night's Work 61. The Captive City
63, etc.

Anthony, Tony (1937–). American leading
man having some success in tough Italian
Westerns.
A Stranger in Town 67. The Stranger Returns
68. Samurai on a Horse 69. Blindman 71, etc.

anti-Semitism was understandably not a
popular subject with film-makers when the
function of movies was simply to entertain.
Amiable comic Jews were permitted, in *Abie's
Irish Rose, Potash and Perlmutter*, and the
Cohen and Kelly series; and it was readily
acknowledged that Jewry provided a flow of star
talent without which show business could not
continue. But thoughtful movies on the Jewish
plight were almost non-existent, unless one
counts such epics as *The Wandering Jew* 33 and
Jew Süss 34. Occasionally came a cry from
Europe, as in *Professor Mamlock* 36, but it was
not really until *The Great Dictator* 40 that the
film-going public was made aware of what was
happening to the Jews in Germany. For
propaganda purposes the Nazis put out a
number of anti-Semitic films such as *Ohm
Krüger* and another version of *Jew Süss*; the
only real reply during World War II was a gentle
British movie called *Mr Emmanuel*. In
Tomorrow the World 44, from the play about an
ex-Nazi youth in America, the subject was
touched on; but not till the reconstruction days
of 1947 could a spade really be called a spade. In
a taut murder thriller called *Crossfire*, the victim
was changed from a homosexual to a Jew; then
came *Gentleman's Agreement*, in which a gentile
reporter posed as a Jew to expose anti-Semitism

in America. Perhaps this interest was stimulated
by the immense popularity of *The Jolson Story*,
with its sympathetic portrait of a Jewish home;
but the confusion in American minds is
demonstrated by the fact that David Lean's
Oliver Twist was banned in 1948 because of Alex
Guinness' 'caricature' of Fagin! During the last
decade or so there seems to have been sporadic
interest in the subject. The birth of Israel
generated such movies as *Sword in the Desert*,
Exodus, Judith and *Cast a Long Shadow*, and
Christopher Isherwood's Berlin stories of the
early thirties became first a play and film called *I
Am a Camera* and later a musical and film called
Cabaret. Poignant recollections of World War II
by a girl who died in Auschwitz produced a
book, play and film called *The Diary of Anne
Frank*, and a little British film called *Reach for
Glory*, which took a swipe at the consequences of
intolerance. In 1971 the world's most successful
stage musical, *Fiddler on the Roof*, was filmed;
dealing with the Russian pogroms, the story has
been filmed many times before in Yiddish,
usually under the title 'Tevye the Milkman'.

Antonioni, Michelangelo (1912–). Italian
director whose reputation was boosted in the
fifties by the ardent support of highbrow film
magazines. Co-scripts all his own films, which
largely jettison narrative in favour of vague
incident and relentless character study.
Cronaca di un Amore 50. Le Amiche 55. Il
Grido 57. L'Avventura 59. La Notte 60.
L'Eclisse 62. The Red Desert 64. Blow-Up (GB)
67. Zabriskie Point (US) 69, etc.

Antony, Scott (1950–). British leading
juvenile of the early seventies.
Baxter 72. Savage Messiah 73. Dead Cert 73.
The Mutations 74.

The Apartment (US 1960) (AA/BFA). A
typically mordant comedy from director Billy
Wilder, scripted by himself and I. A. L.
Diamond. This one lifts the lid off New York
office life, only to discover something not far
removed from a Capra soft centre. Jack
Lemmon finds some sympathy in the part of a
clerk who advances his status by letting out his
apartment to house the amorous affairs of his
bosses.

Applause (US 1929). One of the most
professionally fluent of early talkies, with
director Rouben Mamoulian trying, and usually
bringing off, every cinematic trick in the book as
well as some of his own. On its own level the
story works too: a hokey but powerful
melodrama of mother love against the tawdry

background of burlesque. Written by Garrett Fort from a novel by Beth Brown; photographed by George Folsey. With Helen Morgan, Joan Peers, Henry Wadsworth.

Apted, Michael (1941–). British director, from TV.

□ Triple Echo 72. Stardust 74. The Squeeze 77.

The Arabian Nights. This collection of ancient eastern tales, more properly called *The Arabian Nights' Entertainment*, was first collected around 1450, but Sir Richard Burton's unexpurgated Victorian translation is the one generally used. The tales, presented as told by the heroine Scheherazade, have been plundered innumerable times by film-makers. See the entries under *The Thief of Baghdad* and *Ali Baba*; note also films based on Aladdin, Sinbad the Sailor and various genies in bottles.

Arbeid, Ben (1924–). British producer.
The Barber of Stamford Hill 62. *Private Potter* 63. Children of the Damned 64. Murder Most Foul 65. The Jokers 67. Assignment K 68. The Hireling 71, etc.

Arbuckle, Roscoe 'Fatty' (1887–1933). Grown-up fat boy of American silent cinema whose career was ruined after his involvement in a 1921 scandal in which a girl died. Though he never again appeared before the camera, he directed a few films under the name William Goodrich. The few of his two-reel slapstick comedies which survive are still funny.
The Round-up 20. A Travelling Salesman 21. Gasoline Gus 21. Brewsters Millions 21, etc.

arc. A high-powered lamp used in projectors and studio lighting, its illumination consisting of an electrical discharge between two carbon rods.

Archainbaud, George (1890–1959). American director, mainly of routine westerns.
Single Wives 24. Men of Steel 26. College Coquette 29. The Lost Squadron 32. The Return of Sophie Lang 36. Her Jungle Love 38. Thanks for the Memory 38. Untamed 40. The Kansan 43. Woman of the Town 44. King of the Wild Horses 47. Hunt the Man Down 51, many others.

Archard, Bernard (1922–). Lean, incisive British actor with repertory experience; became famous on TV as *Spy-catcher*.
Village of the Damned 60. The List of Adrian Messenger 63. Face of a Stranger 66. Song of Norway 70. The Horror of Frankenstein 70, etc.

Archer, John (1915–) (Ralph Bowman). American leading man of routine second features.
Flaming Frontier 38. Gangs Inc. 41. Crash Dive 43. The Last Moment 47. White Heat 49. Destination Moon 50. A Yank in Indo-China 52. Rodeo 53. The Stars Are Singing 53. No Man's Woman 55. Emergency Hospital 59. Blue Hawaii 62. Apache Rifles 64, etc.

archive. A vault, usually government-sponsored, containing a selection of films to be preserved for research and for posterity.

Arden, Eve (1912–) (Eunice Quedens). American comedy actress, a tall cool lady who spent a generation as the wisecracking friend of the heroine. Originally a Ziegfeld girl.
Song of Love 29. Dancing Lady 33. Oh Doctor 37. *Stage Door* 37. Having Wonderful Time 38. At the Circus 39. Comrade X 40. Ziegfeld Girl 41. That Uncertain Feeling 41. Whistling in the Dark 41. Let's Face It 43. *Cover Girl* 44. *The Doughgirls* 44. *Mildred Pierce* 45. Night and Day 46. The Unfaithful 47. *The Voice of the Turtle* 47. The Lady Takes a Sailor 49. *Paid in Full* 50. Curtain Call at Cactus Creek 50. *Tea Two* 50. *Three Husbands* 50. *We're Not Married* 52. The Lady Wants Mink 53. Our Miss Brooks 56. *Anatomy of a Murder* 59. *The Dark at the Top of the Stairs* 60. Sergeant Deadhead 65. A Very Missing Person (TV) 71. All My Darling Daughters (TV) 72, etc.
TV series: *Our Miss Brooks* 52–55. The Eve Arden Show 59. *The Mothers in Law* 67–68.

Arden, Robert (1921–). Anglo-American actor resident in Britain; former vocalist.
Two Thousand Women 44. No Orchids for Miss Blandish 48. *Confidential Report* 56, etc.
TV series: *Saber of London* 60.

Argentina has been making films since the turn of the century, many having claim to sophistication, but the only one to receive world distribution and acclaim were those of Leopoldo Torre Nilsson (qv) in the fifties.

Argento, Dario (1943–). Italian thriller director.
The Bird with Crystal Plumage 70. One Night at Dinner 70. Cat O'Nine Tails 71. Four Flies in Grey Velvet 71, etc.

Arise My Love (US 1940). This amiable mock-heroic romantic comedy-drama is notable as Hollywood's most prompt response to the outbreak of World War II in Europe. Claudette Colbert and Ray Milland make an agreeable team as a newspaperwoman and an aviator involved in world events from the Spanish Civil War to the sinking of the *Athenia*, and Billy Wilder's slightly cynical script ends with an implicit command for America to wake up. In the circumstances, Mitchell Leisen's direction is perhaps just a little too impeccable. AA best original story: Benjamin Glazer, John Toldy.

Arkin, Alan (1934–). American leading character actor, from Broadway.
☐ *The Russians are Coming* 66. Woman Times Seven 67. *Wait Until Dark* 67. Inspector Clouseau 68. *The Heart is a Lonely Hunter* 68. Popi 69. The Monitors 69. *Catch 22* 70. *Little Murders* (& d) 71. *Last of the Red Hot Lovers* 72. Freebie and the Bean 74. Rafferty and the Gold Dust Twins 75. Hearts of the West 75.

Arkoff, Samuel Z. (1918–). American executive producer, co-founder with James H. Nicholson of American International Pictures.

Arlen, Harold (1905–). American song composer ('Happiness Is Just a Thing Called Joe', 'That Old Black Magic', 'Blues in the Night', 'Stormy Weather', 'Accentuate the Positive', many others).
Film scores include: Strike Me Pink 36. Love Affair 39. The Wizard of Oz (AA for 'Over the Rainbow') 39. Cabin in the Sky 43. A Star Is Born 54. I Could Go On Singing 63, etc.

Arlen, Richard (1898–1976) (Cornelius van Mattemore). Rugged American leading man who rose from extra to star in the twenties, became the durable hero of scores of 'B' pictures, and later played bits.
In the Name of Love 25. Rolled Stockings 27. *Wings* 27. *The Four Feathers* 28. Thunderbolt 29. *The Virginian* 29. The Sea God 30. Touchdown 31. College Humor 33. Three Cornered Moon 33. She Made Her Bed 34. Heldorado 35. Secret Valley 36. Murder in Greenwich Village 37. Call of the Yukon 38. Mutiny on the Blackhawk 39. Legion of Lost Flyers 39. Hot Steel 40. Men of the Timberland 41. Torpedo Boat 42. Alaska Highway 43. Minesweeper 43. The Lady and the Monster 44. Storm over Lisbon 44. The Phantom Speaks 45. Accomplice 46. Speed to Spare 48. Grand Canyon 49. Kansas Raiders 50. Flaming Feather 52. Sabre Jet 53. Devil's Harbour 54. The Mountain 56. Raymie 60. Cavalry Command 63. Law of the Lawless 64. The Human Duplicators 65. Apache Uprising 66. Red Tomahawk 67. Buckskin 68, many others.

Arletty (1898–) (Leonie Bathiat). Celebrated French actress of stage and screen adept at the portrayal of world-weary, sophisticated women.
Un Chien Qui Rapporte 31. La Guerre des Valses 33. Aloha 37. *Hôtel du Nord* 38. *Le Jour Se Lève* 39. Les Visiteurs du Soir 42. *Les Enfants du Paradis* 44. L'Amour Madame 52. L'Air de Paris 54. Huis Clos 54. Les Petits Matins (Girl on the Road) 61. La Gamberge 62, etc.

Arling, Arthur E. (1906–). American cinematographer.
Gone with the Wind (co-ph) 39. The Yearling (AA) 46. The Homestretch 47. You're My Everything 49. Wabash Avenue 50. Red Garters 54. I'll Cry Tomorrow 55. Pay the Devil 57. The Story of Ruth 60. Notorious Landlady 62. My Six Loves 63. Straitjacket 63. The Secret Invasion 64, many others.

Arliss, George (1868–1946) (George Augustus Andrews). Distinguished British stage actor of the old school who in middle age was persuaded to face the cameras and unexpectedly became a star both in Britain and America, presenting a gallery of kings, statesmen, rajahs, eccentric millionaires and rather unconvincing hoboes.
Autobiographies, *On The Stage* 26. *Up the Years from Bloomsbury* 27. *My Ten Years in the Studios* 40.
☐ The Devil 21. *Disraeli* 21. *The Green Goddess* 23. The Ruling Passion 23. *Disraeli* (sound) 29. *The Green Goddess* (sound) 30. Old English 30. Millionaire 31. Alexander Hamilton 31. The Man Who Played God 32. Successful Calamity 32. The King's Vacation 33. The Working Man 33. Voltaire 33. The House of Rothschild 34. The Tunnel 34. The Last Gentleman 34. Cardinal Richelieu 35. The Iron Duke 35. The Guvnor 35. East Meets West 36. Man of Affairs 37. Dr Syn 37.

Arliss, Leslie (1901–). British writer who worked on Orders Is Orders 32. Jack Ahoy 34. Rhodes of Africa 36. Pastor Hall 39. The Foreman Went to France 42. Then turned director and made some of the popular Gainsborough costume melodramas of the forties.
The Night Has Eyes 42. The Man in Grey 43. Love Story 44. The Wicked Lady 45. A Man about the House 47. Idol of Paris 48. The Woman's Angle 52. Miss Tulip Stays the Night 55. See How They Run 55, etc; recently directing TV films.

Armendariz, Pedro (1912–1963). Massive Mexican actor with expansive personality;

became a star in his own country, then moved on to Hollywood and Europe.
Rosario 36. Isle of Passion 41. *Maria Candelaria* 43. The Pearl 46. The Fugitive 47. Maclovia 48. Fort Apache 48. Three Godfathers 48. Tulsa 48. We Were Strangers 49. The Torch 50. *El Bruto* 52. Lucretia Borgia 52. Border River 54. The Conqueror 56. Manuela 57. The Wonderful Country 59. Francis of Assisi 61. Captain Sinbad 63. *From Russia with Love* 63, etc.

Armetta, Henry (1888–1945). Italian-born character actor, long in US, where he was on stage before going to Hollywood. Typecast as excitable, gesticulating foreigner.
My Cousin 18. The Silent Command 23. Street Angel 28. Romance 30. Strangers May Kiss 31. The Unholy Garden 31. Prosperity 32. What! No Beer? 33. The Man Who Reclaimed His Head 34. After Office Hours 35. Poor Little Rich Girl 36. Make a Wish 37. Everybody Sing 38. Dust be my Destiny 39. *The Big Store* 41. Anchors Aweigh 45. Colonel Effingham's Raid 46, many others.

Arms and the Man. Bernard Shaw's military comedy has only once been filmed straight: this was in 1931 (GB) with Barry Jones as Bluntschli. The stage musical comedy *The Chocolate Soldier* was based on it, but when this was filmed in 1941 Shaw's libretto was abandoned. *The Guardsman*, made in 1932 with Alfred Lunt and Lynn Fontanne, bears some resemblance to it.

Armstrong, Louis (1900–1971). Gravel-voiced black American jazz trumpeter and singer, affectionately known as 'Satchmo' (satchel mouth). Sporadic screen appearances, chiefly in guest spots.
□ Pennies from Heaven 36. Dr Rhythm 38. Artists and Models 38. Going Places 39. *The Birth of the Blues* 41. Cabin in the Sky 43. Jam Session 44. Atlantic City 44. *New Orleans* 47. The Strip 51. *Here Comes The Groom* 51. Glory Alley 51. *The Glenn Miller Story* 54. *High Society* 56. *Satchmo The Great* 57. The Beat Generation 59. *The Five Pennies* 59. *Paris Blues* 61. *Jazz On A Summer's Day* 61. A Man Called Adam 66. Hello Dolly 69.

Armstrong, R. G. (c. 1920–). Tough, serious-looking American supporting actor.
Never Love a Stranger 58. *Ride The High Country* 62. Major Dundee 66. El Dorado 66. The Great White Hope 71, etc.

Armstrong, Robert (1890–1973) (Donald Robert Smith). Tough American character actor

often seen as cop, sheriff, trail boss or shady investigator.
The Main Event 27. Big Money 30. The Tip-Off 31. The Most Dangerous Game 32. *King Kong* (his best role, as foolhardy film producer Carl Denham) 33. Son of Kong 33. G-Men 35. Mystery Man 37. Sky Raiders 41. Outside the Law 41. Dive Bomber 41. The Mad Ghoul 43. Gangs of the Waterfront 45. *Mighty Joe Young* (a continuation of his Kong role) 49. Las Vegas Shakedown 55. For Those Who Think Young 63, many others.

Armstrong, Todd (1939–). Stalwart American leading man of the sixties.
Walk on the Wild Side 62. Jason and the Argonauts 63. King Rat 65. A Time for Killing 68, etc.

army comedies have always been popular, and most well-known comedians have had at least one to their credit. Laurel and Hardy were in *Pack Up Your Troubles* and *Blockheads and Great Guns*; Abbott and Costello in *Buck Privates*; Wheeler and Wolsey in *Half Shot at Sunrise*; Buster Keaton in *The Dough Boys*; Charlie Chaplin in *Shoulder Arms*; Harry Langdon in *A Soldier's Plaything*; Larry Semon in *Spuds*; George Jessel in *Private Izzy Murray*; Joe E. Brown in *Sons of Guns*; Jimmy Durante and Phil Silvers in *You're in the Army Now*; The Ritz Brothers in *We're in the Army Now*; Norman Wisdom in *The Square Peg*; Jerry Lewis in *The Sad Sack*; Martin and Lewis in *At War With The Army*; Bob Hope in *Caught In The Draft*; Frank Randle in *Somewhere In England*; Arthur Lucan in *Old Mother Riley Joins Up*; George K. Arthur and Karl Dane in *Rookies*; Wallace Beery and Raymond Hatton in *Behind The Front*; Alan Carney and Wally Brown in *Adventures Of A Rookie* and *Rookies In Burma*; Joe Sawyer and William Tracy in several comedies including *Tanks a Million, About Face* and *Fall In*; Tom Wilson and Heimie Conklin in *Ham And Eggs At The Front*; George Sidney and Charlie Murray in *Lost At The Front*.
Other American successes in the genre include: *What Did You Do In The War, Daddy?*; *Two Arabian Knights*; *What Price Glory?* ; *The Cockeyed World*; *Top Sergeant Mulligan*; *The Teahouse of The August Moon*; *The Wackiest Ship In the Army*; *Operation Mad Ball*, and above all *M*A*S*H*. Britain has provided *Carry On Sergeant*; *Private's Progress*; *On The Fiddle*; *I Only Arsked*; *Idol On Parade* and *Reluctant Heroes*.
Outstanding TV series: Britain's *The Army Game* and Hollywood's *Bilko* series with Phil

Silvers; *Hogan's Heroes*; *McHale's Navy*; *Gomer Pyle U.S.M.C.*; *M*A*S*H*.

Arnall, Julia (1931–). Austrian-born actress resident in Britain.
Man of the Moment 54. I Am a Camera 55. Lost 56. House of Secrets 56. Man without a Body 57. Mark of the Phoenix 59. The Quiller Memorandum 66. The Double Man 67, etc.

Arnatt, John (1917–). Solid, pipe-smoking British character actor, mostly on TV.
Only Two Can Play 62. Dr Crippen 63. Licensed to Kill 66. The Breaking of Bumbo 70. Crucible of Terror 71, many others.

Arnaud, Yvonne (1892–1958). French actress and pianist, long popular on the British stage.
On Approval 31. A Cuckoo in the Nest 33. The Improper Duchess 36. Stormy Weather 36. Neutral Port 40. Tomorrow We Live 42. Woman to Woman 46. The Ghosts of Berkeley Square 47.

Arnaz, Desi (1915–) (Desiderio Alberto Arnaz y de Acha). Diminutive but explosive Cuban who began his career as a singer and later formed his own Latin-American band. Performed in minor film musicals during forties, then married Lucille Ball, founded Desilu Studios, and appeared in the long-running TV series *I Love Lucy* 50–61. Later films include *The Long Long Trailer* 54. *Forever Darling* 56. Inactive as performer since their divorce but produced TV series *The Mothers-in-Law* 67–69.

Arnaz, Desi Jnr (1951–). American juvenile lead of the early seventies, son of Desi Arnaz and Lucille Ball. Had years of training on his mother's TV series.
Red Sky at Morning 71. Marco 73. Billy Two Hats 74. She Lives (TV) 74, etc.

Arne, Peter (1922–). Unsmiling Anglo-American actor in British films, usually as dastardly villain.
Time Slip 55. The Purple Plain 55. *The Moonraker* 57. Ice Cold in Alex 57. *Danger Within* 58. *The Hellfire Club* 61. The Black Torment 64. Khartoum 66. Battle Beneath the Earth 68. Murders in the Rue Morgue 71. Straw Dogs 71. Antony and Cleopatra 72, etc.

Arness, James (1923–) (James Aurness). Giant (6' 6") American actor who drifted into films from advertising. Played minor parts including the title role in *The Thing* 52; then routine leads in such films as *Them* 54, *The First Travelling Saleslady* 56. Created role of Marshal

Dillon in long-running TV series *Gunsmoke* 55–73, which he later produced and owned.
TV 1976: The MacAhans (How the West was Won).

Arnheim, Rudolf (c. 1900–). German-American critic whose published wriitings include *Film as Art* 32. and *Art and Visual Perception* 58.

Arno, Sig (1895–1975) (Siegfried Aron). German comedy actor in US from early thirties; latterly typecast as funny foreigner.
Manon Lescaut 26. Pandora's Box 28. The Loves of Jeanne Ney 28. Diary of a Lost Girl 29. The Star Maker 38. The Great Dictator 40. The Palm Beach Story 42. Up In Arms 44. The Great Lover 48. On Moonlight Bay 51. The Great Diamond Robbery 53, many others

Arnold, Edward (1890–1956) (Guenther Schneider). Rotund but dynamic American actor who played go-getter leading roles in the thirties. Although he later became typed as kindly father/apoplectic business man, he never lost his popularity.
Autobiography 1940: *Lorenzo Goes To Hollywood*.
☐ When the Man Speaks 16. The Wrong Way 17. Rasputin and the Empress 32. Okay, America 32. Afraid to Talk 32. Whistling in the Dark 33. The White Sister 33. The Barbarian 33. Jennie Gerhardt 33. Her Bodyguard 33. The Secret of the Blue Room 33. *I'm No Angel* 33. *Roman Scandals* 33. Madame Spy 34. Sadie McKee 34. Thirty Day Princess 34. Unknown Blonde 34. Hideout 34. Million Dollar Ransom 34. The President Vanishes 34. Wednesday's Child 34. Biography of a Bachelor Girl 35. Cardinal Richelieu 35. *The Glass Key* 35. *Diamond Jim* 35. *Crime and Punishment* 35. Remember Last Night? 35. Sutter's Gold 36. *Meet Nero Wolfe* 36. *Come and Get It* 36. John Meade's Woman 37. *The Toast of New York* 37. Easy Living 37. Blossoms on Broadway 37. The Crowd Roars 38. *You Can't Take It With You* 38. Let Freedom Ring 39. Idiot's Delight 39. Man About Town 39. *Mr Smith Goes To Washington* 39. Slightly Honourable 40. The Earl of Chicago 40. Johnny Apollo 40. Lillian Russell 40. The Penalty 41. The Lady from Cheyenne 41. Meet John Doe 41. Nothing But the Truth 41. Unholy Partners 41. Design for Scandal 41. Johnny Eager 41. *All That Money Can Buy* (as Daniel Webster) 41. The War Against Mrs Hadley 42. *Eyes in The Night* 42. The Youngest Profession 42. Standing Room Only 44. Janie 44. *Kismet* 44. Mrs Parkington 44. Main Street After Dark 44. Weekend at the

Waldorf 45. The Hidden Eye 45. Ziegfeld Follies 46. Janie Gets Married 46. *Three Wise Fools* 46. No Leave No Love 46. The Mighty McGurk 46. My Brother Talks to Horses 46. *Dear Ruth* 47. *The Hucksters* 47. Three Daring Daughters 48. Big City 48. Wallflower 48. Command Decision 48. John Loves Mary 49. Take Me Out to the Ball Game 49. Big Jack 49. Dear Wife 49. The Yellow Cab Man 50. Annie Get Your Gun 50. The Skipper Surprised His Wife 50. Dear Brat 51. Belles on Their Toes 52. City That Never Sleeps 53. Man of Conflict 53. Living it Up 54. The Houston Story 56. The Ambassador's Daughter 56. Miami Exposé 56.

Arnold, Jack (1916–). American director.
It Came from Outer Space 53. The Glass Web 53. Girls in the Night 53. The Creature from the Black Lagoon 54. Tarantula 55. Red Sundown 56. The Tattered Dress 57. *The Incredible Shrinking Man* 57. Pay the Devil 57. The Lady Takes a Flyer 58. High School Confidential 58. The Mouse That Roared (GB) 59. No Name on the Bullet 59. Bachelor in Paradise 61. A Global Affair 63. Hello Down There 68. Black Eye 73, etc.

Arnold, Malcolm (1921–). British composer.
The Sound Barrier 52. Island in the Sun 56. The Bridge on the River Kwai (AA) 57. Inn of the Sixth Happiness 58. Tunes of Glory 60. The Chalk Garden 64. The Heroes of Telemark 65. The Reckoning 68, etc.

Arnoul, Françoise (1931–) (Françoise Gautsch). Sultry French leading lady of sex melodramas in the fifties.
Quai de Grenelle 50. Forbidden Fruit 52. Companions of the Night 53. La Rage au Corps 53. The Sheep Has Five Legs 54. French Can-Can 55. The Face of the Cat 57. The Devil and the Ten Commandments 61. Le Dimanche de la Vie 66, etc.

Arnt, Charles (1908–). American character actor often seen as snoop, suspicious character, or just plain ordinary fellow.
Ladies Should Listen 34. The Witness Chair 36. Remember the Night 40. Blossoms in the Dust 41. Twin Beds 42. Up in Arms 44. Cinderella Jones 46. *Dangerous Intruder* 46. That Brennan Girl 47. Wabash Avenue 50. Veils of Baghdad Miracle of the Hills 59. Sweet Bird of Youth 62, many others.

Around the World in Eighty Days. Jules Verne's globe-trotting Victorian lark was first filmed by Richard Oswald in Germany in 1919. In 1956 Michael Todd made it the subject of the first of the giant-screen extravaganzas in 70mm, and the impact of location photography, much expense, and 44 stars in cameo roles was enough to gain it the year's best picture Academy Award, despite its many glaring faults. Michael Anderson directed rather uncertainly from a screenplay by S. J. Perelman, James Poe and John Farrow; David Niven as the imperturbable Phileas Fogg led the revels, with Robert Newton as Inspector Fix.

Arsenal (USSR 1929). A notable propaganda piece, written and directed by Dovzhenko, contrasting trench warfare in 1918 with a worker's revolt at home.

Arsène Lupin. The gallant French jewel thief and part-time detective, created at the beginning of the century by Maurice Leblanc, has been the subject of many films, the first being a Vitagraph 1917 version starring Earle Williams. In 1932 the Barrymore brothers were in *Arsène Lupin*, John taking the title role; in 1938 Melvyn Douglas was in *Arsène Lupin Returns*; Charles Korvin took over in 1944 for *Enter Arsène Lupin*; in 1957 there was Robert Lamoureux in *The Adventures of Arsène Lupin*; and in 1962 Jean-Claude Brialy starred in *Arsène Lupin Contre Arsène Lupin.*

Arsenic and Old Lace (US 1944). Joseph Kesselring's black farce about two dotty old ladies who poison lonely gentlemen for their own good, and proceed to have them buried in the cellar, had been a great Broadway success, presumably because it suited audiences in the war years to make fun of death. In Hollywood, however, such an attitude was a tricky innovation, and Frank Capra got it past the Hays Office by directing it at breakneck speed, with Cary Grant as the astonished nephew registering nineteen double takes to the minute. Josephine Hull and Jean Adair were the aunts, John Alexander was mad Uncle Teddy, Peter Lorre was Dr Einstein, and Raymond Massey (because Boris Karloff was regrettably unavailable) took over the gruesome Jonathan.

Artaud, Antonin (1896–1948). French drama critic and writer who dabbled in films.
Napoleon (a) 26. The Passion of Joan of Arc (a) 28. *The Seashell and the Clergyman* (w) 28.

art director. Technician responsible for designing sets, sometimes also costumes and graphics. 'Production designer' is a more pretentious way of saying much the same thing. The importance of this work to the finished product first became noticeable in *Intolerance* and the German expressionist films of the twenties, then in such diverse talking films as *The Old Dark House, Things to Come, The Cat and the Canary* (both versions), *Citizen Kane, Trouble in Paradise, The Mystery of the Wax Museum, A Matter of Life and Death, Les Enfants du Paradis,* and *Kings Row.* Important figures (all qv) include William Cameron Menzies, Anton Grot, Cedric Gibbons, Ken Adam, Vincent Korda, Hans Dreier, Alfred Junge, Carmen Dillon.

art house. American term (now displacing 'specialized hall' in GB) for cinema showing classic revivals and highbrow or off-beat new films of limited commercial appeal.

Arthur. The legendary British king of the 5th or 6th century, central figure of the courtly love tradition and alleged creator not only of the democratic Round Table but of the idyllic city and palace of Camelot, has figured in several movies, especially in recent years when we seem to have had need to cherish our legends. There have been three sound versions, to begin with, of *A Connecticut Yankee at King Arthur's Court* (qv); in the 1949 version Cedric Hardwicke played the King as having a perpetual cold. In 1942, Arthur Askey dreamed he was a member of the Round Table in *King Arthur Was a Gentleman.* In 1964 Disney presented in cartoon form the childhood of Arthur in *The Sword in the Stone.* In slightly more serious vein, Mel Ferrer was Arthur in *Knights of the Round Table* 54, with Robert Taylor as Lancelot and Ava Gardner as Guinevere. Anthony Bushell had the role in *The Black Knight* 54 and Mark Dignam took over in *Siege of the Saxons* 64. In the 1963 *Lancelot and Guinevere,* the three roles were taken respectively by Brian Aherne, Cornel Wilde and Jean Wallace; in the 1967 musical *Camelot* (qv), by Richard Harris, Franco Nero, and Vanessa Redgrave.

TV series on the subject have included *Sir Lancelot,* an Australian cartoon series called *Arthur!,* and a Welsh serial called *Arthur of the Britons.*

Arthur, Beatrice (1924–). Dominant American comedy actress, a big TV hit 1972–76 as *Maude.*
That Kind of Woman 58. Lovers and Other Strangers 69. *Mame* 63, etc.

Arthur, George K. (1899–) (G. K. A. Brest). Small but gamy hero of the British silent screen, popular in such films as *Kipps* 21. *A Dear Fool* 22. Went to Hollywood and was popular for a while.

Madness of Youth 23. Lights of Old Broadway 25. The Salvation Hunters 25. Irene 26. The Boy Friend 26. Rookies (first of a series of comedies with Karl Dane) 27. Baby Mine 28. The Last of Mrs Cheyney 29. Chasing Rainbows 30. Oliver Twist 33. Riptide 34. Vanessa (last to date) 35. Became a financier and distributor of art shorts.

Arthur, Jean (1905–) (Gladys Greene). Petite, squeaky-voiced American leading actress who after a long and dreary apprenticeship was especially notable as the determined feminist heroine of social comedies in the thirties and forties.
□ Cameo Kirby 23. The Temple of Venus 24. Fast and Fearless 24. Seven Chances 25. The Drug Store Cowboy 25. A Man of Nerve 25. Tearing Loose 25. Thundering Through 26. Born to Battle 26. The Hurricane Horseman 26. The Fighting Cheat 26. The Cowboy Cop 26. Twisted Triggers 26. The College Boob 26. The Block Signal 26. Husband Hunters 27. The Broken Gate 27. Horseshoes 27. The Poor Nut 27. Flying Luck 27. The Masked Menace 27. Wallflowers 28. Easy Come Easy Go 28. Warming Up 28. Brotherly Love 28. Sins of the Fathers 29. The Canary Murder Case 29. Stairs of Sand 29. The Mysterious Dr Fu Manchu 29. *The Greene Murder Case* 29. *The Saturday Night Kid* 29. Halfway to Heaven 29. Street of Chance 30. Young Eagles 30. Paramount on Parade 30. The Return of Dr Fu Manchu 30. Danger Lights 30. The Silver Horde 30. The Gang Buster 31. Virtuous Husband 31. The Lawyer's Secret 31. Ex-Bad Boy 31. Get That Venus 33. The Past of Mary Holmes 33. Whirlpool 34. The Defense Rests 34. The Most Precious Thing in Life 34. *The Whole Town's Talking* 35. Public Hero Number One 35. Party Wire 35. *Diamond Jim* 35. The Public Menace 35. *If You Could Only Cook* 35. *Mr Deeds Goes to Town* 36. The Ex Mrs Bradford 36. Adventure in Manhattan 36. *The Plainsman* (as Calamity Jane) 36. More Than a Secretary 36. *History is Made at Night* 37. *Easy Living* 37. *You Can't Take It With You* 38. Only Angels have Wings 39. *Mr Smith Goes to Washington* 39. Too Many Husbands 40. Arizona 40. *The Devil and Miss Jones* 41. *The Talk of the Town* 42. *The More the Merrier* 43. A Lady Takes a Chance 43. The Impatient Years 44. *A Foreign Affair* 48. *Shane* 53.
TV series: *The Jean Arthur Show* 66.

Arthur, Robert (1909–) (R. A. Feder). American producer, mainly with Universal.
Buck Privates Come Home 46. Abbott and Costello Meet Frankenstein 48. The Big Heat 53. Man of a Thousand Faces 57. The Great

Impostor 60. Lover Come Back 60. That Touch of Mink 62. Father Goose 64. Shenandoah 65. Blindfold 66. Hellfighters 68. Sweet Charity 69. One More Train to Rob 73, many others.

Arthur, Robert (1925–) (Robert Arthaud). American actor, former radio announcer, in general supporting roles since 1945.
Roughly Speaking 45. Twelve O'Clock High 49. Ace in the Hole 51. Young Bess 54. Top of the World 55. Hellcats 57. Young and Wild 58, others.

Arundell, Denis (1898–). British character actor (radio's Dr Morelle). Sporadic film roles include: The Show Goes On 35. The Return of Carol Deane 38. Pimpernel Smith 41. Colonel Blimp 43. Carnival 46. The History of Mr Polly 49. Something Money Can't Buy 52.

Arzner, Dorothy (1900–). A former editor who became Hollywood's only woman director of the thirties.
□ The Wild Party 29. Sarah and Son 30. Paramount on Parade (part) 30. Anybody's Woman 30. Honour Among Lovers 31. Working Girls 31. *Merrily We Go to Hell* 32. Christopher Strong 33. *Nana* 34. *Craig's Wife* 36. The Bride Wore Red 37. *Dance Girl Dance* 40. First Comes Courage 43.

A.S.C. Often seen on credit titles after the names of cinematographers, these initials stand for the American Society of Cinematographers, a professional association, membership of which is by invitation only. Its aims since its foundation in 1918 have been 'to advance the art and science of cinematography'.

Ashby, Hal (1936–). American director, former editor.
□ The Landlord 70. Harold and Maude 71. *The Last Detail* 73.

Ashcroft, Dame Peggy (1907–). Distinguished British stage actress who has appeared in films only occasionally.
The Wandering Jew 33. *The Thirty-nine Steps* 35. Rhodes of Africa 36. *Quiet Wedding* 40. The Nun's Story 58. Secret Ceremony 68. Sunday Bloody Sunday 71. Joseph Andrews 77, etc.

Asher, Jack (1916–). British cinematographer, brother of director Robert Asher.
Jassy 47. Lili Marlene 42. The Good Die Young 53. The Young Lovers 54. Reach for the Sky 56. Dracula 58. She'll Have to Go (& co-p) 61. The Intelligence Men 65. The Early Bird 65. That

Riviera Touch 66, many others.

Asher, Jane (1946–). British leading lady, former child performer in films from 1951.
Mandy 52, The Greengage Summer 60. The Girl in the Headlines 63. The Masque of the Red Death 64. Alfie 66. *Deep End* 71. Henry VIII and his Six Wives 72, etc.

Asher, Robert (c. 1917–). British director.
Follow a Star 59. Make Mine Mink 60. She'll Have to Go (co-p, co-w, co-d) 61. On The Beat 62. The Intelligence Men 65.

Asher, William (1919–). American 'B' director.
□ Leather Gloves (co-d) 48. The Shadow on the Window 57. The Twenty-Seventh Day 57. *Beach Party* 63. Johnny Cool 63. Muscle Beach Party 64. Bikini Beach 64. Beach Blanket Bingo 65. How to Stuff a Wild Bikini 65. Fireball 500 66.

Asherson, Renée (1920–). British stage actress in occasional films.
Henry V 44. The Way Ahead 44. The Way to the Stars 44. The Small Back Room 49. The Cure for Love 50. The Day the Earth Caught Fire 62. Rasputin the Mad Monk 65. The Smashing Bird I Used to Know 68, etc.

Ashley, Edward (1904–) (E. A. Cooper). British leading man who went to Hollywood but never did better than third leads.
Men of Steel 33. Underneath the Arches 37. Spies of the Air 39. *Pride and Prejudice* 40. Bitter Sweet 41. The Black Swan 42. Nocturne 46. The Other Love 47. Tarzan and the Mermaids 48. Macao 52. The Court Jester (as the Fox) 56. Herbie Rides Again 73. Won Ton Ton 76, etc.

Ashley, Elizabeth (1939–) (Elizabeth Cole). Cool American leading lady who makes sporadic appearances.
□ *The Carpetbaggers* 64. Ship of Fools 65. The Third Day 65. Marriage of a Young Stockbroker 71. When Michael Calls (TV) 71. The Face of Fear (TV) 71. Second Chance (TV) 71. Paperback Hero 73. One of My Wives is Missing (TV) 74. Golden Needles 74, etc.

Askey, Arthur (1900–). Diminutive (5′ 2″) British comedian with music-hall experience; gained fame as 'Big Hearted Arthur' in radio shows.
Band Wagon 38. Charley's Big-Hearted Aunt 40. *The Ghost Train* 41. Miss London Ltd 42. Back Room Boy 42. King Arthur Was a

Gentleman 42. Bees in Paradise 44. The Love Match 54. Make Mine a Million 58. Friends and Neighbours 59, etc.

Askin, Leon (c. 1920–). Rotund American supporting actor who often plays sinister or comic Russians.
Road to Bali 52. Knock on Wood 54. Son of Sinbad 55. My Gun Is Quick 58. One Two Three 61. Do Not Disturb 65. The Maltese Bippy 69. Dr Death 73, many others.

Askwith, Robin (1950–). British leading man of seventies low comedy.
If 68. Bartleby 70. Nicholas and Alexandra 71. The Four Dimensions of Greta 71. Bless this House 73. Confessions of a Window Cleaner 74. Confessions of a Pop Performer 75. Confessions of a Driving Instructor 76, etc.

Aslan, Grégoire (1908–) (Kridor Aslanian). Franco-Turkish character actor, usually in comic or villainous roles.
Sleeping Car to Trieste 48. Occupe-Toi D'Amélie 49. Last Holiday 50. Cage of Gold 50. Confidential Report 53. He Who Must Die 56. Roots of Heaven 56. The Criminal 60. Cleopatra 62. Paris When It Sizzles 64. The High Bright Sun 65. Moment to Moment 65. Our Man in Marrakesh 66. Lost Command 66. A Flea in Her Ear 68. You Can't Win Them All 70. Sinbad's Golden Voyage 73, many others.

Asner, Edward (c. 1925–). Chubby American character actor who usually plays tough guys, sometimes with a heart of gold.
The Satan Bug 65. The Slender Thread 65. El Dorado 66. The Venetian Affair 67. Gunn 67. The Todd Killings 70. The Skin Game 71. Rich Man Poor Man (TV) 76. Hey I'm Alive (TV) 76, etc.
TV series: *The Mary Tyler Moore Show* 70–72.

aspect ratio. Relative breadth and height of screen. Before 1953 this was 4:3 or 1.33:1. 'Standard' wide screen varies from 1.66:1 to 1.85:1. Anamorphic processes are wider: SuperScope 2:1, CinemaScope and most others 2.35:1 (or 2.55:1 with magnetic stereophonic sound). Vista-Vision, a printing process, was shot in 1.33:1 but recommended for screening at up to 2:1, i.e. with top and bottom cut off and the rest magnified. The TV screen is fixed at 1.33:1, therefore all wide-screen films lose something when played on it.

The Asphalt Jungle (US 1950). W. R. Burnett's crime novel about a robbery that failed was nimbly if coldly directed by John Huston: it

started the long cycle of 'caper' films which included *Rififi* and *The League of Gentlemen*, and was notable for the performances of Sam Jaffe and Louis Calhern as well as for Harold Rosson's photography. It has been remade three times: as *The Badlanders* (in western guise) in 1958, as *Cairo* in 1963, and, with a black cast, as *Cool Breeze* in 1972. It also formed the basis of a short-lived TV series.

Asquith, Anthony (1902–1968). British director, son of Lord Oxford and Asquith, nicknamed 'Puffin'. His films were always civilized and usually entertaining but both the early experiments in technique and the later upper-class comedies and dramas suffered from the same lack of warmth and humanity.
□ *Shooting Stars* (co-d) 28. *Underground* 30. A Cottage on Dartmoor 30. The Runaway Princess 30. Tell England 31. Dance Pretty Lady 31. Lucky Number 33. Unfinished Symphony 34. Moscow Nights 35. *Pygmalion* (co-d) 37. *French Without Tears* 39. Freedom Radio 40. *Quiet Wedding* 40. Cottage to Let 41. Uncensored 42. We Dive at Dawn 43. *The Demi-Paradise* 43. Welcome to Britain (doc) 43. Two Fathers 44. *Fanny by Gaslight* 44. *The Way to the Stars* 45. While the Sun Shines 46. *The Winslow Boy* 48. The Woman in Question 50. *The Browning Version* 50. *The Importance of Being Earnest* 51. The Net 53. The Final Test 53. The Young Lovers 54. Carrington VC 55. On Such a Night (doc) 56. *Orders to Kill* 58. The Doctors' Dilemma 59. Libel 60. The Millionairess 61. Guns of Darkness 62. Two Living One Dead 62. *The VIPS* 63. The Yellow Rolls Royce 64.

assassination has not been a favourite film subject, though historical incidents have been examined in *Julius Caesar, Sarajevo, Nicholas and Alexandra, Nine Hours to Rama* and *The Parallax View*. Assassination attempts have figured in *Suddenly, The Man Who Knew Too Much, Foreign Correspondent, The Manchurian Candidate* and *The Day of the Jackal*.

assistant director. More properly 'assistant to the director', being concerned with details of administration rather than creation.

Associated British is the only British complex of companies which has power comparable to that of the Rank Organization (qv). Its history is tied up with Elstree Studios, originally owned by British International Pictures, which after many mergers emerged as Associated British in 1933. The men involved in the story are producer Herbert Wilcox, John Maxwell, a lawyer who turned film distributor and later founded the ABC cinema chain, and J. D. Williams, a wealthy exhibitor. Distribution was arranged through Pathé Pictures, which became a powerful partner. Elstree was the first British studio to wire for sound (*Blackmail*) and the first to produce a bilingual talkie (*Atlantic*). Throughout the thirties it turned out fifteen films a year, usually unambitious but competent; and unmistakably British. In 1940 a great number of shares were sold to Warner Brothers, and in 1956 the distribution arm became known as Warner-Pathé. Other associated companies include Pathé News, Pathé Laboratories, Pathé Equipment, and ABC Television. In 1969, after several years of comparative inactivity, the complex was taken over by E.M.I.

associate producer. Usually the actual producer or supervisor of the film, the title of 'executive producer' having been taken by the head of the studio.

Association of Cinematograph, Television and Allied Technicians. ACTT: the film-makers' union. Founded 1931.

Asta. A wire-haired fox-terrier who appeared (impersonated by several dogs) in *The Thin Man* and other films between 1934 and 1947.

Astaire, Fred (1899–) (Frederick Austerlitz). American dancing star whose inimitable finesse and good humour delighted two generations. His half-spoken singing was almost equally delightful, and the films in which he was teamed with Ginger Rogers (*) have a magic all their own. Autobiography 1959: *Steps in Time*. Academy Award 1949 'for his unique artistry and his unique contribution to the techniques of motion pictures'. This contrasts amusingly with the studio report on his first screen test: 'Can't act. Can't sing. Can dance a little.'
□ Dancing Lady 33. *Flying Down to Rio 33. The Gay Divorcee 34. *Roberta 35. *Top Hat 35. *Follow the Fleet 36. *Swing Time 36. *Shall We Dance? 37. A Damsel in Distress 37. *Carefree 38. *The Story of Vernon and Irene Castle 39. Broadway Melody 40. Second Chorus 40. You'll Never Get Rich 41. Holiday Inn 42. You Were Never Lovelier 42. The Sky's the Limit 43. Yolanda and the Thief 45. Ziegfeld Follies 46. Blue Skies 46. Easter Parade 48. *The Barkleys of Broadway 48. Three Little Words 50. Let's Dance 50. Royal Wedding 51. The Belle of New York 52. The Band Wagon 53. Deep in my Heart 54. Daddy Long Legs 55. Funny Face 57. Silk Stockings 57. On the Beach (dramatic role) 59. The Pleasure of His*

Company (dr) 61. Notorious Landlady (dr) 62. *Finian's Rainbow* 68. The Midas Run (dr) 69. The Over The Hill Gang Rides Again (dr: TV film) 71. The Towering Inferno (dr) 75. The Amazing Dobermans (dr) 76.
TV series: It Takes a Thief 69–70.

Asther, Nils (1897–). Suave, exotic Swedish leading man in Hollywood from the mid-twenties.
□ *Topsy and Eva* 27. *Sorrell and Son* 27. The Blue Danube 28. Laugh Clown Laugh 28. The Cossacks 28. Loves of an Actress 28. The Cardboard Lover 28. *Our Dancing Daughters* 28. Dream of Love 28. Wild Orchids 29. *The Single Standard* 29. The Wrath of the Seas 29. Letty Lynton 32. The Washington Masquerade 32. *The Bitter Tea of General Yen* 32. Storm at Daybreak 33. The Right to Romance 33. *By Candlelight* 34. Madame Spy 34. The Crime Doctor 34. The Love Captive 34. *Abdul the Damned* (GB) 35. Make Up (GB) 37. Dr Kildare's Wedding Day 41. The Night Before the Divorce 41. The Night of January 16th 41. Sweater Girl 42. Night Monster 42. The Hour Before Dawn 44. *The Man in Half Moon Street* 44. Son of Lassie 45. Jealousy 45. That Man from Tangier 53.

Astin, John (1930–). American comic actor with stage experience.
West Side Story 61. That Touch of Mink 62. Candy 68. Viva Max 68. Evil Roy Slade (TV) 72. Get To Know Your Rabbit 72. The Brothers O'Toole 73.
TV series: I'm Dickens He's Fenster 63. The Addams Family 64.

Astor, Mary (1906–) (Lucille Langehanke). American leading lady who despite a stormy and well-publicized private life remained a star from the mid-twenties to the mid-forties and remained in demand for character roles.
Autobiography: *My Story*. 1959: *A Life on Film*. 1971
Silent films include *The Beggar Maid* 21. The Bright Shawl 23. Puritan Passions 23. *Beau Brummell* 24. Inez from Hollywood 25. *Don Q Son of Zorro* 25. *Don Juan* 26. Rose of the Golden West 27. Two Arabian Knights 27. Heart to Heart 28. Romance of the Underworld 29.
□ Sound: Ladies Love Brutes 30. The Runaway Bride 30. Holiday 30. The Lash 30. The Sin Ship 30. The Royal Bed 30. Other Men's Women 31. Behind Office Doors 31. White Shoulders 31. Smart Woman 31. Men of Chance 31. The Lost Squadron 32. A Successful Calamity 32. Those We Love 32. *Red Dust* 32. The Little Giant 33.

Jennie Gerhardt 33. The Kennel Murder Case 33. Convention City 33. The World Changes 33. Easy to Love 34. The Man with Two Faces 34. Return of the Terror 34. Upper World 34. The Case of the Howling Dog 34. I am a Thief 34. Man of Iron 35. Red Hot Tires 35. Straight from the Heart 35. Dinky 35. Page Miss Glory 35. The Murder of Dr Harrigan 35. The Lady from Nowhere 36. And So They Were Married 36. *Dodsworth* 36. Trapped by Television 36. *The Prisoner of Zenda* 37. *The Hurricane* 37. Paradise for Three 38. No Time to Marry 38. There's Always a Woman 38. Woman against Woman 38. Listen Darling 39. *Midnight* 39. *Turnabout* 40. Brigham Young 40. *The Great Lie* (AA) (her most splendid bitchy performance) 41. *The Maltese Falcon* 41. *Across the Pacific* 42. *The Palm Beach Story* 42. Young Ideas 43. Thousands Cheer 43. *Meet Me in St Louis* 44. Blonde Fever 44. Claudia and David 46. Desert Fury 47. Cynthia 47. Fiesta 47. *Act of Violence* 49. Cass Timberlane 49. *Little Women* (as Marmee) 49. Any Number Can Play 49. A Kiss Before Dying 56. The Power and the Prize 56. The Devil's Hairpin 56. This Happy Feeling 58. Stranger in my Arms 59. *Return to Peyton Place* 61. *Youngblood Hawke* 64. Hush Hush Sweet Charlotte 64.

Astruc, Alexandre (1923–). French director, former film critic.
The Crimson Curtain 51. Les Mauvaises Rencontres 54. Une Vie 56. La Proie Pour l'Ombre 61. L'Education Sentimentale 61. La Longue Marche 65.

L' Atalante (France 1934). A strange, dreamlike, influential film by Jean Vigo about a honeymoon on a barge, with Dita Parlo, Jean Daste, and Michel Simon as the skipper. Music by Maurice Jaubert, photography Boris Kaufmann.

Ates, Roscoe (1892–1962). American comic actor with inimitable nervous stutter.
South Sea Rose 29. The Big House 30. The Champ 31. Alice in Wonderland 33. The People's Enemy 35. Gone with the Wind 39. Captain Caution 40. The Palm Beach Story 42. The Stranger Wore a Gun 53. The Errand Boy 61, many others.

Atherton, William (1947–). American actor of the seventies, with stage background.
□ Class of '44 73. The Sugarland Express 74. The Day of the Locust 74. The Hindenberg 76.

Atkins, Eileen (1934–). British character actress, highly regarded on stage; her only film to date is *Inadmissible Evidence* 68.

Atlantic (GB 1929). Directed by E. A. Dupont, this early talkie was also the first to be made in two language versions (English and German, with different leading actors). There is now very little intrinsic interest in its melodramatics set on the sinking Titanic.

L'Atlantide (France 1921). An exotic adventure film about two wanderers who discover the lost city of Atlantis. Written and directed by Jacques Feyder, its exotic style was highly influential though its length was fatiguing. Pabst made a sound version in 1932.

The Atonement of Gosta Berling (Sweden 1924). Remembered chiefly for introducing Greta Garbo to the screen, this is a strong Scandinavian brew about a clergyman, unfrocked for alcoholism, who dissipates his talents in high society. Solidly well directed by Mauritz Stiller from Selma Lagerlöf's novel; with Lars Hanson.

Attenborough, Richard (1923–). British character actor who escaped from early typecasting as a young coward, revealed an ambitious range of characterizations, and went on to produce and direct.
□ *In Which We Serve* 42. Schweik's New Adventures 42. The Hundred Pound Window 43. Journey Together 43. A Matter of Life and Death 46. School for Secrets 46. The Man Within 47. Dancing with Crime 47. *Brighton Rock* 47. London Belongs to Me 48. *The Guinea Pig* (as a 13-year-old) 49. The Lost People 50. Boys in Brown 50. Morning Departure 50. Hell is Sold Out 51. The Magic Box 51. The Gift Horse 52. Father's Doing Fine 53. Eight O'Clock Walk 54. The Ship that Died of Shame 54. *Private's Progress* 55. The Baby and the Battleship 56. Brothers in Law 56. The Scamp 58. Dunkirk 58. *The Man Upstairs* 58. Danger Within 58. I'm All Right Jack 58. Sea of Sand 58. Jetstorm 59. SOS Pacific 59. *The Angry Silence* (& co-p) 59. *The League of Gentlemen* (& co-p) 59. Only Two Can Play 62. *Whistle Down the Wind* (p only) 62. The Dock Brief 62. All Night Long 62. *The Great Escape* (US) 63. *Seance on a Wet Afternoon* (& p) 64. The Third Secret 64. *Guns at Batasi* (BFA) 64. The Flight of the Phoenix (US) 65. The Sand Pebbles (US) 66. Doctor Dolittle 67. The Bliss of Mrs Blossom 68. *Oh What a Lovely War* (co-p and d only) 69. David Copperfield 69. A Severed Head 70. *Loot* 71. 10 Rillington Place 71. Young Winston (d only) 72. Conduct Unbecoming 75. Brannigan 75. And Then There Were None 75. A Bridge Too Far 77.

Atwill, Lionel (1885–1946). Incisive but rather

stolid British actor who went to Hollywood in 1932 and stayed to play teutonic villains, mad doctors and burgomasters.
□ For Sale 18. The Marriage Price 19. The Highest Bidder 21. Indiscretion 21. The Silent Witness 32. *Doctor X* 32. The Vampire Bat 33. The Secret of Madame Blanche 33. *The Mystery of the Wax Museum* 33. Murders in the Zoo 33. The Sphinx 33. Song of Songs 33. The Secret of the Blue Room 33. The Solitaire Man 33. *Nana* 34. Beggars in Ermine 34. Stamboul Quest 34. One More River 34. The Age of Innocence 34. The Firebird 34. The Man Who Reclaimed His Head 35. Mark of the Vampire 35. *The Devil is a Woman* 35. The Murder Man 35. Rendezvous 35. Captain Blood 35. Lady of Secrets 36. Absolute Quiet 36. Till We Meet Again 36. *The Road Back* 37. Last Train from Madrid 37. The Great Garrick 37. Lancer Spy 37. Three Comrades 38. The Great Waltz 38. *Son of Frankenstein* (memorable as the one-armed police chief) 39. *The Three Musketeers* 39. *The Hound of the Baskervilles* 39. The Gorilla 39. The Sun Never Sets 39. Mr Moto Takes a Vacation 39. The Secret of Dr Kildare 39. Balalaika 39. The Mad Empress 40. Johnny Apollo 40. Charlie Chan's Murder Cruise 40. The Girl in 313 40. Boom Town 40. The Great Profile 40. *Man Made Monster* 41. The Mad Doctor of Market Street 42. *To Be Or Not To Be* 42. The Strange Case of Dr RX 42. The Ghost of Frankenstein 42. Pardon My Sarong 42. Cairo 42. Night Monster 42. Junior G-Men of the Air (serial) 42. *Sherlock Holmes and the Secret Weapon* (as Moriarty) 42. Frankenstein Meets the Wolf Man 43. House of Frankenstein 44, Captain America (serial) 44. Raiders of Ghost City (serial) 44. Lady in the Death House 44. Secrets of Scotland Yard 44. Fog Island 45. Genius at Work 45. Crime Incorporated 45. *House of Dracula* 45. Lost City of the Jungle (serial) 46.

Auberjonois, René (1940–). American character actor.
M*A*S*H. 70. Brewster McCloud 71. McCabe and Mrs Miller 71. Images 72. Pete 'n Tillie 72. Panache (TV) 76, etc.

Aubert, Lenore (c. 1918–). Yugoslavian actress in Hollywood from the late thirties, usually in sinister roles.
Bluebeard's Eighth Wife 38. They Got Me Covered 43. Action in Arabia 44. *Wife of Monte Cristo* 46. The Other Love 47. Return of the Whistler 48. *Abbott and Costello Meet Frankenstein* 48. Abbott and Costello Meet the Killer 49, etc.

Aubrey, Anne (1937–). British leading lady

of a few comedies and adventures in the late fifties.
No Time To Die 58. The Bandit of Zhobe 59. Idle on Parade 59. Killers of Kilimanjaro 59. Let's Get Married 60. The Hellions 61, etc.

Aubrey, Skye (1945–). American leading lady of the seventies.
Skyjacked 72, etc.

Aubry, Cecile (1929–) (Anne-José Benard). Petite French leading lady of the early fifties.
Manon 49. The Black Rose 50. Bluebeard 51. La Ironia 54, etc.

Auclair, Michel (1922–) (Vladimir Vujovic). French leading man.
La Belle et la Bête 46. Les Maudits 47. Manon 49. Justice Est Faite 50. Henriette 52. Funny Face (US) 56. The Fanatics 57. Rendezvous de Minuit 61. Symphony for a Massacre 64. The Day of the Jackal 73, etc.

Audiard, Michel (–). French writer-director. Mr Peek a Boo (w) 51. Babette Goes to War (w) 60. The Big Snatch (w) 63. The Black Flagon (w,d) 71, etc.

Audley, Maxine (1923–). British stage actress who has made occasional film appearances.
The Sleeping Tiger 54. The Barretts of Wimpole Street 57. The Vikings 58. Our Man in Havana 59. The Trials of Oscar Wilde 60. Hell is a City 60. A Jolly Bad Fellow 64. Here We Go Round the Mulberry Bush 67. Frankenstein Must Be Destroyed 69, etc.

Audran, Stephane (1938–). Cool French leading actress.
The Champagne Murders 67. *Les Biches* 68. La Femme Infidèle 69. The Beast Must Die 70. The Lady in the Car 71. *Le Boucher* 70. Without Apparent Motive 71. Dead Pigeon on Beethoven Street 72. The Discreet Charm of the Bourgeoisie 72. And Then There Were None 75. The Black Bird 75, etc.

Audry, Jacqueline (1908–). French director.
Gigi 49. L'Ingénue Libertine 50. *Olivia* 51. Huis Clos 54. In Six Easy Lessons 57. Mitsou 57. Les Petits Matins 62. Soledad 66, etc.

Auer, John H. (1909–1975). Hungarian-born American director, turning out 'B' films since the thirties.
□ Frankie and Johnnie 35. The Crime of D Crespi 35. A Man Betrayed 37. Rhythm in t Clouds 37. Circus Girl 37. Outside of Para 38. Invisible Enemy 38. I Stand Accused 3

Desperate Adventure 38. Orphans of the Street 38. Forged Passport 39. SOS Tidal Wave 39. Smuggled Cargo 39. Calling All Marines 39. Thou Shalt Not Kill 40. Women in War 40. Hit Parade of 1941 40. Pardon My Stripes 42. Moonlight Masquerade 42. Johnny Doughboy 42. Tahiti Honey 43. *Gangway for Tomorrow* 43. Seven Days Ashore 44. Moonlight in Manhattan 44. Pan Americana 45. Beat the Band 47. The Flame 48. I Jane Doe 48. Angel on the Amazon 48. The Avengers 50. Hit Parade of 1951 50. Thunderbirds 52. *City that Never Sleeps* (& p) 53. Hell's Half Acre (& p) 54. The Eternal Sea (& p) 55. Johnny Trouble (& p) 57. Then to TV.

Auer, Mischa (1905–1967) (Mischa Ounskowsky). Lanky Russian comedy actor with prominent eyes and wild gestures. Went to Broadway after the revolution, and in 1928 arrived in Hollywood; after several false starts found himself much in demand for noble idiot roles in broken English.
□ Something Always Happens 28. Marquis Preferred 28. The Benson Murder Case 30. Inside the Lines 30. Just Imagine 30. Women Love Once 30. The Unholy Garden 31. The Yellow Ticket 31. Delicious 31. The Midnight Patrol 32. No Greater Love 32. Mata Hari 32. Scarlet Dawn 32. The Monster Walks 32. Dangerously Yours 33. Sucker Money 33. Infernal Machine 33. Corruption 33. After Tonight 33. Cradle Song 33. Girl Without a Room 33. Wharf Angel 34. Bulldog Drummond Strikes Back 34. Stamboul Quest 34. Mystery Woman 35. Lives of a Bengal Lancer 35. Clive of India 35. Murder in the Fleet 36. The House of a Thousand Candles 36. One Rainy Afternoon 36. The Princess Comes Across 36. *My Man Godfrey* (in which his gorilla impersonation really put him on the map) 36. *The Gay Desperado* 36. Winterset 36. That Girl from Paris 37. Three Smart Girls 37. Top of the Town 37. We Have Our Moments 37. Pick a Star 37. Marry the Girl 37. Vogues of 1938 37. *100 Men and a Girl* 38. Merry Go Round 38. It's All Yours 38. Rage of Paris 38. *You Can't Take It With You* 38. Service de Luxe 38. Little Tough Guys in Society 38. *Sweethearts* 38. *East Side of Heaven* 39. Unexpected Father 39. *Destry Rides Again* 39. Alias the Deacon 40. Sandy is a Lady 40. Public Deb Number One 40. *Spring Parade* 40. Seven Sinners 40. Trail of the Vigilantes 40. The Flame of New Orleans 41. Hold That Ghost 41. Moonlight in Hawaii 41. *Hellzapoppin* 41. *Twin Beds* 42. Around the World 43. *Lady in the Dark* 44. *Up in Mabel's Room* 44. *A Royal Scandal* 45. Brewster's Millions 45. And Then There Were None 45. Sentimental Journey 46.

She Wrote the Book 46. Sofia 48. The Sky is Red 52. Song of Paris 52. *Confidential Report* 53. The Monte Carlo Story 58. Mam'zelle Pigalle 58. The Foxiest Girl in Paris 58. A Dog a Mouse and a Sputnik 60. We Joined the Navy 62. The Christmas that Almost Wasn't 66. Drop Dead Darling 66.

Auger, Claudine (1942–). French leading lady, in occasional films abroad.
In the French Style 63. Thunderball 65. Triple Cross 66. Jeu de Massacre 67. The Devil in Love 67. The Bastard 68.

August, Joseph (1890–1947). Distinguished American cinematographer.
SELECTED SILENTS: The Narrow Trail 17. Tiger Man 18. Square Deal Sanderson 19. Sand 20. O'Melley of the Mounted 21. *Travellin' On* 22. Madness of Youth 23. *Dante's Inferno* 24. *Tumbleweeds* 25. *The Road to Glory* 26. *The Beloved Rogue* 26. Fig Leaves 26. Two Arabian Knights 27. Honor Bound 28. The Black Watch 29.
□ SOUND FILMS: Men Without Women 30. Double Crossroads 30. On Your Back 30. Up the River 30. Seas Beneath 31. Mr Lemon of Orange 31. Quick Millions 31. The Brat 31. Heartbreak 31. Charlie Chan's Chance 31. Silent Witness 32. Mystery Ranch 32. Vanity Street 32. No More Orchids 32. That's My Boy 32. *Man's Castle* 33. Master of Men 33. As the Devil Commands 33. Cocktail Hour 33. Circus Queen Murder 33. The Captain Hates the Sea 34. Among the Missing 34. The Defense Rests 34. Black Moon 34. Twentieth Century 34. No Greater Glory 34. Sylvia Scarlett 35. After the Dance 35. *The Informer* 35. I'll Love You Always 35. The Whole Town's Talking 35. The Plough and the Stars 36. *Mary of Scotland* 36. Every Saturday Night 36. A Damsel in Distress 37. Music for Madame 37. Super Sleuth 37. Fifty Roads to Town 37. *Michael Strogoff* 37. Sea Devils 37. Gun Law 37. This Marriage Business 38. The Saint in New York 38. *The Hunchback of Notre Dame* 39. Gunga Din 39. Nurse Edith Cavell 40. Man of Conquest 40. Melody Ranch 40. Primrose Path 40. *All that Money Can Buy* 41. They Were Expendable 45. *Portrait of Jennie* 48.

Aulin, Ewa (1949–). Scandinavian leading lady in international films.
Candy 68. Start the Revolution without Me 69. This Kind of Love 72, etc.

Ault, Marie (1870–1951) (Mary Cragg). British character actress of stage and screen, usually in dialect comedy roles.

Woman to Woman 24. The Lodger 26. Hobson's Choice 31. Major Barbara 40. Love on the Dole 41. We Dive at Dawn 43. I See a Dark Stranger 46. Madness of the Heart 49, many others.

Aumont, Jean-Pierre (1909–) (J.–P. Salomons). French leading man, in films from 1931, Hollywood from 1941.
Jean de la Lune 32. Maria Chapdelaine 35. Drôle de Drame 36. *Hôtel du Nord* 38. The Cross of Lorraine 42. Assignment in Brittany 43. Heartbeat 46. Song of Scheherazade 48. The First Gentleman (GB) 48. Charge of the Lancers 53. *Lili* 53. Hilda Crane 56. The Seventh Sin 57. The Devil at Four O'Clock 61. Five Miles to Midnight 63. Castle Keep 69. La Nuit Américaine 73, etc.

Aurenche, Jean (1904–). French writer who with Pierre Bost (1901–) wrote many well-known films.
Hôtel du Nord 38. Sylvie et le Fantôme 45. La Symphonie Pastorale 46. *Le Diable au Corps* 46. Occupe-Toi d'Amélie 49. Dieu A Besoin des Hommes 50. *The Red Inn* 51. *Les Jeux Interdits* 51. Ripening Seed 53. Gervaise 56. En Cas de Malheur 57. L'Affaire d'Une Nuit 60. The Clockmaker 76, etc. Aurenche worked alone on the screenplay of *Woman in White* 65.

Auric, Georges (1899–). French composer.
Le Sang d'un Poète 30. *À Nous la Liberté* 31. Lac aux Dames 34. L'Alibi 37. Orage 38. L'Eternel Retour 43. Dead of Night 45. Caesar and Cleopatra 45. La Belle et la Bête 46. It Always Rains on Sunday 47. Corridor of Mirrors 48. Passport to Pimlico 49. *Orphée* 49. *Belles de Nuit* 52. Roman Holiday 53. The Wages of Fear 53. Father Brown 54. Rififi 55. The Witches of Salem 56. Gervaise 56. The Picasso Mystery 56. Heaven Fell That Night 58. Bonjour Tristesse 59. La Chambre Ardente 62, many others.

Aurthur, Robert Alan (1922–). American novelist and screenwriter.
Edge of the City 56. Warlock 59. For Love of Ivy 68. The Lost One 70, etc.

Austen, Jane (1775–1817). The most delightful of English novelists has been oddly neglected by the screen, but the 1940 version of *Pride and Prejudice* is a distinguished and amusing one.

Austin, Charlotte (1933–). American leading lady who moved from musicals to monsters in the fifties.

Sunny Side of the Street 51. The Farmer Takes a Wife 53. How to Marry a Millionaire 53. Gorilla at Large 54. Desirée 54. Daddy Long Legs 55. How to Be Very Very Popular 55. Bride of the Beast 58, etc.

Austin, Jerry (–). Dwarf American actor.
Saratoga Trunk 43. Adventures of Don Juan 47, etc.

Australia has long had a vigorous cinema movement, but it has not suited the rest of the world to take much note of it. Charles Chauvel is the continent's best-known director, but even his films have travelled remarkably little, and after World War Two, Australia leaned very heavily on American imports; though Britain, and especially Ealing Studios, offered encouragement by making a number of films there. More recently Australia's traditional rough-edged action adventures have given way on the one hand to Barry Mackenzie-style smut and on the other to macabre, stylish curiosities such as *The Cars That Ate Paris* and *Picnic At Hanging Rock*; while Australian television doggedly apes Hollywood.

Autant-Lara, Claude (1903–). French director, usually of stylish romantic dramas; former assistant to René Clair.
Ciboulette 33. L'Affaire du Courier de Lyons 37. *Fric Frac* 39. Lettres de l'Amour 42. Douce 43. Sylvie et le Fantôme 45. *Le Diable au Corps* 46. *Occupe-Toi d'Amélie* 49. *The Red Inn* 51. Ripening Seed 53. Le Rouge et le Noir 54. Marguerite de la Nuit 55. La Traversée de Paris 56. *En Cas de Malheur* 57. The Green Mâre's Nest 59. Le Bois des Amants 60. The Count of Monte Cristo 61. Le Meurtrier 62. Thou Shalt Not Kill 62. The Woman in White 65, etc.

authenticator. Studio researcher responsible for establishing accuracy of all script details, ensuring use of 'clear' telephone numbers, etc.

authors as actors are few. Alexander Woolcott once had fun playing opposite Noel Coward in *The Scoundrel*; Irvin S. Cobb tried to take over the mantle of Will Rogers on the latter's death; Mickey Spillane played his own hero Mike Hammer in *The Girl Hunters* and also appeared in *Ring of Fear*. Otherwise literary lions have aspired only to bit parts, such as Compton Mackenzie in *Whisky Galore* and Hugh Walpole in *David Copperfield*. Somerset Maugham did contribute lengthy introductions to three compendiums of his short stories, but they were virtually eliminated from the release prints.

auteur. A term used in the sixties and seventies by egghead critics to denote directors whom they judge to have a discernible message or attitude which runs throughout their work. Oddly enough the term is not applied to authors.

Automobiles with personality enough to become movie titles include *Genevieve, The Fast Lady, La Belle Américaine, The Solid Gold Cadillac, The Yellow Rolls Royce, Chitty Chitty Bang Bang, The Gnome-Mobile* and *The Love Bug.* Other cars with individuality were James Bond's tricksy Aston Martin in *Goldfinger* and the one that ran on two wheels in *Diamonds are Forever*; the Flying Wombat in *The Young at Heart*; the gadget-filled limousine in *Only Two Can Play*; the airborne Model T in *The Absent-minded Professor.* The Model T was also Laurel and Hardy's favourite car, and they wrecked a great many in their time; other old cars were featured in *The Reivers* and TV's *The Beverly Hillbillies.* Multitudes of old and strange cars were featured in *The Great Race, It's a Mad Mad Mad Mad World, Monte Carlo or Bust.* Comic car chases have been featured by Mack Sennett, Abbott and Costello, W. C. Fields and countless other comedians, and a new car was splendidly wrecked in *Tobacco Road.* Realistic chases are becoming more and more violent, as in the progression from *The Silencers* through *Robbery, Bullitt, Vanishing Point, The French Connection* and *Freebie and the Bean.* See *motor racing.*

Autry, Gene (1907–). Easy-going Texan who made innumerable minor Westerns 1934–54 as singing cowboy, usually with his horse Champion.
Boots and Saddles 37. Under Western Stars 38. Carolina Moon 40. Back in the Saddle 41. Sunset in Wyoming 42. Range War 46. Sioux City Sue 47. Guns and Saddles 49. Goldtown Ghost Riders 53, many others.

Avakian, Aram (–). American director.
Cops and Robbers 73. 11 Harrowhouse 74.

Avalon, Frankie (1939–) (Francis Avallone). American light leading man and pop singer, former trumpeter.
Guns of the Timberland 60. The Alamo 60. Voyage to the Bottom of the Sea 62. Beach Blanket Bingo 65. I'll Take Sweden 65. Sergeant Deadhead 66. Fireball 500 66. Pajama Party in a Haunted House 66. How to Stuff a Wild Bikini 66. The Take 74, etc.

avant-garde. An adjective generally used to describe artists 'in advance of their time'; especially used of French surrealists in the twenties, e.g. Kirsanoff, Buñuel, Germaine Dulac.

Avedon, Doe (1928–). American leading lady who had a very short career before retiring to marry.
□ The High and the Mighty 54. Deep in My Heart 55. The Boss 56.

Averback, Hy (c. 1925–). American director with much TV experience, especially in comedy series.
Chamber of Horrors 66. Where Were You When the Lights Went Out? 68. *I Love You Alice B. Toklas* 68. The Great Bank Robbery 69. Suppose They Gave a War and Nobody Came 70, etc.

Avery, Tex (1907–) (Fred Avery). American animator, best known for M.G.M. cartoons which combined savagery with hilarity. He created Droopy.

Avildsen, John G. (–). American director.
Turn on to Love 67. OK Bill 68. Guess What We Learned at School Today 69. *Joe* 70. Cry Uncle 71. Roger the Stoolie 72. Save the Tiger 72. WW and the Dixie Dance Kings 76, etc.

L' Avventura (Italy 1959). Here at great length we see the search for a girl lost on an island; gradually the searchers become pre-occupied with their own problems, and the girl is never found. Highbrow reaction was so favourable to this rather bewildering film by Michelangelo Antonioni that he has since been able to continue exploring life's irrationalities and enigmas, without always communicating his purpose to the audience. Photographed by Aldo Scavarda; with Gabrielle Ferzetti, Monica Vitti.

The Awful Truth (US 1937). A slender but influential and still amiable comedy, one of the first to add a touch of craziness to romantic sophistication. Leo McCarey wrote it and won an Academy Award for directing it; Cary Grant and Irene Dunne played the couple who change their minds about getting divorced, and Ralph Bellamy was a splendid foil as a bemused interloper. In 1953 the script was reshot to considerably less effect by Alexander Hall, with Ray Milland and Jane Wyman, as *Let's Do It Again.*

Axelrod, George (1922–). American comedy writer.
Phffft 54. The Seven Year Itch (oa) 55. Will

Success Spoil Rock Hunter? (oa) 57. Breakfast at Tiffany's 61. The Manchurian Candidate 62. How to Murder Your Wife (& p) 65. Goodbye Charlie 65. Lord Love a Duck (& p-d) 66. The Secret Life of an American Wife (& p) 68, etc.

Aylmer, Felix (1889–) (Felix Edward Aylmer Jones). Distinguished British stage character actor, a respected industry figure who from 1950 was president of Equity, the actors' trade union. In films he mainly played schoolmasters, bankers, bishops, etc.
The Wandering Jew 33. The Iron Duke 35. Tudor Rose 36. As You Like It 36. *Victoria the Great* 37. The Citadel 38. Saloon Bar 40. *The Ghost of St Michael's* 41. Mr Emmanuel 44. Henry V 44. The Ghosts of Berkeley Square 47. *Hamlet* (as Polonius) 48. Edward My Son 49. Quo Vadis 51. Knights of the Round Table 54. The Angel Who Pawned Her Harp 54. Saint Joan 57. *Separate Tables* 58. *Never Take Sweets from a Stranger* 60. The Chalk Garden 64. Becket 64. Decline and Fall 68. Hostile Witness 68, many others.

Ayres, Agnes (1896–1940) (Agnes Hinkle). American leading lady of the silent screen.
Forbidden Fruit 19. The Affairs of Anatol 20. *The Sheik* 21. Racing Hearts 23. When a Girl Loves 24. Morals for Men 25. Her Market Value 26. Son of the Sheik 26. Eve's Love Letters 29, many others.

Ayres, Lew (1908–) (Lewis Ayer). Boyish American leading man of the thirties; he occasionally got a chance to prove himself a comfortable and friendly actor, but his career suffered during World War II when he declared himself a conscientious objector.
☐ *The Kiss* 29. The Sophomore 29. Many a Slip 30. *All Quiet on the Western Front* 30. Common Clay 30. East is West 30. Doorway to Hell 30. Iron Man 31. Up for Murder 31. The Spirit of Notre Dame 31. Heaven on Earth 31.

Mississippi 31. The Impatient Maiden 32. Night World 32. Okay America 32. *State Fair* 33. Don't Bet On Love 33. My Weakness 33. Cross Country Cruise 34. She Learned About Sailors 34. Servants' Entrance 34. Let's Be Ritzy 34. Lottery Lover 35. The Silk Hat Kid 35. The Leathernecks have Landed 36. Panic on the Air 36. Shakedown 36. Lady be Careful 36. Murder with Pictures 36. The Crime Nobody Saw 36. *Last Train from Madrid* 37. Hold 'Em Navy 37. Scandal Street 38. King of the Newsboys 38. *Holiday* (a key performance as Katharine Hepburn's drunken brother) 38. Rich Man Poor Girl 38. *Young Dr Kildare* 38. Spring Madness 38. Ice Follies 39. Broadway Serenade 39. Calling Dr Kildare 39. These Glamour Girls 39. The Secret of Dr Kildare 39. Remember? 39. Dr Kildare's Strange Case 40. Dr Kildare Goes Home 40. The Golden Fleecing 40. Dr Kildare's Crisis 40. Maisie Was a Lady 41. The People vs Dr Kildare 41. Dr Kildare's Wedding Day 41. Fingers at the Window 42. Dr Kildare's Victory 42. *The Dark Mirror* 46. The Unfaithful 47. *Johnny Belinda* 48. The Capture 50. New Mexico 51. No Escape 53. Donovan's Brain 54. *Advise and Consent* 61. *The Carpetbaggers* 64. Earth II (TV) 71. She Waits (TV) 72. The Man (TV) 72. The Biscuit Eater 72. Beneath the Planet of the Apes 73.

Ayres, Robert (1914–1968). Canadian actor of strong silent types, long resident in Britain.
They Were Not Divided 49. Cosh Boy 52. Contraband Spain 55. It's Never Too Late 55. A Night to Remember 57. The Sicilians 63. Battle Beneath the Earth 68, many others

Aznavour, Charles (1924–) (C. Aznavurjan). French leading man of the small but rugged school.
La Tête contre les Murs 58. *Shoot the Pianist* 60. Passage du Rhin 61. Cloportes 65. Candy 68. The Adventurers 70. The Games 70. Un Beau Monstre 70. And Then There Were None 75, etc.

B

'B' picture. A low-budget production usually designed as part of a double bill or to support a more important feature. There are three excellent books on the subject: *B Movies* by Don Miller, *The Wonderful World of B Films* by Alan G. Barbour and *Kings of the Bs* by Todd McCarthy and Charles Flynn.

Babes in Arms (US 1939). Made immediately after *The Wizard of Oz*, this lively teenage musical directed by Busby Berkeley not only established Judy Garland as one of the brightest stars in the MGM sky but was the first of several teaming her with the irrepressible Mickey Rooney: *Strike Up the Band* 40, *Babes on Broadway* 41, *Girl Crazy* 43.

Babes in Toyland. The Victor Herbert fairy tale operetta was filmed by Hal Roach in 1934 as a vehicle for Laurel and Hardy. In 1961 Jack Donohue made a lavish but empty version for Disney, with Ray Bolger as the villain; Laurel and Hardy, curiously, were closely impersonated by Henry Calvin and Gene Sheldon.

babies who have achieved screen stardom include Baby Parsons and Baby Peggy in silent days, Baby Le Roy in the early thirties and Baby Sandy in the early forties. Shirley Temple and the Our Gang cast were scarcely weaned when they hit the big time. Other films about particular babies include *Bachelor Mother*, *Bobbikins*, and *A Diary for Timothy*.

There was a shortlived TV series about a talking baby called *Happy*; and Lucille Ball worked her own confinement into her weekly half-hour. More recently there has been a lamentable fashion for diabolical infants: *Rosemary's Baby*, *It's Alive*, *I Dont Want to be Born* and *The Devil within Her*.

Baby Doll (US 1956). Tennessee Williams wrote and Elia Kazan directed this deliberately shocking comedy about the child-wife of a 'poor white' southerner. Starring Eli Wallach, Karl Malden and Carroll Baker, it is not generally remembered with affection but did its bit towards loosening the Hollywood Production Code, which had been far too restrictive.

Bacall, Lauren (1924–) (Betty Jean Perske). Sultry American leading actress who after stage experience made her film debut opposite Humphrey Bogart ('If you want anything, just whistle . . .') and subsequently married him. Her image gradually changed to that of an astringent and resourceful woman of the world, and in 1970 she made a triumphant return to the Broadway stage in *Applause*.
□ *To Have and Have Not* 44. Confidential Agent 45. *The Big Sleep* 46. Dark Passage 47. Key Largo 48. *Young Man with a Horn* 50. Bright Leaf 50. *How to Marry a Millionaire* 53. Woman's World 54. The Cobweb 55. Blood Alley 55. Written on the Wind 57. Designing Woman 57. The Gift of Love 58. Northwest Frontier (GB) 59. Shock Treatment 64. Sex and the Single Girl 64. *Harper* 66. Murder on the Orient Express 74. The Shootist 76.

Baccaloni, Salvatore (1900–1969). Italian opera singer who played some comedy roles in American films.
Full of Life 56. Merry Andrew 58. Rock a Bye Baby 59. Fanny 61. The Pigeon That Took Rome 62, etc.

Bacharach, Burt (1929–). American composer.
Lizzie (song) 57. What's New Pussycat? (score) 65. Casino Royale (score) 67. *Butch Cassidy and the Sundance Kid* (AA song, AA score) 69. Lost Horizon (songs) 73.

Bachelor Mother (US 1939). A light, bright, romantic comedy showing Hollywood talents at the top of their accomplished form and introducing a new one in the shape of writer-director Garson Kanin who managed to give a fresh aspect to a collection of farcical misunderstandings over a foundling baby. Ginger Rogers, David Niven and Charles Coburn all performed nimbly. The film was reshot in 1955 as *Bundle of Joy*, but without the essential sparkle.

The Bachelor Party (US 1957). A fairly straight filming of Paddy Chayevsky's TV play, this not only showed Hollywood's willingness to learn and profit from its hated rival but was a measure of how adult it had become in a very few years. Nothing, theoretically and indeed actually, could have been more anti-box office than this study of the thwarted lives of New York office workers—a tragedy presented as comedy. With Don Murray, Jack Warden, E. G. Marshall, Carolyn Jones; directed by Delbert Mann.

back projection. A method of producing 'location' sequences in the studio: the players act in front of a translucent screen on which the scenic background is projected.

Back Street. Fannie Hurst's tearful novel has been filmed three times since sound: in 1932 with John Boles and Irene Dunne, directed by John M. Stahl; in 1941 with Charles Boyer and Margaret Sullavan, directed by Robert Stevenson; and in 1961 with Susan Hayward and John Gavin, directed by David Miller. The story of the married man and the woman who sacrificed all for him has worked at the box office every time.

backstage is a term suggesting musicals about putting on a show. But other types of film have taken place mainly or climactically in this area. Thrillers: *The Velvet Touch, Stage Fright, The Phantom of the Opera, Charlie Chan at the Opera, Cover Girl Killer, Murder at the Vanities, The G-String Murders, Theatre of Death.* Dramas: *A Double Life, Applause, The Blue Angel, Limelight, Les Enfants du Paradis, Act One.* Comedies: *A Night at the Opera, Hellzapoppin, The Guardsman, The Royal Family of Broadway, Curtain Up,* etc. Musicals themselves got off to a pretty good start in the early thirties, best and most typical of them being *42nd Street.*

Backus, Jim (1913–). Burly American character comedian, perhaps most famous as the voice of Mr Magoo in UPA cartoons of the fifties. Stock, vaudeville and radio experience. Autobiography 1958: *Rocks on the Roof.*
The Great Lover 49. Hollywood Story 51. His Kind of Woman 51. I Want You 51. Pat and Mike 52. Androcles and the Lion 53. *Rebel Without a Cause* 55. The Great Man 56. Man of a Thousand Faces 57. Macabre 58. Ice Palace 60. Boys' Night Out 62. *It's A Mad Mad Mad Mad World* 63. Advance to the Rear 64. Billie 65. Where Were You When the Lights Went Out? 68. Now You See Him Now You Don't 72, etc.
TV series: *I Married Joan* 53–55. Hot off the Wire 60. *Gilligan's Island* 64–67. Blondie 68.

Baclanova, Olga (1899–1974). Russian actress who played leads in a few American films.
Street of Sin 27. Docks of New York 28. *Freaks* 32. Billion Dollar Scandal 33. Claudia 43, etc.

Bacon, Irving (1892–1965). American character actor in films from 1920, often as not-so-dumb country type or perplexed official.
Street of Chance 30. Million Dollar Legs 32. Private Worlds 35. Sing You Sinners 38. Meet John Doe 41. Pin Up Girl 44. Monsieur Verdoux 47. Room for One More 52. A Star is Born 54. Fort Massacre 58, many others.

Bacon, Lloyd (1890–1955). American director, long under contract to Warner; former actor in Chaplin silents. Competent rather than brilliant, he nevertheless handled several memorable films among the mass of routine.
□ Private Izzy Murphy 26. *The Singing Fool* 28. Stark Mad 29. Honky Tonk 29. No Defense 29. Say it with Songs 29. So Long Lefty 30. She Couldn't Say No 30. A Notorious Affair 30. The Other Tomorrow 30. Moby Dick 30. The Office Wife 30. Kept Husbands 31. Sit Tight 31. Fifty Million Frenchmen 31. Gold Dust Gertie 31. Honor of the Family 31. Manhattan Parade 32. Fireman Save my Child 32. Alias the Doctor 32. The Famous Ferguson Case 32. *Miss Pinkerton* 32. Crooner 32. You Said a Mouthful 32. *42nd Street* 33. *Picture Snatcher* 33. Mary Stevens MD 33. Son of a Sailor 33. *Wonder Bar* 34. A Very Honorable Guy 34. He Was Her Man 34. Six Day Bike Rider 34. *Here Comes the Navy* 34. *Devil Dogs of the Air* 35. In Caliente 35. Broadway Gondolier 35. The Irish In Us 35. Frisco Kid 35. Sons of Guns 36. Cain and Mabel 36. Gold Diggers of 1937 36. Marked Woman 37. Ever Since Eve 37. *San Quentin* 37. Submarine D1 37. *A Slight Case of Murder* 38. Cowboy from Brooklyn 38. *Boy Meets Girl* 38. Racket Busters 38. Wings of the Navy 39. *The Oklahoma Kid* 39. Indianapolis Speedway 39. Espionage Agent 39. A Child is Born 40. Invisible Stripes 40. Three Cheers for the Irish 40. *Brother Orchid* 40. Knute Rockne, All American 40. Honeymoon for Three 41. Footsteps in the Dark 41. Affectionately Yours 41. Larceny Inc 42. Wings for the Eagle 42. Silver Queen 42. Action in the North Atlantic 43. The Sullivans 44. *Sunday Dinner for a Soldier* 44. Captain Eddie 45. Home Sweet Homicide 45. Wake Up and Dream 46. I Wonder Who's Kissing Her Now 47. You were Meant for Me 48. Give My Regards to Broadway 48. Don't Trust Your Husband 48. Mother Is a Freshman 49. It Happens Every Spring 49. Miss Grant Takes Richmond 49. Kill The Umpire 50. The

Good Humor Man 50. The Fuller Brush Girl 50. Call Me Mister 51. Golden Girl 51. The Frogmen 52. The I Don't Care Girl 53. The Great Sioux Uprising 53. Walking my Baby Back Home 53. The French Line 54. She Couldn't Say No 54.

The Bad and the Beautiful (US 1952). A moderately caustic Hollywood self-exposé, this entertaining if ultimately cliché-ridden melodrama was well acted by Kirk Douglas as a talented heel, smoothly written by Charles Schnee (AA) and directed by Vincente Minelli. Gloria Grahame won an Oscar for her supporting performance as did Robert Surtees for his cinematography. Ten years later Douglas played a similar role in a not dissimilar film, *Two Weeks in Another Town*, about a Hollywood film crew in Rome: it even used clips from *The Bad and the Beautiful* to illustrate the character's previous career.

Bad Day at Black Rock (US 1955). Classic suspense melodrama turning on race hatred, with Spencer Tracy as the one-armed stranger who defies violence to prove that the townsfolk of a desert settlement were communally guilty of an old murder. Written by Millard Kaufmann, directed by John Sturges.

bad language. It now seems impossible that in 1938 the phrase 'not bloody likely' in Shaw's *Pygmalion* could have caused a minor sensation; or that in 1942 the seamen in *In Which We Serve* could not say 'Hell' or 'damn' in front of American audiences. But these things happened. Perhaps it was in 1953 that the rot really set in, when Otto Preminger accepted a Legion of Decency 'C' rating and the loss of a production seal for his film of *The Moon Is Blue* rather than rob it of the words 'virgin' and 'mistress'. Three years later, Mickey Shaughnessy in *Don't Go Near the Water* was allowed to mouth obscenities while the sound track amusingly bleeped them out. By the time *Pygmalion* was remade in 1964 as *My Fair Lady* the phrase originally so shocking would have had no dramatic effect; it was replaced by 'Move your bloomin' arse'. In 1967–68 the floodgates really opened. *Poor Cow* and *Who's Afraid of Virginia Woolf?* were the first to allow 'bugger'. In *Here We Go Round the Mulberry Bush* Maxine Audley reproaches her husband as follows: 'Darling, you've got him pissed again'. And in *A Flea in Her Ear* Rex Harrison unchivalrously instructs Rosemary Harris to 'piss off'. That still-notorious four-letter word beginning with F was first uttered by Marianne Faithful in *I'll Never Forget Whatshisname*, and then by Elizabeth

Taylor in *Boom*. And the slang word for defecation was first uttered in *In Cold Blood, Boom, Rosemary's Baby* and *Secret Ceremony*. In general, the effect of such words on the big screen has merely been to show how meaningless, harmless and stupid they are; but over-use of them is worse than pretending they don't exist, and one wonders whether films of the mid-seventies such as *Lenny, Serpico, The Last Detail, Shampoo* and *Dog Day Afternoon* would really have been poorer without them.

Baddeley, Angela (1904–1976). British stage character actress, sister of Hermione Baddeley. Popular on TV as Mrs Bridges in *Upstairs Downstairs* 71–75.
The Speckled Band 31. The Ghost Train 32. Quartet 48. Tom Jones 62, etc.

Baddeley, Hermione (1906–). British character comedienne, adept at blowsy roles; long stage experience.
The Guns of Loos 28. Caste 30. Kipps 41. Brighton Rock 47. Quartet 48. Scrooge 51. Pickwick Papers 52. The Belles of St Trinian's 54. Room at the Top 59. The Unsinkable Molly Brown 64. Mary Poppins 64. Up the Front 72, etc.

Badel, Alan (1923–). British stage and screen actor of considerable sensitivity, not easy to cast in leading roles.
The Stranger Left No Card 53. Salome 53. Three Cases of Murder 55. Magic Fire 56. This Sporting Life 63. Children of the Damned 64. Arabesque 66. Otley 69. Where's Jack? 69. The Adventurers 70. The Day of the Jackal 73, etc.

Baden-Semper, Nina (1945–). West Indian leading lady, popular on British TV
Kongi's Harvest 73. Love Thy Neighbour 74.

Badger, Clarence (1880–1964). American director at his peak in the twenties.
Jubilo 19. Doubling for Romeo 21. Miss Brewster's Millions 26. It 27. Hot News 28. Three Weekends 28. No No Nanette 31. The Bad Man 32. Rangle River 39, etc.

Badham, Mary (1952–). American teenage actress.
□ To Kill a Mockingbird 63. This Property is Condemned 66. Let's Kill Uncle 66.

Badiyi, Reza S. (–). American director from TV.
Trader Horn 73.

Baer, Buddy (1915–) (Jacob Henry Baer).

American heavyweight prizefighter, brother of Max.
Africa Screams 49. Quo Vadis 51. Jack and the Beanstalk 52. Slightly Scarlet 56. Snow White and the Three Stooges 61, etc.

Baer, Max (1909–1959). Prizewinning American boxer who made several films.
The Prizefighter and the Lady 33. Riding High 50. The Iron Road 55. The Harder They Fall 56. Over She Goes 58, etc.

Baer Max Jnr (–). American actor who spent nine years playing Jethro in TV's The Beverly Hillbillies, then became an independent producer.
Macon County Line 74. The McCulloughs (& a,d) 75.

Baggott, King (1874–1948). Tall, powerful American leading man of silent adventure dramas. Made a few early talkies, then retired.
Lady Audley's Secret 12. Ivanhoe 12. Dr Jekyll and Mr Hyde 13. The Corsican Brothers 15. Moonlight Follies 21. Going Straight 22. Tumbleweeds (d only) 25. Notorious Lady 27. The Czar of Broadway 30. Once a Gentleman 30. Scareheads 32. Romance in the Rain 34. Mississippi 35. Come Live with Me 41, many others.

Bailey, Pearl (1918–). Black American entertainer and Broadway star.
Autobiography 1968: *The Raw Pearl*.
Variety Girl 47. *Isn't It Romantic?* 48. *Carmen Jones* 54. *That Certain Feeling* 55. *St Louis Blues* 57. *Porgy and Bess* 59. *All the Fine Young Cannibals* 60. *The Landlord* 69.

Bailey, Raymond (1904–). American small part actor, often a crook or lawyer.
Secret Service of the Air 39. Tidal Wave 40. Picnic 56. The Incredible Shrinking Man 57. Al Capone 59. From the Terrace 60, many others.
TV series: *The Beverly Hillbillies* (as Drysdale) 62–69.

Bailey, Robin (1919–). British character actor, usually in deferential or ineffectual roles.
School for Secrets 46. Private Angelo 49. His Excellency 51. For Better for Worse 55. Hell Drivers 57. The Spy with a Cold Nose 66. The Whisperers 67, etc.

Bainter, Fay (1892–1968). American character actress who came to films from the stage in 1934 and specialized in stalwart but sympathetic matrons.
□ This Side of Heaven 34. *Quality Street* 37. The

Soldier and the Lady 37. Make Way for Tomorrow 37. *Jezebel* (AA) 38. *White Banners* 38. Mother Carey's Chickens 38. The Arkansas Traveller 38. The Shining Hour 39. Yes My Darling Daughter 39. The Lady and the Mob 39. Daughters Courageous 39. Our Neighbours the Carters 39. Young Tom Edison 40. *Our Town* 40. A Bill of Divorcement 40. Maryland 40. Babes on Broadway 42. Woman of the Year 42. *The War Against Mrs Hadley* 42. *Mrs Wiggs of the Cabbage Patch* 42. Journey for Margaret 43. *The Human Comedy* 43. Presenting Lily Mars 43. Salute to the Marines 43. Cry Havoc 43. The Heavenly Body 43. *Dark Waters* (rare villainous role) 44. Three is a Family 44. *State Fair* 45. The Virginian 46. The Kid from Brooklyn 46. *The Secret Life of Walter Mitty* 47. Deep Valley 47. Give My Regards to Broadway 48. *June Bride* 48. Close to my Heart 51. The President's Lady 53. *The Children's Hour* 62.

Baird, Teddy (c. 1900–). British producer, in films since 1928 after journalistic experience.
The Browning Version 51. The Importance of Being Earnest 52. Carrington V.C. 56. Two Living One Dead 62, etc.

Bakaleinikoff, Constantin (1898–1966). Russian music director, long in US. With RKO 1941–52. Own scores include *Notorious* 46. *Mourning Becomes Electra* 47. *Mr Blandings Builds His Dream House* 48. *The Conqueror* 56, many others.

Baker, Art (1898–1966). American general purpose actor.
Once Upon a Time 44. Spellbound 45. The Farmer's Daughter 47. *Cover Up* 48. Take One False Step 49. Cause for Alarm 51. Living It Up 54. Twelve Hours to Kill 60. Young Dillinger 65. The Wild Angels 66, etc.

Baker, Carroll (1931–). American leading lady who tried to vary her sex symbol status via roles of melodramatic intensity.
□ Easy to Love 53. *Giant* 56. *Baby Doll* 56. The Big Country 58. The Miracle 59. But Not for Me 59. Something Wild 61. Bridge to the Sun 61. How the West was Won 63. *The Carpetbaggers* 64. Station Six Sahara 64. Cheyenne Autumn 64. The Greatest Story Ever Told 65. Sylvia 65. Mr Moses 65. *Harlow* 65. Jack of Diamonds 67. The Sweet Body of Deborah 68. Paranoia 68. Captain Apache 71.

Baker, Diane (1938–). Demure-looking American leading actress who can also handle unsympathetic roles. Many TV guest appearances.

☐ *The Diary of Anne Frank* 59. The Best of Everything 59. Journey to the Centre of the Earth 59. The Wizard of Baghdad 61. Hemingway's Adventures of a Young Man 62. The 300 Spartans 62. Nine Hours to Rama 63. Stolen Hours 63. *Strait Jacket* 63. *The Prize* 63. *Marnie* 64. *Mirage* 65. Sands of Beersheba 66. The Horse in the Grey Flannel Suit 68. Krakatoa, East of Java 68. The Badge or the Cross (TV) 70. Do You Take This Stranger? (TV) 70. Congratulations, It's A Boy (TV) 71. TV series: *Here We Go Again* 73.

Baker, George (1929–). British leading man, also on stage and TV.
The Intruder 52. The Dam Busters 55. A Hill in Korea 56. The Woman for Joe 56. *The Moonraker* 57. Tread Softly Stranger 58. No Time for Tears 59. Lancelot and Guinevere 63. Curse of the Fly 65. Mr Ten Per Cent 67. Justine 69. On Her Majesty's Secret Service 69, etc.

Baker, Hylda (1909–). British comedienne in northern music hall tradition.
☐ Saturday Night and Sunday Morning 60. Up the Junction 68. Nearest and Dearest 73.

Baker, Joe Don (1943–). Tough young American leading man of the early seventies.
Cool Hand Luke 67. Guns of the Magnificent Seven 69. Adam at Six a.m. 70. Wild Rovers 71. Mongo's Back in Town (TV) 71. Welcome Home Soldier Boys 72. Junior Bonner 72. *Charley Varrick* 72. *Walking Tall* 72. The Outfit 73. Golden Needles 74. Mitchell 74. Framed 75.

Baker, Kenny (1912–). American crooner, popular in the late thirties but subsequently little heard of.
King of Burlesque 36. The Goldwyn Follies 38. The Mikado (GB: as Nanki Poo) 39. 52nd Street 39. At the Circus 39. Hit Parade of 1941 42. Silver Skates 43. Doughboys in Ireland 43. The Harvey Girls 46, etc.

Baker, Phil (1898–1963). American radio personality who appeared in a few films.
Gift of Gab 34. The Goldwyn Follies 38. The Gang's All Here 43. *Take It or Leave It* 44, etç.

Baker, Robert S. (1916–). British producer: co-founder with Monty Berman of Tempean Films, which since 1948 has produced many co-features, also *The Saint* and other TV series.

Baker, Roy (1916–). Notable British director whose career declined in the sixties. Served apprenticeship at Gainsborough 1934–39, then war service.

The October Man 47. The Weaker Sex 48. *Morning Departure* 50. I'll Never Forget You (US) 51. *Inferno* (US) 52. Don't Bother to Knock (US) 52. Passage Home 54. Jacqueline 56. Tiger in the Smoke 56. *The One That Got Away* 57. *A Night to Remember* 58. The Singer Not the Song (& p) 60. Flame in the Streets (& p) 61. The Valiant 61. Two Left Feet 64. *Quatermass and the Pit* 67. The Anniversary 68. Moon Zero Two 69. The Vampire Lovers 70. Scars of Dracula 70. Dr Jekyll and Sister Hyde 71. Asylum 72. And Now the Screaming Starts 73. Vault of Horror 73. The Legend of the Seven Golden Vampires 74, etc.

Baker, Stanley (1927–1976). Virile Welsh actor who rose from character roles to stardom, projecting honesty or villainy with equal ease.
☐ Undercover 41. All over the Town 48. Your Witness 50. The Rossiter Case 51. Cloudburst 51. Captain Horatio Hornblower 51. Home to Danger 51. Lili Marlene 52. *The Cruel Sea* 53. The Red Beret 53. *Hell Below Zero* 54. Knights of the Round Table 54. The Good Die Young 54. Beautiful Stranger 54. Helen of Troy 55. Alexander the Great 55. A Hill in Korea 56. *Richard III* (as Henry Tudor) 56. Child in the House 56. Checkpoint 57. *Campbell's Kingdom* 57. Violent Playground 57. *Hell Drivers* 57. Sea Fury 58. The Angry Hills 59. Blind Date 60. Jet Storm 60. Yesterday's Enemy 60. Hell is a City 60. *The Criminal* 60. The Guns of Navarone 61. Sodom and Gomorrah 62. A Prize of Arms 62. The Man Who Finally Died 62. Eva 62. In the French Style 63. *Zulu* (& co-p) 63. Dingaka 65. Sands of the Kalahari (& co-p) 65. *Accident* 67. Robbery (& co-p) 67. Where's Jack? 68. Girl with Pistol 68. The Games 69. The Last Grenade 69. Perfect Friday 71. Popsy Pop 71. Innocent Bystanders 72.

Baker, Tom (1941–). British character actor with a larger-than-life air.
Nicholas and Alexandra (as Rasputin) 71. Luther 73. Vault of Horror 73. The Mutations 74. Sinbad's Golden Voyage 75, etc.

Bakewell, William (1908–). American general purpose actor.
The Heart Thief 27. All Quiet on the Western Front 30. Spirit of Notre Dame 31. Three Cornered Moon 33. Cheers for Miss Bishop 41. Davy Crockett 54, many others.

Bakshi, Ralph (–). American animator with a message. Fritz the Cat 71. Heavy Traffic 73. The Nine Lives of Fritz the Cat 75, etc.

Balaban, Barney (1888–1971). American

executive, former exhibitor, president of Paramount 1936–64.

Balaban, Burt (1922–1965). American director.
Lady of Vengeance 57. High Hell 58. Murder Inc. 60, etc.

Balasz, Bela (1884–1949). Hungarian writer.
Wrote book, *Theory of the Film.*
Die Dreigroschenoper 30. *The Blue Light* 31.

Balchin, Nigel (1908–1970). British novelist: books filmed include: *Mine Own Executioner, The Small Back Room, Suspect* ('A Sort of Traitors'). Has also adapted other people's work for the screen: *The Barbarian and the Geisha, The Blue Angel* (remake), etc.

Balcon, Jill (1925–). British actress, daughter of Sir Michael Balcon.
Nicholas Nickleby 47. Good Time Girl 48. Highly Dangerous 50, etc.

Balcon, Sir Michael (1896–). British executive producer. During a long and distinguished career he headed Gainsborough, Gaumont-British, MGM-British, Ealing, Bryanston' and independent production companies, and was directly responsible for the planning and production of many famous films.
Autobiography 1969: *A Lifetime of Films.*
The Thirty-nine Steps 35. Goodbye Mr Chips 38. Next of Kin 41. Dead of Night 45. Kind Hearts and Coronets 49. The Blue Lamp 50. Saturday Night and Sunday Morning 60. Tom Jones 63, many others.

Balderston, John (1889–1954). Anglo-American screenwriter, usually in collaboration, with a penchant for romantic and fantastic themes.
Frankenstein 31. *The Mummy* 32. Smilin' Through 32 and 41. *Berkeley Square* (oa) 33. The Mystery of Edwin Drood 35. *Mad Love* 35. Lives of a Bengal Lancer 35. *Bride of Frankenstein* 35. Beloved Enemy 36. *The Prisoner of Zenda* 37. Victory 40. Tennessee Johnson 42. Gaslight 44. Red Planet Mars 52, others.

Balfour, Betty (1903–). British comedienne of silent days, a popular favourite of the twenties as· pert heroine of *Cinders, Love Life and Laughter* and the *Squibs* series.
The Brat 30. The Vagabond Queen 30. Paddy the Next Best Thing 33. Evergreen 35. Squibs (remake) 36. 29 Acacia Avenue 45.

Balfour, Michael (1918–). American character actor in British films who usually plays dumb gangsters, cabbies, etc.
No Orchids for Miss Blandish 48. Obsession 50. Venetian Bird 53. The Steel Key 55. Breakaway 56. Fiend without a Face 58, many others.

Balin, Ina (1937–) (Ina Rosenberg). American leading lady, with stage experience.
Compulsion 58. The Black Orchid 59. The Comancheros 62. The Patsy 64. The Greatest Story Ever, Told 65. Run like a Thief 68. Charro 69. The Projectionist 71. The Don is Dead 73, etc.

Balin, Mireille (1909–1968). French leading lady.
Don Quixote 33. Pepe le Moko 36. Gueule d'Amour 37, etc.

Ball, Lucille (1910–). American comedienne, a former Goldwyn girl who after a generally unrewarding youth in the movies, turned in middle age to TV and became known as one of the world's great female clowns and a highly competent production executive.
□ Broadway thru a Keyhole 33. Blood Money 33. Roman Scandals 33. Moulin Rouge 33. Nana 34. Bottoms Up 34. Hold that Girl 34. Bulldog Drummond Strikes Back 34. The Affairs of Cellini 34. Kid Millions 34. Broadway Bill 34. Jealousy 34. Men of the Night 34. Fugitive Lady 34. Carnival (first billed role) 35. Roberta 35. Old Man Rhythm 35. Top Hat 35. The Three Musketeers 35. I Dream Too Much 35. Chatterbox 36. Follow the Fleet 36. The Farmer in the Dell 36. Bunker Bean 36. That Girl from Paris 36. Don't Tell the Wife 37. *Stage Door* 37. Joy of Living 38. Go Chase Yourself 38. Having A Wonderful Time 38. *The Affairs of Annabel* 38. Room Service 38. The Next Time I Marry 38. Annabel Takes a Tour 38. Beauty for the Asking 39. Twelve Crowded Hours 39. Panama Lady 39. *Five Came Back* 39. That's Right You're Wrong 39. The Marines Fly High 40. You Can't Fool Your Wife 40. Dance Girl Dance 40. Too Many Girls 40. A Guy, a Girl and Gob 40. Look Who's Laughing 41. Valley of the Sun 42. *The Big Street* (serious role) 42. Seven Days Leave 42. *Du Barry was a Lady* 43. Best Foot Forward 43. Thousands Cheer 43. Meet the People 44. *Without Love* 45. Abbott and Costello in Hollywood 45. Ziegfeld Follies 46. The Dark Corner 46. *Easy to Wed* 46. Two Smart People 46. Lover Come Back 46. Lured 47. *Her Husband's Affairs* 47. *Sorrowful Jones* 49. Easy Living 49. Miss Grant Takes Richmond 49. *Fancy Pants* 50. The Fuller Brush

Girl 50. The Magic Carpet 50. *The Long Long Trailer* 54. Forever Darling 56. *The Facts of Life* 60. Critic's Choice 63. A Guide for the Married Man 67. *Yours Mine and Ours* 68. Mame 73. TV series: *I Love Lucy* 50–. *Here's Lucy* 62–. *The Lucy Show* 68–.

Ball of Fire (US 1941). A zany comedy written by Charles Brackett and Billy Wilder, directed by Howard Hawks. Its plot is cheerfully derived from 'Snow White', the seven dwarfs having become professors writing an encyclopaedia, and Snow White a strip-teaser on the run from gangsters. In view of the talent involved, the fun now seems somewhat slow and obvious despite Gary Cooper, Barbara Stanwyck and a first-rate cast. In 1948 a musical version, *A Song is Born*, became an unsuccessful vehicle for Danny Kaye.

Ball, Suzan (1933–1955). American leading lady of the early fifties.
Untamed Frontier 52. East of Sumatra 53. City Beneath the Sea 53. War Arrow 54. Chief Crazy Horse 55, etc.

Ball, Vincent (–). Australian actor in England.
A Town Like Alice 56. Robbery Under Arms 57. Danger Within 58. Identity Unknown 60, etc.

Ballad of a Soldier (Russia 1959). Pleasant, sentimental, and technically very skilled, this piece of romantic hokum served to show that Soviet film-makers could beat Hollywood at its own game. The simple plot details the mishaps which prevent a soldier from spending his leave in the way he intended before returning to the front and probably death. The leading role is played by Vladimir Ivashov, but the real stars are director Grigori Chukrai and photographers Vladimir Nikolayev and Era Savaleva.

Ballard, Kaye (1926–) (Catherine Balotta). American comedienne with stage experience.
The Girl Most Likely 56. A House is Not a Home 64, etc.
TV series: The Mothers-in-Law 67–68.

Ballard, Lucien (1908–). Distinguished American cinematographer.
Crime and Punishment 35. The King Steps Out 36. Craig's Wife 36. The Shadow 37. Penetentiary 38. *Blind Alley* 39. The Villain Still Pursued Her 40. Wild Geese Calling 41. The Undying Monster 42. Orchestra Wives 42. Holy Matrimony 43. *The Lodger* 44. *Laura* (co-ph) 44. This Love of Ours 45. Temptation 46. Night Song 47. Berlin Express 48. The House on Telegraph Hill 51. O. Henry's Full House 52.

Inferno (3D) 53. New Faces 54. White Feather 55. The Proud Ones 56. *The Killing* 56. Band of Angels 57. Murder by Contract 58. Al Capone 59. Pay or Die 60. The Parent Trap 61. Ride the High Country 62. *The Caretakers* 63. The New Interns 64. Boeing Boeing 65. Nevada Smith 66. *Hour of the Gun* 67. Will Penny 68. *The Wild Bunch* 69. True Grit 69. The Ballad of Cable Hogue 70. The Hawaiians 70. What's the Matter with Helen 71. Junior Bonner 72. The Getaway 72. Breakout 75, etc.

ballet sequences have been a boon to many indifferent films, permitting a brief glimpse into a world that is strange, alarming, but graceful and glamorous. From the time of *The Goldwyn Follies* 38, any Hollywood musical with aspirations had to have a ballet sequence, some of the most memorable being in *The Pirate, On the Town, An American in Paris, Singin' in the Rain*, and *The Band Wagon*. The custom died out in the fifties, since when there has been an over-abundance of unimaginatively presented full-length stage ballets with famous dancing stars. These, filmed at low cost, have found a market, but expensive film ballets like *Tales of Hoffman, Invitation to the Dance* and *Black Tights* had tougher going. Dramatic films set in the ballet world have included *La Mort du Cygne* (remade in Hollywood as *The Unfinished Dance*), *The Red Shoes* and *The Spectre of the Rose*; lighter stories in which the heroine is a ballerina (usually a novice) include *Waterloo Bridge, Carnival, Dance Pretty Lady, On Your Toes* and *St Martin's Lane*. Several comedians have found themselves pursued by plot complications on to a stage and forced to take part clumsily in the ballet in progress: Jack Buchanan in *That's a Good Girl*, Danny Kaye in *Knock on Wood*, Morecambe and Wise in *The Intelligence Men*; while even Laurel and Hardy donned tutus in *The Dancing Masters*.

balloons: See *air balloons*.

ballyhoo. An expressive term, allegedly Irish in origin, used in show business to denote the kind of publicity that has nothing to do with the merits, or indeed the actual contents, of the film in question.

Balsam, Martin (1919–). American character actor of quiet and comfortable presence: range varies from executive to stagecoach driver.
☐ On the Waterfront 54. *Twelve Angry Men* 57. *Time Limit* 57. Marjorie Morningstar 58. Al Capone 59. Middle of the Night 59. *Psycho* (as the ill-fated private detective) 60. Ada 61.

Breakfast at Tiffany's 61. Cape Fear 63. Who's Been Sleeping in My Bed? 63. *The Carpetbaggers* (as the Louis B. Mayer type studio chief) 64. Youngblood Hawke 64. *Seven Days in May* 64. Harlow 65. The Bedford Incident 65. A Thousand Clowns (AA) 65. After the Fox 66. Hombre 67. Me Natalie 69. *The Good Guys and the Bad Guys* 69. Tora! Tora! Tora! 70. Catch 22 70. Little Big Man 70. *The Anderson Tapes* 71. Confessions of a Police Commissioner (It.) 71. The Man (It.) 72. Night of Terror (TV) 72. *Summer Wishes Winter Dreams* 73. The Stone Killer 73. The Taking of Pelham 123 74. Murder on the Orient Express 74. Trapped Beneath the Sea (TV) 74. Miles to Go Before I Sleep (TV) 75. Corruption in the Halls of Justice (It.) 75. Mitchell 75.

Bambi (US 1942). One of Disney's best-loved feature cartoons, virtually excluding the human element from its sentimentalized but charming story of the life of a forest deer, based on the book by Felix Salten.

Bancroft, Anne (1931–) (Anna Maria Italiano). Warm, ambitious and effective American leading actress who after TV experience went to Hollywood in 1952 and made inferior routine films; fled to Broadway stage and after triumph in *The Miracle Worker* returned to films as a star.
□ Don't Bother to Knock 52. Tonight we Sing 53. Treasure of the Golden Condor 53. The Kid from Left Field 53. Demetrius and the Gladiators 54. The Raid 54. Gorilla at Large 54. A Life in the Balance 55. New York Confidential 55. The Naked Street 55. The Last Frontier 55. Walk the Proud Land 56. Nightfall 56. The Restless Breed 57. The Girl in Black Stockings 57. *The Miracle Worker* (AA, BFA) 62. *The Pumpkin Eater* (BFA) 64. *The Slender Thread* 65. Seven Women 65. *The Graduate* 68. *Young Winston* 72. The Prisoner of Second Avenue 75. The Hindenberg 76. Lipstick 76. Silent Movie 76.

Bancroft, George (1882–1956). Burly American actor who after a period in the Navy became popular in Broadway musicals and straight plays. Went to Hollywood in the twenties and found his strong masculine personality much in demand for tough or villainous roles, almost always in run-of-the-mill films.
The Journey's End 21. *Driven* 21. *Pony Express* 25. *Code of the West* 25. *Old Ironsides* 26. *Underworld* 27. White Gold 27. Docks of New York 28. Thunderbolt 29. Derelict 30. Ladies Love Brutes 30. Scandal Sheet 31. Lady and

Gent 33. Blood Money 34. Mr Deeds Goes to Town 36. John Meade's Woman 37. Angels with Dirty Faces 38. *Stagecoach* 39. Each Dawn I Die 39. Young Tom Edison 40. Texas 41. Syncopation 41. Whistling in Dixie 42, many others.

Band, Albert (1924–). French-born director, in Hollywood since the forties.
The Young Guns 56. I Bury the Living (& p) 58. The Tramplers (& p) 66. A Minute to Pray, A Second to Die (& p) 68.

The Bandit (O Cangaceiro) (Brazil 1953). The only Brazilian film to achieve world-wide commercial success, a fact attributable less to writer-director Lima Barreto's routine outlaw story than to the theme music by G. Migliori.

The Band Wagon. 1. British farce of 1939, based on radio show, with Arthur Askey and Richard Murdoch. 2. Hollywood musical of 1953 notable for 'Girl Hunt' ballet, lively Dietz/Schwarz music and lyrics, and star performance of Jack Buchanan.

Bank Holiday (GB 1938). Low-budget 'slice of life' melodrama generally agreed to show the first flowering of Carol Reed's directorial talent. Still enjoyable, in its dated way, for its picture of Brighton on a pre-war summer's day.

Bankhead, Tallulah (1902–1968). Gravel-voiced, highly theatrical leading lady of American stage and screen. The daughter of an eminent politician, she titillated Broadway and London in the twenties by her extravagant performance on stage and off, and later tended to fritter away her considerable talents by living too dangerously. Films never managed to contain her.
Autobiography 1952: *Tallulah.*
□ When Men Betray 18. Thirty a Week 18. A Woman's Law 28. His House in Order 28. *Tarnished Lady* 31. My Sin 31. The Cheat 31. Thunder Below 32. The Devil and the Deep 32. Faithless 32. Stage Door Canteen 43. *Lifeboat* 43. *A Royal Scandal* 45. Main Street to Broadway 53. *Fanatic* (GB) 65.

Banks, Leslie (1890–1952). Distinguished British stage actor who after unsuccessful experiments in home-grown silent films started his film career in Hollywood.
The Most Dangerous Game 32. The Fire-Raisers 33. I am Suzanne 33. Night of the Party 33. *The Man Who Knew Too Much* 34. The Tunnel 35. *Sanders of the River* 35. Fire Over England 36. Farewell Again 37. Wings of the Morning 37.

Twenty-one Days 39. Jamaica Inn 39. The Door with Seven Locks 40. Neutral Port 40. Ships with Wings 41. Cottage to Let 41. The Big Blockade 42. Went the Day Well? 42. *Henry V* (as Chorus) 44. Mrs Fitzherbert 47. The Small Back Room 48. Madeleine 49. Your Witness 50, etc.

Banks, Monty (1897–1950) (Mario Bianchi). Italian comic dancer who appeared in many silent two-reel comedies of the twenties then moved to Britain and later turned director.
Atlantic 30. Weekend Wives 31. Almost a Honeymoon (d) 31. Tonight's the Night (d) 32. No Limit (d) 35. We're Going to be Rich (d) 38. Great Guns (US) (d) 41, etc.

Banky, Vilma (1902–) (Vilma Lonchit). Austro-Hungarian star of American silents, discovered by Sam Goldwyn during a European holiday. Popular in the twenties but could not make the transition to sound.
The Dark Angel 25. The Eagle 25. *Son of The Sheik* 26. The Winning of Barbara Worth 28. A Lady to Love 30, etc.

Bannen, Ian (1928–). British stage and TV actor who has been effective in several films.
Private's Progress 55. The Birthday Present 57. Carlton Browne of the F.O. 58. Macbeth 59. *A French Mistress* 60. *Suspect* 60. On Friday at Eleven 61. Station Six Sahara 63. Rotten to the Core 65. *The Hill* 65. The Flight of the Phoenix 65. Sailor from Gibraltar 66. Penelope 67. Lock Up Your Daughters 69. Too Late the Hero 69. Fright 71. Doomwatch 72. The Offence 72. The Mackintosh Man 73. Bite the Bullet 75, etc.

Banner, John (1910–1973). American character actor of Polish origin; usually played explosive Europeans.
Once upon a Honeymoon 42. The Fallen Sparrow 44. Black Angel 47. My Girl Tisa 48. The Juggler 53. The Rains of Ranchipur 56. The Story of Ruth 60. Hitler 63. Thirty-six Hours 64, etc.
TV series: *Hogan's Heroes* 65–69, Chicago Teddy Bears 71.

Bannon, Jim (1911–). American actor with radio experience: played second feature leads in the forties and starred in a western series as 'Red Ryder' in the fifties.
The Missing Juror 44. I Love a Mystery 45. The Thirteenth Hour 47. Daughter of the Jungle 49. The Man from Colorado 49. Rodeo 53. Chicago Confidential 58. Madame X 65, many others.
TV series: Champion 55.

Bar, Jacques (1921–). French producer,

often in association with American companies.
Where the Hot Wind Blows 60. Vie Privée 61. A Monkey in Winter 62. Joy House 64. Once a Thief 65. The Guns of San Sebastian 67, etc.

Bara, Theda (1890–1955) (Theodosia Goodman). American actress, the first to be called a 'vamp' (because of her absurdly vampirish, man-hungry screen personality). An extra in 1915, she was whisked to stardom on some highly imaginary publicity statistics (she was the daughter of an Eastern potentate, her name was an anagram of 'Arab death', etc.). *A Fool There Was* 16 is remembered for its classic sub-title, 'Kiss Me, My Fool!'; in 1919, her popularity waning, she forsook Hollywood for the Broadway stage, and when she returned in 1925 was forced to accept parts burlesquing her former glories, e.g. *Madame Mystery* 26. Wisely, she soon retired.
☐ The Two Orphans 15. The Clemenceau Case 15. The Stain 15. *A Fool there Was* 16. Sin 16. Carmen 16. Romeo and Juliet 16. The Light 16. Destruction 16. Gold and the Woman 16. The Serpent 16. Eternal Sappho 16. East Lynne 16. Her Double Life 16. *Cleopatra* 17. Madame Du Barry 17. Under Two Flags 17. Camille 17. Heart and Soul 17. The Tiger Woman 17. Salome 18. When a Woman Sins 18. The Forbidden Path 18. The She Devil 18. Rose of the Blood 18. Kathleen Mavourneen 19. La Belle Russe 19. The Price of Silence 21. Her Greatest Love 21. The Hunchback of Notre Dame 23. The Unchastened Woman 25. Madame Mystery 26. The Dancer of Paris 26.

Baratier, Jacques (1918–). French director of shorts and occasional features.
Paris la Nuit 55. Goha 57. La Poupée 62. Dragées au Poivre 63. L'Or du Duc 65, etc.

Barbera, Joe (–). American animator who with William Hanna (qv) created Tom and Jerry at MGM and later formed an independent company which produced dozens of 'semi-animated' cartoon series for TV, including the adventures of Yogi Bear, Huckleberry Hound, the Jetsons, the Flintstones, Magilla Gorilla, Scooby Doo and Snagglepuss.

Barbier, George (1865–1945). American character actor remembered in talkies as a blustery but essentially kindly old man.
Monsieur Beaucaire 24. The Big Bond 30. The Sap from Syracuse 30. The Smiling Lieutenant 31. No Man of her Own 32. One Hour with You 32. Million Dollar Legs 32. The Big Broadcast 32. Mama Loves Papa 33. Tillie and Gus 34. Ladies Should Listen 34. *The Merry Widow* 34.

The Crusades 35. The Cat's Paw 35. The Milky Way 36. The Princess Comes Across 36. *On the Avenue* 37. Hotel Haywire 37. Tarzan's Revenge 38. Little Miss Broadway 38. Sweethearts 38. News is Made at Night 39. The Return of Frank James 40. *The Man Who Came to Dinner* 41. Weekend in Havana 41. The Magnificent Dope 42. Song of the Islands 42. Hello Frisco Hello 43. Weekend Pass 44. Her Lucky Night 45, many others.

Barcroft, Roy (1902–1969). Beefy American character actor, usually seen as a western heavy.
Dakota 45. My Pal Trigger 46. The Fabulous Texan 47. Surrender 50. Man Without a Star 55. Oklahoma! 55. Six Black Horses 62, many others.

Bardem, Juan-Antonio (1922–). Spanish director.
Welcome Mr Marshall 52. *Death of a Cyclist* 54. Calle Mayor 56. Vengeance 57. Sonatas 59. Los Innocentes 62. Los Pianos Mecanicos 64. The Uninhibited 68. Variétés 71, etc.

Bardot, Brigitte (1933–) (Camille Javal). Pulchritudinous French pin-up girl who, given world publicity as a 'sex kitten', used her small but significant talents to make some routine movies very profitable.
Act of Love 54. Doctor at Sea (GB) 55. *The Light across the Street* 55. Helen of Troy 55. *And God Created Woman* 56. Heaven Fell That Night 57. Une Parisienne 57. *En Cas de Malheur* 57. Please Mr Balzac 57. The Devil is a Woman 58. Mam'zelle Pigalle 58. Babette Goes to War 59. Please Not Now 61. *The Truth* 61. *Vie Privée* 61. *Love on a Pillow* 62. *Contempt* 64. Dear Brigitte 65. *Viva Maria* 65. Masculin Feminin 67. Two Weeks in September 67. Shalako 68. *The Novices* 70. The Legend of Frenchy King 72. Don Juan 73, etc.

Bare, Richard (c. 1909–). American director who moved into TV.
Smart Girls Don't Talk 48. Flaxy Martin 48. Return of the Frontiersman 51. Prisoners of the Casbah 53. Shoot-Out at Medicine Bend 57. This Rebel Breed 60, etc.

Bari, Lynn (1915–) (Marjorie Bitzer or Fisher). Pert American 'second lead', often in 'other woman' roles. A chorus graduate, she was given plenty of work in the thirties and forties but almost all of it was routine.
Dancing Lady 33. Stand Up and Cheer 34. Thanks a Million 35. Sing Baby Sing 36. Wee Willie Winkie 37. Josette 38. Return of the Cisco Kid 39. Hollywood Cavalcade 39. Earthbound

40. *Sun Valley Serenade* 41. *Moon Over Her Shoulder* 41. *The Magnificent Dope* 42. *Orchestra Wives* 42. Hello Frisco Hello 43. *The Bridge of San Luis Rey* 44. Tampico 44. Captain Eddie 45. Shock 45. *Margie* 46. The Man from Texas 48. On the Loose 51. Has Anybody Seen My Gal? 52. Francis Joins the WACS 54. Women of Pitcairn Island 56. Damn Citizen 58. Trauma 64. The Young Runaways 68, many others.

Barker, Eric (1912–). British character comedian long popular on radio with his wife Pearl Hackney.
Brothers in Law 57. Happy is the Bride 58. Blue Murder at St Trinian's 58. Carry On Sergeant 58. Left, Right and Centre 59. Carry On Constable 60. Heavens Above 63. The Bargee 65. The Great St Trinian's Train Robbery 66. Maroc 7 67, etc.

Barker, Jess (1914–). Lightweight American leading man of minor forties films.
Cover Girl 44. Keep Your Powder Dry 44. This Love of Ours 45. Take One False Step 49. Shack Out on 101 56, etc.

Barker, Lex (1919–1973). Blond, virile-looking American actor who in 1948 was signed to play Tarzan (qv). After five films the role passed to another actor and Barker's stock slumped, but he continued to make routine action adventures.
Battles of Chief Pontiac 52. The Price of Fear 56. Jungle Heat 57. The Girl in the Kremlin 57. La Dolce Vita 59. Victim Five 63. Kali-Yug, Goddess of Vengeance 64. A Place Called Glory 66. Old Shatterhand 68, etc.

Barker, Ronnie (1929–). Portly but versatile British TV comedian, rarely seen in films.
Doctor in Distress 63. The Bargee 64. The Man Outside 67. *Futtock's End* 70. Robin and Marian 76, etc.

Barker, Will C. (1867–1951). Pioneer British producer.
Henry VIII 11. Sixty Years a Queen 13. East Lynne 13. Jane Shore 15, etc.

Barkworth, Peter (1929–). Smooth British comedy actor, mostly on TV.
Tiara Tahiti 57. A Touch of Larceny 61. No Love for Johnnie 63. Where Eagles Dare 69, etc.

Barnard, Ivor (1887–1953). British character actor of stage and screen, often of henpecked or nosey parker types.
Waltz Time 33. The Wandering Jew 34. Storm in a Teacup 37. Pygmalion 38. The Saint's

Vacation 41. Hotel Reserve 44. The Wicked Lady 45. Great Expectations 46. Oliver Twist 48. *Beat the Devil* (his last and best role, as a vicious killer) 53, many others.

Barnes, Barry K. (1906–1965). Stylish British stage actor, in occasional films.
□ *The Return of the Scarlet Pimpernel* 38. *This Man is News* 38. The Ware Case 38. Prison without Bars 39. The Midas Touch 40. Spies of the Air 40. The Girl in the News 41. Dancing with Crime 46. Bedelia 46.

Barnes, Binnie (1905–)(Gitelle Barnes). Self-confident British light actress who after varied experience made a few early British talkies then went to Hollywood in 1934 and played mainly smart wise-cracking ladies.
Love Lies 31. Murder at Covent Garden 31. Heads We Go 33. *The Private Life of Henry VIII* (as Katherine Howard) 33. The Private Life of Don Juan 34. Diamond Jim 35. The Last of the Mohicans 35. The Magnificent Brute 36. *Three Smart Girls* 37. The Adventures of Marco Polo 38. Three Blind Mice 38. The Divorce of Lady X 38. *The Three Musketeers* 39. Till We Meet Again 40. Tight Shoes 41. Skylark 41. *Three Girls About Town* 41. The Man from Down Under 43. Barbary Coast Gent 44. *Up in Mabel's Room* 44. *It's in the Bag* 45. The Spanish Main 45. If Winter Comes 47. My Own True Love 48. Fugitive Lady 51. Decameron Nights 53. Shadow of the Eagle 55. *The Trouble with Angels* 66. Where Angels Go, Trouble Follows 68. Forty Carats 72, many others.

Barnes, George (1893–1953). Distinguished American cinematographer.
The Haunted Bedroom 19. Silk Hosiery 21. Hairpins 22. Dusk to Dawn 24. *The Eagle* 25. *Son of the Sheik* 26. Janice Meredith 27. Sadie Thompson 28. Our Dancing Daughters 28. *Bulldog Drummond* 29. The Trespasser 29. *Condemned* 29. Raffles 30. Five and Ten 31. The Unholy Garden 31. Street Scene 31. The Wet Parade 32. Sherlock Holmes 32. Peg O' My Heart 33. *Footlight Parade* 33. Massacre 34. *Dames* 34. Flirtation Walk 34. In Caliente 35. The Singing Kid 36. Black Legion 36. *Marked Woman* 37. Hollywood Hotel 37. Gold Diggers in Paris 38. *Jesse James* 39. *Rebecca* (AA) 40. Devil's Island 40. Hudson's Bay 40. *Meet John Doe* 41. *Ladies in Retirement* 41. Rings on Her Fingers 42. Once Upon a Honeymoon 42. Mr Lucky 43. *Frenchman's Creek* 44. *Jane Eyre* 44. None But the Lonely Heart 44. *Spellbound* 45. The Spanish Main 45. The Bells of St Mary's 45. *From This Day Forward* 46. Sinbad the Sailor 47. Mourning Becomes Electra 47. The Emperor

Waltz 48. The Boy with Green Hair 48. *Force of Evil* 49. Let's Dance 50. Mr Music 50. Riding High 50. Here Comes the Groom 51. Something to Live For 52. *The War of the Worlds* 53. Little Boy Lost 53, etc.

Barnes, Joanna (1934–). American actress occasionally seen in cool supporting roles.
Home Before Dark 58. Spartacus 60. The Parent Trap 61. Goodbye Charlie 64. The War Wagon 67. B.S. I Love You 70, etc.

Barnett, Vince (1902–). American character actor, usually of minor gangsters or downtrodden little men.
Scarface 32. I Cover the Waterfront 35. A Star is Born 37. No Leave, No Love 42. The Killers 46. Brute Force 47. The Human Jungle 54, many others.

Barney Oldfield's Race for Life. This oft-quoted film is a twenty-minute Mack Sennett short of 1912, parodying the old railroad melodramas. Mabel Normand and Ford Sterling starred.

Baron Münchhausen (Czechoslovakia 1962). Karel Zeman's stylish if slightly arid semi-animated fantasy is the last of a longish line of movies about the tall-story teller. Méliès made a version in 1911, Emile Cohl in 1913; Hans Albers starred in a German version in 1943. The real Münchhausen (1720–97) was a German army officer, but the collection of stories written by Rudolf Raspe (first published in English in 1785) included much material from other sources.

Barr, Patrick (1908–). British stage, screen and TV actor who has been playing solid dependable types since the thirties.
Norah O'Neale 34. The Return of the Scarlet Pimpernel 38. The Frightened Lady 41. The Blue Lagoon 48. Robin Hood 52. Singlehanded 53. Crest of the Wave 54. Saint Joan 57. Next to No Time 60. The Longest Day 62. Billy Liar 63. Ring of Spies 64. House of Whipcord 74, many others.

Barrat, Robert (1891–1970). American character actor in films from silent days, usually as heavy western villain.
The Picture Snatcher 33. Devil Dogs of the Air 35. Last of the Mohicans 36. The Buccaneer 38. Go West 41. The Adventures of Mark Twain 44. Magnificent Doll 47. Joan of Arc 48. Tall Man Riding 55, many others.

Barrault, Jean-Louis (1910–). Celebrated

French stage actor, in a few rewarding film roles.
Mademoiselle Docteur 36. *Drôle de Drame* 36.
La Symphonie Fantastique 42. *Les Enfants du
Paradis* 44. D'Homme à Hommes 48. La Ronde
50. Le Testament du Docteur Cordelier 59. The
Longest Day 62.

Barreto, Lima (1905–). Brazilian director
responsible for his country's best known film, *O
Cangaceiro (The Bandit)* 53.

Barrett, James Lee (1929–). American
Screenwriter.
The D.I. 58. The Greatest Story Ever Told (co-
w) 65. The Truth About Spring 65. Shenandoah
65. Bandolero 68. The Green Berets 68. The
Cheyenne Social Club (& p) 70, etc.

Barrett, Jane (1923–1969). British leading
lady.
The Captive Heart 45. Eureka Stockade 48.
Time Gentlemen Please 52. The Sword and the
Rose 53, etc.

Barrett, Ray (1926–). Australian leading
actor in British TV and films.
The Sundowners 60. Touch of Death 62. Jigsaw
63. The Reptile 65. Revenge 71, etc.
TV series: *The Troubleshooters* 66–71.

The Barretts of Wimpole Street. Rudolph
Besier's play about the wooing by Robert
Browning of Elizabeth Barrett against her
tyrannical father's opposition was twice filmed
by MGM. The 1934 version with Norma
Shearer, Fredric March and Charles Laughton
was a resounding success; the 1956 version with
Jennifer Jones, Bill Travers and John Gielgud
was a failure. Both versions were directed by
Sidney Franklin. The play was later turned into a
musical, *Robert and Elizabeth*, but no film has so
far materialized.

Barrie, Amanda (1939–) (Amanda
Broadbent). British leading lady with TV
experience.
Carry On Cleo 64. I Gotta Horse 65, etc.

Barrie, Mona (1909–) (Mona Smith).
Australian 'second lead' actress, in Hollywood
from early thirties.
Carolina 34. The House of Connelly 34. A
Message to Garcia 36. I Met Him in Paris 37.
When Ladies Meet 41. Cairo 42. Storm over
Lisbon 44. I Cover Big Town 47. Strange
Fascination 52. Plunder of the Sun 53, many
others.

Barrie, Sir J. M. (1860–1937). British

playwright whose work usually had a
recognizable fey quality, which even survived the
film versions.
The Admirable Crichton (qv) 17. Peter Pan 24
and 53. The Little Minister 34. What Every
Woman Knows 34. Quality Street 37. Darling
How Could You? ('Alice Sit by the Fire') 51.
Forever Female ('Rosalind') 53, etc.

Barrie, Wendy (1912–) (Wendy Jenkins).
Bright British leading lady who went to
Hollywood in 1934 but found only mediocre
roles. Had her own TV show in 1948, and was
later active in local radio.
It's a Boy (GB) 32. *The Private Life of Henry
VIII* (GB) 32. For Love or Money 34. A Feather
in Her Hat 35. Love on a Bet 36. Dead End 37. I
Am the Law 38. The Hound of the Baskervilles
39. Five Came Back 39. The Saint Takes Over
40. Who Killed Aunt Maggie? 40. The Gay
Falcon 41. Eyes of the Underworld 42. Women
in War 42. Forever and a Day 43. It Could
Happen to You (guest appearance) 53, etc.

Barrier, Edgar (1906–1964). American
character actor with stage experience.
Escape 40. Arabian Nights 42. Phantom of the
Opera 43. Flesh and Fantasy 44. *A Game of
Death* 45. Macbeth 48. To the Ends of the Earth
48. Cyrano de Bergerac 50. Princess of the Nile
54. On the Double 61. Irma la Douce 63, many
others.

barring clause. The part of an exhibitor's
contract with a renter preventing him from
showing new films before other specified cinemas
in the area. The showing of a film in London may
thus prevent its exhibition elsewhere within a
radius of fifty miles or more.

Barron, Keith (1934–). British leading actor
of the angry young man type; mostly on TV.
Baby Love 69. Melody 70. The Fire Chasers 70.
The Man Who Had Power over Women 70.
She'll Follow You Anywhere 71. Nothing But
the Night 73, The Land That Time Forgot 75,
etc.

Barry, Don (1912–) (Donald Barry d'Acosta).
Rugged American actor, in Hollywood from
1939 after stage experience and immediately
popular as hero of second feature westerns.
Night Waitress 36. The Crowd Roars 38. Calling
All Marines 39. Remember Pearl Harbor 42. The
Chicago Kid 45. The Dalton Gang 49. Jesse
James' Women (& d) 53. I'll Cry Tomorrow 55.
Walk on the Wild Side 62. Fort Utah 66.
Bandolero 68. Shalako 68, etc.

Barry, Gene (1921–) (Eugene Klass). Poised and debonair American leading man who also does a song and dance act. Films routine, but TV has kept him busy.

□ The Atomic City 52. The Girls of Pleasure Island 52. *The War of the Worlds* 53. Those Redheads from Seattle 53. Alaska Seas 54. *Red Garters* 54. *Naked Alibi* 54. Soldier of Fortune 55. The Purple Mask 55. The Houston Story 56. Back From Eternity 56. The 27th Day 57. China Gate 57. *Thunder Road* 58. Maroc 7 67. Subterfuge 69. Do You Take This Stranger? (TV) 70. The Devil and Miss Sarah (TV) 71. Second Coming of Suzanne 73.

TV series: *Bat Masterson* 59–61. *Burke's Law* 63–65. *The Name of the Game* 68–70. The Adventurer 72.

Barry, Iris (1895–1969). Founder-member of the London Film Society (1925); director of New York Museum of Modern Art Film Library from 1935; president of the International Federation of Film Archives 1946; author of books on the film.

Barry, John (1933–) (J. B. Prendergast). British composer.

Beat Girl 59. The Amorous Prawn 62. The L-shaped Room 62. From Russia with Love 63. Zulu 63. The Man in the Middle 64. Goldfinger 64. The Ipcress File 65. The Knack 65. Thunderball 65. King Rat 65 The Chase 66. Born Free 66. The Wrong Box 66. The Quiller Memorandum 66. Petulia 68. Boom 68. Deadfall 68. The Lion in Winter (AA) 68. Midnight Cowboy 69. Murphy's War 71. They Might Be Giants 71. Diamonds are Forever 72, etc.

Barry, Philip (1896–1949). American playwright, several of whose sophisticated comedies have been filmed.

The Animal Kingdom 32 (remade as One More Tomorrow 46). Holiday 38. The Philadelphia Story 40. Without Love 45.

Barrymore, Diana (1921–1960). American actress, daughter of John Barrymore, She made a few mediocre films in the early forties but was not a successful leading lady and later succumbed to alcoholism. Her autobiography *Too Much Too Soon* was filmed in 1958 with Dorothy Malone (and Errol Flynn as John Barrymore).

□ Eagle Squadron 42. *Between Us Girls* 42. Nightmare 42. Frontier Badmen 43. Fired Wife 43. *Ladies Courageous* 44.

Barrymore, Ethel (1897–1959). Distinguished American actress of regal presence; sister of Lionel and John, daughter of Maurice Barrymore, Made a few silents, then remained on Broadway until 1944 when she made her home in Hollywood and played crotchety old ladies with hearts of gold.

Autobiography 1956: *Memories.*

□ The Nightingale 14. The Final Judgment 15. The Awakening of Helen Ritchie 16. Kiss of Hate 16. The White Raven 17. The Lifted Veil 17. The Eternal Mother 17. The American Widow 17. Life's Whirlpool 17. The Call of Her People 17. Our Miss McChesney 18. The Divorcee 19. Rasputin and the Empress (only film appearance with her brothers) 32. *None but the Lonely Heart* (AA) 44. The Spiral Staircase 46. *The Farmer's Daughter* 47. Moss Rose 47. The Paradine Case 48. Night Song 48. Moonrise 49. Portrait of Jennie 49. The Great Sinner 49. That Midnight Kiss 49. Pinky 49. The Red Danube 49. The Secret of Convict Lake 51. *Kind Lady* 51. It's a Big Country 52. *Deadline* 52. Just for You 52. The Story of Three Loves 53. Main Street to Broadway 53. Young at Heart 54. Johnny Trouble 57.

Barrymore, John (1882–1942). Celebrated American stage and screen actor, brother of Ethel and Lionel Barrymore. A famous matinée idol with a 'great profile', he became a famous romantic movie star of the twenties but later squandered his talents in inferior comedies caricaturing his own alcoholism and debauchery. A great personality and a splendid if often misguided talent.

Autobiography 1926: *Confessions of an Actor.* Best biography by Gene Fowler 1944: *Good Night Sweet Prince.*

□ Are You a Mason? 13. An American Citizen 13. The Man from Mexico 14. The Dictator 15. The Incorrigible Dukane 16. The Lost Bridegroom 16. The Red Widow 16. *Raffles* 17. On the Quiet 18. Here Comes the Bride 18. Test of Honour 19. *Dr Jekyll and Mr Hyde* 20. The Lotus Eater 21. *Sherlock Holmes* 22. *Beau Brummell* 24. *The Sea Beast* 26. *Don Juan* 26. When a Man Loves 27. *The Beloved Rogue* 27. *Tempest* 28. Eternal Love 29. *Show of Shows* (first talkie: recites Richard III) 29. General Crack 29. The Man from Blankley's 30. *Moby Dick* 30. *Svengali* 31. The Mad Genius 31. *Arsène Lupin* 32. *Grand Hotel* 32. State's Attorney 32. *A Bill of Divorcement* 32. *Rasputin and the Empress* 32. *Topaze* 33. *Reunion In Vienna* 33. *Dinner at Eight* 33. Night Flight 33. *Counsellor at Law* 33. Long Lost Father 34. *Twentieth Century* 34. *Romeo and Juliet* (as Mercutio) 36. *Maytime* 37. *Bulldog Drummond Comes Back* (as the inspector) 37. Night Club Scandal 37. Bulldog Drummond's Revenge 37.

Bulldog Drummond's Peril 37. *True Confession* 38. Romance in the Dark 38. *Marie Antoinette* 38. *Spawn of the North* 38. *Hold that Co-Ed* 38. *The Great Man Votes* 39. *Midnight* 39. The Great Profile 40. Invisible Woman 41. World Premiere 41. Playmates 42.

Barrymore, John Jnr (1932–) (John Drew Barrymore). American actor, son of John Barrymore and Dolores Costello. Usually plays weaklings.
The Sundowners 50. The Big Night 51. Thunderbirds 52. While the City Sleeps 56. The Boatmen 59. The Cossacks 60. Nights of Rasputin 61. War of the Zombies 63, etc.

Barrymore, Lionel (1878–1954). Celebrated American character actor, brother of Ethel and John Barrymore. His career was almost entirely devoted to films, including some direction; from the early thirties he was a familiar and well-loved member of the MGM galaxy, playing sentimental grandpas and churlish millionaires. From 1938, arthritis and two falls forced him to act from a wheelchair.
Autobiography 1951: *We Barrymores.*
☐ Friends 09. Fighting Blood 11. Judith of Bethulia 11. The New York Hat 12. The Seats of the Mighty 14. Under the Gaslight 14. Wildfire 15. A Modern Magdalen 15. The Curious Conduct 15. The Flaming Sword 15. Dora 15. A Yellow Streak 15. The Exploits of Elaine 15. Dorian's Divorce 16. The Quitter 16. The Upheaval 16. The Brand of Cowardice 16. His Father's Son 17. The End of the Tour 17. The Millionaire's Double 17. Life's Whirlpool 17. The Valley of Night 19. The Devil's Garden 20. The Copperhead 20. The Master Mind 20. Jim the Penman 21. The Great Adventure 21. Face in the Fog 22. Boomerang 22. Enemies of Women 23. Unseeing Eyes 23. The Eternal City 24. America 24. Meddling Women 24. The Iron Man 25. Children of the Whirlwind 25. The Girl Who Wouldn't Work 25. Fifty Fifty 25. I am the Man 25. The Wrongdoers 25. The Barrier 26. *The Bells* 26. The Splendid Road 26. The Temptress 26. Brooding Eyes 26. The Lucky Lady 26. Paris at Midnight 26. Women Love Diamonds 27. The Show 27. Body and Soul 27. The 13th Hour 27. Drums of Love 27. Love 27. *Sadie Thompson* 28. West of Zanzibar 28. Decameron Nights 28. The Lion and the Mouse 28. Roadhouse 28. The River Woman 28. Alias Jimmy Valentine (first talkie) 29. Mysterious Island 29. Hollywood Revue 29. Confession (d only) 29. Madame X (d only) 29. His Glorious Night (d only) 29. The Unholy Night (d only) 29. The Rogue Song (d only) 30. Free and Easy 30. Ten Cents a Dance (d only) 31. *A Free Soul*

(AA) 31. The Yellow Ticket 31. Guilty Hands 31. Mata Hari 31. *The Man I Killed* 32. *Arsène Lupin* 32. *Grand Hotel* 32. Washington Masquerade 32. *Rasputin and the Empress* (as Rasputin) 32. Sweepings 33. Looking Forward 33. The Stranger's Return 33. Dinner at Eight 33. One Man's Journey 33. Night Flight 33. Christopher Bean 33. Should Ladies Behave? 33. This Side of Heaven 34. Carolina 34. The Girl from Missouri 34. Treasure Island 34. David Copperfield 34. The Little Colonel 35. Mark of the Vampire 35. Public Hero Number One 35. The Return of Peter Grimm 35. *Ah Wilderness* 35. The Voice of Bugle Ann 36. The Road to Glory 36. *The Devil Doll* 36. The Gorgeous Hussy 36. *Camille* 37. *A Family Affair* (first of Hardy Family series) 37. Captains Courageous 37. Saratoga 37. Navy Blue and Gold 37. A Yank at Oxford 38. Test Pilot 38. *You Can't Take It With You* 38. *Young Dr Kildare* (start of series, as Dr Gillespie) 38. Let Freedom Ring 39. Calling Dr Kildare 39. *On Borrowed Time* 39. The Secret of Dr Kildare 39. Dr Kildare's Strange Case 40. Dr Kildare Goes Home 40. Dr Kildare's Crisis 40. The Bad Man 41. The Penalty 41. The People vs Dr Kildare 41. Dr Kildare's Wedding Day 41. Lady Be Good 41. Dr Kildare's Victory 41. *Calling Dr Gillespie* 42. Dr Gillespie's New Assistant 42. Tennessee Johnson 43. Dr Gillespie's Criminal Case 43. Thousands Cheer 43. A Guy Named Joe 43. Three Men in White 44. Since You Went Away 44. Between Two Women 45. The Valley of Decision 45. *Three Wise Fools* 46. *It's a Wonderful Life* 46. The Secret Heart 46. *Duel in the Sun* 46. Dark Delusion 47. *Key Largo* 48. Down to the Sea in Ships 49. Malaya 50. Right Cross 50. Bannerline 51. Lone Star 52. Main Street to Broadway 53.

Bart, Lionel (1930–) (Lionel Begleiter). London-born lyricist and composer who can't read music but has been phenomenally successful with West End Musicals such as *Fings Ain't What They Used To Be, Oliver, Blitz* and *Maggie May.* Has written songs and scores for films since 1957; *Oliver* was filmed in 1968.

Barthelmess, Richard (1895–1963). Presentable American leading man who went straight from college into silent films. Griffith used him memorably, and in 1921 he formed his own company and was popular until the advent of talkies, which made his innocent image seem old-fashioned and condemned him to insipid character roles.
☐ The Hope Chest 19. Boots 19. The Girl Who Stayed Home 19. Three Men and a Girl 19. Peppy Polly 19. *Broken Blossoms* 19. I'll Get

Him Yet 19. Scarlet Days 19. The Idol Dancer 20. The Love Flower 20. Experience 21. *Tol'able David* 21. The Seventh Day 22. Sonny 22. The Bond Boy 22. The Bright Shawl 23. The Fighting Blade 23. Twenty One 24. *The Enchanted Cottage* 24. Classmates 24. New Toys 25. Soul Fire 25. Shore Leave 25. The Beautiful City 25. Just Suppose 26. Ranson's Folly 26. The Amateur Gentleman 26. The White Black Sheep 26. *The Patent Leather Kid* 27. The Drop Kick 27. The Noose 28. Kentucky Courage 28. Wheels of Chance 28. Out of the Ruins 28. Scarlet Seas 28. Weary River 29. Drag 29. Young Nowheres 29. Show of Shows 29. Son of the Gods 30. *The Dawn Patrol* 30. The Lash 31. Way Down East 31. The Finger Points 31. The Last Flight 31. Alias the Doctor 32. *Cabin in the Cotton* 32. Central Airport 33. Heroes for Sale 33. Massacre 33. *A Modern Hero* 34. Midnight Alibi 34. Spy of Napoleon 35. Four Hours to Kill 35. *Only Angels Have Wings* 39. The Man Who Talked Too Much 40. The Mayor of 44th Street 42. *The Spoilers* 42.

Bartholomew, Freddie (1924–) (Frederick Llewellyn). Impeccably well-bred British child actor whose success in Hollywood films of the thirties delighted elderly aunts the world over. His somewhat toffee-nosed image fell from favour during the war and as an adult he moved out of show business into advertising.
□ Fascination (GB) 30. Lily Christine (GB) 32. *David Copperfield* 35. Anna Karenina 35. Professional Soldier 35. *Little Lord Fauntleroy* 36. The Devil is a Sissy 36. Lloyds of London 36. *Captains Courageous* 37. *Kidnapped* 38. Lord Jeff 38. Listen Darling 38. Spirit of Culver 38. Two Bright Boys 39. *The Swiss Family Robinson* 40. *Tom Brown's Schooldays* 40. Naval Academy 41. Cadets on Parade 42. A Yank at Eton 42. The Town Went Wild 44. Sepia Cinderella 47. St Benny the Dip 51.

Bartlett, Hall (1922–). American independent producer whose films seldom seem quite good enough to be independent about.
□ *Navajo* 52. Unchained (& wd) 55. *Drango* (& wd) 56. Zero Hour (& d) 57. All the Young Men (& d) 60. *The Caretakers* (& d) 64. A Global Affair 64. Sol Madrid 68. Jonathan Livingston Seagull (& d, co-w) 73.

Barlett, Sy (1909–) (Sacha Baraniev). American screenwriter, and more recently producer.
The Big Brain (w) 33. Boulder Dam (w) 35. Coconut Grove 38. Road to Zanzibar (co-w) 41. Bullet Scars 42. The Princess and the Pirate 44. 13 Rue Madeleine 46. Down to the Sea in Ships

49. *Twelve O'Clock High* (w) 49. That Lady (wp) 55. *The Big Country* (w) 57. A Gathering of Eagles (wp) 63. Che (p) 69, etc.

Bartok, Eva (1926–) (Eva Sjöke). Agreeable Hungarian leading lady in international films. Autobiography 1959: *Worth Living For.*
A Tale of Five Cities 51. Venetian Bird 52. The Crimson Pirate 52. Front Page Story 54. Ten Thousand Bedrooms 57. Operation Amsterdam 59. SOS Pacific 60. Beyond the Curtain 60. Blood and Black Lace 64, etc.

Barton, Charles (1902–). Routine American director, long at Universal.
□ Wagon Wheels 34. Car 99 35. Rocky Mountain Mystery 35. The Last Outpost (co-d) 35. Timothy's Quest 36. And Sudden Death 36. Nevada 36. Rose Bowl 36. Murder with Pictures 36. The Crime Nobody Saw 37. Forlorn River 37. Thunder Train 37. Born to the West 38. Behind Prison Gates 39. Five Little Peppers and How They Grew 39. My Son is Guilty 40. Five Little Peppers at Home 40. Island of Doomed Men 40. Babies for Sale 40. Out West with the Peppers 40. Five Little Peppers in Trouble 40. Nobody's Children 40. The Phantom Submarine 40. The Big Boss 41. The Richest Man in Town 41. Harmon of Michigan 41. Two Latins from Manhattan 41. Sing for your Supper 41. Honolulu Lu 41. Shut My Big Mouth 42. Tramp Tramp Tramp 42. Hello Anapolis 42. Parachute Nurse 42. Sweetheart of the Fleet 42. A Man's World 42. Lucky Legs 42. The Spirit of Stanford 42. Laugh Your Blues Away 42. *Reveille with Beverly* 43. Let's Have Fun 43. She Has What It Takes 43. What's Buzzin Cousin 43. Is Everybody Happy 43. Beautiful but Broke 44. Hey Rookie 44. Jam Session 44. Louisiana Hayride 44. The Beautiful Cheat 45. Men in her Diary 45. White Tie and Tails 45. *The Time of Their Lives* 46. Smooth as Silk 46. The Wistful Widow of Wagon Gap 47. Buck Privates Come Home 47. Mexican Hayride 48. *Abbott and Costello Meet Frankenstein* 48. The Noose Hangs High 48. Free for All 49. Africa Screams 49. Abbott and Costello Meet the Killer 49. The Milkman 50. Double Crossbones 50. Ma and Pa Kettle at the Fair 52. Dance with Me Henry 56. The Shaggy Dog 59. Toby Tyler 60. Swinging Along 62.

Barton, Dee (–). American composer. High Plains Drifter 73. Thunderbolt and Lightfoot 74.

Barton, James (1902–1962). Grizzled, good-humoured American character actor, a veteran of burlesque and Broadway.

Captain Hurricane 35. Shepherd of the Hills 41. *The Time of Your Life* 48. Yellow Sky 49. The Daughter of Rosie O'Grady 50. Wabash Avenue 50. Here Comes the Groom 51. Golden Girl 51. The Naked Hills 57. Quantez 57. *The Misfits* 61, etc.

Bartosch, Berthold (1893–). Austro-Hungarian animator, best known for his symbolic *L'Idée* 34.

Barzman, Ben (1911–). Canadian writer with Hollywood experience; in Britain from early fifties.
True to Life 42. The Boy with Green Hair 48. He Who Must Die 56. Time Without Pity 57. Blind Date 59. The Ceremony 63. The Heroes of Telemark 65. The Blue Max 66, etc.

baseball has been the subject for occasional films since 1899, when *Casey at the Bat* was first made. (It turned up again in 1927 with Wallace Beery.) Biopics of famous baseball personalities include *The Stratton Story* (James Stewart), *The Babe Ruth Story* (William Bendix), *The Pride of the Yankees* (Gary Cooper as Lou Gehrig), *The Winning Team* (Ronald Reagan as G. C. Alexander), *The Pride of St Louis* (Dan Dailey as Dizzy Dean), *Fear Strikes Out* (Anthony Perkins as Jim Piersall) and *The Jackie Robinson Story*. Serious dramatic films about the sport include *The Bush Leaguer, Slide Kelly Slide* and *The Big Leaguer*. There has been a fantasy, *Angels in the Outfield*, and a who-done-it, *Death on the Diamond*. Musicals are led by *Take Me Out to the Ball Game* and *Damn Yankees*. Comedies include *Elmer the Great, Alibi Ike, Fast Company, Rhubarb, It Happens Every Spring, Speedy* (Harold Lloyd), *College* (Buster Keaton) and *Ladies' Day*. Baseball stadiums have provided memorable scenes in films on other subjects: *The FBI Story, Beau James, The Satan Bug, Experiment in Terror*, etc.

Basehart, Richard (1915–). Thoughtful American leading actor who somehow never achieved his expected stardom; equally adept at honesty, villainy and mental disturbance. Many TV appearances.
□ Cry Wolf 47. Repeat Performance 47. *He Walked by Night* 48. Roseanna McCoy 49. *The Black Book* 49. Tension 49. Outside the Wall 50. *Fourteen Hours* 51. The House on Telegraph Hill 51. Fixed Bayonets 51. Decision Before Dawn 51. The Stranger's Hand 53. Titanic 53. La Strada 54. The Good Die Young 54. Il Bidone (The Swindlers) 55. *Moby Dick* 56. The Intimate Stranger 56. *Time Limit* 57. *The Brothers Karamazov* 58. Five Branded Women 60.

Portrait in Black 60. Passport to China 61. *Hitler* (title role) 63. Kings of the Sun 63. The Satan Bug 65. The Death of Me Yet (TV) 71. City Beneath the Sea (One Hour to Doomsday) (TV) 71. Assignment Munich (TV) 72. The Bounty Man (TV) 72.
TV series: *Voyage to the Bottom of the Sea* 63–67.

Baskett, James (1904–1948). Black American character actor best known for his performance as Uncle Remus in *Song of the South* 48.

Bass, Alfie (1920–). Pint-sized British character comedian, adept at Cockney/Jewish roles.
Johnny Frenchman 45. Holiday Camp 47. It Always Rains on Sunday 47. The Hasty Heart 49. *The Lavender Hill Mob* 51. *The Bespoke Overcoat* 55. A Kid for Two Farthings 55. A Tale of Two Cities 57. I Only Arsked 59. The Millionairess 60. Alfie 66. The Fearless Vampire Killers 67 The Magnificent Seven Deadly Sins 72, etc.
TV series: The Army Game 55–59. Bootsie and Snudge 60–63.

Bass, Saul (1920–). American title designer whose ingenious credits have enlivened such films as *Carmen Jones, The Shrike, The Man with the Golden Arm, Around the World in Eighty Days, Vertigo, The Big Country, Bonjour Tristesse, North by Northwest, Psycho, Ocean's Eleven, A Walk on the Wild Side, It's a Mad Mad Mad Mad World, Bunny Lake is Missing*, many others.

Basserman, Albert (1867–1952). Distinguished German stage actor who came to Hollywood as refugee in 1939 and played sympathetic roles.
□ Der Andere 13. Vorunter Suchung 31. The Last Days Before the War 32. Kadetten 33. Ein Gewisser Herr Gran 33. Alraune 33. Letzte Liebe 38. Le Famille Lefrancois 39. Dr Ehrlich's Magic Bullet 40. *Foreign Correspondent* 40. A Dispatch from Reuters 40. Moon Over Burma 40. Knute Rockne 40. Escape 40. *The Shanghai Gesture* 41. The Great Awakening 41. New Wine 41. A Woman's Face 41. The Moon and Sixpence 42. Invisible Agent 42. Once Upon a Honeymoon 42. Fly by Night 42. Desperate Journey 42. Good Luck Mr Yates 43. Passport to Heaven 43. Reunion in France 43. Madame Curie 44. Since You Went Away 44. *Rhapsody in Blue* 45. Strange Holiday 46. The Searching Wind 46. The Private Affairs of Bel Ami 47. Escape Me Never 47. *The Red Shoes* (GB) 48.

Bassey, Shirley (1937–). Torrid British-born cabaret singer whose film appearances have always been as a performer.

Bassler, Robert (1903–). American producer.
My Gal Sal 42. *The Black Swan* 43. The Lodger 44. Hangover Square 45. Thunder in the Valley 47. *The Snake Pit* 48. Thieves' Highway 49. Halls of Montezuma 50. Kangaroo 52. Beneath the Twelve-mile Reef 53. Suddenly 54, etc.

Bastedo, Alexandra (1946–). Leading lady of Canadian, Italian and English ancestry.
Inside Daisy Clover 66. Casino Royale 67, etc.
TV series: *The Champions* 69.

The Bat. The spooky house melodrama by Mary Roberts Rinehart was first filmed in 1926 with Louise Fazenda and Emily Fitzroy. In 1930 came a sound variation known as *The Bat Whispers*, with Grayce Hampton and some splendid over-acting from Chester Morris. In 1959 there was a somewhat spiritless remake with Agnes Moorehead and Vincent Price.

La Bataille du Rail (France 1944-1945). A remarkable documentary, directed by René Clement shot in occupied France during World War II to show the railwaymen's resistance to the Nazis.

Batchelor, Joy (1914–). British animator, wife of John Halas and co-founder of Halas and Batchelor Cartoon Films.

Bates, Alan (1934–). Leading British actor of stage and screen: tends to play thoughtful toughs with soft centres.
☐ The Entertainer 59. *A Kind of Loving* 62. *Whistle down the Wind* 62. The Caretaker 63. The Running Man 63. *Nothing But the Best* 64. *Zorba the Greek* 65. Georgy Girl 66. King of Hearts 67. *Far from the Madding Crowd* 67. The Fixer 68. *Women in Love* 69. Three Sisters 70. The Go-Between 70. *A Day in the Death of Joe Egg* 71. Impossible Object 73. Butley 73. In Celebration 74. Royal Flash 75.

Bates, Barbara (1925–1969). American leading lady, former model and ballet dancer.
This Love of Ours 45. The Fabulous Joe 48. June Bride 48. *The Inspector General* 49. Cheaper by the Dozen 49. All About Eve 50. Belles on Her Toes 52. Rhapsody 54. House of Secrets (GB) 56. Town on Trial (GB) 57. Apache Territory 58, etc.

Bates, Florence (1888–1954) (Florence Rabe). American character actress, adept at friendly or monstrous matrons. A former lawyer, she was persuaded by Alfred Hitchcock to play the role for which she is best remembered, and remained much in demand for a decade.
☐ The Man in Blue 37. *Rebecca* 40. Calling All Husbands 40. Son of Monte Cristo 40. Hudson's Bay 40. Kitty Foyle 40. Road Show 41. Love Crazy 41. The Chocolate Soldier 41. Strange Alibi 41. The Devil and Miss Jones 41. The Tuttles of Tahiti 42. *The Moon and Sixpence* 42. My Heart Belongs to Daddy 42. Mexican Spitfire at Sea 42. We Were Dancing 42. Slightly Dangerous 43. His Butler's Sister 43. They Got Me Covered 43. Mister Big 43. Heaven Can Wait 43. Mr Lucky 43. The Whistle at Eaton Falls 43. Since You Went Away 44. The Mask of Dimitrios 44. Kismet 44. Belle of the Yukon 44. The Racket Man 44. Saratoga Trunk 45. Tahiti Nights 45. *Tonight and Every Night* 45. San Antonio 45. Out of This World 45. Claudia and David 46. Cluny Brown 46. The Diary of a Chambermaid 46. Whistle Stop 46. The Time the Place and the Girl 46. *The High Window* 47. Love and Learn 47. Desire Me 47. *The Secret Life of Walter Mitty* 47. Texas Brooklyn and Heaven 48. Winter Meeting 48. The Inside Story 48. River Lady 48. My Dear Secretary 48. Portrait of Kennie 48. *I Remember Mama* 48. A Letter to Three Wives 48. The Judge Steps Out 49. The Girl from Jones Beach 49. On The Town 49. Belle of Old Mexico 50. *County Fair* 50. The Second Woman 51. Lullaby of Broadway 51. The Tall Target 51. Havana Rose 51. Father Takes the Air 51. The San Francisco Story 52. Les Miserables 52. Paris Model 53. Main Street to Broadway 53.

Bates, Granville (1882–1940). American general purpose supporting actor of the thirties: storekeepers, doctors and grandpas.
Jealousy 29. The Smiling Lieutenant 31. Woman Wanted 35. 13 Hours by Air 36. They Won't Forget 37. Nancy Steele is Missing 37. Wells Fargo 37. Go Chase Yourself 38. Gold is Where You Find It 38. The Great Man Votes 39. Pride of the Blue Grass 39. Of Mice and Men 39. Jesse James 39. My Favorite Wife 40. The Mortal Storm 40. Brother Orchid 40, many others.

Bates, Michael (1929–). British character actor who specializes in stupid policemen and other caricatures.
Carrington VC 55. I'm All Right Jack 59. Bedazzled 67. *Here We Go Round the Mulberry Bush* 67. Salt and Pepper 68. Don't Raise the Bridge Lower the River 68. Hammerhead 68. Patton 70. The Rise and Rise of Michael Rimmer 70. *A Clockwork Orange* 71. No Sex Please,

We're British 73, etc.

Bates, Ralph (1940–). Incisive British character actor who played Caligula on TV and took the natural step to Hammer horrors.
The Horror of Frankenstein 70. Lust for a Vampire 70. Dr Jekyll and Sister Hyde 71. Fear in the Night 73. Persecution 74. I Don't Want to be Born 75, etc.

bathtubs, though especially associated with Cecil B. de Mille, have been a favourite Hollywood gimmick from early silent days. But de Mille undressed his heroines with the most showmanship, whether it was Gloria Swanson in *Male and Female*, Claudette Colbert in her asses' milk in *The Sign of the Cross* (emulated years later by Frances Day in *Fiddlers Three*) or Paulette Goddard in *Unconquered*. Other ladies who have bathed spectacularly include Joan Crawford in *The Women*, Deanna Durbin in *Can't Help Singing*, Jean Harlow in *Red Dust*, Phyllis Haver in *The Politic Flapper*, Joan Collins in *The Wayward Bus*, Elke Sommer in *The Wicked Dreams of Paula Schultz*, Gina Lollobrigida in *Belles de Nuit*, Carroll Baker in *Harlow* and Sophia Loren (who had Gregory Peck hiding in her shower) in *Arabesque*. Not that the men have had it all their own way: Roger Livesey in *Colonel Blimp* and Gary Cooper in *Love in the Afternoon* suffered in the steamroom; and all the actors who have played coal miners, including Trevor Howard in *Sons and Lovers* and Donald Crisp in *How Green Was My Valley*, know how it feels to be scrubbed all over. Marat in *Marat/Sade* spent the whole film in a tub. The most bathed male star is probably Cary Grant, who had a tub in *The Howards of Virginia*, a shower in *Mr Blandings Builds His Dream House*, another shower, fully clothed this time, in *Charade*, and a Japanese geisha bath in *Walk, Don't Run*. And Hitchcock, with *Psycho*, still takes the prize for the most memorable shower scene.

Battleship Potemkin (Russia 1925). A historical reconstruction of an incident at Odessa in the revolution of 1905. Eisenstein, directing his second film, used the theme not merely as propaganda but as a means to develop his cinematic technique. The editing of the massacre sequence on the steps is justly famous and has been frequently copied. Photographed by Edouard Tisse; assistant to Eisenstein, Grigori Alexandrov.

Baum, L. Frank (1856–1919). American author who published *The Wizard of Oz* in 1900 and started an industry from it and its sequels.

Baum, Vicki (   ). German novelist whose chief gift to Hollywood was the much-filmed and well imitated *Grand Hotel*, which she herself revamped as *Hotel Berlin*.
Autobiography 1964: *It Was All Quite Different*.

Baur, Harry (1881–1941). Celebrated French actor of stage and screen.
Shylock 10. La Voyante 23. David Golder 31. Poil de Carotte 32. Golgotha 34. Moscow Nights 35. Crime and Punishment 35. Taras Bulba 35. Un Carnet de Bal 37. The Rebel Son 38. Volpone 39, etc.

Bava, Mario (1914–). Italian director, former photographer, of period muscleman epics and pseudo-British horror stories, revered by the *cognoscenti* for his tongue-in-cheek attitude towards some of them.
Black Sunday (wphd) 60. Hercules in the Centre of the Earth (wphd) 61. Erik the Conqueror (wd) 63. The Evil Eye (wphd) 62. *Black Sabbath* (wd) 63. *Blood and Black Lace* (wphd) 64. Planet of Blood (d) 65. Dr Goldfoot and the Girl Bombs (d) 66. Curse of the Dead (wd) 67. *Diabolik* (wd) 68. The Antecedent (d) 71, etc.

Baxter, Alan (1908–1976). Cold-eyed American second lead of the forties; graduated to colonels and tough executives.
Mary Burns Fugitive 35. The Last Gangster 37. Gangs of New York 38. Each Dawn I Die 39. Santa Fe Trail 40. Saboteur 42. Submarine Base 43. Winged Victory 44. The Set Up 49. The Devil's Weed 49. End of the Line (in Britain) 56. The True Story of Jesse James 57. The Mountain Road 60. Judgment at Nuremburg 61. This Property is Condemned 66, etc.

Baxter, Anne (1923–). American leading lady who usually played shy and innocent but proved equally at home as a schemer. Trained for the stage but was starring in Hollywood at seventeen. After 1960 found the going tough.
□ Twenty Mule Team 40. The Great Profile 40. Charley's Aunt 41. Swamp Water 41. The Pied Piper 42. *The Mangificient Ambersons* 42. Crash Dive 43. *Five Graves to Cairo* 43. North Star 43. The Sullivans 44. The Eve of St Mark 44. Sunday Dinner for a Soldier 44. *Guest in the House* 45. A Royal Scandal 45. Smoky 46. Angel on My Shoulder 46. *The Razor's Edge* (AA) 46. Blaze of Noon 47. Homecoming 48. The Walls of Jericho 48. The Luck of the Irish 48. Yellow Sky 48. You're My Everything 49. A Ticket to Tomahawk 49. *All About Eve* 50. Follow the Sun 51. The Outcasts of Poker Flat 52. My Wife's Best Friend 52. Full House 52. I Confess 53. The

Blue Gardenia 53. Carnival Story 54. Bedevilled 55. One Desire 55. The Spoilers 55. The Come On 56. The Ten Commandments 56. Three Violent People 57. *Chase a Crooked Shadow* 57. Summer of the Seventeenth Doll 60. Mix Me a Person 61. Cimarron 61. A Walk on the Wild Side 62. The Family Jewels 65. Frontier Woman 66. The Busy Body 67. The Tall Women 68. Fools Parade 71. The Late Liz 71. If Tomorrow Comes (TV) 71. Lisa Bright and Dark (TV) 72. The Money Changers (TV) 76.

Baxter, Beryl (1926–) (Beryl Ivory). British leading lady who was groomed for stardom but starred in only one film, and that notoriously poor: *Idol of Paris* 46. Subsequently: The Man with the Twisted Lip 51. Counterspy 53.

Baxter, Jane (1909–) (Feodora Forde). Gentle-mannered British actress of stage and screen.
The Constant Nymph 32. The Clairvoyant 34. We Live Again (US) 35. The Ware Case 39. Ships with Wings 41. The Flemish Farm 43. Death of an Angel 51, etc.

Baxter, John (1896–). Influential British producer-director of vigorous rough-and-ready dramas and comedies of the thirties and forties which pointed the way to fifties realism and had an amiable style of their own.
Doss House 32. *Song of the Plough* 32. Lest We Forget 34. Music Hall 35. Say It with Flowers 36. Men of Yesterday 37. Crooks' Tour 40. *Love on the Dole* 40. *The Common Touch* 41. *Let the People Sing* 42. *When We are Married* 43. The Shipbuilders 45. The Second Mate 50. Judgment Deferred 51. Ramsbottom Rides Again 56, many others including Old Mother Riley and Flanagan & Allen comedies.

Baxter, Les (1922–). American composer.
Hot Blood 55. The Black Sheep 56. Macabre 58. Goliath and the Barbarians 59. *House of Usher* 60. The Pit and the Pendulum 61. Panic in Year Zero 62. Tales of Terror 62. *The Raven* 63. The Comedy of Terrors 63. Muscle Beach Party 64. Dr G and the Bikini Machine 65. Wild in the Streets 58. Flare Up 69. The Dunwich Horror 70. Cry of the Banshee 70. Frogs 72. I Escaped from Devil's Island 73, many others.

Baxter, Stanley (1928–). Rubber-faced Scottish comedian and impressionist of stage, screen and TV.
□ Geordie 55. *Very Important Person* 61. Crooks Anonymous 62. *The Fast Lady* 63. And Father Came Too 63. Joey Boy 65, etc.

Baxter, Warner (1889–1951). Distinguished-looking American leading man with stage experience. Popular hero of silent melodrama; survived transition to talkies.
□ Her Own Money 14. All Woman 18. Lombardi Ltd. 19. Cheated Hearts 21. First Love 21. The Love Charm 21. Sheltered Daughters 22. If I were Queen 22. The Girl in His Room 22. A Girl's Desire 22. The Ninety and Nine 22. Her Own Money (remake) 22. Blow Your Own Horn 23. In Search of a Thrill 23. St Elmo 23. Alimony 23. Christine of the Hungry Heart 24. The Female 24. The Garden of Weeds 24. His Forgotten Wife 24. Those Who Dance 24. The Golden Bed 25. Air Mail 25. The Awful Truth 25. The Best People 25. Rugged Water 25. A Son of His Father 25. Welcome Home 25. Mannequin 26. Miss Brewsters Millions 26. Mismates 26. Aloma of the South Seas 26. *The Great Gatsby* 26. The Runaway 26. The Telephone Girl 27. The Coward 27. Drums of the Desert 27. Singed 27. Danger Street 28. Three Sinners 28. *Ramona* 28. Craig's Wife 28. The Tragedy of Youth 28. A Woman's Way 28. Linda 29. Far Call 29. Thru Different Eyes 29. Behind that Curtain 29. Romance of the Rio Grande 29. *In Old Arizona* 29. West of Zanzibar 29. Happy Days 29. The Arizona Kid 30. Renegades 30. Such Men are Dangerous 30. The Cisco Kid 31. The Squaw Man 31. Doctors' Wives 31. Their Mad Moment 31. *Daddy Long Legs* 31. Surrender 31. Six Hours to Live 32. Man About Town 32. Amateur Daddy 32. Paddy the Next Best Thing 33. *42nd Street* 33. Dangerously Yours 34. I Loved You Wednesday 34. Penthouse 34. Stand Up and Cheer 34. *Broadway Bill* 34. As Husbands Go 34. Such Women are Dangerous 34. Grand Canary 35. Hell in the Heavens 35. Under the Pampas Moon 35. *One More Spring* 35. King of Burlesque 35. *Prisoner of Shark Island* 36. *The Road to Glory* 36. To Mary with Love 36. White Hunter 36. Robin Hood of El Dorado 36. Slave Ship 37. Vogues of 1938 37. Wife Doctor and Nurse 37. Kidnapped 38. I'll Give a Million 38. Wife Husband and Friend 39. Barricade 39. The Return of the Cisco Kid 39. Earthbound 40. Adam Had Four Sons 41. Crime Doctor 43. The Crime Doctor's Strangest Case 43. Lady in the Dark 44. Shadows in the Night 44. The Crime Doctor's Courage 45. The Crime Doctor's Warning 45. Just Before Dawn 46. The Crime Doctor's Man Hunt 46. The Millerson Case 47. The Crime Doctor's Gamble 47. A Gentleman from Nowhere 48. Prison Warden 49. The Devil's Henchman 49. The Crime Doctor's Diary 49. State Penetentiary 50.

Bayes, Nora (1880–1928) (Dora Goldberg).

American vaudeville singer, impersonated by Ann Sheridan in the biopic *Shine On Harvest Moon* 44.

Bayldon, Geoffrey (1924–). Lanky British character actor with a penchant for absent-minded or eccentric types.
The Stranger Left No Card 53. Dracula 58. Libel 60. The Webster Boy 62. A Jolly Bad Fellow 64. King Rat 65. *Sky West and Crooked* 65. *To Sir With Love* 66. Casino Royale 67. Otley 69. The Raging Moon 70. Scrooge 71. Asylum 72, etc.

Bazin, André (1918–1958). French critic who wrote books on Welles, de Sica and Renoir: 'the spiritual father of the New Wave'. Founded 'Cahiers du Cinema'.

Beacham, Stephanie (1949–). British leading lady.
The Games 69. The Nightcomers 71. Dracula A.D. 1972 72, etc.

Beal, John (1909–) (Alexander Bliedung). American stage actor whose look of boyish innocence was useful in the thirties but tended to hamper him subsequently.
Another Language 33. Hat Coat and Glove 34. *The Little Minister* 34. Les Misérables 35. *Laddie* 35. Break of Hearts 35. The Man Who Found Himself 37. Double Wedding 37. Port of Seven Seas 38. I Am The Law 38. *The Cat and the Canary* 39. Ellery Queen and the Perfect Crime 41. The Great Commandment 42. Edge of Darkness 43. Key Witness 47. Alimony 49. My Six Convicts 52. Remains to Be Seen 53. That Night 57. The Vampire 60. Ten Who Dared 61, etc.

Bean, Judge Roy (1823–1902). American Western badman, a self-appointed lawmaker who kept himself in whisky from his fines. Played by Walter Brennan in *The Westerner* 40; by Edgar Buchanan in a TV series, *Judge Roy Bean* 50; and by Paul Newman in a 1972 movie *The Life and Times of Judge Roy Bean*.

The Beatles. This Liverpudlian pop group achieved astonishing popularity in the early sixties, but the pressures of success caused a split and the members went their rich but somewhat malcontented ways. They were *John Lennon* (1940–), *George Harrison* (1943–), *Paul McCartney* (1942–) and *Ringo Starr* (Richard Starkey) (1940–).
Films together: *A Hard Day's Night* 64. Help! 65. Yellow Submarine 67. Let It Be 70.
Separately, Lennon was in *How I Won The War* 67; Starr in *Candy* 68, *The Magic Christian*

70, *That'll Be the Day* 73.

Beaton, Cecil (1902–). British photographer and designer who has advised on many films, his greatest achievements probably being *Gigi* 58 and *My Fair Lady* 64.

Beatty, Clyde (1903–1965). American animal trainer and circus owner who made a few film appearances.
□ The Big Cage 33. The Lost Jungle 34. Darkest Africa 36. Africa Screams 49. Ring of Fear 54.

Beatty, Robert (1909–). Rugged, good-humoured Canadian leading man long resident in Britain.
San Demetrio, London 43. Appointment with Crime 46. *Odd Man Out* 46. *Against the Wind* 47. Counterblast 48. Another Shore 53. Captain Horatio Hornblower R.N. 51. The Square Ring 53. *Albert R.N.* 53. The Gentle Gunman 53. Tarzan and the Lost Safari 57. Something of Value 57. The Shakedown 59. The Amorous Prawn 62. 2001: A Space Odyssey 68. Where Eagles Dare 69. Man at the Top 73, etc.
TV series: *Dial 999* 57–58.

Beatty, Warren (1937–) (Warren Beaty). Unruly American leading actor of the post-Brando school, with a flair for psychological maladjustment. Brother of Shirley Maclaine.
□ *Splendour in the Grass* 61. The Roman Spring of Mrs Stone 61. *All Fall Down* 62. *Lilith* 65. *Mickey One* 65. Promise Her Anything 66. Kaleidoscope 66. *Bonnie and Clyde* (& p) 67. The Only Game in Town 69. McCabe and Mrs Miller 71. Dollars 72. The Parallax View 74. Shampoo (& p, co-w) 75.

Beau Geste. P. C. Wren's romantic novel of a missing gem, a debt of honour, and savagery in the Foreign Legion, was filmed in 1926 with Ronald Colman as Beau and Noah Beery as the sadistic sergeant. The 1939 version had Gary Cooper and Brian Donlevy; 1966 saw Guy Stockwell and Telly Savalas in the roles (and much of the plot missing).

Le Beau Serge (France 1958). Sometimes claimed as the first 'nouvelle vague' film, this is a quiet, unsensational story about a young man who returns to his native village and tries to help an unhappy friend. Director: Claude Chabrol.

Beaudine, William (1892–1970). Prolific American director of silent family films and, later second features.
Penrod and Sam 23. Little Annie Rooney 25. *Sparrows* 26. The Life of Riley 27. The Cohens

and Kellys in Paris 28. Home James 28. The Girl from Woolworth's 29. The Lady Who Dared 31. *Penrod and Sam* 31. Three Wise Girls 32. The Crime of the Century 33. The Old Fashioned Way 34. Hey Hey USA (in Britain) 36. Says O'Reilly to Macnab (in Britain) 37. Torchy Gets Her Man 38. Torchy Blane in Chinatown 39. Broadway Big Shot 42. The Mystery of the 13th Guest 53. Black Market Babies 46. Kidnapped 48. Blue Grass of Kentucky 50. Westward Ho the Wagons 56. Lassie's Greatest Adventure 63. Billy the Kid versus Dracula 66, etc.

Beaumont, Charles (1929–1967). American writer, chiefly of science fiction.
Queen of Outer Space 58. The Intruder 61. Night of the Eagle 62. The Haunted Palace 63. Seven Faces of Dr Lao 64. Mister Moses 65, etc.

Beaumont, Harry (1893–1966). American director, at his peak in the twenties.
A Man and His Money 19. Lord and Lady Algy 19. *Main Street* 23. *Beau Brummell* 24. *Babbitt* 24. The Lover of Camille 24. *His Majesty Bunker Bean* 25. *Our Dancing Daughters* 28. *Broadway Melody* 29. Lord Byron of Broadway 30. The Floradora Girl 30. Our Blushing Brides 30. Dance Fools Dance 31. Faithless 32. *When Ladies Meet* 33. Enchanted April 35. The Girl on the Front Page 36. When's Your Birthday? 37. Maisie Goes to Reno 44. Twice Blessed 45. The Show-off 47, many others.

Beaumont, Hugh (1909–). American second lead and second feature hero.
Flight Lieutenant 42. The Seventh Victim 43. Objective Burma 45. The Blue Dahlia 46. Bury Me Dead 47. Railroaded 49. Mr Belvedere Rings the Bell 52. Mississippi Gambler 53. The Mole People 57, etc.
TV series: Leave It To Beaver 57-62.

Beaumont, Susan (1936–) (Susan Black). British leading lady of a few fifties films.
Jumping for Joy 55. High Tide at Noon 57. Innocent Sinners 58. Carry On Nurse 59. Web of Suspicion 59, etc.

Beavers, Louise (1902–1962). Black American actress who played innumerable happy housekeepers.
Coquette 29. Girls About Town 32. What Price Hollywood 32. She Done Him Wrong 33. *Imitation of Life* (her best role) 35. Rainbow on the River 36. The Last Gangster 37. Made For Each Other 39. No Time for Comedy 40. Reap the Wild Wind 42. Dubarry was a Lady 43. Delightfully Dangerous 46. *Mr Blandings Builds His Dream House* 48. My Blue Heaven 50.

Teenage Rebel 56. The Goddess 58. The Facts of Life 61, many others.
TV series: *Beulah* 50.

Becker, Jacques (1906–1960). French director, mainly of civilized comedies.
Groupi Mains Rouge 42. Falbalas 44. *Antoine et Antoinette* 47. Rendezvous de Juillet 49. *Edouard et Caroline* 50. *Casque d'Or* 51. Rue de l'Estrapade 52. *Touchez Pas au Grisbi* 53. Ali Baba 55. The Adventures of Arsène Lupin 56. Montparnasse Nineteen 57. The Hole 60, etc.

Becker, Jean (1933–). French director, son of Jacques Becker.
Echappement Libre 62. Pas de Caviare pour Tante Olga 64. Tendre Voyou 66, etc.

Becket (GB 1964). Based on Jean Anouilh's witty if unhistorical play, this was producer Hal Wallis' first bid for prestige and led to the 'intellectual' block-busters of the later sixties. An interesting but unsatisfactory hybrid, its box office success was helped by Richard Burton and Peter O'Toole but not by Peter Glenville's stodgy direction.

Beckett, Scotty (1929–1968). Soulful-looking American child actor of the thirties and forties; one-time member of 'Our Gang'.
Whom the Gods Destroy 34. Dante's Inferno 35. The Charge of the Light Brigade 36. Marie Walewska 38. *The Bluebird* 40. *Kings Row* 42. The Youngest Profession 43. *Ali Baba and the Forty Thieves* 43. Junior Miss 45. *The Jolson Story* (as young Jolson) 46. A Date with Judy 48. Battleground 49. Corky 51. Three for Jamie Dawn 56, many others.

Beckley, Tony (1932–). British actor, often seen as young thug.
The Penthouse 67. Chimes at Midnight 67. The Long Day's Dying 68. The Lost Continent 68. Get Carter 71. Sitting Target 72. Gold 74. Diagnosis Murder 75, etc.

Beckwith, Reginald (1908–1965). Chubby British character actor, whose high voice and impeccable timing were a constant delight. Also wrote successful plays, e.g. *Boys in Brown, A Soldier for Christmas.*
Voice in the Night 41. *Scott of the Antarctic* 48. Another Man's Poison 51. Mr Drake's Duck 52. *Genevieve* 53. *The Runaway Bus* 54. Dance Little Lady 55. *The Captain's Table* 58. The Thirty-nine Steps 59. Double Bunk 61. The Password is Courage 62. Never Put It in Writing 64. A Shot in the Dark 64. Mister Moses 65, many others.

Becky Sharp (US 1935). The first full-length feature in three-colour Technicolor, this version of *Vanity Fair* seems now only a pleasantly-photographed stage play, and director Reuben Mamoulian's experiments in colour are difficult to assess in the prints now available. Miriam Hopkins made a fair shot at the title role, and Cedric Hardwicke was excellent as the Marquis of Steyne. Ray Rennahan was cinematographer.

Beddoe, Don (1891–). American character actor with genial, sometimes startled, look; in hundreds of films, often as sheriff, reporter, or cop.
Golden Boy 39. *The Face behind the Mask* 41. Talk of the Town 42. Crime Inc. 45. O.S.S. 46. The Best Years of Our Lives 46. The Farmer's Daughter 47. Dancing in the Dark 49. Carrie 51. Night of the Hunter 55. *Saintly Sinners* (lead role) 61. *Jack the Giant Killer* (as a leprechaun) 62. Texas Across the River 66. The Impossible Years 68, many others.

Bedelia, Bonnie (1946–). American leading lady.
The Gypsy Moths 69. They Shoot Horses Don't They? 70. *Lovers and Other Strangers* 70. The Strange Vengeance of Rosalie 72. Hawkins on Murder (TV) 73, etc.

Bedford, Brian (1935–). British stage actor who has been in a few films.
Miracle in Soho 58. The Angry Silence 59. The Punch and Judy Man 63. The Pad 66. Grand Prix 67. Robin Hood (voice) 73, etc.

Bedoya, Alfonso (1904–1957). Mexican character actor whose beaming face could provide comedy or menace.
The Treasure of the Sierra Madre (as the bandit) 47. The Pearl 48. Streets of Laredo 49. The Black Rose 50. Sombrero 52. California Conquest 52. The Stranger Wore a Gun 53. Ten Wanted Men 55. *The Big Country* 57, etc.

Beebe, Ford (1888–). American director of low-budget westerns, second features and serials . . . over 200 of them from 1916.
Laughing at Life 33. *Flash Gordon's Trip to Mars* 38. *Riders of Death Valley* 41. Night Monster 42. The Invisible Man's Revenge 44. Enter Arsène Lupin 44. Bomba the Jungle Boy 49, etc.

Beecher, Janet (1884–1955) (J. B. Meysenburg). American character actress usually seen in ladylike roles. Retired 1943.
Gallant Lady 34. The Dark Angel 36. Bitter Sweet 40. Reap the Wild Wind 42. Mrs Wiggs of the Cabbage Patch 43. Henry Gets Glamour 43, etc

Beery, Noah (1884–1946). American character actor, brother of Wallace Beery and one of the silent screen's most celebrated villains.
The Mormon Maid 18. *The Mark of Zorro* 20. The Sea Wolf 20. Tol'able David 21. The Spoilers 22. The Coming of Amos 25. Beau Geste 26. *Don Juan* 26. Beau Sabreur 27. The Four Feathers 29. Noah's Ark 29. Tol'able David 30. The Drifter 31. Out of Singapore 32. She Done Him Wrong 33. King of the Damned (GB) 35. Our Fighting Navy (GB) 37. The Girl of the Golden West 38. Isle of Missing Men 42. This Man's Navy 45, many others.

Beery, Noah Jnr (1913–). American character actor, son of Noah Beery. Started as child actor, and later played easy-going country cousins.
The Mark of Zorro 20. Heroes of the West 26. Father and Son 29. Jungle Madness 31. The Road Back 37. Only Angels Have Wings 39. Of Mice and Men 40. Riders of Death Valley 41. Prairie Chickens 43. Gung Ho 44. Red River 48. Destination Moon 50. White Feather 55. Inherit the Wind 60. The Seven Faces of Dr Lao 64. Incident at Phantom Hill 65. Little Fauss and Big Halsy 70. Walking Tall 73, many others.
TV series: Circus Boy 57–59. Custer 67.

Beery, Wallace (1880/86–1949). American character star with circus and musical comedy experience, long under contract to MGM. Started as a grotesque female impersonator and tried every kind of part before acquiring his best remembered persona: tough, ugly, slow-thinking and easy going.
SELECTED SILENT FILMS: Teddy at the Throttle 16. The Unpardonable Sin 19. The Virgin of Stamboul 20. The Last of the Mohicans 21. *Robin Hood* (as King Richard) 22. *Richard the Lion-Hearted* 23. The Sea Hawk 24. So Big 24. *The Lost World* (as Professor Challenger) 25. The Wanderer 25. Volcano 26. We're in the Navy Now 26. Casey at the Bat 27. Fireman Save My Child 27. Partners of Crime 28. Beggars of Life 28, many others.
□ SOUND FILMS: Chinatown Nights 29. River of Romance 29. *The Big House* 30. Way for a Sailor 30. Billy the Kid 30. A Lady's Morals 30. *Min and Bill* 30. The Secret Six 31. Hell Divers 31. *The Champ* (AA) 31. *Grand Hotel* 32. Flesh 32. *Dinner at Eight* 33. Tugboat Annie 33. *The Bowery* 33. *Viva Villa* 34. *Treasure Island* (as Long John Silver) 34. *The Mighty Barnum* 34. West Point of the Air 35. China Seas 35. O' Shaughnessy's Boy 35. *Ah Wilderness* 35. A

Message to Garcia 36. Old Hutch 36. Good Old Soak 37. *Slave Ship* 37. Bad Man of Brimstone 38. Port of Seven Seas 38. Stablemates 38. Sergeant Madden 39. *Stand Up and Fight* 39. Thunder Afloat 39. The Man from Dakota 40. Twenty Mule Team 40. Wyoming 40. Barnacle Bill 41. The Bad Man 41. The Bugle Sounds 42. Jackass Mail 42. Salute to the Marines 43. Rationing 44. *Barbary Coast Gent* 44. This Man's Navy 45. Bad Bascomb 46. The Mighty McGurk 47. A Date with Judy 48. Alias a Gentleman 48. Big Jack 49.

Beeson, Paul (1921–). British cinematographer.
Kidnapped 70. Jane Eyre 71. A Warm December 73. The Mutations 74. One of our Dinosaurs is Missing 75. Escape from the Dark 76, etc.

The Beggar's Opera. Several attempts have been made to film John Gay's 17th-century operetta of the London underworld. 1. *Die Dreigroschenoper* (Germany 1931) starred Rudolph Forster as Macheath and had music by Kurt Weill. (French version, with Albert Préjean, known as *L'Opéra de Quatr'Sous*.) 2. *The Beggar's Opera* (GB 1952) was a straight version with Laurence Olivier, directed by Peter Brook. 3. *The Threepenny Opera* (Germany/US 1965) starred Curt Jurgens and Sammy Davis Jnr.

Begley, Ed (1901–1970). Blustery American character actor with radio and stage experience; usually seen as jovial uncle or man at the end of his tether.
□ Big Town 47. Boomerang 47. Deep Waters 48. Sitting Pretty 48. The Street with No Name 48. Sorry Wrong Number 48. Tulsa 49. It Happens Every Spring 49. The Great Gatsby 49. Backfire 50. Stars in my Crown 50. Wyoming Mail 50. Convicted 50. Saddle Tramp 50. Dark City 50. Lady from Texas 51. On Dangerous Ground 51. You're In the Navy Now 51. Deadline 52. Boots Malone 52. The Turning Point 52. What Price Glory 52. Lone Star 52. *Patterns* 56. *Twelve Angry Men* 57. *Odds Against Tomorrow* 59. The Green Helmet 61. *Sweet Bird of Youth* (AA) 62. The Unsinkable Molly Brown 64. The Oscar 66. Warning Shot 66. *Billion Dollar Brain* 67. Firecreek 67. Wild in the Streets 68. Hang 'Em High 68. The Violent Enemy 69. The Dunwich Horror 69.

Behan, Brendan (1923–1964). Irish dramatist whose flamboyant behaviour often hit the headlines in the fifties; his only play to be filmed was *The Quare Fellow*.

Behrman, S. N. (1893–). American playwright and screenwriter.
He Knew Women (oa) 30. *Queen Christina* 33. Cavalcade 33. *Anna Karenina* 35. Biography of a Bachelor Girl (oa) 35. A Tale of Two Cities 35. Parnell 37. Conquest 37. *No Time for Comedy* (oa) 40. Waterloo Bridge 40. Two-faced Woman 41. The Pirate (oa) 48. Quo Vadis 51. *Me and the Colonel* (& oa) 56, etc.

Beich, Albert (1919–). American radio and film writer, one of the 'Hollywood Ten' who defied the anti-communist witch-hunt in 1947.
Girls in Chains 44. The Perils of Pauline 47. The Bride Goes Wild 48. Key to the City 50. The Lieutenant Wore Skirts 55. Dead Ringer 64, etc.

Bekassy, Stephen (c.1915–). Hungarian stage actor who came to Hollywood in the forties.
A Song to Remember (as Liszt) 45. Arch of Triumph 48. Black Magic 49. Fair Wind to Java 53. Hell and High Water 54. Interrupted Melody 55. The Light in the Forest 58. Bachelor Flat 61. The Four Horsemen of the Apocalypse 62, etc.

Belafonte, Harry (1927–). Handsome black American ballad singer who has acted strikingly in several films.
□ Bright Road 53. *Carmen Jones* 54. *Island in the Sun* 57. The World the Flesh and the Devil 59. *Odds Against Tomorrow* 59. The Angel Levine 70. Buck and the Preacher 72.

Belasco, Leon (1902–). Wiry Russian-born small-part player of excitable balletmasters, head waiters, landlords, etc.
The Best People (debut) 26. Topper Takes a Trip 39. The Mummy's Hand 40. Nothing But the Truth 41. Pin-up Girl 44. The New Adventures of Don Juan 48. Call Me Madam 53, many others.
TV series: My Sister Eileen.

Bel Geddes, Barbara (1922–) (Barbara Geddes Lewis). American stage actress who makes occasional films, usually as nice placid girls.
□ The Gangster 47. The Long Night 47. *I Remember Mama* 48. Blood on the Moon 48. Caught 49. Panic in the Streets 50. *Fourteen Hours* 51. Vertigo 58. The Five Pennies 59. Five Branded Women 60. By Love Possessed 61. The Todd Killings 70. Summertree 71.

Belita (1924–) (Gladys Jepson-Turner). British ice-skating and dancing star who made a few Hollywood films.
Ice Capades 41. Silver Skates 43. Suspense 46.

The Hunted 47. Never Let Me Go 53. Invitation to the Dance 56. Silk Stockings 57, etc.

Bell, James (1891–). American character actor, usually in benevolent roles.
I Am a Fugitive from a Chain Gang 32. White Woman 33. I Walked with a Zombie 42. The Spiral Staircase 45. Brute Force 47. The Violent Hour 50. The Glenn Miller Story 54. The Lonely Man 57. Twilight of Honor 63, many others.

Bell, Marie (1900–) (Marie-Jeanne Bellon-Downey). Distinguished French actress who appeared in a few well remembered films.
Madame Recamier 28. Le Grand Jeu 34. La Garçonne 35. Carnet de Bal 37. La Charrette Fantôme 40. Colonel Chabert 43. La Bonne Soupe 64. Hotel Paradiso 66, etc.

Bell, Monta (1891–1958). American director whose peak was in the twenties.
A Woman of Paris (co-d) 23. Broadway after Dark 24. The Snob 24. The King on Main Street 27. Torrent 26. After Midnight (& w) 27. Man Woman and Sin (& w) 27. The Bellamy Trial 29. East is West 30. Men in White 33. West Point of the Air 35. China's Little Devils 45, etc.

Bell, Rex (1905–1962) (George F. Beldam). American cowboy star of the thirties: left Hollywood to become Lieut.-Governor of Nevada.
Pleasure Crazed 29. True to the Navy 30. Lightnin' 30. Tombstone 42, many others.

Bell, Tom (1933–). Gaunt British leading man of the sixties.
The Kitchen 61. Payroll 61. HMS Defiant 62. The L-Shaped Room 62. A Prize of Arms 63. Ballad in Blue 65. He Who Rides a Tiger 66. The Long Day's Dying 68. In Enemy Country (US) 68. Lock Up Your Daughters 69. All the Right Noises 69. Quest for Love 71. The Spy's Wife 71. Royal Flash 75, etc.

Bellamy, Earl (1917–). Routine American director, much involved in TV series.
Blackjack Ketchum Desparado 56. Fluffy 65. Gunpoint 65. Incident at Phantom Hill 66. Seven Alone 74. Part Two Walking Tall 75, etc.

Bellamy, Madge (1903–). American general purpose actress of the twenties.
Lorna Doone 23. Bertha the Sewing Machine Girl 27. Mother Knows Best 28, etc.

Bellamy, Ralph (1904–). Soft-voiced, serious-looking American leading man of stage and screen who in the thirties became typecast as the simple-minded rich man who never got the girl. In fact he played most kinds of parts, including detectives and villains, and later became a highly respected stage actor.
The Secret Six 31. West of Broadway 32. Rebecca of Sunnybrook Farm 32. The Narrow Corner 33. Spitfire 34. The Crime of Helen Stanley 35. The Wedding Night 35. Wild Brian Kent 36. The Man Who Lived Twice 36. The Awful Truth 37. The Crime of Dr Hallett 38. Fools for Scandal 38. Boy Meets Girl 38. Trade Winds 38. Blind Alley 39. His Girl Friday 40. Queen of the Mob 40. Ellery Queen Master Detective 40. Footsteps in the Dark 41. Affectionately Yours 41. Dive Bomber 41. The Wolf Man 41. The Ghost of Frankenstein 42. The Great Impersonation 42. Guest in the House 44. Lady on a Train 45. The Court Martial of Billy Mitchell 55. Sunrise at Campobello (as Franklin Roosevelt) 60. The Professionals 66. Rosemary's Baby 67. Doctors' Wives 71. Cancel My Reservation 72. West Side Medical (TV) 77, many others.
TV series: Men Against Crime 49-53. The Eleventh Hour 63. The Survivors 69. The Most Deadly Game 70.

Bellaver, Harry (1905–1970). American character actor, often seen as cop, small-time gangster or cabby.
Another Thin Man 40. The House on 92nd Street 45. No Way Out 50. The Lemon Drop Kid 51. From Here to Eternity 53. Love Me or Leave Me 55. Serenade 56. Slaughter on Tenth Avenue 57. The Old Man and the Sea 58. One Potato Two Potato 64. A Fine Madness 66. Madigan 67, etc.
TV series: Naked City 58-63.

Belle de Jour (France/Italy 1967). Luis Buñuel's brilliant study of a married woman who works off her frustrations at a brothel was much more than that bald summary might make it appear: a penetrating analysis of our society and a fascinating though sometimes confusing blend of fancy and reality. With Catherine Deneuve, Jean Sorel.

La Belle et la Bête (France 1946). Jean Cocteau wrote and directed this highly imaginative film version of Perrault's eighteenth-century fairy tale. There a few plot surprises, but Christian Bérard's decor is uniquely beautiful, Henri Alekan's photography conveys exactly the right sense of mystic trickery, and the taste and charm of the whole enterprise is impeccable. Josette Day and Jean Marais play the title roles. The theme has of course been used in a wide variety of films, including King Kong.

Les Belles de Nuit (France/Italy 1952). A lighter-than-air confection by Rene Clair from a script by himself, Pierre Barillet and Jean-Paul Gredy, about a young music teacher who dreams himself back into a romantic view of history and finds his adventures becoming true when he wakes. A most agreeable, well acted, delicately pointed and civilized entertainment.

Bellocchio, Marco (1940–). Italian director. *Fists in the Pocket* 65. China is Near 67, etc.

Belmondo, Jean-Paul (1933–). Interesting but unhandsome French leading actor.
A Double Tour 59. *A Bout de Souffle* 59. Moderato Cantabile 60. La Viaccia 60. Leon Morin, Priest 61. Two Women 61. Cartouche 62. *Un Singe en Hiver* 62. *That Man from Rio* 64. Weekend in Dunkirk 65. Pierrot le Fou 65. Is Paris Burning? 66. Tendre Voyou 66. Le Voleur 67. The Brain 68. Ho! 68. The Mississippi Mermaid 69. A Man I Like 69. Scoundrel in White 72. Le Magnifique 73. Stavisky 74, etc.

Belmore, Bertha (1882–1953). Ample British character comedienne, a British Margaret Dumont whose dignity was inevitably shattered.
Are You a Mason? 33. Going Gay 34. Broken Blossoms 36. In the Soup 37. Over She Goes 38. Yes Madam 39, etc.

Belmore, Lionel (1875–1940). Portly British character actor in Hollywood in the thirties.
The Love Parade 30. The Warrior's Husband 32. Vanessa 34. Cardinal Richelieu 35. Little Lord Fauntleroy 36. The Prince and the Pauper 37. My Son My Son 40, etc.

Beloin, Edmund (1910–). American comedy writer with radio experience.
Buck Benny Rides Again 40. Love Thy Neighbour 40. Because of Him 45. The Great Lover (& p) 49. A Yankee at King Arthur's Court 49. The Sad Sack 57. G.I. Blues 60. All in a Night's Work 61, etc.

The Beloved Rogue: see *If I Were King.*

Benchley, Robert (1889–1945). American magazine humourist who exploited the small problems of twentieth-century living. He appeared in many films as a loveable bumbler, usually trying to explain something very complicated or to control a patently unmanageable situation. Benchley made many amusing shorts consisting of lectures by him on matters of science or domestic harmony. One of them, *How to Sleep* (1935), won an Academy Award.

Biography 1946: *Robert Benchley* by his son Nathaniel.
□ Feature appearances: Headline Shooter 33. Dancing Lady 33. Rafter Romance 34. Social Register 34. China Seas 35. Piccadilly Jim 36. Live Love and Learn 37. Broadway Melody of 1938 37. Hired Wife 40. *Foreign Correspondent* 40. Nice Girl 41. *The Reluctant Dragon* 41. You'll Never Get Rich 41. Three Girls about Town 41. Bedtime Story 41. Take a Letter Darling 42. The Major and the Minor 42. *I Married a Witch* 42. Flesh and Fantasy 43. Young and Willing 43. Song of Russia 43. The Sky's the Limit 43. Her Primitive Man 44. National Barn Dance 44. See Here Private Hargrove 44. Practically Yours 44. Janie 44. Pan Americana 45. *It's In the Bag* 45. Weekend at the Waldorf 45. Kiss and Tell 45. Duffy's Tavern 45. The Stork Club 45. Road to Utopia 45. The Bride Wore Boots 46. Snafu 46. Janie Gets Married 46. Blue Skies 46.

Bendix, William (1906–1964). Familiar American character actor who usually played the tough guy with the heart of gold; his broken nose, raucous Brooklyn accent and air of amiable stupidity endeared him to a generation.
□ Woman of the Year 42. The McGuerins from Brooklyn 42. Brooklyn Orchid 42. Wake Island 42. *The Glass Key* (as a murderous thug) 42. Who Done It? 42. Star Spangled Rhythm 42. The Crystal Ball 43. Taxi Mister 43. China 43. Hostages 43. Guadalcanal Diary 43. *Lifeboat* 43. *The Hairy Ape* 44. Abroad with Two Yanks 44. Greenwich Village 44. It's in the Bag 45. Don Juan Quilligan 45. A Bell for Adano 45. Sentimental Journey 45. *The Blue Dahlia* 46. The Dark Corner 46. Two Years Before the Mast 46. White Tie and Tails 46. I'll Be Yours 46. Blaze of Noon 47. Calcutta 47. The Web 47. Where There's Life 47. Variety Girl 47. *The Time of Your Life* 48. Race Street 48. The Babe Ruth Story 48. *The Life of Riley* 49. A Connecticut Yankee in King Arthur's Court 49. *The Big Steal* 49. Streets of Laredo 49. Cover Up 49. Johnny Holiday 49. Kill the Umpire 50. Gambling House 50. Submarine Command 51. *Detective Story* 51. Macao 52. A Girl in Every Port 52. Blackbeard the Pirate 52. Dangerous Mission 54. Crashout 55. Battle Stations 56. The Deep Six 58. Idle on Parade (GB) 59. The Rough and the Smooth (GB) 59. Boy's Night Out 62. Johnny Nobody (GB) 62. The Young and the Brave 63. For Love or Money 63. Law of the Lawless 64. The Phoney American 64. Young Fury 65.
TV series: *The Life of Riley* 53-58. Overland Stage 60.

Benedek, Laslo (1907–). Hungarian director in Hollywood; output surprisingly meagre.
□ The Kissing Bandit 48. Port of New York 49. Storm over the Tiber 52. *Death of a Salesman* 52. *The Wild One* 54. Bengal Brigade 54. Kinder Mütter und ein General (Ger.) 55. Affair in Havana 57. Moment of Danger (GB) 58. Malaga (GB) 62. Namu the Killer Whale (& p) 66. The Daring Game 68. The Night Visitor 71.

Benedict, Billy (1917–). American character actor who in his youth was one of the original 'Bowery Boys'; now plays cabbies, bartenders, etc.
The Clock Struck Eight 35. King of the Newsboys 38. Call a Messenger (the first of the 'Bowery Boys' series which ran until 1953) 40. Aerial Gunner 43. The Hallelujah Trail 65, many others.

Benedict, Richard (1916–) (Riccardo Benedetto). American leading man, usually in second features; sometimes plays the heavy.
Till the End of Time 46. Crossfire 47. City across the River 49. State Penitentiary 50. Ace in the Hole 51. Okinawa 52. The Juggler 53. Hoodlum Empire 55. The Shrike 55. Monkey on my Back 57. Ocean's Eleven 60, etc.

Ben Hur. There were several silent versions of Lew Wallace's semi-biblical adventure novel. Best-known is MGM's lavish spectacular of 1926, directed by Fred Niblo with Ramon Novarro and Francis X. Bushman; it was reissued with sound effects in 1931. In 1959 it was remade by MGM and William Wyler, with Charlton Heston and Stephen Boyd: the greatest praise went to the chariot race sequence directed by Andrew Marton.

Benjamin, Arthur (1893–). British composer.
The Man Who Knew Too Much 34. The Scarlet Pimpernel 34. Turn of the Tide 35. Under the Red Robe 36. Master of Bankdam 47, etc.

Benjamin, Richard (1938–). Diffident-seeming American leading man. Married Paula Prentiss.
Thunder over the Plains 53. *Goodbye Columbus* 69. Catch 22 70. *Diary of a Mad Housewife* 70. Marriage of a Young Stockbroker 76. Portnoy's Complaint 72. The Last of Sheila 73. Westworld 73, etc.
TV series: *He and She* 67.

Bennet, Spencer Gordon (1893–). American silent actor and stunt man who became a famous director of serials and made fifty-two in all.

Rogue of the Rio Grande 30. Mysterious Pilot 37. Arizona Bound 42. Batman and Robin 48. Atom Man vs Superman 50. Adventures of Sir Galahad 51. Brave Warrior (feature) 52. The Atomic Submarine (feature) 60. The Bounty Killer (feature) 65, many others.

Bennett, Arnold (1867–1931). British novelist, little of whose work has been filmed. *Buried Alive* has, however, been seen in several versions, under its own title, as *The Great Adventure*, as *His Double Life*, and as *Holy Matrimony*. British studios filmed *The Card* with Alec Guinness, and less successfully *Dear Mr Prohack* with Cecil Parker.

Bennett, Barbara (1902–1958). American leading lady of a few twenties films. Sister of Constance and Joan Bennett.
Syncopation 29. Mother's Boy 29. Love among the Millionaires 30, etc.

Bennett, Belle (1891–1932). American leading lady of the silent screen.
A Soul in Trust 18. His Supreme Moment 25. If Marriage Fails 25. *Stella Dallas* 25. The Fourth Commandment 27. The Way of All Flesh 27. Mother Machree 28. The Iron Mask 29. Courage 30. Recaptured Love 31. The Big Shot 31, etc.

Bennett, Bruce (1909–) (Herman Brix). Athletic American leading man who started in films by playing Tarzan and subsequently settled down as a familiar flannel-suited second lead. Used his own name until 1940.
Student Tour 34. *The New Adventures of Tarzan* 35 (re-edited 1938 as *Tarzan and the Green Goddess*). Danger Patrol 37. Before I Hang 40. Atlantic Convoy 42. The More the Merrier 43. Sahara 43. Mildred Pierce 45. The Treasure of the Sierra Madre 47. Silver River 48. Task Force 49. The Doctor and the Girl 49. Without Honor 50. Sudden Fear 52. Dream Wife 53. Strategic Air Command 55. Three Violent People 57. The Outsider 61, many others.

Bennett, Charles (1899–). British screenwriter who worked on some of Hitchcock's thirties films and later moved to Hollywood. Usually worked in collaboration.
Blackmail 29. The Man Who Knew Too Much 34. The Thirty-nine Steps 35. Secret Agent 36. Sabotage 37. King Solomon's Mines 37. The Young in Heart 38. Balalaika 39. Foreign Correspondent 40. Joan of Paris 42. Reap the Wild Wind 42. The Story of Dr Wassell 44. Ivy 47. Madness of the Heart (& d) 48. Black Magic 49. Where Danger Lives 51. The Green Glove 52. No Escape (& d) 53. The Story of Mankind

57. The Lost World 60. Five Weeks in a Balloon 62. War Gods of the Deep 65, etc.

Bennett, Compton (1900–1974). British director, former editor.
□ *The Seventh Veil* 45. The Years Between 46. Daybreak 48. My Own True Love 49. *That Forsyte Woman* 49. *King Solomon's Mines* 50. So Little Time 52. The Gift Horse 52. It Started in Paradise 52. Desperate Moment 53. That Woman Opposite 57. The Flying Scot 57. Beyond the Curtain 60.

Bennett, Constance (1904–1965). Glamorous American star of the thirties, adept at wordly roles; sister of Barbara and Joan Bennett.
□ Reckless Youth 22. Evidence 22. What's Wrong with the Women? 22. Cytherea 24. Into the Net 24. *The Goose Hangs High* 25. Married 25. Code of the West 25. My Son 25. My Wife and I 25. *The Goose Woman* 25. Sally Irene and Mary 25. Wandering Fires 25. The Pinch Hitter 26. This Thing Called Love 29. Son of the Gods 30. Rich People 30. Common Clay 30. *Three Faces East* 30. Sin Takes a Holiday 30. The Easiest Way 31. Born to Love 31. The Common Law 31. Bought 31. Lady with a Past 32. *What Price Hollywood* 32. Two Against the World 32. Rockabye 32. Our Betters 33. Bed of Roses 33. After Tonight 33. *Moulin Rouge* 33. Affairs of Cellini 34. Outcast Lady 34. After Office Hours 35. Everything is Thunder (GB) 36. Ladies in Love 36. *Topper* (as a ghost) 37. *Merrily We Live* 38. Service de Luxe 38. Topper Takes a Trip 38. Tailspin 39. *Escape to Glory* 40. Law of the Tropics 41. *Two-faced Woman* 41. Wild Bill Hickok Rides 41. Sin Town 42. Madame Spy 42. Paris Underground 46. Centennial Summer 46. *The Unsuspected* 47. Smart Woman 48. Angel on the Amazon 49. As Young as You Feel 51. It Should Happen to You 53. *Madame X* 65.

Bennett, Enid (1895–1969). Australian leading lady in Hollywood films of the twenties.
Princess in the Dark 17. The Vamp 18. The Haunted Bedroom 19. Hairpins 20. Her Husband's Friend 21. Robin Hood 22. Scandalous Tongues 22. The Courtship of Miles Standish 23. The Sea Hawk 24. A Woman's Heart 26. The Wrong Mr Wright 27. Good Medicine 29. Skippy 31. Meet Dr Christian 39. Strike Up the Band 40, many others.

Bennett, Hywel (1944–). Welsh leading man who has usually played roles requiring a feigning of innocence.
□ *The Family Way* 66. Twisted Nerve 68. *The Virgin Soldiers* 69. The Buttercup Chain 70. Loot 71. Percy 71. Endless Night 72. Alice's Adventures in Wonderland 72. The Love Ban 72.

Bennett, Jill (1930–). Unusual-looking British actress who generally plays emancipated roles.
Moulin Rouge 53. Hell Below Zero 54. *Lust for Life* 56. The Criminal 60. The Skull 65. *The Nanny* 65. *Inadmissible Evidence* 68. *The Charge of the Light Brigade* 68. Julius Caesar 70. I Want What I Want 71. Mister Quilp 75, etc.

Bennett, Joan (1910–). Popular American leading lady of the thirties and forties, one of the most attractive stars of her time. Sister of Barbara and Constance Bennett.
□ Power 28. Bulldog Drummond 29. Three Live Ghosts 29. Disraeli 29. Mississippi Gambler 29. Puttin' On the Ritz 30. Crazy that Way 30. Moby Dick 30. Maybe It's Love 30. Scotland Yard 30. Many a Slip 31. Doctors' Wives 31. Hush Money 31. She Wanted a Millionaire 32. Careless Lady 32. The Trial of Vivienne Ware 32. Weekends Only 32. Wild Girl 32. Me and My Gal 32. Arizona to Broadway 32. *Little Women* 33. The Pursuit of Happiness 34. The Man Who Reclaimed His Head 34. *Private Worlds* 35. Mississippi 35. Two for Tonight 35. The Man Who Broke the Bank at Monte Carlo 35. She Couldn't Take It 35. Thirteen Hours by Air 36. Big Brown Eyes 36. Two in a Crowd 36. Wedding Present 36. Vogues of 1938 37. I Met My Love Again 38. The Texans 38. Artists and Models Abroad 38. Trade Winds 39. The Man in the Iron Mask 39. *The Housekeeper's Daughter* 39. Green Hell 40. The House across the Bay 40. The Man I Married 40. Son of Monte Cristo 40. She Knew All the Answers 41. *Man Hunt* 41. Wild Geese Calling 41. Confirm or Deny 42. Twin Beds 42. The Wife Takes a Flyer 42. Girl Trouble 42. Margin for Error 43. *The Woman in the Window* 44. Nob Hill 45. *Scarlet Street* 45. Colonel Effingham's Raid 46. *The Macomber Affair* 47. The Secret Beyond the Door 47. The Woman on the Beach 47. The Scar 47. *The Reckless Moment* 49. *Father of the Bride* 50. For Heaven's Sake 50. Father's Little Dividend 51. The Guy Who Came Back 51. Highway Dragnet 54. We're No Angels 55. There's Always Tomorrow 56. Navy Wife 56. Desire in the Dust 60. The Eyes of Charles Sand (TV) 72.

Bennett, Richard (1873–1944). Dapper American stage actor, a leading figure of his day; father of Barbara, Constance and Joan Bennett. Film appearances rare.
The Eternal City 23. The Home Towners 28. Arrowsmith 32. *If I Had a Million* (as the millionaire) 32. Nana 34. *The Magnificent*

Ambersons 42. Journey into Fear 43, etc.

Bennett, Richard Rodney(1936–). British Composer.
Interpol 57. Indiscreet 58. Only Two Can Play 61. Billy Liar 63. One Way Pendulum 64. The Nanny 65. Far from the Madding Crowd 67.

Benny, Jack (1894–1974) (Benjamin Kubelsky). Celebrated American comedian of radio, TV and occasional films. His inimitable reproachful look, his pretence of meanness and his much maligned violin are among the trademarks which kept him popular for forty years. He graduated from burlesque, and later married his radio leading lady Mary Livingstone (Sadye Marks).
□ *Hollywood Revue of 1929* 29. Chasing Rainbows 30. Medicine Man 30. Transatlantic Merry-Go-Round 34. Broadway Melody of 1936 35. It's in the Air 35. The Big Broadcast of 1937 36. College Holiday 36. Artists and Models 37. Artists and Models Abroad 38. Man About Town 39. Buck Benny Rides Again 39. Love Thy Neighbour 40. *Charley's Aunt* 41. *To Be or Not To Be* (an outstanding performance) 42. George Washington Slept Here 42. The Meanest Man in the World 43. Hollywood Canteen 44. *It's in the Bag* 45. *The Horn Blows at Midnight* 45. A Guide for the Married Man 67.
TV series: *The Jack Benny Show* 50–65.

Benoît-Lévy, Jean (1883–1959). French director who also wrote books on cinema.
La Maternelle 33. Hélène 37, La Mort du Cygne 38. Fire in the Straw 43, etc.

Benson, George (1911–). British character actor of stage, screen and TV, the nervous 'little man' of countless films.
Keep Fit 37. Convoy 40. The October Man 48. Pool of London 50. The Man in the White Suit 51. The Captain's Paradise 53. Doctor in the House 54. Value for Money 56. Dracula 58. A Jolly Bad Fellow 64. A Home of Your Own 65. The Creeping Flesh 72, etc.

Benson, Martin (1918–). British character actor often seen as a smooth foreign-looking crook.
The Blind Goddess 49. West of Zanzibar 54. The King and I (US) 56. Windom's Way 58. The Three Worlds of Gulliver 60. Cleopatra 62. Behold a Pale Horse 64. Goldfinger 64. The Secret of My Success 65. Pope Joan 72, many others.

Benson, Robby (1956–). American juvenile lead of the seventies.

Jory 73. *Jeremy* 73. *Death Be Not Proud* (TV) 75. Lucky Lady 76. The Death of Richie (TV) 76.

Bentine, Michael (1922–). Anglo-Peruvian comedian, popular on stage and TV, who has made several unsuccessful attempts to film his goonish style of humour, most recently in *The Sandwich Man* 66.

Bentley, John (1916–). British leading man who left the stage in 1946 to play in innumerable low-budget crime dramas, including series about Paul Temple and The Toff.
Hills of Donegal 47. Calling Paul Temple 48. The Happiest Days of Your Life 49. The Lost Hours 51. The Scarlet Spear 53. Golden Ivory 55. Istanbul (US) 58. Submarine Seahawk 59. The Singer Not the Song 60. Mary Had a Little 61. The Fur Collar 63, many others.
TV series: African Patrol 59.

Bentley, Thomas (c. 1880–195*). British director, former Dickensian impersonator, who began in films by making silent versions of several Dickens novels.
Young Woodley 30. *Hobson's Choice* 31. The Scotland Yard Mystery 33. *Those Were the Days* 34. The Old Curiosity Shop 35. Music Hath Charms 35. Marigold 38. The Middle Watch 39. Lucky to Me 39. Old Mother Riley's Circus 41, scores of others.

Berenson, Marisa (1947–). International fashion model who has appeared in films.
□ Death in Venice 72. Cabaret 72. Barry Lyndon 75.

Beresford, Harry (1864–1944). British general purpose actor in Hollywood from silent days.
The Quarterback 26. Charles Chan Carries On 31. So Big 32. Dr X 32. The Sign of the Cross 32. Murders in the Zoo 33. Dinner at Eight 33. Cleopatra 34. The Little Minister 34. Seven Keys To Baldpate 35. David Copperfield 35. Follow the Fleet 36. The Prince and the Pauper 37. They Won't Forget 37, many others.

Berg, Gertrude (1899–1966) (Gertrude Edelstein). Plump American character actress famous on TV and radio as Molly of the Goldberg family. She appeared in a film version, *Molly* 51, also in another TV series, *Mrs G Goes to College* 61.

Bergen, Candice (1946–). Stylish American leading lady, daughter of Edgar Bergen.
□ *The Group* 66. The Sand Pebbles 66. The Day

the Fish Came Out 67. Vivre Pour Vivre 67. The Magus 68. Getting Straight 70. Soldier Blue 70. The Adventurers 70. *Carnal Knowledge* 71. The Hunting Party 71. T R Baskin 72. 11 Harrowhouse 74. Bite the Bullet 75. The Wind and the Lion 76.

Bergen, Edgar (1903–). Mild-mannered Swedish-American ventriloquist, manipulator of Charlie McCarthy and Mortimer Snerd (special AA 1937); latterly a character actor.
The Goldwyn Follies 38. Letter of Introduction 38. *You Can't Cheat an Honest Man* 39. *Charlie McCarthy Detective* 39. Look Who's Laughing 41. Here We Go Again 42. Stage Door Canteen 43. Song of the Open Road 44. *I Remember Mama* 48. The Hanged Man 64. One Way Wahine 66. Don't Make Waves 67. The Homecoming (TV) 70, etc.

Bergen, Polly (1929–) (Nellie Burgin). American singer of stage, radio and TV; also pleasing light actress in several films.
□ At War with the Army 50. That's My Boy 51. Warpath 51. The Stooge 53. Arena 53. Escape from Fort Bravo 54. *Cape Fear* 62. Belle Sommers (TV) 62. The Caretakers 63. *Move Over Darling* 63. *Kisses for My President* 64. A Guide for the Married Man 67. Death Cruise (TV) 75.

Berger, Helmut (c. 1942–). Handsome German actor who gives a sinister edge to his performances.
The Damned 69. *Un Beau Monstre* 70. The Garden of the Finzi-Continis 71. Dorian Gray 72. Ash Wednesday 73. Ludwig 73. Conversation Piece 75, etc.

Berger, Ludwig (1892–1969) (Ludwig Bamberger). German director who made some international films.
Ein Glas Wasser 22. The Waltz Dream 26. The Woman from Moscow (US) 28. Sins of the Fathers 29. Die Meistersinger 29. The Vagabond King (US) 30. Playboy of Paris 30. Waltz Time in Vienna 33. Three Waltzes 39. The Thief of Baghdad (GB/US) 40. Ballerina (Fr.) 50, etc.

Berger, Nicole (1934–1967). French leading lady.
Juliette 52. Game of Love 54. Le Premier Mai 57. Love is my Profession 58. Les Dragueurs 59. Shoot the Pianist 62, etc.

Berger, Senta (1941–). Austrian leading lady in international films.
The Secret Ways 61. The Good Soldier Schweik 62. The Victors 63. Major Dundee 65. The Glory Guys 65. Cast a Giant Shadow 66. The Quiller Memorandum 67. Our Man in Marrakesh 67. The Ambushers 67. Treasure of San Gennaro 68. De Sade 69. Percy 70. The Swiss Conspiracy 75, etc.

Bergerac, Jacques (1927–). French leading man, former lawyer, in Hollywood from 1953.
Les Girls 57. Gigi 58. Thunder in the Sun 59. The Hypnotic Eye 60. Taffy and the Jungle Hunter 65, etc.

Berggren, Thommy (1937–). Swedish leading actor.
Sunday in September 63. Raven's End 63. *Elvira Madigan* 67. Joe Hill 71, etc.

Berghof, Herbert (1909–). Austrian character actor long on American stage, also as drama teacher; films rare.
Assignment Paris 52. *Five Fingers* 52. Red Planet Mars 52. Fraulein 58. Cleopatra 62, etc.

Bergman, Henry (1870–1946). American comedy actor, the heavy villain in many a Chaplin film from *His New Job* in 1915 to *The Great Dictator* in 1940.

Bergman, Ingmar (1918–). Swedish writer-director who divides his time between stage and film. In the late fifties his films had world-wide impact because of their semi-mystic, under-explained themes and bravura presentation by a repertory of excellent actors and cameramen; more recently his work has become austere and withdrawn.
□ Crisis 45. It Rains on Our Love 46. A Ship Bound for India 47. Night is Our Future 47. Port of Call 48. *Prison* 48. *Thirst* 49. Till Gladje 49. Summer Interlude 50. Sant Hander inte Har 50. Waiting Women 52. Summer with Monika 52. *Sawdust and Tinsel* 53. A Lesson in Love 54. Journey into Autumn 55. *Smiles of a Summer Night* 55. *The Seventh Seal* 56. *Wild Strawberries* 57. So Close to Life 58. *The Face (The Magician)* 58. *The Virgin Spring* (AA) 59. The Devil's Eye 60. *Through a Glass Darkly* (AA) 61. *Winter Light* 62. *The Silence* 63. Now About these Women 64. *Persona* 66. The Hour of the Wolf 67. The Shame 68. The Touch 70. *Cries and Whispers* 72. Scenes from a Marriage (TV) 74. The Magic Flute (TV) 75. Face to Face (TV) 76.

Bergman, Ingrid (1915–). Gifted Swedish leading actress who went to Hollywood in 1938 and became an international star. In 1948 her romance with Roberto Rossellini (qv) caused a return to Europe where she appeared in mainly inferior films; Hollywood's door opened to her again in 1956.

☐ Munkbrogreven 34. Branningar 35. Swedenhielms 35. Valborgsmassoafton 35. Pa Solsidan 36. *Intermezzo* 36. Juninatten 37. *En Kvinnas Ansikte* 38. En Enda Natt 38. Dollar 38. Die Vier Gesellen 38. *Intermezzo* (US remake) 39. Rage in Heaven 41. Adam Had Four Sons 41. Dr Jekyll and Mr Hyde 41. *Casablanca* 43. *For Whom the Bell Tolls* 43. *Gaslight* (AA) 44. *The Bells of St Mary's* 45. *Spellbound* 45. *Saratoga Trunk* 45. *Notorious* 46. Arch of Triumph 48. *Joan of Arc* 48. Under Capricorn 49. Stromboli 50. Europa 51. We the Women 53. Journey to Italy 54. Joan at the Stake 54. Fear 54. *Anastasia* (AA) 56. Paris Does Strange Things 57. *Indiscreet* 58. *The Inn of the Sixth Happiness* 58. Goodbye Again 61. The Visit 64. The Yellow Rolls Royce 64. Fugitive in Vienna 67. *Cactus Flower* 69. A Walk in the Spring Rain 70. From the Mixed Up Files of Mrs Basil E. Frankweiler 74. Murder on the Orient Express (AA, BFA) 74. A Matter of Time 76.

Bergner, Elisabeth (1898–) (Elizabeth Ettel). German leading actress who settled in Britain in the thirties and married Paul Czinner (qv). Her fey gamine character quickly dated.

☐ Der Evangelimann 24. Nju 24. Der Geiger von Florenz 26. Liebe 27. Queen Louisa 28. Dona Juana 28. Fraulein Else 29. Ariane 31. *Der Traumende Mund* 32. Ariane (GB) 33. *Catherine the Great* (GB) 34. *Escape Me Never* (GB) 35. As You Like It (GB) 36. Dreaming Lips (GB) 37. Stolen Life (GB) 39. Paris Calling (US) 41. Die Glucklichen Jahre der Thorwalds (Ger) 62. Cry of the Banshee (GB) 70. Courier to the Tsar (GB) 71. Der Fussganger (Ger) 73.

Berke, William (1904–1958). American director of second features.

Minesweeper 43. The Falcon in Mexico 44. Splitface 46. Jungle Jim 48. Deputy Marshal 49. Zamba the Gorilla 49. I Shot Billy the Kid (& p) 50. Four Boys and a Gun (& p) 55. Cop Hater (& p) 57, etc.

Berkeley, Ballard (1904–). British light actor of stage and screen.

The Chinese Bungalow 30. London Melody 35. The Outsider 38. In Which We Serve 42. They Made Me a Fugitive 47. The Long Dark Hall 51. Three Steps to the Gallows 56. See How They Run 57. Star! 68, etc.

Berkeley, Busby (1895–1976) (William Berkeley Enos). American song and dance director who in the early thirties invaded Hollywood from Broadway and developed the spectacular, kaleidoscopic girlie numbers which became a feature of all musicals, quickly dated, and were joyously rediscovered in the sixties. Below, (m) signifies that Berkeley directed the musical sequences only. His occasional dramatic films were inconsiderable.

☐ *Whoopee* (m) 30. Kiki (m) 31. Palmy Days (m) 31. Flying High (m) 31. Night World (m) 32. Bird of Paradise (m) 32. *The Kid from Spain* (m) 32. *Forty Second Street* (m) 33. *Gold Diggers of 1933* (m) 33. She Had to Say Yes 33. *Footlight Parade* 33. *Roman Scandals* (m) 33. *Wonder Bar* (m) 34. *Fashions of 1934* (m) 34. Twenty Million Sweethearts (m) 34. *Dames* (m) 34. *Gold Diggers of 1935* 35. Go into Your Dance (m) 35. Bright Lights 35. In Caliente (m) 35. I Live for Love 35. Stars Over Broadway 35. Stage Struck 36. Gold Diggers of 1937 (m) 37. The Go-Getter 37. The Singing Marine (m) 37. Varsity Show (m) 37. Hollywood Hotel 37. Men are Such Fools 38. Gold Diggers in Paris (m) 38. Garden of the Moon 38. Comet over Broadway 38. They Made me a Criminal 39. Broadway Serenade (m) 39. *Babes In Arms* 39. Fast and Furious 39. Forty Little Mothers 40. *Strike Up the Band* 40. Blonde Inspiration 41. *Ziegfeld Girl* (m) 41. *Lady Be Good* (m) 41. Babes on Broadway 41. Born to Sing (m) 41. *For Me and My Gal* 42. Girl Crazy (m) 43. *The Gang's All Here* (first in colour) 43. Cinderella Jones 46. *Take Me Out to the Ball Game* 49. Two Weeks with Love (m) 50. Call me Mister (m) 51. Two Tickets to Broadway (m) 51. Million Dollar Mermaid (m) 52. Small Town Girl (m) 53. Easy to Love (m) 53. Rose Marie (m) 54. Jumbo (m) 62.

Berkeley Square. Based on Henry James' *The Sense of the Past*, this romantic-macabre play by John Balderston concerned a man who enters his own past and falls in love with a girl of two hundred years ago. It was delicately filmed in 1933 by Frank Lloyd, with Leslie Howard in the lead. The 1951 remake with Tyrone Power, under the title, *I'll Never Forget You*, was a nothing.

Berlanga, Luis (1921–). Spanish director. Welcome Mr Marshall 52. Calabuch 56. The Executioner 63, etc.

Berle, Milton (1908–) (Mendel Berlinger). Brash American vaudeville and TV comedian who never quite found his niche in the movies.

☐ New Faces of 1937 37. Radio City Revels 38. Tall Dark and Handsome 41. Sun Valley Serenade 41. Rise and Shine 41. A Gentleman at Heart 42. Whispering Ghosts 42. Over My Dead Body 42. *Margin for Error* 43. *Always Leave Them Laughing* (based on his autobiography)

49. Let's Make Love 60. *It's a Mad Mad Mad Mad World* 63. The Oscar 65. The Happening 67. Who's Minding the Mint? 67. Where Angels Go Trouble Follows 68. For Singles Only 68. Hieronymus Merkin 69. Seven in Darkness (TV) 70. Lepke 75.

Berlin has seemed to film makers a grim grey city, and history provides obvious reasons for this. Standard attitudes are shown in *The Murderers Are Amongst Us, Germany Year Zero, Four Men in a Jeep, Hotel Berlin, Berlin Express, The Man Between, Night People, The Big Lift, I Am a Camera, The Spy Who Came in from the Cold, The Man Who Finally Died, A Prize of Gold, The Quiller Memorandum, Cabaret, Escape from East Berlin, Funeral in Berlin.* But some people have found fun there, notably Billy Wilder in *People on Sunday, A Foreign Affair* and *One Two Three*; and in 1928 Walter Ruttman's stylishly kaleidoscopic documentary, *Berlin: Symphony of a Great City,* showed the place and its people to be just as sympathetic as anywhere else if they are understandingly portrayed.

Berlin, Irving (1888–) (Israel Baline). Prolific American composer and lyricist of tuneful popular songs.
The Awakening 28. The Coconuts 29. Hallelujah 29. Putting on the Ritz 30. Mammy 30. Reaching for the Moon 31. Kid Millions 34. *Top Hat* 35. *Follow the Fleet* 36. *On the Avenue* 37. *Alexander's Ragtime Band* 38. Carefree 38. Second Fiddle 39. Louisiana Purchase 42. *This is the Army* (in which he also appeared and sang 'Oh How I Hate to Get Up in the Morning') 43. *Blue Skies* 46. *Easter Parade* 48. *Annie Get Your Gun* 50. *Call Me Madam* 53. *There's No Business Like Show Business* 54. *White Christmas* 54. Sayonara 57, etc.

Berlin, Jeannie (1949–). American actress, daughter of Elaine May.
☐ On a Clear Day You Can See Forever 70. Getting Straight 70. Move 70. The Strawberry Statement 70. The Baby Maker 70. Bone 72. Why 72. Portnoy's Complaint 71. *The Heartbreak Kid* 73. Sheila Levine 75.

Berlinger, Warren (1937–). American stage and film actor, usually seen as chubby innocent.
Teenage Rebel 56. Three Brave Men 57. Platinum High School 60. The Wackiest Ship in the Army 61. All Hands on Deck 61. Billie 65. Thunder Valley 67, etc.

Berman, Monty (1913–). British second feature producer, former cinematographer.

Jack the Ripper (& d) 56. The Flesh and the Fiends 59. Sea of Sand 59. Blood of the Vampire 60. What a Carve Up 61. *The Hellfire Club* 61, many others.
TV series: *The Saint, Gideon's Way,* The Baron, The Champions, Department S, Randall and Hopkirk (Dec'd), The Adventurer, etc.

Berman, Pandro S. (1905–). Distinguished American producer who spent many years at both RKO and MGM, and maintained a high standard of product.
Morning Glory 32. *The Gay Divorcee* 34. The Little Minister 34. *Top Hat* 35. Sylvia Scarlett 36. Mary of Scotland 36. *Winterset* 36. Quality Street 37. *Stage Door* 37. Room Service 38. *The Hunchback of Notre Dame* 39. *Ziegfeld Girl* 41. Somewhere I'll Find You 42. The Seventh Cross 44. National Velvet 44. Undercurrent 46. *The Three Musketeers* 48. Madame Bovary 49. *Father of the Bride* 50. Ivanhoe 52. The Prisoner of Zenda 52. *The Blackboard Jungle* 55. Tea and Sympathy 56. Jailhouse Rock 57. The Brothers Karamazov 58. Butterfield 8 60. Sweet Bird of Youth 62. *The Prize* 63. A Patch of Blue 65, many others.

Berman, Shelley (1926–). American cabaret monologuist who has made a few film appearances.
☐ *The Best Man* 64. The Wheeler Dealers 64. Divorce Americn Style 67. Every Home Should have One (GB) 70.

Bern, Paul (1889–1932) (Paul Levy). American director whose suicide soon after his marriage to Jean Harlow is still a subject of controversy. (Became MGM executive.)
The North Wind's Malice 20. Worldly Goods 24. Tomorrow's Love 25. The Dressmaker from Paris 25. Grounds for Divorce 25, etc.

Bernard, James (1925–). British composer with a predilection for horror themes. Co-authored film script, *Seven Days to Noon* 50.
The Quatermass Experiment 55. Dracula 58. Windom's Way 58. The Hound of the Baskervilles 59. The Gorgon 64. The Plague of the Zombies 65. Scars of Dracula 70. Frankenstein and the Monster from Hell 72. The Legend of the Seven Golden Vampires 73, etc.

Bernardi, Herschel (1923–). Balding, beaming American general purpose actor, often seen as cop or gangster.
Green Fields 37. Crime Inc. 45. Miss Susie Slagle's 46. Stakeout on Dope Street 58. The Savage Eye 60. A Cold Wind in August 61. Irma La Douce 63. The Honey Pot 67. But I Don't

Want to Get Married (TV) 71. No Place to Run (TV) 72, etc.
TV series: Peter Gunn 58–61. *Arnie* 71.

Bernds, Edward (–). American second feature director, former sound effects man for the Three Stooges.
Blondie Hits the Jackpot 49. Harem Girl (& w) 52. Spy Chasers 55. World Without End (& w) 56. Quantrill's Raiders 58. Return of the Fly (& w) 59. The Three Stooges in Orbit 62. Tickle Me (w only) 65, many others.

Bernhardt, Curtis (or **Kurt**) (1899–). German director; on arrival in Hollywood in 1940, he was generally assigned to 'women's pictures' and approached them with variable style.
Three Loves 29. Thirteen Men and a Girl 31. Die Letzte Kompagnie 32. The Beloved Vagabond (GB) 36. My Love Came Back 40. Lady with Red Hair 40. Million Dollar Baby 41. Juke Girl 42. Happy Go Lucky 43. *Devotion* 44. Conflict 45. My Reputation 45. *A Stolen Life* 46. *Possessed* 47. High Wall 47. The Doctor and the Girl 49. Payment on Demand (& w) 51. Sirocco 51. The Blue Veil 51. Miss Sadie Thompson 53. *Beau Brummell* 54. Interrupted Melody 55. Gaby 56. *Kisses for My President* (& p) 64, etc.

Bernhardt, Sarah (1844–1923) (Rosalie Bernard). Famous French stage tragedienne who lent dignity if nothing else to early silent films.
La Dame aux Camélias 10. Queen Elizabeth 12, etc.

Bernie, Ben (1891–1943) (Benjamin Anzelvitz). American bandleader who worked up a publicity feud with Walter Winchell and consequently appeared in a film or two.
□ Shoot the Works 34. Stolen Harmony 35. *Wake Up and Live* 37. Love and Hisses 37.

Bernstein, Charles (–). American composer.
Hex 73. White Lightning 73. Mr Majestyk 74.

Bernstein, Elmer (1922–). American composer-conductor.
Saturday's Hero 51. Sudden Fear 52. Cat Women of the Moon 53. *The Man with the Golden Arm* 55. The Ten Commandments 56. *The Sweet Smell of Success* 57. The Tin Star 57. God's Little Acre 58. The Buccaneer 59. *The Magnificent Seven* 60. A Walk on the Wild Side 62. To Kill a Mockingbird 62. Baby the Rain Must Fall 65. The Sons of Katie Elder 65. The Reward 65. Return of the Seven 66. *Thoroughly Modern Millie* (AA) 67. A Cannon for Cordoba

70, etc.

Bernstein, Leonard (1918–). American concert musician, conductor and composer.
On the Town 49. On the Waterfront 54. West Side Story 61.

Bernstein, Lord (1899–) (Sidney Bernstein). British executive and producer, founder and chairman of the Granada group, including a television station and a cinema circuit. Founder member of the Film Society (1924). First to institute Saturday morning shows for children and to research audience preferences. During World War II, films adviser to the Ministry of Information and SHAEF. Produced three films with Alfred Hitchcock as director: *Rope* 48. *Under Capricorn* 49. *I Confess* 52.

Berri, Claude (1934–) (Claude Langmann). French director.
Le Vieil Homme et l'Enfant (& w) 66. Mazel Tov ou Le Mariage (& w) 68. Le Pistonne 70. Papa's Cinema 71. Sex Shop 72, etc.

Berry, John (1917–). American director with stage experience.
□ Cross My Heart 45. From This Day Forward 46. Miss Susie Slagle's 46. Casbah 48. Tension 49. He Ran All the Way 51. Ça Va Barder (Fr.) 55. The Great Lover (Don Juan) (Fr.) 55. Je Suis un Sentimental (Fr.) 55. Tamango 57. Oh Que Mambo (It.) 59. Maya 66. Claudine 74.

Berry, Jules (1883–1951) (Jules Paufichet). Saturnine French character actor.
The Crime of Monsieur Lange 34. Carrefour 39. *Le Jour Se Lève* 39. *Les Visiteurs du Soir* 42. La Symphonie Fantastique 47, etc.

Berry, Ken (–). American actor often seen on TV as bird-like comic hero.
Wake Me When The War Is Over (TV) 70. The Reluctant Heroes (TV) 71, etc.

Bertolucci, Bernardo (1940–). Italian director.
Before the Revolution 65. The Grim Reaper 68. The Spider's Stratagem 69. The Conformist 70. *Last Tango in Paris* 72, etc.

Besserer, Eugenie (1870–1934). American character actress.
The Count of Monte Cristo 12. Scarlet Days 19. The Sin of Martha Queed 21. The Rosary 22. Her Reputation 23. The Price She Paid 24. A Fool and His Money 25. The Millionaire Policeman 26. *The Jazz Singer* (as Jolson's mother) 27. Two Lovers 28. Madame X 29.

Thunderbolt 29. In Gay Madrid 30. To the Last Man 33, many others.

Bessie, Alvah (–). American screenwriter, blacklisted in 1949 as one of the Hollywood Ten (qv).
The Very Thought of You 44. Hotel Berlin 45. Objective Burma 45, etc.

Best, Edna (1900–1974). Soft-spoken, maternal British actress, once married to Herbert Marshall. Went to Hollywood in 1939 and stayed.
Tilly of Bloomsbury 21. A Couple of Down and Outs 23. Escape 30. *Tilly of Bloomsbury* 30. The Calendar 31. *Michael and Mary* 32. The Faithful Heart 32. *The Man Who Knew Too Much* 34. Sleeping Partners 37. *South Riding* 38. Prison without Bars 39. *Intermezzo* 39. *The Swiss Family Robinson* 40. A Dispatch from Reuters 40. The Late George Apley 46. The Ghost and Mrs Muir 47. The Iron Curtain 48, etc.

Best, James (1926–). American general purpose actor, often in westerns as sly ranch-hand.
Winchester 73 50. Kansas Raiders 51. Francis Goes to West Point 52. Seven Angry Men 55. Gaby 56. The Left Handed Gun 58. The Mountain Road 60. Shock Corridor 63. Three on a Couch 66. Firecreek 67, etc.

Best, Willie (1916–1962). Goggle-eyed black American comedian, once known as Sleep'n Eat. A memorable frightened man-servant.
The Monster Walks 32. Little Miss Marker 34. Thank you Jeeves 36. Gold is Where You Find It 38. I Take this Woman 40. *The Ghost Breakers* 41. Road Show 41. The Smiling Ghost 41. Nothing But the Truth 41. The Body Disappears 41. A Haunting We Will Go 42. Cabin in the Sky 43. Pillow to Post 45. The Bride Wore Boots 46. Red Stallion 47, many others.
TV series: My Little Margie 52–55.

The Best Man (US 1964). About the best of the serious political films of the early sixties, this bitter comedy-drama about presidential nominations was based on Gore Vidal's play and directed by Franklin Schaffner. Lee Tracy and Henry Fonda were on top form.

The Best Years of Our Lives (US 1946) (AA). On its original release, this film about the resettlement of ex-servicemen in a small American town seemed like an enduring classic. A generation later the mood of the time was impossible to recapture and much of the film seemed humdrum. But it was an important step

in Hollywood's development towards maturity, presented by a highly talented group: director William Wyler (AA), cinematographer Gregg Toland, writer Robert E. Sherwood (AA), from a novel by Mackinlay Kantor. The cast included Fredric March (AA), Myrna Loy, Dana Andrews, Teresa Wright, and a handless veteran, Harold Russell (AA), whose only film this was.

Beswick, Martine (1941–). British pin-up, decorative in occasional films.
From Russia with Love 62. Thunderball 65. One Million Years BC 66. The Penthouse 67. Dr Jekyll and Sister Hyde 71, etc.

La Bête Humaine (France 1938). Based on a novel by Emile Zola, this steamy emotional melodrama with a railway setting was written and directed by Jean Renoir, with photography by Curt Courant and music by Joseph Kosma. In 1954, Fritz Lang directed a perfunctory remake called *Human Desire*, with Glenn Ford, Gloria Grahame and Broderick Crawford in the roles originally taken by Jean Gabin, Simone Simon and Michel Simon.

Bettger, Lyle (1915–). American screen actor who started in 1946 as leading man but seemed more at home in villainous roles.
No Man of Her Own 50. Union Station 50. The First Legion 51. All I Desire 53. The Greatest Show on Earth 53. The Sea Chase 55. Gunfight at the OK Corral 57. Guns of the Timberland 60. Town Tamer 65. Nevada Smith 66. The Fastest Guitar Alive 68. The Seven Minutes 71, many others.
TV series: Grand Jury 58–59.

Betty Boop. Doll-like cartoon creation, a wide-eyed gold-digging flapper created by Max Fleischer in 1915 and popular throughout the twenties and thirties.

Betz, Carl (1920–). American leading man who moved from films to TV.
The President's Lady 53. Inferno 53. Vicki 53. Dangerous Crossing 53. Spinout 66, etc.
TV series: *The Donna Reed Show* 57–64. *Judd for the Defense* 67–70.

Bevan, Billy (1887–1957) (William Bevan Harris). Wide-eyed, moustachioed silent screen comedian, an Australian who moved to Hollywood and became one of Mack Sennett's troupe. Later played many small parts, often that of a bewildered policeman.
Easy Pickings 27. Riley the Cop 28. *Journey's End* 30. Sky Devils 32. *Cavalcade* 33. Alice in Wonderland 33. Limehouse Blues 34. *Dracula's*

Daughter 36. Captain Fury 39. The Long Voyage Home 40. Dr Jekyll and Mr Hyde 41. The Picture of Dorian Gray 45. Cluny Brown 46. The Black Arrow 48, many others.

Bevans, Clem (1880–1963). Long-faced and latterly white-haired American character actor who played a long succession of grandfathers, doorkeepers, oldest inhabitants and gold prospectors.
Way Down East 35. Of Human Hearts 38. Abe Lincoln in Illinois 40. *Saboteur* 42. The Human Comedy 43. Captain Eddie 45. The Yearling 46. The Paleface 48. Streets of Laredo 49. *Harvey* 50. The Stranger Wore a Gun 53. The Kentuckian 55, etc.

Bewes, Rodney (1937–). Chubby British comedy actor.
Billy Liar 63. Decline and Fall 68. Spring and Port Wine 70. Alice's Adventures in Wonderland 72. The Likely Lads 76, etc.
TV series: *The Likely Lads* 66–68. Dear Mother Love Albert 70–72. *Whatever Happened to the Likely Lads* 73.

Bey, Turhan (1920–) (Turhan Selahattin Sahultavy Bey). Dapper Turkish leading man who had a good run in Hollywood during World War II in the absence on war service of more dynamic stars. Later became a stills photographer and moved to Vienna.
Footsteps in the Dark 41. Drums of the Congo 42. The Mummy's Tomb 42. Arabian Nights 42. White Savage 43. Background to Danger 43. The Mad Ghoul 43. Ali Baba and the Forty Thieves 43. Dragon Seed 44. Bowery to Broadway 44. The Climax 44. Frisco Sal 44. A Night in Paradise 46. Out of the Blue 47. Adventures of Casanova 48. Song of India 49. Prisoners of the Casbah 53. Stolen Identity (p only) 53, etc.

Beymer, Richard (1939–). American child actor who in the early sixties seemed about to turn into a major juvenile lead, but somehow never made it.
So Big 52. Indiscretion of an American Wife 52. Johnny Tremain 57. The Diary of Anne Frank 59. High Time 60. *West Side Story* 61. Five Finger Exercise 62. *Hemingway's Adventures of a Young Man* 62. The Longest Day 62. The Stripper 62.

Bezzerides, A. I. (1908–) (Albert Isaac). American screenwriter.
They Drive by Night 40. Northern Pursuit 43. *Thieves' Highway* 49. Sirocco 51. On Dangerous Ground 52. Beneath the 12 Mile Reef 53. Track

of the Cat 54. *Kiss Me Deadly* 55. The Angry Hills 59, etc.

Bianchi, Daniela (1942–). Italian leading lady.
Love is My Profession 59. Sword of El Cid 62. *From Russia With Love* 63. The Balearic Caper 66. Weekend Italian Style 68. The Dirty Heroes 68, etc.

Biberman, Abner (1909–). American character actor who spent many years playing Red Indian braves and dastardly dagoes before turning into a director.
Gunga Din 39. His Girl Friday 40. South of Pago Pago 40. South of Tahiti 41. Broadway 42. The Leopard Man 43. Salome Where She Danced 45. Captain Kidd 45. Back to Bataan 50. Elephant Walk 54. The Golden Mistress 54. The Price of Fear (d) 56. Above all Things 57. Gun for a Coward (d) 57, many others especially in TV.

Biberman, Herbert J. (1900–1971). American director whose career was harmed by his political convictions. Married Gale Sondergaard.
One Way Ticket 35. Meet Nero Wolfe 36. King of Chinatown (w only) 38. *The Master Race* (& d) 44. New Orleans (w only) 47. Abilene Town (p only) 46. Salt of the Earth (& w) 53. Slaves (& w) 69, etc.

The Bible. The extravaganza which claimed to be the 'film of the book' was conceived by Dino de Laurentiis as a nine-hour survey by several directors. It turned up in 1966 as a slow plod through Genesis by and with John Huston. Of the hundreds of films which have been inspired by the Old Testament stories, some of the most memorable are *The Private Life of Adam and Eve, Sodom and Gomorrah, Green Pastures, A Story of David, David and Bathsheba, Samson and Delilah, The Prodigal, The Ten Commandments* (two versions), *Salome, Esther and the King* and *The Story of Ruth*. For the New Testament, see under *Christ*; the immediate effects of whose life have been treated in such assorted films as *The Robe, Demetrius and the Gladiators, The Sign of the Cross, The Big Fisherman, Quo Vadis, Ben Hur, Spartacus, Fabiola, Barabbas, The Silver Chalice*, and *The Fall of the Roman Empire*, not to mention Lord Grade's TV series on his life.

Bickford, Charles (1889–1967). Rugged American character actor who sometimes played stubborn or unscrupulous roles but more often projected sincerity and warmth.

Autobiography 1965: *Bulls, Balls, Bicycles and Actors.*

☐ Dynamite 29. South Sea Rose 29. Hell's Heroes 29. *Anna Christie* 30. The Sea Bat 30. Passion Flower 30. River's End 31. The Squaw Man 31. East of Borneo 31. Pagan Lady 31. Men in Her Life 31. Panama Flo 32. *Thunder Below* 32. Scandal for Sale 32. The Last Man 32. Vanity Street 32. No Other Woman 33. Song of the Eagle 33. This Day and Age 33. White Woman 33. Little Miss Marker 34. A Wicked Woman 34. A Notorious Gentleman 35. Under Pressure 35. The Farmer Takes a Wife 35. East of Java 35. The Littlest Rebel 35. Rose of the Rancho 35. Pride of the Marines 36. The Plainsman 36. Night Club Scandal 37. Thunder Trail 37. Daughter of Shanghai 37. High Wide and Handsome 37. Gangs of New York 38. Valley of the Giants 38. The Storm 39. Stand Up and Fight 39. Romance of the Redwoods 39. Street of Missing Men 39. Our Leading Citizen 39. One Hour to Live 39. Mutiny in the Big House 39. Thou Shalt Not Kill 39. *Of Mice and Men* 40. The Girl from God's Country 40. South to Karanga 40. Queen of the Yukon 40. *Riders of Death Valley* (serial) 41. Burma Convoy 41. Reap the Wild Wind 42. Tarzan's New York Adventure 42. Mr Lucky 43. *The Song of Bernadette* 43. Wing and a Prayer 44. Captain Eddie 45. Fallen Angel 45. *Duel in the Sun* 46. *The Farmer's Daughter* 47. The Woman on the Beach 47. *Brute Force* 47. The Babe Ruth Story 47. Four Faces West 48. *Johnny Belinda* 48. Command Decision 48. Roseanna McCoy 49. Whirlpool 49. *Treason* (as Cardinal Mindzenty) 49. Branded 50. Riding High 50. Jim Thorpe—All American 51. The Raging Tide 51. Elopement 51. *A Star is Born* 54. Prince of Players 55. Not as a Stranger 55. The Court Martial of Billy Mitchell 55. You Can't Run Away from It 56. Mister Cory 57. *The Big Country* 58. The Unforgiven 60. Days of Wine and Roses 62. *A Big Hand for the Little Lady* 66. TV series: *The Virginian* 66.

Bicycle Thieves (Italy 1947). Hailed throughout the world as the fount of Italian post-war realism, this simple tale of a billposter's sad quest for the stolen bicycle essential to his job was actually in a well-established Italian tradition. It was nevertheless an absorbing and brilliant film which influenced film-making in every country where it was seen. Vittorio de Sica directed from Cesare Zavattini's script, and the non-professional performances of Lamberto Maggiorani (the man) and Enzo Staiola (his son) were outstanding.

bicycling. A trade term for the sharing, usually

illegally, of one print between two theatres: the manager had to make frequent bicycle trips!

The Big Broadcast (US 1932). A light-hearted entertainment which used a zany story about a radio station to bring in many radio stars of the day, and was followed by three sequels (1936, 1937, 1938). The films were smoothly made and anticipated the *Hellzapoppin* type humour of the forties.

big business was outside the range of silent movie-makers, but in the thirties, usually personified by Edward Arnold, it became a useful villain for the comedies and dramas of social conscience. A switch was made in *Dodsworth*, in which the businessman became an innocent abroad; but not until the growing affluence of the fifties did Hollywood think it worth while to probe into the personal lives of those who occupy the corridors of power. Then in quick succession we had *Executive Suite*, *Woman's World*, *Patterns of Power*, *The Power and the Prize* and *The Man in the Grey Flannel Suit*; while the inevitable knocking process began as early as *The Man in The White Suit* and continued with *The Solid Gold Cadillac*, *Cash McCall*, *Ice Palace*, *The Apartment* and *The Wheeler Dealers.*

The Big Carnival: see *Ace In The Hole.*

The Big Country (US 1958). Basically a simple, sprawling western about the family feud between two embittered old ranchers, this 165-minute spectacular was enriched by a lush score (Jerome Moross), impeccable direction (William Wyler), and a script (James R. Webb, Sy Bartlett, Robert Wilder) pretentious enough to attempt a parable of the Cold War. The acting of Charles Bickford, Burl Ives, Gregory Peck and Charlton Heston was also a help.

The Big Heat (US 1953). This competent crime film had Glenn Ford as a tough cop out to get gangsters who murdered his wife in mistake for him. It is chiefly notable because both cops and criminals were more humanized than had previously been the case, and because its use of violence (scalding coffee in the heroine's face) was something new and disturbing. Written by Sidney Boehm, photographed by Charles Lang, directed by Fritz Lang.

The Big Parade (US 1925). Though most of it now seems painfully slow and dated, King Vidor's silent film about 'the average guy who went to war' brought home to millions the realities of trench combat. It also established

John Gilbert as a top star, and in two years grossed fifteen million dollars which consolidated the fortunes of MGM. Written by Laurence Stallings, photographed by John Arnold.

bigamists have been prevented by the censorship codes from achieving hero status in more than a few films; perhaps it is significant that although the Italian film called *The Bigamist* is a comedy, the American one is a solemn affair. Over the years, however, scriptwriters have achieved some sympathy and humour for the characters played by William Bendix in *Don Juan Quilligan*, Alec Guinness in *The Captain's Paradise*, Clifton Webb in *The Remarkable Mr Pennypacker*, Rex Harrison in *The Constant Husband*, Jean-Claude Drouot in *Le Bonheur* and Leo McKern in *Decline and Fall*.

Biggers, Earl Derr (1884–1933). American crime novelist, whose chief gift to the movies was Charlie Chan (qv). Also wrote original story of *The Millionaire* 31, and the much filmed play *Seven Keys to Baldpate*.

Bikel, Theodore (1924–). Heavily-built Viennese actor, guitarist and singer; can play most nationalities. International stage, TV, cabaret and film work.
The African Queen 51. The Love Lottery 54. The Pride and the Passion 57. The Defiant Ones 58. The Blue Angel 59. A Dog of Flanders 60. My Fair Lady 64. Sands of the Kalahari 65. The Russians Are Coming, The Russians Are Coming 66. My Side of the Mountain 68. Darker than Amber 70. The Little Ark 71, etc.

Bill, Tony (1940–). American light leading man.
Come Blow Your Horn 63. None But the Brave 65. Marriage on the Rocks 66. Ice Station Zebra 68. Castle Keep 69. Flap 70, etc.
As producer: Deadhead Miles 70. Steelyard Blues 70. The Sting 73. Hearts of the West 75, etc.

billing. The official credits for a film, usually stating the relative sizes of type to be accorded to title, stars, character actors, etc.

Billington, Kevin (1933–). British director, from TV.
Interlude 68. The Rise and Rise of Michael Rimmer 70. The Light at the Edge of the World 71. And No One Could Save Her (TV) 72. Voices 74.

A Bill of Divorcement. Clemence Dane's play about the return of a deranged father from a mental institution was made into a topical film in 1932, with Katharine Hepburn in her film debut playing opposite John Barrymore. It was directed by George Cukor. By the time of John Farrow's scene-for-scene remake in 1940 the material seemed artificial and old-fashioned; Maureen O'Hara lacked Hepburn's intensity, though Adolphe Menjou was surprisingly good as the father.

Billy the Kid, the historical, homicidal western gunslinger, has frequently been turned by the movies into some kind of hero. A favourite character of the silents, he has been seen also in numerous talkie versions. Johnny Mack Brown played him on the wide screen in *Billy the Kid* 30; pious Roy Rogers was the star of *Billy the Kid Returns* 39; in 1940 Robert Taylor was *Billy the Kid*; and in 1943 (or so) came *The Outlaw*, with a happy ending for Jack Buetel who played Billy. In 1949 Audie Murphy played Billy in *The Kid from Texas*; 1950 brought *I Shot Billy the Kid* with Don Barry; 1954 *The Law Versus Billy the Kid* with Scott Brady; 1955 *The Parson and the Outlaw* with Anthony Dexter; 1958 *The Left-handed Gun* with Paul Newman; and in 1966 we were even offered *Billy the Kid Meets Dracula;* and in 1974 Sam Peckinpah's *Pat Garrett and Billy the Kidd* added new refinements of violence. There were also scores of second features in the thirties and forties, with Bob Steele or Buster Crabbe as Billy; whose real name incidentally was William Bonney and who died in 1881 at the age of 21.

Binder, Maurice (1925–). American title artist in Britain.
Indiscreet 58. The Mouse that Roared 59. The Grass is Greener 60. *Dr No* 62. Repulsion 64. The Chase 66. Bedazzled 67. The Private Life of Sherlock Holmes 71. Gold 74. etc.

Bing, Herman (1889–1947). Plump, explosive German comedy actor, former assistant to F. W. Murnau; in Hollywood from 1929.
Married in Hollywood 29. The Guardsman 31. Dinner at Eight 33. The Black Cat 34. Rose Marie 36. The Great Ziegfeld 36. Champagne Waltz 37. The Great Waltz 38. Sweethearts 38. The Devil with Hitler 42. Where Do We Go from Here? 45. Rendezvous 24 46, many others.

Binyon, Claude (1905–). American writer-director.
The Gilded Lily (w) 35. I Met Him in Paris (w) 37. Sing You Sinners (w) 38. Arizona (w) 40. Suddenly It's Spring (w) 44. *The Saxon Charm* (wd) 48. Family Honeymoon (wd) 49. Mother Didn't Tell Me (w) 50. Stella (wd) 50. Aaron

Slick from Punkin Crick (wd) 52. *Dreamboat* (wd) 52. You Can't Run Away from It (w) 56. North to Alaska (w) 60. Satan Never Sleeps (w) 62. Kisses for My President (w) 64, etc.

Biograph. 1. An old name for a cinema projector. 2. Britain's first public cinema, near Victoria Station, London. Opened 1905, still operating. 3. The name of D. W. Griffith's New York studios, 1903–10.

Biopic. A contraction of 'biographical picture', i.e. a film about the life of a real person. For examples see under *Composers, Courtesans, Entertainers, Explorers, Inventors, Kings and Queens, Painters, Politicians, Scientists, Soldiers, Spies, Sportsmen, Writers.*

Birch, Paul (–   ). American general purpose actor.
The War of the Worlds 52. The Fastest Gun Alive 56. The Tattered Dress 57. Portrait in Black 60. The Man Who Shot Liberty Valance 62. *Not Of This Earth* 64, etc.

Bird, Norman (c. 1920–). British character actor, usually of underdogs.
An Inspector Calls 54. *The League of Gentlemen* 59. *Victim* 62. The Hill 65. Sky West and Crooked 65. The Wrong Box 66. A Dandy in Aspic 68. The Virgin and the Gypsy 70. The Rise and Rise of Michael Rimmer 70, many others.

Bird, Richard (1894–). British light actor who played genial middle-aged roles in the thirties.
Tilly of Bloomsbury 31. Mimi 35. Sensation 37. The Terror (& d) 38. The Door with Seven Locks 40. Halfway House 44. Forbidden 49, many others.

birds fit nicely into the glamorous romantic backgrounds of which Hollywood used to be so fond, but a few particular examples have been malevolent, including *The Vulture,* the owner of *The Giant Claw,* the carnivorous birds which nearly pecked *Barbarella* to death, and of course *The Birds* which turned on the human race in Hitchcock's 1963 movie. (In the various versions of Edgar Allan Poe's *The Raven,* the title character has been almost irrelevant.) Other notable birds have been seen in *Treasure Island, Birdman of Alcatraz, The Pigeon That Took Rome, Run Wild Run Free, The Bluebird, Kes, Doctor Dolittle,* and *Bill and Coo*; and in the cartoon field one must remember with affection Donald and Daffy Duck, Tweetie Pie, the Road Runner, and an assortment of other feathered friends. The heroes of *Brewster McCloud* and several other films thought they were birds;

Jonathan Livingston Seagull was.

Birell, Tala (1908–1959) (Natalie Bierle). Polish-Austrian leading lady who made some international films, then settled in Hollywood.
Man in a Cage (GB) 30. Doomed Battalion 32. The Captain Hates the Sea 34. Crime and Punishment 35. Bringing Up Baby 38. Seven Miles from Alcatraz 42. The Song of Bernadette 43. Mrs Parkington 44. Song of Love 47. The House of Tao Ling 47, etc.

Birkett, Michael (1929–) (Lord Birkett). British producer, mainly of specialized entertainments.
The Caretaker 63. The Soldier's Tale 64. Modesty Blaise (associate) 66. The Marat/Sade 66. A Midsummer Night's Dream 68. King Lear 70, etc.

Birney, David (1944–). American leading man.
Caravan to Vaccares 74. Trial by Combat 76. TV series: Bridget Loves Bernie 73. Serpico 76.

Biro, Lajos (1880–1948). Hungarian screenwriter with Hollywood experience in the twenties followed by much work for Korda in Britain.
Forbidden Paradise 24. The Last Command 27. The Way of All Flesh 28. Service for Ladies 32. *The Private Life of Henry VIII* 32. Catherine the Great 34. *The Scarlet Pimpernel* 34. Sanders of the River 35. The Divorce of Lady X 37. The Drum 38. The Four Feathers 39. *The Thief of Baghdad* 40. Five Graves to Cairo 43. A Royal Scandal 45, etc.: mostly in collaboration.

Biroc, Joseph F. (1903–). American cinematographer.
It's a Wonderful Life (co-ph) 46. Magic Town 47. Roughshod 49. Without Warning 52. The Tall Texan 53. Down Three Dark Streets 54. Nightmare 56. Run of the Arrow 56. Attack 57. The Ride Back 57. The Amazing Colossal Man 57. Home Before Dark 58. Hitler 61. The Devil at Four O'Clock 61. Bye Bye Birdie 63. Bullet for a Badman 64. Hush Hush Sweet Charlotte 64. I Saw What You Did 65. The Flight of the Phoenix 65. The Russians Are Coming, The Russians Are Coming 66. The Killing of Sister George 68. Whatever Happened to Aunt Alice? 69. Too Late the Hero 69. The Legend of Lylah Clare 69. The Grissom Gang 71. The Organization 71. Emperor of the North Pole 73. Blazing Saddles 74. The Longest Yard 74, etc.

Birt, Daniel (1907–1955). British director, former editor: busy in late forties.

The Three Weird Sisters 48. No Room at the Inn 49. The Interrupted Journey 49. Circumstantial Evidence 52. Background 53, etc.

The Birth of a Nation (US 1915). D. W. Griffith's monumental melodrama of the American Civil War and its aftermath, supposedly the biggest money-maker of all time (allowing for rising costs), has become something of an embarrassment to Hollywood in view of its anti-Negro bias. It remains exciting to watch, especially during the battle sequences and the final 'heroic' rescue charge of the Ku Klux Klan; and it abounds in technical innovations which became current usage. Various versions have been reissued with sound effects. Written by Griffith and Frank Woods from Thomas Dixon's novel *The Clansman*; photographed by Billy Bitzer.

Bischoff, Samuel (1890–1975). American producer, with Warners in thirties, Columbia in forties, subsequently independent.
The Charge of the Light Brigade 36. A Slight Case of Murder 37. Submarine Zone 41. You'll Never Get Rich 41. Appointment in Berlin 43. None Shall Escape 44. Mr District Attorney 47. Pitfall 48. Mrs Mike 50. The System 53. The Phenix City Story 55. Operation Eichmann 61. King of the Roaring Twenties 61. The Strangler 64, many others.

Bishop, Joey (1918–) (Joseph Abraham Gottlieb). American TV comedian who has made few film appearances.
The Naked and the Dead 58. Sergeants Three 63. Texas across the River 66. A Guide for the Married Man 67. Who's Minding the Mint? 67, etc.
TV series: The Joey Bishop Show 61-64, 67–69.

Bishop, Julie (1917–) (Jacqueline Brown). American leading lady of routine films; also known as Jacqueline Wells.
Alice in Wonderland 33. The Bohemian Girl 36. The Nurse's Secret 41. Northern Pursuit 43. Rhapsody in Blue 45. Sands of Iwo Jima 49. Westward the Women 52. The High and the Mighty 54. The Big Land 57, many others.

Bishop, Terry (1912–). British director. Much TV work.
You're Only Young Twice 52. Model for Murder 58. Cover Girl Killer 59. The Unstoppable Man 61, etc.

Bishop, William (1918–1959). American leading man, mostly in routine features.
Pillow to Post 46. The Romance of Rosy Ridge 47. Anna Lucasta 49. Lorna Doone 51. Cripple Creek 52. The Boss 56. The Oregon Trail 59, etc.

Bissell, Whit (c.1914–). American character actor who plays anything from attorneys to garage attendants.
Holy Matrimony 43. Another Part of the Forest 47. It Should Happen to You 53. The Young Stranger 57. I Was a Teenage Frankenstein 58. The Time Machine 60. Hud 63. Seven Days in May 64. Covenant with Death 67. Airport 69, many others.

Bisset, Jacqueline (1944–). British leading lady, in American films.
□ Cul de Sac 66. Casino Royale 67. Two for the Road 67. The Sweet Ride 67. The Detective 68. Bullitt 68. The First Time 68. L'Echelle Blanche (Fr.) 69. Airport 69. *The Grasshopper* 70. The Mephisto Waltz 71. Believe in Me 71. Secrets 71. Judge Roy Bean 72. Stand Up and Be Counted 72. La Nuit Américaine 73. The Thief Who Came to Dinner 73.

Bitter Sweet. Noel Coward's romantic operetta was twice filmed: in 1933 with Anna Neagle and Fernand Gravet, and in 1940, much altered, with Jeanette MacDonald and Nelson Eddy.

Bitzer, Billy (1874–1944) (George William Bitzer). American cameraman who worked with D. W. Griffith on his most important films and is credited with several major photographic developments.
The New York Hat 12. Judith of Bethulia 13. *Birth of a Nation* 15. *Intolerance* 16. *Hearts of the World* 18. *Broken Blossoms* 19. *Way Down East* 21. *America* 24. The Struggle 30, many others.

Bixby, Bill (1934–). Diffident American light leading man.
Lonely are the Brave 62. Irma la Douce 63. Under the Yum Yum Tree 64. Ride Beyond Vengeance 66. Spinout 67. Speedway 68. Congratulations It's a Boy (TV) 71. The Couple Takes a Wife (TV) 72. Barbary Coast (pilot) (TV) (&d) 75. The Apple Dumpling Gang 75. The Invasion of Johnson County (TV) 76, etc.
TV series: My Favourite Martian 63–65. The Courtship of Eddie's Father 69–70. The Magician 73.

Bjork, Anita (1923–). Swedish actress who made only one English-speaking appearance.
Miss Julie 51. Night People (US) 54. Secrets of Woman 61. Loving Couples 66, etc.

Bjornstrand, Gunnar (1909–). Distinguished Swedish character actor. Frenzy 44. Waiting Women 52. Sawdust and Tinsel 53. *Smiles of a Summer Night* 55. The Seventh Seal 56. *Through a Glass Darkly* 61. Winter Light 62. Loving Couples 65. Persona 66. The Red Mantle 67. The Shame 68. The Rite 69, etc.

Black, Karen (1943–) (Karen Ziegeler). American leading lady.
□ You're a Big Boy Now 67. Hard Contract 68. Easy Rider 69. Five Easy Pieces 70. A Gunfight 71. Drive He Said 71. Born to Win 71. Cisco Pike 71. Portnoy's Complaint 72. The Pyx 73. Rhinoceros 73. The Outfit 73. The Great Gatsby 74. Airport 75 75. Law and Disorder 75. The Day of the Locust 75. Nashville 75. Family Plot 76.

Black, Noel (1937–). American director who graduated to features from shorts.
Pretty Poison 68.

Black, Stanley (1913–). British band-leader and composer, responsible for scoring nearly 200 films.
Rhythm Racketeers 36. Mrs Fitzherbert 47. It Always Rains on Sunday 47. Laughter in Paradise 50. The Trollenberg Terror 57. Hell is a City 60. The Young Ones 61. Summer Holiday 63, etc.

Black Beauty. Anna Sewell's Victorian novel about the life of a horse has been filmed several times since sound; by Hollywood in 1933 and 1947, and in Britain in 1971. 1972 brought a TV series on the subject.

The Black Cat. Two of the best-known films under this title had nothing whatever to do with the Poe story on which they were allegedly based. They were the 1934 melodrama about devil worshippers, with Karloff and Lugosi, and the 1941 thunderstorm mystery with Basil Rathbone. The Poe story was more faithfully treated in *The Living Dead* (Ger.) 33, *Tales of Terror* (US) 62, and *The Black Cat* (US) 67.

black comedy finds humour in serious matters such as death, neurosis and sex perversion. In recent years it has become almost normal, though such films as *A Clockwork Orange* still cause controversy. We were once less sophisticated: in the early thirties, for instance, the comedy element in horror films such as James Whale's *The Bride of Frankenstein* and *The Old Dark House* was not understood, and even now is difficult to maintain on the same level, though Hammer films make sporadic attempts in this direction, and Roger Corman was rather more successful in *The Raven*. (Roman Polanski failed spectacularly in *The Fearless Vampire Killers*.) Comedies of murder date back to *The Front Page* and *Boudu Sauvè des Eaux*, with a progression through *Drôle de Drame*, *A Slight Case of Murder*, *Arsenic and Old Lace*, *Monsieur Verdoux*, *Kind Hearts and Coronets*, *The Red Inn*, *The Criminal Life of Archibaldo de la Cruz*, *The Naked Truth*, *She'll Have to Go*, *Candy* and *The Assassination Bureau*. Death and funerals have been the subject of jest in *Here Comes Mr Jordan*, *Too Many Crooks*, *The Loved One*, *The Wrong Box*, *Loot*, and *Harold and Maude*. On the level of social behaviour, there is black humour in *Who's Afraid of Virginia Woolf?*, *The Anniversary* and *The Honey Pot*, while Luis Buñuel castigates society through similar means in most of his films, notably *El*, *The Exterminating Angel* and *The Diary of a Chambermaid*. *Dr Strangelove* managed to laugh at the destruction of the world. Finally, Laurel and Hardy understood one aspect of the genre in their many grotesque jokes involving physical distortion. Elements of black comedy are to be found in an increasing number of modern films, notably those of Billy Wilder, John Huston and Alfred Hitchcock, and in the adventures of James Bond.

Black Maria. In the history of film this evocative phrase for a police van has a secondary meaning, being the nickname given to Edison's first portable studio.

Black Orpheus (France 1958). The myth of Orpheus and Eurydice was given a Negro setting in this visually splendid but dramatically unsatisfactory piece written and directed by Marcel Camus. With Marpessa Dawn, Breno Mello.

The Black Pirate (US 1926). A typical Douglas Fairbanks silent swashbuckler, involving an experiemental use of colour. Directed by Albert Parker, photographed by Henry Sharp.

The Blackboard Jungle (US 1955). This classroom melodrama, written and directed by Richard Brooks, shocked filmgoers by its revelation of what teachers in big city shcools have to put up with. It also introduced rock-and-roll music (over the credits), and allowed Glenn Ford to give one of his edgiest performances. Eleven years later Sidney Poitier, one of the students here, played the harassed teacher in a British imitation, *To Sir With Love*.

Blacklisting: see *The Hollywood Ten.*

Blackmail (GB 1929). Notable as the first British sound film. Hitchcock had made it as a silent, and remade it hurriedly, with primitive dubbing for the Czech leading lady, Anny Ondra. A typical Hitchcock suspense yarn, the production has now dated badly but still manages several effective moments.

Blackman, Honor (1926–). British leading lady, a Rank 'charm school' product submerged in 'English rose' roles from 1946 until a TV series fitted her up with kinky suits and judo tactics.
Fame is the Spur 47. Quartet 48. Diamond City 49. So Long at the Fair 50. The Rainbow Jacket 53. Breakaway 55. A Night to Remember 58. The Square Peg 58. A Matter of Who 61. *Goldfinger* 64. The Secret of My Success 65. *Life at the Top* 65. Moment to Moment 65. A Twist of Sand 68. Shalako 68. The Last Grenade 69. The Virgin and the Gypsy 70. Fright 71. Something Big 71. To the Devil a Daughter 75, etc.
TV series: *The Avengers* 60–63.

Blackman, Joan (´ –). American leading lady of the sixties.
Visit to a Small Planet 61. The Great Imposter 61. Blue Hawaii 62. Twilight of Honor 63. Intimacy 66, etc.

Blackmer, Sidney (1895–1973). Suave American character actor, often seen as politician or high-class crook but also capable of sympathetic roles.
A Most Immoral Lady 29. Kismet 30. Little Caesar 30. Once a Sinner 31. Cocktail Hour 33. The Count of Monte Cristo 34. The President Vanishes 34. The Little Colonel 35. Smart Girl 35. Early to Bed 36. A Doctor's Diary 37. This is My Affair 37. Charlie Chan at Monte Carlo 37. The Last Gangster 37. Trade Winds 38. Hotel for Women 39. I Want a Divorce 40. Love Crazy 41. The Feminine Touch 41. The Panther's Claw 42. Quiet Please Murder 42. Murder in Times Square 43. Duel in the Sun 46. My Girl Tisa (as Teddy Roosevelt) 48. People will Talk 51. Johnny Dark 54. High Society 56. Tammy and the Bachelor 57. How to Murder Your Wife 65. Covenant with Death 67. Rosemary's Baby 68, many others.

Blacks in Films: see *negroes in films.*

Blackton, J. Stuart (1868–1941). British pioneer producer who spent years in America working with Edison.
Raffles 05. The Life of Moses 10. The Battle Cry

of Peace 15. Womanhood 16. The Glorious Adventure (in Prizmacolour) 21. On the Banks of the Wabash 23. The Clean Heart 24. The Beloved Brute 24. Gypsy Cavalier 24. Tides of Passion 25. The Happy Warrior 25. Bride of the Storm 30, many others.

Blackwell, Carlyle (1888–1955). American stage matinée idol, in demand for romantic roles during the twenties; his declamatory style could scarcely survive the coming of sound.
Uncle Tom's Cabin 09. The Key to Yesterday 14. The Restless Sex 20. Sherlock Holmes 22. The Beloved Vagabond 23. Bulldog Drummond 23. She 25. The Wrecker 29. The Crooked Billet 30. The Calling of Dan Matthews 35, many others.

Blain, Gerard (1930–). French leading man.
Les Fruits Sauvages 53. Crime et Châtiment 55. Desire Takes the Men 56. Les Mistons 57. Le Beau Serge 58. Les Cousins 58. Hatari 62, etc.

Blaine, Vivian (1921–) (Vivienne Stapleton). Vivacious American leading lady and personable songstress. Made comparatively few films, her greatest success being on Broadway.
☐ Thru Different Eyes 42. Girl Trouble 42. He Hired the Boss 43. Jitterbugs 43. Greenwich Village 44. Something for the Boys 44. Nob Hill 45. *State Fair* 45. Doll Face 45. If I'm Lucky 46. *Three Little Girls in Blue* 46. Skirts Ahoy 52. Main Street to Broadway 53. *Guys and Dolls* 55. Public Pigeon Number One 57.

Blair, Betsy (1923–) (Elizabeth Boger). American character actress who often plays shy or nervous women.
☐ The Guilt of Janet Ames 47. A Double Life 47. Another Part of the Forest 48. The Snake Pit 48. Mystery Street 50. Kind Lady 51. *Marty* (BFA) 55. Calle Mayor (Sp.) 56. Il Grido (It.) 57. The Halliday Brand 57. All Night Long (GB) 61. A Delicate Balance 73.

Blair, George (1906–1970). American second feature director.
Duke of Chicago 49. Flaming Fury 49. Daughter of the Jungle 49. Insurance Investigator 51. Jaguar 55. The Hypnotic Eye 60, many others.

Blair, Janet (1921–) (Martha Lafferty). Vivacious American leading lady of co-features in the forties.
☐ Three Girls About Town 41. Blondie Goes to College 42. Two Yanks in Trinidad 42. Broadway 42. My Sister Eileen 42. Something to Shout About 43. Once Upon a Time 44. Tonight

and Every Night 45. Tars and Spars 46. Gallant Journey 46. The Fabulous Dorseys 47. I Love Trouble 48. The Black Arrow 48. The Fuller Brush Man 48. Public Pigeon Number One 57. Boys' Night Out 62. *Night of the Eagle* (GB) 62. The One and Only Genuine Original Family Band 68.
TV series: *The Smith Family* 70–71.

Blair, Linda (1959–). American juvenile lead of the seventies who made a spectacular beginning as a possessed child.
□ *The Exorcist* 74. Born Innocent (TV) 74. Airport 75 75.

Blake, Amanda (1929–) (Beverly Neill). American supporting actress.
Duchess of Idaho 50. Stars in My Crown 50. Lili 53. Sabre Jet 53. A Star is Born 54. About Mrs Leslie 54. High Society 56, etc.
TV series: *Gunsmoke* (as Kitty) 56–74.

Blake, Katherine (1928–). South African actress in Britain, mostly on TV.
Anne of the Thousand Days 70, etc.

Blake, Marie (1896–). American small part actress, sister of Jeanette MacDonald.
Mannequin 37. Young Dr Kildare 38. The Women 39. They Knew What They Wanted 39. A Child Is Born 40. I Married a Witch 42. Abbott and Costello in Hollywood 45. The Snake Pit 49. Love Nest 51. From the Terrace 60, many others.

Blake, Robert (1934–) (Michael Gubitosi). American child actor who later attracted some unusual adult roles.
Andy Hardy's Double Life 43. The Horn Blows at Midnight 45. Treasure of Sierra Madre 47. Revolt in the Big House 58. Battle Flame 59. The Purple Gang 60. The Greatest Story Ever Told 65. *In Cold Blood* 67. *Tell Them Willie Boy Is Here* 69. Corky 72. Electra Glide in Blue 73, etc.
TV series: *Baretta* 74–.

Blakeley, John E. (1889–1958). British producer-director of low-budget Lancashire comedies.
Somewhere in England 40. Somewhere in Camp 42. Demobbed 44. Home Sweet Home 46. Cup Tie Honeymoon 48. It's a Grand Life 53, etc.

Blakeley, Tom (1918–). British producer of second features.
Love's a Luxury 58. Tomorrow at Ten 62. Devils of Darkness 65. Island of Terror 66, etc.

Blakely, Colin (1930–). Stocky British stage actor, in occasional films.
Saturday Night and Sunday Morning 60. This Sporting Life 62. The Informers 63. The Long Ships 64. The Spy with a Cold Nose 67. *The Day the Fish Came Out* 67. Charlie Bubbles 67. The Vengeance of She 68. *Decline and Fall* 68. Alfred the Great 69. *The Private Life of Sherlock Holmes* (as Watson) 70. Something to Hide 72. Young Winston 72.

Blakely, Susan (1949–). American leading lady of the seventies, former model.
□ Savages 72. The Lords of Flatbush 74. The Towering Inferno 74. Report to the Commissioner 75. Shampoo 75. Capone 75. *Rich Man Poor Man* (TV) 76.

Blanc, Mel (1908–). The voice of Warner Brothers' cartoon characters, including Bugs Bunny, Sylvester and Tweetie Pie. Makes occasional cameo appearances in films.
Neptune's Daughter 49. Kiss Me Stupid 64, etc.

Blanchar, Pierre (1892–1963). Distinguished French screen and stage actor.
Jocelyn 23, *L'Atlantide* 31. Le Diable en Bouteille 34. Crime and Punishment 35. Mademoiselle Docteur 36. L'Affaire du Courrier de Lyon 37. *Un Carnet de Bal* 37. Pontcarral 42. La Symphonie Pastorale 46. Rififi Chez les Femmes 58, etc.

Blanchard, Mari (1927–1970). Decorative American leading lady of fifties co-features.
Mr Music 50. Ten Tall Men 51. Veils of Baghdad 53. Black Horse Canyon 54. *Destry* 55. The Crooked Web 56. The Return of Jack Slade 56. Jungle Heat 57. No Place to Land 58. Don't Knock the Twist 62. McLintock 63. Twice Told Tales 64, etc.

Blandick, Clara (1881–1962). American character actress, often seen as sensible servant or no-nonsense aunt.
The Girl Said No 30. Huckleberry Finn 31. The Wet Parade 32. One Sunday Afternoon 33. Broadway Bill 34. The Gorgeous Hussy 36. A Star is Born 37. Huckleberry Finn 39. *The Wizard of Oz* (as Aunt Em) 39. It Started with Eve 41. Can't Help Singing 44. A Stolen Life 46. Live with Father 47. The Bride Goes Wild 48. Love That Brute 50, many others.

Blane, Sally (1910–) (Elizabeth Jung). American leading lady of the early thirties; sister of Loretta Young.
Sirens of the Sea 27. Rolled Stockings 27. The Vagabond Lover 29. Little Accident 30. Once a Sinner 31. Ten Cents a Dance 31. Disorderly

Conduct 31. I am a Fugitive from a Chain Gang 32. Advice to the Lovelorn 33. The Silver Streak 35. One Mile from Heaven 37. Charlie Chan at Treasure Island 39. A Bullet for Joey 54, many others.

Blanke, Henry (1901–). German-American producer, long at Warners.
Female 33. *The Story of Louis Pasteur* 35. Satan Met a Lady 36. The Petrified Forest 36. Green Pastures 36. The Life of Emile Zola 37. Jezebel 38. *The Adventures of Robin Hood* 38. Juarez 39. The Old Maid 39. The Sea Hawk 40. *The Maltese Falcon* 41. Old Acquaintance 43. The Mask of Dimitrios 44. Deception 46. The Treasure of the Sierra Madre 47. The Fountainhead 49. Come Fill the Cup 51. King Richard and the Crusaders 54. Serenade 56. Too Much Too Soon 58. *The Nun's Story* 59. Ice Palace 60. Hell is for Heroes 62, many others.

Blasetti, Alessandro (1900–). Italian director mainly associated with comedy and spectaculars.
Sole 29. Nero 30. Resurrection 31. The Old Guard 33. The Countess of Parma 37. *Four Steps in the Clouds* 42. A Day of Life 46. Fabiola 48. *First Communion* 50. Altri Tempi (Infidelity) 52. Europe by Night 59. I Love You Love 61, many others.

Blatt, Edward A. (1905–). American stage director who worked briefly for Warners in the forties.
□ Between Two Worlds 44. Escape in the Desert 45. Smart Woman 48.

Blatty, William Peter (–). American screenwriter.
The Man from the Diners' Club 63. A Shot in the Dark 64. John Goldfarb Please Come Home 65. Promise Her Anything 66. What Did You Do in the War Daddy? 66. Gunn 67. The Great Bank Robbery 69. Darling Lili 69. The Exorcist (& oa) 73, etc.

Blaustein, Julian (1913–). American producer.
Broken Arrow 50. Mister 880 50. Take Care of My Little Girl 51. Desiree 54. Storm Center 56. Bell Book and Candle 58. The Wreck of the Mary Deare 59. Two Loves 61. The Four Horsemen of the Apocalypse 62. Khartoum 66.

Blier, Bernard (1916–). French actor who makes a virtue of his plumpness and baldness.
Hôtel du Nord 38. *Quai des Orfèvres* 47. *Dédée d'Anvers* 47. L'École Buissonière 48. Manèges (The Wanton) 49. Souvenirs Perdus 50. Les

Misérables 57. Les Grandes Familles 58. Le Cave se Rebiffe 61. Les Saintes Nitouches 63. A Question of Honour (Italy) 66. Breakdown (& d) 67. Catch Me a Spy 71, etc.

blimp. A soundproof cover fixed over a camera during shooting to absorb running noise.

Blind Husbands (US 1919). The start of Erich von Stroheim's brief but spectacular career as a Hollywood actor-writer-director, this bitterly ironic study of a military seducer had all the savage wit for which he is remembered as well as hints of the extravagance which caused his downfall.

blindness, a tragic affliction, has generally been treated by film-makers with discretion, though not without sentimentality. Typical is Herbert Marshall as the blind pianist in *The Enchanted Cottage*, dispensing words of wisdom with piano music in the background and the sounds of nature through the open door. Other sympathetic blind roles include Cary Grant in *Wings in the Dark*; Irene Dunne (later Jane Wyman) in *Magnificent Obsession*; Ronald Colman (later Fredric March) in *The Dark Angel*; Colman also in *The Light That Failed*; John Clements (later Anthony Steel) in *The Four Feathers*; James Cagney in *City for Conquest*; Ida Lupino in *On Dangerous Ground*; Arthur Kennedy in *Bright Victory*; Patricia Neal in *Psyche* 59. John Garfield in *Pride of the Marines*; Jean-Louis Barrault in *La Symphonie Pastorale*; Virginia Cherrill in *City Lights*; Elizabeth Hartmann in *A Patch of Blue*; Michael Wilding in *Torch Song*; and Nicol Williamson in *Laughter in the Dark*. More sinister blind characters came in *Saboteur* and *Victim*; while blind detectives, not forgetting TV's *Longstreet*, include Edward Arnold in *Eyes in the Night* and *The Hidden Eye*, Van Johnson in *23 Paces to Baker Street*, Dick Powell (briefly blinded by cordite fumes) in *Murder My Sweet*; and Karl Malden in *Cat o' Nine Tails*. In thrillers, terrified blind heroines have been useful: Patricia Dainton in *Witness in the Dark*, Audrey Hepburn in *Wait Until Dark* and Mia Farrow in *Blind Terror*. Other tricks with blind characters were played in *Faces in the Dark* and *Silent Dust*, in both of which the hero's condition helped him to outwit his assailants; and *Tread Softly Stranger*, where the murderer gave himself away through fear of the only witness— who turned out to be blind. Genuinely blind actors include Esmond Knight (temporarily) playing a sighted role in *The Silver Fleet*, and Ray Charles in *Ballad in Blue*. A nice ironic point was made in *Bride of Frankenstein*, where O. P. Heggie as a blind hermit was the only human being who did not fear the monster. Finally, in *The Day of the Triffids*, almost everyone on earth was blinded.

Bliss, Sir Arthur (1891–1975). British composer who has occasionally scored films.
Things to Come 36. Christopher Columbus 49. The Beggar's Opera 53, etc.

Blithe Spirit (GB 1945). The nearest British films have come to cocktail comedy, this smooth and glossy version of Noel Coward's ghostly farce was directed by David Lean, photographed in Technicolor by Ronald Neame, and starred Rex Harrison, Kay Hammond, Margaret Rutherford and Constance Cummings.

Bloch, Robert (1917–). American screenwriter dealing almost exclusively in horror themes with trick endings.
Psycho (oa) 60. The Cabinet of Caligari 62. Strait Jacket 63. *The Night Walker* 64. The Psychopath 66. The Deadly Bees 66. The Torture Garden 67. The House that Dripped Blood 70, etc.

block booking. A system supposedly illegal but still practised, whereby a renter forces an exhibitor to book a whole group of mainly mediocre films in order to get the one or two he wants.

Blockade (US 1938). A rare indication (in its period) of Hollywood's awareness of the world outside. Walter Wanger produced this melodrama of the Spanish Civil War, but despite good intentions it wasn't easy to tell whose side the film was on. Henry Fonda and Madeleine Carroll starred.

Blocker, Dan (1928–1972). Heavyweight American character actor.
Come Blow Your Horn 63. Lady in Cement 68. The Cockeyed Cowboys of Calico County 69, etc.
TV series: *Bonanza* (as Hoss Cartwright) 59–72.

Blomfield, Derek (1920–1964). British boy actor of the thirties.
Emil and the Detectives 35. Turn of the Tide 35. The Ghost of St Michael's 41. Alibi 42. Night and the City 50. Hobson's Choice 54. It's Great to be Young 56. Carry On Admiral 57, etc.

Blondell, Joan (1909–). Amiable American comedienne who played reporters, gold-diggers or the heroine's dizzy friend in innumerable comedies and musicals of the thirties. Later graduated to occasional character roles.

Autobiographical novel 1972: *Center Door Fancy.*
The Office Wife 30. God's Gift to Women 31. Public Enemy 31. Night Nurse 31. The Greeks had a Word for Them 32. Make Me a Star 32. Three on a Match 32. Central Park 32. Gold Diggers of 1933 33. *Footlight Parade* 33. Convention City 33. *Dames* 34. Travelling Saleslady 35. Miss Pacific Fleet 35. Bullets or Ballots 36. Three Men on a Horse 36. The King and the Chorus Girl 37. *The Perfect Specimen* 37. *Stand In* 37. East Side of Heaven 39. Good Girls Go to Paris 39. I Want a Divorce 40. *Topper Returns* 41. Lady for a Night 42. Cry Havoc 43. *A Tree Grows in Brooklyn* 45. Adventure 46. *Nightmare Alley* 47. Christmas Eve 47. For Heaven's Sake 50. *The Blue Veil* 51. The Opposite Sex 56. Lizzie 57. The Desk Set 57. Angel Baby 61. Advance to the Rear 64. *The Cincinnati Kid* 65. Ride Beyond Vengeance 66. Waterhole Three 67. Stay Away Joe 68, etc.
TV series: Here Come the Brides 68. Banyon 72.

Blondie. Chic Young's comic strip about dumb but honest family man Dagwood Bumstead and his pretty wife was first filmed in 1938 by Columbia, with Arthur Lake and Penny Singleton, also Jonathan Hale as Mr Dithers, Larry Simms as Baby Dumpling (later Alexander) and a dog (called Daisy) with star quality. It was so successful that Columbia produced an average of one Blondie film every six months for the next ten years; most of them were directed by Frank Strayer or Abby Berlin. All had 'Blondie' in the title except *The Boss Said No* 42, *A Bundle of Trouble* 42, and *Henpecked* 46; the last of all was *Blondie's Hero* 50. Lake and Pamela Britton appeared in a TV series in the early fifties, and the project was unsuccessfully revived in 1968 with Will Hutchins and Patricia Harty.

Blood and Sand. This tragic novel of the bullring by Vicente Blasco Ibanez has twice been filmed in Hollywood. In 1922, directed by Fred Niblo, it became one of Rudolph Valentino's most popular vehicles, with Lila Lee and Nita Naldi as co-stars. In the 1941 colour version directed by Rouben Mamoulian, the leading roles were filled by Tyrone Power, Linda Darnell and Rita Hayworth.

Bloom, Claire (1931–). British leading actress who came to the screen via the Old Vic.
□ The Blind Goddess 48. *Limelight* 52. Innocents in Paris 52. The Man Between 53. Richard III 56. Alexander the Great 56. The Brothers Karamazov 58. *Look Back in Anger* 59. The Buccaneer 59. The Chapman Report 61.

The Wonderful World of the Brothers Grimm 63. *The Haunting* 63. The Outrage 64. High Infidelity 65. *The Spy Who Came in from the Cold* 66. Charly 68. Three into Two Won't Go 69. The Illustrated Man 69. A Severed Head 69. Red Sky at Morning 71. A Doll's House 73.

bloop. To cover a splice in the sound track, usually with thick 'blooping ink'.

Blore, Eric (1887–1959). British comic actor with stage experience; went to Hollywood and played unctuous/insulting butlers and eccentric types in many films.
The Great Gatsby 26. *The Gay Divorcee* 34. *Top Hat* 35. Shall We Dance? 37. Michael Strogoff 37. A Gentleman's Gentleman 39. The Boys from Syracuse 40. The Lone Wolf (series) 40–47. *Sullivan's Travels* 41. *The Moon and Sixpence* 42. Holy Matrimony 43. San Diego I Love You 44. Kitty 46. *Fancy Pants* 50. Love Happy 50. Babes in Baghdad 52. Bowery to Baghdad 54, etc.

blow up. To magnify an image, either a photograph for background purposes, or a piece of film (e.g. from 16mm to 35mm).

Blow-Up (GB 1966). Michelangelo Antonioni's first film in English, a fashionably decorated but empty anecdote in which, as usual, many questions are posed but none answered. David Hemmings plays a selfish photographer who thinks he has witnessed a murder but never finds out whether he imagined the whole thing; the theme is dislocated by irrelevant sex sequences. Carlos di Palma's photography is exquisite and a general sense of style prevents total boredom.

Blue, Ben (1900–1975) (Benjamin Bernstein). Lanky, rubber-limbed American comedian with vaudeville experience; sporadically in films, usually in cameos.
College Rhythm 33. Follow Your Heart 36. High Wide and Handsome 37. College Swing 38. Paris Honeymoon 39. For Me and My Gal 42. Thousands Cheer 43. Easy to Wed 46. One Sunday Afternoon 48. It's a Mad Mad Mad Mad World 63. *The Russians are Coming, The Russians are Coming* 66. *A Guide for the Married Man* 67. Where Were You When the Lights Went Out? 68, etc.

Blue, Monte (1890–1963). Burly American silent hero who later appeared in innumerable bit roles.
Intolerance 16. Till I Come Back to You 18. Pettigrew's Girl 19. The Affairs of Anatol 21.

Orphans of the Storm 22. Main Street 23. *The Marriage Circle* 24. The Black Swan 24. Other Women's Husbands 26. Other Men's Wives 26. So This is Paris 26. Wolf's Clothing 27. *White Shadows of the South Seas* 28. Tiger Rose 29. Isle of Escape 30. The Flood 31. The Stoker 32. Wagon Wheels 34. Lives of a Bengal Lancer 34. G Men 35. Souls at Sea 37. Dodge City 39. Geronimo 40. Across the Pacific 42. The Mask of Dimitrios 44. Life with Father 47. The Iroquois Trail 50. Apache 54, many others.

The Blue Angel (Germany 1930). This heavy melodrama, with Emil Jannings as a professor ignobly infatuated with a tawdry night club singer, was made in both German and English. The latter version made an international star of Marlene Dietrich, whose throaty rendering of 'Falling in Love Again' became a cinema landmark. Sombrely Teutonic in mood and setting, with tirelessly tricksy direction by Joseph von Sternberg, the film still packs a punch for patient audiences. It was written by Karl Zuckmayer from a novel by Heinrich Mann, with music by Frederick Hollander. Remade (unsuccessfully) in Hollywood in 1958, with Curt Jurgens and May Britt.

The Blue Lamp (GB 1950). This documentary-style crime story about the work of the London police is said to have done a great deal of good to the police image. It certainly produced many imitators, and the policeman played by Jack Warner, though killed in the film, was revived on BBC for the long-running series *Dixon of Dock Green*. Directed by Basil Dearden; BFA best British film.

The Bluebird (US 1939). Maurice Maeterlinck's rather eerie child-fantasy, with its moral that happiness is to be found in one's own back-yard, made one of Hollywood's more successful excursions into the supernatural, moving gracefully from the land of the dead to the land of those unborn; but it appealed less widely than its brasher contemporary *The Wizard of Oz*. Filmed in soft colour, it was directed by Walter Lang with Shirley Temple, Gale Sondergaard and Eddie Collins heading the cast. There had been a silent version in 1916, with Robin MacDougall and Tula Belle. The 1976 Russian-American remake was a failure.

Blum, Daniel (1900–1965). American writer, editor and collector; annually produced *Theatre World* and *Screen World* annuals.

Blyden, Larry (1925–1975). American comic actor, on TV and in supporting roles.

The Bachelor Party 57. Kiss Them for Me 57. On a Clear Day You Can See Forever 70, etc.

Blystone, John G. (1892–1938). American director, former actor.
Dick Turpin 25. *Seven Chances* 25. Ankles Preferred 27. Mother Knows Best 28. The Sky Hawk 29. Tolable David 30. Charlie Chan's Chance 32. Shanghai Madness 33. Hell in the Heavens 34. The Magnificent Brute 36. Woman Chases Man 37. Swiss Miss 38. *Blockheads* 38, many others.

Blyth, Ann (1928–). Diminutive American songstress and leading lady who after opera training got her screen break in Donald O'Connor musicals, then graduated to dramatic roles.
☐ Chip off the Old Block 44. The Merry Monahans 44. Babes on Swing Street 44. Bowery to Broadway 44. *Mildred Pierce* (as the abominable daughter) 45. Swell Guy 46. Brute Force 47. Killer McCoy 47. A Woman's Vengeance 47. *Another Part of the Forest* 48. *Mr Peabody and the Mermaid* 48. Red Canyon 49. Once More My Darling 49. Top o' the Morning 49. Free For All 49. Our Very Own 50. *The Great Caruso* 51. Katie Did It 51. Thunder on the Hill 51. I'll Never Forget You 51. The Golden Horde 51. The World in his Arms 51. One Minute to Zero 52. Sally and Saint Anne 52. All the Brothers were Valiant 53. *Rose Marie* 54. The Student Prince 54. The King's Thief 55. Kismet 55. Slander 57. The Buster Keaton Story 57. *The Helen Morgan Story.* 57.

Blythe, Betty (1893–1972) (Elizabeth Blythe Slaughter). American leading lady of the silent era.
Nomads of the North 20. Queen of Sheba 21. Chu Chin Chow 23. The Folly of Vanity 24. She 25. The Girl from Gay Paree 27. Glorious Betsy 28. A Daughter of Israel 28. Eager Lips 30. Tom Brown of Culver 32. Only Yesterday 33. Ever Since Eve 34. The Gorgeous Hussy 36. Gangster's Boy 38. Honky Tonk 41. Jiggs and Maggie in Society 47. My Fair Lady 64, many others.

Blythe, John (1921–). British character actor, often of spiv types.
This Happy Breed 44. Holiday Camp 48. Vote for Huggett 49. Worm's Eye View 51. The Gay Dog 54. Foxhole in Cairo 60. A Stitch in Time 64. The Bed Sitting Room 69, many others.

Boardman, Eleanor (1898–). American leading lady of the twenties.
Souls for Sale 23. Three Wise Fools 23. Sinners in Silk 24. The Wife of the Centaur 25. The Circle 25. Bardelys the Magnificent 26. Tell it to the Marines 28. The Crowd 28. Mamba 30. The Flood 31. The Squaw Man 31, many others.

Bochner, Lloyd (1924–). Canadian leading man, mostly on TV but in occasional films.
Drums of Africa 63. The Night Walker 64. Sylvia 65. Harlow 65. Point Blank 67. Tony Rome 67. The Detective 68. The Young Runaways 68. The Horse in the Grey Flannel Suit 69. Ulzana's Raid 72, etc.

Bodard, Mag (1927–). Swedish producer in France; a rare example of a woman in this job.
The Umbrellas of Cherbourg 64. The Young Girls of Rochefort 66. *Le Bonheur* 66. Mouchette 67. Benjamin 67. Le Viol 68. La Chinoise 68. *Peau d'Ane* 71, etc.

Bodeen, De Witt (1908–). American screenwriter.
The Seventh Victim 43. *The Curse of the Cat People* 44. The Enchanted Cottage 44. *I Remember Mama* 47. Mrs Mike 50. Twelve to the Moon 58. Billy Budd 62, etc.

The Body Snatcher (US 1945). Generally felt to be the most successful of Val Lewton's highly-regarded horror films for RKO, this version of the R. L. Stevenson story had excellent sets of old Edinburgh and a first-class performance by Henry Daniell. The subject matter has, of course, been used in several other films. Directed by Robert Wise.

Boehm, Karl or **Carl** (1928–) (Karlheinz Boehm). Blond, handsome German leading man who has appeared in a few international films.
Peeping Tom 59. Too Hot to Handle 60. The Magnificent Rebel (as Beethoven) 60. The Four Horsemen of the Apocalypse 62. The Wonderful World of the Brothers Grimm 63. Come Fly with Me 63. The Venetian Affair 66, etc.

Boehm, Sidney (1908–). American screenwriter, a reliable hand at crime stories.
High Wall 48. *The Undercover Man* 49. Side Street 50. Mystery Street 50. *Union Station* 50. When Worlds Collide 52. The Savage 53. *The Big Heat* 53. The Secret of the Incas 54. Rogue Cop 54. Black Tuesday 54. Violent Saturday 55. The Tall Men 55. Hell on Frisco Bay 55. The Revolt of Mamie Stover 56. Harry Black 58. A Woman Obsessed (& p) 59. *Seven Thieves* (& p) 60. Shock Treatment 64. Sylvia 65. Rough Night in Jericho 67, etc.

Boetticher, Budd (1916–) (Oscar Boetticher).

American director, former bullfighter. Has not risen above a few striking co-features, but cineastes have made him the centre of a cult.
The Missing Juror 44. Assigned to Danger 47. Sword of D'Artagnan 51. *The Bullfighter and the Lady* (& wp) 51. Red Ball Express 52. Bronco Buster 52. Horizons West 52. East of Sumatra 53. Wings of the Hawk 53. The Man from the Alamo 53. The Magnificent Matador (& w) 55. The Killer is Loose 56. Seven Men from Now 56. Decision at Sundown 57. The Tall T 57. Buchanan Rides Alone 58. Ride Lonesome 59. Westbound 59. *The Rise and Fall of Legs Diamond* 60. *Arruza* 68. A Time for Dying 71, etc.

boffins are research scientists working on hush-hush government projects. Their problems have been dramatized in such films as *The Small Back Room*, *School for Secrets*, *Suspect*, *The Man in the Moon*, *The Satan Bug*, *The Andromeda Strain*, *The Atomic City* and *The Forbin Project*.

Bogarde, Dirk (1920–) (Derek Van Den Bogaerd). British leading actor of Dutch descent. A great success in lightweight homegrown films, he later restricted his appearances and achieved international distinction as a character actor.
Autobiography 1977: *A Postillion Struck by Lightning.*
☐ Esther Waters 47. Once a Jolly Swagman 48. *Quartet* 48. Dear Mr Prohack 49. Boys in Brown 49. So Long at the Fair 49. The Woman in Question 50. The Blue Lamp 50. Blackmailed 51. Penny Princess 51. The Gentle Gunman 52. Hunted 52. *Doctor in the House* 53. Appointment in London 53. They Who Dare 53. Desperate Moment 53. Simba 54. The Sea Shall Not Have Them 54. *The Sleeping Tiger* 54. For Better For Worse 54. Doctor at Sea 55. *Cast a Dark Shadow* 55. Doctor at Large 56. *The Spanish Gardener* 56. Ill Met By Moonlight 57. Campbell's Kingdom 58. The Wind Cannot Read 58. *A Tale of Two Cities* 58. The Doctor's Dilemma 59. Libel 59. Song Without End (as Liszt) (US) 60. The Angel Wore Red 60. The Singer not the Song 60. *Victim* 61. H.M.S. Defiant 62. The Password is Courage 63. I Could Go On Singing 63. The Mind Benders 63. *The Servant* (BFA) 63. Hot Enough for June 64. Doctor in Distress 64. *King and Country* 64. The High Bright Sun 65. *Darling* (BFA) 65. Modesty Blaise 66. Accident 67. Our Mother's House 67. Sebastian 67. The Fixer 68. *The Damned* 69. Justine 69. *Death in Venice* 70. The Serpent 72. The Night Porter 74. Permission to Kill 75.

Bogart, Humphrey (1899–1957). American leading actor who became one of Hollywood's imperishable personalities, a cynical but amiable tough guy in a trench coat who summed up all the *films noirs* of the forties, after a long apprenticeship playing gangsters. Several biographies have been published, but none catch the full flavour of the man who influenced millions. The best are by Nathaniel Benchley, Jonah Ruddy, Clifford McCarty and Ezra Goodman.
☐ A Devil with Women 30. Up the River 30. Body and Soul 30. Bad Sister 30. Women of All Nations 31. A Holy Terror 31. Love Affair 32. Big City Blues 32. Three on a Match 32. Midnight 34. *The Petrified Forest* (his stage role as gangster Duke Mantee) 36. Two Against the World 36. Bullets or Ballots 36. China Clipper 36. Isle of Fury 36. The Great O'Malley 37. Black Legion 37. San Quentin 37. *Marked Woman* 37. Kid Galahad 37. *Dead End* 37. Stand In 37. Swing Your Lady 38. Men Are Such Fools 38. The Amazing Dr Clitterhouse 38. Racket Busters 38: *Angels with Dirty Faces* 38. Crime School 38. King of the Underworld 39. The Oklahoma Kid 39. Dark Victory 39. You Can't Get Away with Murder 39. *The Roaring Twenties* 39. The Return of Dr X (as a vampire) 39. Invisible Stripes 39. Virginia City 40. It All Came True 40. Brother Orchid 40. They Drive by Night 40. *High Sierra* 41. The Wagons Roll at Night 41. *The Maltese Falcon* (his archetypal performance) 41. All Through the Night 42. The Big Shot 42. *Across the Pacific* 42. *Casablanca* 42. Action in the North Atlantic 43. Thank Your Lucky Stars. 43. *Sahara* 43. *To Have and Have Not* 43. Passage to Marseilles 44. Conflict 45. *The Big Sleep* 46. The Two Mrs Carrolls 47. Dead Reckoning 47. Dark Passage 47. *The Treasure of the Sierra Madre* 47. *Key Largo* 48. Knock on any Door 49. Tokyo Joe 49. Chain Lightning 50. In a Lonely Place 50. *The Enforcer* 51. Sirocco 51. *The African Queen* (AA) 52. Deadline 52. Battle Circus 53. *Beat the Devil* 54. *The Caine Mutiny* 54. Sabrina 54. *The Barefoot Contessa* 54. We're No Angels 55. The Left Hand of God 55. The Desperate Hours 55. The Harder they Fall 56.

Bogart, Paul (1925–). American director.
☐ Halls of Anger 68. Marlowe 69. The Skin Game 71. Cancel My Reservation 71. Class of '44 73. Mr Ricco 75.

Bogdanovich, Peter (1939–). American director with a penchant for reworking traditional themes; former film critic.
☐ *Targets* (& w) 68. *The Last Picture Show* (& w) 71. *What's Up Doc?* (& w) 72. Paper Moon 73. Daisy Miller (& p) 74. At Long Last Love 75. Nickelodeon 76.

Bogeaus, Benedict (1904–1968). American independent producer, formerly in real estate; his films were mildly interesting though eccentric.
The Bridge of San Luis Rey 44. Captain Kidd 45. The Diary of a Chambermaid 45. Christmas Eve 47. The Macomber Affair 47. Johnny One Eye 49. Passion 54. Slightly Scarlet 56. The Most Dangerous Man Alive 61, etc.

Bohnen, Roman (1894–1949). American character actor usually seen as hard-working immigrant types.
Vogues of 1938 37. Of Mice and Men 40. So Ends our Night 41. Appointment for Love 41. Edge of Darkness 43. Mission to Moscow 43. The Song of Bernadette 43. *The Hitler Gang* 44. A Bell for Adano 45. The Strange Love of Martha Ivers 46. Mr Ace 46. The Best Years of Our Lives 46. Brute Force 47. Arch of Triumph 48. Night has a Thousand Eyes 48, etc.

Bois, Curt (1900–). Dapper German comedy actor, long in Hollywood playing head waiters and pompous clerks.
Tovarich 37. Hollywood Hotel 38. *The Great Waltz* 38. Boom Town 40. Bitter Sweet 40. Hold Back the Dawn 41. Casablanca 42. The Desert Song 43. The Spanish Main 45. *The Woman in White* 48. The Great Sinner 49. Fortunes of Captain Blood 50. *Herr Puntilla and His Servant Matti* (Ger.) 54, many others.

Boisset, Yves (1939–). French director.
Angel's Leap 69. A Cop 70. Cobra 71. L'Attentat 72. Coplan Saves His Skin 72, etc.

Boland, Bridget (1904–). British playwright and screenwriter.
Gaslight 39. Spies of the Air. 40. The Lost People 48. The Prisoner 54. War and Peace 56, etc.

Boland, Mary (1880–1965). American stage tragedienne who in middle age settled in Hollywood and played innumerable fluttery matrons: appeared in a series of domestic comedies with Charles Ruggles.
The Edge of the Abyss 16. His Temporary Wife 18. Personal Maid 31. *If I had a Million* 32. *Three Cornered Moon* 33. Four Frightened People 34. *Down to Their Last Yacht* 34. *Ruggles of Red Gap* 35. Early to Bed 36. Wives Never Know 36. Mama Runs Wild 37. Little Tough Guys in Society 38. *The Women* 39. New Moon 40. *Pride and Prejudice* (as Mrs Bennett) 40. In Our Time 44. Nothing But Trouble 44. Julia Misbehaves 48. Guilty Bystander 50, many others.

Boles, John (1895–1969). Stalwart American singer and leading man. At his most popular in the early thirties.
So This is Marriage 25. The Loves of Sonya 26. *Rio Rita* 29. *The Desert Song* 29. King of Jazz 30. One Heavenly Night 30. Frankenstein 31. Six Hours to Live 32. *Back Street* 32. My Lips Betray 33. Only Yesterday 33. Bottoms Up 34. Stand Up and Cheer 34. The Life of Vergie Winters 34. Orchids to You 35. Curly Top 35. The Littlest Rebel 35. Rose of the Rancho 35. A Message to Garcia 36. *Stella Dallas* 37. She Married an Artist 38. Sinners in Paradise 38. Between Us Girls 42. Thousands Cheer 43. Babes in Baghdad 52, etc.

Boleslawski, Richard (1889–1937) (Boleslaw Ryszart Srzednicki). Polish stage director, formerly with the Moscow Arts Theatre, who came to Hollywood in 1930 and made a few stylish movies.
□ Three Meetings (USSR) 17. The Gay Diplomat 31. Rasputin and the Empress 32. Storm at Daybreak 33. Beauty for Sale 33. Fugitive Lovers 33. Men in White 34. Operator 13 34. *The Painted Veil* 34. *Clive of India* 35. *Les Misérables* 35. O'Shaughnessy's Boy 35. *Metropolitan* 35. Three Godfathers 36. *Theodora Goes Wild* 36. *The Garden of Allah* 36. The Last of Mrs Cheyney 37.

Bolger, Ray (1904–). Rubber-legged American eccentric dancer, a stage star who has made too few films.
□ The Great Ziegfeld 36. *Rosalie* 37. Sweethearts 38. *The Wizard of Oz* (as the scarecrow) 39. Sunny 41. Stage Door Canteen 43. Four Jacks and a Jill 44. *The Harvey Girls* 46. *Look for the Silver Lining* 49. *Where's Charley* 52. April in Paris 52. Babes in Toyland 60. The Daydreamer 66. The Entertainer (TV) 75. The Captains and the Kings (TV) 76.

Bolkan, Florinda (1945–). Spanish-Indian leading lady.
Candy 68. The Damned 69. Investigation of a Citizen 70. The Last Valley 70. The Anonymous Venetian 71. Detective Belli 71. Romance 71. The Island 72. A Man to Respect 72. Lizard in a Woman's Skin 72. Hearts and Minds 74. Royal Flash 75, etc.

Bologna, Joseph (1938–). American actor who with his wife Renee Taylor usually writes his own material.
Made for Each Other 71. Honor thy Father (TV) 73. Mixed Company 74. Woman of the Year (TV) 75. The Big Bus 76.

Bolt, Robert (1924–). British playwright who

turned to screenwriting and direction.
Lawrence of Arabia 62. *Doctor Zhivago* 65. *A Man For All Seasons* 66. Ryan's Daughter 70. Lady Caroline Lamb (& d) 72.

Bolton, Guy (1885–). American playwright and screenwriter, often associated with P. G. Wodehouse.
Grounds for Divorce 25. The Love Doctor 29. The Love Parade 30. Girl Crazy (oa) 32. Ladies Should Listen (oa) 34. Anything Goes (oa) 35. Rosalie (oa) 37. Weekend at the Waldorf 45. Anastasia (oa) 56, etc.

Bomba the Jungle Boy. This second feature series was devised in 1949, from a comic strip, to use the talents of Johnny Sheffield, who had played Johnny Weissmuller's son in some Tarzan films. It never amounted to much, but twelve films were made until in 1955, after *Lord of the Jungle*, Sheffield became too old and too fat for the role.

Bonanova, Fortunio (1896–1969). Spanish opera singer and impresario who after managing his own repertory company in America in the thirties, settled in Hollywood to play excitable foreigners.
Careless Lady 32. Podoroso Caballero 36. Tropic Holiday 38. La Immaculada 39. I Was an Adventuress 40. *Citizen Kane* (as the music teacher) 41. Blood and Sand 41. The Black Swan 42. Five Graves to Cairo 43. For Whom the Bell Tolls 43. Going my Way 44. Double Indemnity 44. Monsieur Beaucaire 46. The Fugitive 47. Whirlpool 50. September Affair 51. The Moon is Blue 53. An Affair to Remember 57. Thunder in the Sun 59. The Running Man 63. Million Dollar Collar 69, many others.

Bonaparte, Napoleon: see *Napoleon Bonaparte*.

Bond, Derek (1919–). British light leading man with varied pre-film experience including the Grenadier Guards.
The Captive Heart 46. *Nicholas Nickleby* (title role) 47. *Scott of the Antarctic* 48. Broken Journey 48. The Weaker Sex 48. Christopher Columbus 49. Marry Me 49. Uncle Silas 50. The Hour of Thirteen 52. Stranger from Venus 54. Svengali 55. Trouble in Store 55. Gideon's Day 58. The Hand 60. Saturday Night Out 64. Wonderful Life 64. Press for Time 66. When Eight Bells Toll 71, etc.

Bond, Gary (1940–). British leading man.
Zulu 64. Anne of the Thousand Days 70. *Outback* 70, etc.

Bond, Lillian (1910–). American leading lady of the thirties.
Just a Gigolo 31. Fireman Save My Child 32. *The Old Dark House* 32. Hot Pepper 33. Affairs of a Gentleman 34. China Seas 35. The Housekeeper's Daughter 39. The Westerner 40. The Picture of Dorian Gray 45. Man in the Attic 54. Pirates of Tripoli 55, etc.

Bond, Ward (1903–1960). Burly American actor who from the coming of sound distinguished himself in small roles, especially in John Ford films; but it took TV to make him a star.
The Big Trail 30. When Strangers Marry 33. Devil Dogs of the Air 35. You Only Live Once 37. The Oklahoma Kid 39. Young Mr Lincoln 39. Gone with the Wind 39. The Grapes of Wrath 40. *Tobacco Road* 41. The Maltese Falcon 41. Gentleman Jim 42. A Guy Named Joe 43. They Were Expendable 45. My Darling Clementine 46. Fort Apache 48. *Wagonmaster* 50. *The Quiet Man* 52. *Blowing Wild* 53. The Long Gray Line 55. *The Searchers* 56. *The Wings of Eagles* 57. *The Halliday Brand* 57. *Rio Bravo* 59, many others.
TV series: *Wagon Train* 57–60.

Bondartchuk, Sergei (1920–). Russian actor and director.
The Young Guards (a) 48. The Grasshopper (a) 55. Othello (a) 56. *Destiny of a Man* (a, d) 59. *War and Peace* (a, d) (AA) 64. *Waterloo* (d) 70, etc.

Bondi, Beulah (1892–) (Beulah Bondy). Distinguished American character actress who from early middle age played cantankerous or kindly old ladies.
☐ Street Scene 31. Arrowsmith 31. Rain 32. The Stranger's Return 33. Christopher Bean 33. Finishing School 34. The Painted Veil 34. Two Alone 34. Registered Nurse 34. Ready for Love 34. Bad Boy 35. The Good Fairy 35. The Invisible Ray 36. The Trail of the Lonesome Pine 36. The Moon's Our Home 36. The Case Against Mrs Ames 36. Hearts Divided 36. The Gorgeous Hussy 37. *Maid of Salem* 37. *Make Way for Tomorrow* 37. The Buccaneer 38. Of Human Hearts 38. Vivacious Lady 38. The Sisters 38. On Borrowed Time 39. Mr Smith Goes to Washington 39. The Underpup 39. Remember the Night 40. *Our Town* 40. The Captain is a Lady 40. Penny Serenade 41. Shepherd of the Hills 41. One Foot in Heaven 41. Tonight We Raid Calais 43. Watch on the Rhine 43. I Love a Soldier 44. She's a Soldier Too 44. Our Hearts Were Young and Gay 44. And Now Tomorrow 44. The Very Thought of You 44. *The*

Southerner 45. Back to Bataan 45. Breakfast in Hollywood 46. Sister Kenny 46. *It's a Wonderful Life* 46. High Conquest 47. The Sainted Sisters 48. The Snake Pit 48. So Dear to My Heart 48. The Life of Riley 49. Reign of Terror 49. Mr Soft Touch 49. The Baron of Arizona 50. The Furies 50. Lone Star 52. Latin Lovers 53. *Track of the Cat* 54. Back from Eternity 56. The Unholy Wife 57. The Big Fisherman 59. A Summer Place 59. *Tammy Tell Me True* 61. The Wonderful World of the Brothers Grimm 62. Tammy and the Doctor 63. She Lives (TV) 71.

Bonnie and Clyde (US 1967). A milestone film in its sixties-style retelling, with a blend of comedy, poetry and extreme violence, of the oft-recounted life story of two minor desperadoes of the thirties, Bonnie Parker and Clyde Barrow. Comparison with the gangster films of the thirties would be fruitful. Written by Robert Benton and David Newman, photographed by Burnett Guffey (AA), produced by Warren Beatty, directed by Arthur Penn; starring Warren Beatty and Faye Dunaway. Other variations on the story include *Gun Crazy, They Live By Night, Thieves Like Us* and *You Only Live Once.*

Bonzo was a chimpanzee who appeared in *Bedtime for Bonzo* 51 being brought up as a child under an educational experiment. A second and final film of his adventures was *Bonzo Goes to College* 52.

boo-boos occur even in the best-regulated movies; sometimes they pass the eagle eye of editor and director and find their way into the release version. Here are a few which have delighted me.
□ In *Carmen Jones*, the camera tracks with Dorothy Dandridge down a shopping street, and the entire crew is reflected in the windows she passes.
□ In *The Invisible Man*, when the naked but invisible hero runs from the police but is given away by his footprints in the snow, the footprints are of shoes, not feet.
□ In *The Wrong Box*, the roofs of Victorian London are disfigured by TV aerials.
□ In *The Viking Queen*, one character is plainly wearing a wrist watch.
□ In *One Million Years B.C.*, all the girls wear false eyelashes.
□ In *The Group*, set in the thirties, there are several shots of the Pan Am building in New York, built in the sixties.
□ In *Stagecoach*, during the Indian chase across the salt flats one can see the tracks of rubber tyres.
□ In *Decameron Nights*, Louis Jourdan as

Paganino the Pirate stands on the deck of his fourteenth-century ship . . . and down a hill in the distance trundles a large white truck.
□ In *Camelot*, the character played by Lionel Jeffries first meets King Arthur about an hour into the movie; yet twenty minutes earlier he is plainly visible at the king's wedding.
□ In *Son of Frankenstein*, Basil Rathbone during a train journey draws attention to the weirdly stunted trees . . . one of which passes by three times during the conversation.
□ In *Castle of Fu Manchu*, one of the leading characters is referred to in the film as Ingrid, in the synopsis as Anna, and in the end credits as Maria.
□ In *Tea and Sympathy*, a pair of china dogs are back to back in a general view of the scene, but face to face in the close-ups.
□ In *Dracula*, Bela Lugosi refers to Whitby as 'so close to London'. It is in fact 243 miles away.
□ In *The Yellow Mountain* and *A Man Alone*, both westerns set in the last century, aeroplane vapour trails can be seen in the sky.
□ In *The King and I*, while Yul Brynner is singing 'Puzzlement' he is wearing an ear-ring in some shots but not in others.
□ In *Emma Hamilton* (1969) Big Ben is heard to strike in 1804, fifty years before it was built.
□ In *The Lodger* (1944) London's Tower Bridge is shown, ten years before it was built.
□ In *Hello Dolly*, set at the turn of the century, a modern car lies derelict by the side of the railway track.
□ In *Anatomy of a Murder*, Lee Remick in the café scene wears a dress, but when she walks outside she is wearing slacks.
□ In *Hangover Square*, the introductory title gives the date of the action as 1899, but shortly thereafter a theatre programme shows 1903.
□ In *Queen Christina*, the famous final close-up apparently has the wind blowing in two directions at once, one to get the boat under way and the other to arrange Garbo's hair to the best advantage.
□ In *The Desk Set*, Katharine Hepburn leaves her office carrying a bunch of white flowers. By the time she reaches the pavement they are pink.
□ In *Knock on Wood*, Danny Kaye turns a corner in London's Oxford Street, and finds himself in Ludgate Hill, three miles away.
□ In *23 Paces to Baker Street*, Van Johnson has an apartment in Portman Square, with a river view which seems to be that of the Savoy Hotel two miles away.
□ In *Triple Cross*, a World War Two newspaper bears a headline about the cost of Concorde going up again.
□ In *The Lady Vanishes*, Miss Froy writes her name in the steam on a train window, but two or

three shots later the writing is quite different and in another place.

Booke, Sorrell (1926–). American character actor.
Gone are the Days 63. Fail Safe 64. Black Like Me 64. Lady in a Cage 64. Up the Down Staircase 67. Slaughterhouse Five 71. The Take 72. The Iceman Cometh 73. Bank Shot 74, etc.

books on the cinema: see end of book.

boom. A 'long arm' extending from the camera unit and carrying a microphone to be balanced over the actors so that sound can be picked up in a semi-distant shot. A 'camera boom' is a high movable platform strong enough to support the entire camera unit.

Boomerang (US 1947). This who-done-it based on the murder of a priest in a small town set a new style in semi-documentary thrillers. Written by Richard Murphy, directed by Elia Kazan.

Boone, Daniel (1734–1820). American pioneer and Indian scout who helped to open up Kentucky and Missouri. He has been frequently portrayed in films, notably by George O'Brien (*Daniel Boone*, 1936), David Bruce (*Young Daniel Boone*, 1950) and Bruce Bennett (*Daniel Boone, Trail Blazer*, 1956). In 1964 began a long-running TV series, *Daniel Boone*, starring Fess Parker.

Boone, Pat (1934–). Gentle-mannered American pop singer of the fifties; never quite made it as a straight actor, perhaps because he paraded his lack of private vices.
□ *Bernardine* 57. April Love 57. Mardi Gras 58. *Journey to the Centre of the Earth* 59. All Hands on Deck 61. State Fair 62. The Yellow Canary 63. The Main Attraction 63. The Horror of it All (GB) 63. Never Put it in Writing (GB) 64. Goodbye Charlie 64. The Greatest Story Ever Told 65. The Perils of Pauline 67. The Cross and the Switchblade 70.

Boone, Richard (1917–). Craggy American character actor, often in menacing roles.
□ Halls of Montezuma 51. Call Me Mister 51. The Desert Fox 51. Return of the Texan 52. Red Skies of Montana 52. Kangaroo 52. The Way of a Gaucho 52. Man on a Tightrope 53. *Vicki* 53. *The Robe* 53. City of Bad Men 53. Beneath the Twelve-Mile Reef 53. The Siege at Red River 54. Dragnet 54. The Raid 54. Battle Stations 55. *Man Without a Star* 55. Ten Wanted Men 55. Robbers' Roost 55 Star in the Dust 56. Away all

Boats 56. Lizzie 57. Garment Center 57. The Tall T 57. I Bury the Living 58. *The Alamo* 60. A Thunder of Drums 61. *Rio Conchos* 64. *The War Lord* 65. Hombre 67. Kona Coast 68. The Night of the Following Day 69. *The Arrangement* 69. Madron 70. *The Kremlin Letter* 70. Big Jake 71. In Broad Daylight (TV) 72. A Tattered Web (TV) 72. Goodnight My Love (TV) 72. Deadly Harvest (TV) 72. The Great Niagara (TV) 74.
TV series: *Medic* 54–56. *Have Gun Will Travel* 57–61. *The Richard Boone Show* 64.

Boorman, John (1933–). British director, from TV.
□ Catch Us if You Can 65. *Point Blank* (US) 67. *Hell in the Pacific* (US) 69. Leo the Last 70. *Deliverance* 72. Zardoz (& w) 74.

Booth, Anthony (1937–). British general purpose actor: everything from Nazis to layabouts.
Mix Me a Person 62. The L-shaped Room 62. Of Human Bondage 64. Till Death Us Do Part 68. Girl With a Pistol 69. The Garnett Saga 72, etc.
TV series: *Till Death Us Do Part* 67–71.

Booth, Edwina (1909–) (Josephine Constance Woodruff). American leading lady of the late twenties, best known for catching jungle fever while filming in Africa for *Trader Horn* 30. She retired shortly after.

Booth, James (1930–) (David Geeves-Booth). British character actor who can play innocent or villainous.
The Trials of Oscar Wilde 60. The Hellions 61. In the Doghouse 62. Sparrows Can't Sing 63. French Dressing 63. *Zulu* 64. The Secret of My Success 65. Ninety Degrees in the Shade 66. *Robbery* 67. The Bliss of Mrs Blossom 68. The Man Who Had Power over Women 70. Darker than Amber 70. Macho Callahan 71. Revenge 71. That'll Be the Day 74. Brannigan 75, etc.

Booth, Karin (1923–). American leading lady of second features.
Big City 48. Last of the Buccaneers 50. The Texas Rangers 50. Cripple Creek 52. Let's Do It Again 53. Seminole Uprising 55. The Crooked Sky (GB) 56. Beloved Infidel 59, etc.

Booth, Shirley (1907–) (Thelma Ford Booth). Distinguished American stage actress who came to the screen for a few middle-aged roles.
□ *Come Back Little Sheba* (AA) 52. About Mrs Leslie 53. Hot Spell 57. *The Matchmaker* 59.
TV series: *Hazel* 61–66.

Borchers, Cornell (1925–) (Cornelia Bruch).
German leading actress, in a few international
films.
The Big Lift 50. The Divided Heart (BFA) 55.
Never Say Goodbye 56. Istanbul 57. Oasis 60,
etc.

Borden, Olive (1907–1947). American leading
lady of the twenties.
Dressmaker from Paris 25. Three Bad Men 26.
Fig Leaves 26. The Joy Girl 26. Pajamas 26.
Gang War 28. Virgin Lips 28. Love in the Desert
29. Dance Hall 29. Hello Sister 30, etc.

Borg, Veda Ann (1915–1973). American
character actress, the archetypal hard-boiled
blonde of a hundred second features.
Three Cheers for Love 36. Alcatraz Island 37.
She Loved a Fireman 38. Café Hostess 39.
Glamour for Sale 40. The Pittsburgh Kid 41.
Duke of the Navy 42. Isle of Forgotten Sins 43.
Smart Guy 44. What a Blonde 45. Mildred Pierce
45. Accomplice 46. Big Town 47. Blonde Savage
48. Forgotten Women 49. The Kangaroo Kid 50.
Big Jim McLain 52. Three Sailors and a Girl 53.
Bitter Creek 54. Guys and Dolls 55. Frontier
Gambler 56. The Fearmakers 58. Thunder in the
Sun 59. The Alamo 60, many others.

Borgia, Cesare (1476–1507) and **Lucretia**
(1480–1519). The son and daughter of Pope
Alexander VI were suspected of several family
murders. On screen they have been played as
melodramatic figures, notably by MacDonald
Carey and Paulette Goddard (*Bride of
Vengeance*, 1949), Orson Welles (*Prince of
Foxes*, 1949), Pedro Armendariz and Martine
Carol (*Lucretia Borgia*, 1952), and Franco
Fabrizi and Belinda Lee (*Nights of Lucretia
Borgia*, 1959).

Borgnine, Ernest (1915–) (Ermes Borgnino).
Forceful American character actor who after
stage and TV work was typecast by Hollywood
as a heavy until *Marty* gave him star status.
□ China Corsair 51. The Whistle at Eaton Falls
51. The Mob 51. *From Here to Eternity* 53. The
Stranger Wore a Gun 53. Demetrius and the
Gladiators 54. The Bounty Hunter 54. Johnny
Guitar 54. Vera Cruz 54. *Bad Day at Black
Rock* 54. Run for Cover 55. *Marty* (AA, BFA)
55. Violent Saturday 55. The Last Command 55.
The Square Jungle 56. Jubal 56. *The Catered
Affair* 56. *The Best Things in Life Are Free* 56.
Three Brave Men 57. *The Vikings* 58. The
Badlanders 58. Torpedo Run 58. The Rabbit
Trap 58. Man on a String 60. *Pay or Die* 60. Go
Naked in the World 61. Summer of the
Seventeenth Doll 61. Barabbas 62. McHale's

Navy 64. The Flight of the Phoenix 65. McHale's
Navy Meets the Air Force 66. The Oscar 66. *The
Dirty Dozen* 67. Chuka 67. *Ice Station Zebra* 68.
The Split 68. The Legend of Lylah Clare 68. The
Wild Bunch 69. Suppose They Gave a War and
Nobody Came 69. Vengeance is Mine (It.) 69.
The Adventurers 70. Bunny O'Hare 71. Hannie
Caulder 71. Rain for a Dusty Summer 71.
Willard 71. Tough Guy 72. The Revengers 72.
What Happened to the Mysterious Mr Foster?
(TV) 72. The Poseidon Adventure 72. Emperor
of the North Pole 73. The Neptune Factor 73.
Law and Disorder 74. The Devil's Rain 75.
TV series: *McHale's Navy* 62–65. Future Cop
76.

Born Free (GB 1965). Joy Adamson's book
about raising a tame lioness in Kenya was
indifferently filmed by James Hill with Virginia
McKenna and Bill Travers as the Adamsons. In
1971 the sequel, *Living Free*, was made with
Susan Hampshire and Nigel Davenport.
A TV series followed in 1975.

Boros, Ferike (1880–1951). Hungarian
actress in Hollywood.
Little Caesar 30. Svengali 31. Huddle 32.
Humanity 33. The Fountain 34. Make Way for
Tomorrow 37. Love Affair 39. Argentine Nights
40. Caught in the Draft 41. Once Upon a
Honeymoon 42. The Doughgirls 44. The Specter
of the Rose 46, etc.

Borowczyk, Walerian (1923–). French
writer-director.
Dom 58. Le Concert de M et Mme Kabal 62.
Jeux des Anges 64. Goto Island of Love 68.
Blanche 71, etc.

Borradaile, Osmond (c. 1892–). Canadian
cinematographer, in Hollywood from 1914 and
later in Britain.
The Drum 38. The Four Feathers 39. The
Overlanders 46. The Trap 66, etc.

Borzage, Frank (1893–1962). American
director who favoured a soft, sentimental
approach to romantic dramas.
SILENT FILMS INCLUDE: Humoresque 20.
Get Rich Quick Wallingford 21. Children of the
Dust 23. Secrets 24. The Circle 25. The Marriage
Licence 26. Seventh Heaven (AA) 27. Street
Angel 28. The River 29.

□ SOUND FILMS: Song o' My Heart 30.
Liliom 30. Doctors' Wives 31. Young as You
Feel 31. Bad Girl 32. After Tomorrow 32. Young
America 32. *A Farewell to Arms* 32. Secrets 33.
Man's Castle 33. No Greater Glory 34. Little
Man What Now? 34. Flirtation Walk 34. Living

on Velvet 35. Stranded 35. Shipmates Forever 35. *Desire* 36. Hearts Divided 36. The Green Light 37. *History is Made at Night* 37. Big City 38. Mannequin 38. *Three Comrades* 38. The Shining Hour 39. Disputed Passage 39. *Strange Cargo* 40. *The Mortal Storm* 40. Flight Command 41. *Smilin' Through* 41. The Vanishing Virginian 42. Seven Sweethearts 42. Stage Door Canteen 43. His Butler's Sister 43. Till We Meet Again 44. The Spanish Main 45. I've Always Loved You 46. Magnificent Doll 46. That's My Man 47. *Moonrise* 49. China Doll 58. The Big Fisherman 59.

Bose, Lucia (1931–). Italian leading lady, former beauty queen.
No Peace among the Olives 50. Cronaca di un Amore 51. Girls of the Spanish Steps 52. Death of a Cyclist (Sp.) 54. Le Testament d'Orphée 61, etc.

Bosley, Tom (1927–). Plump American character actor with stage and TV experience.
The Street with No Name 46. Call Northside 777 48. The World of Henry Orient 64. *Love with the Proper Stranger* 64. Divorce American Style 67. The Secret War of Harry Frigg 67. Yours Mine and Ours 68. To Find a Man 72, etc.
TV series: *Debbie* 69. Happy Days 75.

Bost, Pierre: see under *Aurenche, Jean*.

Boston Blackie was an American comic strip character, a small-time crook with a weakness for helping people. The first film about his exploits, *Boston Blackie's Little Pal*, was made in 1919. In 1923 there were two Blackie adventures with William Russell. Between 1940 and 1948 the character was revived for thirteen second features starring Chester Morris (with George E. Stone as 'the Runt'). And in 1951–53 Kent Taylor appeared in a TV series.

Bosustow, Stephen (1911–). Founder of UPA cartoons (1943) after working as artist for Disney and others. Later won Academy Awards for creation of Gerald McBoing Boing and Mr Magoo.

Bosworth, Hobart (1867–1943). American character actor with stage experience: films from 1909.
The Country Mouse 14. Joan the Woman 16. Oliver Twist 16. Below the Surface 20. Vanity Fair 23. Captain January 24. Zander the Great 25. The Big Parade 25. The Blood Ship 27. A Woman of Affairs 29. Mammy 30. The Miracle Man 32. Lady for a Day 33. The Crusades 35. Bullets for O'Hara 41. Sin Town 42, many

others.

Boteler, Wade (1891–1943). American general purpose small part actor.
An Old Fashioned Boy 19. The Ghost Patrol 23. High School Hero 26. Top Sergeant Mulligan 28. College Lovers 30. Death Kiss 32. Belle of the Nineties 34. Whipsaw 36. You Only Live Once 37. In Old Chicago 38. Thunder Afloat 39. Castle on the Hudson 40. Kathleen 41. I Was Framed 42. Hi Buddy 43. The Last Ride 44, many others.

Botkin, Perry Jnr (–). American composer.
Bless the Beasts and Children (co-ph) 72. Skyjacked 72. Lady Ice 72. Your Three Minutes are Up 73.

Bottoms, Joseph (1954–). American juvenile of the seventies.
The Dove 74.

Bottoms, Timothy (1949–). Leading American juvenile actor of the early seventies.
□ Johnny Got His Gun 71. *The Last Picture Show* 71. Love, Pain and the Whole Damned Thing 72. The Paper Chase 73. The White Dawn 74. The Crazy World of Julius Vrooder 74.

Bouchet, Barbara (1943–). German-American glamour girl.
In Harm's Way 65. Agent for HARM 66. Casino Royale 67. Danger Route 68, etc.

Bouchey, Willis (1900–). American character actor, often seen as judge or reluctant sheriff.
Elopement 51. Suddenly 54. Johnny Concho 56. The Last Hurrah 58. Sergeant Rutledge 60. Where Love has Gone 64. Support Your Local Sheriff 69, many others.

Bouchier, Chili (1909–) (Dorothy Bouchier). British leading lady, mainly on stage.
Shooting Stars 28. Carnival 31. Get off My Foot 36. The Mind of Mr Reeder 39. The Laughing Lady 47. Old Mother Riley's New Venture 49. The Boy and the Bridge 59, others.

Boudu Sauvé des Eaux (France 1932). Written and directed by Jean Renoir, this wry little piece could qualify as the screen's first black comedy. Michel Simon appears as a pixilated tramp who proceeds to make a family very sorry they saved him from drowning.

Boule de Suif. The chief versions of Guy de Maupassant's story, about the effects of a prostitute on a band of travellers during the 1870s, were by Mikhail Romm in 1934, Robert Wise (as *Mademoiselle Fifi*, with Simone Simon) in 1944, and Christian-Jaque (with Micheline Presle) in 1945. John Ford's *Stagecoach* 39 is based on a very similar situation, as is *The Journey*.

Boulting, John and **Roy** (both 1913–). Twin Britishers who after varied experience set up as writer-producer-directors of films with something to say. After World War II they became somewhat more conventional, and the early fifties were barren, but then they came up with a highly successful series of comedies pillorying national institutions. In the sixties they became directors of British Lion Films, with commercially successful but otherwise disappointing results. (Although they have produced and directed alternately, neither has shown a particular style, and their films below are treated as joint efforts unless mentioned otherwise.

□ Consider Your Verdict 37. Inquest 38. Trunk Crime 38. *Pastor Hall* 39. *Thunder Rock* 42. *Desert Victory* (Roy) 44. Burma Victory (Roy) 45. *Journey Together* (John) 45. *Fame is the Spur* 46. *Brighton Rock* 46. *The Guinea Pig* 49. *Seven Days to Noon* 50. The Magic Box 51. High Treason (Roy) 52. Sailor of the King (Roy) 53. Seagulls Over Sorrento 54. Josephine and Men 54. *Private's Progress* 55. *Brothers in Law* 56. Run for the Sun (Roy) 56. *Lucky Jim* 57. Happy is the Bride 57. Carlton Browne of the F.O. 58. *I'm All Right Jack* 59. Suspect 60. A French Mistress 61. *Heavens Above* 63. Rotten to the Core 65. The Family Way 66. Twisted Nerve 68. There's a Girl in My Soup (John) 70. Endless Night 72. Soft Beds and Hard Battles (Roy) 73.

Boulton, David (–). British cinematographer.
The Password is Courage 62. The Haunting 63. Children of the Damned 65. The Secret of My Success 65. It 66. The Great Waltz 72, etc.

Bourgignon, Serge (1928–). French director of style but little substance.
Sundays and Cybele (AA) 62. The Reward 65. Two Weeks in September 67. The Picasso Summer 69.

Bourvil (1917–1970) (André Raimbourg). Diminutive, expressive French comic actor.
La Ferme du Pendu 45. Mr Peek-a-boo 51. *La Traversée de Paris* 56. The Mirror has Two Faces 58. The Green Mare's Nest 69. Tout l'Or du Monde 62. Heaven Sent 63. The Secret Agents 65. The Big Spree 66. *The Sucker* 66.

Don't Look Now 67. The Brain 68. Monte Carlo or Bust 69. The Red Circle 70, many others.

Bow, Clara (1905–1965). American leading lady, the 'It' girl of the twenties: her films depicted the gay young flapper generation and her wide-eyed vivacity was tremendously popular for a time, but she came to grief through trying to parallel her screen image in her private life.
Down to the Sea in Ships 23. Black Oxen 24. Kiss Me Again 25. Dancing Mothers 26. *Mantrap* 26. The Plastic Age 26. Kid Boots 26. *It* 27. Children of Divorce 27. Rough House Rosie 27. Wings 27. Get Your Man 27. Ladies of the Mob 28. The Fleet's In 28. The Wild Party 29. Dangerous Curves 29. The Saturday Night Kid 29. True to the Navy 30. Her Wedding Night 30. Kick In 31. Call Her Savage 32. Hoopla 33, etc.

Bower, Dallas (1907–). British producer. Originally sound recordist, editor and writer, he became director of BBC TV 1936–1939, supervisor of Ministry of Information film production 1940–42. Associate producer *As You Like It* 36, *Henry V* 44, etc.; produced *Sir Lancelot*, TV series. As director: Alice in Wonderland (Fr.) 50. The Second Mrs Tanqueray 52. Doorway to Suspicion 57.

Bowers, William (1916–). American screenwriter.
My Favorite Spy 42. Night and Day 46. *The Web* 47. Black Bart 48. Larceny 48. *The Gunfighter* 50. Cry Danger 51. *The Mob* 51. Split Second 53. *Five Against the House* 55. The Best Things in Life are Free 56. *The Sheepman* 58. Alias Jesse James 59. *The Last Time I Saw Archie* 61. Advance to the Rear 64. *Support Your Local Sheriff* 69, etc.

The Bowery (US 1933). Wallace Beery and George Raft are the brawling but good-natured protagonists of this rumbustious comedy-melodrama which marked Hollywood's breakaway forever from the static early talkie style. Raoul Walsh's direction abounds in vigour, the screenplay by Howard Estabrook and James Gleason is crisply funny, and the whole production brings to vivid life the teeming side-streets of New York at the turn of the century. It was the first production of Darryl Zanuck's Twentieth Century company, which the following year merged with Fox.

The Bowery Boys. From the original Dead End Kids, one splinter group became known as the Little Tough Guys, another as the East Side

Kids, and yet another as the Bowery Boys (but there is overlapping). The Bowery Boys were led by Leo Gorcey and Huntz Hall; following their zany commands were Bernard Gorcey, David Gorcey, Billy Benedict, Gabriel Dell and Bobby Jordan. Between 1946 and 1948, when most of the comic young hoodlums were actually well into their forties, they made forty-eight low-budget features, at first using fairly realistic themes but later straying into fantasy. Their appeal was based on puns and slapstick, and although the films were basically quite awful they have retained a certain nostalgia. See *Dead End*.

Bowie, Jim (1796–1836). American folk hero who invented the Bowie knife and died at the Alamo. He was played in *The Iron Mistress* by Alan Ladd, in *The Last Command* by Sterling Hayden, in *The First Texan* by Jeff Morrow, in *Davy Crockett* by Kenneth Tobey, in *Man of Conquest* by Robert Armstrong, in *Comanche Territory* by Macdonald Carey, and in *The Alamo* by Richard Widmark. A TV series called *The Adventures of Jim Bowie* 60 starred Scott Forbes.

Bowman, Lee (1910–). Well-groomed American light leading man with stage experience; found a desultory career in films.
Three Men in White 36. *I Met Him in Paris* 37. Love Affair 39. Miracles for Sale 39. Florian 40. Buck Privates 41. *Kid Glove Killer* 42. Three Hearts for Julia 43. Cover Girl 44. *The Impatient Years* 44. Tonight and Every Night 45. The Walls Came Tumbling Down 46. Smash-Up 47. The House by the River 50. Double Barrel Miracle 55. Youngblood Hawke 64, etc.
TV series: Ellery Queen 60.

Box, Betty E. (1920–). British producer, sister of Sydney Box and once assistant to him. For many years she turned out comedies and dramas with box office appeal but little cinematic flavour, usually in association with director Ralph Thomas.
Miranda 48. Here Come the Huggetts 49. *Doctor in the House* 53. The Iron Petticoat 56. A Tale of Two Cities 58. The Thirty-nine Steps 59. No Love for Johnnie 61. A Pair of Briefs 63. No My Darling Daughters 63. The High Bright Sun 65. Deadlier than the Male 66. The High Commissioner 68. Percy 70. The Love Ban 72. Percy's Progress 74, many others.

Box, John (1920–). British production designer.
Lawrence of Arabia (AA) 62. *Doctor Zhivago* (AA) 65. *A Man For All Seasons* 66. *Oliver* (AA) 68. The Looking Glass War (p only) 69. *Nicholas*

and Alexandra (AA) 71. Travels with my Aunt 73. Rollerball 74, etc.

Box, Muriel (1905–). British writer-producer-director, wife of Sydney Box.
The Seventh Veil (w) 46. The Years Between (w) 47. The Man Within (wp) 47. *The Brothers* (w) 48. Dear Murderer (wp) 48. A Girl in a Million (wp) 50. The Happy Family (wd) 52. The Beachcomber (wd) 54. To Dorothy a Son (d) 54. The Truth about Women (pd) 57. Rattle of a Simple Man (d) 64, etc.

Box, Sydney (1907–). British writer-producer who had considerable success in the decade after World War II.
The Seventh Veil 46. The Years Between 47. *Holiday Camp* 47. Jassy 47. *The Brothers* 48. Dear Murderer 48. *Quartet* 48. Don't Take it to Heart (p only) 48. Broken Journey 48. Daybreak 49. A Girl in a Million 50. So Long at the Fair (p only) 51. *The Prisoner* 55, etc.

boxing. Actual prizefighters whose lives have been fictionalized on film include Jim Corbett (Errol Flynn in *Gentleman Jim*), John L. Sullivan (Greg McClure in *The Great John L*), Joe Louis (Coley Wallace in *The Joe Louis Story*), Rocky Graziano (Paul Newman in *Somebody Up There Likes Me*), and Jack Johnson (James Earl Jones in *The Great White Hope*). Purely fictional boxing films have tended to emphasize the corruption of the fight game: *The Ring, The Square Ring, The Square Jungle, Iron Man, Kid Galahad, Kid Nightingale, The Champ, The Crowd Roars, Body and Soul, The Set Up, Champion, Golden Boy, No Way Back, The Good Die Young, Run With the Wind, The Harder They Fall*, and from Europe *Fists in the Pocket* and *Boxer*. Boxing comedy is rare once one discounts the Joe Palooka series, but most comedians have taken part in boxing sequences: Abbott and Costello in *Meet the Invisible Man*, Harold Lloyd in *The Milky Way*, Danny Kaye in *The Kid from Brooklyn*, Chaplin in *The Champion*, etc. The only boxing fantasy was *Here Comes Mr Jordan*, in which Robert Montgomery's soul was transferred into that of a prizefighter.

Boyd, Stephen (1928–) (William Millar). Irish leading man in international films; fairly popular during the sixties.
□ An Alligator Named Daisy 55. A Hill in Korea 56. *The Man Who Never Was* (as the German spy) 56. Seven Waves Away 57. Island in the Sun 57. Seven Thunders 57. Heaven Fell that Night 57. The Bravados 58. *Ben Hur* (as Messala) 59. Woman Obsessed 59. The Best of Everything 59.

The Big Gamble 61. The Inspector 62. Jumbo 62. Imperial Venus 63. *The Fall of the Roman Empire* 64. The Third Secret 64. Genghis Khan 64. The Oscar 66. Fantastic Voyage 66. The Bible 66. The Caper of the Golden Bulls 67. Assignment K 68. Shalako 68. Slaves 69. Carter's Army (TV) 71. The Hands of Cormac Joyce (TV) 71. The Man Called Noon 73. The Squeeze 77.

Boyd, William (1895–1972). Unassuming American leading man, in films from 1919, internationally famous from 1934 as cowboy hero Hopalong Cassidy, in which guise he made scores of second features and TV episodes.
Why Change your Wife? 19. The Temple of Venus 23. Changing Husbands 24. The Volga Boatmen 26. King of Kings 27. *Two Arabian Knights* 27. Skyscraper 28. The Leatherneck 29. The Benson Murder Case 30. The Spoilers 30. The Painted Desert 31. Murder by the Clock 31. Lucky Devils 33. Port of Lost Dreams 34. *Hopalong Cassidy* 35, many others but all subsequent films as Cassidy; last in 1948.

Boyd, William 'Stage' (1890–1935). American stage actor, so known to distinguish him from his Hopalong Cassidy namesake.
Sky Devils 32. Painted Woman 32. *Oliver Twist* (as Sikes) 33, etc.

Boyer, Charles (1899–). Gentlemanly French romantic actor in international films: went to Hollywood first in 1929, and later gained a reputation as the screen's 'great lover'.
☐ L'Homme du Large 20. Chantelouve 21. Le Grillon du Foyer 22. L'Esclave 23. La Ronde Infernale 27. Le Capitain Fracasse 27. *La Barcarolle d'Amour* 28. Le Procès de Mary Dugan 28. The Big House (French version) 30. The Magnificent Lie 31. Tumultes 31. *Redheaded Woman* 32. The Man from Yesterday 32. F.P.I. (French version) 32. The Only Girl 33. L'Impervier 33. The Battle (as a Japanese) 34. *Caravan* 34. Liliom 35. Private Worlds 35. Break of Hearts 35. Shanghai 35. Le Bonheur 36. *The Garden of Allah* 36. *Mayerling* 37. *Tovarich* 37. *Conquest* (as Napoleon) 37. *History is Made at Night* 37. *Algiers* 38. Orage 38. *Love Affair* 39. When Tomorrow Comes 39. Le Corsaire 39. *All This and Heaven Too* 40. Les Amoureux 40. Back Street 41. *Hold Back the Dawn* 41. Appointment for Love 41. Tales of Manhattan 42. The Constant Nymph 43. Flesh and Fantasy (& p) 43. *Gaslight* 44. Confidential Agent 45. Together Again 45. Cluny Brown 46. Arch of Triumph 48. A Woman's Vengeance 48. The Thirteenth Letter 51. The First Legion 52. *The Happy Time* 52. Thunder in the East 53.

Madame de . . . 53. The Cobweb 55. Lucky to Be a Woman 55. Paris Palace Hotel 56. Nana 56. Around the World in Eighty Days 56. La Parisienne 58. The Buccaneer 58. Maxime 62. *Fanny* 62. The Four Horsemen of the Apocalypse 62. Les Démons de Minuit 62. Love is a Ball 63. Adorable Julia 64. *A Very Special Favour* 64. How to Steal a Million 66. Is Paris Burning? 66. Casino Royale 67. *Barefoot in the Park* 68. The April Fools 69. The Madwoman of Chaillot 69. The Day the Hot Line got Hot 69. Lost Horizon 73. Stavisky 74.
TV series: *Four Star Theatre* 56. *The Rogues* 64.

Boyle, Catherine (1929–) (Caterina di Francavilla). Winsome Italian-English TV personality who has made a few film appearances.
Now Wanted on Voyage 52. Intent to Kill 56. The Truth About Women 57, etc.

Boyle, Peter (1933–). Rotund American character actor of the early seventies.
Joe 69. T. R. Baskin 71. Steelyard Blues 71. Dime Box 72. Slither 72. The Candidate 72. The Friends of Eddie Coyle 73. Kid Blue 73. Crazy Joe 74. *Young Frankenstein* (as the monster) 75, etc.

Boyle, Robert (–). American production designer.
The Thrill of it All 63. The Birds 63. Marnie 64. The Russians are Coming, The Russians are Coming 66. How to Succeed in Business 67. In Cold Blood 67. The Thomas Crown Affair 68. Gaily Gaily 69. The Landlord 70. The Fiddler on the Roof 71. Portnoy's Complaint 72, etc.

Boys' Town (US 1938). MGM's highly successful sentimentalized biography of Father Flanagan and his work among juvenile semi-delinquents. Set the Hollywood fashion in boys and priests for years. Spencer Tracy (AA) and Mickey Rooney starred; Norman Taurog directed. The sequel, *Men of Boys Town*, was less interesting.

Bozzuffi, Marcel (1937–). Balding French character actor.
Z 69. The American 69. The Lady in the Car 70. The French Connection 71. Images 72. Nightmare for a Killer 72, etc.

Brabin, Charles (1883–1957). British film director who made a career in Hollywood but retired early.
Stella Maris 18. *So Big* 23. Twinkletoes 26. Hard Boiled Haggerty 27. The Bridge of San Luis Rey 29. Call of the Flesh 30. Sporting Blood 31. Beast

of the City 32. *The Mask of Fu Manchu* 32.
Stage Mother 33. A Wicked Woman 34, many
others.

Brabourne, John (1924–) (Lord Brabourne).
British producer, in films from 1950.
Harry Black 58. Sink the Bismarck 60. HMS
Defiant 62. The Mikado 66. Tales of Beatrix
Potter 71. Murder on the Orient Express 74, etc.

Bracken, Eddie (1920–). American comic
actor, popular in the forties as the nervous
hayseed type; made his best films for Preston
Sturges. Later found stage success.
□ Too Many Girls 40. Life with Henry 41.
Reaching for the Sun 41. Caught in the Draft 41.
Sweater Girl 42. The Fleet's In 42. Star Spangled
Rhythm 42. Happy Go Lucky 43. Young and
Willing 43. *The Miracle of Morgan's Creek* 43.
Hail the Conquering Hero 44. Rainbow Island
44. Out of This World 45. Bring on the Girls 45.
Duffy's Tavern 45. Hold That Blonde 45. Ladies'
Man 47. Fun on a Weekend 47. The Girl from
Jones Beach 49. Summer Stock 50. Two Tickets
to Broadway 51. We're Not Married 52. About
Face 52. A Slight Case of Larceny 53.

Brackett, Charles (1892–1969). American
writer-producer, of generally sophisticated
material; enjoyed long association with Billy
Wilder.
Tomorrow's Love (oa) 25. Pointed Heels (oa) 29.
Secrets of a Secretary (oa) 31. Enter Madame (w)
35. Piccadilly Jim (w) 36. Bluebeard's Eighth
Wife (w) 38. Midnight (w) 39. Ninotchka (w) 39.
Arise My Love (w) 40. Hold Back the Dawn (w)
41. The Major and the Minor (w) 42. *Five Graves
to Cairo* (wp) 43. *The Uninvited* (p) 43. *Double
Indemnity* (wp) 44. *The Lost Weekend* (wp)
(ΛΛ) 45. To Each His Own (wp) 46. *A Foreign
Affair* (wp) 48. *Sunset Boulevard* (wp) (AA) 50.
Niagara (wp) 52. Titanic (wp) 52. Woman's
World (p) 54. The King and I (p) 56. Ten North
Frederick (wp) 58. Journey to the Centre of the
Earth (wp) 59. State Fair (p) 61, many others.

Brackett, Leigh (–). American
screenwriter.
The Big Sleep 46. Rio Bravo 59. 13 West Street
62. Hatari 62. El Dorado 67, etc.

Bradbury, Ray (1920–). American science
fiction writer who has dabbled in films.
It Came from Outer Space (oa) 53. The Beast
from 20,000 Fathoms (oa) 54. Moby Dick (w)
56. Fahrenheit 451 (oa) 66. The Illustrated Man
(oa) 69, etc.

Braden, Bernard (1916–). Canadian TV

personality, in Britain since 1938. Occasional
film appearances. Long married to Barbara
Kelly.
Love in Pawn 52. The Full Treatment 61. The
Day the Earth Caught Fire 62. The War Lover
63, etc.

Bradley, David (1919–). American director
who showed promise as an amateur but never
seemed to make it professionally.
□ Peer Gynt 41. Julius Caesar 50. Talk About a
Stranger 52. Dragstrip Riot 58. Twelve to the
Moon 60. Madmen of Mandoras 64.

Bradna, Olympe (1920–). Slightly-built
American leading lady of the late thirties, former
circus bareback rider.
Three Cheers for Love 36. Souls at Sea 37. Last
Train from Madrid 37. Say It in French 38. Night
of Nights 39. South of Pago Pago 40. The
Knockout 41. International Squadron 41, etc.

Brady, Alice (1892–1939). American stage
actress who in her last few years made many
films, either as a fluttery society matron or as a
drab housewife.
□ La Bohème 16. Bought and Paid for 16. Betsy
Ross 17. Woman and Wife 18. A Dark Lantern
19. The Fear Market 19. The Snow Bride 23.
When Ladies Meet 33. Broadway to Hollywood
33. Beauty for Sale 33. Stage Mother 33. Should
Ladies Behave? 33. Miss Fane's Baby is Stolen
34. *The Gay Divorcee* 34. Let 'Em Have It 34.
Gold Diggers of 1935 35. Lady Tubbs 35.
Metropolitan 35. The Harvester 35. *My Man
Godfrey* 36. Go West Young Man 36. Mind Your
Own Business 36. *Three Smart Girls* 37. Call It a
Day 37. Mama Steps Out 37. Mr Dodd Takes
the Air 37. One Hundred Men and a Girl 37.
Merry Go Round of 1938. *In Old Chicago* (AA)
38. Joy of Living 38. Goodbye Broadway 38.
Zenobia 39. *Young Mr Lincoln* 39.

Brady, Scott (1924–) (Gerald Tierney).
Tough-looking American leading man of the
fifties, brother of Lawrence Tierney.
Canon City 48. He Walked by Night 48. Port of
New York 49. Undercover Girl 50. Kansas
Raiders 51. *The Model and the Marriage Broker*
52. Perilous Journey 53. Johnny Guitar 54.
Gentlemen Marry Brunettes 55. Mohawk 56.
The Maverick Queen 56. They Were So Young
58. Battle Flame 59. Black Spurs 65. Castle of
Evil 66. Red Tomahawk 67. Doctors' Wives 70.
Nightmare in Wax 70. Dollars 71, many others.

Braeden, Eric (–) (Hans Gudegast).
German general purpose actor in international
films.

Colossus of Rhodes 57. The Law and Jake Wade 59. Escape from the Planet of the Apes 70, etc.

Brahm, John (1893–) (Hans Brahm). German director who in the thirties moved first to Britain, then to Hollywood. Films generally competent, but routine.
□ ENGLISH-SPEAKING FILMS: Scrooge 35. The Last Journey 35. *Broken Blossoms* (British remake) 36. Counsel for Crime 37. Penitentiary 38. Girls' School 38. Let Us Live 39. Rio 39. *Escape to Glory* 40. Wild Geese Calling 41. *The Undying Monster* 42. Tonight We Raid Calais 42. Wintertime 43. The Lodger 44. Hangover Square 44. Guest in the House 44. The Locket 46. *The Brasher Doubloon* 47. Singapore 47. The Thief of Venice 51. Face to Face 52. The Miracle of Fatima 52. The Diamond Queen 53. The Mad Magican 54. Special Delivery 55. Bengazi 55. Hot Rods to Hell 67.

Brakhage, Stan (1933–). American underground film-maker.
Flesh of Morning 56. Dog Star Man 64, etc.

Brambell, Wilfrid (1912–). British character actor, specializing in grotesques. Celebrated on TV as old Steptoe in *Steptoe and Son* (64–74); film appearances usually cameos. Autobiography 1976: *All Above Board*.
Another Shore 48. Dry Rot 56. Serious Charge 58. What a Whopper 61. *In Search of the Castaways* 62. The Three Lives of Thomasina 64. *A Hard Day's Night* 64. Crooks in Cloisters 64. Where the Bullets Fly 66. Witchfinder General 68, etc.

Bramble, A. V. (c. 1880–1963). British director, former actor.
Fatal Fingers 16. Wuthering Heights 18. Shooting Stars (p & co-d) 28. The Will 39. An Outcast of the Islands (a only) 51, etc.

Branch, Sarah (1938–). British leading lady of the early sixties.
Sands of the Desert 60. Hell is a City 61. Sword of Sherwood Forest 61, etc.

Brand, Max (1892–1944) (Frederick Faust). American popular novelist whose major bequests to Hollywood were *Destry Rides Again* and the Dr Kildare books. Killed in action as a war correspondent.

Brand, Neville (1920–). Thickset American actor with stage and TV experience; often seen as Red Indian or gangster. In films from 1948 after ten years in the US Army: he was the fourth most decorated soldier.

D.O.A. 49. Halls of Montezuma 51. Stalag 17 53. *Riot in Cell Block Eleven* 54. Mohawk 55. The Tin Star 57. Cry Terror 58. Five Gates to Hell 59. *The Scarface Mob* (as Al Capone) 60. Huckleberry Finn 60. Birdman of Alcatraz 62. That Darn Cat 65. The Desperados 69. The Train Robbers 73. Scalawag 74, many others. TV series: Laredo 65–67.

Brando, Jocelyn (1919–). American character actress, sister of Marlon Brando; film appearances rare.
The Big Heat 53. China Venture 53. Nightfall 56. The Explosive Generation 61. The Ugly American 63. Bus Riley's Back in Town 65. The Chase 66, etc.

Brando, Marlon (1924–). Unsmiling American leading actor whose prototype is the primitive modern male; he has however attempted a wide range of parts which have not always suited his 'method' technique and mumbling accent.
□ *The Men* 50. *A Streetcar Named Desire* 51. *Viva Zapata* (BFA) 52. *Julius Caesar* (as Mark Antony) (BFA) 53. *The Wild One* 53. On the Waterfront (AA. BFA) 54. Desirée (as Napoleon) 54. Guys and Dolls 55. *The Teahouse of the August Moon* 56. Sayonara 57. *The Young Lions* 58. The Fugitive Kind 60. One Eyed Jacks (also directed) 60. Mutiny on the Bounty (as Fletcher Christian) 62. The Ugly American 63. Bedtime Story 64. The Saboteur 65. *The Chase* 66. The Appaloosa 66. A Countess from Hong Kong 67. Reflections in a Golden Eye 67. Candy 68. The Night of the Following Day 68. Queimada 70. The Nightcomers 71. *The Godfather* (AA) 72. *Last Tango in Paris* 73. The Missouri Breaks 76.

Brandon, Henry (1910–) (Henry Kleinbach). American character actor, a reliable menace for thirty years.
Babes in Toyland (as Barnaby) 34. The Garden of Allah 36. I Promise to Pay 37. Son of Monte Cristo 40. Edge of Darkness 43. Canon City 48. Scarlet Angel 52. Scared Stiff 53. Vera Cruz 54. The Searchers 56. The Buccaneer 58. Two Rode Together 61, many others.

Brasselle, Keefe (1923–). American light leading man who later dabbled in TV production.
Fairy Tale Murder 45. Not Wanted 49. A Place in the Sun 51. Bannerline 51. Skirts Ahoy 52. *The Eddie Cantor Story* (title role) 53. Three Young Texans 54. Mad at the World 55. Battle Stations 56, etc.

Brasseur, Pierre (1903–1972). Distinguished

French stage actor in occasional films from 1925.

Claudine à l'École 28. Café de Paris 33. *Quai des Brumes* 38. Lumière d'Été 42. *Les Enfants du Paradis* 44. Les Portes de la Nuit 46. Julie de Carneilhan 50. Bluebeard 51. Porte des Lilas 55. Eyes without a Face 59. Il Bell' Antonio 60. Deux Heures à Tuer 65. A New World 66. Birds in Peru 68, etc.

Bray, Robert (1917–). American actor of the strong silent type.
Blood on the Moon 48. Warpath 52. Bus Stop 56. The Wayward Bus 57. My Gun is Quick (as Mike Hammer) 58. Never So Few 60, etc.
TV series: Man from Blackhawk 54. Stagecoach West 60. Lassie 67-68.

Brazzi, Rossano (1916–). Handsome Italian romantic lead who apart from local work appeared in some successful international films.
Little Women 49. *Three Coins in the Fountain* 54. The Barefoot Contessa 54. *Summertime* 55. The Story of Esther Costello 57. Legend of the Lost 57. *South Pacific* 58. A Certain Smile 58. Count Your Blessings 59. The Light in the Piazza 62. The Battle of the Villa Fiorita 65. The Christmas that Almost Wasn't (& d) 66. The Bobo 67. Krakatoa 68. The Italian Job 69. Psychout for Murder 70. The Great Waltz 72. Master of Love 74, etc.

break figure. A specified amount of takings after which an exhibitor pays a greater percentage to the renter. For the protection of both parties many contracts are on a sliding scale, with the exhibitor paying anything from 25% to 50% of the gross according to the business he does.

breakaway furniture is specially constructed from balsa wood for those spectacular saloon brawls in which so much damage is apparently done to stars and stunt men.

Breakston, George (1922–1973). American who, born in France, went to Hollywood as a child and acted for several years; later went to Africa and produced many routine adventure films and TV series, usually with British backing.
AS ACTOR: Great Expectations 34. Mrs Wiggs of the Cabbage Patch 34. The Dark Angel 35. Love Finds Andy Hardy 38. Jesse James 35. The Courtship of Andy Hardy 42, etc.
AS PRODUCER: Urubu 48, Tokyo File 212 51. The Scarlet Spear (& d) 54. Golden Ivory 55. Escape in the Sun 56. Woman and the Hunter 57. Shadow of Treason (& d) 63. The Boy Cried Murder (& d) 66, etc.

Breathless (À Bout de Souffle) (France 1959). The first film of Jean-Luc Godard, with François Truffaut's story providing a somewhat less anarchic narrative than one finds in Godard's later solo efforts. In the vanguard of the 'new wave', it had an improvised plot apparently dedicated to the proposition that life is just one damned thing after another with death as the end; superficially it was about a small-time gangster's busy life with pauses for sex. Dedicated to Monogram Pictures. With Jean-Paul Belmondo, Jean Seberg.

Brecher, Irving (1914–). American radio writer who moved on to Hollywood and received solo credit for two Marx Brothers scripts.
New Faces of 1937 37. At the Circus 39. Go West 40. Shadow of the Thin Man 41. Dubarry was a Lady 53. *Meet Me in St Louis* 44. Yolanda and the Thief 45. Summer Holiday 47. The Life of Riley (& pd) 49. Somebody Loves Me (& d) 52. Cry for Happy 61. Sail a Crooked Ship (& d) 61. Bye Bye Birdie 63, etc.
TV series: The People's Choice.

Brecht, Bertolt (1898–1956). German poet and playwright whose 'alienation method' (by which audiences are forced by various theatrical devices to remember that they are watching a play) has been influential on films from *Citizen Kane* to *Alfie*. His *Dreigroschenoper*, based on *The Beggar's Opera*, has been filmed twice.

Breck, Peter (1930–). American general purpose actor. From TV's *The Big Valley*.
A Man for Hanging 72. Benji 74, etc.

Breen, Bobby (1927–). American boy singer of the thirties; later gave up films for night club work.
Let's Sing Again 36. Rainbow on the River 36. Make a Wish 37. Hawaii Calls 37. Breaking the Ice 38. Fisherman's Wharf 39. Way Down South 39. Johnny Doughboy 43, etc.

Breen, Joseph (1890–1965). American executive, for many years administrator of the Production Code. (See *censorship*.)

Breen, Richard L. (1919–1967). American scenarist. Former president of Screenwriters' Guild.
A Foreign Affair (co-author) 48. Miss Tatlock's Millions 49. The Model and the Marriage Broker 51. Niagara 53. Titanic (AA) 53. Dragnet 54. Pete Kelly's Blues 55. Stopover Tokyo (& d) 57. Wake Me When It's Over 60. Captain Newman 63. Do Not Disturb 65. Tony Rome 67, many others.

Bremer, Lucille (1922–). American dancer. MGM groomed her for stardom in the forties, but her career was brief.
□ Meet Me in St Louis 44. *Yolanda and the Thief* 45. *Ziegfeld Follies* 45. Till the Clouds Roll By 46. Dark Delusion 47. Adventures of Casanova 48. Ruthless 48. Behind Locked Doors 48.

Brendel, El (1891–1964). Mild-mannered American comic actor, a fake Swede from vaudeville with an attractive way of fracturing the English language.
The Campus Flirt 26. Wings 27. *Sunny Side Up* 29. The Big Trail 30. Just Imagine 30. Mr Lemon of Orange 30. Delicious 31. Hot Pepper 32. My Lips Betray 33. God's Country and the Woman 37. Little Miss Broadway 38. *If I Had My Way* 40. Captain Caution 40. Machine Gun Mama 44. The Beautiful Blonde from Bashful Bend 49. The She Creature 56, many others.

Brennan, Michael (1912–). 'Tough guy' British supporting actor, in films from 1932.
The Clouded Yellow 50. Ivanhoe 52. Trouble in Store 56. The Day They Robbed the Bank of England 60. Thunderball 65. Lust for a Vampire 70, many others.

Brennan, Walter (1894–1974). Popular American character actor who played toothless old men in his thirties, and was still a star in his seventies. Best remembered as a countrified wit, he also played villains and city slickers.
□ The Long Long Trail 29. The Shannons of Broadway 29. Smiling Guns 29. King of Jazz 30. One Hysterical Night 30. Dancing Dynamite 31. Neck and Neck 31. Law and Order 32. Texas Cyclone 32. Two Fisted Law 32. All American 32. Parachute Jumper 32. Man of Action 33. Fighting for Justice 33. Sing Sinner Sing 33. Strange People 33. Silent Men 33. One Year Later 33. Good Dame 34. Half a Sinner 34. Northern Frontier 35. The Wedding Night 35. Bride of Frankenstein 35. Lady Tubbs 35. Man on the Flying Trapeze 35. Metropolitan 35. Barbary Coast 35. Seven Keys to Baldpate 35. These Three 36. Three Godfathers 36. The Moon's Our Home 36. Fury 36. The Prescott Kid 36. *Come and Get It* (AA). 36. Banjo on my Knee 36. She's Dangerous 36. When Love is Young 37. The Affair of Cappy Ricks 37. Wild and Woolly 37. *The Adventures of Tom Sawyer* 38. The Buccaneer 38. The Texans 38. Mother Carey's Chickens 38. *Kentucky* (AA) 38. The Cowboy and the Lady 38. The Story of Vernon and Irene Castle 38. They Shall Have Music 39. *Stanley and Livingstone* 39. Joe and Ethel Turp Call on the President 39. Northwest Passage 40. Maryland 40. *The Westerner* (AA: as Judge Roy

Bean) 40. This Woman is Mine 41. Nice Girl 41. *Meet John Doe* 41. *Sergeant York* 41. *Swamp Water* 41. Rise and Shine 41. Pride of the Yankees 42. Stand By for Action 42. Slightly Dangerous 43. Hangmen also Die 43. North Star 43. Home in Indiana 43. *To Have and Have Not* 44. The Princess and the Pirate 44. Dakota 45. A Stolen Life 46. Centennial Summer 46. Nobody Lives Forever 46. *My Darling Clementine* (as old Clanton) 46. Driftwood 47. Scudda Hoo Scudda Hay 48. Red River 48. Blood on the Moon 48. The Green Promise 49. The Great Dan Patch 49. Brimstone 49. Task Force 49. Singing Guns 50. A Ticket to Tomahawk 50. Curtain Call at Cactus Crick 50. The Showdown 50. Surrender 50. Best of the Bad Men 51. Along the Great Divide 51. The Wild Blue Yonder 51. Return of the Texan 52. Lure of the Wilderness 52. Sea of Lost Ships 53. Drums Across the River 54. Four Guns to the Border 54. Bad Day at Black Rock 55. *Come Next Spring* 56. Glory 56. Goodbye My Lady 56. The Proud Ones 56. Tammy and the Bachelor 57. The Way to the Gold 57. God is my Partner 57. *Rio Bravo* 59. How the West was Won 62. Those Calloways 64. The Oscar 66. *Who's Minding 'the Mint?* 67. The Gnome-mobile 67. The One and Only Genuine Original Family Band 67. Support Your Local Sheriff 69. The Over the Hill Gang (TV) 70. The Over the Hill Gang Rides Again (TV) 71. Smoke in the Wind 71. Home for the Holidays (TV) 72.
TV series: *The Real McCoys* 57–63. Tycoon 64. *The Guns of Will Sonnett* 67–68. To Rome with Love 69.

Brenner, Jules (–). American cinematographer. Johnny Got His Gun 71. The Glass House (TV) 72. Dillinger 73. Posse 75, etc.

Brenon, Herbert (1880–1958). Irish director, in Hollywood after stage experience: a big name of the twenties.
Ivanhoe 13. The Kreuzer Sonata 15. War Brides 16. The Passing of the Third Floor Back 18. The Sign on the Door 21. The Spanish Dancer 23. *Peter Pan* 24. A Kiss for Cinderella 24. *Beau Geste* 26. *Sorrell and Son* (GB) 27. The Great Gatsby 27. Laugh Clown Laugh 28. The Rescue 29. Beau Ideal 29. Oliver Twist 33. Wine Women and Song 34. The Housemaster (GB) 38. At the Villa Rose (GB) 38. Yellow Sands (GB) 38. The Flying Squadron (GB) 40, etc.

Brent, Eve (1930–). American leading lady who played Jane in *Tarzan's Fight for Life* 55. *Tarzan and the Trappers* 57.

Brent, Evelyn (1899–1975) (Mary Elizabeth Riggs). American leading lady of the silent era;

made a few talkies, then retired apart from some bit parts in the forties.
The Other Man's Wife 19. The Shuttle of Life (GB) 20. Sybil (GB) 21. Married to a Mormon (GB) 22. Silk Stocking Sal 24. Smooth as Satin 25. Love 'Em and Leave 'Em 26. Queen of Diamonds 26. *Underworld* 27. Beau Sabreur 28. A Night of Mystery 28. The Mating Call 28. *Broadway* 29. *Slightly Scarlet* 30. Madonna of the Streets 30. The Pagan Lady 31. The World Gone Mad 33. Home on the Range 35. Night Club Scandal 37. Mr Wong Detective 38. The Mad Empress 40. The Seventh Victim 43. Bowery Champs 44. The Golden Eye 48, many others.

Brent, George (1904–) (George Brent Nolan). Irishman who went to Hollywood and after years as a tough hero developed into a light leading man very effective against strong actresses such as Bette Davis and Myrna Loy.
□ SOUND FILMS: Under Suspicion 30. Lightning Warrior 31. Homicide Squad 31. Once a Sinner 31. Fair Warning 31. Charlie Chan Carries On 31. Ex Bad Boy 31. So Big 32. The Rich Are Always With Us 32. Weekend Marriage 32. Miss Pinkerton 32. Purchase Price 32. The Crash 32. They Call it Sin 32. Luxury Liner 33. *Forty Second Street* 33. The Keyhole 33. Lilly Turner 33. Baby Face 33. Female 33. Stamboul Quest 34. Housewife 34. Desirable 34. *The Painted Veil* 34. Living on Velvet 35. Stranded 35. *Front Page Woman* 35. The Goose and the Gander 35. Special Agent 35. In Person 35. The Right to Live 35. Snowed Under 36. The Golden Arrow 36. The Case Against Mrs Ames 36. Give My Your Heart 36. More than a Secretary 37. God's Country and the Woman 37. The Go-getter 37. Mountain Justice 37. Gold is Where you Find It 37. Submarine D-1 37. *Jezebel* 38. Racket Busters 38. Secrets of an Actress 38. Wings of the Navy 39. *Dark Victory* 39. The Old Maid 39. *The Rains Came* 39. The Man who Talked Too Much 40. Till We Meet Again 40. The Fighting 69th 40. South of Suez 40. Honeymoon for Three 41. *The Great Lie* 41. They Dare Not Love 41. International Lady 41. Twin Beds 42. The Gay Sisters 42. In This Our Life 42. You Can't Escape Forever 42. Silver Queen 42. Experiment Perilous 44. *The Affairs of Susan* 45. My Reputation 45. *The Spiral Staircase* 45. Tomorrow is Forever 46. Lover Come Back 46. Temptation 46. Slave Girl 47. Out of the Blue 47. The Corpse Came COD 47. Christmas Eve 47. Luxury Liner 48. Angel on the Amazon 48. Red Canyon 49. Illegal Entry 49. Kid from Cleveland 49. Bride for Sale 49. FBI Girl 51. The Dark Page (GB) 51. Montana Belle 52. Tangier Incident 53.

Brent, Romney (1902–1976) (Romulo Larralde). Dapper Mexican actor in British films in the thirties, later elsewhere.
East Meets West 36. Dreaming Lips 37. School for Husbands 37. Under the Red Robe 37. Dinner at the Ritz (& w) 37. Let George Do It 40. The Adventures of Don Juan 48. The Virgin Queen 55. Don't Go Near the Water 57. The Sign of Zorro 58, etc.

Breon, Edmund (1882–1951) (Edmund McLaverty). Beaming, monocled British stage actor, often seen as amiable bumbler. In Hollywood from late twenties, Britain 1933–42.
The Dawn Patrol 30. I Like your Nerve 31. *Three Men in a Boat* 33. No Funny Business 33. The Scarlet Pimpernel 35. Keep Fit 37. A Yank at Oxford 38. Goodbye Mr Chips 39. The Outsider 39. She Shall Have Music 42. Gaslight 44. Casanova Brown 44. *The Woman in the Window* 45. *Dressed To Kill* 46. Forever Amber 47. Enchantment 48. Challenge to Lassie 50. At Sword's Point 51, etc.

Bresler, Jerry (1912–). American independent producer.
Main Street after Dark 44. Bewitched 45. The Web 47. *Another Part of the Forest* 48. The Flying Missile 50. The Mob 51. Assignment Paris 52. Lizzie 57. *The Vikings* 58. Gidget Goes Hawaiian 61. Diamond Head 63. Major Dundee 65. Pussycat Pussycat I Love You 70, etc.

Bressart, Felix (1890–1949). German character actor in Hollywood from late thirties, usually in downtrodden comic roles; a genuine original.
Drei von der Tankstelle 31. Das Alte Lied 31. Nie Weider Liebe 32. Drei Tage Mittelarrest 33. Der Glückszylinder 34. *Ninotchka* 39. *The Shop Around the Corner* 40. Comrade X 40. Escape 40. Bitter Sweet 40. Blossoms in the Dust 41. *To Be or Not To Be* 42. Crossroads 42. Above Suspicion 43. The Seventh Cross 44. Without Love 45. I've Always Loved You 46. Her Sister's Secret 47. *A Song is Born* 48. *Portrait of Jennie* 48. Take One False Step 49.

Bresslaw, Bernard (1933–). British comic actor who sprang to fame as giant-sized dope in TV series *The Army Game* 55–58, but proved lacking in big screen star quality.
I Only Arsked 57. Too Many Crooks 58. The Ugly Duckling 59. Morgan 66. Carry on Screaming 66. Up Pompeii 70. Vampira 74. One of our Dinosaurs is Missing 76, many others in small roles.

Bresson, Robert (1907–). Elusive French

writer-director of austere, introspective, low-budget films.

☐ Les Anges du Péché 43. *Les Dames du Bois de Boulogne* 44. *Le Journal d'un Curé de Campagne* 50. Un Condamné à Mort s'est Echappé 56. Pickpocket 59. The Trial of Joan of Arc 62. Au Hazard Balthasar 66. Mouchette 67. Une Femme Douce 69. Quatre Nuits d'un Rêveur 71.

Bretherton, Howard (1896–1969). American director of second features.

Hills of Kentucky 27. The Redeeming Sin 29. Isle of Escape 30. The Match King 32. Ladies They Talk About 33. The Return of the Terror 34. The Leathernecks have Landed 36. It Happened out West 37. The Girl Who Dared 44. Prince of Thieves 48. Whip Law 50, many others.

Brett, Jeremy (1935–) (Jeremy Huggins) British light leading man.

War and Peace 56. The Wild and the Willing 61. The Very Edge 63. *My Fair Lady* 64, etc.

Brewster's Millions. This much-filmed comedy, about a man who inherits a vast legacy providing he can spend his first million in secret within twenty-four hours, began as a novel by George McCutcheon which was turned into a play by Winchell Smith and Byron Ongley, and was filmed in 1921 with Fatty Arbuckle, in 1935 with Jack Buchanan, in 1945 with Dennis O'Keefe, and in 1961 (as *Three on a Spree*) with Jack Watling.

Brialy, Jean-Claude (1933–). French leading man.

Éléna et les Hommes 56. Lift to the Scaffold 57. Le Beau Serge 58. The Four Hundred Blows 59. Tiré au Flanc 61. La Chambre Ardente 62. The Devil and Ten Commandments 62. La Ronde 64. Un Homme de Trop 67. King of Hearts 67. Le Rouge et le Noir 70. Claire's Knee 71, etc.

Brian, David (1914–). Stalwart American second lead, a former song-and-dance man who came to Hollywood in 1949 and sank into a groove of toughness and reliability, with a streak of villainy when required.

Flamingo Road 49. Beyond the Forest 49. *Intruder in the Dust* 49. The Damned Don't Cry 50. Breakthrough 50. Inside Straight 51. This Woman is Dangerous 52. Million Dollar Mermaid 52. The High and the Mighty 54. Timberjack 55. The First Travelling Saleslady 56. The Rabbit Trap 59. A Pocketful of Miracles 61. How the West was Won 62. The Rare Breed 68. The Destructors 69. The Seven Minutes 71, many others.

TV series: *Mr District Attorney* 54–55.

Brian, Mary (1908–) (Louise Dantzler). Charming American leading lady of the twenties; her roles diminished with sound and finally petered out.

Peter Pan (as Wendy) 24. The Little French Girl 25. Brown of Harvard 26. Beau Geste 26. Running Wild 27. Shanghai Bound 27. Harold Teen 28. Varsity 28. The Man I Love 29. *The Virginian* 29. The Light of Western Stars 30. *The Royal Family of Broadway* 30. *The Front Page* 31. Blessed Event 32. Girl Missing 33. College Rhythm 34. Charlie Chan in Paris 35. Killer at Large 36. The Amazing Quest of Ernest Bliss (GB) 36. Navy Bound 37. Calaboose 43. The Dragnet 48, many others.

Briant, Shane (1946–). British general purpose actor. Demons of the Mind 70. Straight on till Morning 71. Captain Kronos 72. Frankenstein and the Monster from Hell 72, etc.

Brice, Fanny (1891–1951) (Fanny Borach). American Jewish entertainer who made a virtue of her plainness. Screen appearances rare, but four films were based on her life: *Broadway Thro' a Keyhole* 33, *Rose of Washington Square* 38, *Funny Girl* 68, *Funny Lady* 75.

☐ *My Man* 28. Night Club 29. Be Yourself 30. The Great Ziegfeld 36. Everybody Sing 38. Ziegfeld Follies 45.

Bricusse, Leslie (1931–). British lyricist and composer.

Charley Moon 56. Stop the World I Want to Get Off 65. Doctor Dolittle 67. Goodbye Mr Chips 69, etc.

The Bride of Frankenstein (US 1935). At once the best of the horror films and a gentle mockery of them, this elegant Gothic piece with its eighteenth-century prologue is full of wry humour and pictorial delights. Its reputation rests on James Whale's direction and the script by John Balderston and Anthony Veiller; but Karloff as the monster, Elsa Lanchester as Mary Shelley and Ernest Thesiger as Dr Praetorius are gloriously grotesque.

Bridge, Al (–). Gravel-voiced American character actor chiefly memorable in Preston Sturges comedies.

The Bridge of San Luis Rey. Thornton Wilder's fatalistic twenties novel, tracing the lives of five people who happened to be on a Peruvian rope bridge when it collapsed, was filmed rather unsatisfactorily in 1929 by Charles Brabin and in

1944 by Rowland V. Lee. The many films which have copied its theme and structure include *Friday the Thirteenth* and *Phone Call from a Stranger*.

The Bridge on the River Kwai (GB 1957). Literally adapted by Carl Foreman and Michael Wilson from Pierre Boulle's novel, this anti-heroic war film about the absurdity of behaviour in a Burmese prison camp during World War II is carefully directed by David Lean (AA) and has fascinating performances from Alec Guinness (AA) and Sessue Hayakawa. Despite these assets and its great visual beauty, its plot development is clumsy and its climax confusing, so that its various messages take second place to its spectacular highlights.

Bridges, Alan (1927–). British director, from TV.
□ *An Act of Murder* 65. *Invasion* 66. The Lie (TV) 70. The Hireling 73. Brief Encounter (TV) 75. Out of Season (TV) 75.

Bridges, Beau (1941–). American leading man, son of Lloyd Bridges.
Force of Evil 48. The Red Pony 49. The Incident 67. For Love of Ivy 68. *Gaily Gaily* 69. *The Landlord* 70. Adam's Woman 70. The Christian Licorice Store 71. Hammersmith is Out 72. Child's Play 72. Loving Molly 73. The Other Side of the Mountain 75, etc.

Bridges, James (–). American director.
The Forbin Project (w only) 72. The Baby Maker (& w) 73. The Paper Chase (& w) 73.

Bridges, Jeff (1950–). American leading man of the early seventies, son of Lloyd Bridges.
□ Halls of Anger 70. The Last Picture Show 71. Fat City 71. Bad Company 72. The Last American Hero 73. Lolly Madonna XXX 73. The Iceman Cometh 73. Thunderbolt and Lightfoot 74. Rancho de Luxe 75. *Hearts of the West* 75. Tilt 75.

Bridges, Lloyd (1913–). American general purpose actor and sometimes leading man, who over thirty years has brought a sense of integrity to many westerns and melodramas.
Here Comes Mr Jordan 41. The Lone Wolf Takes a Chance 41. Atlantic Convoy 42. The Heat's On 43. The Master Race 44. Strange Confession 45. Miss Susie Slagle's 46. Canyon Passage 46. Ramrod 47. Sixteen Fathoms Deep 48. Moonrise 49. *Home of the Brave* 49. Trapped 49. Rocketship XM 50. The White Tower 50. *Try and Get Me* 51. Little Big Horn 51. The Whistle at Eaton Falls 51. High Noon 52.

Plymouth Adventure 52. City of Bad Men 53. The Tall Texan 53. The Limping Man (GB) 54. Apache Woman 55. Wetbacks 56. The Rainmaker 56. *The Goddess* 58. Around the World Under the Sea 66. Attack on the Iron Coast 68. *The Love War* (TV) 70. The Silent Gun (TV) 70. To Find a Man 72. Haunts of the Very Rich (TV) 72. Running Wild 73, many others.
TV series: *Sea Hunt* 57–61. The Lloyd Bridges Show 62. *The Loner* 65. San Francisco International 70. Joe Forrester 75.

Bridie, James (1888–1951) (Osborne Henry Mavor). Pawky Scottish dramatist whose works were more suited to stage than screen. Two films which did result were *Flesh and Blood* (from *A Sleeping Clergyman*) and *Folly to Be Wise* (from *It Depends What You Mean*).

Brief Encounter (GB 1946). one of the great post-war British films, this low-key, French-influenced romance between middle-aged people both comfortably married to other partners boasted a discerning script by Noel Coward, impeccable direction by David Lean, gleaming photography by Robert Krasker and poignant performances by Celia Johnson and Trevor Howard. Its stiff-upper-lip Britishness has caused it to be unfairly revalued, but it will certainly be cherished in a more tender age. The 1975 TV remake with Richard Burton and Sophia Loren was abysmal.

Briers, Richard (1934–). Dithery British light comedian who patterns himself after Ralph Lynn; mostly on stage and TV.

Briggs, Harlan (1880–1952). American small part actor.
Dodsworth 36. A Family Affair 37. One Wild Night 38. Calling Dr Kildare 39. Abe Lincoln in Illinois 40. One Foot in Heaven 41. Tennessee Johnson 43. State Fair 45. A Double Life 48. Carrie 52, many others.

Brighton Rock (GB 1947). Graham Greene worked on the screen play of his tough 'entertainment' about a racetrack gang run by a vicious adolescent. The Boulting Brothers produced it in bravura fashion, with a softened ending which was criticized; the film was acclaimed for its new realism and attacked for its new viciousness. Both it and Richard Attenborough's performance now seem rather tame.

Bringing Up Baby (US 1938). This classic example of thirties crazy comedy was full of upper-bracket people behaving in a ridiculous and even anti-social manner in pursuit of a dog, a dinosaur bone, and an escaped pet leopard. Katharine Hepburn was the zany rich girl and Cary Grant the staid archaeologist, with May Robson and Charles Ruggles strong in support. Howard Hawks directed from a script by Hagar Wilde and Dudley Nichols. Hawks re-used portions of the script in *Man's Favourite Sport* 66 and Peter Bogdanovitch virtually remade the film as *What's Up Doc?* 72.

Brisson, Carl (1895–1958) (Carl Pedersen). Danish leading man who made films in Britain. The Ring 28. The Manxman 29. The American Prisoner 29. Song of Soho 30. Murder at the Vanities 34. All the King's Horses 35, etc.

Brisson, Frederick (c.1915–). Danish producer with long experience in Britain (pre-39) and Hollywood. Married Rosalind Russell and subsequently masterminded her appearances. The Pajama Game 57. Under the Yum Yum Tree 64.

The British Empire has provided a useful background for innumerable movies: some comic, some tragic, but most of them plain adventurous. The Elizabethan adventurers roistered through films like *The Sea Hawk, The Virgin Queen* and *Seven Seas to Calais*; the westward voyage occupied *Plymouth Adventure*; Australia provided the canvas for *Under Capricorn, Robbery Under Arms,* and *Botany Bay*; *Mutiny on the Bounty* showed the British in the South Seas; Africa was the subject of *Zulu, The Four Feathers, Khartoum, Sundown, Rhodes of Africa, The Sun Never Sets* and (for the anti-British view) *Ohm Krüger*; and favourite of all far-flung outposts, India provided splendid terrain for such adventures as *The Drum, Northwest Frontier, Gunga Din, King of the Khyber Rifles, The Rains Came, Charge of the Light Brigade* and *Lives of a Bengal Lancer*. When the Empire was at its height, one could view the British influence as benevolent (*Pacific Destiny*), maiden-auntish (*Sanders of the River*), or merely acquisitive (*Victoria the Great*).

The inevitable break-up was rather less well covered. Even American independence has been played down by Hollywood producers with an eye on the British market, though of course it comes into such films as *Last of the Mohicans, Lafayette, Daniel Boone,* and even Disney's *Ben and Me*. Emergent Africa was the theme of *Men of Two Worlds* as long ago as 1946, but between that and the independent state depicted in *Guns at Batasi* came the Mau Mau period shown in *Simba, Safari* and *Something of Value*. The *High Bright Sun* dealt with Cyprus; The

Planter's Wife and *The Seventh Dawn* with Malaya; *Exodus, Judith* and *Cast a Giant Shadow* with Israel; scores of films with the Irish troubles; *Bhowani Junction* and *Nine Hours to Rama* with India. But the emergence of new states is a painful business as a rule, and most of these films give the impression of so much tasteless picking at sore points.
See also: *Ireland.*

British Film Academy. Organization founded 1946 'for the advancement of the film'. Since 1959 amalgamated with the Society of Film and Television Arts. Its award statuette is known as Stella, and is noted in this book by the letters BFA.

British Film Institute. Partly government-subsidized organization founded 1933 'to encourage the use and development of cinema as a means of entertainment and instruction'. Includes the National Film Archive (founded 1935) and the National Film Theatre (founded after the 1951 Festival of Britain). Also library, information section, stills collection, film distribution agency, lecture courses, etc. Chief publications: *Monthly Film Bulletin, Sight and Sound.*

British Lion Film Corporation. A film production company of the twenties which, in the thirties, became mainly a distributor of cheap American product but was revived after World War II by the control of Alexander Korda, then by Michael Balcon, the Boulting Brothers and Frank Launder and Sidney Gilliat. It merged in 1976 with EMI.

Britt, May (1933–) (Maybritt Wilkens). Swedish leading lady, in a few Hollywood films. Affairs of a Model 52. La Lupa 54. The Young Lions 58. The Hunters 58. The Blue Angel 59. Murder Inc. 60. Secrets of Woman 61, etc.

Britton, Barbara (1920–) (Barbara Brantingham Czukor). American leading lady of the forties who went straight from college to Hollywood.
Secret of the Wastelands 40. Louisiana Purchase 41. Wake Island 42. Reap the Wild Wind 42. So Proudly We Hail 43. *Till We Meet Again* 44. The Story of Dr Wassell 44. The Great John L. 45. Captain Kidd 45. The Virginian 46. The Fabulous Suzanne 47. Gunfighters 47. Albuquerque 48. I Shot Jesse James 49. Champagne for Caesar 50. Bandit Queen 50. The Raiders 52. Bwana Devil 53. The Spoilers 55, etc.
TV series: Mr and Mrs North 52.

Britton, Pamela (1923–74). Lightweight American actress, mainly familiar as TV's *Blondie* and in the *My Favorite Martian* series. Anchors Aweigh 45, Key to the City 50, etc.

Britton, Tony (1925–). British stage, screen and TV actor of quiet and polished style.
Salute the Toff 52. Loser Take All 57. The Birthday Present 57. Operation Amsterdam 58. The Rough and the Smooth 59. Suspect 60. Stork Talk 61. The Break 63. There's a Girl in My Soup 70. Sunday Bloody Sunday 71. The Day of the Jackal 73. Night Watch 74, etc.

Broadway Bill (US 1934). A hard-boiled but soft-centred racetrack comedy directed by Frank Capra in the ebullient style which was to become his trademark. From a script by Robert Riskin and a story by Mark Hellinger, it starred Warner Baxter and Myrna Loy. In 1951 Capra remade it as *Riding High*, a semi-musical with Bing Crosby and Coleen Gray.

Broadway Melody (US 1929) (AA). Early sound musical which, imitated, improved and expanded, set the style for all backstage yarns of the thirties. Harry Beaumont directed; Anita Page, Bessie Love and Charles King starred. MGM later used the title but not the plot for *Broadway Melody of 1936* and followed with *Broadway Melody of 1938* and *Broadway Melody of 1940*; there was to have been one for 1944 but the title was changed to *Broadway Rhythm*.

Broccoli, Albert R. ('Cubby') (1909–). American independent producer resident in London since 1951; successful as co-chief of Warwick Productions and later the James Bond films.
Hell Below Zero 54. The Black Knight 54. Cockleshell Heroes 55. Zarak 56. Fire Down Below 57. The Man Inside 59. Dr No 62. Call Me Bwana 63. From Russia With Love 63 (and subsequent Bond films). Chitty Chitty Bang Bang 68, many others.

Broderick, Helen (1890–1959). Wry-faced American stage comedienne whose wisecracks enlivened many thirties comedies. Mother of Broderick Crawford.
Fifty Million Frenchmen 31. *Top Hat* 35. *Murder on a Bridle Path* 36. *Swing Time* 36. We're on the Jury 37. The Rage of Paris 38. *Service De Luxe* 38. Naughty but Nice 39. *No No Nanette* 40. Nice Girl 41. A Chip off the Old Block 44. Her Primitive Man 44. Love Honour and Goodbye 45. Because of Him 46, etc.

Broderick, James (1930–). American TV actor who is typically cast as the worried father in the series *Family*.
Dog Day Afternoon 75.

Brodie, Steve (1919–) (John Stevens). Tough-looking American leading man and character actor, mainly in second features.
This Man's Navy 45. Young Wife 46. Trail Street 47. Home of the Brave 49. Winchester 73 50. Only the Valiant 51. Lady in the Iron Mask 52. The Beast from Twenty Thousand Fathoms 53. The Caine Mutiny 54. Gun Duel in Durango 57. Three Came to Kill 60. Of Love and Desire 63, etc.

Brodine, Norbert (1893–1970). Distinguished American cinematographer.
SELECTED SILENT FILMS: Almost a Husband 19. The Invisible Power 21. A Blind Bargain 22. Brass 23. *The Sea Hawk* 24. The Eagle of the Sea 25. Paris at Midnight 26. The Clown 27. Beware of Bachelors 28. Her Private Affair 29.
□ SOUND FILMS: Rich People 29. This Thing Called Love 29. The Divorcee 30. Holiday 30. Let Us Be Gay 30. Beyond Victory 31. The Guardsman 31. Pagan Lady 31. The Passionate Plumber 32. Beast of the City 32. Night Court 32. Bachelor's Affairs 32. Unashamed 32. Wild Girl 32. Uptown New York 32. The Death Kiss 32. Whistling in the Dark 33. Clear all Wires 33. Made on Broadway 33. Broadway to Hollywood 33. Deluge 33. Counsellor at Law 33. The Crosby Case 34. Love Birds 34. *Little Man What Now* 34. The Human Side 34. There's Always Tomorrow 34. Cheating Cheaters 34. The Good Fairy 35. Princess O'Hara 35. She Gets Her Man 35. Lady Tubbs 35. The Affair of Susan 36. Don't Get Personal 36. Nobody's Fool 36. *Libeled Lady* 36. Nobody's Baby 37. Pick a Star 37. *Topper* 37. *Merrily We Live* 37. Swiss Miss 38. There Goes My Heart 38. Topper Takes a Trip 39. Captain Fury 39. The Housekeeper's Daughter 39. Of Mice and Men 39. *One Million Years B.C.* 40. Turnabout 40. Captain Caution 40. Model Wife 41. Road Show 41. Lady for a Night 41. Dr Gillespie's Criminal Case 43. The Dancing Masters 43. The Bullfighters 45. Don Juan Quilligan 45. *The House on 92nd Street* 45. Sentimental Journey 46. Somewhere in the Night 46. *Thirteen Rue Madeleine* 46. *Kiss of Death* 47. *Boomerang* 47. Sitting Pretty 48. I Was a Male War Bride 49. *Thieves' Highway* 49. *The Frogmen* 51. The Desert Fox 51. Five Fingers 52.

Brodney, Oscar (1905–). American comedy writer, former lawyer. With Universal from the

forties, working mainly on routine series and light costume dramas.
When Johnny Comes Marching Home 43. Are You With It? 48. Yes Sir That's My Baby 49. Francis 50. Little Egypt 53. The Glenn Miller Story 54. Lady Godiva 55. Tammy and the Bachelor 57. Bobbikins (GB) (& p) 59. Tammy and the Doctor 63. The Brass Bottle 64. I'd Rather Be Rich 64, etc.

Brodszky, Nicholas (1905–). Russian-born composer, long in America and Britain.
French Without Tears 39. Quiet Wedding 40. The Way to the Stars 45. A Man About the House 47. The Toast of New Orleans 50. Latin Lovers 53. The Opposite Sex 56, etc.

Broken Arrow (US 1950). A James Stewart western which does not wear particularly well as entertainment but is significant for its renewal of a sympathetic attitude towards the Indians and its depiction of their chief, Cochise, played by Jeff Chandler, as an honourable man. Directed by Delmer Daves from a script by Michael Blankfort.

Broken Blossoms. It suited D. W. Griffith's rather Victorian outlook to film Thomas Burke's *The Chink and the Child*, a sentimental tale of a gentle Chinaman and an innocent waif in a highly imaginary Limehouse, and his 1919 version, being played for every last tear by Richard Barthelmess and Lillian Gish, was a great success. In 1936 Griffith was assigned to do a British remake with Emlyn Williams and Dolly Haas, but he resigned during preparation and Hans (John) Brahm took over. By now the tale was too outmoded for popular success, but it was interestingly done in the arty manner.

Brolin, James (1941–). American leading man.
Take Her She's Mine 63. Goodbye Charlie 64. Von Ryan's Express 65. Morituri 65. Our Man Flint 67. The Boston Strangler 68. Skyjacked 72. Westworld 73. Gable and Lombard (as Gable) 76, etc.
TV series: *Marcus Welby MD* 69–75.

Bromberg, J. Edward (1903–1951). Plump, wide-eyed Hungarian actor, in America from infancy; usually in gentle roles.
Under Two Flags 36. Seventh Heaven 37. Four Men and a Prayer 38. Jesse James 39. Hollywood Cavalcade 39. *Strange Cargo* 40. The Mark of Zorro 40. Pacific Blackout 41. Invisible Agent 42. Phantom of the Opera 43. *Son of Dracula* 43. Chip off the Old Block 44. Salome Where She Danced 45. Cloak and Dagger 46. Arch of Triumph 48. A Song is Born 48. Guilty Bystander 50, many others.

Bromberger, Herve (1918–). French director.
Identité Judiciaire 51. Les Fruits Sauvages 54. Les Loups dans la Bergerie 60. Mort Où Est Ta Victoire? 64, etc.

Bromfield, John (1922–) (Farron Bromfield). American second lead; leading man of second features.
Harpoon 48. Rope of Sand 49. Paid in Full 50. The Furies 50. Flat Top 52. Easy to Love 53. Ring of Fear. 53. Crime Against Joe 55. Manfish 56. Hot Cars 57, etc.
TV series: Sheriff of Cochise 56–57. U.S. Marshal 58–59.

Bromiley, Dorothy (1935–). British leading lady of very few films.
The Girls of Pleasure Island (US) 53. It's Great to be Young 55. A Touch of the Sun 56. The Criminal 60, etc.

Bron, Eleanor (1934–). Bloomsburyish British TV revue actress.
Help 65. Alfie 66. Two for the Road 67. Women in Love 69, etc.

Bronson, Betty (1906–1971) (Elizabeth Bronson). Lively American leading lady of the twenties; did not succeed in talkies.
Peter Pan (title role) 24. The Golden Princess 25. Are Parents People? 25. A Kiss for Cinderella 26. *Ben Hur* 26. The Cat's Pajamas 26. Everybody's Acting 27. Brass Knuckles 27. *The Singing Fool* 28. Companionate Marriage 28. Sonny Boy 29. The Locked Door 29. Medicine Man 30. The Yodelling Kid from Pine Ridge 37. Who's Got the Action? 62. Blackbeard's Ghost 67. Evel Knievel 71, etc.

Bronson, Charles (1922–) (Charles Buchinski). Sombre-looking, deep-featured American character actor who can deal with a variety of types from Russian to Red Indian, from villainous to sturdily heroic. At the age of fifty he suddenly became a star.
You're In the Navy Now 51. Pat and Mike 52. House of Wax 53. Apache 54. *Drumbeat* 54. Vera Cruz 54. Target Zero 55. Jubal 56. Run of the Arrow 57. Machine Gun Kelly 57. When Hell Broke Loose 58. Never so Few 59. *The Magnificent Seven* 60. A Thunder of Drums 61. Lonely are the Brave 62. The Great Escape 63. The Sandpiper 65. Battle of the Bulge 65. This Property is Condemned 66. *The Dirty Dozen* 67. Guns for San Sebastian 68. Once Upon a Time

in the West 69. Rider in the Rain 69. Twinky 69. You Can't Win Them All 70. Cold Sweat 71. The Family 71. *Chato's Land* 72. The Mechanic 72. *The Valachi Papers* 72. Wild Horses 73. The Stone Killer 73. Mr Majestyk 74. *Death Wish* 74. Breakout 75. *Hard Times* 75. Breakheart Pass 76. From Noon Till Three 76. St Ives 76. Raid on Entebbe (TV) 76. Telefon 77, many others.
TV series: Man with a Camera 58–59.

Bronston, Samuel (1910–). American independent producer who in 1959 set up a studio in Madrid and made several international epics but ran into financial difficulty.
Jack London 43. A Walk in the Sun 46. John Paul Jones 59. King of Kings 60. El Cid 61. Fifty Five Days at Peking 62. The Fall of the Roman Empire 64. Circus World 64, etc.

Brontë, Charlotte (1816–1855). British novelist whose *Jane Eyre* has been frequently filmed, most recently in 1934 with Virginia Bruce and Colin Clive, in 1944 with Joan Fontaine and Orson Welles, and in 1971 with Susannah York and George C. Scott. Its central situation, of a governess in the house of a mysterious but romantic tyrant, has also been frequently plagiarized.

Brontë, Emily (1818–1848). British novelist, sister of Charlotte Brontë, and author of *Wuthering Heights* (qv), much filmed in Britain before the definitive 1939 version. A somewhat romantic film about the sisters was filmed in 1943 under the title *Devotion*, with Olivia de Havilland as Charlotte and Ida Lupino as Emily.

Brook, Clive (1887 1974) (Clifford Brook). Distinguished British leading man of stage and screen, for forty years the perfect gentleman (with very occasional caddish lapses). Popular in Hollywood in the twenties and early thirties.
A Debt of Honour 19. Woman to Woman 21. The Royal Oak 23. Seven Sinners 25. You Never Know Women 26. Barbed Wire 27. Underworld 27. The Devil Dancer 27. Forgotten Faces 28. *The Four Feathers* 29. *The Return of Sherlock Holmes* 29. Slightly Scarlet 30. Scandal Sheet 31. East Lynne 31. *Shanghai Express* 32. *Sherlock Homes* 32. *Cavalcade* 33. Gallant Lady 33. Where Sinners Meet 34. For Love of a Queen 35. Action for Slander 37. The Ware Case 39. Convoy 40. Breach of Promise 41. *On Approval* (& pd) 43. The Shipbuilders 44. The List of Adrian Messenger 63, etc.

Brook, Faith (1922–). British actress of stage, screen and TV; daughter of Clive Brook.

Jungle Book 42. Uneasy Terms 48. Wicked as They Come 56. Chase a Crooked Shadow 57. The Thirty-nine Steps 59. To Sir With Love 66, etc.

Brook, Lesley (1916–). British leading lady of a few sentimental dramas of the forties.
The Vulture 37. Dead Men Tell No Tales 39. Rose of Tralee 41. Variety Jubilee 42. I'll Walk Beside You 43. The Trojan Brothers 46. House of Darkness 48, etc.

Brook, Lyndon (1926–). British actor of stage, screen and TV; son of Clive Brook.
Train of Events 49. The Purple Plain 54. Reach for the Sky 56. Innocent Sinners 58. Song Without End (US) 60. Invasion 66. Pope Joan 72, etc.

Brook, Peter (1925–). British stage director whose film experiments have been largely unsuccessful.
☐ The Beggar's Opera 52. Moderato Cantabile 60. Lord of the Flies 63. The Marat/Sade 66. Tell Me Lies 67. King Lear 70.

Brooke, Hillary (1916–) (Beatrice Peterson). Statuesque, blonde American leading lady of forties co-features.
New Faces of 1937. Eternally Yours 39. Unfinished Business 41. Sherlock Holmes and the Voice of Terror 42. Lady in the Dark 44. Practically Yours 44. Ministry of Fear 44. *The Woman in Green* 45. Road to Utopia 45. Strange Journey 46. Big Town 47. Big Town After Dark 47. Let's Live Again 48. Africa Screams 49. The Admiral was a Lady 50. Insurance Investigator 51. Confidence Girl 52. Abbott and Costello Meet Captain Kidd 52. Mexican Manhunt 53. Dragon's Gold 54. The House across the Lake (GB) 54. Bengazi 55. Spoilers of the Forest 57, many others.

Brook-Jones, Elwyn (1911–1962). Thick-set British character actor usually seen in villainous roles.
Dangerous Moonlight 40. Tomorrow We Live 42. Odd Man Out 46. The Three Weird Sisters 48. I'll Get You For This 50. Beau Brummell 54. The Pure Hell of St Trinian's 61, etc.

Brooks, Geraldine (1925–) (Geraldine Stroock). Intense young American actress of the forties; never fulfilled her promise.
Possessed 47. *Cry Wolf* 47. The Younger Brothers 49. *The Reckless Moment* 49. Challenge for Lassie 50. Volcano 50. The Green Glove 52. Street of Sinners 56. Johnny Tiger 66, etc.

Brooks, Jean (1921–). Stylish-looking American leading lady who worked briefly for RKO in the forties.
The Seventh Victim 43. The Leopard Man 43. The Falcon and the Co-Eds 44. Two O'Clock Courage 46. The Falcon's Alibi 46, etc.

Brooks, Leslie (1922–) (Leslie Gettman). American leading lady of the forties.
Undercover Agent 42. Nine Girls 44. Tonight and Every Night 45. The Cobra Strikes 48. Romance on the High Seas 48, etc.

Brooks, Louise (1900–). American leading lady of the twenties who made her best films in Germany and has remained an attractive critical enigma.
The American Venus 26. Evening Clothes 27. A Girl in Every Port 28. Rolled Stockings 28. Beggars of Life 28. *Pandora's Box* 29. *Diary of a Lost Girl* 30. It Pays to Advertise 31. God's Gift to Women 31, etc.

Brooks, Mel (1927–) (Melvin Kaminsky). American writer-producer-director of offbeat comedies.
New Faces (w) 54. *The Producers* (wpd) 68. The Twelve Chairs (wd) 70. *Blazing Saddles* (wp co-d) 74. *Young Frankenstein* (w, pd) 75. *Silent Movie* (w, pd) 76, etc.

Brooks, Phyllis (1914–) (Phyllis Weiler). Blonde American leading lady of co-features in the thirties and forties.
I've Been Around 34. McFadden's Flats 35. You Can't Have Everything 37. Rebecca of Sunnybrook Farm 38. Charlie Chan in Reno 39. Slightly Honourable 40. *The Shanghai Gesture* 41. Hi Ya Sailor 43. The Unseen 45. High Powered 45, etc.

Brooks, Rand (1918–). American leading man, usually in minor films.
Gone with the Wind 39. Florian 40. Son of Monte Cristo 41. Joan of Arc 47. The Steel Fist 52. Man from the Black Hills 56. Comanche Station 60, etc.

Brooks, Ray (1939–). British juvenile leading man with repertory experience.
HMS Defiant 62. Play it Cool 62. Some People 63. *The Knack* 65. Daleks Invasion Earth 2150 AD 66. Alice's Adventures in Wonderland 72. Tiffany Jones 73. House of Whipcord 74, etc.

Brooks, Richard (1912–). American writer-director whose reputation is somewhat higher than his films seem to justify. He wrote however one of the best novels about Hollywood, *The Producer*.
□ White Savage (w only) 42. Cobra Woman (w only) 44. Swell Guy (w only) 46. The Killers (co-w only) 46. Brute Force (w only) 47. Crossfire (oa only) 47. To the Victor (w only) 48. Key Largo (w only) 48. Any Number Can Play (w only) 49. *Crisis* 50. Mystery Street (w only) 50. Storm Warning (co-w only) 50. The Light Touch 51. Deadline 52. Battle Circus 52. The Last Time I Saw Paris (d only) 54. Take the High Ground (d only) 54. The Flame and the Flesh (d only) 54. *The Blackboard Jungle* 55. *The Last Hunt* 56. The Catered Affair (d only) 56. Something of Value 57. The Brothers Karamazov 58. Cat on a Hot Tin Roof 58. *Elmer Gantry* (AA w) 60. Sweet Bird of Youth 62. Lord Jim (& p) 65. The Professionals (& p) 66. *In Cold Blood* (& p) 67. The Happy Ending (& p) 70. Dollars (& p) 72. Bite The Bullet (& p) 75.

Brophy, Edward S. (1895–1960). American character actor, often a gangster or a very odd kind of valet: a rotund, cigar-chewing little man in a bowler hat, oddly likeable despite his pretence of toughness.
Those Three French Girls 30. *The Champ* 31. Freaks 32. What, No Beer? 33. *The Thin Man* 34. Death on the Diamond 34. Mad Love (miscast as a murderer) 35. Remember Last Night 35. Strike Me Pink 36. Kelly the Second 36. *A Slight Case of Murder* 37. You Can't Cheat an Honest Man 39. Calling Philo Vance 40. Buy Me That Town 41. All Through the Night 42. Broadway 42. Cover Girl 44. The Thin Man Goes Home 44. The Falcon in San Francisco (and series) 45. *Wonder Man* 45. It Happened on Fifth Avenue 47. *The Last Hurrah* 58, many others.

brothels were reasonably prominent in silent films, but the Hays Code banished them and for many years one had to look to the French for such revelations as were to be found in *Le Plaisir* and *Adua et sa Compagnie*. In the sixties, however, the doors opened. Comic Victorian brothels were shown in *The Assassination Bureau* and *The Best House in London*, and a French version in *Lady L. Ulysses* showed the Dublin version. *A House is not a Home* told the 'true' story of Polly Adler. The brothel in *The Balcony* was symbolic, in *House of a Thousand Dolls* fantastic, in *How Sweet It Is* charming, in *Games that Lovers Play* whimsical, in *The Last Detail* grimly realistic. *Walk on the Wild Side* concentrated on the depressing aspects and even sported a lesbian madam. Nowadays every western has one, notably *Waterhole Three, Five Card Stud, Hang 'em High, McCabe and Mrs*

Miller, Dirty Dingus Magee, The Cheyenne Social Club and *The Ballad of Cable Hogue*; nor are police thrillers such as *Badge 343* complete without them.

Brother Orchid (US 1939). The virtual end of the thirties gangster cycle was marked by this warm comedy in which Edward G. Robinson plays a gangster who, left for dead after being 'taken for a ride', is cared for by monks and literally sees the light. Directed by Lloyd Bacon.

Brother Rat, a 1936 Broadway success by Fred Finklehoffe and John Monks Jnr, about fun and games at a military institute, was filmed in 1938 by William Keighley, with Ronald Reagan, Wayne Morris and Eddie Albert in the leads. A thin sequel, *Brother Rat and a Baby*, followed in 1940. The original play was remade in 1952 as *About Face*, with Gordon Macrae and Eddie Bracken.

The Brothers Karamazov. Dostoevsky's nineteenth-century novel of Russian family life was filmed by Robert Wiene in Germany in 1921, with Emil Jannings; the same country produced the next version, *The Murder of Dmitri Karamazov*, in 1930, with Fritz Kortner under the direction of Fedor Ozep. In 1958 Richard Brooks made a Hollywood version with Yul Brynner, and the Russian director Pyriev completed a Russian film of the book in 1967.

Brough, Mary (1863–1934). British character comedienne usually seen as battleaxe or suspicious landlady, especially in the Aldwych farces.
The Amazing Quest of Ernest Bliss 22. *Rookery Nook* 30. Tons of Money 32. Turkey Time 33. Thark 33, etc.

Brown, Charles D. (1887–1948). Bland-faced American character actor who played scores of detectives, officials and executives.
The Dance of Life 29. Murder by the Clock 31. The Woman I Stole 33. It Happened One Night 34. Thoroughbreds Don't Cry 37. Charlie Chan in Reno 39. The Grapes of Wrath 39. Fingers at the Window 42. Jam Session 44. The Killers 46. Merton of the Movies 47, many others.

Brown, Clarence (1890–). American director, with MGM and Garbo for many years; most at home with sentimental themes and busy pictorial values.
□ The Great Redeemer 20. The Last of the Mohicans 20. The Light in the Dark 22. Don't Marry for Money 23. The Acquittal 23. The Signal Tower 24. Butterfly 24. Smouldering Fires 25. *The Eagle* 25. *The Goose Woman* 25. Kiki 26. *Flesh and the Devil* 26. Trail of 98 28. A Woman of Affairs 29. Wonder of Women 29. Navy Blues 29. *Anna Christie* 30. Romance 30. Inspiration 31. A Free Soul 31. Possessed 31. Emma 32. Letty Lynton 32. The Son Daughter 32. Looking Forward 33. Night Flight 33. Sadie McKee 34. Chained 34. *Anna Karenina* 35. *Ah Wilderness* 35. Wife versus Secretary 36. The Gorgeous Hussy 36. *Conquest* 37. Of Human Hearts 38. Idiot's Delight 38. *The Rains Came* 39. *Edison the Man* 40. Come Live with Me (& p) 41. They Met in Bombay 41. *The Human Comedy* (& p) 43. The White Cliffs of Dover 44. National Velvet 44. *The Yearling* 46. Song of Love (& p) 47. *Intruder in the Dust* (& p) 49. To Please a Lady (& p) 50. Angels in the Outfield (& p) 51. It's a Big Country (part) 51. When in Rome (& p) 51. Plymouth Adventure 52. Never Let Me Go (p only) 53.

Brown, Ed (–). American cinematographer.
The Hot Rock 72. Lovin' Molly 74. The Education of Sonny Carson 74, etc.

Brown, George H. (1913–). British producer, former production manager.
Sleeping Car to Trieste 48. The Chiltern Hundreds 50. The Seekers 54. Jacqueline 56. Dangerous Exile 57. Tommy the Toreador 60. Murder at the Gallop 63. Guns at Batasi 64. The Trap 66. Finders Keepers 66. Assault 70. Revenge 71. Innocent Bystanders 72. Open Season 74, etc.

Brown, Georgia (1933–). British cabaret songstress in occasional films.
The Fixer 67. Lock Up Your Daughters 69. The Raging Moon 71. Nothing but the Night 73.

Brown, Harry (1917–). American novelist and screenwriter, mainly on war themes.
The True Glory (co-w) 45. A Walk in the Sun (oa) 46. Arch of Triumph 48. Sands of Iwo Jima 49. A Place in the Sun (co-w) 51. Bugles in the Afternoon 52. The Sniper (co-w) 52. Eight Iron Men 52. All the Brothers Were Valiant (co-w) 53. D-Day Sixth of June (co-w) 56. Between Heaven and Hell (co-w) 57. El Dorado (oa) 66, etc.

Brown, Harry Joe (1892–1972). American producer with long experience in all branches of show business; latterly concentrated on Randolph Scott westerns.
Parade of the West (d only) 30. Madison Square Garden (d only) 32. Sitting Pretty (d only) 33. Captain Blood 35. Alexander's Ragtime Band

38. The Rains Came 39. Young People 40. Western Union 41. *Knickerbocker Holiday* (& d) 44. Gunfighters 47. Fortunes of Captain Blood 50. Hangman's Knot 52. Three Hours to Kill 54. Screaming Mimi 58. Ride Lonesome 59, many others.

Brown, James (1920–). Stalwart American supporting actor, in many westerns of the forties and fifties.
The Forest Rangers 42. Corvette K225 44. Objective Burma 45.

Brown, Jim (1936–). Black American leading man, former athlete.
□ Rio Conchos 64. The Dirty Dozen 67. Dark of the Sun 68. The Split 68. Ice Station Zebra 68. Riot 68. *100 Rifles* 69. Tick Tick Tick 70. The Grasshopper 70. Kenner 71. Black Gunn 72. Slaughter 72. Slaughter's Big Rip-off 73. I Escaped from Devil's Island 73. The Slams 74. Three the Hard Way 74. Take a Hard Ride 75.

Brown, Joe (1941–). Amiable British pop singer, in occasional films.
What a Crazy World 63. Three Hats for Lisa 65, etc.

Brown, Joe E. (1892–1973). Wide-mouthed American star comedian of the thirties, with background in circus, vaudeville and basketball.
Autobiography 1956: *Laughter is a Wonderful Thing.*
Crooks Can't Win 28. Sally 29. Hold Everything 30. Sit Tight 31. *You Said a Mouthful* 32. Son of a Sailor 33. *Six Day Bike Rider* 34. *Alibi Ike* 35. *A Midsummer Night's Dream* 35. Sons o' Guns 36. When's Your Birthday? 37. Wide Open Faces 38. Beware Spooks 39. So You Won't Talk 40. Chatterbox 43. Pin Up Girl 44. *Show Boat* (as Cap'n Andy) 51. Around the World in Eighty Days 56. *Some Like It Hot* 59. It's a Mad Mad Mad Mad World 63, many others.

Brown, John Mack (1904–1974). American leading man of the thirties, former football star.
The Bugle Call 26. The Divine Woman 27. *Our Dancing Daughters* 28. Coquette 29. Jazz Heaven 29. *Billy the Kid* 30. The Secret Six 31. *The Last Flight* 31. Saturday's Millions 33. Female 33. Belle of the Nineties 34. Riding the Apache Trail 36. Wells Fargo 37. Bad Man from Red Butte 40. Ride 'Em Cowboy 41. The Right to Live 45. Stampede 49. Short Grass 50. The Bounty Killer 65. Apache Uprising 65, many others.

Brown, John Moulder (1951–). British TV actor, usually seen as callow youth.

The House That Screamed (Sp.) 59. *Deep End* 70, etc.

Brown, Karl (1897–). American cinematographer of the twenties; retired early.
The Birth of a Nation (2nd unit) 15. The Fourteenth Man 20. Gasoline Gus 21. The Dictator 22. *The Covered Wagon* 23. Ruggles of Red Gap 23. Merton of the Movies 24. Beggar on Horseback 25. *Pony Express* 25. Mannequin 26, etc.

Brown, Nacio Herb (1896–1964). American light composer who usually supplied the music for Arthur Freed's lyrics: 'Broadway Melody', 'Singin' in the Rain', 'Good Morning', 'You Are My Lucky Star', many others.

Brown, Pamela (1917–1975). British stage actress in occasional films, usually in haughty or eccentric roles.
One of Our Aircraft is Missing 42. *I Know Where I'm Going* 45. Tales of Hoffman 51. The Second Mrs Tanqueray 52. Personal Affair 53. Richard III 56. The Scapegoat 59. Becket 64. Secret Ceremony 68. Wuthering Heights 70. On a Clear Day You Can See Forever 70. Lady Caroline Lamb 72. Dracula (TV) 73, etc.

Brown, Phil (c. 1916–). American second lead, usually in diffident roles; moved to Europe in 1950.
I Wanted Wings 41. Calling Dr Gillespie 42. The Impatient Years 44. Without Reservations 46. The Killers 46. If You Knew Susie 48. Moonrise 49. *Obsession* 50. The Green Scarf 54. Camp on Blood Island 58. The Bedford Incident 65. Tropic of Cancer 69, etc.

Brown, Robert (c. 1918–). Burly British actor of stage, TV and film.
Helen of Troy 55. A Hill in Korea 56. Campbell's Kingdom 57. Ben Hur 59. Sink the Bismarck 60. The Masque of the Red Death 64. One Million Years BC 66. Private Road 71.

Brown, Rowland (1901–1963). American director whose career waned curiously after a promising start.
□ *Quick Millions* 31. Hell's Highway 32. Blood Money 33. The Devil is a Sissy 37.

Brown, Tom (1913–). American juvenile lead of the thirties; the 'boy next door' type. Re-emerged in the sixties as one of the villagers in the long-running TV series *Gunsmoke*.
The Hoosier Schoolmaster 24. The Lady Lies 29. Queen High 30. *Tom Brown of Culver* 32. Three Cornered Moon 33. Judge Priest 34. Anne

of Green Gables 34. *Freckles* 35. I'd Give My Life 36. Maytime 37. In Old Chicago 38. Duke of West Point 38. Sergeant Madden 39. Sandy is a Lady 40. The Pay Off 43. The House on 92nd Street 45. Buck Privates Come Home 47. Duke of Chicago 49. The Quiet Gun 57, many others.

Brown, Vanessa (1928–) (Smylla Brind). American juvenile leading lady of a few late forties films; usually demure.
Margie 46. *The Late George Apley* 47. Mother Wore Tights 47. The Foxes of Harrow 47. The Heiress 49. Tarzan and the Slave Girl 50. The Bad and the Beautiful 52. Rosie 68. Bless the Beasts and Children 71, etc.

Brown, Wally (1898–1961). American comedian, a fast-talking vaudevillian who teamed with Alan Carney (qv) in a few comedy second features of the forties.
Adventures of a Rookie 44. Rookies in Burma 44. Step Lively 44. Zombies on Broadway 45. Genius at Work 45. As Young As You Feel 51. The High and the Mighty 54. The Absent-minded Professor 61, etc.

Browne, Coral (1913–). Australian stage actress long in Britain, usually in worldly comedy roles; films few.
The Amateur Gentleman 36. Black Limelight 38. Let George Do It 40. Piccadilly Incident 46. *Auntie Mame* (US) 58. The Roman Spring of Mrs Stone 61. Dr Crippen 64. *The Killing of Sister George* 68. Theatre of Blood 73. The Drowning Pool 75, etc.

Browne, Irene (1891–1965). British stage actress, usually in dignified roles; films few.
The Letter 29. Cavalcade 33. Berkeley Square 33. The Amateur Gentleman 36. Pygmalion 38. The Prime Minister 40. *Quartet* 48. Madeleine 50. All at Sea 57. Rooney 58, etc.

Browne, Roscoe Lee (1940–). Black American character actor.
Topaz 69. *The Liberation of L. B. Jones* 70. The Cowboys 72. Cisco Pike 72. Superfly Two 73, etc.

Browning, Ricou (1930–). American diver and stunt man who became a specialist in underwater direction for Ivan Tors.
The Creature from the Black Lagoon (also played title role) 54. Flipper 63. Around the World Under the Sea 66. Lady in Cement 68, etc.

Browning, Tod (1882–1962). American director remembered chiefly for his horror films

of the twenties and early thirties; revaluation has made them less striking than once was thought.
The Brazen Beauty 18. The Virgin of Stamboul 20. Under Two Flags 22. The White Tiger 23. The Unholy Three 25. The Mystic (& w) 25. The Unknown 27. *London After Midnight* 27. West of Zanzibar 28. Where East is East 29. The Thirteenth Chair 29. The Unholy Three (sound remake) 30. *Dracula* 30. Iron Man 31. *Freaks* 32. Fast Workers 33. Mark of the Vampire 35. *The Devil Doll* 36. Miracles for Sale 39, etc.

Brownlow, Kevin (1938–). British producer-director who made his first film, *It Happened Here*, on a shoestring budget over seven years. It was released in 1966. Published 1969 *The Parade's Gone By*, a collection of interviews with silent movie stars.
His 1975 film *Winstanley* was a clever but cheerless historical reconstruction.

Bruce, Brenda (1918–). British stage, TV and occasionally screen actress.
Millions Like Us 43. They Came to a City 45. Piccadilly Incident 46. My Brother's Keeper 48. Marry Me 52. The Final Test 53. Law and Disorder 57. Nightmare 63. The Uncle 65, etc.

Bruce, David (1914–1976) (Marden McBroom). American light leading man familiar in Universal films during World War II.
The Sea Hawk 40. Singapore Woman 42. The Mad Ghoul 43. Ladies Courageous 44. Christmas Holiday 44. Can't Help Singing 44. Salome Where She Danced 45. Lady on a Train 45. Prejudice 48. Masterson of Kansas 55, etc.

Bruce, Nigel (1895–1953). Tubby British comedy actor, mainly in Hollywood from 1934; usually played well-meaning upper class buffoons, and was the screen's most memorable Dr Watson.
□ Red Aces 29. The Squeaker 31. Escape 31. The Calendar 31. Lord Camber's Ladies 32. The Midshipmaid 32. Channel Crossing 32. I Was a Spy 33. Springtime for Henry 34. Stand Up and Cheer 34. Coming Out Party 34. Murder in Trinidad 34. The Lady is Willing 34. Treasure Island 34. The Scarlet Pimpernel 35. *Becky Sharp* 35. Jalna 35. *She* 35. The Man who Broke the Bank at Monte Carlo 35. The Trail of the Lonesome Pine 36. Under Two Flags 36. The White Angel 36. The Charge of the Light Brigade 36. Follow your Heart 36. Make Way for a Lady 36. The Man I Married 36. Thunder in the City 37. The Last of Mrs Cheyney 37. The Baroness and the Butler 38. Kidnapped 38. Suez 38. *The Hound of the Baskervilles* 39. The Adventures of Sherlock Holmes 39. The Rains

Came 39. *Rebecca* 40. Adventure in Diamonds 40. *The Bluebird* 40. Lillian Russell 40. A Dispatch from Reuters 40. Hudson's Bay 40. Playgirl 41. Free and Easy 41. The Chocolate Soldier 41. This Woman is Mine 41. Suspicion 41. Roxie Hart 42. This Above All 42. Eagle Squadron 42. Sherlock Holmes and the Voice of Terror 42. Sherlock Holmes and the Secret Weapon 42. Journey for Margaret 42. Sherlock Holmes in Washington 43. Forever and a Day 43. Sherlock Holmes Faces Death 43. Follow the Boys 44. The Pearl of Death 44. Spider Woman 44. Gypsy Wildcat 44. *The Scarlet Claw* 44. *Frenchman's Creek* 44. Son of Lassie 45. *House of Fear* 45. The Corn is Green 45. The Woman in Green 45. Pursuit to Algiers 45. Terror by Night 46. Dressed to Kill 46. The Two Mrs Carrolls 47. The Exile 47. Julia Misbehaves 48. Vendetta 50. Hong Kong 51. Bwana Devil 53. *Limelight* 53. World for Ransom 53.

Bruce, Virginia (1910–) (Helen Virginia Briggs). American light leading lady of the thirties.
Woman Trap 29. The Love Parade 29. Safety in Numbers 30. Hell Divers 31. The Wet Parade 32. Kongo 32. *Jane Eyre* (title role) 34. Dangerous Corner 34. Escapade 35. Metropolitan 35. The Great Ziegfeld 36. Born to Dance 36. Between Two Women 37. Arsène Lupin Returns 38. Yellow Jack 38. Society Lawyer 39. Flight Angels 40. Invisible Woman 41. Pardon My Sarong 42. Careful Soft Shoulders 42. Action in Arabia 44. Love Honour and Goodbye 45. Night has a Thousand Eyes 48. The Reluctant Bride (GB) 52. Strangers When We Meet 60, many others.

Bruckman, Clyde (1895–1955). American writer-director of many silent comedies; especially associated with Keaton, Lloyd and Fields.
Sherlock Jnr (w) 24. *The Navigator* (w) 24. *The General* (wd) 27. *Feet First* (wd) 30. *Movie Crazy* (d) 32. The Man on the Flying Trapeze (d) 35, many others.

Brummell, Beau (1778–1840). A famous British dandy and politician who has been the subject of two biopics: in 1924 with John Barrymore (directed by Harry Lachman) and in 1954 with Stewart Granger (directed by Curtis Bernhardt).

Brunel, Adrian (1892–1958). British director with pleasant reputation in the twenties as an intellectual at large. Autobiography 1952: *Nice Work*.
Bookworms (short) 21. The Bump (short) 23.

The Man Without Desire 23. Crossing the Great Sagrada (short) 24. *Blighty* 27. *The Constant Nymph* 27. The Vortex 28. While Parents Sleep 35. The City of Beautiful Nonsense 26. Prison Breaker 36. The Lion Has Wings 39. The Girl Who Forgot 40, etc.

Brunius, Jacques (1906–1967). French actor, once critic and assistant to Clair and Renoir; later resident in Britain.
L'Age d'Or 30. Partie de Campagne 37. Sea Devils 53. To Paris with Love 55. Orders to Kill 58, etc.

Brute Force (US 1947). A confected, violent but harrowingly exciting prison melodrama which marked Jules Dassin's debut as a notable director, Photographed by William Daniels, written by Richard Brooks, with powerful performances by Burt Lancaster, Charles Bickford and Hume Cronyn.

Bryan, Dora (1923–) (Dora Broadbent). British stage and film comedienne, specializing in warm-hearted tarts of the cockney or northern variety.
Odd Man Out 46. The Fallen Idol 48. The Cure for Love 48. The Blue Lamp 50. High Treason 51. Lady Godiva Rides Again 51. Mother Riley Meets the Vampire 52. Time Gentlemen Please 53. Fast and Loose 54. See How They Run 55. Cockleshell Heroes 56. The Green Man 57. Desert Mice 59. The Night We Got the Bird 60. *A Taste of Honey* (BFA: leading role) 61. The Great St Trinian's Train Robbery 66. The Sandwich Man 66. Two a Penny 68. Hands of the Ripper 71. Up the Front 72, etc.

Bryan, Jane (1918–) (Jane O'Brien). Sympathetic American leading lady of the later thirties.
□ The Case of the Black Cat 36. Marked Woman 37. Kid Galahad 37. Confession 37. A Slight Case of Murder 38. *The Sisters* 38. Girls on Probation 38. Brother Rat 38. Each Dawn I Die 39. The Old Maid 39. These Glamour Girls 39. *We are not Alone* 39. Invisible Stripes 40. Brother Rat and a Baby 40.

Bryan, John (1911–1969). British producer and production designer.
Great Expectations (des) (AA) 46. Pandora and the Flying Dutchman (des) 51. *The Card* 52. The Purple Plain 54. The Spanish Gardener (& w) 56. Windom's Way 57. The Horse's Mouth 58. There Was a Crooked Man 60. Tamahine 62. After the Fox 66. The Touchables 68, etc.

Bryant, Michael (1928–). Serious-looking

British character actor of stage and TV; films occasionally.

Life for Ruth 62. The Mindbenders 63. Goodbye Mr Chips 69. Nicholas and Alexandra (as Lenin) 71, etc.

Bryant, Nana (1888–1955). Dignified but friendly American character actress who usually played middle-class mums or rich patrons.

A Feather in Her Hat 35. Theodora Goes Wild 36. Mad About Music 38. Espionage Agent 39. Nice Girl 41. Calling Dr Gillespie 42. The Song of Bernadette 43. Brewster's Millions 45. The Unsuspected 47. Harvey 50. Bright Victory 51. About Mrs Leslie 54. The Private War of Major Benson 55, many others.

Brynner, Yul (1915–) (Youl Bryner). Baldheaded international star of somewhat mysterious background: variously alleged to have originated in Switzerland and Russia, but assuredly American by adoption. A Broadway stage success, especially as the king in *The King and I*: long dominant in films though not easy to cast.

☐ Port of New York 49. *The King and I* 56. The Ten Commandments 56. *Anastasia* 56. *The Brothers Karamazov* 58. The Buccaneer 58. The Journey 58. The Sound and the Fury 59. Solomon and Sheba 59. Once More with Feeling 60. Surprise Package 60. *The Magnificent Seven* 60. The Testament of Orpheus 60. Escape from Zahrain 62. *Taras Bulba* 62. Kings of the Sun 63. Flight from Ashiya 64. *Invitation to a Gunfighter* 64. The Saboteur 65. Cast a Giant Shadow 66. Return of the Seven 66. Triple Cross 66. The Double Man 67. The Long Duel 67. Villa Rides 68. The Poppy is also a Flower 68. The Madwoman of Chaillot 69. The File of the Golden Goose 69. The Battle of Neretva 70. The Light at the Edge of the World 71. Romance of a Horsethief 71. Catlow 72. Fuzz 72. The Serpent 72. Westworld 73. The Ultimate Warrior 74. Futureworld 76.

TV series: *Anna and the King* 72.

B.S.C. British Society of Cinematographers, a professional society founded in the fifties, similar in aims to the A.S.C. (qv).

Buchan, John (1875–1940). British adventure novelist oddly neglected by the cinema apart from *The Thirty-nine Steps*, neither version of which bears much resemblance to the original; and a 1927 version of *Huntingtower*.

Buchanan, Edgar (1902–). Jovial American character actor, in innumerable westerns and rustic dramas as hayseed, crooked judge, comic side-kick or straight villain.

My Son is Guilty 39. Arizona 40. The Richest Man in Town 41. The Desperados 42. Destroyer 43. Buffalo Bill 44. The Fighting Guardsman 45. Abilene Town 46. Framed 47. The Black Arrow 48. The Best Man Wins 48. Red Canyon 49. Devil's Doorway 50. The Great Missouri Raid 51. The Big Trees 52. Shane 53. Human Desire 54. Day of the Badman 57. The Sheepman 58. Edge of Eternity 60. Cimarron 61. Ride the High Country 62. McLintock 63. The Rounders 65. Welcome to Hard Times 67, many others.

TV series: Hopalong Cassidy 51–52. Judge Roy Bean 59. Petticoat Junction 63–69. Cade's County 71.

Buchanan, Jack (1891–1957). Debonair British entertainer, a memorable song-and-dance man of stage and screen in the twenties and thirties: good-looking, long-legged, nasal of voice and debonair in appearance.

☐ Bulldog Drummond's Third Round 25. Happy Landing 25. Toni 27. Confetti 28. Paris 29. Show of Shows 29. Monte Carlo 30. Goodnight Vienna 32. A Man of Mayfair 32. Yes Mr Brown 32. Magic Night 32. *Brewster's Millions* 33. That's a Good Girl 33. That Girl 34. Come out of the Pantry 35. Sons o'Guns 35. When Knights were Bold 36. Smash and Grab 37. Break the News 37. This'll Make You Whistle 37. The Sky's the Limit 38. *The Gang's All Here* 39. Alias the Bulldog 39. Bulldog Sees it Through 40. *The Band Wagon* 53. As Long as They're Happy 53. Josephine and Men 55. The Diary of Major Thompson 56.

Buchholz, Horst (1933–). German leading man, in occasional international films.

Tiger Bay 59. *The Magnificent Seven* 60. Fanny 61. One Two Three 61. Nine Hours to Rama 63. The Empty Canvas 64. Marco the Magnificent 65. That Man in Istanbul 66. Cervantes 66. L'Astragale 68. The Great Waltz 72. The Catamount Killing 75, etc.

Buchman, Sidney (1902–1975). American writer-producer of good commercial films.

Matinée Ladies (oa) 27. *The Sign of the Cross* (co-w) 32. I'll Love You Always (w) 35. The King Steps Out (w) 36. *Theodora Goes Wild* (w) 36. *Mr Smith Goes to Washington* (w) 39. The Howards of Virginia (w) 40. *Here Comes Mr Jordan* (w) (AA) 41. *The Talk of the Town* (w) 42. *A Song to Remember* (wp) 45. Over 21 (p) 45. Jolson Sings Again (wp) 49. Saturday's Hero (w) 51. Cleopatra (w) 63. *The Group* (wp) 66, many others.

Buck, Frank (1888–1950). American explorer who made several animal films. Appeared in *Africa Screams* 50.
Bring 'Em Back Alive 32. Fang and Claw 36. Jungle Menace 37. Jacare, Killer of the Amazon 42, etc.

Buck, Jules (1917–). American producer who in the late fifties came to Britain and founded Keep Films with Peter O'Toole.
Fixed Bayonets 51. Treasure of the Golden Condor 53. The Day they Robbed the Bank of England 60. *Becket* 64. Great Catherine 66. The Ruling Class 71, etc.

Buck, Pearl (1892–1973). American novelist and missionary to the Far East. Works filmed include *The Good Earth, Dragon Seed, Satan Never Sleeps.*

Buckner, Robert (1906–). American screenwriter, later producer.
Gold is Where You Find It 38. Jezebel 38. The Oklahoma Kid 39. *Dodge City* 39. Virginia City 39. *Santa Fe Trail* 40. Dive Bomber 41. Yankee Doodle Dandy 42. Gentleman Jim (p) 42. Mission to Moscow (p) 43. Confidential Agent (& p) 45. Rogues' Regiment (& p) 48. Sword in the Desert (& p) 49. Bright Victory (& p) 51. Love Me Tender 56. From Hell to Texas (& p) 58. Return of the Gunfighter 68, etc.

Bucquet, Harold S. (1891–1946). English director in Hollywood.
Young Dr Kildare 39. *On Borrowed Time* 39. The Secret of Dr Kildare 39. We Who Are Young 40. Dr Kildare Goes Home 40. The Penalty 41. Kathleen 41. Calling Dr Gillespie 42. The War Against Mrs Hadley 42. The Adventures of Tartu (GB) 43. Dragon Seed 44. Without Love 45, etc.

Budd, Roy (1949–). British composer.
Zeppelin 71. Get Carter 71. Flight of the Doves 71. Pulp 72. The Internecine Project 74. Paper Tiger 75, etc.

Buetel, Jack (1917–). American western leading man who was little seen after a highly publicized debut.
The Outlaw (as Billy the Kid) 43. Best of the Badmen 51. The Half Breed 52. Jesse James' Women 54. Mustang 59, etc.

Bugs Bunny. Warners' famous cartoon character, the wise-cracking Brooklynesque rabbit who maintained his aplomb in all situations. Voiced by Mel Blanc. Catchphrase: "What's up Doc?" First appearance in *Porky's*

Hare Hunt 1937; 'retired' 1963.
AA 1958: *Knighty Knight Bugs.*

Bujold, Geneviève (1942–). French-Canadian leading lady.
French Can Can 56. La Guerre est Finie 63. King of Hearts 67. Isabel 67. Act of the Heart 70. *Anne of the Thousand Days* (as Anne Boleyn) 70. Earthquake 74. Obsession 76, etc.

Bull, Peter (1912–). Portly British character actor often in haughty, aggressive or explosively foreign roles.
Autobiography 1959: *I Know The Face But . . .*
Sabotage 37. The Ware Case 39. The Turners of Prospect Road 47. Oliver Twist 48. Saraband for Dead Lovers 48. The African Queen 51. The Malta Story 53. Footsteps in the Fog 55. Tom Jones 63. Dr Strangelove 63. The Old Dark House 63. Dr Dolittle 67. Lock Up Your Daughters 69. The Executioner 70. Up the Front 72. Alice's Adventures in Wonderland 72, many others.

Bulldog Drummond. 'Sapper' (Hector McNeil) created this famous character, an amateur James Bond of the twenties with old-fashioned manners and an army background. First portrayed on screen by Carlyle Blackwell in 1922; later by Jack Buchanan (1925 and 1940), Ronald Colman (1928 and 1934), Kenneth McKenna (1930), Ralph Richardson (1934), Atholl Fleming in Jack Hulbert's *Bulldog Jack* (1935), John Lodge (1937), Ray Milland (1937), John Howard, in eight films (1937–39), Ron Randell, in two films (1947), Tom Conway, in two films (1948), Walter Pidgeon in *Calling Bulldog Drummond* (1951) and Richard Johnson in *Deadlier than the Male* (1966) and *Some Girls Do* (1968).

bullfights have understandably not been a popular ingredient of English-speaking films, apart from the romanticism of the two versions of *Blood and Sand* and the cynicism of *The Last Flight* 31 and *The Sun Also Rises*. Several continental films, including *The Moment of Truth*, have tried to convey the mystique of bullfighting, but it has more often been seen as a background for suspense films (*The Caper of the Golden Bulls*) and comedy (*The Kid from Spain*, Laurel and Hardy in *The Bullfighters* and *Tommy the Toreador*, Abbott and Costello in *Mexican Hayride*, Peter Sellers in *The Bobo*, etc). The three more recent American attempts to make a serious drama on the subject (*The Bullfighter and the Lady, The Brave Bulls* and *The Magnificent Matador*) were notably unpopular.

Bunny, John (1863–1915). British actor who became the funny fat man of early American silent comedy; made more than 150 shorts, usually with Flora Finch.

Buñuel, Luis (1900–). Spanish writer-director who worked in France in the twenties and thirties, made many films in Mexico 1945–60, then returned to Europe. A once-notorious surrealist, his later films have mocked hyprocrisy and the shows of religion.

□ Un Chien Andalou 28. *L'Age d'Or* 30. Land Without Bread 32. Grand Casino 46. El Gran Calavera 49. *Los Olvidados* 50. Suzana la Perverse 50. La Hija del Engaño 51. Una Mujer Sin Amor 51. Subida ad Cielo 51. The Brute 52. Wuthering Heights 52. *Robinson Crusoe* 52. El 53. La Ilusión Viaja en Tranvia 53. El Rio y la Muerte 54. The Criminal Life of Archibaldo de la Cruz 55. La Mort en ce Jardin 56. Cela S'Appelle L'Aurore 58. La Fièvre Monte à El Pao 59. Nazarin 59. The Young One 60. *Viridiana* 61. *The Exterminating Angel* 62. Diary of a Chambermaid 64. *Belle de Jour* 66. Simon of the Desert 66. The Milky Way 69. Tristana 70. *The Discreet Charm of the Bourgeoisie* 72. The Phantom of Liberty 74.

Buono, Victor (1938–). Massively bulky American character actor who moved to films via the amateur theatre.

□ *Whatever Happened to Baby Jane?* 62. Four for Texas 63. *The Strangler* 64. Robin and the Seven Hoods 64. The Greatest Story Ever Told 65. Hush Hush Sweet Charlotte 65. Young Dillinger 65. The Silencers 66. Who's Minding the Mint? 67. Beneath the Planet of the Apes 69. The Wrath of God 72. The Mad Butcher 72. Northeast of Seoul 74. High Risk (TV) 76.

Burden, Hugh (1913–). British character actor.

One of Our Aircraft is Missing 41. The Way Ahead 44. Fame is the Spur 46. Sleeping Car to Trieste 48. The Malta Story 53. No Love for Johnnie 61. Funeral in Berlin 66. The Statue 71. Blood from the Mummy's Tomb 71. The House in Nightmare Park 73, etc.

Burge, Stuart (1918–). British director, from TV.

There Was a Crooked Man 60. Othello 66. The Mikado 67. Julius Caesar 70.

Burke, Alfred (1918–). British stage, screen and TV actor usually in cold, unsympathetic or other-worldly roles.

Touch and Go 56. The Man Upstairs 58. The Angry Silence 59. Children of the Damned 64.

The Nanny 65. One Day in the Life of Ivan Denisovitch 71, etc.

TV series: Public Eye 69– .

Burke, Billie (1885–1970) (Mary William Ethelbert Appleton Burke). American stage star who married Florenz Ziegfeld; Myrna Loy played her in *The Great Ziegfeld*. After a few early silents she settled in Hollywood in the thirties and played variations on the dithery matron role she made her own.

Autobiographies: *With A Feather On My Nose* 1949, *With Powder on My Nose* 1959.

□ Gloria's Romance 16. Peggy 16. The Land of Promise 17. Let's Get à Divorce 18. In Pursuit of Polly 18. The Make Believe Wife 18. Good Gracious Annabelle 19. The Misleading Widow 19. *A Bill of Divorcement* 32. Christopher Strong 33. *Dinner at Eight* 33. Only Yesterday 33. Finishing School 34. Where Sinners Meet 34. We're Rich Again 34. Forsaking all Others 34. Society Doctor 35. After Office Hours 35. Becky Sharp 35. Doubting Thomas 35. *A Feather in Her Hat* 35. She Couldn't Take It 35. Splendour 35. My American Wife 36. Piccadilly Jim 36. Craig's Wife 36. Parnell 36. *Topper* 37. The Bride Wore Red 37. Navy Blue and Gold 37. Everybody Sing 38. *Merrily We Live* 38. *The Young in Heart* 38. Topper Takes a Trip 38. Zenobia 39. Bridal Suite 39. The Wizard of Oz 39. Eternally Yours 39. Remember 39. And One Was Beautiful 40. Irene 40. Dulcy 40. Hullaballoo 40. Topper Returns 41. One Night in Lisbon 42. *The Man Who Came to Dinner* 41. What's Cookin'? 42. In This Our Life 42. They All Kissed the Bride 42. Girl Trouble 42. Hi Diddle Diddle 42. So's Your Uncle 44. *The Cheaters* 45. Breakfast in Hollywood 46. The Bachelor's Daughters 46. The Barkleys of Broadway 49. And Baby Makes Three 49. Father of the Bride 50. Three Husbands 51. Father's Little Dividend 51. Small Town Girl 53. The Young Philadelphians 59. Sergeant Rutledge 60. Pepe 60.

Burke, James (1898–1968). Irish-American character actor who played more New York cops than he could count.

A Lady's Profession 33. Little Miss Marker 34. Ruggles of Red Gap 35. Song and Dance Man 36. Dead End 37. Dawn Patrol 38. At the Circus 39. Ellery Queen Master Detective 40. The Maltese Falcon 41. Army Surgeon 42. A Night to Remember 43. The Horn Blows at Midnight 45. Two Years Before the Mast 46. Nightmare Alley 47. June Bride 48. Copper Canyon 50. Lone Star 52. Lucky Me 54, many others.

Burke, Johnny (1908–1964). American

songwriter who often supplied lyrics for Jimmy Van Heusen's music. 'Pennies from Heaven', 'Moonlight Becomes You', 'Swinging on a Star' (AA 44), many others.

Burke, Marie (1894–) (Marie Holt). British actress, mostly on stage.
After the Ball 33. Odette 50. The Constant Husband 55. The Snorkel 58. Rattle of a Simple Man 64, etc.

Burke, Patricia (1917–). British actress, daughter of Marie Burke.
The Lisbon Story 45. The Trojan Brothers 45. Love Story 46. While I Live 47. Forbidden 49. The Happiness of Three Women 54. Spider's Web 60. The Day the Fish Came Out 67, etc.

Burke, Paul (1926–). American leading man, who on TV projected integrity, with great success but has done few movies.
South Sea Woman 53. Screaming Eagles 56. *Valley of the Dolls* 67. The Thomas Crown Affair 68. Daddy's Gone A-Hunting 69. Lt. Schuster's Wife (TV) 72, etc.
TV series: Noah's Ark 60. *Naked City* 60–63. Twelve O'Clock High 67.

Burks, Robert (1910–1968). American cinematographer.
☐ Make Your Own Bed 44. Escape in the Desert 45. To the Victor 48. A Kiss in the Dark 49. *The Fountainhead* 49. Beyond the Forest 49. Task Force 49. The Glass Menagerie 50. Close to My Heart 51. *Strangers on a Train* 51. Tomorrow is Another Day 51. *Come Fill The Cup* 51. *The Enforcer* 51. The Miracle of our Lady of Fatima 52. Room for One More 52. Mara Maru 52. The Desert Song 53. So This is Love 53. Hondo 53. *I Confess* 53. The Boy from Oklahoma 54. Dial M For Murder 54. *Rear Window* 54. *To Catch a Thief* 55. The Trouble with Harry 56. The Man Who Knew Too Much 56. The Vagabond King 56. The Wrong Man 57. The Spirit of St Louis (co-ph) 58. *Vertigo* 58. The Black Orchid 59. *North By Northwest* 59. But Not for Me 59. The Rat Race 60. The Great Imposter 61. The Pleasure of His Company 61. *The Music Man* 62. *The Birds* 63. Marnie 64. Once a Thief 65. A Patch of Blue 66. A Covenant with Death 67. Waterhole Three 67.

burlesque. A word of Italian origin which came to mean an acted 'spoof' of a serious subject. In America it was applied to what the British would call music hall or variety, and eventually connoted striptease and low comedians. It died out as an institution in the thirties: Mamoulian's film *Applause* 29 gives a vivid picture of its latter days. George Watters and Arthur Hopkins' play *Burlesque*, popular in the twenties, concerns a comedian who leaves his long-suffering wife for other women and the demon rum. It was filmed three times, most recently as *When My Baby Smiles at Me* 48, with Betty Grable and Dan Dailey. The heyday of burlesque was also evoked in *The Night They Raided Minsky's* 68, in *Lady of Burlesque* and in *Gypsy*.

The Burmese Harp (Japan 1956). Kon Ichikawa's long, savage epic of the Burmese campaign of 1943–44 centres on a soldier who after horrifying adventures sees that his vocation is to bury the unknown dead. Lead played by Shoji Yasui; written by Natto Wada.

Burnaby, Davy (1881–1949). Heavyweight, monocled British entertainer.
The Co-optimists 29. Three Men in a Boat 33. Are You a Mason? 34. Boys Will Be Boys 35. Feather Your Nest 37. Many Tanks Mr Atkins 39, etc.

Burness, Pete (1910–). American animator who worked his way through *The Little King* and *Tom and Jerry* to U.P.A. and *Bullwinkle*.

Burnett, Carol (1934–). American revue star.
Who's Been Sleeping in My Bed? 63. Pete 'n Tillie 72. The Front Page 74.

Burnett, Frances Hodgson (1849–1924). English novelist whose screen contributions include the much-filmed childrens' stories *Little Lord Fauntleroy* and *The Secret Garden. A Little Princess* made a solid vehicle for Shirley Temple.

Burnett, W. R. (1899–). American writer of gangster novels and screenplays which have been influential.
Little Caesar (oa) 30. *Scarface* (oa) 32. Dr Socrates (oa) 35. *High Sierra* (oa) 40. Crash Dive (w) 43. Nobody Lives Forever (w) 46. The Asphalt Jungle (oa) 50. Captain Lightfoot (w) 54. Sergeants Three (w) 62, many others.

Burnette, Smiley (1911–1967) (Lester Alvin Burnette). Tubby American character comedian who for many years made low-budget westerns as the side-kick of Charles Starrett or Gene Autry.
TV series: Petticoat Junction 63–67.

Burns, Bob ('Bazooka') (1893–1956). Folksy American comedian and humorist who after radio success appeared in several light films.

The Big Broadcast of 1937 37. Waikiki Wedding 37. Wells Fargo 37. Your Arkansas Traveller 38. Tropic Holiday 38. Our Leading Citizen 39. Alias the Deacon 40. Belle of the Yukon 44, etc.

Burns, David (1902–1971). American character actor who often played the hero's buddy, the villain's henchman, or a fast-talking agent.
The Queen's Affair (GB) 34. The Sky's the Limit (GB) 38. A Girl Must Live (GB) 38. Knock On Wood 54. Deep in My Heart 55. Let's Make Love 60. The Tiger Makes Out 67. Who is Harry Kellerman? 71, etc.

Burns, George (1896–) (Nathan Birnbaum). American vaudeville comedian who married his partner Gracie Allen (qv) and spent many successful years on radio and TV, puffing philosophically at his cigar as he suffered her hare-brained schemes.
Autobiography 1955: *I Love Her, That's Why.*
The Big Broadcast 32. International House 32. Love in Bloom 33. We're Not Dressing 34. The Big Broadcast 38. Many Happy Returns 39. The Sunshine Boys (AA) 75, etc.
TV series: The Burns and Allen Show 50–58. The George Burns Show 59–60. Wendy and Me 64.

Burns, Mark (1937–). British leading man.
The Charge of the Light Brigade 67. The Adventures of Gerard 70. A Day on the Beach 70. Death in Venice 70. A Time for Loving 72. Juggernaut 74. The Maids 75, etc.

Burr, Raymond (1917–). Heavily-built Canadian leading man who for years played Hollywood heavies and then achieved TV stardom as Perry Mason.
San Quentin 46. Desperate 47. Sleep My Love 47. Pitfall 48. Bride of Vengeance 49. Love Happy 50. A Place in the Sun 51. Meet Danny Wilson 52. Mara Maru 52. The Blue Gardenia 53. Gorilla at Large 54. *Rear Window* 54. Godzilla 55. Great Day in the Morning 56. A Cry in the Night 56. Crime of Passion 57. Desire in the Dust 60. P. J. 68, many others.
TV series: *Perry Mason* 57–66. *Ironside* 67–74. Kingston 77.

Burroughs, Edgar Rice (1875–1950). American novelist, the creator in 1914 of *Tarzan of the Apes* (qv).

Burrows, Abe (1910–). American librettist: *Guys and Dolls, Can Can, How to Succeed in Business,* etc.

Burstyn, Ellen (1932–) (Edna Gilhooley). Leading American actress of the seventies.
□ Goodbye Charlie 64. For Those who Think Young 65. Pit Stop 69. Tropic of Cancer 69. Alex in Wonderland 70. The Last Picture Show 71. The King of Marvin Gardens 72. Thursdays Game (TV) 73. *The Exorcist* 73. Harry and Tonto 74. *Alice Doesn't Live Here Anymore* (AA) 75.

Burton, Richard (1925–) (Richard Jenkins). Welsh leading actor whose dark brooding good looks did not bring him immediate film success either in Britain or in Hollywood. His 1963 marriage to Elizabeth Taylor, however, helped him climb to the crest of what these days passes for stardom.
□ The Last Days of Dolwyn 48. Now Barabbas was a Robber 49. Waterfront 50. The Woman with No Name 50. Green Grow the Rushes 51. *My Cousin Rachel* 52. The Robe 53. The Desert Rats 53. Prince of Players 54. The Rains of Ranchipur 55. *Alexander the Great* 56. Seawife 57. Bitter Victory 58. *Look Back in Anger* 59. The Bramble Bush 59. Ice Palace 60. The Longest Day 62. *Cleopatra* 62. *The V.I.P.s* 63. *Becket* 64. *The Night of the Iguana* 64. The Sandpiper 65. *The Spy Who Came in from the Cold* 65. *Who's Afraid of Virginia Woolf?* 66. *The Taming of the Shrew* 67. Dr Faustus (& co-d) 67. The Comedians 67. Boom 68. Where Eagles Dare 68. Candy 68. *Staircase* 69. *Anne of the Thousand Days* (as Henry VIII) 70. Raid on Rommel 71. Villain 71. Under Milk Wood 71. The Assassination of Trotsky 72. Hammersmith is Out 72. Bluebeard 72. Divorce His, Divorce Hers (TV) 73. Massacre in Rome 74. The Klansman 74. The Voyage 74. Brief Encounter (TV) 75.

Burton, Wendell (–). American character actor.
The Sterile Cuckoo 69. Fortune and Men's Eyes 70, etc.

Busch, Mae (1897–1946). Cynical-looking American leading lady of the silents who later became an excellent foil for Laurel and Hardy in some of their best two-reelers.
The Grim Game 19. The Devil's Pass-key 20. *Foolish Wives* 21. The Christian (GB) 23. Nellie the Beautiful Cloak Model 24. Married Flirts 24. The Unholy Three 25. San Francisco Nights 27. While the City Sleeps 28. A Man's Man 29. Wicked 31. *Come Clean* 31. Scarlet Dawn 32. Their First Mistake 32. Sucker Money 33. Sons of the Desert 33. The Private Life of Oliver the Eighth 34. The Bohemian Girl 36. Daughter of

Shanghai 37. Prison Farm 38. Women without Names 40. Ziegfeld Girl 40, many others.

Busch, Niven (1903–). American novelist and screenwriter.

Babbitt (w) 34. In Old Chicago (w) 38. The Westerner (w) 40. Duel in the Sun (oa) 46. Pursued (w) 47. The Furies (oa) 50. The Moonlighter (oa & w) 52. Treasure of Pancho Villa (w) 56, etc.

buses have often provided a dramatic background for film plots. *Man-Made Monster* and *The October Man* began with bus accidents, and one of the stories in *Dead of Night* ended with one. Strangers met on a bus in *Friday the Thirteenth*, *It Happened One Night*, *San Diego I Love You* (in which Buster Keaton defied regulations by driving his bus along the seashore), *Bus Stop* and *The Wayward Bus*. Parting at the bus station was featured in *Orchestra Wives*, *Dark Passage*, *Two Tickets to Broadway*, and *Rattle of a Simple Man*; romances were conducted on a bus in *Violent Playground* and *Underground*; a trap was set for a criminal in a bus station in *Down Three Dark Streets*. Passengers on buses broke into song in *Keep Your Seats Please*, *Ride 'Em Cowboy* and *Summer Holiday*. As for comedy effects using buses, there was the little boy whose head stuck in the bus wheel in *Monsieur Hulot's Holiday*, Will Hay driving a bus round a race-track in *Ask a Policeman*, Bob Hope wrecking an Irish bus outing in *My Favourite Blonde*, Frankie Howerd losing his way in the fog in *The Runaway Bus*, Richard Burton escorting his matrons on a bus tour in *The Night of the Iguana*, and Laurel and Hardy driving a bus on to a roller coaster in *The Dancing Masters* ... among others. The only comedies about bus crews were the spinoffs from the British TV series *On the Buses*. *The Big Bus* was a spoof on disaster movies.

Bush, Billy 'Green' (–). American character actor of the seventies.

40 Carats 73. Electra Glide in Blue 74. Alice Doesn't Live Here Anymore 74. Mackintosh and T. J. 75, etc.

Bushell, Anthony (1904–). Bland-faced British leading man of the thirties who started his career in Hollywood; later turned to playing occasional brigadiers and concentrated his efforts on production.

Disraeli 29. *Journey's End* 30. Three Faces East 30. Five Star Final 31. A Woman Commands 32. I Was a Spy 33. The Ghoul 33. Soldiers of the King 33. The Scarlet Pimpernel 34. Dark Journey 37. Farewell Again 37. The Return of

the Scarlet Pimpernel 38. The Lion Has Wings 39. Hamlet (co-p only) 48. The Angel with the Trumpet (& d) 49. The Miniver Story 50. The Long Dark Hall (& pd) 51. High Treason 51. Who Goes There? 52. The Red Beret 53. The Purple Plain 54. The Battle of the River Plate 56. Richard III (co-p only) 56. The Wind Cannot Read 57, etc.

Bushman, Francis X. (1883–1966). Heavily built American leading actor of the silent era, once known as the handsomest man in the world. After a return to the stage, made a brief comeback in 1926 and later played bit parts in unsuitable films of the sixties.

The Magic Wand 12. The Spy's Defeat 13. One Wonderful Night. 14. Under Royal Patronage 14. Graustark 15. The Return of Richard Neal 15. Romeo and Juliet 15. The Great Secret 16. Red White and Blue Blood 17. Social Quicksands 18. The Masked Bride 25. *Ben Hur* (as Messala) 26. The Lady in Ermine 27. The Thirteenth Juror 27. The Grip of the Yukon 29. Once a Gentleman 30. Hollywood Boulevard 36. David and Bathsheba 51. Sabrina 54. The Story of Mankind 57. The Ghost in the Invisible Bikini 66, many others.

Bussières, Raymond (1907–). Long-faced, mournful-looking French character actor.

Nous les Gosses 41. Les Portes de la Nuit 46. Quai des Orfèvres 47. Alice au Pays des Merveilles 51. Ma Pomme 51. Casque d'Or 52. Justice est Faite 52. Belles de Nuit 54. Porte des Lilas 55. Paris Palace Hotel 58. Fanny 61. Paris When It Sizzles 64. Up from the Beach 65, many others.

Butch Cassidy and the Sundance Kid (US 1969). An easy-going, self-parodying western which happened to succeed in all departments and so started a hail of imitations, especially as its amiability formed a necessary contrast to the harshness and violence of most westerns in the late sixties. Directed by George Roy Hill from a script by William Goldman; photographed by Conrad Hall; with Paul Newman and Robert Redford. Its theme song, 'Raindrops Keep Falling on my Head', was an enormous popular success.

Butcher, Ernest (1885–1965). British character actor who spent a lifetime playing mild little men.

Variety Jubilee 42. *Tawny Pipit* 43. *My Brother Jonathan* 48, many others.

Butler, Artie (–). American composer. The Harrad Experiment 73. For Pete's Sake 74.

Butler, Bill (–). American
cinematographer.
The Conversation 74. Jaws 75.

Butler, David (1894–). American director of
light entertainments: occasional promise but
little fulfilment. Former actor.
High School Hero 27. Win That Girl 28. *Sunny
Side Up* 29. *Just Imagine* 30. *A Connecticut
Yankee* 31. Business and Pleasure 32. Hold Me
Tight 33. Bottoms Up 34. Bright Eyes 34. The
Little Colonel 35. The Littlest Rebel 35. Captain
January 36. White Fang 36. Ali Baba Goes to
Town 37. Kentucky 38. East Side of Heaven 39.
That's Right You're Wrong (& p) 39. If I Had
My Way (& p) 40. You'll find Out (& p) 40.
Caught in the Draft 41. Road to Morocco 42.
They Got Me Covered 43. *Thank Your Lucky
Stars* 43. Shine on Harvest Moon 44. The
Princess and the Pirate 44. San Antonio 45. Two
Guys from Milwaukee 46. My Wild Irish Rose
47. Two Guys from Texas 48. Look for the Silver
Lining 49. The Daughter of Rosie O'Grady 50.
Tea for Two 50. Lullaby of Broadway 51.
Painting the Clouds with Sunshine 51. Where's
Charley? 52. By the Light of the Silvery Moon
53. *Calamity Jane* 53. King Richard and the
Crusaders 54. Glory (& p) 56. The Right
Approach 61. C'mon Let's Live a Little 67, etc.

Butler, Frank (1890–1967). British-born
writer, long in Hollywood.
College Humor 33. Babes in Toyland 34. Strike
Me Pink 36. Road to Singapore 40. Road to
Morocco 42. Going My Way (AA) 44.
Incendiary Blonde 45. The Perils of Pauline 47.
Whispering Smith 49. Strange Lady in Town 55,
many others.

Butler, Michael (1944–). American
cinematographer.
Charley Varrick 74. Harry and Tonto 74.

butlers. Hollywood has always been fascinated
by butlers, especially those who give an
impression of British imperturbability. Actors
notably benefiting from this penchant include
Arthur Treacher (who played Jeeves on film in
the thirties), Robert Greig, Charles Coleman,
Aubrey Mather, Melville Cooper, Halliwell
Hobbes, Barnett Parker, Alan Mowbray and
Eric Blore (whose butlers usually had a kind of
suppressed malevolence). The catch-phrase 'the
butler did it' was however seldom true of murder
mysteries, though Bela Lugosi played some very
sinister servants in the forties, Richard Haydn
was guilty of at least one murder in *And Then
There Were None*; the butler in *The Hound of the
Baskervilles* certainly had something to hide.

Another villainous 'man's man' was Philip
Latham in *Dracula Prince of Darkness*: he lured
the count's victims. Comedy butlers are led by
Charles Laughton as *Ruggles of Red Gap* and by
Edward Brophy, who often played an American
imitation of the real thing, Richard Hearne in
The Butler's Dilemma, Edward Rigby in *Don't
Take It to Heart*, and Laurel and Hardy, who in
A Chump at Oxford took literally an instruction
to 'serve the salad undressed'. Jack Buchanan
pretended to be his own butler in *Lord Richard in
the Pantry*, and William Powell and Divid Niven,
who both played *My Man Godfrey*, had their
own reasons for going into service. Other butlers
with something to hide were found in *White Tie
and Tails* and *The Baroness and the Butler*, and
in *Spring in Park Lane* Michael Wilding was a
mysterious footman.

Butterworth, Charles (1896–1946). Balding
American comic actor who through the thirties
played his own style of shy upper-class bachelor,
never getting the girl and sometimes drowning
his sorrows in drink.
The Life of the Party 30. Side Show 31. *Love Me
Tonight* 32. My Weakness 33. Hollywood Party
34. Orchids to You 35. *Baby Face Harrington*
35. The Moon's Our Home 36. Rainbow on the
River 36. Swing High Swing Low 37. *Every
Day's a Holiday* 37. Thanks for the Memory 38.
Let Freedom Ring 39. The Boys from Syracuse
40. Road Show 41. A Night in New Orleans 42.
This is the Army 43. Follow the Boys 44. The
Bermuda Mystery 44, etc.

Butterworth, Donna (1956–). American
child actress.
The Family Jewels 65. Paradise Hawaiian Style
66.

Butterworth, Peter (c. 1923–1979). British
comedian usually seen as well-meaning bumbler.
William Comes to Town 49. Penny Princess 51.
Mr Drake's Duck 52. Carry On series 58– ,
many others.

Buttolph, David (–). American
composer.
Show Them no Mercy 35. Nancy Steele is
Missing 37. Four Sons 40. *The Mark of Zorro*
40. *Tobacco Road* 41. Moontide 42. My Favorite
Blonde 42. Crash Dive 43. The Hitler Gang 44.
The House on 92nd Street 45. Somewhere in the
Night 46. Kiss of Death 47. Rope 48. Roseanna
McCoy 49. Three Secrets 50. The Enforcer 51.
My Man and I 52. *House of Wax* 53. Secret of
the Incas 54. The Lone Ranger 56. The Big Land
57. The Horse Soldiers 59. Guns of the
Timberland 60. The Man from Galveston 64,
many others.

Buttons, Red (1918–) (Aaron Schwatt).
American vaudeville and TV comic who
graduated to strong supporting roles in
occasional movies.
☐ Winged Victory 44. *Sayonara* (AA) 57.
Imitation General 58. The Big Circus 59. Hatari
62. Five Weeks in a Balloon 62. The Longest
Day 62. A Ticklish Affair 63. Your Cheating
Heart 65. Up from the Beach 65. Harlow 65.
Stagecoach 66. They Shoot Horses Don't They?
69. Who Killed Mary What's Her Name? 71.
The Poseidon Adventure 72.
TV series:. *The Red Buttons Show* 52. The
Double Life of Henry Phyfe 66.

Buzzell, Edward (1897–). American director
of competent but not very individual output;
former musical comedy actor.
Virtue 32. Ann Carver's Profession 33. Cross
Country Cruise 34. Transient Lady 35. The
Luckiest Girl in the World 36. As Good as
Married 37. Fast Company 38. Honolulu 39. *At
the Circus* 39. Go West 40. Married Bachelor 41.
Ship Ahoy 42. The Youngest Profession 43.
Keep Your Powder Dry 45. *Easy to Wed* 46.
Three Wise Fools 46. Song of the Thin Man 47.
Neptune's Daughter 49. A Woman of
Distinction 50. Confidentially Connie 53. Ain't
Misbehavin' (& w) 55. Mary Had a Little (GB)
61, etc.

Bwana Devil (US 1953). A poor jungle
adventure which has some historical interest as
the first feature film to be produced in 3-D. As
written, produced and directed by Arch Oboler,
it had little else to offer; Robert Stack and Nigel
Bruce led the struggling cast.

Bygraves, Max (1922–). British entertainer
who has played in several films.
Skimpy in the Navy 49. Tom Brown's
Schooldays 50. Charley Moon 53. A Cry from
the Streets 57. Bobbikins 59. Spare the Rod 61,
etc.

Byington, Spring (1893–1971). American
stage actress who settled in Hollywood in the
thirties and played a long succession of
birdbrained wives, scatty matrons, gossip
columnists, and loving mums.
Little Women (as Marmee) 33. Werewolf of
London 35. Way Down East 35. Mutiny on the
Bounty 35. Ah Wilderness 35. Every Saturday
Night (and ensuing Jones Family series; qv) 36.
Dodsworth 36. Theodora Goes Wild 36. It's
Love I'm After 37. The Adventures of Tom
Sawyer 38. Jezebel 38. *You Can't Take It with
You* 38. The Story of Alexander Graham Bell 39.
A Child is Born 40. The Bluebird 40. Meet John

Doe 41. The Devil and Miss Jones 41. When
Ladies Meet 41. Roxie Hart 42. *Rings on Her
Fingers* 42. Presenting Lily Mars 43. Heaven
Can Wait 43. The Heavenly Body 44. I'll Be
Seeing You 45. The Enchanted Cottage 45.
Dragonwyck 46. Singapore 47. BF's Daughter
48. In the Good Old Summertime 49. Louisa 50.
Walk Softly Stranger 50. According to Mrs
Hoyle 51. Angels in the Outfield 51. Because
You're Mine 52. The Rocket Man 54. Please
Don't Eat the Daisies 60, many others.
TV series: *December Bride* 54–58. Laramie
60–62.

Byrd, Ralph (1909–1952). Tough-looking
American leading man, mainly in second
features.
Hell Ship Morgan 31. Dick Tracy 38. Desperate
Cargo 41. Guadalcanal Diary 43. Mark of the
Claw 47. The Redhead and the Cowboy 51, etc.

Byrne, Eddie (1911–). Irish character actor,
in British films.
Odd Man Out 46. The Gentle Gunman 52. *Time
Gentlemen Please* (leading role) 53. A Kid for
Two Farthings 55. The Admirable Crichton 57.
The Mummy 59. The Bulldog Breed 60. Devils of
Darkness 65. Island of Terror 66. Stardust 74,
many others.

Byrnes, Edd (1933–) (Edward Breitenberger).
American TV juvenile of the fifties; never quite
made it in movies.
Darby's Rangers 58. Up Periscope 59.
Yellowstone Kelly 59. Mutiny on the Bounty 62.
The Secret Invasion 64. Payment in Blood 69,
etc.
TV series: *77 Sunset Strip* 58–62.

Byron, Arthur (1872–1943). American
character actor.
The Mummy 32. Mayor of Hell 33. Marie
Galante 34. Fog Over Frisco 34. Oil for the
Lamps of China 35. Prisoner of Shark Island 36,
many others.

Byron, Lord (1788–1824) (George Gordon).
English poet who has been played on the screen
by Dennis Price in *The Bad Lord Byron*, by
Richard Chamberlain in *Lady Caroline Lamb*
and by Gavin Gordon in *The Bride of
Frankenstein*.

Byron, Kathleen (1922–). British leading
actress of the forties; on stage and screen.
The Young Mr Pitt 41. The Silver Fleet 43. A
Matter of Life and Death 46. *Black Narcissus* (as

a mad nun) 46. The Small Back Room 48.
Madness of the Heart 49. The Reluctant Widow
50. Four Days 51. The Gambler and the Lady
54. Hand in Hand 60. Night of the Eagle 62.
Private Road 71. Twins of Evil 71. One of Our
Dinosaurs is Missing 76, etc.

Byron, Walter (1899–) (Walter Butler)
American actor.
The Awakening 28. The Sacred Flame 29. Not
Damaged 30. Society Girl 32. British Agent 34.
Mary of Scotland 36. Trade Winds 38, many
others.

C

Caan, James (1938–). American leading man who has not quite made the front rank, but continues promising.
Irma La Douce 63. *Lady in a Cage* 64. The Glory Guys 65. Red Line 7000 65. *El Dorado* 67. Countdown 67. Games 67. Journey to Shiloh 68. Submarine XI 68. Man Without Mercy (Gone with the West) 69. The Rain People 69. *Rabbit Run* 70. T. R. Baskin 71. *Brian's Song* (TV) 71. *The Godfather* 72. Slither 73. Cinderella Liberty 75. Freebie and the Bean 75. The Gambler 75. Funny Lady 75. Rollerball 75. The Killer Elite 76. Harry and Walter Go To New York 76, etc.

Cabanne, Christy (1888–1950). American silent film director for Griffith and Fairbanks; declined to second features when talkies came.
Enoch Arden 15. Flirting with Fate 16. Reckless Youth 22. Youth for Sale 24. The Masked Bride 27. Altars of Desire 27. Hotel Continental 32. Daring Daughters 33. A Girl of the Limberlost 34. Keeper of the Bees 35. The Last Outlaw 36. Criminal Lawyer 37. Mutiny on the Blackhawk 39. The Mummy's Hand 40. Scattergood Baines 41. Drums of the Congo 42. Keep 'Em Slugging 43. Scared to Death 46. Robin Hood of Monterey 47. Back Trail 48, many others.

Cabaret (US 1972). A striking musical in its own right, this further variation of *I am a Camera* (qv) by way of a stage musical unwisely tried to be shocking and jettisoned all the middle-aged characters who gave it dramatic strength, but contrived to present a vivid picture of Berlin in the early thirties. Liza Minnelli (AA) and Joel Grey (AA) dealt vibrantly with the musical numbers, but the real star was choreographer/director Robert Fosse (AA). The film won five other Academy Awards.

Cabin in the Sky (US 1943). This all-black musical drama, a variation on the Faust theme, marked an important step forward in Hollywood's humanizing of coloured people, though they still seemed to live in a never-never all-black ghetto. Directed by Vincent Minnelli from the stage play by Lynn Root, John Latouche and Vernon Duke; photographed by Sidney Wagner; with Eddie Anderson, Ethel Waters and Lena Horne.

The Cabinet of Dr Caligari (Germany 1919). Classic horror film, valued not only for its expressionist sets and clever story finally revealed to have been told by a madman, but for its unmistakable influence on German film-making of the twenties. Werner Krauss, Conrad Veidt and Lil Dagover starred, Robert Weine directed from a script by Carl Mayer and Hans Janowitz; Willi Hameister was photographer. Allowing for certain primitive aspects, it still has power to thrill; certainly more so than the inferior American remake of 1962, which used the gimmicks but little else.

Cabiria (Italy 1913). A famous silent spectacle set in Caesarean Rome and concerning the romantic adventures of a lively lady saved as an infant from sacrifice to Baal. Her strong-man servant is one Maciste, who has reappeared as hero of scores of Italian adventure films since. Directed by Pastrone from a scenario by himself and Gabriele d'Annunzio; starring Lidia Quaranta, Bartolomeo Pagano. The original film ran over four hours: a condensed sound version was issued in 1930 and in 1950 came a rather poor remake. Fellini's *Nights of Cabiria* (Italy 1957) is something else again, a wry modern comedy about the ill-luck of a cheerful prostitute, starring Giulietta Masina. This emerged again in 1969 as the Hollywood musical *Sweet Charity*, with Shirley Maclaine.

cable cars have added excitement to the climax of many a film adventure, notably *Night Train to Munich*, *The Trollenberg Terror*, *Edge of Eternity*, *Second Chance*, *Where Eagles Dare*, *Hannibal Brooks* and *The Double Man*.

Cabot, Bruce (1904–1972) (Etienne Pelissier de Bujac). Square-jawed American hero of many a thirties action adventure; later turned up as a western villain.
Roadhouse Murder 32. *King Kong* 33. Murder on the Blackboard 34. Let 'Em Have It 35. Show Them No Mercy 35. Fury 36. Legion of Terror 37. Love Takes Flight 37. Smashing the Rackets

38. Homicide Bureau 39. Dodge City 39. Captain Caution 40. The Flame of New Orleans 41. Wild Bill Hickok Rides 42. The Desert Song 43. Salty O'Rourke 45. Fallen Angel 46. Angel and the Badman 47. Sorrowful Jones 49. Fancy Pants 50. Best of the Badmen 51. Kid Monk Baroni 52. The Quiet American 58. John Paul Jones 59. The Comancheros 61. Hatari 62. Law of the Lawless 64. Cat Ballou 65. The War Wagon 67. The Green Berets 68. Big Jake 71. Diamonds are Forever 71, many others.

Cabot, Sebastian (1918–). Weighty British character actor who became popular on American TV as the incarnation of the pompous but amiable Englishman.
Secret Agent 36. Love on the Dole 41. The Agitator 45. They Made Me a Fugitive 47. Dick Barton Strikes Back 48. Old Mother Riley's Jungle Treasure 50. Ivanhoe 52. Babes in Baghdad 52. Romeo and Juliet 54. *Kismet* 55. Dragoon Wells Massacre 57. Terror in a Texas Town 58. The Time Machine 60. Twice Told Tales 63. The Family Jewels 65, etc.
TV series: *Checkmate* 59–62. *A Family Affair* 66–70.

Cabot, Susan (1927–) (Harriet Shapiro). American leading lady of the fifties.
The Enforcer 50, Flame of Araby 51, Battle at Apache Pass 52. Duel at Silver Creek 52. Ride Clear of Diablo 54. Fort Massacre 58, etc.

Cacoyannis, Michael (1922–). Greek director, trained in England.
Windfall in Athens 53. Stella 54. A Girl in Black 55. A Matter of Dignity 57. One Last Spring 59. The Wastrel 61. Electra 62. *Zorba the Greek* 65. The Day the Fish Came Out 67. The Trojan Women 71.

Cadell, Jean (1884–1967). Sharp-faced Scottish character actress, typically cast as acidulous spinster and latterly dowager.
The Loves of Robert Burns 30. Fires of Fate 33. *David Copperfield* (as Mrs Micawber) 34. Love from a Stranger 37. *Pygmalion* 38. Quiet Wedding 40. The Young Mr Pitt 42. Dear Octopus 43. I Know Where I'm Going 45. Jassy 47. *Whisky Galore* 48. Madeleine 50. The Late Edwina Black 51. Marry Me 52. Rockets Galore 56. *A Taste of Honey* (leading role) 60, many others.

Caesar and Cleopatra (GB 1945). Notorious as Britain's most expensive picture, this entertaining version of Shaw's comedy was produced with unnecessary elaboration and recklessness by Gabriel Pascal. It did not do particularly well at the box office but has strong entertainment value mainly deriving from Shaw and the performances of Claude Rains and Vivien Leigh.

Caesar, Sid (1922–). American comedian, seldom in films but a big TV hit of the fifties.
☐ Tars and Spars 45. The Guilt of Janet Ames 47. It's a Mad Mad Mad Mad World 63. A Guide for the Married Man 67. The Busy Body 67. Ten from Your Show of Shows 74. Airport 75 75.

Cagney, James (1899–). American leading actor whose cocky walk and punchy personality took him out of the vaudeville chorus to become one of the most memorable stars of the thirties and forties. Whether as cop, gangster, western hero or Shakespearean clown, his staccato delivery has had a thousand imitators.
☐ Sinners' Holiday 30. Doorway to Hell 30. The Steel Highway 30. The Millionaire 31. Other Men's Women 31. *The Public Enemy* 31. Illicit 31. Smart Money 31. Blonde Crazy 31. Taxi 32. The Crowd Roars 32. Winner Take All 32. Hard to Handle 33. The Picture Snatcher 33. Mayor of Hell 33. *Footlight Parade* 33. *Lady Killer* 33. Jimmy the Gent 34. He was her Man 34. Here Comes the Navy 34. The St Louis Kid 34. *Devil Dogs of the Air* 35. *G-Men* 35. The Irish in Us 35. *A Midsummer Night's Dream* (as Bottom) 35. The Frisco Kid 35. Ceiling Zero 35. Great Guy 36. Something to Sing About 37. *Boy Meets Girl* 38. *Angels with Dirty Faces* 38. The Oklahoma Kid 39. Each Dawn I Die 39. *The Roaring Twenties* 39. The Fighting 69th 40. Torrid Zone 40. City for Conquest 40. *Strawberry Blonde* 41. The Bride Came C.O.D. 41. Captains of the Clouds 42. *Yankee Doodle Dandy* (AA; as George M. Cohan) 42. Johnny Come Lately 43. Blood on the Sun 45. 13 Rue Madeleine 46. *The Time of Your Life* 48. *White Heat* 49. West Point Story 50. Kiss Tomorrow Goodbye 50. Come Fill the Cup 51. Starlift 51. What Price Glory? 52. A Lion is in the Streets 53. Run for Cover 55. Love Me or Leave Me 55. The Seven Little Foys (guest) 55. *Mister Roberts* 55. Tribute to a Bad Man 56. These Wilder Years 56. *Man of a Thousand Faces* (as Lon Chaney) 57. Short Cut to Hell (d only) 58. Never Steal Anything Small 59. Shake Hands with the Devil 59. The Gallant Hours 60. *One Two Three* 61.

Cagney, Jeanne (1919–) (Jean Cagney), American actress, in occasional films: sister of James Cagney.
Golden Gloves 40. Yankee Doodle Dandy 42. The Time of Your Life 48. Don't Bother to

Knock 52. A Lion is in the Streets 53. Man of a Thousand Faces 57. Town Tamer 65, etc.

Cagney, William (1902–). American producer, brother of James Cagney.
Johnny Come Lately 43. Blood on the Sun 45. The Time of Your Life 48. Kiss Tomorrow Goodbye 50. A Lion is in the Streets 53, etc.

Cahn, Edward L. (1899–1963). American director of second features.
Homicide Squad 31. *Law and Order* 32 (his best film, with Walter Huston as Wyatt Earp). Confidential 35. Main Street After Dark 44. The Checkered Coat 48. Prejudice 48. Experiment Alcatraz (& p) 51. The Creature with the Atom Brain 55. Girls in Prison 56. Curse of the Faceless Man 58. Guns, Girls and Gangsters 58. It, The Terror from Beyond Space 58. Riot in a Juvenile Prison 61. Beauty and the Beast 62. Incident in an Alley 63, many others.

Cahn, Sammy (1913–). American lyricist who has written many film songs, usually with James Van Heusen. Won Academy Awards for four songs: 'Three Coins in the Fountain', 'High Hopes', 'All the Way' and 'Call Me Irresponsible'.
Tonight and Every Night 44. Anchors Aweigh 45. Wonder Man 45. West Point Story 50. April in Paris 53. The Court Jester 55, etc.

Cain, James M. (1892–). American novelist of the hard-boiled school; also worked in Hollywood.
She Made Her Bed (oa) 34. Stand Up and Fight (w) 38. When Tomorrow Comes (oa) 39. *Double Indemnity* (oa) 44. Gypsy Wildcat (w) 44. *Mildred Pierce* (oa) 45. *The Postman Always Rings Twice* (oa) 46. Serenade (oa) 56, etc.

Caine, Michael (1933–) (Maurice Micklewhite). British light leading man with effective mild manner and deliberately unconcealed cockney origin. Played for years in second features before his international appeal was discovered.
How to Marry a Rich Uncle 56. A Hill in Korea 56. Blind Spot 58. Solo for Sparrow 62, etc.
☐ COMPLETE FROM 1963: *Zulu* 63. *The Ipcress File* 65. *Alfie* 66. The Wrong Box 66. Gambit 66. Funeral in Berlin 66. Woman Times Seven 67. Hurry Sundown 67. Billion Dollar Brain 67. Deadfall 68. The Magus 68. Play Dirty 68. The Italian Job 69. The Battle of Britain 69. Too Late the Hero 69. The Last Valley 70. *Get Carter* 71. Zee and Co 71. Kidnapped 72. Pulp 72. *Sleuth* 73. The Black Windmill 73. The

Marseilles Contract 74. The Wilby Conspiracy 75. Peeper 75. The Romantic Englishwoman 75. The Man Who Would Be King 76. Harry and Walter Go To New York 76. The Eagle Has Landed 77.

The Caine Mutiny (US 1954). Humphrey Bogart gave his last notable performance as the paranoiac Captain Queeg in this solid film version by Edward Dmytryk of Herman Wouk's best seller about the courtroom drama following a modern naval mutiny. The film is otherwise significant as an example of the adult but not difficult themes being pursued by Hollywood at this time: long-time idols like the US Navy could be questioned but not yet toppled.

Calamity Jane (c. 1848–1903) (Martha Jane Canary). This rootin' tootin' shootin' woman of the old west has been glamorized many times for the movies, notably by Jean Arthur in *The Plainsman* 36, Frances Farmer in *Badlands of Dakota* 41. Jane Russell in *The Paleface* 48, Yvonne de Carlo in *Calamity Jane and Sam Bass* 49, Evelyn Ankers in *The Texan Meets Calamity Jane* 50, Doris Day in *Calamity Jane* 53, Judi Meredith in *The Raiders* 64, and Abby Dalton in *The Plainsman* 66.

Calder-Marshall, Anna (1949–). British leading actress.
Pussycat Pussycat I Love You 70. *Wuthering Heights* 70.

Caldwell, Erskine (1903–). American novelist who attacked social injustice in several novels which by their sensationalism earned him a fortune. *Tobacco Road* was filmed as a farce; *God's Little Acre* had to be taken straight.

Calhern, Louis (1895–1956) (Carl Vogt). Distinguished American stage actor who was in films occasionally from silent days and later became one of MGM's elder statesmen.
The Blot 21. Stolen Heaven 31. 20,000 Years in Sing Sing 32. Duck Soup 33. The Count of Monte Cristo 34. The Last Days of Pompeii 35. The Gorgeous Hussy 36. The Life of Emile Zola 37. Fast Company 38. Juarez 39. Charlie McCarthy Detective 39. Dr Ehrlich's Magic Bullet 40. Heaven Can Wait 43. The Bridge of San Luis Rey 44. Notorious 46. Arch of Triumph 48. *Annie Get Your Gun* 50. *The Asphalt Jungle* 50. *The Magnificent Yankee* 50. Man with a Cloak 51. We're Not Married 52. The Prisoner of Zenda 52. Julius Caesar 53. *Executive Suite* 54. The Student Prince 54. The Blackboard Jungle 55. The Prodigal 55. High Society 56, many others.

Calhoun, Rory (1922–) (Francis Timothy Durgin). Amiable American leading man of fifties action films; did not make the first rank.
Something for the Boys 44. The Red House 47. Miraculous Journey 48. Massacre River 49. Rogue River 50. I'd Climb the Highest Mountain 51. *With a Song in My Heart* 52. Powder River 53. *How to Marry a Millionaire* 53. Four Guns to the Border 54. Dawn at Socorro 54. Treasure of Pancho Villa 55. The Spoilers 55. Raw Edge 56. The Big Caper 57. The Hired Gun 57. The Colossus of Rhodes 60. Marco Polo 61. A Face in the Rain 62. The Gun Hawk 64. Apache Uprising 65. Finger on the Trigger 67. Dayton's Devils 68. Night of the Lepus 72, many others.
TV series: The Texan 58–60.

Callan, Michael (1935–) (Martin Caliniff). American leading man, former dancer.
They Came to Cordura 58. The Flying Fontaines 59. Mysterious Island 61. Bon Voyage 62. The Interns 63. The Victors 63. Cat Ballou 65. You Must Be Joking 65. Lepke 75, etc.
TV series: Occasional Wife 66.

Calleia, Joseph (1897–1976) (Joseph Spurin-Calleja). Humorous but often sinister Maltese character actor who after world tours as an opera singer settled in Hollywood in the thirties and played several distinguished roles.
His Woman 31, Public Hero Number One 35. After the Thin Man 36. Winner Take All 37. *Algiers* 38. Juarez 39. *Five Came Back* 39. Golden Boy 39. My Little Chickadee 40. The Monster and the Girl 41. Jungle Book 42. *The Glass Key* 42. For Whom the Bell Tolls 43. The Conspirators 44. *Gilda* 46. Lured 47. Four Faces West 48. Noose (GB) 48. Vendetta 50. Branded 51. Valentino 51. When in Rome 52. Treasure of Pancho Villa 55. Hot Blood 56. Serenade 56. Wild is the Wind 57. Touch of Evil 58. Cry Tough 59. The Alamo 60. Johnny Cool 63, many others.

Calloway, Cab (1907–) (Cabell Calloway). High-spirited black American band leader and entertainer, in occasional films.
The Big Broadcast 32. International House 33. The Singing Kid 36. Manhattan Merry Go Round 37. *Stormy Weather* 43. Sensations of 1945 44. St Louis Blues 58. The Cincinnati Kid 65. A Man Called Adam 66, etc.

Calthrop, Donald (1888–1940). Slightly-built British stage actor whose film appearances were usually as nervy villains.
The Gay Lord Quex 18. Nelson 19. *Shooting Stars* 27. *Blackmail* 29. Atlantic 30. Murder 30. The Bells 31. Number Seventeen 32. The Ghost Train 32. Rome Express 32. I Was a Spy 33. Friday the Thirteenth 33. Sorrell and Son 34. The Clairvoyant 34. Scrooge 35. Broken Blossoms 36. Fire Over England 36. Dreaming Lips 37. Let George Do It 40. Major Barbara 40, etc.

Calvert, Phyllis (1915–) (Phyllis Bickle). British leading lady of the forties, former child actress; usually played good girls.
Two Days to Live 39. They Came by Night 39. Charley's Big Hearted Aunt 40. Let George Do It 40. *Kipps* 41. The Young Mr Pitt 42. Uncensored 42. *The Man in Grey* 43. *Fanny by Gaslight* 44. Two Thousand Women 44. *Madonna of the Seven Moons* 44. They Were Sisters 45. Men of Two Worlds 46. The Magic Bow 46. The Root of All Evil 47. Time Out of Mind (US) 47. *My Own True Love* (US) 48. Broken Journey 48. Appointment with Danger (US) 49. The Golden Madonna 49. The Woman with No Name 50. Mr Denning Drives North 51. *Mandy* 52. The Net 53. It's Never Too Late 55. Child in the House 56. Indiscreet 58. Oscar Wilde 60. The Battle of the Villa Fiorita 65. Twisted Nerve 68. Oh What a Lovely War 69. The Walking Stick 69, etc.
TV series: *Kate* 70–71.

Calvet, Corinne (1925–) (Corinne Dibos). French leading lady, a statuesque blonde who had some success in Hollywood in the early fifties.
La Part de l'Ombre 45. Rope of Sand 49. When Willie Comes Marching Home 50. On the Riviera 51. What Price Glory? 52. Powder River 53. Flight to Tangier 53. The Far Country 54. So This Is Paris 55. The Plunderers of Painted Flats 58. Bluebeard's Ten Honeymoons 60. Hemingway's Adventures of a Young Man 62. Apache Uprising 65, etc.

Cambridge, Godfrey (1929–1976). Black American comic actor.
The Last Angry Man 59. Gone are the Days 63. The Busy Body 67. The President's Analyst 67. Bye Bye Braverman 68. The Biggest Bundle of Them All 68. *Watermelon Man 70. Cotton Comes to Harlem* 71. The Biscuit Eater 72. Come Back Charleston Blue 72, etc.

Camelot (US 1967). This overlong film version by Joshua Logan of the Lerner and Loewe stage musical proved to be a deliberately sober retelling of the Arthurian myth, with too few successful flights of fancy and too little of the wit of T. H. White's *The Once and Future King* on which it was based. The music however was splendid, and intelligence was evident though

misapplied. Richard Harris and Vanessa Redgrave were perhaps the last non-singers to be entrusted with major singing roles; they were in any case upstaged by John Truscott's set designs.
See also: *Arthur*.

Camerini, Mario (1895–). Italian director.
I Promessi Sposi 41. Molti Sogni per le Strade 48. Il Brigante Musolino 50. Wife for a Night 50. Honeymoon Deferred 51. Ulysses 55. Kali-Yug Goddess of Vengeance 63, many others.

Cameron, Earl (1925–). Jamaican actor seen in many British films.
Pool of London 50. Emergency Call 51. The Heart of the Matter 53. Simba 55. Safari 56. Sapphire 59. Flame in the Streets 61. Guns at Batasi 64. Thunderball 65. Battle Beneath the Earth 68, etc.

Cameron, John (–). British composer.
Every Home Should Have One 70. Kes 70. Night Watch 73. A Touch of Class 73. Scalawag 73.

Cameron, Rod (1910–) (Nathan Cox). Rugged Canadian star of many a Hollywood second feature; originally labourer, engineer, and stand-in for Fred MacMurray.
Christmas in July 40. Northwest Mounted Police 40. The Monster and the Girl 41. The Remarkable Andrew 42. Wake Island 42. Gung Ho 43. Boss of Boom Town 44. Salome Where She Danced 45. The Runaround 46. The Bride Wasn't Willing 46. The Plunderers 48. Panhandle 49. The Sea Hornet 51. Ride the Man Down 53. Escapement (GB) 57. The Gun Hawk 63. The Bounty Killer 65. Old Firehand (Ger.) 66. The Last Movie 71. Evel Knievel 71, many others.
TV series: City Detective 53–55. Coronado 9 59. State Trooper 60.

Camille. The Dumas *fils* tear-jerker about a courtesan dying of tuberculosis has been a favourite vehicle for many actresses. On screen, Bernhardt did it in 1912, Clara Kimball Young in 1915, Theda Bara in 1917, Nazimova (with Rudolph Valentino) in 1920, Pola Negri in 1920, Norma Talmadge (with Gilbert Roland) in 1927 and Garbo (with Robert Taylor) in 1936. In postwar years many producers must have eyed it longingly before deciding that it belonged to a bygone age: but in 1969 *Camille 2000* arrived, decked out with drugs and heavy sex.

Campanella, Joseph (1927–). American stage and TV actor who makes occasional film appearances.

Murder Inc. 61. The Young Lovers 64. The St Valentine's Day Massacre 67. Ben 72, etc.
TV series: *Mannix* 67–69. The Bold Ones 70.

Campbell, Beatrice (1923–). British leading lady.
Wanted for Murder 46. Things Happen at Night 48. Silent Dust 48. Last Holiday 50. The Mudlark 50. Laughter in Paradise 51. Grand National Night 53. Cockleshell Heroes 55, etc.

Campbell, Eric (1878–1917). Scottish actor who played the bearded heavy in some of Chaplin's most famous two-reelers 1916–17: *Easy Street, The Cure, The Adventurer*, etc.

Campbell, Glen (1935–). American pop singer, venturing into films.
True Grit 69. Norwood 69.

Campbell, Judy (1916–) (Judy Gamble). British leading lady of stage and TV; film appearances infrequent.
Saloon Bar 40. Breach of Promise 41. The World Owes Me a Living 44. Green for Danger 46. Bonnie Prince Charlie 48. There's a Girl in My Soup 70. Forbush and the Penguins 71, etc.

Campbell, Mrs Patrick (1865–1940) (Beatrice Tanner). Leading British stage actress, the original Eliza in *Pygmalion*, who spent her last years playing supporting roles in Hollywood.
The Dancers 30. Riptide 34. One More River 34. Outcast Lady 34. Crime and Punishment 35, etc.

Campbell, Patrick (1907–). British humorist and screenplay writer, the latter usually with Vivienne Knight.
Captain Boycott 47. Helter Skelter 50. The Oracle 54. Lucky Jim 57. Go to Blazes 62. Girl in the Headlines 63, etc.

Campbell, William (1926–). American actor, often seen as personable villain or friend of the hero.
The Breaking Point 50. The People Against O'Hara 52. Escape from Fort Bravo 53. The High and the Mighty 54. Man without a Star 55. Cell 2455 Death Row (as Caryl Chessman) 55. Backlash 56. Eighteen and Anxious 57. The Naked and the Dead 58. The Young Racers 63. The Secret Invasion 64. Hush Hush Sweet Charlotte 64. Dementia 13 65. Blood Bath 66. Black Gunn 72. Dirty Mary Crazy Larry 74, etc.

Camus, Marcel (1912–). French director, chiefly known for *Black Orpheus* 58.

Canada has made strenuous efforts through the

years to promote a native film industry, but the trouble has been that its best talents are easily siphoned off to Hollywood or Britain, and few genuinely Canadian films have earned world acclaim; among those to raise interest have been *Mon Oncle Antoine* and *The Apprenticeship of Duddy Kravitz*. The National Film Board of Canada, however, has had a stimulating effect on world documentary, especially when under the leadership of John Grierson: and Norman McLaren's experimental cartoons are enjoyed the world over.

Films wholly or largely set in Canada have included *Saskatchewan, Quebec, Northwest Mounted Police, The Canadians, River's End, The Naked Heart, Northern Pursuit, Island in the Sky, Hudson's Bay, Rose Marie* and *Jalna*.

Canale, Gianna Maria (1927–). Italian leading lady, occasionally seen in international films.
Rigoletto 49. Go For Broke 51. The Man from Cairo 53. Theodora Slave Empress 54. The Silent Enemy 58. The Whole Truth 58. Queen of the Pirates 60. Scaramouche 63, etc.

cannibalism has been featured in such documentaries as *The Sky Above, The Mud Below*, but it is rare in fiction films. Apart from the Swedish short *Midvinterblot*, the main examples are from the seventies: *Welcome to Arrow Beach* and *Survive!*

Cannon, Dyan (1938–) (Samile Diane Friesen). American leading actress who tends to play floosies.
The Rise and Fall of Legs Diamond 59. *Bob and Carol and Ted and Alice* 69. Doctors' Wives 70. The Anderson Tapes 71. The Love Machine 71. *Such Good Friends* 72. Shamus 72. The Last of Sheila 73, etc.

Cannon, Esma (–1972). Diminutive British character actress often seen in bit parts.
Notable in *Sailor Beware* 56.

Cannon, J. D. (1922–). Cold-eyed American character actor.
An American Dream 66. Cool Hand Luke 67. Cotton Comes to Harlem 71. Lawman 71, etc.
TV series: McCloud 71–.

Cannon, Robert (1901–1964). American animator, a leading figure at UPA during the formative period and the designer of simplified, witty cartoon like *Gerald McBoing Boing* and *Christopher Crumpet*.

Canova, Judy (1916–) (Juliet Canova).

American hillbilly comedienne whose strident yodelling and cornfed humour enlivened a number of forties programmers.
In Caliente 35. Artists and Models 37. Scatterbrain 40. Sis Hopkins 41. Sleepytime Gal 42. Joan of the Ozarks 42. Chatterbox 43. Louisiana Hayride 44. Hit the Hay 45. Singin' in the Corn 46. Honeychile 51. Oklahoma Annie 52. Untamed Heiress 54. Carolina Cannonball 55. The Adventures of Huckleberry Finn 60, etc.

Cantinflas (1911–) (Mario Moreno). Mexican clown, acrobat and bullfighter who made unambitious local comedies for years and was briefly beckoned by Hollywood in the fifties. Immensely popular in Spanish-speaking countries.
Neither Blood Nor Sand 41. Romeo and Juliet 44. *Around the World in Eighty Days* 56. *Pepe* 59, many others.

Cantor, Eddie (1892–1964) (Edward Israel Iskowitz). Rolling-eyed American vaudeville entertainer whose inimitable high-toned voice and sprightly movement made him a big Hollywood star of the thirties. He later made a huge hit in radio, and wrote several autobiographical books including *Take My Life* (57), *The Way I See It* (59) and *As I Remember Them* (62). He appeared briefly in a 1953 biopic, *The Eddie Cantor Story*, in which he was played by Keefe Brasselle, and in 1956 received an Academy Award for distinguished service to the film industry'.
□ Kid Boots 26. Special Delivery 27. Glorifying the American Girl 29. *Whoopee* 30. Palmy Days 31. *The Kid from Spain* 32. Roman Scandals 33. Kid Millions 34. Strike Me Pink 35. Ali Baba Goes to Town 37. Forty Little Mothers 40. *Thank Your Lucky Stars* 43. *Show Business* 44. If You Knew Susie 48. The Story of Will Rogers (guest) 52.

Canty, Marietta (–). Black American character actress.
The Searching Wind 46. Home Sweet Homicide 47. Father of the Bride 50. The I Don't Care Girl 53. My Foolish Heart 53, etc.

Canutt, Yakima (1895–) (Enos Edward Canutt). Famous half-Indian stunt man of American westerns for half a century. Later graduated to second unit direction on epics of the sixties.

Capellani, Albert (1870–1931). French director of silent films, in Hollywood from 1915.
Camille 15. La Vie de Bohème 16. Daybreak 17.

The Red Lantern 19. The Fortune Teller 20. The Young Diana 22. Sisters 22, etc.

Capone, Al (1899–1947). Italian-American gangster, the king of Chicago during the roaring twenties. Has been impersonated many times on screen, notably by Paul Muni (*Scarface*), Edward G. Robinson (*Little Caesar*), Rod Steiger (*Al Capone*), Neville Brand (*The Scarface Mob*), Jason Robards (*The St Valentine's Day Massacre*).

Capote, Truman (1925–). American novelist. Works filmed include *Breakfast at Tiffany's*, *In Cold Blood*. Contributed to scripts of *Beat the Devil*, *The Innocents*. Appeared as actor in *Murder By Death* 76.

Capra, Frank (1897–). Italian-American director who is justly celebrated for a stylish handful of thirties and forties comedies demonstrating a whimsical attachment to the common man and to the belief that even the nastiest of us can be human if given a chance. His best films are masterpieces of timing and organization, but his career ended with sentimental and flabby remakes of his own successes. Autobiography 1971: *The Name Above the Title*.

□ The Strong Man 26. Tramp Tramp Tramp 26. Long Pants 27. For the Love of Mike 27. That Certain Feeling 28. So This is Love 28. The Matinée Idol 28. The Way of the Strong 28. Say it with Sables 28. Submarine 28. Power of the Press 28. The Younger Generation 29. The Donovan Affair 29. Flight 29. Ladies of Leisure 30. Rain or Shine 30. Dirigible 31. The Miracle Woman 31. Forbidden 31. *Platinum Blonde* 32. *American Madness* 32. The Bitter Tea of General Yen 32. *Lady for a Day* 33. *It Happened One Night* (AA) 34. *Mr Deeds Goes to Town* 36. *Lost Horizon* 37. *You Can't Take It With You* (AA) 38. *Mr Smith Goes to Washington* 39. *Meet John Doe* 41. *Why We Fight* (war documentaries) 42–44. Arsenic and Old Lace 44. *It's A Wonderful Life* 46. State of the Union 48. Riding High 50. Here Comes the Groom 51. A Hole in the Head 59. Pocketful of Miracles 61.

Captain Blood. Swashbuckling melodrama from Rafael Sabatini's novel, filmed in 1925 with J. Warren Kerrigan, in 1935 with Errol Flynn. In 1962 Flynn's son Sean starred in an Italian-made *Son of Captain Blood*; and, during the early fifties, Louis Hayward starred in *The Fortunes of Captain Blood* and *Captain Blood Fugitive* (*Captain Pirate*).

Capucine (1933–) (Germaine Lefebvre). Lean and beautiful French model who has been leading lady of a number of international films.
Song Without End 60. A Walk on the Wild Side 62. *The Pink Panther* 63. The Seventh Dawn 64. What's New Pussycat? 65. The Honey Pot 67. The Queens 67. Satyricon 69. Red Sun 72, etc.

Cardiff, Jack (1914–). Superb British colour cinematographer who became an indifferent director of routine films.
AS CINEMATOGRAPHER: *Wings of the Morning* 37. *The Four Feathers* 39. *Western Approaches* 44. Caesar and Cleopatra 45. *A Matter of Life and Death* 46. *Black Narcissus* (AA) 46. *The Red Shoes* 48. Pandora and the Flying Dutchman 51. The Barefoot Contessa 54. *War and Peace* 56. The Vikings 58, many others.
□ AS DIRECTOR: Intent to Kill 58. Beyond this Place 59. Scent of Mystery 60. *Sons and Lovers* 60. My Geisha 62. The Lion 62. The Long Ships 64. Young Cassidy 65. The Liquidator 65. Dark of the Sun 67. Girl on a Motorcycle (& p, & ph) 69. The Mutations 74. Penny Gold 74.

Cardinale, Claudia (1939–). Italian leading lady who was given the international star build-up but did not quite manage the front rank.
Persons Unknown 58. Upstairs and Downstairs (GB) 58. Il Bell'Antonio 59. Rocco and his Brothers 60. Cartouche 61. The Leopard 62. Eight and a Half 63. *The Pink Panther* 63. Circus World 64. Vaghe Stella dell'Orsa 65. Blindfold 65. Lost Command 66. The Professionals 66. Don't Make Waves 67. The Queens 67. Day of the Owl 68. The Hell with Heroes 68. Once Upon a Time in the West 69. A Fine Pair 69. Adventures of Brigadier Gerard 70. Popsy Pop 70. The Red Tent 71. Papal Audience 71. Days of Fury 73, etc.

Carere, Christine (1930–). French leading lady who had a brief Hollywood career.
Olivia 50. Les Collégiennes 57. *A Certain Smile* 57. Mardi Gras 58. A Private Affair 59. I Deal in Danger 66, etc.

Carette (1897–1966) (Julien Carette). Dapper French character actor.
L'Affaire est dans le Sac 32. La Grande Illusion 37. La Bête Humaine 38. La Marseillaise 38. *La Règle du Jeu* 39. Adieu Léonard 43. Sylvie et le Fantôme 45. Les Portes de la Nuit 46. *Occupe-Toi d'Amélie* 49. *The Red Inn* 51. Éléna et les Hommes 55. Archimède le Clochard 59. The Green Mare's Nest 61, many others.

Carew, Arthur Edward (1894–1937). American character actor.

Rio Grande 20. The Ghost Breaker 22. Trilby 23. The Phantom of the Opera 25. The Torrent 26. Uncle Tom's Cabin 27. The Cat and the Canary 27. Sweet Kitty Bellairs 30. Doctor X 32. The Mystery of the Wax Museum 33. Charlie Chan's Secret 36, many others.

Carewe, Edwin (1883–1940) (Jay Fox). American director of silent films noted for their pictorial beauty.
The Final Judgment 15. The Trail to Yesterday 18. Shadow of Suspicion 19. Rio Grande 20. Son of the Sahara 24. Resurrection 27. Ramona 28. Evangeline 29. The Spoilers 30. Are We Civilized? 34, etc.

Carey, Harry (1878–1947). American leading man of silent westerns who later became a character actor in quiet dependable roles.
Riding the Trail 11. Travellin' On 14. Two Guns 17. The Outcasts of Poker Flat 19. Desperate Trails 20. Man to Man 22. Roaring Rails 24. The Texas Trail 25. Trail of 98 27. *Trader Horn* 30. Law and Order 32. Barbary Coast 35. Sutter's Gold 36. Kid Galahad 37. King of Alcatraz 38. *Mr Smith Goes to Washington* 39. They Knew What They Wanted 40. The Spoilers 42. Happy Land 43. The Great Moment 44. Duel in the Sun 46, many others.

Carey, Harry, Jnr (1921–). American light actor, son of Harry Carey; followed his father's example and was seen mostly in westerns.
Pursued 47. Red River 48. So Dear to My Heart 49. Wagonmaster 50. Rio Grande 50. Island in the Sky 53. The Long Gray Line 55. The Searchers 56. The River's Edge 57. Rio Bravo 59. The Great Imposter 61. Alvarez Kelly 66. Bandolero 68. One More Time 71. A Man from the East 74, many others.

Carey, Joyce (1898–) (Joyce Lawrence). British stage actress, daughter of Lilian Braithwaite; made a few silent films then appeared more regularly as upper-class ladies in the forties and fifties.
God and the Man 21. The Newcomes 25. *In Which We Serve* 42. Blithe Spirit 45. *The Way to the Stars* 45. *Brief Encounter* 47. The October Man 48. London Belongs to Me 48. The Chiltern Hundreds 49. The Astonished Heart 50. Happy Go Lovely 51. Cry the Beloved Country 52. The End of the Affair 55. The Eyes of Annie Jones 63. A Nice Girl Like Me 69. The Black Windmill 74, etc.

Carey, Leonard (1893–). British character actor in Hollywood in the forties, best remembered as old Ben in *Rebecca* 40.

Carey, Macdonald (1913–). American leading man, usually the sympathetic good guy in routine romantic comedy-dramas.
Dr Broadway 42. Wake Island 42. Shadow of a Doubt 43. Suddenly It's Spring 46. Dream Girl 47. East of Java 49. Streets of Laredo 49. The Lawless 50. Copper Canyon 50. Let's Make It Legal 51. My Wife's Best Friend 52. Stranger at My Door 56. Blue Denim 59. The Damned (GB) 62. Tammy and the Doctor 63. Broken Sabre 65, etc.
TV series: Dr Christian 56. Lock Up 59–61.

Carey, Phil or **Philip** (1925–). American leading man of the rugged but good-humoured type, in routine films of the fifties and sixties; latterly in senior officer roles.
Operation Pacific 51. *Pushover* 54. Mister Roberts 55. Port Afrique 56. *Wicked As They Come* 56. Screaming Mimi 58. Tonka 59. The Time Travellers 64. The Great Sioux Massacre (as Custer) 65. The Seven Minutes 71, many others.
TV series: 77th Bengal Lancers 56. Philip Marlowe 59. Laredo 66–67.

Carey, Timothy (c. 1925–). Heavy-eyed American character actor, often a loathsome villain.
Hellgate 52. Alaska Seas 54. The Killing 56. Paths of Glory 57. One-Eyed Jacks 61. Reprieve 62. Bikini Beach 64. Waterhole Three 67. Head 68. Minnie and Moskowitz 71. The Conversation 73, etc.

Carfagno, Edward C. (–). American art director.
Skyjacked 73. The Man Who Loved Cat Dancing 73.

Cargill, Patrick (1918–). Impeccable British farce actor with long stage experience.
The Cracksman 60. This is My Street 63. A Stitch in Time 64. *A Countess from Hong Kong* 66. Inspector Clouseau 68. Every Home Should Have One 70. Up Pompeii 71. Father Dear Father 73, etc.
TV series: *Father Dear Father* 69–75.

Carle, Richard (1871–1941) (Charles Carleton). American character actor.
Zander The Great 25. Eve's Leaves 26. The Understanding Heart 27. Madame X 28. Brothers 30. One Hour With You 32. Morning Glory 33. Caravan 34. The Ghost Walks 35. Anything Goes 36. One Rainy Afternoon 36. True Confession 37. Persons in Hiding 39. The Great McGinty 40. The Uncertain Feeling 41, many others.

Carlin, Lynn (1930–). American character actress.
Faces 68. Tick Tick Tick 70. *Taking Off* 71. Wild Rovers 71, etc.

Carlino, Lewis John (–). American screenwriter.
The Mechanic 72. Crazy Joe 74. The Sailor who Fell from Grace with the Sea (& p) 76.

Carlisle, Kitty (1915–) (Catherine Holzman). American operatic singer, briefly with MGM in the thirties.
□ Murder at the Vanities 34. She Loves Me Not 34. Here is my Heart 34. *A Night at the Opera* 35. Hollywood Canteen 43.

Carlisle, Mary (1912–). American leading lady of the thirties.
Justice for Sale 32. College Humor 33. One Frightened Night 35. Love in Exile 36. Dr Rhythm 38. Call a Messenger 40. Baby Face Morgan 42, etc.

Carlo-Rim (1905–) (Jean-Marius Richard). French writer-director, mainly of Fernandel comedies.
L'Armoire Volante 47. Les Truands (Lock Up the Spoons) 56. Le Petit Prof 59, etc.

Carlson, Richard (1912–). American leading man of the forties, mainly in routine films; played the diffident juvenile so long that he had nothing to give to mature roles.
The Young in Heart 38. Winter Carnival 39. The Ghost Breakers 40. No No Nanette 40. Back Street 41. Hold that Ghost 41. *The Little Foxes* 41. White Cargo 42. Presenting Lily Mars 43. So Well Remembered 47. Behind Closed Doors 48. King Solomon's Mines 50. The Blue Veil 51. Valentino 51. Whispering Smith Hits London 52. The Magnetic Monster 53. It Came from Outer Space 53. All I Desire 53. Riders to the Stars (& d) 54. The Creature from the Black Lagoon 54. Four Guns to the Border (d only) 54. Three for Jamie Dawn 56. The Helen Morgan Story 57. Appointment with a Shadow (d only) 59. Kid Rodelo (& d) 66. The Power 68. The Valley of Gwangi 69, many others.
TV series: Mackenzie's Raiders 58.

Carlson, Veronica (1944–). British leading lady, mainly in screamies.
Dracula has Risen from the Grave 68. Frankenstein must be Destroyed 69. The Horror of Frankenstein 70. Pussycat Pussycat I Love You 70, etc.

Carmel, Roger C. (1929–). Rotund American character actor.

Goodbye Charlie 64. The Silencers 66. Gambit 66. The Venetian Affair 66. Skullduggery 69.

Carmen. Prosper Mérimée's high-romantic tale of a fatal gypsy whose worthless attractions wreck men's lives was promptly turned by Bizet into an opera which has been filmed many times, notably as *Carmen Jones* 54. The straight dramatic story, however, probably holds the record for the number of film versions it has spawned:

France	1909 with	Victoria Lepanto
Spain	1910	actress unknown
US	1913	Marguerite Snow
US	1913	Marion Leonard
Spain	1914	actress unknown
US	1915	Geraldine Farrar
US	1915	Edna Purviance (*Burlesque on Carmen*)
US	1916	Theda Bara
US	1918	Pola Negri
US	1921	Raquel Miller
US	1927	Dolores del Rio
France	1942	Vivianne Romance
US	1948	Rita Hayworth
US/WG	1966	Uta Levke

Carmichael, Hoagy (1899–) (Hoagland Howard Carmichael). American song composer and lyricist, best known for 'Stardust' and 'In the Cool, Cool, Cool of the Evening' (AA 1951). Also a slow-speaking actor of light supporting roles, usually involving his singing at the piano.
Autobiographies: *The Stardust Road* 1946. *Sometimes I Wonder* 1965.
As actor/performer: To Have and Have Not 44. Canyon Passage 46. *The Best Years of Our Lives* 46. Young Man with a Horn 50. Belles on Their Toes 52. Timberjack 55, etc.
TV series: Laramie 59–63.

Carmichael, Ian (1920–). British light leading man, adept at nervous novices; long experience in revue.
Meet Mr Lucifer 54. The Colditz Story 54. Storm over the Nile 55. *Simon and Laura* 55. *Private's Progress* 55. *Brothers in Law* 56. *Lucky Jim* 57. Happy is the Bride 57. The Big Money 57. Left, Right and Centre 59. School for Scoundrels 59. *I'm All Right Jack* 59. Light Up the Sky 60. Double Bunk 61. The Amorous Prawn 62. Hide and Seek 63. Heavens Above 63. Smashing Time 67. The Magnificent Seven Deadly Sins 71, etc.

Carminati, Tullio (1894–1971) (Count Tullio Carminati de Brambilla). Italian romantic actor who had a modest career in British and American as well as European films.

The Bat 26. Three Sinners 28. Moulin Rouge 33. *One Night of Love* 34. *The Three Maxims* 35. The Girl in the Street 38. Safari 40. The Golden Madonna 49. La Beauté du Diable 51. Roman Holiday 53. Saint Joan 57. El Cid 61. The Cardinal 63, many others.

Carne, Judy (1939–). Pert British actress who found fame as the 'sock it to me' girl in Hollywood's *Laugh-In* TV series.
A Pair of Briefs 63. The Americanization of Emily 64. All the Right Noises 69, etc.
TV series: Love on a Rooftop 66.

Carné, Marcel (1903–). Certainly the most brilliant of French directors 1937–45; his career later suffered a semi-eclipse.
☐ Jenny 36. *Drôle de Drame* 37. *Quai des Brumes* 38. Hôtel du Nord 38. *Le Jour Se Lève* 39. *Les Visiteurs du Soir* 42. *Les Enfants du Paradis* 44. Les Portes de la Nuit 46. La Marie du Port 48. Juliette Ou La Clef des Songes 51. Thérèse Racquin 53. L'Air de Paris 54. Le Pays d'Où Je Viens 56. Les Tricheurs 58. Terrain Vague 60. Du Mouron pour les Petits Oiseaux 62. Three Rooms in Manhattan 65. The Young Wolves 68. Les Assassins de L'Ordre 71.

Un Carnet de Bal (France 1937). A romantic trifle which found director Julien Duvivier at the top of his cinematic form and was influential because of its linking of several stories through an inanimate object (a dance programme remembered by the heroine). As an entertainment it now seems thin despite its star cast, but it sent Duvivier off to Hollywood where he directed a partial remake (*Lydia*) and some variations (*Tales of Manhattan, Flesh and Fantasy*).

Carney, Alan (1911–73). American comedy supporting actor who in the mid-forties made some second features with *Wally Brown* (qv). His solo appearances were sparse.
Mr Lucky 43. The Pretender 47. Lil Abner 59. It's a Mad Mad Mad Mad World 63. The Love Bug Rides Again 73, etc.

Carney, Art (1918–). American comedy actor, popular on TV.
Pot O'Gold 41. The Yellow Rolls Royce 64. A Guide for the Married Man 67. *Harry and Tonto* (AA) 74. Won Ton Ton 76. Lanigan's Rabbi (TV) 76, etc.

Carney, George (1887–1947). British character actor of stage and screen.
Say It With Flowers 34. Father Steps Out (title role) 37. The Stars Look Down 39. Convoy 40.

Love on the Dole 41. The Common Touch 41. Tawny Pipit 44. I Know Where I'm Going 45. Good Time Girl 47, etc.

carnivals. See *Funfairs.*

Carnovsky, Morris (1898–). Distinguished American stage actor who has appeared in occasional films.
The Life of Emile Zola 37. Tovarich 37. Address Unknown 44. *Rhapsody in Blue* (as Gershwin Snr) 45. Our Vines Have Tender Grapes 45. Dead Reckoning 47. Saigon 48. Thieves' Highway 49. Cyrano de Bergerac 51. A View from the Bridge 61, etc.

Carol, Martine (1922–1967) (Maryse Mourer). French leading lady popular in undressed roles in the early fifties.
Voyage Surprise 48. *Caroline Chérie* 50. A Night with Caroline 52. *Lucrezia Borgia* 52. The Bed 53. The Beach 54. Nana 55. *Lola Montes* 55. Action of the Tiger 57. Ten Seconds to Hell 59. Le Cave Se Rebiffe 61. Hell is Empty 66, etc.

Carol, Sue (1907–) (Evelyn Lederer). American leading lady of the early thirties.
Is Zat So? 27. Girls Gone Wild 29. Dancing Sweeties 30. Her Golden Calf 30. Graft 31. Secret Sinners 34. A Doctor's Diary 37, etc.

Caron, Leslie (1931–). French leading lady and dancer who after being discovered by Gene Kelly followed a successful English-speaking career in light drama and comedy.
☐ *An American In Paris* 51. Man with a Cloak 51. Glory Alley 52. The Story of Three Loves 53. *Lili* (BFA) 53. The Glass Slipper 54. Daddy Longlegs 55. Gaby 56. *Gigi* 58. The Doctor's Dilemma 58. The Man Who Understood Women 59. The Subterraneans 60. Austerlitz 60. *Fanny* 61. Guns of Darkness 63. *The L-Shaped Room* (BFA) 62. Three Fables of Love 63. Father Goose 64. A Very Special Favour 65. Promise Her Anything 66. Is Paris Burning? 66. Head of the Family 68. Madron 69. Chandler 72. QB VII (TV) 74.

Carpenter, Carleton (1926–). American light leading man groomed by MGM in the early fifties.
Lost Boundaries 48. Father of the Bride 50. Summer Stock 51. Fearless Fagan 53. Sky Full of Moon 53. Take the High Ground 53. Up Periscope 59. Some of My Best Friends Are 71.

Carpenter, Paul (1921–1964). Canadian leading man long in Britain as hero of scores of second features.

School for Secrets 46. Albert RN 53. Night People 54. The Sea Shall Not Have Them 55. Fire Maidens from Outer Space 56. The Iron Petticoat 56. Jet Storm 59. Murder Reported 60. Call Me Bwana 63, etc.

The Carpetbaggers (US 1963). The film of Harold Robbins' salacious novel was a watered-down affair but still helped to break the Production Code, and stands also as an example of how Joe Levine's publicity machine could make a mountain out of a molehill. Set in Hollywood in the thirties, the film had George Peppard as a Howard Hughes-type mogul and Carroll Baker as a Jean Harlow-type star, with a remarkably effective last performance from Alan Ladd as the hero's sidekick Nevada Smith, whose unlikely early life in the west was promptly turned into another movie starring Steve McQueen.

Carr, Jane (1909–1957) (Rita Brunstrom). British leading lady, in occasional films.
Taxi to Paradise 33. Lord Edgware Dies 37. Lilac Domino 37. The Lady from Lisbon 37. It's Not Cricket 48. 36 Hours 54, etc.

Carr, John Dickson (1905–1977). American detective story writer, curiously few of whose many novels have been adapted for the screen.
Man with a Cloak 51. That Woman Upstairs 52, etc.

Carr, Mary (1874–1973). Leading American character actress of the twenties; the archetypal white-haired old mother.
Mrs Wiggs of the Cabbage Patch 19. Over the Hill to the Poorhouse 20. Silver Wings 22. Why Men Leave Home 24. The Wizard of Oz 25. Jesse James 27. Lights of New York 28. Beyond Victory 31. Change of Heart 34. East Side of Heaven 36. Friendly Persuasion 56, many others.

Carr, Thomas (1907–). American director, mainly of second feature westerns. Went into TV.
West of the Brazos 50. Captain Scarlett 52. Superman 54. Three for Jamie Dawn 57. Dino 57. Tall Stranger 58. Cast a Long Shadow 59, etc.

Carradine, David (1940–). Lanky American character actor, son of John Carradine.
The Violent Ones 67. Young Billy Young 69. The McMasters 70. Macho Callahan 71. Boxcar Bertha 72. You and Me (& d) 73. Death Race 2000 75. Cannonball 76, etc.
TV series: *Shane* 66. *Kung Fu* 72–74.

Carradine, John (1906–) (Richmond Reed Carradine). Gaunt American actor who scored a fine run of character roles in the thirties and forties but later sank to mad doctors in cheap horror movies, touring meanwhile with one-man Shakespeare readings. Played 1930–35 under the name John Peter Richmond.
Tol'able David 30. The Sign of the Cross 32. Cleopatra 34. Bride of Frankenstein 35. Dimples 36. The Prisoner of Shark Island 36. The Garden of Allah 36. Winterset 36. Captains Courageous 36. The Last Gangster 37. The Hurricane 37. Alexander's Ragtime Band 38. Jesse James 39. Drums along the Mohawk 39. *Five Came Back* 39. *Stagecoach* 39. Brigham Young 40. *The Grapes of Wrath* 40. Blood and Sand 41. Man Hunt 41. Son of Fury 42. *The Black Swan* 42. Hitler's Madman (as Heydrich) 43. Gangway for Tomorrow 43. *Bluebeard* (title Role) 44. The Invisible Man's Revenge 44. It's In the Bag 45. *House of Frankenstein* (as Dracula) 45. Fallen Angel 45. House of Dracula 45. The Face of Marble 46. The Private Affairs of Bel Ami 47. C-Man 49. Casanova's Big Night 54. The Egyptian 54. The Kentuckian 55. The Black Sleep 56. The Ten Commandments 56. Hell Ship Mutiny 57. The Last Hurrah 58. The Cosmic Man 59. Sex Kittens go to College 60. Invasion of the Animal People 62. *The Man Who Shot Liberty Valance* 62. Cheyenne Autumn 64. Billy the Kid vs Dracula 66. Hillbillies in a Haunted House 67. The Fiend with the Electronic Brain 67. The Astro-Zombies 68. The Good Guys and the Bad Guys 69. Bigfoot 69. The McMasters 70. The Seven Minutes 71. Boxcar Bertha 72. The House of the Seven Corpses 73. Silent Night Bloody Night 74. The Shootist 76, many others.

Carradine, Keith (–). American leading man of the seventies, half brother of David Carradine.
□ A Gunfight 71. McCabe and Mrs Miller 71. Hex 73. Emperor of the North 73. Thieves Like Us 74. Nashville 75.

Carreras, James (1910–). British production executive, former exhibitor; chairman of Hammer Films.

Carreras, Michael (1927–). British producer-director for Hammer Films of which he has been managing director since 1971; son of James Carreras.
Blackout (p) 54. The Snorkel (p) 57. Ten Seconds to Hell (p) 58. Passport to China (pd) 61. The Two Faces of Dr Jekyll (d) 61. Maniac (d) 62. What a Crazy World (d) 63. The Curse of the Mummy's Tomb (d) 64. She (p) 65. One Million Years B.C. (p) 67. The Lost Continent (pd) 68, etc.

Carrick, Edward (1905–) (Edward Anthony Craig). British art director, son of Edward Gordon Craig.
Autumn Crocus 34. Jump for Glory 36. Captain Boycott 47. The Divided Heart 54. Tiger Bay 59. What a Crazy World 63. The Nanny 65, many others.

Carriere, Jean-Claude (1931–). French screen writer who began by collaborating with Tati and Etaix.
Viva Maria 65. Le Voleur 67. Borsalino 67. Taking Off 71. The Discreet Charm of the Bourgeoisie 72, etc. (usually in collaboration).

Carrillo, Leo (1880–1961). American light character actor. A Spanish Californian from a wealthy landowning family, he enjoyed many years in Hollywood as an assortment of amiably talkative fellows, usually in fractured English.
Mr Antonio 29. Hell Bound 31. Girl of the Rio 31. The Broken Wing 32. Moonlight and Pretzels 33. Manhattan Melodrama 34. In Caliente 32. *The Gay Desperado* 36. *History is Made at Night* 37. Blockade 38. Rio 39. Lillian Russell 40. Horror Island 41. Riders of Death Valley 41. Sin Town 42. Top Sergeant 43. Ghost Catchers 44. Mexicana 45. The Fugitive 47. The Gay Amigo 48. Pancho Villa Returns 50, many others.

Carroll, Diahann (1935–). Black American entertainer and actress.
Carmen Jones 54. Porgy and Bess 59. Goodbye Again 60. Paris Blues 61. Hurry Sundown 67. The Split 68. Claudine 74, etc.
TV series: *Julia* 68–69.

Carroll, Joan (1932–) (Joan Felt). American child star of the forties.
Primrose Path 40. Laddie 41. Petticoat Larceny 43. Meet Me in St Louis 44. Tomorrow the World 45. The Bells of St Mary's 46, etc.

Carroll, John (1908–) (Julian la Faye). American singing leading man, mostly in second-string musicals of the forties.
Rose of the Rio Grande 38. Susan and God 40. Marx Brothers Go West 41. Rio Rita 42. Flying Tigers 43. A Letter for Evie 43. Bedside Manner 44. Fiesta 47. The Flame 48. Hit Parade of 1951 51. The Reluctant Bride (GB) 52. The Farmer Takes a Wife 53. Decision at Sundown 57. The Plunderers of Painted Flats 59, etc.

Carroll, Leo G. (1892–1972). Distinguished, dry-faced British character actor long based in Hollywood; usually played doctors, judges or academics.

The Barretts of Wimpole Street 34. Clive of India 35. London by Night 37. A Christmas Carol 38. Wuthering Heights 39. *Rebecca* 40. Suspicion 41. Bahama Passage 42. *The House on 92nd Street* 45. *Spellbound* 45. Forever Amber 47. Enchantment 48. Father of the Bride 50. *The First Legion* 51. Strangers on a Train 51. *Rommel Desert Fox* 52. Young Bess 53. We're No Angels 55. The Swan 56. *North by Northwest* 59. The Parent Trap 61. *The Prize* 63, many others.
TV series: *Topper* 53–55. *Going My Way* 62. *The Man from U.N.C.L.E.* (as Mr Waverly) 64–67.

Carroll, Lewis (1832–1898) (Charles Lutwidge Dodgson). British writer, an Oxford lecturer in mathematics who wrote *Alice in Wonderland* (qv).

Carroll, Madeleine (1906–) (Marie Madeleine Bernadette O'Carroll). British leading lady of the thirties and forties; her gentle, well-bred air made her popular in Hollywood for a while.
□ *The Guns of Loos* 28. The First Born 28. What Money Can't Buy 29. The American Prisoner 29. Atlantic 30. *Young Woodley* 30. Escape 30. The W Plan 30. Madame Guillotine 31. Kissing Cup's Race 31. French Leave 31. Fascination 32. School for Scandal 33. Sleeping Car 33. *I Was a Spy* 33. The World Moves On 34. Loves of a Dictator 35. *The Thirty-nine Steps* 35. The Case Against Mrs Ames 36. Secret Agent 36. *The General Died at Dawn* 36. Lloyds of London 36. *On the Avenue* 37. *The Prisoner of Zenda* 37. It's All Yours 38. Blockade 38. Honeymoon in Bali 39. Café Society 39. My Son My Son 40. Safari 40. Northwest Mounted Police 40. Virginia 41. One Night in Lisbon 41. Bahama Passage 42. *My Favourite Blonde* 42. White Cradle Inn 46. Don't Trust Your Husband 48. *The Fan* 49.

Carroll, Nancy (1905–1965) (Ann La Hiff). Warmly-remembered American leading lady of early talkie musicals and light dramas.
□ Ladies Must Dress 27. Abie's Irish Rose 28. Easy Come Easy Go 28. Chicken à la King 28. The Water Hole 28. Manhattan Cocktail 28. *The Shopworn Angel* 29. The Wolf of Wall Street 29. Sin Sister 29. Close Harmony 29. The Dance of Life 29. Illusion 29. Sweetie 29. Dangerous Paradise 30. Honey 30. Paramount on Parade 30. The Devil's Holiday 30. Follow Through 30. *Laughter* 30. Stolen Heaven 31. The Night Angel 31. Personal Maid 31. Broken Lullaby 32. Wayward 32. Scarlet Dawn 32. Hot Saturday 32. Undercover Man 32. Child of Manhattan 33.

The Woman Accused 33. The Kiss Before the Mirror 33. I Love that Man 33. Springtime for Henry 34. Transatlantic Merry-go-round 34. Jealousy 34. I'll Love You Always 35. After the Dance 35. Atlantic Adventure 35. There Goes My Heart 38. That Certain Age 38.

Carry On. This astonishingly successful series of low-budget British farces, with their thin production values and witless emphasis on the physical, began in 1958 with an army comedy called *Carry On Sergeant,* and since then roughly two a year have rolled off the assembly lines of producer Peter Rogers and director Gerald Thomas. The Carry On sequence to date is Nurse, Teacher, Constable, Regardless, Cruising, Cabby, Jack, Spying, Cleo, Cowboy, Screaming, Follow That Camel, Don't Lose Your Head, Doctor, Up the Khyber, Camping, Again Doctor, Loving, Up the Jungle, Henry, At Your Convenience, Matron, Abroad, Girls, Dick, Behind and England. (*Carry On Admiral* and *What A Carry On* are horses of a different colour.) The struggling comedians most likely to be involved are Sid James, Kenneth Williams, Hattie Jacques, Kenneth Connor, Jim Dale and Joan Sims.

Carson, Charles (1885–). British character actor of stage and screen, seen latterly as distinguished old gentlemen.
Leap Year 32. Sanders of the River 35. Victoria the Great 37. Dark Journey 37. Quiet Wedding 40. Pink String and Sealing Wax 45. Cry the Beloved Country 52. Reach for the Sky 56. The Trials of Oscar Wilde 60, many others.

Carson, Jack (1910–1963). Beefy Canadian comedy actor; a former vaudevillian, he usually played 'smart guys' who were really dumber than the suckers they tried to take.
☐ You Only Live Once 37. Stage Door 37. Stand In 37. Too Many Wives 37. It Could Happen To You 37. Music for Madame 37. The Toast of New York 37. Reported Missing 37. The Saint in New York 37. Vivacious Lady 37. Mr Doodle Kicks Off 38. Crashing Hollywood 38. She's Got Everything 38. Night Spot 38. Law of the Underworld 38. This Marriage Business 38. Having Wonderful Time 38. Maids Night Out 38. Everbody's Doing It 38. Quick Money 38. Bringing Up Baby 38. Go Chase Yourself 38. Carefree 38. Destry Rides Again 39. The Kid from Texas 39. Mr Smith Goes to Washington 39. Legion of Lost Flyers 39. The Escape 39. The Honeymoon's Over 39. The Girl in 313 40. Shooting High 40. Young As You Feel 40. Enemy Agent 40. Parole Fixer 40. Alias the Deacon 40. Queen of the Mob 40. Sandy Gets His Man 40. Love Thy Neighbour 40. Lucky Partners 40. I Take this Woman 40. Typhoon 40. *The Strawberry Blonde* 41. Mr and Mrs Smith 41. Love Crazy 41. The Bride Came COD 41. Navy Blues 41. Blues in the Night 41. The Male Animal 42. Gentleman Jim 42. Larceny Inc. 42. Wings for the Eagle 42. The Hard Way 42. Princess O'Rourke 43. Thank Your Lucky Stars 43. Shine On Harvest Moon 44. Arsenic and Old Lace 44. The Doughgirls 44. *Make Your Own Bed* (leading role) 44. *Roughly Speaking* 45. *Mildred Pierce* 45. One More Tomorrow 46. The Time The Place and The Girl 46. Two Guys from Milwaukee 46. Love and Learn 47. April Showers 48. Romance on the High Seas 48. Two Guys from Texas 48. John Loves Mary 49. My Dream is Yours 49. It's a Great Feeling 49. Bright Leaf 50. My Universe 51. The Groom Wore Spurs 51. The Good Humor Man 51. Dangerous When Wet 53. *Red Garters* 54. *A Star is Born* 54. Ain't Misbehavin' 54. The Bottom of the Bottle 56. The Magnificent Roughnecks 56. The Tattered Dress 57. *Cat on a Hot Tin Roof* 58. The Bramble Bush 60. King of the Roaring Twenties 61.

Carson, Jeannie (1928–) (Jean Shufflebottom). Vivacious British entertainer who became popular in America and then surprisingly retired.
Love in Pawn 51. As Long as They're Happy 54. An Alligator Named Daisy 56. Rockets Galore 57. Seven Keys 62, etc.
TV series: *Hey Jeannie!* 56.

Carson, John (1930–). British character actor with a James Mason-like voice. Much on TV, especially heard on commercials.
The Plague of the Zombies 67. The Man Who Haunted Himself 70. Taste the Blood of Dracula 70. Captain Kronos Vampire Hunter 72, etc.

Carson, Kit (1809–1868). American western frontiersman and guide who became a legendary figure and has been portrayed in several films, notably *Kit Carson* 39 in which he was played by Jon Hall.

Carstairs, John Paddy (1912–1970). British director, usually of light-hearted subjects; also comic novelist and painter.
The Saint in London 39. Spare a Copper 40. He Found a Star 40. Dancing with Crime 46. *Sleeping Car to Trieste* 48. *The Chiltern Hundreds* 49. Made in Heaven 52. Trouble in Store 53. Up to His Neck 54. Up in the World 56. Just My Luck 57. The Square Peg 58. Tommy the Toreador 59. Sands of the Desert 60. Weekend with Lulu 61, many others.

Carsten, Peter (1929–) (Pieter Ransenthaler). German character actor in America.
Mr Superinvisible 73, etc.

Carter, Ann (1936–). American child star of the forties.
I Married a Witch 42. North Star 43. *Curse of the Cat People* 44. The Two Mrs Carrolls 46. Song of Love 47. A Connecticut Yankee in King Arthur's Court 49, etc.

Carter, Helena (1923–) (Helen Rickerts). American leading lady of second features in the forties: former model.
Time Out of Mind 46. River Lady 48. Double Crossbones 51. The Golden Hawk 52. Invaders from Mars 53, etc.

Carter, Janis (1921–) (J. Dremann). American leading lady of minor films in the forties; former radio experience.
Cadet Girl 41. Notorious Lone Wolf 43. Paula 44. The Fighting Guardsmen 45. I Love Trouble 47. The Woman on Pier 13 49. My Forbidden Past 51. Flying Leathernecks 51. The Half-Breed 52, etc.

Carter, Mrs Leslie (1862–1937) (Caroline Louise Dudley). American stage actress, a protégée of David Belsco; a 1940 biopic, *Lady with Red Hair*, starred Miriam Hopkins. Film appearances rare.
□ Du Barry 15. The Heart of Maryland 15. The Vanishing Pioneer 34. Rocky Mountain Mystery 34, etc.

cartoon: a film composed of animated drawings, carefully varied to give the appearance of motion. Gertie the Dinosaur, who appeared in 1909, is thought to be the first cartoon character; Mutt and Jeff followed soon after. In the twenties, Pat Sullivan's Felix the Cat and Max Fleischer's Out of the Inkwell series vied for popularity until both were ousted by Walt Disney, who with Ub Iwerks created Mickey Mouse and his familiar friends. In the thirties, Disney went on to Silly Symphonies, Fleischer to Popeye. Other creations were Woody Woodpecker (Walter Lantz), Mighty Mouse, Heckle and Jeckle, Tom and Jerry (Hanna-Barbera for MGM) and Bugs Bunny. Disney's Donald Duck became more popular than Mickey. In the forties, David Hand made British cartoons for the Rank Organisation, but they were not commercially successful. The fifties brought U.P.A. with their new refined lines, intellectual conceptions and sophisticated jokes; Mr Magoo and Gerald McBoing Boing led the new characters but quickly palled. Then the needs of television led to innumerable cartoon series which for the sake of economy had to be only semi-animated and had little vitality; the best of them were The Flintstones and Yogi Bear. These series proliferated into hundreds and not until 1972 did anyone try an adult cartoon series, Hanna-Barbera's *Wait Till Your Father Gets Home*.

Feature-length cartoons were started by Disney in 1937 with *Snow White and the Seven Dwarfs*; Fleischer responded in 1939 with *Gulliver's Travels*. Disney's outstanding serious cartoon was *Fantasia* 40, an interpretation of classical music. Later, French and Japanese cartoons flooded the market, but inspiration was lacking in most of them. Halas and Batchelor's British *Animal Farm* was a fair summation of Orwell's fable, but their later attempts to interpret Gilbert and Sullivan failed. In recent years the cartoon has been put to every kind of serious and comic purpose, including propaganda and advertising, and many prizewinners have come from Europe.

Caruso, Anthony (c. 1913–). American character actor, usually seen as menace.
Johnny Apollo 40. Sunday Punch 42. Objective Burma 45. Wild Harvest 47. Bride of Vengeance 49. Tarzan and the Slave Girl 50. The Iron Mistress 52. Phantom of the Rue Morgue 54. Hell on Frisco Bay 56. The Badlanders 58. The Most Dangerous Man Alive 61. Young Dillinger 65. Flap 70, many others.

Caruso, Enrico (1873–1921). Celebrated Italian operatic tenor who appeared in a few films and was played by Mario Lanza in *The Great Caruso* 51.

Carver, Louise (1898–1956) (Louise Spilger Murray). American character actress, a famous silent comedienne.
The Extra Girl 23. Shameful Behaviour 26. The Fortune Hunter 27. The Man from Blankley's 30. The Big Trail 30. Side Show 31. Hallelujah I'm a Bum 33. Every Night at Eight 35, etc.

Carver, Lynn (1909–1955) (Virginia Reid Sampson). American general purpose actress.
Roberta 35. Maytime 37. A Christmas Carol 38. Calling Dr Kildare 39. Charley's Aunt 41. Tennessee Johnson 42. Law of the Valley 44. Crossed Trails 48, etc.

Casablanca (US 1942). This archetypal Hollywood melodrama of the forties was lucky on several counts. It nearly starred Ronald Reagan and Ann Sheridan instead of Humphrey Bogart and Ingrid Bergman; it happened to provide good parts for Warner regulars such as Greenstreet, Lorre, Sakall and especially Claude Rains; its mood anticipated the *films noirs* which came full flood at war's end; it hit the news accidentally by being released shortly before the Casablanca conference; and almost as an afterthought it had Dooley Wilson singing 'As Time Goes By'. Its intentional merits included a tense and witty script by the Epstein twins and Howard Koch (AA), skilled direction by Michael Curtiz (AA), and the usual A-film Warner lustre. Bogart gave one of his best-remembered good/bad guy performances and set the seal on a comparatively modest professional spy thriller which just happened to wrap up a whole era in an entertaining package.

Casares, Maria (1922–) (Maria Casares Quiroga). Dark-eyed, solemn-looking French-Spanish character actress.
Les Enfants du Paradis 43. Les Dames du Bois de Boulogne 44. La Chartreuse de Parme 47. Bagarres 48 *Orphée* (as Death) 49. Le Testament d'Orphée 59. The Rebel Nun 74, etc.

case histories from medical files, which would once have been considered pretty dull plot material, have recently been presented quite starkly to paying audiences who appear to have relished them. In the forties, *Lady in the Dark* was a richly decorated trifle, and even *The Snake Pit* and *Mandy* had subsidiary love interest, but in recent years we have had such unvarnished studies as *El* (paranoiac jealousy), *Pressure Point* (fascist tendencies), *A Child is Waiting* (mentally handicapped children), *Life Upside Down* (withdrawal), *The Collector* (sex fantasies), *Repulsion*, *In Cold Blood*, *10 Rillington Place* and *The Boston Strangler* (homicidal mania), *Bigger Than Life* (danger from drugs), *The Three Faces of Eve* and *Lizzie* (split personality), *Marnie* (frigidity), *Morgan* (infantile regression), and *Family Life*. At least the pretence of studying a case history relieves writers of the responsibility of providing a dramatic ending.
See also: *dreams; fantasy; amnesia.*

Cash, Johnny (1932–). American folk singer.
Five Minutes to Live 62. *A Gunfight* 70.

Cash, Rosalind (1945–). Black American leading lady.
□ Klute 71. The Omega Man 71. The New Centurions 72. Hickey and Boggs 72. Melinda 72. Uptown Saturday Night 74. Amazing Grace 74. Hit the Open Man 75.

Casino Royale (GB 1966). At once the ultimate in spy kaleidoscopes and the folly that killed off the fashion, this huge shapeless romp is living proof that all the money and talent in the world won't necessarily make a good movie … not, at least, when the script seems to have been put together with paste at a late-night party. If the distinguished directors and actors who made it had fun, they failed to communicate it to the audience.

Caspary, Vera (1904–). American romantic crime novelist.
The Night of June 13th (oa) 32. I'll Love You Always (w) 35. Scandal Street (oa) 38. Lady from Louisiana (w) 41. *Laura* (oa) 44. Claudia and David (w) 46. Bedelia (oa, w) 46. A Letter to Three Wives (w) 48. Three Husbands (oa, w) 51. The Blue Gardenia (oa) 53. Bachelor in Paradise (oa) 61, etc.

Casper the Friendly Ghost. A genial spirit from the Paramount cartoon factory of the forties. The idea of a baby ghost seemed at the time to be in poorish taste.

Casque d'Or (Golden Marie) (France 1952). The flavour and detail of French low-life in the nineties are subtly caught by director Jacques Becker in this much-admired melodrama starring Simone Signoret and Serge Reggiani.

Cass, Henry (1902–). British director with stage experience as actor and producer.
Lancashire Luck 37. 29 Acacia Avenue 45. The Glass Mountain 48. No Place for Jennifer 49. Last Holiday 50. Young Wives' Tale 51. Windfall 55. Blood of the Vampire 59. The Hand 60. Give a Dog a Bone 66, etc.

Cass, Maurice (1884–1954). American character actor of Russian origin; often played old men.
Two for Tonight 35. Charlie Chan at the Opera 37. Son of Monte Cristo 40. Blood and Sand 41. Charley's Aunt 41. Up in Arms 44. Angel on My Shoulder 46. Spoilers of the North 47. We're Not Married 52, many others.

Cassavetes, John (1929–). Slight, intense, American actor who played a variety of parts and later became an experimental director.
□ Taxi 54. The Night Holds Terror 55. Crime in the Streets 56. Edge of the City 57. Saddle the Wind 58. Virgin Island 58. The Webster Boy 61. *Shadows* (d only) 61. Too Late Blues (d only) 62. A Child is Waiting (d only) 62. The Killers 64. The Dirty Dozen 67. The Devil's Angels 67. Rosemary's Baby 68. *Faces* (wd only) 68. Husbands (& wd) 70. Machine Gun McCain 70.

Minnie and Moskowitz (& wd) 71. A Woman Under the Influence (wd only) 74. Capone 75. Two Minute Warning 76.
TV series: *Johnny Staccato* 59.

Cassel, Jean-Pierre (1932–). French leading man.
Les Jeux de l'Amour 60. L'Amant de Cinq Jours 61. The Vanishing Corporal 62. La Ronde 64. Those Magnificent Men in Their Flying Machines 65. Les Fêtes Galantes 65. Is Paris Burning? 66. Jeu de Massacre 67. Baxter 71. The Discreet Charm of the Bourgeoisie 72. The Three Musketeers 74. Murder on the Orient Express 74. That Lucky Touch 75, etc.

cassettes. In 1970–71 the show business world awaited a revolution which despite enormous expense and drum-beating failed to happen ... though in due course it may. The idea was to make available one's favourite film, or any other kind of entertainment, in miniaturized cartridge form which could be played back whenever one wished through new equipment. Unfortunately international agreement on the type of hardware could not be achieved, and none of the prototype gadgets were compatible. Moreover the trade was still busy selling colour TV, so by general consensus the new miracle was deferred, perhaps until the late-seventies.

Cassidy, Jack (1926–1976). American light actor, mostly on TV; husband of Shirley Jones and father of David Cassidy.
Look in any Window 62. FBI Code 98 64. Guide for the Married Man 67. Your Money or Your Wife (TV) 72. Phantom of Hollywood (TV) 74. The Eiger Sanction 75. W. C. Fields and Me (as John Barrymore) 76, etc.

Cassidy, Joanna (1944–). American leading lady of the seventies.
The Laughing Policeman 73. The Outfit 73. Bank Shot 74.

Castellani, Renato (1913–). Italian director.
Un Colpo di Pistola 41. My Son the Professor 46. E Primavera 50. Due Soldi di Speranza 51. Romeo and Juliet (GB) 54. Nella Città l'Inferno 59. Il Brigante 61. Mare Matto 62, etc.

Castellano, Richard (1931–). Fat Italian-American character actor who came to fame in *Lovers and Other Strangers* 69 and in 1972 had his own TV series, *The Super*, as well as appearing in *The Godfather* 72.

Castelnuovo, Nino (1937–). Italian leading man.

La Garçonnière 60. Escapade in Florence 62. Les Parapluies de Cherbourg 64. Camille 2000 69, etc.

Castelnuovo-Tedesco, Mario (1895–1968). Italian composer in America.
The Return of the Vampire 44. The Black Parachute 44. *And Then There Were None* 45. Night Editor 46. Time out of Mind 47. Mark of the Avenger 51, etc.

Castle, Don (1919–1966). American leading man of forties second features.
Love Finds Andy Hardy 38. I Take this Woman 40. Power Dive 41. Tombstone 42. The Guilty 47. The Invisible Wall 47, etc.

Castle, Irene and **Vernon** (Irene Foote, Vernon Blythe). A dancing team who were highly popular in American cabaret 1912–17. Irene (1893–1969) was American, Vernon (1893–1918) was British. Apart from some 1914 shorts, their only feature together was *The Whirl of Life* 15; but Irene alone made a number of dramatic films, especially after Vernon's death in an air crash: *Patria* 17, *The Hillcrest Mystery* 18, *The Invisible Bond* 19, *The Broadway Bride* 21, *No Trespassing* 22, etc. In 1939 Fred Astaire and Ginger Rogers appeared in *The Story of Vernon and Irene Castle*; in 1958 Irene published an autobiography, *Castles in the Air*.

Castle, Mary (1931–). American leading lady.
Criminal Lawyer 51. Eight Iron Men 52. The Lawless Breed 53. The Jailbreakers 61, etc.

Castle, Nick (1910–1968). American dance director.
Swanee River 39. Hellzapoppin 42. Royal Wedding 47. Red Garters 54, others.

Castle, Peggie (1927–1973). American leading lady of fifties second features.
Mr Belvedere Goes to College 49. Buccaneer's Girl 50. Air Cadet 51. I the Jury 53. The Long Wait 54. Jesse James' Women 54. Target Zero 55. Bury Me Dead 57. Seven Hills of Rome 58, etc.
TV series: Lawman 58–62.

Castle, Roy (1933–). British light entertainer, in occasional films.
Dr Terror's House of Horrors 66. Dr Who and the Daleks 66. Carry on Up the Khyber 71. Legend of the Werewolf 75, etc.

Castle, William (1914–) (William Schloss). American director of second features (1941–57)

who became a cheerful purveyor of gimmicky horror films involving give-away insurance policies, mobile skeletons, tingling seats, etc; these he not only produced and directed but introduced in the Hitchcock manner.
□ The Chance of a Lifetime 43. Klondyke Kate 43. *The Whistler* 44. *When Strangers Marry* 44. She's a Soldier Too 44. The Mark of the Whistler 44. Voice of the Whistler 46. Just Before Dawn 46. Mysterious Intruder 46. The Return of Rusty 46. The Crime Doctor's Manhunt 46. The Crime Doctor's Gamble 47. Texas Brooklyn and Heaven 48. The Gentleman from Nowhere 48. Johnny Stool Pigeon 49. Undertow 49. It's a Small World 50. The Fat Man 51. Hollywood Story 51. Cave of Outlaws 51. Serpent of the Nile 53. Fort Ti 53. Conquest of Cochise 53. Slaves of Babylon 53. Charge of the Lancers 54. Drums of Tahiti 54. Jesse James vs the Daltons 54. Battle at Rogue River 54. The Iron Glove 54. The Saracen Blade 54. The Law vs Billy the Kid 54. Masterson of Kansas 54. The Americano 55. New Orleans Uncensored 55. The Gun that Won the West 55. Duel on the Mississippi 55. The Houston Story 56. Uranium Boom 56. *Macabre* 58. *House on Haunted Hill* 59. The Tingler 59. Thirteen Ghosts 60. *Homicidal* 61. Sardonicus 61. Zotz! 62. Thirteen Frightened Girls 63. The Old Dark House 63. Strait Jacket 64. *The Night Walker* 64. I Saw What You Did 65. Let's Kill Uncle 66. The Busy Body 67. The Spirit is Willing 67. Rosemary's Baby (p only) 68. Project X 68. The Sex Symbol (TV) (as actor) 74. Shanks (& p) 74. Shampoo (as actor) 75. Bug (p only) 75. Day of the Locust (as actor) 75.
TV series: Ghost Story 72.

The Cat and the Canary. An eccentric will read at midnight in a spooky house, with secret panels behind which a maniac lurks, are the ingredients of John Willard's stage thriller of 1922, which prompted a host of Hollywood imitations as well as being itself filmed three times. Paul Leni's 1927 version was a semi-surrealist send-up, with Creighton Hale and Laura la Plante. Rupert Julian's sound remake of 1930 was retitled *The Cat Creeps*, and featured Helen Twelvetrees and Raymond Hackett. In 1939 came Elliott Nugent's very satisfactory comedy vehicle for Bob Hope and Paulette Goddard, with Gale Sondergaard as the sinister housekeeper and some elegant photography by Charles Lang. A British remake followed in 1967

Cat Ballou (US 1965). A spoof western directed with some but not quite enough flair by Eliot Silverstein from a joky script by Walter

Newman and Frank Pierson. An amusing ballad by Nat King Cole and Stubby Kaye effectively linked disperate threads of story, and Lee Marvin collected an Oscar for guying a dual role.

Cat People (US 1942). Allegedly the first monster film to refrain from showing its monster, this was the first of the much praised low-budget thrillers produced by Val Lewton at RKO. Directed by Jacques Tourneur from a script by De Witt Bodeen, and atmospherically photographed by Nicholas Musuraca, it begins slowly but builds up to suspenseful set-pieces on a lonely street and in a darkened swimming bath.

Catherine the Great (1762–1798), 'mother of all the Russias', has appeared in the following screen personifications:

Pola Negri	*Forbidden Paradise* 24
Marlene Dietrich	*The Scarlet Empress* 34
Elizabeth Bergner	*Catherine the Great* 34
Tallulah Bankhead	*A Royal Scandal* 45
Viveca Lindfors	*Tempest* 58
Bette Davis	*John Paul Jones* 59
Hildegarde Neff	*Catherine of Russia* 62
Jeanne Moreau	*Great Catherine* 68

What a pity that Mae West's play *Catherine Was Great* never reached the screen . . .

Cates, Gilbert (–   ). American director.
□ *I Never Sang for My Father* 69. Summer Wishes, Winter Dreams 73. The Affair (TV) 73.

Catlett, Walter (1889–1960). Bespectacled American comedian with long vaudeville experience; his flustered gestures often characterized inept crooks, commercial travellers or justices of the peace.
Second Youth 24. Summer Bachelors 29. Why Leave Home? 29. Palmy Days 31. Rain 32. Mama Loves Papa 33. The Captain Hates the Sea 34. Mr Deeds Goes to Town 36. On the Avenue 37. *Bringing Up Baby* 38. Pop Always Pays 40. Horror Island 41. Yankee Doodle Dandy 42. They Got Me Covered 43. Ghost Catchers 44. I'll Be Yours 47. *Look for the Silver Lining* 49. Here Comes the Groom 51. Father Takes the Air 51. Friendly Persuasion 56, many others.

Catto, Max (1907–). Popular British adventure novelist.
Daughter of Darkness (oa) 48. A Prize of Gold (oa) 54. West of Zanzibar (w) 54. Seven Thieves (oa) 60. The Devil at Four O'Clock (oa) 61. Mister Moses (oa) 65, etc.

Caulfield, Joan (1922–). Demure American leading lady of the forties.

□ Miss Susie Slagle's 46. *Monsieur Beaucaire* 46. *Blue Skies* 46. *Dear Ruth* 47. Welcome Stranger 47. The Unsuspected 47. The Sainted Sisters 48. Larceny 48. Dear Wife 50. The Petty Girl 50. The Lady Says No 51. The Rains of Ranchipur 55. Cattle King 63. Red Tomahawk 66. Buckskin 68.

TV series: My Favorite Husband 53.

Cavalcade (US 1933) (AA). Noel Coward's patriotic twentieth-century pageant was brought to the screen by Frank Lloyd (AA) in a spectacular if rather lifeless Hollywood version, with a mainly British cast led by Clive Brook and Diana Wynyard. Art direction by William Darling (AA).

Cavalcanti, Alberto (1897–). Brazilian director who made interesting films in several countries but never quite achieved a masterpiece. *Rien que les Heures* 26. En Rade 27. Sea Fever 29. North Sea 38. Men of the Lightship 41. *Went the Day Well* 42. Champagne Charlie 45. Dead of Night (part) 45. *Nicholas Nickelby* 47. They Made Me A Fugitive 47. The First Gentleman 48. For Them That Trespass 49. O Canto do Mar (Braz.) 53. Herr Puntila (Ger.) 55. La Prima Notte (It.) 58. Yerma (It.) 62, etc.

Cavanagh, Paul (1895–1964). Suave British actor who went to Hollywood in the twenties and spent the rest of his career playing elegant villains, understanding husbands, and murder victims.
The Runaway Princess 29. Grumpy 30. The Devil to Pay 30. The Squaw Man 31. The Devil's Lottery 32. A Bill of Divorcement 32. The Kennel Murder Case 33. Tarzan and his Mate 34. *The Notorious Sophie Lang* 34. *Goin' to Town* (opposite Mae West) 35. Champagne Charlie 36. Romance in Flanders 37. Crime over London 38. Reno 39. The Case of the Black Parrot 40. Maisie was a Lady 41. The Strange Case of Dr RX 42. The Hard Way 43. The Scarlet Claw 44. The Man in Half Moon Street 44. House of Fear 45. The Verdict 46. Humoresque 46. Ivy 47. You Gotta Stay Happy 48. The Iroquois Trail 50. House of Wax 53. Casanova's Big Night 54. The Purple Mask 55. Francis in the Haunted House 56. Diane 57. The Four Skulls of Jonathan Drake 59, many others.

Cavanaugh, Hobart (1886–1950). Mild-mannered, bald and bespectacled American character actor usually seen as clerk, nervous husband or frightened caretaker.
San Francisco Nights 27. I Cover the Waterfront 33. Convention City 33. Housewife 34. I Sell Anything 34. Don't Bet on Blondes 35.

A Midsummer Night's Dream 35. Stage Struck 36. Cain and Mabel 36. Reported Missing 37. *Rose of Washington Square* (as a double act with Al Jolson) 39. An Angel from Texas 40. Meet the Chump 41. Horror Island (as the villain) 41. The Magnificent Dope 42. Sweet Rosie O'Grady 43. Kismet 44. Black Angel 46. You Gotta Stay Happy 48. Stella 50, many others.

Cavani, Liliana (1937–). Italian director who became famous for directing and co-writing *The Night Porter* 74.

Cawthorn, Joseph (1868–1949). American character actor of the thirties.
Very Confidential 27. Silk Legs 28. Jazz Heaven 29. The Taming of the Shrew 29. Dixiana 30. Kiki 31. White Zombie 32. Love me Tonight 32. Whistling in the Dark 33. Housewife 34. The Last Gentleman 34. Go into Your Dance 35. Naughty Marietta 35. The Great Ziegfeld 36. Lillian Russell 40. The Postman Didn't Ring 42, many others.

Cayatte, André (1909–). French lawyer who became writer-director of films with something to say.
Justice est Faite 50. *Nous Sommes Tous les Assassins* 52. An Eye for an Eye 56. The Mirror Has Two Faces 57. The Crossing of the Rhine 60. La Vie Conjugale 63. A Trap for Cinderella 65. Die of Loving 70, etc.

Cazale, John (–). American character actor.
The Godfather 72. The Conversation 74. The Godfather Part Two 74. *Dog Day Afternoon* 75.

Cecchi D'Amico, Suso (1914–) (Giovanna Cecchi D'Amico). Italian screenwriter.
Vivere in Pace 46. Bicycle Thieves 49. Miracle in Milan 51. Bellissima 51. Le Amiche 55. Rocco and his Brothers 60, many others.

Cecil, Jonathan (1939–). British light comic actor usually seen as gangling ineffective types.
The Yellow Rolls Royce 64. Otley 68. The Private Life of Sherlock Holmes 71. Barry Lyndon 75, etc.

Celi, Adolfo (1922–). Solidly-built Italian character actor who followed a Brazilian stage career by playing villains in international films.
Escape into Dreams 50. *That Man from Rio* 64. Von Ryan's Express 65. *Thunderball* 65. El Greco 66. Grand Prix 67. The Honey Pot 67. The Bobo 67. Grand Slam 68. Fragment of Fear 70. Murders in the Rue Morgue 71. Hitler—The

Last Ten Days 73. And Then There Were None 75, etc.

Collier, Frank (1884–1948). British stage actor who seemed to frown a lot and usually played unsympathetic types.
Soldiers of the King 33. The Thirty-nine Steps 35. Rhodes of Africa 36. Tudor Rose 36. Non Stop New York 37. Sixty Glorious Years 38. The Ware Case 39. Quiet Wedding 40. Love on the Dole 41. Give Us the Moon 44. Quiet Weekend 46. The Blind Goddess 48, etc.

censorship. Each country has found it necessary to apply its own rules for film producers; in Britain and America at least these rules were drawn up and enforced at the request of the industry itself. The British Board of Film Censors was founded in 1912. For many years films were classified as 'U' (for universal exhibition), 'A' (adults and accompanied children only) or (from 1933) 'H' (horrific; prohibited for persons under 16). In 1951, with the growing emphasis on sex, 'H' was replaced by 'X', which includes sex *and* horror. In the sixties X came to mean over eighteen, AA no one under 14, and A was simply a warning to parents (children could still get in unaccompanied). In America, the Arbuckle scandal of 1921 precipitated the founding of the 'Hays Office' (named after its first paid president) by the Motion Picture Producers and Distributors of America. The first Production Code was issued in 1930 and has undergone constant amendment especially since *The Moon is Blue* 53, and very rapidly indeed since *Room at the Top* 59; in 1966 *Who's Afraid of Virginia Woolf?* almost swamped it completely and a revised, broadened code was issued. In 1968 this was replaced by a new rating system: 'X', 'R' (restricted), 'PG' (parental guidance advised) and 'G' (general audience). The independent and very strict Catholic Legion of Decency was founded in 1934 and issues its own classifications; it recently changed its name to the National Catholic Office for Motion Pictures.
Best books: Murray Schumach's *The Face on the Cutting Room Floor* and Doug McClelland's *The Unkindest Cuts.*

Cervi, Gino (1901–). Stocky Italian character actor.
Frontier 34. An Ideal Marriage 39. Four Steps in the Clouds 42. Fabiola 47. Furia 48. *The Little World of Don Camillo* (as the mayor) 51. OK Nero 52. Three Forbidden Stories 53. Indiscretion 53. Maddalena 53. The Return of Don Camillo 54. Wife for a Night 55. The Naked Maja 59. Wild Love 60. The Revolt of the Slaves 61. Becket 64, many others.

Chabrol, Claude (1930–). Variable but generally distinguished French director, credited with starting the *nouvelle vague.*
□ *Le Beau Serge* 58. Les Cousins 59. A Double Tour 59. Les Bonnes Femmes 60. Les Godelureaux 60. The Third Lover 61. The Seven Deadly Sins (part) 61. Les Plus Belles Escroqueries du Monde (part) 61. Ophelia 62. Landru 62. Paris vu Par (part) 64. Le Tigre se Parfume à la Dynamite 64. Le Tigre Aime la Chair Fraîche 65. Marie Chantal 65. Line of Demarcation 66. The Champagne Murders 67. The Road to Corinth 68. *Les Biches* 68. La Femme Infidèle 69. *The Beast Must Die* 69. La Rupture 70. *The Butcher* 70. Just Before Night 71. Blood Wedding 71. Ten Days' Wonder 72. The Wolf Trap 72. Scoundrel in White 72. Ophelia 73.

Chaffey, Don (1917–). British director; started in art department at Gainsborough in the early forties.
Time is My Enemy 53. The Girl in the Picture 56. The Flesh is Weak 57. A Question of Adultery 58. *The Man Upstairs* 59. Danger Within 59. Dentist in the Chair 60. Greyfriars Bobby 60. Nearly a Nasty Accident 60. A Matter of Who 61. The Prince and the Pauper 62. *Jason and the Argonauts* 63. A Jolly Bad Fellow 64. One Million Years B.C. ·66. The Viking Queen 67. A Twist of Sand 68. Creatures the World Forgot 71. Persecution 73, etc.

Chagrin, Francis (1905–1972). Russian-born composer in films (mostly British) from 1934; has composed over 200 scores.
Last Holiday 50. An Inspector Calls 54. The Colditz Story 55. The Snorkel 58. Danger Within 59. Greyfriars Bobby 60. In the Cool of the Day 63, etc.

Chakiris, George (1933–). American dancer (from the chorus) and leading man; his star blazed for a while in the early sixties.
Brigadoon 54. Two and Two Make Six (GB) 60. *West Side Story* (AA) 61. Diamond Head 63. Kings of the Sun 63. Flight from Ashiya 64. 633 Squadron 64. The High Bright Sun (GB) 65. Is Paris Burning? 66. The Young Girls of Rochefort 67. The Big Cube 69, etc.

Chaliapin, Feodor (1873–1938). Russian opera singer who appeared in two films and was played by Ezio Pinza in *Tonight We Sing.*
□ Pskovityanka 15. *Don Quixote* 33.

Challis, Christopher (1919–). Distinguished British cinematographer.

☐ Theirs is the Glory 46. End of the River 47. *The Small Back Room* 48. Tales of Hoffman 50. Gone to Earth 50. The Elusive Pimpernel 52. *Genevieve* 53. Angels One Five 53. 24 Hours in a Woman's Life 53. Saadia 54. The Story of Gilbert and Sullivan 54. Twice Upon a Time 54. Malaga 54. The Flame and the Flesh 54. Oh Rosalinda 55. Quentin Durward 55. Raising a Riot 55. The Battle of the River Plate 56. Footsteps in the Fog 56. Ill Met By Moonlight 56. The Spanish Gardener 56. Miracle in Soho 56. Windom's Way 56. Floods of Fear 57. Rooney 57. Sink the Bismarck 60. The Grass is Greener 61. Surprise Package 61. The Captain's Table 62. Never Let Go 62. Blind Date 62. Flame in the Streets 63. HMS Defiant 64. Five Golden Hours 64. The Long Ships 64. Those Magnificent Men in Their Flying Machines 64. *The Victors* 65. A Shot in the Dark 65. The Americanization of Emily 65. Return from the Ashes 65. *Arabesque* 66. Two for the Road 67. Kaleidoscope 67. A Dandy in Aspic 68. Chitty Chitty Bang Bang 69. Staircase 69. The Private Life of Sherlock Holmes 71. Villain 71. Catch Me a Spy 71. Mary Queen of Scots 72. Follow Me 72. The Boy Who Turned Yellow 72. The Little Prince 74. Mister Quilp 75. The Incredible Sarah 76.

Chamberlain, Cyril (1909–). British small-part player often seen as average man, policeman or dull husband.
This Man in Paris 39. London Belongs to Me 48. Trouble in Store 53. Blue Murder at St Trinian's 58. Carry On Constable 60, many others.

Chamberlain, Richard (1935–). Boyish-looking American leading man who used his success in a TV series to establish himself as a serious international actor.

☐ The Secret of the Purple Reef 60. A Thunder of Drums 62. Twilight of Honor 63. Joy in the Morning 65. Petulia 68. The Madwoman of Chaillot 69. Julius Caesar 70. *The Music Lovers* (as Tchaikovsky) 70. *Lady Caroline Lamb* (as Byron) 72. The Three Musketeers 74. The Four Musketeers 75. The Towering Inferno 75. *The Slipper and the Rose* 76. The Count of Monte Cristo (TV) 76.
TV series: *Dr Kildare* 61–65.

The Champ (US 1931). A mawkish tale about a boozy boxer and his small long-suffering son, this now-dated movie won an Academy Award for Wallace Beery and for scriptwriter Francis Marion. It also confirmed the stardom of boy actor Jackie Cooper. It was remade in 1952 as *The Clown*, a vehicle for Red Skelton.

Champion (US 1949). One of the first anti-boxing films, and Stanley Kramer's first big success as producer. Written by Carl Foreman, starring Kirk Douglas, Arthur Kennedy, Lola Albright.

Champion, Gower (1921–). American dancer who appeared with his then wife Marge in several musicals of the early fifties; later turned director.
Till the Clouds Roll By (solo) 46. Mr Music 50. *Show Boat* 51. Lovely to Look At 52. Give a Girl a Break 53. Jupiter's Darling 55. Three for the Show 55. My Six Loves (d) 63. Bank Shot (d) 74, etc.

Champion, Marge (1923–). American dancer who teamed with her then husband Gower (qv). Solo appearances include *The Story of Vernon and Irene Castle* 39; later appeared as character actress.
The Swimmer 67. The Party 68.

Chance, Naomi (1930–). Stylish British leading lady who appeared sporadically in the fifties.
Dangerous Voyage 53. The Saint's Return 54. Operation Bullshine 59. The Trials of Oscar Wilde 60, etc.

Chandler, Chick (1905–). Wiry American hero or second lead of many a second feature in the thirties and forties.
Melody Cruise 33. Murder on a Honeymoon 35. Woman Wise 36. Born Reckless 37. Alexander's Ragtime Band 38. Time Out for Murder 38. Hotel for Women 39. Hollywood Cavalcade 39. Honeymoon Deferred 40. Cadet Girl 41. Hot Spot 41. The Big Shot 42. He Hired the Boss 43. Irish Eyes are Smiling 44. Seven Doors to Death 44. The Chicago Kid 45. Do You Love Me? 46. Lost Continent 47. Family Honeymoon 49. The Great Rupert 50. Aaron Slick from Punkin Crick 52. Battle Cry 55. The Naked Gun 58. It's a Mad Mad Mad Mad World 63, many others.
TV series: Soldiers of Fortune 55.

Chandler, George (1902–). American character actor, an ex-vaudevillian who specialized in sly or comically nervous roles.
The Light of Western Stars 30. Blessed Event 32. Hi Nellie 34. Fury 36. Three Men on a Horse 36. Nothing Sacred 37. Jesse James 39. Arizona 41. *Roxie Hart* 42. It Happened Tomorrow 44. This Man's Navy 45. Dead Reckoning 47. Kansas Raiders 50. Hans Christian Andersen 52. The

High and the Mighty 54. Spring Reunion 57. Dead Ringer 64. One More Time 71, many others.

Chandler, Helen (1909–1968). American leading lady of the thirties: her early retirement robbed Hollywood of an interesting personality.
The Music Master 26. Mother's Boy 29. The Sky Hawk 29. *Outward Bound* 30. *Dracula* 30. Daybreak 31. Salvation Nell 31. *The Last Flight* 31. Vanity Street 32. Christopher Strong 33. The Worst Woman in Paris 33. Long Lost Father 34. Midnight Alibi 34. It's a Bet 35. Unfinished Symphony 35, etc.

Chandler, Jeff (1918–1961) (Ira Grossel). American leading man with the unusual attraction of prematurely grey hair; carved a solid niche for himself by playing an Indian, but his films seldom rose above co-feature level.
□ Johnny O'Clock 47. Invisible Wall 47. Roses are Red 47. Mr Belvedere Goes to College 49. Sword in the Desert 49. Abandoned 49. *Broken Arrow* (as Cochise) 50. Two Flags West 50. Deported 50. Bird of Paradise 51. Smuggler's Island 51. Iron Man 51. Flame of Araby 51. The Battle at Apache Pass 52. Red Ball Express 52. Because of You 52. The Great Sioux Uprising 53. East of Sumatra 53. Yankee Pasha 54. Sign of the Pagan 54. Foxfire 55. The Female on the Beach 55. The Spoilers 55. Toy Tiger 55. Away all Boats 56. Pillars of the Sky 56. Drango 57. The Tattered Dress 57. *Jeanne Eagels* 57. Man in the Shadow 57. The Lady Takes a Flyer 58. Raw Wind in Eden 58. Stranger in My Arms 59. Thunder in the Sun 59. Ten Seconds to Hell 59. The Jayhawkers 59. The Plunderers 60. Return to Peyton Place 61. Merrill's Marauders 61.

Chandler, John Davis (1937–). American character player usually seen as neurotic, twitching villain.
The Young Savages 61. Mad Dog Coll (title tole) 61. Major Dundee 65. Once a Thief 65. The Good Guys and the Bad Guys 69. Barquero 70. Shootout 71. Capone 75, etc.

Chandler, Raymond (1888–1959). American crime novelist to whom literary acclaim came late in life. Several films and a TV series were based on the exploits of his cynical but incorruptible private eye Philip Marlowe.
The Falcon Takes Over (oa) 42. Time to Kill (oa) 42. *Double Indemnity* (w) 44. And Now Tomorrow 44. The Unseen 45. *Murder My Sweet* (oa) 45. *The Big Sleep* (oa) 46. *The Lady in the Lake* (oa) 46. The Blue Dahlia (w) 45. The Brasher Doubloon (oa) 47. *Strangers on a Train* (w) 51. Marlowe (oa) 69. The Long Goodbye (oa) 72.
TV series: Philip Marlowe 59.

Chaney, Lon (1883–1930). American star character actor, known as 'the man of a thousand faces' because of his elaborate disguises in macabre roles; hence the joke, 'Don't step on that spider, it might be Lon Chaney.' A 1957 biopic, *Man of a Thousand Faces*, starred James Cagney.
□ Where the Forest Ends 14. The Chimney Sweep 15. The Oyster Dredger 15. The Stool Pigeon 15. Fires of Rebellion 17. Triumph 17. That Devil Bateese 18. Riddle Gawne 18. The Kaiser, Beast of Berlin 18. Paid in Advance 19. The Rap 19. The Unholy Three 19. *The Miracle Man* 19. False Faces 19. Victory 19. The Wolf Breed 19. The Wicked Darling 19. Nomads of the North 19. Treasure Island 20. Daredevil Jack 20. *The Penalty* 21. Outside the Law 21. The Ace of Hearts 21. Bit o' Life 21. For Those We Love 21. The Night Rose 21. The Trap 22. Quincy Adams Sawyer 22. Shadows 22. *A Blind Bargain* 22. Flesh and Blood 22. Voices of the City 22. The Light in the Dark 22. Oliver Twist 22. *The Hunchback of Notre Dame* 23. The Shock 23. All the Brothers were Valiant 23. While Paris Sleeps 23. He Who Gets Slapped 24. The Next Corner 24. *The Phantom of the Opera* 25. The Tower of Lies 25. The Monster 25. *The Unholy Three* 25. The Black Bird 26. The Road to Mandalay 26. Tell it to the Marines 26. Mr Wu 27. The Unknown 27. Mockery 27. *London After Midnight* 27. The Big City 28. Laugh Clown Laugh 28. While the City Sleeps 28. West of Zanzibar 28. The Thunder 29. Where East is East 29. The Unholy Three 30.

Chaney, Lon, Jnr (1906–1973) (Creighton Chaney). Massive American character actor, who largely followed his father's type of role in progressively inferior films, with many bit parts. In *Man of a Thousand Faces* he was played by Roger Smith.
Bird of Paradise 32. Lucky Devils 33. Sixteen Fathoms Deep 34. The Life of Vergie Winters 35. Accent on Youth 35. Wife, Doctor and Nurse 37. Love and Hisses 37. Charlie Chan on Broadway 37. Road Demon 38. Mr Moto's Gamble 38. Jesse James 39. Frontier Marshal 39. *Of Mice and Men* (his best performance, as Lennie) 39. One Million BC 40. Northwest Mounted Police 40. Man Made Monster 41. *The Wolf Man* 41. North to the Klondike 42. *The Ghost of Frankenstein* (as the monster) 42. The Mummy's Tomb 42. Frankenstein Meets the Wolf Man 43. Son of Dracula 43. Ghost Catchers 44. Weird Woman 44. Dead Man's

Eyes 44. House of Frankenstein 45. Strange Confession 45. My Favourite Brunette 47. Sixteen Fathoms Deep 48. *Abbott and Costello Meet Frankenstein* 48. Captain China 49. Once a Thief 50. Behave Yourself 51. High Noon 52. A Lion is in the Streets 53. Casanova's Big Night 54. Not as a Stranger 55. Manfish 56. The Black Sleep 56. Cyclops 57. The Defiant Ones 58. The Alligator People 59. The Haunted Palace 63. Witchcraft 64. Apache Uprising 66. Hillbillies in a Haunted House 67. Buckskin 68, many others. TV series: *The Last of the Mohicans* (as Chingachgook) 56.

Chang (US 1927). Famous documentary by Merian Cooper and Ernest Schoedsack telling how a tribesman of Siam guards his family against the terrors of the encroaching jungle. Originally ended with a stampede of elephants on the 'Magnascope', an early form of giant screen.

change-over. Transition from one reel of film to another during projection. A reel originally lasted ten minutes but most 35mm projectors now take 20 or 30 minutes. Change-over cues are given in the form of dots which appear on the top right-hand corner of the screen a standard number of seconds before the end of the reel.

Channing, Carol (1921–). Vivacious American cabaret comedienne whose films have been few.
□ Paid in Full 50. The First Travelling Saleslady 56. *Thoroughly Modern Millie* 67. Skidoo 69.

Chapin, Billy (1943–). American child actor of the fifties.
Cluny Brown 48. Tobor the Great 53. Naked Alibi 54. There's No Business Like Show Business 54. A Man Called Peter 55. Violent Saturday 55. *Night of the Hunter* 55, etc.

Chaplin, Charles (1889–). A legendary figure in his own lifetime despite a comparatively limited output, this British pantomimist went to the US in 1910 with Fred Karno's troupe and was invited to join the Keystone company; later also worked for Essanay and Mutual, and these early two-reelers are held by many to be superior to the later, more pretentious features which he produced himself. Honorary AA 1971.
Autobiographical books: *My Trip Abroad* 1922. *My Wonderful Visit* 1930. *My Autobiography* 1964. *My Life in Pictures* 1974.
Other books: *The Little Fellow* by Peter Cotes and Thelma Nicklaus; *Charlie Chaplin* by Theodore Huff; *My Life with Chaplin* by Lita Grey Chaplin.

SHORTS: Making a Living 14. Kid Auto Races at Venice (in which he first wore the improvised tramp costume in which he later became famous) 13. Tillie's Punctured Romance 14. Dough and Dynamite 15. The Tramp 15. Charlie at the Show 15. The Vagabond 16. *The Adventurer* 16. *Easy Street* 16. *The Cure* 16. *The Immigrant* 17. A Dog's Life 18. *Shoulder Arms* 18, many others.
□ FEATURES: *The Kid* 20. The Pilgrim 23. A Woman of Paris (directed only) 23. *The Gold Rush* 24. *The Circus* (AA) 28. *City Lights* 31. *Modern Times* 36. *The Great Dictator* 40. *Monsieur Verdoux* 47. *Limelight* 52. A King in New York (GB) 57. A Countess from Hong Kong (GB) 66.

Chaplin, Geraldine (1944–). Actress daughter of Charles Chaplin.
□ Doctor Zhivago 65. Stranger in the House 67. I Killed Rasputin 68. The Hawaiians 70. Zero Population Growth 72. Innocent Bystanders 72. The Three Musketeers 74. Nashville 75.

Chaplin, Saul (1912–). American songwriter, arranger and producer.
Rookies on Parade (c) 41. Time Out for Rhythm (c) 41. *An American in Paris* (arr) (AA) 51. *Seven Brides for Seven Brothers* (arr) (AA) 54. Can Can (p) 59. *West Side Story* (p) 61. *The Sound of Music* (p) 65. Star! (p) 68, etc.

Chaplin, Syd (1885–1965). British comedian, elder brother of Charles Chaplin; popular internationally in the twenties.
A Submarine Pirate 15. Shoulder Arms 18. King Queen Joker 21. Her Temporary Husband 23. The Perfect Flapper 24. Charley's Aunt 25. Oh What a Nurse 26. The Better 'Ole 27. The Missing Link 27. A Little Bit of Fluff 28, etc.

Chaplin, Sydney (1926–). Actor son of Charles Chaplin; has not achieved the distinction of which he seems capable.
Limelight 52. Confession 55. Land of the Pharaohs 55. Four Girls in Town 56. Quantez 57. Follow that Man 61. A Countess from Hong Kong 66. The Sicilian Clan 70, etc.

Chapman, Edward (1901–). British character actor of solid dependable types, corrupt aldermen and northern millowners.
Juno and the Paycock 29. Murder 30. The Skin Game 31. *Things to Come* 35. Rembrandt 36. The Man Who Could Work Miracles 37. The Citadel 38. The Proud Valley 39. The Briggs Family 40. They Flew Alone 42. Ships with Wings 42. *The October Man* 47. *It Always Rains on Sunday* 47. Mr Perrin and Mr Traill 49. *The*

Card 52. Folly to be Wise 53. A Day to Remember 54. His Excellency 55. School for Scoundrels 60. Oscar Wilde (as Queensberry) 60. A Stitch in Time 63. Joey Boy 64, many others.

Chapman, Marguerite (1916–). Dependable American heroine of many forties co-features.

Charlie Chan at the Wax Museum 40. The Body Disappears 41. Parachute Nurse 42. Destroyer 43. My Kingdom for a Cook 43. Pardon My Past 45. The Walls Came Tumbling Down 46. Mr District Attorney 47. Coroner Creek 48. Kansas Raiders 50. Man Bait 51. Flight to Mars 51. The Seven Year Itch 55. The Amazing Transparent Man 61, etc.

character actor. Usually thought of as one who does not play romantic leads.

The Charge of the Light Brigade. The American film of this name was directed by Michael Curtiz for Warners in 1936 and had a completely fictitious story taking place mainly in India, with the Balaclava events as an afterthought. As a piece of Hollywood stunting, however, the charge has scarcely been surpassed, and Errol Flynn in the lead consolidated his stardom. Tony Richardson's British film of 1968 attempts, and fails, to tell the true story of what happened; the rewards here are a few moments of Victoriana and some splendid bridging animation by Richard Williams.

Charisse, Cyd (1921–) (Tula Ellice Finklea). Stylish, long-legged American dancer and heroine of MGM musical dramas of the fifties.

□ Mission to Moscow 43. Something to Shout About 43. Ziegfeld Follies 45. The Harvey Girls 46. Three Wise Fools 46. Till the Clouds Roll By 46. Fiesta 47. *The Unfinished Dance* 47. On an Island with You 48. Words and Music 48. The Kissing Bandit 49. East Side West Side 49. Tension 49. Mark of the Renegade 51. The Wild North 52. *Singin' in the Rain* 52. Sombrero 53. Easy to Love 53. *The Band Wagon* 53. Brigadoon 54. Deep in My Heart 54. *It's Always Fair Weather* 55. Meet Me in Las Vegas 56. *Invitation to the Dance* 57. Silk Stockings 57. Twilight for the Gods 59. Black Tights 61. *Two Weeks in Another Town* 62. The Silencers 67. Maroc 7 67.

Charlesworth, John (1935–1960). British teenage actor of the fifties.
Tom Brown's Schooldays 51. Scrooge 51. John

of the Fair 54. Yangtse Incident 57. The Angry Silence 59, etc.

Charley's Aunt. Brandon Thomas' 1896 farce has been filmed many times, notably in 1925 with Syd Chaplin, in 1931 with Charles Ruggles, in 1940 with Arthur Askey, in 1941 with Jack Benny, in 1952 (as *Where's Charley*) with Ray Bolger, in 1954 Germany with Heinz Ruhmann and in Australia 1963 with Peter Alexander.

Charlie Bubbles (GB 1967). A small but pleasing bitter comedy about the horrors of being a very rich author with a working-class background. Albert Finney, director, extracts a perfect performance from Albert Finney, actor; he also handles comic set-piece scenes with great bravura and accuracy of mood. Billie Whitelaw (BFA) is a splendidly shrewish ex-wife, and the whole adds up to a fine sardonic comment on the affluent society.

Charlie Chan. Earl Derr Biggers' polite oriental detective with the large family and an even more plentiful supply of wise and witty sayings was first featured by Hollywood in a 1926 serial; George Kuwa played him. Kamiyama Sojin played him once in 1928, E. L. Park once in 1929, Warner Oland sixteen times (1931–37), Sidney Toler twenty-two times (1938–47) and Roland Winters six times (1948–52). J. Carrol Naish then took over for thirty-nine TV films (1957), and in 1971 Ross Martin appeared as Chan in a TV feature. 1972 brought an animated TV cartoon series, *Charlie Chan and the Chan Clan*: Chan was voiced by Keye Luke, who had played Chan's number two son so often in the thirties.

Charrel, Erik (1894–1974). German producer best known abroad for *Congress Dances* 31, which he also directed.

Charteris, Leslie (1907–). Chinese-English crime novelist, creator of 'the Saint' (qv).

Charters, Spencer (1878–1943). American character actor; usually played rural fellows who may have been deaf but not too dumb to outsmart the city slicker.
Little Old New York 23. Janice Meredith 24. Whoopee 30. The Bat Whispers 30. The Front Page 31. The Match King 32. Female 33. Wake up and Dream 34. It's a Gift 34. The Ghost Walks 34. The Raven 35. Colleen 36. Banjo on my Knee 36. Mountain Music 37. In Old Chicago 38. Professor Beware 38. Topper Takes a Trip 38. Jesse James 39. Drums Along the Mohawk 39. Alias the Deacon 40. Our Town 40.

Tobacco Road 41. The Remarkable Andrew 42. Juke Girl 42, many others.

Chase, Borden (c. 1899–1971). American screenwriter.
Under Pressure 35. Blue White and Perfect 41. Destroyer 43. Flame of the Barbary Coast 45. Tycoon 47. Montana 48. Red River 48. The Great Jewel Robber 50. Lone Star 51. Bend of the River 52. The World in his Arms 52. Man without a Star 55. Backlash 56. Night Passage 57. Gunfighters of Casa Grande 65, many others.

Chase, Charlie (1893–1940) (Charles Parrott). Toothbrush-moustached American comedian who made innumerable two-reel comedies from 1924, usually as henpecked husband.

Chase, Ilka (1900–). American columnist who has occasionally brightened films.
Autobiographies: *Past Imperfect* 1945. *Free Admission* 1948.
Why Leave Home? 29. South Sea Rose 29. Free Love 30. The Animal Kingdom 32. Soak the Rich 36. Stronger than Desire 39. *Now Voyager* 42. No Time for Love 43. Miss Tatlock's Millions 48. Johnny Dark 54. The Big Knife 55. Ocean's Eleven 60, etc.

the chase has always been a standard ingredient of film-making, providing a foolproof way of rounding off a comedy or thriller in good style. In silent days it was necessary to every comedian, from the Keystone Kops to Buster Keaton while westerns inevitably concluded with the goodies chasing the baddies, and even *Intolerance* has a four-stranded chase finale. Sound comedies began by using the chase more sparingly, but René Clair's *Le Million* 32 was a superbly sustained example of the fuller orchestration now possible, and later sophisticated comedies like *It Happened One Night, Sullivan's Travels, The Runaround, Sex and the Single Girl, Good Neighbour Sam* and *What's Up Doc?* have not disdained using the chase as a basic theme; nor of course have broader comedians such as Harold Lloyd, W. C. Fields, Laurel and Hardy and Abbott and Costello, and Stanley Kramer devised a super chase in the marathon *It's a Mad Mad Mad Mad World* 63, to be rivalled in 1965 by *The Great Race*. Most of the old chase gags were crammed into the finale of *A Funny Thing Happened on the Way to the Forum* 67. Ealing comedies of the late forties and early fifties (*The Lavender Hill Mob, Whisky Galore, The Man in the White Suit, A Run For Your Money*) also used chases

brilliantly to broaden their shafts of satire.

More serious films using the chase theme include: *You Only Live Once, Stagecoach, Out of the Past, High Sierra, They Live By Night, Odd Man Out, The Capture, The Chase, Tell Them Willie Boy Is Here, Figures in a Landscape*, and the innumerable versions of *Les Misérables*, which also sparked off five television series: *The Fugitive, Run For Your Life, Branded, Run Buddy Run*, and *Kung Fu*. Thrillers which have featured exciting chases include the Bond adventures, many Hitchcocks including *The Thirty-nine Steps* and *North by Northwest, The Naked City, Robbery, Bullitt, Vanishing Point, The French Connection, Puppet on a Chain, Dirty Mary Crazy Larry, Race with the Devil, Escape from Zahrain* and *The Seven-Ups*.

Chatterton, Ruth (1893–1961). Dignified American leading lady, popular in twenties and thirties after stage success; later had success as novelist.
□ Sins of the Fathers 28. The Doctor's Secret 29. The Dummy 29. *Madame X* 29. Charming Sinners 29. The Laughing Lady 29. Sarah and Son 30. Paramount on Parade 30. The Lady of Scandal 30. Anybody's Woman 30. The Right to Love 30. Unfaithful 31. The Magnificent Lie 31. Once a Lady 31. Tomorrow and Tomorrow 32. The Rich are Always with Us 32. The Crash 32. Frisco Jenny 33. Lilly Turner 33. Female 33. Journal of a Crime 33. Lady of Secrets 36. Girls' Dormitory 36. *Dodsworth* 36. The Rat (GB) 38. A Royal Divorce (GB) 38.

Chauvel, Charles (1897–1959). Australian writer-producer-director.
In the Wake of the Bounty 33. Forty Thousand Horsemen 42. The Rats of Tobruk 48. The Rugged O'Riordans 48. Jedda 53, many others.

Chayevsky, Paddy (1923–). Distinguished American writer whose greatest success was in TV.
□ As Young as You Feel (oa) 51. *Marty* (AA) 55. The Catered Affair (oa) 56. *The Bachelor Party* 57. The Goddess (w) 58. Middle of the Night (oa) 59. The Americanization of Emily (w) 64. *The Hospital* (w) (AA) 71. Network 76.

Cheaper by the Dozen (US 1950). Based on the life of Frank Gilbreth, a slightly eccentric efficiency expert and father of twelve children, this very popular film spawned a sequel (*Belles on Their Toes* 52) and caused a resurgence of family movies as well as comedies starring Clifton Webb as an irascible but affectionate father.

The Cheat (US 1915). This melodrama by Hector Turnbull was a huge commercial success in its day, with Sessue Hayakawa as the wily Japanese who loans money to a foolish society dame, ill-treats her when she will not succumb to his lascivious desires, and is killed by her husband. Cecil B. de Mille directed; the film was remade by George Fitzmaurice in 1923, George Abbott in 1931, and in 1937 (in France) by Marcel L'Herbier.

Checker, Chubby (1941–) (Ernest Evans). Endlessly gyrating American pop singer/dancer, briefly popular in the early sixties.
Twist Around the Clock 62. Don't Knock the Twist 62, etc.

Chekhov, Michael (1891–1955). Russian character actor who set up drama schools in London and New York; films sparse.
□ Song of Russia 44. In Our Time 44. *Spellbound* 45. *Spectre of the Rose* 46. Cross My Heart 46. Abie's Irish Rose 46. Arch of Triumph 47. Invitation 51. Holiday for Sinners 52. Rhapsody 54.

Chenal, Pierre (1903–) (Pierre Cohen). French director. Crime and Punishment 35. The Late Mathias Pascal 36. *Alibi* 37. Le Dernier Tournant 39. Sirocco 45. Clochemerle 48. Native Son (US) 51. Sinners of Paris 59, etc.

Cher (1946–) (Cheryl La Piere). American pop singer, with Sonny (Sonny Bono).

Cherkassov, Nicolai (1903–1966). Russian leading actor of epic hero stature.
□ Baltic Deputy 37. *Peter the Great* 37. Ski Battalion 38. Friends 39. Captain Grant's Children 39. The Man with the Gun 38. *Alexander Nevsky* 38. Lenin in October 39. General Suvorov 41. *Ivan the Terrible Part One* 42. In the Name of Life 42. Ivan the Terrible Part Two 44. Spring 48. The First Front 49. Ivan Pavlov 50. Mussorgsky 51. Rimsky Korsakov 54. *Don Quixote 53.*

Cherrill, Virginia (1908–). American leading lady, a society girl who had a brief film career in the early thirties.
□ *City Lights* (as the blind girl) 31. Girls Demand Excitement 31. The Brat 31. Delicious 31. Fast Workers 33. The Nuisance 33. Charlie Chan's Greatest Case 33. White Heat 34. What Price Crime 35. Troubled Waters 35.

Cherry, Helen (1915–). Cool and gracious British actress, mostly on stage; wife of Trevor Howard.

The Courtneys of Curzon Street 48. Adam and Evelyn 49. Morning Departure 50. Young Wives' Tale 51. Castle in the Air 53. Three Cases of Murder 55. High Flight 57. The Naked Edge 61. Flipper's New Adventure 64. Hard Contract 69. 11 Harrowhouse 74, etc.

Chester, Hal E. (1921–). American teenage actor who, as Hally Chester, was one of the 'Little Tough Guys' in 1938–40. Later became producer and settled in Europe.
Joe Palooka Champ 46. The Underworld Story 50. The Highwayman 53. Crashout 55. The Bold and the Brave 56. Night of the Demon 57. School for Scoundrels 60. Hide and Seek 64. The Secret War of Harry Frigg 67. The Double Man 67, etc.

Chesterton, G. K. (1874–1936). English novelist and journalist, an irrepressible wit whose chief bequest to the cinema is the clerical detective Father Brown, played in movies by Walter Connolly and Alec Guinness and on TV by Heinz Roemheld and Kenneth More.

Chevalier, Maurice (1888–1972). Inimitable French singing entertainer, known throughout the world for his accent, his straw hat and his jutting lower lip. Became famous in Paris revues of the twenties, went to Hollywood in the thirties, remained in Europe in the forties, then re-emerged as an international star. Special Academy Award 1958 'for his contributions to the world of entertainment for more than half a century'.
Autobiographies: 1949, The Man in the Straw Hat. 1960, With Love. 1972, I Remember it Well.
□ SOUND FILMS: Innocents in Paris 29. *The Love Parade* 30. Paramount on Parade 30. The Big Pond 30. Playboy of Paris 30. The Smiling Lieutenant 31. *One Hour With You* 32. *Love Me Tonight* 32. Bedtime Story 33. The Way to Love 33. The Merry Widow 34. *Folies Bergère* 35. L'Homme du Jour 36. Avec Le Sourire 36. Break the News 36. The Beloved Vagabond 37. Pièges 39. *Le Silence est d'Or* 47. Le Roi 49. Ma Pomme 50. J'Avais Sept Filles 55. Love in the Afternoon 57. *Gigi* 58. Count Your Blessings 59. Can Can 59. Black Tights 60. A Breath of Scandal 60. Pepe 60. *Fanny* 61. Jessica 62. *In Search of the Castaways* 62. A New Kind of Love 63. Panic Button 64. I'd Rather be Rich 64. Monkeys Go Home 67.

Cheyney, Peter (1896–1951). British mystery writer who created Lemmy Caution and Slim Callaghan, some of whose adventures were filmed.

Deputy Drummer (w) 32. Uneasy Terms (w) 48. Meet Mr Callaghan (w) 50.

Chiari, Mario (1909–). Italian production designer.
Miracle in Milan 51. The Golden Coach 54. Neapolitan Fantasy 54. I Vitelloni 54. The Sea Wall 56, etc.

Chiari, Walter (1924–) (Walter Annichiarico). Italian comic actor, occasionally in international films.
Bellissima 51. OK Nero 51. The Moment of Truth 53. Nana 56. The Little Hut 57. Bonjour Tristesse 58. Pepote 58. Chimes at Midnight 66. They're a Weird Mob 66. Squeeze a Flower 69. The Valachi Papers 72, etc.

Chief Thundercloud (1898–1967) (Scott Williams). American actor of Indian descent who appeared in many second feature westerns and played Tonto on radio.

Chief Thundercloud (1889–1955) (Victor Daniels). American Indian actor who began in films as a stuntman.
Ramona 36. Union Pacific 38. Western Union 41. The Falcon Out West 44. Unconquered 47. The Half Breed 51, many others.

La Chienne (France 1931). Written and directed by Jean Renoir from a novel by La Fouchardière, this bitter melodrama had Michel Simon as an unhappy man who takes up with a prostitute (Janie Mareze), kills her, and allows another man to be condemned in his place. It was remade by Fritz Lang in Hollywood in 1945, as Scarlet Street, with Edward G. Robinson and Joan Bennett. Heavy and unconvincing, this version was important as the first American film in which justice was not seen to be done after a crime ... though Robinson was shown years later, tortured by remorse.

A Child is Waiting (US 1963). From Abby Mann's script, Stanley Kramer produced and John Cassavetes directed this most delicate of problem pictures, exploring the world of mentally handicapped children. Over-tactfulness rendered it rather obvious as a motion picture, but its sincerity is as obvious as its professional polish, and that such a film should have come from Hollywood at all is encouraging. Burt Lancaster, Judy Garland, and Bruce Ritchey as a withdrawn child, give excellent performances.

child stars have been popular with every generation of filmgoers. Throughout the twenties Mary Pickford stayed at the top by remaining a child as long as, and after, she could; with only slight competition from Baby Peggy, Madge Evans, Dawn O'Day (later Anne Shirley) and Wesley Barry. Stronger competititors, perhaps, were Junior Coghlan and, around 1930, Junior Durkin; strongest of all was Jackie Coogan, immortalized by Chaplin as The Kid in 1920 and subsequently cast in all the standard juvenile roles. The child comedians who composed Our Gang for Hal Roach started in the twenties and went on, with cast changes, into the forties: best remembered of them are Joe Cobb, Jean Darling, Johnny Downs, Mickey Daniels, Farina, Spanky Macfarland, Alfalfa Switzer, Darla Hood and Buckwheat Thomas.

Jackie Cooper also started in Our Gang but became a star in his own right after playing in The Champ and Skippy. In the early thirties his main rival was Dickie Moore, a lad of somewhat gentler disposition. Soon both were displaced in popular favour by Freddie Bartholemew in David Copperfield; but no boy could hold a candle to the multi-talented prodigy Shirley Temple, a star in 1933 at the age of five. She capitvated a generation in a dozen or more hurriedly-produced sentimental comedies, and neither the angelic British Binkie Stuart nor the mischievous Jane Withers could cast the same spell.

Noting a splendid performance by twelve-year-old Robert Lynen in the French Poil de Carotte, we next encounter the still irrepressible Mickey Rooney, who popped up variously as Puck, Andy Hardy or a one-man-band. Then in 1937, the year that the Mauch twins appeared in The Prince and the Pauper, an MGM short called Every Sunday introduced two singing teenage girls, Deanna Durbin and Judy Garland, who went on to achieve enormous popularity in maturing roles until both were overtaken by personal difficulties. Another child who went on to musical stardom was vaudeville-bred Donald O'Connor, first seen in Sing You Sinners. But little more was seen of Tommy Kelly, who played Tom Sawyer, or Ann Gillis, or Terry Kilburn, or even Roddy McDowall until he re-emerged as a character actor twenty-five years later.

The early forties saw Edith Fellows as a good girl and Virginia Weidler, so marvellous in The Philadelphia Story, as a bad one. Baby Sandy appeared in a few comedies, as had Baby Le Roy ten years earlier; neither was seen on screen after the toddler stage. Two infant Dead-End Kids, Butch and Buddy, roamed mischievously through several Universal comedies. Margaret O'Brien and Peggy Ann Garner were two truly remarkable child actresses who never quite managed the transition to adult stardom.

Teenagers Ann Blyth and Peggy Ryan partnered Donald O'Connor in many a light musical. Other child actors of the period were Ted Donaldson, Diana Lynn, Darryl Hickman and Sharyn Moffett, while Skippy Homeier gave an electrifying performance as the young Nazi in *Tomorrow the World*. In the post-war years Europe contributed Ivan Jandl in *The Search*; Britain had George Cole and Harry Fowler for cockney roles, Jeremy Spenser for well-bred ones, Anthony Wagner and Jean Simmons in *Great Expectations*, and very memorable performances from Bobby Henrey in *The Fallen Idol* and John Howard Davies in *Oliver Twist*. Hollywood responded with thoughtful Claude Jarman, tearful Bobs Watson, spunky Bobby Driscoll and Tommy Rettig, and pretty little misses Gigi Perreau and Natalie Wood.

The fifties brought William (now James) Fox in *The Magnet*, Brigitte Fossey and Georges Poujouly in *Les Jeux Interdits*, Mandy Miller in *Mandy*, Vincent Winter and Jon Whiteley in *The Kidnappers*, Brandon de Wilde in *Shane*, and Patty McCormack as the evil child in *The Bad Seed*. In 1959 Hayley Mills embarked on a six-year reign (somewhat outshone in *Whistle down the Wind* by Alan Barnes); the similar and equally capable American actress Patty Duke confined herself principally to stage and TV apart from *The Miracle Worker*. Then there have been Disney's over-wholesome Tommy Kirk and Annette Funicello, Fergus McClelland in *Sammy Going South*, Jean-Pierre Léaud in *The Four Hundred Blows*, William Dix in *The Nanny*, Matthew Garber and Karen Dotrice in *Mary Poppins*, Deborah Baxter in *A High Wind in Jamaica*, Mark Lester and Jack Wild in *Oliver*, Tatum O'Neal in *Paper Moon*, Linda Blair in *The Exorcist*, Ando in *Paper Tiger*, Kim Richards and Ike Eisenmann in *Escape to Witch Mountain*, ... and more moppets are inevitably waiting in the wings, though the recent tendency has been for them to make one appearance and disappear from the boards.

The Childhood of Maxim Gorki (Russia 1938). Mark Donskoi's trilogy—the later sections are *Out in the World* and *My Universities*—subordinate propaganda to a highly pictorial evocation of old Russia. They are perhaps the most humane and personal of Soviet films.

Children of Hiroshima (Japan 1953). Written and directed by Kaneto Shindo, this strikingly stylish semi-documentary begins with an unforgettable impressionistic montage of the dropping of the first A-bomb, then continues on a more soberly journalistic note as it follows a young schoolmistress round the stricken city seven years later.

Children's Film Foundation. British company formed in 1951 to produce and distribute specially-devised entertainment films for children's Saturday matinées. Sponsored by trade organizations.

Chin, Tsai (c. 1938–). Chinese leading lady in international films.
The Face of Fu Manchu 65. Invasion 66. The Brides of Fu Manchu 66. You Only Live Twice 67. Rentadick 72, etc.

China was making films of a kind early in the century, but development of the industry was sporadic until the fifties, when the communists churned out many propaganda dramas.

The Chinese Bungalow. A popular British stage melodrama of the twenties, by Marian Osmond and James Corbett, this was first filmed in 1925 by Sinclair Hill, with Matheson Lang repeating his stage performance as the sinister oriental who covets an English rose. He also appeared in the 1930 sound version, with Anna Neagle as his victim; J. B. Williams directed. In 1940 the tale was remade with Paul Lukas and Kay Walsh, directed by George King.

Ching, William (1912–). American general purpose actor of the forties.
Something in the Wind 47. D.O.A. 50. Belle le Grand 51. Pat and Mike 52. Scared Stiff 53, etc.

Chodorov, Edward (1904–). American screenwriter.
The World Changes 33. Kind Lady 35. The Story of Louis Pasteur (co-w) 35. Yellow Jack 38. Undercurrent 46. The Hucksters 47. Roadhouse 48, etc.

Chodorov, Jerome (1911–). American writer, usually with Joseph Fields.
Louisiana Purchase 41. My Sister Eileen 42. Junior Miss 45. Happy Anniversary 59 (all from their plays), etc.

Choureau, Etchika (1923–). French leading lady.
Children of Love 53. The Fruits of Summer 55. Lafayette Escadrille (US) 57. Darby's Rangers (US) 58, etc.

Chrétien, Henri (1879–1956). French inventor of the anamorphic lens subsequently used in CinemaScope and allied processes.

Christ on the screen was for many years a controversial subject: film-makers have usually preferred to imply his presence by a hand, a cloak, or simply reactions of onlookers. However, even in the first ten years of cinephotography there were several versions of his life, and in 1912 Robert Henderson played the role in a 'super' production of *From the Manger to the Cross*. In 1916 came *Civilisation*, with George Fisher as Christ on the battlefields, and in the same year *Intolerance*, in which Howard Gaye was Jesus. In 1927 Cecil B. de Mille's *King of Kings* had H. B. Warner in the role; any offence was minimized by having his first appearance a misty fade-in as the blind girl regains her sight. In 1932 Duvivier made *Golgotha*, with Robert le Vigan; twenty years then went by before Christ's next appearance on the screen, played by a non-professional, Robert Wilson, in a sponsored movie called *Day of Triumph*. In 1961 Jeffrey Hunter appeared as Christ in *King of Kings*, which was unfortunately tagged by the trade *I Was a Teenage Jesus*. George Stevens' disappointing 1965 colossus, *The Greatest Story Ever Told*, cleverly cast Swedish Max von Sydow in the part; in the same year came Pasolini's *The Gospel According to St Matthew*, with Enrique Irazoqui; and in 1969 Buñuel cast Bernard Verley as Christ in *The Milky Way*. Christ-like figures of various kinds have been found in such films as *The Passing of the Third Floor Back*, *The Fugitive*, *Strange Cargo* and *The Face*; while films about the direct influence of Christ's life include *Quo Vadis*, *The Last Days of Pompeii*, *Ben Hur*, *Barabbas*, *The Wandering Jew* and *The Robe*, in which the voice of Christ was provided by Cameron Mitchell. The most recent Christs have been in the pop-operas *Godspell* and *Jesus Christ Superstar*.

Christensen, Benjamin (1879–1959). Danish director whose career faded after a sojourn in Hollywood.
The Mysterious X 13. The Night of Revenge 15. Häxan (Witchcraft through the Ages) 21. Seine Frau Die Unbekannte 23. The Devil's Circus 25. Mockery 27. The Hawk's Nest 28. Seven Footprints to Satan 29, others.

Christian, Linda (1923–) (Blanca Rosa Welter). Mexican-born leading lady who appeared in a few international films, then married into European nobility.
Holiday in Mexico 46. Green Dolphin Street 47. Tarzan and the Mermaids 48. The Happy Time 52. Athena 54. Thunderstorm 56. The House of Seven Hawks 59. The VIPs 63. How to Seduce a Playboy 66, etc.

Christian, Paul: see *Hubschmid, Paul.*

Christian-Jaque (1904–) (Christian Maudet). French writer-director, former journalist.
Les Disparus de Saint-Agil 38. La Symphonie Fantastique 42. Sortilèges 44. *Un Revenant* 46. D'Homme à Hommes 48. Souvenirs Perdus 50. Bluebeard 51. *Fanfan la Tulipe* 51. Lucrezia Borgia 52. Adorables Creatures 52. Nana 54. Si Tous les Gars du Monde (Race for Life) 55. Babette Goes to War 59. Madame Sans Gêne 61. The Black Tulip 63. The Secret Agents (The Dirty Game) (co-director) 66. The Saint Versus . . . 66. Two Tickets to Mexico (Dead Run) 67, etc.

Christians, Mady (1900–1951) (Margarethe Marie Christians). Austrian-born stage actress in occasional Hollywood films.
The Waltz Dream (GB) 26. Slums of Berlin 27. The Runaway Princess (GB) 29. A Wicked Woman 35. Escapade 36. Seventh Heaven 37. Heidi 37. Address Unknown 44. All My Sons 48. Letter from an Unknown Woman 48, etc.

Christie, Dame Agatha (1891–1976). Best-selling British mystery novelist and playwright whose innumerable puzzle plots have been strangely neglected by film-makers.
Lord Edgware Dies (and other films starring Austin Trevor as Hercule Poirot) 36. And Then There Were None 45. Witness for the Prosecution 58. Spider's Web 60. Murder She Said 62. Murder at the Gallop 63. The Alphabet Murders 66. Murder on the Orient Express 74, etc.

Christie, Al (1886–1951). American comedy producer, mainly of two-reelers, in Hollywood from 1914 and a rival of Mack Sennett. Features include *Tillie's Punctured Romance* 17, *Up in Mabel's Room* 26; produced and directed *Charley's Aunt* 25.

Christie, Audrey (–). American supporting actress of the fifties.
Deadline 52. Carousel 56. Splendor in the Grass 61. The Unsinkable Molly Brown 64. The Ballad of Josie 68. Mame 73, etc.

Christie, Howard (1912–). American producer.
Lady on a Train 44. Abbott and Costello Meet the Invisible Man 50. The Purple Mask 55. Away All Boats 56. Gunfight at Abilene 60. Nobody's Perfect 68, other routine films.

Christie, Julie (1940–). Striking British

leading actress whose choice of roles has not always been fortunate.
□ Crooks Anonymous 62. The Fast Lady 63. *Billy Liar* 63. Young Cassidy 64. *Darling* (AA) 65. *Doctor Zhivago* 65. Fahrenheit 451 66. Far From the Madding Crowd 67. Petulia 68. In Search of Gregory 69. The Go-Between 71. McCabe and Mrs Miller 71. *Don't Look Now* 74. Shampoo 75. Demon Seed 77.

Christine, Virginia (1917–). American character actress.
Edge of Darkness 42. The Mummy's Curse 45. The Killers 46. Cyrano de Bergerac 50. Never Wave at a WAC 53. Not as a Stranger 55. Nightmare 56. Invasion of the Body Snatchers 56. The Careless Years 58. Judgment at Nuremberg 61. The Prize 63. Guess Who's Coming to Dinner 67, etc.

Christmas has provided a favourite sentimental climax for many a film. Films wholly based on it include *The Holly and the Ivy, Tenth Avenue Angel, Miracle on 34th Street, White Christmas, Christmas Eve, Christmas in Connecticut, The Bishop's Wife, I'll Be Seeing You*, and the many versions of *Scrooge*. There were happy Christmas scenes in *The Bells of St Mary, The Inn of the Sixth Happiness, The Man Who Came to Dinner, Holiday Inn, Since You Went Away, Three Godfathers, It's A Wonderful Life, Young at Heart, Meet Me in St Louis, On Moonlight Bay, Little Women, The Cheaters, Desk Set* and *Young at Heart* among others; while unhappy Christmases were spent in *Things to Come, Full House* ('The Gifts of the Magi'), *The Apartment, Meet John Doe, The Glenn Miller Story, The Christmas Tree, Christmas Holiday*, and *The Victors*. (Nor was there much for the characters in *The Lion in Winter* to celebrate at the Christmas court of 1189.)
Santa Claus himself put in an appearance in *Miracle on 34th Street* (played by Edmund Gwenn), *The Lemon Drop Kid* (played by Bob Hope), *The Light at Heart* (played by Monty Woolley), and *Robin and the Seven Hoods* (played by the Sinatra clan). Disney features him in *Babes in Toyland* and a short cartoon, *The Night Before Christmas*; and in their 1934 version of *Babes in Toyland* Laurel and Hardy found him an irate employer.
Christmas was celebrated in unlikely settings in *Knights of the Round Table, Conquest of Space, Scott of the Antarctic, Encore* ('Winter Cruise'), *Destination Tokyo* (in a submarine), *The Nun's Story* (in a Congo Mission), and *Black Narcissus* (in an Indian nunnery).

Chrystall, Belle (–). British leading lady of the thirties.
Hindle Wakes 31. Friday the Thirteenth 33. Edge of the World 38, etc.

Chukrai, Grigori (1920–). Russian director.
The Forty First 56. Ballad of a Soldier 59. Clear Sky 61. There Was an Old Man and an Old Woman 65, etc.

Churches have provided a setting for many pretty secular-minded films, from the various versions of *The Hunchback of Notre Dame* to the use of a church as a refuge during a flood in *When Tomorrow Comes*. Other memorable moments include Bogart confessing the plot of *Dead Reckoning* to a priest; Robert Donat's sermon in *Lease of Life* and Orson Welles' in *Moby Dick*; the scandalous confessions in *Les Jeux Interdits* and the dramatic one in *I confess*; the murder of Becket; the bombed but well-used churches in *Mrs Miniver* and *Sundown*; the thing in the rafters of Westminster Abbey in *The Quatermass Experiment*; the attempted murder in Westminster Cathedral in *Foreign Correspondent* and the fall from the church tower in *Vertigo*; the spies in the mission chapel in *The Man Who Knew Too Much*; the arrest of *Pastor Hall*; Arturo de Cordova going mad during a service in *El*; the church-tower climax of *The Stranger*; the Russian services in *Ivan the Terrible* and *We Live Again*; Cagney dying on the church steps in *The Roaring Twenties*; the church used as refuge against the Martians in *The War of the Worlds*; the church used for a town meeting in *High Noon*; the Turkish mosque and espionage rendezvous in *From Russia with Love*; the comic rifling of offertory boxes in *Heaven Sent*; the finale of *Miracle in the Rain* in the church porch; the meeting in church of the protagonists of *The Appaloosa*; the characters finally trapped in a church in *The Exterminating Angel*; the churches swept away by the elements in *The Hurricane* and *Hawaii*; the church rendezvous in *Alice's Restaurant*; the church with the moving statue in *The Miracle of the Bells*; and all the many films in which the protagonists are *priests, monks* and *nuns* (qv).

Churchill, Berton (1876–1940). Forceful Canadian stage actor who in later years settled in Hollywood and played stern bosses and fathers.
Tongues of Flame 24. Nothing but the Truth 29. Secrets of a Secretary 31. The Rich are Always with Us 32. American Madness 32. Master of Men 33. Hi Nellie 34. Dames 34. Babbitt 34. Page Miss Glory 35. Parole 36. Parnell 37. The Singing Marine 37. Sweethearts 38. *Stagecoach*

(as the absconding banker) 39. The Way of All Flesh 40. Turnabout 40, many others.

Churchill, Diana (1913–). British leading lady, mostly on stage.
School for Husbands 36. Housemaster 38. House of the Arrow 40. Eagle Squadron (US) 44. Scott of the Antarctic 48. The History of Mr Polly 49, etc.

Churchill, Donald (1930–). British light actor, usually of callow or nervous young men. Also TV playwright.
Victim 62. The Wild Affair 64, etc.

Churchill, Marguerite (1910–). Pert American leading lady of the thirties.
The Valiant 29. Seven Faces 29. Born Reckless 30. The Big Trail 30. Charlie Chan Carries On 31. Quick Millions 31. Forgotten Commandments 32. Girl without a Room 33. The Walking Dead 36. Dracula's Daughter 36. Legion of Terror 36, etc.

Churchill, Sarah (1914–). British actress, daughter of Sir Winston Churchill.
He Found a Star 40. All Over the Town 47. *Royal Wedding* (US) 51. Serious Charge 58, etc.

Churchill, Sir Winston (1874–1965). British statesman and author who has been the subject of a major documentary, *The Finest Hours* 64, and a TV series, *The Valiant Years* 60. He was impersonated by Dudley Field Malone in *Mission to Moscow* 43, by Patrick Wymark in *Operation Crossbow* 65, by a number of Russian actors in various propaganda pieces, and by Simon Ward in *Young Winston* 72.

Ciannelli, Eduardo (1887–1969). Italian character actor, long in Hollywood; his finely-etched features and incisive speech were usually employed in villainous roles, but he could also strike sympathetic chords.
Reunion in Vienna 33. The Scoundrel 35. *Winterset* 36. Marked Woman 37. Law of the Underworld 38. Gunga Din 39. Foreign Correspondent 40. The Mummy's Hand 40. They Met in Bombay 41. Cairo 42. They Got Me Covered 43. *The Mask of Dimitrios* 44. The Conspirators 44. Dillinger 45. Wife of Monte Cristo 46. Perilous Holiday 47. The Creeper 48. Rapture 50. The People Against O'Hara 51. Volcano 53. Mambo 55. Helen of Troy 55. Houseboat 58. The Visit 64. Mackenna's Gold 68. The Brotherhood 68. The Secret of Santa Vittoria 69, many others.
TV series: *Johnny Staccato* 59.

Cicognini, Alessandro (1906–). Italian composer.
Four Steps in the Clouds 42. Shoeshine 46. I Miserabili 48. Tomorrow is Too Late 50. Miracle in Milan 51. Don Camillo 52. Umberto D 52. Due Soldi di Speranza 52. Gold of Naples 54. Ulysses 54. Summer Madness 55. The Black Orchid 58, etc.

Cilento, Diane (1933–). Versatile Australian leading actress whose talent has not been fully tested in movies.
Wings of Danger 52. The Angel who Pawned Her Harp 54. The Passing Stranger 54. Passage Home 55. The Woman for Joe 56. *The Admirable Crichton* 57. Jet Storm 59. The Full Treatment 60. The Naked Edge 61. I Thank a Fool 62. *Tom Jones* 63. The Third Secret 64. *Rattle of a Simple Man* 64. The Agony and the Ecstasy 65. *Hombre* 67. Negatives 68. Zero Population Growth 72. The Wicker Man 73. Hitler: the Last Ten Days 74, etc.

Cimarron (US 1931) (AA). This famous western was directed by Wesley Ruggles from a script by Howard Estabrook based on Edna Ferber's novel about Yancey Cravat and the opening of the Cimarron Strip. Richard Dix and Irene Dunne starred. In 1961 Anthony Mann, to little effect, directed a remake with Glenn Ford and Maria Schell.

Cimino, Mike (–). American screenwriter.
□ Silent Running (co-w) 72. Magnum Force (co-w) 73. Thunderbolt and Lightfoot (& d) 74.

cinema vérité. A fashionable term of the sixties for what used to be called candid camera. A TV-style technique of recording life and people as they are, in the raw, using handheld cameras, natural sound and the minimum of rehearsal and editing. Chiefly applied to *Chronique d'une Eté* 61, *Le Joli Mai* 62, and the documentaries of Richard Leacock and the Maysles brothers.

cinemas have only rarely provided a background for film situations. A Hollywood première and a sneak preview were shown in *Singin' in the Rain*, and *The Oscar* revealed all about the Academy Awards ceremony. Characters in *Sherlock Junior, Borderlines* and *Merton of the Movies* (Red Skelton version) clambered on to the stage while a film was showing. Projectionists were featured in *Clash by Night, The Blob, The Great Morgan*, and *Hellzapoppin*; also in *The Smallest Show on Earth*, the only film concerned with the running of a cinema as its main plot unless one counts *The Last Picture Show* in which the small town cinema is an essential background to the character development. Fred Allen in *It's in the Bag* had a terrible time trying to find a seat in a full house; Dillinger was killed coming out of a cinema in *The F.B.I. Story*; Bogart was nearly shot in a Chinese cinema in *Across the Pacific*, and Anthony Perkins met Valli in a Siamese one in *This Angry Age* (*The Sea Wall*). A cinema was used as a rendezvous for spies in *The Traitors* and *Sabotage*; a church was used as a cinema in *Sullivan's Travels* when chain-gang convicts watched Mickey Mouse. Mark Stevens and Joan Fontaine in *From This Day Forward* visited a news cinema but were too much in love to heed the warnings of impending war. Louis Jourdan and Linda Christian watched Valentino at the local in *The Happy Time*, and astronauts watched Bob Hope in a space station in *Conquest of Space*. Deanna Durbin got a murder clue in a cinema in *Lady on a Train*; and in *Bullets or Ballots* Humphrey Bogart took Barton MacLane to see a documentary.about his nefarious career. Ray Danton in *The Rise and Fall of Legs Diamond* excused himself during a performance to rob the shop next door. The monster in *The Tingler* escapes into a silent cinema. Linda Hayden in *Baby Love* was accosted in a cinema. Robert Cummings in *Saboteur* started a riot in Radio City Music Hall. In *Brief Encounter*, Celia Johnson and Trevor Howard thought the organist was the best part of the programme. Polly Bergen in *The Caretakers* went crazy and climed up in front of the screen. *Bonnie and Clyde* found time between robberies to see a *Gold Diggers* movie. In *Eye Witness* a cinema manager was killed during the Saturday night performance; and in *Targets* a killer was apprehended by Boris Karloff at a drive-in. A drive-in was used as a rendezvous in *White Heat* and a 42nd Street cinema was a homosexual rendezvous in *Midnight Cowboy*. Home movies figured most notably in *Rebecca* and *Adam's Rib*. See excerpts.

CinemaScope. Wide-screen process copyrighted by Fox in 1953 and first used in *The Robe*; invented many years earlier by Henri Chrétien. Other companies either adopted it or produced their own trade name: WarnerScope, SuperScope, etc. Basically, the camera contains an anamorphic lens which 'squeezes' a wide picture on to a standard 35mm frame (which has a breadth/height ratio of 4:3 or 1.33:1). This, when projected through a complementary lens, gives a picture ratio on screen of 2.55:1 with stereophonic magnetic sound, or 2.35:1 with optical sound. Directors found the new shape

awkward to compose for, the easiest way of handling it being to park the camera and let the actors move, a reversion to early silent methods. Although wide screens are said to have helped the box office, they have effectively prevented the full use of cinematic techniques. Oddly enough Fox in the mid-sixties quietly dropped their own system and moved over to Panavision.

Cinematograph Exhibitors' Association. The British theatre-owners' protective association, founded in 1912 with ten members. In 1922 there were 2000, in 1950, 4000.

cinematographer. Lighting cameraman or chief photographer.

Cinemobile. A massive truck into which everything necessary for location shooting, including dressing rooms and toilets, can be packed.

Cinerama. Extra-wide-screen system, invented by Fred Waller. Three projectors, electronically synchronized, were used to put the picture on the screen in three sections: this gave a disturbing wobble at the joins, though the range of vision was sometimes magnificently wide, as in the aerial shots and roller coaster sequence in *This is Cinerama 52*. After ten years of scenic but cinematically unremarkable travelogues (*Cinerama Holiday*, *Seven Wonders of the World*, *Search for Paradise*, etc.), the first story film in the process, *How the West Was Won*, was made in 1962. Shortly afterwards the three-camera system was abandoned in favour of 'single-lens Cinerama' which is virtually indistinguishable from CinemaScope except for the higher definition resulting from using wider film. 'Cinemiracle', a similar process, was short-lived.

Cioffi, Charles (–). American character actor of the seventies.
The Don is Dead 73. The Thief who Came to Dinner 73. Crazy Joe 74. Dog and Cat (TV) 77.

circuit. A chain of cinemas under the same ownership, often playing the same release programme.

circuses, according to the cinema, are full of drama and passion behind the scenes. So you would think if you judged from *Variety*, *Freaks*, *The Wagons Roll at Night*, *The Greatest Show on Earth*, *The Big Show*, *The Big Circus*, *Sawdust and Tinsel*, *Circus of Horrors*, *Tromba*, *Four Devils*, *The Three Maxims*, *Trapeze*, *Captive Wild Woman*, *Ring of Fear*,

Charlie Chan at the Circus, A Tiger Walks, Circus World, The Trojan Brothers, Circus of Fear, Berserk, The Dark Tower, He Who Gets Slapped, Flesh and Fantasy, Pagliacci and *Far from the Madding Crowd.* But there is a lighter side, as evidenced by *Doctor Dolittle, Yo Yo, Jumbo, High Wide and Handsome, Lady in the Dark, Life is a Circus, The Marx Brothers at the Circus, Three Ring Circus,* Chaplin's *The Circus, The Great Profile, You Can't Cheat an Honest Man,* and *Road Show.*
□ TV Series have included *Circus Boy, Frontier Circus* and *The Greatest Show on Earth.*

The Cisco Kid. This ingratiating Latin rogue was first played by Warner Baxter in Irving Cummings' 1931 film. In 1937 Cesar Romero played him in the first of a series; the role was taken over in 1945 by Duncan Renaldo, who has also been in TV series. The Kid's side-kicks have included Leo Carrillo and Chris-Pin Martin.

The Citadel (GB 1938). Masterly film version of Cronin's novel about a doctor's rise from Welsh slums to Harley Street, directed by King Vidor for MGM-British, with Robert Donat and Ralph Richardson.

Citizen Kane (US 1941). Often acclaimed as the best film of all time: certainly none has used the medium with more vigour and enthusiasm. Herman J. Mankiewicz' script paralleled the career of newspaper magnate William Randolph Hearst, making the point that money isn't everything. Orson Welles, the boy wonder of American radio, produced and directed it as a cinematic box of tricks, often somewhat obscuring the story of a journalist's quest for the truth after Kane's death; nevertheless there isn't a dull scene in the film's 119 minutes. Cameraman Gregg Toland and composer Bernard Herrmann contributed massively to the general effect of a new joyous era in film-making, and many of Welles' Mercury Company of theatre actors launched new careers for themselves: Joseph Cotten, Everett Sloane, Agnes Moorehead, George Coulouris, Ray Collins, Paul Stewart, and Welles himself as Kane. After thirty years the film seems scarcely to have faded at all. See *The Citizen Kane Book* 1971, edited by Pauline Kael.

City Lights (US 1931). Chaplin's depression-period comedy in which the tramp meets a drunken millionaire and a blind flower girl. Comedy over-flooded with sentiment, but some brilliant moments.

Civilisation (US 1916). One of the few films of its time which can stand beside the work of Griffith, Thomas Ince's film is a painstaking anti-war allegory intended to keep America neutral in World War I: Christ returns to earth in human form to work for peace. A very fluent piece of film-making.

Clair, René (1898–) (René Chomette). Distinguished French director of light comedy; he brought to the screen a nimble command of technique, an optimistic outlook, and a total lack of malice or message.
□ Paris Qui Dort 23. Entr'acte 24. *An Italian Straw Hat* 28. Sous Les Toits de Paris 29. Le Million 31. *A Nous la Liberté* 31. Le Quatorze Juillet 33. Le Dernier Milliardaire 34. The Ghost Goes West 35. Break the News 36. The Flame of New Orleans 41. *I Married a Witch* 42. Forever and a Day (part) 43. *It Happened Tomorrow* 44. *And Then There Were None* 45. Le Silence est d'Or 46. La Beauté du Diable 49. *Les Belles de Nuit* 52. Les Grandes Manoeuvres 55. Porte des Lilas 56. Tout l'Or du Monde 60. Les Fêtes Galantes 65.

Claire, Ina (1892–) (Ina Fagan). American stage actress who made occasional films.
The Puppet Crown 15. Wild Goose Chase 15. Polly with a Past 20. The Awful Truth 29. The Royal Family of Broadway 31. Rebound 31. The Greeks Had a Word for Them 32. Ninotchka 39. Claudia 43, etc.

clairvoyance on the screen seems to have caused a remarkable amount of suffering to Edward G. Robinson: he was haunted by the effects of a prophecy in *Flesh and Fantasy, Nightmare* and *Night Has a Thousand Eyes.* Other frightened men for similar reasons were Claude Rains in *The Clairvoyant,* Dick Powell in *It Happened Tomorrow,* George Macready in *I Love a Mystery,* Mervyn Johns in *Dead of Night,* and Michael Hordern in *The Night My Number Came Up.*

clapperboard. A hinged board recording film details. At the beginning of each 'take' it is held before the camera for identification and then 'clapped' to make a starting point in the sound track. This point is then sychronized with the image of the closed board.

Clare, Mary (1894–1970). British character actress, latterly in formidable matron roles.
Becket 24. Hindle Wakes 31. The Constant Nymph 33. The Clairvoyant 34. The Passing of the Third Floor Back 35. Young and Innocent 37. The Lady Vanishes 38. A Girl Must Live 39. Old Bill and Son 40. *Mrs Pym of Scotland Yard*

(title role) 40. Next of Kin 42. *The Night Has Eyes* 42. The Hundred-Pound Window 44. The Three Weird Sisters 48. *Oliver Twist* 48. Moulin Rouge 53. Mambo 55. The Price of Silence 59, many others.

Clarence, O. B. (1870–1955). British stage actor who played benevolent doddering roles in a number of films.
Perfect Understanding 32. Friday the Thirteenth 33. The Scarlet Pimpernel 34. Seven Sinners 36. Pygmalion 38. Inspector Hornleigh Goes To It 41. Penn of Pennsylvania 42. On Approval 43. A Place of One's Own 44. Great Expectations (as the Aged P) 46. Uncle Silas 47, many others.

Clark, Bobby (1888–1960). Bouncy American vaudeville comedian who with Paul McCullough made thirty-six two-reel comedies for RKO between 1928 and 1936, when McCullough died. Clark made only one solo film appearance, in *The Goldwyn Follies* 38.

Clark, Candy (1949–). American leading lady of the seventies.
American Graffiti 73. The Man Who Fell to Earth 76.

Clark, Cliff (1893–1953). Short, stocky American character actor who played tough sheriffs and police inspectors in forties co-features.
Mr Moto's Gamble 38. Kentucky 39. Honolulu 39. The Grapes of Wrath 40. Double Alibi 40. Manpower 41. Kid Glove Killer 42. The Falcon's Brother 42. The Falcon in Danger 43. The Falcon out West 44. Bury Me Dead 47. Deep Waters 48. The Men 50. Cavalry Scout 51. The Sniper 52, many others.

Clark, Dane (1913–) (Bernard Zanville). Pint-sized American tough guy of the forties, a poor man's Garfield.
Tennessee Johnson 43. Destination Tokyo 43. The Very Thought of You 44. God is My Co-Pilot 45. A Stolen Life 46. Her Kind of Man 46. That Way with Women 47. Deep Valley 47. Whiplash 48. *Moonrise* 49. Barricade 50. Without Honour 50. Highly Dangerous (GB) 50. Go Man Go (& co-p) 53. Port of Hell 54. The Toughest Man Alive 55. Murder by Proxy (GB) 55. This Man is Armed 56. The Outlaw's Son 57. The McMasters 70, etc.

Clark, Ernest (1912–). British character actor of all media, usually in cold, tight-lipped roles.
Private Angelo 49. Doctor in the House 53. Beau Brummell 54. The Dam Busters 55. Time without Pity 57. A Tale of Two Cities 58. Sink the Bismarck 60. Nothing but the Best 64. Arabesque 66. Salt and Pepper 68, many others.

Clark, Fred (1914–1968). Bald-domed American character comedian, usually in explosive roles.
□ The Unsuspected 47. Ride the Pink Horse 47. Hazard 48. Cry of the City 48. Two Guys from Texas 48. Fury at Furnace Creek 48. Mr Peabody and the Mermaid 49. Alias Nick Beal 49. Flamingo Road 49. The Younger Brothers 49. Task Force 49. White Heat 49. The Lady Takes a Sailor 49. *Sunset Boulevard* 50. The Eagle and the Hawk 50. Return of the Frontiersman 50. The Jackpot 50. Mrs O'Malley and Mr Malone 50. The Lemon Drop Kid 51. Hollywood Story 51. A Place in the Sun 51. Meet Me After the Show 51. Three for Bedroom C 52. Dreamboat 52. The Stars are Singing 53. The Caddy 53. How to Marry a Millionaire 53. Here Come the Girls 53. Living It Up 54. Abbott and Costello Meet the Keystone Kops 54. Daddy Longlegs 55. How to be Very Very Popular 55. The Court Martial of Billy Mitchell 55. Miracle in the Rain 56. The Birds and the Bees 56. *The Solid Gold Cadillac* 56. Back from Eternity 56. Joe Butterfly 57. The Fuzzy Pink Nightgown 57. *Don't Go Near the Water* 57. Mardi Gras 58. Auntie Mame 58. The Mating Game 59. It Started with a Kiss 59. Visit to a Small Planet 60. Bells are Ringing 60. Zotz 62. Boys' Night Out 62. Hemingway's Adventures of a Young Man 62. Move Over Darling 63. John Goldfarb Please Come Home 64. The Curse of the Mummy's Tomb (GB) 65. Sergeant Deadhead 65. Dr Goldfoot and the Bikini Machine 65. When the Boys meet the Girls 65. War Italian Style 67. The Horse in the Grey Flannel Suit 68. Skidoo 68.
TV series: *The Double Life of Henry Phyfe* 66.

Clark, James B. (–). American director, former editor.
Under Fire 57. Sierra Baron 58. The Sad Horse 59. A Dog of Flanders 60. One Foot in Hell 60. The Big Show 60. Misty 61. Flipper 63. Island of the Blue Dolphins 64. And Now Miguel 66. My Side of the Mountain 68. The Little Ark 71, etc.

Clark, Jim (1931–). British director, former editor.
Every Home Should Have One 70. Madhouse 74.

Clark, Marguerite (1883–1940). American heroine of the silent screen, a rival for Mary Pickford in waif-like and innocent roles. Retired 1921.

Wildflower 14. The Goose Girl 15. Molly Make-Believe 16. Snow White 17. Prunella 18. Mrs Wiggs of the Cabbage Patch 18. Girls 19. All-of-a-Sudden Peggy 20. Scrambled Wives 21.

Clark, Petula (1932–). British child actress who later made it big as a singer and settled in France.
□ Medal for the General 44. Murder in Reverse 45. London Town 46. Strawberry Roan 47. *Here Come the Huggetts* 48. Vice Versa 48. Easy Money 48. Don't Ever Leave Me 49. Vote for Huggett 49. The Huggetts Abroad 50. Dance Hall 50. The Romantic Age 50. White Corridors 51. Madame Louise 51. Made in Heaven 52. *The Card* 52. The Runaway Bus 54. The Gay Dog 54. The Happiness of Three Women 55. Track the Man Down 56. That Woman Opposite 57. Daggers Drawn 64. Finian's Rainbow 68. *Goodbye Mr Chips* 69.

Clark, Robert (1905–). British executive, longtime director (resigned 1969) of Associated British Picture Corporation. Former lawyer; producer of many ABPC films including *the Hasty Heart, The Dam Busters*, etc.

Clark, Susan (1940–). Canadian leading lady in Hollywood.
□ Banning 67. Madigan 68. Coogan's Bluff 68. The Forbin Project 69. Tell Them Willie Boy is Here 69. Skullduggery 69. Valdez is Coming 70. The Skin Game 71. Showdown 73. Trapped (TV) 73. Airport 75 74. The Midnight Man 74. The Apple Dumpling Gang 75. Amelia Earhart (TV) 76.

Clarke, Mae (1910–). Pert American leading lady at her peak in the early thirties; from musical comedy.
Big Time 29. Fall Guy 30. *The Front Page* 31. *Public Enemy* 31. *Waterloo Bridge* 31. Frankenstein 31. Night World 32. The Penguin Pool Murder 32. Parole Girl 33. Penthouse 33. Lady Killer 33. Nana 34. The Silk Hat Kid 35. Wild Brian Kent 36. Trouble in Morocco 37. Women in War 40. Sailors on Leave 41. Flying Tigers 42. Here Come the Waves 44. Kitty 45. Daredevils of the Clouds 48. Annie Get Your Gun 50. The Great Caruso 51. Because of You 52. Women's Prison 55. Mohawk 56. Ask Any Girl 59. Big Hand for a Little Lady 66. Thoroughly Modern Millie 67, many others.

Clarke, Shirley (1925–). American director of the New York *cinema vérité* school.
The Connection 60. Cool World 63. Portrait of Jason 67, etc.

Clarke, T. E. B. (1907–). British screenwriter, former journalist; associated with the heyday of Ealing comedy.
Johnny Frenchman 45. Against the Wind 46. *Hue and Cry* 46. *Passport to Pimlico* 48. The Blue Lamp 50. *The Lavender Hill Mob* 51. *The Titfield Thunderbolt* 53. Barnacle Bill 57. Law and Disorder 58. Gideon's Day 58. Sons and Lovers 60. The Horse Without a Head 63. A Man Could Get Killed 66, etc.

Clarke-Smith, D. A. (1888–1959). British character actor, mainly on stage.
Atlantic 30. The Ghoul 33. Warn London 34. Sabotage 36. The Flying Fifty-Five 39. Frieda 47. Quo Vadis 51. The Baby and the Battleship 56, etc.

Claudia (US 1943). Rose Franken's whimsical book about a child-wife who matures when she hears that her mother is dying was filmed in 1943 with Dorothy McGuire (who played the role on Broadway) and Robert Young. Three years later came a sequel, *Claudia and David*, with the same stars.

Clavell, James (1922–). Australian writer of Anglo-Irish descent.
The Fly 58. Five Gates to Hell (& pd) 58. Walk Like a Dragon (& pd) 60. The Sweet and the Bitter (wpd) (Can.) 62. The Great Escape 63. The Satan Bug 65. King Rat (oa) 65. To Sir With Love (& pd) 66. Where's Jack? (& pd) 69, etc.

Clayburgh, Jill (1945–). American leading lady of the seventies.
Portnoy's Complaint 72. The Thief who Came to Dinner 73. The Terminal Man 74. *Hustling* (TV) 75. *Gable and Lombard* 76. Silver Streak 76.

Clayton, Ethel (1884–1966). American actress.
Her Own Money 12. The College Widow 15. Pettigrew's Girl 19. Sham 21. If I Were Queen 22. The Remittance Woman 23. Wings of Youth 25. Mother Machree 28. Hit the Deck 30. Continental 32. Secrets 33. Artists and Models 37. The Buccaneer 38. Ambush 39, many others.

Clayton, Jack (1921–). British producer-director who worked his way up through the industry.
□ The Bespoke Overcoat (pd) 55. Three Men in a Boat (p) 56. *Room at the Top* (d) 58. *The Innocents* (d) 61. *The Pumpkin Eater* (d) 64. Our Mother's House (d) 67. The Great Gatsby (d) 74.

Cleese, John (1939–). Tall British comic

actor, often on TV satirizing familiar types.
Interlude 68. The Best House in London 68. The
Rise and Rise of Michael Rimmer 70. And Now
for Something Completely Different 71. The
Love Ban 72. Monty Python and the Holy Grail
74, etc.

Clemens, Brian (1931–). British screenwriter
especially associated with *The Avengers*; author
of many TV thrillers.
□ Station Six Sahara 64. The Corrupt Ones 64.
And Soon the Darkness 70. See No Evil 71. Dr
Jekyll and Sister Hyde 71. Captain Kronos
Vampire Hunter (&d) 72. The Golden Voyage of
Sinbad 73.

Clemens, William (1905–). American
director of second features.
□ Man Hunt 36. The Law in Her Hands 36. The
Case of the Velvet Claws 36. Down the Stretch
36. Here Comes Carter 36. Once a Doctor 37.
The Case of the Stuttering Bishop 37. Talent
Scout 37. The Footloose Heiress 37. Missing
Witnesses 37. Torchy Blane in Panama 38.
Accidents will Happen 38. Mr Chump 38.
Nancy Drew Detective 38. Nancy Drew
Reporter 39. Nancy Drew Trouble Shooter 39.
Nancy Drew and the Hidden Staircase 39. The
Dead End Kids on Dress Parade 39. Calling
Philo Vance 40. King of the Lumberjacks 40.
Devil's Island 40. She Couldn't Say No 41.
Knockout 41. The Night of January 16th 41. A
Night in New Orleans 42. Sweater Girl 42. Lady
Bodyguard 43. The Falcon in Danger 43. The
Falcon and the Co-Eds 43. The Falcon Out
West 44. Crime by Night 44. The Thirteenth
Hour 47.

Clement, Dick (1937–). British writer-
director.
The Jokers (co-w) 67. *Otley* (co-w, d) 69. A
Severed Head (d) 70. Villain (w) 71. Catch Me a
Spy (co-, d) 71. The Likely Lads 76, etc.

Clément, René (1913–). Distinguished
French director whose later films have
disappointed.
□ *Bataille du Rail* 43. Les Maudits 46. Le Père
Tranquille 46. Au Dela des Grilles 49. Le
Château de Verre 50. *Les Jeux Interdits* 51.
Knave of Hearts (GB) 53. *Gervaise* 55. The Sea
Wall 56. Plein Soleil 59. Quelle Joie de Vivre 61.
The Day and the Hour 63. The Love Cage 65. Is
Paris Burning? 66. Rider on the Rain 69. The
House under the Trees 71. And Hope to Die 72.

Clements, Sir John (1910–). Distinguished
British actor-manager, on stage from 1930.
Ticker of Leave 35. Things to Come 35.

Rembrandt 36. Knight Without Armour 36.
South Riding 38. The Housemaster 39. *The Four
Feathers* 39. Convoy 40. This England 41. Ships
with Wings 41. Tomorrow We Live 42.
Undercover 42. They Came to a City 45. Call of
the Blood (& wpd) 47. The Silent Enemy 57. *The
Mind Benders* 63. Oh What a Lovely War 69,
etc.

Clements, Stanley (1926–). American actor
familiar in the forties as tough teenager.
Tall Dark and Handsome 41. Going My Way
44. Salty O'Rourke 45. Bad Boy 49. Jet Job 52.
Robbers' Roost 55. Up in Smoke 59. Saintly
Sinners 61. Tammy and the Doctor 63, many
others.

Cléo de 5 à 7 (France 1961). A highly personal
film by Agnes Varda about a young woman who
thinks she is dying and sees the world around her
with heightened perception. With Corinne
Marchand; photographed by Jean Rabier.

Cleopatra (69–30 B.C.). The sultry Egyptian
queen has been portrayed in many films, notably
in a Méliès trick film of 1899; by unspecified
American actresses in 1908 and 1909; by Helen
Gardner in 1911; by Theda Bara in 1917; by
Claudette Colbert in the de Mille version of
1934; by Vivien Leigh in Pascal's 1945 *Caesar
and Cleopatra*; by Rhonda Fleming in *Serpent
of the Nile* 1953; by Hedy Lamarr in *The Story
of Mankind* 1957; by Elizabeth Taylor in the
well-publicized 1962 version; and by Amanda
Barrie in a spoof, *Carry On Cleo*, in 1963. There
seems to be something about the lady that
encourages waste, for the Leigh version was
Britain's most expensive film and the Taylor
version the world's; in neither case did the money
show on the screen.

Cleveland, George (1886–1957). American
character actor, typically cast as grizzled old
prospector.
Keeper of the Bees 35. Revolt of the Zombies 36.
Goldtown Ghost Riders 38. Port of Missing
Girls 38. Mutiny in the Big House 39. Call Out
the Marines 41. The Spoilers 42. Woman of the
Town 44. Can't Help Singing 44. Dakota 45.
The Runaround 46. The Wistful Widow of
Wagon Gap 47. Please Believe Me 50. Trigger
Jnr 52. Untamed Heiress 54, many others.
TV series: *Lassie* 55–57.

Cliff, Laddie (1891–1937) (Laddie Perry).
British light comedian and composer.
The Co-Optimists 30. Sleeping Car 33. Happy
33, etc.

cliffhanger. Trade name for a serial, especially an episode ending in an unresolved situation which keeps one in suspense till next time.

Clift, Montgomery (1920–1966). Romantic American leading actor of stage and screen, usually in introspective roles; his career was jeopardized in 1957 by a car accident which somewhat disfigured him.
□ *The Search* 48. *Red River* 48. The Heiress 49. The Big Lift 50. *A Place in the Sun* 51. I Confess 53. *From Here to Eternity* 53. Indiscretion of an American Wife 54. Raintree County 57. The Young Lions 58. Lonelyhearts 59. Suddenly Last Summer 59. Wild River 60. The Misfits 60. Judgment at Nuremberg 61. *Freud* 63. The Defector 66.

Clifton, Elmer (1890–1949). American director, mainly of second features; started as an actor with Griffith.
Boots 19. Nugget Nell 19. Mary Ellen Comes to Town 21. Down to the Sea in Ships 22. The Wreck of the Hesperus 27. Virgin Lips 28. Six Cylinder Love 31. Crusade against Rackets 37. Isle of Destiny 40. Swamp Woman 41. Seven Doors to Death 44. Not Wanted 49, many others.

Cline, Edward (1892–1961). American comedy director who began with the Sennett bathing beauties.
Summer Girls 18. Three Ages 23. Captain January 24. Old Clothes 25. *Sherlock Junior* 26. Let it Rain 27. Soft Cushions 27. Ladies Night in a Turkish Bath 27, etc.
□ SOUND FILMS COMPLETE: Broadway Fever 29. His Lucky Day 29. The Forward Pass 29. In the Next Room 30. Sweet Mama 30. Leathernecking 30. Hook Line and Sinker 30. The Widow from Chicago 30. Cracked Nuts 31. The Naughty Flirt 31. The Girl Habit 31. *Million Dollar Legs* 32. Parole Girl 33. So This is Africa 33. Peck's Bad Boy 34. The Dude Ranger 34. When a Man's a Man 35. The Cowboy Millionaire 35. It's a Great Life 36. F Man 36. On Again Off Again 37. Forty Naughty Girls 37. High Flyers 37. Hawaii Calls 38. Go Chase Yourself 38. Breaking the Ice 38. Peck's Bad Boy with the Circus 38. *My Little Chickadee* 40. The Villain Still Pursued Her 40. *The Bank Dick* 40. Meet the Chump 41. Cracked Nuts 41. Hello Sucker 41. *Never Give a Sucker an Even Break* 41. Snuffy Smith 32. What's Cookin' 42. Private Buckaroo 42. Give Out Sisters 42. Behind the Eight Ball 42. He's My Guy 43. Crazy House 43. Swingtime Johnny 44. Ghost Catchers 44. Slightly Terrific 44. Moonlight and Cactus 44. Night Club Girl 44.

See My Lawyer 45. Penthouse Rhythm 45. Bringing Up Father 46. Jiggs and Maggie in Society 48. Jiggs and Maggie in Court 48.

Clive, Colin (1898–1937) (Clive Greig). British leading man who looked older than his years; in Hollywood from 1930, playing fraught, serious roles.
□ *Journey's End* 30. Frankenstein (title role) 31. The Stronger Sex (GB) 31. Lily Christine (GB) 32. Christopher Strong 33. Looking Forward 33. The Key 34. *Jane Eyre* (as Rochester) 34. One More River 34. Clive of India 35. The Right to Live 35. *The Bride of Frankenstein* 35. The Girl from Tenth Avenue 35. *Mad Love* 35. The Man who Broke the Bank at Monte Carlo 35. *History is Made at Night* 37. The Woman I Love 37.

Clive, E. E. (1879–1940). British character actor who came late in life to Hollywood and played a succession of sour-faced but often amiable butlers, burgomasters and statesmen, with a sprinkling of lower orders.
The Invisible Man 33. Charlie Chan in London 34. The Mystery of Edwin Drood 35. *The Bride of Frankenstein* 35. A Tale of Two Cities 35. Dracula's Daughter 36. *Piccadilly Jim* 36. The Charge of the Light Brigade 36. Lloyds of London 36. On the Avenue 37. Night Must Fall 37. Bulldog Drummond's Peril 38. Kidnapped 38. The Hound of the Baskervilles 39. The Adventures of Sherlock Holmes 39. *Raffles* 39. Pride and Prejudice 40. Foreign Correspondent 40, many others.

Cloche, Maurice (1907–). French director, in films (as documentarist) from 1933.
La Vie est Magnifique 38. Monsieur Vincent 47. Cage aux Filles 48. Né de Père Inconnu 50. Les Filles de la Nuit 57. Coplan, Secret Agent 64, etc.

Clooney, Rosemary (1928–). Breezy American cabaret singer who made a few film appearances.
□ The Stars are Singing 53. Here Come the Girls 53. *Red Garters* 54. *White Christmas* 54. Deep in My Heart 54.

Closely Observed Trains (Czechoslovakia 1966). Jiri Menzel's oddly likeable little tragi-comedy won the 1968 Academy Award for the best foreign film. Apart from a strangely downbeat ending, it consists of a number of amusing scenes and characters set in a country railway station during World War II.

close-up. Generally applied to a head-and-shoulders shot of a person or any close shot of an object. The first close-up is said to be that of Fred Ott sneezing in an Edison experimental film of 1900. See *long shot*.

Clothier, William H. (1903–). American cinematographer.
Sofia 48. Confidence Girl 52. Track of the Cat 54. Blood Alley 55. The Man in the Vault 56. The Horse Soldiers 59. The Alamo 60. The Deadly Companions 61. The Man Who Shot Liberty Valance 62. A Distant Trumpet 64. Cheyenne Autumn 64. Shenandoah 65. The Way West 67. The War Wagon 67. Firecreek 67. The Devil's Brigade 68. Hellfighters 68. The Cheyenne Social Club 70. Big Jake 71, etc.

Clouse, Robert (–). American director.
Happy Mothers Day, Love George (w only) 73. Enter the Dragon 73. Golden Needles 74. Black Belt Jones 74.

Cloutier, Suzanne (1927–). French-Canadian leading lady.
Temptation (US) 46. Au Royaume des Cieux 47. Juliette ou la Clef des Songes 50. Othello 51. Derby Day (GB) 51. Romanoff and Juliet (US) 61, etc.

Clouzot, Henri-Georges (1907–1977). French writer-director, noted for suspense melodramas.
Un Soir de Rafle (w) 31. Le Dernier des Six (w) 41. Les Inconnus dans la Maison (w) 42. L'Assassin Habite au 21 (wd) 42. *Le Corbeau* (wd) 43. *Quai des Orfèvres* (wd) 47. Manon (wd) 49. Retour à la Vie (wd) 49. *The Wages of Fear* (wd) 53. *Les Diaboliques* (wd) 54. The Picasso Mystery (wd) 56. Les Espions (wd) 57. The Truth (wd) (AA) 60. La Prisonnière (wd) 70, etc.

Clouzot, Vera (1921–1960). Portugese actress, wife of H. G. Clouzot.
The Wages of Fear 53. Les Diaboliques 54. Les Espions 57, etc.

Clunes, Alec (1912–1970). British stage actor who made occasional film appearances.
Convoy 40. Saloon Bar 40. Melba 53. Quentin Durward 56. *Richard III* 56. Tomorrow at Ten 62, etc.

Clurman, Harold (1901–). American stage director chiefly associated with New York's Group Theatre of the thirties. Directed one very pretentious film: *Deadline at Dawn* 46.

Clute, Chester (1891–1956). American character comedian. His startled look, small

stature, tiny moustache and bald pate made him an inimitable henpecked husband or harassed clerk in scores of films.
Dance Charlie Dance 37. Rascals 38. Annabel Takes a Tour 38. Dancing Co-Ed 39. Hired Wife 40. She Couldn't Say No 41. Yankee Doodle Dandy 43. Chatterbox 43. Arsenic and Old Lace 44. Guest Wife 45. Angel on my Shoulder 46. Something in the Wind 47. Mary Ryan Detective 46, many others.

Clyde, Andy (1892–1967). Scottish acrobatic comedian, long in Hollywood as western side-kick and hero of innumerable two-reelers, often as grizzled, toothless old fool.
The Goodbye Kiss 28. Million Dollar Legs 32. The Little Minister 34. McFadden's Flats 35. Two in a Crowd 36. Abe Lincoln in Illinois 39. The Green Years 46, many others.
TV series: *No Time for Sergeants* 64–65.

coal mines and the bravery of the men who work in them formed a theme which commanded the respect of cinema audiences for many years. Apart from *Kameradschaft* (the French-German border), *Black Fury* (US), and *The Molly Maguires* (US) all the major films on this subject have been about Britain: *The Proud Valley*, *The Stars Look Down*, *How Green Was My Valley*, *The Citadel*, *The Corn is Green*, *The Brave Don't Cry*, *Sons and Lovers*, *Women in Love*.

Cobb, Irwin S. (1876–1944). American humorous writer who appeared in a few films and was touted as another Will Rogers after that actor's death.
□ Pardon My French 21. Peck's Bad Boy 21. The Five Dollar Baby 22. The Great White Way 24. Turkish Delight 27. *Steamboat Round the Bend* 34. Everybody's Old Man 36. Pepper 36. Hawaii Calls 38. The Arkansas Traveller 38. The Young in Heart 38.

Cobb, Lee J. (1911–1976) (Leo Jacoby). Powerful American character actor who forsook stage for screen.
□ North of the Rio Grande 37. Ali Baba Goes to Town 37. Rustler's Valley 37. Danger on the Air 38. The Phantom Creeps 39. *Golden Boy* 39. Men of Boys' Town 41. This Thing Called Love 41. Paris Calling 42. Tonight We Raid Calais 43. Buckskin Frontier 43. *The Moon is Down* 43. The Song of Bernadette 43. Winged Victory 44. *Anna and the King of Siam* 46. Boomerang 47. Johnny O'Clock 47. Captain from Castile 47. Call Northside 777 48. The Miracle of the Bells 48. The Luck of the Irish 48. *The Dark Past* 48. Thieves' Highway 49. The Man Who Cheated Himself 50. Sirocco 51. The Family Secret 51.

The Fighter 52. The Tall Texan 53. Yankee Pasha 54. Gorilla at Large 54. *On the Waterfront* 54. Day of Triumph 54. The Racers 55. The Road to Denver 55. The Left Hand of God 55. *The Man in the Grey Flannel Suit* 56. Miami Exposé 56. *Twelve Angry Men* 57. The Garment Jungle 57. The Three Faces of Eve 57. The Brothers Karamazov 58. Man of the West 58. Party Girl 58. The Trap 59. Green Mansions 59. But Not for Me 59. Exodus 60. The Four Horsemen of the Apocalypse 62. How the West Was Won 62. *Come Blow Your Horn* 63. Our Man Flint 66. In Like Flint 67. Mackenna's Gold 68. Coogan's Bluff 68. The Liberation of L. B. Jones 70. Macho Callahan 70. Lawman 70. The Exorcist 73. That Lucky Touch 75.

TV series: *The Virginian* 62–66. The Young Lawyers 70.

Coborn, Charles (1852–1945) (Colin McCallum). British music hall artiste famous for his longevity and his rendering of 'The Man Who Broke the Bank at Monte Carlo'.

Say it with Flowers 34. Music Hall 35. Variety Jubilee 41, etc.

Coburn, Charles (1877–1961). Distinguished American actor. A stage star for many years, he came late in life to Hollywood and delighted audiences for another twenty years in roles of crusty benevolence.

□ Boss Tweed 33. The People's Enemy 35. Of Human Hearts 38. Vivacious Lady 38. Yellow Jack 38. Lord Jeff 38. Idiot's Delight 39. The Story of Alexander Graham Bell 39. Made for Each Other 39. *Bachelor Mother* 39. Stanley and Livingstone 39. In Name Only 39. Road to Singapore 40. Florian 40. Edison the Man 40. Three Faces West 40. The Captain is a Lady 40. *The Lady Eve* 41. *The Devil and Miss Jones* 41. Our Wife 41. Unexpected Uncle 41. H. M. Pulham Esq. 41. Kings' Row 41. In This Our Life 42. George Washington Slept Here 42. *The More the Merrier* (AA) 43. The Constant Nymph 43. *Heaven Can Wait* 43. Princess O'Rourke 43. My Kingdom for a Cook 43. *Knickerbocker Holiday* 44. Wilson 44. The Impatient Years 44. Together Again 44. A Royal Scandal 45. Rhapsody in Blue 45. Over 21 45. Colonel Effingham's Raid 45. Shady Lady 45. *The Green Years* 46. Lured 47. BF's Daughter 48. The Paradine Case 48. Green Grass of Wyoming 48. Impact 49. Yes Sir That's My Baby 49. Everybody Does It 49. The Doctor and the Girl 49. The Gal who Took the West 49. Louisa 50. Peggy 50. Mr Music 50. The Highwayman 51. *Monkey Business* 52. *Has Anybody Seen My Gal?* 52. Gentlemen Prefer Blondes 53. Trouble along the Way 53. The Long Wait 54. The Rocket Man 54. How to Be Very Very Popular 55. The Power and the Prize 56. Around the World in Eighty Days 56. Town on Trial 57. The Story of Mankind 57. How to Murder a Rich Uncle 57. Stranger in My Arms 59. The Remarkable Mr Pennypacker 59. John Paul Jones (as Benjamin Franklin) 59. Pepe 60.

Coburn, James (1928–). American leading man of lithe movement and easy grin; career has been patchy.

□ Ride Lonesome 59. Face of a Fugitive 59. *The Magnificent Seven* 60. Hell is for Heroes 62. The Great Escape 63. *Charade* 63. The Man from Galveston 64. The Americanization of Emily 64. Major Dundee 65. A High Wind in Jamaica 65. The Loved One 65. *Our Man Flint* 66. What Did You Do in the War Daddy? 66. Dead Heat on a Merry Go Round 66. In Like Flint 67. Waterhole Three 67. The President's Analyst 67. Duffy 68. Candy 68. Hard Contract 68. Blood Kin 69. *A Fistful of Dynamite* 71. The Carey Treatment 72. The Honkers 72. A Reason to Live, A Reason to Die 72. Pat Garrett and Billy the Kid 73. The Last of Sheila 73. Harry in Your Pocket 73. The Internecine Project (GB) 74. Hard Times 76. Sky Riders 76. Cross of Iron 77.

TV series: Klondyke 60. Acapulco 60.

Coca, Imogene (1909–). American TV and revue comedienne. Rare film appearance: *Under the Yum Yum Tree* 64.

TV series: *Grindl* 63. It's About Time 66.

Cochise (c. 1818–1874). Peace-loving Apache Indian chief who became a prominent cinema character after Jeff Chandler played him in *Broken Arrow* 50, and later in *Battle at Apache Pass* 52 and *Taza Son of Cochise* 53. John Hodiak took over for *Conquest of Cochise* 53.

Cochran, Steve (1917–1965) (Robert Cochran). American leading man, usually a good-looking heavy, mainly in poor films.

Wonder Man 45. The Best Years of Our Lives 46. The Chase 46. The Kid from Brooklyn 47. A Song is Born 48. White Heat 49. The Damned Don't Cry 50. *Storm Warning* 50. The Tanks are Coming 51. Operation Secret 52. The Desert Song 53. Carnival Story 54. *Come Next Spring* 56. The Weapon (GB) 56. I, Mobster 58. The Beat Generation 59. The Deadly Companions 61. Of Love and Desire 63. Mozambique 65, etc.

Coco, James (1928–). Chubby American comic actor.

Ensign Pulver 64. A New Leaf 71. Such Good Friends 71. Man of la Mancha 72. Murder by Death 76.

Cocteau, Jean (1889–1963). Fanciful French poet and writer who occasionally dabbled in cinema with effective if slightly obscure results.
Le Sang d'un Poète (wd) 30. La Comédie du Bonheur (w) 40, *L'Eternel Retour* (w) 43. *La Belle et la Bête* (w, co-d) 46. L'Aigle a Deux Têtes (wd) 48. Les Parents Terribles (wd) 48. *Les Enfants Terribles* (w) 50. *Orphée* (wd) 50. Le Testament d'Orphée 59, etc.

Codee, Ann (1890–1961). American character actress who played a variety of middle-aged roles for many years.
Hi Gaucho 35. Captain Caution 40. Old Acquaintance 44. The Other Love 47. On the Riviera 51. Kiss Me Kate 53. Daddy Long Legs 55. Can Can 59, etc.

Cody, Lew (1884–1934) (Louis Coté). Smartly-dressed American leading man of the silent screen; his French accccennt affected his sound career.
Comrade John 15. The Demon 18. *Don't Change Your Husband* 19. The Sign on the Door 21. Secrets of Paris 22. Within the Law 23. *Rupert of Hentzau* (title role) 23. The Shooting of Dan McGrew 24. Exchange of Wives 25. Adam and Evil 27. On Ze Boulevard 27. Beau Broadway 28. What a Widow 30. Dishonoured 31. Sporting Blood 31. The Tenderfoot 32. Sitting Pretty 33. Shoot the Works 34, many others.

Cody, William Frederick (Buffalo Bill) (1846–1917). American guide, Indian scout, bison hunter and carnival showman. He has been played in movies by James Ellison in *The Plainsman* 36, Joel McCrea in *Buffalo Bill* 42, Louis Calhern in *Annie Get Your Gun* 50, Charlton Heston in *Pony Express* 52, Clayton Moore in *Buffalo Bill in Tomahawk Territory* 53, Gordon Scott in *Buffalo Bill* (Ger.) 64, Guy Stockwell in *The Plainsman* 66 and Paul Newman in *Buffalo Bill and the Indians* 76. He was a favourite hero of silent movies.

Coe, Barry (–). American juvenile actor of the fifties.
On The Threshold of Space 56. Peyton Place 57. The Bravados 58. One Foot in Hell 60. The 300 Spartans 62, etc.

Coe, Fred (1914–). American producer-director from stage and TV.
The Left-handed Gun (p) 58. The Miracle Worker (p) 62. A Thousand Clowns (pd) 65. Me Natalie (d) 69, etc.

Coe, Peter (1929–). British director with stage experience. First film: *Lock Up Your Daughters* 69.

Co-feature. A moderate-budget production designed (or fated) to form equal half of a double bill.

Coffin, Tristam (–). American actor.
No Greater Sin 41. Blackmail 47. Outrage 50. Undercover Girl 50, etc.
TV series: 26 Men 56.

Coghlan, Junior (1916–) (Frank Coghlan). American boy star of the twenties; previously played baby roles.
Slide, Kelly, Slide 26. The Country Doctor 27. River's End 31. Penrod and Sam 32. Boys' Reformatory 39. Henry Aldrich for President 41. The Adventures of Captain Marvel (serial) 50. The Sand Pebbles 66.

Cohan, George M. (1878–1942). Dapper American actor-dancer-author-composer of the Broadway stage. Songs include: 'Mary's a Grand Old Name', 'Give My Regards to Broadway', 'Over There', 'Yankee Doodle Dandy'; plays include the much-filmed *Seven Keys to Baldpate* (qv). Film appearances: *Broadway Jones* 16. *Hit-the-Trail Holiday* 18. *The Phantom President* 32. *Gambling* 34, etc. Was impersonated by James Cagney in a biopic, *Yankee Doodle Dandy* 42, and in *The Seven Little Foys* 55.

Cohen, Herman (c. 1928–). American producer and director of low-budget horror films.
I Was a Teenage Werewolf 57. Konga 61. Black Zoo 63. Berserk 68. Crooks and Coronets 69. Trog 70. Craze 73, etc.

Cohen, Norman (1936–). Irish director.
□ Brendan Behan's Dublin 67. The London Nobody Knows 68. Till Death Us Do Part 68. Dad's Army 70. Adolf Hitler, My Part in His Downfall 72.

The Cohens and the Kellys. This series of domestic farces about a Jew and an Irishman played by George Sidney and Charlie Murray began in 1926 (title as shown). Subsequent adventures were: (*The Cohens and Kellys*) in *Paris* 28, *in Scotland* 30, *in Africa* 31, *in Hollywood* 33, *in Trouble* 33, etc.

Cohl, Emile (1857–1938) (Emile Courte). Pioneer French cartoonist of the 1908–18 period.
Fantasmagorie 08. Les Allumettes Animées 09.

Don Quichotte 09. Aventures d'une Bout de Papier 11. Monsieur Stop 13. Snookums (series) (US) 13–15. Les Pieds Nickelés 18, many others.

Cohn, Arthur (1928–). Swiss producer.
The Sky Above the Mud Below 63. Woman Times Seven 67. Sunflower 70. *The Garden of the Finzi-Continis* (AA) 71. The Sea Wolf 74, etc.

Cohn, Harry (1891–1958). American executive, chief of Columbia Pictures (qv) for many years; a former song-plugger and vaudevillian who built the company in 1924, reputedly from his sales of a film called *Traffic in Souls*. Biography 1967: *King Cohn*, by Bob Thomas.

cokuloris. A palette with random irregular holes, placed between lights and camera to prevent glare and give a better illusion of real-life light and shadow.

Colbert, Claudette (1905–) (Lily Claudette Chauchoin). French leading lady who went to America as a child and became one of Hollywood's most durable and versatile light actresses of the golden age, most typically cast in smart emancipated roles.
☐ For the Love of Mike 28. The Hole in the Wall 29. The Lady Lies 29. The Big Pond 30. Young Man of Manhattan 30. Manslaughter 30. Honour among Lovers 31. The Smiling Lieutenant 31. Secrets of a Secretary 31. His Woman 31. The Wiser Sex 32. Misleading Lady 32. The Man from Yesterday 32. The Phantom President 32. *The Sign of the Cross* (as Poppaea) 32. Tonight is Ours 33. I Cover the Waterfront 33. *Three Cornered Moon* 33. The Torch Singer 33. Four Frightened People 34. *It Happened One Night* (AA) 34. Cleopatra 34. *Imitation of Life* 34. The Gilded Lily 35. Private Worlds 35. She Married Her Boss 35. The Bride Comes Home 35. Under Two Flags 36. Maid of Salem 37. *I Met Him in Paris* 37. Tovarich 37. Bluebeard's Eighth Wife 38. Zaza 39. *Midnight* 39. It's a Wonderful World 39. Drums along the Mohawk 39. Boom Town 40. *Arise My Love* 40. Skylark 41. Remember the Day 41. *The Palm Beach Story* 42. So Proudly We Hail 43. No Time for Love 43. *Since You Went Away* 44. Practically Yours 45. Guest Wife 45. Tomorrow is Forever 46. Without Reservations 46. The Secret Heart 46. *The Egg and I* 47. Sleep My Love 48. Family Honeymoon 49. Bride for Sale 49. *Three Came Home* 50. The Secret Fury 50. Thunder on the Hill 51. Let's Make it Legal 51. The Planter's Wife (GB) 52. Love and the Frenchwoman 54. Si Versailles M'était Conte 55. Texas Lady 55.

Parrish 60.

the cold war has occupied the cinema right from Churchill's Fulton speech in 1948. For three years diehard Nazis had been the international villains par excellence, but a change was required, and Russians have been fair game ever since, in films like *The Iron Curtain, Diplomatic Courier, I Was a Communist for the FBI, I Married a Communist, The Big Lift, Red Snow, The Red Danube, Red Menace, Red Planet Mars, The Journey, From Russia With Love* and innumerable pulp spy thrillers, as well as such classier productions as *The Third Man, The Man Between* and *The Spy Who Came in from the Cold*. Rather surprisingly none of these caused much escalation of tension between the nations, and cooler feelings have permitted comedies like *One Two Three, Dr Strangelove* and *The Russians are Coming, The Russians are Coming*; while such terrifying panic-button melodramas as *Fail Safe* and *The Bedford Incident* are probably our best guarantee that the dangers are realized on both sides.

Cole, George (1925–). British comedy actor who made his film debut as a cockney child evacuee; usually plays the befuddled innocent.
Cottage to Let 41. Henry V 44. *Quartet* 48. Morning Departure 50. Laughter in Paradise 50. Lady Godiva Rides Again 51. Scrooge 51. *Top Secret* 51. Will Any Gentleman? 52. Happy Ever After 53. Our Girl Friday 53. The Belles of St Trinian's 54. A Prize of Gold 55. The Weapon 56. It's a Wonderful World 56. The Green Man 57. Blue Murder at St Trinian's 58. Too Many Crooks 58. The Bridal Path 59. The Pure Hell of St Trinian's 60. Cleopatra 62. Dr Syn 63. One-Way Pendulum 64. The Legend of Young Dick Turpin 65. The Great St Trinian's Train Robbery 66. The Vampire Lovers 70. Fright 71. Take Me High 73. The Bluebird 76, etc.

Cole, Jack (1914–1974). American dancer and choreographer.
Moon Over Miami (d) 41. Kismet (d) 44. Tonight and Every Night (ch) 45. The Jolson Story (ch) 46. On the Riviera (ch) 51. Designing Woman (dch) 55. Let's Make Love (ch) 61, etc.

Cole, Nat King (1919–1965) (Nathaniel Coles). American Negro pianist and singer who made occasional film appearances.
The Blue Gardenia 53. St Louis Blues (as W. C. Handy) 58. The Night of the Quarter Moon 59. Cat Ballou 65, etc.

Coleman, Charles (1885–1951). Australian character actor in Hollywood; almost always

played the perfect portly butler.
That's My Daddy 28. Bachelor Apartment 31.
Gallant Lady 33. Down to Their Last Yacht 34.
Poor Little Rich Girl 36. That Certain Age 38.
Mexican Spitfire 39. It Started with Eve 41. Twin
Beds 42. The Whistler 44. The Runaround 46.
The Imperfect Lady 47, many others.

Coleman, Nancy (1917–). American leading
lady of the forties, usually in timid roles.
Kings' Row 42. Dangerously They Live 42. The
Gay Sisters 42. Desperate Journey 42. Edge of
Darkness 43. In Our Time 44. *Devotion* (as Anne
Brontë) 45. Her Sister's Secret 46. Mourning
Becomes Electra 47. That Man from Tangier 53.
Slaves 68, etc.

Colette (Gabriel-Sidonie Colette) (1873–1954).
French writer, usually on sex themes.
Claudine à l'Ecole 38. Gigi 48 and 58. Julie de
Carnelihan 50. L'Ingénue Libertine 51. Ripening
Seed 54.

Colicos, John (1928–). Canadian character
actor in occasional films.
Anne of the Thousand Days 70. Raid on
Rommel 71. Red Sky at Morning 71. Doctors'
Wives 71. The Wrath of God 72. Scorpio 73
Drum 76. Breaking Point 76, etc.

Colin, Jean (1905–). British leading lady of
the thirties; appearances sporadic.
The Hate Ship 30. Compromising Daphne 30.
The Mikado 39. Bob's Your Uncle 41. Laxdale
Hall 54, etc.

Colin, Sid (1920–). British TV comedy
scriptwriter.
I Only Arsked 58. The Ugly Duckling 59. Up
Pompeii 70. Up the Chastity Belt 71. Up the
Front 72. Percy's Progress 74, etc.

Colla, Richard J. (–). American
director.
Zigzag 70. *Fuzz* 72. Live Again, Die Again (TV)
74.

Colleano, Bonar (1924–1958) (Bonar
Sullivan). Wise-cracking American actor, from
family of acrobats; worked chiefly in Britain.
The Way to the Stars 45. A Matter of Life and
Death 46. While the Sun Shines 46. Good Time
Girl 47. One Night With You 48. Sleeping Car to
Trieste 48. Pool of London 50. A Tale of Five
Cities 52. Eight Iron Men (US) 52. The Sea Shall
Not Have Them 55. Interpol 57. No Time To Die
58, etc.

colleges: see universities.

Collier, Constance (1878–1955) (Laura
Constance Hardie). Distinguished British stage
actress who spent her later years in Hollywood
playing great ladies with caustic tongues and
eccentric habits.
Autobiography 1929: *Harlequinade.*
□ Intolerance 16. The Code of Marcia Gray 16.
Macbeth 16. Bleak House 20. The Bohemian
Girl 22. *Our Betters* 33. Dinner at Eight 33. Peter
Ibbetson 34. Shadow of Doubt 35. Anna
Karenina 35. Girls' Dormitory 36. Professional
Soldier 36. Little Lord Fauntleroy 36. Thunder
in the City 37. Wee Willie Winkie 37. *Stage Door*
37. She Got What She Wanted 37. A Damsel in
Distress 37. Zaza 39. Susan and God 40. Half a
Sinner 40. Weekend at the Waldorf 45. *Kitty* 45.
Monsieur Beaucaire 46. The Dark Corner 46.
The Perils of Pauline 47. *An Ideal Husband* 48.
Rope 48. The Girl from Manhattan 48.
Whirlpool 50.

Collier, John (1901–). British writer of
polished macabre stories, whose screen work has
been sporadic.
Sylvia Scarlett 35. Her Cardboard Lover 42.
Deception 46. Roseanna McCoy 49. The Story
of Three Loves 53. I Am a Camera 55. The War
Lord 65, etc.

Collier, William (1866–1944). American stage
actor, usually of comedy character roles; moved
to Hollywood in 1929.
Six Cylinder Love 31. The Cheater 34. Josette
38. Thanks for the Memory 38. Invitation to
Happiness 39. There's Magic in Music 41, many
others.

Collin, John (1931–). British character actor.
Star! 68. Before Winter Comes 69. Innocent
Bystanders 72, etc.

Collinge, Patricia (1893–1974). Irish-
American stage actress who made occasional
film appearances.
The Little Foxes 41. Shadow of a Doubt 43.
Casanova Brown 44. Teresa 51. The Nun's
Story 58, etc.

Collings, David (1940–). British character
actor, much on TV.
Mahler 74.

Collins, Anthony (1893–1964). British
composer.
The Rat 37. Victoria the Great 37. Sixty
Glorious Years 38. Nurse Edith Cavell 40. The
Courtneys of Curzon Street 47. Odette 50.
Derby Day 52. Laughing Anne 53, etc.

Collins, Cora Sue (1927–). American child star of the thirties.
They Just Had to Get Married 33. Queen Christina 33. Torch Singer 34. The Scarlet Letter 35. Anna Karenina 35. Magnificent Obsession 36. The Adventures of Tom Sawyer 38, etc.

Collins, Eddie (1884–1940). American character comedian from Vaudeville; crowded a few films into his last years.
In Old Chicago 38. Kentucky Moonshine 38. Charlie Chan in Honolulu 38. Young Mr Lincoln 39. Hollywood Cavalcade 39. *The Bluebird* 39. The Return of Frank James 40.

Collins, Joan (1933–). British leading lady whose sultry charms won her parts in an assortment of international films.
I Believe in You 52. Cosh Boy 53. Our Girl Friday 53. Turn the Key Softly 53. The Good Die Young 54. Land of the Pharaohs 55. The Virgin Queen 55. The Girl in the Red Velvet Swing 55. The Opposite Sex 56. The Wayward Bus 57. Island in the Sun 57. Sea Wife 57. The Bravados 58. Rally Round the Flag Boys 58. Seven Thieves 60. Road to Hong Kong 62. Warning Shot 66. Heironymus Merkin 69. The Executioner 69. Up in the Cellar 70. Drive Hard, Drive Fast (TV) 70. Quest for Love 71. Revenge 71. Tales That Witness Madness 73. Alfie Darling 74. I Don't Want to Be Born 75, etc.

Collins, Ray (1890–1965). American stage actor who came to Hollywood with Orson Welles, stayed to play kindly uncles and political bosses.

Collins, Russell (1897–1965). Hardened-looking American character actor.
Shockproof 49. Niagara 5 53. Miss Sadie Thompson 53. Bad Day at Black Rock 55. Soldier of Fortune 56. The Enemy Below 57. The Matchmaker 58. Fail Safe 64, etc.

Collins, Wilkie (1824–89). British novelist, credited with being the inventor of the detective story via *The Moonstone,* whose complications have resisted filming. *The Woman in White* however was filmed with some fidelity in 1947.

Collinson, Peter (1938–). British director who quickly slumped from arty pretentiousness to routine thrillers.
□ The Penthouse 67. Up the Junction 68. The Long Day's Dying 68. *The Italian Job* 69. You Can't Win 'em All 70. Fright 71. Straight on till Morning 72. Innocent Bystanders 72. The Man Called Noon 73. Open Season 74. The

Spiral Staircase 75. The Sell Out 75.

Collyer, June (1907–1968) (Dorothy Heermance). American leading lady in a few light films of the early thirties; married Stuart Erwin.
Woman Wise 27. East Side West Side 28. Charley's Aunt 31. Alexander Hamilton 31. The Ghost Walks 35, etc.

Colman, Ronald (1891–1958). Distinguished British romantic actor whose gentle manners, intelligence and good looks thrilled two generations. Turned to acting after World War I wounds, and went to Hollywood in 1920.
Biography 1975: *A Very Private Person* by Juliet Benita Colman.
□ The Toilers 19. A Son of David 19. The Snow in the Desert 19. The Black Spider 20. Anna The Adventuress 20. Handcuffs or Kisses 21. The Eternal City 23. *The White Sister* 23. Twenty Dollars a Week 24. Tarnish 24. Romola 24. Her Night of Romance 24. A Thief in Paradise 24. His Supreme Moment 25. The Sporting Venus 25. Her Sister from Paris 25. *The Dark Angel* 25. Stella Dallas 25. Lady Windermere's Fan 25. Kiki 26. *Beau Geste* 26. The Winning of Barbara Worth 26. The Night of Love 27. The Magic Flame 27. The Lovers 28. The Rescue 29. *Bulldog Drummond* 29. Condemned 29. *Raffles* 30. The Devil to Pay 30. The Unholy Garden 31. *Arrowsmith* 31. Cynara 32. The Masquerader 33. Bulldog Drummond Strikes Back 34. Clive of India 35. The Man who Broke the Bank at Monte Carlo 35. *A Tale of Two Cities* 35. Under Two Flags 36. *Lost Horizon* 37. *The Prisoner of Zenda* 37. If I were King 38. The Light that Failed 39. Lucky Partners 40. My Life with Caroline 41. *The Talk of the Town* 42. *Random Harvest* 42. Kismet 44. The Late George Apley 47. *A Double Life* (AA) 48. Champagne for Caesar 50. Around the World in Eighty Days 56. The Story of Mankind 57.
TV series: *Halls of Ivy* 53.

Colonna, Jerry (1903–). American comic actor with strong, high-pitched voice, walrus moustache and bulging eyes.
College Swing 38. Little Miss Broadway 38. Road to Singapore 39. Sis Hopkins 41. True to the Army 42. Star-Spangled Rhythm 42. Ice Capades 42. Atlantic City 44. It's in the Bag 45. Road to Rio 47. Kentucky Jubilee 51. Meet Me in Las Vegas 56. Andy Hardy Comes Home 58, etc.

colour prints of a primitive kind were made as long ago as 1898. During the next few years many films were hand-coloured by stencil, and two unsatisfactory processes, KinemaColor and Gaumont colour, were tried out. D. W. Griffith in *The Birth of a Nation* 14 developed the French practice of tinting scenes for dramatic effect: blue for night, orange for sunshine, etc. In 1918 red-and-green Technicolor was tried out along with half a dozen other processes. 1921: Prizmacolour was used for the British historical film *The Great Adventure*. 1923: de Mille used a colour sequence in *The Ten Commandments*. 1926: *The Black Pirate* was shot in two-colour Technicolor. 1932: first three-colour Technicolor film, Disney cartoon *Flowers and Trees* (AA). 1934: colour used in dramatic sequences of *La Cucaracha* and *The House of Rothschild*. 1935: first feature film entirely in three-strip colour, *Becky Sharp*. 1937: first British Technicolor feature, *Wings of the Morning*. 1939: two-colour Cinecolor, very cheap, became popular for low-budget westerns. 1942: Technicolor introduced monopack process, using one negative instead of three and making equipment less cumbersome and more flexible. 1948: Republic adopted Trucolor. 1949: Anscocolor, later to become Metrocolor, used on *The Man on the Eiffel Tower*. 1951: Supercinecolor (3 colours) adopted by Columbia in *Sword of Monte Cristo*. 1952: Eastmancolor used in *Royal Journey*; Warners adopted it as Warnercolor. 1954: Fox adopted De Luxe Color.

Today, with new colours springing up all the time, effectiveness seems to depend not on the trademark but on how well the film is shot, processed and printed.

colour sequences in otherwise black-and-white movies were used at first experimentally (see above) but have also been employed for dramatic effect. Early examples include *The Ten Commandments* 23, *The Wedding March* 28, *The Desert Song* 29, *Chasing Rainbows* 30; many of the early sound musicals went into colour for their final number, and this went on as late as *Kid Millions* 35. *Victoria the Great* 37 had colour for the final 'Empress of India' scenes. *The Wizard of Oz* 39 had the Oz scenes in colour and the Kansas scenes in sepia. *Irene* 40 went into colour for the 'Alice Blue Gown' number—which made the second half of the film anti-climactic. *The Moon and Sixpence* 42 blazed into colour for the fire at the end . . . and the same director, Albert Lewin, used a similar trick whenever the picture was shown in *The Picture of Dorian Gray* 44. *A Matter of Life and Death* 45 had earth in colour, heaven in a rather metallic monochrome. *Task Force* 49 went into colour for its final battle reels, most of which consisted of blown-up 16mm war footage. *The*

Secret Garden 49 played the same trick as *The Wizard of Oz*. *The Solid Gold Cadillac* 56 had a few final feet of colour to show off the irrelevant car of the title. In 1958 *I Was a Teenage Frankenstein* revived the old dodge of colour for the final conflagration. And *Is Paris Burning?* 66 used colour for the climactic victory sequence, having been forced into black-and-white for the rest of the movie by the necessity of using old newsreel footage. In few of the above cases has reissue printing maintained the original intention: printing short sequences in colour is time consuming. See also: *tinting*.

Colpi, Henri (1921–). French editor *Hiroshima Mon Amour* 59. *Last Year in Marienbad* 61, etc; director *Une Aussi Longue Absence* 61. *Codine* 62.

Columbia Pictures. American production and distribution company long considered one of the 'little two' (the other being Universal) against the 'big five' (MGM, RKO, Fox, Warner and Paramount). Columbia originated with one man, Harry Cohn, who founded it in 1924 after a career as a salesman and shorts producer. Throughout the thirties and forties he turned out competent co-features and second features, apart from prestige pictures such as the Capra comedies and an ill-fated Kramer deal; he was also prepared to spend big money on certainties such as Rita Hayworth and *The Jolson Story*. From the late forties, with films like *All the King's Men, Born Yesterday* and *From Here to Eternity,* the company began to pull itself into the big-time, and when Cohn died in 1958 it was one of the leaders of international co-production, with such major films to its credit as *On the Waterfront* and *The Bridge on the River Kwai,* with *Lawrence of Arabia* and *A Man For All Seasons* to come. It also produces and distributes TV films through its subsidiary Screen Gems (Columbia Television).

Columbo, Russ (1908–1934) (Ruggerio de Rudolpho Columbo). American violinist, vocalist, songwriter and bandleader who appeared in a few films.
Wolf Song 29. The Street Girl 29. Hellbound 31. Broadway through a Keyhole 33. Wake Up and Dream 34, etc.

Colvig, Vance (1892–1967). American actor who spent most of his career at the Disney studio and became the voice for Pluto and Goofy. He was also co-author of the song 'Who's Afraid of the Big Bad Wolf?'

combined print. One on which both sound and

picture (always produced separately) have been 'married', i.e. a standard print as shown in cinemas. See *double-headed print*.

Comden, Betty (1918–) (Elizabeth Cohen). American screenwriter who has collaborated with Adolph Green on books and lyrics of many Broadway shows and films.
Good News 47. The Barkleys of Broadway 49. On the Town 49. Singin' in the Rain 52. Band Wagon 54. Auntie Mame 58. What a Way to Go 64, etc.

comedy: *see comedy teams; crazy comedy; light comedians; satire; sex; social comedy; slapstick.*

comedy teams in the accepted sense began in vaudeville, but, depending so much on the spoken word, could make little headway in films until the advent of the talkies. Then they all tried, and many (Amos 'n Andy, Gallagher and Shean, Olsen and Johnson) didn't quite make it, at least not immediately. Laurel and Hardy, who had been successful in silents by the use of mime, adapted their methods very little and remained popular; during the thirties they were really only challenged by Wheeler and Wolsey, whose style was more frenetic, and briefly by Burns and Allen. From 1940 the cross-talking Abbott and Costello reigned supreme, with an occasional challenge from Hope and Crosby and the splendid *Hellzapoppin* from Olsen and Johnson. Then came Martin and Lewis, who didn't appeal to everybody, Rowan and Martin, who in 1957 didn't appeal to anybody, and sporadic attempts to popularize such teams as Brown and Carney and Allen and Rossi. In Britain, comedy teams were popular even in poor films: the best of them were Jack Hulbert and Cicely Courtneidge, Tom Walls and Ralph Lynn, Lucan and MacShane ('Old Mother Riley'), Arthur Askey and Richard Murdoch, and the Crazy Gang, a bumper fun bundle composed of Flanagan and Allen, Naughton and Gold, and Nervo and Knox. Morecambe and Wise, the latest recruits to the fold, are having trouble adapting their talent to the big screen, but will probably succeed in due course. One should also mention Basil Radford and Naunton Wayne, not cross-talkers but inimitable caricaturists of the Englishman abroad; and others, not strictly comedians, who raised a lot of laughs together: Edmund Lowe and Victor McLaglen, Slim Summerville and Zasu Pitts, Joan Blondell and Glenda Farrell, George Sidney and Charlie Murray, Marie Dressler and Polly Moran, Wallace Beery and Raymond Hatton, James Cagney and Pat O'Brien. See *Movie Comedy Teams* by Leonard

Maltin.
Of larger groups, among the most outstanding are Our Gang, the Keystone Kops, the Marx Brothers, the Three Stooges, the Ritz Brothers, Will Hay with Moore Marriott and Graham Moffat, the 'Carry On' team, and one supposes the Beatles.
See also: *romantic teams*.

Comencini, Luigi (1916–). Italian director.
Bambini in Città 46. Proibito Rubare 48. The Mill on the Po (co-writer only) 49. La Città Si Difende (co-writer only) 51. Persiane Chiuse 51. Bread, Love and Dreams (& w) 53. Bread, Love and Jealousy 54. Mariti in Città 58. Bebo's Girl 63, etc.

Comer, Anjanette (1942–). American leading lady.
Quick Before It Melts 65. The Loved One 65. The Appaloosa 66. Banning 66. Rabbit, Run 70. The Firechasers (TV) 70. The Baby 73. Lepke 74, etc.

Comfort, Lance (1908–1966). British director, formerly cameraman.
Penn of Pennsylvania 41. Hatter's Castle 41. When We Are Married 42. Old Mother Riley, Detective 42. Daughter of Darkness (& p) 45. Great Day 45. Silent Dust 48. Portrait of Clare 50. Eight o'Clock Walk 54. At the Stroke of Nine 57. Make Mine a Million 58. The Ugly Duckling 59. Touch of Death 62. Tomorrow at Ten 62. Devils of Darkness 65, others.
Directed many episodes of TV series, especially *Douglas Fairbanks Presents* which he also co-produced.

comic strips in newspapers have always been avidly watched by film producers with an eye on the popular market. Among films and series so deriving are the following:
Gertie the Dinosaur (cartoon series) 19; The Gumps (two-reelers) 23–28; *Bringing Up Father* 16 (drawn), 20 (two-reeler), 28 (feature with J. Farrell MacDonald and Marie Dressler), 45 (series of 'Jiggs and Maggie' features with Joe Yule and Renee Riano); *The Katzenjammer Kids* (cartoon series) 17 and 38, *Krazy Kat* (various cartoons 16–38); *Ella Cinders* (with Colleen Moore) 22; *Tillie the Toiler* (with Marion Davies) 27; *Skippy* (with Jackie Cooper) 30; *Little Orphan Annie* 32 (with Mitzi Green) and 38 (with Ann Gillis); *Joe Palooka* 34 (with Stu Erwin) and 47–51 (with Joe Kirkwood); *Blondie* (with Penny Singleton) 38–48; *Gasoline Alley* (with James Lydon) 51; *Lil Abner* (qv); *Popeye* (qv); *Jungle Jim* 49–54; *Prince Valiant* 54; *Up Front* 51–53; *Felix the Cat* (qv); *Old Bill*

(GB) 40; *Dick Barton* (GB) in various personifications; *Jane* (GB) in an abysmal 1949 second feature; and, of course, *Modesty Blaise* 66, *Batman* 66, *Barbarella* 68, and *Fritz the Cat* 71.

Strip characters whose adventures were turned into Hollywood serials during the thirties and forties include *Tailspin Tommy, Buck Rogers, Mandrake the Magician, Don Winslow of the Navy, Jet Jackson Flying Commando, Flash Gordon, Batman, Buck Rogers* ('in the 25th century'), *Brick Bradford* ('in the centre of the earth'), *Chandu, Superman, Dick Tracy* (also in forties features), *The Lone Ranger* and *Red Ryder*.

Coming thru the Rye (GB 1924). A sentimental Victorian love story directed by Cecil Hepworth. Slow-moving but pleasantly photographed, it is valued as an example of the 'superior' British silent film of its time. Starred Alma Taylor and James Carew. (Miss Taylor had also starred with Stewart Rome in an earlier 1916 version, also directed by Hepworth.)

Comingore, Dorothy (1913–1971). American actress who made few films but will always be remembered as the second Mrs Kane. Formerly known as Kay Winters and Linda Winters.
□ Campus Cinderella 38. Comet over Broadway 38. Prison Train 38. Trade Winds 38. Blondie Meets the Boss 39. North of the Yukon 39. Scandal Sheet 39. Mr Smith Goes to Washington 39. Café Hostess 39. Pioneers of the Frontier 40. *Citizen Kane* 41. The Hairy Ape 44. Any Number Can Play 49. The Big Night 51.

communism has always been treated by Hollywood as a menace. In the thirties one could laugh at it, in *Ninotchka* and *He Stayed for Breakfast*. Then in World War II there was a respite during which the virtues of the Russian peasantry were extolled in such films as *Song of Russia* and *North Star*. But with the Cold War, every international villain became a commie instead of a Nazi, and our screens were suddenly full of dour dramas about the deadliness of 'red' infiltration: *I Married a Communist, I Was a Communist for the FBI, The Red Menace, The Iron Curtain, Trial, My Son John, Walk East on Beacon, The Red Danube, Red Snow, Red Planet Mars, Blood Alley, Big Jim McLain, The Manchurian Candidate*. In the early sixties a documentary compilation of red aggression was released under the title *We'll Bury You*. The British never seemed to take the peril seriously, though the agitator in *The Angry Silence* was clearly labelled red.

Como, Perry (1912–) (Nick Perido). Italian-American crooner with deceptively relaxed manner which in recent years made him a popular TV star. Appeared in a few musical films of the forties.
Something for the Boys 44. Doll Face 45. If I'm Lucky 46. Words and Music 48, etc.

compilation films have become commonplace on TV through such series as *Twentieth Century, Men of Our Time* and *The Valiant Years*, all using library material to evoke a pattern of the past. Thanks to the careful preservation of original documentary material, film-makers have been able, over the last thirty years or so, to give us such films on a wide variety of subjects and to develop an exciting extra dimension of film entertainment which also serves a historical need.

The first outstanding efforts in this direction were made by H. Bruce Woolfe in his twenties documentaries of World War I, mixing newsreel footage with reconstructed scenes. In 1940 Cavalcanti assembled his study of Mussolini, *Yellow Caesar*; and in 1942 Frank Capra, working for the US Signal Corps, gave a tremendous fillip to the art of the compilation film with his 'Why We Fight' series. Paul Rotha's *World of Plenty* 43 was a clever study of world food shortages using all kinds of film material including animated diagrams and acted sequences. In 1945 Carol Reed and Garson Kanin, in *The True Glory*, gave the story of D-Day to Berlin an unexpected poetry, and in 1946 Don Siegel in his short *Hitler Lives* showed all too clearly what a frightening potential the compilation form had as propaganda. Nicole Védrès in 1947 turned to the more distant past and in *Paris 1900* produced an affectionate portrait of a bygone age; Peter Baylis followed this with *The Peaceful Years*, covering the period between the two wars. In 1950 Stuart Legg's *Powered Flight* traced the history of aviation.
The Thorndikes, working in East Germany, started in 1956 their powerful series *The Archives Testify*, attributing war crimes to West German officials; this aggressive mood was followed in their *Du und Mancher Kamerad* ('The German Story') and *The Russian Miracle*, though in the latter case they seemed somewhat less happy in praising than in blaming. In 1959 George Morrison's *Mise Eire* graphically presented the truth of the much-fictionalized Irish troubles; and in 1960 came the first of the films about Hitler, Erwin Leiser's *Mein Kampf*, to be sharply followed by Rotha's *The Life of Adolf Hitler* and Louis Clyde Stoumen's rather fanciful *Black Fox*. Jack Le Vien, producer of the last-named, went on to make successful films

about Churchill (*The Finest Hours*) and the Duke of Windsor (*A King's Story*). Now every year the compilations come thick and fast. From France, *Fourteen-Eighteen*; from BBC TV, twenty-six half-hours of *The Great War*; from Granada TV, *The Fanatics* (suffragettes), *The World of Mr Wells* (H.G., that is) and a long-running weekly series, *All Our Yesterdays*, which consists entirely of old newsreels; from Associated-British, *Time to Remember*, a series devoting half an hour to each year of the century; from Italy, *Allarmi Siam' Fascisti*, a history of the fascist movement; from Japan, *Kamikaze*, about the suicide pilots; from France, Rossif's *Mourir à Madrid* and *The Fall of Berlin*. The list will be endless, because even though every foot of old newsreel were used up, one could begin again, using different editing, juxtapositions and commentary to achieve different effects.

See also: *documentary*.

composers have frequently been lauded on cinema screens, usually in story lines which bore little relation to their real lives, and the films were not often box office successes. Here are some of the subjects of musical biopics:

George Frederick Handel (1685–1759): Wilfred Lawson, *The Great Mr Handel* 42.

Wolfgang Amadeus Mozart (1756–91): Hannes Steltzer, *Die Kleine Nachtmusik* 39; Gino Cervi, *Eternal Melody* 39; *Whom the Gods Love* 43; Oskar Werner, *The Life of Mozart* 56.

Ludwig van Beethoven (1770–1827): Albert Basserman, *New Wine* 41; Johann Holzmeister, *Eroica* 49; Karl Boehm, *The Magnificent Rebel* 60.

Niccolò Paganini (1782–1840): Stewart Granger, *The Magic Bow* 47.

Franz Schubert (1797–1828): Nils Asther, *Love Time* 34; Richard Tauber, *Blossom Time* 34; Hans Jaray, *Unfinished Symphony* 35; Alan Curtis *New Wine* 41; Tino Rossi, *La Belle Meunière* 47; Claude Laydu, *Symphony of Love* 54; Karl Boehm, *Das Dreimaederlhaus* 58.

Vincenzo Bellini (1801–35); Phillips Holmes, *The Divine Spark* 35.

Hector Berlioz (1803–69): Jean-Louis Barrault, *La Symphonie Fantastique* 40.

Frederic Chopin (1810–49): Jean Servais, *Adieu* 35; Cornel Wilde, *A Song to Remember* 44; Czeslaw Wollejko, *The Young Chopin* 52; Alexander Davion, *Song Without End* 60.

Robert Schumann (1810–56): Paul Henreid, *Song of Love* 47.

Franz Liszt (1811–86): Stephen Bekassy, *A Song to Remember* 44; Henry Daniell, *Song of Love* 47; Will Quadflieg, *Lola Montez* 55; Dirk

Bogarde, *Song Without End* 60; Henry Gilbert, *Song of Norway* 70; Roger Daltrey, *Lizstomania* 75.

Richard Wagner (1813–83): Alan Badel, *Magic Fire* 56; Trevor Howard, *Ludwig* 73.

Johann Strauss Jnr (1825–99): Esmond Knight, *Waltzes from Vienna* 33; Anton Walbrook, *Vienna Waltzes* 34. Fernand Gravet, *The Great Waltz* 38; Kerwin Matthews, *The Waltz King* 60; Horst Buchholz, *The Great Waltz* 72.

Stephen Foster (1826–64): Don Ameche, *Swanee River* 39; Bill Shirley, *I Dream of Jeannie* 52.

Johannes Brahms (1833–97): Robert Walker, *Song of Love* 47.

W. S. Gilbert (1836–1911) and Arthur Sullivan (1842–1900): Nigel Bruce and Claud Allister, *Lillian Russell* 41; Robert Morley and Maurice Evans, *The Story of Gilbert and Sullivan* 53.

Peter Ilich Tchaikovsky (1840–93): Frank Sundstrom, *Song of My Heart* 47; Innokenti Smoktunovsky, *Tchaikovsky* 69; Richard Chamberlain, *The Music Lovers* 70.

Nikolai Rimsky-Korsakov (1844–1908): Jean-Pierre Aumont, *Song of Scheherezade* 47.

Edvard Grieg (1843–1907): Toralv Maurstad, *Song of Norway* 70.

John Philip Sousa (1854–1932): Clifton Webb, *Stars and Stripes Forever* 52.

Victor Herbert (1859–1924): Walter Connolly, *The Great Victor Herbert* 39; Paul Maxey, *Till the Clouds Roll By* 46.

Gustav Mahler (1860–1911): Robert Powell, *Mahler* 74.

Leslie Stuart (1866–1928): Robert Morley, *You Will Remember* 40.

W. C. Handy (1873–1948): Nat King Cole, *St Louis Blues* 57.

Jerome Kern (1885–1945): Robert Walker, *Till the Clouds Roll By* 47.

Sigmund Romberg (1887–1951): Jose Ferrer, *Deep in My Heart* 54.

Irving Berlin (1888–): Tyrone Power, *Alexander's Ragtime Band* 38.

Cole Porter (1892–1964): Cary Grant, *Night and Day* 45.

George Gershwin (1898–1937): Robert Alda, *Rhapsody in Blue* 45.

The list of biopics of lesser modern composers would be long indeed.

composite print: see *combined print* for which it is an alternative term.

Compson, Betty (1896–1974). American leading lady of the twenties, in Christie comedies from 1915.

The Miracle Man 19. Love Call 22. Woman to Woman (GB) 23 and 29. The Enemy Sex 24. The Fast Set 26. The Barker 28. Docks of New York 28. The Great Gabbo 29. On with the Show 30. The Gay Diplomat 31. Destination Unknown 33. Laughing Irish Eyes (GB) 36. A Slight Case of Murder 38. Strange Cargo 40. Mr and Mrs Smith 41. Claudia and David 46. Hard-Boiled Mahoney 48, many others.

Compton, Fay (1894–). British stage actress who has made occasional film appearances.
One Summer's Day 17. A Woman of No Importance 21. The Old Wives' Tale 21. Mary Queen of Scots 22. This Freedom 23. Robinson Crusoe 27. Fashions in Love (US) 29. Tell England 31. Autumn Crocus 34. The Mill on the Floss 35. The Prime Minister 41. Odd Man Out 46. London Belongs to Me 48. Laughter in Paradise 50. Othello 52. Aunt Clara 54. The Story of Esther Costello 57. The Haunting 63. The Virgin and the Gypsy 70, others.

Compton, Joyce (1907–) (Eleanor Hunt). American light second lead of the thirties.
Syncopating Sue 26. Dangerous Curves 29. Three Rogues 31. Only Yesterday 33. Magnificent Obsession 35. The Toast of New York 37. Balalaika 39. City for Conquest 40. Blues in the Night 42. Pillow to Post 45. Grand Canyon 51, etc.

concentration camps, until long after World War II, were thought too harrowing a subject for film treatment; but a few serious reconstructions have emerged, notably *The Last Stage* (Poland) 48, *Kapo* (Italy) 60, *Passenger* (Poland) 61, and *One Day in the Life of Ivan Denisovitch* 71, while the shadow of Auschwitz hangs over *The Diary of Anne Frank* 59 and *The Pawnbroker* 64. An alleged British concentration camp in South Africa was depicted in the Nazi film *Ohm Krüger* 42. The best documentary on the subject was probably Resnais' *Night and Fog.*

concerts of serious music naturally figure largely in films about the lives of composers (qv), and also in those concerned to show off living musicians: *They Shall Have Music, Music for Millions, Battle for Music, Tonight We Sing, Carnegie Hall, A Hundred Men and a Girl, Rhapsody in Blue.* In the forties a string of romantic films were centred on classical musicians and had concert climaxes: *Dangerous Moonlight, Love Story, The Seventh Veil, Intermezzo, The Great Lie*; this style later returned in *Interlude.* Other dramatic and comic concerts were featured in *Unfaithfully Yours, Tales of Manhattan, The Man Who Knew Too Much, The World of Henry Orient, The Bride Wore Black, Counterpoint* and *Deadfall.* The most influential film concert was certainly *Fantasia*, and the most poignant probably Myra Hess' recital in the blitz-beset National Gallery in *Listen to Britain.*

Confessions of a Nazi Spy (US 1939). First of the anti-Hitler films made in Hollywood before World War II began. This Warner melodrama, blending fact with fiction, toned in well with the company's social and biographical output and was often exciting in its own right. While its innovations of technique have since become standard, and its propaganda content now seems naïve, it remains an important landmark pointing the way to *The House on 92nd Street, Boomerang*, etc. Anatole Litvak directed a cast including Edward G. Robinson as the G-man and Francis Lederer and Paul Lukas as spies.

confidence tricksters have figured as minor characters in hundreds of films, but full-length portraits of the breed are few and choice. Harry Baur in *Volpone* and Rex Harrison in *The Honey Pot*; Roland Young, Billie Burke, Janet Gaynor and Douglas Fairbanks Jnr in *The Young in Heart*; Gene Tierney, Laird Cregar and Spring Byington in *Rings on Her Fingers*; Tyrone Power in *Nightmare Alley* and *Mississippi Gambler*; Mai Zetterling in *Quartet*; Paul Newman in *The Hustler*; Charles Coburn and Barbara Stanwyck in *The Lady Eve*; David Niven and Marlon Brando in *Bedtime Story*; George C. Scott in *The Flim Flam Man*; Richard Attenborough and David Hemmings in *Only When I Larf*; James Garner in *The Skin Game*; Newman and Robert Redford in *The Sting*; Ryan and Tatum O'Neal in *Paper Moon*; James Coburn in *Dead Heat on a Merry-go-Round*; Robert Wagner and Eddie Albert in *Switch.*

Congress Dances (Germany 1931). This handsome historical romance, shot in three languages, showed a new face of German film-making and made world stars of Lilian Harvey and Conrad Veidt. Directed by Erik Charell, with music by Werner Heymann.

Conklin, Chester (1888–1971) (Jules Cowles). American silent slapstick comedian, in innumerable short comedies for Keystone and Sennett; features rarer.
Greed 24. Rubber Heels 27. Gentlemen Prefer Blondes 28. Her Majesty Love 31. Hallelujah I'm a Bum 33. *Modern Times* 36. Hollywood Cavalcade 39. The Great Dictator 40. Hail the Conquering Hero 44. The Perils of Pauline 47.

Big Hand for a Little Lady 67, etc.

Conklin, Heinie (1880–1959) (Charles Conklin). American character comedian, one of the original Keystone Kops.

Conlin, Jimmy (1884–1962). Bird-like little American character comedian, in many films, notably those of Preston S SSturges.
College Rhythm 33. And Sudden Death 36. Sullivan's Travels 41. The Palm Beach Story 42. Ali Baba and the Forty Thieves 44. Mad Wednesday 47. The Great Rupert 50. Anatomy of a Murder 59, many others.

A Connecticut Yankee at the Court of King Arthur Three American versions have been made of this Mark Twain fantasy: 1920 with Harry Myers, 1931 with Will Rogers, and 1949 with Bing Crosby.

Connery, Neil (1938–). British leading man who made a brief appearance; Sean Connery's brother.
Operation Kid Brother 66. The Body Stealers 70, etc.

Connery, Sean (1930–) (Thomas Connery). Virile Scots leading man who shot to fame as James Bond and has been unable to escape the image.
□ No Road Back 55. Time Lock 56. Hell Drivers 57. Action of the Tiger 57. Another Time Another Place 58. Darby O'Gill and the Little People 59. Tarzan's Greatest Adventure 59. Frightened City 60. On the Fiddle 61. The Longest Day 62. *Doctor No* 62. *From Russia With Love* 63. Woman of Straw 64. Marnie 64. *Goldfinger* 64. *The Hill* 65. Thunderball 65 A Fine Madness 66. You Only Live Twice 67. Shalako 68. The Molly Maguires 69. The Red Tent 69. The Anderson Tapes 71. Diamonds are Forever 71. The Offence 72. Zardoz 74. Ransom 74. Murder on the Orient Express 74. The Wind and the Lion 75. The Man Who Would Be King 76. Robin and Marian 76. The Next Man 76.

Connolly, Walter (1887–1940). Chubby American character actor who spent his last years in films playing rasping millionaires and choleric editors.
□ No More Orchids 32. Washington Merry Go Round 32. Man Against Woman 32. Lady for a Day 33. East of Fifth Avenue 33. The Bitter Tea of General Yen 33. Paddy the Next Best Thing 33. Master of Men 33. Man's Castle 33. *It Happened One Night* 34. Once to Every Woman 34. Eight Girls in a Boat 34. Twentieth Century 34. Whom the Gods Destroy 34. Servants Entrance 34. Lady by Choice 34. Broadway Bill

34. The Captain Hates the Sea 34. White Lies 34. *Father Brown Detective* 35. She Couldn't Take It 35. So Red the Rose 35. One Way Ticket 35. The Music Goes Round 36. *Soak the Rich* 36. The King Steps Out 36. Libelled Lady 36. The Good Earth 37. Nancy Steele is Missing 37. Let's Get Married 37. The League of Frightened Men 37. First Lady 37. *Nothing Sacred* 37. Penitentiary 38. Start Cheering 38. Four's a Crowd 38. Too Hot to Handle 38. The Girl Downstairs 39. The Adventures of Huckleberry Finn 39. Bridal Suite 39. Good Girls Go to Paris 39. Coast Guard 39. Those High Gray Walls 39. *Fifth Avenue Girl* 39. *The Great Victor Herbert* 39.

Connor, Edric (1915–1968). British West Indian actor and singer.
Cry the Beloved Country 52.   Moby Dick 56. Fire Down Below 57. Four for Texas 63. Nobody Runs Forever 68, many others.

Connor, Kenneth (1918–). British radio and TV comedian adept at nervous or shy roles. A mainstay of the 'Carry On' film series.
There Was a Young Lady 53. The Black Rider 55. Davy 57. Carry On Sergeant 58. Carry On Nurse 59. Dentist in the Chair 60. Carry On Constable 60. What a Carve-up 61. Gonks Go Beat 65. Carry On England 76, etc.

Connors, Chuck (1921–). Tough guy American hero/villain, his thin smile being adaptable to friendship or menace.
Pat and Mike 52. South Sea Woman 53. Naked Alibi 54. Target Zero 55. Three Stripes in the Sun 55. Designing Woman 57. Geronimo 62. Move Over Darling 63. Synanon 65. Broken Sabre 65. Ride Beyond Vengeance 66. Captain Nemo and the Underwater City 69. Kill 'Em All and Come Back Alone 70. The Deserter 70. Pancho Villa 71. Embassy 72. Soylent Green 72. The Mad Bomber 72. 99 44/100% Dead 74, etc. TV series: *Rifleman* 57–62. Arrest and Trial 63. Branded 64–65. Cowboy in Africa 67. The Thrillseekers 72.

Connors, Michael (1925–) (Kreker Ohanian). American action hero of films and TV. Formerly known as Touch Connors.
Sudden Fear 52. The Ten Commandments 56. Where Love has Gone 64. Good Neighbour Sam 64. Situation Hopeless but not Serious 65. Harlow 65. *Stagecoach* 66. Kiss the Girls and Make them Die 67. The Killer who Wouldn't Die (TV) 76, etc.
TV series: *Tightrope* 59. *Mannix* 67– .

Conrad, Jess (1940–). British pop singer and

lightweight actor.
Too Young to Love 59. Konga 61. The Boys 62.
The Golden Head 65. Hell is Empty 67. The
Assassination Bureau 69, etc.

Conrad, Joseph (1857–1924) (Teodor Josef
Konrad Korzeniowski). Polish-Ukrainian
novelist, former seaman, who settled in Britain.
Lord Jim 26 and 65. Sabotage 37. Victory 30
and 40. An Outcast of the Islands 52. Laughing
Anne 53.

Conrad, Robert (1935–) (Conrad Robert
Falk). American leading man, mostly on TV.
Palm Springs Weekend 63. Young Dillinger 65,
etc.
TV series: Hawaiian Eye 63. The Wild Wild
West 66–69. The D.A. 71.

Conrad, William (1920–). Heavily-built
American radio writer and actor who came to
Hollywood to play unpleasant villains, but later
became a producer-director.
The Killers (a) 46. Arch of Triumph (a) 48. One
Way Street (a) 50. Cry Danger (a) 51. Lone Star
(a) 52. The Naked Jungle (a) 54. *Johnny Concho*
(a) 56. The Ride Back (a) 57. Two on a
Guillotine (pd) 64. Brainstorm (pd) 65. Chamber
of Horrors (p) 66. An American Dream (p) 67.
Covenant with Death (p) 67. Countdown (p) 68,
etc.
TV series: *Cannon* (a) 71–75.

Conried, Hans (1917–). Tall, weedy
American comic actor with precise diction and a
richly variable voice.
Dramatic School 37. Crazy House 43. Mrs
Parkington 44. The Senator Was Indiscreet 47.
My Friend Irma 49. The Twonky 53. *The Five
Thousand Fingers of Doctor T* 53. Bus Stop 56.
Rockabye Baby 58. The Patsy 64. The Brothers
O'Toole 73, many others.

Conroy, Frank (1890–1964). British stage
actor who went to Hollywood in the early
thirties, generally played domestic tyrants.
The Royal Family of Broadway 30. Grand Hotel
32. Call of the Wild 35. Wells Fargo 37. *The Ox-
Bow Incident* 42. Naked City 48. Lightning
Strikes Twice 51. The Last Mile 59, etc.

The Constant Nymph. Margaret Kennedy's
popular sentimental novel about the Sanger
family and the handsome tutor has been filmed
three times: in 1927 with Ivor Novello and
Mabel Poulton, directed by Adrian Brunel; in
1933 with Brian Aherne and Victoria Hopper,
directed by Basil Dean (co-author of the play
version); and in 1944 with Charles Boyer and

Joan Fontaine, directed by Edmund Goulding.

Constantine, Eddie (1917–). Tough
American actor popular in France where he
plays Peter Cheyney heroes in crime films.
SOS Pacific 59. Treasure of San Teresa 60. Riff
Raff Girls 62. Alphaville 65, many others.

Constantine, Michael (1927–)
(Constantine Joanides). Greek-American
character actor, mostly on TV.
The Last Mile 59. The Hustler 61. Island of Love
63. Beau Geste 66. Hawaii 66. Skidoo 68. If it's
Tuesday This Must Be Belgium 69. The Reivers
69, etc.
TV series: Hey Landlord. *Room 222.*

Conte, Richard (1911–1975) (Nicholas
Conte). Amiable Italian-American action hero in
films of varying merit; often seen as oppressed
hero or sympathetic gangster.
Heaven with a Barbed Wire Fence 39.
Guadalcanal Diary 43. *The Purple Heart* 44.
Captain Eddie 45. The Spider 46. *A Walk in the
Sun* 46. Somewhere in the Night 46. 13 Rue
Madeleine 46. The Other Love 47. Call
Northside 777 48. Cry of the City 48. House of
Strangers 49. Thieves' Highway 49. The
Sleeping City 50. Hollywood Story 51. The
Fighter 52. The Blue Gardenia 53. New York
Confidential 55. I'll Cry Tomorrow 55. Full of
Life 57. The Brothers Rico 57. They Came to
Cordura 59. Ocean's Eleven 60. Who's Been
Sleeping in My Bed? 63. Circus World
64. Synanon 65. Assault on a Queen 66. Tony
Rome 67. Hotel 67. Lady in Cement 68. The
Godfather 72, many others.
TV series: The Four Just Men 59.

continuity. The development of cinematic
narrative from beginning to end of a film. If
continuity is good the audience will be carried
smoothly from one scene to another without
disturbing breaks or lapses of detail.

contrast. The tone range in a print. Heavy
contrast results in 'soot and whitewash', i.e.
blurry blacks and burnt-out whites.

Converse, Frank (1938–). American general
purpose actor.
Hurry Sundown 67. Hour of the Gun 67. A
Tattered Web (TV) 70. Dr Cook's Garden (TV)
73. The Rowdyman 73.
TV series (leading role): *Movin' On* 74–75.

Conway, Gary (1938–) (Gareth Carmody).
American light leading man.
I was a Teenage Frankenstein (as the monster)

57. Young Guns of Texas 59. Black Gunn 72. Once is not Enough 75, etc.
TV series: *Burke's Law* 63–65. Land of the Giants 68–69.

Conway, Jack (1887–1952). American action director, launched as acting member of D. W. Griffith's stock company; long with MGM.
□ The Old Armchair 12. Bond of Fear 18. Because of a Woman 18. Little Red Decides 18. Her Decision 18. You Can't Believe Everything 18. Diplomatic Mission 19. Desert Law 19. Riders of the Dawn 20. Lombardi Limited 20. Dwelling Place of Light 21. The Money Changers 21. The Spenders 21. The Kiss 21. A Daughter of the Law 21. Step On It 22. A Parisian Scandal 22. The Millionaire 22. Across the Deadline 22. Another Man's Shoes 22. Don't Shoot 22. The Long Chance 22. The Prisoner 23. Sawdust 23. Quicksands 23. What Wives Want 23. Trimmed in Scarlet 23. Lucretia Lombard 23. The Trouble Shooter 24. The Heart Buster 24. The Roughneck 25. The Hunted Woman 25. The Only Thing 25. Brown of Harvard 26. Soul Mates 26. The Understanding Heart 27. Twelve Miles Out 27. Quicksands 27. The Smart Set 28. Bringing Up Father 28. While the City Sleeps 28. Alias Jimmy Valentine 29. *Our Modern Maidens* 29. Untamed 29. They Learned about Women 30. *The Unholy Three* 30. New Moon 30. The Easiest Way 31. Just a Gigolo 31. *Arsène Lupin* 32. But the Flesh is Weak 32. Red-headed Woman 32. Hell Below 33. The Nuisance 33. The Solitaire Man 33. *Viva Villa* 34. The Girl from Missouri 34. The Gay Bride 34. One New York Night 35. *A Tale of Two Cities* 35. *Libelled Lady* 36. Saratoga 37. *A Yank at Oxford* 38. Too Hot to Handle 38. Let Freedom Ring 39. Lady of the Tropics 39. *Boom Town* 40. Love Crazy 40. Honky Tonk 40. Crossroads 42. Assignment in Brittany 43. Dragon Seed 44. High Barbaree 47. *The Hucksters* 47. Julia Misbehaves 48.

Conway, Tom (1904–1967) (Thomas Sanders). British light leading man, brother of George Sanders; well-liked as 'the Falcon' in the forties, but his career declined very suddenly.
Sky Murder 40. The Trail of Mary Dugan 41. Grand Central Murder 42. *The Falcon's Brother* 42. *Cat People* 42. I Walked with a Zombie 43. The Falcon Strikes Back 43. The Seventh Victim 43. The Falcon Out West 44 (and five other Falcon adventures ending in 1946). Criminal Court 46. Repeat Performance 47. One Touch of Venus 48. Confidence Girl 52. Park Plaza 505 (GB) 53. Barbados Quest (GB) 55. The Last Man to Hang (GB) 56. The She-Creature 56.

Twelve to the Moon 60. What a Way to Go (unbilled) 64, many others.
TV series: Mark Saber 52–54.

Conyers, Darcy (1919–1973). British director, former actor.
Ha'penny Breeze (& p) 52. The Devil's Pass (& wp) 56. The Night We Dropped a Clanger 60. Nothing Barred 61. In the Doghouse 62, etc.

Coogan, Jackie (1914–). American child actor of the twenties who achieved outstanding star status but later reappeared as a less appealing adult in minor roles.
The Kid 20. *Peck's Bad Boy* 21. *Oliver Twist* 21. My Boy 22. Trouble 22. Daddy 23. Circus Days 23. Long Live the King 24. A Boy of Flanders 24. The Rag Man 24. Little Robinson Crusoe 25. Johnny Get Your Gun 25. Old Clothes 25. Johnny Get Your Hair Cut 26. The Bugle Call 27. Buttons 27. Tom Sawyer 30. Huckleberry Finn 31. Home on the Range 35. College Swing 38. Kilroy was Here 47. Outlaw Women 52. Lost Women 56. High School Confidential 58. A Fine Madness 66. The Shakiest Gun in the West 68. Marlowe 69. Cahill 73, many others.
TV series: *The Addams Family* 64 (as Uncle Fester).

Cook, Donald (1900–1961). American stage leading man who never quite made it in Hollywood.
The Unfaithful 31. Viva Villa 34. Show Boat 36. The Spanish Cape Mystery 37. Patrick the Great 44. Bowery to Broadway 44. Our Very Own 50, many others.

Cook, Elisha, Jnr (1902–). American character actor adept at cowards and neurotics.
Two in a Crowd 36. They Won't Forget 37. Submarine Patrol 38. Stranger on the Third Floor 40. *The Maltese Falcon* (as Wilmer the gunsel) 41. I Wake up Screaming 41. *Phantom Lady* 44. Dillinger 45. The Big Sleep 46. The Great Gatsby 49. Shane 53. *The Killing* 56. House on Haunted Hill 59. Johnny Cool 63. Welcome to Hard Times 67. The Great Bank Robbery 69. The Great Northfield Minnesota Raid 72. Emperor of the North 73. *The Black Bird* 75, many others.

Cook, Fielder (1923–). American TV director who makes occasional films.
□ *Patterns of Power* 56. Home is the Hero (Eire) 59. *Big Hand for a Little Lady* 66. How to Save a Marriage 67. Prudence and the Pill 68. Eagle in a Cage 71. From the Mixed Up Files of Mrs Basil E. Frankenweiler 73.

Cook, Peter (1937–). British cabaret comedian and writer.
□ The Wrong Box 66. Bedazzled 67. Monte Carlo or Bust 69. The Bed Sitting Room 69. The Rise and Rise of Michael Rimmer 70.

Coop, Denys (1920–). British cameraman.
A Kind of Loving 61. Billy Liar 63. This Sporting Life 63. One Way Pendulum 64. King and Country 65. Bunny Lake is Missing 65. The Double Man 67. My Side of the Mountain 68. 10 Rillington Place 70, etc.

Cooper, Ben (1930–). American light juvenile lead, mainly in westerns.
The Woman They almost Lynched 52. Perilous Journey 53. Johnny Guitar 54. Jubilee Trail 54. The Eternal Sea 55. The Last Command 56. *The Rose Tattoo* 57. Chartroose Caboose 60. Gunfight at Comanche Creek 64. Arizona Raiders 65. Red Tomahawk 67, many others.

Cooper, Gary (1901–1961) (Frank J. Cooper). Slow-speaking, deep-thinking American leading man, a long-enduring Hollywood star who always projected honest determination. Was cowboy and cartoonist before becoming a film extra; progressed to two-reelers and became a star in his first feature, *The Winning of Barbara Worth* 26. Special Academy Award 1960 'for his many memorable screen performances and for the international recognition he, as an individual, has gained for the film industry'.
□ It 27. Children of Divorce 27. Arizona Bound 27. Wings 27. Nevada 27. The Last Outlaw 27. Beau Sabreur 28. Legion of the Condemned 28. Doomsday 28. Half a Bride 28. *Lilac Time* 28. The First Kiss 28. Shopworn Angel 28. Wolf Song 29. The Betrayal 29. The Virginian 29. Only the Brave 29. The Texan 29. Seven Days' Leave 30. A Man from Wyoming 30. The Spoilers 30. Morocco 30. Fightinging Caravans 31. I Take This Woman 31. His Woman 31. The Devil and the Deep 32. *A Farewell to Arms* 32. *City Streets* 32. If I Had a Million 32. One Sunday Afternoon 33. Alice in Wonderland (as the White Knight) 33. Today We Live 33. Design for Living 34. Peter Ibbetson 34. Operator Thirteen 34. The Wedding Night 35. *Lives of a Bengal Lancer* 35. Now and Forever 35. Desire 36. *Mr Deeds Goes to Town* 36. The General Died at Dawn 36. *The Plainsman* 37. Souls at Sea 37. The Adventures of Marco Polo 38. Bluebeard's Eighth Wife 38. The Cowboy and the Lady 39. *Beau Geste* 39. The Real Glory 39. *The Westerner* 40. Northwest Mounted Police 40. *Meet John Doe* 41. *Sergeant York* (AA) 41. Ball of Fire 41. Pride of the Yankees 42. *For Whom the Bell Tolls* 43. The Story of Dr Wassell 44. Saratoga Trunk 44. Casanova Brown 44. Along Came Jones (& p) 45. Cloak and Dagger 46. Unconquered 47. Good Sam 48. The Fountainhead 49. Task Force 49. Bright Leaf 50. Dallas 50. You're in the Navy Now 51. Distant Drums 51. Springfield Rifle 52. *High Noon* (AA) 52. Return to Paradise 52. Blowing Wild 53. Garden of Evil 54. *Vera Cruz* 54. The Court Martial of Billy Mitchell 55. Friendly Persuasion 56. Love in the Afternoon 56. *Ten North Frederick* 58. Man of the West 58. They Came to Cordura 59. The Hanging Tree 59. The Wreck of the Mary Deare 59. The Naked Edge (GB) 61.

Cooper, George A. (1916–). British character actor of vengeful types.
Miracle in Soho 56. Violent Playground 58. Tom Jones 63. Nightmare 64. Life at the Top 65. The Strange Affair 68, etc.

Cooper, Dame Gladys (1888–1971). Distinguished, gracious British stage actress who essentially began her film career in Hollywood at the age of 52, subsequently airing her warm aristocratic personality in many unworthy roles and a few good ones.
Autobiography 1953: *Without Veils*.
□ Masks and Faces 17. The Sorrows of Satan 17. My Lady's Dress 18. The Bohemian Girl 22. Bonnie Prince Charles 23. Dandy Donovan 31. The Iron Duke 35. *Rebecca* 40. Kitty Foyle 40. That Hamilton Woman 41. The Black Cat 41. The Gay Falcon 41. This Above All 42. Eagle Squadron 42. *Now Voyager* 42. Forever and a Day 43. Mr Lucky 43. Princess O'Rourke 43. The Song of Bernadette 43. The White Cliffs of Dover 44. Mrs Parkington 44. The Valley of Decision 45. Love Letters 45. The Green Years 46. The Cockeyed Miracle 46. Green Dolphin Street 47. Beware of Pity 47. The Bishop's Wife 47. Homecoming 48. The Pirate 48. The Secret Garden 49. Madame Bovary 49. Thunder on the Hill 51. At Sword's Point 52. The Man Who Loved Redheads 54. *Separate Tables* 58. The List of Adrian Messenger 63. *My Fair Lady* 64. The Happiest Millionaire 67. A Nice Girl Like Me 69.
TV series: *The Rogues* 64.

Cooper, Jackie (1921–). 'Little tough guy' American child actor who in adult life found roles getting rarer and became a powerful TV executive.
□ *Our Gang* shorts 27–28. Movietone Follies 28. Sunny Side Up 29. *Skippy* 31. Young Donovan's Kid 31. *The Champ* 31. Sooky 31. When a Feller Needs a Friend 32. Divorce in the Family 32. Broadway to Hollywood 33.

The Bowery 33. *Treasure Island* 34. Peck's Bad Boy 34. Lone Cowboy 34. Dinky 35. O'Shaughnessy's Boy 35. Tough Guy 36. The Devil is a Sissy 36. Boy of the Streets 37. White Banners 38. That Certain Age 38. Gangster's Boy. 38. Newsboys' Home 39. Scouts to the Rescue 39. Spirit of Culver 39. Streets of New York 39. Two Bright Boys 39. What a Life 39. The Big Guy 39. Seventeen 40. The Return of Frank James 40. Gallant Sons 40. Life with Henry 41. Ziegfeld Girl 41. Her First Beau 41. Glamour Boys 41. Syncopation 42. Men of Texas 42. The Navy Comes Through 42. Where are your Children? 44. Stork Bites Man 47. Kilroy Was Here 47. French Leave 48. Everything's Ducky 61. The Love Machine 71. Maybe I'll Come Home in the Spring (TV) 71. Stand Up and Be Counted (d only) 72. Chosen Survivors 74. The Invisible Man (TV) 75. Mobile Two (TV) 75.
TV series: The People's Choice. Hennessey.

Cooper, James Fenimore (1789–1851). American adventure novelist whose 'westerns' include *The Last of the Mohicans, The Pathfinder* and *The Deerslayer*, all frequently filmed.

Cooper, Melville (1896–1973). British comedy character actor, long in Hollywood playing pompous upper-class idiots.
The Private Life of Don Juan 34. The Scarlet Pimpernel 34. The Last of Mrs Cheyney 37. Tovarich 37. *The Adventures of Robin Hood* 38. Dawn Patrol 38. The Sun Never Sets 39. Rebecca 40. *Pride and Prejudice* (as Mr Collins) 40. Random Harvest 42. Holy Matrimony 43. Heartbeat 46. Enchantment 48. Father of the Bride 50. It Should Happen to You 53. Moonfleet 55. The Story of Mankind 57. From the Earth to the Moon 58, many others.

Cooper, Merian C. (1893–1973). American executive producer associated with many adventurous films. Special Academy Award 1952 'for his many innovations and contributions to the art of the motion picture'.
Grass 25. *Chang* 27. The Four Feathers 29. *King Kong* 33. The Last Days of Pompeii 35. The Toy Wife 38. Fort Apache 48. Mighty Joe Young 49. Rio Grande 50. The Quiet Man 52. *This is Cinerama* 52. The Searchers 56, etc.

Cooper, Violet Kemble (1886–1961). British stage actress who appeared in a few Hollywood films in the thirties.
Our Betters 33. Vanessa 34. David Copperfield (as Miss Murdstone) 35. The Invisible Ray 36. Romeo and Juliet 36, etc.

Cooper, Wilkie (1911–). British cinematographer, once a child actor.
The Rake's Progress 45. Green for Danger 46. Captain Boycott 47. London Belongs to Me 48. Stage Fright 50. The Admirable Crichton 57. Jason and the Argonauts 63. One Million Years BC 66, etc.

Coote, Robert (1909–). British stage character actor who has filmed mainly in Hollywood; familiar in amiable silly-ass roles.
Sally in Our Alley 31. *A Yank at Oxford* 38. Gunga Din (US) 39. You Can't Fool Your Wife 40. The Commandos Strike at Dawn 43. A Matter of Life and Death 46. The Ghost and Mrs Muir 47. Forever Amber 47. Bonnie Prince Charlie 48. The Three Musketeers 48. The Elusive Pimpernel 49. Rommel, Desert Fox 51. *The Prisoner of Zenda* 52. The Constant Husband 55. Othello (as Roderigo) 55. The Swan 56. Merry Andrew 58. The League of Gentlemen 59. The Golden Head 65. A Man Could Get Killed 66. The Swinger 66. Prudence and the Pill 68. Up the Front 72. Theatre of Blood 73, etc.
TV series: *The Rogues* 64.

Cope, Kenneth (1931–). British TV actor, usually of Liverpudlian types.
The Criminal 60. The Damned 62. Genghis Khan 65. Dateline Diamonds 65. She'll Follow You Anywhere 71, etc.

Copland, Aaron (1900–). American composer.
The City 39. Of Mice and Men 39. Our Town 40. North Star 43. The Red Pony 48. The Heiress (AA) 49. Something Wild 61, etc.

Copley, Peter (1915–). British stage actor who makes occasional film appearances, usually in quiet, downtrodden or slightly sinister roles.
The Golden Salamander 49. The Card 52. The Sword and the Rose 53. Foreign Intrigue 56. Victim 61. King and Country 64, etc.

Coppel, Alec (1910–1972). Australian playwright and screenwriter.
Over the Moon (w) 39. Obsession (oa) 46. Mr Denning Drives North (w) 51. The Captain's Paradise (w) 53. The Gazebo (oa) 59. Moment to Moment (w) 66. The Bliss of Mrs Blossom (w) 69.

Coppola, Francis Ford (1939–). American writer-director who graduated from nudie movies.
□ Dementia 63. This Property is Condemned (w) 65. Is Paris Burning? (w) 66. *You're a Big*

Boy Now (wd) 67. Finian's Rainbow (d) 68. The Rain People (wd) 69. Patton (w only) (AA) 71. *The Godfather* 72. American Graffiti (p only) 73. The Conversation (w, p, d) 74. The Godfather Part Two 75.

copyright. British law relating to film copyright is notably vague, but in practice the owner of a film is protected against piracy for fifty years. In America copyright must be renewed in the 28th year, which has resulted in some fatal errors: e.g. MGM now have no control over *Till the Clouds Roll By* because they forgot to renew it, and Chaplin renewed only the version of *The Gold Rush* including his specially composed forties music track.

Coquillon, John (–). British cinematographer.
Witchfinder General 68. Scream and Scream Again 69. The Oblong Box 69. Triple Echo 72, etc.

Corbett, Glenn (1929–). American second lead.
The Fireball 50. Man on a String 60. The Mountain Road 60. All the Young Men 60. Homicidal 61. Pirates of Blood River (GB) 61. Shenandoah 65. Big Jake 71. Dead Pigeon on Beethoven Street (WG) 72, etc.

Corbett, Harry H. (1925–). British stage actor who played tough guys, regional types and maniacs in an assortment of films before gaining great TV popularity in *Steptoe and Son*; subsequently starred in a number of unsatisfactory comedy vehicles.
Floods of Fear 57. Nowhere to Go 58. Cover Girl Killer 60. Sammy Going South 62. What a Crazy World 63. Ladies Who Do 63. The Bargee 64. Rattle of a Simple Man 64. Joey Boy 65. The Sandwich Man 66. Carry On Screaming 66. Crooks and Coronets 69. The Magnificent Seven Deadly Sins 71. Steptoe and Son 72, etc.

Corbett, Leonora (1907–1960). British stage actress who made few films.
Heart's Delight 32. The Constant Nymph 33. Friday the Thirteenth 33. Farewell Again 36, etc.

Corbett, Ronnie (1930–). Pint-sized British TV comedian.
□ Casino Royale 67. Some Will Some Won't 70. The Rise and Rise of Michael Rimmer 70. No Sex Please We're British 73, etc.

Corbucci, Sergio (1927–). Italian director.
Duel of the Titans 61. Son of Spartacus 62. The Slave 63. Minnesota Clay 64. Django 65. The

Hellbenders 66. The Campanieros 71, etc.

Corby, Ellen (1913–) (Ellen Hansen). American character actress specializing in nosey neighbours and prim spinsters.
The Dark Corner 46. The Spiral Staircase 46. *I Remember Mama* 48. Fighting Father Dunne 48. Madame Bovary 49. On Moonlight Bay 51. About Mrs Leslie 54. The Seventh Sin 57. Macabre 58. Visit to a Small Planet 60. The Strangler 64. The Gnome-Mobile 67, many others.
TV series: The Waltons 72– .

Corcoran, Donna (1943–). American child actress of the fifties.
Angels in the Outfield 51. Don't Bother to Knock 52. Scandal at Scourie 53. Dangerous when Wet 53. Gypsy Colt 54. Violent Saturday 55, etc.

Corcoran, Kevin (1949–). American child actor of the fifties and sixties.
Untamed 55. Old Yeller 59. The Shaggy Dog 59. Toby Tyler 60. The Swiss Family Robinson 61. Babes in Toyland 62. Bon Voyage 63. Savage Sam 64. A Tiger Walks 65, etc.

Cord, Alex (1931–) (Alexander Viespi). Italian-American leading man.
Synanon 65. Stagecoach 66. The Brotherhood 68. Stiletto 69. Dead or Alive 69. The Last Grenade 69. The Dead Are Alive 72. Genesis II (TV) 73. Chosen Survivors 74, etc.

Corday, Mara (1932–) (Marilyn Watts). American leading lady of the fifties.
Sea Tiger 52. So This Is Paris 54. Man Without a Star 55. The Quiet Gun 57. The Black Scorpion 57, etc.

Corday, Paula (1924–) (also known as Paule Croset and Rita Corday). Anglo-Swiss leading lady who went to Hollywood in the forties.
The Falcon Strikes Back 43. The Body Snatcher 45. The Exile 47. Sword of Monte Cristo 51. Because You're Mine 52. The French Line 54, etc.

Cordy, Raymond (1898–1956) (R. Cordiaux). French comedy actor, especially seen in René Clair's films.
Le Million 31. À Nous la Liberté 31. Le Quatorze Juillet 33. Le Dernier Milliardaire 34. Ignace 37. Les Inconnus dans la Maison 42. Le Silence est d'Or 46. La Beauté du Diable 49. Les Belles de Nuit 52. Les Grandes Manoeuvres 55, etc.

Corey, Jeff (1914–). Gaunt American supporting actor seen as farmer, gangster, junkie, wino, convict, cop, and even Wild Bill Hickok.
All that Money Can Buy 41. My Friend Flicka 43. The Killers 46. Brute Force 47. Home of the Brave 49. Bright Leaf 50. Rawhide 51. Red Mountain 52. The Balcony 63. Lady in a Cage 64. Mickey One 65. The Cincinnati Kid 65. *Seconds* 66. In Cold Blood 67. True Grit 69. *Little Big Man* 71. Catlow 72. Paper Tiger 75, many others.

Corey, Wendell (1914–1968). American leading actor who usually played solid dependable types.
☐ Desert Fury 47. I Walk Alone 47. The Search 48. Maneater of Kumaon 48. Sorry Wrong Number 48. The Accused 48. Any Number Can Play 49. The File on Thelma Jordon 49. Holiday Affair 49. No Sad Songs for Me 50. The Furies 50. Harriet Craig 50. The Great Missouri Raid 50. Rich Young and Pretty 51. The Wild Blue Yonder 51. The Wild North 52. Carbine Williams 52. My Man and I 52. Laughing Anne (GB) 53. Jamaica Run 53. Hell's Half Acre 54. Rear Window 54. The Big Knife 55. The Bold and the Brave 56. The Killer is Loose 56. The Rack 56. The Rainmaker 56. Loving You 57. The Light in the Forest 58. Alias Jesse James 59. Blood on the Arrow 64. Agent for Harm 65. Waco 66. Women of the Prehistoric Planet 66. Picture Mommy Dead 66. Red Tomahawk 67. Cyborg 2087 67. The Astro Zombies 68. Buckskin 68.
TV series: Harbor Command 57. The Eleventh Hour 62.

Corfield, John (1893–). British producer in films from 1929; co-founder of British National Films with Lady Yule and J. Arthur Rank.
Turn of the Tide 35. Laugh It Off 40. Gaslight 40. Headline 42. Bedelia 46. The White Unicorn 47. My Sister and I 48, etc.

Corman, Roger (1926–). American director who during the fifties made a record number of grade Z horror films, then presented an interesting series of Poe adaptations; when he seemed poised for better things his career slowed almost to a halt. Has normally produced his own films.
☐ Five Guns West 55. Apache Woman 55. The Day the World Ended 56. Swamp Woman 56. The Gunslinger 56. Oklahoma Woman 56. It Conquered the World 56. Naked Paradise 57. Attack of the Crab Monsters 57. *Not of this Earth* 57. The Undead 57. Rock all Night 57. Carnival Rock 57. Teenage Doll 57. Sorority

Girl 57. The Viking Women and the Sea Serpent 57. War of the Satellites 57. Machine Gun Kelly 58. Teenage Caveman 58. She-Gods of Shark Reef 58. I Mobster 59. Wasp Woman 59. *A Bucket of Blood* 59. Ski Troop Attack 60. *House of Usher* 60. The Little Shop of Horrors 60. The Last Woman on Earth 60. Creature from the Haunted Sea 60. Atlas 60. The Pit and the Pendulum 61. The Premature Burial 62. *The Intruder* 62. Tales of Terror 62. Tower of London 62. *The Raven* 63. The Young Racers 63. The Haunted Palace 63. The Terror 63. X— The Man with X-ray Eyes 63. *The Masque of the Red Death* 64. Secret Invasion 64. *The Tomb of Ligeia* 65. The Wild Angels 66. The St Valentine's Day Massacre 67. The Trip 67. Bloody Mama 70. Gas-s-s! 70. Von Richthofen and Brown 71. Boxcar Bertha (p only) 72. I Escaped from Devil's Island (co-p only) 73. Big Bad Mama (p only) 74. Cockfighter (p only) 74.
In the seventies Corman became a distributor (New World Pictures) and specialized in foreign films.

Cornelius, Henry (1913–1958). British director with a subtle comedy touch.
☐ *Passport to Pimlico* 48. The Galloping Major (& w) 51. *Genevieve* 53. I am a Camera 55. Next to No Time 57.

Cornfield, Hubert (1929–). American director.
☐ Sudden Danger 56. Lure of the Swamp 57. Plunder Road 59. *The Third Voice* 59. Angel Baby (co-d) 61. Pressure Point 62. Night of the Following Day 68.

Corri, Adrienne (1930–) (Adrienne Riccoboni). Tempestuous red-headed British leading lady of Italian descent.
The River 51. The Kidnappers 53. Devil Girl from Mars 54. *Lease of Life* 54. Make Me an Offer 54. The Feminine Touch 55. Three Men in a Boat 56. Corridors of Blood 58. The Rough and the Smooth 59. The Hellfire Club 61. The Tell-Tale Heart 61. A Study in Terror 65. Bunny Lake is Missing 65. The Viking Queen 67. Moon Zero Two 69. A Clockwork Orange 71. Vampire Circus 72. Madhouse 74, etc.

Corrigan, Lloyd (1900–1969). Chubby American character actor, usually in jovial roles; also directed some films in the thirties.
The Splendid Crime 25. Daughter of the Dragon (d) 31. The Broken Wing (d) 32. Murder on a Honeymoon (d) 35. The Dancing Pirate (d) 36. Night Key (d) 37. Young Tom Edison 40. *The Ghost Breakers* 40. The Great Man's Lady 42. Since You Went Away 44. The Bandit of

Sherwood Forest 45. Stallion Road 47. Cyrano de Bergerac 50. Son of Paleface 52. The Bowery Boys Meet the Monsters 54. Hidden Guns 57. The Manchurian Candidate 62, many others.

Corrigan, Ray 'Crash' (1907–1976) (Ray Benard). American leading man, hero of innumerable second feature westerns.
The Three Mesquiteers 36. Wild Horse Rodeo 38. The Purple Vigilantes 38. Three Texas Steers 39. West of the Pinto Basin 40. Wrangler's Roost 41. Rock River Renegades 42.

The Corsican Brothers. The romantic adventure novel by Dumas *père* presents a splendid dual role for an actor. King Baggott starred in the first film version in 1915, followed by Dustin Farnum in 1919 and Douglas Fairbanks Jnr in 1940. *The Return of the Corsican Brothers* (or *Bandits of Corsica*), starring Richard Greene, followed in 1953; and the original was remade in France in 1960, with Geoffrey Toone.

Cort, Bud (1950–). American actor with a tendency to play demented youths.
M*A*S*H. 70. The Travelling Executioner 70. Brewster McCloud 70. Harold and Maude 72, etc.

Cortesa, Valentina (1924–). Italian leading lady in international films.
The Glass Mountain 48. Thieves' Highway 49. Malaya 50. The House on Telegraph Hill 51. Les Misérables 52. The Barefoot Contessa 54. Le Amiche 55. Magic Fire 56. Calabuch 58. Barabbas 62. The Visit 64. Juliet of the Spirits 65. The Legend of Lylah Clare 68. La Nuit Américaine 73, etc.

Cortez, Ricardo (1899–) (Jake Kranz). American leading man, groomed in the twenties as a Latin lover in the Valentino mould. Later developed outside interests and quit movies after a sojourn in routine roles.
Sixty Cents an Hour 23. Pony Express 24. *The Torrent* 26. *The Sorrows of Satan* 27. The Private Life of Helen of Troy 27. Behind Office Doors 28. Ten Cents a Dance 31. Melody of Life 32. The Phantom of Crestwood 33. *Wonder Bar* 34. Special Agent 35. The Walking Dead 36. Talk of the Devil (GB) 36. Mr Moto's Last Warning 38. City Girl (d only) 38. Free, Blonde and Twenty One (d only) 40. World Première 40. I Killed That Man 42. Make Your Own Bed 44. The Locket 46. Blackmail 47. The Last Hurrah 58, many others.

Cortez, Stanley (1908–) (Stanley Kranz).

American cinematographer, brother of Ricardo Cortez; in Hollywood from silent days.
□ Four Days Wonder 37. The Wildcatter 37. Armored Car 37. The Black Doll 38. Lady in the Morgue 38. Danger on the Air 38. Personal Secretary 38. The Last Express 38. For Love or Money 38. The Forgotten Woman 39. They Asked for It 39. Hawaiian Nights 39. Risky Business 39. Laugh It Off 39. Alias the Deacon 39. The Leatherpushers 40. Meet the Wildcat 40. Love Honor and Oh Baby 40. The Black Cat 40. A Dangerous Game 41. San Antonio Rose 41. Moonlight in Hawaii 41. Badlands of Dakota 41. Bombay Clipper 42. Eagle Squadron 42. *The Magnificent Ambersons* 42. Flesh and Fantasy 43. The Powers Girl 43. Since You Went Away (co-ph) 44. Smash Up 47. The Secret Beyond the Door 48. Smart Woman 48. The Man on the Eiffel Tower 49. Underworld Story 50. The Admiral was a Lady 50. The Basketball Fix 51. Fort Defiance 51. Models Inc 52. Abbott and Costello Meet Captain Kidd 52. The Diamond Queen 53. Dragon's Gold 53. Shark River 53. Riders to the Stars 54. Black Tuesday 54. *The Night of the Hunter* 55. Man from Del Rio 56. Top Secret Affair 57. The Three Faces of Eve 57. Thunder in the Sun 59. Vice Raid 60. The Angry Red Planet 60. Dinosaurus 60. Back Street 61. Shock Corridor 63. The Candidate 64. Nightmare in the Sun 64. The Naked Kiss 65. The Navy vs the Night Monsters 66. The Ghost in the Invisible Bikini 66. Blue 68. The Bridge at Remagen 69. The Date 71. Do Not Fold, Spindle or Mutilate (TV) 72.

Cosby, Bill (1938—). Black American leading man and TV personality.
□ Hickey and Boggs 72. Uptown Saturday Night 74. Let's Do It Again 76. Mother, Jugs and Speed 76.
TV series: *I Spy* 66–68. The Bill Cosby Show 69. Fat Albert and the Cosby Kids 72. Cos 76.

Cossart, Ernest (1876–1951). Portly British actor, inevitably cast by Hollywood in butler roles.
The Scoundrel 35. Desire 36. The Great Ziegfeld 36. Angel 37. Zaza 39. The Light That Failed 39. Tom Brown's Schooldays 40. *Charley's Aunt* 41. Casanova Brown 44. Cluny Brown 46. John Loves Mary 49, many others.

Cossins, James (1932–). British character actor, usually of pompous, flustered type.
The Anniversary 68. Lost Continent 68. Melody 70. Villain 71, etc.

Costa-Gavras (1933–). Russo-Greek director, in France from childhood.

□ The Sleeping Car Murders 65. Un Homme de Trop 67. 'Z' (AA) 68. L'Aveu 70. State of Siege 72.

Costello, Dolores (1905–). Gentle American silent screen heroine; married John Barrymore.
Lawful Larceny 23. *The Sea Beast* 25. Bride of the Storm 26. When a Man Loves 27. Old San Francisco 27. Glorious Betsy 28. The Redeeming Sin 29. *Noah's Ark* 29. Show of Shows 29. Second Choice 30. Expensive Women 31. Little Lord Fauntleroy 36. King of the Turf 39. *The Magnificent Ambersons* 42. This is the Army 43, many others.

Costello, Helene (1904–1957). American silent screen leading lady.
The Man on the Box 25. Bobbed Hair 25. Don Juan 26. In Old Kentucky 27. *Lights of New York* 28. Midnight Taxi 28. The Circus Kid 28, etc.

Costello, Lou (1906–1959) (Louis Cristillo). Dumpy American comedian, the zanier half of Abbott and Costello. For films, see *Bud Abbott*. Costello finally made one on his own, *The Thirty-Foot Bride of Candy Rock* 59.

Costello, Maurice (1877–1950). American matinée idol, in films from 1907.
A Tale of Two Cities 11. The Night Before Christmas 12. Human Collateral 20. Conceit 21. Glimpses of the Moon 23. The Mad Marriage 25. Camille 27. Hollywood Boulevard 36. Lady from Louisiana 41, others.

Cottafavi, Vittorio (1914–). Italian director, mainly of cut-rate spectaculars. Has won critical approval for stylish handling of some of them.
Revolt of the Gladiators 58. The Legions of Cleopatra 59. The Vengeance of Hercules 60. Hercules Conquers Atlantis 61.

Cotten, Joseph (1905–). Tall, quiet American leading man, former drama critic and Broadway stage star.
□ *Citizen Kane* 41. *The Magnificent Ambersons* 42. *Journey into Fear* 42. Lydia 41. *Shadow of a Doubt* 43. Hers to Hold 43. Gaslight 44. Since You Went Away 44. Love Letters 45. *I'll Be Seeing You* 45. Duel in the Sun 46. The Farmer's Daughter 47. *Portrait of Jennie* 48. Under Capricorn 49. Beyond the Forest 49. *The Third Man* 49. Two Flags West 50. Walk Softly Stranger 50. September Affair 50. Half Angel 51. Man with a Cloak 51. Peking Express 52. Untamed Frontier 52. The Steel Trap 52. Niagara 52. Blueprint for Murder 53. Special Delivery 54. The Bottom of the Bottle 55. The

Killer is Loose 56. The Halliday Brand 56. From the Earth to the Moon 58. The Angel Wore Red 60. The Last Sunset 61. Hush Hush Sweet Charlotte 64. The Money Trap 65. The Great Sioux Massacre 65. The Tramplers 66. The Oscar 66. I Crudeli (Sp.) 66. The Hell-benders 67. Jack of Diamonds 67. Brighty 67. Some May Live (TV) 67. Petulia 68. Days of Fire (It) 68. Keene 69. Do You Take This Stranger (TV) 70. The Abominable Dr Phibes 71. Doomsday Voyage 71. Tora! Tora! Tora! 71. White Comanche 71. Lady Frankenstein 71. Baron Blood 72. Assault on the Wayne (TV) 72. Doomsday Voyage 72. The Scientific Cardplayer 72. Soylent Green 73. A Delicate Balance 73.

Couffer, Jack (1922–). American director with a penchant for natural history.
□ Ring of Bright Water 69. The Darwin Adventure 72. Jonathan Livingston Seagull 73.

Coulouris, George (1903–). British character actor, in America 1930–50; usually in explosive roles.
Christopher Bean 33. All This and Heaven Too 40. The Lady in Question 40. *Citizen Kane* 41. This Land is Mine 43. *Watch on the Rhine* 43. Between Two Worlds 44. The Master Race 44. Hotel Berlin 45. Confidential Agent 45. The Verdict 46. Sleep My Love 47. A Southern Yankee 48. *An Outcast of the Islands* 51. Doctor in the House 53. The Runaway Bus 54. I Accuse 57. Conspiracy of Hearts 60. King of Kings 61. The Skull 65. Arabesque 66. The Assassinareau 69. Blood from the Mummy's Tomb 71. Papillon 73. Mahler 74. Murder on the Orient Express 74. The Antichrist 75, many others.

The Count of Monte Cristo. This popular adventure yarn by Alexandre Dumas was filmed in 1912 with Hobart Bosworth, and again in the same year with James O'Neill. John Gilbert starred in the 1923 silent film, but the best-remembered version is the 1934 talkie remake with Robert Donat, directed by Rowland V. Lee. Oddly enough it has never since been remade in English, though French versions were made in 1942, 1953 and 1961 starring respectively Pierre Richard Willm, Jean Marais and Louis Jourdan; a TV version starring Richard Chamberlain followed in 1976; and there have been over a dozen films using the name Monte Cristo to cover a multitude of plots, some of them present-day: *Sword of Monte Cristo, Wife of Monte Cristo, Monte Cristo's Revenge*, etc.

Courant, Curt (c. 1895–). German cinematographer who did his best work

elsewhere.
Quo Vadis 24. Woman in the Moon 29. Perfect
Understanding (GB) 33. Amok 34. The Man
Who Knew Too Much (GB) 34. The Iron Duke
(GB) 35. Broken Blossoms (GB) 36. La Bête
Humaine 38. Louise 39. Le Jour Se Lève 39. De
Mayerling à Sarajevo 40. Monsieur Verdoux
(US) 47. It Happened in Athens 61, etc.

Courcel, Nicole (1930–) (Nicole Andrieux).
French leading lady of warm personality.
La Marie du Port 49. Versailles 53. La Sorcière
55. The Case of Dr Laurent 56. Sundays and
Cybele 62, etc.

Court, Hazel (1926–). Red-headed British
leading lady; moved into horror films and went
to live in Hollywood.
Champagne Charlie 44. Dear Murderer 46. My
Sister and I 48. It's Not Cricket 48. Bond Street
50. The Curse of Frankenstein 56. The Man
Who Could Cheat Death 59. Doctor Blood's
Coffin 60. The Premature Burial 62. The
Masque of the Red Death 64, etc.
TV series: Dick and the Duchess 57.

Courtenay, Tom (1937–). Lean young
British actor specializing in under-privileged
roles.
Billy Liar 63. *The Loneliness of the Long
Distance Runner* 63. Private Potter 62. King and
Country 64. Operation Crossbow 65. King Rat
65. Doctor Zhivago 65. The Night of the
Generals 66. The Day the Fish Came Out 67. A
Dandy in Aspic 68. *Otley* 69. One Day in the
Life of Ivan Denisovitch 71, etc.

courtesans have always been viewed by the
cinema through rose-coloured glasses. There
have been innumerable films about Madame du
Barry, Madame Sans Gêne and Nell Gwynne;
Garbo played Camille and Marie Walewska as
well as Anna Christie; even Jean Simmons had a
shot at Napoleon's *Désirée*, and Vivien Leigh
was a decorative Lady Hamilton. Martine Carol
played Lola Montes in the Max Ophüls film,
Yvonne de Carlo in *Black Bart* (in which she
became involved in western villainy during an
American tour).
See also: *prostitutes.*

Courtland, Jerome (1926–). Gangling
young American lead of forties comedies.
Kiss and Tell 45. Man from Colorado 48.
Battleground 49. The Barefoot Mailman 52. The
Bamboo Prison 55. Tonka 59. O Sole Mio (It.)
60. Mary Read, Pirate (It.) 61. Thanis, Son of
Attila (It.) 61. Black Spurs 65. Diamonds on
Wheels (d only) 73, etc.

TV series: Tales of the Vikings 60.

Courtneidge, Dame Cicely (1893–).
Australian comedienne long resident in Britain;
wife of Jack Hulbert. On stage from 1901; her
great vitality made her a musical comedy
favourite.
Autobiography 1953: *Cicely.*
The Ghost Train 32. *Jack's the Boy* 32. Soldiers
of the King 33. Aunt Sally 34. Me and
Marlborough 36. The Imperfect Lady (US) 37.
Take My Tip 38. *Under Your Hat* 40. *The L-
Shaped Room* 62. Those Magnificent Men in
Their Flying Machines 65. The Wrong Box 66.
Not Now Darling 73, etc.

courtroom scenes have been the suspenseful
saving grace of more films than can be counted;
and they also figure in some of the best films ever
made.
British courts best preserve the ancient aura of
the law; among the films they have figured in are
*London Belongs to Me, The Paradine Case,
Eight O'Clock Walk, Life for Ruth, Twenty-one
Days, Brothers in Law, The Winslow Boy,
Witness for the Prosecution, The Blind Goddess*
and *The Dock Brief.* The last four are based on
stage plays, as are the American *Madame X,
Counsellor at Law,* and *The Trial of Mary
Dugan.* Other American films depending heavily
on courtroom denouements include *The Won't
Believe Me, The Unholy Three, The Mouthpiece,
Boomerang, They Won't Forget, The Missing
Juror, Trial, The Young Savages, The Criminal
Code, To Kill a Mockingbird, Criminal Lawyer,
Fury, The Lawyer, A Free Soul, The Seven
Minutes, The People Against O'Hara, The Lady
from Shanghai, Twilight of Honour, An
American Tragedy* (and its remake *A Place in
the Sun*), the several Perry Mason films, and
Young Mr Lincoln. These, even the last-named,
were fictional: genuine cases were reconstructed
in *I Want to Live, Cell 2455 Death Row,
Compulsion, Inherit the Wind, Dr Ehrlich's
Magic Bullet, The Witches of Salem, The Trials
of Oscar Wilde, Judgment at Nuremberg, The
Life of Emile Zola, Dr Crippen, Captain Kidd,
Landru* and *The Case of Charles Peace.*
Comedy courtroom scenes have appeared in *I'm
No Angel, Mr Deeds Goes to Town, You Can't
Take It With You, Roxie Hart, My Learned
Friend, Adam's Rib, Pickwick Papers, Brothers
in Law, What's Up Doc?, Star!* and *A Pair of
Briefs.*
Films in which special interest has centred on
the jury include *Twelve Angry Men, Murder
(Enter Sir John), Perfect Strangers (Too
Dangerous to Love), Justice est Faite* and *The
Monster and the Girl* (in which the criminal

brain inside the gorilla murders the jurors at his trial one by one), Ghostly juries figured in *All That Money Can Buy* and *The Remarkable Andrew*. The judge has been the key figure in *The Judge Steps Out*, *Talk of the Town*, *The Bachelor and the Bobbysoxer*, and *Destry Rides Again*; and we are constantly being promised a film of Henry Cecil's *No Bail for the Judge*. *Anatomy of a Murder* remains the only film in which a real judge (Joseph E. Welch) has played a fictional one. A lady barrister (Anna Neagle) had the leading role in *The Man Who Wouldn't Talk*.

Specialized courts were seen in *M* (convened by criminals), *Saint Joan* and *The Hunchback of Notre Dame* (church courts), *Black Legion* (Ku Klux Klan), *The Devil's Disciple* (18th-century military court), *Kind Hearts and Coronets* (a court of the House of Lords), *The Wreck of the Mary Deare* (mercantile), *Cone of Silence* (civil aviation), *A Tale of Two Cities* and *The Scarlet Pimpernel* (French Revolutionary courts). Courts in other countries were shown in *The Lady in Question*, *The Count of Monte Cristo*, *Crack in the Mirror*, *A Flea in Her Ear*, *La Vérité*, and *Can Can* (French); *The Purple Heart* (Japanese); *The Fall of the Roman Empire* (ancient Roman); *The Spy Who Came in from the Cold* (East German); and *Shoeshine* (Italian). Coroners' courts were featured in *Inquest*, *My Learned Friend* and *Rebecca*.

Courts martial figured largely in *The Caine Mutiny*, *Time Limit*, *The Man in the Middle*, *Across the Pacific*, *The Rack*, *Carrington VC* and *The Court Martial of Billy Mitchell*. There is also a TV series · called *Court Martial* (*Counsellors at War* in the US).

Heavenly courts were convened in *A Matter of Life and Death*, *Outward Bound* and *The Flight That Disappeared*; while other fantasy courts appeared in *Rashomon*, *Morgan*, *One Way Pendulum*, *Alice in Wonderland*, *The Balcony*, *The Wonderful World of the Brothers Grimm*, *The Trial*, *All That Money Can Buy*, and *The Remarkable Andrew*. The court in *Planet of the Apes* is perhaps best classed as prophetic, along with that in *1984*.

TV series based on trials and lawyers include *The Law and Mr Jones*, *Harrigan and Son*, *Sam Benedict*, *The Trials of O'Brien*, *Perry Mason*, *Arrest and Trial*, *The Defenders*, *The D.A.*, *The Verdict is Yours*, *Judd for the Defense*, *Owen Marshall*, *Petrocelli* and *Adam's Rib*.

Cousteau, Jacques-Yves (1910–). French underwater explorer and documentarist.
The Silent World 56. World Without Sun 64, etc.

Coutard, Raoul (1924–). French

cinematographer.
Ranuntcho 50. A Bout de Souffle 59. Shoot the Pianist 60. *Lola* 60. *Jules et Jim* 61. Vivre Sa Vie 61. Bay of Angels 62. Les Carabiniers 63. Silken Skin 63. Pierrot le Fou 65. Made in USA 66. Sailor from Gibraltar 66. The Bride Wore Black 67. 'Z' 68. L'Aveu 70. L'Explosion 70, etc.

The Covered Wagon (US 1923). A big-scale pioneer western which, though it now seems tame, did much to establish the form. Directed by James Cruze, photographed by Karl Brown, edited by Dorothy Arzner, written by Jack Cunningham from a novel by Emerson Hough.

Cowan, Jerome (1897–1972). American character actor with an easy manner. In films from 1936 (*Beloved Enemy*: out of character as a fanatical Irishman). Has played hundreds of supporting roles, typically in *The Maltese Falcon* 41 as the detective killed while searching for the mysterious Floyd Thursby; played the lead in *Crime by Night* 43, *Find the Blackmailer* 44. Recently graduated from jealous rivals to executives, from lawyers to judges.
Claudia and David 46. The Unfaithful 47. Miracle on 34th Street 48. June Bride 48. The Fountainhead 49. Young Man with a Horn 50. Dallas 51. The System 53. Visit to a Small Planet 60. Frankie and Johnny 65. The Gnome-Mobile 67. The Comic 69, many others.
TV series: The Tab Hunter Show 60. Tycoon 64.

Cowan, Lester (c. 1905–). American producer from 1934.
My Little Chickadee 39. Ladies in Retirement 41. The Story of G.I. Joe 45. Love Happy 50. Main Street to Broadway 52, etc.

Cowan, Maurice (1891–1974). British producer of mainly routine films.
Derby Day 52. Turn the Key Softly 55. The Gypsy and the Gentleman 57, etc.

Coward, Sir Noel (1899–1973). British actor-writer-composer-director, the bright young man of international show business in the twenties and thirties.
Autobiographies: *Present Indicative* 1933, *Future Indefinite* 1949. Biography: *A Talent to Amuse* 1969 by Sheridan Morley. Coward was portrayed in *Star!* 68 by Dan Massey.
□ Hearts of the World (a) 18. Private Lives (oa) 31. Cavalcade (oa) 33. Tonight is Ours (oa) 33. Bitter Sweet (oa) 33 and 40. Design for Living (oa) 34. *The Scoundrel* (a) 35. *In Which We Serve* (a,w,pd) (AA) 41. We Were Dancing (oa) 42. *Blithe Spirit* (oa) 45. This Happy Breed (oa) 45. *Brief Encounter* (oa) 46. The Astonished

Heart (a) 49. Meet Me Tonight (oa) 50. Around the World in Eighty Days (a) 56. *Our Man in Havana* (a) 59. Surprise Package (a) 60. Paris When it Sizzles (a) 64. Bunny Lake is Missing (a) 65. Boom (a) 66. The Italian Job (a) 69.

Cowen, William J. (1883–1964). American director.
□ Kongo 32. Oliver Twist 33. Woman Unafraid 34.

Cowl, Jane (1890–1950). American leading stage actress who made very few film appearances.
□ The Garden of Lies 15. The Spreading Dawn 17. Once More My Darling 49. No Man of Her Own 49. The Secret Fury 50. Payment on Demand 50.

Cox, Ronny (–). American character actor with stage background.
The Happiness Cage 72. *Deliverance* 72.
TV series: Apple's Way 74.

Cox, Vivian (1915–). British producer.
Father Brown 54. The Prisoner 55. Bachelor of Hearts 58, etc.

Cox, Wally (1924–1976). American comic actor, usually seen as the bespectacled, weedy character he played in the TV series *Mr Peepers* 52–55 and *Hiram Holliday* 56.
Spencer's Mountain 63. Fate is the Hunter 64. Morituri 65. The Bedford Incident 65. A Guide for the Married Man 67. The One and Only Genuine Original Family Band 68, etc.

Crabbe, Buster (1907–) (Clarence Linden Crabbe). American athlete who became leading man of 'B' pictures.
King of the Jungle 33. Tarzan the Fearless 33. Nevada 36. *Flash Gordon's Trip to Mars* 38. Buck Rogers 39. Queen of Broadway 43. Caged Fury 48. Gunfighters of Abilene 59. Arizona Raiders 65, many others.
TV series: Captain Gallant 55.

Crabtree, Arthur (1900–). British director, former cameraman.
Madonna of the Seven Moons 44. They Were Sisters 45. Dear Murderer 46. Caravan 46. The Calendar 48. Lili Marlene 50. Hindle Wakes 52. The Wedding of Lili Marlene 53. West of Suez 57. Morning Call 58. Horrors of the Black Museum 59, etc.

Craig, Alec (1878–1945). Scottish character actor in Hollywood; often played misers, moneylenders and downtrodden roles.

Mutiny on the Bounty 35. Mary of Scotland 36. Winterset 36. Vivacious Lady 38. Tom Brown's Schooldays 40. Cat People 42. Holy Matrimony 43. Lassie Come Home 43. Spider Woman 44. Kitty 46, many others.

Craig, Edward Gordon (1872–1966) (Henry Edward Wardell). British stage designer, father of Edward Carrick (qv). Though not directly employed in films, his stage designs were influential to people like William Cameron Menzies and Anton Grot.

Craig, H. A. L. (Harold) (–). British screenwriter.
Anzio 68. Waterloo 70, etc.

Craig, James (1912–) (James Meador). American leading man, usually the good-natured but tough outdoor type.
Thunder Trail 37. The Buccaneer 38. The Man They Could Not Hang 39. Zanzibar 40. Kitty Foyle 40. *All That Money Can Buy* (the 'Faust' role, and his best) 41. Valley of the Sun 41. The Omaha Trail 42. The Human Comedy 43. Lost Angel 43. Kismet 44. Our Vines Have Tender Grapes 45. Boys Ranch 45. Little Mister Jim 46. Northwest Stampede 48. Side Street 50. Drums in the Deep South 51. Hurricane Smith 52. Fort Vengeance 53. While the City Sleeps 56. Four Fast Guns 59. The Hired Gun 67, many others.

Craig, Michael (1928–) (Michael Gregson). British light leading man, a former crowd artist groomed by the Rank Organization; latterly attempting more ambitious roles.
Malta Story 53. The Love Lottery 54. Yield to the Night 55. House of Secrets 56. High Tide at Noon 57. Campbell's Kingdom 58. The Silent Enemy 58. Nor the Moon by Night 58. Sea of Sand 59. Sapphire 59. Upstairs and Downstairs 59. *The Angry Silence* (& w) 59. Cone of Silence 60. Doctor in Love 60. Mysterious Island 61. *Payroll* 61. A Pair of Briefs 62. Life for Ruth 62. The Iron Maiden 62. Stolen Hours 63. Of a Thousand Delights (Vaghe Stella dell'Orsa) 65. Life at the Top 65. Modesty Blaise 66. Sandra (It.) 66. *Star!* 68. The Royal Hunt of the Sun 69. Twinky 69. Brotherly Love 70. A Town Called Bastard 71. Vault of Horror 73, etc.

Craig, Wendy (1934–). British stage and TV actress.
The Mind Benders 63. The Servant 63. The Nanny 65. Just Like a Woman 66. I'll Never Forget Whatshisname 67, etc.

Craig, Yvonne (1941–). American leading lady.

The Young Land 60. By Love Possessed 61. Seven Women from Hell 62. Kissin' Cousins 64. One Spy Too Many 66. In Like Flint 67, etc.

Craigie, Jill (1914–). British documentary director.
The Way We Live 46. Blue Scar 48. The Million Pound Note (w only) 51. Windom's Way (w only) 57, etc.

Crain, Jeanne (1925–). American leading lady of the forties; usually the personification of sweetness and light.
□ The Gang's All Here 43. Home in Indiana 44. In the Meantime Darling 44. Winged Victory 44. *State Fair* 45. Leave Her to Heaven 45. Centennial Summer 46. *Margie* 46. Apartment for Peggy 48. You Were Meant for Me 48. A Letter to Three Wives 49. The Fan 49. *Pinky* 49. Cheaper by the Dozen 50. Take Care of My Little Girl 51. People Will Talk 51. The Model and the Marriage Broker 52. Belles on Their Toes 52. Full House 52. Dangerous Crossing 53. City of Bad Men 53. Vicki 53. Duel in the Jungle (GB) 54. Man Without a Star 55. Gentlemen Marry Brunettes 55. The Second Greatest Sex 55. The Fastest Gun Alive 56. The Tattered Dress 57. The Joker is Wild 58. Guns of the Timberland 60. Twenty Plus Two 61. Queen of the Nile (It.) 61. With Fire and Sword (It.) 61. Pontius Pilate (It.) 61. Madison Avenue 62. 52 Miles to Terror 64. Hot Rods to Hell 67. Skyjacked 72.

Crane, Bob (1929–). American light comic actor, popular in TV series *Hogan's Heroes*. Superdad 74.

crane shot. A high-angle shot in which the camera travels up, down or laterally while mounted on a travelling crane.

The Cranes are Flying (Russia 1957). The simple but moving story of a wartime Moscow romance, distinguished by Mikhail Kalatozov's direction, Urusevsky's mobile camerawork, and the performance of Tatiana Samoilova.

Cravat, Nick (1911–). Small, agile American actor, once Burt Lancaster's circus partner.
The Flame and the Arrow 51. The Crimson Pirate 52. King Richard and the Crusaders 54. Three-Ring Circus 55. Kiss Me Deadly 55. Davy Crockett 56. Run Silent, Run Deep 59. The Scalphunters 68. Ulzana's Raid 72, etc.

Craven, Frank (1875–1945). American stage character actor who spent his later years in Hollywood; typically cast as kindly pipe-smoking philosopher.

□ We Americans 28. The Very Idea 29. State Fair 33. That's Gratitude 34. He Was Her Man 34. Let's Talk It Over 34. City Limits 34. Funny Thing Called Love 34. *Barbary Coast* 35. Car 99 35. Vagabond Lady 35. Small Town Girl 36. The Harvester 36. Penrod and Sam 37. Blossoms on Broadway 37. You're Only Young Once 37. Penroad and his Twin Brother 38. Our Neighbours the Carters 39. Miracles for Sale 39. Dreaming Out Loud 40. City for Conquest 40. *Our Town* (his stage role) 40. The Lady from Cheyenne 41. The Richest Man in Town 41. In This Our Life 41. *Thru Different Eyes* 42. Pittsburgh 42. Girl Trouble 42. Son of Dracula 43. Harrigan's Kid 43. Jack London 43. The Human Comedy 43. Keeper of the Flame 43. Destiny 44. My Best Gal 44. They Shall Have Faith 44. The Right to Live 45. Colonel Effingham's Raid 45.

Crawford, Andrew (1917–). Scottish character actor.
The Brothers 46. Dear Murderer 47. London Belongs to Me 48. Morning Departure 50. Shadow of the Cat 61, etc.

Crawford, Anne (1920–1956) (Imelda Crawford). British leading lady with gentle, humorous personality.
They Flew Alone (debut) 42. The Peterville Diamond 42. The Dark Tower 42. The Hundred-Pound Window 43. Millions Like Us 43. Two Thousand Women 44. They Were Sisters 45. Caravan 46. Bedelia 46. Master of Bankdam 47. Daughter of Darkness 48. The Blind Goddess 48. It's Hard To Be Good 49. Tony Draws a Horse 49. Thunder on the Hill (US) 50. Street Corner 52. Knights of the Round Table 53. Mad about Men 55, etc.

Crawford, Broderick (1910–). Beefy American character actor, son of Helen Broderick; began by playing comic stooges and gangsters, with acting performances coming later; after a long spell in TV his popularity waned.
Woman Chases Man 37. The Real Glory 39. Eternally Yours 39. Beau Geste 39. Slightly Honorable 40. When the Daltons Rode 40. The Black Cat 41. Butch Minds the Baby 42. Broadway 42. Sin Town 42. *The Runaround* 46. Slave Girl 47. The Flame 47. The Time of Your Life 48. Anna Lucasta 49. *All the King's Men* (AA) 50. *Born Yesterday* 51. The Mob 51. Lone Star 52. Scandal Sheet 52. Last of the Comanches 52. Stop You're Killing Me 52. Night People 54. Human Desire 54. Down Three Dark Streets 54. New York Confidential 55. Il Bidone (The Swindlers) 55. Not as a Stranger 55.

The Fastest Gun Alive 56. The Decks Ran Red 58. Up from the Beach 65. The Oscar 66. The Texican 66. Red Tomahawk 66. The Vulture 67. Embassy 72. Terror in the Wax Museum 73. Smashing the Crime Syndicate 73, etc.

TV series: *Highway Patrol* 55–59. King of Diamonds 64. The Interns 70.

Crawford, Howard Marion: see *Marion-Crawford, Howard.*

Crawford, Joan (1906–) (Lucille le Sueur; known for a time as Billie Cassin). American leading lady; one of Hollywood's most durable stars, first as a flapper of the jazz age and later as the personification of the career girl and the repressed older woman. Few of her films have been momentous, but she has always been 'box office', especially with women fans, who liked to watch her suffering in mink.

Autobiography 1962: *A Portrait of Joan.*

□ Pretty Ladies 25. The Only Thing 25. Old Clothes 25. Sally, Irene and Mary 25. The Boob 25. Paris 25. Tramp Tramp Tramp 26. The Taxi Dancer 27. Winners of the Wilderness 27. The Understanding Heart 27. The Unknown 27. Twelve Miles Out 27. Spring Fever 27. West Point 28. Rose Marie 28. Across to Singapore 28. The Law of the Range 28. Four Walls 28. *Our Dancing Daughters* 28. Dream of Love 28. The Duke Steps Out 29. Our Modern Maidens 29. Hollywood Revue 29. Untamed 29. Montana Moon 30. Our Blushing Brides 30. Paid 30. Dance Fools Dance 31. Laughing Sinners 31. This Modern Age 31. Possessed 31. Letty Lynton 32. *Grand Hotel* 32. Rain 32. Today We Live 33. *Dancing Lady* 33. Sadie McKee 34. Chained 34. Forsaking All Others 34. No More Ladies 35. I Live My Life 35. *The Gorgeous Hussy* 36. Love on the Run 36. The Last of Mrs Cheyney 37. The Bride Wore Red 37. Mannequin 38. The Shining Hour 38. Ice Follies 39. *The Women* 39. Strange Cargo 40. Susan and God 40. *A Woman's Face* 41. When Ladies Meet 41. They All Kissed the Bride 42. Reunion in France 42. Above Suspicion 43. Hollywood Canteen 44. *Mildred Pierce* (AA) 45. *Humoresque* 46. *Possessed* 47. Daisy Kenyon 47. Flamingo Road 49. The Damned Don't Cry 50. Harriet Craig 50. Goodbye My Fancy 51. This Woman is Dangerous 52. *Sudden Fear* 52. Torch Song 53. Johnny Guitar 54. The Female on the Beach 55. Queen Bee 55. Autumn Leaves 56. The Story of Esther Costello (GB) 57. The Best of Everything 59. *Whatever Happened to Baby Jane?* 62. The Caretakers 63. Strait Jacket 64. Della (TV) 64. I Saw What You Did 65. The Karate Killers (TV) 67. Berserk (GB) 67. Trog 70.

Crawford, Michael (1942–) (Michael Dumble-Smith). Lively British comedy lead, former child actor.

Soap Box Derby 50. Blow Your Own Trumpet 54. Two Living One Dead 62. The War Lover 63. Two Left Feet 63. *The Knack* 65. A Funny Thing Happened on the Way to the Forum 66. *The Jokers* 66. How I Won the War 67. *Hello Dolly* 69. The Games 69. Hello Goodbye 70. Alice's Adventures in Wonderland 72, etc.

TV series: Sir Francis Drake 62.

crazy comedy has two distinct meanings in the cinema. On one hand it encompasses the Marx Brothers, *Hellzapoppin* and custard pies; for this see *Slapstick*. On the other it means the new kind of comedy which came in during the thirties, with seemingly adult people behaving in what society at the time thought was a completely irresponsible way. The Capra comedies, for instance, are vaguely 'agin' the government', upholding Mr Deeds' right to give away his money and play the tuba, the Vanderhofs' right not to work, and Mr Smith's right to be utterly honest. This endearing eccentricity permeated many of the funniest and most modern comedies of the period. William Powell and Myrna Loy in *The Thin Man* were a married couple who upheld none of the domestic virtues. In *Libelled Lady* four top stars behaved like low comedians. In *My Man Godfrey* a rich man pretended to be a tramp and so reformed a party of the idle rich who found him during a 'scavenger hunt'. *Theodora Goes Wild, I Met Him in Paris* and *Easy Living* had what we would now call 'kooky' heroines. In *True Confession* Carole Lombard confessed to a murder she hadn't done, and was told by John Barrymore that she would 'fry'; in *Nothing Sacred* she pretended to be dying of an obscure disease and was socked on the jaw by Fredric March. Hal Roach introduced comedy ghosts, played by two of Hollywood's most sophisticated stars, in *Topper*, and followed it up with two sequels as well as three individual and endearingly lunatic comedies called *The Housekeeper's Daughter* (a battle of fireworks), *Turnabout* (a husband and wife exchange bodies) and *Road Show* (an asylum escapee runs a travelling circus). *The Awful Truth* had no respect for marriage; *You Can't Take It With You* had no respect for law, business, or the American way of life. A film called *Bringing Up Baby* turned out to be about a leopard and a brontosaurus bone; *Boy Meets Girl* was a farcical send-up of Hollywood; and *A Slight Case of Murder* had more corpses than characters. *The Women* had its all-female cast fighting like tiger-cats. *Road to Singapore* began as a romantic comedy but degenerated into snippets from Joe

Miller's gag-book; and any Preston Sturges film was likely to have pauses while the smart and witty hero and heroine fell into a pool. In *Here Comes Mr Jordan* the hero was dead after five minutes or so and spent the rest of the film trying to get his body back.

The genre was by this time well established, and although America's entry into the war modified it somewhat it has remained fashionable and popular ever since. A 1966 film like *Morgan* may seem rather startling, but in fact it goes little further in its genial anarchy than *You Can't Take It With You*; only the method of expression is different. What modern crazy comedies lack is the clear pattern which produced so many little masterpieces within a few years: even direct imitations like *What's Up Doc?* fail to produce the same results.

The Crazy Gang. Three pairs of British music hall comedians made up this famous group which was enormously popular on stage from 1935 till 1962. Bud Flanagan (qv) and Chesney Allen (qv); Jimmy Nervo (James Holloway) (1890–1975) and Teddy Knox (c. 1898–196*); Charlie Naughton (1887–1976) and Jimmy Gold (1886–1967).
☐ OK for Sound 37. Alf's Button Afloat 38. The Frozen Limits 39. Gasbags 40. Life is a Circus 54.

The Creature from the Black Lagoon (US 1954). A poor horror film which spawned one of Universal's more inept monsters, an amphibious chap in a rubber suit who was called the gill man but remained singularly unimpressive and restricted in two sequels: *Revenge of the Creature* 55 and *The Creature Walks Among Us* 56. Ricou Browning played the part, and the underwater photography was the best thing in the film.

credits. Titles at beginning or end of film (nowadays very often five minutes *after* the beginning) listing the names of the creative talents concerned.

creeping title. One which moves up (or sometimes across) the screen at reading pace. Also known as *roller title*.

Cregar, Laird (1916–1944). Heavyweight American character actor who had a tragically brief but impressive career in a rich variety of roles.
☐ Granny Get Your Gun 40. Oh Johnny How You Can Love 40. Hudson's Bay 40. Blood and Sand 41. *Charley's Aunt* 41. *I Wake Up Screaming* 41. Joan of Paris 42. Rings on Her Fingers 42. This Gun for Hire 42. *Ten Gentlemen from West Point* 42. *The Black Swan* 42. Hello Frisco Hello 43. *Heaven Can Wait* 43. Holy Matrimony 43. *The Lodger* 44. Hangover Square 44.

Crehan, Joseph (1884–1966) (Charles Wilson). American character actor, often as sheriff or cop.
Stolen Heaven 31. Before Midnight 33. Identity Parade 34. Boulder Dam 36. Happy Landing 38. Stanley and Livingstone 39. The Roaring Twenties 39. Brother Orchid 40. Texas 42. Phantom Lady 44. Deadline at Dawn 46. The Foxes of Harrow 48. Red Desert 54, many others.

Crenna, Richard (1926–). American leading man, formerly boy actor on radio and TV.
Red Skies of Montana 52. It Grows on Trees 52. Over Exposed 56. John Goldfarb Please Come Home 65. Made in Paris 65. The Sand Pebbles 66. Wait Until Dark 67. Star! 68. Marooned 69. The Deserter 70. Thief (TV) 71. Doctors' Wives 71. Red Sky at Morning 71. Catlow 72. The Man Called Noon 73. Double Indemnity (TV) 73. Nightmare (TV) 75, etc.
TV series: Our Miss Brooks 52–55. The Real McCoys 57–63. Slattery's People 64–65.

Crews, Laura Hope (1880–1942). American stage actress who played character parts in many films, usually as fluttery matron.
Charming Sinners 29. New Morals for Old 32. Escapade 35. *Camille* 36. Thanks for the Memory 38. *Gone with the Wind* (as Aunt Pittypat) 39. The Bluebird 40. The Flame of New Orleans 41. One Foot in Heaven 41, many others.

Cribbins, Bernard (1928–). British comedy character actor and recording star. Played light support roles in several films.
Two Way Stretch 60. The Girl on the Boat 62. The Wrong Arm of the Law 62. Carry On Jack 63. Crooks in Cloisters 64. She 65. The Sandwich Man 66. Daleks Invasion Earth 2150 A.D. 66. The Railway Children 70. Frenzy 72, etc.

Crichton, Charles (1910–). British director, former editor.
For Those in Peril 44. Dead of Night (part) 45. Painted Boats 45. *Hue and Cry* 46. Against the Wind 47. Another Shore 48. Train of Events 49. Dance Hall 50. *The Lavender Hill Mob* 51. Hunted 52. *The Titfield Thunderbolt* 53. The Love Lottery 54. The Divided Heart 54. The Man in the Sky 56. Law and Disorder 57. Floods

of Fear (& w) 58. The Battle of the Sexes 59. The Boy Who Stole a Million 60. The Third Secret 63. He Who Rides a Tiger 65, etc.

Crichton, Michael (1942–). American novelist and screenwriter.
The Andromeda Strain (oa) 71. Westworld (wd) 73.

The Crime Doctor. The hero of this Hollywood-concocted series was a criminal restored by a brain operation to the sober pursuance of his former profession as a doctor. That was in 1943: once the series got under way the premise was forgotten and Warner Baxter was simply a psychiatrist whose involvement in and solution of various complicated crimes was both unlikely and (usually) accidental. The series died with Baxter in 1951.

Crime Does Not Pay. A series of 48 two-reelers, made by MGM between 1935 and 1948 in a very imitable but entertaining hard-hitting style. The first, called *Buried Loot,* introduced Robert Taylor; other budding stars were featured later, and the series proved a valuable training ground for directors, including Jules Dassin and Fred Zinnemann.

The Crime of Monsieur Lange (France 1935). An influential satirical fantasy, written by Jacques Prévert and others, directed by Jean Renoir; about workers who take over a factory when the boss absconds.

Crime Without Passion (US 1934). A melodrama made in New York by writer-directors Ben Hecht and Charles Macarthur, who had hopes of founding a new school of film-making; but the result, despite Claude Rains, was a plain and uncommercial though well-made account of an advocate who murders a young girl and suffers the consequences.

criminals—real-life ones—whose careers have been featured in films include Burke and Hare (*The Flesh and the Fiends, Burke and Hare*), Cagliostro (*Black Magic*), Al Capone (*Little Caesar, The Scarface Mob, Al Capone*), Caryl Chessman (*Cell 2455 Death Row*), Crippen (*Dr Crippen*), John Wilkes Booth (*Prince of Players*), Jack the Ripper (*The Lodger, A Study in Terror, Jack the Ripper,* many others), Landru (*Landru, Bluebeard, Monsieur Verdoux, Bluebeard's Ten Honeymoons*), Leopold and Loeb (*Rope* and *Compulsion*), Christie (*10 Rillington Place*), Charles Peace (*The Case of Charles Peace*), Dick Turpin (qv), Jesse James (qv), Vidocq (*A Scandal in Paris*), Robert

Stroud (*Birdman of Alcatraz*), Barbara Graham (*I Want to Live*), Rasputin (qv), Eddie Chapman (*Triple Cross*), and the various American public enemies of the thirties: *Bonnie and Clyde, Dillinger, Baby Face Nelson, Bloody Mama* (Barker), *A Bullet for Pretty Boy* (Floyd), etc. The clinical sixties also brought accounts of the motiveless murderers of *In Cold Blood* and of *The Boston Strangler.* Criminal movements have been very well explored in fictional films, especially the Mafia, the Thugs, Murder Inc. and the racketeers and bootleggers of the twenties.

Crisp, Donald (1880–1974). Distinguished British screen actor, in Hollywood from 1906; worked with D. W. Griffith and directed some silents, but from 1930 settled on acting and played mainly stern character roles.
Home Sweet Home 14. The Birth of a Nation 15. Broken Blossoms 19. Why Smith Left Home (d) 19. The Bonnie Brier Bush (d) 21. The Mark of Zorro (d) 22. Ponjola (d) 23. *Don Q Son of Zorro* (ad) 25. The Black Pirate 26. Man Bait (d) 27. Stand and Deliver (d) 28. The Return of Sherlock Holmes 29. Runaway Bride (d) 30. Svengali 31. Red Dust 32. Crime Doctor 34. The Little Minister 34. Mutiny on the Bounty 35. Mary of Scotland 36. Beloved Enemy 36. Parnell 37. Jezebel 38. The Sisters 38. *The Dawn Patrol* 38. Wuthering Heights 39. The Old Maid 39. *Brother Orchid* 40. The Sea Hawk 40. Dr Jekyll and Mr Hyde 41. *How Green Was My Valley* (AA) 41. The Gay Sisters 42. Lassie Come Home 43. *The Uninvited* 44. National Velvet 44. Valley of Decision 45. Ramrod 47. Whispering Smith 49. Bright Leaf 50. Prince Valiant 54. The Man from Laramie 55. Saddle the Wind 58. The Last Hurrah 58. Pollyanna 60. Greyfriars Bobby 61. Spencer's Mountain 63, many others.

Cristal, Linda (1936–) (Victoria Maya). Argentinian leading lady, in Hollywood from 1956.
Comanche 56. The Fiend Who Walked the West 58. The Perfect Furlough 58. Cry Tough 59. The Alamo 60. Panic in the City 68. Mr Majestyk 74, etc.
TV series: The High Chaparral 67–69.

Cristaldi, Franco (1924–). Italian producer of good reputation.
La Pattuglia Sperduta 53. La Sfida 59. L'Assassino 60. Salvatori Giuliano 61. Divorce Italian Style 63. The Red Tent 69, etc.

Crockett, Davy (1786–1836). American trapper and Indian scout who became a legendary hero and a politician before dying at the Alamo (qv). He has been portrayed on film by George Montgomery (*Indian Scout*), Fess Parker (*Davy Crockett, Davy Crockett and the River Pirates*), Arthur Hunnicutt (*The Last Command*) and John Wayne (*The Alamo*), among others.

Crompton, Richmal (1890–1969). British writer for children, author of the 'William' books which have been filmed from time to time.

Cromwell, John (1888–). Distinguished American director with stage background.
☐ The Racket 28. The Dummy 29. The Mighty 29. The Dance of Life 29. Close Harmony 29. Street of Chance 30. Tom Sawyer 31. The Texan 30. For the Defense 30. Scandal Street 31. Rich Man's Folly 31. Vice Squad 31. Unfaithful 31. The World and the Flesh 31. Sweepings 33. The Silver Cord 33. Double Harness 33. Ann Vickers 33. Spitfire 34. This Man is Mine 34. *Of Human Bondage* 34. The Fountain 34. Jalna 35. Village Tale 35. I Dream Too Much 35. Little Lord Fauntleroy 36. To Mary With Love 36. Banjo on My Knee 36. *The Prisoner of Zenda* 37. *Algiers* 38. Made for Each Other 38. In Name Only 39. Abe Lincoln in Illinois 39. Victory 40. So Ends Our Night 41. Son of Fury 42. *Since You Went Away* 44. The Enchanted Cottage 45. *Anna and the King of Siam* 46. Dead Reckoning 47. Night Song 47. Caged 50. The Company She Keeps 51. The Racket 51. Hidden Fear 57. The Goddess 58. The Scavengers 60. A Matter of Morals 61.

Cromwell, Richard (1910–1960) (Roy Radebaugh). American leading man, gentle hero of early sound films.
Tol'able David 30. Emma 32. Tom Brown of Culver 33. Carolina 34. *Lives of a Bengal Lancer* 35. Poppy 36. The Road Back 37. Jezebel 38. Young Mr Lincoln 39. Parachute Battalion 41. Riot Squad 42. Baby Face Morgan 42. Bungalow 13 48, etc.

Cronenweth, Jordan (–). American cinematographer.
Brewster McCloud 70. Play it as it Lays 72. Zandy's Bride 74. The Front Page 74, etc.

Cronin, A. J. (1896–). British novelist, former doctor.
Grand Canary 34. The Citadel 38. The Stars Look Down 39. Shining Victory 41. Hatter's Castle 41. The Keys of the Kingdom 44. The Green Years 46. The Spanish Gardener 56.
TV series: Dr Finlay's Casebook 65–71.

Cronjager, Edward (1904–1960). American cinematographer.

The Quarterback 26. The Virginian 30. Cimarron 31. Roberta 35. The Gorilla 39. *Hot Spot* 41. *Heaven Can Wait* 43. Canyon Passage 46. The House by the River 50. Treasure of the Golden Condor 53. Beneath the Twelve-Mile Reef 53, many others.

Cronyn, Hume (1911–) (Hume Blake). Canadian character actor of stage and screen; married Jessica Tandy.
☐ Shadow of a Doubt 43. Phantom of the Opera 43. The Cross of Lorraine 43. *The Seventh Cross* 44. Main Street After Dark 44. Lifeboat 44. A Letter for Evie 45. The Sailor Takes a Wife 45. The Green Years 46. The Postman Always Rings Twice 46. Ziegfeld Follies 46. The Beginning of the End 47. Brute Force 47. The Bride Goes Wild 48. Top o' the Morning 49. People Will Talk 51. Crowded Paradise 56. *Sunrise at Campobello* 60. Cleopatra 63. Hamlet 64. Gaily Gaily 69. The Arrangement 70. There Was a Crooked Man 70. The Parallax View 74.

Crosby, Bing (1903–1978) Harry Lillis Crosby). Star American crooner of the thirties and forties; former band singer, later an agreeable comedian, romantic lead and straight actor.
Autobiography 1953: *Call Me Lucky.*
☐ King of Jazz 30. The Big Broadcast 32. College Humor 33. Too Much Harmony 33. Going Hollywood 33. We're Not Dressing 34. She Loves Me Not 34. Here is My Heart 34. *Mississippi* 35. Two for Tonight 35. The Big Broadcast of 1936 36. *Anything Goes* 36. Rhythm on the Range 36. Pennies from Heaven 36. Waikiki Wedding 37. Double or Nothing 37. Dr Rhythm 38. *Sing You Sinners* 38. Paris Honeymoon 39. East Side of Heaven 39. The Star Maker 39. *Road to Singapore* 40. If I Had My Way 40. Rhythm on the River 40. Road to Zanzibar 41. Birth of the Blues 41. *Holiday Inn* 42. Road to Morocco 42. Star Spangled Rhythm 43. Dixie 43. *Going My Way* (AA) 44. Here Come The Waves 45. Duffy's Tavern 45. Road to Utopia 45. The Bells of St Mary's 45. Blue Skies 46. Variety Girl 47. Welcome Stranger 47. Road to Rio 47. The Emperor Waltz 48. A Connecticut Yankee in King Arthur's Court 49. Top o' the Morning 49. Riding High 50. Mr Music 50. Here Comes the Groom 51. Just for You 52. Road to Bali 52. Little Boy Lost 53. White Christmas 54. *The Country Girl* 54. Anything Goes 56. High Society 56. Man on Fire 57. Say One for Me 59. High Time 60. Pepe 60. Road to Hong Kong 62. Robin and the Seven Hoods 64. Stagecoach 66.
TV series: The Bing Crosby Show 64.

Crosby, Bob (1913–). American bandleader, brother of Bing.
Let's Make Music 40. Reveille with Beverly 43. See Here Private Hargrove 44. Two Tickets to Broadway 51. The Five Pennies 59, etc.

Crosby, Floyd (1899–). American cinematographer who has worked on everything from documentary to horror thrillers.
□ *Tabu* (AA) 31. *The River* (co-ph) 37. The Fight for Life 40. My Father's House 47. Of Men and Music 50. The Brave Bulls 51. *High Noon* 52. Man in the Dark 53. The Steel Lady 53. Man Crazy 53. Stormy 53. The Snow Creature 54. The Monster from the Ocean Floor 54. The Fast and the Furious 54. Five Guns West 55. The Naked Street 55. Shack Out on 101 55. Hell's Horizon 55. Apache Woman 55. Naked Paradise 56. She Gods of Shark Reef 56. Attack of the Crab Monsters 56. Rock all Night 56. Reform School 57. Teenage Doll 57. Ride Out for Revenge 57. Hell Canyon Outlaws 57. Carnival Rock 57. War of the Satellites 57. Suicide Battalion 58. Cry Baby Killer 58. Machine Gun Kelly 58. The Old Man and the Sea (co-ph) 58. Wolf Larsen 58. Hot Rod Gang 58. Teenage Caveman 58. I Mobster 59. Crime and Punishment USA 59. The Miracle of the Hills 59. The Wonderful Country 59. Blood and Steel 59. The Rookie 60. Twelve Hours to Kill 60. *House of Usher* 60. The High Powered Rifle 60. Walk Tall 60. Freckles 60. Operation Bottleneck 61. The Pit and the Pendulum 61. A Cold Wind in August 61. The Purple Hills 61. The Little Shepherd of Kingdom Come 61. The Gambler Wore a Gun 61. Seven Women from Hell 62. The Explosive Generation 62. Woman Hunt 62. The Premature Burial 62. The Two Little Bears 62. Tales of Terror 62. The Firebrand 62. The Broken Land 62. Terror at Black Falls 62. *The Raven* 63. Black Zoo 63. Yellow Canary 63. The Young Racers 63. X— The Man with X-Ray Eyes 63. The Comedy of Terrors 64. Bikini Beach 64. Pajama Party 64. The Haunted Palace 64. Raiders from Beneath the Sea 65. Beach Blanket Bingo 65. How to Stuff a Wild Bikini 65. Sergeant Deadhead 65. Sallah 65. Fireball 500 66. The Cool Ones 67.

Croset, Paule: see *Corday, Paula*.

Crosland, Alan (1894–1936). Routine American director who happened to handle two innovative films.
Enemies of Women 23. Under the Red Robe 23. Three Weeks 24. Bobbed Hair 25. *Don Juan* (first film with synchronized music) 26. The Beloved Rogue 27. Old San Francisco 27. *The Jazz Singer* (first film with talking sequences) 27.

Glorious Betsy 28. General Crack 29. Song of the Flame 30. Captain Thunder 31. Weekends Only 32. The Case of the Howling Dog 34. Lady Tubbs 35. The Great Impersonation 35, many others.

Crosman, Henrietta (1861–1944). American stage actress, a grande dame who made a few films.
How Molly Made Good 15. Broadway Broke 23. Wandering Fires 25. *The Royal Family of Broadway* 30. Pilgrimage 33. Carolina 34. Menace 34. The Dark Angel 35. Charlie Chan's Secret 36. Personal Property 37, etc.

Cross, Eric (1902–). British cinematographer.
Make Up 37. Song of Freedom 38. The First of the Few 42. Don't Take It To Heart 44. The Chance of a Lifetime 49. Hunted 52. The Kidnappers 53. Private's Progress 55. The One That Got Away 57. Behind the Curtain 60, many others.

cross cutting. Interlinking fragments of two or more separate sequences so that they appear to be taking place at the same time. One of the most famous examples is the climax of *Intolerance* which intertwines four stories.

Crosse, Rupert (1927–1973). Black American actor best remembered for *The Reivers* 68, and for the TV series *Partners*.

Crossfire (US 1947). First of the American racialist dramas, a tough adult thriller about the murder of a Jew. (In Richard Brooks' original novel it was a homosexual.) Adapted by John Paxton, directed by Edward Dmytryk, with Robert Ryan as the anti-Semite and Robert Young as the patient cop.

Crossley, Syd (1885–1960). British music hall comedian who played comic supporting roles in many films. In US in twenties.
Keep Smiling 25. Fangs of the Wild 28. Atlantic 29. Tonight's the Night 31. Those were the Days 34. Dandy Dick 35. Music Hath Charms 36. The Ghost Goes West 36. Silver Blaze 37. Penny Paradise 38, many others.

Crothers, Rachel (1878–1958). American playwright; works much filmed.
When Ladies Meet 33 and 41. As Husbands Go 34. Splendour 35. Mother Carey's Chickens 38. Susan and God 40, etc.

The Crowd (US 1928). King Vidor directed and co-wrote this early experiment in social realism, an account of the drab life of a city clerk.

James Murray and Eleanor Boardman starred. In 1933 Vidor made a sequel, *Our Daily Bread*, showing his couple leaving the town for a farming community: Tom Keene and Karen Morley were the stars.

The Crowd Roars. There are two films under this title. Howard Hawks made the first in 1932, with James Cagney as a racing driver; Richard Thorpe made the second with Robert Taylor as a boxer. The plots are dissimilar.

Crowley, Pat (1929–). American leading lady of the fifties.
Forever Female 53. Money from Home 54. Red Garters 54. There's Always Tomorrow 55. Hollywood or Bust 56. Key Witness 60. To Trap a Spy 64, etc.
TV series: Please Don't Eat the Daisies 65–66.

Cruickshank, Andrew (1907–). Scottish stage actor who has appeared in a number of films, usually as doctor or judge. A national figure on TV as Dr Cameron in *Dr Finlay's Casebook* 65–71.
Auld Lang Syne 37. The Mark of Cain 47. Paper Orchid 49. Your Witness 50. The Cruel Sea 53. Richard III 56. Innocent Sinners 58. Kidnapped 60. *There Was a Crooked Man* 60. El Cid 61. Murder Most Foul 64, etc.

Crutchley, Rosalie (1921–). Striking, lean-featured British stage actress who makes occasional film appearances.
Take My Life 47. Give Us This Day 49. Quo Vadis 51. Make Me an Offer 55. The Spanish Gardener 56. *A Tale of Two Cities* (as Madame Lafarge) 58. Beyond This Place 59. Sons and Lovers 60. Freud 62. The Girl in the Headlines 63. Behold a Pale Horse 64. Blood from the Mummy's Tomb 71. Who Slew Auntie Roo? 71. Man of La Mancha 72, etc.

Cruze, James (1884–1942) (Jens Cruz Bosen). Danish-American silent screen actor who broke his leg and turned to direction.
AS ACTOR: A Boy of Revolution 11. She 11. The Star of Bethlehem 12. Joseph in the Land of Egypt 14. *The Million Dollar Mystery* (serial) 14. The Twenty Million Dollar Mystery (serial) 15. Nan of Music Mountain 17. Too Many Millions 18, etc.
AS DIRECTOR: Too Many Millions 18. The Dollar a Year Man 21. One Glorious Day 22. The Dictator 22. *The Covered Wagon* 23. *Hollywood* 23. Ruggles of Red Gap 23. To the Ladies 23. Merton of the Movies 24. The Goose Hangs High 25. *Beggar on Horseback* 25. Pony Express 25. *Old Ironsides* 26. The Mating Call

27. The Great Gabbo 29. Salvation Nell 31. *Washington Merry Go Round* 32. I Cover the Waterfront 33. David Harum 34. Helldorado 34. *Sutter's Gold* 36. Prison Nurse 38. Gangs of New York 38, many others.

Cuba produced its first film in 1897, but native film-making was swamped by American imports until the Communist revolution of 1959, when a politically conscious programme was begun. Tomas Alea is the best known Cuban director.

Cucciolla, Ricardo (1932–). Italian leading actor.
Italia Brava Gente 65. Grand Slam 67. Sacco and Vanzetti 71, etc.

Cugat, Xavier (1900–). Chubby, beaming Spanish-American bandleader and caricaturist, a feature of many MGM musicals of the forties. Autobiography 1948: *Rumba is My Life*.
You Were Never Lovelier 42. Two Girls and a Sailor 44. Holiday in Mexico 46. This Time for Keeps 47. A Date with Judy 48. Neptune's Daughter 49. Chicago Syndicate 55, etc.

Cukor, George (1899–). American director, from the Broadway stage; proved to be one of Hollywood's most reliable handlers of high comedy and other literate material.
□ Grumpy (co-d) 30. Virtuous Sin (co-d) 30. The Royal Family of Broadway 30. Tarnished Lady 30. Girls About Town 31. *One Hour with You* (with Lubitsch) 32. *What Price Hollywood?* 32. A Bill of Divorcement 32. Rockabye 32. Our Betters 33. *Dinner at Eight* 33. *Little Women* 33. *David Copperfield* 34. Sylvia Scarlett 35. Romeo and Juliet 36. *Camille* 36. *Holiday* 38. Zaza 39. *The Women* 39. Susan and God 40. *The Philadelphia Story* 40. A Woman's Face 41. Two-faced Woman 41. Her Cardboard Lover 42. *Keeper of the Flame* 43. Gaslight 44. Winged Victory 44. Desire Me (co-d) 47. A Double Life 47. *Adam's Rib* 49. Edward My Son (GB) 49. A Life of Her Own 50. Born Yesterday 50. The Model and the Marriage Broker 52. The Marrying Kind 52. Pat and Mike 52. The Actress 53. It Should Happen to You 53. *A Star is Born* 54. Bhowani Junction 56. Les Girls 57. Wild is The Wind 57. Heller in Pink Tights 59. Song Without End (part) 60. Let's Make Love 61. The Chapman Report 62. *My Fair Lady* (AA) 64. Justine 69. Travels with My Aunt 73. Love Among the Ruins (TV) 75. The Bluebird 76.

Culp, Robert (1930–). American leading man.
P. T. 109 62. The Raiders 63. Sunday in New

York 64. Rhino! 64. Bob and Carol and Ted and Alice 69. Hannie Caulder 71. Hickey and Boggs (& d) 72. See The Man Run (TV) 72. The Castaway Cowboy 74. A Cry for Help (TV) 75, etc.

TV series: Trackdown 57. *I Spy* 66–68.

Culver, Roland (1900–). British stage actor of impeccable English types, usually comic.
77 Park Lane 32. Nell Gwynn 34. Paradise for Two 37. *French Without Tears* (his stage role) 39. *Quiet Wedding* 40. Night Train to Munich 40. Talk about Jacqueline 42. *On Approval* 43. Dear Octopus 43. *Dead of Night* 45. Wanted for Murder 46. To Each His Own (US) 47. Down to Earth (US) 47. The Emperor Waltz (US) 48. Isn't It Romantic? 48. *Trio* (as Somerset Maugham) 50. The Holly and the Ivy 54. The Man Who Loved Redheads 55. Touch and Go 57. Bonjour Tristesse 58. The Yellow Rolls-Royce 64. A Man Could Get Killed 65. Fragment of Fear 70. Bequest to the Nation 73, others.

Cummings, Constance (1910–) (Constance Halverstadt). American stage actress, long resident in England.
The Criminal Code (US) 31. The Guilty Generation (US) 31. Movie Crazy (US) 32. Channel Crossing 32. Broadway thro' a Keyhole (US) 33. Glamour 34. Looking for Trouble 34. Remember Last Night? (US) 35. Seven Sinners 36. *Busman's Honeymoon* 40. This England 41. The Foreman Went to France 42. *Blithe Spirit* 45. John and Julie 55. The Intimate Stranger 56. The Battle of the Sexes 59. Sammy Going South 62. In the Cool of the Day 63, etc.

Cummings, Irving (1888–1959). American director, former actor; in films from 1909.
SELECTED SILENT FILMS: As Man Desires 25. The Johnstown Flood 26. The Brute 27, etc.
□ In Old Arizona (co-d) 29. Behind the Curtain 29. Cameo Kirby 30. On the Level 30. A Devil with Women 30. A Holy Terror 31. *The Cisco Kid* 31. Attorney for the Defense 32. Night Club Lady 32. Man Against Woman 32. Man Hunt 33. The Woman I Stole 33. The Mad Game 33. I Believed in You 34. Grand Canary 34. The White Parade 34. It's a Small World 35. Curly Top 35. Nobody's Fool 36. Poor Little Rich Girl 36. Girls Dormitory 36. White Hunter 36. Vogues of 1938 37. Merry go Round of 1938 37. Little Miss Broadway 38. Just Around the Corner 38. *The Story of Alexander Graham Bell* 38. *Hollywood Cavalcade* 39. Everything Happens at Night 39. *Lillian Russell* 40. Down Argentine Way 40. *That Night in Rio* 41. Belle Starr 41. Louisiana Purchase 41. My Gal Sal 42.

Springtime in the Rockies 42. Sweet Rosie O'Grady 43. What a Woman 44. The Impatient Years 44. *The Dolly Sisters* 45. Double Dynamite 51.

Cummings, Jack (1900–). American producer, especially of musicals; long with MGM.
The Winning Ticket 35. Born to Dance 36. Go West 40. Ship Ahoy 42. Bathing Beauty 44. Neptune's Daughter 49. Three Little Words 50. Lovely to Look At 52. Kiss Me Kate 53. Seven Brides for Seven Brothers 54. Many Rivers to Cross 55. The Teahouse of the August Moon 56. The Blue Angel 59. Can Can 60. Bachelor Flat 62. Viva Las Vegas 64, many others.

Cummings, Robert (1908–). American light leading man of the forties.
The Virginia Judge 35. Forgotten Faces 36. Last Train from Madrid 37. Souls at Sea 37. Three Smart Girls Grow Up 38. Rio 39. Spring Parade 40. The Devil and Miss Jones 41. Moon over Miami 41. *It Started with Eve* 41. *King's Row* 41. *Saboteur* 42. Princess O'Rourke 43. You Came Along 45. The Bride Wore Boots 46. The Chase 46. Heaven Only Knows 47. The Lost Moment 47. Sleep my Love 48. The Accused 48. Paid in Full 50. For Heaven's Sake 50. The Barefoot Mailman 51. Marry me Again 53. Lucky Me 54. Dial M for Murder 54. How to be Very Very Popular 55. My Geisha 62. Beach Party 63. What a Way to Go 64. *The Carpetbaggers* 64. Promise Her Anything 66. Stagecoach 66. 5 Golden Dragons 67. Partners in Crime (TV) 73, many others.
TV series: *The Bob Cummings Show* 54–61. My Living Doll 64.

Cummins, Peggy (1925–). British leading lady, former teenage star.
Dr O'Dowd 39. The Late George Apley (US) 47. Moss Rose (US) 47. Green Grass of Wyoming (US) 48. Escape (US) 48. My Daughter Joy 50. Who Goes There? 52. To Dorothy a Son 54. The March Hare 55. Night of the Demon 57. Dentist in the Chair 60. In the Doghouse 62, etc.

Cunard, Grace (1893–1967). American silent serial queen.
The Broken Coin 13. The Purple Mask 15. Peg o' the Ring 18. The Last Man on Earth 24. Untamed 29. Resurrection 31. Ladies They Talk About 33, many others.

Cuny, Alain (1908–). Tall, imposing French actor, in occasional films.
Les Visiteurs du Soir 42. Il Cristo Proibito 50. The Hunchback of Notre Dame 56. Les Amants

58. The Milky Way 68. Satyricon 69, etc.

Currie, Finlay (1878–1968) (Finlay Jefferson).
Veteran Scottish actor with stage and music-hall
experience.
The Case of the Frightened Lady 32. Rome
Express 32. Edge of the World 38. The Bells Go
Down 42. *Great Expectations* (as Magwitch) 46.
Sleeping Car to Trieste 48. *The History of Mr
Polly* 49. Trio 50. Treasure Island 50. *The
Mudlark* (as John Brown) 51. Quo Vadis 51.
People Will Talk (US) 52. Ivanhoe 52. Rob Roy
53. The End of the Road (leading role) 54. Make
Me an Offer 55. Dangerous Exile 57. Ben Hur
(US) 59. Kidnapped 60. Billy Liar 63. The Fall of
the Roman Empire 64. Who Was Maddox?
(leading role) 64. The Battle of the Villa Fiorita
65. Bunny Lake is Missing 65, many others.

Curtis, Alan (1909–1953) (Harold Neberroth).
American leading man, and sometimes villain, of
many 'B' pictures of the forties.
Walking on Air 36. Winterset 36. Mannequin
38. Hollywood Cavalcade 39. Buck Privates 40.
The Great Awakening 41. Two Tickets to
London 43. Hitler's Madman 43. *Phantom Lady*
44. Destiny 44. The Invisible Man's Revenge 44.
The Naughty Nineties 45. Philo Vance's Gamble
48. The Masked Pirate 50, etc.

Curtis, Dan (–   ). American producer
specializing in horror themes for TV.
Dark Shadows (serial) 66. The Night Strangler
(TV) 72. *The Norliss Tapes* (TV) 73. Dracula
(TV) (& d) 73. Kolchak, the Night Stalker (TV
series) 74, etc.

Curtis, Tony (1925–) (Bernard Schwarz).
Bouncy American leading man of fifties
actioners who constantly sought a wider range.
□ Criss Cross 49. City Across the River 49. The
Lady Gambles 49. Johnny Stool Pigeon 49.
Francis 49. I was a Shoplifter 50. Winchester 73
50. *The Prince Who Was a Thief* 51. Flesh and
Fury 52. No Room for the Groom 52. Son of Ali
Baba 52. *Houdini* 53. The All American 53.
Forbidden 53. Beachhead 54. The Black Shield
of Falworth 54. Johnny Dark 54. So This is Paris
54. The Purple Mask 54. Six Bridges to Cross
55. The Square Jungle 55. *Trapeze* 56. The
Rawhide Years 56. Mister Cory 57. The
Midnight Story 57. *Sweet Smell of Success* 57.
The Vikings 58. Kings go Forth 58. *The Defiant
Ones* 58. The Perfect Furlough 58. *Some Like It
Hot* 59. Operation Petticoat 59. Pepe 60. Who
Was That Lady? 60. The Rat Race 60.
Spartacus 60. The Great Imposter 60. The
Outsider 61. Forty Pounds of Trouble 62. Taras
Bulba 62. The List of Adrian Messenger 63.

Captain Newman MD 63. Wild and Wonderful
64. Goodbye Charlie 64. Sex and the Single Girl
64. *The Great Race* 65. Boeing Boeing 65. Not
With My Wife You Don't 66. Drop Dead
Darling 67. Don't Make Waves 67. The Chastity
Belt 68. *The Boston Strangler* 68. Those Daring
Young Men in Their Jaunty Jalopies 69. You
Can't Win Them All 70. Suppose They Gave a
War and Nobody Came 71. Third Girl from the
Left (TV) 73. Lepke 75. Casanova 76. The
Count of Monte Cristo (TV) 76. The Last
Tycoon 76.
TV series: *The Persuaders* 71.

Curtiz, Michael (1888–1962) (Mihaly
Kertesz). Hungarian director of more than sixty
films in Europe before settling in Hollywood,
where he made some of the smoothest spectacles
and melodramas of the thirties and forties and
also became famous for his fractured English.
□ ENGLISH-SPEAKING FILMS: The Third
Degree 26. A Million Bid 27. The Desired
Woman 27. Good Time Charley 27. Tenderloin
28. *Noah's Ark* 28. Hearts in Exile 29. Glad Rag
Doll 29. The Madonna of Avenue A 29. The
Gamblers 29. *Mammy* 30. Under a Texas Moon
30. The Matrimonial Bed 30. Bright Lights 30. A
Soldier's Plaything 30. River's End 30. God's
Gift to Women 31. The Mad Genius 31. The
Woman from Monte Carlo 32. Alias the Doctor
32. The Strange Love of Molly Louvain 32.
Doctor X 32. Cabin in the Cotton 32. Twenty
Thousand Years in Sing Sing 33. *The Mystery of
the Wax Museum* 33. The Keyhole 33. Private
Detective 33. Goodbye Again 33. The Kennel
Murder Case 33. Female 33. Mandalay 34.
British Agent 34. Jimmy the Gent 34. The Key
34. *Black Fury* 35. The Case of the Curious
Bride 35. *Front Page Woman* 35. Little Big Shot
35. *Captain Blood* 35. The Walking Dead 36.
The Charge of the Light Brigade 36. Mountain
Justice 37. Stolen Holiday 36. Kid Galahad 37.
The Perfect Specimen 37. Gold is Where You
Find It 38. *The Adventures of Robin Hood* 38.
Four Daughters 38. Four's a Crowd 38. *Angels
with Dirty Faces* 38. Dodge City 39. Daughters
Courageous 39. Four Wives 39. Elizabeth and
Essex 39. Virginia City 40. *The Sea Hawk* 40.
Santa Fe Trail 41. Dive Bomber 41. *The Sea
Wolf* 41. Captains of the Clouds 42. *Yankee
Doodle Dandy* 42. *Casablanca* (AA) 42.
Mission to Moscow 43. This is the Army 43.
Passage to Marseilles 44. Janie 44. Roughly
Speaking 45. *Mildred Pierce* 45. Night and Day
46. Life with Father 47. The Unsuspected 47.
Romance on the High Seas 48. My Dream is
Yours 49. Flamingo Road 49. The Lady Takes a
Sailor 49. Young Man with a Horn 50. Bright
Leaf 50. The Breaking Point 51. Jim Thorpe—

All American 51. Force of Arms 51. I'll See You in My Dreams 52. The Story of Will Rogers 52. The Jazz Singer 53. Trouble Along the Way 53. The Boy from Oklahoma 54. The Egyptian 54. White Christmas 54. *Young at Heart* 55. We're No Angels 55. The Scarlet Hour 56. The Vagabond King 56. The Best Things in Life are Free 56. The Helen Morgan Story 57. The Proud Rebel 58. King Creole 58. The Hangman 59. The Man in the Net 59. The Adventures of Huckleberry Finn 60. A Breath of Scandal 60. Francis of Assisi 61. The Comancheros 62.

Curzon, George (1896–). British stage actor, in occasional films from early thirties, usually in aristocratic or sinister roles.
The Impassive Footman 32. Lorna Doone 35. *Young and Innocent* 37. Sexton Blake and the Hooded Terror 38. Uncle Silas 47. Harry Black 58, etc.

Cusack, Cyril (1910–). Diminutive Irish actor with fourteen years' Abbey Theatre experience. Film Debut as child in 1917.
Odd Man Out 47. The Blue Lagoon 48. The Elusive Pimpernel 49. The Blue Veil (US) 51. Soldiers Three (US) 51. The Man Who Never Was 56. *Jacqueline* 56. The Spanish Gardener 56. Ill Met by Moonlight 57. Floods of Fear 58. Shake Hands with the Devil 59. A Terrible Beauty 59. The Waltz of the Toreadors 62. Eighty Thousand Suspects 63. The Spy Who Came in from the Cold 65. I Was Happy Here 66. *Fahrenheit 451* 66. The Taming of the Shrew 67. Oedipus the King 67. Galileo (It.) 68. David Copperfield 69. King Lear 70. Harold and Maude (US) 71. The Day of the Jackal 73. The Homecoming 73, many others.

Cusack, Sinead (1949–). Irish leading lady, daughter of Cyril Cusack.
□ David Copperfield 60. Hoffman 70. Revenge 71.

Cushing, Peter (1913–). British character actor of stage, TV and screen. His slightly fussy manner at first confined him to mild roles, but since allying himself with the Hammer horror school he has dealt firmly with monsters of all kinds.
□ The Man in the Iron Mask (US) 39. A Chump at Oxford (US) 39. Vigil in the Night (US) 40. Laddie (US) 40. They Dare Not Love (US) 41. Women in War (US) 42. *Hamlet* (as Osric) 47. Moulin Rouge 53. The Black Knight 54. The End of the Affair 55. Magic Fire (US) 56. Time Without Pity 56. Alexander the Great 56. *The Curse of Frankenstein* 57. Violent Playground 57. The Abominable Snowman 57. *Dracula* 58.

The Revenge of Frankenstein 58. Suspect 59. The Hound of the Baskervilles 59. John Paul Jones (US) 59. The Mummy 59. Cone of Silence 60. Brides of Dracula 60. The Hellfire Club 61. Fury at Smugglers Bay 61. The Flesh and the Fiends 61. Sword of Sherwood Forest 61. The Naked Edge 61. Captain Clegg 62. *Cash on Demand* 63. The Man Who Finally Died 63. The Gorgon 64. Dr Terror's House of Horrors 65. She 65. Dr Who and the Daleks 65. Island of Terror 66. Daleks Invasion Earth 66. The Skull 66. Frankenstein Created Woman 67. The Blood Beast Terror 67. Some May Live (TV) 67. Night of the Big Heat 67. The Torture Garden 67. Corruption 68. Frankenstein Must Be Destroyed 69. Scream and Scream Again 69. The House that Dripped Blood 70. The Vampire Lovers 70. One More Time 70. I Monster 70. Twins of Evil 71. Incense for the Damned 71. Dracula AD 1972 72. Dr Phibes Rises Again 72. Nothing But the Night 72. *Tales from the Crypt* 72. The Creeping Flesh 73. Asylum 73. Fear in the Night 73. The Satanic Rites of Dracula 73. Frankenstein and the Monster from Hell 73. From Beyond the Grave 74. The Beast Must Die 74. Horror Express 74. The Legend of the Seven Golden Vampires 74. And Now the Screaming Starts 74. Madhouse 74. The Ghoul 75. Legend of the Werewolf 75. La Grande Trouille 75. Trial by Combat 76. The Uncanny 76. The Devil's Men 76.

custard pies as a comic weapon were evolved at the Keystone studio around 1915, and most silent comedians relied heavily on them. In the thirties Mack Sennett staged a splendid one for a nostalgic farce called *Keystone Hotel*. Other notable pie fighters have included Laurel and Hardy in *The Battle of the Century* 28; the whole cast of *Beach Party* 63; and most of the cast of *The Great Race* 64 and *Smashing Time* 65.

Custer, George Armstrong (1839–1876). American major-general whose romantic eccentricities and foolish death at Little Big Horn have been favourite screen fodder. The screen Custers include Dustin Farnum in *Flaming Frontier* 26, Frank McGlynn in *Custer's Last Stand* 36, Ronald Reagan in *Santa Fe Trail* 40, Addison Richards in *Badlands of Dakota* 41, Errol Flynn in the large-scale Custer biopic *They Died with Their Boots On* 41, James Millican in *Warpath* 51, Sheb Wooley in *Bugles in the Afternoon* 52, Britt Lomond in *Tonka* 58, Phil Carey in *The Great Sioux Massacre* 65, Robert Shaw in *Custer of the West* 67 and Richard Mulligan in *Little Big Man* 70. There has also been a TV series, *The Legend of Custer*, with Wayne Maunder.

cut. Noun: abrupt transition from one shot to another, the first being instantaneously replaced by the second (as opposed to a wipe or a dissolve). Verb: to edit a film, or (during production) to stop the camera running on a scene.

Cuthbertson, Allan (c. 1921–). Australian actor in Britain, adept at supercilious roles.
Carrington VC 55. Law and Disorder 57. *Room at the Top* 59. Tunes of Glory 60. Term of Trial 62. The Informers 63. The Seventh Dawn 64. Life at the Top 65. Press for Time 66, many others.

cutting copy. The first print assembled from the 'rushes'. When this is deemed satisfactory, the negative will be cut to match it, and release prints made.

Cutts, Graham (1885–1958). British director, eminent in silent days.
Flames of Passion 24. Woman to Woman 26. The Rat 27. The Sign of Four 32. Aren't Men Beasts? 37. Just William 39, etc.

Cutts, Patricia (1926–1974). British child actress and leading lady. Daughter of Graham Cutts.
Self Made Lady 31. Just William's Luck 49. Your Witness 50. The Man Who Loved Redheads 55. Merry Andrew 58. The Tingler (US) 58. Private Road 71, etc.

Cybulski, Zbigniew (1927–1967). Polish leading actor.
A Generation 54. *Ashes and Diamonds* 58. He, She or It (La Poupée) 62. To Love 64. Manuscript Found in Saragossa 65, etc.

cyclorama. A smooth, curved giant screen at the back of the set, cunningly lit to give the impression of daylight.

Cyrano de Bergerac. Edmond Rostand's nineteenth-century play about the mock-heroic cavalier with the romantic yearnings and the unfortunately long nose was filmed in Italy in 1909 and 1922, and in France in 1946. In 1950 came Stanley Kramer's American version, directed by Michael Gordon, starring Jose Ferrer (AA); a fair exam crib of the play, it was not much of a motion picture. In 1964 Abel Gance directed a French pastiche, *Cyrano et D'Artagnan*. Charles Laughton, incidentally, played a famous actor in *Because of Him* 45, and at one point was seen as Cyrano. The original Cyrano lived 1619–55 and was a French writer of comedies: whether he had a long nose is uncertain.

Czechoslovakian films were almost unknown in Western countries until recently, when the gentle realistic comedies of Milos Forman (*Peter and Pavla, A Blond in Love*) began winning festival prizes. Other notable Czech films of the last few years include Pavel Juráček's *Josef Kilian*, Jan Kádar and Elmar Klos's *The Shop on the High Street*, and Jan Nemec's *Diamonds of the Night* and Jiři Menzel's *Capricious Summer*.

Czinner, Paul (1890–1972). Hungarian producer-director, long in Britain: husband of Elisabeth Bergner. From 1955 he concentrated on films of opera and ballet, using multiple cameras.
Der Traumende Mund 32. Catherine the Great 33. Escape Me Never 35. As You Like It 36. Dreaming Lips 37. Stolen Life 39. The Bolshoi Ballet 55. The Royal Ballet 59. Der Rosenkavalier 61. Romeo and Juliet 66, etc.

D

DEFA (Deutsches Film Aktien Gesellschaft). The East German party line film production company which absorbed UFA in 1946.

Da Costa, Morton (1914–) (Morton Tecosky). American director of stage musicals and three films.
□ Auntie Mame 58. *The Music Man* 62. Island of Love 64.

Da Silva, Howard (1909–) (Harold Silverblatt). Tough, suspicious-looking American character actor with stage experience. Graduated from bit parts to a peak in the late forties, then had McCarthy trouble.
Abe Lincoln in Illinois 39. The Sea Wolf 41. The Big Shot 43. *The Lost Weekend* 45. The Blue Dahlia 46. Blaze of Noon 47. Unconquered 47. They Live by Night 48. The Great Gatsby 49. Three Husbands 50. Fourteen Hours 51. M 51. David and Lisa 62. The Outrage 65. Nevada Smith 66. '1776' 72. The Great Gatsby 74, etc.

Dade, Stephen (1909–). British cinematographer, in films from 1927.
We'll Meet Again 42. Caravan 46. The Brothers 47. Snowbound 49. A Question of Adultery 57. Bluebeard's Ten Honeymoons 60. Zulu 64. City under the Sea 65. The Viking Queen 66, many others.

Daddy Longlegs. Jean Webster's sentimental novel about a January–May romance against an orphanage setting was filmed in 1919 with Mary Pickford and Mahlon Hamilton; in 1930 with Janet Gaynor and Warner Baxter; in 1935, disguised as *Curly Top*, with Shirley Temple; and in 1955, as a musical, with Leslie Caron and Fred Astaire.

D'Agostino, Albert S. (1893–). American art director, in Hollywood from early silent days; with RKO 1936–58.
The Raven 35. Mr and Mrs Smith 41. The Enchanted Cottage 44. Notorious 46. The Woman on the Beach 47. Mourning Becomes Electra 48. Clash by Night 51. Androcles and the Lion 53. Back from Eternity 56, many others.

Dagover, Lil (1897–) (Marta Maria Liletts). German actress.
The Cabinet of Dr Caligari 19. Chronicles of the Grey House 24. Hungarian Rhapsody 27. The White Devil 30. Congress Dances 31. Kreuzer Sonata 35. Fredericus 39. Karl May 74, etc.

Daguerre, Louis (1787–1851). French pioneer of photography; his original copper-plated prints were known as *daguerrotypes*.

Dahl, Arlene (1924–). Red-haired American leading lady, former model; also beauty columnist.
My Wild Irish Rose 47. A Southern Yankee 48. The Black Book 49. Ambush 50. Three Little Words 50. Inside Straight 51. Sangaree 53. *Woman's World* 54. Slightly Scarlet 56. Wicked as they Come (GB) 56. *Journey to the Centre of the Earth* 59. Kisses for my President 64. The Land Raiders 70, etc.

Dahl, Roald (1916–). Norwegian writer of British adoption; switches from children's books to macabre short stories.
Chitty Chitty Bang Bang (& oa) 69. You Only Live Twice 69. Willy Wonka and the Chocolate Factory 70, etc.

Dahlbeck, Eva (1921–). Swedish actress, often in Ingmar Bergman's films.
Waiting Women 52. The Village (GB) 53. Smiles of a Summer Night 55. So Close to Life 61. Now About These Women 64. Loving Couples 64. Les Creatures 65. The Red Mantle 67. People Meet 69, etc.

Dailey, Dan (1914–). Lanky American actor-dancer with wide experience in vaudeville and cabaret.
The Mortal Storm 40. Dulcy 40. Ziegfeld Girl 41. Moon over Her Shoulder 41. Lady Be Good 41. Panama Hattie 42. Give Out Sisters 42. *Mother Wore Tights* 47. *Give My Regards to Broadway* 48. You Were Meant for Me 48. When My Baby Smiles at Me 48. Chicken Every Sunday 49. My Blue Heaven 50. *When Willie*

Comes Marching Home 50. A Ticket to Tomahawk 50. I Can Get It for You Wholesale 51. Call Me Mister 51. Pride of St Louis 51. What Price Glory? 52. Meet Me at The Fair 53. There's No Business Like Show Business 54. *It's Always Fair Weather* 55. Meet Me in Las Vegas 56. *The Best Things in Life are Free* 56. The Wings of Eagles 56. Oh Men, Oh Women 57. The Wayward Bus 57. Pepe 60. Hemingway's Adventures of a Young Man 62, others.
TV series: The Four Just Men 59. The Governor and J.J. 69. Faraday and Company 73.

dailies: see *rushes*.

Dainton, Patricia (1930–). British leading lady who started as a teenager.
Don't Ever Leave Me 49. The Dancing Years 50. Castle in the Air 52. Operation Diplomat 54. The Passing Stranger 57. Witness in the Dark 60, etc.

Dalby, Amy (c. 1888–1969). British character actress who normally on screen played ageing spinsters.
The Wicked Lady 45. The Man Upstairs 57. The Lamp in Assassin Mews 62. *The Secret of My Success* 65. Who Killed the Cat? 66. The Spy with a Cold Nose 67, etc.

Dale, Charles (1881–1971) (Charles Marks). American vaudevillian who, with Joe Smith (qv), made up Smith and Dale, the inspiration for *The Sunshine Boys*.
□ Manhattan Parade 31. The Heart of New York 32. Two Tickets to Broadway 51.

Dale, Esther (1886–1961). American character actress usually a motherly soul, nurse or grandma.
Crime without Passion 34. Curly Top 35. Fury 36. Dead End 37. Prison Farm 38. Tell No Tales 39. The Mortal Storm 40. Back Street 41. North Star 43. Stolen Life 46. The Egg and I 47. Ma and Pa Kettle 49. No Man of Her Own 50. Ma and Pa Kettle at the Fair 52. The Oklahoman 57, many others.

Dale, Jim (1935–). British pop singer turned light comedian and member of the 'Carry On' team.
Raising the Wind 62. Carry On Spying 64. Carry on Cleo 65. The Big Job 65. Carry On Cowboy 66. Carry On Screaming 66. Lock Up Your Daughters 69. *The National Health* 73. Digby 73, etc.

Daley, Cass (1915–1975) (Catherine Dailey). American comedienne whose shouted songs and acrobatic contortions were a feature of several light musicals of the forties.
The Fleet's In 41. Star Spangled Rhythm 42. Crazy House 43. Out of This World 45. Ladies' Man 46. Here Comes the Groom 51. Red Garters 54. The Spirit Is Willing 67, etc.

Dali, Salvador (1904–). Spanish surrealist painter who collaborated with Luis Buñuel in making two controversial films: *Un Chien Andalou* 29 and *L'Age D'Or* 30. Later designed the dream sequence for *Spellbound* 45.

Dalio, Marcel (1900–). Dapper French comedy actor, frequently in Hollywood.
La Grande Illusion 37. Pepe le Moko 37. *La Règle du Jeu* 39. Unholy Partners 41. Casablanca 42. The Song of Bernadette 43. Temptation Harbour (GB) 46. On the Riviera 51. *The Happy Time* 52. The Snows of Kilimanjaro 52. Lucky Me 54. Sabrina Fair 54. Miracle in the Rain 56. Pillow Talk 59. Can Can 59. Jessica 62. Wild and Wonderful 63. Lady L 65. The 25th Hour 67. How Sweet It Is 68. Catch 22 70, many others.

Dall, Evelyn (c. 1914–). American nightclub singer who appeared in some British film extravaganzas of the forties.
He Found a Star 41. King Arthur Was a Gentleman 42. Miss London Ltd 43. Time Flies 44, etc.

Dall, John (1918–1971). American stage leading man; played in occasional films.
□ For the Love of Mary 45. *The Corn is Green* 46. Something in the Wind 47. *Rope* 48. Another Part of the Forest 48. Gun Crazy 49. The Man Who Cheated Himself 50. Spartacus 60. Atlantis the Lost Continent 61.

Dallesandro, Joe (1948–). American actor associated with 'underground' films.
Heat 72. Warhol's Frankenstein 74. Warhol's Dracula 74.

Dalrymple, Ian (1903–). British writer-producer.
South Riding (w only) 38. The Citadel (w only) 38. The Lion Has Wings 39. Once a Jolly Swagman 46. The Woman in the Hall 48. The Wooden Horse 50. The Heart of the Matter 52. Three Cases of Murder 55. The Admirable Crichton 57. A Cry from the Streets 58, etc.

Dalton, Audrey (1934–). British leading lady in Hollywood.
My Cousin Rachel 52. The Girls of Pleasure Island 53. Titanic 53. Casanova's Big Night 54. The Prodigal 55. Separate Tables 58. Mr

Sardonicus 61. The Bounty Killer 65, etc.

Dalton, Dorothy (1894–1972). American silent screen leading lady with stage experience.
The Disciple 14. Black is White 20. Moran of the Lady Letty 22. The Crimson Challenge 22. Fogbound 23. The Moral Sinner 24. The Lone Wolf 24, etc.

Dalton, Timothy (1944–). Saturnine British stage actor in occasional films.
The Lion in Winter 68. *Wuthering Heights* 70. Mary Queen of Scots 71. Lady Caroline Lamb 72, etc.

Daltrey, Roger (–). British pop singer given dramatic roles by Ken Russell.
□ Tommy 74. Lisztomania 75.

Daly, James (1918–). American stage actor; film appearances rare.
□ The Court Martial of Billy Mitchell 55. The Young Stranger 57. I Aim at the Stars 60. Planet of the Apes 68. The Big Bounce 68. The Five Man Army 69. Wild in the Sky 72.
TV series: *Medical Center* 69– .

Daly, Mark (1887–1957). British character actor, on stage from 1906, screen from 1930 often as cheerful tramp.
The Private Life of Henry VIII 32. A Cuckoo in the Nest 33. The Ghost Goes West 36. Wings of the Morning 37. Next of Kin 42. Bonnie Prince Charlie 49. Lease of Life 54. The Shiralee 57, many others.

Damaged Goods. Eugene Brieux's propaganda play about venereal disease has been popular 'under the counter' fare since it was written in 1903. The chief film versions were in 1919 (British), 1937 (American) and 1961 (American).

Les Dames du Bois de Boulogne (France 1944). Robert Bresson's cold, talky film has over the years become something of a cult. It updates a story by Diderot about a jealous woman's revenge on her lover; but its style is so refined and thin as to be almost the antithesis of cinema. Maria Casares has a splendid stab at the leading role.

Damiani, Damiano (1922–). Italian director.
The Empty Canvas 64. A Bullet for the General 66. Confessions of a Police Captain 71. The Tempter 74. The Genius 75, etc.

Damita, Lili (1901–) (Lilliane Carré). French leading lady who made a few American films and

married Errol Flynn.
The Rescue 28. The Bridge of San Luis Rey 29. The Cockeyed World 29. The Match King 31. This Is the Night 32. Goldie Gets Along 33. The Frisco Kid 35. L'Escadrille de la Chance (Fr.) 36, etc.

The Damned. Films under this title include: 1. René Clement's 1949 melodrama of submarines in the Atlantic during World War II. 2. Joseph Losey's 1964 sceince-fiction extravaganza about other-worldly children kept in a scientific dugout in the Dorset cliffs. 3. Luchino Visconti's 1969 account of a German armaments family under the Nazis.

Damon, Mark (1935–). American leading man in routine films.
Between Heaven and Hell 56. The Fall of the House of Usher 60. The Young Racers 63. Anzio 68, etc.

Damon, Stuart (1937–) (Stuart M. Zonis). American stage and TV leading man.
TV series: The Champions 68.

Damone, Vic (1929–) (Vito Farinola). American light leading man and dancer.
Rich, Young and Pretty 51. The Strip 51. Athena 53. Deep in My Heart 55. Kismet 55. Hell to Eternity 60, etc.

Dampier, Claude (1885–1955) (Claude Cowan). British comedian noted for nasal drawl and country yokel characterization. Long on stage and music hall.
Boys Will Be Boys 35. Mr Stringfellow Says No 37. Riding High 39. Don't Take It to Heart 44. Meet Mr Malcolm 53, etc.

Dana, Leora (1923–). American general purpose actress.
Three-Ten to Yuma 57. Kings Go Forth 58. Some Came Running 58. Pollyanna 60. A Gathering of Eagles 63, etc.

Dana, Viola (1897–) (Violet Flugrath). American silent screen actress, usually in light comedy and fashionable drama.
Molly the Drummer Boy 14. Rosie O'Grady 17. A Chorus Girl's Romance 20. The Willow Tree 20. Open All Night 24. Merton of the Movies 24. Winds of Chance 25. Kosher Kitty Kelly 26. The Sisters 29, etc.

dance bands in the thirties and forties were so popular as to be stars in their own films: Henry Hall's in *Music Hath Charms*, Kay Kyser's in half a dozen films including *That's Right You're*

Wrong, Paul Whiteman's in *King of Jazz*, Tommy and Jimmy Dorsey's in *The Fabulous Dorseys*. Also frequently on hand to assist the stars were the bands of Glenn Miller, Xavier Cugat, Woody Herman and Harry James, to name but a few. In the fifties bands became too expensive to maintain, but *The Glenn Miller Story* and *The Benny Goodman Story* reawakened interest, and Louis Armstrong kept the flag flying till the day he died. The seventies brought signs of a revival of interest in the big bands, in such movies as *W. W. and the Dixie Dancekings*.

Dandridge, Dorothy (1923–1965). Black American leading lady, former child actress.
A Day at the Races 37. Lady from Louisiana 41. Drums of the Congo 42. Bright Road 52. *Carmen Jones* 54. Island in the Sun 57. The Decks Ran Red 58. Porgy and Bess 59. Tamango 59. Moment of Danger 60, etc.

Dane, Karl (1886–1934) (Karl Daen). Lanky Danish character actor who almost accidentally became a popular comedian at the end of the silent period, but could not survive sound.
Lights of Old Broadway 25. *The Big Parade* 25. The Scarlet Letter 26. The Red Mill 27. *Rookies* 27. Baby Mine 28. Circus Rookies 28. Alias Jimmy Valentine 28. Speedway 29. Montana Moon 30. The Big House 30. Billy the Kid 30, etc.

Daneman, Paul (1930–). British light leading man, mainly on stage.
The Clue of the New Pin 61. Zulu 63. How I Won the War 67. Oh What a Lovely War 69, etc.
TV series: Spy Trap.

Dangerous Moonlight (GB 1940). The film which featured Richard Adinsell's 'Warsaw Concerto' and by its success started the crop of concerto movies which finally proved so tiresome in the forties. Basically a romantic melodrama of the Polish Air Force, with Anton Walbrook and Sally Gray; directed by Brian Desmond Hurst.

Daniell, Henry (1894–1963). Incisive, cold-eyed British stage actor, a popular Hollywood villain of the thirties and forties.
Jealousy 29. The Unguarded Hour 30. *Camille* 36. The Thirteenth Chair 37. Madame X 37. Marie Antoinette 38. We are Not Alone 39. *The Sea Hawk* 40. *The Philadelphia Story* 40. The Feminine Touch 41. Sherlock Holmes in Washington 42. Watch on the Rhine 43. Jane Eyre 44. *The Suspect* 45. Hotel Berlin 45. *The*

Body Snatcher 45. The Woman in Green 45. The Bandit of Sherwood Forest 46. Song of Love 47. The Exile 47. Wake of the Red Witch 48. Buccaneer's Girl 50. The Egyptian 54. *The Man in the Grey Flannel Suit* 56. Les Girls 57. Witness for the Prosecution 58. Madison Avenue 62. The Chapman Report 62. My Fair Lady 64, etc.

Daniels, Bebe (1901–1971) (Virginia Daniels). American leading lady of the silent screen. Film debut at seven; played opposite Harold Lloyd and became a popular star; later married Ben Lyon, moved to Britain and appeared with their family on radio and TV.
Male and Female 19. Why Change Your Wife? 20. The Affairs of Anatol 21. Pink Gods 22. Unguarded Women 24. Monsieur Beaucaire 24. Campus Flirt 26. She's a Sheik 27. Rio Rita 29. Alias French Gertie 30. Reaching for the Moon 30. The Maltese Falcon 31. Forty-Second Street 33. Counsellor at Law 33. The Return of Carol Deane 35. Hi Gang (GB) 40. Life with the Lyons (GB) 53. The Lyons in Paris (GB) 55, etc.

Daniels, William (1895–1970). Distinguished American cinematographer.
□ Foolish Wives 21. Merry Go Round (co-ph) 23. Helen's Babies (co-ph) 24. *Greed* (co-ph) 25. Women and Gold 25. The Merry Widow (co-ph) 25. Bardelys the Magnificent 26. The Boob 26. Dance Madness (co-ph) 26. *Flesh and the Devil* 26. Money Talks 26. Monte Carlo 26. The Temptress (co-ph) 26. The Torrent 26. Altars of Desire 27. Captain Salvation 27. Love 27. On Ze Boulevard 27. Tillie the Toiler 27. The Actress 28. Bringing Up Father 28. Dream of Love 28. Lady of Chance 28. The Latest from Paris 28. The Mysterious Lady 28. Sally's Shoulders 28. A Woman of Affairs 28. *The Kiss* 29. The Last of Mrs Cheyney 29. Their Own Desire 29. The Trial of Mary Dugan 29. Wild Orchids 29. Wise Girls 29. Anna Christie 30. Montana Moon 30. Romance 30. Strictly Unconventional 30. Strangers May Kiss 31. The Great Meadow 31. Inspiration 31. A Free Soul 31. Susan Lenox 31. *Mata Hari* 32. Lovers Courageous 32. Grand Hotel 32. As You Desire Me 32. Skyscraper Souls 32. Rasputin and the Empress 33. The White Sister 33. Dinner at Eight 33. The Stranger's Return 33. Broadway to Hollywood 33. Christopher Bean 33. *Queen Christina* 33. The Barretts of Wimpole Street 34. The Painted Veil 34. Naughty Marietta 35. *Anna Karenina* 35. Rendezvous 35. Rose Marie 36. Romeo and Juliet 36. *Camille* 36. Personal Property 37. Broadway Melody of 1938 37. Double Wedding 37. The Last Gangster 37. Beg Borrow or Steal 37. Marie Antoinette 38. Three Loves Has

Nancy 38. Dramatic School 38. Idiot's Delight 39. Stronger Than Desire 39. Ninotchka 39. Another Thin Man 39. The Shop Around the Corner 40. The Mortal Storm 40. New Moon 40. So Ends Our Night 41. Back Street 41. They Met in Bombay 41. Shadow of the Thin Man 41. Dr Kildare's Victory 41. *Keeper of the Flame* 42. Girl Crazy 42. Brute Force 47. Lured 47. *The Naked City* (AA) 48. For the Love of Mary 48. Family Honeymoon 48. The Life of Riley 49. Illegal Entry 49. Abandoned 49. The Gal who Took the West 49. Woman in Hiding 49. Winchester 73 50. Harvey 50. Deported 50. Thunder on the Hill 51. Bright Victory 51. The Lady Pays Off 51. When in Rome 52. Pat and Mike 52. Glory Alley 52. Plymouth Adventure 52. Never Wave at a WAC 53. Forbidden 53. Thunder Bay 53. *The Glenn Miller Story* 53. War Arrow 54. The Far Country 54. Six Bridges to Cross 55. Foxfire 55. The Shrike 55. Strategic Air Command 55. The Girl Rush 55. The Benny Goodman Story 55. Away All Boats (co-ph) 56. The Unguarded Moment 56. Istanbul 56. Night Passage 57. Interlude 57. My Man Godfrey 57. Voice in the Mirror 57. Cat on a Hot Tin Roof 58. Some Came Running 59. Stranger in My Arms 59. A Hole in the Head 60. Never So Few 60. Can Can 60. Ocean's Eleven 60. All the Fine Young Cannibals 60. Come September 61. Jumbo 62. How the West was Won (co-ph) 63. Come Blow Your Horn 63. The Prize 63. Robin and the Seven Hoods (& p) 64. Von Ryan's Express 65. Marriage on the Rocks 65. Assault on a Queen (& p) 66. In Like Flint 67. Valley of the Dolls 67. The Impossible Years 68. Marlowe 68. The Maltese Bippy 69. Move 70.

Daniels, William (1927–). American stage actor in occasional films.
1776 72. The Parallax View 74.

Daniely, Lisa (1930–). Anglo-French leading lady.
Lili Marlene 50. Hindle Wakes 51. The Wedding of Lili Marlene 53. Tiger by the Tail 55. The Vicious Circle 57. An Honourable Murder 60. The Lamp in Assassin Mews 62, etc.

Danischewsky, Monja (1911–). Russian writer-producer, in Britain since twenties. Publicist and writer for Ealing 1938–48. Produced *Whisky Galore* 48. *The Galloping Major* 50. *The Battle of the Sexes* 61, etc. Screenplays, *Topkapi* 64. *Mister Moses* 65. Autobiography 1966: *White Russian, Red Face.*

Danish cinema was one of the first to start production. Nordisk studios were founded in 1906 and from 1910 to 1915 Danish films were as internationally popular as those of any country in the world. But the talent was all drained away, first by the merger with Germany's UFA studios in 1917 and later by a steady trek to Hollywood. Carl Dreyer, one of the wanderers, later returned to Denmark and made there such major films as *Day of Wrath* and *Ordet*; but no Danish school ever emerged again.

Dankworth, Johnny (1927–). British bandleader who has written scores.
The Criminal 60. Saturday Night and Sunday Morning 60. The Servant 64. Return from the Ashes 65. Accident 67. The Last Grenade 69. Ten Rillington Place 70.

Danner, Blythe (–). American young actress of the seventies.
□ 1776 72. To Kill a Clown 72. Lovin' Molly 74. Hearts of the West 75.

Dano, Royal (1922–). American general purpose supporting actor.
The Red Badge of Courage 51. Cahill 73, etc.

Danova, Cesare (1926–). Italian leading man, often in Hollywood.
The Captain's Son 47. The Three Corsairs 52. Don Juan 55. The Man Who Understood Women 59. Cleopatra 63. Viva Las Vegas 64. Chamber of Horrors 66. Che 69, etc.

Dante, Michael (1931–) (Ralph Vitti). American 'second lead' with a screen tendency to villainy.
Fort Dobbs 58. Westbound 59. Seven Thieves 60. Kid Galahad 62. The Naked Kiss 64. Harlow 65, etc.

Dantine, Helmut (1918–). Lean good-looking Austrian actor, in US from 1938. Latterly an executive with the Joseph M. Schenk organization.
International Squadron 41. *Mrs Miniver* 41. Passage to Marseilles 44. Hotel Berlin 45. Escape in the Desert 45. Northern Pursuit 45. Shadow of a Woman 46. Whispering City 48. Call Me Madam 53. Stranger from Venus (GB) 54. War and Peace 56. Fraulein 57. Thundering Jets (d only) 58. Operation Crossbow 65. Garcia 74, etc.

Danton, Ray (1931–). Tall, dark American leading man with radio experience.
Chief Crazy Horse 52. The Spoilers 55. I'll Cry Tomorrow 55. *Too Much Too Soon* 58. *The Rise and Fall of Legs Diamond* 59. Ice Palace 60. A Fever in the Blood 61. *The George Raft Story* 61.

The Chapman Report 62. The Longest Day 62. Sandokan the Great (It.) 63. Tiger of Terror (It.) 64. The Spy Who Went into Hell (Ger.) 65. The Deathmaster (d only) 72. The Centrefold Girls 74, etc.

D'Antoni, Philip (1929–). American producer for cinema and TV.
The French Connection 71. The Connection (TV) 73. Mr Inside Mr Outside (TV) 73. The Seven-Ups (& d) 74.

The Danziger Brothers (Edward and Harry). American producers who after making *Jigsaw* 46, and two or three other films came to England, set up New Elstree Studios and spent fifteen years producing hundreds of second features and TV episodes, hardly any worth recalling.

Darby, Kim (1947–) (Deborah Zenby). American leading lady.
Bus Riley's Back in Town 65. A Time for Living 69. *True Grit* 69. Norwood 69. The Grissom Gang 71. Rich Man Poor Man (TV) 76, etc.

Darc, Mireille (1940–). French leading lady.
Tonton Flingueurs 64. Galia 65. Du Rififi à Paname 66. Weekend 67. Jeff 68. Blonde from Peking 68. There was Once a Cop 72.

Darcel, Denise (1925–) (Denise Billecard). French leading lady, in Hollywood from 1947.
To the Victor 48. Battleground 49. Tarzan and the Slave Girl 50. Westward the Women 51. Dangerous When Wet 53. Flame of Calcutta 53. Vera Cruz 54. Seven Women from Hell 62, etc.

D'Arcy, Alex (1908–) (Alexander Sarruf). Egyptian light actor who has appeared in films of many nations.
Champagne 28. A Nous la Liberté 31. La Kermesse Héroique 35. The Prisoner of Zenda 37. Fifth Avenue Girl 39. Marriage Is a Private Affair 44. How to Marry a Millionaire 53. Soldier of Fortune 56. Way Way Out 66. The St Valentine's Day Massacre 67. Blood of Dracula's Castle (as Dracula) 69. The Seven Minutes 71, etc.

Darden, Severn (1937–). American comedy character actor.
Dead Heat on a Merry Go Round 67. The President's Analyst 67. Luv 68. Pussycat Pussycat I Love You 70. Vanishing Point 71. The Hired Hand 71. Cisco Pike 71. The War Between Men and Women 72. Who Fears the Devil 74, etc.

Darin, Bobby (1936–1974) (Walden Robert Cassotto). American pop singer who alternated lightweight appearances with more serious roles.
Come September 60. Pepe 60. Too Late Blues 61. *Pressure Point* 62. That Funny Feeling 65. Gunfight at Abilene 67. Stranger in the House 67. The Happy Ending 69, etc.

The Dark Angel. Guy Bolton's melodramatic play about a romantic triangle and war blindness was filmed by George Fitzmaurice in 1925, with Ronald Colman, Vilma Banky and Wyndham Standing; Sidney Franklin remade it in 1935 with Fredric March, Merle Oberon and Herbert Marshall.

Dark Victory (US 1939). Romantic drama which began a trend towards unhappy endings: Bette Davis played a socialite dying of a brain tumour. Directed by Edmund Goulding. Remade 1963 as *Stolen Hours*, with Susan Hayward; but the time was past and it did not appeal.

Darling (GB 1965). A scathing but ultimately pointless attack on some worthless members of the affluent society, in particular a selfish girl who gets through men at a rate of knots and leaves despair in her wake. John Schlesinger's direction kept it interesting in a repellent way, but it has already dated alarmingly. With Julie Christie (AA, BFA), Dirk Bogarde (BFA); from a script by Frederic Raphael (AA, BFA); art direction by Ray Simm (BFA).

Darnborough, Anthony (1913–). British producer.
The Calendar 47. Quartet 48. The Astonished Heart 50. The Net 52. To Paris with Love 55. The Baby and the Battleship 56, etc.

Darnell, Linda (1921–1965) (Manetta Eloisa Darnell). Wide-eyed American leading lady of the forties.
□ Hotel for Women 39. Daytime Wife 39. Stardust 40. Brigham Young 40. The Mark of Zorro 40. Chad Hanna 40. Blood and Sand 41. Rise and Shine 41. The Loves of Edgar Allan Poe 42. The Song of Bernadette (as the Virgin Mary) 43. Buffalo Bill 44. *It Happened Tomorrow* 44. Summer Storm 44. Sweet and Lowdown 44. The Great John L 45. Fallen Angel 45. Hangover Square 45. Anna and the King of Siam 46. Centennial Summer 46. My Darling Clementine 46. Forever Amber 47. The Walls of Jericho 48. Unfaithfully Yours 48. A Letter to Three Wives 48. Slattery's Hurricane 49. Everybody Does It 49. No Way Out 50. The Thirteenth Letter 51. The Lady Pays Off 51. The Guy Who Came Back 51. Saturday Island 52.

Night Without Sleep 52. Blackbeard the Pirate 52. Second Chance 53. This Is My Love 54. Forbidden Women (It.) 55. The Last Five Minutes (It.) 56. Dakota Incident 56. Zero Hour 57. Black Spurs 65.

D'Arrast, Harry D'Abbadie (18**–1968). American director of the twenties, with a reputation for style.
Service for Ladies 27. A Gentleman of Paris 27. Serenade 27. The Magnificent Flirt 28. Dry Martini 28. *Raffles* 30. *Laughter* (& w) 30. Topaze 33, etc.

Darren, James (1936–) (James Ercolani). American leading man whose appeal seems to have waned with maturity.
Rumble on the Docks 56. Operation Mad Ball 57. Gidget 59. Let No Man Write My Epitaph 60. *The Guns of Navarone* 61. Diamondhead 63. For Those Who Think Young 64, etc.
TV series: Time Tunnel 66.

Darrieux, Danielle (1917–). Vivacious French leading lady, in films since 1931.
Le Bal 32. *Mayerling* 36. *The Rage of Paris* (US) 38. *Battement de Coeur* 39. Premier Rendezvous 44. *Occupe-Toi d'Amélie* 49. La Ronde 50. Le Plaisir 51. Rich, Young and Pretty (US) 51. Five Fingers (US) 52. Adorables Créatures 52. *Madame De* 53. Alexander the Great (US) 55. Le Rouge et le Noir 57. Marie Octobre 58. Lady Chatterley's Lover 59. Murder at 45 RPM 61. The Greengage Summer (GB) 61. Landru 63. L'Or du Duc 65. Le Dimanche de la Vie 66. The Young Girls of Rochefort 67. L'Homme à la Buick 67. Birds in Peru 68, many others.

Darro, Frankie (1917–) (Frank Johnson). Tough-looking little American actor, former child and teenage player; star of many second features.
So Big 24. The Cowboy Cop 26. Long Pants 27. The Circus Kid 28. The Mad Genius 31. Wild Boys of the Road 33. Broadway Bill 34. Charlie Chan at the Race Track 36. Racing Blood 37. Chasing Trouble 39. Laughing at Danger 40. Freddie Steps Out 45. Heart of Virginia 48. Across the Wide Missouri 51. Operation Petticoat 59, many others.

Darrow, Clarence (1857–1938). Celebrated American defence lawyer, impersonated by Orson Welles in *Compulsion* 58, and by Spencer Tracy in *Inherit the Wind* 60.

Darvi, Bella (1927–1971) (Bayla Wegier). Polish-French leading lady, in a few Hollywood films after being discovered by Darryl Zanuck.

☐ Hell and High Water 54. The Egyptian 54. The Racers 55. Je Suis Un Sentimental 55. Sinners of Paris 59. Lipstick 65.

Darwell, Jane (1880–1967) (Patti Woodward). American character actress, usually in warm-hearted motherly roles.
Rose of the Rancho 14. Brewster's Millions 20. Tom Sawyer 30. Back Street 32. Design for Living 34. Life Begins at Forty 35. Captain January 36. Slave Ship 37. Three Blind Mice 38. Jesse James 39. The Rains Came 39. Gone with the Wind 39 *The Grapes of Wrath* (AA: as the indomitable Ma Joad) 40. *All That Money Can Buy* 41. Private Nurse 41. The Ox Bow Incident 43. The Impatient Years 44. *Captain Tugboat Annie* (title role) 46. My Darling Clementine 46. Three Godfathers 48. Wagonmaster 50. Caged 50. The Lemon Drop Kid 51. Fourteen Hours 51. We're Not Married 52. The Sun Shines Bright 52. Hit the Deck 55. The Last Hurrah 58. Mary Poppins 64, many others.

Dassin, Jules (1911–). American director, former radio writer and actor. Joined MGM 1941 to direct shorts (including a two-reel version of *The Tell-Tale Heart*); moved to features; left for Europe during the McCarthy witch hunt of the late forties.
☐ Nazi Agent 42. The Affairs of Martha 42. Reunion in France 42. Young Ideas 43. The Canterville Ghost 44. A Letter for Evie 44. Two Smart People 46. *Brute Force* 47. *Naked City* 48. *Thieves' Highway* 49. Night and the City (GB) 50. *Rififi* (also acted, as Perlo Vita) 54. He Who Must Die 56. Where the Hot Wind Blows 58. *Never on Sunday* (also acted) 60. Phaedra 62. Topkapi 64. 10.30 p.m. Summer 66. Survival 68. Uptight 68. Promise at Dawn 70.

Daugherty, Herschel (–). American director, from TV.
The Light in the Forest 58. The Raiders 63, etc.

Dauphin, Claude (1903–) (Claude Franc-Nohain). Dapper French actor of stage and screen: in films from 1930.
Entrée des Artistes 38. Battement de Coeur 39. Les Deux Timides 42. English Without Tears (GB) 50. Le Plaisir 51. Casque d'Or 52. Little Boy Lost (US) 53. Innocents in Paris (GB) 54. Phantom of the Rue Morgue (US) 54. The Quiet American (US) 58. The Full Treatment 60. Lady L 65. Two for the Road 67. Hard Contract 69. Rosebud 75, many others.

Davenport, Doris (1915–). American leading lady whose only known role was *The

Westerner 40.

Davenport, Harry (1886–1949). American character actor; long stage career, then in Hollywood as chucklesome, benevolent old man. ☐ Her Unborn Child 30. My Sin 31. His Woman 32. Get That Venus 33. Three Cheers for Love 34. The Scoundrel 35. Three Men on a Horse 36. The Case of the Black Cat 36. King of Hockey 36. Fly Away Baby 36. The Life of Emile Zola 37. Under Cover of Night 37. Her Husband's Secretary 37. White Bondage 37. They Wont Forget 37. Mr Dodd Takes the Air 37. First Lady 37. The Perfect Specimen 37. Paradise Express 37. As Good as Married. 37. Armored Car 37. Wells Fargo 37. Fit for a King 37. Gold is Where You Find It 38. Saleslady 38. The Sisters 38. The Long Shot 38. The First Hundred Years 38. The Cowboy and the Lady 38. Reckless Living 38. The Rage of Paris 38. Tailspin 38. Young Fugitives 38. *You Cant Take It With You* 38. The Higgins Family 38. Orphans of the Street 38. Made for Each Other 39. My Wife's Relatives 39. Should Husbands Work 39. The Covered Trailer 39. Money to Burn 39. Exile Express 39. Death of a Champion 39. The Story of Alexander Graham Bell 39. Juarez 39. Gone with the Wind 39. *The Hunchback of Notre Dame* 39. Dr Ehrlich's Magic Bullet 40. Granny Get Your Gun 40. Too Many Husbands 40. Grandpa Goes to Town 40. Lucky Partners 40. I Want a Divorce 40. All This and Heaven Too 40. Foreign Correspondent 40. That Uncertain Feeling 41. I Wanted Wings 41. Hurricane Smith 41. The Bride Came COD 41. One Foot in Heaven 41. Kings Row 41. *Son of Fury* 42. Larceny Inc 42. Ten Gentlemen from West Point 42. Tales of Manhattan 42. Heading for God's Country 43. We've Never Been Licked 42. Riding High 43. *The Ox Bow Incident* 43. The Amazing Mrs Holliday 43. Gangway for Tomorrow 43. Government Girl 43. Jack London 43. Princess O'Rourke 43. *Meet Me In St Louis* 44. The Impatient Years 44. The Thin Man Goes Home 44. Kismet 44. Music for Millions 45. *The Enchanted Forest* 45. Too Young to Know 45. This Love of Ours 45. She Wouldn't Say Yes 45. Courage of Lassie 46. Blue Sierra 46. A Boy a Girl and a Dog 46. Faithful in My Fashion 46. Three Wise Fools 46. War Brides 46. Lady Luck 46. Claudia and David 46. Pardon My Past 46. Adventure 46. The Farmer's Daughter 47. That Hagen Girl 47. Stallion Road 47. Keeper of the Bees 47. Sport of Kings 47. The Fabulous Texan 47. *The Bachelor and the Bobbysoxer* 47. Three Daring Daughters 48. The Man from Texas 48. For the Love of Mary 48. That Lady in Ermine 48. The Decision of Christopher Blake 48. Down to the Sea in Ships 49. Little Women 49. Tell It To the Judge 49. *That Forsyte Woman* 49. Rising High 50.

Davenport, Nigel (1928–). Breezy, virile British actor, much on TV.
Peeping Tom 59. In the Cool of the Day 63. A High Wind in Jamaica 65. Sands of the Kalahari 65. Where the Spies Are 66. *A Man for All Seasons* 67. Red and Blue 67. Play Dirty 68. Sinful Davey 69. *The Virgin Soldiers* 69. The Royal Hunt of the Sun 69. No Blade of Grass 71. Villain 71. *Living Free* 72. Mary Queen of Scots 72. Dracula (TV) (as Van Helsing) 73. Phase IV 73, etc.

Daves, Delmer (1904–). American writer-producer-director with highly miscellaneous experience. Writer with MGM from 1933, writer-director with Warners from 1943.
Destination Tokyo (w, d) 43. The Red House (w, d) 47. *Dark Passage* (wd) 47. Broken Arrow (d) 50. Bird of Paradise (wd) 51. Never Let Me Go (d) 53. Demetrius and the Gladiators (d) 54. Jubal (wd) 56. The Last Wagon (wd) 56. *3.10 to Yuma* (d) 57. Cowboy (wd) 58. The Hanging Tree (d) 59. Parrish (wd) 61. Spencer's Mountain (wpd) 62. Youngblood Hawke (wd) 64. The Battle of the Villa Fiorita (wpd) 65, many others.

David Copperfield (US 1934). Probably the most successful and satisfactory 'Hollywood classic', an impeccable costume narrative, richly acted, with the true Dickens flavour. George Cukor directed; Hugh Walpole worked on the screenplay (and played the vicar). Cast included W. C. Fields (Micawber), Freddie Bartholomew (young David), Frank Lawton (David as a man), Edna May Oliver (Aunt Betsy), Basil Rathbone (Mr Murdstone), Roland Young (Uriah Heep), Lionel Barrymore (Dan Peggotty), Jessie Ralph (Nurse Peggotty), etc. The 1969 all-star remake was intended for TV in the States, theatres elsewhere; despite interesting performances, it lacked narrative grip.

David, Saul (1921–). American producer.
Von Ryan's Express 65. Our Man Flint 67. Fantastic Voyage 67. Skullduggery 69. The Black Bird 75. Logan's Run 76.

Davies, Betty Ann (1910–1955). British stage actress, usually in tense roles; occasional films from early thirties.
Chick 34. Kipps 41. It Always Rains on Sunday 47. The History of Mr Polly 49. *Trio* 50. Cosh Boy 52. Grand National Night 53. The Belles of St Trinian's 54, etc.

Davies, Jack (1913–). British comedy
scriptwriter, busy since 1932 on Will Hay and
Norman Wisdom comedies, 'Doctor' series, etc.
Laughter in Paradise 51. Top Secret 52. An
Alligator Named Daisy 56. *Very Important
Person* 61. *The Fast Lady* 62. Those Magnificent
Men in Their Flying Machines 65, many others.

Davies, John Howard (1939–). British child
actor, who became a BBC TV director.
Oliver Twist 48. The Rocking-Horse Winner 50.
Tom Brown's Schooldays 51, etc.

Davies, Marion (1897–1961) (Marion
Douras). American leading lady famous less for
her rather mediocre films than for being the
protégée of William Randolph Hearst the
newspaper magnate, who was determined to
make a star out of her. She enjoyed moderate
success 1917–36, then retired.
Biography 1973 by Fred Lawrence Guiles.
□ Runaway Romany 17. Cecilia of the Pink
Roses 18. The Cinema Murder 19. The Dark
Star 19. The Belle of New York 19. The Restless
Sex 20. April Folly 20. Enchantment 21. Buried
Treasure 21. The Bride's Play 22. Beauty Worth
22. When Knighthood was in Flower 22. The
Young Diana 22. Daughter of Luxury 22. Little
Old New York 22. Adam and Eva 23. Janice
Meredith 24. Yolanda 24. Lights of Old
Broadway 25. Zander the Great 25. Beverly of
Graustark 26. Quality Street 27. The Fair Co-ed
27. The Red Mill 27. Tillie the Toiler 27. The
Cardboard Lover 28. The Patsy 28. *Show
People* 28. Hollywood Revue 29. Marianne 29.
The Gay Nineties 29. Not so Dumb 30. The
Floradora Girl 30. It's a Wise Child 31. Five and
Ten 31. Bachelor Father 31. Polly of the Circus
32. Blondie and the Follies 32. The Dark Horse 32.
Peg O' My Heart 33. Operator 13 34. Going
Hollywood 34. *Page Miss Glory* 35. Hearts
Divided 36. Cain and Mabel 36. Ever Since Eve
37.

Davies, Rupert (1916–1976). British
character actor, formerly in small roles, then
famous as TV's *Maigret*.
The Key 58. Sapphire 59. The Uncle 65. The Spy
Who Came in from the Cold 65. Brides of Fu
Manchu 66. House of a Thousand Dolls 67.
Witchfinder General 68. Waterloo 70. Zeppelin
71, etc.

Davies, Windsor (1930–). British character
actor who became a comedy sergeant major on
TV and entered films in *Carry On Behind* 74.

Davion, Alexander (1929–). Anglo-French
leading man, mostly on stage and American TV.

Song Without End (as Chopin) 60. Paranoiac
63. Valley of the Dolls 67. The Royal Hunt of the
Sun 69. Incense for the Damned 71, etc.
TV series: Gideon's Way 64. Custer 67.

Davis, Bette (1908–) (Ruth Elizabeth Davis).
Inimitably intense American dramatic actress; a
box-office queen for ten years from 1937, she
later played eccentric roles.
Autobiographies 1962 *The Lonely Life*. 1975
Mother Goddam.
□ Bad Sister 31. Seed 31. Waterloo Bridge 31.
Way Back Home 31. The Menace 31. *The Man
Who Played God* 32. Hell's House 32. So Big 32.
The Rich are Always with Us 32. The Dark
Horse 32. *Cabin in the Cotton* 32. Three on a
Match 32. Twenty Thousand Years in Sing Sing
32. Parachute Jumper 32. The Working Man 33.
Ex Lady 33. Bureau of Missing Persons 33.
Fashions of 1934 34. The Big Shakedown 34.
Jimmy the Gent 34. Fog over Frisco 34. *Of
Human Bondage* 34. Housewife 34. Bordertown
34. The Girl from Tenth Avenue 35. *Front Page
Woman* 35. Special Agent 35. *Dangerous* (AA)
35. The Petrified Forest 36. The Golden Arrow
36. Satan Met a Lady 36. Marked Woman 37.
Kid Galahad 37. That Certain Woman 37. It's
Love I'm After 37. *Jezebel* (AA) 38. The Sisters
38. *Dark Victory* 39. Juarez 39. *The Old Maid*
39. *The Private Lives of Elizabeth and Essex* 39.
All This and Heaven Too 40. *The Letter* 40. *The
Great Lie* 41. The Bride Came COD 41. *The
Little Foxes* 41. *The Man Who Came to Dinner*
41. In This Our Life 42. *Now Voyager* 42. Watch
on the Rhine 43. Thank Your Lucky Stars 43.
Old Acquaintance 43. *Mr Skeffington* 43.
Hollywood Canteen 44. *The Corn is Green* 45. A
Stolen Life 46. Deception 46. Winter Meeting 48.
June Bride 48. Beyond the Forest 49. *All About
Eve* 50. Payment on Demand 51. Another Man's
Poison 51. Phone Call from a Stranger 52. The
Star 52. The Virgin Queen 55. The Catered
Affair 56. Storm Center 56. John Paul Jones 59.
The Scapegoat 59. A Pocketful of Miracles 61.
Whatever Happened to Baby Jane? 62. Dead
Ringer 64. The Empty Canvas 64. Where Love
Has Gone 64. *Hush Hush Sweet Charlotte* 64.
The Nanny 65. *The Anniversary* 67. Connecting
Rooms 69. Bunny O'Hare 71. Madame Sin (TV)
71. The Judge and Jake Wyler (TV) 73. Scream
Pretty Peggy (TV) 74. Burnt Offerings 76.

Davis, Desmond (1927–). British director,
former cameraman.
□ *Girl with Green Eyes* 64. The Uncle 65. *I Was
Happy Here* 66. Smashing Time 67. A Nice Girl
like Me 69.

Davis, James (or **Jim**) (1915–). Burly

American actor who despite star billing opposite Bette Davis subsided quickly into second feature westerns.
White Cargo 42. Swing Shift Maisie 43. Gallant Bess 46. The Fabulous Texan 47. *Winter Meeting* 48. Brimstone 49. Cavalry Scout 52. Woman of the North Country 52. The Fighting 7th 52. The Last Command 54. Timberjack 55. The Maverick Queen 56. Alias Jesse James 59. Fort Utah 66. Rio Lobo 70. Big Jake 71. The Honkers 72. Bad Company 72. Monte Walsh 72. The Deputies (TV) 76, many others.
TV series: *Rescue 8. The Cowboys.*

Davis, Joan (1908–1961). Rubber-faced American comedienne, in show business from infancy, who enlivened many routine musicals of the thirties and forties.
On the Avenue 37. Wake Up and Live 37. Hold that Co-Ed 38. My Lucky Star 38. Tailspin 39. Sun Valley Serenade 41. Hold That Ghost 42. Sweetheart of the Fleet 42. Around the World 44. She Gets Her Man 44. *Show Business* 44. George White's Scandals 45. If You Knew Susie 48. The Travelling Saleswoman 49. Harem Girl 52, etc.
TV series: *I Married Joan* 53–55.

Davis, John (1906–). British executive, a former accountant who became chairman of the Rank Organization. After the artistic extravagance of the mid-forties, he imposed financial stability; but subsequent film production was comparatively routine and in the late sixties dwindled to nothing as the group was diversified into other fields.

Davis, Nancy (1924–). American leading lady of a few fifties films: married Ronald Reagan.
Shadow on the Wall 50. The Doctor and the Girl 50. Night into Morning 51. It's a Big Country 53. Donovan's Brain 53. Crash Landing 57. Hellcats of the Navy 59, etc.

Davis, Ossie (1917–). Black American actor of massive presence.
No Way Out 50. The Joe Louis Story 53. Gone are the Days (& w) 63. *The Hill* 65. *The Scalphunters* 68. Sam Whiskey 69. Slaves 69. Cotton Comes to Harlem (d only) 70. Kongi's Harvest (d only) 71. Black Girl (d only) 72. Malcolm X 72. Gordon's War (d only) 73, etc.

Davis, Sammy Jnr (1925–). Black American singer and entertainer, a bundle of vitality who describes himself as 'a one-eyed Jewish Negro'. Autobiography 1966: *Yes I Can.*
☐ The Benny Goodman Story 56. *Anna Lucasta*

58. *Porgy and Bess* 59. *Ocean's Eleven* 60. Pepe 60. Sergeants Three 62. Johnny Cool 63. Robin and the Seven Hoods 64. The Threepenny Opera 65. A Man Called Adam 66. Salt and Pepper 68. Sweet Charity 68. Man without Mercy 69. One More Time 70. Poor Devil (TV) 73.

Davis, Stringer (1896–1973). Gentle-mannered British character actor who was usually to be found playing small roles in the films starring his wife Margaret Rutherford.
The Happiest Days of Your Life 50. Curtain Up 53. Murder Most Foul 62. Murder Ahoy 64, etc.

Davison, Bruce (1948–). Slightly-built young American character actor.
Last Summer 69. The Strawberry Statement 70. *Willard* 71. The Jerusalem File 71. Ulzana's Raid 72. Mame 73. The Affair (TV) 73, etc.

Daw, Evelyn (1912–1970). American leading lady of the thirties.
Something to Sing About 37. Panamint's Bad Man 38, etc.

The Dawn Patrol (US 1930). Famous melodrama of World War I flyers, directed by Howard Hawks, starring Richard Barthelmess and Douglas Fairbanks Jnr. Retailored 1938 for Errol Flynn, using much of the same footage and exactly the same script (by John Monk Saunders).

Dawson, Anthony (1916–). Lean-faced British character actor.
The Way to the Stars 45. The Queen of Spades 48. The Long Dark Hall 51. Dial M for Murder (US) 54. Midnight Lace (US) 60. Seven Seas to Calais (US) 63, etc.
The 'Anthony Dawson' who directs Italian costume epics is in fact the nom-de-film of Antonio Margheriti.

Day, Dennis (1921–) (Eugene Patrick McNulty). American singer and light actor of the forties and fifties, most familiar from Jack Benny's radio and TV show.
Buck Benny Rides Again 40. Music in Manhattan 44. One Sunday Afternoon 48. I'll Get By 50. Golden Girl 51. The Girl Next Door 53, etc.

Day, Doris (1924–) (Doris Kappelhoff). Vivacious American dance band singer who achieved instant star status in 1948 and preserved her eminence by transferring to a brand of innocent sex comedy which was all her own and pleased the sixties.
☐ *Romance on the High Seas* 48. My Dream is

Yours 49. It's a Great Feeling 49. Young Man with a Horn 50. Tea for Two 50. West Point Story 50. *Storm Warning* 50. Lullaby of Broadway 51. *On Moonlight Bay* 51. I'll See You in My Dreams 51. Starlift 51. The Winning Team 52. April in Paris 52. By the Light of the Silvery Moon 53. *Calamity Jane* 53. Lucky Me 54. *Young at Heart* 55. Love Me or Leave Me 55. The Man Who Knew Too Much 56. Julie 56. *The Pajama Game* 57. Teacher's Pet 58. The Tunnel of Love 58. It Happened to Jane 59. *Pillow Talk* 59. Please Don't Eat the Daisies 60. Midnight Lace 60. Lover Come Back 62. That Touch of Mink 62. Jumbo 62. The Thrill of It All 63. Move Over Darling 63. Send Me No Flowers 64. Do Not Disturb 65. The Glass Bottom Boat 66. Caprice 67. The Ballad of Josie 68. Where Were You When the Lights Went Out? 68. With Six You Get Egg Roll 68.

TV series: *The Doris Day Show* 68–72.

Day for Night (La Nuit Americaine) (France 1973). An amusing, affectionate and unobtrusively skilful look behind the scenes while a movie is being made with a lot of very temperamental actors. Certainly the best of its kind, and purely for entertainment. Written and directed by Francois Truffaut, with Jean-Pierre Aumont, Valentina Cortesa.

Day, Frances (1908–). Revue star of German and Russian origin, long resident in Britain.
The Price of Divorce 27. The First Mrs Fraser 32. The Girl from Maxim's 34. Who's Your Lady Friend? 37. The Girl in the Taxi 38. Room for Two 40. *Fiddlers Three* (as Poppea) 44. Tread Softly 52. There's Always a Thursday 57, etc.

Day, Jill (1932–). British pop singer and leading lady.
Always a Bride 54. All for Mary 56.

Day, Josette (1914–). French leading lady.
Allo Berlin, Ici Paris 32. La Fille du Puisatier 40. *La Belle et la Bête* 45. Les Parents Terribles 48. Four Days' Leave 50, etc.

Day, Laraine (1917–) (Laraine Johnson). American leading lady of the forties, with stage experience.
Autobiographical book 1952: *Day With The Giants*.
Scandal Sheet 31. Stella Dallas 37. Border G-Men 38. *Young Dr Kildare* (and others in the series) 39. My Son, My Son 40. *Foreign Correspondent* 40. *The Trial of Mary Dugan* 41. Unholy Partners 41. Fingers at the Window 41. Journey for Margaret 42. Mr Lucky 43. The Story of Dr Wassell 43. Bride by Mistake 44. Those Endearing Young Charms 45. Keep Your Powder Dry 45. *The Locket* 46. Tycoon 47. My Dear Secretary 48. I Married a Communist 49. Without Honour 49. The High and the Mighty 54. Toy Tiger 56. Three for Jamie Dawn 57. The Third Voice 59, etc.

Day of Wrath (Denmark 1943). Carl Dreyer's horrifying drama of a medieval witch-hunt, uncannily photographed by Karl Andersson so that every scene looks like a Rembrandt painting. A sombre classic, written by Dreyer and others from a novel by Wiers Jenssons; music by Paul Schierbeck; cast headed by Lisbeth Movin, Thorkild Roose.

Day, Richard (1894–1972). American production designer.
We Live Again 35. *The Dark Angel* (AA) 35. Dodsworth (AA) 36. *The Little Foxes* 41. *How Green Was My Valley* (AA) 41. This Above All (AA) 42. My Gal Sal (AA) 43. *A Streetcar Named Desire* (AA) 51. On the Waterfront 54. Exodus 60. The Greatest Story Ever Told 65. The Chase 66. Valley of the Dolls 67. Tora! Tora! Tora! 70, etc.

Day, Robert (1922–). British director, former cameraman.
The Green Man 57. Grip of the Strangler 58. First Man into Space 58. Corridors of Blood 59. Bobbikins 59. Two-Way Stretch 60. The Rebel 61. Operation Snatch 62. Tarzan's Three Challenges 64. She 65. Tarzan and the Valley of Gold 66. Tarzan and the Great River 69, etc.

De Anda, Peter (–). Black American leading man of the seventies.
Cutter (TV) 72. Come Back Charleston Blue 72. The New Centurions 72 etc.

De Banzie, Brenda (1915–). British character actress who got her big chance on the edge of middle age; later played flouncy matrons.
The Long Dark Hall 51. I Believe in You 52. *Hobson's Choice* 54. The Purple Plain 54. What Every Woman Wants 54. A Kid for Two Farthings 55. The Man Who Knew Too Much 56. The Thirty-nine Steps 59. *The Entertainer* 60. Flame in the Streets 61. The Mark 61. The Pink Panther 63. Pretty Polly 67, etc.

De Bray, Yvonne (1889–1954). French character actress, in films from 1943.
Gigi 48. *Les Parents Terribles* 49. Olivia 50. Caroline Cherie 50. Nous Sommes Tous des Assassins 52, etc.

De Broca, Philippe (1933–). French director.
☐ *Les Jeux de l'Amour* 60. L'Amant de Cinq Jours 61. Cartouche 62. *That Man from Rio* 63. Un Monsieur de Compagnie 64. Tribulations Chinoise en Chine 65. King of Hearts 67. Devil by the Tail 68. Give Her the Moon 70. Chère Louise 72.

De Brulier, Nigel (1878–1948). British actor in Hollywood: career waned with sound.
Intolerance 16. The Four Horsemen of the Apocalypse 21. The Three Musketeers (as Richelieu) 21. Salome 23. The Hunchback of Notre Dame 23. Ben Hur 26. Wings 27. Noah's Ark 29. The Iron Mask 29. Moby Dick 31. Rasputin and the Empress 32. Mary of Scotland 36. The Garden of Allah 36. The Hound of the Baskervilles 39. One Million B.C. 40. The Adventures of Captain Marvel 48, many others.

De Camp, Rosemary (1913–). American character actress specializing in active motherly types.
Cheers for Miss Bishop 41. Jungle Book 42. This is the Army 43. *The Merry Monahans* 44. *Rhapsody in Blue* 45. From this Day Forward 46. Nora Prentiss 47. Night unto Night 49. The Big Hangover 50. *On Moonlight Bay* 51. By the Light of the Silvery Moon 53. Many Rivers to Cross 55. Thirteen Ghosts 60, etc.
TV series: *The Bob Cummings Show*. That Girl.

De Carlo, Yvonne (1922–) (Peggy Middleton). Canadian leading lady, a star in the forties of Hollywood's most outrageous easterns and westerns.
Salome Where She Danced 45. Frontier Gal 45. Song of Scheherezade 47. Brute Force 47. Slave Girl 47. Black Bart (as Lola Montez) 48 Casbah 48. River Lady 48. *Criss Cross* 49. Calamity Jane and Sam Bass 49. The Desert Hawk 50. Tomahawk 51. Hotel Sahara 51. Scarlet Angel 52. Sombrero 53. Sea Devils 52. The Captain's Paradise 53. Passion 54. Magic Fire 56. The Ten Commandments 56. Death of a Scoundrel 56. Band of Angels 57. McLintock 63. Law of the Lawless 64. Munster Go Home 66. The Power 68. The Seven Minutes 71, etc.
TV series: *The Munsters* 64–66.

De Casalis, Jeanne (1896–1966). British revue comedienne and character actress, best known as radio's 'Mrs Feather' in dithery telephone monologues.
Autobiography 1953: *Things I Don't Remember*.
Nell Gwyn 34. Cottage to Let 41. Charley's Big Hearted Aunt 41. Those Kids from Town 42. Medal for the General 44. This Man Is Mine 46. Woman Hater 48, etc.

De Cordoba, Pedro (1881–1950). American stage actor, lean and often sinister, in many silent and sound films.
Carmen 15. Maria Rosa 16. Runaway Romany 20. Young Diana 22. The Crusades 35. Anthony Adverse 36. The Light That Failed 39. The Ghost Breakers 40. The Mark of Zorro 40. Son of Fury 42. For Whom the Bell Tolls 43. The Beast with Five Fingers 47. When the Redskins Rode 50, etc.

De Cordova, Arturo (1908–1973) (Arturo Garcia). Mexican leading man with flashing grin and impudent eyes. Popular in Mexico since 1935; made a few Hollywood films in the forties.
For Whom the Bell Tolls 43. Hostages 43. *Frenchman's Creek* 44. Incendiary Blonde 44. A Medal for Benny 45. Masquerade in Mexico 45. The Flame 47. New Orleans 47. The Adventures of Casanova 48. *El* (Mex.) 51. Kill Him for Me 53, etc.

De Cordova, Frederick (1910–). American director with stage and TV experience.
☐ Too Young to Know 45. Her Kind of Man 46. That Way with Women 47. Love and Learn 47. Always Together 47. Wallflower 48. For the Love of Mary 48. The Countess of Monte Cristo 48. Illegal Entry 49. The Gal who Took the West 49. Buccaneer's Girl 50. Peggy 50. The Desert Hawk 50. Bedtime for Bonzo 51. Katie Did It 51. Little Egypt 51. Finders Keepers 51. Here Come the Nelsons 52. Bonzo Goes to College 52. Yankee Buccaneer 53. Column South 53. I'll Take Sweden 65. Frankie and Johnny 66.

De Corsia, Ted (1906–). American character actor with long vaudeville experience; usually plays surly villains.
The Lady from Shanghai 47. *Naked City* 48. The Enforcer 51. Vengeance Valley 51. Man In the Dark 53. Twenty Thousand Leagues Under The Sea 54. The Big Combo 55. Slightly Scarlet 56. The Killing 56. Baby Face Nelson 57. Gunfight at the O.K. Corral 57. Blood on the Arrow 61. The Quick Gun 64. Nevada Smith 66. Five Card Stud 68, many others.

De Courville, Albert (1887–1960). British stage director who directed a few film comedies.
Wolves 30. The Midshipmaid 32. This is the Life 33. Things Are Looking Up 34. The Case of Gabriel Perry 35. Seven Sinners 36. Crackerjack 38. The Lambeth Walk 38. An Englishman's Home 39, etc.

De Cuir, John (1918–). American production designer.
Naked City 48. The Snows of Kilimanjaro 51.

Call Me Mister 52. The King and I 56. South Pacific 57. Cleopatra 62. The Agony and the Ecstasy 65. Hello Dolly 69. The Great White Hope 70. Once is not Enough 75, etc.

De Filippo, Eduardo (1900–). Italian actor-writer-director, mainly on stage.
Tre Uomini in Frac (a) 32. Il Cappello a tre Punte (a) 34. Napoli Milionaria (awd), 50. Questi Fantasmi (wd) 54. Gold of Naples (a) 54. Fortunella (aw) 58, etc.

De Forest, Lee (1873–1961). American inventor, pioneer of many developments in wireless telegraphy, also the De Forest Phonofilm of the twenties, an early experiment in synchronized sound.

De Funes, Louis (1908–). French character comedian.
Lock up the Spoons 56. Femmes de Paris 58. Taxi 59. A Pied a Cheval et en Spoutnik 61. The Sucker 65. Fantomas 66. Don't Look Now 67. Jo 71. The Mad Adventures of Rabbi Jacob 73, many others.

De Grasse, Robert (1900–1971). American cinematographer, with RKO from 1934.
Three Pals 26. Fury of the Wild 29. Break of Hearts 35. *Stage Door* 37. The Story of Vernon and Irene Castle 39. Bachelor Mother 39. Kitty Foyle 40. Forever and a Day 43. Step Lively 44. *The Body Snatcher* 45. The Miracle of the Bells 48. Home of the Brave 49. The Men 50. Chicago Calling 52, many others.

De Grunwald, Anatole (1910–1967). British producer, in films since 1939.
French Without Tears (w) 39. Quiet Wedding (w) 40. The First of the Few (w) 41. The Demi-Paradise 42. The Way to the Stars 45. The Winslow Boy (& w) 48. The Holly and the Ivy (& w) 54. The Doctor's Dilemma 58. Libel (& w) 61. Come Fly with Me 62. The VIPs 63. The Yellow Rolls-Royce 64. Stranger in the House 67, others.

De Grunwald, Dmitri (c. 1913–). British producer, brother of Anatole de Grunwald.
The Dock Brief 62. Perfect Friday 67. Connecting Rooms 69. The Last Grenade 69. Murphy's War 71. That Lucky Touch 75, etc.

De Haven, Gloria (1925–). American soubrette, in films since 1940: mostly light musicals of no enduring quality.
Susan and God 40. Thousands Cheer 43. *Two Girls and a Sailor* 44. The Thin Man Goes Home 45. Summer Holiday 48. Scene of the

Crime 49. Three Little Words (as her own mother). 50. Two Tickets to Broadway 51. The Girl Rush 55. So This is Paris 55. Call Her Mom (TV) 72. Who is the Black Dahlia (TV) 74, etc.

De Havilland, Olivia (1916–). British-born leading lady, sister of Joan Fontaine. In Hollywood from teenage as leading lady of comedy, romance and costume drama; later proved herself an actress.
Semi-autobiography 1960: *Every Frenchman Has one.*
□ *A Midsummer Night's Dream* 35. The Irish in Us 35. Alibi Ike 35. Captain Blood 35. Anthony Adverse 36. The Charge of the Light Brigade 36. Call It a Day 36. The Great Garrick 36. It's Love I'm After 37. Gold Is Where You Find It 37. Four's a Crowd 38. *The Adventures of Robin Hood* 38. Hard To Get 38. Wings of the Navy 39. Dodge City 39. *Gone with the Wind* 39. Elizabeth and Essex 39. Raffles 40. My Love Came Back 40. Santa Fe Trail 40. Strawberry Blonde 41. Hold Back the Dawn 41. They Died with Their Boots On 41. The Male Animal 42. In This Our Life 42. Government Girl 43. Thank Your Lucky Stars 43. Princess O'Rourke 43. The Well-Groomed Bride 45. *Devotion* (as Charlotte Brontë) 46. *The Dark Mirror* 46. *To Each His Own* (AA) 46. *The Snake Pit* 47. *The Heiress* (AA) 49. My Cousin Rachel 52. That Lady 55. Not as a Stranger 55. The Ambassador's Daughter 56. The Proud Rebel 58. Libel (GB) 60. The Light in the Piazza 62. Lady in a Cage 64. *Hush Hush Sweet Charlotte* 64. The Adventurers 69.

De La Motte, Marguerite (1903–1950). American leading lady of silent films.
The Mark of Zorro 20. The Three Musketeers 21. When a Man's a Man 24. The Beloved Brute 24. Red Dice 26. The Unknown Soldier 26. The Iron Mask 28. Woman's Man 34. Reg'lar Fellers 42, etc.

De La Patelliere, Denys (1921–). French director.
Le Défroque (w only) 52. Les Aristocrates 56. Retour de Manivelle 57. Les Grandes Familles 59. Marco the Magnificent 65. Du Rififi à Paname 66. Black Sun 66, etc.

De Lane Lea, William (1900–1964). British executive, pioneer of sound dubbing processes.

De Laurentiis, Dino (1919–). Italian producer.
Bitter Rice 48. Ulysses 52. La Strada 54. Barabbas 62. The Bible 65. Kiss the Girls and

Make Them Die 67. Anzio 68. Barbarella 68.
Waterloo 69. Wild Horses 73. Death Wish 74.
King Kong 76, etc.

De Luxe Color is the Twentieth Century-Fox
version of Eastmancolor but usually comes out
decidedly blue.

De Marney, Derrick (1906–). Good-looking
British actor with stage experience.
Music Hall 35. Things to Come 36. *Young and
Innocent* 37. Victoria the Great (as Disraeli) 37.
Blonde Cheat (US) 38. The Spider 39. The Lion
Has Wings 40. Dangerous Moonlight 40. The
First of the Few 42. Latin Quarter (& co-p) 46.
Uncle Silas 47. Sleeping Car to Trieste 48. She
Shall Have Murder (& p) 50. Meet Mr Callaghan
(& p) 54. Private's Progress 55. Doomsday at
Eleven 62. The Projected Man 66, etc.

De Marney, Terence (1909–1971). British
actor with stage experience, brother of Derrick
de Marney.
The Mystery of the Marie Celeste 36. I Killed the
Count 38. Dual Alibi 46. No Way Back 49.
Uneasy Terms 49. The Silver Chalice (US) 55.
Death Is a Woman 66. All Neat in Black
Stockings 69.

De Maupassant, Guy (1850–1893). French
short storywriter. Work filmed includes *Diary of
a Madman* , *Une Vie, Le Rosier de Madame
Husson*, and many versions of *Boule de Suif.*

De Mille, Cecil B. (1881–1959). American
producer-director, one of Hollywood's pioneers
and autocrats. Notable in the twenties for sex
comedies, in the thirties and forties for action
adventures, then for biblical epics; all now seem
very stolid, but were enormously successful in
their day.
Autobiography 1959.
☐ *The Squaw Man* 13. The Virginian 14. The
Call of the North 14. What's His Name 14. The
Man from Home 14. Rose of the Rancho 14. The
Girl of the Golden West 15. The Warrens of
Virginia 15. The Unafraid 15. The Captive 15.
Wild Goose Chase 15. The Arab 15. Chimmie
Fadden 15. Kindling 15. Maria Rosa 15.
Carmen 15. Temptation 15. Chimmie Fadden
Out West 15. *The Cheat* 15. The Golden Chance
16. The Trail of the Lonesome Pine 16. Joan the
Woman 16. The Heart of Nora Flynn 16. The
Dream Girl 16. A Romance of the Redwoods 17.
The Little American 17. The Woman God
Forgot 17. The Devil Stone 17. The Whispering
Chorus 18. Old Wives for New 18. We Can't
Have Everything 18. Till I Come Back to You
18. The Squaw Man 18. Don't Change Your
Husband 19. For Better for Worse 19. Male and

Female 19. Why Change your Wife? 20.
Something to Think About 20. Forbidden Fruit
21. *The Affairs of Anatol* 21. Fool's Paradise 22.
Saturday Night 22. Manslaughter 22. Adam's
Rib 23. *The Ten Commandments* 23. Triumph
24. Feet of Clay 24. The Golden Bed 25. The
Road to Yesterday 25. The Volga Boatmen 26.
King of Kings 27. The Godless Girl 28.
Dynamite 29. Madame Satan 30. The Squaw
Man 31. *The Sign of the Cross* 32. This Day and
Age 33. Four Frightened People 34. Cleopatra
34. *The Crusades* 35. *The Plainsman* 36. The
Buccaneer 38. *Union Pacific* 39. Northwest
Mounted Police 40. *Reap The Wild Wind* 42.
The Story of Dr Wassell 44. Unconquered 47.
Samson and Delilah 49. Sunset Boulevard (as
actor) 50. The Greatest Show on Earth 52. The
Ten Commandments 56. The Buccaneer (p only)
59.

De Mille, Katherine (1911–) (Katherine
Lester). American leading lady of the thirties.
Viva Villa 34. Call of the Wild 35. Ramona 36.
Banjo on My Knee 37. Blockade 38. Reap the
Wild Wind 42. The Story of Dr Wassell 44.
Unconquered 47. The Gamblers 50, etc.

De Mille, William (1878–1955). American
director. Elder brother of Cecil B. de Mille, with
theatrical background.
Nice People 22. Craig's Wife 28. Captain Fury
(p only) 39, etc.

De Niro, Robert (1943–). Leading American
actor of the seventies.
Hi Mom 70. The Gang That Couldn't Shoot
Straight 71. Bang the Drum Slowly 73. *Mean
Streets* 73. *The Godfather, Part Two* 74. *Taxi
Driver* 76. The Last Tycoon 76.

De Palma, Brian (1944–). American satirical
director of the semi-underground school.
Greetings 69. Hi Mom 70. Get to Know Your
Rabbit 72. Sisters (& w) 72. *Phantom of the
Paradise* 74, etc.

De Putti, Lya (1901–1931). Hungarian leading
lady of the twenties.
The Phantom (Ger.) 25. *Variety* (Ger.) 25. The
Sorrows of Satan (US) 26. The Heart Thief (US)
27. Buck Privates 28. The Informer (GB) 29, etc.

De Rochemont, Louis (1899–). American
producer, from the world of newsreel. Devised
The March of Time 34; later produced semi-
documentaries like *The House on 92nd Street*
47, *Boomerang* 47, *Martin Luther* 53, and was
involved in many ventures including Cinerama
and Cinemiracle.

De Santis, Giuseppe (1917–). Italian
director.
Caccia Tragica 47. *Bitter Rice* 49. *No Peace
among the Olives* 50. Rome Eleven O'Clock 51.
A Husband for Anna 53. Men and Wolves 56.
La Garconnière 60, etc.

De Santis, Joe (1909–). American character
actor who often plays Italianate gangsters.
Slattery's Hurricane 49. Man with a Cloak 51.
The Last Hunt 56. Tension at Table Rock 57.
And Now Miguel 66. The Professionals 66. Blue
68, etc.

De Sarigny, Peter (1911–). South African-
born producer, in Britain from 1936.
The Malta Story 53. Simba 55. True as a Turtle
56. Never Let Go 61, etc.

De Seta, Vittorio (1923–). Italian director,
mainly of shorts until *Bandits at Orgosolo* 62.

De Sica, Vittorio (1901–1974). Italian actor
and director, in the latter respect an important
and skilful realist. Well known in Italy in the
thirties, but not elsewhere until after World War
II.
Teresa Venerdi (d) 41. I Bambini ci Guardino (d)
42. *Shoeshine* (AA) (d) 46. *Bicycle Thieves* (AA)
(d) 48. *Miracle in Milan* (d) 50. *Umberto D* (d)
52. *Madame De* (a) 52. Stazione Termini
(Indiscretion) (d) 52. Bread, Love and Dreams
(a) 53. Gold of Naples (d) 54. A Farewell to
Arms (a) 57. Il Generale della Rovere (a) 59.
Two Women (d) 61. The Condemned of Altona
(d) 63. Yesterday, Today and Tomorrow (d)
(AA) 64. Marriage Italian Style (d) 64. A New
World (d) 66. The Biggest Bundle of Them All (a)
66. After the Fox (d) 66. Woman Times Seven
(d) 67. The Shoes of the Fisherman (a) 68. A
Place for Lovers (d) 69. Sunflower (d) 70. *The
Garden of the Finzi-Continis* (d) 71. The Voyage
(d) 73, etc.
TV series as actor: *The Four Just Men* (GB) 59.

De Souza, Edward (1933–). British leading
man, mostly on stage.
The Roman Spring of Mrs Stone 61. The
Phantom of the Opera 62. Kiss of the Vampire
63, etc.

De Toth, André (1912–). Hungarian-
American director, mainly of routine actioners.
Oddly enough, directed one of the first 3-D films;
having only one eye, he could not see the effect.
□ Balalaika (Hung.) 39. Toprini Nasz (Hung.)
39. Passport to Suez 43. None Shall Escape 44.
Dark Waters 44. Ramrod 47. The Other Love
47. Pitfall 48. Slattery's Hurricane 49. Man in

the Saddle 51. Carson City 52. Springfield Rifle
52. Last of the Comanches 52. *House of Wax* 53.
The Stranger Wore a Gun 53. Thunder Over the
Plains 53. Crime Wave 54. Riding Shotgun 54.
Tanganyika 54. The Bounty Hunter 54. The
Indian Fighter 55. Monkey on My Back 57.
Hidden Fear 57. The Two Headed Spy (GB) 59.
Day of the Outlaw 59. Man on a String 60.
Morgan the Pirate 61. The Mongols 62. Gold for
the Caesars 64. Play Dirty (GB) 69.

De Vinna, Clyde (1892–1953). American
cinematographer.
SELECTED SILENTS: The Raiders 16.
Madam Who 18. Leave it to Me 20. Yellow Men
and Gold 22. The Victor 23. Ben Hur (co-ph) 26.
California 27. White Shadows in the South Seas
(co-ph) 28. The Pagan 29.
□ SOUND FILMS: *Trader Horn* 31. The Great
Meadow (co-ph) 31. Shipmates 31. Politics 31.
Tarzan the Ape Man (co-ph) 32. Bird of Paradise
(co-ph) 32. Eskimo 33.Tarzan and His Mate (co-
ph) 34. *Treasure Island* 34. West Point of the Air
35.The Last of the Pagans 35. Ah Wilderness 35.
Old Hutch 36. Good Old Soak 36. Bad Man of
Brimstone 38. Of Human Hearts 38. Fast
Company 38. The Girl Downstairs 39. Bridal
Suite 39. Blackmail 39. They All Come Out 39.
Twenty Mule Team 40. Phantom Raiders 40.
Wyoming 40. The Bad Man 41. The People vs
Dr Kildare 41. Barnacle Bill 41. Tarzan's Secret
Treasure 41. The Bugle Sounds 41. Jackass Mail
41. Whistling in Dixie 42. The Immortal
Sergeant 43. Within these Walls 45. The
Caribbean Mystery 45. It's a Joke Son 47.
Sword of the Avenger 48. The Jungle 52.

De Vol, Frank (–). American composer
of background scores.
Ulzana's Raid 71. The Longest Yard 74.

De Wilde, Brandon (1942–1972). American
child actor, later juvenile lead.
□ *The Member of the Wedding* 52. *Shane* 53.
Night Passage 57. Blue Denim 59. All Fall Down
62. *Hud* 63. In Harm's Way 65. Those
Calloways 65. The Deserter 70. Wild in the Sky
72.

De Wolfe, Billy (1907–1974) (William
Andrew Jones).
Toothy, moustachioed American comedy actor,
formerly dancer, with vaudeville and night club
experience. (Famous act: a lady taking a bath.)
Dixie 43. Blue Skies 46. *Dear Ruth* 47. Dear
Wife 50. Tea for Two 50. Lullaby of Broadway
51. *Call Me Madam* 53. Billie 65. The World's
Greatest Athlete 73, etc.
TV series: The Pruitts of Southampton 67. The

Queen and I 69.

De Wolff, Francis (1913–). Bearded, burly, British character actor.
Adam and Evelyne 48. Under Capricorn 49. Treasure Island 50. Scrooge 51. Ivanhoe 53. Scrooge 53. The Master of Ballantrae 55. Geordie 57, many others.

Deacon, Richard (1923–). Bald, bespectacled American character actor who usually plays comic snoops.
Abbott and Costello Meet the Mummy 55. The Power and the Prize 56. The Remarkable Mr Pennypacker 58. Blackbeard's Ghost 68, many others.
TV series: Leave It to Beaver 57–63. *Dick Van Dyke* 61–66. Mothers-in-Law 67–68.

Dead End (US 1937). Set-bound but powerful melodrama from Sidney Kingsley's play about a New York slum. Its success led Hollywood to produce more social dramas; it provided an important part for Humphrey Bogart as the returning gangster; and it introduced the Dead End Kids. As entertainment it has dated, despite Gregg Toland's photography and William Wyler's direction.

Dead of Night (GB 1945). An Ealing omnibus of ghost stories, almost the first serious British treatment of the supernatural. Quality varies, but the Michael Redgrave sequence about a deranged ventriloquist has lost none of its power, and the linking story about an architect caught up in an endless series of recurring dreams is neatly underplayed until its phantasmagoric climax and brilliant trick ending. Directors: Cavalcanti ('Christmas Party' and 'Ventriloquist'), Basil Dearden ('Hearse Driver' and linking story), Charles Crichton ('Golf') and Robert Hamer ('Haunted Mirror').

deaf mutes have been movingly portrayed by Jane Wyman in *Johnny Belinda*, Mandy Miller in *Mandy*, Harry Bellaver in *No Way Out*, and Alan Arkin *The Heart Is a Lonely Hunter*. Dorothy McGuire in *The Spiral Staircase* was mute but not deaf; Patty Duke in *The Miracle Worker* was deaf but could make sounds.

Dean, Basil (1888–). British stage producer who also directed several important films for Associated Talking Pictures, which he founded.
The Impassive Footman 32. The Constant Nymph (& co-w) 33. Java Head 34. Sing As We Go 34. Lorna Doone 35. Twenty-one Days 39, etc.

Dean, Eddie (c. 1908–) (Edgar D. Glossup). American star of western second features in the thirties and fifties.
Renegade Trail 39. Sierra Sue 41. Romance of the West 47. Hawk of Powder River 50, many others.

Dean, Isabel (1918–) (Isabel Hodgkinson). British stage actress, usually in upper-class roles: very occasional film appearances.
The Passionate Friends 47. Twenty-four Hours of a Woman's Life 52. The Story of Gilbert and Sullivan 53. Out of the Clouds 55. Virgin Island 58. The Light in the Piazza 62. A High Wind in Jamaica 65. Inadmissible Evidence 68. Catch Me a Spy 71, etc.

Dean, James (1931–1955). Moody young American actor who after a brief build-up in small roles was acclaimed as the image of the mid-fifties; his tragic death in a car crash caused an astonishing world-wide outburst of emotional necrophilia. A biopic, *The James Dean Story*, was patched together in 1957.
☐ Has Anybody Seen My Gal? 51. Sailor Beware 51. Fixed Bayonets 52. Trouble Along the Way 53. *East of Eden* 55. *Rebel Without A Cause* 55. *Giant* 56.

Dean, Julia (1878–1952). American stage actress who made a few movies after she retired to California.
How Molly Made Good 15. Curse of the Cat People 44. O.S.S. 46. Nightmare Alley 48. People Will Talk 51. Elopement 51, etc.

Dear Ruth (US 1947). Norman Krasna's play, about a teenager who writes love letters to a service man using her elder sister's name and photograph, was pleasantly if unremarkably filmed by William D. Russell with a cast including William Holden, Joan Caulfield, Mona Freeman, Edward Arnold and Billy de Wolfe. So successful was it that two sequels were called for: *Dear Wife* 49. *Dear Brat* 51.

Dearden, Basil (1911–1971). British director, former editor. Began by co-directing Will Hay's last films for Ealing, then formed a writer-producer-director partnership with Michael Relph.
The Bells Go Down 42. The Halfway House 43. Dead of Night (part) 45. Frieda 47. The Captive Heart 47. *Saraband for Dead Lovers* 48. *The Blue Lamp* 50. Pool of London 50. I Believe in You 52. The Gentle Gunman 52. The Rainbow Jacket 54. The Square Ring 55. Out of the Clouds 56. The Smallest Show on Earth 57. *Sapphire* 59. *The League of Gentlemen* 59. Man

in the Moon 60. The Secret Partner 61. *Victim* 62. The Mind Benders 63. Woman of Straw 64. Masquerade 65. *Khartoum* 66. Only When I Larf 68. *The Assassination Bureau* 68. The Man Who Haunted Himself 70, etc.

death has always fascinated film-makers, though the results have often appeared undergraduatish, as fantasy tends to look when brought down to a mass-appeal level. Death has been personified in *Death Takes a Holiday* by Frederic March and in the 1971 TV remake by Monte Markham, in *On Borrowed Time* by Cedric Hardwicke, in *Here Comes Mr Jordan* Claude Rains, in *Orphée* by Maria Casares, in *The Seventh Seal* by Bengt Ekerot, by Richard Burton in *Boom,* by George Jessel in *Heironymous Merkin* and by several actors in *The Masque of the Red Death.* In *Devotion,* Ida Lupino as Emily Brontë dreamed of death on horseback coming to sweep her away; in *The Bluebird* Shirley Temple ventured into the land of the dead to see her grandparents. Most of the characters in *Thunder Rock,* and all in *Outward Bound* (remade as *Between Two Worlds* and later varied for TV as *Haunts of the Very Rich*) were already dead at the start of the story. Other films to involve serious thought about death include *Dark Victory, Jeux Interdits, All the Way Home, Sentimental Journey, No Sad Songs for Me, One Way Passage, Paths of Glory, Wild Strawberries,* and *Ikuru.*

Comedies taking death lightly included *A Slight Case of Murder, Kind Hearts and Coronets, The Trouble with Harry, Too Many Crooks, The Criminal Life of Archibaldo de la Cruz, Send Me No Flowers, The Assassination Bureau, The Loved One, The Wrong Box, Arrivederci Baby,* and *Kiss the Girls and Make Them Die.*

Death of a Salesman (US 1953). Produced by Stanley Kramer and directed by Laslo Benedek, this screen adaptation of Arthur Miller's play about the tragedy of an American 'good guy' for whom life turns sour had an air of being done on the cheap; but Fredric March's performance was peerless and the time-transitions were effected with skill and simplicity.

Death Wish (US 1974). Controversial, unpalatable suspenser about a widower who avenges his wife's death at the hands of New York muggers by becoming an armed back street vigilante. After an unpleasant start it develops almost into a comedy but the handling is not skilful enough to avoid a sour taste. Directed by Michael Winner from a novel by Brian Garfield; with Charles Bronson in typical form.

Debucourt, Jean (1894–1958). French character actor with long stage experience.
Le Petit Chose 22. La Chute de la Maison Usher 28. Douce 43. Le Diable au Corps 46. Occupe-Toi d'Amélie 49, etc.

Decae, Henri (1915–). Distinguished French cinematographer.
Le Silence de la Mer 49. Les Enfants Terribles 49. Crève-Coeur 52. Bob le Flambeur 55. Lift to the Scaffold 57. Le Beau Serge 58. A Double Tour 59. Les Quatre Cents Coups 59. Les Cousins 59. Plein Soleil 59. Les Bonnes Femmes 60. Léon Morin, Priest 61. Sundays and Cybele 62. Dragées au Poivre 63. Viva Maria 65. Weekend at Dunkirk 65. Night of the Generals 66. Le Voleur 67. The Comedians 67. Castle Keep 69. The Sicilian Clan 70. The Light at the Edge of the World 71.

Decker, Diana (1926–). Bright, blonde, American leading lady, in Britain from 1939; became known through toothpaste commercials ('Irium, Miriam?').
Fiddlers Three 44. Meet Me at Dawn 48. Murder at the Windmill 49. Is Your Honeymoon Really Necessary? 53. Lolita 62. Devils of Darkness 65, etc.

Deckers, Eugene (1917–). French character actor who has played continental types in British films since 1946.
Sleeping Car to Trieste 48. The Elusive Pimpernel 50. The Lavender Hill Mob 51. Father Brown 54. Port Afrique 56. Northwest Frontier 59. Lady L 66. The Limbo Line 68, many others.

Decoin, Henri (1896–1969). French director, in films since 1929.
Abus de Confiance 37. Les Inconnus dans la Maison 42. La Fille du Diable 46. Three Telegrams 50. The Truth about Bebe Donge 52. The Lovers of Toledo 53. Razzia sur la Chnouf 55. Charmants Garçons 57. The Face of the Cat 58. Outcasts of Glory 64, many others.

Dee, Frances (1908–) (Jean Dee). American leading lady of the thirties, long married to Joel McCrea; a former extra, she was chosen by Chevalier to play opposite him in her first speaking role.
Playboy of Paris 31. An American Tragedy 31. Rich Man's Folly 32. King of the Jungle 33. Becky Sharp 35. If I Were King 38. So Ends Our Night 41. Meet the Stewarts 42. I Walked with a Zombie 43. Happy Land 43. Bel Ami 48. Four Faces West 48. They Passed This Way 48. Payment on Demand 51. Because of You 53. Mr Scoutmaster 53. Gypsy Colt 54, etc.

Dee, Ruby (1924–). (Ruby Ann Wallace). Black American actress.
No Way Out 50. Tall Target 51. Go Man Go 53. Edge of the City 57. Take a Giant Step 59. *A Raisin in the Sun* 61. The Balcony 62. Buck and the Preacher 72. Black Girl 72.

Dee, Sandra (1942–) (Alexandra Zuck). Petite American leading lady, former model.
Until They Sail 57. The Reluctant Debutante 58. Gidget 59. *Imitation of Life* 59. A Summer Place 59. Portrait in Black 60. Romanoff and Juliet 62. Come September 62. Tammy and the Doctor 63. Take Her She's Mine 64. That Funny Feeling 65. A Man Could Get Killed 66. Doctor, You've Got to be Kidding 67, etc.

Deeley, Michael (1931–). British producer.
The Case of the Mukkinese Battlehorn 61. One Way Pendulum 64. Robbery 67. The Italian Job 69. Murphy's War 70. The Man Who Fell to Earth 75. Nickelodeon 76, etc.

deep focus. Dramatic camera technique which brings both foreground and background objects into equal focus and clarity; notably used in *Citizen Kane* and *Hamlet*.

Defoe, Daniel (c. 1660–1731). English writer whose work included the oft-filmed *Robinson Crusoe* (qv); also *Moll Flanders*, which the 1965 film resembled but slightly.

Defore, Don (1917–). American second lead, the good guy or dumb hearty weserner of dozens of forgettable films in the forties and fifties.
You Can't Escape Forever 42. A Guy Named Joe 43. Thirty Seconds Over Tokyo 44. The Affairs of Susan 45. You Came Along 45. Ramrod 47. Romance on the High Seas 48. Too Late for Tears 48. My Friend Irma 49. Dark City 50. The Guy Who Came Back 51. She's Working Her Way Through College 52. Battle Hymn 57. The Facts of Life 61, etc.
TV series: Ozzie and Harriet. Hazel.

Degermark, Pia (–). Swedish leading lady in international films.
Elvira Madigan 67. The Looking Glass War 71.

Dehn, Paul (1912–1976). British screenwriter, former film critic.
Seven Days to Noon 51. Orders to Kill 58. *Goldfinger* 64. The Spy Who Came in from the Cold 65. The Deadly Affair 66. The Taming of the Shrew 67. *Planet of the Apes* (and four sequels) 67. Fragment of Fear (& p) 69. Murder on the Orient Express 74, etc.

Dehner, John (1915–). American character actor, usually as sympathetic smart alec or dastardly villain.
Captain Eddie 45. The Secret of St Ives 49. Last of the Buccaneers 50. Lorna Doone 51. Scaramouche 52. Apache 54. Carousel 56. The Left-handed Gun (as Pat Garrett) 58. Timbuktu 59. The Chapman Report 62. Youngblood Hawke 63. Stiletto 69. Support Your Local Gunfighter 71, etc.
TV series: The Roaring Twenties 61.

Dekker, Albert (1905–1968). Dutch-American stage actor of long experience.
The Great Garrick 37. Marie Antoinette 38. Beau Geste 39. *Dr Cyclops* 39. Among the Living 41. In Old Oklahoma 43. Woman of the Town 44. The French Key 46. The Killers 46. Gentleman's Agreement 48. The Furies 50. As Young as You Feel 51. Wait Till the Sun Shines, Nellie 53. East of Eden 54. Kiss Me Deadly 55. Illegal 56. Suddenly Last Summer 59. The Wild Bunch 69, many others.

Del Giudice, Filippo (1892–1961). Italian producer who settled in England and became managing director of Two Cities Films.
French without Tears 39. In Which We Serve 42. Henry V 44. The Way Ahead 44. Blithe Spirit 45. Odd Man Out 47. The Guinea Pig 48, many others.

Del Rio, Dolores (1905–) (Dolores Asunsolo). Mexican leading lady with aristocratic background; beautiful and popular star of the twenties and thirties.
Joanna (debut) 25. High Stepper 26. What Price Glory? 27. *The Loves of Carmen* 27. Resurrection 28. Evangeline 29. The Bad One 30. The Dove 31. Bird of Paradise 32. Flying Down to Rio 33. Wonder Bar 34. Madame Du Barry 34. Lancer Spy 37. *Journey into Fear* 42. Portrait of Maria 45, The Fugitive 47. *Cheyenne Autumn* 64. Once upon a Time 67, many others.

Del Ruth, Roy (1895–1961). Very competent American director, former gag writer for Mack Sennett.
□ SOUND FILMS: Conquest 29. The Desert Song 29. The Hottentot 29. Gold Diggers of Broadway 29. The Aviator 29. Hold Everything 30. The Second Floor Mystery 30. Three Faces East 30. The Life of the Party 30. My Past 31. Divorce Among Friends 31. *The Maltese Falcon* 31. Side Show 31. Blonde Crazy 31. Taxi 32. Beauty and the Boss 32. Winner Take All 32. *Blessed Event* 32. Employees Entrance 33. The Mind Reader 33. The Little Giant 33. Captured 33. Bureau of Missing Persons 33. *Lady Killer*

33. Bulldog Drummond Strikes Back 34. Upperworld 34. Kid Millions 34. *Folies Bergere* 35. Broadway Melody of 1936 35. *Thanks a Million* 35. It Had to Happen 36. Private Number 36. Born to Dance 36. *On the Avenue* 37. Broadway Melody of 1938 37. Happy Landing 38. My Lucky Star 38. Tail Spin 39. The Star Maker 39. Here I Am A Stranger 39. He Married His Wife 40. *Topper Returns* 41. Chocolate Soldier 41. Maisie Gets Her Man 42. Dubarry was a Lady 43. Broadway Rhythm 44. Barbary Coast Gent 44. It Happened on Fifth Avenue 47. The Babe Ruth Story 48. The Red Light 49. Always Leave Them Laughing 49. West Point Story 50. On Moonlight Bay 51. Starlift 51. About Face 52. Stop You're Killing Me 52. Three Sailors and a Girl 53. Phantom of the Rue Morgue 54. The Alligator People 59. Why Must I Die 60.

Delair, Suzy (1916–). Vivacious French entertainer, in several films.
Quai des Orfèvres 47. Lady Paname 49. Robinson Crusoe Land 50. Gervaise 55. Rocco and his Brothers 60. Is Paris Burning? 66, etc.

Delaney, Shelagh (1939–). British playwright whose chief contribution to the screen is *A Taste of Honey.*

Delannoy, Jean (1908–). French director, formerly journalist and cutter.
La Symphonie Pastorale 40. *L'Eternel Retour* 43. Les Jeux Sont Faits 47. *Dieu a Besoin des Hommes* 49. Le Garçon Sauvage 51. The Moment of Truth 52. Marie Antoinette 56. Notre Dame de Paris 56. Maigret Sets a Trap 57. Le Soleil des Voyous 67, many others.

Delerue, Georges (1924–). French composer.
Hiroshima Mon Amour 58. Les Jeux de L'Amour 60. Une Aussi Longue Absence 61. Shoot the Pianist 61. Jules et Jim 61. Silken Skin 63. The Pumpkin Eater 64. Viva Maria 65. A Man for All Seasons 66. The 25th Hour 67. Interlude 68, etc.

Delevanti, Cyril (1887–1976). British-born stage actor who played aged gentlemen for many years.
Mary Poppins 64. *Night of the Iguana* 64. The Greatest Story Ever Told 65. Counterpoint 67. The Killing of Sister George 68. Bedknobs and Broomsticks 71. Black Eye 73, many others.

Deliverance (US 1972). A curiously harsh, violent fable about four men who go out to challenge the elements and end up humbled or injured by nature's strength and their own weaknesses. Directed by John Boorman from a novel by James Dickey; with Burt Reynolds, Jon Voight, Ronny Cox, Ned Beatty.

Dell, Gabriel (1920–). American actor, one of the original Dead End Kids (qv) who in the sixties emerged as a TV character actor.

Dell, Jeffrey (1904–). British comedy writer, author in the thirties of *Nobody Ordered Wolves*, a satirical novel of the film industry.
Sanders of the River (c-w) 35. The Saint's Vacation 41. Thunder Rock (co-w) 42. *Don't Take it to Heart* (& d) 44. It's Hard to Be Good (& d) 48. The Dark Man (& d) 50. Brothers-in-Law (co-w) 56. Lucky Jim (co-w) 58. Carlton-Browne of the F.O. (& co-d) 59. A French Mistress (co-w) 61. Rotten to the Core (co-w) 65. The Family Way (co-w) 66, etc.

Delluc, Louis (1892–1924). Pioneer French director of the twenties, associated with the impressionist school.
□ Fièvre 21. La Femme de Nulle Part 22. L'Innondation 24.

Delon, Alain (1935–). Romantic-looking French leading man.
Plein Soleil 59. Rocco and his Brothers 60. The Eclipse 61. The Leopard 62. The Big Snatch 63. The Black Tulip 64. The Yellow Rolls Royce 64. The Love Cage 65. Once a Thief 65. Lost Command 66. Is Paris Burning? 66. Texas Across the River 66. Les Aventuriers 66. Histoires Extraordinaires 67. Diabolically Yours 67. Samurai 67. Girl on a Motorcycle 67. La Pisane 67. Jeff 68. *Borsalino* 70. The Sicilian Clan 70. The Red Circle 70. Red Sun 71. The Assassination of Trotsky 72. Scorpio 72. Borsalino and Co. 73. Shock 74, etc.

Delorme, Daniele (1926–) (Gabrielle Girard). French leading lady.
Gigi 48. La Cage aux Filles 49. Sans Laisser d'Adresse 51. Tempi Nostri 54. Prisons de Femmes 58. La Guerre des Boutons (p only) 62.

Delvaux, André (1926–). Belgian director.
The Man Who Had His Hair Cut Short 67. Un Soir Un Train 68. *Rendezvous at Bray* 73, etc.

Demarest, William (1892–). American character actor, an 'old pro' with vast vaudeville experience before film debut in 1927.
The Jazz Singer 27. Fingerprints 27. The Murder Man 35. Wedding Present 36. Rosalie 38. Mr Smith Goes to Washington 39. Tin Pan Alley 40. The Great McGinty 40. *Sullivan's Travels* 41.

The Palm Beach Story 42. *Hail the Conquering Hero* 43. *The Miracle of Morgan's Creek* (as Officer Kockenlocker) 43. Once upon a Time 44. Pardon My Past 45. Along Came Jones 45. *The Jolson Story* 46. The Perils of Pauline 47. On Our Merry Way 49. Jolson Sings Again 50. *The First Legion* 51. Riding High 51. Dangerous When Wet 52. Escape from Fort Bravo 53. Jupiter's Darling 54. The Rawhide Years 56. Son of Flubber 63. It's a Mad Mad Mad Mad World 63. That Darn Cat 65. The McCullochs 75. Won Ton Ton 76, over a hundred others.
TV series: Wells Fargo 56–58. Love and Marriage 59. My Three Sons 67– .

Demick, Irina (1937–). Franco-Russian leading lady in international films.
The Longest Day 62. Those Magnificent Men in Their Flying Machines 65. Up From The Beach 65. Cloportes 65. Prudence and the Pill 68, etc.

Demongeot, Mylene (1936–). Blonde French leading lady, briefly flaunted as sex symbol.
Les Enfants de L'Amour 44. It's a Wonderful World (GB) 56. *The Witches of Salem* 56. Bonjour Tristesse 57. Upstairs and Downstairs (GB) 59. The Giant of Marathon 60. Gold for the Caesars 62. Uncle Tom's Cabin (Ger.) 65. Fantomas 66. The Vengeance of Fantomas 67. The Private Navy of Sgt O'Farrell 68, etc.

Dempster, Austin (–). British cinematographer.
Bedazzled 67. Otley 69. The Looking Glass War 69, etc.

Dempster, Carol (1901–). American leading lady of the silent screen, especially for D. W. Griffith.
Scarlet Days 19. The Love Flower 20. Dream Street 21. *One Exciting Night* 22. America 24. Isn't Life Wonderful? 24. That Royle Girl 26. The Sorrows of Satan 26, etc.

Demy, Jacques (1931–). French director.
□ *Lola* 60. La Baie des Anges 62. *Les Parapluies de Cherbourg* 64. The Young Girls of Rochefort 67. The Model Shop (US) 70. Peau d'Ane 71.

Dench, Judi (1934–). British stage actress.
□ The Third Secret 64. A Study in Terror 65. He Who Rides a Tiger 66. Four in the Morning (BFA) 66. A Midsummer Night's Dream 68. Luther 73. Dead Cert 74.

Deneuve, Catherine (1943–) (Catherine Dorleac). French leading lady, sister of Françoise Dorleac.
Vice and Virtue 62. *Les Parapluies de Cherbourg* 64. *Repulsion* (GB) 65. Das Liebeskarussel (Who Wants to Sleep?) 65. Les Créatures 66. The Young Girls of Rochefort 67. *Belle de Jour* 67. Benjamin 68. Manon 70 68. Mayerling 68. The April Fools (US) 69. The Mississippi Mermaid 69. *Tristana* 70. Peau d'Ane 71. Hustle 76, etc.

Denham. An English village north of London where in 1936 Korda opened a huge film studio which was later taken over by the Rank Organisation but closed in the fifties so that production could be concentrated at Pinewood a few miles away.

Denham, Maurice (1909–). British character actor with stage experience from 1934.
It's Not Cricket 48. London Belongs to Me 48. The Spider and the Fly 50. The Million Pound Note 54. Simon and Laura 55. Checkpoint 56. Night of the Demon 57. Our Man in Havana 59. Sink the Bismarck 60. HMS Defiant 62. The Seventh Dawn 64. Hysteria 65. The Alphabet Murders 65. After the Fox 66. The Midas Run 69. The Virgin and the Gypsy 70. Countess Dracula 70. Nicholas and Alexandra 71. Luther 73. Shout at the Devil 76, many others.

Denison, Michael (1915–). British leading man with firm but gentle manner; married to Dulcie Gray.
Tilly of Broomsbury 40. Hungry Hill 46. *My Brother Jonathan* 47. *The Glass Mountain* 47. The Blind Goddess 48. The Importance of Being Earnest 51. Angels One Five 51. The Franchise Affair 52. Landfall 53. The Tall Headlines 52. The Truth about Women 56. Faces in the Dark 61, etc.

Denmark: see Danish.

Denner, Charles (c. 1933–). French leading actor.
Landru 62. *Life Upside Down* 63. The Sleeping Car Murder 66. The Two of Us 68. The Bride Wore Black 68. A Gorgeous Bird Like Me 72, etc.

Denning, Richard (1914–) (Louis A. Denninger). American leading man who from 1937 played light romantic roles and manly athletes.
Hold 'Em Navy 37. Persons in Hiding 38. Union Pacific 39. Golden Gloves 40. Adam Had Four Sons 41. Beyond the Blue Horizon 42. The Glass Key 42. Seven Were Saved 46. Black Beauty 46. Caged Fury 48. No Man of Her Own 48.

Weekend with Father 50. Scarlet Angel 51. Hangman's Knot 53. The Creature from the Black Lagoon 54. Assignment Redhead (GB) 56. The Black Scorpion 57. Twice Told Tales 63, many others, mainly second features.
TV series: Mr and Mrs North 53–54. The Flying Doctor 59. Michael Shayne 60.

Dennis, Sandy (1937–). American leading actress.
□ Splendour in the Grass 61. Who's Afraid of Virginia Woolf? (AA) 66. Up the Down Staircase 67. The Fox 68. Sweet November 68. That Cold Day in the Park 69. A Touch of Love 69. The Out-of-Towners 69. The Only Way Out is Dead 72.

Denny, Reginald (1891–1967) (Reginald Leigh Daymore). British actor, on stage from childhood. From 1919 starred in many Hollywood action comedies and when sound came in began to play amiable stiff-upper-lip Britishers. More or less retired after 1950 to devote time to his aircraft company.
49 East 20. Footlights 21. The Leather Pushers 22. The Abysmal Brute 23. Skinner's Dress Suit 25. Oh Doctor 26. California Straight Ahead 27. Embarrassing Moments 29. Madame Satan 30. Private Lives 32. Of Human Bondage 34. Anna Karenina 35. Romeo and Juliet 36. Several Bulldog Drummond films 37–38 (as Algy). Rebecca (as Frank Crawley) 40. Sherlock Holmes and the Voice of Terror 42. Love Letters 45. The Macomber Affair 47. The Secret Life of Walter Mitty 47. Mr Blandings Builds His Dream House (as Mr Simms) 48. Abbott and Costello Meet Dr Jekyll and Mr Hyde 53. Around the World in Eighty Days 56. Fort Vengeance 59. Cat Ballou 65. Batman 66, many others.

Dent, Vernon (1894–1963). American character actor, a pompous butt for the Three Stooges in many of their two-reelers.

dentists are seldom popular chaps, but Preston Sturges made a film about one of them, the inventor of laughing gas: The Great Moment. The Counterfeit Traitor had a spy dentist. Sinister dentists were found in The Man Who Knew Too Much (original version), The Secret Partner, and Footsteps in the Dark, and a comic one, in the person of Bob Hope, in The Paleface. Dentistry is the subject of two British farces: Dentist in the Chair and Dentist on the Job. W. C. Fields once made a film of his sketch The Dentist; and Laurel and Hardy in Leave 'Em Laughing were overcome by laughing gas. The most notable dentist hero was in the twice

remade One Sunday Afternoon; and the most villainous dentist is certainly Laurence Olivier in Marathon Man.

Denver, Bob (1935–). American TV comedian.
Take Her She's Mine 63. For Those Who Think Young 64. Who's Minding the Mint? 67. The Sweet Ride 67. Do You Know The One About the Travelling Saleslady 68, etc.
TV series: Dobie Gillis 59–62. Gilligan's Island 64–66. Dusty's Trail 73.

department stores have usually been a background for comedy. New York store backgrounds have often shown the native superiority of the working girl to snobbish shopwalkers and obtuse management, as in Bachelor Mother and its remake Bundle of Joy, The Devil and Miss Jones and the 1924 Manhandled. Broader comedy elements were to the fore in Miracle on 34th Street, Modern Times, The Big Store, Who's Minding the Store?, Fitzwilly and How to Save a Marriage. British comedies with store settings include Kipps, The Crowded Day, Laughter in Paradise, Keep Fit, and Trouble in Store.

Deray, Jacques (–). French director.
Borsalino 70. Easy Down There 71, etc.

Derek, John (1926–) (Derek Harris). American light-leading man.
I'll Be Seeing You 45. Knock on any Door 49. All The King's Men 49. Rogues of Sherwood Forest 50. Mask of the Avenger 51. Scandal Sheet 51. Mission Over Korea 53. The Adventures of Hajji Baba 54. Prince of Players 55. Run for Cover 55. The Leather Saint 56. The Ten Commandments 56. Omar Khayyam 57. Prisoner of the Volga 60. Exodus 60. Nightmare in the Sun 64. Once Before I Die (& d) 66. Childish Things (& d) 69, etc.

Dern, Bruce (1936–). American general purpose actor, usually seen as tough guy or psychotic.
Wild River 60. Marnie 64. The Wild Angels 66. The Trip 67. The War Wagon 67. Will Penny 68. Castle Keep 69. Number One 69. They Shoot Horses Don't They? 69. Bloody Mama 70. The Incredible Two-headed Transplant 70. Drive He Said 71. The Cowboys 72. Silent Running 72. The King of Marvin Gardens 72. The Laughing Policeman 73. The Great Gatsby 74, many others.

Derr, Richard (1917–). American leading man, usually in minor films.

Ten Gentlemen from West Point 42. Tonight We Raid Calais 43. The Secret Heart 47. Joan of Arc 48. When Worlds Collide 51. Something To Live For 52. Terror is a Man 59. Three in the Attic 68. The Drowning Pool 75, etc.

Desailly, Jean (1920–). French leading man. Le Voyageur de la Toussaint 42. Sylvie et la Fantôme 45. *Occupe-Toi d'Amélie* 49. Les Grandes Manoeuvres 55. Maigret Sets a Trap 59. Le Doulos 62. *Le Peau Douce* 64. The Twenty-Fifth Hour 66, etc.

desert islands have provided the locale of many a film adventure. *Robinson Crusoe* has been filmed several times, with two recent variations in *Robinson Crusoe on Mars* and *Lt. Robin Crusoe USN*. *Treasure Island* too has survived three or four versions, to say nothing of imitations like *Blackbeard the Pirate* and parodies such as *Abbott and Costello Meet Captain Kidd* and *Old Mother Riley's Jungle Treasure*. *The Admirable Crichton* (qv) is perhaps the next most overworked desert island story, with *The Swiss Family Robinson* following on. Dorothy Lamour found a few desert islands in films like *Typhoon* and *Aloma of the South Seas*; the inhabitants of *The Little Hut* had one nearly to themselves; Joan Greenwood and co. were marooned on a rather special one in *Mysterious Island*. *Our Girl Friday* played the theme for sex; *Dr Dolittle* found educated natives on one; Cary Grant lived on one as a reluctant spy in *Father Goose*. *Sea Wife, Lord of the Flies* and *The Day the Fish Came Out* were three recent but not very successful attempts to take the theme seriously: *Hell in the Pacific* was one that did work.

A comic TV series on the subject was *Gilligan's Island* 64–66; a serious one, *The New People* 69.

The Desert Song. The popular operetta by Sigmund Romberg, Otto Harbach and Oscar Hammerstein was filmed in 1929, with John Boles and Carlotta King; in 1943, with Dennis Morgan and Irene Manning, and in 1952, with Gordon Macrae and Kathryn Grayson.

deserts have figured in many a western, from *Tumbleweed* to *Mackenna's Gold*. Other films which have paid particularly respectful attention to the dangers that too much sand can provide include *The Sheik* and *Son of the Sheik*, *Greed*, *The Lost Patrol*, *The Garden of Allah*, *Sahara*, *Five Graves to Cairo*, *Ice Cold in Alex*, *Sea of Sand*, *Desert Rats*, *Play Dirty*, *An Eye for an Eye*, *Inferno*, *Zabriskie Point*, *The Sabre and the Arrow*, *Legend of the Lost*, *The Ten Commandments*, *She*, *Lawrence of Arabia*, *The Black Tent*, *Oasis*, *Sands of The Kalahari*, *The Flight of the Phoenix*, *Garden of Evil* and *The Professionals*.

Desmond, Florence (1905–) (Florence Dawson). British dancer and impersonator, seen in many stage revues but few films. Sally in Our Alley 31. No Limit 35. *Keep Your Seats Please* 37. Hoots Mon 40. Three Came Home (US) 50. Charley Moon 56. Some Girls Do 68, etc.

Desmond, William (1878–1949). Irish leading man of the American silent screen, mostly in westerns. The Sunset Trail 24. Blood and Steel 26. Tongues of Scandal 29. Hell Bent for Frisco 31. Flying Fury 33. Arizona Days 36, etc.

Desmonde, Jerry (1908–1967). British character actor with long music-hall experience, a perfect foil for comedians from Sid Field to Norman Wisdom. London Town 46. Cardboard Cavalier 48. Follow a Star 59. A Stitch in Time 63. The Early Bird 65, many others.

Desni, Tamara (1913–). Russian-born, British-resident leading lady. Jack Ahoy 34. Fire over England 36. The Squeaker 37. Traitor Spy 40. Send for Paul Temple 46. Dick Barton at Bay 50, etc.

Desny, Ivan (1922–). Continental leading man, in films from 1948. *Madeleine* (GB) 50. La Putain Respectueuse 52. Lola Montes 55. The Mirror Has Two Faces 58. The Magnificent Rebel 60. Das Liebeskarussel (Who Wants to Sleep?) 65. The Mystery of Thug Island 66. I Killed Rasputin 68. Mayerling 68. The Adventures of Gerard 70. Paper Tiger 75, etc.

Destry Rides Again (US 1939). Tragi-comic western based on Max Brand's story of the diffident hero who finally buckles on his guns. (Filmed several times, the latest being the 1955 *Destry* with Audie Murphy, it also in 1964 became a TV series with John Gavin.) This version has become a classic for several reasons: Marlene Dietrich's brilliant comeback performance as Frenchy, with songs like 'See What the Boys in the Back Room Will Have'; George Marshall's crisply professional direction; and near-perfect cast including James Stewart, Mischa Auer, Charles Winninger, Samuel S. Hinds, Brian Donlevy and Una Merkel (whose on-screen fight with Dietrich caused a mild censorship problem at the time).

Deutsch, Adolphe (1897–). American composer associated with Warner and MGM.
The Smiling Lieutenant 31. The Great Garrick 37. Indianolis Speedway 39. The Fighting 69th 40. They Drive By Night 40. *The Maltese Falcon* 41. High Sierra 41. Across the Pacific 42. The Mask of Dimitros 43. Uncertain Glory 44. Intruder in the Dust 49. Father of the Bride 50. The Long Long Trailer 53. The Rack 56. Tea and Sympathy 56. The Matchmaker 57. Les Girls 57. Some Like It Hot 59. The Apartment 60, many others.

Deutsch, David (1926–). British producer, in films from 1949.
Blind Date 59. Nothing But the Best 64. Catch Us If You Can 65. Lock Up Your Daughters 69, etc.

the devil has made frequent appearances in movies. There were versions of *Faust* in 1900, 1903, 1904, 1907, 1909, 1911, 1921 and 1925, the last of these featuring Emil Jannings as Mephistopheles. Later variations on this theme include *The Sorrows of Satan* 27, with Adolphe Menjou; *All That Money Can Buy* 41, with Walter Huston as Mr Scratch; *Alias Nick Beal* 49, with Ray Milland; *La Beauté du Diable* 50 with Gérard Philippe. *Damn Yankees* 58 with Ray Walston. *Bedazzled* 67 with Peter Cook; and *Doctor Faustus* 68 with Andreas Teuber. In other stories, Satan was played by Helge Nissen in *Leaves From Satan's Book* 20, Jules Berry in *Les Visiteurs du Soir* 42, Alan Mowbray in *The Devil with Hitler* 42, Rex Ingram in *Cabin in the Sky* 43, Laird Cregar in *Heaven Can Wait* 43, Claude Rains in *Angel on My Shoulder* 46, Stanley Holloway in *Meet Mr Lucifer* 53, Mel Welles in *The Undead* 57, Vincent Price in *The Story of Mankind* 57, Cedric Hardwicke in *Bait* 54, Vittorio Gassman in *The Devil in Love* 67, Stig Järrel in *The Devil's Eye* 60, Donald Pleasence in *The Greatest Story Ever Told* 65, Burgess Meredith in *Torture Garden* 68, Pierre Clement in *The Milky Way* 68, Ralph Richardson in *Tales From the Crypt* 71. In the Swedish *Witchcraft through the Ages* 21 the devil was played by the director, Benjamin Christensen. Devil worship has been the subject of *The Black Cat* 34, *The Seventh Victim* 43, *Night of the Demon* 57, *Back from the Dead* 57, *The Witches* 66, *Eye of the Devil* 66, *The Devil Rides Out* 68, *Rosemary's Baby* 68; while the last-named presaged a rash of diabolically-inspired children in *The Exorcist, I Dont Want to be Born, It's Alive, Devil Within Her* and *The Omen*.

Deville, Michel (1931–). French director.
Ce Soir ou Jamais 60. L'Appartement de Filles 63. Benjamin 67. Bye Bye Barbara 69, etc.

Devil's Island, the French Guianan penal colony, has intermittently fascinated film-makers. Apart from the versions of the Dreyfus case (*Dreyfus, The Life of Emile Zola, I Accuse*), there have been Ronald Colman in *Condemned to Devil's Island*, Donald Woods in *I Was a Prisoner on Devil's Island*, Boris Karloff in *Devil's Island*, Clark Gable in *Strange Cargo*, Humphrey Bogart in *Passage to Marseilles*, Bogart and company in *We're No Angels*, Eartha Kitt in *Saint of Devil's Island*, Steve McQueen in *Papillon*, and Jim Brown in *I Escaped From Devil's Island*.

Devine, Andy (1905–1977). Fat, husky-voiced American character comedian, seen in innumerable westerns.
We Americans 28. Hot Stuff 29. Law and Order 32. Midnight Mary 33. Stingaree 34. Way Down East 35. Romeo and Juliet 36. A Star is Born 37. In Old Chicago 38. *Stagecoach* 39. When the Daltons Rode 40. Badlands of Dakota 41. Sin Town 42. Crazy House 43. Ghost Catchers 44. Frisco Sal 45. Canyon Passage 46. The Vigilantes Return 47. Old Los Angeles 48. *The Red Badge of Courage* 51. New Mexico 51. Montana Belle 52. Island in the Sky 53. Pete Kelly's Blues 55. The Adventures of Huckleberry Finn 60. Two Rode Together 61. The Man who Shot Liberty Valance 62. It's a Mad Mad Mad Mad World 63. Zebra in the Kitchen 65. The Ballad of Josie 68, many others.
TV series: *Wild Bill Hickok*.

Devon, Laura (1940–). American leading lady from TV.
Goodbye Charlie 65. Red Line 7000 66. Gunn 67, etc.

Devry, Elaine (1935–). American leading lady.
Mantrap 61. Diary of a Madman 63. Guide for the Married Man 67. The Boy Who Cried Werewolf 73, etc.

Dewhurst, Colleen (1926–). American general purpose actress.
The Cowboys 72. McQ 74.

Dexter, Anthony (1919–) (Walter Fleischmann). American leading man with stage experience. Cast as Rudolph Valentino, he never lived down the tag, and his subsequent roles have been in small-scale action dramas and science-fiction quickies.

Valentino 51. The Brigand 52. Captain John Smith and Pocahontas 53. Captain Kidd and the Slave Girl 54. Fire Maidens from Outer Space (GB) 54. He Laughed Last 56. The Parson and the Outlaw (as Billy the Kid) 57. Twelve to the Moon 59. Thoroughly Modern Millie 67, etc.

Dexter, Brad (1922–). American character actor often seen as tough hoodlum.
The Asphalt Jungle 50. Macao 52. Untamed 55. The Oklahoman 57. The Magnificent Seven 60. Taras Bulba 62. Bus Riley's Back in Town 64. Von Ryan's Express 65. Blindfold 66. The Naked Runner (p only) 67. The Lawyer 69, etc.

Dexter, John (1935–). British director.
The Virgin Soldiers 69. Sidelong Glances of a Pigeon Kicker 70. I Want What I Want 71, etc.

Dexter, Maury (1927–). American producer-director of second features.
The Third Voice (p) 60. Harbour Lights (pd) 63. The Day Mars Invaded Earth (pd) 63. House of the Damned (pd) 63. The Naked Brigade (d) 65. The Outlaw of Red River (pd) 65. Maryjane (pd) 68. Hell's Belles (pd) 70, etc.

Dheigh, Khigh (1910–). Oriental American character actor familiar on TV as the evil villain of *Hawaii Five-O*.
The Manchurian Candidate 62.

Dhery, Robert (1921–) (Robert Foullcy; born Hery). Dapper French cabaret comedian and pantomimist.
Les Enfants du Paradis 44. Sylvie et la Fantôme 45. La Patronne (d only) 49. *Ah, Les Belles Bacchantes* (Femmes de Paris) (& wp) 54. *La Belle Américaine* (& wp) 61. Allez France (& wp) 64. Le Petit Baigneur (& wp) 67. A Time for Loving 71, etc.

Di Venanzo, Gianni (1920–1966). Italian cinematographer, in films from 1941.
Amore in Città 53. L'Amiche 55. Il Grido 57. I Soliti Ignoti 58. Salvatore Giuliano 61. La Notte 61. L'Eclisse 62. Eva 62. *Eight and a Half* 63. *Juliet of the Spirits* 65, etc.

Le Diable Au Corps (France 1946). A tragic love story of World War I, written by Aurenche and Bost, directed by Claude Autant-Lara, with Gérard Philipe and Micheline Presle. Its international success was a boost for the post-war French cinema.

Les Diaboliques (The Fiends) (France 1954). Suspense thriller which has become a minor classic partly because of the twists of its Boileau-Narcejac plot (frequently copied since), partly because of the acting of Simone Signoret and Vera Clouzot, but chiefly because of Henri-Georges Clouzot's spell-binding direction.

Diamond, I. A. L. (1915–). American screenwriter, his best work being in collaboration with Billy Wilder.
Murder in the Blue Room 44. Never Say Goodbye 46. Always Together 47. The Girl from Jones Beach 49. Something for the Birds 52. That Certain Feeling 56. Love in the Afternoon 57. Merry Andrew 58. *Some Like It Hot* 59. *The Apartment* 60. *One Two Three* 61. Irma la Douce 63. Kiss Me Stupid 64. The Fortune Cookie 66. Cactus Flower 69. *The Private Life of Sherlock Holmes* 70. Avanti 72, etc.

A Diary for Timothy (GB 1945). One of World War II's most brilliantly-assembled documentaries, a picture of Britain in the war's last months, looking to the future through the eyes of four men and a baby. Written by E. M. Forster, produced by Basil Wright, directed by Humphrey Jennings, with commentary by Michael Redgrave. Fifteen years later Granada TV mounted a programme to trace what had happened to the characters in the film.

Diary of a Chambermaid. Octave Mirabeau's eccentric novel of the decadent French squirearchy was filmed rather unsatisfactorily by Jean Renoir in America in 1945, with Paulette Goddard, Francis Lederer and Burgess Meredith. Luis Buñuel directed a French remake in 1964, with Jeanne Moreau and a more sympathetic cast.

Dick, Douglas (1920–). Innocent-looking American 'second lead'.
The Searching Wind 46. Saigon 47. The Accused 48. Home of the Brave 49. The Red Badge of Courage 51. The Gambler from Natchez 55. The Oklahoman 57. North to Alaska 60, etc.

Dick Tracy. The lantern-jawed detective of the comic strips made sporadic film appearances, notably when impersonated by Ralph Byrd in a number of forties second features and serials. The fifties brought a TV cartoon series, and he also appeared in *TV Funnies* 71.

Dickens, Charles (1812–1870). Prolific British novelist whose gusto in characterization and plot-weaving made his books ideal cinema material until the last decade when producers seem to have thought them old-fashioned. Most filmed has perhaps been *A Christmas Carol*, usually personified as *Scrooge* (qv); but *Oliver*

Twist (qv) runs it a close second. There had been several early silent versions of *David Copperfield* before Cukor's splendid 1934 version (qv), and *The Old Curiosity Shop* was popular as the basis of one-reelers before the talkie versions with Hay Petrie (1935) and Anthony Newley (1975). *A Tale of Two Cities* had been a popular stage play under the title *The Only Way*; after many early versions it was directed as a spectacular by Frank Lloyd in 1917, with William Farnum; as a British silent in 1926, with Martin Harvey; as a vehicle for Ronald Colman in 1935; and in a rather uninspired British version of 1958 starring Dirk Bogarde. A 1969 all-star version of *David Copperfield* was primarily intended for American TV.

Other Dickens novels less frequently filmed include *The Mystery of Edwin Drood*, once as an early British silent and again in Hollywood in 1935, with Claude Rains as John Jasper; *Great Expectations*, which had two silent versions, a rather dull Hollywood remake of 1934 and the magnificent David Lean version of 1946 (qv); *Dombey and Son*, under the title *Rich Man's Folly*, starring George Bancroft in 1931; *Nicholas Nickleby*, the only picturization of which was the patchy Ealing version of 1947; and *The Pickwick Papers*, seen in various potted versions in silent days and in Noel Langley's superficial version of 1952.

Dickens' novels which were filmed in the silent period but not since sound include *The Cricket on the Hearth, Martin Chuzzlewit, Our Mutual Friend* and *Barnaby Rudge. Little Dorrit* was made in Germany in 1933 with Anny Ondra.

Dickinson, Angie (1931–) (Angeline Brown). Capable American leading lady, former beauty contest winner, in films from 1954.
Lucky Me 54. *Rio Bravo* 59. The Sins of Rachel Cade 61. Jessica 62. Captain Newman 63. The Killers 64. The Art of Love 65. The Chase 66. Cast a Giant Shadow 66. Pistolero 67. Point Blank 68. Sam Whiskey 68. Young Billy Young 69. Pretty Maids all in a Row 70. Thief (TV) 71. See the Man Run (TV) 72. Big Bad Mama 74, etc.
TV series: *Police Woman* 74– .

Dickinson, Desmond (1902–). British cinematographer. Detective Lloyd (serial) 31. Men of Two Worlds 45. Fame is the Spur 46. *Hamlet* 47. The History of Mr Polly 49. Morning Departure 50. The Browning Version 52. The Importance of Being Earnest 52. Carrington VC 55. Orders to Kill 58. City of the Dead 60. Sparrows Can't Sing 63. A Study in Terror 65. Circus of Blood 67. Decline and Fall 68. Who Slew Auntie Roo? 71. The Fiend 71, etc.

Dickinson, Thorold (1903–). British director, in films since 1925. Retired to teach film theory at Slade School, London.
Book 1971: *A Discovery of Cinema.*
☐ The High Command 36. The Arsenal Stadium Mystery 39. *Gaslight* 39. The Prime Minister 41. *Next of Kin* 41. Men of Two Worlds 45. *The Queen of Spades* 48. The Secret People 52.

Dickson, Dorothy (1902–). American musical comedy star who spent most of her career in Britain.
Money Mad 17. Channel Crossing 32. Danny Boy 34. Sword of Honour 39, etc.

Dickson, Gloria (1916–45) (Thais Dickerson). American leading lady of the thirties.
They Wont Forget 37. Racket Busters 38. No Place to Go 39. They Made Me a Criminal 39. I Want a Divorce 40. The Big Boss 41. Affairs of Jimmy Valentine 42. Lady of Burlesque 43, etc.

Dickson, Paul (1920–). British director, hailed for documentaries. *The Undefeated* 49, *David* 51. His feature films have been less distinguished: *Satellite in the Sky* 56. *The Depraved* 57, many second features and TV episodes.

Dierkes, John (1905–1975). Gaunt American supporting actor.
Macbeth 48. *The Red Badge of Courage* 51. Shane 53. The Naked Jungle 54. Jubal 56. The Alamo 60. The Comancheros 61. The Haunted Palace 63, many others.

Dieterle, William (1893–1972) (Wilhelm Dieterle). Distinguished German director, long in Hollywood; at his best, an incomparable master of crowd scenes and pictorial composition. Formerly an actor in Germany, e.g. in Leni's *Waxworks.*
☐ Faust 26. The Weavers 29. Behind the Altar 29. The Dance Goes On 31. *The Last Flight* 31. Her Majesty Love 31. Man Wanted 32. Jewel Robbery 32. The Crash 32. Six Hours to Live 32. Scarlet Dawn 32. Lawyer Man 32. Grand Slam 33. Adorable 33. Devils in Love 33. Female 33. From Headquarters 33. Fashions of 1934 34. Fog Over Frisco 34. Madame du Barry 34. The Firebird 34. The Secret Bride 35. Dr Socrates 35. *A Midsummer Night's Dream* 35. *The Story of Louis Pasteur* 35. Concealment 35. Men on Her Mind 36. The White Angel 36. Satan Met a Lady 36. The Great O'Malley 37. Another Dawn 37. *The Life of Emile Zola* 37. Blockade 38. *Juarez* 39. *The Hunchback of Notre Dame* 39. *Dr Ehrlich's Magic Bullet* 40. A Dispatch from Reuters 40. *All That Money Can Buy* 41.

Syncopation 42. Tennessee Johnson 42. Kismet 44. *I'll Be Seeing You* 44. Love Letters 45. This Love of Ours 45. The Searching Wind 47. The Accused 48. *Portrait of Jennie* 48. Rope of Sand 49. Paid in Full 50. Dark City 50. September Affair 50. Peking Express 51. Red Mountain 51. Boots Malone 52. The Turning Point 52. Salome 53. Volcano 53. Elephant Walk 54. Magic Fire 56. Omar Khayyam 57. The Confession 66.

Dietrich, Marlene (1901–) (Maria Magdalena von Losch). German singer-actress long in America, a legend of glamour despite many poor films and her domination in the thirties by the heavy style of Josef Von Sternberg. □ The Tragedy of Love 23. Manon Lescaut 26. I Kiss Your Hand Madame 28. *The Blue Angel* 30. Morocco 30. Dishonoured 31. *Shanghai Express* 32. Blonde Venus 32. Song of Songs 33. *The Scarlet Empress* 34. The Devil Is a Woman 35. *Desire* 36. The Garden of Allah 36. Knight Without Armour (GB) 37. Angel 37. *Destry Rides Again* 39. Seven Sinners 40. The Flame of New Orleans 41. Manpower 41. The Lady Is Willing 42. The Spoilers 42. Pittsburgh 42. Follow the Boys 44. Kismet 44. Martin Roumagnac (Fr.) 46. Golden Earrings 47. *A Foreign Affair* 48. Stage Fright (GB) 50. No Highway (GB) 51. Rancho Notorious 52. The Monte Carlo Story 53. Around the World in Eighty Days 56. Witness for the Prosecution 57. Touch of Evil 58. Judgment at Nuremberg 61. Paris When It Sizzles 64.

Dietz, Howard (1896–). American librettist and writer, with MGM from its inception. Best film score: *The Band Wagon* 53.

Diffring, Anton (1918–). German actor, in British films from 1951; often the villainous Nazi or the protagonist of a horror film. State Secret 50. *Albert RN* 53. The Sea Shall Not Have Them 55. The Colditz Story 55. *I Am a Camera* 56. *The Man Who Could Cheat Death* 59. Circus of Horrors 60. Incident at Midnight 63. The Heroes of Telemark 65. Fahrenheit 451 66. The Double Man 67. Counterpoint (US) 67. Where Eagles Dare 68. Zeppelin 71. The Swiss Conspiracy 75. Operation Daybreak 76, etc.

Digges, Dudley (1879–1947). Versatile Irish character actor, with Abbey Theatre experience; played a variety of good roles in Hollywood in the thirties. □ *Condemned* 29. Outward Bound 30. Upper Underworld 30. *The Maltese Falcon* 31. The Ruling Voice 31. Alexander Hamilton 31. Devotion 31. The Honorable Mr Wong 31. The Hatchet Man 32. The Strange Case of Clara

Deane 32. Roar of the Dragon 32. The First Year 32. Tess of the Storm Country 32. The King's Vacation 33. Mayor of Hell 33. Silk Express 33. The Narrow Corner 33. The Invisible Man 33. The Emperor Jones 33. Before Dawn 33. Fury of the Jungle 34. Caravan 34. The World Moves On 34. Massacre 34. What Every Woman Knows 34. I Am a Thief 34. Notorious Gentleman 35. Mutiny on the Bounty 35. China Seas 35. The Bishop Misbehaves 35. Three Live Ghosts 36. The Voice of Bugle Ann 36. The Unguarded Hour 36. *The General Died at Dawn* 36. Valiant is the Word for Carrie 36. Love is News 37. *The Light that Failed* 39. *The Fight for Life* 40. *Raffles* 40. *Son of Fury* 42. The Searching Wind 46.

Dighton, John (1909–). British writer, in films from 1935. Let George Do It 40. Nicholas Nickleby 47. Saraband for Dead Lovers 48. *Kind Hearts and Coronets* 49. *The Happiest Days of Your Life* (from his own play) 49. The Man in the White Suit 51. Roman Holiday 53. Summer of the Seventeenth Doll 60, many others.

Dignam, Basil (1905–). British character actor, in innumerable small parts, often as barrister or other professional man. His Excellency 53. Brothers in Law 57. Room at the Top 59. The Silent Partner 61. Life for Ruth 63. Victim 62, etc.

Dignam, Mark (1909–). British character actor, brother of Basil Dignam. Also plays professional men. Murder in the Cathedral 52. The Maggie 54. The Prisoner 55. Sink the Bismarck 60. No Love for Johnnie 62. Hamlet 69, etc.

Diller, Phyllis (1917–). Zany, grotesque American comedienne who has had trouble adapting her TV style to movies. □ Splendor in the Grass 60. Boy Did I Get a Wrong Number 66. Eight on the Lam 67. The Private Navy of Sergeant O'Farrell 68. Did You Hear the One about the Travelling Saleslady? 68. The Adding Machine (GB) 69. TV series: The Pruitts of Southampton 66. The Beautiful Phyllis Diller Show 68.

Dillinger, John (1903–1934). American gangster of the thirties, public enemy number one; he was shot after leaving a cinema (where he had seen *Manhattan Melodrama*). He has been played in *Dillinger* 45 by Lawrence Tierney, in *Young Dillinger* 64 by Nick Adams, and in *Dillinger* 73 by Warren Oates.

Dillman, Bradford (1930–). Lean American actor.
A Certain Smile 58. *Compulsion* 59. Circle of Deception 61. Francis of Assisi 61. A Rage to Live 65. The Helicopter Spies 67. The Bridge at Remagen 69. Suppose They Gave a War and Nobody Came 71. Brother John 71. Escape from the Planet of the Apes 71. The Way We Were 73. The Iceman Cometh 73, etc.
TV series: Court Martial (GB) 65.

Dillon, Robert (–). American screenwriter.
Prime Cut 72. 99 and 44/100 per cent Dead 74.

Dillon, John Francis (1887–1934). American director.
Children of the Ritz 29. Sally 29. Kismet 30. The Finger Points 31. The Cohens and Kellys in Hollywood 32. Call Her Savage 32. Humanity 33. The Big Shakedown 34, etc.

Dinehart, Alan (1886–1944). American supporting actor who played many bluff-businessman roles.
Wicked 32. Lawyer Man 33. Dante's Inferno 35. This Is My Affair 37. Hotel for Women 39. Girl Trouble 42. Minstrel Man 44, many others.

Dingle, Charles (1887–1956). American stage actor who made occasional screen appearances, usually in cheerfully wicked roles.
One Third of a Nation 39. *The Little Foxes* 41. Johnny Eager 41. Talk of the Town 42. The Song of Bernadette 43. Duel in the Sun 46. The Beast with Five Fingers 47. *State of the Union* 48. Call Me Madam 53. The Court Martial of Billy Mitchell 55, etc.

Dinosaurs: see *Monster Animals*.

The Dionne Quins (1934–) appeared in two films, *Reunion* 36 and *The Country Doctor* 36. They were Cecile, Annette, Emilie (d 1954), Marie (d 1970), Yvonne.

director. Normally the most influential creator of a film, who may not only shoot scenes on the studio floor but also supervise script, casting, editing, etc., according to his standing. In more routine films these functions are separately controlled.

directors' appearances in films are comparatively few. Hitchcock remains the unchallengeable winner, with moments in over thirty of his fifty-odd films, including the confined *Rope* (in which his outline appears on a neon sign) and *Lifeboat* (in which he can be seen in a reducing ad. in a newspaper). Preston Sturges can be glimpsed in *Sullivan's Travels*, and in *Paris Holiday*, as a French resident, gets a whole scene to himself. John Huston, uncredited, plays a tourist in *The Treasure of the Sierra Madre* and a master of foxhounds in *The List of Adrian Messenger*; he has more recently begun to take sizeable credited roles, e.g. in *The Cardinal* and *The Bible*. The Paramount lot became a familiar scene in many forties pictures, with notable guest appearances by Mitchell Leisen in *Hold Back the Dawn* and Cecil B. de Mille in *Sunset Boulevard*, *The Buster Keaton Story*, *Star-Spangled Rhythm*, *Variety Girl*, *Son of Paleface* and others. Jean Cocteau played an old woman in *Orphée* and appeared throughout *The Testament of Orphée*. Nicholas Ray was the American ambassador in *55 Days in Peking*. Jules Dassin played major roles in *Rififi* (as Perlo Vita) and *Never on Sunday*, as did Jean Renoir in *La Règle du Jeu*. Hugo Fregonese was a messenger in *Decameron Nights*, Samuel Fuller a Japanese cop in *House of Bamboo*. Others who can be glimpsed in their own work include Tony Richardson in *Tom Jones*, Michael Winner in *You Must Be Joking*, George Marshall in *The Crime of Dr Forbes*, Frank Borzage in *Jeanne Eagels*, Robert Aldrich in *The Big Knife*, Ingmar Bergman in *Waiting Women*, King Vidor in *Our Daily Bread*, William Castle (producer) in *Rosemary's Baby*, Claude Chabrol in *Les Biches* and *The Road to Corinth*, and Joseph Losey in *The Intimate Stranger* (which he made under the name of Joseph Walton). Huston, Polanski, Truffaut and Bondartchuk are among those who have played major roles in their own and other films.

Disaster films have always been popular. In the thirties large crowds flocked to see *Tidal Wave*, *San Francisco*, *The Last Days of Pompeii*, *In Old Chicago* and *The Rains Came*. World War II was disaster enough for the forties, but the fifties brought *Titanic*, *A Night to Remember*, and *Invasion USA*, and the sixties *The Devil at Four O'Clock* and *Krakatoa East of Java*. It was the seventies, however, that found the killing of large numbers of people to be really top box office. *Earthquake* and *The Towering Inferno* were giants of their kind, and even though *The Hindenberg* was not clever enough to attract, there were plenty of successful imitators.

The Discreet Charm of the Bourgeoisie (France 1972). This hilarious surrealist comedy about a group of friends who just can't seem to get together for dinner is almost certainly director Luis Buñuel's most typical and most likeable film, though it does slightly overstay its welcome.

disguise has featured in many hundreds of films, and was in the twenties the perquisite of Lon Chaney, all of whose later films featured it. Lon Chaney Jnr has also had a tendency to it, as had John Barrymore; while most of the Sherlock Holmes films involved it. Other notable examples include Henry Hull in *Miracles for Sale*; Donald Wolfit in *The Ringer*; Marlene Dietrich in *Witness for the Prosecution*; Jack Lemmon and Tony Curtis in *Some Like It Hot*; Alec Guinness in *Kind Hearts and Coronets*; Peter Sellers in *The Naked Truth* and *After the Fox*; Rod Steiger in *No Way to Treat a Lady*; Tony Randall in *Seven Faces of Dr Lao*; and practically the entire cast of *The List of Adrian Messenger*. Extensions of disguise are the split personality films, from *Dr Jekyll and Mr Hyde* to *The Three Faces of Eve*.

See also: *transvestism*; *multiple roles*.

Diskant, George E. (1907–1965). American cinematographer.
Riff Raff 47. The Narrow Margin 50. On Dangerous Ground 51. The Bigamist 53, others.

Disney, Walt (1901–1966). American animator and executive whose name is a household word all over the world. Formerly a commercial artist, he produced his first Mickey Mouse cartoon in 1928, using his own voice; also Silly Symphonies, one of which (*Flowers and Trees* 33) was the first film in full Technicolor. Donald Duck first appeared in 1936. First full-length cartoon: *Snow White and the Seven Dwarfs* 37, followed by *Pinocchio* 39, *Fantasia* 40, *Dumbo* 41, *Bambi* 43, *The Three Caballeros* (combining cartoon and live action) 44, *Cinderella* 50, *Alice in Wonderland* 51, *Peter Pan* 53, *Lady and the Tramp* 56, *The Sleeping Beauty* 59, *One Hundred and One Dalmatians* 61, *The Sword in the Stone* 63, *Winnie the Pooh and the Honey Tree* 66, *The Jungle Book* 67, *The Aristocats* 70, *Robin Hood* 73. First live-action feature *Treasure Island* 50, followed by a plentiful supply including westerns (*Westward Ho the Wagons, The Nine Lives of Elfego Baca*), adventure classics (*Kidnapped, Dr Syn*), animal yarns (*Greyfriars Bobby, Old Yeller, The Incredible Journey*), cosy fantasies with music (*In Search of the Castaways, Mary Poppins*), trick comedies (*The Absent-Minded Professor, Son of Flubber*) and plain old-fashioned family fun (*Bon Voyage, The Ugly Dachshund*). The patchiness of these films has meant that although the Disney label is still a sure sign of suitability for children, it no longer necessarily indicates

quality of any other kind. In 1948 began the irresistible series of 'True-Life Adventures' (cleverly jazzed-up animal documentaries containing much rare footage) and in 1953 came the first feature of this kind, *The Living Desert*; the series has unfortunately died out.

Disney's long list of Academy Awards are all for shorts, apart from 'special awards' for *Snow White, Fantasia, The Living Desert* and *The Vanishing Prairie*. They include a special award for creating *Mickey Mouse* 32. *Three Little Pigs* 33. *The Tortoise and the Hare* 34. *Three Orphan Kittens* 35. *The Old Mill* 37. *Ferdinand the Bull* 38. *The Ugly Duckling* 39. *Lend a Paw* 41. *Der Fuhrer's Face* 42. *Seal Island* 48. *Beaver Valley* 50. *Nature's Half Acre* 51. *Water Birds* 52. *Toot Whistle Plunk and Boom* 53. *Bear Country* 53. *The Alaskan Eskimo* 53. *Men against the Arctic* 55. *The Wetback Hound* 57. *White Wilderness* 58. *Ama Girls* 58. *The Horse with the Flying Tail* 60. *Winnie the Pooh and the Blustery Day* 68, etc.

A biography, *Walt Disney*, was published in 1958 by his daughter Diane, and in 1968 came Richard Schickel's iconoclastic *The Disney Version*. A massive informational tome is Christopher's Finch's *The Art of Walt Disney* 73.

Disraeli, Benjamin (1804–1881), novelist and prime minister, has been notably portrayed on screen by George Arliss in 1921 and 1930 (in each case his wife Florence Arliss played Mrs Disraeli), by Derrick de Marney in *Victoria the Great* 37 and *Sixty Glorious Years* 38, by John Gielgud in *The Prime Minister* 40; and by Alec Guinness in *The Mudlark* 50.

dissolve (or mix). A change of scene accomplished by gradually exposing a second image over the first while fading the first away.

distributor (or renter). A company which, for a percentage of the profits or a flat fee, undertakes to rent a film to exhibitors on the producing company's behalf. Originally major producers like MGM, Warner and Paramount distributed their own films exclusively, but with the rise of independent producers the situation has become much more fluid, with distributors bidding for the films they consider most likely to succeed at the box office and tying up successful producers to long-term contracts.

Dix, Richard (1894–1949) (Ernest Brimmer). Stalwart American leading man of the twenties and thirties, after which his vehicles declined.
Dangerous Curve Ahead 21. Fools First 22. The Sin Flood 22. The Christian (GB) 23. Souls for

Sale 23. Icebound 24. Unguarded Women 24. Too Many Kisses 25. The Lady who Lied 25. *The Vanishing American* 25. The Quarterback 26. Shanghai Bound 27. Sporting Goods 28. Moran of the Marines 28. Nothing but the Truth 29. *Seven Keys to Baldpate* 29. Shooting Straight 30. *Cimarron* 31. The Public Defender 31. The Lost Squadron 32. Roar of the Dragon 32. The Great Jasper 33. Ace of Aces 33. Stingaree 34. West of the Pecos 34. The Arizonian 35. The Tunnel (GB) 35. Special Investigator 36. The Devil's Playground 37. The Devil is Driving 37. Sky Giant 38. Man of Conquest 39. Here I am a Stranger 39. Cherokee Strip 40. Badlands of Dakota 41. Tombstone 42. Eyes of the Underworld 42. The Kansan 43. Top Man 43. The Ghost Ship 43. The Whistler 44. Mark of the Whistler 44, many others.

Dix, William (1956–). British child actor of the sixties.
The Nanny 65. Doctor Dolittle 67.

Dixon, Thomas (1864–1946). American Baptist minister who wrote the anti-Negro novel *The Clansman*, on which Griffith's *The Birth of a Nation* was based.

Dmytryk, Edward (1908–). American director, in films from 1923. After years of second features he gained a reputation as a stylist with some tough adult thrillers of the forties; but after years of exile due to the McCarthy witch-hunt his more ambitious recent films have seemed impersonal.
☐ The Hawk 35. Television Spy 39. Emergency Squad 40. Golden Gloves 40. Mystery Sea Raider 40. Her First Romance 40. The Devil Commands 41. Under Age 41. Sweetheart of the Campus 41. Blonde from Singapore 41. Confessions of Boston Blackie 41. Secrets of the Lone Wolf 41. Counter Espionage 42. Seven Miles from Alcatraz 42. The Falcon Strikes Back 43. Behind the Rising Sun 43. Captive Wild Woman 43. Tender Comrade 44. *Murder My Sweet* 44. Back to Bataan 45. Cornered 46. Till the End of Time 46. *Crossfire* 47. So Well Remembered (GB) 47. Obsession (GB) 48. Give Us This Day (GB) 49. Mutiny (Fr.) 52. The Sniper 52. Eight Iron Men 52. The Juggler 53. *The Caine Mutiny* 54. Broken Lance 54. The End of the Affair (GB) 54. Soldier of Fortune 55. The Left Hand of God 55. The Mountain (& p) 56. Raintree County 57. The Young Lions 58. Warlock 59. The Blue Angel 59. The Reluctant Saint (It.) 61. A Walk on the Wild Side 62. The Carpetbaggers 63. Where Love Has Gone 64. *Mirage* 65. Alvarez Kelly 66. Anzio 68. Shalako 68. Bluebeard 72.

Dobie, Alan (1932–). British leading actor, usually in astringent roles on stage or TV.
Seven Keys 62. The Comedy Man 64. The Long Day's Dying 68. Alfred the Great 69. The Chairman 69, etc.

Docks of New York (US 1928). A late silent melodrama directed by Josef Von Sternberg in a manner realistic for twenties Hollywood, pretentious in retrospect; from a script by Jules Furthman about a coal stoker who rescues and marries a would-be suicide. With George Bancroft, Betty Compson, Olga Baclanova.

Dr Christian was the kindly country doctor hero, played by Jean Hersholt, of a number of unambitious little films which came out between 1938 and 1940, based on a radio series and inspired by the publicity surrounding Dr Dafoe, who delivered the Dionne Quins in 1937. In 1956 Macdonald Carey featured in a TV series of the same name, but he played the nephew of the original Dr Christian.

Dr Cyclops (US 1939). Horror film making a notable advance in colour trick photography but a disappointing film to come from Ernest Schoedsack. Albert Dekker was the mad scientist who reduced the rest of the cast to midgets.

Dr Ehrlich's Magic Bullet (US 1940). One of the Warner biographical series which also included Pasteur, Zola, Juarez and Reuter, this engrossing production has Edward G. Robinson bearded and unrecognizable as the German research chemist who discovered a cure for syphilis. Directed with great accomplishment by William Dieterle, and splendidly produced and acted. The subject made it a Hollywood milestone.

Doctor in The House (GB 1953). First in a long and still expanding series of comedies adapted from Richard Gordon's collections of anecdotes about a doctor's life. All have been lucrative but only the first had genuine vitality: the TV series which began in 1968 has been better.

Dr Jekyll and Mr Hyde. Robert Louis Stevenson's classic thriller of split personality has become one of the screen's most popular and oft-borrowed themes. There was a Selig version in 1908 and a Danish one in 1909. James Cruze appeared in a Universal version in 1912, and in 1913 King Baggott appeared in a rival production. A British version came out in the same year. 1919 brought Sheldon Lewis as the doctor (copies still exist) and in 1921 John Barrymore gave a brilliant portrayal in the role, with very little use of trick photography or make-up. Meanwhile in Germany in 1920 Conrad Veidt, directed by Murnau, had an equally, splendid shot at the character. In 1932 Fredric March won an Academy Award for his performance in Rouben Mamoulian's version, which was remade in 1941 with Spencer Tracy. Louis Hayward suffered the fatal dose in *Son of Dr Jekyll* 51; Boris Karloff (as well as Lou Costello and Reginald Denny) underwent the transformation in *Abbott and Costello Meet Dr Jekyll and Mr Hyde* 53; Gloria Talbot was *Daughter of Dr Jekyll* 57; and in 1958 Sylvester the cartoon cat was 'translated' in *Dr Jekyll's Hide*. In 1959 Bernard Bresslaw was in a funny version, *The Ugly Duckling*, and in 1960 the same studio, Hammer, had Paul Massie in a serious version called *The Two Faces of Dr Jekyll*, in which for the first time the evil side of the character was handsomer than the good. Another comic version was Jerry Lewis' *The Nutty Professor* 63. In 1970 Hammer produced a transvestite version, *Doctor Jekyll and Sister Hyde*, in which Ralph Bates changed into Martine Beswick. *I, Monster* 71 turned out to be another stab at the original story. Television's first version was Renoir's 1958 *The Testament of Dr Cordelier*; 1973 brought a musical version for TV, with Kirk Douglas, following an excellent straight Canadian TV adaptation in 1968 with Jack Palance.

Dr Kildare. Max Brand's novels about a young intern were first filmed in 1938 with Joel McCrea in the leading role of a film called *Interns Can't Take Money*. In the same year MGM made *Young Dr Kildare* starring Lew Ayres, the first of a popular series of nine films, with Lionel Barrymore as crusty old Dr Gillespie. In 1943 Ayres gave up his role and six films were made starring Barrymore only, with various interns including Van Johnson and Philip Dorn. No movies about Blair Hospital have been made since 1947, but in 1960 MGM revived the characters in a TV series starring Richard Chamberlain and Raymond Massey: it ran five years. In 1972 a half-hour soap opera version began with Mark Jenkins and Gary Merrill.

Dr Mabuse. The master criminal hero-villain of two films directed in Germany by Fritz Lang: *Dr Mabuse the Gambler* 23 and *The Testament of Dr Mabuse* 32. The latter was blatant anti-Nazi propaganda and caused Lang to hurry to Hollywood. In the late fifties the character was revived by Lang and others, but to less effect.

Dr Strangelove (GB/US 1963). The first nuclear comedy, full of black laughter about what might happen if a madman pressed *that* button. Directed by Stanley Kubrick (from Peter George's novel *Red Alert*) to great critical acclaim; but cinematically and dramatically somewhat tortuous and even dull once one knew what it was about. Full credit, however, to the sets of Ken Adam and to Peter Sellers in his three roles. Won three BFA awards: best film, best British film, and United Nations Award.

Dr Syn. Russell Thorndyke's novel about the smuggling vicar of Dymchurch was filmed in 1938 with George Arliss, in 1961 with Peter Cushing, (as *Captain Clegg*) and in 1963 with Patrick McGoohan.

Doctor Zhivago (US 1965). MGM insist on 'Doctor' being spelt out, and this may serve as a key to the pretentiousness of this would-be epic from Boris Pasternak's novel of modern Russia. The story has been simplified until there is almost nothing of it and Zhivago is a nonentity; what's left plays like a thin variant on *Gone with the Wind*. The chief demerit is Robert Bolt's tortuous screenplay, which has characters making inexplicable appearances and disappearances; but David Lean's direction is self-indulgent, wasting time on inessentials, and only Frederick Young's cinematography (AA) emerges with full credit. Maurice Jarre (AA) wrote the score.

doctors (in the medical sense) have been crusading heroes of many movies: fictional epics that come readily to mind include *Arrowsmith, The Citadel, Magnificent Obsession, Private Worlds, Men in White, The Green Light, Disputed Passage, Yellow Jack, The Last Angry Man, Not as a Stranger, Johnny Belinda, The Girl in White, The Doctor and the Girl, Green Fingers, The Outsider, The Crime of Dr Forbes, The Interns, The New Interns, The Young Doctors, Behind the Mask, Doctor Zhivago,* and *White Corridors*. A few have even commanded whole series to themselves: *Dr Kildare, Dr Christian, Dr Gillespie, The Crime Doctor*. Once-living doctors have received the accolade of a Hollywood biopic: *The Story of Louis Pasteur, Dr Ehrlich's Magic Bullet, Prisoner of Shark Island* (Dr Mudd), *L'Enfant Sauvage* (Dr Jean Retard) *The Story of Dr Wassell, Il Est Minuit Dr Schweizer*. Many less single-minded films have had a background of medicine and doctors as leading figures: *The Nun's Story, King's Row, No Way Out, People Will Talk, The Hospital*. More or less villainous doctors were found in *The Flesh and the Fiends, Frankenstein,*

Dr Socrates, Dr Jekyll and Mr Hyde, Green for Danger, Dr Cyclops, The Hands of Orlac, Dr Goldfoot, and *The Amazing Dr Clitterhouse.* TV series on medical subjects have included *Medic* 54–55. *Ben Casey* 60–65. *Dr Kildare* 61–65. *Dr Christian* 56. *Dr Hudson's Secret Journal* 55–56. *The Nurses* 62–63. *The Doctors and the Nurses* 64. *Marcus Welby M.D.* 69. *The Bold Ones* 68–72. *Police Surgeon* 72.
See also: *hospitals.*

documentary was not coined as a word until 1929, but several famous films, including Ponting's *With Scott to the Antarctic,* Lowell Thomas' *With Allenby in Palestine,* and Flaherty's *Nanook of the North,* had before 1921 brought an attitude to their reportage which made them more than mere travel films. In Britain during the twenties, H. Bruce Woolfe made a series of painstaking and still evocative reconstructions of the battles of World War I; while Cooper and Schoedsack went even further afield for the exciting material in ·*Grass* and *Chang.* 1928 brought Eisenstein's *The General Line,* a brilliant piece of farming propaganda, and Turin's *Turksib,* a showy account of the building of the Turko-Siberian railway. John Grierson, who invented the term 'documentary', made in 1929 a quiet little two-reeler about Britain's herring fleet, and called it *Drifters*; for the next ten years Britain's official and sponsored film units produced such brilliant results as *Shipyard, Coalface, Housing Problems, Song of Ceylon, North Sea* and *Night Mail.* In 1931 Vigo made his satirical documentary *A Propos de Nice,* and shortly afterwards Eisenstein was at work on his never-finished *Thunder over Mexico,* brilliant fragments of which survive as *Time in the Sun.* Travel films by explorers like the Martin Johnsons proliferated during the thirties; Flaherty spent two uncomfortable years off the Irish coast to make his *Man of Aran,* and later produced in India the semi-fictional *Elephant Boy.* Pare Lorenz produced cinematic poetry out of America's geographical problems in *The Plow that Broke the Plains* and *The River.*
World War II stimulated documentarists to new urgency and new techniques, brilliantly exemplified by Frank Capra's *Why We Fight* series for the US Signal Corps, turning unpleasant facts into breathtaking entertainment. With a predictably understated approach the British units produced a more sober but equally stirring series of reports on the war (*Western Approaches, Desert Victory, Target for Tonight*) and the home front (*Listen to Britain, Fires Were Started, A Diary for Timothy*), many of them directed by Britain's first documentary poet, Humphrey Jennings.

The two countries combined resources to present a brilliant, high-flying compilation film about the last year of war, *The True Glory.*
Since 1945 the use of documentary for advertising (often very subtly) and teaching has so proliferated that no simple line of development can be shown. Television has relentlessly explored and elaborated every technique of the pioneers, with special attention to 'action stills', compilation films, and hard-hitting popular journalist approaches such as NBC's White Paper series and Granada's *World in Action.* Entertainment films devised a popular blend of fact and fiction in such neo-classics as *Boomerang, The House on 92nd Street* and *Naked City.* At last documentary was accepted as an agreeable blend of instruction and pleasure; and in the changed environment Flaherty's lyrical *Louisiana Story* seemed slow and solemn.

Dodsworth (US 1936). William Wyler made, for its time, a remarkably adult and intelligent film of Sinclair Lewis' novel about a dull but sincere businessman who tries to preserve his marriage to a selfish woman. With Walter Huston and Ruth Chatterton, as the Americans abroad, Mary Astor as the other woman.

Dolan, Robert Emmett (1906–1972). American composer, in Hollywood from 1941.
Scores include: Birth of the Blues 41. Going My Way 44. The Bells of St Mary's 45. My Son John 51, etc. Produced White Christmas 54. Anything Goes 56, etc.

La Dolce Vita (Italy 1959). Federico Fellini's 'exposé' of 'the sweet life', a sprawling persuasive, orgiastic movie assumed by many to have contributed to a decline in standards because it reported without condemning.

Doleman, Guy (1923–). Australian character actor, in British films.
Phantom Stockade 53. The Shiralee 57. The Ipcress File 65. Thunderball 65. The Idol 66, etc.

Dolenz, George (1908–1963). Dullish Trieste-born leading man who played leads in some Hollywood films from 1941.
Unexpected Uncle 41. Enter Arsène Lupin 45. Vendetta 50. My Cousin Rachel 53. The Purple Mask 55. The Four Horsemen of the Apocalypse 62, others.

dolly. A trolley on which a camera unit can be soundlessly moved about during shooting: can usually be mounted on rails. A 'crab dolly' will move in any direction.

Domergue, Faith (1925–). American leading lady, launched in 1950 with a publicity campaign which misfired. However, she played competently in a number of films.
Vendetta 50. Where Danger Lives 50. This Island Earth 55. California 63. Prehistoric Planet Women 66. One on Top of the Other 70. Legacy of Blood 71. The House of the Seven Corpses 73, etc.

Don Juan. The amorous adventures of this legendary rascal, a heartless seducer created in stories by Gabriel Tellez (1571–1641), have been filmed several times, notably with John Barrymore in 1927, Douglas Fairbanks Snr in 1934, Errol Flynn in 1948 and (of all people) Fernandel in 1955. Versions of the opera, *Don Giovanni*, are legion.

Don Quixote. There have been many screen versions of Cervantes' picaresque novel about the adventures of the addled knight and his slow but faithful lieutenant Sancho Panza . . . but none have been entirely successful because the genius of the book is a purely literary one. There was a French production in 1909; an American one in 1916 directed by Edward Dillon; a British one in 1923 directed by Maurice Elvey and starring Jerrold Robertshaw with George Robey. In 1933 Pabst made a British film of the story with Chaliapin and (again) George Robey; meanwhile a Danish director, Lau Lauritzen, had done one in 1926. The next batch of Quixotes began in 1947 with Rafael Gil's Spanish version; but the Russian production of 1957, directed by Kozintsev with Cherkassov in the title role, was probably the best of all. Since 1958 Orson Welles has been filming sections of his own version, which it looks as though we may never see; a Jugoslavian cartoon version appeared in 1961; in 1962 Finland, of all nations, contributed its own Quixote, directed by Eino Ruutsalo; and in 1972 the BBC and Universal made a TV film with Rex Harrison. The popular stage musical *Man of la Mancha*, filmed in 1972, is based on the life of author Miguel de Cervantes (1547–1616) and its correlation with that of his hero. There followed in 1973 a ballet version with Rudolph Nureyev.

Donahue, Troy (1936–) (Merle Johnson). American beefcake hero of the sixties.
Tarnished Angels 57. This Happy Feeling 58. The Perfect Furlough 59. Imitation of Life 59. The Crowded Sky 61. *Parrish* 61. Susan Slade 61. A Summer Place 62. Rome Adventure 62. Palm Springs Weekend 63. A Distant Trumpet 64. My Blood Runs Cold 65. Rocket to the Moon 67. Sweet Saviour 71, etc.
TV series: Surfside Six 60–62.

Donald Duck. Belligerent Disney cartoon character who was introduced in 1936 in *Orphans' Benefit*, was quickly streamlined and became more popular than Mickey Mouse. Still going strong.

Donald, James (1917–). British stage actor who has been in occasional films since 1941; usually plays a man of conscience rather than action.
The Missing Million 41. In Which We Serve 42. The Way Ahead 44. Broken Journey 47. *The Small Voice* 47. Trottie True 49. *White Corridors* 51. Brandy for the Parson 51. The Gift Horse 52. The Pickwick Papers 52. The Net 53. Beau Brummell 54. Lust for Life 56. *The Bridge on the River Kwai* 57. The Vikings 58. The Great Escape 63. King Rat 65. Cast a Giant Shadow 66. *The Jokers* 67. Hannibal Brooks 69. David Copperfield 69. The Royal Hunt of the Sun 69, etc.

Donaldson, Ted (1933–). American child star of the forties.
Once Upon a Time 44. *A Tree Grows in Brooklyn* 45. For the Love of Rusty 47 (and others in this series). The Decision of Christopher Blake 48. Phone Call from a Stranger 52, etc.

Donat, Robert (1905–1958). Distinguished British stage actor with an inimitably melodious voice; he made some impressive films despite asthma which blighted his career.
Biography 1968: *Robert Donat* by J. C. Trewin.
□ Men of Tomorrow 32. That Night in London 32. Cash 32. The Private Life of Henry VIII 33. *The Count of Monte Cristo* 34. *The Thirty-Nine Steps* 35. *The Ghost Goes West* 36. Knight without Armour 37. *The Citadel* 38. *Goodbye Mr Chips* (AA) 39. *The Young Mr Pitt* 42. The Adventures of Tartu 43. Perfect Strangers 45. Captain Boycott (guest appearance) 47. *The Winslow Boy* 48. The Cure for Love (& d) 50. The Magic Box 50. Lease of Life 55. Inn of the Sixth Happiness 58.

Donath, Ludwig (1900–1967). Austrian character actor busy in America from the thirties.
The Strange Death of Adolf Hitler 43. *The Jolson Story* 46. Cigarette Girl 47. Jolson Sings Again 50. The Great Caruso 51. Sins of Jezebel 53. Torn Curtain 66, many others.

Donehue, Vincent J. (1916–1966). American stage director who came to Hollywood to make *Lonelyhearts* 59. *Sunrise at Campobello* 60.

Donen, Stanley (1924–). American director,
former dancer; later branched out from musicals
to sophisticated comedies and thrillers.
☐ *On The Town* (co-d) 49. Royal Wedding 51.
Fearless Fagan 51. Give a Girl a Break 51. Love
is Better than Ever 52. *Singin' in the Rain* (co-d)
52. *Seven Brides for Seven Brothers* 54. Deep in
My Heart 54. It's Always Fair Weather (co-d)
55. *Funny Face* 57. *The Pajama Game* (& co-p)
57. Kiss Them for Me. 57. *Indiscreet* (& p) 58.
Damn Yankees (& co-p) 58. Once More with
Feeling (& p) 60. Surprise Package (& p) 60. The
Grass is Greener (& p) 61. *Charade* (& p) 63.
Arabesque (& p) 66. Two for the Road (& p) 67.
Bedazzled (& p) 67. Staircase (& p) 69. The Little
Prince (& p) 73. Lucky Lady (& p) 76.

Doniger, Walter (1917–). American writer.
Mob Town 41. Red Sundown 49. Cease Fire 52.
The Steel Jungle (& d) 56, etc.

Donlan, Yolande (1920–). American leading
lady who had great success on the British stage
as the dumb blonde in *Born Yesterday*; settled in
England and married Val Guest.
Autobiography 1976: *Shake the Stars Down*.
Turnabout 41. Miss Pilgrim's Progress 50. *Mr
Drake's Duck* 50. Penny Princess 51. They
Can't Hang Me 55. *Expresso Bongo* 59. Jigsaw
62. Eighty Thousand Suspects 63. Seven Nights
in Japan 76, etc.

Donlevy, Brian (1899–1972). Irish-American
leading man, later character actor, in Hollywood
after stage experience; characteristically in fast-
talking tough roles with soft centres.
Mother's Boy 28. Barbary Coast 35. In Old
Chicago 38. We're Going To Be Rich (GB) 38.
Jesse James 39. *Beau Geste* (as the evil sergeant)
39. Destry Rides Again 39. *The Great McGinty*
(leading role) 40. Brigham Young 40. The Great
Man's Lady 40. A Gentleman after Dark 41.
Billy the Kid 41. The Remarkable Andrew 41.
Wake Island 42. *The Glass Key* 42. Nightmare
42. Hangmen Also Die 43. The Miracle of
Morgan's Creek 43. *An American Romance* 44.
Two Years Before the Mast 44. The Virginian 45.
The Trouble with Women 46. The Beginning or
the End 47. Kiss of Death 47. The Lucky Stiff 48.
Shakedown 50. Hoodlum Empire 52. The
Woman They Almost Lynched 53. The Big
Combo 55. The Quatermass Experiment (GB)
55. A Cry in the Night 56. Quatermass II (GB)
56. Cowboy 58. Never So Few 59. The Errand
Boy 61. Curse of the Fly (GB) 65. How to Stuff a
Wild Bikini 65. The Fat Spy 66. Waco 66.
Rogues' Gallery 67, etc.
TV series: Dangerous Assignment 58.

Donnell, Jeff (1921–). Pert American actress
who played the heroine's friend in many routine
comedies of the forties, now plays mothers.
A Night to Remember 43. He's My Guy 45. In a
Lonely Place 50. Thief of Damascus 52. Sweet
Smell of Success 57. Gidget Goes Hawaiian 61.
The Iron Maiden (GB) 62. Stand Up and Be
Counted 72, etc.

Donnelly, Donal (1932–). Irish stage actor, in
occasional films.
The Rising of the Moon 57. Shake Hands with
the Devil 59. Young Cassidy 65. The Knack 65.
Up Jumped a Swagman 65, etc.

Donnelly, Ruth (1896–). American character
actress, a wisecracking girl friend in the thirties,
latterly in maternal roles.
Rubber Heels 27. Transatlantic 31. Ladies They
Talk About 33. Footlight Parade 33. Convention
City 33. Wonder Bar 34. Alibi Ike 35. Mr Deeds
Goes to Town 36. More than a Secretary 36. *A
Slight Case of Murder* 38. *Holiday* 38. Mr Smith
Goes to Washington 39. My Little Chickadee 39.
Rise and Shine 41. Pillow to Post 45. Cinderella
Jones 46. *The Snake Pit* 48. I'd Climb the
Highest Mountain 51. The Spoilers 55. Autumn
Leaves 56. The Way to the Gold 57, many
others.

Donner, Clive (1926–). British director,
former editor, in films since 1942.
☐ The Secret Place 56. Heart of a Child 57. A
Marriage of Convenience 59. The Sinister Man
60. Some People 62. The Caretaker 63. *Nothing
But the Best* 63. What's New Pussycat? 65. Luv
67. *Here We Go Round the Mulberry Bush* 67.
Alfred the Great 69. Vampira 74.

Donner, Jörn (1933–). Finnish writer-
director.
Sunday in September 63. *To Love* 65. Black on
White 67. Portraits of Women 69, etc.

Donner, Richard (–). American
director.
X-15 62. Salt and Pepper (GB) 68. Twinky (GB)
69. *The Omen* 76, etc.

Donohue, Jack (1912–). American director,
former Ziegfeld Follies dancer. Worked on many
MGM musicals.
The Yellow Cab Man 50. Watch the Birdie 51.
Calamity Jane (dances only) 53. Lucky Me 54.
Babes in Toyland 61. Marriage on the Rocks 65.
Assault on a Queen 66, etc.

Donovan, King (c. 1919–). American general
purpose actor, usually in support roles; a

frequent TV guest star.
Cargo to Capetown 50. The Beast from Twenty Thousand Fathoms 53. *Invasion of the Body Snatchers* 56. The Hanging Tree 59, many others.

Donskoi, Mark (1897–). Russian director celebrated for his 'Maxim Gorki trilogy' 1938-40.

Doonan, Patric (1925–1958). British stage and screen actor, usually in honest, put-upon roles. Son of comedian George Doonan.
Once a Jolly Swagman 48. The Blue Lamp 50. The Gentle Gunman 52. The Net 53. Seagulls over Sorrento 54. Cockleshell Heroes 55, many second features.

dope sheet. A list of the contents of a piece of film, usually applied to newsreel libraries.

Doran, Ann (1914–). American character actress, often a friend of the heroine.
Penitentiary 38. Blonde 38. Blue, White and Perfect 42. The More the Merrier 43. Fear in the Night 46. The Snake Pit 48. Rebel without a Cause 55. The Man Who Turned to Stone 58. The Rawhide Trail 60. Rosie 67, many others. TV series: *Longstreet* 71.

Dorfmann, Robert (–   ). French producer.
Jeux Interdits 52. Road to Salina 69. The Red Circle 70. Red Sun 71. Papillon 72. etc.

Dorleac, Françoise (1941–1967). French leading lady, killed in car crash.
That Man from Rio 64. Genghis Khan 65. Where the Spies Are 65. Cul de Sac (GB) 66. The Young Girls of Rochefort 67. Billion Dollar Brain 67, etc.

Dorn, Dolores (1935–) (D. Dorn-Heft). American stage actress briefly in Hollywood.
Phantom of the Rue Morgue 54. Uncle Vanya 58. Underworld USA 60. 13 West Street 62, etc.

Dorn, Philip (1905–1975) (Frits van Dongen). Dutch stage actor who went to Hollywood in 1940 and was used mainly in sincere refugee or thoughtfully professional roles: returned to Holland in the fifties, later settled in California.
Ski Patrol 40. *Escape* 40. Ziegfeld Girl 41. Tarzan's Secret Treasure 41. Calling Dr Gillespie 41. *Random Harvest* 42. Reunion in France 42. Chetniks 43. *Passage to Marseilles* 44. Blonde Fever 44. Escape in the Desert 45. I've Always Loved You 46. *I Remember Mama* 48. Panther's Moon 49. Sealed Cargo 51, etc.

Dorne, Sandra (1925–). British 'platinum blonde', often in tawdry roles.
Eyes That Kill 45. Once a Jolly Swagman 48. The Beggars' Opera 51. Roadhouse Girl 54. The Gelignite Gang 56. The Iron Petticoat 57. Orders to Kill 58. The Devil Doll 64. All Coppers Are . . . 72, etc.

Doro, Marie (1882–1956) (Marie Steward). American leading lady of the silent screen, one of Zukor's 'Famous Players'.
Oliver Twist (title role) 16. The Morals of Marcus 15. The White Pearl 15. The Heart of Nora Flynn 16. The Wood Nymph 16. The Mysterious Princess 19. Twelve Ten 19. Maid of Mystery 20, etc.

Dors, Diana (1931–) (Diana Fluck). British 'blonde bombshell' who has been playing a good-time girl since the mid-forties.
The Shop at Sly Corner 46. Holiday Camp 47. *Oliver Twist* 48. Good Time Girl 48. The Calendar 49. Here Come the Huggetts 49. Dance Hall 50. Lady Godiva Rides Again 51. The Weak and the Wicked 52. Is Your Honeymoon Really Necessary? 52. It's a Grand Life 53. A Kid for Two Farthings 55. Miss Tulip Stays the Night 55. As Long as They're Happy 55. *Yield to the Night* 56. I Married a Woman (US) 56. The Unholy Wife (US) 56. The Long Haul 57. Tread Softly, Stranger 58. Passport to Shame 59. On the Double (US) 60. Mrs Gibbons' Boys 62. West Eleven 63. The Sandwich Man 66. Berserk 67. Baby Love 69. There's a Girl in My Soup 70. Deep End 71. Hannie Caulder 71. The Amazing Mr Blunden 72. The Amorous Milkman 72. Confessions of a Driving Instructor 76, etc.

D'Orsay, Fifi (1907–). Vivacious Canadian leading lady of Hollywood films in the early thirties.
Hot for Paris 30. *Just Imagine* 31. Silk Stockings 32. Wonder Bar 34. Accent on Youth 45. Wild and Wonderful 63. The Art of Love 65, others.

Dorsey, Jimmy (1904–1957) and **Tommy** (1905–1956). American bandleaders and brothers; individually they decorated many musicals of the forties, and came together in a biopic, *The Fabulous Dorseys* 46.

Dorziat, Gabrielle (1880–) (G. Moppert). French character actress.
Mayerling 36. La Fin du Jour 39. Premier Rendezvous 41. Les Parents Terribles 48. Manon 49. Act of Love 54. Les Espions 57. Germinal 63, etc.

Dostoievsky, Fyodor (1821–1881). Russian writer, chiefly of doom-laden novels, of which the most frequently-filmed is *Crime and Punishment*; there have also been attempts at *The Idiot, The Brothers Karamazov, White Nights, The Great Sinner, Pyriev* and others.

Dotrice, Karen (1955–). British child actress.
The Three Lives of Thomasina 63. Mary Poppins 64. The Gnome-Mobile 67.

Dotrice, Michele (1947–). British leading actress, mostly on TV.
And Soon the Darkness 70. Jane Eyre 73.

Dotrice, Roy (1923–). British stage actor with a strong line in senile impersonation.
The Heroes of Telemark 65. A Twist of Sand 68. Lock Up Your Daughters 69. One of Those Things 71. Nicholas and Alexandra 71, etc.

double exposure. This occurs when two or more images are recorded on the same piece of film. Used for trick shots when two characters played by the same actor have to meet; also for dissolves, dream sequences, etc.

double-headed print. One in which sound and picture are recorded on separate pieces of film, usually at cutting copy stage or before OK is received to make combined negative.

Double Indemnity (US 1944). The forties now seem a pretty 'dated' era, but this tawdry crime story, about a man who murders his mistress's husband for his insurance money, still packs a punch by virtue of Billy Wilder's direction and a witty script in which Wilder and Raymond Chandler had a hand. Fred MacMurray and Edward G. Robinson are in good form: Barbara Stanwyck's *femme fatale* has worn less well. From a novel by James Cain; photographed by John Seitz with music by Miklos Rozsa. An undistinguished TV copy was made in 1973, with Richard Crenna and Samantha Eggar.

A Double Life (US 1947). The film for which Ronald Colman belatedly won an Oscar was an arrant piece of nonsense about an actor who got his Othello mixed up with his private life. Neither Garson Kanin's script nor George Cukor's direction could give it the quality it aimed for.

double take. A form of comic reaction to a piece of news or situation. The subject at first fails to take it in, and after a few moments the penny drops with a start. Cary Grant and Oliver Hardy were among the prime exponents of the device, but the comedian who really brought it to

the point of art was James Finlayson, who not only had the most pronounced reactions but added a slow withdrawal of the head, calling the entire effect a 'double take and fade away'.

Douglas, Angela (1940–). British general purpose actress.
Shakedown 59. Some People 61. The Comedy Man 63. Carry On Cowboy 64. Carry On Follow That Camel 66. Carry On Up the Khyber 67. Maroc 7 68. Digby 74.

Douglas, Donald (1905–1945) (Douglas Kinleyside). Quiet-spoken American actor, usually seen as smooth villain or 'good loser'.
Men in White 34. Alexander's Ragtime Band 38. Whistling in the Dark 41. The Crystal Ball 43. Show Business 44. Farewell My Lovely 44. Club Havana 45, etc.

Douglas, Gordon (1909–). American director, former comedy writer for Hal Roach. Jobs have grown in importance but talent remains routine.
Saps at Sea 40. Broadway Limited 41. The Devil with Hitler 43. Zombies on Broadway 45. If You Knew Susie 48. The Doolins of Oklahoma 49. Kiss Tomorrow Goodbye 50. Only the Valiant 51. I Was a Communist for the FBI 51. Come Fill the Cup 51. Mara Maru 52. The Iron Mistress 53. So This is Love 53. The Charge at Feather River 53. *Them* 54. Young at Heart 54. Sincerely Yours 55. The Big Land 56. Bombers B-52 58. Yellowstone Kelly 59. The Sins of Rachel Cade 60. Gold of the Seven Saints 61. Follow That Dream 62. Call Me Bwana 63. Robin and the Seven Hoods 64. Rio Conchos 64. Sylvia 65. Harlow 65. Stagecoach 66. Way Way Out 66. In Like Flint 67. Chuka 67. Tony Rome 67. *The Detective* 68. Lady in Cement 68. Skullduggery 69, etc.

Douglas, Jack (1927–). British comedian who has appeared exclusively in *Carry Ons*. Much on TV.

Douglas, Kirk (1916–). (Issur Danielovitch Demsky). American leading actor with stage experience; started playing weaklings and gangsters but graduated to tense, virile, intelligent heroes in films of many kinds.
□ *The Strange Love of Martha Ivers* 46. *Out of the Past* 47. I Walk Alone 47. My Dear Secretary 47. Mourning Becomes Electra 47. The Walls of Jericho 48. A Letter to Three Wives 48. *Champion* 49. Young Man with a Horn 50. The Glass Menagerie 51. *Ace in the Hole* 51. Along the Great Divide 51. *Detective Story* 51. The Big Trees 52. The Big Sky 52. The Bad and

the Beautiful 52. The Story of Three Loves 53. The Juggler 53. Act of Love 54. Ulysses (It.) 54. Twenty Thousand Leagues under the Sea 54. Man without a Star 55. The Racers 55. The Indian Fighter 55. *Lust for Life* (as Van Gogh) 56. Top Secret Affair 57. *Gunfight at the OK Corral* (as Doc Holliday) 57. *Paths of Glory* 57. The Vikings 58. Last Train from Gun Hill 58. The Devil's Disciple 59. *Spartacus* 60. Town Without Pity 61. The Last Sunset 61. Strangers When We Meet 61. *Lonely Are the Brave* 62. Two Weeks in Another Town 62. *The List of Adrian Messenger* 63. For Love or Money 63. The Hook 63. *Seven Days in May* 64. In Harm's Way 65. The Heroes of Telemark 65. *Cast a Giant Shadow* 66. Is Paris Burning? 66. The Way West 67. The War Wagon 67. A Lovely Way to Die 68. The Brotherhood 68. The Arrangement 69. There Was a Crooked Man 70. A Gunfight 71. The Light at the End of the World 71. Catch Me a Spy 71. Scalawag 73. Mousey (TV) 73. Posse 75. Once is not Enough 75. The Moneychangers (TV) 76.

Douglas, Lloyd C. (1877–1951). American best-selling novelist: a doctor who did not begin writing till in his fifties. Films of his books include *The Green Light, Magnificent Obsession, The Robe, White Banners, Disputed Passage, The Big Fisherman.*

Douglas, Melvyn (1901–) (Melvyn Hesselberg). Suave, polished American leading man of the thirties and forties, most at home in a dinner jacket with an elegant lady on his arm; later spent some years on Broadway and emerged as a fine character actor.
□ Tonight or Never 31. Prestige 32. The Wiser Sex 32. Broken Wing 32. As You Desire Me 32. *The Old Dark House* 32. Nagana 33. The Vampire Bat 33. Counsellor at Law 33. Woman in the Dark 34. *Dangerous Corner* 34. People's Enemy 35. She Married Her Boss 35. Mary Burns Fugitive 35. Annie Oakley 35. *The Lone Wolf Returns* 35. And So They Were Married 36. The Gorgeous Hussy 36. Theodora Goes Wild 36. Women of Glamour 37. Captains Courageous 37. *I Met Him In Paris* 37. Angel 37. I'll Take Romance 37. There's Always a Woman 38. Arsène Lupin Returns 38. The Toy Wife 38. Fast Company 38. *That Certain Age* 38. The Shining Hour 38. There's That Woman Again 38. Tell No Tales 38. Good Girls Go to Paris 39. The Amazing Mr Williams 39. *Ninotchka* 39. Too Many Husbands 40. He Stayed for Breakfast 40. Third Finger Left Hand 40. This Thing Called Love 41. That Uncertain Feeling 41. A Woman's Face 41. Our Wife 41. Two Faced Woman 41. They All Kissed the

Bride 42. Three Hearts for Julia 43. Sea of Grass 47. The Guilt of Janet Ames 47. *Mr Blandings Builds His Dream House* 48. My Own True Love 48. A Woman's Secret 49. The Great Sinner 49. My Forbidden Past 51. On the Loose 51. Billy Budd 62. *Hud* (AA) 63. Advance to the Rear 64. The Americanization of Emily 64. Rapture 65. Hotel 67. *I Never Sang for My Father* 69. Death Takes a Holiday (TV) 71. Companions in Nightmare (TV) 72. One is a Lonely Number 72. The Candidate 72. The Going Up of David Lev (TV) 72.

Douglas, Michael (1945–). American leading man of the seventies, son of Kirk Douglas.
Hail Hero 70. Summertree 71. When Michael Calls (TV) 72. Napoleon and Samantha 72. One Flew Over the Cuckoo's Nest (co-p only) 75, etc.
TV series: *The Streets of San Francisco* 72–75.

Douglas, Paul (1907–1959). Burly American actor with unexpected comedy sense.
□ *A Letter to Three Wives* 48. It Happens Every Spring 49. Everybody Does It 49. The Big Lift 50. Love that Brute 50. Panic in the Streets 50. *Fourteen Hours* 51. The Guy who Came Back 51. When in Rome 52. Clash by Night 52. We're Not Married 52. Never Wave at a WAC 52. Forever Female 53. *Executive Suite* 54. The Maggie 54. Green Fire 54. *Joe Macbeth* 55. The Leather Saint 56. *The Solid Gold Cadillac* 56. The Gamma People 56. This Could Be the Night 57. Beau James 57. The Mating Game 59.

Douglas, Robert (1909–) (Robert Douglas Finlayson). British stage leading man who made some home-grown films during the thirties; moved to Hollywood after the war and played mainly suave villains in routine melodramas, then went into TV direction.
P.C. Josser 31. The Blarney Stone 34. The Street Singer 36. The Challenge 38. Over the Moon 39, etc; war service; The End of the River 47. The Decision of Christopher Blake 48. The New Adventures of Don Juan 48. Sons of the Musketeers 51. Ivanhoe 52. The Prisoner of Zenda 52. Fair Wind to Java 53. King Richard and the Crusaders 54. The Virgin Queen 55. The Scarlet Coat (as Benedict Arnold) 55. Night Train to Paris (GB) (d only) 64, etc.

Dove, Billie (1900–) (Lilian Bohny). American leading lady of the twenties; could not adapt to sound.
Beyond the Rainbow 22. Polly of the Follies 22. Wanderer of the Wasteland 24. The Black Pirate 26. One Night at Susie's 28. Painted Angel 30. Blondie of the Follies 32. Diamond Head 62, etc.

Dovzhenko, Alexander (1894–1956). Russian writer-director, former teacher; in films since 1925.
Arsenal 29. *Earth* 30. *Ivan* 32. *Aerograd* 35. *Life in Blossom* 47, etc.

Dow, Peggy (1928–) (Peggy Varnadow). American leading lady who before retiring to marry made a strong impression in several films of the early fifties.
□ *Undertow* 49. *Woman in Hiding* 50. *Showdown* 50. *The Sleeping City* 50. *Harvey* 50. *Reunion in Reno* 51. *You Never Can Tell* 51. *Bright Victory* 51. *I Want You* 51.

Dowling, Constance (1923–1969). American leading lady who flowered briefly in the forties.
Knickerbocker Holiday 44. *Up in Arms* 44. *The Flame* 47. *Gog* 54, etc.

Dowling, Doris (1921–). American leading lady, sister of Constance Dowling. Briefly in Hollywood character roles, then moved to Italy.
The Lost Weekend 45. *The Blue Dahlia* 46. *Bitter Rice* 48. *Othello* 51. *Running Target* 58, etc.

Dowling, Eddie (1894–1976) (Joseph Nelson Goucher). American singer, comedian and director of the Broadway stage; appeared only in silent films.

Dowling, Joan (1929–1954). British teenage actress who failed to get mature roles.
Hue and Cry 46. *No Room at the Inn* 48. *Landfall* 49. *Pool of London* 51. *Woman of Twilight* 52, etc.

Downs, Cathy (1924–). American leading lady of a few forties films.
Diamond Horseshoe 45. *My Darling Clementine* 46. *The Noose Hangs High* 48. *Short Grass* 50. *Gobs and Gals* 52, etc.

Downs, Johnny (1913–). American light leading man and dancer, former member of 'Our Gang'.
The Clock Strikes Eight 35. *Melody Girl* 40. *All-American Co-Ed* 41. *Harvest Melody* 44. *The Right to Love* 45. *Cruising Down the River* 53, many others.

Doyle, Sir Arthur Conan (1859–1930). British novelist and creator of Sherlock Holmes (qv). His other chief bequest to the screen is the twice-filmed The Lost World.

Doyle, David (–). American character actor.

Parades 72. *Lady Liberty* 72.
TV series: *Bridget Loves Bernie* 73. *Charlie's Angels* 76.

Dozier, William (1908–). American producer, former talent agent. With RKO, Columbia and Goldwyn in the forties; independently made *Two of a Kind* 51. *Harriet Craig* 53; then into TV.

Dracula. The Transylvanian vampire count created by Bram Stoker in his novel published 1897 has been on the screen in many manifestations. Max Schreck played him in Murnau's German silent *Nosferatu* 23. Bela Lugosi first donned the cloak for Universal's *Dracula* 31, was not in *Dracula's Daughter* 36 but reappeared as one of Dracula's relations in *Return of the Vampire* 44 and played the Count in *Abbott and Costello Meet Frankenstein* 48. Lon Chaney starred in *Son of Dracula* 43; John Carradine took over in *House of Frankenstein* 45 and *House of Dracula* 46; Francis Lederer had a go in *The Return of Dracula* 58. Also in 1958 came the British remake of the original *Dracula* (*Horror of Dracula*) with Christopher Lee; David Peel was one of the Count's disciples in *Brides of Dracula* 60 and Noel Willman another in *Kiss of the Vampire* 63; while Lee ingeniously reappeared in 1965 as *Dracula Prince of Darkness*, in 1968 in *Dracula Has Risen from the Grave*; in 1969 in *Taste the Blood of Dracula*, and in 1970 in *Scars of Dracula*. In the same year Ingrid Pitt was *Countess Dracula* and 1972 brought *Vampire Circus*. Meanwhile the Count had American rivals in Count Yorga, in *The House of Dark Shadows* and in *Blacula*. (Hollywood in 1957 had produced a lady vampire in *Blood of Dracula*, and in 1965 *Billy the Kid Meets Dracula*. Polanski's failed satire of 1967, *The Fearless Vampire Killers*, had Ferdy Mayne as Von Krolock, who was Dracula in all but name.) *Dracula AD 1972* and *The Satanic Rites of Dracula* were further variations on the main theme, both with Mr Lee; while Jack Palance in 1973 did a TV film version of the original story for Dan Curtis. It seems that the Count, though officially dead, is unlikely ever to lie down for long.

Drake, Alfred (1914–) (Alfredo Capurro). Italian-American singer-dancer popular in Broadway shows; his only film has been *Tars and Spars* 44.

Drake, Betsy (1923–). American leading lady, formerly on stage; married for a time to Cary Grant, opposite whom she appeared in *Every Girl Should Be Married* 48. *Room for One*

More 52. Also in *Pretty Baby* 50. *The Second Woman* 51. *Clarence the Cross-Eyed Lion* 65, etc.

Drake, Charles (1914–) (Charles Ruppert). American actor usually found in dullish, good-natured 'second leads'.
Dive Bomber 41. The Man Who Came to Dinner 41. Yankee Doodle Dandy 42. Air Force 43. You Came Along 44. Conflict 45. A Night in Casablanca 45. Whistle Stop 46. Tarzan's Magic Fountain 49. Harvey 50. Gunsmoke 52. It Came from Outer Space 53. The Glenn Miller Story 53. All That Heaven Allows 55. The Price of Fear 56. The Third Day 65. Valley of the Dolls 67. The Swimmer 68. The Arrangement 69. The Seven Minutes 71, others.
TV series: Rendezvous (GB) 61.

Drake, Charlie (1925–) (Charles Springall). Diminutive British TV comedian with high-pitched voice and tendency to acrobatic slapstick.
Sands of the Desert 60. Petticoat Pirates 61. The Cracksman 63. Mister Ten Per Cent 66, etc.

Drake, Dona (1920–) (Rita Novella). Mexican singer, dancer and general livewire, former band vocalist as Rita Rio.
Aloma of the South Seas 41. Road to Morocco 42. Salute for Three 43. The House of Tao Ling 47. So This Is New York 48. Beyond the Forest 49. Valentino 51. Princess of the Nile 54, etc.

Drake, Fabia (1904–) (F. D. McGlinchy). British stage and screen character actress: usually plays battleaxes.
Meet Mr Penny 38. All over the Town 48. Young Wives' Tales 51. Fast and Loose 54. The Good Companions 57, many others.

Drake, Tom (1919–) (Alfred Alderdice). American actor, the 'boy next door' of many a forties film.
Two Girls and a Sailor 44. Meet Me in St Louis 44. *The Green Years* 46. I'll Be Yours 47. Master of Lassie 48. Never Trust a Gambler 51. Sudden Danger 55. The Sandpiper 65. Red Tomahawk 67. The Spectre of Edgar Allan Poe 72. The Return of Joe Forrester (TV) 75, etc.

Draper, Peter (1925–). British playwright and screenwriter.
The System 64. I'll Never Forget Whatshisname 67. The Buttercup Chain 70, etc.

Drayton, Alfred (1881–1949) (Alfred Varick). Bald British actor who in later life often played comedy villains in stage farces co-starring

Robertson Hare.
A Scandal in Bohemia 25. Friday the Thirteenth 33. Jack Ahoy 34. The Crimson Circle 36. So This Is London 38. A Spot of Bother 40. The Big Blockade 42. They Knew Mr Knight 44. The Halfway House 44. *Nicholas Nickleby* (as Squeers) 47. Things Happen at Night 48, etc.

dreams, with their opportunities for camera magic and mystery, are dear to Hollywood's heart. The first film with dream sequences followed by a psychological explanation was probably Pabst's *Secrets of a Soul*; the trick caught on very firmly in such later pictures as *Lady in the Dark, A Matter of Life and Death, Spellbound, Dead of Night, Fear in the Night, Farewell My Lovely, The Secret Life of Walter Mitty, Possessed, Dream Girl, Three Cases of Murder* and *The Night Walker*. In *Vampyr* and *Wild Strawberries* the hero dreamed of his own funeral; and in *Devotion* Ida Lupino dreamed of death as a man on horseback coming across the moor to sweep her away. Recently, flashbacks have become less fashionable than a story told as in a series of daydreams by the main character, the past mingling with the present, as in *Death of a Salesman* and *I Was Happy Here*. Roman *Scandals, A Connecticut Yankee at the Court of King Arthur, Ali Baba Goes to Town, Fiddlers Three* and *Dreaming* are but five examples of the many comedies in which a character has been knocked on the head and dreams himself back in some distant time.

In the mid-forties such films as *The Woman in the Window, The Strange Affair of Uncle Harry* and *The Horn Blows at Midnight* set the fashion for getting the hero out of some impossible situation by having him wake up and find he'd been dreaming. This was scarcely fair in adult films, though it had honourable origins in *Alice in Wonderland* and *The Wizard of Oz*. Nor is there much excuse for the other favourite script trick of having one's cake and eating it, as in *Portrait of Jennie* and *Miracle in the Rain*, when some ghostly occurrence to the hero is passed off as dream until he finds some tangible evidence—a scarf, a coin or some other memento—that it was real.

The closest a film dream came to coming true was in *The Night My Number Came Up*, when the foreseen air crash was narrowly averted. In the brilliantly clever frame story of *Dead of Night*, the hero dreams he will commit a murder, and does, only to wake up and find the whole sequence of events beginning again: he is caught in an endless series of recurring nightmares.

See also: *fantasy*.

Dreier, Alex (–). Rotund American

character actor, former news presenter.
Chandler 72. The Carey Treatment 72.
Murdock's Gang (TV) 74.

Dreier, Hans (1884–1966). German art
director, primarily associated with Lubitsch and,
like him, long in Hollywood.
The Hunchback of Notre Dame 23. *Forbidden
Paradise* 24. The Love Parade 29. *Dr Jekyll and
Mr Hyde* 31. *Trouble in Paradise* 32. *Cleopatra*
34. Desire 36. Bluebeard's Eighth Wife 38. Dr
Cyclops 39. Reap the Wild Wind 42. For Whom
the Bell Tolls 43. *Lady in the Dark* 43.
Incendiary Blonde 45. The Emperor Waltz 48.
Samson and Delilah 49. *Sunset Boulevard* 50. A
Place in the Sun 51, many others.

Dreifuss, Arthur (1908–). German-born
American director of second features, former
child conductor and choreographer.
□ Mystery in Swing 40. Reglar Fellers 41. Baby
Face Morgan 42. Boss of Big Town 42. The
Payoff 42. Sarong Girl 43. Melody Parade 43.
Campus Rhythm 43. Nearly Eighteen 43. The
Sultan's Daughter 43. Ever Since Venus 44.
Eadie was a Lady 45. Booked on Suspicion 45.
Boston Blackie's Rendezvous 45. The Gay
Senorita 45. Prison Ship 45. Junior Prom 46.
Freddie Steps Out 46. High School Hero 46.
Vacation Days 47. Betty Co-Ed 47. Little Miss
Broadway 47. Two Blondes and a Redhead 47.
Sweet Genevieve 47. Glamor Girl 48. Mary Lou
48. I Surrender Dear 48. An Old Fashioned Girl
49. Manhattan Angel 49. Shamrock Hill 49.
There's a Girl in My Heart 49. Life Begins at 17
58. The Last Blitzkrieg 58. Juke Box Rhythm 58.
The Quare Fellow 62. Riot on Sunset Strip 67.
The Love Ins 67. For Singles Only 68. A Time to
Sing 68. The Young Runaways 68.

Dreiser, Theodore (1871–1945). Serious
American novelist, a social realist who was
popular in the early part of the century. Films of
his books include *An AmericanTragedy* (remade
as *A Place in the Sun*), *Jennie Gerhardt* and
Carrie.

Dresdel, Sonia (1909–1976) (Lois Obee).
British stage actress usually cast in masterful
roles.
The World Owes Me a Living 42. While I Live
47. This Was a Woman 47. The Fallen Idol 48.
The Clouded Yellow 50. The Third Visitor 51.
Now and Forever 54. The Trials of Oscar Wilde
60. Lady Caroline Lamb 72, etc.

Dresser, Louise (1881–1965) (Louise Kerlin).
American character actress of the thirties,
former vaudevillian.

Prodigal Daughters 23, The Eagle 25. Not Quite
Decent 27. Mammy 30. State Fair 33. The
Scarlet Empress 34. Maid of Salem 37, etc.

Dressler, Marie (1869–1934) (Leila Von
Koerber). American comedy character actress,
the heavyweight heroine of silent comedy and star
of MGM comedy-dramas of the early thirties.
Autobiographical books: *The Life Story of an
Ugly Duckling* 1924, *My Own Story* 1934.
□ *Tillie's Punctured Romance* 14. Tillie's
Tomato Surprise 15. Tillie's Nightmare 15. The
Scriblady 17. The Agonies of Agnes 18. The Red
Cross Nurse 18. The Callahans and the Murphys
27. Breakfast at Sunrise 27. The Joy Girl 27.
Bringing Up Father 28. The Patsy 28. The
Divine Lady 29. The Vagabond Lovers 29.
Hollywood Revue of 1929 29. Road Show 29.
Chasing Rainbows 30. One Romantic Night 30.
Let Us Be Gay 30. Derelict 30. *Anna Christie* 30.
Caught Short 30. The Swan 30. The March of
Time 30. Call of the Flesh 30. The Girl Said No
30. *Min and Bill* 30. Reducing 31. Politics 31.
Emma 32. *Prosperity* 32. *Tugboat Annie* 33.
Dinner at Eight 33. Christopher Bean 33.

Dreville, Jean (1906–). French director.
Cage aux Rossignols 43. La Ferme du Pendu 46.
Le Visiteur 47. Operation Swallow (The Battle
for Heavy Water) 47. Les Casse-Pieds 48.
Horizons Sans Fin 53. A Pied a Cheval et en
Spoutnik 58. Normandie-Niemen 60. Lafayette
61. The Sleeping Sentry 66, etc.

Drew, Ellen (1915–) (Terry Ray). American
light leading lady of the forties.
College Holiday 36. Hollywood Boulevard 36.
Night of Mystery 37. Murder Goes to College
37. The Buccaneer 38. You and Me 38. Sing you
Sinners 38. If I Were King 38. Geronimo 39.
French Without Tears 39. *Christmas In July* 40.
The Mad Doctor 41. Our Wife 41. The
Remarkable Andrew 42. The Impostor 44.
China Sky 45. Isle of the Dead 46. Johnny
O'Clock 47. The Swordsman 47. The Crooked
Way 49. Davy Crockett Indian Scout 50. The
Great Missouri Raid 50. The Outlaw's Son 57,
many others.

Drew, Mr and Mrs Sidney (1864–1920 and
1868–1925) (Sidney White and Lucille McVey).
American stage actors who appeared in a
number of very popular middle-class domestic
film comedies.
Duplicity 16. Hypochondriacs 17. Henry's
Ancestors 17. Her First Love 17. His Deadly
Calm 17. His First Love 18. A Youthful Affair
18. Romance and Rings 19. Once a Mason 19.
Harold the Last of the Saxons 19. The Charming

Mrs Chase 20, etc.

Dreyer, Carl (1889–1968). Celebrated Danish director whose later works were few but notable.
□ *Praesidenten* 20. *Leaves from Satan's Book* 20. Praesteenken 21. Elsker Hverandre 22. Once Upon a Time 22. Michael 24. Du Skal Aere Din Hustru 25. Glomsdal Bruden 26. *The Passion of Joan of Arc* 28. *Vampyr* 32. *Day of Wrath* 43. Tva Manniskor 45. Ordet 55. Gertrud 64.

Dreyfus, Alfred (1859–1935). The French officer unjustly sentenced to Devil's Island, but reprieved by Zola's advocacy, has been played on screen by Cedric Hardwicke in *Dreyfus* (GB 1930), by Joseph Schildkraut in *The Life of Emile Zola* (US 1937) and by Jose Ferrer in *I Accuse* (GB 1957).

Dreyfuss, Richard (1949–). American leading man in Hollywood.
□ Hello Down There 68. The Young Runaways 69. *American Graffiti* 73. *The Apprenticeship of Duddy Kravitz* 74. *Jaws* 75. Inserts 75.

Drifters (GB 1929). John Grierson's first documentary, a study of North Sea herring fishers which now seems dull but on its first screening was a new departure and a revelation.

Driscoll, Bobby (1937–1968). American boy actor of the forties and fifties; AA 1949 as best child actor.
Lost Angel 43. The Sullivans 44. From This Day Forward 46. So Goes My Love 46. Song of the South 46. If You Knew Susie 48. So Dear to My Heart 48. *The Window* 49. *Treasure Island* 50. *The Happy Time* 52. Peter Pan (voice) 54. The Scarlet Coat 55, etc.

Drivas, Robert (–). American leading man, mainly on TV.
Where It's At 69. Janice 73. Road Movie 74, etc.

drive-in. A cinema in the open air, with loudspeakers relaying the sound track into your car. There are 6–7,000 in the USA alone.

Drôle de Drame (France 1937). Intellectual crazy comedy written by Jacques Prevert (from J. Storer Clouston's *The Lunatic at Large*) and directed by Marcel Carne, with a star cast headed by Françoise Rosay, Jean-Louis Barrault, Michel Simon and Louis Jouvet. Made with great vigour, but considerably ahead of its time.

Dru, Joanne (1923–) (Joanne la Cock). American leading lady of the forties, former model.
Abie's Irish Rose 46. *Red River* 48. *All the King's Men* 49. She Wore a Yellow Ribbon 49. Wagonmaster 50. Vengeance Valley 51. Return of the Texan 52. Thunder Bay 53. Three Ring Circus 54. Sincerely Yours 55. The Light in the Forest 58. September Storm 60. Sylvia 65, etc.
TV series: Guestward Ho 61.

drug addiction, long forbidden by the Hays Code, even in Sherlock Holmes films (though it featured in Chaplin's *Easy Street* in 1916), has recently been the subject of many intense reforming movies such as *The Man with the Golden Arm, A Hatful of Rain, Bigger than Life, Monkey on My Back* and *Synanon. Confessions of an Opium Eater,* on the other hand, is a throwback to the Hollywood films of the twenties, when almost every adventure involved a chase through a Chinatown opium den. The addiction has provided plots for many thrillers about the tireless efforts of agents of the US Narcotics Bureau: *Johnny Stool Pigeon, To the Ends of the Earth, Sol Madrid, The Poppy is Also a Flower, The French Connection,* etc. In the late sixties drugs began to be advocated as a permissible opting out, or to be freely and seriously discussed, in such films as *The Trip, Chappaqua* and *Beyond the Valley of the Dolls*; *Panic in Needle Park; Born to Win; Believe in Me; Jennifer on my Mind*; and *Lenny.*

drunk scenes have been the delight of many actors as well as audiences. Who can judge between the charms of the following? Greta Garbo in *Ninotchka*; Robert Montgomery in *June Bride*; Jean Arthur in *Mr Smith Goes to Washington*; Laurel and Hardy in *The Bohemian Girl* and *Scram*; Lionel Barrymore in *A Free Soul*; Eva Marie Saint in *That Certain Feeling*; Errol Flynn in *The Sun Also Rises*; Katharine Hepburn in *The Desk Set*; Leslie Caron in *Father Goose*; Fredric March in *There Goes My Heart*; Lee Marvin in *Cat Ballou* (accompanied by a drunken horse); Albert Finney in *Saturday Night and Sunday Morning*; Alan Bates in *A Kind of Loving*; Bette Davis in *Dark Victory*; Claudia Cardinale in *The Pink Panther*; Charles Laughton in *Hobson's Choice*; Katharine Hepburn in *The Philadelphia Story* and *State of the Union*; Lucille Ball in *Yours Mine and Ours*; Arthur Askey in *The Love Match*; Dan Dailey in *It's Always Fair Weather*; Vanessa Redgrave in *Isadora*; Julie Andrews in *Star!*; Dean Martin and Tony Curtis in *Who Was That Lady?* Martin indeed has deliberately built himself an off-screen alcoholic reputation, as did W. C. Fields.
See also: *alcoholics.*

Drury, James (1934–). American second lead and TV western star.
Forbidden Planet 46. Love Me Tender 56. Bernardine 57. Pollyanna 60. Ride the High Country 62. The Young Warriors 65, etc.
TV series: *The Virginian* 64–69, Firehouse 73.

dry ice. A chemical substance which in water produces carbon dioxide gas and gives the effect of a low-hanging white ground mist, very effective in fantasy sequences.

Dryhurst, Edward (1904–). British producer, former writer, in films from 1920.
So Well Remembered 47. Master of Bankdam 48. Noose 48. While I Live 49. Castle in the Air 52, etc.

Du Maurier, Daphne (1907–). Best-selling British novelist of whose works *Rebecca, Jamaica Inn, Frenchman's Creek, The Years Between, Hungry Hill, My Cousin Rachel, The Scapegoat, The Birds* and *Don't Look Now* have been filmed.

Du Maurier, Sir Gerald (–). British stage actor who appeared in occasional films.

dubbing has several shades of meaning, within the general one of adding sound (effects, music, song, dialogue) to pictures already shot. It can mean re-recording; or replacing original language dialogue by a translation; or having someone else provide top notes for a star who can't sing. Here is an incomplete list of singers who provided uncredited voice-overs for actors who couldn't quite measure up.
Band Wagon India Adams for Cyd Charisse, *The Belle of New York* Anita Ellis for Vera-Ellen, *Brigadoon* Carole Richards for Cyd Charisse, *Call Me Madam* Carole Richards for Vera-Ellen, *Cover Girl* Nan Wynn for Rita Hayworth, *Gigi* Betty Wand for Leslie Caron, *Gilda* Nan Wynn for Rita Hayworth, *The Great Ziegfeld* Allan Jones for Dennis Morgan, *Gypsy* Lisa Kirk for Rosalind Russell, *Happy Go Lovely* Eve Boswell for Vera-Ellen, *The Helen Morgan Story* Gogi Grant for Ann Blyth, *Interrupted Melody* Eileen Farrell for Eleanor Parker, *The Jolson Story* Al Jolson for Larry Parks, *The King and I* Marni Nixon for Deborah Kerr, *The Merry Widow* Trudy Erwin for Lana Turner, *My Fair Lady* Marni Nixon for Audrey Hepburn, *Orchestra Wives* Pat Friday for Lynn Bari, *Pal Joey* Jo Ann Greer for Rita Hayworth, *South Pacific* Muriel Smith for Juanita Hall, *South Pacific* Giorgio Tozzi for Rosanno Brazzi, *Showboat* Annette Warren for Ava Gardner, *A Song is Born* Jeri Sullivan for Virginia Mayo,

The Sound of Music Bill Lee for Christopher Plummer, *State Fair* (1945) Lorraine Hogan for Jeanne Crain, *To Have and Have Not* (believe it nor not) Andy Williams for Lauren Bacall, *Torch Song* India Adams for Joan Crawford, *West Side Story* Marni Nixon for Natalie Wood, *West Side Story* Jim Bryant for Richard Beymer, *West Side Story* Betty Wand for Rita Moreno, *With a Song in My Heart* Jane Froman for Susan Hayward.

Dubbins, Don (1929–). American second lead of the fifties.
From Here to Eternity 53. Tribute to a Bad Man 56. These Wilder Years 57. From the Earth to the Moon 58. The Enchanted Island 58. The Prize 63, etc.

Duck Soup (US 1933). Probably the most perfect, zany and absolute of the vintage Marx Brothers romps, a Ruritanian spy send-up with Margaret Dumont and Louis Calhern as butts. Gags by various hands including Nat Perrin and Arthur Sheekman; music by Bert Kalmar and Harry Ruby.

Dudley-Ward, Penelope (1919–). British leading lady of the forties.
The Case of the Frightened Lady 39. The Demi-Paradise 43. The Way Ahead 44, etc.

Duel in the Sun (US 1946). When first released this was the longest film since *Gone with the Wind*; it became notorious for its emphasis on violence and for casting Gregory Peck and Jennifer Jones as no-good villains who finally shot each other to death. The screenplay, by David Busch and producer David O. Selznick, was tasteless and King Vidor's direction, despite some good western action sequences, unremarkable.

Duel, Pete (1940–1971) (Peter Deuel). American leading man.
A Time for Loving 69. Cannon for Cordoba 70. The Young Country (TV) 71, etc.
TV series: Love on a Rooftop 67. *Alias Smith and Jones* 70.

duels are fought in hundreds of low-budget action dramas, but the well-staged ones are rare enough to be recounted. Basil Rathbone fought Errol Flynn in *The Adventures of Robin Hood* (and later spoofed the occasion in *The Court Jester*). He also lost to Tyrone Power in *The Mark of Zorro*; Flynn also encountered Rathbone in *Captain Blood* and Henry Daniell in *The Sea Hawk*. Douglas Fairbanks Snr fought duels in *The Thief of Baghdad, The Black Pirate* and others; Douglas Fairbanks Jnr was a memorable opponent for Ronald Colman in *The Prisoner of Zenda* (later restaged for James Mason and Stewart Granger and mimicked by Tony Curtis and Ross Martin in *The Great Race*) and duelled again in *The Corsican Brothers* and *Sinbad the Sailor.* Granger also duelled with Mason in *Fanny by Gaslight*, but used pistols this time; it was back to foils again for *Scaramouche* and *Swordsman of Siena*. John Barrymore fought splendid duels in his silent films, notably *Don Juan* and *General Crack*, later opposing Rathbone in *Romeo and Juliet*. In the forties Cornel Wilde became fencer in chief, in such films as *Bandit of Sherwood Forest, Forever Amber* and *Sons of the Musketeers.* All the versions of *The Three Musketeers* involved duelling, but Gene Kelly turned it into a splendid series of acrobatic feats. In more serious films Ferrer duelled in *Cyrano de Bergerac* and Olivier in *Hamlet*, and there was a pistol duel in the Russian *War and Peace* and the Italian *Colpi di Pistola*. The most recent major films to feature duels are *Barry Lyndon* and *Royal Flash.*

Duff, Howard (1917–). American actor with stage experience; usually plays good-looking but shifty types.
Brute Force 47. *Naked City* 48. All My Sons 48. Calamity Jane and Sam Bass 50. Woman in Hiding 50. Shakedown 50. Steel Town 52. Women's Prison 54. While the City Sleeps 56. Boys' Night Out 62. Sardanapalus the Great (It.) 63, etc.
TV series: Mr Adams and Eve 56–57. Dante 60. The Felony Squad 66–68.

Duffell, Peter (1924–). British director.
The House that Dripped Blood 71. England Made Me 72. Inside Out 75.

Dugan, Tom (1889–1955). American supporting comic actor, often seen as Irish cop or minor criminal.
Sharp Shooters 27. Lights of New York 28. Sonny Boy 29. Bright Lights 31. Doctor X 32.Grand Slam 33. Palooka 34. Princess O'Hara 35. Pick a Star 37. Four Daughters 38. The Housekeeper's Daughter 39. The Ghost Breakers 40. The Monster and the Girl 41. *To Be Or Not To Be* 42. Bataan 43. Up in Arms 44. Bringing Up Father 46. Good News 47. Take Me Out to the Ball Game 49. The Lemon Drop Kid 51, many others.

Duggan, Andrew (1923–). American character actor of stalwart types.
Patterns 56. The Bravados 58. The Chapman

Report 62. FBI Code 98 66. The Secret War of Harry Frigg 67. The Skin Game 71. Jigsaw (TV) 72. The Bears and I 74, etc.
TV series: Bourbon Street Beat 59. Room for One More 61. Lancer 68–69.

Duggan, Pat (1910–). American producer, former performer and writer.
Red Garters 54. The Vagabond King 56. The Search for Bridey Murphy 57. The Young Savages 61, etc.

Duke, Ivy (1895–). Star of British silent screen; married to Guy Newall.
The Garden of Resurrection 18. The Lure of Crooning Water 20. The Persistent Lover 22. The Starlit Garden 23. The Great Prince Shan 24. A Knight in London 29, etc.

Duke, Patty (1946–). American child actress who found difficulty in graceful adaptation to adult roles.
□ The Goddess 58. Happy Anniversary 59. *The Miracle Worker* (AA) 62. Billie 65. Valley of the Dolls 67. Me Natalie 69. My Sweet Charlie (TV) 70. Two on a Bench (TV) 71. If Tomorrow Comes (TV) 71. She Waits (TV) 71. You'll Like My Mother 72.
TV series: *The Patty Duke Show* 63.

Dulac, Germaine (1882–1942) (G. Saisset-Schneider). French woman director.
Ames de Fous 18. Le Diable dans la Ville 24. The Seashell and the Clergyman 26. Theme and Variations 30, etc.

Dullea, Keir (1936–). American leading man, usually in roles of nervous tension.
The Hoodlum Priest 61. *David and Lisa* 62. Mail Order Bride 64. The Thin Red Line 64. Bunny Lake is Missing 65. Madame X 66. The Fox 68. De Sade 69. 2001: A Space Odyssey 69. Last of the Big Guns 73. Paperback Hero 73. Paul and Michelle 74. Black Christmas 75, etc.

Dumas, Alexandre, père (1802–1870). Highly industrious French novelist, mainly of swashbuckling adventures. Films resulting include several versions of *The Count of Monte Cristo* and *The Three Musketeers, The Man in the Iron Mask, The Fighting Guardsman* and *The Black Tulip.*

Dumas, Alexandre, fils (1824–1895). French novelist best known for *Camille*, which has been filmed several times.

Dumbrille, Douglass (1890–1974). Canadian character actor, long in Hollywood and typecast

as smooth, suave villain of many a 'B' picture
and an admirable foil for many great comedians.
His Woman 31. That's My Boy 32. Elmer the
Great 33. Voltaire 33. Lady Killer 34. Broadway
Bill 34. Naughty Marietta 35. Crime and
Punishment 35. Lives of a Bengal Lancer 35. *Mr
Deeds Goes to Town* 36. *A Day at the Races* 37.
The Firefly 37. Ali Baba Goes to Town 37. Mr
Moto on Danger Island 38. The Three
Musketeers 39. Charlie Chan at Treasure Island
39. *The Big Store* 41. Ride 'Em Cowboy 42.
Lost in a Harem 44. The Frozen Ghost 45. *Road
to Utopia* 46. The Cat Creeps 46. Christmas Eve
47. Alimony 49. Riding High 50. Son of Paleface
52. Jupiter's Darling 55. The Ten
Commandments 56. The Buccaneer 58. Shock
Treatment 63, many others.
TV series: The Phil Silvers Show 63. Petticoat
Junction 64–65.

Dumke, Ralph (1900–1964). Heavily-built
American supporting actor.
All the King's Men 49. Mystery Street 50. The
Mob 51. Lili 53. Rails into Laramie 54. The Solid
Gold Cadillac 56. The Buster Keaton Story 57,
etc.

Dumont, Margaret (1889–1965). American
character comedienne, the stately butt of many a
comedian, notably Groucho Marx ('Ah, Mrs
Rittenhouse, won't you . . . lie down?').
□ *The Coconuts* 29. *Animal Crackers* 30. The
Girl Habit 30. *Duck Soup* 33. The Gridiron
Flash 34. Fifteen Wives 34. Kentucky Kernels
34. *A Night at the Opera* 35. Orchids to You 35.
Rendezvous 35. The Song and Dance Man 36.
Anything Goes 36. *A Day at the Races* 37. The
Life of the Party 37. High Flyers 37. Youth on
Parole 37. Wise Girl 37. Dramatic School 39. *At
The Circus* 39. *The Big Store* 41. Never Give a
Sucker an Even Break 41. For Beauty's Sake 41.
Born to Sing 41. Sing Your Worries Away 42.
Rhythm Parade 42. About Face 42. The
Dancing Masters 43. Bathing Beauty 44. Seven
Days Ashore 44. Up in Arms 44. The Horn
Blows at Midnight 45. Diamond Horseshoe 45.
Sunset in El Dorado 45. The Little Giant 46.
Susie Steps Out 46. Three for Bedroom C 52.
Stop You're Killing Me 53. Shake Rattle and
Rock 56. Auntie Mame 58. Zotz! 62. What a
Way to Go 64.

Duna, Steffi (1913–) (Stephanie Berindey).
Hungarian dancer who appeared in some
dramatic roles in the thirties.
The Indiscretions of Eve 31. La Cucaracha 35.
The Dancing Pirate 36. Anthony Adverse 36.
Pagliacci 37. Waterloo Bridge 40. River's End
41, etc.

Dunaway, Faye (1941–). American leading
lady.
□ Hurry Sundown 67. The Happening 67.
Bonnie and Clyde 67. The Thomas Crown Affair
68. The Extraordinary Seaman 69. A Place for
Lovers 69. The Arrangement 69. Little Big Man
70. Puzzle of a Downfall Child 71. Doc 71. The
Deadly Trap 71. The Getaway 72. Oklahoma
Crude 73. The Three Musketeers 73. Chinatown
74. *Network* 76. The Disappearance of Aimée
(TV) 76.

Duncan, Archie (1914–). Burly Scottish
actor, the 'Little John' of TV's Robin Hood
series.
Operation Diamond 47. The Bad Lord Byron 48.
The Gorbals Story 51. Robin Hood 53. The
Maggie 53. Laxdale Hall 54. Johnny on the Run
56. Harry Black 58. Lancelot and Guinevere 63.
Ring of Bright Water 69, etc.

Duncan, Sandy (1946–). Tomboyish
American leading lady.
□ Million Dollar Duck 71. *Star Spangled Girl*
71.
TV series: *Funny Face* 71.

Duning, George (1908–). American music
director and composer.
The Corpse Came COD 46. The Dark Past 49.
The Man from Laramie 55. Picnic 56. Cowboy
57. 3.10 to Yuma 57. The World of Suzie Wong
61. Toys in the Attic 63. Dear Brigitte 65, many
others.

Dunn, Emma (1875–1966). British character
actress, long in Hollywood, typically as
housekeeper.
Old Lady 31 20. Pied Piper Malone 23. Side
Street 29. Bad Sister 31. Hard to Handle 33. The
Glass Key 35. Mr Deeds Goes to Town 36.
Thanks for the Memory 38. Son of Frankenstein
39. The Great Dictator 40. Ladies in Retirement
41. I Married a Witch 42. It Happened
Tomorrow 44. Life with Father 47. The Woman
in White 48, many others.

Dunn, James (1905–1967). Genial American
leading man of the thirties; later seized one good
acting chance but slipped into low-budget
westerns.
Bad Girl 31. Over the Hill 31. Sailor's Luck 33.
Hold Me Tight 33. Stand Up and Cheer 34. Baby
Take a Bow 34. Bright Eyes 34. The Daring
Young Man 35. Don't Get Personal 36.
Mysterious Crossing 37. Shadows over
Shanghai 38. Government Girl 43. *A Tree Grows
in Brooklyn* (AA) 45. That Brennan Girl 46.
Killer McCoy 48. The Golden Gloves Story 50.

The Bramble Bush 60. The Nine Lives of Elfego Baca 62. Hemingway's Adventures of a Young Man 62. The Oscar 66, etc.

Dunn, Michael (1935–1973) (Gary Neil Miller). American dwarf actor.
Ship of Fools 65. You're a Big Boy Now 67. No Way to Treat a Lady 68. Madigan 68. Boom 68. Justine 69. Murders in the Rue Morgue 71. Goodnight My Love (TV) 72. The Mutations 74, etc.

Dunne, Irene (1901–). Gracious American leading lady of the thirties and forties, usually in sensible well-bred roles.
☐ Leathernecking 30. *Cimarron* 31. The Great Lover 31. Consolation Marriage 31. Bachelor Apartment 31. *Back Street 32. Symphony of Six Million* 32. Thirteen Women 32. No Other Women 33. The Secret of Madame Blanche 33. The Silver Cord 33. *Ann Vickers* 33. If I Were Free 34. This Man is Mine 34. Stingaree 34. The Age of Innocence 34. Sweet Adeline 35. *Roberta* 35. *Magnificent Obsession* 35. *Show Boat* 36. *Theodora Goes Wild* 36. *The Awful Truth* 37. High Wide and Handsome 37. Joy of Living 38. *Love Affair* 39. Invitation to Happiness 39. When Tomorrow Comes 39. *My Favourite Wife* 40. Penny Serenade 41. Unfinished Business 41. Lady in a Jam 42. A Guy Named Joe 43. The White Cliffs of Dover 44. Together Again 45. Over Twenty One 45. *Anna and the King of Siam* 46. *Life with Father* 47. *I Remember Mama* 48. Never a Dull Moment 50. *The Mudlark* (as Queen Victoria) 51. It Grows on Trees 52.

Dunne, Philip (1908–). American screenwriter.
Student Tour 34. The Last of the Mohicans 36. Lancer Spy 37. Suez 38. Stanley and Livingstone 39. The Rains Came 39. Swanee River 39. How Green was My Valley 41. The Late George Apley 47. Forever Amber 47. The Luck of the Irish 48. Pinky 49. David and Bathsheba 51. The Robe 53. Prince of Players (& pd) 55. Hilda Crane (& d) 56. Ten North Frederick (& d) 58. Blue Denim (& d) 59. Lisa (d only) 62. The Agony and the Ecstasy 65. Blindfold (& d) 66, many others.

Dunnock, Mildred (1904–). American character actress specializing in motherly types.
The Corn is Green 45. Kiss of Death 47. *Death of a Salesman* 51. Viva Zapata 52. The Jazz Singer 53. Love Me Tender 56. Baby Doll 56. Peyton Place 57. The Nun's Story 57. Something Wild 61. Sweet Bird of Youth 62. Behold a Pale Horse 64. Seven Women 66. Whatever

Happened to Aunt Alice? 69. The Spiral Staircase (GB) 75, etc.

dupe negative. One made from the original negative (via a lavender print) to protect it from wear by producing too many copies.

duping print (or **lavender print**). A high quality print made from the original negative. From it dupe negatives can be made.

Dupont, E. A. (Ewald André) (1891–1956). German director who moved with unhappy results to Britain and Hollywood.
Baruh 23. *Variety* 26. Love Me and the World Is Mine 27. Moulin Rouge 28. *Piccadilly* 28. Atlantic 30. Ladies in Love 33. The Bishop Misbehaves 35. Forgotten Faces 36. Hell's Kitchen 39. The Scarf (& w) 50. The Neanderthal Man 53. Return to Treasure Island 54, etc.

Dupree, Minnie (1873–1947). American character actress seen infrequently as sweet old lady.
Night Club 29. *The Young in Heart* 38. Anne of Windy Poplars 40, etc.

Duprez, June (1918–). British leading lady.
The Crimson Circle 36. The Spy in Black 38. The Four Feathers 39. The Thief of Baghdad 41. None But the Lonely Heart (US) 44. *And Then There Were None* (US) 45. Calcutta (US) 46. That Brennan Girl (US) 47. The Kinsey Report (US) 61, etc.

Dupuis, Paul (1916–). French-Canadian leading man popular in British films in the late forties.
Johnny Frenchman 45. The White Unicorn 47. Sleeping Car to Trieste 48. Passport to Pimlico 49. The Reluctant Widow 50, etc.

Durante, Jimmy 'Schnozzle' (1893–). Long-nosed, well-loved American comedian with long career in vaudeville and night clubs. Film appearances spasmodic, and most successful when involving his old routines: 'Umbriago', 'Ink-a-dink', etc.
Biographies: *Schnozzola* 1951 by Gene Fowler; *Goodnight Mrs Calabash* 1963 by William Cahn.
Roadhouse Nights 30. Cuban Love Song 31. The Passionate Plumber 32. Speak Easily 32. The Phantom President 32. The Wet Parade 33. What No Beer? 33. Palooka 33. Hollywood Party 34. Strictly Dynamite 34. Carnival 35. Sally Irene and Mary 38. Little Miss Broadway 38. Melody Ranch 40. *You're in the Army Now*

41. The Man Who Came to Dinner 41. Two Girls and a Sailor 44. Music for Millions 44. Two Sisters from Boston 46. It Happened in Brooklyn 47. This Time for Keeps 47. The Great Rupert 50. The Milkman 50. Pepe 60. Jumbo 62. It's a Mad Mad Mad Mad World 63, etc.

Duras, Marguerite (1914–). French novelist. Works filmed: *The Sea Wall, Hiroshima Mon Amour, Moderato Cantabile* and *Sailor from Gibraltar.*

Durbin, Deanna (1921–) (Edna Mae Durbin). Canadian girl singer who won instant world-wide success as a teenage star; her career faltered after ten years when weight problems added to a change in musical fashion brought about her premature retirement. Special Academy Award 1938 'for bringing to the screen the spirit and personification of youth'.
□ *Three Smart Girls* 36. *One Hundred Men and a Girl* 37. *Mad about Music* 38. *That Certain Age* 38. Three Smart Girls Grow Up 38. First Love 39. It's a Date 39. Spring Parade 40. Nice Girl 40. *It Started with Eve* 41. The Amazing Mrs Holliday 42. Hers to Hold 43. His Butler's Sister 43. Christmas Holiday 44. *Can't Help Singing* 44. Lady on a Train 45. Because of Him 45. I'll Be Yours 46. Something in the Wind 47. Up in Central Park 47. For the Love of Mary 48.

Durfee, Minta (1897–1975). American leading lady of knockabout comedies 1914–16, including some with Chaplin. Married Roscoe Arbuckle and retired, but much later played bit parts.

Durkin, Junior (1915–1935) (Trent Durkin). American juvenile player who was Huck Finn in *Tom Sawyer* 30 and *Huckleberry Finn* 31.

Durning, Charles (–). Burly American TV actor who slowly gained a star footing in movies.
The Connection (TV) 73. The Front Page 74. Dog Day Afternoon 75, etc.

Duryea, Dan (1907–1968). Laconic, long-faced American character actor often typecast as whining villain.
□ *The Little Foxes* 41. Ball of Fire 41. Pride of the Yankees 42. That Other Woman 42. Sahara 43. Man from Frisco 44. Ministry of Fear 44. None but the Lonely Heart 44. *The Woman in the Window* 44. Mrs Parkington 45. Main Street After Dark 44. The Great Flamarion 45. Lady on a Train 45. Scarlet Street 45. Along Came Jones 45. The Valley of Decision 45. *Black Angel* 46. White Tie and Tails 46. Black Bart 48.

River Lady 48. *Another Part of the Forest* 48. Larceny 48. *Criss Cross* 49. Manhandled 49. Too Late for Tears 49. Johnny Stoolpigeon 50. One Way Street 50. The Underworld Story 50. Winchester 73 50. Al Jennings of Oklahoma 51. *Chicago Calling* 51. Sky Commando 53. Thunder Bay 53. 36 Hours 53. World for Ransom 54. Ride Clear of Diablo 54. Silver Lode 54. This is My Love 54. Rails in to Laramie 54. The Marauders 55. Foxfire 55. Storm Fear 56. Battle Hymn 57. The Burglar 57. Night Passage 57. Slaughter on Tenth Avenue 57. Kathy O 58. Platinum High School 60. Six Black Horses 62. He Rides Tall 64. Taggart 64. Walk a Tightrope 64. Do You Know This Voice? 64. The County Killer 65. Incident at Phantom Hill 65. *The Flight of the Phoenix* 65. The Hills Run Red 67. Winchester 73 (TV remake) 67. Stranger on the Run (TV) 67. Five Golden Dragons 67. The Bamboo Saucer 68.
TV series: China Smith 58. Peyton Place 68.

Duse, Eleonora (1858–1924). Eminent Italian tragedienne whose one film appearance was in *Cenere* 16.

Duvall, Robert (1931–). American character actor, often seen as nervous villain.
Captain Newman MD 63. To Kill a Mockingbird 63. The Chase 65. Bullitt 68. The Rain People 69. True Grit 69. M*A*S*H 70. Lawman 71. *The Godfather* 72. The Great Northfield Minnesota Raid 72. Joe Kidd 72. The Godfather Part Two 74. The Outfit 74. Breakout 75. Killer Elite 76. Network 76. The Seven Per Cent Solution 76, etc.

Duvall, Shelley (1949–). American leading lady of the seventies.
Brewster McCloud 70. McCabe and Mrs Miller 71. Thieves Like Us 74. Nashville 75. Three Women 77, etc.

Duvivier, Julien (1896–1967). Celebrated French director of the thirties whose touch seemed to falter after a wartime sojourn in Hollywood.
Hacadelma 19. Poil de carotte 25 and 32. David Golder 30. Maria Chapdelaine 33. Le Golem 35. La Belle Equipe 36. *Pepe Le Moko* 37. *Un Carnet de Bal* 37. The Great Waltz (US) 38. *La Fin de Jour* 39. La Charette Fantôme 39. Lydia (US) 41. Tales of Manhattan (US) 42. Flesh and Fantasy (US) 43. The Imposter (US) 44. *Panique* 46. Anna Karenina (GB) 48. Au Royaume des Cieux 49. Sous le Ciel de Paris 51. *Don Camillo* 52. La Fête à Henriette 54. L'Affaire Maurizius 54. Voici le Temps des Assassins 55. The Man in the Raincoat 57. Pot-Bouille 57. Marie Octobre

59. La Femme et le Pantin 59. La Grande Vie 61.
La Chambre Ardente 62. Chair de Poule 63, etc.

Dvorak, Ann (1912–) (Ann McKim). Smart
but sensitive American leading lady of the
thirties.
Hollywood Revue 29. Way out West 30. The
Guardsman 31. This Modern Age 31. The
Crowd Roars 32. *Scarface* 32. The Strange Love
of Molly Louvain 32. Three on a Match 32. The
Way to Love 33. Heat Lightning 34. Housewife
34. I Sell Anything 34. G Men 35. Folies Bergère
35. *Dr Socrates* 35. We Who Are About to Die
36. Racing Lady 37. The Case of the Stuttering
Bishop 37. Merrily We Live 38. Blind Alley 39.
Café Hostess 40. Girls of the Road 40. Squadron
Leader X (GB) 41. This Was Paris (GB) 42.
Escape to Danger 44. Flame of the Barbary
Coast 45. Abilene Town 46. The Long Night 47.
The Walls of Jericho 48. A Life of Her Own 50. I
Was an American Spy 51. The Secret of Convict
Lake 51, etc.

Dwan, Allan (1885–). Veteran American
director, former writer; has competently handled
commercial movies of every type.
Wildflower 14. The Good Bad Man 15.
Manhattan Madness 16. A Modern Musketeer
18. Luck of the Irish 20. *Robin Hood* 22. Big
Brother 23. Zaza 23. Manhandled 24. Stage
Struck 25. *The Iron Mask* 29. Man to Man 31.
Mayor of Hell 33. Human Cargo 36. Heidi 37.
Suez 38. The Three Musketeers (Ritz Brothers
version) 39. Trail of the Vigilantes 40. Rise and
Shine 41. Abroad with Two Yanks 44. Up in
Mabel's Room 44. Brewster's Millions 45.
Getting Gertie's Garter 46. Angel in Exile 48.
Sands of Iwo Jima 49. The Wild Blue Yonder 51.
Montana Belle 52. The Woman They Almost
Lynched 53. Silver Lode 54. Tennessee's Partner
55. Hold Back the Night 56. Slightly Scarlet 56.
The River's Edge 57. The Most Dangerous Man
Alive 61, scores of others.

Dwyer, Leslie (1906–). Plump cockney
character actor, in films from childhood.

The Fifth Form at St Dominic's 21. The Flag
Lieutenant 31. The Goose Steps Out 41. The
Way Ahead 44. Night Boat to Dublin 46. When
the Bough Breaks 48. The Calendar 48.
Midnight Episode 50. Laughter in Paradise 51.
Hindle Wakes 52. Where There's a Will 53. Act
of Love 54. Left, Right and Centre 59. I've Gotta
Horse 64, many others.

Dyall, Franklin (1874–1950). British stage
actor.
Atlantic 30. The Ringer 32. The Private Life of
Henry VIII 33. The Iron Duke 35. Fire Over
England 36. Bonnie Prince Charlie 49, etc.

Dyall, Valentine (1908–). Gaunt British
actor with resounding voice, famous as radio's
wartime 'Man in Black'. Son of stage actor
Franklin Dyall. Film debut *The Life and Death
of Colonel Blimp* 43; later in many supporting
roles, notably Henry V 44. Caesar and Cleopatra
45. Brief Encounter 46. Vengeance Is Mine 48.
City of the Dead 60. The Haunting 63. The
Horror of It All 65, etc.

Dyer, Anson (1876–). Pioneer British
cartoonist: many entertainment shorts, also
work for government departments.

dynamic frame. A concept invented in 1955
by an American, Glenn Alvey: the screen was
maximum size, i.e. CinemaScope, but individual
scenes were to be masked down to whatever ratio
suited them best, e.g. rather narrow for a
corridor. Only one experimental British film, a
version of H. G. Wells' *The Hole in the Wall*,
was made in dynamic frame, which proved
distracting and has in any case been overtaken
by multiscreen experiments of the sixties.

Dyneley, Peter (1921–). British character
actor.
Beau Brummel 54. The Young Lovers 55. The
Split 60. Call Me Bwana 63. Chato's Land 72,
etc.

E

Eady, David (1924–). British director.
The Bridge of Time (documentary) 52. Three
Cases of Murder (one story) 55. In the Wake of a
Stranger 58. Faces in the Dark 60, etc.

Eagels, Jeanne (1894–1929). American
leading lady of the twenties; her private life was
highly publicized and Kim Novak played her in a
1957 biopic.
Biography 1930: *The Rain Girl by Edward
Doherty*.
□ Man Woman and Sin 27. The Letter 29.
Jealousy 29.

Earp, Wyatt (1848–1928). American frontier
marshal, the most famous lawman of the wild
west. Screen impersonations of him include
Walter Huston in *Law and Order* 31, George
O'Brien in *Frontier Marshal* 35, Randolph Scott
in *Frontier Marshal* 39, Richard Dix in
Tombstone 42, Henry Fonda in *My Darling
Clementine* 46, Joel McCrea in *Wichita* 55, Burt
Lancaster in *Gunfight at the OK Corral* 57,
James Stewart in *Cheyenne Autumn* 64, James
Garner in *Hour of the Gun* 67, Harris Yulin in
Doc 70. There was also a long-running TV series
starring Hugh O'Brian.

Earth (Russia 1930). Dovzhenko's epic drama
on the relation of man to the soil. Written by the
director, photographed by Daniel Demutski.

Earthquake (US 1973). A dreary all-star
disaster melodrama with boring personal stories
backing the razing to the ground of the city of
Los Angeles via very variable trick effects.
Notable for the first use of 'Sensurround', a
stereophonic sound device which created a
frightening rumble and for most people a pain in
the chest.

Easdale, Brian (1909–). British composer:
GPO Film Unit shorts 34–38. Ferry Pilot 42.
Black Narcissus 46. The Red Shoes (AA) 48. An
Outcast of the Islands 51. The Battle of the River
Plate 56, etc.

Eason, B. Reeves (1886–1956). American
action director, mostly of second features.

SELECTED SILENT FILMS include: Moon Rider 20.
Ben Hur (chariot race) 26.
□ SOUND FILMS: The Lariat Kid 29. Winged
Horseman 29. Troopers Three 30. The Roaring
Ranch 30. Trigger Tricks 30. Spurs 30. The
Galloping Ghost 31. The Sunset Trail 32. Honor
of the Press 32. The Heart Punch 32. Cornered
33. Behind Jury Doors 33. Alimony Madness 33.
Revenge at Monte Carlo 33. Her Resale Value
33. Dance Hall Hostess 33. Red River Valley 36.
Land Beyond the Law 37. Empty Holsters 37.
Prairie Thunder 37. Sergeant Murphy 38. The
Kid Comes Back 38. Daredevil Drivers 38. Call
of the Yukon 38. Blue Montana Skies 39.
Mountain Rhythm 39. Men with Steel Faces 40.
Murder in the Big House 42. Spy Ship 42. Truck
Busters 43. Rimfire 49.

East Lynne. Mrs Henry Wood's heavy-going
Victorian novel, in which mother and baby are
literally cast out into the cold, cold snow, was a
favourite silent film subject. There were British
versions in 1912 and 1921, and an American one
in 1925; but the 1931 sound remake, with Ann
Harding, was not a success.

East of Eden (US 1955). Notable for
introducing the young James Dean as a teenage
rebel of yesteryear, this version by Elia Kazan of
John Steinbeck's novel about father-son
relationships in agricultural California before
World War I had emotional power to make up
for its rather sluggish pace and inflated biblical
parallels. Raymond Massey and Jo Van Fleet
(AA) were the mainstays of a film which at least
treated its audience as adults.

Eastman, George (1854–1932). American
pioneer of cinematography: invented the roll
film, which made him a millionaire.

Eastwood, Clint (1930–). American leading
man who after TV success made his big screen
name in Italian westerns, then returned to
Hollywood and became one of the big action
stars of the late sixties.
□ Revenge of the Creature 55. Francis in the
Navy 55. Lady Godiva 55. Tarantula 55. Never
Say Goodbye 56. The First Travelling Saleslady

56. Star in the Dust 56. Escapade in Japan 57. Ambush at Cimarron Pass 58. Lafayette Escadrille 58. *A Fistful of Dollars* 64. *For a Few Dollars More* 65. *The Good The Bad and The Ugly* 66. The Witches 67. Hang 'Em High 68. *Coogan's Bluff* 68. Where Eagles Dare 69. Paint Your Wagon 69. Kelly's Heroes 70. Two Mules for Sister Sara 70. The Beguiled 71. *Play Misty for Me* (& d) 71. *Dirty Harry* 71. Joe Kidd 72. Breezy (d only) 73. High Plains Drifter (& d) 73. Magnum Force 73. Thunderbolt and Lightfoot 74. The Eiger Sanction 75. The Outlaw, Josey Wales 76. The Enforcer 76.
TV series: *Rawhide* 58–65.

Easy Rider (US 1969). A highly influential, cheaply made film which typified a section of America's aimlessly rebellious, death-wishing youth in its casual tale of two motor cyclists trekking across the country and finding nothing to respect, only a meaningless death. By and with Peter Fonda and Dennis Hopper.

Easy Street (US 1917). Perhaps Chaplin's most notable two-reeler, a deft combination of farce and social documentary, with jokes about the Salvation Army, overcrowded slums and drug addiction. Still poignant and funny.

Eaton, Shirley (1936–). Pneumatic blonde British leading lady.
Doctor at Large 56. Sailor Beware 57. Carry on Sergeant 58. Carry on Nurse 59. What a Carve Up 62. The Girl Hunters 63. Goldfinger 64. Rhino 65. Ten Little Indians 65. Around the World Under the Sea 66. Eight on the Lam 67. Sumuru 68, many others.

Ebsen, Buddy (1908–) (Christian Rudolf Ebsen). American actor-dancer of the thirties, usually in 'countrified' parts; later emerged as a character actor and achieved his greatest success in a long-running TV series.
Broadway Melody of 1936. Captain January 36. Born to Dance 36. Banjo on My Knee 36. The Girl of the Golden West 38. Four Girls in White 39. Parachute Battalion 41. Sing Your Worries Away 42. Thunder in God's Country 51. Night People 54. Red Garters 54. Davy Crockett 55. Attack 56. Breakfast at Tiffany's 61. The Interns 62. Mail Order Bride 64. The One and Only Genuine Original Family Band 68. The Daughters of Joshua Cabe (TV) 72. Terror at 37,000 feet (TV) 72, etc.
TV series: *The Beverly Hillbillies* 62–70. *Barnaby Jones* 72–.

Eburne, Maude (1875–1960). Diminutive American character actress who usually played frowning matrons and nosey neighbours.
The Bat Whispers 30. The Guardsman 31. The Vampire Bat 33. Lazy River 34. *Ruggles of Red Gap* 35. Champagne Waltz 37. Meet Doctor Christian 39. West Point Widow 41. Bowery to Broadway 44. The Suspect 45. Mother Wore Tights 47. Arson Inc. 50, many others.

Ecstasy: see *Extase*.

Eddy, Nelson (1901–1967). Romantic American actor-singer with opera background; famous on screen for series of operettas with Jeanette MacDonald.
□ Broadway to Hollywood 31. Dancing Lady 33. Student Tour 34. *Naughty Marietta* 35. *Rose Marie* 36. *Maytime* 37. Rosalie 37. The Girl of the Golden West 38. *Sweethearts* 38. Let Freedom Ring 39. Balalaika 39. *New Moon* 40. Bitter Sweet 40. The Chocolate Soldier 41. I Married an Angel 43. Phantom of the Opera 43. Knickerbocker Holiday 44. Make Mine Music (voice only) 46. Northwest Outpost 47.

Edelmann, Herb (1930–). Bald, lanky American character actor, usually in comic roles.
In Like Flint 67. Barefoot in the Park 67. The Odd Couple 68. The Front Page 74. The Yakuza 75, etc.

Eden, Barbara (1934–) (Barbara Huffman). American leading lady, former chorine.
Back from Eternity 56. Twelve Hours to Kill 60. Flaming Star 60. Voyage to the Bottom of the Sea 61. Five Weeks in a Balloon 62. The Wonderful World of the Brothers Grimm 63. The Brass Bottle 64. Seven Faces of Dr Lao 64. The Feminist and the Fuzz (TV) 71. The Woman Hunter (TV) 72. A Howling in the Woods (TV) 72, etc.
TV series: How to Marry a Millionaire 58. I Dream of Jeannie 65–69.

Edens, Roger (1905–1970). American musical supervisor who moulded many MGM musicals, often as associate to producer Arthur Freed. Academy Awards for Easter Parade 48. On the Town 49. Annie Get Your Gun 50. Produced Deep in My Heart 55. Funny Face 56. Hello Dolly 69, etc.

Edeson, Arthur (1891–1970). American cinematographer.
Wild and Woolly 17. *Robin Hood* 23. *The Thief of Baghdad* 24. *The Lost World* 25. The Bat 26. The Patent Leather Kid 27. In Old Arizona 28. The Big Trail 30. *All Quiet on the Western Front* 30. *Frankenstein* 31. The Big Trail 31. The Old

Dark House 32. *The Invisible Man* 33. Mutiny on the Bounty 35. They Won't Forget 37. Each Dawn I Die 39. They Drive by Night 40. Sergeant York 41. *The Maltese Falcon* 41. *Casablanca* 42. Thank Your Lucky Stars 43. The Mask of Dimitrios 44. The Fighting O'Flynn 48, many others.

Edgar, Marriott (1880–1951). British comedy scenarist, in films from 1935. Worked on many of the best vehicles of Will Hay and the Crazy Gang.
Good Morning Boys 36. Oh Mr Porter 38. Alf's Button Afloat 38. The Frozen Limits 39. The Ghost Train 41, many others; later on children's films. Also author of the 'Sam Small' and 'Albert' monologues made famous by Stanley Holloway.

edge numbers. Serial numbers printed along the edge of all film material to assist identification when re-ordering sections.

Edison, Thomas Alva (1847–1931). American inventor of the phonograph and the incandescent lamp, among over a thousand other devices including the kinetoscope (a combined movie camera and projector), edge perforations and the 35 mm gauge. Biopics: *Young Tom Edison* 39 with Mickey Rooney; *Edison the Man* 40 with Spencer Tracy.

editor. Technician who assembles final print of film from various scenes and tracks available; works closely under director's control except in routine pictures.

Edouard et Caroline (France 1950). Jacques Becker's slight but charming comedy of a tiff between a young married couple was highly influential on later style. Anne Vernon and Daniel Gelin starred.

Edouart, Farciot (–   ). American special effects man, with Paramount for many years.
Alice in Wonderland 33. Lives of a Bengal Lancer 35. Sullivan's Travels 41. Reap the Wild Wind 42. Unconquered 47. Ace in the Hole 51. The Mountain 56, many others.

Edwards, Blake (1922–) (William Blake McEdwards). American writer-producer-director with a leaning for all kinds of comedy.
☐ Panhandle (aw) 47. All Ashore (w) 53. Cruising down the River (w) 53. Drive a Crooked Road (w) 54. Sound Off (w) 54. Bring Your Smile Along (wd) 55. My Sister Eileen (w) 55. He Laughed Last (wd) 55. Mr Cory (wd) 56. Operation Mad Ball (w) 57. This Happy Feeling (wd) 58. The Perfect Furlough (wd) 58.

Operation Petticoat (d) 59. High Time (d) 60. Breakfast at Tiffany's (d) 61. Experiment in Terror (d) 62. Notorious Landlady (w) 62. *Days of Wine and Roses* (d) 62. The Pink Panther (wd) 63. A Shot in the Dark (wpd) 64. *The Great Race* (wpd) 64. What Did You Do in the War, Daddy? (wpd) 66. Waterhole Three (p) 67. Gunn (p, d) 67. The Party (wpd) 68. Darling Lili (wpd) 69. Wild Rovers (wpd) 71. The Carey Treatment (wpd) 72. The Tamarind Seed (wd) 74. The Return of the Pink Panther (wpd) 74. The Pink Panther Strikes Again (wpd) 76.
TV series: Richard Diamond, Dante, Peter Gunn (all as creator).

Edwards, Cliff (1895–1971). Diminutive American entertainer known as 'Ukelele Ike'.
Hollywood Revue 29. Parlour Bedroom and Bath 31. Hell Divers 31. Flying Devils 33. Red Salute 35. Bad Guy 39. Pinocchio (voice of Jiminy Cricket) 40. The Monster and the Girl 41. The Falcon Strikes Back 43. She Couldn't Say No 45. The Avenging Rider 53, many others.

Edwards, Henry (1882–1952). Gentlemanly British romantic lead of the twenties; later directed some films and came back to acting as amiable elderly man.
Broken Threads 18. The Amazing Quest of Ernest Bliss 22. A Lunatic at Large 23. *The Flag Lieutenant* 26. Fear 27. Three Kings 28. Call of the Sea 31. The Flag Lieutenant (talkie) 31. The Barton Mystery (d) 32. General John Regan 33. Discord Driven (d) 33. Scrooge (d) 35. Juggernaut (d) 37. Spring Meeting (d) 41. Green for Danger 46. Oliver Twist 48. London Belongs to Me 48. Madeleine 50. The Long Memory 52, many others.

Edwards, James (1922–1970). Black American actor, on stage from 1945.
The Set-Up 49. *Home of the Brave* 49. The Member of the Wedding 52. The Caine Mutiny 54. The Phoenix City Story 55. Men in War 57. The Sandpiper 65, etc.

Edwards, Jimmy (1920–). Moustachioed British comedian of stage, radio and TV.
Treasure Hunt 48. Murder at the Windmill 48. Three Men in a Boat 55. Bottoms Up 60. Nearly a Nasty Accident 62. Rhubarb 70, etc.

Edwards, Meredith (1917–). Balding Welsh character actor with stage experience.
A Run for Your Money 50. The Blue Lamp 50. Girdle of Gold 53. The Cruel Sea 53. The Long Arm 56. The Trials of Oscar Wilde 60. Only Two Can Play 61. This Is My Street 64, etc.

Edwards, Penny (1919–). American light leading lady of the forties.
Let's Face It 43. That Hagen Girl 47. Two Guys from Texas 48. The Wild Blue Yonder 51. Street Bandits 52. Powder River 53, etc.

Edwards, Vince (1928–). (Vincent Edward Zorrio). American leading man of the tough/sincere kind.
Mr Universe 51. Hiawatha 52. The Killing 56. City of Fear 58. *Murder by Contract* 59. The Victors 63. The Devil's Brigade 68. Hammerhead 68. The Desperadoes 69. The Mad Bomber 72, etc.
TV series: *Ben Casey* 60–65. Matt Lincoln 70.

Egan, Eddie (–). Burly American policeman whose exploits were the basis of *The French Connection* (qv). He subsequently left the force and played small parts in films.
TV series: Joe Forrester 75.

Egan, Peter (–). British TV leading man who has sporadically appeared on stage and in films.
Callan 74. Hennessy 75.

Egan, Richard (1921–). Virile American leading man once thought likely successor to Clark Gable but who has been mainly confined to westerns and action dramas.
The Damned Don't Cry 49. Undercover Girl 50. Split Second 52. Demetrius and the Gladiators 54. Wicked Woman 54. Gog 54. Underwater 55. Untamed 55. Violent Saturday 55. The View from Pompey's Head 55. Seven Cities of Gold 55. Love Me Tender 56. Tension at Table Rock 56. These Thousand Hills 58. A Summer Place 59. Pollyanna 60. Esther and the King 60. The 300 Spartans 62. The Destructors 66. Chubasco 68. The Big Cube 69. The Day of the Wolves (TV) 72, etc.
TV series: Empire 62. Redigo 64.

Ege, Julie (c. 1947–). Decorative Norwegian leading lady in British films of the seventies.
Every Home Should Have One 70. Up Pompeii 70. Creatures the World Forgot 71. The Magnificent Seven Deadly Sins 71. Rentadick 72. The Garnett Saga 72. Not Now Darling 73. Craze 73. The Mutations 74, etc.

Eggar, Samantha (1939–). British leading lady, in international films.
□ The Wild and the Willing 62. Dr Crippen 63. Doctor in Distress 63. Psyche 59 63. *The Collector* 65. Return from the Ashes 65. Walk Don't Run 66. Doctor Dolittle 67. The Molly Maguires 69. The Walking Stick 69. The Lady in

the Car 70. The Light at the Edge of the World 72. Double Indemnity (TV) 73. The Seven Per Cent Solution 76.
TV series: *Anna and the King* 72.

Eight and a Half (Italy 1963). Fellini's beautiful, irresponsible, sometimes incomprehensible but highly cinematic extraganza for our times, about a film director with doubts. Superbly photographed by Gianni de Venanzo, with a fine central part for Marcello Mastroianni. AA 9163: best foreign film.

8mm. A substandard gauge used mostly by amateurs. Sound used to require 9.5mm, but recently 'super 8' was introduced.

Eilers, Sally (1908–). Quiet-spoken American leading lady of the thirties.
The Goodbye Kiss 28. She Couldn't Say No 30. Quick Millions 31. The Black Camel 31. Over the Hill 31. State Fair 33. She Made Her Bed 34. Alias Mary Dow 34. Strike Me Pink 35. Talk of the Devil 36. Danger Patrol 37. Nurse from Brooklyn 38. They Made Her a Spy 39. Full Confession 39. I Was a Prisoner on Devil's Island 41. A Wave and WAC and a Marine 44. Coroner Creek 48. Stage to Tucson 50, many others.

Eisenstein, Sergei (1898–1948). Russian director, one of the cinema giants. Used the camera more vividly and purposefully than almost anyone else.
Biography 1952: *Sergei Eisenstein* by Marie Seton.
□ Strike 24. The Battleship Potemkin 25. October (Ten Days That Shook the World) 27. The General Line 28. Que Viva Mexico (unfinished: sections later released under this title and as *Time in the Sun*) 32. Alexander Nevsky 38. Ivan the Terrible 42–46. Books published include *Film Form, The Film Sense, Notes of a Film Director.* He virtually invented 'montage'.

Eisinger, Jo (–). American screenwriter.
The Spider 45. Gilda 46. The Sleeping City 50. Night and the City 51. The System 53. Bedevilled 55. The Poppy is Only a Flower (Danger Grows Wild) 66, many others.

Eisler, Hanns (1898–1963). German composer who in the forties scored some Hollywood films (*None But the Lonely Heart, The Woman on the Beach,* etc.) In Germany, *Aktion J* 61, many others.

Ekberg, Anita (1931–). Statuesque Swedish blonde who has decorated a number of films in various countries.

The Golden Blade 53. Blood Alley 55. Artists and Models 55. Back from Eternity 56. War and Peace 56. Zarak 56. Interpol 57. Sign of the Gladiator 58. La Dolce Vita 59. Boccaccio 70 61. Call Me Bwana 63. Four for Texas 63. The Alphabet Murders 65. Who Wants to Sleep (Das Liebeskarussel) 65. Way Way Out 66. The Glass Sphinx 67, etc.

Ekk, Nikolai (1902–). Russian director.
The Road to Life 31. The Nightingale 36, etc.

Ekland, Britt (1942–). Swedish leading lady in international films.
□ After the Fox 66. The Bobo 67. The Double Man 68. The Night They Raided Minsky's 68. Stiletto 69. Percy 71. Get Carter 71. A Time for Loving 71. Night Hair Child 71. Baxter 72. Endless Night 72. Asylum 72. The Wicker Man 73. The Man with the Golden Gun 73. Royal Flash 74.

Ekman, Gosta (1887–1937). Swedish leading actor.
Charles XII 24. Faust 26. Intermezzo 36, etc.

El (Mexico 1953). A haunting psychological melodrama written and directed by Luis Buñuel, with Arturo de Cordova as a happily married man who unaccountably goes mad with jealousy.

Elam, Jack (1916–). Laconic, swarthy American character actor, often seen as western villain or sinister comic relief.
Rawhide 50. Kansas City Confidential 52. The Moonlighter 53. Vera Cruz 54. Moonfleet 55. Kiss Me Deadly 55. Gunfight at the OK Corral 57. Baby Face Nelson 57. Edge of Eternity 59. The Comancheros 62. The Rare Breed 66. The Way West 67. Firecreek 67. Once Upon a Time in the West 69. Support Your Local Sheriff 69. Rio Lobo 70. Support Your Local Gunfighter 71. A Knife for the Ladies 74, etc.
TV series: The Dakotas 62. Temple Houston 63.

Eldredge, John (1904–1961). Mild-looking American actor usually cast as weakling brother or bland schemer.
The Man with Two Faces 34. Persons in Hiding 38. Blossoms in the Dust 41. The French Key 47. Champagne for Caesar 50. Lonely Hearts Bandits 52. The First Travelling Saleslady 56, many others.

Eldridge, Florence (1901–) (Florence McKechnie). Distinguished American stage actress, wife of Fredric March. Film appearances occasional.

Six Cylinder Love 23. The Studio Murder Mystery 29. The Matrimonial Bed 30. The Story of Temple Drake 33. Les Misérables 35. Mary of Scotland (as Elizabeth I) 36. An Act of Murder 48. Another Part of the Forest 48. Christopher Columbus 49. Inherit the Wind 60, etc.

Eldridge, John (1917–). British documentary and feature director.
Waverley Steps 47. Three Dawns to Sydney 49. Brandy for the Parson 51. Laxdale Hall 53. Conflict of Wings 54, etc.

the electric chair has figured prominently in innumerable gangster and prison movies, notably Two Seconds, Twenty Thousand Years in Sing Sing, Angels with Dirty Faces and The Last Mile. Front Page Woman concentrated on the reporters ushered in to watch. The death cell scenes in Double Indemnity were deleted before the film's release. The most horrific sequence of this kind was the gas chamber climax of I Want To Live.

electronovision. A much-touted form of transfer from videotape to film, thought likely to save money in putting great stage performances onto the big screen. Unfortunately it proved technically and aesthetically unacceptable, and the two features shot in it in 1965 are only interesting if one can ignore the technical shortcomings. They are Harlow with Carol Lynley and Hamlet with Richard Burton.

Elephant Boy (GB 1937). Directed by Robert Flaherty and Zoltan Korda, this adaptation of Kipling's 'Toomai of the Elephants' had the air of a fictionalized travel film but was a great commercial success because of the popularity of the boy Sabu, who became a star and went to Hollywood. Its Indian backgrounds were charming and authentic. A TV series followed in 1972.

elephants have come closest to starring roles in Zenobia, Elephant Boy and Hannibal Brooks; but they were the subject of concern in Chang, Where No Vultures Fly, Elephant Walk, Maya, and Roots of Heaven, and Tarzan and Dorothy Lamour (in her jungle days) usually had one around as a pet. (Tarzan Goes to India had a splendid elephant stampede.) Circus elephants were stars of Jumbo, and above all of Dumbo.

Eles, Sandor (1946–). Hungarian leading man in Britain.
The Naked Edge 61. The Evil of Frankenstein 64. And Soon the Darkness 70. Countess Dracula 70, etc.

elevators: see *lifts*.

Elg, Taina (1931–). Finnish leading lady in international films.
The Prodigal 55. Diane 56. Gaby 56. Les Girls 57. Imitation General 57. Watusi 58. The Thirty-Nine Steps 59, etc.

Eliot, T. S. (1888–1965). American poet who lived mainly in England. His play *Murder in the Cathedral* was his only work adapted for the cinema.

Elizabeth I, Queen of England (1533–1603), has been notably played by Flora Robson in *Fire Over England* 36 and *The Sea Hawk* 40; by Florence Eldridge in *Mary of Scotland* 36; by Bette Davis in *Elizabeth and Essex* 39 and *The Virgin Queen* 55; by Sarah Bernhardt in *Queen Elizabeth* 12; by Agnes Moorehead in *The Story of Mankind* 57; by Irene Worth in *Seven Seas to Calais* 63; by Catherine Lacey in *The Fighting Prince of Donegal* 65, and by Glenda Jackson in a 1971 TV series followed by *Mary Queen of Scots* 72; Jean Simmons played the young queen in *Young Bess* 53.

Elizondo, Hector (–). American character actor, mainly on stage.
Pocket Money 71. Stand Up and Be Counted 72. The Taking of Pelham One Two Three 74. Report to the Commissioner 75, etc.

Ellery Queen. The fictional American detective was played by four actors between 1935 and 1943: Donald Cook, Eddie Quillan, Ralph Bellamy and William Gargan. The name is a pseudonym for two authors: *Frederick Dannay* (1905–71) and *Manfred Lee* (1905–). In 1971 Peter Lawford turned up on TV in the role.

Ellington, Duke (1899–1974) (Edward Kennedy Ellington). Celebrated black American bandleader and pianist.
Hit Parade 37. New Faces 37. Reveille with Beverly 43. Anatomy of a Murder 59. Paris Blues 61. Change of Mind (m only) 69, etc.

Elliot, Laura (1929–). American supporting actress.
Special Agent 49. Paid in Full 50. *Strangers on a Train* 51. When Worlds Collide 52. Jamaica Run 53. About Mrs Leslie 54, etc.

Elliott, Denholm (1922–). British stage and screen actor, often of well-mannered ineffectual types, latterly in more sophisticated roles.
Dear Mr Prohack 49. The Sound Barrier 52. The

Cruel Sea 53. The Heart of the Matter 53. They Who Dare 54. The Night My Number Came Up 55. Pacific Destiny 56. Scent of Mystery (Holiday in Spain) 59. Station Six Sahara 63. *Nothing but the Best* 64. The High Bright Sun 65. You Must Be Joking 65. King Rat 65. Alfie 66. The Spy with a Cold Nose 67. Maroc 7 67. *Here We Go Round the Mulberry Bush* 67. The Night They Raided Minsky's 68. Too Late the Hero 69. The Rise and Rise of Michael Rimmer 70. Percy 70. Quest for Love 71. A Doll's House 73. Madame Sin 73. The Apprenticeship of Duddy Kravitz 75. Robin and Marian 75. Russian Roulette 76, etc.

Elliott, Sam (–). American leading man of the seventies.
□ The Games 70. Frogs 72. Molly and Lawless John 72. Evel Knievel (TV) 75.

Elliott, 'Wild Bill' (1906–1965) (Gordon Elliott). Burly American leading man of the twenties who later appeared in many second feature westerns and mysteries.
The Private Life of Helen of Troy 27. Broadway Scandals 28. The Great Divide 31. Wonder Bar 34. False Evidence 40. Blue Clay 42. The Plainsman and the Lady 46. The Fabulous Texan 48. Hellfire 49. The Longhorn 51. Dial Red O 55. Chain of Evidence 57, etc.

Ellis, Edward (1872–1952). American stage character actor who made a number of films in the thirties, usually as stern father or judge.
I Am a Fugitive from a Chain Gang 32. From Headquarters 33. The President Vanishes 34. The Return of Peter Grimm 35. Fury 36. Maid of Salem 37. *A Man to Remember* 38. Three Sons 39. A Man Betrayed 41. The Omaha Trail 42, etc.

Ellis, Mary (1900–) (Mary Elsas). American leading lady and singer famous in British stage musicals, especially those of Ivor Novello.
Bella Donna 34. Paris Love Song 35. All the King's Horses 35. Glamorous Night 36. The Three Worlds of Gulliver 61, etc.

Ellis, Patricia (1916–1970) (Patricia Gene O'Brien). American leading lady of the thirties.
Three on a Match 32. 42nd Street 33. Picture Snatcher 33. The St Louis Kid 34. The Case of the Lucky Legs 34. Boulder Dam 36. Melody for Two 37. Blockheads 38. Back Door to Heaven 39. Fugitive at Large 39, etc.

Ellison, James (1910–) (James Ellison Smith). Genial American leading man, mainly seen in routine westerns.

The Play Girl 32. Hopalong Cassidy 35. The Plainsman (as Buffalo Bill) 36. Vivacious Lady 38. Fifth Avenue Girl 39. Ice Capades 41. Charley's Aunt 41. The Undying Monster 42. I Walked with a Zombie 43. The Ghost Goes Wild 46. Calendar Girl 47. Last of the Wild Horses 48. Lone Star Lawman 50. Dead Man's Trail 52, etc.

Elmer Gantry (US 1960). In this lengthy version written (AA) and directed by Richard Brooks, Sinclair Lewis's novel about old-time revivalist religion has its emotions compromised and its satire blunted; but the flavour of the book often filters through; and the film benefits from John Alton's colour photography and the broad, beaming, zestful performance of Burt Lancaster (AA) as the hymn and hellfire salesman.

Elmes, Guy (1920–). British writer.
The Planter's Wife (co-w) 51. The Stranger's Hand 53. Across the Bridge (co-w) 57. Swordsman of Siena 62. A Face in the Rain 63. El Greco 66. The Night Visitor 71, etc.

Elsom, Isobel (1893–) (Isobel Reed). British stage actress who starred in over 60 early British romantic films; went to Hollywood in the late thirties and played innumerable great ladies.
A Debt of Honour 19. Dick Turpin's Ride to York 22. The Sign of Four 23. The Wandering Jew 23. The Love Story of Aliette Brunon 24. Stanglehold 30. Illegal 31. *Ladies in Retirement* 41. You Were Never Lovelier 42. Between Two Worlds 44. The Unseen 45. Of Human Bondage 46. Ivy 47. Love from a Stranger 47. Monsieur Verdoux 47. Desiree 54. 23 Paces to Baker Street 57. The Miracle 59. Who's Minding the Store? 63. My Fair Lady 64, others.

Eltinge, Julian (1882–1941) (William J. Dalton). American female impersonator who appeared in a few silent films.
The Countess Charming 17. Over the Rhine 18. Madame Behave 24, etc.

Elton, Sir Arthur (1906–1973). British producer especially associated with documentary; GPO Film Unit 34–37, Ministry of Information 37–45, Shell Film Unit 45 on. Founder Film Centre, governor BFI, etc.

Elvey, Maurice (1887–1967) (William Folkard). Veteran British director of over Three-Hundred features.
Maria Marten 12. Comradeship 18. Nelson 19. At the Villa Rose 20. The Elusive Pimpernel 20. The Hound of the Baskervilles 21. Dick Turpin's Ride to York 22. The Love Story of Aliette

Brunon 24. The Flag Lieutenant 26. Hindle Wakes 27. Balaclava 28. High Treason 30. The School for Scandal 30. Sally in Our Alley 31. In a Monastery Garden 31. The Water Gypsies 32. The Lodger 32. The Wandering Jew 33. The Clairvoyant 34. *The Tunnel* 34. Heat Wave 35. The Return of the Frog 37. For Freedom 39. Room for Two 39. Under Your Hat 40. The Lamp Still Burns 43. The Gentle Sex (co-d) 43. Medal for the General 44. Salute John Citizen 44. *Beware of Pity* 46. The Third Visitor 51. My Wife's Lodger 52. Fun at St Fanny's 55. Dry Rot 56, many others.

Elvira Madigan (Sweden 1967). Bo Widerberg's ravishingly beautiful film about lovers who would rather starve than live apart caused a small resurgence in romance. Photographed by Jorgen Persson.

Ely, Ron (1938–) (Ronald Pierce). American athlete who in the sixties became Tarzan and played the role in the television series.

Emerson, Faye (1917–). American socialite leading lady popular for a time in the forties.
Between Two Worlds 44. The Mask of Dimitrios 44. Hotel Berlin 45. Danger Signal 45. Nobody Lives Forever 46. Guilty Bystander 50. A Face in the Crowd 57, etc.

Emerson, Hope (1897–1960). Brawny 6′ 2″ American character actress, in films from early thirties.
Smiling Faces 32. Cry of the City 48. Adam's Rib 49. Caged 50. Casanova's Big Night 54. The Day They Gave Babies Away 56. Rock a Bye Baby 58, many others.
TV series: Peter Gunn 58–60.

Emerton, Roy (1892–1944). Long-nosed Canadian character actor in British films: an eminently hissable villain.
The Sign of Four 32. Java Head 34. Lorna Doone (as Carver) 35. Doctor Syn 38. The Drum 38. Busman's Honeymoon 40. The Thief of Baghdad 40. The Man in Grey 43. Henry V 44, etc.

Emery, Dick (1919–). Chubby British TV comedian with a flair for disguise.
Light Up the Sky 60. A Taste of Money 62. The Wrong Arm of the Law 63. Baby Love 69. *Ooh You Are Awful* 72, etc.

Emery, Gilbert (1875–1945) (Gilbert Emery Bensley Pottle). British character actor long in Hollywood as police commissioners, lords of the manor, etc.

Behind that Curtain 29. The Royal Bed 30. A Farewell to Arms 32. The House of Rothschild 34. One More River 34. Clive of India 35. Magnificent Obsession 35. Dracula's Daughter 36. A Man to Remember 38. Nurse Edith Cavell 39. Raffles 39. Rage in Heaven 41. That Hamilton Woman 41. The Loves of Edgar Allan Poe 42. Between Two Worlds 44. The Brighton Strangler 45, many others.

Emery, John (1905–1964). American stage and screen actor of suave and sometimes Mephistophelean types.
Here Comes Mr Jordan 41. Spellbound 45. Blood on the Sun 45. The Woman in White 48. The Gay Intruders 48. Let's Live Again 49. The Mad Magician 54. Ten North Frederick 57. Youngblood Hawke 64, many others.

Emhardt, Robert (c. 1901–). American character actor, short and tubby; once understudied Sidney Greenstreet.
The Iron Mistress 52. 3.10 to Yuma 57. Underworld USA 60. The Stranger 61. Kid Galahad 62. *The Group* 66. Where Were You When the Lights Went Out? 68. Lawman 71, etc.

Emil and the Detectives. Erich Kastner's German novel of schoolboys who track down a thief has been filmed five times: in 1932 (Germany) by Gerhardt Lamprecht; in 1935 (GB) by Milton Rosmer; in 1954 (Germany) by R. A. Stemmle; in 1956 in Japan; and in 1963 (US) by Peter Tewkesbury for Walt Disney.

Emmer, Luciano (1918–). Italian director.
Domenica d'Agosto 50. The Girls of the Spanish Steps 52. The Bigamist 56, etc.

Emmett, E. V. H. (1902–). British commentator, for many years the voice of Gaumont-British and Universal News. Producer of occasional documentaries, also features at Ealing 1946–50.

Emney, Fred (1900–). Heavyweight British comedian, characterized by a growl, a cigar, and a top hat.
Brewster's Millions 35. Yes Madam 39. Just William 40. Let the People Sing 42. Fun at St Fanny's 56. San Ferry Ann 65. The Sandwich Man 66. Lock Up Your Daughters 69, etc.

the end of the world has been fairly frequently considered in movies, and not only in the recent crop of panic button dramas like *Dr Strangelove*, *The Bedford Incident* and *Fail Safe*. Movement of the earth was threatened in *The Day the Earth Stood Still* and stopped (by

Roland Young) in *The Man Who Could Work Miracles*. Plague very nearly ended everything in *Things to Come*. Danger from other planets looming perilously close was only narrowly averted in *Red Planet Mars*, while in *When Worlds Collide* and *The Day the Earth Caught Fire* the worst happened. Another kind of danger was met in *Crack in the World*. The Martians nearly got us in *The War of the Worlds*. In *Five* there were only five people left alive, in *The World, the Flesh and the Devil* only three, and in *On the Beach* none at all.

Endfield, Cy (1914–). American director, in films since 1942. Made second features until 1951; thereafter resident in Britain.
Gentleman Joe Palooka 47. Stork Bites Man (& w) 47. The Argyle Secrets (& w) 48. Underworld Story 50. *The Sound of Fury* 51. Tarzan's Savage Fury 52. The Search 55. Child in the House 56. *Hell Drivers* 57. Sea Fury 58. Jet Storm 59. Mysterious Island 61. *Zulu* 62. Sands of the Kalahari 65. De Sade 69. Universal Soldier 71, etc.

Les Enfants du Paradis (France 1944). A superbly evocative and pictorial romance of Paris's 'theatre street' in the 1830s. Jacques Prevert's script mingles fact and fiction, farce and tragedy; Marcel Carné directs with superb control of the rich detail. The fine cast includes Arletty, Jean-Louis Barrault, Pierre Brasseur and Marcel Herrand, photography by Roger Hubert and Marc Fossard, music by Joseph Kosma and Maurice Thiriet.

Engel, Morris (1918–). American producer-director of off-beat semi-professional features.
The Little Fugitive 53. Lovers and Lollipops 55. Weddings and Babies 58.

Engel, Samuel (1904–). American producer.
Mr Darling Clementine 46. Sitting Pretty 48. Rawhide 50. Belles on Their Toes 52. Daddy Long Legs 55. Boy on a Dolphin 57. The Story of Ruth 60. The Lion 62, others.

Englund, George H. (1926–). American producer-director.
The World, the Flesh and the Devil (p) 59. The Ugly American (pd) 62. Signpost to Murder (d) 64. Dark of the Sun (p) 67. Zachariah (d) 70. Snowjob (d) 71, etc.

Englund, Ken (1914–). American writer, in films from 1938.
Good Sam 47. The Secret Life of Walter Mitty 48. The Caddy 53. The Vagabond King 56, etc.

Ennis, Skinnay (1907–1963). American bandleader who appeared in such thirties films as *College Swing, Sleepytime Gal* and *Follow the Band*.

Enoch Arden was a character in a Tennyson poem who came back to his family after having been long supposed dead. Films with an 'Enoch Arden' theme include *Tomorrow Is Forever* (with Orson Welles), *The Years Between* (with Michael Redgrave), *My Two Husbands* (with Fred MacMurray) and its remake *Three for the Show* (with Jack Lemmon), *My Favourite Wife* (with Irene Dunne) and its remake *Move Over Darling* (with Doris Day), *Piccadilly Incident* (with Anna Neagle), *Return from the Ashes* (with Ingrid Thulin), *Desire Me* (with Robert Mitchum), *Laura* (with Gene Tierney), *Man Alive* (with Pat O'Brien), and *The Man from Yesterday* (with Clive Brook). D. W. Griffith in 1910 and 1911 made short versions of the original story.

Enrico, Robert (1931–). French director.
Incident at Owl Creek 64. Au Coeur de la Vie 65. La Belle Vie 65. Les Aventuriers 67. Zita 67. Ho! 68, etc.

Enright, Ray (1896–1965). American director, former editor and Sennett gagman. Films mostly routine.
Tracked by the Police 27. Dancing Sweeties 30. Havana Widows 33. Twenty Million Sweethearts 34. Dames 34. Alibi Ike 35. Miss Pacific Fleet 35. Earthworm Tractors 36. Slim 37. *Swing Your Lady* 37. Gold Diggers in Paris 38. Angels Wash Their Faces 39. On Your Toes 39.

entertainers, including actors and impresarios, have frequently been the subject of biopics, and if all their stories have seemed much the same, that is Hollywood's fault rather than theirs. Here is a reasonably comprehensive list:
Always Leave Them Laughing Milton Berle, *After the Ball* Pat Kirkwood as Vesta Tilley, *The Buster Keaton Story* Donald O'Connor, *Champagne Charlie* Tommy Trinder as George Leybourne and Stanley Holloway as the Great Vance, *The Dolly Sisters* Betty Grable & June Haver, *The Eddie Cantor Story* Keefe Brasselle, *The Fabulous Dorseys* Tommy and Jimmy Dorsey, *The Five Pennies* Danny Kaye as Red Nichols, *Funny Girl* Barbra Streisand as Fanny Brice, *The Gene Krupa Story* Sal Mineo, *The Glenn Miller Story* James Stewart, *The Great Caruso* Mario Lanza, *The Great Ziegfeld* William Powell, *Gypsy* Natalie Wood as Gypsy Rose Lee, *Harlow* Carroll Baker/Carol Lynley,

The Helen Morgan Story Ann Blyth, *Houdini* Tony Curtis, *The I Don't Care Girl* Mitzi Gaynor as Eva Tanguay, *Incendiary Blonde* Betty Hutton as Texas Guinan, *Interrupted Melody* Eleanor Parker as Marjorie Laurence, *Jeanne Eagels* Kim Novak, *The Joker is Wild* Frank Sinatra as Joe E. Lewis, *The Jolson Story* Larry Parks, *A Lady's Morals* Grace Moore as Jenny Lind, *Lady Sings the Blues* Diana Ross as Billie Holliday. *Lady With Red Hair* Miriam Hopkins as Mrs Leslie Carter and Claude Rains as David Belasco, *Lillian Russell* Alice Faye, *Look for the Silver Lining* June Haver as Marilyn Miller, *Love Me or Leave Me* Doris Day as Ruth Etting, *Man of a Thousand Faces* James Cagney as Lon Chaney, *Melba* Patrice Munsel, *Peg of Old Drury* Anna Neagle as Peg Woffington, *Prince of Players* Richard Burton as Edwin Booth, *The Seven Little Foys* Bob Hope as Eddie Foy, *Shine on Harvest Moon* Ann Sheridan as Nora Bayes, *Somebody Loves Me* Betty Hutton as Blossom Seeley, *So This Is Love* Kathryn Grayson as Grace Moore, *Star!* Julie Andrews as Gertrude Lawrence and Daniel Massey as Noel Coward, *The Story of Vernon and Irene Castle* Fred Astaire and Ginger Rogers, *The Story of Will Rogers* Will Rogers Jnr, *Tonight We Sing* David Wayne as Sol Hurok, *Too Much Too Soon* Dorothy Malone as Diana Barrymore and Errol Flynn as John Barrymore, *With a Song in My Heart* Susan Hayward as Jane Froman, *Yankee Doodle Dandy* James Cagney as George M. Cohan, *Young Man With a Horn* Kirk Douglas as Bix Beiderbecke, *Your Cheatin' Heart* George Hamilton as Hank Williams, *Lenny* Dustin Hoffman as Lenny Bruce, *W.C. Fields and Me* Rod Steiger as W. C. Fields, *Gable and Lombard* James Brolin and Jill Clayburgh.

Ephron, Henry (1912–). American screenwriter who invariably worked as a team with his wife Phoebe Ephron (1914–71). He also produced a few films.
Bride by Mistake 44. Always Together 46. John Loves Mary 49. *The Jackpot* 50. On the Riviera 51. Belles on Their Toes 52. There's No Business Like Show Business 54. Daddy Long Legs 55. Carousel (& p) 56. The Best Things in Life are Free (p only) 56. *Desk Set* 57. Take Her She's Mine 63. Captain Newman MD 64, etc.

epidemics featured memorably in *Jezebel, Yellow Jack, Arrowsmith, The Rains Came, Forever Amber, Panic in the Streets, The Killer That Stalked New York, Elephant Walk, No Blade of Grass, The Andromeda Strain, Eighty Thousand Suspects, The Omega Man, Things to Come, Isle of the Dead, The Satan Bug* and *The*

Seventh Seal.

episodic films in a sense have always been with us—*If I Had a Million*, after all, came out in 1932, and *Intolerance* in 1915—but it was in the forties, possibly spurred by the all-star variety films intended to help the war effort, that they achieved their greatest popularity. *Tales of Manhattan* was linked by a tail coat, *Flesh and Fantasy* by the ramblings of a club bore, *Forever and a Day* by a house, *Easy Money* by football pools, *Train of Events* by a railway accident, *Meet Mr Lucifer* by television. Then came the author complex: *Quartet* (Somerset Maugham), *Le Plaisir* (Maupassant), *Meet Me Tonight* (Noël Coward). The French took over with films like *The Seven Deadly Sins*, *The Devil and Ten Commandments, Life Together*; and the Italians are still at it with *Four Kinds of Love, Made in Italy* and *The Queens*. For English-speaking markets the form was killed in the mid-fifties by the advent of the half-hour TV play, but the sixties saw a brief revival with *How the West Was Won* and *The Yellow Rolls Royce*.

Epstein, Jean (1897–1953). French director since 1922; also wrote books on film theory.
Coeur Fidèle 23. The Fall of the House of Usher 28. Finis Terrae 28. Mor Vran 30. His sister Marie Epstein (1899–) often worked with him, and herself directed La Maternelle 33. La Mort du Cygne 38, etc.

Epstein, Julius J. (1909–) and **Philip G.** (1909–52). American twin screenwriters.
Four Daughters 38. Four Wives 39. No Time for Comedy 40. Strawberry Blonde 41. The Man Who Came to Dinner 41. *Casablanca* (AA) 42, Mr Skeffington (& p) 44. Romance on the High Seas 48. My Foolish Heart 49. Forever Female 53. The Last Time I Saw Paris 54. Then Julius alone: The Tender Trap 55. Tall Story 60. Take a Giant Step (& p) 61. Fanny 61. Send Me No Flowers 64. Any Wednesday (& p) 66, Pete 'n Tillie (& p) 72, etc.

L'Equipage. Directed by Maurice Tourneur in 1927, this was a popular silent drama of a triangular love affair in which the male participants were airmen during World War I. Anatole Litvak remade it in 1935 (with Charles Vanel, Annabella and Jean Pierre Aumont); then went to Hollywood and in 1937 made an English version, *The Woman I Love* (with Paul Muni, Miriam Hopkins and Louis Hayward).

Erdman, Richard (1925–). American actor who began playing callow youths and now takes rather crustier roles.

Thunder across the Pacific 44. Objective Burma 45. The Men 50. The Happy Time 52. Benghazi 55. Bernardine 57. Saddle the Wind 58. Namu the Killer Whale 66. The Brothers O'Toole (d only) 73, others.
TV series: The Tab Hunter Show 60.

Erice, Victor (–). Spanish director.
Spirit of the Beehive 73.

Erickson, Leif (1911–) (William Anderson). American 'second lead', former singer. In unspectacular roles since 1935.
Wanderer of the Wasteland 35. College Holiday 36. Ride a Crooked Mile 38. Nothing But the Truth 41. Eagle Squadron 42. Sorry, Wrong Number 48. Fort Algiers 50. Carbine Williams 52. On the Waterfront 54. The Fastest Gun Alive 56. Tea and Sympathy 57. Straitjacket 63. Mirage 65, many others.
TV series: High Chaparral 67–69.

Ericson, John (1927–) (Joseph Meibes). German-born leading man, long in America.
Teresa (debut) 51. Rhapsody 54. Green Fire 54. Bad Day at Black Rock 54. The Return of Jack Slade 55. Forty Guns 57. Pretty Boy Floyd 59. Under Ten Flags 60. The Seven Faces of Dr Lao 64. The Destructors 66. Operation Bluebook 67. Bedknobs and Broomsticks 71, etc.
TV series: Honey West 65.

Erotikon. There are two films of this title, both dealing with sexual experience and adultery. 1. Sweden 1920, written and directed by Mauritz Stiller, about a scientist who takes up with his niece when his wife proves unfaithful. 2. Czechoslovakia 1929, written and directed by Gustav Machaty, about a poor girl who takes a rich lover.

Errol, Leon (1881–1951). Australian comedian who in 1910 left medicine for Broadway musical comedy and vaudeville, lately becoming familiar to filmgoers as twitchy, bald-pated, henpecked little man in innumerable thirties two-reelers and a number of features, mainly unworthy of his talents.
Paramount on Parade 30. Only Saps Work 30. One Heavenly Night 30. Alice in Wonderland 33. We're Not Dressing 34. Princess O'Hara 35. Make a Wish 37. *Mexican Spitfire* (first of a series with Lupe Velez in which Errol appeared as the drunken Lord Epping) 39. Pop Always Pays 40. Six Lessons from Madame la Zonga 41. Never Give a Sucker an Even Break 41. Higher and Higher 43. Hat Check Honey 44. The Invisible Man's Revenge 44. What a Blonde 45. Mama Loves Papa 45. Joe Palooka Champ (first

of another series) 46. The Noose Hangs High 48, etc.

Erskine, Chester (1905–). American writer-producer-director.
Call it Murder (pd) 34. The Egg and I (wpd) 47. All My Sons (wp) 48. Take One False Step (co-wpd) 49. Androcles and the Lion (wd) 53. Witness to Murder (wp) 57. The Wonderful Country (p) 59, etc.

Erwin, Stuart (1903–1967). American character comedian, who usually played Mr Average or the hero's faithful but slow-thinking friend.
Mother Knows Best 28. The Trespasser 29. Sweetie 29. Men Without Women 30. Dude Ranch 31. Misleading Lady 32. International House 33. Palooka·34. After Office Hours 35. All American Chump 36. Slim 37. Three Blind Mice 38. Hollywood Cavalcade 39. Our Town 40. Cracked Nuts 41. Blondie for Victory 42. He Hired the Boss 43. The Great Mike 44. Pillow to Post 45. Killer Dill 47. Strike it Rich 48. Father is a Bachelor 50. For the Love of Mike 60. Son of Flubber 64. The Misadventures of Merlin Jones 64, many others.
TV series: *The Trouble with Father* 53. The Greatest Show on Earth 63. The Bing Crosby Show 65.

Escape. There are several films under this title.
1. D. W. Griffith 1914; from a play by Paul Armstrong about sex problems in the slums; with Blanche Sweet, Remade 1928 with Virginia Valli. 2. The play by John Galsworthy, about a man on the run from Dartmoor, was filmed by Basil Dean in 1930, with Gerald du Maurier, and by Joseph L. Mankiewicz in 1948, with Rex Harrison. 3. Ethel Vance's novel about an ingenious extrication of the hero's mother from a concentration camp was filmed by Mervyn le Roy in 1940, with Robert Taylor, Nazimova, Norma Shearer and Conrad Veidt. 4. A 1971 TV movie with Christopher George as an escapologist.

Escape Me Never. The two films under this title have no connection. In 1935 Paul Czinner directed Elisabeth Bergner in a tale of an unwed mother and a struggling musician; in 1947 Peter Godfrey had Errol Flynn as a composer torn between two women.

Eskimos have seldom been seriously tackled by the cinema. Documentaries abound, from *Nanook of the North* to *Eskimo*, and *Ukaliq* is a charming cartoon of Eskimo folklore, but the fictional stuff such as *Savage Innocents* and *The White Dawn* has been dull and unsympathetic.

Esmond, Carl (1905–) (Willy Eichberger). Good-looking Austrian actor usually in haughty or arrogant roles, first in Britain and later in Hollywood.
Evensong 33. Invitation to the Waltz 37. Dawn Patrol 38. Thunder Afloat 39. Pacific Rendezvous 42. The Story of Dr Wassell 43. *Ministry of Fear* 44. *Address Unknown* 44. Without Love 45. This Love of Ours 45. Catman of Paris 46. Smash-Up 47. Walk a Crooked Mile 48. The Desert Hawk 50. Mystery Submarine 51. The World in His Arms 52. From the Earth to the Moon 58. Thunder in the Sun 59. Agent for Harm 66. Morituri 66, etc.

Esmond, Jill (–). British leading lady of the thirties, later in Hollywood.
The Skin Game 31. Ladies of the Jury 32. No Funny Business 32. This Above All 42. Random Harvest 42. The White Cliffs of Dover 44. The Bandit of Sherwood Forest 46. Escape 48. Night People 54. A Man Called Peter 55, etc.

Essanay. A production company formed in 1907 by G. K. Spoor and G. M. Anderson (S and A). Mainly remembered for enormous output of early westerns and for Chaplin's first comedies.

Essex, David (–). British pop singer.
That'll Be the Day 73. Stardust 74.

Essex, Harry (1910–). American writer.
Boston Blackie and the Law 43. He Walked by Night 48. The Killer That Stalked New York 50. Kansas City Confidential 52. It Came from Outer Space 53. I The Jury (& d) 55. Mad at the World (& d) 56. The Lonely Man 57. The Sons of Katie Elder (co-w) 64, others; also many TV episodes.

establishing shot. Opening shot of sequence, showing location of scene or juxtaposition of characters in action to follow.

Estabrook, Howard (1894–). American screenwriter.
The Four Feathers 28. Hell's Angels 30. *Cimarron* (AA) 31. A Bill of Divorcement 32. The Masquerader 33. David Copperfield 34. International Lady 39. The Bridge of San Luis Rey 44. The Human Comedy 45. The Girl from Manhattan 48. Lone Star 51. The Big Fisherman 59, others.

Estridge, Robin (1920–). British screenwriter.
Above Us the Waves 54. The Young Lovers 54.

Campbell's Kingdom 57. Northwest Frontier 59. Escape from Zahrain 62. Eye of the Devil 67, etc.

Etaix, Pierre (1928–). French mime comedian, former circus clown and assistant to Tati.
Rupture (short) 61. Happy Anniversary (short) 61. The Suitor 62. Yo Yo 65. As Long As You Have Your Health 67. Le Grand Amour 69, etc.

L'Eternel Retour (France 1943). Jean Cocteau wrote and co-directed (with Jean Delannoy) this modernized, freewheeling but sombre version of the Tristan and Isolde legend. The Nazi occupiers approved its Teutonic appearance, but the French saw in it a message of hope. With Jean Marais, Madeleine Sologne.

Eustrel, Anthony (–). British character actor.
The Silver Fleet 43. Caesar and Cleopatra 45. The Robe 53, etc.

Evans, Barry (1945–). British juvenile lead.
Here We Go Round the Mulberry Bush 67. Die Screaming Marianne 71, etc.

Evans, Clifford (1912–). Welsh actor with stage experience. In films from 1936, at first as leading man and latterly as character actor.
Ourselves Alone 36. The Mutiny on the Elsinore 37. The Luck of the Navy 39. The Proud Valley 39. His Brother's Keeper 39. The Saint Meets the Tiger 40. *Love on the Dole* 41. Penn of Pennsylvania 41. Suspected Person 42. *The Foreman Went to France* 42; war service; The Silver Darlings 47. While I Live 48. Valley of Song 52. The Gilded Cage 55. Passport to Treason 56. Violent Playground 58. SOS Pacific 60. Curse of the Werewolf 62. Kiss of the Vampire 63. The Long Ships 64. Twist of Sand 69. One Brief Summer 70, etc.
TV series: Stryker of the Yard, The Power Game, etc.

Evans, Dale (1912–). (Frances Octavia Evans). American leading lady of the forties, former band singer; appeared frequently with Roy Rogers, and in 1947 married him. Orchestra Wives 42. Swing Your Partner 43. Casanova in Burlesque 44. The Yellow Rose of Texas 44. Utah 45. Belles of Rosarita 45. My Pal Trigger 46. Apache Rose 47. Slippy McGee 48. Susanna Pass 49. Twilight in the Sierras 50. Trigger Jnr 51. Pals of the Golden West 51, many others.

Evans, Dame Edith (1888–1976). Distinguished British stage actress who made occasional films.

Biographies 1977: *Ned's Girl* by Bryan Forbes. *Edith Evans: A Personal Memoir* by Jean Batters.
□ A Welsh Singer 15. East is East 15. *The Queen of Spades* 48. *The Last Days of Dolwyn* 48. *The Importance of Being Earnest* 51. Look Back in Anger 59. The Nun's Story 59. Tom Jones 63. The Chalk Garden 64. Young Cassidy 65. *The Whisperers* (BFA) 67. Fitzwilly (US) 68. Prudence and the Pill 68. Crooks and Coronets 69. David Copperfield 69. Scrooge 70. A Dolls House 73. The Slipper and the Rose 76. Nasty Habits 76.

Evans, Gene (1922–). Stocky American actor in demand for heavy roles since 1947.
Berlin Express 48. Park Row 52. Donovan's Brain 53. The Golden Blade 53. Hell and High Water 54. The Sad Sack 57. Operation Petticoat 59. Apache Uprising 65. Support Your Local Sheriff 69. The Ballad of Cable Hogue 70. Walking Tall 73, etc.
TV series: My Friend Flicka.

Evans, Joan (1934–) (Joan Eunson). American actress who played teenage roles in the early fifties.
Our Very Own 50. On the Loose 51. Roseanna McCoy 51. Skirts Ahoy 52. Edge of Doom 54. The Fortune Hunter 54. No Name on the Bullet 59. The Flying Fontaines 60, etc.

Evans, Madge (1909–). American actress, a child star of silent days, pretty heroine of mainly unremarkable films in the thirties.
The Sign of the Cross 14. The Burglar 16. Classmates 24. Son of India 29. Lovers Courageous 30. The Greeks Had a Word for Them 32. Hallelujah I'm a Bum 33. Dinner at Eight 33. Grand Canary 34. David Copperfield 34. The Tunnel (GB) 35. Piccadilly Jim 37. The Thirteenth Chair 37, etc.

Evans, Maurice (1901–). Eloquent Welsh actor who, long in America, distinguished himself on the Broadway stage.
White Cargo 30. Raise the Roof 30. Wedding Rehearsal 32. Scrooge (GB) 35. Kind Lady 51. The Story of Gilbert and Sullivan (as Sullivan) 53. Androcles and the Lion (as Caesar) 53. Macbeth (title role) 59. The War Lord 65. Jack of Diamonds 67. Planet of the Apes 67. Rosemary's Baby 68. Terror in the Wax Museum 73, etc.
TV series: Bewitched 68–71.

Evans, Norman (1901–1962). British north-country music hall comedian famous for toothless characterisation and female impersonation.

Demobbed 45. Under New Management 46. Over the Garden Wall 50, etc.

Evans, Ray (1915–). American song-writer: 'Buttons and Bows' (AA 48), 'Che Sera Sera' (AA 56), many others.

Evans, Rex (1903–1969). British character actor in Hollywood. Often played stately butlers, as in *The Philadelphia Story* 40. Other appearances include *Camille* 36, *It Should Happen to You* 53, *The Matchmaker* 58. Ran an art gallery in his spare time.

Evans, Robert (1930–). Bland-faced American juvenile of the fifties; gave up acting to become a Paramount production executive, then went independent.
Lydia Bailey 52. *The Man of a Thousand Faces* (as Irving Thalberg) 57. The Sun Also Rises 57. The Fiend Who Walked the West (title Role) 58. The Best of Everything 59, etc.

Evein, Bernard (1929–). French art director.
Les Amants 57. Les Jeux de L'Amour 60. Zazie dans le Métro 61. Lola 61. Cleo de 5 à 7 62. La Baie des Anges 62. Le Feu Follet 63. The Umbrellas of Cherbourg 64. Do You Like Women? 64. Viva Maria 65. The Young Girls of Rochefort 67. Woman Times Seven 67, etc.

Evelyn, Judith (1913–1967) (J. E. Allen). American stage actress; often played neurotic woman.
The Egyptian 54. Rear Window 54. Hilda Crane 56. The Tingler 59, etc.

Everest, Barbara (1891–1967). British stage actress who appeared in many films, latterly in motherly roles.
Lily Christine 31. The Wandering Jew 33. The Passing of the Third Floor Back 35. He Found a Star 40. Mission to Moscow (US) 43. Jane Eyre (US) 43. The Uninvited (US) 44. The Valley of Decision (US) 45. Wanted for Murder 46. Frieda 47. Madeleine 49. Tony Draws a Horse 51. The Man Who Finally Died 62, etc.

Everett, Chad (1937–) (Raymond Cramton). Handsome American leading man of the sixties; films unremarkable.
Claudelle Inglish 61. The Chapman Report 62. Get Yourself a College Girl 65. The Singing Nun 66. First to Fight 67. The Last Challenge 67. The Firechasers (TV) 70, etc.
TV series: *Medical Center* 69–75.

Evergreen (GB 1935). Nostalgic Jessie Matthews vehicle often quoted as Britain's best musical. Victor Saville directed, with script contribution by Emlyn Williams.

Ewell, Tom (1909–) (S. Yewell Tompkins). American comic actor with wide stage experience.
□ *Adam's Rib* 49. A Life of Her Own 50. An American Guerilla in the Philippines 50. Mr Music 50. Up Front 51. Back at the Front 52. Abbott and Costello Lost in Alaska 52. *The Seven Year Itch* 55. The Lieutenant Wore Skirts 55. The Girl Can't Help It 57. Tender is the Night 61. State Fair 62. Suppose They Gave a War and Nobody Came 70. To Find A Man 72. They Only Kill Their Masters 72. The Great Gatsby 74.
TV series: *The Tom Ewell Show* 60. Baretta 75– .

excerpts from films are sometimes incorporated into other films in which characters go to a cinema or watch television. So in *Hollywood Cavalcade* Don Ameche watched a rough-cut of *The Jazz Singer*, just as ten years later Larry Parks in *Jolson Sings Again* watched a rough cut of himself in *The Jolson Story*; an unidentified silent comedy was being played in the room below when the first murder took place in *The Spiral Staircase*; Linda Christian and Louis Jourdan saw *Son of the Sheik* at their local in *The Happy Time*, and Fredric March and Martha Scott watched a William S. Hart film in *One Foot in Heaven*. Prisoners watched *Wings of the Navy* during *Each Dawn I Die* and *The Egg and I* during *Brute Force*; and the chain gang in *Sullivan's Travels* roared with laughter at a Mickey Mouse cartoon. Footage from *Phantom of the Opera* was shown in *Hollywood Story*, from *Comin' thru' the Rye* in *The Smallest Show on Earth*, from *Tol'able David* in *The Tingler*, from *Queen Kelly* in *Sunset Boulevard*, from *Camille* in *Bridge to the Sun*, from *Destination Tokyo* in *Operation Pacific*, and from *Boom Town* in *Watch the Birdie*. Other movies shown in 'cinemas' in later films include: *Uncle Tom's Cabin* in *Abbott and Costello Meet the Keystone Kops*; *Gold Diggers of 1933* in *Bonnie and Clyde*; *Crossroads* in *The Youngest Profession*; *Casablanca* in *First to Fight*; *Red River* in *The Last Picture Show*; *Hell Divers* in *The Wings of Eagles*; *Task Force* in *White Heat*; *The Walking Dead* in *Ensign Pulver*; *Tin Pan Alley* in *Wing and a Prayer*; *Now Voyager* in *Summer of '42*; *Red Dust* in *Heavy Traffic*; various Bogart films in *Play It Again Sam*; *Caprice* in *Caprice* (Doris Day went to the movies, saw herself on the screen, and didn't like it). In *Two Weeks in Another Town*, which had a plot pretty close to that of *The Bad and the Beautiful*, Kirk Douglas

watched himself in–*The Bad and the Beautiful*!
The Bette Davis character in *Whatever
Happened to Baby Jane?* was criticized as a bad
actress on the strength of clips from early Bette
Davis movies, *Ex-Lady* and *Parachute Jumper*.
In the same film Joan Crawford watched herself
on TV in *Sadie McKee*; and in *Walk Don't Run*
there was a flash of James Stewart dubbed in
Japanese in *Two Rode Together*. Finally the
cosmonauts on their space station in *Conquest of
Space* were entertained by a showing of *Here
Come the Girls* ... thus showing, as one critic
remarked, that in 50 years' time TV will still be
relying on old movies!

Other uses for old footage in new films include
such gags as Bob Hope in *Road to Bali* meeting
up with Humphrey Bogart in *The African
Queen*; and economy dictates such measures as
the ten-minute chunk of *The Mummy* at the
beginning of *The Mummy's Hand* and the use in
Singin' in the Rain, as part of a 'new' picture in
production, of sequences from Gene Kelly's
version of *The Three Musketeers*. Similarly bits
of *The Sheik* were in *Son of the Sheik,* and
Topper in *Topper Takes a Trip*. Great chunks of
the *Joan of Arc* battles turned up in *Thief of
Damascus,* as did *The Black Knight* in *Siege of
the Saxons* and *The Four Feathers* in *Storm
Over the Nile* and *East of Sudan*. Universal's
Sword of Ali Baba used so much footage from
their *Ali Baba and the Forty Thieves* that one
actor had to be engaged to replay his original
part! It was however wit rather than economy
that persuaded Preston Sturges to open *Mad
Wednesday* with the last reel of *The Freshman*.

exchange. An American enterprise: a
middleman business which for a commission
deals with the small exhibitors of an area on
behalf of major renters.

Executive Suite (US 1954). In the fifties,
Hollywood took a sudden interest in big
business, notably in this all-star adaptation of
Cameron Hawley's novel about a boardroom
struggle for power. Script by Robert Wise; with
Barbara Stanwyck and Fredric March heading
an all-star cast. The film's success provoked a
rash of boardroom melodramas including
Patterns of Power, The Power and the Prize and
Cash McCall. A TV version followed in 1976.

Exodus (US 1961). Otto Preminger's marathon
film of the birth of Israel, from the book by Leon
Uris. Seldom exciting, it was a good solid plod,
with Paul Newman and Ralph Richardson
leading a good cast. Irresistible is the story that
Mort Sahl at a Hollywood preview stood up after
three hours, turned to the director, and said:

'Otto: let my people go.'

exploitation. A trade word covering all phases
of publicity, public relations and promotion,
especially in the case of 'exploitation pictures'
which have no discernible merit apart from the
capability of being sensationalized.

The Exorcist (US 1974). Sensational
supernatural horror piece about a young girl
possessed by the devil. Apparent seriousness
covered slipshod scripting, but the shocks of bad
language, loud noises and vomit appealed
mightily to an audience in search of new and
greater sensations yet wanting to believe in God.
Written by William Peter Blatty, directed by
William Friedkin; with Ellen Burstyn, Linda
Blair, Jason Miller, Max Von Sydow.

explorers have inspired many documentaries
but surprisingly few features except wholly
fictitious ones like *Trader Horn, She* and *The
Lost World. Marco Polo* has thrice been dealt
with, and *Christopher Columbus* got the full
Rank treatment as well as featuring in the
satirical *Where Do We Go From Here?* The
Pilgrim Fathers were the heroes of *Plymouth
Adventure,* and Drake of *Seven Seas to Calais.*
Lewis and Clark in *The Far Horizons,* were
played by Fred MacMurray and Charlton
Heston. *Scott of the Antarctic* was played by
John Mills, and Amundsen in *The Red Tent* by
Sean Connery; Pierre Radisson in *Hudson's Bay*
by Paul Muni; Cortez in *Captain from Castile* by
Cesar Romero; Pizarro in *The Royal Hunt of the
Sun* by Robert Shaw; Junipero Serra in *Seven
Cities of Gold* by Michael Rennie. *Penn of
Pennsylvania* and *Stanley and Livingstone* were
in the practical sense explorers, though driven by
other motives.

expressionism. A term indicating the fullest
utilization of cinematic resources to give
dramatic larger-than-life effect, as in *Citizen
Kane* or, in a different way, *The Cabinet of Dr
Caligari*.

Extase (Czechoslovakia 1933). Gustav
Machaty directed this mildly experimental,
symbol-crammed erotic drama, widely
publicized on account of Hedy Lamarr's nude
swimming sequence.

exterior. A shot taken in normal lighting
outside the studio.

The Exterminating Angel (Mexico 1962). An
enigmatic but fascinating film exercise, written
and directed by Luis Buñuel, in which a group of

dinner guests find themselves psychologically incapable of going home despite attacks of sickness and violent death. Though it is packed with apparent clues, Buñuel himself says there is 'no rational explanation'.

extra. A crowd player with no lines to speak.

Eythe, William (1918–1947). American leading man of the forties.

The Ox-Bow Incident 42. The Song of Bernadette 43. The Eve of St Mark 44. A Royal Scandal 45. The House on 92nd Street 45. Meet Me at Dawn 47, etc.

F

F.B.I. The US governmental crime fighting agency was set up in 1924 by J. Edgar Hoover and became famous for its heroic stand against the public enemies of the thirties, when its agents became known as G-Men. Surface glamour concealed an immensely painstaking organisation relying heavily on science, but only the glamour was shown in such films as *Show 'Em No Mercy, G-Men, Persons in Hiding, Let 'Em Have It, The FBI Story, FBI Girl, Parole Fixer* and *Queen of the Mob. The House on 92nd Street* in 1945 gave the best impression of the FBI at work, but its sequel *The Street with No Name* reverted to stereotype.

Fabares, Shelley (1942–). American juvenile leading lady of the early sixties.
Never Say Goodbye 56. Summer Love 58. Ride the Wild Surf 64. Girl Happy 65. Hold On 66. Spinout 66. Clambake 67, etc.

Fabian (1942–) (Fabian Forte Bonaparte). American teenage idol, singer and guitarist.
The Hound Dog Man (debut) 59. North to Alaska 60. Mr Hobbs Takes a Vacation 62. Dear Brigitte 65. Ten Little Indians 65. Fireball 500 66. The Devil's Eight 68. A Bullet for Pretty Boy 70. Lovin' Man 72, etc.

Fabray, Nanette (1920–) (Nanette Fabares). American comedy actress and singer, former child star of 'Our Gang' comedies.
Adult films: Elizabeth and Essex 39. Band Wagon 53. The Happy Ending 69, etc.

Fabre, Saturnin (1884–1961). French character actor.
Pepe le Moko 37. Il Etait Neuf Celibataires 42. Un Ami Viendra Ce Soir 46. Les Portes de la Nuit 46. Clochemerle 52. La Fete a Henriette 54, etc.

Fabri, Zoltan (1917–). Hungarian director:
Professor Hannibal 56. The Last Goal 61. Twenty Hours 65, etc.

Fabrizi, Aldo (1905–). Italian character actor, known abroad.
Open City 45. Vivere in Pace 47. First Communion 50. Cops and Robbers 54. Altri Tempi 55. The Birds the Bees and the Italians 65. Made in Italy 68.

A Face in the Crowd (US 1957). Directed by Elia Kazan from a Budd Schulberg story, this was a potent attack on the cult of personality in TV. Andy Griffith made a strong impression as the brash hick intoxicated by his own success; so did Patricia Neal as his mentor who finally destroys him.

fade in. Gradual emergence of a scene from blackness to full definition; opposite of *fade out.*

Fahrenheit 451 (GB 1966). A pale but oddly haunting version by François Truffaut of Ray Bradbury's cynically prophetic vision of a society where books are outlawed and firemen start fires (of literature) rather than putting them out. Ultimately quite moving, it could have been more cinematically paced. Nicolas Roeg's photography gleams; Oskar Werner's performance is a major asset.

Fairbanks, Douglas (1883–1939) (Douglas Ullman). Swashbuckling American star of the silent screen, the acrobatic, zestful, ever-smiling hero of many comedies and costume adventures, almost all of which he produced himself. Despite long stage experience, sound did not suit him, and his thirties films showed a marked decline. He had a famous marriage with Mary Pickford, and in 1919, with Chaplin and Griffith, they were co-founders of United Artists Film Corporation. Posthumous AA 1939 'for his unique and outstanding contribution to the international development of the motion picture'.
Biography 1953: *The Fourth Musketeer* by Elton Thomas.
□ The Lamb 15. Double Trouble 15. His Picture in the Papers 16. The Habit of Happiness 16. The Good Bad Man 16. Reggie Mixes In 16. Flirting with Fate 16. The Mystery of the Leaping Fish 16. The Half Breed 16. Manhattan Madness 16. American Aristocracy 16. The Matrimaniac 16. The Americano 16. In Again Out Again 17. Wild and Woolly 17. Down to Earth 17. The Man from Painted Post 17. Reaching for the Moon

17. A Modern Musketeer 18. Headin' South 18.
Mr Fix-It 18. Say Young Fellow 18. Bound in
Morocco 18. He Comes Up Smiling 18. Arizona
(& wd) 18. Knickerbocker Buckaroo 19. His
Majesty the American 19. When the Clouds Roll
By 20. The Mollycoddle 20. *The Mark of Zorro*
(& w) 20. The Nut (& w) 21. *The Three
Musketeers* 21. *Robin Hood* (& w) 21. *The Thief
of Baghdad* (&w) 23. *Don Q Son of Zorro* 25.
The Black Pirate 26. The Gaucho (& w) 27. The
Iron Mask (& w) 29. The Taming of the Shrew
29. Reaching for the Moon 30. Around the
World in Eighty Minutes (& w) 31. Mr Robinson
Crusoe 32. The Private Life of Don Juan 34.

Fairbanks, Douglas Jnr (1909–). American
leading man who has spent much time in Britain;
of more conventional debonair mould than his
father, he spent as much time in drawing rooms
as on castle battlements, but was at home in any
surroundings. During the early fifties, produced
and sometimes played in innumerable TV half
hours under the title *Douglas Fairbanks
Presents*.
Biography 1955: *Knight Errant* by Brian
Connell.
□ Party Girl 20. Stephen Steps Out 23. Air Mail
25. Wild Horse Mesa 25. Stella Dallas 25. The
American Venus 25. Padlocked 26. Manbait 26.
Is Zat So? 27. A Texas Steer 27. The Barker 28.
A Woman of Affairs 28. *The Jazz Age* 29. Fast
Life 29. Our Modern Maidens 29. The Careless
Age 29. The Forward Pass 29. Show of Shows
29. Loose Ankles 30. *The Dawn Patrol* 30. Little
Accident 30. The Way of All Men 30. *Outward
Bound* 30. Little Caesar 30. One Night at Susie's
30. Chances 31. I Like Your Nerve 31. Union
Depot 32. It's Tough to be Famous 32. Love is a
Racket 32. Parachute Jumper 32. The Narrow
Corner 33. *Morning Glory* 33. Captured 33.
Catherine the Great 34. Success at any Price 34.
Mimi 35. The Amateur Gentleman 35. Accused
36. When Thief Meets Thief 36. *The Prisoner of
Zenda* (as Rupert of Hentzau) 37. Joy of Living
38. The Rage of Paris 38. Having Wonderful
Time 38. *The Young in Heart* 38. *Gunga Din* 39.
The Sun Never Sets 39. Rulers of the Sea 39.
Green Hell 40. Safari 40. Angels over Broadway
40. The Corsican Brothers 41. *Sinbad the Sailor*
47. The Exile 47. That Lady in Ermine 48. The
Fighting O'Flynn 49. *State Secret* 50. Mr
Drake's Duck 51. The Crooked Hearts (TV) 72.

Fairbrother, Sydney (1873–1941) (S.
Tapping). British character actress, in films
occasionally from 1916.
Iron Justice 16. The Third String 31. Chu Chin
Chow 33. The Crucifix 34. The Last Journey 36.
King Solomon's Mines (as Gagool) 37. Little

Dolly Daydream 38, etc.

Fairchild, William (1918–). British
screenwriter.
Morning Departure 50. An Outcast of the
Islands 51. The Gift Horse 52. The Net 53. The
Malta Story 53. Front Page Story 54. John and
Julie (& d) 54. Value for Money 57. The Silent
Enemy (& d) 58. Star! 68. Embassy 72, etc.

Fairhurst, Lyn (1920–). British writer.
Band of Thieves 62. Touch of Death 63. Be My
Guest 64. Devils of Darkness 65, etc.

fairy tales: see *fantasy*.

Faith, Adam (1940–) (Terence Neilhams).
British pop singer turned actor.
Never Let Go 60. Mix Me a Person 62. Stardust
74, etc.

Faith, Percy (1908–76). American orchestral
conductor and composer. Scores include Love
Me or Leave Me 55.

Faithfull, Geoffrey (1894–). British
cinematographer, with Hepworth from 1908.
The Lavender Hill Mob 51. Corridors of Blood
59. Village of the Damned 60. On the Beat 62,
etc.

Faithfull, Marianne (1947–). British leading
lady.
I'll Never Forget Whatshisname 67. Girl on a
Motorcycle 68. Hamlet 69.

The Falcon was a Robin Hood of crime who
appeared in many second features of the forties,
originally inspired by a Michael Arlen character.
At RKO, George Sanders appeared in *A Date
with the Falcon, The Falcon Takes Over* and *The
Falcon's Brother*, in which he was 'killed' and his
role assumed by his real-life brother, Tom
Conway, who proceeded to make nine more
Falcon features of declining merit. In nearly all
these films Edward Brophy appeared as Goldie,
the bumbling valet. Around 1950 John Calvert
made a couple of very inferior Falcon movies for
a small independent company.

Falconetti (1901–1946). French stage actress,
unforgettable in her only film, *The Passion of
Joan of Arc* 28.

Falk, Peter (1927–). Fast-talking, cast-eyed
American actor from the off-Broadway stage.
□ Wind Across the Everglades 58. The Bloody
Brood 59. Pretty Boy Floyd 59. The Secret of the
Purple Reef 60. Murder Inc. 60. Pocketful of

Miracles 61. Pressure Point 62. The Balcony 63. It's a Mad Mad Mad Mad World 63. Robin and the Seven Hoods 64. *The Great Race* 65. Italiano Brava Gente 65. Penelope 66. Luv 67. Anzio 68. Castle Keep 69. Machine Gun McCain 70. Husbands 70. A Woman Under the Influence 76. *Murder by Death* 76.

TV series: *The Trials of O'Brien* 65. *Columbo* 71–.

Falkenburg, Jinx (1919–) (Eugenia Falkenburg). Tall, good-looking American model who made a few light comedies and musicals in the forties.
Biography 1951: *Jinx*.
Two Latins from Manhattan 42. Sing for Your Supper 42. Lucky Legs 43. Tahiti Nights 44. Talk about a Lady 46, etc.

The Fallen Idol (GB 1948). One of Carol Reed's most subtle and successful films, from Graham Greene's story about a boy who sees what he thinks is a murder and tries to cover up for his friend. With Ralph Richardson, Michele Morgan, Bobby Henrey; music by William Alwyn. BFA (best British film).

The Fall of the House of Usher. This grisly tale by Edgar Allan Poe was filmed by Jean Epstein in 1928, by Americans Melville Webber and James Watson in the same year, by British semi-professionals in 1950, and by Roger Corman in 1960.

falling is, of all man's inherited fears, the one most spectacularly played on by Hollywood, where the shot of the villain's hand slipping away from the hero's frenzied grasp, followed by a quick-fading scream, has become a screen stereotype. Harold Lloyd's skyscraper comedies played on this fear, as have the films of many comedians since; in *The Horn Blows at Midnight*, for instance, Jack Benny is only one of six people hanging on to each other's coat-tails from the top of a high building. All circus films, and that includes *The Marx Brothers at the Circus*, base one or two of their thrills on trapeze acts that might go wrong. And whenever a villain starts climbing upwards, as Ted de Corsia did in *Naked City*, or along a ledge, as the same accident-prone Ted de Corsia did in *The Enforcer*, the audience grits its teeth and waits for the inevitable. The whole action of *Fourteen Hours* was based on the question whether a potential suicide would or would not jump from a ledge.

Some of the screen's most spectacular falls include Walter Abel's in *Mirage*, the key to the whole action; Agnes Moorehead's (through a window) in *Dark Passage*; Charlotte Henry's in *Alice in Wonderland*; Cedric Hardwicke's in *Hunchback of Notre Dame*; W. C. Fields' (from an aeroplane) in *Never Give a Sucker an Even Break*; Alan Ladd's (through a roof) in *The Glass Key*; Slim Pickens' (on the bomb) in *Dr Strangelove*; Eleanor Parker's in *An American Dream*; *King Kong*'s (from the top of the Empire State Building); William Bendix's from a skyscraper in *The Dark Corner*. To Alfred Hitchcock falls are a speciality: Edmund Gwenn fell from Westminster Cathedral in *Foreign Correspondent*, Norman Lloyd from the torch of the Statue of Liberty in *Saboteur*, while *Vertigo* not only boasted three falls but based its entire plot on the hero's fear of heights. Falls under trains and buses are legion, but in *The Well* a little girl fell down an old wellshaft, in *The List of Adrian Messenger* a victim fell to his death in a lift (as did characters in *Hotel* and *House of Wax*, while in *Ivy* Joan Fontaine fell down a lift shaft), in Somerset Maugham's *Encore* an acrobat hoped to fall safely into a water tank; and an unnamed gentleman was pushed out of *The High Window* by Florence Bates.

the family is the centre of most people's lives, so naturally there have been many memorable film families. Those popular enough to have warranted a series include the Joneses, the Hardys, the Huggetts, the Wilkinses of *Dear Ruth*, *The Cohens and the Kellys*, the Bumsteads of *Blondie* and the *Four Daughters* saga. World War II brought a sentimental attachment to the family which in Hollywood expressed itself in *Happy Land*, *The Human Comedy*, *Our Town*, *The Happy Time*, *Since You Went Away*, *Meet Me in St Louis*, *A Genius in the Family*, *The Sullivans* and *The Best Years of Our Lives*; in Britain, *Salute John Citizen*, *The Holly and the Ivy*, *Dear Octopus*, *Quiet Wedding*, *This Man is Mine*. Semi-classical treatments of the theme include *Cavalcade*, *The Swiss Family Robinson*, *Pride and Prejudice*, *Little Women*, *Scrooge* and *Whiteoaks*. Odd families, ranging from the merely sophisticated to the downright bizarre, were seen in *Three Cornered Moon*, *The Old Dark House*, *The Royal Family of Broadway*, *My Man Godfrey*, *You Can't Take It With You*, *The Young in Heart*, *The Little Foxes*, *Tobacco Road*, *The Bank Dick*, *House of Strangers*, *An Inspector Calls*, *Sweethearts*, *Treasure Hunt*, *Holiday*, *The Philadelphia Story*, *The Anniversary*, and *The Lion in Winter*. Vaudeville families were seen in *Yankee Doodle Dandy*, *The Merry Monahans*, *The Seven Little Foys*, *The Buster Keaton Story* and *There's No Business Like Show Business*. There has recently been a fashion for the large family, started by *Cheaper*

by the Dozen and *Chicken Every Sunday* in 1949
and reprised by *With Six You Get Egg Roll* and
Yours Mine and Ours in 1968 and a TV series
The Brady Bunch in 1969. Other charming
families have included those in *Our Vines Have
Tender Grapes, Background, The Happy
Family, Four Sons, The Holly and the Ivy, Made
in Heaven, 29 Acacia Avenue, Little Murders,
Never Too Late, This Happy Breed* and *My
Wife's Family*; but the most memorable family of
all is likely to remain the Joads in *The Grapes of
Wrath*, unless it is one of the real families put
under the microscope by American and British
TV.

Famous Players. A production company
founded by Adolph Zukor in New York in 1912,
following his success in distributing Sarah
Bernhardt in *Queen Elizabeth*. The motif was
'famous players in famous plays', which could
not work too well as the films were silent; but the
tag caught on and the company did well enough.
It was later absorbed into Paramount.

Fanny. Originally one of Marcel Pagnol's
1932–34 trilogy (the others: *Marius* and *César*)
about the Marseilles waterfront, this tale of a girl
left pregnant by a sailor was almost
unrecognizable in the MGM version *Port of
Seven Seas* 38. The film was subsequently turned
into a stage musical, and in 1960 Joshua Logan
filmed this – but deleted the songs! The stars
were Leslie Caron, Maurice Chevalier and
Charles Boyer.

Fantasia (US 1940). Disney's ambitious
concert sequence of cartoons caused disension at
first but seems to have established its reputation
and its popularity after thirty years. Despite
lapses of inventiveness and taste, three of its eight
pieces are extremely well done: the Bach Toccata
and Fugue, Stravinsky's Rite of Spring and
Mussorgsky's Night on the Bare Mountain.
Leopold Stokowski conducted the Philadelphia
Symphony Orchestra.

fantasy has always been a popular form of
cinema entertainment because the camera can lie
so well, and trick work is most easily used in an
unrealistic or fanciful story. The early films of
Méliès and his innumerable imitators set a high
standard and were still popular when the sombre
German classics of the twenties – *The Golem,
Nosferatu, Faust, Warning Shadows, The
Niebelungen Saga, Metropolis* – awakened
filmgoers to the possibilities of the medium for
sustaining impossible situations throughout a
whole serious feature.

Although Ince's *Civilisation* showed Christ on

the battlefields, and the twenties brought such
films as *The Four Horsemen of the Apocalypse,
The Lost World* and *The Sorrows of Satan*,
Hollywood did not fully explore the possibilities
of fantasy until sound. Then in quick succession
picturegoers were startled by *Outward Bound,
Dracula, Frankenstein, Berkeley Square, King
Kong* and *The Invisible Man. The Scoundrel*,
with Noel Coward, was the forerunner of the few
serious ghost films: *The Uninvited, The Return of
Peter Grimm, Earthbound, The Ghost and Mrs
Muir, Portrait of Jennie, The Haunting*, etc.
Comic ghosts have, of course, been legion,
notably in the *Topper* films, *The Ghost Breakers,
I Married a Witch, The Canterville Ghost, The
Man in the Trunk, The Remarkable Andrew,
Thirteen Ghosts, The Spirit Is Willing,
Blackbeard's Ghost, Wonder Man*, and so on.
There were even singing ghosts in *Maytime,
Bitter Sweet* and *Carousel*. Britain's
contributions to the genre were few but choice:
*The Ghost Goes West, Blithe Spirit, Things to
Come, The Man Who Could Work Miracles, A
Matter of Life and Death, Dead of Night*.

In 1936 *Green Pastures* showed the Negro
view of heaven, and *On Borrowed Time* three
years later paved the way for the heavenly
comedies of the forties: *Here Comes Mr Jordan,
That's the Spirit, A Guy Named Joe, Heaven
Can Wait, Down to Earth, The Horn Blows at
Midnight, You Never Can Tell*, even *Ziegfeld
Follies* (in which Ziegfeld's shade wrote in his
diary 'Another *heavenly* day . . .'). For many
years the last in this vein was *Carousel* 56; but
1968 brought *Barbarella* with its slightly
tarnished angel, and *The Adding Machine* had its
own perverse view of the hereafter. Meanwhile
objects with magical properties were well served
in *Alf's Button Afloat, A Thousand and One
Nights, The Thief of Baghdad, Turnabout* and
The Picture of Dorian Gray.

Among the many fairy tales filmed are *The
Bluebird, The Wizard of Oz, Alice in
Wonderland, The Glass Slipper, Tom Thumb,
Mary Poppins* and a selection in *Hans Christian
Andersen* and *The Wonderful World of the
Brothers Grimm*. Disney's cartoon versions
included *Pinocchio, Dumbo, The Sleeping
Beauty, Cinderella, Peter Pan*, and, of course,
Snow White and the Seven Dwarfs, which was
cannily adapted for grown-ups by Billy Wilder as
Ball of Fire. Lost Horizon was a kind of grown-
up fairy tale too; and *The Red Shoes* as shown
was certainly not for children. Original fairy tales
for both categories were *The Luck of the Irish*,
with Cecil Kellaway as a leprechaun, and
Miracle on 34th Street, with Edmund Gwenn as
Santa Claus. Modern fairy tales adapted for the
screen include: *Chitty Chitty Bang Bang, Mary*

Poppins, Bedknobs and Broomsticks and *Willy Wonka and the Chocolate Factory.*

In France during the occupation Marcel Carné made *Les Visiteurs du Soir,* a medieval fantasy with allegorical overtones, and after the war poet Jean Cocteau once again turned his attention to the cinema with such results as *La Belle et la Bête, Love Eternal, Orphée,* and *The Testament of Orphée.* More recently Albert Lamorisse has produced fantasies like *Crin Blanc* and *The Red Balloon.* Japan electrified the world with *Rashomon* and other strange, fanciful, stylized entertainments; Russia contributed many solidly-staged versions of old legends like *Sadko* and *Epic Hero and the Beast* (*Ilya Muromets*).

Since 1950, when in Hollywood Dick Powell played an Alsatian dog in *You Never Can Tell* and James Stewart in *Harvey* had a white rabbit six feet high which the script could never quite categorize as fact or hallucination, fantastic elements have been infiltrating into supposedly realistic films to such an extent that it is now difficult to separate them, especially in the films of Fellini, Antonioni, Tony Richardson, Richard Lester and Robert Altman.

See also: *dreams; horror; prophecy; space exploration.*

Fantomas (France 1913–14). Famous thriller serial in five parts, about the exploits of a character reminiscent of Robin Hood, Raffles and the Ringer. Directed by Louis Feuillade (qv). Subsequent versions were made in 1932 by Paul Fejos, 1947 by Jean Sacha, 1949 by Robert Vernay, and 1964/65/66 by André Hunebelle.

Fantoni, Sergio (1930–). Italian leading man in international films.
Esther and the King 60. The Prize 63. Kali-Yug Goddess of Vengeance 63. Von Ryan's Express 65. Do Not Disturb 65. What Did You Do in the War, Daddy? 66. Hornet's Nest 70. Bad Man's River 71, etc.

Fapp, Daniel (–). American cinematographer.
Kitty 45. Golden Earrings 47. Bride of Vengeance 49. Union Station 50. Knock on Wood 54. Living It Up 54. Desire under the Elms 58. One, Two, Three 61. West Side Story (AA) 61. I'll Take Sweden 65. Our Man Flint 65. Lord Love a Duck 66. Sweet November 67. Ice Station Zebra 68. Marooned 69, many others.

Farentino, James (1938–). American leading man, mostly on TV.
Psychomania 64. Ensign Pulver 64. The War Lord 65. The Pad 66. Banning 67. Rosie 68. Me

Natalie 69. The Story of a Woman 70.
TV series: *Cool Million* 72.

A Farewell to Arms. Hemingway's tough-romantic anti-war novel has twice been filmed: in 1933 by Frank Borzage, with Gary Cooper and Helen Hayes, and in 1958 by Charles Vidor, with Rock Hudson and Jennifer Jones. Neither version was a triumph artistically, but the first proved more popular than the second, which was badly inflated by David O. Selznick into a pseudo-epic.

Farmer, Frances (1914–1970). American leading lady of the thirties who retired through ill-health.
Autobiography published 1972: *Will There Ever be a Morning?*
□ Too Many Parents 36. Border Flight 36. Rhythm on the Range 36. *Come and Get It* 36. The Toast of New York 37. Exclusive 37. Ebb Tide 37. Ride a Crooked Mile 38. South of Pago Pago 40. Flowing Gold 40. World Première 41. Badlands of Dakota 41. Among the Living 41. Son of Fury 42. The Party Crashers 58.

Farmer, Mimsy (1945–). American leading lady of the sixties.
Spencer's Mountain 63. Bus Riley's Back in Town 65. Hot Roads to Hell 67. The Devil's Angels 67. Move 69. Road to Salina 69. Four Flies on Gray Velvet 71.

The Farmer's Daughter (US 1947). A lightweight political comedy from a screenplay by Allen Rivkin and Laura Kerr, directed by H. C. Potter, photographed by Milton Krasner, this romantic fable gained an Academy Award for Loretta Young as the Swedish maid who influences her congressman employer. Joseph Cotten, Ethel Barrymore and Charles Bickford were strong in support. In 1963–65 there followed a popular TV series on the subject, with Inger Stevens, William Windom and Cathleen Nesbitt.

Farnon, Robert (1917–). Canadian composer whose many scores include *Captain Hornblower, The Little Hut, Road to Hong Kong,* etc.

Farnum, Dustin (1870–1929). American cowboy star of silent days. Brother of William Farnum.
The Squaw Man 13. The Virginian 14. The Scarlet Pimpernel 17. The Corsican Brothers 19. Flaming Frontier 26, etc.

Farnum, Franklyn (1876–1961). American leading man of the silent screen, especially westerns; appeared in more than a thousand films.

Farnum, William (1876–1953). American leading man of the silent screen.
The Spoilers 14. Les Misérables 17. The Lone Star Ranger 19. If I Were King 20. A Stage Romance 22. The Man Who Fights Alone 24. The Painted Desert 31. Supernatural 33. The Crusades 35. The Spoilers 42. Captain Kidd 45. Samson and Delilah 49. Jack and the Beanstalk 52, many others.

Farr, Derek (1912–). British leading man of stage and screen, married to Muriel Pavlow; former schoolmaster.
The Outsider 40. Spellbound 40. Quiet Wedding 40. Quiet Weekend 46. Wanted for Murder 46. Teheran 47. Bond Street 48. Noose 48. Silent Dust 49. Man on the Run 49. Young Wives' Tale 51. Reluctant Heroes 52. The Dam Busters 55. Town on Trial 56. Doctor at Large 57. The Truth About Women 58. Attempt to Kill 61. The Projected Man 66. Thirty is a Dangerous Age Cynthia 68, etc.

Farr, Felicia (1932–). American leading lady.
Timetable 56. Jubal 56. 3.10 to Yuma 57. The Last Wagon 57. Hell Bent for Leather 60. Kiss Me Stupid 64. The Venetian Affair 67. Charley Varrick 73, etc.

Farrar, David (1908–). Tall, virile-looking British leading man whose career faltered when he went to Hollywood and played villains.
Autobiography 1948: *No Royal Road.*
Return of a Stranger 38. The Sheepdog of the Hills 41. Suspected Person 41. Danny Boy 42. The Night Invader 42. The Dark Tower 43. They Met in the Dark 44. The World Owes Me a Living 44. Meet Sexton Blake (title role) 44. The Echo Murders 45. The Lisbon Story 46. The Trojan Brothers 46. *Black Narcissus* 46. Frieda 47. *Mr Perrin and Mr Traill* 48. *The Small Back Room* 48. Diamond City 49. Night Without Stars 51. The Golden Horde (US) 51. Gone to Earth 52. Duel in the Jungle 54. The Black Shield of Falworth (US) 54. Lilacs in the Spring 55. The Sea Chase (US) 55. Lost 56. I Accuse 57. Solomon and Sheba (US) 59. John Paul Jones (US) 59. Beat Girl 60. The 300 Spartans 62, etc.

Farrar, Geraldine (1882–1967). American operatic star who, unexpectedly, appeared for Samuel Goldwyn as heroine of silent films.
Carmen 15. Maria Rosa 16. The Devil Stone 17. Joan the Woman 17. Flame of the Desert 19. The Riddle Woman 20, etc.

Farrebique (France 1947). A slow-moving drama of peasant life in 1830, marked by a tremendous feeling for the land and for life. Written and directed by Georges Rouquier, photographed (with much use of time-lapse) by André Danton, with music by Henri Languet.

Farrell, Charles (1901–). Gentle-mannered American leading man of the twenties; formed a well-liked romantic team with Janet Gaynor. Retired in middle age to become Mayor of Palm Springs.
The Ten Commandments 23. Wings of Youth 25. Old Ironsides 26. *Seventh Heaven* 27. Street Angel 28. Lucky Star 29. Sunny Side Up 29. High Society Blues 30. Liliom 30. Merely Mary Ann 31. Tess of the Storm Country 32. Aggie Appleby, Maker of Men 33. Change of Heart 34. Fighting Youth 35. Moonlight Sonata (GB) 47. Tailspin 39. The Deadly Game 42, etc.
TV series: My Little Margie 52–55. The Charlie Farrell Show 56.

Farrell, Charles (1901–). Irish character actor who has been playing bit parts in British films since childhood.
Creeping Shadows 31. Meet Mr Penny 38. Meet Sexton Blake 44. Night and the City 50. The Sheriff of Fractured Jaw 58, etc.

Farrell, Glenda (1904–1971). American leading lady and comedienne of the thirties, often seen as wisecracking reporter; made a comeback in the fifties as character actress. Little Caesar (debut) 30. Three on a Match 31. I Am a Fugitive from a Chain Gang 32. *The Mystery of the Wax Museum* 32. Hi Nellie 33. Gold Diggers of 1935 35. In Caliente 36. *Torchy Blane in Chinatown* (and ensuing series) 39. Johnny Eager 41. A Night for Crime 42. Heading for Heaven 47. I Love Trouble 48. Apache War Smoke 52. Girls in the Night 52. Susan Slept Here 54. The Girl in the Red Velvet Swing 55. The Middle of the Night 59. Kissing Cousins 64. The Disorderly Orderly 64, many others.

Farrow, John (1904–1963). Stylish Australian director, former research scientist; in Hollywood from the mid-thirties. Also wrote many of his own scripts.
□ Men in Exile 37. West of Shanghai 37. Fair Warning 37. She Loved a Fireman 38. Little Miss Thoroughbred 38. My Bill 38. Broadway Musketeers 38. Women in the Wind 39. The Saint Strikes Back 39. Sorority House 39. *Five Came Back* 39. Full Confession 39. Reno 39. Married and in Love 40. A Bill of Divorcement 40. Wake Island 42. The Commandos Strike at Dawn (& w) 43. China 43. *The Hitler Gang* (& w) 44. You Came Along 45. Two Years Before

the Mast (& w) 46. California 46. Easy Come
Easy Go 47. Blaze of Noon 47. Calcutta 47. *The
Big Clock* 48. Night Has a Thousand Eyes 48.
Beyond Glory 48. *Alias Nick Beal* 49. Red Hot
and Blue 49. Where Danger Lives 50. Copper
Canyon 50. *His Kind of Woman* (& w) 51.
Submarine Command 51. Ride Vaquero 53.
Plunder of the Sun 53. Botany Bay 53. Hondo
54. A Bullet is Waiting 54. The Sea Chase (& w)
55. Back from Eternity 56. The Unholy Wife 57.
John Paul Jones (& w) 59.

Farrow, Mia (1945–). American leading lady,
daughter of John Farrow and Maureen
O'Sullivan.
□ Guns at Batasi 64. A Dandy in Aspic 67.
Rosemary's Baby 68. Secret Ceremony 68. John
and Mary 69. See No Evil 71. Follow Me 72.
Goodbye Raggedy Ann (TV) 72. Scoundrel in
White 72. The Great Gatsby 73.
TV series: Peyton Place 64–67.

fashions were the basis of many a woman's film
of the thirties: *Roberta, Fashions of 1934,
Vogues of 1938*. Later attempts to recapture this
interest had an air of *deja vu: Maytime in
Mayfair, It Started in Paradise, Lucy Gallant*.
But the wheel turns, and the seventies brought
Mahogany.

Fassbinder, Rainer Werner (1946–).
Fashionable German director of the seventies,
usually with something despairing to say about
the current state of society.
Katzelmacher 69. The Pedlar of Four Seasons
71. The Bitter Tears of Petra Von Kant 72. Fear
Eats the Soul 74.

fast motion: see *accelerated motion*.

Father Brown (GB 1954). The only British
attempt to film the adventures of G. K.
Chesterton's tubby detective-priest was a
civilized comedy with all concerned on the same
wavelength. A quietly witty script by Thelma
Schnee, polished direction by Robert Hamer,
and high comedy acting by Alec Guinness, Peter
Finch, Joan Greenwood and Ernest Thesiger
made it a film with a rare flavour. On television,
Kenneth More played the role in a 1973 series. In
1934 Walter Connolly played the role in a
Hollywood second feature, *Father Brown
Detective*. In West Germany, Heinz Ruhmann
played the role in two sixties films, and Josef
Meinrad in a 1969 TV series.

Father of the Bride (US 1950). The American
domestic comedy *par excellence*, taken from
Edward Streeter's book and starring Spencer

Tracy as the harassed pa. A sequel, *Father's
Little Dividend* 51, was somewhat less effective.
Leon Ames later played the role in a TV series.

Faulds, Andrew (1923–). British character
actor and M.P.
The Card 52. The One That Got Away 56.
Payroll 61. Jason and the Argonauts 64. The
Prince and the Pauper 65. The Devils 70. The
Music Lovers 71, etc.

Faulkner,   William   (1897–1962).
Distinguished American novelist. Works filmed
include *Sanctuary, Intruder in the Dust, The
Sound and the Fury*. Also collaborated on
screenplays:
Road to Glory 36. To Have and Have Not 44.
The Big Sleep 46. Land of the Pharaohs 55, etc.

Faust, Johann (1488–1541). These at least are
the approximate dates of a German conjurer, the
scanty details of whose wandering life were the
basis of plays by Marlowe (1593) and later
Goethe (1831) which turned into classics. The
theme of the man who sells his soul to the devil in
exchange for a rich full life has been seen in
innumerable film versions, including many
musical ones based on Gounod's opera, and a
puppet one from Czechoslovakia. The first
straight version was made in France in 1905; the
most famous silent version is Murnau's of 1926,
with Emil Jannings and Gosta Ekman. 1941
brought Dieterle's *All That Money Can Buy*,
from Stephen Vincent Benet's *The Devil and
Daniel Webster*; René Clair's version, *La Beauté
du Diable*, followed in 1949, *Alias Nick Beal* in
the same year, Autant-Lara's *Marguerite de la
Nuit* in 1955, *Damn Yankees* in 1958 and
Richard Burton's *Dr Faustus* in 1967. There
were modernized versions in France 63, USA 64
and Rumania 66, and a Spanish version of 1957,
Faustina, in which the hero becomes a heroine.
The latest variations on the theme are *Bedazzled*
67, a comic extravaganza with Peter Cook as the
tempter and Dudley Moore as the tempted and
Hammersmith Is Out 72 with Richard Burton
and Peter Ustinov.

Fay, Frank (1894–1961). American light actor
and vaudeville star who made a few
undistinguished films.
Show of Shows 29. God's Gift to Women 31.
Stars over Broadway 35. They Knew What They
Wanted 40. Spotlight Scandals 43. Love Nest 51,
etc.

Faye, Alice (1912–) (Ann Leppert). American
leading lady of the thirties and forties, once a
singer with Rudy Vallee's band. Her wry

expression tended to limit her roles, but she was a key star of her time and commanded a loyal following.

□ George White's Scandals 34. Now I'll Tell 34. She Learned About Sailors 34. 365 Nights in Hollywood 34. George White's 1935 Scandals. Every Night at Eight 35. Music is Magic 35. King of Burlesque 36. Poor Little Rich Girl 36. Stowaway 36. On the Avenue 37. Wake Up and Live 37. You Can't Have Everything 37. You're a Sweetheart 37. Sally Irene and Mary 38. *In Old Chicago* 38. *Alexander's Ragtime Band* 38. Tailspin 39. *Rose of Washington Square* 39. *Hollywood Cavalcade* 39. Barricade 39. Little Old New York 40. *Lillian Russell* 40. Tin Pan Alley 40. That Night in Rio 41. The Great American Broadcast 41. Weekend in Havana 41. *Hello Frisco Hello* 43. The Gang's All Here 43. Fallen Angel 45. State Fair 62.

Faylen, Frank (1907–). American character actor with stage experience. Played scores of bartenders, gangsters, sheriffs, cops, etc., from 1936.

Bullets or Ballots 36. The Grapes of Wrath 40. Top Sergeant Mulligan 42. *The Lost Weekend* (his best role, as the male nurse) 45. Blue Skies 46. Road to Rio 47. Detective Story 51. Riot in Cell Block Eleven 54. Killer Dino 58. The Monkey's Uncle 65. Funny Girl 68, many others.

Fazenda, Louise (1895–1962). American leading lady of the Mack Sennett era: bathing beauty, slapstick comedienne, later a character actress.

The Beautiful and Damned 22. Main Street 23. Cheaper to Marry 25. Bobbed Hair 25. The Bat 26. The Red Mill 27. The Terror 28. Riley the Cop 28. Noah's Ark 29. The Desert Song 29. No No Nanette 30. Leathernecking 30. Cuban Love Song 31. Alice in Wonderland 33. Wonder Bar 34. Colleen 36. The Road Back 37. Swing Your Lady 38. The Old Maid 39, many others.

feature film. Normally accepted to mean a (fictional) entertainment film of more than 3000 feet in length (approx. 34 minutes). Anything less than this is technically a 'short'. NB. In journalism and television a 'feature' usually means a *non*-fiction article or documentary.

featured players. Those next in importance to the stars: usually billed after the title.

Federation of Film Societies. British organization which issues information and arranges screening for film societies; also publishes magazine *Film*.

Fegte, Ernst (1900–1976). German production designer, in Hollywood from the early thirties.

The General Died at Dawn 36. The Palm Beach Story 42. I Married a Witch 42. Five Graves to Cairo 43. Frenchman's Creek 44. Concerto 47. Angel and the Badman 47, etc.

Fehmiu, Bekim (1932–). Stalwart Slav leading man in international films.

The Happy Gypsies 66. *The Adventurers* 70. The Deserter 71. Permission to Kill 75, etc.

Feiffer, Jules (–). American satirical strip cartoonist, venturing into screenwriting.

Little Murders 71. Carnal Knowledge 71, etc.

Feist, Felix E. (1906–1965). American director, at first of short subjects including Pete Smith Specialities; in Hollywood from 1928.

□ Stepping Sisters 32. The Deluge 33. All By Myself 43. You're a Lucky Fellow Mr Smith 43. This is the Life 44. Pardon My Rhythm 44. Reckless Age 44. George White's Scandals 45. The Devil Thumbs a Ride (& w) 47. The Winner's Circle 47. The Threat 49. Treason 49. The Golden Gloves Story 50. The Man Who Cheated Himself 50. Tomorrow is Another Day 51. The Basketball Fix 51. This Woman is Dangerous 52. The Big Trees 52. The Man Behind the Gun 52. Donavan's Brain 53. Pirates of Tripoli 55.

Fejos, Paul (1893–1963). Hungarian director, in America from 1923.

The Last Moment 27. Lonesome 28. Erik the Great 29. Broadway 29. The Big House (co-d) 30. Maria (Hung.) 32. The Golden Smile (Dan.) 35. A Handful of Rice (Swedish) 38.

Feld, Fritz (1900–). Dapper German character comedian, once stage director for Max Reinhardt; long in Hollywood playing temperamental head waiters and clerks.

Broadway 29. I Met Him in Paris 37. Bringing Up Baby 38. Idiot's Delight 39. At the Circus (as Jardinet) 39. Sandy is a Lady 40. World Première 41. Iceland 42. Phantom of the Opera 43. The Great John L 45. Catman of Paris 46. The Secret Life of Walter Mitty 47. My Girl Tisa 48. Mexican Hayride 49. The Jackpot 50. Full House 52. The Patsy 64. Barefoot in the Park 67. Hello Dolly 69. The Love Bug Rides Again 73, many others.

Feldman, Charles K. (1904–1968) (Charles Gould). American producer, former lawyer and talent agent.

Pittsburgh 42. Follow the Boys 44. To Have and

Have Not 44. The Big Sleep 46. Red River 48.
The Red Pony 49. A Streetcar Named Desire 51.
The Seven Year Itch 54. A Walk on the Wild
Side 62. The Seventh Dawn 64. What's New
Pussycat? 65. The Group 66. Casino Royale 67,
etc.

Feldman, Marty (1933–). Pop-eyed British
TV comic. *Every Home Should Have One* 69.
Young Frankenstein 73. The Adventures of
Sherlock Holmes' Smarter Brother 75. Silent
Movie 76, etc.

Feldon, Barbara (1941–). American leading
lady of the seventies who came to notice in the
TV series *Get Smart.*

Felix (The Cat). Cartoon creation of Pat
Sullivan, a perky and indestructible character
highly popular in the twenties; in the fifties
revived for TV by other hands in more
streamlined style.

Felix, Maria (1915–). Mexican actress of
strong personality.
The Devil Is a Woman 52. French Can Can 53.
Les Héros Sont Fatigués 55, many Mexican
films.

Felix, Seymour (1892–1961). American
dance director, in films since 1929.
The Great Ziegfeld (AA) 36. Alexander's
Ragtime Band 38. Cover Girl 44. The I Don't
Care Girl 52, many others.

Fell, Norman (–). Sad-looking American
character actor.
Ocean's Eleven 61. Pork Chop Hill 63. Bullitt 68.
If It's Tuesday This Must Be Belgium 69. The
Stone Killer 73, etc.
TV series: 87th Precinct 61–64. Dan August 71.
Needles and Pins 74.

Fellini, Federico (1920–). Fashionable and
influential Italian director, formerly cartoonist.
Film actor and writer from 1941.
□ AS DIRECTOR: Lights of Variety 50. The
White Sheik 50. I Vitelloni 53. *La Strada* 54. Il
Bidone 55. Notti di Cabiria 57. *La Dolce Vita*
59. Boccaccio 70 (part) 62. *Eight and a Half* 63.
Juliet of the Spirits 65. Histoires Extraordinaires
(part) 68. *Satyricon* 69. The Clowns 70. Fellini
Roma 72. Amarcord 74. Casanova 77.

Fellowes, Rockliffe (1885–1950). Canadian
general purpose actor in Hollywood films of
silent days.
The Easiest Way 17. In Search of a Sinner 20.
The Spoilers 23. The Garden of Weeds 24. East

of Suez 25. Syncopating Sue 26. The Taxi
Dancer 27. The Third Degree 27. The Charlatan
29. Outside the Law 30. Monkey Business 31.
Lawyer Man 32. The Phantom Broadcast 33.
The Black Page 34, many others.

Fellows, Edith (1923–). American teenage
star of the thirties.
Riders of Death Valley 32. Jane Eyre 34. Pennies
from Heaven 36. Five Little Peppers 38. Five
Little Peppers in Trouble 41. Girls' Town 42. Her
First Romance 47, etc.

Fellows, Robert (1903–1969). American
producer.
Virginia City 39. They Died with Their Boots On
41. The Spanish Main 45. A Yankee in King
Arthur's Court 49. Hondo 54. The High and the
Mighty 54, etc.

Felton, Verna (1890–1966). American
character actress, often seen as neighbour or
busybody.
The Gunfighter 50. New Mexico 52. Picnic 55.
Little Egypt 55. The Oklahoman 57, etc.
TV series: December Bride 54–59. Pete and
Gladys 60.

female impersonation: see *transvestism.*

La Femme du Boulanger (*The Baker's Wife*)
(France 1938). Like all Marcel Pagnol's films,
this peasant comedy about a baker whose bread
suffers when his wife leaves him has little
cinematic merit but survives by virtue of
Pagnol's warm script, Raimu's acting and the
affectionate regard for village life.

Fennell, Albert (1920–). British producer
best known for TV's *The Avengers.*
The Green Scarf 54. Next to No Time 57. Tunes
of Glory 59. The Innocents 61. Night of the
Eagle 62. And Soon The Darkness 71. Dr Jekyll
and Sister Hyde 71. The Legend of Hell House
73, etc.

Fenton, Frank (1906–1957). American
general purpose supporting actor.
Lady of Burlesque 42. Buffalo Bill 44. Magic
Town 46. Red River 48. Island in the Sky 53.
Emergency Hospital 56. Hellbound 58, many
others.

Fenton, Leslie (1902–). British-born director
of Hollywood 'B' pictures. (Former actor in
many silent films and early talkies including
*What Price Glory?, The Man I Love, Broadway,
Public Enemy, F.P.1*), etc. Recently inactive.
□ *Tell No Tales* 39. Stronger than Desire 39. The

Man from Dakota 40. The Golden Fleecing 40. The Saint's Vacation 41. Tomorrow the World 46. Pardon My Past 46. On Our Merry Way (co-d) 48. Saigon 48. Lulu Belle 48. Whispering Smith 48. Streets of Laredo 49. The Redhead and the Cowboy 50.

Ferber, Edna (1887–1968). American novelist, some of whose works were filmed.
Our Mrs McChesney 18. Mother Knows Best 28. Showboat 29, 35 and 51. The Royal Family of Broadway 31. Cimarron 31 and 61. So Big 32 and 53. Dinner at Eight 33. Come and Get It 36. Stage Door (with George S. Kaufman) 38. Saratoga Trunk 43. Giant 56. Ice Palace 59.

Ferguson, Elsie (1883–1961). American leading lady of silent melodramas about the upper classes. Popular 1918–27, then retired.
Barbary Sheep 17. The Lie 18. Song of Songs 18. A Society Exile 19. His House in Order 20. Sacred and Profane Love 21. Outcast 22, etc.

Ferguson, Frank (c. 1899–). Toothy American character actor, often in comic bit parts.
This Gun For Hire 42. The Miracle of the Bells 48. Abbott and Costello Meet Frankenstein 49. Elopement 51. Johnny Guitar 54. Andy Hardy Comes Home 58. Raymie 60, many others.
TV series: Peyton Place 65–70.

Fernandel (1903–1971) (Fernand Contandin). Rubber-faced French comedian with toothy grin and music-hall background. Films usually 'naughty but nice'.
Regain (Harvest) 37. Un Carnet de Bal 37. *Fric Frac* 39. *La Fille du Puisatier* 40. *The Red Inn* 51. Forbidden Fruit 52. The *Don Camillo* series from 1952. *The Sheep Has Five Legs* 54. Paris Holiday 57. The Cow and I 59. Croesus 60. La Cuisine au Beurre 63. Le Voyage du Père 66. L'Homme a la Buick 67, etc.

Fernandez, Emilio (1904–). Prolific Mexican director, few of whose films have been seen abroad.
Isle of Passion 41. Maria Candelaria 44. The Pearl 45. Rio Escondido 47. Maclovia 48. The Torch 50. Garcia 74. Breakout 75, etc.

Ferrer, Jose (1909–) (Jose Vicente Ferrer y Centron). Distinguished American stage actor of Puerto Rican origin; film career spotty but interesting.
□ *Joan of Arc* (as the dauphin) 48. Whirlpool 49. Crisis 50. *Cyrano de Bergerac* (AA) 50. Anything Can Happen 52. *Moulin Rouge* (as Toulouse Lautrec) 52. Miss Sadie Thompson 53.

The Caine Mutiny 54. Deep in my Heart 54. The Shrike (& d) 55. Cockleshell Heroes (& d) (GB) 56. The Great Man (& wd) 56. I Accuse (& d) 58. The High Cost of Loving (d) 58. Return to Peyton Place (d only) 61. State Fair (d only) 62. Lawrence of Arabia 62. Nine Hours to Rama 63. Stop Train 349 64. The Greatest Story Ever Told 65. *Ship of Fools* 65. Enter Laughing 67. Cervantes 67. The Aquarians (TV) 68. Banyon (TV) 71. The Marcus Nelson Murders (TV) 73. Orders to Kill 75.

Ferrer, Mel (1917–). Sensitive-looking American leading man, former radio producer and writer.
Girl of the Limberlost (d only) 45. *Lost Boundaries* 49. The Secret Fury (d only) 50. Vendetta (d only) 50. Born to Be Bad 50. The Brave Bulls 51. *Scaramouche* 52. Rancho Notorious 52. Lili 53. Knights of the Round Table (GB) 54. Saadia 54. Oh! Rosalinda (GB) 55. War and Peace 56. The Vintage 57. The Sun Also Rises 57. Fraulein 58. The World the Flesh and the Devil 59. Green Mansions (d only) 59. Blood and Roses 61. The Fall of the Roman Empire 64. Sex and the Single Girl 64. El Greco 65. Wait Until Dark (p only) 67. Every Day's a Holiday (& wdp) (Sp.) 67. A Time for Loving (& p) 71. Embassy (p only) 72. W (p only) 73, etc.

Ferreri, Marco (1928–). Italian director.
El Pisito (Sp.) 56. The Wheelchair (Sp.) 60. Queen Bee 63. The Bearded Lady 64. Wedding March 65. Dillinger Is Dead 68. Blowout 73, etc.

Ferris, Barbara (1940–). British leading lady.
Catch Us If You Can 66. Interlude 68. A Nice Girl Like Me 69.

Ferzetti, Gabriele (1925–) (Pasquale Ferzetti). Italian leading man.
William Tell 48. Cuore Ingrato 51. Three Forbidden Stories 52. Puccini 54. Le Amiche 55. Donatello 56. L'Avventura 59. Torpedo Bay 64. Once Upon a Time in the West 69. On Her Majesty's Secret Service 69. Hitler—The Last Ten Days 73. The Night Porter 74, etc.

festivals. Since World War II a great many cities round the world have derived excellent publicity from annual film festivals. Producers, distributors and actors in search of accolades now diligently trek each year to Cannes, Venice, Berlin, Mar del Plata, Cork, Edinburgh, Karlovy Vary, San Sebastian, Moscow, etc., while London and New York offer résumés in October.

Fetchit, Stepin (1898–) (Lincoln Perry). Gangly, slow-moving American Negro

comedian, popular in films of the thirties.
In Old Kentucky 29. Stand Up and Cheer 33.
Steamboat Round the Bend 35. On the Avenue
37. Elephants Never Forget 39. Bend of the
River 52. The Sun Shines Bright 53, many
others.

Feuillade, Louis (1873–1925). Newly-rediscovered and fêted French director who made marathon silent serials about master criminals.
Fantomas 13. Les Vampires 15. Judex (remade by Franju 63) 16–17. Tih Minh 18. Parisette 21, etc.

Feuillere, Edwige (1907–) (Edwige Cunati). Distinguished French actress, a leading member of the Comédie Française.
Le Cordon Bleu 30. Topaze 32. I Was An Adventuress 38. Sans Lendemain 40. La Duchesse de Langeais 42. *L'Idiot* 46. L'Aigle a Deux Têtes 47. Woman Hater (GB) 48. *Olivia* 50. Adorable Creatures 52. *Le Blé en Herbe* 53. The Fruits of Summer 54. En Cas de Malheur (Love Is My Profession) 57. Crime Doesn't Pay 62. Do You Like Women? 64, etc.

Feydeau, Georges (1862–1921). French writer of stage farces, many of which have become classics and are often filmed, the best cinematic examples being *Occupe Toi d'Amelie* 49 and *Hotel Paradiso* 66.

Feyder, Jacques (1888–1948) (Jacques Frederix). French director, former actor; married Françoise Rosay.
L'Atalantide 21. Crainquebille 22. Thérèse Raquin 28. *Les Nouveaux Messieurs* 29. The Kiss (US) 29. Le Grand Jeu 34. *La Kermesse Héroique* 35. Knight without Armour (GB) 37. Les Gens du Voyage 38. La Loi du Nord 39. Une Femme Disparait 41, Macadam (supervised only) 45, etc.

F.I.D.O. The Film Industry Defence Organization, a body formed by British renters and exhibitors to prevent old feature films being sold to television. It collapsed in 1964 after five years during which no renter dared sell his product for fear of reprisals.

Fiander, Lewis (c. 1940–). Australian-born stage and TV actor in Britain.
Dr Jekyll and Sister Hyde 71. The Abdication, etc.

Fiedler, John (1925–). Mild, bespectacled American character actor.
Twelve Angry Men 57. Stage Struck 58. That

Touch of Mink 62. The World of Henry Orient 64. Kiss Me Stupid 64. Fitzwilly 67. The Odd Couple 68. True Grit 69. Making It 71, etc.

Field, Betty (1918–1973). American character actress who played a variety of roles from neurotic girls to slatternly mums.
☐ What a Life 39. *Of Mice and Men* 39. Seventeen 40. Victory 41. The Shepherd of the Hills 41. Blues in the Night 41. *Kings' Row* 42. Are Husbands Necessary? 42. Flesh and Fantasy 43. The Great Moment 44. Tomorrow the World 44. *The Southerner* 45. The Great Gatsby 49. Picnic 55. Bus Stop 56. Peyton Place 57. The Hound Dog Man 59. Butterfield 8 60. Bird Man of Alcatraz 62. Seven Women 65. How to Save a Marriage 68. Coogan's Bluff 68.

Field, Mary (1896–1968). British executive long associated with films specially made for children. From 1926 worked as continuity girl, editor, etc., also directed some instructional films, including the *Secrets of Nature* series. Well-known writer and lecturer on social aspects of film.

Field, Rachel (1894–1942). American novelist.
☐ All This and Heaven Too 40. And Now Tomorrow 44. Time Out of Mind 47.

Field, Sally (1946–). Diminutive American actress who played the lead in TV series *Gidget* 65, *The Flying Nun* 67–68, The Girl with Something Extra 73.
The Way West 67. Home for the Holidays (TV) 72. Maybe I'll Come Home in the Spring (TV) 72. Marriage Year One (TV) 72, etc.

Field, Shirley Ann (1938–). British leading lady with stage experience; career waned after a promising start.
Dry Rot 56. Once More with Feeling 59. The Entertainer 59. *Saturday Night and Sunday Morning* 60. The Man in the Moon 60. The Damned 61. The War Lover 62. Lunch Hour 63. Kings of the Sun (US) 63. Doctor in Clover 66. *Alfie* 66, etc.

Field, Sid (1904–1950). British comedian who after years in music hall became West End star in 1943. First film, *London Town* 46, valuable as record of his sketches; second and last, *Cardboard Cavalier* 48, a patchy historical farce.

Field, Virginia (1917–) (Margaret Cynthia Field). British-born second lead of Hollywood films in the forties.

The Primrose Path (GB) 35. Lloyds of London 37. Lancer Spy 38. Waterloo Bridge 40. Hudson's Bay 41. The Perfect Marriage 46. Dial 1119 50. The Big Story 58. The Earth Dies Screaming 65, others.

Fielding, Fenella (c. 1930–). Anglo-Rumanian leading lady, usually in outrageously exaggerated roles on stage and TV.
In the Doghouse 62. The Old Dark House 63. Doctor in Clover 66. Carry on Screaming 66. Arrivederci Baby 66. Lock Up Your Daughters 69, etc.

Fielding, Jerry (–). American composer.
The Wild Bunch 69. Johnny Got His Gun 71. Lawman 71. The Nightcomers 71. Straw Dogs 71. Chato's Land 72, etc.

Fielding, Henry (1707–54). Influential English novelist whose chief bequests to films have been *Tom Jones, Lock Up Your Daughters* (indirectly) and *Joseph Andrews*.

Fielding, Marjorie (1892–1956). British stage actress who usually played strict but kindly gentlewomen. Repeated her stage role in *Quiet Wedding* 40 and was subsequently in many films.
The Demi-Paradise 43. Quiet Weekend 46. Spring in Park Lane 47. The Conspirator 49. The Chiltern Hundreds 49. The Franchise Affair 50. The Lavender Hill Mob 51. Mandy 52. Rob Roy 53, etc.

Fields, Benny (1894–1959) (Benjamin Geisenfeld). American vaudevillian whose career was linked with Blossom Seeley. Their story was told (more or less) in *Somebody Loves Me*.
□ Mr Broadway 33. The Big Broadcast of 1937 36. Minstrel Man 44.

Fields, Gracie (1898–) (Grace Stansfield). British singer and comedienne whose Lancashire humour and high spirits helped working-class audiences through the thirties depression. An inimitable voice and personality. Autobiography 1960: *Sing As We Go*.
□ *Sally in our Alley* 31. Looking on the Bright Side 32. This Week of Grace 33. Love Life and Laughter 33. *Sing As We Go* 34. Look Up and Laugh 35. Queen of Hearts 36. The Show Goes On 37. We're Going to Be Rich 38. Keep Smiling 38. Shipyard Sally 39. Stage Door Canteen 43. *Holy Matrimony* 43. Molly and Me 45. Paris Underground 45.

Fields, Stanley (1884–1941) (Walter L.

Agnew). American character actor, former prizefighter and vaudevillian.
Mammy 30. Little Caesar 30. Island of Lost Souls 32. Kid Millions 35. Way Out West 37. Algiers 38. New Moon 40, many others.

Fields, W. C. (1879–1946) (William Claude Dukinfield). Red-nosed, gravel-voiced, bottle-hitting, misogynist American comedian around whose intolerance and eccentric habits many legends have been built. After a hard life as a tramp juggler, his off-beat personality found a niche in silent films, though sound was necessary to his full flowering as a screen personality. Many of his routines were made up as he went along; once he sold for $25,000 a story line written on the back of an envelope. Books on him include *W. C. Fields, His Follies and Fortunes* (Robert Lewis Taylor 1949), *The Films of W. C. Fields* (Donald Deschner 1960). Rod Steiger impersonated him in an inaccurate 1976 film of his life, *W. C. Fields and Me*, from a book by his mistress Carlotta Monti.
□ *Pool Sharks* 15. Janice Meredith 24. Sally of the Sawdust 25. That Royle Girl 26. It's the Old Army Game 26. So's Your Old Man 26. The Potters 27. Running Wild 27. Two Flaming Youths 27. Tillie's Punctured Romance 27. Fools for Luck 28. The Golf Specialist 30. Her Majesty Love 31. Million Dollar Legs 32. If I Had a Million 32. The Dentist 32. The Fatal Glass of Beer 32. The Pharmacist 33. The Barber Shop 33. International House 33. Tillie and Gus 33. Alice in Wonderland (as Humpty Dumpty) 33. Six of a Kind 34. You're Telling Me 34. The Old Fashioned Way 34. Mrs Wiggs of the Cabbage Patch 34. *It's a Gift* 34. *David Copperfield* (as Micawber) 34. Mississippi 35. The Man on the Flying Trapeze 35. Poppy 36. The Big Broadcast of 1938 37. You Can't Cheat an Honest Man 39. *My Little Chickadee* 40. *The Bank Dick* 40. *Never Give a Sucker an Even Break* 41. Follow the Boys 44. Song of the Open Road 44. Sensations of 1945.

Figueroa, Gabriel (1907–). Mexican cinematographer who worked in Hollywood with Gregg Toland and on Luis Buñuel's Mexican films.
The Fugitive 47. Maclovia 50. Night of the Iguana 64. Kelly's Heroes 70, etc.

film making is not too frequently used as a background for movies, as movies about movies are thought to be bad box office. Certainly not too many of the following were big hits: *OK for Sound, The Best Pair of Legs in the Business, Go for a Take, The Comedy Man, The Bad and the Beautiful, Two Weeks in Another Town, It's a*

Great Feeling, Shooting Stars, Pick a Star, A Star is Born, The Carpetbaggers, Eight and a Half, Hellzapoppin, Day for Night, Stand In, Singin' In The Rain, Abbott and Costello Meet the Keystone Kops, Gable and Lombard, Harlow, W. C. Fields and Me, The Big Knife, Once in a Lifetime, Wonderful Life, Hollywood Cavalcade, Hollywood Boulevard, Hollywood Story, Nickelodeon, The Last Tycoon.

film society. A club formed to show high quality revivals and new films not normally found in public cinemas.

Films à Clef are those which appear to be fiction but are really based on factual cases with the names changed. The obvious example is *Citizen Kane*, which parallels the career of William Randolph Hearst. Others are *The Great Dictator*, in which Hynkel is obviously Hitler; *The Miracle Woman*, based on Aimee Semple McPherson; *Compulsion*, based on the Leopold and Loeb murder; *Inherit the Wind*, about the Scopes monkey trial; *The Moon and Sixpence*, in which Charles Strickland stands in for Paul Gaugin; *The Man Who Came to Dinner*, in which Sheridan Whiteside is Alexander Woolcott, Banjo is Harpo Marx, and Beverly Carlton is Noel Coward; *Young Cassidy*, drawn from the early life of Sean O'Casey; *All About Eve*, in which Margo Channing was said to be Tallulah Bankhead and Addison de Witt George Jean Nathan; *Twentieth Century*, in which Oscar Jaffe is an amalgam of Jed Harris and David Belasco; *All the King's Men* and *A Lion is in the Streets*, both essentially about Huey Long; *The Lost Moment*, in which the old lady is allegedly Claire Clairemont, the aged mistress of Byron; *The Adventurers*, in which the characters are supposedly based on Porfirio Rubirosa, Barbara Hutton, Aristotle Onassis and Maria Callas; *The Carpetbaggers*, plainly about Howard Hughes; *Little Caesar*, who was plainly Al Capone; *Major Barbara*, in which Adolphus Cusins was Gilbert Murray; *Call Me Madam*, based on the exploits of Perle Mesta; *The Winslow Boy*, based on the Archer-Shee case, with Sir Robert Morton standing in for Sir Edward Carson; *An American Tragedy*, from the real life Chester Gillette murder case; *Monsieur Verdoux*, who was Landru; *Death of a Scoundrel*, from the career of Charles Rubenstein; *The Prisoner*, inspired by the sufferings of Cardinal Mindzenty; *Fame is the Spur*, in which Homer Radshaw was Ramsay MacDonald; and if you like *Dr Jekyll and Mr Hyde*, whose story was inspired by the burglarious second life of Deacon William Brodie; or even any Sherlock Holmes story, as Holmes was modelled on Dr Joseph Bell.

La Fin du Jour (France 1939). A delightful comedy-drama set in a home for old actors, with subtle direction by Julien Duvivier and effortlessly effective performances from Michel Simon, Louis Jouvet and Victor Francen.

Finch, Flora (1869–1940). British-born actress, formerly on stage; famous as John Bunny's partner in early film comedies. After his death in 1915 she formed her own production company and was in many silent films of the twenties.

Finch, Jon (1941–). British leading man.
□ The Vampire Lovers 70. Horror of Frankenstein 71. Macbeth 71. Sunday Bloody Sunday 71. Frenzy 72. Lady Caroline Lamb 72. The Final Programme 73.

Finch, Peter (1916–1977) (William Mitchell). Thoughtful-looking British leading actor who spent many years in Australia before returning to become an international star.
□ Dad and Dave Come to Town 37. Red Sky at Morning 37. Mr Chedworth Steps Out 38. Rats of Tobruk 44. The Power and the Glory 45. Eureka Stockade 47. Train of Events 49. The Miniver Story 50. *Robin Hood* (as Sheriff) 51. The Heart of the Matter 53. The Story of Gilbert and Sullivan 53. Elephant Walk 54. *Father Brown* (as Flambeau) 54. Make Me an Offer 54. The Dark Avenger 55. Passage Home 55. Josephine and Men 55. *Simon and Laura* 55. *The Battle of the River Plate* (as Langsdorff) 56. *A Town Like Alice* (BFA) 56. The Shiralee 56. Robbery Under Arms 57. Windom's Way 57. Operation Amsterdam 58. Kidnapped 59. *The Nun's Story* 59. The Sins of Rachel Cade 60. *The Trials of Oscar Wilde* 60. *No Love for Johnnie* (BFA) 61. I Thank a Fool 62. In the Cool of the Day 63. Girl with Green Eyes 64. The Pumpkin Eater 64. Judith 65. The Flight of the Phoenix 65. 10.30 pm Summer 67. *Far from the Madding Crowd* 67. The Legend of Lylah Clare 68. The Red Tent 69. *Sunday Bloody Sunday* (BFA) 71. England Made Me 72. *Lost Horizon* 73. A Bequest to the Nation 73. The Abdication 73. Network 76.

fine grain print. One of high quality stock (avoiding the coarseness of silver salt deposit); used for making dupe negatives.

Finklehoffe, Fred F. (1911–). American writer-producer.
Brother Rat (co-w & co-w original stage play) 39. For Me and My Gal (co-w) 42. Meet Me in St Louis (w) 44. The Egg and I (co-wp) 47. At War with the Army (co-wp) 50, etc.

Finland has produced many films for internal consumption, but language and subject barriers have made them unsuitable for international sale. Probably the best known Finnish film is Edvin Laine's *The Unknown Soldier 55*.

Finlay, Frank (1926–). British stage actor who has made tentative screen appearances.
Life for Ruth 62. The Informers 63. Othello (as Iago) 65. Robbery 67. Inspector Clouseau 68. Twisted Nerve 68. Cromwell 69. Assault 71. Gumshoe 71. Danny Jones 71. Sitting Target 72. Shaft in Africa 73. The Three Musketeers 74. The Four Musketeers 75, etc.

Finlayson, James (1877–1953). Scottish comic actor who went to Hollywood in early silent days and became an indispensable comic villain, known for the exaggerated reaction known as a 'double take and fade away'. A memorable opponent for Laurel and Hardy.
Small Town Idol 21. Ladies Night in a Turkish Bath 28. Lady Be Good 28. The Dawn Patrol 30. *Big Business* 30. Pardon Us 31. Fra Diavolo 33. Our Relations 36. *Way Out West* 37. Blockheads 38. The Flying Deuces 39. The Perils of Pauline 47. Grand Canyon Trail 48. Royal Wedding 51, many others.

Finney, Albert (1936–). Leading British actor whose comparatively few films have tended to be controversial.
□ The Entertainer 59. *Saturday Night and Sunday Morning* 60. Tom Jones 63. The Victors 63. Night Must Fall (& p) 63. Two for the Road 67. *Charlie Bubbles* (& pd) 68. The Picasso Summer 69. Scrooge 70. Gumshoe (& p) 71. Alpha Beta 73. Murder on the Orient Express 74.

fire is a standard part of the melodramatist's equipment, whether it be used for disposing of country houses with too many memories (*Dragonwyck, Rebecca, The Lost Moment, The Fall of the House of Usher, The Tomb of Ligeia, Gone with the Wind*) or whole cities (*Forever Amber, In Old Chicago, Quo Vadis*). Sometimes, as in *House of Wax*, it makes a splendid starting point; though to judge from *She* one can't rely on its life-prolonging qualities. Its use in realistic films is rare, though cases of arson were seriously studied in *On the Night of the Fire* and *Violent Playground*. The fires of hell were most spectacularly re-created in the 1935 version of *Dante's Inferno*. Comedies about firemen include *Where's That Fire?* (Will Hay), *Fireman Save My Child, Harvey Middleman Fireman*, and *Go to Blazes* (Dave King); and firemen who start fires instead of putting them out are prophesied in *Fahrenheit 451*. Oil fires were

spectacularly depicted in *Tulsa, Wildcat*, and *Hellfighters*. The classic study of conventional firemen remains *Fires Were Started*; TV series which took up the theme include *Emergency* and *Firehouse*. For many, the greatest screen fire will be the burning of Atlanta in *Gone with the Wind*. Finally fire was always a splendid aid for serial producers, as the oft-used title 'Next Week: Through the Flames' may suggest.
See also: *forest fires.*

Fire Over England (GB 1936). A charade of the Spanish Armada, produced by Alexander Korda with an eye to repeating his 'Henry VIII' success. Directed by William K. Howard. Now chiefly remembered for its gallery of star talents: Flora Robson, Leslie Banks, Laurence Olivier, Vivien Leigh, Raymond Massey, etc.

Fires Were Started (GB 1943). Humphrey Jennings' documentary about the Auxiliary Fire Service during the London blitz is slower and slighter than one might expect from an official tribute, but the treatment gives it an almost poetic quality, and all its people – real firemen – live in the memory.

firing squads have figured chiefly in films about World War I (*Paths of Glory, King and Country*) or those telling the lives of spies, (*Mata Hari, Nurse Edith Cavell, Carve Her Name With Pride*). Other uses have been in *Dishonoured, The Fugitive, Custer of the West, The Victors, The Long Ride Home, Reach for Glory, The Counterfeit Traitor* and *The Ceremony*; and firing squads were given a comic effect in *The Captain's Paradise, Casino Royale, Morgan* and *The Ambushers*.

First National was a Hollywood company founded in 1917. During the next twelve years it was very active, with films featuring Chaplin, Pickford, Milton Sills and Richard Barthelmess. In 1929 it was taken over by Warner Brothers, who however kept the name going for certain product until the mid-thirties.

The First of the Few (GB 1942). Leslie Howard wrote and directed this gentle, cinematically unremarkable but moving film about R. J. Mitchell, inventor of the Spitfire plane. It proved to be one of World War II's most inspirational films, typifying the idealist attitude.

Fischbeck, Harry (–). American cinematographer.
Wives of Men 18. The Devil 21. The Green Goddess 23. Monsieur Beaucaire 24. A Sainted Devil 24. Cobra 25. Sally of the Sawdust 25.

That Royle Girl 25. The Sorrows of Satan 26. Serenade 27. Manhattan Cocktail 28. The Canary Murder Case 29. The Mysterious Dr Fu Manchu 29.Ladies Love Brutes 30. The Spoilers 30. Working Girls 31. Lady and Gent 32. Terror Aboard 33. Search for Beauty 34. Double Door 34. Millions in the Air 35. The Jungle Princess 36. John Meade's Woman 37. Bulldog Drummond's Revenge 37. Prison Farm 38. Persons in Hiding 39. Parole Fixer 40, many others.

Fischer, Gunnar (1911–). Swedish cinematographer who has worked on most of Ingmar Bergman's films.
Smiles of a Summer Night 55. The Seventh Seal 56. Wild Strawberries 57. The Face 58. The Devil's Eye 60, etc.

Fischer, O. W. (1915–). Leading German actor, in films since 1936 but hardly known abroad.
Sommerliebe 42. Heidelberger Romanze 51. El Hakim 57. Uncle Tom's Cabin 65, many others.

Fischinger, Oskar (1900–1967). German animator who pre-dated *Fantasia* in his attempt to illustrate music with abstract forms.
Composition in Blue 33. Allegretto 36. Motion Painting Number One 47, etc.

Fisher, Eddie (1928–). American nightclub singer and actor.
Bundle of Joy 56. Butterfield 8 60, etc.

Fisher, Gerry (1926–). British cinematographer.
AS OPERATOR: The Devil's Disciple 59. Suddenly Last Summer 60. Night Must Fall 63. Guns at Batasi 64. Modesty Blaise 66.
AS CINEMATOGRAPHER: Accident 67. Sebastian 68. Interlude 68. The Go-Between 70. Macho Callahan 71. See No Evil 71. The Amazing Mr Blunden 72. A Bequest to the Nation 73. S.P.Y.S. 74. Juggernaut 74, etc.

Fisher, Terence (1904–). British director, former editor, in films from 1933. Work mainly routine; latterly associated with Hammer horror. Also worked for TV, especially *Douglas Fairbanks Presents*.
To the Public Danger 47. Portrait from Life 48. Marry Me 49. The Astonished Heart 49. So Long at the Fair 50. Home to Danger 51. Kill Me Tomorrow 55. The Curse of Frankenstein 56. Dracula 57. The Hound of the Baskervilles 58. Brides of Dracula 59. The Two Faces of Dr Jekyll 60. The Phantom of the Opera 62. The Gorgon 64. Dracula, Prince of Darkness 65.

Island of Terror 66. The Devil Rides Out 68. Frankenstein and the Monster from Hell 73, etc.

A Fistful of Dollars. The first internationally successful 'spaghetti western', made in Italy in 1964 by Sergio Leone. With a ludicrous plot borrowed from a Japanese Samurai saga, it made a star of Clint Eastwood as the death-dealing 'man with no name', and was rapidly followed by *For a Few Dollars More, The Good the Bad and The Ugly*, and numerous imitations.

Fisz, Benjamin (1922–). Polish-born independent producer, long in England.
Hell Drivers 57. Sea Fury 58. On the Fiddle 61. Heroes of Telemark (co-p) 65. The Battle of Britain (co-p) 69. A Town Called Bastard 71, etc.

Fitzgerald, Barry (1888–1961) (William Shields). Diminutive Irish character actor who found his way to Hollywood and eventually achieved star status, usually in irascible or whimsical 'Oirish' roles.
□ Juno and the Paycock 30. When Knights were Bold 36. *The Plough and the Stars* 36. *Ebb Tide* 37. Bringing Up Baby 38. Marie Antoinette 38. Four Men and a Prayer 38. The Dawn Patrol 38. The Saint Strikes Back 39. Pacific Liner 39. Full Confession 39. *The Long Voyage Home* 40. San Francisco Docks 41. The Sea Wolf 41. How Green Was My Valley 41. Tarzan's Secret Treasure 41. The Amazing Mrs Holliday 43. Two Tickets to London 43. Corvette K225 43. *Going My Way* (AA) 44. I Love a Soldier 44. None but the Lonely Heart 44. Incendiary Blonde 45. *And Then There Were None* 45. Duffy's Tavern 45. The Stork Club 45. Two Years Before the Mast 46. California 46. Easy Come Easy Go 47. Welcome Stranger 47. Variety Girl 47. The Sainted Sisters 48. *The Naked City* 48. Miss Tatlock's Millions 48. Top o' the Morning 49. The Story of Seabiscuit 49. *Union Station* 50. Silver City 51. *The Quiet Man* 52. Happy Ever After 54. The Catered Affair 56. *Rooney* 57. Broth of a Boy 59.

Fitzgerald, Ella (1918–). American Negro singer and entertainer.
Ride Em Cowboy 41. Pete Kelly's Blues 55. St Louis Blues 56. Let No Man Write My Epitaph 60, etc.

Fitzgerald, F. Scott (1896–1940). American novelist and chronicler of 'the jazz age'; was played by Gregory Peck in a biopic, *Beloved Infidel* 59.
The Great Gatsby 48. Tender is the Night 61.

Fitzgerald, Geraldine (1912–). Irish leading

lady who played in British films from 1935; went to Hollywood in 1939 but had rather disappointing roles.

Turn of the Tide 35. The Mill on the Floss 36. Dark Victory 39. *Wuthering Heights* 39. Till We Meet Again 40. Flight from Destiny 41. The Gay Sisters 42. Watch on the Rhine 43. Ladies Courageous 44. *Wilson* 44. Uncle Harry 45. Three Strangers 46. O.S.S. 46. Nobody Lives Forever 47. So Evil My Love (GB) 48. Ten North Frederick 58. The Fiercest Heart 61. The Pawnbroker 65. Rachel Rachel 69. The Last American Hero 73. Harry and Tonto 74, etc.

Fitzgerald, Walter (1896–1977) (Walter Bond). British character actor, on stage from 1922, films from 1930.

Murder at Covent Garden 30. This England 40. Squadron Leader X 41. Strawberry Roan 45. Mine Own Executioner 47. Treasure Island 50. Pickwick Papers 52. Personal Affair 53. Lease of Life 54. Cockleshell Heroes 55. Something of Value 57. Third Man on the Mountain 59. HMS Defiant 62, others.

Fitzmaurice, George (1885–1941). American director of French origin, noted in the twenties for visual style.

A Society Exile 19. On with the Dance 20. Experience 21. *Belladonna* 23. Cytherea 24. *The Dark Angel* 25. *Son of the Sheik* 26. Rose of the Golden West 27. *Lilac Time* 28. His Captive Woman 29. Tiger Rose 29. The Devil to Pay 30. One Heavenly Night 30. The Unholy Garden 31. Mata Hari 32. As You Desire Me 32. Petticoat Fever 36. The Emperor's Candlesticks 37. Arsène Lupin Returns 38. Adventure in Diamonds 40, many others.

Fitzpatrick, James A. (1902–). American documentarist, who from 1925 produced and narrated innumerable travel shorts ('Fitzpatrick Traveltalks'), invariably concluding 'And so we leave ...' Wrote, produced and directed one feature, *Song of Mexico* 45.

Five Fingers (US 1952). L. C. Moyzich's book *Operation Cicero*, about the British Ambassador in Ankara's valet, who during World War II sold secrets to the Germans, can be credited with the post-war reawakening of interest in spying which led eventually to the Bond spoofs. In Joseph L. Mankiewicz's film, Cicero was played by James Mason. There was a TV series of the same name in 1959 with David Hedison.

Five Graves to Cairo (US 1943). Spy story set in the African desert in 1943 and using Rommel as a chief character; a remarkable illustration of writer-director Billy Wilder's penchant for turning headlines into entertainment. Also boasts an ingenious plot and a fascinating performance by Erich von Stroheim.

Five Star Final (US 1932). A famous melodrama of the hardboiled newspaperman school, about a ruthless editor whose probing of a long-dead scandal drives two people to suicide. Directed by Mervyn le Roy, from a play by Louis Weitzenkorn; with Edward G. Robinson.

Fix, Paul (1902–) (Paul Fix Morrison). American general purpose actor who has played hundreds of sheriffs, ranchers, doctors, etc., since the twenties.

The First Kiss 28. Ladies Love Brutes 30. The Last Mile 32. Zoo in Budapest 33. Little Man What Now? 34. Prisoner of Shark Island 36. Souls at Sea 37. News is Made at Night 39. The Ghost Breakers 40. In Old Oklahoma 43. Dakota 45. Tycoon 47. California Passage 50. Hondo 53. The High and the Mighty 54. Blood Alley 55. Giant 56. To Kill a Mockingbird 63. Shenandoah 65. Nevada Smith 66. El Dorado 67. The Day of the Evil Gun 68. Something Big 71, many others.

The Flag Lieutenant. The stiff-upper-lip stage melodrama by W. P. Drury and Lee Trevor, about the intrepid exploits of a naval officer in an outpost of empire, was filmed as a silent in 1919 with George Wynn, and in 1926 with Henry Edwards. In 1932 Edwards appeared in a sound remake, his leading lady being Anna Neagle.

Flagstad, Kirsten (1895–1962). Norwegian operatic soprano whose only film appearance was, surprisingly, in *The Big Broadcast of 1938*.

Flaherty, Robert (1884–1951). Very influential American documentary pioneer, originally an explorer; noted for superb visual sense.

Biography 1963: *The Innocent Eye* by Arthur Calder-Marshall.

□ *Nanook of the North* 20. The Pottery Maker 25. Moana (co-d) 26. 24-Dollar Island 27. *White Shadows in the South Seas* (co-d) 28. Tabu (co-d) 31. Industrial Britain (co-d) 33. *Man of Aran* 34. *Elephant Boy* (co-d) 37. Louisiana Story 48.

Flanagan, Bud (1896–1968) (Robert Winthrop). Genial British comedian, long teamed with Chesney Allen (qv for list of films); they formed part of the Crazy Gang. Wrote and sang catchy, sentimental songs: 'Hometown', 'Underneath the Arches', 'Umbrella Man', 'Strolling'.

Flash Gordon. American newspaper strip hero whose exploits were featured in three famous Hollywood serials starring Buster Crabbe. In the original *Flash Gordon* 36 our hero and his friends saved the Earth from collision with another planet at the cost of being stranded there at the mercy of the wicked Emperor Ming. *Flash Gordon's Trip to Mars* 38 and *Flash Gordon Conquers the Universe* 40 were compounded of similar elements. The directors respectively were Frederick Stephani; Ford Beebe and Robert Hill; and Ray Taylor. A softcore spoof, *Flesh Gordon*, appeared in 1974.

flashback: a break in chronological narrative during which we are shown events of past time which bear on the present situation. The device is as old as the cinema: you could say that *Intolerance* was composed of four flashbacks. As applied to more commonplace yarns, however, with the flashback narrated by one of the story's leading characters, the convention soared into popularity in the thirties until by 1945 or so a film looked very dated indeed if it was not told in retrospect. In the fifties flashbacks fell into absolute disuse, but are now creeping back into fashion again. Some notable uses are:

The Power and the Glory 33, which was advertised as being in 'Narratage' because Ralph Morgan spoke a commentary over the action. *Bride of Frankenstein* 35, which was narrated by Elsa Lanchester as Mary Shelley; the gag was that she also played the monster's mate. *The Great McGinty* 40, in which the flashback construction revealed the somewhat corrupt leading figures finally as penniless, thus mollifying the Hays Office. *Rebecca* 40, in which the introductory narrative, while revealing that Manderley was to go up in flames, also comforted in the knowledge that the hero and heroine would be saved. *Citizen Kane* 41, the complex structure of which was so influential that a whole host of pictures followed in which we tried to get at the truth about a character already dead, by questioning those who knew him: cf. *The Killers, The Rake's Progress, The Moon and Sixpence, The Bridge of San Luis Rey, The Woman in Question, Letter from an Unknown Woman, Rashomon, The Great Man,* even *Doctor Zhivago. Hold Back the Dawn* 41, in which Charles Boyer as a penniless refugee visited Paramount Studios and sold his story to Mitchell Leisen. *The Mummy's Hand* 41, in which the ten-minute chunk telling how the mummy came to be buried alive was lifted straight from the 1932 film *The Mummy.* (Such economies have become commonplace.) *Roxie Hart* 42, in which George Montgomery told a twenty-year-old tale about a notorious lady who

at the end of the film was revealed as the mother of his large family. *Ruthless* 48, a tortuous Zachary Scott melodrama, reviewed as follows by the British critic C. A. Lejeune:

> Beginning pictures at the end
> Is, I'm afraid, a modern trend;
> But I'd find *Ruthless* much more winning
> If it could end at the beginning.

Road to Utopia 45, in which Hope and Lamour appeared as old folks telling the story; as a payoff their 'son' appeared, looking just like Crosby, and Hope told the audience: 'We adopted him.' *Passage to Marseilles* 44, a complex melodrama ranging from Devil's Island to war-torn Britain; it has flashbacks within flashbacks *within flashbacks.* In *Dead of Night* 45, all the characters told supernatural experiences to a psychiatrist, who was then murdered by one of them; the murderer then woke up with no recollection of his nightmare, and proceeded to meet all the other characters again as though for the first time, being caught in an endless series of recurring dreams. *Enchantment* 47, and later *Death of a Salesman* 52, and many films up to *I Was Happy Here* 66, in which characters walk straight out of the present into the past, dispensing with the boring 'I remember' bit. *Edward My Son* 49 and *Teahouse of the August Moon* 56, in which characters step out of the play to tell the story to the audience. *Dead Reckoning* 47, in which Humphrey Bogart confesses the entire plot to a priest. *Kind Hearts and Coronets* 49, in which the story springs from the memoirs of a murderer being written on the night before his execution. *Sunset Boulevard* 50, in which the story is told by the dead hero. *An Inspector Calls* 54, in which a supernatural figure visits a family to make them remember their harsh treatment of a girl who has committed suicide. *Repeat Performance* 47, in which a desperate husband relives the events of the year, leading up to his predicament, and gets a chance to change the outcome. *A Woman's Face* 41, in which the story was based on the recollections of eight courtroom witnesses. *The Locket* and *Lust for Gold,* in which complex flashbacks framed and divided the action.

If the format is to catch on again it will have to be more deftly used than in two sixties films: *Ride Beyond Vengeance,* with its completely irrelevant framing story about a census-taking, and *Lady L,* in which the framing story with the characters as old folks is only marginally less inept than the basic one. Two big-scale musicals, *Star!* and *Funny Girl,* have flashbacks with style but little purpose, and *Little Big Man* barely used its framework except to show that Dustin Hoffman can play a 121-year-old.

Flavin, James (1906–1976). Irish-American supporting actor, usually as genial or bewildered cop.

King Kong 33. The Grapes of Wrath 40. Cloak and Dagger 46. Desert Fury 47. Mighty Joe Young 50. Fighter Attack 53. Mister Roberts 55. The Last Hurrah 58. It's a Mad Mad Mad Mad World 63. Cheyenne Autumn 64. Billwhip Griffin 67, many others.

fleapit. An affectionate British term for the kind of tatty little cinema in which, it was sometimes alleged, the management loaned a hammer with each ticket.

Fleischer, Max (1889–1973). Austrian-born cartoonist and producer, long in Hollywood. Created Betty Boop, Koko, Out of the Inkwell series, Popeye the Sailor, etc. His brother **Dave Fleischer** (1894–) worked as his administrative head.

Gulliver's Travels 39. Mr Bug Goes to Town 41.

Fleischer, Richard (1916–). American director, son of Max Fleischer; former shorts producer. His films usually sound more interesting than they prove to be.

□ Child of Divorce 46. Banjo 47. So This Is New York 49. Make Mine Laughs 49. Trapped 49. Follow Me Quietly 49. The Clay Pigeon 49. The Armored Car Robbery 50. *The Narrow Margin* 51. *The Happy Time* 52. Arena 53. *Twenty Thousand Leagues under the Sea* 54. Violent Saturday 55. The Girl in the Red Velvet Swing 55. Bandido 56. Between Heaven and Hell 56. *The Vikings* 57. These Thousand Hills 58. Compulsion 58. Crack in the Mirror 60. The Big Gamble 61.Barabbas 62. *Fantastic Voyage* 66. Doctor Dolittle 67. *The Boston Strangler* 68. Che! 69. Tora! Tora! Tora! 70. The Last Run 70. Blind Terror 70. The New Centurions 71. 10 Rillington Place 71. Soylent Green 72. The Don is Dead 73. Mr Majestyk 74. The Spikes Gang 74. Mandingo 75. The Incredible Sarah 76. The Prince and the Pauper 77.

Fleming, Eric (1924–1966). Taciturn American general purpose actor.

Conquest of Space 55. Fright 57. Curse of the Undead 59. The Glass Bottom Boat 66, etc.

TV series: *Rawhide* (as Gil Favor, trail boss) 58–65.

Fleming, Ian (1906–1964). Creator of James Bond, whose exploits have been so successfully filmed from the novels.

Fleming, Ian (1888–1969). Australian-born character actor, long in British films as doctors,

civil servants, solicitors, etc. A memorable Dr Watson in the thirties series with Arthur Wontner as Sherlock Holmes.

Fleming, Rhonda (1922–) (Marilyn Louis). Red-haired American leading lady of the forties and fifties.

When Strangers Marry 43. Spellbound 45. The Spiral Staircase 45. Adventure Island 46. Out of the Past (Build My Gallows High) 47. A Yankee in King Arthur's Court 49. Cry Danger 50. The Redhead and the Cowboy 51. The Great Lover 51. Little Egypt 52. The Golden Hawk 52. Serpent of the Nile 53. Inferno 53. Yankee Pasha 54. The Killer Is Loose 56. Slightly Scarlet 56. Gunfight at the OK Corral 57. Gun Glory 57. Home Before Dark 58. Alias Jesse James 59. The Big Circus 59. Run For Your Wife 66, etc.

Fleming, Victor (1883–1949). American director, long with MGM: he was in charge of a few outstanding films, but they seemed to succeed for other reasons.

□ When the Clouds Roll By 20. The Mollycoddle 20. Mamma's Affair 21. Woman's Place 22. Red Hot Romance 22. The Lane That Had No Turning 22. Anna Ascends 22. Dark Secrets 23. Law of the Lawless 23. To the Last Man 23. Call of the Canyon 23. Empty Hands 24. The Call of the Sea 24. A Son of His Father 25. Adventure 25. The Devil's Cargo 25. Lord Jim 25. The Blind Goddess 26. *Mantrap* 26. Rough Riders 27. The Way of all Flesh 27. Hula 27. Abie's Irish Rose 28. The Awakening 28. Wolf Song 29. *The Virginian* 29. Common Clay 30. Renegades 30. Around the World in Eighty Minutes 31. *The Wet Parade* 32. *Red Dust* 32. The White Sister 33. Bombshell 33. *Treasure Island* 34. Reckless 35. The Farmer Takes a Wife 35. Captains Courageous 37. *Test Pilot* 38. *The Wizard of Oz* 39. *Gone with the Wind* (with assistance) 39. *Dr Jekyll and Mr Hyde* 41. Tortilla Flat 42. A Guy Named Joe 43. Adventure 45. Joan of Arc 48.

Flemyng, Gordon (1934–). British director, from TV.

Solo for Sparrow 62. Five to One 63. Dr Who and the Daleks 65. Great Catherine 68. The Split 68. The Last Grenade 69, etc.

Flemyng, Robert (1912–). British actor who usually plays attractive professional men. On stage from 1931, films from 1936 (*Head Over Heels*).

The Guinea Pig 49. The Blue Lamp 50. The Holly and the Ivy 52. The Man Who Never Was 55. Funny Face (US) 56. Windom's Way 57. A Touch of Larceny 59. The Terror of Dr

Hichcock (It.) 63. The Deadly Affair 66. The Spy with a Cold Nose 67. The Blood Beast Terror 67. Young Winston 72. Travels with my Aunt 73, etc.

Flesh and Fantasy (US 1943). One of the earliest compendiums of short stories, linked only by the ramblings of a club bore. In this case, unfortunately; the stories were poorly chosen, and Julien Duvivier's direction somewhat flavourless. The form did not achieve any popularity until 1948 with Somerset Maugham's *Quartet*, and then after three or four years of all-star casts in tenuously linked anecdotes, the advent of television playlets killed the idea stone dead. See also: *Tales of Manhattan*.

Fletcher, Bramwell (1904–). British light leading man of the thirties.
Chick 30. To What Red Hell 30. Raffles (US) 31. Svengali (US) 31. The Mummy (US) 32. The Scarlet Pimpernel 34. Random Harvest (US) 42. White Cargo (US) 42. The Immortal Sergeant (US) 42, etc.

Fletcher, Cyril (1913–). British comedian and entertainer who has made appearances in a few films: *Yellow Canary* 43. *Nicholas Nickleby* 47. *A Piece of Cake* 48, etc.

Fletcher, Louise (1936–). American character actress.
Thieves Like Us 74. Russian Roulette 75. One Flew Over the Cuckoo's Nest (AA) 75, etc.

Flicker, Theodore J. (c. 1929–). American director, former Greenwich Village satirist.
The Troublemaker 64. The President's Analyst 68. Up in the Cellar (& w) 70.

Flippen, Jay C. (1898–1971). Bulky American character actor with vaudeville background; often seen as cop, sergeant or sheriff.
Marie Galante 34. Intrigue 48. Love that Brute 50. Flying Leathernecks 51. Bend of the River 52. The Wild One 53. The Far Country 55. Oklahoma 55. *The Killing* 56. Night Passage 57. From Hell to Texas 58. Studs Lonigan 60. Cat Ballou 65. Firecreek 67. Hellfighters 68. The Seven Minutes 71, many others.
TV series: Ensign O'Toole 62.

Florey, Robert (1900–) French-born director, in Hollywood since 1921.
The Romantic Age 27. The Coconuts 29. *The Murders in the Rue Morgue* 32. Ex Lady 33. The Woman in Red 34. Hollywood Boulevard 36. Hotel Imperial 38. The Face Behind the Mask 40. Lady Gangster 42. Dangerously They Live

43. God Is My Co-Pilot 44. *The Beast with Five Fingers* 46. Monsieur Verdoux (co-d) 47. Rogues' Regiment 48. Out-post in Morocco 48. Johnny One Eye 49. The Gangster We Made 50, many second features; latterly directed hundreds of TV films. Also wrote several scripts, including work on *Frankenstein* 31.

Flowers, Bess (1900–). American bit part player, 'queen of the Hollywood extras', who appeared in literally hundreds of films between 1922 and 1962.

The Fly (US 1958). An unpleasant horror film given big studio treatment in lieu of taste and style, based on an unfortunate mix-up during transmission through space of human and insect atoms. David (then Al) Hedison was the unfortunate victim. There were two sequels: *Return of the Fly* 60 and *Curse of the Fly* 64.

Flying Down to Rio (US 1933). The musical that started the Astaire-Rogers cycle; also notable for a brilliantly-photographed finale with chorus girls on the wings of flying aeroplanes. Nominal stars Dolores del Rio and Gene Raymond; directed by Thornton Freeland.

Flynn, Errol (1909–1959). Tasmanian leading man who led an adventurous life on and off screen and by his handsome impudence maintained a world-wide following for nearly twenty years before hard living got the better of him. Wrote two autobiographical books, *Beam Ends* 34 and *My Wicked Wicked Ways* 59, and a novel, *Showdown*.
□ Murder at Monte Carlo (GB) 34. The Case of the Curious Bride 34. Don't Bet on Blondes 35. *Captain Blood* 35. *The Charge of the Light Brigade* 36. The Green Light 36. The Prince and the Pauper 37. Another Dawn 37. The Perfect Specimen 37. *The Adventures of Robin Hood* 38. Four's a Crowd 38. The Sisters 38. *The Dawn Patrol* 38. Dodge City 39. Elizabeth and Essex 39. Virginia City 39. *The Sea Hawk* 40. Santa Fe Trail 40. Footsteps in the Dark 41. Dive Bomber 41. *They Died with Their Boots On* 41. Desperate Journey 42. *Gentleman Jim* 42. Edge of Darkness 43. Northern Pursuit 43. Thank Your Lucky Stars 43. Uncertain Glory 44. Objective Burma 45. San Antonio 45. Never Say Goodbye 45. Cry Wolf 46. Escape Me Never 47. Silver River 47. The New Adventures of Don Juan 48. *That Forsyte Woman* (as Soames) 49. Montana 50. Rocky Mountain 50. Kim 51. The Adventures of Captain Fabian (& w) 51. Mara Maru 52. Against All Flags 52. The Master of Ballantrae (GB) 53. Crossed Swords (It.) 53. Lilacs in the Spring (GB) 55. The Dark Avenger

(GB) 55. King's Rhapsody (GB) 56. The Big Boodle 56. Istanbul 57. The Sun Also Rises 57. *Too Much Too Soon* (as John Barrymore) 58. Roots of Heaven 58. Cuban Rebel Girls 59.

Flynn, Joe (1925–74). American character comedian, much on TV.
Did You Hear the One about the Travelling Saleslady? 68. Million Dollar Duck 71. Superdad 74, etc.

Foch, Nina (1924–). Cool, Blonde, Dutch-born actress, long in America.
The Return of the Vampire (debut) 43. Nine Girls 43. Cry of the Werewolf 44. Shadows in the Night 44. A Song to Remember 44. I Love a Mystery 44. Prison Ship 45. *My Name Is Julia Ross* 46. Johnny o'Clock 46. The Guilt of Janet Ames 48. The Dark Past 49. Undercover Man 50. *An American in Paris* 51. Young Man with Ideas 51. Scaramouche 52. Fast Company 53. Sombrero 53. Executive Suite 54. You're Never Too Young 55. Illegal 55. The Ten Commandments 56. Three Brave Men 57. Spartacus 60. Cash McCall 60. Such Good Friends 71. Mahogany 76, etc.

fog has been a godsend to many a cinematic entertainment, whether it's the genuine pea-souper inseparable from Hollywood's idea of London, or the ankle-high white mist which used to distinguish heaven and dream sequences. Fog can provide a splendid dramatic background, especially in horror-thrillers like *Dracula, The Wolf Man* and *The Cat and the Canary*; but too often it is simply imposed on a film to force a particular atmosphere, as in *Footsteps in the Fog, Fog over Frisco, Fog Island, Winterset, Out of the Fog* and *The Notorious Landlady. Barbary Coast* seemed to be permanently enveloped in fog, as did the village in *Sherlock Holmes and the Scarlet Claw*: while in *The Adventures of Sherlock Holmes* London had fog in May! Fog was dramatically used in *The VIPs* and *The Divorce of Lady X* (for bringing people together in a hotel); in *The Runaway Bus* (for bringing people together in an abandoned village); in *Midnight Lace* (for masking the identity of the voice threatening Doris Day); in *Twenty-Three Paces to Baker Street* (for hampering the villain but not the blind hero); in *Alias Nick Beal* (as a background for the devil's materialization); in *The Lost Continent* (as a nauseous yellow background for the weird community); in *Random Harvest* (as a means for the hero's escape); and in the various versions of *The Sea Wolf* (for causing the accident that brings hero and heroine together on Wolf Larsen's boat). Even comedies find it useful: the chase through

fog in *After the Fox* results in happy confusion.

Folies Bergère. This innocuous 1935 musical comedy was written by Bess Meredith and Hal Long as a vehicle for Maurice Chevalier, who played a dual role; at the climax his double had to masquerade to his wife as himself. It was too good an idea not to be used again. In 1941 came *That Night in Rio* with Don Ameche; in 1951 *On the Riviera* with Danny Kaye. Kaye apparently liked it so much that he had it altered a little and it served for *On The Double* 61, as well.

Folsey, George J. (1898–). American cinematographer.
The Fear Market 20. Born Rich 24. *Applause* 29. The Smiling Lieutenant 31. Reckless 35. *The Great Ziegfeld* 36. The Shining Hour 38. Lady Be Good 41. Meet Me in St Louis 44. A Guy Named Joe 44. Under the Clock 45. The Green Years 46. Green Dolphin Street 47. State of the Union 48. Take Me Out to the Ball Game 48. The Great Sinner 49. *Adam's Rib* 49. Man with a Cloak 51. Million Dollar Mermaid 53. Executive Suite 54. Seven Brides for Seven Brothers 55. The Fastest Gun Alive 56. Imitation General 58. I Passed for White 60. The Balcony 63, etc.

Fonda, Henry (1905–). American leading actor who used to play gauche young fellows and graduated to roles of amiable wisdom. Long stage experience; father of Jane and Peter Fonda. □ The Farmer Takes a Wife 35. Way Down East 35. I Dream Too Much 36. The Trail of the Lonesome Pine 36. *The Moon's Our Home* 36. Spendthrift 36. Wings of the Morning (GB) 37. You Only Live Once 37. Slim 37. That Certain Woman 37. I Met My Love Again 37. Jezebel 38. Blockade 38. Spawn of the North 38. The Mad Miss Manton 38. Jesse James 39. Let Us Live 39. The Story of Alexander Graham Bell 39. *Young Mr Lincoln* 39. Drums Along the Mohawk 39. *The Grapes of Wrath* 40. Lilian Russell 40. The Return of Frank James 40. Chad Hanna 40. *The Lady Eve* 41. Wild Geese Calling 41. You Belong to Me 41. The Male Animal 42. Rings on Her Fingers 42. *The Ox Bow Incident* 42. The Big Street 42. Tales of Manhattan 42. The Magnificent Dope 42. The Immortal Sergeant 42; war service; *My Darling Clementine* (as Wyatt Earp) 46. The Long Night 47. The Fugitive 47. Daisy Kenyon 47. On Our Merry Way 48. Fort Apache 48; long absence on stage; Mister Roberts 55. The Wrong Man 56. War and Peace 56. *Twelve Angry Men* (BFA) (& p) 57. *Stage Struck* 57. The Tin Star 57. Warlock 59. The Man Who Understood Women 59. Advise and Consent 61. The Longest Day 62. How the West Was Won 62. Spencer's

Mountain 63. The Best Man 64. *Fail Safe* 64. The Dirty Game 64. Sex and the Single Girl 64. The Battle of the Bulge 65. The Rounders 65. In Harm's Way 65. Big Hand for a Little Lady 66. Welcome to Hard Times 67. Firecreek 67. Madigan 68. Yours, Mine and Ours 68. The Boston Strangler 68. Once upon a Time in the West 69. Too Late the Hero 69. There Was a Crooked Man 70. The Cheyenne Social Club 70. Sometimes a Great Notion 71. The Red Pony (TV) 72. The Serpent 72. The Alpha Caper (TV) 73. Ash Wednesday 73. My Name is Nobody (It.) 73. Midway 76.
TV series: The Deputy 59–60. The Smith Family 70–71.

Fonda, Jane (1937–). American leading lady, daughter of Henry Fonda. Stage and modelling experience.
□ Tall Story (debut) 60. Walk on the Wild Side 61. The Chapman Report 62. Period of Adjustment 62. In the Cool of the Day 63. Sunday in New York 63. La Ronde 64. Joy House 65. Cat Ballou 65. The Chase 66. Any Wednesday 66. The Game is Over (Fr.) 66. Hurry Sundown 67. Barefoot in the Park 67. Histoires Extraordinaires 67. Barbarella 68. They Shoot Horses Don't They? 69. *Klute* (AA) 71. Steelyard Blues 72. A Doll's House 74. Fun with Dick and Jane 76. Julia 77.

Fonda, Peter (1939–). American actor, son of Henry Fonda.
Tammy and the Doctor 63. The Victors 63. Lilith 64. The Wild Angels 66. The Trip 67. *Easy Rider* (& p) 69. The Last Movie 71. The Hired Hand (& d) 71. Two People 73. Dirty Mary Crazy Larry 74. Open Season 74. Race with the Devil 75. Fighting Mad 76, etc.

Fontaine, Joan (1917–) (Joan de Havilland; sister of Olivia). British-born leading actress, in America from childhood. Became typed as a shy English rose; later made efforts to play sophisticated roles.
□ No More Ladies 35. Quality Street 37. You Can't Beat Love 37. Music for Madame 37. Maid's Night Out 38. A Damsel in Distress 38. Blonde Cheat 38. The Man Who Found Himself 38. The Duke of West Point 38. Sky Giant 38. Gunga Din 39. Man of Conquest 39. The Women 39. *Rebecca* 40. *Suspicion* (AA) 41. This Above All 42. The Constant Nymph 43. *Jane Eyre* 43. *Frenchman's Creek* 44. The Affairs of Susan 45. *From This Day Forward* 46. Ivy 47. The Emperor Waltz 48. Kiss the Blood off My Hands 48. *Letter from an Unknown Woman* 48. You Gotta Stay Happy 48. Born To Be Bad 50. September Affair 50. Darling How

Could You? 51. Something To Live For 52. Ivanhoe 52. Decameron Nights (GB) 53. Flight to Tangier 53. The Bigamist 53. Casanova's Big Night 54. Serenade 56. Beyond a Reasonable Doubt 56. Island in the Sun 56. Until They Sail 57. A Certain Smile 58. Tender Is the Night 61. Voyage to the Bottom of the Sea 61. The Devil's Own (The Witches) (GB) 66.

Fontanne, Lynn (1887–). Celebrated British-born stage actress, long in America and the wife of Alfred Lunt. Never really took to the screen.
□ Second Youth 26. The Guardsman 32. Stage Door Canteen 43.

Foolish Wives (US 1921). Most typical of Erich Von Stroheim's extravagant, over-charged sex dramas, this tragi-farce is set on the Riviera where a family of swindlers prey on rich women. Stroheim wrote, directed, and gives a rapacious performance. Photographer William Daniels.

footage. Length of a film expressed in feet.

Foran, Dick (1910–) (Nicholas Foran). Burly American leading man of light comedies and westerns in the early forties; often played the good guy who didn't get the girl.
Stand Up and Cheer 34. Shipmates Forever 35. The Petrified Forest 36. The Perfect Specimen 37. Four Daughters 38. Daughters Courageous 39. The Mummy's Hand 40. Horror Island 41. Butch Minds the Baby 42. He's My Guy 43. Guest Wife 45. Fort Apache 48. El Paso 49. Al Jennings of Oklahoma 51. Chicago Confidential 57. Atomic Submarine 60. Taggart 64, many others.

Forbes, Bryan (1926–) (John Clarke). Lively British small-part actor who became a useful scriptwriter, director and production executive.
□ AS ACTOR: The Small Back Room 48. All Over the Town 48. Dear Mr Prohack 49. The Wooden Horse 50. Green Grow the Rushes 51. Appointment in London 52. Sea Devils 53. Wheel of Fate 53. The Million Pound Note 54. *An Inspector Calls* 54. Up to his Neck 54. The Colditz Story 54. Passage Home 55. Now and Forever 55. The Quatermass Experiment 55. The Last Man to Hang 55. The Extra Day 56. It's Great to be Young 56. The Baby and the Battleship 56. Satellite in the Sky 56. Quatermass II 57. The Key 58. I Was Monty's Double 58. Yesterday's Enemy 59. *The League of Gentlemen* 59. The Guns of Navarone 61. A Shot in the Dark 64.
□ AS WRITER/PRODUCER/DIRECTOR: Cockleshell Heroes (w) 56. The Baby and the Battleship (w) 56. The Black Tent (w) 56. House

of Secrets (w) 56. *I Was Monty's Double* (w) 58. The Captain's Table (w) 59. The Angry Silence (w) 59.*The League of Gentlemen* (w) 60. Man in the Moon (w) 60. *Whistle down the Wind* (d) 61. *Only Two Can Play* (w) 62. Station Six Sahara (w) 62. *The L-Shaped Room* (wd) 62. Of Human Bondage (w) 64. The High Bright Sun (w) 64. Seance on a Wet Afternoon (w) 64. King Rat (wd) 65. The Wrong Box (pd) 66. *The Whisperers* (wd) 67. Deadfall (wd) 67. The Madwoman of Chaillot (d) 69. The Raging Moon (wd) 70. The Stepford Wives (d) 74. The Slipper and the Rose (wd) 76.

Forbes, Mary (1882–1974). British character actress in Hollywood, usually as haughty society lady.
Sunny Side Up 29. A Farewell to Arms 32. Blonde Bombshell 33. Les Misérables 35. Wee Willie Winkie 37. The Awful Truth 37. Always Goodbye 38. You Can't Take It With You 38. The Adventures of Sherlock Holmes 40. This Above All 42. The Picture of Dorian Gray 44. Ivy 47. You Gotta Stay Happy 48. The Ten Commandments 56, many others.

Forbes, Meriel (1913–) (M. Forbes-Robertson). British stage actress, wife of Sir Ralph Richardson.
Borrow a Million 35. Young Man's Fancy 39. The Gentle Sex 43. The Captive Heart 46. Home at Seven 52.

Forbes, Ralph (1902–1951). British leading man who became a Hollywood star in the late twenties.
The Fifth Form at St Dominics (GB) 21. Beau Geste 26. Mr Wu 29. The Trail of '98 30. Bachelor Father 31. Smilin' Through 32. The Barretts of Wimpole Street 33. The Three Musketeers 36. Romeo and Juliet 36. If I Were King 39. Elizabeth and Essex 39. Frenchman's Creek 44, etc.

Forbidden Paradise (US 1924). Ernst Lubitsch's famous touch was here applied to the love life of Catherine the Great of Russia, as personified by Pola Negri. A milestone in satire, it was not well served by Lubitsch's own sound remake, *A Royal Scandal* (1945).

Forbidden Planet (US 1956). One of the few science-fiction romps to win critical acclaim, this lively futuristic comic strip, directed by Fred M. Wilcox, was actually a reworking of *The Tempest*, with Walter Pidgeon as Morbius/Prospero fighting monsters from his own *id*. His tame robot Robby also appeared in *The Invisible Boy* 57, and reappeared in a 60s TV series, *Lost in Space*.

Force of Evil (US 1949). A fascinating and influential little thriller about the numbers racket, written and directed by Abraham Polonsky, who was then lost to Hollywood because of the red witch hunt. Photographed by George Barnes; starring John Garfield.

Ford, Alexander (1908–). Polish director who has been making films since 1930. Best known abroad: *The Young Chopin* 51. *Five Boys from Barska Street* 53. *Knights of the Teutonic Order* 60.

Ford, Cecil (1911–). Former Irish actor who turned production manager on some notable films: *Moby Dick* 56. *Around the World in Eighty Days* 57. *The Bridge on the River Kwai* 57. *The Inn of the Sixth Happiness* 58. Produced *The Guns of Navarone* 61. *633 Squadron* 64, others.

Ford, Constance (1929–). American general purpose actress of the fifties.
The Last Hunt 56. A Summer Place 59. Home from the Hill 60. Claudelle Inglish 61. All Fall Down 62. The Cabinet of Caligari 62. The Caretaker 63, etc.

Ford, Francis (1883–1953) (Francis O'Feeney). American character actor, often seen as grizzled, cheery westerner.
In silents and also: Charlie Chan's Greatest Case 33. The Informer 35. Prisoner of Shark Island 36. In Old Chicago 38. Drums across the Mohawk 39. Lucky Cisco Kid 40. The Ox-Bow Incident 42. The Big Noise 44. My Darling Clementine 46. Wagonmaster 50. The Sun Shines Bright 52, many others.

Ford, Glenn (1916–) (Gwyllyn Ford). Stocky Canadian-born star of Hollywood dramas; from the early forties he radiated integrity and determination, and continued his stardom into tortured middle-aged roles.
□ Heaven with a Barbed Wire Fence 39. My Son is Guilty 39. Convicted Woman 40. Men Without Souls 40. Babies for Sale 40. Blondie Plays Cupid 40. The Lady in Question 40. So Ends Our Night 41. Texas 41. Go West Young Lady 41. The Adventures of Martin Eden 42. Flight Lieutenant 42. The Desperadoes 43. Destroyer 43. Gilda 46. A Stolen Life 46. Framed 47. The Mating of Millie 48. The Loves of Carmen 48. The Return of October 48. The Man from Colorado 48. The Undercover Man 49. Mr Soft Touch 49. Lust for Gold 49.The Doctor and the Girl 49. The White Tower 50.

Convicted 50. The Redhead and the Cowboy 50. The Flying Missile 50. Follow the Sun 51. The Secret of Convict Lake 51. The Green Glove 52. Affair in Trinidad 52. Young Man with Ideas 52. Time Bomb 53. The Man from the Alamo 53. Plunder of the Sun 53. *The Big Heat* 53. Appointment in Honduras 53. Human Desire 54. The Americano 55. The Violent Men 55. *The Blackboard Jungle* 55. Interrupted Melody 55. Trial 55. Ransom 56. Jubal 56. *The Fastest Gun Alive* 56. The Teahouse of the August Moon 56. *3.10 to Yuma* 57. Don't Go Near the Water 57. Cowboy 58. *The Sheepman* 58. Imitation General 58. Torpedo Run 58. It Started with a Kiss 59. The Gazebo 59. Cimarron 60. Cry for Happy 61. Pocketful of Miracles 61. The Four Horsemen of the Apocalypse 62. Experiment in Terror 62. Love is a Ball 63. The Courtship of Eddie's Father 63. Advance to the Rear 64. Fate is the Hunter 64. Dear Heart 64. The Rounders 65. The Money Trap 66. Is Paris Burning 66. Rage 67. The Last Challenge 67. A Time for Killing 67. Day of the Evil Gun 68. Heaven with a Gun 69. Smith! 69. Brotherhood of the Bell (TV) 70. Santee 73. Jarrett (TV) 73. The Disappearance of Flight 412 74. The Greatest Gift (TV) 75.
TV series: *Cade's County* 71. Holvak 75. Once an Eagle (TV) 76.

Ford, John (1895–1973) (Sean O'Feeney). Distinguished Irish American director who from 1917 made over 125 features, many of them silent westerns. In the thirties he built up to a handful of incomparable human dramas; in the forties he turned towards roving, brawling, good-natured outdoor action films using a repertory of his favourite actors. His best films are milestones, but he disclaimed any artistic pretensions.
SELECTED SILENT FILMS: The Tornado 17. A Woman's Fool 18. Bare Fists 19. The Wallop 21. Silver Wings 22. The Face on the Bar Room Floor 23. *The Iron Horse* 24. Lightnin' 25. Three Bad Men 26. Four Sons 28. Mother Machree 28. Riley the Cop 28. Strong Boy 29.
□ SOUND FILMS: Black Watch 29. Salute 29. *Men Without Women* 30. Born Reckless 30. Up the River 30. The Seas Beneath 30. The Brat 31. *Arrowsmith* 31. Air Mail 32. Flesh 32. Pilgrimage 33. Doctor Bull 33. *The Lost Patrol* 34. The World Moves On 34. *Judge Priest* 34. The Whole Town's Talking 35. The Informer (AA) 35. *Steamboat Round the Bend* 35. Prisoner of Shark Island 36. Mary of Scotland 36. The Plough and the Stars 36. Wee Willie Winkie 37. *The Hurricane* 37. Four Men and a Prayer 38. Submarine Patrol 38. *Stagecoach* 39. *Young Mr Lincoln* 39. *Drums Along the Mohawk* 39. *The Grapes of Wrath* (AA) 40. The

Long Voyage Home 40. *Tobacco Road* 41. *How Green Was My Valley* (AA) 41. Why We Fight and other war documentaries 42–45. They Were Expendable 45. *My Darling Clementine* 46. The Fugitive 47. Fort Apache 48. Three Godfathers 48. *She Wore A Yellow Ribbon* 49. When Willie Comes Marching Home 50. Wagonmaster 50. Rio Grande 50. This is Korea 51. *The Quiet Man* 52. What Price Glory? 52. Mogambo 53. *The Shines Bright* 54. The Long Gray Line 55. Mister Roberts 55. *The Searchers* 56. The Wings of Eagles 57. The Rising of the Moon 57. *The Last Hurrah* 58. Gideon's Day 59. The Horse Soldiers 59. Sergeant Rutledge 60. Two Rode Together 61. The Man Who Shot Liberty Valance 62. How the West Was Won (part) 63. Donovan's Reef 63. Cheyenne Autumn 64. Young Cassidy (part) 64. Seven Women 66.

Ford, Paul (1901–1976). American character actor best known on TV as the harassed colonel in the Bilko series and star of *The Baileys of Balboa*.
The House on 92nd Street 45. Lust for Gold 49. Perfect Strangers 50. *The Teahouse of the August Moon* 56. The Matchmaker 58. Advise and Consent 61. *The Music Man* 62. *Never Too Late* 65. Big Hand for a Little Lady 66. The Russians Are Coming, The Russians Are Coming 66. The Spy with a Cold Nose (GB) 67. The Comedians 67, etc.

Ford, Wallace (1897–1966) (Sam Grundy). British general purpose actor who went to Hollywood in the early thirties and after a few semi-leads settled into character roles.
Freaks 32. Lost Patrol 34. *The Informer* 35. OHMS (GB) 36. The Mummy's Hand 40. Inside the Law 42. Shadow of a Doubt 43. The Green Years 46. Embraceable You 48. *Harvey* 50. The Nebraskan 53. Destry 55. Johnny Concho 56. The Last Hurrah 58. A Patch of Blue 66, etc.

Forde, Eugene (1898–). American director of second features, former silent screen actor.
Charlie Chan in London 33. Buy Me That Town 41. Berlin Correspondent 42. Jewels of Brandenberg 46. Invisible Wall 47, Many others.

Forde, Walter (1896–) (Thomas Seymour). British director, formerly a popular slapstick comedian of the silents: *Wait and See, Would You Believe It*, many shorts, one of which was featured in *Helter Skelter* 49. Directed some high-speed farces and several thrillers and melodramas.
The Silent House 28. Lord Richard in the Pantry 30. *The Ghost Train* 31. Jack's the Boy 32. *Rome Express* 32. Orders Is Orders 33. Jack Ahoy 34.

Chu Chin Chow 34. *Bulldog Jack* 35. King of the Damned 35. Land Without Music 36. The Gaunt Stranger 38. The Four Just Men 39. Inspector Hornleigh on Holiday 39. *Saloon Bar* 40. Sailors Three 40. The Ghost Train 41. Atlantic Ferry 41. Charley's Big-Hearted Aunt 41. *It's That Man Again* 42. Time Flies 44. Master of Bankdam 47. Cardboard Cavalier 48, many others.

Foreign Correspondent (US 1940). Hitchcock's first American thriller, a welcome return to his best form apart from the final message: 'Don't let the lights go out all over Europe!' Splendid moments in a Dutch windmill, a crashing aeroplane, and Westminster Cathedral.

the foreign legion has been taken reasonably seriously in the three versions of *Beau Geste*, the two versions of *Le Grand Jeu, Beau Sabreur, China Gate, Rogue's Regiment, Ten Tall Men,* and *The Legion's Last Patrol.* It was sent up something wicked by Laurel and Hardy in *Beau Hunks* and *The Flying Deuces*; by Abbott and Costello *In the Foreign Legion*; and by the Carry On gang in *Follow That Camel.*

Foreman, Carl (1914–). American writer-producer-director, latterly resident in Britain.
So This Is New York (w) 48. The Clay Pigeon (w) 49. Home of the Brave (w) 49. *Champion* (w) 49. The Men (w) 50. Cyrano de Bergerac (w) 50. *High Noon* (w) 52. *The Bridge on the River Kwai* (w) 57. The Key (wp) 58. *The Guns of Navarone* (wp) 61. The Victors (wpd) 63. Born Free (p) 65. Mackenna's Gold (p) 68. The Virgin Soldiers (p) 69. Young Winston (wp) 72.

Forest, Mark (1933–) (Lou Degni). American athlete and gymnast who has appeared in many Italian muscle-man epics.
The Revenge of Hercules, Maciste in the Valley of Kings, Goliath and the Giant, etc.

forest fires have made a roaring climax for many films including *The Blazing Forest, Red Skies of Montana, Guns of the Timberland, The Bluebird, The Big Trees* and *Ring of Fire.* None was more dramatic than the cartoon version in *Bambi.*

Forester, C. S. (1899–1966). British adventure novelist. Works filmed include *Captain Horatio Hornblower, The African Queen, Payment Deferred, The Pride and the Passion* ('The Gun').

Forever and a Day (US 1942). Originally conceived as a World War II charity appeals film called *Let the Rafters Ring*, this all-star production finally consisted of episodes in the life of an English family (and their house) from 1804 to 1942. Many hands were involved in the script, and there was a different director for each episode: René Clair, Edmund Goulding, Cedric Hardwicke, Frank Lloyd, Victor Saville, Robert Stevenson, Herbert Wilcox. Almost every Hollywood-based actor with English connections took part.

Forman, Milos (1932–). Czech director of realistic comedies.
□ Peter and Pavla 64. *A Blonde in Love* 65. The Fireman's Ball 68. *Taking Off* (US) 71. *One Flew Over the Cuckoo's Nest* 75.

Formby, George (1905–1961) (George Booth). Lancashire comedian with a toothy grin and a ukelele, long popular in music halls.
□ Boots Boots (debut) 33. On the Dole 34. *No Limit* 35. *Keep Your Seats Please* 36. Feather Your Nest 37. *Keep Fit* 37. I See Ice 38. *It's in the Air* 38. Trouble Brewing 39. Come On, George 39. *Let George Do It* 40. Spare a Copper 41. Turned Out Nice Again 41. South American George (dual role) 42. Much Too Shy 42. Get Cracking 43. Bell-Bottom George 43. He Snoops To Conquer 44. I Didn't Do It 45. George in Civvy Street 46.

Forrest, Frederic (–). American leading man of the seventies.
□ Where the Legends Die 72. The Don is Dead 74. The Conversation 74. The Gravy Train 74. Permission to Kill 75.

Forrest, Sally (1928–) (Katharine Scully Feeney). American leading lady of the early fifties.
Not Wanted 49. Mystery Street 50. Never Fear 50. Hard Fast and Beautiful 51. Excuse My Dust 51. The Strange Door 51. The Strip 51. Son of Sinbad 55. Ride the High Iron 57, etc.

Forrest, Steve (1924–) (William Forrest Andrews). American leading man, brother of Dana Andrews.
The Bad and the Beautiful 52. Phantom of the Rue Morgue 54. Prisoner of War 54. Bedevilled 55. The Living Idol 57. Heller in Pink Tights 60. The Yellow Canary 63. Rascal 69. The Wild Country 71. Wanted the Sundance Woman (TV) 76, etc.
TV series: The Baron 65. S.W.A.T. 74–5.

Forst, Willi (1903–) (Wilhelm Frohs). Austrian director.

Maskerade 34. Bel Ami 39. etc.

Forster, Robert (1942–). Sardonic-looking American leading man with echoes of John Garfield.
□ *Reflections in a Golden Eye* 67. The Stalking Moon 68. Justine 69. Medium Cool 69. Pieces of Dreams 70. Cover Me Babe 72.
TV series: *Banyon* 72.

Forster, Rudolph (1884–1968). German leading actor of heavy personality, seen abroad chiefly in *Die Dreigroschenoper* (*The Threepenny Opera*; as Macheath) 32.

Forsyth, Bruce (1921–). Bouncy, beaming, British TV comedian whose film appearances have been scant.
□ Star! 68. Hieronymus Merkin 69. The Magnificent Seven Deadly Sins 71. Bedknobs and Broomsticks 71.

Forsyth, Rosemary (1944–). American leading actress.
Shenandoah (debut) 65. The War Lord 65. Texas Across the River 66. Where It's At 69. Whatever Happened to Aunt Alice? 69. How Do I Love Thee? 70. City Beneath the Sea (TV) 71. One Little Indian 73. Black Eye 74, etc.

Forsythe, John (1918–) (John Freund). Smooth American leading man with Broadway experience.
Destination Tokyo 43. Captive City 52. Escape from Fort Bravo 53. The Trouble with Harry 56. *The Ambassador's Daughter* 56. See How They Run (TV) 64. Kitten with a Whip 65. Madame X 66. In Cold Blood 67. Topaz 69. The Happy Ending 69. Murder Once Removed (TV) 71. The Healers (TV) 75, etc.
TV series: Bachelor Father 57–62. The John Forsythe Show 65. To Rome with Love 69.

Forty-Ninth Parallel (GB 1941). Producer-director team Michael Powell and Emeric Pressburger made this impressive all-star propaganda piece about a stranded submarine-load of Nazis on the run through Canada. Laurence Olivier, Leslie Howard and Anton Walbrook starred as assorted democrats; Eric Portman leapt to stardom as the chief Nazi.

Forty-Second Street (US 1933). Classic 'putting-on-a-show' musical from Hollywood's 'golden age', with a genuine backstage atmosphere and a fairly caustic script. Music by Al Dubin and Harry Warren; directed by Lloyd Bacon with a cast including Warner Baxter, Ruby Keeler, Dick Powell, Ginger Rogers and Bebe Daniels.

For Whom the Bell Tolls (US) 1943). Ernest Hemingway's novel about an American living with guerillas during the Spanish Civil War, and sacrificing his life for their cause, was made by Sam Wood into a disappointingly tedious and self-satisfied film in which the whole cast struck unconvincing attitudes, mostly in broken English. Katina Paxinou won an Oscar for her performance; Gary Cooper and Ingrid Bergman seemed to wish they were elsewhere. The basic situation, incidentally, was borrowed ten years later by a Sterling Hayden second feature called *Fighter Attack*.

Fosse, Bob (1927–). American dancer who became a Broadway director.
□ Give a Girl a Break 52. The Affairs of Dobie Gillis 52. Kiss Me Kate 53. My Sister Eileen (& c) 55. *The Pajama Game* (choreographed only) 57. Damn Yankees (ch only) 58. *Sweet Charity* (directed and choreographed) 68. *Cabaret* (dc) (AA) 72. Lenny (d) 74. The Little Prince (a only) 75.

Fossey, Brigitte (1945–). French juvenile actress of the fifties.
Jeux Interdits 52. Le Grand Meaulnes 55. Adieu L'Ami 60. M Comme Mathieu 71, etc.

Foster, Barry (1931–). British light actor, usually figuring as comic relief.
Sea of Sand 56. Yesterday's Enemy 59. King and Country 64. The Family Way 66. Robbery 67. Twisted Nerve 68. Ryan's Daughter 70. Frenzy 72. Divorce His Divorce Hers (TV) 73, etc.

Foster, Dianne (1928–) (D. Laruska). Canadian leading lady who has made British and American films.
The Quiet Woman (GB) 51. Isn't Life Wonderful? (GB) 53. Drive a Crooked Road (US) 54. The Kentuckian (US) 55. The Brothers Rico (US) 57. Gideon's Day (GB) 58. The Last Hurrah (US) 58. King of the Roaring Twenties (US) 61. Who's Been Sleeping in My Bed (US) 63, etc.

Foster, Jodie (1962–). American child actress who has been precociously cast.
Tom Sawyer 73, One Little Indian 73. *Alice Doesn't Live Here Any More* 74. *Bugsy Malone* 76. *Taxi Driver* 76. The Little Girl Who Lives Down the Lane 76. Candleshoe 77. Freaky Friday 77, etc.

Foster, Julia (1941–). British leading lady.
The Small World of Sammy Lee 63. Two Left Feet 63. The System 64. The Bargee 64. One-Way Pendulum 64. Alfie 66. Half a Sixpence 67. All Coppers Are 72, etc.

Foster, Lewis (1899–1974). American director, former Hal Roach gag writer.
The Lucky Stiff (& w) 48. Manhandled (& w) 49. Captain China 49. The Eagle and the Hawk (& w) 40. Crosswinds 51. Those Redheads from Seattle (& w) 53. Top of the World 55. The Bold and the Brave 56. Tonka (& w) 58, etc.

Foster, Norman (1900–1976). American leading man of the early thirties; became a director and had a rather patchy career.
Gentlemen of the Press 29. It Pays to Advertise 31. Reckless Living 31. Alias the Doctor 32. Skyscraper Souls 32. State Fair 33. Professional Sweetheart 33. Orient Express 34. Behind the Green Lights 35. High Tension 36. I Cover Chinatown (& d) 36.
□ DIRECTED ONLY:
Fair Warning 37. Think Fast Mr Moto 37. Thank You Mr Moto 37. Walking Down Broadway 38. Mysterious Mr Moto 38. Mr Moto's Last Warning 39. Charlie Chan in Reno 39. Mr Moto Takes a Vacation 39. *Charlie Chan at Treasure Island* 39. Charlie Chan in Panama 40. Viva Cisco Kid 40. Ride Kelly Ride 41. Scotland Yard 41. *Journey Into Fear* 42. Rachel and the Stranger 48. Kiss the Blood off My Hands 48. Tell It to the Judge 49. Father is a Bachelor 50. Woman on the Run 50. Navajo 52. Sky Full of Moon 52. Sombrero 53. Davy Crockett 55. The Sign of Zorro 60. Indian Paint 66. Brighty 67.

Foster, Preston (1901–1970). Handsome American leading man of the thirties, former clerk and singer.
Nothing But the Truth (debut) 30. Life Begins 31. *The Last Mile* 31. Wharf Angel 34. The Informer 35. The Last Days of Pompeii 35. Annie Oakley 36. The Plough and the Stars 37. First Lady 38. News Is Made at Night 38. Geronimo 39. Moon over Burma 40. Northwest Mounted Police 40. Unfinished Business 41. Secret Agent of Japan 42. My Friend Flicka 43. The Bermuda Mystery 44. The Valley of Decision 45. The Last Gangster 45. The Harvey Girls 46. Ramrod 47. Green Grass of Wyoming 48. Tomahawk 49. The Tougher They Come 51. The Big Night 52. Kansas City Confidential 53. I the Jury 55. Destination 60,000 58. Advance to the Rear 64. The Time Travellers 65. Chubasco 68, many others.
TV series: Waterfront 54–56. Gunslinger 60.

Foster, Stephen (1826–1864). American songwriter of popular sentimental ballads: 'Old Folks at Home', 'Beautiful Dreamer', etc. Impersonated on screen by Douglass Montgomery in *Harmony Lane* 35, Don Ameche in *Swanee River* 39, and Bill Shirley in *I Dream of Jeannie* 52.

Foster, Susanna (1924–) (Suzan Larsen). American operatic singer and heroine of several forties films.
The Great Victor Herbert 40. *There's Magic in Music* 41. The Hard Boiled Canary 42. Top Man 43. *Phantom of the Opera* 43. The Climax 44. Bowery to Broadway 44. This Is the Life 44. Frisco Sal 45. That Night with You 45, etc.

Foulger, Byron (1900–1970). American small-part actor, the prototype of the worried, bespectacled clerk.
The Prisoner of Zenda 37. Edison the Man 40. Sullivan's Travels 41. Since You Went Away 44. Champagne for Caesar 49. The Magnetic Monster 53. The Long Hot Summer 59. The Gnome-Mobile 67, innumerable others.

Four Daughters. The three Lane sisters and Gale Page appeared as Claude Rains' musical daughters in this dollop of sweetness and light which despite its computerized script was a big hit in 1938. It can be credited with introducing the angry-young-man hero, and at the same time a new actor, John Garfield. All these components were reproduced the following year in a film called *Daughters Courageous* which however dealt with different people in a different milieu; the original characters then reappeared in *Four Wives* 39 and *Four Mothers* 40. *Four Sons* 40 was something else again, an anti-Nazi propaganda piece about the break-up of a German family. In 1955 the original *Four Daughters* was remade as a semi-musical, *Young at Heart*, with Doris Day and Frank Sinatra.

The Four Feathers. A. E. W. Mason's novel of the old Empire, with heroism and cowardice in the Sudan after General Gordon's death, was magnificently filmed by Alexander Korda in 1939, with John Clements and Ralph Richardson. Much of the same footage reappeared in Zoltan Korda's 1955 remake *Storm over the Nile*, stretched into CinemaScope and not improved thereby. (The action scenes have also been used in several other films, e.g. *Zarak* 57, *Master of the World* 61, *East of Sudan* 64.) There was a British silent version in 1921 starring Harry Ham and Cyril Perceval, and a Hollywood one in 1928 starring Richard Arlen and Clive Brook.

The Four Horsemen of the Apocalypse. In 1921 Rex Ingram directed a spectacular version of Ibanez' novel about love, war and death, notable for introducing Rudolph Valentino as a star. Vincente Minnelli remade it in 1962 with Glenn Ford and an updated script by Robert Ardrey and John Gay, but by now the entire conception seemed to belong to a Victorian novelette.

The Four Hundred Blows (France 1958). This influential 'new wave' film, written and directed by François Truffaut, was basically a moving account of a small boy's adventures in the big city while on the run from an unhappy home and school life. Henri Decae's location photography was masterly.

Four Steps in the Clouds (Italy 1942). A still enjoyable and historically significant step forward in Italian light realist comedy; a film full of sunshine and *joie de vivre* with little relation to the war then raging. Gino Cervi plays a young commuter who by a series of mischances spends twenty-four hours in complicated excitements before returning to his wife and family. Written by Giuseppe Amato, directed by Alessandro Blasetti.

Fourteen Hours (US) 1951). This suspenser, based on the real case of a man who stood on a ledge threatening suicide and defied police to come and get him, was well written (John Paxton from an article by Joel Sayre) and directed (Henry Hathaway); it seemed at the time to point to new profitable combinations of actuality and entertainment, though there was some over-dramatization and a happy outcome was substituted for the real tragic one. Richard Basehart was in his element as the unfortunate central figure.

Fowler, Gene (–). American writer, close friend of John Barrymore and author of his biography *Good Night Sweet Prince*.

Fowler, Gene Jnr (–). American director.
□ I Was a Teenage Werewolf 56. Gang War 58. Showdown at Boot Hill 58. I Married a Monster from Outer Space 59. Here Come the Jets 59. The Rebel Set 59. The Oregon Trail 59.

Fowler, Harry (1926–). British cockney actor on screen since the early forties, often in cameo roles.
Those Kids from Town 42. Champagne Charlie 44. Hue and Cry 46. For Them That Trespass 48. I Believe in You 52. Pickwick Papers 53. Home and Away 56. Idle on Parade 59. Ladies Who Do 63. Doctor in Clover 66, many others.
TV series: The Army Game, Our Man at St Mark's.

Fowley, Douglas (1911–). American character actor often seen as nervous or comic gangster.
Let's Talk it Over 34. Crash Donovan 36. Charlie Chan on Broadway 37. Mr Moto's Gamble 38. Dodge City 39. Ellery Queen Master Detective 40. Tanks a Million 41. Jitterbugs 42. The Kansan 43. One Body Too Many 44. The Hucksters 47. If You Knew Susie 48. Battleground 49. Edge of Doom 50. Criminal Lawyer 51. *Singin' in The Rain* (as the hysterical director) 52. The High and the Mighty 54. Macumba Love (p and d only) 59. Desire in the Dust 60. Barabbas 62, many others.
TV series: Pistols and Petticoats 67.

Fox, Edward (1937–). British leading man of the seventies.
The Naked Runner 67. The Long Duel 67. Oh What a Lovely War 69. Skullduggery 69. The Breaking of Bumbo 70. The Go-Between 71. *The Day of the Jackal* 73. Doll's House 73. The Cat and the Canary 77, etc.

Fox, James (1939–). British leading man, who usually plays a weakling. Once a child actor, notable in *The Magnet* 50 (as William Fox).
The Servant 63. Tamahine 64. Those Magnificent Men in Their Flying Machines 65. King Rat 65. The Chase 65. Thoroughly Modern Millie 67. Duffy 68. Isadora 68. Arabella 69. Performance 70, etc.

Fox, Sidney (1910–1942). American leading lady of the early thirties.
Bad Sister 31. The Mouthpiece 32. Once In a Lifetime 32. Murders in the Rue Morgue 32. Midnight 34, etc.

Fox, Wallace (1898–1958). American director.
The Amazing Vagabond 29. Cannonball Express 32. Powdersmoke Range 35. The Last of the Mohicans (co-d) 36. Racing Lady 37. Pride of the Plains 40. Bowery Blitzkrieg 41. Kid Dynamite 43. Riders of the Santa Fe 44. Mr Muggs Rides Again 45. Gunman's Code 46. Docks of New York 48. Six Gun Mesa 50. Montana Desperado 51, many others.

Fox, William (1879–1952) (W. Friedman). Hungarian-American pioneer and executive, the Fox of 20th Century Fox. Moved from the garment industry into exhibition, production and distribution. *Upton Sinclair Presents William Fox*, a biography, was published in 1933.

Foxwell, Ivan (1914–). British producer, in films since 1933.

No Room at the Inn 47. The Intruder 51. The Colditz Story 54. Manuela 56. A Touch of Larceny 59. Tiara Tahiti 62. The Quiller Memorandum 66. Decline and Fall (also wrote) 68, etc.

Foy, Bryan (1900–). American producer, mostly of low budgeters at Warner. Wrote song, 'Mr Gallagher & Mr Shean'.
The Home Towners (d) 28. Little Old New York (d) 28. The Gorilla (d) 31. Berlin Correspondent 42. Guadalcanal Diary 43. Doll Face 46. Trapped 49. Breakthrough 50. Inside the Walls of Folsom Prison 51. The Miracle of Fatima 52. *House of Wax* 53. The Mad Magician 54. Women's Prison 55. Blueprint for Robbery 61. PT 109 63, many others.

Foy, Eddie Jnr (1905–). American vaudeville entertainer, son of another and one of the 'seven little Foys'.
Fugitive from Justice 40. The Farmer Takes a Wife 53. Lucky Me 54. The Pajama Game 57. Bells Are Ringing 60. Thirty Is a Dangerous Age, Cynthia 67, etc.
TV series: Fair Exchange 63.

Foy, Eddie Snr (1854–1928) (Edward Fitzgerald). Famous American vaudeville comedian who made few film appearances but was several times impersonated by Eddie Foy Jnr: in *Yankee Doodle Dandy, Wilson, Bowery to Broadway*, etc. Bob Hope played him in *The Seven Little Foys*.
Films include A Favourite Fool 15.

Fraker, William A. (–). American cinematographer.
Games 67. The Fox 67. The President's Analyst 67. *Bullitt* 68. Rosemary's Baby 68. Paint Your Wagon 69. *Monte Walsh* (& d) 70. Day of the Dolphin 73, etc.

frame. A single picture on a strip of film. At normal sound projection speed, 24 frames are shown each second.

France's national film history falls into a pattern of clearly-defined styles. First of note was that of Louis Feuillade, whose early serials had tremendous panache. In the twenties came René Clair, with his inimitable touch for fantastic comedy, and a little later Jean Renoir, whose view of the human comedy was wider but equally sympathetic. Sacha Guitry contributed a series of rather stagey but amusing high comedies; Jean Vigo in his brief career introduced surrealism. Marcel Pagnol made a number of self-indulgent regional comedies which were hugely enjoyable but had little to do with cinema. Then beginning in the thirties came an unsurpassed group of adult entertainments from the writer-director team of Jacques Prevert and Marcel Carné; these were widely copied by less talented hands and the resulting stream of sex dramas, seldom less than competent, preserved the legend of the naughty French. Other notable directors were Julien Duvivier, the romantic; Jacques Becker, at his happiest in comedy; and Jacques Feyder, who generally made melodramas with flashes of insight. Henri-Georges Clouzot developed into the French Hitchcock, and Cocteau's art films reached a wide public. In the forties Robert Bresson, Rene Clement and Jacques Tati all began to make themselves felt. The fifties were in danger of becoming a dull period, with no new talent of note, when the 'new wave' (qv) changed the whole direction of French film-making and made some of the older hands look suddenly and undeservedly old-fashioned. Directors well-regarded in the sixties include Jacques Demy, François Truffaut, Jean-Luc Godard, Louis Malle, Jean-Pierre Melville, Claude Lelouch and Georges Franju.

Among French male stars of note are Raimu, Michel Simon, Harry Baur, Fernandel, Louis Jouvet, Jean Gabin, Pierre Fresnay, Jean-Louis Barrault, Gérard Philippe, Pierre Brasseur, Maurice Chevalier, Charles Boyer and Jean-Paul Belmondo. Of the women, the most influential have been Ginette Leclerc, Michele Morgan, Danielle Darrieux, Arletty, Simone Signoret, Brigitte Bardot, Jeanne Moreau, Françoise Dorleac and Catherine Deneuve.

France, C. V. (1868–1949). British stage character actor, most typically seen in films as dry lawyer or ageing head of household.
Lord Edgware Dies 35. Scrooge 35. Victoria the Great 37. A Yank at Oxford 38. If I Were King (US) 39. Night Train to Munich 40. Breach of Promise 41. The Halfway House 44, etc.

Francen, Victor (1888–). Belgian stage actor, occasionally in French films from 1921, but most familiar in Hollywood spy dramas during World War II.
Crepuscule d'Epouvante 21. Après l'Amour 31. Nuits de Feu 36. Le Roi 36. J'Accuse 38. Sacrifice d'Honneur 38. La Fin du Jour 39. Tales of Manhattan 42. Mission to Moscow 43. Devotion 43. The Mask of Dimitrios 44. The Conspirators 44. Passage to Marseilles 44. Confidential Agent 45. The Beast with Five Fingers 46. La Nuit s'achève 49. The Adventures of Captain Fabian 51. Hell and High Water 54. Bedevilled 55. A Farewell to Arms 58. Fanny 61. Top-Crack 66, many others.

Francis. The talking mule of several Universal comedies (1950–56) was the direct ancestor of TV's talking palomino *Mister Ed*, also produced by Arthur Lubin. Francis' first master was Donald O'Connor, but later Mickey Rooney took over the reins. Francis was 'voiced' by Allan Lane, Ed by Chill Wills.

Francis, Alec B. (c 1864–1934). British born character actor in Hollywood films as elderly gentleman.
Flame of the Desert 19. Smiling Through 22. Three Wise Fools 23. Charley's Aunt 25. Tramp Tramp Tramp 26. The Terror 28. Outward Bound 30. Arrowsmith 31. The Last Mile 32. Oliver Twist 33. Outcast Lady 34, many others.

Francis, Anne (1932–). American leading lady of several fifties films: formerly model, with radio and TV experience.
Summer Holiday (debut) 48. So Young So Bad 50. Elopement 52. Lydia Bailey 52. Susan Slept Here 54. Bad Day at Black Rock 54. The Blackboard Jungle 55. Forbidden Planet 56. Don't Go Near the Water 57. Girl of the Night 60. The Satan Bug 65. Funny Girl 68. The Love God 69. More Dead than Alive 70. Pancho Villa 71. Haunts of the Very Rich (TV) 72, etc.
TV series: Honey West 64.

Francis, Arlene (1908–). American TV personality who has appeared in a few films.
Stage Door Canteen 43. All My Sons 48. One Two Three 61. The Thrill of it All 63, etc.

Francis, Connie (1938–) (Constance Franconero). American pop singer who has had some light films built around her.
Where the Boys Are 63. Follow the Boys 64. Looking for Love 65, etc.

Francis, Freddie (1917–). British cinematographer who turned to direction with less distinguished results.
Mine Own Executioner 47. Time without Pity 57. Room at the Top 59. *Sons and Lovers* (AA) 60. The Innocents 61, etc.
AS DIRECTOR ONLY: Two and Two make Six 61. Vengeance 62. Paranoiac 63. Nightmare 63. The Evil of Frankenstein 64. Traitor's Gate 65. The Skull 65. The Deadly Bees 66. They Came from Beyond Space 66. The Torture Garden 67. Dracula has Risen from the Grave 68. Mumsy Nanny Sonny and Girlie 69. Tales from the Crypt 71. Asylum 72. Tales that Witness Madness 73. Legend of the Werewolf 74, etc.

Francis, Kay (1899–1968) (Katherine Gibbs).

Lady-like, serious-faced American star of women's films in the thirties.
□ Gentlemen of the Press 29. The Coconuts 29. Dangerous Curves 29. Illusion 29. The Marriage Playground 29. Behind the Makeup 30. *Street of Chance* 30. Paramount on Parade 30. A Notorious Affair 30. Raffles 30. For the Defence 30. Let's Go Native 30. The Virtuous Sin 30. Passion Flower 30. Scandal Sheet 31. Ladies' Man 31. The Vice Squad 31. Transgression 31. Guilty Hands 31. Twenty-Four Hours 31. Girls about Town 31. The False Madonna 32. Strangers in Love 32. Man Wanted 32. Street of Women 32. Jewel Robbery 32. *One Way Passage* 32. *Trouble in Paradise* 32. *Cynara* 32. The Keyhole 33. Storm at Daybreak 33. Mary Stevens MD 33. I Loved a Woman 33. The House on 56th Street 33. Mandalay 34. Wonder Bar 34. Doctor Monica 34. British Agent 34. Stranded 34. The Goose and the Gander 35. Living on Velvet 35. I Found Stella Parish 35. *The White Angel* (as Florence Nightingale) 36. Give Me Your Heart 36. Stolen Holiday 37. Confession 37. Another Dawn 37. *First Lady* 37. Women are Like That 38. My Bill 38. Secrets of an Actress 38. Comet over Broadway 38. King of the Underworld 39. Women in the Wind 39. In Name Only 39. It's a Date 40. Little Men 40. When the Daltons Rode 40. Play Girl 40. The Man Who lost Himself 40. *Charley's Aunt* 41. The Feminine Touch 41. Always in My Heart 42. Between Us Girls 42. Four Jills in a Jeep 44. Divorce 45. Allotment Wives 45. Wife Wanted 46.

Francis, Robert (1930–1955). American leading man whose budding career was cut short by an air crash.
The Caine Mutiny 54. The Long Gray Line 55, etc.

Franciscus, James (1934–). American leading man.
Four Boys and a Gun 56. I Passed for White 60. The Outsider 61. The Miracle of the White Stallions 63. Youngblood Hawke 64. The Valley of Gwangi 69. Marooned 69. Beneath the Planet of the Apes 69. Cat O'Nine Tails 71. The Dream Makers (TV) 75, etc.
TV series: Naked City 58. Mr Novak 63–64. Longstreet 71. Hunter 77.

Franciosa, Anthony or **Tony** (1928–) (Anthony Papaleo). Italian-American leading actor with lithe movement and ready grin.
A Face in the Crowd (debut) 57. This Could Be the Night 57. *A Hatful of Rain* (his stage role) 57. Wild Is the Wind 58. *The Long Hot Summer* 58. The Naked Maja 59. Career 59. The Story on

Page One 59. Go Naked in the World 60. Period of Adjustment 62. Rio Conchos 64. The Pleasure Seekers 65. A Man Could Get Killed 65. Assault on a Queen 66. The Swinger 66. Fathom (GB) 67. The Sweet Ride 68. In Enemy Country 68. A Man Called Gannon 68. Across 110th Street 72, etc.

TV series: Valentine's Day 61. *The Name of the Game* 68–69. Search 72.

Francks, Don (1932–). Canadian singer whose first notable film role was in *Finian's Rainbow* 68.

Franju, Georges (1912–). French director, former set designer. Co-founder of Cinémathèque Française. Best-known documentaries: *Le Sang des Bêtes* 49. *Hôtel des Invalides* 51. *Le Grand Melies* 51. Features: *La Tête contre les Murs* (*The Keepers*) 58. *Eyes without a Face* 59. Spotlight on a Murderer 61. Thérèse Desqueyroux 62. Judex 63. Thomas the Impostor 64. Les Rideaux Blancs 65.

Frank, Charles (1910–). British director, former dubbing expert.
Uncle Silas 47. Intimate Relations 53, etc.

Frank, Harriet: see *Ravetch, Irving*.

Frank, Melvin (1917–). American comedy scriptwriter and latterly producer/director.
WITH NORMAN PANAMA: *My Favourite Blonde* 42. Thank Your Lucky Stars 43. Road to Utopia 45. Monsieur Beaucaire 46. *Mr Blanding Builds His Dream House* 48. The Reformer and the Redhead 50. Above and Beyond 52. White Christmas 56. That Certain Feeling 56. Lil Abner 59. *The Facts of Life* 61. Road to Hong Kong 62. Strange Bedfellows 65, etc.
SOLO: A Funny Thing Happened on the Way to the Forum (wp) 66. Buona Sera Mrs Campbell (wpd) 68. A Touch of Class (wpd) 72. The Duchess and the Dirtwater Fox (wpd) 76.

Frankau, Ronald (1894–1951). British stage and radio comedian with an 'idle rich' characterization.
The Calendar 31. His Brother's Keeper 39. Double Alibi 46. The Ghosts of Berkeley Square 47, etc.

Frankel, Benjamin (1906–1973). British composer. Scores include The Seventh Veil 46. Mine Own Executioner 47, etc.

Frankel, Cyril (1921–). British director, former documentarist with Crown Film Unit.
Devil on Horseback 54. Make Me an Offer 55. It's Great To Be Young 56. No Time for Tears 57. She Didn't Say No 58. Alive and Kicking 58. Never Take Sweets from a Stranger 61. Don't Bother To Knock 61. On the Fiddle 61. The Very Edge 63. The Witches (The Devil's Own) 66. The Trygon Factor 67. Persmission to Kill 75, etc.

Frankenheimer, John (1930–). Ebullient American director, formerly in TV.
□ *The Young Stranger* 57. The Young Savages 61. All Fall Down 61. *The Manchurian Candidate* 62. *Birdman of Alcatraz* 62. *Seven Days in May* 64. The Train 64. *Seconds* 66. Grand Prix 67. The Extraordinary Seaman 68. The Fixer 68. The Gypsy Moths 69. I Walk the Line 70. The Horsemen 71. Impossible Object 73. The Iceman Cometh 73. 99 44/100 Dead 74. French Connection II 75.

Frankenstein. The man/monster theme was explored in American movies of 1908 (with Charles Ogle) and 1916 (*Life Without Soul*), also in Italy in 1920 (*Master of Frankenstein*). The 1931 Hollywood film, written by Robert Florey and directed by James Whale, borrowed as much from Wegener's *The Golem* 22 as from Mary Shelley's early 19th-century novel; but despite censorship problems the elements jelled, with Boris Karloff a great success as the monster composed from dead bits and pieces, and a legend was born. Sequels included *Bride of Frankenstein* (qv) 35. *Son of Frankenstein* 39. *Ghost of Frankenstein* 41. *Frankenstein Meets the Wolf Man* 43. *House of Frankenstein* 45. *House of Dracula* 45. *Abbott and Costello Meet Frankenstein* 48; among those who took over from Karloff were Lon Chaney, Bela Lugosi and Glenn Strange. In 1956 the original story was remade in Britain's Hammer Studios under the title *The Curse of Frankenstein*; colour and gore were added, and sequels, with various monsters, came thick and fast: *The Revenge of Frankenstein* 58. *The Evil of Frankenstein* 63. *Frankenstein Created Woman* 67. *Frankenstein Must Be Destroyed* 69. *Horror of Frankenstein* 70. *Frankenstein and the Monster from Hell* 73. A variation on the original monster make-up was used by Fred Gwynne in the TV comedy series, *The Munsters* 64–65. There have also been several recent American, Japanese and Italian attempts to cash in on the name of Frankenstein in cheap exploitation pictures: *I Was a Teenage Frankenstein* 57. *Frankenstein 1970* 58. *Frankenstein Versus the Space Monsters* 65. *Frankenstein Conquers the World* 68. *Lady Frankenstein* 70, etc.

Franklin, Pamela (1949–). British juvenile actress of the sixties.

The Innocents 61. The Lion 62. The Third Secret 64. The Nanny 65. Our Mother's House 67. The Night of the Following Day 68. *The Prime of Miss Jean Brodie* 69. Sinful Davey 69. David Copperfield 69. And Soon the Darkness 70. Necromancy 72. The Legend of Hell House 73. Food for the Gods 76, etc.

Franklin, Sidney (1893–1972). American producer-director, in Hollywood since leaving school. Academy Award 1942 'for consistent high achievement'.
Martha's Vindication (d) 16. Heart o' the Hills (d) 19. Dulcy (d) 23. Beverly of Graustark (d) 26. The Last of Mrs Cheyney (d) 29. Private Lives (d) 31. The Guardsman (d) 32. Smiling Through (d) 32. Reunion in Vienna (d) 33. The Barretts of Wimpole Street (d) 33. The Dark Angel (d) 35. The Good Earth (d) 37. On Borrowed Time (p) 39. Waterloo Bridge (p) 40. Mrs Miniver (p) 42. Random Harvest (p) 42. The White Cliffs of Dover (p) 44. The Yearling (p) 46. The Miniver Story (p) 50. Young Bess (p) 54. The Barretts of Wimpole Street (d) 57, many others.

Franklyn, William (1926–). Smooth British character actor, popular on TV.
Quatermass II 57. Fury at Smugglers' Bay 58. Pit of Darkness 62. The Legend of Young Dick Turpin 64. The Intelligence Men 65. The Satanic Rites of Dracula 73, etc.

Frankovich, Mike (1910–). American producer, a former sports commentator and screenwriter. During the fifties he ran Columbia's British organization, and in the sixties became their head of world production, then turned independent again.
Fugitive Lady 51. Decameron Nights 53. Footsteps in the Fog 55. Joe Macbeth 56. Marooned 69. Bob and Carol and Ted and Alice 69. Cactus Flower 69. Butterflies are Free 72. Forty Carats 73, etc.

Franz, Arthur (1920–). American leading man, latterly character actor; radio, stage and TV experience.
Jungle Patrol (debut) 48. Sands of Iwo Jima 49. Abbott and Costello Meet the Invisible Man 51. The Sniper 52. Eight Iron Men 52. The Caine Mutiny 54. The Unholy Wife 57. Running Target 58. Hellcats of the Navy 59. Alvarez Kelly 66. Anzio 68, etc.

Franz, Eduard (1902–). American character actor, often seen as foreign dignitary, Jewish elder, or psychiatrist.
The Iron Curtain 48. Francis 50. The Thing 51. The Jazz Singer 52. Dream Wife 53. Broken

Lance 54. The Ten Commandments 56. Man Afraid 57. A Certain Smile 58. The Story of Ruth 60. Hatari 62. The President's Analyst 67, many others.
TV series: *The Breaking Point* 63.

Fraser, Bill (1907–). British comic character actor, TV's 'Snudge'. Wide stage experience; film parts since 1938 usually bits till recently.
Meet Me Tonight 52. The Americanization of Emily 65. Joey Boy 65. Masquerade 65. I've Gotta Horse 65. Up the Chastity Belt 71. That's Your Funeral 72, etc.

Fraser, John (1931–). British leading man with stage experience, sporadically in films.
The Good Beginning 53. Touch and Go 55. The Good Companions 57. Tunes of Glory 59. *The Trials of Oscar Wilde* (as Lord Alfred Douglas) 60. El Cid 61. Fury at Smugglers Bay 61. The Waltz of the Toreadors 62. Repulsion 65. Operation Crossbow 65. Isadora 68, etc.

Fraser, Liz (1933–). British character actress, specializing in dumb cockney blondes.
Wonderful Things 58. I'm All Right, Jack 59. Two-Way Stretch 60. The Rebel 61. Double Bunk 61. Carry On Regardless 61. The Painted Smile (leading role) 61. Raising the Wind 62. Live Now Pay Later 63. The Americanization of Emily 64. The Family Way 66. Up the Junction 68. Dad's Army 70. Confessions of a Driving Instructor 76, etc.

Fraser, Moyra (1923–). Australian comedienne in British stage and TV.
Here We Go Round the Mulberry Bush 67. Prudence and the Pill 68. The Boy Friend 71, etc.

Fraser, Richard (1913–1971). Scottish-born leading man of some American second features in the forties.
How Green Was My Valley 41. The Picture of Dorian Gray 44. Fatal Witness 46. The Cobra Strikes 48. Alaska Patrol 51, etc.

Fraser, Ronald (1930–). Stocky British character actor, in films and TV since 1954.
The Sundowners 59. The Pot Carriers 62. The Punch and Judy Man 63. Crooks in Cloisters 64. The Beauty Jungle 64. The Flight of the Phoenix 65. The Whisperers 67. The Killing of Sister George 68. Sinful Davey 69. Too Late the Hero 69. The Rise and Rise of Michael Rimmer 70. The Magnificent Seven Deadly Sins 71. Rentadick 72. Ooh You Are Awful 72. Swallows and Amazons 74. Paper Tiger 75.

Frawley, William (1887–1966). Stocky, cigar-

chewing American comedy character actor from vaudeville, in innumerable films as taxi driver, comic gangster, private detective or incompetent cop.
Moonlight and Pretzels 33. Crime Doctor 34. Alibi Ike 35. Desire 36. High Wide and Handsome 37. Professor Beware 38. Persons in Hiding 39. One Night in the Tropics 40. Footsteps in the Dark 42. *Roxie Hart* 42. Whistling in Brooklyn 43. Going My Way 44. Lady on a Train 45. The Crime Doctor's Manhunt 46. Miracle on 34th Street 47. The Babe Ruth Story 48. East Side West Side 49. Kill the Umpire 50. The Lemon Drop Kid 51. Rancho Notōrious 52. Safe at Home 62, etc.
TV series: *I Love Lucy* 51–60. My Three Sons 60–63.

Frazee, Jane (1918–) (Mary Jane Frahse). Vivacious American singer and leading lady of minor musicals in the forties.
Rookies 41. Moonlight in Havana 42. Swing and Sway 44. Incident 48. Rhythm Inn (last to date) 51, etc.

Freaks (US 1932). Tod Browning's macabre drama set in a circus and with real freaks in the cast enjoyed a greater reputation than it deserved because it was unseen for thirty years owing to a censor's ban. Now it seems interesting but unsatisfactory, a curious aberration of the Irving Thalberg regime at MGM.

Frears, Stephen (1931–). British director.
Gumshoe 71.

Freda, Riccardo (1909–). Egyptian-Italian director who brings some style to exploitation pictures; former art critic.
Les Misérables 46. Theodora, Slave Express 54. I Vampiri 57. The Giant of Thessaly 61. The Terror of Dr Hitchcock 62. The Spectre 63. Coplan FX 18 Casse Tout (The Exterminators) 65, etc.

Frederick, Pauline (1883–1938) (Pauline Libbey). American leading lady of silent days.
Bella Donna 15. The Slave Island 16. Sleeping Fires 17. Her Final Reckoning 18. The Peace of Roaring River 19. *Madame X* 20. La Tosca 21. Married Flirts 24. Her Honour the Governor 26. On Trial 28. The Sacred Flame 29. This Modern Age 31. The Phantom of Crestwood 32. My Marriage 36. Thank You Mr Moto 38, etc.

Fredericks, Ellsworth (–). American cinematographer.
Invasion of the Body Snatchers 55. The Friendly Persuasion 56. Sayonara 57. High Time 60.

Seven Days in May 64. Pistolero 66. The Power 67. Mister Buddwing 67, etc.

free cinema. A term applied to their own output by a group of British documentarists of the fifties, e.g. Lindsay Anderson, Karel Reisz. Their aim was to make 'committed' films which cared about the individual and the significance of the everyday. The resulting films were not always better than those produced by professional units with more commercial intent. The most notable were *O Dreamland, Momma Don't Allow, The March to Aldermaston, Every Day Except Christmas* and *We Are the Lambeth Boys*, the two latter films being sponsored by commercial firms.

Freed, Arthur (1894–1973) (Arthur Grossman). American producer, mainly of musicals for MGM, many of them featuring his own music.
Hold Your Man (m only) 33. Hollywood Party (m only) 34. Broadway Melody of 1936 (m only). Broadway Melody of 1938 (m only). *Babes In Arms* (& m) 39. Strike Up the Band 40. Lady Be Good (& m) 41. Cabin in the Sky 43. Meet Me in St Louis 44. Ziegfeld Follies 46. The Pirate 48. On the Town 49. Annie Get Your Gun 50. Showboat 51. *An American in Paris* 51. *Singin' in The Rain* (& m) 52. *Band Wagon* 53. Kismet 55. Invitation to the Dance 56. *Gigi* 58. Bells are Ringing 60. The Light in the Piazza 62, many others.

Freeland, Thornton (1898–). American director, former cameraman.
Three Live Ghosts 29. Whoopee 30. *Flying Down to Rio* 33. Brewster's Millions (GB) 35. The Amateur Gentleman (GB) 36. Jericho (GB) 37. The Gang's All Here (GB) 39. Over the Moon (GB) 39. Too Many Blondes 41. Meet Me at Dawn 47. The Brass Monkey (Lucky Mascot) (GB) 48. Dear Mr Prohack (GB) 49, etc.

Freeman, Al Jnr (1934–). Black American leading man.
Black Like Me 64. Dutchman 67. The Detective 68. Finian's Rainbow 68. Castle Keep 69. The Lost Man 70. A Fable (& d) 71, etc.

Freeman, Everett (1911–). American writer, usually in collaboration.
Larceny Inc. 42. Thank Your Lucky Stars 43. The Secret Life of Walter Mitty 47. Million Dollar Mermaid 52. My Man Godfrey 57. The Glass Bottom Boat 66. Where Were You When the Lights Went Out? (& co-p) 68, many others.

Freeman, Howard (1899–1967). American

character actor, usually in comic roles as businessman on the make.
Pilot Number Five 43. Once Upon a Time 44. Take One False Step 49. Scaramouche 52. Remains To Be Seen 53. Dear Brigitte 65, many others.

Freeman, Kathleen (c. 1919–). American character actress.
Naked City 47. Lonely Heart Bandits 52. Bonzo Goes To College 52. Full House 52. Athena 54. The Fly 58. The Ladies' Man 61. The Disorderly Orderly 65. Three on a Couch 66. Support Your Local Gunfighter 71. Stand Up and Be Counted 72, etc.

Freeman, Leonard (1921–1974). American TV producer best known for *Hawaii Five-O.*

Freeman, Mona (1926–) (Monica Freeman). American leading lady, at her peak as a troublesome teenager in the forties.
□ National Velvet 44. Our Hearts were Young and Gay 44. Till We Meet Again 44. Here Come the Waves 44. Together Again 44. Roughly Speaking 45. Junior Miss 45. Danger Signal 45. Black Beauty 46. That Brennan Girl 46. Our Hearts Were Growing Up 46. Variety Girl 47. *Dear Ruth* 47. Mother Wore Tights 47. Isn't It Romantic? 48. Streets of Laredo 49. The Heiress 49. Dear Wife 49. Branded 50. Copper Canyon 50. I Was a Shoplifter 50. Dear Brat 51. Darling How Could You? 51. The Lady from Texas 51. Flesh and Fury 52. Jumping Jacks 52. Angel Face 52. Thunderbirds 52. Battle Cry 55. The Road to Denver 55. The Way Out (GB) 56. Before I Wake (GB) 56. Hold Back the Night 56. Huk 56. Dragoon Wells Massacre 57. The World was his Jury 58.

Freeman, Robert (c. 1935–). British director, former fashion director and title artist (*A Hard Day's Night, Help*).
The Touchables 68. World of Fashion (short) 68. L'Echelle Blanche 69.

Freeman, Frank Y. (1890–). American executive, vice president of Paramount in charge of the studio from 1938 until his retirement.

freeze frame. A printing device whereby the action appears to 'freeze' into a still, this being accomplished by printing one frame many times.

Fregonese, Hugo (1908–). Argentine-born director, former journalist, in Hollywood from 1945.
One-Way Street 50. Saddle Tramp 51. Apache Drums 51. Mark of the Renegade 52. My Six

Convicts 52. Decameron Nights 53. Blowing Wild 54. The Man in the Attic 54. The Raid 53. Black Tuesday 54. Seven Thunders (GB) 57. Harry Black 58. Marco Polo 61. Apaches Last Battle (Old Shatterhand) (Ger.) 64. Savage Pampas (Sp.) 66, etc.

The French Connection (US 1971) (AA). Moderate police yarn about New York cops tracking down heroin smugglers. Its success was due to a splendid car chase, a strong performance by Gene Hackman as a brutish cop, and a fashionable use of bad language and wild sound (which often rendered the dialogue unintelligible). Directed by William Friedkin from a script by Ernest Tidyman. A 1975 sequel, *French Connection II,* continued the chase to Marseilles, but the storyline was pointless and repetetive.

French, Harold (1897–). British stage actor and producer, in films since 1931.
Biography 1970: *I Swore I Never Would.*
AS DIRECTOR: The House of the Arrow 39. Jeannie 41. Unpublished Story 42. The Day Will Dawn 42. Secret Mission 42. *Dear Octopus* 43. English Without Tears 44. Mr Emmanuel 44. Quiet Weekend 46. My Brother Jonathan 47. The Blind Goddess 48. Quartet (part) 48. The Dancing Years 49. Trio (part) 50. Encore (part) 51. The Hour of 13 52. Isn't Life Wonderful 53. Rob Roy 53. Forbidden Cargo 54. The Man Who Loved Redheads 55, etc.

French, Leslie (1899–). Diminutive British character player.
This England 41. *Orders to Kill* 58. The Leopard 63. More than a Miracle 67. Death in Venice 70, etc.

French, Valerie (1931–). British actress, in occasional Hollywood films.
Jubal 56. Garment Center 57. Decision at Sundown 57. The Four Skulls of Jonathan Drake 59. Shalako 68, etc.

Frend, Charles (1909–1977). British director.
The Foreman Went to France 42. *San Demetrio, London* 43. Johnny Frenchman 45. *Scott of the Antarctic* 48. *The Cruel Sea* 52. Lease of Life 55. Barnacle Bill 57. Cone of Silence 60. Torpedo Bay (It.) 62. Ryan's Daughter (2nd unit) 70, many TV films, etc.

Fresnay, Pierre (1897–1974) (Pierre Laudenbach). Distinguished French stage actor who made many films.
Marius (debut) 31. Fanny 32. César 34. The Man Who Knew Too Much (GB) 34. *La Grand*

Illusion 37. Le Corbeau 43. *Monsieur Vincent* 47. *God Needs Men* 50. The Fanatics 57, others.

Freud (US 1962). A biographical film written by Charles Kaufman and Wolfgang Reinhardt, directed by John Huston in the actual Viennese locations, with a cast including Montgomery Clift, Susannah York and Larry Parks; but to little avail in terms of public response despite the sensational incidents depicted. Significant as a contrast to the Warner biographical films of the late thirties, which were very similar but hugely successful.

Freud, Sigmund (1856–1939). Viennese physician who became the virtual inventor of psychoanalysis and the discoverer of sexual inhibition as a mainspring of human behaviour; a gentleman, therefore, to whom Hollywood has every reason to be grateful.

Freund, Karl (1890–1969). Czech-born cinematographer, famous for his work in German silents like The Last Laugh 24. Metropolis 26. Variety 26. Berlin 27, etc.
SINCE IN USA: *The Mummy* (& d) 33. Moonlight and Pretzels (d only) 33. Madame Spy (d only) 33. Mad Love (d only) 35. Camille 36. *The Good Earth* (AA) 37. Marie Walewska 38. Pride and Prejudice 40. The Seventh Cross 44. Key Largo 48. Bright Leaf 50, many others.

Frey, Leonard (1938–). American character actor.
The Magic Christian 70. Tell Me That You Love Me Junie Moon 70. *The Boys in the Band* 70. Fiddler on the Roof 71.

Fried, Gerald (1926–). American composer. Killer's Kiss 55. Terror in a Texas Town 58. A Cold Wind in August 60. The Cabinet of Caligari 62. One Potato Two Potato 64. The Killing of Sister George 68. Too Late the Hero 69. The Grissom Gang 71. Soylent Green 73, many others.

Friedhofer, Hugo (1902–). American composer.
The Adventures of Marco Polo 38. China Girl 42. The Lodger 44. The Woman in the Window 45. The Best Years of Our Lives (AA) 46. Joan of Arc 48. Ace in the Hole 51. Above and Beyond 52. Vera Cruz 54. The Rains of Ranchipur 55. One-Eyed Jacks 59. The Secret Invasion 64, etc.

Friedkin, William (1939–). American director, from TV.
Good Times 67. The Birthday Party 68. The Night They Raided Minsky's 68. The Boys in the Band 70. *The French Connection* (AA) 71. The Exorcist 73.

Friend, Philip (1915–). British leading man with stage experience.
Pimpernel Smith 41. Next of Kin 42. The Flemish Farm 43. Great Day 45. My Own True Love (US) 48. Panthers' Moon (US) 50 The Highwayman (US) 51. Background 53. Son of Robin Hood 59. Stranglehold 62, etc.

Friese-Greene, William (1855–1921). Pioneer British inventor who built the first practical movie camera in 1889. Died penniless; his life was the subject of *The Magic Box* 51.

Friml, Rudolf (1879–1972). Viennese-American composer of operettas which were frequently filmed: *The Firefly, Naughty Marietta, The Vagabond King*, etc.

Frings, Ketti (–) (Catherine Frings). American scenarist.
Hold Back the Dawn (& original novel) 41. Guest in the House 44. The Accused 48. Dark City 50. Because of You 52. Come Back Little Sheba 53. Foxfire 55, etc.

Fritz the Cat (US 1971). Satirical animated feature by Ralph Bakshi from his comic strip for adults only; the feline hero gets into some pretty repellent adventures in the urban underground. The contrast between the subject and the old-fashioned Tom and Jerry style were striking, but a sequel was less effective.

Fritsch, Willy (1901–). Popular German leading man, in films since 1921.
The Spy 28. Congress Dances 31. Drei Von Der Tankstelle 31 (and 55). Amphitryon 35. Film Ohne Titel 47, many others.

Frobe, Gert (1912–). German character actor first seen abroad as the downtrodden little man of *Berliner Ballade* 48; later put on weight and emerged in the sixties as an international semi-star, usually as villain.
The Heroes Are Tired 55. He Who Must Die 56. The Girl Rosemarie 58. The Testament of Dr Mabuse 64. *Goldfinger* 64. Those Magnificent Men in Their Flying Machines 65. Is Paris Burning? 66. De Rififi à Paname 67. Rocket to the Moon 67. Monte Carlo or Bust 69. Dollars 71. And Then There Were None 75, etc.

Frohlich, Gustav (1902–). German actor (from *Metropolis* 26) and director (*The Sinner* 51, etc.). Few of his films have been exported.

From Here to Eternity (US 1953) (AA). A seething melodramatic attack on the US Army, this over-sexed, over sentimentalized and thoroughly unattractive picture, from James Jones' 'realistic' novel, was extremely well directed by Fred Zinneman (AA) from a scenario by Daniel Taradash (AA). Photographed by Burnett Guffey (AA), with solid performances from Burt Lancaster, Frank Sinatra (AA), Deborah Kerr, Montgomery Clift, Donna Reed (AA) and Ernest Borgnine.

From This Day Forward (US 1945). An early example of American romantic realism, a simple love story shot on the streets of New York. Written by Hugo Butler; photographed by George Barnes; directed by John Berry; with Joan Fontaine and Mark Stevens.

The Front Page. Ben Hecht and Charles MacArthur's tough, hard-boiled Broadway comedy was first filmed in 1930 by Lewis Milestone, with Pat O'Brien as the fast-talking reporter who shields an escaped murderer, and Adolphe Menjou as his scheming editor. In 1940 Howard Hawks remade it as *His Girl Friday*, with a sex switch: Rosalind Russell played the reporter and Cary Grant her boss. 1974 brought Billy Wilder's freewheeling version with Jack Lemmon and Walter Matthau.

Frontiere, Dominic (1931–). American composer.
Giant 56. The Marriage Go Round 60. Hero's Island 62. Billie 65. Hang 'Em High 68. Popi 69. Chisum 70. Cancel My Reservation 72. Hammersmith is Out 72, etc.

frost on movie windows is usually produced from a mixture of epsom salts and stale beer.

Frye, Dwight (1899–1943). American character actor who made a corner in crazed hunchbacks.
Dracula 30. Frankenstein 31. The Vampire Bat 33. Bride of Frankenstein 35. Something to Sing About 38. Son of Monte Cristo 41. Frankenstein Meets the Wolf Man 43, etc.

Fryer, Robert (1920–). American producer, former casting director.
The Boston Strangler 68. The Prime of Miss Jean Brodie 69. Myra Breckenridge 69. The Salzburg Connection 71. Travels with My Aunt 73. Mame 73. The Abdication 73. Voyage of the Damned 76.

Fuest, Robert (1927–). British director, from TV.
□ Just Like a Woman 66. And Soon the Darkness 70. *Wuthering Heights* 70. The Abominable Dr Phibes 71. Dr Phibes Rises Again 72. The Final Programme (& w) 73. The Devil's Rain (US) 76.

The Fugitive. Under this title there have been at least two silent adventures, two second feature westerns, one Polish and one Indian film. John Ford's *The Fugitive* 47 is deservedly the best known of all, a pictorially beautiful if depressing account of the last struggles of a 'whisky priest' in Mexico, from Graham Greene's book *The Power and the Glory*. There was also a successful modern TV series of the same title.

Fuller, Leslie (1889–1948). Beefy British concert-party comedian who was popular in broad comedy films of the thirties.
Not So Quiet on the Western Front 31. Kiss Me, Sergeant 31. The Pride of the Force 33. The Stoker 35. Captain Bill 36. Two Smart Men 40. The Middle Watch 40. Front Line Kids 42, etc.

Fuller, Robert (1934–). American leading man, mostly on TV.
Return of the Seven 66. Incident at Phantom Hill 67. The Hard Ride 70. The Gatling Gun 72, etc.
TV series: *Laramie* 59–62. Wagon Train 63–64. Emergency 70–.

Fuller, Samuel (1911–). American writer-director who has also produced most of his own pictures; which have normally been violent melodramas on topical subjects.
□ I Shot Jesse James 49. The Baron of Arizona 50. Fixed Bayonets 51. The Steel Helmet 51. Park Row 52. Pickup on South Street 52. Hell and High Water 54. House of Bamboo 55. Run of the Arrow 55. China Gate 56. Forty Guns 57. Verboten 58. The Crimson Kimono 59. Underworld USA 60. Merrill's Marauders 62. Shock Corridor 64. The Naked Kiss 66. Shark 67. Dead Pigeon on Beethoven Street 72 (West Ger.).

Fullerton, Fiona (1955–). British juvenile actress of the seventies.
Run Wild Run Free 69. Nicholas and Alexandra 71. Alice's Adventures in Wonderland 72, etc.

Fulton, John P. (1902–1965). American special effects photographer, responsible for the tricks in most of the *Invisible Man* series and other fantasy movies.

Fu Manchu. Sax Rohmer's oriental master-criminal was played by Harry Agar Lyons in a series of British two-reelers in the twenties.

Warner Oland played him in *The Mysterious Fu Manchu* 29, *The Return of Fu Manchu* 30 and *Daughter of the Dragon* 31; Boris Karloff in *Mask of Fu Manchu* 32, and Henry Brandon in *Drums of Fu Manchu* 41. Otherwise he was oddly neglected until the sixties series starring Christopher Lee, beginning with *The Face of Fu Manchu* 65 and *Brides of Fu Manchu* 66: it degenerated into shambling nonsense.

funerals provided a starting point for *The Third Man, Frankenstein, The Great Man, Death of a Salesman, The Bad and the Beautiful, Citizen Kane,* and *Keeper of the Flame;* figured largely in *The Premature Burial, The Mummy, The Egyptian, The Fall of the House of Usher, The Counterfeit Traitor, Funeral in Berlin, The Godfather, The Glass Key, I Bury the Living, Miracle in Milan, Doctor Zhivago* and *Hamlet;* and formed a climax for *Our Town.* In *Vampyr* and *Wild Strawberries* the hero dreamed of his own funeral; and in *Holy Matrimony* Monty Woolley attended his own funeral, having arranged to have his valet's body mistaken for his. Funerals were taken lightly in *I See a Dark Stranger, Little Caesar, Kind Hearts and Coronets, Too Many Crooks, A Comedy of Terrors, Charade, The Wrong Box, I Love You Alice B. Toklas, Robin and the Seven Hoods, Monsieur Hulot's Holiday, Entr'acte, Ocean's Eleven, Comrade X, What a Way to Go, The Private Life of Sherlock Holmes,* and above all *The Loved One.*

funfairs have provided fascinating settings for many a bravura film sequence. *The Wagons Roll at Night, Nightmare Alley, Dante's Inferno* and Hitchcock's *The Ring* were set almost entirely on fairgrounds. Tawdry or 'realistic' funfairs were shown in *Jeanne Eagels, Saturday Night and Sunday Morning, East of Eden, Picnic,* and *Inside Daisy Clover;* glamorized or sentimentalized ones cropped up in *The Wolf Man, My Girl Tisa, State Fair, Roseanna McCoy, The Great Ziegfeld* and *Mr and Mrs Smith.* Musicals like *On the Town, On the Avenue, Coney Island, Centennial Summer, State Fair* and *Down to Earth* had funfair sequences and they are also used to excellent advantage in thrillers: *Brighton Rock, Spider Woman, Horrors of the Black Museum, Gorilla at Large, The Third Man, Lady from Shanghai, Strangers on a Train.* Naturally funfairs are also marvellous places for fun: though not for Eddie Cantor in *Strike Me Pink,* Tony Curtis in *Forty Pounds of Trouble,* Laurel and Hardy in *The Dancing Masters,* or Bob Hope (fired from a cannon) in *Road to Zanzibar. The Beast from 20,000 Fathoms* was finally cornered in a

funfair; *Dr Caligari* kept his cabinet in one. The star who made the most of a funfair sequence was undoubtedly Mae West as the carnival dancer in *I'm No Angel,* in which she delivered her famous line: 'Suckers!'

Funicello, Annette (1942–). American leading lady, former juvenile actress; was host of Disney's TV Mickey Mouse Club, and in his films is known simply as 'Annette'.
Johnny Tremain 57. The Shaggy Dog 61. Babes in Toyland 61. The Misadventures of Merlin Jones 63. Bikini Beach 64. The Monkey's Uncle 65. Fireball 500 66, etc.

Funt, Allen (1914–). American TV trickster who appeared for years on *Candid Camera* and in 1970 produced and starred in a film version, *What Do You Say to a Naked Lady?*

Furie, Sidney J. (1933–). Canadian director with a restless camera; came to Britain 1959, Hollywood 1966.
□ A Dangerous Age 57. A Cool Sound from Hell 58. The Snake Woman 60. Doctor Blood's Coffin 61. During One Night 61. Three on a Spree 61. The Young Ones 61. The Boys 62. The Leather Boys 63. Wonderful Life 64. *The Ipcress File* 65. Day of the Arrow 65. The Appaloosa 66. The Naked Runner 67. The Lawyer 69. Little Fauss and Big Halsy 70. Lady Sings the Blues 72. Gable and Lombard 76.
TV series: Hudson's Bay 59.

Furneaux, Yvonne (1928–). French leading lady in British films.
Meet Me Tonight 52. The Dark Avenger 55. Lisbon 56. The Mummy 59. La Dolce Vita 59. Enough Rope (Fr.) 63. *Repulsion* 64. The Scandal (Fr.) 66, etc.

Furrer, Urs (1934–1975). Swiss-born American cinematographer.
Pigeons 70. Desperate Characters 71. Shaft 71. Shaft's Big Score 72. Dr Cook's Garden (TV) 72. The Seven Ups 73, etc.

Furse, Judith (1912–). British character actress who often plays district nurses, matrons, heavy schoolmistresses, etc.
Goodbye Mr Chips 39. English Without Tears 44. Black Narcissus 46. The Man in the White Suit 51. Doctor at Large 57. Serious Charge 59, etc.

Furse, Margaret (1911–1974). British costume designer.
Oliver Twist 48. The Mudlark 50. The Inn of the Sixth Happiness 58. Sons and Lovers 60. Young

Cassidy 64. Anne of the Thousand Days 70. Mary Queen of Scots 72. Love Among the Ruins (TV) 75, etc.

Furse, Roger (1903–1972). British stage designer.
Henry V (costumes only) 44. The True Glory 45. Odd Man Out 47. Hamlet 47. Ivanhoe 52. Richard III 56. The Prince and the Showgirl 57. Saint Joan 57. Bonjour Tristesse 58. The Roman Spring of Mrs Stone 61. Road to Hong Kong 62, etc.

Furthman, Jules (1888–1966). American writer, usually in collaboration.
Treasure Island 20. The Way of All Flesh 27. *Shanghai Express* 32. *Mutiny on the Bounty* 35. Spawn of the North 38. Only Angels Have Wings 39. The Outlaw 43. To Have and Have Not 44. The Big Sleep 46. Nightmare Alley 48. Jet Pilot 50 (released 57). Peking Express 51, many others.

Fury (US 1936). Fritz Lang's first and best indictment of lynch law, but with a happy ending. Important and influential, coming two years before *They Won't Forget*, it was also highly commercial, with a suspenseful plot and a star performance from Spencer Tracy as the man unjustly accused. Written by Lang and Bartlett Cormack from a novel by Norman Krasna; photographed by Joseph Ruttenberg, with music by Franz Waxman.

Fusco, Giovanni (1906–). Italian composer, especially associated with Antonioni.
Cronaca di un Amore, Le Amiche. Il Grido. Hiroshima Mon Amour. L'Avventura. The Eclipse. The Red Desert. The War is Over, etc.

Fyffe, Will (1884–1947). Pawky Scots comedian, famous in the halls for his song 'I Belong to Glasgow'.
Happy 34. Annie Laurie 36. Cotton Queen 37. Owd Bob 38. The Mind of Mr Reeder 39. Rulers of the Sea (US) 39. For Freedom 40. Neutral Port 40. Heaven Is Round the Corner 44. The Brothers 47, etc.

G

Gaal, Franceska (1909–) (Fanny Zilveritch). Hungarian leading lady who made three American films: The Buccaneer 38. Paris Honeymoon 39. The Girl Downstairs 39.

Gabel, Martin (1912–). Balding, rotund American character actor, mostly on stage.
The Lost Moment (d only) 47. Fourteen Hours 51. M 51. The Thief 52. Tip on a Dead Jockey 57. Marnie 64. Lord Love a Duck 66. Divorce American Style 67. Lady in Cement 68. There was a Crooked Man 70. The Front Page 75, etc.

Gabel, Scilla (1937–). Buxom Italian leading lady in international films.
Queen of the Pirates 60. Village of Daughters 62. Sodom and Gomorrah 62. Revenge of the Gladiators 65. Modesty Blaise 66, etc.

Gabin, Jean (1904–1976) (Alexis Moncourge). Distinguished French actor, former Folies Bergère extra, cabaret entertainer, etc. His stocky virility and world-weary features have kept him a star from the early thirties.
Les Bas Fonds 36. *Pepe Le Moko* 36. *La Grande Illusion* 37. *Quai des Brumes* 38. *La Bête Humaine* 38. Remorques 39. *Le Jour Se Lève* 39. Moontide (US) 42. Martin Roumagnac 45. Au Delà des Grilles 48. *Touchez Pas au Grisbi* 53. French Can Can 54. Crime and Punishment 56. Les Grandes Familles 58. Le President 60. Le Cave Se Rebiffe 61. Le Baron de l'Ecluse 62. The Big Snatch (Melodie en Sous-Sol) 62. Maigret Voit Rouge 63. Monsieur 64. De Rififi à Paname 66. Le Jardinier d'Argenteuil 66. Le Soleil des Voyous 67. Le Tatoué 68. Fin de Journée 69, many others.

Gable, Christopher (c. 1940–). British actor, ex-ballet dancer.
Women in Love 69. The Music Lovers 70. The Boy Friend 71. The Slipper and the Rose 76.

Gable, Clark (1901–1960). American leading man who kept his popularity for nearly thirty years, and was known as the 'king' of Hollywood. His big ears were popular with caricaturists; his impudent grin won most female hearts.
□ The Painted Desert 30. The Easiest Way 31. Dance Fools Dance 31. A Free Soul 31. The Finger Points 31. The Secret Six 31. Laughing Sinners 31. Night Nurse 31. Sporting Blood 31. Susan Lenox 32. Possessed 32. Hell's Divers 32. Polly of the Circus 32. *Red Dust* 32. Strange Interlude 32. No Man of Her Own 32. The White Sister 32. Dancing Lady 33. Hold Your Man 33. Night Flight 33. *It Happened One Night* (AA) 34. Men in White 34. Manhattan Melodrama 34. Chained 34. After Office Hours 35. Forsaking All Others 35. *Mutiny on the Bounty* 35. China Seas 35. Call of the Wild 35. Wife Versus Secretary 36. *San Francisco* 36. Cain and Mabel 36. Love on the Run 37. Parnell 37. Saratoga 37. Test Pilot 38. Too Hot to Handle 38. Idiot's Delight 39. *Gone with the Wind* 39. Strange Cargo 40. Boom Town 40. Comrade X 40. They Met in Bombay 41. Honky Tonk 41. Somewhere I'll Find You 41; war service; Adventure 45. *The Hucksters* 47. Homecoming 48. Command Decision 48. Any Number Can Play 49. Key to the City 50. To Please a Lady 50. Across the Wide Missouri 51. Lone Star 52. Never Let Me Go (GB) 53. Mogambo 53. Betrayed 54. The Tall Men 55. Soldier of Fortune 55. The King and Four Queens 56. Band of Angels 57. Teacher's Pet 58. Run Silent Run Deep 58. But Not for Me 59. It Started in Naples 59. *The Misfits* 60.

Gabor, Eva (1921–). Hungarian leading lady, sister of Zsa Zsa Gabor.
Autobiography 1954: *Orchids and Salami*.
Pacific Blackout 41. Forced Landing 41. A Royal Scandal 45. Wife of Monte Cristo 46. Song of Surrender 49. The Mad Magician 64. Tarzan and the Slave Girl 54. The Truth about Women 56. Gigi 58. A New Kind of Love 63. Youngblood Hawke 63, etc.
TV series: *Green Acres* 65–68.

Gabor, Zsa Zsa (1919–) (Sari Gabor). Exotic international leading lady, Miss Hungary of 1936, who has decorated films of many nations.
Autobiography 1961: *My Story*.
Lovely To Look At (US) 52. Lili (US) 53. Moulin Rouge (GB) 53. Public Enemy Number One (Fr.) 54. Diary of a Scoundrel (US) 56. The Man

Who Wouldn't Talk (GB) 57. Touch of Evil (US) 58. Queen of Outer Space (US) 59. Arrivederci Baby 66. Picture Mommy Dead (US) 66. Up the Front (GB) 72, etc.

Gainsborough. A British film company of the thirties, associated with costume drama and Aldwych farces. Subsequently merged with Rank.

Gallagher, Skeets (1891–1955) (Richard). Cheerful American vaudevillian, in some films of the early talkie period.
The Racket 28. It Pays to Advertise 31. Merrily We Go to Hell 32. Riptide 34. Polo Joe 37. Idiot's Delight 39. Zis Boom Bah 42. The Duke of Chicago 50, etc.

Galeen, Henrik (1881–1949). Dutch writer-director, a leading figure of German silent cinema.
The Student of Prague (wd) 12. The Golem (wd) 14. The Golem (w) 20. Nosferatu (w) 22. Waxworks (w) 25. The Student of Prague 26. Alraune 27. After the Verdict 30. Salon Dora Greene 36, many others.

Gallico, Paul (1897–1976). Hungarian novelist, whose work has been much adapted.
Wedding Present 36. Joe Smith American 42. Pride of the Yankees 42. The Cock 45. Never Take No for an Answer 52. Lili 53. Merry Andrew 58. Next to No Time 58. The Three Lives of Thomasina 63. The Snow Goose (TV) 71. The Poseidon Adventure 72, etc.

Gallone, Carmine (1886–1973). Veteran Italian director who ranged from opera to action epics.
Pawns of Passion 28. Un Soir de Rafle 30. My Heart is Calling 34. Madame Butterfly 39. Manon Lescaut 40. La Traviata 47. Faust and the Devil 49. La Forza del Destino 51. Tosca 56. Michael Strogoff 59. Carthage in Flames 59, many others.

Galloway, Don (–). American TV leading man, familiar in Ironside.
Rough Night in Jericho 68. Lt Schuster's Wife (TV) 72, etc.

Gallu, Samuel (1918–). American director, former opera singer.
Theatre of Death 66. The Man Outside 67. The Limbo Line 68.

Galsworthy, John (1867–1933). British novelist who wrote about the upper middle class. Works filmed include Escape 30 and 48. The Skin Game 31. Loyalties 34. Twenty-one Days 39. That Forsyte Woman 49, etc.

Galton, Ray (1930–). British comedy writer; with Alan Simpson, co-author of successful TV series, e.g. Hancock's Half-Hour, Steptoe and Son; films include The Rebel 61. The Wrong Arm of the Law 62. The Bargee 64. The Spy with a Cold Nose 67, etc.

Galvani, Dino (1890–1960). Distinguished-looking Italian actor, in films (mainly British) from 1908.
Atalantic 30. In a Monastery Garden 32. Midnight Menace 35. Mr Satan 38. It's That Man Again (as Signor So-So) 42. Sleeping Car to Trieste 49. Father Brown 54. Checkpoint 57. Bluebeard's Ten Honeymoons 60, many others.

Gam, Rita (1928–). American stage leading lady in occasional films.
The Thief 52. Sign of the Pagan 54. Night People 54. Magic Fire 55. Mohawk 56. King of Kings 61. Klute 71. Such Good Friends 71, etc.

gambling, in the indoor sport sense, is quite a preoccupation of film-makers. Gregory Peck in The Great Sinner played a man who made a great career of it, as did James Caan in The Gambler and George Segal in California Split; while in The Queen of Spades Edith Evans learnt the secret of winning at cards from the devil himself. Other suspenseful card games were played in The Cincinnati Kid, Lucky Jordan, The Lady Eve, Hazard, and Big Hand for a Little Lady; snooker pool was the game in The Hustler; old-time Missisippi river-boats were the setting for Mississippi Gambler, The Naughty Nineties, Frankie and Johnny and a sequence in The Secret Life of Walter Mitty. Roulette, however, is the most spectacular and oft-used film gambling game, seen in The Shanghai Gesture, Robin and the Seven Hoods, Ocean's Eleven, The Big Snatch, Doctor No, La Baie des Anges, Quartet (the 'Facts of Life' sequence), Seven Thieves, The Las Vegas Story, The Big Sleep, Gilda, Kaleidoscope, and many others. Second features with such titles as Gambling House, Gambling Ship and Gambling on the High Seas were especially popular in the forties. Musically, the filmic high-point was undoubtedly the 'biggest floating crap game in the world' number in Guys and Dolls. This stemmed from the writings of Damon Runyon, also adapted in such films as Sorrowful Jones and The Lemon Drop Kid.

Gance, Abel (1889–). French producer-director, in films since 1910. Pioneer of wide-screen techniques.

Baberousse 16. *J'Accuse* 19 and 37. La Roue 21. *Napoleon* 26. La Fin du Monde 31. Lucrezia Borgia 35. Une Grande Amour de Beethoven 36. Paradis Perdu 39. La Tour de Nesle 54. The Battle of Austerlitz 60, etc.

gangsters, a real-life American menace of the twenties, provided a new kind of excitement for early talkies like *Little Caesar* and *Public Enemy*, which told how their heroes got into criminal activities but didn't rub in the moral very hard. The pace of the action, however, made them excellent movies, and critics defended them against religious pressure groups. *Quick Millions, Scarface, Lady Killer, The Little Giant* and *Public Enemy's Wife* were among the titles which followed; then Warner Brothers cleverly devised a way of keeping their thrills while mollifying the protesters: they made the policeman into the hero, in films like *G-Men, I Am the Law, Bullets or Ballots*. By 1938 it seemed time to send up the whole genre in *A Slight Case of Murder*, with its cast of corpses, and in the later *Brother Orchid* the gangster-in-chief became a monk; yet in 1940 the heat had cooled off sufficiently to allow production of *The Roaring Twenties*, one of the most violent gangster movies of them all. The war made gangsters old-fashioned, but in the late forties Cagney starred in two real psychopathic toughies, *White Heat* and *Kiss Tomorrow Goodbye*. After that the fashion was to parody gangsterism, in *Party Girl, Some Like It Hot*, and a couple of Runyon movies; but the success of a French film called *Rififi* and a TV series called *The Untouchables* left the field wide open for redevelopment. Successes in the sixties included *Bonnie and Clyde, The St Valentine's Day Massacre, Pay or Die, The Rise and Fall of Legs Diamond, King of the Roaring Twenties*, and from the French *Borsalino* and various *Rififi* sequels. The seventies brought British gang violence in *Get Carter, Villain, The Squeeze* and *Sweeney*, and in 1972 the gigantic success of *The Godfather* spawned sequels, rivals (*The Valachi Papers*) and parodies (*The Gang That Couldn't Shoot Straight*).

Garas, Kaz (–). American leading man. The Last Safari 68. Ben 72, etc.

Garber, Matthew (1956–). British child actor.
The Three Lives of Thomasina 63. Mary Poppins 64. The Gnomobile 67.

Garbo, Greta (1905–) (Greta Gustafson). Swedish leading actress who was taken to Hollywood by her director Mauritz Stiller and

became a goddess of the screen, her aloof beauty carefully nurtured by MGM through the late twenties and early thirties. Her early retirement enhanced the air of mystery which has always surrounded her. Special Academy Award 1954 'for her unforgettable screen performances'.
Biographies: 1954, *Garbo* by John Bainbridge. 1970, *Garbo* by Norman Zierold.
☐ Peter the Tramp 22. The Atonement of Gösta Berling 24. Joyless Street 25. The Torrent 26. The Temptress 26. *Flesh and the Devil* 27. Love 27. The Mysterious Lady 27. The Divine Woman 28. The Kiss 29. A Woman of Affairs 29. Wild Orchids 29. The Single Standard 29. *Anna Christie* 30. Romance 30. Inspiration 31. Susan Lennox 31. Mata Hari 31. *Grand Hotel* 32. As You Desire Me 32. *Queen Christina* 33. The Painted Veil 34. *Anna Karenina* 35. *Camille* 36. Conquest 37. *Ninotchka* 39. Two Faced Woman 41.

The Garden of Allah. Robert Hichens' novel about a sophisticated woman whose husband turns out to be an escaped Trappist monk was filmed as a silent in 1917, with Tom Santschi and Helen Ware, and again in 1927 with Ivan Petrovitch and Alice Terry. The 1936 sound remake had excellent early colour, elegant direction by Richard Boleslawski, and exotic performances from Charles Boyer and Marlene Dietrich.

Gardenia, Vincent (1922–). American comic character actor.
Mad Dog Coll 61. A View from the Bridge 61. The Pursuit of Happiness 71. Cold Turkey 71. Hickey and Boggs 72. *Death Wish* 74, etc.

Gardiner, Reginald (1903–). British actor who perfected the amiable silly ass type, in Hollywood from 1936.
The Lovelorn Lady 32. Borrow a Million 34. *Born to Dance* 36. Everybody Sing 37. Marie Antoinette 38. Sweethearts 39. *The Great Dictator* 40. My Life with Caroline 41. *The Man Who Came to Dinner* 41. Captains of the Clouds 42. The Immortal Sergeant 43. Molly and Me 44. Christmas in Connecticut 45. Cluny Brown 46. Fury at Furnace Creek 48. Wabash Avenue 50. Halls of Montezuma 51. The Black Widow 54. Ain't Misbehaving 55. The Birds and the Bees 56. Mr Hobbs Takes a Vacation 62. Do Not Disturb 65, many others.
TV series: The Pruitts of Southampton 65.

Gardner, Ava (1922–). American leading lady of the forties and fifties, once voted the world's most beautiful woman.
Biography 1960: *Ava* by David Hanna.

☐ We Were Dancing 42. Joe Smith American 42. Sunday Punch 42. This Time for Keeps 42. Calling Dr Gillespie 42. Kid Glove Killer 42. Pilot No. 5 43. Hitler's Madman 43. Ghosts on the Loose 43. Reunion in France 43. Dubarry was a Lady 43. Young Ideas 43. Lost Angel 43. Swing Fever 44. Music for Millions 44. Three Men in White 44. Blonde Fever 44. Maisie Goes to Reno 44. Two Girls and a Sailor 44. She Went to the Races 45. Whistle Stop 46. *The Killers* 46. *The Hucksters* 47. Singapore 47. One Touch of Venus 48. The Great Sinner 49. East Side West Side 49. The Bribe 49. My Forbidden Past 52. *Show Boat* 51. *Pandora and the Flying Dutchman* 51. Lone Star 52. The Snows of Kilimanjaro 52. Ride Vaquero 53. *Mogambo* 53. Knights of the Round Table 53. *The Barefoot Contessa* 54. Bhowani Junction 56. The Little Hut 57. *The Sun Also Rises* 57. The Naked Maja 59. On the Beach 59. The Angel Wore Red 60. 55 Days at Peking 63. Seven Days in May 64. *The Night of the Iguana* 64. The Bible 66. Mayerling 68. Tam Lin 70. Judge Roy Bean 72. Earthquake 74. The Sentinel 77.

Gardner, Erle Stanley (1889–1970). American best-selling crime novelist, the creator of Perry Mason (qv).

Gardner, Joan (1914–). British leading lady of the thirties who married Zoltan Korda.
Men of Tomorrow 32. Catherine the Great 34. The Scarlet Pimpernel 35. The Man Who Could Work Miracles 36. Dark Journey 39. The Rebel Son (last to date) 39, etc.

Garfein, Jack (1930–). American stage and screen director, married to Caroll Baker.
End as a Man 47. Something Wild 62.

Garfield, Allen (1939–). American character actor.
Get to Know Your Rabbit 72. Slither 73. Busting 74. The Conversation 74. The Front Page 74. Mother Jugs and Speed 76, etc.

Garfield, John (1913–1952) (Julius Garfinkle). American leading actor, usually in aggressive or embittered roles; formerly a star of New York's leftish Group Theatre.
☐ *Four Daughters* 38. Blackwell's Island 38. *They Made Me a Criminal* 39. Juarez 39. Daughters Courageous 39. Dust Be My Destiny 39. Saturday's Children 40. East of the River 40. Castle on the Hudson 40. Flowing Gold 40. *The Sea Wolf* 41. Out of the Fog 41. Tortilla Flat 42. Dangerously They Live 42. Air Force 43. The Fallen Sparrow 43. Thank Your Lucky Stars 43. Between Two Worlds 44. Destination Tokyo 44.

Pride of the Marines 45. Nobody Lives Forever 46. The Postman Always Rings Twice 46. *Humoresque* 46. *Body and Soul* 47. *Gentleman's Agreement* 48. We Were Strangers 48. *Force of Evil* 49. Under My Skin 50. The Breaking Point 50. He Ran All the Way 51.

Garfunkel, Arthur (1937–). American pop singer, half of Simon and Garfunkel; as actor, *Catch 22* 70. *Carnal Knowledge* 71.

Gargan, Ed (1902–1964). American character actor, brother of William Gargan; often seen as comedy cop or prizefighter's manager.
Gambling Ship 34. My Man Godfrey 36. Thanks for the Memory 38. We're in the Army Now 40. A Haunting We Will Go 42. Wonder Man 45. Gallant Bess 50. Cuban Fireball 52, etc.

Gargan, William (1905–). American light leading man of the thirties and forties, usually in 'good guy' roles; retired when left voiceless after operation. Brother of Ed Gargan.
Autobiography 1969: *Why Me?*
The Misleading Lady 32. *Rain* 32. The Story of Temple Drake 33. Four Frightened People 34. Black Fury 35. The Milky Way 36. You Only Live Once 37. The Crowd Roars 38. *The Housekeeper's Daughter* 39. Turnabout 40. *They Knew What They Wanted* 40. Bombay Clipper 41. Miss Annie Rooney 42. The Canterville Ghost 44. The Bells of St Mary's 45. Till the End of Time 46. Night Editor 46. The Argyle Secrets 48. Miracle in the Rain 56, many others.
TV series: *Martin Kane* 57.

Garland, Beverly (1926–) (Beverly Fessenden). Pert and pretty leading lady of some fifties Hollywood films; more successful on TV.
DOA 49. The Glass Web 53. The Miami Story 54. The Desperate Hours 55. It Conquered the World 56. Not of this Earth 56. The Joker is Wild 57. The Alligator People 59. Twice Told Tales 63. Pretty Poison 68. The Mad Room 69. Airport 75 74, etc.
TV series: *Decoy* 57. The Bing Crosby Show 64. My Three Sons 66–69.

Garland, Judy (1922–1969) (Frances Gumm). American entertainer and leading lady who for many years radiated the soul of show business. The child of vaudeville performers, on stage from five years old, she later seemed unable to stand the pace of her own success; but her resultant personal difficulties only accentuated the loyalty of her admirers. Special Academy Award 1939 'for her outstanding performance as a screen juvenile'. Biographical books include *The Other*

Side of the Rainbow 1971 by Mel Torme.

□ Every Sunday (short) 36. Pigskin Parade 36. Broadway Melody of 1938 37. Thoroughbreds Don't Cry 38. Everybody Sing 38. Listen Darling 38. Love Finds Andy Hardy 38. *The Wizard of Oz* 39. *Babes in Arms* 39. Andy Hardy Meets a Debutante 39. Strike Up the Band 40. Little Nellie Kelly 40. Ziegfeld Girl 41. Life Begins for Andy Hardy 41. Babes on Broadway 41. *For Me and My Gal* 42. Presenting Lily Mars 42. Girl Crazy 42. Thousands Cheer (guest) 43. *Meet Me in St Louis* 44. Ziegfeld Follies 45. *The Clock* 45. The Harvey Girls 46. Till the Clouds Roll By (guest) 46. The Pirate 47. *Easter Parade* 48. Words and Music (guest) 48. In the Good Old Summertime 49. Summer Stock 50. *A Star Is Born* 54. Judgment at Nuremberg 60. A Child Is Waiting 62. I Could Go On Singing (GB) 63.

Garmes, Lee (1897–). Distinguished American cinematographer, in Hollywood from 1916.
The Grand Duchess and the Waiter 26. The Private Life of Helen of Troy 27. Disraeli 29. Lilies of the Field 30. Whoopee 30. Morocco 30. Dishonoured 31. City Streets 31. An American Tragedy 31. *Shanghai Express* (AA) 32. *Scarface* 32. Smilin' Through 32. *Zoo in Budapest* 33. Crime without Passion 34. The Scoundrel 34. Dreaming Lips (GB) 37. Gone with the Wind (co-ph) (uncredited) 39. Angels over Broadway 40. *Lydia* 41. Jungle Book 42. Guest in the House 44. Since You Went Away 44. *Love Letters* 45. *Duel in the Sun* 46. The Spectre of the Rose (& co-p) 46. The Secret Life of Walter Mitty 47. The Paradine Case 48. Our Very Own 50. Detective Story 51. Actors and Sin (& co-d) 52. The Desperate Hours 55. Land of the Pharaohs 55. The Big Fisherman 59. Hemingway's Adventures of a Young Man 62. Lady in a Cage 64. Big Hand for a Little Lady 66. How to Save a Marriage 68, etc.

Garner, James (1928–) (James Baumgarner). Amiable, good-looking American leading man of the sixties; showed a sense of humour among the action and romance, but did not quite measure up as a substitute for Clark Gable.
□ Toward the Unknown 56. The Girl He Left Behind 56. Shoot out at Medicine Bend 57. Sayonara 57. Darby's Rangers 58. Up Periscope 59. Cash McCall 59. The Children's Hour 62. Boys' Night Out 62. *The Great Escape* 63. *The Thrill of It All* 63. The Wheeler Dealers 63. Move Over Darling 63. *The Americanization of Emily* 64. *Thirty Six Hours* 64. The Art of Love 65. Duel at Diablo 66. A Man Could Get Killed

66. Mister Buddwing 66. Grand Prix 66. Hour of the Gun (as Wyatt Earp) 67. The Pink Jungle 68. How Sweet It Is 68. *Support Your Local Sheriff* 69. Marlowe 69. A Man Called Sledge 70. *The Skin Game* 71. Support Your Local Gunfighter 71. They Only Kill Their Masters 72. Our Little Indian 73. The Castaway Cowboy 74.
TV series: *Maverick* 57–61. Nichols 71. The Rockford Files 74.

Garner, Peggy Ann (1931–). American child star of the forties; Academy Award 1944 as 'outstanding child actress'. Did not make it as adult star.
□ Little Miss Thoroughbred 38. Blondie Brings Up Baby 39. In Name Only 39. Abe Lincoln in Illinois 40. The Pied Piper 42. Eagle Squadron 42. *Jane Eyre* 44. *A Tree Grows in Brooklyn* 45. The Keys of the Kingdom 45. Nob Hill 45. Junior Miss 45. Home Sweet Homicide 46. Daisy Kenyon 47. Thunder in the Valley 47. The Sign of the Ram 48. The Lovable Cheat 49. Bomba the Jungle Boy 49. The Big Cat 49. Teresa 51. The Black Widow 54. Eight Witnesses 54. The Black Forest 54. The Cat 67.

Garnett, Tay (1895–). American director, a light professional talent.
□ Celebrity 28. The Spieler 28. Flying Fools 29. Oh Yeah 29. Officer O'Brien 30. *Her Man* (& w) 30. Bad Company 31. *One Way Passage* (& w) 32. Prestige 32. Okay America 32. Destination Unknown 33. SOS Iceberg 33. China Seas (& w) 35. She Couldn't Take It 35. Professional Soldier 35. Love is News (& w) 37. *Slave Ship* (& w) 37. Stand In 37. Joy of Living 38. Trade Winds (& w) 38. Eternally Yours (& p) 39. Slightly Honorable (& wp) 40. Seven Sinners 40. Cheers for Miss Bishop (& w) 41. My Favorite Spy 42. Bataan 43. The Cross of Lorraine 43. Mrs Parkington 44. The Valley of Decision 45. The Postman Always Rings Twice 46. Wild Harvest 47. A Connecticut Yankee in King Arthur's Court 49. The Fireball (& w) 50. Soldiers Three 51. Cause for Alarm 51. One Minute to Zero 52. Main Street to Broadway 53. The Black Knight 54. Seven Wonders of the World 56. A Terrible Beauty 60. Cattle King 63. The Temper Tramp 73.

Garnett, Tony (1936–). British producer.
□ *Kes* 69. The Body 70. *Family Life* 71.

Garrett, Betty (1919–). Peppy American singer and actress with musical comedy experience.
□ Big City (debut) 46. Words and Music 48. Take Me Out to the Ball Game 48. Neptune's Daughter 49. *On the Town* 49. My Sister Eileen

55. The Shadow on the Window 57.
TV series: All in the Family 73–75.

Garrett, Oliver H. P. (1897–1952). American screenwriter.
Forgotten Faces 28. *Street of Chance* 30. She Couldn't Take It 35. One Third of a Nation 39. The Man I Married 40. Flight for Freedom 43. Duel in the Sun 46. Dead Reckoning 47. Sealed Cargo 51, etc.

Garrett, Otis (c. 1895–1941). American director.
□ The Black Doll 37. The Last Express 38. Personal Secretary 38. Danger on the Air 38. *Lady in the Morgue* 38. The Witness Vanishes 39. The Mystery of the White Room 39. Exile Express 39. Margie 40. Sandy Gets Her Man 41.

Garrick, David (1717–1779). Famous English actor who has been impersonated on screen by Cedric Hardwicke in *Peg of Old Drury* 34 and Brian Aherne in *The Great Garrick* 37.

Garrick, John (1902–) (Reginald Doudy). British stage actor of the twenties and thirties; made some film appearances, usually as 'the other man'.
The Lottery Bride (US) 31. Chu Chin Chow 33. Rocks of Valpre 35. Sunset in Vienna 37. The Great Victor Herbert (US) 39, etc.

Garrison, Sean (1937–). American leading man of the sixties.
Moment to Moment 66. Banning 67, etc.
TV series: Dundee and the Culhane 67.

Garson, Greer (1908–). Red-haired Anglo-Irish leading lady who after stage experience was cast as Mrs Chipping in *Goodbye Mr Chips* 39 and promptly went to Hollywood, where her gentle aristocratic good looks enabled her to reign as a star for ten years.
□ Remember 39. *Pride and Prejudice* 40. *Blossoms in the Dust* 41. When Ladies Meet 41. *Mrs Miniver* (AA) 42. *Random Harvest* 42. *Madame Curie* 43. Mrs Parkington 44. The Valley of Decision 45. Adventure 45. Desire Me 47. Julia Misbehaves 48. *That Forsyte Woman* 49. The Miniver Story 50. The Law and the Lady 51. Scandal at Scourie 52. Julius Caesar 53. Her Twelve Men 53. Strange Lady in Town 54. Sunrise at Campobello (as Eleanor Roosevelt) 60. Pepe 60. The Singing Nun 66. The Happiest Millionaire 67.

Gaslight. Patrick Hamilton's stage suspense thriller, about a Victorian wife deliberately being driven insane by her murderous husband, was perfectly filmed in Britain in 1939 by Thorold Dickinson with Anton Walbrook, Diana Wynyard and Frank Pettingell. MGM promptly bought and destroyed the negative, and in 1943 produced an opulent and inferior remake with Charles Boyer, Ingrid Bergman (AA) and Joseph Cotten, directed by George Cukor. In Britain this version was known as *The Murder in Thornton Square*; prints of the original version did survive and have been shown in America as *Angel Street*.

Gasnier, Louis J. (1882–1963). American director: mostly of foreign language versions.
Darkened Rooms 29. The Lawyer's Secret 31. Forgotten Commandments 32. Gambling Ship 33. The Last Outpost 35. Bank Alarm 37. Murder on the Yukon 40. Fight On Marines 42, etc.

Gassman, Vittorio (1922–). Italian actor and matinée idol, in occasional films since 1946.
Bitter Rice 48. Sombrero (US) 53. Rhapsody (US) 54. War and Peace 56. Tempest 57. The Love Specialist 60. Barabbas 62. The Devil in Love 66. Woman Times Seven 67, etc.

Gastoni, Lisa (1935–). Italian leading lady in British films of the fifties.
The Runaway Bus 54. Man of the Moment 55. The Baby and the Battleship 56. Intent to Kill 58. Hello London 59. Passport to China 64. Maddalena 72. The Last Days of Mussolini 74, etc.

Gate of Hell (Jigokumon) (Japan 1953). Known principally for its outstanding use of Eastmancolor, this medieval legend was directed by Teinosuke Kinugasa and photographed by Kohei Suziyama. Academy Award 1954: 'best foreign film'.

Gates, Larry (1915–). American character actor, often seen as small town merchant or middle-aged good guy.
Has Anybody Seen My Gal? 52. The Girl Rush 54. Invasion of the Body Snatchers 56. Jeanne Eagels 57. Cat on a Hot Tin Roof 58. One Foot in Hell 60. The Hoodlum Priest 62. Toys in the Attic 63. The Sand Pebbles 67. Airport 69, etc.

Gates, Nancy (1926–). American leading lady of the forties and fifties.
The Great Gildersleeve 42. The Spanish Main 45. The Atomic City 52. The Member of the Wedding 53. Suddenly 54. The Search for Bridey Murphy 56. The Brass Legend 56. Death of a Scoundrel 56. Some Came Running 59. Comanche Station 60, etc.

Gaudio, Tony (1885–1951) (Gaetono Gaudio). Italian cinematographer, long in Hollywood.
The Mark of Zorro 20. Secrets 24. The Temptress 25. Two Arabian Knights 27. *Hell's Angels* 30. Sky Devils 32. Bordertown 35. The Story of Louis Pasteur 35. *Anthony Adverse* (AA) 36. *The Life of Emile Zola* 37. *The Adventures of Robin Hood* 38. Juarez 39. *The Letter* 40. The Great Lie 41. The Constant Nymph 43. A Song to Remember 45. Love From a Stranger 47. The Red Pony 49, many others.

Gauge, Alexander (1914–1960). Heavyweight British actor, Friar Tuck in TV's *Robin Hood* series.
The Interrupted Journey (debut) 49. Murder in the Cathedral 51. Pickwick Papers 52. Fast and Loose 54. Martin Luther 55. The Iron Petticoat 56. The Passing Stranger 57, etc.

Gaumont, Leon (1863–1946). Pioneer French inventor, producer and exhibitor. Founder of Gaumont Studios at Shepherds Bush, also Gaumont circuit, both later sold to Rank. Invented sound on disc in 1902.

Gautier, Dick (1939–). American leading man of the seventies.
Wild in the Sky 72.
TV series: *Here We Go Again* 72.

Gavin, John (1928–). American leading man.
A Time To Live and a Time To Die 58. Imitation of Life 59. Spartacus 60. Psycho 60. A Breath of Scandal 61. Back Street 61. Romanoff and Juliet 62. Thoroughly Modern Millie 67. The Madwoman of Chaillot 69. Pussycat Pussycat I Love You 70. Rich Man Poor Man (TV) 76, etc.
TV series: Destry 62. Convoys 65.

Gawthorne, Peter (1884–1962). Splendidly pompous-looking British stage actor, often seen as general, admiral or chief constable in comedies of the thirties.
Sunny Side Up (US) 29. Charlie Chan Carries On (US) 31. Jack's the Boy 32. The Iron Duke 35. Wolf's Clothing 36. Alf's Button Afloat 38. *Ask a Policeman* 40. Much Too Shy 42. The Case of Charles Peace 49. Five Days 54, many others.

Gaxton, William (1893–1963). American entertainer who made a few film appearances.
Fifty Million Frenchmen 31. Something to Shout About 42. Best Foot Forward 43. Tropicana 44. Diamond Horseshoe 45, etc.

Gaye, Gregory (c. 1900–). American character actor.
Dodsworth 36. Hollywood Boulevard 36. Ninotchka 39. Cash 42. The Bachelor and the Bobbysoxer 47. The Eddy Duchin Story 56. Auntie Mame 58, etc.

Gaynor, Janet (1906–) (Laura Gainer). American leading lady of the twenties and thirties, immensely popular in simple sentimental films, especially when teamed with Charles Farrell. Played in many short comedies and westerns before achieving star status. Retired 1939 apart from a mother role in *Bernardine* 57.
The Johnstown Flood 26. *Seventh Heaven* (AA) 27. *Sunrise* 27. Street Angel 28. Lucky Star 29. Sunny Side Up 29. High Society Blues 30. *Daddy Longlegs* 31. Delicious 31. Merely Mary Ann 31. Tess of the Storm Country 32. *State Fair* 33. Paddy the Next Best Thing 33. Carolina 34. The Farmer Takes a Wife 35. Ladies in Love 36. *A Star Is Born* 37. Three Loves Has Nancy 38. *The Young in Heart* 39, etc.

Gaynor, Mitzi (1930–) (Francesca Mitzi von Gerber). American light leading lady with singing and dancing talents.
□ My Blue Heaven 50. Take Care of My Little Girl 51. *Golden Girl* 51. We're Not Married 51. Bloodhounds of Broadway 51. The I Don't Care Girl 53. Down Among the Sheltering Palms 53. Three Young Texans 54. There's No Business Like Show Business 54. Anything Goes 56. The Birds and the Bees 56. The Joker is Wild 57. Les Girls 57. *South Pacific* 58. Happy Anniversary 59. Surprise Package 60. For Love or Money 63.

Gayson, Eunice (1931–). British leading lady, also on stage.
Dance Hall 50. Street Corner 53. Out of the Clouds 54. Zarak 57. The Revenge of Frankenstein 58, etc.

Gazzara, Ben (1930–). American actor, usually of rebellious types.
□ The Strange One 57. *Anatomy of a Murder* 59. The Young Doctors 61. Convicts Four 62. A Rage to Live 65. The Bridge at Remagen 69. Husbands 70. When Michael Calls (w) 72. Pursued (TV) 72. The Family Rico (TV) 72. Indict and Convict (TV) 73. The Neptune Factor 73. Maneater (TV) 73. Capone 75. High Velocity 76.
TV series: *Arrest and Trial* 63. *Run for Your Life* 65–67.

Geer, Will (1902–). American character actor with a penchant for sinister old men.
The Misleading Lady 32. Deep Waters 48. Intruder in the Dust 49. Broken Arrow 50. The

Tall Target 51. Salt of the Earth 53. Advise and Consent 61. *Seconds* 66. In Cold Blood 67. Bandolero 68. The Reivers 70. Brother John 70. Napoleon and Samantha 72. Executive Action 73, etc.
TV series: *The Waltons* 72–.

Geesink, Joop (1913–). Dutch puppeteer who in the late thirties made several shorts under the general heading of 'Dollywood'.

Geeson, Judy (1948–). British leading lady who started with sexy teenage roles.
Berserk 67. To Sir With Love 67. Here We Go Round the Mulberry Bush 67. Prudence and the Pill 68. Hammerhead 68. Three into Two Won't Go 69. The Executioner 69. 10 Rillington Place 70. One of Those Things 71. Who Killed the Mysterious Mr Foster? (TV) 71. Doomwatch 72. Fear in the Night 72, etc.

Geeson, Sally (1950–). British juvenile actress of the sixties, sister of Judy Geeson.
□ What's Good for the Goose 68. Cry of the Banshee 70. Forbush and the Penguins 71.

Gelin, Daniel (1921–). French leading man with stage experience. In films since 1941.
Rendezvous de Juillet 49. *Edouard et Caroline* 50. *La Ronde* 50. Les Mains Sales 51. Rue de l'Estrapade 53. Les Amants du Tage (The Lovers of Lisbon) 54. The Man Who Knew Too Much (US) 55. Charmants Garçons 57. There's Always a Price Tag 58. Carthage in Flames 60. The Season for Love 65. Black Sun 66. Le Souffle au Coeur 71, etc.

Gemma, Giuliano (1940–). Italian leading man of spaghetti westerns.
The Titans 62. Goliath and the Sins of Babylon 63. Adios Gringo 65. A Pistol for Ringo 65. Day of Anger 67. A Man to Respect 72, etc.

The General (US 1926). Famous Buster Keaton silent comedy-adventure with a Civil War setting and a train as co-hero. Basically a succession of impeccably-timed gags devised by Keaton himself. The story was used by Walt Disney in somewhat more serious vein for *The Great Locomotive Chase* 56.

The General Died at Dawn (US 1936). A rather pretentious melodrama which gave the impression of being backed by political thought, concerning an idealistic American's fight against a Chinese warlord. It paved the way for Hollywood involvement in the Spanish Civil War. Directed by Lewis Milestone, with Gary Cooper, Madeleine Carroll and Akim Tamiroff.

The General Line (The Old and the New) (Russia 1928). A brilliant semi-documentary, photographed by Tissé and directed by Eisenstein, intended as propaganda to introduce the newest and most productive methods to Soviet peasant farmers.

A Generation (Poland 1954). Andrzej Wajda's famous trilogy (the other two titles being *Kanal* 56, *Ashes and Diamonds* 58) gave a vivid picture of life in wartime Poland. Its impact is largely responsible for the resurgence of that country's film industry during sixties.

Genevieve (GB 1953). A sophisticated comedy, written by William Rose and directed by Henry Cornelius, which marked a turn away from Ealing's polished innocence towards a more realistic Chelsea-based robustness. Despite many imitations its freshness and *joie de vivre* have not been equalled. Larry Adler's harmonica score immensely assisted the frolicsome story of a vintage car race from London to Brighton, and there were made to measure parts for Kenneth More, Kay Kendall, Dinah Sheridan and John Gregson.

Genina, Augusto (1892–1957). Italian pioneer director.
La Gloria 13. Prix de Beauté 30. The White Squadron 35. Bengasi 42. Heaven Over the Marshes 49. Three Forbidden Stories 52. Maddalena 54. Frou Frou 55, many others.

Genn, Leo (1905–). Bland British character actor, formerly a practising barrister.
Immortal Gentleman 35. Dream Doctor 36. Jump for Glory 37. Kate Plus Ten 38. Contraband 40. The Way Ahead 44. *Henry V* 46. Caesar and Cleopatra 45. *Green for Danger* 46. Mourning Becomes Electra (US) 48. The Velvet Touch (US) 48. *The Snake Pit* (US) 48. The Wooden Horse 50. The Miniver Story 50. *Quo Vadis* 51. Plymouth Adventure (US) 52. Personal Affair 53. The Green Scarf 55. Beyond Mombasa 56. Lady Chatterley's Lover (Fr.) 56. Moby Dick 56. I Accuse 57. No Time To Die 58. Too Hot To Handle 60. The Longest Day 62. Fifty-Five Days at Peking 62. Ten Little Indians 65. Circus of Fear 67. Connecting Rooms 69. Die Screaming Marianne 70, etc.

Gentleman's Agreement (US 1948) (AA). An earnest indictment of anti-Semitism, written by Moss Hart from Laura Hobson's novel, and directed by Elia Kazan, with Gregory Peck and John Garfield. Not very lively as a film, but immensely significant to Hollywood as the first of a series of anti-racialist pictures.

Gentlemen Prefer Blondes. Anita Loos' comic novel about a gold-digging twenties chorus girl on the make in the millionaire set was filmed in 1928 by Mal St Clair, with Ruth Taylor and Alice White, then in 1953 by Howard Hawks with Marilyn Monroe and Jane Russell.

George, Chief Dan (1899–). Canadian Indian actor.
□ Smith! 69. *Little Big Man* 70. Alien Thunder 73. Harry and Tonto 74. The Bears and I 74. The Outlaw Josey Wales 76.

George, Christopher (1929–). American TV leading man.
El Dorado 68. Tiger by the Tail 69. Escape (TV) 69. The Immortal (TV) 69. Man on a String (TV) 72. I Escaped from Devil's Island 73. Grizzly 76, etc.
TV series: The Rat Patrol 66. The Immortal 69, etc.

George, Gladys (1900–1954) (Gladys Clare). American leading actress with stage experience.
□ Red Hot Dollars 20. Home Spun Folks 20. The Easy Road 21. Chickens 21. The House that Jazz Built 21. Straight is the Way 34. *Valiant is the World for Carrie* 36. They Gave Him a Gun 37. *Madame X* 37. Love is a Headache 38. Marie Antoinette 38. *The Roaring Twenties* 39. Here I Am a Stranger 39. I'm from Missouri 39. A Child is Born 40. The Way of all Flesh 40. The House Across the Bay 40. *The Maltese Falcon* 41. The Lady from Cheyenne 41. Hit the Road 41. The Hard Way 42. Nobody's Darling 43. The Crystal Ball 43. Minstrel Man 44. Christmas Holiday 44. Steppin In Society 45. The Best Years of Our Lives 46. Millie's Daughter 47. Alias a Gentleman 48. Flamingo Road 49. Undercover Girl 50. Bright Leaf 50. He Ran all the Way 51. Detective Story 51. Lullaby of Broadway 51. Dark City 51. Silver City 53. It Happens Every Thursday 54.

George, Grace (1879–1961). American stage actress whose one film, in 1943, was *Johnny Come Lately*.

George, Muriel (1883–1965). Plump, motherly British character actress who often played charladies or landladies. Music-hall background.
His Lordship (debut) 32. Yes Mr Brown 33. Dr Syn 37. A Sister to Assist 'Er (leading role) 38. Quiet Wedding 40. Dear Octopus 43. The Dancing Years 49. Simon and Laura 55, many others.

George, Susan (1950–). British leading lady,

former child actress; usually typed as sexpot.
Billion Dollar Brain 67. The Strange Affair 68. Twinky 68. All Neat in Black Stockings 69. Spring and Port Wine 69. The Looking Glass War 69. Die Screaming Marianne 70. Eye Witness 70. Fright 71. The Straw Dogs 71. Dirty Mary Crazy Larry 73. Sonny and Jed 74. Mandingo 75. Out of Season 75, etc.

Georgy Girl (GB 1966). The dying fall of Britain's 'new wave', this eccentric comedy cast Lynn Redgrave as a plain Jane who envies her glamorous but selfish girl friend; she finally settles for adopting the friend's unwanted baby and marriage to a lecherous businessman. Touches of zany black comedy did not give the wanted illusion of freshness. With James Mason and Charlotte Rampling; directed by Silvio Narizzano from Peter Nichols' rather desperate screenplay.

Gerald, Jim (1889–1958) (Jacques Guenod). French actor, in occasional films from 1911.
An Italian Straw Hat 27. La Chant au Marin 31. French Without Tears (as le professeur) 39. Boule de Suif 45. The Crimson Curtain 52. Father Brown 54. Fric Frac en Dentelles 57, etc.

Gerald McBoing Boing (US 1951). The first Stephen Bosustow cartoon for UPA, whose spareness of line and sharpness of wit contrasted happily with Disney's chocolate-box period. It concerned a little boy who could speak only sounds. There were a couple of less successful sequels.

Gerasimov, Sergei (1906–). Russian director, best known abroad for *And Quietly Flows the Don* 57. Formerly an actor.

Geray, Steve (1904–1976) (Stefan Gyergyay). Hungarian character actor of stage and screen, usually seen as mild-mannered little fellow. In London from 1934, Hollywood from 1941.
Dance Band 34. Inspector Hornleigh 39. Man at Large 41. *The Moon and Sixpence* (as Dirk Stroeve) 42. Night Train from Chungking 43. The Mask of Dimitrios 44. *So Dark the Night* (leading role) 46. *Gilda* 46. I Love Trouble 48. The Big Sky 52. Call Me Madam 53. The Birds and the Bees 56. Count Your Blessings 59. Dime with a Halo 63, many others.

Gering, Marion (1901–). Polish-Russian director with long stage experience; in America from 1925.
The Devil and the Deep 32. Madame Butterfly 33. Rumba 35. Lady of Secrets 36. Thunder in the City (GB) 37. She Married an Artist 38.

Sarumba (& co-p) 50, etc.

Germaine, Mary (1933–). British leading lady of the fifties.
Laughter in Paradise 51. Where's Charley? 52. Women of Twilight 53. The Green Buddha (last to date) 54, etc.

German cinema had its most influential period in the years following World War I, when depression and despair drove directors into a macabre fantasy world and produced films like *The Golem, The Cabinet of Dr Caligari, Nosferatu, Warning Shadows* and *Waxworks*; it is also notable that many of the makers of these films later went to Hollywood and exerted a strong influence there. G. W. Pabst was somewhat more anchored to reality, apart from the stylish *Die Dreigroschenoper*; Fritz Lang seemed primarily interested in the criminal mentality, though he produced masterworks of prophecy and Teutonic legend. With the advent of Hitler most of Germany's genuine creative talent was forced abroad; the main achievements of the thirties were Leni Riefenstahl's colossal propaganda pieces *Triumph of the Will* and *Olympische Spiele*. The anti-British war-time films have their interest, but the post-war German cinema was not producing competent thrillers and comedies for the home market. In the seventies however a new realistic school developed in the hands of Rainer Fassbinder, Werner Herzog, etc. Notable German players include Werner Krauss, Conrad Veidt, Marlene Dietrich, Anton Walbrook and Gert Frobe.

Germi, Pietro (1914–1974). Italian director, in films since 1945.
In the Name of the Law 49. The Road to Hope 50. Man of Iron 56. Maledotto Imbroglio (A Sordid Affair) 59. Divorce Italian Style 61. Seduced and Abandoned 63. The Birds the Bees and the Italians 65. Alfredo Alfredo 73, many others.

Geronimo (1829–1909). Apache Indian chief who dealt destruction to the whites. Memorably impersonated by Chief Thundercloud in *Geronimo* 38, Jay Silverheels in *The Battle at Apache Pass* 52, Chuck Connors in *Geronimo* 62.

Gerrard, Gene (1892–1971) (Eugene O'Sullivan). British music hall comedian with engaging light style: starred in several comedy musicals of the thirties.
Let's Love and Laugh 31. *My Wife's Family* 31. *Out of the Blue* (& d) 31. Let Me Explain Dear (& d) 32. The Love Nest 33. It's a Bet 35. No

Monkey Business 35. Where's Sally? 36. Glamour Girl 37, etc.

Gershenson, Joseph (1904–). Russian musician, long in US. In films from 1920; head of Universal music department from 1941.

Gershwin, George (1889–1937). American popular composer of scores of songs and concert pieces. Contributed to many films. His biography was told in *Rhapsody in Blue* 45, and his music was used exclusively in *An American in Paris* 51. Three hitherto unpublished songs were even used in *Kiss Me Stupid* 64.

Gershwin, Ira (1896–). American lyricist, brother of George Gershwin. Has written for stage since 1918, films since 1931.
Delicious 31. Goldwyn Follies 39. Cover Girl 44. An American in Paris 51. Kiss Me Stupid 64, many others.

Gertie the Dinosaur. Early American cartoon character created by Winsor McKay in 1909.

Gertsman, Maury (c. 1910–). American cinematographer.
Strange Confession 45. Terror by Night 46. Singapore 47. Rachel and the Stranger 48. One Way Street 50. Meet Danny Wilson 52. The World in My Corner 55. Kelly and Me 57. Gunfight in Abilene 66, many others.

Gervaise (France 1956). Written by Jean Aurenche and Pierre Bost from Zola's novel, directed by René Clement, this seamy story presented a vivid picture of 19th-century Paris, comparable with David Lean's Dickens films. Delightfully acted by Maria Schell, François Perier and Suzy Delair.

The Ghost Breaker. This American stage thriller by Paul Dickey and Charles W. Goddard, about an heiress's voodoo-haunted castle, was filmed in 1915 with H. B. Warner and in 1922 (directed by Alfred E. Green) with Wallace Reid. In 1940 George Marshall directed a talkie version as a vehicle for Bob Hope, and the result was an oddly successful combination of laughs and horror, with contributions from Willie Best, Paulette Goddard and Paul Lukas. (The title, incidentally, was made plural.) In 1953 Marshall remade it, with remarkable fidelity to the 1940 script, as a vehicle for Martin and Lewis under the title *Scared Stiff*, with Lizabeth Scott and Carmen Miranda; the results were hardly stimulating.

The Ghost Goes West. (GB 1936). René

Clair showed British films a lighter touch than they had known before in this fantasy of a gay Scottish ghost who follows his castle when it is moved stone by stone to America. Robert Donat shone in a dual role.

The Ghost Train. This hugely successful British stage comedy-thriller by Arnold Ridley, about stranded passengers at a lonely Cornish station being used by gun-runners, was first filmed in 1928, directed by C. Bolvary, with Guy Newall as the silly-ass hero who turns out to be a policeman. A talkie version followed in 1931 with Jack Hulbert, directed by Walter Forde, who also directed the 1941 remake in which the leading role was split between Arthur Askey and Richard Murdoch.

ghosting. Another word for dubbing, especially when a star apparently singing is actually miming to the voice of the real artist. See *dubbing.*

ghosts: see *fantasy.*

Giallelis, Stathis (1939–). Greek actor who went to Hollywood.
America America 63. Cast a Giant Shadow 66. The Eavesdropper 67, etc.

giants are infrequently encountered in films, but Harold Lloyd met one in *Why Worry?*, as did Abbott and Costello in *Lost in a Harem.* Costello also met *The Thirty Foot Bride of Candy Rock,* not to be confused with *The Attack of the Fifty Foot Woman.* Then there was *The Giant of Marathon,* and Glenn Langan played *The Amazing Colossal Man* in two films. Back to Abbott and Costello again: it was they who appeared with Buddy Baer in *Jack and The Beanstalk.*

Gibbons, Cedric (1895–1960). American art director; worked for Edison 1915–17, Goldwyn 1918–24, MGM 1924 on. Co-directed one film, *Tarzan and His Mate* 34. Designed the 'Oscar' statuette.
The Bridge of San Luis Rey (AA) 29. Pride and Prejudice (AA) 40. Blossoms in the Dust (AA) 41. Gaslight (AA) 44. The Yearling (AA) 46. Little Women (AA) 49. An American in Paris (AA) 51, hundreds of others.

Gibbs, Gerald (c. 1910–). British cinematographer.
Whisky Galore 49. Fortune Is a Woman 57. The Man Upstairs 58. The Leather Boys 63. A Jolly Bad Fellow 64. Mister Ten Per Cent 67, etc.

Gibson, Alan (1938–). Canadian director in Britain.
□ Crescendo 69. Goodbye Gemini 70. Dracula AD 1972 72. The Satanic Rites of Dracula 73.

Gibson, Helen (1892–) (Rose August Wenger). American leading lady of the silent screen; of Swiss descent; married to Hoot Gibson. Former stunt girl. Appeared in *Hollywood Story* 51.
The Hazards of Helen (serial) 15. No Man's Woman 20. The Wolverine 21, etc.

Gibson, Hoot (1892–1962) (Edward Gibson). American cowboy hero of silent films; in Hollywood from 1911 after real cowpunching experience. Films good-humoured but not memorable.
The Hazards of Helen 15. The Cactus Kid 19. The Denver Dude 22. Surefire 24. Galloping Fury 27. Points West 29. Spirit of the West 32. Powdersmoke Range 33. Sunset Range 35. The Marshal's Daughter 53. The Horse Soldiers 59. Ocean's Eleven 61, hundreds of others.

Gibson, Wynne (1899–). American leading lady, from the chorus.
Nothing But the Truth 30. Ladies of the Big House 32. I Give My Love 34. The Captain Hates the Sea 34. Gangs of New York 38. Café Hostess 40. The Falcon Strikes Back 43, many others.

Gidding, Nelson (c. 1915–). American screenwriter.
I Want To Live 58. Odds against Tomorrow 59. Nine Hours to Rama 61. The Inspector 62. The Haunting 64. Lost Command 66, The Andromeda Strain 70, etc.

Gidget: an American teenager of the early sixties, a kind of female Andy Hardy. The first film was released in 1959 and starred Sandra Dee. Then in 1961 came *Gidget Goes Hawaiian* with Deborah Walley, and in 1963 *Gidget Goes to Rome* with Cindy Carol. In 1971 there were TV movies called *Gidget Grows Up* with Karen Valentine, and *Gidget Gets Married* with Monie Ellis; in 1972 came a cartoon version, *Gidget Makes the Wrong Connection.* In 1965 there was also a TV series with Sally Field.

Gielgud, Sir John (1904–). Distinguished British stage actor who has made occasional films.
□ Who Is the Man? 24. The Clue of the New Pin 29. Insult 32. The Good Companions 32. Secret Agent 36. The Prime Minister (as Disraeli) 40. *Julius Caesar* (as Cassius) 53. Richard III 56.

The Barretts of Wimpole Street 57. Saint Joan 57. Becket 64. The Loved One 65. Chimes at Midnight 66. Around the World In Eighty Days 66. Sebastian 67. *The Charge of the Light Brigade* 68. Assignment to Kill 68. The Shoes of the Fisherman 68. Oh What a Lovely War 69. Julius Caesar 70. Eagle in a Cage 71. Probe (TV) 72. Lost Horizon 73. Frankenstein, the True Story (TV) 73. QB VII 73. 11 Harrowhouse 74. Luther 74. Gold 74. *Murder on the Orient Express* 74. Galileo 75.

Gifford, Alan (1905–). American character actor in British films.
It Started in Paradise 52. Lilacs in the Spring 54. The Iron Petticoat 56. A King in New York 57. Too Young to Love 60. Carry On Cowboy 66, Arrivederci Baby 66. Phase IV 73, etc.

Gifford, Frances (1922–). American leading lady of the forties, trained as lawyer. Career subsequently halted by ill-health.
Hold That Woman 40. Jungle Girl 41. My Son Alone 42. Tarzan Triumphs 43. She Went to the Races 45. Little Mister Jim 46. Luxury Liner 48. Riding High 49. Sky Commando 53, etc.

Gigi (US 1958) (AA). Colette's novel of a *fin-de-siècle* Parisian cocotte was filmed straight in the forties with Daniele Delorme, but is now best known in the form of the American musical, directed by Vincente Minnelli (AA) with a Lerner and Loewe score (AA). Cecil Beaton's designs (AA) shared honours with Leslie Caron, Maurice Chevalier and Louis Jourdan. The film won nine Academy Awards.

Gigli, Beniamino (1890–1957). Famous Italian tenor who starred in several films.
Forget Me Not 35. Ave Maria 37. Pagliacci 42. Night Taxi 50, etc.

Gigolos are figures from another age, when women could be imposed on, but they were memorably played by David Niven in *Dodsworth*, Montgomery Clift in *The Heiress*, Fred MacMurray in *The Lady is Willing*, Burt Lancaster in *Sorry Wrong Number*, William Holden in *Sunset Boulevard*, Van Johnson in *Invitation*, Bekim Fehmiu in *The Adventurers*, Jon Voight in *Midnight Cowboy*, Charles Grodin in *The Heartbreak Kid* and Helmet Berger in *Ash Wednesday*.

Gilbert, Billy (1893–1971). American character comedian usually seen as a fat, excitable Italian. In films since 1929, after vaudeville experience: a memorable stooge for Laurel and Hardy, the Three Stooges and the Marx Brothers.
Noisy Neighbours (debut) 29. The Music Box 32. Sutter's Gold 37. Snow White and the Seven Dwarfs (as the voice of Sneezy) 37. Blockheads 38. Destry Rides Again 39. *The Great Dictator* (as Goering) 40. *His Girl Friday* 40. Tin Pan Alley 41. Anchors Aweigh 45. Down Among the Sheltering Palms 52. Five Weeks in a Balloon 62, many others.

Gilbert, John (1895–1936) (John Pringle). American leading man of the twenties. From a theatrical family, he worked his way up from bit parts to romantic leads, but sound revealed his voice to be less dashing than his looks.
Princess of the Dark 17. Should a Woman Tell 19. Ladies in Love 21. The Count of Monte Cristo 22. A Man's Mate 23. Cameo Kirby 23. The Merry Widow 25. *The Big Parade* 25. La Bohème 26. Love 27. *Flesh and the Devil* 27. Man, Woman and Sin 28. The Cossacks 28. Desert Nights 29. Redemption 30. The Way of a Sailor 32. Queen Christina 33. The Captain Hates the Sea 34, etc.

Gilbert, Lewis (1920–). British director, former actor and documentarist.
□ The Little Ballerina 47. Marry Me (w only) 49. Once a Sinner 50. There Is another Sun 50. The Scarlet Thread 51. Emergency Call 52. Time Gentlemen Please 52. Cosh Boy 53. Johnny on the Run 53. *Albert RN* 53. The Sea Shall Not Have Them 54. *The Good Die Young* 54. Cast a Dark Shadow 55. *Reach for the Sky* 56. The Admirable Crichton 57. Carve Her Name with Pride 57. A Cry from the Streets 58. Ferry to Hong Kong 59. *Sink The Bismarck* 60. Light Up the Sky 60. The Greengage Summer 61. HMS Defiant 62. The Seventh Dawn 64. Alfie 66. You Only Live Twice 67. The Adventurers 70. Friends (& w) 71. Paul and Michelle 73. Operation Daybreak 75. Seven Nights in Japan 76. The Spy Who Loved Me 77.

Gilbert, Paul (1917–) (Paul MacMahon). American comedy dancer, former trapezist.
So This Is Paris 55. The Second Greatest Sex 55. You Can't Run Away from It 56. Women of the Prehistoric Planet 66, etc.

Gilbert, W. S. (1836–1911) (William Schwenck) and **Sullivan, Sir Arthur** (1842–1900). Celebrated British composers (words and music respectively) of the Savoy operas of the eighties, most cherished for their comic aspects and still performed all over the world by the D'Oyly Carte Company. Many film versions have been made, notably of *The*

Mikado. In 1954 came a moderate biopic, *The Story of Gilbert and Sullivan,* with Robert Morley and Maurice Evans.

Gilchrist, Connie (1901–). American character actress of stage and screen.
Billy the Kid 41. The Hucksters 47. A Letter to Three Wives 49. The Man in the Grey Flannel Suit 56. Some Came Running 58. Auntie Mame 59. Say One For Me 59. A House Is Not a Home 64. Sylvia 65. Tickle Me 65. Fuzz 70, etc.
TV series: Long John Silver 56.

Gilda (US 1946). A highly professional example of the glossy *film noir* coming out of Hollywood in the somewhat dejected period following World War II, when victory had turned to ashes. Everyone in this tale is cynical and at least partly corrupt: George Macready as the nominal villain evokes more sympathy than hero (Glenn Ford) or heroine (Rita Hayworth). Charles Vidor's direction is showy but controlled, and Hayworth's song numbers (including 'Put the Blame on Mame') show her at her most torrid. Other films of this time and genre include *Till the End of Time, The Blue Dahlia, Johnny O'Clock, Build My Gallows High* and *The Strange Love of Martha Ivers.*

Giler, David (–). American screenwriter with many TV credits.
Myra Breckinridge (co-w) 70. The Parallax View (co-w) 74. The Black Bird (& d) 75.

Gilford, Jack (1907–). American comic actor with long stage career.
Hey Rookie 53. Main Street to Broadway 53. A Funny Thing Happened on the Way to the Forum 66. Mister Buddwing 66. Enter Laughing 67. The Happening 67. Who's Minding the Mint? 67. They Might Be Giants 71. Catch 22 71. Save the Tiger 73, etc.

Gilles, Genevieve (1946–) (Genevieve Gillaizeau). French leading lady, protégée of Darryl Zanuck.
□ World of Fashion (short) 67. Hello-Goodbye 69.

Gillette, William (1855–1937). American stage actor famous for his personification of *Sherlock Holmes,* which he played on film in 1916.

Gilliat, Leslie (1917–). British producer, brother of Sidney Gilliat, with whom he usually works.

Gilliat, Sidney (1908–). British comedy

screenwriter usually in collaboration with Frank Launder (qv); they have also produced most of their films since the forties.
Rome Express 33. *Friday the Thirteenth* 33. Jack Ahoy 34. Chu Chin Chow 34. Bulldog Jack 35. Where There's a Will 36. Seven Sinners 36. Take My Tip 37. *A Yank at Oxford* 38. *The Lady Vanishes* 38. The Gaunt Stranger 38. Jamaica Inn 39. *Ask a Policeman* 39. They Came by Night 40. *Night Train to Munich* 40. *Kipps* 41. *The Young Mr Pitt* 42. Millions Like Us (& d) 43. *Waterloo Road* (& d) 44. *The Rake's Progress* (& d) 45. *Green for Danger* (& d) 46. London Belongs to Me (& d) 48. *State Secret* (& d) 50. The Story of Gilbert and Sullivan (& d) 53. The Constant Husband (& d) 55. Fortune is a Woman (& d) 57. Left Right and Centre (& d) 59. *Only Two Can Play* (& d) 62. The Great St Trinian's Train Robbery (& d) 65, etc.

Gilliatt, Penelope (1933–). British critic and screenwriter: Sunday Bloody Sunday 72.

Gillie, Jean (1915–1949). British leading lady, former chorine.
School for Stars 35. Brewster's Millions 35. While Parents Sleep 36. Sweet Devil 38. Tilly of Bloomsbury 40. Sailors Don't Care 40. The Gentle Sex 43. *Tawny Pipit* 44. Decoy (US) 47. The Macomber Affair (US) 47, etc.

Gilling, John (1912–). British writer-director who has turned out dozens of crime and adventure pot-boilers since the war.
The Greed of William Hart (w) 48. The Man from Yesterday (wd) 49. No Trace (wd) 50. Mother Riley Meets the Vampire (wd) 52. The Voice of Merrill (d) 52. The Gamma People (wd) 55. Odongo (wd) 56. Interpol (wd) 57. High Flight (d) 57. The Man Inside (wd) 58. Idle on Parade (d) 59. The Flesh and the Fiends (wd) 59. The Challenge (wd) 60. Fury at Smuggler's Bay (wd) 61. Shadow of the Cat (wd) 62. Pirates of Blood River (wd) 62. The Scarlet Blade (wd) 63. The Brigand of Kandahar (wd) 64. The Plague of the Zombies (wd) 65. The Mummy's Shroud (wd) 67, many others.

Gillingwater, Claude (1870–1939). American stage actor who came to films to play irascible old men.
Little Lord Fauntleroy 21. Dulcy 23. Daddies 24. Daddy Long Legs 31. The Captain Hates the Sea 34. A Tale of Two Cities 36. Prisoner of Shark Island 36. Conquest 37. Café Society 39, etc.

Gillis, Ann (1927–) (Alma O'Connor).

American child star of the thirties; adult roles routine.

The Garden of Allah 37. Off to the Races 37. *The Adventures of Tom Sawyer* 38. The Underpup 39. Little Men 40. Nice Girl 41. In Society 44. Since You Went Away 44. Janie Gets Married 46, etc.

Gillmore, Margalo (1897–). American stage actress in occasional films.
Wayward 32. Perfect Strangers 50. The Law and the Lady 51. Skirts Ahoy 52. Woman's World 54. Gaby 56. High Society 56, etc.

Gilmore, Lowell (1907–1960). American general purpose actor.
Calcutta 47. Dream Girl 48. Tripoli 50. Lone Star 52. Plymouth Adventure 52. Saskatchewan 54, etc.

Gilmore, Virginia (1919–) (Sherman Poole). American leading lady of the forties; films routine.
Winter Carnival 39. Laddie 40. Swamp Water 41. The Loves of Edgar Allan Poe 42. Orchestra Wives 42. Chetniks 43. Wonder Man 45. Close Up 48. Walk East on Beacon 52, etc.

gimmicks. There are those who would classify such developments as 3-D, CinemaScope and even talkies under this heading. The genuine gimmick however is a more fleeting affair, a momentary method for getting audiences into cinemas for reasons that have little to do with the quality of the film. William Castle is the established master. For *Macabre* he offered free insurance if one died of heart failure. For *Homicidal*, a fright break before the climax when cowards could leave—and even get their money back if they could stand to go home without learning the awful secret. For *The House on Haunted Hill*, 'Emergo', in which a skeleton on wires shot above the audience's head at a suitable point in the film. For *The Tingler*, a device which wired up certain seats to give people a small electric shock. In competition, the producers of *Chamber of Horrors* thought up the fear flasher and the horror horn to warn weak spirits when a nasty moment was coming.

Gingold, Hermione (1897–). British revue comedienne who delights in grotesque characters.
Autobiography 1958: *The World is Square*.
Someone at the Door 36. Meet Mr Penny 39. The Butler's Dilemma 43. Cosh Boy 52. *Pickwick Papers* 52. Our Girl Friday 53. Around the World in Eighty Days 56. *Bell, Book and Candle* (US) 58. *Gigi* (US) 58. *The Music Man*

(US) 61. I'd Rather Be Rich (US) 64. Harvey Middlemann, Fireman (US) 65. Munster Go Home (US) 66. Banyon (TV) 71. *A Little Night Music* 76, etc.

Girard, Bernard (c. 1929–). American director.
□ Ride Out for Revenge 57. Green Eyed Blonde 57. The Party Crashers 58. As Young as we Are 58. Dead Heat on a Merry Go Round 68. The Mad Room 69. Gone with the West 69. The Happiness Cage 72.

Girardot, Annie (1931–). French leading lady.
Thirteen at Table 56. Maigret Sets a Trap 58. Vice and Virtue 63. Vivre pour Vivre 67. Les Gauloises Bleues 68. Dillinger Is Dead 69. A Man I Like 69. The Novices 70, etc.

Girardot, Etienne (1856–1939). Dapper Anglo-French character actor, in many American plays and films.
The Violin of Monsieur 12. The Kennel Murder Case 33. *Twentieth Century* 34. Clive of India 35. Metropolitan 35. Go West Young Man 36. *The Great Garrick* 37. Professor Beware 38. The Hunchback of Notre Dame 39. Isle of Destiny 40, many others.

Girotti, Massimo (1918–). Italian leading man.
Obsession 42. Caccia Tragica 47. Fabiola 47. Bellissima 51. Aphrodite 57. Theorem 68, etc.

Gish, Dorothy (1898–1968) (Dorothy de Guiche). Famous American silent star, in films for D. W. Griffith from 1912: *Hearts of the World, Orphans of the Storm*, etc. On stage between 1928 and 1944.
Our Hearts Were Young and Gay 44. The Whistle at Eaton Falls 51. The Cardinal 63, etc.

Gish, Lillian (1896–) (Lillian de Guiche). Famous American silent star, sister of Dorothy Gish, and also a D. W. Griffith discovery. From mid-twenties spent much time on stage, but filmed occasionally.
Autobiography 1969: *The Movies, Mr Griffith, and Me*.
Birth of a Nation 14. *Intolerance* 16. *Broken Blossoms* 18. *Way Down East* 20. Orphans of the Storm 22. The Scarlet Letter 26. Annie Laurie 27. His Double Life 34. The Commandos Strike at Dawn 43. Miss Susie Slagle's 46. *Duel in the Sun* 46. Portrait of Jennie 48. *Night of the Hunter* 55. Orders to Kill 58. The Unforgiven 59. Follow Me Boys 66. The Comedians 67. Twin Detectives (TV) 76, etc.
Special AA 1970.

Gist, Robert (1924–). American general purpose actor; turned director once, then went into TV.
Jigsaw 49. I Was a Shoplifter 50. The Band Wagon 53. D Day Sixth of June 56. Operation Petticoat 59. Blueprint for Robbery 61. An American Dream (d only) 66, etc.

Givot, George (1903–). American character actor, usually in hearty roles.
When's Your Birthday? 37. Marie Walewska 38. Dubarry Was a Lady 43. Riff Raff 46. Captain Blood Fugitive 52. Miracle in the Rain 56, etc.

glass shot. Usually a scenic shot in which part of the background is actually painted on a glass slide held in front of the camera and carefully blended with the action. In this way castles, towns, etc., may be shown on a location where none exist, without the expense of building them.

Gleason, Jackie (1916–). Heavyweight American TV comedian who as a young man played small movie roles, then returned as a star but never found his niche.
Biography 1956: *The Golden Ham* by Jim Bishop.
Navy Blues 41. Orchestra Wives 42. Springtime in the Rockies 42. The Desert Hawk 50. *The Hustler* (as Minnesota Fats) 61. Gigot (& w) 62. Requiem for a Heavyweight 62. Papa's Delicate Condition 63. Soldier in the Rain 63. Skidoo 68. How to Commit Marriage 69. Don't Drink the Water 69. How Do I Love Thee? 70, etc.
TV series: The Life of Riley 52–54. *The Honeymooners* 55. The Jackie Gleason Show 62–68.

Gleason, James (1886–1959). American character actor noted for hard-boiled comedy roles, usually in Brooklynese. On stage from infancy; also wrote several plays.
A Free Soul 30. Her Man 30. Oh Yeah (& oa) 30. Orders Is Orders (GB) 33. Murder on the Bridle Path 36. The Higgins Family 38. On Your Toes 39. Meet John Doe 41. *Here Comes Mr Jordan* 41. A Guy Named Joe 43. Arsenic and Old Lace 44. *Once Upon a Time* 44. A Tree Grows in Brooklyn 44. This Man's Navy 45. Captain Eddie 45. Down to Earth 47. The Bishop's Wife 48. The Life of Riley 49. Come Fill the Cup 51. *Suddenly* 54. The Last Hurrah 58, many others.

Gleason, Lucille (1886–1947). American character actress, wife of James Gleason, with whom she often appeared.
The Shannons of Broadway 39. Nice Women 32. Beloved 33. Klondike Annie 36. First Lady 37. *The Higgins Family* (& four subsequent episodes) 38. Lucky Partners 40. The Clock 45, etc.

Gleason, Russell (1908–1945). American juvenile actor, son of James and Lucille Gleason.
Strange Cargo 29. All Quiet on the Western Front 30. Nice Women 32. Private Jones 33. Off to the Races 37. Big Business (as Jones Family member) 37. *The Higgins Family* (& four subsequent episodes) 38. News is Made at Night 39. Unexpected Uncle 41. Salute to the Marines 43. The Adventures of Mark Twain 44, etc.

The Glenn Miller Story. (US 1953). Influential in giving a strong nostalgic twist to the aimless pop music of the fifties, this sentimental biography of the well-liked bandleader was otherwise a routine production, with a characteristic performance from James Stewart.

Glenn, Roy Snr (1915–1971). American Negro character actor.
Guess Who's Coming to Dinner 67. The Great White Hope 70, etc.

Glennon, Bert (1893–1967). Distinguished American cinematographer.
Ramona 16. The Torrent 20. *The Ten Commandments* 23. Woman of the World 26. The Patriot 28. Java Head 34. *The Hurricane* 37. Drums along the Mohawk 39. *Stagecoach* 39. They Died with Their Boots On 41. Dive Bomber 42. Destination Tokyo 44. The Red House 47. *Wagonmaster* 50. Operation Pacific 50. The Big Trees 52. *House of Wax* 53. The Mad Magician 54. Sergeant Rutledge 60, many others.

Glenville, Peter (1913–). British stage director who has made occasional films, usually of theatrical successes.
□ The Prisoner 54. Me and the Colonel 58. Summer and Smoke 60. Term of Trial 61. *Becket* 64. Hotel Paradiso 66. The Comedians 67.

The Glorious Adventure (GB 1921). A restoration drama directed by J. Stuart Blackton, notable as the first British feature in a colour process (Prizmacolour). Not an artistic success.

Glover, Julian (1935–). British general purpose actor chiefly on stage and TV.
Tom Jones 63. Girl with Green Eyes 64. I Was Happy Here 66. Alfred the Great 69. The Adding Machine 69. Wuthering Heights 70. Nicholas and Alexandra 71. Dead Cert 74. Juggernaut 75, etc.

Glyn, Elinor (1864–1943). Extravagant British romantic novelist whose 'daring' *Three Weeks* was filmed in Hollywood in 1924 and proved both sensational and influential. Her grandson Anthony Glyn wrote her biography in 1968.

Glynne, Mary (1898–1954). British stage actress of the well-bred school.
The Cry of Justice 19. The Hundredth Chance 20. The Good Companions (as Miss Trant) 32. Emil and the Detectives 34. Scrooge 35. The Heirloom Mystery (last film) 37, etc.

G Men (US 1935). Following public outcry about glamorized gangster films, James Cagney went over to the law in this competent semi-documentary about J. Edgar Hoover's men. Directed by William Keighley, with a shoot-'em-up climax which is still rousing.

Gobel, George (1919–). American TV comedian of 'little man' appeal.
□ The Birds and the Bees 56. I Married a Woman 57.

Godard, Jean-Luc (1930–). Semi-surrealist French writer-director of the 'new wave', his talent often muffled by incoherent narrative.
À Bout de Souffle (Breathless) (d only) 60. Une Femme Est Une Femme 61. Vivre Sa Vie 62. Le Petit Soldat 63. Les Carabiniers 63. Bande à Part 64. Une Femme Mariée 64. Alphaville 65. Pierrot Le Fou 66. Made in USA 66. Weekend 67. Tout va Bien 72, etc.

Goddard, Paulette (1911–) (Marion Levy). Pert, pretty American leading lady of the early forties; started as a Goldwyn girl, married Charlie Chaplin and Burgess Meredith, and when her not inconsiderable career petered out married Erich Maria Remarque.
□ The Girl Habit 31. The Mouthpiece 32. The Kid from Spain 32. *Modern Times* 36. The Young in Heart 38. Dramatic School 38. The Women 39. *The Cat and the Canary* 39. *The Ghost Breakers* 40. The Great Dictator 40. Northwest Mounted Police 40. Second Chorus 40. Pot o' Gold 41. Nothing But the Truth 41. Hold Back the Dawn 41. The Lady Has Plans 42. *Reap The Wild Wind* 42. The Forest Rangers 42. Star Spangled Rhythm 43. The Crystal Ball 43. So Proudly We Hail 43. Standing Room Only 44. I Love a Soldier 44. Duffy's Tavern 45. *Kitty* 45. *The Diary of a Chambermaid* 46. Suddenly It's Spring 47. Variety Girl 47. Unconquered 47. An Ideal Husband (GB) 47. On Our Merry Way 48. Hazard 48. Bride of Vengeance 49. Anna Lucasta 49. The Torch 50. Babes in Baghdad 52. Vice Squad 53. Paris Model 53. Sins of Jezebel 53. Charge of the Lancers 54. The Stranger Came Home (GB) 54. Time of Indifference 66. The Snoop Sisters (TV) 72.

Goddard, Willoughby (1932–). Heavyweight British character actor, mostly on TV.
In the Wake of a Stranger 59.
TV series: *William Tell* 59.

Godden, Rumer (1907–). Much-filmed British novelist.
Black Narcissus 46. Enchantment 48. The River 51. The Greengage Summer 61. Battle of the Villa Fiorita 65, etc.

The Godfather. (US 1972) (AA). An enormously commercial picturization of a violent Mafia-whitewashing gangster novel by Mario Puzo. Francis Ford Coppola's movie worked in sequences rather than as a whole, but was marked by some distinguished photography (Gordon Willis) and a notable star debut by Al Pacino. Marlon Brando's much-touted performance in the rather small title role seemed more a triumph of make-up and facial wiring than of acting. *The Godfather Part Two* was released in 1974, but proved too complex for general audiences.

Godfrey, Bob (1921–). British animator: shorts include *Polygamous Polonius, The Do-It-Yourself Cartoon Kit, The Plain Man's Guide to Advertising, Great*, etc.

Godfrey, Peter (1899–1970). British stage actor and producer who in the thirties directed two quickies, subsequently went to Hollywood and remained to direct routine films.
□ The Lone Wolf Spy Hunt 39. Unexpected Uncle 41. Highways by Night 42. Make Your Own Bed 44. Hotel Berlin 45. Christmas in Connecticut 45. One More Tomorrow 46. The Two Mrs Carrolls 47. Cry Wolf 47. That Hagen Girl 47. Escape Me Never 47. *The Woman in White* 48. The Decision of Christopher Blake 48. The Girl from Jones Beach 49. One Last Fling 49. Barricade 50. The Great Jewel Robber 50. He's a Cockeyed Wonder 50. One Big Affair 52. Please Murder Me 56.

Godsell, Vanda (c. 1919–). British character actress, usually in blowsy roles.
The Large Rope 54. Hour of Decision 57. Hell Is a City 60. This Sporting Life 63. The Earth Dies Screaming 64. Who Killed the Cat? 66, etc.

Godzilla. A Japanese monster creation first seen in the film of that name in 1955. Apparently closely related to *tyrannosaurus rex*, he has since suffered at the hands of King Kong and the Thing in inferior sequels. He remained rather plainly a man in a rubber suit.

Goetz, Ben (1891–). American executive, long with MGM and in charge of their British studios in the forties.

Goetz, William (1903–1969). American producer, in films since 1923, chiefly with Fox and Universal. As independent, he latterly produced the following.
The Man from Laramie 55. Sayonara 57. They Came to Cordura 58. Me and the Colonel 58. Song Without End 60, etc.

Goff, Ivan (1910–). Australian-born screenwriter; usually in collaboration with Ben Roberts (qv).
My Love Came Back 40. *White Heat* 49. Captain Horatio Hornblower 51. Come Fill the Cup 51. Full House 52. King of the Khyber Rifles 53. Green Fire 54. Serenade 56. Man of a Thousand Faces 57. Shake Hands with the Devil 59. Portrait in Black 60, etc.
TV series: *The Rogues* 64.

Going My Way (US 1944) (AA). Produced and directed by Leo McCarey (AA) from his own story, this chunk of sweetness and light about a singing priest in a poor district was immensely popular and had several imitators. Bing Crosby (AA) and Barry Fitzgerald (AA) each won new laurels. A TV series of the same name, made in 1963, starred Gene Kelly, but he neither sang nor danced in it. *The Bells of St Mary's* 45 also starred Crosby as Father O'Malley and was a kind of sequel.

Golan, Gila (c. 1940–). Hollywood leading lady of indeterminate background, being a European war orphan of probably Polish-Jewish parentage.
Ship of Fools 65. Our Man Flint 66. Three on a Couch 66. The Valley of Gwangi 69, etc.

Golan, Menahem (1931–). Israeli director.
Sallah 66. Tevye and His Seven Daughters 68. What's Good for the Goose? (GB) 69. Lepke 74. Diamonds 76, etc.

The Gold Diggers. This Broadway play by Avery Hopwood, about a group of girls in search of millionaire husbands, was filmed in 1923 under its original title, in 1929 as *Gold Diggers of Broadway* and in 1951 as *Painting the Clouds with Sunshine*. It also figured largely in the plot of *The Greeks Had a Word for Them* (1932), which was the basis of *How to Marry a Millionaire* 53 and the resulting TV series of the latter title. *Gold Diggers of 1933* was the first of five annual Warner musicals loosely based on the theme, their lethargic plots being more or less compensated for by Busby Berkeley's kaleidoscopic dance ensembles.

Gold, Ernest (1921–). Viennese-American composer.
Too Much Too Soon 57. On the Beach 59. Exodus (AA) 60. Judgment at Nuremberg 60. A Child Is Waiting 62. Pressure Point 62. It's a Mad Mad Mad Mad World 63. Ship of Fools 65. The Secret of Santa Vittoria 69, etc.

Gold, Jack (1930–). British TV director who moved into films.
□ *The Bofors Gun* 68. The Reckoning 69. The National Health 73. *Catholics* (TV) 73. Man Friday 75. *The Naked Civil Servant* (TV) 75. Aces High 76.

Gold, Jimmy: see *The Crazy Gang*.

The Gold Rush. (US 1924). Often accepted as Chaplin's greatest comedy, this sentimental farce played against a background of snow and ice has wonderfully-timed moments, though most of the fun is near the beginning and pathos takes over too firmly later on. Photographed by Rollie Totheroh.

Goldbeck, Willis (–). American director, former writer (co-author of *Freaks*).
Dr Gillespie's New Assistant 42. Between Two Women 44. She Went to the Races 45. Love Laughs at Andy Hardy 46. Johnny Holiday 50. Ten Tall Men 51, etc.

Golden, Michael (1913–). British character actor.
Send for Paul Temple 46. Hungry Hill 47. Escape 48. The Blue Lamp 50. The Green Scarf 55, etc.

Goldman, James (–). American playwright and screenwriter.
The Lion in Winter (oa & w) 68. *They Might Be Giants* 71. Nicholas and Alexandra 72.

Goldman, William (1931–). American screenwriter.
Soldier in the Rain (oa) 63. Masquerade 65. Harper 66. No Way to Treat a Lady (oa) 67. *Butch Cassidy and the Sundance Kid* 69. The Hot Rock 71. The Great Waldo Pepper 75, etc.

Goldner, Charles (1900–1955). Austrian character actor, in Britain from the thirties.

Room for Two 40. Brighton Rock 47. One Night With You 48. Third Time Lucky 48. Give Us This Day 49. Black Magic 49. Shadow of the Eagle 50. *The Captain's Paradise* 54, etc.

Goldoni, Lelia (c. 1938–). American actress. *Shadows* 59. Hysteria 64. The Italian Job 69. Alice Doesn't Live Here Any More 74. The Day of the Locust 75.

Goldsmith, Jerry (1930–) (Jerrald Goldsmith). American composer.
Lonely Are the Brave 62. The Prize 63. Seven Days in May 64. Lilies of the Field 64. In Harm's Way 65. The Trouble with Angels 66. Stagecoach 66. The Blue Max 66. Seconds 66. The Sand Pebbles 66. In Like Flint 67. Planet of the Apes 68. Patton 70. Tora! Tora! Tora! 71. The Mephisto Waltz 71. Papillon 73. The Reincarnation of Peter Proud 75, etc.

Goldstein, Robert (1903–1974). American producer, with Twentieth Century-Fox for many years.

Goldstone, James (1931–). American director, from TV.
□ Jigsaw (TV) 68. A Man Called Gannon 69. Winning 69. Brother John 70. Red Sky at Morning 71. The Gang that Couldn't Shoot Straight 72.

Goldstone, Richard (1912–). American producer.
The Outriders 50. Inside Straight 51. The Tall Target 51. The Devil Makes Three 52. Cinerama's South Seas Adventure 58. No Man is an Island (& wd) 62. The Sergeant 68, etc.

Goldwyn, Samuel (1882–1974) (Samuel Goldfish). Polish-American producer, in Hollywood from 1910. Co-produced *The Squaw Man* (1913); a top producer ever since, with a high reputation for star-making; he always refused to make any but family films; famous for 'Goldwynisms' like 'Include me out', mostly invented. Films since sound include *Arrowsmith* 31. *Roman Scandals* 33. *Barbary Coast* 35. *Dodsworth* 36. *Dead End* 37. The Adventures of Marco Polo 38. *Wuthering Heights* 39. *The Westerner* 40. *The Little Foxes* 41. *Up In Arms* 44. *The Best Years of Our Lives* (special AA) 46. *The Bishop's Wife* 48. *Hans Christian Andersen* 52. *Guys and Dolls* 55. *Porgy and Bess* 59, scores of others.

Goldwyn, Samuel Jnr. (1926–). American producer.
The Man with the Gun 55. The Proud Rebel 58.

Huckleberry Finn 60. The Young Lovers (& d) 65, etc.

The Golem. (Germany 1920). This classic legend, previously filmed in 1914, was written and directed by Henrik Galeen and Paul Wegener; the latter also played the clay monster brought to life by a rabbi to save the persecuted Jews. Brilliant Grimm-like medieval sets, photographed by Karl Freund, make the second part of the film still fresh, and both in detail and general development it was closely copied in *Frankenstein* 31. The story was remade in France in 1936 (with Harry Baur) and in Czechoslovakia in 1953, and in 1922 a British film called *It* borrowed the idea.

Golitzen, Alexander (–). American production designer.

Gombell, Minna (1900–1973) (also known as Winifred Lee and Nancy Carter). American character actress of the thirties and forties, usually in hard-boiled roles.
Doctors' Wives (debut) 31. The Thin Man 34. Babbitt 35. Banjo on My Knee 37. The Great Waltz 38. The Hunchback of Notre Dame 39. Boom Town 40. A Chip Off the Old Block 44. Man Alive 46. Pagan Love Song 51. I'll See You in My Dreams 52, etc.

Gomez, Thomas (1905–1971). Bulky American stage character actor who became a familiar villain or detective in Hollywood films.
Who Done It? 42. *Phantom Lady* 44. *The Dark Mirror* 46. Singapore 47. *Ride the Pink Horse* 47. Key Largo 48. *Force of Evil* 49. That Midnight Kiss (rare comedy role) 49. Anne of the Indies 51. Macao 52. Sombrero 52. Las Vegas Shakedown 54. The Magnificent Matador 55. The Conqueror 55. Trapeze 56. But Not for Me 59. John Paul Jones 59. Summer and Smoke 61. Stay Away Joe 68. Beneath the Planet of the Apes 69, many others. Also on TV.

Gone with the Wind (US 1939) (AA). For many years the longest film (220 minutes) ever to be released in the western hemisphere, this enormously successful romance of the American Civil War, from Margaret Mitchell's novel, was a splendidly professional job. It starred Vivien Leigh (AA), Clark Gable, Leslie Howard and Olivia de Havilland; Victor Fleming (AA) directed most of it, with contributions from George Cukor and Sam Wood. Ernest Haller (AA) and Ray Rennahan (AA) were cinematographers, and the production was designed by William Cameron Menzies. The Technicolor which was so splendid at the time now seems less impressive. Producer David O. Selznick had to release through MGM in order to get Gable's services, and that company has reissued it many times with immense profit. In 1968 an 'adapted' negative was made for showing in 70 mm: it was successful financially if not aesthetically.

The Good Companions. (GB 1932). J. B. Priestley's sprawling comic novel of English life was filmed by Victor Saville in rather primitive style, but its very *naiveté* remains infectious, and there are attractive performances by Edmund Gwenn, Jessie Matthews, Max Miller and others. Remade by J. Lee-Thompson in 1957, with Eric Portman and Janette Scott, with only fair success.

Goodbye Mr Chips (GB 1939). A highly successful product of MGM's short-lived British studio under Michael Balcon 1937–39, this sentimental biography of a schoolmaster, from James Hilton's novel, was impeccably produced, with a brilliant performance from Robert Donat (AA). Directed by Sam Wood. Remade in 1969 as an overlong and lifeless semi-musical with Peter O'Toole, directed by Herbert Ross.

Goodliffe, Michael (1914–1976). British stage actor often cast as officer, professional man or diplomat.
The Small Back Room (debut) 48. The Wooden Horse 50. Rob Roy 53. The Adventures of Quentin Durward 55. The Battle of the River Plate 56. A Night To Remember 58. Sink the Bismarck 60. The Trials of Oscar Wilde 60. Jigsaw 62. The Seventh Dawn 64. The Man with the Golden Gun 73, many others.

Goodman, Benny (1909–). American clarinettist and bandleader, the 'King of Swing'.
Hollywood Hotel 38. Hello Beautiful 42. The Gang's All Here 44. Sweet and Lowdown 44. A Song Is Born 48, etc.
Provided the music for The Benny Goodman Story 55, in which he was portrayed by Steve Allen.

Goodrich, Frances (1901–). American screenwriter, almost always in collaboration with her husband Albert Hackett.
Scripts since 1933 include:Naughty Marietta 35. Another Thin Man 38. The Hitler Gang 44. It's a Wonderful Life 46. Summer Holiday 47. Father of the Bride 50. Seven Brides for Seven Brothers 54. The Diary of Anne Frank (also stage play) 60, many others.

Goodwin, Bill (1910–1958). American

character actor, usually of genial type in routine films.
Wake Island 42. So Proudly We Hail 43. Bathing Beauty 44. Spellbound 45. House of Horrors 46. *The Jolson Story* 46. Heaven Only Knows 47. Jolson Sings Again 49. Tea for Two 50. The Atomic Kid 54. The Big Heat 54. The Opposite Sex 56, etc.

Goodwin, Harold (1917–). British character actor usually seen as cockney serviceman or small-time crook.
Dance Hall 50. The Card 52. The Cruel Sea 53. The Dam Busters 55. Sea of Sand 58. The Mummy 59. The Bulldog Breed 61. The Comedy Man 63. The Curse of the Mummy's Tomb 64. Frankenstein Must Be Destroyed 69, many others.

Goodwin, Ron (c. 1930–). British composer.
I'm All Right Jack 59. The Trials of Oscar Wilde 60. Postman's Knock 62. Murder She Said 62. Lancelot and Guinevere 63. 633 Squadron 64. Operation Crossbow 65. Those Magnificent Men in Their Flying Machines 65. The Alphabet Murders 65. Where Eagles Dare 68. Battle of Britain 70. Frenzy 72. The Happy Prince 74. One of Our Dinosaurs is Missing 75, etc.

Goodwins, Leslie (1899–1969). British-born director, in Hollywood for many years. Films mainly routine second features.
'Mexican Spitfire' series 39–44: Glamour Boy 39. Pop Always Pays 40. Silver Skates 43. Murder in the Blue Room 44. What a Blonde 45. The Mummy's Curse 46. Gold Fever 52. Fireman Save My Child 54. Paris Follies of 1956 56.

Goolden, Richard (1895–). British character actor, on stage and screen for many years, usually in henpecked or bewildered roles; created the radio character of Old Ebenezer the night watchman.
Whom the Gods Love 38. Meet Mr Penny 38. Mistaken Identity 43, etc.

Gorcey, Bernard (1888–1955). American character actor and ex-vaudevillian, father of Leo Gorcey, with whom he often appeared in the Bowery Boys series.
Abie's Irish Rose 28. The Great Dictator 40. Out of the Fog 41. No Minor Vices 49. Pick-Up 51, many others.

Gorcey, Leo (1915–1969). Pint-sized American second feature star, one of the original Dead End Kids; his screen personality was that of a tough, fast-talking, basically kindly

Brooklyn layabout, and he developed this in scores of routine films, mostly under the Bowery Boys banner.
Dead End 37. Mannequin 38. Crime School 38. *Angels With Dirty Faces* 38. Hell's Kitchen 39. Angels Wash Their Faces 39. Invisible Stripes 40. Pride of the Bowery 40. Spooks Run Wild 41. Mr Wise Guy 42. Destroyer 43. Midnight Manhunt 45. Bowery Bombshell 46. Spook Busters 46. Hard Boiled Mahoney 47. Jinx Money 48. Angels in Disguise 49. Lucky Losers 50. Crazy over Horses 51. No Holds Barred 52. Loose in London 52. The Bowery Boys Meet the Monsters 54. Bowery to Bagdad 55. Crashing Las Vegas 56. The Phynx 69, many others.

Gordon, Bert (1898–1974). American comedian known as 'the Mad Russian'.

Gordon, Bert I. (1922–). American producer-director of small independent horror exploitation films.
The Beginning of the End 57. The Amazing Colossal Man 57. Cyclops 57. The Boy and the Pirates 60. The Magic Sword 62. Picture Mommy Dead 66. How to Succeed with Sex (wd only) 69. Necromancy (pd) 73, etc.

Gordon, Bruce (1919–). American character actor, invariably a heavy.
Love Happy 50. The Buccaneer 58. Rider on a Dead Horse 61. Slow Run 68, etc.
TV series: *The Untouchables* (as Frank Nitti) 59–62.

Gordon, C. Henry (1884–1940). American character actor, often seen as maniacally evil villain or Indian rajah.
Charlie Chan Carries On 31. Rasputin and the Empress 32. Mata Hari 32. Lives of a Bengal Lancer 35. *The Charge of the Light Brigade* 36. The Return of the Cisco Kid 38. Kit Carson 40. Charlie Chan at the Wax Museum 40, etc.

Gordon, Colin (1911–1972). British light comedy actor, on stage from 1931; often seen as mildly cynical civil servant or schoolmaster.
Bond Street 47. The Winslow Boy 48. The Man in the White Suit 51. *Folly To Be Wise* 52. Escapade 55. The Safecracker 58. Please Turn Over 59. Night of the Eagle 62. The Pink Panther 63. The Family Way 66. Casino Royale 67, many others.

Gordon, Gale (1906–) (Gaylord Aldrich). Plump, fussy American comedy actor, best known on TV.
Here We Go Again 42. A Woman of Distinction 50. Don't Give Up the Ship 59. Visit to a Small

Planet 60. Sergeant Deadhead 65. Speedway 68, etc.
TV series: My Favorite Husband 51. Our Miss Brooks 52, 55. The Brothers 57. Dennis the Menace 62–64. *The Lucy Show* 64–74.

Gordon, Gavin (1901–1970). American general purpose actor.
Romance (lead) 30. The Bitter Tea of General Yen 32. The Scarlet Empress 34. Bride of Frankenstein 35. Windjammer 38. Paper Bullets 41. Centennial Summer 46. Knock on Wood 54. The Bat 59, etc.

Gordon, Hal (1894–*). Hearty British comedy actor, often seen as good-natured foil to star comedian.
Adam's Apple 31. Happy 34. Captain Bill 36. Keep Fit 37. It's in the Air 38. Old Mother Riley, Detective 43. Give Me the Stars 45 (last appearance), etc.

Gordon, Leo (1922–). Thick-set American character actor, usually in tough guy roles.
China Venture 53. Riot in Cell Block 11 53. Seven Angry Men 55. The Conqueror 55. The Man Who Knew Too Much 56. Cry Baby Killer (& w) 57. The Big Operator 59. The Stranger 62. The Terror (& w) 63. The Haunted Palace 64. Beau Geste 66. Tobruk (& w) 66. The St Valentine's Day Massacre 67. You Can't Win 'Em All 71, etc.

Gordon, Mary (1882–1963). Tiny Scottish character actress in Hollywood; best remembered as the perfect Mrs Hudson in many a Sherlock Holmes film.
The Home Maker 25. The Black Camel 31. The Little Minister 34. The Bride of Frankenstein 35. The Plough and the Stars 36. Kidnapped 38. The Hound of the Baskervilles 39. Tear Gas Squad 40. Appointment for Love 41. The Mummy's Tomb 42. Sherlock Holmes Faces Death 43. The Woman in Green 45. Little Giant 46. The Invisible Wall 47, many others.

Gordon, Michael (1909–). American director with stage experience.
□ Boston Blackie Goes to Hollywood 42. Underground Agent 42. One Dangerous Night 43. Crime Doctor 43. *The Web* 47. Another Part of the Forest 48. An Act of Murder 48. The Lady Gambles 49. Woman in Hiding 49. Cyrano de Bergerac 50. I Can Get It for You Wholesale 51. The Secret of Convict Lake 51. Wherever She Goes 53. *Pillow Talk* 59. Portrait in Black 60. Boys' Night Out 62. For Love of Money 63. Move Over Darling 63. A Very Special Favor

65. Texas Across the River 66. The Impossible Years 68. How Do I Love Thee 70.

Gordon, Ruth (1896–) (Ruth Gordon Jones). Distinguished American stage actress who wrote several screenplays with her husband Garson Kanin, saw two of her own plays filmed, and had a long sporadic career as film actress.
□ AS WRITER: Over 21 (oa/solo) 45. *A Double Life* 48. *Adam's Rib* 49. The Marrying Kind 52. Pat and Mike 52. The Actress (oa/solo) 53. Rosie (oa/solo) 58.
□ AS ACTRESS: Camille 15. The Wheel of Life 16. Abe Lincoln in Illinois 40. Dr Ehrlich's Magic Bullet 40. Two Faced Woman 41. Edge of Darkness 43. Action in the North Atlantic 43. Inside Daisy Clover 66. Lord Love a Duck 66. *Rosemary's Baby* (AA) 68. Whatever Happened to Aunt Alice? 69. Where's Poppa? 70. *Harold and Maude* 72. The Big Bus 76.

Goring, Marius (1912–). British stage and screen actor adept at neurotic or fey roles.
Consider Your Verdict (debut) 36. Rembrandt 37. *The Case of the Frightened Lady* 38. *A Matter of Life and Death* 45. The Red Shoes 48. Mr Perrin and Mr Traill 49. So Little Time 52. *Ill Met by Moonlight* 57. Exodus 60. The Inspector (Lisa) 62. Up From the Beach 65. Girl on a Motorcycle 68. Subterfuge 69. First Love 70. Zeppelin 71, etc.

Gorky, Maxim (1868–1936) (Alexei Maximovitch Peshkov). Russian writer whose autobiography was filmed by Donskoi as *The Childhood of Maxim Gorky* (qv), *Out in the World* and *My Universities*. Other filmed works include *The Lower Depths* (many times) and *The Mother*.

Gorman, Cliff (–). American leading man of the seventies.
Cops and Robbers 73. Rosebud 75, etc.

Gorshin, Frank (1935–). Wiry American impressionist and character actor, popular as 'The Riddler' in TV's Batman series.
The True Story of Jesse James 57. Warlock 59. Studs Lonigan 60. Ring of Fire 61. The George Raft Story 61. Batman 65, etc.

Gortner, Marjoe (1941–). American evangelist turned actor (following a 1972 documentary on his life called *Marjoe*).
□ The Marcus Nelson Murders (TV) 73. Earthquake 74. The Gun and the Pulpit (TV) 74. Food of the Gods 76.

Gosho, Heinosuke (1901–). Japanese

director, best known for *Four Chimneys* 52. *Adolescence* 55. *When a Woman Loves* 59.

Goudal, Jetta (1898–). French leading lady of American silent films.
The Bright Shawl 24. Open All Night 24. Spanish Love 25. Road to Yesterday 25. 3 Faces East 26. White Gold 27. Forbidden Woman 28. Her Cardboard Lover 28. Lady of the Pavements 30. Plutocrat 31. Business and Pleasure 32, etc.

Gough, Michael (1917–). Tall British stage (since 1936) and screen (since 1946) actor; has recently gone in for homicidal roles.
Blanche Fury (debut) 46. The Small Back Room 48. The Man in the White Suit 51. Richard III 56. Dracula 57. Horrors of the Black Museum 58. The Horse's Mouth 59. Konga 61. Black Zoo 63. Dr Terror's House of Horrors 65. Circus of Blood 67. Trog 70. The Corpse 70. The Go-Between 70. Henry VIII and His Six Wives 72, many others.

Gould, Elliott (1938–) (Elliot Goldstein). American actor whose very unhandsomeness made him the man for the early seventies.
□ The Confession 66. The Night They Raided Minsky's 68. *Bob and Carol and Ted and Alice* 69. M*A*S*H. 70. Getting Straight 70. Move 70. I Love My Wife 70. The Touch 70. Little Murders 71. The Long Goodbye 72. Busting 73. S.P.Y.S. 74. California Split 74. Who? 74. Nashville 74. Whiffs 76. I will . . . I Will . . . for Now 76. Harry and Walter Go to New York 76.

Goulding, Alfred J. (1896–1972). American director; active with Harold Lloyd in the twenties and later with Laurel and Hardy (*A Chump at Oxford*).

Goulding, Edmund (1891–1959). British director in Hollywood; a safe handler of the big female stars of the thirties and forties.
□ Sun Up 25. Sally Irene and Mary 25. Love 27. *The Trespasser* (& w) 29. The Devil's Holiday (& w) 30. Reaching for the Moon (& w) 30. The Night Angel (& w) 31. *Grand Hotel* 32. Blondie of the Follies 32. Riptide 34. The Flame Within (& wp) 35. That Certain Woman (& w) 37. White Banners 38. The Dawn Patrol 38. *Dark Victory* 39. *The Old Maid* 39. We Are Not Alone 39. Till We Meet Again 40. *The Great Life* 41. Forever and a Day (co-d) 43. The Constant Nymph 43. *Claudia* 43. Of Human Bondage 46. *The Razor's Edge* 46. *Nightmare Alley* 47. Everybody Does It 49. Mister 880 50. We're Not Married 52. Down Among the Sheltering Palms 53. Teenage Rebel 56. Mardi Gras 58.

Goulet, Robert (1933–). Canadian singer and leading man, with experience mainly on TV.
Honeymoon Hotel 63. I'd Rather Be Rich 64. Underground 70.
TV series: The Blue Light 64.

governesses have most frequently been personified by Deborah Kerr: in *The King and I*, *The Innocents*, and *The Chalk Garden*. Julie Andrews runs a close second with *Mary Poppins* and *The Sound of Music*; as does Bette Davis with *All This and Heaven Too* and *The Nanny*. Joan Fontaine's contribution to the gallery was *Jane Eyre*, and Susannah York later followed in her footsteps.

Gowland, Gibson (1872–1951). English character actor in mainly American films.
The Birth of a Nation 15. Blind Husbands 19. Ladies Must Love 21. Shifting Sands 23. *Greed* 24. The Phantom of the Opera 25. Don Juan 26. Topsy and Eva 27. Rose Marie 28. The Mysterious Island 29. The Sea Bat 30. Doomed Battalion 32. SOS Iceberg 33. The Secret of the Loch 34. The Mystery of the Marie Celeste 36. Cotton Queen 37, many others.

Gozzi, Patricia (1950–). French juvenile actress of the sixties.
Sundays and Cybele 62. Rapture 65, etc.

Grable, Betty (1916–1973). American leading lady who personified the peaches-and-cream appeal which was required in the forties but which later seemed excessively bland. She performed efficiently in a series of light musicals and dramas, and was the most famous pin-up of World War II.
☐ Let's Go Places 30. New Movietone Follics of 1930 30. Whoopee 30. Kiki 31. Palmy Days 31. The Greeks had a Word for Them 32. The Kid from Spain 32. Child of Manhattan 32. Probation 32. Hold 'Em Jail 32. Cavalcade 33. What Price Innocence 33. Student Tour 34. *The Gay Divorcee* 34. The Nitwits 35. Old Man Rhythm 35. Collegiate 35. Follow the Fleet 36. Pigskin Parade 36. Don't Turn 'Em Loose 36. This Way Please 37. Thrill of a Lifetime 37. College Swing 38. Give Me a Sailor 38. Campus Confessions 38. Man About Town 39. Million Dollar Legs 39. The Day the Bookies Wept 39. *Down Argentine Way* 40. *Tin Pan Alley* 40. *Moon Over Miami* 41. A Yank in the RAF 41. *I Wake Up Screaming* 41. Footlight Serenade 42. Song of the Islands 42. Springtime in the Rockies 42. *Coney Island* 43. Sweet Rosie O'Grady 43. Four Jills in a Jeep 44. Pin Up Girl 44. Diamond Horseshoe 45. The Dolly Sisters 45 The Shocking Miss Pilgrim 47. *Mother Wore Tights*

47. That Lady in Ermine 48. When My Baby Smiles at Me 48. The Beautiful Blonde from Bashful Bend 49. Wabash Avenue 50. My Blue Heaven 50. Call Me Mister 51. Meet Me After the Show 51. The Farmer Takes a Wife 53. *How To Marry A Millionaire* 53. Three for the Show 54. How to be Very Very Popular 55.

grading: the laboratory process of matching the density and brightness of each shot to the next.

The Graduate (US 1967). Set in the well-to-do suburbs of Los Angeles, and concerning an aimless young man whose protest at society takes the form of being seduced by one of his father's friends and then falling in love with her daughter, this beautifully photographed film (Robert Surtees) from a book by Charles Webb was filled with bitter hilarity and showed that a wide-screen film can still look good. Its enormous commercial success was presumably due to its comparative frankness on sexual matters; its direction (Mike Nichols: AA) and acting (Dustin Hoffman, Anne Bancroft) were impeccable.

Graetz, Paul (1901–1966). Franco-Austrian independent producer.
Le Diable au Corps 46. Monsieur Ripois (Knave of Hearts) 53. Is Paris Burning? 66, etc.

Graham, Morland (1891–1949). Stocky Scottish character actor, on stage and screen from twenties.
The Scarlet Pimpernel 35. Jamaica Inn 39. Old Bill and Son (as Old Bill) 40. The Ghost Train 41. The Shipbuilders 44. The Brothers 47. Bonnie Prince Charlie 48. Whisky Galore 48, etc.

Graham, Sheilah (c. 1912–). British gossip columnist in America, widow of F. Scott Fitzgerald.

Graham, William (c. 1930–). American director, from TV.
Waterhole Three 67. Submarine X-1 68. Change of Habit 69.

Grahame, Gloria (1924–) (Gloria Hallward). Blonde American leading lady, usually in offbeat roles.
Blonde Fever (debut) 44. Without Love 45. It's a Wonderful Life 46. *Crossfire* 47. Roughshod 48. A Woman's Secret 48. *In a Lonely Place* 50. *The Bad and the Beautiful* (AA) 52. Prisoners of the Casbah 53. The Greatest Show on Earth 53. *The Big Heat* 54. The Good Die Young (GB) 54. Human Desire 55. The Man Who Never Was (GB) 55. Not as a Stranger 55. The Cobweb 55.

Oklahoma 56. Odds Against Tomorrow 59. Ride Beyond Vengeance 66. The Todd Killings 70. Blood and Lace 72. The Girl on the Late Late Show (TV) 75. Rich Man Poor Man (TV) 76, etc.

Grahame, Margot (1911–). British leading lady of the thirties, with stage experience.
The Love Habit 30. Rookery Nook 30. Sorrell and Son 34. The Informer (US) 35. The Three Musketeers (US) 36. Michael Strogoff (US) 37. The Shipbuilders 44. Broken Journey 48. The Romantic Age 49. Venetian Bird 52. Orders Are Orders 55. Saint Joan 57, etc.

Grainer, Ron (c. 1925–). Australian composer in Britain.
A Kind of Loving 62. Nothing But the Best 64. To Sir with Love 67. Lock Up Your Daughters 68. In Search of Oregon 70. The Omega Man 71. Yellow Dog 73. I Don't Want to Be Born 75, many others.

Grainger, Edmund (1906–). American producer and executive, long with RKO. Specialized in quality action pictures.
Diamond Jim 35. Sutter's Gold 36. International Squadron 41. Wake of the Red Witch 48. Sands of Iwo Jima 49. Flying Leathernecks 50. One Minute to Zero 52. Treasure of Pancho Villa 55. Green Mansions 59. Home from the Hill 60. Cimarron 61, many others.

Granach, Alexander (1890–1945). Polish character actor who went to Hollywood in the late thirties.
Biography 1945: *There Goes An Actor*.
Warning Shadows 23. Kameradschaft 31. *Ninotchka* 39. Hangmen Also Die 43. For Whom the Bell Tolls 43. The Hitler Gang 44. A Voice in the Wind 44. The Seventh Cross 44, etc.

Grand Hotel (US 1932–33). The Hollywood all-star film *par excellence*, from Vicki Baum's novel; it allowed effective parts for Garbo, the Barrymore brothers, Joan Crawford and Wallace Beery. Not very cinematic, as directed by Edmund Goulding, but immensely popular. AA best picture of its year. More or less remade in 1945 as *Weekend at the Waldorf*, but with no impact whatever. A 1959 West German remake, *Menschen im Hotel*, had Michele Morgan in Garbo's role and O. W. Fischer in John Barrymore's.

Le Grand Jeu (France 1933). This melodrama by Charles Spaak and Jacques Feyder about the off-duty problems of Foreign Legionnaires was filmed by Feyder in 1933 and had memorable performances by Françoise Rosay and Marie

Bell. Robert Siodmak's 1953 remake was flavourless despite the presence of Arletty and Gina Lollobrigida.

Grand Prix (US 1966). An absurdly cliché-ridden and poorly scripted motor-racing spectacular decorated by half a dozen brilliantly exciting race sequences directed by John Frankenheimer and photographed by Lionel Lindon with all the showmanship – and showing off – they could muster. (These sequences were also notable for experimental use of multiscreen effects.) The actors paled into complete insignificance.

La Grande Illusion (France 1937). Jean Renoir's great anti-war film, set in a German prison camp for officers in 1917, commanded by Erich Von Stroheim. A subtler piece than most of the recent variations on this theme, it was written by Charles Spaak and Renoir, with music by Joseph Kosma and photography by Christian Matras and Claude Renoir.

Granger, Farley (1925–). American leading man who began his film career straight from school.
North Star (debut) 43. They Live By Night 47. *Rope* 48. *Strangers on a Train* 51. Hans Christian Andersen 52. Senso (It) 53. The Girl in the Red Velvet Swing 55. Rogues' Gallery 68. Something Creeping in the Dark (It.) 71. The Serpent 72. Confessions of a Sex Maniac (It.) 72. They Call Me Trinity (It.) 72. The Man Called Noon 73. Arnold 75, etc.

Granger, Stewart (1913–) (James Stewart). British leading man, on stage from 1935.
Give Her a Ring 34. So This Is London 38. *The Man in Grey* 43. The Lamp Still Burns 43. Fanny by Gaslight 43. *Waterloo Road* 44. *Love Story* 44. Madonna of the Seven Moons 44. *Caesar and Cleopatra* 45. Caravan 46. The Magic Bow (as Paganini) 46. *Captain Boycott* 47. Blanche Fury 48. Saraband for Dead Lovers (as Koenigsmark) 48. Woman Hater 49. Adam and Evelyne 49. *King Solomon's Mines* (US) 50. The Light Touch (US) 51. *Scaramouche* (US) 52. The Prisoner of Zenda (US) 52. Young Bess (US) 53. Salome (US) 53. All the Brothers Were Valiant (US) 54. *Beau Brummell* (US) 54. Green Fire (US) 55. Moonfleet (US) 55. Footsteps in the Fog 55. Bhowani Junction 56. The Last Hunt (US) 56. The Little Hut 57. The Whole Truth 58. Harry Black 58. North to Alaska (US) 60. The Secret Partner 61. Sodom and Gomorrah 62. Swordsman of Siena (It.) 62. The Legion's Last Patrol (It.) 63. Among Vultures (Ger.) 64. Der Oelprinz (Ger.) 65. Old Surehand (Ger.) 65. The

Trygon Factor 67. The Last Safari 67. The Flaming Frontier 68. The Hound of the Baskervilles (TV) (as Holmes) 71, etc. TV series: The Men from Shiloh 70.

Grangier, Gilles (1911–). French director. Le Cavalier Noir 44. L'Amour Madame 52. Archimède le Clochard 58. Le Cave Se Rebiffe 61. La Cuisine au Beurre 63. Train d'Enfer 65. L'Homme à la Buick 67. Fin de Journée 69, etc.

Grant, Arthur (1915–1972). British cinematographer. Hell Is a City 60. Jigsaw 62. Eighty Thousand Suspects 63. The Tomb of Ligeia 64. Blood from the Mummy's Tomb 71, etc.

Grant, Cary (1904–) (Archibald Leach). Debonair British-born leading man with a personality and accent all his own; varied theatrical experience before settling in Hollywood. Special AA 1969.
□ This Is the Night 32. Sinners in the Sun 32. Hot Saturday 32. Merrily We Go to Hell 32. The Devil and the Deep 32. Madame Butterfly 32. Blonde Venus 33. *She Done Him Wrong* 33. Alice in Wonderland (as the Mock Turtle) 33. The Eagle and the Hawk 33. Woman Accused 33. Gambling Ship 33. I'm No Angel 33. Thirty Day Princess 34. Born To Be Bad 34. Kiss and Make Up 34. Enter Madame 34. Ladies Should Listen 34. Wings in the Dark 35. The Last Outpost 35. Sylvia Scarlett 35. Big Brown Eyes 35. Suzy 36. Wedding Present 36. The Amazing Quest of Mr Ernest Bliss (GB) 36. When You're in Love 36. *The Awful Truth* 37. The Toast of New York 37. *Topper* 37. *Bringing Up Baby* 38. Holiday 38. *Gunga Din* 39. Only Angels Have Wings 39. In Name Only 39. *My Favorite Wife* 40. The Tree of Liberty 40. *His Girl Friday* 40. *The Philadelphia Story* 40. Penny Serenade 41. Suspicion 41. Talk of the Town 42. Once upon a Honeymoon 42. Destination Tokyo 43. Mr Lucky 43. Once upon a Time 44. None But the Lonely Heart 44. *Arsenic and Old Lace* 44. Night and Day (as Cole Porter) 45. Notorious 46. *The Bachelor and the Bobbysoxer* 47. The Bishop's Wife (as an angel) 48. Every Girl Should Be Married 48. *Mr Blandings Builds His Dream House* 48. I Was a Male War Bride 49. Crisis 50. Room for One More 52. Dream Wife 53. To Catch a Thief 55. The Pride and the Passion 57. *An Affair to Remember* 57. Kiss Them for Me 57. *Indiscreet* (GB) 58. Houseboat 58. *North by Northwest* 59. Operation Petticoat 59. The Grass Is Greener 60. That Touch of Mink 62. Charade 63. Father Goose 64. Walk Don't Run 66.

Grant, James Edward (1902–66). American writer. Whipsaw 35. We're Going to Be Rich 38. Belle of the Yukon 44. The Great John L. 45. Angel and the Bad Man (& d) 46. Sands of Iwo Jima 49. Big Jim McLain 52. Hondo 54. Ring of Fear (co-w and d) 54. The Alamo 60. McLintock 63, etc.

Grant, Kathryn (1933–) (Olive Grandstaff). American leading lady who retired to marry Bing Crosby. Arrowhead 53. Living it Up 54. The Phoenix City Story 55. Mister Cory 56. Gunman's Walk 58. Operation Mad Ball 58. The Seventh Voyage of Sinbad 58. The Big Circus 60, etc.

Grant, Kirby (1914–) (K. G. Horn). Dutch-Scottish-American leading man, former bandleader. Red River Range 39. Ghost Catchers 44. The Lawless Breed 47. Trail of the Yukon 50. Snow Dog 51. Yukon Gold 52. The Court Martial of Billy Mitchell 55. Yukon Vengeance 55, etc.

Grant, Lawrence (1870–1952). British character actor in American films. The Great Impersonation 21. His Hour 24. The Grand Duchess and the Waiter 26. Doomsday 28. The Canary Murder Case 29. *Bulldog Drummond* 29. The Cat Creeps 30. Daughter of the Dragon 31. The Unholy Garden 31. Jewel Robbery 32. The Mask of Fu Manchu 32. Grand Hotel 32. Shanghai Express 32. Queen Christina 33. By Candlelight 34. Nana 34. Werewolf of London 34. The Devil is a Woman 35. Little Lord Fauntleroy 36. The Prisoner of Zenda 37. Bluebeard's Eighth Wife 38. Son of Frankenstein 39. Women in War 40. Dr Jekyll and Mr Hyde 41. Confidential Agent 45, many others.

Grant, Lee (1929–) (Lyova Rosenthal). Dynamic American stage actress, sporadically seen in films.
□ *Detective Story* 51. Storm Fear 55. Middle of the Night 59. The Balcony 63. An Affair of the Skin 63. Terror in the City 66. Divorce American Style 67. In the Heat of the Night 67. Valley of the Dolls 67. Buona Sera Mrs Campbell 68. There Was a Crooked Man 70. *The Landlord* 70. *Plaza Suite* 71. Ransom for a Dead Man (TV) 71. Portnoy's Complaint 72. Lt Schuster's Wife (TV) 72. The Neon Ceiling (TV) 72. Partners in Crime (TV) 72. The Internecine Project 74. Shampoo 75. Airport 77 77.

Granville, Bonita (1923–). American child actress of the thirties; adult career gradually petered out but she became a producer. Westward Passage 32. Cradle Song 33. Ah

Wilderness 35. *These Three* 36. Maid of Salem 37. Call it a Day 37. Merrily We Live 38. Nancy Drew Detective (and subsequent series) 38. Angels Wash Their Faces 39. Escape 40. H.M. Pulham Esq 41. The Glass Key 42. Now Voyager 42. *Hitler's Children* 43. Youth Runs Wild 44. Love Laughs at Andy Hardy 46. The Guilty 47. Treason 50. The Lone Ranger 56. Lassie's Greatest Adventure (p) 63, etc.
TV series: Lassie (p) 55–67.

The Grapes of Wrath (US 1940). John Ford's (AA) film of John Steinbeck's novel about the migration of poor workers from the mid-western dustbowl to the Californian fruit valleys is not only one of the earliest Hollywood exposés of social injustice but one of the most moving and beautiful films to come out of America. Gregg Toland's soft, warm photography, Alfred Newman's music and Nunnally Johnson's screenplay provide a perfect background for the performances of Henry Fonda, Jane Darwell (AA) and a fine cast.

Grapewin, Charley (1869–1956). American character actor best remembered in movies for his range of grizzled old gentlemen.
Only Saps Work 30. The Night of June 13th 32. Heroes for Sale 33. Judge Priest 34. Ah Wilderness 35. Alice Adams 35. Libelled Lady 36. The Good Earth 37. Captains Courageous 37. Big City 37. Three Comrades 38. The Wizard of Oz 39. *The Grapes of Wrath* 40. Ellery Queen Master Detective 40. *Tobacco Road* (as Jeeter Lester) 41. They Died With Their Boots On 41. Crash Dive 42. The Impatient Years 44. Gunfighters 47. Sand 49. When I Grow Up 51, many others.

Grass (US 1925). Cooper and Schoedsack's feature-length documentary was shot among the Baktyari tribe of north-west Persia during their twice-yearly migration in search of grass. Though an impressive achievement at the time, it was less stirring than the same team's *Chang*, which followed in 1927.

Grauman, Walter (1922–). American director, from TV.
Lady in a Cage 63. 633 Squadron 64. A Rage to Live 65. I Deal in Danger 66. The Last Escape 69.
TV series include The Untouchables, Naked City, Route 66, The Felony Squad.

Graves, Peter (1925–) (Peter Aurness). American leading man, usually in 'B' action pictures: brother of James Arness.
Rogue River (debut) 50. Fort Defiance 52. Red

Planet Mars 52. Stalag 17 53. Beneath the Twelve-Mile Reef 53. Black Tuesday 55. It Conquered the World 56. Wolf Larsen 59. A Rage to Live 65. The Ballad of Josie 67. The Five Man Army 68. Call to Danger (TV) 73, etc.
TV series: Fury 55–59. Whiplash 60. Court Martial (Counsellors at War) 66. Mission Impossible 67–72.

Graves, Peter (1911–). British light leading man, tall and suave, usually in musical comedy.
Kipps (debut) 41. King Arthur Was a Gentleman 42. Bees in Paradise 44. I'll Be Your Sweetheart 44. Waltz Time 45. The Laughing Lady 46. Spring Song 47. Mrs Fitzherbert (as the Prince Regent) 47. Spring in Park Lane 48. Maytime in Mayfair 50. Derby Day 52. Lilacs in the Spring 54, etc.: latterly in cameo roles, e.g. The Wrong Box 66, The Slipper and the Rose 76.

Graves, Ralph (1901–1977). American silent star of heroic roles.
Talkies include: Submarine 28. Dirigible 30. Ladies of Leisure 30.
Later became writer and producer of minor films.

Graves, Teresa (c. 1938–). Black American leading lady.
Black Eye 73. Get Christie Love (TV) (and series) 74. Vampira 74.

Gravet, Fernand (1904–1970) (Fernand Martens). Debonair French leading man with some Hollywood experience.
Bitter Sweet 33. The Great Waltz 38. Fools for Scandal 38. Le Dernier Tournant 38. La Ronde 50. Short Head 53. How to Steal a Million 66. The Madwoman of Chaillot 69, etc.

Gray, Carole (1940–). South African leading lady in British films of the sixties.
The Young Ones 61. Curse of the Fly 64. Rattle of a Simple Man 64. Island of Terror 66, etc.

Gray, Charles (1928–) (Donald M. Gray). British stage and TV actor usually seen in smooth unsympathetic roles.
The Entertainer 60. The Man in the Moon 61. Masquerade 65. The Night of the Generals 66. The Secret War of Harry Frigg (US) 67. *The Devil Rides Out* 68. The File of the Golden Goose 69. Cromwell 69. *Diamonds are Forever* 71. The Beast Must Die 74. Seven Nights in Japan 76. The Seven Per Cent Solution 76.

Gray, Colleen (1922–) (Doris Jensen). American leading lady of the forties.
Kiss of Death 47. Nightmare Alley 47. Fury at Furnace Creek 48. *Red River* 48. Sand 49.

Riding High 50. The Sleeping City 51. Kansas City Confidential 52. Sabre Jet 53. Arrow in the Dust 54. The Killing 56. Hell's Five Hours 57. The Leech Woman 60. Town Tamer 65. PJ 68, etc.

Gray, Dolores (1924–). Statuesque American singer-dancer, on stage in musical comedy (played *Annie Get Your Gun* in London).
□ It's Always Fair Weather 54. Kismet 55. The Opposite Sex 56. Designing Woman 57.

Gray, Donald (1914–)(Eldred Tidbury). One-armed British leading man, former radio actor and announcer; best known as TV's Mark Saber. Films include Strange Experiment 37. The Four Feathers 39. Idol of Paris 48. Saturday Island (Island of Desire) 52. Timeslip 55. Satellite in the Sky 56, etc.

Gray, Dulcie (1919–)(Dulcie Bailey). Gentle-mannered British leading lady, married to Michael Denison.
A Place of One's Own 44. They Were Sisters 45. Mine Own Executioner 47. The Glass Mountain 48. Angels One Five 51. A Man Could Get Killed 65, etc.

Gray, Gary (1936–). American boy actor of the forties.
A Woman's Face 41. Address Unknown 44. The Great Lover 47. Rachel and the Stranger 48. Father Is a Bachelor 49. The Next Voice You Hear 50. The Painted Hills 51. The Party Crashers 58, others.

Gray, Gilda (1901–1959) (Marianna Michalska). Polish dancer who went to America and is credited with inventing the shimmy.
Aloma of the South Seas 26. The Devil Dancer 28. Rose Marie 36, etc.

Gray, Nadia (1923–) (Nadia Kujnir-Herescu). Russian-Roumanian leading lady, in European and British films.
The Spider and the Fly 49. Night Without Stars 51. Valley of Eagles 51. Neapolitan Fantasy 54. Folies Bergère 56. The Captain's Table 58. Parisienne 59. La Dolce Vita 59. Maniac 63. Two for the Road 67. The Naked Runner 67, etc.

Gray, Sally (1916–) (Constance Stevens). Popular British screen heroine of thirties and forties, with stage experience from 1925.
School for Scandal 30. Radio Pirates 35. Cheer Up 35. The Saint in London 38. The Lambeth Walk 38. Dangerous Moonlight 40. Carnival 46. *Green for Danger* 46. They Made Me a Fugitive 47. The Mark of Cain 48. Silent Dust 49.

Obsession 49. Escape Route 52, etc.

Grayson, Kathryn (1922–) (Zelma Hedrick). American singing star in Hollywood from 1940 (as one of Andy Hardy's dates).
The Vanishing Virginian 41. Rio Rita 42. Seven Sweethearts 42. Thousands Cheer 43. Ziegfeld Follies 44. Anchors Aweigh 45. Two Sisters from Boston 45. Till the Clouds Roll By 46. The Kissing Bandit 48. That Midnight Kiss 49. Showboat 51. Lovely To Look At 52. The Grace Moore Story (So This Is Love) 53. Kiss Me Kate 53. The Vagabond King 55, etc.

Great Britain had been making films for more than fifty years when finally a 'British school' emerged capable of influencing world production. Hollywood films had invaded British cinemas during World War I, and British audiences liked them; so the battle for power was won with only faint stirrings of resistance. British films were tepid, shoddy, stilted, old-fashioned in acting and production; and for many years they were kept that way by short-sighted government legislation, intended to help the industry, ensuring that at least a proportion (usually a third) of local product must be shown in every British cinema. Thus began the long list of 'quota quickies', deplorable B pictures whose producers knew they could not fail to get their money back. In the mid-thirties, Britain was producing 200 films a year, but they reflected nothing of life and offered little in the way of entertainment.

Exceptions to this general rule were the suspense thrillers of Alfred Hitchcock; a couple of promising dramas from Anthony Asquith; some well-produced entertainments from Victor Saville, such as *The Good Companions* and *South Riding*; Herbert Wilcox's popular view of such historical figures as Nell Gwyn and Queen Victoria; and the ambitious and often masterly, but not particularly British, productions of Alexander Korda, whose *Rembrandt* and *Things to Come* could still justify their inclusion in any list of the world's ten best. The British music-hall tradition also survived remarkably well in skilful low-budget productions with such stars as Gracie Fields, George Formby, Will Hay and the Crazy Gang; the two directors most concerned, Marcel Varnel and Walter Forde, had much to tell anyone who cared to listen about the art of screen comedy, as had writers Val Guest, Frank Launder and Sidney Gilliat.

In 1939 MGM had achieved three notable British productions – *A Yank at Oxford, Goodbye Mr Chips* and *The Citadel* – but the war swept away all plans and British studios started anew. Their renaissance began through the splendid documentaries of Humphrey

Jennings, Harry Watt and Basil Wright, graduates of the GPO Film Unit which had been turning out excellent short films in the thirties but failing to secure cinema bookings for them. The strong feelings of national pride and urgency percolated to the fiction film, first in stories of social comment (*The Proud Valley, The Stars Look Down, Love on the Dole*), then in topical entertainments like Carol Reed's *Night Train to Munich* and Thorold Dickinson's *Next of Kin*. Noel Coward's *In Which We Serve* came as a revelation of style and substance, and what it did for the navy was done for the army by Reed's *The Way Ahead* and for the air force by Asquith's *The Way to the Stars*. The home front was covered with equal sensitivity by Launder and Gilliat's *Millions Like Us*, Leslie Howard's *The Gentle Sex*, and Coward's *This Happy Breed*.

Even non-war films had a fresh impetus. Gabriel Pascal made an excellent *Major Barbara* to follow the success of his 1938 *Pygmalion*. Dickinson's *Gaslight*, Reed's *Kipps*, and Asquith's *Quiet Wedding* were all excellent of their kind. The new team of Michael Powell and Emeric Pressburger brought a fresh command and insight to some unlikely but ambitious themes in *The Life and Death of Colonel Blimp* and *A Matter of Life and Death*. Korda supplied *The Thief of Baghdad, Lady Hamilton* and *Perfect Strangers*. The Boulting Brothers followed up *Pastor Hall* with the thoughtful *Thunder Rock*. Launder and Gilliat followed the realistic *Waterloo Road* with sparkling comedy-dramas (*The Rake's Progress, I See a Dark Stranger*), and a classic who-done-it (*Green for Danger*). Gainsborough Studios turned out several competent costume dramas on the Hollywood model. In 1945 the future of British films seemed bright indeed with Olivier's *Henry V*, Coward and Lean's *Blithe Spirit*, and Ealing Studios' supernatural omnibus *Dead of Night* earning popular approval, and such films as *Brief Encounter* and *Odd Man Out* in the works.

In the next few years the industry was beset by financial problems and diminishing audiences. Then Britain's leading film magnate, J. Arthur Rank, set out to conquer by means which proved regrettable. Originally attracted to the cinema as a means for spreading the Methodist religion, he now determined to impress world markets by a series of enormously expensive and generally arty productions, few of which recovered their costs: *Caesar and Cleopatra* is the most notorious. The more modestly-budgeted pictures proved to have little to say now that the end of the war had removed their main subject; and with exceptions like *Mine Own Executioner, The*

Red Shoes, and *The Third Man* the field was thin until the celebrated Ealing comedies (*Passport to Pimlico, Whisky Galore, The Man in the White Suit, Kind Hearts and Coronets*) began to attract world audiences. But these too had their day, and all through the fifties British studios were trying in vain to find subjects to replace them. During this period many stars found their way to Hollywood, and then gradually began to drift back as kingpins of international co-productions, ventures which seldom turned out very happily. It was not till the relaxed hand of censorship permitted *Room at the Top, Saturday Night and Sunday Morning, The Leather Boys, Tom Jones, Georgy Girl, Blow Up,* James Bond and *Alfie* that British films at last set the world afire by showing just what you could get away with if you did it with sufficient skill and truth. Unfortunately even sex and violence must pall . . . so what next? The stopgap answer of the late sixties and early seventies was low comedy, much of it borrowed from TV; but that presumably can't last.

The Great Caruso (US 1951). The film which confirmed Mario Lanza on his brief but triumphant career as a top singing star and also proved to a surprised Hollywood that opera can be big business if given the right sugar coating.

The Great Dictator (US 1940). Chaplin's satire on Hitler has many moments of bitter hilarity but is marred by the sentimentality of the ghetto scenes. The first film in which Chaplin spoke coherently, and the last in which he used his famous tramp character.

Great Expectations (GB 1946). Dickens' novel has been filmed several times, but never with such definition, pace and attention to detail as in the *de luxe* version directed by David Lean and photographed by Ronald Neame. Most outstanding in an excellent cast were John Mills, Jean Simmons, Alec Guinness, Finlay Currie and Martita Hunt; Guy Green (AA) was cinematographer and John Bryan (AA) was production designer. The best previous version was made in Hollywood in 1934, with Philips Holmes and Jane Wyatt.

The Great Gatsby. F. Scott Fitzgerald's mordant story of an ex-gangster who meets his death among the Long Island high livers was filmed in 1926 with Warner Baxter, in 1949 with Alan Ladd, and in 1974 with Robert Redford. The first was by all accounts the most successful, the second being merely surprising for biting off more than it could chew and the third swamped by decoration and overlength.

The Great Impersonation. E. Phillips Oppenheim's cunningly-constructed spy thriller was filmed in 1921 with James Kirkwood; in 1935 with Edmund Lowe; and in 1942 with Ralph Bellamy.

The Great Race (US 1965). A lavish and often splendid period comedy about a 1908 auto race from New York to Paris, this engaging Blake Edwards film was written by Arthur Ross with nods to Valentino, Laurel and Hardy and *The Prisoner of Zenda*. Some of the gags are prolonged, but the film is always good to look at, and the zany leading roles are comfortably filled by Tony Curtis, Jack Lemmon, Natalie Wood, Peter Falk and Ross Martin.

The Great Train Robbery (US 1903). An eleven-minute western sometimes inaccurately hailed as the first story film; but it was the longest of its time, and it did have all the elements of its modern descendants, with careful editing and a sense of cinema showmanship. Directed by Edwin S. Porter.

The Great Ziegfeld (US 1936). A mammoth musical drama of its time, running three hours and recounting the life story of Broadway's great showman. William Powell played the part, and Robert Z. Leonard directed. Academy Awards went to the film (best picture), to Luise Rainer, and to Seymour Felix for the dance direction of the closing number with its enormous revolving set.

The Greatest Story Ever Told (US 1965). George Stevens' immensely long life of Christ (in Cinerama) was plainly a labour of love: he was quoted as hoping that it would still be showing 'at the end of the century and after'. But despite beautiful moments it was fatally compromised by the casting of stars in bit parts and by the heavy-handedness evident in all Stevens' later films. The publicity about deciding to shoot it in Utah (because Utah was 'more like Palestine than Palestine') didn't help; but Max Von Sydow was an excellent Christ. At the box office, the picture died.

Greco, Juliette (1927–). French singer who acted in several films both at home and abroad.
Au Royaume des Cieux 49. The Green Glove 52. *The Sun Also Rises* 57. Naked Earth 58. Roots of Heaven 59. Whirlpool 59. Crack in the Mirror 60, etc.

Greece has had a film industry since 1912, but its development has been affected by political upheavals, and the results have had little international appeal, the best known directors being Michael Cacoyannis and Greg Tallas. The personality of Melina Mercouri and the music of Mikis Thodorakis were however more successfully exported.

Greed (US 1923). Originally an estimated nine hours long, cut by June Mathis to two, this realistic study of money as the root of all evil, set in contemporary American settings, was both Erich Von Stroheim's triumph and his downfall; for it made his extravagance a talking-point in Hollywood and a few years later he was forced to retire from directing. Here he also wrote the scenario, from Frank Norris' novel *McTeague*; his cinematographers were Ben Reynolds, William Daniels and Ernest Schoedsack and his leading actors Zasu Pitts, Gibson Gowland and Jean Hersholt.

Green, Adolph (1915–). American writer of books and lyrics for many Broadway shows and musical films, usually with Betty Comden (qv).

Green, Alfred E. (1889–1960). American director of mainly routine but generally competent films; in Hollywood from 1912.
Little Lord Fauntleroy 20. Ella Cinders 23. Through the Back Door 26. The Green Goddess 30. Old English 31. Smart Money 31. Disraeli 31. The Rich Are Always with Us 32. Parachute 33. Dangerous 35. Duke of West Point 38. South of Pago Pago 40. Badlands of Dakota 41. Meet the Stewarts 42. A Thousand and One Nights 44. *The Jolson Story* 46. The Fabulous Dorseys 47. They Passed This Way 48. Four Faces West 48. Cover Up 49. Invasion USA 52. The Eddie Cantor Story 53, many others.

Green, Danny (1903–). Heavyweight British character actor usually in cheerful—or sometimes menacing—cockney roles. Appeared in some American silents.
Crime over London 37. Fiddlers Three 44. The Man Within 47. No Orchids for Miss Blandish 48. Little Big Shot 52. A Kid for Two Farthings 55. The Lady Killers 55. Beyond This Place 59, many others.

Green, Guy (1913–). British cinematographer who became a useful director.
AS CINEMATOGRAPHER: In Which We Serve 42. The Way Ahead 44. *Great Expectations* (AA) 46. Take my Life 47. *Oliver Twist* 48. Captain Horatio Hornblower 51. The Beggar's Opera 52. Rob Roy 53, etc.
□ AS DIRECTOR: River Beat 54. Portrait of Alison 55. Postmark for Danger 56. Lost 56. House of Secrets 56. The Snorkel 58. Sea of Sand

58. SOS Pacific 59. *The Mark* 60. *The Angry Silence* 60. The Light in the Piazza 62. Diamond Head 63. A Patch of Blue 65. Pretty Polly 67. The Magus 68. A Walk in the Spring Rain 70. Luther 73. Once is Not Enough 75.

Green, Harry (1892–1958). American comedian, primarily on stage; former lawyer.
Bottoms Up 34. The Cisco Kid and the Lady 37. Joe MacBeth (GB) 55. A King in New York (GB) 57, etc.

Green, Hughie (1920–). Canadian actor in Britain, former juvenile, now popular TV quizmaster and talent scout.
Little Friend 34. Midshipman Easy 36. Tom Brown's Schooldays (US) 39. If Winter Comes (US) 48. Paper Orchid 49, etc.

Green, Janet (1914–). British screenwriter.
The Clouded Yellow 49. Cast a Dark Shadow (oa) 54. Lost 55. The Long Arm 56. *Sapphire* (BFA) 59. Midnight Lace (oa) 60. Life for Ruth 62. *Victim* 62. Seven Women 66, etc.

Green, Johnny (1908–). American composer, band leader, songwriter; in Hollywood from 1933. Scored Easter Parade (AA) 47. An American in Paris (AA), 51. Oliver (AA) 68, many others.

Green, Martyn (1899–1975). British light opera singer, with the D'Oyly Carte Company for many years; settled in America.
Autobiography 1952: *Here's A How De Do*.
□ *The Mikado* 39. The Story of Gilbert and Sullivan 53. A Lovely Way to Die 68.

Green, Mitzi (1920–1969) (Elizabeth Keno). American child performer of the thirties.
Honey 30. Tom Sawyer 30. Little Orphan Annie 32. Transatlantic Merry-Go-Round 34, etc.: later appeared in Lost in Alaska 52. Bloodhounds of Broadway 52.

Green, Nigel (1924–1972). Dominant British character actor with stage experience.
Reach for the Sky 56. Bitter Victory 58. The Criminal 60. Jason and the Argonauts 63. *Zulu* 64. *The Ipcress File* 65. *The Face of Fu Manchu* 65. The Skull 66. Let's Kill Uncle (US) 66. *Deadlier than the Male* 66. *Tobruk* (US) 67. Africa Texas Style 67. Play Dirty 68. Wrecking Crew (US) 69. The Kremlin Letter 69. Countess Dracula 70. The Ruling Class 71, etc.

Green Pastures (US 1936). A fairly lavish and sympathetic film version, directed by William Keighley, of the Marc Connelly play from Roark

Bradford's stories showing the simple Negro interpretation of the Bible, with Heaven as a gigantic 'fish fry' and 'De Lawd' played by Rex Ingram as a dignified old Negro. The first film since *Hallelujah* 29 to give a fairly serious account of Negro thought, it did not entirely avoid a patronizing air.

Green, Philip (c. 1917–). British composer.
The March Hare 54. John and Julie 55. Rooney 57. Innocent Sinners 58. Operation Amsterdam 59. Sapphire 59. The Bulldog Breed 61. Victim 62. It's All Happening (& co-p) 63. The Intelligence Men 65. Masquerade 65, etc.

Greenberg, Stanley R. (–). American screenwriter.
Welcome Home Johnny Bristol (TV) 72. Skyjacked 72. Soylent Green 73, etc.

Greene, Clarence (c. 1918–). American writer-producer, usually in collaboration with Russel Rouse.
The Town Went Wild 45. D.O.A. 48. The Well 51. New York Confidential 55. A House Is Not a Home 64. The Oscar 66. Caper of the Golden Bulls 67, etc.
TV series: Tightrope 59.

Greene, David (1924–). British director, former small-part actor; became a TV director in Canada and the U.S.
□ The Shuttered Room 66. Sebastian 68. The Strange Affair 68. I Start Counting (& p) 69. The People Next Door 70. Madame Sin (TV) 72. *Godspell* 73. Rich Man Poor Man (TV) (co-d) 76.

Greene, Graham (1904–). Distinguished British novelist who has provided material for many interesting films.
Stamboul Train (Orient Express) 34. This Gun for Hire 42. The Ministry of Fear 43. Confidential Agent 45. The Man Within 46. Brighton Rock 47. The Fugitive 48. The Fallen Idol 48. The Third Man 49. The Heart of the Matter 53. The Stranger's Hand 54. The End of the Affair 55. The Quiet American 58. Our Man in Havana 59. The Comedians 67. Travels with My Aunt 73, etc.

Greene, Leon (–). Stalwart British supporting actor, former opera singer.

Greene, Lorne (1915–). Solidly-built Canadian character actor.
The Silver Chalice 54. Tight Spot 55. Autumn Leaves 56. Peyton Place 57. The Gift of Love 58. The Trap 58. Legacy of a Spy (TV) 68. The

Harness (TV) 71. Earthquake 74, etc.
TV series: Sailor of Fortune 56. *Bonanza* (as Ben Cartwright) 59–72. Griff 73.

Greene, Max (1896–1968) (Mutz Greenbaum). German cinematographer, long in Britain.
The Stars Look Down 39. Hatter's Castle 41. Spring in Park Lane 48. Maytime in Mayfair 49. Night and the City 50, etc.

Greene, Richard (1918–). Good-looking, lightweight British leading man with brief stage experience before 1938 film debut (*Four Men and a Prayer*) resulted in Hollywood contract.
My Lucky Star 38. Submarine Patrol 38. Kentucky 38. The Little Princess 39. The Hound of the Baskervilles 39. Stanley and Livingstone 39. Little Old New York 40. Unpublished Story 41. Flying Fortress 42. Yellow Canary 43. Don't Take It to Heart 44. Gaiety George 46. Forever Amber 47. Lady Windermere's Fan 49. Now Barabbas 50. Shadow of the Eagle 50. Lorna Doone 51. The Black Castle 52. Captain Scarlett 52. The Return of the Corsican Brothers 53. Contraband Spain 55. Beyond the Curtain 60. Sword of Sherwood Forest 61. Dangerous Island 67. Blood of Fu Manchu 68, etc. Also starred in 165 TV episodes of Robin Hood.

Greene, W. Howard (–1956). American colour cinematographer.
Trail of the Lonesome Pine 36. *The Garden of Allah* 36. *A Star is Born* 37. Nothing Sacred 37. *The Adventures of Robin Hood* 38. Jesse James 39. Elizabeth and Essex 39. Northwest Mounted Police 40. Blossoms in the Dust 41. The Jungle Book 42. Arabian Nights 42. *Phantom of the Opera* (AA) 43. Ali Baba and the Forty Thieves 44. Cant Help Singing 44. Salome Where she Danced 45. A Night in Paradise 46. Tycoon 47. High Lonesome 50. Quebec 51. The Brigand 52. Gun Belt 53, etc.

Greenleaf, Raymond (1892–1963). American character actor, usually seen as benevolent elderly man.
Storm Warning 51. Angel Face 53. Violent Saturday 54. *When Gangland Strikes* (leading role) 56. The Story on Page One 60, many others.

Greenstreet, Sidney (1879–1954). Immense British stage actor long in America; a sensation in his first film, made at the age of 61, he became a major star of the forties.
□ *The Maltese Falcon* 41. They Died with Their Boots On 41. *Across the Pacific* 42. Casablanca 42. Background to Danger 42. Passage to Marseilles 44. *Between Two Worlds* 44. The Mask of Dimitrios 44. The Conspirators 44. Hollywood Canteen 44. Pillow to Post 45. Conflict 45. Christmas in Connecticut 45. *Three Strangers* 46. Devotion (as Thackeray) 46. The Verdict 46. That Way with Women 47. *The Hucksters* 47. *The Woman in White* 48. The Velvet Touch 48. Ruthless 48. Flamingo Road 49. It's a Great Feeling 49. Malaya 50.

Greenwood, Charlotte (1893–). Tall American comedienne and eccentric dancer, on stage from 1905.
Jane 18. Baby Mine 27. So Long Letty 30. Palmy Days 32. Down Argentine Way 40. Springtime in the Rockies 43. Up in Mabel's Room 44. Home in Indiana 47. Peggy 50. Dangerous When Wet 52. Glory 55. Oklahoma 56. The Opposite Sex 56, etc.

Greenwood, Jack (1919–). British producer, responsible for second-feature crime series: Edgar Wallace, Scales of Justice, Scotland Yard, etc.

Greenwood, Joan (1921–). Plummy-voiced British leading lady of the forties.
□ John Smith Wakes Up 40. My Wife's Family 40. He Found a Star 41. *The Gentle Sex* 42. They Knew Mr Knight 44. Latin Quarter 44. A Girl in a Million 45. The Man Within 46. *The October Man* 47. The White Unicorn 47. *Saraband for Dead Lovers* 48. The Bad Lord Byron 48. Whisky Galore 49. *Kind Hearts and Coronets* 49. Flesh and Blood 50. The Man in the White Suit 50. Young Wives' Tale 51. Mr Peek-a-Boo 51. *The Importance of Being Earnest* 52. Knave of Hearts 54. *Father Brown* 54. Moonfleet (US) 55. Mysterious Island 62. The Amorous Prawn 62. Tom Jones 63. The Moon Spinners 64. Girl Stroke Boy 71.

Greenwood, John (1889–). British composer.
To What Red Hell? 30. The Constant Nymph 33. Elephant Boy 37. Pimpernel Smith 41. San Demetrio, London 44. Frieda 47. Quartet 48, others.

Greenwood, Walter (1903–1974). British writer who chronicled industrial life, notably in *Love On the Dole*.

Greer, Jane (1924–) (Bettyjane Greer). Cool American leading lady of the forties; could play good-humoured dames, well-bred ladies or *femmes fatales*.
□ Pan Americana 45. Two O'Clock Courage 45. George White's Scandals 45. Dick Tracy 45. The

Falcon's Alibi 46. Bamboo Blonde 46. Sunset Pass 46. Sinbad the Sailor 46. *They Won't Believe Me* 47. *Out of the Past* 47. Station West 48. *The Big Steal* 49. You're in the Navy Now 51. The Company She Keeps 51. The Prisoner of Zenda 52. Desperate Search 52. You for Me 52. The Clown 53. Down Among the Sheltering Palms 53. *Run for the Sun* 56. *Man of a Thousand Faces* 57. Where Love Has Gone 64. Billie 65.

Gregg, Hubert (1914–). British songwriter, screenwriter, and light actor, married to Pat Kirkwood. On stage from 1933, films from 1942. In Which We Serve 42. 29 Acacia Avenue 45. Vote for Huggett 49. Robin Hood 52. The Maggie 54. Simon and Laura 55. Stars in My Eyes 57, etc.

Gregory, James (1911–). American character actor with stage experience, a familiar Hollywood 'heavy' or senior cop.
Naked City 47. The Frogmen 51. The Scarlet Hour 56. The Young Stranger 57. Al Capone 59. Two Weeks in Another Town 62. *The Manchurian Candidate* 62. P.T.109 63. A Distant Trumpet 64. The Sons of Katie Elder 65. A Rage To Live 65. *The Silencers* 66. Clambake 68. The Hawaiians 70. Million Dollar Duck 71. Shootout 71, etc.
TV series: The Lawless Years 59.

Gregory, Paul (c. 1905–) (Jason Lenhart). American impresario who teamed with Charles Laughton in the forties to present dramatized readings: also produced *Night of the Hunter* 55, which Laughton directed, and *The Naked and the Dead* 58.

Gregson, John (1919–1975). Scottish leading man, a likeable and dependable star of British comedies and action dramas in the fifties.
□ Saraband for Dead Lovers 48. Scott of the Antarctic 48. Whisky Galore 49. Train of Events 49. Treasure Island 50. Cairo Road 50. *The Lavender Hill Mob* 51. Angels One Five 51. *The Brave Don't Cry* 51. Venetian Bird 52. The Holly and the Ivy 52. The Titfield Thunderbolt 53. *Genevieve* 53. The Weak and the Wicked 53. Conflict of Wings 54. To Dorothy a Son 54. The Crowded Day 54. Above Us the Waves 55. Value for Money 55. *Jacqueline* 56. The Battle of the River Plate 56. True as a Turtle 56. Miracle in Soho 57. *Rooney* 57. Sea of Sand 58. *The Captain's Table* 58. SOS Pacific 59. Faces in the Dark 60. Hand in Hand 60. Treasure of Monte Cristo 61. Frightened City 61. *Live Now Pay Later* 62. Tomorrow at Ten 62. The Longest Day 62. The Night of the Generals 66. Fright 71.

TV series: Gideon's Way 65. Shirley's World 71.

Greig, Robert (1880–1958). Australian character actor, long in Hollywood; the doyen of portly pompous butlers.
Animal Crackers 30. Tonight or Never 31. Love Me Tonight 32. Trouble in Paradise 32. Horse Feathers 32. Merrily We Go to Hell 33. Pleasure Cruise 33. Clive of India 35. Lloyds of London 36. Easy Living 37. Algiers 38. No Time for Comedy 40. The Lady Eve 41. Sullivan's Travels 42. *The Moon and Sixpence* 42. I Married a Witch 42. The Palm Beach Story 42. The Great Moment 44. The Picture of Dorian Gray 45. The Cheaters 45. Unfaithfully Yours 48, many others.

Gremillon, Jean (1901–59). French director with limited but interesting output since 1929.
Remorques 39. Lumière d'Eté 42. Pattes Blanches 48, etc.

Grenfell, Joyce (1910–) (Joyce Phipps). Angular British comedienne adept at refined gaucherie; a revue star and solo performer, on stage since 1939.
The Demi-Paradise 42. The Lamp Still Burns 43. While the Sun Shines 46. *The Happiest Days of Your Life* 49. Stage Fright 50. *Laughter in Paradise* 51. Genevieve 53. The Million Pound Note 54. The Belles of St Trinian's 54. Happy Is the Bride 57. Blue Murder at St Trinian's 58. The Pure Hell of St Trinian's 60. The Old Dark House 63. The Americanization of Emily 64. The Yellow Rolls Royce 64, etc.

Greville, Edmond (1906–1966). French director; assistant to Dupont on *Piccadilly* 30, to Clair on *Sous les Toits de Paris* 32.
Remous 34. Mademoiselle Docteur 37. L'Ile du Pêché 39. Passionelle 46. Noose (GB) 48. The Romantic Age (GB) 49. But Not In Vain (also wrote and produced) (GB) 49. Port du Désir 56. Guilty (GB) 56. Beat Girl (GB) 60. The Hands of Orlac (GB) 61. Les Menteurs 61, etc.

Grey, Joel (1932–) (Joe Katz). American singing entertainer who took a long time to hit stardom, managed it on the New York stage in *Cabaret*, but proved difficult to cast.
□ About Face 52. Come September 63. *Cabaret* 72. Man on a String 74. Buffalo Bill and the Indians 76. The Seven Per Cent Solution 76.

Grey, Nan (1918–) (Eschal Miller). American leading lady of the late thirties.
Dracula's Daughter 36. Three Smart Girls 36. Three Smart Girls Grow Up 38. Tower of London 39. The Invisible Man Returns 40.

Sandy Is a Lady 41, etc.

Grey, Virginia (1917–). American leading lady of minor films in the thirties and forties.
Uncle Tom's Cabin (debut) 27. Misbehaving Ladies 31. Secrets 33. Dames 34. The Firebird 34. The Great Ziegfeld 36. Rosalie 37. Test Pilot 38. The Hardys Ride High 39. Hullaballoo 40. Blonde Inspiration 41. The Big Store 41. Grand Central Murder 42. Idaho 43. Strangers in the Night 44. Blonde Ransom 45. House of Horrors 46. Unconquered 47. Who Killed Doc Robbin? 48. Jungle Jim 49. Slaughter Trail 51. Desert Pursuit 52. Target Earth 54. The Last Command 55. Crime of Passion 56. The Restless Years 58. Portrait in Black 60. Back Street 61. Black Zoo 63. Love Has Many Faces 65. Madame X 66. Rosie 68. Airport 69, many others.

Grey, Zane (1875–1939). American novelist whose western yarns provided the basis of hundreds of silent and sound movies. He lacked sophistication, but as late as 1958 TV had its *Zane Grey Playhouse*.

Greyfriars Bobby (US 1960). Elinor Atkinson's sentimental novel of old Edinburgh, about a dog who lies on his master's grave, was filmed agreeably enough by Disney. It had also been used as the plot of *Challenge to Lassie* 49.

Griem, Helmut (1940–). German leading man in international films.
The Damned 69. The Mackenzie Break 70. *Cabaret* 72. Ludwig 73, etc.

Grier, Pam (–). Black American leading lady.
Beyond the Valley of the Dolls 70. Twilight People 72. Blacula 72. Hit Man 72. Coffy 74. Black Mama White Mama 74. The Arena 75, etc.

Grier, Roosevelt (–). Black American footballer, cousin of Pam Grier; makes occasional showbiz appearances.
The Thing with Two Heads 72.

Grierson, John (1898–1972). Distinguished British documentarist. Founded Empire Marketing Board Film Unit 30. GPO Film Unit 33; Canadian Film Commissioner 39–45, etc. Produced *Drifters* 29. *Industrial Britain* 33. *Song of Ceylon* 34. *Night Mail* 36, etc. In 1957–63 he had his own weekly TV show *This Wonderful World* showing excerpts from the world's best non-fiction films.

Gries, Tom (1922–1977). American producer

and co-writer with varied Hollywood experience from 1946.
□ Hell's Horizon 55. The Girl in the Woods 58. *Will Penny* (& w) 68. 100 Rifles 69. Number One 69. The Hawaiians 70. Fools 71. Lady Ice 73. QB VII (TV) 74. Breakout 75. Breakheart Pass 76. Helter Skelter (TV) 76.

Griffies, Ethel (1878–1975) (Ethel Woods). Angular British character actress, in Hollywood for many years.
Waterloo Bridge 31. Love Me Tonight 32. The Mystery of Edwin Drood 35. Kathleen 37. We are Not Alone 39. Irene 40. Great Guns 41. *Time to Kill* 42. Jane Eyre 44. The Horn Blows at Midnight 45. Devotion 46. The Homestretch 47. The Birds 63. *Billy Liar* (GB) 63, many others.

Griffin, Josephine (1928–). British leading lady.
The Weak and the Wicked 54. The Purple Plain 54. The Man Who Never Was 56. The Spanish Gardener (last to date) 56, etc.

Griffith, Andy (1926–). Tall, slow-speaking American comic actor, adept at wily country-boy roles.
A Face in the Crowd (debut) 57. No Time for Sergeants 58. Onionhead 58. Winter Kill (TV) 73. Hearts of the West 75.
TV series: The Andy Griffith Show 60–68.

Griffith, Corinne (1898–). American leading lady of the twenties.
The Yellow Girl 22. Six Days 23. Lilies of the Field 24. Love's Wilderness 24. The Marriage Whirl 25. Infatuation 25. Syncopating Sue 26. Three Hours 27. The Garden of Eden 28. The Divine Lady 29. Saturday's Children 29. Back Pay 30. Lily Christine 30. Papa's Delicate Condition (oa only) 52, etc.

Griffith, D. W. (David Wark) (1874–1948). American film pioneer, the industry's first major producer-director; he improved the cinema's prestige, developed many aspects of technique, created a score of stars, and was only flawed by his sentimental Victorian outlook, which in the materialistic twenties put him prematurely out of vogue and in the thirties out of business. Best book about him: *The Movies, Mr Griffith, and Me*, by Lillian Gish.
SELECTED EARLY FILMS: For the Love of Gold 08. The Song of the Shirt 08. Edgar Allan Poe 09. The Medicine Bottle 09. The Drunkard's Reformation 09. The Cricket on the Hearth 09. What Drink Did 09. The Violin Maker of Cremona 09. Pippa Passes 09. In the Watches of the Night 09. Lines of White on a Sullen Sea 09.

Nursing a Viper 09. The Red Man's View 09. In Old California 10. Ramona 10. In the Season of Buds 10. The Face at the Window 10. The House with Closed Shutters 10. The Usurer 10. The Chink at Golden Gulch 10. Muggsy's First Sweetheart 10. The Italian Barber 10. The Manicure Lady 11. What Shall We Do with Our Old? 11. *The Lonedale Operator* 11. The Spanish Gypsy 11. Paradise Lost 11. Enoch Arden 11. Through Darkened Vales 11. The Revenue Man and the Girl 11. A Mender of Nets 12. The Goddess of Sagebrush Gulch 12. The Old Actor 12. *Man's Genesis* 12. The Sands of Dee 12. *The Musketeers of Pig Alley* 12. My Baby 12. *The New York Hat* 12. The God Within 12. The One She Loved 12. The Mothering Heart 13. The Sheriff's Baby 13. The Battle at Elderbrush Gulch 13. *Judith of Bethulia* 13. The Escape 14. The Avenging Conscience 14. The Mother and the Law 14. Home Sweet Home 14, many others.

□ FROM 1915: *The Birth of a Nation* 15. *Intolerance* 16. *Hearts of the World* 18. The Great Love 18. The Greatest Thing in Life 18. A Romance of Happy Valley 19. *Broken Blossoms* 19. The Girl Who Stayed at Home 19. True Heart Susie 19. Scarlet Days 19. The Greatest Question 19. The Idol Dancer 20. The Love Flower 20. *Way Down East* 20. Dream Street 21. *One Exciting Night* 22. *Orphans of the Storm* 22. The White Rose 23. America 24. Isn't Life Wonderful 25. Sally of the Sawdust 26. That Royle Girl 26. *The Sorrows of Satan* 26. Drums of Love 28. The Battle of the Sexes 28. Lady of the Pavements 29. Abraham Lincoln 29. The Struggle 30. One Million Years B.C. (reputed contribution) 40.

Griffith, Edward H. (1894–). American director. Scrambled Wives 21. Unseeing Eyes 23. Bad Company 25. Afraid to Love 27. Paris Bound 29. Holiday 30. Rebound 31. The Animal Kingdom 32. Another Language 33. Biography of a Bachelor Girl 35. No More Ladies 35. Ladies in Love 36. Café Metropole 37. Café Society 39. Safari 40. Virginia 40. One Night in Lisbon 41. Bahama Passage 42. The Sky's the Limit 43. Perilous Holiday 46, etc.

Griffith, Hugh (1912–). Flamboyant Welsh actor, former bank clerk.
Neutral Port (debut) 40; war service; The Three Weird Sisters 48. London Belongs to Me 48. The Last Days of Dolwyn 48. A Run for Your Money 49. Laughter in Paradise 51. The Galloping Major 51. The Beggar's Opera 52. *The Titfield Thunderbolt* 53. The Sleeping Tiger 54. Passage Home 55. *Lucky Jim* 57. Ben Hur (AA) 59. The Day They Robbed the Bank of

England 60. Exodus 61. The Counterfeit Traitor 62. *Tom Jones* 63. The Bargee 64. Moll Flanders 65. Oh Dad, Poor Dad 66. Sailor from Gibraltar 66. How to Steal a Million 66. The Chastity Belt 67. Oliver 68. The Fixer 68. Start the Revolution Without Me 69. Cry of the Banshee 70. Wuthering Heights 70. The Abominable Dr Phibes 71. Who Slew Auntie Roo? 72. What 72. Craze 73. Take Me High 73, others.

Griffith, James (1919–). American general purpose actor.
Bright Leaf 50. Rhubarb 51. The Law vs Billy the Kid (as Pat Garrett) 54. Anything Goes 56. The Big Fisherman 59. The Amazing Transparent Man 61, etc.

Griffith, Kenneth (1921–). Sharp-eyed Welsh actor of stage and screen, often the envious 'little man'.
Love on the Dole 41. The Shop at Sly Corner 45. Bond Street 48. High Treason 50. Lucky Jim 57. I'm All Right, Jack 59. Circus of Horrors 59. *Only Two Can Play* 61. Rotten to the Core 65. The Bobo 67. The Whisperers 67. Revenge 71. The House in Nightmare Park 73, many others.

Griffith, Raymond (1894–1937). Dapper American comedian of the twenties.
Fools First 22. The Eternal Three 23. Changing Husbands 24. Poisoned Paradise 24. Open All Night 24. Miss Bluebeard 24. A Regular Fellow 25. *Fine Clothes* 25. *Hands Up* 25. *Wet Paint* 26. You'd Be Surprised 27. Time to Love 27. Wedding Bills 27. *All Quiet on the Western Front* (as the dying soldier) 30, etc.

Griffith, Richard (1912–1969). American film critic and curator of New York's Museum of Modern Art.

Griffiths, Jane (1930–). British leading lady of the fifties.
The Million Pound Note 54. The Green Scarf 54. Dead Man's Evidence 62. The Traitors 63, etc.

Griggs, Loyal (   ). American cinematographer.
Shane (AA) 53. Elephant Walk 54. We're No Angels 55. The Ten Commandments 56. The Hangman 59. Walk Like a Dragon 60. The Slender Thread 66. Hurry Sundown 67. P.J. 68, others.

Grimault, Paul (1905–). French animator.
Le Petit Soldat 47, many shorts.

Grimes, Gary (1955–). American juvenile lead of the seventies.

□ *Summer of 42* 71. The Culpeper Cattle Co. 72. Class of 44 73. Cahill 73. The Spikes Gang 74.

Grimm, Jakob (1785–1863) and **Wilhelm** (1786–1859). German writers of philology and—especially—fairy tales. The latter are familiar throughout the world and have been the basis of many children's films by Walt Disney and others. A thin biopic, *The Wonderful World of the Brothers Grimm*, was made in 1962.

Grinde, Nick (1891–). American director.
Excuse Me 25. Upstage 26. Beyond the Sierra 28. *The Bishop Murder Case* 30. Good News 30. This Modern Age 31. Vanity Street 32. Ladies Crave Excitement 35. Public Enemy's Wife 36. White Bondage 37. King of Chinatown 39. The Man They Could Not Hang 39. Behind the Door 40. Hitler Dead or Alive 43. Road to Alcatraz 45, etc.

grip. A technician who builds or arranges the film set; a specialized labourer. The chief grip on a picture is usually credited as 'Key Grip'.

Grizzard, George (1925–). American stage actor, usually in sneaky roles in films.
From the Terrace 60. *Advise and Consent* 62. Warning Shot 66. Happy Birthday Wanda June 71, etc.

Grock (1880–1959) (Adrien Wettach). Swiss clown who made a few silent films in Britain, and later in Germany. A biopic, *Farewell Mr Grock*, was made in 1954.

Grodin, Charles (1935–). American leading man.
The Heartbreak Kid 73. 11 Harrowhouse (& w) 74.

Grot, Anton (1884–) (Antocz Franziszek Groszewski). Polish art director, in Hollywood from the twenties: the driving force of Warner's thirties dream machine.
Robin Hood 20. Svengali 31. Doctor X 32. *The Mystery of the Wax Museum* 33. Gold Diggers of 1933 33. Footlight Parade 33. Gold Diggers of 1935 35. *A Midsummer Night's Dream* 35. The Sea Hawk 40. The Conspirators 44, many others.

The Group (US 1966). A faithful and entertaining film version of Mary McCarthy's immensely detailed novel about the lives of some young women graduates in the thirties. Sidney Buchman's script and Sidney Lumet's direction keep the stories nicely contrasted. Of a cast of near-unknowns, impressive performances come from Joan Hackett, Jessica Walter, Elizabeth Hartman, Kathleen Widdoes and others.

Group 3. A British production company set up in 1951 by the National Film Finance Corporation. In charge were John Baxter, John Grierson and Michael Balcon, and their aim was to make low-budget films employing young talent. The venture was regarded with suspicion by the trade, and the results were not encouraging—a string of mildly eccentric comedies and thrillers lucky to get second feature circuit bookings. Some of the titles: *Judgement Deferred, Brandy for the Parson, The Brave Don't Cry, You're Only Young Twice, The Oracle, Laxdale Hall, Time Gentlemen Please.*

Gruber, Frank (1904–1969). American screenwriter.
Death of a Champion (oa) 39. The Kansan (oa) 43. *The Mask of Dimitrios* 44. Terror by Night 47. Fighting Man of the Plains 49. The Great Missouri Raid 51. Denver and Rio Grande 52. Hurricane Smith 52, etc.

Grune, Karl (1890–1962). Czech-Austrian director in German films.
The Street 23. At the Edge of the World 27. Waterloo 28. Abdul the Damned (GB) 35. Pagliacci (GB) 37, etc.

Grusin, Dave (–). American composer.
Divorce American Style 67. The Graduate 67. Candy 68. The Mad Room 69. Tell them Willie Boy is Here 69. The Pursuit of Happiness 71. The Great Northfield Minnesota Raid 72.

Guardino, Harry (1925–). Leading American TV actor, in occasional films.
Houseboat 58. Pork Chop Hill 59. The Five Pennies 59. King of Kings 61. Hell is for Heroes 62. Rhino 64. Bullwhip Griffin 67. Madigan 68. Lovers and Other Strangers 69. Red Sky at Morning 71. Dirty Harry 71, etc.
TV series: The Reporter 65. Monty Nash 71.

Guareschi, Giovanni (1908–68). Italian author of the 'Don Camillo' stories about a parish priest's comic struggles with a communist mayor. Several have been filmed with Fernandel and Gino Cervi.

Guess Who's Coming to Dinner (US 1967). A commercially successful sugar-coated race relations pill, showing the genteel and sympathetic reactions of an enlightened and wealthy couple to the news that their daughter is going to marry a distinguished black man. All bets are hedged, and the characters do little more than sit around and chat on a single set, but so much talent is involved that the effect is strangely enjoyable if traumatic. Spencer Tracy, whose last film this was, and Katharine Hepburn, who won an Academy Award for her performance, played the parents, with Sidney Poitier (who else?) as the bone of contention. William Rose (AA) wrote the screenplay; Stanley Kramer produced and directed with his usual bloodless competence.

Guest, Val (1911–). British writer-producer-director, former journalist. Worked on screenplays of thirties comedies for Will Hay, Arthur Askey, the Crazy Gang, etc. Married to Yolande Donlan.
Miss London Ltd (d) 43. Just William's Luck (wd) 47. Mr Drake's Duck (wd) 50. Penny Princess (wpd) 51. The Runaway Bus (wpd) 54. Quatermass II (wd) 56. Hell Is a City (wd) 59. The Day the Earth Caught Fire (wpd) 62. Jigsaw (wpd) 62. The Beauty Jungle (wpd) 64. Where the Spies are (wpd) 65. Assignment K (wd) 67.When Dinosaurs Ruled the Earth (wd) 69. Confessions of a Window Cleaner 74. The Diamond Mercenaries 76, many others.

Guetary, Georges (1915–) (Lambros Worloou). Greek/Egyptian singer who became popular in French cabaret and musical comedy. Only American film: An American in Paris 51.

Guffey, Burnett (1905–). Distinguished American cinematographer.
Cover Girl 44. Johnny O'Clock 46. Gallant Journey 46. The Reckless Moment 48. *All the King's Men* 49. In a Lonely Place 50. The Sniper 52. *From Here to Eternity* (AA) 53. Human Desire 55. The Harder They Fall 56. Edge of Eternity 59. Birdman of Alcatraz 62. King Rat 65. *Bonnie and Clyde* (AA) 67. The Split 68. The Madwoman of Chaillot 69. The Great White Hope 70, etc.

Guild, Nancy (1926–). American leading lady.
Somewhere in the Night 46. The High Window 47. Give My Regards to Broadway 49. Abbott and Costello Meet the Invisible Man 51. Francis Covers the Big Town 54. Such Good Friends 71, etc.

Guilaroff, Sydney (1910–). American star hairdresser, long at MGM.

Guilfoyle, Paul (1902–1961). American character actor usually in sly or sinister roles.
Special Agent 36. Blind Alibi 38. Time to Kill 42. Sweetheart of Sigma Chi 46. Miss Mink of 1949.

Mighty Joe Young 50. Torch Song 52. Julius Caesar 53. Valley of Fury 55, many others.
AS DIRECTOR: Captain Scarface 53. A Life at Stake 54. Tess of the Storm Country 60.

Guillermin, John (1925–). British director who started in second features and graduated to international spectaculars.
□ Torment 49. Smart Alec 50. Two on the Tiles 51. Four Days 51. Song of Paris 52. Miss Robin Hood 52. Operation Diplomat 53. Adventure in the Hopfields 54. The Crowded Day 54. Thunderstorm 55. *Town on Trial* 56. The Whole Truth 57. *I Was Monty's Double* 58. Tarzan's Greatest Adventure 59. The Day They Robbed the Bank of England 60. Never Let Go (& w) 60. Waltz of the Toreadors 62. Tarzan Goes to India 62. Guns at Batasi 64. Rapture 65. *The Blue Max* 66. P.J. 68. House of Cards 68. The Bridge at Remagen 69. El Condor 70. Skyjacked 72. Shaft in Africa 74. The Towering Inferno 74. King Kong 76.

the guillotine, that French instrument of execution, cast its shadow over a variety of films including *Mata Hari, Marie Antoinette, A Tale of Two Cities, Uncertain Glory, The Scarlet Pimpernel,* and *Mad Love.* The Carry On gang managed to make fun with it in *Don't Lose Your Head.* Private guillotines were employed for diabolical purposes in *The Mystery of the Wax Museum, House of Wax, Chamber of Horrors* and *Two on a Guillotine.*

Guinan, Texas (188*–1933) (Mary Louise Guinan). American star entertainer of twenties speakeasies: her catchphrase was 'Hello, sucker!'. Betty Hutton played her in *Incendiary Blonde* 45.
□ The Gun Woman 18. Little Miss Deputy 19. I am the Woman 21. The Stampede 21. Queen of the Night Clubs 29. Glorifying the American Girl 29. Broadway through a Keyhole 33.

Guinness, Sir Alec (1914–). Distinguished British stage actor, who in the late forties started a spectacular film career, first as a master of disguise, then as a young hero and later as any character from an Arab king to Hitler.
□ Evensong 33. Great Expectations (as Herbert Pocket) 46. *Oliver Twist* (as Fagin) 48. *Kind Hearts and Coronets* (playing eight roles) 49. A Run for Your Money 49. Last Holiday 50. *The Mudlark* (as Disraeli) 50. *The Lavender Hill Mob* 51. *The Man in the White Suit* 51. *The Card* 52. The Captain's Paradise 52. The Malta Story 53. *Father Brown* 54. To Paris with Love 54. The Prisoner 55. The Ladykillers 55. The Swan 56. Barnacle Bill 57. *The Bridge on the*

River Kwai (AA, BFA) 57. The Scapegoat 58. The Horse's Mouth (& w) 58. Our Man in Havana 59. *Tunes of Glory* 60. A Majority of One 61. HMS Defiant 62. Lawrence of Arabia 62. The Fall of the Roman Empire 64. Situation Hopeless but Not Serious 64. Doctor Zhivago 66. Hotel Paradiso 66. The Quiller Memorandum 66. The Comedians 67. Cromwell (as Charles I) 69. Scrooge 70. Hitler: The Last Ten Days (as Hitler) 73. Brother Sun and Sister Moon 73. Murder by Death 76. Star Wars 77.

Guiol, Fred (1898–). American director, mainly of second features; also worked as assistant on many of George Stevens pictures.
Live and Learn 30. The Cohens and Kellys in Trouble 33. The Nitwits 35. Hayfoot 41. Here Comes Trouble 48, many others.

Guitry, Sacha (1885–1957). Distinguished French writer-director, in films occasionally over a long period. Autobiography 1956: *If Memory Serves*. Biography 1968: *The Last Boulevardier* by James Harding.
Ceux de Chez Nous 15. Les Deux Couverts 32. Bonne Chance 35. Le Roman d'un Tricheur 36. Quadrille 38. Ils Etaient Neuf Célibataires 39. Donne-moi tes yeux 43. Le Comedien 49. Deburau 51. Versailles 54. Napoleon 55. La Vie à Deux 57, etc.

Gulager, Clu (1935–). American leading man, mostly on TV.
The Killers 64. Winning 69. San Francisco International (TV) 70. The Last Picture Show 71. McQ 74, etc.
TV series: The Tall Man 60–62.

Gulliver's Travels. Jonathan Swift's savage allegory was naturally seen by Hollywood as merely a child's fantasy. Max Fleischer's 1939 feature cartoon seemed at the time to have as much charm and skill as a Disney production, but it has worn disappointingly. Jack Sher's 1960 live action version, *The Three Worlds of Gulliver*, had neat trick work but a less than absorbing screenplay.

Gunfight at the OK Corral (US 1957). A somewhat psychologically-motivated version of the celebrated if semi-legendary confrontation between Wyatt Earp and the Clanton gang in 1881 at Tombstone, Arizona. Here Burt Lancaster was Earp, with Kirk Douglas as Doc Holliday, roles played in *My Darling Clementine* 46 by Henry Fonda and Victor Mature. Jon Hall also played Earp in an earlier version, *Frontier Marshal* 39. and the TV series *Wyatt Earp* starred Hugh O'Brian.

Gunga Din. Rudyard Kipling's narrative poem of the northwest frontier was re-written in 1939 by Joel Sayre and Fred Guiol as a rousing combination of high adventure and barrack room comedy, directed by George Stever and starring Douglas Fairbanks Jnr, Cary Gran. and Victor McLaglen. In 1951 *Soldiers Three*, directed by Tay Garnett with Stewart Granger, David Niven and Walter Pidgeon, amounted almost to a remake; while in 1961 John Sturges directed Frank Sinatra, Dean Martin and Peter Lawford in a pastiche called *Sergeants Three*, set in the American west.

Gunn, Gilbert (c. 1912–). British director, former documentarist.
The Elstree Story 51. The Strange World of Planet X 57. Girls at Sea 58. Operation Bullshine 59. What a Whopper 62, etc.

Gunn, Moses (c. 1938–). Blac American actor.
The Great White Hope 70. Carter's Army (TV) 70. The Wild Rovers 71. Shaft 72. The Hot Rock 72. Haunts of the Very Rich (TV) 73. Rollerball 75.

The Guns of Navarone. Typical of the expensive multi-star action adventures of the early sixties, this entertaining yarn of World War II was reasonably suspenseful and certainly typical of the international co-productions of this time.

Gurie, Sigrid (1911–1969) (S. G. Haukelid). American/Norwegian leading lady of the late thirties.
The Adventures of Marco Polo 38. Algiers 38. Rio 40. Three Faces West 40. Dark Streets of Cairo 41. A Voice in the Wind 44. Sword of the Avenger (last to date) 48, etc.

Gutowski, Gene (1925–). Polish producer with US TV experience.
Four Boys and a Gun 56. Station Six Sahara (GB) 63. Repulsion (GB) 65. Cul-de-Sac (GB) 66. The Fearless Vampire Killers (GB) 66, etc.

Guy-Blache, Alice (1873–1965). The first French woman director, at work in the early 1900s.
La Fée aux Choux 00. Le Voleur Sacrilège 03. Paris La Nuit 04. La Vie du Christ 06, etc.

Gwenn, Edmund (1875–1959). Stocky English stage actor who in middle age became a Hollywood film star and gave memorable comedy portrayals into his eighties.
□ SOUND FILMS: How He Lied to Her

Husband 31. Money for Nothing 31. Condemned to Death 31. Frail Women 31. Hindle Wakes 31. Tell Me Tonight 32. The Admiral's Secret 32. Love on Wheels 32. *The Skin Game* 32. *The Good Companions* 33. I Was a Spy 33. Early to Bed 33. Cash 33. *Friday the Thirteenth* 33. Marooned 33. Java Head 34. Spring in the Air 34. Channel Crossing 34. Passing Shadows 34. Waltzes from Vienna 34. Father and Son 34. Warn London 34. The Bishop Misbehaves 35. Sylvia Scarlett 35. The Walking Dead 36. Anthony Adverse 36. All American Chump 36. Mad Holiday 36. *Laburnum Grove* 36. Parnell 37. A Yank at Oxford 38. *South Riding* 38. Penny Paradise 38. An Englishman's Home 38. Cheer Boys Cheer 39. The Earl of Chicago 40. Madmen of Europe 40. The Doctor Takes a Wife 40. *Pride and Prejudice* 40. *Foreign Correspondent* (rare villainous role) 40. Scotland Yard 41. Cheers for Miss Bishop 41. The Devil and Miss Jones 41. *Charley's Aunt* 41. One Night in Lisbon 41. A Yank at Eton 42. The Meanest Man in the World 43. Forever and a Day 43. *Lassie Come Home* 43. *Between Two Worlds* (his original 'Outward Bound' stage role) 44. The Keys of the Kingdom 45. Bewitched 45. Dangerous Partners 45. She Went to the Races 45. Of Human Bondage 46. Undercurrent 46. *Miracle on 34th Street* (AA) 46. Thunder in the Valley 47. Life with Father 47. Green Dolphin Street 47. Apartment for Peggy 48. Hills of Home 48. Challenge to Lassie 49. A Woman of Distinction 50. Louisa 50. *Pretty Baby* 50. *Mister 880* 50. For Heaven's Sake 50. Peking Express 51. Sally and St Anne 52. Bonzo Goes to College 52. Les Misérables 52. Something for the Birds 52. Mister Scoutmaster 52. The Bigamist 53. *Them* 54. The Student Prince 54. *The Trouble with Harry* 55. It's a Dog's Life 55. Calabuch 57.

Gwynn, Michael (1916–1976). British stage actor in occasional films.

The Runaway Bus 54. The Secret Place 57. The Revenge of Frankenstein (as the monster) 58. Village of the Damned 60. The Virgin Soldiers 69, etc.

Gwynne, Anne (1918–) (Marguerite Gwynne Trice). American leading lady of the forties, former model.
Sandy Takes a Bow 39. Jailhouse Blues 41. The Strange Case of Doctor RX 42. Weird Woman 44. House of Frankenstein 45. Fear 46. The Ghost Goes Wild 46. Dick Tracy Meets Gruesome 48. Call of the Klondike 51. Breakdown 52. The Meteor Monster 57, etc.

Gwynne, Fred (c. 1924–). Lanky, lugubrious American comic actor who appeared in TV series Car 54 Where Are You? 61–62, and The Munsters 64–66.
On the Waterfront 54. Munster Go Home 66.

Gynt, Greta (1916–) (Greta Woxholt). Norwegian leading lady, popular in British films of the forties.
The Arsenal Stadium Mystery 39. Dark Eyes of London 39. Tomorrow We Live 42. It's That Man Again 42. Mr Emmanuel 44. London Town 46. Dear Murderer 47. Take My Life 47. The Calendar 48. Mr Perrin and Mr Traill 48. Shadow of the Eagle 50. Soldiers Three (US) 51. Forbidden Cargo 54. Bluebeard's Ten Honeymoons 60. The Runaway 66, others.

gypsies have not been a favourite subject for movies but glamorized versions have turned up in *Gypsy Wildcat, Golden Earrings, Caravan, Hot Blood,* and *The Man in Grey*. Something closer to the real thing, perhaps, was on view in *Sky West and Crooked* and *The Gypsy and the Gentleman*. The screens most memorable gypsy was probably Maria Ouspenskaya as Maleva in *The Wolf Man* and *Frankenstein Meet the Wolf Man*.

H

Haanstra, Bert (1916–). Dutch documentarist.
Mirror of Holland 50. The Rival World 55. Rembrandt Painter of Man 56. Glass 58. Fanfare (feature) 58. Zoo 62. The Human Dutch 64. The Voice of the Water 66, etc.

Haas, Charles (–). American director.
□ Star in the Dust 56. Screaming Eagles 56. Showdown at Abilene 56. Summer Love 58. Wild Heritage 58. The Beat Generation 59. The Big Operator 59. Girls' Town 59. Platinum High School 60.

Haas, Dolly (1911–). German leading lady of the thirties, in a few international films.
Dolly's Way to Stardom 30. Liebes-Commando 32. Der Page vom Dalmasse Hotel 34. *Broken Blossoms* (GB) 36. Spy of Napoleon (GB) 37. I Confess (US) 53, etc.

Haas, Hugo (1901–1968). Czech character actor, in Hollywood from the late thirties; later took to writing and directing low-budget melodramas as vehicles for himself.
Skeleton on Horseback 39. Summer Storm 44. A Bell for Adano 45. Dakota 45. Holiday in Mexico 46. The Foxes of Harrow 47. My Girl Tisa 48. King Solomon's Mines 50. Vendetta 50. The Girl on the Bridge (& wd) 51. Pickup (& wd) 51. Strange Fascination (& wd) 52. Thy Neighbour's Wife (& wd) 53. Hold Back Tomorrow (& wd) 55. The Other Woman (& wd) 55. Edge of Hell (& wd) 56. *Lizzie* (& wd) 57. Born to be Loved (& wd) 59. Night of the Quarter Moon (& wd) 59. Paradise Alley (& wd) 61, etc.

Hackett, Albert (1900–). American writer, usually with his wife Frances Goodrich (qv).

Hackett, Buddy (1924–) (Leonard Hacker). Tubby American comedian with vaudeville experience.
Walking My Baby Back Home 53. God's Little Acre 58. *The Music Man* 62. It's a Mad Mad Mad Mad World 63. The Golden Head 65. The Love Bug 69, etc.
TV series: Stanley 56.

Hackett, Joan (1934–). American leading lady usually seen in unglamorous roles.
□ *The Group* 66. Will Penny 67. Support Your Local Sheriff 69. Assignment to Kill 69. The Rivals 72. The Young Country (TV) 72. The Last of Sheila 73. Class of '63 (TV) 73. Reflections of Murder (TV) 75.

Hackett, Raymond (1902–1958). American leading man who had brief popularity during the changeover from silent to sound.
The Loves of Sunya 28. Madame X 29. Our Blushing Brides 29. The Trial of Mary Dugan 30. The Sea Wolf 30. The Cat Creeps 31. Seed 31, etc.

Hackman, Gene (1930–). Virile American character actor who unexpectedly became a star of the early seventies.
□ Lilith 64. Hawaii 66. First to Fight 67. A Covenant with Death 67. Banning 67. *Bonnie and Clyde* 67. The Split 68. Riot 69. Downhill Racer 69. *I Never Sang For My Father* 69. The Gypsy Moths 69. Marooned 70. Shadow on the Land (TV) 71. Doctors' Wives 71. The Hunting Party 71. *The French Connection* (AA) 71. Cisco Pike 72. Prime Cut 72. The Poseidon Adventure 72. The Conversation 73. Scarecrow 73. Zandy's Bride 74. Young Frankenstein 74. Bite the Bullet 75. French Connection II 75. Lucky Lady 75. Night Moves 76. The Domino Principle 77.

Hackney, Alan (1924–). British comedy writer.
Private's Progress 55. I'm All Right, Jack 59. Two-way Stretch (c-w) 60. Swordsman of Siena 62. You Must Be Joking 65, etc.

Haddon, Peter (1898–1962) (Peter Tildsley). British light actor, usually in silly-ass roles.
Death at Broadcasting House 34. The Silent Passenger (as Lord Peter Wimsey) 35. Kate Plus Ten 38. Helter Skelter 49. The Second Mrs Tanqueray 54, etc.

Haden, Sara (1899–). American actress of quiet, well-spoken parts, best remembered as the spinster aunt of the Hardy family.

Spitfire (debut) 34. Magnificent Obsession 35. First Lady 38. H. M. Pulham Esquire 41. Lost Angel 43. Mr Ace 45. Our Vines Have Tender Grapes 45. She-Wolf of London (as villainess) 46. The Bishop's Wife 48. A Life of her Own 50. A Lion is in the Streets 53. Andy Hardy Comes Home 58, many others.

Hadjidakis, Manos (1925–). Greek composer.
Stella 55. A Matter of Dignity 57. *Never On Sunday* (AA) 59. America America 63. Blue 68, etc.

Hadley, Reed (1911–1974) (Reed Herring). American 'second lead'.
Fugitive Lady 38. The Bank Dick 41. Guadalcanal Diary 43. Leave Her to Heaven 46. The Iron Curtain 48. Captain from Castile 49. Dallas 51. Big House USA 55. The St Valentine's Day Massacre 68, etc.

Hageman, Richard (1882–1966). Dutch-American composer.
Stagecoach 39. Paris Calling 40. The Fugitive 47. Fort Apache 48. She Wore a Yellow Ribbon 48. Three Godfathers 49. Wagonmaster 50, etc.

Hagen, Jean (1924–) (Jean Verhagen). American comedy character actress, usually of Brooklynesque dames; also minor leading lady.
□ Side Street 49. *Adam's Rib* 49. Ambush 50. The Asphalt Jungle 50. A Life of Her Own 50. Night into Morning 50. No Questions Asked 51. *Singin' In the Rain* (a splendid performance as the silent star with the ghastly voice) 52. Shadow in the Sky 52. Carbine Williams 52. Latin Lovers 53. Arena 53. Half a Hero 53. The Big Knife 55. Spring Reunion 57. The Shaggy Dog 59. Sunrise at Campobello 60. Panic in Year Zero 62. Dead Ringer 64.

Haggar, William (1851–1924). British pioneer producer, a former fairground showman who made short sensational films featuring himself and his family.
The Maniac's Guillotine 02. The Wild Man of Borneo 02. Mirthful Mary 03. A Dash for Liberty 03. The Sign of the Cross 04. The Life of Charles Peace 05. Desperate Footpads 07. Maria Marten 08. The Dumb Man of Manchester 08, etc.

Haggard, Piers (1939–). British director.
□ Wedding Night 69. Satan's Skin 70, etc.

Haggard, Sir H. Rider (1856–1925). British adventure novelist, whose most famous novel, *She*, has been filmed at least nine times. There have also been two versions of *King Solomon's Mines*.

Hagman, Larry (1930–). American comedy leading man, much on TV; son of Mary Martin.
Ensign Pulver 64. Fail Safe 64. In Harm's Way 65. The Group 65. Vanished (TV) 70. Up in the Cellar 70. Beware the Blob (TV) 71. A Howling in the Woods (TV) 72. The Alpha Caper (TV) 73. Stardust 74. Harry and Tonto 74. Mother Jugs and Speed 76, etc.
TV series: *I Dream of Jeannie* 65–68. The Good Life 71. Here We Go Again 72.

Hagmann, Stuart (1939–). American director.
The Strawberry Statement 70. Believe in Me 71, etc.

Haigh, Kenneth (1929–). British stage actor, the original lead of *Look Back in Anger*, has tended to remain in angry young man roles.
My Teenage Daughter 56. High Flight 56. Saint Joan 57. Cleopatra 63. A Hard Day's Night 64. The Deadly Affair 66. A Lovely Way to Die (US) 68. Eagle in a Cage 71. Man at the Top 73, etc.
TV series: *Man at the Top* 70.

Haines, William (1900–1973). American leading man of the silents.
Three Wise Fools 23. Tower of Lies 24. Brown of Harvard 25. Tell It to the Marines 27. Alias Jimmy Valentine 28. Navy Blues 30. The Adventures of Get-Rich-Quick Wallingford 31. The Fast Life 33. The Marines Are Coming 35, etc.

Hakim, André (1915–). Egyptian-born producer, long in US.
Mr Belvedere Rings the Bell 52. The Man Who Never Was 56, etc.

Hakim, Robert (1907–) and **Raymond** (1909–). Egyptian-born brothers who have been producing films since 1927.
Pepe Le Moko 36. La Bête Humaine 38. Le Jour Se Lève 39. The Southerner 44. Her Husband's Affairs 47. The Long Night 47. The Blue Veil 52. Belle de Jour 67. Isadora 68, many others.

Halas, John (1912–). Hungarian-born animator, long in Britain producing in association with his wife Joy Batchelor (1914–) a stream of efficient short cartoons, many sponsored by official organizations.
FEATURES: *Animal Farm* 54. Ruddigore 67.

Hale, Alan (1892–1950) (Rufus Alan McKahan). Jovial American actor, a hero of

silent action films from 1911 and a familiar cheerful figure in scores of talkies.
The Cowboy and the Lady (debut) 11. The Four Horsemen of the Apocalypse 21. Robin Hood (as Little John) 22. The Covered Wagon 23. Main Street 24. She Got What She Wanted 27. The Rise of Helga 30. So Big 32. It Happened One Night 34. The Last Days of Pompeii 35. Jump for Glory (GB) 36. Stella Dallas 37. *The Adventures of Robin Hood* (as Little John) 38. Dodge City 39. The Man in the Iron Mask 40. The Sea Hawk 40. Tugboat Annie Sails Again 41. *Strawberry Blonde* 41. Manpower 41. *Desperate Journey* 42. Action in the North Atlantic 43. Destination Tokyo 44. Hotel Berlin 45. Escape in the Desert 45. Night and Day 45. My Wild Irish Rose 47. Pursued 48. The New Adventures of Don Juan 48. *My Girl Tisa* 49. Rogues of Sherwood Forest (as Little John) 50, many others.

Hale, Alan, Jnr (1918–). American character actor who bids fair to be his father's double.
To the Shores of Tripoli 42. One Sunday Afternoon 48. The Gunfighter 50. The Big Trees 52. Rogue Cop 54. Young at Heart 54. The Indian Fighter 55. The Killer is Loose 56, many others.
TV series: *Casey Jones* 57. *Gilligan's Island* 64–66.

Hale, Barbara (1922–). Pleasant American leading lady of the forties.
Higher and Higher 43. The Falcon in Hollywood 44. First Yank into Tokyo 45. Lady Luck 46. The Boy with Green Hair 48. The Window 48. *Jolson Sings Again* 49. The Jackpot 50. Lorna Doone 51. A Lion is in the Streets 53. Unchained 54. The Far Horizons 55. The Oklahoman 57. Airport 69, many others.
TV series: *Perry Mason* (as Della Street) 57–66.

Hale, Binnie (1899–) (Bernice Hale Monro). British revue comedienne of the thirties, sister of Sonnie Hale. Films rare.
The Phantom Light 35. Hyde Park Corner 36. Love from a Stranger 37. Take a Chance 37, etc.

Hale, Creighton (1882–1965) (Patrick Fitzgerald). American leading man of the twenties, sometimes in meek-and-mild comedy roles.
The Exploits of Elaine 15. The Thirteenth Chair 19. Way Down East 20. Trilby (as Little Billee) 23. *The Marriage Circle* 24. The Circle 25. Beverly of Graustark 26. Annie Laurie 27. *The Cat and the Canary* 27. Rose Marie 28. Holiday 30. The Masquerader 33. Hollywood Boulevard 36. The Return of Dr X 39. The Gorilla Man 42.

Bullet Scars 45. The Perils of Pauline 47, many others.

Hale, Jonathan (1892–1966) (J. Hatley). American character actor, former consular attaché, in films from 1934, usually as mildly exasperated business man or hero's boss.
Lightning Strikes Twice 34. Alice Adams 35. Fury 36. The Blondie series (as Mr Dithers) 38–50. Her Jungle Love 39. Johnny Apollo 40. Call Northside 777 48. The Steel Trap 52. The Night Holds Terror 56. Jaguar 58, many others.

Hale, Louise Closser (1872–1933). American character actress with long stage experience.
The Hole in the Wall 29. Dangerous Nan McGrew 30. Platinum Blonde 31. Rasputin and the Empress 33. Shanghai Express 32. Today We Live 33. Dinner at Eight 33, etc.

Hale, Sonnie (1902–1959) (Robert Hale Monro). British light comedian of the thirties, mostly on stage.
Tell Me Tonight 32. Friday the Thirteenth 33. Evergreen 34. Are You a Mason? 34. Marry the Girl 35. Head over Heels (d only) 37. Gangway (d only) 37. Sailing Along (d only) 38. The Gaunt Stranger 38. Let's Be Famous 39. Fiddlers Three 44. London Town 46, etc.

Hale, William (1928–). American director, from TV.
The Naked Hunt 58. Gunfight in Abilene 66. Journey to Shiloh 67, etc.

Hale's Tours. In 1902 at the St Louis Exposition, George C. Hale, ex-chief of the Kansas City Fire Department, had the bright idea of shooting a film from the back of a moving train and screening the result in a small theatre decorated like an observation car. During the screening bells clanged, train whistles sounded and the 'coach' rocked slightly. The idea was so successful that it toured for several years in the United States.

Haley, Jack (1899–). Diffident American light comedian, popular in the thirties and forties.
Follow Thru 30. Sitting Pretty 33. The Girl Friend 35. *Poor Little Rich Girl* 36. Wake Up and Live 37. Pick a Star 37. Rebecca of Sunnybrook Farm 38. *Alexander's Ragtime Band* 38. Hold that Co-ed 38. *The Wizard of Oz* (as the Tin Man) 39. Moon over Miami 41. Beyond the Blue Horizon 42. Higher and Higher 43. Scared Stiff 44. George White's Scandals 45. People are Funny 45. Vacation in Reno 47. Norwood 69, etc.

Haley, Jack Jnr (1934–). American executive, best known for marrying Liza Minnelli and assembling *That's Entertainment.*

Hall, Alexander (1894–1968). American director from 1932, previously on Broadway.
□ Sinners in the Sun 32. Madame Racketeer 32. The Girl in 419 33. Midnight Club 33. Torch Singer 33. Miss Fane's Baby is Stolen 34. Little Miss Marker 34. The Pursuit of Happiness 34. Limehouse Blues 34. Going to Town 35. Annapolis Farewell 35. Give Us This Night 36. Yours for the Asking 36. Exclusive 37. There's Always a Woman 38. I am the Law 38. There's That Woman Again 38. The Lady's From Kentucky 39. Good Girls Go to Paris 39. The Amazing Mr Williams 39. The Doctor Takes a Wife 40. He Stayed for Breakfast 40. This Thing Called Love 40. *Here Comes Mr Jordan* 41. Bedtime Story 41. They All Kissed the Bride 42. My Sister Eileen 42. The Heavenly Body 43. Once Upon a Time 44. She Wouldn't Say Yes 45. Down to Earth 47. The Great Lover 49. Love that Brute 50. Louisa 50. Up Front 51. Because You're Mine 52. Let's Do it Again 53. Forever Darling 56.

Hall, Charles (1899–1959). American character actor, often in comedy two-reelers; memorable as the victim of many a Laurel and Hardy mishap culminating in a tit-for-tat disaster.

Hall, Charles D. (1899–). British-born production designer, long in Hollywood.
Frankenstein 31. *Bride of Frankenstein* 35. Diamond Jim 35. *Showboat* 36. *Modern Times* 36. Captain Fury 39. The Vicious Years 51, etc.

Hall, Conrad (1926–). American cinematographer.
Morituri 65. Harper 66. The Professionals 66. *Cool Hand Luke* 67. In Cold Blood 67. Hell in the Pacific 69. *Butch Cassidy and the Sundance Kid* 69. Tell Them Willie Boy is Here 69. The Happy Ending 70. Fat City 72, etc.

Hall, Henry (1899–). British bandleader of the thirties, popular on radio. Appeared in a few films including *Music Hath Charms* 36.
Autobiography 1955: *Here's to the Next Time.*

Hall, Huntz (1920–) (Henry Hall). Long-faced American character actor, the 'dumb-bell' second lead of the original Dead End Kids and later of the Bowery Boys.
Dead End 37. Crime School 38. Angels with Dirty Faces 38. The Return of Doctor X 39. Give Us Wings 40. Spooks Run Wild 41. Private

Buckaroo 42. Wonder Man 45. Bowery Bombshell 46. Bowery Buckaroos 47. Jinx Money 48. Angels in Disguise 49. Lucky Losers 50. Ghost Chasers 51. No Holds Barred 52. Loose in London 53. Paris Playboys 54. High Society 55. Dig That Uranium 56. Spook Chasers 57. In the Money 58. The Gentle Giant 67. The Love Bug Rides Again 73, many others.
TV series: Chicago Teddy Bears 71.

Hall, James (1900–1940) (James Brown). American leading man of the early talkie period.
The Campus Flirt 26. Stranded in Paris 27. Rolled Stockings 27. Four Sons 28. Smiling Irish Eyes 29. The Canary Murder Case 29. The Saturday Night Kid 29. Dangerous Nan Mc Grew 30. *Hells Angels* 30. Millie 31. The Good Bad Girl 31. Divorce Among Friends 31. Manhattan Tower 33, etc.

Hall, Jon (1913–) (Charles Locher). Athletic American leading man who became a star in his first year as an actor but whose roles gradually diminished in stature; he retired to a photography business.
Charlie Chan in Shanghai 36. Mind Your Own Business 36. The Girl from Scotland Yard 37. *The Hurricane* 37. Kit Carson 40. South of Pago Pago 40. Aloma of the South Seas 41. Eagle Squadron 42. Invisible Agent 42. Arabian Nights 42. White Savage 43. Ali Baba and the Forty Thieves 44. Cobra Woman 44. The Invisible Man's Revenge 44. San Diego I Love You 45. Sudan 45. The Michigan Kid 47. Last of the Redmen 47. Prince of Thieves 48. Deputy Marshal 49. Hurricane Island 50. When the Redskins Rode 51. Last Train from Bombay 52. The Beachgirls and the Monster (& d) 65. Five the Hard Way (co-p & ph only) 69, etc.
TV series: Ramar of the Jungle 52–53.

Hall, Juanita (1901–1968). American Negro character actress and singer, best remembered in the stage and screen versions of *South Pacific* (as Bloody Mary) and *Flower Drum Song.*

Hall, Peter (1930–). British theatrical producer recently venturing into films.
□ Work is a Four-Letter Word 68. A Midsummer Night's Dream 68. Three Into Two Won't Go 69. Perfect Friday 70. The Homecoming 73. Akenfield 74.

Hall, Porter (1888–1953). Wry-faced American character actor with stage experience before settling in Hollywood.
The Thin Man (debut) 34. The Story of Louis Pasteur 36. Mr Smith Goes to Washington 39. Sullivan's Travels 41. The Miracle of Morgan's

Creek 44. Mad Wednesday 47. Intruder in the Dust 49. Ace in the Hole 51. The Half Breed 52. Pony Express 53. Return to Treasure Island 53, many others.

Hall, Thurston (1883–1958). American character actor adept at choleric executives. Long stage experience; ran his own touring companies.
Cleopatra (as Mark Antony) 18. Theodora Goes Wild 36. Professor Beware 38. The Great McGinty 40. He Hired the Boss 43. Brewster's Millions 45. The Secret Life of Walter Mitty 47. Affair in Reno 56, scores of others.

Hall, Willis (1929–). British playwright and screenwriter (in collaboration with Keith Waterhouse).
The Long and the Short and the Tall 61. Whistle Down the Wind 61. A Kind of Loving 62. Billy Liar 63, etc.

Hallatt, May (1882–*). British character actress, mainly on stage.
No Funny Business 33. The Lambeth Walk 39. Painted Boats 45. *Black Narcissus* 46. The Pickwick Papers 52. *Separate Tables* 58. Make Mine Mink 60, etc.

Hallelujah (US 1929). This famous film, directed by King Vidor, was probably the first serious screen treatment of Negro life, but despite an all-coloured cast it now seems exaggerated, patronizing and sentimental. The story concerns a Negro murderer who becomes a priest.

Haller, Daniel (1928–). American director, former art director on Roger Corman's Poe films, etc.
□ Die Monster Die 67. The Devil's Angels 68. The Wild Racers 68. Paddy 70. The Dunwich Horror 70. Pieces of Dreams 70.

Haller, Ernest (1896–1970). Distinguished American cinematographer.
Neglected Wives 20. Outcast 22. Stella Dallas 25. Weary River 29. The Dawn Patrol 31. The Emperor Jones 33. Dangerous 35. Jezebel 38. *Gone with the Wind* (AA) 39. Dark Victory 39. All This and Heaven Too 40. Saratoga Trunk 43. Mr Skeffington 44. *Mildred Pierce* 45. Humoresque 46. *My Girl Tisa* 47. The Flame and the Arrow 50. Rebel without a Cause 55. Back from the Dead 57. God's Little Acre 58. Man of the West 58. The Third Voice 59. Whatever Happened to Baby Jane? 62. Lilies of the Field 64. Dead Ringer 64, many others.

Halliday, John (1880–1947). Suave and dapper Scottish actor, long in Hollywood.
□ The Woman Gives 20. East Side Sadie 29. Father's Sons 30. Recaptured Love 30. Scarlet Pages 30. Smart Women 31. Consolation Marriage 31. The Ruling Voice 31. Millie 31. Once a Sinner 31. Captain Applejack 31. Fifty Million Frenchmen 31. The Spy 31. Transatlantic 31. Men of Chance 32. The Impatient Maiden 32. The Age of Consent 32. Weekends Only 32. Bird of Paradise 32. Perfect Understanding 33. Terror Aboard 33. Bed of Roses 33. The House on 56th Street 33. Woman Accused 33. Return of the Terror 34. Housewife 34. A Woman's Man 34. Happiness Ahead 34. Registered Nurse 34. The Witching Hour 34. Desirable 34. Finishing School 34. Myster Woman 35. The Dark Angel 35. The Melody Lingers On 35. Peter Ibbetson 35. *Desire* 36. Fatal Lady 36. Three Cheers for Love 36. *Hollywood Boulevard* 36. Arsene Lupin Returns 38. Blockade 38. That Certain Age 39. The Light that Failed 39. Hotel for Women 39. Intermezzo 39. *The Philadelphia Story* 40. Lydia 41. Escape to Glory 41.

Halop, Billy (1920–1976). American actor, the erstwhile leader of the Dead End Kids: stardom failed to materialize, and he descended to bit parts.
Dead End 37. Crime School 38. Little Tough Guy 38. Angels with Dirty Faces 38. You Can't Get Away with Murder 39. Angels Wash Their Faces 39. Call a Messenger 39. Tom Brown's Schooldays 40. Hit the Road 41. Mob Town 41. Junior Army 43. Dangerous Years 47. Mister Buddwing 66. Fitzwilly 66, many others.

Halperin, Victor (1895–). American director.
Party Girl 29. Ex Flame 30. *White Zombie* 32. Supernatural 33. I Conquer the Sea 36. Revolt of the Zombies 36. Nation Aflame 37. Torture Ship 39. Buried Alive 40. Girls' Town 42.

Halton, Charles (1876–1959). American character actor, inimitable as a sour-faced bank clerk, professor or lawyer.
Dodsworth 36. Dr Cyclops 39. Jesse James 39. H. M. Pulham, Esq. 41 Tobacco Road 41. Up in Arms 44. The Best Years of Our Lives 46. Carrie 51. The Moonlighter 53, many others.

Hamer, Gerald (1886–1973). British character actor in Hollywood.
Swing Time 36. Bulldog Drummond's Bride 39. Sherlock Holmes Faces Death 43. The Scarlet Claw 44. The Sign of the Ram 48, etc.

Hamer, Robert (1911–1963). British director,

erratic but at his best impeccably stylish.

□ San Demetrio London (w only) 43. Dead of Night (mirror sequence & w) 45. Pink String and Sealing Wax 45. *It Always Rains on Sunday* (& w) 47. *Kind Hearts and Coronets* (& w) 49. The Spider and the Fly 49. His Excellency (& w) 52. The Long Memory (& w) 52. *Father Brown* 54. To Paris With Love 54. The Scapegoat 59. *School for Scoundrels* 60. A Jolly Bad Fellow (w only) 63.

Hamilton, George (1939–). American leading man, usually in serious roles.
Crime and Punishment USA (debut) 58. Home from the Hill 60. All the Fine Young Cannibals 60. Angel Baby 61. By Love Possessed 61. A Thunder of Drums 61. The Light in the Piazza 62. The Victors 63. *Act One* (as Moss Hart) 63. Viva Maria 65. Your Cheating Heart 65. Doctor, You've Got To Be Kidding 67. The Long Ride Home 67. Jack of Diamonds 67. The Power 67. Evel Knievel 72. The Man Who Loved Cat Dancing 73. Once is not Enough 75, etc.
TV series: The Survivors 69.

Hamilton, Guy (1922–). British director, former assistant to Carol Reed.
□ The Ringer 52. The Intruder 53. *An Inspector Calls* 54. The Colditz Story 54. Charley Moon 56. Manuela 57. The Devil's Disciple 58. A Touch of Larceny 59. The Best of Enemies 62. The Party's Over 63. The Man in the Middle 64. *Goldfinger* 64. Funeral in Berlin 66. The Battle of Britain 70. Diamonds are Forever 71. Live and Let Die 72. The Man with the Golden Gun 73.

Hamilton, John (1916–). American actor whose career was affected by the communist witch hunt; made a comeback in *Seconds* 67.

Hamilton, Margaret (1902–). American character actress, a former kindergarten teacher who came to films via Broadway and usually played hatchet-faced spinsters or maids.
Another Language 33. These Three 36. Nothing Sacred 37. *The Wizard of Oz* 39. Invisible Woman 41. *Guest in the House* 44. Mad Wednesday 47. State of the Union 48. The Great Plane Robbery 50. Thirteen Ghosts 60. The Daydreamer 66. Rosie 67. The Anderson Tapes 71. Brewster McCloud 71, etc.

Hamilton, Murray (1923–). American general purpose actor.
Bright Victory 50. No Time for Sergeants 58. The FBI Story 59. Seconds 66. The Graduate 67. No Way to Treat a Lady 68. The Boston Strangler 68. If It's Tuesday This Must Be Belgium 69. The Way We Were 73, etc.

Hamilton, Neil (1899–). Stalwart American leading man of silent days.
White Rose 23. America 24. Isn't Life Wonderful? 25. Beau Geste 26. The Great Gatsby 27. Why Be Good? 28. Keeper of the Bees 29. The Dawn Patrol 30. The Wet Parade 31. The Animal Kingdom 32. Tarzan the Ape Man 32. One Sunday Afternoon 33. Tarzan and His Mate 34. Federal Fugitives 41. The Little Shepherd of Kingdom Come 61. Madame X 66, many others.
TV series: Batman 65–68.

Hamlet (GB 1948). This, the most celebrated of the screen Hamlets (for others, see under Shakespeare), won Academy Awards as the best picture of its year, for Laurence Olivier's performance, for Roger Furse's art direction and costume design, and for Carmen Dillon's set decoration. Those critics not overwhelmed by its prestige value, however, have often found it cold and empty, marred by injudicious text-cutting and a tendency to rove pointlessly and endlessly down corridors at the expense of action. Notable in the cast were Basil Sydney as Claudius, Eileen Herlie as Gertrude, Jean Simmons as Ophelia, Felix Aylmer as Polonius and Stanley Holloway as the gravedigger. Olivier produced and directed.

Hamlisch, Marvin (1946–). American composer.
Flap 70. The Sting (AA) 73. The Way We Were 73.

Hammer, Will (1887–*). British producer, the original founder of Hammer films.

Hammerstein II, Oscar (1895–1960). Immensely successful American lyricist who wrote many stage musicals, usually with Richard Rodgers (qv). *The King and I, South Pacific, The Sound of Music*, etc.

Hammett, Dashiell (1894–1961). American writer of detective novels and occasional screenplays.
City Streets (& w) 31. The Maltese Falcon 31. The Thin Man 34. The Glass Key 35. The Maltese Falcon 41. The Glass Key 42. Watch on the Rhine (w) 43, etc.

Hammid, Alexander (c. 1910–) (Alexander Hackenschmied). German documentarist in America.
Hymn of the Nations 46. Of Men and Music 51. To the Fair 65, etc.

Hammond, Kay (1909–) (Dorothy

Standing). Plummy-voiced British leading lady, mostly on stage; married to John Clements.
Children of Chance 30. A Night in Montmartre 31. Almost a Divorce 32. Out of the Blue 32. A Night Like This 32. Sally Bishop 32. Yes Madam 33. Sleeping Car 33. Bitter Sweet 33. Two on a Doorstep 36. Jeannie 41. *Blithe Spirit* (as Elvira) 45. Call of the Blood 48. Five Golden Hours 61, etc.

Hammond, Peter (1923–). British juvenile player of the forties; became a TV and film director.
They Knew Mr Knight 46. Holiday Camp 47. Fly Away Peter 48. Morning Departure 50. Vote for Huggett 50. The Adventurers 51. Spring and Port Wine (d only) 69, etc.

Hampden, Walter (1879–1955) (Walter Hampden Dougherty). American stage actor with a long career behind him when he came to Hollywood.
The Hunchback of Notre Dame (debut) 40. Reap the Wild Wind 42. All About Eve 50. Five Fingers 52. The Silver Chalice 54. The Vagabond King 55, etc.

Hampshire, Susan (1938–). Talented British leading lady, somewhat handicapped by her own demureness.
□ Upstairs and Downstairs 59. During One Night 61. The Long Shadow 61. The Three Lives of Thomasina 63. Night Must Fall 64. Wonderful Life 64. The Fighting Prince of Donegal 66. The Trygon Factor 67. Monte Carlo or Bust 69. David Copperfield (TV) 69. A Time for Loving 72. Living Free 72. Baffled (TV) 72. Malpertuis 72.
TV series: *The Forsyte Saga* (as Fleur) 67. *The Pallisers* 74.

Hampton, Hope (1899–). American leading lady of the silents.
The Bait 21. The Gold Diggers 23. Hollywood 23. The Truth About Women 24. Lover's Island 25. The Unfair Sex 26, etc.

Hancock, John (1939–). American director.
□ Let's Scare Jessica to Death 73. Bang the Drum Slowly 74. Baby Blue Marine 76.

Hancock, Sheila (1933–). British comic actress of stage and TV.
Light Up the Sky 58. The Girl on the Boat 61. Night Must Fall 63. The Anniversary 67. Take a Girl Like You 70, etc.

Hancock, Tony (1924–1968). Popular British radio and TV comedian.

Orders Is Orders 55. The Rebel 61. The Punch and Judy Man 63. Those Magnificent Men in Their Flying Machines 65. The Wrong Box 66, etc.

Hand, David (1900–). American animator, formerly with Disney; came to Britain 1945 to found cartoon unit for Rank. Some pleasing results (*Musical Paintbox* series, etc); but it was a financial failure and Hand returned to America in 1950.

Handl, Irene (1902–). Dumpy British character comedienne, frequently seen as maid or charlady; became a star in her later years.
The Girl in the News 41. Pimpernel Smith 41. Temptation Harbour 46. Silent Dust 48. One Wild Oat 51. The Belles of St Trinian's 54. A Kid for Two Farthings 56. Brothers in Law 57. *I'm All Right Jack* 59. Make Mine Mink 60. The Rebel 61. Heavens Above 63. Morgan 66. Smashing Time 67. On a Clear Day You Can See Forever 70. The Private Life of Sherlock Holmes 71. For the Love of Ada 72. Adventures of a Private Eye 76, etc.
TV series: *For the Love of Ada* 70.

Handley, Tommy (1894–1949). British radio comedian most famous for his long-running, morale-building *Itma* series during World War II.
Elstree Calling 30. Two Men in a Box 38. *It's That Man Again* 42. Time Flies 43. Tom Tom Topia (short) 46.

hands. The clutching hand was long a staple of melodrama; usually hairy, with long fingernails, it came out of shadowed panelling and menaced the heroine in hundreds of thrillers such as *The Cat and the Canary*. Severed hands were also a favourite: passing fancies in most of the mummy films, they received more detailed attention in *The Beast with Five Fingers, Chamber of Horrors, The Hand,* and the various versions of *The Hands of Orlac*.

The Hands of Orlac. This improbable thriller by Maurice Renard, about a pianist who loses his hands in an accident and has the hands of a murderer grafted on, has been the basis of three film versions: 1. Directed by Robert Wiene in 1924 (Ger.), with Conrad Veidt and Werner Krauss. 2. Directed by Karl Freund in 1934 (US), as *Mad Love*, with Colin Clive and Peter Lorre. 3. Directed by Edmond Greville in 1961 (GB), with Mel Ferrer and Donald Wolfit.

Haney, Carol (1928–1964). American dancer, former assistant to Gene Kelly.

☐ Kiss Me Kate 53. Invitation to the Dance 54. *The Pajama Game* 57.

Hanley, Jimmy (1918–1970). Former British child actor developed as 'the boy next door' type by Rank in the forties.
Little Friend 34. Boys Will Be Boys 35. Night Ride 37. There Ain't No Justice 39. Salute John Citizen 42. For You Alone 44. The Way Ahead 44. Henry V 44. 29 Acacia Avenue 45. The Heart 46. Master of Bankdam 47. It Always Rains on Sunday 48. It's Hard To Be Good 49. Here Come the Huggetts (and ensuing series) 49–52. The Blue Lamp 50. The Black Rider 54. The Deep Blue Sea 56. Lost Continent 58, etc.

Hanna, William (1911–). American animator who with his partner **Joe Barbera** created Tom and Jerry for MGM, later founding their own successful company creating innumerable semi-animated series for TV: Huckleberry Hound, Yogi Bear, The Flintstones, The Jetsons, Wait Till Your Father Gets Home, etc.

Hanson, Lars (1887–1965). Swedish stage actor who made silent films abroad but after the coming of sound remained in Sweden.
Ingeborg Holm (debut) 13. Dolken 16. Erotikon 19. The Atonement of Gosta Berling 24. The Scarlet Letter (US) 26. The Divine Woman (US) 27. The Wind (US) 28. The Informer (GB) 28, etc.

Harareet, Haya (c. 1934–) (Haya Hararit). Israeli leading lady.
Hill 24 Does Not Answer 55. Ben Hur 59. The Secret Partner 61, etc.

hard ticket. A phrase used in the sixties to describe film exhibition of the type once called 'road show': separate performances, reserved seats, long runs and high prices.

Hardin, Ty (1930–) (Orton Hungerford). Muscular leading man of the sixties, mostly on TV.
I Married a Monster from Outer Space 58. The Chapman Report 62. PT 109 63. Battle of the Bulge 65. Berserk (GB) 67. Custer of the West 68. The Last Rebel 71, etc.
TV series: *Bronco* 58–61. Riptide 69.

Harding, Ann (1902–) (Dorothy Gatley). Gentlewomanly American leading lady of thirties romances.
☐ Paris Bound 29. Her Private Affair 29. Condemned 29. *Holiday* 30. Girl of the Golden West 30. East Lynne 31. Devotion 31. Prestige 31. Westward Passage 32. The Conquerors 32.

The Animal Kingdom 32. When Ladies Meet 33. Double Harness 33. Right to Romance 33. Gallant Lady 33. The Life of Vergie Winters 34. The Fountain 34. *Biography of a Bachelor Girl* 35. Enchanted April 35. The Flame Within 35. Peter Ibbetson 35. The Lady Consents 36. The Witness Chair 36. *Love from a Stranger* (GB) 37. Eyes in the Night 42. Mission to Moscow 43. North Star 43. Janie 44. Nine Girls 44. Those Endearing Young Charms 45. Janie Gets Married 46. It Happened on Fifth Avenue 47. Christmas Eve 47. The Magnificent Yankee 50. Two Weeks with Love 50. The Unknown Man 51. The Man in the Grey Flannel Suit 56. I've Lived Before 56. Strange Intruder 56.

Harding, Lyn (1867–1952) (David Llewellyn Harding). British stage actor who made a splendid 'heavy' in some films of the twenties and thirties.
The Barton Mystery 20. When Knighthood Was in Flower (as Henry VIII) 21. The Speckled Band (as Moriarty) 31. *The Triumph of Sherlock Holmes* (as Moriarty) 35. Spy of Napoleon 36. Fire Over England 36. Knight without Armour 37. *Goodbye Mr Chips* (as Chips' first headmaster) 39. The Prime Minister 40, etc.

Hardwicke, Sir Cedric (1893–1964). Distinguished British stage actor who settled in Hollywood and too frequently allowed his talents to be squandered on inferior material.
Autobiography 1961: *A Victorian in Orbit.*
☐ Nelson 26. Dreyfus 31. Rome Express 32. Orders is Orders 32. The Ghoul 33. *Nell Gwyn* (as Charles II) 34. The Lady is Willing 34. Jew Süss 34. King of Paris 34. Bella Donna 34. Peg of Old Drury 35. Les Misérables 35. *Becky Sharp* 35. Things to Come 36. Tudor Rose 36. Laburnum Grove 36. The Green Light 37. *King Solomon's Mines* (as Allan Quartermain) 37. *On Borrowed Time* (as Death) 39. *Stanley and Livingstone* (as Livingstone) 39. The Hunchback of Notre Dame (as Frollo) 39. The Invisible Man Returns 40. *Tom Brown's Schooldays* (as Dr Arnold) 40. The Howards of Virginia 40. Victory 40. Suspicion 41. Sundown 41. The Ghost of Frankenstein 42. Valley of the Sun 42. Invisible Agent 42. The Commandos Strike at Dawn 42. Forever and a Day 43. *The Moon is Down* 43. The Cross of Lorraine 43. The Lodger 44. Wing and a Prayer 44. Wilson 44. The Keys of the Kingdom 45. Sentimental Journey 46. The Imperfect Lady 47. Ivy 47. Lured 47. Song of My Heart 47. Beware of Pity 47. *Nicholas Nickleby* 47. Tycoon 47. *I Remember Mama* 48. *The Winslow Boy* 48. Rope 48. A Connecticut Yankee in King Arthur's Court 49. Now Barabbas 49. The White Tower 50. Mr

Imperium 51. The Desert Fox 51. The Green Glove 52. Caribbean 52. Salome 53. Botany Bay 53. Bait 54. *Richard III* 55. Helen of Troy 55. Diane 56. Gaby 56. The Vagabond King 56. The Power and the Prize 56. The Ten Commandments 56. Around the World in Eighty Days 56. The Story of Mankind 57. Baby Face Nelson 57. Five Weeks in a Balloon 62. The Pumpkin Eater 64.

TV series: Mrs G Goes to College 61.

The Hardy Family. Between 1937 and 1947 fifteen highly successful modest-budget films were made by MGM about the vicissitudes of a 'typical family' in a small midwestern town: father just happened to be a judge who enjoyed man-to-man talks with his teenage son, the wildly untypical Mickey Rooney. Everyone was insufferably nice in these films: father Lewis Stone (Lionel Barrymore did the first episode), mother Fay Holden, daughter Cecilia Parker, aunt Sara Haden. Perhaps because of this they did not last into the post-war period, and an attempt to revive them in 1958 (*Andy Hardy Comes Home*) failed rather miserably. The series was given a special Academy Award in 1942 for 'furthering the American way of life'.

Hardy, Oliver (1892–1957). Ample-figured American comedian, the fat half of the screen's finest comedy team, noted for his genteel pomposity, tie twiddle and long-suffering look at the camera.
Biography 1961: *Mr Laurel and Mr Hardy* by John McCabe.
SELECTED SOLO APPEARANCES: Outwitting Dad 13. Playmates 15. Lucky Dog 17. He Winked and Won 17. The Chief Cook 18. The Three Ages 23. Rex, King of the Wild Horses 24. The Wizard of Oz (as the Tin Man) 25. The Nicklehopper 25. Zenobia 39. The Fighting Kentuckian 49. Riding High 50, many others.
□ LAUREL AND HARDY FILMS: Slipping Wives 26. With Love and Hisses 27. Sailors Beware 27. Do Detectives Think? 27. Flying Elephants 27. Sugar Daddies 27. Call of the Cuckoo 27. The Rap 27. Duck Soup 27. Eve's Love Letters 27. Love 'Em and Weep 27. Why Girls Love Sailors 27. Should Tall Men Marry? 27. Hats Off 27. Putting Pants on Philip 27. *The Battle of the Century* 27. Leave 'Em Laughing 28. From Soup to Nuts 28. *The Finishing Touch* 28. *You're Darn Tootin'* 28. Their Purple Moment 28. Should Married Men Go Home? 28. Early to Bed 28. *Two Tars* 28. Habeas Corpus 28. We Faw Down 28. Liberty 28. Wrong Again 29. That's My Wife 29. *Big Business 29. Double Whoopee 29. Berth Marks 29. Men O'War 29.*

The Perfect Day 29. They Go Boom 29. Bacon Grabbers 29. Angora Love 29. Unaccustomed as We Are 29. Hollywood Revue of 1929. The Hoosegow 29. Night Owls 30. Blotto 30. The Rogue Song (feature) 30. Brats 30. Be Big 30. Below Zero 30. The Laurel and Hardy Murder Case 30. *Hog Wild* 30. Another Fine Mess 30. Chickens Come Home 30. *Laughing Gravy* 31. Our Wife 31. *Come Clean* 31. Pardon Us (f) 31. One Good Turn 31. Beau Hunks 31. *Helpmates* 31. Any Old Port 31. *The Music Box* (AA) 32. The Chimp 32. *County Hospital* 32. *Scram* 32 Pack Up Your Troubles (f) 32. Their First Mistake 32. *Towed in a Hole* 33. Twice Two 33. Me and My Pal 33. *Fra Diavolo* (f) 33. *The Midnight Patrol* 33. *Busy Bodies* 33. *Dirty Work* 33. *Sons of the Desert* (f) 33. Oliver the Eighth 33. Hollywood Party (f) 34. *Going Bye Bye* 34. *Them Thar Hills* 34. *Babes in Toyland* (f) 34. The Live Ghost 34. *Tit for Tat* 35. The Fixer Uppers 35. Thicker than Water 35. Bonnie Scotland (f) 35. The Bohemian Girl (f) 36. *Our Relations* (f) 36. *Way out West* (f) 36. Pick a Star (f) 37. Swiss Miss (f) 38. *Blockheads* (f) 38. *The Flying Deuces* (f) 39. *A Chump at Oxford* (f) 40. Saps at Sea (f) 40. Great Guns (f) 41. A Haunting We Will Go (f) 42. Air Raid Wardens (f) 43. Jitterbugs (f) 43. The Dancing Masters (f) 43. The Big Noise (f) 44. Nothing but Trouble (f) 44. The Bullfighters (f) 45. Robinson Crusoeland (Atoll K) (f) 52.
□ COMPILATION FEATURES: The Golden Age of Comedy 58. When Comedy was King 60. Days of Thrills and Laughter 61. Thirty Years of Fun 62. MGM's Big Parade of Comedy 65. Laurel and Hardy's Laughing Twenties 65. The Crazy World of Laurel and Hardy 66. The Further Adventures of Laurel and Hardy 69. Four Clowns 69.

Hardy, Robert (1925–). British character actor, mostly on TV.
The Spy Who Came in from the Cold 65. How I Won the War 67. 10 Rillington Place 70, etc.
TV series: *Elizabeth R* 71.

Hardy, Thomas (1840–1928). British novelist of dour country stories. Works principally filmed, neither satisfactorily, are *Tess of the D'Urbervilles* and *Far From the Madding Crowd*.

Hare, Lumsden (1875–1964). Irish character actor, long in Hollywood.
Charlie Chan Carries On 31. Clive of India 35. She 35. Gunga Din 39. Rebecca 40. The Lodger 44. Challenge to Lassie 49. Julius Caesar 53. The Four Skulls of Jonathan Drake 59, many others.

Hare, Robertson (1891–). Bald-headed British comedian, the put-upon little man of the Aldwych farces of the twenties and thirties, transferred intact from stage to screen.
Rookery Nook 30. A Cuckoo in the Nest 33. Thark 33. Fishing Stock 35. Aren't Men Beasts? 38. Banana Ridge 41. He Snoops To Conquer 45. Things Happen at Night 48. *One Wild Oat* 51. Our Girl Friday 53. Three Men in a Boat 56. The Young Ones 61, etc.

Harker, Gordon (1885–1967). British comic actor, the jutting-lipped Cockney of many a thirties comedy.
The Ring (debut) 27. The Calendar 31. *Rome Express* 33. Friday the Thirteenth 33. Boys Will Be Boys 35. Millions 37. The Return of the Frog 38. *Inspector Hornleigh* 40. *Saloon Bar* 41. Warn That Man 43. 29 Acacia Avenue 45. Happen at Night 48. Her Favourite Husband 50. The Second Mate 50. Derby Day 52. Small Hotel 58. Left, Right and Centre 59, etc.

Harlan, Kenneth (1895–1967). American leading man of the silent screen.
Cheerful Givers 17. The Hoodlum 19. The Beautiful and the Damned 22. The Broken Wing 23. Bobbed Hair 24. Twinkletoes 26. San Francisco 36. Paper Bullets 41. The Underdog 44, many others.

Harlan, Otis (1865–1940). Tubby American character actor with long stage experience.
What Happened to Jones? 25. Lightnin' 26. Man to Man 31. The Hawk 32. Married in Haste 34. Diamond Jim 35. A Midsummer Night's Dream 35. Mr Boggs Steps Out 38, many others.

Harlan, Russell (1903–1974). American cinematographer, former stunt man.
Hopalong Rides Again 37. Stagecoach War 40. The Kansan 43. *A Walk in the Sun* 45. *Red River* 48. The Big Sky 52. *Riot in Cell Block Eleven* 54. The Blackboard Jungle 55. This Could Be the Night 57. Witness for the Prosecution 57. Run Silent Run Deep 58. King Creole 58. The Spiral Road 62. Hatari 62. To Kill a Mockingbird 62. Quick Before It Melts 65. Tobruk 66. Darling Lili 70, etc.

Harlan, Veit (1899–1964). German director.
Kreutzer Sonata 36. Jew Süss 40. Der Grosse Konig 41. Offergang 43. Die Blaue Stunde 52. The Third Sex 57, etc.

Harline, Leigh (1907–1969). American screen composer.
Snow White and the Seven Dwarfs (songs) 37. Pinocchio (songs) (AA) 39. His Girl Friday 40.

The More the Merrier 43. Road to Utopia 45. The Farmer's Daughter 47. The Big Steal 49. Monkey Business 52. Broken Lance 54. The Wayward Bus 57. Ten North Frederick 58, etc.

Harlow, Jean (1911–1937) (Harlean Carpentier). American leading lady and most sensational star of the early thirties, a wisecracking 'platinum blonde' with a private life to suit her public image.
Biographies: 1937 *Hollywood Comet* by Dentner Davies.1964, *Harlow* by Irving Shulman. □ Moran of the Marines 28. Double Whoopee (short) 29. The Unkissed Man 29. The Fugitive 29. Close Harmony 29. New York Nights 29. The Love Parade 29. Weak but Willing 29. Bacon Grabbers (short) 29. The Saturday Night Kid 29. The Love Parade 30. Hell's Angels 30. City Lights 31. The Secret Six 31. Iron Man 31. *Public Enemy* 31. Goldie 31. Platinum Blonde 31. Three Wise Girls 32. Beast of the City 32. *Red Headed Woman* 32. *Red Dust* 32. *Dinner at Eight* 33. Hold Your Man 33. *Bombshell* 33. The Girl from Missouri 34. Reckless 35. *China Seas* 35. Riffraff 35. Wife vs Secretary 35. Suzy 36. *Libelled Lady* 36. Personal Property 37. Saratoga 37.

Harlow, John (1896–). British writer-director, former music-hall performer.
Spellbound (d) 40. Candles at Nine (d) 43. Meet Sexton Blake (d) 44. The Agitator (d) 45. Appointment with Crime (wd) 46. Green Fingers (wd) 47. *While I Live* (Dream of Olwen) (wd) 48. Old Mother Riley's New Venture (d) 49. Those People Next Door (d) 52, etc.

Harolde, Ralf (1899–1974) (R. H. Wigger). American supporting actor often seen as thin-lipped crook.
Night Nurse 32. A Tale of Two Cities 35. Horror Island 41. Baby Face Morgan 42. Farewell My Lovely (as the doctor) 44. Alaska Patrol (last film) 51, many others.

Harper, Gerald (1929–). Aristocratic-looking British actor familiar on TV as *Adam Adamant* and *Hadleigh*.
The Admirable Crichton 57. A Night to Remember 58. The League of Gentlemen 59. The Punch and Judy Man 64, etc.

Harrigan, William (1894–1966). American general purpose actor of the thirties and forties.
On the Level 17. Cabaret 27. Nix on Dames 27. Born Reckless 30. Pick Up 33. The Invisible Man 33. G Men 35. The Silk Hat Kid 35. Federal Bullets 37. Hawaii Calls 38. Back Door to Heaven 39. The Farmer's Daughter 47. Flying

Leathernecks 51. Street of Sinners 55, etc.

Harrington, Curtis (1928–). American director who made experimental shorts before graduating to features.
☐ Night Tide 63. Queen of Blood 66. Games 67. What's the Matter with Helen? 71. Who Slew Auntie Roo? 73. The Dead Don't Die (TV) 74. The Deadly Bees (TV) 74.

Harris, Barbara (1936–). American leading lady.
A Thousand Clowns 65. Oh Dad . . . 66. Plaza Suite 71. Who is Harry Kellerman . . . ? 71. The War Between Men and Women 72, etc.

Harris, James B. (1924–). American producer, associated with director Stanley Kubrick.
The Killing 56. Paths of Glory 57. Lolita 62. The Bedford Incident (& d) 65. Some Call It Loving 71, etc.

Harris, Jonathan (c. 1919–). American character actor, popular in prissy roles in TV series *The Third Man* 59–61, *The Bill Dana Show* 63–64, *Lost in Space* 65–68.
Botany Bay 54. The Big Fisherman 59, etc.

Harris, Julie (1925–). American stage actress, adept at fey roles. Films occasional.
☐ *The Member of the Wedding* 53. East of Eden 55. I am a Camera 56. The Truth about Women 56. Sally's Irish Rogue 60. Requiem for a Heavyweight 62. *The Haunting* 63. Harper 66. You're a Big Boy Now 66. *Reflections in a Golden Eye* 67. The Split 68. The People Next Door 70. Home for the Holidays (TV) 72.

Harris, Julie (–). British production designer.
The Naked Edge 61. The Fast Lady 62. The Chalk Garden 64. Darling 65. The Wrong Box 65. Casino Royale 67. Goodbye Mr Chips 69. Live and Let Die 73. Rollerball 74. The Slipper and the Rose 76, many others.

Harris, Phil (1906–). American bandleader and comic singer; in occasional films.
Melody Cruise 33. Man about Town 39. Buck Benny Rides Again 40. Here Comes the Groom 51. The Glenn Miller Story 54. The High and the Mighty 54. Anything Goes 56. The Wheeler Dealers 63. The Cool Ones 67, etc.

Harris, Richard (1932–). Gaunt Irish leading actor. Usually cast as a rebel, he tries to match the part in real life.
☐ Alive and Kicking 58. Shake Hands with the Devil 59. The Wreck of the Mary Deare 59. A Terrible Beauty 60. All Night Long 61. The Long the Short and the Tall 61. The Guns of Navarone 61. *Mutiny on the Bounty* 62. *This Sporting Life* 63. The Red Desert 64. I Tre Volti 64. Major Dundee 65. The Heroes of Telemark 65. The Bible 66. Hawaii 66. Caprice 66. *Camelot* (as King Arthur) 67. The Molly Maguires 69. A Man Called Horse 69. Bloomfield (& d) 70. *Cromwell* (title role) 70. The Snow Goose (TV) 71. Man in the Wilderness 71. The Deadly Trackers 73. 99 44/100 Dead 74. Juggernaut 75. Robin and Marian 75. The Return of a Man Called Horse 76.

Harris, Robert (1900–). British classical actor who has played occasional film roles.
How He Lied to Her Husband 31. The Life and Death of Colonel Blimp 43. The Bad Lord Byron 48. That Lady 55. Oscar Wilde 60. Decline and Fall 68, etc.

Harris, Robert H. (c. 1909–). American character actor, usually in pompous comedy roles.
Bundle of Joy 56. How to Make a Monster 58. America America 63. Mirage 65. Valley of the Dolls 67, etc.

Harris, Rosemary (1930–). British leading lady, chiefly on stage.
Beau Brummel 54. The Shiralee 55. A Flea in Her Ear 68.

Harris, Vernon (c. 1910–). British screenwriter.
Albert RN (co-w) 53. The Sea Shall Not Have Them (co-w) 55. Reach for the Sky 56. Ferry to Hong Kong 57. The Admirable Crichton 57 Light up the Sky 61. Oliver 68, etc.

Harrison, Joan (1911–). British writer-producer, assistant for many years to Alfred Hitchcock.
Jamaica Inn (w) 39. Rebecca (w) 40. Foreign Correspondent (w) 40. Suspicion (w) 41. Saboteur (w) 42. Dark Waters (w) 44. Phantom Lady (p) 44. Uncle Harry (p) 45. Ride the Pink Horse (p) 47. Circle of Danger (p) 51, etc.
TV series: *Alfred Hitchcock Presents* (p) 55–63.

Harrison, Kathleen (1898–). British character actress, usually seen as a cockney but born in Lancashire. On stage from 1926; films have made her an amiable, slightly dithery but warm-hearted national figure.
Hobson's Choice (debut) 31. The Ghoul 33. Broken Blossoms 36. Night Must Fall (US) 37. *Bank Holiday* 38. The Outsider 39. *The Ghost*

Train 41. Kipps 41. *In Which We Serve* 42. Dear Octopus 43. Great Day 45. *Holiday Camp* 47. *The Winslow Boy* 48. Bond Street 48. Oliver Twist 48. *Here Come the Huggetts* (and ensuing series) 49–52. Waterfront 50. Scrooge 51. Pickwick Papers 52. *Turn the Key Softly* 53. Cast a Dark Shadow 54. Where There's a Will 54. Lilacs in the Spring 54. *All for Mary* 55. Home and Away 56. A Cry from the Streets 58. Alive and Kicking 58. Mrs Gibbons' Boys 62. West Eleven 63. Lock Up Your Daughters 69, many others.

Harrison, Rex (1908–) (Reginald Carey). Debonair British leading actor of pleasant if limited range, on stage since 1924; films have only occasionally given him the right material. Autobiography 1974: *Rex*.
□ The Great Game 30. The School for Scandal 30. All at Sea 34. Get Your Man 34. Leave It to Blanche 35. Men Are Not Gods 36. *Storm in a Teacup* 37. School for Husbands 37. St Martin's Lane 38. The Citadel 38. Over the Moon 39. The Silent Battle 39. Ten Days in Paris 39. *Night Train to Munich* 40. *Major Barbara* 40. I Live in Grosvenor Square 45. *Blithe Spirit* 45. *The Rake's Progress* 46. Anna and the King of Siam (US) 46. The Ghost and Mrs Muir (US) 47. The Foxes of Harrow (US) 47. Unfaithfully Yours (US) 48. Escape 48. The Long Dark Hall 51. The Fourposter (US) 52. King Richard and the Crusaders (as Saladin) (US) 54. The Constant Husband 55. The Reluctant Debutante (US) 58. Midnight Lace (US) 60. The Happy Thieves (US) 62. Cleopatra (US) 62. *My Fair Lady* (AA) (US) 64. The Yellow Rolls Royce 64. The Agony and the Ecstasy (US) (as a medieval pope) 65. The Honey Pot (US) 67. Doctor Dolittle (US) 67. A Flea in Her Ear (US/Fr.) 68. Staircase 69. Don Quixote (TV) 72. The Prince and the Pauper 67.

Harron, Robert (Bobby) (1894–1920). American juvenile lead who joined D. W. Griffith's company almost from school; died in shooting accident.
Man's Genesis 12. The Birth of a Nation 14. Intolerance 16. Hearts of the World 18. True Heart Susie 19, many others.

Harryhausen, Ray (c. 1920–). American trick film specialist and model maker; invented 'Superdynamation'. 1972: published *Film Fantasy Scrapbook*.
Mighty Joe Young 50. It Came from Beneath the Sea 52. Twenty Million Miles to Earth 57. The Three Worlds of Gulliver 60. *Jason and the Argonauts* 63. The First Men in the Moon 64. One Million Years B.C. 66. The Valley of Gwangi 69. Sinbad's Golden Voyage 73, etc.

Hart, Dolores (1938–) (D. Hicks). American lady of a few films in the late fifties.
Loving You 56. Wild is the Wind 57. Lonelyhearts 59. Sail a Crooked Ship 60. Lisa 62, etc.

Hart, Harvey (1928–). Canadian director, from TV, now in Hollywood.
□ Dark Intruder 65. Bus Riley's Back in Town 65. Sullivan's Empire 67. The Sweet Ride 68. Fortune and Men's Eyes 71. The Pyx 73.

Hart, Moss (1904–1961). American playwright (usually in collaboration with George S. Kaufman) and theatrical producer. Wrote occasional screenplays.
Autobiography 1958: *Act One* (filmed 1963).
Once in a Lifetime (oa) 32. You Can't Take It With You (oa) 38. *The Man Who Came to Dinner* (oa) 41. George Washington Slept Here (oa) 42. Lady in the Dark (oa) 44. Winged Victory (w) 44. *Gentleman's Agreement* (w) 47. Hans Christian Andersen (w) 52. A Star Is Born (w) 54. Prince of Players (w) 55, etc

Hart, Richard (1915–1951). American leading man with a very brief Hollywood career.
□ Green Dolphin Street 47. Desire Me 47. B.F.'s Daughter 48. The Black Book 49.

Hart, William S. (1870–1946). Mature, solemn-faced hero of innumerable silent westerns; one of the key performers of the twenties. The initial 'S' is variously reputed to have stood for 'Shakespeare' and 'Surrey'.
Autobiography 1929: *My Life East and West*.
The Disciple 15. The Captive God 16. The Return of Draw Egan 16. Hell's Hinges 17. Truthful Tolliver 17. Blue Blazes Rawden 18. Selfish Yates 18. Riddle Gawne 18. The Border Wireless 18. Wagon Tracks 18. The Poppy Girl's Husband 19. The Toll Gate 20. Sand 20. Cradle of Courage 20. O'Malley of the Mounted 21. White Oak 21. Travellin' On 22. Hollywood 23. Wild Bill Hickok 23. Singer Jim McKee 24. *Tumbleweeds* 25, many others.

Hartford-Davis, Robert (1923–). British producer-director, in films since 1939.
That Kind of Girl 62. The Yellow Teddybears 63. Saturday Night Out 63. Black Torment 64. Gonks Go Beat 65. The Sandwich Man 66. Corruption 68. The Smashing Bird I Used to Know 69. The Fiend 71. Black Gunn (US) 72. The Take (US) 74, etc.

Hartman, Don (1901–1958) (Samuel Hartman). American comedy screenwriter.
The Gay Deception 35. The Princess Comes

Across 35. Waikiki Wedding 37. Tropic Holiday 38. Paris Honeymoon 39. The Star Maker 39. *Road to Singapore* 40. Life with Henry 41. *Road to Zanzibar* 41. Nothing but the Truth 41. *Road to Morocco* 42. True to Life 42. Up in Arms 44. The Princess and the Pirate 44. Down to Earth (& p) 47. It Had to be You (& d) 47. Every Girl Should Be Married (& pd) 48. Mr Imperium (& d) 51. Desire Under the Elms (p) 57. The Matchmaker (p) 58, many others.

Hartman, David (c. 1940–). Tall, gangling TV leading man.
The Feminist and the Fuzz (TV) 71. The Island at the Top of the World 75, etc.
TV series: *Lucas Tanner.*

Hartman, Elizabeth (1941–). American leading actress.
□ A Patch of Blue 66. The Group 66. You're a Big Boy Now 67. The Fixer 68. The Beguiled 71. Walking Tall 73.

Hartnell, William (1908–1975). Thin-lipped British character actor who rose briefly to star status in the forties after playing many small-time crooks and tough sergeants.
Follow the Lady 33. While Parents Sleep 35. Murder at Madame Tussaud's 36. Farewell Again 37. They Drive by Night 39. Flying Fortress 40. Suspected Person 41. The Peterville Diamond 42. The Bells Go Down 43. Headline 43. *The Way Ahead* 44. The Agitator 44. Murder in Reverse 45. Strawberry Roan 46. Appointment with Crime 46. Odd Man Out 46. Temptation Harbour 47. *Brighton Rock* 47. Now Barabbas 49. The Lost People 49. The Dark Man 50. The Magic Box 51. The Holly and the Ivy 52. The Ringer 52. Will any Gentleman? 53. Footsteps in the Fog 54. Private's Progress 55. Hell Drivers 57. Carry on Sergeant 58. Piccadilly Third Stop 60. This Sporting Life 62. Heaven's Above 63, many others.

Harvey (US) 1950). It was fashionable at the time to despise this as inferior to the stage play about a genial alcoholic who is accompanied by an invisible white rabbit six feet high. But James Stewart coped admirably with most of the googly lines; Josephine Hull was a positive delight as his much-abused sister; the supporting cast included gems from Cecil Kellaway, Wallace Ford, and Jesse White; and Henry Koster's direction, while not exciting, gave Mary Chase's script its full head.

Harvey, Anthony (1931–). British director, former editor.
□ Dutchman 66. *The Lion in Winter* 68. They

Might Be Giants 71. The Abdication 74. The Glass Menagerie (TV) 74.

Harvey, Forrester (1890–1945). Irish character actor, long in Hollywood.
The White Sheik 26. Tarzan the Ape Man 32. Shanghai Express 32. The Invisible Man 33. David Copperfield 34. Lloyds of London 37. A Chump at Oxford 40. Dr Jekyll and Mr Hyde 41. Devotion 44, many others.

Harvey, Frank (1912–). British playwright and screenwriter.
Saloon Bar (oa) 40. Things Happen at Night (oa) 48. Seven Days to Noon (w) 50. High Treason (w) 52. Private's Progress (w) 55. I'm All Right Jack (w) 59. Heaven's Above (w) 63. No My Darling Daughter (pa/w) 63, etc.

Harvey, Laurence (1928–1973) (Larushka Mischa Skikne). Lithuanian-born leading man who worked his way slowly from British second features to top Hollywood productions, but was only briefly in fashion.
Biographies: 1976, *One Tear is Enough* by Pauline Stone. 1974, *The Laurence Harvey Story* by Hans Borgett. 1973, *The Prince* by Emmett and Des Hickey.
House of Darkness 48. Man on the Run 49. The Scarlet Thread 51. The Good Die Young 54. Storm Over the Nile 55. *Three Men in a Boat* 56. The Silent Enemy 58. *Room at the Top* 59. Expresso Bongo 59. The Alamo 60. Butterfield 8 61. A Walk on the Wild Side 62. *The Manchurian Candidate* 62. The Running Man 63. The Ceremony (& pd) 63. Of Human Bondage 64. The Outrage 64. Darling 65. Life at the Top 65. The Spy with a Cold Nose 67. A Dandy in Aspic 68. He and She (& p) 69. WUSA 70. Night Watch 73. Welcome to Arrow Beach, etc.

Harvey, Lilian (1906–1968). British leading lady who in the thirties became star of German films.
Leidenschaft 25. Die Tolle Lola 27. Drei von der Tankstelle 30. *Congress Dances* 31. Happy Ever After 32. My Weakness (US) 33. I Am Suzanne (US) 34. Invitation to the Waltz (GB) 35. Capriccio 38. Serenade (Fr.) last film 39, etc.

Harvey, Paul (1884–1955). American character actor who often played the choleric executive or kindly father.
Advice to the Lovelorn 34. Rebecca of Sunnybrook Farm 38. Algiers 38. Stanley and Livingstone 39. Maryland 40. Pillow to Post 45. The Late George Apley 47. Father of the Bride

50. The First Time 52. Three for the Show 55, hundreds of others.

Haskin, Byron (1899–). American director with a penchant for science fiction; some interesting films among the routine. Cameraman and special effects expert through the thirties.
□ Matinée Ladies 27. Ginsberg the Great 27. Irish Hearts 27. The Siren 28. *I Walk Alone* 47. Maneater of Kumaon 48. Too Late for Tears 49. Treasure Island 50. Tarzan's Peril 51. Warpath 51. Silver City 51. Denver and Rio Grande 52. *The War of the Worlds* 53. His Majesty O'Keefe 53. The Naked Jungle 54. Long John Silver 55. Conquest of Space 55. The First Texan 56. The Boss 56. From the Earth to the Moon 58. The Little Savage 59. September Storm 60. Armored Command 61. *Captain Sindbad* 63. *Robinson Crusoe on Mars* 64. The Power 67.

Hasso, Signe (1910–). Swedish leading lady of the forties, in Hollywood.
Assignment in Brittany 43. The Seventh Cross 44. *The House on 92nd Street* 45. Johnny Angel 45. A Scandal in Paris 46. Where There's Life 47. *To the Ends of the Earth* 48. A Double Life 48. Outside the Wall 50. Crisis 50. Picture Mommy Dead 66. Reflection of Fear 71. The Black Bird 75, etc.

Hatfield, Hurd (1918–). American leading man whose coldly handsome face proved to be his misfortune.
□ Dragon Seed 44. *The Picture of Dorian Gray* 45. The Diary of a Chambermaid 46. The Beginning or the End 47. The Unsuspected 47. The Checkered Coat 48. Joan of Arc 48. Chinatown at Midnight 48. Tarzan and the Slave Girl 50. The Left Handed Gun 58. King of Kings 61. El Cid 61. Mickey One 65. The Boston Strangler 68. Von Richthofen and Brown 71.

Hathaway, Henry (1898–). American director, in films (as child actor) from 1907. Acted till 1932, then directed westerns. Later became known as a capable handler of big action adventures and thrillers.
□ Wild Horse Mesa 32. Heritage of the Desert 33. Under the Tonto Rim 33. Sunset Pass 33. Man of the Forest 33. To the Last Man 33. Come On Marines 34. The Last Round-Up 34, Thundering Herds 34. The Witching Hour 34. Now and Forever 34. *Lives of a Bengal Lancer* 35. Peter Ibbetson 35. Trail of the Lonesome Pine 36. Go West Young Man 36. Souls at Sea 37. Spawn of the North 38. The Real Glory 39. Johnny Apollo 40. Brigham Young 40. Shepherd of the Hills 41. Sundown 41. Ten Gentlemen from West Point 42. China Girl 43. Home in

Indiana 44. A Wing and a Prayer 44. Nob Hill 45. *The House on 92nd Street* 45. The Dark Corner 46. 13 Rue Madeleine 46. *Kiss of Death* 47. Call Northside 777 48. Down to the Sea in Ships 49. The Black Rose 50. You're in the Navy Now 51. Rawhide 51. Fourteen Hours 51. *Rommel, Desert Fox* 51. Diplomatic Courier 52. *Niagara* 52. White Witch Doctor 53. Prince Valiant 54. Garden of Evil 54. The Racers 54. The Bottom of the Bottle 55. Twenty-three Paces to Baker Street 56. Legend of the Lost 57. From Hell to Texas 58. A Woman Obsessed 59. Seven Thieves 60. *North to Alaska* 60. How the West Was Won (part) 62. Circus World 64. The Sons of Katie Elder 65. Nevada Smith 66. The Last Safari 67. Five Card Stud 68. True Grit 69. Raid on Rommel 71. Shootout 72.

Hatton, Raymond (1887–1971). American character actor, the comic side-kick of a hundred minor westerns; in Hollywood from 1911. Formed a comedy team with Wallace Beery 1926–29.
Oliver Twist 16. Whispering Chorus 18. Male and Female 19. Jes' Call Me Jim 20. The Affairs of Anatol 21. Ebb Tide 22. The Hunchback of Notre Dame 23. The Fighting American 24. In the Name of Love 25. Born to the West 26. *Behind the Front* 26. *We're In the Navy Now* 26. Fireman Save My Child 27. The Woman God Forgot 27. We're in the Air Now 27. Partners in Crime 28. Hell's Heroes 29. Midnight Mistery 30. Woman Hungry 31. The Squaw Man 31. Polly of the Circus 32. Terror Trail 33. Wagon Wheels 34. Laughing Irish Eyes 36. Roaring Timber 37. Love Finds Andy Hardy 38. Kit Carson 40. Tall in the Saddle 44. Black Gold 47. Operation Haylift 50. Shake Rattle and Rock 56. In Cold Blood 67, many others.

Hatton, Rondo (1894–1946). American actor who suffered from facial and bodily deformity as a result of acromegaly; he was rather tastelessly cast as a monstrous killer in several low-budget mysteries of the early forties.
In Old Chicago 38. The Ox Bow Incident 42. Pearl of Death 44. Jungle Captive 45. House of Horrors 46. Spider Woman Strikes Back 46. The Brute Man 46, etc.

Havelock-Allan, Anthony (1905–). British producer.
This Man Is News 38. In Which We Serve (associate) 42. Blithe Spirit 45. Brief Encounter 46. Great Expectations 46. Oliver Twist 48. The Small Voice 49. Never Take No for an Answer 51. The Young Lovers 54. Orders to Kill 58. The Quare Fellow 61. An Evening with the Royal Ballet 64. Othello 65. The Mikado 67, etc.

Haver, June (1926–) (June Stovenour). American leading lady of the forties, mostly in musicals; married Fred McMurray. Retired.
□ The Gangs All Here 43. Home in Indiana 44. Irish Eyes Are Smiling 44. Where Do We Go from Here? 45. *The Dolly Sisters* 45. Three Little Girls in Blue 46. Wake Up and Dream 46. I Wonder Who's Kissing Her Now 47. Scudda Hoo Scudda Hay 48. Oh You Beautiful Doll 49. *Look for the Silver Lining* (as Marilyn Miller) 49. The Daughter of Rosie O'Grady 50. I'll Get By 50. Love Nest 51. The Girl Next Door 53.

Haver, Phyllis (1899–1960). American leading lady of the silent screen, a former Sennett bathing beauty.
Small Town Idol 20. Temple of Venus 23. Fig Leaves 25. Up in Mabel's Room 26. The Way of All Flesh 28. Hard Boiled 29. Hell's Kitchen 29, many others.

Havoc, June (1916–) (June Hovick). American leading lady, former child actress; sister of Gypsy Rose Lee.
Autobiography 1960: *Early Havoc.*
Four Jacks and a Jill 42. Brewster's Millions 45. The Story of Molly X 49. Once a Thief 50. A Lady Possessed 51. Three for Jamie Dawn 57, etc.

Hawkins, Jack (1910–1973). Dominant British actor; after long apprenticeship, became an international star in middle age, but in 1966 lost his voice after an operation; his subsequent minor appearances were dubbed.
Autobiography 1974: *Anything For a Quiet Life.*
Birds of Prey 30. The Lodger 32. The Good Companions 32. The Lost Chord 33. I Lived with You 33. The Jewel 33. A Shot in the Dark 33. Autumn Crocus 34. Death at Broadcasting House 34. *Peg of Old Drury* 35. Beauty and the Barge 37. The Frog 37. Who Goes Next 38. A Royal Divorce 38. Murder Will Out 39. The Flying Squad 40. Next of Kin 42. *The Fallen Idol* 48. Bonnie Prince Charlie 48. The Small Back Room 48. *State Secret* 50. The Black Rose 50. The Elusive Pimpernel 50. The Adventurers 51. No Highway 51. Home at Seven 51. *Angels One Five* 52. The Planter's Wife 52. Mandy 52. *The Cruel Sea* 52. Twice Upon a Time 53. The Malta Story 53. The Intruder 53. Front Page Story 54. The Seekers 54. The Prisoner 55. Touch and Go 55. The Long Arm 56. The Man in the Sky 56. Fortune is a Woman 57. *The Bridge on the River Kwai* 57. Gideon's Day 58. The Two Headed Spy 58. *The League of Gentlemen* 59. *Ben Hur* (US) 59. Two Loves (US) 61. Five Finger Exercise (US) 62. *Lawrence of Arabia* 62. Lafayette 63. *Rampage* (US) 63.

Zulu 63. The Third Secret 64. Guns at Batasi 64. Masquerade 65. Lord Jim 65. Judith 65. Great Catherine 67. Shalako 68. Oh What a Lovely War 69. Monte Carlo or Bust 69. Waterloo 70. The Adventures of Gerard 70. Nicholas and Alexandra 71. Kidnapped 72. Young Winston 72. Theatre of Blood 73. Tales that Witness Madness 73, etc.
TV series: *The Four Just Men* 59.

Hawks, Howard (1896–). American director, at his best an incomparable provider of professional comedies and action dramas. In films from 1918, at first as writer and editor.
□ Tiger Love (w only) 24. The Road to Glory (& w) 26. Fig Leaves (& w) 26. The Cradle Snatchers 27. Paid to Love 27. A Girl in Every Port (& w) 28. Fazil 28. The Air Circus 28. Trent's Last Case (& w) 29. *The Dawn Patrol* 30. The Criminal Code 31. The Crowd Roars 32. *Scarface* 32. Tiger Shark 32. Today We Live 33. *Twentieth Century* 34. Viva Villa (part) 34. *Barbary Coast* 35. Ceiling Zero 36. Road to Glory 36. Come and Get It (co-d) 36. *Bringing Up Baby* 38. Only Angels Have Wings 39. *His Girl Friday* 40. Sergeant York 41. Ball of Fire 41. Air Force 42. Corvette K 225 (p only) 44. *To Have and Have Not* 44. *The Big Sleep* 46. A Song Is Born 48. *Red River* 48. I Was a Male War Bride 49. The Thing from Another World (p only) 52. The Big Sky 52. Monkey Business 52. Full House (one episode) 52. Gentlemen Prefer Blondes 53. Land of the Pharaohs 55. *Rio Bravo* 58. Hatari 62. Man's Favourite Sport 64. Red Line 7000 65. El Dorado 66. Rio Lobo 70.

Hawn, Goldie (1945–). American leading lady who scored as blonde dimwit on TV's *Laugh-In.*
□ The One and Only Genuine Original Family Band 68. *Cactus Flower* (AA) 69. *There's a Girl in My Soup* 70. Butterflies are Free 72. Dollars 72. The Sugarland Express 73. The Girl from Petrovka 74. Shampoo 75. The Duchess and the Dirtwater Fox 76.

Haworth, Jill (1945–). British leading lady in Hollywood.
Exodus 60. In Harm's Way 65. It 66. Home for Holidays (TV) 72. The Mutations 74.

Hawthorne, Nathaniel (1804–1864). American novelist whose books *The Scarlet Letter, Twice-Told Tales* and *The House of Seven Gables* have been much adapted for the screen.

Hawtrey, Charles (1914–). Spindle-shanked British comic actor, long cast as ageing

schoolboy in Will Hay and other comedies; in the sixties, a familiar member of the 'Carry On' team.
Good Morning Boys 37. Where's That Fire 40. The Goose Steps Out 42. A Canterbury Tale 48. The Galloping Major 50. Brandy for the Parson 52. *You're Only Young Twice* 53. Carry on Sergeant 58. Carry on Nurse 59. Carry on Jack 54. Carry on Cowboy 67. Carry on at Your Convenience 71. Carry on Abroad 72, many others.

Hay, Alexandra (c. 1944–). American leading lady.
Skidoo 68. The Model Shop 69. The Love Machine 71. 1000 Convicts and a Woman 71, etc.

Hay, Will (1888–1949). British character comedian, one of the screen's greats; after many years in the music halls, starred in several incomparable farces playing variations on his favourite role of an incompetent, seedy schoolmaster.
□ Those Were the Days 34. Dandy Dick 34. Radio Parade 35. Boys will be Boys 35. Where There's a Will 36. Windbag the Sailor 36. *Good Morning Boys* 37. Convict 99 38. *Old Bones of the River* 38. *Oh Mr Porter* 38. *Ask a Policeman* 39. Where's that Fire? 39. *The Ghost of St Michael's* 41. The Black Sheep of Whitehall 41. The Big Blockade 42. The Goose Steps Out 42. *My Learned Friend* 44.

Hayakawa, Sessue (1889–1973). Japanese actor, a popular star of American silents; more recently in occasional character roles.
The Typhoon 14. *The Cheat* 15. Forbidden Paths 17. The Tong Man 19. Daughter of the Dragon 29. Tokyo Joe 49. Three Came Home 50. *The Bridge on the River Kwai* 57. The Geisha Boy 59. The Swiss Family Robinson 60. Hell to Eternity 61, etc.

Hayden, Linda (1951–). British leading lady; started by playing teenage sexpots.
Baby Love 69. Taste the Blood of Dracula 69. Satan's Skin 70. Something to Hide 72. Confessions of a Window Cleaner 74, etc.

Hayden, Russell (1912–) (Pate Lucid). American 'second string' leading man, for many years Hopalang Cassidy's faithful side-kick. Now produces TV westerns.
Hills of Old Wyoming (debut) 37. Range War 39. Lucky Legs 42. 'Neath Canadian Skies 46. Seven Were Saved 47. Silver City 49. Valley of Fire 51, many others.

Hayden, Sterling (1916–) (John Hamilton). Rangy American leading man and part-time explorer.
Autobiography 1963: *Wanderer*.
Virginia 40. Bahama Passage 41. Blaze of Noon 47. El Paso 49. Manhandled 49. *The Asphalt Jungle* 50. Denver and Rio Grande 52. The Golden Hawk 52. The Star 52. So Big 53. Prince Valiant 54. Arrow in the Dust 54. Johnny Guitar 54. Suddenly 54. Timberjack 55. The Eternal Sea 55. The Last Command 55. *The Killing* 56. Crime of Passion 56. Five Steps to Danger 56. Zero Hour 57. Terror in a Texas Town 58. Dr Strangelove 63. Hard Contract 69. Loving 70. The Godfather 72. The Long Goodbye 73, etc.

Haydn, Richard (1905–). British revue star of the thirties, in Hollywood from 1941, usually in adenoidal character cameos.
Ball of Fire (debut) 41. Charley's Aunt 41. Forever and a Day 43. And Then There Were None 45. *Cluny Brown* 46. *Sitting Pretty* 47. Miss Tatlock's Millions (& d) 48. Mr Music (& d) 50. Dear Wife (d only) 50. Jupiter's Darling 54. Please Don't Eat the Daisies 60. *The Lost World* 60. Mutiny on the Bounty 62. Five Weeks in a Balloon 62. The Sound of Music 65. Clarence the Cross-Eyed Lion 65. Bullwhip Griffin 66. Young Frankenstein 74, many others.

Haye, Helen (1874–1957) (Helen Hay). Distinguished British stage actress (debut 1898), in occasional films, usually as kindly dowager.
Tilly of Bloomsbury 21. Atlantic 30. Congress Dances 31. *The Spy in Black* 39. Kipps 41. *Dear Octopus* 43. Anna Karenina 48. Richard III 56, many others.

Hayers, Sidney (1921–). British director, in films since 1942. Former editor and second unit director.
□ Violent Moment 58. The White Trap 59. Circus of Horrors 59. Echo of Barbara 60. *Payroll* 61. *Night of the Eagle* 62. This Is My Street 63. Three Hats for Lisa 65. The Trap 66. Finders Keepers 66. The Southern Star 69. The Firechasers 70. Assault 71. Revenge 71.

Hayes, Allison (1930–) (Mary Jane Hayes). American leading lady of a few films in the fifties.
Francis Joins the WACs 54. The Purple Mask 55. The Blackboard Jungle 55. Mohawk 56. The Zombies of Mora Tau 57. Attack of the Fifty-Foot Woman (title role) 58. Who's Been Sleeping in My Bed? 63. Tickle Me 65.

Hayes, George 'Gabby' (1885–1969). Bewhiskered American character comedian, in minor westerns from silent days.

The Rainbow Man 29. Beggars in Ermine 34. The Lost City 35. Three on the Trail 36. Mountain Music 37. Hopalong Rides Again 38. Gold is Where You Find It. 38. Man of Conquest 39. Wagons Westward 40. Melody Ranch 41. In Old Oklahoma 43. Tall in the Saddle 44. Utah 45. My Pal Trigger 46. Wyoming 47. Return of the Badmen 48. El Paso 49. The Cariboo Trail 50, many others.

Hayes, Margaret (1915–1977). American character actress, also in TV and public relations.
The Blackboard Jungle 55. Violent Saturday 55. Omar Khayyam 57. Fraulein 57, etc.

Hayes, Helen (1900–) (Helen Brown). Distinguished American stage actress who made a few film appearances. Autobiographical books: 1940 *Letters to Mary Catherine Hayes Brown*. 1969 *On Reflection*.
□ The Weavers of Life 17. Babs 20. *The Sin of Madelon Claudet* (AA) 31. Arrowsmith 31. *A Farewell to Arms* 32. The Son Daughter 33. The White Sister 33. Another Language 33. Night Flight 33. What Every Woman Knows 34. Vanessa 35. Stage Door Canteen 43. My Son John 51. Main Street to Broadway 53. *Anastasia* 56. *Airport* (AA) 69. Do Not Fold Spindle or Mutilate (TV) 71. Herbie Rides Again 73. The Snoop Sisters (TV) 73 (and series). One of Our Dinosaurs is Missing 75.

Hayes, John Michael (1919–). American screenwriter.
Rear Window 54. To Catch a Thief 55. The Trouble with Harry 56. Peyton Place 57. *The Carpetbaggers* 63. Where Love Has Gone 64. Harlow 65. Judith 66. Nevada Smith 66, etc.

Haymes, Dick (1916–). Argentine-born crooner, former radio announcer.
Irish Eyes Are Smiling (debut) 44. Diamond Horseshoe 45. *State Fair* 45. Do You Love Me? 46. The Shocking Miss Pilgrim 47. Up in Central Park 48. One Touch of Venus 48. St Benny the Dip 51. All Ashore 53, etc.

Hays, Will H. (1879–1954). American executive, for many years (1922–45) president of the Motion Picture Producers and Distributors Association of America, and author of its high-toned Production Code (1930), which for many years put producers in fear of 'the Hays office'. *The Memoirs of Will H. Hays* was published in 1955.

Hayter, James (1907–). Portly, jovial British character actor, on stage from 1925, films from 1936.

Sensation 36. Sailors Three 41. School for Secrets 46. *Nicholas Nickleby* (as the Cheeryble twins) 47. The Blue Lagoon 48. *Trio* 50. Tom Brown's Schooldays 51. Robin Hood (as Friar Tuck) 52. *Pickwick Papers* (title role) 53. The Great Game 53. A Day to Remember 54. Touch and Go 56. Port Afrique 58. The Thirty-Nine Steps 59. Stranger in the House 67. Oliver 68. David Copperfield 69. Song of Norway 70, many others.

Haythorne, Joan (1915–) (Joan Haythornthwaite). British stage actress, usually in aristocratic roles.
School for Secrets 46. Jassy 47. Highly Dangerous 50. Svengali 54. The Weak and the Wicked 54. The Feminine Touch 56. Three Men in a Boat 56. Shakedown 59. So Evil So Young 61, etc.

Hayward, Leland (1902–1971). American talent agent and stage producer. Recently produced films.
Mister Roberts 55. The Spirit of St Louis 57. The Old Man and the Sea 58, etc.

Hayward, Louis (1909–) (Seafield Grant). Mild-mannered, South African-born leading man with stage experience; in Hollywood from 1935.
□ Chelsea Life (GB) 33. *Sorrell and Son* (GB) 34. The Flame Within 35. Anthony Adverse 36. The Luckiest Girl in the World 36. Midnight Intruder 37. The Rage of Paris 38. *The Saint in New York* 38. *Duke of West Point* 39. *The Man in the Iron Mask* 39. *My Son, My Son* 40. Son of Monte Cristo 40. Ladies in Retirement 41. And Then There Were None 45. Monte Cristo's Revenge 47. Young Widow 47. Repeat Performance 47. The Black Arrow 48. Walk a Crooked Mile 48. Pirates of Capri 49. The Fortunes of Captain Blood 50. Son of Dr Jekyll 51. Dick Turpin's Ride 51. Lady in the Iron Mask 52. Captain Pirate 52. Fire Over Africa 53. The Saint's Return (GB) 53. Duffy of San Quentin 54. *The Search for Bridey Murphy* 56. Chuka 67. Terror in the Wax Museum 73.
TV series: The Lone Wolf 54. The Pursuers 62. The Survivors 69.

Hayward, Susan (1918–1975) (Edythe Marrener). Vivacious American leading lady, in films from 1938 after modelling experience: often in agressive roles.
□ Girls on Probation 38. Our Leading Citizen 39. $1000 A Touchdown 39. Beau Geste 39. Adam Had Four Sons 41. Sis Hopkins 41. Among the Living 41. Reap the Wild Wind 42. The Forest Rangers 42. I Married a Witch 42.

Star Spangled Rhythm 42. Change of Heart 43. Jack London 43. Young and Willing 43. The Fighting Seabees 44. And Now Tomorrow 44. The Hairy Ape 44. Canyon Passage 45. Deadline at Dawn 46. Smash-Up 47. They Won't Believe Me 47. The Lost Moment 47. Tap Roots 48. The Saxon Charm 48. *Tulsa* 49. *My Foolish Heart* 49. House of Strangers 49. I'd Climb the Highest Mountain 50. *I Can Get It For You Wholesale* 51. Rawhide 51. David and Bathsheba 51. *With a Song in My Heart* 52. The Lusty Men 52. The Snows of Kilimanjaro 52. The President's Lady 53. White Witch Doctor 53. Demetrius and the Gladiators 54. Garden of Evil 54. Untamed 55. Soldier of Fortune 55. The Conqueror 55. *I'll Cry Tomorrow* (as Lilian Roth) 55. Top Secret Affair 57. *I Want To Live* (as Barbara Graham) (AA) 58. A Woman Obsessed 59. Thunder in the Sun 59. The Marriage-Go Round 60. Ada 61. Back Street 61. Stolen Hours (GB) 63. I Thank a Fool (GB) 63. Where Love Has Gone 64. The Honey Pot 67. Valley of the Dolls 67. Fitzgerald and Pride (TV) 71. The Revengers 72. Say Goodbye Maggie Cole (TV) 72.

Hayworth, Rita (1918–) (Margarita Carmen Cansino). Star American leading lady and dancer of the forties, often in tempestuous roles; on stage from six years old; of Latin-Irish ancestry.
□ Dante's Inferno 35. Under the Pampas Moon 35. Charlie Chan in Egypt 35. Paddy O'Day 35. Human Cargo 36. A Message to Garcia 36. Meet Nero Wolfe 36. Rebellion 36. Old Louisiana 37. Hit the Saddle 37. Trouble in Texas 37. Criminals of the Air 37. Girls Can Play 37. The Game that Kills 37. Paid to Dance 37. The Shadow 37. Who Killed Gail Preston? 38. There's Always a Woman 38. Convicted 38. Juvenile Court 38. Homicide Bureau 38. The Lone Wolf's Spy Hunt 39. Renegade Ranger 39. *Only Angels Have Wings* 39. Special Inspector 39. Music in My Heart 40. Blondie on a Budget 40. Susan and God 40. *The Lady in Question* 40. Angels over Broadway 40. *The Strawberry Blonde* 41. Affectionately Yours 41. Blood and Sand 41. *You'll Never Get Rich* 41. My Gal Sal 42. Tales of Manhattan 42. You Were Never Lovelier 42. *Cover Girl* 44. Tonight and Every Night 45. *Gilda* 46. Down to Earth 47. *The Lady from Shanghai* 48. The Loves of Carmen 48. Affair in Trinidad 52. Salome 53. *Miss Sadie Thompson* 53. Fire Down Below 57. *Pal Joey* 57. *Separate Tables* 58. They Came to Cordura 59. The Story on Page One 59. The Happy Thieves 62. Circus World 64. The Money Trap 66. The Poppy is also a Flower 67. The Rover 68. Sons of Satan 68. The Road to Salina 70. The Wrath of God 72.

Hazell, Hy (1920–1970) (Hyacinth Hazel O'Higgins). British revue and musical comedy artist.
Meet Me at Dawn 46. Paper Orchid 49. Celia 49. The Lady Craved Excitement 50. The Night Won't Talk 52. Up in the World 56. The Whole Truth 58, etc.

Head, Edith (1907–). American dress designer, in Hollywood since the twenties. First solo credit *She Done Him Wrong* 33; later won Academy Awards for The Heiress 49. Samson and Delilah 51. A Place in the Sun 52, etc. Appears in *The Oscar* 66.
Autobiography 1940: *The Dress Doctor*.

Healy, Ted (1886–1937). Tough-looking, cigar-chewing American vaudevillian who originated the Three Stooges and took them to Hollywood.
Soup to Nuts 30. Dancing Lady 33. The Band Plays On 34. Mad Love 35. San Francisco 36. Hollywood Hotel 37, etc.

Hearne, Richard (1908–). British acrobatic comedian, in music hall and circus practically from the cradle. Has made occasional films, often in his character of 'Mr Pastry'.
Dance Band 35. Millions 37. Miss London Ltd 42. The Butler's Dilemma 43. One Night with You 48. Helter Skelter 49. Captain Horatio Hornblower 50. Madame Louise 51. Miss Robin Hood 52. Something in the City 53. Tons of Trouble 56, etc.

Hearst, William Randolph (1863–1950). American newspaper magnate thought to have been the original of *Citizen Kane*. Also noted for pushing his protégée Marion Davies (qv) to film stardom by buying a production company solely for her vehicles.
Biography 1961: *Citizen Hearst* by W. A. Swanberg.

Heatherton, Joey (1944–). American leading lady, former child stage performer.
Twilight of Honor 64. Where Love Has Gone 64. My Blood Runs Cold 64. Bluebeard 72, etc.

Heaven: see *fantasy*.

Heaven Can Wait (US 1943). One of the most charming, polished and unexpected comedies of Ernst Lubitsch, this half-forgotten film drew surprisingly warm performances from Don Ameche and Gene Tierney, the former as a lately deceased gentleman describing his youthful follies to a sauve and sympathetic Satan in a very luxurious version of Hell. Script by Samson Raphaelson from Laslo Bus-Fekete's play *Birthday*. The period settings and fantasy endpapers, all in colour, made it a great success in the middle of World War II.

Heavens Above (GB 1963). The Boulting Brothers' long-awaited satire on the church turned out to be a long-drawn-out sentimental comedy which pulled its punches and drifted too often into tedious irrelevance. Peter Sellers made a dull fellow of the proletarian parson, but there were compensations in the contributions of Cecil Parker, Miles Malleson and Ian Carmichael as church dignitaries.

Hecht, Ben (1894–1964). American writer and critic with screenplay credits going back to silent days. Often worked in collaboration with Charles MacArthur.
Autobiographies: *A Child of the Century, Gaily Gaily*.
Underworld (w) (AA) 28. The Great Gabbo (oa) 29. *The Front Page* (oa) 31. Topaze (w) 33. Twentieth Century (oa) 34. *Crime Without Passion* (wd) 34. *The Scoundrel* (wd) (AA) 35. *Soak the Rich* (wpd) 36. *Nothing Sacred* (w) 37. The Goldwyn Follies (w) 38. *Wuthering Heights* (w) 39. *Angels Over Broadway* (wpd) 40. Lydia (w) 41. Tales of Manhattan (w) 42. The Black Swan (w) 42. *Spellbound* (w) 45. *Notorious* (w) 46. The Specter of the Rose (wpd) 46. Her Husband's Affairs (w) 47. The Miracle of the Bells (w) 48. Whirlpool (w) 49. Actors and Sin (wpd) 52. Monkey Business (w) 52. Miracle in the Rain (w) 56. Legend of the Lost (w) 58. Circus World (w) 64, etc.

Hecht, Harold (1907–). American producer, formerly dance director and literary agent. From 1947 produced jointly with Burt Lancaster and later James Hill.
Vera Cruz 54. Marty 55. Trapeze 56. Separate Tables 58. Taras Bulba 63. Cat Ballou 65. The Way West 67, etc.

Heckart, Eileen (1919–). American character actress, mainly on stage.
Miracle in the Rain 56. The Bad Seed 56. Somebody Up There Likes Me 57. Hot Spell 57. Heller in Pink Tights 60. Up the Down Staircase 68. No Way to Treat a Lady 68. Butterflies Are Free (AA) 72, etc.

Heckroth, Hein (1901–1970). German art director who did work in Britain, mainly for Powell and Pressburger.
Caesar and Cleopatra 45. *A Matter of Life and*

Death 46. *The Red Shoes* (AA) 48. Tales of Hoffman 51. The Story of Gilbert and Sullivan 53. The Battle of the River Plate 56. Torn Curtain (US) 66, etc.

Hedison, David (formerly **Al Hedison**) (1928–) (Ara Heditsian). American leading man, mostly on TV.
The Enemy Below 57. *The Fly* 58. Son of Robin Hood 59. The Lost World 60. Marines Let's Go 61. The Greatest Story Ever Told 65. Live and Let Die 73, etc.
TV series: *Five Fingers* 59. *Voyage to the Bottom of the Sea* 63–67.

Hedley, Jack (1930–). Amiable British leading man best remembered as TV's 'Tim Frazer'.
Room at the Top (debut) 59. Make Mine Mink 60. Lawrence of Arabia 62. In the French Style 63. The Scarlet Blade 63. *Of Human Bondage* 64. Witchcraft 65. The Anniversary 67. Goodbye Mr Chips 69. Brief Encounter (TV) 74, etc.

Hedren, Tippi (1935–). American leading lady, former TV model.
□ *The Birds* 63. Marnie 64. A Countess from Hong Kong 66. The Man with the Albatross 69. Tiger by the Tail 69. Satan's Harvest 69. Mr Kingstreet's War 73. The Harrad Experiment 73.

Heerman, Victor (1892–). American director.
□ Personality 30. Animal Crackers 30. Sea Legs 30. Paramount on Parade (co-d) 30.

Heffron, Richard (–). American director, from TV.
Newman's Law 73.

Heflin, Van (1910–1971) (Emmett Evan Heflin). Purposeful American leading man of the forties, craggy character actor of the fifties and sixties.
□ A Woman Rebels 36. The Outcasts of Poker Flat 37. Flight from Glory 37. Saturday's Heroes 37. Annapolis Salute 37. Back Door to Heaven 39. *Santa Fe Trail* 40. The Feminine Touch 41. H. M. Pulham Esq 41. *Johnny Eager* (AA) 41. *Kid Glove Killer* 42. Seven Sweethearts 42. Grand Central Murder 42. Tennessee Johnson 42. Presenting Lily Mars 43. *The Strange Love of Martha Ivers* 46. Till the Clouds Roll By 46. Possessed 47. Green Dolphin Street 47. Tap Roots 48. B.F.'s Daughter 48. The Three Musketeers 48. Act of Violence 48. Madame Bovary 48. East Side West Side 49. Tomahawk

51. *The Prowler* 51. Weekend with Father 51. My Son John 52. Wings of the Hawk 53. *Shane* 53. Tanganyika 54. South of Algiers (GB) 54. The Raid 54. Woman's World 54. The Black Widow 54. Count Three and Pray 55. Battle Cry 55. *Patterns* 56. *3.10 to Yuma* 57. Gunman's Walk 58. They Came to Cordura 59. Tempest 59. Five Branded Women 60. Under Ten Flags 60. Cry of Battle 63. The Wastrel 64. To Be a Man 64. The Greatest Story Ever Told 65. Once a Thief 65. Stagecoach 66. The Man Outside (GB) 67. Each Man for Himself 68. *Airport* 69. The Big Bounce 69. The Last Child (TV) 71.

Heggie, O. P. (1879–1936). Scottish character actor of stage and, latterly, screen.
The Mysterious Dr Fu Manchu 29. East Lynne 31. Smiling Through 32. Midnight 34. Bride of Frankenstein (as the blind hermit) 35. Prisoner of Shark Island 36, etc.

Heifits, Joseph (1904–). Russian director, from 1928. Known in thirties for *Baltic Deputy*, but did not come to western notice again until *The Lady with the Little Dog* 59. In the Town of S 65. Salute Marya 70.

Heindorf, Ray (c. 1910–). American musical director.
Hard to Get 38. Strawberry Blonde 41. Yankee Doodle Dandy (AA) 42. Calamity Jane 53. A Star is Born 54. The Music Man 62. Finian's Rainbow 68, many others.

Heinz, Gerard (1903–1972). German character actor, mainly in British movies.
Thunder Rock 42. Went the Day Well? 42. Caravan 46. His Excellency 51. The Man Inside 57. House of the Seven Hawks 59. The Guns of Navarone 61. The Cardinal 63. The Dirty Dozen 67, many others.

The Heiress (US 1949). Oscars for best actress (Olivia de Havilland) and best art direction and costume design were won by this adaptation of the play by Ruth and Augustus Goetz from Henry James' novel *Washington Square*, about an unattractive spinster who finally turns the tables on her money-seeking suitor. With Montgomery Clift, Ralph Richardson; directed by William Wyler.

Heisler, Stuart (1894–). Competent American director.
□ The Biscuit Eater 40. *The Monster and The Girl* 41. Among the Living 41. The Remarkable Andrew 42. *The Glass Key* 42. Along Came Jones 45. *Blue Skies* 46. *Smash Up* 47. Tulsa 49. Tokyo Joe 49. Chain Lightning 50. Dallas 50.

Storm Warning 50. Journey into Light 51. Saturday Island 52. *The Star* 53. Beachhead 54. This is My Love 54. I Died a Thousand Times 55. The Lone Ranger 56. The Burning Hills 56. Hitler 62.

Heiss, Carol (1940–). German-Swiss skating star: she came to Hollywood for one movie, *Snow White and the Three Stooges* 61.

helicopters, restricted in scope, have been put to sound dramatic use in two films about helicopter services, *Battle Taxi* and *Flight from Ashiya*; while their potential for thrill sequences was well explored in *The Bridges at Toko-Ri*, *Experiment in Terror*, *From Russia with Love*, *Arabesque*, *Caprice*, *You Only Live Twice*, *The Satan Bug*, *Fathom*, *The Las Vegas Story*, *Where Eagles Dare*, *Masquerade*, *Tarzan in the Valley of Gold*, *That Riviera Touch*, *The Wrecking Crew*, *Figures in a Landscape*, *Birds of Prey*, *Breakout* and *Russian Roulette*. TV series on the subject include *Chopper One* and *Chopper Squad*. See also *airplanes*.

hell has been used more figuratively than realistically in movies; but what passed for the real thing did appear in *Dante's Inferno*, *Heaven Can Wait*, *Hellzapoppin* and *Angel on My Shoulder*, not to mention a Sylvester cartoon called *Satan's Waitin'*.

Heller, Lukas (1930–). German-born screenwriter, associated chiefly with Robert Aldrich.
Whatever Happened to Baby Jane? 62. Hush Hush Sweet Charlotte (co-w) 64. The Dirty Dozen (co-w) 67. The Killing of Sister George 68. The Deadly Trackers 73, etc.

Heller, Otto (1896–1970). Czech-born cinematographer, in Britain since early thirties. Had more than 300 features to his credit.
The High Command 36. Tomorrow We Live 42. Mr Emmanuel 44. I Live in Grosvenor Square 45. *The Queen of Spades* 48. The Winslow Boy 48. Never Take No for an Answer 51. The Divided Heart 54. Manuela 57. The Light in the Piazza 62. West Eleven 63. The Ipcress File 65. Alfie 66. Funeral in Berlin 66. Duffy 68. Bloomfield 70, etc.

Hellinger, Mark (1903–1947). American journalist who scripted some films and later turned producer.
Biography 1952: *The Mark Hellinger Story* by Jim Bishop.
The Killers 46. Brute Force 47. Naked City 47.

Hellman, Lillian (1905–). American playwright who has adapted much of her own work for the screen and also written other screenplays.
Autobiographies: 1969, *An Unfinished Woman*. 1974, *Pentimento* 74.
These Three 36. *The Little Foxes* 41. Watch on the Rhine 43. North Star 43. The Searching Wind 46. *Another Part of the Forest* 48. *The Children's Hour* 62. Toys in the Attic 63. The Chase 66, etc.

Hellman, Marcel (1898–). Rumanian producer, long in Britain.
The Amateur Gentleman 36. Jeannie 41. Happy Go Lucky 51. Northwest Frontier 59. Moll Flanders 65, many others.

Hellman, Monte (1931–). American director of cheapies.
□ The Beast from Haunted Cave 59. Flight to Fury 65. Back Door to Hell 65. The Shooting 65. Ride the Whirlwind 71. Two Lane Blacktop 71. Cockfighter 74. Shatter 74.

Hell's Angels (US 1927–1930). Started as a silent and re-shot for sound, this aerial spectacular of World War I, produced and directed by Howard Hughes, still survives by virtue of its highly dramatic combat scenes, including a zeppelin raid over London. The personal story is badly dated, though the scene in which Jean Harlow allures Ben Lyon by changing into 'something more comfortable' is not to be missed.

Hellzapoppin (US 1942). Directed by H. C. Potter from the stage show starring Ole Olsen and Chic Johnson, this crazy farce now seems insufficiently daring: there's actually a plot and a love interest! Many of the gags, however, still work, and as a whole it was more successful in popularizing this kind of entertainment than the Marx Brothers had been.

Helm, Brigitte (1906–) (Gisele Eve Schittenhelm). German star actress of the twenties.
Metropolis 26. *The Loves of Jeanne Ney* 27. Alraune 28. Countess of Monte Cristo 31. L'Atlantide 31. Gold 33. The Blue Danube 34, etc.

Helm, Fay (c. 1910–). American actress.
Racket Busters 38. Dark Victory 39. A Child Is Born 40. Night Monster 42. Phantom Lady (title role) 44. Sister Kenny 46. The Locket 47, etc.

Helpmann, Robert (1909–). Australian ballet dancer and actor of stage and screen, in Britain since 1930.
One of Our Aircraft Is Missing 42. Henry V 44. The Red Shoes 48. Tales of Hoffman 50. 55 Days in Peking 62. The Quiller Memorandum 66. Chitty Chitty Bang Bang 68. Alice's Adventures in Wonderland 72. Don Quixote (& co-d) 73, others.

Helton, Percy (1894–1971). Chubby little American comedy actor; his round face expressed surprise and dismay in innumerable small roles.
Silver Wings 22. Miracle on 34th Street 47. The Set Up 49. My Friend Irma 49. Call Me Madam 52. A Star is Born 54. Butch Cassidy and the Sundance Kid 69, many others.

Hemingway, Ernest (1899–1961). Distinguished American novelist. Works filmed include *A Farewell to Arms* 32 and 57. *Spanish Earth* (original screenplay and production) 37. *For Whom the Bell Tolls* 43. *The Killers* 46 and 64. *The Macomber Affair* 47. *The Snows of Kilimanjaro* 53. *The Sun Also Rises* 57. *The Old Man and the Sea* 58. *Hemingway's Adventures of a Young Man* 62. *To Have and Have Not* was filmed three times (inaccurately); in 1944, 1951 (as *The Breaking Point*) and 1956 (as *The Gun Runner*).

Hemmings, David (1941–). Slightly-built British leading man who after appearing in many second features suddenly seemed to have the acceptable image for the late sixties.
No Trees in the Street 59. The Wind of Change 60. Some People 62. Live It Up 63. Dateline Diamonds 65. Eye of the Devil 66. *Blow Up* 66. Camelot 67. *The Charge of the Light Brigade* 68. A Long Day's Dying 68. Only When I Larf 68. Barbarella 68. Alfred the Great 69. The Walking Stick 69. Fragment of Fear 69. Unman Wittering and Zigo 70. The Love Machine 71. Running Scared (d only) 72. The Squeeze 77, etc.

Henabery, Joseph (1886–1976). American silent actor who played Lincoln in *The Birth of a Nation* and later directed Gish and Fairbanks.
His Majesty the American 19. A Sainted Devil 24, etc.

Henderson, Florence (–). American singer and actress.
Song of Norway 70. The Brady Bunch (TV series) 71–74.

Henderson, Marcia (1950–). American leading lady of the fifties.
Thunder Bay 53. The Glass Web 53. Naked

Alibi 54. Back to God's Country 54, etc.

Hendrix, Wanda (1928–). American leading lady.
Confidential Agent 45. Ride the Pink Horse 47. Miss Tatlock's Millions 48. Prince of Foxes 49. Captain Carey USA 50. The Highwayman 52. The Last Posse 53. The Black Dakotas 54. Johnny Cool 63. Stage to Thunder Rock 65, etc.

Hendry, Ian (1931–). Virile, aggressive, British leading actor, mostly on TV.
In the Nick 60. Live Now Pay Later 62. The Girl in the Headlines 53. Children of the Damned 63. This is My Street 63. *The Beauty Jungle* 64. Repulsion 65. The Hill 65. The Sandwich Man 66. Casino Royale 67. Doppelganger 69. The Southern Star 69. The Mackenzie Break 70. Get Carter 71. The Jerusalem File 72. All Coppers Are . . . 72. Tales from the Crypt 72. Theatre of Blood 73. Assassin 73. The Internecine Project 74, etc.

Henie, Sonja (1910–1969). Norwegian skating star who appeared in light Hollywood musicals of the thirties and forties.
Autobiography 1940: *Wings on My Feet*.
□ *One in a Million* 36. Thin Ice 37. Happy Landing 38. My Lucky Star 38. Second Fiddle 39. Everything Happens at Night 39. Sun Valley Serenade 41. Iceland 42. Wintertime 43. It's a Pleasure 45. The Countess of Monte Cristo 48. Hello London (GB) 58.

Henreid, Paul (1907–) (Paul von Hernreid). Austrian leading man of the thirties; fled to Britain, then to Hollywood, where his immobile good looks made him a suitable leading man, in the absence at war of home-grown talent, for a number of strong-willed leading ladies.
□ *Goodbye Mr Chips* 39. *Night Train to Munich* 40. Joan of Paris 41. *Now Voyager* 42. Casablanca 42. In Our Time 44. Between Two Worlds 44. The Conspirators 44. The Spanish Main 45. Devotion 46. Of Human Bondage 46. Deception 46. Song of Love 47. The Scar 48. Rope of Sand 49. So Young So Bad 50. Last of the Buccaneers 50. For Men Only (& pd) 51. Thief of Damascus 52. Siren of Baghdad 53. Pirates of Tripoli 55. A Woman's Devotion (& d) 57. Holiday for Lovers 59. The Four Horsemen of the Apocalypse 62. Dead Ringer (d only) 64. Operation Crossbow 65. Mrs R (TV) 75, etc.

Henrey, Bobby (1939–). British child actor, notable in *The Fallen Idol* 48. Retired after *The Wonder Kid* 50.

Henry Aldrich, the accident-prone American

teenager of the forties, created on radio by Ezra Stone, was played by Jimmy Lydon in a number of small-town comedies of the forties, with Charles Smith as his friend Dizzy.

Henry, Buck (1930–) (B. Zuckerman). Mild-looking American actor-writer of abrasive comedy.
The Troublemaker (w) 64. The Graduate (w) 67. Candy (w) 68. *Catch 22* (w) 70. The Owl and the Pussycat (w) 70. *Taking Off* (a) 71. The Day of the Dolphin (w) 73.

Henry, Charlotte (1916–). American juvenile actress of the early thirties.
Rebecca of Sunnybrook Farm 32. Alice in Wonderland 33. Babes in Toyland 34. Charlie Chan at the Opera 37. Stand and Deliver (last to date) 41, etc.

Henry, Mike (1939–). American ex-athlete who came to the screen briefly as Tarzan.
Tarzan and the Valley of Gold 65. Tarzan and the Great River 67. Tarzan and the Jungle Boy 68. Skyjacked 72, etc.

Henry, O. (1862–1910) (William Sydney Porter). American story writer who for the last ten years of his life wrote a weekly story for the *New York World*. A compendium of them was used in *O. Henry's Full House* 52, and there followed a TV series, *The O. Henry Playhouse* 56.

Henry V (GB 1944). Laurence Olivier directed this Shakespearean spectacular, timed for victory, and also starred in it. The method of starting in the Globe Theatre, moving gradually into reality for the battle and then returning was controversial, but in general the production could not have been more splendid. Leslie Banks, Robert Newton and Leo Genn stood out in a remarkable cast, and the Agincourt charge sequence is justly famous. Photographed in Technicolor by Robert Krasker, with music by William Walton.

Henry, William (1918–). American leading man, former child actor, later in callow roles.
Lord Jim 26. The Thin Man 34. Tarzan Escapes 36. Four Men and a Prayer 38. Blossoms in the Dust 41. Women in Bondage 44. Federal Man 49. Jungle Moonmen 54. Mister Roberts 55. The Lone Ranger and the Lost City of Gold 58. How the West Was Won 62, etc.

Henson, Gladys (1897–) (Gladys Gunn). Irish character actress often seen as plump, homely mum, or latterly grand-mum. On stage

from 1910.
The Captive Heart 45. It Always Rains on Sunday 47. *London Belongs to Me* 48. *The Blue Lamp* 50. Lady Godiva Rides Again 51. Those People Next Door 52. Cockleshell Heroes 55. The Leather Boys 63, etc.

Henson, Leslie (1891–1957). British stage comedian with bulging eyes; often in musical farces.
The Sport of Kings 30. It's a Boy 33. A Warm Corner 34. Oh Daddy 35. The Demi-Paradise 43. Home and Away 56, etc.

Henson, Nicky (1945–). British general purpose actor.
Witchfinder General 68. There's a Girl in My Soup 70. All Coppers Are 71. Penny Gold 72. Vampira 74. The Bawdy Adventures of Tom Jones 76.

Hepburn, Audrey (1929–) (Audrey Hepburn-Ruston). Belgian-born star actress of Irish-Dutch parentage; after small parts in English films, rose rapidly to Hollywood stardom as elegant gamine.
☐ One Wild Oat 51. Young Wives' Tale 51. Laughter in Paradise 51. The Lavender Hill Mob 51. Monte Carlo Baby 52. The Secret People 52. *Roman Holiday* (AA, BFA) 53. Sabrina 54. *War and Peace* 56. *Funny Face* 57. Love in the Afternoon 57. *The Nun's Story* (BFA) 59. Green Mansions 59. The Unforgiven 60. Breakfast at Tiffany's 61. The Children's Hour 62. Charade 63. Paris When it Sizzles 64. My Fair Lady 64. How to Steal a Million 66. Two for the Road 66. *Wait Until Dark* 67. Robin and Marian 76.

Hepburn, Katharine (1907–). Dominant American star actress with Bryn Mawr personality; one of the most durable, talented and likeable interpreters of emancipated feminine roles.
Biographies 1973, *Tracey and Hepburn* by Garson Kanin. 1976, *Kate* by Charles Higham.
☐ *A Bill of Divorcement* 32. Christopher Strong 33. *Morning Glory* (AA) 33. *Little Women* 33. Spitfire 34. Break of Hearts 34. The Little Minister 34. Alice Adams 35. Sylvia Scarlett 35. Mary of Scotland 36. A Woman Rebels 36. Quality Street 37. *Stage Door* 37. *Bringing Up Baby* 38. Holiday 38. *The Philadelphia Story* 40. *Woman of the Year* 42. Keeper of the Flame 42. Stage Door Canteen 43. Dragon Seed 44. Without Love 45. Undercurrent 46. Sea of Grass 47. Song of Love 47. State of the Union 48. *Adam's Rib* 49. *The African Queen* 51. *Pat and Mike* 52. *Summer Madness* 55. The Rainmaker 56. The Iron Petticoat (GB) 56. *Desk Set* 57.

Suddenly Last Summer 59. *Long Day's Journey Into Night* 62. *Guess Who's Coming to Dinner* (AA) 67. *The Lion in Winter* (AA, BFA) 68. The Madwoman of Chaillot 69. The Trojan Women 71. A Delicate Balance 73. Rooster Cogburn 75.

Hepworth, Cecil (1874–1953). Pioneer British film producer-director. For many years had his own stock company of stars and was financially successful, though his films were old-fashioned and sentimental. Wrote first book on Cinema 1897: *Animated Photography*.
Autobiography 1951: *Came the Dawn*.
The Quarrelsome Anglers 98. Two Cockneys in a Canoe 99. Wiping Something off the Slate 00. How it Feels to be Run Over 00. The Glutton's Nightmare 01. Alice in Wonderland 03. Firemen to the Rescue 03. Rescued by Rover 05. Blind Fate 12. His Country's Bidding 14. The Canker of Jealousy 14. The Man Who Stayed at Home 15. Trelawney of the Wells 16. Annie Laurie 16. Comin' Through the Rye 16. Nearer My God to Thee 17. The Touch of a Child 18. The Forest on the Hill 19. Alf's Button 20. Wild Heather 21. The Pipes of Pan 22. Strangling Threads 22. *Comin' Through the Rye* (remake) 24. The House of Marney 27, many others.

Herbert, F. Hugh (1897–1957). American comedy screenwriter.
Adam and Evil 27. Hotel Continental 32. If You Could Only Cook (oa) 35. That Certain Age (oa) 38. Melody Ranch 40. West Point Widow 41. Together Again 44. *Kiss and Tell* (& oa) 45. Home Sweet Homicide 46. *Margie* 46. Scudda Hoo Scudda Hay (& d) 48. *Sitting Pretty* 48. Our Very Own 50. The Girls of Pleasure Island (& d) 53. *The Moon is Blue* (& oa) 53. The Little Hut 57, many others.

Herbert, Holmes (1882–1956) (Edward Sanger). British stage actor, on the Hollywood screen from 1917, usually in quiet British roles—butler, lawyer or clerk.
Gentlemen Prefer Blondes 27. The Terror 28. Dr Jekyll and Mr Hyde 32. The Mystery of the Wax Museum 33. Mark of the Vampire 35. Lloyds of London 37. Stanley and Livingstone 39. This Above All 42. The Uninvited 44. Sherlock Holmes and the Secret Code (Dressed to Kill) 46. David and Bathsheba 51. The Brigand 52, etc.

Herbert, Hugh (1887–1952). American eccentric comedian, remembered for nervous 'woo woo' exclamation.
Caught in the Fog 28. Laugh and Get Rich 31. The Lost Squadron 32. Strictly Personal 33. Convention City 33. Wonder Bar 34. Dames 34. A Midsummer Night's Dream 35. One Rainy

Afternoon 36. Top of the Town 37. Gold Diggers in Paris 38. The Great Waltz 38. Eternally Yours 39. La Conga Nights 40. The Black Cat 41. *Hellzapoppin* 41. Cracked Nuts 42. Mrs Wiggs of the Cabbage Patch 42. There's One Born Every Minute 43. Kismet 44. Men in Her Diary 45. Carnegie Hall 46. A Song is Born 48. The Beautiful Blonde from Bashful Bend 49. Havana Rose 51, many others.

Herbert, Percy (1925–). British character actor, usually seen as cockney rating or private.
The Baby and the Battleship 56. The Bridge on the River Kwai 57. *Tunes of Glory* 61. Mysterious Island 62. Mutiny on the Bounty 63. One Million Years BC 66. Tobruk (US) 66. The Viking Queen 67. The Royal Hunt of the Sun 69. Man in the Wilderness 71. Captain Apache 71. Doomwatch 72. Craze 73.
TV series: Cimarron Strip 67.

Here Comes Mr Jordan (US 1941). This 'heavenly' comedy, from Harry Segal's play about a boxer who dies too early and is sent back to earth only to find that his body has been cremated, was a great success in wartime America and had several imitators. Directed by Alexander Hall, with Robert Montgomery, Claude Rains, Edward Everett Horton, James Gleason.

Herlie, Eileen (1919–) (Eileen Herlihy). Scottish stage actress who has made occasional films.
Hungry Hill (debut) 47. Hamlet 48. The Angel with the Trumpet 49. The Story of Gilbert and Sullivan 53. Isn't Life Wonderful? 53. For Better For Worse 54. She Didn't Say No 58. Freud 62. The Seagull 68.

Hernandez, Juano (1900–1970). Black American character actor with powerful presence.
Intruder in the Dust 48. The Breaking Point 50. *Young Man with a Horn* 50. Kiss Me Deadly 55. Trial 55. Ransom 56. Something of Value 57. The Pawnbroker 64. The Extraordinary Seaman 68, etc.

Herrmann, Bernard (1911–1975). American composer and orchestral conductor.
□ *Citizen Kane* 41. *All that Money Can Buy* (AA) 41. *The Magnificent Ambersons* 42. Jane Eyre 43. Hangover Square 45. Anna and the King of Siam 46. The Ghost and Mrs Muir 47. The Day the Earth Stood Still 51. On Dangerous Ground 51. Five Fingers 52. The Snows of Kilimanjaro 52. White Witch Doctor 53. Beneath the 12-mile Reef 53. King of the Khyber

Rifles 53. Garden of Evil 54. The Egyptian 54. Prince of Players 55. The Kentuckian 55. *The Trouble with Harry* 56. The Man in the Grey Flannel Suit 56. The Man who Knew Too Much 56. The Wrong Man 57. A Hatful of Rain 57. Vertigo 58. The Naked and the Dead 58. The Seventh Voyage of Sinbad 58. *North by Northwest* 59. Blue Denim 59. Journey to the Centre of the Earth 59. *Psycho* 60. The Three Worlds of Gulliver 60. Mysterious Island 61. Cape Fear 61. Tender is the Night 62. Jason and the Argonauts 63. Marnie 64. Joy in the Morning 65. Fahrenheit 451 66. The Bride wore Black 67. Twisted Nerve 69. Obsessions 69. The Battle of Neretva 70. The Night Diggers 71. Sisters 73. It's Alive 74. *Taxi Driver* 76.

Hershey, Barbara (1948–) (Barbara Hertzstein: now known as Barbara Seagull). American leading lady of the seventies.
With Six You Get Egg Roll 68. Last Summer 69. The Liberation of L. B. Jones 69. The Pursuit of Happiness 69. The Baby Maker 71. Boxcar Bertha 72, etc.
TV series: *The Monroes* 66.

Hersholt, Jean (1886–1956). Phlegmatic Danish character actor in Hollywood.
Princess Virtue 16. The Four Horsemen of the Apocalypse 21. *Greed* 23. Stella Dallas 25. The Secret Hour 28. Abie's Irish Rose 28. The Rise of Helga 30. Transatlantic 31. *Grand Hotel* 32. The Mask of Fu Manchu 32. Christopher Bean 35. Mark of the Vampire 35. Seventh Heaven 35. Heidi 37. Alexander's Ragtime Band 38. Meet Doctor Christian (and ensuing series) 38–40. They Meet Again 41. Stage Door Canteen 43. Dancing in the Dark 49. Run for Cover 55, others.

Herzog, Werner (1942–). German director.
Signs of Life 67. Even Dwarfs Started Small 70. Fata Morgana 71. The Land of Darkness and Silence 71. *Aguirre Wrath of God* 73.

Hervey, Irene (c. 1916–) (Irene Herwick). American leading lady of light films in the forties.
Three on a Honeymoon 34. East Side of Heaven 39. Destry Rides Again 39. Unseen Enemy 42. Half Way to Shanghai 43. My Guy 44. Mr Peabody and the Mermaid 49. Teenage Rebel 56. Going Steady 59. Cactus Flower 69, etc.
TV series: Honey West 64.

Heslop, Charles (1884–1966). British comic actor, longtime star of stage farces.
Waltzes from Vienna 33. The Lambeth Walk 39. Flying Fortress 42. The Late Edwina Black 51. Follow a Star 59.

Hessler, Gordon (1930–). American director
in Britain.
The Last Shot You Hear 64. The Oblong Box (&
p) 69. Scream and Scream Again 70. Cry of the
Banshee (& p) 70. Murders in the Rue Morgue
(& p) 71. Embassy 72. Sinbad's Golden Voyage
73, etc.

Heston, Charlton (1924–). Stalwart
American leading actor with stage experience;
seemed likely for a time to become typed in
biblical and medieval epics.
☐ Dark City 50. The Greatest Show on Earth 52.
The Savage 52. Ruby Gentry 52. The President's
Lady (as Andrew Jackson) 52. Pony Express 53.
Arrowhead 53. Bad for Each Other 54. The
Naked Jungle 54. The Secret of the Incas 54. The
Far Horizons 55. The Private War of Major
Benson 55. Lucy Gallant 55. *The Ten
Commandments* (as Moses) 56. Three Violent
People 56. Touch of Evil 58. The Big Country
58. The Buccaneer 58. The Wreck of the Mary
Deare 59. Ben Hur (AA) 59. El Cid 61. The
Pigeon that Took Rome 62. Diamond Head 62.
55 Days at Peking 63. The Greatest Story Every
Told 65. Major Dundee 65. The Agony and the
Ecstasy (as Michelangelo) 65. *The War Lord* 65.
Khartoum (as General Gordon) 66.
Counterpoint 67. *Planet of the Apes* 67. *Will
Penny* 68. Number One 69. Beneath the Planet of
the Apes 69. Julius Caesar 70.The Hawaiians 70.
The Omega Man 71. Antony and Cleopatra (&
d) 71. Skyjacked 72. Soylent Green 73. The
Three Musketeers 73. The Four Musketeers 74.
The Last Hard Men 76. Two Minute Morning
76.

Heydt, Louis Jean (1905–1960). American
character actor, often seen as a man with
something to hide.
Test Pilot 38. Each Dawn I Die 39. Gone with
the Wind 39. Dive Bomber 41. Our Vines Have
Tender Grapes 45. The Furies 50. The Eternal
Sea 55, many others.

Heyer, John (1916–). Australian
documentarist, former cameraman; with the
Shell Film Unit 1948–56.
The Back of Beyond 54. Playing with Water 54.
The Forerunner 57. Tumult Pond 62, etc.

Heyes, Douglas (1923–). American director,
from TV.
Kitten with a Whip 65. Beau Geste 67, etc.

Heyman, John (1933–). British agent and
producer.
Privilege 66. Boom! 68. Secret Ceremony 69.
Twinky 70. Bloomfield 71. The Go-Between 71,
etc.

Heywood, Anne (1931–) (Violet Pretty).
British leading lady, former beauty contestant.
Find the Lady 55. Checkpoint 56. Dangerous
Exile 56. The Depraved 57. Violent Playground
58. Floods of Fear 58. Upstairs and Downstairs
59. A Terrible Beauty 60. Petticoat Pirates 61
Stork Talk 62. Vengeance 62. The Very Edge 62.
Ninety Degrees in the Shade 66. *The Fox* 68. The
Chairman 69. The Awful Story of the Nun of
Monza (It) 69. The Midas Run 69. I Want What
I Want 71. Trader Horn 73. The Nun and the
Devil (It) 73, etc.

Heywood, Pat (1927–). British character
actress.
Romeo and Juliet 68. All the Way Up 69. 10
Rillington Place 71. Who Slew Auntie Roo? 72,
etc.

Hibbert, Geoffrey (1922–1969). British actor
who played callow youths around 1940 but
turned rather quickly into a character man.
Love on the Dole 41. The Common Touch 42.
Next of Kin 42. Orders to Kill 58. Crash Drive
59, etc.

Hibbs, Jesse (1906–). American director,
mainly of routine 'B' features.
☐ The All American 53. Ride Clear of Diablo 54.
Black Horse Canyon 54. Rails into Laramie 54.
The Yellow Mountain 54. To Hell and Back 55.
The Spoilers 55. World in My Corner 56. Walk
the Proud Land 56. Joe Butterfly 57. Ride a
Crooked Trail 58.

Hibler, Winston (1911–1976). American
producer, almost entirely of wild life material for
Disney.

Hickman, Darryl (1931–). American juvenile
actor who has more recently been seen in heavy
roles.
The Grapes of Wrath 40. Hearts in Springtime
41. Boys' Ranch 45. Dangerous Years 46.
Prisoner of War 53. Tea and Sympathy 54, etc.
TV series: The Blue and the Gold 58.

Hickman, Dwayne (1934–). American
juvenile, former child actor.
Captain Eddie 45. The Return of Rusty 46. The
Sun Comes Up 49. Rally Round the Flag Boys
59. Beach Party 64, others.
TV series: The Affairs of Dobie Gillis 59.

Hickok, Wild Bill (1837–1876). American
frontier gunfighter of wild west days, frequently
personified on screen.
Wild Bill Hickok 21: William S. Hart. *The
Plainsman* 36: Gary Cooper. *Badlands of*

Dakota 41: Richard Dix. *Wild Bill Hickok Rides* 41: Bruce Cabot. *Dallas* 50: Reed Hadley. *Pony Express* 52: Forrest Tucker. *The Lawless Breed* 52: Rock Hudson. *Calamity Jane* 53: Howard Keel. *The Raiders* 55: Robert Culp. *The Plainsman* 66: Don Murray. *Little Big Man* 70: Jeff Corey. Guy Madison starred as Hickok in a TV series (51–57).

Hickox, Douglas (1929–). British director.
□ It's All Over Town 64. Just for You 64. Les Bicyclettes de Belsize 69. Entertaining Mr Sloane 70. Sitting Target 72. Theatre of Blood 73.

Hicks, Russell (1895–1957). American character actor who almost always played executive types. Actor and director from silent days; in hundreds of films.
Laughing Irish Eyes 36. In Old Chicago 38. The Three Musketeers 39. The Big Store 41. His Butler's Sister 43. Bandit of Sherwood Forest 46. Bowery Battalion 51. Seventh Cavalry 56, many others.

Hicks, Sir Seymour (1871–1949). British stage farceur, also writer and producer. Occasional film appearances.
Autobiography 1938: *Night Lights*.
Always Tell Your Wife 22. Sleeping Partners 26. The Secret of the Loch 34. Vintage Wine 35. *Scrooge* 35. Pastor Hall 39. *Busman's Honeymoon* 40. Silent Dust 48, etc.

Hickson, Joan (1906–). British character actress, in innumerable films as understanding mum or slightly dotty aunt.
Widow's Might 34. Love from a Stranger 37. I See a Dark Stranger 45. The Guinea Pig 48. Seven Days to Noon 50. The Card 52. The Man Who Never Was 56. Happy is the Bride 57. The 39 Steps 59. Murder She Said 61. A Day in the Death of Joe Egg 70. Theatre of Blood 73, many others.

High Noon (US 1952). An influential western of classic economy and some symbolism, the action ranging over a few hours during which one man searches desperately for support against a gang of revengeful outlaws. Written by Carl Foreman, directed by Fred Zinnemann, with Gary Cooper and a first-rate cast. The ballad was written by Dmitri Tiomkin.

High Sierra (US 1941). Modish melodrama with Humphrey Bogart as a gangster on the run and Ida Lupino as the girl who befriends him too late. Gloomily directed by Raoul Walsh, from a script by W. R. Burnett and John Huston; chiefly notable for its early example of an anti-hero.

Remade 1955 by Stuart Heisler as *I Died a Thousand Times*, with Jack Palance, Shelley Winters, and no flair.

Hildyard, Jack (1908–). British cinematographer.
School for Secrets 46. While the Sun Shines 46. Vice Versa 48. The Sound Barrier 52. Hobson's Choice 54. The Deep Blue Sea 55. Summertime 55. *The Bridge on the River Kwai* (AA) 57. The Journey 59. Suddenly Last Summer 59. The Millionairess 60. 55 Days at Peking 62. The VIPs 63. The Yellow Rolls Royce 64. Battle of the Bulge 66. Casino Royale 67. The Long Duel 67. Villa Rides 68. Topaz 70. Puppet on a Chain 71. The Beast Must Die 74. The Message 76, etc.

The Hill (GB 1965). An engagingly arrant melodrama, played mostly for laughs, about brutalities in a North African prison camp during World War II. This raucous but stylish film unfortunately has pretensions which, coupled with poor sound recording, finally make it seem overblown and empty. But there are compensations in Sidney Lumet's direction, Oswald Morris' harsh photography, and the performances of Harry Andrews, Ian Hendry and Ossie Davis.

Hill, Arthur (1922–). Canadian actor, on British and American stage and screen.
Miss Pilgrim's Progress 49. I Was a Male War Bride 49. Salute the Toff 52. Life with the Lyons 54. The Deep Blue Sea 55. The Ugly American 63. In the Cool of the Day 63. Moment to Moment 65. *Harper* 66. Petulia 68. The Chairman 69. *The Andromeda Strain* 70. The Pursuit of Happiness 70. Futureworld 76, etc.
TV series: *Owen Marshall Counsellor at Law* 71–73.

Hill, Benny (1925–). British vaudeville comedian and mimic.
□ Who Done It? 56. Light Up the Sky 59. Those Magnificent Men in Their Flying Machines 65. Chitty Chitty Bang Bang 68. The Italian Job 69.

Hill, George (1888–1934). American director.
Through the Dark 23. The Midnight Express 24. Zander the Great 25. Tell It to the Marines 26. The Cossacks 28. The Flying Fleet 29. *The Big House* 30. *Min and Bill* 30. The Secret Six 31. Hell Divers 31. Clear all Wires 33, etc.

Hill, George Roy (1922–). American director with New York stage background.
□ Period of Adjustment 63. Toys in the Attic 63. *The World of Henry Orient* 64. Hawaii 66. Thoroughly Modern Millie 67. *Butch Cassidy*

and the Sundance Kid 69. *Slaughterhouse Five*
72. The Sting 73. The Great Waldo Pepper 75.

Hill, James (1919–). British director, former
documentarist.
Journey for Jeremy 47. The Stolen Plans (& w)
52. The Clue of the Missing Ape (& w) 53.
Giuseppina (& w) (AA) 61. The Kitchen 62. The
Dock Brief 62. Every Day's a Holiday 64. A
Study in Terror 65. Born Free 66. Captain Nemo
and the Underwater City 69. Black Beauty 71.
The Belstone Fox 73, etc.

Hill, James (1916–). American producer.
Vera Cruz 54. *The Kentuckian* 55. *Trapeze* 56,
etc.

Hill, Sinclair (1894–1945). British director
most eminent in the twenties.
The Tidal Wave 20. Don Quixote 23. Indian
Love Lyrics 23. Boadicaea 25. Beyond the Veil
25. The Chinese Bungalow 26. The King's
Highway 27. A Woman Redeemed 27. *The Guns
of Loos* 28. *The Price of Divorce* 28. The First
Mrs Fraser 30. The Man from Toronto 33. My
Old Dutch 34. Follow Your Star 38, etc.

Hill, Steven (1924–) (Solomon Berg).
American stage actor.
A Lady without Passport 50. The Goddess 58. A
Child is Waiting 62. The Slender Thread 67.
TV series: Mission Impossible 67.

Hill, Terence (1931–) (Mario Girotti). Italian
leading man of spaghetti westerns.
The Leopard 63. Seven Seas to Calais 63. Blood
River 67. Boot Hill 69. They Call Me Trinity 70.
Man of the East 72. My Name is Nobody 73.
Watch Out, We're Mad 74, etc.

Hill, Walter (–). American screenwriter.
□ Hickey and Boggs 72. The Thief Who Came
to Dinner 72. The Getaway 72. The Mackintosh
Man 73. Hard Times 75.

hillbillies became a stereotype of the thirties
cinema, and subsequently made infrequent
appearances before the enormous success of the
TV series *The Real McCoys* 57–63 and *The
Beverly Hillbillies* 62–69. Notable hillbillies
through the years include the Kettles, Lum and
Abner, the Weaver Brothers and Elviry; the Ritz
Brothers in *Kentucky Moonshine*; Annie in
Annie Get Your Gun; and the characters in
*Roseanna McCoy, Thunder Road, Lil Abner,
Guns in the Afternoon, Feudin' Fussin' and A-
Fightin', The Moonshine War, I Walk the Line,*
and *Coming Round the Mountain*; while the
denizens of *Tobacco Road*, geographically not

hillbillies, splendidly personified the image.
Cartoon-wise, Elmer Fudd in the Bugs Bunny
series is an old-fashioned hillbilly, and Disney
produced a twenty-minute version of *The
Martins and the Coys*, followed in 1975 by a TV
movie, *The Hatfields and the McCoys*.

Hiller, Arthur (1923–). Canadian-American
director, from TV.
□ The Careless Years 57. Miracle of the White
Stallions 63. The Wheeler Dealers 63. The
Americanization of Emily 64. Promise Her
Anything 66. Penelope 66. Tobruk 67. The Tiger
Makes Out 67. Popi 69. The Out-of-Towners 70.
Love Story 70. Plaza Suite 70. The Hospital 71.
Man of La Mancha 72. The Crazy World of
Julius Vrooder 74. The Man in the Glass Booth
75. Silver Streak 76.

Hiller, Wendy (1912–). Distinguished British
stage actress with inimitable voice and clarity of
diction; her films have been fewer than one would
like.
□ Lancashire Luck 37. *Pygmalion* 38. *Major
Barbara* 40. *I Know Where I'm Going* 45. An
Outcast of the Islands 51. Single Handed 52.
Something of Value 57. How to Murder a Rich
Uncle 57. *Separate Tables* (AA) 58. *Sons and
Lovers* 60. Toys in the Attic 63. *A Man for All
Seasons* 66. David Copperfield 69. The Cat and
the Canary 77.

Hilliard, Harriet (1914–) (Peggy Lou
Snyder). American leading lady of thirties
romantic comedies and musicals, e.g. *Follow the
Fleet* 36. *She's My Everything* 38. *Sweetheart of
the Campus* 41. *Canal Zone* 42, etc. Married
Ozzie Nelson and for ten years from 1954
appeared with him in their weekly TV show
Ozzie and Harriet; they also appeared with their
family in the film *Here Come the Nelsons* 52. TV
series: *Ozzie's Girls* 73. TV movie 1976: *Smash-
up on Interstate Five.*

Hillier,   Erwin   (1911–).   British
cinematographer.
The Lady from Lisbon 41. The Silver Fleet 43.
Great Day 45. *I Know Where I'm Going* 45.
London Town 47. *The October Man* 48. Mr
Perrin and Mr Traill 49. Where's Charley? 52.
The Dam Busters 55. Shake Hands with the
Devil 59. A Matter of Who 62. Sammy Going
South 63. Operation Crossbow 65. Sands of the
Kalahari 65. Eye of the Devil 66. The Quiller
Memorandum 66. The Shoes of the Fisherman
68, etc.

Hillyer, Lambert (1889–). American director
of westerns which declined in stature after his

days of writing and directing for William S. Hart.
The Toll Gate 20. *Travellin' On* 22. *White Oak*
23. *The Spoilers* 23. The Branded Sombrero 28.
Beau Bandit 30. Master of Men 33. *Dracula's
Daughter* 36. The Invisible Ray 37. Batman
(serial) 41. Blue Clay 42. The Case of the Baby
Sitter 47. Sunset Pass 49, many others.

Hilton, James (1900–1953). British novelist
whose work was turned by himself and others
into several highly successful films. Also worked
as scenarist on other films, including *Mrs
Miniver* 42.
Knight Without Armour 37. *Lost Horizon* 37.
Goodbye Mr Chips 39. We Are Not Alone 39.
Random Harvest 42. The Story of Dr Wassell
43. So Well Remembered 47, etc.

Hindle Wakes. This now dated Lancashire
drama by Stanley Houghton, about the mill-girl
who gets pregnant by the boss's son, has been a
staple of British films. There were silent versions
in 1918 with Ada King and in 1926 with Estelle
Brody; in 1931 Belle Chrystall starred in a sound
remake, and as late as 1951 it was popular again
with Lisa Daniely.

Hinds, Anthony (1922–). British producer, in
films since 1946, latterly associated with
Hammer's horror films. Also writes screenplays
under the name 'John Elder'.

Hinds, Samuel S. (1875–1948). Dignified
American character actor, formerly a lawyer for
thirty-five years; specialized in kindly fathers and
crooked lawyers.
Gabriel over the White House 33. She 35. Trail
of the Lonesome Pine 36. Test Pilot 38. *You
Can't Take It with You* 38. *Destry Rides Again*
39. The Strange Case of Doctor RX 41. The
Spoilers 42. A Chip off the Old Block 44. The
Boy with Green Hair 48, many others.

Hines, Johnny (1895–). American star
comedian of the twenties; roles declined as sound
came in.
Little Johnny Jones 23. The Speed Spook 24.
The Crackerjack 25. The Brown Derby 26.
Home Made 27. The Runaround 31. Whistling in
the Dark 32. Her Bodyguard 33. Society Doctor
35. Too Hot to Handle 38, etc.

Hingle, Pat (1923–). Burly American
character actor with stage and TV experience.
On the Waterfront 54. The Strange One 57. No
Down Payment 57. Splendor in the Grass 61.
The Ugly American 63. Invitation to a
Gunfighter 64. Nevada Smith 66. Hang 'Em
High 68. Bloody Mama 69. Norwood 69.

W.U.S.A. 70. The Carey Treatment 72. One
Little Indian 73. Run Wild 73, etc.

Hird, Thora (1914–). British north-country
character comedienne, mother of Janette Scott;
often plays acidulous landladies, etc.
Autobiography 1976: *Seen and Hird.*
The Black Sheep of Whitehall 41. Corridor of
Mirrors 46. The Blind Goddess 48. Conspirator
50. The Long Memory 53. Simon and Laura 55.
The Entertainer 60. *A Kind of Loving* 62. Rattle
of a Simple Man 64. The Nightcomers 71, many
others.

Hiroshima Mon Amour (France/Japan
1959). Alain Resnais' cinematically explorative
study of the effect of our war-torn past on the
love affair of a Frenchwoman and a Japanese
businessman. Original, influential, generally
rewarding. Written by Marguerite Duras, with
Emmanuele Riva, Eiji Okada.

Hirsch, Robert (1929–). French character
actor of the Comédie Française.
No Questions on Saturday 64. Kiss Me General
66, etc.

Hirschfeld, Gerald (–). American
cinematographer.
Goodbye Columbus 69. Last Summer 69. Diary
of a Mad Housewife 71. Doc 71. Summer
Wishes Winter Dreams 73. *Young Frankenstein*
74, etc.

Hiscott, Leslie (1894–1968). British director,
in films from 1919.
The Passing of Mr Quinn 28. Black Coffee 32.
While London Sleeps 33. The Triumph of
Sherlock Holmes 35. She Shall Have Music 35.
Tilly of Bloomsbury 40. The Seventh Survivor
41. Welcome Mr Washington 44. The Time of
His Life 52, etc.

Hitchcock, Alfred (1899–). British director,
in Hollywood more or less since 1940. His name,
his profile, and his lugubrious voice are a
trademark around the world for suspense
thrillers with a touch of impudence, using
techniques which are purely cinematic; though of
course he has frequently fallen below his own
high standards. Of innumerable books written
about him, the most detailed and typical is
probably *Le Cinema Selon Hitchcock* by
François Truffaut 1966.
□ The Pleasure Garden 25. The Mountain Eagle
25. *The Lodger* 26. Downhill 27. Easy Virtue 27.
The Ring 27. The Farmer's Wife 28. Champagne
28. The Manxman 29. *Blackmail* 29. Elstree
Calling (sketches) 30. Juno and the Paycock 30.

Murder 30. The Skin Game 31. Rich and Strange 31. *Number Seventeen* 32. Waltzes from Vienna 33. *The Man Who Knew Too Much* 34. *The Thirty-Nine Steps* 35. Secret Agent 36. Sabotage 37. Young and Innocent 37. *The Lady Vanishes* 38. Jamaica Inn 39. *Rebecca* 40. *Foreign Correspondent* 40. Mr and Mrs Smith 41. Suspicion 41. Saboteur 42. *Shadow of a Doubt* 43. Lifeboat 43. *Spellbound* 45. *Notorious* 46. The Paradine Case 47. Rope 48. Under Capricorn 49. Stage Fright 50. *Strangers on a Train* 51. I Confess 53. Dial M For Murder 54. *Rear Window* 54. To Catch a Thief 55. *The Trouble with Harry* 55. The Man Who Knew Too Much 56. The Wrong Man 57. Vertigo 58. *North by Northwest* 59. *Psycho* 60. *The Birds* 63. Marnie 64. Torn Curtain 66. Topaz 69. Frenzy 72. Family Plot 76.
TV series: *Alfred Hitchcock Presents* 55–65.

Hitler, Adolf (1889–1945) (Adolf Schickelgruber). German fascist dictator, subject of many screen documentaries, notably *Mein Kampf* 63 and *The Life of Adolf Hitler* 65. Actors who have impersonated him include Chaplin in *The Great Dictator* 40; Luther Adler in *The Magic Face* 51 and *The Desert Fox* 52; Ludwig Donath in *The Strange Death of Adolf Hitler* 43: Tom Dugan in *To Be or Not To Be* 42 and *Star Spangled Rhythm* 42; Albin Skoda in *The Last Act* 55; Richard Basehart in *Hitler* 61; Billy Frick in *Is Paris Burning?* 66; Kenneth Griffith in *The Two Headed Spy* 59; and Sidney Miller in *Which Way to the Front?* 69 and Alec Guinness in *Hitler: The Last Ten Days* 73. Most frequent Hitler-player, however, is Robert Watson, who in the forties seemed to do little else: apart from an excellent serious portrayal in *The Hitler Gang* 44, he supplied Hitler walk-ons in *The Devil with Hitler* 42, *That Nazty Nuisance* 43, *Hitler Dead or Alive* 43, *The Miracle of Morgan's Creek* 44, *The Story of Mankind* 57, and many others.

Hively, Jack (c. 1907–). American director.
□ They Made Her a Spy 39. Panama Lady 39. The Spellbinder 39. Three Sons 39. Two Thoroughbreds 39. The Saint's Double Trouble 40. The Saint Takes Over 40. Anne of Windy Poplars 40. Laddie 40. The Saint in Palm Springs 41. They Met in Argentina 41. Father Takes a Wife 41. Four Jacks and a Jill 41. Street of Chance 42. Are You With It? 48.

Hobart, Rose (1906–) (Rose Keefer). American actress, usually in character roles.
Liliom 30. Dr Jekyll and Mr Hyde 32. Tower of London 39. Nothing but the Truth 41. Ziegfeld Girl 41. The Soul of a Monster 44. The Farmer's Daughter 46. Mickey 48, etc.

Hobbes, Halliwell (1877–1962). British character actor, long the impeccable butler, on stage from 1898, films from 1929 (after which he lived in Hollywood).
Charley's Aunt 30. Dr Jekyll and Mr Hyde 32. *The Masquerader* 33. Bulldog Drummond Strikes Back 35. Dracula's Daughter 36. *You Can't Take It with You* 38. Lady Hamilton 41. *Sherlock Holmes Faces Death* 43. If Winter Comes 47. That Forsyte Woman 49. Miracle in the Rain 56, scores of others.

Hobbs, Jack (1893–1968). British actor on screen from silent days, usually in genial roles.
The Sin Game 30. Trouble in Store 34. No Limit 35. Millions 37. *It's in the Air* 38. Behind These Walls 48. *Worm's Eye View* 51, etc.

Hobson, Valerie (1917–). British leading lady with 'upper-class' personality.
Path of Glory (debut) 34. The Bride of Frankenstein (US) 35. The Mystery of Edwin Drood (US) 35. The Great Impersonation (US) 36. The Drum 38. This Man Is News 38. Q Planes 39. *The Spy in Black* 39. Contraband 40. The Adventures of Tartu 42. The Years Between 46. *Great Expectations* 46. The Small Voice 48. Kind Hearts and Coronets 49. *The Card* 52. The Voice of Merrill 53. Background 53. Knave of Hearts 54, etc.

Hobson's Choice. This famous stage comedy by Harold Brighouse, set in industrial Salford at the turn of the century and showing how a heavy father gets his come-uppance, has been filmed three times in Britain. The 1920 version, directed by Percy Nash, with Joe Nightingale and Joan Ritz, was much improved on by the 1931 sound remake directed by Thomas Bentley, with Frank Pettingell and Viola Lyel. This was eclipsed, however, by David Lean's brilliant 1954 production, with Charles Laughton as the tyrant shoeseller, Brenda de Banzie as his stubborn daughter, and John Mills as her intended.

Hoch, Winton C. (c. 1908–). American cinematographer, former research physicist.
Dr Cyclops 40. Captains of the Clouds 42. So Dear to My Heart 48. Joan of Arc (co-ph) (AA) 48. *She Wore a Yellow Ribbon* (AA) 49. Tulsa 49. Halls of Montezuma 51. *The Quiet Man* (co-ph) (AA) 52. Mr Roberts 55. *The Searchers* 56. Darby O'Gill and the Little People 59. The Lost World 60. Five Weeks in a Balloon 62. *Robinson Crusoe on Mars* 64. The Green Berets 68, etc.

Hodges, Ken (1922–). British cinematographer.
Faces in the Dark 60. The Comedy Man 63. The Jokers 67. Negatives 68. Every Home Should Have One 70. A Day in the Death of Joe Egg 70. The Ruling Class 72. Bedevilled 73, etc.

Hodges, Mike (1932–). British director, from TV.
□ Suspect (TV) 69. Rumour (TV) 70. Get Carter 71. Pulp 72. The Terminal Man (US) (& p) 73.

Hodiak, John (1914–1955). Serious-looking American leading man of the forties, of Ukrainian descent.
Lifeboat 43. Marriage Is a Private Affair 44. *Sunday Dinner for a Soldier* 44. *A Bell for Adano* 45. The Harvey Girls 46. Somewhere in the Night 46. The Miniver Story 50. Night into Morning 51. The People against O'Hara 51. Battle Zone 52. Conquest of Cochise 53. On the Threshold of Space 55, etc.

Hoellering, George (c. 1900–). Austrian producer of *Hortobagy*, long in Britain as specialized distributor and exhibitor; also producer of *Murder in the Cathedral* 51.

Hoey, Dennis (1893–1960) (Samuel David Hyams). British character actor, mostly in Hollywood; a memorably obtuse Lestrade to Basil Rathbone's Sherlock Holmes.
Tell England 30. The Good Companions 32. Chu Chin Chow 34. The Wandering Jew 34. Brewster's Millions 35. Maria Marten 36. This Above All 42. Sherlock Holmes and the Secret Weapon 42. Spider Woman 44. Pearl of Death 44. House of Fear 45. Kitty 46. Where There's Life 47. If Winter Comes 47. Wake of the Red Witch 48. David and Bathsheba 51, many others.

Hoffenstein, Samuel (1890–1947). Lithuanian-American screenwriter, always in collaboration.
An American Tragedy 31. *Dr Jekyll and Mr Hyde* 31. *Love Me Tonight* 32. Song of Songs 33. Marie Galante 34. Desire 36. Conquest 38. The Great Waltz 39. Lydia 41. Flesh and Fantasy 43. Phantom of the Opera 43. Laura 44. Cluny Brown 46. Give My Regards to Broadway 48.

Hoffman, Dustin (1937–). Diffident American leading actor who suited the mood of the late sixties.
□ Madigan's Millions 66. Un Dollaro per Sette Vigliacchi 67. The Tiger Makes Out 67. *The Graduate* 67. *Midnight Cowboy* 69. John and Mary 69. Little Big Man 70. Who is Harry Kellerman . . . ? 71. Alfredo Alfredo 72. Straw Dogs 72. Papillon 73. Lenny 74. *All the President's Men* 76.

Hogan, James P. (1891–1943). American director.
Last Train from Madrid 37. Ebb Tide 38. The Texans 39. Power Dive 41. The Mad Ghoul 43. The Strange Death of Adolf Hitler 44, etc.

Hohl, Arthur (1889–). Staring-eyed American character actor who often played rustic types.
The Cheat 31. Island of Lost Souls 32. Man's Castle 33. Cleopatra 34. Show Boat 36. The Road Back 37. Kidnapped 38. Blackmail 39. Moontide 42. The Scarlet Claw 44. The Yearling 46. The Vigilantes Return 47, many others.

Holbrook, Hal (1925–). American general purpose stage and TV actor, also Mark Twain impersonator.
The Group 66. Wild in the Streets 68. A Clear and Present Danger (TV) 69. The People Next Door 70. Suddenly Single (TV) 71. *That Certain Summer* (TV) 72. Magnum Force 73. All the President's Men 76, etc.
TV series: *The Bold Ones* 70–71.

Holden, Fay (1894–1973) (Fay Hammerton). British stage actress who went to Hollywood in the thirties and found a niche as the mother of the Hardy family. Once known as Dorothy Clyde.
Wives Never Know 36. Exclusive 37. Judge Hardy's Children 38. Sweethearts 38. The Hardys Ride High 39. Bitter Sweet 40. Andy Hardy's Private Secretary 41. Ziegfeld Girl 41. Blossoms in the Dust 41. Andy Hardy's Double Life 43. Andy Hardy's Blonde Trouble 44. Canyon Passage 46. Love Laughs at Andy Hardy 46. Samson and Delilah 49. The Big Hangover 50. Andy Hardy Comes Home 58, many others.

Holden, Gloria (1908–). London-born leading lady, long in Hollywood.
Dracula's Daughter (title Role) 36. The Life of Émile Zola 37. Test Pilot 38. A Child Is Born 40. The Corsican Brothers 41. Behind the Rising Sun 43. The Hucksters 47. Dream Wife 53. The Eddy Duchin Story 57. This Happy Feeling 68, etc.

Holden, William (1918–) (William Beedle). Good-looking American leading man who hit his greatest popularity in the fifties.
□ Golden Boy 39. Invisible Stripes 40. Our Town 40. Those were the Days 40. Arizona 40. I Wanted Wings 41. Texas 41. The Fleet's In 42.

The Remarkable Andrew 42. Meet the Stewarts 42. Young and Willing 43. Blaze of Noon 47. Dear Ruth 47. Variety Girl 47. *Rachel and the Stranger* 48. Apartment for Peggy 48. The Man from Colorado 48. The Dark Past 49. The Streets of Laredo 49. Miss Grant Takes Richmond 49. Dear Wife 49. Father is a Bachelor 50. *Sunset Boulevard* 50. Union Station 50. *Born Yesterday* 50. Force of Arms 51. Submarine Command 51. Boots Malone 52. The Turning Point 52. *Stalag 17* (AA) 53. The Moon is Blue 53. Forever Female 53. Escape from Fort Bravo 53. Executive Suite 54. Sabrina 54. The Country Girl 54. The Bridges at Toko-Ri 54. *Love is a Many-Splendored Thing* 55. Picnic 55. The Proud and Profane 56. Toward the Unknown 56. *The Bridge on the River Kwai* 57. The Key 58. The Horse Soldiers 59. The World of Suzie Wong 60. Satan Never Sleeps 62. The Counterfeit Traitor 62. The Lion 62. Paris When it Sizzles 64. The Seventh Dawn 64. Alvarez Kelly 66. Casino Royale 67. The Devil's Brigade 68. The Christmas Tree 69. *The Wild Bunch* 69. Wild Rovers 71. The Revengers 72. The Blue Knight (TV) 72. Breezy 73. Open Season 74. Network 76.

Holiday (US 1938). A slightly bitter comedy of manners, more refined than the well-known crazy comedies of the thirties but in a similar mood, about a thinking man who marries into the idle rich, but at the last minute swaps his conventional intended for her eccentric sister. Directed by George Cukor from Philip Barry's play, with typically graceful performances from Katharine Hepburn and Cary Grant, and almost equally memorable contributions from Edward Everett Horton, Lew Ayres and Henry Kolker. Edward H. Griffith had directed a previous version in 1930, with Ann Harding, Mary Astor, Robert Ames and Edward Everett Horton in the same role as in 1938.

Holland has produced two major documentarists: Joris Ivens and Bert Haanstra. Fiction films have not been the country's forte, though Fons Rademakers has his adherents.

Hollander, Frederick (1892–1976). German song composer, long in America.
The Blue Angel 30. Desire 36. *Destry Rides Again* 39. The Man Who Came to Dinner 42. A Foreign Affair 48. The Five Thousand Fingers of Dr T 53, etc.

Holles, Antony (1901–1950). British actor who often played excitable foreigners.
The Lodger 32. Brewster's Millions 35. Dark Journey 37. Neutral Port 41. Warn That Man

43. Carnival 46. Bonnie Prince Charlie 49. The Rocking-Horse Winner 50, others.

Holliday, Doc (1849–1885). American wild west character; a tubercular dentist and poker-player who oddly changed to the right side of the law when he teamed up with Wyatt Earp in *Tombstone*. Played inaccurately but picturesquely on screen by Cesar Romero in *Frontier Marshal* 39; Walter Huston in *The Outlaw* 41; Kent Taylor in *Tombstone* 42; Victor Mature in *My Darling Clementine* 46; James Griffith in *Masterson of Kansas* 55; Kirk Douglas in *Gunfight at the OK Corral* 56; Arthur Kennedy in *Cheyenne Autumn* 64; Jason Robards in *Hour of the Gun* 67; and Stacy Keach in *Doc* 70.

Holliday, Judy (1922–1965) (Judith Tuvim). American revue star who shot to fame in the fifties as a slightly daffy blonde in a handful of well-scripted comedies.
□ Greenwich Village 44. Something for the Boys 44. Winged Victory 44. Adam's Rib 49. *Born Yesterday* (AA) 50. The Marrying Kind 52. *It Should Happen to You* 53. Phffft 54. *The Solid Gold Cadillac* 56. Full of Life 56. Bells are Ringing 60.

Holliman, Earl (1928–). American general purpose actor who can play innocent or villainous.
Destination Gobi 53. The Bridges at Toko-Ri 54. Broken Lance 54. The Big Combo 55. Forbidden Planet 56. Trooper Hook 57. Hot Spell 58. Last Train from Gun Hill 59. Visit to a Small Planet 60. Summer and Smoke 61. Armored Command 61. The Sons of Katie Elder 65. Covenant with Death 67. Anzio 68. Smoke 69. Trapped (TV) 73.
TV series: Hotel de Paree 61. The Wide Country 62. Police Woman 74– .

Holloway, Stanley (1890–). British north-country comedian, entertainer, singer and character actor with a long list of international credits in revue, musical comedy and variety as well as films.
Autobiography 1969: *Wiv' a Little Bit of Luck*.
□The Rotters 21. *The Co-Optimists* 30. Sleeping Car 33. The Girl from Maxim's 33. Lily of Killarney 34. Love at Second Sight 34. Sing as We Go 34. Road House 34. D'Ye Ken John Peel? 35. In Town Tonight 35. *Squibs* 35. Play Up the Band 35. Song of the Forge 36. *The Vicar of Bray* 36. Cotton Queen 37. Sam Small Leaves Town 37. Our Island Nation 37. Major Barbara 41. *Salute John Citizen* 42. *The Way Ahead* 44. *Champagne Charlie* 44. *This Happy Breed* 44.

The Way to the Stars 45. *Brief Encounter* 45. Caesar and Cleopatra 45. Wanted for Murder 46. Carnival 46. Meet Me at Dawn 46. *Nicholas Nickleby* (as Mr Crummles) 47. Saraband for Dead Lovers 48. One Night with You 48. Noose 48. The Winslow Boy 48. *Hamlet* (as the gravedigger) 48. Another Shore 48. Passport to Pimlico 49. The Perfect Woman 49. Midnight Episode 50. One Wild Oat 50. *The Lavender Hill Mob* 51. Lady Godiva Rides Again 51. The Magic Box 51. The Happy Family 52. Meet Me Tonight 52. *The Titfield Thunderbolt* 52.*The Beggar's Opera* 53. A Day to Remember 53. *Meet Mr Lucifer* 53. Fast and Loose 53. An Alligator Named Daisy 55. Jumping for Joy 55. Alive and Kicking 58. No Trees in the Street 58. Hello London 58. *No Love for Johnnie* 61. On the Fiddle 61. *My Fair Lady* (as Dolittle) 64. In Harm's Way 64. Ten Little Indians 64. The Sandwich Man 66. Mrs Brown You've Got a Lovely Daughter 68. The Private Life of Sherlock Holmes 70. The Flight of the Doves 71. TV series: *Our Man Higgins* 62.

Holloway, Sterling (1905–). Slow-speaking American comic actor, usually of yokels or hillbillies. Busiest in the thirties; latterly the voice of many Disney characters.
Casey at the Bat 27. Alice in Wonderland 33. Life Begins at Forty 35. Professor Beware 38. The Bluebird 40. A Walk in the Sun 46. The Beautiful Blonde from Bashful Bend 49. Shake, Rattle and Rock 56. Live a Little Love a Little 68, many others.
TV series: The Life of Riley 53–58. The Baileys of Balboa 64.

Hollywood. The American film city, nominally a suburb of Los Angeles, was founded in 1912 when a number of independent producers headed west from New York to avoid the effects of a patents trust. The site was chosen because of its nearness to the Mexican border in case of trouble, and because the weather and location possibilities were excellent. By 1913 Hollywood was established as the film-maker's Mecca, and continued so for forty years. Several factors combined in the late forties to affect its unique concentration. Actors transformed themselves into independent producers and reduced the power of the 'front office'; stars now made the films they liked instead of the ones to which they were assigned. The consequent break-up of many big studios, which now simply sold production space to independent outfits, weakened continuity of product. Each production now had to start from scratch; there was no longer a training ground for new talent, nor was the old production gloss always in

evidence. The communist witch hunt unfortunately drove many leading talents to Europe, and some found they preferred Shepperton or Cinecitta to California. The coming of CinemaScope, a device to halt the fall in box office returns which resulted from the beginning of commercial TV, meant that real locations were now necessary, as studio sets would show up on the screen. So began the world-wide trekking now evident in American production: generally speaking only routine product and TV episodes are made in the film city itself, but each distribution set-up will have up to a dozen films being made in various parts of the globe.

Hollywood on film has generally been shown as the brassy, gold-digging, power-conscious society which, in the nature of things, it can hardly fail to be. There was a somewhat sentimental period in the twenties and thirties, with *Ella Cinders*, *Hollywood*, *Going Hollywood*, *Hollywood Cavalcade*, and *Hollywood Boulevard*; but satire had already struck in such films as *The Last Command*, *Merton of the Movies*, *Show People*, *The Lost Squadron*, *What Price Hollywood*, *Lady Killer*, *Something to Sing About*, *Once in a Lifetime*, *Stardust*, *Hollywood Hotel*, *Stand In*, *A Star Is Born* and *Boy Meets Girl*. The moguls didn't seem to mind the film city being shown as somewhat zany, as in *The Goldwyn Follies*, Disney's *Mother Goose Goes Hollywood*, *The Cohens and Kellys in Hollywood*, *Abbott and Costello in Hollywood*, *The Jones Family in Hollywood*, *Movie Crazy*, *Never Give a Sucker an Even Break*, and *Hellzapoppin*; but they preferred the adulatory attitude best expressed in *The Youngest Profession*, which concerned the autograph hunters who lay in wait at the studio exits.

During the forties Paramount was the studio most addicted to showing itself off, though the front office can't have relished watching Preston Sturges bite the hand that fed him in *Sullivan's Travels*. The story of *Hold Back the Dawn* was supposedly told to sentimental Mitchell Leisen during a lunch break on the studio floor; Crosby and Hope based a score of gags on Paramount; and the studio was the setting for *Star Spangled Rhythm*, an all-star musical which encouraged other studios to emulate it, with Warner's *Thank Your Lucky Stars* and *It's a Great Feeling*, Universal's *Follow the Boys*, the independent *Stage Door Canteen*, and later Paramount's less successful reprise, *Variety Girl*.

In 1950 *Sunset Boulevard* took a really sardonic look at the film city, and set a fashion for scathing movies like *The Star*, *The Bad and* the Beautiful, The Barefoot Contessa and The Big Knife. As though to atone, almost every studio threw in a light-hearted, nostalgic look at Hollywood's golden era: Singin' in the Rain, The Perils of Pauline, Jolson Sings Again, The Eddie Cantor Story. But in the last few years the only really affectionate review of Hollywood's past has been in the Cliff Richard musical Wonderful Life, though Jerry Lewis continued to paint zany pictures of studio life in The Errand Boy, The Ladies' Man and The Patsy. The rest was all denunciation and bitterness: Hollywood Boulevard, Hollywood Story, The Wild Party, The Day of the Locust, Inserts, The Big Knife, The Goddess, Two Weeks in Another Town, The Carpetbaggers, Harlow, Inside Daisy Clover, The Loved One and The Oscar. A 1969 TV series, Bracken's World, was set in a film studio (20th Century Fox) and saw it as a kind of valley of the dolls—and the studio scenes in that movie were none too convincing.

The Hollywood Ten. Alvah Bessie, Herbert Biberman, Lester Cole, Edward Dmytryk, Ring Lardner Jnr, John Howard Lawson, Albert Maltz, Sam Ornitz, Adrian Scott and Dalton Trumbo were the famous band of writers, producers and directors who in 1947 refused to tell Unamerican Activities Committee whether or not they were communists. All served short prison sentences and had difficulty getting work in Hollywood for several years.

Holm, Celeste (1919–). Cool, calm, American stage actress whose films have usually provided her with wisecracking roles.
□ Three Little Girls in Blue 46. Carnival in Costa Rica 47. Gentleman's Agreement (AA) 47. Road House 48. The Snake Pit 48. Chicken Every Sunday 48. Come to the Stable 49. Everybody Does It 49. A Letter to Three Wives (narrator only) 49. All About Eve 50. Champagne for Caesar 50. The Tender Trap 55. High Society 56. Bachelor Flat 61. Doctor You've Got to be Kidding 67. The Delphi Bureau (TV) 72. Tom Sawyer 73.
TV series: Nancy 70.

Holm, Ian (1932–). British stage actor recently emerging in films.
□ The Bofors Gun (BFA) 68. A Midsummer Night's Dream 68. The Fixer 68. A Severed Head 70. Nicholas and Alexandra 71. Mary Queen of Scots 72. Young Winston 72. The Homecoming 73. Regan (TV) 73. Shout at the Devil 76.
TV series: The Sweeney 73– .

Holmes, Phillips (1909–1942). American

juvenile lead who went straight from college to Hollywood; son of Taylor Holmes. His rather stiff personality soon lost its appeal.
Varsity 28. The Return of Sherlock Holmes 29. The Criminal Code 31. An American Tragedy 32. The Man I Killed 32. Nana 34. Great Expectations 34. The House of a Thousand Candles 36. The Housemaster (GB) 38, many others.

Holmes, Taylor (1872–1959). Veteran American character actor with long stage experience; latterly seen as amiably crooked politician or confidence trickster.
Efficiency Edgar's Courtship 17. Ruggles of Red Gap (title role) 18. One Hour of Love 28. The First Baby 36. Boomerang 47. Nightmare Alley 47. Father of the Bride 50. The First Legion 51. Beware My Lovely 52. The Maverick Queen 56, many others.

Holt, Charlene (1939–). American leading lady, former star of TV commercials (and The Tom Ewell Show).
Man's Favourite Sport? 64. Red Line 7000 66. El Dorado 67, etc.

Holt, Jack (1888–1951). Tough-looking American leading man of silent and sound action films.
A Cigarette—That's All 14. The Little American 16. The Woman Thou Gavest Me 18. Held by the Enemy 20. Bought and Paid For 22. Empty Hands 24. Wanderer of the Wasteland 25. Vengeance 28. Hell's Island 30. Dirigible 31. War Correspondent 32. The Forgotten Man 33. The Littlest Rebel 35. San Francisco 36. Alien Sabotage 40. Holt of the Secret Service 43. They Were Expendable 45. Flight to Nowhere 46. Brimstone 49. Task Force 49. Across the Wide Missouri 51, many others.

Holt, Nat (1892–1971). American independent producer.
Badman's Territory 46. Trail Street 47. Return of the Badmen 48. Fighting Man of the Plains 49. The Great Missouri Raid 51. Denver and Rio Grande 52. Pony Express 53. Flight to Tangier 53, etc.
TV series: Tales of Wells Fargo 57–61. Overland Trail 61.

Holt, Patrick (1912–) (Patrick Parsons). Bland British leading man of the forties, later in character roles.
The Return of the Frog 38. Sword of Honour 39. Convoy 41. Hungry Hill 47. Master of Bankdam 47. The Mark of Cain 48. Portrait from Life 49. Marry Me 49. Guilt is My Shadow 50. The Dark

Avenger 55. Miss Tulip Stays the Night 56. Thunderball 65. Murderers' Row 66. Hammerhead 68. No Blade of Grass 71, many others.

Holt, Seth (1923–1971). British director, formerly editor and associate producer for Ealing.

☐ Nowhere to Go 58. Taste of Fear 61. Station Six Sahara 63. *The Nanny* 65. Danger Route 67. Blood from the Mummy's Tomb 71.

Holt, Tim (1918–1973). American leading man, son of Jack Holt. In films from 1937, and was hero of many low-budget westerns.

History Is Made at Night 37. The Law West of Tombstone 38. Stagecoach 39. The Swiss Family Robinson 40. *The Magnificent Ambersons* 42. Hitler's Children 42. My Darling Clementine 46. *The Treasure of the Sierra Madre* 47. The Mysterious Desperado 49. His Kind of Woman 51. The Monster That Challenged the World 57, etc.

Homeier, Skip (1929–). American child actor of the forties, later in a variety of supporting roles.

Tomorrow the World 44. Boys' Ranch 46. Mickey 48. The Gunfighter 50. Fixed Bayonets 51. Sailor Beware 52. Beachhead 54. At Gunpoint 56. Comanche Station 60. The Ghost and Mr Chicken 66, etc.

TV series: *Dan Raven* 60.

Un Homme et une Femme (France 1966). A slight, sophisticated modern love story which achieved international box-office success because audiences were waiting for a reversion from the kitchen sink school and found it in this glossy accumulation of television commercial tricks. Critics busied themselves with theories as to why certain scenes were shot in colour and others in black and white, until director Claude Lelouch admitted that he ran out of funds and simply couldn't afford any more colour stock. Anouk Aimée and Jean-Louis Trintignant were the protagonists; Francis Lai's music helped immeasurably.

Homoki-Nagy, Istvan (1914–). Hungarian naturalist who has made many films of wild life including *From Blossom Time Till Autumn Frost*.

Homolka, Oscar (1899–). Viennese-born character actor, a fine 'heavy'. On stage from 1918, international films from mid-thirties.

Rhodes of Africa 36. *Sabotage* 37. *Ebb Tide* 37. Comrade 40. Ball of Fire 41. Rage in Heaven 41.

Mission to Moscow 43. *The Shop at Sly Corner* 46. *I Remember Mama* 48. Anna Lucasta 49. Top Secret 52. House of the Arrow 53. The Seven Year Itch 55. *War and Peace* 56. Tempest 59. Mr Sardonicus 63. The Long Ships 63. Joy in the Morning 65. Funeral in Berlin 66. The Happening 67. Jack of Diamonds 67. *Billion Dollar Brain* 68. Song of Norway 70, etc.

homosexuality can be said to have arrived during the late sixties as a fit subject for the western cinema, producers having toyed gingerly with it for the previous three decades. During the forties, there were clear intimations of it in *The Maltese Falcon, Victory,* and *Rope.* The fifties brought *Strangers on a Train, I Vitelloni, Serious Charge,* Germany's *The Third Sex,* and *Suddenly Last Summer,* and the decade was rounded off with two productions of the life of Oscar Wilde. *Cat on a Hot Tin Roof* 58 and *Spartacus* 60 were probably the last Hollywood movies to have homosexual inferences deliberately removed from the original. In 1962 the subject came right out into the open with *Victim,* a well-intentioned thriller about the blackmail of homosexuals; *A Taste of Honey* featured a sympathetic homosexual; and both *Advise and Consent* and *The Best Man* concerned allegations of homosexuality against American politicians. On the other hand *Lawrence of Arabia* was so reticent about its hero's sexual make-up that it was difficult to know what estimate was being made; but for good measure Peter O'Toole was raped a second time in *Lord Jim.* Universal romantic comedies now began to make fun of the subject: in *That Touch of Mink* Gig Young's psychiatrist thought he was in love with Cary Grant, and in *A Very Special Favour* Rock Hudson deliberately made Leslie Caron think him effeminate so that she would 'rescue him'. The floodgates were now open: in rapid succession we had *A View From the Bridge,* with its male kiss; *The Servant,* with its odd relationship between master and man; *The Leather Boys; Stranger in the House; The Fearless Vampire Killers,* with its young homosexual bloodsucker; the miscast and unhappy *Staircase; The Detective,* which made New York appear to be a very gay city; *The Gay Deceivers,* in which two young men avoided the draft by pretending to be queer; *Reflections in a Golden Eye; Midnight Cowboy; The Boys in the Band,* the first sympathetic homosexual comedy; *The Boston Strangler* and *Funeral in Berlin,* with scenes in transvestite bars; *If, Riot, The Sergeant* and *Villain,* which revealed camp goings-on in school, prison, the army and gangland. *Girl Stroke Boy* revealed the plight of parents who could not tell whether their son was engaged to a girl or a boy. In *Myra Breckenridge* homosexuality was almost lost in a welter of more spectacular perversions. Historical figures such as Richard the Lionheart and Tchaikovsky had their sexual pecadilloes explored in *The Lion in Winter* and *The Music Lovers*, and Billy Wilder jokingly investigated *The Private Life of Sherlock Holmes*. It seems likely that, having secured public sympathy for their plight, homosexuals will now overstep the mark in merely sordid productions such as *Fortune and Men's Eyes*, *The Queens*, *Some of My Best Friends Are*, and the semi-underground ramblings of Andy Warhol and his clan. TV movies invaded the territory in 1973 with *That Certain Summer*.

See also: *Lesbianism*.

Honegger, Arthur (1892–1955). Swiss composer who worked on French and British pictures.

La Roue 22. Napoleon 27. Les Miserables 34. L'Idée 34. Mayerling 36. *Pygmalion* 38. *Pacific 231* 46.

Hooks, Robert (1937–). Black American leading man.

Sweet Love Bitter 66. Hurry Sundown 67. Crosscurrent (TV) 71. Trapped (TV) 73, etc. TV series: N.Y.P.D. 67.

Hopalong Cassidy, the genial black-garbed hero of scores of western second features since 1935, was created by novelist Clarence E. Mulford. William Boyd (qv) was his only screen and TV personification.

Hope, Anthony (1863–1933) (Sir Anthony Hope Hawkins). British adventure novelist whose *The Prisoner of Zenda* and its sequel *Rupert of Hentzau* have frequently been filmed.

Hope, Bob (1903–) (Leslie Townes Hope). Wisecracking American star comedian, a major name in entertainment for nearly forty years. Born in Britain, he spent years in American vaudeville and musical comedy before establishing himself as a big star of the forties, usually as a comic coward who makes good. Special Academy Awards in 1940, 1944 and 1952, mainly in appreciation of his troop shows and charitable ventures.

Autobiographical Books: 1958, *Have Tux Will Travel*. 1963; *I Owe Russia $2000*. 1976, *The Last Christmas Show*.

□ The Big Broadcast of 1938. College Swing 38. Give Me a Sailor 38. *Thanks for the Memory* 38. Never Say Die 39. Some Like It Hot 39. *The Cat and the Canary* 39. *Road to Singapore* 40. The

Ghost Breakers 40. *Road to Zanzibar* 41. Caught in the Draft 41. Nothing But the Truth 41. Louisiana Purchase 41. *My Favorite Blonde* 42. *Road to Morocco* 42. Star Spangled Rhythm 42. They Got Me Covered 42. Let's Face It 43. The Princess and the Pirate 44. Road to Utopia 45. Monsieur Beaucaire 46. My Favorite Brunette 47. Where There's Life 47. Variety Girl 47. Road to Rio 48. *The Paleface* 48. Sorrowful Jones 48. The Great Lover 49. *Fancy Pants* 50. The Lemon Drop Kid 51. My Favorite Spy 51. Son of Paleface 52. Road to Bali 52. Off Limits 53. Here Come the Girls 53. Casanova's Big Night 54. The Seven Little Foys 54. That Certain Feeling 56. The Iron Petticoat 56. Beau James 57. Paris Holiday 58. Alias Jesse James 59. *The Facts of Life* 60. Bachelor in Paradise 61. Road to Hong Kong 62. Critics Choice 63. Call Me Bwana 63. A Global Affair 64. I'll Take Sweden 65. Boy Did I Get a Wrong Number 66. The Oscar 66. Eight on the Lam 67. The Private Navy of Sgt O'Farrell 68. How to Commit Marriage 69. Cancel My Reservation 72.

Hope, Vida (1918–1962). British character actress, usually in comic proletarian roles; also stage director.

English Without Tears 44. Nicholas Nickelby 47. It Always Rains on Sunday 48. *The Man in the White Suit* 51. Lease of Life 54. Family Doctor 58, etc.

Hopkins, Anthony (1941–). British character actor.

The Lion in Winter 68. The Looking Glass War 70. *When Eight Bells Toll* 71. Young Winston (as Lloyd George) 72. A Doll's House 73. All Creatures Great and Small 74. QB VII (TV) 74. The Girl from Petrovka 74. Juggernaut 74. The Lindbergh Kidnapping Case (TV) 76. Dark Victory (TV) 76, etc.

Hopkins, Bo (–). Towering American leading man of the seventies.

The Wild Bunch 69. Monte Walsh 70. The Culpeper Cattle Company 72. The Getaway 72. American Graffiti 73. White Lightning 73. The Nickel Ride 74. The Day of the Locust 75. Breaking Point 76, etc.

Hopkins, John (1931–). British writer, mostly for TV.

The Virgin Soldiers (w) 69. The Offence (w) 72, etc.

Hopkins, Miriam (1902–1972). American leading lady of the thirties; her rather brittle style has dated.

□ Fast and Loose 30. The Smiling Lieutenant

31. Twenty Four Hours 31. Dr Jekyll and Mr Hyde 32. Two Kinds of Women 32. Dancers in the Dark 32. The World and the Flesh 32. *Trouble in Paradise* 32. *The Story of Temple Drake* 33. Design for Living 33. The Stranger's Return 33. All of Me 34. She Loves Me Not 34. The Richest Girl in the World 34. *Becky Sharp* 35. Barbary Coast 35. Splendor 35. *These Three* 36. Men Are Not Gods (GB) 37. The Woman I Love 37. Woman Chases Man 37. Wise Girl 37. The Old Maid 39. Virginia City 40. *Lady With Red Hair* 41. A Gentleman After Dark 42. *Old Acquaintance* 43. The Heiress 49. The Mating Season 51. Carrie 52. The Outcasts of Poker Flat 52. The Children's Hour 62. Fanny Hill 65. The Chase 66.

Hopper, Dennis (1935–). American juvenile of the fifties who later blossomed into a fashionable actor and director.
I Died a Thousand Times 35. Rebel Without a Cause 55. Giant 56. The Story of Mankind 57. Key Witness 60. Night Tide 63. The Sons of Katie Elder 65. The Trip 67. Cool Hand Luke 67. *Easy Rider* (& d) 69. The Last Movie (& wd) 71. Kid Blue 72.

Hopper, Hedda (1890–1966) (Elda Furry). American general purpose actress, mainly in silent days; in later life became a powerful Hollywood columnist.
Autobiographies: 1952, *From Under My Hat*. 1963, *The Whole Truth and Nothing But*. Biography 1972: *Hedda and Louella*, by George Eels.
Virtuous Wives 19. Heedless Moths 21. Sherlock Holmes 22. Has the World Gone Mad? 23. Reno 24. The Teaser 25. Don Juan 26. Wings 27. Harold Teen 28. His Glorious Night 29. Holiday 30. The Common Law 31. Speak Easily 32. Beauty For Sale 33. Little Man What Now? 34. Alice Adams 35. Dracula's Daughter 36. Topper 37. Thanks for the Memory 38. The Women 39. Queen of the Mob 40. Reap the Wild Wind 42. Sunset Boulevard 50. Pepe 60. The Oscar 66, many others.

Hopper, Jerry (1907–). American director of routine action films and TV series.
□ The Atomic City 52. Hurricane Smith 52. Pony Express 53. Alaska Seas 54. The Secret of the Incas 54. Naked Alibi 54. Smoke Signal 55. The Private War of Major Benson 55. One Desire 55. The Square Jungle 55. Never Say Goodbye 56. Toy Tiger 56. The Sharkfighters 56. Everything but the Truth 56. The Missouri Traveller 58. Blueprint for Robbery 61. Madron 70. *Kung Fu* (TV) 72, etc.

Hopper, Victoria (1909–). Canadian leading lady of a few British films of the thirties.
□ *The Constant Nymph* 33. *Lorna Doone* 34. Whom the Gods Love 36. Laburnam Grove 36. The Lonely Road 36. The Mill on the Floss 37. Escape from Broadmoor 38.

Hopper, William (1915–1969) (William Furry). American general purpose supporting actor, son of Hedda Hopper.
Footloose Heiress 37. Torchy Blane 38. Track of the Cat 54. Rebel Without a Cause 55. The Bad Seed 56. Twenty Million Miles to Earth (lead) 57, etc.
TV series: *Perry Mason* (as Paul Drake) 57–66.

Hordern, Michael (1911–). British character actor, on stage from 1937; film appearances usually as careworn official.
The Girl in the News (debut) 39: war service: School for Secrets 46. Mine Own Executioner 47. Good Time Girl 48. Passport to Pimlico 48. The Hour of Thirteen 51. The Heart of the Matter 53. The Baby and the Battleship 55. *The Spanish Gardener* 56. Sink the Bismarck 60. El Cid 61. The VIPs 63. Dr Syn 63. Genghis Khan 65. The Spy Who Came In from the Cold 66. Khartoum 66. *A Funny Thing Happened on the Way to the Forum* 66. The Taming of the Shrew 67. Where Eagles Dare 68. *The Bed-Sitting Room* 69. Anne of the Thousand Days 70. Futtock's End 70. Girl Stroke Boy 71. England Made Me 72. Alice's Adventures in Wonderland (as the Mock Turtle) 72. Theatre of Blood 73. The Mackintosh Man 73. Mister Quilp 74. Royal Flash 74. Lucky Lady 75. *The Slipper and the Rose* 76, others.

Horn, Camilla (1906–). German actress who had brief careers in Hollywood and Britain before retiring.
Faust 26. Tempest 28. The Return of Raffles 32. Luck of a Sailor (GB) 34, etc.

Horn, Leonard (1926–1975). American director, from TV.
Rogues' Gallery 68. The Magic Garden of Stanley Sweetheart 70. Going All Out 71. Corkey 71, etc.

Hornblow, Arthur Jnr (1893–1976). American producer, in Hollywood from 1926.
Bulldog Drummond 29. Ruggles of Red Gap 34. The Cat and the Canary 39. Gaslight 44. Weekend at the Waldorf 45. The Hucksters 47. The Asphalt Jungle 50. Oklahoma 56. Witness for the Prosecution 57. The War Lover 63, many others.

Horne, David (1898–1970). Portly British character actor, mainly on stage; almost always in pompous roles.
General John Regan 33. The Mill on the Floss 36. The First of the Few 42. The Seventh Veil 45. The Rake's Progress 45. The Man Within 46. It's Hard To Be Good 49. Madeleine 50. Lust for Life 56. The Devil's Disciple 59, many others.

Horne, Geoffrey (–). British general purpose actor.
The Bridge on the River Kwai 57. Tempest 58. Bonjour Tristesse 58, etc.

Horne, James V. (1880–1942). American director, in Hollywood from 1911. Made some of Laurel and Hardy's best two-reelers, and appeared as the villain in *Beau Hunks*.
The Third Eye 20. American Manner 24. *College* 27. Bonnie Scotland 35. The Bohemian Girl 36. *Way Out West* 37. Holt of the Secret Service 42, many others.

Horne, Lena (1917–). Lithe and sultry black American singer whose best appearances were in forties musicals.
Autobiographies: 1950, *In Person*. *1966* (with Richard Schickel), *Lena*.
□ Panama Hattie 42. *Cabin in the Sky* 43. *Stormy Weather* 43. Thousands Cheer 43. I Dood It 43. Swing Fever 43. Broadway Rhythm 44. Two Girls and a Sailor 44. Ziegfeld Follies 46. Till the Clouds Roll By 46. Words and Music 48. Duchess of Idaho 50. Meet Me In Las Vegas 56. *Death of a Gunfighter* (dramatic role) 69.

Horne, Victoria (c. 1920–). American comedienne.
The Scarlet Claw 44. The Ghost and Mrs Muir 47. The Snake Pit 48. Abbott and Costello Meet the Killer 49. *Harvey* 50. Affair with a Stranger 53, etc.

Horner, Harry (1910–). Czech-born production designer with stage experience in Vienna and New York.
Our Town 40. *The Little Foxes* 41. A Double Life 47. *The Heiress* (AA) 49. Born Yesterday 50. *The Hustler* (AA) 61, many others.
AS DIRECTOR: Beware My Lovely 52. Red Planet Mars 52. New Faces 54. A Life in the Balance 55. The Wild Party 56. Man from Del Rio 56, etc.

horror as a staple of screen entertainment really emanates from Germany (although Edison shot a picture of *Frankenstein* as early as 1908). Before World War I Wegener had made a version of *The Golem*, which he improved on in

1920: it was this second version which directly influenced the Hollywood horror school stimulated by James Whale. What is surprising is that Hollywood took so long to catch on to a good idea, especially as the Germans, in depressed post-war mood, relentlessly turned out such macabre films as *The Cabinet of Dr Caligari* (with Veidt as a hypnotically-controlled monster), *Nosferatu* (Murnau's brilliantly personal account of Bram Stoker's 'Dracula'), *Waxworks* (Leni's three-part thriller about Ivan the Terrible, Haroun-al-Raschid and Jack the Ripper); *The Hands of Orlac* and *The Student of Prague*. Most of the talents involved were exported to Hollywood by 1927; but the only horror film directly resulting was Leni's *The Cat and the Canary*, which was a spoof. California did encourage Lon Chaney, but his films were grotesque rather than gruesome; and John Barrymore had already been allowed in 1921 to impersonate *Dr Jekyll and Mr Hyde* (a role to be played even more for horror by Fredric March in 1932). By the end of the twenties, the European horror film was played out except for Dreyer's highly individual *Vampyr*; the ball was in Hollywood's court.

In 1930 Tod Browning filmed the stage version of *Dracula*, using a Hungarian actor named Bela Lugosi; shortly after, Robert Florey wrote and James Whale directed a version of *Frankenstein* that borrowed freely from *The Golem*. Both films (see individual entries) were wildfire successes, and the studio involved, Universal, set out on a steady and profitable progress through a series of sequels. In 1932 Karloff appeared in *The Mummy*, and in 1933 Claude Rains was *The Invisible Man*; these characters were added to the grisly band. In 1935 the studio made *Werewolf of London*, which led five years later to *The Wolf Man* giving Lon Chaney Jnr a useful sideline. By 1945, despite the upsurge in supernatural interest during the war, these characters were thought to be played out, and in the last two 'serious' episodes they appeared *en masse*. In 1948 they began to meet Abbott and Costello, which one would have thought might ensure their final demise; but more of that later.

Meanwhile other landmarks had been established. Browning made the outlandish *Freaks*, and in 1935 the spoof *Mark of the Vampire*. James Whale in 1932 made *The Old Dark House*, an inimitably entertaining mixture of disagreeable ingredients. Warners in 1932 came up with *Doctor X* and *The Mystery of the Wax Museum* (remade as *House of Wax*) and later got some mileage out of *The Walking Dead*. Paramount went in for mad doctors, from *The Island of Dr Moreau* (*Island of Lost Souls*) to

Doctor Cyclops, and at the beginning of World War II produced scary remakes of *The Cat and the Canary* and *The Ghost Breakers*. RKO were busy with *King Kong* and *She*, MGM with *The Devil Doll*. In the early forties Universal began a listless anthology series under the title *Inner Sanctum*, and later failed in *The Creature from the Black Lagoon* to add another intriguing monster to their gallery. By far the most significant extension of the genre was the small group of depressive but atmospheric thrillers produced by Val Lewton at RKO in 1942–45, the best of them being *The Body Snatcher, The Cat People* and *I Walked with a Zombie*.

After the war, little was heard of horror until the advent of science fiction in 1950. After this we heard a very great deal of nasty visitors from other planets (*The Thing, Invasion of the Body Snatchers*), mutations (*The Fly, This Island Earth*), robots (*The Day the Earth Stood Still, Forbidden Planet*) and giant insects (*Them, Tarantula*). To please the teenage audience, fly-by-night producers thought up fantastic horror-comic variations and came up with titles like *The Blob, I Married a Monster from Outer Space* and *I Was a Teenage Werewolf*; such crude and shoddy productions cheapened the genre considerably. The Japanese got into the act with rubber-suited monsters like *Godzilla* and *Rodan*; then, surprisingly, it was the turn of the British. Hammer Films, a small independent outfit with an old Thames-side house for a studio, impudently remade the sagas of Frankenstein, Dracula *et alia*, and the results have been flooding the world's screens for more than twenty years now, marked by a certain bold style, lack of imagination, and such excess of blood-letting that several versions have to be made for each film (the bloodiest for Japan, the most restrained for the home market). Britain also produced commendable screen versions of *The Quatermass Experiment* and other TV serials.

Since 1955 horror has been consistently in fashion, at least in the world's mass markets, and film-makers have been busy capping each other by extending the bounds of how much explicit physical shock and horror is permissible. (This, of course, does not make for good films.) If Franju was revolting in the detail of *Eyes Without a Face*, Hitchcock certainly topped him in *Psycho* and was himself outdone by William Castle in *Homicidal*, and by the perpetration in the seventies of films like *Blood Feast* and *Death Line*. (*Psycho* also gave the screen an inventive horror-writing talent in Robert Bloch, who has since been kept as busy as he could wish.) And the cheapjack American nasties at least provided a training ground for producer-director Roger

Corman, who between 1960 and 1964 made a series of Poe adaptations much admired for style and enthusiasm if not for production detail. The trend in the early seventies was towards the compendiums of graveyard horror typified by *Tales from the Crypt* and *The House that Dripped Blood*, and towards such combinations of spoof and nastiness as *Theatre of Blood, Shivers* and *Squirm*.

Best books: *An Illustrated History of Horror Films* (1968) by Carlos Clarens; *A Pictorial History of Horror Films* (1973) by Dennis Gifford.

Horsley, John (–). British character actor, often seen as plain clothes man or executive.

Highly Dangerous 48. The Long Memory 51. The Runaway Bus 54. Father Brown 54. Above Us the Waves 55, Bond of Fear 56, etc.

Horsfall, Bernard (1930–). British character actor.

On Her Majesty's Secret Service 69. Gold 74. Shout at the Devil 76, etc.

Horton, Edward Everett (1886–1970). American star comic actor with inimitable crooked smile and diffident manner; a favourite throughout the twenties, thirties and forties.

Too Much Business 22. Ruggles of Red Gap (title role) 23. Marry Me 25. The Nutcracker 26. The Terror 28. Sonny Boy 29. The Hottentot 29. The Sap 29. Take the Heir 30. *Holiday* 30. Once a Gentleman 30. Kiss Me Again 31. The Front Page 31. Six Cylinder Love 31. *Trouble in Paradise* 32. A Bedtime Story 33. Soldiers of the King (GB) 33. *Alice in Wonderland* (as the Mad Hatter) 33. It's a Boy (GB) 34. The Merry Widow 34. *The Gay Divorcee* 35. The Devil is a Woman 35. In Caliente 35. *Top Hat* 35. Your Uncle Dudley 35. The Private Secretary (GB) 35. The Man in the Mirror (GB) 36. *Lost Horizon* 37. Shall We Dance? 37. Angel 37. The Great Garrick 37. Bluebeard's Eighth Wife 38. *Holiday* (repeat of 1930 role) 38. That's Right You're Wrong 39. Ziegfeld Girl 41. Sunny 41. *Here Comes Mr Jordan* 41. The Body Disappears 41. The Magnificent Dope 42. Forever and a Day 43. *Thank Your Lucky Stars* 43. The Gang's All Here 43. Her Primitive Man 44. *Summer Storm* 44. *San Diego I Love You* 44. Arsenic and Old Lace 44. Lady on a Train 45. Cinderella Jones 46. Down to Earth 47. Her Husband's Affairs 47. The Story of Mankind 57. *Pocketful of Miracles* 61. Sex and the Single Girl 64. The Perils of Pauline 67. 2000 Years Later 69. Cold Turkey 70, many others.

TV series: *F Troop* (as a Red Indian chief) 65.

Horton, Robert (1924–) (Mead Howard Horton). Good looking American leading man who made it big on TV in the late fifties but could not manage the transfer to the big screen.
The Tanks are Coming 51. Bright Road 53. Prisoner of War 54. This Man is Armed 56. The Dangerous Days of Kiowa Jones 66. The Green Slime 69, etc.
TV series: *Wagon Train* 57–61. *A Man Called Shenandoah* 65.

hospitals have been the setting of many films. *Life Begins* and its remake *A Child is Born* were set in the maternity wards, *No Time for Tears* in the children's wards. *Young Dr Kildare* started a whole series about a general hospital, and soon they were *Calling Dr Gillespie*. Other general hospital dramas include *White Corridors, The Lamp Still Burns, Behind the Mask, Life in Emergency Ward Ten, Emergency Hospital*; thrillers set among the wards include *Intent to Kill, The Sleeping City, Green for Danger* (the best of all), *Eye Witness* and *The Carey Treatment*, which last is in the vein of savage black humour evidenced in the early seventies by such films as *The Hospital* and *Where Does It Hurt?* Gentler hospital comedy has been found in *Doctor in the House, Twice Round the Daffodils, Trio*, and several episodes of the 'Carry On' series which have specialized in bedpan humour. TV series on the subject include *Medic, The Nurses, The Doctors and the Nurses, Doctor Kildare, Ben Casey, Dr Hudson's Secret Journal, Dr Christian, General Hospital, West Side Medical*.

Hossein, Robert (1927–). French actor.
Rififi 55. The Wicked Go to Hell (& d) 55. Girls Disappear 58. La Musica 60. Enough Rope 63. Marco the Magnificent 65. I Killed Rasputin (& d) 68. The Burglars (& d) 71, etc.

hotels have frequently formed a useful setting for films wanting to use the 'slice of life' technique. Thus *Grand Hotel, Hotel for Women, Stage Door, Hotel Berlin, Weekend at the Waldorf, Separate Tables* and *Hotel* itself; while *Ship of Fools* is a variation on the same theme. The hotel background was a valuable dramatic asset to films as varied as *The Last Laugh, The October Man, Don't Bother to Knock, Hotel du Nord, Pushover, Honeymoon Hotel, Room Service* (and its remake *Step Lively*), *Hotel Reserve, Hotel Sahara, The Horn Blows at Midnight, Hotel for Women, Hollywood Hotel, Paris Palace Hotel, Bedtime Story, The Best Man, The Greengage Summer, A Hole in the Head*, and *The Silence*. Hotel security did not prevent attempts on the hero's life in *Journey into*

Fear and *Foreign Correspondent*. The most bewildering hotel was certainly that in *So Long at the Fair*; the most amusing hotel sequences may have been in *Ninotchka, The Bellboy, A Flea in Her Ear*, or *The Perfect Woman*. And hotels that have no accommodation left sparked off quite a few Hollywood comedies during the war, including *Government Girl, Standing Room Only*, and *The More the Merrier* (recently remade as *Walk Don't Run*).

Houdini, Harry (1873–1926) (Ehrich Weiss). American escapologist and magician extraordinary, in films from 1918. A biopic in 1953 starred Tony Curtis, and a 1976 TV movie, *The Great Houdinis*, Paul Michael Glaser.
Biography: 1969, *Houdini, the Unknown Story* by Christopher Milbourne.
The Master Mystery (serial) 18. The Grim Game 19. Terror Island 20. The Man from Beyond 21. Haldane of the Secret Service 23, etc.

Hough, John (1941–). British director in international films.
□ Wolfshead 69. Eye Witness 70. Twins of Evil 71. Treasure Island 72. The Legend of Hell House 73. Dirty Mary Crazy Larry 74. Escape to Witch Mountain 75.

Houghton, Katharine (1945–). American leading lady of *Guess Who's Coming to Dinner* 67; niece of Katharine Hepburn.

The Hounds of Zaroff: see *The Most Dangerous Game*.

House of Wax (US 1953). The film which seemed to gain public approval for 3-D (until CinemaScope proved the stronger card) was actually a simplified remake of the old horror film *The Mystery of the Wax Museum* 32, with Vincent Price in Lionel Atwill's old part as the disfigured madman who creates a new wax face for himself.

The House on 92nd Street (US 1946). Producer Louis de Rochemont here brought his March of Time technique to bear on a semi-fictional spy story with a clever mystery plot and a myriad of new documentary tricks. The brisk journalistic method was highly influential, and Henry Hathaway's direction neared his best.

Houseman, John (1902–) (Jacques Haussmann). American producer. After varied experience, helped Orson Welles to found his Mercury Theatre in New York in 1937, later followed him to Hollywood.
Autobiography 1972: *Runthrough*.

The Blue Dahlia 46. Letter from an Unknown Woman 48. They Live by Night 48. The Bad and the Beautiful 52. Julius Caesar 53. Executive Suite 54. Lust for Life 56. Two Weeks in Another Town 62. This Property is Condemned 66, etc.

AS ACTOR: *Paper Chase* (AA) 74. Three Days of the Condor 75. Rolerball 75. Meeting at Potsdam (TV) (as Churchill) 76. Fear on Trial (TV) 76.

houses have been the dramatic centre of many films: there was even one, *Enchantment*, in which the house itself told the story. The films of Daphne du Maurier's novels usually have a mysterious old house at the crux of their plots, as in *Rebecca, Frenchman's Creek, Jamaica Inn, My Cousin Rachel.* So in *Dragonwyck*; so in *House of Fear*; so, of course, in *Jane Eyre* and *Wuthering Heights.* Both *Citizen Kane* and *The Magnificent Ambersons* are dominated by unhappy houses, as is *Gaslight.* Thrillers set in lonely houses full of secret panels and hidden menace are exemplified by *The Spiral Staircase, The Black Cat, Night Monster, The House on Haunted Hill, The Cat and the Canary, The Ghost Breakers, The House that Dripped Blood, Whatever Happened to Baby Jane?, The Beast with Five Fingers, Ladies in Retirement* and *And Then There Were None.* Haunted houses are rarer, but those in *The Uninvited, The Unseen, The Innocents, The Enchanted Cottage* and *The Haunting* linger vividly in the memory. So for a different reason does the Bates' house in *Psycho.* Happier houses of note include the rose-covered cottage in *Random Harvest,* the family mansions of *Forever and a Day* and *Enchantment,* the red-decorated Denver house in *The Unsinkable Molly Brown,* the laboriously built country seat of *Mr Blandings Builds His Dream House,* the labour-saving modern house of *Mon Oncle,* the broken-down houses of *George Washington Slept Here* and *Father Came Too,* and dear old *Rookery Nook.* And filmgoers have various reasons to remember *The House on 92nd Street, The House on Telegraph Hill, House of Strangers, House of Horrors, House of Bamboo, House of Numbers, House of the Damned, House of the Seven Hawks, House of Women, House by the River, House of Seven Gables, House of Dracula, House of Frankenstein, House of Wax, Sinister House, The Red House, Crazy House, The Old Dark House* and *The Fall of the House of Usher.*

Housman, Arthur (1888–1942). American character actor, usually seen as incoherent but gentlemanly drunk in comedies of the early thirties.

Under the Red Robe 23. Manhandled 24. The Bat 26. Sunrise 27. Fools for Luck 28. The Singing Fool 28. Broadway 29. The Squealer 30. Five and Ten 31. *Scram* (Laurel and Hardy two-reeler) 32. She Done Him Wrong 33. Mrs Wiggs of the Cabbage Patch 34. Our Relations 36. Step Lively Jeeves 37, etc.

Houston, Donald (1923–). Burly, capable Welsh leading man of the early fifties. Later a useful character actor.

□ *The Blue Lagoon* 48. A Run for Your Money 49. Dance Hall 50. My Death is a Mockery 51. Crow Hollow 52. The Red Beret 53. Small Town Story 53. The Large Rope 53. The Happiness of Three Women 54. Doctor in the House 54. The Flaw 55. Double Cross 55. Find the Lady 56. Yangtse Incident 57. The Surgeon's Knife 57. A Question of Adultery 58. The Man Upstairs 58. Danger Within 58. *Room at the Top* 58. The Mark 61. Twice Round the Daffodils 62. The Prince and the Pauper 62. Maniac 62. The 300 Spartans 63. Doctor in Distress 63. Carry on Jack 63. 633 Squadron 64. A Study in Terror 65. The Viking Queen 66. My Lover My Son 70. Tales that Witness Madness 73.

Houston, Glyn (1926–). Welsh character actor, brother of Donald Houston.

The Blue Lamp 50. Payroll 60. Solo for Sparrow (lead role) 62. The Secret of Blood Island 65. Invasion 66, etc.

Houston, Renée (1902–) (Katherina Houston Gribbin). British vaudeville and revue artiste, once teamed with her sister Billie, later with Donald Stewart; more recently character actress of screen and TV.

Mr Cinders 34. A Girl Must Live 38. Old Bill and Son 40. Two Thousand Women 44. The Bells of St Trinians 54. *A Town Like Alice* 56. *Time Without Pity* 57. The Horse's Mouth 59. The Flesh and the Fiends 60. Three on a Spree 61. Repulsion 64. Carry On at Your Convenience 71, etc.

Houston, Sam (1793–1863). An American hero of the early days of Texas, played on film by Richard Boone in *The Alamo,* William Farnum in *The Conqueror,* Richard Dix in *Man of Conquest,* Moroni Olsen in *Lone Star,* Hugh Sanders in *The Last Command* and Joel McCrea in *The First Texan.*

Hovey, Tim (1945–). American child actor of the mid-fifties.

The Private War of Major Benson 55. Toy Tiger 56. Man Afraid 57, etc. Later on TV.

How Green Was My Valley (US 1941) (AA best picture). A stagey but oddly moving film version of Richard Llewellyn's novel about a Welsh mining family several decades ago. The elaborate village set was used again in other movies including *The Moon Is Down*. Directed by John Ford (AA); with Walter Pidgeon, Donald Crisp (AA) and Maureen O'Hara; photographed by Arthur Miller (AA).

How the West Was Won (US 1962). Historically notable as the first story film—and almost the last—in three-lens Cinerama. (*The Wonderful World of the Brothers Grimm* followed on, but the single-lens system, almost indistinguishable from other wide-screen methods, was introduced in 1963.) A patchy western directed by George Marshall, Henry Hathaway and John Ford, it has spectacular action sequences which dwarf the chatter of an all-star cast. Photographers: Charles Lang Jnr, William Daniels, Milton Krasner, Joseph la Shelle, Harold A. Wellman.

How to Marry a Millionaire (US 1953). The second released film, and the first comedy, in CinemaScope. Showed no master of the technique but provided Marilyn Monroe with a good comedy part. Written by Nunnally Johnson, directed by Jean Negulesco.

Howard, Arthur (1910–). British character actor, brother of Leslie Howard, often seen as schoolmaster, clerk, etc.
Passport to Pimlico 48. *The Happiest Days of Your Life* 49. The Intruder 53. The Shoes of the Fisherman 68. Zeppelin 70. Steptoe and Son 72. One of Our Dinosaurs Is Missing 75, etc.

Howard, Cy (1915–). American director.
Lovers and Other Strangers 69. Every Little Crook and Nanny 75.

Howard, Esther (1893–1965). American character actress, usually in blowsy roles.
Ladies of the Big House 31. Ready for Love 35. Serenade 39. Sullivan's Travels 41. Farewell My Lovely 44. The Lady Gambles 49, etc.

Howard, John (1913–) (John Cox). Good-looking, useful American leading man of the thirties and forties, mainly in routine films.
Annapolis Farewell 35. Soak the Rich 36. *Lost Horizon* 37. *Bulldog Drummond Comes Back* (and ensuing series) 37. Penitentiary 38. Prison Farm 38. Disputed Passage 39. Green Hell 40. *The Philadelphia Story* 40. The Invisible Woman 40. The Mad Doctor 41. Tight Shoes 41. The Undying Monster 42. Isle of Missing Men

43. Love from a Stranger 47. I Jane Doe 48. The Fighting Kentuckian 49. Experiment Alcatraz 51. The High and the Mighty 54. Unknown Terror 58, etc.
TV series: *Dr Hudson's Secret Journal* 55–56. Adventures of Seahawk 58.

Howard, Joyce (1922–). British leading lady of the forties.
Freedom Radio 40. Love on the Dole 41. The Gentle Sex 43. They Met in the Dark 43. Woman to Woman 46. Mrs Fitzherbert 47. Shadow of the Past 50, etc.

Howard, Kathleen (1879–1956). Canadian character actress, former opera singer; memorable as W. C. Fields' frequent screen wife.
Death Takes a Holiday 34. You're Telling Me 34. The Man on the Flying Trapeze 35. It's a Gift 35. Laura 44. The Late George Apley 47, etc.

Howard, Ken (1944–). Hulking American leading man who came to the fore in TV series *Adam's Rib* and *Manhunter*.
□ Tell Me That You Love Me Junie Moon 70. Such Good Friends 71. The Strange Vengeance of Rosalie 72. 1766 72.

Howard, Leslie (1890–1943) (Leslie Stainer). Distinguished British actor of Hungarian origin; his image was that of the romantic intellectual who had only to ignore women to be idolized. He was equally successful in American films.
Biography 1959: *A Very Remarkable Father*, by his daughter Ruth Howard.
□ *Outward Bound* 30. Never the Twain Shall Meet 31. A Free Soul 31. Five and Ten 31. Devotion 31. Service for Ladies 32. Smilin' Through 32. The Animal Kingdom 32. Secrets 33. Captured 33. *Berkeley Square* 33. The Lady is Willing 34. *Of Human Bondage* 34. British Agent 34. *The Scarlet Pimpernel* 35. *The Petrified Forest* 36. Romeo and Juliet 36. It's Love I'm After 36. Stand-In 37. *Pygmalion* (& co-d) 38. *Gone with the Wind* 39. *Intermezzo* 39. Pimpernel Smith (& p) 41. 49th Parallel 41. *The First of the Few* (& oa) 42. The Gentle Sex (pd only) 43. The Lamp Still Burns (p only) 43.

Howard, Ron: see *Ronny Howard*.

Howard, Ronald (1918–). British actor, son of Leslie Howard; formerly reporter.
While the Sun Shines (debut) 46. The Queen of Spades 48. Tom Brown's Schooldays 51. Drango (US) 56. Babette Goes to War 59. Spider's Web 60. The Curse of the Mummy's Tomb 64. Africa Texas Style 67. The Hunting Party 71, many others.
TV series: *Sherlock Holmes* 58.

Howard, Ronny (1953–). American child actor of the sixties.
The Music Man 62. The Courtship of Eddie's Father 63. Smoke 69. The Wild Country 71. American Graffiti 73.
TV series: The Andy Griffith Show 60–68. The Smith Family 70–71.

Howard, Shemp (1901–1955). American character comedian, brother of Moe Howard of the Three Stooges and occasional substitute for him; usually played tramps and bartenders.
Soup to Nuts 30. Headin' East 37. *The Bank Dick* 40. Buck Privates 41. *Hellzapoppin* 41. Pittsburgh 42. Crazy House 43. Blondie Knows Best 46. Africa Screams 49, many others.

Howard, Sidney (1891–1939). American playwright whose chief contributions to Hollywood were *The Late Christopher Bean, They Knew What They Wanted, Yellow Jack,* and most of the script of *Gone with the Wind.*

Howard, Sydney (1884–1946). Plump British comedian famous for fluttering gestures. On stage from 1912, films from 1930.
French Leave (debut) 30. *Up for the Cup* 33. Splinters in the Navy 34. *Night of the Garter* 36. Chick 36. Shipyard Sally 39. *Tilly of Bloomsbury* 40. Once a Crook 41. *When We Are Married* 42. Flight from Folly 45, etc.

Howard, Trevor (1916–). Distinguished British leading man, on stage from 1934; later concentrated on films.
□ The Way Ahead (debut) 44. The Way to the Stars 45. *Brief Encounter* 46. I See a Dark Stranger 46. *Green for Danger* 46. So Well Remembered 47. They Made Me a Fugitive 47. The Passionate Friends 48. *The Third Man* 49. The Golden Salamander 49. Odette 50. The Clouded Yellow 51. An Outcast of the Islands 52. The Gift Horse 52. *The Heart of the Matter* 53. The Lovers of Lisbon (Fr.) 54. The Stranger's Hand 54. Cockleshell Heroes 55. Around the World in Eighty Days 56. Run for the Sun (US) 56. Interpol 57. Manuela 57. *The Key* (BFA) 58. Roots of Heaven 59. Moment of Danger 60. *Sons and Lovers* 60. *Mutiny on the Bounty* (as Captain Bligh) 62. The Lion 62. The Man in the Middle 64. Father Goose 64. Von Ryan's Express 65. Operation Crossbow 65. Morituri 65. The Liquidator 65. The Poppy is Also a Flower 66. Triple Cross 66. The Long Duel 67. Pretty Polly 68. *The Charge of the Light Brigade* 68. The Battle of Britain 69. Twinky 69. *Ryan's Daughter* 70. *The Night Visitor* 71. Catch Me a Spy 71. Mary Queen of Scots 72. Kidnapped 72. Pope Joan 72. Ludwig

72. The Offence 72. *Catholics* (TV) 73. Craze 73. Persecution 74. 11 Harrowhouse 74. Conduct Unbecoming 75. The Bawdy Adventures of Tom Jones 76.

Howard, William K. (1899–1954). American director who made some interesting films in the thirties.
East of Broadway 24. Code of the West 25. Gigolo 26. The Main Event 27. The River Pirate 28. Live Love and Laugh 29. Scotland Yard 30. Don't Bet on Women 31. Transatlantic 31. *Sherlock Holmes* 32. *The Power and the Glory* 33. The Cat and the Fiddle 34. Evelyn Prentice 34. Vanessa 35. *Mary Burns Fugitive* 35. The Princess Comes Across 36. *Fire Over England* (GB) 36. Back Door to Heaven 39. Bullets for O'Hara 41. Johnny Come Lately 43, etc.

Howe, James Wong (1899–1976) (Wong Tung Jim). Distinguished Chinese cinematographer, in Hollywood from 1917.
□ Drums of Fate 23. The Woman with Four Faces 23. Call of the Canyon 23. The Spanish Dancer 23. To the Last Man 23. The Trail of the Lonesome Pine 23. The Alaskan 24. The Breaking Point 24. The Side Show of Life 24. The Best People 25. The Charmer 25. The King on Main Street 25. Not So Long Ago 25. Mantrap 26. Padlocked 26. Sea Horses 26. The Song and Dance Man 26. The Rough Riders 27. Sorrell and Son 27. Four Walls 28. The Perfect Crime 28. Laugh Clown Laugh 28. Desert Nights 29. Today 30. The Criminal Code 31. Transatlantic 31. The Spider 31. The Yellow Ticket 31. Surrender 31. Dance Team 32. After Tomorrow 32. Amateur Daddy 32. Man about Town 32. Chandu the Magician 32. Hello Sister 33. Beauty for Sale 33. The Power and the Glory 33. The Show Off 34. *The Thin Man* 34. Hollywood Party 34. Stamboul Quest 34. Have a Heart 34. Biography of a Bachelor Girl 34. The Night is Young 35. Mark of the Vampire 35. The Flame Within 35. O'Shaughnessy's Boy 35. Three Live Ghosts 35. Whipsaw 36. Fire Over England 36. Farewell Again 36. Under the Red Robe 37. *The Prisoner of Zenda* 37. The Adventures of Tom Sawyer 37. Algiers 38. Comet Over Broadway 38. They Made Me a Criminal 39. The Oklahoma Kid 39. Daughters Courageous 39. Dust Be My Destiny 39. On Your Toes 39. Abe Lincoln in Illinois 39. *Dr Ehrlich's Magic Bullet* 40. Saturday's Children 40. Torrid Zone 40. City for Conquest 40. A Dispatch from Reuter's 40. The Strawberry Blonde 41. Shining Victory 41. Navy Blues 41. Out of the Fog 41. *King's Row* 41. Yankee Doodle Dandy 42. The Hard Way 42. Hangmen also Die 43. Air Force 43. North Star 43.

Passage to Marseille 44. Objective Burma 45. Counterattack 45. Confidential Agent 45. Danger Signal 45. My Reputation 46. Nora Prentiss 47. Pursued 47. Body and Soul 47. Mr Blandings Builds His Dream House 48. The Time of Your Life 48. The Eagle and the Hawk 49. The Baron of Arizona 50. Tripoli 50. The Brave Bulls 51. He Ran All the Way 51. Behave Yourself 51. The Lady Says No 52. Main Street to Broadway 53. Come Back Little Sheba 54. The Rose Tattoo (AA) 55. *Picnic* 56. Death of a Scoundrel 56. Drango 56. *Sweet Smell of Success* 57. The Old Man and the Sea 58. Bell Book and Candle 58. The Last Angry Man 59. The Story on Page One 60. Song Without End 60. Tess of the Storm Country 61. *Hud* (AA) 63. The Outrage 64. The Glory Guys 65. This Property is Condemned 66. *Seconds* 67. Hombre 67. The Heart is a Lonely Hunter 69. The Molly Maguires 70. Last of the Mobile Hotshots 70. Funny Lady 75.
Directed *Go Man Go* 52.

Howells, Ursula (1922–). British actress, mainly on stage and TV. Film roles infrequent.
Flesh and Blood 51. The Constant Husband 55. They Can't Hang Me 55. The Long Arm 56. Dr Terror's House of Horrors 65. Mumsy Nanny Sonny and Girly 68. Crossplot 69, etc.

Howerd, Frankie (1921–) (Francis Howerd). British eccentric comedian of stage and TV.
Autobiography 1977: *On My Way I Lost It.*
☐ *The Runaway Bus* 54. Jumping for Joy 55. The Ladykillers 55. A Touch of the Sun 56. Further Up the Creek 59. The Cool Mikado 63. The Great St Trinian's Train Robbery 66. Carry On Doctor 68. *Up Pompeii* 70. Up the Chastity Belt 71. Up the Front 72. *The House in Nightmare Park* 73, etc.

Howes, Bobby (1895–1972). Diffident, diminutive British leading man of stage musical comedies in the thirties.
☐ The Guns of Loos 28. Third Time Lucky 31. Lord Babs 32. For the Love of Mike 32. Over the Garden Wall 34. Please Teacher 37. Sweet Devil 38. *Yes Madam* 38. Bob's Your Uncle 41. The Trojan Brothers 45. Happy Go Lovely 51. The Good Companions 57. Watch It Sailor 61.

Howes, Sally Ann (1930–). British child actress of the forties, later an occasional leading lady. Daughter of Bobby Howes.
☐ *Thursday's Child* 43. Halfway House 44. *Dead of Night* 45. Pink String and Sealing Wax 45. Nicholas Nickleby 47. My Sister and I 48. Anna Karenina 48. *The History of Mr Polly* 48. Fools Rush In 49. Stop Press Girl 50.

Honeymoon Deferred 51. The Admirable Crichton 57. Chitty Chitty Bang Bang 68. The Hound of the Baskervilles (TV) 72.

Howlett, Noel (1901–). British stage actor who has appeared in small film roles since 1936, often as solicitor, auctioneer or civil servant.
A Yank at Oxford 46. Corridor of Mirrors 47. The Blind Goddess 49. Father Brown 54. The Scapegoat 59. Some Will Some Won't 70, etc.

Howlin, Olin (1896–1959) (formerly known as **Olin Howland**). American character actor, in innumerable small film roles since the early talkies.
So Big 32. Nothing Sacred 37. This Gun for Hire 42. The Wistful Widow 47. Them 54. The Blob 58, etc.

Hoyt, John (1905–) (John Hoysradt). Incisive American character actor, sometimes cast as German officer or stylish crook.
O.S.S. 46. *Rommel, Desert Fox* 51. New Mexico 52. When Worlds Collide 52. Androcles and the Lion 53. Julius Caesar 53. The Blackboard Jungle 55. Trial 55. The Conqueror 56. Six Inches Tall 58. Never So Few 60. Duel at Diablo 66. Flesh Gordon 74, many others.

Hubbard, John (1914–). American light leading man who starred in several Hal Roach comedies.
The Housekeeper's Daughter 39. *Turnabout* 40. Road Show 41. Gunfight at Comanche Creek 63. Fate Is the Hunter 64. Duel at Diablo 66. Herbie Rides Again 73, etc.

Hubbard, Lucien (1888–1971). American screenwriter.
The Perils of Pauline 14. Wild Honey 22. The Vanishing American 25. Wings 27. Five Star Final 22. 42nd Street 33. The Casino Murder Case (& p) 35. A Family Affair (& p) 37. Ebb Tide (p) 37. Nick Carter Master Detective (p) 39, etc.

Huber, Harold (1904–1959). American character actor, former lawyer; often seen as sly crook or dumb detective.
The Bowery 33. G-Men 35. San Francisco 36. A Slight Case of Murder 38. Kit Carson 40. The Lady from Chungking 43. Let's Dance 50, many others.

Hubley, John (1914–1977). American animator, associated with the early days of UPA; a co-creator of Mr Magoo. Latterly worked on experiemental documentary cartoons: *Of Stars and Men*, etc.

Hubley, Season (–   ). American leading lady of the seventies.
Lolly Madonna XXX 73. Catch My Soul 74. She Lives (TV) 74.

Hubschmid, Paul (1917–) (known in US as **Paul Christian**). German-Swiss leading man, in international films.
Maria Ilona 40. Baghdad 49. The Thief of Venice 52. The Beast from 20,000 Fathoms 53. Journey to the Lost City 60. Mozambique 66. *Funeral in Berlin* 66. Skullduggery 69, many others.

Huckleberry Finn. Mark Twain's lively Mississippi boy had film adventures in 1919, when he was played by Lewis Sargent; in 1931, by Junior Durkin; in 1939, by Mickey Rooney; and in 1960, by Eddie Hodges. He also turned up in several of the films about Tom Sawyer (qv).

Hud (US 1962). This realistic, ambling melodrama of a modern western ne'er-do-well was refreshingly off-beat for Hollywood. Written by Irving Ravetch and Harriet Frank Jnr; directed by Martin Ritt; photographed by James Wong Howe (AA); with Paul Newman, Patricia Neal (AA), Melvyn Douglas (AA).

Hudd, Walter (1898–1963). British character actor of stage and screen; usually played aloof characters and in 1936 was cast as T. E. Lawrence but the production was abandoned.
Rembrandt 36. Black Limelight 37. Elephant Boy 37. The Housemaster 38. Major Barbara 40. I Know Where I'm Going 45. Paper Orchid 49. Life For Ruth 62, etc.

Hudson, Rochelle (1914–1972). American leading lady who played *ingénue* roles in the thirties.
Laugh and Get Rich 30. She Done Him Wrong 33. Les Misérables 35. Way Down East 36. Smuggled Cargo 39. Island of Doomed Men 40. Meet Boston Blackie 41. Rubber Racketeers 42. Queen of Broadway 43. Skyliner 49. Rebel without a Cause 55. The Night Walker 65. Broken Sabre 65, etc.

Hudson, Rock (1925–) (Roy Scherer). Giant-sized American leading man who did very well in Hollywood despite lack of acting training, moving from westerns to sob stories to sophisticated comedies.
□ Fighter Squadron 48. Double Crossbones 48. Undertow 49. I Was a Shoplifter 50. One Way Street 50. Winchester 73 50. Peggy 50. The Desert Hawk 50. Shakedown 50. The Fat Man 50. Air Cadet 51. Tomahawk 51. Iron Man 51. Bright Victory 51. Bend of the River 52. Here

Come the Nelsons 52. Scarlet Angel 52. Has Anybody Seen My Gal? 52. Horizons West 52. The Lawless Breed 52. Gun Fury 53. Seminole 53. Sea Devils (GB) 53. The Golden Blade 53. Back to God's Country 53. Taza Son of Cochise 53. *Magnificent Obsession* 54. Bengal Brigade 54. Captain Lightfoot 55. One Desire 55. All That Heaven Allows 55. Never Say Goodbye 56. *Giant* 56. Battle Hymn 56. *Written on the Wind* 56. Four Girls in Town 56. Something of Value 57. *The Tarnished Angels* 57. A Farewell to Arms 57. Twilight for the Gods 58. This Earth is Mine 59. *Pillow Talk* 59. The Last Sunset 61. Come September 61. Lover Come Back 61. The Spiral Road 62. A Gathering of Eagles 63. Marilyn (narrator) 63. Man's Favourite Sport? 64. Send Me No Flowers 64. Strange Bedfellows 64. A Very Special Favor 65. Blindfold 66. *Seconds* 66. Tobruk 67. Ice Station Zebra 68. A Fine Pair 69. The Undefeated 69. Darling Lili 69. Hornet's Nest 70. Pretty Maids all in a Row 71. Showdown 73.
TV series: *McMillan and Wife* 71–76.

Hue and Cry (GB 1946). One of the first post-war Ealing comedies, typical in its use of London bomb-site locations and its exhilarating spoof of authority; basically a lively 'tupenny blood' boys' adventure about crooks in Covent Garden. Written by T. E. B. Clarke, directed by Charles Crichton; with Alastair Sim and Jack Warner; music George Auric; photography Douglas Slocombe.

Huffaker, Clair (–   ). American screenwriter.
Flaming Star 60. Seven Ways from Sundown 60. Rio Conchos 64. Tarzan and the Valley of Gold 47. The War Wagon 67, etc.

Huggins, Roy (1914–). American screenwriter.
I Love Trouble 48. The Lady Gambles 49. Sealed Cargo 51. Hangman's Knot (& d) 52. *Pushover* 54. A Fever in the Blood (& p) 61, etc.
TV series: *The Fugitive* (p) 63–66. Run for Your Life (p) 65–67, etc.

Hughes, Barnard (1915–). American character actor familiar on TV as *Doc*.
Rage 72. Sisters 73, etc.

Hughes, Howard (1905–1976). American businessman and celebrated recluse of eccentric habits; once an enthusiastic film-maker. A character based on him was played by George Peppard in *The Carpetbaggers* 64. Biographies: 1967, *The Bashful Billionaire* by Albert Gerber. 1967, *Howard Huges* by John Keats.

Two Arabian Knights (p) 27. *Hell's Angels* (pd) 30. The Front Page (p) 31. *Scarface* (p) 32. Sky Devils 32. *The Outlaw* (pd) 43. Jet Pilot 56, etc.

Hughes, Kathleen (1929–) (Betty von Gerlean). Blonde American leading lady of the fifties.
Mother is a Freshman 49. For Men Only 51. The Golden Blade 53. It Came from Outer Space 53. The Glass Web 53. Dawn at Socorro 54. Cult of the Cobra 55. Promise Her Anything 66. The President's Analyst 67, etc.

Hughes, Ken (1922–). British director who has tackled a great variety of projects with variable success.
□ Wide Boy 52. Black Thirteen 53. Little Red Monkey (& w) 53. Confession (& w) 53. Timeslip (& w) 53. The House Across the Lake (& w) 54. *Joe Macbeth* (& w) 55. Wicked as They Come (& w) 56. The Long Haul 57. Jazzboat 60. In the Nick 60. *The Trials of Oscar Wilde* (& w) 60. The Small World of Sammy Lee (& w) 63. Of Human Bondage 64. Drop Dead Darling (& w) 66. Casino Royale (co-d) 67. Chitty Chitty Bang Bang (& w) 69. *Cromwell* (& w) 70. The Internecine Project 74. Alfie Darling 74. Sextet 77.

Hughes, Lloyd (1896–1958). American leading man of the twenties.
The Turn in the Road 19. Hail the Woman 21. Tess of the Storm Country 22. *The Sea Hawk* 24. *The Lost World* 24. The Desert Flower 25. Ella Cinders 26. Loose Ankles 26. The Stolen Bride 27. The Mysterious Island 29. Moby Dick 30. Hell Bound 31. The Miracle Man 32. Harmony Lane 35. Romance of the Redwoods 39, many others.

Hughes, Mary Beth (1919–). American leading lady of the forties, mainly in second features.
These Glamour Girls 39. Lucky Cisco Kid 40. Orchestra Wives 42. *The Ox-Bow Incident* 43. I Accuse My Parents 44. Caged Fury 47. Gun Battle at Monterey 57, etc.

Hughes, Roddy (1891–). Welsh character actor in films from 1934, often in roly-poly comedy roles.
The Stars Look Down 39. The Ghost of St Michael's 41. Hatter's Castle 41. Nicholas Nickleby 47. Scrooge 51. Sea Wife 57, etc.

Hulbert, Claude (1900–1963). British 'silly ass' comedian, brother of Jack Hulbert.
Champagne 28. Naughty Husbands 30. A Night Like This 32. The Mayor's Nest 32. *Thark* 32.

Radio Parade 33. A Cup of Kindness 34. *Bulldog Jack* 34. Wolf's Clothing 36. The Vulture 37. His Lordship Regrets 38. *Sailors Three* 40. *The Ghost of St Michael's* 41. The Dummy Talks 43. *My Learned Friend* 44. London Town 46. The Ghosts of Berkeley Square 47. Cardboard Cavalier 48. Fun at St Fanny's 55. Not a Hope in Hell 60, etc.

Hulbert, Jack (1892–). Jaunty, long-chinned British light comedian, popular in films of the thirties.
Autobiography 1976: *The Little Woman's Always Right.*
□ Elstree Calling 30. *The Ghost Train* 31. Sunshine Susie 31. *Jack's the Boy* 32. Love on Wheels 32. Happy Ever After 32. Falling for You 33. Jack Ahoy 34. The Camels are Coming 34. *Bulldog Jack* 34. Jack of all Trades 36. Take My Tip 37. Paradise for Two 37. Kate Plus Ten 38. Under Your Hat 40. Into the Blue 51. The Magic Box 51. Miss Tulip Stays the Night 55. Spider's Web 60. The Cherry Picker 72. Not Now Darling 73.

Hull, Henry (1890–1977). Versatile American character actor.
The Volunteer 17. One Exciting Night 22. The Hoosier Schoolmaster 24. For Woman's Favour 24. Midnight 34. Great Expectations 34. *Werewolf of London* (leading role) 35. Yellow Jack 38. Boys' Town 38. The Great Waltz 38. Jesse James 39. Miracles for Sale 39. Judge Hardy and Son 39. My Son My Son 40. High Sierra 40. Lifeboat 43. Woman of the Town 44. Objective Burma 45. Mourning Becomes Electra 47. The Walls of Jericho 48. The Great Gatsby 49. Hollywood Story 51. Inferno 53. The Man with the Gun 55. The Proud Rebel 58. The Sheriff of Fractured Jaw 58. Master of the World 61. The Chase 66. Covenant with Death 67, many others.

Hull, Josephine (1884–1957) (Josephine Sherwood). Bubbly little American stage actress who gave two memorable film performances.
□ After Tomorrow 32. Careless Lady 32. *Arsenic and Old Lace* 44. *Harvey* (AA) 50. The Lady from Texas 51.

Hull, Warren (1903–1974). American leading man of many second features: also radio hero of such serials as Mandrake the Magician and The Spider.
Miss Pacific Fleet 35. The Walking Dead 36. Night Key 37. Wagons Westward 40. Bowery Blitzkrieg 41, etc.

Humberstone, H. Bruce (1903–).

American director, a competent craftsman of action films and musicals.
If I Had a Million (part) 32. The Crooked Circle 32. Pack Up Your Troubles 32. Charlie Chan in Honolulu 37. Lucky Cisco Kid 40. Tall, Dark and Handsome 41. *Sun Valley Serenade* 41. Hot Spot 41. To the Shores of Tripoli 42. *Hello, Frisco Hello* 43. *Wonder Man* 45. Three Little Girls in Blue 46. *Fury at Furnace Creek* 48. East of Java 49. Happy Go Lovely (GB) 51. She's Working Her Way Through College 52. The Desert Song 53. The Purple Mask 55. Tarzan and the Lost Safari 57. Madison Avenue 61, etc.

Hume, Benita (1906–1967). British leading lady of the thirties; in Hollywood from 1935; retired to marry Ronald Colman.
The Constant Nymph 28. High Treason 29. Service for Ladies 32. The Flying Fool 32. Lord Camber's Ladies 33. Jew Süss 34. The Garden Murder Case 36. Tarzan Escapes 36. The Last of Mrs Cheyney 37. Peck's Bad Boy with the Circus 39, etc.

Hume, Alan (1924–). British cinematographer.
The Legend of Hell House 72. Carry on Girls 73. The Land that Time Forgot 74. Trial by Combat 76, etc.

Hume, Kenneth (1926–1967). British producer, former editor.
Cheer the Brave (wpd) 50. Hot Ice (wd) 51. Sail into Danger (wd) 57. Mods and Rockers (pd) 64. I've Gotta Horse (pd) 65, etc.

The Hunchback of Notre Dame. Victor Hugo's novel *Notre Dame de Paris* has been filmed three times under this title; in 1923 with Lon Chaney, in 1939 with Charles Laughton, and in 1956 with Anthony Quinn. The last of these was disappointing; the earlier two are considerable cinematic achievements, William Dieterle's 1939 version in particular standing out as a masterpiece of studio technique.

Hungary has had one of the most flourishing film histories in Europe, and many of its talents found their way to Hollywood, including Michael Curtiz, Alexander Korda and Bela Lugosi. The native films were seldom exported, oddly enough, until after a strong Soviet influence made itself felt: Zoltan Fabri and Miklos Jancso are now respected names.

Hunnicutt, Arthur (1911–). American actor of slow-speaking country characters.
Wildcat 42. Lust for Gold 49. Broken Arrow 50. The Red Badge of Courage 51. The Big Sky 52.

The French Line 54. The Last Command 56. The Kettles in the Ozarks 56. Apache Uprising 65. Cat Ballou 65. El Dorado 66. Million Dollar Duck 71. The Revengers 72. Harry and Tonto 74. The Spikes Gang 74. Moonrunners 75, etc.

Hunnicutt, Gayle (1942–). American leading lady of the sixties.
□ The Wild Angels 66. P. J. 68. Marlowe 69. Eye of the Cat 69. Fragment of Fear 70. Running Scared 72. The Legend of Hell House 73. The Sellout 76.

Hunt, Marsha (1917–) (Marcia Hunt). American leading lady who usually plays gentle characters.
Virginia Judge (debut) 35. Hollywood Boulevard 36. The Hardys Ride High 38. These Glamour Girls 39. *Pride and Prejudice* 40. Blossoms in the Dust 41. Kid Glove Killer 42. Seven Sweethearts 42. The Human Comedy 43. *Lost Angel* 43. None Shall Escape 43. Cry Havoc 44. The Valley of Decision 45. A-Letter for Evie 45. Carnegie Hall 46. Take One False Step 49. Mary Ryan, Detective 50. The Happy Time 52. No Place to Hide 56. Blue Denim 59. The Plunderers 60. Johnny Got His Gun 71, etc.

Hunt, Martita (1900–1969). British stage and screen actress who graduated from nosy spinsters to *grandes dames*.
I Was a Spy (debut) 33. Spare a Copper 39. The Man in Grey 43. The Wicked Lady 45. *Great Expectations* (as Miss Havisham) 46. The Ghosts of Berkeley Square 47. My Sister and I 48. The Fan 49. *Treasure Hunt* 52. Melba 53. Three Men in a Boat 56. Anastasia 56. *Brides of Dracula* 60. The Unsinkable Molly Brown 64. Bunny Lake Is Missing 65, others.

Hunt, Peter (1928–). British director, former editor.
□ On Her Majesty's Secret Service 69. 1776 72. Shout at the Devil 76.

Hunter, Evan (1926–). American novelist and screenwriter who also writes as *Ed McBain*.
The Blackboard Jungle (oa) 55. Strangers When We Meet (w) 60. The Young Savages (w) 61. The Birds (w) 63. Mister Buddwing (oa) 66, etc.
TV series: *87th Precinct* 61.

Hunter, Glenn (1897–1945). American leading man of the twenties.
The Case of Becky 21. The Country Flapper 22. Smilin' Through 22. The Scarecrow 22. Puritan Passions 23. *Merton of the Movies* 24. The Pinch Hitter 25. For Beauty's Sake 41, etc.

Hunter, Ian (1900–1976). British actor of
dependable characters: on stage from 1919, films
soon after.
Mr Oddy 22. Not for Sale 24. Confessions 25.
The Ring 27. Something Always Happens 31.
The Sign of Four (as Dr Watson) 32. Death at
Broadcasting House 34. A Midsummer Night's
Dream (US) 35. The White Angel (US) 36. Call
It a Day (US) 37. *52nd Street* (US) 38. The
Adventures of Robin Hood (as King Richard)
(US) 38. Tower of London (US) 39. Strange
Cargo (US) 40. Bitter Sweet (US) 40. Billy the
Kid (US) 41. *Dr Jekyll and Mr Hyde* (as
Lanyon) (US) 41. A Yank at Eton (US) 42.
Bedelia 46. White Cradle Inn 47. The White
Unicorn 48. *Edward My Son* 49. Appointment
in London 52. Don't Blame the Stork 53. The
Battle of the River Plate 56. Fortune Is a Woman
57. Northwest Frontier 59. The Bulldog Breed
60. Dr Blood's Coffin 61. Guns of Darkness 63,
many others.

Hunter, Jeffrey (1925–1969) (Henry H.
McKinnies). American leading man, in films
from 1951 after radio experience.
Fourteen Hours (debut) 51. Red Skies of
Montana 52. Singlehanded 53. White Feather
55. The Searchers 56. A Kiss Before Dying 56.
The True Story of Jesse James 57. No Down
Payment 57. The Last Hurrah 57. Hell to
Eternity 60. *King of Kings* (as Jesus) 61. The
Longest Day 62. Vendetta 65. Brainstorm 65.
The Private Navy of Sgt O'Farrell 68. Custer of
the West 68, many others.

Hunter, Kim (1922–) (Janet Cole). Pert,
dependable American leading lady who after
brief stage experience started a rather desultory
film career.
▢ The Seventh Virgin 43. Tender Comrade 43.
When Strangers Marry 44. You Came Along 45.
A Matter of Life and Death (GB) 45. A
Canterbury Tale (GB) 46. *A Streetcar Named
Desire* (AA) 51. *Deadline U.S.A.* 52. Anything
Can Happen 52. Storm Center 56. The Young
Stranger 57. Bermuda Affair 58. Money Women
and Guns 58. Lilith 64. Planet of the Apes 67.
The Swimmer 68. Beneath the Planet of the Apes
70. Escape from the Planet of the Apes 71. The
Magician (TV) 73.

Hunter, Ross (1921–) (Martin Fuss).
American producer; a former actor, he has
specialized in remakes of glossy dramas from
Hollywood's golden age, and has seldom failed
to make hot commercial properties of them.
AS ACTOR: A Guy a Gal and a Pal 45.
Sweetheart of Sigma Chi 47, The Bandit of
Sherwood Forest 47. The Groom Wore Spurs

51, etc.
AS PRODUCER: Take Me to Town 53.
Magnificent Obsession 54. One Desire 55. The
Spoilers 55. All that Heaven Allows 56. Battle
Hymn 57. My Man Godfrey 57. *Pillow Talk* 58.
Imitation of Life 59. Portrait in Black 60.
Tammy Tell Me True 61. Back Street 61. Flower
Drum Song 61. The Thrill of it All 63. The Chalk
Garden 64. Madame X 66. The Pad 66.
Thoroughly Modern Millie 67. *Airport* 69. *Lost
Horizon* 73, etc.

Hunter, T. Hayes (1881–1944). American
director, in Britain in the thirties.
Desert Gold 19. Earthbound 20. The Triumph of
the Scarlet Pimpernel 29. The Silver King 29.
The Frightened Lady 31. Sally Bishop 33. *The
Ghoul* 33, etc.

Hunter, Tab (1931–) (Art Gelien). Athletic
American leading man, a teenage rave of the
fifties.
The Lawless (debut) 48. Saturday Island 52.
Gun Belt 53. Return to Treasure Island 53.
Track of the Cat 54. Battle Cry 55. The Sea
Chase 55. The Burning Hills 56. The Girl He
Left Behind 57. Gunman's Walk 57. *Damn
Yankees* 58. That Kind of Woman 59. The
Pleasure of His Company 60. The Golden
Arrow (It.) 62. City under the Sea 65. Birds Do It
66. Hostile Guns 67. Judge Roy Bean 72. The
Temper Tramp 73, etc.
TV series: The Tab Hunter Show 60.

Huntington, Lawrence (1900–1968). British
director, mainly of routine thrillers.
Suspected Person (& w) 41. Night Boat to
Dublin 41. *Wanted for Murder* 46. *The
Upturned Glass* 47. When the Bough Breaks 48.
Mr Perrin and Mr Traill 48. Man on the Run (&
w) 49. The Franchise Affair (& w) 51. There Was
a Young Lady (& w) 53. Contraband Spain (&
w) 55. Stranglehold 62. The Fur Collar (& wp)
63, etc.

Huntley, Raymond (1904–). British
character actor, often of supercilious types or
self-satisfied businessmen: on stage from 1922,
screen from 1934.
Rembrandt 37. *Night Train to Munich* 40. *The
Ghost of St Michael's* 41. School for Secrets 45.
Mr Perrin and Mr Traill 49. *Trio* 50. Room at the
Top 59. Only Two Can Play 62. Rotten to the
Core 65. Hostile Witness 67. Destiny of a Spy
(TV) 69. *That's Your Funeral* 73, many others.

Hurndall, Richard (1910–). Incisive British
character actor.
Joanna 67. I Monster 71, etc.

Hurok, Sol (1889–1974). Distinguished American impresario whose life in classical music was recounted in *Tonight we Sing* 53.

Hurst, Brian Desmond (1900–). Irish director who has made many kinds of film.
Sensation 36. Glamorous Night 37. Prison Without Bars 39. On the Night of the Fire 40. *Dangerous Moonlight* 41. Alibi 42. The Hundred Pound Window 43. Theirs Is the Glory 45. Hungry Hill 47. The Mark of Cain 48. Tom Brown's Schooldays (p only) 51. *Scrooge* 51. The Malta Story 53. Simba 55. The Black Tent 56. Dangerous Exile 57. Behind the Mask 58. His and Hers 60. The Playboy of the Western World 62, etc.

Hurst, David (1925–). Austrian actor who played some comedy roles in British films.
The Perfect Woman 49. So Little Time 52. Mother Riley Meets the Vampire 52. As Long As They're Happy 53. The Intimate Stranger 56. After the Ball 57. Hello Dolly (US) 69, etc.

Hurst, Fannie (1889–1968). American popular novelist, several of whose romantic novels, usually with a tragic finale, have been filmed more than once: *Humoresque, Imitation of Life, Back Street*, etc.

Hurst, Paul (1889–1953). American character actor in hundreds of cameo roles from 1912, usually as gangster, bartender, outlaw or cop.
The Red Raiders 27. Tugboat Annie 32. Riff Raff 34. Gone with the Wind 39. Caught in the Draft 41. Jack London 44. Yellow Sky 49. The Sun Shines Bright 53, many others.

Hurst, Veronica (1931–). British light leading lady of the fifties.
Laughter in Paradise 51. Angels One Five 51. The Maze (US) 53. Will Any Gentleman? 53. The Yellow Balloon 54. Peeping Tom 58. Dead Man's Evidence 62. Licensed to Kill 64. The Boy Cried Murder 66, etc.

Hurt, John (1940–). Offbeat British stage and film leading man.
The Wild and the Willing 62. *A Man for All Seasons* 66. Before Winter Comes 69. Sinful Davey 69. In Search of Gregory 70. *10 Rillington Place* 71. Forbush and the Penguins 71. Little Malcolm and His Struggle against the Eunuchs 74. *The Naked Civil Servant* (TV) 75, etc.

Hussein, Waris (–). Director.
Melody 71. The Six Wives of Henry VIII 72.

Hussey, Olivia (1951–). British leading lady, born in Argentina.
□ The Battle of the Villa Fiorita 65. Cup Fever 65. *Romeo and Juliet* 68. All the Right Noises 69. Summertime Killer 72. Lost Horizon 73. Black Christmas 75. Jesus of Nazareth (TV) 77. The Cat and the Canary 77.

Hussey, Ruth (1914–) (Ruth Carol O'Rourke). Smart, competent, sometimes wisecracking American leading lady of the early forties.
□ Madame X 37. Judge Hardy's Children 38. Man Proof 38. Marie Antoinette 38. Hold that Kiss 38. Rich Man Poor Girl 38. Time Out for Murder 38. Spring Madness 38. Honolulu 39. Within the Law 39. Maisie 39. The Women 39. Another Thin Man 39. Blackmail 39. *Fast and Furious* 39. Northwest Passage 40. Susan and God 40. *The Philadelphia Story* 40. Flight Command 40. Free and Easy 41. Our Wife 41. Married Bachelor 41. *H. M. Pulham Esq* 41. Pierre of the Plains 42. Tennessee Johnson 42. Tender Comrade 43. *The Uninvited* 44. Marine Raiders 44. Bedside Manner 45. I Jane Doe 48. The Great Gatsby 49. Louisa 50. Mr Music 50. That's My Boy 51. Woman of the North Country 52. Stars and Stripes Forever 52. The Lady Wants Mink 53. The Facts of Life 60.

The Hustler (US 1961) (BFA best film). Robert Rossen wrote, produced and directed this unusual film from Walter Tevis' novel, with Paul Newman as a professional pool player who meets his match in Minnesota Fats, played by Jackie Gleason. Other key roles are cleverly played by George C. Scott and Myron McCormick, and the the CinemaScope photography by Eugene Shuftan (AA), together with Harry Horner's (AA) art direction, adds immeasurably to the total effect. A tragic subplot involving Piper Laurie is less successful.

Huston, Anjelica (1952–). American leading lady, daughter of John Huston.
Sinful Davey 69. A Walk With Love and Death 69. The Last Tycoon 76.

Huston, John (1906–). Unpredictable but occasionally splendid American director, son of Walter Huston.
Biography 1965: *King Rebel* by W. F. Nolan.
AS SCREENWRITER ONLY: Murders in the Rue Morgue 32. The Amazing Dr Clitterhouse 38. Jezebel 38. High Sierra 40. Sergeant York 41. Three Strangers 46, etc.
□ AS DIRECTOR: *The Maltese Falcon* (& w) 41. In This Our Life 42. Across the Pacific 42. Report from the Aleutians 43. Battle of San

Pietro 45. Let There Be Light 45 (four other official war documentaries 44–45). *Treasure of Sierra Madre* (& w) (AA) 47. *Key Largo* (& w) 48. We Were Strangers 49. *The Asphalt Jungle* (& w) 50. The Red Badge of Courage (& w) 51. *The African Queen* (& w) 52. Moulin Rouge (& w) 53. Beat the Devil (& w) 54. Moby Dick (& w) 56. Heaven Knows Mr Alison (& w) 57. The Barbarian and the Geisha 58. The Roots of Heaven (& w) 58. The Unforgiven 60. The Misfits 60. *Freud* 62. The List of Adrian Messenger 63. *The Night of the Iguana* (& w) 64. The Bible 66. Casino Royale (part) 67. Reflections in a Golden Eye 67. Sinful Davey 69. A Walk with Love and Death 69. The Kremlin Letter 70. *Fat City* 72. Judge Roy Bean 72. The Mackintosh Man 73. The Man Who Would Be King 75.

□ AS ACTOR: The Treasure of the Sierra Madre (uncredited) 47. The List of Adrian Messenger (uncredited) 63. *The Cardinal* 63. *The Bible* (as Noah) 66. Casino Royale 67. Candy 68. De Sade 69. Myra Breckinridge 70. The Deserter 70. Man in the Wilderness 71. Judge Roy Bean 72. Battle for the Planet of the Apes 73. Chinatown 74. Breakout 75. The Wind and the Lion 75.

Huston, Walter (1884–1950) (W. Houghston). Distinguished American character actor of stage and screen: latterly projected roguery and eccentricity with great vigour. He also played bit parts in his son John's first two films, as Captain Jacoby in *The Maltese Falcon* 41, and a bartender in *In This Our Life* 42. After his death his stage recording of 'September Song', played in *September Affair* 50, became a big hit.

□ Gentlemen of the Press 28. The Lady Lies 29. *The Virginian* 30. The Bad Man 30. The Virtuous Sin 30. *Abraham Lincoln* 30. The Criminal Code 31. Star Witness 31. The Ruling Voice 31. A Woman from Monte Carlo 31. A House Divided 32. *Law and Order* (as Wyatt Earp) 32. Beast of the City 32. The Wet Parade 32. Night Court 32. *American Madness* 32. Kongo 32. *Rain* 32. Hell Below 32. Gabriel over the White House 33. The Prizefighter and the Lady 33. Storm at Daybreak 33. Ann Vickers 33. Keep 'Em Rolling 33. The Tunnel (GB) 34. Rhodes of Africa (GB) 36. *Dodsworth* 36. Of Human Hearts 38. The Light That Failed 39. *All That Money Can Buy* (as the devil) 41. Swamp Water 41. The Shanghai Gesture 42. Always in My Heart 42. Yankee Doodle Dandy 42. Mission to Moscow 42. Edge of Darkness 42. North Star 43. *The Outlaw* (as Doc Holliday) 43. Dragon Seed 44. *And Then There Were None* 45. Dragonwyck 46. Duel in the Sun 46. *The*

Treasure of the Sierra Madre (AA) 47. Summer Holiday 47. The Great Sinner 49. The Furies 50.

Hutcheson, David (1905–). British light comedian who has often played monocled silly-asses, mainly on stage.
This'll Make You Whistle 35. Sabotage at Sea 41. Convoy 42. School for Secrets 46. *Vice Versa* 48. Sleeping Car to Trieste 48. The Elusive Pimpernel 50. The Evil of Frankenstein 64. The National Health 73, etc.

Hutchins, Will (1932–). Bland-faced American leading man who came to fame in 57–60 as TV's *Sugarfoot*.
No Time for Sergeants 58. Merrill's Marauders 62. The Shooting 66. Clambake 67, etc.

Hutchinson, Josephine (1904–). American actress who has usually played sweet or maternal types.
Happiness Ahead 34. The Story of Louis Pasteur 36. Son of Frankenstein 39. Somewhere in the Night 46. Ruby Gentry 52. Miracle in the Rain 56. North By Northwest 59. Huckleberry Finn 60. Baby the Rain Must Fall 64. Nevada Smith 66. Rabbit Run 70, etc.

Huth, Harold (1892–1967). British light leading man of silent days; later became producer-director.
One of the Best 27. Balaclava 28. The Silver King 29. Leave it to Me 30. The Outsider 31. Sally Bishop 32. Rome Express 32. The Ghoul 33. The Camels are Coming 34. Take My Tip 37. Hell's Cargo (d) 39. East of Piccadilly (d) 40. Busman's Honeymoon (p) 40. Breach of Promise (d) 42. Love Story (p) 44. They Were Sisters (p) 45. Caravan (p) 46. Night Beat (pd) 47. My Sister and I (pd) 48. Look Before You Love (pd) 48. One Wild Oat (p) 51. Police Dog (p) 55. The Hostage (d) 56. Idle on Parade (p) 59. The Trials of Oscar Wilde (p) 60. The Hellions (p) 61, etc.

Hutton, Betty (1921–) (Betty Jane Thornburg). Blonde and bouncy American leading lady of many singing/dancing light entertainments of the forties.
□ *The Fleet's In* 42. Star Spangled Rhythm 42. Happy Go Lucky 43. Let's Face It 43. *The Miracle of Morgan's Creek* 44. And the Angels Sing 44. Here Come the Waves 44. *Incendiary Blonde* (as Texas Guinan) 45. Duffy's Tavern 45. The Stork Club 45. Cross My Heart 46. *The Perils of Pauline* 47. Dream Girl 48. Red Hot and Blue 49. *Annie Get Your Gun* 50. Let's Dance 50. Somebody Loves Me 52. The Greatest Show on Earth 52. Spring Reunion 57.

Hutton, Brian G. (1935–). American director.
□ Fargo 65. The Pad 66. Sol Madrid 67. *Where Eagles Dare* 68. Kelly's Heroes 70. Zee and Co 71. Night Watch 73.

Hutton, Jim (1938–). American leading man who usually plays gangly types.
A Time to Love and a Time to Die 58. Bachelor in Paradise 61. The Horizontal Lieutenant 62. The Honeymoon Machine 62. Period of Adjustment 63. The Hallelujah Trail 65. Never Too Late 65. *Walk Don't Run* 66. Who's Minding the Mint 67. The Green Berets 68. Hellfighters 69, etc.
TV series: Ellery Queen 75.

Hutton, Marion (1920–) (Marion Thornburg). American singer, with the Glenn Miller band; appeared in a few forties musicals. Sister of Betty Hutton.
Orchestra Wives 42. Crazy House 44. In Society 44. Babes on Swing Street 45. Love Happy 50, etc.

Hutton, Lauren (1943–) (Mary Hutton). American leading lady.
Little Fauss and Big Halsy 71. The Gambler 74, etc.

Hutton, Robert (1920–) (Robert Bruce Winne). American leading man of the forties.
Destination Tokyo 44. Janie 44. Too Young To Know 45. Time Out of Mind 47. Always Together 48. The Steel Helmet 51. Casanova's Big Night 54. Invisible Invaders 58. Cinderfella 60. The Slime People (& pd) 62. The Secret Man (GB) 64. Finders Keepers (GB) 66. They Came from Beyond Space (GB) 68, etc.

Huxley, Aldous (1894–1963). Distinguished British novelist who spent some time in Hollywood and worked on the screenplays of *Pride and Prejudice* 40 and *Jane Eyre* 43.

Hyams, Leila (1905–). Vivacious, blonde American leading lady of the twenties.
Sandra 24. Summer Bachelors 26. The Brute 27. The Wizard 27. Alias Jimmy Valentine 28. Spite Marriage 29. The Idle Rich 29. The Bishop Murder Case 30. The Big House 30. The Flirting Widow 30. Men Call it Love 31. The Phantom of Paris 31. Red Headed Woman 32. Freaks 32. Island of Lost Souls 32. Sing Sinner Sing 33. Affairs of a Gentleman 34. Ruggles of Red Gap 35. Yellow Dust 36, many others.

Hyams, Peter (–). American director.
Busting (& w) 74. Our Time 74.

Hyde-White, Wilfrid (1903–). Impeccably British character actor of stage and screen, mainly in comedy roles.
Murder by Rope 37. *The Third Man* 49. The Story of Gilbert and Sullivan 54. See How They Run 55. The Adventures of Quentin Durward 56. *North-West Frontier* 59. Carry On Nurse 59. Two-Way Stretch 61. *My Fair Lady* 64. John Goldfarb Please Come Home 64. You Must Be Joking 65. Ten Little Indians 65. The Liquidator 65. Out Man in Marrakesh 66. Chamber of Horrors 66. Skullduggery 69. Gaily Gaily 69. Fragment of Fear 70, etc.

Hyer, Martha (1929–). American light leading lady of the fifties, in mainly routine films.
The Locket 46. The Woman on the Beach 47. The Velvet Touch 48. The Clay Pigeon 49. The Lawless 50. Salt Lake Raiders 50. Abbott and Costello Go to Mars 52. So Big 53. Riders to the Stars 54. Sabrina 54. Francis in the Navy 55. Red Sundown 56. Battle Hymn 57. Mister Cory 57. My Man Godfrey 57. Paris Holiday 58. Houseboat 58. Some Came Running 59. The Best of Everything 59. Ice Palace 60. The Last Time I Saw Archie 61. A Girl Named Tamiko 62. Wives and Lovers 63. The Carpetbaggers 64. The First Men in the Moon 64. The Sons of Katie Elder 65. The Chase 66. The Happening 67. Massacre at Fort Grant 68. Crossplot 69. Once You Kiss a Stranger 70, many others.

Hyland, Diana (1936–1977). American stage and TV actress.
One Man's Way 64. The Boy in the Plastic Bubble (TV) 76.

Hylton, Jane (1926–). British actress, in films since 1945.
When the Bough Breaks 47. Here Come the Huggetts 49. *It Started in Paradise* 52. The Weak and the Wicked 53. House of Mystery 59, many others.

Hylton, Richard (1921–1962). American actor with stage experience.
Lost Boundaries 48. The Secret of Convict Lake 51. Fixed Bayonets 51. The Pride of St Louis 52, etc.

Hyman, Kenneth (1928–). American executive producer; formerly with Allied Artists and Seven Arts in Britain, now independent.
The Hound of the Baskervilles 59. The Roman Spring of Mrs Stone 61. Gigot 62. The Small World of Sammy Lee 63. The Hill 65. The Dirty Dozen 66, etc.

Hymer, Warren (1906–1948). American

character actor with stage experience; usually seen as dim-witted gangster.

Up the River 30. Charlie Chan Carries On 31. Twenty Thousand Years in Sing Sing 32. Kid Millions 35. San Francisco 36. Tainted Money 37. Destry Rides Again 39. Meet John Doe 41. Baby Face Morgan 42. Joe Palooka Champ 46, many others.

hypnosis on the screen has mainly been a basis for melodrama. *Svengali* was its most demonic exponent, but others who followed in his footsteps were Jacques Bergerac in *The Hypnotic Eye,* Boris Karloff in *The Climax,* Bela Lugosi in *Dracula,* Charles Gray in *The Devil Rides Out,* Erich Von Stroheim in *The Mask of Diijon,* Christopher Lee in *The Face of Fu Manchu,* Orson Welles in *Black Magic,* and Jose Ferrer in *Whirlpool* (in which, immediately after major surgery, he hypnotized himself into leaving his bed and committing a murder). In *Fear in the Night* and its remake *Nightmare,* De Forrest Kelley and Kevin McCarthy were hypnotized into becoming murderers. Comic uses are legion, the perpetrators including Lugosi in *Abbott and Costello Meet Frankenstein,* Karloff in *The Secret Life of Walter Mitty,* Gale Sondergaard in *Road to Rio,* the cast of *How to be Very Very Popular,* Yves Montand in *On a Clear Day You Can See Forever,* Alan Badel in *Will Any Gentleman,* Mildred Natwick in *The Court Jester,* and Pat Collins in *Divorce American Style.* The chief serious study of the subject has been *Freud,* though one might also count *The Search for Bridey Murphy.*

Hyson, Dorothy (1915–). British leading lady of the thirties, with stage experience (mainly in Aldwych farces).

Soldiers of the King 33. The Ghoul 33. Turkey Time 33. Sing As We Go 34. A Cup of Kindness 34. Spare a Copper 40, etc.

Hytten, Olaf (1888–1955). Scottish character actor in American films.

It Is the Law 24. The Salvation Hunters 27. Daughter of the Dragon 31. Berkeley Square 33. Becky Sharp 35. The Good Earth 37. The Adventures of Robin Hood 38. Our Neighbours The Carters 40. The Black Swan 42. The Lodger 44. Three Strangers 46. Perils of The Jungle 53, etc.

I Am a Camera: see *Cabaret*.

I Am a Fugitive from a Chain Gang (US 1932). Arguably the first American social melodrama to urge actual reforms; also the first of Warner's 'prestige' films of the thirties. Paul Muni played the man forced against his will into a life of crime. Written by Sheridan Gibney and Brown Holmes; directed by Mervyn Le Roy.

I, Claudius (GB 1937). Alexander Korda's ambitious epic · of ancient Rome, based on Robert Graves' highly readable book, was never finished: star Merle Oberon was injured in a car crash and the production, which had presented Korda with many problems, was abandoned after two or three reels were in the can. Nearly thirty years later, in 1965, a television film, *The Epic That Never Was*, pieced the story together and made one wish that more had been shot, if only for the sake of George Perinal's photography and the performances of Charles Laughton and Emlyn Williams. Director Josef Von Sternberg seemed less at home with the material. A TV serial starring Derek Jacobi followed in 1976.

I Married a Witch (US 1942). Generally considered René Clair's best American film, this gay fantasy starred Fredric March and Veronica Lake, with Cecil Kellaway as a most delightful old sorcerer. It directly inspired the more recent TV series *Bewitched*, *I Dream of Jeannie* and *The Girl With Something Extra*.

Ibbetson, Arthur (1922–). British cinematographer.
The Horse's Mouth 58. The Angry Silence 59. The League of Gentlemen 60. *Tunes of Glory* 61. Whistle Down the Wind 61. The Inspector 62. Nine Hours to Rama 63. I Could Go On Singing 63. The Chalk Garden 64. Sky West and Crooked 65. A Countess from Hong Kong 66. Inspector Clouseau 68. Where Eagles Dare 68. The Walking Stick 69. Anne of the Thousand Days 70. The Railway Children 70. Willie Wonka and the Chocolate Factory 71. A Doll's House 73. Frankenstein: the True Story (TV) 73.

11 Harrowhouse 74. It Shouldn't Happen to a Vet 76, etc.

Ibert, Jacques (1890–1962). French composer.
Don Quixote 34. Golgotha 35. La Charette Fantome 38. Macbeth 48, etc.

Ichikawa, Kon (1915–). Distinguished Japanese director.
The Heart 54. The Punishment Room 55. *The Burmese Harp* 55. Odd Obsessions 58. *Fires on the Plain* 59. The Sin 61. An Actor's Revenge 63. *Alone on the Pacific* 66, etc.

Idiot's Delight (US 1939). Robert Sherwood's play marked Broadway's earliest reaction to the war clouds looming over Europe. This hasty film version, with Clark Gable as the eager hoofer and Norma Shearer as the fake duchess, managed to be as false as its continental backcloths, despite Clarence Brown's direction, and probably made the danger seem remote instead of imminent to many Americans. In the early sixties a short-lived TV series called *Harry's Girls* borrowed the central character if little else.

If . . . (GB 1967). An agreeably anarchic though overlong and formless attack on the British public school system, written by David Sherwin and directed by Lindsay Anderson. Much of it seemed as meaningless as its random alternation between colour and monochrome, but its box office success (partly due to some full frontal nudity) was undoubted and led to a flurry of surrealist movies with much less in the way of observation to commend them.

If I Had a Million (US 1933). Probably the first short story compendium; this one had the connecting link of a sudden windfall to a variety of people. The most quoted episode (each had a different director) is that in which Charles Laughton, as a down-trodden clerk, blows a raspberry to his boss.

If I Were King. Justin McCarthy's play, a historical adventure about François Villon, was filmed in 1920 with William Farnum and in 1938 with Ronald Colman. On it was based Rudolf Friml's operetta *The Vagabond King*, filmed in 1930 with Dennis King and Jeanette Macdonald, and in 1955 with Oreste Kirkop and Kathryn Grayson.

If Winter Comes. A. S. M. Hutchinson's sentimental romance about the effect of malicious gossip in a village community was first filmed in 1923 with Percy Marmont and Ann Forrest, directed by Harry Millarde. In 1947 MGM unconvincingly up-dated it for Walter Pidgeon and Deborah Kerr, with direction by Victor Saville.

Ifield, Frank (1936–). British-born ballad singer who grew up in Australia.
Only film: *Up Jumped a Swagman* 65.

Ihnat, Steve (1934–1972). Czech-born general purpose actor in Hollywood, mostly in TV.
□ The Chase 66. Countdown 67. The Hour of the Gun 67. Kona Coast 68. Madigan 69. Fuzz 72. *The Honkers* (wd only) 72, etc.

Illing, Peter (1899–1966). German-born character actor, in British films since the forties.
The End of the River 46. Eureka Stockade 48. I'll Get You for This 51. The Young Lovers 54. Zarak 56. Whirlpool 59. Sands of the Desert 60. The Twenty-fifth Hour 66, many others.

Image, Jean (1911–). French animator, best known abroad for his cartoon feature *Johnny Lionheart (Jeannot I.'Intrépide)* 50.

I'm All Right Jack (GB 1959). An ironic comedy on the serious subject of labour relations, with Peter Sellers as the communist shop steward and Ian Carmichael as the innocent who precipitates a strike. The Boulting Brothers produced and directed from an enjoyable if uneven script by themselves and Frank Harvey based on Alan Hackney's novel *Private Life*.

Imitation of Life. Fannie Hurst's romantic novel, with its naïve but moving early depiction of a race problem (a black girl tries to pass for white), was filmed in 1934 with Claudette Colbert, Warren William and Louise Beavers; director John M. Stahl. In 1959 it was glossily refashioned for Lana Turner, John Gavin and Juanita Moore; directed by Douglas Sirk, photography by Russell Metty.

impresarios presented on film include Sol Hurok, by David Wayne in *Tonight We Sing*;

Rupert D'Oyly Carte, by Peter Finch in *The Story of Gilbert and Sullivan*; Walter de Frece, by Laurence Harvey in *After the Ball*; David Belasco, by Claude Rains in *Lady With Red Hair*; Lew Dockstatter, by John Alexander in *The Jolson Story*; Noel Coward by Daniel Massey, and André Charlot by Alan Oppenheimer, in *Star!*; and Florenz Ziegfeld, by William Powell in *The Great Ziegfeld* and by Walter Pidgeon in *Funny Girl*. Of fictional impresarios, the most memorable were those played by John Barrymore in *Maytime* and Anton Walbrook in *The Red Shoes*.

impressionism. Generally understood to mean contriving an effect or making a point by building up a sequence from short disconnected shots or scenes.

in-jokes were especially frequent when Hollywood was a parochial society, and many must have been so private as to escape the general eye. The following, however, seem reasonably typical. *The Black Cat* (34): Boris Karloff as a devil worshipper has to be heard reciting an invocation to Satan, which to please the Hays Code is made up of such Latin phrases as 'cave canem' (beware of the dog), 'cum grano salis' (with a grain of salt), 'in vino veritas' (in wine is truth) and 'reductio ad absurdum est' (it is shown to be impossible). *Bride of Frankenstein*: Ernest Thesiger repeats a line ('It's my only weakness') from his previous role for the same director in *The Old Dark House*. *Mad Love*: a statue apparently comes to life, and a frightened onlooker says 'It went for a little walk', which is a line used of the monster in *The Mummy*, the same director's previous film. *His Girl Friday*: Cary Grant refers to the execution of a fellow named Archie Leach, which is Grant's own real name. *Hellzapoppin*: Olsen and Johnson see a sledge on a film set and remark 'I thought they burned that', a reference to Rosebud in *Citizen Kane*. *Song of the Thin Man*: William Powell finds a razor blade and remarks 'Somerset Maugham has been here', a reference to the author's current best seller *The Razor's Edge*. *The Maltese Falcon* and *In This Our Life*: Walter Huston plays uncredited bit parts under his son John's direction. (One of innumerable similar instances.) *On the Town*: Frank Sinatra is subjected to good-natured joshing about his real-life marriage to Ava Gardner. *Arise My Love*: Ray Milland, asked whether he was a test pilot, replies 'No, that was Clark Gable', referring to the recently released *Test Pilot*. *Northern Pursuit*: Errol Flynn, then in the middle of a real-life rape case, tells the heroine she is the only girl he has ever loved, then looks at the audience and says: 'What am I saying?' *How to Marry a Millionaire*: Lauren Bacall, then married to Humphrey Bogart, says in conversation 'That old man in *The African Queen*, I'm crazy about him'. *The Big Store*: Groucho tells the audience: 'This scene should have been in Technicolor but Mr Mayer said it was too expensive'. (Again, many similar instances exist, notably in the *Road* films, which are full of studio gags such as 'Paramount will protect us 'cause we're signed for five more years'.) *Another Dawn*: in the thirties, whenever a cinema canopy was shown, it usually advertised a non-existent film under this title; but in 1938 Warners were stuck for a title for their new Errol Flynn film, so they irrelevantly and cynically called it *Another Dawn*. *Some Like It Hot*: Tony Curtis has to impersonate a millionaire and as part of the disguise gives a devastatingly accurate impression of Cary Grant's voice, only be told scathingly by Jack Lemmon 'Nobody talks like that!' In the same movie, and also in *Singin' in the Rain*, a gangster tosses a coin in imitation of George Raft in *Scarface*. *The VIPs*: asked for her home phone number, Elizabeth Taylor gives 'Grosvenor 7060', which is the number of MGM's London office. *Star Spangled Rhythm*: the harassed and excitable producer played by Walter Abel is named G. B. de Soto, in imitation of B. G. de Sylva, then a Paramount producer. *The Wings of Eagles*: the film director, John Dodge, is played by Ward Bond as an imitation of John Ford, who directed *The Wings of Eagles*. *Irma La Douce*: the pimps' union is called the Mecs' Paris Protective Association, or MPPA, which also stands for Motion Picture Producers Association, an organization which gave director Billy Wilder some trouble. *Caprice*: heroine Doris Day goes to the movies and sees a Doris Day movie. *One Two Three*: James Cagney threatens a girl with a grapefruit, mimicking his own action thirty years before in *Public Enemy*: he also steals from *Little Caesar* the line 'Mother of mercy, is this the end of Rico?' *The Entertainer*: reference is made to Sergeant Ossie Morris; the film was photographed by Ossie Morris. *Finian's Rainbow*: Fred Astaire has a short speech which consists, with different emphasis, of the words of one of his old songs. *The House that Dripped Blood*: Geoffrey Bayldon as a mad scientist is made up to look like Ernest Thesiger in *Bride of Frankenstein*. *How to Marry a Millionaire*: Betty Grable fails to recognize a Harry James recording, (she was married to him at the time). *For The First Time*: there is reference to a convict named Cocozza, which happens to be star Mario Lanza's real name. *Connecting Rooms*: Bette Davis passes a poster mentioning

stage star Margot Channing, the name of the character she played in *All About Eve*. (The name is also used for one of the unseen characters in *Sleuth*.) *Pete 'N Tillie*: Walter Matthau takes his girl to a cinema showing *Lonely Are the Brave*, one of his own earlier films. *Aaron Slick From Punkin Crick*: a waiter in a café scene calls 'Give that Perlberg-Seaton order special attention'. (Perlberg and Seaton produced and directed the film.) *Road to Utopia*: Bob Hope says Bing Crosby's voice is 'just right for selling cheese', a reference to Bing's then-current radio show, *Kraft Music Hall*. *Godfather II*: Troy Donahue plays a character called Merle Johnson, which is his own real name. *Dames*: Dick Powell is told 'Miss Warren, Miss Dubin and Miss Kelly are outside', a reference to song writers Al Dubin and Harry Warren and dress designer Orry-Kelly.

In the Heat of the Night (US 1967; AA). Basically a rather unconvincing murder mystery set in a sweltering small town in the deep south, this screenplay by Sterling Silliphant (AA) benefited from fine colour photography by Haskell Wexler and splendid acting from Rod Steiger (AA) and Sidney Poitier, whose conflict (as lazy sheriff and arrogant Philadelphia detective) was intensified by race bitterness. Norman Jewison produced and directed. Two 'sequels' starring Poitier, *They Call Me Mister Tibbs* and *The Organization*, were disappointing.

In Which We Serve (GB 1942). The first really important film about naval aspects of World War II, this was very much a Noel Coward enterprise. He surprised everyone at the time not only by producing, co-directing, and writing the script and music, but by his serious and effective performance as the captain of a doomed destroyer. Highly effective propaganda in Britain, the film was given a special Academy Award. Cast included Bernard Miles, John Mills, Richard Attenborough and Celia Johnson.

Ince, Ralph (1887–1937). American leading man of the twenties who rather oddly ended his career in Britain directing quota quickies.

AS ACTOR: The Land of Opportunity 20. The Sea Wolf 25. Bigger than Barnum's 26. Wall Street 29. Little Caesar 30. The Big Gamble 31. The Hatchet Man 32. The Tenderfoot 32. Havana Widows 33, etc.
AS DIRECTOR: A Man's Home 21. Homeward Bound 23. A Moral Sinner 24. Smooth as Satin 25. Bigger than Barnum's 26. South Sea Love 28. Lucky Devils 33. What's in a Name? 34. Murder at Monte Carlo 34. Blue

Smoke 35. It's You I Want 35. Hail and Farewell 36. The Vulture 36. The Man Who Made Diamonds 37, many others.

Ince, Thomas (1882–1924). American director, a contemporary of D. W. Griffith and some say an equal innovator; he certainly systematized production methods. Best remembered now for *Custer's Last Fight* 12. *Civilization* 15. *Human Wreckage* 23.

incest has scarcely been fashionable film fare, though the theatrical acceptance of it goes back to *Oedipus Rex* (filmed in 1969) and one supposes *The Bible* (filmed in 1966) which fails to explain how else Adam and Eve's two sons propagated the species. It has been implied in a handful of American films from *Scarface* to *Toys in the Attic*, and more or less clearly stated in *Mourning Becomes Electra, A View from the Bridge* and *Chinatown*. Its full flowering came with the British *Brotherly Love*, but as expected the French had beaten us to it with *Souffle au Coeur*.

India has provided the setting for English-speaking films mainly of the military kind: *King of the Khyber Rifles, The Drum, Lives of a Bengal Lancer, Gunga Din, Soldiers Three, The Charge of the Light Brigade* (1936 version), *Bengal Brigade,* and *Conduct Unbecoming.* Civilian interests were the concern of *They Met in Bombay, The Rains Came, Elephant Boy, Bhowani Junction, Monsoon, The River Song of India, Calcutta, Thunder in the East, Northwest Frontier, Nine Hours to Rama* and *The Guru.* Of native Indian films only a few have percolated to western cinemas, mostly directed by Mehboob, Satyajit Ray, or James Ivory.

Indians: see *Red Indians.*

Inescort, Frieda (1901–1976). Scottish-born actress of well bred roles, once secretary to Lady Astor; on stage from 1922. Went to Hollywood to begin film career.
If You Could Only Cook 35. Call it a Day 37. Beauty for the Asking 38. Woman Doctor 39. Pride and Prejudice 40. The Amazing Mrs Holliday 43. The Return of the Vampire 43. The Judge Steps Out 47. Foxfire 55. The Crowded Sky 60, etc.

The Informer (US 1935). Despite, or perhaps because of, its murky expressionist studio look, this film of Liam O'Flaherty's novel about Dublin during the troubles was able to turn melodrama into something approaching a tragedy. It won Academy Awards for director John Ford, Max Steiner's music, Dudley Nichols' script, and Victor McLaglen's performance as the half-witted brute who betrays his friend for a handful of silver. Joseph H. August's photography was also notable. There was a previous British silent version in 1928, starring Lars Hanson; and in 1968 Jules Dassin made a black variation called *Uptight.*

Inge, William (1913–1973). American playwright, most of whose work has been translated to the screen.
Come Back Little Sheba 52. Picnic 56. Bus Stop 56. The Dark at the Top of the Stairs 60. Splendor in the Grass (w) 61. The Stripper 63, etc.

Ingels, Marty (1936–). American character comedian.
Ladies' Man 60. Armored Command 61. The Horizontal Lieutenant 62. Wild and Wonderful 64. The Busy Body 67. For Singles Only 68, etc.
TV series: *I'm Dickens He's Fenster* 62.

Ingham, Barrie (1934–). British light leading man and general purpose actor.
Tiara Tahiti 62. Invasion 66. Dr Who and the Daleks 66. A Challenge for Robin Hood (title role) 68, etc.

Ingram, Rex (1892–1950). (Reginald Hitchcock). Irishman who went to Hollywood and became first an actor and screenwriter, then a noted director of silent spectaculars.
AS ACTOR: The Great Problem 16. Reward of the Faithless 17. Under Crimson Skies 19. Trifling Women 22, etc.
AS DIRECTOR: *The Four Horsemen of the Apocalypse* 21. The Conquering Power 21. *The Prisoner of Zenda* 22. Where the Pavement Ends 23. *Scaramouche* 23. The Arab 24. *Mare Nostrum* 26. The Magician 26. The Garden of Allah 27. Baroud 31. Love in Morocco 33, etc.

Ingram, Rex (1895–1969). Impressive black actor, in films from 1919; former doctor.
The Ten Commandments 23. The Big Parade 26. The Four Feathers 29. *The Emperor Jones* 33. Captain Blood 35. *Green Pastures* (as De Lawd) 36. Huckleberry Finn 38. *The Thief of Baghdad* (as the genie) 40. *Cabin in the Sky* (as Satan) 43. Sahara 43. A Thousand and One Nights 44. God's Little Acre 59. Watusi 59. Hurry Sundown 67, etc.

Ingster, Boris (c. 1913–). American writer-director.
The Last Days of Pompeii (co-w) 35. Happy Landings (w) 38. Stranger on the Third Floor (d)

40. Paris Underground (w) 45. The Judge Steps Out (wd) 49. Forgery (d) 50. Something for the Birds (co-w) 52, etc.

Inherit the Wind (US 1960). Although essentially a filmed play, this is probably the most satisfactory cinematic example of Stanley Kramer's work as a producer-director. Based on Jerome Laurence and Robert E. Lee's dramatization of the Scopes' 'monkey trial' of the twenties, when a schoolmaster in a God-fearing community was put in the dock for teaching evolution, the film benefits enormously from the performances of Spencer Tracy and Fredric March as defence and prosecution counsels (in real life Clarence Darrow and William Jennings Bryan). An absorbing entertainment, cleanly photographed by Ernest Laszlo.

Inner Sanctum. A series of second features made by Universal in the early forties, starring Lon Chaney Jnr and offering apparently supernatural phenomena which are explained away in the last reel. Based on a radio series; introduced for no very clear reason by a spiel from a misshapen head within a crystal ball on a boardroom table! Titles were *Calling Dr Death, Weird Woman, Pillow of Death, Dead Man's Eyes, The Frozen Ghost, Strange Confession.*

The Inn of the Sixth Happiness (GB 1958). A glamorized but generally successful version of the life of Gladys Aylward, an indomitable British missionary to China in the thirties. Ingrid Bergman, theoretically miscast, gave a commanding star performance; Robert Donat in his last film was most moving as a mandarin converted to Christianity. Directed by Mark Robson, photographed by Frederick Young, this was hailed as a reversion to 'family entertainment' after what seemed at the time a period of over-sophistication.

insanity in the cinema has usually been of the criminal kind: Robert Montgomery (and Albert Finney) in *Night Must Fall*, Keir Dullea in *Bunny Lake Is Missing*, Bette Davis in *Whatever Happened to Baby Jane?* and *The Nanny*, Franchot Tone in *Phantom Lady*, George Brent in *The Spiral Staircase*, Joseph Cotten in *Shadow of a Doubt*, Edward G. Robinson in *The Sea Wolf*, Robert Ryan in *Beware My Lovely*, Ivan Kirov in *Spectre of the Rose*, Robert Mitchum in *Night of the Hunter*, Douglass Montgomery in *The Cat and the Canary*, Anthony Perkins in *Psycho*, Hywel Bennett in *Twisted Nerve*, Oliver Reed in *Paranoiac*, Brember Wills in *The Old Dark House* and

hundreds of others. Indeed, most screen villains have been, if not psychopathic, at least subject to an *idée fixé*: and many a tortured hero has had a mad wife in the attic. Insanity has however been played quite frequently for comedy, notably in *Harvey, Miss Tatlock's Millions, The Criminal Life of Archibaldo de la Cruz* and *Drôle de Drame*. Serious studies of insanity and its effects are on the increase, not only through fictitious situations as shown in *A Bill of Divorcement, The Shrike, Suddenly Last Summer, Of Mice and Men, David and Lisa, Shock Corridor, Shock Treatment, Diary of a Madman, One Flew over the Cuckoo's Nest* and *Cul de Sac*, but also in more clinical investigations such as *The Snake Pit, El, Labyrinth, La Tête contre les Murs, Morgan, Pressure Point, A Child Is Waiting, Lilith* and *Repulsion*. A mixture of attitudes is found in the scientific fantasy of *Charly*; while *Bedlam* was a curious attempt at a horror film set entirely in an asylum, a setting later used by *The Marat/Sade*. In *King of Hearts* the insane are shown to be wiser than the rest, like Mr Dick in *David Copperfield*.

insects on the screen have generally been of the monstrous kind: *Tarantula, The Black Scorpion, The Wasp Woman, The Fly, Them*, and *The Monster That Challenged the World* come to mind. Of course, normal-sized ants can be monstrous enough if seen in quantity, as in *The Naked Jungle*, or if you are as small as *The Incredible Shrinking Man*. Giant spiders are perhaps the most popular breed: there was a particularly loathsome one in *The Thief of Baghdad*. Friendly insects have included those who went to the 'ugly bug ball' in *Summer Magic*; and the dancing caterpillar of *Once upon a Time*. The most symbolic insect was certainly the butterfly in *All Quiet on the Western Front*; the most abundant, the locust in *The Good Earth*. A documentary feature about insects of the most dramatic kind was *The Hellstrom Chronicle*.

insert shot. One inserted into a dramatic scene, usually for the purpose of giving the audience a closer look at what the character on screen is seeing, e.g. a letter or a newspaper headline.

Intermezzo. A simple romantic tale, larded with classical music, this was originally filmed in Sweden in 1936 by Gustav Molander, with Gosta Ekman and Ingrid Bergman. In 1939 Bergman recreated the role in Hollywood opposite Leslie Howard; the film, known in Britain as *Escape to Happiness*, was directed by Gregory Ratoff.

Intolerance (US 1916). D. W. Griffith's epic film, sub-titled 'Love's Struggle Through the Ages', is a sentimentally-conceived examination of intolerance in four periods of history. The narrative moves constantly from one story to another, with frenzied cross-cutting at the climax. The spectacle of the Babylon sequence is on a massive scale, but the public were confused and the film was long considered a commercial failure. Written by Griffith, photographed by Billy Bitzer.

Invasion of the Body Snatchers (US 1956). A catch-penny title obscures the most subtle film in the science-fiction cycle, with no visual horror whatever; about a small town whose population is taken over by 'duplicates' from outer space. Directed by Don Siegel; from Jack Finney's novel; with Kevin McCarthy and Dana Wynter.

inventors have been the subject of many screen biographies; indeed, Don Ameche had to live down his invention of the telephone in *The Story of Alexander Graham Bell* and of the sub-machine gun in *A Genius in the Family*. Mickey Rooney appeared as *Young Tom Edison* and Spencer Tracy as *Edison the Man*; James Stewart was *Carbine Williams*; Robert Donat played William Friese-Greene, inventor of the movie camera, in *The Magic Box*. Joel McCrea in *The Great Moment* invented laughing gas; *The Sound Barrier* covered Sir Frank Whittle's invention of the jet engine, and *The Dam Busters* has Michael Redgrave as the inventor of the bouncing bomb, Dr Barnes Wallis. That prolific inventor Galileo was played in an Italian film by Cyril Cusack and more recently by Topol. In *I Aim At the Stars* Curt Jurgens was Wernher von Braun. Benjamin Franklin was portrayed not by an actor but by Disney's cartoonists in *Ben and Me*. Charles Coburn later took over in *John Paul Jones* and Howard da Silva in *1776*.

The Invisible Man. The rights to H. G. Wells' tragi-comic fantasy novel were bought by Universal in 1933; the resulting film, directed by James Whale with splendid trick effects by Arthur Edeson, made a star of Claude Rains although his face was seen only briefly, in death. Universal later made a sporadic low-budget series alternating between farce and melodrama: *The Invisible Man Returns* (Vincent Price) 40, *The Invisible Woman* (Virginia Bruce) 40, *Invisible Agent* (Jon Hall) 42, *The Invisible Man's Revenge* (Jon Hall) 44, *Abbott and Costello Meet the Invisible Man* (Arthur Franz) 51. Meanwhile invisibility had been put to excellent comic effect in the *Topper* series (qv) and many other movies. *Invisible Boy* 57 was

something else again, a sequel to *Forbidden Planet*; but in the early sixties a new series of 'invisible man' movies emanated from Argentina and Mexico: there was a TV series in 1958; and in 1972 the Disney studios had fun with invisibility in *Now You See Him, Now You Don't*.

Invitation to the Dance (US/GB 1956). This ambitious ballet film in three parts was devised and directed by Gene Kelly, who also starred. Its lack of commercial success harmed his career, especially as it was not quite the masterpiece which had been anticipated. The cartoon sequence has been shown separately as *The Magic Lamp*.

The Ipcress File (GB 1965). A 'realistic' espionage picture which offered a useful corrective to the adventures of James Bond, this astringent movie was more coherent than the Len Deighton novel from which it sprang, but suffered from director Sidney Furie's apparent determination to smother it in weird camera angles. However, it clearly marked out Michael Caine for stardom; and it won BFA awards as the best British picture, also for Ken Adam's art direction and Otto Heller's photography.

Ireland to film-makers has rather too often meant 'the troubles', which were celebrated in *Beloved Enemy*, *The Informer*, *The Gentle Gunman*, *Shake Hands with the Devil*, and the films of Sean O'Casey's plays, including *Juno and the Paycock* and *The Plough and the Stars*. (Rod Taylor played O'Casey, lightly disguised, in *Young Cassidy*.) More romantic or whimsical views of Eire were expressed in *The Luck of the Irish*, *The Rising of the Moon*, *Top of the Morning*, *Broth of a Boy*, *Home is the Hero*, *The Quiet Man*, *I See a Dark Stranger*, *Happy Ever After*, *Hungry Hill*, *The Search for Bridey Murphy*, *Jacqueline*, *Rooney*, *Never Put It In Writing* and *Ulysses*; realism was sought in *Odd Man Out*, *Parnell*, *Captain Boycott*, *No Resting Place*, *A Terrible Beauty*, and *Ryan's Daughter*. The number of Irish characters on the screen is of course legion, the most numerous and memorable varieties being priests, drunks, New York cops, and Old Mother Riley. The new 'troubles' of the early seventies have been, at the time of writing, too horrifying to provoke a response from makers of fiction films, apart from a TV movie called *War of Children*.

Ireland, Jill (1936–). British leading lady of the fifties.
Oh Rosalinda 55. Three Men in a Boat 55. Hell Drivers 57. Robbery under Arms 57. Carry On

Nurse 59. Raising the Wind 61. Twice Round the Daffodils 62. Villa Rides (US) 68. Rider on the Rain (US) 70. The Mechanic (US) 72. Wild Horses (US) 73. The Valachi Papers (It). 73. Breakheart Pass (US) 76. From Noon Till Three (US) 76, etc.
TV series: Shane 66.

Ireland, John (1914–). Canadian leading man in Hollywood; a popular tough-cynical hero of the early fifties, he declined with unaccountable rapidity to bit parts and second features.
A Walk in the Sun 45. Behind Green Lights 46. The Gangster 47. Raw Deal 48. Red River 48. I Shot Jesse James 49. Anna Lucasta 49. The Doolins of Oklahoma 49. *All the King's Men* 49. Cargo to Capetown 50. The Scarf 51. Red Mountain 51. Hurricane Smith 52. Outlaw Territory 53. Security Risk 54. *The Good Die Young* (GB) 54. Queen Bee 55. Gunfight at the OK Corral 57. Party Girl 58. No Place to Land 59. Spartacus 60. Brushfire 62. The Ceremony 63. The Fall of the Roman Empire 64. I Saw what you Did 65. Fort Utah 67. Caxambu 67. Arizona Bushwackers 68. One on Top of the Other 70. The House of the Seven Corpses 73, many others.

Irene (1901–1962). Long-standing MGM costume designer.

iris. An adjustable diaphragm in the camera which opens or closes from black like an expanding or contracting circle, giving a similar effect on the screen. So called because it resembles the iris of the human eye.

Israel's native films have been few owing to problems of finance and language: *Hill 24 Does Not Answer* 55 is still the most notable, though a few comedies have been exported. The country's problems however have been fully aired in *Exodus, Judith, Cast a Giant Shadow* and *QB VII.*

Isherwood, Christopher (1904–) (William Bradshaw). English novelist of the thirties who wrote the stories on which *I Am a Camera* and *Cabaret* were based. He later settled in California and wrote a few screenplays.

It Always Rains on Sunday (GB 1947). A once-praised example of early English realism which cannot now stand comparison with the *Saturday Night and Sunday Morning* school. Basically a cliché-ridden slice of hokum about an escaped convict in London's East End, its often effective low-life atmosphere was chiefly attributable to Douglas Slocombe's photography and to the cosy familiarity of its long list of British players led by Jack Warner and Googie Withers.

It Happened Here (GB 1957–1963). A remarkable first film by two semi-professionals, Kevin Brownlow and Andrew Mollo, shot on a tiny budget over a period of seven years. In dramatically unwieldy but frequently vivid fashion it paints a grim picture of what might have happened if the Nazis had invaded London in 1942, and although sometimes let down by its dialogue sequences, the fake newsreel montages alone make it an achievement of more than mere cleverness.

It Happened One Night (US 1934). This enormously successful romantic comedy was written by Robert Riskin (AA), directed by Frank Capra (AA), starred Claudette Colbert (AA) as a runaway heiress and Clark Gable (AA) as a wandering journalist. (It also won the Award for the best picture.) Its lively good humour and piquant dialogue endeared it to all comers; if today it seems on the slow side, it is infinitely preferable to the 1956 remake, *You Can't Run Away From It*, with June Allyson and Jack Lemmon.

Italian Cinema was an international force in the early years of the century with spectaculars like *Cabiria* and *Quo Vadis*. It later succumbed to the power of Hollywood and was little heard from until the post-war realist movement brought de Sica to world eminence. *Bicycle Thieves* was the high water mark of achievement; afterwards came a slow slide into the commercialism of the fifties, which however re-established Rome—and Cinecitta Studios—as a world force in film making, together with the idiosyncratic fancies of Fellini and Antonioni. Now many big Hollywood films are made on Italian locations, as well as the familiar cut-rate spectaculars peopled by mythical strong-men and the 'spaghetti westerns' which ape Hollywood traditions but add an extra helping of violence.

An Italian Straw Hat (Un Chapeau de Paille d'Italie) (France 1928). Probably René Clair's most famous silent comedy, this account of a hilariously impeded marriage, though now occasionally ponderous, set a new style in fast-paced yet stylish visual fun. Written by Clair from a play by Eugene Labiche.

It's a Mad Mad Mad Mad World (US 1963). A marathon attempt to revive silent slapstick comedy and combine it with the modern taste for violence, all in colour and single-lens Cinerama. A large star cast played second fiddle to the stunt men; Stanley Kramer produced and directed from a script by William and Tania Rose.

It's a Wonderful Life (US 1946). Frank Capra's own favourite among his films, this frantic but sentimental comedy concerns a would be suicide (James Stewart) saved by an elderly angel (Henry Travers) who points out in vivid form how his small town friends would have missed him had he not lived. A splendid piece of film pyrotechnics, with a host of familiar actors in full throttle; written by Frances Goodrich, Albert Hackett, and Capra, whose last film in this vein it proved to be.

Iturbi, Jose (1895–). Spanish pianist and conductor who made his American concert debut in 1929; in the forties appeared in a number of MGM musicals and helped to popularise classical music.
□ Thousands Cheer 43. Two Girls and a Sailor 44. Music for Millions 44. A Song to Remember (dubbed piano for Cornel Wilde; his recording of a Chopin Polonaise sold over one million copies) 44. Anchors Aweigh 45. Holiday in Mexico 46. Three Daring Daughters 48. That Midnight Kiss 49.

Ivan, Rosalind (1884–1959). American character actress, mainly on stage.
The Suspect 44. Three Strangers 46. The Corn Is Green 46. Ivy 47. The Robe 53. Elephant Walk 54, etc.

Ivan the Terrible (USSR 1942–1946). Eisenstein's two-part historical film is full of splendidly grotesque imagery. Part One was released in 1942; Part Two was banned temporarily for political reasons and when eventually released proved somewhat disappointing because its colour experiments compared unfavourably with the brilliant black and white of Part One.

Ivano, Paul (1900–). American cinematographer.
The Dancers 25. No Other Woman 28. Atlantic Flight 37. *The Shanghai Gesture* 41. See My Lawer 44. Spider Woman Strikes Back 46. Champagne for Caesar 50. For Men Only 52. Hold Back Tomorrow 55. Lizzie 57. Chubasco 68, many others, especially second unit shooting.

Ivens, Joris (1898–). Dutch writer-director best known for documentaries.
Autobiography 1969: *The Camera and I.*
Rain 29. Zuidersee 30. New Earth 34. Spanish Earth 37. The 400 Millions 39. The Power and the Land 40. Song of the Rivers 53. The Threatening Sky 66, etc.

Ives, Burl (1909–) (Burl Icle Ivanhoe). American actor and ballad-singer, once itinerant worker and professional footballer. His paunchy figure, beard and ready smile are equally adaptable to villainous or sympathetic parts.
Smoky (debut) 46. East of Eden 54. *Cat on a Hot Tin Roof* 57. *The Big Country* (AA) 58. Our Man in Havana 59. The Brass Bottle 64. Rocket to the Moon 67. The McMasters 70. The Only Way Out is Dead 70, etc.
TV series: O.K. Crackerby 65. The Bold Ones 69.

Ivory, James (1928–). American director who makes films in India.
□ The Householder 62. *Shakespeare Wallah* 64. The Guru 69. Bombay Talkie 70. Savages (US) 72. The Wild Party (US) 75.

Iwerks, Ub (1900–71). American animator, long associated with Disney (he drew the first Mickey Mouse cartoon, *Plane Crazy*). Formed own company in 1930 to create Flip the Frog; went back to Disney 1940 as director of technical research. AA 1959 for improvements in optical printing, 1965 for advancing techniques of travelling matte. Iwerks did much of the complex trick work for Hitchcock's *The Birds.*

J

Jack the Ripper. The unknown murderer of London prostitutes in 1888–89 has stimulated several flights of film fancy. Pabst brought him in to carry off the heroine of *Pandora's Box* 28. Two years earlier Alfred Hitchcock had directed the first film adaptation of Mrs Belloc Lowndes' novel *The Lodger*, but in this version Ivor Novello was found not to be the Ripper after all. Further versions were offered by Maurice Elvey in 1932 (Ivor Novello), John Brahm in 1944 (Laird Cregar) and Hugo Fregonese in 1953 (Jack Palance as *The Man in the Attic*). Further slight variations were posed in *The Phantom Fiend* 35 and *The Strangler* 64, while the long-standing puzzle was 'solved' in *Jack the Ripper* 58, *A Study in Terror* 65 and a TV 'Thriller' episode called *Yours Truly Jack the Ripper*. The Ripper was used as an alibi by *Dr Jekyll and Sister Hyde* 71, and the sins of the fathers were passed on in *Hands of the Ripper* 72, with Angharad Rees as the Ripper's daughter.

Jacks, Robert L. (1922–). American producer, long with Fox.
Man on a Tightrope 53. White Feather 55. A Kiss Before Dying 56. Bandido 57. Roots of Heaven 59. Man in the Middle 64. Zorba the Greek 65. Bandolero 68, many others.

Jackson, Anne (1925–). American actress, wife of Eli Wallach; films rare.
□ So Young So Bad 50. The Journey 58. Tall Story 60. The Tiger Makes Out 67. How to Save a Marriage 67. *The Secret Life of an American Wife* 68. Lovers and Other Strangers 70. Zigzag 70. Dirty Dingus Magee 70.

Jackson, Freda (1909–). British character actress with a penchant for melodrama; on stage from 1934, films from 1942.
A Canterbury Tale 42. Henry V 44. Beware of Pity 46. Great Expectations 46. *No Room at the Inn* 47. Women of Twilight 49. The Crowded Day 53. Brides of Dracula 60. The Third Secret 64. Monster of Terror 65, etc.

Jackson, Glenda (1937–). British star actress.

□ The Marat/Sade 66. Negatives 68. *Women in Love* (AA) 69. The Music Lovers 70. *Sunday Bloody Sunday* 71. The Boy Friend (uncredited) 71. Mary Queen of Scots (as Queen Elizabeth) 71. A Touch of Class (AA) 72. The Triple Echo 72. A Bequest to the Nation 73. Hedda 76. The Incredible Sarah 76.
TV series: *Elizabeth R* 71.

Jackson, Gordon (1923–). Scottish actor whose rueful expression got him typecast as a weakling; now getting more interesting roles.
The Foreman Went to France (debut) 42. Millions Like Us 43. Nine Men 43. San Demetrio, London 44. Pink String and Sealing Wax 45. The Captive Heart 46. Against the Wind 47. Eureka Stockade 48. *Whisky Galore* 48. The Lady with a Lamp 51. Meet Mr Lucifer 54. Pacific Destiny 56. *Tunes of Glory* 60. The Great Escape (US) 62. *The Ipcress File* 65. Cast a Giant Shadow (US) 66. The Fighting Prince of Donegal 66. The Prime of Miss Jean Brodie 69. Run Wild Run Free 69. Kidnapped 72. Russian Roulette 75, others.
TV series: *Upstairs Downstairs* 71–.

Jackson, Pat (1916–). British director, a war documentarist whose later output has been disappointing.
Ferry Pilot 41. *Western Approaches* 44. The Shadow on the Wall (US) 48. *White Corridors* 50. Something Money Can't Buy 52. The Feminine Touch 55. Virgin Island 58. Snowball 60. What a Carve Up 62. Seven Keys 62. Don't Talk to Strange Men 62. Seventy Deadly Pills 64, etc.

Jackson, Thomas E. (1886–1967). American character actor often seen as police officer.
Little Caesar 30. Doctor X 32. Terror Aboard 33. The Mystery of the Wax Museum 33. Call of the Wild 35. Hollywood Boulevard 36. The Westland Case 37. Torchy Gets Her Man 38. Golden Gloves 40. Law of the Tropics 41. The Woman in the Window 44. The Big Sleep 46. Dead Reckoning 47. Stars and Stripes Forever 52. Attack of the Fifty Foot Woman 58. Synanon 65, many others.

Jacobi, Derek (1939–). British actor who played the lead in *I Claudius* on TV.
The Day of the Jackal 73. Blue Blood 74. The Odessa File 74, etc.

Jacobs, Arthur P. (1918–1973). American independent producer, former publicist.
□ What a Way to Go 64. Dr Dolittle 67. Planet of the Apes 68. The Chairman 69. Goodbye Mr Chips 69. Beneath the Planet of the Apes 69. Escape from the Planet of the Apes 71. Conquest of the Planet of the Apes 72.

Jacobs, W. W. (1863–1943). British short story writer: *The Monkey's Paw* has been filmed many times.

Jacobsson, Ulla (1929–). Leading Swedish actress.
One Summer of Happiness 51. Smiles of a Summer Night 55. Love is a Ball 63. Zulu 64. The Heroes of Telemark 65, etc.

Jacoby, Scott (1956–). American juvenile lead.
Baxter 72. Rivals 73. The Little Girl Who Lived Down the Lane 76, etc.

Jacoves, Felix (1907–). American director.
Homicide 48. Embraceable You 49, etc.

Jacques, Hattie (1924–). Plump British comedienne, well known at the Players' Theatre and on TV. In most of the 'Carry On' films.
Nicholas Nickleby 47. Oliver Twist 48. Trottie True 49. The Pickwick Papers 52. Make Mine Mink 61. In the Doghouse 62. The Bobo 67. Crooks and Coronets 69, etc.

Jaeckel, Richard (1926–). American actor, former Fox mail boy, who made a name playing frightened youths in war films.
Guadalcanal Diary 43. Jungle Patrol 48. Sands of Iwo Jima 49. The Gunfighter 50. Come Back Little Sheba 52. The Violent Men 55. Attack! 55. 3.10 to Yuma 57. The Gallant Hours 60. Town Without Pity 61. Four for Texas 63. Town Tamer 65. The Dirty Dozen 67. The Devil's Brigade 68. The Green Slime 69. Chisum 70. Sometimes a Great Notion 71. Chosen Survivors 74, many others.

Jaffe, Carl (1902–). Aristocratic-looking German actor, long in England.
Over the Moon 39. The Lion Has Wings 40. The Life and Death of Colonel Blimp 43. Gaiety George 46. Appointment in London 53. Operation Crossbow 65. The Double Man 67, many others.

Jaffe, Sam (1897–). American character actor of eccentric appearance and sharp talent. On stage from 1916, films from 1933.
The Scarlet Empress 34. *Lost Horizon* (as the High Lama) 37. *Gunga Din* 39. Gentleman's Agreement 48. *The Asphalt Jungle* 50. The Barbarian and the Geisha 58. Ben Hur 59. Guns for San Sebastian 68. The Kremlin Letter 69. Bedknobs and Broomsticks 71, etc.
TV series: Ben Casey 60–64.

Jagger, Dean (1903–) (Dean Jeffries). American star character actor of the forties, usually in sympathetic roles; later seen as colonels, fathers, town elders, etc.
Women from Hell 29. College Rhythm 34. Home on the Range 34. Men without Names 35. Revolt of the Zombies 36. Exiled to Shanghai 37. *Brigham Young* (title Role) 40. Western Union 41. The Men in Her Life 41. The Omaha Trail 42. North Star 43. When Strangers Marry 44. I Live in Grosvenor Square (GB) 45. Sister Kenny 46. Pursued 47. Twelve O'Clock High (AA) 49. Dark City 50. Denver and Rio Grande 52. It Grows on Trees 52. The Robe 53. *Executive Suite* 54. Bad Day at Black Rock 55. The Great Man 56. X the Unknown (GB) 57. The Proud Rebel 58. The Nun's Story 59. Elmer Gantry 60. Parrish 61. The Honeymoon Machine 62. First to Fight 67. Firecreek 68. The Kremlin Letter 70. Vanishing Point 71. The Glass House (TV) 72, many others.
TV series: Mr Novak 63–65.

Jagger, Mick (1939–). Heavy-faced British pop idol whose film career did not get off the ground.
□ Ned Kelly 69. Performance 70.

James Bond, the over-sexed one man spy machine created by Ian Fleming, first came to the screen in the guise of Sean Connery in *Dr No* 62. Connery continued in *From Russia with Love* 63, *Goldfinger* 64, *Thunderball* 65, *You Only Live Twice* 67; David Niven appeared as 'Sir James' in *Casino Royale* 67. George Lazenby took over for *On Her Majesty's Secret Service* 69; Connery came back for *Diamonds Are Forever* 71; Roger Moore signed on for *Live and Let Die, The Man with the Golden Gun* and *The Spy who Loved Me.*

James, Clifton (–   ). Corpulent American character actor.
David and Lisa 64. Cool Hand Luke 67. Tick Tick Tick 70. Live and Let Die 72. The Man with the Golden Gun 73. The Bank Shot 74. Silver Streak 76, etc.

James, Harry (1916–). American bandleader and trumpeter who has appeared in occasional films.
Springtime in the Rockies 42. Best Foot Forward 43. Bathing Beauty 44. Do You Love Me 46. Carnegie Hall 47. I'll Get By 50. The Benny Goodman Story 56, etc.

James, Henry (1843–1916). American novelist who lived in Europe. Film versions include *Berkeley Square, The Lost Moment, The Heiress, The Innocents, Daisy Miller.*

James, Jesse (1847–1882). American wild west outlaw who has acquired the legend of a Robin Hood but in fact plundered ruthlessly as head of a gang which also included his sanctimonious elder brother **Frank James** (1843–1915). Among the many screen personifications of Jesse are Tyrone Power in *Jesse James* 39; Lawrence Tierney in *Badman's Territory* 46; Macdonald Carey in *The Great Missouri Raid* 52; Audie Murphy in *Kansas Raiders* 53; Willard Parker in *The Great Jesse James Raid* 53; Robert Wagner in *The True Story of Jesse James* 56; Dale Robertson in *Fighting Man of the Plains* 59; Ray Stricklyn in *Young Jesse James* 60; Chris Jones in a TV series *The Legend of Jesse James* 65; Robert Duvall in *The Great Northfield Minnesota Raid* 72; and Clayton Moore in several Republic serials. Henry Fonda was in *The Return of Frank James* 40.

James, Sid (or **Sidney**) (1913–1976). Crumple-faced South African comedy actor, in Britain from 1946. A familiar face on TV and in scores of movies, including most of the 'Carry On' series (1958 to date).
Black Memory 46. Once a Jolly Swagman 48. The Man in Black 49. The Lavender Hill Mob 51. The Titfield Thunderbolt 53. Joe Macbeth 55. The Silent Enemy 57. Too Many Crooks 58. Tommy the Toreador 59. Double Bunk 60. What a Carve Up 62. The Big Job 65. Don't Lose Your Head 67. Bless This House 73, many others.

Jamison, Bud (1894–1944). American character actor, a stock Columbia player who played the heavy in most of the Three Stooges two-reelers.

James, M. R. (1862–1936). English ghost story writer, an academic with a splendid command of language. *The Night of the Demon* is a fairly satisfactory film version of *Casting the Runes.*

Jancso, Miklos (1921–). Hungarian director.
Cantata 63. My Way Home 64. The Round Up 65. The Red and the White 67. Silence and Cry 68. Winter Wind 70. The Pacifist 71. Agnus Dei 71. Red Psalm 72, etc.

Jane Eyre. Charlotte Brontë's romantic melodrama ('Reader, I married him') was screened in various silent versions, including one in 1913 with Ethel Grandin as Jane and Irving Cummings as the gloomy Mr Rochester; another in 1915 with Louise Vale and Alan Hale; and in 1921 with Mabel Ballin and Norman Trevor. There have been three sound versions: in 1934 with Virginia Bruce and Colin Clive, in 1943 with Joan Fontaine and Orson Welles, and in 1972 with Susannah York and George C. Scott.

Janis, Conrad (1926–). American teenage player of the forties.
Snafu 45. Margie 46. The High Window 46. Beyond Glory 48. Keep it Cool 58, etc.

Janis, Elsie (1889–1956) (Elsie Bierbauer). American musical comedy star who made a few silent movies such as *Betty in Search of a Thrill* and *A Regular Girl*; only talkie, *Women in War* 42.

Janni, Joseph (1916–). Italian producer, in England from 1939.
The Glass Mountain 48. Romeo and Juliet 53. *A Town Like Alice* 56. *A Kind of Loving* 62. Darling 65. Modesty Blaise 66. Far From the Madding Crowd 67. *Poor Cow* 68. *Sunday Bloody Sunday* 71. Made 72, etc.

Jannings, Emil (1884–1950) (Theodor Emil Janenz). Distinguished German actor, on stage from ten years old. Entered films through his friend Ernst Lubitsch.
Madame Dubarry 18. *Peter the Great* 23. *The Last Laugh* 24. *Variety* 25. *Faust* 26. *The Way of All Flesh* (US) (AA) 28. Sons of the Fathers (US) 28. The Last Command (US) 28. *The Blue Angel* 30. The Old and the Young King 35. The Broken Jug 37. Ohm Kruger 41, many others.

Janssen, David (1930–) (David Meyer). American leading man, very successful on TV; film roles routine, persona doggedly glum.
Yankee Buccaneer 52. Chief Crazy Horse 54. The Square Jungle 55. Toy Tiger 56. The Girl He Left Behind 56. Hell to Eternity 60. Ring of Fire 60. Mantrap 61. *King of the Roaring Twenties* (as Arnold Rothstein) 61. My Six Loves 63. Warning Shot 67. The Green Berets 68. The Shoes of the Fisherman 68. Where It's At 69. A Time for Giving 69. Macho Callahan 70. Fer de

Lance (TV) 74. Once is not Enough 75. Farrell (TV) 76, etc.
TV series: *Richard Diamond* 59. *The Fugitive* 63–67. O'Hara U.S. Treasury 71. Harry O 73–75.

Janssen, Eileen (1937–). American child actress of the forties.
The Green Years 46. About Mrs Leslie 54. The Search for Bridie Murphy 56, etc.

Japan has a cinema tradition all of its own, based on No plays and samurai epics, both with a style quite alien to the west. The first breakthrough was made in the fifties by the vivid films of Kurosawa, such as *Rashomon* and *Seven Samurai*; other directors who came to be respected if not entirely understood are Gosho, Ozu, Mizoguchi, Ichikawa, Kinugasa and Kobayashi.

Jarman, Claude, Jnr (1934–). American boy actor of the forties.
The Yearling (special AA) 46. High Barbaree 47. Intruder in the Dust 49. Rio Grande 51. Fair Wind to Java 53. The Great Locomotive Chase 56, etc.

Jarre, Maurice (1924–). French composer.
Hôtel des Invalides 52. La Têtre contre les Murs 59. Eyes Without a Face 59. Crack in the Mirror 60. *The Longest Day* 62. *Lawrence of Arabia* (AA) 62. Weekend at Dunkirk 65. *Dr Zhivago* (AA) 65. Is Paris Burning? 66. The Professionals 66. The 25th Hour 67. Five Card Stud 68. Isadora 68. The Damned 69. *Ryan's Daughter* 70.

Jarrott, Charles (1927–). British director, from TV.
□ Time to Remember 62. *Anne of the Thousand Days* 70. Mary Queen of Scots 72. Lost Horizon 73. The Dove 74. Escape from the Dark 76.

Jason, Leigh (1904–). American director, mainly of second features.
High Gear 33. The Mad Miss Manton 38. Lady for a Night 39. Model Wife 41. Three Girls About Town 41. Lost Honeymoon 46. Out of the Blue 48. Okinawa 52, etc.

Jason, Rick (1929–). American leading man of the fifties.
Sombrero 53. The Saracen Blade 54. The Lieutenant Wore Skirts 55. The Wayward Bus 57, etc.
TV series: The Case of the Dangerous Robin 60. *Combat* 62–67.

Jason, Sybil (1929–). South African child actress of the thirties.
Barnacle Bill (GB) 35. Little Big Shot (GB) 36. The Singing Kid (US) 36. The Little Princess (US) 39. The Bluebird (US) 40, etc.

Jason, Will (1899–1970). American second feature director.
The Soul of a Monster 44. Thief of Damascus 52, many others.

Jaubert, Maurice (1900–1940). French composer.
L'Affaire Est dans le Sac 32. Le Quatorze Juillet 33. Zéro de Conduite 33. L'Atalante 34. Drôle de Drame 37. *Un Carnet du Bal* 37. *Quai des Brumes* 38. *Le Jour Se Lève* 39. La Fin du Jour 39, etc.

Jaws A 1975 box-office sensation about a killer shark, lurking near a seaside resort, this modest shocker proved slow moving, and only moderately well-made, but hit the big time simply because of the barrage of publicity with which it was launched and because sharks were a new fad.

Jay, Ernest (1894–1957). British stage character actor.
Tiger Bay 34. Broken Blossoms 36. Don't Take It to Heart 44. Vice Versa 47. The History of Mr Polly 49. Edward My Son 49. I Believe in You 52. Who Done It? 55. The Curse of Frankenstein 56.

Jayston, Michael (1936–). British stage actor commanding reputable film roles.
□ Cromwell 70. *Nicholas and Alexandra* 71. Follow Me 72. Alice's Adventures in Wonderland 72. A Bequest to the Nation 73. Tales that Witness Madness 73. The Homecoming 73. Craze 73. The Internecine Project 74.

Jazz has been featured in American movies since they began to talk; Al Jolson always acknowledged its influence on his style. Jazz bands featured as specialties through the thirties, but in the forties began a line of films purporting to investigate the origins of jazz: *Birth of the Blues, New Orleans, Syncopation* and *St Louis Blues*. Fictional stories relying on a jazz background include *Young Man with a Horn, Paris Blues, Pete Kelly's Blues, Blues in the Night* and *Cabin in the Sky*; while most of the famous dance bands of the forties were to some extent indebted to the inspiration of jazz, the American Negro's musical idiom.

The Jazz Singer (US 1927). The 'first talking film' has only a few patches of dialogue and some songs; but Al Jolson's personality is so vibrant that one can imagine the sensation he originally caused. The well-worn sentimental story is efficiently directed by Alan Crosland. There was a 1953 remake starring Danny Thomas.

Jean, Gloria (1928–) (Gloria Jean Schoonover). Former American child singer, on screen from 1939 as second-feature rival to Deanna Durbin.
The Underpup 39. Pardon My Rhythm 40. If I Had My Way 40. Moonlight in Vermont 41. She's My Lovely 42. I'll Remember April 44. Fairy Tale Murder 45. Copacabana 47. I Surrender, Dear 48. There's a Girl in My Heart 49. The Ladies' Man 61, etc.

Jeanmaire, Zizi (Renee) (1924–). French leading lady and ballet dancer, in occasional films.
Hans Christian Andersen 51. Anything Goes 56. Folies Bergère 56. Charmants Garçons 57. Black Tights 60, etc.

Jeans, Isabel (1891–). British stage actress, invariably in aristocratic roles.
Tilly of Bloomsbury 21. The Rat 25. Downhill 27. Easy Virtue 28. Sally Bishop 33. Tovarich (US) 38. Suspicion (US) 41. Banana Ridge 41. Great Day 45. It Happened in Rome 57. Gigi 58. A Breath of Scandal 60. Heavens Above 63, etc.

Jeans, Ursula (1906–1973) (Ursula McMinn). British stage actress, long married to Roger Livesey; in occasional films.
The Gypsy Cavalier (debut) 31. Cavalcade 33. Dark Journey 37. Mr Emmanuel 44. The Woman in the Hall 46. The Weaker Sex 48. The Dam Busters 55. Northwest Frontier 59. The Queen's Guards 61. The Battle of the Villa Fiorita 65, etc.

Jeanson, Henri (1900–). French writer.
Pepe le Moko 37. Carnet du Bal 37. Prison Without Bars 38. Carmen 42. Nana 55. L'Affaire d'une Nuit 60, etc.

Jeayes, Allan (1885–1963). British stage actor of dignified heavy presence; played supporting roles in many films.
The Impassive Footman 32. The Scarlet Pimpernel 34. Rembrandt 37. Elephant Boy 37. The Four Feathers 39. The Thief of Baghdad 40. The Man Within 46. Saraband for Dead Lovers 48. Waterfront 50, many others.

Jefford, Barbara (1931–). British state

actress, more recently in films.
Ulysses 67. The Bofors Gun 68. A Midsummer Night's Dream 68. The Shoes of the Fisherman 68. Lust for a Vampire 70, etc.

Jeffrey, Peter (1929–). British general purpose actor.
Becket 64. If 67. The Abominable Dr Phibes 71. The Horsemen 71. Dr Phibes Rises Again 72, etc.

Jeffreys, Anne (1923–). American leading lady of the forties, formerly in opera.
I Married an Angel 42. Step Lively 44. Dillinger 45. Riff Raff 47. Return of the Badmen 49. Boys Night Out 62, etc.
TV series: Topper 53. Love That Jill 58.

Jeffries, Lionel (1926–). Bald British character comedian, in films from 1952.
Stage Fright 50. Windfall 54. The Baby and the Battleship 55. Law and Disorder 57. The Nun's Story 58. Idol on Parade 59. Two-Way Stretch 60. The Trials of Oscar Wilde 60. The Hellions 61. The Notorious Landlady 61. The Wrong Arm of the Law 63. Call Me Bwana 63. The Long Ships 64. The First Men in the Moon 64. The Truth about Spring 65. The Secret of My Success 65. You Must Be Joking 65. Arrivederci Baby 66. The Spy with a Cold Nose 67. Rocket to the Moon 67. Camelot 67. Chitty Chitty Bang Bang 68. Eyewitness 70. Who Slew Auntie Roo 71. Royal Flash 74, etc.
□ AS DIRECTOR: The Railway Children 70. The Amazing Mr Blunden 72. Baxter 72. The Water Babies 77.

Jenkins, Allen (1900–1974) (Alfred McGonegal). 'Tough guy' American comic actor, a staple of Warners' repertory in the thirties.
The Girl Habit 31. Rackety Rax 32. I am a Fugitive from a Chain Gang 32. 42nd Street 33. Professional Sweetheart 33. Jimmy the Gent 34. The St Louis Kid 34. Page Miss Glory 35. Miss Pacific Fleet 35. The Singing Kid 36. Three Men on a Horse 36. The Perfect Specimen 37. Dead End 37. Swing Your Lady 37. A Slight Case of Murder 38. The Amazing Dr Clitterhouse 38. Five Came Back 39. Destry Rides Again 39. Tin Pan Alley 40. Footsteps in the Dark 41. Maisie Gets Her Man 42. Wonder Man 45. Wild Harvest 47. Bodyhold 49. Behave Yourself 51. Pillow Talk 59. Robin and the Seven Hoods 64. Doctor You've Got to be Kidding 67. The Front Page 74, many others.
TV series: Hey Jeannie 56.

Jenkins, Jackie 'Butch' (1938–). Buck-toothed American child star of the forties, son of Doris Dudley; retired because he developed a stutter.

☐ *The Human Comedy* 43. National Velvet 44. An American Romance 44. Abbott and Costello in Hollywood 45. Our Vines Have Tender Grapes 45. Boys' Ranch 46. Little Mister Jim 46. My Brother Talks to Horses 46. Big City 48. The Bride Goes Wild 48. Summer Holiday 48.

Jenkins, Megs (1917–). Plump British actress of kindly or motherly roles, on stage from 1933.

The Silent Battle 39. *Green for Danger* 46. The Brothers 47. The Monkey's Paw 48. *The History of Mr Polly* 49. White Corridors 51. Ivanhoe 52. The Cruel Sea 53. The Gay Dog 54. John and Julie 55. The Man in the Sky 56. Conspiracy of Hearts 59. *The Innocents* 61. The Barber of Stamford Hill 62. Bunny Lake Is Missing 65. Stranger in the House 67. Oliver 68. David Copperfield 69, etc.

Jenks, Frank (1902–1962). American character comedian, usually seen as Runyonesque stooge, cop or valet.

When's Your Birthday? 37. You Can't Cheat an Honest Man 39. Dancing on a Dime 40. Rogues' Gallery 45. Loonies on Broadway 46. The She-Creature 56, many others.

TV series: Colonel Flack 59–61.

Jennings, Al (1864–1961). American outlaw of the old west who among other pursuits became a silent screen actor.

The Lady of the Dugout 18. Fighting Fury 24. The Sea Hawk 24. The Demon 26. Loco Luck 27. Land of Missing Men 30, etc.

Jennings, Humphrey (1907–1950). Distinguished British documentarist, with the GPO Film Unit from 1934. Responsible for a fine World War II series of sensitive film records of the moods of the time.

The First Days (co-d) 39. *London Can Take It* (co-d) 40. *Listen to Britain* 41. The Silent Village 43. *Fires Were Started* 43. *A Diary for Timothy* 45, etc. Also: The Cumberland Story 47. *Dim Little Island* 49. Family Portrait 50, etc.

Jens, Salome (1935–). American leading lady, in very occasional films.

☐ *Angel Baby* 61. The Fool Killer 65. Seconds 66. Me Natalie 69.

Jergens, Adele (1922–). American leading lady, mainly in second features.

A Thousand and One Nights 44. Ladies of the Chorus 48. Blonde Dynamite 50. Somebody

Loves Me 52. The Cobweb 55. Girls in Prison 56. The Lonesome Trail 58, etc.

Jerome, Jerome K. (1859–1927). British humorist and essayist. His *Three Men in a Boat* and *The Passing of the Third Floor Back* were filmed several times.

Jerrold, Mary (1877–1955) (Mary Allen). British character actress, mainly on stage; in films, played mainly sweet old ladies.

Alibi 31. Friday the Thirteenth 33. The Man at the Gate 41. *The Way Ahead* 44. *The Queen of Spades* 48. Mr Perrin and Mr Traill 49. Top of the Form 52, etc.

Jessel, George (1898–). American entertainer, in vaudeville from childhood. After making the mistake of turning down *The Jazz Singer*, he had a very spasmodic film career, but in the fifties he produced a number of musicals for Fox.

Autobiographies: 1946, *So Help Me*. 1955, *This Way Miss*. 1975, *The World I Live In*.

AS ACTOR: The Other Man's Wife 19. Private Izzy Murphy 26. Lucky Boy (My Mother's Eyes) 29. Love Live and Laugh 29. Stage Door Canteen 43. Four Jills in a Jeep 44. The I Don't Care Girl 53. The Busy Body 57. Heironymus Merkin 69, etc.

AS PRODUCER: Do You Love Me 46. When My Baby Smiles at Me 48. Dancing in the Dark 49. Meet Me After the Show 51. Golden Girl 51. Wait Till the Sun Shines Nellie 52. The I Don't Care Girl 53. Tonight We Sing 53, etc.

Jessel, Patricia (1921–1968). British character actress, mostly on stage.

Quo Vadis 51. *City of the Dead* 61. A Jolly Bad Fellow 64. A Funny Thing Happened on the Way to the Forum 66, etc.

Jessua, Alain (1932–). French writer-director of off-beat films.

Life Upside Down 63. Jeu de Massacre 67, etc.

Jeux Interdits (France 1952). A powerful anti-war film and a plea for innocence with a fresh angle: two children whose parents have been killed in an air raid are sheltered by peasants and invent their own game of death. Their world is shown as the only innocent one, all adults being in some way corrupt; but the world does not understand. Directed by René Clement from a novel by Françoise Boyer; with Brigitte Fossey and Georges Poujouly.

Jew Süss (Germany 1940). This remake of the legend of a Jew who, inspired by a demonaical

Rabbi, takes over Wurtemberg but is finally toppled from power, was a natural theme for Nazi Germany, and Veit Harlan's film is said to have been dictated and supervised by Goebbels. There were earlier, more temperate versions, including a British one in 1934.

jewel thieves were fashionable with Hollywood film-makers in the thirties, the heyday of Raffles, the Lone Wolf, and Arsène Lupin; they were the subject of Lubitsch's best comedy, *Trouble in Paradise*. In the sixties they seemed to come into their own again, with *To Catch a Thief, The Greengage Summer, Topkapi, The Pink Panther* and *Jack of Diamonds*.

Jewell, Isabel (1913–1972). Diminutive American leading lady of the thirties, a minor 'platinum blonde' who graduated to character parts.
Blessed Event 33. Counsellor at Law 33. Manhattan Melodrama 34. A Tale of Two Cities 36. The Man Who Lived Twice 37. Marked Woman 37. *Lost Horizon* 37. Gone with the Wind 39. The Leopard Man 43. The Bishop's Wife 48. The Story of Molly X 48. Bernardine 57, many others.

Jewison, Norman (1926–). Canadian director, from TV.
□ Forty Pounds of Trouble 63. The Thrill of It All 63. Send Me No Flowers 64. The Art of Love 65. *The Cincinnati Kid* 65. *The Russians Are Coming* (& p) 66. *In the Heat of the Night* (pd) 67. The Thomas Crown Affair (pd) 68. The Landlord (p) 69. Gaily, Gaily (pd) 69. Fiddler on the Roof (pd) 71. Jesus Christ Superstar (pd) 73.

Jews and their plight in Europe under the Nazis were the subject of *So Ends Our Night, The Great Dictator, Professor Mamlock, Mr Emmanuel* and *The Diary of Anne Frank*. The problems of the new state of Israel were treated in *Sword in the Desert, Exodus, The Juggler, Judith* and *Cast a Giant Shadow*; while looking further back in history we find many versions of *Jew Süss* and *The Wandering Jew*, also *The Fixer* and the *Fiddler on the Roof*. American films about Jews used to show them as warm-hearted comic figures: *Kosher Kitty Kelly, Abie's Irish Rose, The Cohens and the Kellys*. Gertrude Berg continued this tradition on TV in the fifties. Recently films set in Jewish milieux have treated their characters more naturally, if with a touch of asperity: *No Way to Treat a Lady, I Love You Alice B. Toklas, Bye Bye Braverman, Funny Girl, The Night They Raided Minsky's, Goodbye Columbus, Portnoy's Complaint, Hester Street,*

Lies My Father Told Me, The Apprenticeship of Duddy Kravitz. See also: *anti-semitism.*

Joan of Arc has had her story told several times on film. In 1916 Geraldine Farrar played her in *Joan the Woman*. Dreyer's classic *The Passion of Joan of Arc*, with Falconetti, came in 1928; and in 1930 Marco de Gastyne directed *Saint Joan the Maid* with Simone Genevois. In Germany, Angela Salloker had the role in 1935. The next two were Hollywood failures: Victor Fleming's *Joan of Arc* 48, with Ingrid Bergman, and Otto Preminger's *Saint Joan* 57, with Jean Seberg. Hedy Lamarr also made a brief appearance as Joan in *The Story of Mankind* 57. In 1962 Robert Bresson made his highly specialized *The Trial of Joan of Arc* with Florence Carrez.

Jobert, Marlène (1943–). French leading lady.
Masculin Feminin 66. Le Voleur 66. L'Astragale 68. Rider on the Rain 69. Last Known Address 70. Catch Me a Spy 72. Ten Days' Wonder 72.

Joe Palooka. The dumb boxer hero of the famous American comic strip was first on screen in 1934, played by Stuart Erwin. Ten years later Joe Kirkwood, an amateur golfer, played him in a Monogram series, with Leon Errol (later James Gleason) as his manager Knobby Walsh.

Johann, Zita (1904–). American leading lady of the early thirties.
The Struggle 31. Tiger Shark 32. *The Mummy* 32. Luxury Liner 33. Grand Canary 34, etc.

John, Rosamund (1913–) (Nora Jones). Gentle-mannered British leading lady who turned in several pleasing performances in the forties.
□ The Secret of the Loch 34. The First of the Few 42. *The Gentle Sex* 43. The Lamp Still Burns 43. Tawny Pipit 44. *The Way to the Stars* 45. Green for Danger 46. The Upturned Glass 47. Fame is the Spur 47. When the Bough Breaks 47. No Place for Jennifer 49. She Shall Have Murder 50. Never Look Back 52. Street Corner 53. Operation Murder 56.

Johns, Glynis (1923–). Husky-voiced British actress, daughter of Mervyn Johns; on stage (as child) from 1935.
South Riding (debut) 36. Prison Without Bars 38. 49th Parallel 41. Halfway House 44. *Perfect Strangers* 45. This Man Is Mine 46. Frieda 47. *Miranda* (as a mermaid) 47. An Ideal Husband 47. State Secret 50. Appointment with Venus 51. *The Card* 52. The Sword and the Rose 53.

Personal Affair 53. Rob Roy 53. The Weak and
the Wicked 54. The Beachcomber 55. Mad
About Men 55. *The Court Jester* (US) 56. The
Day They Gave Babies Away (US) 56. Shake
Hands with the Devil 59. The Sundowners 60.
The Spider's Web 61. *The Chapman Report* (US)
62. Mary Poppins (US) 64. Dear Brigitte (US)
65. Don't Just Stand There (US) 68. Lock Up
Your Daughters 69. Under Milk Wood 71. Vault
of Horror 73, etc.
TV series: Glynis 63.

Johns, Mervyn (1899–). Welsh character
actor, on stage from 1923; usually plays mild-
mannered roles.
Lady in Danger (debut) 34. Jamaica Inn 39.
Saloon Bar 40. *Next of Kin* 41. Went the Day
Well? 42. Halfway House 44. *My Learned
Friend* 44. *Dead of Night* 45. *Pink String and
Sealing Wax* 45. Scrooge 51. The Intimate
Stranger 56. No Love for Johnnie 61. 80,000
Suspects 63. The Heroes of Telemark 65. Who
Killed the Cat? 66, many others.

Johnson, Arte (–). Small-scale
American comic actor.
Miracle in the Rain 56. The Subterraneans 60.
The President's Analyst 67, etc.

Johnson, Ben (1919–). American character
actor, a staple of John Ford and other westerns
for years. Former stunt rider.
Three Godfathers 49. Mighty Joe Young 49. She
Wore a Yellow Ribbon 49. *Wagonmaster* 50.
Rio Grande 50. Fort Defiance 51. Shane 53.
Slim Carter 57. Fort Bowie 60. One Eyed Jacks
61. Major Dundee 65. The Rare Breed 66. Will
Penny 67. The Wild Bunch 69. The Undefeated
69. *The Last Picture Show* (AA) 71. Corky 72.
Junior Bonner 72. Dillinger 73. The Sugarland
Express 73. Bite the Bullet 75. Hustle 76, many
others.

Johnson, Celia (1908–). Distinguished
British actress, on stage from 1928, usually in
well-bred roles: films rare.
□ *In Which We Serve* (debut) 42. *Dear Octopus*
42. This Happy Breed 44. *Brief Encounter* 46.
The Astonished Heart 49. I Believe In You 52.
The Captain's Paradise 53. The Holly and the
Ivy 54. A Kid for Two Farthings 56. The Good
Companions 57. The Prime of Miss Jean Brodie
69.

Johnson, Chic (1891–1962). Portly American
vaudeville comedian (with partner Ole Olsen).
Oh Sailor Behave 30. Fifty Million Frenchmen
31. *Hellzapoppin* 41. Crazy House 43. Ghost
Catchers 43, etc.

Johnson, Katie (1878–1957). British
character actress who became a star in her old
age.
Jeannie 41. The Years Between 46. I Believe in
You 52. *The Ladykillers* 55. How to Murder a
Rich Uncle 56, many others.

Johnson, Kay (1904–). American leading
lady of the thirties.
Dynamite 29. The Spoilers 30. Madame Satan
30. American Madness 32. Of Human Bondage
34. Jalna 35. White Banners 38. Son of Fury 42.
Mr Lucky 43, etc.

Johnson, Lamont (1920–). American
director, from TV.
□ Covenant with Death 67. The Mackenzie
Break 70. A Gunfight 71. The Groundstar
Conspiracy 72. You'll Like My Mother 72. The
Last American Hero 73. Lipstick 76.

Johnson, Martin (1884–1937) and **Osa**
(1894–1953). American explorers who made
several feature-length films.
Jungle Adventure 21. Simba 28. Congorilla 32.
Baboona 35. I Married Adventure 38, etc.

Johnson, Noble (1897–). Black American
actor who played a multitude of fearsome native
chiefs.
Robinson Crusoe (as Friday) 22. The Ten
Commandments 23. The Navigator 24. Hands
Up 26. Vanity 27. Redskin 28. The Four
Feathers 29. Moby Dick 30. The Mummy 32.
King Kong 33. She 35. Conquest 37. The Ghost
Breakers 40. Jungle Book 42. A Game of Death
45. She Wore a Yellow Ribbon 49. North of the
Great Divide 50, many others.

Johnson, Nunnally (1897–1977). American
screenwriter, producer and director.
The House of Rothschild (w) 34. Cardinal
Richelieu (w) 35. Jesse James (w) 39. *The Grapes
of Wrath* (w) 40. Tobacco Road (w) 41. *The
Moon Is Down* (wp) 43. Holy Matrimony (wp)
43. The Keys of the Kingdom (w) 44. *The Dark
Mirror* (w) 46. The Mudlark (wp) 51. *Rommel,
Desert Fox* (wp) 51. How to Marry a Millionaire
(wp) 53. Night People (wpd) 54. The Man in the
Grey Flannel Suit (wd) 56. Oh Men, Oh Women
(wpd) 57. The Three Faces of Eve (wpd) 57. The
Man Who Understood Women (wpd) 59. Take
Her She's Mine (wp) 63. The World of Henry
Orient (p) 64. *The Dirty Dozen* (w) 67, many
others.

Johnson, Rafer (1935–). American black
actor, formerly Olympic athlete.
The Fiercest Heart 61. The Sins of Rachel Cade

61. Wild in the Country 61. The Lion 63, etc.

Johnson, Richard (1927–). British leading man of stage and screen.
Captain Horatio Hornblower 51. Never So Few (US) 59. Cairo (US) 62. *The Haunting* 63. Eighty Thousand Suspects 63. The Pumpkin Eater 64. Operation Crossbow 65. Moll Flanders 65. Khartoum 66. *Deadlier Than the Male* (as Bulldog Drummond) 66. Danger Route 67. La Strega in Amore (It.) 67. Oedipus The King 68. A Twist of Sand 68. Lady Hamilton (as Nelson) (German) 68. Some Girls Do 68. Julius Caesar 70. Hennessy 75. Aces High 76, etc.

Johnson, Rita (1912–1965). American actress who usually played 'the other woman'.
Serenade 39. Edison the Man 40. Here Comes Mr Jordan 41. Thunderhead, Son of Flicka 44. They Won't Believe Me 47. Family Honeymoon 49. Susan Slept Here 54. Emergency Hospital 56. The Day They Gave Babies Away 57, etc.

Johnson, Van (1916–). American light leading man, in films since 1941 after stage experience.
Murder in the Big House debut) 41. *Dr Gillespie's New Assistant* 42. The Human Comedy 43. A Guy Named Joe 43. The White Cliffs of Dover 44. Two Girls and a Sailor 44. Thirty Seconds over Tokyo 44. Thrill of a Romance 45. Weekend at the Waldorf 45. Easy to Wed 45. No Leave, No Love 45. High Barbaree 46. The Romance of Rosy Ridge 47. State of the Union 48. The Bride Goes Wild 48. In the Good Old Summertime 49. *Battleground* 50. Go for Broke 51. When in Rome 52. Plymouth Adventure 52. *The Caine Mutiny* 54. Brigadoon 55. The Last Time I Saw Paris 55. The End of the Affair (GB) 55. *Miracle in the Rain* 56. Twenty-Three Paces to Baker Street 57. Kelly and Me 57. Beyond This Place (GB) 59. Subway in the Sky (GB) 60. Wives and Lovers 63. Divorce American Style 67. Where Angels Go Trouble Follows 68. Battle Squadron (It.) 69. Company of Killers (TV) 70. Rich Man Poor Man (TV) 76, others.

Johnston, Eric A. (1895–1963). American executive, successor to Will H. Hays as President of the M.P.A.A. (Motion Picture Association of America) (1945–63).

Johnston, Margaret (1917–). Australian actress who has made occasional British films, notably in mid-forties.
The Prime Minister (debut) 40. *The Rake's Progress* 45. A Man About the House 47. Portrait of Clare 50. The Magic Box 51. Knave of Hearts 53. Touch and Go 55. *Night of the Eagle* 62. Life at the Top 65. The Psychopath 66. Sebastian 67, etc.

Johnston, Oliver (1888–1966). British character actor.
Room in the House 55. *A King in New York* 57. A Touch of Larceny 60. Dr Crippen 62. Cleopatra 63. A Countess from Hong Kong 67, etc.

Jolson, Al (1886–1950) (Asa Yoelson). Celebrated Jewish-American singer and entertainer, of inimitable voice and electric presence. After years as a big Broadway attraction, he starred in the first talking picture and although his fortunes subsequently declined, a biopic using his voice made him a world celebrity again in his sixties.
Biographies: *The Immortal Jolson* (1962) by Pearl Sieben; *Al Jolson* (1972) by Michael Friedland; *Sonny Boy* (1975) by Barrie Anderton.
☐ *The Jazz Singer* 27. *The Singing Fool* 28. Sonny Boy 29. Say It with Songs 29. Mammy 30. Big Boy 30. Hallelujah I'm a Bum 33. Wonder Bar 34. Go into Your Dance 35. The Singing Kid 36. *Rose of Washington Square* 39. Hollywood Cavalcade 39. Swanee River 39. Rhapsody in Blue 45. *The Jolson Story* (voice only) 46. *Jolson Sings Again* (voice only) 49.

Jones, Allan (1907–). American singing star of the thirties.
☐ Reckless 35. *A Night at the Opera* 35. Rose Marie 36. Showboat 36. A Day at the Races 37. *The Firefly* 37. Everybody Sing 38. Honeymoon in Bali 39. The Great Victor Herbert 39. The Boys from Syracuse 40. One Night in the Tropics 40. There's Magic in Music 42. True to the Army 42. When Johnny Comes Marching Home 43. Honeymoon Ahead 45. Stage to Thunder Rock 67.

Jones, Barry (1893–). British character actor, usually in diffident roles; a well-known stage actor from 1921.
Arms and the Man (as Bluntschli) 31. Squadron Leader X 42. Dancing with Crime 46. Frieda 47. The Calendar 48. *Seven Days to Noon* (leading role) 50. White Corridors 51. Plymouth Adventure (US) 52. Prince Valiant (US) 54. Brigadoon (US) 55. War and Peace 56. *The Safecracker* 58. A Study in Terror 65, etc.

Jones, Buck (1889–1942) (Charles Gebhardt). Popular American western star of the twenties and thirties, mainly in second features.
Straight from the Shoulder 20. Skid Proof 23.

Hearts and Spurs 25. Riders of the Purple Sage 26. The Flying Horseman 27. The Lone Rider 30. Border Law 32. The California Trail 33. When a Man Sees Red 34. Boss Rider of Gun Creek 36. Unmarried 39. Riders of Death Valley 41, many others.

Jones, Carolyn (1929–). Dark-eyed American leading lady, usually in off-beat roles.
Road to Bali 52. House of Wax 52. The Big Heat 53. Invasion of the Body Snatchers 55. The Opposite Sex 56. *The Bachelor Party* 57. Marjorie Morningstar 58. Last Train from Gun Hill 58. A Hole in the Head 59. Ice Palace 60. A Ticklish Affair 63. Heaven with a Gun 68. Color Me Dead 70, etc.
TV series: *The Addams Family* (as Morticia) 64–65.

Jones, Christopher (1941–). American leading man.
Chubasco 67. Wild in the Streets 68. The Looking Glass War 69. Three in the Attic 69. *Ryan's Daughter* 70, etc.
TV series: *The Legend of Jesse James* 65.

Jones, Chuck (1915–) (Charles M. Jones). American animator, long with Warners directing Daffy Duck, Bugs Bunny and Sylvester. Features include *Gay Purree* 62. *The Phantom Tollbooth* 69.

Jones, Dean (1933–). American leading man who usually plays well-behaved fellows.
Tea and Sympathy 56. Handle with Care 58. Never So Few 60. *Under the Yum Yum Tree* 64. The New Interns 64. Two on a Guillotine 64. That Darn Cat 65. The Ugly Duckling 66. Any Wednesday 66. Monkeys Go Home 67. Blackbeard's Ghost 67. The Love Bug 69. Million Dollar Duck 71. Snowball Express 73. Mr Superinvisible 76, etc.
TV series: Ensign O'Toole 62. Chicago Teddy Bears 71.

Jones, Emrys (1915–1972). British stage actor.
One of Our Aircraft is Missing 42. The Rake's Progress 45. The Wicked Lady 46. Nicholas Nickleby 47. The Small Back Room 48. Three Cases of Murder 55. Oscar Wilde 60, etc.

The Jones Family. A 1936 second feature called *Every Saturday Night* started off a series of seventeen about a comicalized small town American family in which Pa was Jed Prouty and Ma was Spring Byington. They had four years of popularity without ever quite equalling MGM's Hardy family, which had more

sentimentality.

Jones, Freddie (1927–). Clever British character actor who has yet to control a tendency towards twitchy caricatures.
The Bliss of Mrs Blossom 68. Otley 69. Frankenstein Must be Destroyed 70. Goodbye Gemini 70. Antony and Cleopatra 72. Sitting Target 72. The Satanic Rites of Dracula 73, etc.

Jones, Griffith (1910–). British light leading man, on stage from 1930.
The Faithful Heart (debut) 32. Catherine the Great 34. The Mill on the Floss 36. A Yank at Oxford 38. *The Four Just Men* 39. Young Man's Fancy 39. Atlantic Ferry 40. This Was Paris 41. Henry V 44. The Wicked Lady 45. *The Rake's Progress* 45. *They Made Me a Fugitive* 47. Good Time Girl 48. Miranda 48. Look Before You Love 49. Honeymoon Deferred 51. Star of My Night 53. The Sea Shall Not Have Them 55. Face in the Night 57. Kill Her Gently 59. Strangler's Web 63. Decline and Fall 68, many others.

Jones, Harmon (1911–1972). Canadian director in Hollywood.
□ As Young As You Feel 51. The Pride of St Louis 52. Bloodhounds of Broadway 52. The Silver Whip 53. City of Bad Men 53. The Kid from Left Field 53. Gorilla at Large 54. Princess of the Nile 54. Target Zero 55. A Day of Fury 56. Canyon River 56. The Beast of Budapest 58. Bullwhip 58. Wolf Larsen 58. Dont Worry We'll Think of a Title 58.

Jones, Henry (1912–). American character actor of stage, TV, and occasional films; usually plays the guy next door or the worm who turns.
The Lady Says No 51. *The Bad Seed* 56. The Girl Can't Help It 57. Vertigo 58. The Bramble Bush 60. Angel Baby 60. Never Too Late 65. Project X 67. Stay Away Joe 68. Support Your Local Sheriff 69. The Skin Game 71, etc.
TV series: Phyllis 75– .

Jones, James Earl (1931–). Black American leading actor.
The Great White Hope 70. The Man (TV) 73. Claudine 74. The Bingo Long Travelling All Stars 76, etc.

Jones, Jennifer (1919–) (Phyllis Isley). Intense, variable American leading actress, in small film roles from 1939.
□ Dick Tracy's G Men 39. The New Frontier 39. *The Song of Bernadette* (AA) 43. Since You Went Away 44. Love Letters 45. Cluny Brown 46. Duel in the Sun 46. *Portrait of Jennie* 48. We

Were Strangers 49. Madame Bovary 49. *Carrie* 51. Gone to Earth (GB) 51. Ruby Gentry 52. Indiscretion 54. Beat the Devil 54. *Love Is a Many-Splendored Thing* 55. Good Morning, Miss Dove 55. The Man in the Grey Flannel Suit 56. The Barretts of Wimpole Street 57. A Farewell to Arms 58. Tender Is the Night 61. The Idol (GB) 66. Angel Angel Down We Go 69. The Towering Inferno 74.

Jones, L. Q. (1936–). American character actor.
The Wild Bunch 69. The Ballad of Cable Hogue 70. The Hunting Party 71. The Brotherhood of Satan (& p) 71.

Jones, Marcia Mae (1924–). American child actress of the thirties.
King of Jazz 31. These Three 36. Heidi 37. The Little Princess 39. Tomboy 40. Nice Girl 41. Nine Girls 44. Arson Inc. 50. Chicago Calling (under the name of Marsha Jones) 52. Rogue's Gallery 68, etc.

Jones, Paul (1943–). British leading man, former pop singer.
Privilege 66. Demons of the Mind 71, etc.

Jones, Paul (1901–1968). American producer, long with Paramount.
The Great McGinty 40. Sullivan's Travels 41. Road to Morocco 42. The Virginian 46. Dear Ruth 47. Here Come the Girls 53. Living It Up 54. Pardners 56. The Disorderly Orderly 64, many others.

Jones, Peter (1920–). British character comedian.
Fanny by Gaslight 44. The Yellow Balloon 53. Albert R.N. 53. Danger Within 58. Never Let Go 61. Romanoff and Juliet 61. Press for Time 66. Just Like a Woman 66, etc.

Jones, Quincy (1935–). Black American character actor.
The Pawnbroker 65. The Deadly Affair 66. In Cold Blood 67. MacKenna's Gold 69. Bob and Carol and Ted and Alice 70. Cactus Flower 71. The Anderson Tapes 72.

Jones, Shirley (1934–). American singer and leading lady who blossomed into a substantial actress.
Oklahoma 55. Carousel 56. April Love 57. Bobbikins (GB) 59. Pepe 60. *Elmer Gantry* (AA) 60. Two Rode Together 61. *The Music Man* 62. A Ticklish Affair 63. Bedtime Story 64. Dark Purpose 64. Fluffy 65. The Secret of My Success 65. Silent Night Holy Night (TV) 69. The

Cheyenne Social Club 70. The Happy Ending 70. But I Dont Want to Get Married (TV) 71. Winner Take All (TV) 75.
TV series: *The Partridge Family* 70–73.

Jones, Spike (1911–1965) (Lindley Armstrong Jones). Pint-sized American bandleader ('Spike Jones and his City Slickers'), popular in the forties for crazy variations on well-known songs.
Thank Your Lucky Stars 43. Bring on the Girls 45. Variety Girl 47. Fireman Save My Child 55, etc.

Jordan, Bobby (1923–1965). American actor, one of the original Dead End Kids.
Dead End 37. Angels with Dirty Faces 38. They Made Me a Criminal 39. That Gang of Mine 40. Pride of the Bowery 41. Let's Get Tough 42. Clancy Street Boys 43. Bowery Champs 44. Bowery Bombshell 46. Hard Boiled Mahoney 47. Treasure of Monte Cristo 49. This Man is Armed 56, many others.

Jordan, Richard (1938–). American leading actor.
The Yakuza 75. Kamouraska 75. Rooster Cogburn 75. *Captains and the Kings* (TV) 76, etc.

Jory, Victor (1902–). Saturnine Canadian actor, on stage from mid-twenties. Usually a villain on screen.
Sailor's Luck (debut) 32. A Midsummer Night's Dream (as Oberon) 35. *The Adventures of Tom Sawyer* (as Injun Joe) 38. Gone with the Wind 39. Unknown Guest 44. The Gallant Blade 48. Canadian Pacific 49. Cat Women of the Moon 53. Valley of the Kings 54. Diary of a Scoundrel 56. The Man Who Turned to Stone 58. The Fugitive Kind 60. *The Miracle Worker* 63. Cheyenne Autumn 64. Mackenna's Gold (narration only) 69. A Time for Dying 69. Flap 70. Papillon 73, many others.
TV series: Manhunt 59–61.

Joseph, Robert (1913–1969). American producer.
The Third Secret (& w) 63, etc.

Joslyn, Allyn (1905–). American character comedian whose crumpled features admirably portray bewilderment.
They Won't Forget (debut) 37. Bedtime Story 41. A Yank in Dutch 42. *Heaven Can Wait* 43. Bride by Mistake 44. Junior Miss 45. *It Shouldn't Happen to a Dog* 47. If You Knew Susie 48. As Young As You Feel 51. Titanic 53. The Fastest Gun Alive 56. The Brothers O'Toole

73, many others.
TV series: The Addams Family 64. Don't Call
Me Charlie 66.

Jourdan, Louis (1919–) (Louis Gendre).
Smooth French leading man who has made films
also in Britain and Hollywood.
Le Corsaire (debut) 39. The Paradine Case 48.
Letter from an Unknown Woman 48. Madame
Bovary 49. Bird of Paradise 50. Anne of the
Indies 51. *The Happy Time* 52. *Rue de
l'Estrapade* 52. Decameron Nights 53. *Three
Coins in the Fountain* 54. The Swan 56. Julie 56.
Gigi 58. The Best of Everything 59. Can-Can 60.
The Count of Monte Cristo 61. *The VIPs* 62.
Made in Paris 65. Peau d'Espion 67. A Flea in
Her Ear 68. Run a Crooked Mile (TV) 71. The
Count of Monte Cristo (TV) 76. The Silver Bears
77, etc.
TV series: Paris Precinct 53.

Jour de Fête (France 1949). The first full-
length comedy written and directed by Jacques
Tati, who stars as the rural postman with a
sudden ambition to be efficient. The climactic
sequence of visual gags is hilarious, but as in his
later films Tati needs stronger control.

Le Jour Se Lève (France 1939). This
memorable melodrama may have been over-
praised because it was subsequently bought up
and threatened with destruction to make way for
an inferior American remake (*The Long Night*
47). Nevertheless it drew great tension from
Jacques Prevert's tragic story of a man who kills
a girl's persecutor and, cornered by the police,
commits suicide. Directed by Marcel Carne, with
music by Maurice Jaubert and photography by
Curt Courant; also first-rate performances by
Jean Gabin, Arletty and Jules Berry.

Journal d'Un Curé de Campagne (France
1950). Written and directed by Robert Bresson
from Georges Bernanos' novel, this spare,
ascetic film tells of a young priest's difficulties
and early death in his first parish. Claude
Laydu's withdrawn performance is exactly in
keeping.

Journey into Fear (US 1942). Set up by Orson
Welles before he fell out of favour with RKO,
this tight little thriller from Eric Ambler's book
bears unmistakable signs of his influence though
technically directed by Norman Foster.
Brilliantly atmospheric in its Constantinople
settings, it provides excellent roles for Joseph
Cotten, Dolores del Rio and Welles himself as
Colonel Haki of the Turkish Secret Police. Its
influence can be seen in *The Third Man*. The

1974 remake went sadly awry.

Journey to the Center of the Earth (US
1959). Jules Verne's fantastic novel was here
adapted by Charles Brackett and Walter Reisch,
directed by Henry Levin and photographed by
Leo Tover. Despite some cardboard sets, it
successfully set a light whimsical trend in science
fiction, with James Mason as an earnest
professor and Arlene Dahl as a Victorian lady
who makes tea several miles down.

Journey's End (GB/US 1930). This film
version of R. C. Sheriff's play set in the World
War I trenches was an early example of Anglo-
American co-production. It was also the last
major film of producer George Pearson, and it
took to Hollywood two interesting talents: actor
Colin Clive and director James Whale, both of
whom were involved in these capacities in the
London stage production. In 1976 came an
'aerial version', *Aces High*.

Jouvet, Louis (1887–1951). Distinguished
French actor of stage and screen.
Topaze 32. *Doctor Knock* 33. *La Kermesse
Héroïque* 35. Les Bas Fonds 36. *Un Carnet de
Bal* 37. Hôtel du Nord 38. *La Fin du Jour* 38.
Volpone 41. *Quai des Orfèvres* 47. Retour à la
Vie 49. Doctor Knock (remake) 50. Un Histoire
d'Amour 51, etc.

Joy, Leatrice (1899–) (Leatrice Joy Zeidler).
Vivacious, self-confident American leading lady
of the twenties.
Bunty Pulls the Strings 20. The Marriage Cheat
21. Manslaughter 22. You Can't Fool Your Wife
23. The Ten Commandments 23. Triumph 24.
The Dressmaker from Paris 25. For Alimony
Only 26. Angel of Broadway 27. The Blue
Danube 28. A Most Immoral Lady 29. First
Love 39. Red Stallion in the Rockies 49. Love
Nest 52, etc.

Joy, Nicholas (1894–1964). American small
part actor often seen as beaming toff or
benevolent father.
Daisy Kenyon 47. If Winter Comes 47. The
Great Gatsby 49. And Baby Makes Three 50.
Man with a Cloak 51. Affair with a Stranger 53.
Desk Set 57, etc.

Joyce, Alice (1889–1955). American leading
lady of the silent screen.
Womanhood 17. The Lion and the Mouse 19.
Cousin Kate 21. The Green Goddess 23.
Daddy's Gone a-Hunting 25. The Squall 29.
Song o' My Heart 30, etc.

Joyce, Brenda (1918–) (Betty Leabo). American leading lady, former model. Played innocent types in the forties, then retired.
The Rains Came (debut) 39. Little Old New York 40. Maryland 40. Marry the Boss's Daughter 41. Whispering Ghosts 42. The Postman Didn't Ring 42. Little Tokyo USA 43. Strange Confession 45. The Enchanted Forest 46. Tarzan and the Huntress 47. Shaggy 48. Tarzan's Magic Fountain 49, etc.

Joyce, Yootha (1927–). Angular British character actress, popular in TV comedy series.
Sparrows Can't Sing 62. The Pumpkin Eater 64. Stranger in the House 67. Burke and Hare 71.

Joyless Street (Germany 1925). Much-censored study of prostitution and other vices, a rare German film of the period to centre on squalid fact rather than romantic fantasy. Directed by G. W. Pabst, with a cast including Greta Garbo, Asta Nielsen and Werner Krauss.

Judd, Edward (1932–). British general purpose actor.
The Day the Earth Caught Fire 61. Stolen Hours 63. The Long Ships 63. *The First Men in the Moon* 64. Strange Bedfellows 65. Island of Terror 66. Invasion 66. The Vengeance of She 68. Living Free 71. Universal Soldier 71. Vault of Horror 73. Assassin 73, The Incredible Sarah 76, etc.

Judex (France 1916). A super-serial by Louis Feuillade, enjoying belated recognition (in a six-hour version) as a primitive precursor of James Bond. A remake was directed by Georges Franju in 1963.

Judge, Arline (1912–1974). American general purpose leading lady.
Bachelor Apartment 31. Girl Crazy 32. Name This Woman 35. King of Burlesque 36. Valiant Is the Word for Carrie 37. The Lady Is Willing 42. From This Day Forward 45. Two Knights in Brooklyn 49, etc.

Judge Priest (US 1934). Directed by John Ford, this southern-state comedy-drama fairly oozed with local colour and provided a fat part for Will Rogers as a kindly old local judge. (Irvin S. Cobb, from whose writings it was taken, took over a couple of Will Rogers' roles after the actor died in an air crash in 1935.) In 1952 Ford remade the film as *The Sun Shines Bright*, with Charles Winninger.

Juillard, Robert (1906–). French cinematographer.
Germany Year Zero 48. Jeux Interdits 52. Les Belles de Nuit 52. Les Grandes Manoeuvres 55. Austerlitz 60, etc.

Jules et Jim (France 1961). François Truffaut's affectionate recreation of a period (pre-1914) and a curious triangular love affair has been enthusiastically adopted as a credo by sophisticted young people in many countries. Jeanne Moreau's performance transcends the lumpiness of the script, which ends in uneasy gloom.

Julian, Rupert (1886–1943). American director of the twenties.
Merry Go Round 23. Love and Glory 24. Hell's Highroad 25. *The Phantom of the Opera* 25. Three Faces West 26. Yankee Clipper 27. The Leopard Lady 28. Love Comes Along 30. The Cat Creeps 30, etc.

Julius Caesar (102–44 B.C.). The Roman emperor has been memorably portrayed by Claude Rains in *Caesar and Cleopatra*, Warren William in the 1934 *Cleopatra* and Rex Harrison in the 1962 remake. The Shakespeare play was filmed many times in silent days, but the only notable sound versions in English have been Joseph L. Mankiewicz's 1953 production with Louis Calhern as Caesar, James Mason as Brutus, and John Gielgud as Cassius, and the 1970 version with Gielgud as Caesar, Richard Johnson as Cassius, and Charlton Heston as Mark Antony. A British second feature of 1959, *An Honourable Murder*, brought the story up to date as a melodrama of boardroom intrigue.

jump-cutting. Moving abruptly from one scene to another to make a dramatic point, e.g. from cause to effect.

June, Ray (c. 1908–1958). American cinematographer.
Wandering Husbands 24. The Silent Avenger 27. Alibi 29. Arrowsmith 31. Horse Feathers 32. Riptide 34. I Cover the Waterfront 35. Night Must Fall 37. Test Pilot 38. The Hoodlum Saint 46. A Southern Yankee 48. Crisis 50. The Reformer and the Redhead 51. Sombrero 53. The Court Jester 55. Funny Face 56. Houseboat 58, many others.

Junge, Alfred (1886–). German art director with long experience at UFA; in Britain from the twenties.
Piccadilly 28. The Good Companions 32. *The Man Who Knew Too Much* 34. Bulldog Jack 35. *King Solomon's Mines* 37. The Citadel 38. *Goodbye Mr Chips* 39. The Silver Fleet 42. *The*

Life and Death of Colonel Blimp 43. I Know Where I'm Going 45. *A Matter of Life and Death* 45. *Black Narcissus* (AA) 46. Edward My Son 49. The Miniver Story 50. Ivanhoe 52. Mogambo 53. *Invitation to the Dance* 56. The Barretts of Wimpole Street 57. A Farewell to Arms 58, many others.

Jungle Jim. This sub-Tarzan character began as a comic strip, and in 1937 Forde Beebe directed a serial on his exploits. In 1948 began the rather tired series tossed off for Columbia with a paunchy Johnny Weissmuller in the title role: it started ineptly and quickly became ridiculous.

The Jungle Princess (US 1936). This Paramount programmer about a beautiful female Tarzan, directed by William Thiele, put Dorothy Lamour in a sarong for the first time and started her off on a series of similar exploits: *Her Jungle Love, Aloma of the South Seas, Typhoon, Beyond the Blue Horizon, Rainbow Island*, etc.

Jurado, Katy (1927–) (Maria Jurado Garcia). Spirited Mexican actress who has made Hollywood films.
The Bullfighter and the Lady 51. High Noon 52. Arrowhead 53. Broken Lance 54. Trial 55. Trapeze 56. One-Eyed Jacks 59. Barabbas 61. Smoky 66. Covenant With Death 67. Stay Away Joe 68. Pat Garrett and Billy the Kid 72, etc.

Juran, Nathan (1907–). Austrian art director, long in the US. Won Academy Award for *How Green Was My Valley* 41. Later became a director of action films.
☐ The Black Castle 52. Gunsmoke 53. Law and Order 53. The Golden Blade 53. Tumbleweed 53. Highway Dragnet 54. Drums along the River 54. The Crooked Web 55. The Deadly Mantis 57. Hellcats of the Navy 57. Twenty Million Miles to Earth 57. The Seventh Voyage of Sinbad 58. Good Day for a Hanging 58. Flight of the Lost Balloon 61. *Jack the Gaint Killer* 62. Siege of the Saxons 63. First Men in the Moon 64. East of Sudan 65. The Land Raiders 70. The Boy Who Cried Werewolf 73.

Jurgens, Curt (1912–). German stage leading man, in films from 1939; since the war

has played internationally.
The Devil's General 54. Les Héros Sont Fatigués 55. *An Eye for an Eye* 56. Without You It Is Night (& d) 56. And Woman Was Created 57. *Me and the Colonel* 57. The Enemy Below 57. Inn of the Sixth Happiness 58. The Blue Angel 58. Ferry to Hong Kong 58. *I Aim at the Stars* (as Wernher von Braun) 59. Tamango 60. Lord Jim 64. The Threepenny Opera 65. Das Liebeskarussel (Who Wants to Sleep) 65. The Assassination Bureau 68. The Battle of Neretva 70. Nicholas and Alexandra 71. Vault of Horror 73. The Spy Who Loved Me 77, etc.

Jurow, Martin (1914–). American producer.
The Hanging Tree 58. The Fugitive Kind 60. Breakfast at Tiffany's 61. Soldier in the Rain 63. The Great Race 65, etc.

Justice est Faite (France 1950). Written and directed by André Cayatte, this study of a jury during a murder trial managed to provide entertaining drama while questioning points of law. Cayatte's subsequent films mostly followed a similar pattern, but not so successfully.

Justice, James Robertson (1905–1975). Bearded Scottish actor and personality, former journalist and naturalist.
Fiddlers Three (debut) 44. *Scott of the Antarctic* 48. Christopher Columbus 49. *Whisky Galore* 49. David and Bathsheba 51. The Voice of Merrill 52. *Doctor in the House* 54. Storm over the Nile 55. Land of the Pharaohs 55. Moby Dick 56. Campbell's Kingdom 57. Seven Thunders 57. Doctor at Large 58. *Very Important Person* 61. *The Fast Lady* 62. Crooks Anonymous 62. You Must Be Joking 65. Doctor in Clover 66. Hell is Empty 67. Mayerling 68. Chitty Chitty Bang Bang 68, many others.

Justin, John (1917–). British leading man, on stage from 1933.
The Thief of Baghdad (film debut) 40. The Gentle Sex 43. Journey Together 45. Call of the Blood 47. The Sound Barrier 51. Melba 53. Seagulls over Sorrento 54. The Man Who Loved Redheads 55. The Teckman Mystery 55. Safari 56. Island in the Sun 56. The Spider's Web 61. Candidate For Murder 64. Savage Messiah 72, etc.

K

Kadar, Jan (1918–). Czech director who invariably works with writer Elmer Klos (1910–).
Kidnap 56. Death Is Called Engelchen 58. The Accused 64. *A Shop on the High Street* (AA) 64. The Angel Levine (US) 70. Adrift 71, etc.

Kahn, Madeleine (1942–). American comic actress who tends to overplay her hand; the darling of the Mel Brooks clique.
What's Up Doc? 72. Paper Moon 73. Blazing Saddles 74. Young Frankenstein 74. The Adventure of Sherlock Holmes' Smarter Brother 75. At Long Last Love 75, etc.

Kalem. An early American production company founded in 1907, taking its name from the initials of its three principals, George Klein, Sam Long and Frank Marion (K-L-M). Its most famous production is *From the Manger to the Cross* 12.

Kalatozov, Mikhail (1903–1973). Russian director and executive.
Their Kingdom 28. Salt for Svenetia 30. A Nail in a Boot 32. The Conspiracy of the Doomed 50. *The Cranes are Flying* 57. The Unsent Letter 60. I Am Cuba 66. The Red Tent 69.

Kalmar, Bert (1884–1947). American vaudevillian, song-writer (with Harry Ruby) and music executive.
Check and Double Check (& w) 30. The Kid from Spain (& w) 32. *Horse Feathers* (& w) 32. *Duck Soup* (& w) 33. Kentucky Kernels (& w) 34. Everybody Sing 38. Wake Up and Dream 46. Carnival in Costa Rica 48, many others.

Kalmus, Herbert T. (1881–1963). American pioneer photographic expert, later president of Technicolor. His wife *Natalie Kalmus* (1892–1965) was adviser on all Technicolor films from 1933.

Kameradschaft (Germany 1931). G. W. Pabst's most acclaimed film shows how a mine disaster in a French town near the German border breaks down the barriers of hatred between the two nations. The original version

had a cynical ending. Photographed by Fritz Arno Wagner.

Kaminska, Ida (1899–). Polish character actress.
The Shop on High Street 66. The Angel Levine (US) 70, etc.

Kane, Joseph (1894–1975). American director since 1935, mainly of competent but unambitious Republic westerns.
The Man from Music Mountain 38. The Man from Cheyenne 42. Flame of the Barbary Coast 44. The Cheaters 45. The Plainsman and the Lady 46. The Plunderers (& p) 48. California Passage (& p) 50. Hoodlum Empire (& p) 51. Jubilee Trail (& p) 53. Spoilers of the Forest (& p) 57, many others.

Kanin, Garson (1912–). American writer and raconteur who has spent time in Hollywood as director, also as screenwriter, especially in collaboration with his wife Ruth Gordon.
□ AS DIRECTOR: A Man to Remember 38. Next Time I Marry 38. *The Great Man Votes* 38. *Bachelor Mother* 39. My Favorite Wife 40. They Knew What They Wanted 40. *Tom, Dick and Harry* 41. The True Glory (w co-d) 45. *Where It's At* (& w) 69. *Some Kind of a Nut* (& w) 70.
AS WRITER: From This Day Forward 46. A Double Life 48. *Adam's Rib* 49. *Born Yesterday* (oa) 50. The Marrying Kind 52. Pat and Mike 52. It Should Happen to You 53, etc.

Kanin, Michael (1910–). American writer brother of Garson Kanin; often works with his wife Fay.
Anne of Windy Poplars 40. *Woman of the Year* 42. The Cross of Lorraine 44. Centennial Summer 46. Rhapsody 54. The Opposite Sex 56. Teacher's Pet 58. The Outrage 64, etc.

Kann, Lily (c. 1898–). German character actress, long in England.
The Flemish Farm 43. Latin Quarter 45. Mrs Fitzherbert 47. A Tale of Five Cities 51. Betrayed (US) 54. A Kid for Two Farthings 55. No Trees in the Street 59, many others.

Kanner, Alexis (1942–). British character
actor.
Reach for Glory 63. Crossplot 69. Connecting
Rooms 69. Goodbye Gemini 70, etc.

Kanter, Hal (1918–). American writer-
director with TV background.
I Married a Woman (d) 55. Loving You (wd) 56.
Once Upon a Horse (wd) 58. Pocketful of
Miracles (co-w) 61. Move Over Darling (w) 63.
Dear Brigitte (w) 65, etc.

Kantor, Mackinlay (1904–). American
writer full of sentiment and patriotism.
The Voice of Bugle Ann 37. Happy Land 43. The
Best Years of Our Lives 46. The Romance of
Rosy Ridge 47. Follow Me Boys 66.

Kaper, Bronislau (1902–). Polish composer
now resident in US.
Gaslight 44. Without Love 45. Green Dolphin
Street 47. The Forsyte Saga 49. *The Red Badge
of Courage* 51. *Lili* (AA) 53. *Them* 54. The Swan
56. The Brothers Karamazov 58. Butterfield 8
61. Mutiny on the Bounty 62. Kisses for My
President 64. Lord Jim 64. Tobruk 66. A Flea in
Her Ear 68, etc.

Kaplan, Marvin (1924–). Owlish little
American comedy actor.
The Reformer and the Redhead 50. I Can Get It
for You Wholesale 51. Angels in the Outfield 51.
Behave Yourself 61. Wake Me When It's Over
60. A New Kind of Love 63. It's a Mad Mad
Mad Mad World 63. The Great Race 65, etc.
TV series: Chicago Teddybears 71.

Kaplan, Sol (–). American composer.
Tales of Manhattan 42. Port of New York 49.
Rawhide 51. Niagara 53. Happy Anniversary
59. The Victors 63. The Spy Who Came in from
the Cold 65. Explosion 69. Living Free 72, etc.

Karina, Anna (1940–) (Hanne Karin Beyer).
Danish leading lady, mostly in French films,
especially those of Jean-Luc Godard.
She'll Have To Go (GB) 61. *Une Femme Est une
Femme* 61. *Vivre Sa Vie* 62. Le Petit Soldat 63.
Bande à Part 64. Alphaville 65. Made in USA
66. The Magus 68. Before Winter Comes 68.
Laughter in the Dark 69. Justine 69. The
Salzburg Connection 72, etc.

Karlin, Miriam (1925–) (M. Samuels).
Rasping voiced British revue comedienne and
character actress.
The Deep Blue Sea 55. The Entertainer 59. On
the Fiddle 61. The Small World of Sammy Lee
63. Heavens Above 63. The Bargee 64. Ladies

Who Do 64. A Clockwork Orange 71. Barry
Lyndon 75, etc.

Karloff, Boris (1887–1969) (William Pratt).
Gaunt British character actor, on stage from
1910, films from 1919, mainly in US. Achieved
world fame as the monster in *Frankenstein* 31,
and became typed in horrific parts despite his
gentle, cultured voice.
Biographies: *Horror Man* (1972) by Peter
Underwood. *Karloff, the Man, the Monster, the
Movies* (1973) by Denis Gifford. *The Films of
Boris Karloff* by Richard Bojarski and Kenneth
Beals.
SELECTED SILENTS: His Majesty the
American 19. The Last of the Mohicans 20. The
Man from Downing Street 22. A Woman
Conquers 23. Parisian Nights 25. Never the
Twain Shall Meet 25. The Bells 26. Valencia 26.
Tarzan and the Golden Lion 27. Two Arabian
Knights 27. Vultures of the Sea 28. Phantoms of
the North 29, many others.
□ SOUND FILMS: Behind that Curtain 29.
King of the Kongo 29. The Unholy Night 29.
The Bad One 30. The Sea Bat 30. The Utah Kid
30. Mothers Cry 30. The Criminal Code 30.
Cracked Nuts 31. Young Donovan's Kid 31.
King of the Wild 31. Smart Money 31. The
Public Defender 31. I Like Your Nerve 31. Graft
31. Five Star Final 31. The Mad Genius 31. The
Yellow Ticket 31. Guilty Generation 31.
Frankenstein 31. Tonight or Never 31. Behind
the Mask 32. Business and Pleasure 32. Scarface
32. The Cohens and Kellys in Hollywood 32.
The Miracle Man 32. Night World 32. The Old
Dark House 32. *The Mask of Fu Manchu* 32.
The Mummy 32. The Ghoul 33. The Lost Patrol
34. The House of Rothschild 34. The Black Cat
34. The Gift of Gab 34. *The Bride of
Frankenstein* 35. *The Black Room* 35. *The
Raven* 35. The Invisible Ray 36. The Walking
Dead 36. The Man Who Lived Again 36.
Juggernaut 36. *Charlie Chan at the Opera* 37.
Night Key 37. West of Shanghai 37. The
Invisible Menace 37. Mr Wong Detective 38.
Son of Frankenstein 39. The Mystery of Mr
Wong 39. Mr Wong in Chinatown 39. The Man
they could not Hang 39. Tower of London 39.
The Fatal Hour 40. British Intelligence 40. Black
Friday 40. The Man with Nine Lives 40. Devil's
Island 40. Doomed to Die 40. Before I Hang 40.
The Ape 40. You'll Find Out 40. The Devil
Commands 41. The Boogie Man will Get You
42. The Climax 44. *House of Frankenstein* 44.
The Body Snatcher 45. Isle of the Dead 45.
Bedlam 46. The Secret Life of Walter Mitty 47.
Lured 47. Unconquered 47. Dick Tracy meets
Gruesome 47. Tap Roots 48. Abbott and
Costello Meet the Killer 49. The Strange Door

51. The Black Castle 52. Abbott and Costello Meet Dr Jekyll and Mr Hyde 53. Monster of the Island 53. The Hindu 53. Voodoo Island 58. Grip of the Strangler 58. Corridors of Blood 58. Frankenstein 70 58. *The Raven* 63. The Terror 63. Comedy of Terrors 63. Black Sabbath 64. Bikini Beach 64. Die Monster Die 65. Ghost in the Invisible Bikini 66. The Venetian Affair 67. The Sorcerers 67. *Targets* 68. Curse of the Crimson Altar 68. The Snake People 70. The Incredible Invasion 70. Cauldron of Blood 70. The Fear Chamber 70. House of Evil 70.
TV series: Colonel March of Scotland Yard 55. Thriller 58–59.

Karlson, Phil (1908–) (Philip Karlstein). American director, in Hollywood from 1932. Mainly low-budget actioners until he suddenly gained stature in the fifties.
□ A Wave a WAC and a Marine 44. GI Honeymoon 45. There Goes Kelly 45. Shanghai Cobra 45. Swing Parade 46. Live Wires 46. Dark Alibi 46. Behind the Mask 46. Bowery Bombshell 46. The Missing Lady 46. Wife Wanted 46. Black Gold 47. Kilroy was Here 47. Louisiana 47. Rocky 48. Adventures in Silverado 48. Thunderhoof 48. Ladies of the Chorus 49. The Big Cat 49. Down Memory Lane 49. The Iroquois Trail 50. Lorna Doone 51. The Texas Rangers 51. Mask of the Avenger 51. *Scandal Sheet* 52. The Brigand 52. *Kansas City Confidential* 53. 99 River Street 53. They Rode West 54. Tight Spot 55. Hell's Island 55. Five Against the House 55. *The Phoenix City Story* 55. The Brothers Rico 57. Gunman's Walk 58. Hell to Eternity 60. Key Witness 60. The Secret Ways 61. The Young Doctors 61. Kid Galahad 62. Rampage 63. *The Silencers* 66. A Time for Killing 67. Wrecking Crew 69. Hornet's Nest 70. Ben 72. Walking Tall 73. Framed 75.

Karno, Fred (1866–1941). English impresario from whose team of slapstick comedians sprang several stars including Stan Laurel and Charles Chaplin.

Karns, Roscoe (1893–1970). American character actor, very active in the thirties, usually in hard-boiled comedy roles.
Beggars of Life 28. *The Front Page* 30. Undercover Man 32. *Night After Night* 32. *Twentieth Century* 34. *It Happened One Night* 34. Thanks for the Memory 38. They Drive by Night 40. *His Girl Friday* 40. His Butler's Sister 43. Will Tomorrow Ever Come? 47. Inside Story 48. Onionhead 58, mnay others.
TV series: Hennessey 63.

Kasket, Harold (c. 1916–). British character actor of mixed descent, originally stage impressionist.
Hotel Sahara 51. Moulin Rouge 53. Interpol 57. Sands of the Desert 60. Arabesque 66, etc.

Kastner, Elliott (1930–). American producer, former literary agent.
Bus Riley's Back in Town 65. Harper 66. Kaleidoscope 66. The Night of the Following Day 68. Where Eagles Dare 68. The Walking Stick 69. A Severed Head 70. When Eight Bells Toll 71. Villain 71. Zee and Co. 72. The Nightcomers 72. The Long Goodbye 73. Harrowhouse 74. Farewell My Lovely 75. The Missouri Breaks 76, etc.

Kastner, Erich (1899–1974). German novelist whose *Emil and the Detectives* has been much filmed. He also wrote the original of *The Parent Trap.*

Kastner, Peter (1944–). Canadian actor who made a corner in frustrated adolescents.
Nobody Waved Goodbye (Can.) 65. *You're a Big Boy Now* (US) 66. B.S. I Love You 70, etc.
TV series: The Ugliest Girl in Town 68.

Kasznar, Kurt (1913–). Chubby Austrian character actor, in US from 1936.
The Light Touch (debut) 51. The Happy Time 52. Lili 53. Sombrero 53. My Sister Eileen 55. Anything Goes 56. A Farewell to Arms 58. For the First Time 59. Casino Royale 66. The King's Pirate 67. The Ambushers 67, etc.
TV series: Land of the Giants 68–69.

Katch, Kurt (1896–1958) (Isser Kac). Bald Polish character actor, in Hollywood from 1942.
Ali Baba and the Forty Thieves 43. *The Mask of Dimitrios* 44. Salome Where She Danced 45. The Mummy's Curse 45. Song of Love 47. The Secret of the Incas 54. Abbott and Costello Meet the Mummy 55. Pharaoh's Curse 57, etc.

Katzin, Lee H. (–). American director.
Heaven with a Gun 69. Whatever Happened to Aunt Alice? 69. The Phynx 70. Le Mans 71. The Salzburg Connection 72, etc.

Katzman, Sam (1901–1973). American producer, chiefly of low-budget co-features including the *Jungle Jim* series, *Rock Around the Clock* 56, many others.

Kaufman, Boris (c. 1906–). Polish cinematographer, in France from 1928, US from 1942.
□ La Marche des Machines 28. A Propos de

Nice (& co-d) 30. Les Halles 30. *Zero de Conduite* 32. Seine 33. *L'Atalante* 34. Pere Lampion 36. Fort Delores 37. Serenade 38. Better Tomorrow 45. Capital Story 45. The Southwest 45. Journey into Medicine 47. The Tanglewood Story 50. The Garden of Eden 54. *On the Waterfront* (AA) 54. Crowded Paradise 56. *Baby Doll* 56. Patterns 56. *Twelve Angry Men* 57. That Kind of Woman 59. The Fugitive Kind 60. Splendor in the Grass 61. Long Day's Journey into Night 62. All the Way Home 63. Gone are the Days 63. *The World of Henry Orient* 64. The Pawnbroker 65. *The Group* 66. *Bye Bye Braverman* 67. Uptight 68. The Brotherhood 68. Tell Me That You Love Me Junie Moon 70.

Kaufman, George S. (1889–1961). American comedy playwright, often in collaboration with Moss Hart (qv). Most of his works were filmed.
Biography 1972: *George S. Kaufman* by Howard Teichman.
Dulcy 23. Beggar on Horseback 25. *Animal Crackers* 30. The Royal Family of Broadway 30. *Once in a Lifetime* 32. Dinner at Eight 33. Stage Door 37. *You Can't Take It With You* 38. *The Man Who Came to Dinner* 41. George Washington Slept Here 42. The Late George Apley 47. The Senator was Indiscreet (wd) 49. The Solid Gold Cadillac 56, etc.

Kaufman, Millard (–). American screenwriter.
Gun Crazy 50. Take the High Ground 53. *Bad Day at Black Rock* 55. Raintree County 57. Never So Few 59. Convicts Four (& d) 62. The War Lord 65, etc.

Kaufmann, Christine (1944–). German leading lady in international films.
Town without Pity 61. Taras Bulba 62. Wild and Wonderful 64. Tunnel 28 64. Murders in the Rue Morgue 71, etc.

Kaufmann, Maurice (1928–). British supporting actor.
A Shot in the Dark 64. Fanatic 65. Bloomfield 70. The Abominable Dr Phibes 71, etc.

Kautner, Helmut (1908–). German director who had an unhappy experience in Hollywood in the fifties.
Kitty and the World Conference 39. Adieu Franciska 41. Romanze in Moll 43. Unter Den Brücken 45. In Jenen Tagen 47. Der Apfel Ist Ab 48. Epilog 50. The Last Brigade 54. Himmel Ohne Sterne 55. The Wonderful Years (US) 58. Stranger in My Arms (US) 59, etc.

Kawalerowicz, Jerzy (1922–). Polish director.
Gromada 51. Cien 54. The True End of the Great War 57. *Pociag* (Night Train) 59. *Mother Jeanne of the Angels* (The Devil and the Nun) 60. *The Pharaoh* 64, etc.

Kaye, Danny (1913–) (David Daniel Kaminsky). Ebullient American star entertainer of stage, screen and TV. After making several unpromising two reelers in the thirties (later compiled as *The Danny Kaye Story*) he was given the big build up by Sam Goldwyn and gained enormous popularity, though his recent films have been disappointing. Special Academy Award in 1954 'for his unique talents, his service to the industry and the American People'.
Biography 1948: *The Danny Kaye Saga* by Kurt Singer.
Up in Arms 44. *Wonder Man* 45. The Kid from Brooklyn 46. *The Secret Life of Walter Mitty* 47. A Song Is Born 48. The Inspector General 49. On the Riviera 51. *Hans Christian Andersen* 52. *Knock on Wood* 53. White Christmas 54. Assignment Children (UN short) 54. *The Court Jester* 56. Me and the Colonel 57. Merry Andrew 58. The Five Pennies 59. On the Double 62. The Man from the Diners' Club 63. The Madwoman of Chaillot 69. Peter Pan (TV) 75.

Kaye, Stubby (1918–). Rotund American comic actor.
Guys and Dolls 55. Lil Abner 59. 40 Pounds of Trouble 62. Cat Ballou 65. Sweet Charity 68, etc.

Kazan, Elia (1909–) (Elia Kazanjoglous). Distinguished American stage and screen director of Greek/Turkish descent. Intermittently an actor; with New York's Group Theatre in the thirties.
AS ACTOR: City for Conquest 40. Blues in the Night 41, etc.
AS DIRECTOR: *A Tree Grows in Brooklyn* 45. The Sea of Grass 47. *Boomerang* 47. *Gentleman's Agreement* (AA) 47. Pinky 49. Panic in the Streets 50. A Streetcar Named Desire 51. *Viva Zapata* 52. Man on a Tightrope 53. *On the Waterfront* (AA) 54. East of Eden 55. Baby Doll 56. *A Face in the Crowd* (& p) 57. Wild River (& p) 60. Splendor in the Grass (& p) 61. America America (& wp) 63. The Arrangement (& wp) 69. The Visitors (& w) 72. The Last Tycoon 76.

Keach, Stacy (1941–). American general purpose actor.
□ The Heart is a Lonely Hunter 68. End of the Road 68. The Travelling Executioner 69.

Brewster McCloud 70. Doc 70. Judge Roy Bean 72. The New Centurions 72. Fat City 72. The Gravy Train 73. The Killer inside Me 74. *Conduct Unbecoming* 75. The Squeeze 77.
TV series: Caribe 74.

Keane, Robert Emmett (1883–). Toothbrush-moustached American character actor who played travelling salesmen and fall guys in scores of light comedies and dramas.
Men Call It Love 31. Boys' Town 38. We're in the Army Now 40. Tin Pan Alley 41. Jitterbugs 43. When My Baby Smiles at Me 50. When Gangland Strikes 56, etc.

Kearton, Cherry (1871–1940). Pioneer British travel film producer whose success lasted from 1912 to the mid-thirties.

Keating, Larry (1897–1963). American character actor, often as executive or uppity neighbour.
Whirlpool 49. Three Secrets 50. Come Fill the Cup 51. About Face 52. Inferno 53. Daddy Longlegs 55. The Buster Keaton Story 57. Who was that Lady? 60. Boys' Night Out 62, many others.
TV series: *The Burns and Allen Show* 56–58. *Mister Ed* 60–62.

Keaton, Buster (1895–1966) (Joseph Francis Keaton). One of America's great silent clowns, the unsmiling but game little fellow who always came out on top whatever the odds. In two-reelers with Fatty Arbuckle from 1917, but soon began to shape his own material. Special Academy Award 1959 'for his unique talents which brought immortal comedies to the screen'. Trained in vaudeville with family act. Did not easily survive sound, but later came back in featured roles and was gaining a fresh popularity at the time of his death.
Autobiography 1960: *My Wonderful World of Slapstick*. Biographies: *Keaton* (1966) by Rudi Blesh; *Buster Keaton* (1969) by Derek Robinson. Keaton was played by Donald O'Connor in a 1957 biopic, *The Buster Keaton Story*.
The Playhouse 20. Daydreams 21. *Cops* 22. Balloonatic 23. *Our Hospitality* 23. *Sherlock Junior* 24. *The Navigator* 24. Seven Chances 25. *The General* 26. *Steamboat Bill Junior* 27. *The Cameraman* 28. Hollywood Revue of 1929. Doughboys 30. Sidewalks of New York 31. The Passionate Plumber 32. Hollywood Cavalcade 39. *San Diego I Love You* 45. God's Country 47. In the Good Old Summertime 49. Sunset Boulevard 50. *Limelight* 52. Huckleberry Finn 60. It's a Mad Mad Mad Mad World 63. How to

Stuff a Wild Bikini 65. *The Railroader* 65. Film 65. A Funny Thing Happened on the Way to the Forum 66, many others.

Keaton, Diane (1949–). American leading lady of the seventies.
□ Lovers and Other Strangers 70. The Godfather 72. Play it Again Sam 72. Sleeper 74. Godfather Two 74. Love and Death 75. Harry and Walter Go to New York 76. I Will, I Will . . . For Now 76.

Kedrova, Lila (1918–). Russian-French character actress, known internationally.
Zorba the Greek (AA) 64. A High Wind in Jamaica 65. Torn Curtain 66. Penelope 67. The Kremlin Letter 69. Soft Beds, Hard Battles 74. March or Die 77, etc.

Keel, Howard (1917–) (Harold Keel). Stalwart American leading man and singer whose career faltered when musicals went out of fashion.
□ The Small Voice (GB) 48. *Annie Get Your Gun* 50. Pagan Love Song 50. Three Guys Named Mike 51. *Showboat* 51. Texas Carnival 51. Callaway Went Thataway 51. Lovely to Look At 52. Desperate Search 52. Fast Company 53. Ride Vaquero 53. *Calamity Jane* 53. *Kiss Me Kate* 53. Rose Marie 54. *Seven Brides for Seven Brothers* 54. Deep in My Heart 54. Jupiter's Darling 54. Kismet 55. Floods of Fear (GB) 58. The Big Fisherman 59. Armored Command 61. The Day of the Triffids 63. Waco 66. Red Tomahawk 67. The War Wagon 67. Arizona Bushwhackers 68.

Keeler, Ruby (1909–) (Ethel Keeler). Petite American singer-dancer who made a small talent go a long way in musicals of the early thirties.
□ *42nd Street* 33. Gold Diggers of 1933. Footlight Parade 33. *Dames* 34. Flirtation Walk 35. Go Into Your Dance 35. Shipmates Forever 35. Colleen 36. Ready Willing and Able 37. Mother Carey's Chickens 38. Sweetheart of the Campus 41. The Phynx 70.

Keen, Geoffrey (1918–). Incisive British character actor, son of Malcolm Keen (stage actor).
His Excellency 50. Genevieve 53. The Long Arm 56. No Love for Johnnie 61. The Spiral Road 62. Live Now Pay Later 63. The Heroes of Telemark 65. Dr Zhivago 65. Born Free 66. Taste the Blood of Dracula 70. Living Free 71. Doomwatch 72, many others.

Keene, Ralph (1902–1963). British documentarist, in films from 1934. With

Ministry of Information, British Transport, etc.: emphasis on animal studies. *Cyprus Is an Island, Crofters, Journey into Spring, Between the Tides, Winter Quarters, Under Night Streets,* etc.

Keene, Tom (1896–1963) (also known at times as George Duryea and Richard Powers). American western star, mainly in second features of the thirties and forties.
Golden Girl 28. The Dude Wrangler 30. Saddle Buster 32. Our Daily Bread 33. Where the Trails Divide 37. Dynamite Cargo 41. Up in Arms 44. If You Knew Susie 48. Red Planet Mars 52. Plan 9 from Outer Space 56, many others.

Keighley, William (1889–). American director with stage experience: made many highly polished entertainments for Warners.
The Match King 32. Big-Hearted Herbert 33. Babbitt 34. *G-Men* 35. *Green Pastures* 36. Bullets or Ballots 36. The Prince and the Pauper 37. *The Adventures of Robin Hood* (co-d) 38. Brother Rat 39. The Fighting 69th 40. Torrid Zone 40. No Time for Comedy 40. *The Man Who Came to Dinner* 41. George Washington Slept Here 42. The Bride Came C.O.D. 42. The Street with No Name 48. Close to My Heart 51. The Master of Ballantrae 53, many others.

Keir, Andrew (1926–). Scottish character actor, usually in stern roles.
The Lady Craved Excitement 50. The Brave Don't Cry 52. The Maggie 54. Heart of a Child 57. Pirates of Blood River 60. Dracula, Prince of Darkness 65. Daleks Invasion Earth 2500 AD 65. The Viking Queen 67. *Quatermass and the Pit* 67. The Royal Hunt of the Sun 69. Zeppelin 70. Blood from the Mummy's Tomb 71, etc.
TV series: The Outsiders 77.

Keitel, Harvey (1947–). American actor.
Alice Doesn't Live Here Any More 74. That's The Way of the World 75. Mother Jugs and Speed 76, etc.

Keith, Brian (1921–) (Robert Keith Jnr). American actor of easy-going types, understanding fathers and occasional villains.
Arrowhead (debut) 52. Alaska Seas 53. The Violent Men 54. Five Against the House 55. Storm Centre 56. Run of the Arrow 57. Sierra Baron 58. The Young Philadelphians 59. The Deadly Companions 61. The Parent Trap 61. Moon Pilot 62. Savage Sam 63. Those Calloways 65. The Hallelujah Trail 65. *Nevada Smith* 66. The Russians Are Coming 66. *Reflections in a Golden Eye* 67. With Six You Get Eggroll 68. Krakatoa 68. Suppose They

Gave a War and Nobody Came 69. The Mackenzie Break 70. Scandalous John 71. Something Big 72. The Yakuza 75. *The Wind and the Lion* (as Theodore Roosevelt) 76. The Quest (TV) 76, etc.
TV series: Crusader 56. The Westerner 63. *Family Affair* 64–68. The Little People 72–73. Archer 75.

Keith, Ian (1899–1960) (Keith Ross). American actor, latterly in character roles.
Manhandled 24. The Divine Lady 27. Abraham Lincoln 31. The Sign of the Cross 32. Queen Christina 33. The Crusades 35. The Three Musketeers (as de Rochefort) 36. The Sea Hawk 40. The Chinese Cat 44. Nightmare Alley 48. The Black Shield of Falworth 54. Prince of Players 55. The Ten Commandments (as Rameses I) 56, many others.

Keith, Robert (1896–1966). American character actor with concert and stage experience. Spent some time as a Hollywood writer in the thirties but did not act in films until the late forties.
Boomerang 47. My Foolish Heart 49. Fourteen Hours 51. I Want You 51. *The Wild One* 53. *Young at Heart* 54. Guys and Dolls 55. My Man Godfrey 57. Tempest 58. Cimarron 61, etc.

Kellaway, Cecil (1891–1973). British character actor born in South Africa, who spent many years acting in Australia; came to Hollywood in 1939 and became an endearing exponent of roguish benevolence.
Wuthering Heights 39. Intermezzo 39. *I Married a Witch* 42. My Heart Belongs to Daddy 42. The Good Fellows (leading role) 43. Practically Yours 44. *Frenchman's Creek* 44. Love Letters 45. *Kitty* (as Gainsborough) 45. Monsieur Beaucaire 46. The Postman Always Rings Twice 46. Unconquered 47. Portrait of Jennie 48. *The Luck of the Irish* (as a leprechaun) 48. Joan of Arc 48. *Harvey* 50. The Beast from 20,000 Fathoms 53. The Female on the Beach 55. The Shaggy Dog 59. The Cardinal 63. *Hush Hush, Sweet Charlotte* 64. Spinout 66. Fitzwilly 67. Guess Who's Coming to Dinner 67. Getting Straight 70, many others.

Keller, Harry (1913–). American director.
Blonde Bandit 49. Rose of Cimarron 52. The Unguarded Moment 56. The Female Animal 57. Quantez 58. Voice in the Mirror 58. Six Black Horses 61. Tammy and the Doctor 63. Kitten with a Whip 65. In Enemy Country (& p). The Skin Game 71, etc.

Kellerman, Annette (1888–1975). Australian

dancer and swimming star who pioneered the one-piece bathing suit. Esther Williams played her in a biopic, *Million Dollar Mermaid* 52.
Neptune's Daughter 14. Daughter of the Gods 16. Queen of the Sea 18. What Women Love 20, etc.

Kellerman, Sally (1941–). American leading lady of the seventies.
The Third Day 65. The Boston Strangler 68. The April Fools 69. M*A*S*H 69. Brewster McCloud 70. Last of the Red Hot Lovers 72. Lost Horizon 73. Slither 73. Rafferty and the Gold Dust Twins 75. The Big Bus 76, etc.

Kellett, Bob (1927–). British director.
A Home of Your Own 64. San Ferry Ann 65. Girl Stroke Boy 71. Up the Chastity Belt 71. Up the Front 72. The Garnett Saga 72. Our Miss Fred 72. Spanish Fly 76, etc.

Kelley, Barry (1908–). Tough-looking Irish-American supporting actor, usually in gangster roles.
Boomerang 47. The Asphalt Jungle 50. The Killer That Stalked New York 51. 711 Ocean Drive 52. The Long Wait 54. The Buccaneer 59. The Manchurian Candidate 62, many others.

Kelley, De Forrest (1920–). American general purpose actor.
Fear in the Night (leading role) 47. Duke of Chicago 50. House of Bamboo 55. Gunfight 57. Warlock 59. Johnny Reno 66, etc.
TV series: *Star Trek* 66–69.

Kellin, Mike (–). American actor.
Freebie and the Bean 74.

Kellino, Pamela (1916–) (Pamela Ostrer). British actress, married first to Roy Kellino and then to James Mason. Now columnist and TV personality.
Jew Süss 34. I Met A Murderer 38. They Were Sisters 45. The Upturned Glass 47. Lady Possessed 51, etc.

Kellino, Roy (1912–1956). British cinematographer and director whose talent never quite displayed itself.
AS CINEMATOGRAPHER: The Phantom Light 37. The Last Adventurers 38. Johnny Frenchman 35, etc.
AS DIRECTOR: Catch as Catch Can 38. *I Met a Murderer* (& ph) 39. Guilt is My Shadow 49. Lady Possessed (US) 51. Charade 53. The Silken Affair 55, etc.

Kellino, Will P. (1873–1958) (William P.

Gislingham). British circus clown and acrobat, father of Roy Kellino. Made many early shorts as Pimple and Bumbles, characters from his stage act. Later became a director.

Kelly, Emmett (1895–). American character actor, former circus clown.
The Fat Man 51. The Greatest Show on Earth 52. Wind Across the Everglades 58, etc.

Kelly, Gene (1912–). Breezy, bouncy American dancer who became one of Hollywood's great star personalities of the forties and fifties, although his acting and singing abilities were minimal and his 'good guy' characterization wore a little thin. When musicals lamentably went out of fashion, he turned to direction. Special Academy Award 1951 'in appreciation of his versatility as an actor, singer, director and dancer, and specially for his brilliant achievements in the art of choreography on film'.
Biography 1974: *Gene Kelly* by Clive Hirschhorn.
□ *For Me and My Gal* 42. Pilot Number Five 42. Dubarry was a Lady 43. Thousands Cheer 43. The Cross of Lorraine 43. *Cover Girl* 44. Christmas Holiday 44. Anchors Aweigh 45. Ziegfeld Follies 46. Living in a Big Way 47. *The Pirate* 48. *The Three Musketeers* 48. Words and Music 48. *Take Me Out to the Ball Game* 49. *On the Town* (& co-d) 49. Black Hand 50. Summer Stock 50. It's A Big Country 51. *An American in Paris* 51. *Singin' in the Rain* (& co-d) 52. The Devil Makes Three 52. Love is Better than Ever 52. Brigadoon 54. Seagulls over Sorrento (GB) 54. Deep in My Heart 54. It's Always Fair Weather 55. *Invitation to the Dance* (& d) 56. The Happy Road (& pd) 57. Les Girls 57. Marjorie Morningstar 58. The Tunnel of Love (d only) 58. Inherit the Wind 60. Let's Make Love (cameo) 60. What a Way to Go 64. The Young Girls of Rochefort 67. A Guide for the Married Man (d only) 67. Hello Dolly (d only) 69. The Cheyenne Social Club (pd only) 70. Forty Carats 73. That's Entertainment 74. That's Entertainment Two 76.
TV series: Going My Way 62.

Kelly, Grace (1928–). American leading lady of the fifties: her 'iceberg' beauty quickly made her a top star, but she retired to become Princess of Monaco.
Biography 1976: *Princess Grace* by Gwen Robyns.
□ Fourteen Hours 51. High Noon 52. Mogambo 53. Dial M for Murder 54. *Rear Window* 54. *The Country Girl* (AA) 54. Green Fire 54. The Bridges at Toko-Ri 54. To Catch a Thief 55. The

Swan 56. *High Society* 56.

Kelly, Jack (1927–). Irish-American actor who usually plays wryly humorous roles; notably in TV series *King's Row* and *Maverick*.
Where Danger Lives 51. Drive a Crooked Road 54. To Hell and Back 56. Hong Kong Affair 58. Love and Kisses 65. Young Billy Young 69, etc.

Kelly, Judy (1913–). Australian leading lady, in British films.
Lord Camber's Ladies 32. His Night Out 35. Make Up 37. At the Villa Rose 40. Tomorrow We Live 43. The Butler's Dilemma 43. Dead of Night 45. Warning to Wantons 48, etc.

Kelly, Nancy (1921–). American leading lady, former child model; in films 1938–47, then on Broadway stage.
Submarine Patrol 38. *Tailspin* 38. Jesse James 39. Stanley and Livingstone 39. Parachute Battalion 41. Tornado 43. Show Business 44. Woman in Bondage 45. Betrayal from the East 45. Friendly Enemies 47. *The Bad Seed* 56. Crowded Paradise 56. The Impostor (TV) 73, etc.

Kelly, Patsy (1910–). Dumpy American comedienne of the thirties, often a pert wisecracker or a frightened maid.
Going Hollywood 33. The Girl from Missouri 34. Go Into Your Dance 35. Page Miss Glory 35. Kelly the Second 36. Sing Baby Sing 36. Pigskin Parade 36. Wake and Live 37. Merrily We Live 38. The Gorilla 39. Road Show 41. Topper Returns 41. *Broadway Limited* 41. Sing Your Worries Away 42. My Son the Hero 43. Please Don't Eat the Daisies 60. The Naked Kiss 64. The Ghost in the Invisible Bikini 66. Rosemary's Baby 68, etc.
TV series: Valentine's Day 64.

Kelly, Paul (1899–1956). Wiry American leading man of the thirties and forties, almost always in 'B' pictures.
Uncle Sam of Freedom Ridge 20. The New Klondike 26. Slide Kelly Slide 27. The Girl from Calgary 32. Broadway Thro' a Keyhole 33. Side Streets 34. Public Hero Number One 35. The Silk Hat Kid 35. The Accusing Finger 36. Navy Blue and Gold 37. Island in the Sky 38. Within the Law 39. The Roaring Twenties 39. Invisible Stripes 40. Queen of the Mob 40. Mystery Ship 41. Tarzan's New York Adventure 42. Flying Tigers 42. The Man from Music Mountain 43. Dead Man's Eyes 44. China's Little Devils 45. The Cat Creeps 46. Spoilers of the North 47. Fear in the Night 47. *Crossfire* 47. The File on Thelma Jordon 49. The Secret Fury 50. The

Painted Hills 51. Springfield Rifle 52. Split Second 53. The High and the Mighty 54. The Square Jungle 55. Storm Center 56. Bail Out at 43,000 57, many others.

Kelly, Tommy (1928–). American child actor of the thirties.
The Adventures of Tom Sawyer 38.

Kelsall, Moultrie (c. 1901–). Scottish character actor of stage and screen.
Landfall 49. The Lavender Hill Mob 51. The Master of Ballantrae 53. The Maggie 54. The Man Who Never Was 56. Violent Playground 58. The Battle of the Sexes 60, etc.

Kelsey, Fred (1884–1961). American small part actor, often seen as lugubrious sheriff or cop on the beat.
The Four Horsemen of the Apocalypse 21. The Eleventh Hour 23. The Gorilla 27. The Last Warning 29. Guilty as Hell 32. One Frightened Night 35. The Lone Wolf Keeps a Date 40. The Adventures of Mark Twain 44. Bringing Up Father 46. Hans Christian Andersen 52. Racing Blood 54, many others.

Kelton, Pert (1907–1968). American character comedienne, usually in hard-boiled roles.
Sally 29. *The Bowery* 33. Mary Burns Fugitive 35. Annie Oakley 35. Kelly the Second 36. Cain and Mabel 36. The Hit Parade 37. *The Music Man* 62. Love and Kisses 65. The Comic 69, etc.

Kemp, Jeremy (1934–) (Edmund Walker). British leading man who resigned from TV series *Z Cars* and has had some success in films.
Dr Terror's House of Horrors 65. Operation Crossbow 65. Cast a Giant Shadow 66. The Blue Max 66. Face of a Stranger 66. Assignment K 67. The Strange Affair 68. Darling Lili 70. The Games 70. Eyewitness 70. The Belstone Fox 73, etc.

Kemper, Victor J. (–). American cinematographer.
Last of the Red Hot Lovers 72. The Candidate 72. Shamus 73. The Gambler 74. The Reincarnation of Peter Proud 75. Dog Day Afternoon 75. The Last Tycoon 76, etc.

Kempson, Rachel (1910–). British actress, wife of Michael Redgrave.
The Captive Heart 46. A Woman's Vengeance (US) 48. Georgy Girl 66. The Jokers 66. Jennie (TV) 76, etc.

Kemp-Welch, Joan (1906–). British

character actress who used to play shy girls and spinsters on stage and screen. During the fifties emerged as a TV director of distinction.
Once a Thief 35. The Girl in the Taxi 37. Busman's Honeymoon 40. Pimpernel Smith 41. Jeannie 41 (last film to date), etc.

Kendall, Cyrus Q. (1898–1953). American character actor, a splendid cigar-chewing 'heavy' of the thirties.
The Dancing Pirate 36. Hot Money 36. They Won't Forget 37. The Shadow Strikes 37. Hawaii Calls 38. Stand Up and Fight 38. Angels Wash Their Faces 39. Men without Souls 40. Billy the Kid. Johnny Eager 42. The Whistler 44. She Gets Her Man 45, many others.

Kendall, Henry (1897–1962). British entertainer, immaculate star of London revues in the thirties and forties. On stage from 1914; occasional films.
Autobiography 1960: *I Remember Romano's*.
Tilly of Bloomsbury 21. French Leave 30. Rich and Strange 32. King of the Ritz 33. Death at Broadcasting House 34. The Amazing Quest of Ernest Bliss 36. School for Husbands 37. The Butler's Dilemma 43. 29 Acacia Avenue 45. The Voice of Merrill 52. An Alligator Named Daisy 55, etc.

Kendall, Kay (1926–1959) (Justine McCarthy). Vivacious, stylish British leading lady of the fifties.
□ Fiddlers Three 44. Dreaming 44. Champagne Charlie 44. Waltz Time 45. *London Town* 46. Dance Hall 50. Happy Go Lovely 51. Lady Godiva Rides Again 51. Wings of Danger 52. Curtain Up 52. It Started in Paradise 52. Mantrap 52. Street of Shadows 53. The Square Ring 53. *Genevieve* 53. Meet Mr Lucifer 53. Fast and Loose 54. Doctor in the House 54. The Constant Husband 54. *Simon and Laura* 55. Quentin Durward 56. Les Girls 57. *The Reluctant Debutante* 58. Once More with Feeling 59.

Kendall, Suzy (c. 1943–) (Frieda Harrison). British leading lady.
Circus of Fear 67. To Sir With Love 67. Penthouse 67. *Up the Junction* 68. Thirty is a Dangerous Age, Cynthia 68. Fraulein Doktor 68. The Betrayal 69. Darker than Amber (US) 70. The Bird with the Crystal Plumage (It.) 70. Assault 71. Tales that Witness Madness 73. Craze 73. Fear is the Key 73.

Kennaway, James (1928–1968). British novelist and screenwriter.
Tunes of Glory 61. The Mind Benders 63. The

Shoes of the Fisherman (co-w) 68. The Battle of Britain (co-w) 69, etc.

Kennedy, Arthur (1914–). American leading actor who despite many intelligent performances failed to achieve stardom.
□ City for Conquest 40. High Sierra 41. Strange Alibi 41. Knockout 41. Highway West 41. Bad Men of Missouri 41. They Died with Their Boots On 41. Desperate Journey 42. Air Force 43. *Devotion* (as Branwell Brontë) 46. Boomerang 47. Too Late for Tears 49. *Champion* 49. *The Window* 49. The Walking Hills 49. Chicago Deadline 49. *The Glass Menagerie* 50. *Bright Victory* 41. Red Mountain 52. *Rancho Notorious* 52. The Girl in White 52. Bend of the River 52. The Lusty Men 52. Impulse (GB) 54. The Man from Laramie 55. The Naked Dawn 55. The Desperate Hours 55. Crashout 55. The Rawhide Years 56. Peyton Place 57. Twilight for the Gods 58. Some Came Running 58. A Summer Place 59. Elmer Gantry 60. Home is the Hero 61. Claudelle Inglish 61. Murder She Said (GB) 62. Hemingway's Adventures of a Young Man 62. Barrabas 62. *Lawrence of Arabia* 62. Cheyenne Autumn 64. Joy in the Morning 65. Murieta 65. Fantastic Voyage 66. Nevada Smith 66. The Movie Murderer (TV) 67. The Prodigal Gun 68. Anzio 68. The Day of the Evil Gun 68. Dead or Alive 68. Hail Hero 69. Glory Boy 71. Crawlspace (TV) 72. Nakia (TV) 74. The Sentinel 77.

Kennedy, Burt (c. 1923–). American director, originally radio writer (from 1947), later TV writer-director (*Combat* series, etc.).
The Canadians (wd) 61. Mail Order Bride (wd) 63. The Rounders (wd) 64. The Money Trap (d) 65. *Return of the Seven* 66. Welcome to Hard Times (wd) 67. *The War Wagon* 67. Monday's Child ((Arg.) 67. *Support Your Local Sheriff* 69. Young Billy Young 69. The Good Guys and the Bad Guys 69. The Dubious Patriots 70. Support Your Local Gunfighter 71. The Deserter 71. Hannie Caulder 71. The Train Robbers (& w) 75, etc.

Kennedy, Douglas (1915–1973) (formerly known as Keith Douglas). American leading man of action features, later character actor.
The Way of All Flesh 40. Women without Names 41. Dark Passage 47. Chain Gang 50. I Was an American Spy 51. Ride the Man Down 53. Bomba and the Lion Hunters 54. The Amazing Transparent Man 59, many others.
TV series: Steve Donovan Western Marshal, etc.

Kennedy, Edgar (1890–1948). Bald, explosive American comedian with vaudeville experience.

A former Keystone Kop, he continued in demand for supporting roles and also starred in innumerable domestic comedy two-reelers, his exasperated gestures being familiar the world over. His brother Tom Kennedy (1885–1965), also a Keystone Kop, became a professional wrestler, and later played bit parts in movies and TV right up to his death.
Tillie's Punctured Romance 15. The Leather Pushers 22. Midnight Patrol 31. Duck Soup 33. King Kelly of the USA 34. Captain Tugboat Annie 46. Unfaithfully Yours 48, scores of others.

Kennedy, George (1925–). American character actor, usually seen as menace but graduating to sympathetic roles.
Little Shepherd of Kingdon Come (debut) 60. Lonely Are the Brave 62. The Man from the Diners Club 63. *Charade* 63. Straitjacket 64. Mirage 65. Shenandoah 65. *The Flight of the Phoenix* 65. Hurry Sundown 67. The Dirty Dozen 67. *Cool Hand Luke* (AA) 67. Bandolero 68. The Boston Strangler 68. Guns of the Magnificent Seven 69. The Good Guys and the Bad Guys 69. Airport 69. Tick Tick Tick 70. Fool's Parade 71. A Great American Tragedy (TV) 72. Lost Horizon 73. Cahill 73. Airport 75 74. Thunderbolt and Lightfoot 74. Earthquake 74. The Human Factor 75.
TV series: *Sarge* 71. The Blue Knight 75–76.

Kennedy, Margaret (1896–1967). British best-selling sentimental novelist; *The Constant Nymph* and her play *Escape Me Never* were each filmed more than once.

Kennedy, Merna (1908–1944) (Maude Kahler). American leading lady of the late twenties. Retired to marry Busby Berkeley.
The Circus 28. Broadway 30. Laughter in Hell 32. Arizona to Broadway 33. Police Call 33. I Like It That Way 34, etc.

Kenney, James (1930–). British juvenile actor of the late forties, son of vaudeville comedian Horace Kenney.
Circus Boy 47. Captain Horatio Hornblower 50. The Gentle Gunman 52. *Cosh Boy* 53. The Sea Shall Not Have Them 54. The Gelignite Gang 56. Son of a Stranger 58, etc.

Kent, Jean (1921–) (Joan Summerfield). British leading lady of the forties, formerly in the Windmill chorus.
Rocks of Valpre 35. Hullo Fame 40. It's That Man Again 42. Fanny by Gaslight 44. *Waterloo Road* 45. The Rake's Progress 45. Caravan 46. *Good Time Girl* 48. Trottie True 49. The Woman

in Question 50. The Browning Version 52. Before I Wake 55. Bonjour Tristesse 58. Please Turn Over 60, etc.

Kent, Keneth (1882–1963). British actor and singer, mostly on stage.
House of the Arrow 39. Night Train to Munich 40.

Kenton, Erle C. (1896–). American director, from 1914.
Small Town Idol 20. The Leather Pushers 22. Street of Illusion 25. Father and Son 27. Isle of Lost Souls 32. Remedy for Riches 39. Petticoat Politics 41. North to the Klondike 41. Ghost of Frankenstein 42. Who Done It? 42. Frisco Lil 42. House of Frankenstein 45. *House of Dracula* 45. Should Parents Tell? 49. Killer with a Label 50, etc.

Kenyon, Doris (1897–). American silent-screen leading lady who was married to Milton Sills.
The Pawn of Fate 16. A Girl's Folly 17. The Hidden Hand 18. The Ruling Passion 22. Monsieur Beaucaire 24. Blonde Saint 26. The Hawk's Nest 28. Alexander Hamilton 31. Voltaire 33. Counsellor at Law 33. The Man in the Iron Mask 39, etc.

Kerima (1925–). Algerian actress.
An Outcast of the Islands 51. La Lupa 52. The Quiet American 58, etc.

La Kermesse Héroique (France 1935). Also known as *Carnival in Flanders*, this broad but polished comedy about the occupation by Spanish troops of a 16th-century Flemish town seemed at the time delightfully spontaneous and had world-wide success unprecedented for a French film since sound. Written by Charles Spaak, directed by Jacques Feyder, photographed by Harry Stradling, with Françoise Rosay and Louis Jouvet.

Kern, James V. (1909–1966). American director, former lawyer.
That's Right You're Wrong 39. You'll Find Out 40. *Thank Your Lucky Stars* 43. The Doughgirls (wd) 44. Never Say Goodbye (wd) 46. Stallion Road 47. April Showers 48. Two Tickets to Broadway 52, etc.

Kern, Jerome (1885–1945). Celebrated American songwriter. His Academy Award songs are 'The Way You Look Tonight' and 'The Last Time I Saw Paris'.
Roberta 33. Showboat 36 and 51. Swing Time 36. Cover Girl 44. Can't Help Singing 44.

Centennial Summer 46. Till the Clouds Roll By (in which he was played by Robert Walker) 46.

Kerr, Deborah (1921–) (Deborah Kerr-Trimmer). British leading lady usually cast in well-bred roles.
□ Major Barbara (debut) 40. *Love on the Dole* 41. Penn of Pennsylvania 41. Hatter's Castle 41. The Day Will Dawn 42. *The Life and Death of Colonel Blimp* 43. *Perfect Strangers* 45. *I See a Dark Stranger* 45. *Black Narcissus* 46. The Hucksters 47. If Winter Comes 48. Edward My Son 49. Please Believe Me 49. King Solomon's Mines 50. Quo Vadis 51. Thunder in the East 51. The Prisoner of Zenda 52. Dream Wife 52. Julius Caesar 53. *From Here to Eternity* 53. Young Bess 53. The End of the Affair 55. *The King and I* 56. The Proud and Profane 56. *Tea and Sympathy* 56. Heaven Knows Mr Alison 56. *An Affair to Remember* 57. *Separate Tables* 58. Bonjour Tristesse 58. Count Your Blessings 59. The Journey 59. Beloved Infidel 59. *The Sundowners* 60. The Grass is Greener 61. *The Innocents* 61. The Naked Edge 61. The Chalk Garden 63. *The Night of the Iguana* 64. Marriage on the Rocks 65. Eye of the Devil 66. Casino Royale 67. *Prudence and the Pill* 68. The Gypsy Moths 69. The Arrangement 69.

Kerr, Frederick (1858–1933) (Frederick Keen). British character actor of stage and, latterly, American screen; delightful as slightly doddering old man.
The Honour of the Family 27. Raffles 29. *The Devil to Pay* 30. Frankenstein (as the old baron) 31. Waterloo Bridge 31. The Midshipman 32. The Man from Toronto 33, etc.

Kerr, John (1931–). American leading man.
The Cobweb 55. Gaby 56. *Tea and Sympathy* 56. *South Pacific* 58. The Pit and the Pendulum 61. Seven Women from Hell 62, etc.

Kerrigan, J. M. (1885–1964). Irish character actor who went with the Abbey players to Hollywood in 1935, and stayed there.
Little Old New York 23. Song of My Heart 30. The Informer 35. Laughing Irish Eyes 36. Little Orphan Annie 39. Captains of the Clouds 42. Black Beauty 46. The Wild North 52. The Fastest Gun Alive 56, many others.

Kerrigan, J. Warren (1880–1947). American actor of the silent screen.
Samson 13. Landon's Legacy 16. A Man's Man 18. The Covered Wagon 23. Captain Blood 24, etc.

Kerry, Norman (1889–1956) (Arnold Kaiser).

American actor of the silent screen.
The Black Butterfly 16. Merry Go Round 23. The Hunchback of Notre Dame 23. Phantom of the Opera 26. The Unknown 28. Air Eagles 31, many others.

Kershner, Irvin (1923–). American director.
□ Stakeout on Dope Street 58. The Young Captives 59. The Hoodlum Priest 61. Face in the Rain 63. The Luck of Ginger Coffey 64. A Fine Madness 66. The Flim Flam Man 67. Loving 70. Up The Sandbox 72. S.P.Y.S. 74. The Return of a Man Called Horse 76.

The Kettles (Ma and **Pa).** Hillbilly couple played in *The Egg and I* 47, and in a subsequent long-running series of comedy second features, by Marjorie Main and Percy Kilbride. Highly successful in US, less so in Britain.

Key Largo (US 1948). Maxwell Anderson's preachy melodrama about gangsters hiding out in a remote Florida hotel was obviously intended to say something about the post-war human condition, and borrowed quite a bit from Sherwood's *The Petrified Forest*. But the film is remembered chiefly as a display of acting pyrotechnics, with Edward G. Robinson as the relentless baddie, Humphrey Bogart as the war veteran who realised that being good is not enough, and Lauren Bacall, Lionel Barrymore and Claire Trevor (AA) as assorted relevant attitudes. John Huston wrote (with Richard Brooks) and directed.

Keyes, Evelyn (1919–). American leading lady of the forties, originally dancer.
Autobiography 1977: *Scarlet O'Hara's Younger Sister.*
The Buccaneer (debut) 38. Gone with the Wind 39. Before I Hang 40. The Face behind the Mask 41. Here Comes Mr Jordan 41. Ladies in Retirement 41. Flight Lieutenant 42. The Adventures of Martin Eden 42. The Desperadoes 43. Nine Girls 44. A Thousand and One Nights 44. *The Jolson Story* 46. Renegades 46. Johnny O'Clock 47. The Mating of Millie 46. Enchantment 48. Mrs Mike 48. House of Settlement 49. The Killer That Stalked New York 50. Smugglers' Island 51. *The Prowler* 51. Rough Shoot (GB) 52. The Seven Year Itch 54. Hell's Half Acre 54. Around the World in Eighty Days 56, etc.

The Keystone Kops. A troupe of slapstick comedians led by Ford Sterling who, from 1912–20 under the inspiration of Mack Sennett at Keystone Studios, made innumerable violent comedies full of wild chases and trick effects.

Abbott and Costello Meet the Keystone Kops 55
was a somewhat poor tribute.

Kibbee, Guy (1882–1956). Bald-headed
American character comedian, usually in
flustered, shifty or genial roles.
Stolen Heaven (debut) 31. City Streets 32. Forty-
Second Street 33. *Dames* 34. *Babbitt* 34.
Captain January 35. Mr Smith Goes to
Washington 39. Chad Hanna 41. Scattergood
Baines 41. The power of the Press 43. The Horn
Blows at Midnight 45. Gentleman Joe Palooka
47. Fort Apache 48. Three Godfathers 49.

Kibbee, Roland (1914–). American radio,
TV and screen writer.
A Night in Casablanca 45. Angel on My
Shoulder 46. *Vera Cruz* 54. Top Secret Affair
57. The Appaloosa 66. Valdez is Coming (& p)
71. The Midnight Man (& co-w, co-d) 75, etc.

Kid Galahad (US 1937). Thought at the time to
be one of the best of boxing dramas, this was
directed by Michael Curtiz, starred Edward G.
Robinson and Bette Davis, and introduced
Wayne Morris. It was remade in a disguised
form as *The Wagons Roll at Night* 41, with
Humphrey Bogart; then it turned up again in
1962 as an Elvis Presley vehicle, directed by Phil
Karlson.

Kidd, Michael (1919–). American dancer.
Where's Charley? (choreography only) 52. Band
Wagon 53. Seven Brides for Seven Brothers 54.
It's Always Fair Weather 54. Guys and Dolls 55.
Merry Andrew (& d) 58. Hello Dolly 69. Smile
75, etc.

Kidder, Margot (1948–). Canadian leading
lady of the seventies.
Sisters 72. The Gravy Train 74. The Great
Waldo Pepper 75. The Reincarnation of Peter
Proud 75. 92 in the Shade 77, etc.
TV series: Nichols 72.

kidnapping has been the subject of a great
number of films; apart from the various versions
of Robert Louis Stevenson's *Kidnapped*,
examples include *Nancy Steele is Missing, No
Orchids for Miss Blandish, Ransom, The
Kidnappers, A Cry in the Night, Cry Terror,
Tomorrow at Ten, High and Low, My Name is
Julia Ross, Seance on a Wet Afternoon, The
Collector, The Happening, Bunny Lake is
Missing, Bonnie and Clyde, Big Jake, The Night
of the Following Day, The Grissom Gang,
Murder on the Orient Express, The Man Who
Loved Cat Dancing, Night People, Funeral in
Berlin, Sugarland Express, The Wind and the*

Lion, and on TV *The Longest Night* and *The
Lindbergh Kidnapping Case.*

Kiepura, Jan (1902–1966). Polish operatic
tenor.
Farewell to Love (GB) 30. *My Song for You*
(GB) 31. Be Mine Tonight (GB) 32. Give Us This
Night (US) 36. Her Wonderful Lie (It.) 50.

Kilbride, Percy (1888–1964). American
character actor of wiley hayseed roles.
White Woman 33. Soak the Rich 36. George
Washington Slept Here 42. Knickerbocker
Holiday 44. She Wouldn't Say Yes 45. The Well-
Groomed Bride 45. The Egg and I 47. Ma and Pa
Kettle (series) 47–59.

Kilburn, Terry (1926–). British boy actor of
the thirties; never quite made it as adult.
A Christmas Carol 38. The Boy from
Barnardo's 38. Sweethearts 39. Goodbye Mr
Chips (as three generations of Colley) 39. The
Swiss Family Robinson 40. A Yank at Eton 42.
National Velvet 45. Bulldog Drummond at Bay
47. Only the Valiant 51. The Fiend without a
Face 58, etc.

Kiley, Richard (1922–). American general
purpose actor with stage experience: has latterly
become a Broadway musical star.
The Mob 51. The Sniper 52. Pick Up on South
Street 52. The Blackboard Jungle 55. The
Phoenix City Story 56. Spanish Affair 58.
Pendulum 69. AKA Cassius Clay 70. Murder
Twice Removed (TV) 71. The Little Prince 73,
etc.

Kilian, Victor (1891–). American character
actor, usually as suspicious or downright
villainous characters.
The Wiser Sex 32. Air Hawks 35. Seventh
Heaven 36. Dr Cyclops 39. Reap the Wild Wind
42. Spellbound 45. Gentleman's Agreement 47.
The Flame and the Arrow 50. Tall Target 51, etc.
1976: on TV in *Mary Hartman, Mary Hartman.*

The Killers (US 1946). A brilliantly intricate
and explosive crime melodrama elaborated by
writer Anthony Veiller from a Hemingway
sketch, photographed by Woody Bredell, and
directed with tremendous verve by Robert
Siodmak. It introduced Burt Lancaster to the
screen and also had an excellent performance by
Edmond O'Brien. In 1964 it was remade by Don
Siegel in a version originally intended for colour
TV had it not proved too violent; the star was
Lee Marvin and the film had plenty of
fashionable violence but little style.

Kilpatrick, Lincoln (–). Black American
actor.

Cool Breeze 72. Soul Soldier 72. Soylent Green 73. Chosen Survivors 74. Uptown Saturday Night 74, etc.

Killiam, Paul (1916–). American collector of silent movies, clips from which he introduces on TV in various series.

Kimmins, Anthony (1901–1963). British actor-writer-producer-director, almost entirely of light comedy subjects.
The Golden Cage (a) 33. White Ensign (a) 34. While Parents Sleep (w) 35. Keep Your Seats Please (w) 36. Talk of the Devil (w) 36. *Keep Fit* (wd) 37. The Show Goes On (w) 37. I See Ice (wd) 38. It's In the Air (wd) 38. Trouble Brewing (wd) 39. Under Your Hat (wd) 40. *Mine Own Executioner* (pd) 47. Bonnie Prince Charlie (d) 48. Flesh and Blood (d) 50. Mr Denning Drives North (d) 51. Who Goes There? (d) 52. *The Captain's Paradise* (wpd) 53. Aunt Clara (d) 54. Smiley (pd) 56. *The Amorous Prawn* (wpd) 62, etc.

Kind Hearts and Coronets (GB 1949). Robert Hamer directed this witty comedy of Edwardian bad manners from a script by himself and John Dighton. Despite dull patches it remains supreme of its stylish kind, with Dennis Price as the most elegant of murderers and Alec Guinness as eight aristocratic victims.

A Kind of Loving (GB 1962). The first British film to take a genuinely realistic view of working-class life, without the sophistication of *Look Back in Anger* or the high good humour of *Saturday Night and Sunday Morning*. From a depressingly truthful novel by Stan Barstow, it had Alan Bates and June Ritchie as the young couple driven into a make-do-and-mend marriage; John Schlesinger directed as though it were a documentary.

Kinematograph Renters' Society (K.R.S.). This British organization was founded by film distributors in 1915 for their own protection and collective bargaining power, chiefly against exhibitors.

Kinescope. American term for what the British call a telerecording, i.e. a live or tape show transferred for convenience on to tape. The technical quality is seldom satisfactory, and the process was gradually discontinued in favour of electronic tape conversion from one line standard to another.

Kinetoscope. An early film viewing apparatus (1893) in which a continuous loop of film could be viewed by one person only.

King, Alan (1924–) (Irwin Kniberg). American cabaret comedian who has made a few film appearances.
Hit the Deck 55. Miracle in the Rain 56. The Helen Morgan Story 57. On the Fiddle (GB) 61. Bye Bye Braverman 68. The Anderson Tapes 71, etc.

King, Allan (1933–). Canadian documentarist.
Warrendale 67. A Married Couple 69, etc.

The King and I: see *Anna and the King of Siam.*

King, Andrea (1915–) (Georgetta Barry). French-American leading lady with experience on the New York stage.
The Very Thought of You 44. Hotel Berlin 45. The Man I Love 46. Shadow of a Woman 46. The Violent Hour 50. The Lemon Drop Kid 51. Red Planet Mars 53. Band of Angels 57. Darby's Rangers 58. Daddy's Gone A-Hunting 69, etc.

King, Anita (1889–1963). American leading lady of the silent screen, who came to fame in *The Virginian* 14.

King Arthur: see *Arthur.*

King, Charles (1889–1944). American song and dance man of the twenties.
Broadway Melody 28. Hollywood Revue 29. Chasing Rainbows 30, etc.

King, Charles (1899–1957). American character actor, usually a western heavy.
Range Law 32. Mystery Ranch 34. O'Malley of the Mounted 36. The Mystery of the Hooded Horsemen 37. Son of the Navy 40. Gunman from Bodie 42. Ghost Rider 43, etc.

King, Dave (1929–). British TV comedian of the sixties; made a few film appearances.
Pirates of Tortuga 61. Go to Blazes 62. Strange Bedfellows 65, etc.

King, Dennis (1897–1971) (Dennis Pratt). British-born opera singer who in the early thirties starred in Hollywood films.
The Vagabond King 30. Fra Diavolo 33.

King, George (1900–1966). British producer-director, mainly of independent quota quickies and melodramas.
Too Many Crooks (d) 31. John Halifax Gentleman (p) 36. The Chinese Bungalow (pd)

39. The Case of the Frightened Lady (pd) 40. The Face at the Window (pd) 40. The First of the Few (p) 42. Tomorrow We Live (pd) 42. Candlelight in Algeria (pd) 44. Gaiety George (pd) 45. The Shop at Sly Corner (pd) 46. Forbidden (pd) 48. Eight O'Clock Walk (p) 54, etc.

King, Henry (1892–) (some sources say 1888). Veteran American director with experience in most branches of show business. In Hollywood, became a skilful exponent of the well-made expensive family entertainment, usually with a sentimental streak.
Who Pays? 16. A Sporting Chance 19. *Tol'able David* 21. Romola 24. Stella Dallas 25. The Winning of Barbara Worth 26. Lightin' 30. Over the Hill 31. *State Fair* 33. Carolina 34. Marie Galante 34. Ramona 36. Seventh Heaven 36. Lloyds of London 37. *In Old Chicago* 38. *Alexander's Ragtime Band* 38. Jesse James 39. *Stanley and Livingstone* 39. Little Old New York 40. Maryland 40. Chad Hanna 40. A Yank in the R.A.F. 41. *The Black Swan* 42. *The Song of Bernadette* 43. *Wilson* 44. A Bell for Adano 45. *Margie* 46. Captain from Castile 47. Prince of Foxes 49. *Twelve O'Clock High* 49. *The Gun Fighter* 50. I'd Climb the Highest Mountain 51. *David and Bathsheba* 51. Wait Till the Sun Shines Nellie 52. *The Snows of Kilimanjaro* 52. King of the Khyber Rifles 53. *Love Is a Many-Splendored Thing* 55. Carousel 56. *The Sun Also Rises* 57. The Bravados 58. This Earth Is Mine 59. *Tender Is the Night* 61, many others.

King Kong (US 1932–33). The most famous of screen monsters remains after thirty years the most impressive. Willis H. O'Brien's trick photography has not been surpassed, and the film holds together as a splendid adventure for grown-up school-boys; even the acting of Robert Armstrong and Fay Wray is delightfully of its period. Produced and directed by Merian Cooper and Ernest Schoedsack, with suitably throbbing music by Max Steiner. The production team made a further visit to the mysterious island for *Song of Kong* 33, but here the giant gorilla was played for laughs and the trick effects were skimpy. The 1976 remake of the original story was inoffensive but totally lacked the charisma of the 1933 film.

King, Louis (1898–1962). American director in films from 1919; brother of Henry King.
Persons in Hiding 38. Typhoon 40. The Way of All Flesh 40. Moon over Burma 41. Thunderhead, Son of Flicka 44. Smoky 46. Bob, Son of Battle 47. Green Grass of Wycoming 48. Mrs Mike 49. The Lion and the Horse 52.

Powder River 53. Dangerous Mission 54, etc.

King of Jazz (US 1930). A famous early revue directed by John Murray Anderson, produced by Carl Laemmle Jnr and photographed by Hal Mohr; with Paul Whiteman and his band and guest stars. For its age, an astonishing triumph of style.

King of Kings: see under *Christ*.

King, Perry (–). American juvenile of the mid seventies.
Mandingo 75. The Wild Party 75, etc.

King Solomon's Mines. Rider Haggard's African adventure novel was more than adequately filmed in Britain in 1937, with Cedric Hardwicke as Allan Quartermain: the director was Robert Stevenson. MGM's 1951 remake with Stewart Granger was an unsatisfactory mishmash in which the plot thread was all but lost and there was so much spare location footage that a semi-remake, *Watusi*, used it up in 1959.

King, Walter Woolf (1899–). American actor, Broadway singing star who went to Hollywood and was gradually relegated to villain roles.
A Night at the Opera 35. Call It a Day 37. Swiss Miss 38. Balalaika 39. Marx Brothers Go West 41. Today I Hang 42. Tonight We Sing 53. Kathy 'O 58, etc.

kings and queens, of England at least, have been lovingly if not very accurately chronicled in the cinema. We still await an epic of the Norman Conquest, but in 1925 Phyllis Neilson-Terry went still further back to play *Boadicea*, and in 1969 David Hemmings played *Alfred the Great*. Henry II, played by Peter O'Toole, was protagonist of *Becket* and *The Lion in Winter*. Richard I (Lionheart), also in the latter, was a shadowy figure of do-goodery in scores of films from *Robin Hood* to *King Richard and the Crusaders*; his brother John was just as frequently the villain of the piece, as in *The Adventures of Robin Hood*. Edward IV made an appearance in *Tower of London* and *Richard III*, but only as a pawn in the scheming hands of Richard III (Crookback). Henry IV appeared in *Chimes at Midnight*; *Henry V* was a notable role for Laurence Olivier; Henry VII-to-be was played in *Richard III* by Stanley Baker. Henry VIII was for long personified by Charles Laughton, who played him in 1933, but there have been other contenders: Montagu Love in *The Prince and the Pauper*, Robert Shaw in *A*

Man for All Seasons, Richard Burton in *Anne of the Thousand Days*, Keith Michell in *Henry VIII and his Six Wives*, and James Robertson Justice in *The Sword and the Rose*. Similarly Elizabeth I was identified with Bette Davis (*Elizabeth and Essex, The Virgin Queen*) until Glenda Jackson played her on TV and in *Mary Queen of Scots*, though she was also personified by Flora Robson (*Fire over England, The Sea Hawk*), Florence Eldridge (*Mary of Scotland*), Irene Worth (*Seven Seas to Calais*) and others. The unfortunate *Mary of Scotland* was notably played by Katharine Hepburn and Vanessa Redgrave. Young Edward VI was in *The Prince and the Pauper*. The early Stuarts were a dour lot, but Charles I was impersonated by Alec Guinness in *Cromwell*; Charles II, the merry monarch, has been personified by a number of actors including Cedric Hardwicke (*Nell Gwyn*), George Sanders (*Forever Amber*), Vincent Price (*Hudson's Bay*) and Douglas Fairbanks Jnr (*The Exile*). Of the Hanoverians, George I was played by Eric Pohlmann in *Rob Roy* and Peter Bull in *Saraband for Dead Lovers*, George III by Raymond Lovell in *The Young Mr Pitt*, and by Robert Morley in *Beau Brummell*. Prinny, the Prince Regent, later George IV, was undertaken by Cecil Parker in *The First Gentleman* and Peter Ustinov in *Beau Brummell*. Victoria to many people still looks like Anna Neagle, who played her three times; other actresses in the role have included Irene Dunne (*The Mudlark*), Fay Compton (*The Prime Minister*) and Mollie Maureen (*The Private Life of Sherlock Holmes*). James Robertson Justice played Edward VII in *Mayerling*, and Richard Chamberlain Edward VIII in a TV film, *The Woman I Love*.

Foreign monarchs who have been notably impersonated include Catherine the Great of Russia (Pola Negri, Elizabeth Bergner, Tallulah Bankhead, Bette Davis, Marlene Dietrich); Russia's last Czar and Czarina, *Nicholas and Alexandra* (Michael Jayston and Janet Suzman); *Peter the Great*; *Ivan the Terrible*; *Queen Christina* of Sweden (Greta Garbo, and Liv Ullmann in *The Abdication*); Francis I of France (Harry Davenport in *The Hunchback of Notre Dame*); Louis XI of France (Basil Rathbone in *If I Were King*); Charles VII of France, by Jose Ferrer in *Joan of Arc*; *Marie Antoinette* (Norma Shearer); Louis XIV, by John Barrymore in *Marie Antoinette*; Louis XVI, by Robert Morley in *Marie Antoinette* and by Pierre Renoir in *La Marseillaise*; Louis XVII, by Jean-Pierre Cassel in *The Three Musketeers*; Philip II of Spain (Paul Scofield in *That Lady*; Raymond Massey in *Fire Over England*).

King's Row (US 1942). An unusually adult film to come from Hollywood in the middle of the war, this strong period drama from Henry Bellamann's novel of small-town life was directed with bravura by Sam Wood and acted with relish by Claude Rains, Betty Field, Ann Sheridan, Charles Coburn, and Maria Ouspenskaya, with Ronald Reagan and Robert Cummings making surprisingly interesting heroes. Musical score by Erich Wolfgang Korngold. An undistinguished TV series of 1957 used the title and some of the characters.

Kingsford, Walter (1882–1958). British character actor, in Hollywood from the thirties after long stage experience; usually played kindly professional men. Was Dr Carew in the *Kildare* series.
The Mystery of Edwin Drood 35. Captains Courageous 37. Algiers 38. Kitty Foyle 40. My Favorite Blonde 42. The Velvet Touch 49. Loose in London 53. Merry Andrew 58, many others.

Kingsley, Dorothy (1909–). American scenarist, former radio writer for Bob Hope.
Neptune's Daughter 49. When In Rome 52. Kiss Me Kate 53. Seven Brides For Seven Brothers 54. Pal Joey 57. Can Can 59. Pepe 60. Half a Sixpence 67. Valley of the Dolls 67, etc.

Kingsley, Sidney (1906–) (Sidney Kieschner). American playwright.
Plays filmed include: Men in White 35. Dead End 37. Detective Story 51.

Kinnear, Roy (1934–). Bulbous British character comedian whose perspiring bluster is a quickly overplayed hand.
Sparrows Can't Sing 62. Heavens Above 63. French Dressing 65. The Hill 65. Help! 66. A Funny Thing Happened on the Way to the Forum 67. How I Won the War 67. Lock Up Your Daughters 67. Willy Wonka and the Chocolate Factory 71. The Three Musketeers 74. Juggernaut 74. One of Our Dinosaurs is Missing 75, etc.

Kinnoch, Ronald (c. 1911–). British producer, former scenarist and production manager.
Escape Route 52. How to Murder a Rich Uncle 57. The Secret Man (& wd) 58. Village of the Damned 60. Invasion Quartet 61. Cairo 62. The Ipcress File (ap) 65, etc.

Kinskey, Leonid (1903–). Lanky Russian character actor, long in US. Was playing intense but not over-bright revolutionaries in 1932 (*Trouble in Paradise*) and still does it on TV.

The Great Waltz 38. Down Argentine Way 40. Can't Help Singing 44. Monsieur Beaucaire 46. The Man with the Golden Arm 55, many others.

Kinski, Klaus (1926–). German character actor of intense roles.
Ludwig II 54. Kali Yug Goddess of Vengeance 63. For a Few Dollars More 65. Dr Zhivago 65. Circus of Fear 67. *Aguirre Wrath of God* 72. The Bloody Hands of the Law 73, etc.

Kinsolving, Lee (1938–1974). American actor best remembered as the juvenile lead in *The Dark at the Top of the Stairs* 60.

Kinugasa, Teinosuke (1896–). Japanese director. Crossways 28. Joyu 47. Gate of Hell 53. The White Heron 58, etc.

Kipling, Rudyard (1865–1936). British novelist who mainly concerned himself with the high days of the British in India.
Films from his works include *Gunga Din, Soldiers Three, Elephant Boy, Wee Willie Winkie, Captains Courageous, The Light That Failed, The Jungle Book, Kim, The Man Who Would Be King* (in which he was played by Christopher Plummer).

Kipps. H. G. Wells' comic-sentimental 'story of a simple soul' was first filmed in 1921 (GB) with George K. Arthur as the draper's assistant who comes into money and has an unhappy encounter with high society. In 1941 Carol Reed made a very stylish and satisfying sound version with Michael Redgrave; and 1967 brought the inevitable musical version, *Half a Sixpence*, with Tommy Steele vivacious but somewhat miscast in the lead.

Kirk, Phyllis (1926–) (Phyllis Kirkegaard). American leading lady of the fifties, former model and dancer.
Our Very Own 50. The Iron Mistress 52. House of Wax 53. Canyon Crossroads 55. The Sad Sack 57. That Woman Opposite (GB) 58. City after Midnight 59, etc.
TV series: The Thin Man 57.

Kirk, Tommy (1941–). American juvenile lead, former Disney child actor.
Old Yeller 57. The Shaggy Dog 59. The Swiss Family Robinson 60. The Absent-Minded Professor 60. Babes in Toyland 61. Bon Voyage 62. Son of Flubber 63. The Misadventures of Merlin Jones 63. The Monkey's Uncle 65. How to Stuff a Wild Bikini 65, etc.

Kirkland, Muriel (1903–1971). American stage actress, briefly in films in the thirties.
Fast Workers 33. Hold Your Man 33. The Secret of the Blue Room 33. Nana 34. Little Man What Now? 34, etc.

Kirkop, Oreste (1926–). Maltese operatic tenor whose sole film appearance to date has been in *The Vagabond King* 55.

Kirkwood, Pat (1921–). British leading lady and entertainer, in variety since her teens; married to Hubert Gregg.
Come On, George 38. No Leave No Love (US) 42. Once a Sinner 50. After the Ball 56, etc.

Kirsanov, Dmitri (1899–1957). Russian émigré film-maker, at the forefront of France's avant-garde movement of the twenties.
☐ Autumn Mists 25. *Menilmontant* 26. Rapt 35.

Kismet. Edward Knoblock's rather stolid Arabian Nights play has been filmed five times. In 1920 Louis Gesnier directed Otis Skinner; in 1931 (in Germany) William Dieterle directed Gustav Fröhlich; in 1931 Otis Skinner played in a talkie version directed by John Francis Dillon; in 1944 Dieterle had another crack at it, with Ronald Colman in the lead; and in 1955 the stage version with musical themes by Borodin was filmed by Vincente Minnelli, with Howard Keel.

Kiss Me Deadly (US 1955). A Mickey Spillane thriller directed by Robert Aldrich. Quite incomprehensible and extremely violent but with brilliantly entertaining moments. A phantasmagoria of Hollywood thriller clichés, its arty direction made it a considerable influence on Truffaut and the 'new wave'.

Kiss Me Kate (US 1953). This film of the stage musical based on *The Taming of the Shrew* was probably the best production shot in 3-D; it was, however, released 'flat'. Apart from its Cole Porter score it had lively performances from Howard Keel, Kathryn Grayson and Ann Miller; directed by George Sidney.

Kiss of Death (US 1947). A gangster thriller influential in its violence, despair and incisiveness; also notable for the first appearance of Richard Widmark in the role of a sadistic laughing killer. Written by Ben Hecht and Charles Lederer, photographed by Norbert Brodine, directed by Henry Hathaway. A disguised remake, *The Fiend Who Walked the West*, was issued in 1958 but had nothing to offer except blood-letting.

Kitt, Eartha (1928–). American Creole cabaret singer whose essential vibrance was captured only in her first film.
Autobiography 1956: *Thursday's Child.*
□ New Faces 54. St Louis Blues 57. Mark of the Hawk 58. Anna Lucasta 58. Saint of Devil's Island 61. Synanon 65. Uncle Tom's Cabin (wg) 65. Up the Chastity Belt (GB) 71. Lt Schuster's Wife (TV) 72. Friday Foster 75.

Kitzmiller, John (1913–1965). Negro character actor, in Italy from 1945 (after army service).
Paisa 46. To Live In Peace 46. Senza Pieta 48. The Naked Earth 57. Doctor No 62. Uncle Tom's Cabin (title role) (Ger.) 65, etc.

Kjellin, Alf (1920–). Swedish actor who went to Hollywood and worked mostly in TV, turning his talents to direction.
Frenzy 44. My Six Convicts 52. The Iron Mistress 53. The Juggler 63. Ship of Fools 65. Assault on a Queen 66. The Midas Run (d) 69. The McMasters (d) 70, etc.

Klein, William (1929–). American director, in Paris.
Far From Vietnam (part) 66. Qui Etes-Vous Polly Magoo? 67. Mr Freedom 68.

Kleiner, Harry (1916–). American screenwriter.
Fallen Angel 46. The Street with No Name 48. Red Skies of Montana 51. Salome 53. Miss Sadie Thompson 53. *Carmen Jones* 54. The Garment Jungle (& p) 56. Ice Palace 60. Fantastic Voyage 66. *Bullitt* 68, etc.

Klein-Rogge, Rudolf (1889–1955). German actor who appeared in some of the most famous German films of the twenties.
Der Mude Tod 21. Dr Mabuse 22. Siegfried 24. Metropolis 26. The Testament of Dr Mabuse 32, etc.

Klemperer, Werner (1919–). Bald-pated German-American character actor, often seen as comic or sinister Nazi.
Death of a Scoundrel 56. Five Steps to Danger 56. The Goddess 58. Operation Eichmann (title role) 61. Judgment at Nuremberg 61. Escape from East Berlin 62. Youngblood Hawke 64. Ship of Fools 65. The Wicked Dreams of Paula Schultz 67, etc.
TV series: *Hogan's Heroes* 65–68.

Kline, Herbert (1909–). American director, sometimes of documentaries.
Crisis 39. Lights out in Europe 40. The Forgotten Village (& p) 41. My Father's House (& p) 47. The Kid from Cleveland 49. The Fighter (& wp) 52, etc.

Kline, Richard (1926–). American cinematographer.
Camelot 67. *The Boston Strangler* 69. A Dream of Kings 69. The Andromeda Strain 70. Kotch 71. Black Gunn 72. The Harrad Experiment 73. Mandingo 75. King Kong 76, etc.

Klinger, Michael (1921–). British producer.
Repulsion 64. Cul de Sac 66. The Yellow Teddy Bears 66. A Study in Terror 67. Baby Love 69. Get Carter 71. Pulp 73. Gold 74. Shout at the Devil 76, etc.

Klos, Elmar: see *Kadar, Jan.*

Kluge, Alexander (1932–). German director.
Abschied von Gestern 66. Artists at the Top of the Big Top 68. Willy Tobler 71. Occasional Work of a Female Slave 74, etc.

Klugman, Jack (1922–). Lean American actor who can be comically henpecked, tragically weak, or just sinister.
Timetable 56. *Twelve Angry Men* 57. Days of Wine and Roses 62. Act One 63. Yellow Canary 63. The Detective 68. The Split 68. Goodbye Columbus 69. Who Says I Can't Ride a Rainbow? 71.
TV series: Harris against the World 64. *The Odd Couple* 70–74. Quincy 76–.

The Knack (GB 1965). Richard Lester's free-wheeling film version of Ann Jellicoe's sex play was dull only while it stuck to the script; the running gags and visually inventive interludes shot in London streets were almost undiluted joy. Photographed by David Watkin, with a spirited young cast, the film unfortunately encouraged less talented film-makers, and even Lester himself, to think that anything goes providing you keep moving.

Kneale, Nigel (1922–). Manx writer, best known for BBC TV serials about Professor Quatermass, all three of which were filmed.
Look Back in Anger 59. The Entertainer 60. The First Men in the Moon 64. The Devil's Own 66, etc.

Knef, Hildegarde: see *Neff, Hildegarde.*

Knight, Castleton (1894–1972). British newsreel producer (Gaumont British). Directed some films in the thirties, including *Kissing Cup's Race* and *The Flying Scotsman*; also various compilations such as *Theirs Is the Glory* and *Fourteenth Olympiad*.

Knight, David (1927–) (David Mintz). American leading man, on London stage since 1953.
The Young Lovers (debut) 55. Lost 57. Across the Bridge 57. Battle of the V.1 58. Nightmare 63, etc.

Knight, Esmond (1906–). Welsh actor, on stage since 1925, screen since 1931. Partially blinded during World War II.
The Silver Fleet 42. *Henry V* 44. End of the River 47. Hamlet 47. The Red Shoes 48. Richard III 56. Sink the Bismarck 60. Where's Jack? 69. Anne of the Thousand Days 70, etc.

Knight, Fuzzy (1901–1976) (J. Forrest Knight). American night club musician who found himself a niche in Hollywood as comic relief in innumerable westerns.
She Done Him Wrong 33. The Trail of the Lonesome Pine 36. Johnny Apollo 40. Trigger Trail 44. Down to the Sea in Ships 50. Topeka 54. These Thousand Hills 59. Waco 66, etc.

Knight, Shirley (1937–). American leading actress, also on stage and TV; latterly known as Shirley Knight Hopkins.
Five Gates to Hell 59. The Dark at the Top of the Stairs 60. Sweet Bird of Youth 62. *The Group* 66. Dutchman 67. *Petulia* 68. The Rain People 69. Secrets 71. Juggernaut 74, etc.

Knopf, Edwin H. (1899–). American producer, sometimes writer and director.
Border Legion (d) 30. Bad Sister (w) 31. The Wedding Night (w) 35. Piccadilly Jim (w) 36. The Trial of Mary Dugan (p) 41. The Cross of Lorraine (p) 44. The Valley of Decision (p) 45. BF's Daughter (p) 48. Edward My Son (p) 49. The Law and the Lady (d) 51. Lili (p) 53. The Vintage (p) 57, many others.

Knotts, Don (1924–). American 'hayseed' comedian, from TV.
Wake Me Up When It's Over 60. The Last Time I Saw Archie 61. The Incredible Mr Limpet 62. *The Ghost and Mr Chicken* 66. The Reluctant Astronaut 67. The Shakiest Gun in the West 68. The Love God 69. How to Frame a Figg 71. The Apple Dumpling Gang 75, etc.
TV series: *The Andy Griffith Show* 60–68.

Knowles, Bernard (1900–). British cinematographer who became a competent director.
AS CINEMATOGRAPHER: Dawn 29. The

Good Companions 32. Jew Süss 34. The Thirty-Nine Steps 35. Gaslight 39. Quiet Wedding 40, etc.
□ AS DIRECTOR: *A Place of One's Own* 45. The Magic Bow 46. The Man Within 47. The White Unicorn 47. Jassy 47. Easy Money 48. The Lost People 49. The Perfect Woman 49. The Reluctant Widow 50. Park Plaza 605 53. Barbados Quest 54. Frozen Alive 64. Spaceflight IC-1 65. Hell is Empty 68.

Knowles, Patric (1911–) (Reginald Knowles). British light 'second lead' who went to Hollywood in 1936 and stayed.
Irish Hearts (GB) 34. Abdul the Damned (GB) 34. The Guvnor (GB) 35. The Charge of the Light Brigade 36. The Adventures of Robin Hood 38. Storm over Bengal 39. Anne of Windy Poplars 40. How Green Was My Valley 41. The Wolf Man 41. Lady in a Jam 42. Eyes of the Underworld 42. Frankenstein Meets the Wolf Man 43. Always a Bridesmaid 43. Pardon My Rhythm 44. Kitty 45. Of Human Bondage 46. Monsieur Beaucaire 46. Ivy 47. The Big Steal 49. Three Came Home 50. Mutiny 52. Flame of Calcutta 53. Band of Angels 57. Auntie Mame 59. The Devil's Brigade 68. In Enemy Country 68. Chisum 71. Terror in the Wax Museum 73, others.

Knox, Alexander (1907–). Quiet-spoken Canadian actor, on British stage from 1930, films from 1938; also in Hollywood.
The Gaunt Stranger 38. *The Sea Wolf* 40. This Above All 42. None Shall Escape 43. *Wilson* (title role) 44. Over Twenty-One 45. Sister Kenny 46. *The Judge Steps Out* 47. The Sign of the Ram 48. I'd Climb the Highest Mountain 50. Paula 52. The Sleeping Tiger 53. The Divided Heart 54. Reach for the Sky 56. High Tide at Noon 57. The Wreck of the Mary Deare 59. The Man in the Middle 64. Crack in the World 65. Mister Moses 65. The Psychopath 66. Accident 66. How I Won the War 67. Villa Rides 68. Shalako 68. Skullduggery 69. Nicholas and Alexandra 71. Puppet on a Chain 71. Meeting at Potsdam (TV) 76, etc.

Knox, Teddy: see *The Crazy Gang*.

Knudsen, Peggy (1925–). American leading lady of the forties.
Stolen Life 46. Humoresque 47. Trouble Preferred 48. Copper Canyon 50. Unchained 53. Good Morning Miss Dove 55, etc.

Kobayashi, Masaki (1916–). Japanese director.
Ningen No Joker 61. Hara Kiri 63. Kwaidan 64. Rebellion 67, etc.

Koch, Howard (1902–). American screenwriter.
The Sea Hawk (co-w) 40. The Letter (co-w) 40. Casablanca (co-w) (AA) 42. Mission to Moscow (co-w) 43. Letter from an Unknown Woman 47. The Thirteenth Letter 51. The War Lover 63. The Fox (co-wp) 68, many others.

Koch, Howard W. (1916–). American executive, from 1965–66 Paramount's vice-president in charge of production. Former producer and director.
Big House USA (d) 54. Beachhead (p) 55. The Black Sleep (p) 56. Frankenstein 70 (d) 58. Sergeants Three (p) 62. The Manchurian Candidate (p) 62. Come Blow Your Horn (p) 63. None But the Brave (p) 65. The Odd Couple (p) 68. On a Clear Day You Can See Forever (p) 70. Badge 373 73. Once Is Not Enough 75, etc.

Koenekamp, Fred (–). American cinematographer.
Kansas City Bomber 72. Papillon 73. The Towering Inferno 74. Uptown Saturday Night 74. Posse 75. Doc Savage 75, etc.

Kohlmar, Fred (1905–1969). American producer in Hollywood from the early thirties, at first with Goldwyn.
That Night in Rio 41. The Glass Key 42. Kiss of Death 47. When Willie Comes Marching Home 50. It Should Happen to You 53. Picnic 55. Pal Joey 57. The Last Angry Man 59. The Notorious Landlady 62. How To Steal a Million 66. A Flea in Her Ear 68. The Only Game in Town 69, many others.

Kohner, Susan (1936–). American leading lady.
To Hell and Back 55. Imitation of Life 58. All the Fine Young Cannibals 60. Freud 62, etc.

Kolb, Clarence (1875–1964). Veteran character actor, usually of explosive executive types; formerly in vaudeville.
Carefree 38. Nothing but the Truth 41. Hellzapoppin 42. True to Life 43. The Kid from Brooklyn 46. Christmas Eve 47. Adam's Rib 49. The Rose Bowl Story 53. Man of a Thousand Faces 57, many others.

Kolker, Henry (1874–1947). American stage actor who played lawyers and heavy fathers in many films.
How Molly Made Good 15. Any Woman 25. Soft Living 28. Dubarry 31. Wonder Bar 34. Now and Forever 35. Romeo and Juliet 36. Theodora Goes Wild 37. *Holiday* 38. A Woman's Face 41. Blue beard 45, etc.

Korda, Sir Alexander (1893–1956) (Sandor Corda). Hungarian producer-director who worked in Paris, Berlin and Hollywood before settling in London 1930. More than any other man the saviour of the British film industry. Formed London Films and sealed its success with *The Private Life of Henry VIII* 32; built Denham Studios.
Catherine the Great 33. *The Scarlet Pimpernel* 34. Sanders of the River 35. *Things to Come* 35. The Ghost Goes West 36. *Rembrandt* (pd) 37. Knight Without Armour 37. *Elephant Boy* 37. The Drum 38. *The Four Feathers* 39, others; in Hollywood: *The Thief of Baghdad* 40. Lady Hamilton (pd) 41. Jungle Book 42, etc.; back in Britain: Perfect Strangers (pd) 45. An Ideal Husband (pd) 47. Anna Karenina 48. The Fallen Idol 48. *The Third Man* 49. Seven Days to Noon 50. *The Sound Barrier* 51. Hobson's Choice 54. Richard III 56, etc.

Korda, Vincent (1896–). Hungarian art director who usually worked on the films of his brothers Alexander and Zoltan.
The Private Life of Henry VIII 32. Sanders of the River 35. Things to Come 36. The Four Feathers 39. The Thief of Baghdad 40. To Be or Not To Be 42. The Fallen Idol 48, etc.

Korda, Zoltan (1895–1961). Hungarian director, brother of Alexander Korda; spent most of his career in Britain and Hollywood.
Cash 32. Sanders of the River 35. The Drum 38. *The Four Feathers* 39. Jungle Book 42. Sahara 43. Counterattack 43. *The Macomber Affair* 47. A Woman's Vengeance 48. Cry the Beloved Country 51, etc.

Korjus, Miliza (1908–). Polish operatic soprano who settled in America but did not pursue what looked like being a popular film career.
□ *The Great Waltz* 38. Imperial Cavalry (Mexico) 42.

Korngold, Erich Wolfgang (1897–1957). Czech composer-conductor, a child prodigy. To Hollywood in 1935 with Warners.
□ Captain Blood 35. *Anthony Adverse* (AA) 36. The Green Pastures 36. A Midsummer Night's Dream 36. The Story of Louis Pasteur 36. Another Dawn 37. The Prince and the Pauper 37. *The Adventures of Robin Hood* 38. Juarez 39. Elizabeth and Essex 39. The Sea Wolf 41. *King's Row* 41. The Constant Nymph 43. Between Two Worlds 44. Devotion 44. Deception 46. Of Human Bondage 46. Escape Me Never 47. Magic Fire 56.

Korris, Harry (1888–1971). British music-hall comedian who became popular on radio and made several slapdash film farces.
Somewhere in England 40. Somewhere in Camp 41. Happidrome 43, etc.

Kortner, Fritz (1892–1970) (Fritz Nathan Kohn). Austrian character actor, in films of many nations.
Beethoven 26. Warning Shadows 27. *Pandora's Box* 28. The Murder of Dimitri Karamazov 30. Dreyfus 30. Chu Chin Chow 34. Evensong 34. Abdul the Damned 35. The Crouching Beast 36. The Strange Death of Adolf Hitler 43. The Hitler Gang 44. Somewhere in the Night 46. The Brasher Doubloon 47. Berlin Express 48, many others.

Korty, John (1941–). American director.
□ The Crazy Quilt 65. Funnyman 67. Riverrun 68. The Autobiography of Miss Jane Pittman (TV) 73. Silence 74.

Korvin, Charles (1907–) (Geza Kaiser). Czech-born leading man with varied experience before Hollywood debut.
Enter Arsène Lupin 44. This Love of Ours 45. Temptation 47. The Killer That Stalked New York 50. Lydia Bailey 52. Sangaree 53. Zorro the Avenger 60. Ship of Fools 65. The Man Who Had Power Over Women 70, etc.
TV series: Interpol Calling 59.

Koscina, Sylva (1935–). Jugoslavian leading lady in international films.
Hercules Unchained 60. Jessica 62. Hot Enough for June (GB) 63. Juliet of the Spirits (It.) 65. Three Bites of the Apple (US) 66. Deadlier than the Male (GB) 67. A Lovely Way to Die 68. The Battle for Neretva 70. Hornet's Nest 70, etc.

Kosleck, Martin (1907–) (Nicolai Yoshkin). Russian character actor with experience on the German stage; in America from mid-thirties.
Confessions of a Nazi Spy (as Goebbels) 39. Nurse Edith Cavell 39. A Date with Destiny 40. Foreign Correspondent 40. North Star 43. *The Hitler Gang* (as Goebbels) 44. The Frozen Ghost 44. The Mummy's Curse 45. House of Horrors 46. Hitler (as Goebbels) 61. Something Wild 62. Thirty-Six Hours 64. Morituri 65. The Flesh Eaters 67. Which Way to the Front? 70, etc.

Kosma, Joseph (1905–1969). Hungarian composer, in France from 1933.
La Grande Illusion 37. *La Bête Humaine* 38. *Partie de Campagne* 38. La Règle du Jeu 39. *Les Enfants du Paradis* 44. Les Portes de la Nuit 45. Les Amants de Vérone 48. The Green Glove 52.

Huis Clos 54. Calle Mayor 56. The Doctor's Dilemma 59. Lunch on the Grass 59. La Poupée 62. In the French Style 64. The Little Theatre of Jean Renoir 69, etc.

Kossoff, David (1919–). British character actor and stage monologuist.
The Good Beginning 50. The Young Lovers 55. *A Kid for Two Farthings* 56. *The Bespoke Overcoat* 57. The Journey 59. Freud 62. Ring of Spies 64, many others.

Kostal, Irwin (c. 1915–). American musician who has scored several films.
West Side Story (AA) 61. Mary Poppins 64. *The Sound of Music* (AA) 65. Half a Sixpence 67.

Koster, Henry (1905–) (Hermann Kosterlitz). German director, in Hollywood from mid-thirties, adept at sentimental comedy.
□ Thea Roland (Ger.) 32. Peter (Ger.) 33. Little Mother (Ger.) 33. Peter (Hung.) 35. Marie Bashkirtzeff (Ger.) 36. *Three Smart Girls* 36. One Hundred Men and a Girl 37. The Rage of Paris 38. Three Smart Girls Grow Up 38. First Love 39. Spring Parade 40. *It Started with Eve* 41. Between Us Girls 42. Music for Millions 44. Two Sisters from Boston 45. The Unfinished Dance 47. *The Bishop's Wife* 48. The Luck of the Irish 38. Come to the Stable 49. *The Inspector General* 49. Wabash Avenue 50. My Blue Heaven 50. *Harvey* 50. No Highway (GB) 51. Mr Belvedere Rings the Bell 52. Elopement 52. Stars and Stripes Forever 52. My Cousin Rachel 52. *The Robe* 53. Désirée 54. A Man Called Peter 55. The Virgin Queen 55. Good Morning, Miss Dove 55. D-Day the Sixth of June 56. The Power and the Prize 56. My Man Godfrey 57. Fraulein 58. The Naked Maja 59. The Story of Ruth 60. Flower Drum Song 60. Mr Hobbs Takes a Vacation 62. Take Her She's Mine 63. Dear Brigitte 65. The Singing Nun 66.

Kotcheff, Ted (1931–). Canadian director resident in Britain.
□ Tiara Tahiti 62. Life at the Top 65. Two Gentlemen Sharing 70. Outback 71. Billy Two Hats 73. The Apprenticeship of Duddy Kravitz 74.

Kotto, Yaphet (1937–). Black American actor.
Across 110th Street 72. Live and Let Die 73. Truck Turner 74. Report to the Commissioner 75. Drum 76, etc.

Kovack, Nancy (1935–). American leading lady with stage and TV experience.
Strangers When We Meet 60. Diary of a

Madman 62. Jason and the Argonauts 63. The Outlaws Is Coming 65. Frankie and Johnny 66. The Silencers 66. Tarzan and the Valley of Gold 66. Marooned 69, etc.

Kovacs, Ernie (1919–1962). Big, cigar-smoking American comedian and TV personality.
Biography 1976: *Nothing in Moderation* by David G. Walley.
□ *Operation Mad Ball* 57. Bell, Book and Candle 58. It Happened to Jane 58. *Our Man in Havana* 59. Wake Me When It's Over 60. Strangers When We Meet 60. North to Alaska 60. Pepe 60. Five Golden Hours 61. Sail à Crooked Ship 62.

Kovacs, Laszlo (–). American cinematographer given to experimentation which seldom pleases the eye.
Targets 68. The Savage Seven 68. Easy Rider 69. Getting Straight 70. Five Easy Pieces 70. Alex in Wonderland 70. The Last Movie 71. Marriage of a Young Stockbroker 71. Pocket Money 72. What's Up Doc? 72. Paper Moon 73. Freebie and the Bean 74. Shampoo 75. At Long Last Love 75. Nickelodeon 76, etc.

Kowalski, Bernard (1931–). American director, from TV.
Hot Car Girl 58. Attack of the Giant Leeches 58. Night of the Blood Beast 58. Blood and Steel 59. Krakatoa East of Java 69. Stiletto 70. Macho Callahan 70. Sssss 73, etc.

Kozintsev, Grigori (1905–1973). Russian director, in films since 1924.
The Youth of Maxim 35. *Don Quixote* 57. *Hamlet* 64. King Lear 69, etc.

Kramer, Larry (1935–). American screenwriter.
Women in Love (& p) 69. Lost Horizon 72, etc.

Kramer, Stanley (1913–). American producer of clean-cut, well-intentioned films which sometimes fall short on inspiration.
□ So Ends our Night 41. *The Moon and Sixpence* 42. So This Is New York 48. Home of the Brave 49. *The Men* 50. Cyrano de Bergerac 50. *Death of a Salesman* 51. *High Noon* 52. The Sniper 52. The Happy Time 52. My Six Convicts 52. The Member of the Wedding 52. Eight Iron Men 52. The Fourposter 53. The Juggler 53. The 5000 Fingers of Dr T 53. The Wild One 54. *The Caine Mutiny* 54. Not as a Stranger (& d) 55. The Pride and the Passion (& d) 57. The Defiant Ones (& d) 58. *On the Beach* (& d) 59. *Inherit the Wind* (& d) 60. Judgment at Nuremberg (& d)

61. Pressure Point 62. A Child is Waiting 62. It's a Mad Mad Mad Mad World (& d) 63. Invitation to a Gunfighter 64. *Ship of Fools* (& d) 65. *Guess Who's Coming to Dinner* (& d) 67. The Secret of Santa Vittoria (& d) 69. R.P.M. (& d) 71. Bless the Beasts and Children (& d) 71. *Oklahoma Crude* (& d) 73.

Krampf, Gunter (1899–195*). German cinematographer, in Britain from 1931.
The Student of Prague 24. The Hands of Orlac 24. *Pandora's Box* 28. Rome Express 32. Little Friend 34. Latin Quarter 45. Fame is the Spur 46. Portrait of Clare 50. The Franchise Affair 52, many others.

Krasker, Robert (1913–). Australian cinematographer, long in Britain.
Dangerous Moonlight 40. *Henry V* 44. Caesar and Cleopatra 45. *Brief Encounter* 46. *Odd Man Out* 47. *The Third Man* (AA) 49. Romeo and Juliet 53. Trapeze 56. The Quiet American 58. The Criminal 60. El Cid 61. Billy Budd 62. The Running Man 63. The Fall of the Roman Empire 64. The Heroes of Telemark 65, many others.

Krasna, Norman (1909–). American playwright who has worked on many films since 1932, including adaptations of his own plays.
Fury 36. *Bachelor Mother* 39. The Flame of New Orleans 41. The Devil and Miss Jones 41. *Princess O'Rourke* (AA) (& d) 43. The Big Hangover (& pd) 50. The Ambassador's Daughter (& d) 56. *Indiscreet* 58. Who Was That Lady? (& d) 60. Let's Make Love 61. Sunday in New York 64, many others.

Krasner, Milton (c. 1898–). American cinematographer.
I Love That Man 33. The Crime of Dr Hallett 36. The House of the Seven Gables 40. *The Woman in the Window* 44. Scarlet Street 45. *The Dark Mirror* 46. The Farmer's Daughter 47. *The Set Up* 49. Rawhide 50. *All About Eve* 50. Monkey Business 51. *Three Coins in the Fountain* (AA) 54. The Rains of Ranchipur 55. Bus Stop 56. An Affair to Remember 57. The Four Horsemen of the Apocalypse 62. Two Weeks in Another Town 62. Love with the Proper Stranger 64. The Sandpiper 65. The Singing Nun 66. Hurry Sundown 67. The Epic of Josie 67. The St Valentine's Day Massacre 68. The Sterile Cuckoo 69. Beneath the Planet of the Apes 70, many others.

Kraushaar, Raoul (–). American composer.
Melody Ranch 40. Stardust on the Sage 42. Stork Bites Man 47. Bride of the Gorilla 51. The

Blue Gardenia 53. Mohawk 56. Mustang 59, etc.

Krauss, Werner (1884–1959). Distinguished German actor.
The Cabinet of Dr Caligari 19. *Waxworks* 24. The Student of Prague 25. Secrets of a Soul 26. Jew Süss 40, etc.

Kreuger, Kurt (1917–). Swiss actor, former ski instructor, who appeared in many Hollywood films as smooth continental heart-throb or menace.
Sahara 43. The Moon Is Down 43. Mademoiselle Fifi 44. Madame Pimpernel 45. Unfaithfully Yours 48. The Enemy Below 58. What Did You Do in the War, Daddy? 66. The St Valentine's Day Massacre 67, etc.

Krish, John (1923–). British director who began in sponsored documentary field.
□ Unearthly Stranger 61. The Wild Affair 65. Decline and Fall 68. The Man Who Had Power Over Women 70.

Kristofferson, Kris (1936–). American leading man of the seventies, former folk singer and musician.
Cisco Pike 72. Pat Garrett and Billy the Kid 73. Bring Me the Head of Alfredo Garcia 74. Alice Doesn't Live Here Any More 75. The Sailor Who Fell from Grace with the Sea 76. A Star is Born 76, etc.

Kruger, Alma (1872–1960). American stage actress who made many films in later life and is specially remembered as the head nurse in the Dr Kildare series.
These Three 36. One Hundred Men and a Girl 37. Marie Antoinette 38. Balalaika 39. Saboteur 42. A Royal Scandal 46. Forever Amber (last film) 47, etc.

Kruger, Hardy (1928–). Blond German leading man who has filmed internationally.
The One That Got Away 57. Bachelor of Hearts 58. Blind Date 59. Sundays and Cybèle 60. Hatari 62. The Flight of the Phoenix 65. The Defector 66. The Secret of Santa Vittoria 69. The Red Tent 70. Night Hair Child 71. Paper Tiger 75. Barry Lyndon 75, etc.

Kruger, Otto (1885–1974). Suave American actor with long stage experience.
The Intruder (debut) 32. *Chained* 34. Springtime for Henry 34. Treasure Island 35. *Dracula's Daughter* 36. They Won't Forget 37. *The Housemaster* (GB) 38. Thanks for the Memory 38. Dr Ehrlich's Magic Bullet 40. This Man Reuter 40. The Big Boss 41. *Saboteur* 42.

Murder My Sweet 44. Escape in the Fog 45. Duel in the Sun 46. Smart Woman 48. Payment on Demand 51. High Noon 52. Magnificent Obsession 54. The Last Command 56. The Wonderful World of the Brothers Grimm 63. Sex and the Single Girl 64, many others.

Krushchen, Jack (1922–). American chracter comedian of stage and TV.
Red Hot and Blue 49. The Last Voyage 60. The Apartment 60. Lover Come Back 62. The Unsinkable Molly Brown 64. Million Dollar Duck 71. Freebie and the Bean 74, etc.

The Ku Klux Klan was sympathetically portrayed in Griffith's *The Birth of a Nation*, a fact which has never ceased to provoke controversy. The villainous actuality has, however, been displayed in *Black Legion* 36, *Legion of Terror* 37, *The Burning Cross* 47, *Storm Warning* 51, *The FBI Story* 59, *The Cardinal* 63 and *The Klansman* 74, among others. See also: *Lynch Law.*

Kubrick, Stanley (1928–). American writer-producer-director, in whose psyche independence seems equated with excess.
□ Fear and Desire (wdph) 53. Killer's Kiss (wd) 55. *The Killing* (wd) 56. *Paths of Glory* (wd) 58. Spartacus (d) 60. Lolita (d) 62. *Dr Strangelove* (wdp) 63. *2001: A Space Odyssey* (wdp) 69. A Clockwork Orange (wdp) 71. Barry Lyndon 75.

Kulik, Buzz (c. 1923–). American director, from TV.
□ The Explosive Generation 61. The Yellow Canary 63. Warning Shot (& p) 66. Villa Rides 68. Riot 68. Vanished (TV) 71. To Find a Man 72. The Lindbergh Kidnapping Case (TV) 76.

Kurnitz, Harry (1907–1968). American screenwriter, in Hollywood from 1938.
Fast and Furious 38. The Thin Man Goes Home 44. The Web 47. A Kiss in the Dark (& p) 48. Pretty Baby 49. The Inspector General 49. Melba 53. The Man Between 53. Land of the Pharaohs 55. *Witness for the Prosecution* 57. Goodbye Charlie 64. How To Steal a Million 66, many others.

Kurosawa, Akira (1910–). Distinguished Japanese director.
Tora-No-O 45. *Rashomon* 50. *Living* 52. *Seven Samurai* 54. The Lower Depths 57. *Throne of Blood* 57. The Hidden Fortress 58. High and Low 62. Redbeard 64, etc.

Kwan, Nancy (1938–). Chinese-English leading lady.

The World of Suzie Wong 60. Flower Drum Song 61. Tamahine 63. Fate Is the Hunter 64. The Wild Affair 65. Lt Robin Crusoe 65. Arrivederci Baby 66. Nobody's Perfect 67. The Wrecking Crew 68. The Girl Who Knew Too Much 69. The McMasters 70. Wonder Woman (TV) 73, etc.

Kwouk, Burt (1930–). Chinese-English character actor.
Goldfinger 64. You Only Live Twice 68. The Most Dangerous Man in the World 69. Deep End 71. The Return of the Pink Panther 75, etc.

Kydd, Sam (1917–). British character comedian whose sharp features have been seen in many films since 1945.
The Captive Heart 45. The Small Back Room 48. Treasure Island 50. The Cruel Sea 53. The Quatermass Experiment 55. I'm All Right Jack 59. Follow That Horse 60. Island of Terror 66, etc.

Kyo, Machiko (1924–). Japanese actress.
Rashomon 50. Gate of Hell 52. The Teahouse of the August Moon 56. Ugetsu Monogatari 58, etc.

Kyser, Kay (1897–). Mild-mannered American bandleader who made a number of comedy films in the early forties, then retired to become an active Christian Scientist.
□ That's Right You're Wrong 39. You'll Find Out 40. Playmates 41. My Favorite Spy 42. Around the World 43. Swing Fever 44. Carolina Blues 44.

L

La Cava, Gregory (1892–1952). American director, former cartoonist and writer: a delicate talent for comedy usually struggled against unsatisfactory vehicles.

Womanhandled 25. Running Wild 27. Feel My Pulse 28. Laugh and Get Rich 31. Symphony of Six Million 32. The Half-Naked Truth 32. Gabriel over the White House 32. Affairs of Cellini 34. What Every Woman Knows 34. Private Worlds 35. She Married Her Boss 35. *My Man Godfrey* 36. *Stage Door* 37. Fifth Avenue Girl 39. The Primrose Path 40. Unfinished Business 41. Lady in a Jam 42. Living in a Big Way 47, etc.

La Marr, Barbara (1896–1926) (Reatha Watson). American leading lady of silent films from 1920.

The Prisoner of Zenda 22. The Eternal City 23. Thy Name Is Woman 24. The Shooting of Dan McGrew 24. The Girl from Montmartre 26, etc.

La Planche, Rosemary (1923–). American leading lady of the forties.

Mad about Music 38. The Falcon in Danger 43. Prairie Chickens 43. Devil Bat's Daughter 46, etc.

La Plante, Laura (1904–). American leading lady of the silent screen.

The Old Swimming Hole 21. Skinner's Dress Suit 24. The Cat and the Canary 27. Smouldering Fires 28. King of Jazz 30. Widow's Might 35. Little Mister Jim 46. Spring Reunion 57, etc.

La Rocque, Rod (1896–1969) (Roderick la Rocque de la Rour). Popular American leading man of the silent screen, in Hollywood from 1917 after circus experience.

Efficiency Edgar's Courtship 17. The Venus Model 18. The Ten Commandments 23. Forbidden Paradise 25. Resurrection 26. Our Modern Maidens 28. Let Us Be Gay 29. One Romantic Night 30. SOS Iceberg 33. Till We Meet Again 36. The Hunchback of Notre Dame 40. Dr Christian Meets the Women 41. Meet John Doe 41, others.

La Rue, Danny (1928–) (Daniel Patrick Carroll). British revue star and female impersonator.

□ Our Miss Fred 72.

La Rue, Jack (1903–) (Gaspare Biondolillo). Grim-faced American actor, typed as gangster since the early thirties.

Lady Killer 34. Captains Courageous 37. Paper Bullets 41. Gentleman from Dixie (a rare sympathetic part) 41. Machine Gun Mama 44. No Orchids for Miss Blandish (GB) (as the maniacal Slim Grisson) 48. Robin Hood of Monterey 49. Ride the Man Down 53. Robin and the Seven Hoods 64. Won Ton Ton 76, many others.

La Shelle, Joseph (1903–). American cinematographer.

Happy Land 43. *Laura* (AA) 44. *Hangover Square* 44. The Foxes of Harrow 47. Come to the Stable 49. Mister 880 50. Les Misérables 52. Marty 55. Storm Fear 55. *The Bachelor Party* 57. I Was a Teenage Werewolf 57. No Down Payment 57 The Naked and the Dead 58. The Apartment 60. Irma La Douce 63. The Fortune Cookie 66. The Chase 66. Barefoot in the Park 67. Kona Coast 68, many others.

Laage, Barbara (1925–) (Claire Colombat). French leading lady of several fifties films.

La Putain Respecteuse 52. L'Esclave Blanche 54. Act of Love 54. Un Hmme à Vendre 58, etc.

labour relations is too downbeat a subject to be very popular on the screen; but strikes have been treated with seriousness in *Strike, The Crime of Monsieur Lange, Black Fury, How Green Was My Valley, The Agitator, Love on the Dole, Chance of a Lifetime, The Whistle at Eaton Falls,* and *The Angry Silence*; with humour in *A Nus la Liberté, Modern Times, Carry On at Your Convenience, The Pajama Game,* and *I'm All Right Jack.* The classical comical strike of women against their husbands, led by Lysistrata, was depicted in the French *Love, Soldiers and Women* and Americanized in *The Second Greatest Sex.*

Lacey, Catherine (1904–). British stage and screen actress, adept at sympathetic spinsters and eccentric types.
The Lady Vanishes (debut) 38. Cottage to Let 41. I Know Where I'm Going 45. *The October Man* 47. Whisky Galore 49. Rockets Galore 56. Crack in the Mirror 60. The Fighting Prince of Donegal (as Queen Elizabeth I) 66. The Sorcerers 67, etc.

Lachman, Harry (1886–1975). Anglo-American director, at his best in the thirties.
Weekend Wives 28. Under the Greenwood Tree 29. The Yellow Mask 30. The Outsider 30. The Compulsory Husband 30. Aren't We All 32. Insult 32. Paddy the Next Best Thing 33. Baby Take a Bow 34. *Dante's Inferno* 35. Charlie Chan at the Circus 36. *Our Relations* 36. The Devil is Driving 37. No Time to Marry 38. They Came by Night 40. Dead Men Talk 41. The Loves of Edgar Allan Poe 42, etc.

Ladd, Alan (1913–1964). Unsmiling, pint-sized tough-guy American star who proved to be just the kind of hero the forties wanted.
□ Once in a Lifetime 32. Pigskin Parade 36. Last Train from Madrid 37. Souls at Sea 37. Hold 'em Navy 37. The Goldwyn Follies 38. Come on Leathernecks 38. The Green Hornet 39. Rulers of the Sea 39. Beast of Berlin 39. Light of Western Stars 40. Gangs of Chicago 40. In Old Missouri 40. The Howards of Virginia 40. Those were the Days 40. Captain Caution 40. Wildcat Bus 40. Meet the Missus 40. Great Guns 41. Citizen Kane 41. Cadet Girl 41. Petticoat Politics 41. The Black Cat 41. The Reluctant Dragon 41. Paper Bullets 41. Joan of Paris 42. *This Gun for Hire* 42. *The Glass Key* 42. Lucky Jordan 42. Star Spangled Rhythm 42. China 43. And Now Tomorrow 44. Salty O'Rourke 45. Duffy's Tavern 45. *The Blue Dahlia* 46. O.S.S. 46. Two Years Before the Mast 46. Calcutta 47. Variety Girl 47. Wild Harvest 47. Saigon 48. Beyond Glory 48. Whispering Smith 48. *The Great Gatsby* 49. Chicago Deadline 49. Captain Carey USA 50. Branded 51. Appointment with Danger 51. Red Mountain 52. The Iron Mistress 53. Thunder in the East 53. Desert Legion 53. *Shane* 53. Botany Bay 53. The Red Beret (GB) 53. Saskatchewan 54. Hell Below Zero (GB) 54. The Black Knight (GB) 54. Drum Beat 54. The McConnell Story 55. Hell on Frisco Bay 55. Santiago 56. The Big Land 57. Boy on a Dolphin 57. The Deep Six 58. The Proud Rebel 58. The Bandleaders 58. The Man in the Net 58. Guns of the Timberland 60. All the Young Men 60. One Foot in Hell 60. Duel of the Champions (It.) 61. 13 West Street 62. *The Carpetbaggers* 64.

Ladd, Diane (1932–) (Diane Ladnier). American character actress.
White Lightning 73. Chinatown 74. *Alice Doesn't Live Here Any More* 75, etc.

The Lady Eve (US 1941). Written and directed by Preston Sturges, this amusing trifle about a bashful millionaire landed by the daughter of a confidence trickster was a sparkling example of the Sturges penchant for mixing sophisticated romance with pratfall farce. Henry Fonda, Barbara Stanwyck and Charles Coburn were the leads. In 1956 the plot was warmed over as a vehicle for George Gobel, with the assistance of Mitzi Gaynor and David Niven; but *The Birds and the Bees* was merely flatfooted.

Lady for a Day (US 1933). Robert Riskin wrote, and Frank Capra directed, this Runyonesque fantasy about an old flowerseller who is helped by gangster friends to deceive her visiting daughter into thinking she is comfortably placed. Deftly handled, with a vigorous performance from May Robson, it was agreeable Hollywood moonshine. In 1961 Capra remade it as *Pocketful of Miracles*, but it was now dated and not even Bette Davis and a host of good character actors could save it from tedium, especially as its length was nearly doubled and Capra's direction seemed tired.

The Lady from Shanghai (US 1948). The Orson Welles film which first showed his fatal fault as a solo director: inattention to detail. Even in this Hollywood-produced thriller the lighting is as murky as the plot and most of the dialogue is inaudible, with a dull performance from Welles himself. There are, however, some brilliantly-handled sequences, and the final shoot-up in a hall of mirrors has not been surpassed.

Lady Hamilton: see *That Hamilton Woman*.

Lady in the Dark (US 1944). Moss Hart's now-dated stage play, with songs by Kurt Weill, was about a career girl who was psychologically going to pieces, because she was torn between her work and three different men. The film version by Mitchell Leisen was good to look at but artificial, with dry-ice dream sequences largely replacing the songs. It did however mark the beginning of Hollywood's interest in psychiatry, and its colour photography was coolly superior to any we had seen before.

The Lady in the Lake (US 1946). The suspense and wit of Raymond Chandler's mystery novel were dissipated in this version by the experiment with subjective camera: the entire action was seen as through the hero's eyes, and he did not appear except in mirrors. Robert Montgomery played the role and also directed; but the film was not liked.

Lady Killer (US 1933). Directed by Roy del Ruth, this Warner programmer marks an attempt to spoof gangster movies three years before *A Slight Case of Murder* and a year before the turnaround which put James Cagney on the side of the *G-Men*. Here he plays a cinema usher who turns con-man and gangster, then escapes his pursuers by becoming a Hollywood star. The pace is fast and furious, and the casting of Mae Clarke seems to indicate a direct aping of the *Public Enemy* image.

The Lady Killers (GB 1955). An odd little black farce in which a fang-toothed Alec Guinness and his sinister gang move in on a little old lady who neatly parries their sinister designs and innocently brings about their doom. With Katie Johnson and many familiar British faces; directed by Alexander Mackendrick from a script by William Rose. Memorable but somehow dislikeable.

The Lady Vanishes (GB 1938). Despite model sets and obvious back projection this remains the most likeable and probably the most entertaining of Hitchcock's films, a suspenseful comedy-thriller about a disappearing lady on a train. Scripted by Sidney Gilliat from a novel by Ethel Lina White, it featured Michael Redgrave, Margaret Lockwood, Dame May Whitty, Paul Lukas, Linden Travers, Mary Clare and Cecil Parker, and was notable as the film which introduced Basil Radford and Naunton Wayne as Charters and Caldicott, the Englishmen abroad *par excellence*.

The Lady with a Little Dog (Russia 1959). This highly pictorial love story, set at Yalta in the nineties, came as a mild revelation to western audiences conditioned for years to Russian films stuffed with propaganda. Full of Chekhovian charm, it was directed by Josif Heifits and photographed by Andrej Moskvine.

Laemmle, Carl (1867–1939). German-American pioneer, in films from 1906; produced *Hiawatha* 09, founded Universal Pictures 1912. A biography (1931) by John Drinkwater.

Laemmle, Carl, Jnr (1908–). Son of Carl Laemmle; executive producer at Universal for many years. Credited with the success of *Frankenstein, Dracula*, and *All Quiet on the Western Front*.

Laffan, Patricia (1919–). British stage actress.
The Rake's Progress 45. Caravan 46. Quo Vadis (as Poppea) 51. Devil Girl From Mars 54. Twenty-Three Paces to Baker Street 56, etc.

Lahr, Bert (1895–1968) (Irving Lahrheim). Wry-faced American vaudeville comedian who made occasional film appearances.
Biography 1969: *Notes on a Cowardly Lion* by John Lahr (his son).
Faint Heart 31. Flying High 31. Love and Hisses 37. Josette 38. Just Around the Corner 38. Zaza 39. *The Wizard of Oz* 39. Ship Ahoy 42. Meet the People 44. Always Leave Them Laughing 49. Mr Universe 51. Rose Marie 54. The Second Greatest Sex 56. The Night They Raided Minsky's 68, etc.

Lai, Francis (c. 1933–). French film composer.
Un Homme et Une Femme (AA) 66. Mayerling 68. House of Cards 68. Rider on the Rain 70. *Love Story* (AA) 71. Le Petit Matin 71, etc.

Laine, Frankie (1913–) (Frank Paul Lo Vecchio). American pop singer who made several light musicals in the fifties.
When You're Smiling 50. Make Believe Ballroom 50. The Sunny Side of the Street 51. Rainbow Round My Shoulder 52. Bring Your Smile Along 55. He Laughed Last 56. Viva Las Vegas 56, etc.

Laird, Jenny (1917–). British character actress.
Just William 39. The Lamp Still Burns 43. Black Narcissus 46. *Painted Boats* 47. The Long Dark Hall 51. Conspiracy of Hearts 60, etc.

Lake, Arthur (1905–) (Arthur Silverlake). Harassed, crumple-faced American light comedy actor, best remembered as Dagwood Bumstead in the Blondie series of 28 films in twelve years.
Jack and the Beanstalk 17. Skinner's Dress Suit 26. The Irresistible Lover 27. *Harold Teen* 28. On with the Show 29. Indiscreet 31. Midshipman Jack 33. Orchids to You 35. Topper 37. *Blondie* (and subsequent series) 38. Three is a Family 44. Sixteen Fathoms Deep 48, many others.

Lake, Veronica (1919–1973) (Constance Ockleman). Petite American leading lady who now, with her limited acting ability and her 'peek a boo bang' (long blonde hair obscuring one eye), seems an appropriately artificial image for the

Hollywood of the early forties.
Autobiography 1968: *Veronica*.
□ All Women Have Secrets 39. Sorority House
39. Forty Little Mothers 40. *I Wanted Wings* 41.
Sullivan's Travels 41. *This Gun for Hire* 42. The
Glass Key 42. *I Married a Witch* 42. Star
Spangled Rhythm 42. So Proudly We Hail 43.
The Hour Before the Dawn 44. Bring on the
Girls 45. Out of this World 45. Duffy's Tavern
45. Hold that Blonde 45. Miss Susie Slagle's 45.
The Blue Dahlia 46. Ramrod 47. Variety Girl
47. The Sainted Sisters 48. Saigon 48. Isn't It
Romantic? 48. Slattery's Hurricane 49.
Stronghold 52. Footsteps in the Snow 66. Flesh
Feast 70.

Lamarr, Hedy (1913–) (Hedwig Kiesler).
Austrian leading lady of the thirties and forties,
in Hollywood from 1937 after creating a
sensation by appearing nude in the Czech film
Extase 33. She became a household word for
glamour, but lacked the spark of personality.
Autobiography 1966: *Ecstasy and Me*.
□ AMERICAN FILMS: *Algiers* 38. Lady of the
Tropics 39. I Take this Woman 40. Boom Town
40. Comrade X 40. Come Live with Me 41.
Ziegfeld Girl 41. H.M. Pulham Esq 41. Tortilla
Flat 42. Crossroads 42. *White Cargo* (as
Tondelayo) 42. The Heavenly Body 43. The
Conspirators 44. Experiment Perilous 44. Her
Highness and the Bellboy 45. The Strange
Woman 46. Dishonoured Lady 47. Let's Live a
Little 48. *Samson and Delilah* 49. A Lady
without Passport 50. Copper Canyon 50. My
Favourite Spy 51. The Face That Launched a
Thousand Ships 54. The Story of Mankind 57.
The Female Animal 57.

Lamas, Fernando (1915–). Argentinian
leading man, in Hollywood from 1950 in routine
musicals and comedies.
Rich, Young and Pretty 51. The Law and the
Lady 51. The Merry Widow 52. The Girl Who
Had Everything 53. Sangaree 53. Rose Marie 54.
The Girl Rush 55. The Lost World 60. The
Violent Ones (& d) 67. 100 Rifles 69. Powder
Keg 71, etc.

Lamb, Gil (1906–). Rubber-boned American
comic, seen in many forties musicals.
The Fleet's In (debut) 42. Rainbow Island 44.
Practically Yours 44. Humphrey Takes a
Chance 50. Terror in a Texas Town 58.
Blackbeard's Ghost 67, others.

Lambert, Gavin (1924–). British critic and
novelist, in Hollywood since 1956. Stories about
Hollywood: *The Slide Area*.
AS SCRIPTWRITER: Bitter Victory 57. The

Roman Spring of Mrs Stone 61. Inside Daisy
Clover 65, etc.

Lambert, Jack (1899–). Scottish character
actor.
The Ghost Goes West 36. Nine Men 43. Hue and
Cry 46. Eureka Stockade 47. The Brothers 47.
The Lost Hours 50. The Sea Shall Not Have
Them 54. Storm over the Nile 56. Reach for the
Sky 56. Greyfriars Bobby 60. Modesty Blaise
66, many others.

Lambert, Jack (1920–). American character
actor, usually an evil-eyed heavy.
The Cross of Lorraine 43. The Killers 46. The
Unsuspected 47. The Enforcer 51. Scared Stiff
53. Kiss Me Deadly 55. Machine Gun Kelly 57.
The George Raft Story 61. Four for Texas 63,
many others.

Lamble, Lloyd (1914–). Australian light actor
who has been in many British films as detective,
official, or other man.
The Story of Gilbert and Sullivan 53. The Belles
of St Trinian's 54. The Man Who Never Was 56.
Quatermass II 57. Blue Murder at St Trinian's
58. No Trees in the Street 59. The Trials of Oscar
Wilde 60, etc.

Lamont, Charles (1898–). American
director, in Hollywood from silent days. With
Universal from mid-thirties, making comedies
featuring Abbott and Costello, the Kettles, etc.
Love, Honour and Oh Baby 41. The Merry
Monahans 44. Bowery to Broadway 44. Frontier
Gal 45. The Runaround 46. Slave Girl 47.
Baghdad 49. Flame of Araby 51. Abbott and
Costello Meet Dr Jekyll and Mr Hyde 53. Ma
and Pa Kettle in Paris 53. Untamed Heiress 54.
Abbott and Costello Meet the Mummy 55.
Francis in the Haunted House 56. The Kettles in
the Ozarks 56, many others.

Lamont, Duncan (1918–). Scottish actor
with stage experience, in films since World War
II.
The Golden Coach 53. *The Adventures of
Quentin Durward* 56. Ben Hur 59. Mutiny on the
Bounty 62. Murder at the Gallop 63. The
Brigand of Kandahar 65. Arabesque 65. Decline
and Fall 68. Pope Joan 72. Escape from the Dark
76, many others.

Lamorisse, Albert (1922–1970). French
director known for short fantasy films.
Bim 49. *Crin Blanc* 52. *The Red Balloon* 55.
Stowaway in the Sky 61. Fifi La Plume 64, etc.

Lamour, Dorothy (1914–) (Dorothy

Kaumeyer). Good-humoured American leading lady of the thirties and forties: became typed in sarong roles, and happily guyed her own image.

□ *The Jungle Princess* 36. Swing High Swing Low 37. Last Train from Madrid 37. High Wide and Handsome 37. *The Hurricane* 37. The Big Broadcast of 1938: Her Jungle Love 38. Spawn of the North 38. Tropic Holiday 38. St Louis Blues 39. Man About Town 39. Disputed Passage 39. Johnny Apollo 40. Typhoon 40. *Road to Singapore* 40. Moon over Burma 40. Chad Hanna 40. Road to Zanzibar 41. Caught in the Draft 41. Aloma of the South Seas 41. The Fleet's In 42. Beyond the Blue Horizon 42. Road to Morocco 42. Star Spangled Rhythm 42. They Got Me Covered 43. Dixie 43. Riding High 43. And the Angels Sing 43. Rainbow Island 44. Road to Utopia 45. A Medal for Benny 45. Duffy's Tavern 45. Masquerade in Mexico 45. My Favorite Brunette 47. Road to Rio 47. Wild Harvest 47. Variety Girl 47. On Our Merry Way 48. Lulu Belle 48. The Girl from Manhattan 48. Slightly French 48. Manhandled 48. The Lucky Stiff 49. The Greatest Show on Earth 52. Road to Bali 52. Road to Hong Kong 62. Donovan's Reef 63. Pajama Party 64. Death at Love House (TV) 76.

Lampert, Zohra (1936–). American TV actress, heroine of 60s series *The Nurses*.

Lancaster, Burt (1913–). Athletic American leading man and latterly distinguished actor. Former circus acrobat; acted and danced in soldier shows during World War II.

□ *The Killers* 46. Desert Fury 47. I Walk Alone 47. *Brute Force* 47. Sorry, Wrong Number 48. Kiss the Blood Off My Hands 48. All My Sons 48. Criss Cross 49. Rope of Sand 49. Mister 880 50. *The Flame and the Arrow* 50. Vengeance Valley 51. Ten Tall Men 51. Jim Thorpe All-American 51. The Crimson Pirate 52. *Come Back Little Sheba* 53. South Sea Woman 53. From Here to Eternity 53. His Majesty O'Keefe 54. Apache 54. *Vera Cruz* 54. The Kentuckian (& d) 55. The Rose Tattoo 55. Trapeze 56. The Rainmaker 57. *Gunfight at the OK Corral* (as Wyatt Earp) 57. Sweet Smell of Success 57. Separate Tables 58. The Devil's Disciple (GB) 58. Run Silent Run Deep 58. The Unforgiven 59. *Elmer Gantry* (AA) 60. The Young Savages 61. Judgment at Nuremberg 60. *Birdman of Alcatraz* 62. A Child Is Waiting 62. The Leopard 63. The List of Adrian Messenger 63. Seven Days in May 64. The Train 64. The Hallelujah Trail 65. *The Professionals* 66. *The Swimmer* 67. The Scalphunters 68. Castle Keep 69. The Gypsy Moths 69. Airport 69. Lawman 70. Valdez is Coming 71. Ulzana's Raid 72. Scorpio

73. The Midnight Man (& co-p, co-d) 74. Conversation Piece 75. Buffalo Bill and the Indians 76. *1900* 76. Twilight's Last Gleaming 76.

Lanchester, Elsa (1902–) (Elizabeth Sullivan). British character actress, widow of Charles Laughton. On stage and screen in Britain before settling in Hollywood 1940.

Autobiography 1938: *Charles Laughton and I.*

Bluebottles 28. The Private Life of Henry VIII 32. David Copperfield 35. *The Bride of Frankenstein* 35. The Ghost Goes West 36. *Rembrandt* 37. Vessel of Wrath 38. Ladies in Retirement 41. Tales of Manhattan 42. The Spiral Staircase 45. End of the Rainbow 47. The Inspector-General 49. Androcles and the Lion 53. Bell, Book and Candle 57. *Witness for the Prosecution* 57. Mary Poppins 64. Blackbeard's Ghost 67. Me, Natalie 69. Willard 71. Terror in the Wax Museum 73. *Murder by Death* 76, many others.

Landau, Ely (1920–). American producer, former distributor.

Long Day's Journey Into Night 62. The Pawnbroker 64; etc; plus all productions of the American Film Theatre 1972–74.

Landau, Martin (1933–). Gaunt American actor often in sinister roles.

North by Northwest 59. The Gazebo 59. Cleopatra 62. The Hallelujah Trail 65. Nevada Smith 66. They Call Me Mr Tibbs 70. Savage (TV) 72. Black Gunn 72, etc.

TV series: Mission Impossible 66–68. Space 1999 75–76.

Landers, Lew (1901–1962) (Lewis Friedlander). American director of 'B' pictures, especially westerns, from silent days.

The Raven 35. The Man Who Found Himself 37. Canal Zone 39. Pacific Liner 39. The Boogie Man Will Get You 42. Return of the Vampire 43. The Enchanted Forest 46. State Penitentiary 49. Man in the Dark (in 3-D) 53. Captain Kidd and the Slave Girl 53. Hot Rod Gang 58. Terrified 62, many others.

Landi, Elissa (1904–1948) (Elizabeth Zanardi-Landi). Austrian-Italian leading lady, in international films of the thirties.

Underground 29. Children of Chance 30. Always Goodbye 31. The Yellow Ticket 31. Passport to Hell 32. *The Sign of the Cross* 32. The Masquerader 32. The Warrior's Husband 33. By Candlelight 34. Sisters under the Skin 34. The Count of Monte Cristo 34. Without Regret 35. Enter Madame 35. The Amateur Gentleman

36. After the Thin Man 36. The Thirteenth Chair 37. Corregidor 43, etc.

Landi, Marla (c. 1937–). Italian leading lady and model, in British films.
Across the Bridge 57. First Man into Space 58. The Hound of the Baskervilles 59. Pirates of Blood River 61. The Murder Game 65, etc.

Landis, Carole (1919–1948) (Frances Ridste). American leading lady, in films from 1937 (as extra).
Man and His Mate (One Million B.C.) 40. *Turnabout* 40. Road Show 41. Topper Returns 41. Hot Spot 41. Orchestra Wives 42. Wintertime 43. Having Wonderful Crime 44. Behind Green Lights 45. It Shouldn't Happen to a Dog 46. A Scandal in Paris 46. Out of the Blue 47. The Brass Monkey (GB) 48. Noose (GB) 48, etc.

Landis, Cullen (1896–1975). American silent screen hero.
Who Is Number One 17. Beware of Blondes 18. Almost a Husband 19. Born Rich 24, many others.

Landis, Jessie Royce (1904–1972) (Jessie Royce Medbury). American character actress of long stage experience; usually in fluttery comedy roles.
Autobiography 1954: *You Wont Be So Pretty*.
□ Derelict 30. Mr Belvedere Goes to College 49. It Happens Every Spring 49. My Foolish Heart 49. Mother Didn't Tell Me 30. Meet Me Tonight (GB) 51, *To Catch a Thief* 55. The Swan 56. The Girl He Left Behind 56. My Man Godfrey 57. I Married a Woman 58. *North by Northwest* 59. A Private Affair 59. Goodbye Again 61. Bon Voyage 62. Boys' Night Out 62. Critic's Choice 63. Gidget Goes To Rome 63. Airport 69.

Landon, Michael (1937–) (Michael Orowitz). American leading man best known as Little Jo in TV series *Bonanza*.
I Was a Teenage Werewolf 57. God's Little Acre 58. The Legend of Tom Dooley 59, etc.
TV series co-producer: Little House on the Prairie 74–.

Landone, Avice (1910–1976). British stage actress, usually in cool, unruffled roles.
My Brother Jonathan 48. The Franchise Affair 51. An Alligator Named Daisy 55. Reach for the Sky 56. Carve Her Name with Pride 58. Operation Cupid 60, etc.

Landres, Paul (1912–). American director, former editor.

Oregon Passage 57. The Miracle of the Hills 58. The Flame Barrier 58. The Vampire 59. The Return of Dracula 58. Son of a Gunfighter 65, etc.

Lane, Allan 'Rocky' (1901–1973) (Harry Albershart). American cowboy star of the thirties, former athlete.
Night Nurse 32. Maid's Night Out 38. The Dancing Masters 44. Trail of Robin Hood 51. The Saga of Hemp Brown 58. Hell Bent for Leather 60, scores of second features.

Lane, Charles (1899–). American character actor seen since early thirties as comedy snoop, salesman or tax inspector.
Mr Deeds Goes to Town 36. In Old Chicago 38. You Can't Take It With You 38. The Cat and the Canary 39. Hot Spot 41. Arsenic and Old Lace 44. Intrigue 49. The Juggler 53. Teacher's Pet 58. The Gnome-Mobile 67. What's So Bad About Feeling Good? 68, many others.
TV series: Petticoat Junction 64–69.

Lane, Lupino (1892–1959) (Henry George Lupino). Diminutive, dapper British stage comedian and master of the pratfall, member of a family who had been clowns for generations. His American two-reelers of the twenties were little masterpieces of timing and hair-raising stunts, but he failed to develop a personality for sound.
Biography 1957: *Born to Star* by James Dillon White.
The Reporter 22. Isn't Life Wonderful? 24. The Love Parade 29. Bride of the Regiment 30. The Golden Mask 30. The Deputy Drummer (GB) 35. Me and My Gal (GB) 39, etc.

Lane, Richard (1900–). American supporting player, formerly sports announcer; frequently seen in the forties as reporter, tough cop, or exasperated executive.
The Outcasts of Poker Flat 37. Union Pacific 39. Hellzapoppin 41. Meet Boston Blackie 41. What a Blonde 45. Gentleman Joe Palooka 46. Take Me Out to the Ball Game 48. I Can Get It For You Wholesale 51, etc.

The Lane Sisters. American leading ladies, real name Mulligan. Three of the five sisters (all actresses) had sizeable roles in Hollywood films: Lola (1909–), Rosemary (1913–1974) and Priscilla (1917–).
TOGETHER: Four Daughters 38. Four Wives 39. Four Mothers 40.
OTHER APPEARANCES FOR LOLA: Speakeasy 29. Death from a Distance 35. Marked Woman 37. Zanzibar 40. Why Girls Leave Home 36.

ROSEMARY: Hollywood Hotel 38. The Oklahoma Kid 38. The Return of Dr X 40. Time Out for Rhythm 42. The Fortune Hunter 45.
PRISCILLA: Brother Rat 39. Dust be My Destiny 39. Yes My Darling Daughter 39. The Roaring Twenties 40. Blues in the Night 41. Saboteur 42. Arsenic and Old Lace 44. Fun on a Weekend 46. Bodyguard 48, etc.

Lanfield, Sidney (1900–1972). American director from 1932; former jazz musician.
Hat Check Girl 32. Moulin Rouge 34. Sing Baby Sing 36. *The Hound of the Baskervilles* 39. Swanee River 39. You'll Never Get Rich 41. The Lady Has Plans 41. *My Favorite Blonde* 42. The Meanest Man in the World 42. Let's Face It 43. Standing Room Only 44. Bring on the Girls 45. The Well-Groomed Bride 45. Stations West 47. The Lemon Drop Kid 50. Follow the Sun 51. Skirts Ahoy 52, etc.

Lang, Charles (1915–). American writer.
The Magnificent Matador 56. Desire in the Dust 62, etc.

Lang, Charles (1902–). Distinguished American cinematographer.
Shopworn Angel 29. *A Farewell to Arms* (AA) 33. Death Takes a Holiday 34. Lives of a Bengal Lancer 35. *Desire* 36. *The Cat and the Canary* 39. Nothing But the Truth 41. Practically Yours 44. The Uninvited 44. The Ghost and Mrs Muir 47. A Foreign Affair 47. *Ace in the Hole* 51. Sudden Fear 52. The Big Heat 53. The Female on the Beach 55. The Man from Laramie 55. Autumn Leaves 56. The Solid Gold Cadillac 56. Gunfight at the OK Corral 57. Some Like It Hot 59. One-Eyed Jacks 59. The Facts of Life 60. The Magnificent Seven 60. Blue Hawaii 61. A Girl Named Tamiko 62. *Charade* 63. Inside Daisy Clover 65. How to Steal a Million 66. Not With My Wife You Don't 66. Hotel 67. The Flim Flam Man 67. Wait Until Dark 67. A Flea in Her Ear 68. Cactus Flower 69. Bob and Carol and Ted and Alice 70. The Love Machine 71, many others.

Lang, Fritz (1890–1976). German director of distinguished silent films. Went to Hollywood 1934 and tended thereafter to make commercial though rather heavy-handed thrillers.
□ Halblut 19. Der Herr der Liebe 19. Die Spinnen 19. Hara Kiri 19. Das Wanderne Bild 21. *Destiny* 21. Vier um die Frau 20. Der Mude Tod 21. *Dr Mabuse der Spieler* 22. Inferno 22. *Siegfried* 23. Krimhild's Revenge 24. *Metropolis* 26. *The Spy* 27. Frau im Mond 28. *M* 31. The Testament of Dr Mabuse 32. Liliom 33. *Fury* 36. *You Only Live Once* 37. You and Me 38. The

Return of Frank James 40. Western Union 41. Man Hunt 41. Confirm or Deny (part) 42. Hangmen Also Die 43. *The Woman in the Window* 44. Ministry of Fear 44. Scarlet Street 45. Cloak and Dagger 46. The Secret Beyond the Door 48. House by the River 49. An American Guerrilla in the Philippines 51. Rancho Notorious 52. Clash by Night 52. The Blue Gardenia 52. *The Big Heat* 53. Human Desire 54. Moonfleet 55. While the City Sleeps 55. Beyond a Reasonable Doubt 56. Der Tiger von Ischnapur (Ind.) 58. Das Indische Grabmal (Ger.) 58. The Thousand Eyes of Dr Mabuse (Ger.) 60.

Lang, Harold (1923–1970). British actor and drama teacher.
Flood Tide 49. Cairo Road 50. Laughing Anne 53. The Quatermass Experiment 55. Carve Her Name with Pride 58. The Nanny 63, etc.

Lang, June (1915–) (June Vlasek). American leading lady, former dancer.
Chandu the Magician 32. Bonnie Scotland 35. Ali Baba Goes to Town 38. Redhead 41. Flesh and Fantasy 44. Lighthouse 48, etc.

Lang, Jennings (1915–). American executive, long near the top of MCA TV and latterly executive producer of many Universal films.

Lang, Matheson (1879–1948). Scottish-Canadian stage actor, a London matinée idol of the twenties who made occasional films.
Autobiography 1940: *Mr Wu Looks Back*.
Mr Wu 21. Carnival 21 & 31. Dick Turpin's Ride to York 22. The Wandering Jew 23. The Chinese Bungalow 25 & 30. Beyond the Veil 25. Island of Despair 26. The Triumph of the Scarlet Pimpernel 29. Channel Crossing 32. Little Friend 34. Drake of England 35. The Cardinal 36, etc.

Lang, Robert (1934–). British character actor, mainly on stage.
Night Watch 73. Savage Messiah 73. Shout at the Devil 76, etc.

Lang, Walter (1896–1972). American director of competent but seldom outstanding entertainments.
□ The Satin Woman 27. The College Hero 27. Brothers 30. Hell Bound 30. Women Go On for Ever 31. No More Orchids 32. The Warrior's Husband 33. Meet the Baron 33. Whom the Gods Destroy 34. The Mighty Barnum 34. Carnival 35. Hooray for Love 35. Love Before Breakfast 36. *Wife, Doctor and Nurse* 37.

Second Honeymoon 37. The Baroness and the Butler 38. I'll Give a Million 38. The Little Princess 39. *The Bluebird* 40. Star Dust 40. The Great Profile 40. *Tin Pan Alley* 40. Moon over Miami 41. Weekend in Havana 41. Song of the Islands 42. The Magnificent Dope 42. Coney Island 43. Greenwich Village 44. *State Fair* 45. Sentimental Journey 46. Claudia and David 46. Mother Wore Tights 47. *Sitting Pretty* 48. When My Baby Smiles at Me 48. You're My Everything 49. Cheaper by the Dozen 50. The Jackpot 50. On the Riviera 51. *With a Song in My Heart* 51. *Call Me Madam* 53. There's No Business like Show Business 54. *The King and I* 56. The Desk Set 57. But Not for Me 59. Can Can 60. The Marriage Go Round 61. Snow White and the Three Stooges 61.

Langan, Glenn (1917–). American light leading man, in films from the early forties after stage experience.
Four Jills in a Jeep 44. *Margie* 46. Forever Amber 47. The Snake Pit 48. Treasure of Monte Cristo 59. Rapture (Swedish) 50. Hangman's Knot 52. 99 River Street 54. The Amazing Colossal Man 57, etc.

Langdon, Harry (1884–1944). Baby-faced, melancholy American clown who was a great hit in the twenties but could not reconcile his unusual image with sound.
Picking Peaches 23. *Tramp Tramp Tramp* 26. *The Strong Man* 26. *Long Pants* 26. His First Flame 27. Three's a Crowd 27. The Chaser (& d) 28. See America Thirst 30. A Soldier's Plaything 31. Hallelujah I'm a Bum 33. My Weakness 33. There Goes My Heart 38. *Zenobia* 39. Misbehaving Husbands 40. House of Errors 42. Spotlight Scandals 44, etc.

Langdon, Sue Ane (1940–). American leading lady and comedienne.
The Outsider 61. The Rounders 65. A Fine Madness 66. A Guide for the Married Man 67. The Cheyenne Social Club 70, etc.
TV series: *Arnie* 70–71.

Lange, Hope (1931–). American leading lady of the fifties who developed into a mature and pleasing comedienne.
□ Bus Stop 56. The True Story of Jesse James 57. Peyton Place 57. The Young Lions 58. In Love and War 58. The Best of Everything 59. Wild in the Country 61. Pocketful of Miracles 61. Love is a Ball 63. Crowhaven Farm (TV) 70. That Certain Summer (TV) 72. Death Wish 74. TV series: *The Ghost and Mrs Muir* 68. *The New Dick Van Dyke Show* 71.

Langella, Frank (1944–). American leading man of the seventies.
The Twelve Chairs 70. Diary of a Mad Housewife 70. The Wrath of God 72, etc.

Langford, Frances (1914–). American band singer, popular in the forties, mainly in guest spots. Appeared mainly in light musicals.
Every Night at Eight 35. Broadway Melody 36. Hollywood Hotel 37. Too Many Girls 40. Swing It, Soldier 41. The Girl Rush 44. The Bamboo Blonde 45. Beat the Band 46. No Time For Tears 52. The Glenn Miller Story 54, etc.

Langley, Noel (1911–). South African playwright and screenwriter, in Britain and Hollywood.
Maytime (co-w) 38. The Wizard of Oz (co-w) 39. They Made Me a Fugitive 47. Tom Brown's Schooldays 51. Scrooge 52. The Pickwick Papers (& d) 53. Our Girl Friday (& d) 53. The Search for Bridey Murphy (& d) 56, others.

Langlois, Henri (1914–1977). Idiosyncratic French archivist, instigator of the Cinematheque Française. His methods annoyed some, but his good intentions were never in question. Received special Academy Award in 1974.

Langtry, Lillie (1853–1929) (Emilie Charlotte Le Breton). American vaudeville entertainer who charmed, among others, Judge Roy Bean and Edward VII. Sole film appearance in 1913: *His Neighbour's Wife*.

Lansbury, Angela (1925–). British character actress who has always seemed older than her years. Evacuated to Hollywood during World War II, she played a long succession of unsympathetic parts, but in the sixties became a Broadway musical star.
□ Gaslight 44. National Velvet 44. *The Picture of Dorian Gray* 45. The Harvey Girls 46. The Hoodlum Saint 46. The Private Affairs of Bel Ami 47. Till the Clouds Roll By 47. If Winter Comes 47. Tenth Avenue Angel 48. State of the Union 48. The Three Musketeers 48. The Red Danube 49. Samson and Delilah 49. Kind Lady 51. Mutiny 52. Remains to Be Seen 53. A Lawless Street 55. A Life at Stake 55. The Purple Mask 55. Please Murder Me 56. The Court Jester 56. The Reluctant Debutante 58. The Long Hot Summer 58. *The Dark at the Top of the Stairs* 60. A Breath of Scandal 61. Blue Hawaii 61. Summer of the Seventeenth Doll 61. All Fall Down 62. *The Manchurian Candidate* 62. In the Cool of the Day 63. The World of Henry Orient 64. Dear Heart 64. The Greatest Story Ever Told 65. Harlow 65. Moll Flanders

65. Mister Buddwing 66. Something for Everyone 70. *Bedknobs and Broomsticks* 71.

Lansing, Joi (1936–72) (Joy Brown). American leading lady of the sixties; films minor. The Brave One 57. A Hole in the Head 59. Who Was That Lady? 60. Marriage on the Rocks 63, etc.

Lansing, Robert (1929–) (Robert H. Broom). Cold-eyed, virile American leading man of the sixties.
The 4-D Man 59. A Gathering of Eagles 63. Under the Yum Yum Tree 64. The Grissom Gang 71. Wild in the Sky 72. Bittersweet Love 76, etc.
TV series: 87th Precinct 61. 12 O'clock High 64. The Man Who Never Was 66.

Lantz, Walter (1900–). American animator, in charge of Universal cartoons since 1928 and the creator of Woody Woodpecker.

Lanza, Mario (1921–1959) (Alfredo Cocozza). American opera singer, popular in MGM musicals until overcome by weight problem.
□ That Midnight Kiss 49. The Toast of New Orleans 50. *The Great Caruso* 51. Because You're Mine 52. The Student Prince (voice only) 54. Serenade 56. Seven Hills of Rome 58. For the First Time 58.

Larsen, Keith (1925–). American secondstring leading man.
Flat Top 52. Hiawatha 52. Arrow in the Dust 54. Wichita 55. Dial Red O 56. Fury River 61. Caxambu 67, etc.
TV series: Northwest Passage 57.

Lasky, Jesse (1880–1958). American pioneer. Formed his first production company in 1914 and had a big hit with *The Squaw Man*; in 1916 gained control of Famous Players and later Paramount. Later produced for Fox, Warner, RKO.
Autobiography 1958: *I Blow My Own Horn*.
Sergeant York 41. The Adventures of Mark Twain 44. Rhapsody in Blue 45. The Miracle of the Bells 49. The Great Caruso 51, many others.

Lasky, Jesse Jnr (1910–). American screenwriter, son of Jesse Lasky.
Autobiography 1974: *Whatever Happened to Hollywood?*
Union Pacific (co-w) 39. Reap the Wild Wind (co-w) 42. Unconquered (co-w) 48. Samson and Delilah (co-w) 49. The Thief of Venice 50. The Brigand 52. The Ten Commandments (co-w) 56. Seven Women from Hell (co-w) 61, etc.

Lassally, Walter (1926–). German cinematographer, long in Britain.
We Are the Lambeth Boys 58. *A Taste of Honey* 61. The Loneliness of the Long-Distance Runner 62. *Tom Jones* 63. *Zorba the Greek* (AA) 65. The Day the Fish Came Out 67. Oedipus the King 67. Joanna 68. Turnkey 70, etc.

Lasser, Louise (c. 1940–). American TV actress popular in 76 serial *Mary Hartman, Mary Hartman.*
Everything You Always Wanted to Know About Sex 72. Slither 73, etc.

Lassie. The first film featuring this intelligent collie (actually a laddie) was *Lassie Come Home* 42, based on Eric Knight's novel; the dog, born in 1940, was called Pal, and continued his masquerade in several subsequent 'Lassie' adventures, though more recently different dogs have been used. The latest addition is *Lassie's Great Adventure* 62, and there has been a long-running TV series since 1955, followed in 1973 by a cartoon series, *Lassie's Rescue Rangers.*

The Last Chance (Switzerland 1945). Almost the only Swiss film of international repute, this story of escape from Italy at the end of the 1943 campaign was directed by Leopold Lindtberg.

The Last Days of Pompeii. Lord Lytton's novel climaxing in the catastrophic eruption of Vesuvius was filmed in Italy in 1912 ('10,000 people, 260 scenes'), 1925 and 1960. In 1935 Cooper and Schoedsack filmed it in Hollywood, with a cast including Basil Rathbone and Preston Foster.

The Last Hurrah (US 1958). Edwin O'Connor's amusing novel about the last days of a lovably roguish politician was turned by director John Ford into a sentimental reunion for a number of veteran character actors including Spencer Tracy, Edward Brophy, James Gleason, Basil Rathbone, John Carradine, Pat O'Brien, Donald Crisp, Ricardo Cortez, Wallace Ford, Frank McHugh and Jane Darwell. As a film it was fair.

The Last Laugh (Der Letzte Mann) (Germany 1925). A silent drama dispensing entirely with sub-titles. Emil Jannings gave one of his most characteristic and clever performances as the lordly hotel porter degraded to washroom attendant;
F. W. Murnau directed from a script by Karl Mayer; photography by Karl Freund.

The Last of the Mohicans. Fenimore

Cooper's adventure novel of American colonization was filmed in 1920 by Maurice Tourneur, with George Hackathorne; in 1936 by George Seitz, with Randolph Scott, and in 1952, as *The Last of the Redskins*, by George Sherman with Jon Hall. A Canadian TV series in 1956, starred John Hart.

The Last Picture Show (US 1971). The movie which rocketed director Peter Bogdanovich to fame and set him off on a number of flawed nostalgic retrospectives was a potent distillation of small town sexual mores circa 1951: it was itself aped by *American Graffiti* two years later. Cloris Leachman and Ben Johnson distinguished themselves among a generally able cast.

Last Year in Marienbad (US 1961). Written by Alain Robbe-Grillet and directed by Alain Resnais, this curious film was hailed by many critics as a masterpiece, while others suspected a leg-pull. It had only three characters of note, but the problem for audiences was to find out how they were interrelated and what the film was about. Sacha Vierney's photography, in and around a baroque hotel, added its share of mystery.

Laszlo, Andrew (1926–). Hungarian-American cinematographer.
You're a Big Boy Now 67. The Night They Raided Minsky's 68. Popi 69. Teacher Teacher 70. The Out of Towners 70. Lovers and other Strangers 71. The Owl and the Pussycat 71. Class of 44 73. The Man without a Country (TV) 74.

Laszlo, Ernest (1905–). American cinematographer.
The Hitler Gang 44. Two Years Before the Mast 44. The Girl from Manhattan 48. Dead on Arrival 49. The Steel Trap 52. The Star 52. Stalag 17 53. *Vera Cruz* 54. The Big Knife 55. Judgment at Nuremberg 60. *Inherit the Wind* 60. It's A Mad Mad Mad Mad World 63. Ship of Fools (AA) 65. Fantastic Voyage 66. Star! 68. The First Time 69. Daddy's Gone A-Hunting 69. *Airport* 69. Showdown 73. Logan's Run 76, many others.

Lathrop, Philip (1916–). American cinematographer.
The Monster of Piedras Blancas 57. Experiment in Terror 62. Lonely are the Brave 62. Days of Wine and Roses 63. The Pink Panther 63. The Americanization of Emily 64. Thirty-Six Hours 65. The Cincinnati Kid 65. What Did You Do in the War Daddy? 66. The Russians are Coming

66. The Happening 67. Point Blank 68. *Finian's Rainbow* 69. The Gypsy Moths 69. The Illustrated Man 69. They Shoot Horses Don't They? 69. Von Richthofen and Brown 71. Airport 77 77, etc.

Latimer, Jonathan (–). American writer, usually in collaboration.
Topper Returns 41. They Won't Believe Me 47. Alias Nick Beal 49. Plunder of the Sun 51. Botany Bay 54. The Unholy Wife 57, etc.

Latimore, Frank (1925–) (Frank Kline). American leading man with stage experience.
In the Meantime, Darling 44. Three Little Girls in Blue 46. Black Magic 49. Three Forbidden Stories (Italian) 50. John Paul Jones 59. The Sergeant 68, etc.

Lattuada, Alberto (1914–). Italian director.
The Mill on the Po 48. Without Pity 48. Lights of Variety (co-d) 50. Il Capotto 52. The Wolf 53. The Beach 53. Guendalina 56. Tempest 58. The Adolescents 61. La Steppa 62. The Mandrake 65. The Betrayal 68.

Lauder, Sir Harry (1870–1950). Scottish music-hall entertainer.
Autobiography 1928: *Roamin' in the Gloamin'*.
Huntingtower 27. Auld Lang Syne 33. Song of the Road 36.

Laughlin, Tom (1938–). American independent director.
The Young Sinner 65. Born Losers (& ap) 67. Billy Jack (& apw) 71. The Trial of Billy Jack (& apw) 72. The Master Gunfighter (& apw) 75, etc.

Laughton, Charles (1899–1962). Distinguished British character actor, whose plump wry face was one of the most popular on screen in the thirties. His later Hollywood roles showed a regrettable tendency to ham, but he was always worth watching.
Biographies: *Charles Laughton and I* (1938) by his wife Elsa Lanchester; *The Charles Laughton Story* (1952) by Kurt Singer; *Charles Laughton* (1976) by Charles Higham.
□ Wolves 27. Bluebottles 28. Daydreams 28. Piccadilly 29. Comets 30. Down River 30. *The Old Dark House* 32. The Devil and the Deep 32. Payment Deferred 32. *The Sign of the Cross* (as Nero) 32. If I Had a Million 32. Island of Lost Souls 32. *The Private Life of Henry VIII* (AA) 33. White Woman 33. *The Barretts of Wimpole Street* 34. Ruggles of Red Gap 35. Les Misérables 35. Mutiny on the Bounty (as Captain Bligh) 35. Rembrandt 36. *I Claudius* (unfinished) 37. Vessel of Wrath 37. St Martin's

Lane 38. Jamaica Inn 39. *The Hunchback of Notre Dame* 39. They Knew What They Wanted 40. It Started with Eve 41. The Tuttles of Tahiti 42. Tales of Manhattan 42. Stand by for Action 43. Forever and a Day 43. This Land is Mine 43. The Man from Down Under 43. The Canterville Ghost 44. *The Suspect* 44. Captain Kidd 45. Because of Him 46. The Paradine Case 48. The Big Clock 48. Arch of Triumph 48. The Girl from Manhattan 49. The Bribe 49. The Man on the Eiffel Tower (as Maigret) 49. The Blue Veil 51. The Strange Door 51. Full House 52. Abbott and Costello Meet Captain Kidd 52. Salome 53. Young Bess 53. *Hobson's Choice* 54. *Witness for the Prosecution* 57. Under Ten Flags 60. Spartacus 60. *Advise and Consent* 62.
AS DIRECTOR: *Night of the Hunter* 55.

Launder, Frank (1907–). British comedy scriptwriter, from 1938 usually in collaboration with Sidney Gilliat (qv); they have produced most of their own films.
Under the Greenwood Tree 29. The W Plan 30. Children of Chance 30. After Office Hours 31. Josser in the Army 31. Facing the Music 33. Those were the Days 34. Emil and the Detectives 35. Seven Sinners 36. Educated Evans 36. *Oh Mr Porter* 38. *The Lady Vanishes* 38. A Girl must Live 39. They Came by Night 40. *Night Train to Munich* 40. Kipps 41. The Young Mr Pitt 42. Millions Like Us (& d) 43. 2000 Women (& d) 43. *I See a Dark Stranger* (& d) 45. Captain Boycott (& d) 47. The Blue Lagoon (& d) 48. *The Happiest Days of Your Life* (& d) 50. Lady Godiva Rides Again (& d) 51. *The Belles of St Trinian's* (& d) 54. Geordie (& d) 55. The Bridal Path (& d) 59. Joey Boy (& d) 65. The Great St Trinian's Train Robbery (& d) 66, etc.

Laura (US 1944). A superior mystery from a novel by Vera Caspary, this was notable for Otto Preminger's spare direction of his small cast, and for Clifton Webb's first star performance as the acidulous Waldo Lydecker. Cinematography: Joseph La Shelle (AA).

Laurel, Stan (1890–1965) (Arthur Stanley Jefferson). British-born comedian, the thin half and gag deviser of the Laurel and Hardy team. Went to USA with Fred Karno's troupe, with short comedies from 1915, teamed with Hardy 1926. He had director credit on some of their films and virtually directed many others. Special Academy Award 1960 'for his creative pioneering in the field of cinema comedy'. For list of films see *Oliver Hardy*.

Laurenson, James (1935–). New Zealand actor in British and Australian TV, especially

series *Boney*.
The Magic Christian 69. Assault 70, etc.

Laurents, Arthur (1918–). American playwright.
Caught (original screenplay) 48. Home of the Brave 49. Summertime 55. West Side Story (co-w) 61. The Way We Were (original screenplay) 73.

Laurie, John (1897–). Scottish character actor, often in dour roles. On stage from 1921.
Juno and the Paycock 30. Red Ensign 34. *The Thirty-Nine Steps* 35. Tudor Rose 36. As You Like It 36. Farewell Again 37. Edge of the World 38. Q Planes 39. Sailors Three 40. *The Ghost of St Michael's* 41. Old Mother Riley Cleans Up 41. The Gentle Sex 43. Fanny by Gaslight 43. *The Way Ahead* 44. *Henry V* 44. I Know Where I'm Going 45. Caesar and Cleopatra 45. The Brothers 47. Uncle Silas 47. Bonnie Prince Charlie 48. Hamlet 48. Trio 50. Laughter in Paradise 51. The Fake 53. Hobson's Choice 54. The Black Knight 55. Campbell's Kingdom 57. Kidnapped 60. Siege of the Saxons 63. Mr Ten Per Cent 66, etc.

Laurie, Piper (1932–) (Rosetta Jacobs). Pert American leading lady of fifties costume charades.
Louisa (debut) 49. The Prince Who Was a Thief 51. Son of Ali Baba 52. The Golden Blade 54. Ain't Misbehavin' 55. *The Hustler* 61, etc.

Lauter, Ed (1936–). American general purpose actor.
The Last American Hero 73. Executive Action 73. Lolly Madonna XXX 74. The Longest Yard 75. Last Hours Before Morning (TV) 75. King Kong 76, etc.

Lauter, Harry (1920–). American supporting actor.
The Gay Intruders 48. Tucson 49. Whirlwind 51. The Sea Tiger 52. Dragonfly Squadron 54. The Crooked Web 55. Hellcats of the Navy 57. Gunfight at Dodge City 59. Posse from Hell 61. Ambush Bay 66. More Dead than Alive 68, many others.

Laven, Arnold (1922–). American director, former dialogue coach.
Without Warning 52. Down Three Dark Streets 54. The Rack 56. The Monster That Challenged the World 57. Slaughter on Tenth Avenue 58. Anna Lucasta 58. Geronimo (& p) 62. The Glory Guys 66. Rough Night in Jericho 67. Sam Whiskey 68. The Scalphunters (p only) 68, etc.

The Lavender Hill Mob (GB 1950). One of the most affectionately remembered Ealing comedies, a skit on *The Blue Lamp* with Alec Guinness and Stanley Holloway as unlikely gangsters almost getting away with the bullion. Lightly and amusingly scripted by T. E. B. Clarke, directed by Charles Crichton.

lavender print. A high quality, well-contrasted print, sometimes called a 'fine grain', struck from the original negative for the purpose of making duplicates.

Laverick, June (1932–). British leading lady, groomed for stardom by the Rank charm school of the fifties.
Doctor at Large 56. The Gypsy and the Gentleman 57. Son of Robin Hood 58. Follow a Star 59, etc.

Lavery, Emmet (–). American writer.
The First Legion 51.

Lavery, Emmet Jnr (1927–). American TV executive producer, mainly with Paramount.
Delancy Street 75. Serpico (and series) 76, etc.

Lavi, Daliah (1940–). Israeli leading lady in international films.
Il Demonio (Italian) 63. Old Shatterhand (WG) 64. Lord Jim 65. Ten Little Indians 65. The Silencers 66. The Spy with a Cold Nose 67. Some Girls Do 67. Nobody Runs Forever 68. Catlow 72, etc.

Law, John Phillip (1937–). American leading man.
The Russians Are Coming 66. Hurry Sundown 67. Barbarella 68. Skidoo 68. The Sergeant 68. Danger: Diabolik 68. The Hawaiians 70. Von Richthofen and Brown 71. The Love Machine 71. The Last Movie 71. Sinbad's Golden Voyage 73.

Lawford, Peter (1923–). British light leading man, former child actor, in Hollywood from 1938.
Poor Old Bill 31. The Boy from Barnardo's 38. Mrs Miniver 42. The White Cliffs of Dover 44. Cluny Brown 46. It Happened in Brooklyn 47. Easter Parade 48. Little Women 49. Royal Wedding 52. Exodus 60. Advise and Consent 61. Sylvia 65. Harlow 65. Dead Run (Austria) 67. Salt and Pepper (GB) 68. Buona Sera Mrs Campbell 68. The April Fools 69. One More Time 70. Don't Look Behind You (TV) 71. Phantom of Hollywood (TV) 74. Rosebud 75, etc.
TV series: Dear Phoebe 55. The Thin Man 58.

Lawrance, Jody (1930–) (Josephine Lawrence Goddard). American leading lady.
Mask of the Avenger 51. Son of Dr Jekyll 51. The Brigand 52. Captain John Smith and Pocahontas 53. The Scarlet Hour 55. Stagecoach to Dancer's Rock 62.

Lawrence, Barbara (1928–). American comedy actress, usually seen as wise-cracking friend of the heroine.
Margie 46. You Were Meant for Me 47. Thieves' Highway 49. Two Tickets to Broadway 51. Jesse James Versus the Daltons 54. *Oklahoma* 55. Joe Dakota 57, etc.

Lawrence, D. H. (1885–1930). Introspective British novelist whose novels have been adapted with varying success for the screen.
Lady Chatterley's Lover 58. Sons and Lovers 60. The Fox 68. Women in Love 69. The Virgin and the Gypsy 70, etc.

Lawrence, Delphi (c. 1927–). Anglo-Hungarian actress, in British films.
Blood Orange 54. Barbados Quest 55. It's Never Too Late 56. Too many Crooks 59. Cone of Silence 60. Farewell Performance 63. Pistolero (US) 67, others.

Lawrence, Florence (1886–1938). American leading lady of the silent screen; one of the industry's chief stars, she was known at first as 'the Biograph Girl'. Retired in the early twenties.
Miss Jones Entertains 09. Resurrection 10. A Singular Cynic 14. The Enfoldment 20, many others.

Lawrence, Gertrude (1898–1952) (Alexandre Dagmar Lawrence-Klasen). Vivacious British revue star of the twenties, especially associated with Noel Coward. Despite sporadic attempts, her quality never came across on the screen. She was impersonated by Julie Andrews in *Star!* 68.
Autobiography 1949: *A Star Danced.*
☐ The Battle of Paris 29. No Funny Business 32. Mimi 35. Rembrandt 36. Men are Not Gods 36. *The Glass Menagerie* 50.

Lawrence, Marc (1910–). American character actor, former opera singer; usually seen as Italian gangster.
White Woman 33. Dr Socrates 35. Penitentiary 38. The Housekeeper's Daughter 39. Johnny Apollo 40. The Monster and the Girl 41. Hold That Ghost 42. Dillinger 45. I Walk Alone 47. The Asphalt Jungle 50. My Favorite Spy 51. Helen of Troy 55. Kill Her Gently 58. Johnny Cool 64. Nightmare in the Sun (wd only) 64.

Savage Pampas 66. Custer of the West 67. Krakatoa East of Java 69, many others.

Lawrence of Arabia (GB 1962). David Lean's epic account of a finally mysterious character: beautiful, careful, over-long. The supreme example of the modern multi-million-dollar international epic, several years in the making and shot on the actual locations. Peter O'Toole leads an all-star cast; production by Sam Spiegel, script by Robert Bolt. AA best picture, director, etc.

Lawrence, Quentin (c. 1923–). British director, from TV.
The Trollenberg Terror 55. Cash on Demand 62. The Man Who Finally Died 63. The Secret of Blood Island 65, etc.

Lawrence, T. E. (1888–1935). British adventurer and soldier whose book *Seven Pillars of Wisdom* made him a cult and remotely inspired the film *Lawrence of Arabia*.

Lawson, John Howard (1886–). American writer with Marxist affiliations.
Heart of Spain 37. Algiers 38. Blockade 38. Five Came Back 39. *Sahara* 43. Counter-Attack 43. Smash-Up 47, etc.

Lawson, Leigh (1944–). British leading man of the seventies.
Ghost Story 74. Percy's Progress 74. Love Among the Ruins (TV) 75, etc.

Lawson, Sarah (1928–). British leading lady of the fifties.
The Browning Version 50. Street Corner 52. Blue Peter 54. It's Never Too Late 55, etc.

Lawson, Wilfrid (1900–1966) (Wilfrid Worsnop). British character actor, on stage from 1916; revelled in eccentric parts.
Turn of the Tide (film debut) 36. Ladies in Love (US) 36. The Terror 37. The Gaunt Stranger 38. Yellow Sands 38. Bank Holiday 38. *Pygmalion* (as Dolittle) 38. Stolen Life 39. *Pastor Hall* 39. The Long Voyage Home (US) 40. Tower of Terror 41. Hard Steel 41. The Night Has Eyes 42. Danny Boy 42. *The Great Mr Handel* 42. Thursday's Child 43. Fanny by Gaslight 43. The Turners of Prospect Road 47. The Prisoner 55. Tread Softly Stranger 58. Room at the Top 59. *The Wrong Box* 66, etc.

Lawton, Charles Jnr (–1965). American cinematographer.
My Dear Miss Aldrich 36. Miracles for Sale 39. Gold Rush Maisie 41. Fingers at the Window 42.

Abroad with Two Yanks 44. The Thrill of Brazil 46. *The Lady from Shanghai* 48. Shockproof 49. Rogues of Sherwood Forest 50. Mask of the Avenger 51. *The Happy Time* 52. Miss Sadie Thompson 53. Drive a Crooked Road 54. The Long Gray Line 55. Jubal 56. *3.10 to Yuma* 57. The Last Hurrah 58. It Happened to Jane 59. Two Rode Together 61. 13 West Street 62. Spencer's Mountain 63. Youngblood Hawke 64. A Rage to Live 65, many others.

Lawton, Frank (1904–1969). Charming but undynamic British leading man of the thirties, husband of Evelyn Laye; in British and American films.
Young Woodley 28. Birds of Prey 30. The Skin Game 31. The Outsider 31. Michael and Mary 31. After Office Hours 32. Cavalcade 33. Heads We Go 33. Friday the Thirteenth 33. One More River 34. *David Copperfield* (title role) 34. The Invisible Ray 36. The Devil Doll 36. The Mill on the Floss 37. The Four Just Men 39. Went the Day Well? 42. The Winslow Boy 48. Rough Shoot 52. The Rising of the Moon 57. A Night to Remember 57. Gideon's Day 57, etc.

Laydu, Claude (1927–). Undernourished-looking French leading actor.
Diary of a Country Priest 50. Nous Sommes Tous les Assassins 52. Symphonie d'Amour 55. Le Dialogue des Carmelites 59, etc.

Laye, Evelyn (1900–). British musical comedy star of the twenties and thirties; films rare. Married Frank Lawton.
Autobiography 1958: *Boo to My Friends*.
□ Luck of the Navy 29. One Heavenly Night (US) 31. Waltz Time 33. Princess Charming 33. *Evensong* 34. The Night is Young 34. Make Mine a Million 59. Theatre of Death 66. Say Hello to Yesterday 71.

Lazenby, George (1939–). Australian leading man who made the big jump from TV commercials to playing James Bond.
On Her Majesty's Secret Service 69. Universal Soldier 71. The Man from Hong Kong 75.

Le Borg, Reginald (1902–). Austrian-born director, in Hollywood from 1937, at first as shorts director. Output mainly routine with occasional flashes of talent.
She's For Me 42. The Mummy's Ghost 44. Calling Dr Death 44. *San Diego I Love You* 45. Joe Palooka, Champ 46. Young Daniel Boone 47. Wyoming Trail 49. Bad Blonde 51. Sins of Jezebel 53. The Black Sleep 56. The Dalton Girls 57. The Flight That Disappeared 61. The Diary of a Madman 62, many others.

Le Breton, Auguste (1915–). French writer.
Razzia sur la Chnouf 54. Rififi 55. Bob le
Flambeur 56. Rafles sur la Ville 57, etc.

Le Chanois, Jean-Paul (1909–) (J.-P.
Dreyfus). French director.
l'École Buissonière 48. La Belle Que Voilà 51.
Papa, Mama, the Maid and I 54. The Case of Dr
Laurent 56. Les Misérables 58. Monsieur 64. Le
Jardinier d'Argenteuil 66, etc.

Le Fanu, J. Sheridan (1814–1873). Irish
novelist specializing in mystery and the occult.
His story *Carmilla*, about lesbian vampires, has
been filmed as *Blood and Roses* and *The
Vampire Lovers*; *Uncle Silas* was filmed in 1949.

Le Galienne, Eva (1899–). Distinguished
American stage actress.
□ Prince of Players 54. The Devil's Disciple 59.

Le Roy, Baby (1931–) (Le Roy Overacker).
American toddler who appeared to general
delight in comedies of the early thirties. The story
goes that W. C. Fields once spiked his orange
juice with gin . . .
A Bedtime Story 33. Tillie and Gus 33. Miss
Fane's Baby is Stolen 33. The Old Fashioned
Way 34. The Lemon Drop Kid 34. It's a Gift 35,
etc.

Le Roy, Mervyn (1900–). American director,
former actor, in Hollywood from 1924.
Autobiography 1975: *Take One*.
Hot Stuff 27. Top Speed 28. Broken Dishes 29.
Little Caesar 30. Broadminded 31. *Five Star
Final* 32. Three on a Match 32. *I Am a Fugitive
from a Chain Gang* 32. Two Seconds 32.
Tugboat Annie 32. Gold Diggers of 1933. Hi
Nellie 33. Oil for the Lamps of China 33. Hot to
Handle 33. Sweet Adeline 34. Page Miss Glory
34. I Found Stella Parish 35. Anthony Adverse
36. Three Men on a Horse 36. *They Won't
Forget* 37. Fools for Scandal 38. Stand Up and
Fight (p only) 38. The Wizard of Oz (p only) 39.
At the Circus (p only) 39. *Waterloo Bridge* 40.
Escape 40. Blossoms in the Dust 41. Unholy
Partners 41. Johnny Eager 41. *Random Harvest*
42. Madame Curie 43. Thirty Seconds over
Tokyo 44; war service; Without Reservations
47. Homecoming 48. Little Women 49. Any
Number Can Play 49. East Side West Side 50.
Quo Vadis 51. Lovely To Look At 52. Million
Dollar Mermaid 53. Rose Marie 54. Mister
Roberts (co-d) 55. Strange Lady in Town (& p)
55. The Bad Seed (& p) 56. Toward the
Unknown (& p) 56. No Time for Sergeants (& p)
58. Home Before Dark (& p) 59. The FBI Story
(& p) 59. A Majority of One (& p) 60. The Devil

at Four O'Clock 61. Gypsy (& p) 62. Mary
Mary (& p) 63. Moment to Moment (& p) 65,
etc.

Leachman, Cloris (1926–). American
character actress, mostly on TV.
Kiss Me Deadly 54. The Rack 56. The Chapman
Report 62. Butch Cassidy and the Sundance Kid
69. *The Last Picture Show* (AA) 71. Haunts of
the Very Rich (TV) 72. Dillinger 73. Charley and
the Angel 74. Daisy Miller 74. Hitch Hike (TV)
74. Crazy Mama 75. A Girl Named Sooner (TV)
75. Death Sentence (TV) 75, etc.
TV series: Lassie (in fifties). The Mary Tyler
Moore Show 70–73. *Phyllis* 74– .

Leacock, Philip (1917–). British director,
noted for his way with children; lost to American
television.
□ *The Brave Don't Cry* 52. Appointment in
London 52. *The Kidnappers* 53. Escapade 55.
The Spanish Gardener 56. High Tide at Noon
57. Innocent Sinners 58. The Rabbit Trap 58.
Let No Man Write My Epitaph 59. Hand in
Hand 60. Take a Giant Step 61. Reach for Glory
61. 13 West Street 62. The War Lover 63.
Tamahine 63. Adam's Woman 70. The Birdmen
(TV) 71. The Great Man's Whiskers (TV) 72.
When Michael Calls (TV) 72. Key West (TV) 72.
The Daughters of Joshua Cabe (TV) 72. Baffled
(TV) 72.

Leacock, Richard (1921–). British-born
cameraman and director, brother of Philip
Leacock. Worked with Flaherty and became
associated with the 'cinema vérité' school.
Primary 60. The Chair 62. Quints 63. Chiefs 68,
etc.

leader. Length of blank film joined to the
beginning of a reel for lacing up in projector.
'Academy' leaders give a numbered countdown
to the start of action.

Lean, David (1908–). Distinguished British
director, former editor, in films from 1928.
□ In Which We Serve (co-d) 42. This Happy
Breed 44. *Blithe Spirit* 45. *Brief Encounter* 46.
Great Expectations 46. *Oliver Twist* 48. The
Passionate Friends 48. Madeleine 49. *The Sound
Barrier* (& p) 51. *Hobson's Choice* (& p) 54.
Summer Madness 55. *The Bridge on the River
Kwai* (AA) 57. *Lawrence of Arabia* (AA) 62. *Dr
Zhivago* 65. *Ryan's Daughter* 70.

Lear, Norman (1926–). American producer.
Divorce American Style 67. The Night They
Raided Minsky's 68. Start The Revolution
Without Me 69, etc.

TV series: *All in the Family* 70. *Maude* 72, many others.

Leaves from Satan's Book (Denmark 1921). A compendium of stories illustrating the work of the devil through the ages; written and directed by Carl Dreyer.

Leavitt, Sam (1917–). American cinematographer.
The Thief 52. *A Star is Born* 54. Carmen Jones 54. The Man with the Golden Arm 55. *The Defiant Ones* 58. Anatomy of a Murder 59. Exodus 60. Advise and Consent 62. Two on a Guillotine 64. Major Dundee 65. Brainstorm 65. An American Dream 66. Guess Who's Coming to Dinner 67. The Desperados 68. The Grasshopper 70. Star Spangled Girl 71. The Man in the Glass Booth 75, etc.

Lebedeff, Ivan (1899–1953). Russian character actor, former diplomat, in US from 1925.
The Sorrows of Satan 27. Midnight Mystery 30. Blonde Bombshell 33. China Seas 35. History Is Made at Night 37. Hotel for Women 39. The Shanghai Gesture 41. They Are Guilty 45. The Snows of Kilimanjaro 52, many others.

Leclerc, Ginette (1912–). Sulky-looking French stage and screen actress.
Prison sans Barreaux 38. *La Femme du Boulanger* 38. *Le Corbeau* 43. Le Plaisir 51. Les Amants du Tage 54. Gas-Oil 55. Le Cave Se Rebiffe 61. Goto, Island of Love 68. Tropic of Cancer 69.

Leaud, Jean-Pierre (1944–). French leading actor who began as a boy star.
Les Quatre Cents Coups 59. Love at Twenty 61. Masculin-Feminin 66. La Chinoise 67. Stolen Kisses 68. Pigsty 69. Last Tango in Paris 62. Day for Night 73, etc.

Ledebur, Friedrich (–). Austrian actor of eccentric roles.
Moby Dick 56. The Blue Max 66. Alfred the Great 69. Juliet of the Spirits 69, etc.

Lederer, Charles (1911–1976). American screenwriter, in Hollywood since 1931.
The Front Page 31. Topaze 33. Comrade X 40. His Girl Friday 40. Ride the Pink Horse 47. *Kiss of Death* 48. The Thing 52. It Started with a Kiss 58. The Spirit of St Louis 58. Can Can 59. Ocean's Eleven 61. Mutiny on the Bounty 62, many others.
AS DIRECTOR : Fingers at the Window 42. On the Loose 51. Never Steal Anything Small (& w) 58, etc.

Lederer, Francis (1906–). Czech-born leading man, in Hollywood from 1933, after European stage and film experience.
Pandora's Box (Ger.) 28. Atlantic (Ger.) 30. The Bracelet (Ger.) 32. The Pursuit of Happiness 34. It's All Yours 36. The Lone Wolf in Paris 37. Midnight 38. *Confessions of a Nazi Spy* 39. The Man I Married 40. The Bridge of San Luis Rey 44. A Voice in the Wind 45. The Diary of a Chambermaid 45. Million Dollar Weekend 48. Captain Carey USA 49. A Woman of Distinction 50. Stolen Identity 53. Lisbon 56. The Return of Dracula 58. Terror Is a Man 59, etc.

Lederman, D. Ross (1895–1972). American director, former prop man for Mack Sennett.
Man Hunter 30. Riding Tornado 32. Glamour for Sale 40. The Body Disappears 41. Strange Alibi 41. Shadows on the Stairs 43. Key Witness 47, etc.

Lee, Anna (1914–) (Joanna Winnifrith). British leading lady, in US since 1939.
Ebb Tide 32. The Camels Are Coming 36. King Solomon's Mines 37. The Four Just Men 39. My Life with Caroline 41. Summer Storm 44. Fort Apache 48. Whatever Happened to Baby Jane? 62. The Sound of Music 65. Seven Women 65. In Like Flint 67, many others.

Lee, Belinda (1935–1961). Blonde British starlet trained for stardom by Rank but given poor material: appeared in continental semi-spectaculars and died in car crash.
The Runaway Bus 54. The Belles of St Trinian's 54. Man of the Moment 55. Who Done It? 55. The Feminine Touch 56. The Secret Place 56. The Big Money 56. Miracle in Soho 57. Dangerous Exile 57. Nor the Moon by Night 58. Les Drageurs 59. Nights of Lucretia Borgia 59. Carthage in Flames 61, etc.

Lee, Bernard (1908–). British character actor with solid, friendly personality, on stage from 1926. In films, often a sergeant or a superintendent ... or 'M' in the James Bond films.
The River House Mystery 35. The Terror 37. Spare a Copper 40. Once a Crook 41; war service; The Courtneys of Curzon Street 47. *The Fallen Idol* 48. Quartet 48. *The Third Man* 49. The Blue Lamp 50. Appointment with Venus 51. The Gift Horse 52. The Purple Plain 54. *Father Brown* 54. The Battle of the River Plate 56. Dunkirk 58. Danger Within 59. The Angry Silence 59. The Secret Partner 60. Whistle Down

the Wind 61. *Dr No* 62. Two Left Feet 63. From Russia with Love 63. Ring of Spies 63. Goldfinger 64. The Legend of Young Dick Turpin 65. Thunderball 65. The Spy Who Came In from the Cold 65. You Only Live Twice 66. The Raging Moon 70. Dulcima 71. Frankenstein and the Monster from Hell 73. The Man with the Golden Gun 74. The Spy who Loved Me, many others.

Lee, Billy (1930–). American child star of the thirties.
Wagon Wheels 34. Coconut Grove 38. The Biscuit Eater 40. Hold Back the Dawn 41. Mrs Wiggs of the Cabbage Patch 42, etc.

Lee, Bruce (1940–1973). Diminutive Chinese-American leading man and practitioner of the martial arts.
After comparative failure in Hollywood (a bit part in *Marlowe* 69, a supporting role in a TV series *The Green Hornet* 68) he went to Hong Kong and became a sensation in ' chop socky ' movies.
Fist of Fury 72. The Big Boss 72. Enter The Dragon 73. The Way of the Dragon 73, etc.

Lee, Canada (1907–1952). (Lionel Canegata). Black American actor.
□ Lifeboat 43. Body and Soul 47. Lost Boundaries 49. Cry the Beloved Country 52.

Lee, Christopher (1922–). Gaunt British actor whose personality lends itself best to sinister or horrific parts. Seems to have made more films than any other living actor, and has certainly played most of the known monsters.
Corridor of Mirrors 47. Hamlet 48. They Were Not Divided 49. Prelude to Fame 50. Valley of Eagles 51. The Crimson Pirate 52. Moulin Rouge 53. The Dark Avenger 54. Private's Progress 55. Alias John Preston 56. Moby Dick 56. Ill Met by Moonlight 57. *The Curse of Frankenstein* (as the monster) 56. The Traitor 57. A Tale of Two Cities 57. *Dracula* (title role) 58. Corridors of Blood 58. The Hound of the Baskervilles (as Sir Henry) 59. The Man Who Could Cheat Death 59. *The Mummy* (title role) 59. Beat Girl 60. City of the Dead 60. The Hands of Orlac 60. Taste of Fear 61. The Terror of the Tongs 61. The Devil's Daffodil 62. Pirates of Blood River 62. Sherlock Holmes and the Deadly Necklace (Ger.) 62. The Gorgon 63. Dr Terror's House of Horrors 63. She 65. The Face of Fu Manchu 65. The Skull 65. Dracula Prince of Darkness 65. Rasputin the Mad Monk 65. Theatre of Death 66. Night of the Big Heat 67. The Devil Rides Out 68. Curse of the Crimson Altar 68. Julius Caesar 70. I Monster 71.

Dracula AD 1972 72. The Wicker Man 73. The Satanic Rites of Dracula 73. The Three Musketeers 74. The Man with the Golden Gun 74. Dragnoi's Murder 75. To the Devil a Daughter 75. Killer Force 75. Airport 77 77, etc.

Lee, Davey (1925–). American child actor of the early talkies.
The Singing Fool 28. Sonny Boy 29. The Squealer 30, etc.

Lee, Dixie (1911–1952) (Wilma Wyatt). American leading lady, former wife of Bing Crosby.
Not for Sale 24. Movietone Follies 29. The Big Party 30. No Limit 31. Manhattan Love Song 34. Love in Bloom 35, etc.

Lee, Dorothy (1911–). American leading lady of the thirties, especially associated with Wheeler and Wolsey.
Syncopation 29. Rio Rita 29. The Cuckoos 30. Half Shot at Sunrise 30. Cracked Nuts 31. Caught Plastered 31. Girl Crazy 32. Take a Chance 33. Hips, Hips Hooray 34. The Rainmakers 35. Silly Billies 36. Twelve Crowded Hours 39, etc.

Lee, Gypsy Rose (1913–1970) (Louise Hovick). American burlesque artiste, on stage from six years old: her early life, glamorized, is recounted in *Gypsy* 62.
□ You Can't Have Everything 37. Ali Baba Goes to Town 38. My Lucky Star 39. Belle of the Yukon 44. Babes in Baghdad 52. Screaming Mimi 57. Wind Across the Everglades 58. The Stripper 62. The Trouble with Angels 66.

Lee, Jack (1913–). British director, originally in documentaries.
Close Quarters 44. Children on Trial 46. The Woman in the Hall 47. *The Wooden Horse* (co-d) 50. Turn the Key Softly 53. *A Town Like Alice* 56. Robbery under Arms 57. The Captain's Table 58. Circle of Deception 61, etc.

Lee, Lila (1902–1973) (Augusta Apple). Demure American leading lady of the twenties.
The Cruise of the Make Believes 18. Male and Female 19. Terror Island 20. Blood and Sand 22. Million Dollar Mystery 25. Queen of the Night Clubs 29, etc.

Lee, Michele (1942–) (Michele Dusiak). American leading lady and singer, with stage experience.
How to Succeed in Business 67. The Love Bug 69. The Comic 69.

Lee, Peggy (1920–) (Norma Egstrom). American night-club singer, in occasional films. Mr Music 50. The Jazz Singer 53. Pete Kelly's Blues 55. Lady and the Tramp (voice only) 56, etc.

Lee, Rowland V. (1891–1975). American director, in films from 1918.
Alice Adams 26. Barbed Wire 26. The Mysterious Dr Fu Manchu 29. *Zoo in Budapest* 33. *The Count of Monte Cristo* 34. Cardinal Richelieu 35. The Three Musketeers 36. Service de Luxe 38. *Son of Frankenstein* 39. Tower of London 39. Son of Monte Cristo 41. The Bridge of San Luis Rey 44. Captain Kidd 45. The Big Fisherman (p only) 59, etc.

Lee-Thompson, J. (1914–). British director, former actor and playwright.
□ The Middle Watch (w) 36. For Them That Trespass (w) 48. Murder without Crime (wd) 50. *The Yellow Balloon* (wd) 52. The Weak and the Wicked (wd) 53. As Long As They're Happy (d) 54. For Better For Worse (d) 54. An Alligator Named Daisy (d) 55. Yield to the Night (d) 56. The Good Companions (co-pd) 57. Woman in a Dressing Gown (d) 59. Tiger Bay (d) 59. Northwest Frontier (d) 59. I Aim at the Stars (d) (US) 60. *The Guns of Navarone* (d) 61. Cape Fear (d) (US) 61. Taras Bulba (d) (US) 62. Kings of the Sun (d) (US) 63. What a Way To Go (d) (US) 64. John Goldfarb Please Come Home (d) (US) 65. Return from the Ashes (pd) 65. Eye of the Devil (d) 66. Mackenna's Gold (d) (US) 68. Before Winter Comes (d) 68. The Chairman (d) 69. Country Dance (d) 70. Conquest of The Planet of the Apes (d) (US) 72. Huckleberry Finn (d) (US) 74. The Reincarnation of Peter Proud (d) (US) 74. The White Buffalo (d) (US) 77.

Leech, Richard (1922–). British character actor, often as army or air force officer.
The Dam Busters 55. A Night to Remember 57. The Good Companions 57. Ice Cold in Alex 59. The Horse's Mouth 59. Tunes of Glory 60. The Wild and the Willing 62. I Thank a Fool 63. The Fighting Price of Donegal 66, etc.

Leeds, Andrea (1914–) (Antoinette Lees). American leading lady of the late thirties.
Come and Get It 36. *Stage Door* 37. The Goldwyn Follies 39. Letter of Introduction 39. Swanee River 39, etc.

Leeds, Herbert I. (c. 1900–1954) (Herbert I. Levy). American director of second features, former editor.
Mr Moto in Danger Island 38. Island in the Sky 38. The Cisco Kid and the Lady 39. Manila Calling 42. *Time to Kill* 43. It Shouldn't Happen to a Dog 46. Let's Live Again 48. Father's Wild Game 51, etc.

Legg, Stuart (1910–). British documentarist and administrator. From 1932 with GPO Film Unit and Empire Marketing Board. 1939–45: National Film Board of Canada. 1953 on: director of Film Centre Ltd.

Leggatt, Alison (1904–). British character actress, mainly on stage.
This Happy Breed 44. Marry Me 47. The Card 52. Touch and Go 55. Never Take Sweets from a Stranger 60, etc.

Legrand, Michel (1931–). French composer.
Lola 61. Eva 62. Vivre sa Vie 62. La Baie des Anges 63. *The Umbrellas of Cherbourg* 64. Bande à Part 64. Une Femme Mariée 65. Les Demoiselles de Rochefort 67. Ice Station Zebra 68. Peau d'Ane 70. *Summer of 42* (AA) 71. A Time for Loving (& a) 71. One is a Lonely Number 72. Portnoy's Complaint 72. Cops and Robbers 73. The Three Musketeers 74, etc.

Lehman, Ernest (c. 1920–). American screenwriter.
Inside Story 48. Executive Suite 54. Sabrina 54. *The Sweet Smell of Success* 57. North by Northwest 59. *The Prize* 63. The Sound of Music 65. Who's Afraid of Virginia Woolf? (& p) 66. Hello Dolly (& p) 69. Portnoy's Complaint (& pd) 72. Family Plot 76, etc.

Lehmann, Beatrix (1898–). British character actress, often of withdrawn eccentrics; film appearances few.
The Passing of the Third Floor Back 36. Black Limelight 38. The Rat 38. The Key 58. Psyche 59 64. The Spy who Came in from the Cold 66. Staircase 69, etc.

Lehmann, Carla (1917–). Canadian leading lady, in British films of the forties.
So This Is London 39. Cottage to Let 41. Talk About Jacqueline 42. Candlelight in Algeria 44. 29 Acacia Avenue 45. Fame Is the Spur 47, etc.

Leiber, Fritz (1883–1949). American Shakespearean actor who played many supporting roles in films.
A Tale of Two Cities 35. Anthony Adverse 36. The Hunchback of Notre Dame 40. Phantom of the Opera 43. Humoresque 46. Another Part of the Forest 48, etc.

Leibman, Ron (1937–). American character actor of the seventies.

The Hot Rock 72. Slaughterhouse Five 72. The Super Cops 73. Your Three Minutes Are Up 74. Won Ton Ton 76, etc.

Leigh, Janet (1927–) (Jeanette Morrison). Capable American leading lady of the fifties and sixties; began as a peaches-and-cream heroine but graduated to sharper roles.
□ The Romance of Rosy Ridge 47. If Winter Comes 47. Hills of Home 47. Words and Music 48. Act of Violence 48. Little Women 49. *That Forsyte Woman* 49. The Doctor and the Girl 49. The Red Danube 49. Holiday Affair 49. Strictly Dishonourable 51. Angels in the Outfield 51. Two Tickets to Broadway 51. It's a Big Country 51. Just this Once 52. Scaramouche 52. Fearless Fagan 52. The Naked Spur 53. Confidentially Connie 53. *Houdini* 53. Walking My Baby Back Home 54. Prince Valiant 54. Living it Up 54. The Black Shield of Falworth 54. Rogue Cop 54. Pete Kelly's Blues 55. *My Sister Eileen* 55. Safari (GB) 56. Jet Pilot 57. Touch of Evil 58. The Vikings 58. The Perfect Furlough 58. Who was that Lady? 60. *Psycho* 60. Pepe 60. The Manchurian Candidate 62. Bye Bye Birdie 62. Wives and Lovers 63. Three on a Couch 66. Harper 66. Kid Rodelo 66. An American Dream 66. Hello Down There 68. Grand Slam 68. The House on Greenapple Road (TV) 70. The Monk (TV) 70. One is a Lonely Number 72. Night of the Lepus 74.

Leigh, Suzanna (1945–). British leading lady. Boeing Boeing 66. Paradise Hawaiian Style 66. Deadlier Than the Male 67. Lost Continent 68. Lust for a Vampire 70. The Fiend 71, etc.

Leigh, Vivien (1913–1967) (Vivien Hartley). Distinguished British leading lady whose stage and screen career was limited by delicate health; for many years the wife of Laurence Olivier.
Biography 1973: *Light of a Star* by Gwen Robyns.
□ Things Are Looking Up 34. The Village Squire 35. Gentleman's Agreement 35. Look Up and Laugh 35. Fire Over England 36. *Dark Journey* 37. Storm in a Teacup 37. St Martin's Lane 38. Twenty-One Days 38. *A Yank at Oxford* 38. *Gone with the Wind* (AA: as Scarlett O'Hara) (US) 39. Waterloo Bridge (US) 40. *Lady Hamilton* (US) 41. *Caesar and Cleopatra* 45. Anna Karenina 48. *A Streetcar Named Desire* (AA) (US) 51. The Deep Blue Sea 55. The Roman Spring of Mrs Stone 61. Ship of Fools (US) 65.

Leigh-Hunt Barbara (1941–). British character actress.
Frenzy 72. Henry VIII and his Six Wives 72. A Bequest to the Nation 73, etc.

Leigh-Hunt, Ronald (c. 1916–) Smooth British supporting actor.
Tiger by the Tail 53. Shadow of a Man 55. A Touch of Larceny 59. Sink the Bismarck 60. Piccadilly Third Stop 61. The Truth About Spring 65. Hostile Witness 67. Le Mans 71, many others.

Leighton, Margaret (1922–1976). British leading actress on stage from 1938.
Bonnie Prince Charlie 48. Under Capricorn 49. The Astonished Heart 50. The Holly and the Ivy 54. The Constant Husband 55. *The Sound and the Fury* 58. The Waltz of the Toreadors 61. The Best Man 64. Seven Women 65. The Go-Between 70. Zee & Co. 71. Lady Caroline Lamb 72. A Bequest to the Nation 73. Frankenstein: The True Story (TV) 73. Great Expectations 75, etc.

Leisen, Mitchell (1898–1972). American director, former set designer; his films are mostly romantic trifles, but many have considerable pictorial style.
Biography 1972: *Hollywood Director* by David Chierichelti.
□ *Cradle Song* 33. *Death Takes a Holiday* 34. Murder at the Vanities 34. Behold My Wife 35. Four Hours to Kill 35. Hands across the Table 35. Thirteen Hours by Air 36. The Big Broadcast of 1937 36. Swing High Swing Low 37. *Easy Living* 37. The Big Broadcast of 1938 37. Artists and Models Abroad 38. *Midnight* 39. Remember the Night 40. *Arise My Love* 40. I Wanted Wings 41. *Hold Back the Dawn* 41. The Lady Is Willing 42. Take a Letter Darling 42. No Time for Love (& p) 43. *Lady in the Dark* (also w) 44. *Frenchman's Creek* 44. Practically Yours (& p) 44. *Kitty* 45. Masquerade in Mexico 45. To Each His Own 46. Suddenly It's Spring 46. Golden Earrings 47. Dream Girl 48. Bride of Vengeance 49. Song of Surrender 49. Captain Carey USA 50. No Man of Her Own (& w) 50. The Mating Season (51). Darling How Could You? 51. Young Man with Ideas 52. Tonight We Sing 53. Bedevilled 55. The Girl Most Likely 57.

Leiser, Erwin (1923–). Swedish documentarist.
Mein Kampf (Blodige Tiden) 59. Murder by Signature (Eichmann and the Third Reich) 61, etc.

Leister, Frederick (1885–). British character actor, on stage from 1906, screen from twenties. Usually played distinguished and kindly professional men.

Dreyfus 30. The Iron Duke 35. Goodbye Mr Chips 39. The Prime Minister 41. *Dear Octopus* 43. *The Hundred Pound Window* 43. The Captive Heart 46. Quartet 48. The End of the Affair 54. Left, Right and Centre 59. A French Mistress 63, many others.

Leith, Virginia (1932–). American leading lady of the fifties.
Black Widow 54. Violent Saturday 55. White Feather 55. A Kiss Before Dying 56. On the Threshold of Space 56. The Beast that Wouldn't Die 63, etc.

Lelouch, Claude (1937–). French director with lush visual style; internationally fashionable in the mid-sixties, but overreached himself.
□ Le Propre de l'Homme 60. Une Fille et des Fusils 63. Avec des Si 64. Secret Paris 64. *Un Homme et Une Femme* 66.*Vivre Pour Vivre* 67. Challenge in the Snow 68. Far from Vietnam 69. A Man I Like 69. Life Love Death 69. Le Rose et le Noir 70. The Crook 71. Smic, Smac, Smoc 71. Simon the Swiss 71. Adventure is Adventure 72. *La Bonne Année* 73. And Now My Love 75.

Le May, Alan (1899–). American writer.
Reap the Wild Wind 42. The Adventures of Mark Twain 44. Tap Roots 48. High Lonesome (& d) 50. Thunder in the Dust 51. I Dream of Jeannie 53. The Searchers (oa) 56, etc.

Lembeck, Harvey (1925–). American character actor.
The Frogmen 51. You're In the Navy Now 53. Back at the Front 53. Stalag 17 54. Life after Dark 55. Sail a Crooked Ship 62. Bikini Beach 65, etc.

Le Mesurier, John (1912–). British character actor. Usually plays bewildered professional men; a favourite for cameo roles since 1946.
Death in the Hand 48. Beautiful Stranger 54. Private's Progress 55. *Happy Is the Bride* 57. I Was Monty's Double 58. *School for Scoundrels* 60. *Only Two Can Play* 61. Invasion Quartet 62. The Pink Panther 63. The Moonspinners 64. Masquerade 65. Where the Spies Are 65. The Wrong Box 66. The Midas Run 69. *The Magic Christian* 70. Dad's Army 71. The Garnett Saga 72. Confessions of a Window Cleaner 75. Stand Up Virgin Soldiers 77, many others.
TV series: *Dad's Army* 68-77.

Lemmon, Jack (1925–). American light comedy leading actor with Broadway experience: sometimes typed in mildly lecherous or otherwise sex-fraught roles.

Biography 1975: *Lemmon* by Don Widener.
□ *It Should Happen to You* 53. Three for the Show 53. Phffft 54. My Sister Eileen 55. *Mister Roberts* (AA) 55. You Can't Run Away From It 56. Cowboy 57. Fire Down Below 57. Operation Mad Ball 57. Bell, Book and Candle 58. It Happened to Jane 58. *Some Like It Hot* 59. The Wackiest Ship in the Army 60. *The Apartment* 60. The Notorious Landlady 62. Days of Wine and Roses 62. *Irma La Douce* 63. Under the Yum Yum Tree 64. Good Neighbour Sam 64. How to Murder Your Wife 65. *The Great Race* 65. The Fortune Cookie 66. Luv 67. *The Odd Couple* 68. The April Fools 69. The Out-of-Towners 69. *Kotch* (d only) 71. The War Between Men and Women 72. Avanti 72. Save the Tiger (AA) 73. The Front Page 74. The Prisoner of Second Avenue 75. The Entertainer 75. Alex and the Gypsy 76. Airport 77 77.

Leni, Paul (1885–1929). German director, former set designer; died in Hollywood.
Waxworks 24. *The Rat and the Canary* 27. The Man Who Laughs 28. The Chinese Parrot 28. The Last Warning 29, etc.

Lenica, Jan (1928–). Polish animator.
Dom 58. Monsieur Tete 59. Janko the Musician 60. Rhinosceros 63. A 64, etc.

Lenin (1870–1924) (Vladimir Ilyich Ulyanov). Russian statesman, the power behind the revolution. Little footage of him exists, but he has been played by various actors in such politically-based semi-fictions as *Lenin in October*, *Lenin in 1918* and *Lenin in Poland*.

Lennart, Isabel (1915–1971). American screenwriter.
Lost Angel 44. Anchors Aweigh 45. East Side West Side 49. Skirts Ahoy 52. Latin Lovers 54. Inn of the Sixth Happiness 58. The Sundowners 60. Period of Adjustment 62. Funny Girl 68, many others.

Lenya, Lotte (1900–) (Caroline Blamauer). Austrian character actress; also inimitable singer of her late husband Kurt Weill's songs.
Die Dreigroschenoper 31. The Roman Spring of Mrs Stone 61. *From Russia with Love* 63. The Appointment 69, etc.

Lenz, Kay (1953–). American leading lady of the seventies.
Breezy 73. Lisa Bright and Dark (TV) 73. White Line Fever 75. The Great Scout and Cathouse Thursday 76, etc.

Lenz, Rick (1939–). American actor.
Cactus Flower 70. Where Does It Hurt? 72.

Leonard, Herbert B. (1922–). American independent TV producer best known series include *Rin Tin Tin, Circus Boy, Naked City, Route 66*.

Leonard, Robert Z. (1889–1968). American director (former actor), in Hollywood from 1915. Showed care but not much imagination.
The Waning Sex 27. The Demi-Bride 27. Adam and Evil 28. Tea for Three 29. Susan Lenox 31. *Strange Interval* 32. *Dancing Lady* 33. Peg O' My Heart 33. Outcast Lady 34. *The Great Ziegfeld* 36. Piccadilly Jim 37. Escapade 37. *Maytime* 38. The Firefly 38. New Moon (& p) 40. *Pride and Prejudice* 40. Ziegfeld Girl 41. When Ladies Meet (& p) 41. We Were Dancing 42. Stand By for Action 42. The Man from Down Under 43. Marriage Is a Private Affair 44. Weekend at the Waldorf 45. The Secret Heart 46. B.F.'s Daughter 48. The Bride 48. In the Good Old Summertime 49. Nancy Goes to Rio 49. Duchess of Idaho 50. Everything I Have Is Yours 52. The Clown 53. The King's Thief 55. Kelly and Me 56. Beautiful But Dangerous (It.) 56, others.

Leonard, Sheldon (1907–) (Sheldon Bershad). American character actor who played Runyonesque gangsters for years; finally quit to produce TV series.
Another Thin Man 39. Buy Me that Town 41. Street of Chance 42. *Lucky Jordan* 42. To Have and Have Not 44. Zombies on Broadway 45. Somewhere in the Night 46. Violence 47. The Gangster 47. Take One False Step 49. Behave Yourself 51. *Stop You're Killing Me* 52. Money from Home 54. Guys and Dolls 55. Pocketful of Miracles 61, many others.

Leone, Sergio (1921–). Italian director who came to the fore internationally via his savage westerns on the American pattern.
The Colossus of Rhodes 61. *A Fistful of Dollars* 64. For a Few Dollars More 65. The Good The Bad and The Ugly 67. Once Upon a Time in the West 69. A Fistful of Dynamite 72, etc.

Leontovich, Eugenie (1894–). Russian stage actress in American.
Four Sons 40. The Men in Her Life 41. Anything Can Happen 52. The World in His Arms 53. Homicidal 61, etc.

The Leopard (Italy 1963). An ambitious production based on Lampedusa's complex historical novel about Italian politics and noble life at the time of Garibaldi. Burt Lancaster made a somewhat unconvincing Italian nobleman, and the film in its international version was not popular; but Luchino Visconti's direction and Giuseppe Rotunno's cinematography were praised.

leprechauns have made rare but effective screen appearances in the persons of Cecil Kellaway (*Luck of the Irish*), Jimmy O'Dea (*Darby O'Gill and the Little People*), Don Beddoe (*Jack the Giant Killer*) and Tommy Steele (*Finian's Rainbow*).

Lerner, Alan Jay (1918–). American composer and writer.
An American in Paris (w) (AA) 51. Gigi (score) (AA) 58. My Fair Lady (script and score in collaboration) (AA) 64. Camelot (script and score in collaboration) 67. On a Clear Day You Can See Forever (& p) 70. The Little Prince 74, others.

Lerner, Irving (1909–1977). American director, former cameraman and documentarist.
□ Man Crazy 54. Edge of Fury 58. *Murder by Contract* 58. City of Fear 59. Studs Lonigan 60. Cry of Battle 63. The Royal Hunt of the Sun 69.

Les Misérables. Film versions of Victor Hugo's classic novel about escaped convict Jean Valjean were made in 1909 (US), 1913 (France), 1918 (US), 1922 (GB), 1925 (France), 1934 (France), 1935 (US, with Fredric March and Charles Laughton); 1946 (Italy); 1952 (US, with Michael Rennie and Robert Newton) and 1957 (France, with Jean Gabin and Bernard Blier). The recent TV series, *The Fugitive* and *Kung Fu*, acknowledge their indebtedness to the theme.

lesbianism has now come into its own with the filming of *The Killing of Sister George*; but for many years it was unthinkable as a screen subject. *These Three* in 1936 had to be so changed that it was almost unrecognizable as a version of *The Children's Hour*; and the matter was scarcely broached again until the fifties, when the French brought it up in *Olivia* and *The Girl with the Golden Eyes*. The first Hollywood film to bring the subject to our notice was *A Walk on the Wild Side* 62; since then there have been more or less discreet references in *The Haunting, The Balcony, Lilith, The Silence, Alyse and Chloe, The Vampire Lovers, Beyond the Valley of the Dolls, La Religieuse, The Group, Tony Rome, The Fox, Therese and Isabelle, Baby Love, The Smashing Bird I Used to Know,* and *Once Is Not Enough*; while *The Children's Hour* was filmed again, this time with its full force.

Lesley, Carole (1935–1974) (Maureen

Rippingdale). British leading lady briefly groomed for stardom.
Those Dangerous Years 57. Woman in a Dressing-Gown 57. No Trees in the Street 59. Doctor in Love 60. What a Whopper 62. The Pot Carriers 62, etc.

Leslie, Bethel (1930–). American leading actress, mainly on TV.
The Rabbit Trap 58. Captain Newman 63. A Rage to Live 65. The Molly Maguires 69, etc.

Leslie, Joan (1925–) (Joan Brodell). Pert, pretty American leading lady of the forties; in vaudeville from childhood.
Camille (debut) 36. Men with Wings 38. Foreign Correspondent 40. High Sierra 41. *Sergeant York* 41. The Male Animal 42. Yankee Doodle Dandy 42. The Hard Way 42. This Is the Army 43. Thank Your Lucky Stars 43. Hollywood Canteen 44. *Rhapsody in Blue* 45. Where Do We Go From Here? 45. Too Young to Know 45. Cinderella Jones 46. Royal Flush 46. Repeat Performance 47. Northwest Stampede 49. Born To Be Bad 51. The Toughest Man in Arizona 52. The Woman They Almost Lynched 53. Jubilee Trail 54. The Revolt of Mamie Stover 57. The Keegans (TV) 76, etc.

Lesser, Sol (1890–). American pioneer exhibitor of silent days, later producer: many Tarzan films.
Thunder Over Mexico 33. Our Town 40. Kontiki 52, etc.

Lester, Bruce (1912–) (Bruce Lister). South African leading man who made some British and American films; now plays support roles.
Death at Broadcasting House 34. Crime over London 37. If I Were King 39. Pride and Prejudice 40. Above Suspicion 43. Golden Earrings 47. King Richard and the Crusaders 54, etc.

Lester, Dick or **Richard** (1932–). American director who found his spurt to fame in Britain doing zany comedies full of fast fragmented action. As soon as commercial backing was available his style went way over the top.
□ It's Trad Dad 61. The Mouse on the Moon 63. *A Hard Day's Night* 64, *The Knack* 65. Help 65. A Funny Thing Happened on the Way to the Forum 66. How I Won the War 67. Petulia 68. The Bed Sitting Room 69. The Three Musketeers 73. Juggernaut 74. The Four Musketeers 75. Royal Flash 75. Robin and Marian 76. The Ritz 76.

Lester, Mark (1958–). Innocent-looking

British child star of the sixties.
Allez France 64. Spaceflight IC–1 65. Our Mother's House 67. *Oliver* (title role) 68. Run Wild Run Free 69. Eye Witness 70 Melody 71. Black Beauty 71. Night Hair Child 71. Who Slew Auntie Roo? 72. Scalawag 73. Little Adventurer 75. The Prince and the Pauper 77, etc.

Letter from an Unknown Woman (US 1948). Out of Stefan Zweig's romantic novelette Max Ophuls fashioned a finely decorated though studio-bound piece of middle-European nostalgia; elegant, tragic and luxurious. With Joan Fontaine, Louis Jourdan.

letters have provided a starting point or climax for several films. Undelivered ones for *Address Unknown*, *The Postman Didn't Ring*; misdelivered ones for *Dear Ruth*, *The Go-Between*, *A Letter for Evie*; an incriminating one in *Suspicion*; lost ones for *Cause for Alarm*, *Never Put It In Writing*; indiscreet ones for *A Letter To Three Wives*, *So Evil My Love*, *The Last of Mrs Cheyney*, *The Letter*; posthumous ones for *Letter from an Unknown Woman*, *Love Letters*, *The Lost Moment*, *Mister Roberts*.

Lettieri, Al (1927–1975). American actor.
The Bobo 68. The Godfather 72. Getaway 73. Mr Majestyk 74. Deadly Trackers 75, etc.

Levant, Oscar (1906–1972). American pianist and master of insult who appeared in several films as his grouchy, neurotic self.
Autobiographical books: *A Smattering of Ignorance* 1944. *Memoirs of an Amnesiac* 1965. *The Unimportance of Being Oscar* 68.
□ The Dance of Life 29. Rhythm on the River 40. Kiss the Boys Goodbye 41. *Rhapsody in Blue* 45. Humoresque 46. You Were Meant for Me 47. Romance on the High Seas 48. The Barkleys of Broadway 49. *An American in Paris* 51. *The Band Wagon* 53. The I Don't Care Girl 53. The Cobweb 55.

Leven, Boris (c. 1900–). Russian-born production designer, long in US.
Alexander's Ragtime Band 38. *The Shanghai Gesture* 41. Mr Peabody and the Mermaid 48. Sudden Fear 52. *Giant* 56. Anatomy of a Murder 59. *West Side Story* (AA) 61. The Sound of Music 65. The Sand Pebbles 67. Star! 68. The Andromeda Strain 70. Jonathan Livingston Seagull 73. Mandingo 75. New York, New York 77, many others.

Levene, Sam (1905–). American stage actor, often in Runyonesque film roles.
Three Men on a Horse (debut) 36. Golden Boy

39. The Purple Heart 44. *Crossfire* 47. Boomerang 47. Guilty Bystander 50. Three Sailors and a Girl 53. Sweet Smell of Success 57. Act One 63. A Dream of Kings 69. Such Good Friends 71, etc.

LeVien, Jack (1918–). American documentarist responsible for several distinguished compilation films.
Black Fox 62. The Finest Hours 64. A King's Story 67.
TV series on Churchill: *The Valiant Years* 60.

Levien, Sonya (1888–1960). American writer, former lawyer. Story editor at various times for Fox, MGM, Paramount.
Cavalcade 33. *State Fair* 33. *Berkeley Square* 33. In Old Chicago 38. *The Hunchback of Notre Dame* 40. Ziegfeld Girl 41. Rhapsody in Blue 45. Cass Timberlane 48. Quo Vadis 51. *Interrupted Melody* (AA) 55. *Jeanne Eagels* 58, etc.

Levin, Henry (1909–). American director, in Hollywood from 1943 after stage experience.
Cry of the Werewolf 44. I Love a Mystery 45. The Guilt of Janet Ames 47. Jolson Sings Again 49. The Petty Girl 50. Convicted 50. Belles on Their Toes 52. The President's Lady 52. Mister Scoutmaster 53. Gambler from Natchez 54. The Mating of Millie 55. The Lonely Man 57. Bernardine 57. Let's Be Happy (GB) 57. The Remarkable Mr Pennypacker 58. Holidays for Lovers 59. *Journey to the Centre of the Earth* 59. Where the Boys Are 60. The Wonderful World of the Brothers Grimm 62. Come Fly with Me 63. Honeymoon Hotel 64. Genghis Khan 65. Kiss the Girls and Make Them Die 66. Murderers' Row 67. The Desperados 70. That Man Bolt 73, others.

Levine, Joseph E. (1905–). American production executive and showman, former theatre owner. Formed Embassy Pictures in late fifties, originally to exploit cheap European spectacles; also set up finance for films like *Eight and a Half, Divorce Italian Style, Boccaccio* 70.
AS PRODUCER: The Carpetbaggers 63. Where Love Has Gone 64. Harlow 65. A Bridge Too Far 77, etc.

Levy, Louis (1893–). British musical director and composer, in films since 1916. Scored *Nanook of the North* 20. With Gaumont and Gainsborough 1928–47, supervising all musical productions.
Pygmalion 38. The Citadel 38, many others.

Levy, Ralph (1919–). American director, in TV from 1947.

Bedtime Story 64. Do Not Disturb 65.

Levy, Raoul (1922–67). French producer.
Les Orgueilleux 53. And God Created Woman (& w) 56. Heaven Fell That Night 57. En Cas de Malheur 58. Babette Goes to War (& co-w) 59. Moderato Cantabile 60. The Truth 60. The Defector (& wd) 66, etc.

Lewin, Albert (1895–1968). American writer-producer-director with something of an Omar Khayyam fixation. Production executive 1931–41.
□ *The Moon and Sixpence* (wd) 42. *The Picture of Dorian Gray* (wd) 44. The Private Affairs of Bel Ami (wpd) 47. *Pandora and the Flying Dutchman* (wpd) 51. Saadia (wpd) 54. The Living Idol (wpd) 57.

Lewis, Fiona (1946–). British leading lady.
The Fearless Vampire Killers 67. Where's Jack? 69. Villain 71. Dracula (TV) 73. Lisztomania 75, etc.

Lewis, Herschell (1926–). American director of exploitation films.
The Living Venus 61. Goldilocks and the Three Bares 63. Blood Feast 63. Monster a Go Go 65. The Gruesome Twosome 67. A Taste of Blood 67. The Ecstasies of Women 69. The Wizard of Gore 70. Stick it in Your Ear 72, many others.

Lewis, Jay (1914–1969). British producer, in films from 1933.
Morning Departure 50. The Gift Horse 52, etc.
AS DIRECTOR: The Baby and the Battleship 55. Invasion Quartet 61. Live Now Pay Later 62. A Home of Your Own 65, etc.

Lewis, Jerry (1926–) (Joseph Levitch). Goonish American comedian whose style is a mixture of exaggerated mugging and sticky sentiment. Until 1958 he formed a popular partnership with Dean Martin, but his increasingly indulgent solo films since then have gradually reduced his once-fervent band of admirers.
□ *My Friend Irma* 49. My Friend Irma Goes West 50. At War with the Army 51. That's My Boy 51. Sailor Beware 52. Jumping Jacks 52. The Stooge 53. Scared Stiff 53. The Caddy 53. Money from Home 54. Living it Up 54. Three Ring Circus 54. You're Never Too Young 54. Artists and Models 55. Pardners 56. Hollywood or Bust 56. The Delicate Delinquent 57. The Sad Sack 58. Rock a Bye Baby 58. The Geisha Boy 58. Don't Give up the Ship 59. Visit to a Small Planet 60. *The Bellboy* 60. Cinderfella 60. Ladies' Man 61. The Errand Boy 61. It's Only

Money 62. The Nutty Professor 63. Who's Minding the Store? 64. The Patsy 64. The Disorderly Orderly 64. The Family Jewels 65. Boeing-Boeing 65. Three on a Couch 66. Way Way Out 66. The Big Mouth 67. Don't Raise the Bridge, Lower the River 68. Hook Line and Sinker 69. Which Way to the Front? 70. One More Time (d only) 71.

Lewis, Joe E. (1901–1971). American nightclub comedian. Only film, *Private Buckaroo* 42; but Frank Sinatra appeared as him in a biopic, *The Joker is Wild* 58.

Lewis, Joseph H. (1900–). American director, mainly of second features, some of them well above average.
Two-Fisted Rangers 40. The Mad Doctor of Market Street 41. Bombs over Burma 42. Minstrel Man 44. *My Name Is Julia Ross* 45. *So Dark the Night* 46. *The Jolson Story* (musical numbers only) 46. The Swordsman 47. The Return of October 48. *The Undercover Man* 49. A Lady without Passport 50. Gun Crazy 50. Retreat Hell 52. Cry of the Hunted 53. The Big Combo 55. A Lawless Street 55. Seventh Cavalry 56. The Halliday Brand 56. *Terror in a Texas Town* 58, etc.

Lewis, Michael J. (1939–). British composer.
The Madwoman of Chaillot 69. The Man Who Haunted Himself 70. Unman Wittering and Zigo 72. Theatre of Blood 73. 11 Harrowhouse 74. Russian Roulette 75, etc.

Lewis, Ronald (1928–). British leading man, in films from 1953.
The Prisoner 55. Storm over the Nile 55. A Hill in Korea 56. Bachelor of Hearts 59. The Full Treatment 61. Twice Round the Daffodils 62. Mr Sardonicus 63. The Brigand of Kandahar 65. Friends 71. Paul and Michelle 74, etc.

Lewis, Sheldon (1868–1958). American character actor of stage and screen.
The Exploits of Elaine 15. Dr Jekyll and Mr Hyde (title role) 16. Orphans of the Storm 21. The Red Kimono 26. Black Magic 29. The Monster Walks 32. The Cattle Thief (last film) 36, many others.

Lewis, Sinclair (1885–1951). American novelist.
Arrowsmith 32. Ann Vickers 33. Babbitt 34. Dodsworth 36. Untamed 40. Elmer Gantry 60.

Lewis, Ted (1889–1971) (Theodore Friedman). American bandleader and

entertainer ('Me and My Shadow') who appeared in a few movies.
□ Is Everybody Happy? 28. Show of Shows 29. Here Comes the Band 35. Manhattan Merry Go Round 37. Hold That Ghost 42. Follow the Boys 44.

Lewton, Val (1904–1951) (Vladimir Leventon). American producer, remembered for a group of low-budget, high quality horror films made for RKO in the forties.
Biography 1973: *The Reality of Terror* by Joel E. Siegel.
□ *Cat People* 42. I Walked with a Zombie 43. The Leopard Man 43. The Seventh Victim 43. The Ghost Ship 43. Mademoiselle Fifi 44. Curse of the Cat People 44. Youth Runs Wild 44. *The Body Snatcher* 45. Isle of the Dead 45. Bedlam 46. My Own True Love 49. Please Believe Me 50. Apache Drums 51.

Lexy, Edward (1897–) (Edward Gerald Little). British character actor in films from 1936, usually as sergeant-major, police inspector or irascible father.
Farewell Again 37. South Riding 38. Laugh It Off 40. Spare a Copper 40. Piccadilly Incident 46. It's Not Cricket 48. Miss Robin Hood 52. Orders Are Orders 55. The Man Who Wouldn't Talk 58, many others.

Leyton, John (1939–). British pop singer who transferred to dramatic roles.
The Great Escape 63. Von Ryan's Express 65. Krakatoa 68, etc.
TV series: Jericho 67.

L'Herbier, Marcel (1890–). French director.
Rose France 19. Eldorado 22. The Late Mathias Pascal 25. L'Epervier 33. Nuits de Feu 37. La Nuit Fantastique 42. The Last Days of Pompeii 49. Le Père de Mademoiselle 53, etc.

Liberace (1919–) (Wladziu Valentino Liberace). American pianist-showman of stage, night clubs and TV. Starred in his only major appearance, *Sincerely Yours* 55; also seen as a pianist in *East of Java* 49 and as a coffin salesman in *The Loved One* 65.

library shot. see *stock shot*.

Licudi, Gabriella (1943–). Italian leading lady in international films.
The Liquidators 65. The Jokers 66. Casino Royale 66. The Last Safari 67. Separate Beds 73, many others.

Liebelei (Austria 1933). A sentimental love

story culminating in a duel in which the hero is killed by the husband of an ex-mistress. All the film's merit is in the style of director Max Ophuls and cinematographer Franz Planer.

Lieven, Albert (1906–1971). German actor in films from 1933, including many British productions.

Victoria the Great 37. Night Train to Munich 40. *Jeannie* 40. Yellow Canary 43. *The Seventh Veil* 45. *Beware of Pity* 46. Frieda 47. *Sleeping Car to Trieste* 48. Hotel Sahara 50. Conspiracy of Hearts 60. Foxhole in Cairo 61. The Victors 63. Traitor's Gate 65, many others.

The Life and Death of Colonel Blimp (GB 1943). This amiable and quite ambitiously staged biography of a fictitious military man, whose career ranged from the Boer War to the London blitz, had delightful incidental detail even though it made no very obvious point and had the oddities one was coming to expect from films written, produced and directed by Michael Powell and Emeric Pressburger. Running three hours in its original form, in what then seemed exquisite colour, it had Roger Livesey in the title role, Deborah Kerr as the three women in his life, and Anton Walbrook as a sympathetic German friend.

The Life of Emile Zola (US 1937) (AA best film). This, the only Warner Brothers biographical film to win an award as the best film of its year, was probably the best of them. Stylishly directed by William Dieterle, it also gained Academy Awards for Joseph Schildkraut (as Dreyfus) and for the scenarists Norman Reilly Raine, Heinz Herald and Geza Herczeg. Paul Muni played Zola.

Life Upside Down (La Vie a L'Envers) (France 1964). A simple but curiously haunting little film in the introspective manner of the sixties, about a young man who withdraws from life into the simplicity and solitude of a small white room. Written and directed by Alain Jessua; with Charles Denner.

Lifeboat (US 1943). An Alfred Hitchcock movie notable for confining itself to the smallest acting space of any film ever made: a lifeboat on the open sea. John Steinbeck wrote the script and Tallulah Bankhead and Walter Slezak made the most of the acting chances.

lifts (or elevators) provided a convenient means of murder in *Garment Center*, *The List of Adrian Messenger* and *House of Wax*, and of unwitting suicide in *Ivy*. Sean Connery in *Diamonds are*

Forever had a spectacular fight in a lift. People were trapped in lifts in *Cry Terror*, *A Night in Casablanca*, *Love Crazy*, *Sweet Charity*, *Towering Inferno* and *Lady in a Cage*, in which last the lift was of the domestic variety used by Katharine Hepburn in *Suddenly Last Summer*. Michael Rennie had more trouble in lifts than any other actor — in *The Power*, *The Day the Earth Stood Still*, and *Hotel*. Invalid chair-lifts were sported by Ethel Barrymore in *The Farmer's Daughter*, Charles Laughton in *Witness for the Prosecution*, and Eugenie Leontovich in *Homicidal*.

light comedians, the lithe and dapper heroes who can be funny and romantic at the same time, have added a great deal to the mystique and nostalgia of the screen. Linder and Chaplin both partly belong to this debonair tradition, and indeed did much to mould it; but only sound could enable its full realization. Maurice Chevalier had the field pretty well to himself in Hollywood during the early thirties, with strong support from such stalwarts as Roland Young, Edward Everett Horton and Charles Butterworth. Soon Cary Grant entered the lists along with David Niven, William Powell, Louis Hayward, Melvyn Douglas and Ronald Colman when he felt in lighter mood. Britain scored with Jack Buchanan, Jack Hulbert, and the ineffable Aldwych team of Tom Walls and Ralph Lynn; while Leslie Howard scored a major hit in *Pygmalion* and Rex Harrison, who was to play the same role twenty-five years later in *My Fair Lady*, was already demonstrating his talent in less important comedies.

Back in Hollywood *The Philadelphia Story* was a milestone in light comedy and set Katharine Hepburn firmly on the road she later followed in her splendid series with Spencer Tracy. Bette Davis, too, had her moments in this field, and so did Rosalind Russell. Bob Hope and Danny Kaye both clowned around a good deal but still got the girl in the end ... but Britishers Basil Radford and Naunton Wayne were bachelors born and bred. The more realistic approach of the fifties was stifling the genre, but Dennis Price managed a notable performance in *Kind Hearts and Coronets* before Ian Carmichael cornered the diminishing market. In more recent years actors have had to turn comic or tragic at the drop of a hat: among those best able to manage the light touch are Jack Lemmon, Tony Curtis, Frank Sinatra and Peter O'Toole.

lighthouses formed dramatic settings for such movies as *Thunder Rock*, *The Seventh Survivor*, *The Phantom Light* and *Back Room Boy*, and dominated key scenes of *Portrait of Jennie*, *A*

Stolen Life and *The Beast from 20,000 Fathoms.*

Lightner, Winnie (1901–1971) (Winifred Hanson). American vaudeville comedienne who appeared in several early talkies.
Gold Diggers of Broadway 30. Playgirl 32. Dancing Lady 32. I'll Fix It 34, etc.

Lights of New York (US 1928). The first all-talking film, a backstage gangster drama notable for little except its continuous nasal chatter (still separated by sub-titles). Directed by Bryan Foy from a many-handed script.

Lil Abner. Al Capp's comic strip about the hillbilly inhabitants of Dogpatch was first filmed, unsuccessfully, in 1940 with Granville Owen; masks were rather oddly used for some characters. In 1957 Panama and Frank made a successful musical version with Peter Palmer, based on the Broadway show. Also, Paramount made a few Lil Abner cartoons in the late forties.

Liliom. Ferenc Molnar's play about the here and the hereafter was filmed in Hollywood in 1930 by Frank Borzage and in Germany in 1933 by Fritz Lang. In 1956 it turned up again, via a stage musical, as *Carousel*, directed by Henry King.

Lillie, Beatrice (1898–) (Constance Sylvia Munston, later Lady Peel). Sharp-faced, mischievous British revue star of the twenties and thirties who graced only a few films with her wit.
Biography 1973: *Every Inch a Lady.*
□ *Exit Smiling* 26. Show of Shows 29. Are You There? 30. Dr Rhythm 38. *On Approval* 43. Around the World in Eighty Days 56. Thoroughly Modern Millie 67.

Limelight (US 1952). Chaplin's last major film, a sentimental old-fashioned back-stage story which succeeded by its sheer aplomb but overdid the pathos. His theme song, 'Eternally', made it a hit.

Lincoln, Abbey (1930–) (Anna Marie Woolridge). Black American character actress.
For Love of Ivy 68.

Lincoln, Abraham (1809–1865). Sixteenth American president, a familiar screen figure with his stovepipe hat, bushy whiskers, and his assassination during a performance of 'Our American Cousin'. More or less full length screen portraits include *Abraham Lincoln's Clemency* 10; *Lincoln the Lover* 13; Joseph Henabery in *Birth of a Nation* 14; Frank McGlynn in *The Life of Abraham Lincoln* 15; George A. Billings in *Abraham Lincoln* 25;

Walter Huston in *Abraham Lincoln* 30; John Carradine in *Of Human Hearts* 38; Henry Fonda in *Young Mr Lincoln* 39; Raymond Massey in *Abe Lincoln in Illinois* 39.

Lincoln, Elmo (1889–1952) (Otto Elmo Linkenhelter). American silent actor who became famous as the first *Tarzan of the Apes* 18, and played small roles up to his death.
Birth of a Nation 14. Elmo the Mighty 19, etc.

Lindblom, Gunnel (1939–). Leading Swedish actress.
The Seventh Seal 56. Wild Strawberries 57. The Virgin Spring 60. Winter Light 62. *The Silence* 63. Rapture 65. Loving Couples 66.

Linden, Eric (1909–). American juvenile lead of the thirties.
Are These Our Children? 32. The Silver Cord 33. Girl of the Limberlost 34. The Voice of Bugle Ann 36. Gone with the Wind 39, etc.

Linden, Hal (1932–) (Harold Lipshitz). American character actor, best known as TV's *Barney Miller.*

Linden, Jennie (1939–). British leading actress.
Nightmare 63. Dr Who and the Daleks 66. *Women in Love* 69. A Severed Head 70. Hedda 75, etc.

Linder, Cec (–). Canadian character actor, long in British films.
Crack in the Mirror 59. Jetstorm 59. Too Young to Love 60. SOS Pacific 60. Goldfinger 64. Explosion 71. A Touch of Class 73. Sunday in the Country 74, many others.

Linder, Max (1883–1925) (Gabriel Levielle). Dapper French silent comedian, a probable source for Chaplin. Scripted and directed most of his own films (1906–25), of which three were recently reissued by his daughter under the title *Laugh with Max Linder.*

Lindfors, Viveca (1920–). Swedish actress, in films from 1941, Hollywood from 1946.
To the Victor 47. Night Unto Night 48. The New Adventures of Don Juan 48. No Sad Songs for Me 50. Dark City 50. The Flying Missile 51. Four in a Jeep 51. The Raiders 52. Run for Cover 55. Moonfleet 55. I Accuse 57. Tempest 58. King of Kings 61. Sylvia 65. Brainstorm 65. The Way We Were 73, others.

Lindgren, Lars Magnus (1922–). Swedish director.

Do You Believe in Angels? 60. Dear John 64.
The Coffin (The Sadist) 66.

Lindo, Olga (1898–1968). Anglo-Norwegian
character actress, on British stage and screen.
The Shadow Between 32. The Last Journey 35.
When We Are Married 42. Bedelia 46. Train of
Events 49. *An Inspector Calls* 54. Woman in a
Dressing Gown 57. Sapphire 59, etc.

Lindon, Lionel (1905–1971). American
cinematographer.
Going My Way 44. A Medal for Benny 45. Road
to Utopia 46. *Alias Nick Beal* 49. Destination
Moon 50. Conquest of Space 55. *Around the
World in Eighty Days* (AA) 56. The Lonely Man
57. The Black Scorpion 57. Too Late Blues 61.
The Manchurian Candidate 62. The Trouble
with Angels 66. Boy Did I Get a Wrong
Number 66. *Grand Prix* 66. Generation 69, etc.

Lindsay, Howard (1889–1968). American
actor-playwright-stage director. With Russell
Crouse wrote *Life with Father* and *State of the
Union*, both filmed. Acted in and directed *Dulcy*
21, co-authored *She's My Weakness* 31.

Lindsay, Margaret (1910–) (Margaret Kies).
American leading lady of the thirties, with stage
experience; in Hollywood from 1931.
West of Singapore 32. Lady Killer 34.
Bordertown 35. G-Men 35. The Green Light 37.
Jezebel 38. The House of Seven Gables 40.
There's Magic in Music 41. A Close Call for
Ellery Queen 42. No Place for a Lady 43. Crime
Doctor 43. Alaska 44. Club Havana 45. Scarlet
Street 45. Her Sister's Secret 47. Cass
Timberlane 47. Emergency Hospital 56. Jet over
the Atlantic 59. Tammy and the Doctor 63,
many others.

Lindtberg, Leopold (1902–). Swiss director.
Marie Louise 44. *The Last Chance* 45. Four
Days Leave 48. The Village 52.

The Lion in Winter (GB/US 1968). This
curious treatment of the court of Henry II in the
vein of *Who's Afraid of Virginia Woolf?* won
Oscars for Katharine Hepburn, in her element as
the wily Eleanor of Aquitaine, for John Barry's
music and for James Goldman's screenplay from
his off-Broadway original. Anthony Harvey's
direction ensured good clear talk at the expense
of cinema; Peter O'Toole was an amusingly
rampant Henry.

Lipman, Jerzy (1922–). Polish
cinematographer.
A Generation 54. Kanal 57. The Eighth Day of

the Week 58. Lotna 59. Knife in the Water 62.
No More Divorces 63. Ashes 65, etc.

Lippert, Robert L. (1909–). American
exhibitor, latterly head of company making
second features for 20th Century-Fox, many of
them produced by his son *Robert L. Lippert Jnr*
(1928–).

Lipscomb, W. P. (1887–1958). British
screenwriter who spent some years in
Hollywood.
French Leave 27. The Good Companions 32. I
Was a Spy 33. Clive of India (co-w) 34. A Tale of
Two Cities 35. The Garden of Allah 36.
Pygmalion (co-w) 38. A Town Like Alice 56.
Dunkirk (co-w) 58, many others.

Lisi, Virna (1937–) (Virna Pieralisi).
Voluptuous Italian leading lady who after
starring in innumerable local spectaculars came
on to the international market.
The Black Tulip 63. Eva 63. How to Murder
Your Wife (US) 65. Casanova 70 65. Signore e
Signori 65. Assault on a Queen (US) 66. Not
with My Wife You Don't (US) 66. The Girl and
the General 67. The Twenty-fifth Hour 67.
Arabella 68. The Secret of Santa Vittoria 69. Un
Beau Monstre 70. The Statue 71. The Serpent 72.
Bluebeard 72, etc.

Listen to Britain (GB 1941). A classic
impressionist documentary by Humphrey
Jennings, blending the sights and sounds of a
country at war.

Lister, Francis (1899–1951). Suave British
character actor, mainly on stage.
Comin' Thro' the Rye 24. Atlantic 30. Jack's the
Boy 32. Clive of India 35. The Return of the
Scarlet Pimpernel 38. Henry V 44. The Wicked
Lady 45. Home to Danger 51, etc.

Lister, Moira (1923–). South African leading
lady and character actress, in British films.
My Ain Folk 44. Uneasy Terms 48. Another
Shore 48. *A Run for Your Money* 49. Grand
National Night 53. John and Julie 55. Seven
Waves Away 57. The Yellow Rolls Royce 64.
Stranger in the House 67, etc.

Litel, John (1895–1972). American character
actor, in films since 1929; often seen as judge,
lawyer or stern father.
Marked Woman 37. The Life of Emile Zola 37.
Virginia City 40. Men Without Souls 40. They
Died with Their Boots On 41. Sealed Lips 41.
Boss of Big Town 43. Kiss Tomorrow Goodbye
50. Houseboat 58. A Pocketful of Miracles 61.

The Sons of Katie Elder 65, many others.

Little Caesar (US 1930). The first talking gangster film glorifying the gang wars of the twenties, this powerful melodrama with its famous last line ('... is this the end of Rico?') caused a long-lasting controversy but sold a lot of tickets and produced a host of imitators. (The genre wore itself out in the forties but was revived in the late fifties.) Edward G. Robinson was suddenly a star after his performance; Mervyn Le Roy directed.

Little, Cleavon (1939–). Black American comedy actor.
What's So Bad About Feeling Good 68. Cotton Comes to Harlem 70. Vanishing Point 71. *Blazing Saddles* 74, etc.
TV series: *Temperatures Rising* 72.

The Little Foxes (US 1941). This admirable adaptation of Lilian Hellman's play about a grasping family after the Civil War was an example of Hollywood at its best, with beautiful photography by Gregg Toland, subtle direction by William Wyler, and a gallery of first-rate performances: Bette Davis, Herbert Marshall, Ray Collins, Charles Dingle, Dan Duryea, Patricia Collinge and others. An unusual kind of sequel, *Another Part of the Forest*, was filmed in 1947: this showed the earlier lives of the Hubbard family.

Little Lord Fauntleroy. The well-known children's novel by Frances Hodgson Burnett, about an American boy who becomes a British earl, was filmed in 1922 as a transvestite vehicle for Mary Pickford; direction appears to have been shared between Alfred E. Green, Jack Pickford and Alfred Werker. In 1936 it was remade by John Cromwell for Selznick, with Freddie Bartholemew in the title role.

Little Women. Louisa M. Alcott's cosy 19th-century saga of a nice widow's even nicer daughters was a major success when filmed in 1933 by George Cukor, with Katharine Hepburn and Paul Lukas. Remade in 1949 with June Allyson and Rossano Brazzi, it seemed calculated and coy. A sequel, *Little Men*, was filmed in 1940 as a vehicle for Kay Francis.

Littlefield, Lucien (1895–1960). American character actor, in Hollywood from 1913 in supporting roles.
The Sheik 22. Miss Pinkerton 32. Ruggles of Red Gap 34. Rose Marie 36. The Great American Broadcast 40. Scared Stiff 44. Susanna Pass 51. Pop Girl 56, etc.

Littlewood, Joan (1916–). British stage director whose only film to date is *Sparrows Can't Sing* 63. Created London's 'Theatre Workshop'.

Litvak, Anatole (1902–1974). Russian-born director in Germany and France from 1927, Hollywood from 1937.
□ Dolly Gets Ahead (Ger.) 31. Nie Wieder Liebe (Ger.) 32. Coeur de Lilas (Fr.) 32. Be Mine Tonight (Ger.) 33. Sleeping Car (GB) 33. Cette Vielle Canaille (Fr.) 35. L'Equipage (Fr.) 36. *Mayerling* (Fr.) 36. *The Woman I Love* 37. Tovarich 38. The Amazing Dr Clitterhouse 38. The Sisters 38. Castle on the Hudson 39. *Confessions of a Nazi Spy* 39. All This and Heaven Too 40. *City for Conquest* 40. Out of the Fog 41. Blues in the Night 41. This Above All 42. The Long Night 47. Sorry Wrong Number 48. *The Snake Pit* 48. Decision Before Dawn 52. Act of Love 53. The Deep Blue Sea 55. Anastasia 56. The Journey 59. Goodbye Again 61. Five Miles to Midnight 63. The Night of the Generals 67. The Lady in the Car 70.

Livesey, Jack (1901–). British actor, brother of Roger Livesey.
The Wandering Jew 33. The Passing of the Third Floor Back 35. Old Bill and Son 40. The First Gentleman 47. Paul Temple's Triumph 51, etc.

Livesey, Roger (1906–1976). Husky-voiced, often roguish British character star who divided his time between stage and screen.
□ The Old Curiosity Shop 20. Where the Rainbow Ends 21. The Four Feathers 21. Married Love 23. East Lynne on the Western Front 31. A Veteran of Waterloo 33. A Cuckoo in the Nest 33. Blind Justice 34. The Price of Wisdom 35. Lorna Doone 35. Midshipman Easy 35. *Rembrandt* 36. *The Drum* 38. Keep Smiling 38. Spies of the Air 39. The Rebel Son 39. The Girl in the News 40. 49th Parallel 41. *The Life and Death of Colonel Blimp* 43. *I Know Where I'm Going* 45. *A Matter of Life and Death* 46. *Vice Versa* 47. That Dangerous Age 49. Green Grow the Rushes 50. The Master of Ballantrae 53. The Intimate Stranger 56. The League of Gentlemen 59. The Entertainer 60. No My Darling Daughter 61. Of Human Bondage 64. Moll Flanders 65. Oedipus the King 68. Hamlet 69. Futtock's End 70.

Livesey, Sam (1873–1936). British actor, father of Jack and Roger Livesey.
Young Woodley 30. The Flag Lieutenant 32. The Private Life of Henry VIII 32. Jew Süss 34. Turn of the Tide 36. Dark Journey 37, etc.

Living (Ikiru) (Japan 1952). Edited, part-written, and directed by Akira Kurosawa, this step-by-step account of an elderly clerk dying of cancer could hardly have been made in the west at this time; certainly not with so fine and finally uplifting a touch.

The Living Desert (US 1953). The first of Walt Disney's feature-length 'True Life Adventures', an absorbing animal documentary despite the facetious Fitzpatrick-type monotone commentary and many suspect 'dramatic' sequences which must have been either staged or cleverly edited. (By reverse printing, Disney even made scorpions do a square dance.) Outraged scientific critics could not deny the charm and fascination of the piece, nor its popularity; and many of the shots were extremely rare. Disney followed it with *The Vanishing Prairie, The African Lion, Secrets of Life, The Jungle Cat*, and several two-reelers of the same kind: *Seal Island, Beaver Valley, Bear Country, Water Birds, Nature's Half Acre*, etc.

Livingston, Jay (1915–). American songwriter, usually of words and music; often worked with Ray Evans.
To Each His Own 47. Golden Earrings 48. The Paleface (AA for 'Buttons and Bows') 49. Captain Carey (USA) (AA for 'Mona Lisa') 50. The Man Who Knew Too Much (AA for 'Que Sera Sera') 56. All Hands on Deck 62, many others. Wrote themes for *Bonanza, Mister Ed*, etc.

Lizzani, Carlo (1922–). Italian director.
Caccia Tragica (co-w only) 47. Bitter Rice (co-w only) 49. Achtung Banditi 51. Ai Margini Della Metropoli 54. The Great Wall 58. Hunchback of Rome 60. The Hills Run Red 66. The Violent Four 68. Crazy Joe 73. The Last Days of Mussolini 74, etc.

Lloyd, Doris (1899–1968). British actress with repertory experience; in Hollywood from the twenties.
Charley's Aunt (as Donna Lucia) 30. Disraeli 30. Tarzan the Ape Man 32. Oliver Twist 33. Clive of India 35. Vigil in the Night 39. Phantom Lady 44. The Secret Life of Walter Mitty 47. A Man Called Peter 55. The Time Machine 60. The Notorious Landlady 62. Rosie 67, etc.

Lloyd, Euan (1923–). British independent producer, former publicist.
Genghis Khan 65. Murderers' Row 66. Shalako 68. Catlow 71. The Man Called Noon 73. Paper Tiger 75, etc.

Lloyd, Frank (1887–1960). Scottish-born director, in Hollywood from 1913 after acting experience.
Les Misérables 18. Madame X 20. Oliver Twist 22. The Eternal Flame 23. The Sea Hawk 24. Dark Streets 26. *The Divine Lady* (AA) 29. East Lynne 30. Sin Flood 31. Passport to Hell 32. *Cavalcade* (AA) 33. *Berkeley Square* 33. *Mutiny on the Bounty* 35. Under Two Flags 36. Maid of Salem 37. Wells Fargo 37. If I Were King (& p) 39. Rulers of the Sea 39. The Tree of Liberty (& d) 40. The Lady from Cheyenne (& p) 41. This Woman Is Mine 41. *Blood on the Sun* 45. The Shanghai Story (& p) 54: The Last Command (& p) 55, many others.

Lloyd, Harold (1893–1971). American silent comedian, famous for his timid bespectacled 'nice boy' character and for thrill-comedy situations involving dangerous stunts. In hundreds of two-reelers from 1916.
Autobiography 1928: *An American Comedy*.
☐ A Sailor-Made Man 21. *Grandma's Boy* 22. Dr Jack 22. *Safety Last* 23. Why Worry? 23. Girl Shy 24. Hot Water 24. *The Freshman* 25. For Heaven's Sake 26. *The Kid Brother* 27. Speedy 28. Welcome Danger 29. *Feet First* 30. *Movie Crazy* 32. The Catspaw 34. The Milky Way 36. Professor Beware 38. Mad Wednesday (The Sins of Harold Diddlebock) 47. Later produced two compilations of his comedy highlights: *World of Comedy* and *Funny Side of Life*. Special Academy Award 1952 as 'master comedian and good citizen'.

Lloyd, Norman (1914–). British character actor in Hollywood, usually in mean or weak roles; gave up acting to become TV producer, mainly for Alfred Hitchcock.
Saboteur (as the villain who fell from the statue of Liberty) 42. The Unseen 45. The Southerner 45. Spellbound 45. The Green Years 46. The Beginning or the End 47. Scene of the Crime 49. The Flame and the Arrow 60. He Ran all the Way 51. Limelight 52, etc.

Lloyd, Sue (1939–). British leading lady of the sixties.
The Ipcress File 66. Where's Jack? 68. Percy 71. TV series: *The Baron*.

Lloyd-Pack, Charles (1905–). British character actor of stage and screen, usually in self-effacing roles; butlers, etc.
High Treason 51. *The Importance of Being Earnest* 52. The Constant Husband 55. Night of the Demon 57. Dracula 58. *Victim* 62. If 68. Song of Norway 70. Madame Sin 72, etc.

Loach, Ken (1936–). British director from TV.
Poor Cow 67. *Kes* 69. *Family Life* 72. Days of Hope (TV) 75.

Lo Bianco, Tony (　–). American character actor.
The French Connection 72. The Seven Ups 73, etc.

location. A shooting site away from the studios.

Lockhart, Calvin (1934–). Black West Indian leading man.
Joanna 68. Cotton Comes to Harlem 69. Leo the Last 69. Myra Breckinridge 70. The Beast Must Die 74, etc.

Lockhart, Gene (1891–1957). Canadian character actor at home in genial or shifty parts. Also writer: in films since 1922.
Star of Midnight 34. Something to Sing About 37. *Algiers* 38. Blackmail 39. *All That Money Can Buy* 41. Meet John Doe 41. Hangmen Also Die 43. Going My Way 44. *The House on 92nd Street* 45. A Scandal in Paris 46. Miracle on 34th Street 47. *The Inspector General* 49. Rhubarb 51. Androcles and the Lion 53. Carousel 56, others.

Lockhart, June (1925–). American supporting actress, daughter of Gene.
All This and Heaven Too 40. Meet Me in St Louis 44. Keep Your Powder Dry 45. Bury Me Dead 47. Time Limit 47, etc.
TV series: *Lassie* 56–66.

Lockwood, Gary (1937–) (John Gary Yusolfsky). American leading man of the sixties, mostly on TV.
Splendor in the Grass 61. Wild in the Country 61. It Happened at the World's Fair 63. Firecreek 67. 2001: A Space Odyssey 68. The Model Shop 69. RPM 70. Stand Up and Be Counted 72, etc.
TV series: *Follow the Sun* 61. *The Lieutenant* 63.

Lockwood, Julia (1941–). British leading lady, daughter of Margaret Lockwood.
My Teenage Daughter 56. Please Turn Over 59. No Kidding 60, etc.

Lockwood, Margaret (1916–) (Margaret Day). Durable, indomitable British leading lady who was an appealing ingénue in the thirties, a rather boring star villainess in the forties, and later a likeable character actress of stage and TV. Autobiography 1955: *Lucky Star*.

□ Lorna Doone 35. The Case of Gabriel Perry 35. Some Day 35. Honours Easy 35. Man of the Moment 35. Midshipman Easy 35. Jury's Evidence 36. The Amateur Gentleman 36. The Beloved Vagabond 36. Irish for Luck 36. The Street Singer 37. Who's Your Lady Friend? 37. Dr Syn 37. Melody and Romance 37. Owd Bob 38. Bank Holiday 38. *The Lady Vanishes* 38. A Girl Must Live 39. The Stars Look Down 39. Susannah of the Mounties (US) 39. Rulers of the Sea (US) 39. *Night Train to Munich* 40. The Girl in the News 40. Quiet Wedding 41. Alibi 42. *The Man in Grey* 43. Dear Octopus 43. Give us the Moon 44. Love Story 44. A Place of One's Own 45. I'll Be Your Sweetheart 45. *The Wicked Lady* 45. Bedelia 46. Hungry Hill 46. Jassy 47. The White Unicorn 47. Look Before You Love 48. Cardboard Cavalier 49. Madness of the Heart 49. Highly Dangerous 50. Trent's Last Case 52. Laughing Anne 53. Trouble in the Glen 54. *Cast a Dark Shadow* 57. The Slipper and the Rose 76.

Loder, John (1898–) (John Lowe). Handsome British leading man, in international films from 1927 after varied experience.
The First Born 29. Java Head 34. Lorna Doone 35. Murder Will Out 38. Meet Maxwell Archer 39. How Green Was My Valley 41. *Now Voyager* 42. Gentleman Jim 42. The Gorilla Man 42. Old Acquaintance 43. The Hairy Ape 44. The Brighton Strangler 45. A Game of Death 46. Wife of Monte Cristo 46. Dishonoured Lady 47. Woman and the Hunter 57. Gideon's Day 58, etc.

Lodge, David (c. 1922–). British character actor, with music-hall and stage experience.
Private's Progress 56. Two Way Stretch 60. The Dock Brief 61. Yesterday's Enemy 61. The Long Ships 63. Guns at Batasi 64. Catch Us If You Can 65. Press For Time 66. Corruption 69. Doctors Wear Scarlet 70. The Railway Children 71. Go For a Take 72. The Amazing Mr Blunden 72. The Return of the Pink Panther 74, etc.

Lodge, John (1903–). American leading man of the thirties, mainly European films. Retired to take up politics.
A Woman Accused (debut) 32. Little Women 33. The Scarlet Empress 34. Koenigsmark 35. Sensation 36. Bulldog Drummond at Bay 37. Bank Holiday 38. L'Esclave Blanche 39.

The Lodger: see *Jack the Ripper*.

Loesser, Frank (1910–1969). American songwriter, in films since 1930. 'Baby It's Cold Outside', 'Jingle Jangle', many others. Scores for *Hans Christian Andersen, Where's Charley?*

Guys and Dolls, How to Succeed in Business Without Really Trying, etc.

Loew, Marcus (1870–1927). Austrian-American exhibitor and distributor, co-founder and controller of MGM, which is still run by Loews Inc.

Loewe, Frederick (1901–). Austrian composer in America, usually of musicals with Alan Jay Lerner.
Gigi, My Fair Lady, Camelot, Paint Your Wagon, etc.

Loftus, Cecilia (1876–1943). British character actress who went to Hollywood with a Shakespearean company in 1895, and stayed.
East Lynne 31. The Old Maid 39. The Bluebird 40. Lucky Partners 40. The Black Cat 41, etc.

Logan, Joshua (1908–). American stage director whose occasional films have tended towards stodginess.
Autobiography 1976: *Josh.*
□ I Met My Love Again 38. *Picnic* 56. *Bus Stop* 56. *Sayonara* 57. South Pacific 58. Tall Story 60. Fanny 61. Ensign Pulver 64. *Camelot* 67. Paint Your Wagon 69.

Loggia, Robert (1930–). American leading man.
Somebody Up There Likes Me 56. Cop Hater 58. The Nine Lives of Elfego Baca 59. Cattle King 63. Che! 69, etc.
TV series: *T.H.E. Cat* 66.

Lohr, Marie (1890–1975). Distinguished Australian stage actress, on London stage from 1901; since 1930 in dowager roles.
Aren't We All? (debut) 32. Pygmalion 38. *Major Barbara* 40. The Winslow Boy 48. A Town Like Alice 56, many others.

Lola Montes (France/Germany 1955). This last film by Max Ophuls, treating the life of the famous courtesan in a series of complex flashbacks from the circus act in which she later toured, was a bravura piece of cinema in typically tortuous but often stimulating style. Unfortunately it was generally shown in an atrocious dubbed and shortened version with the circus sequences removed and the remainder in roughly chronological order. Photographed in colour by Christian Matras; with Martine Carol, Anton Walbrook and Peter Ustinov.

Lollobrigida, Gina (1927–). Italian glamour girl and international leading lady, in films since 1947.

Pagliacci 47. Fanfan la Tulipe 51. *Belles de Nuit* 52. The Wayward Wife 52. *Bread, Love and Dreams* 53. Beat the Devil 54. Le Grand Jeu 54. Trapeze 56. Where the Hot Wind Blows 58. Solomon and Sheba 59. Come September 61. Woman of Straw 64. Strange Bedfellows 65. Four Kinds of Love (Bambole) 65. Hotel Paradiso 66. Buona Sera, Mrs Campbell 68. Bad Man's River 71. King Queen Knave 72, many others.

Lom, Herbert (1917–) (Herbert Charles Angelo Kuchacevich ze Schluderpacheru). Czech actor whose personality adapts itself equally well to villainy or kindliness; in Britain from 1939.
Mein Kampf 40. The Young Mr Pitt (as Napoleon) 41. The Dark Tower 43. Hotel Reserve 44. *The Seventh Veil* 46. Night Boat to Dublin 46. *Dual Alibi* 47. Good Time Girl 48. The Golden Salamander 49. *State Secret* 50. The Black Rose 50. Hell Is Sold Out 51. The Ringer 52. The Net 53. The Love Lottery 54. *The Ladykillers* 55. War and Peace (as Napoleon) 56. Chase a Crooked Shadow 57. Hell Drivers 57. No Trees in the Street 58. Roots of Heaven 58. Northwest Frontier 59. I Aim at the Stars (US) 59. Mysterious Island 61. El Cid 61. Phantom of the Opera (title role) 62. A Shot in the Dark 64. Return from the Ashes 65. Uncle Tom's Cabin (Ger.) 65. Gambit 66. Assignment to Kill 67. Villa Rides 68. Doppelganger 69. Murders in the Rue Morgue 71. Asylum 72. And Now the Screaming Starts 73. The Return of the Pink Panther 74. And Then There Were None 75. The Pink Panther Strikes Again 77, others.
TV series: *The Human Jungle.*

Lomas, Herbert (1887–1961). Gaunt, hollow-voiced British stage actor.
The Sign of Four 32. Lorna Doone 35. Rembrandt 36. Jamaica Inn 39. Ask a Policeman 39. *The Ghost Train* 41. I Know Where I'm Going 45. Bonnie Prince Charlie 48. The Net 53, etc.

Lombard, Carole (1908–1942) (Jane Peters). American leading lady of the thirties, a fine comedienne with an inimitable rangy style.
Biography 1976: *Screwball* by Larry Swindell.
□ A Perfect Crime 21. Hearts and Spurs 25. Marriage in Transit 25. Me Gangster 28. Power 28. Show Folks 28. Ned McCobb's Daughter 29. High Voltage 29. Big News 29. The Racketeer 29. The Arizona Kid 30. Safety in Numbers 30. Fast and Loose 30. It Pays to Advertise 31. Man of the World 31. Ladies' Man 31. Up Pops the Devil 31. I Take this Woman 31. No One Man 32. Sinners in the Sun 32. Virtue 32. No More

Orchids 32. *No Man of Her Own* 32. From Heaven to Hell 33. Supernatural 33. The Eagle and the Hawk 33. Brief Moment 33. White Woman 33. *Bolero* 34. We're Not Dressing 34. *Twentieth Century* 34. Now and Forever 34. Lady by Choice 34. The Gay Bride 34. *Rumba* 34. Hands Across the Table 35. Love Before Breakfast 36. *My Man Godfrey* 36. The Princess Comes Across 36. Swing High Swing Low 37. True Confession 37. *Nothing Sacred* 37. Fools for Scandal 38. Made for Each Other 38. In Name Only 39. Vigil in the Night 40. *They Knew What They Wanted* 40. *Mr and Mrs Smith* 41. *To Be or Not To Be* 42.

London has provided a background, usually highly inaccurate, for innumerable movies, but few have really explored it, though *The Ipcress File* and *The Pumpkin Eater* found some unusual angles. *London Town* was a half-hearted musical; twenty years later *Three Hats for Lisa* captured the mood better but managed to seem old-fashioned. *Pygmalion* and *My Fair Lady* embodied the spirit of London in some theatrical sets. *Indiscreet* prowled lovingly around the Embankment, and *A Run for Your Money* made good use of the Paddington area as well as suburban Twickenham. The City was the venue of part of *You Must Be Joking*, while *Morgan* used Hampstead to good advantage. The East End, especially the street markets and the railway sidings, were exploited in *Waterloo Road, A Kid for Two Farthings* and *It Always Rains on Sunday*. The docks had *Pool of London* to themselves. Hollywood's idea of London in geography can be pretty weird, as in *Knock on Wood*, when Paramount went to the trouble of having special location material shot with Jon Pertwee doubling for Danny Kaye, but showed the star turning off Marble Arch into Fleet Street two miles away. Similarly in *Twenty-three Paces to Baker Street* the river frontage of the Savoy Hotel could be entered from Portman Square, in actuality another two-mile jaunt. London fog has been a useful cover for many a scrappy set, especially in films presenting the Victorian London associated with Sherlock Holmes. Going further back, *Henry V* presented in model form the London of 1600, and attempts at historical recreation were also made in *Tower of London, Fire over England, Elizabeth and Essex, Nell Gwyn, Forever Amber, Mrs Fitzherbert, The First Gentleman, Victoria the Great, Cromwell* and *The Mudlark*. It was probably Hitchcock who began the fashion of making London a stately background for thrillers, with his East End mission in *The Man Who Knew Too Much*, the music hall in *The Thirty-nine Steps*, the bus journey and the Lord Mayor's Show in *Sabotage*, the fall from Westminster Cathedral in *Foreign Correspondent*, the theatrical garden party in *Stage Fright*, and Covent Garden in *Frenzy*. Others in this tradition have included *Brannigan, Hennessy, Villain, Robbery*, and innumerable TV series such as *The Sweeney*.
See also: *Swinging London*.

London Films. Production company founded by Alexander Korda and associated with his own major films of the thirties and later with other leading names operating under his banner.

London, Jack (1876–1916). American adventure novelist, whose most-filmed stories include *The Sea Wolf, Adventures of Martin Eden, Call of the Wild* and *White Fang*.

London, Julie (1926–) (Julie Peck). American leading lady and singer.
Jungle Woman 44. The Red House 47. The Fat Man 51. The Great Man 56. Saddle the Wind 58. Man of the West 58. The Third Voice 60. The George Raft Story 62, etc.
TV series: *Emergency* 71– .

London Town (GB 1946). An attempt by the Rank Organization to make a British musical, often quoted as proof that success in this genre is impossible outside Hollywood (a maxim not disproved till the sixties). Despite an imported American director, Wesley Ruggles, it's all lamentably dull except for Sid Field's sketches, here preserved intact.

The Lone Ranger. This western Robin Hood originally featured in a radio serial, later became a comic strip in 1935; twenty years later Clayton Moore played the hero in a successful TV series and a couple of feature films, with Jay Silverheels as Tonto.

The Lone Wolf was a gentleman thief created by Louis Joseph Vance. He reached the screen in silent days and was played by H. B. Warner, Jack Holt, and Bert Lytell; in the thirties Melvyn Douglas and Francis Lederer each played him once and then Warren William took over for eight episodes, usually with Eric Blore as his manservant. In 1946 Gerald Mohr played in the first of three episodes, and in 1949 Ron Randell personified Michael Lanyard for the last time on the big screen. In 1954 Louis Hayward played him in a TV series, *The Lone Wolf*, also known as *Streets of Danger*.

Long, Audrey (1924–). American leading lady of the forties.

A Night of Adventure 44. Pan Americana 45. Song of My Heart 47. The Petty Girl 50. Indian Uprising 52, etc.

Long, Richard (1927–1974). American leading man, mainly in second features.
Tomorrow Is Forever 44. The Stranger 45. The Egg and I 47. Criss Cross 49. Saskatchewan 54. Cult of the Cobra 55. Home from the Hills 59. The Tenderfoot 64, etc.
TV series: *77 Sunset Strip* 58–60. *Bourbon Street Beat* 61. *The Big Valley* 64–67. *Nanny and the Professor* 70–71.

long shot. One taken from a distance, usually to establish a scene or a situation but sometimes for dramatic effect. Opposite of close-up.

Long, Walter (1879–1952). Burly, evil-faced American character actor of silent days; usually played a bestial Hun in World War I films, and was later a memorable foil for Laurel and Hardy.
Intolerance 16. The Little American 17. Scarlet Days 19. Moran of the Lady Letty 22. The Shock Punch 25. Yankee Clipper 27. Moby Dick 30. The Maltese Falcon 31. Pardon Us 31. Six of a Kind 34. Pick a Star 37, etc.

Longden, John (1900–). British leading man of the early thirties; later graduated to character roles.
Blackmail 30. Atlantic 30. The Ringer 31. Born Lucky 33. French Leave 37. The Gaunt Stranger 38. The Lion Has Wings 39. The Common Touch 41. The Silver Fleet 43. Bonnie Prince Charlie 48. The Man with the Twisted Lip (as Sherlock Holmes) 51. Quatermass II 56. An Honourable Murder 60, many others.

Longden, Terence (1922–). British actor, in secondary roles.
Never Look Back 52. Simon and Laura 55. Doctor at Large 57. Carry On Sergeant 58. Ben Hur 59. The Return of Mr Moto 65, etc.

The Longest Day (US 1962). Darryl F. Zanuck master-minded this detailed reconstruction of D-Day 1944. Long and very noisy, it has some brilliantly handled action sequences, and the all-star cast provided box office insurance at the cost of verisimilitude.

Longstreet, Stephen (1907–). American screenwriter.
The Jolson Story 46. The Greatest Show on Earth (co-w) 52. The First Travelling Saleslady 55. The Helen Morgan Story 57, etc.

Loo, Richard (c. 1903–). Hawaiian-Chinese

actor who turned to films after business depression. Has played hundreds of oriental roles.
Dirigible 31. The Good Earth 37. The Keys of the Kingdom 44. Rogues' Regiment 48. Love is a Many-Splendored Thing 54. The Quiet American 58. The Sand Pebbles 66. One More Time 71, etc.

Looney Tunes and **Merrie Melodies** are the two umbrella titles under which Warners have long released their cartoon shorts featuring such characters as Bugs Bunny, Daffy Duck, Porky Pig, Pepe le Pew, Sylvester and Tweetie Pie. They have won Academy Awards for *Tweetie Pie* 47, *For Scentimental Reasons* 49, *Speedy Gonzales* 55, *Birds Anonymous* 57, *Knighty Knight Bugs* 58.

Loos, Anita (1893–). American humorous writer who spent years in Hollywood studios.
Autobiography 1966: *A Girl Like I.* 1974: *Kiss Hollywood Goodbye.*
Intolerance (subtitles) 16. Let's Get a Divorce (w) 18. A Temperamental Wife (oa) 19. Mama's Affair (d) 20. In Search of a Sinner (p) 20. Red Hot Romance (w) 22. Learning to Love (w) 25. Gentlemen Prefer Blondes (oa) 31. Midnight Mary (oa) 33. *San Francisco* (w) 36. Saratoga (w) 37. The Women (w) 39. When Ladies Meet (oa) 41. *Gentlemen Prefer Blondes* (oa) 52, etc.

Lopez, Trini (c. 1933–). American character actor, ex-bandleader.
Marriage on the Rocks 66. The Dirty Dozen 67, etc.

Lord, Del (1895–). American second feature director who handled most of the Three Stooges shorts.

Lord, Jack (1922–) (John Joseph Ryan). Craggy-faced American leading man who found his greatest success in television.
Cry Murder 51. The Court Martial of Billy Mitchell 55. God's Little Acre 58. Walk Like a Dragon 60. Doctor No 62. The Road to Hangman's Tree 67. The Name of the Game is Kill 68, etc.
TV series: *Stony Burke* 62. *Hawaii Five-O* 68– .

Lord Jim. Joseph Conrad's saga of a man in search of himself all over the Far East was filmed as a 1925 silent in Hollywood with Percy Marmont. In 1965 Richard Brooks wrote and directed a slap-up international version with Peter O'Toole, but it proved singularly dreary.

Lord, Marjorie (1922–). American leading

lady of minor films in the forties.
Forty Naughty Girls 38. Timber 42. Sherlock Holmes in Washington 42. Flesh and Fantasy 44. The Argyle Secrets 48. New Orleans 49. Port of Hell 55. Boy Did I Get a Wrong Number 66, etc.

Lord, Pauline (1890–1950). American stage actress who made only two films.
□ Mrs Wiggs of the Cabbage Patch 35. A Feather in Her Hat 36.

Lord, Robert (1900–1976). American writer and producer associated with Warner Brothers throughout the thirties and forties; later joined Humphrey Bogart in Santana Productions.

Loren, Sophia (1934–) (Sophia Scicoloni). Statuesque Italian leading lady, latterly an accomplished international actress. In films from 1950 (as extra).
Biography 1975: *Sophia* by Donald Zec.
Aida 53. The Sign of Venus 53. Tempi Nostri 54. Attila 54. The Gold of Naples 54. *Woman of the River* 55. Too Bad She's Bad 55. The Miller's Wife 55. Scandal in Sorrento 55. Lucky To Be a Woman 56. The Pride and the Passion 57. *Boy on a Dolphin* 57. Legend of the Lost 57. Desire under the Elms 58. *The Key* 58. Houseboat 58. Black Orchid 59. That Kind of Woman 59. Heller in Pink Tights 60. A Breath of Scandal 61. *Two Women* (AA, BFA) 61. *The Millionairess* 61. El Cid 61. Boccaccio 70 61. The Condemned of Altona 62. Madame Sans Gêne 62. Five Miles to Midnight 62. Yesterday, Today and Tomorrow 63. The Fall of the Roman Empire 64. Marriage Italian Style 64. Operation Crossbow 65. Judith 65. Arabesque 66. Lady L 66. A Countess from Hong Kong 66. More than a Miracle 69. Sunflower 70. Cinderella Italian Style 70. Ghosts Italian Style 71. Man of La Mancha 72. Lady Liberty 74. Brief Encounter (TV) 74. The Voyage 75. The Cassandra Crossing 77, etc.

Lorentz, Pare (1905–). American documentarist and film critic.
The Plow that Broke the Plains 36. The River 37.

Lorne, Marion (1886–1968) (M. L. MacDougal). American character comedienne with long stage experience, latterly seen as eccentric old lady.
Strangers on a Train 51. The Girl Rush 55. The Graduate 68, etc.
TV series *Bewitched* (as the dotty witch-aunt) 64–67.

Lorre, Peter (1904–1964) (Laszlo Loewenstein). Highly individual Hungarian character actor who filmed in Germany and Britain before settling in Hollywood. His rolling eyes, timid manner and mysterious personality could adapt to either sympathetic or sinister roles; a weight problem restricted his later appearances.
□ M 31. Bomben auf Monte Carlo 31. Die Koffer des Herrn O.F. 31. Funf von der Jazzband 32. Schuss im Morgengrauen 32. Der Weisse Damon 32. F.P.I. 32. Was Frauen Traumen 33. Unsichtbare Gegner 33. De Haut en Bas 34. *The Man Who Knew Too Much* 34. *Mad Love* 35. *Crime and Punishment* (as Raskolnikov) 35. *The Secret Agent* 36. Crack Up 36. Nancy Steele is Missing 37. Lancer Spy 37. Think Fast Mr Moto 37. Thank You Mr Moto 37. Mr Moto's Gamble 38. I'll Give a Million 38. Mr Moto Takes a Chance 38. Mysterious Mr Moto 38. Mr Moto on Danger Island 39. Mr Moto Takes a Vacation 39. Mr Moto's Last Warning 39. Strange Cargo 40. I Was an Adventuress 40. Island of Doomed Men 40. Stranger on the Third Floor 40. You'll Find Out 40. Mr District Attorney 41. *The Face Behind the Mask* 41. They Met in Bombay 41. *The Maltese Falcon* 41. All through the Night 42. Invisible Agent 42. The Boogie Man Will Get You 42. Casablanca 42. Background to Danger 43. The Cross of Lorraine 43. Passage to Marseilles 44. *The Mask of Dimitrios* 44. Arsenic and Old Lace 44. The Conspirators 44. Hollywood Canteen 44. Hotel Berlin 45. Confidential Agent 45. Three Strangers 46. Black Angel 46. The Chase 46. The Verdict 46. *The Beast with Five Fingers* 46. My Favorite Brunette 47. Casbah 48. Rope of Sand 49. Quicksand 50. Double Confession 50. Der Verlorene (& d) 50. Beat the Devil 53. 20,000 Leagues under the Sea 54. *Congo Crossing* 56. Around the World in Eighty Days 56. The Buster Keaton Story 56. Silk Stockings 57. The Story of Mankind (as Nero) 57. Hell Ship Mutiny 57. The Sad Sack 58. The Big Circus 59. Scent of Mystery 59. Voyage to the Bottom of the Sea 61. *Tales of Terror* 62. Five Weeks in a Balloon 62. *The Raven* 63. The Comedy of Terrors 63. The Patsy 64.

Lorring, Joan (1926–) (Magdalen Ellis). English-Russian actress, evacuated to US in 1939; played some nasty teenagers.
Girls under Twenty-One 41. Song of Russia 44. The Bridge of San Luis Rey 44. The Corn Is Green 45. The Verdict 46. The Lost Moment 47. Good Sam 49. Stranger on the Prowl 53, etc.

Los Angeles, being the home of the film studios, was the anonymous background of ninety per cent of Hollywood films from the very beginning. Only more recently, however, has the actual city been explored, usually in a cynical Chandleresque manner as in *The Long Goodbye* and *Marlowe*, or as a vivid sunlit background for police thrillers with their screaming car chases, especially in such TV series as *Police Story, The Blue Knight, Police Woman, The Rookies, Chase, Emergency, The Smith Family* and *Dragnet*. The city's seamy side was shown in *M* and *The Savage Eye*, its future in *The Omega Man*, its sophisticated present in *Divorce American Style*, its sewers in *Them*, and its past in *Chinatown*. Perhaps the most vivid picture of the growing sprawl is to be found as background to the comedies of the Keystone Kops and Laurel and Hardy.

Losch, Tilly (1901–1975). Austrian exotic dancer, in Hollywood in the thirties and forties.
□ The Garden of Allah 36. The Good Earth 37. Duel in the Sun 46.

Losey, Joseph (1909–). American director of somewhat pretentious movies, in Britain since 1952 after the communist witch-hunt.
□ The Boy with Green Hair 48. The Lawless 50. *The Prowler* 50. M 51. The Big Night 51. Stranger on the Prowl 53. The Sleeping Tiger 54. The Intimate Stranger 56. Time without Pity 57. The Gypsy and the Gentleman 57. Blind Date 59. The Criminal 60. *The Damned* 61. Eva 62. *The Servant* 63. King and Country 64. Modesty Blaise 66. *Accident* 67. Boom 68. Secret Ceremony 68. Figures in a Landscape 70. The Go-Between 71. The Assassination of Trotsky 72. A Doll's House 73. Galileo 74. The Romantic Englishwoman 75. Mr Klein 76.

Lost Horizon (US 1937). Frank Capra's uneven but attractive film, from the James Hilton novel about a Tibetan Utopia, made Shangri-La a household word. The actors were perfectly cast, with Ronald Colman as Conway, H. B. Warner as Chang and Sam Jaffe as the High Lama. In 1973 Ross Hunter remade the story as a semi-musical, with Peter Finch, John Gielgud and Charles Boyer, and an unhappy result.

The Lost Patrol (US 1934). An unconvincing but savage and relentless melodrama about a British desert patrol picked off one by one by Arabs until rescuers find the one survivor raving mad. Notable for photography by Harold Wendstrom, directed by John Ford (here on the brink of his best period), and heavily overacted but enjoyable performances from Victor McLaglen, Boris Karloff and Reginald Denny. From a novel by Philip MacDonald which later inspired *Sahara* 43, *Bataan* 46 and *Last of the Comanches* 51.

The Lost Weekend (US 1945; AA best picture). Three days in the life of a dipsomaniac, cunningly dramatized by its producer and director, Charles Brackett and Billy Wilder, from a novel by Charles Jackson. Ray Milland (AA) gave the performance of his life, and the film's success gave Hollywood realism a big stride forward.

The Lost World. The 1924 silent version of Arthur Conan Doyle's exciting adventure story was notable for the first efforts of Willis O'Brien in animating prehistoric dinosaurs.
The 1960 remake was notable for nothing except doing everything wrong, including the hilarious miscasting of Claude Rains as Professor Challenger.

Lotinga, Ernie (1876–1951). British vaudeville comedian formerly known as Dan Roy. Made a few slapstick comedies which had their followers. The Raw Recruit 28. PC Josser 31. Josser Joins the Navy 32. Josser in the Army 33. Love Up the Pole 36, etc.

Louise, Anita (1915–1970) (Anita Louise Fremault). American leading lady, usually in gentle roles. Played child parts from 1924.
What a Man 30. A Midsummer Night's Dream 35. The Story of Louis Pasteur 35. Anthony Adverse 36. The Green Light 37. Marie Antoinette 38. The Sisters 39. Phantom Submarine 41. The Fighting Guardsman 45. The Bandit of Sherwood Forest 46. Retreat, Hell! 52. TV series: *My Friend Flicka* 56.

Louise, Tina (1934–). Statuesque American leading lady of routine films in the sixties.
God's Little Acre 58. Day of the Outlaw 59. Armored Command 61. For Those Who Think Young 64. Wrecking Crew 68. The Good Guys and the Bad Guys 69. How to Commit Marriage 70. The Stepford Wives 75, etc.
TV series: *Gilligan's Island* 64–66.

Lourie, Eugene (c. 1905–). French designer. Les Bas Fonds 36. *La Grande Illusion* 37. La Règle du Jeu 39. This Land Is Mine (US) 42. *The Southerner* (US) 44. The River 51, etc.
AS DIRECTOR: The Beast from Twenty Thousand Fathoms 53. The Colossus of New York 58. Gorgo (GB) 60, etc.

Love, Bessie (1898–) (Juanita Horton). Vivacious, petite American leading lady of the twenties. In films from childhood; since the mid-thirties resident in London, playing occasional cameo parts.

Intolerance 15. The Aryan 16. A Sister of Six 17. The Dawn of Understanding 18. The Purple Dawn 20. The Vermilion Pencil 21. Human Wreckage 23. Dynamite Smith 24. The Lost World 25. Lovey Mary 26. Sally of the Scandals 27. Broadway Melody 28. Chasing Rainbows 30. Morals for Women 31. Conspiracy 32. Atlantic Ferry 42. Journey Together 45. Touch and Go 55. The Wild Affair 64. Isadora 68. Sunday Bloody Sunday 71. Mousey (TV) 74, many others.

Love, Montagu (1877–1943). Heavily built British character actor, long in Hollywood, latterly as stern fathers.

Bought and Paid For 16. The Gilded Cage 19. The Case of Becky 21. A Son of the Sahara 24. Son of the Sheik 26. Don Juan 26. King of Kings 27. Jesse James 27. The Haunted House 28. The Divine Lady 29. Bulldog Drummond 29. Outward Bound 30. The Cat Creeps 30. Midnight Lady 32. Clive of India 35. The White Angel 36. The Prince and the Pauper (as Henry VIII) 37. The Adventures of Robin Hood 38. Gunga Din 39. All This and Heaven Too 40. Shining Victory 41. The Constant Nymph 43. Devotion 44, many others.

Love Me Tonight (US 1932). An early sound musical with an apparent 'Lubitsch touch' which actually belongs to director Rouben Mamoulian, who also manages to provide a René Clair view of Paris as a place where everybody sings. Visual and aural experiments jostle the wit and good humour, and memorable songs like 'Mimi' and 'Isn't It Romantic?' complete a masterpiece of light cinema. With Maurice Chevalier, Jeanette MacDonald, Myrna Loy, Charles Butterworth, Charles Ruggles. What plot there is concerns a tailor who makes it in high society.

The Love Parade (US 1930). An early sound comedy by Ernst Lubitsch which set his style, and that of other directors influenced by him, for many years to come. Brittle, sophisticated, finely mounted, with the story told in visual terms, it was written by Ernest Vajda and Guy Bolton, with sets designed by Hans Dreier and music by Victor Schertzinger; and it started Maurice Chevalier, Jeanette MacDonald, Lupino Lane and Lilian Roth. Its impact cannot now be recaptured.

Love Story (US 1970). A remarkable box office success from the novel by Erich Segal, this very ordinarily made film turned out to be a piece of abject thirties sentimentality dressed up with fashionable four-letter words. About a couple of young marrieds and their parent trouble, it featured a heroine who died of an incurable disease without losing a shred of her beauty. In its wake a flood of similar films was expected, but few materialized and none was successful. Directed by Arthur Hiller, with Ali MacGraw and Ryan O'Neal.

The Loved One (US 1965). Advertised as the film with something to offend everybody, this too-free adaptation of Evelyn Waugh's satirical account of the burial customs of southern California got itself tangled up with a number of extraneous matters, including over-eating, film production and military bureaucracy. Despite central miscasting and some pretentious writing, a number of the bravura passages come off amusingly; but the film remains notable for effort rather than achievement. Directed by Tony Richardson, photographed by Haskell Wexler, with John Gielgud, Liberace, Rod Steiger, Milton Berle and others.

Lovejoy, Frank (1912–1962). American actor of tough roles, with stage and radio experience.

Black Bart 48. Home of the Brave 49. In a Lonely Place 50. The Sound of Fury 51. I Was a Communist for the FBI 51. Force of Arms 51. The Hitch Hiker 52. Retreat Hell 52. The System 53. House of Wax 53. The Charge at Feather River 54. Beachhead 54. The Americano 55. Top of the World 55. Strategic Air Command 55. The Crooked Web 56, etc.

TV series: Meet McGraw 57–58.

Lovell, Raymond (1900–1953). Canadian stage actor long in Britain: often in pompous or sinister roles.

Warn London 34. Contraband 40. 49th Parallel 41. Alibi 42. Warn That Man 43. The Way Ahead 44. Caesar and Cleopatra 45. The Three Weird Sisters 48. Time Gentlemen Please 52. The Steel Key 53, etc.

Lowe, Arthur (1904–). Rotund British character actor who after a career of bit parts achieved star status on TV in a variety of tape shows from Coronation Street to Dad's Army.

Stormy Crossing 48. Kind Hearts and Coronets 49. This Sporting Life 63. The Rise of Michael Rimmer 70. Dad's Army 71. The Ruling Class 71. Theatre of Blood 73. O Lucky Man 73. No Sex Please, We're British 73. Royal Flash 75.

Lowe, Edmund (1890–1971). Suave American leading man of the twenties and thirties who did not manage to age into a character actor.

The Spreading Dawn 17. The Devil 20. Peacock Alley 21. The Silent Command 23. The Fool 25. *What Price Glory?* 26. Is Zat So? 27. Dressed to Kill 28. In Old Arizona 29. The Cockeyed World 29. Scotland Yard 30. Transatlantic 31. Chandu the Magician 32. Dinner at Eight 33. Gift of Gab 34. Mr Dynamite 35. The Great Impersonation 35. Seven Sinners (GB) 36. The Squeaker (GB) 37. Secrets of a Nurse 38. Our Neighbours the Carters 39. Wolf of New York 40. Call out the Marines 41. Murder in Times Square 43. Dillinger 45. Good Sam 48. Around the World in Eighty Days 56. The Wings of Eagles 57. Heller in Pink Tights 60, etc.

TV series: *Front Page Detective* 52.

The Lower Depths. Gorki's doss-house study has had two notable filmings. As *Les Bas Fonds*, it provided in 1936 memorable roles for Jean Gabin and Louis Jouvet, with direction by Jean Renoir. In 1958 in Japan, Akira Kurosawa directed Toshiro Mifune in a surprisingly faithful adaptation.

Lowery, Robert (1916–1971) (R. L. Hanks). American leading man of the forties, mainly in routine films.
Wake Up and Live 37. Young Mr Lincoln 39. Lure of the Islands 42. A Scream in the Dark 44. Prison Ship 45. The Mummy's Ghost 46. Death Valley 48. Batman and Robin (serial) (as Batman) 50. Crosswinds 51. Cow Country 53. The Rise and Fall of Legs Diamond 60. Johnny Reno 66, many others.

Loy, Myrna (1905–) (Myrna Williams). Likeable American lady of the thirties; began her career in villainous oriental roles but later showed a great flair for sophisticated and warm domestic drama.
SELECTED SILENT FILMS: The Cave Man 26. Don Juan 26. The Climbers 27. Beware of Married Men 28. State Street Sadie 28. The Midnight Taxi 28. Noah's Ark 29, etc.
□ SOUND FILMS: The Jazz Singer 27. The Desert Song 29. The Squall 29. Black Watch 29. Hard Boiled Rose 29. Evidence 29. Show of Shows 29. The Great Divide 30. The Jazz Cinderella 30. Cameo Kirby 30. Isle of Escape 30. Under a Texas Moon 30. Cock of the Walk 30. Bride of the Regiment 30. Last of the Duanes 30. The Truth about Youth 30. Renegades 30. Rogue of the Rio Grande 30. The Devil to Pay 30. The Naughty Flirt 31. Body and Soul 31. A Connecticut Yankee 31. Hush Money 31. Transatlantic 31. Rebound 31. Skyline 31. Consolation Marriage 31. Arrowsmith 31. Emma 32. The Wet Parade 32. Vanity Fair 32.

The Woman in Room 13 32. New Morals for Old 32. *Love Me Tonight* 32. Thirteen Women 32. *The Mask of Fu Manchu* 32. The Animal Kingdom 32. Topaze 33. The Barbarian 33. The Prizefighter and the Lady 33. *When Ladies Meet* 33. Penthouse 33. Night Flight 33. Men in White 34. Manhattan Melodrama 34. *The Thin Man* 34. Stamboul Quest 34. Evelyn Prentice 34. *Broadway Bill* 34. Wings in the Dark 35. Whipsaw 35. Wife versus Secretary 36. Petticoat Fever 36. The Great Ziegfeld 36. To Mary with Love 36. Libeled Lady 36. After the Thin Man 36. Parnell 37. *Double Wedding* 37. Man Proof 38. Test Pilot 38. Too Hot to Handle 38. Lucky Night 39. *The Rains Came* 39. Third Finger Left Hand 39. Another Thin Man 39. I Love You Again 40. Love Crazy 41. Shadow of the Thin Man 41. The Thin Man Goes Home 44. So Goes My Love 46. *The Best Years of Our Lives* 46. The Bachelor and the Bobby Soxer 47. Song of the Thin Man 47. *Mr Blandings Builds His Dream House* 48. The Red Pony 49. *Cheaper by the Dozen* 50. My Daughter Joy (GB) 50. Belles on Their Toes 52. The Ambassador's Daughter 56. Lonelyhearts 58. From the Terrace 60. Midnight Lace 60. The April Fools 69. Death Takes a Holiday (TV) 70. Do Not Fold Spindle or Mutilate (TV) 71. Airport 75 74.

Loy, Nanni (1925–). Italian director.
Parola di Ladra 56. The Four Days of Naples 62. Made in Italy 68, etc.

Lubin, Arthur (1901–). American director from 1935, mainly of light comedy, and with a penchant for eccentric animals.
□ A Successful Failure 34. The Great God Gold 35. Honeymoon Limited 35. Two Sinners 35. Frisco Waterfront 35. The House of a Thousand Candles 36. Yellowstone 37. Mysterious Crossing 37. *California Straight Ahead* 37. I Cover the War 37. Idol of the Crowds 37. Adventure's End 37. Midnight Intruder 38. Beloved Brat 38. Prison Break 38. Secrets of a Nurse 38. Risky Business 38. Big Town Czar 39. Mickey the Kid 39. Call a Messenger 39. The Big Guy 40. *Black Friday* 30. Gangs of Chicago 40. I'm Nobody's Sweetheart Now 40. Meet the Wildcat 40. Who Killed Aunt Maggie? 40. San Francisco Docks 41. Where Did You Get That Girl? 41. *Buck Privates* 41. In the Navy 41. Hold That Ghost 41. Keep 'Em Flying 41. Ride 'Em Cowboy 42. Eagle Squadron 42. White Savage 43. *Phantom of the Opera* 43. Ali Baba and the Forty Thieves 44. Delightfully Dangerous 45. Spider Woman Strikes Back 46. A Night in Paradise 46. New Orleans 47. Impact 49. *Francis* 50. Queen for a Day 51. Francis Goes to the Races 51. *Rhubarb* 51. Francis Goes to West

Point 52. It Grows on Trees 52. South Sea Woman 53. Francis Covers Big Town 53. Francis Joins the WACS 54, Francis in the Navy 55. Footsteps in the Fog 55. Lady Godiva 55. Star of India 56. The First Travelling Saleslady 56. Escapade in Japan 57. Thief of Baghdad 61. The Incredible Mr Limpet 64. Hold On 66. Rain for a Dusty Summer 71.
TV series: *Mister Ed* 58–64.

Lubitsch, Ernst (1892–1947). German director, once a comic actor, in a series of silent farces starring him as 'Meyer'. After a variety of subjects he settled for a kind of sophisticated sex comedy that became unmistakably his: the 'Lubitsch touch' was a form of visual innuendo, spicy without ever being vulgar. His greatest period came after 1922, when he settled in Hollywood and became Paramount's leading producer. Early films include many 'shorts. Awarded special Oscar 1946 'for his distinguished contributions to the art of the motion picture'. A splendid biographical book, *The Lubitsch Touch* (1968), was written by Herman G. Weinberg.
SELECTED EUROPEAN FILMS: Carmen 18. Madame du Barry 19. Sumurun 20. Anne Boleyn 20. Pharaoh's Wife 21. The Flame 21, etc.
□ AMERICAN FILMS: Rosita 23. *The Marriage Circle* 24. Three Women 24. *Forbidden Paradise* 24. Kiss Me Again 25. Lady Windermere's Fan 25. So This Is Paris 26. The Student Prince 27. The Patriot 28. Eternal Love 29. *The Love Parade* (first sound film) 29. Paramount on Parade (Chevalier sequences) 30. Monte Carlo 30. The Smiling Lieutenant 31. The Man I Killed 32. *One Hour With You* 32. *Trouble in Paradise* 32. If I Had a Million (Laughton sequence) 32. Design for Living 33. The Merry Widow 34. *Desire* (p only) 36. Angel 37. Bluebeard's Eighth Wife 38. *Ninotchka* 39. *The Shop Around the Corner* 40. That Uncertain Feeling 41. *To Be or Not To Be* 42. *Heaven Can Wait* 43. A Royal Scandal (produced only) 45. Cluny Brown 46. That Lady in Ermine (finished by Otto Preminger) 48.

Lucan, Arthur (1887–1954) (Arthur Towle). British music hall comedian famous for his impersonation of Old Mother Riley, a comic Irish washerwoman. Made fourteen films featuring her, usually with his wife Kitty McShane (1898–1964) playing his daughter.
Stars on Parade 35. Kathleen Mavourneen 36. Old Mother Riley 37. Old Mother Riley in Paris 38. Old Mother Riley Joins Up 39. Old Mother Riley in Business 40. Old Mother Riley's Ghosts 41. Old Mother Riley Detective 43. Old Mother

Riley at Home 45. Old Mother Riley Headmistress 50. Mother Riley Meets the Vampire 52, etc.

Lucas, George (1945–). American director.
□ THX 1138 72. *American Graffiti* (& co-w) 73.

Lucas, Leighton (1903–). British composer and musical director; former ballet dancer.
Target for Tonight 41. Stage Fright 50. A King in New York 57. Ice Cold in Alex 58. The Millionairess 61, many others.

Lucas, Wilfred (1871–1940). Canadian character actor in Hollywood, best remembered as a foil for Laurel and Hardy.
The Barbarian 08. The Spanish Gypsy 11. Cohen's Outing 13. Acquitted 16. The Westerners 18. The Barnstormer 22. The Fatal Mistake 24. Her Sacrifice 26. Just Imagine 30. *Pardon Us* 31. Fra Diavolo 33. The Count of Monte Cristo 34. Modern Times 36. The Baroness and the Butler 38. Zenobia 39. A Chump at Oxford 40. The Sea Wolf 41, many others.

Lucas, William (1926–). British leading man of stage, TV and occasional films.
Timeslip 55. X the Unknown 56. Breakout 59. Sons and Lovers 60. The Devil's Daffodil 61. Calculated Risk 63, etc.

Luchaire, Corinne (1921–1950). French actress who was a big hit in *Prison Without Bars* 38. After World War II was convicted as a collaborator and died in poverty.

Ludwig, Edward (1895–). American director, from 1932.
They Just Had To Get Married 33. Friends of Mr Sweeney 34. *The Man Who Reclaimed His Head* 34. Age of Indiscretion 36. That Certain Age 38. The Last Gangster 39. The Swiss Family Robinson 40. The Man Who Lost Himself 41. They Came To Blow Up America 43. The Fighting Seabees 44. Three's a Family 45. The Fabulous Texan 47. *Wake of the Red Witch* 48. Smuggler's Island 51. Big Jim McLain 52. Sangaree 53. Flame of the Islands 56. The Black Scorpion 57. The Gun Hawk 63, etc.

Ludwig, William (1912–). American writer.
The *Hardy Family* films 38–44. Challenge to Lassie 49. Shadow on the Wall 50. The Great Caruso 51. *Interrupted Melody* (AA) 55. Back Street 61, etc.

Lugosi, Bela (1882–1956) (Bela Lugosi Blasko). Hungarian stage actor of chilling presence and voice; became famous in films as Dracula, but his accent was a handicap for normal roles and he became typecast in inferior horror films.

Biographies: *The Count* (1974) by Arthur Lennig. *Lugosi, the Man behind the Cape* (1976) by Robert Cremer.

The Silent Command 23. The Rejected Woman 24. The Thirteenth Chair 29. Renegades 30. Oh For a Man 30. *Dracula* 30. Broad Minded 31. The Black Camel 31. *The Murders in the Rue Morgue* 31. *White Zombie* 32. *Chandu the Magician* 32. Island of Lost Souls 33. The Death Kiss 33. *The Black Cat* 34. Mysterious Mr Wong 35. The Mystery of the Marie Celeste (GB) 35. Mark of the Vampire 35. The Raven 35. The Invisible Ray 35. Postal Inspector 36. Dark Eyes of London (GB) 38. The Phantom Creeps 39. *Son of Frankenstein* (as Igor) 39. The Saint's Double Trouble 40. Black Friday 40. The Wolf Man 41. Spooks Run Wild 41. Night Monster 42. The Ghost of Frankenstein 42. The Ape Man 43. Frankenstein Meets the Wolf Man (as the monster) 43. The Return of the Vampire 43. One Body Too Many 44. Zombies on Broadway 45. The Body Snatcher 45. Scared to Death 47. *Abbott and Costello Meet Frankenstein* (as Dracula) 48. Bela Lugosi Meets a Brooklyn Gorilla 52. Mother Riley Meets the Vampire (GB) 52. Bride of the Monster 56. Plan 9 from Outer Space 56, etc.

Lukas, Paul (1887–1971) (Pal Lukacs). Suave Hungarian leading actor, in Hollywood from the late twenties, first as a romantic figure, then as a smooth villain, finally as a kindly old man.

Two Lovers 28. Three Sinners 28. Manhattan Cocktail 28. Half Way to Heaven 29. Slightly Scarlet 30. The Benson Murder Case 30. Slightly Dishonorable 31. City Streets 31. Thunder Below 32. Rockabye 32. The Kiss Before the Mirror 33. The Secret of the Blue Room 33. *Little Women* 33. By Candlelight 33. Affairs of a Gentleman 34. I Give My Love 34. The Fountain 34. The Casino Murder Case 34. The Three Musketeers 35. I Found Stella Parish 35. *Dodsworth* 36. Dinner at the Ritz (GB) 37. *The Lady Vanishes* (GB) 38. The Chinese Bungalow (GB) 38. *Confessions of a Nazi Spy* 39. Strange Cargo 40. The Ghost Breakers 40. They Dare Not Love 41. Lady in Distress 32. *Watch on the Rhine* (AA) 43. Hostages 43. Uncertain Glory 44. *Address Unknown* 44. *Experiment Perilous* 44. Deadline at Dawn 46. Berlin Express 48. Kim 50. 20,000 Leagues Under the Sea 54. Roots of Heaven 58. Tender is the Night 61. 55 Days at Peking 63. Lord Jim 65. Sol Madrid 68, etc.

Luke, Keye (1909–). Chinese-American actor who was popular in the thirties as Charlie Chan's number two son.

Charlie Chan in Paris 34. Oil for the Lamps of China 35. King of Burlesque 36. Charlie Chan at the Opera 36. Charlie Chan on Broadway 37. International Settlement 38. Mr Moto's Gamble 38. Disputed Passage 39. Bowery Blitzkrieg 41. Invisible Agent 42. Salute to the Marines 43. Three Men in White 44. First Yank into Tokyo 45. Sleep My Love 47. Hell's Half Acre 54. Battle Hell 57. Yangtse Incident (GB) 57. Nobody's Perfect 67. The Chairman (GB) 69, many others.

TV series: *Anna and the King* 72. *Kung Fu* 72–74.

Lulli, Folco (1912–1970). Italian character actor.

The Bandit 47. Caccia Tragica 48. Without Pity 49. Flight into France 49. No Peace Under the Olives 50. Infidelity 52. *The Wages of Fear* 54. An Eye for an Eye 60. Lafayette 63. Marco the Magnificent 66, many others.

Lulu (1948–) (Marie Lawrie). British pop singer.
□ Gonks Go Beat 65. To Sir With Love 68. The Cherry Picker 72.

Lum and Abner: Chester Lauch (1902–) and Norris Goff (1906–). American comedy actors of hillbilly characters.

Dreaming Out Loud 40. Bashful Bachelors 42, etc.

Lumet, Sidney (1924–). American director, former child actor and TV producer.
□ *Twelve Angry Men* 57. Stage Struck 58. That Kind of Woman 59. The Fugitive Kind 60. A View from the Bridge 61. Long Day's Journey into Night 62. *Fail Safe* 64. *The Pawnbroker* 65. *The Hill* 65. *The Group* 65. The Deadly Affair 66. Bye Bye Braverman 68. The Seagull 68. The Appointment 69. Blood Kin 69. The Anderson Tapes 71. The Offence 72. Child's Play 72. Lovin' Molly 73. Serpico 74. Murder on the Orient Express 74. *Dog Day Afternoon* 75. *Network* 76. Equus 77.

Lumière, Louis (1864–1948). Pioneer French cinematographer, with brother Auguste Lumière (1862–1954). Gave first public demonstration 1895, including *Arrival of Train at Station* and other simple events; later made short comedies, e.g. *L'Arrosseur Arrossé* 1897.

Luna, Barbara (1937–). American actress who usually plays beautiful foreigners.

The Devil at Four O'Clock 60. Five Weeks in a Balloon 62. Synanon 64. Ship of Fools 65. Firecreek 67. Che! 69, etc.

Lund, John (1913–). American leading man with Broadway experience; film roles mainly stodgy.
To Each His Own 46. The Perils of Pauline 47. A Foreign Affair 47. Night Has a Thousand Eyes 48. Miss Tatlock's Millions 48. My Friend Irma 49. Duchess of Idaho 50. Darling, How Could You? 51. Steel Town 52. Bronco Buster 52. The Woman They Almost Lynched 53. Chief Crazy Horse 54. White Feather 55. Battle Stations 56. High Society 56. Affair in Reno 57. The Wackiest Ship in the Army 60, etc.

Lundigan, William (1914–1975). American leading man of routine features, formerly in radio.
Three Smart Girls Grow Up 38. The Old Maid 39. The Sea Hawk 40. Sunday Punch 42. What Next, Corporal Hargrove? 45. Pinky 49. *I'd Climb the Highest Mountain* 51. Down among the Sheltering Palms 52. *Inferno* 53. Serpent of the Nile 53. The White Orchid 54. The Underwater City 61. The Way West 67, etc.
TV series: *Men into Space* 59.

Lunt, Alfred (1892–). Distinguished American stage actor, husband of Lynne Fontanne.
□ Backbone 23. The Ragged Edge 23. Second Youth 24. Lovers in Quarantine 25. Sally of the Sawdust 26. *The Guardsman* 31.

Lupino, Ida (1914–). British leading lady, daughter of Stanley Lupino, who went to Hollywood and played a variety of mainly fraught roles; later became a director.
□ AS ACTRESS: Her First Affaire 33. Money for Speed 33. High Finance 33. The Ghost Camera 33. I Lived with You 34. Prince of Arcadia 34. Search for Beauty 34. Come on Marines 34. Ready for Love 34. Paris in Spring 35. Smart Girl 35. Peter Ibbetson 35. Anything Goes 36. One Rainy Afternoon 36. Yours for the Asking 36. The Gay Desperado 36. Sea Devils 37. Let's Get Married 37. Artists and Models 37. Fight for your Lady 37. The Lone Wolf Spy Hunt 39. The Lady and the Mob 39. The Adventures of Sherlock Holmes 39. The Light that Failed 40. *They Drive by Night* 40. *High Sierra* 41. The Sea Wolf 41. Out of the Fog 41. *Ladies in Retirement* 41. Moontide 42. *The Hard Way* 42. Life Begins at 8.30 42. Forever and a Day 43. Thank your Lucky Stars 43. In Our Time 44. Hollywood Canteen 44. Pillow to Post 45. *Devotion* (as Emily Brontë) 46. The

Man I Love 47. Deep Valley 47. Escape Me Never 47. *Roadhouse* 48. Lust for Gold 49. Woman in Hiding 50. On Dangerous Ground 51. Beware My Lovely 52. Jennifer 53. The Bigamist 53. Private Hell 36 54. Women's Prison 55. The Big Knife 55. While the City Sleeps 56. Strange Intruder 56. Women in Chains (TV) 71. Junior Bonner 72. The Devil's Rain 75. The Food of the Gods 76.
TV series: *Mr Adams and Eve* 56.
AS DIRECTOR: Not Wanted (wp only) 49. Outrage (& w) 50. Never Fear 51. Hard, Fast and Beautiful 51. The Hitch Hiker (& w) 53. The Bigamist 53. Private Hell 36 (w only) 54. The Trouble with Angels 66, plus many TV episodes.

Lupino, Stanley (1893–1942). British comedian on stage from 1900, especially in musical comedy.
The Love Race 32. Sleepless Nights 33. Happy 34. Cheer Up 36. Sporting Love 37. Over She Goes 38. Lucky to Me 39, etc.

Lydon, James (or **Jimmy**) (1923). American actor familiar in the early forties as gangling adolescent.
Back Door to Heaven 39. *Tom Brown's Schooldays* (title role) 40. Little Men 40. Henry Aldrich for President (and subsequent series of ten) 41. Aerial Gunner 43. The Town Went Wild 45. Life with Father 47. Bad Boy 49. September Affair 51. Island in the Sky 53. Battle Stations 56. I Passed for White 60. The Last Time I Saw Archie 61. Brainstorm 65. Death of a Gunfighter 69. Scandalous John 71, etc.

Lye, Len (1901–). New Zealander animator, remembered for British GPO and other shorts of the thirties. Went to US and was associated for a while with *The March of Time*.
Tusalava 29. Colour Box 34. Birth of a Robot 36. Rainbow Dance 36. Kaleidoscope 36. Trade Tattoo 37. Swinging the Lambeth Walk 39. Colour Cry 52. Rhythm 53. Free Radicals 58. Particles in Space 66, etc.

Lyel, Viola (1900–1972) (Violet Watson). British character actress, mainly on stage in comedy roles.
Hobson's Choice (leading role) 30. Channel Crossing 32. Quiet Wedding 40. Wanted for Murder 46. No Place for Jennifer 50. Isn't Life Wonderful? 53. See How They Run 56, etc.

Lyles, A. C. (1918–). American producer, former publicist; noted for his second-feature westerns using veteran talent.
Short Cut to Hell 57. Raymie 60. The Young and the Brave 61. Law of the Lawless 64. Stagecoach

to Hell 64. Young Fury 65. Black Spurs 65. Town Tamer 65. Apache Uprising 66. Johnny Reno 66. Waco 66. Red Tomahawk 67. Buckskin 68, etc.

Lynch, Alfred (1933–). Raw-boned British actor, usually as cockney private.
□ On the Fiddle 61. Two and Two Make Six 61. West Eleven 63. 55 Days at Peking 63. The Hill 65. The Taming of the Shrew 67. The Seagull 68.

lynch law has been condemned in many outstanding dramatic movies from Hollywood. Fury 36. They Won't Forget 37. Young Mr Lincoln 39. The Ox-Bow Incident 43. Storm Warning 51. The Sound of Fury 51. The Sun Shines Bright 52. Rough Night in Jericho 68. See also: *Ku Klux Klan.*

Lynde, Paul (1926–). American TV comedian who usually plays a flustered character with a funny voice.
New Faces 54. Bye Bye Birdie 63. Send Me No Flowers 64. The Glass Bottom Boat 66. How Sweet It Is 68.
TV series: *The Paul Lynde Show* 72. *Temperatures Rising* 74.

Lyndon, Barre (1896–1972) (Alfred Edgar). British playwright, long in Hollywood as scriptwriter.
The Amazing Dr Clitterhouse (oa) 38. Sundown 41. The Lodger 44. The Man in Half Moon Street (oa) 44. The House on 92nd Street 45. Night has a Thousand Eyes 48. The Greatest Show on Earth 51. The War of the Worlds 53. Conquest of Space 54. Sign of the Pagan 55. Omar Khayyam 57. Dark Intruder 65, etc.

Lynley, Carol (1942–). Talented American leading lady of the sixties.
□ The Light in the Forest 58. Holiday for Lovers 59. *Blue Denim* 59. The Hound Dog Man 60. Return to Peyton Place 61. The Last Sunset 61. The Stripper 63. Under the Yum Yum Tree 63. The Cardinal 63. Shock Treatment 64. The Pleasure Seekers 64. *Harlow* (TV) 65. *Bunny Lake is Missing* (GB) 65. The Shuttered Room (GB) 68. Danger Route (GB) 68. The Smugglers (TV) 68. The Maltese Bippy 69. Norwood 69. Once You Kiss a Stranger 70. Weekend of Terror (TV) 70. Crosscurrent (TV) 71. The Night Stalker (TV) 72. The Poseidon Adventure 72. Cotter 73. Death Stalk (TV) 75.

Lynn, Ann (c. 1934–). British actress, mainly on TV; grand-daughter of Ralph Lynn.
Piccadilly Third Stop 60. The Wind of Change 61. Strongroom 61. Flame in the Streets 62.

Black Torment 64. Four in tne Morning 65. Baby Love 69, etc.

Lynn, Diana (1926–1971) (Dolores Loehr). Pert, witty American leading lady of the forties, former child actress and pianist.
□ They Shall Have Music 39. There's Magic in Music 41. Star Spangled Rhythm 42. *The Major and the Minor* 43. Henry Aldrich Gets Glamour 43. *The Miracle of Morgans Creek* 44. And the Angels Sing 44. Henry Aldrich Plays Cupid 44. *Our Hearts were Young and Gay* 44. Out of this World 45. Duffy's Tavern 45. Our Hearts were Growing Up 46. The Bride Wore Boots 46. Easy Come Easy Go 47. Variety Girl 47. Ruthless 48. Texas Brooklyn and Heaven 48. Every Girl Should Be Married 48. My Friend Irma 49. Paid in Full 50. My Friend Irma Goes West 50. Rogues of Sherwood Forest 50. Peggy 50. Bedtime for Bonzo 51. The People against O'Hara 51. Meet Me at the Fair 52. Plunder of the Sun 53. Track of the Cat 54. An Annapolis Story 55. The Kentuckian 55. You're Never Too Young 55. Company of Killers (TV) 71.

Lynn, Jeffrey (1909–) (Ragnar Lind). American leading man with varied experience, in films from 1938.
Four Daughters 38. Yes, My Darling Daughter 39. Espionage Agent 39. The Roaring Twenties 40. A Child Is Born 40. All This and Heaven Too 40. Four Mothers 40. Million Dollar Baby 41. The Body Disappears 41. Whiplash 47. Black Bart 48. A Letter to Three Wives 49. Up Front 51. Captain China 52. Come Thursday 64. Tony Rome 67, many others.

Lynn, Leni (1925–). American girl singer who after debut in *Babes in Arms* 39 came to England and starred in several low-budget musicals.
Heaven Is Round the Corner 43. Give Me the Stars 44. Spring Song 46, etc.

Lynn, Ralph (1882–1964). Incomparable British comedy actor of the silly ass school; his monocled face, limp hands and mastery of timing were essential ingredients of several films of the Aldwych farces of the thirties.
□ *Rookery Nook* 30. Tons of Money 31. Plunder 31. Chance of a Night-Time 31. Mischief 31. A Night like This 32. Thark 32. Just My Luck 33. Summer Lightning 33. Up to the Neck 33. Turkey Time 33. *A Cuckoo in the Nest* 33. A Cup of Kindness 34. Dirty Work 34. Fighting Stock 35. Stormy Weather 35. Foreign Affairs 35. In the Soup 36. Pot Luck 36. All In 36. For Valour 37.

Lynn, Robert (1918–). British director, in

films from 1936 as camera assistant. Son of Ralph Lynn.
Postman's Knock 61. Dr Crippen 62. Victim Five 65. Change Partners 66. The Railway Children (p only) 71, etc.

Lynn, Vera (1921–). British singing star, 'The Forces' Sweetheart' of World War II.
Autobiography 1976: *Vocal Refrain*.
We'll Meet Again 44. One Exciting Night 45, etc.

Lyon, Ben (1901–). Amiable American leading man of the twenties and thirties; came to Britain with his wife Bebe Daniels and stayed to become popular radio personality; later became casting director for 20th-Century Fox.
Biography 1976: *Bebe and Ben* by Jill Allgood.
Open Your Eyes 19. Potash and Perlmutter 23. So Big 24. Bluebeard's Seven Wives 25. The Prince of Tempters 26. Dance Magic 27. The Air Legion 28. Alias French Gertie 30. *Hell's Angels* 30. The Hot Heiress 31. Her Majesty Love 31. Hat Check Girl 32. I Cover the Waterfront 33. Crimson Romance 34. Dancing Feet 36. I Killed the Count (GB) 38. Hi Gang (GB) 40. Life with the Lyons (GB) 54, etc.

Lyon, Francis D. (1905–). American director, former editor.
□ Crazylegs 53. The Bob Mathias Story 54. Cult of the Cobra 55. The Great Locomotive Chase 56. The Oklahoman 56. Bale Out at 43,000 57. Gunsight Ridge 57. South Seas Adventure (co-d) 58. Escort West 59. The Tomboy and the Champ 61. The Young and the Brave 63. Destination Inner Space 66. Castle of Evil 67. The Destructors 68. The Money Jungle 68. The Girl Who Knew Too Much 69.

Lyon, Sue (1946–). American juvenile actress.
Lolita 62. *Night of the Iguana* 64. Seven Women 65. The Flim Flam Man 67. Tony Rome 67. Evel Knievel 72, etc.

Lytell, Bert (1888–1954). American leading man of silent films.
To Have and to Hold 17. The Lone Wolf 21. A Message from Mars 23. *Rupert of Hentzau* 23. Lady Windermere's Fan 25. Steele of the Royal Mounted 27. Blood Brothers 30. The Single Sin 31. Stage Door Canteen 43, etc.

M

M. Fritz Lang was the first, in 1931, to film this story of a child-murderer finally hunted down by the city's organized criminal element, and Peter Lorre had his first great success as the psychopath. In 1950 Joseph Losey directed an almost scene-for-scene American remake starring David Wayne, but it generated no particular atmosphere.

m and e track. A sound track giving music and effects but not dialogue, necessary in dubbing stages.

McAndrew, Marianne (1938–). American leading lady.
Hello Dolly 69. The Seven Minutes 71, etc.

MacArthur, Charles (1895–1956). American playwright and screenwriter, long married to Helen Hayes; often collaborated with Ben Hecht (qv).
Biography 1957: *Charlie* by Ben Hecht.
The Front Page (oaw) 31. The Unholy Garden 31. Rasputin and the Empress 32. 20th Century 34. Crime Without Passion (wpd) 35. Barbary Coast 35. Soak the Rich (wpd) 36. Once in a Blue Moon (wpd) 36. Gunga Din (w) 39. Wuthering Heights (w) 39. His Girl Friday 40. The Senator was Indiscreet (w) 47. Perfect Strangers (oa) 50, etc.

MacArthur, James (1937–). American leading man, former juvenile; adopted son of Charles MacArthur and Helen Hayes.
The Young Stranger 57. The Light in the Forest 58. The Third Man on the Mountain 59. Kidnapped 60. The Swiss Family Robinson 60. The Interns 62. Spencer's Mountain 63. The Truth about Spring 65. The Bedford Incident 65. Ride Beyond Vengeance 66. The Love-Ins 67. Hang 'Em High 68, etc.
TV series: *Hawaii Five-O* 68– .

McAvoy, May (1901–). American leading lady of the twenties, a casualty of sound.
Hate 17. Sentimental Tommy 21. Clarence 22. The Enchanted Cottage 24. Ben Hur 26. The Jazz Singer 27. The Lion and the Mouse 28. No Defense 29, etc.

McBain, Diane (–). American leading lady of the sixties.
Ice Palace 60. Claudelle Inglish 61. A Distant Trumpet 64, etc.

Macbeth. Among many attempts to film Shakespeare's Scottish tragedy, none of them wholly successful, have been the following: 1. In 1915 John Emerson directed and D. W. Griffith produced a straightforward version starring Sir Herbert Beerbohm Tree and Constance Collier. 2. In 1948 Orson Welles directed and starred in his own adaptation, shot in 21 days for Republic; the would-be Scottish burr in which the cast was drilled completely obscured the poetry, but despite papier-maché sets there were some striking effects. 3. In 1956 Ken Hughes wrote and directed a modernized version, *Joe Macbeth*, in which the kings and princes became rival gangsters; Paul Douglas starred. 4. In 1957 Akira Kurosawa directed *Throne of Blood*, a stylized Japanese version. 5. In 1960 George Schaefer directed an honest G.C.E.-type rendering in colour with Maurice Evans and Judith Anderson; destined for American television, it was released theatrically in Britain. 6. In 1971 Jon Finch and Francesca Annis starred in a blood-spattered version by Roman Polanski.

McBride, Donald (1894–1957). American character comedian adept at explosive editors, dumb policemen, etc. Made debut in his stage role as the harassed hotel manager in *Room Service* 38.
The Story of Vernon and Irene Castle 39. *Here Comes Mr Jordan* 41. *Topper Returns* 41. Invisible Woman 41. They Got Me Covered 42. The Glass Key 42. Two Yanks in Trinidad 42. Abbott and Costello in Hollywood 45. Good News 48. Bowery Battalion 51. The Seven Year Itch 55, many others.

McCallister, Lon (1923–). American leading man, usually in callow roles.
Souls at Sea 37. Babes in Arms 39. *Stage Door Canteen* 43. *Home in Indiana* 44. Winged Victory 44. The Red House 47. The Big Cat 50. Letter from Korea 50. Combat Squad 54, etc.

McCallum, David (1933–). Slightly built Scottish juvenile lead of the fifties and sixties; became popular on American television as Ilya Kuriakin in the UNCLE series.

Prelude to Fame 50. The Secret Place 56. Robbery Under Arms 57. Violent Playground 58. The Long the Short and the Tall 61. Billy Budd 62. Freud 62. *The Great Escape* 63. The Greatest Story Ever Told 65. Around the World Under the Sea 66. Three Bites of the Apple 67. Sol Madrid 68. Mosquito Squadron 69. Frankenstein, The True Story (TV) 73. Dogs 76, etc.

TV series: *The Man from UNCLE* 64–67 (plus eight feature films 'amplified' from TV material for cinema release). *Colditz* 72. *Invisible Man* 75.

McCallum, John (1917–). Australian leading man of stage and screen, in England 1945–55; married Googie Withers.

Joe Goes Back 44. The Root of All Evil 47. The Loves of Joanna Godden 47. The Woman in Question 50. Trent's Last Case 52. Trouble in the Glen 53. Port of Escape 55. The Nickel Queen (d only) 71, etc.

McCallum, Neil (1929–1976). Beefy Canadian actor in British films.

The Inspector 62. The Longest Day 62. The War Lover 63. Witchcraft 64, etc.

McCambridge, Mercedes (1918–). Intense, unpredictable American character actress, often in cynical or hard-bitten roles. Autobiography 1960: *The Two of Us*.

□ *All the King's Men* (AA) 50. Lightning Strikes Twice 51. The Scarf 51. Inside Straight 51. Johnny Guitar 54. *Giant* 56. A Farewell to Arms 57. Suddenly Last Summer 59. Cimarron 60. Angel Baby 61. 99 Women 69. The Counterfeit Killer (TV) 70.

McCarey, Leo (1898–1969). American director with above-average talent and a sentimental streak. Before graduating to features he directed many silent shorts, including Laurel and Hardy as *Two Tars*.

□ The Sophomore 29. Red Hot Rhythm 29. Let's Go Native 30. Wild Company 30. Part Time Wife 30. Indiscretion 31. The Kid from Spain 32. *Duck Soup* 33. Six of a Kind 34. Belle of the Nineties 34. *Ruggles of Red Gap* 35. The Milky Way 36. *Make Way for Tomorrow* (& wp) 37. *The Awful Truth* (& w) (AA) 37. *Love Affair* (& w) (AA screenplay) 39. Once Upon a Honeymoon 42. *Going My Way* (AA) (& p) 44. The Bells of St Mary's (& p) 45. Good Sam (& p) 48. My Son John (& wp) 52. An Affair to

Remember (& wp) 57. Rally Round the Flag Boys (& wp) 58. Satan Never Sleeps (& wp) 62.

McCarey, Ray (1904–1948). American director of second features, formerly making Hal Roach shorts.

Pack Up Your Troubles 32. Millions in the Air 36. That Other Woman 42. Atlantic City 44. The Falcon's Alibi 46, etc.

McCarthy, Frank (1912–). American producer.

Decision Before Dawn 51. Sailor of the King 53. A Guide for the Married Man 67. *Patton* 70, etc.

McCarthy, Senator Joseph (1905–1957). American politician who after the Hollywood witch hunt of the late forties sought communists everywhere in government but was finally discredited when he took on the army.

McCarthy, Kevin (1914–). American leading man and latterly character actor, with stage experience.

Death of a Salesman (debut) 52. Stranger on Horseback 55. *Invasion of the Body Snatchers* 56. The Misfits 61. *The Prize* 63. The Best Man 64. Mirage 65. A Big Hand for the Little Lady 66. Hotel 67. If He Hollers Let Him Go 68. Revenge in El Paso 69. Kansas City Bomber 72. Alien Thunder 73. Buffalo Bill and the Indians 76, etc.

TV series: *The Survivors* 69.

McCarthy, Michael (1917–1959). British director, in films from 1934.

Assassin for Hire 51. Mystery Junction 51. Crow Hollow 52. Shadow of a Man 54. It's Never Too Late 56. Smoke Screen 57. The Traitor 57. Operation Amsterdam 58, etc.

McClory, Kevin (1926–). Irish production executive, former sound technician. Wrote, produced and directed *The Boy and the Bridge* 59; produced *Thunderball* 65.

McClory, Sean (1923–). Irish actor with Abbey Theatre experience; long in Hollywood. Beyond Glory 49. Rommel, Desert Fox 51. Les Misérables 52. Ring of Fear 54. Moonfleet 55. Diane 57. Bandolero 68, etc.

McClure, Doug (1935–). American leading man, from TV.

Because They're Young 59. The Unforgiven 60. Shenandoah 65. Beau Geste 66. The King's Pirate 67. Nobody's Perfect 68. The Judge and Jake Wyler (TV) 71. The Land That Time Forgot 75. At The Earth's Core 76, etc.

TV series: *Checkmate* 59–61. *Overland Trail* 60. *The Virginian* 64–69. *Search* 72.

McClure, Greg (1918–) (Dale Easton). American leading man who starred in his first film but did little thereafter.
The Great John L 45. Bury Me Dead 47. Lulu Belle 48. Joe Palooka in the Squared Circle 50. Stop That Cab 51, etc.

McCord, Ted (1910–1976). American cinematographer.
Treasure of Sierra Madre 48. *Johnny Belinda* 48. The Breaking Point 50. Young at Heart 54. East of Eden 54. The Proud Rebel 58. War Hunt 61. Two for the Seesaw 63. *The Sound of Music* 65. A Fine Madness 66, etc.

McCormack, John (1884–1945). Irish tenor. Song O'My Heart 30. Wings of the Morning 37.

McCormack, Patty (1945–). American juvenile actress who went to Hollywood to repeat her stage role as the evil child of *The Bad Seed* 56.
The Day They Gave Babies Away 57. Kathy 'O 58. The Adventures of Huckleberry Finn 60. The Explosive Generation 61. The Young Runaways 68, etc.

McCormick, F. J. (1891–1947) (Peter Judge). Irish character actor, long on the Abbey Theatre stage. Well remembered as Shell in *Odd Man Out* 46.
The Plough and the Stars 37. Hungry Hill 46.

McCormick, Myron (1908–1962). Wry-faced American character actor, with stage experience.
Winterset 37. One Third of a Nation 39. Jigsaw 49. Jolson Sings Again 50. No Time for Sergeants 58. *The Hustler* 61, etc.

McCowan, George (–). American TV director who made a Hollywood start with *Frogs* 72.

McCowen, Alec (1925–). Youthful-looking British stage actor, in occasional films.
Time without Pity 57. Town on Trial 57. The Loneliness of the Long Distance Runner 62. In the Cool of the Day 63. The Agony and the Ecstasy 65. The Witches 66. The Hawaiians (US) 70. Frenzy 72. *Travels With My Aunt* 72, etc.

McCoy, Tim (1891–). American cowboy star, in films from 1923 when, an ex-army officer, he went to Hollywood as adviser on The Covered Wagon.
War Paint 26. The Indians Are Coming 30. The Fighting Fool 31. Texas Cyclone 32. Whirlwind 33. Hell Bent for Love 34. Square Shooter 35, many others. Later played bit parts: Around the World in Eighty Days 56. Run of the Arrow 57. Requiem for a Gunfighter 65, etc.

McCrea, Joel (1905–). Athletic, good-humoured, dependable American hero of the thirties and forties.
□ Penrod and Sam 23. The Jazz Age 29. So This is College 29. Dynamite 29. The Silver Horde 29. Lightnin' 30. Once a Sinner 30. Kept Husbands 31. Born to Love 31. Girls about Town 31. Business and Pleasure 32. The Lost Squadron 32. *Bird of Paradise* 32. *The Most Dangerous Game* 32. Rockabye 32. The Sport Parade 32. The Silver Cord 33. Bed of Roses 33. One Man's Journey 33. Chance at Heaven 33. Gambling Lady 34. Half a Sinner 34. The Richest Girl in the World 35. Private Worlds 35. Our Little Girl 35. Woman Wanted 35. Barbary Coast 35. Splendour 35. These Three 36. Two in a Crowd 36. Adventure in Manhattan 36. Come and Get It 36. Banjo on My Knee 36. Internes Can't Make Money 37. Wells Fargo 37. Woman Chases Man 37. *Dead End* 37. Three Blind Mice 38. Youth Takes a Fling 38. Union Pacific 39. They Shall Have Music 39. Espionage Agent 39. He Married His Wife 40. The Primrose Path 40. *Foreign Correspondent* 40. Reaching for the Sun 41. *Sullivan's Travels* 41. The Great Man's Lady 42. *The Palm Beach Story* 42. The More the Merrier 43. Buffalo Bill 44. The Great Moment 44. The Unseen 45. The Virginian 46. Ramrod 47. Four Faces West 48. South of St Louis 49. Colorado Territory 49. Stars in My Crown 50. The Outriders 50. Saddle Tramp 50. Frenchie 50. Cattle Drive 51. The San Francisco Story 52. Lone Hand 53. Rough Shoot (GB) 53. Border River 54. Stranger on Horseback 55. Wichita 55. The First Texan 56. The Oklahoman 57. Trooper Hook 57. Gunsight Ridge 57. The Tall Stranger 57. Cattle Empire 58. Fort Massacre 58. Gunfight at Dodge City 59. *Ride the High Country* 62. Cry Blood Apache 71. Mustang Country 76.
TV series: *Wichita Town* 59.

McCullers, Carson (1917–1967). American novelist, usually on themes pertaining to her homeland, the deep south.
The Member of the Wedding, Reflections in a Golden Eye, The Heart is a Lonely Hunter.

McCullough, Paul (1884–1936). American farce comedian, with Bobby Clark in two-reelers 1928–35.

McDaniel, Hattie (1895–1952). Black American character actress of cheerful and immense presence; once a radio vocalist.

The Story of Temple Drake 33. Judge Priest 35. Showboat 36. Nothing Sacred 37. *Gone with the Wind* (AA) 39. *The Great Lie* 41. Thank Your Lucky Stars 43. Margie 46. Song of the South 47. Family Honeymoon 49, many others.

TV series: *Beulah* 52.

McDermott, Hugh (1908–1972). Scottish-born character actor, in British films from mid-thirties, specializing in hearty transatlantic types.

The Wife of General Ling 38. Pimpernel Smith 41. The Seventh Veil 45. No Orchids for Miss Blandish 48. Trent's Last Case 52. A King in New York 57. The First Men in the Moon 64. Captain Apache 71. Chato's Land 72, many others.

McDevitt, Ruth (1895–1976) (Ruth Shoecraft). American character actress.

The Parent Trap 62. The Birds 63. The Out of Towners 69, many others.

MacDonald, David (1904–). British director who showed promise in the thirties and forties but declined to second features.

Double Alibi 27. It's Never Too Late to Mend 37. Dead Men Tell No Tales 38. A Spot of Bother 38. *This Man is News* 38. This Man in Paris 39. Spies of the Air 39. Law and Disorder 40. Men of the Lightship 40. This England 40. *The Brothers* 47. Good Time Girl 48. Snowbound 48. Christopher Columbus 49. Diamond City 49. The Bad Lord Byron 49. Cairo Road 50. The Adventurers 51. The Lost Hours 52. Tread Softly 53. Devil Girl from Mars 54. Alias John Preston 56. Small Hotel 57. *The Moonraker* 58. Petticoat Pirates 61, etc.

McDonald, Frank (1899–). American director of second features; former stage actor and author.

The Murder of Dr Harrigan 38. Carolina Moon 40. One Body Too Many 44. My Pal Trigger 46. Father Takes the Air 51. The Treasure of Ruby Hills 55. The Underwater City 61, etc.

McDonald, Grace (1921–). American singing and dancing second lead of many a forties 'B'.

MacDonald, Jeanette (1902/3–1965). American concert singer and leading lady of the thirties. Popular on her own account, she made a fondly remembered series of film operettas with Nelson Eddy, and these are noted (E) below.

Biography 1976: *The Jeanette MacDonald Story* by Robert Parish.

□ *The Love Parade* 29. The Vagabond King 30. Monte Carlo 30. Let's Go Native 30. The Lottery Bride 30. Oh For a Man 30. Don't Bet on Women 31. Annabelle's Affairs 31. *One Hour With You* 32. *Love Me Tonight* 32. The Cat and the Fiddle 32. The Merry Widow 34. *Naughty Marietta* (E) 35. *Rose Marie* (E) 36. *San Francisco* 36. Maytime (E) 37. The Firefly 37. The Girl of the Golden West (E) 38. Sweethearts (E) 39. Broadway Serenade 39. New Moon (E) 40. Bitter Sweet (E) 40. Smilin' Through 41. I Married an Angel (E) 42. Cairo 42. Follow the Boys 44. Three Daring Daughters 48. The Sun Comes Up 49.

MacDonald, J. Farrell (1875–1952). American minstrel singer who became a familiar Hollywood character actor.

The Maltese Falcon 31. The Thirteenth Guest 32. The Cat's Paw 34. The Irish in Us 36. Topper 37. Little Orphan Annie 39. Meet John Doe 41. My Darling Clementine 46. Mr Belvedere Rings the Bell 51, etc.

MacDonald, Joseph (1906–1968). American cinematographer.

Charlie Chan in Rio 41. Sunday Dinner for a Soldier 44. *Yellow Sky* 48. Panic in the Streets 50. *Viva Zapata* 52. Niagara 53. Titanic 53. How to Marry a Millionaire 53. Broken Lance 54. A Hatful of Rain 57. Ten North Frederick 57. Pepe 60. Kings of the Sun 63. The Carpetbaggers 63. Rio Conchos 64. Invitation to a Gunfighter 64. Mirage 65. Blindfold 65. The Sand Pebbles 66. Mackenna's Gold 68, many others.

McDonald, Marie (1923–1965) (Marie Frye). American leading lady, publicized as 'The Body'; former model.

Pardon My Sarong 42. A Scream in the Dark 44. Getting Gertie's Garter 46. Living in a Big Way 47. Tell It to the Judge 49. Geisha Boy 59. Promises Promises 63, etc.

McDonald, Ray (1920–1959). American actor-dancer of lightweight forties musicals.

Babes in Arms 39. Presenting Lily Mars 43. Good News 47. Till the Clouds Roll By 48, etc.

McDonell, Fergus (1910–1968). British director.

The Small Voice 48. Prelude to Fame 50. Private Information 52, etc.

MacDougall, Ranald (1915–1973). American screenwriter.

Objective Burma 45. Possessed 47. The

Unsuspected 47. June Bride 48. The Hasty Heart 49. Bright Leaf 50. I'll Never Forget You 51. The Naked Jungle 54. Queen Bee (& d) 55. The Mountain 56. Man on Fire (& d) 57. The World the Flesh and the Devil (& d) 59. Go Naked in the World (& d) 61. The Cockeyed Cowboys of Calico County (& d) 69, etc.

MacDougall, Roger (1910–). British screenwriter and playwright.
This Man is News (w) 38. The Foreman went to France (w) 42. *The Man in the White Suit* (oaw) 51. To Dorothy a Son (oa) 54. *Escapade* (oa) 56. The Mouse that Roared (w) 59. A Touch of Larceny (w) 60, etc.

McDowall, Roddy (1928–). British child actor of the forties, in Hollywood from 1940. Developed into an unpredictable adult performer, but made a reputation as a photographer.
Murder in the Family 36. Just William 37. This England 40. Man Hunt 41. *How Green Was My Valley* 41. Confirm or Deny 41. The Pied Piper 42. My Friend Flicka 43. Lassie Come Home 43. The White Cliffs of Dover 44. Thunderhead 45. Holiday in Mexico 46. Macbeth 50. Killer Shark 50. The Subterraneans 60. The Longest Day 62. Cleopatra 63. Shock Treatment 64. The Loved One 65. That Darn Cat 65. Lord Love a Duck 66. The Cool Ones 67. It 67. Planet of the Apes 67. Five Card Stud 68. Angel Angel Down You Go 69. Beneath the Planet of the Apes 70. Tam Ling (d only) 70. Escape from the Planet of the Apes 71. Bedknobs and Broomsticks 71. Pretty Maids all in a Row 71. Conquest of the Planet of the Apes 72. The Poseidon Adventure 72. The Legend of Hell House 73. Battle for the Planet of the Apes 73. Arnold 74. Funny Lady 75, etc.
TV series: *Planet of the Apes* 74.

McDowell, Malcolm (1944–). Fashionable British leading actor of the early seventies.
If 69. Figures in a Landscape 70. The Raging Moon 71. *A Clockwork Orange* 71. *O Lucky Man* 73. Royal Flash 75. Aces High 76, etc.

McEachin, James (1934–). Black American actor of the seventies, TV's *Tenafly*.
The Alpha Caper (TV) 73.

McEnery, John (1945–). British light leading man of the seventies.
Romeo and Juliet 68. The Lady in a Car 70. *Bartleby* 71. Nicholas and Alexandra 71. Days of Fury 73. The Land that Time Forgot 74. Little Malcolm 74, etc.

McEnery, Peter (1940–). British leading man with TV experience.
Tunes of Glory 60. Victim 62. The Moonspinners 64. The Fighting Prince of Donegal 66. The Game Is Over 66. I Killed Rasputin 68. Negatives 68. Entertaining Mr Sloane 70. The Adventures of Gerard 70. Tales that Witness Madness 73, etc.

McEveety, Bernard (–). American director, from TV.
Broken Sabre 65. Ride Beyond Vengeance 66. The Brotherhood of Satan 70. Napoleon and Samantha 72. One Little Indian 73, etc.

McEveety, Joseph L. (1926–1976). American producer, long with Disney.

McEveety, Vince or **Vincent** (–). American director.
Firecreek 68. Million Dollar Duck 71, etc.

McEwan, Geraldine (1933–). Leading British stage actress.
Escape from the Dark 76. The Bawdy Adventures of Tom Jones 76.

McFadden, Hamilton (1901–). American director of 'B' features.
Harmony at Home 30. Charlie Chan Carries On 31. Second Hand Wife 33. Stand Up and Cheer 34. Elinor Norton 35. The Three Legionnaires 37. Sea Racketeers 39. Inside the Law 42, etc.

McFarland, Spanky (1928–) (George Emmett McFarland). American child actor of the thirties, the fat boy of the 'Our Gang' one-reelers.
Day of Reckoning 33. Kentucky Kernels 35. O'Shaughnessy's Boy 35. Trail of the Lonesome Pine 36. Peck's Bad Boy with the Circus 39. Johnny Doughboy 43, etc.

McGann, William (1895–). American director of second features.
I Like Your Nerve 31. Illegal 32. The Case of the Black Cat 36. Penrod and Sam 37. Blackwell's Island 39. The Parson of Panamint 41. Tombstone 42. Frontier Badmen 43, etc.

McGavin, Darren (1922–). American 'character lead' who can play unpleasant villains or tough heroes.
Fear 46. Summer Madness 55. The Court Martial of Billy Mitchell 55. *The Man with the Golden Arm* 56. The Delicate Delinquent 57. Beau James 57. The Case Against Brooklyn 58. Bullet for a Badman 64. The Great Sioux Massacre 65. Mrs Pollifax—Spy 70. Happy

Mother's Day Love George 73. The Night Stalker (TV) 74. The Night Strangler (TV) 74. No Deposit No Return 76, etc.
TV series: *Mike Hammer* 58. *Riverboat* 60. *The Outsider* 68. *The Night Stalker* 74.

McGee, Fibber (1897–) (James Jordan). American radio comedian, always with his wife 'Molly' (Marion: 1898–1961).
This Way Please 38. Look Who's Laughing 40. Here We Go Again 41. Heavenly Days 44, etc.

McGill, Barney (–1941). American cinematographer.
Breezy Jim 19. The Critical Age 23. Casey at the Bat 27. The Terror 28. Show of Shows 29. Doorway to Hell 30. Mammy 30. *Svengali* 31. The Mouthpiece 32. Cabin in the Cotton 32. Twenty Thousand Years in Sing Sing 33. Mayor of Hell 33. *The Bowery* 33. The President Vanishes 34. My Marriage 35. Thank You Jeeves 36. Lancer Spy 37. Sharpshooters 38. The Cisco Kid and the Lady 40, many others.

McGinn, Walter (c. 1939–). American character actor of the seventies.
The Parallax View 74. Delancy Street (TV) 75.

MacGinnis, Niall (1913–). Irish-born actor, in films since 1935.
Turn of the Tide 35. Edge of the World 38. 49th Parallel 41. We Dive at Dawn 43. Henry V 44. No Highway 51. *Martin Luther* (title role) 53. The Battle of the River Plate 55. *Night of the Demon* 57. The Nun's Story 58. Billy Budd 62. A Face in the Rain 62. Becket 64. Island of Terror 66. Sinful Davey 69, etc.

McGiver, John (1913–1975). American character comedian with worried, owl-like features.
Love in the Afternoon 57. *Breakfast at Tiffany's* 61. Mr Hobbs Takes a Vacation 62. The Manchurian Candidate 62. Who's Minding the Store? 63. Man's Favourite Sport? 64. Marriage on the Rocks 65. The Spirit is Willing 67. Fitzwilly 67. Midnight Cowboy 69. Lawman 70. The Great Man's Whiskers (TV) 71. The Apple Dumpling Gang 75, etc.
TV series: *Many Happy Returns* 64. *The James Stewart Show* 71.

McGlynn, Frank (1867–1951). American character actor, adept at portraying Abraham Lincoln.
Min and Bill 31. Little Miss Marker 34. The Littlest Rebel 35. Trail of the Lonesome Pine 36. Prisoner of Shark Island 37. Wells Fargo 37. Union Pacific 39. Boom Town 40, many others.

McGoohan, Patrick (1928–). American-born leading man with individual characteristics; in British films, after stage experience, from the mid-fifties.
Passage Home 55. Zarak 55. *High Tide at Noon* 56. *Hell Drivers* 57. The Gypsy and the Gentleman 57. Nor the Moon by Night 58. Two Living One Dead 60. All Night Long 61. The Quare Fellow 62. *Life For Ruth* 62. Dr Syn 63. Ice Station Zebra 68. The Moonshine War 70. Mary Queen of Scots 72. Catch My Soul (d only) 73. The Genius (It.) 75. Silver Streak 76, etc.
TV series: *Danger Man* (Secret Agent) 60–66. *The Prisoner* 67.

MacGowan, Kenneth (1888–1963). American film theorist and teacher (at UCLA) who was also a notable producer. Author of several film textbooks.
Little Women 33. Becky Sharp 35. Young Mr Lincoln 39. Man Hunt 41. Lifeboat 43. Jane Eyre 43, etc.

McGowan, Robert A. (1901–). American producer who devised the original 'Our Gang' comedies.

MacGowran, Jack (1916–1973). Irish character actor, usually of mean, sharp-featured fellows. Also on stage and TV.
The Quiet Man 52. The Gentle Gunman 52. The Titfield Thunderbolt 53. The Rising of the Moon 57. Darby O'Gill and the Little People 59. Blind Date 60. Mix Me a Person 61. Lord Jim 65. Cul de Sac 66. The Fearless Vampire Killers 67. How I Won the War 67. Wonderwall 68. The Exorcist 73, etc.

McGrath, Frank (1903–1967). Grizzled American stunt man who appeared in countless westerns but achieved his greatest popularity as the trail cook in TV's *Wagon Train* series.

McGrath, Joe (1930–). Scottish director whose TV style of goonish comedy has adapted less successfully to film.
Casino Royale (part) 67. Thirty is a Dangerous Age Cynthia 68. The Bliss of Mrs Blossom 68. The Magic Christian 70. Digby 73. The Great McGonagall 74, etc.

MacGraw, Ali (1938–). American leading lady.
□ A Lovely Way to Die 68. *Goodbye Columbus* 69. *Love Story* 71. Getaway 72.

McGraw, Charles (1914–). American actor, invariably in tough roles.
The Moon Is Down 43. The Killers 46. The

Armored Car Robbery 50. *The Narrow Margin* 50. His Kind of Woman 51. The Bridges at Toko-Ri 51. Away All Boats 56. Slaughter on Tenth Avenue 58. The Defiant Ones 58. The Wonderful Country 59. Spartacus 60. Cimarron 61. In Cold Blood 67. Pendulum 69. Johnny Got His Gun 71, etc.

McGuane, Thomas (–). American screenwriter.
Rancho de Luxe 75. 92 in the Shade (& d) 75. The Missouri Breaks 76, etc.

McGuire, Don (1919–). American writer-director, former press agent. Then to TV as producer-director of the *Hennessey* series.
Meet Danny Wilson (w) 51. Walking My Baby Back Home (w) 52. Three Ring Circus (w) 54. Bad Day at Black Rock (co-w) 54. Johnny Concho (wd) 56. The Delicate Delinquent (wd) 57.

McGuire, Dorothy (1919–). American leading lady of the forties, latterly playing mothers; always in gentle, sympathetic roles.
□ Claudia 43. *A Tree Grows in Brooklyn* 44. The Enchanted Cottage 44. *The Spiral Staircase* 45. Claudia and David 46. Till the End of Time 46. Gentleman's Agreement 47. Mother Didn't Tell Me 50. Mister 880 50. Callaway Went Thataway 50. I Want You 51. Invitation 52. Make Haste to Live 53. *Three Coins in the Fountain* 54. Trial 55. Friendly Persuasion 56. Old Yeller 57. The Remarkable Mr Pennypacker 59. This Earth Is Mine 59. A Summer Place 60. *The Dark at the Top of the Stairs* 60. The Swiss Family Robinson 60. Susan Slade 61. Summer Magic 63. The Greatest Story Ever Told (as the Virgin Mary) 65. Flight of the Doves 71. She Waits (TV) 71. Rich Man Poor Man (TV) 76.

Machaty, Gustav (1898–1963). Czech director best remembered for exposing Hedy Lamarr's naked charms in *Extase* 33.
The Kreutzer Sonata 26. Erotikon 29. From Saturday to Sunday 31. Nocturno 35. Within the Law (US) 39. Jealousy (US) 45, etc.

McHugh, Frank (1899–). Amiable American character actor with surprised look, frequently in Irish-American roles.
If Men Played Cards as Women Do 28. Dawn Patrol 30. The Mystery of the Wax Museum 33. Footlight Parade 33. Havana Widows 34. A Midsummer Night's Dream 35. Three Men on a Horse 36. Swing Your Lady 38. Going My Way 44. State Fair 45. Mighty Joe Young 49. My Son John 51. There's No Business Like Show Business 54. Career 59. A Tiger Walks 64. Easy

Come Easy Go 67, many others.
TV series: *The Bing Crosby Show 64*.

McHugh, Jimmy (1895–1969). American song-writer: 'I Can't Give You Anything But Love, Baby', 'I Feel a Song Comin' On', 'On the Sunny Side of the Street', etc.
You'll Find Out 40. Seven Days Ashore 43. Do You Love Me? 46, etc.

McIntire, John (1907–). Spare, laconic American character actor with radio and stage experience, in Hollywood from the mid-forties, often as sheriff, editor, politician, cop.
The Asphalt Jungle 50. Lawless Breed 52. A Lion Is in the Streets 53. Apache 54. The Far Country 54. The Kentuckian 55. Backlash 56. The Phoenix City Story 56. The Tin Star 57. Flaming Star 60. Psycho 60. Summer and Smoke 62. Rough Night in Jericho 67. Herbie Rides Again 73. Rooster Cogburn 75, etc.
TV series: *Naked City* 59. *Wagon Train* 61–64. *The Virginian* 67–69.

Maciste. A legendary hero of the Italian cinema, a strong man originating in *Cabiria* (14). Such of his adventures as have been dubbed into English usually translate him as Samson.

Mack, Helen (1913–). American leading lady of the thirties, former child actress.
Zaza 24. Grit 28. The Silent Witness 31. Son of Kong 34. She 35. The Return of Peter Grimm 35. The Milky Way 36. Last Train from Madrid 37. Gambling Ship 39. His Girl Friday 40. Divorce (last to date) 45, etc.

Mack, Russell (1892–1972). American director of the thirties.
Second Wife 30. Heaven on Earth 31. Once in a Lifetime 32. Private Jones 33. The Band Plays On 34. The Meanest Girl in Town 35, etc.

Mackaill, Dorothy (1903–). British leading lady of the American silent screen, former Ziegfeld chorine.
The Face at the Window (GB) 21. Twenty-one 26. Dancer of Paris 27. Children of the Ritz 29. Once a Sinner 30. Kept Husbands 31. No Man of Her Own 32. Bulldog Drummond at Bay 37, etc.

Mackay, Barry (1906–). British stage leading man and singer.
Evergreen 34. Oh Daddy 35. Forever England 35. Glamorous Night 37. Gangway 37. Sailing Along 38. Smuggled Cargo 40. Pickwick Papers 52. Orders Are Orders 55.

McKellen, Ian (1935–). British stage actor, in occasional films.
Alfred the Great 69. A Touch of Love 69. The Promise 69, etc.

Mackendrick, Alexander or **Sandy** (1912–). American director, long in Britain; pursued an erratic career with a couple of brilliant spots.
□ Midnight Menace (w only) 37. Saraband for Dead Lovers (w only) 48. *Whisky Galore* (& w) 49. Dance Hall (w only) 50. *The Man in the White Suit* (& w) 51. *Mandy* 52. The Maggie 54. The Ladykillers 55. *Sweet Smell of Success* 56. Sammy Going South 62. A High Wind in Jamaica 65. Don't Make Waves 67.

MacKenna, Kenneth (1899–1962) (Leo Mielziner). American general purpose actor (also director).
Miss Bluebeard 25. The Lunatic at Large 27. Crazy that Way 30. Those We Love 32. High Time 60. 13 West Street 62, etc.

McKenna, Siobhan (1923–). Fiery Irish actress, on stage from 1940, and in very occasional films.
□ Hungry Hill 46. Daughter of Darkness 48. The Lost People 49. King of Kings 61. Playboy of the Western World 62. Of Human Bondage 64. Doctor Zhivago 65, etc.

McKenna, T. P. (1931–). Irish general purpose actor.
Anne of the Thousand Days 70. The Beast in the Cellar 70. Perfect Friday 70. Villain 71, etc.

McKenna, Virginia (1931–). Demure-looking but spirited British leading lady with stage experience; married to Bill Travers.
□ The Second Mrs Tanqueray 52. Father's Doing Fine 52. The Oracle 53. *The Cruel Sea* 54. Simba 55. The Ship That Died of Shame 55. *A Town Like Alice* (BFA) 56. The Smallest Show on Earth 57. The Barretts of Wimpole Street 57. *Carve Her Name with Pride* 58. The Passionate Summer 58. The Wreck of the Mary Deare 59. Two Living One Dead 62. *Born Free* 66. Ring of Bright Water 69. An Elephant Called Slowly 70. Waterloo 70. Swallows and Amazons 74.

Mackenzie, Sir Compton (1883–1974). Scottish novelist. His *Carnival* was twice filmed, but he became best known for *Whisky Galore*, in which he also played a part.

McKern, Leo (1920–). Australian character actor with wide stage experience and usually

explosive personality. On stage from 1942, in England from 1946.
All for Mary 55. X the Unknown 56. *Time without Pity* 57. The Mouse That Roared 59. Mr Topaze 61. The Day the Earth Caught Fire 62. *A Jolly Bad Fellow* 64. King and Country 64. Moll Flanders 65. Help! 65. *A Man for All Seasons* 66. Decline and Fall 68. Ryan's Daughter 71. The Adventure of Sherlock Holmes' Smarter Brother 76. The Omen 76, etc.

McKinney, Nina Mae (1909–1968). Black American actress.
Hallelujah 29. Sanders of the River 35. Dark Waters 44. Without Love 45. Pinky 49, etc.

MacKenzie, John (1932–). British director, ex TV.
□ One Brief Summer 69. Unman Wittering and Zigo 71. Made 72.

McLaglen, Andrew (1925–). American director, son of Victor McLaglen; has made several big-scale westerns in the manner of John Ford.
□ Gun the Man Down 56. *The Abductors* 56. The Man in the Vault 57. The Little Shepherd of Kingdom Come 61. *McLintock* 63. *Shenandoah* 65. The Rare Breed 66. Monkeys Go Home 67. The Way West 67. The Ballad of Josie 68. The Devil's Brigade 68. Bandolero 68. The Undefeated 69. Something Big (& p) 71. Fool's Parade (& p) 71. The Train Robbers 73. The Oregon Trail (TV) 76.

McLaglen, Victor (1883–1959). Burly, good-humoured star of British silent films; later became popular in Hollywood.
Autobiography 1935: *Express to Hollywood*.
The Call of the Road 20. The Glorious Adventure 21. The Beloved Brute 23. Beau Geste 26. *What Price Glory?* 26. Captain Lash 27. Mother Macree 28. The Cockeyed World 29. *Dishonoured* 30. Wicked 31. Rackety Rax 32. Hot Pepper 33. *Dick Turpin* 33. *The Lost Patrol* 34. *The Informer* (AA) 35. Under Two Flags 36. The Magnificent Brute 37. *Gunga Din* 39. Broadway Limited 41. Call Out the Marines 42. Powder Town 42. The Princess and the Pirate 44. The Michigan Kid 47. Fort Apache 48. *She Wore a Yellow Ribbon* 49. Rio Grande 50. *The Quiet Man* 52. Fair Wind to Java 53. Prince Valiant 54. Lady Godiva 55. Many Rivers to Cross 55. Bengazi 56. The Abductors 57. Sea Fury 58, many others.

Maclaine, Shirley (1934–) (Shirley Maclean Beaty). Impish American leading lady, sister of Warren Beatty. Was signed for films while

dancing in a Broadway chorus.
Autobiographies: 1970, *Don't Fall Off The Mountain*. 1975, *You Can't Get There from Here*.
□ *The Trouble with Harry* 55. Artists and Models 56. Around the World in Eighty Days 56. Hot Spell 57. *The Matchmaker* 58. Some Came Running 58. The Sheepman 58. *Ask Any Girl* (BFA) 59. Career 59. Can-Can 59. *The Apartment* (BFA) 59. All in a Night's Work 61. Spinster 61. My Geisha 62. The Children's Hour 62. Two for the Seesaw 63. *Irma La Douce* 63. What a Way To Go 64. The Yellow Rolls Royce 64. John Goldfarb Please Come Home 64. Gambit 66. Woman Times Seven 67. *Sweet Charity* 68. The Bliss of Mrs Blossom (GB) 68. Two Mules for Sister Sara 69. Desperate Characters 71. The Possession of Joel Delaney 72.
TV series: *Shirley's World* 71.

MacLane, Barton (1900–1969). Tough-looking American character actor, often seen as crooked cop, sheriff or gangster. In hundreds of films since 1924 debut.
Tillie and Gus 33. Black Fury 34. Ceiling Zero 36. You Only Live Once 37. Gold Is Where You Find It 38. The Maltese Falcon 41. Bombardier 43. San Quentin 46. The Treasure of the Sierra Madre 47. Kiss Tomorrow Goodbye 51. Captain Scarface (leading role) 53. Backlash 56. Geisha Boy 58. Gunfighters of Abilene 59. Law of the Lawless 63. Town Tamer 65. Buckskin 68, many others.
TV series: *Outlaws* 60.

McLaren, Norman (1914–). British-born Canadian animator-director of notable shorts, especially for the National Film Board, mainly with sound as well as picture drawn directly onto the celluloid; occasionally uses live action with stop motion, and a variety of other techniques.
Allegro 39. *Dots and Loops* 40. Boogie Doodle 41. Hoppity Pop 46. Fiddle-de-dee 47. *Begone Dull Care* 49. Around is Around 51. *Neighbours* 52. Blinkety Blank 55. Rhythmetic 56. A Chairy Tale 57. Blackbird 58. Parallels 60. *Pas de Deux* 62. Mosaic 65, etc.

McLaughlin, Gibb (1884–197*). British character actor of stage and screen, once a stage monologuist and master of disguise; used his splendidly emaciated features to great advantage.
Carnival 21. Nell Gwyn 24. The Farmer's Wife 27. Kelly 29. Sally in Our Alley 31. The Private Life of Henry VIII 32. No Funny Business 33. The Scarlet Pimpernel 34. Where There's a Will 36. Mr Reeder in Room Thirteen (title role) 40.

My Learned Friend 43. Caesar and Cleopatra 45. Oliver Twist 48. The Black Rose 51. The Card 52. Hobson's Choice 54. Sea Wife 57, many others.

MacLean, Alistair (1922–). Best-selling British adventure novelist whose works suddenly became popular as screen fodder.
The Guns of Navarone 60. When Eight Bells Toll 70. Puppet on a Chain 71. Fear is the Key 72. Caravan to Vaccares 75. Breakheart Pass 76, etc.

MacLean, Douglas (1890–1967). American silent screen comedian. Later became writer/producer. Retired 1938.
As Ye Sow 19. Captain Kidd Jnr 19. 23½ Hours' Leave 21. The Hottentot 22. Never Say Die 24. Introduce Me 25. Seven Keys to Baldpate 25, etc.

McLeod, Catherine (c. 1924–). American leading lady of the forties.
I've Always Loved You 46. Will Tomorrow Ever Come? 47. So Young So Bad 50. The Fortune Hunter 54. Ride the Wild Surf 64, etc.

McLeod, Norman Z. (1898–1964). American director, in Hollywood from the early twenties. Originally an animator; later wrote screenplays (e.g. *Skippy* [31]); then turned to direction.
Monkey Business 31. *Horse Feathers* 32. If I Had a Million (part) 33. Alice in Wonderland 33. *It's a Gift* 34. Pennies from Heaven 36. *Topper* 37. Merrily We Live 38. Panama Hattie 41. The Kid from Brooklyn 46. *The Secret Life of Walter Mitty* 47. *The Paleface* 47. My Favorite Spy 51. Never Wave at a WAC 53. Casanova's Big Night 54. Alias Jesse James 59, etc.

McLerie, Allyn (1926–). Canadian-born dancer and leading lady who made a few films amid stage work.
Words and Music 48. Where's Charley? 52. The Desert Song 53. Phantom of the Rue Morgue 54. Battle Cry 55. The Cowboys 72. Cinderella Liberty 74, etc.

MacLiammoir, Micheal (1901–). Irish character actor of the old school; film roles very occasional.
Autobiography 1961: *Each Actor on His Ass*.
Othello 52. The Kremlin Letter 70. What's the Matter with Helen? 71, etc.

MacMahon, Aline (1899–). Sad-faced, gentle-mannered American character actress, mostly in films of the thirties.
Five Star Final 31. The Mouthpiece 32. Life

Begins 32. Once in a Lifetime 32. *Golddiggers of 1933* 33. Heroes for Sale 33. *Babbitt* 34. Kind Lady 35. I Live My Life 35. Ah Wilderness 35. When You're in Love 37. Back Door to Heaven 39. Out of the Fog 41. The Lady is Willing 42. Dragon Seed 44. Guest in the House 44. The Mighty McGurk 46. The Search 48. Roseanna McCoy 49. The Flame and the Arrow 50. The Eddie Cantor Story 53. The Man from Laramie 55. Cimarron 60. I Could Go on Singing 63. All the Way Home 63, etc.

MacMahon, Horace (1907–1971). American character actor, likely to be best remembered as the older cop in the TV series *Naked City*. In films from 1937, often as cop or gangster.
Navy Blues 37. King of the Newsboys 38. Rose of Washington Square 39. Lady Scarface 41. Lady Gangster 45. Waterfront at Midnight 48. *Detective Story* 51. Man in the Dark 53. Susan Slept Here 54. My Sister Eileen 55. Beau James 57. The Swinger 66. *The Detective* 68, many others.

MacMurray, Fred (1907–). Likeable, durable American leading man of the thirties and forties; found a new lease of life in Walt Disney comedies of the early sixties.
☐ Friends of Mr Sweeney 34. Grand Old Girl 35. *The Gilded Lily* 35. Car 99 35. Men without Names 35. Alice Adams 35. Hands Across the Table 35. The Bride Comes Home 35. *The Trail of the Lonesome Pine* 36. 13 Hours by Air 36. The Princess Comes Across 36. The Texas Rangers 36. Maid of Salem 37. Champagne Waltz 37. Swing High Swing Low 37. Exclusive 37. True Confession 37. Coconut Grove 38. *Sing You Sinners* 38. Men With Wings 38. Café Society 39. Invitation to Happiness 39. Honeymoon in Bali 39. Little Old New York 40. Remember the Night 40. Too Many Husbands 40. Rangers of Fortune 40. Virginia 41. One Night in Lisbon 41. New York Town 41. Dive Bomber 41. The Lady is Willing 42. Take a Letter Darling 42. The Forest Rangers 42. Star Spangled Rhythm 42. Flight for Freedom 43. Above Suspicion 43. No Time for Love 43. Standing Room Only 44. And the Angels Sing 44. *Double Indemnity* 44. Murder He Says 44. Practically Yours 45. Where do We Go from Here? 45. Captain Eddie 45. Pardon My Past 46. Smoky 46. Suddenly it's Spring 47. The Egg and I 47. Singapore 47. The Miracle of the Bells 48. On Our Merry Way 48. Don't Trust Your Husband 48. Family Honeymoon 48. Father was a Fullback 48. Borderline 50. Never a Dull Moment 50. A Millionaire for Christy 51. Callaway went Thataway 51. Fair Wind to Java 53. The Moonlighter 53. *The Caine Mutiny* 54.

Pushover 54. Woman's World 54. The Far Horizons 55. The Rains of Ranchipur 55. At Gunpoint 55. There's Always Tomorrow 56. Gun for a Coward 57. Quantez 57. Day of the Badman 57. Good Day for a Hanging 58. *The Shaggy Dog* 59. Face of a Fugitive 59. The Oregon Trail 59. *The Apartment* 60. *The Absent Minded Professor* 61. Bon Voyage 62. Son of Flubber 63. Kisses for My President 64. Follow Me Boys 66. The Happiest Millionaire 67. Charlie and the Angel 73. The Chadwick Family (TV) 75. Beyond the Bermuda Triangle (TV) 76.
TV series: *My Three Sons* 60– .

McNally, Stephen (1913–) (Horace McNally). American leading man and sometimes 'heavy', in films from 1942. Former lawyer.
The Man from Down Under 43. The Harvey Girls 45. Johnny Belinda 48. Rogues' Regiment 48. No Way Out 50. Winchester 73 50. The Raging Tide 51. Devil's Canyon 53. Black Castle 53. Make Haste to Live 54. A Bullet Is Waiting 54. Tribute to a Bad Man 56. Hell's Five Hours 58. The Fiend Who Walked the West 58. Hell Bent for Leather 59. Requiem for a Gunfighter 65. Panic in the City 68. Black Gunn 72, etc.
TV series: *Target the Corruptors* 61.

McNamara, Maggie (1928–). Capable but short-staying American leading lady of the fifties.
☐ *The Moon is Blue* 53. Three Coins in the Fountain 54. Prince of Players 55. The Cardinal 63.

McNaught, Bob (1915–). British director, also associate producer on many films.
Grand National Night 53. Sea Wife 57. A Story of David 61, etc.

McNaughton, Gus (1884–1969) (Augustus Howard). British comedy actor, once a Fred Karno singer.
Murder 30. The Thirty-Nine Steps 35. Keep Your Seats Please 37. The Divorce of Lady X 38. Trouble Brewing 39. Jeannie 41. Much Too Shy 42. Here Comes the Sun 46, etc.

McNear, Howard (1905–1969). American comedy actor, familiar on the Burns and Allen TV show as a nosey and mean-spirited neighbour.
The Long Long Trailer 54. Bundle of Joy 56. Voyage to the Bottom of the Sea 61. Follow that Dream 62. Irma La Douce 63. Kiss Me Stupid 64. The Fortune Cookie 66, etc.

MacNee, Patrick (1922–). Smooth British leading man, best-known on TV.

The Life and Death of Colonel Blimp 43. Hamlet 48. Flesh and Blood 51. Three Cases of Murder 55. The Battle of the River Plate 56. Les Girls 58. Mr Jericho (TV) 70. Incense for the Damned 70, etc.

TV series: *The Avengers* 60–68. *The New Avengers* 76.

Macowan, Norman (1877–1961). Scottish character actor.

Whisky Galore 48. Laxdale Hall 53. X the Unknown 56. Tread Softly Stranger 58. The Boy and the Bridge 59. Kidnapped 60, etc.

MacPhail, Douglas (1910–1944). American singer.

Born to Dance 36. Maytime 37. Sweethearts 38. *Babes in Arms* 39. Little Nellie Kelly 40. Born to Sing 42, etc.

McQueen, Butterfly (1911–) (Thelma McQueen). Black American character actress.

Gone with the Wind (as the weeping maid) 39. Cabin in the Sky 43. Flame of the Barbary Coast 45. Mildred Pierce 45. Duel in the Sun 46. The Phynx 70, etc.

McQueen, Steve (1930–). Unconventional but fashionable American leading man of the sixties and seventies; usually plays tough, sexy and determined.

Biography 1974: *Steve McQueen* by Malachy McCoy.

□Never Love a Stranger 58. The Blob 58. Never So Few 59. The Great St Louis Bank Robbery 59. *The Magnificent Seven* 60. The Honeymoon Machine 61. Hell is for Heroes 61. The War Lover 62. *The Great Escape* 63. *Love with the Proper Stranger* 63. Soldier in the Rain 63. Baby the Rain Must Fall 65. *The Cincinnati Kid* 65. Nevada Smith 66. The Sand Pebbles 66. The Thomas Crown Affair 68. *Bullitt* 68. The Reivers 70. Le Mans 71. Junior Bonner 72. Getaway 72. Papillon 73. The Towering Inferno 74. An Enemy of the People 76.

TV series: Wanted Dead or Alive 58.

Macquitty, William (1905–). British producer who came to feature films via wartime MOI shorts.

The Happy Family 52. The Beachcomber 54. Above Us the Waves 55. A Night to Remember 58. The Informers 64, etc.

Macrae, Duncan (1905–1967). Craggy-faced Scottish stage actor who made some impressive film appearances.

□ *The Brothers* 47. Whisky Galore 48. The Woman in Question 50. *The Kidnappers* 53. You're Only Young Twice 53. The Maggie 54. Geordie 55. Rockets Galore 56. The Bridal Path 58. Kidnapped 59. Our Man in Havana 59. Greyfriars Bobby 60. *Tunes of Glory* 60. The Best of Enemies 61. A Jolly Bad Fellow 64. Thirty is a Dangerous Age Cynthia 67. Casino Royale 67.

Macrae, Gordon (1921–). American actor-singer, a former child performer who broke into films from radio.

□ Look for the Silver Lining 49. Backfire 49. The Daughter of Rosie O'Grady 50. Return of the Frontiersman 50. Tea for Two 50. West Point Story 51. On Moonlight Bay 51. Starlift 51. About Face 52. By the Light of the Silvery Moon 53. Three Sailors and a Girl 53. The Desert Song 53. Oklahoma 55. Carousel 56. The Best Things in Life Are Free 56.

Macready, George (1909–1973). American character actor, a descendant of Macready the tragedian. A splendid villain, neurotic or weakling, he ran an art gallery before coming to films in 1942.

The Commandos Strike at Dawn 42. The Seventh Cross 44. Wilson 45. I Love a Mystery 45. A Song to Remember 46. *Gilda* 46. Knock on Any Door 49. *Alias Nick Beal* 49. Detective Story 51. Julius Caesar 53. Vera Cruz 54. *Paths of Glory* 58. Seven Days in May 64. The Great Race 65. Tora! Tora! Tora! 70. The Return of Count Yorga 71.

TV series: Peyton Place 66–68.

McShane, Ian (1942–). British general purpose leading man.

The Wild and the Willing 62. The Pleasure Girls 65. Sky West and Crooked 66. The Battle of Britain 69. If It's Tuesday This Must Be Belgium (US) 69. Pussycat Pussycat I Love You (US) 70. Tam Lin 70. Villain 71. Sitting Target 72. The Last of Sheila 73. Ransom 74. Journey into Fear 75, etc.

McTaggart, James (1928–1975). British TV director.

All the Way Up 69.

MacWilliams, Glen (1898–). American cinematographer.

Ever Since Eve 21. Captain January 24. Ankles Preferred 27. Hearts in Dixie 29. The Sea Wolf 30. Hat Check Girl 32. Evergreen (GB) 34. Great Guns 41. He Hired the Boss 43. Lifeboat 44. Wing and a Prayer 44. If I'm Lucky 46, many others.

Madame De (France/Italy 1952). Elegant adaptation by Max Ophuls of Louise de Vilmorin's novella about a -pair of jewelled earrings which are passed back and forth between a husband, a wife and a lover. Photographed by Christian Matras with music by Georges Van Parys and Oscar Straus; star performances from Danielle Darrieux, Charles Boyer and Vittorio de Sica.

Madame du Barry. Lubitsch's German film of 1919, combining realism with spectacle, is probably still the best film made about the 18th century French courtesan. Starring Pola Negri, it was the first post-war German film to find international favour. Other Du Barrys have included Mrs Leslie Carter in *Du Barry* 15; Theda Bara in *Du Barry* 17; Norma Talmadge in *Du Barry, Woman of Passion* 30; Dolores del Rio in *Madame du Barry* 34; Lucille Ball in *Du Barry Was a Lady* 43; and Martine Carol in *Mistress Du Barry* 54.

Madame X. This sentimental tear-jerker about the woman whose son grows up without knowing her, from the play by Alexander Bisson, has been filmed six times. The lead was played by Jane Harding in 1909, Dorothy Donnelly in 1916, Pauline Frederick in 1920, Ruth Chatterton in 1929, Gladys George in 1937, and Lana Turner in 1966.

Madden, Peter (c. 1910–). Gaunt British character actor of TV and films.
Counterblast 48. Tom Brown's Schooldays 51. The Battle of the V.1 58. Hell Is a City 60. Saturday Night and Sunday Morning 60. The Loneliness of the Long Distance Runner 62. The Very Edge 63. Doctor Zhivago 66, etc.

Maddern, Victor (1926–). Stocky Cockney character actor, formerly on stage and radio.
Seven Days to Noon (debut) 49. Cockleshell Heroes 55. Private's Progress 56. Blood of the Vampire 58. I'm All Right Jack 59. HMS Defiant 61. Rotten to the Core 65. Circus of Fear 67, many others.
TV series: Fair Exchange (US) 62.

Madison, Guy (1922–) (Robert Moseley). American leading man, in films since 1944 after naval career.
Since You Went Away (debut) 44. Till the End of Time 46. The Charge at Feather River 53. The Command 54. Five Against the House 55. The Last Frontier 56. Hilda Crane 57. Bullwhip 58. Gunmen of the Rio Grande 65. The Mystery of Thug Island 66, etc.
TV series: *Wild Bill Hickok* 54–57.

Madison, Noel (1898–1975) (Nathaniel Moscovitch). American actor of sinister roles, especially gangsters. Formerly known as Nat Madison; son of actor Maurice Moscovitch.
Sinners' Holiday 30. Manhattan Melodrama 34. G-Men 35. The Man Who Made Diamonds 37. Crackerjack (GB) 39. Footsteps in the Dark 41. Jitterbugs 43. Gentleman from Nowhere 49, etc.

The Mafia. A Sicilian secret society which emerged spectacularly in the urban Italian sections of the US and is believed to control most organised crime and rackets in that country. Films which have seized on the subject with glee include *The Godfather, The Black Hand, The Don is Dead, Pay or Die, The Sicilian Clan, The Brotherhood, Johnny Cool, New York Confidential, The Brothers Rico,* and *Honor Thy Father.*

Magee, Patrick (1924–). British general purpose actor, often in sinister roles.
The Criminal 60. The Servant 63. Zulu 64. Masque of the Red Death 64. The Skull 65. *The Marat/Sade* 67. *The Birthday Party* 68. King Lear 70. You Can't Win 'em All 71. The Fiend 71. A Clockwork Orange 71. Demons of the Mind 72, etc.

The Magic Box (GB 1951). The British film industry's ambitious but uninspired contribution to the Festival of Britain: a sentimental biography of film pioneer William Friese-Greene, played by Robert Donat. An all-star cast appeared in cameo roles, including Laurence Olivier as the startled policeman who saw the first moving picture. Written by Eric Ambler, photographed by Jack Cardiff, produced by Ronald Neame, directed by John Boulting.

magicians have always had a fascination for film-makers, who on the whole preferred to have their tricks finally discredited, as with Cesar Romero in *Charlie Chan on Treasure Island* and *Two on a Guillotine*, Dante in *A Haunting We Will Go*, Vincent Price in *The Mad Magician*, Jules Berry in *Lee Jour Se Lève*, Harold Lloyd in *Movie Crazy* and Tony Curtis in *Houdini*. The most splendidly genuine magician was the sorcerer in *Fantasia*, but Cecil Kellaway was an amiable warlock in *I Married a Witch*, and Bela Lugosi was chilling as *Chandu*. The 1927 version of Somerset Maugham's book *The Magician* contributed a caricature of Aleister Crowley; *The Magician* is also the title of a 1973 TV series starring Bill Bixby.

Magnani, Anna (1907–1973). Volatile Italian

star actress (Egyptian-born).
The Blind Woman of Sorrento 34. Tempo Massimo 36. *Open City* 45. Angelina 47. *The Miracle* 50. Volcano 53. The Golden Coach 54. Bellissima 54. *The Rose Tattoo* (AA) 55. Wild is the Wind 57. The Fugitive Kind 59. Mamma Roma 62. Made in Italy 67. The Secret of Santa Vittoria 69, etc.

The Magnificent Ambersons (US 1942). Orson Welles' fascinating but only partially successful follow-up to *Citizen Kane*. Besides directing, he adapted Booth Tarkington's novel about the decline of a mid-Western family in the early years of the century, and the eventual come-uppance of its arrogant son. The early scene-setting is brilliant, but the later reels and hurried happy ending seem unbalanced: Welles himself has said that his last three reels were cut by the RKO-Radio chiefs and a final scene tacked on by other hands. Photographed by Stanley Cortez, with impeccable performances from Joseph Cotten, Dolores Costello, Tim Holt, Agnes Moorehead, Anne Baxter and Ray Collins. Welles' end-credits are highly entertaining.

Magnificent Obsession. This tear-jerking novel by Lloyd C. Douglas, about an irresponsible playboy who becomes a surgeon and not only cures but falls in love with the woman he accidentally blinded, was filmed in 1935 by John M. Stahl, with Robert Taylor and Irene Dunne, and again in 1954 by Douglas Sirk, with Rock Hudson and Jane Wyman.

The Magnificent Seven (US 1961). Lively Hollywood remake of the Japanese *Seven Samurai*, transferring the action to a standard western setting but preserving the essential story of a group of mercenaries who defend a village from plundering by bandits. Yul Brynner leads the goodies with Eli Wallach as a memorably murderous bandit. Directed by John Sturges, photographed by Charles Lang, music by Elmer Bernstein. A 1966 sequel, *Return of the Seven*, proved to be only a routine western, as did *Guns of the Magnificent Seven* 70, and *The Magnificent Seven Ride* 72.

Maharis, George (1928–). Intense-looking American leading man who has been most successful on TV.
□ Exodus 60. Sylvia 65. Quick Before it Melts 65. The Satan Bug 65. Covenant with Death 67. The Happening 67. The Land Raiders 69. Rich Man Poor Man (TV) 76.
TV series: *Route 66* 60–73. The Most Deadly Game 70.

Mahin, John Lee (1907–). American scriptwriter.
Naughty Marietta 35. Captains Courageous 37. Too Hot to Handle 38. Dr Jekyll and Mr Hyde 41. Tortilla Flat 42. Down to the Sea in Ships 49. Quo Vadis 51. Elephant Walk 54. Heaven Knows Mr Allison 57. The Horse Soldiers (& p) 59. The Spiral Road 62. Moment to Moment 66, many others.

Mahoney, Jock (1919–) (Jacques O'Mahoney). Athletic American leading man who apart from playing Tarzan was confined to routine roles.
The Doolins of Oklahoma 49. A Day of Fury 55. Away All Boats 56. I've Lived Before 56. A Time to Love and a Time to Die 58. The Land Unknown 58. Tarzan the Magnificent 60. Tarzan Goes to India 62. Tarzan's Three Challenges 64. The Walls of Hell 66, etc.
TV series: The Range Rider 51–52. Yancey Derringer 58.

Maibaum, Richard (1909–). American scriptwriter.
They Gave Him a Gun 37. Ten Gentlemen from West Point 40. O.S.S. 46. *The Great Gatsby* 49. Cockleshell Heroes 55. Zarak 57. The Day They Robbed the Bank of England 60. *Dr No* 62. From Russia with Love 63. Goldfinger 64. Thunderball 65. Jarrett (TV) 73, etc.

Mailer, Norman (1923–). American sensational novelist. Works filmed include *The Naked and the Dead, An American Dream. The Deer Park* was an 'expose' of Hollywood.

Main, Marjorie (1890–1975) (Mary Tomlinson). American character actress, probably best remembered as Ma Kettle in the long-running hillbilly series.
Take a Chance (debut) 33. *Dead End* 37. Stella Dallas 37. Test Pilot 38. Angels Wash Their Faces 39. The Women 39. Turnabout 40. Bad Man of Wyoming 40. A Woman's Face 41. Honky Tonk 41. Jackass Mail 42. Tish 42. Heaven Can Wait 43. Rationing 43. *Meet Me in St Louis* 44. *Murder He Says* 44. The Harvey Girls 45. Bad Bascomb 45. Undercurrent 46. *The Egg and I* 47. The Wistful Widow of Wagon Gap 47. Ma and Pa Kettle 49. Ma and Pa Kettle Go to Town 50 (then one Kettle film a year till 1956). Mrs O'Malley and Mr Malone 50. The Belle of New York 52. Rose Marie 54. Friendly Persuasion 56, many others.

Maisie. The hard-boiled (but soft-centred) gold-digging heroine of ten MGM comedy-dramas between 1939 and 1947; played in all of them by Ann Sothern.

Maitland, Marne (1920–). Anglo-Indian actor in British films; adept at sinister orientals.
Cairo Road 50. Father Brown 54. Bhowani Junction 56. The Camp on Blood Island 58. The Stranglers of Bombay 59. Sands of the Desert 60. Nine Hours to Rama 62. Lord Jim 65. The Reptile 65. Khartoum 66, etc.

Major Barbara (GB 1940). Accomplished screen version of the Bernard Shaw play about a militant young Salvationist. Produced and directed by Gabriel Pascal, who even persuaded Shaw to write additional scenes. Cast includes Wendy Hiller, Rex Harrison, Robert Morley, Robert Newton, Marie Lohr, Emlyn Williams, Sybil Thorndike and Deborah Kerr.

Majors, Lee (c. 1940–). American leading man.
Will Penny 67. The Liberation of L. B. Jones 70. The Six Million Dollar Man (TV) 73. Gary Francis Powers (TV) 76, etc.
TV series: *The Big Valley* 65–68. The Men from Shiloh 70. Owen Marshall 71–72. Six Million Dollar Man 73– .

Makeham, Eliot (1882–1956). British character actor of stage and screen, former accountant. For years played bespectacled little bank clerks who sometimes surprised by standing up for themselves.
Rome Express 32. Orders Is Orders 32. Lorna Doone 35. Dark Journey 37. Farewell Again 37. Saloon Bar 40. *Night Train to Munich* 40. The Common Touch 42. The Halfway House 44. Jassy 47. Trio 50. Scrooge 51. Doctor in the House 53. Sailor Beware 56, etc.

Mako (–). Japanese-American character actor.
The Sand Pebbles 66. Hawaii 67. The Island at the Top of the World 74.

Malden, Karl (1913–) (Mladen Sekulovich). Respected American stage actor whose film career has been generally disappointing because Hollywood has not seemed to know what to do with him.
□ They Knew What They Wanted 40. Winged Victory 44. 13 Rue Madeleine 46. Boomerang 47. The Gunfighter 50. Where the Sidewalk Ends 50. Halls of Montezuma 50. *A Streetcar Named Desire* (AA) 52. Decision Before Dawn 52. Diplomatic Courier 52. Operation Secret 52. Ruby Gentry 52. I Confess 53. Take the High Ground 53. Phantom of the Rue Morgue 54. *On the Waterfront* 54. *Baby Doll* 56. Fear Strikes Out 57. Time Limit (d only) 57. Bombers B52 57. The Hanging Tree 59. Pollyanna 60. The

Great Imposter 60. Parrish 61. One Eyed Jacks 61. All Fall Down 62. Bird Man of Alcatraz 62. Gypsy 62. How the West was Won 63. Come Fly with Me 63. Dead Ringer 64. Cheyenne Autumn 64. The Cincinnati Kid 65. Nevada Smith 66. The Silencers 66. Murderers Row 66. *Hotel* 67. The Adventures of Bullwhip Griffin 67. Billion Dollar Brain 67. Blue 68. Hot Millions 68. Patton 69. Cat O'Nine Tails 69. Wild Rovers 71.
TV series: *Streets of San Francisco* 72– .

Malick, Terrence (1945–). American director.
□ *Badlands* (& w, p) 73. The Gravy Train (w only) 74.

Malle, Louis (1932–). French 'new wave' director, former assistant to Robert Bresson.
World of Silence (co-d) 56. Lift to the Scaffold 57. *The Lovers* 58. *Zazie dans le Metro* 61. Le Feu Follet 63. Viva Maria 65. Le Voleur 67. *Souffle au Coeur* 71. Lacombe Lucien 75, etc.

Malleson, Miles (1888–1969). British playwright, screen writer and actor whose credits read like a potted history of the British cinema.
AS WRITER: *Nell Gwyn* 34. Peg of Old Drury 35. Rhodes of Africa 36. *Victoria the Great* 37. The First of the Few 42. They Flew Alone 43. Mr Emmanuel 44, etc.
AS ACTOR: Knight without Armour 37. Sixty Glorious Years 38. The Thief of Baghdad 40. Dead of Night 45. The Magic Box 51. *The Importance of Being Earnest* 52. The Man Who Never Was 56. Dracula 58. I'm All Right Jack 59. Heavens Above 63. The Magnificent Showman 64, many others.

Mallory, Boots (1913–1958) (Patricia Mallory). American leading lady of the thirties.
Handle with Care 32. Hello Sister 33. Sing Sing Nights 35. Here's Flash Casey 37, etc.

Malo, Gina (1909–1963) (Janet Flynn). Irish-German-American leading lady of the thirties, usually in tempestuous roles. Filmed in Britain; married Romney Brent.
In a Monastery Garden 32. Good Night Vienna 32. Waltz Time 33. The Private Life of Don Juan 34. Jack of All Trades 36. Over She Goes 38. The Door with Seven Locks 40, etc.

Malone, Dorothy (1925–) (Dorothy Maloney). American leading lady of the fifties, often in sultry roles.
□ The Falcon and the Co-Eds 43. One Mysterious Night 44. Show Business 44. Seven

Days Ashore 44. Hollywood Canteen 44. Too Young to Know 45. Janie Gets Married 46. *The Big Sleep* 46. Night and Day 48. To the Victor 48. Two Guys from Texas 48. One Sunday Afternoon 48. Flaxy Martin 49. South of St Louis 49. Colorado Territory 49. The Nevadan 50. Convicted 50. Mrs O'Malley and Mr Malone 50. The Killer that Stalked New York 50. Saddle Legion 51. The Bushwhackers 52. Scared Stiff 53. Torpedo Alley 53. Law and Order 54. Jack Slade 54. Loophole 54. Pushover 54. The Fast and Furious 54. Private Hell 36 54. Young at Heart 54. The Lone Gun 54. Five Guns West 55. Battle Cry 55. Tall Man Riding 55. Sincerely Yours 55. Artists and Models 55. At Gunpoint 55. Pillars of the Sky 56. Tension at Table Rock 56. *Written on the Wind* (AA) 56. Quantez 57. Man of a Thousand Faces 57. *The Tarnished Angels* 57. Tip on a Dead Jockey 57. *Too Much Too Soon* (as Diana Barrymore) 58. Warlock 59. The Last Voyage 60. The Last Sunset 61. Beach Party 63. Fate is the Hunter 64. Exzess (WG) 70. The Man Who Would Not Die 75.
TV series: *Peyton Place* 64–69.

Maltby, H. F. (1880–1963). British comedy playwright (*The Rotters, The Right Age to Marry*, etc.). Screenwriter (*Over the Garden Wall* 44, etc.) and actor of choleric characters. Autobiography 1950: *Ring Up The Curtain*.
Those Were The Days 34. Jack of All Trades 36. Pygmalion 38. Under Your Hat 40. A Canterbury Tale 44. The Trojan Brothers 45, etc.

The Maltese Falcon. Dashiell Hammett's brilliantly written crime story was filmed three times by Warners. In 1931 it starred Bebe Daniels and Ricardo Cortez and was directed by Roy del Ruth; in 1936 it appeared as *Satan Met a Lady*, directed by William Dieterle, with Bette Davis and Warren William. The definitive version, however, did not come till 1941, when John Huston directed it (his first film) from his own script. Humphrey Bogart was the private eye, and the rogues' gallery included Mary Astor, Sidney Greenstreet, Peter Lorre, and Elisha Cook Jnr. It was highly influential on later crime films, and is often claimed as Huston's best film: he spoofed it unsuccessfully in his *Beat the Devil* 54.

Maltz, Albert (1908–). American screenwriter who suffered from the anti-communist witch hunt.
Afraid to Talk 32. This Gun for Hire 42. Destination Tokyo 43. The Man in Half Moon Street 44. Cloak and Dagger 46. *Naked City* 48, etc.

Mamoulian, Rouben (1897–). American stage director of Armenian origin. Over the years he made a number of films which vary in quality but at their best show a fluent command of the medium.
□ *Applause* 29. *City Streets* 31. *Dr Jekyll and Mr Hyde* 32. *Love Me Tonight* 32. Song of Songs 33. *Queen Christina* 33. We Live Again 34. *Becky Sharp* 35. *The Gay Desperado* 36. High, Wide and Handsome 37. Golden Boy 39. *The Mark of Zorro* 40. Blood and Sand 41. Rings on Her Fingers 42. Summer Holiday 48. Silk Stockings 57. Began work on *Cleopatra* 62 but was replaced.

A Man and a Woman: see *Un Homme et une Femme*.

A Man For All Seasons (AA) (GB 1966). A deceptively simple and straightforward piece of film-making by Fred Zinnemann (AA), based on Robert Bolt's play about Sir Thomas More but shedding its stylization in favour of a plain chronological treatment. The result was a triumph of sheer excellence in every department. Paul Scofield (AA) had the role of his life, with effective contributions from Wendy Hiller and Robert Shaw; the cinematography of Ted Moore (AA) was a constant delight. The film also marked an encouraging example of a sober, literate and thoughtful work gaining wide public acceptance.

The Man in Grey (GB 1943). Though fairly flat and unimaginative, this Regency melodrama from Lady Eleanor Smith's novel was so popular that it provoked a rash of similar costume pieces: *Madonna of the Seven Moons* 44, *The Wicked Lady* 45, *Caravan* 46, *Jassy* 47, *Blanche Fury* 47, etc. It also did much for the careers of Margaret Lockwood, James Mason, Phyllis Calvert and Stewart Granger. Leslie Arliss directed.

The Man in the Iron Mask. No one knows what mixture of fact and fiction exists in the famous story of Louis XIV's mysterious prisoner who languished for years in the Bastille, his face always covered (actually with velvet). Some said it was Louis' bastard brother, others an Italian diplomat. Anyway, Dumas wrote an exciting novel on the subject, and it has been twice filmed: in 1929 (as *The Iron Mask*) with Douglas Fairbanks, and in 1939 (by James Whale) with Louis Hayward.

The Man in the White Suit (GB 1951). Bubbly Ealing satire, nimbly directed by Alexander Mackendrick, about a scientist who manages to antagonize both management and labour by inventing a fabric which never gets dirty and never wears out. Written by Mackendrick, Roger Macdougall and John Dighton; starring Alec Guiness, Joan Greenwood, Cecil Parker, Ernest Thesiger. A small classic.

Man of Aran (GB 1934). Influential documentarist Robert Flaherty came to Britain and took three years to film this sympathetic account of fisherfolk on a barren island off Ireland's west coast. It encouraged later films like *Edge of the World* 38, and generally opened the way for British film-makers to look more closely at their natural surroundings.

The Man Who Came to Dinner (US 1941). George S. Kaufman and Moss Hart based their hilarious stage success on the real-life figure of Alexander Woolcott, who perfectly fitted the character of the cantankerous, megalomaniac broadcaster who is confined by a broken hip to a normal mid-western home which he turns into bedlam. Monty Woolley was just right in the film version, and had perfect support from Bette Davis, Reginald Gardiner, Jimmy Durante, Billie Burke and others. William Keighley directed.

The Man Who Knew Too Much. Alfred Hitchcock twice filmed this thriller about a child held hostage by a gang planning to assassinate an international political figure: GB 1934, with Leslie Banks, Edna Best and Peter Lorre; and US 1956, with James Stewart, Doris Day and Bernard Miles. The first version, despite (or perhaps because of) its curious studio sets, made incomparably better entertainment.

The Man with the Golden Arm (US 1956). Otto Preminger produced and directed this film about drug addiction, from Nelson Algren's novel; at the time it not only flew in the face of the Hollywood production code, but also marked the first time the Rank circuit played an 'X' film since *Detective Story*, after the poor returns of which they had announced that 'X' films were for sensation-seekers and Rank theatres would henceforth play nothing but family entertainment. Frank Sinatra, Eleanor Parker and Kim Novak starred; Elmer Bernstein supplied the music. As a film it was rather a drag.

Mancini, Henry (1924–). American composer.
AS ARRANGER: The Glenn Miller Story 53. The Benny Goodman Story 56, etc.
AS COMPOSER: Touch of Evil 58. High Time

60. *Breakfast at Tiffany's* (AA) 61. Bachelor in Paradise 61. *Hatari* 62. *The Pink Panther* 63. Charade 63. A Shot in the Dark 64. Dear Heart 65. What Did You Do in the War, Daddy? 66. Two for the Road 67. Darling Lili 69. The White Dawn 73, others.
Academy Award songs: 'Moon River', 'Days of Wine and Roses'.

Mancunian Films. A small but dauntless little British studio which throughout the forties and early fifties earned its keep locally with a stream of wild farces starring home-grown music hall talent: Frank Randle, Harry Korris, Sandy Powell, Tessie O'Shea, Betty Jumel, Nat Jackley, Josef Locke, Jewel and Warriss, Suzette Tarri and Norman Evans. Neither art nor craft entered into the matter.

Mander, Miles (1888–1946) (Lionel Mander). British character actor, a former theatre manager with long experience of all kinds of stage work.
The Pleasure Garden 26. The First Born (& wd) 28. Loose Ends (wd only) 30. The Missing Rembrandt (wd only) 31. The Private Life of Henry VIII 32. Loyalties 33. The Morals of Marcus (d only) 35, etc.; then settled in Hollywood as actor. *The Three Musketeers* (as Richelieu) 36. Lloyds of London 37. Slave Ship 37. Suez 38. The Three Musketeers (musical version; as Richelieu again) 39. *Wuthering Heights* 39. Tower of London 39. Lady Hamilton 41. *Five Graves to Cairo* 43. *Farewell My Lovely* 44. The Scarlet Claw 44. Pearl of Death 45. The Bandit of Sherwood Forest 46. The Walls Came Tumbling Down 46, many others.

Mandy (GB 1952). A delicately handled mixture of fiction and documentary about the teaching of a congenitally deaf child. Directed by Alexander Mackendrick from a novel, *The Day Is Ours*, by Hilda Lewis; with Jack Hawkins, Phyllis Calvert and the child actress Mandy Miller.

Mangano, Silvana (1930–). Italian actress, wife of producer Dino de Laurentiis. Former model.
L'Elisir D'Amore 49. Bitter Rice 51. Ulysses 55. The Sea Wall 57. Tempest 59. Five Branded Women 61. Barabbas 62. Theorem 68. The Decameron 70. Death in Venice 71.

Manhunt (US 1941). This then topical, though now dated, adventure melodrama from Geoffrey Household's *Rogue Male* told of a big game hunter's 'stalk' of Hitler and the consequent espionage intrigues. Fritz Lang's directorial style was ponderous, the foggy London settings hilarious; Walter Pidgeon and George Sanders, however, had polish as hero and villain.

Mankiewicz, Don (1922–). American scriptwriter and novelist, son of Herman Mankiewicz.
Trial 55. House of Numbers 57. I Want to Live 58.

Mankiewicz, Herman (1897–1953). American screenwriter, also journalist and noted wit; brother of Joseph L. Mankiewicz.
The Road to Mandalay 26. After Office Hours 35. John Meade's Woman 37. Citizen Kane (AA) (contribution disputed: some say he wrote most of it) 41. Pride of the Yankees 42. Stand By for Action 43. Christmas Holiday 44. The Enchanted Cottage 44. The Spanish Main 45. A Woman's Secret 48. Pride of St Louis 52, etc.

Mankiewicz, Joseph L. (1909–). American film creator of many talents.
AS WRITER: The Mysterious Dr Fu Manchu 29. Million Dollar Legs 32. Forsaking All Others 34. The Keys of the Kingdom 44, etc.
AS PRODUCER: Fury 36. The Bride Wore Red 37. Three Comrades 38. Huckleberry Finn 39. Strange Cargo 40. The Philadelphia Story 40. Woman of the Year 42. The Keys of the Kingdom 44, etc.
☐ AS WRITER-DIRECTOR: Dragonwyck 46. Somewhere in the Night 46. The Late George Apley 47. The Ghost and Mrs Muir 47. Escape 48. A Letter for Three Wives (AA script) 49. House of Strangers (d only) 50. No Way Out 50. All About Eve (AA script and direction) 50. People will Talk 51. Five Fingers (d only) 52. Julius Caesar 53. The Barefoot Contessa 54. Guys and Dolls 55. The Quiet American (& p) 57. Suddenly Last Summer (d only) 59. Cleopatra 63. The Honey Pot 67. There was a Crooked Man 70. Sleuth (d only) 72.

Mankowitz, Wolf (1924–). British novelist and screenwriter.
A Kid for Two Farthings 56. Expresso Bongo 59. Waltz of the Toreadors 62. The Day the Earth Caught Fire 63. Where the Spies Are 65. Casino Royale 66. Dr Faustus 67. The 25th Hour 67. Bloomfield 71. The Hireling 73.

Mann, Abby (1927–). American playwright and screenwriter.
Judgment at Nuremburg (oaw) 61. A Child is Waiting (w) 63. The Condemned of Altona (w) 63. Ship of Fools (w) 65. The Detective (w) 68. The Marcus Nelson Murders (TV) 73, etc.

Mann, Anthony (1906–1967) (Emil Bundesmann). American director, usually of outdoor films; his best work was concerned with the use of violence by thoughtful men.
☐ Dr Broadway 42. Moonlight in Havana 42. Nobody's Darling 43. My Best Gal 44. Strangers in the Night 44. The Great Flamarion 45. Two O'Clock Courage 45. Sing Your Way Home 45. Strange Impersonation 46. The Bamboo Blonde 46. Desperate 47. Railroaded 47. T-Men 47. Raw Deal 48. The Black Book 49. Border Incident 49. Side Street 49. Devil's Doorway 50. The Furies 50. Winchester 73 50. The Tall Target 51. Bend of the River 51. The Naked Spur 52. Thunder Bay 53. The Glenn Miller Story 54. The Far Country 55. Strategic Air Command 55. The Man from Laramie 55. The Last Frontier 56. Serenade 56. Men in War 57. The Tin Star 57. God's Little Acre 58. Man of the West 58. Cimarron 60. El Cid 61. The Fall of the Roman Empire 64. The Heroes of Telemark 65. A Dandy in Aspic (completed by Lawrence Harvey) 68.

Mann, Daniel (1912–). American director, ex stage and TV.
☐Come Back Little Sheba 52. About Mrs Leslie 54. The Rose Tattoo 55. I'll Cry Tomorrow 55. The Teahouse of the August Moon 56. Hot Spell 58. The Last Angry Man 59. The Mountain Road 60. Butterfield 8 60. Ada 61. Who's Got the Action? 62. Who's Been Sleeping in my Bed? 63. Judith 65. Our Man Flint 66. For Love of Ivy 68. A Dream of Kings 69. Willard 71. The Revengers 72. Maurie 73. Interval 73. Lost in the Stars 73.

Mann, Delbert (1920–). American director, ex TV.
☐ Marty (AA) 55. The Bachelor Party 57. Desire Under the Elms 58. Separate Tables 58. Middle of the Night 59. The Dark at the Top of the Stairs 60. Lover Come Back 61. The Outsider 62. Five Finger Exercise 62. That Touch of Mink 62. A Gathering of Eagles 63. Dear Heart 65. Quick Before it Melts 65. Mister Buddwing 66. Fitzwilly 67. The Pink Jungle 68. David Copperfield (TV) 69. Kidnapped 72. Jane Eyre (TV) 72. Man Without a Country (TV) 73. A Girl Named Sooner (TV) 75.

Mann, Hank (1887–1971) (David Liebermann). Gargantuan American supporting player of silent days, especially with Chaplin; one of the Keystone Kops.
Modern Times 36. Hollywood Cavalcade 39. The Great Dictator 40, etc.

Mann, Ned (1893–1967). American special-

effects director, a one-time professional roller skater who entered films in 1920 as an actor. Best remembered for his long association with Alexander Korda.
The Man Who Could Work Miracles 35. The Ghost Goes West 36. Things to Come 36. The Thief of Baghdad 40. Anna Karenina 47. Bonnie Prince Charlie 48. Around the World in Eighty Days 56.

Manners, David (1901–) (Rauff de Ryther Duan Acklom). Canadian leading man of Hollywood films in the thirties; claimed to be descended from William the Conqueror.
Journey's End 30. Dracula 30. A Bill of Divorcement 32. The Mummy 32. The Warrior's Husband 33. Roman Scandals 33. The Mystery of Edwin Drood 35. A Woman Rebels 37, etc.

Mannheim, Lucie (1895–1976). German-born character actress, married to Marius Goring.
The Thirty-Nine Steps (as the mysterious victim) 35. The High Command 37. Yellow Canary 43. Hotel Reserve 44. So Little Time 52. Beyond the Curtain 60. Bunny Lake Is Missing 65, etc.

Manning, Irene (1917–) (Inez Harvuot). American leading lady of the forties, former café singer.
Two Wise Maids 37. The Big Shot 42. Yankee Doodle Dandy 42. The Desert Song 44. Shine On, Harvest Moon 44. Escape in the Desert 45. Bonnie Prince Charlie (GB) 48, etc.

Mansfield, Jayne (1932–1967) (Vera Jane Palmer). Amply proportioned American leading lady whose superstructure became the butt of many jokes.
Biography 1973: *Jayne Mansfield* by May Mann.
The Female Jungle 55. Illegal 56. Pete Kelly's Blues 56. The Burglar 57. The Girl Can't Help It 57. The Wayward Bus 57. Will Success Spoil Rock Hunter? 57. Kiss Them For Me 57. The Sheriff of Fractured Jaw 59. Too Hot to Handle (GB) 60. The Challenge (GB) 60. It Happened in Athens 62. Panic Button 64. Country Music USA 65. The Fat Spy 66. A Guide for the Married Man 67, etc.

Mantz, Paul (1903–1965). American stunt pilot who died in a crash during the filming of *The Flight of the Phoenix*.
Biography 1967: *Hollywood Pilot* by Don D. Wiggins.

Manvell, Roger (1909–). British film historian. Director of the British Film Academy since 1947 and author of many books on cinema, the most influential being the Penguin *Film* 44.

Manx, Kate (1930–1964). American leading lady.
□ Private Property 60. Hero's Island 62.

Mara, Adele (1923–) (Adelaida Delgado). Spanish-American dancer who played leads in Hollywood co-features of the forties.
Alias Boston Blackie 42. Bells of Rosarita 45. Tiger Woman 46. Diary of a Bride 48. The Sea Hornet 51. Back from Eternity 56. Curse of the Faceless Man 58. The Big Circus 59, etc.

Marais, Jean (1913–) (Jean Marais-Villain). French romantic actor well remembered in several Cocteau films. Later films less notable; recently in cloak-and-sword epics, also playing 'The Saint', 'Fantomas' and various secret agents.
Autobiography 1975: *Histoires de ma Vie*.
L'Eternel Retour 43. La Belle et la Bête 45. L'Aigle a Deux Têtes 47. Les Parents Terribles 48. Orphée 49, etc.

March, Fredric (1897–1975) (Frederick McIntyre Bickel). One of America's most respected stage and screen actors, who always projected intelligence and integrity and during the thirties and forties was at times an agreeable light comedian. Long married to Florence Eldridge.
□ The Dummy 29. The Wild Party 29. The Studio Murder Mystery 29. Paris Bound 29. Jealousy 29. Footlights and Fools 29. The Marriage Playground 29. Sarah and Son 30. Ladies Love Brutes 30. Paramount on Parade 30. True to the Navy 30. Manslaughter 30. Laughter 30. *The Royal Family of Broadway* 30. Honour among Lovers 30. Night Angel 31. My Sin 31. Merrily We Go to Hell 32. *Dr Jekyll and Mr Hyde* (AA) 32. Smiling Through 32. Strangers in Love 32. The Sign of the Cross 33. The Eagle and the Hawk 33. The Affairs of Cellini 34. All of Me 34. Good Dame 34. Design for Living 34. *Death Takes a Holiday* 34. The Barretts of Wimpole Street (as Robert Browning) 34. We Live Again 34. *Les Misérables* 35. The Dark Angel 35. Anna Karenina 35. Mary of Scotland 36. Anthony Adverse 36. The Road to Glory 36. *A Star Is Born* 37. *Nothing Sacred* 37. The Buccaneer 38. There Goes My Heart 38. Trade Winds 39. Susan and God 40. Victory 40. So Ends Our Night 41. *One Foot in Heaven* 41. Bedtime Story 42. *I Married a Witch* 42. Tomorrow the World

44. *The Adventures of Mark Twain* 44. *The Best Years of Our Lives* (AA) 46. Another Part of the Forest 48. An Act of Murder 48. Christopher Columbus (GB) 49. It's a Big Country 51. *Death of a Salesman* 52. Man on a Tightrope 53. *Executive Suite* 54. The Bridges at Toko Ri 54. The Desperate Hours 55. Alexander the Great 55. The Man in the Grey Flannel Suit 56. Middle of the Night 59. *Inherit the Wind* 60. The Young Doctors 62. The Condemned of Altona 63. *Seven Days in May* 64. Hombre 67. Tick Tick Tick 70. The Iceman Cometh 73.

March, Hal (1920–1970). American comic actor who never quite made it.
Outrage 50. Yankee Pasha 54. My Sister Eileen 55. *Hear Me Good* 57. Send Me No Flowers 64, etc.

The March of Time. A highly influential series of two-reelers on current affairs, started and financed in 1934 by the founders of *Time* Magazine in association with film-maker Louis de Rochemont. The raucous American commentary marred it for European consumption, but its contents were a first-class in-depth examination of what was happening in the world. It ran with great success until the late forties, when it was gradually replaced by TV series such as *NBC White Paper*, *CBS Reports*, Granada's *World in Action*, and the BBC's *Panorama*.

Marchand, Corinne (1928–). French leading lady of the sixties.
Cleo de 5 à 7 62. Seven Deadly Sins 63. The Milky Way 69. Rider on the Rain 70. Borsalino 70, etc.

Marchand, Henri (1898–1959). French comedy actor.
À Nous la Liberté 31. Je Vous Aimerai Toujours 33. Volga en Flammes 35. Les Deux Combinards 38. L'Ennemi sans Visage 46. La Sorcière 50. Operation Magali 53. Till Eulenspiegel 56, many others.

Marcuse, Theodore (1920–1967). Shaven-pated American character actor, usually in sinister roles.
The Glass Bottom Boat 65. The Cincinnati Kid 65. Last of the Secret Agents 66. The Wicked Dreams of Paula Schultz 67, etc.

Margetson, Arthur (1897–1951). British stage actor, former stockbroker's clerk, who went to Hollywood in 1940 and played supporting roles.
Other People's Sins 31. His Grace Gives Notice

33. Little Friend 34. Broken Blossoms 36. Juggernaut 37. Action for Slander 38. Return to Yesterday 40. Random Harvest 43. Sherlock Holmes Faces Death 44, etc.

Margo (1918–) (Maria Marguerita Guadelupe Boldao y Castilla). Spanish-born actress, a one-time professional dancer who has been in occasional Hollywood films since 1933.
Crime without Passion 34. Winterset 36. Lost Horizon 37. The Leopard Man 43. Behind the Rising Sun 43. Gangway for Tomorrow 44. Viva Zapata 52. I'll Cry Tomorrow 57. Who's Got the Action? 63, etc.

Margolin, Janet (1943–). American leading lady.
David and Lisa 62. Bus Riley's Back in Town 65. The Greatest Story Ever Told 65. The Saboteur 65. Nevada Smith 66. Enter Laughing 67. Buona Sera Mrs Campbell 68. Take the Money and Run 70, etc.

Margolin, Stuart (–). American character actor.
Limbo 72. The Stone Killer 73. Death Wish 74, etc.

Marin, Edwin L. (1901–1951). American director.
The Death Kiss 32. A Study in Scarlet 33. Paris Interlude 34. The Casino Murder Case 35. I'd Give My Life 36. Everybody Sing 38. A Christmas Carol 38. Fast and Loose 39. Maisie 39. Florian 40. A Gentleman After Dark 42. *Show Business* 44. Tall in the Saddle 44. Johnny Angel 45. The Young Widow 46. Nocturne 46. Christmas Eve 47. Race Street 48. Canadian Pacific 49. Fighting Man of the Plains 49. The Cariboo Trail 50. Fort Worth 51, etc.

Marin, Jacques (1919–). French character actor.
The Island at the Top of the World 64.

Marion, Frances (1888–1973). American screenwriter.
Autobiography 1972: *Off With Their Heads*.
Daughter of the Sea 16. Humoresque 22. Stella Dallas 25. The Winning of Barbara Worth 26. The Scarlet Letter 27. *Love* 27. The Wind 28. *The Big House* (AA) 30. *The Champ* (AA) 32. *Dinner at Eight* 33. Riff Raff 36. *Knight without Armour* 37. Green Hell 40, etc.

Marion-Crawford, Howard (1914–1969). British actor often seen in Watsonian roles or as jovial, beefy, sporting types.
Forever England 32. Freedom Radio 40. The

Rake's Progress 45. The Hasty Heart 49. The Man in the White Suit 51. Where's Charley? 52. Reach for the Sky 56. Virgin Island 58. The Brides of Fu Manchu 66, etc.

Maris, Mona (1903–) (Maria Capdevielle). Franco-Argentinian 'second lead' in Hollywood films.
Romance of the Rio Grande 29. Secrets 33. Law of the Tropics 41. Tampico 44. Heartbeat 46. The Avengers 50, etc.

Marius (France 1931). The first of a trilogy (the others: *Fanny* 32, *César* 34), written by Marcel Pagnol about characters of the Marseilles waterfront: saloon-owner César; his wayward son Marius; Fanny, the mother of Marius' child; Panisse, an ageing widower who marries Fanny. In 1938 James Whale directed *Port of Seven Seas*, a Hollywood remake with Wallace Beery in Raimu's role; in 1960 Joshua Logan directed another remake, *Fanny*, with Boyer and Chevalier but without the songs which had been used in a Broadway musical version shortly before.

Marken, Jane (1895–). French character actress with long stage experience.
Fioritures 15. Camille 34. *Partie de Campagne* 37. Hôtel du Nord 38. *Lumière d'Eté* 42. Les Enfants du Paradis 44. L'Idiot 46. Clochemerle 47. Une Si Jolie Petite Plage 48. Manèges 49. Ma Pomme 50. Les Compagnes de la Nuit 52. Marie Antoinette 55. And God Created Woman 56. Pot Bouille 57. The Mirror Has Two Faces 58, etc.

Marker, Chris (1921–). French documentary director. Leader of the modernist 'left bank' school.
Olympia 52. Toute la Memoire du Monde 56. Letter from Siberia 58. Description d'un Combat 60. Cuba Si 61. Le Joli Mai 62. La Jetée 63. If I Had Four Dromedaries 66, etc.

Markham, Monte (1935–). American leading man, mostly on TV.
Death Takes a Holiday (TV) 71. One is a Lonely Number 72. Midway 76, etc.
TV series: The Second Hundred Years 67. Mr Deeds Goes to Town 68. The New Perry Mason 73.

Markle, Fletcher (1921–). Canadian director, briefly in Hollywood.
□ Jigsaw 49. Night into Morning 51. The Man with a Cloak 51. The Incredible Journey 63.

Marks, Alfred (1921–). Bald-pated British

comedian, in films from 1950 but more usually seen on TV and stage.
Desert Mice 59. There Was a Crooked Man 60. Weekend with Lulu 62. Frightened City 63. She'll Have to Go 63. Scream and Scream Again 70. Our Miss Fred 72. Valentino 77, etc.

Marley, J. Peverell (1899–1964). American cinematographer who worked on de Mille's silent epics.
The Ten Commandments 23. The Volga Boatmen 25. *King of Kings* 27. House of Rothschild 34. Clive of India 35. *Alexander's Ragtime Band* 38. *The Hound of the Baskervilles* 39. Night and Day 46. Life with Father 47. The Greatest Show on Earth 52. House of Wax 53. Serenade 56. The Left-Handed Gun 58. A Fever in the Blood 61, many others.

Marley, John (1916–). American character actor.
My Six Convicts 52. Timetable 56. I Want to Live 58. America America 65. Cat Ballou 66. Faces 68. *Love Story* 70. A Man Called Sledge 70. The Godfather 72. Blade 73. W. C. Fields and Me 76, etc.

Marlowe, Hugh (1914–) (Hugh Hipple). American actor, former radio announcer, in films from 1937.
Mrs Parkington 44. Meet Me In St Louis 44. *Twelve O'Clock High* 50. *All about Eve* 50. The Day the Earth Stood Still 51. Monkey Business 52. Garden of Evil 54. Earth Versus the Flying Saucers 56. Thirteen Frightened Girls 64. Castle of Evil 66. The Last Shot You Hear 68, etc.

Marly, Florence (1918–) (Hana Smekalova). Franco-Czech leading lady, married to Pierre Chenal. Made a few films in Hollywood.
Sealed Verdict 48. Tokyo Joe 49. Tokyo File 212 51. Gobs and Gals 52. Undersea Girl 58. Queen of Blood 65. Games 67. Doctor Death 73, etc.

Marmont, Percy (1883–1977). Veteran British romantic actor of silent era, in films since 1913.
SILENT FILMS: Lord Jim (US) 25. Mantrap (US) 26. The Silver King (GB) 24. Rich and Strange (GB) 27, etc.
SOUND FILMS: The Silver Greyhound 32. Secret Agent 36. Action for Slander 38. I'll Walk Beside You 41. Loyal Heart 45. No Orchids for Miss Blandish 48. Lisbon 56, many others.

Marquand, Christian (1927–). French leading man, who turned director with *Candy* 68.
Lucretia Borgia 53. Senso 54. And God Created

Woman 56. Sait-on Jamais? 57. Une Vie 58, etc.

Marquand, John P. (1893–1960). American novelist who wrote solid popular books about middle-aged men regretting their lost youth; also the Mr Moto series (filmed in the late thirties with Peter Lorre).

H. M. Pulham Esquire 41. The Late George Apley 47. B. F.'s Daughter 49. Top Secret Affair (Melville Goodwin USA) 56. Stopover Tokyo 57, etc.

The Marriage Circle (US 1924). Ernst Lubitsch's famous silent comedy was adapted by Paul Bern from a play by Lothar Schmidt. Basically a very small comedy of adultery, it was impeccably done and gave new screen personas to Monte Blue, Marie Prevost and Adolphe Menjou, as well as bringing forth many imitators anxious to equal Lubitsch's flair for sophisticated sex. In 1932 Lubitsch remade it, equally delightfully, with dialogue, songs, recitative, and characters who frequently addressed the camera, as *One Hour With You*; with Maurice Chevalier, Genevieve Tobin, Jeanette MacDonald and Roland Young.

Marriott, Moore (1885–1949) (George Thomas Moore-Marriott). British character comedian specializing in hoary rustics, chiefly beloved as the ancient but resilient old Harbottle of the Will Hay comedies: *Convict 99* 36, *Oh Mr Porter* 38, *Ask a Policeman* 39, *Where's That Fire?* 40. etc. Also notable with the Crazy Gang in *The Frozen Limits* 39, and *Gasbags* 40. Made over 300 films in all.

Dick Turpin 08. Passion Island 26. The Lyons Mail 31. The Water Gypsies 32. As You Like It 36. Time Flies 44. Green for Danger 46. The History of Mr Polly 49. High Jinks in Society 49.

Mars, Kenneth (1936–). American character comedian who is usually way over the top.
The Producers 67. Desperate Characters 71. What's Up Doc? 72. Paper Moon 73. The Parallax View 74. Young Frankenstein 74. Night Moves 75, etc.

La Marseillaise (France 1938). A revered but patchy and overlong account of the French Revolution, directed and co-written by Jean Renoir, with Pierre Renoir as Louis XVI.

Marsh, Carol (1926–) (Norma Simpson). British leading lady whose career faltered when she outgrew *ingénue* roles.
Brighton Rock 47. Marry Me 49. Helter Skelter 50. Alice in Wonderland (French puppet

version) 50. Salute the Toff 51. Dracula 58. Man Accused 59, etc.

Marsh, Garry (1902–) (Leslie March Geraghty). Robust, balding British character actor; in films since 1930, usually as harassed father, perplexed policeman or explosive officer.
Night Birds 30. Dreyfus 30. Number Seventeen 32. The Maid of the Mountains 32. Scrooge 35. When Knights Were Bold 36. Bank Holiday 38. It's in the Air 38. The Four Just Men 39. Hoots Mon 40. I'll Be Your Sweetheart 45. The Rake's Progress 45. Dancing with Crime 46. Just William's Luck 48. Murder at the Windmill 49. Worm's Eye View 51. Mr Drake's Duck 53. Who Done It? 55. Where the Bullets Fly 66, many others.

Marsh, Mae (1895–1968) (Mary Warne Marsh). American leading lady of the silent screen; later played small character roles.
Man's Genesis 12. The Birth of a Nation 14. Intolerance 15. Polly of the Circus 17. Spotlight Sadie 18. The Little 'Fraid Lady 20. Flames of Passion 22. The White Rose 23. Daddies 24. The Rat (GB) 25. Tides of Passion 26. Over the Hill 32. Little Man What Now 34. Jane Eyre 43. A Tree Grows in Brooklyn 44. The Robe 53. Sergeant Rutledge 60, many others.

Marsh, Marion (1913–) (Violet Krauth). American leading lady of English, German, French and Irish descent. Began in Hollywood as an extra; chosen by John Barrymore to play Trilby to his *Svengali* 31.
The Mad Genius 32. Five Star Final 32. The Eleventh Commandment 33. Love at Second Sight (GB) 34. The Black Room 35. When's Your Birthday? 37. Missing Daughters 40. House of Errors 42, etc.

Marsh, Oliver H. T. (1893–1941). American cinematographer.
The Floor Below 18. Good References 19. Lessons in Love 21. Jazzmania 23. The Dove 27. The Divine Woman 28. Not So Dumb 30. The Sin of Madelon Claudet 31. Arsene Lupin 32. Today We Live 33. The Merry Widow 34. *David Copperfield* 35. *A Tale of Two Cities* 35. The Great Ziegfeld 36. His Brother's Wife 36. After the Thin Man 36. Maytime 37. The Firefly 37. Sweethearts 38. It's a Wonderful World 39. Bitter Sweet 40. Rage in Heaven 41. Lady Be Good 41, many others.

Marshal, Alan (1909–1961). Australian-born actor of light romantic leads: came to films in 1936 after New York stage experience.
The Garden of Allah 36. Night Must Fall 38.

The Hunchback of Notre Dame 40. Tom, Dick and Harry 40. *Lydia* 41. The White Cliffs of Dover 43. The Barkleys of Broadway 48. The Opposite Sex 56. The House on Haunted Hill 59.

Marshall, Brenda (1915–) (Ardis Ankerson Gaines). American leading lady who married William Holden and retired.

Espionage Agent 39. The Sea Hawk 40. Footsteps in the Dark 41. Singapore Woman 41. Background to Danger 43. The Constant Nymph 44. Strange Impersonation 45. Whispering Smith 49. The Tomahawk Trail 50, etc.

Marshall, Connie (1938–). American child actress of the forties.

Sunday Dinner for a Soldier 44. *Sentimental Journey* 45. Dragonwyck 46. Home Sweet Homicide 47. Mother Wore Tights 48. Kill the Umpire 50, etc.

Marshall, E. G. (1910–) (Everett G. Marshall). American character actor with long Broadway experience.

The House on 92nd Street 45. The Caine Mutiny 54. Pushover 55. *Twelve Angry Men* 57. *The Bachelor Party* 57. Town Without Pity 61. The Poppy is Also a Flower (TV) 64. The Chase 66. The Bridge at Remagen 69. The Pursuit of Happiness 71. Collision Course (TV) (as Harry Truman) 76, etc.

TV series: The Defenders 61–65. The Bold Ones 69.

Marshall, George (1891–1975). American director with over 400 features to his credit. Entered films 1912 as an extra; graduated to feature roles in early serials and comedies; began directing 1917 with a series of Harry Carey westerns.

Pack Up Your Troubles 32. A Message to Garcia 34. The Crime of Dr Forbes 37. In Old Kentucky 38. The Goldwyn Follies 38. You Can't Cheat an Honest Man 39. *Destry Rides Again* 39. *The Ghost Breakers* 40. When the Daltons Rode 40. The Forest Rangers 42. Star Spangled Rhythm 43. And the Angels Sing 43. *Murder He Says* 44. Incendiary Blonde 45. Hold That Blonde 45. The Blue Dahlia 46. The Perils of Pauline 47. Tap Roots 48. *Fancy Pants* 50. The Savage 52. Scared Stiff 53. *Red Garters* 54. The Second Greatest Sex 55. Beyond Mombasa (GB) 56. The Sad Sack 57. The Sheepman 58. Imitation General 58. The Gazebo 59. Cry for Happy 61. How the West Was Won (part) 62. Advance to the Rear 64. Boy, Did I Get a Wrong Number 66. Eight on the Lam 67. Hook Line and Sinker 69.

Marshall, Herbert (1890–1966). Urbane British actor who despite the loss of a leg in World War I invariably played smooth, sometimes diffident but always gentlemanly roles. In Hollywood from early thirties.

□ Mumsie 27. The Letter 29. Murder 30. The Calendar 31. Secrets of a Secretary 31. *Michael and Mary* 32. The Faithful Heart 32. Blonde Venus 32. *Trouble in Paradise* 32. Evenings for Sale 32. The Solitaire Man 33. I Was a Spy 33. Four Frightened People 34. Outcast Lady 34. The Painted Veil 34. Riptide 34. The Good Fairy 35. The Flame Within 35. Accent on Youth 35. *The Dark Angel* 35. If You Could Only Cook 35. The Lady Consents 36. Forgotten Faces 36. Till We Meet Again 36. Girls' Dormitory 36. A Woman Rebels 36. Make Way for a Lady 36. *Angel* 37. Breakfast for Two 37. Mad About Music 38. Always Goodbye 38. Woman against Woman 38. Zaza 39. A Bill of Divorcement 40. *Foreign Correspondent* 40. *The Letter* 40. When Ladies Meet 41. *The Little Foxes* 41. Kathleen 41. Adventure in Washington 41. *The Moon and Sixpence* (as Somerset Maugham) 42. Young Ideas 43. Forever and a Day 43. Flight for Freedom 43. Andy Hardy's Blonde Trouble 44. The Unseen 45. *The Enchanted Cottage* 44. Crack up 46. *The Razor's Edge* (as Somerset Maugham) 46. Duel in the Sun 46. High Wall 47. Ivy 47. The Secret Garden 49. The Underworld Story 50. Anne of the Indies 51. Black Jack 52. Angel Face 53. The Black Shield of Falworth 54. Gog 54. Riders to the Stars 54. The Virgin Queen 55. Wicked as They Come 56. The Weapon 67. *Stage Struck* 57. The Fly 58. A Fever in the Blood 60. Midnight Lace 60. Five Weeks in a Balloon 62. The List of Adrian Messenger 63. The Third Day 65.

Marshall, Herbert (1900–). British documentarist, married to Fredda Brilliant. Associate of John Grierson; worked on English dubbing of Russian films. Produced and directed feature, *Tinker* 49.

Marshall, Trudy (1922–). American leading lady of minor films in the forties.

Secret Agent of Japan 42. Girl Trouble 44. Sentimental Journey 46. Disaster 48. Mark of the Gorilla 50. The President's Lady 53, etc.

Marshall, Tully (1864–1943) (William Phillips). American silent screen actor; stage experience from boyhood.

Intolerance 15. Oliver Twist (as Fagin) 16. Joan the Woman 16. The Slim Princess 20. The Hunchback of Notre Dame 23. The Merry Widow 25. The Red Mill 27. The Cat and the Canary 28. Trail of '98 29. Show of Shows 29.

The Unholy Garden 31. Scarface 32. Grand Hotel 33. Diamond Jim 35. Souls at Sea 37. A Yank at Oxford 38. Brigham Young 40. Chad Hanna 41. This Gun for Hire 42, many others.

Marshall, William (c. 1915–). Black American character actor.
Lydia Bailey 52. Something of Value 57. The Boston Strangler 68. Blacula 72. Scream Blacula Scream 73, etc.

Marshall, Zena (1926–). British leading lady with French ancestry; stage experience.
Caesar and Cleopatra (debut) 45. Good Time Girl 47. Miranda 48. Sleeping Car to Trieste 48. Marry Me 49. Hell Is Sold Out 51. The Embezzler 54. My Wife's Family 56. The Story of David 61. Dr No 62, etc.

Martelli, Otello (1903–). Italian cinematographer, especially associated with Fellini.
Paisa 46. Bitter Rice 49. La Dolce Vita 50. I Vitelloni 52. La Strada 54. Il Bidone 55. I Tre Volti 63, etc.

Martin, Chris-Pin (1894–1953). Rotund Mexican actor who provided comic relief in many a western.
Four Frightened People 34. The Gay Desperado 36. The Return of the Cisco Kid 39 (and ensuing series). The Mark of Zorro 41. Weekend in Havana 42. Mexican Hayride 49. Ride the Man Down 53, etc.

Martin, Dean (1917–) (Dino Crocetti). Heavy-lidded, self-spoofing American leading man and singer. Teamed with Jerry Lewis until 1956, then enjoyed spectacular solo success in sixties.
Biography (of Martin and Lewis) 1976: *Everybody Loves Somebody Sometime* by Arthur Marx.
□ My Friend Irma 49. My Friend Irma Goes West 50. At War with the Army 51. That's My Boy 51. Sailor Beware 51. Jumping Jacks 52. The Stooge 52. Scared Stiff 53. The Caddy 53. Money from Home 53. Living It Up 54. Three Ring Circus 54. You're Never Too Young 55. Artists and Models 55. Pardners 56. Hollywood or Bust 56. Ten Thousand Bedrooms 57. *The Young Lions* 58. Some Came Running 58. *Rio Bravo* 59. Career 59. Who was that Lady? 60. Bells are Ringing 60. Ocean's Eleven 60. All in a Night's Work 61. Ada 61. Sergeants Three 62. Who's Got the Action? 62. Toys in the Attic 63. Who's Been Sleeping in my Bed? 63. Four For Texas 64. What a Way to Go 64. Robin and the Seven Hoods 64. *Kiss Me Stupid* 64. The Sons

of Katie Elder 65. *The Silencers* 66. Texas Across the River 66. Murderers' Row 67. Rough Night in Jericho 67. The Ambushers 67. Bandolero 68. How to Save a Marriage 68. Five Card Stud 68. Wrecking Crew 68. Airport 69. Something Big 71. Showdown 73.

Martin, Dewey (1923–). American leading man.
Knock On Any Door (debut) 49. Kansas Raiders 50. The Thing 52. The Big Sky 52. Tennessee Champ 54. Prisoner of War 54. Land of the Pharaohs 55. The Desperate Hours 55. Ten Thousand Bedrooms 57. Wheeler and Murdoch (TV) 72, etc.

Martin, Dick (1923–). See *Rowan, Dan.*

Martin, Edie (1880–1964). The frail, tiny old lady of scores of British films. On stage from 1886, films from 1932.
The History of Mr Polly 49. The Lavender Hill Mob 51. The Man in the White Suit 52. The Titfield Thunderbolt 53. The Ladykillers 55, etc.

Martin, Marion (1916–). American leading lady of 'B' pictures, a statuesque blonde who graduated from the Ziegfeld chorus.
Boom Town 40. Mexican Spitfire at Sea 41. The Big Store 41. They Got Me Covered 42. Abbot and Costello in Hollywood 45. Queen of Burlesque 47. Oh You Beautiful Doll 50. Thunder in the Pines 54, etc.

Martin, Mary (1913–). American musical comedy star; her film career did not seem satisfactory.
Autobiography 1977: *My Heart Belongs.*
□ The Great Victor Herbert 39. Rhythm on the River 40. Love Thy Neighbour 40. Kiss the Boys Goodbye 41. New York Town 41. *Birth of the Blues* 41. Star Spangled Rhythm 42. Happy Go Lucky 42. True to Life 43. Night and Day 46. Main Street to Broadway 53.

Martin, Millicent (1934–). British songstress of stage and TV.
The Horsemasters 60. The Girl on the Boat 62. Nothing But the Best 64. Those Magnificent Men in Their Flying Machines 65. Alfie 66. Stop the World I Want To Get Off 66, etc.
TV series: From a Bird's Eye View 69.

Martin, Ross (1920–) (Martin Rosenblatt). Polish-American character actor: film appearances sporadic.
Conquest of Space 55. The Colossus of New York 58. Experiment in Terror 62. The Ceremony 64. The Great Race 65. Charlie

Chan: Happiness is a Warm Clue (TV: title role) 70.
TV series: *The Wild Wild West* 65–68.

Martin, Strother (1920–). American character actor, often in grizzled western roles.
The Asphalt Jungle 50. Storm over Tibet 52. The Big Knife 55. The Shaggy Dog 59. The Deadly Companions 61. The Man Who Shot Liberty Valance 62. The Sons of Katie Elder 65. Harper 66. True Grit 69. Butch Cassidy and the Sundance Kid 69. The Ballad of Cable Hogue 70. The Brotherhood of Satan 70. Fool's Parade 71. Pocket Money 72. Sssss 73. Rooster Cogburn 75. Hard Times 75. The Great Scout and Cathouse Thursday 76, many others.

Martin, Tony (1912–) (Alfred Norris). American cabaret singer and leading man, in Hollywood from 1936 after years of touring with dance bands.
Sing, Baby, Sing 36. Banjo on My Knee 37. Ali Baba Goes to Town 38. Music in My Heart 40. The Big Store 41. Ziegfeld Girl 41. Till the Clouds Roll By 46. Casbah 48. Two Tickets to Broadway 51. Here Come the Girls 53. Deep in My Heart 54. Hit the Deck 55. Let's Be Happy (GB) 57, etc.

Martin Harvey, Sir John (–). British actor manager of the old school who appeared in a film or two.
Scaramouche 12. A Tale of Two Cities 13. The Cigarette Maker's Romance 13.

Martinelli, Elsa (1933–). Italian leading lady, in films from 1950.
The Indian Fighter (US) 55. Manuela (GB) 57. The Boatmen 60. Hatari (US) 62. The Trial 63. Marco the Magnificent 65. De l'Amour 65. The Tenth Victim 65. Candy 68, etc.

Martini, Nino (1904–). Italian actor-singer, who made a few English-speaking films.
Here's to Romance (US) 35. The Gay Desperado (US) 36. One Night With You (GB) 48, etc.

Martins, Orlando (1899–). West African actor in British films.
Sanders of the River 35. Jericho 37. The Man from Morocco 44. Men of Two Worlds (as the witch doctor) 46. End of the River 47. Where No Vultures Fly 52. Simba 55. Sapphire 59. Mister Moses 65, etc.

Martinson, Leslie H. (–). American director, from TV.
PT 109 62. For Those Who Think Young 64.

Batman 66. Fathom 67. Mrs Pollifax—Spy 70, etc.

Marton, Andrew (1904–). Hungarian-born director, in Hollywood from 1923; settled there after return visits to Europe. Co-directed *King Solomon's Mines* 50.
SOS Iceberg 32. The Demon of the Himalayas 34. Wolf's Clothing (GB) 37. Secrets of Stamboul (GB) 37. Gentle Annie 45. The Wild North 52. Prisoner of War 54. Green Fire 55. The Thin Red Line 64. *Crack in the World* 65. Around the World under the Sea 65, etc.
AS SECOND-UNIT DIRECTOR: *The Red Badge of Courage* 51. A Farewell to Arms 57. *Ben Hur* 59. 55 Days at Peking 62. *The Longest Day* 62. Cleopatra 62, etc.

Marty (US 1956) (AA). The film which started Hollywood's TV invasion. From Paddy Chayefsky's small-screen play about a shy butcher who courts an equally shy schoolteacher, its success started an influx of fresh talent from New York. Directed by Delbert Mann (AA), produced by Harold Hecht, with Ernest Borgnine (AA) and Betsy Blair. Chayefsky also won the best screenplay award.

Marvin, Lee (1924–). Ruthless-looking American actor who lately switched from unpleasant villains to unsympathetic heroes.
You're in the Navy Now 51. Duel at Silver Creek 52. The Big Heat 53. The Wild One 54. Gorilla at Large 54. The Caine Mutiny 54. Bad Day at Black Rock 54. Violent Saturday 55. Not as a Stranger 55. Pete Kelly's Blues 55. Shack Out on 101 55. I Died a Thousand Times 56. Seven Men from Now 57. *Attack* 57. Raintree County 57. The Missouri Traveller 58. The Comancheros 61. The Man Who Shot Liberty Valance 62. Donovan's Reef 63. *The Killers* 64. *Cat Ballou* (AA) 65. Ship of Fools 65. The Professionals 66. The Dirty Dozen 67. Point Blank 67. Hell in the Pacific 68. Paint Your Wagon 69. Monte Walsh 70. Prime Cut 72. Emperor of the North Pole 73. The Iceman Cometh 73. Shout at the Devil 76. The Great Scout and Cathouse Thursday 76, etc.
TV series: M Squad 58–60. Lawbreaker 64.

The Marx Brothers. A family of American comedians whose zany humour convulsed minority audiences in its time and influenced later comedy writing to an enormous extent. *Chico* (1886–1961) (Leonard Marx) played the piano eccentrically and spoke with an impossible Italian accent; *Harpo* (1888–1964) (Adolph Marx) was a child-like mute who also played the harp; *Groucho* (1890–) (Julius Marx) had a

painted moustache, a cigar, a loping walk and the lion's share of the wisecracks. In vaudeville from childhood, they came to films after Broadway success. Originally there were two other brothers: *Gummo* (1897–) (Milton Marx), who left the act early on, and *Zeppo* (1901–) (Herbert Marx), who didn't fit in with the craziness and left them after playing romantic relief in their first five films. These first five films contain much of their best work: later their concentrated anarchy was dissipated by musical and romantic relief. Harpo published his autobiography 1961: *Harpo Speaks!* Among Groucho's semi-autobiographical works are *Groucho and Me* 59, *Memoirs of a Mangy Lover* 64 and *The Groucho Letters* 67. His son Arthur published *Life With Groucho* 52 and *Son of Groucho* 72. In 1974 Richard Anobile and Groucho came up with *The Marx Brothers Scrapbook.* The films are examined in detail in *The Marx Brothers at the Movies* by Paul D. Zimmerman and Burt Goldblatt.
□ The Coconuts 29. *Animal Crackers* 30. *Monkey Business* 31. *Horse Feathers* 32. *Duck Soup* 33. *A Night at the Opera* 35. *A Day at the Races* 37. Room Service 38. *At the Circus* 39. Go West 40. The Big Store 41. *A Night in Casablanca* 46. Love Happy (a curious and unhappy failure) 50. *The Story of Mankind* (guest appearances) 57.
GROUCHO ALONE: Copacabana 47. Mr Music 50. Double Dynamite 51. A Girl in Every Port 52. Skidoo 68.

Mary Poppins (US 1964). Walt Disney's most successful film for years, a tricksy fantasy from the books by P. L. Travers about a magical nanny who descends on a family in Edwardian London. Over-long, but with pleasant songs and brilliant trick effects. With Julie Andrews (AA), Dick Van Dyke, David Tomlinson, etc.; directed by Robert Stevenson.

M*A*S*H (US 1970). A bitter farce by Richard Hooker and Ring Lardner Jnr, directed by Robert Altman, about high jinks in the face of death at an army hospital in Korea. Highly influential, it spawned a toned-down TV series in 1972 as well as a number of other films holding nothing sacred.

Masina, Giulietta (1921–). Italian gamin-like actress, married to Federico Fellini. In films since 1941.
Senza Pieta 47. *Lights of Variety* 48. *La Strada* 54. Il Bidone 55. *Nights of Cabiria* 57. Juliet of the Spirits 65, etc.

mask. A technical device for blocking out part of the image. *Masking* is the black cloth which surrounds the actual cinema screen: these days it has to be electrically adjustable to encompass the various screen sizes.

The Mask of Dimitrios (US 1944). Amusingly entangled and well-staged mystery film about a writer who sets out to uncover the truth about the career of an international crook. It boasted a splendid array of character actors in their best form: Sidney Greenstreet, Peter Lorre, Victor Francen, Steve Geray, Eduardo Cianelli, Kurt Katch, Florence Bates and John Abbott. It was stylishly directed by Jean Negulesco, who subsequently failed to live up to his promise, and introduced actor Zachary Scott, of whom likewise. Frank Gruber wrote the screenplay from Eric Ambler's novel.

Maskell, Virginia (1936–1968). British leading lady.
Our Virgin Island 58. The Man Upstairs 59. Doctor in Love 60. The Wild and the Willing 62. *Only Two Can Play* 62. Interlude 68, etc.

Mason, A. E. W. (1865–1948). British novelist whose *The House of the Arrow* and *The Four Feathers* have been filmed several times. *Fire Over England* and *At the Villa Rose* also came to the screen.

Mason, Elliott (1897–1949). Scottish character actress with repertory experience.
The Ghost Goes West 36. Owd Bob 38. The Ghost of St Michael's 41. The Gentle Sex 43. The Captive Heart 46, etc.

Mason, Herbert (1891–1960). British director.
His Lordship 36. Strange Boarders 38. Back Room Boy 41. Flight from Folly 45, etc.

Mason, James (1909–). Leading British and international actor who became a star at home in saturnine roles during World War II, went to Hollywood and initially had a thin time but during the fifties became a respected interpreter of varied and interesting characters.
□ Late Extra 35. Twice Branded 36. Troubled Waters 36. Prison Breaker 36. Blind Man's Bluff 36. The Secret of Stamboul 36. Fire Over England 36. The Mill on the Floss 37. The High Command 37. Catch as Catch Can 37. The Return of the Scarlet Pimpernel 38. *I Met a Murderer* 39. This Man is Dangerous (The Patient Vanishes) 41. Hatter's Castle 42. *The Night Has Eyes* 42. Alibi 42. Secret Mission 42. Thunder Rock 43. The Bells Go Down 43. *The Man in Grey* (a key role as an 18th-century

villain) 43. They Met in the Dark 43. Candlelight in Algeria 44. Fanny by Gaslight 44. Hotel Reserve 44. A Place of One's Own 45. They Were Sisters 45. *The Seventh Veil* 45. *The Wicked Lady* 46. *Odd Man Out* 46. The Upturned Glass 47. Caught 49. Madame Bovary 49. The Reckless Moment 49. East Side West Side 49. One Way Street 50. *Pandora and the Flying Dutchman* 51. *The Desert Fox* (as Rommel) 51. Lady Possessed 52. *Five Fingers* 52. The Prisoner of Zenda (as Rupert) 52. Face to Face 52. The Desert Rats 53. *Julius Caesar* (as Brutus) 53. The Story of Three Loves 53. Botany Bay 53. The Man Between 53. Charade 53. Prince Valiant 54. *20,000 Leagues under the Sea* (as Captain Nemo) 54. *A Star is Born* 54. Forever Darling 56. Bigger than Life (& p) 56. Island in the Sun 57. Cry Terror 58. The Decks Ran Red 58. North by Northwest 59. *Journey to the Center of the Earth* 59. A Touch of Larceny 60. The Trials of Oscar Wilde 60. The Marriage Go Round 61. The Land We Love 62. Tiara Tahiti 62. *Lolita* (as Humbert) 62. The Fall of the Roman Empire 64. Torpedo Bay 64. *The Pumpkin Eater* 64. Lord Jim 65. The Player Pianos 65. Genghis Khan 65. *The Blue Max* 66. Georgy Girl 66. *The Deadly Affair* 67. Stranger in the House 67. Duffy 68. Mayerling 68. Age of Consent 69. The Seagull 69. Spring and Port Wine 70. Kill! 70. Cold Sweat 70. Bad Man's River 71. Child's Play 72. The Last of Sheila 73. Frankenstein, the True Story (TV) 73. 11 Harrowhouse 74. The Marseilles Contract 74. Inside Out 76. Cross of Iron 77.

Mason, Shirley (1900–) (Leona Flugrath). American leading lady of the silent screen, sister of Viola Dana.
Vanity Fair 15. Goodbye Bill 18. Treasure Island 20. Merely Mary Ann 20. Lights of the Desert 22. What Fools Men 25. Don Juan's Three Nights 26. Sally in Our Alley 27. Show of Stars 29, etc.

Massari, Lea (–). French-Italian leading lady.
Les Choses de la Vie 69. Le Souffle au Coeur 71, etc.

Massen, Osa (1915–). Danish-born actress in Hollywood from the late thirties.
Honeymoon in Bali 39. The Devil Pays Off 41. The Master Race 44. Tokyo Rose 44. Cry of the Werewolf 44. Deadline at Dawn 47. Rocketship XM 50, etc.

Massey, Anna (1937–). British character actress, daughter of Raymond Massey.
Gideon's Day 58. Bunny Lake is Missing 65. De Sade 69. Frenzy 72. A Doll's House 73. Vault of Horror 73, etc.

Massey, Daniel (1933–). British actor, son of Raymond Massey, usually seen on stage or TV.
Girls at Sea 57. Upstairs and Downstairs 59. The Queen's Guard 61. Go to Blazes 62. Moll Flanders 65. The Jokers 66. *Star!* (as Noel Coward) 68. Fragment of Fear 70. Mary Queen of Scots 72. Vault of Horror 73. The Incredible Sarah 76, etc.

Massey, Ilona (1912–1974) (Ilona Hajmassy). Hungarian-born leading lady, in Hollywood from the mid-thirties.
Rosalie 37. Balalaika 39. International Lady 41. Invisible Agent 42. Frankenstein Meets the Wolf Man 43. End of the Rainbow 47. Love Happy 50. Jet over the Atlantic 59, etc.

Massey, Raymond (1896–). Canadian-born actor, on stage (in Britain) from 1922. In films, has played saturnine, benevolent or darkly villainous, with a penchant for impersonations of Abraham Lincoln.
Autobiography, When I Was Young 1977.
□ The Speckled Band (as Sherlock Holmes) 31. The Face at the Window 31. *The Old Dark House* 32. *The Scarlet Pimpernel* 34. *Things to Come* 36. Fire over England 36. Under the Red Robe 37. *The Prisoner of Zenda* 37. Dreaming Lips 37. The Hurricane 38. The Drum 38. Black Limelight 39. *Abe Lincoln in Illinois* 39. Santa Fe Trail (as John Brown) 40. 49th Parallel 41. Dangerously They Live 41. Desperate Journey 42. Reap the Wild Wind 42. Action in the North Atlantic 43. *Arsenic and Old Lace* 44. The Woman in the Window 44. Hotel Berlin 45. God Is My Co-Pilot 45. A Matter of Life and Death 46. Possessed 47. Mourning Becomes Electra 47. The Fountainhead 48. Roseanna McCoy 49. Chain Lightning 49. Barricade 50. Dallas 50. Sugarfoot 51. Come Fill the Cup 51. David and Bathsheba 51. Carson City 52. The Desert Song 53. Prince of Players 55. Battle Cry 55. *East of Eden* 55. Seven Angry Men 55. Omar Khayyam 57. The Naked and the Dead 58. The Great Impostor 60. The Fiercest Heart 61. The Queen's Guard 61. How the West Was Won 62. Mackenna's Gold 68. All My Darling Daughters (TV) 72.
TV series: Dr Kildare (as Dr Gillespie) 61–65.

Massie, Paul (1932–). Canadian-born actor, on British stage and screen.
High Tide at Noon 57. *Orders to Kill* 58. Sapphire 59. Libel 60. The Two Faces of Dr Jekyll 60. The Pot Carriers 62, many others.

Massingham, Richard (1898–1953). British actor-producer-director: a qualified doctor who abandoned his medical career to make numerous short propaganda films for government departments during World War II and after, infusing them with quiet wit and sympathy. Gratefully remembered as the stout party bewildered by government restrictions: bathing in five inches of water, collecting salvage, avoiding colds, preventing rumours, wearing a gas mask, etc.

Masterson, Bat (–). American western gunman who reformed; played in films by Albert Dekker in *Woman of the Town*, Randolph Scott in *Trial Street*, George Montgomery in *Masterson of Kansas*, Kenneth Tobey in *Gunfight at the OK Corral*, Joel McCrea in *Gunfight at Dodge City*, and Gene Barry in a long-running TV series.

Mastroianni, Marcello (1923–). Italian leading man, a former clerk who broke into films with a bit part in *I Miserabili* 47. Now Italy's most respected and sought-after lead.
Sunday in August 49. Girls of the Spanish Steps 51. The Bigamist 55. *White Nights* 57. I Soliti Ignoti 58. La Dolce Vita 59. *Il Bell' Antonio* 60. La Notte 61. *Divorce Italian Style* (BFA) 62. Family Diary 62. Eight and a Half 63. *Yesterday, Today and Tomorrow* (BFA) 63. Marriage Italian Style 64. Casanova 70 65. The Tenth Victim 65. The Organizer 65. Shoot Loud, Louder, I Don't Understand 66. The Stranger 67. Diamonds for Breakfast (GB) 68. A Place for Lovers 69. Sunflower 70. What? 72. Blowout 73, etc.

Mata Hari. Three films have been made about the French spy executed during World War I: by Friedrich Feher in 1927, with Magda Sonia; by George Fitzmaurice in 1931, with Greta Garbo; by Jean-Louis Richard in 1964, with Jeanne Moreau.

Mate, Rudolph (1899–1964). Polish-born cameraman.
The Passion of Joan of Arc 26. *Vampyr* 31. Liliom 33. *Dante's Inferno* 35. Dodsworth 36. Love Affair 39. *Foreign Correspondent* 40. To Be or Not To Be 42. Cover Girl 44, etc.
□LATER DIRECTOR: It had to Be You (co-d) 47. The Dark Past 49. D.O.A. 50. No Sad Songs for Me 50. *Union Station* 50. Branded 50. The Prince Who Was a Thief 51. When Worlds Collide 51. The Green Glove 52. Paula 52. Sally and Saint Anne 52. Mississippi Gambler 53. Second Chance 53. Forbidden 53. The Siege At Red River 54. *The Black Shield of Falworth* 54.

The Violent Men 55. The Far Horizons 55. Miracle in the Rain 56. The Rawhide Years 56. Port Afrique 56. Three Violent People 57. The Deep Six 58. For the First Time 59. The 300 Spartans 62. Aliki 63. Seven Seas to Calais 64.

Mather, Aubrey (1885–1958). British character actor, on stage from 1905, films from 1931. Settled in Hollywood and became useful member of English contingent, playing butlers and beaming, bald-headed little men.
Young Woodley 31. As You Like It 36. When Knights Were Bold 36. Jane Eyre 44. The Keys of the Kingdom 44. The Forsyte Saga 49. The Importance of Being Earnest 52, many others.

Matheson, Murray (c. 1910–). Soft-spoken English actor in Hollywood, mostly on TV.
Hurricane Smith 52. Botany Bay 53. Love Is a Many Splendored Thing 55. Assault On a Queen 66. How To Succeed In Business 67, etc.

Matheson, Richard (–). American science-fiction novelist and screenwriter.
The Incredible Shrinking Man (oaw) 57. The House of Usher (w) 60. The Pit and the Pendulum (w) 61. The Raven (w) 63. The Comedy of Terrors (w) 63. The Last Man on Earth (oa) 64. The Young Warriors (oaw) 68. The Devil Rides Out (w) 68. De Sade (w) 69. The Omega Man (oa) 71. The Legend of Hell House (w) 73. Dracula (TV) 73, etc.

Mathews, Kerwin (1926–). American leading man, former teacher.
Five Against the House 55. The Seventh Voyage of Sinbad 58. Man on a String 60. The Three Worlds of Gulliver 60. Jack the Giant Killer 61. Pirates of Blood River 62. Maniac (GB) 63. Battle Beneath the Earth (GB) 68. Barquero 69. The Boy Who Cried Werewolf 73, etc.

Mathieson, Muir (1911–1975). British musical director, in films from 1931.
Things to Come 36. Dangerous Moonlight 40. In Which We Serve 42. Brief Encounter 46. The Sound Barrier 52. The Swiss Family Robinson 60. Becket 64, many others.

Mathis, June (1892–1927). American screenwriter.
An Eye for an Eye 18. The Four Horsemen of the Apocalypse 21. Blood and Sand 22. Three Wise Fools 23. Greed 23. Ben Hur 27, etc.

Matras, Christian (1903–). French cinematographer, in films from 1928.
La Grande Illusion 37. Boule de Suif 45. Les Jeux Sont Faits 47. La Ronde 50. Madame De

53. *Lola Montes* 55. Les Espions 57. Paris Blues 61. Les Fêtes Galantes 65. The Milky Way 68, many others.

matt or **matte**. A technique (sometimes known as *travelling matt*) for blending actors in the studio with location or trick scenes. The actor is photographed against a non-reflective background (e.g. black velvet) and a high-contrast negative of this image is combined with the desired background. Thus men can move among animated monsters, and ghosts can slowly disappear.

Matt Helm. The laconic hero of a number of self-spoofing private-eye dime novels by Donald Hamilton, personified on screen by a droopy-eyed Dean Martin. Over-sexed and witless, the series represents a rather miserable but commercial sixties blend of high camp, self-indulgence, comic strip and semi-pornography. *The Silencers* 66, *Murderers' Row* 66, *The Ambushers* 67 and *Wrecking Crew* 69 were the titles, and it seemed to be a point of honour with the producer that the title should have no relevance whatever to the movie.

A Matter of Life and Death (GB 1946) (American title: *Stairway to Heaven*). The first film to be selected for the Royal Film Performance. Damned in some quarters and exalted in others, it was a typical product of the Archers (Michael Powell and Emeric Pressburger) and of its time, when war deaths turned the thoughts of many people towards religion. An RAF pilot undergoes a brain operation and dreams the outcome as the result of a trial conducted in heaven: the theme seems curiously unthought through and full of irrelevances, but the production is full of enjoyable lapses of taste as well as flashes of sheer brilliance and incomparable imagination. Décor by Hein Heckroth; acting by David Niven, Roger Livesey, Marius Goring and Raymond Massey; colour and monochrome photography by Jack Cardiff.

Matthau, Walter (1920–) (Walter Matasschanskayasky). American character actor with a penchant for wry comedy; his lugubrious features and sharp talent made him a star in the late sixties.
□ The Kentuckian 55. The Indian Fighter 55. Bigger than Life 56. *A Face in the Crowd* 57. Slaughter on Tenth Avenue 57. King Creole 58. Ride a Crooked Trail 58. The Voice in the Mirror 58. Onionhead 58. Strangers when We Meet 60. Gangster Story (& d) 60. Lonely are the Brave 62. Who's Got the Action? 62. Island

of Love 63. *Charade* 63. Ensign Pulver 64. Fail Safe 64. Goodbye Charlie 64. *Mirage* 65. *The Fortune Cookie* (AA) 66. *A Guide for the Married Man* 67. *The Odd Couple* 68. The Secret Life of an American Wife 68. Candy 68. *Hello Dolly* 69. Cactus Flower 69. A New Leaf 71. Plaza Suite 71. *Kotch* 71. Pete'n Tillie 72. Charley Varrick 73. The Laughing Policeman 73. Earthquake 74. The Taking of Pelham One Two Three 74. The Front Page 75. The Sunshine Boys 75. The Bad News Bears 76. Casey's Shadow 77.
TV series: Tallahassee 7000 59.

Matthews, A. E. (1869–1960). British actor, on stage from 1886, films from the mid-twenties; in his youth a suave romantic lead, he was later famous for the crotchety cheerfulness of his extreme longevity.
Autobiography 1953: *Matty*.
Quiet Wedding 40. The Life and Death of Colonel Blimp 43. Piccadilly Incident 46. Just William's Luck 48. *The Chiltern Hundreds* (in his stage role as Lord Lister) 49. The Galloping Major 51. Made in Heaven 52. The Million Pound Note 54. Three Men in a Boat 56. Inn for Trouble 60, many others.

Matthews, Francis (1927–). British leading man with TV and repertory experience.
Bhowani Junction 56. The Revenge of Frankenstein 58. The Lamp in Assassin Mews 62. Dracula, Prince of Darkness 65. That Riviera Touch 66. Just Like a Woman 66. Crossplot 69, etc.

Matthews, Jessie (1907–). Vivacious British singing and dancing star of light musicals in the thirties; on stage from 1917.
Autobiography 1975: *Over My Shoulder*.
□ The Beloved Vagabond 24. Straws in the Wind 24. Out of the Blue 31. There Goes the Bride 32. The Midshipmaid 32. The Man from Toronto 32. *The Good Companions* 32. Friday the Thirteenth 33. Waltzes from Vienna 33. *Evergreen* 34. First a Girl 35. It's Love Again 36. Head over Heels 37. Gangway 37. Sailing Along 38. Climbing High 39. Forever and a Day 43. Candles at Nine 43. Tom Thumb 58.

Matthews, Lester (1900–). British stage actor, in Hollywood from 1934.
Creeping Shadows 31. Facing the Music 34. Blossom Time 34. Werewolf of London 35. Thank You, Jeeves 35. The Prince and the Pauper 37. The Adventures of Robin Hood 38. Northwest Passage 40. Man Hunt 41. Between Two Worlds 44. The Invisible Man's Revenge 44. Lorna Doone 51, many others.

Mattsson, Arne (1919–). Swedish director, in films from 1942.
She Only Danced One Summer 51. The Girl in Tails 56. Mannequin in Red 59. The Doll 62, etc.

Mature, Victor (1915–). American leading man of the forties; once known as 'the Hunk', but beneath the brawn lurked some style and a sense of humour.
□ The Housekeeper's Daughter 39. One Million BC 40. Captain Caution 40. No No Nanette 40. I Wake Up Screaming 41. The Shanghai Gesture 41. Song of the Islands 42. My Gal Sal 42. Footlight Serenade 42. Seven Days' Leave 42. *My Darling Clementine* (as Doc Holliday) 46. Moss Rose 47. Kiss of Death 47. Fury at Furnace Creek 48. Cry of the City 48. Red Hot and Blue 49. Easy Living 49. *Samson and Delilah* 49. Wabash Avenue 50. Stella 50. Gambling House 50. The Las Vegas Story 52. Androcles and the Lion 52. Something for the Birds 52. Million Dollar Mermaid 52. The Glory Brigade 53. Affair with a Stranger 53. *The Robe* 53. Veils of Baghdad 53. Dangerous Mission 54. Demetrius and the Gladiators 54. Betrayed 54. *The Egyptian* 54. Chief Crazy Horse 55. Violent Saturday 55. The Last Frontier 55. Safari (GB) 56. The Sharkfighters 56. Zarak (GB) 57. Interpol (GB) 57. The Long Haul (GB) 57. China Doll 57. No Time to Die (GB) 58. Escort West 59. The Bandit of Zhobe (GB) 59. The Big Circus 59. Timbuktu 59. Hannibal 60. *After The Fox* 66. Head 68. Every Little Crook and Nanny 72. Won Ton Ton 76.

Mau mau. The terrorist activities in Kenya during the fifties were the subject of three very savage movies: *Simba* 55, *Safari* 56, *Something of Value* 56.

Mauch, Billy and Bobby (1925–). American twins, boy actors who appeared in several films in the mid-thirties, notably a 'Penrod' series and the Errol Flynn version of *The Prince and the Pauper* 37.

Maugham, W. Somerset (1874–1965). Distinguished British novelist, short story writer and playwright whose works have often been filmed.
Smith 17. A Man of Honour 19. The Circle 25 and 30 (as *Strictly Unconventional*). Rain 28 (as *Sadie Thompson*). 32 and 53 (as *Miss Sadie Thompson*). Our Betters 33. The Painted Veil 34 and 57 (as *The Seventh Sin*). Of Human Bondage 34, 46 and 64. Ashenden (as *Secret Agent*) 36. Vessel of Wrath 37 and 54 (as *The Beachcomber*). The Letter 40 (also very freely adapted as *The Unfaithful* 47). The Moon and Sixpence 42. Christmas Holiday 44. The Razor's Edge 46. Theatre (as *Adorable Julia*) 63, etc.
He also introduced three omnibus films of his stories: *Quartet* 48, *Trio* 50 and *Encore* 51; a film of his life is promised.

Maunder, Wayne (1942–). American leading man of the sixties.
The Seven Minutes 71.
TV series: *Custer* 68. Lancer 69.

Maurey, Nicole (1925–). French leading lady.
Little Boy Lost (US) 51. The Secret of the Incas (US) 54. The Weapon (GB) 56. Me and the Colonel (US) 58. The House of the Seven Hawks (GB) 59. High Time (US) 60. The Day of the Triffids (GB) 62, etc.

Maxwell, Edwin (1886–1948). Stocky, balding American character actor, frequently cast as shady businessman.
The Jazz Singer 27. The Taming of the Shrew 29. Daddy Longlegs 31. Scarface 32. Cleopatra 34. Fury 36. Young Mr Lincoln 39. His Girl Friday 40. I Live on Danger 42. Holy Matrimony 43. Wilson 44. The Jolson Story 46. The Gangster 47, many others.

Maxwell, Elsa (1883–1963). Dumpy, talkative American columnist and party-giver.
Autobiographical books: *My Last Fifty Years* 1943. *I Married the World* 1955. *Celebrity Circus* 1961.
FILM APPEARANCES: Hotel for Women 39. Public Deb Number One 40. Stage Door Canteen 43, etc.

Maxwell, John (1875–1940). Scottish lawyer who turned distributor and became co-founder of Associated British productions and the ABC cinema chain.

Maxwell, Lois (1927–) (Lois Hooker). Canadian leading lady who had a brief Hollywood career (1946–48) before settling in England.
The Decision of Christopher Blake 47. Corridor of Mirrors 48. Women of Twilight 49. Domano E Troppo Tardi (It.) 50. The Woman's Angle 52. Aida (It.) 53. Passport to Treason 55. The High Terrace 56. Kill Me Tomorrow 57. Operation Kid Brother 67, etc.; plays Miss Moneypenny in the James Bond films.

Maxwell, Marilyn (1921–1972) (Marvel Maxwell). Blonde American radio singer and actress, formerly child dancer.

Stand By For Action 42. Swing Fever 42. Thousands Cheer 43. Lost in a Harem 44. Summer Holiday 47. The Lemon Drop Kid 51. Off Limits 54. New York Confidential 55. Rock-a-bye-Baby 58. Critic's Choice 62. Stagecoach to Hell 64, etc.
TV series: Bus Stop 61.

May, Elaine (1932–). American cabaret star of the fifties (with Mike Nichols); also screenwriter.
□ Luv (a) 67. Enter Laughing (a) 67. A New Leaf (awd) 71. Such Good Friends (w) 72.

May, Hans (1891–1959). Viennese composer who settled in Britain in the early thirties.
The Stars Look Down 39. Thunder Rock 42. The Wicked Lady 45. Brighton Rock 46. The Gypsy and the Gentleman 57, etc.

May, Joe (1880–1954) (Joseph Mandel). German director of early serials and thrillers.
Stuart Webb 15. Veritas Vincit 16. The Hindu Tomb 21, etc. Best German film probably *Asphalt* 29.
IN HOLLYWOOD: Music in the Air 34. The Invisible Man Returns 40. The House of Seven Gables 40. Hit the Road 41. Johnny Doesn't Live Here Any More 44, etc.

Mayehoff, Eddie (1911–). American comic actor, former dance band leader.
That's My Boy 51. Off Limits 52. How to Murder Your Wife 65, etc.

Mayer, Carl (1894–1944). German screen writer.
The Cabinet of Dr Caligari 19. *The Last Laugh* 24. Tartuffe 26. Berlin 27. *Sunrise* 27, etc.

Mayer, Gerald (1919–). American director.
□ Dial 1119 50. Inside Straight 51. The Sellout 52. Holiday for Sinners 52. Bright Road 53. The Marauders 55. Diamond Safari 57.

Mayer, Louis B. (1885–1957). American executive, former production head of MGM. Once a scrap merchant, he became a cinema manager and later switched to distribution. With Sam Goldwyn, formed Metro-Goldwyn-Mayer in 1924, and when Goldwyn bought himself out became one of Hollywood's most flamboyant and powerful tycoons until the fifties when he found himself less in touch and responsible to a board. Special Academy Award 1950 'for distinguished service to the motion picture industry'.
Biographies: *Holywood Rajah* 1954 by Bosley Crowther. *Mayer and Thalberg* 1975 by Sam Marx.

Mayerling (France 1936). A well-remembered tragic-romantic movie about the love of Austrian Archduke Rudolph for Marie Vetsera. The pair were eventually found dead in a hunting lodge, but the suicide alleged by the film is not totally justified by historical facts: it derives from a novel by Claude Anet. The film made international stars of Charles Boyer and Danielle Darrieux, and led to a Hollywood career for director Anatole Litvak, who in 1956 remade it for TV with Mel Ferrer and Audrey Hepburn. Meanwhile in 1949 Jean Delannoy had made another French version under the title *The Secret of Mayerling*. In 1968 Terence Young concocted an expensive European rehash with Omar Sharif and Catherine Deneuve; despite its length and tedium, there are indications that public fashion is in its favour.

Mayes, Wendell (–). American screenwriter.
Bank Shot 74. Death Wish 74, etc.

Maylon, Eily (1879–1961). English character actress in Hollywood, a familiar supporting face from *His Greatest Gamble* 34 to *The Secret Heart* 46, typically as the acidulous aunt in *On Borrowed Time* 38.

Maynard, Ken (1895–1973). American cowboy star, mainly seen in low-budget features. Once a rodeo rider; broke into films as a stunt man.
Janice Meredith 24. Señor Daredevil 26. The Red Raiders 27. Branded Men 31. Texas Gunfighter 32. Come on, Tarzan 32. Wheels of Destiny 34. Heir to Trouble 34. Wild Horse Stampede 45, many others.

Maynard, Kermit (1898–1971). American action player, brother of Ken Maynard. Once doubled for George O'Brien, Victor McLaglen, Warner Baxter and Edmund Lowe.
The Fighting Trooper 34. Sandy of the Mounted 34. Wild Bill Hickok 38. Golden Girl 51, many others.

Mayne, Ferdy (1916–). German-born actor, long in Britain; often seen as smooth villain.
Meet Sexton Blake 44. You Know What Sailors Are 53. Storm over the Nile 55. Ben Hur 59. Freud 62. Operation Crossbow 65. The Bobo 67. *The Fearless Vampire Killers* 68. Where Eagles Dare 69. When Eight Bells Toll 71. Innocent Bystanders 72, many others.

Mayo, Archie (1891–1968). American director of very variable output.

Money Talks 26. The College Widow 27. Beware of Married Men 28. Sonny Boy 29. Is Everybody Happy? 29. The Sacred Flame 29. Doorway to Hell 30. *Svengali* 31. Under Eighteen 31. The Expert 32. Night after Night 32. Mayor of Hell 33. Convention City 33. Desirable 34. *Bordertown* 34. *Go Into Your Dance* 35. The Case of the Lucky Legs 35. *The Petrified Forest* 36. Give Me Your Heart 36. Black Legion 36. Call it a Day 37. It's Love I'm After 37. Youth Takes a Fling 38. They Shall Have Music 39. The House Across the Bay 40. Four Sons 40. The Great American Broadcast 41. Charley's Aunt 41. Confirm or Deny 41. Moontide 42. Orchestra Wives 42. Crash Dive 43. Sweet and Low Down 44. A Night in Casablanca 46. Angel on My Shoulder 46. The Beast of Budapest (p only) 57, etc.

Mayo, Virginia (1920–) (Virginia Jones). American 'peaches and cream' leading lady of the forties; played a few bit parts before being cast as decoration in colour extravaganzas.
The Adventures of Jack London 43. *Up In Arms* 44. *The Princess and the Pirate* 44. Wonder Man 45. The Best Years of Our Lives 46. Out of the Blue 47. *The Secret Life of Walter Mitty* 47. A Song is Born 48. Smart Girls Don't Talk 48. The Girl from Jones Beach 49. White Heat 49. Backfire 50. The Flame and the Arrow 50. Along the Great Divide 51. Captain Horatio Hornblower 51. She's Working Her Way through College 52. South Sea Woman 53. King Richard and the Crusaders 54. Pearl of the South Pacific 55. Congo Crossing 56. The Story of Mankind 57. Fort Dobbs 58. Jet over the Atlantic 59. Young Fury 65. Castle of Evil 66. Fort Utah 67. Won Ton Ton 76, etc.

Maysles, David (1931–) and **Albert** (1933–). American film-making brothers, semi-professional and semi-underground; apart from a number of shorts their main achievements are *Showman* 63, a study of Joe Levine, and *Salesman* 69.

Mazurki, Mike (1909–) (Mikhail Mazurkski). Immense American character actor of Ukrainian descent; former heavyweight wrestler. Began in Hollywood as an extra.
The Shanghai Gesture (debut) 41. *Farewell My Lovely* 44. The French Key 46. Unconquered 47. Rope of Sand 49. Ten Tall Men 51. My Favorite Spy 52. Blood Alley 55. Davy Crockett 56. Donovan's Reef 63. Cheyenne Autumn 64. Seven Women 66, many others.
TV series: It's About Time 66. Chicago Teddy Bears 71.

Mazursky, Paul (c. 1938–). American writer-director.
□ I Love you Alice B. Toklas (co-w) 68. *Bob and Carol and Ted and Alice* (co-wd) 70. Alex in Wonderland (co-wd) 70. Blume in Love (wd) 73. Harry and Tonto (co-w, p, d) 74. Next Stop Greenwich Village (w, p, d) 76.

Mc: see under *Mac*.

Meara, Anne (–). American comedienne who turned straight actress in a 1975 TV series, *Kate McShane*.
Nasty Habits 76.

Medak, Peter (–). Hungarian director in Britain.
Negatives 68. *A Day in the Death of Joe Egg* 70. The Ruling Class 71.

Medford, Don (c. 1920–). American director.
□ The Hunting Party 71. The Organization 71.

Medina, Patricia (1921–). British-born leading lady of the forties and fifties, in routine international films.
The Day will Dawn 42. They Met in the Dark 42. The First of the Few 42. Dont Take It To Heart 44. Hotel Reserve 44. Waltz Time 45. The Secret Heart 46. Moss Rose 47. The Three Musketeers 48. The Fighting O'Flynn 49. Abbott and Costello in the Foreign Legion 50. The Magic Carpet 51. Lady in the Iron Mask 52. Siren of Baghdad 53. Phantom of the Rue Morgue 54. Pirates of Tripoli 55. Uranium Boom 56. Buckskin Lady 57. Count Your Blessings 59. The Killing of Sister George 68, etc.

medium shot. One taking in the full body of the actor, not so close as a close-up not so far off as a long shot.

Medwin, Michael (1923–). British light character comedian, usually seen as Cockney.
Piccadilly Incident 46. Boys in Brown 49. Top Secret 52. Above Us the Waves 55. A Hill in Korea 56. I Only Arsked 58. Night Must Fall 63. Rattle of a Simple Man 64. I've Gotta Horse 65. The Sandwich Man 66. Scrooge 70, many others.
AS PRODUCER: Charlie Bubbles 67. If 68. Spring and Port Wine 69. Gumshoe 71. Alpha Beta 73. O Lucky Man 73. Law and Disorder 73.

Meek, Donald (1880–1946). Scottish-born character actor, long in Hollywood; a bald,

worried and timidly respectable little man was his invariable role.
The Hole in the Wall (debut) 28. Mrs Wiggs of the Cabbage Patch 34. Barbary Coast 35. Captain Blood 35. Pennies from Heaven 36. The Adventures of Tom Sawyer 38. *Stagecoach* 39. Tortilla Flat 42. They Got Me Covered 43. State Fair 45. Magic Town 46, many others.

Meeker, Ralph (1920–) (Ralph Rathgeber). American leading man of the Brando type, with Broadway experience.
Teresa (debut) 51. Four in a Jeep 51. Shadow in the Sky 51. Glory Alley 52. The Naked Spur 53. Jeopardy 53. Code Two 53. Big House USA 54. *Kiss Me Deadly* (as Mike Hammer) 55. Desert Sands 56. *Paths of Glory* 58. Ada 61. Something Wild 62. The Dirty Dozen 67. The St Valentine's Day Massacre 67. Gentle Giant 67. The Detective 68. I Walk the Line 70. The Anderson Tapes 71. The Happiness Cage 73. The Food of the Gods 76, etc.

Meerson, Lazare (1900–1938). Russian-born production designer.
An Italian Straw Hat 28. Sous les Toits de Paris 29. Le Million 31. A Nous la Liberté 32. La Kermesse Héroique 35. As You Like It 36. The Citadel 38, etc.

Meet John Doe (US 1941). An interesting Frank Capra film in which pessimism almost won the upper hand: the one sane man nearly had to commit suicide in order to bring the grasping connivers to their senses. Otherwise a typically big, sprawling, superbly proficient Capra production with a newspaper setting, written by Robert Riskin with a cast headed by Barbara Stanwyck and Gary Cooper.

Meet Me in St Louis (US 1944). A somewhat overrated but enjoyable period musical which purveyed charm at a time when it was most needed and can now be seen to have contained much of the best Hollywood talent of the forties. Simply concerned with the ups-and-downs of a middle-class family at the turn of the century, it was directed by Vincente Minnelli from a script by Irving Brecher and Fred Finklehoffe; the songs were by Hugh Martin and Ralph Blane, and included 'The Trolley Song', 'Have Yourself a Merry Little Christmas', and 'The Boy Next Door'. The cast included Judy Garland, Margaret O'Brien, Leon Ames, Mary Astor and Harry Davenport; and the colour at the time seemed rich and luscious.

Mehboob (1907–) (Ramjankhan Mehboobkhan). Prolific Indian director, few of

whose films have been seen in the west.
Aan 49. Mother India 56. A Handful of Grain 59, etc.

Meighan, Thomas (1879–1936). American leading man of the silent screen.
The Trail of the Lonesome Pine 16. Male and Female 19. The Miracle Man 19. The New Klondyke 21. Conrad in Quest of His Youth 22. Manslaughter 23. The Alaskan 24. Tin Gods 26. The Racket 27. Young Sinners 31. Peck's Bad Boy 34, etc.

Meillon, John (1933–). Austalian character actor, in Britain from 1960.
On the Beach 59. The Sundowners 59. Offbeat 60. The Valiant 61. Billy Budd 62. The Running Man 63. They're a Weird Mob 66, etc.

Mekas, Adolfas (1925–). Lithuanian underground film-maker, in US.
Hallelujah the Hills (wd) 63. Guns of the Trees (a) 64. Windflowers (wd) 68, etc.

Mekas, Jonas (1922–). Lithuanian underground film-maker in US, brother of Adolfas Mekas.
The Secret Passions of Salvador Dali 61. The Brig 64. Guns of the Trees 64. Hare Krishna 66. Report from Millbrook 66, etc.

Melcher, Martin (1915–1968). American producer, married to Doris Day and from 1952 the co-producer of all her films.
Calamity Jane 53. Julie 56. Pillow Talk 59. Jumbo 62. Move Over, Darling 63. Send Me No Flowers 64. Where Were You When the Lights Went Out? 68, etc.

Melchior, Ib (1917–). Danish-born writer-director, long in US; former actor and set designer. Son of Lauritz Melchior.
□ Angry Red Planet (wd) 59. Reptilicus (wd) 61. The Time Travellers (wd) 64. Robinson Crusoe on Mars (w) 65.

Melchior, Lauritz (1890–1973). Danish operatic tenor, in a few Hollywood films.
Thrill of a Romance 45. Two Sisters from Boston 46. This Time for Keeps 47. Luxury Liner 48. The Stars Are Singing 53, etc.

Méliès, Georges (1861–1938). French film pioneer, an ex-conjuror who produced the cinema's first trick films, most of them ambitious and still effective. Credited with being the first to use the dissolve, double exposure, and fades. After World War I he found his films out of date and his talents unwanted.

Biography 1973: *Méliès Enchanteur* by Madeleine Méliès.
Une Partie de Cartes (debut) 96. The Artist's Dream 98. The Dreyfus Affair 99. Cinderella (1900). Indiarubber Head 01. Voyage to the Moon 02. The Kingdom of the Fairies 03. The Impossible Voyage 04. Twenty Thousand Leagues under the Sea 07. Baron Munchausen 11. The Conquest of the Pole 12, many others.

Mellor, William C. (1904–1963). American cinematographer.
Wings in the Dark 35. Disputed Passage 39. The Great MgGinty 40. Dixie 43. Abie's Irish Rose 46. Love Happy 49. *A Place in the Sun* (AA) 51. The Naked Spur 52. Give a Girl a Break 53. Bad Day at Black Rock 54. *Giant* 55. The Diary of Anne Frank 59. State Fair 62, etc.

Melton, James (1904–1961). American operatic tenor, in a few Hollywood films.
Stars over Broadway 35. Sing Me a Love Song 36. Melody for Two 37. Ziegfeld Follies 45.

Melville, Jean-Pierre (1917–1973) (J. P. Grumbach). French director, with stage experience.
Le Silence de la Mer 47. Les Enfants Terribles 48. Quand Tu Liras Cette Lettre 52. Bob le Flambeur 55. *Leon Morin Priest* 61. Second Wind 66. *The Samurai* 67. The Red Circle 70, etc.

Melvin, Murray (1932–). British light character actor with stage experience in Theatre Workshop.
The Criminal (debut) 60. *A Taste of Honey* 61. HMS Defiant 62. Sparrows Can't Sing 63. The Ceremony 64. Alfie 66. A Day in the Death of Joe Egg 70. The Boy Friend 71. Ghost Story 74. Barry Lyndon 75. The Bawdy Adventures of Tom Jones 76, etc.

The Men (US 1950). A typical early Stanley Kramer production, making drama out of an urgent real-life problem, in this case that of paraplegics—war veterans paralysed below the waist. Direct by Fred Zinnemann from a script by Carl Foreman, with Marlon Brando, Teresa Wright, Jack Webb and Everett Sloane.

Mendes, Lothar (1894–1974). Hungarian director, mainly in US.
A Night of Mystery 27. The Four Feathers 29. Payment Deferred 32. Jew Süss (GB) 34. *The Man Who Could Work Miracles* (GB) 36. Moonlight Sonata (GB) 38. International Squadron 41. Flight for Freedom 43. The Walls Came Tumbling Down 46, etc.

Menges, Chris (–). British cinematographer.
Black Beauty 71. Gumshoe 71, etc.

Menjou, Adolphe (1890–1963). Dapper French-American leading man of the twenties, later a polished, sharp-spoken character actor; had the reputation of being Hollywood's best-dressed man.
Autobiography 1952: *It Took Nine Tailors*.
SELECTED SILENT FILMS: The Kiss 16. The Faith Healer 21. The Three Musketeers 21. Bella Donna 23. *A Woman of Paris* 23. *The Marriage Circle* 24. *Forbidden Paradise* 24. The Swan 25. The Grand Duchess and the Waiter 26. Service for Ladies 27. Serenade 27. His Private Life 28. Marquis Preferred 28.
□ SOUND FILMS: Fashions in Love 29. Morocco 30. New Moon 30. Men Call it Love 31. The Easiest Way 31. *The Front Page* 31. The Great Lover 31. Friends and Lovers 31. Prestige 32. Forbidden 32. Two White Arms 32. The Man From Yesterday 32. Bachelor's Affairs 32. Night Club Lady 32. A Farewell to Arms 32. Blame the Woman 32. The Circus Queen Murder 33. *Morning Glory* 33. The Worst Woman in Paris 33. Convention City 33. Journal of a Crime 34. Easy to Love 34. The Trumpet Blows 34. *Little Miss Marker* 34. Flirtation 34. The Human Side 34. The Mighty Barnum 34. Gold Diggers of 1935. Broadway Gondolier 35. The Milky Way 36. Sing Baby Sing 36. Wives Never Know 36. One in a Million 36. *A Star is Born* 37. Café Metropole 37. *A Hundred Men and a Girl* 37. Stage Door 37. The Goldwyn Follies 38. Letter of Introduction 38. Thanks for Everything 38. King of the Turf 39. That's Right You're Wrong 39. Golden Boy 39. *The Housekeeper's Daughter* 39. *A Bill of Divorcement* 40. Turnabout 41. Road Show 41. Father Takes a Wife 41. *Roxie Hart* 42. Syncopation 42. You Were Never Lovelier 42. Hi Diddle Diddle 43. Sweet Rosie O'Grady 43. *Step Lively* 44. Man Alive 45. Heartbeat 46. The Bachelor's Daughters 46. I'll Be Yours 47. Mr District Attorney 47. The Hucksters 47. *State of the Union* 48. My Dream is Yours 49. Dancing in the Dark 49. To Please a Lady 50. Tall Target 51. Across the Wide Missouri 51. *The Sniper* 52. Man on a Tightrope 53. Timberjack 55. The Ambassador's Daughter 56. Bundle of Joy 56. The Fuzzy Pink Nightgown 57. *Paths of Glory* 57. I Married a Woman 58. Pollyanna 60.

Menzel, Jiri (1938–). Czech director.
Closely Observed Trains (AA) 66. Capricious Summer 68.

Menzies, William Cameron (1896–1957). American art director who did much memorable work, especially with louring, impressionistic skyscapes. Also directed a few rather disappointing low-budget films.

AS ART DIRECTOR: Robin Hood 22. *The Thief of Baghdad* 24. Tempest 27. *The Dove* (AA) 28. Bulldog Drummond 29. Alice in Wonderland 33. *Things to Come* (& co-d) 36. The Adventures of Tom Sawyer 38. Gone with the Wind 39. Our Town 40. Foreign Correspondent 40. *King's Row* 41. For Whom the Bell Tolls 43. Ivy 47. Arch of Triumph 48. Around the World in Eighty Days 56, etc.

□ AS DIRECTOR: Always Goodbye 31. The Spiders 31. Almost Married 32. Chandu the Magician 32. Wharf Angel 34. *Things to Come* 36. The Green Cockatoo 40. Address Unknown 44. Drums in the Deep South 51. The Whip Hand 51. The Maze 53. Invaders from Mars 54.

Merande, Doro (c. 1898–1975). American character actress who specialized in acidulous, eccentric and whimsical spinsters.

Our Town 40. Sullivan's Travels 41. Mr Belvedere Rings the Bell 52. The Seven Year Itch 55. The Cardinal 63. Hurry Sundown 67, many others.

Mercer, Beryl (1882–1939). British character actress, of small stature, in Hollywood from 1923; played mothers, maids, landladies.

The Christian 23, Seven Days' Leave 29. *Outward Bound* 30. Merely Mary Ann 31. Supernatural 32. *Cavalcade* 33. Berkeley Square 33. The Little Minister 34. Night Must Fall 37. The Hound of the Baskervilles 39, etc.

Mercer, Johnny (1909–1976). American lyricist and composer, active in Hollywood from the early thirties. Songs include 'Blues in the Night', 'Black Magic', 'Something's Got to Give', 'Accentuate the Positive', etc.

The Harvey Girls (AA) 46. Here Comes the Groom (AA) 51. Seven Brides for Seven Brothers (AA) 54. Lil Abner 59, etc.

Merchant, Vivien (1929–) (Ada Thompson). British leading actress, mainly on TV: wife of Harold Pinter.

Alfie 66. Accident 67. Under Milk Wood 71. Frenzy 72. The Offence 72. The Homecoming 73, etc.

Mercier, Michele (1942–). French leading lady, seen abroad in *Retour de Manivelle* 61, *A Global Affair* (US) 63, more recently in a series about the amorous historical adventures of *Angelique*.

Mercouri, Melina (1923–). Volatile Greek star actress with flashing smile and dominant personality; married Jules Dassin and appeared in international films.

Autobiography 1971: *I Was Born Greek*.

□ *Stella* 54. He Who Must Die 56. The Gypsy and the Gentleman 58. The Law 59. *Never on Sunday* 60. Il Giudizio Universale 61. Phaedra 61. The Victors 63. *Topkapi* 64. A Man Could Get Killed 65. 10.30 pm Summer 66. Gaily Gaily 69. Promise at Dawn 71. Once Is Not Enough 75. Nasty Habits 76.

Meredith, Burgess (1908–) (George Burgess). American star character actor who was famous on Broadway in the thirties, but never seemed to find the right Hollywood outlet for his enthusiastic, eccentric portrayals.

□ *Winterset* 36. There Goes the Groom 37. Spring Madness 38. Idiot's Delight 39. *Of Mice and Men* 39. Castle on the Hudson 40. Second Chorus 40. San Francisco Docks 41. *That Uncertain Feeling* 41. Tom Dick and Harry 41. Street of Chance 42. *The Story of GI Joe* (as Ernie Pyle) 45. The Diary of a Chambermaid 46. Magnificent Doll 46. On Our Merry Way 48. *Mine Own Executioner* (GB) 48. The Man on the Eiffel Tower 49. The Gay Adventure 53. Joe Butterfly 57. Advise and Consent 62. The Cardinal 63. In Harm's Way 65. A Big Hand for the Little Lady 66. Madame X 66. Batman 66. Hurry Sundown 67. The Torture Garden (GB) 67. Mackenna's Gold 68. Stay Away Joe 68. There Was a Crooked Man 70. Probe (TV) 71. Such Good Friends 71. Golden Needles 74. The Day of the Locust 74. The Hindenberg 76. Rocky 77.

TV series: Mr Novak 65. Search 72.

Merivale, Philip (1886–1946). British stage actor who moved to Hollywood in the late thirties.

The Passing of the Third Floor Back 35. Give Us This Night 36. Rage in Heaven 41. This Above All 42. This Land Is Mine 43. Lost Angel 44. The Stranger 45, etc.

Merkel, Una (1903–). American character actress who started in the thirties as heroine's girlfriend type, later played mothers and aunts.

Abraham Lincoln 30. Daddy Longlegs 31. Whistling in the Dark 33. The Merry Widow 34. Saratoga 37. Destry Rides Again 39. Road to Zanzibar 41. This Is the Army 43. Twin Beds 44. With a Song in My Heart 52. The Kentuckian 55. The Mating Game 59. Summer and Smoke 62. A Tiger Walks 63. Spinout 66, many others.

Merman, Ethel (1908–) (Ethel

Zimmermann). Brassy, vibrant, much-loved American star entertainer who has an incomparable way with a song that can be belted across. Her style was too outsize for Hollywood. Autobiography 1955: *Who Could Ask For Anything More?* (UK: *Don't Call Me Madam*).
□ Follow the Leader 30. We're Not Dressing 34. Kid Millions 34. *Anything Goes* 36. The Big Broadcast of 1936. Strike Me Pink 36. Happy Landing 38. *Alexander's Ragtime Band* 38. Straight Place and Show 38. Stage Door Canteen 43. *Call Me Madam* 53. There's No Business Like Show Business 54. It's a Mad Mad Mad Mad World 63. The Art of Love 65. Won Ton Ton 76.

Merrall, Mary (1890–) (Mary Lloyd). British character actress, on stage from 1907; often in fey or absent-minded roles.
The Duke's Son 20. You Will Remember 39. *Love on the Dole* 41. Squadron Leader X 42. *Dead of Night* 45. Nicholas Nickleby 47. Badger's Green 48. The Late Edwina Black 51. The Pickwick Papers 52. *The Belles of St Trinian's* 54. It's Great To Be Young 56. The Camp on Blood Island 58. Spare the Rod 61. Who Killed the Cat? 66, many others.

Merrie Melodies: see *Looney Tunes*.

Merrill, Dina (1928–) (Nedenia Hutton Rumbough). American leading lady of the sixties, and leading socialite.
The Desk Set 57. The Sundowners 59. The Courtship of Eddie's Father 63. The Pleasure Seekers 64. I'll Take Sweden 65. Running Wild 73, etc.

Merrill, Gary (1914–). Dependable, tough-looking American actor.
Winged Victory 44. Slattery's Hurricane 48. Twelve O'Clock High 49. *All About Eve* 50. Decision Before Dawn 51. Another Man's Poison (GB) 51. Phone Call from a Stranger 53. Night Without Sleep 52. Blueprint for Murder 53. The Human Jungle 54. The Black Dakotas 54. Bermuda Affair 56. The Pleasure of His Company 61. The Woman Who Wouldn't Die 65. Around the World Under the Sea 66. Destination Inner Space 66. Catacombs (GB) 66. The Power 68. Huckleberry Finn 74, others.

Merritt, George (1890–). British character actor of solid presence, usually seen as trades unionist, policeman, or gruff north-country type.
Dreyfus 30. The Lodger 32. I Was a Spy 33. Dr Syn 37. Q Planes 39. He Found a Star 41. Hatter's Castle 41. Waterloo Road 45. I'll Be Your Sweetheart 45. I'll Turn to You 46.

Nicholas Nickleby 47. Marry Me 49. The Green Scarf 54. Quatermass II 57. Tread Softly Stranger 58. I Monster 70, etc.

Merrow, Jane (1941–). British leading lady.
Don't Bother to Knock 61. The Wild and the Willing 62. The System 63. *The Lion in Winter* 68. Hands of the Ripper 70. The Horror at 37,000 Feet (TV) 73. Diagnosis Murder 75, etc.

The Merry Widow, Franz Lehar's operetta has been filmed at least three times. 1. US 1925; as silent, by Erich Von Stroheim, with John Gilbert, Mae Murray and Roy d'Arcy. 2. US 1934: by Ernst Lubitsch, with Maurice Chevalier and Jeanette MacDonald; added lyrics by Gus Khan and Lorenz Hart. 3. US 1952: by Curtis Bernhardt, with Fernando Lamas, Lana Turner and Richard Haydn; added lyrics by Paul Francis Webster.

Merton of the Movies. This American comic novel by Harry Leon Wilson, about an innocent in Hollywood in early silent days, has been filmed three times: in 1924 with Glenn Hunter, in 1932 (as *Make Me a Star*) with Stuart Erwin, and in 1947 with Red Skelton.

Mervyn, William (1912–1976). Portly, plummy-voiced British character actor, much on TV in high comedy roles.
The Blue Lamp 52. The Long Arm 56. Invasion Quartet 61. Murder Ahoy 64. The Jokers 67. The Railway Children 70. The Ruling Class 71. Up The Front 72, many others.

Mescall, John (1899–). American cinematographer.
Hold Your Horses 20. So This Is Paris 26. *The Black Cat* 34. *Bride of Frankenstein* 35. *Showboat* 36. The Road Back 37. Josette 38. Kit Carson 40. Dark Waters 44. Bedside Manner 45. The Desperadoes Are In Town 56. Not of This Earth 57, many others.

Messel, Oliver (1904–). British stage designer who has occasionally worked in films.
The Scarlet Pimpernel 34. Romeo and Juliet 36. The Thief of Baghdad 40. Caesar and Cleopatra 45. The Queen of Spades 48, etc.

Methot, Mayo (1904–1951). American actress who is best remembered for her stormy marriage with Humphrey Bogart.
Corsair 31. The Mind Reader 33. Jimmy the Gent 33. Side Streets 34. Dr Socrates 35. Mr Deeds Goes to Town 36. Marked Woman 37. The Sisters 38. Unexpected Father 39. Brother Rat and a Baby 40, etc.

Metro-Goldwyn-Mayer. For many years the undoubted leader of the industry, this famous American production company has lately suffered most from the lack of 'front office' control and the proliferation of independent productions: now that it doesn't own the racecourse, it can't seem to pick the winners. The company stems from Loew's Inc., an exhibiting concern which in 1920 bought into Metro Pictures, which then produced two enormous money-spinners, *The Four Horsemen of the Apocalypse* and *The Prisoner of Zenda*. In 1924 Metro was merged with the Goldwyn production company (though Samuel Goldwyn himself promptly opted out and set up independently); and the next year Louis B. Mayer Pictures joined the flourishing group to add further power. Mayer himself became studio head and remained the dominant production force for over twenty-five years. Ideas man and executive producer in the early years was young Irving Thalberg, whose artistic flair provided a necessary corrective to Mayer's proletarian tastes, and who, before his death in 1936, had established a lofty pattern with such successes as *Ben Hur*, *The Big Parade*, *Anna Christie*, *Grand Hotel*, *The Thin Man*, *David Copperfield* and *Mutiny on the Bounty*, and stars like Garbo, Gable, Beery, Lionel Barrymore, Joan Crawford, John Gilbert, Lon Chaney, William Powell, Jean Harlow, Spencer Tracy, Lewis Stone, Nelson Eddy, Jeannette MacDonald, Laurel and Hardy and the Marx Brothers. (MGM's motto was in fact 'more stars than there are in heaven . . .') The success story continued through the forties with *Goodbye Mr Chips*, Greer Garson, *The Wizard Of Oz*, Judy Garland, the Hardy Family, Gene Kelly and Esther Williams. Such continuity of product is a thing of the past, but MGM keeps its end up with occasional big guns like *Dr Zhivago*, *When Eagles Dare* and *Network*.

Metropolis (Germany 1926). Fritz Lang's futuristic fantasy, from a script by himself and Thea Von Harbou, details the horrors of a mechanized Utopia. The actual story is a dull revamping of the struggle between capital and labour; but the great geometric sets are imaginatively handled. With Brigitte Helm (as a robot) and Rudolph Klein-Rogge; photographed by Karl Freund.

Metty, Russell (1906–). American cinematographer.
Sylvia Scarlett 35. Bringing Up Baby 38. Music in Manhattan 44. The Story of G.I. Joe 45. *The Stranger* 45. *Ivy* 47. All My Sons 48. We Were Strangers 49. Magnificent Obsession 54. Man

without a Star 55. *Miracle in the Rain* 56. Written on the Wind 56. Man with a Thousand Faces 57. A Time to Love and a Time to Die 58. The Misfits 60. *Spartacus* (AA) 61. The Art of Love 65. The War Lord 65. Madame X 66. The Appaloosa 66. The Secret War of Harry Frigg 67. Madigan 68. Eye of the Cat 69. The Omega Man 71. Ben 72, many others.

Metzger, Radley (1930–). American director.
Dark Odyssey 61. The Dirty Girls 64. Carmen Baby 67. Therese and Isabelle 68. Camille 2000 69. The Lickerish Quartet 70. Little Mother 72. Score 73, etc.

Meurisse, Paul (1912–). French general purpose actor.
Montemartre sur Seine 41. Marie la Misère 45. Diabolique 54. La Tête contre les Murs 58. Lunch on the Grass 59. La Vérité 60, etc.

Mexican Spitfire. This was the first (1939) of a series of American second-feature comedies which ran till 1943 with such titles as *Mexican Spitfire Sees a Ghost*, *Mexican Spitfire at Sea*. (The series had virtually begun with a 1938 entry called *The Girl from Mexico*.) Donald Woods was a young businessman with a temperamental wife (Lupe Velez), a scheming Uncle Matt (Leon Errol) and a drunken English client, Lord Epping (also played by Leon Errol). The films were only tolerably well made, but always managed a hectic finale of impersonation and mistaken identity which allowed full play to Mr Errol's jerky convulsions.

Mexico was a late starter in the feature film market, but made a few from about 1920, hampered by competition from Hollywood, which also plundered most of its best actors. The late thirties saw an improvement, with Emilio Fernandez as leading director, and in the forties Buñuel settled there and made some small stylish films. More recent productions have varied between cheap Hollywood-aping hokum and dour politically conscious social dramas.

Meyer, Emile (c. 1903–). American character actor typically cast as crooked cop or prizefight manager; but sometimes an honest Joe.
The People Against O'Hara 51. Shane 53. The Blackboard Jungle 55. *Riot in Cell Block 11* 55. The Man with the Golden Arm 56. *Sweet Smell of Success* 57. Baby Face Nelson 57. Paths of Glory 58. The Fiend Who Walked the West 59. Young Jesse James 60. Taggart 64. Young Dillinger 65. Hostile Guns 67. More Dead Than Alive 70, etc.

Meyer, Russ (1923–). American director of erotic films who broke briefly into the big time.
□ The Immoral Mr Teas 59. Eroticon 61. Eve and the Handyman 61. Naked Gals of the Golden West 62. Europe in the Raw 63 Heavenly Bodies 63. Laura 64. Mudhoney 65. Motor Psycho 65. Fanny Hill 65. Faster Pussycat Kill Kill 66. Mondo Topless 66. Good Morning and Goodbye 67. Common Law Cabin 67. Finders Keepers Lovers Weepers 68. *Vixen* 68. Cherry Harry and Raquel 69. Beyond the Valley of the Dolls 70. The Seven Minutes 71. Black Snake 73. The Supervixens 73. *Up* 76.

Meyer, Torben (1885–1965). German-American character actor who played many waiters, music teachers and petty officials, especially memorable in the films of Preston Sturges.
Roberta 35. The Prisoner of Zenda 37. Christmas in July 40. Edge of Darkness 42. The Miracle of Morgans Creek 43. Mad Wednesday 47, many others.

Michael, Gertrude (1911–1964). American actress usually seen in secondary roles.
I'm No Angel 33. The Notorious Sophie Lang (lead) 37. Women in Bondage 44. Caged 50. Women's Prison 55. Twist All Night 62, etc.

Michael, Ralph (1907–) (Ralph Champion Shotter). British character actor of stage and screen, often in stiff-upper-lip roles.
John Halifax Gentleman 38. San Demetrio, London 43. For Those in Peril 44. *Dead of Night* 45. Johnny Frenchman 45. The Captive Heart 46. Eureka Stockade 48. The Astonished Heart 49. The Sound Barrier 52. King's Rhapsody 56. Seven Waves Away 57. A Night To Remember 58. A Jolly Bad Fellow 64. House of Cards 68, others.

Michael Shayne. The American private eye created by Brett Halliday in a string of thirties novels was a lightly shaded character at best, but sufficed for a number of second feature thrillers in the early forties, with Lloyd Nolan as star. (One of them, *Time to Kill*, was actually adapted from Raymond Chandler's *The High Window*, not from a Halliday original.) In 1960 Richard Denning played the lead in a television series.

Michael Strogoff. Jules Verne's historical adventure novel, about espionage in war-torn Russia of 1870, has been a favourite with film makers. Tourjansky made a version with Mosjoukine in 1926. George Nicholls Jnr directed a Hollywood version with Anton

Walbrook in 1937. Carmine Gallone made the story again in colour in 1956, with an international cast headed by Curt Jurgens, who continued in 1961 in *The Triumph of Michael Strogoff*. In 1971 John Phillip Law appeared in a new version, *Courier of the Tsar*.

Michaels, Beverly (1927–). American leading lady of sultry dramas in the early fifties.
East Side West Side 49. Pick Up 51. Wicked Woman 53. Crashout 55, etc.

Michaels, Dolores (1930–). American leading lady of the late fifties; retired early.
The Wayward Bus 57. April Love 57. Fraulein 58. Warlock 59. Five Gates to Hell 59. One Foot in Hell 60. The Battle at Bloody Beach 61, etc.

Michell, Keith (1926–). Australian leading man, on British stage and screen from the mid-fifties.
True as a Turtle 57. Dangerous Exile 57. The Gypsy and the Gentleman 58. *The Hellfire Club* 61. Seven Seas to Calais 63. Prudence and the Pill 68. House of Cards 68. *Henry VIII and His Six Wives* 72. Moments 73, etc.

Michener, James A. (1907–). American adventure-epic novelist. Works filmed include: *South Pacific, Return to Paradise, The Bridges at Toko Ri, Sayonara, Hawaii.*

Middleton, Charles (1874–1949). American character actor usually in villainous roles; especially remembered as Ming the Merciless in the Flash Gordon serials.
Mystery Ranch 32. Mrs Wiggs of the Cabbage Patch 34. Kentucky 39. The Grapes of Wrath 40. Our Vines Have Tender Grapes 45. The Black Arrow 49, many others.

Middleton, Guy (1906–1973). Hearty-type British light character actor, in films as amiable idiot or other man since the early thirties after Stock Exchange career.
A Woman Alone 32. Fame 34. Keep Fit 37. French Without Tears 39. Dangerous Moonlight 40. The Demi-Paradise 43. Champagne Charlie 44. The Rake's Progress 45. The Captive Heart 46. One Night with You 48. The Happiest Days of Your Life 49. Never Look Back 52. Albert RN 53. The Belles of St Trinian's 54. The Passionate Summer 58. The Waltz of the Toreadors 62. The Magic Christian 70, etc.

Middleton, Noelle (c. 1928–). British leading lady of the fifties.
Carrington V.C. 55. The Iron Petticoat 56.

Middleton, Ray (1908–). American actor-singer.
Gangs of Chicago 40. Lady For A Night 41. The Girl From Alaska 42. I Dream of Jeannie 52. Jubilee Trail 54. The Road To Denver 55, etc.

Middleton, Robert (1911–) (Samuel G. Messer). Weighty American character actor usually cast as villain.
The Silver Chalice 55. The Big Combo 55. The Desperate Hours 55. The Court Jester 55. The Friendly Persuasion 56. The Tarnished Angels 58. Career 59. Gold of the Seven Saints 61. For Those Who Think Young 64. Big Hand for a Little Lady 66. Which Way to the Front? 71, many others.

Midnight Cowboy (US 1968). A glossy film about sleazy New York was bound to leave a bad taste in the mouth, which is presumably what director John Schlesinger intended when he adapted this skilful but ultimately pointless film exercise from James Leo Herlihy's novel. Jon Voight and Dustin Hoffman give surprisingly attractive performances as the stud and the bum who sit freezing in a tenement all winter instead of going out to get jobs. On its release the film marked a considerable step forward—or backward—into permissiveness.

A Midsummer Night's Dream. Shakespeare's fairy play was filmed in America in 1929 by J. Stuart Blackton, starring Maurice Costello; and there is a Czechoslovakian puppet version by Jiri Trnka. But the best-known version is Max Reinhardt's lavish production for Warners in 1935, directed by Reinhardt and William Dieterle, with a surprising cast including James Cagney as Bottom, Mickey Rooney as Puck, Hugh Herbert, Arthur Treacher, Dick Powell, Anita Louise, Victor Jory and Olivia de Havilland. Peter Hall's 'realistic' version of 1968, aimed primarily at American TV, was generally thought unsuccessful.

Mifune, Toshiro (1920–). Versatile Japanese actor with a ferocious style, seen in many films by Kurosawa and others.
The Drunken Angel 48. The Stray Dog 49. Rashomon 50. Seven Samurai 54. The Lower Depths 57. Throne of Blood 57. The Hidden Fortress 58. The Bad Sleep Well 59. Yojimbo 61. Red Beard 64. The Lost World of Sinbad 64. Grand Prix (US) 66. Rebellion 67. Hell in the Pacific (US) 68. Red Sun 71. Paper Tiger 75. Midway 76, etc.
AS DIRECTOR: Legacy of the Five Hundred Thousand 63.

Mike Hammer. The tough, immoral private eye created by Mickey Spillane (qv for list of films).

Miles, Sir Bernard (1907–). British actor specializing in slow-speaking countryfolk and other ruminating types. An ex-school master, on stage since 1930. Founder of London's Mermaid Theatre (1959) with which he is nowadays mainly concerned.
Channel Crossing 32. Quiet Wedding 40. In Which We Serve 42. Tawny Pipit (& co-w and d) 44. Carnival 46. Great Expectations 46. Nicholas Nickleby 47. The Guinea Pig 48. Chance of a Lifetime (& wpd) 49. Never Let Me Go 53. The Man Who Knew Too Much 56. Moby Dick 56. The Smallest Show on Earth 57. Tom Thumb 58. Sapphire 59. Heavens Above 63. Run Wild Run Free 69, etc.

Miles, Christopher (1939–). British director, brother of Sarah Miles.
Six-sided Triangle 64. Up Jumped a Swagman 65. The Virgin and The Gypsy 70. Time for Loving 71. The Maids 74. That Lucky Touch 75.

Miles, Joanna (1949–). American leading lady of the seventies.
Bug 75.

Miles, Peter (1938–) (Gerald Perreau). American child actor of the forties, brother of Gigi Perreau.
Passage to Marseilles 44. The Red Pony 48. Roseanna McCoy 50. Quo Vadis 51, etc.

Miles, Sarah (1941–). Vivacious British leading actress; married Robert Bolt.
□ Term of Trial 62. The Servant 63. The Ceremony 64. Those Magnificent Men in Their Flying Machines 65. I Was Happy Here 65. Blow Up 66. Ryan's Daughter 70. Lady Caroline Lamb 72. The Hireling 73. The Man Who Loved Cat Dancing 73. Great Expectations (TV) 75. Dynasty (TV) 76. The Sailor Who Fell with Grace from the Sea 76.

Miles, Sylvia (1932–). American character actress.
Heat 72. Farewell My Lovely 75. 92 in the Shade 75. The Great Scout and Cathouse Thursday 76. The Sentinel 77, etc.

Miles, Vera (1929–) (Vera Ralston). Dependable American leading lady who came from TV to films.
For Men Only (debut) 52. Charge at Feather River 54. 23 Paces to Baker Street 55. The Searchers 56. The Wrong Man 57. The FBI Story 59. Psycho 60. A Tiger Walks 63. Those

Calloways 65. Follow Me, Boys 66. The Spirit is Willing 66. Hell-fighters 68. The Castaway Cowboy 74. One Little Indian 75, many others.

Milestone, Lewis (1895–). Veteran American director whose later films never quite matched up to his early achievements. Former editor, in Hollywood from 1918.
□ Seven Sinners 25. The Cave Man 26. The New Klondike 26. *Two Arabian Knights* (AA) 27. The Garden of Eden 28. The Racket 28. Betrayal 29. New York Nights 29. *All Quiet on the Western Front* (AA) 30. *The Front Page* 31. Rain 32. *Hallelujah I'm a Bum* 33. The Captain Hates the Sea 34. Paris in Spring 35. Anything Goes 36. *The General Died at Dawn* 36. *Of Mice and Men* 39. Night of Nights 40. Lucky Partners 40. My Life with Caroline (& p) 41. Edge of Darkness 43. North Star 43. The Purple Heart 44. The Strange Love of Martha Ivers 46. *A Walk in the Sun* 46. No Minor Vices 47. Arch of Triumph 48. The Red Pony 48. Halls of Montezuma 51. Kangaroo 52. Les Misérables 52. Melba 53. They Who Dare (GB) 54. Pork Chop Hill 59. Ocean's Eleven 61. Mutiny on the Bounty 62.

Milhollin, James (1920–). Crumple-faced American character comedian, mostly on TV. No Time For Sergeants 58. Bon Voyage 62, etc.
TV series: *Grindl* 64.

Milian, Tomas (–). Cuban character actor in spaghetti westerns.
The Bounty Killer 66. Face to Face 67. The Big Gundown 67. Run Man Run 68. Django Kill 68. Apache 70. The Companeros 70. The Counsellor 74, etc.

Milius, John (1945–). American director.
The Devil's Eight (w only) 68. Evel Knievel (w only) 72. Jeremiah Johnson (w only) 72. Judge Roy Bean (w only) 73. Magnum Force (co-w only) 73. *Dillinger* (& w) 73. The Wind and the Lion (& w) 75.

Miljan, John (1893–1960). American character actor with stage experience; often played the suave villain.
Love Letters 23. The Amateur Gentleman 26. The Painted Lady 29. The Ghost Walks 35. Double Cross 41. The Merry Monahans 44. The Killers 46. Samson and Delilah 50. Pirates of Tripoli 55, etc.

Milland, Ray (1905–) (Reginald Truscott-Jones). Welsh-born light leading man of ready smile and equable disposition; carved a pleasant niche for himself in Hollywood in the thirties,

and later surprised many by becoming an actor and director of some repute before stepping on the inevitable downhill slope.

□ The Plaything (GB) 29. The Flying Scotsman (GB) 29. Bachelor Father 31. Just a Gigolo 31. Bought 31. Ambassador Bill 31. Blonde Crazy 31. Polly of the Circus 31. The Man Who Played God 32. Payment Deferred 32. This is the Life (GB) 33. Orders is Orders (GB) 33. Bolero 34. We're Not Dressing 34. Many Happy Returns 34. Menace 34. Charlie Chan in London 34. The Gilded Lily 35. One Hour Late 35. Four Hours to Kill 35. The Glass Key 35. Alias Mary Dow 35. Next Time We Love 36. The Return of Sophie Lang 36. The Big Broadcast of 1937. *The Jungle Princess* 36. Three Smart Girls 37. Wings Over Honolulu 37. Easy Living 37. Ebb Tide 37. Wise Girl 37. Bulldog Drummond Escapes 37. Her Jungle Love 38. Men with Wings 38. Say It In French 38. Hotel Imperial 39. *Beau Geste* 39. Everything Happens at Night 39. *French Without Tears* (GB) 39. Irene 40. The Doctor Takes a Wife 40. Untamed 40. *Arise My Love* 41. I Wanted Wings 41. Skylark 41. The Lady Has Plans 42. Are Husbands Necessary 42. The Major and the Minor 42. Reap the Wild Wind 42. Star Spangled Rhythm 42. Forever and a Day 43. The Crystal Ball 43. *The Uninvited* 44. Lady in the Dark 44. Till We Meet Again 44. *Ministry of Fear* 44. *The Lost Weekend* (AA) 45. Kitty 45. The Well Groomed Bride 46. California 46. The Imperfect Lady 47. The Trouble with Women 47. Golden Earrings 47. Variety Girl 47. The Big Clock 48. So Evil My Love 48. Sealed Verdict 48. *Alias Nick Beal* 49. It Happens Every Spring 49. A Woman of Distinction 50. A Life of Her Own 50. Copper Canyon 50. Circle of Danger (GB) 51. Night into Morning 51. Rhubarb 52. Close to My Heart 51. Bugles in the Afternoon 52. Something to Live For 52. *The Thief* 52. Jamaica Run 53. Let's Do It Again 53. *Dial M for Murder* 54. A Man Alone (& d) 55. The Girl in the Red Velvet Swing 55. Lisbon (& d) 56. Three Brave Men 57. The River's Edge 57. The Safecracker (& d) (GB) 58. High Flight (GB) 58. The Premature Burial 62. Panic in Year Zero (& d) 62. The Man with X-Ray Eyes 63. The Confession 65. Hostile Witness (& d) (GB) 68. River of Gold (TV) 69. Daughter of the Mind (TV) 69. Love Story 70. Company of Killers (TV) 70. Black Noon (TV) 71. Embassy 72. The Thing with Two Heads 72. Frogs 72. Terror in the Wax Museum 73. The House in Nightmare Park (GB) 73. Gold 74. The Student Connection 74. Escape to Witch Mountain 76. Rich Man Poor Man (TV) 76. The Last Tycoon 76.

TV series: Markham 59.

Millar, Stuart (1929–). American producer.
The Young Stranger 57. Stage Struck 58. The
Young Doctors 61. I Could Go On Singing 63.
The Best Man 64. Paper Lion 68. When the
Legends Die (& d) 72. Rooster Cogburn (d only)
75.

Miller, Ann (1919–) (Lucy Ann Collier).
Long-legged American dancer, in films from
mid-thirties.
Autobiography 1974: *Miller's High Life.*
New Faces of 1937. *You Can't Take It With
You* 38. Go West, Young Lady 41. *Reveille with
Beverly* 43. Jam Session 44. Eve Knew Her
Apples 45. Easter Parade 48. *On the Town* 49.
Two Tickets to Broadway 51. *Kiss Me Kate* 53.
The Opposite Sex 56, etc.

Miller, Arthur (1915–). American playwright
whose work has been adapted for the cinema.
All My Sons 48. Death of a Salesman 52. The
Witches of Salem 56, etc.
Wrote scenes for *Let's Make Love* 60, starring
his then wife Marilyn Monroe; also complete
screenplay *The Misfits* 61.

Miller, Arthur (1894–1971). Distinguished
American cinematographer.
Selected Silent Films: At Bay 15. The Iron
Heart 17. The Profiteers 19. His House in Order
20. Kick In 22. The Cheat 23. The Coming of
Amos 24. The Clinging Vine 26. The Fighting
Eagle 28. The Spieler 29, etc.
☐ SOUND FILMS: Oh Yeah 30. Sailor's
Holiday 30. Strange Cargo 30. The Lady of
Scandal 30. Officer O'Brien 30. The Truth about
Youth 30. Behind the Make Up 30. Father's Son
30. Bad Company 31. Panama Flo 32. Big Shot
32. The Young Bride 32. Breach of Promise 32.
Me and My Gal 32. Okay America 32. Sailor's
Luck 33. Hold Me Tight 33. The Man Who
Dared 33. The Last Trail 33. The Mad Game 33.
My Weakness 33. Bottoms Up 34. Ever Since
Eve 34. Handy Andy 34. Love Time 34. The
White Parade 34. Bright Eyes 34. The Little
Colonel 35. It's a Small World 35. Black Sheep
35. Welcome Home 35. Paddy O'Day 35. White
Fang 36. 36 Hours to Kill 36. Pigskin Parade 36.
Stowaway 36. *Wee Willie Winkie* 37. Heidi 37.
The Baroness and the Butler 38. Rebecca of
Sunnybrook Farm 38. Little Miss Broadway 38.
Submarine Patrol 38. *The Little Princess* 39.
Susannah of the Mounties 39. Here I Am a
Stranger 39. *The Rains Came* 39. *The Blue Bird*
40. Johnny Apollo 40. On Their Own 40. *The
Mark of Zorro* 40. Brigham Young 40. *Tobacco
Road* 41. The Men in Her Life 41. Man Hunt 41.
How Green was My Valley (AA) 41. *This Above
All* 42. Iceland 42. The Moon is Down 43. The

Immortal Sergeant 43. The Ox Bow Incident 43.
The Song of Bernadette (AA) 43. The Purple
Heart 44. The Keys of the Kingdom 45. A Royal
Scandal 45. Dragonwyck 46. *Anna and the King
of Siam* 46. The Razor's Edge 46. Gentleman's
Agreement 47. The Walls of Jericho 48. A Letter
to Three Wives 49. Whirlpool 49. *The
Gunfighter* 50. The Prowler 51.

Miller, Colleen (1932–). American leading
lady.
The Las Vegas Story 52. The Purple Mask 55.
Man with a Shadow 57. Step Down to Terror 59,
etc.

Miller, David (1909–). American director,
formerly editor, in Hollywood from 1930.
☐ Billy the Kid 41. Sunday Punch 42. Flying
Tigers 43. Top o' the Morning 49. Love Happy
50. Our Very Own 51. Saturday's Hero 52.
Sudden Fear 53. Twist of Fate 54. Diane 55. The
Opposite Sex 56. The Story of Esther Costello
57. Happy Anniversary 59. Midnight Lace 60.
Back Street 61. *Lonely Are the Brave* 62.
Captain Newman 63. Hammerhead (GB) 68.
Hail Hero 69. Executive Action 73. Bittersweet
Love 76, etc.

Miller, Glenn (1904–1944). American
bandleader and composer, whose 'new sound'
was immensely popular during World War II.
Appeared in *Orchestra Wives* 42. *Sun Valley
Serenade* 42. Was impersonated by James
Stewart in *The Glenn Miller Story* 53.

Miller, Jason (1939–). American playwright
who turned actor in *The Exorcist* 74.

Miller, Jonathan (1936–). British satirist and
director.
☐ Alice in Wonderland (TV) 67. Take a Girl
Like You 70.

Miller, Mandy (1944–). British child star.
The Man in the White Suit 51. *Mandy* 52. Dance
Little Lady 54. A Child in the House 56. The
Secret 57. The Snorkel 61, etc.

Miller, Marilyn (1898–1936) (Mary Ellen
Reynolds). American dancing and singing star of
Broadway musicals in the twenties. Films
include *Sally* 30. *Sunny* 31. *Her Majesty Love*
32. She was impersonated by June Haver in a
biopic, *Look for the Silver Lining* 49, and by
Judy Garland in *Till the Clouds Roll By* 46.

Miller, Martin (1899–) (Rudolph Muller).
Czechoslovakian character actor active in
Britain from the late thirties.

Squadron Leader X 40. The Huggetts Abroad 51. Front Page Story 53. Libel 60. 55 Days at Peking 62. Children of the Damned 64. Up Jumped a Swagman 65, many others.

Miller, Marvin (1913–) (M. Mueller). American tough guy supporting actor who has represented menaces of various nations.
Johnny Angel 45. Intrigue 47. The High Window 47. Off Limits 53. The Shanghai Story 54, etc.

Miller, Max (1895–1963) (Harold Sargent). Ribald British music-hall comedian ('the Cheeky Chappie'). Starred in several vehicles during the thirties but his style had to be considerably toned down for the screen.
The Good Companions 32. Friday the Thirteenth 33. Princess Charming 34. *Educated Evans* 36. Hoots Mon 40. Asking for Trouble 43, etc.

Miller, Patsy Ruth (1905–). American leading lady of the silent screen, former juvenile player.
Camille 15. Judgment 18. The Hunchback of Notre Dame 23. Lorraine of the Lions 24. Why Girls Go Back Home 27. The Hottentot 28. Lonely Wives 31. Quebec 51, etc.

Miller, Robert Ellis (1927–). American director, from TV.
□ Any Wednesday 66. Sweet November 68. The Heart is a Lonely Hunter 68. The Buttercup Chain 70.

Miller, Seton I. (1902–1974). American silent actor (*Brown of Harvard* 26, etc.) who turned into one of Hollywood's most prolific screenwriters.
Dawn Patrol 30. The Criminal Code 32. *Scarface* 32. G-Men 35. *The Adventures of Robin Hood* 38. The Sea Hawk 40. *Here Comes Mr Jordan* (AA) 41. The Black Swan 42. The Ministry of Fear 43. Two Years Before the Mast (& p) 46. Istanbul 57, etc.

Millhauser, Bertram (1892–1958). American screenwriter mainly engaged on second features, some of them better than average.
The Garden Murder Case 36. Sherlock Holmes in Washington 42 (and others in this series including Pearl of Death 44). The Invisible Man's Revenge 44. Patrick the Great 45. Walk a Crooked Mile 48. Tokyo Joe 48, etc.

Millican, James (1910–1955). American general purpose actor, often in low-budget westerns.

The Remarkable Andrew 42. Bring on the Girls 44. Hazard 47. Rogues' Regiment 48. Carson City 52. The Man from Laramie 55, etc.

Millichip, Roy (1930–). British independent producer.
The Uncle 65. I Was Happy Here 66. A Nice Girl Like Me 69, etc.

Milligan, Spike (1918–). Irish comedian and arch-goon of stage, TV and radio.
The Case of the Mukkinese Battlehorn 56. Watch Your Stern 60. Suspect 60. Invasion Quartet 61. Postman's Knock 62. The Magic Christian 70. Rentadick 72, Alice's Adventures in Wonderland 72. Adolf Hitler, My Part in His Downfall (& oa) 72. The Three Musketeers 74. The Great McGonagall 74. The Last Remake of Beau Geste 77, etc.

Le Million (France 1930). Brilliant early sound comedy with music, ranging from slapstick to satire in a zany tale about a search for a lost lottery ticket. Written and directed by René Clair: probably his best film and certainly his most engaging. With René Lefebre, Annabella; photography by Georges Perinal; music by Georges Van Parys, Armand Bernard, Phillipe Pares.

Mills, Hayley (1946–). Tomboy British juvenile actress, daughter of John Mills.
Tiger Bay 59. *Pollyanna* (US) (special AA) 60. *The Parent Trap* (US) 61. Whistle Down the Wind 61. Summer Magic (US) 62. In Search of the Castaways 63. The Chalk Garden 64. The Moonspinners 65. The Truth about Spring 65. Sky West and Crooked 66. The Trouble with Angels 66. The Family Way 66. Pretty Polly 67. Twisted Nerve 68. Take a Girl Like You 70. Forbush and the Penguins 71. Endless Night 72. Deadly Strangers 75. What Changed Charley Farthing? 75. The Kingfisher Caper 75, etc.

Mills, Hugh (c. 1913–). British screen writer.
Blanche Fury 47. Blackmailed (co-w) 50. Knave of Hearts 52. The House by the Lake 54. Prudence and the Pill 68, etc.

Mills, John (1908–). Popular British leading actor with musical comedy experience; overcame short stature to become a useful stiff upper lip type in the forties, and later a character actor of some versatility.
□ The Midshipmaid 32. Britannia of Billingsgate 33. The Ghost Camera 33. River Wolves 34. A Political Party 34. *Those Were the Days* 34. The Lash 34. Blind Justice 34. Doctor's Orders 34. Royal Cavalcade 35. Forever England 35.

Charing Cross Road 35. Car of Dreams 35. First Offence 36. Tudor Rose 36. OHMS 37. The Green Cockatoo 37. Goodbye Mr Chips 39. Old Bill and Son 40. *Cottage to Let* 41. The Black Sheep of Whitehall 41. The Big Blockade 42. The Young Mr Pitt 42. *In Which We Serve* 42. We Dive at Dawn 43. This Happy Breed 44. *Waterloo Road* 44. *The Way to the Stars* 45. *Great Expectations* 46. So Well Remembered 47. *The October Man* 47. *Scott of the Antarctic* 48. *The History of Mr Polly* (& p) 49. The Rocking Horse Winner 50. Morning Departure 50. Mr Denning Drives North 51. The Gentle Gunman 52. The Long Memory 52. *Hobson's Choice* 53. The Colditz Story 54. The End of the Affair 54. Above Us the Waves 55. Escapade 55. It's Great to be Young 56. The Baby and the Battleship 56. War and Peace 56. Around the World in 80 Days 56. *Town On Trial* 57. Vicious Circle 57. Dunkirk 58. I Was Monty's Double 58. Ice Cold in Alex 58. *Tiger Bay* 59. Summer of the Seventeenth Doll 60. *Tunes of Glory* 60. *The Swiss Family Robinson* (US) 61. Flame in the Streets 61. The Singer Not the Song 61. The Valiant 62. Tiara Tahiti 62. The Chalk Garden 63. The Truth About Spring 64. Operation Crossbow 65. *Sky West and Crooked* (d only) 65. King Rat (US) 66. *The Wrong Box* 66. The Family Way 66. Cowboy in Africa (US) 67. Chuka (US) 67. Oh What a Lovely War 69. Run Wild Run Free 69. Emma Hamilton (Ger.) 69. A Black Veil for Lisa 69. Return of the Boomerang 70. *Ryan's Daughter* (AA) 71. Dulcima 71. Young Winston 72. Lady Caroline Lamb 72. Tom Brown's Schooldays 73. Oklahoma Crude 73. The Human Factor 76. Trial by Combat 76. The Water Babies 77.

TV series (US): Dundee and the Culhane 67.

Mills, Juliet (1941–). British leading lady, daughter of John Mills and sister of Hayley.
No My Darling Daughter 61. Twice Round the Daffodils 62. Nurse on Wheels 63. Carry on Jack 64. The Rare Breed (US) 66. Oh What a Lovely War 69. Avanti 72, etc.

TV series: *Nanny and the Professor* 70–71.

Milner, Martin (1927–). American general purpose actor.
Life with Father (debut) 47. Our Very Own 50. I Want You 52. Pete Kelly's Blues 55. The Sweet Smell of Success 57. Marjorie Morningstar 58. Thirteen Ghosts 60. Sullivan's County 67. Valley of the Dolls 67, etc.

TV series: The Trouble With Father 53–55. The Life of Riley 56–57. Route 66 63–64. Adam 12 68– .

Milner, Victor (1893–). Distinguished

American cinematographer, with Paramount for many years.
Hiawatha 14. The Velvet Hand 18. Haunting Shadows 20. The Cave Girl 22. Thy Name is Woman 24. Lady of the Harem 26. Rolled Stockings 27. Wolf of Wall Street 29. *The Love Parade* 29. Monte Carlo 30. Daughter of the Dragon 31. *Trouble in Paradise* 32. Song of Songs 33. Design for Living 33. *Cleopatra* (AA) 34. The Crusades 35. *The General Died at Dawn* 36. The Plainsman 36. Artists and Models 37. The Buccaneer 39. Union Pacific 39. The Great Victor Herbert 39. Northwest Mounted Police 40. Christmas in July 40. The Lady Eve 41. The Monster and the Girl 41. The Palm Beach Story 42. Hostages 43. The Story of Dr Wassell 44. The Mummy's Curse 44. The Strange Love of Martha Ivers 46. The Other Love 47. Unfaithfully Yours 48. The Furies 50. September Affair 50. *Carrie* 51. Jeopardy 53, many others.

Milton, Billy (1905–). British light actor of the thirties, now in small parts. Also singer, pianist and composer.
Young Woodley 30. Three Men in a Boat 33. Someone at the Door 36. Aren't Men Beasts? 37. Yes Madam 39, etc.

Milton, Ernest (1890–). American-born Shakespearean actor with long theatrical history on both sides of the Atlantic. Few film appearances, in small parts.
A Wisp in the Woods 17. The Scarlet Pimpernel 34. Fiddlers Three 44.

Mimieux, Yvette (1939–). American leading lady signed up for films almost straight from college.
The Time Machine (debut) 60. Where the Boys Are 61. The Four Horsemen of the Apocalypse 62. *The Light in the Piazza* 62. The Wonderful World of the Brothers Grimm 63. Diamondhead 63. Joy in the Morning 65. Monkeys Go Home 66. The Caper of the Golden Bulls 67. Dark of the Sun 67. Three in an Attic 68. Black Noon (TV) 71. Skyjacked 72. The Neptune Factor 73. Hit Lady (& w) (TV) 74. Jackson County Jail 76, etc.

TV series: The Most Deadly Game 70.

Minciotti, Esther (1883–1962). Italian-American character actress, wife of Silvio Minciotti.
□ House of Strangers 49. Shockproof 49. The Undercover Man 50. Strictly Dishonorable 51. *Marty* 55. Full of Life 56. The Wrong Man 57.

Minciotti, Silvio (1883–1961). Italian-

American character actor.
House of Strangers 49. Deported 49. The Great
Caruso 51. Clash by Night 52. Kiss Me Deadly
54. Marty 55, etc.

Mine Own Executioner (GB 1947). Hailed
as the first 'adult' film to come out of post-war
Britain, this interesting melodrama from Nigel
Balchin's novel had Burgess Meredith as a lay
psychiatrist unsure how to handle a homicidal
patient. Directed by Anthony Kimmins.

Mineo, Sal (1939–1976). Diminutive
American actor, on Broadway as a child before
going to Hollywood.
Six Bridges to Cross (debut) 55. Rebel without a
Cause 55. Giant 56. Somebody Up There Likes
Me 57. Tonka 58. The Gene Krupa Story 60.
Exodus 60. Escape from Zahrain 62. Cheyenne
Autumn 64. The Greatest Story Ever Told 65.
Who Killed Teddy Bear? 66. Krakatoa 68.
Escape from the Planet of the Apes 71, etc.

Miner, Allen H. (–). American director.
Ghost Town 55. The Ride Back 57. Black Patch
(& p) 57. Chubasco 67, etc.

miniaturization. Making people small is a
theme obviously likely to appeal to the cinema's
trick photographers. Characters were reduced
by 'scientific' or magic means in *The Devil Doll,
Dr Cyclops, The Incredible Shrinking Man*, and
Fantastic Voyage. Land of the Giants showed
the other side of the coin. Laurel and Hardy were
miniaturized into their own children in *Brats*;
other small humans were in *Darby O'Gill and
the Little People, The Adventures of Mark
Twain* and *The Bride of Frankenstein*.

Minnelli, Liza (1946–). American singer,
daughter of Judy Garland; her gamine looks and
vibrant voice made her a fashionable figure of the
early seventies.
□ Charlie Bubbles 67. The Sterile Cuckoo 69.
Tell Me that You Love Me Junie Moon 70.
Cabaret (AA) 72. Lucky Lady 76. A Matter of
Time 76. New York New York 77.

Minnelli, Vincente (1910–). American
director who earned a reputation as a stylist with
MGM musicals but whose other output has been
very variable. Stage experience as art director
and producer.
Autobiography 1974: *I Remember It Well*.
□ *Cabin in the Sky* 43. I Dood It 43. Ziegfeld
Follies 44. Meet Me in St Louis 44. *The Clock*
44. Yolanda and the Thief 45. Undercurrent 46.
The Pirate 47. Madame Bovary 49. *Father of the
Bride* 50. Father's Little Dividend 51. *An*

American in Paris 51. The Bad and the Beautiful
52. The Story of Three Loves (part) 52. *The
Band Wagon* 53. The Long, Long Trailer 54.
Brigadoon 54. Kismet 55. The Cobweb 55. Lust
for Life 56. Tea and Sympathy 56. Designing
Woman 57. *Gigi* (AA) 58. The Reluctant
Debutante 58. Some Came Running 58. Home
from the Hill 59. Bells Are Ringing 60. The Four
Horsemen of the Apocalypse 62. Two Weeks in
Another Town 62. The Courtship of Eddie's
Father 63. Goodbye Charlie 65. The Sandpiper
65. On A Clear Day You Can See Forever 70. A
Matter of Time 76.

Minevitch, Borrah (1904–1955). Russian-
American harmonica player who with his
Rascals enlivened a few thirties musicals.
One in a Million 36. Love Under Fire 37.
Rascals 38. Always in My Heart 42, etc.

Minney, R. J. (1895–). British producer and
screenwriter, former journalist, in films since
1934.
AS WRITER: Clive of India 35. Dear Octopus
42. Carve Her Name with Pride 58, many
others.
AS PRODUCER: Madonna of the Seven
Moons 44. The Wicked Lady 45. The Final Test
53. Carve Her Name with Pride 58, etc.

Minter, George (1911–1966). British
producer-distributor, in films from 1938. Made
films for his company, Renown.
The Glass Mountain 48. Tom Brown's
Schooldays 50. Pickwick Papers 52. The Rough
and the Smooth 58, scores of others.

Minter, Mary Miles (1902–) (Juliet Reilly).
American silent screen heroine.
The Nurse 12. Barbara Frietchie 15.
Environment 16. Lovely Mary 16. Melissa of the
Hills 17. The Ghost of Rosy Taylor 17. Anne of
Green Gables 19. Nurse Marjorie 20. Moonlight
and Honeysuckle 21. South of Suva 22. The
Trail of the Lonesome Pine 23. The Drums of
Fate 23, many others.

Miracle in Milan (Italy 1951). Beguiling
fantasy about a colony of shantytown poor led
by a young idealist whose fervour gives him the
power to work miracles and finally flies them all
on broomsticks to another, better place.
Directed by Vittorio de Sica with a strong
element of René Clair; written by Cesare
Zavattini and others; with special effects by Ned
Mann. By its indirect methods the film managed
to make as much protest about post-war
conditions as its predecessor *Bicycle Thieves*.

The Miracle of Morgan's Creek (US 1943). An outrageous satirical farce, written and directed in whirlwind style by Preston Sturges, about a small-town girl who gets drunk at an army party, marries a soldier whose name she thinks is Ratskywatsky, can't find him, and has terrible trouble getting someone else to marry her without admitting she's pregnant; finally becomes a heroine by presenting the nation with sextuplets. Funny? Oddly enough, very, and fast enough to stop tastelessness from creeping in. Apart from the usual Sturges repertory company, the film is well served by Betty Hutton and Eddie Bracken, by Diana Lynn as the heroine's sharp young sister, and especially William Demarest as her father, the outraged Officer Kockenlocker. Prudes could console themselves with the thought that the film made quite a comment on the morals of the nation in time of war.

Miracle on 34th Street (US 1947). A charming, endearing piece of whimsy in Hollywood's best style, with Edmund Gwenn (AA) as a benevolent old fellow who may or may not be Santa Claus. Never nauseating in its abundance of goodwill towards men, the film moves smoothly to a hilarious courtroom climax in the Capra manner. Written and directed by George Seaton (AA) against pleasantly observed New York backgrounds.

Miranda (GB 1948). A mild British comedy about a mermaid (played by Glynis Johns) which had sufficient moments of hilarity to call for a sequel (*Mad about Men*) and a Hollywood imitation (*Mr Peabody and the Mermaid*).

Miranda, Carmen (1913–1955) (Maria de Carmo Miranda de Cunha). Portuguese singer, the 'Brazilian Bombshell'; always fantastically over-dressed and harshly made-up, yet emitting a force of personality which was hard to resist.
□ Down Argentine Way (debut) 40. That Night in Rio 41. Weekend in Havana 41. Springtime in the Rockies 42. *The Gang's All Here* 43. Four Jills in a Jeep 44. Greenwich Village 44. Something for the Boys 44. Doll Face 46. If I'm Lucky 46. Copacabana 47. A Date with Judy 48. Nancy Goes to Rio 50. Scared Stiff 53.

Miranda, Isa (1909–) (Ines Isabella Sanpietro). Italian star actress. Occasional films.
Adventure in Diamonds (US) 38. Hotel Imperial (US) 40. La Ronde (Fr.) 50. Summertime (GB) 55. The Yellow Rolls Royce (GB) 64.

The Mirisch Brothers: *Harold* (1907–1968), *Marvin* (1918–), *Walter* (1921–). American producers, founders in 1957 of the Mirisch company, one of the most successful independent production groups since the decline of the big studios. Formerly the two elder brothers had been exhibitors, the youngest a producer of cheap second features: the 'Bomba' series, etc.
Man of the West 58. The Magnificent Seven 60. West Side Story 61. Two for the See-Saw 62. The Great Escape 63. Toys in the Attic 63. The Satan Bug 65. The Russians Are Coming 66. What Did You Do in the War, Daddy? 66. Hawaii 66. The Fortune Cookie 66. In the Heat of the Night 68. The Organization 70. Midway 76, etc.

Miroslava (1926–1955) (Miroslava Stern). Czech-born actress who became popular in Mexico.
The Brave Bulls 51. Stranger on Horseback 55.

mirrors have a clear psychological fascination, and cameramen have frequently derived dramatic compositions from the use of them. Innumerable characters have talked to their reflections, and *The Man in the Mirror* changed places with his. *Dracula* and his kind cast no reflection; a switch on this was provided in *The Gorgon*, where looking at the monster turned one to stone, but looking at her through a mirror was OK. In *The Lady In the Lake* Robert Montgomery played the lead from the position of the camera lens, so the only time we saw him was when he looked in a mirror. Eric Portman in *Corridor of Mirrors* was surrounded by them: the hero of *The Student of Prague* shot his reflection in one. Then there was the magic mirror in *Snow White and the Seven Dwarfs*, which told the queen all she wanted to hear; and the more evil magic mirror in *Dead of Night*, which had belonged to a murderer and caused Ralph Michael when he looked in it to strangle his wife. Two-way mirrors are now familiar, especially since *From Russia With Love*; but they were used as long ago as 1946 in *The House on 92nd Street*. In *Orphée* a full-length mirror proved liquid to the touch and was the doorway to the other world. *The Lady from Shanghai* had a splendidly confusing finale in a mirror maze which was gradually shot to pieces; *Up Tight* made dramatic use of a distorting mirror arcade. The most-used mirror joke is that in which the glass is broken and a 'double' tries to take the place of the reflection: Max Linder performed it in 1919 in *Seven Years Bad Luck*, and it was superbly reprised by the Marx Brothers in *Duck Soup* 44, and by Abbott and Costello in *The Naughty Nineties* 45.

Les Miserables: see under *L*.

The Misfits (US 1961). A sad film, over-loaded with talent, notable chiefly for the last appearance of both Clark Gable and Marilyn Monroe, whose then husband Arthur Miller wrote the heavy-going script about cowboys on a savage hunt for wild mustangs. John Huston's direction was lethargic. This kind of pseudo-highbrow non-money-maker would in the old days have been vetoed at script stage by the studio's front office; failures like this are the price of independence.

Misraki, Paul (1908–). French composer. Retour à l'Aube 38. Battement de Coeur 39. Manon 48. Confidential Report 55. Les Cousins 59. Alphaville 65. A Murder Is . . . 72, etc.

missionaries have not been popular cinema heroes: the most lauded real-life ones were David Livingstone in *Stanley and Livingstone* and Gladys Aylward in *The Inn of the Sixth Happiness*. Over-zealous ones appeared in *Zulu, Hawaii, Seven Women* and the various versions of *Rain*.

Miss Julie. Strindberg's play about a nobleman's daughter who commits suicide because she loves a valet was filmed in 1912 (Sweden), 1921 (Germany) and 1947 (Argentina). The best-known version was written and directed by Alf Sjoberg in Sweden (1951) with Anita Bjork and Ulf Palme; in 1972 came a draggy British extension directed by Robin Phillips, with Helen Mirren and Donal McCann.

Mission to Moscow (US 1942). A remarkable semi-documentary made by Warners as a modern addendum to their biographical series. Based on US Ambassador Joseph Davies' account of his dealings with the Russians between 1936 and 1941, it was notable for its impersonations of living politicians: Churchill, Stalin, Roosevelt, etc. Walter Huston was ideally cast as Davies, and Michael Curtiz directed with his usual expertise. During the anti-communist era at the end of the forties, Jack Warner had to apologize for making it.

Mr Blandings Builds His Dream House (US 1948). A highly civilized and likeable American domestic comedy from the delightful book by Eric Hodgins; it shows Hollywood in the late forties getting its humour a little nearer to life and away from the studio. H. C. Potter directed with quiet aplomb, and no one would wish for a better husband, wife and friend of the family than Cary Grant, Myrna Loy and Melvyn Douglas as they doggedly build a house in Connecticut.

Mr Deeds Goes to Town (US 1936). The first of the big social comedies of the thirties, directed by Frank Capra (AA), demonstrating the victory of small-town innocence and good intentions over big city sophistication. Gary Cooper was perfectly cast as the naïve hero who refuses to be swindled out of a huge legacy even though he may be a little 'pixillated'. Robert Riskin wrote the script, which today seems slow-moving. In 1969 a TV series starring Monte Markham was based on the original script.

Mr Magoo. Myopic, bumbling cartoon character created by UPA in the early fifties and voiced by Jim Backus. He quickly became a bore, but some of the early shorts were outstandingly funny: *Barefaced Flatfoot, Fuddy Duddy Buddy, Spellbound Hound*, etc.

Mr Moto. A mild-mannered Japanese detective and master of disguise created by novelist John P. Marquand and played in nearly a dozen films by Peter Lorre: from *Think Fast Mr Moto* in 1937 to *Mr Moto Takes a Vacation* in 1939. In 1965 Henry Silva played the role in an unsuccessful second feature.

Mr Smith Goes to Washington (US 1939). Another of Frank Capra's thirties social comedies, a kind of 'Mr Deeds in Politics' with James Stewart as the idealistic young senator from Wisconsin who uproots the evil of Claude Rains. This is a beautifully made picture which judges all its effects exactly and remains consistently entertaining for over two hours. It was the last of its type: World War II made America's country cousins more sophisticated than Capra could have imagined. Among a superb cast were Jean Arthur, Guy Kibbee, Thomas Mitchell, H. B. Warner, Edward Arnold, Harry Carey, Eugene Pallette and William Demarest. Sidney Buchman wrote the script.

Mr Wong (James Lee Wong, that is) was a Chinese detective thought up in 1938 by Monogram from stories by Hugh Riley, as a counter to Mr Moto who was doing so well for Fox. He was played five times in 1938–39 by the physically unsuitable Boris Karloff, in rather feeble second feature productions: in 1940 Keye Luke took over for *Phantom of Chinatown*.

Mrs Miniver (US 1942). Hollywood's emotional tribute to England's women in wartime was never a good film, but its sentimentality and its never-never picture of the English middle-class scene made it an enormous box office hit even though most people privately jibed at it afterwards and it had absolutely no reissue value. It now seems a quaint curiosity, with Greer Garson tending the roses while Walter Pidgeon dashes off to rescue some chaps from Dunkirk. William Wyler directed fluently in the circumstances; among the many contributors to the script were Arthur Wimperis and James Hilton, who should have known better. However, the film won Academy Awards for Garson, Wyler, the scriptwriters, and the photographer Joe Ruttenberg; it was also named best film. In 1950 a sequel was made showing Mrs Miniver dying of cancer, but not surprisingly *The Miniver Story* flopped.

Mrs Wiggs of the Cabbage Patch. The sentimental shanty-town novel by Olive Higgins Prouty was filmed three times: in 1919 with Mary Carr, in 1934 with Pauline Lord, and in 1943 with Fay Bainter.

Mitchell, Cameron (1918–) (Cameron Mizell). American actor, ex-radio commentator and Broadway player.
They Were Expendable 45. Command Decision 48. *Death of a Salesman* 52. How to Marry a Millionaire 53. Love Me or Leave Me 55. Monkey On My Back 57. The Last of the Vikings 61. Unstoppable Man 61. Blood and Black Lace 65. Minnesota Clay (It.) 66. Hombre 67. Monster of the Wax Museum 67. Ride the Whirlwind 68. Buck and the Preacher. 71. The Midnight Man 74, etc.
TV series: High Chaparral 67–68.

Mitchell, Grant (1874–1957). American character actor, often seen as a worried father, lawyer or small-town politician.
Man to Man 31. Dinner at Eight 33. The Life of Emile Zola 37. New Moon 40. Tobacco Road 41. The Man Who Came to Dinner 41. Orchestra Wives 42. Father is a Prince 43. Arsenic and Old Lace 44. Blondie's Anniversary 48, many others.

Mitchell, Guy (1925–) (Al Cernick). Boyish, stocky American singer with a brief career in films.
□ Those Redheads from Seattle 53. Red Garters 54.
TV series: Whispering Smith 62.

Mitchell, James (1920–). American dancer and character actor.
Cobra Woman 44. Colorado Territory 49. Stars in My Crown 50. Deep in My Heart 54. Oklahoma 55, etc.

Mitchell, Julien (1884–1954). British stage

character actor who made film debut as a crazed train driver in *The Last Journey* 36.
It's In the Air 37. The Drum 38. The Sea Hawk (US) 40. Hotel Reserve 44. Bedelia 46. Bonnie Prince Charlie 48. The Galloping Major 51. Hobson's Choice 54, etc.

Mitchell, Leslie (1905–). British commentator and broadcaster; the voice of British Movietone News from 1938; co-author of a 1946 book *The March of the Movies*.

Mitchell, Margaret (1900–1949). American author of the novel on which Hollywood's most famous film, *Gone with the Wind*, was based.

Mitchell, Millard (1900–1953). Nasal-voiced, rangy American character actor, in films from 1940.
Mr and Mrs Smith 40. Grand Central Murder 42. *A Double Life* 47. *A Foreign Affair* 48. Twelve O'Clock High 49. The Gunfighter 50. My Six Convicts 52. *Singin' in the Rain* 52. The Naked Spur 52. Here Come the Girls 53, etc.

Mitchell, Oswald (c. 1890–1949). British director.
Old Mother Riley 37. Danny Boy 41. The Dummy Talks 43. Loyal Heart 46. Black Memory 47. The Greed of William Hart 47. The Man From Yesterday 49, etc.

Mitchell, Thomas (1892–1962). Irish-American character actor of great versatility; could be tragic or comic, evil or humane. Former reporter, Broadway star and playwright; in Hollywood from the mid-thirties.
Craig's Wife (debut) 36. Theodora Goes Wild 36. *Lost Horizon* 37. Make Way for Tomorrow 37. The Hurricane 38. Mr Smith Goes to Washington 39. *Stagecoach* (AA) 39. Gone with the Wind 39. Only Angels Have Wings 39. The Hunchback of Notre Dame 40. Three Cheers for the Irish 40. Our Town 40. The Long Voyage Home 40. Angels over Broadway 40. Out of the Fog 41. Song of the Islands 42. This Above All 42. Moontide 42. The Black Swan 42. The Immortal Sergeant 43. The Outlaw 43. Bataan 43. *The Sullivans* 44. Wilson 44. Buffalo Bill 44. Dark Waters 44. The Keys of the Kingdom 44. The Dark Mirror 45. It's a Wonderful Life 45. Adventure 46. High Barbaree 47. Silver River 47. *Alias Nick Beal* 49. The Big Wheel 50. High Noon 52. The Secret of the Incas 54. Destry 55. While the City Sleeps 56. Too Young for Love (GB) 59. A Pocketful of Miracles 61, others.
TV series: O. Henry Playhouse 56. Glencannon 58.

Mitchell, Warren (1926–). British comedy character actor, mainly on TV, especially in series *Till Death Us Do Part*.
Tommy the Toreador 60. Postman's Knock 62. Where Has Poor Mickey Gone? 63. The Intelligence Men 65. Arrivederci Baby 66. *Till Death Us Do Part* 68. The Assassination Bureau 68. The Best House in London 69. All the Way Up 70. Innocent Bystanders 72. The Alf Garnett Saga 72. Stand Up Virgin Soldiers 77, many others.

Mitchell, Yvonne (1925–). British actress and playwright, on stage from 1940.
Autobiography 1957: *Actress*.
The Queen of Spades (film debut) 48. Turn the Key Softly 53. *The Divided Heart* 54. Yield to the Night 56. *Woman in a Dressing Gown* 57. The Passionate Summer 58. Tiger Bay 59. Sapphire 59. The Trials of Oscar Wilde 61. The Main Attraction 63. Genghis Khan 65. The Corpse 70. The Great Waltz 72. The Incredible Sarah 76, etc.

Mitchum, James (1938–). American actor, son of Robert Mitchum.
Thunder Road (debut) 58. The Young Guns of Texas 62. The Victors 63. The Tramplers 66. Ambush Bay 67, etc.

Mitchum, Robert (1917–). Sleepy-eyed American leading man who has sometimes hidden his considerable talent behind a pretence of carelessness.
Biography 1975: *It Sure Beats Working* by Mike Tomkies.
□ Hoppy Serves a Writ 43. The Leather Burners 43. Border Patrol 43. Follow the Band 43. Colt Comrades 43. The Human Comedy 43. We've Never Been Licked 43. Beyond the Last Frontier 43. Bar 20 43. Doughboys in Ireland 43. Corvette K-225 43. Aerial Gunner 43. The Lone Star Trail 43. False Colors 43. The Dancing Masters 43. Riders of the Deadline 43. Cry Havoc 43. Gung Ho 43. Johnny Doesn't Live Here Any More 44. When Strangers Marry 44. The Girl Rush 44. Thirty Seconds Over Tokyo 44. Nevada 44. West of the Pecos 45. *The Story of G.I. Joe* 45. Till the End of Time 46. Undercurrent 46. The Locket 46. *Pursued* 47. *Crossfire* 47. Desire Me 47. *Out of the Past* 47. Rachel and the Stranger 48. Blood on the Moon 48. The Red Pony 49. *The Big Steal* 49. Holiday Affair 49. Where Danger Lives 50. My Forbidden Past 51. His Kind of Woman 51. The Racket 51. Macao 52. One Minute to Zero 52. The Lusty Men 52. Angel Face 53. White Witch Doctor 53. Second Chance 53. She Couldn't Say No 54. River of No Return 54. Track of the Cat

54. Not as a Stranger 55. *Night of the Hunter* 55. The Man with the Gun 55. Foreign Intrigue 56. Bandido 56. Heaven Knows Mr Alison 57. Fire Down Below 57. The Enemy Below 57. Thunder Road 58. The Hunters 58. The Angry Hills 59. The Wonderful Country 59. Home from the Hill 60. A Terrible Beauty 60. The Grass is Greener 60. *The Sundowners* 60. The Last Time I Saw Archie 61. Cape Fear 62. The Longest Day 62. Two for the Seesaw 62. The List of Adrian Messenger 63. Rampage 63. Man in the Middle 64. What a Way to Go 64. Mr Moses 65. The Way West 67. El Dorado 67. Anzio 68. Villa Rides 68. Five Card Stud 68. Secret Ceremony 68. Young Billy Young 69. The Good Guys and the Bad Guys 69. *Ryan's Daughter* 71. Going Home 71. The Wrath of God 72. The Friends of Eddie Coyle 73. The Yakuza 75. *Farewell My Lovely* 75. Midway 76. The Last Tycoon 76.

Mitry, Jean (1907–). French director, former critic.
Pacific 231 49. Images Pour Debussy 51. Symphonie Mecanique 55, etc.

Mix, Tom (1880–1940). A US Marshal who turned actor and starred in over four hundred low-budget westerns.
Biographies: 1972, *The Life and Legend of Tom Mix* by Paul E. Mix. 1957, *The Fabulous Tom Mix* by Olive Stokes.
The Ranch Life in the Great Southwest 10. Child of the Prairie 13. Cupid's Round-Up 18. Tom Mix in Arabia 22. North of Hudson Bay 24. The Last Trail 27. Destry Rides Again 27. Painted Post 28. My Pal the King 32. The Terror Trail 33. The Fourth Horseman 33, etc.

Mizoguchi, Kenji (1898–1956). Japanese director, former actor. Directed from 1923, though few of his films were seen in the West.
A Paper Doll's Whisper of Spring 25. The Gorge Between Love and Hate 32. The Story of the Last Chrysanthemums 39. Woman of Osaka 40. The Forty-Nine Ronin 42. The Life of O'Haru 52. *Ugetsu Monogatari* 52. Street of Shame 56, many others.

Mobley, Mary Ann (1939–). American leading lady, former 'Miss America'.
Girl Happy 65. Three on a Couch 66. For Singles Only 68, etc.

Moby Dick. Herman Melville's allegorical novel about the pursuit by an obsessed sea captain of a white whale, has been seen on the screen in at least three versions, all American. 1. *The Sea Beast* 26, directed by Millard Webb, with John Barrymore, Dolores Costello and

George O'Hara. 2. *Moby Dick* 30, directed by
Lloyd Bacon, with John Barrymore, Joan
Bennett and Lloyd Hughes. 3. *Moby Dick* 56,
directed by John Huston, with Gregory Peck,
Richard Basehart and no feminine lead.

Mockridge, Cyril (1896–). British-born
composer, in American from 1921, films from
1932.
The Sullivans 44. Mr Darling Clementine 46.
How to Marry a Millionaire 53. Many Rivers to
Cross 55. Flaming Star 60, many others.

Mocky, Jean-Pierre (1929–) (Jean
Mokiejeswki). French director.
Un Couple 60. Snobs 62. Les Vierges 63. La
Bourse et la Vie 65. Les Compagnons de la
Marguerite 67, etc.

Modern Times (US 1936). The film in which
Chaplin's voice was first heard—though only in
a gibberish song. Basically this is a dated—
almost period—sociological comedy about how
to be happy though poor in the machine age.
Best to forget the propaganda and see it as a
series of gags, impeccably timed and edited. As
usual, he wrote (words and music), directed,
produced and starred; Paulette Goddard played
the waif.

Modot, Gaston (1887–1970). French
character actor.
Fievre 21. L'Age d'Or 30. Sous Les Toits de
Paris 30. La Grande Illusion 37. Pepe le Moko
37. La Regle du Jeu 39. Les Enfants du Paradis
44. French Can Can 55. Le Testament du
Docteur Cordelier 59, many others.

Moffatt, Graham (1919–1965). British actor,
fondly remembered as the impertinent fat boy of
the Will Hay comedies: *Oh Mr Porter* 38. *Ask a
Policeman* 39. Where's That Fire 40, etc. Other
films include A Cup of Kindness (debut) 34. Dr
Syn 38. I Thank You 41. I Know Where I'm
Going 45, many others. Retired to keep a pub,
but made very occasional appearances: The
Second Mate 50. Inn for Trouble 59. Eighty
Thousand Suspects 63.

Moffett, Sharyn (1936–). American child
actress of the forties.
My Pal Wolf 44. The Body Snatcher 45. Child of
Divorce 47. The Judge Steps Out 47. Mr
Blandings Builds His Dream House 48. Girls
Never Tell 51, etc.

Moguy, Leonide (1899–1976) (L.
Maguilevsky). Russian newsreel producer, later
in France and US as director.

Prison Without Bars 38. The Night Is Ending
43. Action in Arabia 44. Whistle Stop 46.
Tomorrow Is Too Late 50. Les Enfants de
l'Amour 54, etc.

Mohner, Carl (1921–). Austrian actor in
films from 1949.
Rififi 55. He Who Must Die 56. The Key 58.
Camp on Blood Island 58. The Kitchen 61. Hell
is Empty 67. Callan 74, etc.

Mohr, Gerald (1914–1968). Suave American
actor, in films from 1941; played the 'Lone
Wolf', a gentleman crook, in a mid-forties series.
Also on TV.
The Monster and the Girl 41. Ten Tall Men 51.
Detective Story 53. The Eddie Cantor Story 53.
Angry Red Planet 59. Funny Girl 68, many
others.

Mohr, Hal (1894–1974). American
cinematographer, in Hollywood from 1915.
The Last Night of the Barbary Coast 13. Money
14. The Deceiver 21. Bag and Baggage 23. The
Monster 24. The High Hand 26. The Jazz Singer
27. The Last Warning 28. Broadway 29. Big Boy
30. Woman of Experience 31. A Woman
Commands 32. State Fair 33. David Harum 34.
A Midsummer Night's Dream (AA) 35. *Captain
Blood* 35. *Green Pastures* 36. The Walking
Dead 36. I Met My Love Again 38. Rio 39.
Destry Rides Again 39. When the Daltons Rode
40. International Lady 41. Twin Beds 42.
Phantom of the Opera 43. Ladies Courageous
44. Salome Where She Danced 45. Because of
Him 46. The Lost Moment 47. Another Part of
the Forest 48. Johnny Holiday 49. Woman on
the Run 50. The Big Night 51. The Fourposter
52. *The Wild One* 54. The Boss 56. Baby Face
Nelson 57. The Gun Runners 58. The Last
Voyage 60. The Man from the Diner's Club 63.
Bamboo Saucer 68, many others.

Molander, Gustaf (1888–*). Veteran
Swedish director, former actor and writer
(including *Sir Arne's Treasure* 19). Directing
since 1922, but few of his films have been seen
abroad.
Sin 28. Intermezzo 36. A Woman's Face 38.
Woman Without a Face 47. Sir Arne's Treasure
(remake) 55, many others.

Molinaro, Edouard (1928–). French
director.
Evidence in Concrete (Le Dos au Mur) 57. Girls
for the Summer 60. A Ravishing Idiot 63. The
Gentle Art of Seduction 64, etc.

Molnar, Ferenc (–). Hungarian

dramatist whose comedies were the basis of many Hollywood films including *The Shop Around the Corner* and *One Two Three*.

Monash, Paul (c. 1916–). American producer, former TV writer.
Peyton Place (TV series) 64–69. Butch Cassidy and the Sundance Kid 69. Slaughterhouse Five 72. The Friends of Eddie Coyle (& w) 74. The Front Page 74. Carrie 76, etc.

Mondo Cane (Italy 1961). The first of many so-called documentaries consisting of a ramshackle collection of true incidents showing humanity at its most ignorant and depraved, mostly involving sex, sadism or paranoia. Director Jacopetti meanwhile found the business very profitable, and after watching his many imitators, produced in 1965 his *Mondo Cane 2*, showing that the field of degradation is far from exhausted.

Mondy, Pierre (1925–) (Pierre Cuq). French actor.
Rendezvous de Juillet 49. Sans Laisser d'Adresse 50. Les Louves 57. Austerlitz (as Napoleon) 60. Bebert et l'Omnibus 63, etc.

Monicelli, Mario (1915–). Italian director.
Cops and Robbers (co-d) 51. Persons Unknown 58. Boccaccio 70 (part) 61. The Organizer 63. Casanova 70 66. Girl With a Pistol 69, etc.

The Monkees sprang to fame in an American TV series of that title 66–67. They are a pop quartet deliberately recruited by Screen Gems to emulate the Beatles in crazy comedy with music; their ensuing popularity surprised not only themselves but their sponsors, and in 1969 they made a movie called *Head*. Individually they are: **Peter Tork** (1942–) (Peter Torkelson); **Mike Nesmith** (1943–); **Micky Dolenz** (1945–), who is the son of George Dolenz and previously starred in the TV series *Circus Boy* 56–57; **Davy Jones** (1944–), the only Britisher in the group.

Monkhouse, Bob (1928–). British comedian of TV, radio and occasional films.
Carry On Sergeant 58. Dentist in the Chair 59. Weekend with Lulu 61. She'll Have to Go 61. The Bliss of Mrs Blossom 68, etc.
TV series: Mad Movies.

monks in films have usually been caricatures of the Friar Tuck type; Tuck himself turned up, personified by Eugene Pallette or Alexander Gauge, in most of the versions of Robin Hood (qv). The funny side of monastery life was presented in *Crooks in Cloisters*, while milder humour came from Edward G. Robinson's conversion to the simple life in *Brother Orchid*. Serious crises of the monastic spirit have been treated in two American films, *The Garden of Allah* and *The First Legion*; but on the whole monks have appealed less than priests to filmmakers in search of an emotional subject. See also: *nuns; priests; churches*.

Monogram Pictures: see *Allied Artists*.

Monroe, Marilyn (1926–1962) (Norma Jean Baker or Mortenson). American leading lady, a former model whose classic rags-to-riches story was built on a super-sexy image which quickly tarnished, leaving her a frustrated, neurotic and tragic victim of the Hollywood which created her. The pity was that she had real talent as well as sex appeal. *Marilyn*, a compilation feature, was released after her death. Several biographies have been published. In 1976 Misty Rowe played her in *Goodbye Norma Jean*.
□ Dangerous Years 48. Ladies of the Chorus 48. Love Happy 50. A Ticket to Tomahawk 50. *The Asphalt Jungle* 50. All About Eve 50. The Fireball 50. Right Cross 50. Home Town Story 51. As Young as You Feel 51. Love Nest 51. Let's Make It Legal 51. We're Not Married 52. Clash by Night 52. Full House 52. Monkey Business 52. Don't Bother to Knock 52. *Niagara* (here the build-up really started) 52. *Gentlemen Prefer Blondes* 53. *How to Marry a Millionaire* 53. River of No Return 54. There's No Business Like Show Business 54. *The Seven-Year Itch* 55. Bus Stop 56. The Prince and the Showgirl (GB) 57. *Some Like It Hot* 59. Let's Make Love 60. The Misfits 61.

Monroe, Vaughan (1911–1973). American bandleader who unexpectedly appeared as hero of a few westerns.
Meet the People 44. Carnegie Hall 47. Singing Guns 50. The Toughest Man in Arizona 52, etc.

Monsieur Beaucaire. Booth Tarkington's light novel about a barber who impersonates the King of France was filmed as a straight romantic vehicle for Rudolph Valentino and Bebe Daniels in 1924, directed by Sidney Olcott. In 1946 Bob Hope had his way with it in a version directed by George Marshall.

Monsieur Hulot's Holiday (France 1952). Written and directed by Jacques Tati, this comedy in which he also stars as an accident-prone do-gooder on a seaside holiday will probably be remembered as his best. It has no story, just a collection of tiny incidents: many are hilarious, but some so untidily executed as to make one suspect that Tati would be even more marvellous under someone else's direction.

monster animals. The 1924 version of *The Lost World* set a persisting fashion for giant animals operated by technical ingenuity. The supreme achievement in the genre was of course *King Kong*, who carried on in *Son of Kong* and (more or less) in *Mighty Joe Young*. Dinosaurs and other creatures which once did exist were featured in such films as *Man and His Mate* (in which what we saw were actually magnified lizards), *The Land Unknown*, *Dinosaurus*, *The Lost Continent*, *Gorgo*, *The Beast from Twenty Thousand Fathoms*, *Godzilla*, *Rodan*, *One Million Years B.C.* and *When Dinosaurs Ruled the Earth*. Other films concentrated on normal species which had been giantized by radiation or some other accident of science: *The Black Scorpion*, *Them*, *The Deadly Mantis*, *The Giant Claw*, *Tarantula*, *Mysterious Island*, *Bug*, *Night of the Lepus*, *Squirm*, *Jaws*, *Food of the Gods*. More fanciful giant animals were created for *Jason and the Argonauts*, *Jack the Giant Killer* and *The Seventh Voyage of Sinbad*. The 1976 *King Kong* remake mainly featured a man in a gorilla suit.

montage. In the most general sense, the whole art of editing or assembling scenes into the finished film. Specifically, 'a montage' is understood as an impressionistic sequence of short dissolve-shots either bridging a time gap, setting a situation or showing the background to the main story. Classic montages which come to mind are in *The Battleship Potemkin*, *The Roaring Twenties* and *Citizen Kane*.

Montagu, Ivor (1904–). British producer, director and film theorist. In films from 1925; was associate of Hitchcock on several of his mid-thirties thrillers; produced *Behind the Spanish Lines* 38, *Spanish ABC* 38, etc.; co-authored many screenplays including *Scott of the Antarctic* 48. Latest publication *Film World* 64. Autobiography 1970: *The Youngest Son*.

Montague, Lee (1927–). British actor, mainly seen on stage and TV.
Savage Innocents 59. The Secret Partner 60. Billy Budd 61. The Horse without a Head 62. You Must Be Joking 65, etc.

Montalban, Ricardo (1920–). Mexican leading man in Hollywood.
Fiesta 47. The Kissing Bandit 49. Border Incident 49. *Battleground* 50. Right Cross 50. Across the Wide Missouri 51. My Man and I 52.

Sombrero 53. Latin Lovers 54. A Life in the Balance 55. *Sayonara* 57. Adventures of a Young Man 62. Love Is a Ball 63. The Money Trap 65. Madame X 66. Sol Madrid 68. Blue 68. *Sweet Charity* 68. Desperate Mission (TV) 72. Fantasy Island (TV) 77, others.

Montana, Bull (1887–1950) (Luigi Montagna). Italian-American strong man who played ape men and heavies in the twenties.
Brass Buttons 19. Go and Get It 20. Painted People 23. The Lost World 24. Son of the Sheik 26. Good Morning Judge 28. Show of Shows 29. Tiger Rose 29, etc.

Montand, Yves (1921–) (Ivo Levi). French actor-singer in films from the mid-forties; married to Simone Signoret.
Les Portes de la Nuit 46. Lost Property 50. *The Wages of Fear* 53. The Heroes Are Tired 55. The Witches of Salem 56. *Let's Make Love* (US) 60. Sanctuary (US) 61. My Geisha (US) 62. The Sleeping Car Murders 65. The War Is Over 66. Is Paris Burning? 66. Grand Prix 67. Vivre Pour Vivre 67. 'Z' 68. On a Clear Day You Can See Forever 69. L'Aveu 70. The Red Circle 70. The Son 72, etc.

Montes, Lola (1818–1861) (Eliza Gilbert). Irish dancer who became world-famous as the mistress of King Ludwig I of Bavaria. Max Ophuls made a film about her in 1955, with Martine Carol, and Yvonne de Carlo played her in *Black Bart* 48. There was also a Spanish biopic in 1944 with Conchita Montenegro.

Montez, Maria (1919–1951) (Maria de Santo Silas). Exotic Hollywood leading lady mainly seen in hokum adventures.
The Invisible Woman (debut) 41. South of Tahiti 41. The Mystery of Marie Roget 42. *Arabian Nights* 42. White Savage 43. *Cobra Woman* 44. Ali Baba and the Forty Thieves 44. Gypsy Wildcat 44. Sudan 45. Tangier 46. Pirates of Monterey 47. The Exile 47. Siren of Atlantis 48. The Thief of Venice 51, etc.

Montgomery, Douglass (1908–1966) (Robert Douglass Montgomery). Canadian leading man with stage experience; once known as *Kent Douglass*.
Paid (debut) 31. Waterloo Bridge 31. Little Women 33. A House Divided 33. Little Man, What Now? 34. The Mystery of Edwin Drood 35. Counsel for Crime 37. *The Cat and the Canary* 39. *The Way to the Stars* (GB) 45. Woman to Woman (GB) 47. Forbidden (GB) 48, etc.

Montgomery, Elizabeth (1933–). Pert American leading lady, daughter of Robert Montgomery; most familiar as the witch-wife of the TV series *Bewitched* 64-71.
The Court Martial of Billy Mitchell 55. Who's Been Sleeping in My Bed? 63. Johnny Cool 63. The Victim (TV) 72. Cry Rape (TV) 74.

Montgomery, George (1916–) (George M. Letz). Genial American leading man, mostly in low-budgeters; former boxer and stunt man who later had ambitions to direct.
The Cisco Kid and the Lady 39. Young People 40. *Roxie Hart* 42. *Ten Gentlemen from West Point* 42. Orchestra Wives 42. Coney Island 43. Bomber's Moon 43. Three Little Girls in Blue 46. The Brasher Doubloon 47. Lulu Belle 48. Dakota Lil 50. Sword of Monte Cristo 51. The Texas Rangers 51. Fort Ti 53. Street of Sinners 55. Huk 56. Black Patch 57. Watusi 59. The Steel Claw (& d) 61. Samar (& d) 62. From Hell to Borneo (& d) 64. Battle of the Bulge 65. Hallucination Generation 66. Huntsville 67, many others.
TV series: Cimarron City 58.

Montgomery, Robert (1904–) (Henry Montgomery). Smooth, smart American leading man of the thirties; later became a director, then forsook show business for politics.
□ So This is College 29. Untamed 29. Three Live Ghosts 29. The Single Standard 29. Their Own Desire 29. Free and Easy 30. The Divorcee 30. The Big House 30. Our Blushing Brides 30. Sins of the Children 30. Love in the Rough 30. War Nurse 30. The Easiest Way 31. Strangers May Kiss 31. Inspiration 31. Shipmates 31. The Man in Possession 31. Private Lives 31. Lovers Courageous 31. But the Flesh is Weak 32. Letty Lynton 32. Blondie of the Follies 32. Faithless 32. Hell Below 33. Made on Broadway 33. *When Ladies Meet* 33. Night Flight 33. Another Language 33. Fugitive Lovers 34. Riptide 34. The Mystery of Mr X 34. Hideout 34. Forsaking All Others 35. Vanessa, Her Love Story 35. Biography of a Bachelor Girl 35. No More Ladies 35. Petticoat Fever 36. Trouble for Two 36. Piccadilly Jim 36. The Last of Mrs Cheyney 37. *Night Must Fall* 37. Ever Since Eve 37. Live Love and Learn 37. The First Hundred Years 37. *Yellow Jack* 38. Three Loves has Nancy 38. Fast and Loose 39. The Earl of Chicago 40. *Busman's Honeymoon* (GB) (as Lord Peter Wimsey) 40. Rage in Heaven 41. Mr and Mrs Smith 41. *Here Comes Mr Jordan* 41. Unfinished Business 41. They Were Expendable 45. *The Lady in the Lake* (& d) 46. Ride the Pink Horse (& d) 47. The Saxon Charm 48. June Bride 48. Once More My Darling (& d) 49. Your Witness (GB) 50. The Gallant Hours (d only) 60.
TV series: Robert Montgomery Presents 50–57.

Montiel, Sarita (1927–) (Maria Antonia Abad). Spanish leading lady in Mexican and American films.
Vera Cruz 54. Serenade 56. She Gods of Shark Reef 57. Run of the Arrow 57, etc.

Monty Python. An ensemble name for a group of British nonsense comedians who had much influence on television comedy of the sixties and seventies. They include John Cleese, Michael Palin, Terry Gilliam, Eric Idle and Graham Chapman.
□ And Now for Something Completely Different 71. *Monty Python and the Holy Grail* 75.

Moody, Ron (1924–) (Ronald Moodnick). British character comedian of stage and TV.
□ Make Mine Mink 59. Summer Holiday 63. The Mouse on the Moon 63. Ladies Who Do 63. Murder Most Foul 64. Every Day's a Holiday 64. San Ferry Ann 65. The Sandwich Man 65. Oliver (as Fagin) 68. David Copperfield 69. The Twelve Chairs 70. Flight of the Doves 71. Dogpound Shuffle 74. Legend of the Werewolf 75.

The Moon and Sixpence (US 1942). A remarkable first film written and directed by Albert Lewin, whose exotic literary talent later got out of control. From the novel by Somerset Maugham based on the life of Gauguin, it was remarkable in remaining more faithful to its original than most Hollywood films of the period, while still managing to do well at the box office. Herbert Marshall appeared (not for the last time) as Maugham, George Sanders made the most of his meaty role as Strickland, and Steve Geray had his best part as Dirk Stroeve.

The Moon is Blue (US 1953). This straightforward version by Otto Preminger of F. Hugh Herbert's frothy Broadway comedy marked the first breaking-down of the Hollywood Production Code and the Legion of Decency, which Preminger defied by retaining the words 'virgin', 'mistress' and 'seduction' and treating these matters as a great joke. After the film's enormous box office success, Hollywood's mind quickly broadened. The actors involved were David Niven, William Holden and Maggie McNamara.

Moore, Clayton (1908–). Tall American leading man of forties serials such as *The Crimson Ghost, G-Men Never Forget, The Ghost* *of Zorro.* Later famous on TV as *The Lone Ranger.*

Moore, Cleo (1928–1973). American leading lady who appeared chiefly in Hugo Haas's low-budget emotional melodramas.
This Side of the Law 50. On Dangerous Ground 50. One Girl's Confession 53. Bait 54. Women's Prison 55. Over-Exposed 56, etc.

Moore, Colleen (1900–) (Kathleen Morrison). American leading lady of the silent screen.
Autobiography 1968: *Silent Star.*
The Bad Boy 17. Little Orphan Annie 18. So Long Letty 20. Come On Over 22. Flaming Youth 23. So Big 25. Synthetic Sin 28. Lilac Time 28. Why Be Good? 29. The Power and The Glory 33. The Scarlet Letter 34.

Moore, Constance (1919–). American leading lady and singer, mildly popular in the forties; usually in 'sensible' roles.
Prison Break 38. You Can't Cheat an Honest Man 39. La Conga Nights 40. Ma, He's Making Eyes at Me 40. I Wanted Wings 41. Take a Letter, Darling 42. *Show Business* 43. *Atlantic City* 44. Delightfully Dangerous 45. Earl Carroll's Vanities 45. In Old Sacramento 46. Hit Parade of 1947. Hats Off to Rhythm 47, etc.

Moore, Dickie (1925–). American child actor of the thirties, first on screen when one year old.
The Beloved Rogue 26. Passion Flower 30. Blonde Venus 32. Oliver Twist 33. Peter Ibbetson 34. Sergeant York 41. Miss Annie Rooney 42. Dangerous Years 47. Out of the Past (Build My Gallows High) 48. Killer Shark 50. The Member of the Wedding (last to date) 52, etc.

Moore, Dudley (1935–). British cabaret pianist and comedian, often teamed with Peter Cook.
□ The Wrong Box 66. Thirty is a Dangerous Age Cynthia 67. Bedazzled 68. Monte Carlo or Bust 69. The Bed Sitting Room 69. Alice's Adventures in Wonderland 72.

Moore, Eva (1870–1955). British stage actress who made a few films in the thirties.
Chu Chin Chow 22. Brown Sugar 31. The Old Dark House (splendid in her cries of 'No beds! They can't have beds!') (US) 32. I Was a Spy 33. A Cup of Kindness 34. Vintage Wine 35. Old Iron 39. The Bandit of Sherwood Forest (US) 46, etc.

Moore, Grace (1901–1947). American operatic singer who appeared in occasional films; Kathryn Grayson played her in a 1953 biopic, *So This is Love.*
Autobiography 1946: *You're Only Human Once.*
□ A Lady's Morals (as Jenny Lind) 30. New Moon 30. *One Night of Love* 34. Love Me Forever 35. The King Steps Out 36. When You're In Love 37. I'll Take Romance 37. Louise 40.

Moore, Ida (1883–1964). American character actress.
The Merry Widow 25. She's a Soldier Too 44. To Each His Own 46. The Egg and I 47. Manhattan Angel 49. Harvey 50. Honeychile 51. Scandal At Scourie 53. The Country Girl 54. Ma and Pa Kettle at Waikiki 55. The Desk Set 57. Rock a Bye Baby 58, etc.

Moore, Juanita (1922–). Black American character actress.
Lydia Bailey 52. Witness to Murder 54. Ransom 55. The Girl Can't Help It 57. *Imitation of Life* 59. Walk on the Wild Side 62. The Singing Nun 66. Rosie 68, etc.

Moore, Kieron (1925–) (Kieron O'Hanrahan). Hangdog Irish leading man with stage experience.
The Voice Within 44. *A Man about the House* 46. *Mine Own Executioner* 47. Anna Karenina 48. Ten Tall Men 51. The Key 58. The Day They Robbed the Bank of England 60. Dr Blood's Coffin 61. The Day of the Triffids 63. The Thin Red Line 64. Crack in the World 65. Arabesque 66. Custer of the West 67, etc.

Moore, Mary Tyler (1936–). Pert American leading lady who has been most successful on TV.
□ X15 61. Thoroughly Modern Millie 67. What's So Bad About Feeling Good? 68. Don't Just Stand There 68. Change of Habit 69. Run a Crooked Mile (TV) 70.
TV series: Richard Diamond 57. Steve Canyon 58. *The Dick Van Dyke Show* 61–66. *The Mary Tyler Moore Show* 70– .

Moore, Richard (–). American cinematographer.
The Wild Angels 65. Wild in the Streets 67. Winning 69. The Reivers 70. WUSA 70. A Complete State of Death 73, etc.

Moore, Roger (1928–). British light leading man, most successful on TV; film debut in Hollywood.

☐ The Last Time I Saw Paris 54. Interrupted Melody 55. The King's Thief 55. Diane 55. The Miracle 59. The Sins of Rachel Cade 61. Gold of the Seven Saints 61. Crossplot 69. The Man Who Haunted Himself 70. Live and Let Die (as James Bond) 73. The Man with the Golden Gun 74. Gold 74. Street People 76. The Spy Who Loved Me 77.

TV series: Ivanhoe 57. The Alaskans 59. Maverick 61. *The Saint* 63–68. *The Persuaders* 71.

Moore, Ted (1914–). South African cinematographer, in British films.
The Black Knight 54. Cockleshell Heroes 56. *A Man for All Seasons* (AA) 66. Shalako 68. The Prime of Miss Jean Brodie 69. The Most Dangerous Man in the World 69. Country Dance 70. Diamonds are Forever 71. Live and Let Die 73, etc.

Moore, Terry (1929–) (Helen Koford). American leading lady, former child model, in films from infancy.
The Murder in Thornton Square 43. Mighty Joe Young 50. The Sunny Side of the Street 53. King of the Khyber Rifles 54. Bernardine 57. A Private's Affair 59. Why Must I Die? 60. Town Tamer 65, etc.
TV series: Empire 63.

Moore, Victor (1876–1962). Veteran American vaudeville comedian with hesitant, bumbling manner, in films occasionally from 1915.
Snobs 15. The Clown 16, many one-reelers through the twenties, Romance in the Rain 34. Swing Time 36. Gold Diggers of 1937. *Louisiana Purchase* 41. Star Spangled Rhythm 42. Duffy's Tavern 45. It's in the Bag 45. It Happened on Fifth Avenue 47. We're Not Married 52. *The Seven-Year Itch* 55, etc.

Moorehead, Agnes (1906–1974). Sharp-featured American character actress, often seen in waspish or neurotic roles.
☐ Citizen Kane 41. *The Magnificent Ambersons* 42. Journey into Fear 42. The Big Street 42. The Youngest Profession 43. Government Girl 43. Jane Eyre 43. Since You Went Away 44. Dragon Seed 44. The Seventh Cross 44. Mrs Parkington 44. Tomorrow the World 44. Keep Your Powder Dry 45. Our Vines Have Tender Grapes 45. Her Highness and the Bellboy 45. Dark Passage 47. *The Lost Moment* (as a centenarian) 47. Summer Holiday 48. *The Woman in White* 48. Stations West 48. Johnny Belinda 48. The Stratton Story 49. The Great Sinner 49. Without Honor 49. Caged 50.

Fourteen Hours 51. Show Boat 51. The Blue Veil 51. The Adventures of Captain Fabian 51. Captain Blackjack 52. The Blazing Forest 52. The Story of Three Loves 53. Scandal at Scourie 53. Main Street to Broadway 53. Those Redheads from Seattle 53. Magnificent Obsession 54. Untamed 55. The Left Hand of God 55. All that Heaven Allows 56. Meet Me in Las Vegas 56. The Conqueror 56. The Revolt of Mamie Stover 56. The Swan 56. Pardners 56. The Opposite Sex 56. Raintree County 57. The True Story of Jesse James 57. Jeanne Eagels 57. The Story of Mankind 57. Night of the Quarter Moon 59. Tempest 59. *The Bat* 59. Pollyanna 60. Twenty Plus Two 61. Bachelor in Paradise 61. Jessica 62. How the West was Won 63. Who's Minding the Store? 63. Hush Hush Sweet Charlotte 64. The Singing Nun 66. What's the Matter with Helen? 71. Suddenly Single (TV) 71. Rolling Man (TV) 72. Night of Terror (TV) 72. Frankenstein: the True Story (TV) 73.
TV series: *Bewitched* 64–71.

Morahan, Christopher (c. 1930–). British director with stage and TV experience.
☐ Diamonds for Breakfast 68. All Neat in Black Stockings 69.

Moran, Peggy (1918–). American leading lady of the forties, with radio experience; married Henry Koster and retired.
Girls' School 39. The Mummy's Hand 40. Horror Island 41. Drums of the Congo 42. Seven Sweethearts 42, etc.

Moran, Polly (1884–1952). American vaudeville comedienne who made some early sound films, notably in partnership with Marie Dressler.
Hollywood Revue 29. Caught Short 29. Reducing 30. Politics 31. The Passionate Plumber 32. Alice in Wonderland 33; later played smaller roles in Two Wise Maids 37. Tom Brown's Schooldays 39. Petticoat Politics 41. Adam's Rib 49, etc.

More, Kenneth (1914–). Breezy British leading actor, a recognizable World War II type who later gave compassionate interpretations of middle-aged dreamers; film-makers forsook him after his great fifties success, and he turned to stage and TV.
Autobiography 1959: *Happy Go Lucky*.
☐ Look Up and Laugh 35. Windmill Revels 38. Carry on London 38. Scott of the Antarctic 48. Man on the Run 49. Now Barabbas 49. Stop Press Girl 49. Morning Departure 50. Chance of a Lifetime 50. The Clouded Yellow 50. The Franchise Affair 50. No Highway 51.

Appointment With Venus 51. Brandy for the Parson 52. The Yellow Balloon 52. Never Let Me Go 53. *Genevieve* 53. Our Girl Friday 53. *Doctor In the House* 54. Raising a Riot 54. *The Deep Blue Sea* 55. *Reach For the Sky* (as Douglas Bader) 56. The Admirable Crichton 57. A Night to Remember 58. Next to No Time 58. The Sheriff of Fractured Jaw 58. The 39 Steps 59. Northwest Frontier 59. *Sink The Bismarck* 60. Man in the Moon 60. The Greengage Summer 61. The Longest Day 62. Some People 62. We Joined the Navy 62. The Comedy Man 63. The Mercenaries 67. Oh What a Lovely War 69. Fraulein Doktor 69. Battle of Britain 69. Scrooge 70.
TV series: Father Brown 73.

More O'Ferrall, George (c. 1906–). British director who was mainly successful in TV.
AS ASSISTANT DIRECTOR: Midshipman Easy 34 to No Highway 51.
AS DIRECTOR: Angels One Five 52. The Holly and the Ivy 53. The Heart of the Matter 53. The Green Scarf 53. A Woman for Joe 55. The March Hare 56.

The More the Merrier (US) 1943). Perhaps the best of the several farces about overcrowding in Washington hotels during World War II, this amiable movie starred Charles Coburn, Jean Arthur and Joel McCrea, was written by Robert Russell and Frank Ross, and directed by George Stevens. In 1966 it was lethargically remade by Charles Walters, its setting changed to the Tokyo Olympics, as *Walk Don't Run*; Cary Grant took over as ageing Cupid to Samantha Eggar and Jim Hutton.

Moreau, Jeanne (1928–). French actress of stage and screen; the Bette Davis of her time.
The She-Wolves 55. Lift to the Scaffold 57. *The Lovers* 59. Le Dialogue des Carmelites 59. Les Liaisons Dangereuses 60. Moderato Cantabile 60. La Notte 61. *Jules et Jim* 61. Eva 62. The Trial 63. The Victors 63. Le Feu Follet 64. *Diary of a Chambermaid* 64. The Yellow Rolls-Royce 64. The Train 64. Mata Hari 65. *Viva Maria* 65. Mademoiselle 65. Chimes at Midnight 66. Sailor from Gibraltar 66. The Bride Wore Black 67. Great Catherine 68. Le Corps de Diane 68. Monte Walsh 70. Alex in Wonderland 70. Louise 72. Mr Klein 76. The Last Tycoon 76, etc.

Morecambe, Eric (1926–) (Eric Bartholomew) and **Wise, Ernie** (1925–) (Ernest Wiseman). British comedy team with music-hall experience since 1943. In the sixties they became immensely popular on TV, but their films have been rather less than satisfactory.

☐ The Intelligence Men 64. That Riviera Touch 66. The Magnificent Two 67.

Moreland, Mantan (1902–1973). Chubby American black actor, long cast as frightened valet.
Frontier Scout 38. Laughing at Danger 40. King of the Zombies 41. The Strange Case of Doctor RX 41. Charlie Chan in the Secret Service (and many others in this series) 44. Murder at Malibu Beach 47. The Feathered Serpent 49. Enter Laughing 68. Watermelon Man 70, etc.

Morell, André (1909–) (André Mesritz). Dignified British character actor.
Thirteen Men and a Gun (debut) 38. No Place for Jennifer 49. Seven Days to Noon 50. High Treason 51. Summer Madness 55. The Bridge on the River Kwai 57. Ben Hur 59. The Hound of the Baskervilles 59. Cone of Silence 60. Mysterious Island 61. Shadow of the Cat 62. Cash on Demand 64. She 65. Plague of the Zombies 65. The Mummy's Shroud 67. 10 Rillington Place 70. Barry Lyndon 75. The Message 76, etc.

Moreno, Antonio (1886–1967). Romantic Spanish star of Hollywood.
SILENT FILMS: Voice of the Million 12. House of Hate 18. The Trail of the Lonesome Pine 23. The Spanish Dancer 24. Mare Nostrum 25. Beverly of Graustark 26. The Temptress 26. It 27. Synthetic Sin 28, etc.
CHARACTER PARTS: One Mad Kiss 30. Storm over the Andes 35. Rose of the Rio Grande 38. Valley of the Giants 42. The Spanish Main 45. Captain from Castile 47. Thunder Bay 53. The Creature from the Black Lagoon 54. The Searchers 56, many others.

Moreno, Rita (1931–) (Rosita Dolores Alverio). Puerto Rican actress-dancer, in films sporadically since 1950, between stage appearances.
Pagan Love Song 50. Singin' in the Rain 52. Garden of Evil 54. The Vagabond King 55. The King and I 56. The Deerslayer 57. *West Side Story* (AA) 61. The Night of the Following Day 68. Popi 69. Carnal Knowledge 71. *The Ritz* 76, etc.

Morgan: A Suitable Case for Treatment (GB 1966). A serio-comedy which takes the *Lucky Jim/Look Back in Anger* type of fifties hero to the logical conclusion of madness, wretched by his own selfishness, nihilism and fantasy. David Mercer's script, extended from his own TV play, had very little to say, but there are intermittent enjoyments coupled with uneasy moments of flashy editing and slapstick. (The actual ending is borrowed from Buñuel.) David Warner enjoys himself in the title role; Karel Reisz directs rather uncertainly.

Morgan, Dennis (1910–) (Stanley Morner). American leading man, former opera singer.
Suzy (debut) 36. The Great Ziegfeld 36. Kitty Foyle 40. Captains of the Clouds 42. Thank Your Lucky Stars 43. Two Guys from Texas 46. My Wild Irish Rose 47. Painting the Clouds with Sunshine 51. The Gun That Won the West 55. Uranium Boom 56. Rogues' Gallery 68, etc.
TV series: 21 Beacon Street 58.

Morgan, Frank (1890–1949) (Francis Wupperman). American character actor. In films from 1916, usually playing his endearing if slightly fuddled self, but his real popularity came with sound, when he was an MGM contract player for over twenty years.
A Modern Cinderella 17. Queen High 26. Dangerous Dan McGrew 30. Reunion in Vienna 33. Hallelujah I'm a Bum 33. Naughty Marietta 35. The Great Ziegfeld 35. *The Last of Mrs Cheyney* 37. The Crowd Roars 38. Sweethearts 38. Serenade 39. Balalaika 39. *The Wizard of Oz* (title role) 39. *The Shop Around the Corner* 40. *Boom Town* 40. Washington Melodrama (leading role) 41. Honky Tonk 41. Tortilla Flat 42. White Cargo 42. *The Human Comedy* 43. The White Cliffs of Dover 43. Yolanda and the Thief 45. Courage of Lassie 45. The Great Morgan (leading role) 46. Mr Griggs Returns (leading role) 46. *Summer Holiday* 48. The Stratton Story 49. The Great Sinner 49. Any Number Can Play 49, many others.

Morgan, Harry (1915–) (Harry Bratsburg). Mild-looking American character actor with stage experience.
To the Shores of Tripoli (debut) 42. From This Day Forward 45. The Saxon Charm 49. Moonrise 50. The Well 51. High Noon 52. The Glenn Miller Story 53. Not as a Stranger 55. The Teahouse of the August Moon 56. Inherit the Wind 60. John Goldfarb Please Come Home 64. What Did You Do in the War, Daddy? 66. Support Your Local Sheriff 69. The Barefoot Executive 71. Snowball Express 73. The Apple Dumpling Gang 75, many others.
TV series: December Bride 54–58. Pete and Gladys 60–61. The Richard Boone Show 64. Kentucky Jones 65. Dragnet 69. The D.A. 71.

Morgan, Helen (1900–1941). American café singer of the thirties; film appearances few.
Biopic 1956 with Ann Blyth: *The Helen Morgan Story*.

Biography 1974: *Helen Morgan, Her Life and Legend* by Gilbert Maxwell.
□ *Applause* 29. Roadhouse Nights 30. You Belong to Me 34. Marie Galante 34. Sweet Music 35. Go Into Your Dance 36. *Show Boat* 36. Frankie and Johnnie 36.

Morgan, Michele (1920–) (Simone Roussel). French leading lady, in films from mid-thirties.
Orage 36. *Quai des Brumes* 38. Remorques 39. La Loi du Nord 39. La Symphonie Pastorale 40. Joan of Paris (US) 41. Higher and Higher (US) 43. Passage to Marseilles (US) 44. *The Fallen Idol* (GB) 48. Les Orgeuilleux 50. The Seven Deadly Sins 51. Les Grandes Manoeuvres 55. Marguerite de la Nuit 56. The Mirror Has Two Faces 60. Landru 63. Lost Command 66. Benjamin 68, etc.

Morgan, Ralph (1882–1956) (Ralph Wupperman). American character actor, brother of Frank Morgan. Former lawyer; went on stage, then to films in the twenties.
Charlie Chan's Chance 31. Rasputin and the Empress 32. Strange Interlude 32. *The Power and the Glory* 33. Anthony Adverse 36. The Life of Emile Zola 37. Forty Little Mothers 40. Black Market Babies 45. The Monster Maker 45. Sleep My Love 48. Gold Fever 52, many others.

Morgan Terence (1921–). British leading man.
Hamlet (debut) 48. Mandy 52. Turn the Key Softly 53. They Can't Hang Me 55. The Scamp 56. Shakedown 58. Piccadilly Third Stop 61. The Curse of the Mummy's Tomb 64, others.
TV series: Sir Francis Drake 62.

Moriarty, Michael (1941–). American leading man of the seventies.
Hickey and Boggs 72. The Last Detail 73. Bang the Drum Slowly 73. Shoot It Black Shoot It Blue 74. Report to the Commissioner 75, etc.

Morison, Patricia (1915–) (Eileen Morison). Slightly sulky-looking American leading lady of the forties; never quite made it but did well later on stage.
□ *Persons in Hiding* 39. I'm from Missouri 39. The Magnificent Fraud 39. Untamed 40. Rangers of Fortune 40. One Night in Lisbon 41. Romance of the Rio Grande 41. The Roundup 41. A Night in New Orleans 42. Beyond the Blue Horizon 42. Are Husbands Necessary? 42. Silver Skates 43. Hitler's Madman 43. Calling Dr Death 43. The Fallen Sparrow 43. The Song of Bernadette 43. Where are Your Children? 44. Without Love 45. Lady on a Train 45. Dressed to Kill 46. Danger Woman 46. Queen of the

Amazons 47. Tarzan and the Huntress 47. Song of the Thin Man 47. Prince of Thieves 47. Walls of Jericho 48. The Return of Wildfire 48. Sofia 48. Song Without End 60.

Morlay, Gaby (1897–1964) (Blanche Fumoleau). French character actress.
La Sandale Rouge 13. Les Nouveaux Messieurs 28. Derrière la Façade 38. Le Voile Bleu 42. Gigi 48. Le Plaisir 51. Mitsou 55. Ramuntcho 58, many others.

Morley, Karen (1905–) (Mildred Linton). American leading lady of the thirties.
Inspiration 31. *Scarface* 32. Dinner at Eight 33. Our Daily Bread 34. Beloved Enemy 36. Kentucky 39. Pride and Prejudice 40. Jealousy 45. The Unknown 46. 'M' 51, others.

Morley, Robert (1908–). Portly British character actor (and playwright), on stage from 1929, films from 1938.
Autobiography 1966: *Robert Morley, Responsible Gentleman.*
Marie Antoinette (US) 38. *Major Barbara* 40. *The Young Mr Pitt* 42. I Live in Grosvenor Square 45. An Outcast of the Islands 51. *Gilbert and Sullivan* 53. *Beat the Devil* 53. Around the World in Eighty Days 56. The Doctor's Dilemma 59. *Oscar Wilde* 60. The Young Ones 61. Murder at the Gallop 63. Those Magnificent Men in Their Flying Machines 65. The Alphabet Murders 65. Genghis Khan 65. A Study in Terror 65. Hotel Paradiso 66. Way Way Out (US) 66. The Trygon Factor 67. Sinful Davey 69. When Eight Bells Toll 71. Theatre of Blood 73. The Blue Bird 76, etc.

Morning Glory (US 1933). Zoe Akins' play about a maddening but talented young actress in New York was filmed by Lowell Sherman with Katharine Hepburn (who won an Academy Award) and Adolphe Menjou. In 1957 Sidney Lumet remade it as *Stage Struck*, with Susan Strasberg and Henry Fonda.

Morocco (US 1930). The film in which Marlene Dietrich made her American debut, directed by Josef Von Sternberg. Remembered chiefly for the impudence of the scenes in which Marlene (*a*) dressed in a tuxedo, kisses a young woman on the lips, and (*b*) strides into the Sahara in high heels to follow her departed lover.

Moross, Jerome (1913–). American composer.
When I Grow Up 51. The Sharkfighters 56. The Big Country 57. The Proud Rebel 58. The Jayhawkers 59. The Cardinal 63. The War Lord 65. Rachel Rachel 68, etc.

Morricone, Ennio (1928–). Italian composer and arranger.
A Fistful of Dollars 64. El Greco 64. Fists in the Pocket 65. The Good the Bad and the Ugly 66. The Big Gundown 66. Matchless 67. Theorem 69. Once Upon a Time in the West 69. Investigation of a Citizen 69. Fraulein Doktor 69. The Bird with the Crystal Plumage 70. Cat O'Nine Tails 71. The Red Tent 71. Four Flies in Grey Velvet 71. The Decameron 71. The Burglars 71. The Black Belly of the Tarantula 72. Bluebeard 72. The Serpent 72, etc.

Morris, Chester (1901–1970). Jut-jawed American leading man of the thirties, an agreeable 'B' picture lead who later became a considerable stage and TV actor.
Alibi 29. She Couldn't Say No 30. The Divorcee 30. *The Big House* 30. The Bat Whispers 31. The Miracle Man 32. Red Headed Woman 32. Blondie Johnson 33. The Gift of Gab 34. I've Been Around 35. Society Doctor 35. Moonlight Murder 36. They Met in a Taxi 36. Flight from Glory 37. Law of the Underworld 38. Smashing the Rackets 38. Blind Alibi 39. *Five Came Back* 39. The Marines Fly High 40. No Hands on the Clock 41. Meet Boston Blackie 41 (and subsequent series of 12 films until 1949). I Live on Danger 42. Wrecking Crew 43. Secret Command 44. Double Exposure 45. Unchained 55, etc.

Morris, Ernest (1915– -). British director, mainly of second features for the Danzigers.
The Tell-Tale Heart 60. Echo of Diana 64. The Return of Mr Moto 65, etc.

Morris, Howard (1919–). American comedy director.
Boys Night Out (a only) 62. Who's Minding the Mint? 67. With Six You Get Egg Roll 68. Don't Drink the Water 69, etc.

Morris, Lana (1930–). British leading lady of the fifties.
Spring in Park Lane 47. The Weaker Sex 48. Trottie True 49. The Chiltern Hundreds 49. The Woman in Question 50. Trouble in Store 53. Man of the Moment 55. Home and Away 56. I Start Counting 70, others.

Morris, Mary (1915–). British character actress with dominant personality, on stage from 1925.
Prison without Bars (film debut) 38. The Spy in Black 39. The Thief of Baghdad 40. *Pimpernel Smith* 41. Undercover 43. The Man from

Morocco 45. Train of Events 49. High Treason 51, others.

Morris, Mary (1895–1970). American stage actress who played her stage role of the evil old lady in *Double Door* 34.

Morris, Oswald (1915–). British cinematographer, in films from 1932.
Green for Danger 46. *Moulin Rouge* 53. Knave of Hearts 53. Beat the Devil 53. Beau Brummell 54. Moby Dick 56. A Farewell to Arms 57. The Key 58. Roots of Heaven 59. Look Back in Anger 59. Our Man in Havana 59. The Entertainer 60. Lolita 62. Of Human Bondage 64. *The Pumpkin Eater* (BFA) 64. The Hill (BFA) 65. Life at the Top 65. The Spy Who Came In from the Cold 65. Stop the World I Want To Get Off 66. *The Taming of the Shrew* 67. Oliver! 68. Goodbye Mr Chips 69. Scrooge 70. Fiddler on the Roof (AA) 71. Lady Caroline Lamb 72. The Mackintosh Man 73. The Odessa File 74. The Man Who Would Be King 75, many others.

Morris, Wayne (1914–1959) (Bert de Wayne Morris). Brawny American leading man with stage experience.
China Clipper (debut) 36. *Kid Galahad* 37. Brother Rat and a Baby 39. Bad Men of Missouri 40. The Smiling Ghost 41. Deep Valley 47. The Time of Your Life 47. The Tougher They Come 50. The Master Plan 55. The Crooked Sky 57. Paths of Glory 58, etc.

Morrissey, Paul (1939–). American 'underground' director associated with Andy Warhol.
Flesh 68. Trash 70. *Heat* 72, etc.

Morros, Boris (1891–1963) (Boris Milhailovitch). Russian-born independent producer in America from the late thirties. Later revealed as an American agent via his 1957 book *Ten Years a Counterspy*, filmed in 1960 as *Man on a String*, with Ernest Borgnine as Morros.
The Flying Deuces 39. Second Chorus 41. Tales of Manhattan 42. Carnegie Hall 48, others.

Morrow, Jeff (1913–). Mature American leading man, from Broadway and TV actor, in Hollywood from 1953.
The Robe 53. Flight to Tangier 53. Siege of Red River 54. Tanganyika 54. Sign of the Pagan 54. *This Island Earth* 55. The Creature Walks Among Us 56. The Giant Claw 57. The Story of Ruth 60. Harbour Lights 63, etc.
TV series: Union Pacific 58.

Morrow, Jo (1940–). American leading lady of the sixties.
Because They're Young 56. Brushfire 57. The Legend of Tom Dooley 59. Our Man in Havana 59. The Three Worlds of Gulliver 60. He Rides Tall 63. Sunday in New York 64. Doctor Death 73, etc.

Morrow, Vic (1932–). American actor formerly cast as a muttering juvenile delinquent. Stage experience.
The Blackboard Jungle (film debut) 55. Tribute to a Bad Man 56. Men in War 57. God's Little Acre 58. Cimarron 61. Portrait of a Mobster 61. Sledge (d only) 69. The Glass House (TV) 72. The Take 74. Captains and the Kings (TV) 76. Treasure of Matecumbe 76. The Bad News Bears 76. Roots (TV) 77, etc.
TV series: Combat 62–66.

Morse, Barry (1919–). British leading man who moved to Canada and became star of stage and TV there.
The Goose Steps Out 42. When We Are Married 42. There's a Future in It 43. Late at Night 46. Daughter of Darkness 48. No Trace 50, then after long gap—Kings of the Sun 63. Justine 69. Asylum 72, etc.
TV series: The Fugitive (as Lieut. Gerard) 63–67. Zoo Gang 71. The Adventurer 73. Space 1999 75–76.

Morse, Robert (1931–). American comedy actor who usually plays the befuddled innocent.
The Matchmaker 58. Honeymoon Hotel 64. Quick Before It Melts 65. *The Loved One* 65. Oh Dad, Poor Dad 66. *How to Succeed in Business without Really Trying* 67. Where Were You When the Lights Went Out? 68. The Boatniks 69, etc.
TV series: That's Life 68.

Morse, Terry (1906–). American second feature director.
☐ Jane Arden 39. On Trial 39. Waterfront 39. Smashing the Money Ring 39. No Place to Go 39. British Intelligence 40. Tear Gas Squad 40. Fog Island 45. Danny Boy 46. Shadows over Chinatown 46. Dangerous Money 46. Bells of San Fernando 47. Unknown World 51. Godzilla (US version) 56. Taffy and the Jungle Hunter 65. Young Dillinger 65.

morticians: see *undertakers*.

Mortimer, John (1923–). British playwright who has worked in films. Originally scriptwriter for Crown Film Unit.
The Innocents 61. Guns of Darkness 63. The

Dock Brief 63. The Running Man 63. Bunny Lake Is Missing 65, etc.

Morton, Clive (1904–1975). Straight-faced British character actor on stage from 1926, films from 1932, usually in slightly pompous roles.
The Blarney Stone 32. Dead Men Tell No Tales 39. While the Sun Shines 46. Scott of the Antarctic 48. The Blue Lamp 49. His Excellency 51. Carrington VC 54. Richard III 56. Shake Hands with the Devil 59. Lawrence of Arabia 62. Stranger in the House 67, many others.

Mosjoukine, Ivan (1889–1939). Russian actor of the old school, who appeared in many international films.
The Defence of Sebastopol 11. Satan Triumphant 22. Tempest (Fr.) 22. Shadows That Mass (Fr.) 23. Casanova (Fr./It.) 27. Sergeant X (Fr.) 30. Nitchevo (Fr.) 36, etc.

Moss, Arnold (1910–). American character actor often seen in sly or sinister roles.
Temptation 47. The Black Book (as Napoleon) 49. Kim 51. Viva Zapata 52. Casanova's Big Night 54. The Twenty-Seventh Day 57. The Fool Killer 64. Gambit 66. Caper of the Golden Bulls 67, many others.

The Most Dangerous Game (US 1932). Richard Connell's well-known short story concerned a mad sportsman who trapped human beings on a tropical island in order to hunt them and display their heads in his trophy room. This first and best film version was produced by Merian C. Cooper, directed by Ernest Schoedsack and Irving Pichel, photographed by Henry Gazzara; it had a thumping Max Steiner score and starred Leslie Banks. In 1945 it was remade as *A Game of Death*, with Edgar Barrier; in 1948 *Johnny Allegro* borrowed liberally from it, with George Macready shooting arrows at George Raft; *Kill or Be Killed* in 1950 had George Coulouris as the menace; *Run For the Sun* in 1956 made Trevor Howard a refugee Nazi in the Brazilian jungle, pursuing unwary intruders with savage hounds. 1966 found Cornel Wilde on the run from African headhunters in *The Naked Prey*, which used basically the same story; and in the same year an exploitation item called *Blood Lust* borrowed the plot once more.

Mostel, Zero (1915–). Heavyweight American comedian principally seen on Broadway stage.
Panic in the Streets 50. *The Enforcer* 51. A Funny Thing Happened on the Way to the Forum 66. Great Catherine 68. *The Producers*

68. The Great Bank Robbery 69. The Angel Levine 69. The Hot Rock 72. Marco 73. Rhinoceros 73. The Front 76, etc.

mother love has been the driving force of many of the screen's most popular, and therefore most remade, melodramas, such as *Imitation of Life, Madame X, Stella Dallas, Over the Hill, Mrs Wiggs of the Cabbage Patch* and *To Each His Own*. Britain chipped in with *The Woman in the Hall, The White Unicorn*, and *When the Bough Breaks*. Some say that Hitchcock made *Psycho* as the ultimate riposte to this sentimental tendency; but *The Anniversary* came a close second. Nor should mother-motivated gangsters such as those in *White Heat* and *Villain* be forgotten, while Melina Mercouri in *Promise At Dawn* and Rosalind Russell in *Gypsy* were perhaps the most sinister mothers of all.

Motion Picture Association of America. A trade guild in which distributors meet to set tariffs and deal with complaints, also set a censorship code.

motor-cycles, hideous and unbearably noisy machines, have become a badge of aggressive youth, and since *The Wild Angels* in 1966 American drive-in screens have been filled with a host of cheap movies extolling the pleasures of leather-jacketed speed with a bird on the back. All of these appear to have been banned in Britain, as was *The Wild One*, an early example of the genre, in 1954. But we did let through Elvis Presley in *Roustabout*, and Steve McQueen doing his own stunt sequence in *The Great Escape*, and *Easy Rider*, and *Coogan's Bluff*, and *Little Fauss and Big Halsy*, and we even made *The Leather Boys*, about our own ton-up teenagers. As for *Girl on a Motorcycle*, in which the bike becomes the ultimate sex symbol, words fail one. There was a good British film about speedway racing, *Once a Jolly Swagman*, and one about the fairground called *Wall of Death*. Comedian George Formby went in for the TT races in *No Limit*, and rode a motor-bike also in *It's In the Air*. Groucho Marx used one to comic effect in *Duck Soup*, as did Horst Bucholz in *One, Two, Three*. In American films, the motor-cycle cops are too familiar to warrant individual attention but *Electra Glide in Blue* took one seriously. *Easy Rider*, almost an *hommage* to the machine, is also the most successful film to feature it.

motor racing has been the subject of many a routine melodrama, and always seems to reduce the writer to banalities, even in a spectacular like *Grand Prix*. Some other examples of the genre include *The Crowd Roars, Indianapolis Speedway, Checkpoint, The Green Helmet, The Devil's Hairpin, Red Line 7000, Le Mans*, and *Winning*. The funniest comedy use of the sport was probably in *Ask a Policeman*, when Will Hay accidentally drove a bus on to Brooklands racetrack in the middle of a race.

Moulder Brown, John (1945–). British actor, usually of intense roles.
Deep End 69. Vampire Circus 71. King Queen Knave 72. Ludwig 72, etc.

Moulin Rouge. The three films made under this title are unconnected with each other. 1. US 1928: a drama directed by E. A. Dupont, with Eve Grey. 2. US 1933: a romantic comedy directed by Sidney Lanfield, with Constance Bennett and Franchot Tone. 3. GB 1953: a life of Toulouse Lautrec, from Pierre la Mure's novel, directed by John Huston and starring Jose Ferrer; mainly notable for its period atmosphere and Oswald Morris' colour photography.

Mount, Peggy (1916–). British character comedienne with long experience in repertory before starring as the termagant mother-in-law in *Sailor Beware*, filmed in 1956.
Dry Rot 57. The Naked Truth 58. Inn for Trouble 60. Ladies Who Do 63. One Way Pendulum 65. Hotel Paradiso 66. Finders Keepers 66. Oliver! 68, etc.
TV series: The Larkins, George and the Dragon.

mountains have provided a challenge in innumerable movies including *The Challenge, The White Tower, The Mountain, The White Hell of Pitz Palu, The Gold Rush, Trail of 98, The Eiger Sanction, The Snows of Kilimanjaro, The Abominable Snowman, Lost Horizon* and *Goodbye Mr Chips*.

Mowbray, Alan (1893–1969). Imperious-mannered British character actor, in America since early 1920s; appeared later in nearly 400 films, often as butler or pompous emissary.
Alexander Hamilton 31. Sherlock Holmes 32. Roman Scandals 33. Becky Sharp 35. Desire 36. My Man Godfrey 36. Topper 37. Stand In 37. The Villain Still Pursued Her 40. Lady Hamilton 41. That Uncertain Feeling 41. A Yank at Eton 42. His Butler's Sister 43. Holy Matrimony 43. Where Do We Go from Here? 45. *Terror by Night* 45. Merton of the Movies 46. *My Darling Clementine* 46. Prince of Thieves 47. The Jackpot 50. Wagonmaster 50. Dick Turpin's Ride 51. Androcles and the Lion 53. The King's Thief 55. The King and I 56, many others.
TV series: Colonel Flack 57–58.

Moxey, John (1920–). British TV director who has made occasional films and many TV movies in America.
City of the Dead 59. The £20,000 Kiss 63. Ricochet 63. Strangler's Web 65. Circus of Fear 67, etc.

Mudie, Leonard (1884–1965) (Leonard M. Cheetham). British Character actor in Hollywood.
The Mummy 32. The House of Rothschild 34. Clive of India 35. Lancer Spy 37. Dark Victory 39. Berlin Correspondent 42. My Name is Julia Ross 45. Song of My Heart 48. The Magnetic Monster 53. The Big Fisherman 59, many others.

Mueller, Elizabeth (1926–). German leading lady who made some Hollywood films.
The Power and the Prize 56. El Hakim 58. Confess Dr Corda 58. The Angry Hills 59, etc.

Muhl, Edward E. (1907–). American executive, an ex-accountant who has been in charge of Universal production since 1953.

Muir, Esther (1895–). American character actress usually seen as hard-faced blonde.
A Dangerous Affair 31. So This is Africa 33. The Bowery 33. Fury 36. *A Day at the Races* (in which she suffered memorably at the hands of Groucho Marx) 37. The Law West of Tombstone 38. Stolen Paradise 41. X Marks the Spot 42, etc.

Muir, Gavin (1907–1972). Quiet-spoken American actor with a British accent, usually a smooth villain.
Lloyds of London 36. Wee Willie Winkie 37. Eagle Squadron 41. *Nightmare* 42. The Master Race 44. Salome Where She Danced 45. California 46. Ivy 47. Abbott and Costello Meet the Invisible Man 51. King of the Khyber Rifles 54. The Sea Chase 55. The Abductors 57. Johnny Trouble 59, many others.

Muir, Jean (1911–) (J. M. Fullerton). American leading lady of the thirties.
Female 34. A Midsummer Night's Dream 35. Jane Steps Out (GB) 37. And One Was Beautiful 40. The Lone Wolf Meets a Lady 40. The Constant Nymph 44, etc.

Muldaur, Diana (c. 1943–). Sensitive-looking American leading lady, McCloud's girl friend on TV; adept at nice sophisticated types; also on TV in 1974, played Joy Adamson in Born Free.
□ The Swimmer 68. Number One 69. The Lawyer 70. The Other 71. One More Train to

Rob 72. McQ 73. The Chosen Survivors 74. Charlie's Angels (TV) 76.

Mulford, Clarence E. (1895–1970). American western novelist, the creator of Hopalong Cassidy.

Mulhall, Jack (1891–). American silent-screen leading man.
Sirens of the Sea 17. Mickey 18. All of a Sudden Peggy 20. Molly'O 21. The Bad Man 23. The Goldfish 24. Friendly Enemies 25. The Poor Nut 27. Just Another Blonde 28. Dark Streets 29, many others; appeared as an 'old-timer' in Hollywood Boulevard 36.

Mulhare, Edward (1923–). Irish leading man who has been on American stage.
Hill Twenty-Four does Not Answer 55. Signpost to Murder 64. Von Ryan's Express 65. Our Man Flint 65. Eye of the Devil 67. *Caprice* 67. Gidget Grows Up (TV) 72.
TV series: The Ghost and Mrs Muir 68–69.

Mullard, Arthur (1920–). Big, bluff cockney character comedian who became a British television star of the seventies.
The Wrong Arm of the Law 63. The Great St Trinian's Train Robbery 67, many others.

Mullen, Barbara (1914–1979). Irish actress, former dancer, who came to films as star of *Jeannie* 42.
Thunder Rock 42. A Place of One's Own 44. The Trojan Brothers 45. Corridor of Mirrors 48. So Little Time 52. The Challenge 60, etc.
TV series: Dr Finlay's Casebook.

Muller, Renate (1907–1974). German leading lady best known abroad for *Sunshine Susie* 31.
Biography 1944: *Queen of America?* by R. E. Clements.
Liebling der Götter 30. Viktor und Viktoria 34. Allotria 36.

Mulligan, Richard (1932–). Lanky American leading man.
The Group 66. The Undefeated 69. Little Big Man 70. The Big Bus 76, etc.
TV series: The Hero 66.

Mulligan, Robert (1925–). American director, from TV.
□ Fear Strikes Out 57. The Rat Race 60. Come September 61. The Great Impostor 61. The Spiral Road 62. *To Kill a Mockingbird* 62. Love with the Proper Stranger 64. Baby the Rain Must Fall 65. Inside Daisy Clover 65. Up the Down Staircase 67. The Stalking Moon 68. The Pursuit

of Happiness 70. *Summer of '42* 71. The Other 73. The Nickel Ride 75.

multi-screen techniques are nothing new, but the Montreal Exhibition of 1967 made them fashionable again, so that in such films as *The Boston Strangler*, *Grand Prix* and *The Thomas Crown Affair* the audience was supposed to look at up to a dozen different images at the same time, which became mighty exhausting. Mercifully, the fashion soon wore off.

multiplane. A word introduced by Walt Disney to explain his new animation process for *Fantasia* 40. Instead of building up a drawing by laying 'cells' directly on top of each other, a slight illusion of depth was obtained by leaving space between the celluloid images of foreground, background, principal figure, etc.

multiple roles. The record for the number of characters played by one actor in a film is held not by Alec Guinness in *Kind Hearts and Coronets* but (probably) by Lupino Lane, who played twenty-four parts in a 1929 comedy called *Only Me*, by Buster Keaton in *The Playhouse*, or by George S. Melies in his 1900 film *The One Man Band*. Others with high scores, apart from Guinness' eight, include Robert Hirsch's dozen in *No Questions on Saturday*, Paul Muni's seven in *Seven Faces*, Jerry Lewis' seven in *The Family Jewels*, Tony Randall's seven in *The Seven Faces of Dr Lao*, Hugh Herbert's six in *La Conga Nights*, Fernandel's six in *The Sheep Has Five Legs*, Anna Neagle's four in *Lilacs in the Spring*, Françoise Rosay's four in *Une Femme Disparait*, Louis Jourdan's and Joan Fontaine's four each in *Decameron Nights*, Rod Steiger's and Claire Bloom's four each in *The Illustrated Man*, Lionel Jeffries' four in *The Secret of My Success*, Alan Young's four in *Gentlemen Prefer Brunettes*, Terry Kilburn's four generations of boy in *Goodbye Mr Chips*, Moira Shearer's three in *The Man Who Loved Redheads*, Deborah Kerr's three in *The Life and Death of Colonel Blimp*, Peter Sellers' three in *The Mouse That Roared* and *Dr Strangelove*, Leon Errol's three in some episodes of the *Mexican Spitfire* series, Joanne Woodward's three in *The Three Faces of Eve* and Eleanor Parker's three in *Lizzie*. One should perhaps also count Danny Kaye's various dream selves in *The Secret Life of Walter Mitty*.

Dual roles have frequently been of the schizophrenic type of which *Dr Jekyll and Mr Hyde* (qv) is the most obvious example. This category includes Henry Hull in *Werewolf of London* and Lon Chaney Jnr in *The Wolf Man*,

Phyllis Calvert in *Madonna of the Seven Moons*, Phyllis Thaxter in *Bewitched*, Jerry Lewis in *The Nutty Professor*, and Alec Guinness in *The Captain's Paradise*. Two-character roles include Ronald Colman in *The Masquerader* and *The Prisoner of Zenda*, Lon Chaney in *London After Midnight*, Edward G. Robinson in *The Man with Two Faces*, Laurel and Hardy in *Our Relations*, Allan Jones and Joe Penner in *The Boys from Syracuse*, Chaplin in *The Great Dictator*, Louis Hayward in *The Man in the Iron Mask*, Olivia de Havilland in *The Dark Mirror*, Boris Karloff in *The Black Room*, Herbert Lom in *Dual Alibi*, George M. Cohan in *The Phantom President*, Jack Palance in *House of Numbers*, Peter Whitney in *Murder He Says*, Elisabeth Bergner (and later Bette Davis) in *Stolen Life*, Bette Davis in *Dead Ringer*, Yul Brynner in *The Double Man*, Stanley Baxter in *Very Important Person*, Peter Lawford in *One More Time*, George Arliss in *His Lordship*, Alain Delon in *The Black Tulip*, John McIntire in *The Lawless Breed*, Valentino in *Son of the Sheik*, Jack Mulhall in *Dark Streets* (allegedly the first to use the split-image technique) and Larry Parks (playing Jolson *and* himself) in *Jolson Sings Again*.

multiple-story films probably began in 1916 with *Intolerance*, which audiences rejected as too complicated. Later attempts made sure that the stories were clearly woven into a common thread; *The Bridge of San Luis Rey* in 1929, *Grand Hotel* in 1932, *Friday the Thirteenth* and *Dinner at Eight* in 1933. *Un Carnet de Bal* (also known as *Christine*) in 1936. *Tales of Manhattan* in 1942, *Forever and a Day* in 1942, *Flesh and Fantasy* in 1943, *Weekend at the Waldorf* and *Dead of Night* in 1945. In 1948–50 three Somerset Maugham compendiums, introduced by the author, emerged as *Quartet*, *Trio* and *Encore*; this inspired *O. Henry's Full House* in 1952. In 1963 we had *The VIPs* and in 1964 *The Yellow Rolls Royce*, the stories in the latter being very casually linked. Meanwhile horror compendiums were becoming popular, 1962's *Tales of Terror* being followed between 1967 and 1972 by *Dr Terror's House of Horrors*, *The Torture Garden*, *The House that Dripped Blood*, *Tales From the Crypt*, *Asylum* and *Vault of Horror*.

The Mummy. Interest in avenging mummies was aroused during the twenties by the widespread stories of the curse of Tutankhamen whose tomb had recently been discovered and opened. In 1932 Karl Freund directed a rather strange romantic film on the subject with Boris Karloff as a desiccated but active three-thousand-year-old still on the track of his lost love. Despite good box office it was not reprised until 1940, when *The Mummy's Hand*, a pure hokum thriller, appeared with Tom Tyler in the role. Between 1942 and 1944 there were three increasingly foolish sequels starring (if it really *was* him under the bandages) Lon Chaney Jnr: they were *The Mummy's Tomb*, *The Mummy's Ghost* and *The Mummy's Curse*. In 1959 Hammer took over the character and remade *The Mummy* with an English Victorian setting: Christopher Lee was the monster. There have been two poor sequels, *The Curse of the Mummy's Tomb* 64 and *The Mummy's Shroud* 66. *Blood From The Mummy's Tomb* 71 did not feature a monster; it was based on a Bram Stoker story. The lighter side of the subject was viewed by Wheeler and Woolsey in *Mummy's Boys* 35, the Three Stooges in *Mummie's Dummies* 38, and Abbott and Costello in *Meet the Mummy* 54.

Mundin, Herbert (1898–1939). British character actor with stage experience, in British films in the twenties, Hollywood from 1930.
The Devil's Lottery 31. Sherlock Holmes 32. Cavalcade 33. *David Copperfield* (as Barkis) 34. Mutiny on the Bounty 35. Another Dawn 37. *The Adventures of Robin Hood* (as Much the Miller) 38. Society Lawyer 39, etc.

Muni, Paul (1896–1967) (Muni Weisenfreund). Distinguished American actor of Austrian parentage. Long stage experience.
Biography 1974: *Actor* by Jerome Lawrence.
□ The Valiant (film debut) 28. Seven Faces 29. *Scarface* 32. *I Am a Fugitive from a Chain Gang* 32. The World Changes 33. Hi Nellie 33. Bordertown 34. Black Fury 35. Dr Socrates 35. *The Story of Louis Pasteur* (AA) 36. *The Good Earth* 37. *The Life of Emile Zola* 37. The Woman I Love 38. Juarez 39. We Are Not Alone 39. Hudson's Bay 40. The Commandos Strike at Dawn 42. Stage Door Canteen 43. *A Song to Remember* 44. Counter Attack 45. Angel on My Shoulder 46. Stranger on the Prowl 51. The Last Angry Man 59.

Munk, Andrzej (1921–1961). Polish director.
Men of the Blue Cross 55. Eroica 57. Bad Luck 60. The Passenger (incomplete) 61, etc.

Munro, Janet (1934–1972). Scottish leading lady with brief stage experience before films in both GB and US.
The Trollenberg Terror 57. The Young and the Guilty 57. Darby O'Gill and the Little People 58. Third Man on the Mountain 59. The Swiss Family Robinson 60. The Day the Earth Caught Fire 62. Life for Ruth 62. Bitter Harvest 63. A

Jolly Bad Fellow 64. Sebastian 67, etc.

Munsel, Patrice (1925–). American operatic soprano who played the title role in *Melba* 53.

Munshin, Jules (1915–1970). Rubber-limbed American comedian, in occasional films from the mid-forties.
Easter Parade 48. Take Me Out to the Ball Game 48. *On the Town* 49. Ten Thousand Bedrooms 56. Silk Stockings 57. Wild and Wonderful 64, etc.

Munson, Ona (1906–1955) (Ona Wolcott). American character actress, former dancer.
Going Wild 30. Five Star Final 32. Gone with the Wind 39. Drums of the Congo 40. *The Shanghai Gesture* (as Mother Gin Sling) 41. The Cheaters 45. The Red House 47, etc.

Murder on the Orient Express (GB 1973). This old-fashioned, twenties-set Agatha Christie thriller came in on a wave of publicity and was decently enough done but proved disappointing and slow in its second half, despite an all-star cast: the set was too restrictive and Albert Finney as Poirot was way over the top. Surprisingly in view of its box office success, no cycle of detective stories resulted, only the spoof *Murder By Death*.

murderers abound in fictional films, but only a handful of real-life cases have been analysed with any seriousness. There have been several 'lives' of Charlie Peace and Landru, and fantasies about the earlier French 'Bluebeard'. More recently a cold clinical eye was applied to Barbara Graham in *I Want to Live* 57, *Dr Crippen* 64, *The Boston Strangler* 68, John Christie in *Ten Rillington Place* 71. Ruth Ellis was said to have inspired *Yield to the Night* 56 and Leopold and Loeb were plainly the subject of *Compulsion* 58.

Murdoch, Richard (1907–). British radio entertainer, long partnered with Arthur Askey and Kenneth Horne.
Band Wagon 39. *The Ghost Train* 41. It Happened in Soho 48. Golden Arrow 52. Not a Hope in Hell 59. Strictly Confidential 61, etc.

Murnau, F. W. (or **Friedrich**) (1889–1931) (F. W. Plumpe). German director in films from 1919; Hollywood from 1927.
Satanas 19. Dr Jekyll and Mr Hyde 20. *Nosferatu* (Dracula) 22. *The Last Laugh* 24. Tartuffe 24. *Faust* 26. *Sunrise* 27. Four Devils 28. Our Daily Bread (City Girl) 30. Tabu (co-d) 31, etc.

Murphy, Audie (1924–1971). Boyish American leading man of the fifties; came to films on the strength of his war record as America's most decorated soldier, but despite some talent was soon relegated to low-budget westerns.
□ Beyond Glory 48. Texas Brooklyn and Heaven 48. Bad Boy 49. Sierra 50. The Kid from Texas 50. Kansas Raiders 50. *The Red Badge of Courage* 51. The Cimarron Kid 51. The Duel at Silver Creek 52. Gunsmoke 52. Column South 53. Tumbleweed 53. Ride Clear of Diablo 54. Drums Across the River 54. *Destry* 55. *To Hell and Back* (based on his autobiography) 55. The World in My Corner 56. Walk the Proud Land 56. The Guns of Fort Petticoat 57. Joe Butterfly 57. Night Passage 57. *The Quiet American* 58. Ride a Crooked Trail 58. The Gun Runners 58. No Name on the Bullet 59. The Wild and the Innocent 59. Cast a Long Shadow 59. Hell Bent for Leather 60. The Unforgiven 60. Seven Ways from Sundown 60. Posse from Hell 61. The Battle at Bloody Beach 61. Six Black Horses 62. Showdown 63. Gunfight at Comanche Creek 63. The Quick Gun 64. Bullet for a Badman 64. Apache Rifles 64. Arizona Raiders 65. Gunpoint 66. Trunk to Cairo 66. The Texican 66. Forty Guns to Apache Pass 67.
TV series: Whispering Smith 61.

Murphy, Ben (1941–). Athletic American TV hero of *Alias Smith and Jones, Griff, Gemini Man*, etc.
Sidecar Racers 75, etc.

Murphy, George (1902–). Amiable Irish-American actor and dancer, a pleasant light talent who left the screen for politics and became senator for California. Special Academy Award 1940 'for interpreting the film industry to the nation at large'.
Autobiography 1970: *Say, Didn't You Use to be George Murphy?*
Kid Millions 34. After the Dance 35. Woman Trap 36. London by Night 37. You're a Sweetheart 37. Little Miss Broadway 38. Hold that Co-Ed 38. Risky Business 39. Broadway Melody of 1940. *Little Nellie Kelly* 40. Ringside Maisie 41. *Tom Dick and Harry* 41. Rise and Shine 41. For Me and My Gal 41. The Navy Comes Through 42. The Powers Girl 42. Bataan 43. This is the Army 43. Broadway Rhythm 44. *Show Business* 44. *Step Lively* 44. Having Wonderful Crime 44. Up Goes Maisie 46. The Arnelo Affair 47. Tenth Avenue Angel 48. The Big City 48. Border Incident 49. Battleground 49. No Questions Asked 51. It's a Big Country 51. Walk East on Beacon 52. Talk About a Stranger 52, etc.

Murphy, Mary (1931–). American leading lady.
The Lemon Drop Kid (debut) 51. The Wild One 54. Beachhead 54. Hell's Island 55. The Desperate Hours 55. The Intimate Stranger (GB) 56. Crime and Punishment USA 59. Forty Pounds of Trouble 63. Junior Bonner 72, etc.

Murphy, Ralph (1895–1967). American director, in Hollywood from silent days.
The Gay City 41. Hearts in Springtime 41. Mrs Wiggs of the Cabbage Patch 42. Rainbow Island 44. The Man in Half Moon Street 44. Red Stallion in the Rockies 49. Dick Turpin's Ride 51. Captain Blood, Fugitive 52. Desert Rats 53. The Lady in the Iron Mask 53. Three Stripes in the Sun (& w) 55, etc.

Murphy, Richard (1912–). American writer, in Hollywood from 1937.
Boomerang 47. Cry of the City 48. Panic in the Streets 50. Les Misérables 52. Broken Lance 54. Compulsion 58. The Wackiest Ship in the Army (& d) 60, etc.

Murphy, Rosemary (1925–). American stage actress in occasional films.
☐ The Young Doctors 61. Any Wednesday 66. Ben 72. You'll Like My Mother 72. Walking Tall 73. Forty Carats 73. Ace Eli and Rodgers of the Skies 73.

Murray, Barbara (1929–). British leading lady with stage experience.
Anna Karenina 48. Passport to Pimlico 48. Doctor at Large 56. Campbell's Kingdom 58. A Cry from the Streets 58. Girls in Arms 60, many others.

Murray, Charlie (1872–1941). American vaudeville comedian long with Mack Sennett. In *Tillie's Punctured Romance* 15, and later played with George Sidney in a long series about the Cohens and Kellys.

Murray, Don (1929–). Ambitious American actor who graduated from innocent to tough roles but does not seem to have received the attention he sought and merited.
☐ *Bus Stop* 56. *The Bachelor Party* 57. A Hatful of Rain 57. From Hell to Texas 58. These Thousand Hills 59. Shake Hands with the Devil 59. One Foot in Hell 60. *The Hoodlum Priest* (& co-p) 61. *Advise and Consent* 62. Escape from East Berlin 62. One Man's Way 64. Baby the Rain Must Fall 65. Kid Rodelo 66. The Plainsman 66. Sweet Love, Bitter 67. The Viking Queen 67. Tale of the Cock 67. Childish Things (& wp) 70. The Intruders (TV) 70. Conquest of the Planet of the Apes 72. Happy Birthday Wanda Jane 72. The Girl on the Late Late Show (TV) 75. Deadly Hero 76.
TV series: *The Outcasts* 68.

Murray, James (1901–1936). American leading man, a former extra who was chosen by King Vidor to play the hero of *The Crowd* 28, but subsequently took to drink and died in obscurity.
The Big City 28. Thunder 29. Bright Lights 30. The Reckoning 32. Heroes for Sale 32. Skull and Crown 35, etc.

Murray, Ken (1903–) (Don Court). American comedy actor, radio and TV entertainer, especially as collector of old 'home movies' of the stars. Collected special Oscar for his 1947 bird fantasy *Bill and Coo*.
Autobiography 1960: *Life on a Pogo Stick*.
Half Marriage 29. A Night at Earl Carroll's 41. Follow Me Boys 66.

Murray, Mae (1889–1965) (Marie Adrienne Koenig). American leading lady of the silent screen; former dancer; usually in flashy roles. Retired to marry.
Biography 1959: *The Self-Enchanted* by Jane Ardmore.
Sweet Kitty Bellairs 17. Her Body in Bond 18. The Mormon Maid 20. Jazz Mania 21. Fashion Row 23. The Merry Widow 25. Circe the Enchantress 27. Peacock Alley 31, etc.

Murray, Stephen (1912–). British character actor, on stage from 1933.
The Prime Minister 41. *Next of Kin* 42. Undercover 43. *Master of Bankdam* 46. *London Belongs to Me* 48. The Magnet 50. Four-Sided Triangle 53. Guilty 55. A Tale of Two Cities 57. The Nun's Story 59, etc.

Murray-Hill, Peter (1908–1957). British leading man of stage and screen; was married to Phyllis Calvert.
A Yank at Oxford 38. The Outsider 39. Jane Steps Out 40. The Ghost Train 41. Madonna of the Seven Moons 44. They Were Sisters (last film) 45, etc.

Murton, Lionel (1915–). Canadian character actor resident in Britain.
Meet the Navy 46. The Long Dark Hall 51. The Runaway Bus 54. The Battle of the River Plate 55. Up the Creek 58. Northwest Frontier 59, many others.

Musante, Tony (1941–). American character actor.
Once a Thief 65. The Detective 68. The Bird with

the Crystal Plumage 70. The Grissom Gang 71.
The Last Run 71, etc.
TV series: *Toma* 73.

Muse, Clarence (1889–). Black American
character actor.
Hearts in Dixie 28. Cabin in the Cotton 32.
Showboat 36. Tales of Manhattan 42. An Act of
Murder 48. So Bright the Flame 52, many others.

musical remakes are becoming thicker on the
ground than musical originals. All the following
had been filmed at least once before, as straight
dramas or comedies with music:
Where's Charley? as *Charley's Aunt*; *Three for
the Show* as *My Two Husbands*; *Living It Up* as
Nothing Sacred; *Carmen Jones* as *Carmen*;
Scrooge as *A Christmas Carol*; *Step Lively* as
Room Service; *In the Good Old Summertime* as
The Shop Around The Corner; *Meet Me After
The Show* as *He Married His Wife*; *Annie Get
Your Gun* as *Annie Oakley*; *Kismet* as *Kismet*;
The King and I as *Anna and the King of Siam*;
Carousel as *Liliom*; *High Society* as *The
Philadelphia Story*; *Silk Stockings* as
Ninotchka; *Gigi* as *Gigi*; *My Fair Lady* as
Pygmalion; *The Sound of Music* as *The Trapp
Family*; *Funny Girl* as *Rose of Washington
Square*; *Sweet Charity* as *Nights of Cabiria*;
Camelot as *Lancelot and Guinevere*; *Oliver!* as
Oliver Twist; *Hello Dolly* as *The Matchmaker*;
Cabaret as *I Am a Camera*; *Fiddler on the Roof*
as *Tevye the Milkman*; *Mame* as *Auntie Mame*;
Lost Horizon as *Lost Horizon*; *Goodbye Mr
Chips* as *Goodbye Mr Chips*. *A Star Is Born* as
What Price Hollywood?

musicals obviously could not exist before Al
Jolson sang 'Mammy', in 1927. During the first
two or three years of talkies, however,
Hollywood produced so many gaudy back-stage
stories and all-star spectacles that the genre
quickly wore out its welcome: *Broadway
Melody, The Singing Fool, The Desert Song,
Showboat, Chasing Rainbows, Show of Shows,
Hollywood Revue, Lights of New York, On with
the Show, King of Jazz, Gold Diggers of
Broadway, Sunny Side Up* ... all these before
the end of 1930, and there were many poorer
imitations. Discipline was needed, and the
disciplinarian who emerged was Broadway
dance director Busby Berkeley. His
kaleidoscopic ensembles first dazzled the eye in
Goldwyn-Cantor extravaganzas like *Whoopee*
and *Palmy Days*, and came to full flower in the
Warner musicals which brought to the fore stars
like Joan Blondell, Ruby Keeler and Dick
Powell, filling the years from 1933 to 1937 with
such shows as *Footlight Parade, Forty-Second*

Street, Dames, Wonder Bar, Flirtation Walk
and the annual *Gold Digger* comedies.
Meanwhile at Paramount Lubitsch had been
quietly establishing a quieter style, using
recitative, with *The Love Parade* and *One Hour
with You*; Mamoulian was equally successful
with *Love Me Tonight*; and the Marx Brothers
contributed their own brand of musical anarchy.
From 1933 to 1939 at RKO Fred Astaire and
Ginger Rogers were teamed in an affectionately-
remembered series of light comedy-musicals.
MGM made sporadic efforts with creaky
vehicles like *Cuban Love Song* but did not come
into their own until 1935, when they started the
Jeanette MacDonald/Nelson Eddy series of
operettas; these were followed by a dramatic
musical, *The Great Ziegfeld*, by the Eleanor
Powell spectaculars like *Rosalie*, by a revived
Broadway Melody series, and by *The Wizard of
Oz* and the early Judy Garland/Mickey Rooney
teenage extravaganzas, *Babes in Arms* and
Strike Up the Band. Fox had Shirley Temple,
Sonja Henie and Alice Faye; Goldwyn
contributed Cantor and *The Goldwyn Follies*.
Paramount concentrated on Maurice Chevalier,
Bing Crosby and the all-star *Big Broadcast*
series.
   The popularity of musicals continued into the
war-torn forties, when escapism was *de rigueur*.
Universal, whose only major pre-war musical
was *Showboat*, continued to build up Deanna
Durbin and threw in Donald O'Connor and
Gloria Jean for good measure. Warners had *This
Is the Army* and several musical biopics: *Yankee
Doodle Dandy, Night and Day, Rhapsody in
Blue*. RKO had a young man named Sinatra.
Fox found goldmines in Carmen Miranda and
Betty Grable, but their vehicles were routine;
Columbia did slightly better by Rita Hayworth,
and then surprised everyone with *The Jolson
Story*, which set the musical back on top just
when it was flagging. Paramount was doing very
nicely with Bing Crosby and Bob Hope.
Everybody did at least one big morale-building
musical with all the stars on the payroll blowing
kisses to the boys out there: *Star Spangled
Rhythm, Thank Your Lucky Stars, Hollywood
Canteen, Thousands Cheer* and so on.
   Top dog in the forties and fifties was
undoubtedly MGM. Specialities like *Ziegfeld
Follies, Till the Clouds Roll By* and *Words and
Music* came side by side with more routine
productions starring Gene Kelly, Judy Garland,
and Esther Williams (in aqua-musicals, of
course). The decade ended in a blaze of glory
with *On the Town*, which led to the even more
spectacular heights of *An American in Paris* and
Singin' in the Rain. By this time Mario Lanza
and Howard Keel were needing new vehicles for

themselves, *The Great Caruso* and *Seven Brides for Seven Brothers* being outstanding productions in their own right. But by the mid-fifties the demand, or the fashion, for musicals was dying. It lasted longest at Metro, who doggedly remade pictures like *The Belle of New York* and *Rose Marie*, added music to *Ninotchka* and *The Philadelphia Story* and *Gigi*. Warners plugged on until their bright star of 1948, Doris Day, signed with another studio and turned dramatic; Fox had two mammoth tries in *Call Me Madam* and *There's No Business Like Show Business*; Paramount came up with *White Christmas*, the enterprising *Red Garters* and *Funny Face*, and even *Lil' Abner*. But the risk was becoming too great in a chancy market, with expenses growing by the minute; and for the last ten years no original musicals have been written in Hollywood, with the exception of the family-aimed *Mary Poppins, Thoroughly Modern Millie* and the twenty-odd look-alike vehicles of Elvis Presley. Copper-bottomed Broadway hits like *Pal Joey, Oklahoma, Carousel, The Pajama Game, South Pacific, The King and I, West Side Story, Guys and Dolls, Hello Dolly, On a Clear Day You Can See Forever, Fiddler on the Roof, Man of La Mancha, The Sound of Music* and *My Fair Lady* are still filmed, at gargantuan cost, but as cinema they all too often disappoint filmgoers with memories of Berkeley and Kelly and Donen. The most inventive screen musicals have been Bob Fosse's *Sweet Charity* and *Cabaret.*

In Britain, the thirties were a highpoint of the light musical starring such talents as Jack Buchanan, Jessie Matthews, Gracie Fields, George Formby and Anna Neagle; Miss Neagle indeed carried on, dauntless, into the less favourable climate of the fifties. The forties were pretty barren apart from the Rank spectacular *London Town*, which flopped; and it wasn't until the sixties that Elstree struck something like the right note with its energetic though derivative series starring Cliff Richard. In 1968 the old-fashioned though energetic *Oliver!* proved that Britain can handle a really big musical. The seventies brought little but rock operas and one or two curiously old-fashioned stagings of such as *Mame* and *1776.*

Books: *Gotta Sing Gotta Dance* by John Kobal; *The Hollywood Musical* by John Russell Taylor; *All Talking, All Singing, All Dancing* by John Springer.

See also: *entertainers.*

The Musketeers of Pig Alley (US 1912). A D. W. Griffith melodrama starring Lillian Gish, often quoted as the screen's first step towards social realism; set in the teeming slums of New York.

Mustin, Burt (1884–1977). American comedy character actor who was 67 when he made his first film.
Detective Story 51. The Lusty Men 53. The Desperate Hours 55. The Big Country 57. Huckleberry Finn 61. The Thrill of It All 63. Cat Ballou 65. Speedway 68. Hail Hero 70. The Skin Game 71, etc.
TV series: Phyllis 76.

Musuraca, Nicholas (c. 1900–). American cinematographer.
Bride of the Storm 24. Lightning Lanats 25. Tyrant of Red Gulch 27. The Cuckoos 31. Cracked Nuts 33. Long Lost Father 34. Murder on a Bridle Path 36. Blind Alibi 38. Five Came Back 39. Golden Boy 39. The Swiss Family Robinson 40. Tom Brown's Schooldays 40. *Cat People* 42. The Seventh Victim 43. Curse of the Cat People 44. *The Spiral Staircase* 45. The Locket 46. The Bachelor and the Bobbysoxer 47. *Out of the Past* 47. Blood on the Moon 48. Where Danger Lives 51. Clash by Night 52. Devil's Canyon 53. The Story of Mankind 57. Too Much Too Soon 58, many others.

mute print. One with only the picture, no sound track.

Mutiny on the Bounty. Two films have been made of this semi-historical account of how Captain Bligh was cast adrift in an open boat in 1789. 1. US 1935 (AA): directed by Frank Lloyd, with Clark Gable and Charles Laughton. 2. US 1962: directed by Carol Reed (who resigned) and Lewis Milestone, with Marlon Brando and Trevor Howard. The first remains the most impressive despite its technical limitations.

Muybridge, Edward or **Eadweard** (1830–1904). British photographer who in 1877, in America, succeeded in analysing motion with a camera by taking a series of pictures of a horse in motion. (He used twenty-four cameras attached to a trip wire.) Later he invented a form of projector which reassembled his pictures into the appearance of moving actuality.

My Darling Clementine (US 1946). A highly atmospheric, semi-literary western based (remotely) on Stuart N. Lake's book *Wyatt Earp Frontier Marshal* which had been previously filmed as *Frontier Marshal* with Randolph Scott in 1939. Excellent performances by Henry Fonda as Earp, Victor Mature as Doc Holliday, and Walter Brennan as the head of the Clantons who get shot up in the OK corral. John Ford directs affectionately. *Gunfight at the OK Corral*

57, with Burt Lancaster and Kirk Douglas, is a partial remake.

My Fair Lady (US 1964) (AA, BFA). A professional but uninspired celluloid version of the fabulous Lerner-Loewe musical play from Shaw's *Pygmalion* (qv). A prodigious expenditure of talent, and to a lesser degree money, is evident, and there is plenty to enjoy; but more might have been packed into the most eagerly anticipated musical of the decade. With Audrey Hepburn, Rex Harrison (AA), Stanley Holloway; directed by George Cukor (AA); designed by Cecil Beaton (AA); photographed by Harry Stradling (AA). A special word is surely due for Marni Nixon, whose singing voice Audrey Hepburn mimes.

My Girl Tisa (US 1947). A charming, neglected, period romance set in New York's immigrant quarter at the turn of the century, with special reference to the political scene and an amusing if unlikely ending with Teddy Roosevelt as *deus ex machina*. Delightfully played by Lilli Palmer, Sam Wanamaker, Alan Hale, Stella Adler and a large cast; written by Allen Boretz, photographed by Ernest Haller, directed by Elliott Nugent.

My Little Chickadee (US 1940). An outlandish comedy-western starring, and written by, W. C. Fields and Mae West, the former as Cuthbert J. Twillie, the latter as Flower Belle Lee. Edward Cline was faced with the task of directing these strange personalities, and didn't quite manage it; the result is one of those engaging Hollywood freaks which no one can afford to have happen any more.

My Man Godfrey. Twice-filmed crazy comedy about a family of bored millionaires brought to heel by a butler they pick up in the gutter. 1936: directed by Gregory La Cava, with William Powell and Carole Lombard. 1957: directed by Henry Koster, with David Niven and June Allyson.

My Sister Eileen. Another twice-filmed comedy, from the book by Ruth McKinney about two sisters on the hunt for fame and men in New York. 1942: directed by Alexander Hall, with Rosalind Russell and Janet Blair. 1955: a semi-musical directed by Richard Quine, with Betty Garrett and Janet Leigh. There has also been a TV series with Elaine Stritch and Shirley Bonne. The men in the case were (1) Brian Aherne, (2) Jack Lemmon, (3) Jack Weston (later replaced by Stubby Kaye).

Mycroft, Walter (1891–1959). British director. Chief scriptwriter and director of productions at Elstree in the thirties.
Spring Meeting 40. My Wife's Family 41. Banana Ridge 41. The Woman's Angle (p only) 52, etc.

Myers, Carmel (1901–). American leading lady of the twenties, in the 'vamp' tradition.
Sirens of the Sea 16. The Famous Mrs Fair 23. Beau Brummell 24. Ben Hur 25. Sorrell and Son 27. Svengali 31. Lady for a Night 42, etc.

mystery has always been a popular element of motion picture entertainment. Always providing scope for sinister goings-on and sudden revelations, mystery films divide themselves into two basic genres: who done it, and how will the hero get out of it? Silent melodramas like *The Perils of Pauline* were full of clutching hands and villainous masterminds, devices adopted by the German post-war cinema for its own purposes: *The Cabinet of Dr Caligari, Dr Mabuse* and *Warning Shadows* are all mysteries, peopled by eccentrics and madmen. American silent who-done-its like *The Cat and the Canary, The Thirteenth Chair* and *One Exciting Night* set a pattern for thrillers which could not come fully into their own until music and sound were added. In the thirties the 'thunderstorm mystery', with its spooky house and mysterious servants (the butler usually did it) quickly became a cliché; but this is not to denigrate the entertainment value of such movies as *The Bat, The Terror, Murder by the Clock, The Gorilla, Seven Keys to Baldpate, Double Door, You'll Find Out, Topper Returns, The House on Haunted Hill,* and the Bob Hope remakes of *The Cat and the Canary* and *The Ghost Breakers.*

The thirties also saw a movement to relegate the puzzle film to the detective series, a genre later taken over eagerly by TV. These films were built around such protagonists as Charlie Chan, Sherlock Homes, Hercule Poirot, Inspector Hanaud, Ellery Queen, Perry Mason, Inspector Hornleigh, Nero Wolfe, Philo Vance, Nick Carter, The Crime Doctor, The Saint, The Falcon, Bulldog Drummond, Mrs Pym, the 'Thin Man' (the thin man was actually the victim of the first story, but the tag stuck to William Powell), Mr Moto, Michael Shayne, Hildegarde Withers, Mr Wong, Arsène Lupin, Dick Barton, The Baron, The Toff, Gideon, Slim Callaghan, Lemmy Caution and Maigret ... all soundly spoofed by Groucho Marx as Wolf J. Flywheel in *The Big Store.* The best of these fictional detectives were the creations of Dashiell Hammett (Sam Spade in *The Maltese Falcon*) and Raymond Chandler (Philip Marlowe in *The*

Big Sleep, Farewell My Lovely and *The High Window*); and after a twenty-year hiatus the threads were picked up by Ross Macdonald's *Harper*, Craig Stevens as *Gunn*, Frank Sinatra as *Tony Rome*, films of Chandler's *Marlowe* and J. D. Macdonald's *Darker Than Amber*, and Richard Roundtree as *Shaft*. Single who-doneits of great merit were *Gaslight, Laura, Green for Danger* (one ached for a whole series starring Alastair Sim as Inspector Cockrill), *The Spiral Staircase, Crossfire, Boomerang, Bad Day at Black Rock, Les Diaboliques, Charade, Mirage, Taste of Fear, The List of Adrian Messenger*, and the two verisons of *Ten Little Niggers*. Two gentler detectives were provided by Alec Guinness' *Father Brown* and Margaret Rutherford's Miss Marple.

The other type of mystery, with a hero on the run, usually suspected of murder, finally uncovering the real villain after many narrow escapes from death, was developed by Alfred Hitchcock in such films as *The Thirty-Nine Steps, The Lady Vanishes, Saboteur, Spellbound, Strangers on a Train, North by Northwest* and *Torn Curtain*. But stars as various as Alan Ladd, Bob Hope, Danny Kaye, Robert Mitchum, and Paul Newman have also found the device useful.

The recent vogue for tongue -in-cheek spy thrillers is to all intents and purposes a reversion to the Pearl White school, with the hero menaced at every turn but, of course, finally triumphant.

See also: *spies*; *private eyes*.

The Mystery of the Wax Museum (US 1933). A badly-structured but interesting shocker in two-colour Technicolor, with sets by Anton Grot and direction by Michael Curtiz. Thought for years to be a lost film, it survives as a milestone of its era, with Glenda Farrell and Frank McHugh as wisecracking news hawks, Fay Wray as a frightened lady and Lionel Atwill as a mad sculptor who uses a wax face to disguise his hideously burned features. In 1953 the story was remade in 3-D as *House of Wax*, and in 1966 most of it turned up again in *Chamber of Horrors*.

N

Nader, George (1921–). American leading man who after TV experience starred in many Universal action films of the fifties but has lately been less active.

Monsoon (debut) 52. Four Guns to the Border 54. The Second Greatest Sex 55. Away All Boats 56. Congo Crossing 56. Four Girls in Town 57. Joe Butterfly 57. Nowhere to Go (GB) 58. The Human Duplicators 65. The Million Eyes of Su-Muru 66, etc.

TV series: Ellery Queen 56. The Man and the Challenge 59. Shannon 61.

Nagel, Anne (1912–1966) (Anne Dolan). American supporting actress, the heroine's friend in countless movies of the forties.

Hot Money 36. Black Friday 40. Man Made Monster 41. Women in Bondage 44. Spirit of West Point 47, etc.

Nagel, Conrad (1896–1970). American leading man of the twenties who came to Hollywood after stage experience; latterly ran acting school.

Little Women 19. Fighting Chance 20. Three Weeks 24. The Exquisite Sinner 26. Slightly Used 27. Quality Street 27. One Romantic Night 30. Bad Sister 31. East Lynne 31. Dangerous Corner 34. Navy Spy 37. I Want a Divorce 40. The Woman in Brown 48. All That Heaven Allows 55. Stranger in My Arms 58. The Man Who Understood Women 59, many others.

Naish, J. Carrol (1900–1973). American character actor with stage experience, in films from 1930.

The Hatchet Man 32. Lives of a Bengal Lancer 35. Anthony Adverse 36. *Beau Geste* 39. Birth of the Blues 41. Blood and Sand 41. The Corsican Brothers 41. The Pied Piper 42. Dr Renault's Secret 42. Batman (serial) 43. Behind the Rising Sun 43. Gung Ho! 44. *A Medal for Benny* 45. House of Frankenstein 45. The Southerner 45. Enter Arsène Lupin 45. The Beast with Five Fingers 46. Joan of Arc 48. Black Hand 49. Annie Get Your Gun 50. Across the Wide Missouri 51. Sitting Bull 54. Violent Saturday 54. New York Confidential 54. The Young Don't Cry 57. The Hanged Man 64. Blood of

Frankenstein 70, many others.

TV series: Life With Luigi 54. The New Adventures of Charlie Chan 57. Guestward Ho! 60.

Naismith, Laurence (1908–) (Lawrence Johnson). Amiable British character actor with wide stage experience.

Trouble in the Air 47. A Piece of Cake 48. I Believe in You 51. The Beggar's Opera 52. Mogambo 53. Carrington VC 55. *Richard III* 56. Boy on a Dolphin 57. Tempest 58. A Night to Remember 58. Sink the Bismarck 60. The Singer Not the Song 61. Jason and the Argonauts 63. The Three Lives of Thomasina 63. Sky West and Crooked 65. The Scorpio Letters 67. The Long Duel 67. Fitzwilly 67. *Camelot* 67. The Valley of Gwangi 68. Eye of the Cat 69. Scrooge 70. Diamonds are Forever 71. *The Amazing Mr Blunden* 72.

TV series: *The Persuaders* 71.

Naked City (US 1948). Mark Hellinger's last production was a highly influential police thriller shot on location in New York and using a development of the semi-documentary approach first seen in such films as *The House on 92nd Street* two years earlier. It ended with the famous tag used in all 99 episodes of the TV series which followed twelve years later: 'There are eight million stories in the naked city: this has been one of them.' Barry Fitzgerald played the leading cop and Don Taylor his aide; Jules Dassin directed, enlivening a basically routine story with striking detail; the script was by Albert Maltz and Marvin Wald with photography by William Daniels (AA). Despite hundreds of imitations the 'authentic' crime thriller is still popular.

Naldi, Nita (1899–1961) (Anita Donna Dooley). Italian-American leading lady of the twenties, formerly in the Ziegfeld Follies.

Dr Jekyll and Mr Hyde 20. The Unfair Sex 22. Blood and Sand 22. The Ten Commandments 23. Cobra 25. A Sainted Devil 25. The Marriage Whirl 26. The Lady Who Lied 27, etc.

Namath, Joe (–). American professional sportsman who made a few films.

Norwood 69. C. C. and Company 70.

Nana. Zola's novel of the Paris demimonde in the eighties has been seen in four major film versions. 1. Jean Renoir directed a silent French version in 1926, with Catherine Hessling and Werner Krass. 2. Dorothy Arzner directed an American version, sometimes known as *Lady of the Boulevards*, in 1934 with Anna Sten, Lionel Atwill and Phillips Holmes. 3. Christian-Jaque directed a second French version in 1955, this time in colour, with Martine Carol and Charles Boyer. 4. Mac Ahlberg directed a Franco-Swedish 1970 version called *Take Me, Love Me*, with Anna Gael.

Nancy Drew. The teenage heroine of a number of American second features made in 1938–39; all were directed by William Clemens and starred Bonita Granville. The titles included *Nancy Drew Detective, Nancy Drew Reporter, Nancy Drew and the Hidden Staircase, Nancy Drew Trouble Shooter.* A TV series followed in 1977.

Nanook of the North (US 1921). This classic documentary was made by explorer-director Robert Flaherty, who was commissioned by Revillon Frères, a fur company, and spent years in the Arctic among the Eskimos while amassing his material. It is virtually the first significant documentary in the history of the cinema, and even today remains watchable.

Napier, Alan (1903–) (Alan Napier-Clavering). Dignified British character actor, in Hollywood since 1940; usually plays butlers or noble lords.
In a Monastery Garden 31. Loyalties 32. For Valour 37. The Four Just Men 39. The Invisible Man Returns 40. Random Harvest 42. Ministry of Fear 43. Lost Angel 44. Forever Amber 47. Tarzan's Magic Fountain 50. Julius Caesar 53. The Court Jester 55. Journey to the Centre of the Earth 59. Marnie 64, scores of others.
TV series: Batman 65–67.

Napier, Diana (1908–) (Molly Ellis). British leading lady of the thirties; married Richard Tauber.
Wedding Rehearsal 33. Catherine the Great 34. The Private Life of Don Juan 34. Mimi 35. Land Without Music 36. Pagliacci 37, then retired until *I was a Dancer* 48.

Napier, Russell (1910–1974). Australian-born actor, long in Britain. Appeared in numerous small parts, usually as officials; also played the chief inspector in many of the 3-reel 'Scotland Yard' series.

Napoleon, Art (1923–). American director.

Man on the Prowl (& w) 57. Too Much Too Soon 58. Ride the Wild Surf (w only) 64.

Napoleon Bonaparte has been impersonated on screen by Charles Boyer in *Marie Walewska* (*Conquest*), Esmé Percy in *Invitation to the Waltz*, Emile Drain in *Madame sans Gêne* and *Les Perles de la Couronne*, Rollo Lloyd in *Anthony Adverse*, Julien Berthau in *Madame*, Marlon Brando in *Désirée*, Arnold Moss in *The Black Book*, Pierre Mondy in *Austerlitz*, Herbert Lom in several films including *The Young Mr Pitt* and *War and Peace*, Eli Wallach in *The Adventures of Gerard*, and Rod Steiger in *Waterloo*, and Kenneth Haigh in *Eagle in a Cage*.
Abel Gance's 1925 film *Napoleon* (with Albert Dieudonne) is noted for the first use of a triptych screen corresponding very closely to Cinerama.

Nardini, Tom (1945–). Young American character actor.
Cat Ballou 65. Africa Texas Style 67. The Young Animals 68, etc.
TV series: Cowboy in Africa 68.

Nares, Owen (1888–1943) (O. N. Ramsay). British matinée idol and silent screen star.
Dandy Donovan 14. God Bless the Red, White and Blue 18. Indian Love Lyrics 23. Young Lochinvar 23. The Sorrows of Satan 27. Milestones 28. The Middle Watch 30. Sunshine Susie 31. The Impassive Footman 32. The Private Life of Don Juan 34. The Show Goes On 37. The Prime Minister 41, etc.

Narizzano, Silvio (c. 1927–). Canadian director in Britain, from TV.
□ Under Ten Flags (co-d) 60. Fanatic 65. *Georgy Girl* 66. Blue (US) 67. Loot 70.

narrators are heard at the beginning of many important movies. Well-known actors are normally used, but sometimes take no credit. Here is a selected checklist to silence nagging doubts.
The Big Knife: Richard Boone.
Dragon Seed: Lionel Barrymore.
Duel in the Sun: Orson Welles.
The Hallelujah Trail: John Dehner.
How the West was Won: Spencer Tracy.
It's a Big Country: Louis Calhern.
King of Kings: Orson Welles.
A Letter to 3 Wives: Celeste Holm.
Mackenna's Gold: Victor Jory.
Mother Wore Tights: Anne Baxter.
The Mummy's Shroud: Peter Cushing.
The Night They Raided Minsky's: Rudy Vallee.
The Picture of Dorian Gray: Cedric Hardwicke.

Quo Vadis: Walter Pidgeon.
The Red Badge of Courage: James Whitmore.
The Secret Heart: Hume Cronyn.
The Solid Gold Cadillac: George Burns.
The Swiss Family Robinson: Orson Welles.
Those Magnificent Men in Their Flying Machines: James Robertson Justice.
To Kill a Mockingbird: Kim Stanley.
Tom Jones: Micheal MacLiammoir.
The Unseen: Ray Collins.
The Vikings: Orson Welles.
The Wild Heart: Joseph Cotten.
The War of the Worlds: Cedric Hardwicke.
Zulu: Richard Burton.

Nascimbene, Mario (1916–). Italian composer.
OK Nero 51. The Barefoot Contessa 54. Alexander the Great 55. A Farewell to Arms 57. The Vikings 58. Room at the Top 58. Solomon and Sheba 59. Sons and Lovers 60. Barabbas 61. Jessica 62. One Million Years BC 66. Dr Faustus 67. When Dinosaurs Ruled the Earth 70, many others.

Nash, Mary (1885–1976). American stage actress.
Come and Get It 36. Heidi 37. *The Philadelphia Story* 40. The Human Comedy 43. Cobra Woman 44. Monsieur Beaucaire 46, etc.

National Film Archive. A government-financed museum of films of artistic and historical value. Operated by the British Film Institute.

The National Film Board of Canada was set up in 1939, with John Grierson at its head, to show Canada's face to the world. Many excellent documentaries ensued, not to mention the brilliant animation films of Norman McLaren, but by the end of the sixties the Board's fortunes were at a lower ebb.

The National Film Finance Corporation was founded in 1949 to provide loans for film production, but began to withdraw its facilities in the early seventies, at a time when financial encouragement had never been more needed for British production.

The National Film Theatre on London's South Bank is an extension of the British Film Institute; founded in 1951, it runs a daily repertory in two theatres of films of all nationalities and types.

Natwick, Mildred (1908–). American character actress, at her best in eccentric roles.

☐ The Long Voyage Home 40. The Enchanted Cottage 45. Yolanda and the Thief 45. The Late George Apley 47. A Woman's Vengeance 47. Three Godfathers 48. The Kissing Bandit 40. She Wore a Yellow Ribbon 49. Cheaper by the Dozen 50. The Quiet Man 52. Against All Flags 52. *The Trouble With Harry* 55. *The Court Jester* 56. Teenage Rebel 56. Tammy and the Bachelor 57. *Barefoot in the Park* 67. If It's Tuesday This Must be Belgium 69. The Maltese Bippy 69. Do Not Fold Spindle or Mutilate (TV) 71. The Snoop Sisters (TV) 72. Daisy Miller 74. At Long Last Love 75.

Naughton, Charles: see *The Crazy Gang.*

naval comedy in British movies usually has a thirties look about it, may well be written by Ian Hay, and almost always concerns the officers; as in *The Middle Watch, Carry on Admiral, The Midshipmaid, The Flag Lieutenant* and *Up the Creek* (though the other ranks had their look in with *The Bulldog Breed, The Baby and the Battleship* and *Jack Ahoy*). In Hollywood movies the focus of interest is set firmly among the other ranks: *Follow the Fleet, Abbott and Costello in the Navy, Anchors Aweigh, Operation Petticoat, Mr Roberts, South Pacific, Ensign Pulver, On the Town, You're in the Navy Now, The Fleet's In, Onion-head, Don't Go near the Water, Don't Give Up the Ship, The Honeymoon Machine.*

The Navigator (US 1924). One of Buster Keaton's classic silent comedies, a succession of brilliant sight gags showing the comedian marooned with a girl at sea on an otherwise empty luxury liner. Written by Clyde Bruckman and Joseph Mitchell; directed by Keaton and Donald Crisp.

Nazarin (Mexico 1959). An arresting and imaginative fantasy about the misadventures of a Roman Catholic priest hounded by the sins of the world. Directed and co-written by Luis Buñuel; with Francisco Rabal.

Nazarro, Ray (–). American director of second features.
The Tougher They Come 50. The Return of the Corsican Brothers 53. Top Gun 55. The Hired Gun 57, etc.; then into TV.

Nazimova, Alla (1879–1945) (Alla Nazimoff). Russian-born stage actress who made a number of films in America.
War Brides 16. Camille 21. A Doll's House 22. Salome 23. Escape 40. The Bridge of San Luis Rey 44, etc.

Nazzari, Amedeo (1907–). Virile Italian leading man, in films since 1935 although few have travelled.
The Wolf of Sila 47. The Brigand 51. Nights of Cabiria 57. Labyrinth 59. The Best of Enemies 61. The Valachi Papers 72, etc.

Neagle, Dame Anna (1904–) (Marjorie Robertson). British leading lady, a former chorus dancer who after her marriage in the thirties to producer Herbert Wilcox built up a formidable film gallery of historical heroines, and when film roles grew hard to find returned successfully to the theatre.
Autobiography 1974: *There's Always Tomorrow*.
□ Should a Doctor Tell? 30. The Chinese Bungalow 31. Goodnight Vienna 32. The Flag Lieutenant 32. The Little Damozel 33. *Bitter Sweet* 33. The Queen's Affair 33. *Nell Gwyn* 34. Peg of Old Drury 35. Limelight 36. The Three Maxims 36. London Melody 37. *Victoria the Great* 37. Sixty Glorious Years 38. *Nurse Edith Cavell* 39. Irene (US) 40. No No Nanette (US) 40. Sunny (US) 41. They Flew Alone (as Amy Johnson) 42. Forever and a Day 43. Yellow Canary 43. I Live in Grosvenor Square 45. *Piccadilly Incident* 46. The Courtneys of Curzon Street 47. *Spring in Park Lane* 48. Elizabeth of Ladymead 49. Maytime in Mayfair 49. *Odette* 50. *The Lady with a Lamp* 51. Derby Day 52. Lilacs in the Spring 55. King's Rhapsody 56. My Teenage Daughter 56. No Time for Tears 57. The Man Who Wouldn't Talk 58. The Lady is a Square 58. In 1958–61 produced three Frankie Vaughan films; returned to stage.

Neal, Patricia (1926–). American leading actress who handled some interesting roles before illness caused her semi-retirement.
□ John Loves Mary 49. *The Fountainhead* 49. It's a Great Feeling 49. *The Hasty Heart* (GB) 50. Bright Leaf 50. Three Secrets 50. The Breaking Point 50. Operation Pacific 51. Raton Pass 51. Diplomatic Courier 51. The Day the Earth Stood Still 51. Weekend with Father 51. Washington Story 52. Something for the Birds 52. Stranger from Venus (GB) 54. *A Face in the Crowd* 57. Breakfast at Tiffany's 61. *Hud* (AA, BFA) 63. Psyche 59 (GB) 64. In Harm's Way (BFA) 64. The Subject was Roses 68. The Homecoming (TV) 71. The Night Digger 71. Happy Mother's Day Love George 73. Things in Their Season (TV) 75.

Neal, Tom (1914–1972). American leading man, mainly in second features; former athlete.
Out West with the Hardys 39. One Thrilling Night 42. The Racket Man 45. Detour 47. Navy Bound 51. Red Desert 54, etc.

Neame, Ronald (1911–). Outstanding British cinematographer who became a rather disappointing director.
SELECTED FILMS AS CINEMA-TOGRAPHER: Drake of England 34. The Gaunt Stranger 37. The Crimes of Stephen Hawke 39. Major Barbara 40. In Which We Serve 42. Blithe Spirit 45.
□AS DIRECTOR: Take My Life 47. The Golden Salamander 50. *The Card* (& p) 52. The Million Pound Note 53. The Man Who Never Was 56. Windom's Way 58. The Horse's Mouth 59. *Tunes of Glory* 60. I Could Go On Singing 62. The Chalk Garden 64. Mister Moses 65. A Man Could Get Killed (co-d) 66. Gambit 66. The Prime of Miss Jean Brodie 68. The Poseidon Adventure 72.

Nebenzal, Seymour (1899–1961). Distinguished German producer who had a disappointing career after going to Hollywood in the late thirties.
Westfront 30. M 31. Kameradschaft 32. The Testament of Dr Mabuse 33. Mayerling 36. We Who are Young 40. Summer Storm 44. Whistle Stop 46. Heaven Only Knows 47. Siren of Atlantis 48. M (remake) 51, etc.

Nedell, Bernard (1898–1972). American character actor.
The Serpent 16. The Return of the Rat (GB) 29. Shadows (GB) 31. Lazybones (GB) 35. The Man Who could Work Miracles (GB) 36. Mr Moto's Gamble 38. Angels Wash Their Faces 39. Strange Cargo 40. The Desperadoes 43. One Body Too Many 44. Monsieur Verdoux 47. The Loves of Carmen 48. Heller in Pink Tights 60. Hickey and Boggs 72, many others.

Neff, Hildegarde (1925–) (Hildegarde Knef). German leading lady, former artist and film cartoonist. Briefly on German stage, then to films, and for a time in Hollywood.
Autobiography 1971: *The Gift Horse*.
The Murderers are Amongst Us 46. *Film without Title* 47. The Sinner 50. Decision before Dawn 51. *The Snows of Kilimanjaro* 52. Diplomatic Courier 52. Henriette 52. The Man Between 53. The Girl from Hamburg 57. And So to Bed 63. Landru 63. Mozambique 65. The Lost Continent (GB) 68, etc.

Negri, Pola (1897–) (Appolonia Chalupek). Polish-born leading lady with experience on German stage and screen; went to Hollywood in twenties and was popular until sound came in.
Autobiography 1970: *Memories of a Star*.
Die Bestie 15. Madame du Barry 18. The Flame 20. Bella Donna (US) 23. *Forbidden Paradise*

24. Hotel Imperial 26. Three Sinners 28. A Woman Commands 31. Madame Bovary 35. Hi Diddle Diddle 43. The Moonspinners 64, etc.

Negroes in films have only slowly attained equal status with whites. In early silents they were invariably depicted as slaves, a fact encouraged by the several popular versions of *Uncle Tom's Cabin*. If a film had a Negro role of consequence, it was usually played by a white man in blackface. But Negroes began to make their own films for their own audiences, and still do, though these seldom get a general showing. The first all-Negro film was *Darktown Jubilee* in 1914 . . . the year that Griffith made *The Birth of a Nation*, with its strong anti-Negro bias. Griffith atoned for this in *The Greatest Thing in Life* 18, in which a white soldier and a Negro embraced, but in 1922 he again incurred the wrath of colour-sensitive critics by making *One Exciting Night*, the first film to boast the quickly stereotyped figure of the terrified Negro manservant. Early talkies included such all-Negro films as *Hearts in Dixie* and Vidor's *Hallelujah*, and in 1933 Paul Robeson appeared in a version of Eugene O'Neill's *The Emperor Jones*. Much of the interest of *Imitation of Life* 34 centred on the problems of Negro servant Louise Beavers and her half-white daughter. In 1936 the screen version of *Green Pastures*, depicting the simple Negro's idea of the Bible, was widely acclaimed but tended to perpetuate a patronizing attitude. The feeling of the South for its Negroes was strongly outlined in *They Won't Forget* 37 and *Gone with the Wind* 39. *Stormy Weather* 42 and *Cabin in the Sky* 43 were all-Negro musicals in Hollywood's best manner, but *Tales of Manhattan* 42 was retrogressive in showing Negroes as inhabitants of a vast shanty town. In *Casablanca* 42, however, Dooley Wilson was accepted on equal terms by Humphrey Bogart. Disney's *Song of the South* 46, despite an engaging performance by James Baskett, brought back the old Uncle Remus image. The post-war period generally permitted the emergence of serious Negro actors like James Edwards and Sidney Poitier, and films on racial themes such as *Intruder in the Dust* and *Pinky*. At last, in 1965, came films in which a Negro could play a straight part utterly unrelated to his colour. Poitier did so in *The Bedford Incident*, then used colour defiantly in *In the Heat of the Night* and *Guess Who's Coming to Dinner*. Remakes of well known 'white' movies were one way to bring in a wide range of coloured actors: *The Lost Man* (*Odd Man Out*), *Uptight* (*The Informer*), *Cool Breeze* (*The Asphalt Jungle*). Even *Barefoot in the Park* became a black TV series, and *Steptoe and Son* in the US became the black *Sanford and Son*. The subject was rather self-consciously aired in such films as *Change of Mind*, *Watermelon Man*, *The Landlord* and *Medium Cool*. In 1970 came *Cotton Goes to Harlem*, perhaps the first black thriller with no chip on its shoulder; in 1972 the seal of approval was set up by *Shaft*, a violent private eye thriller with an all-black cast which proved not only acceptable to all audiences but highly commercial. The floodgates opened and before 1972 was out we even had *Blacula* and *Blackenstein*. Wholly black films which followed included *Sounder*, *The Autobiography of Miss Jane Pittman*, *Uptown Saturday Night*, *Let's Do It Again*; and in 1977 a sensational impact was achieved by a TV serialization of Alex Haley's *Roots*, by watching which half of America sought to atone for a century of bad white behaviour towards the blacks.

Britain, less affected by Negro problems, moved in parallel fashion. In the early thirties, films of *The Kentucky Minstrels*; then Paul Robeson dominating somewhat insulting material in *Sanders of the River* and subsequently earning three or four serious film vehicles of his own; the post-war attempt to understand in *Men of Two Worlds*; and problem pictures like *Simba*, about the Mau-Mau, and *Flame in the Streets*, about the prospect of a Negro in an East End family.

Negulesco, Jean (1900–). Rumanian-born director, in US from 1927.

□ Kiss and Make Up 34. Singapore Woman 41. *The Mask of Dimitrios* 44. The Conspirators 44. Three Strangers 46. Nobody Lives Forever 46. *Humoresque* 46. Deep Valley 47. *Roadhouse* 48. *Johnny Belinda* 48. Britannia Mews 49. Under My Skin 50. *Three Came Home* 50. *The Mudlark* 51. Take Care of My Little Girl 51. Phone Call from a Stranger 52. Lydia Bailey 52. Lure of the Wilderness 52. Full House (part) 52. Titanic 53. *How to Marry a Millionaire* 53. Three Coins in the Fountain 54. Woman's World 54. Daddy Longlegs 55. The Rains of Ranchipur 55. Boy on a Dolphin 57. A Certain Smile 58. The Gift of Love 58. Count Your Blessings 59. The Best of Everything 59. Jessica 62. The Pleasure Seekers 65. The Invincible Six 68. Hello and Goodbye 70.

Neil, Hildegarde (1939–). South African leading lady.
The Man Who Haunted Himself 70. Antony and Cleopatra 71. England Made Me 72, etc.

Neilan, Marshall (1891–1958). American director who had meteoric success in the twenties and just as suddenly failed in the mid-thirties.

Also acted from 1912; last role *A Face in the
Crowd* 57.
The Cycle of Fate 16. Freckles 17. Rebecca of
Sunnybrook Farm 17. M'Liss 18. Daddy
Longlegs 19. The Lotus Eater 21. Tess of the
D'Urbervilles 25. Her Wild Oat 27. Three Ring
Marriage 28. The Awful Truth 29. Sweethearts
on Parade 30. The Lemon Drop Kid 34. Swing
It, Professor 37, many others.

Neill, Roy William (1890–1946) (Roland de
Gostrie). Irish-born director, long in Hollywood;
never rose above low-budget thrillers but often
did them well.
Love Letters 17. Good References 21. Toilers of
the Sea 23. The Good Bad Girl 31. The Black
Room 34. The Good Old Days (GB) 35. Dr Syn
(GB) 37. · Eyes of the Underworld 41.
Frankenstein Meets the Wolf Man 43. Gypsy
Wildcat 44. Black Angel 46, etc.; also produced
and directed most of the *Sherlock Holmes* series
starring Basil Rathbone 42–46.

Neilson, James (1918–). American director,
former war photographer, who has worked
mostly for Walt Disney.
☐ Night Passage 57. The Country Husband
(TV) 58. Moon Pilot 62. Bon Voyage 62.
Summer Magic 63. Dr Syn 63. The Moon
Spinners 63. Return of the Gunfighter (TV) 66.
The Adventures of Bullwhip Griffin 67. The
Gentle Giant 67. Where Angels Go 68. The First
Time 69. Flare Up 69.

Nell Gwyn. Charles II's orange-seller has
appeared briefly in many films, but the two
devoted to her story were both made in Britain by
Herbert Wilcox: in 1927 with Dorothy Gish and
in 1934 with Anna Neagle. Both caused
censorship problems, the latter because of the
lady's cleavage.

Nelson, Barry (1920–) (Robert Neilson).
Stocky American leading man who makes films
between stage shows.
China Caravan 42. A Guy Named Joe 43.
Winged Victory 44. The Beginning of the End
45. The Man with My Face 51. The First
Travelling Saleslady 56. Mary Mary 63. The
Borgia Stick (TV) 68. Airport 69. Pete 'n Tillie
72, others.
TV series: My Favorite Husband 55. Hudson's
Bay 59.

Nelson, Ed (1928–). American actor who
played gangsters, brothers-in-law and boy
friends in innumerable fifties second features,
then went into TV and found himself a secure
niche as Dr Rossi in *Peyton Place* 63–68, and in
The Silent Force 70. Midway 76.

Nelson, Gene (1920–) (Gene Berg).
American actor-dancer, on stage from 1938,
films from 1950.
I Wonder Who's Kissing Her Now 47.
Gentleman's Agreement 48. The Daughter of
Rosie O'Grady 50. Tea for Two 51. Lullaby of
Broadway 52. She's Working Her Way through
College 52. So This is Paris 55. Oklahoma 55.
20,000 Eyes 62. The Purple Hills 63, etc.
☐ AS DIRECTOR: Hand of Death 62.
Hootenanny Hoot 63. Kissin' Cousins 64. Your
Cheatin' Heart 64. Harum Scarum 65. The Cool
Ones 67.

Nelson, Lord Horatio (1758–1805), the hero
of Trafalgar, was portrayed in *Nelson* 19 by
Donald Calthrop; in *Nelson* 26 by Cedric
Hardwicke; in *The Divine Lady* 29 by Victor
Varconi; in *Lady Hamilton* 42 by Laurence
Olivier; in *Lady Hamilton* (Ger.) 68 by Richard
Johnson; and in *Bequest to the Nation* 73 by
Peter Finch.

Nelson, Lori (1933–). American light leading
lady of the fifties.
Ma and Pa Kettle at the Fair 52. Bend of the
River 52. Walking My Baby Back Home 53.
Destry 55. Mohawk 56. Hot Rod Girl 56. The
Day the World Ended 56, etc.

Nelson, Ozzie (1906–1975). American
bandleader whose genial, diffident personality
became familiar in long-running domestic
comedy series on TV.
Sweetheart of the Campus 41. Hi Good Lookin'
44. People are Funny 45. Here Come the
Nelsons 52. Love and Kisses (& wpd) 65. The
Impossible Years 68, etc.
TV series: *Ozzie and Harriet* 52–65. Ozzie's
Girls 73– .

Nelson, Ralph (1916–). American director.
☐ Requiem for a Heavyweight 62. *Lilies of the
Field* 63. Soldier in the Rain 64. Fate is the
Hunter 64. Father Goose 64. Once a Thief 65.
Duel at Diablo 66. Counterpoint 67. Charly 68.
Tick Tick Tick 70. Soldier Blue 70. Flight of the
Doves 71. The Wrath of God 72. The Wilby
Conspiracy 75. Embryo 76.

Nelson, Rick (1940–). American singer and
light actor, son of bandleader Ozzie Nelson and
his wife Harriet (formerly Harriet Hilliard: qv)
with whom he appeared in the long-running TV
series *The Adventures of Ozzie and Harriet*
54–64. Films on his own include:
Here Come the Nelsons 52. Rio Bravo 59. The
Wackiest Ship in the Army 60. Love and Kisses
65.

Nemec, Jan (1936–). Czech director.
Diamonds of the Night 64. The Party and the Guests 66. The Martyrs of Love 67, etc.

neo-realism is a term mainly applied to the Italian post-war films which seemed to present a fresh and vivid kind of social realism. The essentials were real locations and at least a proportion of amateur actors. The most famous neo-realist film is *Bicycle Thieves*.

Nero, Franco (1942–). Italian leading man in international films.
The Tramplers 66. The Bible 66. *Camelot* 67. The Day of the Owl 68. A Quiet Place in the Country 68. Tristana 70. The Virgin and the Gypsy 70. The Battle of Neretva 70. Pope Joan 72. The Monk 72, etc.

Nervo, Jimmy: see *The Crazy Gang*.

Nesbitt, Cathleen (1889–). British character actress, on stage from 1910; very occasional films.
Autobiography 1975: *A Little Love and Good Company*.
The Case of the Frightened Lady 32. The Passing of the Third Floor Back 36. Fanny by Gaslight 43. Nicholas Nickleby 47. Three Coins in the Fountain 54. Désirée 54. *An Affair to Remember* 57. Promise Her Anything 66. The Trygon Factor 67. Staircase 69. Villain 71, etc.
TV series: *The Farmer's Daughter* 65.

Nesbitt, Derren (c. 1932–). British character actor, usually a smiling villain.
The Man in the Back Seat 60. *Victim* 62. Strongroom 62. *The Naked Runner* 67. Nobody Runs Forever 68. Where Eagles Dare 68. Innocent Bystanders 72. Ooh You are Awful 72. The Amorous Milkman (wd) 74, etc.

Nettleton, Lois (c. 1929–). American character actress.
□ Period of Adjustment 62. Come Fly with Me 63. Mail Order Bride 64. Valley of Mystery 66. Bamboo Saucer 68. The Good Guys and the Bad Guys 69. Dirty Dingus Magee 70. Sidelong Glances of a Pigeon Kicker 71. The Forgotten Man (TV) 71. The Honkers 72. Echoes of a Summer 75.

Neumann, Kurt (1908–1958). German director, in Hollywood from 1925.
My Pal the King 32. The Big Cage 33. Rainbow on the River 36. Island of Lost Men 39. Ellery Queen Master Detective 40. The Unknown Guest 43. Tarzan and the Leopard Woman 46. Bad Boy 49. Rocketship XM (& wp) 50. Son of Ali Baba 53. Carnival Story 54. Mohawk 56. Kronos 57. *The Fly* 58. Watusi 58, etc.

Never Give a Sucker an Even Break (US 1941). The wildest of W. C. Fields' comedies, known in GB as *What a Man!*; Fields himself suggested the billing should be shortened to *Fields: Sucker*. The ridiculous plot, reputedly written by Fields on the back of an envelope and sold to Universal for 25,000 dollars, concerns his experiences when, after dropping a bottle of whisky from a plane and diving out after it, he lands on a mountain top where there lives a girl who has never seen a man and promptly falls in love with him, despite the disapproval of her guardian Mrs Haemoglobin. ... As with all Fields, the humour is a matter of taste.

Never on Sunday (Greece 1960). An inexpensive but highly commercial location comedy made by Jules Dassin, who also played the shy American tourist who 'improves' a vivacious Greek prostitute. The music score by Manos Hadjidakis was as great an asset as Melina Mercouri's performance, and the film as a whole was another significant nail in the coffin of the Hays code, as vice remained triumphant.

Neville, John (1925–). British leading man, primarily on stage.
□ Oscar Wilde 60. Billy Budd 62. Unearthly Stranger 63. *A Study in Terror* (as Sherlock Holmes) 65. The Adventures of Gerard 70.

'new wave' or **'nouvelle vague'**. Term given (by themselves?) to a group of new, exploring young French directors towards the end of the fifties: François Truffaut, Jean-Luc Godard, Louis Malle, Alain Resnais, etc. As their talents were widely divergent, the term meant very little. It was coined by Françoise Giroud.

New York has provided a vivid backcloth for films of many types, and its skyscrapers allegedly gave Fritz Lang the inspiration for *Metropolis*. Studio re-creations provided the period flavour of *Little Old New York, New York Town, One Sunday Afternoon, A Tree Grows in Brooklyn, Incendiary Blonde, My Girl Tisa*, and *The Bowery*; and it was a studio city which was wrecked by *King Kong*. But the camera has also explored the real article, notably in thrillers like *Saboteur, Naked City, Union Station, The FBI Story* and *North by Northwest*; in realistic comedy dramas like *From This Day Forward, So This is New York, Miracle on 34th Street, Lovers and Lollipops, Marty, It Should Happen to You, Sunday in New York, Breakfast at*

Tiffany's, The Lost Weekend, The Bachelor Party, A Man Ten Feet Tall, A Fine Madness, Love with the Proper Stranger, The World of Henry Orient, Midnight Cowboy, The Pawnbroker, Barefoot in the Park, Beau James, The French Connection, Cotton Goes to Harlem, Shaft, The Out-of-Towners, Any Wednesday, Serpico, Bye Bye Braverman, Sweet Charity, The Seven-Ups, The Taking of Pelham One Two Three, The Prisoner of Second Avenue, Mean Streets, Taxi Driver, Death Wish and *Three Days of the Condor*; in hard-hitting social melodramas like *On the Waterfront, Sweet Smell of Success,* and *The Young Savages*; and in musicals like *On the Town* and *West Side Story.* Other films which concern the effect of New York without showing much of the actuality include *Mr Deeds Goes to Town, Bachelor Mother, Lady on a Train, Bell, Book and Candle, Portrait of Jennie, Kid Millions, Dead End, The Apartment, Patterns of Power, The Garment Jungle, Mr Blandings Builds His Dream House* and *America, America.* Finally Mahattan Island was bought from the Indians by Groucho Marx in *The Story of Mankind, Knickerbocker Holiday* pictured the city in its Dutch colonial days as New Amsterdam and *Godspell* used it as a novel background for its revised version of the Life of Christ.

Television series with authentic New York locations include *Naked City, The Defenders, East Side West Side, N.Y.P.D., Madigan, McCloud, Kojak.*

Newall, Guy (1885–1937). British stage actor who became a popular leading man in silent sentimental dramas, especially with his wife Ivy Duke. Also directed most of his films.
Comradeship 18. The Garden of Resurrection 19. The Lure of Crooning Water 20. The Duke's Son 20. Beauty and the Beast 22. Boy Woodburn 22. The Starlit Garden 23. The Ghost Train 27. The Eternal Feminine 30. The Marriage Bond 30. Grand Finale 37, etc.

Newbrook, Peter (1916–). British producer, former cinematographer.
The Yellow Teddy Bears 63. Black Torment 64. Gonks Go Beat 65. The Sandwich Man 66. Press for Time 66. Corruption 69. She'll Follow You Anywhere 70. The Asphyx 72.

Newfeld, Sam (1900–1964). American director of second features.
Reform Girl 33. Big Time or Bust 34. Northern Frontier 35. Timber War 36. Trail of Vengeance 37. Harlem on the Prairie 38. Secrets of a Model 40. Billy the Kid's Fighting Pals 41. The Mad Monster 42. Nabonga 44. Ghost of Hidden

Valley 46. The Counterfeiters 48. Motor Patrol 50. Three Desperate Men 51. Thunder Over Sangoland 55. Wolf Dog 58, many others.

Newhart, Bob (1923–). American TV and record comedian who has appeared in a few movies.
Hell is for Heroes 62. Hot Millions 68. On a Clear Day You Can See Forever 70. Catch 22 70. Cold Turkey 70.
TV series: *The Bob Newhart Show* 71–74.

Newland, John (c. 1916–). American TV actor (the host of *One Step Beyond*) who also directed a few films.
That Night 57. The Violators 57. The Spy with My Face 65. Hush-a-Bye Murder 70.
Played Algy in the Tom Conway Bulldog Drummond films 1948–49.

Newlands, Anthony (1926–). British character actor, mainly on TV; usually plays schemers.
Beyond This Place 59. The Trials of Oscar Wilde 60. Hysteria 64. Theatre of Death 67, etc.

Newley, Anthony (1931–). Versatile but dislikeable British actor, composer, singer, comedian; former child star.
Oliver Twist 48. Vice Versa 48. Those People Next Door 53. *Cockleshell Heroes* 56. X the Unknown 57. High Flight 57. *No Time to Die* 58. Idol on Parade 60. In the Nick 61. The Small World of Sammy Lee 63. Dr Dolittle (US) 67. Sweet November (US) 68. Can Heironymus Merkin Ever Forget Mercy Humpe and Find True Happiness? (& wd) 69. Summertree (d only) 72, etc.

Newman, Alfred (1901–1970). American composer, former child pianist; an eminent Hollywood musical director since early sound days, he composed over 250 film scores.
The Devil To Pay 30. Whoopee 31. *Arrowsmith* 31. Cynara 32. *The Bowery* 33. Nana 34. Dodsworth 36. *Dead End* 37. *Alexander's Ragtime Band* (AA) 38. *Gunga Din* 39. *Tin Pan Alley* (AA) 40. *The Grapes of Wrath* 40. Son of Fury 42. The Song of Bernadette 43. The Razor's Edge 46. *Mother Wore Tights* (AA) 47. Unfaithfully Yours 48. *With a Song in My Heart* (AA) 52. *Call Me Madam* (AA) 53. Love is a Many Splendored Thing (AA) 55. *The King and I* (AA) 56. Flower Drum Song 61. The Counterfeit Traitor 62. How the West was Won 62. Nevada Smith 66, many others.

Newman, Barry (1940–). American leading actor.

☐ Pretty Boy Floyd 60. *The Lawyer* 69. *Vanishing Point* 71. The Salzburg Connection 72. Fear is the Key 72.
TV series: Petrocelli 73–74.

Newman, Joseph M. (1909–). American director, in films from 1931.
Jungle Patrol 48. 711 Ocean Drive 50. The Outcasts of Poker Flats 52. Red Skies of Montana 52. Pony Soldier 53. The Human Jungle 54. Dangerous Crossing 54. Kiss of Fire 55. *This Island Earth* 55. Flight to Hong Kong (& p) 56. Gunfight at Dodge City 58. The Big Circus 59. Tarzan the Ape Man 59. King of the Roaring Twenties 61. A Thunder of Drums 61. The George Raft Story 61, etc.

Newman, Lionel (–). American composer.
The Street with No Name 48. Cheaper by the Dozen 50. Diplomatic Courier 52. Dangerous Crossing 53. Gorilla at Large 54. How to Be Very Very Popular 55. A Kiss Before Dying 56. Mardi Gras 58. Compulsion 59. North to Alaska 60. Move Over Darling 63. Do Not Disturb 65. The Salzburg Connection 72, many others.

Newman, Nanette (–). British leading lady, married to Bryan Forbes.
Personal Affair 53. House of Mystery 58. Faces in the Dark 59. The League of Gentlemen 59. Twice Round the Daffodils 62. The Wrong Arm of the Law 63. Of Human Bondage 64. Séance on a Wet Afternoon 64. The Wrong Box 66. The Whisperers 66. The Madwoman of Chaillot 69. *The Raging Moon* 70. The Love Ban 72. Man at the Top 73, etc.

Newman, Paul (1925–). American leading actor who suffered initially from a similarity to Marlon Brando but later developed a lithe impertinence which served him well in his better films.
Biography 1975: *Paul Newman* by Charles Humblett.
☐ The Silver Chalice 54. *Somebody Up There Likes Me* 56. The Rack 56. Until They Sail 57. The Helen Morgan Story 57. *The Long Hot Summer* 58. The Left Handed Gun 58. Rally Round the Flag Boys 58. Cat on a Hot Tin Roof 58. The Young Philadelphians 59. From the Terrace 60. Exodus 60. *The Hustler* (BFA) 61. Paris Blues 61. Sweet Bird of Youth 62. Hemingway's Adventures of a Young Man 62. *Hud* 63. A New Kind of Love 63. *The Prize* 63. What a Way to Go 64. The Outrage 64. Lady L 64. Torn Curtain 66. *Harper* 66. *Hombre* 67. *Cool Hand Luke* 67. The Secret War of Harry Frigg 67. Rachel Rachel (d only) 68. Winning 69.

Butch Cassidy and the Sundance Kid 69. W.U.S.A. 70. Sometimes a Great Notion (& d) 71. The Effect of Gamma Rays on Man-in-the-Moon Marigolds (d only) 72. *Judge Roy Bean* 72. The Mackintosh Man 73. The Sting 73. The Towering Inferno 74. The Drowning Pool 75. Buffalo Bill and the Indians 76. Slap Shot 77.

Newmar, Julie (1930–) (Julia Newmeyer). Tall American blonde.
The Marriage Go Round 60. Mackenna's Gold 68. The Maltese Bippy 69, etc.
TV series: My Living Doll 63.

newsreels were part of the very earliest cinema programme, and the nine-minute round up of topical events filmed by roving cameramen was a feature of programmes in cinemas throughout the world until the mid-sixties, when it was clear that the newsreel had been replaced by television. Most newsreel companies have looked after their libraries, and the result is a vivid history of the twentieth century, frequently plundered by producers of compilation films.

Newton, Robert (1905–1956). British star character actor with a rolling eye and a voice to match; a ham, but a succulent one.
☐ Reunion 32. Dark Journey 37. Fire Over England 37. *Farewell Again* 37. The Squeaker 37. The Green Cockatoo 37. Twenty One Days 38. Vessel of Wrath 38. Yellow Sands 38. Dead Men are Dangerous 39. Jamaica Inn 39. Poison Pen 39. Hell's Cargo 39. Bulldog Sees It Through 40. Gaslight 40. Busman's Honeymoon 40. *Major Barbara* 40. *Hatter's Castle* 41. They Flew Alone 42. *This Happy Breed* 44. *Henry V* (as Pistol) 45. Night Boat to Dublin 46. *Odd Man Out* 46. Temptation Harbour 47. Snowbound 48. *Oliver Twist* (as Bill Sikes) 48. Kiss the Blood off My Hands (US) 48. Obsession 49. *Treasure Island* (as Long John) 50. Waterfront 50. *Tom Brown's Schooldays* (as Dr Arnold) 51. Soldiers Three (US) 51. Les Misérables (US) 52. Blackbeard the Pirate (US) 52. *Androcles and the Lion* (US) 53. Desert Rats (US) 53. The High and the Mighty (US) 54. *The Beachcomber* 54. Long John Silver 55. Around the World in Eighty Days (US) 56.
TV series: *Long John Silver* 54.

Next of Kin (GB 1942). An official wartime film on the dangers of careless talk, treated as a documentary thriller but intended for military audiences, this was successful enough to be sent on general release and proved very popular. It still makes good cinema. Directed by Thorold Dickinson, with Mervyn Johns and Stephen Murray.

Ney, Marie (1895–). British stage actress in occasional films.
Escape 30. The Wandering Jew 34. Scrooge 37. Jamaica Inn 39. Seven Days to Noon 50. Simba 54. Yield to the Night 55. Witchcraft 64, etc.

Ney, Richard (1917–). American financier who almost accidentally went into acting but appears only occasionally.
Mrs Miniver 42. The Late George Apley 46. Joan of Arc 48. Babes in Baghdad 52. The Premature Burial 61, etc.

Niblo, Fred (1874–1948) (Federico Nobile). American director of silent films; had stage experience.
The Marriage Ring 18. Sex 20. *The Mark of Zorro* 20. *The Three Musketeers* 21. *Blood and Sand* 23. Thy Name is Woman 24. The Temptress 26. *Ben Hur* 27. Camille 27. Redemption 29. The Big Gamble 33. Three Sons o' Guns 41.

Nicholls, Anthony (1902–1977). Distinguished-looking British stage actor, in occasional films.
The Laughing Lady 47. The Guinea Pig 49. The Hasty Heart 49. The Dancing Years 50. The Franchise Affair 50. The Weak and the Wicked 54. Make Me an Offer 55. The Safecracker 58. Victim 62. Mister Ten Per Cent 66, etc.

Nichols, Barbara (1932–). American comedy actress, former model; adept at portraying not-so-dumb blondes.
Miracle in the Rain 56. The King and Four Queens 57. The Scarface Mob 60. The George Raft Story 61. Where the Boys Are 63. The Disorderly Orderly 64. Dear Heart 65. The Loved One 65. The Swinger 66, etc.

Nichols, Dandy (1907–). British character comedienne, often seen as nervous maid or cockney char. Became famous on TV as the long-suffering Else in *Till Death Us Do Part* 66–68; appeared in the film version 68.
Hue and Cry 46. Here Come the Huggetts 49. Street Corner 52. The Deep Blue Sea 55, many others.

Nichols, Dudley (1895–1960). Distinguished American screenwriter, in Hollywood from 1929.
Born Reckless 30. The Sign of the Cross 32. *The Lost Patrol* 34. Steamboat round the Bend 34. *The Informer* (AA) 35. Mary of Scotland 36. The Hurricane 37. *Bringing Up Baby* 38. *Stagecoach* 39. The Long Voyage Home 40. For Whom the Bell Tolls 43. The Bells of St Mary's 45. *It Happened Tomorrow* 44. *And Then There Were None* 45. Scarlet Street 45. Sister Kenny (& d) 46. Mourning Becomes Electra (& pd) 47. Pinky 49. Prince Valiant 54. The Tin Star 57. The Hangman 59, many others.

Nichols, Mike (1931–) (Michael Igor Peschkowsky). German-born American cabaret entertainer and latterly film director.
☐ *Who's Afraid of Virginia Woolf?* 66. *The Graduate* (AA) 67. Catch 22 70. Carnal Knowledge 71. The Day of the Dolphin 73. The Fortune 76.

Nicholson, Jack (1937–). American leading actor, a fashionable figure of the early seventies.
Cry Baby Killer 58. The Little Shop of Horrors 60. The Raven 63. The Terror 63. The Trip (w only) 67. *Easy Rider* 69. Five Easy Pieces 70. On a Clear Day You Can See Forever 70. Drive He Said (w, d only) 70. *Carnal Knowledge* 71. The King of Marvin Gardens 72. *The Last Detail* 74. *Chinatown* 74. Tommy 74. The Passenger 75. The Fortune 76. *One Flew Over the Cuckoo's Nest* (AA) 76. The Missouri Breaks 76. The Last Tycoon 76, etc.

Nicholson, James H. (1916–1972). American executive, former theatre owner and distributor, who became president of American International Pictures.

Nicholson, Nora (1892–1973). British stage character actress whose film roles have usually been fey or eccentric.
The Blue Lagoon 48. Treat Softly 48. Crow Hollow 52. Raising a Riot 54. A Town Like Alice 56. The Captain's Table 59. Diamonds for Breakfast 69, etc.

nickelodeon. A humorous term applied to early American cinemas once they had become slightly grander than the converted stores which were used for the purpose at the turn of the century.

Nicol, Alex (1919–). American leading man with stage experience, mainly in Universal action pictures.
The Sleeping City 50. Because of You 52. Law and Order 54. The Man from Laramie 55. Sincerely Yours 55. Under Ten Flags 60. Three Came Back (& pd) 60. Look in Any Window 61. The Savage Guns 62. Ride and Kill 63. Gunfighters of Casa Grande 65. Bloody Mama 69. Point of Terror (d only) 71. The Night God Screamed 75, etc.

Nielsen, Asta (1882–1972). Danish stage actress.

☐ Der Abgrund 10. Enelein 13. Kurfurstendamm 19. Reigen 20. Hamlet 20. Fraulein Julie 21. Vanina Vanini 22. Erdgeist 23. Hedda Gabler 24. Joyless Street 25. Secrets of a Soul 26.

Nielsen, Leslie (1925–). Canadian leading man, former radio disc jockey; much TV work.
The Vagabond King 55. Forbidden Planet 56. Ransom 56. Tammy and the Bachelor 57. Harlow 65. Beau Geste 66. The Poseidon Adventure 72, etc.
TV series: The Bold Ones 72.

Nigh, Jane (1926–). American leading lady of minor films in the forties and fifties.
Something for the Boys 44. State Fair 45. Dragonwyck 46. Give My Regards to Broadway 48. Red Hot and Blue 49. Fighting Man of the Plains 49. County Fair 50. Blue Blood 51. Fort Osage 53, etc.

Nigh, William (1881–1955). American director.
Marriage Morals 23. Mr Wu 27. The Single Sin 31. Crash Donovan 35. The Ape 40. Corregidor 42. The Right to Live 45. Divorce 45, etc.

A Night at the Opera (US 1935). The Marx Brothers' first film for MGM. Given a big budget, they also had to suffer romantic and musical interludes which made their fans impatient; but the film contained some of their best routines, including the cabin scene, and the final sabotaging of *Il Trovatore* is brilliantly timed. As usual, Margaret Dumont stood the brunt of the insults.

Night Mail (GB 1936). A highly influential two-reel documentary made by Harry Watt and Basil Wright for the GPO Film Unit, building up an exciting pattern of images and sounds as the night mail train steams from London to Scotland. The verse which largely replaces commentary was written by W. H. Auden.

Night Must Fall. Emlyn Williams' macabre play about the homicidal Welsh pageboy who keeps his victim's head in a hatbox was filmed in 1938 by Richard Thorpe for MGM, with Robert Montgomery. When Karel Reisz produced a somewhat modernized version in 1963 with Albert Finney, the critics all yearned for the 1938 film, which they hadn't seen for twenty years. One doubts whether either version really pleased the author.

The Night of the Demon (GB 1957) (US title: *Curse of the Demon*). Charles Bennett adapted M. R. James' story 'Casting the Runes' for this unassuming little thriller which was directed by Jacques Tourneur with a strong Hitchcock flavour. It remains one of the screen's best ventures into the supernatural, though not helped by the colourless playing of the romantic leads. Niall MacGinnis, however, gives a roistering performance as the evil Karswell, and the final train sequence is genuinely exciting.

The Night of the Hunter (US 1955). One of the strangest films to come out of Hollywood, an allegory of good and evil from Davis Grubb's novel about the escape of two children from a psychopathic preacher (Robert Mitchum). Impeccably directed by Charles Laughton so that, although the film does not satisfy as a whole, fragments of it linger in the memory; enhanced by Stanley Cortez' splendid photography.

Nightingale, Florence (1820–1910). English nurse who organized hospitals at the front during the Crimean War, with little official help and under appalling conditions. There have been two biopics of her: *The White Angel* (US) 35, with Kay Francis, and *The Lady with a Lamp* (GB) 51, with Anna Neagle.

Nights of Cabiria: see under *Cabiria*.

Nilsson, Anna Q. (1889–1974). Swedish-born actress, long in America and popular in silent films from 1919.
The Love Burglar 19. Kingdom of Dreams 20. Soldiers of Fortune 20. Hollywood 22. The Isle of Lost Ships 23. Inez of Hollywood 24. The Masked Woman 25. The Greater Glory 26. Sorrell and Son 27. The World Changes 34. Prison Farm 38. Girls' Town 42. The Farmer's Daughter 47. Sunset Boulevard 50, etc.

Nilsson, Leopold Torre: see *Torre-Nilsson, Leopold*.

Nimmo, Derek (1931–). British character comedian who gets laughs from toe-twiddling and funny voices (especially of the comedy curate kind).
The Millionairess 61. The Amorous Prawn 62. The Bargee 64. Joey Boy 65. The Liquidator 65. Casino Royale 66. Mister Ten Per Cent 66. A Talent for Loving 69. One of Our Dinosaurs is Missing 75, etc.
TV series: All Gas and Gaiters 67. The World of Wooster 68. Oh Brother 70. Oh Father 73.

Nimoy, Leonard (1932–). Lean-faced American character actor.

Queen for a Day 51. Rhubarb 51. The Balcony 63. Catlow 72. The Alpha Caper (TV) 73, etc.
TV series: *Star Trek* (as Mr Spock) 66–68. Mission Impossible 70–72.

Ninotchka (US 1939). A blithe satire about communism meeting capitalism in Paris, in the shapes of Greta Garbo and Melvyn Douglas. For the most part a felicitous though over-long comedy, with engaging performances from the principals and from Sig Ruman, Alexander Granach and Felix Bressart as the incompetent Russian emissaries. Directed by Ernst Lubitsch from a script by Charles Brackett, Billy Wilder and Walter Reisch. The film in which 'Garbo laughs!'. Remade in 1957 as a musical, *Silk Stockings*, with Cyd Charisse and Fred Astaire.

Nissen, Greta (1939–) (Grethe Rutz-Nissen). Norwegian leading lady in American films.
The Wanderer 25. The Popular Sin 26. Women of All Nations 31. Rackety Rax 32. Melody Cruise 33. Red Wagon 36, etc.

nitrate. Until 1950 film stock had a nitrate base, which helped give a splendid sheen, but was very inflammable. The change was made to safety stock, which burns much more slowly, but black and white films at least never looked so good again.

Niven, David (1909–). Debonair British leading man whose natural enthusiasm found several outlets before he accidentally arrived in Hollywood and was signed up as an extra. His light-hearted approach to life is reflected in his 1972 autobiography *The Moon's a Balloon* and its 1975 sequel *Bring On the Empty Horses*.
☐ Barbary Coast 35. Without Regret 35. A Feather in Her Hat 35. Splendor 35. Rose Marie 36. *Thank You Jeeves* 36. Palm Springs 36. The Charge of the Light Brigade 36. *Dodsworth* 36. Beloved Enemy 36. We Have Our Moments 37. Dinner at the Ritz 37. *The Prisoner of Zenda* (as Fritz von Tarlenheim) 37. Four Men and a Prayer 38. Bluebeard's Eighth Wife 38. Three Blind Mice 38. The Dawn Patrol 38. Wuthering Heights 39. *Bachelor Mother* 39. The Real Glory 39. Eternally Yours 39. *Raffles* 40. The First of the Few 41. *The Way Ahead* 44. *A Matter of Life and Death* 46. The Perfect Marriage 46. Magnificent Doll 46. The Other Love 47. The Bishop's Wife 47. Bonnie Prince Charlie 47. Enchantment 48. A Kiss in the Dark 49. A Kiss for Corliss 49. The Elusive Pimpernel 50. The Toast of New Orleans 50. Soldiers Three 51. Happy Go Lovely 51. The Lady Says No 52. Appointment with Venus 52. The Moon is Blue 53. The Love Lottery 54. Happy Ever After 54.

The King's Thief 55. *Carrington V.C.* 55. The Birds and the Bees 56. *Around the World in Eighty Days* (as Phileas Fogg) 56. Oh Men Oh Women 57. The Little Hut 57. My Man Godfrey 57. The Silken Affair 57. Bonjour Tristesse 58. *Separate Tables* (AA) 58. Ask Any Girl 59. Happy Anniversary 50. Please Don't Eat the Daisies 60. The Guns of Navarone 61. Guns of Darkness 62. The Best of Enemies 62. 55 Days at Peking 63. The Pink Panther 64. Bedtime Story 64. Where the Spies Are 65. Lady L 66. Casino Royale 67. Eye of the Devil 67. The Extraordinary Seaman 68. Prudence and the Pill 68. The Impossible Years 68. Before Winter Comes 68. The Brain 69. The Statue 70. King Queen Knave 72. Vampira 74. Paper Tiger 75. Murder by Death 76. No Deposit No Return 76. Candleshoe 77.
TV series: *The David Niven Show* 59. *The Rogues* 64.

Nixon, Marian (1904–). American leading lady.
What Happened to Jones? 26. Rosita 27. General Crack 29. Adios 30. After Tomorrow 32. Rebecca of Sunnybrook Farm 32. Walking Down Broadway 32.

Nixon, Marni (c. 1929–). American singer, former MGM messenger, who has dubbed in high notes for many stars including Margaret O'Brien in *Big City*, Deborah Kerr in *The King and I*, Natalie Wood in *West Side Story* and Audrey Hepburn in *My Fair Lady*. Has made only one film appearance, as a nun in *The Sound of Music* 65.

Noel, Magali (1932–). French leading lady.
Seul dans Paris 51. Razzia sur la Chnouf 55. Rififi 55. Elena et les Hommes 56. Desire Takes the Men 58. La Dolce Vita 59. The Man Who Understood Women 70. Amarcord 74, etc.

Noel-Noel (1897–) (Lucien Noel). Dapper French character comedian.
Octave 32. A Case of Nightingales 43. Le Pere Tranquille 46. The Seven Deadly Sins 51. The Diary of Major Thompson 56. Jessica 62, etc.

Noiret, Philippe (1931–). Chubby French character actor in international films.
Zazie dans le Métro 60. Les Copains 62. The Night of the Generals 66. Topaz 69. Murphy's War 70. A Time for Loving 71. The Serpent 72, etc.

Nolan, Doris (1916–). American leading lady who married Alexander Knox and retired.
The Man I Married 37. Holiday 38. Irene 40. Moon over Burma 41. Follies Girl 44, etc.

Nolan, Jeanette (c. 1911–). American character actress, much on TV.
Macbeth (as Lady Macbeth) 48. The Secret of Convict Lake 51. The Happy Time 52. The Big Heat 53. The Guns of Fort Petticoat 57. The Rabbit Trap 58.
TV series: The Richard Boone Show 64.

Nolan, Lloyd (1902–). Dependable American character actor, with stage experience from 1927.
Stolen Harmony (film Debut) 34. G Men 35. Ebb Tide 37. Gangs of Chicago 40. Michael Shayne, Private Detective 40. Blues in the Night 41. Bataan 43. *A Tree Grows in Brooklyn* 44. *The House on 92nd Street* 45. The Lady in the Lake 46. The Street with No Name 48. The Last Hunt 56. Peyton Place 58. Circus World 64. Never Too Late 65. An American Dream 66. The Double Man (GB) 67. Ice Station Zebra 68. Airport 69. Earthquake 74, many others.
TV series: Julia 68–69.

Nolbandov, Sergei (1895–1971). Russian-born writer-producer, in Britain from 1926.
City of Song (w) 30. Fire over England (w) 36. Ships with Wings (wd) 42. This Modern Age (series) (p) from 1946. The Kidnappers (p) 53. Mix Me a Person (p) 62, many others.

Nolte, Nick (1941–). Virile American leading man of the mid-seventies.
Return to Macon County 75. Death Sentence (TV) 76. The Runaway Barge (TV) 76. *Rich Man Poor Man* (TV) 76. The Deep 77, etc.

non-theatrical. A descriptive adjective usually applied to film showings at which there is no paid admission on entrance, e.g. schools, clubs, etc. Some distributors apply the term to all 16mm showings.

Noonan, Tommy (1921–1968) (Thomas Noon). Ebullient American comedian.
Starlift 51. Gentlemen Prefer Blondes 53. A Star is Born 54. How to Be Very Very Popular 55. Bundle of Joy 56. *The Ambassador's Daughter* 56. The Rookie (& p) 60, etc.

Norden, Christine (1923–). British leading lady, a sex symbol of the late forties.
Night Beat 47. *Mine Own Executioner* 48. Idol of Paris 48. A Case for PC 49 51. Reluctant Heroes 51, etc.

Norman, Leslie (1911–). British producer-director, former editor, in films from late twenties.
Where No Vultures Fly (p) 51. The Cruel Sea (p)

54. The Night My Number Came Up (d) 56. X the Unknown (d) 57. The Shiralee (d) 58. Dunkirk (d) 58. The Long, the Short and the Tall (d) 60. Mix Me a Person (d) 61. Summer of the 17th Doll (d) 61, etc.

Normand, Mabel (1894–1930) (Mabel Fortescue). American comedienne, a leading player of Vitagraph and Keystone comedies from 1911, and a Chaplin co-star.
Barney Oldfield's Race for Life 12. Fatty and Mabel Adrift 15. Mickey 17. Sis Hopkins 18. Molly O 21. Suzanna 22. The Extra Girl 24, many others.

Norris, Edward (1910–). American leading man of second features; former reporter.
Queen Christina 33. Boys' Town 38. The Man with Two Lives 41. End of the Road 44. Decoy 47. Forbidden Women 49. Inside the Walls of Folsom Prison 51. The Man from the Alamo 53. The Kentuckian (last to date) 55, many others.

North, Alex (1910–). American composer.
□ *A Streetcar Named Desire* 51. The Thirteenth Letter 51. Death of a Salesman 51. Viva Zapata 52. Les Miserables 52. Pony Soldier 52. The Member of the Wedding 53. Desiree 54. Go Man Go 54. The Racers 55. Unchained 55. The Man with the Gun 55. The Rose Tattoo 55. I'll Cry Tomorrow 56. The Bad Seed 56. The Rainmaker 56. Four Girls in Town 56. The King and Four Queens 56. The Bachelor Party 57. The Long Hot Summer 58. Stage Struck 58. Hot Spell 58. South Seas Adventure 58. The Sound and the Fury 59. The Wonderful Country 59. *Spartacus* 60. The Children's Hour 61. Sanctuary 61. The Misfits 61. All Fall Down 62. Cleopatra 63. The Outrage 64. Cheyenne Autumn 64. The Agony and the Ecstasy 65. Who's Afraid of Virginia Woolf 66. The Devil's Brigade 68. The Shoes of the Fisherman 68. A Dream of Kings 69. Hard Contract 69. Willard 71.

North by Northwest (US 1959). A blithe comedy-thriller, possibly Hitchcock's most likeable film if only because it is an over-size bag of his best old tricks. Cary Grant is irresistibly debonair as the innocent hero chased by spies over the great stone faces of Mount Rushmore and savaged by an aeroplane in a cornfield; Leo G. Carroll and James Mason smoothly represent law and disorder respectively. Written by Ernest Lehman, photographed by Robert Burks, with music by Bernard Herrmann.

North, Jay (1953–). American juvenile actor, popular as a child on TV in *Dennis the Menace* 59–63 and later *Maya* 67.
Film appearance: *Zebra in the Kitchen* 65.

North, Michael (c. 1920–). American leading man of the forties. Formerly known as Ted North; changed and was reintroduced for *The Unsuspected* 48.

North, Sheree (1933–) (Dawn Bethel). Blonde American leading lady, former dancer. Excuse My Dust 51. *How to Be Very Very Popular* 55. The Best Things in Life are Free 56. The Way to the Gold 57. No Down Payment 57. Mardi Gras 58. Destination Inner Space 66. Madigan 68. The Gypsy Moths 69. Lawman 71. Charley Varrick 73. Breakout 75. The Shootist 76, etc.

Northwest Passage (US 1940). Actually this was only part one of Kenneth Roberts' novel, and bore the subtitle 'Rogers' Rangers'; part two unfortunately was never made, and in the film as it stands the northwest passage is never seen and barely talked about. Spencer Tracy gives a splendid performance as the indomitable major exacting retribution from the Indians and nearly killing off his own men in the process. Directed by King Vidor, and beautifully photographed in fairly early Technicolor, it remains one of the screen's most invigorating westerns.

Norton, Jack (1889–1958) (Mortimer J. Naughton). American character actor, invariably seen as an amiable well-dressed drunk with a sour expression; he rarely had a coherent speaking part.
Cockeyed Cavaliers 34. Thanks for the Memory 38. The Ghost Breakers 40. The Bank Dick 40. The Fleet's In 41. The Palm Beach Story 42. Hail the Conquering Hero 44. Hold that Blonde 45. Bringing Up Father 46, many others.

Norwood, Eille (1870–*). British stage actor who played Sherlock Holmes in a score of twenties two-reelers and a few features.

Nosferatu: see under *Dracula*.

Nosseck, Max (1902–1972) (Alexander Norris). Polish director in Hollywood from 1939; former stage and film actor/director in Europe.
□ AMERICAN FILMS: Girls Under Twenty One 40. Gambling Daughters 41. *Dillinger* 45. The Brighton Strangler 45. Black Beauty 46. The Return of Rin Tin Tin 47. Kill or Be Killed 50. Korea Patrol 51. The Hoodlum 51. The Body Beautiful 53. Garden of Eden 57.

Nothing But the Truth. James Montgomery's Broadway comedy about a man who takes a bet to tell the absolute truth for twenty-four hours was filmed in 1920 with Taylor Holmes in 1929, with Richard Dix; and in 1941, with Bob Hope.

Nothing Sacred (US 1937). One of Hollywood's most successful satirical comedies, perhaps because the bitterness was mixed with slapstick. Carole Lombard plays the girl who thinks she is dying of a rare disease and is propelled by reporter Fredric March to the status of a national heroine; Walter Connolly is a magnificently wrathful editor. Most memorable moment: March finds himself in an unfriendly small town, where the natives are all surly and mutter at him in monosyllables; suddenly a small boy darts out from behind a picket fence and bites him in the leg. Written by Ben Hecht; directed by William Wellman; in Technicolor. Remade 1954, with Jerry Lewis (!) in the Lombard part, as *Living It Up*.

Novak, Eva (–). American silent screen leading lady, sister of Jane.
The Lost Trail 21. Society Secrets 21. The Man From Hells River 22. Boston Blackie 23. A Fight for Honor 24. The Forlorn Lover 25. Irene 26. Red Signals 27. Phantom of the Desert 30, etc.

Novak, Jane (–). American silent screen leading lady, sister of Eva.
The Barbarian 21. Colleen of the Pines 22. Jealous Husbands 23. The Lullaby 24. Lure of the Wilds 25. Whispering Canyon 26. What Price Love? 27. Free Lips 28. Redskin 29, etc.

Novak, Kim (1933–) (Marilyn Novak). Artificially-groomed American blonde star who never managed to give a natural performance, though she did try.
□ The French Line 53. *Pushover* 54. Phfft 54. Five against the House 55. Son of Sinbad 55. Picnic 55. The Man with the Golden Arm 56. The Eddy Duchin Story 56. *Jeanne Eagles* 57. Pal Joey 58. Vertigo 58. Bell Book and Candle 58. Middle of the Night 59. Strangers When We Meet 60. Pépé 60. Boys' Night Out 62. The Notorious Landlady 62. Of Human Bondage 64. Kiss Me Stupid 64. The Amorous Adventures of Moll Flanders 65. The Legend of Lylah Clare 68. The Great Bank Robbery 69. Tales That Witness Madness 73. Third Girl from the Left (TV) 74. Satan's Triangle (TV) 75.

Novarro, Ramon (1899–1968) (Ramon Samaniegos). Romantic Mexican leading man of the twenties in Hollywood; later came back as character actor.
The Prisoner of Zenda (as Rupert) 22. Where the Pavement Ends 23. *Scaramouche* 23. The Arab

24. The Midshipman 25. *Ben Hur* 25. The
Student Prince 27. Across to Singapore 28.
Forbidden Hours 28. The Pagan 29. Call of the
Flesh 30. Son of India 31. Mata Hari 31. The
Son-Daughter 32. The Barbarian 33. The Cat
and the Fiddle 34. The Night is Young 35. The
Sheik Steps Out 37. *We Were Strangers* 48. The
Big Steal 49. Crisis 50. Heller in Pink Tights 60,
etc.

Novello, Ivor (1893–1951) (Ivor Davies).
Welsh matinée idol with an incredibly successful
career in stage musical comedy; also prolific
playwright and composer.
Biographies: 1951, *Ivor* by MacQueen Pope.
1951, *Ivor Novello* by Peter Noble. 1974,
Perchance to Dream by Richard Rose. 1975,
Ivor by Sandy Wilson.
Carnival 22. The Bohemian Girl 22. The White
Rose 23. *The Man without Desire* 23. *The Rat*
25. *The Lodger* 26. The Triumph of the Rat 27.
The Constant Nymph 27. Downhill 27. The
Vortex 28. Once a Lady 31. The Lodger
(remake) 32. Sleeping Car 33. I Lived with You
34. Autumn Crocus 34, etc.

Novello, Jay (1905–). Wiry little American
actor, familiar in films from Tenth Avenue Kid
38 to Atlantis the Lost Continent 61, usually as
scruffy little crook.

Nugent, Elliott (1899–). American stage
actor, producer and playwright who only
dabbled in films but proved a good director of
comedies.
Autobiography 1965: *Events Leading Up to the
Comedy*.
AS ACTOR: So This is College 29. The Unholy
Three 30. Romance 30. The Last Flight 31, etc.
AS DIRECTOR: The Mouthpiece 32. Whistling
in the Dark 33. *Three Cornered Moon* 33. She
Loves Me Not 34. Love in Bloom 35. And So
They Were Married 36. Professor Beware 38.
The Cat and the Canary 39. Nothing but the
Truth 40. The Male Animal (& oa) 42. The
Crystal Ball 43. Up in Arms 44. My Favorite
Brunette 47. *My Girl Tisa* 48. *The Great Gatsby*
49. My Outlaw Brother 51. Just for You 52, etc.

Nugent, Frank (1908–1966). American
screenwriter, former reporter and critic.
Fort Apache 48. *She Wore a Yellow Ribbon* 49.
The Quiet Man 52. Trouble in the Glen 53. *The
Searchers* 56. The Last Hurrah 58. Donovan's
Reef 63, etc.

nuns have been popular figures on the screen,
though only in *The Nun's Story* and the Polish

The Devil and the Nun has any real sense of
dedication been achieved; the French *Dialogue
des Carmélites* tried hard but failed.
Sentimentalized nuns were seen in *The Cradle
Song, Bonaventure, The White Sister,
Conspiracy of Hearts, The Bells of St Mary's,
Come to the Stable, Portrait of Jennie, Heaven
Knows Mr Allison, Black Narcissus, Lilies of the
Field, The Miracle, The Song of Bernadette* and
The Sound of Music; while nuns who combined
modern sophistication with sweetness and light
afflicted us in *The Singing Nun* and *The Trouble
with Angels*, and in *Two Mules for Sister Sara*
Shirley Maclaine played a prostitute disguised as
a nun. A nun was raped in *Five Gates to Hell*.
The most sinister nun was perhaps Catherine
Lacey, with her high heels, in *The Lady
Vanishes*, but the nuns in *The Trygon Factor*
also count. The most agonized nuns were in *The
Devils, La Religieuse*, and *The Awful Story of
the Nun of Monza*. The weirdest was TV's *The
Flying Nun*.

The Nun's Story (US 1959). Written by
Robert Anderson from Kathryn Hulme's book,
and directed by Fred Zinnemann, this long and
sincere film lapsed into conventional melodrama
after a brilliant first half showing the training of a
novice. But at least it marked an advance in the
kind of subject that can be tackled by a big,
expensive movie. Photographed by Franz
Planer, with music by Franz Waxman; with
Audrey Hepburn in the leading role.

nurses have inspired biopics (*Sister Kenny, The
White Angel, The Lady with a Lamp, Nurse
Edith Cavell*); sentimental low-key studies of the
profession (*The Lamp Still Burns, The Feminine
Touch, Vigil in the Night, No Time for Tears,
White Corridors, Prison Nurse, Private Nurse,
Night Nurse*); even comedies (*Carry On Nurse,
Twice Round the Daffodils, Nurse on Wheels*).
Green For Danger is probably still the only
thriller in which both victim and murderer were
nurses. The best satire has been *The National
Health* (or *Nurse Norton's Affair*). There was a
popular TV series called *Janet Dean Registered
Nurse* 53, and later *The Nurses* 62–64. See also
hospitals; *doctors*.

Nuyen, France (1939–). Franco-Chinese
leading lady, former model, who made some
Hollywood films.
In Love and War 57. *South Pacific* 58. Satan
Never Sleeps 61. The Last Time I Saw Archie 62.
A Girl Named Tamiko 63. Diamondhead 63.
The Man in the Middle 64. Dimension Five 66.
One More Train to Rob 71. The Horror at
37,000 Feet (TV) 73, etc.

Nyby, Christian (1919–). American director.
□ *The Thing* 52. Hell on Devil's Island 57. Six-Gun Law 62. Young Fury 64. Operation CIA 65. First to Fight 66.

Nykvist, Sven (1922–). Distinguished Swedish cinematographer.
Sawdust and Tinsel 53. Karin Mansdotter 53. The Virgin Spring 60. Winter Light 62. *The Silence* 64. Loving Couples 65. Persona 66. Hour of the Wolf 67. The Last Run 71. One Day in the Life of Ivan Denisovitch 71, etc.

nymphomaniacs are still fairly rare in normal commercial movies. The fullest studies have been by Suzanne Pleshette in *A Rage to Live*, Françoise Arnoul in *La Rage au Corps*, Claire Bloom in *The Chapman Report*, Merle Oberon in *Of Love and Desire*, Sue Lyon in *Night of the Iguana*, Lee Remick in *The Detective*, Melina Mercouri in *Topkapi*, Maureen Stapleton in *Lonelyhearts*, Jean Seberg in *Road to Corinth*, Elizabeth Taylor in *Butterfield 8*, and Sandra Jullien in *I Am a Nymphomaniac*; but one should not forget Myrna Loy's comic nympho in *Love Me Tonight*.

O

Oakie, Jack (1903–) (Lewis D. Offield). Cheerful American comic actor well known for a startled 'double take'; formerly in vaudeville.
Finders Keepers (debut) 27. Paramount on Parade 30. Million Dollar Legs 32. College Humor 33. If I Had a Million 33. Call of the Wild 35. The Texas Rangers 36. The Toast of New York 37. Rise and Shine 39. *The Great Dictator* (a caricature of Mussolini) 40. Tin Pan Alley 40. Footlight Serenade 42. Song of the Islands 42. Something to Shout About 43. Hello Frisco Hello 43. *It Happened Tomorrow* 44. That's the Spirit 44. The Merry Monahans 44. On Stage Everybody 45. When My Baby Smiles at Me 48. Thieves' Highway 49. Last of the Buccaneers 50. The Battle of Powder River 52. Around the World in Eighty Days 56. The Wonderful Country 59. The Rat Race 60. Lover Come Back 62, many others.

Oakland, Simon (1922–). American general purpose actor with stage experience.
The Brothers Karamazov 58. I Want to Live 58. Psycho 60. West Side Story 61. Follow That Dream 62. Wall of Noise 63. The Satan Bug 65. The Plainsman 66. The Sand Pebbles 67. Tony Rome 67. Chubasco 68. On a Clear Day You Can See Forever 70. Chato's Land 72. Happy Mother's Day Love George 73, etc.

Oakland, Vivian (1895–1958) (V. Anderson). American child star and vaudeville artiste, who later became familiar as wife to the leading comic in many a two-reeler.
Gold Dust Gertie 31. Only Yesterday 32. The Bride Walks Out 36. Way Out West 37. The Man in the Trunk 42. Bunco Squad 51, many others.

Oakley, Annie (1859–1926) (Phoebe Annie Oakley Mozee). American sharpshooter who gained fame in her teens as star of Buffalo Bill's wild west show. Played on screen by Barbara Stanwyck in *Annie Oakley* 35, and by Betty Hutton in *Annie Get Your Gun* 50.

Oates, Warren (c. 1932–). American supporting actor who has tended towards psychopathic heavies.

Yellowstone Kelly 59. Private Property 60. Hero's Island 61. Mail Order Bride 64. Major Dundee 65. Return of the Seven 67. In the Heat of the Night 67. The Split 68. Crooks and Coronets (GB) 69. The Wild Bunch 69. There was a Crooked Man 70. Two Lane Blacktop 71. The Hired Hand 71. Tom Sawyer 73. Dillinger (title role) 73. The White Dawn 73. Badlands 73. 92 in the Shade 75. Race with the Devil 75. Drum 76, etc.

Ober, Philip (1902–). American general purpose character actor.
The Secret Fury 50. From Here to Eternity 53. Tammy 56. North by Northwest 59. Let No Man Write My Epitaph 60. The Brass Bottle 64. The Ghost and Mr Chicken 66, etc.

Oberon, Merle (1911–) (Estelle O'Brien Merle Thompson). British leading lady. Educated in India; came to Britain 1928, worked as dance hostess until signed up by Korda. Mainly in Hollywood from 1936.
□ Service for Ladies 32. Ebb Tide 32. Wedding Rehearsal 32. Men of Tomorrow 32. The Private Life of Henry VIII 33. The Battle 34. The Broken Melody 34. The Private Life of Don Juan 34. *The Scarlet Pimpernel* 34. Folies Bergere 35. The Dark Angel 35. These Three 36. Beloved Enemy 36. I Claudius (unfinished) 37. Over the Moon 37. *The Divorce of Lady X* 38. The Cowboy and the Lady 38. *Wuthering Heights* 39. The Lion Has Wings 39. 'Til We Meet Again 40. That Uncertain Feeling 41. Affectionately Yours 41. Lydia 41. Forever and a Day 43. Stage Door Canteen 43. First Comes Courage 43. The Lodger 44. Dark Waters 44. *A Song to Remember* 45. This Love of Ours 45. A Night in Paradise 46. Temptation 46. Night Song 47. Berlin Express 48. Pardon My French 51. 24 Hours of a Woman's Life 52. All is Possible in Granada 54. Desiree 54. Deep in My Heart 54. The Price of Fear 56. Of Love and Desire 63. The Oscar 66. Hotel 67. Interval 73.
TV series: Assignment Foreign Legion 56.

Objective Burma (US 1945). The film which brought to a head British resentment about America appearing to have won the war singlehanded; in this case it was Errol Flynn who took Burma without any British help. The outcry was so great that the film was withdrawn in Britain. In fact it tells a good yarn efficiently if at too great length, with photography by James Wong Howe and direction by Raoul Walsh. Ranald MacDougall and Lester Cole wrote the script.

Oboler, Arch (1909–). American writer-producer-director with a long career in radio. Has made mainly stunt films.
□ Bewitched 45. Strange Holiday 46. The Arnelo Affair 47. Five 51. Bwana Devil 52. The Twonky 53. One Plus One 61. The Bubble 67.

O'Brian, Hugh (1925–) (Hugh Krampke). Leathery American leading man, former athlete.
Never Fear 50. On the Loose 51. Red Ball Express 52. Seminole 54. There's No Business Like Show Business 54. White Feather 55. The Brass Legend 56. The Fiend Who Walked the West 58. Come Fly with Me 62. In Harm's Way 65. Love Has Many Faces 65. Ten Little Indians 65. Ambush Bay 66. Africa Texas Style 67. Probe (TV) 72. Killer Force 75. The Shootist 76. Murder at the World Series (TV) 77.
TV series: *Wyatt Earp* 56–59. Search 72.

O'Brien, Dave (1912–1969) (David Barclay). American light character actor, in Hollywood from the early thirties. Played supporting roles in innumerable films; most familiar as the hero/victim of the Pete Smith comedy shorts of the forties.
Jennie Gerhardt 33. East Side Kids 39. Son of the Navy 40. 'Neath Brooklyn Bridge 43. Tahiti Nights 44. Phantom of 42nd Street 45. The Desperadoes are in Town 56, etc.

O'Brien, Edmond (1915–). Anglo-Irish leading man of the forties, latterly character actor; long in Hollywood.
The Hunchback of Notre Dame 39. Parachute Battalion 41. Powder Town 42, etc.; war service; *The Killers* 46. The Web 47. A Double Life 47. Another Part of the Forest 48. An Act of Murder 48. White Heat 49. *D.O.A.* 49. Between Midnight and Dawn 50. Two of a Kind 51. Denver and Rio Grande 52. Julius Caesar 53. The Hitch Hiker 53. Man in the Dark 53. The Bigamist 53. Cow Country 53. *The Barefoot Contessa* (AA) 54. Shield for Murder (& co-d) 54. 1984 (GB) 55. The Girl Can't Help It 57. *The Third Voice* 59. The Last Voyage 60. Mantrap (pd only) 61. The Great Imposter 61. The Man Who Shot Liberty Valance 62. Birdman of Alcatraz 62. *Seven Days in May* 64. Sylvia 65. Fantastic Voyage 66. The Viscount (Fr.) 67. The Wild Bunch 69. The Love God 69. Jigsaw (TV) 72. 99 44/100 Dead 74, etc.
TV series: Sam Benedict 63. The Long Hot Summer 64.

O'Brien, George (1900–). American cowboy star, who entered films as stunt man.
The Iron Horse (first starring role) 24. Sunrise 27. Noah's Ark 28. Lone Star Ranger 30. Riders of the Purple Sage 31. The Last Trail 33. O'Malley of the Mounted 36. Daniel Boone 36. The Painted Desert 38. Stage to Chino 40. Legion of the Lawless 42. She Wore a Yellow Ribbon 49. Cheyenne Autumn 64, others.

O'Brien, Margaret (1937–) (Angela Maxine O'Brien). Stunningly talented American child actress of the forties; won special Academy Award in 1944. Had no luck with adult comeback.
□ Babes on Broadway 41. *Journey for Margaret* 42. Dr Gillespie's Criminal Case 43. Thousands Cheer 43. *Lost Angel* 43. Madame Curie 43. Jane Eyre 43. The Canterville Ghost 44. *Meet Me in St Louis* 44. Music for Millions 45. *Our Vines Have Tender Grapes* 45. Bad Bascomb 45. Three Wise Fools 46. The Unfinished Dance 47. Tenth Avenue Angel 47. Big City 48. *Little Women* 49. The Secret Garden 49. Her First Romance 51. Glory 56. Heller in Pink Tights 60.

O'Brien, Pat (1899–). Easy-going, gentle but tough-looking Irish-American character actor, a popular star of the thirties.
Autobiography 1964: *The Wind at My Back*.
The Front Page 31. Honour among Lovers 31. Final Edition 32. Hell's House 32. American Madness 32. Air Mail 32. Bureau of Missing Persons 33. Bombshell 33. Gambling Lady 34. Here Comes the Navy 34. I Sell Anything 34. Devil Dogs of the Air 35. Oil for the Lamps of China 35. Page Miss Glory 35. The Irish in Us 35. Ceiling Zero 35. Public Enemy's Wife 36. China Clipper 36. The Great O'Malley 37. Slim 37. San Quentin 37. *Boy Meets Girl* 38. *Angels with Dirty Faces* 38. Indianapolis Speedway 39. The Fighting 69th 40. Slightly Honorable 40. Castle on the Hudson 40. Torrid Zone 40. Knute Rockne, All American 41. Submarine Zone 41. Broadway 42. The Navy Comes Through 42. Bombardier 43. The Iron Major 43. His Butler's Sister 43. Secret Command 44. Having Wonderful Crime 45. Man Alive 45. Perilous Holiday 46. Riffraff 47. Fighting Father Dunne 48. The Boy with Green Hair 48. A Dangerous Profession 49. Johnny One Eye 50. The People against O'Hara 51. Okinawa 52. Jubilee Trail 54. Inside Detroit 55. Kill Me Tomorrow (GB) 57. The Last Hurrah 58. Some Like It Hot 59. Town Tamer 65. Nick Carter (TV) 72, many others.
TV series: Harrigan and Son 60.

O'Brien, Virginia (1921–). American comedienne, the 'dead pan' singer of the forties.

Hullaballoo 40. *The Big Store* 41. Ship Ahoy 42. Thousands Cheer 43. Dubarry was a Lady 44. The Harvey Girls 45. Till the Clouds Roll By 46. Merton of the Movies 47, etc.

O'Brien, Willis (1886–1962). American specialist in the creation of monster animals for use in stop-motion techniques.
The Ghost of Slumber Mountain 20. *The Lost World* 24. *King Kong* 33. Son of Kong 33. Mighty Joe Young 49. The Animal World 56. The Black Scorpion 58, etc.

O'Casey, Sean (1880–1964). Irish playwright, much preoccupied by 'the troubles'. Works filmed include *Juno and the Paycock* and *The Plough and the Stars*; an alleged biopic, *Young Cassidy*, was made in 1964 with Rod Taylor.

Occupe-Toi d'Amélie (France 1949). High-speed film version of a Feydeau farce, flawlessly and wittily put together by Claude Autant-Lara. Like *Henry V* it begins and ends with a stage performance of the play, but every minute is highly cinematic. Scripted by Jean Aurenche and Pierre Bost, photographed by André Bac; with Danielle Darrieux, Jean Desailly and a nimble cast.

O'Connell, Arthur (1908–). American character actor with long Broadway experience; usually mildly bewildered roles.
Law of the Jungle 42. Countess of Monte Cristo 49. The Whistle at Eaton Falls 51. *Picnic* 55. The Solid Gold Cadillac 56. *The Man in the Grey Flannel Suit* 56. Bus Stop 56. Operation Mad Ball 57. Operation Petticoat 59. Anatomy of a Murder 59. Follow That Dream 61. Kissin' Cousins 64. The Monkey's Uncle 65. Your Cheating Heart 65. The Great Race 65. The Silencers 66. Fantastic Voyage 66. The Power 68. There Was a Crooked Man 70. Ben 72. The Poseidon Adventure 72. Huckleberry Finn 74. The Hiding Place 75, etc.

O'Connolly, Jim (1926–). British director.
The Traitors (wp only) 62. Smokescreen 63. *The Little Ones* 64. Berserk 67. The Valley of Gwangi 68. Crooks and Coronets 69, etc.

O'Connor, Carroll (1922–). Burly American character actor, often in blustery military roles.
By Love Possessed 61. Lonely are the Brave 62. Cleopatra 63. In Harm's Way 65. What Did You Do in the War Daddy? 65. Waterhole Three 67. Point Blank 67. The Devil's Brigade 68. Marlowe 69. Doctors' Wives 70. Law and Disorder 74, etc.
TV series: *All In the Family* (as Archie Bunker) 70– .

O'Connor, Donald (1925–). Snappy American light comedian, singer and dancer, a teenage star of the forties whose film career suffered with the decline of musicals.
□ *Sing You Sinners* 38. Sons of the Legion 38. Men With Wings 38. *Tom Sawyer Detective* 38. Unmarried 39. Death of a Champion 39. Million Dollar Legs 39. Night Work 39. On Your Toes 39. Beau Geste 39. Private Buckaroo 42. Give Out Sisters 42. Get Hep to Love 42. When Johnny Comes Marching Home 42. Strictly in the Groove 43. It Comes Up Big 43. *Mister Big* 43. Top Man 43. *Chip off the Old Block* 44. This is the Life 44. Follow the Boys 44. The Merry Monahans 44. Bowery to Broadway 44. *Patrick the Great* 45. Something in the Wind 47. Are You With It 48. Feudin' Fussin' and a-Fightin' 48. Yes Sir That's My Baby 49. *Francis* 49. Curtain Call at Cactus Creek 50. The Milkman 50. Double Crossbones 50. Francis Goes to the Races 51. *Singin' In the Rain* 52. Francis Goes to West Point 52. *Call Me Madam* 53. I Love Melvin 53. Francis Covers Big Town 53. Walking My Baby Back Home 53. Francis Joins the WACS 54. There's No Business Like Show Business 54. Francis in the Navy 55. Anything Goes 56. *The Buster Keaton Story* 57. Cry for Happy 61. The Wonders of Aladdin 61. That Funny Feeling 65.

O'Connor, Robert Emmett (1885–1962). American small part player, often as snoop or policeman, on screen from 1909 after circus and vaudeville experience.
Public Enemy 31. A Night at the Opera 35. Tight Shoes 41. Whistling in Brooklyn 44. Boys' Ranch 46, many others.

O'Connor, Una (1893–1959). Sharp-featured Irish character actress with stage experience before film debut in 1929; in Hollywood from 1932.
Cavalcade 33. *The Invisible Man* 33. The Barretts of Wimpole Street 34. *Bride of Frankenstein* 35. The Informer 35. The Plough and the Stars 36. The Adventures of Robin Hood 38. The Sea Hawk 40. Random Harvest 42. Holy Matrimony 43. *Cluny Brown* 46. The Corpse Came C.O.D. 48. *Witness for the Prosecution* 57, many others.

O'Conor, Joseph (c. 1910 –). British character actor, mainly on stage and TV.
Crooks in Cloisters 63. Oliver! 68. Doomwatch 72. The Black Windmill 74.
TV series: The Forsyte Saga (as Old Jolyon) 66.

October (Ten Days that Shook the World) (Russia 1928). Eisenstein's spectacular and exciting reconstruction of the Russian revolution, brilliantly photographed by Tisse. The screen's most persuasive re-creation of fact, and one of its most powerful pieces of propaganda.

Odd Man Out (GB 1947) (BFA). The film which established Carol Reed as a major director; with considerable help from the Abbey Theatre players he created a moving and cinematic impression of the last hours of an IRA gunman on the run. The more theatrical aspects of the picture have not worn well, but it has enough brilliant moments to preserve its reputation. R. C. Sheriff and F. L. Green wrote the script from the latter's novel; photography by Robert Krasker. James Mason played the pathetic central figure, with notable contributions from F. J. McCormick, Robert Newton and many others. The film was more or less remade in 1969 as *The Lost Man*, with Sidney Poitier.

O'Dea, Denis (1905–). Irish stage actor who has been in occasional films.
The Informer 35. The Plough and the Stars 47. Odd Man Out 47. The Fallen Idol 48. Under Capricorn 49. Treasure Island 50. Niagara 52. Mogambo 53. The Rising of the Moon 57. The Story of Esther Costello 58, etc.

O'Dea, Jimmy (1899–1965). Irish character comedian.
Let's Be Famous 39. The Rising of the Moon 57. Darby O'Gill and the Little People 59, etc.

Odets, Clifford (1903–1963). American playwright and occasional scriptwriter.
The General Died at Dawn (w) 36. Golden Boy (oa) 39. None But the Lonely Heart (wd) 44. Deadline at Dawn (w) 46. Humoresque (w) 46. Clash by Night (oa) 52. The Country Girl (oa) 54. The Big Knife (oa) 55. Sweet Smell of Success (w) 57. The Story on Page One (wd) 60, etc.

Odette, Mary (1901–) (Odette Goimbault). French actress in many British silent films from 1915, at first as juvenile. *Dombey and Son, A Spinner of Dreams, With All Her Heart, Mr Gilfil's Love Story*, etc.

O'Donnell, Cathy (1923–1970) (Ann Steely). American leading lady with brief stage experience.
☐ The Best Years of Our Lives (debut) 46. Bury Me Dead 47. The Spiritualist 47. *They Live by Night* 48. Side Street 50. The Miniver Story 50. Detective Story 51. Never Trust a Gambler 53.

The Woman's Angle (GB) 52. Eight O'Clock Walk (GB) 54. The Man from Laramie 55. The Story of Mankind 58. Ben Hur 59.

O'Driscoll, Martha (1922–). American leading lady of the forties, mainly in second features.
The Secret of Dr Kildare 40. The Lady Eve 41. My Heart Belongs to Daddy 42. Follow the Boys 44. Ghost Catchers 44. House of Dracula 45. Criminal Court (last to date) 47, etc.

Of Human Bondage. Somerset Maugham's novel has been filmed three times. 1. US 1934, directed by John Cromwell, with Leslie Howard and Bette Davis. 2. US 1946, directed by Edmund Goulding, with Paul Henreid and Eleanor Parker. 3. GB 1964, directed by Ken Hughes and Henry Hathaway, with Laurence Harvey and Kim Novak. None could prevent the hero's tribulations with a tart from seeming mawkishly unlikely, but the first version was the best acted.

Of Mice and Men (US 1940). A curious film to come from comedy producer Hal Roach, this spare little morality about a gentle but homicidal giant who has to be killed by his best friend seemed striking at the time but has dated badly. From John Steinbeck's novel; directed by Lewis Milestone; with Lon Chaney Jnr, Burgess Meredith and Betty Field.

O'Farrell, Bernadette (1926–). British leading lady who married her director, Frank Launder.
Captain Boycott 48. The Happiest Days of Your Life 49. Lady Godiva Rides Again 51. The Story of Gilbert and Sullivan 53, etc.

offices have provided the setting for many a film. *The Crowd* in 1926 and *The Rebel* in 1961 chose pretty much the same way of stressing the dreariness of daily routine; but *Sunshine Susie* in 1931 and *How to Succeed in Business without Really Trying* in 1967 both saw the office as a gay place full of laughter and song. Satyajit Ray in *Company Limited* and Ermanno Olmi in *Il Posto* and *One Fine Day* took a realistic look at office life. Billy Wilder took a jaundiced view of it in *The Apartment*, as did the makers of *Patterns of Power, Executive Suite, Bartleby* and *The Power and the Prize*. Romantic comedies of the thirties like *Wife versus Secretary, After Office Hours* and *Take a Letter Darling* saw it as ideal for amorous intrigue, and in 1964 *The Wild Affair* took pretty much the same attitude. Orson Welles in *The Trial* made it nightmarish; Preston Sturges in *Christmas in July* made it friendly;

The Desk Set made it computerized; *The Bachelor Party* made it frustrating. Perhaps the best film office is that of Philip Marlowe in the Raymond Chandler films: there's seldom anyone in it but himself. The most spectacular was that of Alfred Abel in *Metropolis*.

Ogilvy, Ian (1943–). Slightly-built British leading man.
Stranger in the House 67. The Sorcerers 67. Witchfinder General 68. Wuthering Heights 70. And Now the Screaming Starts 72. No Sex Please We're British 73, etc.
TV series: *Son of the Saint* 77.

Ogle, Charles (1865–1926). American silent actor.
The Honour of His Family 09. The Ironmaster 14. Joan the Woman 17. Treasure Island 20. The Covered Wagon 23. The Alaskan 24. Contraband 25. The Flaming Forest 26, many others.

Oh Mr Porter (GB 1938). One of the funniest British comedies in the music-hall tradition of the thirties. About an incompetent stationmaster who clears an Irish branch line of gun-runners posing as ghosts, it is superbly written around the talents of Will Hay, with Graham Moffatt (the fat boy) and Moore Marriott (old Harbottle) as foils. Written by Val Guest, Marriott Edgar and J. O. C. Orton, directed by Marcel Varnel.

Oh What a Lovely War (GB 1969). A musical fantasia on World War I, directed with variable wit and imagination by Richard Attenborough, from Joan Littlewood's stage production. Mediocrity and dullness mingled with brilliant sequences such as the final backtrack from war graves; the actors were swamped by the concept. The songs were fine.

O'Hanlon, George (1917–) (George Rice). American comedy actor with stage experience; played Joe McDoakes in the one-reeler 'Behind the Eight Ball' series.
The Great Awakening 41. The Hucksters 47. The Tanks are Coming 51. Battle Stations 55. Bop Girl 57. The Rookie 59. Charley and the Angel 73, etc.

O'Hara, Gerry (c. 1925–). British director.
That Kind of Girl 61. The Pleasure Girls 64. Maroc 7 67. Amsterdam Affair 68. All the Right Noises (& w) 69. The Spy's Wife, etc.

O'Hara, John (1905–1970). American best-selling novelist who wrote chiefly about sex in suburbia. Works filmed include *Pal Joey, From the Terrace, A Rage to Live, Butterfield 8*. Also co-wrote screenplays. In 1976 a TV series was based on his *Gibbsville* stories.
I was an Adventuress 40. Moontide 42. Strange Journey 46. On Our Merry Way 48. The Best Things in Life are Free 56, etc.

O'Hara, Maureen (1920–) (Maureen Fitzsimmons). Striking red-haired Irish leading lady who survived in Hollywood less through acting talent than through pleasing, unassuming personality.
□ My Irish Molly 38. Kicking the Moon Around 38. Jamaica Inn 39. *The Hunchback of Notre Dame* 39. A Bill of Divorcement 40. Dance Girl Dance 40. They Met in Argentina 41. How Green Was My Valley 41. To the Shores of Tripoli 42. Ten Gentlemen from West Point 42. *The Black Swan* 42. The Immortal Sergeant 43. This Land is Mine 43. The Fallen Sparrow 43. Buffalo Bill 44. The Spanish Main 45. Sentimental Journey 46. Do You Love Me 46. Sinbad the Sailor 47. The Homestretch 47. Miracle on 34th Street 47. The Foxes of Harrow 47. Sitting Pretty 48. Britannia Mews 49. A Woman's Secret 49. Father was a Fullback 49. Baghdad 49. Comanche Territory 50. Tripoli 50. Rio Grande 50. Flame of Araby 51. At Sword's Point 52. Kangaroo 52. *The Quiet Man* 52. Against All Flags 52. Redhead from Wyoming 52. War Arrow 53. Fire over Africa 54. The Long Gray Line 55. The Magnificent Matador 55. Lady Godiva 55. Lisbon 56. Everything But the Truth 56. The Wings of Eagles 57. Our Man in Havana 59. The Parent Trap 61. The Deadly Companions 61. Mr Hobbs Takes a Vacation 62. Spencer's Mountain 63. McLintock 63. The Battle of the Villa Fiorita 65. The Rare Breed 66. How to Commit Marriage 69. How Do I Love Thee 70. Big Jake 71. The Red Pony (TV) 72.

O'Herlihy, Dan (1919–). Irish character actor and occasional off-beat leading man, with Abbey Theatre and radio experience.
Odd Man Out (GB) 46. Hungry Hill (GB) 46. Kidnapped 48. Macbeth 48. Actors and Sin 50. Rommel, Desert Fox 51. The Blue Veil 51. The Highwayman 52. *The Adventures of Robinson Crusoe* 52. Bengal Brigade 53. The Black Shield of Falworth 54. The Purple Mask 55. The Virgin Queen 55. That Woman Opposite (GB) 57. Home before Dark 58. Imitation of Life 59. *The Cabinet of Caligari* 61. Fail Safe 64. 100 Rifles 69. Waterloo 69. The Carey Treatment 72. QB VII (TV) 73. The Tamarind Seed 74, others.
TV series: The Travels of Jaimie McPheeters 63.

O'Herlihy, Michael (1929–). Irish director in Hollywood, with TV experience.

The Fighting Prince of Donegal 66. The One and Only Genuine Original Family Band 68. Smith! 69.

Ohmart, Carol (1928–). American leading lady with stage experience, whose career in films did not develop.
The Scarlet Hour (debut) 55. The House on Haunted Hill 58. Born Reckless 59. The Scavangers 60. Wild Youth 60. One Man's Way 64. Caxambu 67. The Spectre of Edgar Allan Poe 72, etc.

O'Keefe, Dennis (1908–1968) (Edward 'Bud' Flanagan). Cheerful American leading man of the forties; began as an extra after vaudeville experience with his parents.
Bad Man of Brimstone 38. That's Right, You're Wrong 39. La Conga Nights 40. You'll Find Out 40. Lady Scarface 41. *Topper Returns* 41. Broadway Limited 41. The Affairs of Jimmy Valentine 42. Good Morning Judge 42. The Leopard Man 43. The Fighting Seabees 43. Up in Mabel's Room 44. Abroad with Two Yanks 44. *The Affairs of Susan* 45. Brewster's Millions 45. Come Back to Me 46. Dishonoured Lady 47. T-Men 47. Mr District Attorney 47. Raw Deal 48. Walk a Crooked Mile 49. Woman on the Run 50. The Company She Keeps 51. Follow the Sun 52. The Fake (GB) 53. The Diamond Wizard (GB) (& d) 54. Angela (& d) 55. Inside Detroit 56. Dragoon Wells Massacre 57. Graft and Corruption 58. All Hands on Deck 61, many others.
TV series: The Dennis O'Keefe Show 59.

Oland, Warner (1880–1938). Swedish character actor in Hollywood who oddly enough became the screen's most popular Chinese detective.
The Yellow Ticket 18. Witness for the Defense 19. His Children's Children 23. Don Q Son of Zorro 25. Don Juan 26. The Jazz Singer 27. Old San Francisco 27. Chinatown Nights 29. The Mysterious Dr Fu Manchu 29. The Vagabond King 30. *Charlie Chan Carries On* 31 (and 15 other episodes in this series). Shanghai Express 32. The Painted Veil 34. *Werewolf of London* 35. Shanghai 35, many others.

Olcott, Sidney (1873–1949) (John S. Alcott). Irish-Canadian director, in Hollywood from the beginning.
Ben Hur (one reel) 07. Florida Crackers 08. Judgement 09. The Miser's Child 10. The O'Neil (Irish) 11. From the Manger to the Cross 12. Madame Butterfly 15. The Innocent Lie 17. Scratch My Back 20. Little Old New York 21. The Humming Bird 23. The Green Goddess 23.

Monsieur Beaucaire 24. The Amateur Gentleman 26. The Claw 27, etc.

old age on the screen has seldom been explored, and the commercial reasons for this are obvious. Among the serious studies are *The Whisperers*, with Edith Evans; *Umberto D*, with Carlo Battisti; *The Shameless Old Lady*, with Sylvie; *Ikuru*, with Takashi Shimura; *The End of the Road*, with Finlay Currie: *I Never Sang for My Father*, with Melvyn Douglas; *Make Way for Tomorrow*, with Beulah Bondi; *Alive and Kicking*, with Sybil Thorndike and Estelle Winwood; *Kotch* with Walter Matthau and *Harry and Tonto* with Art Carney. Sentimentality crept in in *Mr Belvedere Rings the Bell*; and *The Old Man and the Sea* was merely pretentious.
There was an element of black comedy in the attitudes expressed towards the old people in *Grapes of Wrath, Tobacco Road* and *Night of the Iguana*; and more melodramatic caricatures were presented in *The Lost Moment* (Agnes Moorehead), *The Queen of Spades* (Edith Evans), *Little Big Man* (Dustin Hoffman), and *The Old Dark House* (John Dudgeon). Fantasy crept in with *Lost Horizon*, in which the lamas grew incredibly old by natural processes, and *The Man in Half Moon Street*, in which Nils Asther was assisted by science. Other actors who have specialized in geriatric portraits include A. E. Matthews, Edie Martin, Clem Bevans, Andy Clyde, Maria Ouspenskaya, Jessie Ralph, Nancy Price and Adeline de Walt Reynolds, who did not become an actress until she was eighty. Perhaps the Screen's most delightful senior citizens were the capering Harbottle, played by Moore Marriott in Will Hay comedies, and Barry Fitzgerald in *Broth of a Boy*; the most horrific was Cathleen Nesbit in *Staircase;* the most commercially successful were George Burns and Walter Matthau in *The Sunshine Boys*.

The Old Dark House (US 1932). A connoisseur's horror film, from J. B. Priestley's novel about an assorted group of people marooned in an inhospitable old mansion on a stormy night. Directed by James Whale with a rare sense of the eccentric and bizarre; acted by a splendid cast including Ernest Thesiger ('Have some gin: it's my only weakness'), Eva Moore ('No beds—they can't have beds'), Melvyn Douglas, Charles Laughton, Raymond Massey, Boris Karloff and Brember Wills. The Hammer remake (GB 1963) proved completely unsatisfactory.

Old Mother Riley. The vociferous Irish

washerwoman was impersonated by Arthur Lucan for years in the music halls and in a dozen or more films between 1937 and 1952, the last one being *Mother Riley Meets the Vampire*. Daughter Kitty was played by the resistible Kitty McShane. Most of the films were atrociously made but all of them made a sizeable profit from British provincial showings.

Oldfield, Barney (1878–1946) (Berna Eli Oldfield). American racing driver, the first to travel a mile a minute; featured in *Barney Oldfield's Race for Life* 16.

Oldland, Lilian (1905–). British leading lady of the silents, who later changed her name to Mary Newland.
The Secret Kingdom 25. The Flag Lieutenant 26. Troublesome Wives 27. Jealousy 31. Ask Beccles 34. Death at Broadcasting House 34. The Silent Passenger (last to date) 35, etc.

Oliver!: see *Oliver Twist*.

Oliver, Anthony (1923–). Welsh general purpose actor, in British films and TV.
Once a Jolly Swagman 48. The Clouded Yellow 50. The Runaway Bus 54. Lost 56. The Fourth Square 61, others.

Oliver, Edna May (1883–1942) (Edna May Cox-Oliver). American character actress, usually of acidulous but often warm-hearted spinsters; on stage from 1912.
Icebound 23. The American Venus 26. Saturday Night Kid 29. Half Shot at Sunrise 31. Cimarron 31. *Fanny Foley Herself* 31. The Penguin Pool Murder 32. Little Women 33. Alice in Wonderland 33. *David Copperfield* (as Aunt Betsy) 34. A Tale of Two Cities 35. Romeo and Juliet (as the Nurse) 36. Parnell 37. Rosalie 38. Second Fiddle 38. The Story of Vernon and Irene Castle 39. Nurse Edith Cavell 39. *Pride and Prejudice* (as Lady Catherine de Bourgh) 40. Lydia 41, etc.

Oliver, Susan (1937–). American leading TV actress whose film roles have been few.
Green-Eyed Blonde 57. The Gene Krupa Story 60. Looking for Love 64. The Disorderly Orderly 65. Your Cheating Heart 66. A Man Called Gannon 68. Change of Mind 69, etc.

Oliver Twist. Dickens' novel was filmed many times in the early silent period: in 1909 by Pathé, in 1910 by Vitagraph, in 1912 by an independent company with Nat C. Goodwin as Fagin. A famous American version of 1916 had Tully Marshall as Fagin and Marie Doro as Oliver; in 1922 the roles were played by Lon Chaney and Jackie Coogan, and in 1933 by Irving Pichel and Dickie Moore. The definitive version to date, however, is the British one directed by David Lean in 1948, with John Howard Davies in the title role. Alec Guinness' brilliant performance as Fagin caused a hold-up in American distribution as it was accused of anti-semitism. Technically a remarkable evocation of the book's melodramatic realism, the film was photographed by Guy Green, designed by John Bryan, with music by Arnold Bax. *Oliver!*, a 1968 musical version, won six Oscars: best film, best director (Carol Reed), best art direction (John Box and Terence Marsh), best score (John Green), best sound (Shepperton Studios), best choreography (Onna White).

Oliver, Vic (1898–1964) (Victor von Samek). Austrian-born comedian, pianist, violinist and conductor, long in Britain. Occasional films. Autobiography 1954: *Mr Show Business*.
Rhythm in the Air 37. Room for Two 40. He Found a Star 41. Hi Gang 41. Give Us the Moon 44. I'll Be Your Sweetheart 45, etc.

Olivier, Laurence (1907–) (Lord Olivier). Distinguished British stage actor whose film appearances have been reasonably frequent.
Biographies: 1969, *Cry God for Larry* by Virginia Fairweather. 1975, *Laurence Olivier* by John Cottrell.
□ Too Many Crooks 30. The Temporary Widow 30. Potiphar's Wife 30. The Yellow Ticket 31. Friends and Lovers 31. Westward Passage 31. No Funny Business 32. Perfect Understanding (US) 32. Conquest of the Air 35. Moscow Nights 35. As You Like It (as Orlando) 36. Fire over England 36. *The Divorce of Lady X* 38. Twenty-One Days 39. Q Planes 39. *Wuthering Heights* (US) 39. *Rebecca* (US) 40. *Pride and Prejudice* (US) 40. *Lady Hamilton* (US) (as Nelson) 41. 49th Parallel 41. The Demi-Paradise 43. *Henry V* (& p, co-d) (special AA) 44. *Hamlet* (& pd) (AA) 48. The Magic Box (cameo Role) 51. *Carrie* (US) 52. The Beggar's Opera (as Macheath) 52. *Richard III* (& pd) 56. The Prince and the Showgirl (& d) 58. *The Devil's Disciple* 59. Spartacus (US) 60. *The Entertainer* 60. Term of Trial 62. Bunny Lake is Missing 65. Othello 65. Khartoum 66. The Shoes of the Fisherman 68. Oh What a Lovely War 69. The Dance of Death 69. The Battle of Britain 69. David Copperfield 69. Three Sisters (& d) 70. Nicholas and Alexandra 71. Lady Caroline Lamb 72. *Sleuth* 72. Love Among the Ruins (TV) 74. *Marathon Man* 76. The Seven Per Cent Solution 76. Jesus of Nazareth (TV) 77.

Olmi, Ermanno (1931–). Italian director.
Il Posto (*The Job*) 61. I Fidanzati 62. And There Came a Man 65. One Fine Day 69. Diary of Summer 71, etc.

O'Loughlin, Gerald S. (1923–). American TV actor, prominent in series *The Rookies* 72–76.

Olsen, Ole (1892–1965) (John Sigurd Olsen). Norwegian-American comedian, in vaudeville from 1914, almost always with partner Chic Johnson.
Gold Dust Gertie 31. Fifty Million Frenchmen 31. The Country Gentleman 37. Hellzapoppin 42. Crazy House 44. Ghost Catchers 44. See My Lawyer 45, etc.

Olsen, Moroni (1889–1954). Heavily-built American character actor, with stage experience.
The Three Musketeers (as Porthos) 36. The Witness Chair 38. The Three Musketeers (as Bailiff) 39. Kentucky 39. The Glass Key 42. Call Northside 777 48. Father of the Bride 50. The Long, Long Trailer 54, many others.

Olson, James (1932–). American general purpose actor.
The Sharkfighters 56. The Strange One 57. Rachel Rachel 67. The Andromeda Strain 70. Moon Zero Two 70. Wild Rovers 71. The Groundstar Conspiracy 72, etc.

Olson, Nancy (1928–). American leading lady who came to films from college, retired after a few years and recently reappeared in more mature roles.
Canadian Pacific 49. Union Station 50. *Sunset Boulevard* 50. Submarine Command 51. Force of Arms 52. So Big 52. Battle Cry 55. Pollyanna 60. The Absent-Minded Professor 61. Son of Flubber 63. Smith! 69. Snowball Express 73, etc.

Los Olvidados (Mexico 1950). Luis Buñuel's study of depraved and deprived adolescents in Mexico: the young anti-hero ends up dead on a dung heap. Photographed by Figueroa, it is a comfortless film, but important in the history of social realism.

Olympische Spiele (Germany 1936). Leni Riefenstahl's brilliantly-photographed and edited account of the Olympic Games of 1936, is a hymn to the human body and a superb example of film reporting.

O'Malley, J. Pat (1901–). British character actor in Hollywood.
Go and Get It 20. Happiness 24. The Fall Guy

30. Frisco Jenny 33. Hollywood Boulevard 36. A Little Bit of Heaven 40. Lassie Come Home 43. The Rugged O'Riordans 49. Kind Lady 51. The Long Hot Summer 58. *Blueprint for Robbery* 60. The Cabinet of Caligari 62. A House is Not a Home 64. Gunn 67. Hello Dolly 69. Willard 70, many others.

O'Malley, Rex (1901–1976). American light actor who was little heard from after giving nice performances in *Camille* 36 and *Midnight* 39.

O'Mara, Kate (1939–). British leading lady.
Great Catherine 68. The Limbo Line 68. The Desperados 69. Horror of Frankenstein 70, etc.

On Approval (GB 1944). A curious but very successful one-shot at directing by Clive Brook, who with Googie Withers, Beatrice Lillie and Roland Culver made up the romantic quartet involved in this unexpected version of Frederick Lonsdale's Edwardian comedy. There was a touch of the Marx Brothers about the semi-mocking treatment of the faded material, but it certainly came off even though it had no imitators at the time.

On the Beach (US 1959). Stanley Kramer's bleak film about the end of the world, from Nevil Shute's novel, was about the most downbeat production ever to come from Hollywood. Although interesting it seemed in the long run over-slow and rather pointless, but the last rites of mankind were glossily photographed by Sam Leavitt.

On the Town (US 1949). One of Hollywood's most exhilarating and influential musicals. A tale of three sailors on a day's leave in New York, it had a sextet of principals who lit up the screen with their sheer vivacity and well-nigh perpetual motion: Gene Kelly, Frank Sinatra, Jules Munshin, Betty Garrett, Ann Miller and Vera-Ellen. No one talks in this film when song or dance will do. Direction by Kelly and Stanley Donen; music by Leonard Berstein; words by Adolph Green and Betty Comden; photography by Harold Rossen.

On the Waterfront (US 1954). Basically a good location thriller about the docks protection rackets, this film from Budd Schulberg's novel had enough pretensions to win it several Academy Awards: best actor (Marlon Brando), best supporting actress (Eva Marie Saint), best art direction (Richard Day), best picture, best cinematography (Boris Kaufman), best direction (Elia Kazan), best editing (Gene Milford). It wasn't really all that good; but it did bring the method to the masses, mumblings and all.

Ondra, Anny (1903–) (A. Ondrakova). German-Czech leading lady of British silent films; her accent killed her career when sound came. Returned to Europe and appeared in a few German films.

Chorus Girls 28. The Manxman 29. Blackmail 30. Glorious Youth 31. Schön Muso Man Sein 50. Die Zuercher Verlorung 57, etc.

Ondricek, Miroslav (1934–). Czech cinematographer in international films.

Diamonds of the Night 64. Intimate Lighting 66. Peter and Pavla 68. The White Bus 67. If 67. The Firemen's Ball 69. Taking Off 71, etc.

One Hour with You: see *The Marriage Circle.*

One Hundred and One Dalmatians (US 1960). Disney's most pleasing post-war full length cartoon, with a strength and delicacy of line which the studio was not able to maintain. Based on an amusing story by Dodie Smith, it makes play with a well-observed London background.

One Million B.C. (US 1939). This curious film, also known as *The Cave Dwellers* and *Man and His Mate*, was produced and directed in 1939 by Hal Roach with assistance from D. W. Griffith, upon whose 1912 *Man's Genesis* it was based. A highly unscientific account of the tribulations of primitive man, it featured Carole Landis and Victor Mature, whose dialogue consisted largely of grunts, and who came up against a remarkable variety of pre-historic monsters which were rather obviously normal reptiles crudely decorated and magnified. In 1966 Hammer remade it in a rather pedestrian colour version with Raquel Welch and John Richardson, directed by Don Chaffey; this time the monsters were plastic animations. 1970 brought a kind of sequel, *When Dinosaurs Ruled the Earth*, directed by Val Guest, and *Creatures the World Forgot* followed in 1971.

One Sunday Afternoon (US 1933). This pleasant romantic comedy-drama, set in Brooklyn in the nineties, was made three times within fifteen years by the same company, Warners. The first version, directed by Stephen Roberts, had Gary Cooper, Neil Hamilton, Fay Wray and Frances Fuller. The second version, made in 1941 under the title *Strawberry Blonde*, was directed by Raoul Walsh and starred James Cagney, Jack Carson, Olivia de Havilland and Rita Hayworth. In 1948 Raoul Walsh again directed under the original title, this time with songs added; the stars were Dennis Morgan,

Don Defore, Dorothy Malone and Janis Paige. The scripts stemmed from a play by James Hagan, about a dentist who fell for a glamorous girl but eventually returned to his artless sweetheart.

One, Two, Three (US 1961). Billy Wilder has always liked to take his stories from the newspaper headlines, but this frantic comedy was his most daring, being all about the Berlin Wall at a time when it seemed we were in for a third world war over it. Based on a Molnar play, brought up to date by Wilder and I. A. L. Diamond, it scuttles along with tremendous zip until round about the third act, when the pace flags. James Cagney as an exuberant Coca-Cola salesman makes it practically a one-man show. Photographed by Daniel Fapp.

One Way Passage (US 1932). A popular tear-jerker of its time, about a dying beauty (Kay Francis) and a convicted murderer (William Powell) who meet on an ocean liner and fall in love while keeping their secrets; written and directed by Tay Garnett. In 1940 it was remade by Edmund Goulding as *Till We Meet Again*, with Merle Oberon and George Brent.

O'Neal, Frederick (1905–). Powerful American Black character actor, mainly on stage.

Pinky 49. No Way Out 50. Something of Value 56. Anna Lucasta 58. Take a Giant Step 59, etc. TV series: Car 54 Where Are You? 61–62.

O'Neal, Patrick (1927–). American general purpose actor with stage and TV experience.

The Mad Magician 54. From the Terrace 60. The Cardinal 63. In Harm's Way 65. King Rat 65. A Fine Madness 66. Chamber of Horrors 66. Alvarez Kelly 66. *Assignment to Kill* 67. Where Were You When the Lights Went Out? 68. The Secret Life of an American Wife 68. Castle Keep 69. Stiletto 69. The Kremlin Letters 69. Corky 72. The Way We Were 73. The Stepford Wives 75, etc.

TV series: Dick and the Duchess 58.

O'Neal, Ron (1937–). Black American leading man.

Superfly 72. Superfly TNT 73. The Master Gunfighter 75, etc.

O'Neal, Ryan (1941–) (Patrick Ryan O'Neal). Bland American leading man of the late sixties and seventies.

□ The Big Bounce 69. *Love Story* 70. Love Hate Love (TV) 70. Wild Rovers 71. *What's Up Doc* 72. The Thief Who Came to Dinner 73. *Paper*

Moon 73. Barry Lyndon 75. Nickelodeon 76.
TV series: Empire 61. *Peyton Place* 64–68.

O'Neal, Tatum (1962–). Abrasive child
actress of the seventies, daughter of Ryan
O'Neal.
□ *Paper Moon* (AA) 73. The Bad News Bears
76. Nickelodeon 76.

O'Neil, Barbara (1909–). American
character actress who made a corner in mad
wives and other neurotic roles.
Stella Dallas 37. *When Tomorrow Comes* 39.
Tower of London 39. Gone with the Wind 39. *All
This and Heaven Too* 40. Shining Victory 41. I
Remember Mama 47. Whirlpool 49. Angel Face
52. Flame of the Islands 55. The Nun's Story 58,
many others.

O'Neil, Sally (1913–1968) (Virginia Noonan).
American leading lady of the twenties.
Sally Irene and Mary 25. Battling Butler 26. Slide
Kelly Slide 27. The Lovelorn 27. The Mad Hour
28. Jazz Heaven 29. Hold Everything 30.
Salvation Nell 31. Murder by the Clock 31.
Sixteen Fathoms Deep 33. Kathleen 37, etc.

O'Neill, Eugene (1888–1953). Irish-American
playwright of self-pitying disposition and a
tendency in his plays to tragic despair. His
gloominess led Hollywood to regard his works as
art, which killed many of the film versions stone
dead.
Anna Christie 23 with Blanche Sweet, 30 with
Garbo, Strange Interlude 32. The Emperor
Jones 33. Ah Wilderness 35. The Long Voyage
Home 40. The Hairy Ape 44. Summer Holiday
47. Mourning Becomes Electra 48. Desire under
the Elms 57. Long Day's Journey into Night 62.
The Iceman Cometh 73, etc.

O'Neill, Henry (1891–1964). American
character actor with stage experience, in
Hollywood from early thirties. Played scores of
judges, guardians, fathers, lawyers, etc.
I Loved a Woman 33. Wonder Bar 34. Black
Fury 35. The White Angel 36. First Lady 37.
Brother Rat 38. Juarez 39. Billy the Kid 41.
White Cargo 43. The Virginian 46. Alias Nick
Beal 49. The Milkman 50. Untamed 55. The
Wings of Eagles 57, over a hundred others.

O'Neill, James (1847–1920). American stage
actor, father of Eugene. Best film part 1913: *The
Count of Monte Cristo*.

O'Neill, Jennifer (1947–). American leading
lady of the seventies.
Rio Lobo 70. *Summer of 42* 71. Such Good

Friends 71. The Carey Treatment 72. Glass
Houses 72. Lady Ice 73. The Reincarnation of
Peter Proud 75. Whiffs 75, etc.

O'Neill, Maire (1885–1952) (Maire Allgood).
Irish character actress, an Abbey player; sister of
Sara Allgood.
Juno and the Paycock 30. Sing As We Go 34.
Farewell Again 37. Love on the Dole 41. Gaiety
George 46. Someone at the Door 50. Treasure
Hunt 52, etc.

Onibaba (Japan 1964). A stylish medieval
horror comic set entirely within a forest of tall
reeds by a river, where two penniless women
murder strangers for their clothing, finally
coming to grief through lust and jealousy. Its
remarkable holding power is attributable to
Kaneto Shindo's direction and Kyomi Kuroda's
photography.

Opatoshu, David (1918–). American general
purpose actor, often seen as villain.
Exodus 60. Guns of Darkness 63. Torn Curtain
66. The Defector 67. Enter Laughing 67. Death
of a Gunfighter 69, etc.

Open City (Italy 1945). A semi-documentary
record, shot under the noses of the retreating
German army by Italian patriots, of what Italy
had suffered under the occupation. Occasionally
melodramatic but always moving, with a
rawness fresh to the western cinema at the time.
Also the film which introduced Anna Magnani to
a wider audience. Directed by Roberto Rossellini
from a script by Sergei Amidei and Federico
Fellini; photographed by Uberto Arato.

opera has never been a successful commodity
on the screen, although many operas have been
filmed as from the stalls, and appear to have
succeeded with minority audiences. The
occasional big opera production such as *Porgy
and Bess, Pagliacci* or *Carmen Jones*, however,
can expect to meet with only moderate success.
Opera does, however, make an excellent
background for thrillers (*Charlie Chan at the
Opera*), farces (*A Night at the Opera*) and
melodramas (*Metropolitan*). Opera singers who
have succeeded as film stars include Grace
Moore, Lily Pons, Mario Lanza, Tito Gobbi,
Richard Tauber, Lauritz Melchior, Ezio Pinza
and Gladys Swarthout. Oddly enough the singer
Mary Garden was a big hit in *silent* films.

Ophuls, Marcel (1927–). French director,
son of Max Ophuls; mainly associated with
elaborate documentaries.
Peau de Banane 63. *The Sorrow and the Pity* 69.
A Sense of Loss 73. A Memory of Justice 76.

Ophuls, Max (1902–1957) (Max Oppenheimer). German director of international highly decorated, romantic films.
☐ Dan Schön Lieber Lebertran 30. Die Lachende Erben 31. Die Verliebte Firma 31. Der Verkaufte Braute 32. *Liebelei* 32. Une Histoire d'Amour 33. On a Volé un Homme 34. La Signora Di Tutti 34. Trouble with Money 34. Divine 35. La Tendre Ennemie 36. Yoshimara 37. Werther 38. Sans Lendemain 39. De Mayerling à Sarajevo 40. The Exile 47. *Letter from an Unknown Woman* 48. Caught 48. *The Reckless Moment* 49. *La Ronde* 50. Le Plaisir 51. *Madame De* 53. *Lola Montes* 55.

opticals. A general term indicating all the visual tricks such as wipes, dissolves, invisibility, mattes, etc., which involve laboratory work.

Orchard, Julian (1930–). Lugubrious British revue comedian who has enlivened a number of bit parts.
Crooks Anonymous 58. On the Beat 60. Kill or Cure 62. The Spy with a Cold Nose 66. Carry On Doctor 68. Heironymus Merkin 69. Perfect Friday 70, others.

orchestral conductors have figured as leading men in *Intermezzo*, *Interlude*, *Once More with Feeling*, *Unfaithfully Yours*, *Song of Russia*, *Break of Hearts*, *Prelude to Fame*, *Counterpoint*; Charles Laughton cut a tragicomic figure in *Tales of Manhattan*. Real conductors who have played dramatic roles in movies include Leopold Stokowski, José Iturbi and many swing and jazz figures such as Paul Whiteman, Tommy Dorsey, Henry Hall, Glenn Miller, Benny Goodman, Xavier Cugat.

Oreste: see *Kirkop, Oreste*.

original version. In European countries, this indicates a foreign language film which is subtitled and not dubbed.

Ornadel, Cyril (–). British composer.
Some May Love 67. Die Screaming Marianne 71. Not Now Darling 72. Brief Encounter (TV) 75. Edward the Seventh (TV series) 75, etc.

Ornitz, Arthur J. (–). American cinematographer.
The Anderson Tapes 71. Serpico 73. Next Stop Greenwich Village 76.

O'Rourke, Brefni (1889–1945). Irish stage actor, an Abbey player, who made some British films, usually as testy types.
The Ghost of St Michael's 41. Hatter's Castle 41.

The Lamp Still Burns 43. Don't Take It to Heart 44. I See a Dark Stranger 45, etc.

Orphee (France 1949). A strange poetic fantasy written and directed by Jean Cocteau, based on the myth of Orpheus and Eurydice but with twists of his own. Its real meaning is almost as obscure as that of his 1930 surrealist film *Le Sang d'un Poète*, but there is much pleasure to be gained from watching it purely as a piece of instinctively successful cinema using all the devices of the medium. Photographed by Nicolas Hayer, music by Georges Auric, with Jean Marais as Orpheus and Maria Casares as Death. Cocteau in 1960 made an even stranger sequel, *Le Testament D'Orphée*.

Orry-Kelly (1897–1964). Australian designer, in Hollywood from 1923 after Broadway experience. For many years with Warner, then with Fox. Won Academy Award for costumes of *An American in Paris* 51, *Some Like It Hot* 59.

Orth, Frank (1880–1962). American small part actor who must have played more bartenders than he could count.
Hot Money 36. Serenade 39. The Lost Weekend 45. Father of the Bride 50. Here Come the Girls 54, many others.

Ortolani, Riz (–). Italian composer.
Mondo Cane 63. The Seventh Dawn 64. Woman Times Seven 67. Buona Sera Mrs Campbell 68. The Mackenzie Break 70. Say Hello to Yesterday 71. The Valachi Papers 72, etc.

Orwell, George (1903–1950) (Eric Blair). British satirist and novelist whose chief bequests to the cinema are *Animal Farm* and *1984*.

Osborn, Andrew (1912–). British stage and film actor. More recently BBC TV producer: Maigret series, etc.
Who Goes Next? 38. Idol of Paris 48. Dark Interval 50. Angels One Five 51. The Second Mrs Tanqueray 53, etc.

Osborne, John (1929–). British dramatist. Plays filmed: *Look Back in Anger* 59. *The Entertainer* 60. *Inadmissible Evidence* 68. Also wrote screenplay for *Tom Jones* 63.

'Oscar'. An affectionate name given to the Academy Award statuette; reputedly because when the figure was first struck in 1927 a secretary said: 'It reminds me of my Uncle Oscar.'

Oscar, Henry (1891–1970) (Henry Wale). British character actor, on stage from 1911, films from 1932, usually as meek or scheming fellows.
After Dark (debut) 32. I was a Spy 33. The Man Who Knew Too Much 34. Fire over England 37. *The Return of the Scarlet Pimpernel* (as Robespierre) 39. Hatter's Castle 41. They Made Me a Fugitive 47. The Greed of William Hart 48. The Black Rose 50. Private's Progress 55. Foxhole in Cairo 60, etc.

Oscarsson, Per (1927–). Swedish leading actor.
The Doll 62. Hunger 66. My Sister My Love 66. Who Saw Him Die? 67. Dr Glas 67. A Dandy in Aspic 68. The Last Valley 71. Secrets 72. The Emigrants 72. Endless Night 72, etc.

O'Shea, Michael (1906–1973). American actor with a 'good guy' personality, who, after circus and vaudeville experience, made several films in the forties and fifties.
Jack London 42. Striptease Lady 43. The Eve of St Mark 44. It's a Pleasure 45. Circumstantial Evidence 45. The Big Wheel 49. The Model and the Marriage Broker 52. It Should Happen to You 55, etc.

O'Shea, Milo (1926–). Irish character actor, usually in slightly bumbling comic roles.
Never Put It in Writing 64. *Ulysses* (as Bloom) 67. Romeo and Juliet 68. Barbarella 68. The Adding Machine 69. Loot 70. The Angel Levine 70, etc.

O'Shea, Tessie (1917–). Amply-proportioned British music hall singer.
The Shiralee 58. The Russians are Coming, The Russians are Coming 66. The Best House in London 68. Bedknobs and Broomsticks 71.

Osmond, Cliff (–). Heavyweight American comedy actor.
Kiss Me Stupid 64. The Fortune Cookie 67. The Front Page 74. Sharks Treasure 75, etc.

O'Sullivan, Maureen (1911–). Irish leading lady in Hollywood, always in shy, gentle roles. Mother of Mia Farrow.
□ Song of My Heart 30. So This is London 30. Just Imagine 30. The Princess and the Plumber 30. A Connecticut Yankee 31. Skyline 31. *Tarzan the Ape Man* 32 (she was his most famous Jane). The Silver Lining 32. Big Shot 32. Information Kid 32. Strange Interlude 32. Skyscraper Souls 32. Payment Deferred 32. The Fast Companions 32. Robbers Roost 33. The Cohens and Kellys in Trouble 33. Tugboat Annie 33. Stage Mother 33. Tarzan and His Mate 34. The Thin Man 34. *The Barretts of Wimpole Street* 34. Hideout 34. West Point of the Air 34. David Copperfield 34. Cardinal Richelieu 35. The Flame Within 35. Anna Karenina 35. Woman Wanted 35. The Bishop Misbehaves 35. Tarzan Escapes 36. The Voice of Bugle Ann 36. The Devil Doll 36. A Day at the Races 37. Between Two Women 37. The Emperor's Candlesticks 37. My Dear Miss Aldrich 37. A Yank at Oxford 38. Hold that Kiss 38. The Crowd Roars 38. Port of Seven Seas 38. Spring Madness 38. Let Us Live 38. Tarzan Finds a Son 39. *Pride and Prejudice* 40. Sporting Blood 40. Maisie was a Lady 41. Tarzan's Secret Treasure 41. Tarzan's New York Adventure 42. The Big Clock 48. Where Danger Lives 50. Bonzo Goes to College 52. All I Desire 53. Mission Over Korea 53. Duffy of San Quentin 54. The Steel Cage 54. The Tall T 57. Wild Heritage 58. *Never Too Late* 65. The Phynx 69. The Crooked Hearts (TV) 72.

O'Sullivan, Richard (1943–). British juvenile, formerly child actor.
The Stranger's Hand 53. Dangerous Exile 56. A Story of David 60. The Young Ones 61. Wonderful Life 64. Father Dear Father 73, etc.

Oswald, Gerd (1916–). German-American director, son of Richard Oswald.
□ A Kiss before Dying 56. The Brass Legend 57. Crime of Passion 57. Fury at Sundown 57. Valerie 57. Paris Holiday 57. Screaming Mimi 58. Brainwashed 61. Agent for H.A.R.M. 66. 80 Steps to Jonah 69. Bunny O'Hare 71.

Oswald, Richard (1880–1963) (R. Ornstein). German director, father of Gerd Oswald.
Pagu 16. Round the World in Eighty Days 19. Victoria and Her Hussar 31. Der Hauptmann von Köpenick 32. I Was a Criminal (US) 41. Isle of Missing Men (US) 42. The Lovable Cheat (US) 49, etc.

O'Toole, Peter (1932–). British leading man who after stage and TV experience had fairly meteoric rise to stardom in films.
□ Kidnapped (debut) 59. Savage Innocents 59. The Day They Robbed the Bank of England 60. *Lawrence of Arabia* 62. *Becket* 64. Lord Jim 65. What's New Pussycat? 65. How to Steal a Million 66. The Night of the Generals 66. The Bible 66. Great Catherine 67. *The Lion in Winter* 68. *Goodbye Mr Chips* 69. Country Dance 70. Murphy's War 70. Under Milk Wood 71. The Ruling Class 71. Man of la Mancha 72. Rosebud 75. Man Friday 75. Foxtrot 75. Rogue Male (TV) 76.

Ottiano, Rafaela (1894–1942). Italian-born stage actress who went to Hollywood and played sinister housekeepers, etc.
As You Desire Me 32. Grand Hotel 32. She Done Him Wrong 33. Great Expectations 34. Maytime 37. Topper Returns 41, etc.

Oulton, Brian (1908–). British stage and film comedy actor, usually in unctuous or prim roles.
Too Many Husbands 39. Miranda 48. Last Holiday 50. Castle in the Air 52. The Million Pound Note 54. Private's Progress 55. Happy is the Bride 57. The Thirty-Nine Steps 59. A French Mistress 60. Kiss of the Vampire 62. Carry On Cleo 64. The Intelligence Men 64. Carry On Camping 69. On the Buses 71. Ooh You are Awful 72.

Our Daily Bread (US 1933). King Vidor wrote and directed this sequel to his 1928 urban movie *The Crowd*; he now showed his downtrodden hero making good during the depression years by taking to collective farming. Photographed by Robert Planck; with Tom Keene and Karen Morley.

'Our Gang'. A collection of child actors first gathered together in short slapstick comedies by producer Hal Roach in the mid-twenties. They remained popular through the thirties and forties, though the personnel of the team naturally changed. The originals included Mary Kornman, Farina, Joe Cobb, Mickey Daniels and Jackie Condon; a later generation included Spanky Macfarland, Darla Hood and Buckwheat Thomas. Robert McGowan directed most of the films, many of which have been revived on TV.

Oury, Gerard (1919–) (Max-Gerard Tannenbaum). Dapper French character actor.
Antoine et Antoinette 46. La Belle Que Voilà 49. Sea Devils (GB) 52. *Father Brown* (GB) 54. House of Secrets (GB) 56. The Journey (US) 58. The Mirror Has Two Faces 59, etc.
NOW DIRECTOR: La Main Chaude 60. *The Sucker* (*Le Corniaud*) 64. The Big Spree 66. The Brain 69. Adventures of Rabbi Jacob 72, etc.

Ouspenskaya, Maria (1876–1949). Distinguished, diminutive European character actress who enlivened some Hollywood films after the mid-thirties.
□ Dodsworth 36. Conquest 37. *Love Affair* 39. *The Rains Came* 39. Judge Hardy and Son 39. Dr Ehrlich's Magic Bullet 40. Waterloo Bridge 40. The Mortal Storm 40. The Man I Married 40. Dance Girl Dance 40. Beyond Tomorrow 40. *The Wolf Man* 41. The Shanghai Gesture 41. *King's Row* 42. The Mystery of Marie Roget 42.

Frankenstein Meets the Wolf Man 43. Tarzan and the Amazons 45. I've Always Loved You 46. Wyoming 47. A Kiss in the Dark 49.

Out of the Inkwell (US 1920–1924). An influential series of silent cartoons by Max Fleischer, in which the artist's hands and drawing pad were in normal photography and the cartoon characters, superimposed, appeared to animate themselves.

The Outlaw (1943). This notorious censor-baiting western, with its advertising campaign based on Jane Russell's cleavage, has historical interest as an example of how producer-director Howard Hughes managed to fool all of the people all of the time. The movie is neither sensational nor very entertaining, but by withholding it from release for three years and getting into a lot of argument with censor boards, Hughes made the world's press believe it was. Basically a fanciful tale of an encounter between Billy the Kid and Doc Holliday, it needed firmer handling than Hughes was able to supply. The full story of the film's making can be found in the recent biographies of Hughes (qv).

Outward Bound. Sutton Vane's 1923 play concerns a group of people who find themselves travelling on a luxurious but mysterious ship and slowly realize they are dead. It was filmed in 1930 by Robert Milton, with Leslie Howard and Douglas Fairbanks Jnr, and ran into considerable censor trouble. In 1944 an updated and extremely dreary version was directed by Edward A. Blatt under the title *Between Two Worlds*: Paul Henreid and John Garfield had the leads, and Sidney Greenstreet livened up the last half as the heavenly examiner. In 1972 a TV movie called *Haunts of the Very Rich* unofficially brought it up to date.

The Overlanders (GB 1946). Made on location in Australia, this story of an arduous cattle drive seemed to open new horizons for colonial film-making, but they did not develop significantly and the later Australian productions proved disappointing. Even star Chips Rafferty waned in appeal. But this was a good western in a fresh locale, written and directed by Harry Watt and photographed by Osmond Borrodaile.

Overman, Lynne (1887–1943). American character actor with stage experience. Memorable in cynical comedy roles for his relaxed manner and sing-song voice.
Midnight 34. Rumba 35. The Jungle Princess 36. Spawn of the North 38. Typhoon 40. Aloma of the South Seas 40. Caught in the Draft 41. *Roxie Hart* 42. Reap the Wild Wind 42. Dixie 43, etc.

Owen, Bill (1914–) (Bill Rowbotham). British character comedian, former dance band musician and singer.

The Way to the Stars (debut) 45. When the Bough Breaks 47. The Girl Who Couldn't Quite 49. Trottie True 49. Hotel Sahara 51. The Square Ring 53. The Rainbow Jacket 54. Davy 57. Carve Her Name with Pride 58. The Hellfire Club 61. The Secret of Blood Island 65. Georgy Girl 66. O Lucky Man 72. In Celebration 74, etc.

Owen, Cliff (1919–). British director, in films from 1937.

Offbeat 60. A Prize of Arms 62. The Wrong Arm of the Law 63. A Man Could Get Killed 66. That Riviera Touch 66. The Magnificent Two 67. Steptoe and Son 72. Ooh You Are Awful 72. No Sex Please We're British 73. The Bawdy Adventures of Tom Jones 76, etc.

Owen, Reginald (1887–1972). British character actor, on stage from 1905, films (in Hollywood) from 1929.

The Letter (debut) 29. Platinum Blonde 32. Queen Christina 33. Call of the Wild 35. Anna Karenina 35. The Great Ziegfeld 36. A Tale of Two Cities 36. *Trouble for Two* 36. Conquest 37. The Earl of Chicago 39. Florian 40. Charley's Aunt 41. Tarzan's Secret Treasure 41. *Mrs Miniver* 42. Random Harvest 42. White Cargo 42. Madame Curie 43. Lassie Come Home 43. The Canterville Ghost 44. *Kitty* 45. The Diary of a Chambermaid 45. Cluny Brown 46. If Winter Comes 47. The Three Musketeers 48. The Miniver Story 50. Kim 51. Red Garters 54. The Young Invaders 58. Voice of the Hurricane (MRA film) 63. Mary Poppins 64. Rosie 68. Bedknobs and Broomsticks 71, hundreds of others.

Owen, Seena (1894–1966) (Signe Auen). American silent screen lady.

Intolerance 16. The Sheriff's Son 19. Victory 19. Shipwrecked 23. Flame of the Yukon 25. The Rush Hour 28. Marriage Playground 29, others.

Owens, Patricia (1925–). Canadian leading lady who made films in Britain and America.

Miss London Ltd 43. While the Sun Shines 46. The Happiest Days of Your Life 49. Mystery Junction 52. The Good Die Young 53. Windfall 55. Island in the Sun 56. Sayonara (US) 57. *No Down Payment* (US) 57. The Fly (US) 58. Five Gates to Hell (US) 59. Hell to Eternity (US) 60. Seven Women from Hell 62. Black Spurs 65, etc.

The Ox-Bow Incident (US 1943). A striking western indictment of lynch law, from the novel by Walter Van Tilburg Clark. A remarkably sombre and atmospheric film to come out of Hollywood in the middle of World War II, it had no popular success. Henry Fonda led an excellent cast; William Wellman directed from a script by Lamar Trotti.

Oxley, David (c. 1929–). British actor.

Ill Met by Moonlight 57. Saint Joan 58. Yesterday's Enemy 58. The Hound of the Baskervilles 59. Life at the Top 64, etc.

Ozep, Fedor (1895–1949). Russian director.

The Crime of Dmitri Karamazov 31. The Living Dead 33. Amok 34. Gibraltar 38. She Who Dares (US) 44. Whispering City (Can.) 48, etc.

Ozu, Yasujiro (1903–1963). Japanese director, since 1927.

A Story of Floating Weeds 34. Late Spring 49. Early Summer 51. Tokyo Story 53. Early Spring 56. Late Autumn 61. Early Autumn 62, etc.

P

Pabst, G. W. (1885–1967) (George Wilhelm). Distinguished German director who usually tackled pessimistic themes.

☐ Der Schatz 23. Gräfin Donelli 24. *Joyless Street* 25. *Secrets of a Soul* 26. Man Spielt Nicht mit der Liebe 26. *The Love of Jeanne Ney* 27. *Pandora's Box* 28. Abwege 28. *Diary of a Lost Girl* 29. The White Hell of Pitz Palu (co-d) 29.*Westfront 1918* 30. Skandal um Eva 30. *The Threepenny Opera* (*Die Dreigroschenoper*) 31. *Kameradschaft* 31. L'Atlantide 32. Don Quixote 33. A Modern Hero (US) 34. De Haut en Bas 34. Mademoiselle Docteur 37. Le Drama de Shanghai 39. Mädchen in Uniform 39. Komodianten 41. Paracelsus 43. Der Fall Molander 45. Der Prozess 48. Geheimnisvolle Tiefe 49. The Voice of Silence 52. Cose da Pazzi 53. *Ten Days to Die* 54. Das Bekenntnis der Ina Kahr 54. Jackboot Mutiny 55. The Last Act 55. Roses for Bettina 56. Durch die Walder 56.

Pace, Judy (1946–). Black American leading lady of the seventies.

Three in the Attic 68. Up in the Cellar 70. Cool Breeze 72. Frogs 72, etc.

Pacino, Al (1939–) (Alfredo Pacino). American leading actor of the seventies, of New York/Sicilian descent.

Me Natalie 68. The Panic in Needle Park 71. *The Godfather* 72. Scarecrow 73. Serpico 74. The Godfather — Part Two 74. *Dog Day Afternoon* 75, etc.

Paderewski, Ignace (1860–1941). Polish prime minister and classical pianist. Appeared in a few films including the British *Moonlight Sonata* 37.

Padovani, Lea (1920–). Italian leading actress, in films from 1945.

Give Us This Day (GB) 49. Three Steps North (US) 51. Tempi Nostri 53. Montparnasse 19 57. The Naked Maja (US) 58, etc.

Page, Anthony (1935–). British director, with stage experience.

☐ *Inadmissible Evidence* 68. Alpha Beta 73.

Page, Gale (1913–) (Sally Rutter). American leading lady.

Four Daughters 38. Crime School 38. They Drive by Night 40. Four Wives 40. Four Mothers 41. The Time of Your Life 48. About Mrs Leslie 54, etc.

Page, Genevieve (1931–). French leading lady who has made American films.

Foreign Intrigue 56. Trapped in Tangiers 60. Song Without End 60. El Cid 61. L'Honorable Stanislas 63. Youngblood Hawke 64. Les Corsaires 65. Belle de Jour 67. Decline and Fall 68, etc.

Page, Geraldine (1924–). American leading actress, on stage from 1940.

☐ Taxi 53. Hondo 54. *Summer and Smoke* 61. Sweet Bird of Youth 62. Toys in the Attic 63. *Dear Heart* 65. The Happiest Millionaire 67. You're a Big Boy Now 67. Whatever Happened to Aunt Alice? 69. The Beguiled 71. Pete 'n Tillie 72. J. W. Coop 73. The Day of the Locust 75.

Page, Patti (1927–) (Clara Ann Fowler). American TV singer.

☐ Elmer Gantry 60. Dondi 61. Boys' Night Out 63.

Paget, Debra (1933–) (Debralee Griffin). American leading lady with brief stage experience.

Cry of the City 48. House of Strangers 49. Broken Arrow 50. Les Misérables 52. Prince Valiant 54. Love Me Tender 56. From the Earth to the Moon 58. Tales of Terror 62. The Haunted Palace 64, others.

Pagett, Nicola (1948–). British leading lady of the seventies, much on TV.

Frankenstein, the True Story (TV) 73. Operation Daybreak 75, etc.

Pagnol, Marcel (1894–1974). French writer-director noted for sprawling comedy dramas which strongly evoke country life without being very cinematic.

Autobiographies: 1962, *The Time of Secrets*. 1960, *The Days Were Too Short*.

Marius (script only) 31. *Fanny* (script only) 32. *César* 34. Joffroi 34. Regain (Harvest) 37. *La Femme du Boulanger* 38. *La Fille du Puisatier* 40. La Belle Meunière 48. Manon des Sources 53. Lettres de Mon Moulin 55, etc.

Paige, Janis (1922–) (Donna Mae Jaden). American leading lady with operatic training.
Hollywood Canteen (debut) 44. Cheyenne 46. Romance on the High Seas 48. Mr Universe 51. Remains to be Seen 53. Please Don't Eat the Daisies 61. The Caretakers 63. Welcome to Hard Times 67. Gibbsville (TV) 75.

Paige, Mabel (1879–1954). American character actress.
My Heart Belongs to Daddy 42. *Lucky Jordan* 43. The Good Fellows 43. *Someone to Remember* (lead role) 43. If You Knew Susie 48. The Sniper 52. Houdini 53.

Paige, Robert (1910–) (John Arthur Page). American leading man, former radio announcer, in many films of the forties, little since.
Cain and Mabel 37. Hellzapoppin 42. Shady Lady 42. Son of Dracula 43. Can't Help Singing 44. Red Stallion 47. The Flame 48. Raging Waters 51. Abbott and Costello Go to Mars 53. The Big Payoff 58. The Marriage Go Round 61. Bye Bye Birdie 63, etc.

Painlevé, Jean (1902–). French documentarist, famous for short scientific naturalist studies of sea horses, sea urchins, shrimps, etc.

painters have frequently had their lives glamorized to provide film-makers with drama to counterpoint art. Among the most notable are Charles Laughton as *Rembrandt*, George Sanders as Gauguin in *The Moon and Sixpence*, José Ferrer as Toulouse Lautrec in *Moulin Rouge*, Anthony Franciosa as Goya in *The Naked Maja*, Kirk Douglas as Van Gogh and Anthony Quinn as Gauguin in *Lust for Life*, Gerard Philipe as Modigliani in *Montparnasse 19*, Cecil Kellaway as Gainsborough in *Kitty*, Charlton Heston as Michelangelo in *The Agony and the Ecstasy*, and Mel Ferrer as *El Greco*.

Paisa (Italy 1946). Episodic story film, a kind of sequel to *Open City*, dramatizing incidents in the German retreat through Italy. Directed by Roberto Rossellini from a script by himself, Fellini, and others. Its success encouraged later short story compendiums such as *Quartet* 48.

Paiva, Nestor (1905–1966). American

character actor of assorted foreign peasant types.
Ride a Crooked Mile 38. The Marines Fly High 40. The Falcon in Mexico 44. Fear 46. Road to Rio 46. Five Fingers 52. The Creature from the Black Lagoon 55. The Deep Six 57. The Nine Lives of Elfego Baca 59. The Spirit is Willing 66, many others.

The Pajama Game (US 1957). A wholly successful—and cinematic—version of the stage musical with the unlikely subject of labour unrest in a pajama factory. Stanley Donen's lively direction and Bob Fosse's choreography survive disagreeable colour, and the songs by Richard Adler and Jerry Ross are among the brightest ever written for one show. Book by Richard Bissell and George Abbott; Doris Day, John Raitt and Eddie Foy Jnr head the cast.

Pakula, Alan J. (1928–). American producer who turned director.
☐ AS PRODUCER: Fear Strikes Out 57. To Kill a Mockingbird 63. Love with the Proper Stranger 63. Baby the Rain Must Fall 65. Inside Daisy Clover 66. Up the Down Staircase 67. The Stalking Moon 68.
☐ AS PRODUCER-DIRECTOR: The Sterile Cuckoo 69. *Klute* 71. Love, Pain and the Whole Damn Thing 73. The Parallax View 74. *All The President's Men* 76.

Pal, George (1908–). Hungarian puppeteer whose short advertising films enlivened programmes in the late thirties; went to Hollywood 1940 and produced series of 'Puppetoons'; later produced many adventure films involving trick photography. Special Academy Award 1943 'for the development of novel methods and techniques'.
Destination Moon (AA) 50. *When Worlds Collide* (AA) 51. *The War of the Worlds* (AA) 53. The Naked Jungle 55. *Tom Thumb* (AA) 58. *The Time Machine* (AA) 61. The Wonderful World of the Brothers Grimm 63. The Power 68.

Palance, Jack (1920–) (Walter Palanuik). Gaunt American leading man with stage experience; started in films playing villains.
Panic in the Streets 50. Halls of Montezuma 51. Shane 53. Sign of the Pagan 54. *The Big Knife* 55. I Died a Thousand Times 56. Attack 56. The Man Inside 57. The Lonely Man 57. House of Numbers 57. Ten Seconds to Hell 58. The Mongols 60. Barabbas 62. Warriors Five 62. Le Mépris 63. Once a Thief 65. The Professionals 66. The Torture Garden (GB) 67. Kill a Dragon 67. A Professional Gun 68. Ché! 69. The Desperados 69. They Came to Rob Las Vegas

69. The Companeros 70. Monte Walsh 70. The McMasters 70. The Horsemen 72. Chato's Land 72. Oklahoma Crude 73. Dracula (TV) 73. Craze 73, etc.
TV series: The Greatest Show on Earth 63. Bronk 75.

The Paleface (US 1948). A western romp written by Edmund Hartman and Frank Tashlin, directed by Norman Z. McLeod, this had Bob Hope as a cowardly dentist and Jane Russell as Calamity Jane. In 1952 these stars were joined by Roy Rogers for an even crazier extravaganza called *Son of Paleface*. In 1968 the original was revamped for Don Knotts under the title *The Shakiest Gun in the West*.

Pallette, Eugene (1889–1954). Rotund, gravel-voiced American character actor, at his peak as an exasperated father or executive in the thirties and forties.
Intolerance 16. Alias Jimmy Valentine 20. The Three Musketeers 21. To the Last Man 23. Light of the Western Stars 25. Lights of New York 28. The Canary Murder Case 29. The Sea God 30. It Pays to Advertise 31. Shanghai Express 32. The Kennel Murder Case 33. Bordertown 34. Steamboat Round the Bend 35. *The Ghost Goes West* 36. My Man Godfrey 36. One Hundred Men and a Girl 37. Topper 37. *The Adventures of Robin Hood* (as Friar Tuck) 38. Mr Smith Goes to Washington 39. The Mark of Zorro 40. The Lady Eve 41. Tales of Manhattan 42. It Ain't Hay 43. Heaven Can Wait 43. Step Lively 44. Lake Placid Serenade 45. In Old Sacramento 46, many others.

Pallos, Stephen (1902–). Hungarian producer who worked with Korda in England from 1942, later as independent.
Call of the Blood 46. The Golden Madonna 48. Jet Storm 59. Foxhole in Cairo 60. A Jolly Bad Fellow 64. Where the Spies Are 65, others.

Palmer, Betsy (1929–) (Patricia Brumek). American light actress and TV panellist.
The Long Gray Line 55. Queen Bee 55. The Tin Star 57. The Last Angry Man 59. It Happened to Jane 59, etc.

Palmer, Ernest (1885–). American cinematographer.
Ivanhoe 12. Lothar 17. Ladies Must Live 21. The Wanters 23. The Kiss Barrier 25. The Palace of Pleasure 26. Seventh Heaven 27. The River 29. City Girl 30. A Connecticut Yankee 31. The Painted Woman 32. Cavalcade 33. Berkeley Square 33. Music in the Air 34. Charlie Chan in Paris 35. Banjo on My Knee 36. Slave Ship 37.

Four Men and a Prayer 38. News is Made at Night 39. The Great Profile 40. Blood and Sand 41. Song of the Islands 42. Coney Island 43. Pin Up Girl 44. The Dolly Sisters 45. Centennial Summer 46. I Wonder Who's Kissing Her Now 47. Broken Arrow 50, many others.

Palmer, Gregg (1927–) (Palmer Lee). American 'second lead', former disc jockey.
Son of Ali Baba 51. Veils of Baghdad 53. Magnificent Obsession 54. The Creature Walks among Us 56. Forty Pounds of Trouble 62. The Undefeated 69. Big Jake 71.

Palmer, Lilli (1914–) (Lilli Peiser). Austrian leading actress, on stage from childhood, in films from teenage.
Autobiography 1975: *Change Lobsters and Dance*.
Crime Unlimited (GB) 34. Good Morning, Boys (GB) 36. Secret Agent (GB) 36. A Girl Must Live (GB) 38. The Door with Seven Locks (GB) 40. *Thunder Rock* (GB) 42. The Gentle Sex (GB) 43. English without Tears (GB) 44. *The Rake's Progress* (GB) 45. Beware of Pity (GB) 46. Cloak and Dagger (US) 46. *My Girl Tisa* (US) 47. Body and Soul (US) 48. No Minor Vices (US) 48. The Long Dark Hall (GB) 51. The Fourposter (US) 52. Is Anna Anderson Anastasia? (Ger.) 56. La Vie à Deux (Fr.) 58. But Not for Me (US) 58. Conspiracy of Hearts (GB) 60. Rendezvous at Midnight (Fr.) 60. *The Pleasure of His Company* (US) 61. The Counterfeit Traitor (US) 62. Adorable Julia (Ger.) 63. The Flight of the White Stallions (US) 64. Operation Crossbow (GB) 65. Moll Flanders (GB) 65. Sebastian (GB) 67. Oedipus the King (GB) 67. Nobody Runs Forever (GB) 68. The Dance of Death (Swed.) 68. De Sade (US) 69. Hard Contract (US) 69. Murders in the Rue Morgue (GB) 71. Night Hair Child (GB) 71, others.
TV series: *Zoo Gang* 73.

Palmer, Maria (1924–). Austrian leading lady, sister of Lilli Palmer. Wide stage experience at home, TV and films in America.
Mission to Moscow 42. Lady on a Train 44. Rendezvous 24 46. Slightly Dishonourable 51. Three for Jamie Dawn 56, others.

Palmer, Peter (1931–). American actor-singer who repeated his stage role as *Lil Abner* 59.
TV series: Custer 67.

Paluzzi, Luciana (1939–). Italian leading lady in international films.
Three Coins in the Fountain 54. Sea Fury 58.

Thunderball 65. The Venetian Affair 66. Chuka 67. 99 Women 69. The Green Slime 69. Black Gunn 72. War Goddess 74, etc.
TV series: Five Fingers 59.

pan. A shot in which the camera rotates horizontally. Also used as a verb.

Pan, Hermes (1905–). American dance director.
Top Hat 35. Swing Time 36. Damsel in Distress (AA) 37. Let's Dance 50. Lovely to Look At 52. Silk Stockings 57. Can Can 59. My Fair Lady 64. Lost Horizon 73, many others.

Panama, Norman (1914–). Writer-producer-director who has long worked in collaboration with Melvin Frank, (qv) for note on films. Now working solo.
Not with My Wife You Don't (wpd) 66. How to Commit Marriage (d only) 69. The Maltese Bippy (wd) 69. I Will, I Will . . . For Now (co-w, d) 76.

panavision. A wide-screen system which outdistanced CinemaScope because of its improved anamorphic lens. Super-Panavision and Panavision 70 are 'road show' processes involving projection on wide film: in the first case the film is shot on 65mm, in the second blown up after photography. Great confusion was caused in the seventies by the company insisting on the credit 'filmed with Panavision equipment' even on non-anamorphic films.

Pangborn, Franklin (1894–1958). American character comedian with long stage experience; in scores of films from the twenties, typically as flustered hotel clerk or organizer.
My Friend from India 27. My Man 30. International House 33. My Man Godfrey 36. Stage Door 37. Christmas in July 41. *The Bank Dick* 41. *The Palm Beach Story* 42. The Carter Case 42. Now Voyager 42. *Hail the Conquering Hero* 44. Mad Wednesday 47. Romance on the High Seas 48. The Story of Mankind 57, etc.

Papas, Irene (1926–). Greek stage actress who has made films at home and abroad.
Necripolitia (debut) 51. Theodora Slave Empress 54. Attila the Hun 54. Tribute to a Bad Man (US) 55. The Power and the Prize (US) 56. The Guns of Navarone 61. Electra 62. *Zorba the Greek* 64. Beyond the Mountains 66. The Brotherhood (US) 68. 'Z' 68. A Dream of Kings (US) 69. Anne of the Thousand Days 70. The Trojan Women 71. The Message 76, etc.

paper prints were made of most films between 1895 and 1912 because the US Copyright Act did not allow for celluloid. This quirk of the law meant the preservation of hundreds of early titles which could otherwise have been lost, and in the sixties they were all copied for the archives of the motion picture academy on to 16mm film.

Paramount Pictures Corporation was basically the creation of Adolph Zukor (qv), a nickelodeon showman who in 1912 founded Famous Players, with the intention of presenting photographed versions of stage successes. In 1914 W. W. Hodkinson's Paramount Pictures took over distribution of Famous Players and Lasky products, and in the complex mergers which resulted, Zukor came out top man. Through the years his studio more than any other gave a family atmosphere, seldom producing films of depth but providing agreeable light entertainment with stars like Valentino, Maurice Chevalier, the Marx Brothers, Mary Pickford, Claudette Colbert, Bob Hope, Bing Crosby, Dorothy Lamour, Alan Ladd, and directors like Lubitsch, De Mille and Wilder. Notable films include *The Sheik, The Covered Wagon, The Ten Commandments* (both versions), *Trouble in Paradise, The Crusades, Union Pacific*, the Road films, *Going My Way, The Greatest Show on Earth*, etc. In recent years, since Zukor's retirement, the company had many difficulties, but was helped by a takeover by Gulf and Western Industries which spurred the commercial instinct, and produced two enormous winners in *Love Story* and *The Godfather*.

Les Parents Terribles (France 1948). A straight film version by Jean Cocteau of his own claustrophobic play about a family always on the verge of hysteria who come to an emotional crisis when the son announces his intention to marry. With Yvonne de Bray, Jean Marais, Gabrielle Dorziat. Disastrously remade in English by Charles Frank as *Intimate Relations* 53, with Marian Spencer, Russell Enoch and Ruth Dunning.

Paris has usually figured in films as the centre of sophistication, romance and luxury: thus *Ninotchka, I Met Him in Paris, The Last Time I Saw Paris, Innocents in Paris, April in Paris, How to Steal a Million, To Paris With Love, Paris When it Sizzles, A Certain Smile, Funny Face, Paris Holiday, Can Can, Parisienne, Paris Palace Hotel, Two for the Road* and innumerable others. The bohemian aspect is another favourite, as depicted in *An American in Paris, Latin Quarter, Paris Blues, What's New, Pussycat?, Svengali, French Cancan, Moulin*

Rouge, What a Way to Go, The Moon and Sixpence, etc. The tourists' Paris has provided a splendid backcloth for films as diverse as *The Great Race, The Man on the Eiffel Tower, Charade, Those Magnificent Men in Their Flying Machines, Zazie dans le Metro, Pig Across Paris, The Red Balloon, Father Brown, Take Her She's Mine, Dear Brigitte, Bon Voyage*, and *Paris Nous Appartient*. French film-makers seem particularly fond of showing the city's seamy side in thrillers about vice, murder and prostitution: *Quai de Grenelle, Quai des Orfèvres, Les Compagnes de la Nuit, Le Long des Trottoirs, Rififi*, etc. René Clair has always had his own slightly fantastic view of Paris, from *Paris Qui Dort* through *Sous les Toits de Paris, A Nous la Liberté, Le Million, Le Quatorze Juillet*, and *Porte des Lilas*. Rouben Mamoulian re-created this vision in *Love Me Tonight*, and *The Mad Woman of Chaillot* lived in a city of similar nuances. Historical Paris has been re-created for *The Hunchback of Notre Dame, The Scarlet Pimpernel, The Three Musketeers, Camille, A Tale of Two Cities, Marie Antoinette, So Long at the Fair* and *Les Enfants du Paradis*; while Paris under fire in World War II was depicted in *Is Paris Burning?* As for *Last Tango in Paris*, its emphasis was hardly on the city.

Paris, Jerry (1925–). American supporting actor: *The Caine Mutiny* 54. *Marty* 55. *Unchained* 55, many others; also played the neighbour in *The Dick Van Dyke Show* 61–66. Turned director: *Never a Dull Moment* 68. *Don't Raise the Bridge Lower the River* 68. *Viva Max* 69. *The Grasshopper* 70.

Paris Qui Dort (France 1924). Also known as *The Crazy Ray*, this first film to be written and directed by René Clair is an amusing trifle mostly shot on the Eiffel Tower, about a mad professor whose new invention reduces Paris to silence and sleep.

Parker, Barnett (1890–1941). British character actor in Hollywood, one of the perfect butlers of the thirties.
The President's Mystery 36. Espionage 37. Wake Up and Live 37. Listen Darling 38. At the Circus 39. Love Thy Neighbour 40. The Reluctant Dragon 41, etc.

Parker, Cecil (1897–1971) (Cecil Schwabe). British character actor with upper-class personality which could be amiable or chill.
The Silver Spoon (film debut) 33. A Cuckoo in the Nest 33. Storm in a Teacup 37. Dark Journey 37. *The Lady Vanishes* 38. The Citadel 38. *Caesar and Cleopatra* 45. Hungry Hill 46.

Captain Boycott 47. *The First Gentleman* (as the Prince Regent) 47. *Quartet* 48. Dear Mr Prohack 49. *The Chiltern Hundreds* 49. Tony Draws a Horse 51. The Man in the White Suit 52. His Excellency 52. I Believe in You 52. Isn't Life Wonderful? 54. *Father Brown* 54. The Constant Husband 55. The Ladykillers 55. The Court Jester (US) 55. It's Great to be Young 56. The Admirable Crichton 57. Indiscreet 58. I was Monty's Double 58. Happy is the Bride 58. A Tale of Two Cities 58. The Navy Lark 59. A French Mistress 60. On the Fiddle 61. Petticoat Pirates 62. Heavens Above 63. The Comedy Man 64. Guns at Batasi 64. Moll Flanders 65. A Study in Terror 65. Circus of Fear 67. Oh What a Lovely War 69, others.

Parker, Cecilia (1915–). Canadian leading lady who played many Hollywood roles but is best remembered as Andy's sister in the *Hardy Family* series 37–44.
Young as you Feel 31. The Painted Veil 34. Naughty Marietta 35. A Family Affair (first of the Hardy films) 37. Seven Sweethearts 42. Andy Hardy Comes Home 58, etc.

Parker, Clifton (1905–). British composer.
Yellow Canary 43. Johnny Frenchman 46. Blanche Fury 47. Treasure Island 50. The Gift Horse 52. Hell below Zero 54. Night of the Demon 57. Sea of Sand 59. Sink the Bismarck 60. Taste of Fear 62. The Informers 64, etc.

Parker, Dorothy (1893–1967) American short story writer, reviewer and wit who spent some years in Hollywood as an associate scriptwriter of undistinguished films.
Biography 1971: *You Might as well Live* by John Keats.

Parker, Eleanor (1922–). American leading lady with brief stage experience before a Hollywood contract; her career followed a typical pattern, with increasingly good leading roles followed by a decline, with a later comeback in character parts.
□ They Died with Their Boots On (debut as extra) 41. Buses Roar 42. Mysterious Doctor 43. Mission to Moscow 43. The Very Thought of You 44. Crime by Night 44. Between Two Worlds 44. The Last Ride 44. Pride of the Marines 45. Of Human Bondage (as Mildred) 46. Never Say Goodbye 46. Escape Me Never 47. *The Voice of the Turtle* 47. The Woman in White 48. Chain Lightning 49. Three Secrets 50. *Caged* 50. Valentino 51. A Millionaire for Christy 51. *Detective Story* 51. Scaramouche 52. Above and Beyond 52. Escape from Fort Bravo 53. The Naked Jungle 54. Valley of the Kings 54. Many

Rivers to Cross 54. *Interrupted Melody* 55. The Man with the Golden Arm 56. The King and Four Queens 56. Lizzie 57. The Seventh Sin 57. A Hole in the Head 59. Home from the Hill 60. Return to Peyton Place 61. Madison Avenue 62. Panic Button 64. The Sound of Music 65. The Oscar 66. An American Dream 66. Warning Shot 66. The Tiger and the Pussycat 67. How to Steal the World 68. Eye of the Cat 69. Maybe I'll Come Home in the Spring 70. Vanished (TV) 71. Home for the Holidays (TV) 72.
TV series: Bracken's World 69.

Parker, Fess (1925–). American leading man with some stage experience.
Untamed Frontier 52. *Davy Crockett* 55 (and two sequels). The Great Locomotive Chase 56. Westward Ho the Wagons 56. Old Yeller 57. The Hangman 59. Hell is for Heroes 62. Smoky 66, etc.
TV series: Mr Smith Goes to Washington 62. Daniel Boone 64–68.

Parker, Jean (1915–) (Mae Green). Once-demure American leading lady, popular in the thirties; latterly playing hard-boiled roles.
Rasputin and the Empress 32. *Little Women* 33. *Sequoia* 34. The Ghost Goes West (GB) 36. Princess O'Hara 37. The Flying Deuces 39. Beyond Tomorrow 40. No Hands on the Clock 42. One Body Too Many 42. Minesweeper 43. Bluebeard 44. Detective Kitty O'Day 44. Lady in the Death House 44. The Gunfighter 50. Those Redheads from Seattle 53. Black Tuesday 54. A Lawless Street 55. Apache Uprising 65, others.

Parker, Suzy (1932–) (Cecelia Parker). Statuesque American leading lady, former model.
Kiss Them for Me (debut) 57. *Ten North Frederick* 58. The Best of Everything 59. Circle of Deception 61. The Interns 62. Chamber of Horrors 66, etc.

Parker, Willard (1912–) (Worster van Eps). Tall American 'second lead', in films from 1938 after stage experience.
A Slight Case of Murder (debut) 38. The Fighting Guardsman 43. You Gotta Stay Happy 48. Sangaree 53. The Great Jesse James Raid 53. The Earth Dies Screaming 64, etc.
TV series: Tales of the Texas Rangers 55–57.

Parkins, Barbara (1942–). Canadian leading lady whose major success was TV.
Valley of the Dolls 67. The Kremlin Letters 69. The Mephisto Waltz 71. Puppet on a Chain 72. Asylum 72. Captains and the Kings (TV) 76, etc.
TV series: *Peyton Place* 63–67.

Parks, Gordon (1925–). Black American director, former stills photographer.
The Learning Tree 68. *Shaft* 71. Shaft's Big Score 72. Leadbelly 76, etc.

Parks, Gordon Jnr (1948–). American director, son of Gordon Parks.
Superfly 72.

Parks, Larry (1914–1975) (Samuel Klausman Parks). American light leading man whose career in 'B' pictures was interrupted by his highly successful impersonation of Al Jolson. He subsequently proved difficult to cast, and was forced out of Hollywood after testifying to the Unamerican Activities Committee.
Mystery Ship 41. Canal Zone 42. The Boogie Man will Get You 42. Reveille with Beverly 43. Counter Attack 45. Renegades 46. *The Jolson Story* 46. Down to Earth 47. The Swordsman 47. The Gallant Blade 48. *Jolson Sings Again* 49. Jealousy 50. The Light Fantastic 51. Love Is Better than Ever 52. Tiger by the Tail (GB) 55. Freud 63, etc.

Parks, Michael (1938–). Brooding American leading man.
Wild Seed 64. Bus Riley's Back in Town 65. The Bible (as Adam) 66. The Idol (GB) 66. The Happening 67. Can Ellen Be Saved (TV) 73. The Last Hard Men 76, etc.
TV series: Bronson 69.

Parkyakarkus (1904–1958) (Harry Einstein). American radio comedian formerly known as Harry Parke.
Strike Me Pink 36. Night Spot 38. Glamour Boy 40. Earl Carroll's Vanities 45.

Parkyn, Leslie (–). British executive producer, associated with Sergei Nolbandov 1951–57, subsequently with Julian Wintle.
The Kidnappers 53. Tiger Bay 59. The Waltz of the Toreadors 62. Father Came Too 64, many others.

Parlo, Dita (1906–1971) (Gerthe Kornstadt). German star actress of the thirties.
Homecoming 28. Melody of the Heart 30. Secrets of the Orient 31. L'Atalante 34. The Mystic Mountain 36. Mademoiselle Docteur 37. La Grande Illusion 37. Ultimatum 39. Justice est Faite 50. Quand le Soleil Montera 56, etc.

Parnell, Emory (1894–). American general purpose character actor: could be villain, prison warden, weakling or kindly father.
King of Alcatraz 39. I Married a Witch 42. Mama Loves Papa 46. Words and Music 48.

Call Me Madam 53. Man of the West 58, many others.

parody without satire was never prominent among film genres until the seventies, when the easygoing talents of such as Mel Brooks and Gene Wilder produced films such as *Blazing Saddles, Sherlock Holmes' Smarter Brother, Young Frankenstein, Murder By Death, The Black Bird, The Big Bus* and *Phantom of the Paradise.*

Parrish, Helen (1922–1959). American leading lady, former baby model and child actress.
The Big Trail 31. A Dog of Flanders 34. Mad about Music 38. You'll Find Out 40. They All Kissed the Bride 42. The Mystery of the Thirteenth Guest 44. The Wolf Hunters 50, etc.

Parrish, Robert (1916–). American director, former editor.
Autobiography 1976: *Growing Up in Hollywood.*
□ Cry Danger 51. The Mob 51. My Pal Gus 52. The San Francisco Story 52. Rough Shoot (GB) 52. Assignment Paris 52. The Purple Plain 54. Lucy Gallant 55. Fire Down Below 57. Saddle the Wind 58. The Wonderful Country 59. In the French Style (& p) 63. Up from the Beach 65. The Bobo 67. Duffy 68. Journey to the Far Side of the Sun 69. A Town Called Bastard 71. The Marseilles Contract 74.

Parrott, James (1892–1939). American director, mainly of two-reelers featuring Laurel and Hardy (*Blotto, The Music Box, County Hospital*, etc), Charlie Chase and Max Davidson. Features include *Jailbirds* 31, *Sing, Sister, Sing* 35.

Parry, Gordon (1908–). British director of mainly secondary films: former actor, production manager, etc.
Bond Street 48. Third Time Lucky 48. Now Barabbas 49. Midnight Episode 50. Innocents in Paris 52. Women of Twilight 52. A Yank in Ermine 55. Sailor Beware 56. Tread Softly Stranger 58. The Navy Lark 60, etc.

Parry, Natasha (1930–). British leading lady, married to Peter Brook. Appears occasionally on stage and screen.
Dance Hall 49. The Dark Man 50. Crow Hollow 52. Knave of Hearts 53. Windom's Way 57. The Rough and the Smooth 59. Midnight Lace 60. The Fourth Square 62. The Girl in the Headlines 64. Romeo and Juliet 68. Oh What a Lovely War 69, etc.

Parsons, Estelle (1927–). American character actress with stage background.
Bonnie and Clyde (AA) 67. Rachel Rachel 68. I Never Sang for My Father 69. Don't Drink the Water 69. I Walk the Line 70. Watermelon Man 71. Two People 73. For Pete's Sake 74. Foreplay 75, etc.

Parsons, Louella (1880–1972) (L. Oettinger). Hollywood columnist whose gossip rivalled in readership that of Hedda Hopper. In occasional films as herself, e.g. *Hollywood Hotel* 37, *Starlift* 51.
Autobiographical books: *The Gay Illiterate* 44. *Tell It to Louella* 62.
Biography 1973: *Hedda and Louella* by George Eels.

Parsons, Milton (–). Lugubrious American character actor often seen as undertaker.
The Hidden Hand 42. Margie 44, many others.

Parsons, Nicholas (1928–). British light actor and entertainer.
Master of Bankdam 48. Brothers in Law 57. Too Many Crooks 59. Doctor in Love 62. Don't Raise the Bridge Lower the River 68, etc.

Une Partie de Campagne (France 1936). A rare instance of a film which is unfinished and all the better for it. Based on a Maupassant story, it describes a romantic idyll in the countryside; the spot is revisited fourteen years later by the protagonists, who are of course unable to recapture their original feeling. The film's first and last sequences were filmed by Renoir before production was halted for various reasons. It proved impossible to get the actors together again to film the middle sequence showing how the lives of the characters diverge, and the incomplete film was issued in 1946 to general acclaim. The cast included Sylvia Bataille, Georges Saint-Saens and Jeanne Marken.

parties in movies have often been wild, as for instance in *The Wild Party*, also *The Party's Over, I'll Never Forget Whatshisname, Breakfast at Tiffany's, I Love You Alice B. Toklas, The Impossible Years, Skidoo, Beyond the Valley of the Dolls, Camille 2000, The Pursuit of Happiness, The Party Crashers*, and *The Party* itself, which started out sedately but finished with an elephant in the swimming pool. Some of the more amusing film parties, however, were better behaved, as in *The Apartment, Only Two Can Play, All About Eve* and *Citizen Kane*.

Pascal, Gabriel (1894–1954). Hungarian

producer-director who came to Britain in the thirties, won the esteem of Bernard Shaw, and was entrusted with the filming of several of his plays.

□ Pygmalion (p) 38. Major Barbara (pd) 40. Caesar and Cleopatra (pd; a notoriously extravagant production) 45. Androcles and the Lion (p) (US) 53.

Pasco, Richard (1926–). British character actor, mainly on stage and TV.
Room at the Top 59. Yesterday's Enemy 60. The Gorgon 64. Rasputin the Mad Monk 66, etc.

Pasolini, Pier Paolo (1922–1975). Italian director.
Accattone 61. Mamma Roma 62. The Witches (part) 63. *The Gospel According to St Matthew* 64. Oedipus Rex 67. *Theorem* 68. Pigsty 69. Medea 70. Decameron 70, etc.

Passer, Ivan (1933–). Czech director, latterly in Hollywood.
A Boring Afternoon 64. Intimate Lighting 66. Born to Win 71. Law and Disorder 74, etc.

The Passing of the Third Floor Back. Jerome K. Jerome's popular novel and play, about a Christ-like stranger who has a benign influence on the down-at-heel inhabitants of a boarding house, was filmed in 1918 with Johnston Forbes-Robertson and in 1935 with Conrad Veidt.

The Passing Parade. A series of one-reel interest films, mostly historical cameos enacted in corners of MGM's great sets, devised and produced by John Nesbitt in the thirties and forties.

La Passion de Jeanne D'Arc (France 1928). A notable silent film directed by Carl Dreyer and photographed by Rudolph Maté. It tells the familiar story as a series of Rembrandtesque tableaux, with stark white décor by Herman Warm. Falconetti gives a remarkable performance in this her only film.

Passport to Pimlico (GB 1948). The first of the 'Ealing comedies', whose special quality was to find humour and wit in the lives of ordinary people who are not music-hall caricatures. This one concerns the discovery that part of London belongs to France, and is acted by a notable gallery of character players. Directed by Henry Cornelius from a script by T. E. B. Clarke.

Pasternak, Joe (1901–). Hungarian producer in Hollywood during the golden years;

especially identified with cheerful light musicals. Autobiography 1956: *Easy the Hard Way.*
Three Smart Girls 36. *One Hundred Men and a Girl* 37. Mad About Music 38. *Destry Rides Again* 39. Seven Sinners 40. It Started with Eve 41. Presenting Lily Mars 42. Song of Russia 43. Two Girls and a Sailor 44. Anchors Aweigh 45. Holiday in Mexico 46. The Unfinished Dance 47. On an Island with You 48. In the Good Old Summertime 49. The Duchess of Idaho 50. *The Great Caruso* 51. Skirts Ahoy 52. Latin Lovers 53. The Student Prince 54. Love Me or Leave Me 55. The Opposite Sex 56. Ten Thousand Bedrooms 57. Party Girl 58. Ask Any Girl 59. Please Don't Eat the Daisies 60. The Horizontal Lieutenant 61. Jumbo 62. The Courtship of Eddie's Father 63. Girl Happy 65. Penelope 66. The Sweet Ride 68, many others.

Patch, Wally (1888–1971) (Walter Vinicombe). Burly British Cockney character actor, in films since 1920 after varied show business experience.
Shadows 31. The Good Companions 32. Get Off My Foot 35. Not So Dusty 36. Bank Holiday 38. Quiet Wedding 40. Gasbags 40. The Common Touch 41. Old Mother Riley at Home 45. The Ghosts of Berkeley Square 47. The Guinea Pig 49. Will Any Gentleman? 53. Private's Progress 55. I'm All Right, Jack 59. Sparrows Can't Sing 63, scores of others.

Pate, Michael (1920–). Australian actor in Hollywood in the fifties and sixties, often as Red Indian chief or second-string villain.
The Rugged O'Riordans 49. The Strange Door 51. Five Fingers 52. Houdini 53. The Silver Chalice 54. The Court Jester 56. Congo Crossing 56. The Oklahoman 57. Green Mansions 59. The Canadians 61. McLintock 63. Major Dundee 65, etc.
TV series: Matlock Police 71.

Paterson, Neil (1916–). British screenwriter (and novelist).
The Kidnappers 53. High Tide at Noon 57. *Room at the Top* (AA) 59. The Spiral Road 62. Mister Moses 65.

Pathé, Charles (1863–1957). Pioneer French executive and producer, founder of Pathé Frères and later Pathé Gazette. Also credited with making the first 'long' film: Les Misérables. (Made in 1909, it ran four whole reels.)

Pather Panchali (India 1954). The first of a trilogy written and directed by Satyajit Ray (the other titles are *The Unvanquished* 56 and *The World of Apu* 59) showing the hero's development from childhood to manhood against a background of the poverty of modern India. The three films provide the best documentation available on a country whose films have normally been too traditional to interest western audiences.

Paths of Glory (US 1957). A harsh attack on the futility of war in general and in particular the cynical manoeuvrings of World War I. Full of brilliant dialogue and action sequences. Directed by Stanley Kubrick from a script by Calder Willingham and Jim Thompson and a novel by Humphrey Cobb; photographed by George Krause; with Kirk Douglas, Adolphe Menjou and George Macready.

Patrick, Gail (1911–) (Margaret Fitzpatrick). American leading lady in Hollywood from early thirties, usually in routine smart woman roles.
The Phantom Broadcast 32. Cradle Song 33. No More Ladies 35. Artists and Models 37. Reno 40. Quiet, Please, Murder 43. Women in Bondage 44. Twice Blessed 45. The Plainsman and the Lady 46. Calendar Girl 47, many others. Retired from acting and became a TV producer, notably of the successful *Perry Mason* series.

Patrick, Lee (1906–). American character actress with stage experience, in Hollywood from 1937, usually as hard-bitten blondes.
Strange Cargo (debut) 29. *The Maltese Falcon* 41. Now Voyager 42. Mother Wore Tights 47. Caged 50. There's No Business Like Show Business 54. Vertigo 58. Summer and Smoke 61. The New Interns 64. *The Black Bird* 75, many others.
TV series: Topper 53–55. Mr Adams and Eve 56–57.

Patrick, Nigel (1913–). Debonair British leading actor, on stage from 1932.
Mrs Pym of Scotland Yard (film debut) 39. *Spring in Park Lane* 47. *Noose* 47. The Perfect Woman 49. *Trio* 50. The Browning Version 51. The Sound Barrier 52. *The Pickwick Papers* 53. Who Goes There? 53. The Sea Shall Not Have Them 55. All for Mary 56. Raintree County (US) 57. How to Murder a Rich Uncle (& d) 57. Sapphire 59. *The League of Gentlemen* 60. The Trials of Oscar Wilde 60. Johnny Nobody (& d) 61. The Informers 63. The Virgin Soldiers 69. The Executioner 69. The Great Waltz 72. The Mackintosh Man 73, etc.
TV series: Zero One 62.

Patten, Luana (1938–). American teenage actress of the fifties.
Song of the South 46. So Dear to My Heart 48.

Johnny Tremain 57. The Little Shepherd of Kingdom Come 61. A Thunder of Drums 61. Follow Me Boys 66, etc.

Patterson, Elizabeth (1876–1966). American character actress with stage experience; in Hollywood from the late twenties, usually as kindly or shrewish elderly ladies.
Daddy Longlegs 30. A Bill of Divorcement 32. Miss Pinkerton 32. Dinner at Eight 33. So Red the Rose 36. Sing You Sinners 38. *The Cat and the Canary* 39. *Tobacco Road* 41. Hail the Conquering Hero 43. Lady on a Train 45. *Intruder in the Dust* 48. Little Women 49. Bright Leaf 50. Pal Joey 57. The Oregon Trail 59, many others.

Patterson, Lee (1929–). Sturdy Canadian leading man of minor British and American films.
36 Hours 51. The Passing Stranger 54. Above Us the Waves 55. Soho Incident 56. Cat and Mouse 58. Jack the Ripper 60. The Ceremony 63. Valley of Mystery 67. Chato's Land 72, etc.
TV series: Surfside Six 60–61.

Patterson, Neva (1929–). American character actress.
Desk Set 57. Too Much Too Soon 58, etc.
TV series: The Governor and JJ 63. Nichols 71.

Patterson, Pat (c. 1910–). British leading lady who went to Hollywood and married Charles Boyer.
Bitter Sweet 33. Bottoms Up 34. Charlie Chan in Egypt 35. 52nd Street 37. Idiot's Delight 39, etc.

Paul, Robert (1869–1943). Pioneer British movie camera inventor (1895). The following year he invented a projector, which he called a theatrograph. Later turned showman.

Pavan, Marisa (1932–) (Marisa Pierangeli). Italian leading lady, sister of Pier Angeli. In Hollywood from 1950.
What Price Glory? (debut) 52. The Rose Tattoo 55. The Man in the Grey Flannel Suit 56. Solomon and Sheba 59. John Paul Jones 59, etc.

Pavlow, Muriel (1921–). British leading lady, on stage and screen from 1936; her youthful appearance enabled her to continue in juvenile roles for many years.
A Romance in Flanders (debut) 36. Quiet Wedding 40. Night Boat to Dublin 45. The Shop at Sly Corner 47. Malta Story 53. Doctor in the House 54. *Reach for the Sky* 56. Tiger in the Smoke 57. Rooney 58. Murder She Said 62, etc.

Pawle, Lennox (1872–1936). British character actor, mainly on stage.
The Admirable Crichton (GB) 18. The Great Adventure (GB) 21. Married in Hollywood (US) 29. The Sin of Madeleine Claudet (US) 32. *David Copperfield* (as Mr Dick) 34. Sylvia Scarlett (US) 35, etc.

The Pawnbroker (US 1964). A somewhat overheated but impressive modern morality with Rod Steiger (BFA) as a Jewish pawnbroker in New York, drained of humanity by his experiences in a Nazi concentration camp. Striking scenes and moments somehow fail to add up to more than a well-meaning melodrama. Photographed by Boris Kaufman; directed by Sidney Lumet from a script by David Friedkin and Morton Fine.

Paxinou, Katina (1900–1973). Greek actress with international experience; played in some Hollywood films.
For Whom the Bell Tolls (AA) 43. Confidential Agent 44. Uncle Silas (GB) 47. *Mourning Becomes Electra* 47. Confidential Report 55. Rocco and His Brothers 60. Zita 68, etc.

Paxton, John (1911–). American screenwriter.
Farewell My Lovely 43. So Well Remembered 47. *Crossfire* 47. Fourteen Hours 51. The Wild One 54. On the Beach 59, etc.

Payne, John (1912–). General purpose American leading man, mostly of forties musicals and fifties westerns.
Dodsworth 36. Fair Warning 37. Love on Toast 38. Wings of the Navy 39. *Kid Nightingale* 39. Maryland 40. The Great Profile 40. *Tin Pan Alley* 40. *The Great American Broadcast* 41. Weekend in Havana 41. Remember the Day 41. Sun Valley Serenade 41. To the Shores of Tripoli 42. Springtime in the Rockies 42. Hello Frisco Hello 43. The Dolly Sisters 45. Sentimental Journey 46. The Razor's Edge 46. Miracle on 34th Street 47. The Saxon Charm 48. The Crooked Way 49. Captain China 49. Tripoli 50. Crosswinds 51. Caribbean 52. Kansas City Confidential 52. Raiders of the Seven Seas 53. 99 River Street 53. Rails into Laramie 54. Santa Fé Passage 55. Hell's Island 55. Slightly Scarlet 56. *The Boss* 56. Bailout at 43,000 57. Hidden Fear 57. Gift of the Nile 68, etc.
TV series: *The Restless Gun* 58–59.

Payne, Laurence (1919–). British leading man, on stage and (occasionally) screen from 1945.
Train of Events 49. Ill Met by Moonlight 57. The

Tell Tale Heart 61. The Court Martial of Major Keller 61. Vampire Circus 72, etc.

Payton, Barbara (1927–1967). American leading lady.
Once More My Darling 49. Dallas 50. Kiss Tomorrow Goodbye 51. Drums in the Deep South 51. Bride of the Gorilla 52. The Great Jesse James Raid 53. Four-Sided Triangle (GB) 54. The Flanagan Boy (GB) 55, etc.

Peach, Mary (1934–). British leading lady, in films from 1957.
Follow That Horse 59. Room at the Top 59. *No Love for Johnnie* 61. A Pair of Briefs 62. A Gathering of Eagles (US) 63. Ballad in Blue 65. The Projected Man 66. Scrooge 70, etc.

Pearce, Alice (1913–1966). American character comedienne, usually in adenoidal roles.
On the Town 49. The Opposite Sex 56. The Disorderly Orderly 64. Dear Brigitte 65. The Glass Bottom Boat 66, etc.
TV series: Bewitched 65–66.

Pearson, Beatrice (1920–). American leading lady with a brief career.
□ Force of Evil 49. Lost Boundaries 49.

Pearson, George (1875–1973). British writer-producer-director who came to films at the age of 37 after being a schoolmaster. Hundreds of films to his credit.
Autobiography 1957: *Flashback*.
The Fool 12. A Study in Scarlet 14. Ultus the Man from the Dead 15. The Better Ole 18. The Old Curiosity Shop 20. *Squibs* 21. Squibs Wins the Calcutta Sweep 22. Satan's Sister 25. Huntingtower 27. The Silver King 28. Journey's End (p) 30. The Good Companions (p) 32. Four Marked Men 34. The Pointing Finger 38, many others.

Pearson, Lloyd (1897–1966). Portly British character actor, usually of bluff Yorkshire types.
The Challenge 38. Tilly of Bloomsbury 40. Kipps 41. *When We Are Married* 42. Schweik's New Adventures (leading role) 43. My Learned Friend 44. Mr Perrin and Mr Traill 49. Hindle Wakes 52. The Good Companions 57. The Angry Silence 59, etc.

Peary, Harold (–). American character comedian who for years in the forties played The Great Gildersleeve on radio and in a short-lived film series.

Peck, Gregory (1916–). Durable and likeable

American leading actor, with stage experience before sudden success in Hollywood.

☐ Days of Glory 43. *The Keys of the Kingdom* 44. The Valley of Decision 44. *Spellbound* 45. The Yearling 46. *Duel in the Sun* 46. *The Macomber Affair* 47. *Gentleman's Agreement* 47. The Paradine Case 47. Yellow Sky 48. The Great Sinner 49. *Twelve O'Clock High* 49. *The Gunfighter* 50. David and Bathsheba 51. Captain Horatio Hornblower (GB) 51. Only the Valiant 52. The World in His Arms 52. The Snows of Kilimanjaro 52. Roman Holiday 53. Night People 54. The Million Pound Note (GB) 54. The Purple Plain (GB) 55. *The Man in the Grey Flannel Suit* 56. Moby Dick 56. Designing Woman 57. The Bravados 58. *The Big Country* 58. Pork Chop Hill 59. Beloved Infidel (as Scott Fitzgerald) 59. On the Beach 59. The Guns of Navarone (GB) 61. Cape Fear 62. How the West was Won 62. *To Kill a Mockingbird* (AA) 63. Captain Newman 63. Behold a Pale Horse 64. Mirage 65. Arabesque 66. Mackenna's Gold 68. The Stalking Moon 68. The Most Dangerous Man in the World 69. Marooned 69. I Walk the Line 70. Shootout 71. Billy Two Hats 73. The Dove (p only) 75.*The Omen* 76. MacArthur 77.

Peckinpah, Sam (1926–). American director of tough westerns.
☐ The Deadly Companions 61. *Ride the High Country* 62. Major Dundee 65. *The Wild Bunch* 69. The Ballad of Cable Hogue 69. Straw Dogs 71. Junior Bonner 72. The Getaway 72. Pat Garrett and Billy the Kid 73. Bring Me the Head of Alfredo Garcia 74. The Killer Elite 76. Cross of Iron 77.

Peerce, Larry (–). American writer-director, son of opera singer Jan Peerce.
One Potato Two Potato 66. Goodbye Columbus 69. A Separate Peace 73. Ash Wednesday 74. The Other Side of the Mountain 76. Two Minute Warning 76.

Peg O' My Heart. This sentimental play by J. Hartley Manners, about an Irish servant girl who stays with her English relatives, was filmed in 1922 by King Vidor with Laurette Taylor, and in 1932 by Robert Z. Leonard, with Marion Davies.

Pelissier, Anthony (1912–). British director with stage experience; son of Fay Compton.
The History of Mr Polly 49. The Rocking Horse Winner 50. Night without Stars 50. Meet Me Tonight 52. Meet Mr Lucifer 54, etc.

Pendleton, Nat (1895–1967). American character actor, formerly professional wrestler,

usually seen in 'dumb ox' roles. In films from c. 1930.
You Said a Mouthful 32. The Sign of the Cross 32. Manhattan Melodrama 34. The Great Ziegfeld 36. The Marx Brothers at the Circus 39. Young Dr Kildare (and series) 39. On Borrowed Time 39. Northwest Passage 40. Top Sergeant Mulligan 42. Rookies Come Home 45. Scared to Death 47. Death Valley 49, many others.

Penn, Arthur (1922–). American director, from TV.
☐ The Left Handed Gun 58. The Miracle Worker 62. Mickey One 65. The Chase 66. *Bonnie and Clyde* 67. Alice's Restaurant 69. Little Big Man 70. Night Moves 75. The Missouri Breaks 76.

Penner, Joe (1904–1941) (J. Pinter). Hungarian-American radio comedian who made a few films.
College Rhythm 33. Go Chase Yourself 38. Glamour Boy 40. The Boys from Syracuse 40, etc.

Pennick, Jack (1895–1964). American small part actor and horse trainer, often in John Ford westerns.
Four Sons 28. Under Two Flags 36. Stagecoach 39. Northwest Mounted Police 40. My Darling Clementine 46. Fort Apache 48. Rio Grande 50. The Alamo 60.

Pennington-Richards, C. M. (1911–). British director, former photographer.
The Oracle 54. Inn for Trouble 60. Double Bunk 62. Ladies Who Do 63. A Challenge for Robin Hood 67, etc.

Penrod. Booth Tarkington's American boy character, in his mid-west small town setting, was for many years a favourite Hollywood subject. Marshall Neilan directed Gordon Griffith in a 1922 version. In 1923 William Beaudine directed Ben Alexander in the role in *Penrod and Sam*, which was remade by Beaudine in 1931 with Leon Janney, and again by William McGann in 1937 with Billy Mauch. Mauch and his twin brother Bobby appeared in two sequels: *Penrod's Double Trouble* 38 directed by Lewis Seiler, and *Penrod and His Twin Brother* 38 directed by McGann. Two Doris Day musicals, *On Moonlight Bay* 51 and *By the Light of the Silvery Moon* 53, were also lightly based on the Tarkington stories: Penrod, unaccountably disguised as 'Wesley', was played by Billy Gray.

People on Sunday (Mennschen am Sonntag) (Germany 1930). A rare combination of talents made this attractive comedy-drama showing how Berliners spent their weekends in pre-Hitler days. Written by Robert Siodmak and Billy Wilder, it was directed by Siodmak with assistance from Fred Zinnemann and Edgar G. Ulmer, photographed by Eugene Schufftan.

Pépé le Moko: see *Algiers*.

Peppard, George (1929–). American leading man with Broadway experience; began interestingly, but developed into an acceptable tough lead of hokum adventures.
□ *The Strange One* 57. Pork Chop Hill 59. Home from the Hill 60. The Subterraneans 60. *Breakfast at Tiffany's* 61. How the West was Won 62. The Victors 63. The Carpetbaggers 64. Operation Crossbow 65. The Third Day 65. *The Blue Max* 66. Tobruk 67. Rough Night in Jericho 67. P.J. 68. What's So Bad about Feeling Good? 68. House of Cards 68. Pendulum 68. The Executioner 69. Cannon for Cordoba 70. The Bravos (TV) 71. One More Time 71. The Groundstar Conspiracy 72. Newman's Law 74. One of Our Own (TV) 75. Guilty or Innocent: The Sam Sheppard Murder Case. TV 75. Damnation Alley. 77 *Banacek* 72–73.

Pepper, Barbara (1912–1969). American second-lead actress who usually played tramps.
Our Daily Bread 33. Winterset 36. Lady in the Morgue 38. Brewster's Millions 45. Terror Trail 47. Inferno 53. The D.I. 57. A Child is Waiting 63. Kiss Me Stupid 64, many others.

Percival, Lance (1933–). British light comedian.
Twice Round the Daffodils 62. The VIPs 63. Carry On Cruising 63. The Yellow Rolls-Royce 64. The Big Job 65. Darling Lili 69. Up Pompeii 71. Our Miss Fred 72, etc.

Percy, Esmé (1887–1957). Distinguished British stage actor, especially of Shavian parts. On stage from 1904; occasional films from twenties.
Murder 30. Bitter Sweet 33. *The Frog* 36. Pygmalion 38. Caesar and Cleopatra 45. The Ghosts of Berkeley Square 46. Death in the Hand 48, etc.

Perelman, S. J. (1904–). Renowned American humorist whose name appeared on a few films, mostly in collaboration.
Monkey Business 31. Horse Feathers 32.

Ambush 39. The Golden Fleecing 40. Around the World in Eighty Days 56, etc.

Périer, Etienne (1931–). French director.
Bobosse 59. Murder at 45 RPM 60. Bridge to the Sun 61. Swordsman of Siena 63. When Eight Bells Toll 71. Zeppelin 71. Five against Capricorn 72. A Murder is a Murder 72, etc.

Perier, François (1919–) (François Pilu). Sturdy French actor, in films from mid-thirties.
Hotel du Nord 38. Un Revenant 46. Le Silence est d'Or 48. *Orphée* 49. The Bed 53. *Gervaise* 55. Nights of Cabiria 56. Charmants Garçons 57. Weekend at Dunkirk 65. The Samurai 67. The Red Circle 70. Just Before Nightfall 73, many others.

The Perils of Pauline. Pearl White's famous 1914 serial was directed by Donald Mackenzie, co-starred Crane Wilbur, and concerned the heroine's evasion of attempts on her life by her dastardly guardian. The 1947 film of the same name was a lightly fictionalized biography of Pearl White, with Betty Hutton in the role; George Marshall directed. The 1967 film was vaguely based on the original serial, with Pamela Austin as the heroine, now involved in goings-on zanier than anything Pearl White dreamed of. Direction was by Herbert Leonard and Joshua Shelley.

Perinal, Georges (1897–1965). French cinematographer, in films from 1913.
Les Nouveaux Messieurs 28. Sous les Toits de Paris 30. *Le Sang d'un Poète* 30. *Le Million* 31. *A Nous la Liberté* 32. The Private Life of Henry VIII 32. *Rembrandt* 36. *The Thief of Baghdad* (AA) 40. *The Life and Death of Colonel Blimp* 43. *Nicholas Nickleby* 47. An Ideal Husband 47. *The Fallen Idol* 48. Lady Chatterley's Lover 55. A King in New York 57. Saint Joan 57. Bonjour Tristesse 58. Oscar Wilde 60, many others.

Perkins, Anthony (1932–). Gangly American juvenile lead of the fifties, son of Osgood Perkins. Found mature roles scarce.
□ *The Actress* 53. Friendly Persuasion 56. The Lonely Man 57. *Desire Under the Elms* 57. *Fear Strikes Out* 57. The Tin Star 57. *This Angry Age* 58. The Matchmaker 58. Green Mansions 58. On the Beach 59. Tall Story 60. *Psycho* 60. Goodbye Again 61. Phaedra 62. Five Miles to Midnight 62. The Trial 62. Two are Guilty 64. The Fool Killer 64. Is Paris Burning? 66. The Champagne Murders 68. Pretty Poison 68. Catch 22 70. *WUSA* 70. How Awful About (TV) 70. Ten Days Wonder 71. Judge Roy Bean 72. Play It as It Lays 72. Lovin' Molly 73. Mahogany 75.

Perkins, Millie (1939–). American leading lady who went to Hollywood from dramatic school.
The Diary of Anne Frank 59. Wild in the Country 61. Wild in the Streets 68. Lady Cocoa 75, etc.

Perkins, Osgood (1892–1937). American character actor, mainly on stage.
The Cradle Buster 22. Puritan Passions 23. Knockout Reilly 27. Mother's Boy 29. Tarnished Lady 31. Scarface 32. Kansas City Princess 34. I Dream Too Much 35, etc.

Perlberg, William (1899–1969). American producer, often in conjunction with George Seaton; came from agency business, in Hollywood from mid-thirties.
Golden Boy 39. The Song of Bernadette 43. Forever Amber 47. The Country Girl 54. Teacher's Pet 58. The Counterfeit Traitor 62. Thirty-Six Hours 64, many others.

Perreau, Gigi (1941–) (Ghislaine Perreau-Saussine). American child actress of the forties who seems not quite to have managed the transition to adult stardom.
Madame Curie 43. Song of Love 47. My Foolish Heart 49. Has Anybody Seen My Gal? 51. The Man in the Grey Flannel Suit 56. Wild Heritage 58. Look in Any Window 61, others.

Perrine, Valerie (1946–). American leading lady of the seventies.
Slaughterhouse Five 72. The Last American Hero 73. Lenny 74. W. C. Fields and Me 76, etc.

Perrins, Leslie (1902–1962). British character actor, often seen as a smooth crook.
The Sleeping Cardinal 31. The Pointing Finger 34. Tudor Rose 36. Old Iron 39. The Woman's Angle 43. A Run for Your Money 49. Guilty 56, many others.

Perry, Frank (1930–). American director.
☐ David and Lisa 63. Ladybug, Ladybug 64. The Swimmer 68. Trilogy 68. Last Summer 69. Diary of a Mad Housewife 70. Doc 71. Play It as it Lays 72. Man on a Swing 74. Rancho de Luxe 76.

Perry, Paul P. (1891–1963). Pioneer American cinematographer who experimented with colour.
Rose of the Rancho 14. The Cheat 15. Hidden Pearls 17. The Sea Wolf 21. Rosita 23. Souls for Sables 26, many others.

persistence of vision. The medical explanation for our being able to see moving pictures. Twenty-four ordered still pictures are shown to us successively each second, and our sense of sight is slow enough to merge them into one continuous action. The retina of the eye retains each still picture just long enough for it to be replaced by another only slightly different.

Persoff, Nehemiah (1920–). Israeli actor, long in America; trained at Actors' Studio.
On the Waterfront 54. The Harder They Fall 56. *This Angry Age* 57. The Badlanders 58. Never Steal Anything Small 58. Al Capone 59. Some Like It Hot 59. The Big Show 61. The Comancheros 62. The Hook 63. *Fate is the Hunter* 64. The Greatest Story Ever Told 65. Panic in the City 68. Red Sky at Morning 71. Psychic Killer 75, etc.

Persson, Essy (1945–). Swedish leading lady.
I a Woman 67. Thérèse and Isabelle 68. Cry of the Banshee 70, etc.

Pertwee, Jon (1919–). British comic actor, brother of Michael Pertwee, son of Roland.
Murder at the Windmill 48. Mr Drake's Duck 51. Will Any Gentleman? 53. A Yank in Ermine 56. Carry On Cleo 64. Carry On Screaming 66. The House that Dripped Blood 70. One of Our Dinosaurs is Missing 75, etc.

Pertwee, Michael (1916–). British playwright who has been involved in many screenplays.
Silent Dust (from his play) 48. The Interrupted Journey 49. *Laughter in Paradise* 51. Top Secret 52. Now and Forever 54. *The Naked Truth* 58. In the Doghouse 62. The Mouse on the Moon 62. Ladies Who Do 63. A Funny Thing Happened on the Way to the Forum 66. Finders Keepers 66. The Magnificent Two 67. Salt and Pepper 68. One More Time 70. Digby 73, etc.

Peters, Brock (1927–). Black American actor in American films.
To Kill a Mockingbird 62. The L-Shaped Room 62. *Heavens Above* (GB) 63. The Pawnbroker 64. Major Dundee 65. P. J. 67. The McMasters 70. Black Girl 73. Framed 75, etc.

Peters, House (1880–1967). American silent screen leading man.
Leah Kleschna 12. The Pride of Jennico 14. The Great Divide 15. Mignon 15. The Storm 22. Held to Answer 23. Raffles 25. Head Winds 25, many others.

Peters, Jean (1926–). Attractive American

leading lady of the fifties; retired to marry Howard Hughes.

□ Captain from Castile 47. Deep Waters 48. It Happens Every Spring 49. Love That Brute 50. Take Care of My Little Girl 51. As Young as You Feel 51. Anne of the Indies 52. Viva Zapata 52. Wait Till the Sun Shines Nellie 52. Lure of the Wilderness 52. Full House 52. Niagara 53. Pickup on South Street 53. Blueprint for Murder 53. Vicki 53. *Three Coins in the Fountain* 54. Apache 54. Broken Lance 54. *A Man Called Peter* 55.

Peters, Susan (1921–1952) (Suzanne Carnahan). American leading lady of the forties; badly injured in an accident, she continued her career from a wheelchair.
Santa Fé Trail 40. *Random Harvest* 42. Assignment in Brittany 43. Song of Russia 44. Keep Your Powder Dry 45. The Sign of the Ram 48, etc.

Petersen, Colin (1946–). British child actor of the fifties.
Smiley 56. The Scamp 57. A Cry from the Streets 57, etc.

Petit, Pascale (1938–) (Anne-Marie Petit). French leading lady.
The Witches of Salem 57. Les Tricheurs 58. Girls for the Summer 59. L'Affaire d'Une Nuit 60. Demons at Midnight 62, etc.

Petri, Elio (1929–). Italian director.
The Assassin 61. The Tenth Victim 65. We Still Kill the Old Way 68. A Quiet Place in the Country 68. Investigation of a Citizen above Suspicion (AA) 69. The Working Class Goes to Heaven 71, etc.

Petrie, Daniel (1920–). American director with academic background; stage and TV experience.
□ The Bramble Bush 59. A Raisin in the Sun 61. The Main Attraction 62. Stolen Hours 63. The Idol 66. The Spy with a Cold Nose 67. A Howling in the Woods (TV) 71. The Neptune Factor 73. Buster and Billie 74. Lifeguard 75.

Petrie, Hay (1895–1948). Scots character actor of stage and screen, specializing in eccentrics.
Suspense 30. The Private Life of Henry VIII 32. Nell Gwyn 34. *The Old Curiosity Shop* (as Quilp) 34. The Ghost Goes West 36. *Twenty-One Days* 38. The Spy in Black 39. Q Planes 39. Jamaica Inn 39. Crimes at the Dark House 40. The Thief of Baghdad 40. One of Our Aircraft is Missing 42. A Canterbury Tale 44. Great Expectations 46. The Red Shoes 48. The Guinea Pig 48, etc.

The Petrified Forest (US 1936). A simple photographed version of Robert Sherwood's talkative play about an idealist, held captive by a gangster in a remote inn, who finally gives his life to save the other hostages. Remarkable chiefly for the opportunities it gave to three talents: Leslie Howard, Humphrey Bogart and Bette Davis. Directed by Archie Mayo.

Petrov, Vladimir (1896–1966). Russian director.
Thunderstorm 34. *Peter the Great* 38, etc.

Petrova, Olga (1886–) (Muriel Harding). British-born leading lady of Hollywood silents in which she played *femmes fatales*.
Autoiography 1942: *Butter with My Bread*.
The Tigress 14. The Soul Market 16. The Undying Flame 17. Daughter of Destiny 18. The Panther Woman 18, etc.

Pettet, Joanna (1944–). Anglo-American leading lady.
The Group 65. Night of the Generals 66. Robbery 67. Blue 68. The Weekend Nun (TV) 74. Captains and the Kings (TV) 76, etc.

Pettingell, Frank (1891–1966). British north-country character actor who dispensed rough good humour on stage from 1910; films from 1931.
Hobson's Choice (as Mossop) 31. Jealousy 31. *The Good Companions* 32. *Sing As We Go* 34. The Last Journey 36. Fame 36. Millions 36. Sailing Along 38. *Gaslight* 39. Busman's Honeymoon 40. The Seventh Survivor 41. This England 41. Kipps 41. Once a Crook 41. *When We are Married* 42. The Young Mr Pitt 42. Get Cracking 44. Gaiety George 46. The Magic Box 51. Meet Me Tonight 52. Value for Money 57. Becket 64, many others.

Pevney, Joseph (1920–). American director, former stage actor.
Shakedown 50. Undercover Girl 50. Iron Man 51. The Strange Door 51. Meet Danny Wilson 51. Just across the Street 52. Because of You 54. Desert Legion 54. The Female on the Beach 55. Three Ring Circus 55. Away All Boats 56. Congo Crossing 56. Tammy 57. *Man of a Thousand Faces* 57. Twilight for the Gods 58. Cash McCall 60. Night of the Grizzly 66, etc.

Peyton Place (US 1957). The film version of Grace Metalious' novel started a fashion for small-town sex exposés on the screen. A well-made film with particularly good colour photography by William Mellor, it was carefully produced by Jerry Wald, directed by Mark Robson and scripted by John Michael Hayes. A sequel, *Return to Peyton Place*, followed in 1961, and in 1964 came a TV serial of two half-hours a week; it proved so popular that from 1965 it was given three half-hours, and lasted until 1969.

The Phantom of the Opera. The melodramatic tale of the embittered disfigured composer who haunts the sewers beneath the Paris Opera House and takes a pretty young singer as his protégée has been filmed three times. 1. US 1925; directed by Rupert Julian; with Lon Chaney and Mary Philbin. 2. US 1943; directed by Arthur Lubin; with Claude Rains and Susanna Foster. 3. GB 1962; directed by Terence Fisher; with Herbert Lom and Heather Sears. The first version is without doubt the most interesting.

The Philadelphia Story (US 1940). This glossy cocktail comedy, not without its serious points, stands out as by far the most adult and successful film of its type. Adapted by Donald Ogden Stewart from the play by Philip Barry, it stars Katharine Hepburn in her stage role as Tracy Lord the idle rich heiress with the wrong kind of standards; Cary Grant as C. K. Dexter Haven, her ex-husband; James Stewart (AA) as Macaulay Connor, her would-be next, and in sterling support, Ruth Hussey, Roland Young, John Halliday, Mary Nash, Virginia Weidler and Henry Daniell. George Cukor directed with his accustomed dexterity. In 1956 the script was shortened and devitalized to permit the inclusion of some poor Cole Porter numbers under the title *High Society*. Grace Kelly filled Hepburn's shoes comfortably but Bing Crosby and Frank Sinatra were miscast and the whole thing was a fairly complete disaster; at least for anyone who remembered the original.

Philbin, Mary (1903–). American leading lady of the silent screen.
The Blazing Trail 21. Merry Go Round 23. Phantom of the Opera 25. The Man Who Laughs 28. After the Fog 30, etc.

Philip Marlowe was the weary but incorruptible private eye creation of Raymond Chandler, treading the seamier streets of Los Angeles in a dogged hunt for suspects. On television he was played in a poor series by Phil Carey, on screen by Humphrey Bogart, Robert Montgomery, George Montgomery, Dick Powell, James Garner and (badly) Elliott Gould.

Philipe, Gérard (1922–1959). France's leading young actor of the fifties, who alternated stage and screen activities.
Biography 1964: *No Longer Than a Sigh* by Anne Philipe.
Le Diable au Corps 46. L'Idiot 46. *Une Si Jolie Petite Plage* 48. *La Beauté du Diable* 49. La Ronde 50. Fanfan la Tulipe 51. *Belles de Nuit* 52. Les Orgeuilleux 53. Knave of Hearts (Monsieur Ripois) (GB) 53. Le Rouge et le Noir 54. Les Grandes Manoeuvres 55. Till Eulenspiegel (& co-d) 56. Pot-Bouille 58. *Les Liaisons Dangereuses* 59, etc.

Philips, Conrad (1930–). British leading man, mostly on TV.
The White Trap 59. Chamber of Horrors 60. The Fourth Square 61. No Love for Johnnie 62. Stopover Forever 64. Who Killed the Cat? 66, etc.
TV series: *William Tell* 58.

Philips, Mary (1900–1975). American stage actress who made very occasional film appearances.
Life Begins 32. A Farewell To Arms 33. That Certain Women 37. Lady in the Dark 44. Leave Her to Heaven 46. Dear Wife 47, etc.

Philips, Robin (1941–). British juvenile lead.
Decline and Fall 68. David Copperfield 69. Two Gentlemen Sharing 70.

Philiber, John (1872–1944). Slightly-built American character actor in a few early forties films; best remembered for *It Happened Tomorrow* 44.

Phillips, Frank (–). American cinematographer.
The Island at the Top of the World 74. Escape to Witch Mountain 75, etc.

Phillips, Leslie (1924–). British light comedian, former child actor, on stage from 1935, occasional films from 1936.
The Citadel 38. Train of Events 49. The Sound Barrier 52. Value for Money 57. *Carry On Nurse* 59. Carry On Constable 60. Doctor in Love 60. Watch Your Stern 60. *Very Important Person* 61. Raising the Wind 61. In the Doghouse 62. Crooks Anonymous 62. *The Fast Lady* 62. And Father Came Too 64. Doctor in Clover 66. Maroc 7 (& p) 66. Doctor in Trouble 70. The Magnificent Seven Deadly Sins 71. Not Now Darling 73, others.

Phillips, Sian (1934–). Dignified British stage actress.

Becket 64. Young Cassidy 64. Laughter in the Dark 69. Goodbye Mr Chips 69. Murphy's War 70. Under Milk Wood 72.

Philo Vance: see *Van Dine, S. S.*

Philpotts, Ambrosine (1912–). British character actress, mainly on stage.
This Man is Mine 46. The Franchise Affair 51. The Captain's Paradise 53. Up in the World 56. Room at the Top 59. Doctor in Love 60. Life at the Top 65, etc.

Phipps, Nicholas (1913–). British light comedian often seen in cameo roles. On stage from 1932. Has also scripted or co-scripted many films:
Piccadilly Incident 46. Spring in Park Lane 48. Doctor in the House 53. Doctor in Love 60. The Wild and the Willing 62, many others. He appeared in most of these.

Piazza, Ben (1934–). Canadian actor who went to Hollywood, but was little heard from.
A Dangerous Age (Can.) 58. The Hanging Tree 59, etc.

Piccoli, Michel (1925–). Franco-Italian leading man.
French Cancan 55. The Witches of Salem 56. Le Bal des Espions 60. Le Mépris 63. Diary of a Chambermaid 64. De L'Amour 65. Lady L. 65. La Curée 66. The Young Girls of Rochefort 67. Un Homme de Trop 67. Belle de Jour 67. Dillinger is Dead 68. The Milky Way 69. Topaz 69. Blowout 73. The Infernal Trio 74, others.

Picerni, Paul (1922–). American leading man, usually in second features.
Saddle Tramp (debut) 50. Maru Maru 52. House of Wax 53. Drive a Crooked Road 54. Hell's Island 55. Omar Khayyam 57. Strangers When We Meet 60. The Scalphunters 68. The Land Raiders 69, etc.
TV series: The Untouchables.

Pichel, Irving (1891–1954). American actor-director, in Hollywood from 1930.
AS ACTOR: The Right to Love 30. The Miracle Man 31. Oliver Twist (as Fagin) 33. Cleopatra 34. Jezebel 38. Jaurez 40. Sante Fé 51, many others.
□ AS DIRECTOR: *The Most Dangerous Game* (co-d) 32. Before Dawn 33. *She* (co-d) 35. The Gentleman from Louisiana 36. Beware of Ladies 37. Larceny of the Air 37. The Sheik Steps Out 37. The Duke Comes Back 37. The Great Commandment 39. Earthbound 40. The Man I Married 40. Hudson's Bay 40. Dance Hall 41..

Secret Agent of Japan 42. The Pied Piper 42. Life Begins at 8.30 42. *The Moon is Down* 43. *Happy Land* 43. And Now Tomorrow 44. A Medal for Benny 45. Colonel Effingham's Raid 45. Tomorrow is Forever 46. The Bride Wore Boots 46. O.S.S. 46. Temptation 46. They Won't Believe Me 47. Something in the Wind 47. The Miracle of the Bells 48. Mr Peabody and the Mermaid 48. Without Honor 49. The Great Rupert 50. Quicksand 50. Destination Moon 50. Santa Fe 51. Martin Luther 53. Day of Triumph 54.

Pickens, Slim (1919–) (Louis Bert Lindley). Slow-talking American character actor, in scores of low-budget westerns from mid-forties, more recently in bigger films.
The Sun Shines Bright 53. The Great Locomotive Chase 56. One-Eyed Jacks 59. Dr Strangelove 63. Major Dundee 65. Rough Night in Jericho 67. The Cowboys 72. Blazing Saddles 74. The Apple Dumpling Gang 75. The White Buffalo 77, etc.
TV series: Custer 67.

Pick, Lupu: see *Lupu-Pick*

Pickford, Jack (1896–1933). American light actor, brother of Mary Pickford.
Tom Sawyer 17. Sandy 18. Just Out of College 21. The Goose Woman 25. The Bat 26. Brown of Harvard 26. Gang War 28, etc.

Pickford, Mary (1893–) (Gladys Smith). Canadian actress who in the heyday of silent films was known as 'the world's sweetheart'; became co-founder of United Artists Films and one of America's richest women. Acting on stage from five years old; was brought into films by D. W. Griffith.
Autobiography 1955: *Sunshine and Shadow*. Biography 1974: *Sweetheart* by Robert Windeler. Special Academy Award 1976.
Her First Biscuits 09. The Violin Maker of Cremona 10. The Paris Hat 13. Madame Butterfly 15. Less Than the Dust 16. The Little Princess 17. Rebecca of Sunnybrook Farm 17. Stella Maris 18. *Pollyanna* 19. Suds 20. *Little Lord Fauntleroy* 21. The Love Light 21. *Tess of the Storm Country* 22. Rosita 23. Dorothy Vernon of Haddon Hall 24. Little Annie Rooney 25. My Best Girl 27. The Taming of the Shrew 29. Secrets 29. *Coquette* (AA) 29. Kiki 31. Secrets 33, many others.

Pickles, Vivian (1933–) British character actress.
Play Dirty 68. Nicholas and Alexandra 71. Harold and Maude 71. Sunday Bloody Sunday 72. O Lucky Man 73, etc.

Pickles, Wilfred (1904–). British radio personality and latterly character actor; plays Yorkshiremen.
Autobiography 1949: *Between You and Me*.
The Gay Dog 53. Billy Liar 63. The Family Way 66. For the Love of Ada 72, etc.

Picnic (US 1955). Based on the play by William Inge, this over-heated melodrama of small town American sex life—or rather the lack of it—seemed at the time to be starting an American 'new wave'. It had the new sex symbol Kim Novak; the popular William Holden as the virile young stranger; Rosalind Russell as the repressed schoolmistress; and an insistent theme tune called 'Moonglow' by George Duning. Joshua Logan's direction was generally lethargic, but James Wong Howe's colour photography did a lot to compensate. The success of the movie led to a long spate of imitations: *The Long Hot Summer, Peyton Place, The Bramble Bush, A Summer Place*, etc.

Picon, Molly (–). American stage actress; films very occasional.
Come Blow Your Horn 63. For Pete's Sake 74, etc.

The Picture of Dorian Gray (US 1944). Albert Lewin adapted and directed Oscar Wilde's macabre fantasy about a man who stays young while his portrait shows his debauchery, and a remarkably successful film it was, like an exotic Victorian hothouse, with Hurd Hatfield suitably impassive in the lead and George Sanders uttering epigrams in the background. The director's obvious passion for Egyptian cats and Omar Khayyam, however, was a signpost to the absurdity of his later films. A German remake in 1969 had little quality.

Pidgeon, Walter (1897–). Good-looking, quiet-spoken Canadian leading man in Hollywood; during the thirties and forties he gave gentlemanly support to several dominant leading ladies.
□ Mannequin 25. Old Loves and New 26. The Outsider 26. Miss Nobody 26. Marriage License 26. The Girl from Rio 27. The Heart of Salome 27. The Gorilla 27. The Thirteenth Juror 27. Gateway of the Moon 27. Clothes Make the Woman 28. Woman Wise 28. Turn Back the Hours 28. Melody of Love 28. A Most Immoral Lady 29. Her Private Life 29. Bride of the Regiment 30. Sweet Kitty Bellairs 30. Viennese Nights 30. Kiss Me Again 30. Going Wild 30. The Gorilla 31. The Hot Heiress 31. Rockabye 32. The Kiss Before the Mirror 33. Journal of a Crime 34. Big Brown Eyes 36. Fatal Lady 36.

Girl Overboard 37. Saratoga 37. A Girl with Ideas 37. She's Dangerous 37. As Good as Married 37. My Dear Miss Aldrich 37. Man Proof 38. The Girl of the Golden West 38. Shopworn Angel 38. Too Hot to Handle 38. Listen Darling 38. *Society Lawyer* 39. Six Thousand Enemies 39. Stronger than Desire 39. Nick Carter Master Detective 39. The House across the Bay 40. It's a Date 40. Dark Command 40. Phantom Raiders 40. Sky Murder 40. Flight Command 40. *Man Hunt* 41. *Blossoms in the Dust* 41. *How Green was My Valley* 41. Design for Scandal 42. *Mrs Miniver* 42. White Cargo 42. The Youngest Profession 43. *Madame Curie* 43. Mrs Parkington 44. Weekend at the Waldorf 45. Holiday in Mexico 46. The Secret Heart 46. Cass Timberlane 47. If Winter Comes 47. Julia Misbehaves 48. Command Decision 48. *That Forsyte Woman* (as Young Jolyon) 49. The Red Danube 49. The Miniver Story 50. Soldiers Three 51. Calling Bulldog Drummond 51. The Unknown Man 51. The Sellout 52. Million Dollar Mermaid 52. The Bad and the Beautiful 52. Scandal at Scourie 53. Dream Wife 53. *Executive Suite* 54. Men of the Fighting Lady 54. The Last Time I Saw Paris 54. Deep in My Heart 54. Hit the Deck 55. The Glass Slipper 55. *Forbidden Planet* 56. These Wilder Years 56. The Rack 56. Voyage to the Bottom of the Sea 61. *Advise and Consent* 62. The Two Colonels 62. Big Red 62. The Shortest Day 63. Cosa Nostra (TV) 67. Warning Shot 67. Funny Girl (as Ziegfeld) 68. Rascal 69. The Mask of Sheba (TV) 69. The Vatican Affair 69. Skyjacked 72. The Neptune Factor 73. Harry in Your Pocket 73. Yellow Headed Summer 74. Live Again Die Again (TV) 75. You Lie So Deep My Love (TV) 75. The Lindbergh Kidnapping Case (TV) 76. Murder at 40,000 Feet (TV) 76.

Pierce, Jack (1889–1968). American make-up artist who worked at Universal for many years and created the familiar images of Dracula, the Wolf Man, the Mummy and the Frankenstein monster.

Pierlot, Francis (1876–1955). American character actor, usually of mild professorial types.
Night Angel 31. The Captain is a Lady 40. Night Monster 42. The Doughgirls 44. Dragonwyck 46. The Late George Apley 47. That Wonderful Urge 48. My Friend Irma 49. Cyrano de Bergerac 50. The Robe 53, many others.

Pierson, Frank (1945–). American director, from TV.
Cat Ballou (co-w) 65. The Looking Glass War 69. The Anderson Tapes (w only) 71. Dog Day

Afternoon (d only) 75. A Star Is Born (d only) 76. etc.
TV series: *Nichols* 71.

Pilbeam, Nova (1919–). British teenage star of the thirties.
Little Friend 34. The Man Who Knew Too Much 34. *Tudor Rose* 35. *Young and Innocent* 37. Spring Meeting 40. Banana Ridge 41. This Man is Mine 46. Counterblast 47. The Three Weird Sisters 48, etc.

pilot: in television terminology, a film which is made as a trial, to see whether a series on the same premise will be ordered.

pin screen animation: a curious and short-lived means of animation by photographing pins pushed through a rubber sheet. The shadows caused by the varying height of the pins gives the single picture. The best example is Alexieff's *Night on Bald Mountain* 33.

Pine, William H. (1896–195) and **Thomas, William C.** (1892–). An American production executive and an exhibitor-writer who banded together in the early forties to make scores of second features for Paramount. *Power Dive, Wildcat, Midnight Manhunt, They Made Me a Killer, Wrecking Crew, Torpedo Boat, I Cover Big Town,* etc. Continued into the fifties with larger-scale adventures: *Sangaree, Jamaica Run, The Far Horizons,* etc., but never managed a top-notcher.

Pinero, Sir Arthur Wing (1855–1934). British playwright who dealt mainly with the upper middle class. Many films were made of his work in silent days; the most popular later were *The Second Mrs Tanqueray* and *The Enchanted Cottage,* though his farce *The Magistrate* had several incarnations, notably as *Those Were the Days* 34.

Pinewood Studios, seventeen miles northwest of London, was built in 1935 and opened in 1936 by a millionaire named Charles Boot as Britain's reply to Hollywood. It rapidly came under the control of the Rank Organisation, and its fortunes have fluctuated, but on the whole it has been fairly well used.
History published 1976: *Movies from the Mansion* by George Perry.

Pink, Sidney (1916–). American director.
Journey to the Seventh Planet 61. Reptilicus 62. Finger on the Trigger 65. The Tall Women 66.

The Pink Panther (US 1963). An amiable star-studded romp about jewel robbers, this rather patchy comedy by Blake Edwards surprisingly triggered off a cartoon series featuring the Pink Panther (who does not appear in the film except as a title design: the title refers to a jewel) as well as four sequels about the accident-prone detective created by Peter Sellers: *A Shot in the Dark* 64 (with Sellers), *Inspector Clouseau* 68 (with Alan Arkin), *The Return of the Pink Panther* 75 (Sellers) and *The Pink Panther Smiles Back* 76.

Pinky (US 1949). A moderately pioneering Hollywood contribution to race relations, this quiet tale of a negress who 'passed' for white but felt bound to tell the truth about herself was somewhat compromised by the casting of white Jeanne Crain in the role. But the script by Philip Dunne and Dudley Nichols was generally intelligent and thoughtful, and both the photography by Joe Macdonald and the direction by Elia Kazan were more than competent.

Pinsent, Gordon (1933–). Canadian leading actor, much on TV.
The Thomas Crown Affair 68. The Forbin Project 69. Quarantined (TV) 69. The Rowdy Man 72. Newman's Law 74, etc.
TV series: *Quentin Durgens* 69.

Pinter, Harold (1930–). British playwright, and juggler of nonsense plotting and obscure motivation. His film scripts have been more straightforward.
☐ The Servant (w) 63. The Caretaker (oaw) 64. The Pumpkin Eater (w) (BFA) 64. The Quiller Memorandum (w) 67. Accident (w) 67. The Birthday Party (woa) 69. The Go Between (w) 71. The Homecoming (oa) 73. Butley (d) 73. Rogue Male (TV) (a) 76. The Last Tycoon (w) 76.

Pintoff, Ernest (1931–). Modernist American cartoon maker: Flebus 57. *The Violinist* 59. *The Interview* 60. *The Critic* 63, etc. Also wrote and directed one live-action feature, *Harvey Middlemann, Fireman* 64.

Pinza, Ezio (1893–1957) (Fortunato Pinza). Italian-American opera singer who graced a few films.
☐ Carnegie Hall 48. Mr Imperium 50. Slightly Dishonorable 51. Tonight We Sing 53.

Pious, Minerva (1909–). American radio comedienne of the forties, famous with Fred Allen as Mrs Nussbaum.
It's In the Bag 45. The Ambassador's Daughter 56. Love in the Afternoon 57, etc.

Piper, Frederick (1902–). British character actor, mostly on stage: usually played the average man or police inspector.
The Good Companions 32. Jamaica Inn 39. Hue and Cry 46. Passport to Pimlico 49. The Blue Lamp 50. Doctor at Sea 55. Very Important Person 61. One Way Pendulum 64. He Who Rides a Tiger 65, etc.

The Pirate (US 1948). One of the first signs of the new trend in musicals which was to come with On the Town and An American in Paris, this stage-bound operetta didn't manage as a whole to rise above its conventions, but it did have splendid moments. Judy Garland, Gene Kelly and the Nicholas Brothers were involved, and although Cole Porter's songs were below his best, they were put over with vigour. Directed by Vincente Minnelli, photographed by Harry Stradling, book by Albert Hackett and Frances Goodrich.

pirates have regularly appeared on the screen. Stories with some claim to historical authenticity, or at least based on the exploits of a pirate who once lived, include Captain Blood (and its various sequels), The Black Swan, Morgan the Pirate, Seven Seas to Calais, Blackbeard the Pirate, Captain Kidd, The Buccaneer, and Anne of the Indies (a rare female pirate: one other was depicted in The Pirate Queen). Totally fictitious stories are of course headed by Treasure Island (qv) in its various versions; other swashbuckling yarns included The Sea Hawk, The Black Pirate, The Crimson Pirate, The Golden Hawk, Fair Wind to Java, A High Wind in Jamaica, Pirates of Tortuga, Yankee Buccaneer, The Spanish Main, Pirates of Tripoli, Devil Ship Pirates, Pirates of Blood River, Prince of Pirates, and Raiders of the Seven Seas. The only notable musical pirate was Gene Kelly in The Pirate; comic pirates are also rare, but they do include The Princess and the Pirate, Blackbeard's Ghost, Double Crossbones, The Dancing Pirate and Old Mother Riley's Jungle Treasure.

Pirosh, Robert (1910–). American writer-director.
The Winning Ticket (oa) 35. A Day at the Races (w) 37. I Married a Witch (w) 42. Rings on Her Fingers (w) 42. Up In Arms (w) 44. Battleground (w) (AA) 49. Go for Broke (wd) 51. Washington Story (wd) 52. Valley of the Kings (wd) 54. The Girl Rush (wd) 55. Spring Reunion (wd) 57. Hell is for Heroes (w) 62. A Gathering of Eagles (w) 63. What's so Bad about Feeling Good? (w) 68, etc.

Pitt, Ingrid (1944–) (Ingrid Petrov). Polish-born leading lady in British films.
Where Eagles Dare 69. The Vampire Lovers 70. The House that Dripped Blood 71. Countess Dracula 71. Nobody Ordered Love 72. The Wicker Man 73, etc.

plastic surgery was long a staple of horror films, but improved techniques have made it a subject for 'woman's pictures' such as Ash Wednesday and Once is Not Enough. Arsenic and Old Lace made a comedy point of it, and Seconds took it seriously.

Pitts, Zasu (1898–1963). American actress, a heroine of the twenties and a tearful comedienne of the thirties.
The Little Princess 17. Early to Wed 21. Greed 23. Twin Beds 27. The Wedding March 28. Seed 30. Bad Sister 31. The Guardsman 32. Back Street 32. Walking Down Broadway 32. many two-reeler comedies with Thelma Todd (32–34), Dames 34. Mrs Wiggs of the Cabbage Patch 34. So's Your Aunt Emma 38. Buck Privates 39. Nurse Edith Cavell 40. Niagara Falls 41. Let's Face It 43. Life with Father 47. Francis 50. Francis Joins the WACS 55. This Could be the Night 57. It's a Mad Mad Mad Mad World 63, many others.
TV series: Oh Susanna 56–59.

Pizer, Larry (–). British cinematographer.
The Party's Over 63. Four in the Morning 65. Morgan 65. Our Mother's House 66. Isadora 68. All Neat in Black Stockings 69. Phantom of the Paradise 74, etc.

A Place in the Sun (US 1951). Now almost forgotten, this version of Theodore Dreiser's An American Tragedy (previously filmed in 1931 with Phillips Holmes) was hailed by some critics at the time of its release as one of the greatest films of all time. It is now difficult to see why. Slowly and pretentiously directed by George Stevens, its story of a young man's efforts to get into high society at any cost even then seemed dated and empty. Montgomery Clift did what he could with an unsympathetic role, and William C. Mellor's photography was luxurious.

The Plainsman (US 1937). Cecil B. de Mille's well-remembered western starred Gary Cooper as Wild Bill Hickok, James Ellison as Buffalo Bill, and Jean Arthur as Calamity Jane. It was poorly remade in 1966 with Don Murray, Guy Stockwell and Abby Dalton.

Planck, Robert (1894–). American cinematographer.

Our Daily Bread 33. *Jane Eyre* 43. Cass Timberlane 47. The Three Musketeers 48. Little Women 50. Rhapsody 54. Moonfleet 55, etc.

Planer, Franz (1894–1963). German cinematographer, in Hollywood from 1937.
Drei von Der Tankstelle 30. *Liebelei* 33. Maskerade 34. The Beloved Vagabond (GB) 36. Holiday 38. The Face Behind the Mask 41. The Adventures of Martin Eden 42. Once Upon a Time 44. The Chase 47. *Letter from an Unknown Woman* 48. Criss Cross 48. The Scarf 51. The Blue Veil 51. *Death of a Salesman* 52. Twenty Thousand Leagues under the Sea 54. Not as a Stranger 55. The Pride and the Passion 57. The Big Country 58. The Nun's Story 59. The Unforgiven 60. The Children's Hour 62, etc.

Planet of the Apes (US 1967). Adapted by Paul Dehn from a novel by Pierre Boulle and stylishly directed by Franklin Schaffner, this distinctive piece of science fiction had Charlton Heston as an astronaut who, caught in a time warp, finds himself on a planet where the humans have degenerated and the apes rule with wisdom. A last minute twist reveals the planet to be Earth at some time in the future, when war has reduced our present civilizations to ruins. Taken up by the young as a moral parable, the film had great success and spawned four sequels of increasing violence and decreasing interest: *Beneath the Planet of the Apes* 69, *Escape from the Planet of the Apes* 70, *Conquest of the Planet of the Apes* 72. *Battle for the Planet of the Apes* 73. A TV series in 1974 was shortlived. Mention should be made of the splendidly flexible ape make-up by John Chambers.

Platt, Edward (1916–1974). American character actor who usually plays generals, stern fathers and similar types.
The Shrike 55. Rebel Without a Cause 55. Serenade 56. The Great Man 56. Designing Woman 57. The Gift of Love 58. North by Northwest 59. Pollyana 60. A Ticklish Affair 63, many others.
TV series: *Get Smart* 66–69.

Platt, Louise (1914–). American leading lady who retired after a brief career.
Spawn of the North 38. *Stagecoach* 39. Forgotten Girls 40. Captain Caution 40. Street of Chance 41, etc.

Platt, Marc (1913–). American dancer and lightweight actor: few appearances.
Tonight and Every Night 44. Tars and Spars 45. Down to Earth 47. Seven Brides for Seven Brothers 54. Oklahoma 55, etc.

Platts-Mills, Barney (1944–). British independent director of low-budget films.
□ Bronco Bullfrog 70. Private Road 71.

Pleasence, Donald (1919–). Bald, pale-eyed British character actor usually seen in villainous or eccentric roles.
Manuela 57. A Tale of Two Cities 57. The Flesh and the Fiends 59. Hell Is a City 60. No Love for Johnnie 61. Dr Crippen 62. The Great Escape 63. *The Caretaker* 64. The Greatest Story Ever Told 65. The Hallelujah Trail 65. Fantastic Voyage 66. Cul de Sac 66. The Night of the Generals 66. Eye of the Devil 67. Will Penny 67. The Madwoman of Chaillot 69. Soldier Blue 70. Outback 71. The Jerusalem File 72. Henry VIII and His Six Wives 72. Innocent Bystanders 72. Tales That Witness Madness 73. The Mutations 73. The Black Windmill 74. Hearts of the West 75. Trial by Combat 76. The Last Tycoon 76, etc.

Pleschkes, Otto (1931–). Austrian producer, in Britain.
Georgy Girl 66. The Bofors Gun 68. The Homecoming 73, etc.

Pleshette, Suzanne (1937–). Intelligent American leading actress whose roles have been generally disappointing.
□ The Geisha Boy 58. Rome Adventure 62. Forty Pounds of Trouble 63. The Birds 63. Wall of Noise 63. A Distant Trumpet 64. Fate is the Hunter 64. Youngblood Hawke 64. A Rage to Live 65. The Ugly Dachshund 66. Nevada Smith 66. Mister Buddwing 66. The Adventures of Bullwhip Griffin 67. Blackbeard's Ghost 68. The Power 68. If Its Tuesday This Must Be Belgium 69. Suppose They Gave a War and Nobody Came 69. Support Your Local Gunfighter 71.
TV series: The Bob Newhart Show 72.

Plummer, Christopher (1927–). Canadian leading man with stage experience including Shakespeare.
□ Stage Struck 58. Wind Across the Everglades 58. *The Fall of the Roman Empire* 64. *The Sound of Music* 65. Inside Daisy Clover 65. The Night of the Generals 67. Triple Cross 67. Oedipus the King 67. Nobody Runs Forever 68. Lock Up Your Daughters 69. The Royal Hunt of the Sun 69. The Battle of Britain 69. *Waterloo* (as the Duke of Wellington) 70. The Pyx 73. Conduct Unbecoming 75. The Spiral Staircase 75. The Man Who Would be King 75. The Return of the Pink Panther 75. Jesus of Nazareth (TV) 77.*

Plunkett, Patricia (1928–). British leading lady of the early fifties.

It Always Rains on Sunday 47. Bond Street 48. For Them That Trespass 48. Landfall 50. Murder Without Crime 52. Mandy 53. The Crowded Day 55. Dunkirk 58, etc.

Plunkett, Walter (1902–). American costume designer.
Hit the Deck 29. Rio Rita 29. Cimarron 31. *Little Women* 33. The Gay Divorcee 34. Of Human Bondage 34. Mary of Scotland 36. Quality Street 37. *Gone with the Wind* 39. The Hunchback of Notre Dame 39. Stagecoach 39. Ladies in Retirement 41. To Be or Not to Be 42. A Song to Remember 45. Duel in the Sun 46. The Three Musketeers 48. That Forsyte Woman 49. *An American in Paris* (AA) 51. The Prisoner of Zenda 52. Kiss Me Kate 53. Seven Brides for Seven Brothers 54. Lust for Life 56. Pollyanna 60. How the West was Won 63. Seven Women 66, many others.

Podesta, Rossana (1934–). Italian leading lady who has been in international films.
Cops and Robbers 51. La Red 53. Ulysses 54. Helen of Troy 56. Santiago 58. The Golden Arrow 65. Il Prete Sposato 70, many others.

Poe, Edgar Allan (1809–1849). American poet, story-writer and manic depressive, whose tortured life as well as his strange tales have been eagerly seized upon by film-makers. Griffith made *The Life of Edgar Allan Poe* in 1909, and in 1912 another version was disguised as *The Raven*. In 1915 Charles Brabin made another film called *The Raven* with Henry B. Walthall as Poe; a few months earlier Griffith had released his own alternative version under the title *The Avenging Conscience*. The next film called *The Raven*, in 1935, starred Karloff and Lugosi and had nothing to do with Poe's life, being merely an amalgam of his stories; but in 1942 Fox brought out *The Loves of Edgar Allan Poe* starring Shepperd Strudwick; and in 1951 MGM made a curious melodrama called *Man with a Cloak*, in which the dark stranger who solved the mystery signed himself 'Dupin' and was played by Joseph Cotten in the Poe manner.
Of the stories, *The Mystery of Marie Roget* was filmed by Universal in 1931 and 1942; *The Tell-Tale Heart* was told as an MGM short directed by Jules Dassin in 1942, by a British company with Stanley Baker in 1950, by UPA as a cartoon narrated by James Mason in 1954, by an independent American company in a film known as both *Manfish* and *Calypso* in 1956 (the film also claimed to be partly based on *The Gold Bug*) and by the Danzigers in Britain in 1960. *The Fall of the House of Usher* was filmed in France by Jean Epstein in 1929, in Britain by

semi-professionals in 1950, and in Hollywood by Roger Corman in 1960. Universal released films called *The Black Cat* in 1934 and 1941, both claiming to be 'suggested' by Poe's tale; in fact, neither had anything at all to do with it, but the genuine story was told in a German film called *The Living Dead* in 1933, and in Corman's 1962 *Tales of Terror*. *The Pit and the Pendulum* was filmed in 1913 and 1961, and the central idea has been borrowed by many film-makers without credit, most recently by the 'Uncle' boys in *One Spy Too Many*. *The Premature Burial* was filmed straight in 1962, and around the same time TV's *Thriller* series presented a fairly faithful adaptation; the idea was also used in 1934 in *The Crime of Dr Crespi*, a low-budgeter starring Erich Von Stroheim. *The Murders in the Rue Morgue* was filmed in 1914 and 1932, turned up again in 3-D in 1954 under the title *Phantom of the Rue Morgue*, and was remade under the original title in 1971. Other Poe stories filmed once include *The Bells* 13, *The Facts in the Case of M. Valdemar* (in *Tales of Terror* 62), *The Masque of the Red Death* 64, and *The Tomb of Ligeia* 64.

Poe, James (1923–). American writer, from radio and TV.
Around the World in Eighty Days (co-w) 56. Attack 57. Cat on a Hot Tin Roof 58. Last Train from Gun Hill 59. Summer and Smoke 61. Toys in the Attic 63. Lilies of the Field 64. The Bedford Incident 65, etc.

Pogostin, S. Lee (1926–). American writer-director.
Synanon (w) 65. Hard Contract (d) 69. Golden Needles (co-d) 74, etc.

Pohlmann, Eric (1913–). Viennese character actor, on British stage and radio from 1948; also a familiar bald, portly villain on screen.
The Constant Husband 55. House of Secrets 56. Expresso Bongo 59. The Kitchen 62. Carry On Spying 64. The Million Dollar Collar (US) 67. The Horsemen 71, many others.

Poil de Carotte (France 1932). Julien Duvivier, who had also directed a silent version of the same story in 1925, made his international reputation with this sensitive, grim story of an unwanted boy being driven to the brink of suicide. It shows a French countryside quite different from Pagnol's: sunlit but bleak and inhospitable. Jules Renard's screenplay and Thirard Monniot's photography enhanced the performances of Harry Baur as the father and Robert Lynen (who was later killed in the Maquis) as the boy.

Poitier, Sidney (1924–). Handsome black American leading actor; his success in the late sixties helped to break the race barrier.

☐ *No Way Out* 50. Cry the Beloved Country 52. Red Ball Express 52. Go Man Go 54. *The Blackboard Jungle* 55. Goodbye, My Lady 56. *Edge of the City* 57. Something of Value 57. Band of Angels 58. Mark of the Hawk 58. *The Defiant Ones* 58. *Porgy and Bess* 59. Virgin Islands 60. All the Young Men 60. A Raisin in the Sun 61. Paris Blues 61. Pressure Point 62. *Lilies of the Field* (AA) 63. The Long Ships 64. The Greatest Story Ever Told 65. *The Bedford Incident* (for the first time his colour was not mentioned or relevant) 65. A Patch of Blue 65. The Slender Thread 65. Duel at Diablo 66. *In the Heat of the Night* 67. To Sir with Love 67. *Guess Who's Coming to Dinner* 67. For Love of Ivy 68. The Lost Man 69. They Call Me Mister Tibbs 70. The Organization 71. Brother John 71. Buck and the Preacher (& d) 72. A Warm December (& d) 73. Uptown Saturday Night (& d) 74. The Wilby Conspiracy 75. Let's Do It Again (& d) 76.

Poland had a vigorous cinema school from the earliest days, but subjects were dominated by Russian influence. After World War II Alexander Ford led a new vigorous group of film makers including Wajda and Munk, whose films of post-war problems became world famous. Later directors of note include Polanski, Kawalerowicz, and Skolimowski.

Polanski, Roman (1933–). Polish director, former actor. Gained a reputation with shorts such as *Two Men and a Wardrobe* 58.

☐ FEATURES: Knife in the Water 61. *Repulsion* 65. Cul de Sac 66. The Fearless Vampire Killers 67. *Rosemary's Baby* 68. Macbeth 71. What? 72. *Chinatown* 74. The Tenant 76.

Polglase, Van Nest (1898–). American art director, in films from 1919. With RKO 1932–43, since then with Columbia.

police in the forties and earlier were offered in British films only for our admiration; in the fifties they began to have human frailties; and in the sixties many of them were shown, truthfully or not, to be corrupt. *The Blue Lamp, The Long Arm,* and *Gideon of Scotland Yard* are only three of many of the first kind, *Violent Playground* one of the second, and *The Strange Affair* a corking example of the last. But the *Z Cars* series on British TV will long uphold the best traditions of the force . . . as will *Maigret* for France.

American cops have always been tougher, but even so a gradual change can be traced through *Naked City, The Big Heat, Detective Story, Shield for Murder, Experiment in Terror, Madigan, The Detective, The French Connection, Fuzz* and *The New Centurions.* TV series which have been influential include *Dragnet* 52–59 and 67–69, *Naked City* 58–62, *87th Precinct* 61, *M Squad* 57–60, *The Detectives* 60–61, *The Line Up* 54–59, *Hawk* 66, *The New Breed* 61, *Adam 12* 68– , *Hawaii Five O* 68– . *The Rookies* 72. *Police Story* 73 , Police Woman 74– , Starsky and Hutch 75– .

Comic policemen go right back to the Keystone Kops. Other examples: Will Hay in *Ask a Policeman,* George Formby in *Spare a Copper,* Norman Wisdom in *On the Beat,* Alastair Sim in *Green for Danger,* Peter Sellers in *The Pink Panther,* Lionel Jeffries in *The Wrong Arm of the Law,* 'Officer Krupke' in *West Side Story,* Donald McBride in *Topper Returns,* Dennis Hoey as Inspector Lestrade in the Sherlock Holmes films, Sidney James and crew in *Carry On, Constable,* Laurel and Hardy in *Midnight Patrol,* Buster Keaton's cast in *Cops,* Charles Chaplin in *Easy Street* . . . and on TV, *Car 54 Where are You?*

politics, as any exhibitor will tell you, is the kiss of death to a film as far as box office is concerned. Nevertheless many films with serious political themes have been made. Among those presenting biographies of actual political figures, the American ones include *Young Mr Lincoln, Abe Lincoln in Illinois, Tennessee Johnson, The Man with Thirty Sons* (Oliver Wendell Holmes), *Magnificent Doll* (Dolly Madison and Aaron Burr), *The President's Lady* (Andrew Jackson), *Wilson,* Teddy Roosevelt (in *My Girl Tisa* and others), Franklin Roosevelt (in *Sunrise at Campobello*), *Beau James* (Jimmy Walker) and John Kennedy (*PT 109*), while *All the King's Men* and *A Lion Is in the Streets* are clearly based on Huey Long, and there was a real-life original for the idealistic young senator from Wisconsin in *Mr Smith Goes to Washington.* Fictional presidencies have been involved in *Gabriel over the White House, First Lady, The Tree of Liberty* (*The Howards of Virginia*), *Advise and Consent, The Manchurian Candidate, Seven Days in May, Dr Strangelove, Kisses for My President,* and *Fail Safe.* Among the many films alleging political graft and corruption in the US are *Mr Smith Goes to Washington, Confessions of a Nazi Spy, Louisiana Purchase, Alias Nick Beal, State of the Union, Lil' Abner, The Great McGinty, The Glass Key, Citizen Kane, All the King's Men, Bullets or Ballots, A Lion Is in the Streets, The Last Hurrah, The Best Man, The Senator was

Indiscreet and *The Candidate*. The witch-hunts of 1948 produced a series of right-wing melodramas like *I Was a Communist for the FBI, I Married a Communist* and *My Son John* ... a striking contrast to 1942, when *Mission to Moscow* could be made. In 1971 TV produced a four-hour thriller called *Vanished* about a president with doubtful motives. The mid-seventies brought a number of TV drama-documentaries about political matters: *Eleanor and Franklin, Collision Course* (Truman and MacArthur), *The Missiles of October, Fear On Trial, Tail Gunner Joe* (McCarthy), *Meeting at Potsdam*.

The British House of Commons and its characters have been involved in many a film with Disraeli (qv) coming out as favourite. Pitt the Younger was impersonated by Robert Donat, and Charles James Fox by Robert Morley, in *The Young Mr Pitt*; Gladstone was played by Ralph Richardson in *Khartoum*, Malcolm Keen in *Sixty Glorious Years* and Stephen Murray in *The Prime Minister*; *Cromwell* by Richard Harris; Canning by John Mills and William Lamb by Jon Finch in *Lady Caroline Lamb*; while Ramsay MacDonald was allegedly pictured in *Fame is the Spur*. MPs were also the leading figures of the fictional *No Love for Johnnie, Three Cases of Murder* and *The Rise and Rise of Michael Rimmer*.

Political films from other countries abound; one might almost say that every Soviet film is political. But politics do not export well, so that for the life of Villa, Zapata, Juarez and Che Guevara we have to turn to glamorized Hollywood versions of the truth; ditto for Parnell, Richelieu and even Hitler. Lenin has been pictured in innumerable Soviet films, and Richard Burton starred in *The Assassination of Trotsky*.

That politics is not entirely a serious matter can be seen from the number of comedies about it. The best of them is the already mentioned *State of the Union*, but one can also instance the *Don Camillo* series, *Old Mother Riley MP, Angelina MP, Dad Rudd MP, Louisiana Purchase, Kisses for My President, The Great Man Votes, Left Right and Centre* and *Vote for Huggett*.

Polito, Gene (–). American cinematographer.
Prime Cut 72. Westworld 73. Five on the Black Hand Side 73, etc.

Polito, Sol (1892–1960). American cinematographer.
Treason 18. Hard-Boiled Haggerty 27. Five Star Final 31. *I Am a Fugitive from a Chain Gang* 32.

Forty-Second Street 33. G Men 35. *The Petrified Forest* 36. *The Charge of the Light Brigade* 36. *The Adventures of Robin Hood* 38. Confessions of a Nazi Spy 39. *The Sea Hawk* 40. The Sea Wolf 41. Now Voyager 42. Arsenic and Old Lace 44. Rhapsody in Blue 45. The Long Night 47. Sorry, Wrong Number 48. Anna Lucasta 48, many others.

Poll, Martin H. (1922–). American producer.
Love is a Ball 62. Sylvia 65. The Lion in Winter 68. Night Watch 73. The Man Who Loved Cat Dancing 73, etc.

Pollack, Sydney (–). American director, from TV.
□ *The Slender Thread* 65. This Property is Condemned 66. The Scalphunters 68. Castle Keep 69. *They Shoot Horses Don't They?* 69. Jeremiah Johnson 72. The Way We Were 73. The Yakusa 75. *Three Days of the Condor* 76.

Pollard, Harry (1883–1934). American silent-screen director.
Motherhood 14. The Leather Pushers 22. Oh Doctor 24. California Straight Ahead 25. Uncle Tom's Cabin 27. Showboat (first talkie) 29. The Prodigal 31. Fast Life 32, etc.

Pollard, Michael J. (1939–) (M. J. Pollack). Pint-sized American character actor.
Adventures of a Young Man 62. Summer Magic 62. The Stripper 64. *Bonnie and Clyde* 67. Hannibal Brooks 69. Little Fauss and Big Halsy 70. Dirty Little Billy 72. Sunday in the Country 74, etc.

Pollard, Snub (1886–1962) (Harold Fraser). Australian comedian, in America from early silent film days. In many silent slapstick shorts, and later continued to play bit parts, the last being in *A Pocketful of Miracles* 61.

Pollock, Ellen (1903–). British stage actress, in occasional films.
Non Stop New York 37. The Street Singer 37. Sons of the Sea 39. Kiss the Bride Goodbye 44. The Galloping Major 51, etc.

Pollock, George (1907–). British director, former assistant, in films since 1933.
A Stranger in Town 56. Rooney 58. Don't Panic Chaps 60. Murder She Said 63. Murder at the Gallop 63. Murder Most Foul 64. Ten Little Indians 65, etc.

Polonsky, Abraham (c. 1910–). American writer who fell foul of the communist witch-hunt.
Body and Soul 47. *Force of Evil* (& d) 49. I Can

Get It for You Wholesale 50. Tell Them Willie Boy is Here (& d) 69, etc.

Pommer, Erich (1889–1966). German producer since 1915. During the thirties worked briefly in the US and also, with Charles Laughton, formed Mayflower Films in Britain.
The Cabinet of Dr Caligari 19. Dr Mabuse 22. Die Nibelungen 24. *Variety* 25. *Metropolis* 26. *The Blue Angel* 30. Congress Dances 31. Liliom 34. Fire over England 36. Vessel of Wrath 38. Jamaica Inn 39. They Knew What They Wanted 40. Illusion in Moll 52. Kinder, Mutter und Ein General 55, etc.

Pons, Lily (1904–1976). French-born operatic singer who starred in some Hollywood films.
I Dream Too Much 35. That Girl from Paris 36. Hitting a New High 37. Carnegie Hall 47, etc.

Pontecorvo, Gillo (1919–). Italian director.
Kapo 60. *The Battle of Algiers* 66. The Wide Blue Road 68. Burn! 70, etc.

Ponti, Carlo (1913–). Italian producer, now involved in international productions.
I Miserabili 47. Attila the Hun 52. Ulysses 54. War and Peace 56. Black Orchid 58. That Kind of Woman 59. Marriage, Italian Style 65. Operation Crossbow 65. Smashing Time 67. Sunflower 70. Lady Liberty 72. The Passenger 74. etc.

Ponting, Herbert G. (1870–1935). British explorer and film-maker, a maker of quality documentaries in the cinema's early days.
With Captain Scott R.N. to the South Pole 13, etc.

Popeye. Tough sailorman hero of over 250 cartoon shorts produced by Max Fleischer c. 1933–50. Other characters involved were girlfriend Olive Oyl and tough villain Bluto, against whose wiles Popeye fortified himself with tins of spinach. The films were so popular on TV that a newly-drawn series was produced c. 1959 by King Features—but the old vulgar panache was missing.

Popkin, Harry M. (–). American independent producer.
And Then There Were None 45. Impact 48. *D.O.A.* 49. Champagne for Caesar 49. The Thief 52, etc.

Porcasi, Paul (1880–1946). Sicilian character actor in Hollywood films; former opera singer.
The Devil and the Deep 32. Maytime 37. Torrid

Zone 40. Quiet Please Murder 43. I'll Remember April 45, etc.

Porter, Cole (1893–1964). American songwriter and composer whose lyrics were probably the wittiest ever appended to popular songs. Cary Grant played Porter in a biopic, *Night and Day* 46; other films using Porter scores are: *Anything Goes* 36 and 56. *Rosalie* 38. *Broadway Melody of 1940. Something to Shout About* 42. *The Pirate* 48. *Kiss Me Kate* 53. *High Society* 56. *Can Can* 59, etc.
Biography 1967: *The Life That Late He Led* by George Eels.

Porter, Don (1912–). American leading man of second features, latterly character actor.
Top Sergeant 42. Night Monster 43. The Curse of the Allenbys 48. 711 Ocean Drive 50. Because You're Mine 52. The Racket 52. Our Miss Brooks 56. Bachelor in Paradise 61. Youngblood Hawke 64. The Candidate 72. Forty Carats 73. White Line Fever 75, etc.
TV series: Private Secretary. Our Miss Brooks. The Ann Sothern Show.

Porter, Edwin S. (1869–1941). America's first notable director, who later found himself in D. W. Griffith's shadow and left the industry.
The Life of an American Fireman 02. *The Great Train Robbery* 03. The Ex-Convict 05. Rescued from an Eagle's Nest 07. Alice's Adventures in Wonderland 10. The Count of Monte Cristo 12. The Eternal City 15, etc.

Porter, Eric (1928–). British stage actor who became nationally known as Soames in the TV version of *The Forsyte Saga*.
The Heroes of Telemark 65. Kaleidoscope 66. The Lost Continent 68. Hands of the Ripper 71. Antony and Cleopatra 71. Nicholas and Alexandra 71. The Day of the Jackal 73. The Belstone Fox 73. Callan 74. Hennessy 75, etc.

Porter, Nyree Dawn (1940–). New Zealand leading lady in British films and TV.
Two Left Feet 63. The Cracksman 63. Jane Eyre 70. The House that Dripped Blood 70. From Beyond the Grave 73, etc.
TV series: *The Forsyte Saga* (as Irene) 67. *The Protectors* 72.

Portman, Eric (1903–1969). Distinguished British stage actor who appeared sporadically in films.
□ The Murder in the Red Barn (debut) 35. Hyde Park Corner 35. The Prince and the Pauper (US) 37. Moonlight Sonata 37. The Crimes of Stephen Hawke 38. *49th Parallel* 41. One of Our Aircraft

is Missing 42. Uncensored 42. Squadron Leader X 43. We Dive at Dawn 43. *Millions Like Us* 43. A Canterbury Tale 44. Great Day 45. Men of Two Worlds 46. *Wanted for Murder* 46. Dear Murderer 47. Daybreak 48. The Mark of Cain 48. Corridor of Mirrors 48. The Blind Goddess 48. The Spider and the Fly 50. His Excellency 51. The Colditz Story 54. *The Deep Blue Sea* 55. Child in the House 56. The Good Companions 57. The Naked Edge 61. The Man Who Finally Died 62. West Eleven 63. The Bedford Incident 65. The Whisperers 66. The Spy with a Cold Nose 67. Assignment to Kill 67. Deadfall 68.

Portrait of Jennie (US 1948). A pretentious but enjoyable fantasy in Hollywood's lushest manner, about a penniless artist who meets a fey young girl in Central Park and discovers not only that she grows much older every time he sees her but that she actually died many years ago. She finally dies again in a storm off Cape Cod. Not even the author could possibly understand this plot, and even the light relief is of a whimsical nature; but the acting (Joseph Cotten, Jennifer Jones, Ethel Barrymore, David Wayne, Lilian Gish) is so good, the direction (William Dieterle) so accomplished and the photography (Joseph August) so striking that the thing comes off.

The Poseidon Adventure (US 1972). The film which brought the disaster genre back with a bang was directed by Ronald Neame from a story by Paul Gallico about a ship which turns upside down after an explosion, and makes it difficult for survivors to escape. Routine melodramatics were handled by a capable cast.

Post, Ted (1925–). American director, from TV.
□ The Peacemaker 56. The Legend of Tom Dooley 59. Hang 'Em High 68. Beneath the Planet of the Apes 70. The Baby 73. The Harrad Experiment 73. Magnum Force 73. Whiffs 75.

Posta, Adrienne (1948–) (Adrienne Poster). British juvenile actress specializing in cheeky teenagers.
No Time for Tears 59. To Sir With Love 67. Here We Go Round the Mulberry Bush 67. Up the Junction 68. Some Girls Do 69. Percy 70. Up Pompeii 71. Percy's Progress 74, etc.

Poston, Tom (1927–). American light comedian.
□ City That Never Sleeps 53. Zotz! 62. Soldier in the Rain 63. The Old Dark House 63. Cold Turkey 70. The Happy Hooker 75.

post-synchronization. Adding sound, by dubbing, to visuals already shot. Sound can only rarely be recorded at the time of shooting because of extraneous noise and requirements of volume, pitch, etc.; actors must usually repeat their lines in accordance with their image on screen.

Potter, H. C. (1904–). American director with stage experience, in Hollywood from 1935; an expert at comedy.
□ Beloved Enemy 36. Wings Over Honolulu 37. Romance in the Dark 38. Shopworn Angel 38. The Cowboy and the Lady 38. *The Story of Vernon and Irene Castle* 39. Blackmail 39. Congo Maisie 40. Second Chorus 40. *Hellzapoppin* 41. Mr Lucky 43. *The Farmer's Daughter* 47. A Likely Story 47. *Mr Blandings Builds His Dream House* 48. The Time of Your Life 48. You Gotta Stay Happy 48. The Miniver Story 50. Three for the Show 55. Top Secret Affair 57.

Potter, Martin (1944–). British juvenile lead of the early seventies.
Fellini Satyricon 70. Goodbye Gemini 71. Nicholas and Alexandra 71. All Coppers Are 71. Craze 73, etc.

Poujouly, Georges (1940–). French boy actor of the early fifties.
Jeux Interdits 52. Nous Sommes Tous des Assassins 52. Les Diaboliques 54. Lift to the Scaffold 57. Girls for the Summer 59, etc.

Poulton, Mabel (1905–). British leading lady of the twenties.
The Heart of an Actress 24. Virginia's Husband 25. The Constant Nymph 28. The Return of the Rat 28.

poverty in America and Britain is rare enough now to be little discussed, but in the days when film-makers began to have social conscience a number of films memorably examined the problem in different milieus. American hoboes and shanty town dwellers were revealed in *Sullivan's Travels, Hallelujah I'm a Bum, Man's Castle, My Man Godfrey, One More Spring*; the rural poor were the subject of *Our Daily Bread, The Grapes of Wrath, Tobacco Road*. Hollywood's regretful gaze wandered to China for *The Good Earth* and for *Tortilla Flat* to Mexico, which was more memorably covered by Bruñuel in *Los Olvidados*. Poverty in Italy was the subject of *Bicycle Thieves*, and in England of *Love on the Dole, Doss House* and *The Whisperers*.

Powell, Dick (1904–1963). American

crooning juvenile of the thirties who later suffered a sea-change and emerged as a likeable tough leading man, a competent director and an ambitious producer, the founder of Four Star Television.

Blessed Event 32. Too Busy to Work 32. The King's Vacation 33. *Forty-Second Street* 33. Gold Diggers of 1933. Footlight Parade 33. College Coach 33. Convention City 33. *Dames* 34. Wonder Bar 34. Twenty Million Sweethearts 34. Happiness Ahead 34. Flirtation Walk 34. Gold Diggers of 1935. Page Miss Glory 35. Broadway Gondoliers 35. A Midsummer Night's Dream 35. Shipmates Forever 35. Thanks a Million 35. Colleen 36. Hearts Divided 36. Stage Struck 36. Gold Diggers of 1937. *On the Avenue* 37. The Singing Marine 37. Varsity Show 37. Hollywood Hotel 38. Cowboy from Brooklyn 38. Hard to Get 38. Going Places 38. Naughty but Nice 39. *Christmas in July* 40. I Want a Divorce 40. Model Wife 41. In the Navy 41. Star Spangled Rhythm 42. Happy Go Lucky 42. True to Life 43. Riding High 43. *It Happened Tomorrow* 44. Meet the People 44. *Murder My Sweet* (as Philip Marlowe) 44. Cornered 45. Johnny O'Clock 47. To the Ends of the Earth 48. Pitfall 48. Station West 48. Rogues Regiment 48. Mrs Mike 49. The Reformer and the Redhead 50. Right Cross 50. Callaway Went Thataway 51. Cry Danger 51. The Tall Target 51. You Never Can Tell 51. The Bad and the Beautiful 52. Split Second (d only) 53. Susan Slept Here 54. The Conqueror (pd only) 56. The Enemy Below (d only) 57. The Hunters (d only) 58, etc.

TV series: *Dick Powell Theatre* 59–61.

Powell, Eleanor (1910–). Long-legged American tap dancer whose vitality enhanced a few films.

☐ George White's Scandals 35. Broadway Melody of 1936. *Born to Dance* 36. Broadway Melody of 1938. *Rosalie* 38. Honolulu 39. Broadway Melody of 1940. Lady Be Good 41. Ship Ahoy 42. I Dood It 43. Thousands Cheer 43. Sensations of 1945 44. The Duchess of Idaho 50.

Powell, Jane (1929–) (Suzanne Burce). Diminutive American singing and dancing leading lady; former child performer.

☐ Song of the Open Road 44. Delightfully Dangerous 45. Holiday in Mexico 46. Three Daring Daughters 48. A Date with Judy 48. Luxury Liner 48. Nancy Goes to Rio 50. Two Weeks with Love 50. Royal Wedding 51. Rich Young and Pretty 51. Small Town Girl 53. Three Sailors and a Girl 53. *Seven Brides for Seven Brothers* 54. Athena 54. Deep in My Heart 54. Hit the Deck 55. The Girl Most Likely 57. The Female Animal 58. Enchanted Island 58.

Powell, Michael (1905–). Important British writer-producer-director whose highly imaginative work, especially in his collaboration with Emeric Pressburger ('The Archers' 42–57), was sometimes marred by a streak of tastelessness.

AS WRITER ONLY: Caste 30. 77 Park Lane 31. The Star Reporter 31. Hotel Splendide 32. The Fire Raisers 33. Night of the Party 34. Lazybones 35. The Phantom Light 35. The Man Behind the Mask 36, many others.

☐ AS EXECUTIVE wholly or jointly in charge, including work as WRITER-PRODUCER-DIRECTOR: The Edge of the World 37. *The Spy in Black* 38. The Lion Has Wings 39. The Thief of Baghdad 39. Contraband 40. 49th Parallel 41. One of Our Aircraft is Missing 42. *The Life and Death of Colonel Blimp* 43. The Silver Fleet 43. A Canterbury Tale 44. *I Know Where I'm Going* 45. *A Matter of Life and Death* 46. Black Narcissus 46. End of the River 47. *The Red Shoes* 48. The Small Back Room 48. Gone to Earth 50. The Elusive Pimpernel 51. The Tales of Hoffman 51. Oh Rosalinda 55. The Battle of the River Plate 56. Ill Met by Moonlight 57. Peeping Tom 60. Honeymoon 61. The Queen's Guards 61. They're a Weird Mob 66. Sebastian (p only) 67. Age of Consent 69. The Boy Who Turned Yellow 72.

Powell, Robert (1946–). Sad-looking British leading man of the seventies.

Secrets 71. Running Scared 72. Asylum 72. The Asphyx 73. Mahler 73. Tommy 75. Jesus of Nazareth (TV) 77, etc.

Powell, Sandy (1898–). British music-hall comedian who made some knockabout films using his radio catch-phrase 'Can you hear me, mother?'

The Third String 32. Leave It to Me 36. I've Got a Horse 38. Cup Tie Honeymoon 48, etc.

Powell, William (1892–). Mature, debonair American leading man of the thirties and forties; a pillar of MGM for many years, he began as a cowboy villain but is probably best remembered as Nick Charles in *The Thin Man.*

SELECTED SILENT FILMS: Sherlock Holmes 22. The Bright Shawl 23. Romola 24. Too Many Kisses 25. Faint Perfume 25. Desert Gold 26. Aloma of the South Seas 26. Beau Geste 26. Señorita 27. Nevada 27. Feel My Pulse 28. The Last Command 28. The Vanishing Pioneer 28, etc.

☐ SOUND FILMS: Interference 29. *The Canary Murder Case* (as Philo Vance) 29. The Greene Murder Case 29. Charming Sinners 29. The Four Feathers 29. The Benson Murder Case

30. Paramount on Parade 30. Shadow of the Law 30. Pointed Heels 30. Behind the Make-up 30. *Street of Chance* 30. For the Defense 30. Man of the World 31. Ladies' Man 31. The Road to Singapore 31. High Pressure 32. Jewel Robbery 32. *One Way Passage* 32. Lawyer Man 32. Double Harness 33. Private Detective 62 33. The Kennel Murder Case 33. Fashions of 1934. The Key 34. Manhattan Melodrama 34. *The Thin Man* 34. Evelyn Prentice 34. Reckless 35. Star of Midnight 35. Escapade 35. Rendezvous 35. *The Great Ziegfeld* 36. The Ex Mrs Bradford 36. *My Man Godfrey* 36. Libelled Lady 36. After the Thin Man 36. The Last of Mrs Cheyney 37. The Emperor's Candlesticks 37. Double Wedding 37. The Baroness and the Butler 38. Another Thin Man 39. I Love You Again 40. Love Crazy 41. Shadow of the Thin Man 41. Crossroads 42. The Youngest Profession 43. The Heavenly Body 44. The Thin Man Goes Home 44. Ziegfeld Follies 45. The Hoodlum Saint 46. Song of the Thin Man 47. *Life With Father* 47. The Senator was Indiscreet 47. Mr Peabody and the Mermaid 48. Take One False Step 49. Dancing in the Dark 49. Treasure of Lost Canyon 51. It's a Big Country 51. The Girl Who had Everything 53. How to Marry a Millionaire 53. *Mister Roberts* (as Doc) 55.

Power, Hartley (1894–1966). Bald-headed American character actor who settled in Britain and was often seen as general, con man or brash agent.
Friday the Thirteenth 33. Evergreen 34. Lady in Distress 42. The Way to the Stars 45. *Dead of Night* 45. A Girl in a Million 47. Roman Holiday 53. To Dorothy a Son 54. Island in the Sun 56, many others.

Power, Tyrone (1913–1958). American leading man, of theatrical family; in films from 1932, usually deploying smooth gentle personality.
□ Tom Brown of Culver 32. Girls' Dormitory 36. Ladies in Love 36. *Lloyds of London* 37. Love is News 37. Café Metropole 37. Thin Ice 37. Second Honeymoon 37. *In Old Chicago* 38. *Alexander's Ragtime Band* 38. Marie Antoinette 38. Suez 38. *Rose of Washington Square* 39. *Jesse James* 39. Second Fiddle 39. The Rains Came 39. Daytime Wife 39. Johnny Apollo 40. Brigham Young 40. *The Mark of Zorro* 40. A Yank in the RAF 41. Blood and Sand 41. This Above All 42. Son of Fury 42. *The Black Swan* 42. Crash Dive 42; war service; The Razor's Edge 46. Captain from Castile 47. Nightmare Alley 47. The Luck of the Irish 48. That Wonderful Urge 48. Prince of Foxes 49. The Black Rose 50. An American Guerilla in the

Philippines 51. Rawhide 51. I'll Never Forget You 51. Diplomatic Courier 52. Pony Soldier 52. Mississippi Gambler 53. King of the Khyber Rifles 53. The Long Gray Line 54. Untamed 55. The Eddy Duchin Story 56. Seven Waves Away 57. The Rising of the Moon (narrated only) 57. *The Sun Also Rises* 57. Witness for the Prosecution 57.

Power, Tyrone, Snr (1869–1931). American stage actor, father of Tyrone Power: played heavy in a few films.
A Texas Street 15. Where are My Children? 16. Footfalls 21. The Lone Wolf 24. Bride of the Storm 26. The Big Trail 30 Tom Brown of Culver 32, etc.

Powers, Mala (–) (Mary Ellen Powers). American leading lady, former child actress.
Tough as They Come 41. Outrage 50. Cyrano de Bergerac 50. Rose of Cimarron 52. Rage at Dawn 55. Benghazi 55. The Storm Rider 57. Daddy's Gone A-Hunting 69. Doomsday 72, etc.

Powers, Stefanie (1942–) (Stefania Federkiewicz). American leading lady of the sixties.
Experiment in Terror 62. The Interns 62. Palm Springs Weekend 63. *Fanatic* (GB) 64. Stagecoach 66. Warning Shot 67. Herbie Rides Again 73, etc.
TV series: *The Girl from UNCLE* 66.

Powers, Tom (1890–1955). American general purpose supporting actor.
Double Indemnity 44. Two Years Before the Mast 46. Up in Central Park 48. Chicago Deadline 49. Destination Moon 50. Horizons West 52. Julius Caesar 53. The Americano 54, etc.

pratfall. Something in which all silent comedians were skilled: the art of falling on one's fundament without getting hurt.

pre-credits sequence. It has recently become fashionable to start films with an explosive opening scene, sometimes running seven of eight minutes, before the titles appear. This now over-worked device, used by almost all American TV series, is generally traced back to *Rommel, Desert Fox* 51, which had a long pre-credits sequence showing a commando raid; but the titles come quite late in *The Egg and I* 47, and even in *Destry Rides Again* 39 there is nearly a minute of shooting before they appear; while in *The Magnificent Ambersons* 42 they are not seen at all, only spoken at the end of the picture.

Preisser, June (–). Vivacious teenage leading lady of the forties.
The Fleet's In 41. Sweater Girl 43, etc.

Préjean, Albert (1898–). French light character actor who was in most of René Clair's early successes.
Le Voyage Imaginaire 25. An Italian Straw Hat 27. Sous les Toits de Paris 30. Die Dreigroschenoper (L'Opéra de Quat'Sous) 31. Jenny 36. Métropolitain 40. L'Etrange Suzy 43. Les Nouveaux Maîtres 49. Les Amants du Tage 54, etc.

Preminger, Ingo (–). Austrian American producer, brother of Otto.
M*A*S*H 70, etc.

Preminger, Otto (1906–). Austrian American director with theatrical background. Always a good craftsman, he has latterly applied heavy-handed treatment to potentially interesting subjects.
Biography 1973: *Behind the Scenes of Otto Preminger* by Willi Frischauer.
□ Die Grosse Liebe (Austrian) 32, then to US: Under Your Spell 36. Danger, Love at Work 37. They Got Me Covered (acted only) 42. The Pied Piper 42. Margin for Error (& a) 43. In the Meantime, Darling 44. *Laura* 44. Royal Scandal 45. Centennial Summer 46. Fallen Angel 46. Forever Amber 47. Daisy Kenyon 47. That Lady in Ermine (part) 48. The Fan 49. Whirlpool 50. Where the Sidewalk Ends 50. The Thirteenth Letter 51. Angel Face 52. *The Moon is Blue* 53. *Stalag 17* (acted only) 53. River of No Return 54. *Carmen Jones* 54. The Court Martial of Billy Mitchell 55. *The Man with the Golden Arm* 56. Bonjour Tristesse 57. Saint Joan (GB) 57. Porgy and Bess 59. *Anatomy of a Murder* 59. Exodus 60. *Advise and Consent* 61. The Cardinal 63. In Harm's Way 65. Bunny Lake is Missing (GB) 65. Hurry Sundown 67. Skidoo 68. Tell Me That You Love Me, Junie Moon 70. Such Good Friends 72. Rosebud 75.

Prentiss, Paula (1939–) (Paula Ragusa). Tall American leading lady who came almost straight from college to Hollywood.
Where the Boys Are 61. The Honeymoon Machine 62. Bachelor in Paradise 62. The Horizontal Lieutenant 63. *Man's Favorite Sport?* 64. The World of Henry Orient 64. In Harm's Way 65. What's New Pussycat? 65. Catch 22 69. Last of the Red Hot Lovers 72. Crazy Joe 73. The Parallax View 74. The Stepford Wives 75, etc.
TV series: *He and She* 67.

Presle, Micheline (1922–) (Micheline Chassagne). French leading actress with stage experience.
Jeunes Filles en Détress 38. La Nuit Fantastique 41. Boule de Suif 45. *Le Diable au Corps* 46. Les Jeux Sont Faits 47. Under My Skin (US) 50. The Adventures of Captain Fabian (US) 51. La Dame aux Camélias 52. Villa Borghese 54. The She Wolves 57. Blind Date (GB) 59. The Prize 63. La Religieuse 65. King of Hearts 67. Peau d'Ane 70, etc.

Presley, Elvis (1935–1978). Heavy-lidded American pop singer and guitarist, once known as 'the Pelvis' because of his swivel-hipped style. His popularity with teenagers survived a host of bad movies.
□ Love Me Tender 56. Loving You 57. Jailhouse Rock 57. King Creole 58. G.I. Blues 60. Flaming Star 60. Wild in the Country 61. Blue Hawaii 61. Kid Galahad 62. Girls Girls Girls 62. Follow That Dream 62. Fun in Acapulco 63. It Happened at the World's Fair 63. Kissin' Cousins 64. Viva Las Vegas 64. Roustabout 64. Girl Happy 65. Tickle Me 65. Harem Scarem 65. Frankie and Johnny 66. Paradise Hawaiian Style 66. Spinout 66. Easy Come Easy Go 67. Double Trouble 67. Stay Away Joe 68. Speedway 68. Clambake 68. Live a Little Love a Little 68. Charro 69. Change of Habit 70. The Trouble with Girls 70. Elvis—that's the Way It Is 70.

Presnell, Harve (1933–). American light opera singer, now in occasional films.
□ The Unsinkable Molly Brown 64. The Glory Guys 65. Where the Boys Meet the Girls 66. Paint Your Wagon 69.

Presnell, Robert, Jnr (1914–). American writer.
The Man in the Attic 53. Legend of the Lost 57. Conspiracy of Hearts (GB) 59. Let No Man Write My Epitaph 60. The Third Day 65, etc.

Presnell, Robert, Snr (1894–). American writer, usually in collaboration.
Hi Nellie 32. My Man Godfrey 36. The Real Glory 39. Meet John Doe 41. Second Chance 53. 13 West Street 62, etc.

Pressburger, Arnold (1885–1951). Hungarian producer who worked in Germany, Britain and Hollywood.
City of Song 30. Tell Me Tonight 32. The Return of the Scarlet Pimpernel 38. The Shanghai Gesture 41. Hangmen Also Die 43. It Happened Tomorrow 44. A Scandal in Paris 46, etc.

Pressburger, Emeric (1902–). Hungarian

journalist and scriptwriter in Britain from 1935. Worked on script of *The Challenge* 37 and met Michael Powell, qv for list of their joint films as 'The Archers'.
SOLO: Twice Upon a Time (wpd) 52. Miracle in Soho (wp) 56. Behold a Pale Horse (from his novel) 64. Operation Crossbow (w) (as Richard Imrie) 65. They're a Weird Mob (w) 66. The Boy Who Turned Yellow (w) 72.

Preston, Robert (1917–) (Robert Preston Messervey). American leading man who made routine films from 1938, became a theatre star of great vitality in the fifties.
☐ King of Alcatraz 38. Illegal Traffic 38. Disbarred 38. Union Pacific 39. *Beau Geste* 39. Typhoon 39. Moon over Burma 39. Northwest Mounted Police 40. New York Town 40. The Lady from Cheyenne 40. The Night of January 16th 41. Parachute Battalion 41. · Pacific Blackout 41. Reap the Wild Wind 42. *This Gun for Hire* 42. Wake Island 42. Night Plane to Chungking 42; war service; Wild Harvest 47. *The Macomber Affair* 47. Variety Girl 47. Whispering Smith 47. Blood on the Moon 48. Big City 48. The Lady Gambles 48. *Tulsa* 49. The Sundowners 49. Best of the Badmen 51. When I Grow Up 51. Face to Face 52. Cloudburst (GB) 53. The Last Frontier 56. *The Dark at the Top of the Stairs* 60. *The Music Man* (his stage role) 61. Island of Love 63. *All the Way Home* 63. How the West was Won 63. Junior Bonner 72. Child's Play 72. Mame 73. My Father's House (TV) 75.

Prévert, Jacques (1900–1977). French screenwriter whose most memorable work was in conjunction with Marcel Carné.
Drôle de Drame 37. *Quai des Brumes* 38. *Le Jour Se Lève* 39. *Les Visiteurs du Soir* 42. *Les Enfants du Paradis* 44. *Les Portes de la Nuit* 46. Les Amants de Verone 48. Other scripts include *L'Affaire est dans le Sac* (& a) 32. *Le Crime de Monsieur Lange* 35. *Une Partie de Campagne* 36. *Lumière d'Eté* 42. Notre Dame de Paris 56, etc.

Prevert, Pierre (1906–). French director, brother of Jacques Prevert.
L'Affaire est Dans Le Sac 32. Adieu Leonard 43. Voyage Surprise 46, etc.

Prévin, André (1929–). German composer and arranger, long in Hollywood. Settled in Britain and became orchestral conductor.
Scene of the Crime 49. Three Little Words 51. Bad Day at Black Rock 54. The Fastest Gun Alive 56. Designing Woman 57. Gigi (AA) 58. Porgy and Bess (AA) 59. Elmer Gantry 60. One, Two, Three 62. Irma La Douce (AA) 63. My Fair Lady (AA) 64.

Prévost, Marie (1898–1937) (Marie Bickford Dunn). Anglo-French leading lady of American silent films.
East Lynne with Variations 20. Her Night of Nights 22. The Marriage Circle 24. Red Lights 24. The Loves of Camille 25. Up in Mabel's Room 26. Getting Gertie's Garter 27. Lady of Leisure 28. Side Show 30. Sporting Blood 31. Parole Girl 33. Tango (last film) 36, etc.

Price, Dennis (1915–1973) (Dennistoun Franklyn John Rose-Price). British light leading man and latterly equally light character actor; on stage from 1937.
A Canterbury Tale (debut) 44. *A Place of One's Own* 44. The Magic Bow 46. Hungry Hill 46. Dear Murderer 47. Jassy 47. *Holiday Camp* 47. Master of Bankdam 47. The White Unicorn 47. Good Time Girl 48. *The Bad Lord Byron* 48. *Kind Hearts and Coronets* (his best role) 49. The Dancing Years 49. The Adventurers 50. Lady Godiva Rides Again 51. The House in the Square 52. Song of Paris 52. The Intruder 52. That Lady 54. Oh Rosalinda 55. *Private's Progress* 55. Charley Moon 56. The Naked Truth 58. I'm All Right, Jack 59. Tunes of Glory 60. *Victim* 61. Play It Cool 62. Tamahine 63. A High Wind in Jamaica 65. Ten Little Indians 65. Horror of Frankenstein 70. Twins of Evil 71. Alice's Adventures in Wonderland 72. Theatre of Blood 72, many others.
TV series: *The World of Wooster* (as Jeeves).

Price, Nancy (1880–1970). Dominant British character actress with long stage experience, especially remembered as Grandma in *Whiteoaks*. Also an indefatigable traveller, naturalist and semi-mystic.
The Stars Look Down 39. Madonna of the Seven Moons 44. I Live in Grosvenor Square 45. The Three Weird Sisters 48. Mandy 52, etc.

Price, Vincent (1911–). Tall, gentle-voiced American character actor, lately typed in horror films. On stage since 1934; also a well-known art expert.
Autobiography 1959: *I Like What I Know.*
Biography 1976: *Vincent Price Unmasked* by J. R. Parish and Steven Whitney.
Service de Luxe (debut) 38. Elizabeth and Essex 39. Green Hell 40. *Tower of London* (as Clarence) 40. Brigham Young 40. The Song of Bernadette 43. The Keys of the Kingdom 44. Laura 44. Czarina 45. *Dragonwyck* 46. Shock 46. The Long Night 47. The Three Musketeers 49. Champagne for Caesar 49. *His Kind of Woman* 51. *House of Wax* 53. The Mad Magician 54. The Ten Commandments 56. *The Story of Mankind* 57. The Fly 58. The Bat 59.

The House on Haunted Hill 60. *The Fall of the House of Usher* 61. The Pit and the Pendulum 61. Tales of Terror 62. *The Raven* 63. A Comedy of Terrors 63. *The Tomb of Ligeia* 64. City under the Sea 65. Dr Goldfoot and the Sex Machine 65. House of a Thousand Dolls 67. The Oblong Box 69. Scream and Scream Again 69. Cry of the Banshee 70. The Abominable Dr Phibes 71. Dr Phibes Rises Again 71. Theatre of Blood 73. Madhouse 73, etc.

Pride and Prejudice (US 1940). A delightful example of Hollywood 'Englishness'. Though Aldous Huxley's script was a simplification of Jane Austen and advanced the period forty years to take advantage of the fuller fashions, this remains a splendid romantic comedy of a more polite age, full of richly satisfying performances: Greer Garson as Elizabeth, Laurence Olivier as Darcy, Edmund Gwenn as Mr Bennet, Edna May Oliver as Lady Catherine, Melville Cooper as Mr Collins. Directed by Robert Z. Leonard in just the right unhurried style.

Priestley, J. B. (1894–). Prolific British novelist. There have been film versions of *The Good Companions, Benighted* (The Old Dark House), *Let the People Sing*, and also of his plays *Dangerous Corner, Laburnum Grove, When We Are Married* and *An Inspector Calls*. His autobiographical *Midnight on the Desert* (1937) says much about Hollywood.

priests have been a godsend to film makers. Most male stars have played them occasionally: the combination of masculine attractiveness and non-availability apparently works at the box office. Thus Frank Sinatra in *The Miracle of the Bells*; William Holden and Clifton Webb in *Satan Never Sleeps*; Bing Crosby in *Going My Way, The Bells of St Mary's* and *Say One for Me*; Richard Dix in *The Christian*; Pat O'Brien in a dozen films including *Angels with Dirty Faces, The Fighting 69th* and *Fighting Father Dunne*; ditto Spencer Tracy, in *Boys' Town, San Francisco, The Devil at Four O'Clock*, and others; George Arliss in *Cardinal Richelieu*; Don Murray in *The Hoodlum Priest*; Karl Malden in *On the Waterfront* and *The Great Impostor*; Pierre Fresnay in *Monsieur Vincent*; Claude Laydu in *Diary of a Country Priest*; Jean-Paul Belmondo in *Leon Morin Priest*; John Mills in *The Singer Not the Song*; Tom Tryon in *The Cardinal*; Gregory Peck in *The Keys of the Kingdom*; Geoffrey Bayldon in *Sky West and Crooked*; Richard Burton in *Becket*; David Warner in *The Ballad of Cable Hogue*; Ward Bond in *The Quiet Man*; Mickey Rooney in *The Twinkle in God's Eye*; Montgomery Clift in *I*

Confess; Alec Guinness in *Father Brown* and *The Prisoner*; Trevor Howard in *Ryan's Daughter*; Donald Sutherland in *Act of the Heart*; and Marcello Mastroianni in *The Priest's Wife*.

Protestant priests included Anthony Quayle in *Serious Charge*; Richard Burton in *The Sandpiper*; Robert Donat in *Lease of Life*; Wilfred Lawson in *Pastor Hall*; Peter Sellers in *Heavens Above*; Richard Todd in *A Man Called Peter*; David Niven in *The Bishop's Wife*. Actors who have got to play pope include Anthony Quinn and John Gielgud in *The Shoes of the Fisherman*, Rod Steiger in *A Man Called John*, Paolo Stoppa in *Becket* and Rex Harrison in *The Agony and the Ecstasy*.

False priests were Humphrey Bogart in *The Left Hand of God*, Rod Steiger in *No Way to Treat a Lady*, Dennis Price in *Kind Hearts and Coronets*, and Peter Sellers in *After the Fox*; while priestly villains were Ralph Richardson in *The Ghoul*, George Arliss in *Dr Syn* (followed by Peter Cushing in *Captain Clegg*), Keenan Wynn in *Johnny Concho*, Cedric Hardwicke in *The Hunchback of Notre Dame* and Robert Mitchum in *Night of the Hunter*. Classifiable as fallen priests were Henry Fonda in *The Fugitive*, Richard Burton in *Night of the Iguana*, Max Von Sydow in *Hawaii*, Burt Lancaster in *Elmer Gantry*, Lars Hanson in *The Scarlet Letter*, and Pierre Fresnay in *Le Défroqué* and *Dieu a Besoin des Hommes*.

Priests have come into their own again in the recent spate of diabolical thrillers: Max Von Sydow and Jason Miller in *The Exorcist*, Patrick Troughton in *The Omen*, Oliver Reed in *The Devils*.

Priggen, Norman (1924–). British producer, with Ealing Studios from 1939, later independent.
The Professionals 61. Payroll 61. The Servant 64. Secret Ceremony (co-p) 68. Tales That Witness Madness 73, etc.

Primus, Barry (–). American director.
The Gravy Train 74.

The Prince and the Pauper. Mark Twain's medieval story, about a prince and a commoner who change places, was filmed in 1909; in 1915 with Marguerite Clark; in 1923 with Tibi Lubin; in 1937 with the Mauch twins (and Errol Flynn); and in 1962 with Sean Scully.

Prince, Harold (1924–). American stage producer who dabbles in films.
□ Something for Everyone 70. A Little Night Music 77.

Prince, William (1913–). American stage leading man who has been less successful in films.
Destination Tokyo 44. Pillow to Post 46. Dead Reckoning 47. Carnegie Hall 48. Cyrano de Bergerac 51. The Vagabond King 55. Macabre 58. The Stepford Wives 75, etc.

Prine, Andrew (1936–). American leading man.
The Miracle Worker 62. Company of Cowards 64. The Devil's Brigade 68. Bandolero 68. Generation 69. One Little Indian 73. Grizzly 76, etc.

Pringle, Aileen (1895–) (Aileen Bisbee). American actress of the silent screen, best remembered for her performance in Elinor Glyn's *Three Weeks* 24.
Redhead 19. The Christian 23. Wife of a Centaur 24. Dance Madness 24. Adam and Evil 27. Soldiers and Women 30. Convicted 32. Jane Eyre 33. Piccadilly Jim 36. Nothing Sacred 37. The Girl from Nowhere (last film) 39, etc.

Pringle, Bryan (1935–). British character actor of stage and TV.
Saturday Night and Sunday Morning 60. The Boy Friend 71, etc.

Prinz, Le Roy (1895–). American choreographer who after adventurous early life came to Hollywood and worked on many Paramount and Warner films.
The Sign of the Cross 32. The 'Road' films 39–42. Yankee Doodle Dandy 42. Night and Day 46. The Ten Commandments 56. South Pacific 58, many others. Directed short subject *A Boy and His Dog* (AA) 48.

prison films have always had an audience, but did not reach their full potential until sound. Then and through the thirties, film-makers took us on a conducted tour of American prisons. *The Big House, The Last Mile, I Was a Fugitive from a Chain Gang, Twenty Thousand Years in Sing Sing, Front Page Woman* (with its gas chamber scene), *Angels with Dirty Faces, San Quentin, Blackwell's Island, Each Dawn I Die, Invisible Stripes, King of Alcatraz, Prison Ship, Prison Doctor, Mutiny in the Big House* and many others. During the war prison films were surpassed in excitement, but they came back with a bang in *Brute Force*, the toughest of them all, and *White Heat*. The fifties brought *Behind the High Wall, Duffy of San Quentin, Riot in Cell Block Eleven, Inside the Walls of Folsom Prison, Black Tuesday, I Want to Live, Cell 2455 Death Row*, and a remake of *The Last*

Mile. More recently Burt Lancaster appeared in the factual *Bird Man of Alcatraz*; and in the second half of the sixties the subject became popular again with *The Brig, The Ceremony, Reprieve, Point Blank, The Dirty Dozen, Triple Cross, Riot, There was a Crooked Man, A Clockwork Orange* and *Fortune and Men's Eyes*.
British studios have produced few prison films until the realist wave of the sixties which brought with it *The Criminal, The Pot Carriers*, and the army prison film *The Hill*.
Unusual prisons were shown in *Sullivan's Travels, Devil's Canyon, One Day in the Life of Ivan Denisovich*, and *Nevada Smith*; while among the films poking fun at prison life are *Up the River, Pardon Us* (Laurel and Hardy), *Convict 99* (Will Hay), *Jailhouse Rock* and *Two-Way Stretch*.
Prisons for women crop up quite regularly in such films as *Prison without Bars, Caged* (American), *Caged* (Italian), *Au Royaume des Cieux, Women's Prison, Girls behind Bars, So Evil So Young, The Weak and the Wicked, Yield to the Night* and *The Smashing Bird I Used to Know* and *Women in Chains* (TV).

The Prisoner of Zenda. At least three versions have been made of Anthony Hope's classic Ruritanian romance about a great impersonation, all in Hollywood. 1. 1922: directed by Rex Ingram, with Lewis Stone and Ramon Novarro. 2. 1937: directed by John Cromwell, with Ronald Colman and Douglas Fairbanks Jnr. 3. 1952: directed by Richard Thorpe, with Stewart Granger and James Mason. The 1937 version remains a model of its kind, with a fine cast including C. Aubrey Smith, David Niven, Raymond Massey and Madeleine Carroll; the 1952 version is a mechanical scene-for-scene remake. A parody on the story was included in *The Great Race* 65.

prisoners of war were featured in many films after World War II. The British examples often made the camps seem almost too comfortable, despite the possibility of being shot while attempting to escape; this was perhaps because they were all filled with the same familiar faces. *Albert RN, The Captive Heart, The Colditz Story, The Betrayal, Danger Within, Reach for the Sky* and *The Password is Courage* all found humour in the situation at any rate; whereas the American counterparts, *The Purple Heart, Prisoner of War, Stalag 17* and *The Mackenzie Break* saw the harsher side which doubtless existed. The co-production, *The Bridge on the River Kwai*, gave a mixed picture of a Japanese camp; Britain's Hammer horror studio then produced *The Camp on Blood Island*, a fictitious record of atrocity, followed some years later by *The Secret of Blood Island*. Meanwhile the British in *The One That Got Away* paid tribute to the one German to escape from a British camp; and more recently *The Great Escape* showed the Americans coming some way towards the British idea of how jolly life in a camp can be. The ultimate absurdity was reached by an American TV series, *Hogan's Heroes*, which has a camp almost entirely controlled by the prisoners. The best serious film about prisoners of war remains undoubtedly Renoir's *La Grande Illusion*, made in 1937; though *King Rat* in 1965 made a fair bid to reveal the squalor and futility of the life. Recently comic adventure stories about the escape of POWs have included *Very Important Person*, *The Secret War of Harry Frigg*, *Where Eagles Dare* and *Hannibal Brooks*.

Women's camps were shown in *Two Thousand Women* (GB 1944), *Three Came Home* (US 1950), *A Town Like Alice* (GB 1956) and *Kapo* (It. 1960).

private eyes: see *mystery*.

The Private Life of Henry VIII (GB 1932). Credited with being the first British film to win success in the American market, this enjoyable historical romp was directed by Alexander Korda from a script by Lajos Biro and Arthur Wimperis. Charles Laughton (AA) gave one of his richest performances, with memorable assistance from Robert Donat, Elsa Lanchester and Binnie Barnes. Design by Vincent Korda, photography by Georges Perinal. 1972's *Henry VIII and his Six Wives* was a semi-remake.

Private's Progress (GB 1955). The first of the Boulting Brothers' anti-establishment comedies, this took a sound swipe at the army, with Ian Carmichael as the innocent involved in red tape and regulations. Directed by John Boulting, written by himself and Frank Harvey from Alan Hackney's novel. Subsequent Boulting films attacked the unions (*I'm All Right, Jack*) 59, and the Church (*Heavens Above*) 63.

prizefighting: see *boxing*.

Prizmacolour. An early American colour process used for *The Glorious Adventure* 21. Crude in effect, in using orange and turquoise filters, it anticipated Cinecolor.

producer. On the stage this term may be equivalent to 'director', i.e. the man who actually marshals the actors and whose conception of the show is supreme. In the film world it almost always indicates the man in control of the budget, whether an independent or working for a big studio. He controls all personnel including the director, and though the film may originally be his overall conception, he normally delegates his artistic responsiblities, remaining responsible chiefly for the film's ultimate commercial success or failure.

Production Designer. Technician responsible for the overall 'look' of a film, ranging from actual set design to photographic style.

production manager. The person responsible for administrative details of a production, e.g. salaries, transport, departmental expenditure.

programmer. Trade term for a routine feature of only moderate appeal, likely to form half a bill; similar to 'co-feature'.

Prokoviev, Sergei (1891–1953). Russian composer whose main film scores were *Alexander Nevsky* 39, *Lermontov* 43 and *Ivan the Terrible* 42 and 46.

propaganda: see under *documentary*.

prophecy has interested film-makers only occasionally, but at least two outstanding films have resulted: *Metropolis* and *Things to Come*. *Just Imagine* painted a light-hearted picture, and *Seven Days in May* was not too frightening about what might be happening politically a few years from now; but one hopes not to take too seriously the predictions in *1984*, *The Time Machine*, *Fahrenheit 451*, *Alphaville*, *When Worlds Collide*, *The World, the Flesh and the Devil*, *The War Game*, *Dr Strangelove*, *Punishment Park*, *Beyond the Time Barrier*, *No Blade of Grass*, *Barbarella*, *A Clockwork Orange*, *Planet of the Apes*, *Westworld*, *Futureworld*, *Logan's Run*, *Star Wars*, *The Final Programme*, *Death Race 2000*, *Soylent Green* and *The Ultimate Warrior*.

prostitutes for many years could not be so labelled in Hollywood films, which featured a surprising number of 'café hostesses'. It was however fairly easy to spot the real profession of the various ladies who played Sadie Thompson in *Rain*, of Marlene Dietrich in *Dishonoured* and *Shanghai Express*, of Clara Bow in *Call Her Savage*, of Greta Garbo in *Anna Christie*, of Miriam Hopkins in *Dr Jekyll and Mr Hyde*, of Tallulah Bankhead in *Faithless*, of Bette Davis in *Of Human Bondage*, of Vivien Leigh in *Waterloo Bridge*, and of Joan Bennett in *Man*

Hunt, to name but a few. The French, who have always called a spade a spade, flaunted the calling in hundreds of films including *Dedée D'Anvers, La Ronde, Le Plaisir, Boule de Suif, Le Long des Trottoirs, La Bonne Soupe, Adua et sa Compagnie* and *Les Compagnons de la Nuit*; Italy chipped in with *Mamma Roma* and Japan with *Street of Shame*. In the fifties Britain moved into the field with surprising eagerness—every other movie seemed to feature Dora Bryan in a plastic mac—and there were several alleged exposés of Soho corruption under such titles as *The Flesh is Weak, Passport to Shame* and *The World Ten Times Over*. Hollywood half-heartedly followed with some double-talking second features about call girls—*Why Girls Leave Home, Call Girl, Girls in the Night*—and some 'medical case histories' such as *The Three Faces of Eve, Girl of the Night*. Around 1960 the floodgates opened, eased by the sensationally successful Greek comedy *Never on Sunday* (and some continental imitators like *Always on Saturday* and *Every Night of the Week*). Among English-speaking stars who have lately played prostitutes are Shirley Maclaine in *Some Came Running* and *Irma La Douce*, Sophia Loren in *Lady L, Yesterday, Today and Tomorrow, Marriage Italian Style, Boccaccio 70* and *Man of La Mancha*, Anna Karina in *Vivre sa Vie*, Lee Grant in *Divorce American Style* and *The Balcony*, Catherine Deneuve in *Belle de Jour*, Carroll Baker in *Sylvia*, Shirley Jones in *Elmer Gantry*, Nancy Kwan in *The World of Suzie Wong*, Elizabeth Taylor in *Butterfield 8*, Diane Cilento in *Rattle of a Simple Man*, Carol White in *Poor Cow*, Inger Stevens in *Five Card Stud*, Margot Kidder in *Gaily, Gaily*, Kitty Wynn in *Panic in Needle Park*, Jane Fonda in *Klute*. Brothels have been shown in *Lady L, A Walk on the Wild Side, The Revolt of Mamie Stover, A House is not a Home, Ulysses, The Balcony, A Funny Thing Happened on the Way to the Forum, The Assassination Bureau, The Best House in London, Games That Lovers Play, The Reivers, Gaily, Gaily*, and an increasing number of westerns. In *Our Man Flint*, girls were described as 'pleasure units' . . .

See also: *courtesans*.

Prouty, Jed (1879–1956). American character actor with stage experience, in films from the mid-twenties. Best remembered as father of *The Jones Family*; he appeared in over a dozen episodes of this domestic comedy series between 1935 and 1940.
Broadway Melody 28. George White's Scandals 35. The Texas Rangers 36. Roar of the Press 41. Mug Town 43. Guilty Bystander 49, many others.

Prouty, Olive Higgins (1882–1974). American novelist, best known to filmgoers for *Now Voyager* and *Stella Dallas*.

Provine, Dorothy (1937–). American leading lady who became well known as night club entertainer in TV series *The Roaring Twenties*.
The Bonnie Parker Story 58. Wall of Noise 63. It's a Mad Mad Mad Mad World 63. Good Neighbour Sam 64. That Darn Cat 65. The Great Race 65. One Spy Too Many 66. Kiss the Girls and Make Them Die 66. Who's Minding the Mint? 67, etc.

Prowse, Juliet (1937–). South African leading lady, in Hollywood from 1958, at first as dancer.
Can Can 59. G.I. Blues 60. The Fiercest Heart 61. The Right Approach 61. The Second Time Around 61. Run For Your Wife 66, etc.
TV series: *Meet Mona McCluskey* 65.

Pryor, Richard (1940–). Black American night club comedian.
Wattstax 73. Uptown Saturday Night 74. The Bingo Long Travelling All Stars and Motor Kings 76. Silver Streak 77.

Pryor, Roger (1901–1974). American leading man of minor movies, also stage and radio actor.
Moonlight and Pretzels 33. Belle of The Nineties 34. Ticket to Paradise 36. Money and the Woman 40. She Couldn't Say No 41, etc.

Psycho (US 1960). Alfred Hitchcock's horror comic, which he appears to have made as a joke, in the spirit of seeing whether he could get away with its nastiness. The critics found it revolting at first, but some later came round and admitted that once you were used to the idea of vivid bathtub murders, etc., it was done in Hitchcock's usual accomplished manner. Unfortunately it enabled less talented producers subsequently to indulge in similar shock tactics and is partly responsible for the low ebb of the thriller today with its emphasis on gore. Written by Joseph Stefano from a novel by Robert Bloch which is rather more subtle than the film; photographed by John L. Russell; with Anthony Perkins.

psychology is featured most prominently in American films—quite naturally since the United States is the home of the psychiatrist. However, one of the best serious psychological films, *Mine Own Executioner*, did come from Britain and showed the doctor to be more in need of help than the patient; while two other notable British films, *Thunder Rock* and *Dead of Night*, centred on the depiction of psychological states.

Although films about psychology can be firmly traced back to *The Cabinet of Dr Caligari* and *Secrets of a Soul*, the subject took its firmest hold in the middle of World War II, when so many people needed reassurance; the recounting of dreams to an analyst could even take the place of musical numbers in a romantic trifle like *Lady in the Dark*. Soon we were inundated with melodramas like *Spellbound, The Dark Mirror* and *Possessed*, in which the question to be answered was not so much who or how but why; and it wasn't until about 1950, with *Harvey*, that analysts could be laughed at; they are still being analysed in the seventies in such films as *Taking Off*. In the fifties the schizophrenic drama took on a new lease of life (*The Three Faces of Eve, Lizzie, Vertigo*), as did the tendency to guy individual psychiatrists while still claiming to respect the profession (*Oh Men Oh Women, Mirage, A Fine Madness, The Group, What a Way to Go, Marriage of a Young Stockbroker*). Of course, films were still made which took the whole matter with deadly seriousness, as in *The Cobweb, The Mark, Captain Newman MD, The Third Secret* and *Pressure Point*. John Huston's under-rated film on the life of *Freud* may have been unlucky to arrive at a time of change: the fashion is now for case histories in which no solution is offered (*Repulsion, Morgan, Cul-de-Sac*) or psychological horror comics such as *Psycho, Homicidal*, and *The Night Walker*, while in *Promise Her Anything* we were finally shown a psychiatrist (Robert Cummings) who doesn't believe in psychiatry.

See also *dreams; fantasy; amnesia; case histories*.

The Public Enemy (US 1931). One of the most violent of the early sound gangster films; it helped to swell official opinion against them, and James Cagney, who dispensed a lot of sudden death in this one, had to reform in *G-Men* 35, in which he stays on the right side of the law. Directed by William Wellman from a script by Harvey Thew; photographed by Dev Jennings. It still has powerful sequences despite its undeniably dated air.

Pudovkin, V. (Vsevolod) (1893–1953). Russian film theorist, writer and actor. Best remembered as director.
Mother 26. The End of St Petersburg 27. Storm over Asia 28. The Deserter 33. General Suvorov 41, many others which have not travelled.

Puglia, Frank (1892–1962). American character actor with vaudeville experience.
Viva Villa 34. Maisie 39. The Mark of Zorro 40.

Jungle Book 42. Phantom of the Opera 43. Blood on the Sun 45. The Desert Hawk 50. The Burning Hills 56. Cry Tough 59, many others.

Pulver, Lilo or **Liselotte** (1929–). Swiss-German leading lady.
A Time to Live and a Time to Die (US) 59. One, Two, Three (US) 61. A Global Affair (US) 63. La Religieuse (Fr.) 65. Le Jardinier d'Argentueil (Fr.) 66.

The Pumpkin Eater (GB 1964). A flashily-made, kaleidoscopic film by Jack Clayton about an unhappily married well-to-do woman in London; from Penelope Mortimer's novel. Despite the tiresomeness of the character, there are many brilliantly-handled sequences and Anne Bancroft gives a superb performance. The whole film, indeed, has the feel of life about it. With Peter Finch, James Mason; scripted by Harold Pinter; photographed by Oswald Morris; music by Georges Delerue.

Purcell, Dick (1908–1944). American leading man of second features.
Man Hunt 36. Navy Blues 37. Air Devils 38. Nancy Drew, Detective 39. King of the Zombies 41. Phantom Killer 42. The Mystery of the Thirteenth Guest 43. Timber Queen 44, etc.

Purcell, Noel (1900–). Tall, usually bearded, Irish character actor and comedian.
Captain Boycott 47. The Blue Lagoon 48. Doctor in the House 53. Moby Dick 56. Watch Your Stern 60. Mutiny on the Bounty 62. Lord Jim 65. Arrivederci Baby 66, many others.

Purdell, Reginald (1896–1953) (R. Grasdorf). British light character actor, mostly on stage and music hall.
Congress Dances 31. Q Planes 38. Many Thanks Mr Atkins 40. Pack Up Your Troubles 40. Variety Jubilee 43. We Dive at Dawn 43. 2000 Women 44. Holiday Camp 47. Captain Boycott 48, etc.

Purdom, Edmund (1924–). British light leading man who in the fifties was given the full Hollywood treatment but failed to emerge as a star.
Titanic 53. The Student Prince 54. The Egyptian 54. The Prodigal 55. The King's Thief 55. The Cossacks 60. Herod the Great 60. Nights of Rasputin 61. The Comedy Man 63. Suleiman the Conqueror 63. The Beauty Jungle 64. The Yellow Rolls Royce 64. The Man in the Golden Mask 69. The Black Corsair 69. Evil Fingers 72, etc.

Purviance, Edna (1894–1958). American leading lady of silent days.

A Night Out 15 (and other early Chaplin films including *Easy Street, The Count, The Cure, The Adventurer, Shoulder Arms*). Sunnyside 19. The Kid 21. The Pilgrim 23. A Woman of Paris 23. The Seagull 26. Limelight 52, many others.

Pygmalion (GB 1938). Despite 1964's *My Fair Lady*, this straight version of Shaw's play, directed by Anthony Asquith and Leslie Howard, remains the most satisfying and perfectly cast: Howard as Higgins, Wendy Hiller as Eliza, Scott Sunderland as Pickering and Wilfrid Lawson as Dolittle. Produced by Gabriel Pascal, photographed by Harry Stradling, with music by Arthur Honegger, it remains one of the cinema's most civilized comedies.

Pyle, Denver (1920–). American character actor, mostly in TV and big-screen westerns.

The Man from Colorado 48. To Hell and Back 55. Shenandoah 65. Bonnie and Clyde 67. Five Card Stud 68. Something Big 71. Cahill 73. Escape to Witch Mountain 75, etc.

TV series: The Doris Day Show 68–69.

Q

Quai des Brumes (France 1938). A highly influential study in poetic pessimism, directed by Marcel Carné from Jacques Prévert's script. Romance of the highest order is distilled from a squalid situation in foggy Le Havre, with Jean Gabin as a victim of circumstances on the run from the police, and Michèle Morgan there to comfort him briefly before the inevitable tragic finale. Music by Maurice Jaubert.

Quaid, Randy (1953–). American actor who has been seen in gangling, awkward roles.
□The Last Picture Show 71. What's Up Doc? 72. The Last Detail 73. Lolly Madonna XXX 73. Paper Moon 73. Breakout 75.

Qualen, John (1899–) (John Oleson). Canadian-born Norwegian character actor, in Hollywood from the thirties playing amiably ineffectual foreign types.
Arrowsmith (debut) 32. Black Fury 35. Seventh Heaven 37. *The Grapes of Wrath* 40. Out of the Fog 41. *All That Money Can Buy* 41. Jungle Book 42. Casablanca 42. Fairy Tale Murder 45. Adventure 46. The Fugitive 48. The Big Steal 49. Hans Christian Andersen 52. The High and the Mighty 54. The Searchers 56. Two Rode Together 60. The Man Who Shot Liberty Valance 62. The Prize 63. The Seven Faces of Dr Lao 64. Cheyenne Autumn 64. The Sons of Katie Elder 65. A Big Hand for the Little Lady 66. Firecreek 67, many others.

Quarry, Robert (1923–). American character actor bidding fair to be the horror man of the seventies.
A Kiss Before Dying 56. Count Yorga Vampire 69. The Return of Count Yorga 71. Dr Phibes Rises Again 72. The Revenge of Dr Death 73. The Midnight Man 73, etc.

Quayle, Anna (1937–). British comedienne. Drop Dead Darling 67. Smashing Time 67. Chitty Chitty Bang Bang 68. Up the Chastity Belt 71, etc.

Quayle, Anthony (1913–). Distinguished British stage actor and director, in occasional films as actor.
□ Hamlet 48. Saraband for Dead Lovers 48. Oh Rosalinda 55. The Battle of the River Plate 56. The Wrong Man (US) 57. Woman in a Dressing-Gown 57. *Ice Cold in Alex* 58. Serious Charge 59. Tarzan's Greatest Adventure 59. The Challenge 60. The Guns of Navarone 61. Lawrence of Arabia 62. HMS Defiant 62. The Fall of the Roman Empire 64. East of Sudan 64. Operation Crossbow 64. A Study in Terror 65. Before Winter Comes 69. Anne of the Thousand Days 70. Everything You Always Wanted to Know About Sex 72. A Bequest to the Nation 73. Jarrett (TV) 73. QB VII (TV) 73. The Tamarind Seed 74. Great Expectations (TV) 75. Moses 76.
TV series: Strange Report 69.

Que Viva Mexico (Mexico 1932). Eisenstein's famous epic of Mexican history, based on funds supplied and later withdrawn by Upton Sinclair, was to have been an episodic semi-documentary. It was never completed, but fragments have been bought up and shown as *Thunder Over Mexico* (by Sol Lesser), *Death Day* (by Upton Sinclair) and *Time in the Sun* (by Marie Seton).

Queen Christina (US 1933). This historical romance seemed less a calculated box-office film than an act of homage by its production company (MGM) towards its star (Greta Garbo). Expensively presented, directed with care and craft by Rouben Mamoulian, it makes a flawless example of bespoke tailoring from Hollywood's golden age. The plot, concerning a royal love affair in 16th century Sweden, is fictitious. John Gilbert co-starred at Garbo's own request, but it was his last major role.

Queen Kelly (US 1928). A typical unfinished extravagance written and directed by Erich Von Stroheim, about an ill-fated romance between a young convent girl and the consort of the mad queen of a petty European principality. Further fragments keep on turning up, taking the story into a brothel and to Africa. Gloria Swanson starred, with Walter Byron and Seena Owen.

The Queen of Spades (GB 1948). The Pushkin story has been filmed several times in Russia. This atmospheric version by Rodney Ackland and Arthur Boys, directed by Thorold Dickinson, goes all out to surpass Eisenstein in imagery but despite brilliant moments is finally too slow to have the necessary grip. Edith Evans plays the aged countess who has reputedly sold her soul to the devil in exchange for the secret of winning at faro, Anton Walbrook the soldier desperate to˙learn the trick.

The Quiet Man (US 1952). Typically easygoing romantic comedy of John Ford's later period, enjoyably set in a never-never Ireland and concerning an ex-boxer's Petruchio-like courtship of a fiery colleen. John Wayne, Maureen O'Hara, Victor McLaglen and Barry Fitzgerald head a hand-picked cast; music by Victor Young; original story by Maurice Walsh.

Quillan, Eddie (1907–). Bouncy, beaming American comic actor, in Hollywood from 1930.
Big Money 30. Mutiny on the Bounty 35. Young Mr Lincoln 39. The Grapes of Wrath 40. Dark Streets of Cairo 40. Flying Blind 41. Sideshow 50. Brigadoon 54. The Ghost and Mr Chicken 66; latterly on TV.

Quimby, Fred (1886–1965). American producer, head of MGM's short subjects department 1926–56. Specially known for development of Tom and Jerry cartoons.

Quine, Richard (1920–). American director, former leading man. (*The World Changes* 32 as juvenile also *Babes on Broadway* 40, *My Sister Eileen* 41, *For Me and My Gal* 42, etc.)

The Sunny Side of the Street 51. Drive a Crooked Road 54. Pushover 54. My Sister Eileen 55. *The Solid Gold Cadillac* 56. Operation Mad Ball 58. Bell, Book and Candle 58. The World of Suzie Wong 60. The Notorious Landlady 62. Paris When It Sizzles 64. How to Murder Your Wife 65. Oh Dad, Poor Dad 66. Hotel 67. A Talent for Loving 69. The Moonshine War 70. 'W' 74, etc.

Quinn, Anthony (1915–). Mexican-born leading actor, in films since 1936, latterly noted for full-blooded performances.
Autobiography: *The Original Sin* 72.
Parole 36. The Plainsman 37. Last Train from Madrid 37. Union Pacific 39. Blood and Sand 41. Ghost Breakers 41. The Black Swan 42. The Ox-Bow Incident 43. Buffalo Bill 44. China Sky 45. Tycoon 48. The Brave Bulls 51. *Viva Zapata* (AA) 52. The World in His Arms 52. Ride Vaquero 53. Blowing Wild 54. The Long Wait 54. *La Strada* (It.) 54. Attila the Hun (It.) 54. Ulysses 55. *Lust for Life* (AA) 56. The Man from Del Rio 56. The Hunchback of Notre Dame 56. The River's Edge 57. Hot Spell 58. Black Orchid 58. Last Train from Gun Hill 58. Warlock 59. The Buccaneer (d only) 59. Heller in Pink Tights 60. Savage Innocents 60. The Guns of Navarone 61. Lawrence of Arabia 62. Barabbas 62. Requiem for a Heavyweight 63. The Visit 63. *Zorba the Greek* 64. A High Wind in Jamaica 65. Lost Command 66. The Happening 67. The Twenty-Fifth Hour 67. The Rover 67. *The Shoes of the Fisherman* 68. The Magus 68. The Secret of Santa Vittoria 69. R.P.M. 69. A Walk in the Spring Rain 69. Flap 70. Across 110th Street 72. The Marseilles Contract 74. Mohammed (The Message) 76. Jesus of Nazareth (TV) 77, etc.
TV series: *The Man and the City* 71.

Quo Vadis? The biblical epic by Henryk Sienkiewicz has been filmed three times: in Italy in 1912 and 1924, and in the US in 1951. The third version, though less impressive as a product of its period than the others, was certainly the most spectacular, with the appropriate cast of thousands and a well-drilled squad of Christian-gorging lions. Robert Taylor and Deborah Kerr suffered under Peter Ustinov's Nero; Mervyn Le Roy directed.

quota. By Act of Parliament renters are obliged

to sell, and exhibitors to show, a varying proportion of British-made films. There has not always been enough British talent to fill the necessary number of releases: hence the notorious 'quota quickies' of the twenties and thirties, and much second-feature material more recently, which however bad can invariably get a circuit booking providing it has a British quota ticket. The normal quota which an exhibitor has to fill is 30% for features, 25% for supporting programme. This contrasts markedly with independent television contractors, whose programmes must be 86% British.

R

Rabier, Jean (1927–). French cinematographer.
Cleo de 5 à 7 61. Ophelia 62. Landru 62. *La Baie des Anges* 63. *Les Parapluies de Cherbourg* 64. Le Bonheur 65. The Champagne Murders 66. Les Biches 68. *Le Boucher* 70, etc.

Rackin, Martin (1918–1976). American screenwriter.
Air Raid Wardens 43. Riff Raff 47. Fighting Father Dunne 48. Three Secrets 50. The Enforcer 51. Sailor Beware 52. The Stooge 53. Santiago (& p) 56. The Helen Morgan Story (p only) 57. The Horse Soldiers (& p) 59. North to Alaska 60. Stagecoach (p only) 66. Rough Night in Jericho (p only) 67. The Revengers (p only) 72, etc.

Radd, Ronald (1924–1976). British character actor, usually in heavy roles. Much on TV.
The Camp on Blood Island 58. The Small World of Sammy Lee 62. Up Jumped a Swagman 65. Where the Spies Are 65. Mr Ten Per Cent 66. The Offence 72. The Spiral Staircase 74, etc.

Rademakers, Fons (1921–). Dutch director, with stage experience.
Doctor in the Village 58. The Knife 61, etc.

Radford, Basil (1897–1952). British light character comedian, on stage from 1922, films from 1929 (*Barnum Was Right*). Became popular when he and Naunton Wayne played two imperturbable Englishmen abroad in *The Lady Vanishes* 38.
Just William 38. *Night Train to Munich* 40. *Crooks Tour* 40. Next of Kin 42. Millions Like Us 43. The Way to the Stars 45. *Dead of Night* 45. *The Captive Heart* 46. Girl in a Million 46. It's Not Cricket 48. Passport to Pimlico 48. The Winslow Boy 48. Quartet 48. *Whisky Galore* 48. Chance of a Lifetime 50. The Galloping Major 51, etc.

Radnitz, Robert B. (1925–). American producer of 'family' films.
A Dog of Flanders 60. Misty 62. Island of the Blue Dolphins 64. And Now Miguel 66. My Side of the Mountain 68. The Little Ark 70. *Sounder* 72, etc.

Rafelson, Bob (1935–). American director.
Head (co-w only) 68. Five Easy Pieces 71. The King of Marvin Gardens 72. Stay Hungry 76, etc.

Rafferty, Chips (1909–1971) (John Goffage). Rangy Australian character actor with varied experience before coming to films.
Dad Rudd, M.P. 39. Forty Thousand Horsemen 40. The Rats of Tobruk 42. *The Overlanders* 46. The Loves of Joanna Godden (GB) 46. Eureka Stockade 47. Bitter Springs 51. Kangaroo 52. King of the Coral Seal 54. Walk into Paradise 56. *The Sundowners* 60. Mutiny on the Bounty 62. They're a Weird Mob 66. Kona Coast 68. Skullduggery 69. Outback 70, many others.

Rafferty, Frances (1922–). American leading lady.
Seven Sweethearts 42. Dragon Seed 44. Abbott and Costello in Hollywood 45. The Hidden Eye 45. Lady at Midnight 48. Rodeo 52. The Shanghai Story 54, etc.
TV series: December Bride 54–58.

Rafkin, Alan (–). American director.
Ski Party 65. The Ghost and Mr Chicken 66. Nobody's Perfect 68. The Shakiest Gun in the West 68, etc.

Raft, George (1895–) (George Rauft). Smooth, rather sinister American leading man of the thirties and forties; formerly a professional athlete, gambler, night club dancer and companion of gangsters. In 1961 Ray Danton appeared in the title role of *The George Raft Story*.
□ Queen of the Night Clubs 29. Quick Millions 31. Hush Money 31. Palmy Days 31. Dancers in the Dark 32. *Scarface* 32. Night World 32. Madame Racketeer 32. Night after Night 32. If I Had a Million 32. Undercover Man 32. Pick Up 33. Midnight Club 33. *The Bowery* 33. All of Me 34. *Bolero* 34. The Trumpet Blows 34. Limehouse Blues 34. *Rumba* 35. Stolen Harmony 35. *The Glass Key* 35. Every Night at

Eight 35. She Couldn't Take It 35. It Had to Happen 36. Yours for the Asking 36. *Souls at Sea* 37. You and Me 38. Spawn of the North 38. The Lady's from Kentucky 38. *Each Dawn I Die* 39. I Stole a Million 39. Invisible Stripes 40. The House across the Bay 40. They Drive by Night 40. Manpower 41. Broadway 42. Stage Door Canteen 43. Background to Danger 43. Follow the Boys 44. Nob Hill 45. Johnny Angel 45. Whistle Stop 46. Mr Ace 46. Nocturne 46. Christmas Eve 47. Intrigue 48. Race Street 48. Outpost in Morocco 49. Johnny Allegro 49. A Dangerous Profession 49. The Red Light 50. Lucky Nick Cain 51. Loan Shark 52. The Man from Cairo 53. Rogue Cop 54. Black Widow 54. A Bullet for Joey 55. Around the World in Eighty Days 56. Some Like It Hot 59. Jet over the Atlantic 59. Ocean's Eleven 60. Ladies' Man 64. The Patsy 64. For Those Who Think Young 64. Casino Royale 67. Du Rififi à Paname 67. Five Golden Dragons 67. Skidoo 68. Hammersmith is Out 72.

TV series: I Am the Law 55. Sextette 77.

Ragland, Rags (1905–1946). American character comedian, former boxer.
Whistling in the Dark 41. The War against Mrs Hadley 42. Panama Hattie 42. Girl Crazy 43. Her Highness and the Bellboy 45. Anchors Aweigh 45, etc.

railway stations have provided a major setting for some memorable films including *The Ghost Train, Doctor Zhivago, Knight without Armour, I'll Never Forget Whatshisname* (with its white 'dream' station), *Union Station, 3.10 to Yuma, Last Train from Madrid, Bhowani Junction, Northwest Frontier, 100 Rifles, The Mercenaries, Waterloo Road, Anna Karenina, Grand Central Station, Under the Clock, Brief Encounter, Oh Mr Porter, The Titfield Thunderbolt, High Noon, In the Heat of the Night* and *The Train* ... while Orson Welles made *The Trial* almost entirely within a deserted station, and de Sica made *Indiscretion* among the crowds of Rome's Stazione Termini.
See also: *trains.*

Raimu (1883–1946) (Jules Muraire). French character actor and comedian with music-hall background.
Marius 31. *Fanny* 32. *César* 34. Un Carnet de Bal 37. *La Femme du Boulanger* 39. La Fille du Puisatier 40. Heart of a Nation 40. Les Inconnus dans la Maison 42. Colonel Chabert 44. L'Homme au Chapeau Rond 46, etc.

Rain. Somerset Maugham's story of the conflict between a missionary and a woman of highly doubtful character has been filmed three times in Hollywood: in 1928 with Gloria Swanson and Lionel Barrymore, in 1932 with Joan Crawford and Walter Huston, and in 1957 (as *Miss Sadie Thompson*) with Rita Hayworth and José Ferrer. In each case the Production Code made you guess what the lady's actual profession was.

rain has been put to many uses by film scenarists. It was the direct cause of dramatic situations in *Rebecca* (a shower flattened Joan Fontaine's hair-do just as she arrived at Manderley); in *The Loneliness of the Long Distance Runner* (it revealed evidence which the hero was trying to conceal); in *Floods of Fear* (it permitted the escape of three convicts, one of whom then rescued the heroine); in *The African Queen* (it raised the water level and so released the boat from the reeds which held it captive); in *Desk Set* (it persuaded Spencer Tracy to accept Katharine Hepburn's offer of hospitality); in *Pygmalion* (it caused the meeting of Higgins and Eliza); in *Sands of the Kalahari* (it flooded a pit in which Stuart Whitman was imprisoned and permitted his escape); in *When Tomorrow Comes* (it stranded Charles Boyer and Irene Dunne in a remote church for the night); and in many others. Two splendid symbolic uses were in *Saraband for Dead Lovers* (a raindrop made a stained glass madonna appear to weep at the ill-fated wedding) and *The Stars Look Down* (as the hero and heroine make love, two raindrops intertwine on the window pane).

Rain has often been used symbolically as a relief from tension and heat, in films as diverse as *Night of the Iguana, Passport to Pimlico, The Long Hot Summer, Key Largo, Twelve Angry Men, Black Narcissus, The Good Earth* and *Rain* itself. It has provided a solemn or ominous background in *Psycho, Term of Trial, Rashomon, It Always Rains on Sunday, Room at the Top, The Robe, Fires on the Plain, The Collector* and many others. It has a particularly depressing effect at a funeral, as shown in *The Glass Key* and *Our Town*; or at an assassination (*Foreign Correspondent*). But it can also be used for farcical purposes: in *Three Men in a Boat, The Silencers, Fraternally Yours, Oh Mr Porter*, etc. And it can provide a comedy twist, as at the end of *The Lady Vanishes*, when the English travellers so eager to get back to the test match find that rain has stopped play.

It can produce a decorative effect (*Les Parapluies de Cherbourg, Miracle in the Rain, Breakfast at Tiffany's*). It can be spectacular (the climax of *Journey into Fear*, the glistening streets in *The Third Man*, the downpours in *The Rains Came*, and *Pather Panchali*, the battles in the rain in *Tower of London* and *Seven Samurai*). And it can provide a cue for song: 'Isn't it a Lovely Day to be Caught in the Rain' in *Top Hat*, the title songs of *Singin' in the Rain* and *Stormy Weather*, 'The Rain in Spain' in *My Fair Lady*, 'April Showers' in *The Jolson Story*, 'Little April Shower' in *Bambi*. In fact, it seems to be by far the most versatile of all the film-maker's effects.

Raine, Norman Reilly (1895–1971). American screenwriter.
Tugboat Annie 33. White Woman 33. God's Country and the Woman 36. *The Life of Emile Zola* (AA) 38. The Adventures of Robin Hood 38. Elizabeth and Essex 39. The Fighting 69th 39. Captains of the Clouds 42. Ladies Courageous 44. A Bell for Adano 45. Woman of the North Country 52. Sea of Lost Ships 53, etc.

Rainer, Luise (1909–). Austrian actress on stage from 1930; later in Hollywood films.
Escapade 35. *The Great Ziegfeld* (AA) 36. *The Good Earth* (AA) 37. The Emperor's Candlesticks 37. The Big City 37. The Great Waltz 38. The Toy Wife 38. Dramatic School 38. Hostages 43.

Raines, Ella (1921–) (Ella Raubes). American leading lady of the forties, with brief stage experience.
Phantom Lady 43. Hail the Conquering Hero 43. Enter Arsène Lupin 44. The Suspect 45. The Runaround 46. Time out of Mind 47. Brute Force 47. Mr Ashton was Indiscreet 48. Ride the Man Down 52. Man in the Road (GB) 54, etc.
TV series: Janet Dean Registered Nurse 57.

The Rains Came. Louis Bromfield's novel of the high days of British India was filmed in 1939 with Myrna Loy and Tyrone Power, and in 1955 with Lana Turner and Richard Burton. (The title was changed to *The Rains of Ranchipur*.)

Rains, Claude (1889–1967). Suave, incisive British character actor, long resident in America. Wide stage experience.
□ *The Invisible Man* 33. *Crime without Passion* 34. The Man Who Reclaimed His Head 34. The Mystery of Edwin Drood 35. The Clairvoyant (GB) 35. The Last Outpost 35. Anthony Adverse 36. Hearts Divided 36. Stolen Holiday 36. The Prince and the Pauper 37. They Won't Forget 37. Gold is Where You Find It 38. *The Adventures of Robin Hood* 38. White Banners 38. Four Daughters 38. They Made Me a Criminal 39. Juarez 39. *Mr Smith Goes to Washington* 39. Four Wives 39. Daughters Courageous 39. Saturday's Children 39. The Sea

Hawk 40. Lady with Red Hair (as David Belasco) 40. Four Mothers 40. *Here Comes Mr Jordan* 41. The Wolf Man 41. *King's Row* 41. Moontide 42. Now Voyager 42. *Casablanca* 42. Forever and a Day 43. Phantom of the Opera (title role) 43. Passage to Marseilles 44. *Mr Skeffington* 44. This Love of Ours 45. *Caesar and Cleopatra* (GB) 45. Angel on My Shoulder 46. *Deception* 46. *Notorious* 46. The Unsuspected 47. Strange Holiday 47. *The Passionate Friends* (GB) 47. Rope of Sand 49. Song of Surrender 49. The White Tower 50. Where Danger Lives 50. Sealed Cargo 51. The Man Who Watched Trains Go By (GB) 52. Lisbon 56. This Earth is Mine 59. The Lost World 60. Battle of the Worlds (It.) 61. Lawrence of Arabia 62. Twilight of Honor 63. The Greatest Story Ever Told 65.

Raitt, John (1921–). American stage singer whose only film has been *The Pajama Game* 57.

Rakoff, Alvin (1927–). Canadian TV director resident in Britain.
Passport to Shame 58. Treasure of San Teresa 59. On Friday at Eleven 61. The Comedy Man 64. Hoffman 70. Say Hello to Yesterday 70. Don Quixote (TV) 72, etc.

Raksin, David (1912–). American composer, in Hollywood from mid-thirties. Arranged Chaplin's score for *Modern Times* 36.
Laura 44. The Secret Life of Walter Mitty 47. The Bad and the Beautiful 52. Separate Tables 58. Too Late Blues 62. Two Weeks in Another Town 62. Invitation to a Gunfighter 65. A Big Hand for the Little Lady 66. Will Penny 67. What's the Matter with Helen? 71, etc.

Ralli, Giovanna (1935–). Italian leading lady.
The Children are Watching Us 43. Lights of Variety 49. La Lupa 53. The Bigamist 56. Il Generale Della Rovere 59. Deadfall 68. Cannon for Cordoba 70, many others.

Ralph, Jessie (1864–1944) (Jessie Ralph Chambers). American character actress who came to Hollywood late in life and played many endearing granny roles.
Child of Manhattan 33. *David Copperfield* (as Peggotty) 34. Captain Blood 35. Camille 36. *San Francisco* 36. Café Society 39. The Bluebird 40. They Met in Bombay (last film) 41, etc.

Ralston, Esther (1902–). American leading lady of the twenties and thirties.
The Phantom Fortune (serial) 23. Peter Pan 24. A Kiss for Cinderella 25. Lucky Devil 26. Old Ironsides 26. Figures Don't Lie 27. The Sawdust

Paradise 28. The Prodigal 31. Sadie McKee 33. Hollywood Boulevard 36. Tin Pan Alley 40, etc.

Ralston, Jobyna (1901–1967). American leading lady of the twenties, especially with Harold Lloyd.
Why Worry 23. Girl Shy 24. The Freshman 24. For Heaven's Sake 26. Wings 27, many others.

Ralston, Vera Hruba (1921–). Czech actress, former skating champion. In US from late thirties, films from 1942. Married Herbert Yates, boss of Republic Studios, and appeared exclusively in his pictures. Now retired.
□ Ice Capades 41. Ice Capades Revue 42. The Lady and the Monster 44. Storm Over Lisbon 44. Lake Placid Serenade 44. Dakota 45. Murder in the Music Hall 46. The Plainsman and the Lady 46. The Flame 47. Wyoming 47. I Jane Doe 48. Angel on the Amazon 48. The Fighting Kentuckian 49. Surrender 50. Belle Le Grand 51. The Wild Blue Yonder 51. Hoodlum Empire 52. Fair Wind to Java 53. A Perilous Journey 53. Jubilee Trail 54. Timberjack 55. Accused of Murder 56. Spoilers of the Forest 57. Gunfire at Indian Gap 57. The Notorious Mr Monks 58. The Man Who Died Twice 58.

Rambeau, Marjorie (1889–1970). American character actress.
The Dazzling Miss Davison 16. Her Man 30. Man's Castle 33. The Rains Came 39. Twenty Mule Team 40. Tugboat Annie Sails Again (title role) 41. So Ends Our Night 41. Tobacco Road 41. Broadway 42. Army Wives 45. Abandoned 49. Torch Song 53. The View from Pompey's Head 56. Man of a Thousand Faces 57, others.

Ramona. Helen Hunt Jackson's novel about an Indian girl was filmed four times: by Griffith in 1910, with Mary Pickford and Henry B. Walthall; by Donald Crisp in 1916, with Adda Gleason and Monroe Salisbury; by Edwin Carewe in 1928, with Dolores del Rio and Warner Baxter; and by Henry King in 1936, with Loretta Young and Don Ameche.

Rampling, Charlotte (1945–). British leading lady.
Rotten to the Core 65. Georgy Girl 66. The Long Duel 67. The Damned 69. Corky 72. The Ski Bum 72. Henry VIII and His Six Wives 72. Asylum 72. Zardoz 73. Caravan to Vaccares 74. The Night Porter 74. Farewell My Lovely 75. Foxtrot 76, etc.

Rand, Sally (1904–). American dancer and fan dancer, in a few films.
The Dressmaker from Paris 24. Getting Gertie's

Garter 27. King of Kings 27. The Fighting Eagle 28. Bolero 34, etc.

Randall, Tony (1920–). Sardonic American comedy actor, adept at light drunks, depressives and friends of the hero.
□ Oh Men Oh Women 57. Will Success Spoil Rock Hunter? 57. No Down Payment 58. The Mating Game 59. *Pillow Talk* 59. The Adventures of Huckleberry Finn 60. Let's Make Love 61. Lover Come Back 61. Boys Night Out 62. Island of Love 63. The Brass Bottle 63. *Send Me No Flowers* 64. *Seven Faces of Dr Lao* 64. Fluffy 65. The Alphabet Murders (hilariously miscast as Hercule Poirot) 66. Our Man in Marrakesh 66. Hello Down There 68.
TV series: *Mr Peepers* 52–55. *The Odd Couple* 70–74. Tony Randall Show 76– .

Randell, Ron (1918–). Australian leading man with radio experience; has appeared in films and TV episodes all over the world.
It Had to be You 47. Lorna Doone 50. Kiss Me Kate 53. Bulldog Drummond at Bay 54. I Am a' Camera 55. Beyond Mombasa 56. The Story of Esther Costello 58. King of Kings 61. The Longest Day 62. Gold for the Caesars 63. The Seven Minutes 71, many others.

Randle, Frank (1901–1957) (Arthur McEvoy). Lancashire music-hall comedian of immense vulgarity; made his own slapdash but highly popular films in the forties.
Somewhere in England 40. Somewhere in Camp 42. Somewhere in Civvies 43. School for Randle 47. Home Sweet Home 47. Holidays with Pay 48. It's a Grand Life 53, etc.

Randolph, Elsie (1904–). British revue artiste, often teamed in the thirties with Jack Buchanan.
Rise and Shine 32. Yes, Mr Brown 33. *That's a Good Girl* 33. *This'll Make You Whistle* 35. Smash and Grab 38. Cheer the Brave 50. Frenzy 72, etc.

Randolph, Jane (1919–). American leading lady of the forties.
Highways by Night 42. Cat People 42. In the Meantime, Darling 44. Jealousy 46. T Men 48. Abbott and Costello Meet Frankenstein (last to date) 48, etc.

Randolph, John (1917–). American character actor usually seen as pompous business man.
Seconds 67. Pretty Poison 68. There Was a Crooked Man 70. Little Murders 71. Serpico 73.

Random Harvest (US 1942). Immensely popular in the drab wartime days of its release, this romantic film was taken from a James Hilton novel about a man who marries while suffering from amnesia; he gets his memory back, is restored to his former position in life, and fails to recognize his wife when she comes to work as his secretary. Sheer hokum complete with roses round the door, but persuasively produced in MGM's best manner, carefully directed by Mervyn le Roy, and with irresistible star performances from Ronald Colman and Greer Garson.

Rank, J. Arthur (Lord Rank) (1888–1972). British flour magnate who entered films in the mid-thirties in the hope of promoting interest in religion. Formed or took over so many companies including production, distribution and exhibition that by the mid-forties he was accused of monopolistic tendencies. His influence was generally excellent, and he encouraged independent producers (sometimes unwisely), but his organization generally suffered from a preponderance of accountants unable to understand the ingredients of a good film. Without their financial advice, however, the empire might well have perished altogether. At its height it fostered such production companies as the Archers, Cineguild, Wessex, Individual and Two Cities. In recent years the film side of the organization has proved less important than its hotels, bowling alleys and such developments as Xerox-copying; but it includes Odeon and Gaumont Theatres, Rank Film Distributors, Pinewood Studios, Denham Laboratories, etc. A biography, *Mr Rank* by Alan Wood, was published in 1952.

Ransohoff, Martin (1927–). American writer and executive. Longtime chairman of Filmways, producers of such TV series as *The Beverly Hillbillies* and *The Addams Family*. Has also produced films.
Boys Night Out 62. The Wheeler Dealers 63. The Americanization of Emily 64. Topkapi 64. The Sandpiper 65. The Loved One 65. The Cincinnati Kid 65. Don't Make Waves 67. Ice Station Zebra 68. The Moonshine War 70. The White Dawn 73. Silver Streak 76, etc.

Ransome, Prunella (1943–). British leading lady.
Far from the Madding Crowd 67. Alfred the Great 69. Man in the Wilderness 71. Who Can Kill A Child? (Sp.) 75, etc.

rape was virtually unmentionable in English-speaking films until Warners got away with it in *Johnny Belinda* in 1947. Then it became the centre of attention in *Outrage, Peyton Place, Wicked as They Come, A Streetcar Named Desire, Last Train from Gun Hill, Two Women, To Kill a Mockingbird, Satan Never Sleeps, Shock Corridor, Assault, Trial, Five Gates to Hell, The Chapman Report, The Mark, Anatomy of a Murder, Town without Pity, The Party's Over* (in which the victim proved to be dead), and *The Penthouse*. In *Waterhole Three* James Coburn, accused of the crime, shrugged it off as 'assault with a friendly weapon'. There was much talk of rape in *The Knack* and *Lock Up Your Daughters*, threat of rape in *Experiment in Terror* and *Cape Fear*, and an accusation of rape in *Term of Trial*. Foreign language films on the subject have included *Rashomon, The Virgin Spring, Two Women, Viridiana* and the Greek *Amok*. In the seventies films it became too commonplace to be worth mentioning, outstanding fictional instances being *Straw Dogs, A Clockwork Orange, Lipstick,* and *Death Wish*, with *Cry Rape* and *A Case of Rape* adopting a documentary treatment.

Raphael, Frederic (1931–). British writer.
Nothing But the Best 64. Darling (AA, BFA) 65. Two for the Road 67. Far from the Madding Crowd 67, etc.

Raphaelson, Samson (1896–). American playwright whose best screenplays were for Lubitsch: he led the saucy, stylish European trends of the thirties.
☐ The Jazz Singer (& oa) 27. Boudoir Diplomat 30. The Smiling Lieutenant 31. The Magnificent Lie 31. *One Hour with You* 32. Broken Lullaby 32. *Trouble in Paradise* 32. The Merry Widow 34. Caravan 34. Servants' Entrance 34. Ladies Love Danger 35. Dressed to Thrill 35. *Accent on Youth* (& oa) 35. The Last of Mrs Cheyney 37. *The Shop around the Corner* 40. Suspicion 41. Skylark (& oa) 41. *Heaven Can Wait* 43. The Perfect Marriage (& oa) 46. Green Dolphin Street 47. That Lady in Ermine 48. Bannerline 51. Main Street to Broadway 53. Hilda Crane (oa) 56.

Rapper, Irving (c. 1898–). American director with stage experience, long associated with Warner films.
Shining Victory 41. One Foot in Heaven 41. The Gay Sisters 42. *Now Voyager* 42. The Adventures of Mark Twain 44. Rhapsody in Blue 45. The Corn is Green 46. *Deception* 46. *The Voice of the Turtle* 48. The Glass Menagerie 50. Another Man's Poison (GB) 51. Forever Female 52. The Brave One 56. Strange Intruder

57. Marjorie Morningstar 58. The Miracle 59. The Christine Jorgenson Story 70, others.

Rashomon (In the Woods) (Japan 1951). The film which after many years opened western cinemas to Japanese films; America has even paid it the compliment of remaking it (1964) as *The Outrage*. Concerning the different views of the four people concerned about a moment of violence, it was a stylistic revelation and established Akira Kurosawa as an OK name though his subsequent films seldom got beyond the very specialized halls.

Rasp, Fritz (1891–). German character actor. Jugend 22. Warning Shadows 23. Metropolis 27. The Loves of Jeanne Ney 27. Spione 28. Diary of a Lost Girl 29. Die Dreigroschenoper 33. Lina Braake 76, many others.

Rasputin, the mysterious monk who dominated members of the Tsar's family just before the Russian revolution, has been a popular film subject. Conrad Veidt played him in *Rasputin* (Germany 1930); Lionel Barrymore in *Rasputin and the Empress* (US 1932); Harry Baur in *Rasputin* (France 1938); Edmund Purdom in *Nights of Rasputin* (Italy 1960); and Christopher Lee in *Rasputin the Mad Monk* (Britain 1966); while 1968 brought Gert Frobe in the role in *I Killed Rasputin*, and 1971 had Tom Baker as Rasputin in *Nicholas and Alexandra*.

Rasulala, Thalmus (1939–) (Jack Crowder). Black American character actor.
Cool Breeze 71. Blacula 72. Willie Dynamite 73. Mr Ricco 75. Bucktown 75, etc.

Rasumny, Mikhail (1890–1956). Russian character actor with stage experience, long in Hollywood.
Comrade X 40. This Gun for Hire 42. For Whom the Bell Tolls 43. Saigon 47. The Kissing Bandit 49. Hot Blood 55, many others.

Rathbone, Basil (1892–1976). Incisive British actor, on stage since 1911, in American from the mid-twenties. An excellent villain and a fine Sherlock Holmes.
Autobiography 1962: *In and Out of Character.*
□ Innocent 21. The Fruitful Vine 21. The School for Scandal 23. Trouping with Ellen 24. The Masked Bride 25. The Great Deception 24. The Last of Mrs Cheyney 29. The Bishop Murder Case 30. A Notorious Affair 30. The Lady of Scandal 30. This Mad World 30. The Flirting Widow 30. A Lady Surrenders 30. Sin Takes a Holiday 30. A Woman Commands 31. One Precious Year 33. After the Ball 33. Loyalties 33.

David Copperfield (as Murdstone) 35. *Anna Karenina* (as Karenin) 35. The Last Days of Pompeii 35. A Feather in Her Hat 35. A Tale of Two Cities 35. *Captain Blood* 35. Kind Lady 35. Private Number 36. Romeo and Juliet 36. The Garden of Allah 36. Confession 37. Love from a Stranger 37. Make a Wish 37. Tovarich 37. The Adventures of Marco Polo 38. *The Adventures of Robin Hood* (as Gisbourne) 38. If I Were King 38. The Dawn Patrol 38. Son of Frankenstein 39. *The Hound of the Baskervilles* 39. The Sun Never Sets 39. The Adventures of Sherlock Holmes 39. Rio 39. Tower of London 39. Rhythm on the River 40. The Mark of Zorro 40. The Mad Doctor 41. The Black Cat 41. International Lady 41. Paris Calling 41. Fingers at the Window 41. Crossroads 42. Sherlock Holmes and the Voice of Terror 42. Sherlock Holmes and the Secret Weapon 42. Sherlock Holmes in Washington 43. Above Suspicion 43. Sherlock Holmes Faces Death 43. *Spider Woman* 44. The Scarlet Claw 44. Bathing Beauty 44. The Pearl of Death 44. Frenchman's Creek 44. The House of Fear 45. The Woman in Green 45. Pursuit to Algiers 45. Terror by Night 45. *Heartbeat* 46. Dressed to Kill 46. Casanova's Big Night 54. We're No Angels 55. *The Court Jester* 56. The Black Sleep 56. The Last Hurrah 58. The Magic Sword 62. Tales of Terror 62. Two Before Zero 62. The Comedy of Terrors 64. Pontius Pilate 64. Queen of Blood 66. The Ghost in the Invisible Bikini 66. Voyage to a Prehistoric Planet 67. Autopsy of a Ghost 67. Hillbillies in a Haunted House 67.

ratio (screen): see *aspect ratio.*

Ratoff, Gregory (1897–1960). English-fracturing Russian actor and impresario, in Hollywood and Britain from mid-thirties as actor or director.
I'm No Angel (a) 33. Under Two Flags (a) 36. Lancer Spy (d) 37. Rose of Washington Square (d) 39. Intermezzo (d) 39. I Was an Adventuress (d) 40. Adam Had Four Sons (d) 41. The Corsican Brothers (a) 41. The Men in Her Life (d) 42. Song of Russia (d) 44. Where Do We Go from Here? (d) 45. Moss Rose (d) 47. *All about Eve* (a) 50. My Daughter Joy (d) 50. Abdullah the Great (ad) 57. *Oscar Wilde* (d) 60. The Big Gamble (a) 61, many others.

Rattigan, Sir Terence (1912–). Distinguished British playwright, many of whose successes have been filmed.
French without Tears 39. While the Sun Shines 46. The Winslow Boy 48. The Browning Version 51. The Deep Blue Sea 55. Separate Tables 58, etc.

AS SCREENWRITER: English without Tears 43. The Way to the Stars 45. The Sound Barrier 52. The VIPs 63. The Yellow Rolls-Royce 64. Goodbye Mr Chips 69. Bequest to the Nation 73, others.

Ravetch, Irving (c. 1915–). American writer who with his wife Harriet Frank has frequently worked with director Martin Ritt on scripts that include *Hud* 63, and *Hombré* 67. Turned writer-producer with *The Reivers* 69.

Rawi, Ousama (1940–). Iranian cinematographer.
Pulp 73. The Black Windmill 74. Gold 74. Rachel's Man 75. Alfie Darling 75. Sky Riders 76, etc.

Rawlins, John (1902–). American director, mainly of second features.
State Police 38. Six Lessons from Madame La Zonga 41. Halfway to Shanghai 42. Sherlock Holmes and the Voice of Terror 42. The Great Impersonation 42. Ladies Courageous 44. Sudan 45. Dick Tracy Meets Gruesome 47. Fort Defiance 52. Shark River 53. The Lost Legion 57, etc.

Rawnsley, David (1909–). British art director (*49th Parallel, In Which We Serve, The Rake's Progress, I See a Dark Stranger*, etc). Inventor of the Independent Frame system, intended as a production economy; it caused constriction in practice and was quickly abandoned.

Rawsthorne, Alan (1905–1971). British composer.
Burma Victory 45. The Captive Heart 46. Uncle Silas 47. Saraband for Dead Lovers 48, etc.

Ray, Aldo (1926–) (Aldo da Re). Beefy American actor, in local politics before film career.
Saturday's Heroes 51. *The Marrying Kind* 51. Pat and Mike 52. Let's Do It Again 53. Miss Sadie Thompson 54. We're No Angels 55. The Gentle Sergeant 56. Men in War 57. God's Little Acre 58. The Naked and the Dead 58. The Siege of Pinchgut (GB) 58. The Day They Robbed the Bank of England (GB) 60. Johnny Nobody (GB) 61. Nightmare in the Sun 64. Sylvia 65. What Did You Do in the War, Daddy? 66. Dead Heat on a Merry-Go-Round 66. Welcome to Hard Times 67. Riot on Sunset Strip 67. The Power 67. The Green Berets 68. Man Without Mercy 69. And Hope to Die 72. Inside Out 75, etc.

Ray, Andrew (1939–). British juvenile lead, son of Ted Ray.
The Mudlark (debut) 50. The Yellow Balloon 52. Escapade 55. Woman in a Dressing-Gown 57. Serious Charge 59. Twice Round the Daffodils 62. The System 64. Great Expectations (TV) 75, etc.

Ray, Charles (1891–1943). American leading man of the silent screen, often in country boy roles.
SILENT FILMS: Bill Henry 19. The Old Swimming Hole 20. The Barnstormer 22. The Girl I Love 23. Sweet Adeline 23. The Courtship of Miles Standish (& p) 23. Vanity 25. Getting Gertie's Garter 27. The Garden of Eden 28, etc.
SOUND FILMS: Ladies Should Listen 34. By Your Leave 35. Just My Luck 37, etc.

Ray, Johnnie (1927–). American 'crying' singer of the fifties who played a leading role in *There's No Business Like Show Business* 54.

Ray, Man (1890–). American photographer, dadaist and surrealist, long resident in France; made a few strange films.
Retour à la Raison (wd) 23. Entr'acte (a) 24. L'Etoile de Mer (wd) 28. The Mystery of the Château of the Dice (wd) 29. Dreams that Money Can Buy (oa) 46, etc.

Ray, Nicholas (1911–) (Raymond N. Kienzle). American director, former writer and stage director. Acclaimed for his first film, he later seemed to lack a particular style.
□ *They Live by Night* 47. A Woman's Secret 49. Knock on Any Door 49. Born to be Bad 50. *In a Lonely Place* 50. Flying Leathernecks 51. On Dangerous Ground 51. The Lusty Men 52. Johnny Guitar 54. Run for Cover 55. *Rebel without a Cause* 55. Hot Blood 56. Bigger than Life 56. The True Story of Jesse James 57. Bitter Victory 57. Wind Across the Everglades 58. Party Girl 58. Savage Innocents 59. King of Kings 61. 55 Days at Peking 62. Dreams of Thirteen 76.

Ray, René (1912–) (Irene Creese). British actress, on stage from childhood; has often played downtrodden waifs.
Young Woodley 30. *The Passing of the Third Floor Back* 35. Crime over London 36. Farewell Again 37. *The Rat* 38. Bank Holiday 38. The Return of the Frog 39. They Made Me a Fugitive 47. If Winter Comes (US) 47. Women of Twilight 52. The Good Die Young 53. Vicious Circle 57, etc.

Ray, Satyajit (1921–). Indian director, famous

for the 'Apu' trilogy of a child growing up in modern India.
Pather Panchali 54. *The Unvanquished* (Aparajito) 56. The Music Room 58. *The World of Apu* 59. The Goddess 60. Kanchenjunga 62. The Adventures of Goopy and Bagha 68. The Adversary 71. Company Limited 72. Distant Thunder 74. The Middle Man 76, etc.

Ray, Ted (c. 1909–) (Charles Olden). British music-hall comedian and violinist who has been in occasional films.
Autobiography 1952: *Raising The Laughs*.
Elstree Calling 30. Radio Parade of 1935. A Ray of Sunshine 47. Meet Me Tonight 50. Escape by Night 52. My Wife's Family 54. Carry On, Teacher 59. Please Turn Over 60, etc.

Raye, Carol (1923–) (Kathleen Corkrey). Australian leading lady of British films of the forties.
Strawberry Roan 45. Spring Song 46. While I Live 48, etc.

Raye, Martha (1916–) (Maggie O'Reed). Wide-mouthed American comedienne and vocalist, popular on radio and TV.
Rhythm on the Range (debut) 36. Waikiki Wedding 37. Artists and Models 38. The Boys from Syracuse 40. Keep 'Em Flying 41. *Hellzapoppin* 42. Pin-Up Girl 43. Four Jills in a Jeep 44. *Monsieur Verdoux* 47. Jumbo 62. *Pufnstuf* 70, etc.
TV series: The Martha Raye Show 59. The Bugaloos 68. McMillan 76.

Raymond, Cyril (c. 1897–1973). British stage and screen actor often seen as the dull husband or professional man.
The Shadow 32. Mixed Doubles 33. The Tunnel 35. Dreaming Lips 37. Come On George 39. Brief Encounter 46. This was a Woman 47. Jack of Diamonds 48. Angels One Five 51. Lease of Life 53. Charley Moon 56, etc.

Raymond, Gary (1935–). British 'second lead'.
The Moonraker 58. *Look Back in Anger* 59. Suddenly Last Summer 59. The Millionairess 61. El Cid 61. Jason and the Argonauts 63. The Greatest Story Ever Told 65. Traitors' Gate 65. The Playboy of the Western World 66, etc.
TV series: The Rat Patrol 65.

Raymond, Gene (1908–) (Raymond Guion). American leading man of the thirties; was married to Jeanette MacDonald. On stage from childhood. Directed one film, *Million Dollar Weekend* (& a) 48.

Personal Maid (debut) 31. *Zoo in Budapest* 33. Flying Down to Rio 33. I Am Suzanne 34. Seven Keys to Baldpate 34. That Girl from Paris 37. Stolen Heaven 38. Mr and Mrs Smith 41. Smilin' Through 41. The Locket 46. Assigned to Danger 49. Hit the Deck 55. The Best Man 64, etc.

Raymond, Jack (1892–1953). British producer, mainly lightweight comedy films.
Sorrell and Son 34. Up for the Cup 34. The Frog 36. Splinters 37. The Rat 38. The Mind of Mr Reeder (& d) 39. You Will Remember 41. Worm's Eye View 51. Reluctant Heroes 52, many others.

Raymond, Paula (1923–) (Paula Ramona Wright). American leading lady, former model.
Devil's Doorway 49. Crisis 50. The Tall Target 51. The Beast from Twenty Thousand Fathoms 53. The Human Jungle 54. The Gun that Won the West 55. The Flight That Disappeared 62. Blood of Dracula's Castle 70, etc.

Reagan, Ronald (1911–). American leading man of the forties, former sports reporter. Went into politics and in 1966 was elected Governor of California; in 1976 narrowly missed the Republican presidential nomination.
Published autobiography 1965: *Where's the Rest of Me?*
Love is on the Air 37. Accidents Will Happen 38. Dark Victory 39. Hell's Kitchen 39. Brother Rat and a Baby 40. Santa Fé Trail 40. International Squadron 41. Nine Lives are Not Enough 41. *King's Row* 41. Juke Girl 42. *Desperate Journey* 42. This is the Army 43. Stallion Road 47. That Hagen Girl 47. The Voice of the Turtle 47. Night unto Night 48. John Loves Mary 49. The Hasty Heart (GB) 49. Louisa 50. Storm Warning 51. Hong Kong 52. Prisoner of War 54. Law and Order 54. Tennessee's Partner 55. Hellcats of the Navy 57. The Killers 64, etc.

Rear Window (US 1954). Alfred Hitchcock here set himself the task of making a thriller in which the action is all confined to one room— and the block of flats opposite at whose inhabitants the peeping-tom hero peers through his binoculars and uncovers a murder. Successful less because of Cornell Woolrich's story than because of John Michael Hayes' witty dialogue; Hitchcock's own talent seemed cramped. Photographed by Robert Burks, with music by Franz Waxman; with James Stewart, Grace Kelly.

Reason, Rex (1928–) (formerly known as **Bart Roberts**). American leading man, mainly in routine films.

Storm over Tibet 52. Salome 53. Yankee Pasha 54. This Island Earth 55. Raw Edge 56. Band of Angels 57. The Rawhide Trail 60, etc.
TV series: *The Roaring Twenties*.

Reason, Rhodes (1930–). American leading man, mainly in second features.
Crime against Joe 56. Jungle Heat 57. Yellowstone Kelly 59. King Kong Escapes (Jap.) 68, etc.
TV series: *White Hunter*.

Rebecca (US 1940). A splendid example of the cinema as a popular storyteller. From Daphne du Maurier's smash-hit novel of passion and mystery in a Cornish stately home, Hitchcock fashioned an impeccable film, with the help of a clever screenplay by Robert E. Sherwood and Joan Harrison, and a cast including Laurence Olivier, Joan Fontaine, Judith Anderson, Reginald Denny, George Sanders, Florence Bates, Gladys Cooper, C. Aubrey Smith and Nigel Bruce. Commercial film-making at its best. AA best film, best photography (George Barnes).

Rebecca of Sunnybrook Farm. The American children's classic by Kate Douglas Wiggin was filmed in 1917 by Marshall Neilan, with Mary Pickford; in 1932 by Alfred Santell, with Marian Nixon; and in 1938 (much changed) by Allan Dwan, with Shirley Temple.

Rebel without a Cause (US 1955). This story of teenage restlessness directed by Nicholas Ray and starring James Dean was felt to be of some significance because for the first time the hoodlums were shown as coming from rich, comfortable homes. Otherwise it was a straightforward star vehicle.

The Red Badge of Courage (US 1951). The story of the making of this film is told in hilarious detail by Lillian Ross in her book *Picture*, and it is a classic example of what happens to artistic intentions when the commercial element of film-making gets its teeth into them. The film as released did not do justice to Stephen Crane's civil war history, or to the box office; director John Huston had tired of the unhappy compromise, and all the viewer could salvage were some stirring battle scenes directed by Andrew Marton, with accomplished photography by Harold Rosson and music by Bronislau Kaper.

The Red Balloon (France 1956). A thirty-six minute fantasy written and directed by Albert Lamorisse, about a boy's pursuit of a balloon

through the streets of Paris. A uniquely charming and happy film which succeeds in a field the cinema should tackle more often.

Red Dust (US 1932). This Malayan rubber plantation melodrama is remembered for the electric teaming of Clark Gable and Jean Harlow, and for the scene in which Harlow takes a primitive shower. It was remade in 1939 as *Congo Maisie*, with Ann Sothern and John Carroll; and in 1954 Gable himself appeared opposite Ava Gardner in a lavish restyling under the title *Mogambo*.

Red Garters (US 1954). Only a minor musical, but it set out with fair success to stylize the western form, and if the pretty Technicolor sets hadn't got so monotonous it might have had more recognition. Michael Fessier's script was lively and pleasant, George Marshall's direction smooth, and the songs by Jay Livingston and Ray Evans very hummable. With Rosemary Clooney, Gene Barry, Jack Carson, Guy Mitchell.

Red Indians, it is generally thought, were always portrayed as villains on screen until *Broken Arrow* in 1950, when Jeff Chandler played Cochise. But in fact there were many silent films in which Indians were not only on the side of right but the leading figures in the story. In 1911 one finds titles like *An Indian Wife's Devotion, A Squaw's Love, Red-Wing's Gratitude*; *Ramona* (qv) had already been made once and was to survive three remakes; 1913 brought *Heart of an Indian* and *The Squaw Man*. Later there were versions of *In the Days of Buffalo Bill* 21, *The Vanishing American* 25, and *Redskin* 28. It seems to have been sound that made the Indians villainous, and kept them that way for twenty-two years.

After *Broken Arrow* there was a deluge of pro-Indian films. *Devil's Doorway, Across the Wide Missouri, The Savage, Arrowhead, The Big Sky, Apache, Taza—Son of Cochise, Chief Crazy Horse, Sitting Bull, White Feather, Navajo, Hiawatha*, all came within four years. There were even biopics of modern Indians: *The Outsider* (Ira Hayes) and *Jim Thorpe, All American*. In recent years the Indians have been slipping back into villainy: but the sixties brought *Flaming Star, Cheyenne Autumn, Tell them Willie Boy is Here, A Man called Horse, Flap, Little Big Man, The Stalking Moon*; and TV in 1966 boasted a series based on a Red Indian cop in New York (the name is *Hawk*) as well as comic Indians in *F Troop*; and Elvis Presley played a Red Indian hero in *Stay Away Joe*.

The Red Inn (France 1951). A direction-pointing black comedy which came somewhat ahead of its time. The script by Aurenche and Bost satirizes society, religion and everything else within sight in its nineteenth-century fable of two inn-keepers (Carette and Françoise Rosay) who murder travellers for money. A monk (Fernandel) gets one batch safely away, only to see their carriage topple over a precipice. Claude Autant-Lara directed.

The Red Shoes (GB 1948). Michael Powell and Emeric Pressburger always aimed high in their choice of subject, and here their aim was to give us the feel of the world of ballet: the backstage and private lives of those concerned in it. The detail remains fascinating, the colour evocative, the dancing superb; only the story is rather trite and lumpy. Moira Shearer made a hit as the tragic heroine, Anton Walbrook spat superbly as the impresario; Jack Cardiff's photography was near his best.

Redfield, William (1927–1976). American general purpose actor with long stage experience; former boy actor.
I Married a Woman 58. Fantastic Voyage 66. Duel at Diablo 66. A New Leaf 70. Death Wish 74, etc.

Redford, Robert (1936–). Blond, athletic American leading actor of the early seventies.
□ War Hunt 61. Situation Hopeless but not Serious 65. Inside Daisy Clover 65. *The Chase* 66. This Property is Condemned 66. Barefoot in the Park 67. Tell Them Willie Boy is Here 69. *Butch Cassidy and the Sundance Kid* 69. Downhill Racer 69. Little Fauss and Big Halsy 70. The Hot Rock 72. Jeremiah Johnson 72. *The Candidate* 72. The Way We Were 73. *The Sting* 73. The Great Gatsby 74. The Great Waldo Pepper 75. Three Days of the Condor 75. *All the President's Men* 76.

Redgrave, Corin (–). British supporting actor, son of Sir Michael Redgrave.
A Man for All Seasons 66. Charge of the Light Brigade 68. Oh What a Lovely War 69. David Copperfield 69. Von Richthofen and Brown 71, etc.

Redgrave, Lynn (1943–). British actress, daughter of Sir Michael Redgrave; has tended to play gauche comedy roles.
□ Tom Jones 63. Girl with Green Eyes 64. *Georgy Girl* 66. The Deadly Affair 67. Smashing Time 67. The Virgin Soldiers 69. Blood Kin 69. Killer from Yuma 71. Every Little Crook and Nanny 72. Everything You Always Wanted to Know about Sex 72. The National Health 73. The Happy Hooker 75. The Big Bus 76.

Redgrave, Sir Michael (1908–). Tall, distinguished British actor, former schoolmaster, on stage from 1934.
Biography 1956: *Michael Redgrave, Actor* by Richard Findlater.
Secret Agent 36. *The Lady Vanishes* 38. Climbing High 38. A Stolen Life 39. *The Stars Look Down* 39. *Kipps* 41. *Jeannie* 41. *Thunder Rock* 42. The Way to the Stars 45. *Dead of Night* 45. The Captive Heart 46. The Man Within 47. *Fame is the Spur* 47. Mourning Becomes Electra (US) 47. The Secret Beyond the Door (US) 48. *The Browning Version* 51. *The Importance of Being Earnest* 52. Oh Rosalinda 55. Confidential Report 55. *The Dam Busters* 55. Nineteen Eighty-Four 56. Time without Pity 57. *The Quiet American* 58. Law and Disorder 58. The Innocents 61. The Loneliness of the Long Distance Runner 63. Young Cassidy 64. The Hill 65. The Heroes of Telemark 65. Department K 67. Oh What a Lovely War 69. Goodbye Mr Chips 69. The Battle of Britain 69. David Copperfield 69. Connecting Rooms 69. Goodbye Gemini 70. Nicholas and Alexandra 71. The Go-Between 71, etc.

Redgrave, Vanessa (1937–). British leading lady of the sixties, daughter of Sir Michael Redgrave; as well known for her espousal of causes as for her acting.
□ Behind the Mask 58. *Morgan* 66. Red and Blue 66. Sailor from Gibraltar 66. A Man for all Seasons (uncredited) 66. Blow Up 66. *Camelot* 67. The Charge of the Light Brigade 68. *Isadora* 68. A Quiet Place in the Country (It.) 68. Dropout (It.) 69. Vacation (It.) 69. The Seagull 69. Oh What a Lovely War 69. The Trojan Women 71. The Devils 71. *Mary Queen of Scots* 72. Murder on the Orient Express 74. Out of Season 75. The Seven Per Cent Solution 76. Julia 77.

Redman, Joyce (1918–). Irish stage actress whose most memorable film role was in the eating scene in *Tom Jones* 63.

Redmond, Liam (1913–). Irish character actor, an Abbey player.
I See a Dark Stranger 45. Captain Boycott 48. High Treason 51. The Gentle Gunman 52. The Divided Heart 54. Jacqueline 56. Night of the Demon 57. The Boy and the Bridge 59. The Ghost and Mr Chicken (US) 65. Tobruk (US) 66. The Twenty-Fifth Hour 66. The Last Safari 67, etc.

Redmond, Moira (–   ). British actress.
Doctor in Love 58. *Nightmare* 62. Jigsaw 62.
The Limbo Line 66, etc.

reduction print: one optically reduced from
35mm to 16mm.

Reece, Brian (1913–1962). British light actor
whose success was mainly on stage.
A Case for PC 49 51. Fast and Loose 54. Orders
are Orders 55. Carry on Admiral 58, etc.

Reed, Donna (1921–) (Donna Mullenger).
American leading lady of the forties, later star of
long-running TV series *The Donna Reed Show*.
Won screen test after a beauty contest while still
at college.
The Getaway (debut) 41. Shadow of the Thin
Man 42. The Courtship of Andy Hardy 42.
Calling Dr Gillespie 42. The Human Comedy
43. See Here, Private Hargrove 44. The Picture
of Dorian Gray 44. It's a Wonderful Life 46.
Green Dolphin Street 47. Chicago Deadline 49.
From Here to Eternity (AA) 53. The Last Time I
Saw Paris 55. Ransom 56. Backlash 56. The
Benny Goodman Story 56. Beyond Mombasa
57, etc.

Reed, Maxwell (1920–). Brooding Irish
leading man in British films from 1946, after
repertory experience.
The Years Between 46. Daybreak 47. *The
Brothers* 48. Holiday Camp 48. The Dark Man
49. The Square Ring 53. Before I Wake 56.
Notorious Landlady 62. Picture Mommy Dead
66, etc.

Reed, Michael (1929–). British
cinematographer.
October Moth 60. Linda 61. The Gorgon 64.
Dracula Prince of Darkness 66. On Her
Majesty's Secret Service 69. The Mackenzie
Break 71. The Groundstar Conspiracy 73. The
Hireling 73. Galileo 75. Shout at the Devil 76,
etc.

Reed, Oliver (1938–). Burly British leading
man, usually in sullen roles.
The Rebel 60. No Love for Johnnie 61. Curse of
the Werewolf 62. Pirates of Blood River 62. *The
Damned* 62. Paranoic 63. *The System* 64. The
Scarlet Blade 64. The Party's Over 64. The
Brigand of Kandahar 65. *The Trap* 66. The
Shuttered Room 66. *The Jokers* 66. I'll Never
Forget Whatshisname 67. The Assassination
Bureau 68. Oliver! 68. Hannibal Brooks 68.
Women in Love 69. Take a Girl Like You 69.
The Lady in the Car 70. The Devils 71. The
Hunting Party 71. Z.P.G. 72. Sitting Target 72.

Triple Echo 72. Days of Fury 73. The Three
Musketeers 73. The Four Musketeers 74. And
Then There Were None 74. Royal Flash 74.
Tommy 75. The Sellout 75. Great Scout and
Cathouse Thursday 76. Burnt Offerings 76. The
Prince and the Pauper 77, etc.

Reed, Philip (1908–). American leading man
with long stage experience.
Female 34. Last of the Mohicans 36. Aloma of
the South Seas 41. Old Acquaintance 44. I Cover
Big Town 47. Unknown Island 50. The Tattered
Dress 57. Harem Scarem 67, etc.

Reed, Sir Carol (1906–1976). Distinguished
British director who after a peak in the late forties
seemed to lose his way; his infrequent later films,
though always civilized, were generally
disappointing.
□ Midshipman Easy 34. Laburnum Grove 36.
Talk of the Devil 36. Who's Your Lady Friend?
37. *Bank Holiday* 38. Penny Paradise 38.
Climbing High 38. A Girl Must Live 39. *The
Stars Look Down* 39. *Night Train to Munich* 40.
The Girl in the News 40. *Kipps* 41. The Young
Mr Pitt 41. *The Way Ahead* 44. The True Glory
(co-d) 45. *Odd Man Out* 46. *The Fallen Idol* 48.
The Third Man 49. *An Outcast of the Islands* 51.
The Man Between 53. A Kid for Two Farthings
55. Trapeze 56. The Key 58. Our Man in
Havana 59. The Running Man 63. The Agony
and the Ecstasy 65. *Oliver!* (AA) 68. Flap 70.
Follow Me 72.

reel. A loose term generally taken to mean
1,000 feet of 35mm film, i.e. the amount which
would fit on to a reel of the old-fashioned kind,
running about ten minutes. Thus short films were
spoken of as two-reelers, three-reelers, etc., and
charged accordingly. But modern 35mm
projector spools will take 2,000 feet and
sometimes 3,000 feet, so the term is slowly falling
into disuse ... especially as 16mm projectors
have always taken spools of either 400, 800 or
1,600 feet.

Rees, Angharad (1949–). Welsh leading
lady.
Hands of the Ripper 72. Under Milk Wood 72.
The Love Ban 73. Moments 74, etc.

Reese, Tom (1930–). American character
actor, a notable 'heavy'.
Flaming Star 60. Marines Let's Go 61. Forty
Pounds of Trouble 62. Murderers' Row 66, etc.

Reeve, Ada (1874–1966). British character
actress with long stage career.
Autobiography 1964: *Take It for a Fact*.

They Came to a City 44. When the Bough Breaks 47. Night and the City 50. Eye Witness 56, etc.

Reeve, Geoffrey (1932–). British director. Puppet on a Chain 71. Caravan to Vaccares 74.

Reeves, George (1914–1959) (George Besselo). American leading man.
Gone with the Wind (debut) 39. Strawberry Blonde 41. Blood and Sand 42. Bar 20 44. Jungle Jim 49. Samson and Delilah 50. Sir Galahad (serial) 50. From Here to Eternity 53.
TV series: Superman 51.

Reeves, Kynaston (1893–1971). British character actor of stage and screen, often seen as academic.
The Lodger 32. The Housemaster 38. The Prime Minister 40. Vice Versa 48. The Guinea Pig 49. The Mudlark 50. Top of the Form 53. Brothers in Law 57. School for Scoundrels 60, many others.

Reeves, Michael (1944–1969). British director whose promising career barely got started.
□ Sister of Satan (Revenge of the Blood Beast) (It.) 65. The Sorcerers 67. Witchfinder General 68.

Reeves, Steve (1926–). American actor, formerly 'Mr World' and 'Mr Universe'; found stardom from 1953 in Italian muscleman spectacles.
□ Athena 54. The Labours of Hercules 57. Hercules and the Queen of Sheba 58. Goliath and the Barbarians 59. The Giant of Marathon 59. The White Devil 59. Thief of Baghdad 59. Morgan the Pirate 60. The Last Days of Pompeii 61. Romulus and Remus 61. The War of Troy 61. The Legend of Enea 62. Son of Spartacus 62. Sandokan 63. Vivo per la Tua Morte 68.

Reggiani, Serge (1922–). Slightly-built French-Italian actor with stage experience.
Les Portes de la Nuit 46. Manon 48. Les Amants de Vérone 48. La Ronde 50. Secret People (GB) 51. *Casque d'Or* 51. The Wicked Go to Hell 55. Les Misérables 57. Marie Octobre 58. Paris Blues 60. The Leopard 63. The 25th Hour 67. Les Aventuriers 67. Day of the Owl (It.) 68, etc.

La Règle Du Jeu (France 1939). A satire on the decadence of the pre-1939 French aristocracy, directed by Jean Renoir from a script by himself and Carl Koch. Only a butchered version was released after his flight to America, and not until 1958 was the original

version pieced together. Not an easy film for any but Frenchmen to understand fully; but well worth the effort if only to appreciate its curious mixture of comedy and farce. Photographed by Claude Renoir; with Marcel Dalio, Nora Gregor and Jean Renoir himself.

Reichenbach, François (1922–). French documentarist with an ironic viewpoint.
L'Amérique Insolite 59. Un Coeur Gros Comme Ça 61. Les Amoureux du France 64. Hollywood through a Keyhole 66. Love of Life (co-d) 68, etc.

Reicher, Frank (1875–1965). German-born character actor, long in Hollywood.
Her Man O' War 26. Mata Hari 32. *King Kong* 33. Kind Lady 36. Anthony Adverse 36. Lancer Spy 38. They Dare Not Love 41. House of Frankenstein 45. The Mummy's Ghost 46. The Secret Life of Walter Mitty 47. Samson and Delilah 50, many others.
AS DIRECTOR: The Eternal Mother 17. Behind Masks 21. Wise Husbands 21, etc.

Reid, Alastair (1939–). British director.
□ Baby Love 69. The Night Digger 71. Something to Hide 72.

Reid, Beryl (1918–). British revue comedienne who has latterly weathered a transition to character acting.
The Belles of St Trinian's 54. The Extra Day 56. The Dock Brief 62. Star! 68. Inspector Clouseau 68. The Assassination Bureau 68. *The Killing of Sister George* (her stage role) (US) 68. Entertaining Mr Sloane 70. The Beast in the Cellar 71. Dr Phibes Rises Again 72. Psychomania 72. Father Dear Father 73. No Sex Please We're British 73. Joseph Andrews 76, etc.

Reod, Carl Benton (1894–1973). American character actor with stage career before settling in Hollywood.
The Little Foxes 41. In a Lonely Place 50. Convicted 50. The Great Caruso 51. Lorna Doone 51. Carbine Williams 52. The Egyptian 54. The Left Hand of God 55. The Gallant Hours 59, etc.
TV series: Amos Burke—Secret Agent 65.

Reid, Kate (–). Canadian actress.
This Property is Condemned 66. The Andromeda Strain 71.
TV series: Jalna 72.

Reid, Wallace (1890–1923). American leading man of the silent screen.

The Deerslayer 11. The Birth of a Nation 14. The Love Mask 16. House of Silence 18. The Dancing Fool 20. The Affairs of Anatol 21. The Ghost Breaker 22. Adam's Rib 23, many others.

reincarnation has seldom been seriously tackled in the cinema: *The Search for Bridey Murphy*, *I've Lived Before* and *The Reincarnation of Peter Proud* are almost the only examples. Many characters of farce and melodrama have *thought* they were reincarnated, including the hero of *She* and heroine of *The Vengeance of She*. The real thing happened to Oliver Hardy in *The Flying Deuces* (he came back as a horse); to a dog in *You Never Can Tell* (he came back as Dick Powell); and to the luckless heroine of *The Bride and the Beast*, who found that in a former existence she had been a gorilla. Reincarnation was also the basis of *Here Comes Mr Jordan*, and of *The Mummy*. A man came back as Debbie Reynolds in *Goodbye Charlie*, and in *Quest for Love* there were parallel love stories two centuries apart. In 1968 a version was made of Elmer Rice's *The Adding Machine*, with its celestial laundry for souls; and in 1970 there was even a musical on the subject, *On a Clear Day You Can See Forever*.

Reiner, Carl (1922–). Balding, genial American comedy writer and actor.
AS ACTOR: Happy Anniversary 59. The Gazebo 59. Gidget Goes Hawaiian 61. *It's a Mad Mad Mad Mad World* 63. The Art of Love 65. The Russians are Coming 66. A Guide for the Married Man 67. The Comic 69. Heaven Help Us (TV series) 76, etc.
AS WRITER: The Thrill of It All 63. The Art of Love 65. Enter Laughing 67. The Comic 69. Also TV's *The Dick Van Dyke Show* 61–66.
AS DIRECTOR: Enter Laughing 67. The Comic 69. Where's Poppa? 70, etc.

Reinhardt, Gottfried (1911–). Austrian producer, son of theatrical producer Max Reinhardt. Went to US with his father and became assistant to Walter Wanger. Has since produced and occasionally directed.
The Great Waltz (script) 37. Comrade X (p) 40. Two-Faced Woman (p) 41. Command Decision (p) 48. The Red Badge of Courage (p) 51. Invitation (d) 52. The Story of Three Loves (d) 53. Betrayed (d) 54. The Good Soldier Schweik (p) 59. Town without Pity (pd) 61. Situation Hopeless But Not Serious (pd) 65, etc.

Reinhardt, Max (1873–1943). Austrian theatrical producer of great pageants. His only screen direction (with William Dieterle) was *A Midsummer Night's Dream* 35, from his stage production.

Reiniger, Lotte (1899–). German animator, well-known for her silhouette cartoons.
The Adventures of Prince Achmed 26. Dr Dolittle (series) 28. Carmen 33. Papageno 35. The Brave Little Tailor 55, etc.

Reis, Irving (1906–1953). American director, with radio experience.
□ One Crowded Night 40. I'm Still Alive 40. Weekend for Three 41. A Date with the Falcon 41. The Gay Falcon 41. The Falcon Takes Over 42. The Big Street 43. Hitler's Children 43. Crack Up 46. *The Bachelor and the Bobby-soxer* 47. *Enchantment* 48. All My Sons 48. Roseanna McCoy 49. Dancing in the Dark 49. Three Husbands 50. New Mexico 51. The Fourposter 52.

Reisch, Walter (1900–). Austrian writer who in the thirties came to Britain, then Hollywood.
Men Are Not Gods (& d) 36. Ninotchka 39. Comrade X 40. The Heavenly Body 43. Song of Scheherezade (& d) 46. Titanic 52. The Girl in the Red Velvet Swing 55. Journey to the Centre of the Earth 59, etc.

Reisner, Allen (–). American director, from TV.
□ St Louis Blues 58. All Mine to Give 56.

Reisz, Karel (1926–). Czech director, in Britain from childhood. Former film critic.
□ We are the Lambeth Boys 58. *Saturday Night and Sunday Morning* 60. Night Must Fall 63. This Sporting Life (p only) 63. *Morgan: A Suitable Case for Treatment* 66. Isadora 68. The Gambler 74.

rejuvenation is not a theme the cinema has frequently explored. *She* tried it several times with unhappy results, as did Laurel and Hardy in *Dirty Work* (Olly came back as a chimpanzee). *The Man in Half Moon Street* and *Countess Dracula* both kept young on the blood of others; *Dorian Gray* did it by keeping a picture of himself in the attic. Most successful were *Lost Horizon*'s inhabitants of Shangri-La, but once the cold winds of the outside world blew they were done for. Rock Hudson had worse luck in *Seconds*.

religion has inspired film-makers from the beginning—as a commercial trump card. In the early years of the century it was the Italians who produced vast semi-biblical spectacles like *Quo Vadis* and *Cabiria*, but Hollywood was not slow to catch on, and producers soon found that religious shorts gave them extra prestige. There were several versions of *From the Manger to the Cross*; Griffith, in *Judith of Bethulia* and *Intolerance*, contributed his share; *Ben Hur* was the biggest spectacular of all; but it was Cecil B. de Mille in the twenties who brought the Bible to full commercial flower with *The Ten Commandments* and *King of Kings*. (His 1932 *The Sign of the Cross*, 1950 *Samson and Delilah* and 1956 remake of *The Ten Commandments* show that for him at least time continued to stand still.) In 1929, though *Noah's Ark* was spectacle pure and simple, Vidor's *Hallelujah* at least partially transmitted Negro religious fervour. In the thirties Hollywood was seeking fresh ways to combine religion with sentiment or spectacle, in *The Cradle Song, Dante's Inferno, The Garden of Allah, The Green Light* and *Boy's Town*. One result was a new characterization of priests (qv) as jolly good fellows: stars like Spencer Tracy and Pat O'Brien were eager to play them. Yet none had the quiet dignity of Rex Ingram as De Lawd in *Green Pastures*, a Negro version of the Scriptures.

The war naturally brought a religious revival. Every film set in England seemed to end with a service in a bombed church, and religious figures became big time in films like *The Song of Bernadette, Going My Way, The Keys of the Kingdom* and *The Bells of St Mary's*. Savage war films masqueraded under such titles as *God Is My Co-Pilot* and *A Wing and a Prayer*. And heaven was used as a background for lighthearted fantasy films about death and judgement day, such as *Here Comes Mr Jordan, Heaven Can Wait*, and *The Horn Blows at Midnight*. The only film of this period to question religion at all was the British *Major Barbara*. What price salvation now?

In the cynical post-war years religion was at a low ebb. An expensive *Joan of Arc* in 1948 failed disastrously, and an attempt to bring God into our everyday life, *The Next Voice You Hear*, fared no better. A sincere performance by Robert Donat could not bring people to see *Lease of Life*. Indeed, the only religious films to break even at the box office were those with a direct Roman Catholic appeal, such as *Monsieur Vincent* and *The Miracle of Fatima*. True religion, to Hollywood, was out, and the Bible became once more a source book for a string of tawdry commercial epics: *Quo Vadis, Salome, The Prodigal, The Robe*, a remake of *Ben Hur, Barabbas, The Silver Chalice, Sodom and Gomorrah* and many cut-rate dubbed Italian spectacles of a similar kind (most with Hollywood stars). Occasionally a spark of sincerity would flash through, as in the otherwise

dull *David and Bathsheba*; while small independent companies could produce interesting films like *The First Legion*. Towards the end of the fifties there were occasional attempts to see religion afresh: *A Man Called Peter, The Nun's Story, Inn of the Sixth Happiness, Whistle Down the Wind*. Otto Preminger, despite a 1957 failure with *Saint Joan*, tried again in 1963 with *The Cardinal*. In 1965 George Stevens unveiled *The Greatest Story Ever Told*, a tepid life of Jesus which found little box office favour, being overtaken in some quarters by Pasolini's *The Gospel According to St Matthew*. 1966 brought the long-promised Italian-American epic known as *The Bible*: in fact it dealt only with the Book of Genesis, and that at such a dull pace and inordinate length that it is doubtful whether sequels will be called for. 1969 offered a drama of modern popes, *The Shoes of the Fisherman*, but it died. The most fashionable film interpretations of religion in the early seventies were the pop operas exemplified by *Godspell* and *Jesus Christ Superstar*; but in 1977 Lew Grade's mammoth six-hour *Jesus of Nazareth*, directed by Franco Zeffirelli, achieved record viewing figures and pointed to a benighted world's requirement to believe in *something*.

Relph, George (1888–1960). British character actor mainly seen on stage.
Nicholas Nickleby 47. I Believe in You 52. *The Titfield Thunderbolt* (leading role as the vicar) 53. Doctor at Large 57. Davy 57, etc.

Relph, Michael (1915–). British producer-director, son of George Relph. Former art director and production designer; from 1947 to 1969 he worked almost exclusively with Basil Dearden, usually producing while Dearden directed.
The Captive Heart 46. Frieda 47. Saraband for Dead Lovers 48. *The Blue Lamp* 50. I Believe in You (& co-w) 52. The Rainbow Jacket 54. Davy (d) 57. Rockets Galore (d) 57. Violent Playground 58. Sapphire 59. *The League of Gentlemen* 59. *Victim* 61. Life for Ruth 62. The Mind Benders 63. Woman of Straw 63. Masquerade 65. The Assassination Bureau 68, etc.

Remarque, Erich Maria (1898–1970). German novelist.
All Quiet on the Western Front 30. The Road Back 37. Three Comrades 38. So Ends Our Night 41. Arch of Triumph 48. A Time to Love and a Time to Die (& a) 57, etc.

Rembrandt (GB 1937). Perhaps the most satisfying film ever produced about a painter, its hypnotic effect stemming from Charles Laughton's brilliant performance. Script by Carl Zuckmayer, direction by Alexander Korda, design by Vincent Korda, photography by Georges Perinal.

Remick, Lee (1935–). American leading lady with stage and TV experience.
A Face in the Crowd (film debut) 57. The Long Hot Summer 58. *Anatomy of a Murder* 59. Sanctuary 61. Experiment in Terror 62. *Days of Wine and Roses* 63. The Wheeler Dealers 64. Baby the Rain Must Fall 65. The Hallelujah Trail 65. No Way to Treat a Lady 68. A Severed Head 70. Loot 70. Sometimes a Great Notion 72. A Delicate Balance 73. QB VII 74. The Blue Knight (TV) 74. Hennessy 75. *Jennie* (TV) 75. The Omen 76, etc.

Renaldo, Duncan (1904–) (Renault Renaldo Duncan). American actor and painter with varied experience. In many films from *Trader Horn* 30 to *For Whom the Bell Tolls* 42; later more famous as The Cisco Kid in a series of second feature westerns (1945–50). Directed some films in the twenties.

Rennahan, Ray (1896–). American cinematographer, in Hollywood from 1917; an expert on colour.
Fanny Foley Herself 31. *The Mystery of the Wax Museum* 33. *Becky Sharp* 35. *Wings of the Morning* 37. *Gone with the Wind* (co-ph) (AA) 39. *The Blue Bird* 40. Down Argentine Way 40. *Blood and Sand* (co-ph) (AA) 42. *For Whom the Bell Tolls* 43. Belle of the Yukon 44. The Perils of Pauline 47. The Paleface 48. A Yankee at King Arthur's Court 49. Arrowhead 53. Terror in a Texas Town 58, many others.

Rennie, James (1890–1965). American hero of the twenties.
Remodelling Her Husband 20. The Dust Flower 22. His Children's Children 23. Clothes Make the Pirate 25. The Girl of the Golden West 30. Illicit 31, etc.

Rennie, Michael (1909–1971). Lean, good-looking British leading man best known as TV's *The Third Man*. Varied experience before going into repertory and film stand-in work.
Secret Agent 36. The Divorce of Lady X 38. Dangerous Moonlight 40. Ships with Wings 41. I'll be Your Sweetheart 45. *The Wicked Lady* 45. The Root of All Evil 47. Idol of Paris 48. The Black Rose 50; Then to US; Five Fingers 52. Les Misérables 52. *The Day the Earth Stood Still* 52. The Robe 53. Désirée 54. The Rains of Ranchipur 55. Island in the Sun 56. Omar

Khayyam 57. Third Man on the Mountain 59. *The Lost World* 60. Mary, Mary 63. Ride beyond Vengeance 65. The Power 67. Hotel. The Devil's Brigade 68. The Battle of El Alemain (as Montgomery) 68. Subterfuge 69, etc.

Renoir, Claude (1914–). French cinematographer.
Toni 34. *Une Partie de Campagne* 36. La Règle du Jeu 39. Monsieur Vincent 47. *The River* 51. The Green Glove 52. *The Golden Coach* 53. *Eléna et les Hommes* 55. Crime and Punishment 56. The Witches of Salem 56. Les Tricheurs 58. *Blood and Roses* 60. Lafayette 61. Circus World 64. The Game is Over 66. Barbarella 68. The Madwoman of Chaillot (co-ph) 69. The Horsemen 71. Paul and Michelle 74. The Spy Who Loved Me 77, many others.

Renoir, Jean (1894–). Distinguished French director, son of painter Auguste Renoir, brother of Pierre Renoir. Stage experience in productions of his own plays.
Autobiography 1973: *My Life and My Films*.
La Fille de L'Eau 24. Nana 26. Charleston 27. The Little Match-Seller 28. *Le Chienne* 31. *Boudu Sauvé des Eaux* 32. Toni 34. Madame Bovary 34. *Le Crime de Monsieur Lange* 35. *Les Bas Fonds* 36. *Une Partie de Campagne* 36. *La Grande Illusion* 37. *La Marseillaise* 38. *La Bête Humaine* 38. *La Règle de Jeu* (& a) 39; To US; Swamp Water 41. This Land Is Mine 43. *The Southerner* 44. Diary of a Chambermaid 45. The Woman on the Beach 47; Back to Europe; The River 51. The Golden Coach 53. French Cancan 55. Eléna et les Hommes 56. Lunch on the Grass 59. The Vanishing Corporal 61. C'est la Revolution 67. Le Petit Theatre de Jean Renoir 69, etc.

Renoir, Pierre (1885–1952). French character actor, brother of Jean Renoir.
Madame Bovary 34. La Marseillaise 38. Les Enfants du Paradis 44. Doctor Knock 50, many others.

Renzi, Eva (1944–). German leading lady in international films.
Funeral in Berlin 66. The Pink Jungle 68. Beiss Mich Liebling 70, etc.

reporters in American films have since the beginning of the sound era been pictured as trench-coated, trilby-hatted, good-looking guys with a smart line in wisecracks. Among the outstanding examples of this tradition are Pat O'Brien in *The Front Page*, Robert Williams in

Platinum Blonde, Clark Gable in *It Happened One Night* and *Teacher's Pet*, Fredric March in *Nothing Sacred*, Lee Tracy in *Doctor X*, Joel McCrea in *Foreign Correspondent*, David Janssen in *The Green Berets*, James Stewart in *The Philadelphia Story*, Lynne Overman in *Roxie Hart*, Gene Kelly in *Inherit the Wind*; while on the distaff side one can't overlook Glenda Farrell in *The Mystery of the Wax Museum*, Bette Davis in *Front Page Woman*, Jean Arthur in *Mr Deeds Goes to Town*, Rosalind Russell in *His Girl Friday* or Barbara Stanwyck in *Meet John Doe*. Presented somewhat more realistically were William Alland in *Citizen Kane*, James Stewart in *Call Northside 777*, Burgess Meredith as Ernie Pyle in *The Story of G.I. Joe*, Kirk Douglas in *Ace in the Hole*, and Arthur Kennedy in *Lawrence of Arabia*. British films have used their newshawks more flippantly, especially in the case of *This Man Is News* with Barry K. Barnes and *A Run for Your Money* with Alec Guinness. Just as well; for Edward Judd in *The Day the Earth Caught Fire*, Jack Hawkins in *Front Page Story*, Sidney James in *Quatermass II* and Norman Wooland in *All Over the Town* were a pretty dull lot, and Colin Gordon's imitation of the American model in *Escapade* was hardly convincing. Television series, of course, have found the reporter a convenient peg, as in the British *Deadline Midnight* and the American *Saints and Sinners* and *The Reporter*.

Republic Pictures Corporation. A small Hollywood production and distribution company founded in 1935 by a former tobacco executive named Herbert J. Yates (qv) who had spent some years building up a film laboratory. Republic continued as a one-man concern, producing innumerable competently-made second feature westerns and melodramas with such stars as Roy Rogers, Vera Hruba Ralston (Yates' wife), John Carroll, Constance Moore. The studio also churned out the majority of Hollywood's serials. Very occasionally there would be a major production such as *Rio Grande* or *The Quiet Man*. Production stopped in the mid-fifties, when 'bread and butter' pictures were no longer needed, and the company's interests moved into TV.

Repulsion (GB 1965). A curious film setting down in detail the horrifying case history of a homicidal girl repelled by sex. Shot by Roman Polanski almost entirely in a London flat, the film has clever cinematic shock-effects but little ear for dialogue. With Catherine Deneuve.

Rescher, Gayne (–). American cinematographer.
Rachel Rachel 68. John and Mary 69, etc.

Resnais, Alain (1922–). Controversial French director, former editor.
☐ Statues Also Die 51. Nuit et Brouillard (short) 55. Toute la Memoire du Monde 56. *Hiroshima Mon Amour* 59. *Last Year at Marienbad* 61. Muriel 62. The War is Over 66. Je n'Aime, Je t'Aime 69. Stavisky 74, etc.

Rettig, Tommy (1941–). American boy actor of the fifties.
Panic in the Streets 50. The Five Thousand Fingers of Dr T 53. The Egyptian 54. The Last Wagon 56. At Gunpoint 57, etc.
TV series: Lassie.

Revere, Anne (1903–). American character actress, mainly on stage.
Double Door 34. The Devil Commands 41. The Gay Sisters 42. *The Song of Bernadette* 43. The Keys of the Kingdom 44. *National Velvet* (AA) 45. Dragonwyck 46. Body and Soul 47. *Gentleman's Agreement* 48. A Place in the Sun 51. Macho Callahan 70, etc.

Revill, Clive (1930–). New Zealander in Britain playing mainly comic character roles.
Bunny Lake is Missing 65. Modesty Blaise 66. A Fine Madness (US) 66. The Double Man 66. Fathom 67. Nobody Runs Forever 68. A Severed Head 70. Avanti 72. The Legend of Hell House 73. The Black Windmill 74. One of Our Dinosaurs Is Missing 75, etc.

Reville, Alma (1900–). British screenwriter, married to Alfred Hitchcock; worked on many of his films.
The Ring 27. Rich and Strange 32. The Thirty-Nine Steps 35. Secret Agent 36. Sabotage 37. Young and Innocent 37. The Lady Vanishes 38. Suspicion 41. Shadow of a Doubt 43. The Paradine Case 47. Stage Fright 50, etc.

Rey, Alejandro (–). Mexican actor in American TV and films.
The Wild Pack 72. The Stepmother 73. Mr Majestyk 74. Breakout 75, many others.

Rey, Fernando (1915–) (Fernando Arambillet). Suave Spanish actor in international films, a favourite of Luis Buñuel.
Welcome Mr Marshall 52. The Adventurers 70. The French Connection 72. The Discreet Charm of the Bourgeoisie 72. French Connection II 75, many others.

Reynolds, Adeline de Walt (1862–1961). American character actress with long stage experience; for many years Hollywood's oldest bit player.
Come Live with Me (film debut) 41. The Human Comedy 43. Going My Way 44. A Tree Grows in Brooklyn 45. The Girl from Manhattan 48. Lydia Bailey 52. Witness to Murder 54, etc.

Reynolds, Burt (1936–). Lithe, virile American leading man who after years in television became a 'bankable' box office star of the early seventies.
Angel Baby 61. Armored Command 61. Operation CIA 65. Navajo Joe 67. Shark 68. Impasse 68. Skullduggery 69. Sam Whiskey 69. 100 Rifles 69. Fuzz 72. *Deliverance* 72. Shamus 72. White Lightning 73. The Man Who Loved Cat Dancing 73. The Longest Yard 74. WW and the Dixie Dancekings 75. At Long Last Love 75. Hustle 76. Lucky Lady 76. Gator (& d) 76. Nickelodeon 76, etc.
TV series: Riverboat 59–60. Hawk 67. Dan August 70.

Reynolds, Debbie (1932–) (Mary Frances Reynolds). Petite, vivacious American leading lady of fifties musicals; later a pleasing comedienne.
□ June Bride 48. The Daughter of Rosie O'Grady 50. Three Little Words 50. Two Weeks with Love 50. Mr Imperium 51. *Singin' in the Rain* 52. Skirts Ahoy 52. I Love Melvin 53. The Affairs of Dobie Gillis 53. Give a Girl a Break 53. *Susan Slept Here* 54. Athena 54. Hit the Deck 55. The Tender Trap 55. The Catered Affair 56. Bundle of Joy 56. Meet Me in Las Vegas 56. Tammy and the Bachelor 57. This Happy Feeling 58. The Mating Game 59. Say One for Me 59. It Started with a Kiss 59. The Gazebo 59. The Rat Race 60. Pépé 60. The Pleasure of His Company 61. The Second Time Around 61. How the West was Won 62. My Six Loves 63. Mary Mary 63. *The Unsinkable Molly Brown* 64. Goodbye Charlie 64. The Singing Nun 66. Divorce American Style 67. How Sweet It Is 68. *What's the Matter with Helen?* 71. Charlotte's Web (voice only) 72.
TV series: *Debbie* 69.

Reynolds, Joyce (1924–). Vivacious American leading lady of the forties, usually in teenage roles.
George Washington Slept Here 42. Janie 44. Always Together 48. Dangerous Inheritance 50, etc.

Reynolds, Marjorie (1921–) (Marjorie Goodspeed). American leading lady of the forties. Former child actress.

Up in the Air 40. Holiday Inn 42. Star Spangled Rhythm 43. Ministry of Fear 43. Dixie 43. Three is a Family 44. Bring on the Girls 45. Meet Me on Broadway 46. Heaven Only Knows 47. Home Town Story 51. The Great Jewel Robber 51. The Silent Witness 54, etc.
TV series: The Life of Riley 52–57. Our Man Higgins 62.

Reynolds, Peter (1926–1975) (Peter Horrocks). British light character actor, given to shifty roles.
The Captive Heart 46. Guilt is My Shadow 49. Smart Alec 50. Four Days 51. The Last Page 52. Devil Girl from Mars 54. You Can't Escape 55. The Delavine Affair 56. Shake Hands with the Devil 59. West Eleven 63. Nobody Runs Forever 68, etc.

Reynolds, Sheldon (1923–). American radio and TV writer who wrote, produced and directed two films.
□ Foreign Intrigue 56. Assignment to Kill 68.

Rhodes, Erik (1906–). American comic actor from the musical comedy stage, best remembered as the excitable Italian in two Astaire-Rogers films, *The Gay Divorcee* 34 and *Top Hat* 35. ('Your wife is safe with Tonetti—he prefers spaghetti.')
One Rainy Afternoon 36. *Criminal Lawyer* 37. Woman Chases Man 37. Dramatic School 38. On Your Toes 39, etc.

Rhodes, Marjorie (1902–). Homely British character actress, on stage from 1920; usually plays warm-hearted mums, nosey neighbours, etc.
Poison Pen (debut) 39. *Love on the Dole* 40. World of Plenty 41. *When We are Married* 43. Uncle Silas 47. *The Cure for Love* 50. Those People Next Door 53. Hell Drivers 58. Watch It, Sailor 62. *The Family Way* 66. Mrs Brown You've Got a Lovely Daughter 68. Hands of the Ripper 71, many others.

Rhue, Madlyn (1934–). American supporting actress.
Operation Petticoat 59. Escape from Zahrain 62. It's a Mad Mad Mad Mad World 63. He Rides Tall 64. Stand Up and Be Counted 72, etc.
TV series: Bracken's World 69. Executive Suite 76.

Rice, Elmer (1892–1967) (Elmer Reizenstern). American playwright. Works filmed include *Street Scene, The Adding Machine, Dream Girl* and *Counsellor at Law.*

Rice, Florence (1907–1974). American leading lady of the late thirties, always in sweet-tempered roles.
The Best Man Wins 34. Sweethearts 39. Miracles for Sale 39. *At the Circus* 39. Fighting Marshal 41. The Ghost and the Guest 43, etc.

Rice, Joan (1930–) British leading lady, former waitress, briefly popular in the fifties.
Blackmailed 50. One Wild Oat 51. The Story of Robin Hood and His Merrie Men 52. A Day to Remember 54. His Majesty O'Keefe (US) 55. One Good Turn 56. Payroll 61. Horror of Frankenstein 70, etc.

Rich, David Lowell (c. 1923–). American director, from TV.
Senior Prom 58. Hey Boy, Hey Girl 59. Have Rocket Will Travel 59. Madame X 66. The Plainsman 66. Rosie 67. A Lovely Way to Die 68. *Eye of the Cat* 69. The Sex Symbol (TV) 74, etc.

Rich, Irene (1891–) (Irene Luther). American silent screen heroine, little seen since sound.
Stella Maris 18. Beau Brummell 24. So This is Paris 26. *Craig's Wife* 28. Lady Windermere's Fan 28. Shanghai Rose 29. That Cetain Age 38. The Lady in Question 41. New Orleans 47. Joan of Arc 48, etc.

Rich, John (1925–). American director, from TV.
Wives and Lovers 63. The New Interns 64. Boeing Boeing 65. Easy Come Easy Go 67, etc.

Rich, Roy (1909–1970). British producer, director and executive, with widely varied experience including radio and TV.
My Brother's Keeper (d only) 47. It's Not Cricket (d only) 48. Double Profile (d only) 54. Phantom Caravan (d only) 54, etc.

Richard, Cliff (1940–) (Harold Webb). Boyish British pop singer who succeeded by restricting his film appearances.
☐ Serious Charge 59. Expresso Bongo 60. *The Young Ones* 61. Summer Holiday 62. Wonderful Life 64. Finders Keepers 66. Two a Penny 68. Take Me High 73.

Richard III (GB 1956). Laurence Olivier's third Shakespearean production has a more direct popular appeal than either *Henry V* or *Hamlet*, perhaps because it centres firmly on Olivier's rich caricature of Crookback. It tells its story in a leisurely fashion, production values are economical, and the battle skimped, but Shakespeare and the acting win the day, with an especially fascinating performance from Ralph Richardson as Buckingham. The only other talking version of the story, oddly enough, is Rowland V. Lee's outrageous but amusing *Tower of London* 39, with Basil Rathbone as Richard and Boris Karloff as Mord the Executioner: this was remade in 1963 by Roger Corman, with Vincent Price as Richard. (He played Clarence in the earlier version.)

Richards, Addison (1887–1964). American character actor with long stage experience; in Hollywood from early thirties, usually as professional man; later in TV series.
Riot Squad 34. Coleen 36. Black Legion 37. Boom Town 40. My Favorite Blonde 42. Since You Went Away 44. The Mummy's Curse 46. Indian Scout 50. Illegal 56. The Oregon Trail 59, hundreds of others.

Richards, Ann (1918–). Australian leading lady.
Tall Timbers 38. The Rudd Family 39, etc. Then to Hollywood: Random Harvest 42. Dr Gillespie's New Assistant 43. An American Romance 44. Love Letters 45. The Searching Wind 46. Sorry, Wrong Number 48. Breakdown 52, etc.

Richards, Beah (–). Black American actress.
The Miracle Worker 62. In the Heat of the Night 67. *Guess Who's Coming to Dinner* 67. Mahogany 76, etc.

Richards, Dick (c.1936–). American director.
Farewell My Lovely 75. Rafferty and the Gold Dust Twins 76.

Richards, Jeff (–) (Richard Mansfield Taylor). American general purpose actor.
Johnny Belinda 48. Kill the Umpire 50. The Strip 51. Above and Beyond 52. Seven Brides for Seven Brothers 55, many others.

Richards, Paul (1924–1974). American general purpose actor.
The Black Whip 55. Tall Man Riding 56. Battle for the Planet of the Apes 71, etc.

Richardson, John (1936–). British leading man, mainly in fancy dress.
Bachelor of Hearts 58. She 65. One Million Years BC 66. The Vengeance of She 68. The Chastity Belt 68. On a Clear Day You Can See Forever 70. Duck in Orange Sauce (It.) 75, etc.

Richardson, Sir Ralph (1902–).

Distinguished British stage actor, in occasional films. Despite his splendid theatrical voice and thespian mannerisms, he has been at his best playing ordinary chaps, though his gallery includes plenty of eccentrics.

☐ The Ghoul 33. Friday the Thirteenth 33. The Return of Bulldog Drummond 34. Java Head 34. King of Paris 34. *Bulldog Jack* 35. Things to Come 36. The Man who Could Work Miracles 36. Thunder in the City 37. *South Riding* 38. The Divorce of Lady X 38. The Citadel 38. *Q Planes* 39. *The Four Feathers* 39. The Lion has Wings 39. On the Night of the Fire 39. The Day Will Dawn 42. The Silver Fleet 43. School for Secrets 46. *Anna Karenina* 48. The Fallen Idol 48. *The Heiress* 49. An Outcast of the Islands 51. Home at Seven (& d) 52. The Sound Barrier 52. The Holly and the Ivy 53. *Richard III* (as Buckingham) 56. Smiley 57. The Passionate Stranger 57. Our Man in Havana 59. *Oscar Wilde* (as Sir Edward Carson) 60. Exodus 61. The 300 Spartans 62. *Long Day's Journey into Night* 62. woman of Straw 64. Doctor Zhivago 66. The Wrong Box 66. Khartoum 67. Oh What a Lovely War 69. The Midas Run 69. The Bed Sitting Room 69. The Battle of Britain 69. The Looking Glass War 69. David Copperfield (as Micawber) 69. Eagle in a Cage 71. Who Slew Auntie Roo? 71. Tales from the Crypt 71. Lady Caroline Lamb 72. Alice's Adventures in Wonderland (as the Caterpillar) 72. A Doll's House 73. O Lucky Man 73. Frankenstein: The True Story (TV) 73. Rollerball 75. Jesus of Nazareth (TV) 77.

Richardson, Tony (1928–). British director of stage and screen.

☐ Momma Don't Allow (short: co-d) 55. Look Back in Anger 58. The Entertainer 60. Sanctuary (US) 61. *A Taste of Honey* 61. The Loneliness of the Long Distance Runner 63. *Tom Jones* 63. The Loved One (US) 65. Sailor from Gibraltar 66. Mademoiselle 66. Red and Blue 67. The Charge of the Light Brigade 68. Laughter in the Dark 69. Hamlet 69. Ned Kelly 70. A Delicate Balance 73. Dead Cert (& co-w) 74. Joseph Andrews 77.

Richman, Harry (1895–1972). American entertainer, in occasional films.

☐ Putting on the Ritz 30. The Music Goes Round 36. Kicking the Moon Around 38.

Richman, Mark (1927–). American general purpose actor, much on TV.

Friendly Persuasion 56. The Strange One 57. The Black Orchid 58. The Crime Busters 61. Dark Intruder 65. For Singles Only 68, etc.

TV series: *Cain's Hundred* 61.

Richmond, Anthony (1942–). British cinematographer.

Only When I Larf 67. Let It Be 70. Madame Sin 73. *Don't Look Now* 73. Vampira 74. Stardust 74. The Man Who Fell to Earth 76. The Eagle Has Landed 77, etc.

Richmond, Kane (1906–1973) (Frederick W. Bowditch). American leading man of second features.

The Leather Pushers (serial) 30. Nancy Steele is Missing 36. Hard Guy 41. Action in the North Atlantic 43. Tiger Woman 45. Black Gold 47, many others.

Richmond, Ted (1912–). American producer, former writer.

So Dark the Night 46. The Milkman 50. The Strange Door 51. Desert Legion 53. Forbidden 54. Count Three and Pray 55. Seven Waves Away 57. Solomon and Sheba 59. Advance to the Rear 64. Return of the Seven 66. Villa Rides 68, others.

Richter, Hans (1888–1976). German dadaist director of animated and surrealist films, most active in twenties.

Prelude and Fugue 20. Film is Rhythm 20. Rhythm 23. Rhythm 25. Film Study 26. Inflation 26. Twopenny Magic 27. Vormittagspuk 28. Everything Revolves 30. Dreams That Money Can Buy 44. 8×8 57, etc.

Rickles, Don (1926–). American general purpose actor.

Run Silent Run Deep 58. The Rabbit Trap 59. The Rat Race 60. Enter Laughing 67. The Money Jungle 68. Where It's At 69. Kelly's Heroes 70, etc.

Riddle, Nelson (–). American composer.

A Kiss Before Dying 55. St Louis Blues 58. Ocean's Eleven 60. Lolita 62. Robin and the Seven Hoods 64. Marriage on the Rocks 65. El Dorado 66. Paint Your Wagon 69. The Great Gatsby 74, etc.

Ridgeley, John (1909–1968) (John Huntingdon Rea). American supporting actor generally cast as gangster.

Invisible Menace 38. They Made Me a Fugitive 39. Brother Orchid 40. The Big Shot 42. Destination Tokyo 44. My Reputation 46. The Big Sleep 46. Possessed 47. Command Decision 48. The Blue Veil 52, many others.

Ridges, Stanley (1892–1951). Incisive, heavy-featured British character actor who appeared in many Hollywood films.

The Scoundrel 34. Yellow Jack 38. If I were King 39. Black Friday 40. Sergeant York 41. *To Be Or Not To Be* 42. The Big Shot 42. The Master Race 45. Possessed 47. No Way Out 50. The Groom Wore Spurs 51, others.

Riefenstahl, Leni (1902–). German woman director, former dancer, who made brilliant propaganda films for Hitler.
The White Hell of Pitz Palu (acted) 29. The Blue Light (ad) 32. S.O.S. Iceberg (a) 33. *Triumph of the Will* (the Nuremberg Rally) (d) 34. *Olympische Spiele 1936*. Tiefland 45, etc.

Riesner, Charles (1887–1962). American director.
The Man in the Box 25. Reducing 32. The Show-Off 34. Sophie Lang Goes West 37. *The Big Store* 41. Meet the People 44. Lost in a Harem 44. The Cobra Strikes 48. The Travelling Saleswoman 50, many others, mainly second features.

Rififi (France 1955). The film which re-established Jules Dassin as an international director after years of inactivity following his blacklisting by the Un-American Activities tribunals; also the film which triggered off an unending series of stories about big-scale robberies which come unstuck. Its particular selling-point was that the entire twenty-minute robbery sequence took place in complete silence. Written by René Wheeler and Dassin from a novel by Auguste le Breton; photographed by Philippe Agostini; music by Georges Auric; with Jean Servais, Carl Mohner, Dassin. Several inferior sequels were made by other directors.

Rigby, Edward (1879–1951). British stage character actor in films since 1934; became a familiar figure in endearingly doddery roles.
Lorna Doone 35. Mr Smith Carries On 37. The Proud Valley 39. *Kipps* 41. The Common Touch 41. *Let the People Sing* 42. *Salute John Citizen* 42. Get Cracking 43. *Don't Take It to Heart* 44. Quiet Weekend 47. *Easy Money* 48. It's Hard to be Good 49. *The Happiest Days of Your Life* 49. *The Mudlark* 50, many others.

Rigg, Diana (1938–). British leading actress who came to fame in *The Avengers* TV series 65–67.
☐ The Assassination Bureau 68. A Midsummer Night's Dream 68. On Her Majesty's Secret Service 69. Julius Caesar 70. The Hospital 71. Theatre of Blood 73. In This House of Brede (TV) 75. A Little Night Music 77.
TV series: The Diana Rigg Show 73.

Rilla, Walter (1895–). German actor on stage from 1921; to Britain in mid-thirties.
Der Geiger von Florenz 26. The Scarlet Pimpernel 35. Victoria the Great 37. At the Villa Rose 39. The Adventures of Tartu 43. The Lisbon Story 46. State Secret 50. Behold the Man (pd) 51. Cairo 61. The Thousand Eyes of Dr Mabuse 63. The Face of Fu Manchu 65, etc.

Rilla, Wolf (1920–). British director, son of Walter Rilla
Noose for a Lady 53. The End of the Road 54. Pacific Destiny 56. The Scamp 57. Bachelor of Hearts 58. Witness in the Dark 50. Piccadilly Third Stop 60. *Village of the Damned* 62. Cairo 63. The World Ten Times Over (& w) 63. Secrets of a Door to Door Salesman 73, etc.

Rin Tin Tin (1916–1932). An ex-German Army dog which became one of the biggest box office draws of the American silent screen; also in serials.
Where the North Begins 23. The Night Cry 23. The Clash of the Wolves 24. Jaws of Steel 27. The Frozen River 29. A Dog of the Regiment 30, etc.

Rio Rita. The operetta by Joseph McCarthy and Henry Tierney became, in 1929, one of the first musicals to be filmed, and Bebe Daniels and John Boles are remembered for their work in what was necessarily a very primitive production. In 1942 the work was retailored for Abbott and Costello, with John Carroll and Kathryn Grayson doing the singing.

Ripley, Arthur (1895–1961). American director whose films are oddly sparse.
☐ I Met My Love Again 38. Prisoner of Japan 42. *A Voice in the Wind* 44. The Chase 47. Thunder Road 58.

Ripper, Michael (1913–). British character actor, often in comic roles.
Captain Boycott 48. Treasure Hunt 52. The Belles of St Trinian's 54. Richard III 56. Quatermass II 57. The Revenge of Frankenstein 58. Brides of Dracula 60. Captain Clegg 62. The Secret of Blood Island 65. The Reptile 66. The Plague of the Zombies 66. Where the Bullets Fly 66. Scars of Dracula 70, etc.

Riscoe, Arthur (1896–1954). British stage comedian with rare film appearances.
Going Gay 34. Paradise for Two 38. *Kipps* (as Chitterlow) 41, etc.

Risdon, Elizabeth (1887–1958) (E. Evans). British stage actress who in later life went to

Hollywood and played many character roles.
Guard That Girl 35. Crime and Punishment 36.
The Great Man Votes 39. Lost Angel 44.
Grissly's Millions 44. Mama Loves Papa 45. Life
with Father 47. Bannerline 51. Scaramouche 52,
etc.

Risi, Dino (1916–). Italian director.
The Sign of Venus 55. Poveri ma Belli 56. Il
Sorpasso 62, etc.

Riskin, Robert (1897–1955). Distinguished
American screenwriter.
Illicit 31. The Miracle Woman 31. *Lady for a
Day* 33. *It Happened One Night* (AA) 34.
Broadway Bill 34. The Whole Town's Talking
35. *Mr Deeds Goes to Town* 36. *Lost Horizon*
37. *You Can't Take It with You* 38. The Real
Glory 39. *Meet John Doe* 41. The Thin Man
Goes Home 44. Magic Town 46. Riding High
50. Mister 880 50. The Groom Wore Spurs 51,
etc.

Ritchard, Cyril (1896–). British dancer and
light comedian, mainly on stage.
Piccadilly 29. Blackmail 30. I See Ice 38. Half a
Sixpence 67.

Ritchie, June (1939–). British leading lady,
mainly in 'realist' films.
A Kind of Loving 61. Live Now Pay Later 63.
The Mouse on the Moon 63. The World Ten
Times Over 63. This is My Street 64. The
Syndicate (GB) 67, etc.

Ritchie, Michael (1939–). American
director.
□ Downhill Racer 69. Prime Cut 72. *The
Candidate* 72. *Smile* 75. The Bad News Bears
76.

Ritt, Martin (1919–). American director with
stage and TV experience.
□ *Edge of the City* 56. *No Down Payment* 57.
The Long Hot Summer 58. The Sound and the
Fury 59. The Black Orchid 59. Five Branded
Women 60. Paris Blues 61. Hemingway's
Adventures of a Young Man 62. *Hud* 63. The
Outrage 64. *The Spy Who Came in from the
Cold* 65. Hombre 67. The Brotherhood 68. The
Molly Maguires 69. The Great White Hope 71.
Sounder 72. Pete 'n Tillie 72. Conrack 74. The
Front 76. Casey's Shadow 77.

Ritter, Tex (1907–) (Woodward Ritter).
American singing cowboy star of innumerable
second features.
Song of the Gringo 36. Sing, Cowboy, Sing 38.
The Old Chisholm Trail 43. Marshal of
Gunsmoke 46, etc.

Ritter, Thelma (1905–1969). Wry-faced
American character actress and comedienne;
she provided a sardonic commentary on the
antics of the principals in many fifties comedies.
□ Miracle on 34th Street 47. Call Northside 777
48. A Letter to Three Wives 49. City across the
River 49. Father was a Fullback 49. Perfect
Strangers 50. *All About Eve* 50. I'll Get By 50.
The Mating Season 51. As Young as You Feel
51. *The Model and the Marriage Broker* 51.
With a Song in My Heart 52. Titanic 53. The
Farmer Takes a Wife 53. *Pickup on South Street*
53. Rear Window 54. Daddy Longlegs 55. Lucy
Gallant 55. The Proud and Profane 56. A Hole in
the Head 59. Pillow Talk 59. The Misfits 61. The
Second Time Around 61. Birdman of Alcatraz
62. How the West was Won 62. For Love or
Money 63. A New Kind of Love 63. Move Over
Darling 63. Boeing Boeing 65. The Incident 67.

The Ritz Brothers: Al (1901–1965), **Jim**
(1903–) and **Harry** (the leader) (1906–). Zany
American night club comedians who made many
enjoyable appearances in musicals of the thirties.
Their real surname was Joachim.
□ Hotel Anchovy (short) 34. Sing Baby Sing 36.
One in a Million 37. *On the Avenue* 37. You
Can't Have Everything 37. Life Begins at
College 37. *The Goldwyn Follies* 38. Kentucky
Moonshine 38. Straight Place and Show 38. *The
Three Musketeers* 39. The Gorilla 39. Pack Up
Your Troubles 39. Argentine Nights 40. Behind
the Eight Ball 42. Hi Ya Chum 43. Never a Dull
Moment 43. Won Ton Ton (guest appearance by
Harry and Jim) 76.

Riva, Emmanuele (1932–). French leading
actress.
Hiroshima Mon Amour 58. Adua et sa
Compagnie (Hungry for Love) 58. Kapo 59.
Leon Morin Priest 60. Climats 61. Thérèse
Desqueyroux 63. Soledad 66, etc.

The River. There are two famous films of this
title. 1. US 1938: a documentary by Pare
Lorenz, with free-verse commentary, about the
Tennessee Valley Authority and its effect on the
dwellers in the Mississippi Basin. Words by
Thomas Chalmers, music by Virgil Thompson.
2. India 1951: Jean Renoir's colour romance in
which the story serves as a slender thread on
which to hold the decoration; with Adrienne
Corri, Esmond Knight.

Rivette, Jacques (1928–). French director,
former critic.
Le Coup du Berger 56. Paris Nous Appartient
60. La Religieuse (& w) 65. L'Amour Fou (& w)
68, etc.

Rix, Brian (1924–). British actor-manager associated with the Whitehall farces.
Reluctant Heroes 51. What Every Woman Wants 54. Up to His Neck 54. Dry Rot 55. The Night We Dropped a Clanger 59. And the Same to You 60. Nothing Barred 61. Don't Just Lie There Say Something 73, etc.

RKO Radio Pictures Inc was for many years one of Hollywood's 'big five' production companies, with its own distribution arm. It started in 1921 as a joint enterprise of the Radio Corporation of America and the Keith-Orpheum cinema circuit. Despite severe financial vicissitudes, it struggled on for twenty-seven years, buoyed by a generally decent production standard; stars like Cary Grant, Katharine Hepburn, Wheeler and Woolsey, Leon Errol; individual films such as *Cimarron, King Kong, The Informer, Suspicion, Mr Blandings Builds His Dream House* and *Fort Apache*; and the participation of Goldwyn, Disney and Selznick, all released through RKO at its peak. In 1948 Howard Hughes (qv) acquired a large share of the stock; but after a period of uncertainty RKO ceased production in 1953 and the studio was sold to Desilu TV.

Roach, Bert (1891–*). American silent screen actor.
The Millionaire 21. The Rowdy 21. The Flirt 22. Excitement 24. Don't 25. Money Talks 26. The Taxi Dancer 27. The Desert Rider 29. No No Nanette 30. Viennese Nights 30. Hallelujah I'm a Bum 33. San Francisco 36. Algiers 38. Hi Diddle Diddle 43. The Perils of Pauline 47, etc.

Roach, Hal (1892–). American producer chiefly associated with gag comedies. Varied early experience before he teamed with Harold Lloyd 1916; later made films with Our Gang, Laurel and Hardy, etc.
SOUND FILMS: *Fraternally Yours* 33. *Way Out West* 36. *Topper* 37. *Of Mice and Men* 40. *Turnabout* 40. One Million BC 40. *Tooper Returns* 41, many others.

road show. A term which used to mean a travelling show; latterly in cinema terms it indicates the special, prolonged pre-release at advanced prices of a big-screen attraction, e.g. *My Fair Lady* or *The Sound of Music*, which may in this way run for years in a big city before being released to local theatres.

Road to Singapore (US 1940). This modest studio-made romantic comedy happened to star three Paramount contract players: Bing Crosby, Bob Hope and Dorothy Lamour. They worked so well together, with successful ad-libbing and an easy style, that several other 'Road' comedies were made, getting crazier each time and using every kind of gag the writers could think of. The only thing you were sure of in these pictures was that Bob wouldn't get the girl; otherwise anything could happen, from inside gags about Paramount to talking camels. They all date badly. *Road to Zanzibar* 41, *Road to Morocco* 42, *Road to Utopia* 46, *Road to Rio* 47, *Road to Bali* 52, *Road to Hong Kong* 62.

Robards, Jason (1893–1963). American stage actor. Few film appearances.
□ On Trial 28. Abraham Lincoln 30. The Crusades 35. I Stole a Million 39. Riff Raff 47.

Robards, Jason, Jnr (1920–). American stage actor, son of Jason Robards.
The Journey 58. By Love Possessed 59. *Tender is the Night* 61. Long Day's Journey into Night 62. A Big Hand for the Little Lady 66. A Thousand Clowns 66. Any Wednesday 66. Divorce American Style 67. *The Hour of the Gun* 67. The St Valentine's Day Massacre 67. The Night They Raided Minsky's 68. Isadora 68. Once Upon a Time in the West 69. Tora! Tora! Tora! 70. Julius Caesar 70. The Ballad of Cable Hogue 70. Murders in the Rue Morgue 71. Johnny Got His Gun 71. The War Between Men and Women 72. Pat Garrett and Billy the Kid 73. Play It As It Lays 73. All The President's Men (AA) 76. Julia 77, etc.

Robbe-Grillet, Alain (1922–). French writer, associated with Resnais in *Last Year at Marienbad* 60. Also wrote and directed *L'Immortelle* 62, *Trans-Europe Express* 66.

robberies have been a commonplace of film action fare since *The Great Train Robbery* itself; but of late there has been a fashion for showing the planning and execution of robberies through the eyes of the participants. Perhaps this started in 1950 with *The Asphalt Jungle* (and its two remakes *The Badlanders* and *Cairo*); anyway, some of the films built on this mould are *Rififi, Five against the House, Seven Thieves, The Killing, Payroll, Piccadilly Third Stop, The Day They Robbed the Bank of England, A Prize of Gold, On Friday at Eleven, Once a Thief, He Who Rides a Tiger, Robbery, Charley Varrick, Cops and Robbers, The Taking of Pelham One Two Three, The Getaway, 11 Harrowhouse, The Bank Shot, Gambit, Dog Day Afternoon* and *Inside Out*; while films treating the same subject less seriously included *The Lavender Hill Mob, The Lady Killers, Ocean's Eleven, Persons Unknown, The League of Gentlemen, Topkapi,*

The Big Job, Assault on a Queen, The Biggest Bundle of Them All, Grand Slam, They Came to Rob Las Vegas, The Italian Job, The Hot Rock and *The Anderson Tapes.* The biggest attempted robbery of all was probably the raid on Fort Knox in *Goldfinger.* Sometimes one longs for a return to the days of the dapper jewel thieves: Ronald Colman or David Niven in *Raffles,* Herbert Marshall in *Trouble in Paradise,* John Barrymore or even Charles Korvin as Arsène Lupin, Cary Grant in *To Catch a Thief.* The closest we have come to this style for many years, apart from William Wyler's *How to Steal a Million,* is 1973's *The Thief Who Came to Dinner* with Ryan O'Neal. In 1964 TV made a gallant effort with *The Rogues.*

Robbins, Harold (1916–). American best-selling novelist whose over-sexed tales have been readily transcribed to the screen.
The Carpetbaggers 63. Where Love Has Gone 64. Nevada Smith 66. Stiletto 69. The Adventurers 69. The Betsy 77, etc.
TV series: *The Survivors* 69.

Robbins, Jerome (1918–). American dancer and ballet-master who has choreographed several films.
The King and I 56. *West Side Story* (AA) (& co-d) 61, etc.

The Robe (US 1953). This solemn epic from Lloyd C. Douglas' novel about the aftermath of the Crucifixion is unremarkable except as the first film in CinemaScope (qv). Photographer Leon Shamroy operated under difficulties with a lens as yet imperfect. Victor Mature, who gave the best performance, appeared next year in a sequel, *Demetrius and the Gladiators.*

Rober, Richard (1906–1952). American general purpose actor with stage experience.
Smart Girls Don't Talk 48. Deported 50. The Well 52. The Devil Makes Three 52, etc.

Robert, Yves (1920–). French director, former actor. Gained fame with *The War of the Buttons* 61; then *Bébert et l'Omnibus* 63, *Copains* 64, *Follow the Guy with One Black Shoe* 72.

Roberti, Lyda (1910–1938). German-Polish leading lady, former child café singer, in several Hollywood films of the thirties.
□ Million Dollar Legs 32. The Kid from Spain 32. Dancers in the Dark 32. Torch Singers 33. Three-Cornered Moon 33. College Rhythm 34. The Big Broadcast of 1936 35. George White's Scandals 35. Pick a Star 37. Nobody's Baby 37. Wide Open Faces 37.

Roberts, Ben (1916–) (Benjamin Eisenberg). American writer, almost always with Ivan Goff (qv).

Roberts, Florence (1860–1940). American character actress best remembered as Granny in the Jones Family series 1936–40.

Roberts, Lynne (1922–) (Mary Hart). American leading lady of forties second features.
Dangerous Holiday 37. Winter Wonderland 39. Call of the Klondike 41. Quiet Please Murder 42. The Great Plane Robbery 47. The Blazing Forest 52, many others.

Roberts, Pernell (1930–). American general purpose actor; became famous as one of the brothers in TV's *Bonanza,* but left after four years and never regained the limelight.
Ride Lonesome 58. The Silent Gun (TV) 69, etc.

Roberts, Rachel (1927–). British stage actress.
Valley of Song 52. The Good Companions 57. Our Man in Havana 59. *Saturday Night and Sunday Morning* (BFA) 60. *This Sporting Life* (BFA) 63. A Flea in Her Ear 68. Doctors' Wives 71. Wild Rovers 71. *O Lucky Man* 73. The Belstone Fox 73. Murder on the Orient Express 74. Picnic at Hanging Rock 76, etc.

Roberts, Roy (1900–1975). American character actor who once played cops but graduated to senior executives.
Guadalcanal Diary 43. My Darling Clementine 46. Flaming Fury 49. The Big Trees 52. The Glory Brigade 53. The Boss 56, many others.
TV series: Petticoat Junction 64–68.

Roberts, Stephen (1895–1936). American director.
□ Sky Bride 32. Lady and Gent 32. The Night of June 13th 32. If I Had a Million (part) 32. The Story of Temple Drake 33. *One Sunday Afternoon* 33. The Trumpet Blows 34. Romance in Manhattan 34. *Star of Midnight* 35. The Man Who Broke the Bank at Monte Carlo 35. The Lady Consents 36. The Ex Mrs Bradford 36.

Roberts, Theodore (1861–1928). American character actor, the grand old man of the silent screen.
Where the Trail Divides 14. The Trail of the Lonesome Pine 16. Male and Female 19. The Affairs of Anatol 21. Our Leading Citizen 22. *The Ten Commandments* (as Moses) 23.

Grumpy 23. Locked Doors 25. Masks of the Devil 28, many others.

Robertshaw, Jerrold (1866–1941). Gaunt British stage actor who made several film appearances.
Dombey and Son 18. She 25. Downhill 27. Kitty 29. Don Quixote (title role) 33, etc.

Robertson, Cliff (1925–). Ambitious American leading man with long stage experience before being spotted for films.
□ Picnic (debut) 55. Autumn Leaves 56. The Girl Most Likely 57. The Naked and the Dead 58. Gidget 59. Battle of the Coral Sea 59. As the Sea Rages 60. All in a Night's Work 61. The Big Show 61. Underworld USA 61. The Interns 62. My Six Loves 63. PT 109 (as President Kennedy) 63. Sunday in New York 64. The Best Man 64. 633 Squadron 64. Love Has Many Faces 65. Masquerade (GB) 65. Up from the Beach 65. The Honey Pot 67. The Devil's Brigade 68. Charly (AA) 68. Too Late the Hero 69. The Great Northfield Minnesota Raid 72. J. W. Coop (& pd) 72. Ace Eli and Rodger of the Skies 73. Man on a Swing 74. My Father's House (TV) 75. Three Days of the Condor 76. Midway 76. Shoot 76. Obsession 76.
TV series: Rod Brown of the Rocket Rangers 53.

Robertson, Dale (1923–). American western star, former schoolteacher.
Fighting Man of the Plains (debut) 49. Two Flags West 50. Lydia Bailey 52. The Silver Whip 53. Sitting Bull 54. A Day of Fury 56. Law of the Lawless 65. Blood on the Arrow 65. Coast of Skeletons 65, etc.
TV series: Tales of Wells Fargo 57–61. The Iron Horse 66.

Robeson, Paul (1898–1976). Black American actor and singer, on stage including concerts from mid-twenties.
Biographies, all entitled Paul Robeson: 1958 by Marie Seton; 1968 by Edwin P. Hoyt; 1974 by Virginia Hamilton.
□ Body and Soul 24. The Emperor Jones 33. Sanders of the River 35. Showboat 36. Song of Freedom 37. Jericho 38. Big Fella 38. King Solomon's Mines 38. The Proud Valley 39. Tales of Manhattan 42.

Robey, Sir George (1869–1954) (George Edward Wade). British music-hall comedian, 'the prime minister of mirth'. Appeared in silent farcical comedies, later in character roles.
Autobiography 1933: Looking Back on Life.
The Rest Cure 23. Don Quixote (as Sancho Panza) 23 and 33. Her Prehistoric Man 24. Chu

Chin Chow 33. Marry Me 33. Birds of a Feather 36. A Girl Must Live 39. Variety Jubilee 40. Salute John Citizen 42. Henry V 44. The Trojan Brothers 45. The Pickwick Papers 52, etc.

Robin, Dany (1927–). French leading lady.
Le Silence est d'Or 46. Histoire d'Amour 52. Act of Love 54. In Six Easy Lessons 60. The Waltz of the Toreadors 62. Topaz 69, etc.

Robin Hood. The legendary outlaw leader of Plantagenet England is one of literature's most oft-filmed characters. There were film versions in 1909 (GB), 1912 (GB), 1912 (US), 1913 (US), and 1913 (GB). Douglas Fairbanks made his big-scale Robin Hood in 1922, with Wallace Beery as King Richard. In 1938 came The Adventures of Robin Hood, one of Hollywood's most satisfying action adventures, with Errol Flynn as Robin, Claude Rains as Prince John and Basil Rathbone as Guy of Gisbourne; directed by William Keighley and Michael Curtiz, from a script by Norman Reilly Raine and Seton I. Miller. Its exhilaration has not diminished with time. In 1946 (US) Cornel Wilde played Robin's son in Bandit of Sherwood Forest; in 1948 (US) Jon Hall was Robin in Prince of Thieves; in 1950 (US) John Derek was Robin's son in Rogues of Sherwood Forest; Robert Clarke played Robin in an odd concoction called Tales of Robin Hood (US 1952). Also in 1952, in Britain, Disney filmed Richard Todd in The Story of Robin Hood and His Merrie Men, with only fair success, though the real Sherwood Forest was used for the first time. Robin also appeared briefly (played by Harold Warrender) in Ivanhoe 52. Men of Sherwood Forest (GB 1956) had Don Taylor as Robin; Son of Robin Hood (GB 1959) turned out to be a daughter, played by June Laverick. Most durable Robin is Richard Greene, who played the role not only in 165 half-hour TV films but in a feature, Sword of Sherwood Forest (GB 1961). In 1967 Barrie Ingham took over in A Challenge for Robin Hood, in 1973 the Disney studios produced a cartoon version, and in 1976 came Robin and Marian, which traced the sad fortunes of the protagonists twenty years later.

Robin, Leo (1899–). American lyricist. Songs include 'Louise', 'Beyond the Blue Horizon', 'June in January', 'No Love No Nothing'.
Innocents of Paris 29. Monte Carlo 30. One Hour with You 32. Little Miss Marker 34. The Big Broadcast of 1938 (AA for 'Thanks for the Memory'). Gulliver's Travels 39. My Gal Sal 43. Meet Me after the Show 50. My Sister Eileen 55, etc.

Robinson, Bill (1878–1949). Black American tap-dancer and entertainer, famous for his stairway dance.
The Little Colonel 35. In Old Kentucky 36. Rebecca of Sunnybrook Farm 38. *Stormy Weather* 43, etc.

Robinson, Casey (1903–). American screenwriter, in Hollywood from 1921.
I Love That Man 33. Captain Blood 35. Call it a Day 37. It's Love I'm After 37. Four's a Crowd 39. *King's Row* 42. Passage to Marseilles 44. Days of Glory 44. *The Macomber Affair* 47. Under My Skin (& p) 50. Two Flags West (& p) 50. Diplomatic Courier (& p) 52. The Snows of Kilimanjaro 52. While the City Sleeps 56. This Earth is Mine (& p) 59, etc.

Robinson Crusoe. There have been many film variations on Defoe's novel. The closest to the original have been Luis Buñuel's *The Adventures of Robinson Crusoe* (Mexico 1953) with Dan O'Herlihy, and oddly enough, Byron Haskin's *Robinson Crusoe on Mars* (US 1964) with Paul Mantee. *Man Friday* (GB 1975) tried to be satirical by showing the situation from Friday's viewpoint.

Robinson, Edward G. (1893–1973) (Emanuel Goldenberg). Dynamic American star actor of Rumanian origin. On stage from 1913; later settled in Hollywood. Special Academy Award 1972.
Autobiography 1973: *All My Yesterdays*.
□ The Bright Shawl 23. The Hole in the Wall 29. Night Ride 30. A Lady to Love 30. Outside the Law 30. East is West 30. Widow from Chicago 30. *Little Caesar* (which made him a star) 30. *Five Star Final* 31. Smart Money 31. The Hatchet Man 31. Two Seconds 32. Tiger Shark 32. Silver Dollar 32. The Little Giant 33. I Loved a Woman 33. Dark Hazard 34. The Man with Two Faces 34. *The Whole Town's Talking* 34. Barbary Coast 35. Bullets or Ballots 36. Thunder in the City (GB) 37. Kid Galahad 37. The Last Gangster 38. *A Slight Case of Murder* 38. *The Amazing Dr Clitterhouse* 38. I Am the Law 38. Confessions of a Nazi Spy 39. Blackmail 39. *Dr Ehrlich's Magic Bullet* 40. *Brother Orchid* 40. A Dispatch from Reuters 41. *The Sea Wolf* 41. Manpower 41. Unholy Partners 41. Larceny Inc. 42. Tales of Manhattan 42. Destroyer 43. Flesh and Fantasy 43. Tampico 44. *Double Indemnity* 44. Mr Winkle Goes to War 44. *The Woman in the Window* 44. Our Vines Have Tender Grapes 45. *Scarlet Street* 45. Journey Together (GB) 45. The Stranger 46. The Red House 47. *All My Sons* 48. *Key Largo* 48. Night Has a Thousand Eyes 48. *House of Strangers* 49. My Daughter

Joy (GB) 50. Actors and Sin 52. Vice Squad 53. Big Leaguer 53. The Glass Web 53. Black Tuesday 54. The Violent Men 55. Tight Spot 55. A Bullet for Joey 55. Illegal 55. Hell on Frisco Bay 56. Nightmare 56. The Ten Commandments 56. A Hole in the Head 59. Seven Thieves 59. Pépé 60. My Geisha 62. *Two Weeks in Another Town* 62. Sammy Going South (GB) 62. The Prize 63. Good Neighbour Sam 64. Robin and the Seven Hoods 64. Cheyenne Autumn 64. The Outrage 64. *The Cincinnati Kid* 65. Who Has Seen the Wind 65. The Biggest Bundle of Them All 66. Never a Dull Moment 67. Grand Slam 67. Mackenna's Gold 68. It's Your Move 68. Operation St Peter's 68. Song of Norway 69. Operation Heartbeat (TV) 69. The Old Man Who Cried Wolf (TV) 71. Soylent Green 73.

Robinson, Frances (1916–1971). American supporting actress, usually in smart roles.
Forbidden Valley 25. The Last Warning 28. Tim Tyler's Luck 35. The Lone Wolf Keeps a Date 37. The Invisible Man Returns 39. Tower of London 39. Smilin' Through 41. Suddenly It's Spring 46. Keeper of the Bees 47. Backfire 50, many others.

Robinson, Jay (1930–). American stage actor of eccentric roles.
The Robe 53. Demetrius and the Gladiators 54. The Virgin Queen 55. My Man Godfrey 57. Bunny O'Hare 71. Shampoo 75, etc.

Robinson, John (1908–). British stage actor, familiar in heavy father or tough executive roles.
The Scarab Murder Case 36. The Lion Has Wings 40. Uneasy Terms 49. Hammer the Toff 51. The Constant Husband 55. Fortune is a Woman 58. And the Same to You 61, etc.

Robinson, Madeleine (1916–) (Madeleine Svoboda). French stage and film actress.
Soldats sans Uniformes 43. Douce 43. Une Si Jolie Petite Plage 48. Dieu a Besoin des Hommes 50. Le Garçon Sauvage 51. The She Wolves 57. A Double Tour 59. The Trial 64. A Trap for Cinderella 65. A New World 66. Le Voyage du Père 66. Le Petit Matin 70, etc.

Robison, Arthur (1888–). Chicago-born director of German films.
Warning Shadows 24. The Informer (GB) 29. The Student of Prague 35, etc.

Robots have been sparingly used in movies. Brigitte Helm memorably played one in *Metropolis*; so did Patricia Roc in *The Perfect Woman*. Robby the Robot featured sympathetically in *Forbidden Planet* and *Invisible Boy*; then there was *Kronos*, and Gort in *The Day the Earth Stood Still*. *Westworld* and *Futureworld* brought in a whole race of robots, one of whom looked like Yul Brynner; while in TV, *The Avengers* have frequently encountered the Cybernauts and *Dr Who* the Daleks.

Robson, Dame Flora (1902–). Distinguished British stage actress.
Biography 1960: *Flora Robson* by Janet Dunbar.
☐ Dance Pretty Lady 31. One Precious Year 33. Catherine the Great 34. *Fire Over England* 36. Farewell Again 37. Wuthering Heights 39. Poison Pen 39. We Are Not Alone 39. Invisible Stripes 39. The Sea Hawk 40. Bahama Passage 41. Saratoga Trunk 43. 2000 Women 44. Great Day 45. Caesar and Cleopatra 45. *Black Narcissus* 46. Good Time Girl 47. Holiday Camp 47. Saraband for Dead Lovers 48. The Malta Story 52. Romeo and Juliet 54. *Innocent Sinners* 57. High Tide at Noon 57. No Time for Tears 57. The Gypsy and the Gentleman 58. 55 Days at Peking 62. Murder at the Gallop 63. Guns at Batasi 64. Those Magnificent Men in Their Flying Machines 64. Young Cassidy 65. Seven Women 65. The Shuttered Room 66. A Cry in the Wind 66. Eye of the Devil 67. Fragment of Fear 69. The Beloved 70. The Beast in the Cellar 71. Alice's Adventures in Wonderland 72. Comedy, Tragedy and All That 72.

Robson, Mark (1913–). American director, former editor: began with Lewton and Kramer but progressed to more solidly commercial subjects.
☐ *The Seventh Victim* 43. The Ghost Ship 43. Youth Runs Wild 44. Isle of the Dead 45. Bedlam 46. *Champion* 49. Home of the Brave 49. Roughshod 49. My Foolish Heart 50. Edge of Doom 50. Bright Victory 51. I Want You 51. Return to Paradise 53. Hell Below Zero (GB) 54. The Bridges at Toko-Ri 54. Phffft 54. A Prize of Gold 55. Trial 55. The Harder They Fall 56. The Little Hut (& p) 57. Peyton Place 58. The Inn of the Sixth Happiness (GB) 58. From the Terrace (& p) 59. Lisa (The Inspector) (p only) 62. Nine Hours to Rama (GB) (& p) 63. The Prize 63. *Von Ryan's Express* (& p) 65. Lost Command (& p) 66. Valley of the Dolls (& p) 67. Daddy's Gone A-Hunting (& p) 69. Happy Birthday Wanda June 71. Limbo 73. Earthquake 74.

Robson, May (1858–1942). Australian actress, in America from childhood. Long experience on stage tours before coming to

Hollywood, where she played domineering but kindly old ladies.
The Rejuvenation of Aunt Mary 27. Mother's Millions 29. Strange Interlude 32. Letty Lynton 32. *If I Had a Million* 32. *Lady for a Day* 33. Alice in Wonderland 33. Dinner at Eight 33. Grand Old Girl 35. The Baxter Millions 36. Rhythm on the River 37. A Star Is Born 37. *Four Daughters* 38. *Bringing Up Baby* 38. The Adventures of Tom Sawyer 38. Nurse Edith Cavell 39. Irene 40. *Granny Get Your Gun* 40. Million Dollar Baby 41. Playmates 42, many others.

Roc, Patricia (1918–) (Felicia Riese). British leading lady of the forties, signed for films after brief stage experience.
The Rebel Son (Taras Bulba) 38. The Gaunt Stranger 39. The Mind of Mr Reeder 39. Three Silent Men 40. Let the People Sing 42. Millions Like Us 43. 2000 Women 44. Love Story 44. Madonna of the Seven Moons 44. The Wicked Lady 45. Johnny Frenchman 45. Canyon Passage (US) 46. *The Brothers* 47. Jassy 47. When the Bough Breaks 48. One Night with You 48. The Perfect Woman 49. Circle of Danger 50. The Man on the Eiffel Tower 51. Something Money Can't Buy 53. The Hypnotist 55. Bluebeard's Ten Honeymoons 60, etc.

Rocco and His Brothers (Italy 1960). A super-realistic story of a peasant family in the big city, this film by Luchino Visconti was highly acclaimed on its first appearance but seems to have left little mark. Written by Suso Cecchi d'Amico, Vasco Pratolini and Luchino Visconti; photographed by Giuseppe Rotunno.

Roddenberry, Gene (–). American TV producer of science fiction series *Star Trek* and *Galaxy Two*. Wrote and produced *Pretty Maids All in a Row* 70.

Rodgers, Anton (1927–). British comic character actor.
Rotten to the Core 65. Scrooge 70. The Day of the Jackal 73.

Rodgers, Richard (1901–). American composer who has worked variously with lyricists Lorenz Hart and Oscar Hammerstein II.
Love Me Tonight 32. *Hallelujah I'm a Bum* 33. On Your Toes 38. Babes in Arms 39. The Boys from Syracuse 40. State Fair 45. *Oklahoma!* 55. *The King and I* 56. *Pal Joey* 57. *South Pacific* 58. *The Sound of Music* 65, many other complete scores and single songs.

Rodrigues, Percy (1924–). Black Canadian character actor.
The Plainsman 67. The Sweet Ride 68. The Heart is a Lonely Hunter 70. Genesis II (TV) 73, etc.

Roeg, Nicolas (1928–). British cinematographer and director.
AS CINEMATOGRAPHER: The System 63. Nothing But the Best 64. The Caretaker 66. Petulia 67. A Funny Thing Happened on the Way to the Forum 68. *Far from the Madding Crowd* 68, etc.
□ AS DIRECTOR: Performance (co-d) 72. Walkabout 72. *Don't Look Now* 73. The Man Who Fell to Earth 76.

Rogell, Albert S. (1901–). American director of second features, former cameraman.
Señor Daredevil 26. Mamba 30. Riders of Death Valley 32. Argentine Nights 40. Trouble Chaser 40. The Black Cat 41. Tight Shoes 41. In Old Oklahoma 43. Heaven Only Knows 47. Northwest Stampede 48. The Admiral was a Lady (& p) 50. Men against Speed 58, etc.

Rogers, Charles 'Buddy' (1904–). American light leading man of the twenties and thirties; married to Mary Pickford.
Fascinating Youth 26. Wings 27. Abie's Irish Rose 29. Paramount on Parade 30. Varsity 30. Young Eagles 31. This Reckless Age 32. Old Man Rhythm 35. Once in a Million 36. This Way Please 38. Golden Hooves 41. Mexican Spitfire's Baby 43. Don't Trust Your Husband 48, many others.

Rogers, Ginger (1911–) (Virginia McMath). American leading actress, comedienne and dancer, affectionately remembered for her thirties musicals with Fred Astaire. Former band singer; then brief Broadway experience before being taken to Hollywood.
Young Man of Manhattan 30. The 13th Guest 32. *Gold Diggers of 1933. Forty-Second Street* 33. *Flying Down to Rio* 33. *The Gay Divorcee* 34. *Roberta* 34. *Top Hat* 35. In Person 36. *Follow the Fleet* 36. *Shall We Dance?* 37. Having Wonderful Time 38. *Stage Door* 38. *Carefree* 38. Vivacious Lady 38. *The Story of Vernon and Irene Castle* 39. *Bachelor Mother* 39. Fifth Avenue Girl 39. The Primrose Path 40. Lucky Partners 40. *Kitty Foyle* (AA) 40. Tom, Dick and Harry 41. *Roxie Hart* 42. Once upon a Honeymoon 42. *The Major and the Minor* 43. *Lady in the Dark* 43. I'll Be Seeing You 44. Weekend at the Waldorf 45. Magnificent Doll 47. It Had to be You 48. The Barkleys of Broadway 48. Storm Warning 51. We're Not

Married 52. Monkey Business 53. Black Widow 54. Tight Spot 55. Oh Men, Oh Women 57. Harlow (electrono-vision version) 65. The Confession 65, etc.

Rogers, Maclean (1899–). British director, mainly of low-budget features for which he has often written his own unambitious scripts.
The Third Eye 29. Busman's Holiday 36. Old Mother Riley Joins Up 39. Gert and Daisy's Weekend 42. Variety Jubilee 43. The Trojan Brothers 45. Calling Paul Temple 48. The Story of Shirley Yorke 49. Johnny on the Spot 54. Not so Dusty 56. Not Wanted on Voyage 57. Not a Hope in Hell 60, many others.

Rogers, Paul (1917–). British character actor, on stage from 1938, occasional films from 1932.
Beau Brummell 53. Our Man in Havana 59. The Trials of Oscar Wilde 60. No Love for Johnnie 61. Billy Budd 62. The Wild and the Willing 63. The Third Secret 64. He Who Rides a Tiger 65. A Midsummer Night's Dream 68. The Looking Glass War 69. The Reckoning 69. I Want What I Want 72. The Homecoming 73. The Abdication 75. Mr Quilp 75, etc.

Rogers, Peter (1916–). British producer, in films from 1942; wrote and co-produced many comedies during forties and early fifties; conceived and produced the 'Carry On' series (qv) 58– .

Rogers, Roy (1912–) (Leonard Slye). American singing cowboy star, usually seen with horse **Trigger** (1932–65). Varied early experience; formed 'Sons of the Pioneers' singing group; in small film roles from 1935, a star from 1938 till 1953.
Under Western Skies 38. The Carson City Kid 40. Dark Command 40. Robin Hood of the Pecos 42. The Man from Music Mountain 44. Along the Navajo Trail 46. Roll on Texas Moon 47. Night Time in Nevada 49. Trail of Robin Hood 51. Son of Paleface 52. Pals of the Golden West 53. Mackintosh and T.J. 75, etc.
TV series: The Roy Rogers Show 52–54.

Rogers, Will (1879–1935). American rustic comedian, ex-Ziegfeld Follies, whose cracker barrel philosophy almost moved nations.
Biography 1953: *Our Will Rogers* by Homer Croy. Biopic 1972 (starring his son): *The Story of Will Rogers.*
□ Laughing Bill Hyde 18. Almost a Husband 19. *Jubilo* 19. Jes' Call Me Jim 20. Cupid the Cowpuncher 20. Honest Hutch 20. Guile of Women 21. Boys will be Boys 21. Doubling for

Romeo 21. One Glorious Day 21. The Headless Horseman 22. Fruits of Faith 22. A Texas Steer 27. They Had to See Paris 29. Happy Days 30. So This is London 30. Lightnin' 30. A Connecticut Yankee 31. Young as You Feel 31. Ambassador Bill 31. Business and Pleasure 32. Too Busy to Work 32. *State Fair* 33. Doctor Bull 33. Mister Skitch 33. *David Harum* 34. *Handy Andy* 34. *Judge Priest* 34. County Chairman 35. *Life Begins at Forty* 35. Doubting Thomas 35. In Old Kentucky 35. *Steamboat round the Bend* 35.

Rohmer, Eric (1920–) (Jean Maurice Scherer). French director of rarefied conversation pieces.
Le Signe du Lion 59. La Boulangère de Monceau 63. La Carrière de Suzanne 64. La Collectioneuse 67. Ma Nuit chez Maude 69. Le Genou de Claire 70. Love in the Afternoon 72, etc.

Rohmer, Sax (1886–1959) (Arthur Sarsfield Ward). British novelist, the creator of the much filmed Dr Fu Manchu.

Roizman, Owen (–). American cinematographer.
The Taking of Pelham One Two Three 74. The Stepford Wives 75, etc.

Roland, Gilbert (1905–) (Luis Antonio Damaso De Alonso). Mexican leading man, trained as bullfighter, who gatecrashed Hollywood in the mid-twenties and became immediately popular.
The Plastic Age (debut) 25. Camille 27. Men of the North 29. Call Her Savage 32. *She Done Him Wrong* 33. Last Train from Madrid 37. Juarez 39. The Sea Hawk 40. My Life with Caroline 41. Isle of Missing Men 42. Captain Kidd 45. Pirates of Monterey 47. Riding the California Trail 48. *We Were Strangers* 49. The Furies 50. The Bullfighter and the Lady 51. The Bad and the Beautiful 52. The Racers 54. Treasure of Pancho Villa 56. Guns of the Timberland 58. The Big Circus 59. Cheyenne Autumn 64. The Reward 65. The Poppy is also a Flower 66. Johnny Hamlet 72. Running Wild 73, many others.

Roland, Ruth (1893–1937). American leading lady, a silent serial queen.
The Red Circle 15. The Neglected Wife 17. Hands Up 18. Tiger's Trail 19, etc.
FEATURES: While Father Telephoned 13. The Masked Woman 26. Reno 30. From Nine to Nine 36, many others.

Rolfe, Guy (1915–). Lean British leading man and character actor, former racing driver and boxer.
Hungry Hill (debut) 46. Nicholas Nickleby 47. Uncle Silas 47. Broken Journey 47. Portrait from Life 49. *The Spider and the Fly* 50. Prelude to Fame 51. Ivanhoe 52. King of the Khyber Rifles 54. It's Never Too Late 56. Snow White and the Three Stooges 62. Taras Bulba 62. Mr Sardonicus 63. The Fall of the Roman Empire 64. The Alphabet Murders 65. The Land Raiders 69. Nicholas and Alexandra 71. And Now the Screaming Starts 73, etc.

Romain, Yvonne (1938–). French leading lady in British films.
The Baby and the Battleship 56. Seven Thunders 57. Corridors of Blood 58. Chamber of Horrors 60. Curse of the Werewolf 61. Village of Daughters 61. Devil Doll 63. The Brigand of Kandahar 65. The Swinger (US) 66. Double Trouble (US) 67. The Last of Sheila 73, etc.

Roman, Leticia (1939–). American leading lady of the sixties.
Pirates of Tortuga 61. Gold of the Seven Saints 61. Fanny Hill 64. The Evil Eye 65, etc.

Roman, Ruth (1924–). American actress; leading lady of the fifties, then a plumpish character player.
Ladies Courageous 44. Jungle Queen 45. You Came Along 45. A Night in Casablanca 45. The Big Clock 48. Good Sam 48. *The Window* 49. Champion 49. Barricade 50. Three Secrets 50. Lightning Strikes Twice 51. *Strangers On a Train* 51. Maru Maru 52. Blowing Wild 53. Down Three Dark Streets 54. The Far Country 55. Joe Macbeth 56. Five Steps to Danger 57. Bitter Victory 58. Desert Desperadoes 59. Look in Any Window 61. Love Has Many Faces 65. The Baby 72. Go Ask Alice (TV) 73, etc.
TV series: *The Long Hot Summer* 64.

Romance, Vivianne (1909–). French leading lady of the thirties and forties.
La Belle Equipe 35. Gibraltar 37. The White Slave 38. Blind Venus 39. Box of Dreams 39. Carmen 42, etc.

Romanoff, Mike (1890–1972) (Harry Gerguson). Amiable American con man who posed as a Russian prince (but 'renounced' his title in 1958). Best known as proprietor of Hollywood's most famous and expensive restaurant. Played occasional bit parts.
Arch of Triumph 48. Do Not Disturb 65. Tony Rome 67, etc.

romantic teams who have been popular enough to make several films together are headed by William Powell and Myrna Loy, who made 12 joint appearances. Runners-up include Janet Gaynor and Charles Farrell (11 appearances); Dick Powell and Joan Blondell (10); Fred Astaire and Ginger Rogers (10); Spencer Tracy and Katharine Hepburn (9); Judy Garland and Mickey Rooney (8); Clark Gable and Joan Crawford (8); Nelson Eddy and Jeanette MacDonald (8); Greer Garson and Walter Pidgeon (8); Errol Flynn and Olivia de Havilland (8); Bette Davis and George Brent (7); Clark Gable and Jean Harlow (6); James Cagney and Joan Blondell (6). Even though most of these teamings began because both stars happened to be under contract to the same studio, they would not have continued had they not been felicitous. Other teams who struck notable sparks off each other but have fewer films to their credit include Humphrey Bogart and Lauren Bacall; Ronald Colman and Greer Garson; Cary Grant and Irene Dunne; Greta Garbo and John Gilbert; Greta Garbo and Melvyn Douglas; Bob Hope and Paulette Goddard; Danny Kaye and Virginia Mayo; Alan Ladd and Veronica Lake; Donald O'Connor and Peggy Ryan; Marie Dressler and Wallace Beery; Rita Hayworth and Glenn Ford; John Barrymore and Carole Lombard; Charlie Ruggles and Mary Boland; Rock Hudson and Doris Day; Jack Hulbert and Cicely Courtneidge; Richard Burton and Elizabeth Taylor; John Payne and Betty Grable; James Dunn and Sally Eilers; David Niven and Loretta Young; Van Johnson and June Allyson; Louis Hayward and Patricia Medina; Bob Hope and Dorothy Lamour.

Romberg, Sigmund (1887–1951). Hungarian composer of light music. Scores include *The Desert Song* 29 and 43, *New Moon* 31 and 40, *Blossom Time* 34, *Maytime* 37, *Balalaika* 39, *The Student Prince* 54. (Most of these began as stage operettas.) José Ferrer played him in a biopic, *Deep in My Heart* 54.

Rome in its ancient days was reconstructed for *Quo Vadis, The Sign of the Cross, Ben Hur, The Last Days of Pompeii, Androcles and the Lion, The Fall of the Roman Empire, The Robe, I Claudius, Julius Caesar, Cleopatra* and *Spartacus*. The funny side of its life was depicted in *Roman Scandals, Fiddlers Three, Carry On Cleo, Scandal in the Roman Bath* and *A Funny Thing Happened on the Way to the Forum*. Modern Rome has been seen hundreds of times in Italian movies, notably *Bicycle Thieves, Paisa, La Dolce Vita, The Girls of the Spanish Steps,*

Sunday in August, Rome Eleven o'Clock and the American co-production *Indiscretion* which was shot entirely within Rome's railway station. American views of Rome include *Three Coins in the Fountain, Seven Hills of Rome, Roman Holiday, Two Weeks in Another Town, The Pigeon That Took Rome* and *The Roman Spring of Mrs Stone;* while the Colosseum was used for the finale of films as various as *House of Cards* and *Twenty Million Miles to Earth*. The Vatican was well shown in *Never Take No for an Answer,* about the small boy who persists in getting an audience with the Pope.

Rome Express. A British train thriller directed by Walter Forde in 1933, starring Conrad Veidt; John Paddy Carstairs remade it in 1948, almost word for word and scene for scene, starring Albert Lieven, as *Sleeping Car to Trieste*. Finlay Currie played the same supporting role in both versions.

Rome, Stewart (1887–1965) (Septimus William Ryott). British stage matinée idol who made several romantic films in the twenties and later appeared in character roles.
The Prodigal Son 25. Sweet Lavender 26. The Gentleman Rider 27. Thou Fool 28. Dark Red Roses 29. The Man Who Changed His Name 30. Designing Women 33. Men of Yesterday 34. Wings of the Morning 37. Banana Ridge 41. The White Unicorn 47. Woman Hater 48, etc.

Romeo and Juliet. Apart from the numerous silent versions of Shakespeare's play, and the ballet adaptations, there have been three major straight versions since sound. In 1936 George Cukor directed Leslie Howard and Norma Shearer in a lavish studio-bound semi-pop version for MGM; in 1953 Renato Castellani came to Britain and made for Rank a more sober, but duller film in colour, with Laurence Harvey and Susan Shentall; and in 1968 came Franco Zeffirelli's version with Leonard Whiting and Olivia Hussey. (This won Oscars for Pasqualina de Santis' cinematography and Danilo Donati's costumes.) In the late 1940's, a French *film noir, Les Amants de Verone,* transposed the story to a modern setting. The musical *West Side Story* 61, is a violent modernization of Shakespeare's tale, and *Romanoff and Juliet* a satirical rendering.

Romero, Cesar (1907–). Handsome Latin-American leading man, former dancer and Broadway actor. Also on TV.
Metropolitan (film debut) 35. Wee Willie Winkie 37. The Return of the Cisco Kid (and others in

this series) 39. The Gay Caballero 40. Weekend in Havana 41. Tales of Manhattan 42. Orchestra Wives 42. Coney Island 43. Carnival in Costa Rica 47. That Lady in Ermine 48. Happy Go Lovely 51. Prisoners of the Casbah 53. Vera Cruz 54. The Racers 55. The Leather Saint 56. Villa 58. Two on a Guillotine 64. Marriage on the Rocks 65. Batman 66. Hot Millions 68. Crooks and Coronets (GB) 69. The Midas Run (GB) 69. A Talent for Loving 69. Now You See Him Now You Don't 72 The Strongest Man in the World 74, etc.
TV series: *Batman* (as the Joker) 67–70.

Romero, George (1939–). American director of exploitation pictures.
Night of the Living Dead 68. The Crazies 73. Hungry Wives 73, etc.

Romm, Mikhail (1901–1971). Russian director.
Boule de Suif 34. *Lenin in October* 37. Lenin in 1918 39. The Russian Question 48. Nine Days of One Year 61. Ordinary Fascism 64, etc.

Romney, Edana (1919–) (E. Rubenstein). South African-born leading lady, in three British films of the forties.
□ East of Piccadilly 41. Alibi 42. Corridor of Mirrors 48.

La Ronde. There had been earlier continental films of Arthur Schnitzler's *Reigen*, a light play about love's merry-go-round; but Max Ophuls' 1950 French version was so piquantly presented by a highly sophisticated cast that it seemed to expand suddenly the possibilities of sex comedy on British and American screens. Previously this sort of thing had always been left to the French, but *La Ronde* was so internationally popular that everyone wanted to get in on the act. Jacques Natanson and Ophuls wrote the screenplay. Christian Matras was photographer, Oscar Straus wrote the music, and the top-flight cast included Anton Walbrook, Jean-Louis Barrault, Danielle Darrieux, Simone Signoret, Daniel Gelin, Simone Simon, Fernand Gravet and Gerard Philipe. Roger Vadim's 1964 remake, with colour but less interesting performers, substituted sensation for subtlety.

Ronet, Maurice (1927–). French leading man.
Rendezvous de Juillet 49. La Sorcière 56. He Who Must Die 56. Lift to the Scaffold 47. Carve Her Name with Pride (GB) 58. Plein Soleil 59. Rendezvous de Minuit 61. *Le Feu Follet* 63. Enough Rope 63. The Victors 63. La Ronde 64. Three Weeks in Manhattan 65. Lost Command

66. The Champagne Murders (La Scandale) 67. The Road to Corinth 68. How Sweet It Is (US) 68. The Marseilles Contract 74, etc.

Rookery Nook (GB 1930). Although this early talkie was a straight transference of the popular Aldwych farce, directed by Tom Walls as though the camera were in the front row of the stalls, it admirably preserves Ben Travers' very clever dialogue and stage business along with the best performances of a classic team of farceurs: Walls with a perpetually roving eye, Ralph Lynn dropping his monocle at every untoward event, Robertson Hare moaning calamitously and losing his trousers, Mary Brough sniffing suspiciously, and whoever played Poppy Dickey selling flags for the lifeboat in her cami-knickers. No later farce was ever quite so hilariously well-judged.

Rooks, Conrad (–). American experimental director.
□ Chappaqua 66. Siddhartha 72.

Room, Abram (1894–1976). Russian director, former journalist, with stage experience.
In Pursuit of Moonshine 24. The Haven of Death 26. Bed and Sofa 27. The Ghost that Never Returns 29. The Five Year Plan 30. Invasion 44. Silver Dust 53, etc.

Room at the Top (GB 1959). This raw version of John Braine's novel about a young man's burning ambition to get to the top in a northern town was significant on several counts. It was franker about sex than any previous British movie. It introduced a new directorial talent in Jack Clayton. And it was the spearhead of a new and successful drive to get British films a wider showing in the US. Simone Signoret was imported from France to put the sex over, and won an Academy Award; so did Neil Paterson who wrote the screenplay. *Room at the Top* was logically followed by an overdose of equally raw films about British provincial life: *Saturday Night and Sunday Morning* 60, *A Taste of Honey* 62, *The Leather Boys* 63, etc.; also by its own sequel *Life at the Top* 65, showing what happened to the same characters ten years after. A later TV series, *Man at the Top*, spawned a third film about the character in 1973.

Room Service (US 1938). This George Abbott farce about a theatrical troupe stranded without cash in a smart hotel made too restricted a vehicle for the Marx Brothers but permitted a splendid comedy performance from Donald McBride as the frantic manager. William Seiter directed. It was remade in 1944 by Tim Whelan as a musical, *Step Lively*, with Frank Sinatra and George Murphy.

Rooney, Mickey (1920–) (Joe Yule). Diminutive, aggressively talented American performer, on stage from the age of two (in parents' vaudeville act). In films from 1926 (short comedies) as Mickey McGuire, then returned to vaudeville; came back as Mickey Rooney in 1932.
Autobiography 1965: *I.E.*
My Pal the King 32. The Hide-Out 34. *A Midsummer Night's Dream* (as Puck) 35. *Ah Wilderness* 35. Little Lord Fauntleroy (not in title role) 36. Captains Courageous 37. *A Family Affair* (as Andy Hardy) 37. *Judge Hardy's Children* 38. Love Finds Andy Hardy 38. *Boys' Town* (special AA) 38. The Adventures of Huckleberry Finn 39. *Babes in Arms* 39. Young Tom Edison 40. Strike Up the Band 40. Men of Boys' Town 41. Babes on Broadway 41. A Yank at Eton 42. Andy Hardy's Double Life 42. *The Human Comedy* 43. Girl Crazy 43. Andy Hardy's Blonde Trouble 44. National Velvet 44. Love Laughs at Andy Hardy 46. Summer Holiday 47. The Fireball 50. A Slight Case of Larceny 53. *The Bold and the Brave* 56. Andy Hardy Comes Home 58. Baby Face Nelson 58. The Big Operator 59. Breakfast at Tiffany's 61. It's a Mad Mad Mad Mad World 63. Twenty-Four Hours to Kill 65. Ambush Bay 66. The Extraordinary Seaman 68. Skidoo 68. The Comic 69. Pulp 73. The Domino Principle 77, others.
TV series: The Mickey Rooney Show (Hey Mulligan) 54. Mickey 64, etc.

Roosevelt, Franklin Delano (1882–1945). American president 1933–45, exponent of the 'New Deal'. He was played by Ralph Bellamy in Dore Schary's play and film of his life, *Sunrise at Campobello* 60, by Capt. Jack Young in *Yankee Doodle Dandy* and by Godfrey Tearle in *The Beginning of the End*. In TV's *Eleanor and Franklin* (1976) he was played by Edward Herrmann.

Roosevelt, Theodore (Teddy) (1858–1919). American president 1901–1909. His extrovert personality and cheerful bullish manners have been captured several times on screen, notably by John Alexander in *Arsenic and Old Lace* (a parody) and *Fancy Pants*, by Wallis Clark in *Yankee Doodle Dandy*, by John Merton in *I Wonder Who's Kissing Her Now*, and by Sidney Blackmer in *My Girl Tisa, This is My Affair* and *Buffalo Bill*.

Rope (US 1948). The first film from Transatlantic Pictures, the Alfred Hitchcock–Sidney Bernstein company, showed Hitchcock trying out a new trick: confining the action to one continuous take by using a constantly roving camera and passing something black at reel changes. Patrick Hamilton's suspenseful one-room play about a body in a chest was as suitable for the method as anything ever would be, but the 'ten-minute take' was in fact the negation of cinema and even took away the play's theatrical impact by incessant bewildering movement. It was never tried again. The photographers were Joseph Valentine and William V. Skall.

Rosay, Françoise (1891–1974) (Francoise de Naleche). Distinguished French actress in films from the mid-twenties.
Gribiche 25. *Le Grand Jeu* 33. *La Kermesse Heroïque* 35. Jenny 36. *Un Carnet de Bal* 37 Les Gens du Voyage 38. *Une Femme Disparait* 41. Johnny Frenchman (GB) 45. Macadam 46. *The Red Inn* 51. The Thirteenth Letter (US) 51. That Lady (GB) 54. The Seventh Sin (US) 57. Le Joueur 58. The Sound and the Fury (US) 58. The Full Treatment (GB) 60. Up from the Beach (US) 65, etc.

Rose, Billy (–). American nightclub owner and songwriter, husband of Fanny Brice. Biography 1968: *Manhattan Primitive* by Earl Rogers.

Rose, David (1910–). British-born composer, long in US.
Winged Victory 44. Texas Carnival 51. Jupiter's Darling 54, many others.

Rose, David E. (1895–). American producer, in films from 1930, long in charge of United Artists productions. More recently in Britain.
The End of the Affair 55. The Safecracker 58. The House of the Seven Hawks 59, etc.

Rose, George (1920–). British stage and screen character actor.
Pickwick Papers 52. Grand National Night 53. The Sea Shall Not Have Them 54. The Night My Number Came Up 56. Brothers in Law 57. A Night to Remember 58. Jack the Ripper 59. The Flesh and the Fiends 60. Hawaii (US) 66. A New Leaf 71, etc.

Rose, Jack; see *Shavelson, Melville*.

Rose Marie. The Rudolph Friml/Oscar Hammerstein operetta about the mounties getting their man was first filmed in 1928 by Lucien Hubbard as a silent: Joan Crawford had the title role. In 1936 W. S. Van Dyke made the well-remembered version with Jeannette MacDonald and Nelson Eddy, and in 1954 Mervyn le Roy directed a remake with Ann Blyth and Howard Keel.

Rose, Reginald (1921–). American writer who has created numerous TV plays, also a series, *The Defenders*.
Crime in the Streets 56. *Twelve Angry Men* 57. The Man in the Net, etc.

Rose, William (1918–). American screenwriter who spent some years in Britain.
Once a Jolly Swagman (co-w) 48. The Gift Horse 51. *Genevieve* 53. *The Maggie* 54. The Lady Killers 55. The Smallest Show on Earth 57. *It's a Mad Mad Mad Mad World* 63. The Russians are Coming 66. The Flim Flam Man 67. *Guess Who's Coming to Dinner* (AA) 67. The Secret of Santa Vittoria 69, etc.

Rosen, Phil (1888–1951). Russian-born American director of second features.
The Single Sin 21. The Young Rajah 22. Abraham Lincoln 25. Burning Up Broadway 28. Two-Gun Man 31. Beggars in Ermine 34. Two Wise Maids 37. Double Alibi 40. Forgotton Girls 40. Spooks Run Wild 41. Prison Mutiny 43. Step by Step 46. The Secret of St Ives 49, many others.

Rosenberg, Aaron (1912–). American producer, in Hollywood from 1934; working for Universal from 1946.
Johnny Stool Pigeon 47. Winchester 73 50. The Glenn Miller Story 54. To Hell and Back 55. The Great Man 57. Morituri 65. The Reward 65. Tony Rome 67, many others.

Rosenberg, Stuart (1925–). American director with long TV experience.
□ Murder Inc. 60. Question 7 61. *Cool Hand Luke* 67. The April Fools 69. Move 70. W.U.S.A. 70. Pocket Money 72. The Laughing Policeman 73. The Drowning Pool 75.

Rosenbloom, 'Slapsie' Maxie (1906–1976). American 'roughneck' comedian, ex-boxer, in occasional comedy films as gangster or punch drunk type.
Mr Broadway 33. Nothing Sacred 37. Louisiana Purchase 41. Hazard 48. Mr Universe 51. Abbott and Costello Meet the Keystone Kops 55. The Beat Generation 59, etc.

Rosenman, Leonard (–). American composer.
The Cobweb 55. East of Eden 55. Rebel Without

a Cause 55. Lafayette Escadrille 58. The Chapman Report 62. Fantastic Voyage 66. Hellfighters 68. Beneath the Planet of the Apes 71, etc.

Rosher, Charles (1885–1974). Distinguished American cinematographer.
The Clown 16. The Love Night 20. Smilin' Through 22. Sparrows 26. *Sunrise* (AA) 27. *Tempest* 28. What Price Hollywood? 32. Our Betters 33. The Affairs of Cellini 34. Little Lord Fauntleroy 36. White Banners 38. A Child Is Born 40. Kismet 44. *The Yearling* (co-ph) (AA) 46. *Show Boat* 51. Scaramouche 52. Kiss Me Kate 53. Young Bess 54, many others.

Rosi, Francesco (1922–). Italian director.
La Sfida 57. Salvatore Giuliano (& w) 61. Hands over the City 63. The Moment of Truth 64. More than a Miracle 68, etc.

Rosmer, Milton (1881–1971) (Arthur Milton Lunt). British stage actor, in many films from 1913.
General John Regan 21. The Passionate Friends 22. The Phantom Light 35. South Riding 38. Goodbye Mr Chips 39. Atlantic Ferry 41. Fame is the Spur 47. The Monkey's Paw 48. The Small Back Room 49, etc.
AS DIRECTOR: Dreyfus 31. Channel Crossing 32. The Guvnor 36. The Challenge 37.

Ross, Diana (1944–). Black American singer and actress.
□ *Lady Sings the Blues* (as Billie Holiday) 72. Mahogany 76.

Ross, Frank (1904–). American producer, in Hollywood from early thirties.
Of Mice and Men (associate) 39. The Devil and Miss Jones 41. The Robe 53. The Rains of Ranchipur 55. Kings Go Forth 58. Mister Moses 65. Where It's At 70, others.

Ross, Herbert (1927–). American choreographer.
Doctor Dolittle 67. Funny Girl 69, etc.
□ AS DIRECTOR: Goodbye Mr Chips 69. The Owl and the Pussycat 70. T. R. Baskin 71. Play It Again Sam 72. The Last of Sheila (& p) 73. Funny Lady 75. The Sunshine Boys 75. The Seven Per Cent Solution 76.

Ross, Katharine (1942–). American leading lady.
□ Shenandoah 65. Mr Buddwing 66. The Singing Nun 66. Games 67. *The Graduate* 67. Hellfighters 68. Tell Them Willie Boy is Here 69. Butch Cassidy and the Sundance Kid 69. Fools

70. They Always Kill Their Masters 72. The Stepford Wives 75. Wanted, the Sundance Woman (TV) 77.

Ross, Shirley (1909–1975) (Bernice Gaunt). American pianist and singer who appeared as leading lady in a few films.
The Age of Indiscretion 35. San Francisco 36. *Thanks for the Memory* 38. Paris Honeymoon 39. Kisses for Breakfast 41. A Song for Miss Julie 45, etc.

Rossellini, Roberto (1906–). Italian director, in films from 1938. Started as writer; co-scripts his own films.
Open City 45. *Paisa* 46. Germany Year Zero 48. Stromboli 49. Europa 51. General Della Rovere 59. Louis XIV Seizes Power 66, others.

Rossen, Robert (1908–1966). American writer-producer-director, in Hollywood from 1936 after stage experience.
□ Marked Woman (w) 37. They Won't Forget (w) 37. Racket Busters (w) 38. Dust be My Destiny (w) 39. *The Roaring Twenties* (w) 39. A Child is Born (w) 39. The Sea Wolf (w) 41. Blues in the Night (w) 41. Edge of Darkness (w) 42. *A Walk in the Sun* (w) 45. The Strange Love of Martha Ivers (w) 46. Desert Fury (w) 47. Johnny O'Clock (wd) 47. *Body and Soul* (d) 47. *All the King's Men* (wpd) (AA) 49. The Brave Bulls (pd) 50. Mambo (wd) 54. Alexander the Great (wpd) 56. Island in the Sun (d) 57. They Came to Cordura (wd) 59. *The Hustler* (wpd) 61. Billy Budd (co-w) 62. Lilith (wpd) 64.

Rossi, Franco (1919–). Italian writer-director.
I Falsari 52. Il Seduttore 54. *Amici per la Pelle* (Friends for Life) 55. Morte di un Amico 60. Smog 62, etc.

Rossi-Drago, Eleonora (1925–) (Palmina Omiccioli). Italian leading lady.
Pirates of Capri 48. Persiane Chiuse 50. Three Forbidden Stories 51. The White Slave 53. Le Amiche 55. Maledetto Imbroglio 59. David and Goliath 59. Under Ten Flags 60. Uncle Tom's Cabin (Ger.) 65. Camille 2000 69, etc.

Rossif, Frederic (1922–). French documentarist.
Les Temps du Ghetto 61. Mourir à Madrid 62. The Fall of Berlin 65, etc.

Rossington, Norman (1928–). British character actor of stage, TV and films.
A Night to Remember 58. Carry On Sergeant 58. *Saturday Night and Sunday Morning* 60.

Go to Blazes 62. The Comedy Man 63. Tobruk (US) 66. The Adventures of Gerard 70. Deathline 72. Go for a Take 72, etc.

Rossiter, Leonard (1927–). British comic actor.
King Rat 64. Hotel Paradiso 66. The Devil's Own 67. Oliver 68. Butley 73. The Pink Panther Strikes Again 77, etc.

Rosson, Hal or **Harold** (1895–). Distinguished American cinematographer.
The Cinema Murder 19. Manhandled 24. Gentlemen Prefer Blondes 28. *Tarzan of the Apes* 32. *The Scarlet Pimpernel* 35. The Ghost Goes West 36. The Garden of Allah (AA) 36. *The Wizard of Oz* 39. Johnny Eager 42. The Hucksters 47. *On the Town* 49. *The Red Badge of Courage* 51. *Singin' in the Rain* 52. The Bad Seed 56. No Time for Sergeants 58. El Dorado 67, many others.

Rota, Nino (1911–). Italian composer.
My Son the Professor 46. Flight into France 48. *The Glass Mountain* 48. E Primavera 49. Anna 52. I Vitelloni 53. La Strada 54. Amici per la Pelle 56. *War and Peace* 56. Il Bidone 56. Cabiria 58. La Dolce Vita 59. Plein Soleil 60. Rocco and His Brothers 60. Boccaccio 70 62. Eight and a Half 63. Juliet of the Spirits 65. Shoot Loud, Louder, I Don't Understand 66. Satyricon 69. The Abdication 74, etc.

Roth, Lillian (1910–) (Lillian Rutstein). American leading lady who began her professional career as the baby in the Educational Pictures trademark. After a few films in the early thirties, personal problems caused her retirement. Her story was filmed in 1955 as *I'll Cry Tomorrow*, with Susan Hayward.
The Love Parade 20. The Vagabond King 30. *Madame Satan* 30. Animal Crackers 31. Sea Legs 31. Ladies They Talk About 33. Take a Chance 33, etc.

Rotha, Paul (1907–). British documentarist and film theorist. With GPO Film Unit in thirties, later independent. Author of *The Film till Now, Documentary Film*, etc.
Shipyard 30. Contact 33. The Rising Tide 33. The Face of Britain 34. The Fourth Estate 40. *World of Plenty* 42. Land of Promise 46. The World is Rich 48. No Resting Place 50. World without End (co-d) 52. Cat and Mouse 57. *The Life of Adolf Hitler* 62. The Silent Raid 62, etc.

Rotunno, Giuseppe (–). Italian cinematographer.

Scandal in Sorrento 55. White Nights 57. Anna of Brooklyn 58. The Naked Maja 59. The Angel Wore Red 60. Rocco and His Brothers 60. The Best of Enemies 61. The Leopard 62. Yesterday, Today and Tomorrow 63. Anzio 68. The Secret of Santa Vittoria 69. Satyricon 69. Sunflower 70. Carnal Knowledge 71. Man of La Mancha 72. Amarcord 74, etc.

rough cut. The first assembly of shots in the order in which they will be seen in the finished film, used to show those involved what work still needs to be done.

Roundtree, Richard (1937–). Black American leading man of the seventies.
Shaft 71. Embassy 72. Charley One Eye 72. Shaft's Big Score 72. Earthquake 74. Man Friday 75, etc.
TV series: Shaft 73.

Rounseville, Robert (1914–1974). American opera singer.
☐ Tales of Hoffman 51. Carousel 56.

Rouquier, Georges (1909–). French documentarist.
Le Tonnelier 42. Farrébique 46. Salt of the Earth 50. Lourdes and Its Miracles 56, etc.

Rouse, Russel (c.1916–). American director and co-writer, usually in partnership with Clarence Greene (qv).
D.O.A. 50. The Well 51. The Thief 52. New York Confidential 55. The Fastest Gun Alive 56. Thunder in the Sun 59. A House is Not a Home 64. The Oscar 66. Caper of the Golden Bulls 67, etc.

Rowan, Dan (1922–). American comedian, one-half of *Rowan and Martin*, the other being *Dick Martin* (1922–). Belatedly successful on TV with *Laugh In* 68–72, they have not been popular in films.
☐ Once upon a Horse 57. The Maltese Bippy 69.

Rowland, Roy (c.1910–). American director, mainly of routine features, in Hollywood from mid-thirties. Many shorts, including *Benchley, Pete Smith, Crime Does Not Pay.*
Lost Angel 44. *Our Vines Have Tender Grapes* 45. Killer McCoy 48. Tenth Avenue Angel 48. Scene of the Crime 49. Two Weeks with Love 50. Bugles in the Afternoon 53. The Moonlighter 53. Rogue Cop 53. The Five Thousand Fingers of Doctor T 53. Affair with a Stranger 53. Many Rivers to Cross 55. Hit the Deck 55. Meet Me in Las Vegas 56. These Wilder Years 56. Gun Glory 57. Seven Hills of Rome 58. The Girl

Hunters 64. Gunfighters of Casa Grande 66. They Called Him Gringo 68, others.

Rowlands, Gene (1934–) (Virginia Rowlands). American leading actress, mostly on stage.
The High Cost of Loving 58. A Child is Waiting 62. Lonely are the Brave 62. Tony Rome 67. Faces 68. The Happy Ending 69. Minnie and Moskowitz 71, etc.
TV series: 87th Precinct 61.

Roxie Hart (US 1942). Brilliantly scathing, zippy and entertaining satire, now unjustly forgotten, of Chicago in the twenties, with Ginger Rogers as a chorus girl who confesses to a murder for the sake of the publicity. She is splendidly abetted by Adolphe Menjou, Lynne Overman and George Montgomery; script and production are by Nunnally Johnson, music by Alfred Newman, direction by William Wellman.

Royle, Selena (1904–). American character actress.
The Misleading Lady 32. Mrs Parkington 44. The Fighting Sullivans 44. Gallant Journey 47. Cass Timberlane 47. Joan of Arc 48. Branded 50. Robot Monster 53. Murder is My Beat 55, etc.

Rozsa, Miklos (1907–). Hungarian composer, in Hollywood from 1940.
Knight without Armour 37. *The Four Feathers* 39. *The Thief of Baghdad* 40. Lady Hamilton 41. Five Graves to Cairo 43. Double Indemnity 44. A Song to Remember 44. The Lost Weekend 45. *Spellbound* (AA) 45. *The Killers* 46. Brute Force 47. *A Double Life* (AA) 47. Naked City 48. Adam's Rib 49. The Asphalt Jungle 50. Quo Vadis 51. Ivanhoe 52. Julius Caesar 53. Moonfleet 55. Lust for Life 56. *Ben Hur* (AA) 59. King of Kings 61. El Cid 61. Sodom and Gomorrah 62. The VIPs 63. The Power 65. The Green Berets 68, many others.

Rub, Christian (1887–1956). Austrian character actor, long in Hollywood. Was the model and voice for Gepetto the woodcarver in Disney's *Pinocchio*.
The Trial of Vivienne Ware 32. The Kiss beind the Mirror 33. A Dog of Flanders 35. Dracula's Daughter 36. Heidi 37. Mad about Music 38. The Great Waltz 38. The Swiss Family Robinson 40. Tales of Manhattan 42. Fall Guy 48. Something for the Birds 52, many others.

Rubens, Alma (1897–1931) (Alma Smith). American leading lady of the silent screen: her career was prematurely ended by drug addiction. Intolerance 15. The Firefly of Tough Luck 17. Humoresque 20. Cytherea 24. Fine Clothes 25. Siberia 26. Masks of the Devil 28. Showboat 29, etc.

Ruby, Harry (1895–1974). American songwriter (with Bert Kalmar). See *Kalmar, Bert* for credits.

Ruddy, Albert S. (–   ). American producer.
The Godfather 72. The Longest Yard 74. The McAhans (TV) 76, etc.

Rudley, Herbert (1911–   ). American supporting actor.
Abe Lincoln in Illinois 39. The Seventh Cross 44. *Rhapsody in Blue* (as Ira Gershwin) 45. A Walk in the Sun 46. Joan of Arc 48. The Silver Chalice 55. The Black Sleep 56. Beloved Infidel 59, etc.
TV series: The Mothers-in-Law 68.

Ruggles, Charles (1886–1970). American character comedian, brother of Wesley Ruggles. In films from 1928 after stage experience; quickly became popular for his inimitably diffident manner.
□ Peer Gynt 15. The Majesty of the Law 15. The Reform Candidate 15. The Heart Raider 23. Gentlemen of the Press 29. The Lady Lies 29. The Battle of Paris 29. Roadhouse Nights 30. Young Man of Manhattan 30. Queen High 30. Her Wedding Night 30. *Charley's Aunt* 30. Honor Among Lovers 31. The Girl Habit 31. The Smiling Lieutenant 31. Beloved Bachelor 31. Husband's Holiday 31. This Reckless Age 32. One Hour with You 32. This is the Night 32. Make Me a Star 32. *Love Me Tonight* 32. 70,000 Witnesses 32. The Night of June 13th 32. *Trouble in Paradise* 32. Evenings for Sale 32. If I Had a Million 32. Madame Butterfly 32. Murders in the Zoo 33. Terror Aboard 33. Melody Cruise 33. Mama Loves Papa 33. Girl without a Room 33. Alice in Wonderland 33. Six of a Kind 34. Goodbye Love 34. Melody in Spring 34. Murder in the Private Car 34. Friends of Mr Sweeney 34. The Pursuit of Happiness 34. *Ruggles of Red Gap* 35. People will Talk 35. No More Ladies 35. The Big Broadcast of 1936 35. Anything Goes 36. *Early to Bed* 36. Hearts Divided 36. Wives Never Know 36. Mind Your Own Business 36. Turn Off the Moon 37. Exclusive 37. *Bringing Up Baby* 38. Breaking the Ice 38. Service De Luxe 38. His Exciting Night 38. Boy Trouble 39. Sudden Money 39. Invitation to Happiness 39. Night Work 39. Balalaika 39. The Farmer's Daughter 40.

Opened by Mistake 40. Maryland 40. Public Deb Number One 40. No Time for Comedy 40. Invisible Woman 41. Honeymoon for Three 41. Model Wife 41. The Parson of Panamint 41. Go West Young Lady 41. The Perfect Snob 41. Friendly Enemies 42. Dixie Dugan 43. Our Hearts were Young and Gay 44. The Doughgirls 44. Three is a Family 44. Bedside Manner 45. Incendiary Blonde 45. A Stolen Life 46. Gallant Journey 46. The Perfect Marriage 46. My Brother Talks to Horses 46. *It Happened on Fifth Avenue* 47. Ramrod 47. Give My Regards to Broadway 48. The Loveable Cheat 49. *Look for the Silver Lining* 49. Girl on the Subway (TV) 58. All in a Night's Work 61. *The Pleasure of His Company* 61. The Parent Trap 61. Son of Flubber 63. Papa's Delicate Condition 63. *I'd Rather be Rich* 64. The Ugly Dachshund 66. Follow Me Boys 66.
TV series: The World of Mr Sweeney 53.

Ruggles of Red Gap. This well-known story by Harry Leon Wilson, about a British butler exported to the American mid-west, was filmed with Edward Everett Horton in 1923 and with Charles Laughton in 1935. Bob Hope's *Fancy Pants* in 1950 bore more than a passing resemblance to it.

Ruggles, Wesley (1889–1972). American director, in Hollywood from 1914. One of the original Keystone Kops: brother of Charles Ruggles.
Wild Honey 22. The Plastic Age 26. Silk Stockings 27. Are These Our Children? 30. *Cimarron* 31. No Man of Her Own 32. College Humour 33. *I'm No Angel* 33. Bolero 34. The Gilded Lily 35. Valiant is the Word for Carrie 36. *I Met Him in Paris* 37. True Confession 37. *Sing You Sinners* (& p) 38. Invitation to Happiness 39. My Two Husbands 40. Arizona (& p) 40. Good Morning Doctor 41. Somewhere I'll Find You 42. See Here Private Hargrove 44. London Town (GB) 46, etc.

Ruhmann, Heinz (1902–   ). German actor whose films have rarely been seen abroad.
Drei von der Tankstelle 30. *Ship of Fools* (US) 65, etc.

Rule, Janice (1931–   ). American leading lady with stage and TV experience.
Goodbye My Fancy 51. Holiday for Sinners 52. Rogues' March 53. Gun for a Coward 57. Bell, Book and Candle 58. The Subterraneans 60. Invitation to a Gunfighter 64. *The Chase* 66. Alvarez Kelly 66. The Ambushers 67. The Swimmer 68. Doctors' Wives 71. Gumshoe 71. Kid Blue 73, etc.

Ruman, Sig (or Siegfried Rumann)
(1884–1967). German character actor, usually
of explosive roles, in Hollywood from 1934.
The Wedding Night 35. *A Night at the Opera* 35.
A Day at the Races 37. *Ninotchka* 39. Bitter
Sweet 41. *To Be or Not To Be* 42. The Hitler
Gang 44. *A Night in Casablanca* 45. On The
Riviera 49. *Stalag 17* 53. The Glenn Miller Story
54. Three-Ring Circus 56. The Wings of Eagles
57. Robin and the Seven Hoods 64. Last of the
Secret Agents 66, many others.

running shot. One in which the camera,
mounted on wheels, keeps pace with its subject, a
moving actor or vehicle.

running speed. In silent days, 35 mm ran
through the projector at 16 frames per second or
60 feet per minute. When sound came, this was
amended for technical reasons to 24 frames per
second or 90 feet per minute. No normal 35 mm.
projector can now operate at silent speed, which
is why silent films look jerky when you see them
(unless a special and very expensive laboratory
process is adopted). It is said that many films
made in the later silent period were in fact
intended for showing at about 20 frames per
second, and as machines were variable this was
easily accomplished: such films now seem
unduly slow when projected at 16 frames per
second.
See: *slow motion, accelerated motion.*

Runyon, Damon (1884–1946). Inimitable
American chronicler of the ways of a never-
never New York inhabited by good-hearted and
weirdly-named guys and dolls who speak a
highly imaginitive brand of English. Among the
films based on his stories are *Lady for a Day* 33
(and its remake *Pocketful of Miracles* 61), *The
Lemon Drop Kid* 34 and 51, *A Slight Case of
Murder* 38 (and *Stop You're Killing Me* 52), *The
Big Street* 42, and *Guys and Dolls* 55.

Rush, Barbara (1927–). American leading
lady who came to Hollywood from college.
The First Legion 51. When Worlds Collide 51.
Flaming Feather 52. It Came from Outer Space
53. Magnificent Obsession 54. The Black Shield
of Falworth 54. Captain Lightfoot 55. The
World in My Corner 56. Bigger Than Life 57.
Oh Men! Oh Women! 58. Harry Black 58. The
Young Philadelphians (The City Jungle) 59. The
Bramble Bush 60. Strangers When We Meet 60.
Come Blow Your Horn 63. Robin and the Seven
Hoods 64. Hombre 67. The Eyes of Charles
Sand (TV) 72. Superdad 74, others.

Rush, Richard (–). American director.

Psych-Out 68. Hell's Angels on Wheels 69.
Getting Straight 70. The Stunt Man 71. Freebie
and the Bean 74, etc.

rushes. A day's shooting on film when it comes
back from the laboratories and is ready for
viewing by those involved.

Russell, Gail (1924–1961). American leading
lady of the forties; came to Hollywood straight
from dramatic training.
Henry Aldrich Gets Glamour (debut) 43. Lady
in the Dark 43. *The Uninvited* 44. Our Hearts
were Young and Gay 44. Salty O'Rourke 45.
Night Has a Thousand Eyes 47. Moonrise 48.
Wake of the Red Witch 49. Air Cadet 51. The
Tattered Dress 57. The Silent Call 61, etc.

Russell, Harold (1914–). Canadian
paratroop sergeant who lost both hands in an
explosion during World War II and
demonstrated his ability not only to use hooks in
their place but to act as well in *The Best Years of
Our Lives* 45, for which he won two Oscars.
Published autobiography 1949: *Victory in My
Hands.* Became a public relations executive.

Russell, Jane (1921–). American leading
lady who came to Hollywood when an agent sent
her photo to producer Howard Hughes; he
starred her in *The Outlaw* 43 but it was held up
for three years by censor trouble. The publicity
campaign emphasized the star's physical
attributes.
□ The Young Widow 47. *The Paleface* 48.
Double Dynamite 50. Macao 51. Montana Belle
51. His Kind of Woman 51. Son of Paleface 52.
The Las Vegas Story 52. Gentlemen Prefer
Blondes 53. The French Line 54. Underwater 55.
Gentlemen Marry Brunettes 55. Foxfire 55. Hot
Blood 56. The Tall Men 56. The Revolt of
Mamie Stover 57. The Fuzzy Pink Nightgown
57. Fate is the Hunter (guest appearance) 64.
Waco 66. Darker than Amber 70.

Russell, John (1921–). American 'second
lead'.
Jesse James 39. The Bluebird 40. A Bell for
Adano 45. The Fat Man 51. The Sun Shines
Bright 53. The Last Command 55. Rio Bravo
59. Fort Utah 66. Cannon for Cordoba 70,
many others.
TV series: Soldiers of Fortune 55. Lawman
58–60.

Russell, Ken (1927–). British director, a
middle-aged *enfant terrible* of the seventies who
after a rigorous training in BBC art films turned

out to want to shock people, and did so with flair but no subtlety.
☐ French Dressing 64. Billion Dollar Brain 67. *Women In Love* 69. *The Music Lovers* 70. The Devils 71. The Boy Friend 71. Savage Messiah 72. Mahler 74. Tommy 75. Lisztomania 75. Valentino 77.

Russell, Kurt (1947–). American boy actor of the sixties, usually in Disney films.
The Absent-Minded Professor 60. Follow Me Boys 66. The Horse in the Grey Flannel Suit 68. Charley and the Angel 73. Superdad 74, etc.

Russell, Lillian (1861–1922) (Helen Louise Leonard). Statuesque American singer-entertainer, highly popular around the turn of the century. Made no films, but was played by Alice Faye in a 1940 biopic, by Ruth Gillette in *The Great Ziegfeld*, by Andrea King in *My Wild Irish Rose* and by Binnie Barnes in *Diamond Jim*.

Russell, Rosalind (1908–1976). Dominant American leading lady of the thirties and forties, usually as career women; later attempted character roles, but her choice was sometimes unwise.
☐ Evelyn Prentice 34. The President Vanishes 34. West Point of the Air 35. The Casino Murder Case 35. Reckless 35. China Seas 35. Rendezvous 35. Forsaking All Others 35. The Night is Young 35. It Had to Happen 36. Under Two Flags 36. Trouble for Two 36. Craig's Wife 36. *Night Must Fall* 37. Live Love and Learn 37. Manproof 38. *The Citadel* 38. Four's a Crowd 38. Fast and Loose 39. *The Women* 39. *His Girl Friday* 40. No Time for Comedy 40. Hired Wife 40. This Thing Called Love 41. They Met in Bombay 41. The Feminine Touch 41. Design for Scandal 41. Take a Letter Darling 42. *My Sister Eileen* 42. Flight for Freedom 43. What a Woman 43. Roughly Speaking 45. She Wouldn't Say Yes 45. Sister Kenny 46. The Guilt of Janet Ames 47. Mourning Becomes Electra 48. The Velvet Touch 48. Tell it to the Judge 49. A Woman of Distinction 50. Never Wave at a WAC 52. The Girl Rush 55. Picnic 56. Auntie Mame 58. A Majority of One 61. Gypsy 62. Five-Finger Exercise 62. The Trouble with Angels 66. Oh Dad, Poor Dad 67. Where Angels Go Trouble Follows 68. Rosie 68. The Unexpected Mrs Pollifax 70. The Crooked Hearts (TV) 72.

Russell, William D. (1908–1968). American director.
☐ Our Hearts were Growing Up 46. Ladies' Man 47. *Dear Ruth* 47. The Sainted Sisters 48.

The Green Promise 49. Bride for Sale 49. Best of the Badmen 51.

the Russian cinema has been one of the most influential in the world, chiefly owing to a small group of highly talented men. Before the revolution Russian films were old-fashioned and literary; but the Bolsheviks saw the great potential of the film as propaganda and actively encouraged the maturing talents of such men as Eisenstein (*Battleship Potemkin, October, The General Line, Alexander Nevsky, Ivan the Terrible*), Pudovkin (*Mother, The End of St Petersburg, The Deserter, General Suvorov*), Dovzhenko (*Arsenal, Earth*), Turin (*Turksib*) and Petrov (*Peter the Great*). Donskoi in *The Childhood of Maxim Gorki* and its two sequels were allowed to be nostalgic, but this vein only occasionally comes to the surface, most recently in *The Lady with a Little Dog*. The light touch comes hard to Russian film-makers, but Alexandrov achieved it in *Volga Volga*, and recently there have been signs of greater effort in this direction, at least for home consumption. The stolidity of most Russian films since World War II should not blind anyone to the enormous influence which the best Soviet work has had on film-makers the world over, especially in its exploration of the potentialities of camera movement, editing and sound; all these techniques were seen at their best in the mid-sixties in a seven-hour version of *War and Peace*.

Rutherford, Ann (1920–). American leading lady of the forties, former child stage star.
Love Finds Andy Hardy 38. The Hardys Ride High 39. Gone with the Wind 39. Pride and Prejudice 40. Happy Land 43. Two O'Clock Courage 45. *The Secret Life of Walter Mitty* 47. The Adventures of Don Juan 48. They Only Kill Their Masters 72, etc.

Rutherford, Dame Margaret (1892–1972). Inimitable, garrulous, shapeless, endearing British comedy character actress, who usually seemed to be playing somebody's slightly dotty spinster aunt.
Published *An Autobiography* 1972.
☐ Talk of the Devil 36. Dusty Ermine 38. Beauty and the Barge 38. *The Demi Paradise* 43. Yellow Canary 43. English without Tears 44. *Blithe Spirit* (as Madame Arcati) 45. While the Sun Shines 46. Meet Me at Dawn 47. *Miranda* 47. Passport to Pimlico 48. *The Happiest Days of Your Life* 50. Her Favourite Husband 51. The Magic Box 51. Castle in the Air 51. *The Importance of Being Earnest* 52. Curtain Up 52. Miss Robin Hood 53. Innocents in Paris 53. Trouble in Store 53. The Runaway Bus 54. Mad

about Men 55. Aunt Clara 55. An Alligator Named Daisy 56. The Smallest Show on Earth 57. I'm All Right Jack 59. Just My Luck 59. *Murder She Said* (as Miss Marple) 62. Mouse on the Moon 63. Murder at the Gallop 63. *The VIPs* (AA) 63. Murder Most Foul 63. Murder Ahoy 64. Chimes at Midnight 66. A Countess from Hong Kong 67. Arabella 68.

Ruttenberg, Joseph (1889–). Russian cinematographer, in Hollywood from 1915.
Over the Hill 28. Fury 36. *The Great Waltz* (AA) 38. *Dr Jekyll and Mr Hyde* 41. *Mrs Miniver* (AA) 42. Madame Curie 43. Adventure 46. BF's Daughter 48. Side Street 49. The Forsyte Saga 49. The Great Caruso 51. Julius Caesar 53. The Last Time I Saw Paris 54. The Swan 56. *Somebody Up There Likes Me* (AA) 56. *Gigi* (AA) 58. The Reluctant Debutante 58. Butterfield 8 60. Bachelor in Paradise 61. Who's Been Sleeping in My Bed? 63. Sylvia 63. Harlow 65. Love Has Many Faces 65. The Oscar 66. Speedway 68, many others.

Ruttman, Walter (1887–1941). German director most famous for his experimental film *Berlin* 27.
Weekend 30, Mannesmann 37. Deutsche Panzer 40, etc.

Ruysdael, Basil (1888–1960). Authoritative Russian-American character actor, former opera singer.
The Coconuts 29. Come to the Stable 49. Broken Arrow 50. My Forbidden Past 51. Carrie 52. The Blackboard Jungle 56. The Last Hurrah 58. The Story of Ruth 60, many others.

Ryan, Frank (1907–1947). American director.
Hers to Hold 43. Can't Help Singing 44. Patrick the Great 45. A Genius in the Family 46, etc.

Ryan, Irene (1903–1973) (Irene Riordan). Wiry American comedienne, was famous as Granny in TV's *The Beverly Hillbillies*.
Melody for Three 41. San Diego I Love You 44. Diary of a Chambermaid 45. Meet Me after the Show 51. Blackbeard the Pirate 52. Spring Reunion 57, etc.

Ryan, Kathleen (1922–). Irish leading lady with stage experience.
Odd Man Out (debut) 47. Captain Boycott 47. Esther Waters 48. Give Us This Day 50. The Yellow Balloon 52. Captain Lightfoot 53. Laxdale Hall 53. *Jacqueline* 56. Sail into Danger 58, etc.

Ryan, Mitchell or **Mitch** (1928–). Stalwart American character actor, mostly on TV.
TV series: Chase 74. Executive Suite 76.

Ryan, Peggy (1924–). American teenage comedienne of the early forties, often teamed with Donald O'Connor. In vaudeville from childhood.
Top of the Town 37. Give Out Sisters 42. Top Man 43. The Merry Monahans 44. Bowery to Broadway 44. That's the Spirit 54. On Stage Everybody 45. All Ashore 52, etc.
TV series: Hawaii Five-O 68– .

Ryan, Robert (1909–1973). Strong-featured American leading actor who never seemed to get the roles he deserved.
□ Golden Gloves 40. Queen of the Mob 40. Northwest Mounted Police 40. Bombardier 43. *Gangway for Tomorrow* 43. The Sky's the Limit 43. Behind the Rising Sun 43. The Iron Major 43. Tender Comrade 43. Marine Raiders 44. Trail Street 47. The Woman on the Beach 47. *Crossfire* 47. Berlin Express 48. Return of the Badmen 48. The Boy with Green Hair 48. Act of Violence 49. Caught 49. *The Set-Up* 49. The Woman on Pier 13 49. The Secret Fury 50. Born to be Bad 50. Best of the Badmen 51. Flying Leathernecks 51. The Racket 51. On Dangerous Ground 51. *Clash by Night* 52. Beware My Lovely 52. Horizons West 52. City beneath the Sea 53. The Naked Spur 53. Inferno 53. Alaska Seas 54. About Mrs Leslie 54. Her Twelve Men 54. Bad Day at Black Rock 55. Escape to Burma 55. House of Bamboo 55. The Tall Men 55. The Proud Ones 56. Back from Eternity 56. Men in War 57. *God's Little Acre* 58. Lonelyhearts 59. Day of the Outlaw 59. *Odds against Tomorrow* 59. Ice Palace 60. The Canadians 61. King of Kings 61. The Longest Day 62. *Billy Budd* 62. The Crooked Road 65. Battle of the Bulge 65. The Dirty Game 66. The Professionals 66. The Busy Body 67. The Dirty Dozen 67. Hour of the Gun 67. Custer of the West 67. Dead or Alive 67. Anzio 68. Captain Nemo and the Underwater City 68. The Wild Bunch 69. Lawman 71. The Love Machine 71. And Hope to Die 72. The Iceman Cometh 73. Executive Action 73. Lolly Madonna XXX 73. The Outfit 74.

Ryan, Sheila (1921–1975) (Katherine McLaughlin). American light leading lady of the forties.
Something for the Boys 44. The Lone Wolf in London 46. Caged Fury 47. Mask of the Dragon 51. Pack Train 53, etc.

Ryan, Tim (1889–1956). American comedy

supporting actor, very adept at drunks, wisecracking reporters, dumb cops, etc.
Brother Orchid 40. The Mystery of the Thirteenth Guest 43. Crazy Knights 45. The Shanghai Chest 48. Sky Dragon 49. Cuban Fireball 51. From Here to Eternity 53. Fighting Trouble 56, etc.

Ryan's Daughter (US 1971). The biggest butterfly ever broken on the wheel of David Lean's talent, a tiny village drama stretched out to the length of *Gone with the Wind*. Directorial style almost keeps the interest, though sadly despite the two years of Irish locations the village is a set and some of the beach scenes were shot in South Africa. Robert Bolt's stuffy dialogue hardly helps, but the playing of Sarah Miles, Trevor Howard and Robert Mitchum does.

Rydell, Bobby (1942–). American pop star who appeared to no great advantage in *Bye Bye Birdie* 63.

Rydell, Mark (1934–). American director.
□ The Fox 68. The Reivers 69. The Cowboys (& p) 72. Cinderella Liberty (& p) 74. Harry and Walter Go To New York (& p) 76.

Ryskind, Morrie (1895–). American comedy writer.
Animal Crackers 31. Palmy Days 31. *A Night at the Opera* 35. *My Man Godfrey* 36. Stage Door 37. Room Service 38. Man About Town 39. Penny Serenade 41. Where Do We Go from Here? 45. Heartbeat 46, etc.

S

Sabatini, Rafael (1875–1950). Anglo-Italian author of swashbuckling historical novels, several of which have been filmed more than once: *The Sea Hawk, Scaramouche, Captain Blood, The Black Swan, Bardelys the Magnificent*, etc.

Sabu (1924–1963) (Sabu Dastagir). Boyish Indian actor, a stable lad in Mysore when he was noticed by director Robert Flaherty and appeared in *Elephant Boy* 37. Came to England, later America.
□ The Drum 38. *The Thief of Baghdad* 40. *The Jungle Book* 42. Arabian Nights 42. White Savage 43. Cobra Woman 44. Tangier 46. Black Narcissus 46. *The End of the River* 47. Maneater of Kumaon 48. Song of India 49. Hello, Elephant 52. Jaguar 56. Herrin der Welt (WG) 60. Rampage 63. A Tiger Walks 63.

Sackheim, Jerry (–). American screenwriter.
The Night Before the Divorce 42. The Last Crooked Mile 46. The Strange Door 51. Paula 52. The Black Castle 52. Young Jesse James 60, etc.

Sackheim, William (1919–). American writer.
Smart Girls Don't Talk 48. A Yank in Korea 51. Column South 53. Border River 54. The Human Jungle 54, etc.

safety film took over from nitrate stock in 1950–51. It burns much more slowly and therefore reduces fire risk, but its acetate base also reduces the possibility of gleaming black and white photography, tending instead to a matt look.

Safety Last (US 1923). One of Harold Lloyd's classic gag-and-thrill comedies, probably the best of them, culminating with his climb up a building and many predictable but hilarious mishaps. Directed by Sam Taylor and Fred Newmeyer.

Sagal, Boris (1923–). American director, from TV.
□ Dime with a Halo 63. Twilight of Honor 64. Girl Happy 65. Made in Paris 66. The Thousand Plane Raid 69. Mosquito Squadron 70. The Omega Man 71.
TV series as executive producer: T.H.E. Cat 67.

Sagan, Françoise (1935–) (F. Quoirez). French novelist very popular in the late fifties. Works filmed include *Bonjour Tristesse, A Certain Smile, Aimez-Vous Brahms? (Goodbye Again)*.

Sagan, Leontine (1899–1974). German lady director.
Maedchen in Uniform 31. Men of Tomorrow 32, etc.

Sahl, Mort (1926–). Sardonic American political comedian fashionable in early sixties. Films untypical.
In Love and War 58. All the Young Men 60. Don't Make Waves 67. Doctor You've Got to be Kidding 68, etc.

sailors of whom screen accounts have been given include Christopher Columbus (1446–1506), by Fredric March in *Christopher Columbus* 49; Horatio Nelson (qv); Captain Bligh, by Charles Laughton, and later by Trevor Howard, in *Mutiny on the Bounty* (qv); John Paul Jones (1747–92), by Robert Stack in *John Paul Jones* 59; Francis Drake (1540–96), by Matheson Lang in *Drake of England* 35 and by Rod Taylor in *Seven Seas to Calais* 62; Walter Raleigh by Richard Todd in *The Virgin Queen* 55; and Admiral Halsey, by James Cagney in *The Gallant Hours* 61.

The Saint. Among the actors who have played Leslie Charteris' 'Robin Hood of crime' in both British and American films since 1937 are Louis Hayward, Hugh Sinclair and George Sanders. One feels that 'the Falcon', a series character played in the forties by George Sanders and later Tom Conway, was heavily indebted to the Saint, who more recently made a strong comeback on television in the person of Roger Moore. In France, a barely recognizable 'Saint' has been played in several films by Jean Marais.

Saint, Eva Marie (1924–). Cool, intelligent American stage actress who played heroine in a variety of films.
□ *On the Waterfront* (AA) 54. That Certain Feeling 56. *A Hatful of Rain* 57. Raintree County 57. North by Northwest 59. Exodus 60. All Fall Down 62. 36 Hours 64. The Sandpiper 65. The Russians are Coming, The Russians are Coming 66. Grand Prix 66. The Stalking Moon 68. A Talent for Loving 69. Loving 70. Cancel My Reservation 72.
TV series: How the West Was Won 76–.

St Clair, Malcolm or **Mal** (1897–1952). American director with a reputation for style in the twenties; in the forties however he almost ruined the reputation of Laurel and Hardy.
Find Your Man 24. On Thin Ice 25. A Woman of the World 25. *The Grand Duchess and the Waiter* 26. Breakfast at Sunrise 27. *Gentlemen Prefer Blondes* 28. The Canary Murder Case 29. Dangerous Nan McGrew 30. The Boudoir Diplomat 30. Olsen's Big Moment 33. She Had to Eat 37. A Trip to Paris 38 (and several other Jones Family episodes 36–40). Hollywood Cavalcade 39. Man in the Trunk 42. Over My Dead Body 42. Jitterbugs 43. The Dancing Masters 43. The Big Noise 44. The Bullfighters 45, etc.

St Jacques, Raymond (1930–) (James Johnson). Black American leading man.
Black like Me (debut) 64. Mister Moses 65. Mister Buddwing 66. The Comedians 67. The Green Berets 68. If He Hollers Let Him Go 68. Uptight 68. Change of Mind 70. Cotton Comes to Harlem 70. The Book of Numbers (& pd) 73. Lost in the Stars 73, etc.

Saint James, Susan (1946–) (Susan Miller). American leading lady of the seventies, who is mostly seen on TV playing slightly kooky but determined young ladies.
PJ 68. Where Angels Go Trouble Follows 68. The Magic Carpet (TV) 72, etc.
TV series: *The Name of the Game* 68–71. *McMillan and Wife* 71–75.

St John, Al ('Fuzzy') (1893–1963). American character comedian in many silents from 1913; latterly played comic side-kick in numerous second-feature westerns.
Mabel's Strange Predicament 13. Special Delivery 27. Dance of Life 29. Wanderer of the Wasteland 35. Call of the Yukon 37. Arizona Terrors 42. Frontier Revenge 49, hundreds of others.

St John, Betta (1930–) (Betty Streidler). American leading lady with stage experience.
Dream Wife (debut) 53. The Robe 53. The Student Prince 54. The Naked Dawn 55. High Tide at Noon (GB) 57. Tarzan the Magnificent (GB) 60. City of the Dead (GB) 61, etc.

St John, Howard (1905–1974). American character actor on stage from 1925, films from 1948, usually as father, executive or military commander.
Born Yesterday 50. David Harding, Counterspy 50. Counterspy Meets Scotland Yard 51. The Tender Trap 55. *Lil Abner* 59. Straitjacket 63. Sex and the Single Girl 64. Strange Bedfellows 65. Don't Drink the Water 69, many others.

St John, Jill (1940–) (Jill Oppenheim). American leading lady.
Summer Love 57. The Lost World 60. Come Blow Your Horn 62. Who's Been Sleeping in My Bed? 63. The Liquidator (GB) 65. The Oscar 66. Eight on the Lam 67. Banning 67. Tony Rome 67. Diamonds are Forever 71. Sitting Target 72, etc.

St Trinian's. This school full of little female horrors was originally conceived by cartoonist Ronald Searle. From his formula Frank Launder and Sidney Gilliat made four commercially successful if disappointing farces: *The Belles of St Trinian's* 54, *Blue Murder at St Trinian's* 57, *The Pure Hell of St Trinian's* 60, *The Great St Trinian's Train Robbery* 66.

Sakall, S. Z. (1884–1955) (Eugene Gero Szakall). Hungarian character actor with vaudeville and stage experience. In films from 1916, Hollywood from 1939; became popular comic support and was nicknamed 'Cuddles'. Autobiography 1953: *The Story of Cuddles*.
It's a Date 40. Ball of Fire 41. Casablanca 42. *Thank Your Lucky Stars* 43. *Wonder Man* 45. Cinderella Jones 46. Whiplash 48. Tea for Two 50. The Student Prince 54, many others.

Saks, Gene (1921–). American director, from Broadway.
Barefoot in the Park 67. The Odd Couple 67. Cactus Flower 70. Last of the Red Hot Lovers 72. Mame 74. The Prisoner of 2nd Avenue (a only) 74.

Sale, Richard (1911–). Prolific American writer of stories and screenplays, none very memorable.
Rendezvous With Annie 46. Spoilers of the North (d only) 47. A Ticket to Tomahawk 49. Meet Me After the Show 51. Half Angel (d only) 51. Let's Make It Legal (d only) 51. My Wife's

Best Friend (d only) 52. Suddenly 54. Woman's World 54. Gentlemen Marry Brunettes (& wrote words and music and co-p) 55. Seven Waves Away (& d) 56. The White Buffalo 77, etc.

Sales, Soupy (1926–) (Milton Hines). American entertainer, popular on children's TV. Film debut in *Birds Do It* 66.

Salkow, Sidney (1909–). American director of second features from mid-thirties.
Woman Doctor 39. Café Hostess 40. The Lone Wolf Strikes 40 (and others in this series). The Adventures of Martin Eden 42. Millie's Daughter 46. Bulldog Drummond at Bay 47. Shadow of the Eagle (GB) 50. Sitting Bull 52. The Golden Hawk 52. Jack McCall, Desperado 53. Raiders of the Seven Seas 53. College Confidential 57. Twice Told Tales 63. The Great Sioux Massacre 65, many others.

Sallis, Peter (1921–). Bemused-looking British character actor, often in 'little man' roles.
Anastasia 56. The Doctor's Dilemma 58. Saturday Night and Sunday Morning 60. Charlie Bubbles 67. Inadmissible Evidence 68, many others.

Salmi, Albert (1928–). Chubby American character actor, mainly on stage.
The Brothers Karamazov 58. The Unforgiven 59. Wild River 60. The Ambushers 67. The Deserter 70. Lawman 71. The Take 74, etc.

Salt, Waldo (1914–). American screenwriter.
The Shopworn Angel 38. Tonight We Raid Calais 43. Mr Winkle Goes to War 44. Rachel and the Stranger 48. The Flame and the Arrow 50. Taras Bulba 62. Flight from Ashiya 64. Midnight Cowboy 68. The Gang That Couldn't Shoot Straight 72. Serpico 74. The Day of the Locust 75, etc.

Salter, Hans J. (–). German composer in Hollywood.
Call a Messenger 39. It Started with Eve 41. The Mummy's Tomb 42. The Spoilers 42. Frankenstein Meets the Wolf Man 43. Sherlock Holmes Faces Death 44. Scarlet Street 45. The Web 47. The Reckless Moment 49. The Prince Who was a Thief 51. The Far Horizons 55. The Mole People 56. Raw Wind in Eden 58. Come September 61. Hitler 62. Bedtime Story 64. Beau Geste 66, many others.

Saltzman, Harry (1915–). Canadian-born independent producer with TV experience. Recently very successful in Britain with *Look*

Back in Anger, the James Bond films, *The Ipcress File, The Battle of Britain*, etc.

Samoilova, Tatania (1934–). Russian leading actress.
The Cranes are Flying 57. The Letter that was not Sent 60. Anna Karenina 67, etc.

Samuelson, G. B. (1887–1945). British producer and distributor of silent films. His sons now operate an international production organization.
A Study in Scarlet 14. Little Women 17. Hindle Wakes 18. Quinneys 19. The Last Rose of Summer 21. Should a Doctor Tell? 23. She 25, many others.

San Francisco, replete with cable cars, steep streets, Golden Gate Bridge and Alcatraz out there in the bay, has provided a picturesque location for innumerable movies, outstandingly *Vertigo, What's Up Doc?, The Glenn Miller Story, The Well Groomed Bride, Bullitt, Guess Who's Coming io Dinner, Point Blank, Yours Mine and Ours, The House on Telegraph Hill, Sudden Fear, Experiment in Terror, Flower Drum Song, The Maltese Falcon, The Conversation, Daddy's Gone A-Hunting, Dirty Harry, Pete 'n Tillie, The Laughing Policeman, Dark Passage* and *Petulia*. TV series have also used it ad nauseum: *The Line Up, Sam Benedict, Ironside, McMillan and Wife, Streets of San Francisco, Phyllis*. The Barbary Coast days were well caught in *San Francisco, Nob Hill, Barbary Coast, Flame of the Barbary Coast*, and many other movies.

San Francisco (US 1936). A large-scale Hollywood entertainment of the thirties, its melodramatic story built round a reconstruction of the 1906 earthquake. Typically good performances from Clark Gable, Jeanette MacDonald, Spencer Tracy and Jack Holt; direction by W. S. Van Dyke; special effects, including a still-unsurpassed earthquake sequence, by John Hoffman and others; script by Anita Loos; lavish production values by MGM.

San Juan, Olga (1927–). Vivacious American dancer and comedienne, with radio experience.
Rainbow Island 44. Blue Skies 46. The Beautiful Blonde from Bashful Bend 49. Countess of Monte Cristo 49. The Third Voice 60, etc.

Sanda, Dominique (1948–) (Dominique Varaigne). Leading actress of the seventies.
Une Femme Douce 70. The Garden of the Finzi-

Continis 71. The Conformist 71. Without
Apparent Motive 72.

Sande, Walter (1906–1972). American
character actor, usually a background heavy.
The Goldwyn Follies 38. Confessions of Boston
Blackie 41. To Have and Have Not 44. Wild
Harvest 47. Dark City 50. Red Mountain 52.
Bad Day at Black Rock 55. The Gallant Hours
60, many others.

Sanders, Denis (1929–) and **Terry**
(1931–). American producer brothers who for
many years have been promising great things but
never quite fulfilling them.
A Time Out of War (short) 54. Crime and
Punishment USA 58. War Hunt 61. Shock
Treatment 63, etc.

Sanders, George (1906–1972). Suave British
actor who played scoundrels, cads and crooks
for thirty years. Varied early experience
including London revue.
Autobiography 1960: *Memoirs of a
Professional Cad.*
□ The Man Who Could Work Miracles 36.
Dishonour Bright 37. Lloyds of London 37.
Lancer Spy 37. Four Men and a Prayer 38. The
Outsider 39. Nurse Edith Cavell 39. Confessions
of a Nazi Spy 39. The House of Seven Gables 40.
Rebecca 40. Foreign Correspondent 40. *The
Saint* (series) 40–42. The Falcon (series) 41–43.
Rage in Heaven 41. Man Hunt 41. Son of Fury
42. *The Moon and Sixpence* 42. Quiet Please,
Murder 43. The Lodger 44. Action in Arabia 44.
Summer Storm 44. *The Picture of Dorian Gray*
44. Hangover Square 44. Uncle Harry 45. *A
Scandal in Paris* 46. The Strange Woman 47.
The Ghost and Mrs Muir 47. *Forever Amber* 47.
Bel Ami 48. Personal Column 48. *Lady
Windermere's Fan* 49. Samson and Delilah 49.
All About Eve (AA) 50. I Can Get It For You
Wholesale 51. Ivanhoe 52. Call Me Madam 53.
Witness to Murder 54. King Richard and the
Crusaders 54. Jupiter's Darling 54. Moonfleet
55. The King's Thief 55. Never Say Goodbye 56.
While the City Sleeps 56. Death of a Scoundrel
56. The Whole Truth (GB) 57. From the Earth to
the Moon 58. Solomon and Sheba 59. That Kind
of Woman 59. A Touch of Larceny (GB) 60.
Bluebeard's Ten Honeymoons 60. *Village of the
Damned* (GB) 62. A Shot in the Dark 64. The
Golden Head 64. Moll Flanders 65. The Quiller
Memorandum 66. The Kremlin Letter 69. The
Candy Man 69. Endless Night 72. Doomwatch
72. Psychomania 72.
TV series: George Sanders Mystery Theatre 58.

Sandford, Christopher (1939–). Emaciated
British character actor.
Half a Sixpence 67. Before Winter Comes 70,
etc.

Sandford, Tiny (1894–) (Stanley J.
Sandford). American character actor who is best
remembered as a foil for Laurel and Hardy:
traffic cop or other nemesis.
The Immigrant 17. The World's Champion 22.
The Circus 28. The Iron Mask 29. Our Relations
36. Modern Times 36, many others.

Sandrich, Mark (1900–1945). American
director who came to Hollywood in 1927 as
director of Lupino Lane two-reelers; later
associated with musicals.
□ The Talk of Hollywood 30. Melody Cruise 33.
Aggie Appleby, Maker of Men 33. Hips Hips
Hooray 34. Cockeyed Cavaliers 34. *The Gay
Divorce* 34. *Top Hat* 35. Follow the Fleet 36. A
Woman Rebels 36. Shall we Dance 37. Carefree
38. Man About Town 39. Buck Benny Rides
Again 40. Love Thy Neighbour 40. Skylark 41.
Holiday Inn 42. So Proudly we Hail 43. I Love a
Soldier 44. Here Come the Waves 44.

Sands, Tommy (1937–). American 'teenage
rave' singer.
Sing Boy Sing 57. Love in a Goldfish Bowl 59.
Babes in Toyland 60. The Longest Day 62.
None But the Brave 65, etc.

Sanford, Erskine (1880–1950). American
character actor, playing elderly gents in the
forties.
Pop Always Pays 40. *Citizen Kane* (as flustered
editor) 41. The Magnificent Ambersons 42.
Ministry of Fear 44. Possessed 47. Lady from
Shanghai 48. Macbeth 50, etc.

Sandy or **Baby Sandy** (1938–) (Sandra
Henville). Infant actress who achieved brief
stardom in the early forties.
□ East Side of Heaven 39. Unexpected Father
39. Little Accident 39. Sandy Gets Her Man 40.
Sandy is a Lady 40. Bachelor Daddy 41. Melody
Lane 41. Johnny Doughboy 41.

Sanford, Ralph (1899–1963). American
supporting player, usually in burly 'good guy'
roles.
Give Me a Sailor 38. Thunderhead, Son of
Flicka 45. Champion 49. Blackjack Ketchum
Desperado 56. The Purple Gang 59, many
others.

Le Sang d'un Poète (France 1930). Jean Cocteau's first film was short and surrealist, full of nightmare images with a tendency to the erotic, all sandwiched between shots of a chimney falling. Full of interesting pointers to his later work.

Sangster, Jimmy (1924–). British horror screenwriter, long associated with Hammer Films.
The Trollenberg Terror 55. *The Curse of Frankenstein* 56. *Dracula* 58. *The Mummy* 59. Jack the Ripper 59. Brides of Dracula 60. Taste of Fear (& p) 61. Maniac (& p) 63. Hysteria (& p) 65. *The Nanny* (& p) 65. Deadlier than the Male 67. The Anniversary (& p) 68. Horror of Frankenstein (& pd) 70. Lust for a Vampire (& d) 70. Fear in the Night (& pd) 72, etc.

Santell, Alfred (1895–). American director, former architect. With Mack Sennett as writer and director in the twenties.
Wildcat Jordan 22. Subway Sadie 26. The Patent Leather Kid 27. The Little Shepherd of Kingdom Come 28. *Daddy Long Legs* 30. The Sea Wolf 30. Tess of the Storm Country 33. A Feather in Her Hat 35. *Winterset* 36. Having Wonderful Time 38. Aloma of the South Seas 41. Beyond the Blue Horizon 42. Jack London 44. The Hairy Ape 44. That Brennan Girl 46, etc.

Santley, Joseph (1889–1971). American director, former child actor and vaudevillian.
The Smartest Girl in Town 32. Spirit of Culver 37. Swing, Sister, Swing 41. Hitting the Headlines 42. Brazil 44. Shadow of a Woman 47. Make Believe Ballroom 49, etc.

Santoni, Reni (1939–). American actor, of French/Spanish ancestry; ex TV writer.
Enter Laughing 67. Anzio 68. Dirty Harry 71, etc.

Santschi, Tom (1879–1931). American leading man of the silents.
The Sultan's Power 09. The Spoilers 14. The Garden of Allah 16. Little Orphan Annie 19. Three Bad Men 26. In Old Arizona 29. Ten Nights in a Bar-Room 31, etc.

Sarafian, Richard C. (c. 1927–). American director, of Armenian descent; much TV experience.
□ Andy 65. Run Wild Run Free 69. Fragment of Fear 70. *Vanishing Point* 71. Man in the Wilderness 71. The Man Who Loved Cat Dancing 73. Lolly Madonna XXX 73.

Sarandon, Chris (1942–). American character actor.
Dog Day Afternoon 75. Lipstick 76. The Sentinel 77.

Sarandon, Susan (1946–) (Susan Tomaling). American leading lady, ex-wife of Chris Sarandon.
The Front Page 74. The Great Waldo Pepper 75. Dragonfly 77, etc.

Sargent, Dick (c. 1937–). American screen actor who once specialized in gangling youths.
Bernardine 57. Operation Petticoat 59. That Touch of Mink 62. The Ghost and Mr Chicken 66. The Private Navy of Sergeant O'Farrell 68, etc.

Sargent, Joseph (1925–). American director.
The Forbin Project 69. White Lightning 73. Sunshine (TV) 74. The Taking of Pelham One Two Three 74. MacArthur 77, etc.

Sarne, Michael (1939–). British director, former light actor.
AS ACTOR: Sodom and Gomorrah 60. The Guns of Navarone 61. A Place to Go 64. Every Day's a Holiday 65. Two Weeks in September 67, etc.
□ AS DIRECTOR: The Road to St Tropez 66. Joanna 68. Myra Breckinridge 69.

Saroyan, William (1908–). American writer, mainly of fantasies about gentle people.
The Human Comedy 43. The Time of Your Life 48, etc.

Sarrazin, Michael (1940–). Canadian leading man of the early seventies, usually seen as the young innocent.
□ Gunfight in Abilene 67. *The Flim Flam Man* 67. Journey to Shiloh 67. The Sweet Ride 68. A Man Called Gannon 68. Eye of the Cat 68. They Shoot Horses Don't They? 69. In Search of Gregory 70. The Pursuit of Happiness 71. Believe in Me 71. Sometimes a Great Notion 71. The Groundstar Conspiracy 72. Believe in Me 72. Frankenstein: the True Story (TV) (as the creature) 73. Harry in Your Pocket 74. For Pete's Sake 74. The Reincarnation of Peter Proud 75. The Gumball Rally 76.

Sartre, Jean-Paul (1905–). French existentialist writer. Works filmed include:
Huis Clos (No Exit) 48. Crime Passionel 51. La Putain Respectueuse 52. Les Jeux Sont Faits 54. The Condemned of Altona 63.

Sasdy, Peter (–   ). Hungarian director in England.
□ Taste the Blood of Dracula 69. Countess Dracula 70. Hands of the Ripper 71. Doomwatch 72. Nothing But the Night 72.

Sassard, Jacqueline (1940–). French leading lady.
Accident 67. Les Biches 68.

satire, being defined in theatrical circles as 'what closes Saturday night', has seldom been encouraged by Hollywood, and the few genuinely satirical films have not been commercially successful, from *A Nous la Liberté* through *American Madness*, *Nothing Sacred* and *Roxie Hart* to *The Loved One*. However, the odd lampoon in the middle of an otherwise straightforward comedy has often brought critical enthusiasm for films as diverse as *Modern Times*, *Boy Meets Girl*, *I'm All Right, Jack*, *The President's Analyst* and *The Groove Tube*; and in future it looks as though one can at least expect that the range of permissible targets will become even wider. The spotty but considerable success in 1976 of *Network*, the screen's most hysterical satire of all, was at least partly due to its sexy scenes and uninhibited language.

Saturday Night and Sunday Morning (GB 1960). Alan Sillitoe's raw, humorous wallow in the sub-life of Nottingham was filmed by Karel Reisz, whose directorial talent has oddly found no satisfactory expression since. The film broadened still further the British attitude to illicit sex and taught us that the subject needn't be treated very seriously. It also introduced a new star in Albert Finney. Photographed by Freddie Francis. BFA for the best British film.

Saunders, Charles (1904–). British director, former editor.
Tawny Pipit (co-d) 44. Fly Away Peter 47. One Wild Oat 51. Meet Mr Callaghan 54. Kill Her Gently 57. Womaneater 58. Danger by My Side 62, etc.

Saunders, John Monk (1895–1940). American screenwriter with a special interest in aviation.
Wings 28. *Dawn Patrol* 30. *The Last Flight* 31. Devil Dogs of the Air 35. I Found Stella Parish 35.

Sautet, Claude (1924–). French director.
The Big Risk 60. Head First 64. Les Choses de la Vie 69.

The Savage Eye (US 1959). One of the first of the exposé pictures which have since flooded the market, this semi-professional job with flashes of brilliance attempts to take the lid off a big American city, with scenes of faith healing, striptease and wrestling to show its decadence. The connecting narration by a neurotic woman is unfortunate. Produced and directed by Ben Maddow and Joseph Strick.

Savalas, Telly (1924–) (Aristotle Savalas). Greek-American character actor with TV experience; former academic.
The Young Savages 59. Birdman of Alcatraz 62. The Interns 63. Cape Fear 63. The Man from the Diners' Club 63. The New Interns 64. Genghis Khan 65. *The Battle of the Bulge* 65. The Slender Thread 66. Beau Geste 66. The Dirty Dozen 67. *The Scalphunters* 68. Buona Sera Mrs Campbell 68. The Assassination Bureau (GB) 68. Crooks and Coronets (GB) 69. The Land Raiders 69. Mackenna's Gold 69. Kelly's Heroes 70. A Town Called Bastard 71. Pretty Maids All in a Row 71. Pancho Villa 71. The Marcus Nelson Murders (TV) 73. A Reason to Live a Reason To Die 72. The Killer is on the Phone 72. She Cried Murder (TV) 73. The Diamond Mercenaries 75. Inside Out 75, etc.
TV series: *Kojak* 73– .

Saville, Victor (1897–). British director who after making some outstanding films in the thirties went to Hollywood with very meagre results. Former film salesman and exhibitor.
The Arcadians 27. Roses of Picardy 28. *Woman to Woman* (US) 29. Hindle Wakes 31. Sunshine Susie 31. *The Good Companions* 32. I Was a Spy 33. *Friday the Thirteenth* 33. *Evergreen* 34. The Iron Duke 36. Dark Journey 37. Storm in a Teacup 37. *South Riding* 38. The Citadel (p only) 38. Goodbye Mr Chips (p only) 39. Bitter Sweet (p) 40. Dr Jekyll and Mr Hyde (p) 41. White Cargo (p) 42. Tonight and Every Night (pd) 44. The Green Years (pd) 46. If Winter Comes (d) 47. The Conspirator (d) 47. Kim (p) 51. I the Jury (p) 53. The Long Wait (pd) 54. The Silver Chalice (pd) 55. Kiss Me Deadly (p) 55. The Greengage Summer (p) 61.

Sawdust and Tinsel (Sweden 1953). The first of writer-director Ingmar Bergman's films to be internationally noticed, this deftly handled melodrama has Ake Gromberg as the foolish owner of a travelling circus and Harriet Andersson as his repressed wife.

Sawtell, Paul (–   ). American composer.
The Gay Falcon 41. Tarzan Triumphs 43. The Scarlet Claw 44. Dick Tracy Meets Gruesome

47. Black Magic 49. Son of Dr Jekyll 51. Inferno 53. Texas Lady 55. Stopover Tokyo 57. The Lost World 60. Five Weeks in a Balloon 62. Island of the Blue Dolphins 64. The Christine Jorgenson Story 70, many others.

Sawyer, Joseph (1901–) (Joseph Sauer). American comedy actor usually seen as tough cop or army sergeant.
College Humour 33. The Marines Have Landed 36. About Face 42. The McGuerins from Brooklyn 42. Fall In 44. Joe Palooka, Champ 46. Fighting Father Dunne 49. It Came from Outer Space 53. The Killing 56, many others.

Saxon, John (1935–) (Carmen Orrico). American leading man, former model.
Running Wild (debut) 55. The Unguarded Moment 56. The Reluctant Debutante 58. Portrait in Black 59. The Unforgiven 59. The Plunderers 60. Posse from Hell 61. War Hunt 62. The Cardinal 63. The Evil Eye (It.) 63. The Appaloosa 66. The Night Caller (GB) 67. Death of a Gunfighter 69. Joe Kidd 72. Enter the Dragon 73. Black Christmas 75. Mitchell 75.
TV series: The Bold Ones 69.

Sayonara (US 1957). A solemn burying of the hatchet between two countries in the form of a romantic idyll between an American air force officer and a Japanese girl after World War II. Immensely good to look at but extremely long drawn out by director Joshua Logan, with little meat to be had from Paul Osborn's script or James Michener's original novel, and a mumbling Southern-accented performance from Marlon Brando. The armchair travelogue elements come off best, via Ellsworth Fredericks' cinematography. AA best art direction, sound recording, supporting actors Red Buttons and Miyoshi Umeki.

Scaife, Ted (1912–). British cinematographer.
Bonnie Prince Charlie 48. An Inspector Calls 54. Sea Wife 57. *Night of the Demon* 57. 633 Squadron 64. *Khartoum* 66. The Dirty Dozen 67. Play Dirty 68. Sinful Davey 69. Forbush and the Penguins 71. Hannie Caulder 71. Sitting Target 72. Catlow 72, many others.

Scala, Gia (1934–1972) (Giovanna Scoglio). Italian leading lady who made a few American films.
The Price of Fear 56. Four Girls in Town 56. Don't Go Near the Water 56. The Garment Jungle 57. The Two-Headed Spy (GB) 58. I Aim at the Stars 59. The Guns of Navarone 61, etc.

Scaramouche. Rafael Sabatini's tongue-in-cheek French Revolutionary romance, about a nobleman who, to outwit his enemies, disguises himself as a clown in a travelling theatre, was filmed in 1922 by Rex Ingram, with Ramon Novarro, and in 1952 by George Sidney, with Stewart Granger.

Scarface (US 1932). A highly professional and exciting gangster film based on the career of Al Capone. Written by Seton I. Miller, John Lee Mahin, W. R. Burnett and Ben Hecht, directed by Howard Hawks, it made crime so attractive that the moralists were subsequently able to curb Hollywood's freedom by means of a tougher code. Photography by Lee Garmes and L. W. O'Connell, production by Howard Hughes; cast headed by Paul Muni and George Raft, who have been associated with these roles ever since.

The Scarlet Empress (US 1934). For its superb visual flair rather than its dramatic sense, this highly romanticized biography of Catherine the Great remains a cinema classic. Fantastically baroque décor, a hypnotic performance from Sam Jaffe as the mad prince, and the mysterious depths of Marlene Dietrich's personality (here suggested but not plumbed) are brought together by Josef Von Sternberg into a fantasy he relishes to the last hysterical note. See also: *Catherine the Great.*

The Scarlet Letter. Nathaniel Hawthorne's story of puritanical eighteenth-century New England was filmed in 1917 with Mary Martin as the adultress and Stuart Holmes as her priest-lover forced to accuse her. In 1926 came Victor Sjostrom's more famous version with Lillian Gish and Lars Hanson. 1934 brought a talkie remake with Colleen Moore and Hardie Albright.

The Scarlet Pimpernel. Baroness Orczy's foppish hero of the French Revolution has been filmed three times since sound. GB 1935: by Harold Young, with Leslie Howard, opposing Raymond Massey as Chauvelin. GB 1938: by Hans Schwarz, with Barry K. Barnes winning out over Francis Lister. GB 1950: by Michael Powell and Emeric Pressburger, with David Niven as Sir Percy. There has also been a TV series starring Marius Goring. Silent versions included one in 1917 starring Dustin Farnum and one in 1929 starring Matheson Lang. The idea was modernized in Leslie Howard's *Pimpernel Smith* 41.

Scarlet Street (US 1945). This sombre drama directed by Fritz Lang concerns a professor

(Edward G. Robinson) who is taken in by a tart, finally murders her, and allows her gigolo friend to be executed for the crime. A remake of Renoir's 1931 French film *La Chienne*, it was notable as the first American film in which a character is allowed to commit murder and get away with it—although he is shown to be still tortured by remorse many years later.

Scattergood Baines, an amiable small-town busybody created by Clarence Buddington Kelland, was personified by Guy Kibbee in six second features (41–42), all directed by Christy Cabanne.

scenario: see *shooting script.*

Schaefer, George (1920–). American director with TV experience.
□ Macbeth 61. Pendulum 68. Doctors' Wives 71.

Schafer, Natalie (1912–). American comedienne usually seen as a dizzy rich woman.
Marriage is a Private Affair 43. Wonder Man 45. The Snake Pit 48. Caught 49. Anastasia 56. Oh Men Oh Women 57. Susan Slade 61. Forty Carats 73, etc.
TV series: *Gilligan's Island* 64–66.

Schaffner, Franklin (1920–). Stylish American director, from TV.
□ The Stripper 63. *The Best Man* 64. *The War Lord* 65. The Double Man 67. *Planet of the Apes* 68. *Patton* (AA) 69. Nicholas and Alexandra 71. *Papillon* 73.

Scharf, Walter (–). American composer.
Chatterbox 43. Dakota 45. The Saxon Charm 48. Deported 50. Hans Christian Andersen 52. Living It Up 54. Hollywood or Bust 56. King Creole 58. A Pocketful of Miracles 61. Where Love Has Gone 64. Pendulum 69. The Cheyenne Social Club 70. Ben 72, many others.

Schary, Dore (1905–). American writer-producer with newspaper and theatrical experience. AA best screenplay *Boys' Town* 38; produced for MGM 1941–45; head of production RKO 1945–48; head of production MGM 1948–56; since then independent.
Lonely Hearts 59. Sunrise at Campobello 60. Act One (wpd) 63, etc.

Schatzberg, Jerry (–). American director, former fashion photographer.
□ Puzzle of a Downfall Child 71. The Panic in

Needle Park 71. Scarecrow 73. Dandy, the All American Girl 76.

Scheider, Roy (1934–). Lean American character actor.
The Curse of the Living Corpse 64. Klute 71. Assignment Munich (TV) 72. The French Connection 72. The Seven-Ups 73. Jaws 75. Marathon Man 76, etc.

Schell, Maria (1926–). Austrian leading lady who has been in British and American films.
The Angel with the Trumpet 49. The Magic Box 51. So Little Time 52. The Heart of the Matter 52. Der Traumende Mund 53. The Last Bridge (Aus.) 54. Die Ratten 55. White Nights (It.) 57. Une Vie (Fr.) 58. The Brothers Karamazov 58. Cimarron 61. The Mark (GB) 61. 99 Women 69. The Odessa File 74, etc.

Schell, Maximilian (1930–). Austrian leading man who has been in international films. Brother of Maria Schell.
Kinder, Mütter und Ein General 58. The Young Lions 58. *Judgment at Nuremberg* (AA) 61. Five-Finger Exercise 62. The Condemned of Altona 63. The Reluctant Saint 63. Topkapi 64. Return from the Ashes 65. The Deadly Affair 66. Beyond the Mountains 66. Counterpoint 67. The Castle 68. Krakatoa 68. First Love (wpd only) 70. The Passenger (pd) 73. The Odessa File 74. First Love (& d) 75. The Man in the Glass Booth 75. Julia 77. Cross of Iron 77, etc.

Schenck, Aubrey (1908–). American producer.
Shock 46. Repeat Performance 48. Beachhead 53. Up Periscope 58. Frankenstein 70 59. Robinson Crusoe on Mars 64. Don't Worry We'll Think of a Title 66. The Alpha Caper (TV) 73, etc.

Schenck, Joseph M. (1878–1961). Russian-born executive, in America from 1900, at first as pharmacist, then as fairground showman and owner. By 1924 was chairman of United Artists and creator of its theatre chain. In 1933 he founded Twentieth Century Productions and by 1935 was head of Twentieth-Century Fox. In 1953 he created Magna Productions with Mike Todd. In 1950 he was voted a special Academy Award.

Schenck, Nicholas M. (1881–1969). Russian-born executive, brother of Joseph M. Schenck, with whom after arrival in America in 1900 he ran an amusement park. Later developed theatre chain which emerged as Loew's Consolidated Enterprises; became president of Loew's and thus financial controller of MGM.

Schertzinger, Victor (1880–1941). American director, former concert violinist. Wrote the first film music score, for *Civilisation* 15.
AS DIRECTOR: Forgotten Faces 29. Nothing but the Truth 31. Uptown New York 32. The Cocktail Hour 33. One Night of Love 34. Love Me Forever 35. The Music Goes Round 36. Something to Sing About 36. The Mikado (GB) 39. Road to Singapore 40. Rhythm on the River 41. Road to Zanzibar 41. Kiss the Boys Goodbye 41, etc.

Schiaffino, Rosanna (1939–). Italian leading lady in international films.
Two Weeks in Another Town 62. The Victors 63. El Greco 66. Arrivederci Baby 66. The Man Called Noon 73. The Heroes 75, etc.

Schifrin, Lalo (–). Argentinian composer in Hollywood.
Joy House 64. The Cincinnati Kid 64. The Liquidator 66. Cool Hand Luke 67. The Brotherhood 68. Bullitt 68. Kelly's Heroes 70. The Beguiled 71. Dirty Harry 71. Prime Cut 72. The Wrath of God 72. The Four Musketeers 75, many others.

Schildkraut, Joseph (1895–1964). Austrian leading man and character actor, of theatrical family. On American stage from early twenties. Autobiography 1959: *My Father and I*.
Orphans of the Storm 21. Dust of Desire 23. The Road to Yesterday 25. *King of Kings* 27. *Show Boat* 29. Mississippi Gambler 30. Night Ride 31. Carnival (GB) 32. The Blue Danube 32. Garden of Allah 36. *The Life of Émile Zola* (as Dreyfus) (AA) 37. Suez 38. Idiot's Delight 38. The Man in the Iron Mask 39. Flame of the Barbary Coast 44. *The Cheaters* 45. Monsieur Beaucaire 46. End of the Rainbow 47. Gallant Legion 48. *The Diary of Anne Frank* 59, etc.

Schilling, Gus (1908–1957). Wry-faced American comic actor from musical comedy and burlesque.
Citizen Kane (debut; as the waiter) 41. A Thousand and One Nights 44. Lady from Shanghai 47. On Dangerous Ground 52. Glory 56, etc.

Schlesinger, John (1926–). British director, former small-part actor and TV director.
□ *Terminus* 60. *A Kind of Loving* 62. *Billy Liar* 63. *Darling* 65. Far from the Madding Crowd 67. *Midnight Cowboy* (US) 69. *Sunday Bloody*

Sunday 72. The Day of the Locust 75. Marathon Man 76.

Schnee, Charles (1916–1963). American screenwriter.
I Walk Alone 47. The Furies 50. *The Bad and the Beautiful* (AA) 52. Butterfield 8 60. The Crowded Sky 61. Two Weeks in another Town 62, etc.

Schneer, Charles (1920–). American producer, mainly of trick films using 'Superdynamation'.
The Seventh Voyage of Sinbad 58. The Three Worlds of Gulliver 59. I Aim at the Stars 61. Mysterious Island 62. *Jason and the Argonauts* 63. The First Men in the Moon 64. You Must Be Joking 65. Half a Sixpence 67. The Executioner 69. Sinbad's Golden Voyage 74. Sinbad and the Eye of the Tiger 77, etc.

Schneider, Marie (–). German leading actress.
Last Tango in Paris 73. The Passenger 73, etc.

Schneider, Romy (1938–) (Rosemarie Albach-Retty). Austrian leading lady in international films.
The Story of Vicki (Ger.) 58. Forever My Love 61. Boccaccio 70. 62. The Cardinal 63. The Trial 63. The Victors 63. Good Neighbour Sam 64. What's New Pussycat? 65. 10.30 p.m. Summer 66. Triple Cross 66. Les Choses de la Vie 69. Don't You Cry 70. Bloomfield 70. The Assassination of Trotsky 72. The Infernal Trio 74, etc.

Schneiderman, George (c. 1890–1964). American cinematographer.
Love is Love 19. Bare Knuckles 21. Boston Blackie 23. *The Iron Horse* 24. The Johnstown Flood 26. Three Bad Men 26. Four Sons 28. Born Reckless 30. Charlie Chan Carries On 31. Young America 32. Doctor Bull 33. *Judge Priest* 34. Steamboat Round the Bend 35. The Devil is a Sissy 36. The Gladiator 38. Michael Shayne Private Detective 40, many others.

Schnitzler, Arthur (1862–1931). Austrian playwright whose chief bequests to the cinema are *Liebelei* and *La Ronde*.

Schoedsack, Ernest B. (1893–). American director, former cameraman, who with Merian C. Cooper made the following.
Grass 26. *Chang* 27. *The Four Feathers* 29. Rango 31. *The Hounds of Zaroff* 32. *King Kong* 33. Son of Kong 34. Long Lost Father 34.

Outlaws of the Orient 37. Dr Cyclops 39. Mighty Joe Young 49, etc.

schooldays have often been depicted in films with a thick sentimental veneer, as in *Goodbye Mr Chips*, *Good Morning Miss Dove* and *Blossoms in the Dust*. But more usually the pupils have serious problems to worry about, as in *Young Woodley*, *The Guinea Pig*, *Friends for Life*, *Tea and Sympathy* and *Tom Brown's Schooldays*; while with at least equal frequency our sympathies are elicited on behalf of the staff: *The Housemaster*, *Bright Road*, *The Blackboard Jungle*, *The Browning Version*, *Spare the Rod*, *Edward My Son*, *The Blue Angel*, *The Children's Hour*, *The Corn is Green*, *Term of Trial*, *To Sir With Love*, *Spinster*, *The Prime of Miss Jean Brodie*, *Please Sir*, *Unman Wittering and Zigo*. More light-hearted treatment of the whole business is evident in *The Trouble with Angels* and *Margie*, and in some cases the treatment has undeniably been farcical: *Boys Will Be Boys*, *The Ghost of St Michael's*, *Good Morning Boys*, *A Yank at Eton*, *Vice Versa*, *Bottoms Up* and *The Happiest Days of Your Life*; with the St Trinians saga wildest of all. The strangest schools on film are those depicted in *Zéro de Conduite* and its semi-remake *If . . .* while very special schools are seen in *Battement de Coeur* (for pickpockets), *School for Secrets* (for 'boffins'), *Old Bones of the River* (for African tiny tots), *The Goose Steps Out* (for young Nazis), *Orders to Kill*, *The House on 92nd Street*, *Carve Her Name with Pride* and *From Russia with Love* (for spies).

Schreck, Max (1879–1936). German actor best known for his eerie portrayal of the vampire count in *Nosferatu* 22.

Schufftan, Eugene (1893–). German cinematographer. Invented the Schufftan process, a variation on the 'glass shot' (qv), by which mirror images are blended with real backgrounds.
People on Sunday 30. *L'Atlantide* 32. *Drôle de Drame* 37. *Quai des Brumes* 38. *It Happened Tomorrow* 44. *Ulysses* 54. *Eyes without a Face* 59. *Something Wild* 61. *The Hustler* (AA) 62. *Lilith* 64, etc.

Schulberg, B. P. (1892–1957). American executive, former publicist; general manager of Paramount (1926–32), then independent producer.

Schulberg, Budd (1914–). American novelist whose work has been adapted for the screen. Son of B. P. Schulberg.

On the Waterfront (AA) 54. The Harder They Fall 56. A Face in the Crowd 57. Wind Across the Everglades 59, etc.

Schunzel, Reinhold (1886–1954). German actor and director who came to Hollywood in the thirties.
Rich Man, Poor Girl (d) 38. Balalaika (d) 39. The Great Awakening (d) 41. Hostages (a) 43. The Man in Half Moon Street (a) 44. The Woman in Brown (a) 48. Washington Story (a) 52, etc.

Schuster, Harold (1902–). American director, former editor.
Wings of the Morning 37. Dinner at the Ritz 37. Zanzibar 40. My Friend Flicka 43. The Tender Years 47. So Dear to My Heart 49. Kid Monk Baroni 52. Slade 53. Dragoon Wells Massacre 57. The Courage of Black Beauty 58, etc.

Schwartz, Arthur (1900–). American producer and composer, former lawyer.
Navy Blues (c) 42. Thank Your Lucky Stars (c) 43. Cover Girl (p) 44. The Band Wagon (c) 53. You're Never Too Young (c) 55, others.

Schwarz, Maurice (1891–1960). American actor famous in the Yiddish theatre; many of his successes, such as *Tevya the Milkman*, were filmed for limited circulation. Appeared in Hollywood's version of *Salome* 53.

science fiction, a term incapable of precise definition, may perhaps be taken as that kind of fantasy which depends not on legend only, like Dracula, but involves the work of man. Thus King Kong and the 'natural' monsters would not qualify, but Frankenstein and the Invisible Man would. Space exploration and prophecy, considered elsewhere, are branches of it, as are all the films about mad doctors and colliding worlds.

scientists have been the subject of many films, though few real-life ones have led sufficiently dramatic lives to warrant filming. Warners led the way in the thirties with *The Story of Louis Pasteur* and *Dr Ehrlich's Magic Bullet*. In 1939 Mickey Rooney played *Young Tom Edison*, followed by Spencer Tracy as *Edison the Man*. Then in 1943, Greer Garson played *Madame Curie*. At this point the movie fan's thirst for scientific knowledge died out, and John Huston's *Freud* in 1962 did not revive it.
See also: *inventors*.

Scofield, Paul (1922–). Distinguished British stage actor whose films have been infrequent.

☐ That Lady 55. Carve Her Name with Pride 58. The Train 64. *A Man For All Seasons* (AA, BFA) 66. King Lear 69. Bartleby 71. Scorpio 73. A Delicate Balance 73.

score. The music composed for a film.

Scorsese, Martin (–). American director.
☐ Who's That Knocking at My Door? 70. Boxcar Bertha 72. *Mean Streets* 73. *Alice Doesn't Live Here Any More* 74. *Taxi Driver* 76. New York, New York 77.

Scott, Adrian (1912–1972). American producer.
Murder My Sweet 44. My Pal Wolf 44. Cornered 46. So Well Remembered 47. Crossfire 47, etc.

Scott, George C. (1926–). Distinguished but taciturn American actor; usually plays tough or sardonic characters and was the first actor to refuse an Oscar.
☐ The Hanging Tree 58. *Anatomy of a Murder* 59. *The Hustler* 62. *The List of Adrian Messenger* 63. Dr Strangelove 63. The Yellow Rolls Royce 64. The Bible 66. Not with My Wife You Don't 66. The Flim Flam Man 67. Petulia 69. *Patton* (AA) 70. They Might Be Giants 71. The Last Run 71. *The Hospital* 72. The New Centurions 72. Jane Eyre (TV) 72. Oklahoma Crude 73. The Day of the Dolphin 73. Rage (& d) 73. The Savage is Loose (& d) 74. Bank Shot 75. The Hindenberg 75. The Prince and the Pauper 77.
TV series: East Side West Side 63.

Scott, Gordon (1927–) (Gordon M. Werschkul). American leading man who after being fireman, cowboy and lifeguard was signed to play Tarzan in *Tarzan's Hidden Jungle* 55; made four further episodes, has lately been in Italy making muscleman epics.
Romulus and Remus 61. Maciste against the Vampires 61. Zorro and the Three Musketeers 62. Goliath and the Black Hercules 63. Arm of Fire 64. The Tramplers 66, etc.

Scott, Gordon L. T. (1920–). British producer, former production manager.
Look Back in Anger 58. Petticoat Pirates 61. The Pot Carriers 63. Crooks in Cloisters 64, etc.

Scott, Janette (1938–). British leading lady, former child star.
Went the Day Well? 42. No Place for Jennifer 49. No Highway 50. The Magic Box 51. As Long As They're Happy 52. Now and Forever 55. The Good Companions 57. The Devil's Disciple 59. The Old Dark House 63. *The Beauty Jungle* 64. Crack in the World 65, etc.

Scott, Lizabeth (1922–) (Emma Matzo). Sultry American leading lady of the forties, a box office concoction of blonde hair, defiant expression and immobile upper lip.
☐ *You Came Along* 45. The Strange Love of Martha Ivers 46. Dead Reckoning 47. Desert Fury 47. I Walk Alone 47. Variety Girl 47. Pitfall 48. Too Late for Tears 49. Easy Living 49. Paid in Full 50. Dark City 50. The Racket 51. The Company She Keeps 51. Two of a Kind 51. Red Mountain 51. Stolen Face 52. Scared Stiff 53. Bad for Each Other 54. Silver Lode 54. Loving You 57. The Weapon 57. Pulp 72.

Scott, Margaretta (1912–). British stage (from 1929) and screen (from 1934) actress who usually plays upper-middle-class women.
Dirty Work 34. Things to Come 36. Quiet Wedding 40. Sabotage at Sea 42. Fanny by Gaslight 43. The Man from Morocco 45. Mrs Fitzherbert 47. Idol of Paris 48. Where's Charley? 52. Town on Trial 56. The Last Man to Hang 56. A Woman Possessed 58. An Honourable Murder 60. Crescendo 69. Percy 71, etc.

Scott, Martha (1914–). American actress with stage experience.
Our Town 40. Cheers for Miss Bishop 41. The Howards of Virginia 41. Hi Diddle Diddle 42. One Foot in Heaven 42. In Old Oklahoma 43. So Well Remembered 47. The Desperate Hours 55. The Ten Commandments 56. Ben Hur 59. Airport 75 74, etc.

Scott, Peter Graham (1923–). British director, from TV.
Panic in Madame Tussauds 48. Sing Along with Me 52. The Headless Ghost 59. Captain Clegg 62. The Pot Carriers 63. Bitter Harvest 63. Father Came Too 64. Mister Ten Per Cent 67. The Promise 69, etc.

Scott, Pippa (–). American actress.
Auntie Mame 58. Petulia 68. Cold Turkey 70, etc.

Scott, Randolph (1903–) (Randolph Crane). Rugged American outdoor star, in films from 1931 after stage experience.
Sky Bride 31. Supernatural 32. Home on the Range 33. Roberta 34. *She* 35. So Red the Rose 35. Follow the Fleet 36. Go West Young Man 36. *Last of the Mohicans* 36. High, Wide and Handsome 37. Rebecca of Sunnybrook Farm

38. The Texans 38. Jesse James 39. Virginia City 40. My Favourite Wife 40. When the Daltons Rode 40. Western Union 41. Belle Starr 41. Paris Calling 41. To the Shores of Tripoli 42. The Spoilers 42. Pittsburgh 42. Bombardier 43. Gung Ho 43. The Desperadoes 43. Belle of the Yukon 44. China Sky 44. Captain Kidd 45. Badman's Territory 46. Abilene Town 47. Christmas Eve 47. Fighting Man of the Plains 49. Sugarfoot 51. Santa Fe 51. Hangman's Knot 53. The Stranger Wore a Gun 53. The Bounty Hunter 54. A Lawless Street 55. Seven Men from Now 56. Decision at Sundown 57. Ride Lonesome 58. Ride the High Country 62, many others.

Scott, Sir Walter (1771–1832). Scottish novelist, mainly of period adventure stories. His *Ivanhoe, The Talisman* and *Rob Roy* have received most attention from film makers.

Scott, Zachary (1914–1965). American leading man with considerable stage experience. *The Mask of Dimitrios* (film debut) 44. *The Southerner* 45. Mildred Pierce 46. Stallion Road 47. The Unfaithful 48. Shadow on the Wall 50. Born To Be Bad 51. Let's Make It Legal 53. Appointment in Honduras 53. Bandido 56. The Young One 60. It's Only Money 62, others.

Scotto, Vincente (1876–1952). French composer.
Jofroi 34. Pepe le Moko 36. La Fille du Puisatier 40. Domino 43. L'Ingénue Libertine 50, etc.

Scourby, Alexander (1913–). American stage character actor.
Affair in Trinidad 52. *The Big Heat* 53. The Silver Chalice 55. Giant 56. Seven Thieves 59. The Big Fisherman 59. Confessions of a Counterspy 60.

screenplay: see *shooting script*.

Scrooge. Dickens' *A Christmas Carol*, the tale of miser Scrooge haunted by his past, has been filmed countless times. Among the best-remembered are the Essanay version of 1908; the Edison version of 1910; the Seymour Hicks versions of 1913 and 1935; the 1916 version with Rupert Julian, who also directed; the MGM 1938 version with Reginald Owen; the 1951 version with Alastair Sim; and the 1970 musical with Albert Finney.

The Sea Hawk. Rafael Sabatini's swashbuckling Elizabethan romance about a feuding family was screened with reasonable fidelity in 1924 with Milton Sills. The Errol Flynn pirate yarn of 1940 jettisoned almost everything but the title.

The Sea Wolf. Jack London's stark psychological novel of an obsessed sea captain, Wolf Larsen, has been filmed seven times. In 1913 it starred Hobart Bosworth, in 1920 Noah Beery, in 1925 Ralph Ince, in 1930 Milton Sills, and in 1941 Edward G. Robinson. 1950 brought a disguised western version, *Barricade*, with Raymond Massey, and in 1957 yet another straight version, under the title *Wolf Larsen*, was made with Barry Sullivan.

Seagull, Barbara (1948–) (formerly Barbara Hershey). American leading lady.
The Crazy World of Julius Vrooder 74. You and Me 75. Diamonds 75, etc.

Seal, Elizabeth (1935–). British dancer and occasional actress.
Town on Trial 56. Cone of Silence 60. Vampire Circus 72, etc.

seances on the screen have often been shown to be fake, as in *Seance on a Wet Afternoon, Bunco Squad, Palmy Days, The Spiritualist, Houdini,* and *The Medium*. But just occasionally they do result in something being called up from over there: it happened in *Blithe Spirit, The Haunting, The Uninvited, Night of the Demon, Thirteen Ghosts, Hands of the Ripper,* and *The Legend of Hell House.*

Searle, Francis (1909–). British director.
A Girl in a Million 46. Things Happen at Night 48. Cloudburst (& w) 51. Wheel of Fate (& w) 53, many second features.

Searle, Jackie (1920–). American boy actor of the thirties, usually in mean roles.
Tom Sawyer 31. Skippy 31. Peck's Bad Boy 35. Little Lord Fauntleroy 36. That Certain Age 38. Little Tough Guys in Society 39. The Hard Boiled Canary 41. The Paleface 49, many others.

Sears, Fred F. (1913–1957). American director of second features.
Desert Vigilante 49. Raiders of Tomahawk Creek 50. Snake River Desperadoes 51. Last Train from Bombay 52. Ambush at Tomahawk Gap 53. El Alamein 53. The Miami Story 54. Wyoming Renegades 55. Chicago Syndicate 55. Rock around the Clock 56. Earth versus the Flying Saucers 56. Don't Knock the Rock 56. The Giant Claw 57. The World was His Jury 58, etc.

Sears, Heather (1935–). British actress with repertory experience.
Dry Rot 56. *The Story of Esther Costello* 57. *Room at the Top* 59. Sons and Lovers 60. Phantom of the Opera 62. Saturday Night Out 64. Black Torment 64, etc.

The Seashell and the Clergyman (France 1928). For many years this surrealist fantasy filled with sexual symbols was justly cited as the cinema's furthest excursion into the avant-garde. Its creator, Germaine Dulac, produced nothing else of equal interest. The film is also notable for provoking a famous remark by the British Board of Film Censors in banning the picture: 'It is so obscure as to have no apparent meaning. If there is a meaning, it is doubtless objectionable.'

seaside resorts have provided lively settings for many British comedies: Douglas in *No Limit*, Brighton in *Bank Holiday*, Blackpool in *Sing As We Go*, and a variety of south coast resorts in *The Punch and Judy Man, French Dressing, All Over the Town, Barnacle Bill*. Sometimes the resort has provided a contrast to more serious goings-on, as in *The Entertainer, Brighton Rock, Room at the Top, The Dark Man, A Taste of Honey, I Was Happy Here, Family Doctor, The System, The Damned*. Hollywood usually comes a cropper when depicting British resorts, either comically as in *The Gay Divorcee* or seriously as in *Separate Tables*; its own resorts have a monotonous look, whether viewed romantically in *Moon Over Miami* and *Fun in Acapulco*, nostalgically in *Some Like It Hot*, trendily in *Beach Party* and its many sequels, or morosely in *Tony Rome*. The French Riviera has never been notably well captured on film since Vigo's *A Propos de Nice*, but among the movies to have a go with the aid of back projection are *On the Riviera, That Riviera Touch* and *Moment to Moment*. Hitchcock got some picture postcard views but little else out of *To Catch a Thief*, while the French had a go for themselves in· *St Tropez Blues* and others. A Mediterranean resort was the setting of the climax of *Suddenly Last Summer*; other European watering-places featured memorably in *Une Si Jolie Petite Plage, Sunday in August* and *The Lady with the Little Dog*. The most ingenious use of the seaside for purposes of film fantasy was certainly in *Oh What a Lovely War*.

Seastrom (or **Sjostrom**), **Victor** (1879–1960). Distinguished Swedish actor-director with stage experience.
Ingeborg Holm 13. Terje Vigen (ad) 16. Jerusalem (d) 18. *Ordet* (The Word) (a) 21. *The Phantom Carriage* (Thy Soul Shall Bear

Witness) (d) 20. The Master of Man (US) (d) 23. He Who Gets Slapped (US) (d) 24. *The Scarlet Letter* (US) (d) 26. Tower of Lies (US) (d) 26. The Divine Woman (US) (d) 28. The Wind (US) (d) 28. Under the Red Robe (GB) (d) 36. Ordet (remake) (a) 43. *Wild Strawberries* (a) 57, many others.

Seaton, George (1911–). American writer-director, Acted and produced on stage; joined MGM writing staff 1933; later independent or working with producer William Perlberg.
A Day at the Races (co-w) 37. *The Song of Bernadette* (w) 43. Diamond Horseshoe (wd) 45. Junior Miss (wd) 45. The Shocking Miss Pilgrim (wd) 47. *Miracle on 34th Street* (wd) (AA) 47. The Big Lift (wd) 51. For Heaven's Sake (wd) 51. Anything Can Happen (wd) 53. Little Boy Lost (wd) 53. *The Country Girl* (wd) (AA) 54. The Proud and Profane (wd) 56. The Tin Star (p) 57. Teacher's Pet (d) 58. The Pleasure of His Company (d) 61. The Counterfeit Traitor (wd) 63. Thirty-Six Hours (wd) 64. What's So Bad About Feeling Good? (wpd) 68. *Airport* (wd) 69. Showdown (wpd) 73, many others.

Seberg, Jean (1938–). American leading lady who won contest for role of Preminger's *Saint Joan* 57, after which her career faltered but has picked up in French films.
Bonjour Tristesse 57. The Mouse That Roared 59. *Breathless* (A Bout de Souffle) 60. Playtime 62. In the French Style 63. Lilith 64. Moment to Moment 65. Estouffade à la Caraïbe 66. The Road to Corinth 68. Pendulum 69. Paint Your Wagon 69. Airport 69. Macho Callahan 71. Mousey (TV) 73, etc.

Secombe, Harry (1921–). Burly Welsh comedian and singer, who apart from a number of second-feature appearances in the early fifties has filmed only rarely.
Davy 57. Jet Storm 59. Oliver! 68. Song of Norway 70. The Magnificent Seven Deadly Sins 71. Sunstruck 73, etc.

second unit director. One who directs not the actors but the spectacular location sequences, stunt men, scenic backgrounds, etc., and is thus sometimes responsible for a film's most striking effects; e.g. Andrew Marton's chariot race sequence in *Ben Hur* 59.

Sedgwick, Edward (1893–1953). American director of mainly routine films.
Live Wires 21. The First Degree 23. Two Fisted Jones 25. Spring Fever 27. The Cameraman 28. The Passionate Plumber 32. I'll Tell the World 34. Pick a Star 37. Beware Spooks 39. Ma and

Pa Kettle Back on the Farm 50, many others.

Seeley, Blossom (1892–1974). American nightclub entertainer, married to Benny Fields. Played by Betty Hutton in *Somebody Loves Me* 52.
□ Broadway Through a Keyhole 33.

Segal, Alex (1915–). American director, from TV.
□ Ransom 56. All the Way Home 63. Joy in the Morning 65. Harlow (electronovision) 66.

Segal, George (1934–). Leading American actor more at home with thought than with action, which may account for a somewhat fitful career.
□ The Young Doctors 61. The Longest Day 62. Act One 62. The New Interns 64. Invitation to a Gunfighter 64. Ship of Fools 65. *King Rat* 65. Lost Command 65. Who's Afraid of Virginia Woolf? 66. The Quiller Memorandum 66. The St Valentine's Day Massacre 67. Bye Bye Braverman 68. No Way to Treat a Lady 68. The Southern Star 69. The Girl who Couldn't Say No 69. The Bridge at Remagen 69. Loving 70. *The Owl and the Pussycat* 70. Where's Poppa? 70. Born to Win 72. The Hot Rock 72. Blume in Love 73. *A Touch of Class* 73. The Terminal Man 74. California Split 75. The Black Bird 75. Russian Roulette 76. The Duchess and the Dirtwater Fox 76. Rollercoaster 77.

Segall, Harry (1897–1975). American writer who started the heavenly fantasies of the forties with his play 'Halfway to Heaven'.
Fatal Lady 36. Here Comes Mr Jordan 41. Angel on My Shoulder 46. For Heaven's Sake 50. Monkey Business 52, etc.

Seiler, Lewis (1891–1964). American director. Many Tom Mix silents; then *Air Circus* (co-d) 28, second features through thirties.
Dust Be My Destiny 39. It All Came True 40. South of Suez 41. The Big Shot 42. Guadalcanal Diary 43. Molly and Me 44. If I'm Lucky 46. Whiplash 48. The Tanks are Coming 51. The Winning Team 52. The System 53. Women's Prison 55. Battle Stations 56. The True Story of Lynn Stuart 58, many others.

Seiter, William A. (1891–1964). American director, in Hollywood from 1918, then directing shorts.
Boy Crazy 22. The Teaser 25. Skinner's Dress Suit 26. Good Morning Judge 28. The Love Racket 30. Girl Crazy 32. If I Had a Million (part) 33. Diplomaniacs 33. Professional Sweetheart 33. *Sons of the Desert* 33. Roberta

35. *The Moon's Our Home* 36. Dimples 36. *This is My Affair* 37. *Room Service* 38. It's a Date 40. *Broadway* 42. You Were Never Lovelier 42. Destroyer 43. *The Affairs of Susan* 45. I'll Be Yours 47. One Touch of Venus 48. Dear Brat 51. Make Haste to Live 54, many others.

Seitz, George B. (1888–1944). American director, known as the serial king. A writer-director from 1913, he worked on *The Perils of Pauline*, and directed *The Fatal Ring* 17 and all subsequent Pearl White serials. In the twenties, he acted in his own serials: *Velvet Fingers, The Sky Ranger*, etc. Turning to features, he directed nearly forty between 1927 and 1933, then moved to MGM and kept up an even more rapid output, including episodes of the Hardy Family series.
The Woman in His Life 35. Andy Hardy Meets a Debutante 39. Kit Carson 40. Sky Murder 40. Andy Hardy's Private Secretary 41. China Caravan 42, etc.

Seitz, John F. (1893–). American cinematographer, in Hollywood from 1916.
SILENT FILMS: *The Four Horsemen of the Apocalypse* 21. *The Prisoner of Zenda* 23, etc.
SOUND FILMS: She Wanted a Millionaire 32. Huckleberry Finn 39. *Sullivan's Travels* 41. Hail the Conquering Hero 44. *Double Indemnity* 44. *The Lost Weekend* 45. *Sunset Boulevard* 50. The San Francisco Story 52. Hell on Frisco Bay 55. The Man in the Net 58. Guns of the Timberland 60, etc.

Sekely, Steve (1899–) (Istvan Szekely). Hungarian director, in Hollywood from the mid-thirties.
Women in Bondage 44. The Scar 48. Stronghold 51. The Blue Camellia 54. The Day of the Triffids 68. Kenner 69, etc.

Selander, Lesley (1900–). American director who has been making low-budget westerns and other action pictures since 1936.
Cattle Pass 37. The Round-Up 41. The Vampire's Ghost 46. Belle Starr's Daughter 48. I Was an American Spy 51. Flight to Mars 51. The Highwayman 52. Tall Man Riding 54. The Lone Ranger and the Lost City of Gold 58. Town Tamer 65. Fort Utah 67, many others.

Selig, William N. (1864–1948). Pioneer American producer; many serials.
The Count of Monte Cristo 08. The Spoilers 13, etc.

Sellars, Elizabeth (1923–). British leading actress on stage from 1941.
Floodtide (debut) 48. Madeleine 50. Cloudburst

51. The Gentle Gunman 52. The Barefoot Contessa 54. Three Cases of Murder 55. The Shiralee 57. The Day They Robbed the Bank of England 61. The Chalk Garden 64. The Mummy's Shroud 67. The Hireling 73, etc.

Sellers, Peter (1925–). British comic actor who became an international star, then faltered. From variety stage and radio's 'Goon Show'.
Biography 1969: *Peter Sellers, The Mask Behind the Mask* by Peter Evans.
□ Penny Points to Paradise 51. Down Among the Z Men 52. Orders Are Orders 54. John and Julie 55. The Lady Killers 55. *The Smallest Show on Earth* 57. *The Naked Truth* 58. Tom Thumb 58. Up the Creek 58. Carlton-Browne of the F.O. 58. *The Mouse That Roared* 59. *I'm All Right, Jack* 59. The Battle of the Sexes 60. Two-Way Stretch 60. Never Let Go 61. The Millionairess 61. Mr Topaze (& d) 61. *Only Two Can Play* 62. Lolita 62. Waltz of the Toreadors 62. The Dock Brief 63. Heavens Above 63. The Wrong Arm of the Law 63. *The Pink Panther* 63. *Dr Strangelove* 63. The World of Henry Orient 64. A Shot in the Dark 64. What's New, Pussycat? 65. The Wrong Box 66. After the Fox 66. Casino Royale 67. The Bobo 67. Woman Times Seven 67. The Party 68. *I Love You Alice B. Toklas* 68. The Magic Christian 69. Hoffman 70. There's a Girl in My Soup 70. Where Does it Hurt? 72. Alice's Adventures in Wonderland (as the March Hare) 72. The Optimists of Nine Elms 72. Soft Beds and Hard Battles 73. Ghost in the Noonday Sun 73. The Great McGonagall (as Queen Victoria) 74. The Return of the Pink Panther 75. Murder by Death 76. The Pink Panther Strikes Again 77.

Selten, Morton (1860–1940) (Morton Stubbs). British stage actor who played distinguished old gentlemen in some thirties films.
Service for Ladies 32. Ten Minute Alibi 35. The Ghost Goes West 36. Fire over England 36. A Yank at Oxford 38. The Divorce of Lady X 38. The Thief of Baghdad 40, etc.

Seltzer, David (–). American screenwriter.
One is a Lonely Number 72. The Other Side of the Mountain 75. *The Omen* 76, etc.

Seltzer, Walter (1914–). American producer.
One Eyed Jacks 58. The Naked Edge 61. The War Lord 65. Will Penny 67. Darker than Amber 70. Skyjacked 72, etc.

Selwyn, Edgar (–). American director.

Night Life of New York 25. The Girl in the Show 29. War Nurse 30. The Sin of Madelon Claudet 31. Turn Back the Clock 33. The Mystery of Mr X 34. Pierre of the Plains (wp only) 42.

Selznick, David O. (1902–1965). American independent producer, former writer. Worked for RKO from 1931, MGM from 1933; founded Selznick International Pictures in 1936.
Biographical books: *Selznick* by Bob Thomas, 1970; *Memo From David O. Selznick*, 1972.
A Star is Born 37. *The Prisoner of Zenda* 37. *Nothing Sacred* 37. Tom Sawyer 38. Intermezzo 39. *Gone with the Wind* 39. *Rebecca* 40. Since You Went Away 43. Spellbound 45. *Duel in the Sun* 46. *The Third Man* (co-p) 49. Indiscretion (Stazione Termini) 51. A Farewell to Arms 57. Tender is the Night 62, many others.

Semon, Larry (1889–1928). American silent slapstick comedian, popular in innumerable two-reelers of the twenties; also some features.
The Simple Life 18. The Wizard of Oz 24. The Sawmill 25. Spuds 27, etc.

Semple, Lorenzo Jnr (–). American screenwriter.
Pretty Poison 69. Marriage of a Young Stockbroker 71. Papillon (co-w) 73. The Drowning Pool (c-w) 75. Three Days of the Condor (co-w) 75. King Kong 76, etc.

Sennett, Mack (1880–1960) (Michael Sinnott). American 'king of comedy' who in the twenties produced countless slapstick shorts featuring the Keystone Kops, Chester Conklin, Louise Fazenda, Charlie Chaplin, Mack Swain, Billy West, Fred Mace, Heinie Conklin, Slim Summerville and others. By the time sound came, Sennett had exhausted all the possible tricks of his 'fun factory' and found the new methods not to his taste. His output waned almost to nothing, but he was given a special Academy Award in 1937: 'For his lasting contribution to the comedy technique of the screen ... the Academy presents a Special Award to that master of fun, discoverer of stars, sympathetic, kindly, understanding genius—Mack Sennett.'
A biography, *King of Comedy*, was published in 1955.

sequence: a film paragraph, usually starting and ending with a fade to black.

serials demand a book to themselves. They began in the early years of the century and continued until the early fifties, their plethora of adventurous and melodramatic incident being usually divided into fifteen or twenty chapters of about twenty minutes each. They were the domain of mad doctors, space explorers, clutching hands, mysterious strangers, diabolical villains and dewy-eyed heroines. Each chapter ended with a 'cliffhanger' in which the hero or heroine was left in some deadly danger from which it was plain he could not escape; but at the beginning of the next chapter escape he did. A few favourite serials are *Fantomas, The Perils of Pauline, Batman, Flash Gordon's Trip to Mars* and *Captain Marvel*. Almost all of them were American. They were finally killed by the advent of TV and by the increasing length of the double-feature programme.

Books on the subject include *To Be Continued* by Weiss and Goodgold; *Days of Thrills and Adventure* by Alan Barbour; and *The Great Movie Serials* by Harmon and Glut.

series of feature films used to be popular enough, and many are individually noted in this book; in recent years the series concept has been taken over by TV, and in any case low-budget movies featuring cut-to-pattern characters could no longer be made to pay their way in theatres. When one looks back over these old heroes, who flourished chiefly in the thirties and forties, most of them turn out to be sleuths of one kind or another. They included *Sherlock Holmes, The Saint, The Lone Wolf, Father Brown, Nero Wolfe, Duncan McLain, The Crime Doctor, Sexton Blake, Mr Moto, Perry Mason, Bulldog Drummond, Nancy Drew, Mr Wong, Charlie Chan, Ellery Queen, Boston Blackie, The Falcon, Hildegarde Withers, Hercule Poirot, Dick Tracy, Torchy Blane, Michael Shayne, Philip Marlowe* and, more recently, *Inspector Clouseau, Tony Rome, Virgil Tibbs, Coffin Ed Johnson* and *Shaft*. Nor should one forget crime anthologies like *Inner Sanctum* and *The Whistler*. The spy vogue, a recent happening, is naturally headed by *James Bond*: in his wake you may discern *Counterspy, Coplan, Flint, The Tiger, The Man from Uncle, Harry Palmer*, and *Superdragon*. Among the more muscular outdoor heroes may be counted *Hopalong Cassidy, The Three Mesquiteers, The Lone Ranger, Captain Blood, Zorro, Robin Hood, Tarzan, Jungle Jim, The Cisco Kid, Bomba, The Man with No Name* and the Italian giants who go under such names as *Maciste, Goliath, Hercules* and *Ursus*. The longest surviving series villain is certainly *Fu Manchu*. As for monsters, take your pick from *Frankenstein, Dracula, The Mummy, The Creature from the Black Lagoon, The Invisible Man, The Wolf Man, Dr X*; while if you prefer comedy freaks there are *Topper* and *Francis*. There have been a goodly number of

domestic comedies and dramas, including *Squibs, The Jones Family, The Hardy Family, The Cohens and the Kellys, Blondie, Ma and Pa Kettle, Maisie, Henry Aldrich, Scattergood Baines, Lum and Abner, Jeeves, Mr Belvedere, Gidget* and the *Four Daughters* saga. Other comedy series have ranged from the subtleties of *Don Camillo* to the prat-falls of *Old Mother Riley, Mexican Spitfire*, the *Doctor* series, and *Carry On* films. Animals have had series to themselves, as for instance *Rin Tin Tin, Flicka, Lassie, Rusty* and *Flipper*. So have children of various ages: *Our Gang, Gasoline Alley, The Dead End Kids, The East Side Kids, The Bowery Boys*. The best-established musical series were *Broadway Melody* and *The Big Broadcast*. And three cheers for *Dr Kildare, Dr Christian, Dr Defoe, Dr Mabuse* and *Dr Goldfoot* . . . to say nothing of Professor *Quatermass*.

Serling, Rod (1924–1975). American TV playwright who contributed scores of scripts to such series as *Twilight Zone* and *Night Gallery* (which he also introduced).
Patterns of Power 56. Saddle the Wind 58. Requiem for a Heavyweight (Blood Money) 63. Yellow Canary 63. Seven Days in May 64. Assault on a Queen 66. Planet of the Apes 67.

Sernas, Jacques (1925–). Lithuanian-born leading man, in international films.
The Golden Salamander (GB) 50. Jump into Hell (US) 55. Helen of Troy (US/It.) 55. Maddalena (Fr.) 56. The Sign of the Gladiator (It.) 60. Son of Spartacus (It.) 62. Goliath Against the Vampires 67, etc.

Sersen, Fred (1890–1962). American special effects photographer, long with Fox, for whom he produced such spectacles as the fire in *In Old Chicago*, the storm in *The Rains Came*, and the canal-building in *Suez*.

Servais, Jean (1910–1976). French character actor with stage experience.
Criminel 31. La Valse Eternelle 36. La Danse de Mort 47. Une Si Jolie Petite Plage 48. Le Plaisir 51. *Rififi* 55. Les Jeux Dangereux 58. That Man from Rio 64. Lost Command 66. They Came to Rob Las Vegas 69, etc.

servants in movies have provided great pleasure, mainly because the vast majority of the audience has been unlikely to encounter the breed in person. Actors who spent their lives playing stately butlers include Eric Blore, Charles Coleman, Robert Greig, Barnett Parker, Halliwell Hobbes and Arthur Treacher. Louise Beavers and Hattie McDaniel were the leading coloured maids, and many black comedians played frightened valets: Mantan Moreland, Stepin Fetchit, Willie Best. Sinister housekeepers are led by Gale Sondergaard and Judith Anderson. Even more eccentric servants were played by Edward Rigby in *Don't Take it to Heart*, Cantinflas in *Around the World in Eighty Days*, Seymour Hicks in *Busman's Honeymoon*, Edward Brophy in the Falcon series; and downright villianous ones by Dirk Bogarde in *The Servant*, Philip Lathrop in *Dracula Prince of Darkness*, Boris Karloff in *The Old Dark House* and Bela Lugosi in *The Body Snatcher*. Romantic comedies in which servants have had liaisons with their masters (or mistresses) include *History is Made at Night*, *When Tomorrow Comes*, *Common Clay*, *What Price Hollywood? The Farmer's Daughter*, *If You Could Only Cook*, *Lord Richard in the Pantry* and *Upstairs Downstairs*; while thirties comedies in which Russian exiles and new poor took jobs as servants are exemplified by *Tovarich* and *My Man Godfrey*.

Sessions, Almira (1888–1974). American character actress, often seen in fluttery or eccentric bit parts.
Little Nellie Kelly 41. The Diary of a Chambermaid 46. The Fountainhead 49. The Boston Strangler 67. Rosemary's Baby 69, many others.

Seton, Bruce (1909–1969). British leading man, later character actor; military background.
Blue Smoke 34. Sweeney Todd 36. Love from a Stranger 38. The Curse of the Wraydons 46. Bonnie Prince Charlie 48. Whisky Galore 49. John Paul Jones (US) 59, etc.
TV series: Fabian of the Yard 54.

Setton, Maxwell (1909–). British independent producer, former lawyer. Recently held executive posts for Bryanston and Columbia.
The Spider and the Fly 50. So Little Time 52. They Who Dare 54. Footsteps in the Fog 55. Town on Trial 56. I Was Monty's Double 58, etc.

Seven Brides for Seven Brothers (US 1954). A highly successful MGM musical which appeared at the end of the peak period spurred by Gene Kelly, and somehow failed to prolong it. Marred by obvious budget economies, it nevertheless brought tremendous gusto to its western retelling of the story of the rape of the Sabine women. Produced by Jack Cummings, directed by Stanley Donen, with music by Gene de Paul, lyrics by Johnny Mercer, choreography by Michael Kidd; book by Albert Hackett,

Frances Goodrich and Dorothy Kingsley. Howard Keel and Jane Powell led a talented cast.

Seven Days in May (US 1964). A fine political melodrama directed by John Frankenheimer and written by Rod Serling from a novel by Fletcher Knebel and Charles W. Bailey II. About a militarist attempt to depose a weak president, it gives first-class opportunities to Fredric March as the president, Burt Lancaster as the ambitious general and Kirk Douglas as his bewildered aide; and apart from an unnecessary sex interest it moves with tremendous pace and attack.

Seven Keys to Baldpate. The famous stage comedy-thriller by Earl Derr Biggers and George M. Cohan has been filmed five times; with Cohan himself in 1917, Douglas Maclean in 1926, Richard Dix in 1929, Gene Raymond in 1935, and Philip Terry in 1947.

Seven Samurai (Japan 1954). The film on which *The Magnificent Seven* (qv) was based; a spellbinding piece of oriental savagery which runs nearly three hours even in the abbreviated western version but never allows the eye to wander. Director Akira Kurosawa and actor Toshiro Mifune share the credit. AA best foreign film 1955.

Seventh Heaven. Frank Borzage directed Janet Gaynor (AA) and Charles Farrell in the immensely popular 1927 version of this simple garret love story set in Paris before the 1914 war, from which the hero returns blinded. Henry King remade it in 1937, with Simone Simon and James Stewart. The story has its origins in a play by Austin Strong.

The Seventh Seal (Sweden 1957). Ingmar Bergman's most fascinating and infuriating film, on outpouring of medieval religious images of life and death, pain and joy. Its meaning probably can't be fully analysed, even by Bergman himself, but almost every scene is in some way memorable, and the film stands as a textbook of filmcraft. Photographed by Gunnar Fischer, with music by Eric Nordgren. The cast includes Nils Poppe, Gunnar Bjornstrand, Max Von Sydow, and Bengt Ekerot as Death.

The Seventh Veil (GB 1945). An incredibly successful piece of commercial film-making, one of the first post-war returns to the pre-war novelette school; about a concert pianist undergoing psychiatric treatment because she can't decide which of three men to marry. Expertly concocted by producer Sidney Box, glossily directed by Compton Bennett. With Ann Todd, James Mason, Herbert Lom, Albert Lieven. When the film was televised in Britain over ten years later, cinemas all over the country suffered, and the event helped to toughen the attitude of the film trade to television.

Sewell, George (1924–). British character actor of tough roles, familiar on TV in *Special Branch*.
Sparrows Can't Sing 63. Robbery 67. Get Carter 71, etc.

Sewell, Vernon (1903–). British director, former engineer, photographer, art director and editor.
The Silver Fleet 43. *Latin Quarter* 46. The Ghosts of Berkeley Square 47. Uneasy Terms 48. The Ghost Ship 52. Where There's a Will 55. Battle of the V1 58. House of Mystery 61. Strongroom 62. The Curse of the Crimson Altar 68. Burke and Hare 71, etc.

sewers have figured in several thrillers, most notably *The Third Man* with its exciting final chase; its sewer complex was recently spoofed in *Carry On Spying*. In 1948 in *He Walked by Night* Richard Basehart played a criminal who invariably escaped through the sewers; and our old friend *The Phantom of the Opera* was similarly skilled, as was Lee Marvin in *Point Blank*. As recently as the British thriller *Invasion* a sewer detour was used; while the Frankenstein monster was saved from the burning windmill by falling through to the sewer, where he was found at the beginning of *Bride of Frankenstein*. As for more serious films, sewers are of course featured in the many versions of *Les Misérables*, while the Polish resistance film *Kanal* takes place entirely—and nauseatingly—in the sewers of Warsaw. Fred MacMurray had a comic sewer escape in *Bon Voyage*, and the giant ants of *Them!* were cornered in the sewers of Los Angeles.

sex. This was once called 'romance': the beginnings of corruption set in with de Mille's silent comedies such as *Why Change Your Wife?* and Lubitsch's classics *Forbidden Paradise* and *The Marriage Circle*. These gentlemen carried their sophistication into the early sound period, assisted by such stars as Valentino, Harlow, Dietrich, Clara Bow and Ginger Rogers; and there was considerable help from a film called *The Private Life of Henry VIII*, a lady named Mae West and a director named Josef Von Sternberg; but around 1934 the Hays Code and the Legion of Decency forced innocence upon Hollywood to such an extent that the smart hero

and heroine of 1934's *It Happened One Night* just wouldn't dream of sharing a bedroom without a curtain between them. The later thirties, perforce, were the heyday of the boy next door and the *ingénue*: nice people all, personified by such stars as Gary Cooper, Dick Powell, Ray Milland, David Niven, Ruby Keeler, Janet Gaynor, Deanna Durbin and Irene Dunne. Meanwhile a strong reaguard action was being fought by actors like William Powell, Myrna Loy, Melvyn Douglas, Ann Sheridan and Cary Grant, but usually the blue pencil had been wielded so heavily on their scripts that it was difficult to tell what was really being implied. The best way out was found in such comedies as *The Philadelphia Story*, which were basically earthy but gave every appearance of keeping it all in the mind. The war years produced a certain slackening of restrictions; for instance, the pin-up girl became not only permissible but desirable as a way of building up military morale. Preston Sturges brought sex out into the open in *The Palm Beach Story* and *The Miracle of Morgan's Creek*; Spencer Tracy and Katharine Hepburn started (in *Woman of the Year*) a series of films portraying the battle of the sexes in a recognizably human way. The 'love goddesses' became progressively more blatant in their appeal: Jane Russell, Marilyn Monroe, Jayne Mansfield. (But in the fifties it turned out that one of the earthiest of them, Sophia Loren, was also the best actress.) By now the production code had been broken down to the extent of permitting words like 'virgin' and 'mistress' (*The Moon is Blue*), the recognition of adultery and prostitution as human facts (*Wives and Lovers, Kiss Me Stupid*), depiction of the lustfulness of males (*Tom Jones, Alfie*), 'realistic' dramas like *Room at the Top*, erotic romances like *Les Amants*, and the presentation, albeit in a fantasy, of girls as 'pleasure units' (*Our Man Flint*). Indeed, after *Georgy Girl, Night Games* and *Who's Afraid of Virginia Woolf?*, it seemed that public frankness could go very little further; but along came *Blow Up, Midnight Cowboy, Satiricon, Flesh, The Music Lovers, Percy, Last Tango in Paris* and *Deep Throat* to prove the opposite. There even emerged an X-rated cartoon *Fritz the Cat*; and by the mid-seventies pornographic films on view in most cities outnumbered the other kind.

sex changes have not been a profitable line of inquiry for the cinema, though the gimmick thriller *Homicidal* depended on one, as did *Myra Breckinridge*. *The Christine Jorgenson Story* was an account of a genuine case, and *I Want What I Want* presented a fictitious case history.

Sexton Blake. The lean, ascetic detective hero of several generations of British boys was the creation of Harry Blyth ('Hal Meredith') (1852–98). On screen he was first portrayed in 1914 in *The Clue of the Wax Vesta*. He was played in the twenties by Langhorne Burton, in the thirties by George Curzon, in the forties by David Farrar and in the fifties by Geoffrey Toone; while 1962's *Mix Me a Person* was taken from a Blake story but cast Anne Baxter in the role.

Seyler, Athene (1889–). British comedy actress with long stage career dating from 1908. This Freedom 22. The Perfect Lady 32. The Citadel 38. *Quiet Wedding* 40. *Dear Octopus* 43. Nicholas Nickleby 47. Queen of Spades 48. Young Wives' Tale 51. *Pickwick Papers* 53. Yield to the Night 56. Campbell's Kingdom 58. The Inn of the Sixth Happiness 58. Make Mine Mink 59. Nurse on Wheels 63, many others.

Seymour, Anne (1909–). American character actress.
All the King's Men 49. Man on Fire 57. Home from the Hill 59. The Subterraneans 60. Sunrise at Campobello 60. Mirage 65. Blindfold 66, etc. TV series: Empire 60.

Seymour, Dan (1915–). Burly American character actor, the scowling menace of countless films.
Casablanca 42. To Have and Have Not 44. Cloak and Dagger 46. Key Largo 48. Rancho Notorious 52. The Big Heat 53. Moonfleet 55. The Sad Sack 57. Watusi 59. Escape to Witch Mountain 75, etc.

Seyrig, Delphine (1932–). French leading actress.
Pull My Daisy 58. *Last Year in Marienbad* 61. Muriel 63. La Musica 66. Accident (GB) 67. Mr Freedom 68. Stolen Kisses 68. Daughters of Darkness 70. Peau d'Ane 70. The Discreet Charm of the Bourgeoisie 72. The Day of the Jackal 73. The Black Windmill 74. Aloise 75, etc.

Shadow of a Doubt (US 1943). A very effective, and pleasingly understated, Hitchcock thriller about a small-town family visited by a romantic big-city uncle who turns out to be the Merry Widow Murderer. Hitch's technique has never been more supple, and Thornton Wilder's script is a great asset. Joseph Cotten and Teresa Wright give responsive performances. The film was remade, inadequately, in 1959 as a second feature called *Step Down to Terror*.

Shadows (US 1959). An improvised film shot on 16mm in New York by John Cassavetes with unknown actors. About young people in the big city, its chief interest was in its technique, which influenced the 'cinema vérité' school.

Shakespeare, William (1564–1616). British poet and dramatist whose plays have received plenty of attention from film-makers. *The Taming of the Shrew* was filmed in 1908 by D. W. Griffith; in 1929 with Douglas Fairbanks, Mary Pickford, and the immortal credit line 'additional dialogue by Sam Taylor'; in 1953, more or less, as *Kiss Me Kate*; and in 1966 with Elizabeth Taylor, Richard Burton, and script credits to three writers none of whom is Shakespeare. As You Like It was filmed in 1912 with Rose Coghlan and Maurice Costello; the only sound filming was in 1936 by Paul Czinner, with Elisabeth Bergner and Laurence Olivier. *A Midsummer Night's Dream* was tackled in major fashion by Warners in 1935, but the elaborate Max Reinhardt production failed to please at the box-office; in 1968 a 'realistic' version by Peter Hall was equally unsuccessful.

Of the tragedies, *Othello* has been frequently attempted, by Emil Jannings in 1922, Orson Welles in 1952, Sergei Bondartchuk in 1955 and Laurence Olivier in 1966; a 1961 British film called *All Night Long* was a modern up-dating of the plot, and Ronald Colman's Academy Award-winning performance in *A Double Life* 47 had him as an actor who starts playing the Moor in private life, as did Sebastian Shaw in *Men Are Not Gods* 36. *Hamlet* was played by Sir Johnston Forbes Robertson in 1913, Asta Nielsen in 1922, Olivier in 1948, and Innokenti Smoktunovsky in 1964. (Note also a 1972 western called *Johnny Hamlet*.) *Macbeth* is thought to be an unlucky play; but Sir Herbert Beerbohm Tree appeared in a version for Griffith in 1916; Orson Welles directed himself in the role in 1948, Paul Douglas in 1955 was an updated *Joe Macbeth*, in 1960 Maurice Evans appeared in a version originally intended for TV but shown theatrically, and in 1971 Roman Polanski presented a bloodthirsty version with Jon Finch. One should also mention *The Siberian Lady Macbeth* and the Japanese *Throne of Blood*. In 1969 *King Lear* was filmed with Paul Scofield; there was a one-reel Vitagraph version in 1909 and Frederic Warde starred in a 1916 production. *Romeo and Juliet* was also made in 1916, starring Francis X. Bushman and Beverly Bayne; this superseded several one-reel versions. In 1936 MGM produced its Leslie Howard/Norma Shearer version directed by George Cukor; in 1954 Renato Castellani directed an unsuccessful colour version with Laurence Harvey and Susan Shentall; in 1961 came the inevitable modernization in *West Side Story*: and 1968 brought another expensive production by Franco Zeffirelli. (There have also been several ballet versions.) There were early potted versions of *Julius Caesar* before the spectacular Italian production of 1914; the play was not filmed again until MGM's excellent 1953 version. The plot was used in a curious British second feature called *An Honourable Murder* 59, with the action moved to a modern executive suite; an all-star version in colour followed in 1970, starring Charlton Heston and finding more action than is normally evident in the play.

Of the histories, most of *Henry IV* has been compressed by Orson Welles into his *Chimes at Midnight, Henry V* was splendidly dealt with by Olivier in 1944, *Richard III* existed in several primitive versions, and John Barrymore recited a speech from it in *Show of Shows* 28; but again it was left to Olivier to do it properly.

The oddest screen fate of a Shakespeare play was surely that of *The Tempest*, which in 1956 yielded its entire plot to that winning bit of science fiction *Forbidden Planet*.

The best book on the subject is 1971's *Shakespeare and the Film* by Roger Manvell.

Shamroy, Leon (1901–1974). Distinguished American cinematographer.
Catch as Catch Can 27. Out with the Tide 28. The Women Men Marry 31. Jennie Gerhardt 33. Three Cornered Moon 33. Thirty Day Princess 34. Private Worlds 35. Soak the Rich 36. You Only Live Once 37. *The Young In Heart* 38. The Story of Alexander Graham Bell 39. *The Adventures of Sherlock Holmes* 40. Lillian Russell 40. Tin Pan Alley 40. A Yank in the RAF 41. Roxie Hart 42. *Ten Gentlemen from West Point* 42. *The Black Swan* (AA) 42. *Stormy Weather* 43. Buffalo Bill 44. *Wilson* (AA) 44. *A Tree Grows in Brooklyn* 45. State Fair 45. *Leave Her to Heaven* (AA) 46. Forever Amber 47. That Lady in Ermine 48. Prince of Foxes 49. Twelve O'Clock High 49. Cheaper by the Dozen 50. On the Riviera 51. David and Bathsheba 51. The Snows of Kilimanjaro 53. Call Me Madam 53. *The Robe* 53. The Egyptian 54. Love is a Many Splendored Thing 55. *The King and I* 56. Desk Set 57. South Pacific (co-ph) 58. Porgy and Bess 59. North to Alaska 60. Tender is the Night 61. Cleopatra 63. The Cardinal 63. The Agony and the Ecstasy 65. The Glass Bottom Boat 66. Caprice (also appeared) 67. *Planet of the Apes* 67. Justine 69, many others.

Shane (US 1953). A serious, atmospheric western about a pioneer family protected by a mysterious stranger; written by A. B. Guthrie Jnr from Jack Schaefer's novel. George Stevens directed it with great feeling and turned it into a classic. Photographed by Loyal Griggs (AA), music by Victor Young; with Alan Ladd, Jean Arthur, Van Heflin.

Shane, Maxwell (1905–). American writer-director, former publicist.
You Can't Beat Love (co-w) 37. One Body Too Many (w) 43. Fear in the Night (wd) 46 (remade as Nightmare in 1956). City across the River (wdp) 49. The Naked Street (wd) 55, etc.

Shanghai Express (US 1932). This nostalgic melodrama, which even when new seemed to be spoofing itself, has over the years acquired the patina of a Hollywood classic. All about the intertwining of the lives of a Chinese war lord, a high class prostitute, and a stiff-upper-lip British officer on a train beset by rebels, it had suitable performances from Warner Oland, Marlene Dietrich and Clive Brook. Josef Von Sternberg directed from a script by Jules Furthman; Lee Garmes (AA) was cinematographer. There was one direct remake, *Peking Express* 52, but many films borrowed the basic situations: *Half Way to Shanghai, Night Plane from Chungking, The House of Tao Ling*, even *The General Died at Dawn* and *The Lady Vanishes*.

Shannon, Harry (1890–1964). American character actor, often seen as sympathetic father or rustic; musical comedy experience.
Hands Up 31. Young Tom Edison 40. The Eve of St Mark 44. The Gunfighter 50. High Noon 52. Executive Suite 54. Come Next Spring 56. Hell's Crossroads 57, many others.

Shapiro, Stanley (1925–). American writer-producer associated with glossy comedies; long experience in radio and TV.
The Perfect Furlough (w) 58. Pillow Talk (co-w) (AA) 59. Operation Petticoat (co-w) 59. Come September (co-w) 60. That Touch of Mink (co-w) 62. Bedtime Story (wp) 64. How to Save a Marriage (p) 68. For Pete's Sake (co-wp) 74, etc.

Sharaff, Irene (c. 1910–). American costume designer, long with Fox.
An American in Paris (AA) 51. The King and I (AA) 56. West Side Story (AA) 61. Hello Dolly 69.

Sharif, Omar (1932–) (Michel Shalhouz). Egyptian leading man now in international films.
Goha 59. *Lawrence of Arabia* 62. The Fall of the Roman Empire 64. Behold a Pale Horse 64. The Yellow Rolls-Royce 64. Genghis Khan 65. *Dr Zhivago* 65. The Night of the Generals 66. Marco the Magnificent 66. More Than a Miracle

67. Funny Girl 68. Mayerling 68. Mackenna's Gold 68. The Appointment 69. Che! 69. The Last Valley 70. The Horsemen 71. The Burglars 71. The Tamarind Seed 74. Juggernaut 74. The Mysterious Island of Captain Venus 74. Funny Lady 75. Crime and Passion 75, etc.

Sharp, Don (1922–). Australian-born director, in British film industry from 1952, at first as writer.
Ha'penny Breeze (w) 52. Robbery Under Arms (w) 56. The Professionals 59. Linda 60. Kiss of the Vampire 62. Devil Ship Pirates 63. *Witchcraft* 64. Those Magnificent Men in Their Flying Machines (second unit) 65. Rasputin the Mad Monk 65. *The Face of Fu Manchu* 65. Our Man in Marrakesh 66. The Million Eyes of Su Muru 66. Rocket to the Moon 67. Psychomania 72. Callan 74. Hennessy 75, etc.

Sharp, Henry (c. 1890–1966). American cinematographer.
Homespun Folks 20. The Hottentot 22. A Girl of the Limberlost 24. Don Q Son of Zorro 25. *The Black Pirate* 26. The Lovelorn 27. *The Crowd* 28. The Iron Mask 29. Lord Byron of Broadway 30. The False Madonna 31. The Devil is Driving 32. Duck Soup 33. Six of a Kind 34. The Glass Key 35. Lady be Careful 36. Hotel Haywire 37. Booloo 38. Geronimo 39. Dr Cyclops (co-ph) 40. Broadway Limited 41. The Hidden Hand 42. Ministry of Fear 44. Jealousy 45. It Happened on Fifth Avenue 47. Perilous Waters 48. Daughter of the West 49. The Young Land (co-ph) 59, many others.

Shatner, William (1931–). Canadian leading actor, seen mostly on TV.
The Brothers Karamazov 58. The Explosive Generation 61. The Intruder (The Stranger) 61. The Outrage 64. Go Ask Alice (TV) 73. The Horror at 37,000 feet (TV) 74, Big Bad Mama 74, etc.
TV series: *Star Trek* 66–69; *Barbary Coast* 75.

Shaughnessy, Alfred (1916–). British producer.
Brandy for the Parson 51. Cat Girl 57. Heart of a Child 57. Just My Luck (script only) 59. The Impersonator (script and direction only) 61. Lunch Hour 63, etc.

Shaughnessy, Mickey (1920–). Tough-looking American comic actor with stage experience.
The Last of the Comanches (debut) 52. From Here to Eternity 53. Conquest of Space 55. Jailhouse Rock 57. *Don't Go Near the Water* 57. North to Alaska 60. A Global Affair 63. A

House Is Not a Home 64. Never a Dull Moment 68, etc.
TV series: Chicago Teddy Bears 71.

Shavelson, Melville (1917–). American screenwriter, in Hollywood from early forties.
The Princess and the Pirate 44. Always Leave Them Laughing 50. Room for One More 52. The Seven Little Foys (& d) 56. Beau James (& d) 57. Houseboat (& d) 58. The Five Pennies (& d) 59. The Pigeon That Took Rome (& pd) 62. A New Kind of Love (& pd) 63. Cast a Giant Shadow (& pd) 66. The War Between Men and Women (co-wd) 72, many others, usually in collaboration with *Jack Rose* (1911–).

Shaw, Artie (c. 1904–). American bandleader and trumpeter.
□ Dancing Co-Ed 39. Second Chorus 40.

Shaw, Bernard (1856–1950). Distinguished Irish playwright who for many years refused to allow film versions of his works: he was reconciled to the idea by Gabriel Pascal. The following versions have been made.
How He Lied to Her Husband 30. Arms and the Man 31. Pygmalion 38. Major Barbara 40. Caesar and Cleopatra 45. Androcles and the Lion 53. Saint Joan 57. The Doctor's Dilemma 58. The Devil's Disciple 59. Helden (Arms and the Man) (WG) 59. The Millionairess 61. My Fair Lady (from Pygmalion) 64. Great Catherine 67.

Shaw, Irwin (1912–). American novelist and screenwriter.
Talk of the Town 42. I Want You 51. Fire Down Below 57. The Young Lions (& oa) 58. Tip on a Dead Jockey 58. Two Weeks in Another Town (novel only) 62. *Rich Man Poor Man* (novel only) (TV) 76, etc.

Shaw, Robert (1927–). British actor, mainly on stage from 1954.
The Dam Busters (film debut) 55. Sea Fury 59. The Valiant 61. Tomorrow at Ten 62. *From Russia with Love* 63. The Caretaker 63. The Luck of Ginger Coffey 64. The Battle of the Bulge 65. *A Man For All Seasons* (as Henry VIII) 66. Custer of the West 67. The Battle of Britain 69. The Royal Hunt of the Sun 69. Figures in a Landscape 70. A Town Called Bastard 71. The Hireling 73. The Sting 73. The Taking of Pelham One Two Three 74. Jaws 75. Diamonds 76. Swashbuckler 76. The Deep 77, etc.
TV series: The Buccaneers 56.

Shaw, Sebastian (1905–). British leading

man of the thirties, latterly character actor. On stage from 1913 (as child).
Caste 30. Taxi to Paradise 33. Men are not Gods 36. The Squeaker 37. The Spy in Black 39. East of Piccadilly 41. The Glass Mountain 48. It Happened Here 64. A Midsummer Night's Dream 68, etc.

Shaw, Susan (1929–) (Patsy Sloots). British leading lady groomed by the Rank 'charm school'.
London Town 46. The Upturned Glass 47. Holiday Camp 47. London Belongs to Me 48. The Woman in Question 50. The Intruder 51. The Good Die Young 52. Stock Car 54. Carry On Nurse 59. The Switch 63, etc.

Shaw, Victoria (1935–) (Jeanette Elphick). Australian leading lady in American films.
Cattle Station (Aust.) 55. The Eddy Duchin Story 56. Edge of Eternity 59. The Crimson Kimono 60. Alvarez Kelly 66. Westworld 73, etc.

Shaw, Wini (1899–). American singer of Hawaiian descent, used as voice of non-singing stars in many Warner musicals of the thirties. Actually appeared in the following.
Three on a Honeymoon 34. Gold Diggers of 1935 35. In Caliente 35. Melody for Two 37, etc.

Shawlee, Joan (1929–) (formerly Joan Fulton). American character comedienne with night club and stage experience.
Men in Her Diary 45. Cuban Pete 46. I'll Be Yours 47. The Marrying Kind 52. Conquest of Space 54. A Star is Born 54. *Some Like It Hot* 59. The Apartment 60. Irma La Douce 63. The Wild Angels 66. The St Valentine's Day Massacre 67. One More Time 71. Willard 71, etc.
TV series: Aggie 57.

Shawn, Dick (c. 1929–) (Richard Schulefand). American comedian, in occasional films.
Wake Me When It's Over 60. It's a Mad Mad Mad Mad World 63. A Very Special Favor 65. What Did You Do in the War, Daddy? 66. Penelope 66. The Producers 68, etc.

Shayne, Robert (c. 1910–) (Robert Shaen Dawe). American general purpose actor.
Keep 'Em Rolling 34. Shine On Harvest Moon 44. The Swordsman 47. The Neanderthal Man (lead role) 53. Spook Chasers 58. Valley of the Redwoods 61, etc.

She. Seven silent versions are said to have been

made of Rider Haggard's adventure fantasy about a lost tribe, an ageless queen and a flame of eternal life in darkest Africa. Only the last remains, made in London and Berlin by G. B. Samuelson, with Betty Blythe and Carlyle Blackwell. In 1934 in Hollywood, Merian Cooper and Ernest Schoedsack remade the story in a North Pole setting, with Helen Gahagan and Randolph Scott. In 1965 came a lifeless Hammer version directed by Robert Day, with Ursula Andress and John Richardson; this was followed in 1968 by a sequel, *The Vengeance of She*, that was more than slightly potty.

She Only Danced One Summer (Sweden 1951). This glum romantic tragedy came complete with nude bathing scene and dour puritan priests, amounting to almost a parody of itself. But it was commercial enough to cause a renewal of interest in European films. Arne Matsson directed: Ulla Jacobson and Folke Sundquist were the doomed lovers.

Shean, Al (1868–1949) (Alfred Schoenberg). German-born entertainer, long in American vaudeville; part of the famous 'Mr Gallagher and Mr Shean' act. After his partner's death he played character roles in Hollywood films.
Murder in the Air 35. San Francisco 36. The Great Waltz 38. Ziegfeld Girl 41. Atlantic City 44, etc.

Shear, Barry (–). American director.
□ Wild in the Streets 68. The Todd Killings 71. Across 110th Street 72. The Deadly Trackers 73.

Shearer, Douglas (1899–1971). American sound engineer, brother of Norma Shearer; at MGM for many years, he won twelve Academy Awards, and developed a new sound head.
The Big House 30. Naughty Marietta 35. San Francisco 36. Strike Up the Band 40. Thirty Seconds Over Tokyo 44. Green Dolphin Street 47. The Great Caruso 51, many others.

Shearer, Moira (1926–) (Moira King). Scottish-born ballet dancer who came to films for the leading role in *The Red Shoes* 48.
□ Tales of Hoffman 52. The Story of Three Loves 53. The Man Who Loved Redheads 55. Peeping Tom 59. Black Tights 60.

Shearer, Norma (1900–). American star actress of the twenties and thirties, widow of Irving Thalberg, MGM executive producer.
The Stealers (debut) 20. The Snob 24. He Who Gets Slapped 24. The Tower of Lies 25. The Waring Sex 26. The Student Prince 27. The

Actress 28. The Trial of Mary Dugan (first sound film) 29. The Divorcee (AA) 29. The Last of Mrs Cheyney 29. Hollywood Revue 29. Their Own Desire 30. Let Us Be Gay 30. Strangers May Kiss 30. Private Lives 31. A Free Soul 31. Strange Interlude 31. Smilin' Through 32. Riptide 34. The Barretts of Wimpole Street 34. Romeo and Juliet 36. Marie Antoinette 38. Idiot's Delight 39. The Women 39. Escape 40. We Were Dancing 42. Her Cardboard Lover 42.

Sheekman, Arthur (1892–). American comedy writer, often in collaboration.
Monkey Business 31. Roman Scandals 33. Dimples 36. Wonder Man 45. Welcome Stranger 46. Saigon 47. Young Man with Ideas 52. Bundle of Joy 56. Ada 61, etc.

Sheen, Martin (1940–) (Ramon Estevez). American leading actor of the seventies.
□ The Incident 67. The Subject was Roses 68. Catch 22 69. Goodbye Raggedy Ann (TV) 71. Rage 72. Message to My Daughter (TV) 72. Pursuit (TV) 73. That Certain Summer (TV) 73. Letters for Three Lovers (TV) 73. Sweet Hostage (TV) 73. *Badlands* 73. Catholics (TV) 74. The Execution of Private Slovik (TV) 74. The Missiles of October (TV) 74. The California Kid (TV) 75. The Legend of Earl Durand 75. No Drums No Bugles (TV) 77.

Sheffield, Johnny (1931–). American boy actor of the thirties, especially in the *Tarzan* and later the *Bomba* series.
Babes in Arms 39. Roughly Speaking 45, etc.

The Sheik. Rudolph Valentino first appeared as the romantic Arab in 1922, with Agnes Ayres as his willing co-star, in an adaptation of E. M. Hull's novelette. It was one of his most successful roles, and Son of the Sheik came out in 1926 with Vilma Banky partnering him. His death prevented further episodes, but in 1937 Ramon Novarro made fun of the idea in The Sheik Steps Out, and in 1962 came an Italian spoof called The Return of the Son of the Sheik with Gordon Scott.

Sheldon, Sidney (1917–). American writer-director.
The Bachelor and the Bobbysoxer (w) (AA) 47. Dream Wife (co-w, d) 53. You're Never Too Young (w) 55. Pardners (w) 56. The Buster Keaton Story (wpd) 57. Jumbo (w) 62, etc.

Shelley, Barbara (1933–). British leading lady who has filmed in Italy; latterly associated with horror films.
Cat Girl 57. Blood of the Vampire 59. Village of

the Damned 61. Shadow of the Cat 62. Postman's Knock 62. The Gorgon 64. The Secret of Blood Island 65. Rasputin the Mad Monk 65. Dracula, Prince of Darkness 65. *Quatermass and the Pit* 67. Ghost Story 74, etc.

Shelley, Mary Wollstonecraft (1797–1851). British writer (wife of the poet) who somewhat unexpectedly is remembered as the creator of *Frankenstein*, which she composed to pass the time during a wet summer. She was played in *Bride of Frankenstein* by Elsa Lanchester.

Shelton, Joy (1922–). British leading lady.
Millions Like Us 43. Waterloo Road 44. No Room at the Inn 48. A Case for PC 49 51. Impulse 54. No Kidding 60. HMS Defiant 62, etc.

Shenson, Walter (c. 1921–). American producer, former publicist; based in Britain.
Korea Patrol 53. The Mouse That Roared 59. A Matter of Who 61. *A Hard Day's Night* 64. Help! 65. A Talent for Loving 69. Welcome to the Club (d) 70. Digby 73, etc.

Shepherd, Cybill (1949–). American leading lady of the seventies.
□ The Last Picture Show 71. The Heartbreak Kid 72. Daisy Miller 74. At Long Last Love 75. Taxi Driver 76. Special Delivery 76.

Shepley, Michael (1907–1961) (Michael Shepley-Smith). British stage actor who usually played amiable buffoons.
Black Coffee 30. Goodbye Mr Chips 39. Quiet Wedding 40. The Demi Paradise 43. Maytime in Mayfair 49. An Alligator Named Daisy 56. Don't Bother to Knock 61, etc.

Shepperd, John (1907–) (also known as Shepperd Strudwick). American leading man and latterly character actor, usually in gentle, understanding roles.
Congo Maisie (debut) 40. *Remember the Day* 41. The Loves of Edgar Allan Poe 42. Enchantment 47. Joan of Arc 48. All the King's Men 50. A Place in the Sun 51. Autumn Leaves 56. The Sad Sack 57. The Unkillables 67. Cops and Robbers 73, etc.

Sher, Jack (1913–). American writer-director, former columnist.
My Favorite Spy (w) 52. Off Limits (w) 53. Four Girls in Town (wd) 56. Kathy 'O (wd) 58. The Wild and the Innocent (wd) 59. The Three Worlds of Gulliver (wd) 60. Paris Blues (co-w)

61. Critic's Choice (w) 63. Move Over Darling (co-w) 63, etc.

Sheridan, Ann (1915–1967) (Clara Lou Sheridan). American leading lady at her peak in the early forties; a cheerful beauty contest winner who developed a tough style and became known as the 'oomph' girl.

□ Search for Beauty 34. Bolero 34. Come on Marines 34. Murder at the Vanities 34. Kiss and Make Up 34. Shoot the Works 34. The Notorious Sophie Lang 34. Ladies Should Listen 34. Wagon Wheels 34. Mrs Wiggs of the Cabbage Patch 34. College Rhythm 34. You Belong to Me 34. Limehouse Blues 34. Enter Madame 35. Home on the Range 35. Rumba 35. Behold My Wife 35. Car 99 35. Rocky Mountain Mystery 35. Mississippi 35. The Glass Key 35. The Crusades 35. The Red Blood of Courage 35. Fighting Youth 35. Sing Me a Love Song 35. Black Legion 36. The Great O'Malley 37. San Quentin 37. Wine, Women and Horses 37. The Footloose Heiress 37. Alcatraz Island 37. She Loves a Fireman 38. The Patient in Room 18 38. Mystery House 38. Cowboy from Brooklyn 38. Little Miss Thoroughbred 38. Letter of Introduction 38. Broadway Musketeers 38. *Angels with Dirty Faces* 38. They Made Me a Criminal 39. Dodge City 39. Naughty but Nice 39. Winter Carnival 39. Indianapolis Speedway 39. Angels Wash Their Faces 39. Castle on the Hudson 40. It All Came True 40. *Torrid Zone* 40. *They Drive by Night* 40. City for Conquest 40. Honeymoon for Three 41. Navy Blues 41. *Kings' Row* 41. *The Man Who Came to Dinner* 41. Juke Girl 42. Wings for the Eagle 42. George Washington Slept Here 42. Edge of Darkness 43. *Thank Your Lucky Stars* 43. *Shine on Harvest Moon* 44. The Doughgirls 44. One More Tomorrow 46. Nora Prentiss 47. *The Unfaithful* 47. Silver River 48. Good Sam 48. *I Was a Male War Bride* 49. Stella 50. Woman on the Run 50. Steel Town 52. Just Across the Street 52. Take Me to Town 53. Appointment in Honduras 53. *Come Next Spring* 56. The Opposite Sex 56. Woman and the Hunter 57.

TV series: Pistols and Petticoats 67.

Sheridan, Dinah (1920–). British leading lady.

Irish and Proud of It 36. Full Speed Ahead 39. Salute John Citizen 42. For You Alone 44. Hills of Donegal 47. Calling Paul Temple 48. The Story of Shirley Yorke 48. Paul Temple's Triumph 50. Where No Vultures Fly 51. Genevieve 53. The Railway Children 71, etc.

Sheriff, Paul (1903–1962) (Paul Shouvalov). Russian art director in Britain since mid-thirties.

French Without Tears 39. Quiet Wedding 40. The Gentle Sex 43. The Way to the Stars 45. Vice Versa 48. Flesh and Blood 51. Gentlemen Marry Brunettes 55. Interpol 57. The Doctor's Dilemma 58. The Grass is Greener 60, etc.

Sherin, Edwin (–). American director.
Valdez is Coming 70. Glory Boy 71, etc.

Sherlock Holmes. Conan Doyle's classic fictional detective, around whom a detailed legend has been created by ardent followers, has a long screen history. There were American one-reel films featuring him in 1903, 1905 and 1908. Also in 1908 there began a series of twelve Danish one-reelers starring Forrest Holger-Madsen. In 1910 there were two German films and in 1912 six French. A second French series began in 1913; also in this year an American two-reel version of *The Sign of Four* featured Harry Benham. British six-reelers were made of *A Study in Scarlet* 14, and *Valley of Fear* 16; also in 1916 the famous stage actor William Gillette put his impersonation of Holmes on film for Essanay. In 1917 came a German version of *The Hound of the Baskervilles*; then nothing till 1922, when John Barrymore played Holmes and Roland Young was Watson in Goldwyn's *Sherlock Holmes*, based on Gillette's stage play. In Britain in the same year Maurice Elvey directed a full-length version of *The Hound of the Baskervilles* and followed it with over 25 two-reelers starring Eille Norwood, remaining faithful to the original stories. In 1929 Carlyle Blackwell played Holmes in a German remake of *The Hound of the Baskervilles*; and in the same year Clive Brook played in a talkie, *The Return of Sherlock Holmes*, with H. Reeves-Smith as Watson. Arthur Wontner, a perfect Holmes, first played the role in *Sherlock Holmes' Final Hour* (GB) 31, later appearing in *The Sign of Four* 32, *The Missing Rembrandt* 33, *The Triumph of Sherlock Holmes* 35, and *The Silver Blaze* 36 (Ian Fleming was Watson). Raymond Massey was Holmes in *The Speckled Band* (GB) 31, with Athole Stewart as Watson; in 1932 Robert Rendel was in *The Hound of the Baskervilles* (GB). Clive Brook again appeared in *Sherlock Holmes* (US) 32, with Reginald Owen as Watson; Owen then played Holmes in *A Study in Scarlet* (US) 33. The Germans made three more Holmes films in the mid-thirties, including yet another remake of *The Hound*, which in 1939 was again tackled by Fox in Hollywood, this time with Basil Rathbone as the detective and Nigel Bruce as Watson. Its success led to a hurried remake of the Gillette play under the title *The Adventures of Sherlock Holmes* 39; two years later the same two actors began a series of twelve films in which the settings were modernized and most of the stories unrecognizable, although the acting and much of the writing were well in character. The titles were *Sherlock Holmes and the Voice of Terror* 41, *Sherlock Homes and the Secret Weapon* 42, *Sherlock Holmes in Washington* 42, *Sherlock Holmes Faces Death* 43, *Spider Woman* 44, *The Scarlet Claw* 44, *Pearl of Death* 44, *House of Fear* 45, *Woman in Green* 45, *Pursuit to Algiers* 45, *Terror by Night* 46, *Dressed to Kill* (*Sherlock Holmes and the Secret Code*) 46. Then a long silence was broken by Peter Cushing and André Morell in the leads of a British remake of *The Hound of the Baskervilles* 59. In 1962 Christopher Lee and Thorley Walters played Holmes and Watson in a German film, *Sherlock Holmes and the Deadly Necklace*; and in 1965 John Neville and Donald Houston appeared in an original story involving the famous pair with Jack the Ripper: *A Study in Terror*. Also in 1965 a BBC TV series featured Douglas Wilmer and Nigel Stock, with Peter Cushing later taking over as Holmes; the period atmosphere was carefully sought but the stories suffered from being padded out to the standard TV length. (There was also a Franco-American TV series in 1954 with Ronald Howard and Howard Marion-Crawford.) In 1969 Billy Wilder made *The Private Life of Sherlock Holmes* with Robert Stephens, apparently intending a send-up but producing only a further pleasant variation. In 1970 George C. Scott thought he was Sherlock Holmes in *They Might Be Giants*, so did Larry Hagman in a 1976 TV movie, *The Return of the World's Greatest Detective*. Nicol Williamson as Holmes was treated by Sigmund Freud in 1976's *The Seven Per Cent Solution*.

Sherman, George (1908–). American director who graduated slowly from second feature westerns.
Wild Horse Rodeo 37. Death Valley Outlaws 41. Outside the Law 41. Mantrap 43. Mystery Broadcast 44. The Lady and the Monster 44. *The Bandit of Sherwood Forest* 46. Renegades 46. Last of the Redskins 48. Sword of the Desert 49. Panther's Moon 48. The Golden Horde 51. Against All Flags 52. War Arrow 54. Dawn at Socorro 54. Count Three and Pray 55. Comanche 56. Son of Robin Hood 58. The Enemy General 60. Panic Button 64. Smoky 66. Big Jake 71, many others.

Sherman, Lowell (1885–1934). American leading man with stage experience.
Way Down East 20. Monsieur Beaucaire 24. The Divine Woman 27. Mammy 30. The Greeks Had a Word for Them 32. False Faces 32. She

Done Him Wrong (directed only) 33. Morning Glory 33. Broadway Through a Keyhole 33, etc.

Sherman, Richard (1928–) and **Robert** (1925–). Americans songwriting brothers who have worked mainly for Disney.
Mary Poppins (AA) 64. The Happiest Millionaire 67. The One and Only Genuine Original Family Band 68. Bedknobs and Broomsticks 71. Huckleberry Finn (& w) 74. The Slipper and the Rose (& w) 76, etc.

Sherman, Vincent (1906–). American director, formerly stage actor.
The Return of Doctor X 39. *All Through the Night* 41. The Hard Way 42. Old Acquaintance 43. In Our Time 44. Mr Skeffington 45. The Unfaithful 47. The New Adventures of Don Juan 48. The Hasty Heart 49. Lone Star 51. Affair in Trinidad 52. The Garment Jungle 57. Naked Earth 57. The Young Philadelphians 59. Ice Palace 60. The Second Time Around 61. Cervantes 66, etc.

Sherriff, R. C. (1896–1975). Prolific British playwright and screenwriter.
Autobiography 1969: *No Leading Lady*.
AS PLAYWRIGHT: Journey's End 30. Badger's Green 47. Home at Seven 52.
AS SCREENWRITER: The Invisible Man 33. Goodbye Mr Chips 39. Lady Hamilton 41. Odd Man Out 47. Quartet 48. No Highway 50. The Dam Busters 55, many others.

Sherrin, Ned (1931–). British ex-barrister who became a BBC producer and performer, then turned to producing movies.
The Virgin Soldiers 69. Every Home Should Have One 70. Girl Stroke Boy 71. Up Pompeii 71. Rentadick 72. Up the Chastity Belt 72. The Alf Garnett Saga 72, etc.

Sherwood, Madeleine (1926–). American character actress.
Cat on a Hot Tin Roof 58. Hurry Sundown 67. Pendulum 69, etc.
TV series: The Flying Nun 67–68.

Sherwood, Robert (1896–1955). American dramatist. Plays filmed:
Reunion in Vienna 32. The Petrified Forest 36. Tovarich 38. Idiot's Delight 39. Abe Lincoln in Illinois 39, etc.
OTHER SCRIPTS: Waterloo Bridge 32. The Adventures of Marco Polo 38. Rebecca 40. The Best Years of Our Lives 45. The Bishop's Wife 48. Jupiter's Darling (The Road to Rome) 54.

Sheybal, Vladek (1928–). Intense-looking Polish character actor in Britain.
Kanal 56. Women in Love 69. The Music Lovers 70. The Boy Friend 71. QB VII 74. The Wind and the Lion 75, etc.

Shields, Arthur (1895–1970). Irish character actor, an Abbey player, long in Hollywood; brother of Barry Fitzgerald.
The Plough and the Stars 37. Drums along the Mohawk 39. The Long Voyage Home 40. The Keys of the Kingdom 44. The Corn is Green 45. The River 51. The Quiet Man 52. The King and Four Queens 56. Night of the Quarter Moon 59. The Pigeon That Took Rome 62, etc.

Shigeta, James (1933–). Hawaiian leading man who usually plays Japanese in Hollywood films.
The Crimson Kimono 60. Cry for Happy 60. Walk Like a Dragon 60. Bridge to the Sun 61. Flower Drum Song 61. Paradise Hawaian Style 66. Nobody's Perfect 68. Lost Horizon 73. Midway 76, etc.

Shimkus, Joanna (1943–). Canadian leading lady in American and European films.
Paris vu Par 66. Les Aventuriers 67. Zita 68. Ho! 68. Boom 68. The Lost Man 69. *The Virgin and the Gypsy* 70. The Marriage of a Young Stockbroker 71. A Time for Loving 71, etc.

Shimura, Takashi (1905–). Japanese leading actor.
Rashomon 50. Seven Samurai 54. Godzilla 56. Throne of Blood 57. The Hidden Fortress 58. Yojimbo 62. Stray Dog 64, etc.

Shindo, Kaneto (1912–). Japanese director.
Children of Hiroshima 53. The Wolf 56. *The Island* 62. Ningen 63. *Onibaba* 64. Kuroneko 67, etc.

Shine, Bill (1911–). Amiable British small part actor often seen as vacuous dandy.
The Scarlet Pimpernel 34. Farewell Again 37. Let George Do It 40. Perfect Strangers 45. Melba 53. Father Brown 54. Jack the Ripper 58, many others.

Shiner, Ronald (1903–1966). British comedy actor, on stage from 1928, films from 1934, at first in bit parts, later as star.
King Arthur Was a Gentleman 42. The Way to the Stars 45. *Worm's Eye View* 50. *Reluctant Heroes* 51. Laughing Anne 53. Top of the Form 54. Up to His Neck 55. Keep It Clean 56. Dry Rot 56. Girls at Sea 58. Operation Bullshine 59. The Night We Got the Bird 60, etc.

Ship of Fools (US 1965). A rather splendid sixties reversion to the star-studded 'Grand Hotel' type of film, with sociological overtones added. The period is 1933, the ship is full of Germans and Jews, and most of the ironies are naïvely and quaintly based on hindsight; but the dramatic situations are well handled, Stanley Kramer's direction of the several stories is well controlled if rather stately, and there is a feast of good acting, notably from Simone Signoret, Oskar Werner, Vivien Leigh and Heinz Ruhmann.

ships, of the modern passenger kind, have provided a useful setting for many films, most recently in *Ship of Fools* (see above). Three notable versions of the Titanic disaster were *Atlantic* 30, *Titanic* 53 and *A Night to Remember* 58; while sinking ships also figured in *We're Not Dressing* 34, *Souls at Sea* 37, *History is Made at Night* 37, *The Blue Lagoon* 48, *Our Girl Friday* 52, *The Admirable Crichton* 57 (and earlier versions), *The Last Voyage* 60 and *The Poseidon Adventure* 72. A sinister time was had on board ship in *Journey into Fear*, *Across the Pacific*, *King Kong*, *My Favorite Blonde*, *The Ghost Ship*, *The Mystery of the Marie Celeste*, *The Sea Wolf*, *The Hairy Ape*, *Dangerous Crossing*, *Ghost Breakers*, *The Wreck of the Mary Deare*, *Juggernaut*, and *Voyage of the Damned*; laughter, however, was to the fore in *Monkey Business* 31, *The Lady Eve* 41, *Luxury Liner* 48, *Doctor at Sea* 55, *The Captain's Table* 58, *A Countess from Hong Kong* 66, and *A Night at the Opera* 35 with its famous cabin scene. The romance of a cruise was stressed in *Dodsworth* 36, *The Big Broadcast of 1938*, *Now Voyager* 42, and the two versions of *Love Affair* 39 (the second being *An Affair to Remember* 56); while in the 'Winter Cruise' section of *Encore* 51, it was almost forced on Kay Walsh. In *Assault on a Queen* 66 the leading characters plan to hi-jack the Queen Mary. The weirdest ship was the ship of the dead in *Outward Bound* 30, and its remake *Between Two Worlds* 44.

Mississippi riverboats have featured in *Mississippi*, *Rhythm on the River*, *Mississippi Gambler*, *The Secret Life of Walter Mitty*, *The Naughty Nineties*, *The Adventures of Mark Twain*, *Four for Texas*, *Frankie and Johnny*, and the several versions of *Showboat*; also in the TV series *Riverboat*.

Sailing ships of olden days are too numerous to detail.

Shirley, Anne (1918–) (Dawn Paris). American child star of the twenties (under the name Dawn O'Day) who later graduated to leading lady roles.

So Big 32. *Anne of Green Gables* 35. Stella Dallas 37. Vigil in the Night 39. Anne of Windy Poplars 40. West Point Widow 41. All that Money Can Buy 41. *Farewell My Lovely* 44, etc.

Shoemaker, Ann (1895–). American character actress with stage experience.
A Dog of Flanders 35. Alice Adams 35. Stella Dallas 37. Babes in Arms 39. Conflict 45. A Woman's Secret 49. Sunrise at Campobello 60. The Fortune Cookie 66, many others.

Sholem, Lee (c. 1900–). American director.
Tarzan's Magic Fountain 48. Redhead from Wyoming 52. Tobor the Great 53. Emergency Hospital 56. Pharoah's Curse 56. Sierra Stranger 57, etc.

Shonteff, Lindsay (–). British director, from TV.
The Curse of Simba 63. Devil Doll 64. Licensed to Kill 65. Run with the Wind 66, etc.

shooting script. This differs from a screenplay, which concentrates on dialogue, in that it includes camera directions and breaks up the script into shots; it is an instruction manual for technicians rather than a work of art.

The Shop around the Corner (US 1939). Written by Samson Raphaelson from a play by Nikolaus Laszlo, produced and directed by Ernst Lubitsch, this was a charming piece of Hollywood schmaltz, though none of the cast really suggested Budapest shop assistants. James Stewart and Margaret Sullavan were the couple who disliked each other by day but fell in love through a lonely hearts bureau; in support were Frank Morgan, Joseph Schildkraut, Felix Bressart. In 1949 Robert Z. Leonard remade it as a musical, *In the Good Old Summertime*, with Judy Garland and Van Johnson.

Shopworn Angel (US 1929). A well-remembered comedy-drama about a hard-boiled Broadway gold-digger (Nancy Carroll) who ultimately gave up her rich provider (Paul Lukas) for a poor doughboy on his way to war (Gary Cooper). This version was directed by Richard Wallace, H. C. Potter remade it in 1938, with Margaret Sullavan, Walter Pidgeon and James Stewart. In 1959 it turned up again as *That Kind of Woman*, with Sidney Lumet directing Sophia Loren, George Sanders and Tab Hunter. It had originally been a silent film of 1919 called *Pettigrew's Girl*, written by Dana Burnett and Ethel Clayton.

Shore, Dinah (1917–) (Frances Rose Shore).

American cabaret singer, in very occasional films; latterly running a daily TV chat show for women.
□ Thank Your Lucky Stars 43. Up in Arms 44. Follow the Boys 44. Belle of the Yukon 45. Till the Clouds Roll By 46. Aaron Slick from Punkin Crick 52.

shorts are officially any films running less than 3000 feet (about 33 minutes). In the thirties most programmes consisted of a feature and several one-reelers, but the big studios first found shorts uneconomic and then closed down altogether. Shorts fell into the hands of independent producers, who found that the longer they made them the more money they could demand, even if the quality was not high. Double-feature programmes also contributed to their demise.

Shostakovich, Dmitri (1906–). Russian composer.
The New Babylon 28. The Youth of Maxim 35. The Fall of Berlin 47. Hamlet 64. War and Peace 64.

Shotter, Winifred (1904–). British leading lady of the thirties, chiefly remembered in the Aldwych farces beginning with *Rookery Nook* 30.

Showalter, Max (1917–) (formerly known as Casey Adams). American supporting actor often seen as reporter, newscaster or good guy friend.
Always Leave Them Laughing 50. With a Song in My Heart 52. Bus Stop 56. The Naked and the Dead 58. Elmer Gantry 60. Bon Voyage 62. Fate is the Hunter 64. The Moonshine War 70. The Anderson Tapes 71, etc.

Showboat. Jerome Kern and Oscar Hammerstein II's operetta from Edna Ferber's novel was filmed by Harry Pollard in 1929 with Laura la Plante and Joseph Schildkraut; by James Whale in 1936 with Irene Dunne, Allan Jones and Paul Robeson; and by George Sidney in 1951 with Kathryn Grayson, Howard Keel and William Warfield.

Schuck, John (–). American character actor familiar as the dumb sergeant on *McMillan and Wife*.
M*A*S*H 70. Blade 73. Thieves Like Us 74, etc.

Shuken, Leo (1906–1976). American composer.
Waikiki Wedding 37. The Flying Deuces 39. *Stagecoach* (AA) 39. The Lady Eve 41. *Sullivan's Travels* 41. The Miracle of Morgan's

Creek 44. The Fabulous Dorseys 47. The Greatest Story Ever Told 64, etc.

Shumlin, Herman (1898–). American stage producer who directed two films in the forties.
□ Watch on the Rhine 43. Confidential Agent 45.

Shurlock, Geoffrey (1895–1976). Film administrator, an Englishman who became the power behind the MPEA Production Code 1954–68.

Shute, Nevil (1899–1960). Australian best-selling novelist.
The Pied Piper 43. Landfall 54. A Town Like Alice 56. On the Beach 59, etc.

Sidney, George (1878–1945) (Sammy Greenfield). American comedian, once popular in vaudeville.
Potash and Perlmutter 23. Millionaires 26. Clancy's Kosher Wedding 27. The Cohens and Kellys in Paris 28. Manhattan Melodrama 34. Good Old Soak 37, others.

Sidney, George (1911–). American director, former musician and MGM shorts director.
Free and Easy 41. Thousands Cheer 43. Bathing Beauty 44. Anchors Aweigh 45. *The Harvey Girls* 46. Cass Timberlane 47. *The Three Musketeers* 48. The Red Danube 49. Annie Get Your Gun 50. *Showboat* 51. Scaramouche 52. Young Bess 53. *Kiss Me Kate* 53. Jupiter's Darling 54. The Eddy Duchin Story 56. *Jeanne Eagels* 57. Pal Joey 57. Who Was That Lady? 59. Pepe 60. Bye Bye Birdie 62. Viva Las Vegas 63. The Swinger 66. Half a Sixpence 67, etc.

Sidney, Sylvia (1910–) (Sophia Kosow). Fragile, dark-eyed American heroine of the thirties.
□ Thru Different Eyes 29. *City Streets* 31. Confessions of a Co-Ed 31. An American Tragedy 31. *Street Scene* 31. Ladies of the Big House 32. The Miracle Man 32. Merrily We Go to Hell 33. Madame Butterfly 33. Pick Up 33. Jennie Gerhardt 33. Good Dame 34. Thirty Day Princess 34. Behold My Wife 34. Accent on Youth 35. Mary Burns Fugitive 35. Trail of the Lonesome Pine 36. Fury 36. Sabotage (GB) 37. *You Only Live Once* 37. Dead End 37. You and Me 37. One Third of a Nation 39. The Wagons Roll at Night 41. Blood on the Sun 45. The Searching Wind 46. Mr Ace 46. Love from a Stranger 47. Les Misérables 53. Violent Saturday 55. Behind the High Wall 56. Do Not Fold Spindle or Mutilate (TV) 71. Summer

Wishes Winter Dreams 73. Death at Love House (TV) 76.

Siegel, Don (1912–). American director, former editor; an expert at crime thrillers, he has recently been attracting the attention of highbrow critics.
□ *Hitler Lives* (short) (AA) 45. Star in the Night (short) (AA) 45. The Verdict 46. Night Unto Night 48. The Big Steal 49. Duel at Silver Creek 52. No Time for Flowers 52. Count the Hours 53. China Venture 54. *Riot in Cell Block 11* 54. Private Hell 36 55. An Annapolis Story 55. *Invasion of the Body Snatchers* 56. Crime in the Streets 57. Spanish Affair 57. *Baby Face Nelson* 57. The Line Up 58. The Gun Runners 58. The Hound Dog Man 59. Edge of Eternity 59. Flaming Star 60. Hell is for Heroes 62. The Killers 64. The Hanged Man 64. Madigan 67. *Coogan's Bluff* 68. Two Mules for Sister Sara 69. Death of a Gunfighter (co-d) 69. The Beguiled 71. *Dirty Harry* 72. *Charley Varrick* 73. The Black Windmill 74. *The Shootist* 76. Telefon 77.

Siegel, Sol C. (1903–). American producer, in films from 1929.
Kiss and Tell 44. Blue Skies 46. House of Strangers 49. Fourteen Hours 51. Call Me Madam 53. High Society 56. Les Girls 57. Home from the Hill 59. Walk Don't Run 66. Alvarez Kelly 66. No Way to Treat a Lady 68, etc.

Siegfried (Germany 1924). This, with its sequel *Kriemhilde's Revenge*, is Fritz Lang's version of the Niebelungen saga, full of dragons and national heroes. Heavy-going Teutonic spectacle, but in its day a triumph of filmcraft.

Signoret, Simone (1921–) (Simone Kaminker). Distinguished French leading actress, married to Yves Montand.
Bolero 42. Les Démons à l'Aube 45. Macadam 46. *Dédée d'Anvers* 47. *Manèges* 49. Four Days' Leave 49. *La Ronde* 50. *Casque d'Or* (BFA) 51. Thérèse Raquin 53. *Les Diaboliques* 54. *The Witches of Salem* (BFA) 56. *Room at the Top* (AA, BFA) 59. Term of Trial 62. Ship of Fools 65. The Sleeping-Car Murder 66. Is Paris Burning? 66. The Deadly Affair 66. Games 68. The Seagull 68. Le Rose et le Noir 70. L'Aveu 70. Le Chat 74, etc.

silent films began to grow unfashionable during 1927, though for eighteen months or so producers continued to put out so called 'silent versions' of their talkies: these versions were unspeakably bad, as the new talkies used very little camera movement and a great deal of dialogue which had to be given in sub-titles. By

1930 silents had all but disappeared, with exceptions such as Flaherty's *Tabu* 32, Chaplin's *City Lights* 31, and *Modern Times* 36, and an unsuccessful 1952 experiment called *The Thief*, which eschewed dialogue though it did have a music and effects track.

Silliphant, Sterling (1918–). American writer-producer with much TV experience (*Naked City, Route 66*, etc.). Former advertising executive.
The Joe Louis Story (w) 53. Five Against the House (w, co-p) 55. Nightfall (w) 56. Damn Citizen (w) 57. The Slender Thread (w) 66. In the Heat of the Night (w) (AA) 67. Charly 68. A Walk in the Spring Rain 69. The Killer Elite (w) 75, etc.

Sillitoe, Alan (1928–). British north-country novelist best known to filmgoers for *Saturday Night and Sunday Morning* and *The Loneliness of the Long Distance Runner*. His less successful novel *The General* was filmed as *Counterpoint*.

Sills, Milton (1882–1930). Stalwart American leading man of the silent screen.
The Rack 15. The Claw 17. Eyes of Youth 19. The Weekend 20. Burning Sands 22. Adam's Rib 23. Madonna of the Streets 24. The Sea Hawk 24. Paradise 26. Valley of the Giants 27. His Captive Woman 29. The Sea Wolf 30, many others.

Silly Symphony. The name given by Walt Disney to all his short cartoon fables of the thirties which did not feature Mickey Mouse, Pluto or Donald Duck.

Silva, Henry (1928–). Pale-eyed Puerto Rican actor, often seen as sadistic villain or assorted Latin types.
Viva Zapata 52. Crowded Paradise 56. A Hatful of Rain 57. The Bravados 58. Green Mansions 59. Cinderfella 60. *The Manchurian Candidate* 62. *Johnny Cool* (leading role) 63. The Return of Mr Moto 65. The Reward 65. The Plainsman 66. The Hills Ran Red (It.) 66. Never a Dull Moment 68. Five Savage Men 70. The Kidnap of Mary Lou 75. Shoot 76, etc.

Silver, Joan Macklin (–). American director.
Hester Street 74. Between the Lines 76.

Silvera, Frank (1914–1970). American general purpose actor with stage experience.
Viva Zapata 52. Killer's Kiss 55. Crowded Paradise 56. The Mountain Road 60. Mutiny on the Bounty 62. The Appaloosa 66. Che! 69. Valdez is Coming 71, etc.

Silverheels, Jay (1920–). Canadian Red Indian actor, mainly in western films.
The Prairie 47. Fury at Furnace Creek 48. Broken Arrow 50. War Arrow 53. The Lone Ranger 55. Indian Paint 65. The Phynx 70. Santee 73, others.
TV series: The Lone Ranger 48–61.

Silvers, Phil (1912–). American vaudeville star comedian in occasional films from 1941.
Tom, Dick and Harry (debut) 41. *You're in the Army Now* 42. Roxie Hart 42. My Gal Sal 42. Coney Island 43. *Cover Girl* 44. A Thousand and One Nights 45. Where Do We Go from Here? 45. Summer Stock 50. Lucky Me 54. Forty Pounds of Trouble 63. *It's a Mad Mad Mad Mad World* 63. A Funny Thing Happened on the Way to the Forum 66. Follow That Camel (GB) 67. Buona Sera, Mrs Campbell 68. Deadly Tide (TV) 75. Won Ton Ton 76, etc.
TV series: *You'll Never Get Rich* (as Bilko) 55–58. *The New Phil Silvers Show* 64.

Silverstein, Eliot (c. 1925–). American director, from TV.
□ Belle Sommers (TV) 62. *Cat Ballou* 65. The Happening 67. A Man Called Horse 69.

Sim, Alastair (1900–1976). Lugubrious Scottish comedy actor of stage and screen; his diction and gestures were inimitable.
□ Riverside Murder 35. The Private Secretary 35. A Fire Has Been Arranged 35. Late Extra 35. Troubled Waters 36. Wedding Group 36. The Big Noise 36. Keep Your Seats Please 36. The Man in the Mirror 36. The Mysterious Mr Davis 36. Strange Experiment 37. Clothes and the Woman 37. Gangway 37. The Squeaker 37. A Romance in Flanders 37. Melody and Romance 37. Sailing Along 38. *The Terror* 38. Alf's Button Afloat 38. *This Man is News* 38. Climbing High 38. *Inspector Hornleigh* 39. This Man in Paris 39. Inspector Hornleigh on Holiday 39. Law and Disorder 40. Inspector Hornleigh Goes to It 41. *Cottage to Let* 41. *Let the People Sing* 42. Waterloo Road 44. *Green for Danger* 46. Hue and Cry 47. Captain Boycott 47. *London Belongs to Me* 48. *The Happiest Days of Your Life* 49. Stage Fright 50. *Laughter in Paradise* 51. *Scrooge* 51. Lady Godiva Rides Again 51. Folly to be Wise 52. Innocents in Paris 53. *An Inspector Calls* 54. *The Belles of St Trinian's* 54. Escapade 55. Geordie 55. The Green Man 56. Blue Murder at St Trinian's 57. The Doctor's Dilemma 59. Left, Right and Centre 59. School for Scoundrels 60.

The Millionairess 60. The Ruling Class 71. Escape from the Dark 76. Rogue Male (TV) 76.

Sim, Gerald (1925–). British supporting actor, often in well bred and slightly prissy roles.
Fame is the Spur 47. The Wrong Arm of the Law 63. The Pumpkin Eater 64. King Rat 64. The Whisperers 66. Oh What a Lovely War 68. Dr Jekyll and Sister Hyde 71. No Sex Please We're British 73. The Slipper and the Rose 76, many others.

Sim, Sheila (1922–). British leading lady, married to Richard Attenborough.
A Canterbury Tale 44. Great Day 45. Dancing with Crime 47. The Guinea Pig 48. Dear Mr Prohack 49. The Magic Box 51. The Night My Number Came Up 55, etc.

Simenon, Georges (1903–). French crime novelist, creator of Inspector Maigret.
Les Inconnus dans la Maison 43. Panique 46. Temptation Harbour (GB) 46. La Marie du Port 50. The Man on the Eiffel Tower (US) 50. Le Fruit Défendu 52. The Brothers Rico (US) 57. Maigret Sets a Trap 58, etc.
TV series: Maigret 63. Thirteen Against Fate 67.

Simmons, Anthony (c. 1924–). British writer-director, known for short films.
Sunday by the Sea 53. Bow Bells 54. The Gentle Corsican 56. Your Money or Your Wife 59. Four in the Morning 65. The Optimists of Nine Elms 73.

Simmons, Jean (1929–). Self-possessed and beautiful British leading lady who married Stewart Granger (later Richard Brooks) and settled in Hollywood to make films which have generally been unworthy of her talents.
□ Give Us the Moon 43. Mr Emmanuel 44. Meet Sexton Blake 44. Kiss the Bride Goodbye 44. The Way to the Stars 45. Caesar and Cleopatra 45. Hungry Hill 45. The Woman in the Hall 45. *Great Expectations* 46. *Black Narcissus* 46. Uncle Silas 47. *Hamlet* 48. The Blue Lagoon 48. Adam and Evelyne 49. Trio 50. Cage of Gold 50. So Long at the Fair 50. The Clouded Yellow 50. Angel Face 52. Androcles and the Lion 53. Young Bess 53. Affair with a Stranger 53. The Robe 53. The Actress 53. She Couldn't Say No 54. The Egyptian 54. A Bullet is Waiting 54. Désirée 54. Footsteps in the Fog 55. Guys and Dolls 56. Hilda Crane 56. This Could Be the Night 57. Until They Sail 57. *The Big Country* 58. Home Before Dark 58. This Earth is Mine 59. *Elmer Gantry* 60. Spartacus 60. *The Grass is Greener* 61. All the Way Home 63. Life at the Top 65. Mister Buddwing 66. Rough Night in

Jericho 67. Divorce American Style 67. The Happy Ending 69. Say Hello to Yesterday 71. Mr Sycamore 75.

Simms, Ginny (1916–) (Virginia Sims). Glamorous American vocalist, with Kay Kyser's band.
That's Right You're Wrong 39. You'll Find Out 40. Playmates 42. Hit the Ice 43. Broadway Rhythm 44. Shady Lady 45. Night and Day 46, etc.

Simms, Larry (1934–). American boy actor, notably in the *Blondie* series 1938–48. (He was Baby Dumpling.)
The Last Gangster 37. Mr Smith Goes to Washington 39. Madame Bovary 49, etc.

Simon, Michel (1895–1975) (François Simon). Heavyweight French character actor, in films from the twenties after music hall experience.
Feu Mathias Pascal 25. The Passion of Joan of Arc 28. La Chienne 31. *Boudu Sauvé des Eaux* 32. Lac aux Dames 34. *L'Atalante* 34. Jeunes Filles de Paris 36. Drôle de Drame 37. Les Disparus de Saint-Agil 38. Quai des Brumes 38. Fric Frac 39. *La Fin du Jour* 39. Circonstances Attenuantes 39. Vautrin 43. Un Ami Viendra Ce Soir 45. *Panique* 46. Fabiola 48. *La Beauté du Diable* 49. The Strange Desire of Monsieur Bard 53. Saadia 53. La Joyeuse Prison 56. It Happened in Broad Daylight 58. The Head 59. Austerlitz 59. Candide 60. The Devil and Ten Commandments 62. The Train 64. Two Hours to Kill 65. *The Two of Us* 67, many others.

Simon, Neil (1927–). American comedy playwright whose Broadway success has been remarkable.
Come Blow Your Horn 63. After the Fox (oa) 66. Barefoot in the Park 67. The Odd Couple 68. Sweet Charity 68. The Out of Towners 70. Plaza Suite 71. Last of the Red Hot Lovers 72. The Sunshine Boys (oa) 75. Murder by Death 76.

Simon, S. Sylvan (1910–1951). American director with radio experience.
A Girl with Ideas 37. Four Girls in White 39. Whistling in the Dark 41. Rio Rita 42. Song of the Open Road 44. Son of Lassie 45. Her Husband's Affairs 47. I Love Trouble 48. The Lust for Gold 49. Born Yesterday (p) 50, etc.

Simon, Simone (1910–). Pert French leading lady with brief stage experience.
Le Chanteur Inconnu (début) 31. Lac aux Dames 34; to US: Girls' Dormitory 36. *Seventh Heaven* 37. Josette 38. *La Bête Humaine* 38. *All*

That Money Can Buy 41. *Cat People* 42. Tahiti Honey 43. Mademoiselle Fifi 44. Temptation Harbour (GB) 47. Donna Senza Nome (It.) 49. La Ronde 50. Olivia 50. Le Plaisir 51. Double Destin 54. The Extra Day (GB) 56, etc.

Simpson, Alan (1929–). British TV and film comedy writer, with *Ray Galton* (qv).

Simpson, Russell (1878–1959). American character actor, in Hollywood from silent days. Billy the Kid 31. Way Down East 36. Ramona 37. Dodge City 39. The Grapes of Wrath 40. Outside the Law 41. They Were Expendable 45. My Darling Clementine 46. The Beautiful Blonde from Bashful Bend 49. Seven Brides for Seven Brothers 54. Friendly Persuasion 56. The Horse Soldiers 59, many others.

Sims, Joan (1930–). British stage, TV and film comedienne, often in cameo roles.
Colonel March Investigates 53. Meet Mr Lucifer 54. The Belles of St Trinian's 54. Dry Rot 56. The Naked Truth 58. Carry On Regardless 60. Twice Round the Daffodils 62. Strictly for the Birds 64. Follow that Camel 67. The Alf Garnett Saga 72. One of Our Dinosaurs is Missing 75, many others.

Sinatra, Frank (1915–). American leading actor and vocalist, former band singer. A teenage rave in the forties, he later became respected as an actor and a powerful producer.
□ Las Vegas Nights 41. Ship Ahoy 42. Reveille with Beverly 43. Higher and Higher (acting debut) 43. *Step Lively* 44. *Anchors Aweigh* 45. Till the Clouds Roll By 46. It Happened in Brooklyn 46. The Kissing Bandit 47. The Miracle of the Bells 48. *Take Me Out to the Ball Game* 48. *On the Town* 49. Double Dynamite 50. Meet Danny Wilson 51. *From Here to Eternity* (AA) 53. Suddenly 54. Young at Heart 54. The Tender Trap 55. Not as a Stranger 55. *The Man with the Golden Arm* 56. Johnny Concho 56. The Pride and the Passion 56. Around the World in Eighty Days 56. Guys and Dolls 56. *High Society* 56. *Pal Joey* 57. The Joker is Wild 57. Kings Go Forth 58. Some Came Running 58. A Hole in the Head 59. Can Can 59. Never So Few 59. Pepe 60. Ocean's Eleven 60. The Devil at Four O'Clock 61. Sergeants Three 62. *The Manchurian Candidate* 62. Four for Texas 63. The List of Adrian Messenger 63. Come Blow Your Horn 63. Robin and the Seven Hoods 64. None But the Brave (& d) 65. Von Ryan's Express 65. Marriage on the Rocks 65. Cast a Giant Shadow 66. Assault on a Queen 66. The Naked Runner (GB) 67. Tony Rome 67. *The Detective* 68. Lady in Cement 68. Dirty Dingus Magee 70.

Sinatra, Nancy (1940–). American leading lady and singer, daughter of Frank Sinatra.
For Those Who Think Young 64. The Last of the Secret Agents 66. Speedway 68, etc.

Sinclair, Andrew (1935–). British director.
The Breaking of Bumbo 69. Before Winter Comes (w only) 70. Under Milk Wood 72. Blue Blood 73, etc.

Sinclair, Hugh (1903–1962). British stage leading man, in occasional films.
Our Betters 33. Escape Me Never 35. A Girl Must Live 39. Alibi 42. They Were Sisters 45. Corridor of Mirrors 48. The Rocking Horse Winner 50. The Second Mrs Tanqueray 52, etc.

Sinclair, Robert (1905–1970). American director.
Woman Against Woman 38. Dramatic School 38. Mr and Mrs North 41. Mr District Attorney 46. That Wonderful Urge 48, etc.

Sinden, Donald (1923–). British leading man, on stage from mid-thirties.
The Cruel Sea (film debut) 53. Doctor in the House 54. Simba 55. Eyewitness 57. Doctor at Large 58. Operation Bullshine 59. Twice Round the Daffodils 62. Decline and Fall 68. Villain 71. Rentadick 72. The National Health 73. The Day of the Jackal 73. The Island at the Top of the World 74. That Lucky Touch 75, etc.

Sing As We Go (GB 1934). You can almost smell the tripe and onions in this cheerful Gracie Fields vehicle scripted by J. B. Priestley. As things have happened, it also preserves the most authentic flavour on film of Britain's industrial north in the thirties.

Singer, Alexander (1932–). American director.
□ *A Cold Wind in August* 62. Psyche 59. 64. Love Has Many Faces 65. Captain Apache 71.

Singer, Campbell (1909–). British character actor, often seen as heavy father, commissionaire, sergeant-major or policeman.
Première 37. Take My Life 47. The Ringer 52. Simba 55. The Square Peg 58. The Pot Carriers 63, many others.

The Singing Fool (US 1928). Remembered because Al Jolson sang 'Sonny Boy' in it, this early talkie is otherwise a dismal tear-jerker about a brash entertainer who comes to his senses when his little boy dies. Directed by Lloyd Bacon from a play by Leslie S. Barrows.

Singin' in the Rain (US 1952). One of the most exhilarating and fast-moving comedy-musicals ever to come out of Hollywood, this enjoyably professional piece is also a gentle satire on the movie modes and manners of the twenties. Adolph Green and Betty Comden wrote the script, Arthur Freed and Nacio Herb Brown the words and music, Harold Rosson was cinematographer, and Gene Kelly and Stanley Donen directed. Kelly also starred, along with Donald O'Connor, Debbie Reynolds, Millard Mitchell and Jean Hagen.

Singleton, Penny (1908–) (Dorothy McNulty). American leading lady, formerly in vaudeville, who from 1938 played the comic strip heroine 'Blondie' in two films a year for ten years. First film *After the Thin Man* 36; others negligible.

Siodmak, Curt (1902–). German writer-director, in films from 1929, Hollywood from 1937.
People on Sunday (co-w) 29. The Tunnel (co-w) 34. Her Jungle Love (co-w) 38. Frankenstein Meets the Wolf Man (w) 42. Son of Dracula (w) 43. The Beast with Five Fingers (w) 47. Bride of the Gorilla (wd) 51. *The Magnetic Monster* (d) 51. Love Slaves of the Amazon (wd) 57. Ski Fever (wd) 66, etc.

Siodmak, Robert (1900–1973). American director with early experience in Germany and France.
People on Sunday 29. The Weaker Sex 32. La Vie Parisienne 35. *Pièges* 39. West Point Widow 41. Son of Dracula 43. *Phantom Lady* 44. *The Suspect* 44. Christmas Holiday 44. *The Spiral Staircase* 45. The Strange Affair of Uncle Harry 45. *The Killers* 46. *The Dark Mirror* 46. Cry of the City 48. Criss Cross 48. The File on Thelma Jordon 49. The Great Sinner 49. Deported 50. The Whistle at Eaton Falls 51. The Crimson Pirate 52. Le Grand Jeu 53. Mein Vater der Schauspieler 56. Jatja 59. The Rough and the Smooth 59. Tunnel 28 (Escape from East Berlin) 62. Custer of the West 67, others.

Sir Arne's Treasure (Sweden 1919). A famous silent film directed by Mauritz Stiller from the novel by Selma Lagerlöf. It tells a 16th century tale of three Scottish mercenaries in the Swedish army who rob a priest but are prevented from escaping by an icy winter which freezes up their ship; also of the girl Estelle who falls in love with one of them but is killed. The story was remade by Gustav Molander in 1954.

Sirk, Douglas (1900–) (Detlef Sierck). German director, with stage experience; in America from early forties.
Der Letzte Akkord 36. La Habanera 37. Summer Storm 44. Hitler's Madman 44. A Scandal in Paris 46. Personal Column 47. *Sleep My Love* 48. The First Legion (& p) 51. No Room for the Groom 52. Magnificent Obsession 54. All That Heaven Allows 55. *Written on the Wind* 56. Battle Hymn 56. *The Tarnished Angels* 57. A Time to Love and a Time to Die 58. Imitation of Life 59, others.

Sitting Bull (1831–1890). Sioux Indian chief, almost always on the warpath. The villain of countless westerns; J. Carrol Naish played him in a 1954 biopic, also in *Annie Get Your Gun* 50.

Sitting Pretty. This title was used for a 1933 comedy directed by Harry Joe Brown, with Jack Oakie and Jack Haley as two songwriters hitch-hiking their way to Hollywood. It is however chiefly associated with the 1947 comedy starring Clifton Webb as Lynn Belvedere, baby-sitter extraordinary. Webb appeared in two sequels, *Mr Belvedere Goes to College* 49 and *Mr Belvedere Rings the Bell* 51.

16mm. A 'sub-standard' gauge to which feature films are reduced for private hire and in many countries for television. Many sponsored documentaries not intended for cinema showing are filmed in 16mm, as are television news and features. The smaller frame and greater magnification do not always lead to unsatisfactory results, but the dangers are obvious.

Sjoberg, Alf (1903–). Swedish director, former stage actor and director.
The Road to Heaven 42. *Frenzy* 44. Only a Mother 49. *Miss Julie* 51. Barabbas 53. Karin Mansdotter 54. Wild Birds 55. The Judge 60. The Island 66, others.

Sjoman, Vilgot (1924–). Swedish director, chiefly famous (and notorious) for '*491*' 66. *I Am Curious: Blue* 67, *I Am Curious: Yellow* 67, and *Blushing Charlie* 71.

Sjostrom, Victor: see *Seastrom, Victor*.

Skala, Lilia (–). German actress in America.
Lilies of the Field 64. Deadly Hero 76, etc.

Skall, William V. (1898–1976). American cinematographer.
Victoria the Great 37. The Mikado 39. Northwest Passage 40. Life with Father 47. *Joan of Arc* (AA) 48. Quo Vadis 51. The Silver Chalice 55, many others.

Skelton, Red (1910–) (Richard Skelton). American comedian of radio and TV; made numerous films in forties, very few since.
Having Wonderful Time (debut) 38. Lady Be Good 40. *Whistling in the Dark* 41. Ship Ahoy 42. *Whistling in Dixie* 42. Du Barry Was a Lady 43. Whistling in Brooklyn 43. Bathing Beauty 44. The Show-Off 46. Merton of the Movies 47. *Three Little Words* 50. The Clown 53. The Great Diamond Robbery 54. Public Pigeon Number One 57. Those Magnificent Men in Their Flying Machines 65, etc.

skiing has formed a pleasant background in many romantic comedies including *I Met Him in Paris* and *Two-Faced Woman*; in farces including *The Pink Panther* and *Snowball Express*; dramas including *Last of the Ski Bums, Ski Fever* and *Downhill Racer*; and in a plethora of spy stories, including *Caprice, The Double Man* and a couple of Bonds.

Skiles, Marlin (1906–). American composer.
The Impatient Years 44. Gilda 46. Dead Reckoning 47. Callaway Went Thataway 51 The Maze 53. Bowery to Bagdad 55. Fort Massacre 58. The Hypnotic Eye 60. The Strangler 64. The Resurrection of Zachary Wheeler 71, many others.

Skinner, Cornelia Otis (1901–). American stage actress, daughter of Otis Skinner the tragedian. Toyed with Hollywood occasionally. Her autobiographical book *Our Hearts Were Young and Gay* (co-written with Emily Kimbrough) was filmed with Gail Russell.
The Uninvited 44. The Girl in the Red Velvet Swing 55. The Swimmer 67.

Skinner, Frank (1898–). American composer.
Son of Frankenstein 39. Destry Rides Again 39. Hellzapoppin 41. Back Street 41. Saboteur 42. Gung Ho 43. The Suspect 44. The Egg and I 47. Abbott and Costello Meet Frankenstein 48. Francis 49. Harvey 50. The World in His Arms 52. Thunder Bay 53. Battle Hymn 56. Imitation of Life 58. Back Street 61. Shenandoah 65. Madame X 66, many others.

Skinner, Otis (1858–1942). American stage actor who appeared in films. Only in two versions of *Kismet* 20 & 30. Charles Ruggles played him in *Our Hearts Were Young and Gay* 44.

Skipworth, Alison (1875–1952) (Alison Groom). Chubby British character actress, long in Hollywood; a favourite foil for W. C. Fields.
Raffles 30. Outward Bound 30. Devotion 31. Night After Night 32. *If I Had a Million* 32. Song of Songs 33. *Tillie and Gus* 33. Six of a Kind 34. The Captain Hates the Sea 34. Becky Sharp 35. Shanghai 35. Satan Met a Lady 36. Stolen Holiday 37. Wide Open Faces 38, many others.

Skirball, Jack H. (1896–). American independent producer, former salesman.
Miracle on Main Street 38. Lady from Cheyenne 41. Saboteur 42. Shadow of a Doubt 43. It's in the Bag (The Fifth Chair) 45. Guest Wife 46. Payment on Demand 51, etc.

Skolimowski, Jerzy (1938–). Polish director.
The Barrier 66. The Departure 67. Hands Up 67. Dialogue 69. The Adventures of Gerard 70. Deep End 71. King, Queen, Knave 72, etc.

Skouras, Spyros (1893–1971). Greek-American executive, former hotelier. President of Twentieth-Century Fox 1943–62; instigator of CinemaScope.

slapstick. One of the earliest (1895) Lumière shorts, *L'Arroseur Arrosé*, was a knockabout farce, and in 1966 *A Funny Thing Happened on the Way to the Forum* was keeping the tradition going. Out of simple slapstick developed the great silent clowns, each with his own brand of pathos: Harold Lloyd, Charlie Chaplin, Buster Keaton, Fatty Arbuckle, Harry Langdon, Mabel Normand, Larry Semon, Laurel and Hardy. Pure destructive slapstick without humanity was superbly dispensed by Mack Sennett, especially in his Keystone Kops shorts. France had produced Max Linder; Britain lagged behind, but in the twenties Betty Balfour, Monty Banks and Lupino Lane kept the flag flying. Many of these names survived in some degree when sound came, but cross-talk was an added factor in the success of Wheeler and Woolsey, Charlie Chase, Edgar Kennedy, Leon Errol, Hugh Herbert, Joe E. Brown, W. C. Fields, Eddie Cantor, Abbott and Costello and above all the Marx Brothers. Similarly in Britain there was an influx of stage comics with firm music-hall traditions: George Formby, Will Hay, Max Miller, Gracie Fields, Leslie Fuller, the Crazy Gang, Arthur Askey, Gordon Harker, Sandy Powell, Frank Randle and Old Mother Riley. The forties in Hollywood brought the more sophisticated slapstick of Danny Kaye, writer-director Preston Sturges, and the Bob Hope gag factory, with extreme simplicity keeping its end up via Olsen and Johnson and Jerry Lewis. In the fifties, TV finally brought a female clown, Lucille Ball, to the top; though competition was thin. France since the war has had Fernandel, Louis de Funes, Jacques Tati and Pierre Etaix; Britain Norman Wisdom and Morecambe and Wise; Italy Totò and Walter Chiari. In Hollywood romantic stars now take turns at donning the clown's hat, without making a career of it; and the fashion has recently been for epic comedies of violence and destruction, such as *It's a Mad Mad Mad Mad World*, *The Great Race*, and *Those Magnificent Men in Their Flying Machines*.

Slate, Jeremy (1925–). American general purpose actor.
Wives and Lovers 63. I'll Take Sweden 65. The Sons of Katie Elder 66. The Devil's Brigade 68, etc.

Slater, John (1916–1975). British cockney character actor and comedian of stage and TV, occasionally in films.
Love on the Dole (debut) 40. Went the Day Well? 42. A Canterbury Tale 44. Passport to Pimlico 48. Johnny You're Wanted 54. Violent Playground 58. Three on a Spree 61. A Place to Go 63, many others.

Slaughter, Tod (1885–1956) (N. Carter Slaughter). Barnstorming British actor who toured the provinces with chop-licking revivals of outrageous old melodramas, all of which he filmed after a fashion.
Maria Marten 35. Sweeney Todd 36. Sexton Blake and the Hooded Terror 38. *The Face at the Window* 39. The Curse of the Wraydons 43. The Greed of William Hart 48, etc.

sleeper: a trade term for a film which suddenly does much better at the box office than was expected.

Slezak, Walter (1902–). Austrian character actor, of theatrical family; in America since 1930.
Autobiography 1962: *What Time's the Next Swan?*
Once Upon a Honeymoon (English-speaking debut) 42. *Lifeboat* 44. Step Lively 44. The Spanish Main 45. Cornered 45. Sinbad the Sailor 47. The Pirate 48. *The Inspector General* 49. Call Me Madam 53. White Witch Doctor 54. The Steel Cage 54. Come September 61. Emil

and the Detectives 64. Wonderful Life (GB) 64. Twenty-Four Hours to Kill 65. A Very Special Favor 65. Caper of the Golden Bulls 67. Dr Coppelius 68. Black Beauty 71, etc.

A Slight Case of Murder (US1938). This black comedy by Damon Runyon, directed by Lloyd Bacon, was Warners' way of eating their cake and having it. In face of mounting official criticism of gangster films, they made one with the highest death-rate of all but turned it into a comedy and left star Edward G. Robinson with clean hands. (A year later, in *Brother Orchid*, they made him see the light and become a monk.) In 1952 the movie was remade as *Stop You're Killing Me*, with Broderick Crawford.

Sloane, Everett (1909–1965). Incisive American character actor, brought to Hollywood by Orson Welles.
□ Citizen Kane 41. *Journey into Fear* 42. *The Lady from Shanghai* 48. Prince of Foxes 49. *The Men* 50. Bird of Paradise 51. The Enforcer 51. Sirocco 51. The Prince Who Was a Thief 51. The Blue Veil 51. The Desert Fox 51. The Sellout 51. Way of a Gaucho 52. *The Big Knife* 55. *Patterns* 56. Somebody Up There Likes Me 56. Lust for Life 56. Marjorie Morningstar 58. The Gun Runners 58. Home from the Hill 60. By Love Possessed 61. Brushfire 62. The Man from the Diners Club 63. The Patsy 64. Ready for the People 64. The Disorderly Orderly 64.

Sloane, Olive (1896–1963). British character actress of stage and screen whose best role was in *Seven Days to Noon* 50. Countless other small roles since film debut in *Soldiers of the King* 33.

Slocombe, Douglas (1913–). British cinematographer, former journalist.
Dead of Night 45. The Captive Heart 46. Hue and Cry 46. The Loves of Joanna Godden 47. *It Always Rains on Sunday* 47. *Saraband for Dead Lovers* 48. Kind Hearts and Coronets 49. Cage of Gold 50. The Lavender Hill Mob 51. Mandy 52. The Man in the White Suit 52. *The Titfield Thunderbolt* 53. Man in the Sky 56. The Smallest Show on Earth 57. Tread Softly Stranger 58. Circus of Horrors 59. The Young Ones 61. The L-Shaped Room 62. *Freud* 63. The Servant 63. Guns at Batasi 64. A High Wind in Jamaica 65. The Blue Max 66. Promise Her Anything 66. The Vampire Killers 67. Fathom 67. Robbery 67. Boom 68. The Lion in Winter 68. The Italian Job 69. *The Music Lovers* 70. Murphy's War 70. The Buttercup Chain 70. Travels with My Aunt 73. The Great Gatsby 74. Love Among the Ruins (TV) 75. Rollerball 75. Hedda 76, etc.

slow motion. An effect obtained by running the camera faster than usual. When the film passes through the projector at normal speed, each movement appears slower, as it occupies more frames of film. For scientific purposes (e.g. recording the growth of plants) cameras are so arranged that a single frame of film is exposed at regular intervals, thus giving an impression of accelerated growth.

Small, Edward (1891–). Veteran American independent producer, former actor and agent, in Hollywood from 1924.
I Cover the Waterfront 35. The Man in the Iron Mask 39. The Corsican Brothers 41. Brewster's Millions 45. Down Three Dark Streets 55. Witness for the Prosecution 57. Jack the Giant Killer 62. I'll Take Sweden 65. Forty Guns to Apache Pass 66, many others; also TV series.

small towns were for many years the staple of the American cinema. Most audiences were small-town folk, and wanted to see slightly idealized versions of themselves. Thus the popularity of the happy families, the Hardys and the Joneses; thus *Our Town*, *The Human Comedy*, *Ah Wilderness*, *The Music Man* and *The Dark at the Top of the Stairs*. The darker side of small-town life was shown in *The Chase*, *Kings Row*, *Peyton Place* and *Invasion of the Body Snatchers*. British small towns did not have the same aura; most of the comparable stories were set against industrial backgrounds.

Smart, Ralph (1908–). British producer-director, latterly of TV series *The Invisible Man*, *Danger Man*, etc. Former editor and writer.
DIRECTOR: Bush Christmas 46. A Boy, a Girl and a Bike 48. Bitter Springs 50. Never Take No for an Answer (co-d) 51. Curtain Up 52. Always a Bride 54, etc.

Smedley-Aston, E. M. (1912–). British producer.
The Extra Day 56. Two-Way Stretch 60. Offbeat 61. The Wrong Arm of the Law 63. Ooh You Are Awful 72, etc.

Smight, Jack (1926–). American director, from TV.
□ I'd Rather Be Rich 64. The Third Day 65. *Harper* 66. Kaleidoscope 66. The Secret War of Harry Frigg 67. No Way to Treat a Lady 68. The Illustrated Man 69. The Travelling Executioner 70. Frankenstein: The True Story (TV) 73. Airport 75 74. Midway 76. Damnation Alley 77.

Smilin' Through. The popular sentimental

stage play by Jane Cowl and Jane Murfin, about a tragedy affecting the romances of two generations, was filmed in 1922 by Sidney Franklin, with Norma Talmadge, Wyndham Standing and Harrison Ford; in 1932, again Sidney Franklin, with Norma Shearer, Leslie Howard and Fredric March. In 1941 Frank Borzage remade it with Jeanette MacDonald, Brian Aherne and Gene Raymond.

Smith, Alexis (1921–). American leading lady of the forties who won an acting contest from Hollywood high school. Married to Craig Stevens.
Lady with Red Hair 41. Dive Bomber 41. The Smiling Ghost 41. Gentleman Jim 42. The Constant Nymph 42. The Doughgirls 44. Conflict 45. Rhapsody in Blue 45. San Antonio 45. Night and Day 46. Of Human Bondage 46. Stallion Road 47. The Woman in White 47. The Decision of Christopher Blake 48. Any Number Can Play 50. Undercover Girl 52. Split Second 53. The Sleeping Tiger (GB) 55. The Eternal Sea 56. The Young Philadelphians (The City Jungle) 59. Once Is Not Enough 75. Casey's Shadow 77, etc.

Smith, Bernard (c. 1905–). American producer, ex publisher and story editor.
Elmer Gantry (AA) 60. How the West Was Won 62. Seven Women 65. Alfred the Great 69.

Smith, Sir C. Aubrey (1863–1948). Distinguished British character actor who after a long stage career settled in Hollywood to play crusty, benevolent or authoritarian old gentlemen.
SELECTED SILENT FILMS: The Witching Hour 16. The Bohemian Girl 23. The Rejected Woman 24.
□ SOUND FILMS: Trader Horn 31. Never the Twain Shall Meet 31. Bachelor Father 31. Daybreak 31. Just a Gigolo 31. Son of India 31. The Man in Possession 31. Phantom of Paris 31. Guilty Hands 31. Surrender 31. Polly of the Circus 31. Tarzan the Ape Man 32. But the Flesh is Weak 32. *Love Me Tonight* 32. Trouble in Paradise 32. No More Orchids 32. They Just Had to Get Married 32. Luxury Liner 33. Secrets 33. The Barbarian 33. Adorable 33. The Monkey's Paw 33. *Morning Glory* 33. Bombshell 33. Queen Christina 33. The House of Rothschild 34. Gambling Lady 34. Curtain at Eight 34. The Tunnel (GB) 34. Bulldog Drummond Strikes Back 34. Cleopatra 34. Madame Du Barry 34. One More River 34. Caravan 34. The Firebird 34. The Right to Live 35. *Lives of a Bengal Lancer* 35. The Florentine Dagger 35. The Gilded Lily 35. Clive of India 35.

China Seas 35. Jalna 35. The Crusades 35. Little Lord Fauntleroy 36. Romeo and Juliet 36. The Garden of Allah 36. Lloyds of London 36. Wee Willie Winkie 36. *The Prisoner of Zenda* 37. Thoroughbreds Don't Cry 37. The Hurricane 37. Four Men and a Prayer 38. Kidnapped 38. Sixty Glorious Years (GB) 38. East Side of Heaven 39. Five Came Back 39. *The Four Feathers* (GB) 39. The Sun Never Sets 39. Eternally Yours 39. Another Thin Man 39. The Underpup 39. Balalaika 39. *Rebecca* 40. City of Chance 40. A Bill of Divorcement 40. Waterloo Bridge 40. Beyond Tomorrow 40. A Little Bit of Heaven 40. Free and Easy 41. Maisie was a Lady 41. Dr Jekyll and Mr Hyde 41. Forever and a Day 43. Two Tickets to London 43. Flesh and Fantasy 43. Madame Curie 43. The White Cliffs of Dover 44. The Adventures of Mark Twain 44. Secrets of Scotland Yard 44. Sensations of 1945 44. They Shall Have Faith 44. *And Then There Were None* 45. Scotland Yard Investigator 45. Cluny Brown 46. Rendezvous with Annie 46. High Conquest 47. Unconquered 47. *An Ideal Husband* (GB) 47. Little Women 49.

Smith, Charles (c. 1920–). American character actor who in the forties played Dizzy in the *Henry Aldrich* series and other amiably doltish roles.
The Shop Around the Corner 40. Tom Brown's Schooldays 40. Three Little Girls in Blue 45. Two Weeks with Love 50. City of Bad Men 53, many others.

Smith, Constance (1929–). British leading lady.
Brighton Rock 47. Don't Say Die 50. The Thirteenth Letter (US) 51. Red Skies of Montana (US) 52. Treasure of the Golden Condor (US) 53. Tiger by the Tail 55, etc.

Smith, Cyril (1892–1963). British character actor of stage and screen, often a henpecked husband but equally likely to be a grocer, dustman or policeman. On stage from 1900, films from 1908, and was in over 500 of the latter.
Friday the Thirteenth 33. School for Secrets 46. It's Hard To Be Good 48. Mother Riley Meets the Vampire 52. John and Julie 54. *Sailor Beware* (his stage role) 56, etc.

Smith, G. A. (1864–1959). British pioneer cinematographer who invented a cine-camera in 1896 and made some trick films.
The Corsican Brothers 97. The Fairy Godmother 98. Faust 98, etc.

Smith, John (1931–) (Robert Van Orden). Boyish American leading man.
The High and the Mighty 54. Ghost Town 56. The Bold and the Brave 57. Circus World 64. Waco 66, etc.
TV series: Cimarron City 58. Laramie 59–62.

Smith, Kent (1907–). Smooth, quiet American leading man of the forties; latterly a useful character actor.
Cat People 42. Hitler's Children 43. This Land is Mine 43. *The Spiral Staircase* 46. *Nora Prentiss* 47. The Decision of Christopher Blake 48. The Fountainhead 49. The Damned Don't Cry 50. Paul 52. Comanche 56. Party Girl 58. Strangers When We Meet 60. Moon Pilot 62. A Distant Trumpet 64. The Touble with Angels 66. Assignment to Kill 68. Death of a Gunfighter 69. Pete'n Tillie 72. Cops and Robbers 73, many others.
TV series: *Peyton Place* 64–67.

Smith, Maggie (1934–). Leading British actress with a taste for eccentric comedy.
□ Nowhere to Go 58. Go to Blazes 62. *The VIPs* 63. The Pumpkin Eater 64. Young Cassidy 65. Othello 66. *The Honey Pot* 67. Hot Millions 68. Oh What a Lovely War 69. *The Prime of Miss Jean Brodie* (AA) 69. Love Pain and the Whole Damn Thing 73. Travels with My Aunt 73. Murder by Death 76.

Smith, Pete (1892–). American producer of punchy one-reel shorts on any and every subject from 1935 to the fifties, all narrated by 'a Smith named Pete'. Former publicist. Special Academy Award 1953 'for his witty and pungent observations on the American scene'.

Smith, Roger (1932–). American leading man.
The Young Rebels 56. Operation Mad Ball 57. Man with a Thousand Faces (as Lon Chaney Jnr) 57. Never Steal Anything Small 59. Auntie Mame 59. Rogues' Gallery 68. The First Time (wp) 70.
TV series: 77 Sunset Strip 58–64. Mr Roberts 65.

Smith, Thorne (1892–1934). American humorous novelist. Works filmed include *Topper, Turnabout, I Married a Witch*.

smoking has served as the springboard of a few plots. *No Smoking* and *Cold Turkey* concerned cures for it, and one also figured in *Taking Off*. In *On a Clear Day You Can See Forever*, Barbra Streisand launched the plot by taking psychiatric advice about it. The most fashionable smoking habit was Paul Henreid's in *Now Voyager*, lighting two cigarettes and passing one to Bette Davis; this was mimicked with eight cigarettes by Bob Hope in *Let's Face It*. The longest cigarette holder was sported by Harpo Marx in *A Night in Casablanca*.

Smoktunovsky, Innokenti (1925–). Leading Russian stage actor, seen in a few films including *Nine Days of One Year* 60. *Hamlet* 64. *Tchaikovsky* 69. *Crime and Punishment* 75.

smugglers of the old-fashioned type are almost entirely a British concern, figuring in *Fury at Smugglers' Bay, Jamaica Inn, The Ghost Train, Oh Mr Porter, Ask a Policeman, I See a Dark Stranger, Moonfleet*, and others. Smuggling in American films has been a much more modern and less picturesque affair.

The Snake Pit (US 1948). Directed by Anatole Litvak from the novel by Mary Jane Ward, this deliberately unsensational study of mental illness did not entirely escape the problem of dramatizing a subject too serious for fiction. But Olivia de Havilland gave a fine performance and the film did much to assist Hollywood's new 'adult' post-war image. Photographed by Leo Tover, with music by Alfred Newman.

sneak preview. An unheralded tryout of a film at a public performance, usually in place of a second feature. Intended to gauge audience reaction, it is often followed by considerable re-editing before the official première.

Snodgress, Carrie (1946–). American leading lady of the seventies.
The Forty-Eight Hour Mile (TV) 68. Silent Night Holy Night (TV) 69. Rabbit Run 71. *Diary of a Mad Housewife* 72, etc.

snow, when needed for a movie scene, has been known to consist of a variety of ingredients including bleached cornflakes, soapflakes, chopped feathers, shredded asbestos, balsa chips, sawdust, and a wide range of plastic products.

Snow White and the Seven Dwarfs (US 1937). The first full-length Disney cartoon has remained popular through the years, perhaps because it so admirably suits its creator's Grimm-like imagination. He has certainly never again presented so precisely differentiated a group of comedians as Bashful, Sleepy, Grumpy, Sneezy, Happy, Dopey and Doc.

soap opera. A term used disparagingly of TV domestic drama serials. Originated because such offerings were invariably sponsored by the big soap companies who needed to attract the housewife.

social comedy. Silent romantic comedies were completely unrealistic, though they sometimes found it prudent to pretend satirical intent to cloak their lowbrow commercialism. Social comedy really came in as a substitute for sex comedy when the Hays Office axe fell in 1934. Frank Capra took by far the best advantage of it, with his series of films showing an America filled to bursting point with good guys who only wanted a simple and comfortable home life in some small town where corruption never raised its ugly head. The best of these films were *Mr Deeds Goes to Town, You Can't Take It with You* and *Mr Smith Goes to Washington*; by the time *Meet John Doe* came along in 1941 war had soured the mood again. There was no British equivalent to Capra, unless one counts a few attempts by Priestley (*The Good Companions, Let the People Sing*) and such amusing depictions of the middle class as *Quiet Wedding* and *Dear Octopus*; but in the late forties came the Ealing comedies, delightful and apparently realistic, but presenting a picture of England just as false as Capra's America. In both countries the fifties saw the development of an affluent society in which cynicism was fashionable and few reforms seemed worth urging except in bitterly serious fashion.

social conscience has long been a feature of Hollywood film production. Other countries have presented the odd feature pointing to flaws in their national make-up, but American has seemed particularly keen to wash its own dirty linen on screen, perhaps because this is rather easier than actually cleaning up the abuses.

The evolution of this attitude can be traced back as far as 1912 and Griffith's *The Musketeers of Pig Alley*, showing slum conditions, a theme developed in *Intolerance* 16; and, of course, Chaplin was a master at devising humour and pathos out of the unpleasant realities of poverty, a fact which endeared him to poor people all over the world. But it was not till the late twenties that the flood of socially conscious films began in earnest. Vidor's *The Crowd* investigated the drabness of everyday life for a city clerk. John Baxter's British *Dosshouse* was a lone entry on the lines of *The Lower Depths. City Streets* and *One-Third of a Nation* treated slum conditions; Vidor's *Our Daily Bread* concerned a young couple driven out of the city by poverty only to find farming just as precarious. *Little Caesar* and the gangster dramas which followed always assumed a crusading moral tone deploring the lives of vice and crime which they depicted; there was a somewhat more honest ring to *I Was a Fugitive from a Chain Gang*, which showed how circumstance can drive an honest man into anti-social behaviour. Capra sugared his pill with comedy: *American Madness* (the madness was money) and the popular comedies which followed all pitted common-man philosophy against urban sophistication and corruption.

In the mid-thirties there were certainly many abuses worth fighting. *Black Legion* began Hollywood's campaign against the Ku Klux Klan, later followed up in *The Flaming Cross, Storm Warning* and *The Cardinal*. Lynch law, first tackled in *Fury*, was subsequently the subject of *They Won't Forget, The Ox Bow Incident* and *The Sound of Fury*. Juvenile delinquency was probed in *Dead End, Angels with Dirty Faces* and *They Made Me a Criminal*, but the 'Dead End Kids' were later played for comedy. Prison reform was advocated in *Each Dawn I Die, Castle on the Hudson*, and many other melodramas of questionable integrity. *The Good Earth* invited concern for the poor of other nations; *Mr Smith Goes to Washington* and *The Glass Key* were among many dramas showing that politicians are not incorruptible; *Love on the Dole* depicted the poverty of industrial Britain; *The Grapes of Wrath* and *Tobacco Road* pondered the plight of farming people deprived of a living by geographical chance and thoughtless government. In *Sullivan's Travels*, Preston Sturges came to the curious conclusion that the best thing you can do for the poor is make them laugh.

During World War II the nations were too busy removing the abuse of Nazidom to look inward, and indeed much poverty was alleviated by conscription and a fresh national awareness which, together with the increased need for industrial manpower, greatly improved the lot of the lower classes. But with victory came a whole crop of films, led by *The Best Years of Our Lives* and *Till the End of Time*, about the rehabilitation of war veterans. Concern about mental illness was shown in *The Snake Pit*, about paraplegia in *The Men* and about labour relations in *The Whistle at Eaton Falls*. Alcoholism was treated in *The Lost Weekend* and *Smash-Up*, and the racial issues were thoroughly aired in *Lost Boundaries, Crossfire, Home of the Brave, No Way Out, Gentleman's Agreement* and *Pinky*. A plea was for nations to help and understand each other made in the French *Race for Life*.

With the development in the fifties of the affluent society, the number of reforms worth urging was drastically reduced. Teenage hoodlums figured largely in a score of films of which the best were *The Wild One* and *Rebel without a Cause*. Mentally handicapped children were sympathetically portrayed in *A Child is Waiting*. In recent years, however, it is one world issue which has dominated the film-makers' social consciousness, that of the panic button; and this has manifested itself in films as diverse as *On the Beach, Dr Strangelove, Fail Safe* and *The Bedford Incident*.

Social consciousness has been apparent in almost every drama of the seventies, but used as a top dressing, sometimes to permit the exploitation of violence. In films like *A Clockwork Orange* and *O Lucky Man* it is difficult enough to discover what point is being made.

Sofaer, Abraham (1896–). Burmese actor, on British stage since 1921.
Dreyfus (debut) 31. Rembrandt 36. *A Matter of Life and Death* 46. Judgment Deferred 51. *Elephant Walk* (US) 54. The Naked Jungle (US) 54. Bhowani Junction 56. King of Kings 61. Captain Sinbad (US) 63. Head 68. Che! 69, etc.

soft focus. A diffused effect used in photographing ageing leading ladies who can't stand good definition; also frequently used for exotic shots in musical numbers, etc.

Sokoloff, Vladimir (1889–1962). Russian character actor, in Hollywood from 1936.
The Loves of Jeanne Ney 27. West Front 1918 30. Die Dreigroschenoper 31. L'Atlantide 32. Mayerling 35. The Life of Emile Zola 37. Spawn of the North 38. Juarez 39. Road to Morocco 42. For Whom the Bell Tolls 43. Cloak and Dagger 46. Back to Bataan 46. Istanbul 56. Confessions of a Counterspy 60. Sardonicus 62, many others.

Soldati, Mario (1906–). Italian director.
Scandal in the Roman Bath 51. The Wayward Wife 53. The Stranger's Hand 54. Woman of the River 55, many others.

soldiers depicted at length in films include Alexander the Great (by Richard Burton), Hannibal (by Victor Mature), Ghenghis Khan (by John Wayne and Omar Sharif), Alexander Nevsky (by Cherkassov), Clive of India (by Ronald Colman), Napoleon (by Charles Boyer, Marlon Brando, Herbert Lom, and others), Bonnie Prince Charlie (by David Niven), Wellington (by George Arliss), General Gordon (by Charlton Heston), Custer (by Errol Flynn and Robert Shaw), La Fayette (by Michel le Royer), Davy Crockett (by Fess Parker and others), Sergeant York (by Gary Cooper), Audie Murphy (by Audie Murphy), Rommel (by Erich Von Stroheim and James Mason), Che Guevara (by Omar Sharif), General Patton (by George C. Scott), and General Macarthur (by Gregory Peck).

Solon, Ewen (c. 1923–). New Zealand character actor in Britain, especially on TV in series *Maigret* (as Lucas).
The Sundowners 59. Jack the Ripper 60. The Hound of the Baskervilles 60. The Terror of the Tongs 61, etc.

Somlo, Josef (1885–1973), Hungarian producer with long experience at UFA; in Britain from 1933.
Dark Journey 37. The Mikado 39. Old Bill and Son 40. Uncle Silas 47. The Man Who Loved Redheads 55. Behind the Mask 59, etc.

Sommer, Elke (1940–) (Elke Schletz). German leading lady now in international films.
Don't Bother to Knock (GB) 60. The Victors (GB) 63. *The Prize* (US) 63. A Shot in the Dark (US) 64. The Art of Love (US) 65. Four Kinds of Love (It.) 65. The Money Trap (US) 65. The Oscar (US) 66. Boy, Did I Get a Wrong Number (US) 66. Deadlier than the Male (GB) 66. The Venetian Affair (US) 66. The Corrupt Ones 67. The Wicked Dreams of Paula Schultz (US) 68. Zeppelin (US) 71. Percy (GB) 71. Carry on Behind (GB) 76, etc.

Sondergaard, Gale (1899–) (Edith Sondergaard). Tall, dark American character actress with a sinister smile; career harmed by the anti-communist witch hunt of the early fifties.
□ *Anthony Adverse* (AA) 36. Maid of Salem 37. Seventh Heaven 37. The Life of Emile Zola 37. Lord Jeff 38. Dramatic School 38. Never Say Die 38. Juarez 38. *The Cat and the Canary* 39. The Llano Kid 40. *The Bluebird* 40. The Mark of Zorro 40. The Letter 40. The Black Cat 41. Paris Calling 41. My Favorite Blonde 42. Enemy Agent Meets Ellery Queen 42. A Night to Remember 43. Appointment in Berlin 43. Isle of Forgotten Sins 43. The Strange Death of Adolf Hitler 43. *Spider Woman* 44. Follow the Boys 44. Christmas Holiday 44. The Invisible Man's Revenge 44. Gypsy Wildcat 44. The Climax 44. Enter Arsène Lupin 44. Spider Woman Strikes Back 46. A Night in Paradise 46. Anna and the King of Siam 46. The Time of Their Lives 46. *Road to Rio* 47. Pirates of Monterey 47. East Side West Side 49. Slaves 69. The Cat Creature (TV) 74. The Return of a Man Called Horse 76.

The Song of Bernadette (US 1943). An enormous box office success in the middle of World War II, this calculated piece of Hollywood religion turned Franz Werfel's book into sentimental hokum. The miracles of Lourdes have since been more movingly and convincingly treated; Henry King's direction was lethargic; and attempts at acting were smothered by syrupy music and phoney sets. Jennifer Jones' debut as Bernadette was highly successful, but Linda Darnell as the Virgin Mary took some swallowing. The film began a cycle of religious epics, including *Going My Way, The Bells of St Mary's, The Miracle of the Bells*, etc. (See *religion.)*

Song of Ceylon (GB 1934). A documentary written, photographed and directed by Basil Wright for the Ceylon Tea Marketing Board, who must have been very surprised when they saw what they had got: a leisurely 40-minute poetic impression of the island without any direct propaganda. As an 'art house' picture it remains fascinating. Produced by John Grierson, with music by Walter Leigh.

Sonny (1935–) (Salvatore Bono). American singer, with *Cher* (qv).

Sons and Lovers (GB 1960). A decent and enjoyable film adaptation of D. H. Lawrence's autobiographical novel about growing up in the Nottinghamshire coalfields fifty years ago. Surprisingly produced by Jerry Wald, with Dean Stockwell making a reasonable attempt at the central part and more assured performances coming from Trevor Howard and Wendy Hiller, the film was perhaps most of all enjoyable for the background detail and for Freddie Francis' black-and-white photography. Jack Cardiff directed with care.

Sons of the Desert (Fraternally Yours) (US 1933). The quintessential Laurel and Hardy comedy, in which the boys, hen-pecked as always, devise frantic schemes to get to a weekend convention—and then wish they hadn't. Sociologically, the movie pinpoints its period with total precision.

Sordi, Alberto (1919–). Italian leading man and comic actor.
I Vitelloni 53. The Sign of Venus 55. A Farewell to Arms 57. The Best of Enemies 60. Those Magnificent Men in Their Flying Machines 65. To Bed or Not To Bed 65, etc.

Sorel, Jean (1934–) (Jean de Rochbrune). French leading man.
The Four Days of Naples 62. A View from the

Bridge 62. Vaghe Stella dell'Orsa 65. Le Bambole 66. Belle de Jour 67, etc.

Sorel, Louise (1944–). French leading lady of occasional films.
The Party's Over 65. B.S. I Love You 70. Plaza Suite 71.

Sorrell and Son. H. B. Warner played Sorrell in both British versions of Warwick Deeping's family novel; in 1927 the son was Nils Asther and the director Herbert Brenon, while in 1933 Hugh Williams replaced Asther and Jack Raymond directed.

Sorvino, Paul (1939–). Chubby American comedy actor.
I Will, I Will . . . For Now 76.
TV series: Bert D'Angelo 75.

Sothern, Ann (1909–) (Harriette Lake). Pert American comedienne and leading lady with stage experience.
Let's Fall in Love (debut) 34. Kid Millions 35. Trade Winds 38. Hotel for Women 39. *Maisie* 39. Brother Orchid 40. Congo Maisie 40. Gold Rush Maisie 41 (and seven others in series before 1947). Lady Be Good 41. Panama Hattie 42. Cry Havoc 43. The Judge Steps Out 47. *A Letter to Three Wives* 49. Nancy Goes to Rio 50. Lady in a Cage 63. The Best Man 64. Sylvia 65. Chubasco 67. The Great Man's Whiskers (TV) 71. Golden Needles 74. Crazy Mama 75. Captains and the Kings (TV) 76, etc.
TV series: *Private Secretary* 52–54. The Ann Sothern Show 58–60.

sound. The first really successful experiments with synchronized sound had the track on gramophone discs; cylinders were also employed. These systems obviously led to maddening breakdowns, and editing was next to impossible. Fox, using the De Forrest Phonofilm system combined with a German process called Tri-Ergon, contrived in 1926 to record sound directly on to film next to the picture, forming the first sound track. It was this system which by 1930 had superseded the others and is still with us.

The Sound of Music (AA) (US 1965). The huge commercial success of this sentimental Rodgers and Hammerstein musical with its simple story, happy ending and sumptuous Austrian locations seemed to mark a genuine public desire for less sophisticated fare than the sixties have been giving; but producers have been either unwilling or unable to satisfy it. It won Academy Awards for Robert Wise's direction,

William Reynolds' editing, Jane Corcoran's sound recording, Irwin Kostal's scoring, and Ted McCord's photography. Julie Andrews played the spunkie heroine.

Sous les Toits de Paris (France 1930). This early sound film, a light romantic drama of the Paris garrets, has a well-remembered title and established the fame of writer-director René Clair, but it now seems rather heavier than his usual style, with his accustomed humour breaking through only occasionally. Albert Préjean and Pola Illery had the leading roles.

The Southerner (US 1945). Jean Renoir's most successful American film, comparable to *The Grapes of Wrath* in its feeling for a poor Texas family scratching a living from cotton-growing. Zachary Scott and Betty Field are man and wife, with Beulah Bondi magnificent as the cantankerous granny and J. Carrol Naish as a suspicious neighbour. Photographed by Lucien Andriot, with music by Werner Janssen; from a novel, *Hold Autumn in Your Hand*, by George Sessions Perry.

Spaak, Catherine (1945–). Belgian leading lady, daughter of Charles Spaak.
Le Trou 60. The Empty Canvas 64. Weekend at Dunkirk 65. Hotel 67. Libertine 68. Cat O' Nine Tails 71, etc.

Spaak, Charles (1903–1975). Belgian screenwriter associated with many French films.
La Kermesse Héroïque 35. Les Bas-Fonds 36. *La Grande Illusion* 37. *La Fin du Jour* 39. Panique 46. Justice est Faite (co-w) 50. Thérèse Raquin 53. Crime and Punishment 56. Charmants Garçons 57. The Vanishing Corporal 61. Cartouche 62, etc.

space exploration on screen began in 1899 with Méliès; in the twenties Fritz Lang made *The Woman in the Moon* and in the thirties there was *Buck Rogers in the Twenty-Fifth Century*, but not until 1950 did the subject seem acceptable as anything but fantasy. In that year an adventure of the comic strip type, *Rocketship XM*, competed for box office attention with George Pal's semi-documentary *Destination Moon*, and suddenly the floodgates were opened. During the years that followed we were offered such titles as *Riders to the Stars, Fire Maidens from Outer Space, Satellite in the Sky, From the Earth to the Moon, Conquest of Space, Forbidden Planet, It!, The Terror from Beyond Space, Robinson Crusoe on Mars, The First Men in the Moon* and *2001: A Space Odyssey*. Nor was the traffic all one way: Earth had many strange visitors from other planets, notably in *The Thing from Another World, The Day the Earth Stood Still, Devil Girl from Mars, Stranger from Venus, It Came from Outer Space, Invasion of the Body Snatchers* (the best and subtlest of them all), *The War of the Worlds, The Quatermass Experiment, Quatermass II, Visit to a Small Planet, This Island Earth,* and *The Man Who Fell to Earth.* On television, the most imaginative exploits have been in *Star Trek* and *Space 1999.*

Spacek, Sissy (–). American leading lady of the seventies.
Badlands 73. Carrie 76.

spaghetti westerns: a dismissive name for the blood-spattered Italian imitations of American westerns which became popular in the sixties, using such actors as Lee Van Cleef and Clint Eastwood.

Spain produced few distinguished films before the Civil War, Buñuel having settled in France, and afterwards the product was dictated by politics apart from a few pleasing comedies and melodrama by such directors as Berlanga and Bardem. Buñuel made a few visits in the sixties.

The Spanish Civil War featured in a few Hemingway picturizations, notably *For Whom the Bell Tolls* and *The Snows of Kilimanjaro;* in *The Fallen Sparrow, Blockade, The Angel Wore Red, Love Under Fire, Last Train from Madrid, Arise My Love, Confidential Agent* and (remotely) *The Prime of Miss Jean Brodie.*

Spark, Muriel (1918–). British novelist feted by the intelligentsia. Two films of her work, *The Prime of Miss Jean Brodie* and *The Driver's Seat,* have both been unsatisfactory.

Sparks, Ned (1883–1957) (Edward Sparkman). Hard-boiled, cigar-chewing Canadian comic actor often seen in Hollywood films of the thirties as grouchy reporter or agent.
The Big Noise 27. The Miracle Man 30. Forty-Second Street 33. Two's Company (GB) 37. The Star Maker 39. For Beauty's Sake 40. Magic Town 46, etc.

Sparkuhl, Theodor (1894–). German cinematographer in Hollywood from the early thirties.
Carmen 18. Manon Lescaut 26. La Chienne 31. Too Much Harmony 33. Enter Madame 35. Beau Geste 39. The Glass Key 42. Star Spangled Rhythm 43. Blood on the Sun 46. Bachelor Girls 47, many others.

Sparv, Camilla (1943–). Swedish-born leading lady in Hollywood films.
The Trouble with Angels 66. Murderers' Row 66. Dead Heat on a Merry-go-Round 66. Department K 67. Mackenna's Gold 68. Downhill Racer 69. The Italian Job 69, etc.

special effects: a general term covering the many tricks of film-making which cannot be achieved by direct photography: optical wipes, dissolves, sub-titles, invisibility, mattes, etc.

speeches of any length are the antithesis of good film-making, but sometimes a long monologue has been not only an actor's dream but absolutely right, memorable and hypnotic in its context. The record (twenty minutes) is probably held by Edwige Feuillère in *The Eagle Has Two Heads,* but more effective, and somewhat shorter, were Sam Jaffe in *Lost Horizon,* Alec Guinness in *The Mudlark,* Orson Welles in *Compulsion,* Spencer Tracy in *Inherit the Wind,* Anne Baxter in *The Walls of Jericho,* James Stewart in *Mr Smith Goes to Washington,* Paul Muni in *The Life of Emile Zola,* Don Murray in *One Man's Way,* Orson Welles in *Moby Dick,* and Charles Chaplin in *The Great Dictator.*

Spellbound. There are two films of this title. In 1940 John Harlow made a low-budget British attempt to explore spiritualism, with Derek Farr as a distraught young man attempting to get in touch with his dead sweetheart. The years have been unkind to this naïve little movie, but it broke fresh ground at the time. In 1945 Alfred Hitchcock in Hollywood used the title for his glossy adaptation of Francis Beeding's *The House of Dr Edwardes,* with Ingrid Bergman and Gregory Peck, in loving close-up, discovering whether or not Peck, a psychiatrist, is in fact a murderous amnesiac. Full of tricks, but satisfying, the movie had a memorable dream sequence designed by Salvador Dali.

Spencer, Bud (–) (Carlo Pedersoli). Italian character actor in many spaghetti westerns.
Blood River 67. Beyond the Law 68. Boot Hill 69. They Call Me Trinity 70. Four Flies in Grey Velvet 71. Watch Out We're Mad 74, etc.

Spenser, Jeremy (1937–). British leading man, former child actor, also on stage.
Portrait of Clare 48. *Prelude to Fame* 50. Appointment with Venus 51. Summer Madness 55. The Prince and the Showgirl 57. Wonderful Things 58. Ferry to Hong Kong 58. *The Roman Spring of Mrs Stone* 61. King and Country 64.

He Who Rides a Tiger 65. Fahrenheit 451 66, etc.

Sperling, Milton (1912–). American producer.
Cloak and Dagger 46. Three Secrets 50. Murder Inc. 51. Blowing Wild 54. The Court Martial of Billy Mitchell (& co-w) 55. The Bramble Bush (& co-w) 59. The Battle of the Bulge 65. Captain Apache (wp) 71, etc.

Spewack, Sam (1899–1971). American playwright who with his wife Bella turned out several scripts for Hollywood.
The Secret Witness 31. Rendezvous 35. *Boy Meets Girl* 38. Three Loves has Nancy 38. My Favorite Wife 40. Weekend at the Waldorf 45. Kiss Me Kate 53. Move Over Darling 63, etc.

Spiegel, Sam (1901–). Polish-born producer, in Hollywood from 1941. Also known as S. P. Eagle.
Tales of Manhattan 42. *The Stranger* 45. *We Were Strangers* 48. *The African Queen* 51. *On the Waterfront* 54. The Strange One 57. *The Bridge on the River Kwai* 57. *Lawrence of Arabia* 62. The Chase 66. *The Night of the Generals* 66. The Happening 67. The Swimmer 68. Nicholas and Alexandra 71. The Last Tycoon 76, etc.

Spielberg, Steven (1946–). American director.
□ Amblin' (short) 69. *Duel* (TV) 71. Something Evil (TV) 72. Sugarland Express 73. *Jaws* 75. Close Encounters of the Third Kind 77.

spies are currently enjoying enormous popularity as the heroes of over-sexed, gimmick-ridden melodramas. Real-life spies have been less frequently depicted, the world of James Bond being much livelier than those of Moyzich (*Five Fingers*), Odette Churchill (*Odette V.C.*), Nurse Edith Cavell, Violette Szabo (*Carve Her Name with Pride*), *Mata Hari*, or the gangs in *The House on 92nd Street, 13 Rue Madeleine*, and *Ring of Spies*.

Fictional spy films first became popular during and after World War I: they added a touch of glamour to an otherwise depressing subject, even though the hero often faced the firing squad in the last reel. Right up to 1939 romantic melodramas on this theme were being made: *I Was a Spy, The Man Who Knew Too Much, The Thirty-Nine Steps, Lancer Spy, The Spy in Black, Dark Journey, British Agent, Secret Agent, The Lady Vanishes, Espionage Agent, Confessions of a Nazi Spy*. The last-named brought the subject roughly up to date,

and with the renewed outbreak of hostilities new possibilities were hastily seized in *Foreign Correspondent, Night Train to Munich, Casablanca, The Conspirators, They Came to Blow Up America, Berlin Correspondent, Across the Pacific, Escape to Danger, Ministry of Fear, Confidential Agent, Sherlock Holmes and the Secret Weapon, Hotel Reserve*, and innumerable others. (It was fashionable during this period to reveal that the villains of comedy-thrillers and who-done-its were really enemy agents.) During the post-war years two fashions in film spying became evident: the downbeat melodrama showing spies as frightened men and women doing a dangerous job (*Notorious, Cloak and Dagger, Hotel Berlin, Orders to Kill*) and the 'now it can be told' semi-documentary revelation (*O.S.S., Diplomatic Courier, The Man Who Never Was, The Two-Headed Spy, The Counterfeit Traitor, Operation Crossbow*). In the late forties Nazis and Japs were replaced by reds, and we had a spate of melodramas under such titles as *I Married a Communist, I Was a Communist for the FBI, I Was an American Spy, Red Snow* and *The Red Danube*.

There had always been spy comedies. Every comedian made one or two: the Crazy Gang in *Gasbags*, Duggie Wakefield in *Spy for a Day*, Jack Benny in *To Be or Not To Be*, Bob Hope in *They Got Me Covered*, Radford and Wayne in *It's Not Cricket*, George Cole in *Top Secret*, right up to the 'Carry On' Team in *Carry On Spying* and Morecambe and Wise in *The Intelligence Men*. There were also occasional burlesques like *All Through the Night* and sardonic comedies like *Our Man in Havana*. But it was not until the late fifties that the spy reasserted himself as a romantic figure who could be taken lightly; and not until 1962 was the right box-office combination of sex and suspense found in *Dr No*. Since then we have been deluged with pale imitations of James Bond to such an extent that almost every leading man worth his salt has had a go. Cary Grant in *Charade*, David Niven in *Where the Spies Are*, Rod Taylor and Trevor Howard in *The Liquidator*, Dirk Bogarde in *Hot Enough for June*, Michael Caine in *The Ipcress File*, Paul Newman in *Torn Curtain*, James Coburn in *Our Man Flint*, Gregory Peck in *Arabesque*, Yul Brynner in *The Double Man*, George Peppard in *The Executioner*, Stephen Boyd in *Assignment K*, Frank Sinatra in *The Naked Runner*, Anthony Hopkins in *When Eight Bells Toll*, Kirk Douglas in *Catch Me a Spy*, Tom Adams in *Licensed to Kill*. There have also been elaborations such as the extreme sophistication of *The Manchurian Candidate*, the cold realism of *The Spy Who Came in from the Cold*, the op-art spoofing of

Modesty Blaise, even the canine agent of *The Spy with a Cold Nose* and spies from outer space in *This Island Earth*. And the TV screens of 1970 were filled with such tricky heroes as those in *Danger Man* (Secret Agent), *The Man from U.N.C.L.E.*, *Amos Burke Secret Agent*, *The Baron, I Spy* and *The Avengers*. The trend of the seventies was towards sour and disenchanted looks at the whole business, such as *Callan, The Killer Elite, Permission to Kill* and *Three Days of the Condor*.

Spillane, Mickey (1918–) (Frank Morrison). Bestselling American crime novelist of the love-'em and kill-'em variety.
I the Jury 53. The Long Wait 54. Kiss Me Deadly 55.
AS ACTOR: Ring of Fear 54. The Girl Hunters (as Mike Hammer) (& w) 64.
Darren McGavin played Hammer in a 1960 TV series.

Spinetti, Victor (1932–). British comic actor with stage experience.
A Hard Day's Night 64. The Wild Affair 64. Help! 65. The Taming of the Shrew 66. Heironymus Merkin 69. Unman Wittering and Zigo 71, etc.

The Spiral Staircase (US 1945). Basically a superior 'thunderstorm mystery', this admirably cinematic extension of a suspense novel by Ethel Lina White was notable for Robert Siodmak's direction, Nicholas Musuraca's photography, and the performance of Dorothy McGuire as a deaf-mute servant girl terrorized by a maniac in a lonely house. The 1975 remake by Peter Collinson is best forgotten.

The Spoilers. Rex Beach's action novel has been filmed five times, with interest centring on its climactic fight scene between the two male leads, who were as follows. 1914: William Farnum and Tom Santschi. 1922: Milton Sills and Noah Beery. 1930: William Boyd and Gary Cooper. 1942: John Wayne and Randolph Scott. 1956: Jeff Chandler and Rory Calhoun.

Spoliansky, Mischa (1898–). Russian composer, in Germany from 1930, Britain from 1934.
Don Juan 34. *Sanders of the River* 35. The Ghost Goes West 36. *King Solomon's Mines* 37. Jeannie 42. Don't Take It To Heart 44. Mr Emmanuel 44. Wanted for Murder 46. *The Happiest Days of Your Life* 50. Trouble in Store 53. Saint Joan 57. Northwest Frontier 59. The Battle of the Villa Fiorita 65. Hitler: The Last Ten Days 73, many others.

sportsmen who have been the subject of biopics include Babe Ruth (William Bendix) in *The Babe Ruth Story*; Grover Cleveland Alexander (Ronald Reagan) in *The Winning Team*; Lou Gehrig (Gary Cooper) in *The Pride of the Yankees*; Monty Stratton (James Stewart) in *The Stratton Story*; Jim Piersall (Anthony Perkins) in *Fear Strikes Out*; Jim Corbett (Errol Flynn) in *Gentleman Jim*; John L. Sullivan (Greg McClure) in *The Great John L.*; Knute Rockne (Pat O'Brien) in *Knute Rockne All-American*; Jim Thorpe (Burt Lancaster) in *Jim Thorpe All-American* (*Man of Bronze*); Ben Hogan (Glenn Ford) in *Follow the Sun*; Annette Kellerman (Esther Williams) in *Million Dollar Mermaid*.

Spring, Howard (1889–1965). British novelist. Works filmed include *Fame is the Spur* and *My Son My Son*.

Spring in Park Lane (GB 1947). An unexpectedly successful light comedy with music, this agreeable but witless affair about a footman who—of course—is really an earl in disguise was dated even when released, but coasted to fame on a blithe teaming of talents. Anna Neagle and Michael Wilding were a popular romantic team, Tom Walls and Nigel Patrick furnished light relief, and the palatial settings were lapped up by the British public after six years of total war. It was directed by Herbert Wilcox from a script by Nicholas Phipps. In the following year the same team attempted a sequel, *Maytime in Mayfair*, but this time the soufflé fell flat.

Springsteen, R. G. (1904–). American director who has been making efficient low-budget westerns since 1930.
Honeychile 48. Hellfire 49. The Enemy Within 49. The Toughest Man in Arizona 53. Track the Man Down 53. Come Next Spring 56. Cole Younger, Gunfighter 58. Battle Flame 59. Black Spurs 64. Taggart 65. Waco 66. Johnny Reno 66. Red Tomahawk 66, many others.

The Spy Who Came in from the Cold (GB 1965). A deliberately dour and chilling look at the spy game, made as a corrective to the James Bond cult. John le Carré's tale provided a splendid series of doublecrosses, and Richard Burton and Oskar Werner extracted plenty of feeling from skeletal parts, but Ossie Morris' photography was perhaps a little too grainy and harsh to be fair. Martin Ritt directed.

The Squaw Man (US 1913). A western generally considered as a milestone in Hollywood's history, being the first major film to be produced there. An enormous success, it starred Dustin Farnum (who later regretted his refusal to take a percentage of the profits instead of salary) and was directed by Cecil B. de Mille for Jesse L. Lasky. A remake starring Jack Holt was made in 1918, and a talkie version starring Warner Baxter appeared in 1931.

Squibs. The cockney flower-seller heroine of George Pearson's silent comedy put in her first successful appearance in 1921. Public acclaim produced three sequels: *Squibs Wins the Calcutta Sweep* 22, *Squibs MP* 23, *Squibs' Honeymoon* 23. Pearson then grew tired of the tomboyish character and cast Betty Balfour in other rôles, but she reappeared in a not-too-successful talkie version in 1936, with Gordon Harker and Stanley Holloway.

Squire, Ronald (1886–1958) (Ronald Squirl). Jovial British character actor of stage (since 1909) and screen (since 1934).
Don't Take It to Heart 44. While the Sun Shines 46. Woman Hater 48. The Rocking-Horse Winner 50. Encore 52. My Cousin Rachel (US) 53. The Million Pound Note 54. Now and Forever 55. Count Your Blessings 58, etc.

Stack, Robert (1919–) (Robert Modini). Personable, cold-eyed American leading man of the fifties, later successful in television.
☐ First Love 39. The Mortal Storm 40. A Little Bit of Heaven 40. *Nice Girl* (in which he gave Deanna Durbin her first screen kiss) 41. Badlands of Dakota 41. To Be or Not To Be 42. Eagle Squadron 42. Men of Texas 42. A Date with Judy 48. Miss Tatlock's Millions 48. Fighter Squadron 48. Mr Music 50. My Outlaw Brother 51. Bwana Devil 53. War Paint 53. Conquest of Cochise 53. Sabre Jet 53. The High and the Mighty 54. The Iron Glove 54. House of Bamboo 55. Good Morning Miss Dove 55. Great Day in the Morning 56. *Written on the Wind* 56. *The Tarnished Angels* 57. The Gift of Love 58. *John Paul Jones* 59. The Last Voyage 60. The Caretakers 63. Is Paris Burning? 66. The Corrupt Ones 67. Le Soleil des Voyous 68. The Story of a Woman 70. The Action Man 70. TV series: *The Untouchables* 59–62. *The Name of the Game* 68–70. Most Wanted 76.

Stafford, Frederick (1928–). Austrian leading man who after many he-man roles in European movies imitating James Bond was signed by Alfred Hitchcock to play the lead in *Topaz* 69.

Stagecoach (US 1939). A classic western which cleverly utilizes not only the usual ingredients but the never-failing trick of putting a miscellaneous group of people together in a dangerous situation. (Ernest Haycox's original story 'Stage to Lordsburg' clearly patterned itself after Maupassant's 'Boule de Suif'.) Directed by John Ford from Dudley Nichols' screenplay, with John Wayne, Claire Trevor, Thomas Mitchell, Donald Meek, etc. Remade in 1966 to little effect.

Stahl, John M. (1886–1950). American director, former stage actor; in films from 1914.
Wives of Men 18. Husbands and Lovers 23. The Child Thou Gavest Me 24. The Naughty Duchess 28. Seed 31. *Back Street* 32. *Imitation of Life* 34. *Magnificent Obsession* 35. Parnell 37. Letter of Introduction 38. *When Tomorrow Comes* 39. Our Wife 41. *Holy Matrimony* 43. The Immortal Sergeant 43. The Eve of St Mark 44. *The Keys of the Kingdom* 44. Leave Her to Heaven 45. The Foxes of Harrow 47. The Walls of Jericho 47. Oh You Beautiful Doll 49, many others.

Stainton, Philip (1908–1963). Rotund British actor with surprised expression; often played policemen.
Scott of the Antarctic 47. Passport to Pimlico 48. The Quiet Man 52. Angels One Five 52. Hobson's Choice 54. The Woman for Joe 56, many others.

staircases have provided dramatic backgrounds for many films. Martin Balsam was murdered on one in *Psycho*; the climax of *The Spiral Staircase* took place just there; Vivien Leigh was carried up one by a lustful Clark Gable in *Gone with the Wind*; Jerry Lewis danced down one in *Cinderfella*; Errol Flynn and Basil Rathbone duelled on one in *The Adventures of Robin Hood*; Ann Todd rode a horse up one in *South Riding*; Joan Fontaine in *Rebecca* descended one in delight and ascended it in tears; Raymond Massey ascended a particularly shadowy one in *The Old Dark House*, and later a very sinister character came down it; the entire cast of *Ship of Fools* came down one at the end, like a musical finale; a severed head bumped down one in *Hush Hush Sweet Charlotte*; Gene Tierney threw herself down one in *Leave Her to Heaven*; an old lady was tossed down one in a wheelchair in *Kiss of Death*; Bela Lugosi in *Dracula* passed through the cobwebs on one without breaking them; Laurel and Hardy in *Blockheads* had to descend and ascend innumerable flights of stairs in pursuit of a lost ball; Anna Sten was killed on one in *The Wedding Night*; the lighthouse staircase was a dramatic feature of *Thunder*

Rock; James Cagney danced down the White House staircase in *Yankee Doodle Dandy*; and the main feature of *A Matter of Life and Death*, was a moving stairway to heaven. Universal and Paramount both had very striking and oft-used staircase sets in the forties; the latter was most dramatically used for Kirk Douglas' death in *The Strange Love of Martha Ivers*. Oddly enough in the film called *Staircase* the staircase was not an essential feature.

Stallings, Laurence (1894–1968). American screenwriter.
The Big Parade 25. *What Price Glory?* (co-w) 26. So Red the Rose (co-w) 35. Northwest Passage (co-w) 39. Jungle Book 42. Salome Where She Danced 45. *She Wore a Yellow Ribbon* (co-w) 49. The Sun Shines Bright 52, etc.

Stallone, Sylvester (1946–). Solemn-looking American star who shot to the top in a modest film which he wrote himself.
□ The Lords of Flatbush 73. Capone 73. Bananas 73. The Prisoner of Second Avenue 75. *Rocky* 76.

Stamp, Terence (1940–). British juvenile lead of the sixties.
Billy Budd 62. Term of Trial 62. The Collector 65. Modesty Blaise 66. Far from the Madding Crowd 67. Poor Cow 67. Blue 68. Theorem (It.) 68. The Mind of Mr Soames 69.

Stamp-Taylor, Enid (1904–1946). British character actress with stage experience.
Feather Your Nest 37. Action for Slander 37. The Lambeth Walk 38. Hatter's Castle 41. The Wicked Lady 45. Caravan 46, etc.

Stander, Lionel (1908–). Gravel-voiced American character actor, on stage and screen from the early thirties.
The Scoundrel 34. Mr Deeds Goes to Town 36. *A Star is Born* 37. Guadalcanal Diary 42. The Spectre of the Rose 46. Unfaithfully Yours 48. St Benny the Dip 51. *Cul de Sac* (GB) 66. Promise Her Anything (GB) 66. A Dandy in Aspic (GB) 68. The Gang That Couldn't Shoot Straight 72. The Con Men 73. The Black Bird 75, etc.

Standing, Sir Guy (1873–1937). British stage actor, father of Kay Hammond, in some Hollywood films.
The Eagle and the Hawk 33. Double Door 34. Lives of a Bengal Lancer 35. The Return of Sophie Lang 36. Lloyds of London 37, etc.

Standing, John (1934–). British character actor, son of Kay Hammond.

The Wild and the Willing 62. A Pair of Briefs 63. King Rat 65. Walk Don't Run 66. The Psychopath 66. Torture Garden 67. Zee and Co. 71, etc.

Stanley, Kim (1921–) (Patricia Reid). American stage actress.
The Goddess 57. Seance on a Wet Afternoon 64.

Stanwyck, Barbara (1907–) (Ruby Stevens). Durable American star actress, a sultry lady usually playing roles in which she is just as good as a man, if not better.
□ Broadway Nights 27. The Locked Door 29. Mexicali Rose 29. Ladies of Leisure 30. Ten Cents a Dance 31. Illicit 31. *Miracle Woman* 31. *Night Nurse* 31. Forbidden 32. Shopworn 32. *So Big* 32. The Purchase Price 32. *The Bitter Tea of General Yen* 33. Ladies They Talk About 33. *Baby Face* 33. Ever in My Heart 33. A Lost Lady 34. Gambling Lady 34. The Secret Bride 35. The Woman in Red 35. Red Salute 35. *Annie Oakley* 35. A Message to Garcia 36. The Bride Walks Out 36. His Brother's Wife 36. Banjo on My Knee 36. The Plough and the Stars 36. Internes Can't Take Money 37. This is My Affair 37. *Stella Dallas* 37. Breakfast for Two 38. The Mad Miss Manton 38. Always Goodbye 38. Union Pacific 39. Golden Boy 39. Remember the Night 40. *The Lady Eve* 41. *Meet John Doe* 41. You Belong to Me 41. *Ball of Fire* 41. The Great Man's Lady 42. The Gay Sisters 42. Lady of Burlesque 42. Flesh and Fantasy 43. *Double Indemnity* 44. Hollywood Canteen 44. Christmas in Connecticut 45. My Reputation 45. The Bride Wore Boots 46. *The Strange Love of Martha Ivers* 46. California 46. The Other Love 47. The Two Mrs Carrolls 47. Cry Wolf 47. BF's Daughter 48. *Sorry Wrong Number* 48. The Lady Gambles 49. East Side West Side 49. Thelma Jordon 50. No Man of Her Own 50. *The Furies* 50. To Please a Lady 50. Man with a Cloak 51. Clash by Night 52. Jeopardy 53. Titanic 53. All I Desire 53. The Moonlighter 53. Blowing Wild 53. *Executive Suite* 54. Witness to Murder 54. Cattle Queen of Montana 54. The Violent Men 55. Escape to Burma 55. There's Always Tomorrow 56. The Maverick Queen 56. These Wilder Years 56. Crime of Passion 57. Trooper Hook 57. Forty Guns 57. Walk on the Wild Side 62. Roustabout 64. The Night Walker 65. The House That Would Not Die (TV) 70. A Taste of Evil (TV) 71. The Letters (TV) 73. TV series: *The Big Valley* 65–68.

Stapleton, Jean (–). American actress familiar from TV's *All in the Family*.
Cold Turkey 70. Klute 71, etc.

Stapleton, Maureen (1925–). American character actress.
Lonelyhearts 59. The Fugitive Kind 60. A View from the Bridge 62. Bye Bye Birdie 62. Airport 69. Plaza Suite 70, etc.

Stapley, Richard: see *Wyler, Richard*.

star is a word coined by some forgotten publicist in the early years of the century who presumably touted his leading actors as twinkling heavenly lights. It came in the thirties to mean any actor who was billed above the title; but nowadays real stars are hard to find, and the word is generally applied only to those thought likely actually to draw patrons to the box office.

Star! (US 1968). A supremely professional if unconvincing account of the life of Gertrude Lawrence, done in the musical style of the thirties and forties and all the better for it. Meticulously directed by Robert Wise on a mammoth budget, with skilled cinematography by Ernest Laszlo. Julie Andrews shows great stamina but her numbers somehow disappoint; Daniel Massey as Noel Coward steals the show.

A Star is Born. This 1937 screenplay by Dorothy Parker, Alan Campbell and Robert Carson has become a Hollywood legend and in some cases a reality: the marriage of two stars goes on the rocks because one of them is on the way up and the other on the way down. It was then tailored for Janet Gaynor and Fredric March with strong support from Adolphe Menjou and Lionel Stander as Hollywood types; William Wellman directed, Howard Greene was photographer, and Max Steiner wrote the music. In 1954 George Cukor directed Judy Garland and James Mason in the star roles, with Charles Bickford and Jack Carson; it was a long and lumpy film but with moments of magic including a couple of show-stopping musical numbers which seemed to distil the essence of Garland. In 1976 it was revamped for Barbra Streisand. The theme is in fact traceable back to a 1930 film called *What Price Hollywood?*

Stark, Graham (1922–). British comedy actor of films and TV, mostly in cameo roles.
The Millionairess 61. Watch It, Sailor 62. A Shot in the Dark 64. Becket 64. Alfie 66. Finders Keepers 66, etc.

Stark, Ray (c. 1914–). American producer.
The World of Suzie Wong 60. Oh Dad, Poor Dad 66. This Property is Condemned 66. Funny Girl 67. Reflections in a Golden Eye 68. The Way We Were 73. Funny Lady 75, etc.

Starke, Pauline (1901–). American silent screen actress.
Intolerance 16. Salvation Nell 19. A Connecticut Yankee 21. Shanghai 24. Twenty Cents a Dance 26, etc.

Starr, Belle (–). American female outlaw of the wild west period. On screen she has been glamorized by Gene Tierney in the film of that name, by Jane Russell in *Montana Belle* and by Isabel Jewell in *Badman's Territory*.

Starrett, Charles (1904–). American cowboy star of innumerable second features in the thirties and forties. Inactive since 1952.
The Quarterback (debut) (playing himself, a professional footballer) 26. Fast and Loose 30. Sky Bride 32. Green Eyes 34, etc.

Starrett, Jack (–). American director.
Race with the Devil 74. A Small Town in Texas 76.

State Fair. This agreeable piece of rural Americana was first filmed in 1933 by Henry King, from a script by Sonya Levien and Paul Green. Will Rogers, Lew Ayres, Janet Gaynor and Sally Eilers were the stars. In 1945, with the benefit of added songs by Rodgers and Hammerstein, it was remade by Walter Lang with Charles Winninger, Dick Haymes, Jeanne Craine and Vivian Blaine, and again, with a different score, in 1961 by Jose Ferrer, with Tom Ewell, Pat Boone, Pamela Tiffin and Ann-Margret.

statesmen who have frequently been depicted in films include Disraeli (most often), Gladstone, Melbourne, Ramsay Macdonald (disguised in *Fame is the Spur*), Woodrow Wilson, Churchill, Roosevelt (notably in *Sunrise at Campobello*), Lincoln (qv) and Parnell. Fleeting glimpses of famous leaders were also given in *Mission to Moscow* and some Russian wartime films.

statues have come to life in *Night Life of the Gods, Animal Crackers, Turnabout* and *One Touch of Venus*. They were central to the plots of *The Light that Failed, Latin Quarter, Song of Songs* and *Mad Love*, while *A Taste of Honey* involved them in an attractive title sequence. In horror films, they came murderously alive in *Night of the Eagle, The Norliss Tapes* (TV) and that grand-daddy of them all, *The Golem*.

Steel, Anthony (1920–). Athletic British leading man with slight stage experience.
Saraband for Dead Lovers (film debut) 48. Marry Me 49. *The Wooden Horse* 50. Laughter

in Paradise 51. The Malta Story 52. *Albert RN* 53. The Sea Shall Not Have Them 55. Storm over the Nile 56. The Black Tent 56. Checkpoint 56. A Question of Adultery 57. Harry Black 58. Honeymoon 60. The Switch 63. Hell is Empty 67. Anzio 68. Massacre in Rome 74, etc.

Steele, Barbara (1938–). British leading lady who has appeared mainly in Italian horror films. Bachelor of Hearts 58. Sapphire 59. Black Sunday (The Devil's Mask) 60. The Pit and the Pendulum (US) 61. The Terror of Dr Hichcock 62. Eight and a Half 63. The Spectre 64. Sister of Satan (The Revenge of the Blood Beast) 65, etc.

Steele, Bob (1907–) (Robert Bradbury). American actor on stage from two years old. Since 1920 he has played cowboy roles in over 400 second features, and was one of the 'Three Mesquiteers'.

Steele, Tommy (1936–) (Tommy Hicks). Energetic British cockney performer and pop singer.
Kill Me Tomorrow 55. The Tommy Steele Story 57. The Duke Wore Jeans 59. Light Up The Sky 59. Tommy the Toreador 60. It's All Happening 62. The Happiest Millionaire (US) 67. *Half a Sixpence* 67. Finian's Rainbow (US) 68. Where's Jack? 69.

Steiger, Rod (1925–). Burly American leading character actor who became known on stage and TV after training at New York's Theatre Workshop.
☐ Teresa 51. *On the Waterfront* 54. The Big Knife 55. Oklahoma 55. *The Court Martial of Billy Mitchell* 55. The Unholy Wife 56. Jubal 56. *The Harder They Fall* 56. Back from Eternity 57. Run of the Arrow 57. Across the Bridge (GB) 57. *Al Capone* 58. Cry Terror 58. Seven Thieves 59. The Mark 61. 13 West Street 61. On Friday at Eleven 61. The Longest Day 62. Convicts Four 62. Time of Indifference 63. Hands Over the City (It.) 63. *The Pawnbroker* (BFA) 65. The Loved One 65. Doctor Zhivago 65. The Girl and the General 66. *In the Heat of the Night* (AA, BFA) 67. A Man Called John 68. No Way to Treat a Lady 68. The Sergeant 68. The Illustrated Man 69. Three into Two Won't Go 69. Waterloo (as Napoleon) 71. A Fistful of Dynamite 71. Happy Birthday Wanda June 72. Lolly Madonna XXX 72. Lucky Luciano 73. Hennessy 74. W. C. Fields and Me 76. Jesus of Nazareth (TV) 77.

Stein, Paul (1891–1952). Austrian director who made films in America and Britain.
Ich Liebe Dich 23. My Official Wife (US) 26.

Forbidden Woman (US) 27. Sin Takes a Holiday (US) 30. One Romantic Night 30. Born to Love 31. A Woman Commands (US) 31. Lily Christine (GB) 32. The Outsider (GB) 38. The Saint Meets the Tiger (GB) 41. Talk about Jacqueline (GB) 42. Kiss the Bride Goodbye (GB) 43. Twilight Hour (GB) 44. The Lisbon Story (GB) 46. Counterblast (GB) 48. The Twenty Questions Murder Mystery (GB) 49, etc.

Steinbeck, John (1902–1968). American novelist.
Of Mice and Men 40. The Grapes of Wrath 40. Tortilla Flat 42. The Moon is Down 43. The Red Pony 49. East of Eden 54. The Wayward Bus 57, etc.

Steiner, Max (1888–1971). Austrian composer, in American from 1924; became one of Hollywood's most reliable and prolific writers of film music.
Cimarron 31. A Bill of Divorcement 32. *King Kong* 33. The Lost Patrol 34. *The Informer* (AA) 35. *She* 35. The Charge of the Light Brigade 36. A Star is Born 37. *Gone with the Wind* 39. *The Letter* 40. *The Great Lie* 41. *Now Voyager* (AA) 42. *Casablanca* 42. *Since You Went Away* (AA) 44. Rhapsody in Blue 45. The Big Sleep 46. The Treasure of the Sierra Madre 47. Johnny Belinda 48. The Fountainhead 49. The Glass Menagerie 50. Room for One More 52. The Charge at Feather River 53. The Caine Mutiny 54. Battle Cry 55. Come Next Spring 56. Band of Angels 57. The FBI Story 59. The Dark at the Top of the Stairs 60. Parrish 61. Youngblood Hawke 64, scores of others.

Stella Dallas. This weepy novel of frustrated mother-love, written by Olive Higgins Prouty, was filmed by Henry King in 1925, with Belle Bennett and Ronald Colman, and by King Vidor in 1937, with Barbara Stanwyck and John Boles.

Sten, Anna (1908–) (Anjuschka Stenski Sujakevitch). Russian leading actress imported to Hollywood by Goldwyn in 1933 in the hope of rivalling Garbo; but somehow she didn't click.
Storm over Asia (Russ.) 28. Trapeze 31. The Brothers Karamazov 31. *Nana* 34. We Live Again 34. The Wedding Night 35. A Woman Alone 38. So Ends Our Night 41. They Came to Blow Up America 43. She Who Dares 44. Let's Live a Little 48. Soldier of Fortune 55. The Nun and the Sergeant 62, etc.

Stepanek, Karel (1899–). Czech character actor, in Britain from 1940. Usually plays Nazis or other villains.
They Met in the Dark 43. *The Captive Heart* 46.

The Fallen Idol 48. State Secret 50. Cockleshell Heroes 55. *Sink the Bismarck* 60. Operation Crossbow 65. Before Winter Comes 69, many others.

Stephen, Susan (1931–). British leading lady of the fifties.
His Excellency 51. The Red Beret 53. For Better For Worse 54. Golden Ivory 54. The Barretts of Wimpole Street 57. Carry On Nurse 59. Return of a Stranger 61. The Court Martial of Major Keller 63, etc.

Stephens, Ann (1931–). British juvenile actress of the forties.
In Which We Serve 42. Dear Octopus 43. The Upturned Glass 47. The Franchise Affair 51. Intent to Kill 58, others.

Stephens, Martin (1949–). British juvenile player.
The Hellfire Club 61. *Village of the Damned* 62. *The Innocents* 62. Battle of the Villa Fiorita 65. The Witches 66, etc.

Stephens, Robert (1931–). British stage actor, in occasional films.
Circle of Deception 60. Pirates of Tortuga (US) 61. A Taste of Honey 61. The Inspector 62. Cleopatra 62. The Small World of Sammy Lee 63. Morgan 66. Romeo and Juliet 68. The Prime of Miss Jean Brodie 69. *The Private Life of Sherlock Holmes* 69. The Asphyx 72. Travels with My Aunt 73, etc.

Stephenson, Henry (1871–1956) (H. S. Garroway). British stage actor who came to Hollywood films in his sixties and remained to play scores of kindly old men.
Cynara (debut) 32. Little Women 33. Mutiny on the Bounty 35. Little Lord Fauntleroy 36. The Charge of the Light Brigade 36. Conquest 38. The Young in Heart 39. The Adventures of Sherlock Holmes 40. This above All 42. The Green Years 46. Oliver Twist (GB) 48. Challenge to Lassie 49, etc.

Stephenson, James (1888–1941). Suave British-born stage actor, in Hollywood from 1938.
When Were You Born? (debut) 38. Boy Meets Girl 38. Confessions of a Nazi Spy 38. Beau Geste 39. Calling Philo Vance 40. The Sea Hawk 40. *The Letter* 40. Shining Victory 41. International Squadron 41, etc.

Steppat, Ilse (1917–1970). German character actress.
Marriage in the Shadow 47. The Bridge 51. The Confessions of Felix Krull 62. On Her Majesty's Secret Service 69.

stereophony: hearing sound from more than one source at the same time, a gimmick used to 'put you in the picture' by surrounding you with loudspeakers when CinemaScope was first introduced.

stereoscopy: viewing in three-dimensions, usually accomplished by watching through polaroid glasses, two films projected one on top of the other after being photographed from slightly different angles corresponding to one's two eyes.

Sterling, Ford (1883–1939) (George F. Stitch). American comic actor, a leading Keystone Kop and slapstick heavy.
Drums of the Desert 26. Gentlemen Prefer Blondes 28. Kismet 30. Alice in Wonderland 33. The Black Sheep 35, etc.

Sterling, Jan (1923–) (Jane Sterling Adriance). Blonde American leading lady with slight stage experience.
Johnny Belinda 48. Rhubarb 51. *Ace in the Hole* 51. Split Second 52. Pony Express 53. Alaska Seas 54. The High and the Mighty 54. Women's Prison 55. The Female on the Beach 55. 1984 56. The Harder They Fall 56. Kathy O 58. Love in a Goldfish Bowl 61, etc.

Sterling, Robert (1917–) (William Sterling Hart). American leading man of the forties, mainly in second features.
Only Angels Have Wings 39. I'll Wait for You 41. Somewhere I'll Find You 42. The Secret Heart 46. Bunco Squad 48. Roughshod 50. Thunder in the Dust 51. Column South 53. Return to Peyton Place 61. Voyage to the Bottom of the Sea 62, etc.
TV series: Topper 53–55. Ichabod and Me 61.

Stevens, Connie (1938–) (Concetta Ingolia). American leading lady with mixed Italian, English, Irish and Mohican blood.
Eighteen and Anxious 57. Rockabye Baby 58. Parrish 61. Susan Slade 61. Two on a Guillotine 64. Never Too Late 65. Mr Jericho (TV) 70. The Grissom Gang 71. The Sex Symbol (TV) 73. Scorchy 76, etc.
TV series: Hawaian Eye 59–62.

Stevens, Craig (1918–) (Gail Shekles). American leading man, married to Alexis Smith.
Affectionately Yours 41. Since You Went Away 43. The Lady Takes a Sailor 47. The French Line 54. Abbott and Costello Meet Dr Jekyll and

Mr Hyde 55. Gunn 66. The Limbo Line 68. The Snoop Sisters (TV) 72. Rich Man Poor Man (TV) 76, etc.
TV series: Peter Gunn 58–60. Man of the World 62. Mr Broadway 64.

Stevens, George (1904–1975). American director, in Hollywood from 1923. In the late thirties and early forties he made smooth and lively entertainments, but his infrequent later productions tended towards elephantiasis.
□ The Cohens and Kellys in Trouble 33. Bachelor Bait 34. Kentucky Kernels 34. Laddie 34. The Nitwits 34. Alice Adams 34. Annie Oakley 35. Swing Time 36. A Damsel in Distress 37. *Quality Street* 37. Vivacious Lady 38. *Gunga Din* 39. Vigil in the Night 40. Penny Serenade 40. *Woman of the Year* 41. *Talk of the Town* 42. *The More the Merrier* 43. *I Remember Mama* 47. *A Place in the Sun* (AA) 51. Something to Live For 52. *Shane* 53. *Giant* (AA) 56. The Diary of Anne Frank 59. The Greatest Story Ever Told 65. The Only Game in Town 69.

Stevens, Inger (1935–1970) (Inger Stensland). Pert and pretty Swedish leading lady, in America from childhood.
Man on Fire (film debut) 57. Cry Terror 58. The World the Flesh and the Devil 58. The Buccaneer 59. The New Interns 64. *A Guide for the Married Man* 67. Firecreek 67. Madigan 68. Five Card Stud 68. Hang 'Em High 68. House of Cards 68. The Borgia Stick (TV) 68. A Dream of Kings 69. Run Simon Run (TV) 70, etc.
TV series: *The Farmer's Daughter* 63–65.

Stevens, K. T. (1919–) (Gloria Wood). American leading lady of a few forties films; daughter of director Sam Wood.
Kitty Foyle 40. The Great Man's Lady 41. Address Unknown 44. Vice Squad 53. Tumbleweed 53. Missile to the Moon 58, etc.

Stevens, Leith (1909–1970). American musical arranger and composer.
The Wild One 52. Julie 56. The Five Pennies 49. A New Kind of Love 63, many others for Fox and Paramount, including TV series.

Stevens, Leslie (1924–). American screenwriter.
The Left-Handed Gun 58. Private Property (& pd) 59. The Marriage-Go-Round (from his play) 60. Hero's Island (& pd) 62, etc.
TV series as creator-producer-director: Stony Burke, The Outer Limits.

Stevens, Mark (1916–) (also known as Stephen Richards). American leading man with varied early experience; usually in routine roles.
Objective Burma 45. *From This Day Forward* 45. The Dark Corner 46. I Wonder Who's Kissing Her Now 47. The Snake Pit 48. The Street with No Name 48. Sand 49. Mutiny 53. Cry Vengeance (also pd) 54. Timetable (also pd) 55. September Storm 60. Fate is the Hunter 64. Frozen Alive 66. Sunscorched 66.

Stevens, Onslow (1902–1977) (Onslow Ford Stevenson).
American stage actor occasionally seen in film character roles.
Heroes of the West (debut) 32. Counsellor at Law 33. The Three Musketeers 36. Under Two Flags 36. When Tomorrow Comes 39. Mystery Sea Raider 40. *House of Dracula* 45. O.S.S. 46. Night Has a Thousand Eyes 48. The Creeper 48. State Penitentiary 50. Them 54. Tarawa Beachhead 58. All the Fine Young Cannibals 60. Geronimo's Revenge 63, etc.

Stevens, Rise (1913–). American opera singer, seen in a few films.
□ The Chocolate Soldier 41. Going My Way 44. Carnegie Hall 47.

Stevens, Robert (c. 1925–). American director, from TV.
□ The Big Caper 57. Never Love a Stranger 58. I Thank a Fool 62. In the Cool of the Day 63. Change of Mind 69.

Stevens, Ronnie (1925–). British comic actor with stage and TV experience.
Made in Heaven 52. An Alligator Named Daisy 55. I Was Monty's Double 58. I'm All Right, Jack 59. Dentist in the Chair 60. San Ferry Ann 65. Give a Dog a Bone 66. Some Girls Do 68, etc.

Stevens, Stella (1936–) (Estelle Eggleston). American leading lady.
Say One For Me (debut) 58. Lil Abner 59. Too Late Blues 61. The Courtship of Eddie's Father 63. The Nutty Professor 63. Synanon 65. The Secret of My Success 65. The Silencers 66. How to Save a Marriage 67. The Mad Room 69. The Ballad of Cable Hogue 70. A Town Called Bastard 71. Stand Up and be Counted 71. The Poseidon Adventure 72. Arnold 74. Cleopatra Jones and the Casino of Gold 74, etc.

Stevens, Warren (1919–). American general purpose actor.
The Frogmen 51. The Barefoot Contessa 54. Forbidden Planet 56. Hot Spell 58. No Name on the Bullet 59. Forty Pounds of Trouble 62. An

American Dream 66. Madigan 68, many others. TV series: 77th Bengal Lancers 56. The Richard Boone Show 64.

Stevenson, Houseley (1879–1953). American character actor, latterly familiar as a gaunt, usually unshaven, old man.
Native Land 42. Somewhere in the Night 46. Dark Passage 47. Casbah 48. Moonrise 49. All the King's Men 49. The Sun Sets at Dawn 51. The Wild North 52, etc.

Stevenson, Robert (1905–). British director, in Hollywood from 1939.
☐Tudor Rose 36. The Man Who Changed His Mind 36. Jack of all Trades 37. *King Solomon's Mines* 37. Non Stop New York 37. Owd Bob 38. The Ware Case 39. Young Man's Fancy 40. *Tom Brown's Schooldays* 40. *Back Street* 41. Joan of Paris 43. Forever and a Day (co-d) 43. *Jane Eyre* 43. Dishonored Lady 47. *To the Ends of the Earth* 48. The Woman on Pier 13 49. Walk Softly Stranger 50. My Forbidden Past 51. The Last Vegas Story 52. Johnny Tremain 57. Old Yeller 57. Darby O'Gill and the Little People 59. Kidnapped 60. The Absent-Minded Professor 61. In Search of the Castaways 62. Son of Flubber 63. The Misadventures of Merlin Jones 64. *Mary Poppins* 64. The Monkey's Uncle 65. That Darn Cat 65. The Gnome-Mobile 67. Blackbeard's Ghost 67. The Love Bug 69. Bedknobs and Broomsticks 71. Herbie Rides Again 73. The Island at the Top of the World 74. One of Our Dinosaurs is Missing 75. The Shaggy D.A. 77.

Stevenson, Robert Louis (1850–1894). British novelist and short story writer. Works filmed include *Dr Jekyll and Mr Hyde* (many versions), *Treasure Island* (many versions), *The Body Snatcher, The Suicide Club, Kidnapped, The Master of Ballantrae, Ebb Tide, The Wrong Box.*

Steward, Ernest (–). British cinematographer.
Carry on Camping 71. Callan 74. Hennessy 75, many others.

Stewart, Alexandra (1939–). Canadian leading lady who has filmed mainly in Europe.
Exodus 60. Le Feu Follet 63. Dragees au Poivre 65. The Bride Wore Black 67. The Man Who Had Power Over Women 70. The Marseilles Contract 74, etc.

Stewart, Anita (1895–1961) (Anna May Stewart). American silent screen leading lady.
A Million Bid 13. The Goddess 15. Mary Regan 19. Her Kingdom of Dreams 20. Never the Twain Shall Meet 25. Sisters of Eve 28, many others.

Stewart, Athole (1879–1940). British stage character actor.
The Speckled Band 31. The Clairvoyant 34. Dusty Ermine 37. The Spy in Black 39. Tilly of Bloomsbury 40, etc.

Stewart, Donald Ogden (1894–). American playwright and screenwriter. Autobiography 1974: *By a Stroke of Luck.*
Tarnished Lady 31. Smilin' Through 32. The Barretts of Wimpole Street 34. *The Prisoner of Zenda* 37. Holiday 38. Love Affair 39. *The Philadelphia Story* (AA) 40. Keeper of the Flame 42. Life with Father 47. Edward, My Son 49, etc.

Stewart, Elaine (1929–) (Elsy Steinberg). American leading lady of a few fifties films; former usherette.
Sailor Beware 51. The Bad and the Beautiful 52. Young Bess 53. Brigadoon 54. The Tattered Dress 56. The Adventures of Hajji Baba 57. The Rise and Fall of Legs Diamond 60. The Most Dangerous Man Alive 61, etc.

Stewart, Hugh (1910–). British producer, former editor.
Trottie True 49. The Long Memory 52. Man of the Moment 55 (and all subsequent Norman Wisdom comedies). The Intelligence Men 65, etc.

Stewart, James (1908–). American leading actor of inimitable slow drawl and gangly walk; portrayed slow-speaking, honest heroes for thirty-five years.
☐ Murder Man 35. Rose Marie 36. Next Time We Love 36. Wife versus Secretary 36. Small Town Girl 36. Speed 36. The Gorgeous Hussy 36. Born to Dance 36. After the Thin Man 36. *Seventh Heaven* 37. The Last Gangster 37. Navy Blue and Gold 37. Of Human Hearts 38. Vivacious Lady 38. Shopworn Angel 38. *You Can't Take It with You* 38. Made for Each Other 38. Ice Follies of 1939. It's a Wonderful World 39. *Mr Smith Goes to Washington* 39. *Destry Rides Again* 39. *The Shop around the Corner* 39. The Mortal Storm 40. No Time for Comedy 40. *The Philadelphia Story* (AA) 40. Come Live with Me 40. Pot O' Gold 41. Ziegfeld Girl 41; war service; *It's a Wonderful Life* 46. Magic Town 47. *Call Northside 777* 47. On Our Merry Way 48. Rope 48. You Gotta Stay Happy 48. The Stratton Story 49. Malaya 49. *Winchester 73* 50. *Broken Arrow* 50. The Jackpot 50.

Harvey 50. No Highway (GB) 51. The Greatest Show on Earth 51. Bend of the River 52. Carbine Williams 52. The Naked Spur 53. Thunder Bay 53. *The Glenn Miller Story* 53. *Rear Window* 54. The Far Country 54. Strategic Air Command 55. *The Man from Laramie* 55. The Man Who Knew Too Much 56. The Spirit of St Louis 57. Night Passage 57. Vertigo 58. Bell, Book and Candle 58. *Anatomy of a Murder* 59. The FBI Story 59. The Mountain Road 60. Two Rode Together 61. The Man Who Shot Liberty Valance 62. *Mr Hobbs Takes a Vacation* 62. How the West Was Won 62. Take Her She's Mine 63. Cheyenne Autumn 64. Dear Brigitte 65. *Shenandoah* 65. The Flight of the Phoenix 65. The Rare Breed 66. Firecreek 67. Bandolero 68. The Cheyenne Social Club 70. Fool's Parade 71. The Shootist 76. Airport 77 77.
TV series: The Jimmy Stewart Show 71. Hawkins on Murder 73.

Stewart, Paul (1908–). American character actor, often in clipped, sinister roles.
Citizen Kane 41. Johnny Eager 42. Government Girl 44. *Champion* 49. *The Window* 49. Walk Softly Stranger 50. The Bad and the Beautiful 52. Prisoner of War 54. The Cobweb 55. King Creole 58. A Child is Waiting 62. The Greatest Story Ever Told 65. In Cold Blood 67. The Day of the Locust 75. Bite the Bullet 75. W. C. Fields and Me 76, others.

Stewart, Sophie (1909–). British stage and radio actress, in occasional films.
Maria Marten 35. As You Like It 36. The Return of the Scarlet Pimpernel 38. Nurse Edith Cavell 39. The Lamp Still Burns 43. Uncle Silas 47. Yangtse Incident 56, etc.

Stiller, Mauritz (1883–1928). Swedish director who went to Hollywood in the twenties with Garbo, but died shortly after.
Vampyren 12. *Sir Arne's Treasure* 19. Erotikon 20. *The Atonement of Gosta Berling* 24. The Blizzard (US) 26. Hotel Imperial 27. Street of Sin 28, etc.

The Sting (US 1973) (AA). A lucky film which brought together the old confidence trickster routines, the happy combination of Robert Redford and Paul Newman, a piano rag music score by Scott Joplin, and cheerful fadeout after much suspense. The box office reaction was terrific, but attempts to imitate the formula failed apart from a moderate TV series called *Switch*, with Robert Wagner and Eddie Albert.

Stock, Nigel (1919–). British character actor, former boy performer.

Lancashire Luck 38. Brighton Rock 46. Derby Day 51. The Dam Busters 55. Eye Witness 57. HMS Defiant 62. The Lost Continent 68. The Lion in Winter 68. A Bequest to the Nation 73. Russian Roulette 75, many others.

stock shot. One not made at the time of filming but hired from a library. It can be either newsreel, specially shot material such as planes landing at an airport, views of a city, etc., or spectacular material lifted from older features. (e.g. *Storm over the Nile* 55 had a large proportion of action footage from the original *Four Feathers* 39, and the same shots have turned up in several other films including *Master of the World* 61 and *East of Sudan* 64.)

Stockfield, Betty (1905–1966). British stage actress, in occasional films.
City of Song 30. The Impassive Footman 32. The Beloved Vagabond 36. Derrière la Façade (Fr.) 40. Flying Fortress 42. Edouard et Caroline (Fr.) 50. The Lovers of Lisbon 55. True As a Turtle 57, etc.

Stockwell, Dean (1936–). American boy actor of the forties, later leading man.
□ The Valley of Decision 45. Anchors Aweigh 45. Abbott and Costello in Hollywood 45. *The Green Years* 46. Home Sweet Homicide 46. The Mighty McGurk 47. The Arnelo Affair 47. Song of the Thin Man 47. The Romance of Rosy Ridge 47. Gentleman's Agreement 48. *The Boy with Green Hair* 48. Deep Waters 48. Down to the Sea in Ships 49. The Secret Garden 49. Stars in My Crown 50. The Happy Years 50. Kim 50. Cattle Drive 51. Gun for a Coward 57. The Careless Years 57. *Compulsion* 59. *Sons and Lovers* 60. Long Day's Journey into Night 62. Rapture 65. Psych-Out 68. The Dunwich Horror 70. The Failing of Raymond (TV) 71. The Loners 72. Another Day at the Races 73. Win, Place or Steal 75.

Stockwell, Guy (1938–). American leading actor.
The War Lord 65. *Blindfold* 65. And Now Miguel 66. *Beau Geste* 66. The Plainsman 66. Tobruk 66. The King's Pirate 67. The Million Dollar Collar 67. In Enemy Country 68. The Gatling Gun 72. Airport 75 74, etc.

Stoker, Bram (1847–1912). Irish novelist, the creator of *Dracula*. Was also Henry Irving's manager.

Stokowski, Leopold (1882–) (Leopold Stokes or Boleslowowicz). British-born orchestral conductor.

□ One Hundred Men and a Girl 37. The Big Broadcast of 1937 37. Fantasia 40. Carnegie Hall 47.

Stoll, George (1905–). American musical director, with MGM from 1945.
Anchors Aweigh (AA) 45. Neptune's Daughter 49. I Love Melvin 53. The Student Prince 54. Hit the Deck 55. Meet Me in Las Vegas 56, many others.

Stoloff, Morris (1893–). American musical director, in Hollywood from 1936.
Lost Horizon 37. You Can't Take It With You 38. Cover Girl (AA) 44. A Song to Remember 45. The Jolson Story (AA) 46. The 5000 Fingers of Dr T 52. Picnic 55, many others.

Stone, Andrew (1902–). American producer-director (latterly with his wife Virginia) who made it a rule since the mid-forties not to shoot in a studio, always on location. Formed Andrew Stone Productions 1943.
The Great Victor Herbert 39. *Stormy Weather* (d only) 42. Hi Diddle Diddle 43. Sensations of 1945. Highway 301 51. The Steel Trap 52. The Night Holds Terror 54. Julie 56. *Cry Terror* 58. The Decks Ran Red 59. The Last Voyage 60. Ring of Fire 61. The Password is Courage 62. Never Put It in Writing 64. The Secret of My Success 65. *Song of Norway* 69. *The Great Waltz* 72, etc.

Stone, George E. (1903–1967) (George Stein). Polish-born character actor, who in Hollywood films played oppressed little men; formerly in vaudeville.
The Front Page 30. Little Caesar 30. Cimarron 31. Anthony Adverse 36. *The Housekeeper's Daughter* 38. His Girl Friday 41. The Boston Blackie series. Dancing in the Dark 50. The Robe 53. Guys and Dolls 55. The Man with the Golden Arm 56, many others.

Stone, Harold J. (1911–). American character actor.
The Harder They Fall 56. Garment Center 57. Man Afraid 57. Spartacus 60. The Chapman Report 62. The Man with X-Ray Eyes 63. Which Way to the Front? 70. Mitchell 75, etc.
TV series: My World and Welcome To It 68. Bridget Loves Bernie 74.

Stone, Lewis (1879–1953). Distinguished American stage actor, a leading man of silent films and later a respected character actor.
Honour's Altar (debut) 15. *The Prisoner of Zenda* 22. Scaramouche 23. *The Lost World* 24. Madame X 30. The Mask of Fu Manchu 32.

Mata Hari 32. Grand Hotel 33. Queen Christina 33. *David Copperfield* 34. *Treasure Island* 35. The Thirteenth Chair 37. *You're Only Young Once* 37. Judge Hardy's Children 38. Love Finds Andy Hardy 38. Out West with the Hardys 39 (and ten further episodes of this series, ending in 1947). Yellow Jack 39. The Bugle Sounds 41. Three Wise Fools 46. The State of the Union 48. Key to the City 50. Scaramouche 52. The Prisoner of Zenda 52. All the Brothers Were Valiant 53, many others.

Stone, Milburn (1904–). American character actor, in Hollywood from the mid-thirties; has been in hundreds of low-budget action features, usually as villain or tough hero; more recently became famous as 'Doc' in the *Gunsmoke* TV series.

Stone, Peter (1930–). American screenwriter.
Charade 63. Father Goose (AA) 64. Mirage 65. Sweet Charity 68. The Skin Game 71. '1776' 72. The Taking of Pelham One Two Three 74, etc.

The Three Stooges. A trio of American knockabout comics specializing in a peculiarly violent form of slapstick. They originally went from vaudeville to Hollywood with Ted Healy (as Ted Healy and his Stooges) but broke away to become world famous in hundreds of two-reelers throughout the thirties, forties and fifties. The original trio were Larry Fine (1911–1975), Moe Howard (1895–1975) and his brother Jerry (Curly) Howard (1906–1952). In 1947 Curly was replaced by yet another brother, Shemp Howard (Samuel Howard) (1891–1955). On Shemp's death he was replaced by Joe Besser, who in 1959 was replaced by Joe de Rita. Towards the end of their popularity the Stooges appeared in a few features.
Stop Look and Laugh 61. Snow White and the Three Stooges 61. The Three Stooges Meet Hercules 63. The Outlaws is Coming 64. The Three Stooges Go Around the World in a Daze 65, etc.

stop motion. The method by which much trick photography is effected: the film is exposed one frame at a time, allowing time for rearrangement of models, etc., between shots, and thus giving the illusion in the completed film of motion by something normally inanimate. The monsters in *King Kong* 33 are the supreme example of this method.
See: *time-lapse photography.*

Stoppa, Paolo (1906–). Italian character actor, in films from 1932.

La Beauté du Diable 49. Miracle in Milan 50. The Seven Deadly Sins 52. Love Soldiers and Women 55. La Loi 59. The Leopard 63. Becket 64. After the Fox 66. Once Upon a Time in the West 67, etc.

Storch, Larry (–). American comic actor.
Captain Newman MD 63. Wild and Wonderful 64. The Monitors 69. The Couple Takes a Wife (TV) 72, etc.
TV series: F Troop.

Storck, Henri (1907–). Belgian documentarist.
Pour Vos Beaux Yeux 29. The Story of the Unknown Soldier 32. Symphonie Paysanne 42. Au Carrefour de la Vie 49. Les Belges de la Mer 54. Les Gestes du Silence 61. La Musée Vivante 65, etc.

Storm, Gale (1922–) (Josephine Cottle). American leading lady of the forties.
Tom Brown's Schooldays 39. Foreign Agent 42. Nearly Eighteen 43. The Right to Live 45. Sunbonnet Sue 46. It Happened on Fifth Avenue 47. Abandoned 49. Underworld Story 50. The Texas Rangers 51, etc.
TV series: The Gale Storm Show 56–59. My Little Margie 61.

Storm over Asia (Russia 1930). Also known as *The Heir to Genghis Khan*, this beautifully-made propagandist melodrama concerned a Mongol fur trapper found in 1918 to be a descendant of Genghis Khan. Tried and half-executed for treason, he is reprieved to become a puppet monarch. Directed by V. I. Pudovkin.

storms of one kind or another have been brilliantly staged in *The Hurricane, The Wizard of Oz, When Tomorrow Comes, Reap the Wild Wind, Typhoon, Lord Jim, A High Wind in Jamaica, The Blue Lagoon, Sunrise, Key Largo, Ryan's Daughter, Portrait of Jennie, Noah's Ark* and *The Bible*, to name but a handful; they have also been essential situation-builders in such films as *Five Came Back, Hatter's Castle, Our Man Flint, The Card, Storm Fear* and *The Blue Lagoon*. A whole genre of films, known as the 'thunderstorm mystery', grew up in the thirties when every screen murder took place in a desolate mansion during a terrifying storm with no means of communication with the outside world; typical of these are *The Black Cat, The Cat and the Canary, The Ghost Breakers, Night Monster, Hold That Ghost, You'll Find Out* and *The Spiral Staircase*. Finally there is nothing like a good electrical storm for breathing life into

a monster, as evidenced in a score of films from *Frankenstein* to *The Electric Man* and after.

The Story of Louis Pasteur (US 1936). The first of Warner Brothers' famous series of historical biographies: later films dealt with Zola, Reuter, Dr Ehrlich, Juarez, etc. In this case popularization managed to make scientific research remarkably exciting. Paul Muni (AA) was Pasteur, William Dieterle directed from a script by Sheridan Gibney and Pierre Collings, and Erich Wolfgang Korngold wrote the music. These films were very successful commercially; but when John Huston revived the form in 1962 with *Freud*, it was a box office disaster.

Stossel, Ludwig (1883–1973). Austrian character actor in Hollywood from the mid-thirties.
Four Sons 39. Man Hunt 41. Woman of the Year 41. Hitler's Madman 43. Cloak and Dagger 46. A Song is Born 48. Call Me Madam 53. Me and the Colonel 58. G.I. Blues 60, many others.

Stout, Archie (1886–). American cinematographer in Hollywood from 1914.
Fort Apache 48. Hard Fast and Beautiful 51. *The Quiet Man* (AA) 52. The Sun Shines Bright 53. The High and the Mighty 54.

Stowe, Harriet Beecher (1811–1896). American novelist, author of the much-filmed *Uncle Tom's Cabin* (qv).

Stradling, Harry (1907–1970). British-born cinematographer, long in US.
La Kermesse Héroïque 35. *Knight without Armour* 37. *Pygmalion* 38. The Citadel 38. Jamaica Inn 39. Suspicion 41. *The Picture of Dorian Gray* (AA) 44. The Pirate 48. The Barkleys of Broadway 49. *A Streetcar Named Desire* 51. Valentino 51. Hans Christian Andersen 52. Helen of Troy 55. Guys and Dolls 55. The Eddy Duchin Story 56. The Pajama Game 57. A Face in the Crowd 57. The Dark at the Top of the Stairs 60. *My Fair Lady* (AA) 64. How to Murder Your Wife 65. Moment to Moment 65. Walk, Don't Run 66. Funny Girl 68. Hello Dolly 69, many others.

Stradling, Harry Jnr (–). American cinematographer, son of Harry Stradling.
Welcome to Hard Times 67. Support Your Local Sheriff 69. The Mad Room 69. Something Big 71. Fools Parade 71. The Way We Were 73. McQ 74. Bite the Bullet 75. Midway 76. The Big Bus 76. Airport 77 77, etc.

Stradner, Rose (1913–1958). Austrian actress who made a few Hollywood films.
The Last Gangster 38. Blind Alley 39. The Keys of the Kingdom 44, etc.

Strange, Glenn (1899–1973). Giant-size American character actor, in Hollywood from 1937, mainly in cowboy roles. Also played the monster. in *House of Frankenstein* 45, *Abbott and Costello meet Frankenstein* 48, etc.

Strange Interlude (US 1932). Eugene O'Neill's sombre romantic drama, with its sense of time and opportunity wasted, was a strange choice for MGM to film at the time, but Norma Shearer and Clark Gable provided powerful box office lure, and the long monologues were overcome by billing the movie as 'the film in which you hear the characters THINK!' Robert Z. Leonard directed unobtrusively.

Strasberg, Lee (1901–). American drama teacher, founded the Actors' Studio which in the fifties taught The Method.
The Godfather Part Two 74.

Strasberg, Susan (1938–). American leading lady, daughter of Lee Strasberg, founder of the New York Actors' Studio. Stage and TV experience.
Picnic (film debut) 55. Stage Struck 57. Taste of Fear 59. Kapo 60. Hemingway's Adventures of a Young Man 62. The High Bright Sun 65. Psych-Out 68. The Brotherhood 68, etc.

Stratton, John (1925–). British general purpose actor.
The Cure for Love 49. Appointment with Venus 52. The Cruel Sea 54. The Long Arm 55, etc.

Straub, Jean-Marie (1933–). French director in German films.
Machorka Muff 63. Nicht Versohnt 65. *The Chronicle of Anna-Magdalena Bach* 67. Othon 72. History Lessons 73, etc.

Strauss, Peter (1942–). American leading man who became well known in *Rich Man Poor Man* (TV) 76.
Soldier Blue 71. The Last Tycoon 76, etc.

Strauss, Robert (1913–1975). American comedy actor (occasionally in menacing roles); former salesman.
Sailor Beware 52. Stalag 17 53. The Seven Year Itch 54. Attack 57. The Last Time I Saw Archie 61. The Family Jewels 65, etc.

Strayer, Frank (1891–1964). American director of second features.
Rough House Rosie 27. Enemy of Men 30. The Monster Walks 32. The Vampire Bat 33. The Ghost Walks 35. Blondie (and many others in this series) 38. The Daring Young Man 42. Messenger of Peace 50. etc.

Streeter, Edward (1892–1976). American humorous novelist: *Father of the Bride* and *Mr Hobbs Takes a Vacation* were filmed.

Streisand, Barbra (1942–). American singer and entertainer who made a virtue of her odd looks.
□ *Funny Girl* (as Fanny Brice) (AA) 68. Hello Dolly 69. On a Clear Day You Can See Forever 70. The Owl and the Pussycat 70. What's Up Doc? 72. Up the Sandbox 72. The Way We Were 73. For Pete's Sake 74. Funny Lady 75. A Star is Born 76.

stretch-printing. The reason silent films look jerky is that they were shot at 16 frames a second whereas modern sound projectors operate at 24, making everything move half as fast again as normal. One means of overcoming this jerkiness is stretch-printing in the lab: every second frame is printed twice. This still gives a curious effect, as for every two frames slower than normal sound speed we still get one frame faster.

Strick, Joseph (1923–). American director.
The Savage Eye 59. The Balcony 64. Ulysses 67. Ring of Bright Water (GB) (p only) 69. Tropic of Cancer 69. The Darwin Adventure (p) 71. Janice 73.

Stricklyn, Ray (1930–). American 'second lead' with stage experience.
The Proud and the Profane 56. The Last Wagon 57. Ten North Frederick 58. Young Jesse James 60. Arizona Raiders 65, etc.

Stride, John (1936–). British supporting actor, much on TV.
Bitter Harvest 63. Macbeth 72. Juggernaut 74. Brannigan 75, etc.
TV series: The Main Chance.

strikes: see *Labour Relations*.

Stritch, Elaine (1922–). Sharp, lanky American character comedienne, mainly on stage.
□ The Scarlet Hour 55. Three Violent People 57. A Farewell to Arms 57. The Perfect Furlough 58. Who Killed Teddy Bear? 65. Sidelong

Glances of a Pigeon Kicker 70. The Spiral Staircase 75.
TV series: *My Sister Eileen* 62. Two's Company 75–76.

Strock, Herbert L. (1918–). American director, former publicist and editor.
The Magnetic Monster 52. Riders to the Stars 54. Battle Taxi 55. Teenage Frankenstein 57. How to Make a Monster 58. Rider on a Dead Horse 62. The Crawling Hand 63, etc.

Strode, Woody or **Woodrow** (c. 1923–). Tall black American actor.
The Lion Hunters 51. The Ten Commandments 56. *Sergeant Rutledge* 60. Spartacus 60. Two Rode Together 62. The Man Who Shot Liberty Valance 62. Genghis Khan 65. The Professionals 66. Shalako 68. Che! 69. The Revengers 72. The Gatling Gun 72. Winterhawk 76, etc.

Stromberg, Hunt (1894–1968). American producer, long with MGM, who went independent in the forties.
Breaking into Society (as d) 24. Fire Patrol (as d) 26. Torrent 27. Our Dancing Daughters 28. Red Dust 32. *The Thin Man* 34. *The Great Ziegfeld* (AA) 36. Maytime 38. Marie Antoinette 38. Idiot's Delight 39. *The Women* 39. Northwest Passage 40. *Pride and Prejudice* 41. Guest in the House 44. Lured 47. Too Late for Tears 49. Betweeen Midnight and Dawn 50. Mask of the Avenger 51, many others.

Stross, Raymond (1916–). British producer, in films from 1933; married to Anne Heywood.
As Long as They're Happy 52. An Alligator Named Daisy 56. The Flesh is Weak 56. A Question of Adultery 58. A Terrible Beauty 59. The Very Edge 62. The Leather Boys 63. Ninety Degrees in the Shade 65. The Midas Run 69. I Want What I Want 72, etc.

Stroud, Don (1937–). American leading man.
Madigan 68. Games 68. What's So Bad about Feeling Good 68. Coogan's Bluff 69. Bloody Mama 70. Explosion 70. Von Richtofen and Brown 70. Tick Tick Tick 70. Joe Kidd 72. Scalawag 73.

Strudwick, Shepperd: see *Shepperd, John.*

Struss, Karl (c. 1890–). American cinematographer.
Ben Hur 26. *Sunrise* (AA) 27. Abraham Lincoln 30. The Sign of the Cross 32. *Dr Jekyll and Mr Hyde* 32. The Great Dictator 40. Bring on the Girls 44. Suspense 46. The Macomber Affair 47.

Rocketship XM 50. *Limelight* 52. Tarzan and the She-Devil 53, many others.

Stuart, Binkie (c. 1932–). British child actress of the thirties.
Moonlight Sonata 37. Little Dolly Daydream 38. My Irish Molly 39, etc.

Stuart, Gloria (1909–) (Gloria Stuart Finch). American leading lady of the thirties.
The Old Dark House 32. The Invisible Man 33. Roman Scandals 33. Prisoner of Shark Island 36. Rebecca of Sunnybrook Farm 38. The Three Musketeers 39. She Wrote the Book (last to date) 46, etc.

Stuart, John (1898–1972?) (John Croall). British leading man of the twenties, character actor of the forties and after.
Her Son (debut) 20. We Women 25. The Pleasure Garden 26. Blackmail 29. Elstree Calling 30. Atlantic 30. Number Seventeen 31. Taxi for Two 32. The Pointing Finger 34. Abdul the Damned 35. Old Mother Riley's Ghost 41. The Phantom Shot 46. Mine Own Executioner 47. The Magic Box 51. Quatermass II 57. Blood of the Vampire 58. Sink the Bismarck 60, etc.

Stuart, Mel (–). American director.
If It's Tuesday This Must Be Belgium 69. I Love My Wife 70. Willie Wonka and the Chocolate Factory 71. One is a Lonely Number 72.

The Student of Prague. The old German legend, about a man who sold his reflection to the devil and bought it back only at the expense of his life, was filmed in 1913 by Stellan Rye, with Paul Wegener; in 1926 by Henrik Galeen, with Conrad Veidt; and in 1936 by Arthur Robison, with Anton Walbrook.

The Student Prince. The Sigmund Romberg/Dorothy Donnelly operetta about a Ruritanian prince who loves a barmaid was filmed by Lubitsch in 1927 with Ramon Novarro and Norma Shearer. There was no sound version until 1954, when Richard Thorpe directed Ann Blyth and Edmund Purdom (the latter using Mario Lanza's voice).

student protest was a feature of a few films of the late sixties. They were not successful, with the exception of *If.* For the record the other main titles were *Flick, The Strawberry Statement, Getting Straight, R.P.M.* and *The Revolutionary.*

stunt men, who risk their lives doubling for the stars when the action gets too rough, have been featured in remarkably few movies: *Hollywood Stunt Men, Lucky Devils, The Lost Squadron, Sons of Adventure, Callaway Went Thataway* and *Singin' in the Rain. Hell's Angels* was said to be the film on which most stunt men were killed; more recently Paul Mantz lost his life while stunt-flying for *The Flight of the Phoenix*, which was subsequently dedicated to him. Most famous stunt men are probably Yakima Canutt, who later became a famous second-unit director; Richard Talmadge, who doubled for Douglas Fairbanks and also directed a few films himself; and Cliff Lyons, who stood in for most of the western stars. Stunt men who became famous in their own right include George O'Brien, Jock Mahoney, Rod Cameron and George Montgomery.

Sturges, John (1911–). American director of smooth if increasingly pretentious action films, former editor and documentarist.

□ The Man Who Dared 46. Shadowed 46. Alias Mr Twilight 47. For the Love of Rusty 47. Keeper of the Bees 48. The Best Man Wins 48. The Sign of the Ram 48. The Walking Hills 49. The Capture 49. Mystery Street 50. The Magnificent Yankee 50. Right Cross 50. Kind Lady 51. The People Against O'Hara 51. It's a Big Country (part) 51. The Girl in White 52. Fast Company 52. Jeopardy 53. Escape from Fort Bravo 53. *Bad Day at Black Rock* 54. Underwater 55. The Scarlet Coat 55. Backlash 56. *Gunfight at the OK Corral* 57. The Law and Jake Wade 58. The Old Man and the Sea 58. Last Train from Gun Hill 58. Never So Few 59. *The Magnificent Seven* 60. By Love Possessed 61. Sergeants Three 62. A Girl Named Tamiko 63. *The Great Escape* 63. The Satan Bug 65. The Hallelujah Trail 65. The Hour of the Gun 67. Ice Station Zebra 68. Marooned 69. Joe Kidd 72. McQ 74. The Eagle Has Landed 77.

Sturges, Preston (1898–1959) (Edmund P. Biden). American writer-director who in the early forties was Hollywood's wonder boy who never lost the common touch despite his free-wheeling witty style and subject matter. By 1950 his talent had disappeared, and he retired unhappily to France.

AS WRITER: *The Power and the Glory* 33. We Live Again 34. The Good Fairy 35. Diamond Jim 35. Easy Living 37. Port of Seven Seas 38. If I Were King 39. Never Say Die 39. Remember the Night 40, etc.

□ AS WRITER-DIRECTOR: *The Great McGinty* (AA) 40. *Christmas in July* 40. *Sullivan's Travels* 41. The Lady Eve 41. *The Palm Beach Story* 42. *The Great Moment* 43. *The Miracle of Morgan's Creek* 43. Hail the Conquering Hero 44. Mad Wednesday 46. Unfaithfully Yours 48. The Beautiful Blonde from Bashful Bend 49. The Diary of Major Thompson 56.

Styne, Jule (1905–) (Jules Styne). British-born composer, in US from childhood. Former pianist and conductor. Film songs include 'There Goes That Song Again', 'Give Me Five Minutes More', 'It's Magic', 'Three Coins in the Fountain'. Shows filmed include *Gentlemen Prefer Blondes, Bells Are Ringing, Gypsy, Funny Girl.*

submarines have been the setting for so many war action films that only a few can be noted. Pure entertainment was the object of *Submarine Patrol, Submarine Command, Torpedo Run, Destination Tokyo, Run Silent Run Deep, Crash Dive, The Deep Six* and *Ice Station Zebra.* Somewhat deeper thoughts were permitted in *Morning Departure, The Silent Enemy, Les Maudits*, and *We Dive at Dawn.* Submarines became objects of farce in *Jack Ahoy, Let's Face It*, and *Operation Petticoat.*

More unusual submarine vehicles appeared in *Voyage to the Bottom of the Sea, Around the World Under the Sea, Twenty Thousand Leagues Under the Sea, Thunderball, You Only Live Twice, Above Us the Waves* and *The Beast from 20,000 Fathoms.*

Subotsky, Milton (1921–). American independent producer and writer.
Rock Rock Rock 56. The Last Mile 58. City of the Dead (GB) 60. It's Trad Dad (GB) 63. Dr Terror's House of Horrors (GB) 64. Dr Who and the Daleks (GB) 65. The Skull (GB) 66. The Psychopath (GB) 66. Daleks Invasion Earth 2150 AD (GB) 66. Torture Garden (GB) 67. The House That Dripped Blood (GB) 70. Tales from the Crypt (GB) 71. Asylum (GB) 72. Madhouse (GB) 73. The Land That Time Forgot (GB) 75. At the Earth's Core (GB) 76, etc.

subways: see *Underground Railways.*

subtitles in silent days came *after* the scene in which the actors mouthed the dialogue. When talkies came the less cumbersome method was evolved of superimposing the dialogue at the foot of the screen, which considerably sharpened up the audience's reading speed.

Sucksdorff, Arne (1917–). Swedish documentarist who has normally written and photographed his own films, which vary from six minutes to feature length.
The West Wind 42. Shadows on the Snow 45.

Rhythm of a City 47. *A Divided World* 48. The Road 48. The Wind and the River 51. *The Great Adventure* 53. The Flute and the Arrow 57. The Boy in the Tree 60. My Home is Copacabana 65. Forbush and the Penguins 71, etc.

suicide became the central subject of two sixties films; *Le Feu Follet* and *The Slender Thread*, in which the motives for it in two particular cases are examined. It has, of course, been part of countless other plots, including factual or legendary ones such as *Cleopatra, Romeo and Juliet* and *Scott of the Antarctic*. Innumerable melodramas have begun with apparent suicides which have been proved by the disbelieving hero to be murder; the latest of these is probably *The Third Secret*. In *An Inspector Calls* a girl's suicide caused guilt complexes in an entire family for different reasons. In *An American Dream* the hero virtually commits suicide by walking into a room full of gangsters out to kill him. In *Leave Her to Heaven* the leading character commits suicide in such a way that her husband will be blamed for her murder. Several Japanese films have been based on the suicide pilots or Kamikaze, and there has also been a graphic account of the principles of *Hara Kiri*. Suicide has often been the way out for villains in mystery pictures: drowning for Herbert Marshall in *Foreign Correspondent*, shooting for Leo G. Carroll in *Spellbound*, poison for Rosamund John in *Green for Danger* and Barry Fitzgerald in *Ten Little Niggers*. And one could not begin to count the films in which characters have been narrowly saved from suicide, like Ray Milland in *The Lost Weekend*. Attempted suicide was even played for comedy by Laurel and Hardy in *The Flying Deuces*, and by Jack Lemmon in *Luv*, while in *It's a Wonderful Life* James Stewart was dissuaded from suicide by a friendly angel.

Sullavan, Margaret (1911–1960). American leading actress in light films of the thirties and forties; she had a special whimsical quality which was unique.
□ Only Yesterday 33. Little Man What Now? 34. So Red the Rose 35. *The Good Fairy* 35. Next Time We Love 36. The Moon's Our Home 36. *Three Comrades* 38. Shopworn Angel 38. The Shining Hour 39. *The Shop around the Corner* 39. *The Mortal Storm* 40. So Ends Our Night 40. Back Street 41. Appointment for Love 41. Cry Havoc 43. No Sad Songs for Me 50.

Sullivan, Barry (1912–) (Patrick Barry). American leading man with stage experience.
Lady in the Dark 43. Two Years before the Mast 44. And Now Tomorrow 44. Suspense 46. The Gangster 47. Tension 49. The Great Gatsby 49.

The Outriders 50. Three Guys Named Mike 51. *The Bad and the Beautiful* 52. Jeopardy 54. Queen Bee 55. Forty Guns 57. Wolf Larsen 57. Seven Ways from Sundown 60. The Light in the Piazza 62. Stagecoach to Hell 64. My Blood Runs Cold 64. Harlow (electronovision version) 65. An American Dream (See You in Hell, Darling) 66. Intimacy 66. Buckskin 68. Willie Boy 69. Earthquake 74. The Human Factor 75, etc.
TV series: Harbourmaster 57. The Road West 66.

Sullivan, C. Gardner (1885–1965). American screenwriter.
The Battle of Gettysburg 14. The Wrath of the Gods 15. Civilization 16. The Aryan 16. Carmen of the Klondike 18, many others.

Sullivan, Francis L. (1903–56). Heavyweight British character actor, often seen as advocate. On stage from 1921, films from 1933.
The Missing Rembrandt (debut) 33. Chu Chin Chow 33. Great Expectations (US) 35. *The Mystery of Edwin Drood* (US) 35. Sabotage 36. Action for Slander 37. Dinner at the Ritz 37. Twenty-One Days 38. The Citadel 38. The Four Just Men 39. *Pimpernel Smith* 41. *Fiddlers Three* 44. Caesar and Cleopatra 45. *Great Expectations* 46. *Oliver Twist* 48. Night and the City 51. Plunder of the Sun (US) 51. The Prodigal (US) 55. Hell's Island (US) 55, many others.

Sullivan, Pat (1887–1933). Australian newspaper cartoonist who settled in the US and invented Felix the Cat, the most popular character in film cartoons of the twenties.

Sullivan's Travels (US 1941). Perhaps the most meaningful, eccentric and devastating of all Preston Sturges' comedies. About a film director who goes off in search of truth but finally discovers that all people want is to laugh, it is a remarkably sure-footed combination of farce, melodrama and sentiment, and its appeal seems to have increased over the years. Written and directed by Sturges, produced by Paul Jones, photographed by John F. Seitz; with memorable performances by Joel McCrea, Veronica Lake, and the familiar Sturges repertory of supporting players.

Sully, Frank (1910–1975). American small part actor often seen as farmer or dumb crook.
Mary Burns Fugitive 35. The Grapes of Wrath 40. Escape to Glory 41. Thousands Cheer 43. Renegades 46. With a Song in My Heart 52. The Naked Street 56, many others.

Sumac, Yma (1928–). Peruvian singer with wide octave range.
The Secret of the Incas 54.

Summerfield, Eleanor (1921–). British character comedienne, on stage from 1939.
London Belongs to Me (film debut) 47. Scrooge 51. It's Great To Be Young 56. Dentist in the Chair 59. On the Beat 62. Guns of Darkness 63. Some Will Some Won't 70, many others.

Summers, Jeremy (1931–). British director, from TV.
The Punch and Judy Man 62. Crooks in Cloisters 64. Ferry Cross the Mersey 64. House of a Thousand Dolls 67. Vengeance of Fu Manchu 67, etc.

Summers, Walter (1896–). British director of the twenties and thirties.
Ypres 25. Mons 26. The Battle of the Coronel and Falkland Islands 31. Deeds Men Do 32. The Return of Bulldog Drummond 33. Mutiny on the Elsinore 36. Music Hath Charms (co-d) 36. At the Villa Rose 38. Dark Eyes of London 38. Traitor Spy 40, etc.

Summertime (Summer Madness) (US 1955). This adaptation of Arthur Laurents' play *The Time of the Cuckoo* successfully balanced its slight emotional story against the exotic background of Venice. Katharine Hepburn gave a brilliant performance as the lonely spinster tourist attracted by a handsome but married Italian (Rossano Brazzi); David Lean's direction was subtle and witty, and Jack Hildyard's colour photography proved a major asset.

Summerville, Slim (1892–1946) (George J. Summerville). Lanky, mournful-looking American character comedian, former gagman and director for Mack Sennett.
The Beloved Rogue 27. All Quiet on the Western Front 30. The Front Page 31. Life Begins at Forty 35. White Fang 36. The Road Back 37. Rebecca of Sunnybrook Farm 38. Jesse James 39. Tobacco Road 41. Miss Polly 41. Niagara Falls 42. The Hoodlum Saint 46, many others.

Sumner, Geoffrey (1908–). British comic actor of silly ass types.
Helter Skelter 49. The Dark Man 52. A Tale of Five Cities 53. Traveller's Joy 55, etc.

Sundberg, Clinton (1919–). American character actor, former teacher; usually plays flustered clerk or head waiter.
Undercurrent 46. Living in a Big Way 47. Annie Get Your Gun 50. Main Street to Broadway 52.

The Caddy 53. The Birds and the Bees 56. The Wonderful World of the Brothers Grimm 63. Hotel 67, many others.

Sunrise (US 1927). An interesting example of the German influence on Hollywood (written by Karl Mayer, directed by F. W. Murnau), this melodrama won a special Academy Award for 'artistic quality of production'. There were awards too for the camerawork (Charles Rosher, Karl Struss) and for Janet Gaynor as the young wife whose life is threatened by her temporarily unbalanced husband (George O'Brien). The story takes place during a journey, and the use of locations to this extent was rare for Hollywood at the time.

Sunset Boulevard (US 1950). A harsh look at Hollywood directed by Billy Wilder from a script by himself, Charles Brackett and D. M. Marsham Jnr. Gloria Swanson enjoys herself as the faded star who makes a tragic comeback, but she, Erich Von Stroheim, Anna Q. Nilsson and Buster Keaton come so close to playing themselves it's macabre. William Holden plays the star's kept man who encourages her false hopes. Photographed by John F. Seitz with music by Franz Waxman.

superdynamation. A term coined by Ray Harryhausen for his method of animating rubber monsters.

Super-8. Improved 8mm film which can take a sound track, therefore replacing the old 9.5mm.

superimpose: place one image on top of another, usually during a dissolve when one is fading out and the other fading in.

Superman. A comic strip character of the thirties, a being of giant powers from the planet Krypton; until they are needed he masquerades as Clark Kent, a timid newspaperman. Superman has never been out of fashion—1977 brings a multi-million dollar live version to follow the various cartoons and serials which have been popular over the years—and along the way he has inspired Batman, Spiderman, Doc Savage, the Six Million Dollar Man, the Bionic Woman, etc, etc.

Surtees, Bruce (–). American cinematographer.
The Beguiled 71. Play Misty for Me 71. Dirty Harry 72. The Great Northfield Minnesota Raid 72. Blume in Love 73. Night Moves 75.

Surtees, Robert L. (1906–). Distinguished

American cinematographer, in Hollywood from 1927.
Thirty Seconds over Tokyo 44. Our Vines Have Tender Grapes 45. The Unfinished Dance 47. Act of Violence 48. *Intruder in the Dust* 49. *King Solomon's Mines* (AA) 50. Quo Vadis 51. *The Bad and the Beautiful* (AA) 52. Escape from Fort Bravo 53. Trial 55. *Oklahoma!* 55. The Swan 56. Raintree County 57. Merry Andrew 58. *Ben Hur* (AA) 59. Mutiny on the Bounty 62. The Hallelujah Trail 65. The Collector 65. The Satan Bug 65. Lost Command 66. Doctor Dolittle 67. *The Graduate* 67. *Sweet Charity* 68. The Arrangement 69. Summer of 42 71. The Last Picture Show 71. The Cowboys 72. The Other 72. Oklahoma Crude 73. The Sting 73. The Great Waldo Pepper 75. The Hindenberg 75. A Star Is Born, etc.

Susann, Jacqueline (1921–1974). American best-selling novelist. Films of her books include *Valley of the Dolls, The Love Machine* and *Once is Not Enough.*

Suschitsky, Peter (–). British cinematographer.
It Happened Here 65. Privilege 66. Charlie Bubbles 67. A Midsummer Night's Dream 68. Lock Up Your Daughters 68. Leo the Last 70. Valentino 77, etc.

Suschitsky, Wolfgang (1912–). Austrian cinematographer in Britain.
No Resting Place 51. Cat and Mouse 57. The Small World of Sammy Lee 63. Ulysses 67. Theatre of Blood 73, etc.

Suspicion (US 1941). The film for which Joan Fontaine won an Academy Award was toned down from a novel by Francis Iles: the ending was changed as it was felt that no one would accept Cary Grant as a wife-murderer. Hitchcock directed rather coldly, and the production was only average.

Susskind, David (1920–). American TV and theatre personality and producer who has also produced a few films.
Edge of the City 57. A Raisin in the Sun 61. Requiem for a Heavyweight 62. All the Way Home 63. Lovers and Other Strangers 70, etc.

Sutherland, A. Edward (1895–1974). American director, in Hollywood from 1914.
Wild Wild Susan 25. Dance of Life 29. Palmy Days 31. Mississippi 35. Diamond Jim 35. Champagne Waltz 37. Every Day's a Holiday 38. The Flying Deuces 39. *The Boys from*

Syracuse 40. Beyond Tomorrow 41. Invisible Woman 41. Nine Lives Are Not Enough 42. Dixie 43. Follow the Boys 44. Abie's Irish Rose 46. Having Wonderful Crime 46. Bermuda Affair 56, many others.

Sutherland, Donald (1935–). Gaunt Canadian actor who became very fashionable at the end of the sixties.
□ The World Ten Times Over 63. Castle of the Living Dead 64. Dr Terror's House of Horrors 65. Fanatic 65. The Bedford Incident 65. Promise Her Anything 66. The Dirty Dozen 67. Billion Dollar Brain 67. Oedipus the King 68. Interlude 68. Joanna 68. The Split 68. Start the Revolution Without Me 69. Act of the Heart 70. M*A*S*H 70. Kelly's Heroes 70. Alex in Wonderland 71. Little Murders 70. *Klute* 71. Johnny Got His Gun (as Christ) 71. Steelyard Blues 72. Lady Ice 72. Alien Thunder 73. Don't Look Now 73. S*P*Y*S 74. The Day of the Locust 75. 1900 76. Casanova 76. The Eagle Has Landed 77.

Sutton, Dudley (1933–). British character actor.
The Leather Boys 63. Rotten to the Core 65. Crossplot 69. The Walking Stick 70. The Devils 71, etc.

Sutton, Grady (1908–). American character comedian usually seen as vacuous country cousin; in Hollywood from 1926.
The Story of Temple Drake 32. Alice Adams 35. Stage Door 37. Alexander's Ragtime Band 38. The Bank Dick 41. The Great Moment 44. My Wild Irish Rose 48. White Christmas 54. My Birds and the Bees 56. My Fair Lady 64. Paradise Hawaiian Style 66. The Great Bank Robbery 69. Myra Breckinridge 70, many others.
TV series: The Pruitts of Southampton 66.

Sutton, John (1908–1963). British actor with stage experience; in Hollywood from 1937, usually as second lead or smooth swashbuckling villain.
Bulldog Drummond Comes Back 37. The Adventures of Robin Hood 38. The Invisible Man Returns 40. A Yank in the RAF 41. *Ten Gentlemen from West Point* 42. Jane Eyre 43. Claudia and David 46. The Three Musketeers 48. The Golden Hawk 52. East of Sumatra 54. The Bat 59, many others.

Suzman, Janet (1939–). South African stage actress in Britain.

□ A Day in the Death of Joe Egg 70. *Nicholas and Alexandra* 72. The Black Windmill 74.

Svengali, the evil genius of George du Maurier's Victorian romance *Trilby,* has been seen at least five times on screen. In 1915 Wilton Lackaye and Clara Kimball Young appeared in a version under the title *Trilby.* There was a British one-reeler in 1922 in the 'Tense Moments with Great Authors' series, and in 1923 James Young directed a second Hollywood version with Arthur Edmund Carewe and Andrée Lafayette. In 1931, under the title *Svengali,* Archie Mayo directed a sound remake with John Barrymore as the hypnotist to Marian Marsh's heroine, and in 1954 Donald Wolfit and Hildegarde Neff appeared in a British version directed by Noel Langley.

Svenson, Bo (–). American leading man of the seventies.
The Great Waldo Pepper 75. Part Two Walking Tall 75.

Swain, Mack (1876–1935). American silent actor, a Mack Sennett heavy from 1914; most memorable in *The Gold Rush* 24. Last part, *Midnight Patrol* 32.

Swanson, Gloria (1897–) (Josephine Swenson). American leading lady of the silent screen who started as a Mack Sennett bathing beauty and is still making comebacks.
The Meal Ticket 15. Teddy at the Throttle 17. The Pullman Bride 17. Shifting Sands 18. Don't Change Your Husband 18. *Male and Female* 19. Why Change Your Wife? 19. *The Affairs of Anatol* 21. Adam's Rib 23. Prodigal Daughters 23. Madame Sans Gene 25. Untamed Lady 26. *Sadie Thompson* 28. *Queen Kelly* (unfinished) 28. Indiscreet 31. Perfect Understanding 33. Music in the Air 34. Father Takes a Wife 41. *Sunset Boulevard* 50. Three for Bedroom C 52. Nero's Mistress (It.) 56. Deadly Bees (TV) 73. Airport 75 74, many others.

Swanson, Maureen (1932–). British leading lady who retired to marry after a brief career.
Moulin Rouge 53. A Town Like Alice 56. The Spanish Gardener 56. Robbery under Arms 57. The Clue of the Twisted Candle 61. The Malpas Mystery 63, etc.

Swarthout, Gladys (1904–1969). American opera singer who acted in a few films.
Rose of the Rancho 35. Give Us This Night 36. Champagne Waltz 37. Romance in the Dark 38. Ambush 39, etc.

Swedish cinema was at the forefront of world production as early as 1910. Famous directors such as Victor Sjostrom and Mauritz Stiller were well known by 1912, and tended to make films of Swedish legends, which appealed by their very strangeness. *Sir Arne's Treasure* 19, *Thy Soul Shall Bear Witness* 20, *The Atonement of Gosta Berling* 24, are among the best-known titles of the Swedish silent period; but in the mid-twenties all Sweden's best talent—including the newly-discovered Greta Garbo—moved towards Hollywood and the home industry was eclipsed until the late forties saw the appearance of talents like Werner (*Midvinterblot*), Sucksdorff (*Rhythm of a City*) and Sjoberg (*Frenzy*). In the fifties the Swedish vein of romantic pessimism was developed to its ultimate in the semi-mystic but commercial films of Ingmar Bergman, who remains the most significant name in the Scandinavian cinema.

Sweet, Blanche (1895–) (Daphne Wayne). American silent heroine.
The Lonedale Operator 11. Judith of Bethulia 13. The Secret Sin 15. The Deadliest Sex 20. In the Palace of the King 23. Anna Christie 23. Tess of the D'Urbervilles 24. Bluebeard's Seven Wives 26. Singed 27. The Woman Racket 30. The Silver Horde 30, etc.

Sweet Smell of Success (US 1957). An odd, unexpected and harsh attack on Broadway columnists written in venom by Clifford Odets and Ernest Lehman, directed with tremendous polish by Alexander Mackendrick, fresh from Ealing. Not very likeable but highly cinematic, with photography by James Wong Howe, music by Elmer Bernstein, and arresting performances by Burt Lancaster and Tony Curtis.

Swenson, Inga (1932–). American actress.
□ Advise and Consent 61. The Miracle Worker 62.

Swerling, Jo (1894–) (Joseph Swerling). Russian-American writer, long in Hollywood.
Dirigible 31. Platinum Blonde 32. Man's Castle 35. Made for Each Other 38. The Westerner 40. Blood and Sand 42. Lifeboat 43. Leave Her to Heaven 46. Thunder in the East 52. King of the Roaring Twenties 61, many others.

Swift, David (1919–). American radio and TV writer-producer-director (TV series include *Mr Peepers, Grindl*). Recently turned to films.
Pollyanna 60. The Parent Trap 61. Love is a Ball 63. The Interns 63. Under the Yum Yum Tree

64. Good Neighbour Sam 64. How to Succeed in Business without Really Trying (wpd) 67, etc.

Swift, Jonathan (1667–1745). Irish satirist best known for the much-filmed *Gulliver's Travels*, which is *not* a children's book.

Swinburne, Nora (1902–). British actress on stage from 1914, screen occasionally from 1921. Alibi 30. Potiphar's Wife 31. Fanny by Gaslight 43. *Quartet* 48. The River 51. The End of the Affair 55. Conspiracy of Hearts 59. Interlude 68. Up the Chastity Belt 71, many others.

swinging London was a myth, a creation of *Time Magazine* which rebounded through the world's press and lasted for several silly seasons from 1965. It also helped British production finances by persuading American impresarios that London was where the action is, and its influence was felt in scores of trendy and increasingly boring films, including *Georgy Girl, Alfie, The Jokers, Kaleidoscope, Smashing Time, Help!, The Knack, Blow Up, Casino Royale, I'll Never Forget Whatshisname, To Sir With Love, Up the Junction, Bedazzled, Poor Cow, The Strange Affair, Salt and Pepper, Joanna, Darling* and *Otley*.

The Swiss Family Robinson. The classic children's novel by Johann Wyss was filmed in Hollywood in 1940 by Edward Ludwig, with Thomas Mitchell, Edna Best, Freddie Bartholemew and Terry Kilburn. In 1960 Ken Annakin remade it as a Walt Disney spectacular, with John Mills, Dorothy McGuire, James MacArthur and Tommy Kirk as the desert island castaways.

Swit, Loretta (–). American comic actress of the seventies, familiar as Hot Lips Houlihan from TV's M.A.S.H.
Freebie and the Bean 74. Race with the Devil 75.

Switzer, Carl ('Alfalfa') (1926–1959). American boy actor of the thirties, a graduate of 'Our Gang'; later in character roles.
General Spanky 37. The War Against Mrs Hadley 42. State of the Union 48. Track of the Cat 54. The Defiant Ones 58, many others.

Sydney, Basil (1894–1968). British actor of heavy roles, on stage from 1911.
Romance (film debut) 20. The Midshipmaid 32. The Tunnel 35. Rhodes of Africa 36. The Four Just Men 39. Ships with Wings 41. Went the Day

Well? 42. *Caesar and Cleopatra* 45. The Man Within 47. *Hamlet* 48. Treasure Island 50. Ivanhoe 52. Hell Below Zero 54. The Dam Busters 55. The Three Worlds of Gulliver 60, etc.

Sykes, Eric (1923–). British TV comedian. Invasion Quartet 61. Village of Daughters 62. Kill or Cure 63. Heavens Above 63. The Bargee 63. One-Way Pendulum 64. Those Magnificent Men in Their Flying Machines 65. Rotten to the Core 65. The Liquidator 65. The Spy with a Cold Nose 67. The Plank (& d) 67. Shalako 68. Monte Carlo or Bust 69. Rhubarb (& d) 70. Theatre of Blood 73.

Sylbert, Richard (–). American art director.
Baby Doll 56. Splendor in the Grass 61. Walk on the Wild Side 62. The Manchurian Candidate 62. How to Murder Your Wife 64. The Pawnbroker 64. Who's Afraid of Virginia Woolf? 66. The Graduate 67. Rosemary's Baby 68. Catch 22 70. Carnal Knowledge 71. The Fortune 75, etc.

Sylvester. The celebrated cartoon cat with the lisping Bronx accent, always in pursuit of Tweetie Pie but never quite managing to win, appeared from the forties to the sixties in Warner shorts, voiced by the inimitable Mel Blanc.

Sylvester, William (1922–). American leading man, in British films since 1949.
Give Us This Day 50. The Yellow Balloon 52. Albert RN 53. High Tide at Noon 57. Gorgo 59. Offbeat 60. Ring of Spies 63. Devil Doll 64. Devils of Darkness 65. The Syndicate 67. The Hand of Night 67. 2001: A Space Odyssey 68, many others.
TV series: Gemini Man 76.

Sylvie (1887–1970). French character actress. Un Carnet de Bal 37. Le Corbeau 43. Le Diable au Corps 46. Dieu a Besoin des Hommes 51. Nous Sommes Tous des Assassins 56. *The Shameless Old Lady* 64.

Syms, Sylvia (1934–). British leading lady with brief stage and TV experience.
My Teenage Daughter (film debut) 56. Ice Cold in Alex 58. Flame in the Streets 60. Victim 61. The Quare Fellow 62. The World Ten Times Over 63. East of Sudan 64. Operation Crossbow 65. The Big Job 65. Run Wild Run Free 69. Hostile Witness 70. Asylum 72. The Tamarind Seed 74, etc.

synchronization. The arranging of sound and picture to match. Only rarely is this done by shooting them simultaneously; the normal process involves re-recording and much laboratory work to give the optimum results.

Szabo, Istvan (1938–). Hungarian director. Age of Illusion 65. Father 66, etc.

Szwarc, Jeannot (–). American director, mainly on TV.
Extreme Close Up 74. Bug 75, etc.

Tafler, Sidney (1916–). British character actor on stage from 1936.
The Little Ballerina (film debut) 46. It Always Rains on Sunday 47. Passport to Pimlico 48. Mystery Junction 51. Venetian Bird 53. The Sea Shall Not Have Them 55. *Carve Her Name with Pride* 58. Sink the Bismarck 60. The Bulldog Breed 61. The Seventh Dawn 64. *The Birthday Party* 69. The Adventurers 71, many others.

take. A take is a single recording of a scene during the making of a film. Sometimes one take is enough; but directors have been known to shoot as many as fifty before they are satisfied with the results.

Talbot, Lyle (1904–) (Lisle Henderson). Square-built American leading man and sometimes heavy, busy from the early thirties.
Love is a Racket 32. Three on a Match 32. Havana Widows 33. The Dragon Murder Case 34. Red Hot Tyres 35. Trapped by Television 36. Three Legionaires 37. One Wild Night 38. Second Fiddle 39. Parole Fixer 40. Mexican Spitfire's Elephant 42. Up in Arms 44. Champagne for Caesar 50. With a Song in My Heart 52. There's No Business Like Show Business 54. The Great Man 56. Sunrise at Campobello 60, many others.

Talbot, Nita (1930–). Smart, wise-cracking American leading comedienne of the sixties.
Bundle of Joy 56. Once upon a Horse 58. Who's Got the Action? 62. Girl Happy 65. That Funny Feeling 65. *A Very Special Favour* 65. The Cool Ones 67. Buck and the Preacher 71. The Day of the Locust 75, etc.
TV series: *Hot off the Wire* 61. *Here We Go Again* 72.

A Tale of Two Cities. Apart from three very early one-reel versions, Dickens' novel of the French Revolution was filmed in 1917 with William Farnum, in 1926 (as *The Only Way*) with Martin Harvey, in 1935 with Ronald Colman and in 1958 with Dirk Bogarde.

Tales of Hoffman (GB 1951). An ambitious if rather foolhardy attempt to combine opera and ballet in a popular form. Lacking a modern story, it did not have the box-office value of *The Red Shoes*, made three years earlier by the same team, Michael Powell and Emeric Pressburger. All very Teutonic, with heavy colour, music by Offenbach, décor by Hein Heckroth, choreography by Frederick Ashton, photography by Christopher Challis; and dancing and singing by the best talent money can buy.

Tales of Manhattan (US 1942). Directed by Julien Duvivier, this string of anecdotes linked by the travels of one tail coat can be credited with starting or revivifying the short story compendium form, later developed in such movies as *Flesh and Fantasy, Quartet, Full House, The Story of Three Loves, It's a Great Country* and many others. In itself it was unremarkable apart from Charles Laughton's splendid bit of pathos as a poor conductor; the Negro sequence was incredibly 'Uncle Tom'; and what might have been the best story, starring W. C. Fields, was removed before release because the film was too long. The film's inspiration was Duvivier's own *Un Carnet de Bal*, made in 1937, which gave him his ticket to hollywood.

talkies caused the biggest revolution the film industry has known, and provoked critical resentment difficult to understand until one sees a very early talkie and realizes what a raucous and unpleasant experience it must have been until Hollywood caught up with itself. The main steps of development were as follows. In 1923 Lee de Forrest (qv) made primitive shorts. In 1926 Warners created Vitaphone, a disc process, and Fox pioneered sound on film with Movietone. Also in 1926 came *Don Juan*, the first film with synchronized music and effects. The first speaking and singing came in 1927 with Al Jolson in *The Jazz Singer*. In 1928 the first all-talking film, *Lights of New York*, set the seal of popular success on the new medium.

Talmadge, Constance (1899–1974). American silent heroine and comedienne, sister of Norma Talmadge.

Intolerance 15. Matrimaniac 16. The Honeymoon 17. Happiness à la Mode 19. Lessons in Love 21. Her Primitive Lover 22. The Goldfish 24. Her Sister from Paris 25. Venus 29, many others.

Talmadge, Natalie (1898–1969). American leading lady of a few silent comedies; retired to marry Buster Keaton. Younger sister of Norma and Constance Talmadge.

Talmadge, Norma (1893–1957). American silent heroine, sister of Constance Talmadge. Battle Cry of Peace 14. Going Straight 15. Forbidden City 18. The Sign on the Door 21. Within the Law 23. Secrets 24. The Lady 25. Camille 27. The Dove 28. Dubarry Woman of Passion (last film) 30, many others.

Talmadge, Richard (1896–) (Ricardo Metzetti). American stunt man of the twenties, who doubled for Fairbanks, Lloyd, etc., and later became a star of action films such as *The Speed King, Laughing at Danger* and *Fighting Demon*. In the thirties became a director of stunt sequences, and has recently worked on *How the West Was Won, What's New Pussycat? Hawaii* and *Casino Royale*.

Talman, William (1915–1968). American character actor usually seen as a crook or cop: for seven years was well occupied in TV's *Perry Mason* series as the D.A. who never won a case. Red Hot and Blue 49. The Armored Car Robbery 50. One Minute to Zero 52. *The Hitch Hiker* 52. City That Never Sleeps 53. This Man Is Armed 56. Two-Gun Lady 59. The Ballad of Josie 67.

Tamba, Tetsuro (c. 1929–). Japanese actor who has appeared in occidental films. Bridge to the Sun 61. The Seventh Dawn 64. You Only Live Twice 67. The Five Man Army 70.

Tamblyn, Russ (1934–). Buoyant American dancer and tumbler, in small film roles from 1949. Father of the Bride 50. Father's Little Dividend 51. *Seven Brides for Seven Brothers* 54. Hit the Deck 55. Don't Go Near the Water 56. Peyton Place 57. *Tom Thumb* 58. Cimarron 61. *West Side Story* 61. The Wonderful World of the Brothers Grimm 63. The Haunting 63. Son of a Gunfighter 65. Blood of Frankenstein 70. Win, Place or Steal 75, etc.

Tamiroff, Akim (1899–1972). Russian leading character actor, in America from 1923. Sadie McKee (film debut) 34. Lives of a Bengal

Lancer 35. Naughty Marietta 35. China Seas 36. The Story of Louis Pasteur 36. *The General Died at Dawn* 36. *The Great Gambini* 37. Spawn of the North 38. Union Pacific 39. Geronimo 40. *The Way of All Flesh* 40. The Great McGinty 40. The Corsican Brothers 41. *For Whom the Bell Tolls* 43. The Bridge of San Luis Rey 44. A Scandal in Paris 46. The Gangster 47. My Girl Tisa 48. Outpost in Morocco 50. You Know What Sailors Are (GB) 53. Confidential Report 55. The Black Sleep 56. Me and the Colonel 57. Topkapi 64. The Liquidator 65. Alphaville 65. Lieut. Robin Crusoe 66. After the Fox 66. Great Catherine 68, scores of others.

Tandy, Jessica (1909–). British-born actress wife of Hume Cronyn. The Seventh Cross 44. Dragonwyck 46. The Green Years 46. Forever Amber 48. A Woman's Vengeance 48. Rommel, Desert Fox 51. The Light in the Forest 58. Hemingway's Adventures of a Young Man 62. The Birds 63. Butley 73, etc.

Tani, Yoko (1932–). Japanese leading lady, in international films. The Wind Cannot Read 57. The Quiet American 58. Savage Innocents 59. Piccadilly Third Stop 60. Marco Polo 61. Who's Been Sleeping in My Bed? 63. Invasion 66, etc.

Tanner, Tony (1932–). British light actor and revue artiste. Strictly for the Birds 64. A Home of Your Own 65. The Pleasure Girls 65. Stop the World I Want to Get Off 66, etc.

Tapley, Colin (1911–). New Zealand character actor who has played a few stalwart types in international pictures. Search for Beauty 34. The Black Room 35. Samson and Delilah 49. Angels One Five 52. The Dam Busters 56, etc.

Taradash, Daniel (1913–). American screenwriter. Golden Boy 39. Rancho Notorious 48. *From Here to Eternity* (AA) 53. Désirée 54. Storm Centre (& d) 55. Picnic 55. Bell, Book and Candle 58. Morituri 65. Hawaii 66. Doctors' Wives 71, etc.

Target for Tonight (GB 1941). A feature-length documentary about an RAF bombing raid. Using no actors, it seemed at the time an amazing realistic achievement; but the slang and the understatement have dated it badly, and the aerial photography has since been surpassed. Produced by Ian Dalrymple, written and directed by Harry Watt, with music by Leighton Lucas.

Tarkington, Booth (1869–1946). American novelist. Films of his books include *Alice Adams, Penrod* (qv), *Monsieur Beaucaire* (qv), *The Magnificent Ambersons* (qv).

Tarkovsky, Andrei (1932–). Russian director.
Ivan's Childhood 62. *Andrei Rublev* 66. *Solaris* 71, etc.

Tarzan. The brawny jungle hero, an English milord lost in Africa as a child and grown up with the apes, was a creation of novelist Edgar Rice Burroughs (1875–1950); the first Tarzan story was published in 1914. The films quickly followed. *Tarzan of the Apes* 18 starred Elmo Lincoln with Enid Markey as Jane; so did *Romance of Tarzan* 18. *The Return of Tarzan* 20 had Gene Polar and Karla Schramm. *Son of Tarzan* 20 was a serial with Kamuela C. Searle in the title role; Tarzan was P. Dempsey Tabler. Elmo Lincoln returned in another serial, *The Adventures of Tarzan* 21, with Louise Lorraine. *Tarzan and the Golden Lion* 27 starred James Pierce and Dorothy Dunbar. Another serial, *Tarzan the Mighty* 28, had Frank Merrill and no Jane; a runner-up, *Tarzan the Tiger* 30, had the same crew. In 1932 came Johnny Weissmuller in the first of MGM's long line of Tarzan pictures: *Tarzan the Ape Man*, with Maureen O'Sullivan as Jane. There followed *Tarzan and His Mate* 34, *Tarzan Escapes* 36, *Tarzan Finds a Son* 39, *Tarzan's Secret Treasure* 41, and *Tarzan's New York Adventure* 42. Meanwhile in 1935 an independent company had made a serial starring Herman Brix which was later released as two features, *Tarzan and the Green Goddess* and *New Adventures of Tarzan*; and in 1933 producer Sol Lesser had started his Tarzan series with *Tarzan the Fearless*, starring Buster Crabbe; he followed this up with *Tarzan's Revenge* 38 starring Glenn Morris. In 1943 Lesser took over Weissmuller (but not O'Sullivan or any other Jane) for *Tarzan Triumphs*, followed by *Tarzan's Desert Mystery* 44, *Tarzan and the Amazons* (reintroducing Jane in the shape of Brenda Joyce) 45, *Tarzan and the Leopard Woman* 46, *Tarzan and the Huntress* 47, and *Tarzan and the Mermaids* 48. Then Weissmuller was replaced by Lex Barker for *Tarzan's Magic Fountain* 48, *Tarzan and the Slave Girl* 49, *Tarzan's Peril* 50, *Tarzan's Savage Fury* 51, and *Tarzan and the She-Devil* 52. Gordon Scott next undertook the chore in *Tarzan's Hidden Jungle* 55, *Tarzan and the Lost Safari* 57, *Tarzan's Fight for Life* 58,

Tarzan's Greatest Adventure 59 and *Tarzan the Magnificent* 60. MGM now remade *Tarzan the Ape Man* 60 starring Denny Miller; and, with Jock Mahoney, *Tarzan Goes to India* 62 and National General presented *Tarzan's Three Challenges* 64. The latest additions are *Tarzan and the Valley of Gold* 66, *Tarzan and the Great River* 67, and *Tarzan and the Jungle Boy* 68, all with Mike Henry. A TV series 66–67 starred Ron Ely.

Tashlin, Frank (1913–1972). American comedy writer-director, former cartoonist.
The Fuller Brush Man (w) 48. *The Paleface* (w) 48. The Good Humour Man (w) 50. Kill the Umpire (w) 51. Susan Slept Here (d) 54. Artists and Models (wd) 55. *The Girl Can't Help It* (wpd) 57. Will Success Spoil Rock Hunter? (wpd) 57. Rockabye Baby (wd) 58. Say One for Me (pd) 59. Cinderfella (wd) 60. It's Only Money (d) 63. The Man from the Diners Club (d) 64. The Alphabet Murders (d) 65. The Glass Bottom Boat (d) 66. Caprice (d) 67. The Private Navy of Sgt O'Farrell (wd) 68, etc.

Tashman, Lilyan (1899–1934). American silent screen sophisticate.
Experience 21. Manhandled 24. Don't Tell the Wife 27. New York Nights 29. Murder by the Clock 31. Scarlet Dawn 32. Frankie and Johnny 33, etc.

A Taste of Honey (GB 1961). A strange and influential little film produced and directed by Tony Richardson from a play by Shelagh Delaney, and lovingly photographed by Walter Lassally. Finding humour and compassion in the depressing background of industrial Lancashire, viewed through the eyes of a gawky adolescent schoolgirl, it paints vivid sketches of her tarty mum and the harmless homosexual who looks after her when a sailor leaves her pregnant. With the help of excellent performances from Rita Tushingham, Dora Bryan (BFA) and Murray Melvin, it succeeds in its determination to wring poetry out of squalor.

Tate, Reginald (1896–1955). British character actor, mainly on stage.
Riverside Murder 35. Dark Journey 37. Next of Kin 42. The Life and Death of Colonel Blimp 43. Uncle Silas 47. Robin Hood 52. King's Rhapsody 55, etc.

Tate, Sharon (1943–1969). American leading lady, victim of a sensational murder.
Eye of the Devil 67. The Fearless Vampire Killers 67. Valley of the Dolls 67. Wrecking Crew 69, etc.

Tati, Jacques (1908–) (Jacques Tatischeff). French pantomimist and actor who after years in the music halls and in small film roles began to write and direct his own quiet comedies which were really little more than strings of sight gags on a theme.
□ *Jour de Fête* 49. *Monsieur Hulot's Holiday* 52. Mon Oncle 58. Playtime 68. Traffic 71.

Tauber, Richard (1892–1948). Austrian operatic singer, long in Britain where he made a number of artless musical comedy films.
Blossom Time 32. Land without Music 35. Pagliacci 37. The Lisbon Story 45, etc.

Taurog, Norman (1899–). American director, former child actor, in Hollywood from 1917.
Lucky Boy 28. *Skippy* (AA) 31. Huckleberry Finn 33. We're Not Dressing 34. Mrs Wiggs of the Cabbage Patch 35. Strike Me Pink 36. *Mad about Music* 38. The Adventures of Tom Sawyer 38. Boys' Town 38. Broadway Melody of 1940 40. Young Tom Edison 40. A Yank at Eton 42. Girl Crazy 42. The Hoodlum Saint 46. The Bride Goes Wild 48. Please Believe Me 50. Room for One More 52. Living It Up 54. The Birds and the Bees 56. Bundle of Joy 57. Don't Give Up the Ship 59. Palm Springs Weekend 63. Tickle Me 65. Sergeant Deadhead 65. Speedway 67, many others.

Taylor, Alma (1895–1974). British actress of the silent screen.

Taylor, Deems (1886–1966). American journalist and musician whose chief connection with films was to act as narrator for *Fantasia* 40 and to help write *A Pictorial History of the Movies* 48.

Taylor, Don (1920–). American light leading man, with stage experience.
Naked City 48. For the Love of Mary 48. Ambush 49. Father of the Bride 50. Submarine Command 51. The Blue Veil 51. Stalag 17 53. Men of Sherwood Forest 54. I'll Cry Tomorrow 57, etc.
AS DIRECTOR: The Savage Guns 62. Ride the Wild Surf 64. Jack of Diamonds 67. The Five Man Army 70. Escape from the Planet of the Apes 71. Tom Sawyer 73. Echoes of a Summer 75. The Great Scout and Cathouse Thursday 76, etc.

Taylor, Elizabeth (1932–). British-born leading lady with a well-publicized private life. Was evacuated to Hollywood during World War II and began as a child star. Scored eight husbands so far, including several helpings of Richard Burton.
□ There's One Born Every Minute 42. Lassie Come Home 43. Jane Eyre 43. The White Cliffs of Dover 44. *National Velvet* 44. Courage of Lassie 45. Cynthia 47. Life with Father 47. A Date with Judy 48. Julia Misbehaves 48. *Little Women* 49. Conspirator 49. The Big Hangover 49. *Father of the Bride* 50. Father's Little Dividend 51. Quo Vadis 51. Love is Better Than Ever 51. *A Place in the Sun* 51. The Light Fantastic 51. Ivanhoe 52. The Girl Who Had Everything 53. Rhapsody 54. Elephant Walk 54. Beau Brummell 54. The Last Time I Saw Paris 55. *Giant* 56. *Raintree County* 57. *Cat on a Hot Tin Roof* 58. *Suddenly Last Summer* 59. *Butterfield 8* (AA) 60. Scent of Mystery 60. *Cleopatra* 62. The VIPs 63. The Sandpiper 65. *Who's Afraid of Virginia Woolf?* (AA) 66. The Taming of the Shrew 67. Doctor Faustus 67. The Comedians 67. Reflections in a Golden Eye 67. Boom 68. Secret Ceremony 68. The Only Game in Town 69. Under Milk Wood 71. Zee and Co 71. Hammersmith is Out 72. Night Watch 73. Ash Wednesday 73. The Driver's Seat 75. The Blue Bird 76.

Taylor, Estelle (1899–1958) (Estelle Boylan). American stage actress who made some silent films.
While New York Sleeps 22. The Ten Commandments 23. Don Juan 26. The Whip Woman 27. When East is East 28, etc.

Taylor, Gilbert (1914–). British cinematographer, in films since 1929.
The Guinea Pig 48. Seven Days to Noon 50. The Yellow Balloon 52. It's Great To Be Young 55. The Good Companions 57. Ice Cold in Alex 58. The Rebel 60. Dr Strangelove 63. Repulsion 65. The Bedford Incident 65. Before Winter Comes 69. Macbeth 71. The Omen 76, etc.

Taylor, Kent (1907–) (Louis Weiss). Suave American leading man of second features since the early thirties.
Two Kinds of Women 32. I'm No Angel 33. Double Door 34. Two Fisted 35. The Accusing Finger 36. The Jury's Secret 37. I Take this Woman 40. Frisco Lil 42. Bombers Moon 43. The Daltons Ride Again 45. The Crimson Key 47. Payment on Demand 51. Playgirl 54. Slightly Scarlet 56. Ghost Town 56. Harbour Lights 64. The Day Mars Invaded Earth 64. Smashing the Crime Syndicate 73, etc.
TV series: *Boston Blackie* 51–52.

Taylor, Laurette (1884–1946) (Laurette Cooney). American stage leading lady who filmed her great success *Peg O'My Heart* 22 and stayed in Hollywood for a few more silent films: *Happiness, One Night in Rome*, etc.

Taylor, Robert (1911–1969) (Spangler Arlington Brugh). Durable American leading man signed by MGM while still a medical student. His boyish good looks turned rather set and grim in middle age, but he remained a star.
□ Handy Andy 34. There's Always Tomorrow 36. Wicked Woman 34. Society Doctor 34. West Point of the Air 35. Times Square Lady 35. Murder in the Fleet 35. Broadway Melody of 1936 36. *Magnificent Obsession* 35. Small Town Girl 36. Private Number 36. His Brother's Wife 36. The Gorgeous Hussy 36. *Camille* 36. Personal Property 37. This is My Affair 37. Broadway Melody of 1938 38. *A Yank at Oxford* 38. Three Comrades 38. The Crowd Roars 38. Stand Up and Fight 39. Lucky Night 39. Lady of the Tropics 39. Remember 39. *Waterloo Bridge* 40. Escape 40. Flight Command 40. Billy the Kid 41. When Ladies Meet 41. Johnny Eager 42. Her Cardboard Lover 42. Stand By for Action 43. *Bataan* 43. Song of Russia 44. Undercurrent 46. High Wall 47. The Bribe 49. Ambush 49. Devil's Doorway 50. Conspirator 50. *Quo Vadis* 51. Westward the Women 51. *Ivanhoe* 52. Above and Beyond 52. Ride Vaquero 53. All the Brothers were Valiant 53. *Knights of the Round Table* 53. Valley of the Kings 54. Rogue Cop 54. Many Rivers to Cross 55. Quentin Durward 55. The Last Hunt 56. D Day Sixth of June 56. The Power and the Prize 56. Tip on a Dead Jockey 57. Saddle the Wind 58. The Law and Jake Wade 58. Party Girl 58. The Hangman 59. The House of the Seven Hawks 59. Killers of Kilimanjaro 60. The Miracle of the White Stallions 61. Cattle King 63. A House is Not a Home 64. The Night Walker 65. Savage Pampas 66. The Return of the Gunfighter 66. Johnny Tiger 66. Where Angels Go Trouble Follows 68. The Day the Hot Line Got Hot 68. Devil May Care 68. The Glass Sphinx 68.
TV series: *The Detectives* 59–61.

Taylor, Rod (1929–) (Robert Taylor). Australian-born, Hollywood-based leading man with stage experience.
King of the Coral Sea 54. Long John Silver 55. The Catered Affair 56. Giant 56. Raintree County 57. Separate Tables 58. *The Time Machine* 60. *The Birds* 63. *The VIPs* 63. Sunday in New York 63. Fate Is the Hunter 64. *Thirty-Six Hours* 64. Young Cassidy 65. Do Not Disturb 65. The Liquidator 65. The Glass Bottom Boat 66. Hotel 67. Dark of the Sun 67. Chuka 67. Nobody Runs Forever 68. Hell is for Heroes 69. The Man Who Had Power Over

Women 70. Darker than Amber 70. The Train Robbers 72. Family Flight (TV) 72. Trader Horn 73. Deadly Trackers 73. Shamus (TV) 73. The Heroes 75, etc.
TV series: Hong Kong 60. Bearcats 71.

Taylor, Sam (1895–1958). American screenwriter of the twenties: *The Freshman, Exit Smiling*, etc. Remembered chiefly for the credit line to the 1928 version of *The Taming of the Shrew*: 'By William Shakespeare, with additional dialogue by Sam Taylor.'

Taylor-Young, Leigh (1944–). American leading lady of the early seventies.
□ I Love You Alice B. Toklas 68. The Big Bounce 68. The Adventurers 69. The Buttercup Chain 70. The Horsemen 71. The Gang That Couldn't Shoot Straight 72. Soylent Green 73.

Tazieff, Haroun (1914–). French explorer-photographer, best known for *Rendezvous du Diable* (*Volcano*) 58, *The Forbidden Volcano* 67.

teachers have been notably played by Robert Donat in *Goodbye Mr Chips*; Jennifer Jones in *Good Morning Miss Dove*; Greer Garson in *Her Twelve Men*; Michael Redgrave in *The Browning Version*; Aline MacMahon in *Back Door to Heaven*; Claudette Colbert in *Remember the Day*; Bette Davis in *The Corn is Green*; Jack Hawkins in *Mandy*; Judy Garland in *A Child is Waiting*; Anne Bancroft in *The Miracle Worker*; Shirley Maclaine in *Spinster*; Glenn Ford in *The Blackboard Jungle*; Sidney Poitier in *To Sir With Love*; Sandy Dennis in *Up the Down Staircase*; Dorothy Dandridge in *Bright Road*; Max Bygraves in *Spare the Rod*; Otto Kruger in *The Housemaster*; Cecil Trouncer in *The Guinea Pig*; Maggie Smith in *The Prime of Miss Jean Brodie*; Joanne Woodward in *Rachel, Rachel*; Robert Mitchum in *Ryan's Daughter*; Laurence Olivier in *Term of Trial*; Richard Todd in *The Love-Ins*; James Whitmore in *The Harrad Experiment*.
    Comic teachers were to the fore in *Boys Will Be Boys* (Will Hay, the best of them all); the *St Trinian's* films; *Carry On Teacher*; *Old Mother Riley Headmistress*; *Bottoms Up* (Jimmy Edwards); *Fun at St Fanny's* (Fred Emney); *The Happiest Days of Your Lives*; *Please Sir*; and *Vice Versa* (James Robertson Justice). See also: *Schools*.

Teal, Ray (1902–). American character actor often seen as sheriff, good or bad. In films from 1938 after stage experience.
The Cherokee Strip 40. A Wing and a Prayer 44. Captain Kidd 45. Joan of Arc 48. The Men 50.

Ace in the Hole 51. The Lion and the Horse 53. Montana Belle 53. Hangman's Knot 54. Ambush at Tomahawk Gap 54. Run for Cover 55. The Indian Fighter 55. Saddle the Wind 57. One-Eyed Jacks 61. Cattle King 63. Taggart 64. The Liberation of L. B. Jones 71, many others.

Teams: see *Romantic Teams*.

Tearle, Conway (1878–1938) (Frederick Levy). American leading actor of silent days; half-brother of Godfrey Tearle.
Stella Maris 18. The Virtuous Vamp 20. Woman of Bronze 23. Bella Donna 25. Gold Diggers of Broadway 29. Vanity Fair 32. Should Ladies Behave? 34. Klondike Annie 36. Romeo and Juliet 36, etc.

Tearle, Sir Godfrey (1884–1953). Distinguished British stage actor, on stage from 1893; occasional films from 1906, when he played Romeo in a one-reeler.
If Youth But Knew 30. The Thirty-Nine Steps 35. One of Our Aircraft is Missing 42. The Rake's Progress 45. The Beginning of the End 47. Private Angelo 48. *The Tiffield Thunderbolt* 53, etc.

Teasdale, Verree (1904–). American general purpose actress, mostly in comedy.
Syncopation 29. Fashions of 1934 34. The Milky Way 36. Topper Takes a Trip 38. Turnabout 40, many others.

teaser. A poster, trailer, or other piece of publicity which whets the appetite for a forthcoming film without giving full details about it, sometimes not even the title. The term was also applied to early pornographic films 1900–05, e.g. *Lovers Interrupted, Making Love in a Hammock,* etc.

Technicolor. Colour process which existed from 1915, though the various improvements virtually amounted to completely new versions. The first had separate red and green films projected simultaneously; the second combined them on panchromatic film; the third used dye transfer. In 1932 came the three-strip process which gave the rich full tones familiar to filmgoers of the forties, but a link with Eastmancolor in 1951 made it difficult to pick out Technicolor from any other process.

Technirama. A process similar to Vistavision for producing extreme clarity of image.

Techniscope. A process saving money by printing two wide images one below the other on the old 4 × 3 frame, then blowing them up to CinemaScope size; the results were awful.

telecine: the machine which enables film to be 'projected' electronically on television. Theoretically it is capable of panning from side to side across the CinemaScope image, picking out the optimum sections of each scene, but the results are usually dire unless the process has been carefully rehearsed.

the telephone has been a very useful instrument to film scenarists. The saga of its invention was told in *The Story of Alexander Graham Bell.* It brought sinister, menacing and threatening calls in *Sorry—Wrong Number, The Small World of Sammy Lee, Midnight Lace, I Saw What You Did, Experiment in Terror, Sudden Fear, Strangers on a Train,* and *Dirty Harry. Chicago Calling* and *The Slender Thread* were among the films based entirely on someone trying to contact another character by telephone. *Bells Are Ringing, The Glenn Miller Story* and *Bye Bye Birdie* had musical numbers based on telephones. Shelly Berman, Jeanne de Casalis and Billy de Wolfe are among the revue artists famous for telephone sketches. Single phone calls were of high dramatic significance in *The Spiral Staircase, Little Caesar, Fail Safe, Dr Strangelove, Murder Inc., Dial M for Murder, The Silencers, 2001: A Space Odyssey, No Way to Treat a Lady, Call Northside 777,* and *Phone Call from a Stranger,* while the phone had a special inference in several call girl pictures including *Butterfield 8. Our Man Flint, Indiscreet, Strange Bedfellows, Come Blow Your Horn* and *It's a Mad Mad Mad Mad World* are among the many films deriving comedy from the telephone ... while the most chilling moment in many a thriller has been the discovery that the phone is disconnected. In *The President's Analyst* the telephone company turned out to be the supreme enemy of civilization.

telephoto lens. One which brings far-off objects apparently very close, but has the disadvantage of distorting and flattening perspective.

television, arch-enemy of the film-makers, was used during the fifties as an object of derision (*The Tiffield Thunderbolt, Happy Anniversary, No Down Payment, Meet Mr Lucifer*), or totally ignored. Yet it had featured in films even before World War II: *International House, Television Spy, Murder by Television, Raffles,* and a host of science fiction serials. More recently, television studios have provided a useful background for comedy (*You Must Be Joking, A Hard Day's Night*), for thrillers (*The Glass Web, Arabesque, The Barefoot Executive*) and for melodramas (*Seven Days in May, The Third Secret, The Love Machine*). The only serious movie study of the effects of television is *A Face in the Crowd*; and the funniest scenes about television programmes are probably those in *The Apartment*. Closed circuit TV is extensively used in *The Forbin Project, The Andromeda Strain, Loving* and *The Anderson Tapes*. In *THX 1138* television is used as a mass opiate for the workers of the subterranean world of the future.

television movies became prevalent in the late sixties. For four or five years mediocre movies had failed to get theatrical release and were seen first on television; from this it was a short step to making feature films specifically for television exposure. Aaron Spelling and Universal were the main providers; costs were kept low by assembly line methods, and it soon became just like the old days at the big studios, with stars making fast appearances in superficially glossy vehicles tailored to a specific time requirement. The quality obtained was roughly that of a Universal co-feature of the fifties. Middle-aged or elderly stars who still meant something to the home viewing circle were coaxed back to the studios: Barbara Stanwyck, Susan Hayward, Ray Milland, Bette Davis, Shelley Winters, Broderick Crawford, Myrna Loy, Milton Berle and their peers all starred again in the new forms, some in two-hour slots (97 minutes actual) but most successfully in 90-minute slots (73 minutes actual). By 1972 such films were appearing at the rate of two or three a week, more if one includes long-form series such as *Mystery Movie*, which gave new life to George Peppard, Rock Hudson, Richard Boone, Peter Falk and others. Crime was the most popular element of these films, with a strong flavouring of the supernatural, an occasional western or sob story, and a modicum of comedy. Art was not sought after, but as the touch became more assured, a few films received crical acclaim, notably *Brian's Song, Short Walk to Daylight, Duel*, and *That Certain Summer*. One such film, *My Sweet Charlie*, was sent on theatrical release after its TV exposure, but the experiment failed. In Britain, several of the films went out on theatrical release before TV exposure, and one of them, *Duel*, received rave reviews. By the mid-seventies the trend in TV movies had turned to drama documentaries (*Eleanor and Franklin. Fear On Trial*) and to character drama, with an unfortunate stress on heroes and heroines dying of leukemia, tumours and similar afflictions. Then the success of two serialized novels (*Rich Man, Poor Man* and

Roots) started a stampede to climb on this new bandwagon.

television series based on motion picture originals almost outnumber the other kind. They include *The Thin Man, The Whistler, King's Row, Casablanca, My Friend Flicka, How to Marry a Millionaire, Margie, The Roaring Twenties, I Remember Mama, Blondie, Claudia, Jungle Jim, Hawkeye, The Invisible Man, Hudson's Bay, The Asphalt Jungle, Mr Smith Goes to Washington, Father of the Bride, Life with Father, National Velvet, Bus Stop, No Time for Sergeants, Going My Way, The Greatest Show on Earth, Les Girls, Peyton Place, The Naked City, Rin Tin Tin, Topper, The Virginian, Hopalong Cassidy, The Munsters* (indirectly), *The Wackiest Ship in the Army, Mr Roberts, Gidget, Please Don't Eat the Daisies, Twelve O'Clock High, Dr Kildare, The Farmer's Daughter, The Long Hot Summer, Tarzan, The Rounders, The Saint, Gideon's Way, The Man Who Never Was, Batman, Mr Deeds Goes to Town, The Courtship of Eddie's Father, The Odd Couple, Barefoot in the Park, Anna and the King, Perry Mason, M.A.S.H., Shane, Lassie, Bob and Carol and Ted and Alice, Shaft, Adam's Rib, How the West Was Won, Planet of the Apes, Alice Doesn't Live Here Any More.*

Tellegen, Lou (1881–1934). Dutch matinée idol who made many silent films in Hollywood. Autobiography 1931: *Women Have Been Kind*. Queen Elizabeth 12. The Explorer 15. The World and Its Women 19. Single Wives 23. The Redeeming Sin 25, etc.

Tempest, Dame Marie (1864–1942) (Marie Susan Etherington). British stage actress whose very rare films included *Moonlight Sonata* 37, *Yellow Sands* 38.

Temple, Shirley (1928–). American child star of the thirties, performing in short films at three; a genuine prodigy.
☐ The Red-Haired Alibi 32. To the Last Man 33. Out All Night 33. Carolina 34. Mandalay 34. *Stand Up and Cheer* 34. Now I'll Tell 34. Change of Heart 34. *Little Miss Marker* (her first star vehicle) 34. Baby Take a Bow 34. Now and Forever 34. Bright Eyes 34. The Little Colonel 35. Our Little Girl 35. *Curly Top* 35. The Littlest Rebel 35. Captain January 36. Poor Little Rich Girl 36. *Dimples* 36. Stowaway 36. *Wee Willie Winkie* 37. *Heidi* 37. Rebecca of Sunnybrook Farm 38. Little Miss Broadway 38. Just around the Corner 38. *The Little Princess* 39. Susannah of the Mounties 39. The Blue Bird 40. Young People 40. Kathleen 41. Miss Annie

Rooney 42. Since You Went Away 44. I'll Be Seeing You 44. Kiss and Tell 45. Honeymoon 47. The Bachelor and the Bobbysoxer 47. That Hagen Girl 47. Fort Apache 48. Mr Belvedere Goes to College 49. Adventure in Baltimore 49. The Story of Seabiscuit 49. A Kiss for Corliss 49.

Later appeared on TV in *Shirley Temple Storybook*, and in the sixties went into local California politics. Won special Academy Award 1934 'in grateful recognition of her outstanding contribution to screen entertainment'.

The Ten Commandments. Cecil B. de Mille made two films under this title. The 1923 version spent only half its length on the biblical story, paralleling this with a modern tale about what happens when the moral laws are broken nowadays. It starred Richard Dix, Rod la Rocque and Estelle Taylor. The 1956 version spent nearly four hours on the Bible story alone, and with less cinematic flair than the silent picture. Charlton Heston was Moses and Yul Brynner Pharaoh.

tennis has accounted for some memorable scenes in the cinema, among them the suspenseful match in *Strangers on a Train* and the hilarious one in *Monsieur Hulot's Holiday*. Professional tennis was the subject of *Hard Fast and Beautiful*. Nor should one forget the championship between Tom and Jerry in *Tennis Chumps*, or the weird game with no ball in *Blow Up*. Other tennis sequences figured in *The System, Nobody Runs Forever* and *Come to the Stable*.

Terhune, Max (1890–1973). American small-time western star, one of the Three Mesquiteers in 30s second features; also appeared in the Range Busters series.

La Terra Trema (Italy 1948). A famous dramatic film written and directed by Luchino Visconti and photographed by G. R. Aldo, about a family of poor Sicilian fishermen and their struggle against exploitation.

Terriss, Ellaline (1871–1971). British stage actress, widow of Sir Seymour Hicks; in a few films.
Blighty 27. Glamour 31. The Iron Duke 35. The Four Just Men 39, etc.

Terry, Alice (1899–) (Alice Taafe). American leading lady of the silent screen.
Not My Sister 16. The Four Horsemen of the Apocalypse 21. The Prisoner of Zenda 23. Mare Nostrum 27. The Garden of Allah 28, etc.

Terry, Don (1902–) (Donald Locher). American hero of serials and second features in the thirties.
Me Gangster 28. The Valiant 29. Whistlin' Dan 32. Paid to Dance 37. Who Killed Gail Preston? 38 The Secret of Treasure Island (serial) 38. Don Winslow of the Navy (serial) 41. Drums of the Congo 42. White Savage 43. Top Sergeant 43. Don Winslow of the Coastguard (serial) 43, etc.

Terry, Paul (1887–1971). American animator, the creator of 'Terry-toons' (starring Mighty Mouse, Heckle and Jeckle, etc.) which filled Fox supporting programmes for over thirty years.

Terry, Philip (1909–). American leading man of the forties, mainly in second features.
The Parson of Panamint 41. The Monster and the Girl 41. Bataan 43. Music in Manhattan 44. Pan-Americana 45. *The Lost Weekend* 45. Seven Keys to Baldpate 47. Born to Kill 47, etc.

Terry-Thomas (1911–) (Thomas Terry Hoar-Stevens). British comedian with inimitable gap-toothed manner; has recently become Hollywood's favourite idea of the English silly ass. Also on stage and TV.
Private's Progress 56. Blue Murder at St Trinian's 57. The Naked Truth 58. Tom Thumb 58. *Carleton Browne of the FO* 58. *I'm All Right, Jack* 59. School for Scoundrels 60. His and Hers 61. A Matter of Who 62. Bachelor Flat 62. The Wonderful World of the Brothers Grimm 63. Kill or Cure 63. It's a Mad Mad Mad Mad World 63. The Mouse on the Moon 63. *Those Magnificent Men in Their Flying Machines* 65. *How to Murder Your Wife* 65. You Must be Joking 65. Munster Go Home 66. Kiss the Girls and Make Them Die 66. Rocket to the Moon 67. The Perils of Pauline 67. Don't Look Now 68. Where Were You When the Lights Went Out? 68. 2000 Years Later 69. Monte Carlo or Bust 69. The Abominable Dr Phibes 71. Vault of Horror 73. Spanish Fly 76. The Last Remake of Beau Geste 77, etc.

Terzieff, Laurent (1935–). French leading man.
Les Tricheurs 58. Le Bois des Amants 59. La Notte Brava 60. Kapo 60. Thou Shalt Not Kill 61. The Seven Deadly Sins 62. Ballade pour un Voyou 64. Le Triangle 65. Le Voyage du Père 66. Two Weeks in September 67. The Milky Way 68. Medea 69, etc.

Tester, Desmond (1919–). British boy actor of the thirties; went to Australia.
Midshipman Easy 35. Tudor Rose 36. Sabotage 37. The Drum 38. The Stars Look Down 39. The

Turners of Prospect Road 47. Barry Mackenzie Holds His Own 74, etc.

Tetzel, Joan (1924–). American leading actress with stage experience, married to Oscar Homolka.
Duel in the Sun 46. The Paradine Case 47. The File on Thelma Jordon 50. Joy in the Morning 65, etc.

Tetzlaff, Ted (1903–). American director, formerly cinematographer.
World Première 41. *Riff Raff* 46. *The Window* 48. Johnny Allegro 48. The White Tower 50. The Treasure of Lost Canyon 52. Time Bomb 53. Son of Sinbad 55. The Young Land 57, etc.

Tewksbury, Peter (1924–). American director, from TV (*Father Knows Best*, *My Three Sons*, etc.).
□ *Sunday in New York* 64. Emil and the Detectives 65. Doctor You've Got to be Kidding 67. Stay Away Joe 68. The Trouble with Girls 69.

Thackery, Bud (1903–). American cinematographer, especially for Republic, where he photographed innumerable westerns and serials. Moved into TV. Recently: *Coogan's Bluff* 68.

Thalberg, Irving (1899–1936). American producer, MGM's boy wonder of the early thirties, responsible for the literary flavour of films like *The Barretts of Wimpole Street* 34, *Mutiny on the Bounty* 35, *Romeo and Juliet* 36; also for hiring the Marx Brothers. A biography by Bob Thomas, *Thalberg*, was published in 1969. *Mayer and Thalberg* by Samuel Marx followed in 1976. Thalberg was played by Robert Evans in *Man of a Thousand Faces*.

Thank Your Lucky Stars (US 1943). A typical example of the all-star musicals mounted by the big Hollywood studios during World War II—and the best of them. The idea was to gather together all the stars on the payroll doing sketches or numbers joined by a thin story line and ending in a patriotic morale-boost for the boys overseas. In the same year MGM did *Thousands Cheer* and Paramount *Star-Spangled Rhythm*; this Warner job has better songs, a more amusing story, and the bright idea of making most of the stars do things one wouldn't expect from them. Eddie Cantor, Edward Everett Horton and S. Z. Sakall did the linking.

That Hamilton Woman (US 1942). A rather stiff saga of Nelson's famous love affair. This famous film paired Laurence Olivier and Vivien Leigh at their peak, and had the distinction of being Winston Churchill's favourite film. Alexander Korda, directing it in Hollywood, managed to turn it into anti-invasion propaganda.

Thatcher, Torin (1905–). Tough-looking British character actor, on stage from 1923; latterly on stage again after some years in Hollywood.
General John Regan (film debut) 34. Major Barbara 40. The Captive Heart 45. Great Expectations 46. The Crimson Pirate 52. The Robe 53. Love is a Many-Splendored Thing 55. Witness for the Prosecution 57. The Canadians 60. Jack the Gaint Killer 62. The Sandpiper 65. Hawaii 66. The King's Pirate 67, many others.

Thaxter, Phyllis (1921–). American leading lady of the forties, recently back in character roles.
Thirty Seconds Over Tokyo (debut) 44. Weekend at the Waldorf 45. Bewitched 45. Tenth Avenue Angel 47. Blood on the Moon 48. Come Fill the Cup 51. Springfield Rifle 53. Women's Prison 54. The World of Henry Orient 64. The Longest Night (TV) 72, etc.

theatres have provided an effective setting for many films apart from the countless putting-on-a-show musicals. Films concerned exclusively with matters theatrical include *The Royal Family of Broadway, Twentieth Century, The Great Profile, The Country Girl, Stage Door, Morning Glory, Queen of Hearts, Heller in Pink Tights, Take the Stage, To Be or Not To Be, Main Street to Broadway, Les Enfants du Paradis, Prince of Players, The Velvet Touch, All About Eve, Curtain Up, Kiss Me Kate, The Producers, The Boyfriend* and *Variety Jubilee*, while a theatre was also the principal setting for *Those Were the Days, Henry V, Occupe-Toi d'Amélie, The Lost People, The High Terrace, Four Hours to Kill, The Phantom of the Opera* and *The Climax.* Thrillers with climaxes in a theatre include *The Thirty-Nine Steps, Torn Curtain, Charlie Chan at the Opera, Cover Girl Killer, The Westerner, Stage Fright, Charade, Scaramouche, The Deadly Affair, No Way to Treat a Lady* and *King Kong;* comedies include *A Night at the Opera, A Haunting We Will Go, Knock On Wood, The Intelligence Men, Trouble in Paradise, The Secret of My Success, My Learned Friend* and *Meet Mr Lucifer.* Less frequent are uses of the theatre as a setting for romance, but it served this purpose in *All This and Heaven Too, The Lady with a Little Dog,* and *Letter from an Unknown Woman*. The scariest theatre was *Theatre of Death*, with Vincent Price as an actor murdering all the critics who had given him bad notices.

These Three (US 1936). This was a disguised version, directed by William Wyler, of Lillian Hellman's play *The Children's Hour* about a lesbian relationship between two schoolmistresses and the scandal caused by a malicious girl. The affair had to be changed to a more normal one. In 1962 Wyler had another go, censorship being more relaxed, and filmed the original more or less intact, with Audrey Hepburn and Shirley Maclaine.

Thesiger, Ernest (1879–1961). Witty, skeletal-looking British character actor, on stage from 1909.
West End Wives 29. *The Old Dark House* 32. The Ghoul 33. Heart Song 34. *The Bride of Frankenstein* 35. The Man Who could Work Miracles 36. *They Drive By Night* 38. Henry V 44. Caesar and Cleopatra 45. A Place of One's Own 46. The Ghosts of Berkeley Square 47. Quartet 48. Laughter in Paradise 51. *The Man in the White Suit* 52. *Father Brown* 54. Make Me an Offer 55. The Battle of the Sexes 59. The Roman Spring of Mrs Stone 61, many others.

They Won't Forget (US 1937). Among the first of Hollywood's anti-lynching melodramas, this was a stark and shattering affair to come from Warners in the escapist years. Convincingly set in the deep south, diligently directed by Mervyn le Roy, and not shirking a tragic ending, it was somewhat marred by the miscasting of Claude Rains as a southern senator. Notable for the debut of sweater girl Lana Turner as the murder victim.

The Thief of Baghdad. This Arabian Nights tale was superbly filmed with Douglas Fairbanks in 1924 (US); again in 1940 (GB/US) with Sabu and some remarkable trick photography, directed by Michael Powell, Tim Whelan and Ludwig Berger; and in 1961 (Italy) with Steve Reeves and a much altered plot.

Thiele, William (1890–1975). German director who went to Hollywood in the thirties but found little work.
His Late Excellency 29. Liebeswalzer 31. *Drei von der Tankstelle* 31. Le Bal 32. The Jungle Princess 36. London by Night 37. Bridal Suite 39. Tarzan Triumphs 43. Tarzan's Desert Mystery 43. The Madonna's Secret 46, etc.

Thiess, Ursula (1929–). German leading lady, in a few American films.
Monsoon 52. The Iron Glove 54. Bengal Brigade 55. The Americano 55, etc.

Thimig, Helene (1889–1974). German character actress, widow of Max Reinhardt, in a few American films.
None But the Lonely Heart 44. Cloak and Dagger 46. The Locket 47, etc.

The Thin Man. In Dashiell Hammett's crime novel of the twenties, the thin man is the murderer's first victim. Oddly enough the tag stuck to William Powell (not all that thin) who played Nick Charles the detective, and he starred in five sequels: *After the Thin Man* 37, *Another Thin Man* 38, *Shadow of the Thin Man* 42, *The Thin Man Goes Home* 44, *Song of the Thin Man* 46. (There was also, later, a TV series with Peter Lawford and Phyllis Kirk.) Myrna Loy played Nora Charles in all the features, and it was said that her domestic scenes with Powell in the original film marked the first time a sophisticated, affectionate marriage had been realistically portrayed on the screen.

The Thing from Another World (US 1952). Interesting as one of the first films to combine the old horror with the new science fiction, this was a competent job but disappointingly thin and tame considering its credits. Written by Charles Lederer and photographed by Russell Harlan, it was produced by Howard Hawks (and some say also directed by him despite the credit to Christian Nyby; there are also rumours that Orson Welles had a hand). The gripping early scenes about a USAF base at the North Pole threatened by a temporarily frozen 'intellectual carrot' from a flying saucer weakened when the visitor thawed out and proved to be James Arness in a metallic suit.

Things to Come (GB 1936). This film from H. G. Wells' prophetic tract, though naïve in some of its dialogue scenes, provided not only a tolerably accurate forecast of World War II and the atomic bomb but splendid imaginative spectacle and a musical theme by Sir Arthur Bliss which remains fresh and stirring. William Cameron Menzies directed, and among a cast who refused to be dwarfed were Raymond Massey and Ralph Richardson.

Thinnes, Roy (1938–). Stocky American leading man of some successful television series: *The Long Hot Summer* 64. *The Invaders* 66–67. The Psychiatrist 70.
Journey to the Far Side of the Sun 69. Charlie

One Eye 72. The Horror at 37,000 Feet (TV) 73. The Norliss Tapes (TV) 73. Airport 75 74. The Hindenberg 75, etc.

Thirard, Armand (1899–). French cinematographer.
Remorques 41. Quai des Orfèvres 47. Manon 49. The Wages of Fear 52. Act of Love 54. Les Diaboliques 54. And God Created Woman 56. The Truth 60, etc.

The Third Man (GB 1949). A lucky combination of talents gave this romantic thriller set in war-torn Vienna an almost poetic quality and an excitement which have kept it vivid. The photogenic ruins provided a suitable background for all four star actors, Joseph Cotten, Valli, Trevor Howard and Orson Welles; Graham Greene wrote a bitter, well-timed script; Robert Krasker photographed lovingly; and Carol Reed directed every scene with the surest of touches except the last one, which was perhaps misjudged. And then there was that insistent zither music by Anton Karas. ... BFA best British film. (A sixties TV series with Michael Rennie borrowed the title but little else.)

35mm. The standard commercial film gauge or width.

The Thirty-Nine Steps. Neither film version has borne much resemblance to John Buchan's lively spy yarn apart from the hero's initial predicament and the Scottish setting for the chase. Hitchcock, however (GB 1935), working from Charles Bennett's pacy script, scattered touches of macabre comedy and romantic banter which hit just the right note; Ralph Thomas (GB 1959) reworked the same ideas stolidly and without flair. And Kenneth More, Taina Elg and Barry Jones were somehow no match for Robert Donat, Madeleine Carroll and Godfrey Tearle.

This Gun for Hire (US 1942). This was not only a moderately intelligent though considerably reshaped version of Graham Greene's A Gun for Sale: it was also notable for giving Alan Ladd his first starring role as the professional killer, a role which catapulted him into the front rank of box office attractions. Frank Tuttle directed. The story was remade in 1956 as Short Cut to Hell, directed by James Cagney: Robert Ivers played the gunman, but both he and the movie passed without comment.

This Modern Age. A series of current affairs two-reelers sponsored in 1946 by Rank as the British answer to The March of Time. Although decently produced by Sergei Nolbandov, the monthly issues were not a popular addition to already overlong programmes, and the attempt was given up in 1949.

Thomas, Danny (1914–) (Amos Jacobs). American night club comedian and star of his own seven-year TV series.
The Unfinished Dance 47. Big City 48. Call Me Mister 51. I'll See You in My Dreams 52. The Jazz Singer 53.

Thomas, Dylan (1914–1953). Welsh poet whose drama Under Milk Wood has been filmed. He also worked on the scripts of a number of British films in the late forties, including The Three Weird Sisters.

Thomas, Gerald (1920–). British director, former editor, in films from 1946.
Time Lock 57. Vicious Circle 57. The Duke Wore Jeans 58. Carry On Sergeant 58 (and all the subsequent 'Carry Ons'). Watch Your Stern 60. Twice Round the Daffodils 62. The Big Job 65. Don't Lose Your Head 66. Follow that Camel 67. Carry On Living 70. Carry On Girls 73. Carry On England 76, etc.

Thomas, Jameson (1892–1939). British actor who usually played 'the other man'. Went to Hollywood in the early thirties but did not command leading roles.
Blighty 27. A Daughter of Love 28. Piccadilly 29. High Treason 30. Hate Ship 30. Elstree Calling 30. The Phantom President 32. It Happened One Night 34. Lives of a Bengal Lancer 35. Mr Deeds Goes to Town 36. Death Goes North 38, etc.

Thomas, Lowell (1892–). American broadcaster and lecturer who partly controlled Cinerama and appeared as travelling commentator in some of its episodes: Search for Paradise 58, etc.

Thomas, Olive (1898–1920) (Olive Elaine Duffy). American 'Ziegfeld girl' who played a few comedy roles in films.
Beatrice Fairfax 16. Limousine Life 18. The Follies Girl 19. The Glorious Lady 19. Footlights and Shadows 20, etc.

Thomas, Ralph (1915–). British director, former trailer maker, who with producer Betty Box has tackled some ambitious subjects in a rather stolid manner.
Helter Skelter 48. Traveller's Joy 49. The Clouded Yellow 51. Appointment with Venus 51. Venetian Bird 53. Doctor in the House 54. Above Us the Waves 55. The Iron Petticoat 56.

Campbell's Kingdom 57. A Tale of Two Cities 57. The Wind Cannot Read 58. The Thirty-Nine Steps 59. No Love for Johnnie 61. The Wild and the Willing 62. Hot Enough for June 64. The High Bright Sun 65. Deadlier than the Male 66. Some Girls Do 68. Percy 71. Quest for Love 71. The Love Ban 73. Percy's Progress 74, etc.

Thomas, Richard (1951–). American juvenile lead of the early seventies.
Winning 69. Last Summer 70. Cactus in the Snow 70. Red Sky at Morning 71. You'll Like My Mother 72.
TV series: *The Waltons* 72–76.

Thomas, Terry: see *Terry-Thomas.*

Thomas, William C.: see *Pine, William H.*

Thompson, Alex (–). British cinematographer.
Here We Go Round the Mulberry Bush 67. The Strange Affair 68. Alfred the Great 69.

Thompson, Carlos (1916–) (Juan Carlos Mundanschaffter). Argentinian stage and screen matinée idol who has made some Hollywood films.
Fort Algiers 53. The Flame and the Flesh 54. Valley of the Kings 54. Magic Fire 56, etc.
TV series: Sentimental Agent 62.

Thompson, Marshall (1926–). American leading man who began by playing quiet juvenile roles.
Reckless Age 44. Gallant Bess 45. The Romance of Rosy Ridge 46. Homecoming 48. Words and Music 48. The Violent Hour 50. My Six Convicts 52. Battle Taxi 55. To Hell and Back 55. Clarence the Cross-Eyed Lion 65. Around the World Under the Sea 66, many others.
TV series: Angel 60. Daktari 66–68.

Thorburn, June (1931–1967). British leading lady with repertory experience.
The Pickwick Papers (film debut) 53. The Cruel Sea 53. True as a Turtle 56. Tom Thumb 59. The Three Worlds of Gulliver 59. The Scarlet Blade 63, etc.

Thorndike, Andrew (1909–). East German director who with his wife Annelie made the strident anti-Nazi documentary series *The Archives Testify*; also *The German Story, The Russian Miracle*, etc.

Thorndike, Dame Sybil (1882–1976). Distinguished British stage actress who appeared in occasional films.

Biography 1950: *Sybil Thorndike* by Russell Thorndike.
Moths and Rust (debut) 21. Dawn 29. To What Red Hell 30. Hindle Wakes 31. Tudor Rose 36. Major Barbara 40. *Nicholas Nickleby* 47. Stage Fright 50. The Magic Box 51. Melba 53. *Alive and Kicking* 58. Shake Hands with the Devil 59. Hand in Hand 61, etc.

Thornton, Frank (1921–). British comic actor, much on TV.
Crooks and Coronets 68. All the Way Up 70. Our Miss Fred 72. Digby 73. No Sex Please We're British 73. The Three Musketeers 73.

Thorpe, Jerry (c. 1930–). American director from TV.
The Venetian Affair 66. The Day of the Evil Gun (& p) 68, etc.
TV series: *Kung Fu* 72–74.

Thorpe, Richard (1896–) (Rollo Smolt Thorpe). American director, formerly in vaudeville.
The Feminine Touch 28. Forgotten Woman 32. The Last of the Pagans 35. *Night Must Fall* 38. Huckleberry Finn 39. Tarzan Finds a Son 39. Wyoming 40. The Earl of Chicago 40. Tarzan's New York Adventure 42. Above Suspicion 43. Her Highness and the Bellboy 45. Fiesta 47. The Sun Comes Up 48. Malaya 49. *The Great Caruso* 51. The Prisoner of Zenda 52. Ivanhoe 52. The Student Prince 54. Knights of the Round Table 54. The Prodigal 55. *The Adventures of Quentin Durward* 56. Jailhouse Rock 57. The House of the Seven Hawks 59. The Tartars 60. Fun in Acapulco 63. The Golden Head 65. That Funny Feeling 65. The Truth about Spring 65. The Scorpio Letters 67. Pistolero 67, etc.

Those Magnificent Men in Their Flying Machines (GB 1965). This amiable romp about the first London-to-Paris air race was only moderately well written by Jack Davies and directed by Ken Annakin; but it serves as an example of a big budget and a lot of stars on a wide screen being acceptable in the mid-sixties in place of real talent. The primitive airplanes were the real stars. In 1969 a follow-up by the same team, this time about vintage car racing, came off less well: it was known in Britain as *Monte Carlo or Bust* and in the States as *Those Daring Young Men in Their Jaunty Jalopies.*

Three Coins in the Fountain (US 1954). This highly commercial film taught Hollywood the travelogue possibilities of CinemaScope to freshen up a tired story, and encouraged the trek of producers from Hollywood to locations all over the world, thus changing the face of film-making. A simple trio of romantic stories, from John Secondari's novel, the action was deftly directed by Jean Negulesco, who ten years later attempted a disguised remake under the title *The Pleasure Seekers*. But by now there was no novelty left and the picture crept by almost unnoticed.

3-D. Three-dimensional film-making had been tried in 1935 by MGM, as a gimmick involving throwaway paper glasses with one red and one green eyepiece to match the double image on the screen. In 1953, Hollywood really got the idea that this device would save an ailing industry, and a number of cheap exploitation pictures were shot in 3-D before anyone got down to the practical problem of renting out and collecting the necessary polaroid spectacles, which threw cinema managers into fits. *Bwana Devil* was an awful picture; *Man in the Dark* and *Fort Ti* were a shade better, except that the action kept stopping for something to be hurled at the audience; *House of Wax*, a Warner horror remake of *The Mystery of the Wax Museum*, had better production values and seemed to catch on with the public. All the studios began to make 3-D films—*Kiss Me Kate, The Charge at Feather River, Dial M for Murder, Sangaree*—but by the time these were ready, interest had shifted to Fox's new CinemaScope process, which although it gave no illusion of depth was at least a different shape and didn't need glasses. Nor did it entail such problems as running both projectors at once, with consequent intervals every twenty minutes; or long pauses when the film broke in order to mutilate the second copy in precisely the same way; or one machine running a little slower than the other, with gradual loss of synchronization. The remaining 3-D films were released 'flat', and the industry breathed a sigh of relief. So did the critics, who had wondered whether they would ever again see a film which did not involve frequent violent action. The Russians did claim at the time that they were inventing a 3-D process which would not require the use of glasses, but we are still waiting for that. In 1970–71 there was a brief revival of interest in 3-D as a promotion gimmick for cheap pornographic films.

The Three Musketeers. Apart from numerous European versions, Alexandre Dumas' classic swashbuckler has been a Hollywood favourite too. Edison made a version in 1911; so did Edward Laurillard in 1913, C. V. Heinkel in 1914, and Fred Niblo (the Douglas Fairbanks spectacular) in 1921. In the last-named production the musketeers were played by Eugene Pallette, Leon Barry and George Siegmann. Walter Abel was D'Artagnan in a 1936 version for RKO, with Paul Lukas, Moroni Olsen and Onslow Stevens: Rowland V. Lee directed. Don Ameche *sang* in a 1939 musical comedy version (sometimes known as *The Singing Musketeer*) with the Ritz Brothers, no less, as lackeys impersonating the famous trio. Directed by Allan Dwan, it was very, very funny. Gene Kelly made an acrobatic D'Artagnan for MGM in 1948, with Van Heflin, Gig Young and Robert Coote; and 1973 brought an all-star international version directed by Richard Lester, with Michael York, Oliver Reed, Frank Finlay and Richard Chamberlain.

Three Smart Girls (US 1937). A minor domestic comedy about three teenagers who save Dad from the clutches of a gold digger and restore him to the arms of Mum, this was notable as the first feature appearance, and a highly successful one, of Deanna Durbin. Henry Koster directed this and the 1939 sequel, *Three Smart Girls Grow Up*. In 1943 followed a third film on the adventures of the Durbin character only, *Hers to Hold*.

The Three Stooges: see *Stooges*.

Thring, Frank (–). Australian actor in occasional films.
Ben Hur 59. King of Kings 61, etc.

Thulin, Ingrid (1929–). Swedish leading actress, often in Ingmar Bergman's films.
Foreign Intrigue 55. *Wild Strawberries* 57. So Close to Life 58. The Face 59. The Four Horsemen of the Apocalypse (US) 62. Winter Light 62. *The Silence* 63. Return from the Ashes (US) 65. The War is Over (Fr.) 66. Night Games 66. The Damned 69. The Rite 69. Cries and Whispers 72. Moses 76, etc.

Thunder Rock (GB 1942). Rather belated in its message, but still one of World War II's most thoughtful films, this intriguing fantasy was about an isolationist in a lighthouse spurred to get back into the world's affairs by the ghosts of passengers drowned near the rock a hundred years before. Memorably acted by Michael Redgrave, Barbara Mullen, Lilli Palmer, Frederick Valk and James Mason: produced and directed by the Boulting brothers from Robert Ardrey's play.

Thundercloud, Chief (1900–1955) (Victor Daniels). American Indian actor.
Ramona 36. Renfrew of the Royal Mounted 37. Geronimo 39. Typhoon 40. Northwest Mounted

Police 41. Buffalo Bill 44. The Senator was Indiscreet 47. Ambush 49. Davy Crockett Indian Scout 50, etc.

Thurber, James (1894–1961). American humorist whose chief gifts to Hollywood were the original stories of *The Secret Life of Walter Mitty* and *The Male Animal*. TV series based on his cartoons: *My World and Welcome to It* 69.

Thy Soul Shall Bear Witness (Sweden 1920). A fantasy directed by Victor Sjostrom, who also played the leading role of a drunkard whose soul is taken in death's wagon to review the misery he has caused. Remade recently in Sweden, also in France in 1940 by Julien Duvivier, as *La Charrette Fantôme*, with Pierre Fresnay as the drunkard.

Tibbett, Lawrence (1896–1960). American opera star who made some films in the thirties.
□ Rogue Song 30. New Moon 30. The Prodigal 31. Cuban Love Song 32. Metropolitan 36. Under your Spell 37.

Tidyman, Ernest (–). American novelist who scripted the *Shaft* films from his own novels. *The French Connection* 72. High Plains Drifter 74. Report to the Commissioner (co-w), etc.

Tierney, Gene (1920–). Gentle-featured American leading lady of the forties, typically a smooth socialite.
□ The Return of Frank James 40. Hudson's Bay 40. Tobacco Road 41. *Belle Starr* 41. Sundown 41. The Shanghai Gesture 41. Son of Fury 42. Rings on Her Fingers 42. Thunder Birds 42. China Girl 42. *Heaven Can Wait* 43. *Laura* 44. A Bell for Adano 45. Leave Her to Heaven 45. Dragonwyck 46. *The Razor's Edge* 46. The Ghost and Mrs Muir 47. The Iron Curtain 48. That Wonderful Urge 48. Whirlpool 48. Night and the City 50. Where the Sidewalk Ends 50. The Mating Season 51. On the Riviera 51. The Secret of Convict Lake 51. Close to My Heart 51. Way of a Gaucho 51. The Plymouth Adventure 52. Never Let Me Go (GB) 53. Personal Affair (GB) 53. Black Widow 54. The Egyptian 54. *The Left Hand of God* 54. Advise and Consent 62. Toys in the Attic 63. The Pleasure Seekers 64. Daughter of the Mind (TV) 69.

Tierney, Lawrence (1919–). American 'tough-guy' actor, brother of Scott Brady.
The Ghost Ship 44. *Dillinger* (title role) 45. Step by Step 46. San Quentin 47. The Devil Thumbs a Ride 47. Shakedown 50. The Hoodlum 51. A

Child is Waiting 62. Custer of the West 67. Such Good Friends 71, etc.

Tiffin, Pamela (1942–). American leading lady, former child model.
Summer and Smoke 60. One Two Three 61. State Fair 61. The Hallelujah Trail 65. Viva Max 69, etc.

Tilbury, Zeffie (1863–1950). American character actress.
The Marriage of William Ashe 21. Werewolf of London 35. The Last Days of Pompeii 35. Maid of Salem 37. Balalaika 39. Tobacco Road 41. She Couldn't Say No 45, etc.

Till, Eric (1929–). Canadian director, from TV.
Hot Millions 68. The Walking Stick 69. A Fan's Notes 72.

Tiller, Nadja (1929–). Austrian leading lady, in international films.
Rosemary 59. Portrait of a Sinner 61. The World in My Pocket 62. And So to Bed 65. The Upper Hand 67, etc.

tilt. An upward or downward camera movement.

Tilton, Martha (1915–). American singer, in occasional films.
Sunny 41. Swing Hostess 44. Crime Inc 45. The Benny Goodman Story 56, etc.

time-lapse photography. The method by which one can obtain such fascinating results as a flower growing and blooming before one's eyes. The camera is set up and regulated to expose one frame of film at pre-arranged intervals. See also: *stop motion.*

Tingwell, Charles (1917–). Australian actor, now in British TV and films; usually in self-effacing roles.
Always Another Dawn 48. Bitter Springs 50. Life in Emergency Ward Ten 58. Cone of Silence 60. Murder She Said 63. The Secret of Blood Island 65. Dracula—Prince of Darkness 65. Nobody Runs Forever 68, etc.
TV series: Homicide 74–75.

Tinling, James (c. 1899–1955). American second-feature director.
Silk Legs 27. Arizona 30. Broadway 33. Charlie Chan in Shanghai 35. Pepper 36. 45 Fathers 37. Mr Moto's Gamble 38. Riders of the Purple Sage 41. Sundown Jim 42. The House of Tao Ling 47.

Night Wind 48. Trouble Preferred 49. Tales of
Robin Hood 52.

tinting has plainly gone out of fashion now that
virtually all films are in colour, but in black-and-
white days the use of single colours could lead to
interesting effects. In the twenties and earlier it
was common practice to tint night scenes blue,
sunlit scenes yellow, etc.; I saw one Russian film
made in 1917 in which the only scene in black-
and-white was that in which the hero hanged
himself! When talkies came in these colour
effects were forgotten, but towards the mid-
thirties when colour was threatening, a tint
seemed better than nothing. Films released
wholly in sepia included *The Ghost Goes West,
Bad Man of Brimstone, The Firefly, Maytime,
The Girl of the Golden West, The Oklahoma
Kid, Of Mice and Men* and *The Rains Came*:
while the 'real' scenes of *The Wizard of Oz* were
also sepia, leaving full colour until we landed
over the rainbow. *A Midsummer Night's Dream*
was released with a blue rinse, as were the water
ballet reels of *A Day at the Races*. Other colours
have been used for short sequences. Green for
Portrait of Jennie (the storm), *Luck of the Irish*
(the leprechaun forest) and *Lost Continent* (to
obscure the poor monster animation). Red for
the *Hell's Angels* battle scenes and for the flash at
the end of *Spellbound* when the villain turns a
gun on himself. Even monochrome has its
effectiveness, as shown in *A Matter of Life and
Death* and *Bonjour Tristesse*.

Tiomkin, Dmitri (1899–). Russian-American
composer of innumerable film scores.
Autobiography 1959: *Please Don't Hate Me*.
Alice in Wonderland 33. *Lost Horizon* 37. The
Great Waltz 38. *The Moon and Sixpence* 42.
Shadow of a Doubt 43. Duel in the Sun 46.
Portrait of Jennie 48. The Men 50. *High Noon*
(AA) 52. *The High and the Mighty* (AA) 54.
Land of the Pharaohs 55. Friendly Persuasion
56. *Giant* 56. Night Passage 57. *Gunfight at the
O.K. Corral* 57. The Old Man and the Sea (AA)
58. The Unforgiven 60. The Alamo 60. The
Guns of Navarone 61. 55 Days at Peking 62.
The Fall of the Roman Empire 64. Tschaikovsky
71, etc.

Tissé, Edouard (1897–1961). Franco-Russian
cinematographer who worked closely with
Eisenstein.
Strike 24. *The Battleship Potemkin* 25. *The
General Line* (The Old and the New) 27. *Que
Viva Mexico* 32. Aerograd 36. *Alexander
Nevsky* 39. *Ivan the Terrible* 42 and 46. Glinka
54, etc.

To Be or Not to Be (US 1942). A bitter farce
remarkable for the furore it caused on its release
because it found humour in the Nazi occupation
of Warsaw. Dealing with a troupe of actors who
outwit the Nazis, it seems now not only
inoffensive but funnier than it was at the time,
with a string of running jokes put over as only
Ernst Lubitsch knew how. Carole Lombard,
whose last film this was, and Jack Benny were
perfect comedy leads, and the cast included Sig
Ruman, Stanley Ridges, Lionel Atwill, Felix
Bressart and Tom Dugan.

To Have and Have Not. Ernest Hemingway's
tough, soft-hearted adventure novel has been
filmed three times; in 1944 by Howard Hawks,
with Bogart, Bacall, and not much left of the plot;
in 1951 by Michael Curtiz, as *The Breaking
Point*, with John Garfield and Patricia Neal; and
in 1958, as *The Gun Runners*, with Audie
Murphy.

Tobacco Road (US 1941). Generally regarded
as a minor film in the John Ford canon, this
adaptation of Erskine Caldwell's savage picture
of the southern 'poor whites' was successfully
played for laughs and a few tears, and has grown
more pleasing with the years. Among the
apathetic, even stupid, but delightfully resilient
characters, Charley Grapewin's performance as
Jeeter stands out as something rare and wholly
attractive; there is interesting work, too, by
Marjorie Rambeau, Elizabeth Patterson,
William Tracy and Slim Summerville.

Tobey, Kenneth (1919–). American
character actor of dependable types.
Kiss Tomorrow Goodbye 49. About Face 51.
The Thing 52. The Beast from 20,000 Fathoms
55. The Man in the Grey Flannel Suit 56, many
others.

Tobias, George (1901–). American
character actor with stage experience.
Saturday's Children (debut) 40. City for
Conquest 40. Sergeant York 41. Yankee Doodle
Dandy 42. This is the Army 43. Thank Your
Lucky Stars 43. Between Two Worlds 44.
Objective Burma 45. Mildred Pierce 45. Sinbad
the Sailor 47. Rawhide 50. The Glenn Miller
Story 53. The Seven Little Foys 55. A New Kind
of Love 63. The Glass Bottom Boat 66, many
others.
TV series: Hudson's Bay. Adventures in
Paradise. Bewitched.

Tobin, Dan (c. 1909–). Lightweight American
character actor.
Woman of the Year 41. Undercurrent 46. The

Big Clock 48. The Velvet Touch 49. Dear Wife 52. Wedding Breakfast 56. The Love Bug Rides Again 73, etc.
TV series: Perry Mason 57–66.

Tobin, Genevieve (1901–). Vivacious American actress of French parentage. Mainly stage experience; made some films during thirties.
The Lady Surrenders (debut) 31. One Hour With You 32. Easy to Wed 34. The Petrified Forest 36. The Great Gambini 37. Dramatic School 38. Zaza 39, etc.

Todd, Ann (1909–). Blonde British leading actress, a big star of the forties. Later produced and directed short travel films.
□ Keepers of Youth 31. These Charming People 31. The Ghost Train 31. The Water Gypsies 31. The Return of Bulldog Drummond 34. Things to Come 36. The Squeaker 37. Action for Slander 37. *South Riding* 38. Poison Pen 39. Danny Boy 41. Ships with Wings 41. Perfect Strangers 45. *The Seventh Veil* 45. Gaiety George 46. Daybreak 47. So Evil my Love 47. The Paradine Case (US) 48. *The Passionate Friends* 48. Madeleine 49. The Sound Barrier 52. The Green Scarf 54. Time without Pity 57. Taste of Fear 61. Son of Captain Blood 62. Ninety Degrees in the Shade 65. The Fiend 71.

Todd, Ann (1932–) (A. T. Mayfield). American child star of the thirties and forties.
Zaza 39. Blood and Sand 41. King's Row 42. The Jolson Story 46. Bomba and the Lion Hunters 52, etc.

Todd, Bob (1922–). Bald British comic actor, much on TV.
The Intelligence Men 65. Hot Millions 68, etc.

Todd, Mike (1907–1958) (Avrom Goldenborgen). Dynamic American producer of Broadway spectacles. His one personally produced film was in similar vein: *Around the World in Eighty Days* 56. The wide-screen system *Todd-AO* is named after him. A biography, *The Nine Lives of Mike Todd*, by Art Cohn, was published in 1959.

Todd, Richard (1919–). British leading man, in repertory from 1937 until spotted by a film talent scout.
For Them That Trespass (debut) 48. *The Hasty Heart* 49. Stage Fright 50. Lightning Strikes Twice (US) 51. *Robin Hood* 52. Venetian Bird 53. The Sword and the Rose 54. Rob Roy 54. *A Man Called Peter* 55. The Virgin Queen (US) 55. *The Dam Busters* 55. Yangtse Incident 56.

Chase a Crooked Shadow 57. Danger Within 58. The Long, the Short and the Tall 59. The Hellions 60. Never Let Go 61. The Longest Day 62. The Boys 62. The Very Edge 63. Operation Crossbow 65. The Battle of the Villa Fiorita 65. Coast of Skeletons 65. Death Drums along the River 66. Last of the Long-Haired Boys 68. Subterfuge 69. Dorian Gray 70. Asylum 72, etc.

Todd, Thelma (1905–1935). Perky American leading blonde of the early thirties, heroine of many two-reel comedies. Died in mysterious circumstances.
Fascinating Youth 26. Rubber Heels 27. The Haunted House 28. Her Private Life 29. Aloha 30. The Hot Heiress 31. *Monkey Business* 31. The Maltese Falcon 31. *Horse Feathers* 32. Air Hostess 33. Sitting Pretty 33. Hips Hips Hooray 34. Bottoms Up 34. Two for Tonight 35. The Bohemian Girl 35, many others.

Tognazzi, Ugo (1922–). Italian leading actor.
His Women (Il Mantenuto) (& d) 61. The Fascist (Il Federale) 62. Queen Bee (Ape Regina or The Conjugal Bed) 63. The Magnificent Cuckold 64. An American Wife 65. A Question of Honour 66. Barbarella 68. Property is No Longer a Theft 73. Blowout 73. Duck in Orange Sauce 75, etc.

Tokar, Norman (1920–). American director, from radio; in films, has worked exclusively for Disney.
Big Red 62. Savage Sam 63. Sammy the Way Out Seal 63. A Tiger Walks 64. Those Calloways 65. Follow Me Boys 65. The Ugly Dachshund 66. The Happiest Millionaire 67. The Horse in the Grey Flannel Suit 68. Rascal 69. Snowball Express 73. The Apple Dumpling Gang 75, etc.

Tokyo Olympiad (Japan 1964). This documentary by Kon Ichikawa and a score of photographers is in its quiet way as remarkable as Leni Riefenstahl's film of the 1936 games. Here the athletes are seen not as gods but as men and women suffering the ultimate in physical stress; the probing cameras achieve many remarkable effects.

Tol'able David. This novel by Joseph Hergesheimer was first, and most successfully, filmed in 1921, with Richard Barthelmess as the gentle youth making good in the tough outdoor life; it was directed by Henry King from a scenario by Edmund Goulding. In 1931 John G. Blystone directed a disappointing sound remake with Richard Cromwell.

Toland, Gregg (1904–1948). Distinguished

American cinematographer who worked mainly with Goldwyn.

The Unholy Garden 31. Roman Scandals 33. Tugboat Annie 33. *Nana* 34. *We Live Again* 34. *Mad Love* 35. Les Misérables 35. These Three 36. *Dead End* 37. The Goldwyn Follies 38. Intermezzo 39. *Wuthering Heights* (AA) 39. Raffles 40. *The Grapes of Wrath* 40. The Long Voyage Home 40. *The Westerner* 40. *Citizen Kane* 41. *The Little Foxes* 41; war service; *The Best Years of Our Lives* 46. The Kid from Brooklyn 47. The Bishop's Wife 48. *Enchantment* 48, many others.

Toler, Sidney (1874–1947). Chubby American character actor who in 1928 took over the part of Charlie Chan and played it twenty-five times.

Madame X 29. Is My Face Red? 32. Spitfire 35. Call of the Wild 35. Our Relations 36. Wide Open Faces 38. Charlie Chan in Honolulu 38. Law of the Pampas 39. Charlie Chan at the Wax Museum 40. Castle in the Desert 42. White Savage 43. The Scarlet Clue 45. Dark Alibi 46. The Trap 47, many others.

Tolstoy, Leo (1828–1910). Russian novelist whose *Anna Karenina* and *War and Peace* have been frequently filmed.

Tom and Jerry. Short cartoons featuring the mean-minded, accident-prone cat and his inventive and likeable little adversary were in production at MGM, with a break in the fifties, from 1937, with Fred Quimby (qv) as executive producer until his death. They have been much criticized for their excessive violence, but their humour, coupled with the impossibility of the situations, has won the day. The Academy Award-winning titles are *The Milky Way* 40, *Yankee Doodle Mouse* 43, *Mouse Trouble* 44, *Quiet Please* 45, *Cat Concerto* 46, *The Little Orphan* 48, *The Two Mouseketeers* 51, *Johann Mouse* 52. The original cartoons were drawn by William Hanna and Joe Barbera.

Tom Brown's Schooldays. The two major film versions of this famous Victorian story of life at Rugby School were: 1. US 1939, with Cedric Hardwicke as Dr Arnold and Jimmy Lydon as Tom, directed by Robert Stevenson. 2. GB 1951, with Robert Newton and John Howard Davies, directed by Gordon Parry.

Tom Jones (GB 1963). Bawdy, rollicking, phenomenally popular adaptation of Fielding's eighteenth-century novel about the misfortunes of a foundling. Produced and directed by Tony Richardson, scripted by John Osborne,

photographed by Walter Lassally, designed by Ralph Brinton, with a cast led by Albert Finney, Hugh Griffith and Edith Evans. For the most part vivid and hilarious, it runs out of breath before the end; and the colour process sometimes looks like an awful mistake while at other points perfectly capturing the texture of an old print. AA best film, best direction, best music (John Addison); BFA best film.

Tom Sawyer. Mark Twain's boy hero has been played on film by Jack Pickford in 1917 (also in *Huck and Tom* 18), Jackie Coogan in 1920, Tommy Kelly in 1938 (the Selznick production), also in 1938, by Billy Cook in *Tom Sawyer, Detective*, and in 1972 by Johnny Whitaker.

Tombes, Andrew (1889–197*). American supporting actor often seen as cop, undertaker, bartender or harassed official.

Moulin Rouge 33. Charlie Chan at the Olympics 37. Too Busy to Work 39. Phantom Lady 44. Can't Help Singing 44. Oh You Beautiful Doll 49. How To Be Very Very Popular 55, many others.

Tomelty, Joseph (1910–). Irish character actor, in British films since 1945.

Odd Man Out 46. The Sound Barrier 52. Meet Mr Lucifer 54. Simba 55. A Kid for Two Farthings 56. The Black Torment 64, many others.

Tomlinson, David (1917–). Amiable British leading man and comedian, a latter-day Ralph Lynn.

Quiet Wedding 40. Journey Together 45. The Way to the Stars 45. Master of Bankdam 47. *Miranda* 48. Sleeping Car to Trieste 48. *The Chiltern Hundreds* 49. Hotel Sahara 51. *Three Men in a Boat* 55. Up the Creek 58. Follow That Horse 60. Tom Jones 63. *Mary Poppins* 64. The Truth about Spring 65. City in the Sea 65. The Liquidator 66. The Love Bug 69. Bedknobs and Broomsticks 71, many others.

Tone, Franchot (1905–1968). American leading man of stage and screen.

The Wiser Sex (film debut) 32. Gabriel over the White House 33. Moulin Rouge 34. Mutiny on the Bounty 35. Suzy 36. Quality Street 36. *They Gave Him a Gun* 37. Three Comrades 39. The Trail of the Vigilantes 40. Nice Girl 41. The Wife Takes a Flyer 42. *Five Graves to Cairo* 43. His Butler's Sister 43. *Phantom Lady* 44. Dark Waters 44. That Night with You 45. Because of Him 46. Her Husband's Affairs 47. I Love Trouble 48. Every Girl Should Be Married 48. The Man on the Eiffel Tower 50. *Advise and*

Consent 62. La Bonne Soupe 64. In Harm's Way 65. Nobody Runs Forever 68, etc.

Tonti, Aldo (1910–). Italian cinematographer.
Ossessione 44. Europe 51 50. The Mill on the Po 51. War and Peace 56. Cabiria 57. Reflections in a Golden Eye 67, etc.

Toomey, Regis (1902–). American character actor, on screen since 1928, usually as cop or victim in routine crime dramas.
Framed 29. Murder by the Clock 32. G-Men 35. The Big Sleep 46. The Nebraskan 53. Guys and Dolls 55. Man's Favorite Sport? 63. Peter Gunn 67, scores of others.
TV series: Burke's Law.

Top Hat (US 1935). The most delightful and enduring of the Astaire-Rogers musicals of the thirties, with an agreeable wisp of plot and amusing if dated comedy dialogue handled by an expert team of supporting comics: Edward Everett Horton, Eric Blore, Helen Broderick and Erik Rhodes. Irving Berlin's score, one of his best, includes 'The Piccolino', 'Cheek to Cheek' and 'Isn't it a Lovely Day' as well as the title number; and Astaire and Rogers are at their peak. Script by Dwight Taylor and Alan Scott, photography by David Abel, direction by Mark Sandrich, production by Pandro S. Berman.

Topol (1935–) (Chaim Topol). Israeli leading actor who gained fame with London stage run of *Fiddler on the Roof.*
Cast a Giant Shadow 65. Sallah 66. Before Winter Comes 69. *Fiddler on the Roof* 71. Follow Me 72. Galileo 74, etc.

Topper (US 1937). Hal Roach produced this mixture of slapstick, sophistication and the supernatural, from Thorne Smith's novel, and started a new trend in Hollywood comedy. Roland Young was perfectly cast as the henpecked businessman beset by jovial ghosts in the forms of Cary Grant and Constance Bennett; only Norman McLeod's direction tended to lack the necessary lightness of touch. Young also appeared in two sequels, *Topper Takes a Trip* 39 and *Topper Returns* 41. In the fifties *Topper* was personified by Leo G. Carroll in a TV series.

Topper, Burt (1934–). American director.
Diary of a High School Bride 61. The Strangler 64. The Devil's Eight 69. Wild in the Streets (p) 68. The Hard Ride 71. Lovin' Man 72.

Torchy Blane. A series of half a dozen second features, made in 1939–48, starring Glenda Farrell as a wisecracking girl reporter and Barton MacLane as the puzzled policeman who gets the comeback for her zany ideas. Most of the films were directed by William Beaudine.

Toren, Marta (1926–1957). Swedish leading lady signed by Hollywood scout while at dramatic school.
Casbah (debut) 48. Rogues' Regiment 49. One-Way Street 50. Panthers' Moon 51. Sirocco 51. The Man Who Watched the Trains Go By 52. Maddalena 54, etc.

Tormé, Mel (1923–). Amiable American ballad singer who has made occasional films.
Higher and Higher 43. Let's Go Steady 45. Junior Miss 45. Good News 47. Duchess of Idaho 50. The Big Operator 59. Walk like a Dragon 60. The Patsy 64. A Man Called Adam 66, etc.

Torn, Rip (1931–) (Elmore Torn). American general purpose actor, mainly on stage and TV.
Baby Doll 56. Time Limit 57. Cat on a Hot Tin Roof 58. King of Kings 61. Sweet Bird of Youth 62. The Cincinnati Kid 65. You're a Big Boy Now 66. Beach Red 67. The Rain People 69. Tropic of Cancer 69. Payday 73. Crazy Joe 73. Birch Interval 76. The Man Who Fell To Earth 76, etc.

Torrence, David (–). American silent screen actor.
The Inside of the Cup 21. Sherlock Holmes 22. The Abysmal Brute 23. Surging Seas 24. The Reckless Sex 25. Laddie 26. Annie Laurie 27. The Little Shepherd of Kingdom Come 28. Untamed Justice 29. Raffles 30. Voltaire 33. Mandalay 34. The Dark Angel 35, etc.

Torrence, Ernest (1878–1933). Scottish actor, in American silent films, usually as villain; former opera singer.
Tol'able David 21. The Hunchback of Notre Dame 23. The Trail of the Lonesome Pine 23. The Covered Wagon 23. Peter Pan 24. King of Kings 27. The Cossacks 28. The Bridge of San Luis Rey 29. The New Adventures of Get-Rich-Quick Wallingford 31. Cuban Love Song 32. Sherlock Holmes 33, many others.

Torre-Nilsson, Leopoldo (1924–). Argentinian director, usually of sharp-flavoured melodramas which he also writes.
The House of the Angel 57. *The Fall* 59. The Hand in the Trap 60. Summer Skin 61. Four Women for One Hero 62. The Roof Garden 63. The Eavesdropper 65. Monday's Child 67. Martin Fierro 68, etc.

Torres, Raquel (1908–) (Paula Marie Osterman). American leading lady who played fiery sirens in the early thirties.
White Shadows in the South Seas 28. The Bridge of San Luis Rey 29. Under a Texas Moon 30. The Woman I Stole 33. Duck Soup 33. The Red Wagon 36, etc.

Tors, Ivan (1916–). Hungarian writer-producer-director, in Hollywood from 1941.
Song of Love (w) 47. The Forsyte Saga (w) 49. Storm over Tibet (wp) 52. The Magnetic Monster (wp) 53. Gog (wp) 54. Riders to the Stars (p) 55. Battle Taxi (p) 56. Flipper (p) 60. Rhino (pd) 63. Zebra in the Kitchen 65. Around the World Under the Sea 65, etc.
TV series as producer include *The Man and the Challenge*, *Sea Hunt*, *Flipper*, *Primus*.

torture has figured in *Arabian Nights, Thief of Baghdad*, and other of this genre; in witchcraft dramas such as *Witchfinder General, The Devils* and *Day of Wrath*; in medieval epics such as *El Cid, Ivanhoe* and *Tower of London*; further back to Roman times, in *The Robe, Barabbas, Spartacus* and *Demetrius and the Gladiators*; in World War II yarns such as *13 Rue Madeleine, OSS, Carve Her Name with Pride, The Seventh Cross* and *633 Squadron*; in cold war melodramas such as *Treason, The Prisoner*, and *The Manchurian Candidate*; in historical mysteries such as *The Man in the Iron Mask* and in documentary adventures such as *A Man Called Horse*.

Totheroh, Rollie (1891–1967). American cinematographer who worked notably for Charles Chaplin.
The Pilgrim 24. City Lights 31. The Great Dictator 40. Monsieur Verdoux 47, etc.

Toto (1897–1967) (Antonio Furst de Curtis-Gagliardi). Italian comedian, from music hall and revue.
Fermo con le Mani 36. Toto Le Moko 49. Cops and Robbers 53. Gold of Naples 54. Racconti Romani 55. Persons Unknown 58. Toto of Arabia 63. The Commander 67, many others.

Totter, Audrey (1918–). American leading lady of the 'hard-boiled' type, with stage and radio experience.
Main Street after Dark (debut) 44. Her Highness and the Bellboy 45. The Postman Always Rings Twice 45. *The Lady in the Lake* 46. Tenth Avenue Angel 47. The Unsuspected 48. Alias Nick Beal 49. The Set-Up 49. Tension 51. The Blue Veil 52. Assignment Paris 53. Women's Prison 54. A Bullet for Joey 55. The Carpetbaggers 64. Harlow (electronovision version) 65. Chubasco 68, others.
TV series: Our Man Higgins 62.

Toumanova, Tamara (1917–). Russian ballerina who has made occasional appearances in American films.
Days of Glory 43. Torn Curtain 67, etc.

Tourneur, Jacques (1904–). Franco-American director, son of Maurice Tourneur, with a special flair for the macabre.
Nick Carter, Master Detective 39. *Cat People* 42. *I Walked with a Zombie* 43. *The Leopard Man* 43. Days of Glory 44. *Experiment Perilous* 44. *Out of the Past* 47. Berlin Express 48. Stars in My Crown 50. The Flame and the Arrow 51. Appointment in Honduras 53. Wichita 55. Great Day in the Morning 56. *Night of the Demon* 57. Timbuktu 59. The Giant of Marathon 61. A Comedy of Terrors 63. City under the Sea 65, etc.

Tourneur, Maurice (1876–1961) (Maurice Thomas). French director who made some American films.
Mother 14. Man of the Hour 15. Trilby 15. Poor Little Rich Girl 17. The Bluebird 18. The Last of the Mohicans 20. Treasure Island 20. The Christian (GB) 23. Aloma of the South Seas 26. Mysterious Island 26. L'Équipage 27. Maison de Danses 31. Koenigsmark 35. Volpone 40. The Devil's Hand 42. L'Impasse des Deux Anges 48, etc.

Tover, Leo (1902–). American cinematographer in Hollywood from 1918.
Dead Reckoning 47. *The Snake Pit* 48. *The Heiress* 49. The Secret of Convict Lake 51. The President's Lady 53. Soldier of Fortune 55. The Sun Also Rises 57. *Journey to the Centre of the Earth* 59. Follow That Dream 62. Sunday in New York 63. Strange Bedfellows 64. A Very Special Favor 65, many others.

Tower of London (US 1939). A historical melodrama notable chiefly for treating the story of Richard III as a horror yarn: Basil Rathbone and Boris Karloff, who played Richard and his executioner, had just finished *Son of Frankenstein*. Rowland V. Lee directed. Vincent Price, who played Clarence, played Richard in an inferior 1962 remake by Roger Corman.

The Towering Inferno (US 1974). This all-star Irwin Allen extravaganza, with most of the cast dying in flames at the top of a burning skyscraper, was the apex of the seventies disaster cycle and had special effects to match.

Dramatically, at nearly three hours, it was far too much. The inevitable TV imitation was *Terror on the Fortieth Floor*.

Towers, Harry Alan (1920–). British executive producer with varied experience in films and TV. Recently making popular crime and adventure films with international casts and finance.
Victim Five (& w) 64. Mozambique (& w) 64. The Face of Fu Manchu 65. Ten Little Indians 65. Our Man in Marrakesh (Bang, Bang, You're Dead) 66. The Brides of Fu Manchu 66. Rocket to the Moon 67. Treasure Island 72. Call of the Wild 73, etc.

Towne, Robert (–). American screenwriter.
The Tomb of Ligeia 64. Villa Rides 67. The Last Detail 73. *Chinatown* 74. Shampoo (co-w) 75. The Yakuza (co-w) 75, etc.

Toye, Wendy (1917–). British director, former dancer. Drew attention with two ingenious short films, *The Stranger Left No Card* 52 and *On the Twelfth Day* 55. Features: *Three Cases of Murder* 54. *All for Mary* 55. *True as a Turtle* 56. *We Joined the Navy* 62, etc.

Track of the Cat (US 1954). An interesting but unsuccessful experiment by William Wellman to create a fresh filmic texture and atmosphere by shooting in colour but restricting his subjects to black and white—in this case snowy landscapes and forests—with the very occasional flash of colour. Unfortunately the story in this case, a kind of backwoods *Cold Comfort Farm*, was laborious and unappealing, and the cast led by Robert Mitchum looked understandably glum. William Clothier was the cinematographer.

tracking shot. One taken with a moving camera, usually forwards or backwards, and often on an actual track.

Tracy, Arthur (1903–) (Harry Rosenberg). American singer who made his greatest success in England, especially with his rendering of 'Marta'.
The Big Broadcast 32. Limelight (GB) 36. The Street Singer (GB) 37. Follow Your Star (GB) 38, etc.

Tracy, Lee (1898–1968). American leading actor of stage (from 1919) and screen (sporadically from 1929): had inimitable nasal delivery.
Big Time (debut) 29. Liliom 30. Love is a Racket 32. *Doctor X* 32. Blessed Event 32. Clear All Wires 33. *Dinner at Eight* 33. Bombshell 33. I'll Tell the World 34. *The Lemon Drop Kid* 34. Two-Fisted 35. Sutter's Gold 36. Criminal Lawyer 37. Spellbinder 39. The Power of the Press 43. I'll Tell the World 45. High Tide 47. *The Best Man* 64, etc. Also TV appearances.

Tracy, Spencer (1900–1967). Distinguished American actor with stage experience from 1922; exclusively on screen from 1930. His uneven features gained him gangster roles to begin with, then he made a corner in priests and friends of the hero; but his chief mature image was that of a tough, humorous fellow who was also a pillar of integrity.
Biography 1970: *Spencer Tracy* by Larry Swindell. 1973: *Tracy and Hepburn* by Garson Kanin.
☐ Up the River 30. Quick Millions 31. Six-Cylinder Love 31. Goldie 31. She Wanted a Millionaire 32. Sky Devils 32. Disorderly Conduct 32. Young America 32. Society Girl 32. Painted Woman 32. Me and My Girl 32. *Twenty Thousand Years in Sing Sing* 32. Face in the Sky 33. *The Power and the Glory* 33. Shanghai Madness 33. The Mad Game 33. *A Man's Castle* 33. Looking for Trouble 34. The Show-Off 34. Bottoms Up 34. Now I'll Tell 34. Marie Galante 34. It's a Small World 35. Dante's Inferno 35. The Murder Man 35. Whipsaw 35. Riff Raff 36. *Fury* 36. *San Francisco* 36. *Libeled Lady* 36. *Captains Courageous* (AA) 37. They Gave Him a Gun 37. The Big City 38. Mannequin 38. Test Pilot 38. *Boys' Town* (AA) 38. *Stanley and Livingstone* 39. I Take This Woman 39. *Northwest Passage* 40. *Edison the Man* 40. Boom Town 40. Men of Boys' Town 41. Dr Jekyll and Mr Hyde 41. *Woman of the Year* 42. Tortilla Flat 42. Keeper of the Flame 43. A Guy Named Joe 43. *The Seventh Cross* 44. Thirty Seconds over Tokyo 44. Without Love 45. Sea of Grass 46. Cass Timberlane 47. *State of the Union* 48. Edward My Son (GB) 49. *Adam's Rib* 49. Malaya 49. *Father of the Bride* 50. The People against O'Hara 51. Father's Little Dividend 51. Pat and Mike 52. Plymouth Adventure 52. The Actress 53. Broken Lance 54. *Bad Day at Black Rock* 55. The Mountain 56. The Desk Set 57. The Old Man and the Sea 58. *The Last Hurrah* 58. *Inherit the Wind* 60. The Devil at Four O'Clock 61. *Judgment at Nuremberg* 61. It's a Mad Mad Mad Mad World 63. *Guess Who's Coming to Dinner* (BFA) 67.

Tracy, William (1917–1967). American actor who used to play sly or dumb young fellows.
Brother Rat 38. Strike Up the Band 40. Tobacco Road 41. About Face 42. Fall In 44. The Walls

of Jericho 49. Mr Walkie Talkie 54. The Wings of Eagles 56, etc.

Trader Horn (US 1930). MGM's safari to darkest Africa to shoot scenes, with actors, for this picture was the first such expedition by a major Hollywood studio. The result, though directed by W. S. Van Dyke, showed that there was much to learn, and the film now seems very naïve. 1973 brought a remake with Rod Taylor, so bad it was barely released.

The Trail of the Lonesome Pine. This backwoods melodrama was first filmed in 1916 with Charlotte Walker and Earle Foxe. In 1923 it was remade with Mary Miles Minter, Antonio Moreno and Ernest Torrence. In 1936 Henry Hathaway made a sound version with Sylvia Sidney, Henry Fonda and Fred MacMurray, and this version was significant as the first outdoor film in the newly-perfected three-colour Technicolor.

trains have above all served film-makers as a splendid background for suspense thrillers. Scores of sequences crowd to mind, all enhanced by the dramatic background of a speeding train: *The Lady Vanishes, North by Northwest, From Russia with Love, The Narrow Margin, The Tall Target, How the West Was Won, 3.10 to Yuma, Lady on a Train, Cat Ballou, Jesse James, Bad Day at Black Rock, Night of the Demon, Time Bomb, Rome Express, Sleeping Car to Trieste, Northwest Frontier, Man without a Star, The Thirty-Nine Steps, Secret Agent, Shanghai Express, Number 17, Last Train from Madrid, Last Train to Bombay, Ministry of Fear, Von Ryan's Express, Across the Bridge, Double Indemnity, Strangers on a Train, The Iron Horse, Union Pacific, Canadian Pacific, Next of Kin, Berlin Express, The Great Locomotive Chase, Terror by Night, Crack-Up, Rampage, Fool's Parade, The Train, Breakheart Pass, Murder on the Orient Express* ... the list could be almost endless. More serious films using trains include *La Bête Humaine* (and its remake *Human Desire*), *Metropolitan* and its remake *A Window in London*), *Brief Encounter, The Last Journey, Sullivan's Travels, Indiscretion of an American Wife, Anna Karenina, Terminus, Night Mail, The Manchurian Candidate, The Railway Children, Doctor Zhivago, Boxcar Bertha,* and *Emperor of the North*; while spectacular crashes were featured in *The Greatest Show on Earth, Hatter's Castle, Seven Sinners, The Young in Heart, Mad Love, The Wrong Box, Lawrence of Arabia, Crack in the World, The Ghost Train,* and *King Kong.* Murder was seen from a train in *Metropolitan*

and *Lady in a Train*, and *through* a train in *Twelve Angry Men*. The subway, elevated or underground railway was featured in *Practically Yours, On the Town, The Bachelor Party, Boys' Night Out, Union Station, The FBI Story, The Young Savages, Underground, Bulldog Jack, Daleks Invasion Earth 2150 A.D., The French Connection, Beneath the Planet of the Apes,* and *The Liquidator.* The back platforms of American trains have become familiar, especially in political films like *Abe Lincoln in Illinois, Wilson* and *All the King's Men*; but also in *Hail the Conquering Hero, Double Indemnity, The Merry Monahans* and *Mr Deeds Goes to Town.* Comedy train sequences include the Marx Brothers chopping up moving carriages for fuel in *Go West,* the Ale and Quail Club in *The Palm Beach Story,* Buster Keaton's splendidly inventive *Our Hospitality* and *The General, The Great St Trinian's Train Robbery,* Laurel and Hardy going to sleep in the same bunk in *The Big Noise,* Hal Roach's *Broadway Limited,* John Barrymore in *Twentieth Century,* Peter Sellers in *Two-Way Stretch,* the western sequence of *Around the World in Eighty Days,* the pullman car sequence of *Some Like It Hot,* Monty Banks in *Play Safe,* Morecambe and Wise in *The Magnificent Two, The Private Life of Sherlock Holmes,* the whole of *The Titfield Thunderbolt* and *Oh Mr Porter* ... and many scenes of jaywalking on top of moving carriages, including *Professor Beware, The Merry Monahans* and *Fancy Pants.* Musical sequences with a train motif or setting are found in *A Hard Day's Night, Monte Carlo, Some Like It Hot, The Harvey Girls* ('The Atchison, Topeka and the Santa Fe'), *At the Circus* ('Lydia the Tattooed Lady'), *Sun Valley Serenade* ('Chattanooga Choo Choo'), *Dumbo* ('Casey Junior'), *The Jazz Singer* ('Toot Toot Tootsie, Goodbye'), *Easter Parade* ('When the Midnight Choo Choo Leaves for Alabam'), *Forty-second Street* ('Shuffle off to Buffalo').
TV series involving trains as a regular motif include *Casey Jones, The Wild Wild West, The Iron Horse, Petticoat Junction* and *Union Pacific.*

tramps or hoboes who have figured largely in films include those played by William Powell in *My Man Godfrey,* Joel McCrea in *Sullivan's Travels,* George Arliss in *The Guv'nor,* Jean Gabin in *Archimède le Clochard,* practically the whole cast of *Hallelujah I'm a Bum,* and of course Charlie Chaplin in all his earlier comedies.

transvestism. There have been many films, mostly lightweight ones, making effective use of situations in which men dress up as women.

Charley's Aunt has proved a perennial, and in silent days Julian Eltinge, a female impersonator, made several popular films: his 1972 successor was Danny la Rue, in *Our Miss Fred*. Well-known actors in female attire have included Wallace Beery as 'Swedy' in a series of silent comedies, Lon Chaney in *The Unholy Tree*, Lionel Barrymore in *The Devil Doll*, William Powell in *Love Crazy*, Cary Grant in *I Was a Male War Bride*, Joe E. Brown as his own grandma in *The Daring Young Man*, Cook and Moore as leaping nuns in *Bedazzled*, Alec Guinness in *The Comedians*, Brian Deacon in *Triple Echo*, Alec Guinness in *Kind Hearts and Coronets*, Peter Sellers in *The Mouse That Roared*, William Bendix and Dennis O'Keefe in *Abroad with Two Yanks*, Jimmy Durante in *You're in the Army Now*, Lee J. Cobb in *In Like Flint*, Ray Walston in *Caprice*, Jerry Lewis in *Three on a Couch*, Stan Laurel in *That's My Wife* and *Jitterbugs*, Bing Crosby in *High Time*, Bob Hope in *Casanova's Big Night*, Tony Curtis and Jack Lemmon in *Some Like It Hot*, Tony Perkins in *Psycho*, Dick Shawn in *What Did You Do in the War, Daddy?*, Phil Silvers and Jack Gilford in *A Funny Thing Happened on the Way to the Forum*; and the device seems to have become a standard ingredient of recent spy stories including *Thunderball, Licensed to Kill, Where the Bullets Fly*, and *Gunn. Myra Breckenridge* also fits in somewhere, as does *Dr Jekyll and Sister Hyde*.

Women disguised as men are rarer; but one can instance such notable examples as Katharine Hepburn in *Sylvia Scarlett*, Annabella in *Wings of the Morning*, Signe Hasso in *The House on 92nd Street*, Nita Talbot in *A Very Special Favor*, Marlene Dietrich in *Morocco*, Greta Garbo in *Queen Christina*, Mary Pickford in *Kiki*, Debbie Reynolds in *Goodbye Charlie*, Jesse Matthews in *Gangway*, and the ambiguous hero-heroine-villain of *Homicidal*. In *Turnabout* a husband and wife exchanged bodies, with dire results.

Traubel, Helen (1899–1972). American soprano.
□ Deep in My Heart 54. The Ladies' Man 61. Gunn 67.

Trauner, Alexander (1906–). French art director who has worked on international films.
Quai des Brumes 38. Le Jour Se Lève 39. *Les Visiteurs du Soir* 42. *Les Enfants du Paradis* 44. Les Portes de la Nuit 45. Manèges 49. Othello 52. Love in the Afternoon 56. *The Nun's Story* 58. The Apartment 60. One Two Three 61. Irma La Douce 63. The Night of the Generals 66. *A Flea in Her Ear* 68, many others.

travelling matte: a masking film overlaid with another in the optical printer so as to produce a trick effect.

Travers, Ben (1886–). British playwright responsible for the Tom Walls/Ralph Lynn Aldwych farces which were all filmed in the early thirties.
Rookery Nook 30. *A Cuckoo in the Nest* 33. A Cup of Kindness 33. Turkey Time 34. Banana Ridge 41, etc.
Also wrote film scripts: Fighting Stock 36. Just My Luck 37. Uncle Silas 47, etc.

Travers, Bill (1922–). Tall British leading man, married to Virginia McKenna; stage experience from 1947.
The Square Ring 54. Geordie 55. Bhowani Junction 56. The Barretts of Wimpole Street 57. *The Smallest Show on Earth* 57. The Seventh Sin (US) 58. The Bridal Path 49. Gorgo 60. Invasion Quartet 61. Two Living, One Dead (Swed.) 62. Born Free 66. Duel at Diablo (US) 66. A Midsummer Night's Dream 68. Ring of Bright Water 69. The Belstone Fox 73, etc.

Travers, Henry (1874–1965) (Travers Heagerty). British character actor, on stage from 1894, in America from 1901. Came to films in the thirties and usually played benign old gentlemen.
The Invisible Man 33. Reunion in Vienna 33. Seven Keys to Baldpate 35. On Borrowed Time 38. Dark Victory 39. Anne of Windy Willows 40. High Sierra 41. Ball of Fire 41. Mrs Miniver 42. *The Moon is Down* 43. The Naughty Nineties 45. The Bells of St Mary's 46. *It's a Wonderful Life* (as an angel) 46. The Yearling 47. The Girl from Jones Beach (last appearance) 49, etc.

Travers, Linden (1913–) (Florence Lindon-Travers). British leading lady of stage (from 1931), screen shortly after.
Children of the Fog 35. Double Alibi 36. The Lady Vanishes 38. The Terror 39. The Stars Look Down 39. *The Ghost Train* 41. The Missing Million 42. Beware of Pity 46. No Orchids for Miss Blandish 48. *Quartet* 48. Christopher Columbus 49, etc.

Travis, Richard (1913–) (William Justice). American leading man of forties and fifties second features.
The Man Who Came to Dinner 41. The Big Shot 42. Buses Roar 43. Jewels of Brandenberg 44. Alaska Patrol 46. Skyliner 48. Operation Haylift 50. Mask of the Dragon 51. Fingerprints Don't Lie 51. City of Shadows 55, etc.

Treacher, Arthur (1894–1975) (A. T. Veary). Tall British character comedian, the perfect butler for 30 years. On stage from twenties, Hollywood from 1933.
David Copperfield 34. A Midsummer Night's Dream 35. *Thank You Jeeves* 36. The Little Princess 39. National Velvet 44. Delightfully Dangerous 45. The Countess of Monte Cristo 48. Love That Brute 50. Mary Poppins 64, many others.

Treasure Island. Robert L. Stevenson's adventure classic for boys was filmed three times by American companies. In 1920 Charles Ogle was Long John and Jim Hawkins was played by a girl—Shirley Mason. Maurice Tourneur directed. In 1935, in a splendid production for MGM, Victor Fleming directed Wallace Beery and Jackie Cooper; in 1950, in Britain for Disney, Byron Haskin directed Robert Newton, who was born to play Long John, and Bobby Driscoll. Newton afterwards played the role in a feature, *Long John Silver* 54, and 26 TV half-hours filmed in Australia. In 1972 Orson Welles starred in a European remake, using such a thick accent that he had to be dubbed; and in 1973 Kirk Douglas appeared in *Scalawag*, which borrowed the plot for a modern story.

The Treasure of the Sierra Madre (US 1948). Written and directed by John Huston from the novel by the mysterious B. Traven, this sombre but gripping saga of thieves falling out over gold, after an arduous search in bandit country, won Academy Awards for Huston on both counts and for his father Walter Huston who played the oldest of the rascals. Humphrey Bogart and Tim Holt were also involved, the photography was by Ted McCord and the music by Max Steiner. The film has not worn too well—it has a studio look—but at the time it was hailed as another stride forward by Hollywood towards productions of adult appeal and integrity.

treatment. The first expansion of a script idea into sequence form, giving some idea of how the story is to be told, i.e. with examples of dialogue, camera angles, etc.

Tree, David (1915–). British comedy actor with stage experience.
Knight Without Armour 37. *Pygmalion* (as Freddy Eynsford-Hill) 38. Q Planes 39. *French Without Tears* 39. Major Barbara 40. Then war service, in which he lost an arm; subsequently retired.

Treen, Mary (1907–). American comedy actress who usually plays nurses, office girls, or the heroine's plain friend.
Babbitt 35. Colleen 36. First Love 40. I Love a Soldier 44. From This Day Forward 45. Let's Live a Little 48. The Caddy 53. The Birds and the Bees 56. Rockabye Baby 58. Paradise Hawaiian Style 56, many others.

Tremayne, Les (–). American small part actor.
The Racket 51. Dream Wife 53. A Man Called Peter 55. The Story of Ruth 60. The Fortune Cookie 66, etc.

Trenchard-Smith, Brian (1946–). British director in Australia.
The World of Kung Fu 74. Man from Hong Kong 75, etc.

Trevelyan, John (1904–). British executive, secretary of the British Board of Film Censors 1958–1970, responsible for a more liberal policy allowing such controversial films as *Saturday Night and Sunday Morning, Tom Jones, The Servant, The Silence, Repulsion* and *Who's Afraid of Virginia Woolf?* Published memoirs 1973: *What the Censor Saw.*

Trevor, Austin (1897–) (A. Schilsky). British character actor with long stage experience.
At the Villa Rose 30. *Alibi* (as Hercule Poirot) 31. Lord Edgware Dies (as Hercule Poirot) 34. Dark Journey 37. Goodbye Mr Chips 39. Champagne Charlie 44. The Red Shoes 48. Father Brown 54. The Horrors of the Black Museum 59, etc.

Trevor, Claire (1909–) (Claire Wemlinger). American character actress on stage from childhood. Made many routine films before gaining critical notice.
Life in the Raw (debut) 33. Hold That Girl 34. Dante's Inferno 35. Career Woman 36. Dead End 37. The Amazing Dr Clitterhouse 38. *Stagecoach* 39. I Stole a Million 39. Dark Command 40. Honky Tonk 41. Crossroads 42. Street of Chance 42. Woman of the Town 43. *Murder My Sweet* 44. Johnny Angel 45. Crack Up 46. Bachelor Girls 47. *Key Largo* (AA) 48. The Lucky Stiff 49. Best of the Badmen 50. Hard, Fast and Beautiful 51. The Stranger Wore a Gun 52. The High and the Mighty 54. The Man without a Star 55. The Mountain 56. Marjorie Morningstar 58. Two Weeks in Another Town 62. How to Murder Your Wife 65. Capetown Affair 67, etc.

The Trial (France 1962). Orson Welles' attempt to put Kafka on the screen was mainly filmed in a

French railway station and offered some opportunity for bravura direction and photography; but there were obvious technical inadequacies as well as an all-pervading portentousness, so that as a whole it didn't work except as a vehicle for the off-beat talents of Anthony Perkins as the victimized 'K' and Welles himself as a lawyer.

Triesault, Ivan (1902–). Estonian character actor, former dancer, in Hollywood for many years, usually as frowning villainous henchman.
Mission to Moscow 43. The Hitler Gang 44. Notorious 46. To the Ends of the Earth 48. Five Fingers 52. Fräulein 58. The 300 Spartans 62. Barabbas 62. Von Ryan's Express 65. Batman 66, many others.

Trinder, Tommy (1909–). British cockney music-hall comedian, in occasional films.
Laugh It Off 40. Sailors Three 41. The Bells Go Down 42. *The Foreman Went to France* 42. Champagne Charlie 44. *Fiddlers Three* 44. Bitter Springs 49. You Lucky People 54. The Beauty Jungle 64, etc.

Trintignant, Jean-Louis (1930–). French leading man.
Race for Life 55. And God Created Woman 56. Austerlitz 59. Château en Suède 63. Mata Hari 64. Angélique 64. *A Man and a Woman* 66. Trans-Europe Express 66. The Sleeping Car Murders 66. The Libertine 68. Les Biches 68. 'Z' 68. Ma Nuit Chez Maud 69. The American 70. The Conformist 70. Simon the Swiss 71. Aggression 75.

Triumph of the Will (Germany 1934). A pictorial record of the sixth Nazi congress at Nuremberg, this controversial film still has a sensational impact and is probably the most powerful propaganda film ever made. Leni Riefenstahl's direction and editing, abetted by Sepp Allgeier's luminous photography, make the Nazis seem more like gods than men; and for this reason the film has been denied a commercial reissue in Britain. The early sequence showing Hitler's plane coming down from the clouds is perhaps the cleverest of all.

Trivas, Victor (1896–1970). Russian writer in America.
War is Hell (d) 31. Song of Russia 44. The Stranger 45, etc.

Trnka, Jiři (1910–1969). Czech animator and puppeteer, many of whose short films have been shown abroad.
The Emperor's Nightingale 49. Song of the

Prairie 49. The Good Soldier Schweik 54. Jan Hus 56. A Midsummer Night's Dream 57, etc.

Troell, Jan (1931–). Swedish director.
Here is Your Life 66. Who Saw Him Die 67. *The Emigrants* 72. The New Land 73, etc.

Tronson, Robert (1924–). British director, from TV.
The Man at the Carlton Tower 62. The Traitors 62. On the Run 63. Ring of Spies 64, etc.

Trotti, Lamar (1900–1952). Prolific American scriptwriter and producer.
Judge Priest (co-w) 34. Steamboat Round the Bend (co-w) 35. Ramona (w) 36. Slave Ship (w) 37. *In Old Chicago* (w) 38. *Young Mr Lincoln* (w) 39. Hudson's Bay (w) 41. *The Ox Bow Incident* (wp) 42. Wilson (wp) 43. The Razor's Edge (wp) 46. Mother Wore Tights (wp) 47. Yellow Sky (wp) 48. *Cheaper by the Dozen* (wp) 50. I'd Climb the Highest Mountain (wp) 51. Stars and Stripes Forever (wp) 52. With a Song in My Heart (wp) 52, many others.

Trouble in Paradise (US 1932). One feels that Ernst Lubitsch probably enjoyed making this more than any of his other American films: a roguish, pacy tale of cross and double cross among society jewel thieves, it is told with a lively visual wit and has such a gallery of attractive performances as to make it a sophisticated classic. Herbert Marshall, Miriam Hopkins, Kay Francis, C. Aubrey Smith, Charles Ruggles, Edward Everett Horton are all at their best. Written by Samson Raphaelson with sets designed by Hans Dreier.

The Trouble with Harry (US 1956). Alfred Hitchcock's second favourite of his own films is a determinedly gay black comedy which lacks cinematic spontaneity, all its humour coming straight from Jack Trevor Story's original novel about a corpse on the heath which villagers keep burying and digging up again for their own reasons. The autumnal Vermont setting, delightful in itself, is a distraction to a movie which would have worked better in black and white. Mildred Natwick, Edmund Gwenn and Shirley Maclaine make the most of the macabre situations.

Troughton, Patrick (1920–). British character actor, mainly on TV.
Escape 48. Hamlet 48. Treasure Island 50. The Black Knight 52. Richard III 56. The Gorgon 64. The Omen 76, many others in small roles.

Trouncer, Cecil (1898–1953). British stage

character actor with splendidly resonant diction.
Pygmalion 38. While the Sun Shines 46. London
Belongs to Me 48. *The Guinea Pig* 49. The Lady
with a Lamp 51. Pickwick Papers 52. The Weak
and the Wicked 54.

Trowbridge, Charles (1882–1967).
American character actor, former architect;
usually played professors or kindly fathers.
I Take This Woman 31. The Thirteenth Chair
36. Confessions of a Nazi Spy 39. The Mummy's
Hand 40. Mildred Pierce 45. The Wings of
Eagles 57, many others.

The True Glory (GB 1945). This brilliantly-
made, rather too literary documentary,
composed of newsreel material from D-Day to
the fall of Berlin, still has that brilliant surface
polish which at the time of its release made it by
far the best compilation film to have been seen,
Directed by Carol Reed and Garson Kanin, with
music by William Alwyn.

True-life Adventures: see under *The Living
Desert*.

Truex, Ernest (1890–1973). American
character actor of 'little man' roles, in films since
the twenties.
Whistling in the Dark 33. *The Adventures of
Marco Polo* 38. Christmas in July 40. His Girl
Friday 41. Always Together 48. The Leather
Saint 56. Twilight for the Gods 58. Fluffy 65,
many others; latterly much on TV.

Truffaut, François (1932–). French 'new
wave' director, former critic.
□ Les Mistons 58. *Les Quatre Cents Coups* 59.
Shoot the Pianist 60. *Jules and Jim* 61. Love at
Twenty (part) 62. *Silken Skin* 64. Fahrenheit
451 66. The Bride Wore Black 67. Stolen Kisses
68. Mississippi Mermaid 69. L'Enfant Sauvage
(& a) 69. Domicile Conjugale 70. *Soufflé au
Coeur* 71. Anne and Muriel 72. A Gorgeous Bird
Like Me 72. La Nuit Américaine 73. The Story
of Adele H 75.

Truman, Michael (1916–). British director,
former editor.
Touch and Go 54. Go to Blazes 62. The Girl in
the Headlines 63, etc.

Truman, Ralph (1900–). British stage
character actor who makes occasional film
appearances.
Henry V 44. Beware of Pity 46. Oliver Twist 48.
Quo Vadis 51. The Man Who Knew Too Much
56. El Cid 61. Nicholas and Alexandra 71, many
others.

Trumbo, Dalton (1905–1976). American
screenwriter, one of the 'Hollywood Ten' who
were blacklisted in the forties.
The Remarkable Andrew 42. A Guy Named Joe
43. Our Vines Have Tender Grapes 45. Exodus
60. The Sandpiper 65. Hawaii 66. The Fixer 68.
Johnny Got His Gun (&d) 71. Executive Action
73. Papillon (co-w, a) 73, many others.

Trundy, Natalie (–). American leading
lady in occasional films.
The Careless Years 57. The Monte Carlo Story
58. Mr Hobbs Takes a Vacation 62. Conquest
of the Planet of the Apes 71, etc.

Tryon, Tom (1919–). American leading man
with stage and TV experience.
The Scarlet Hour (debut) 55. Three Violent
People 56. I Married a Monster from Outer
Space 57. Moon Pilot 61. Marines Let's Go 61.
The Cardinal 63. In Harm's Way 65. The Glory
Guys 65. The Horsemen 71. Johnny Got His
Gun (& pd) 71. The Others (oa only) 72, etc.

Tsu, Irene (1943–). Chinese glamour girl in
Hollywood.
Caprice 66. The Green Berets 67. Paper Tiger
75, etc.

Tuchner, Michael (–). British director.
□ Villain 71. Fear is the Key 72. Mister Quilp 75.
The Likely Lads 76.

Tucker, Forrest (1919–). Rugged American
leading man, mostly in routine action pictures
from 1940.
The Westerner (debut) 40. Keeper of the Flame
42. The Yearling 47. The Big Cat 49. Sands of
Iwo Jima 50. The Wild Blue Yonder 52.
Crosswinds 53. Trouble in the Glen (GB) 54.
Break in the Circle (GB) 56. *The Abominable
Snowman* (GB) 57. Auntie Mame 58. The Night
They Raided Minsky's 68. Cancel My
Reservation 72. The Wild McCullochs 75, many
others.
TV series: Crunch and Des 55. F Troop 65–67.
Dusty's Trail 73.

Tucker, Sophie (1884–1966) (Sophia Abuza)
American popular singer, the heavyweight 'red
hot momma' of vaudeville.
□ Honky Tonk 29. Gay Love (GB) 34. Gay
Time (GB) 34. Broadway Melody of 1937 37.
Thoroughbreds Don't Cry 37. Atlantic City 44.
Follow the Boys 44. Sensations of 1945.

Tufts, Sonny (1911–1970) (Bowen Charleston
Tufts). Tall, good-humoured American 'second
lead', in Hollywood from the early forties.

□ So Proudly We Hail 43. Government Girl 43. In The Meantime Darling 44. I Love a Soldier 44. Here Come the Waves 45. Bring on the Girls 45. Duffy's Tavern 45. Miss Susie Slagle's 45. The Virginian 46. The Well-Groomed Bride 46. Cross My Heart 46. Easy Come Easy Go 47. Blaze Of Noon 47. Variety Girl 47. Swell Guy 47. The Untamed Breed 48. The Crooked Way 49. Easy Living 49. The Gift Horse (GB) 52. No Escape 53. Cat Women of the Moon 53. Run for the Hills 53. Serpent Island 54. The Seven Year Itch 55. Come Next Spring 56. The Parson and the Outlaw 57. Town Tamer 65. Cottonpicking Chickenpicker 67.

Tugboat Annie. This aggressive, middle-aged lady of the waterfront was devised by Norman Reilly Raine and personified in the 1933 film by Marie Dressler. Subsequent films include *Tugboat Annie Sails Again* 40 with Marjorie Rambeau and *Captain Tugboat Annie* 45 with Jane Darwell. A 1958 TV series featured Minerva Urecal.

Tully, Montgomery (1904–). British writer and director.
Murder in Reverse (wd) 45. Spring Song (wd) 47. Boys in Brown (d) 49. A Tale of Five Cities (d) 51. The Glass Cage (d) 55. The Hypnotist (d) 57. Escapement (d) 58. Clash by Night (d) 63. Who Killed the Cat? (wd) 66. Battle Beneath the Earth (d) 68, many other second features and TV episodes.

Tully, Tom (1896–). American character actor with stage experience; usually tough-looking but soft-hearted roles.
Destination Tokyo 44. Adventure 45. The Town Went Wild 45. June Bride 48. Where the Sidewalk Ends 50. The Caine Mutiny 54. Ten North Frederick 57. The Wackiest Ship in the Army 61. Coogan's Bluff 68, etc.
TV series: The Line-Up 59.

Tunberg, Karl (1908–). American screenwriter, in Hollywood from 1937.
My Lucky Star 38. Down Argentine Way 40. Orchestra Wives 42. Kitty 45. You Gotta Stay Happy 47. Scandal at Scourie 53. The Scarlet Coat 55. *Ben Hur* 59. Libel 59. Taras Bulba 62. Harlow (electronovision version) 65. Where Were You When the Lights Went Out? 68, many others.

Turman, Laurence (1926–). American producer.
The Young Doctors 61. The Flim Flam Man 66. *The Graduate* 67. Pretty Poison 69. The Great White Hope 70. Marriage of a Young Stockbroker (& d) 71, etc.

The Turn of the Tide (GB 1935). This small, well-intentioned little drama about family rivalry in a Yorkshire fishing village is said to have persuaded Lord Rank to enter the film industry because it showed that a fiction film could be a teaching instrument. Norman Walker directed: John Garrick and Geraldine Fitzgerald were the leading players.

Turner, Florence (1887–1946). American actress who in 1907 became the first 'movie star' known by name; also as 'the Vitagraph Girl'.
A Dixie Mother 10. Francesca da Rimini 12. The Welsh Singer (GB) 13. My Old Dutch (GB) 15. East is East (GB) 15. The Old Wives' Tale (GB) 21, etc. Went back to Hollywood in roles of diminishing stature; retired in the mid-twenties.

Turner, John (1932–). British leading man with stage experience, also known as TV's 'Knight Errant'.
Behemoth, the Sea Monster 60. Petticoat Pirates 61. Sammy Going South 62. The Black Torment 64, etc.

Turner, Lana (1920–) (Julia Turner). American leading lady of the forties; began as the 'girl next door' type but became increasingly sophisticated.
They Won't Forget (debut) 37. The Great Garrick 37. Four's a Crowd 38. The Adventures of Marco Polo 38. Calling Dr Kildare 39. *Love Finds Andy Hardy* 39. Rich Man Poor Girl 39. Dramatic School 39. These Glamour Girls 39. Dancing Co-Ed 39. Two Girls on Broadway 40. We Who Are Young 40. Choose Your Partner 40. Ziegfeld Girl 41. Dr Jekyll and Mr Hyde 41. Honky Tonk 41. Johnny Eager 41. *Somewhere I'll Find You* 42. Slightly Dangerous 43. Marriage is a Private Affair 44. Keep Your Powder Dry 44. Weekend at the Waldorf 45. The Postman Always Rings Twice 45. Green Dolphin Street 46. Cass Timberlane 47. Homecoming 48. The'Three Musketeers 48. A Life of Her Own 50. Mr Imperium 51. The Merry Widow 52. The Bad and the Beautiful 52. Latin Lovers 53. The Flame and the Flesh 54. Betrayed 55. The Prodigal 55. The Rains of Ranchipur 55. The Sea Chase 55. Diane 56. Another Time Another Place (GB) 57. *Peyton Place* 57. The Lady Takes a Flyer 58. *Imitation of Life* 59. Portrait in Black 60. By Love Possessed 61. Bachelor in Paradise 62. Who's Got the Action? 63. Love Has Many Faces 65. Madame X 66. The Big Cube 69. Persecution 74. Bittersweet Love 76, etc.
TV series: The Survivors 69.

Turpin, Ben (1874–1940). Cross-eyed American silent comedian, mainly popular in short slapstick skits of the twenties. In films from 1915 after vaudeville experience.
Uncle Tom's Cabin 19. Small Town Idol 21. Show of Shows 29. The Love Parade 30, scores of others.

Turpin, Dick (1705–1739) was a seasoned criminal without too many obvious redeeming characteristics. Film-makers have seized on his ride to York and his affection for his horse as an excuse to view him through rose-tinted glasses. So he was played as a hero by Matheson Lang in 1922, Tom Mix in 1925, Victor McLaglen in 1933, Louis Hayward in 1951, and David Weston (for Walt Disney) in 1965.

Turpin, Gerry (c. 1930–). British cinematographer.
The Queen's Guards 61. Seance on a Wet Afternoon 64. The Whisperers 67. Deadfall 68. Oh What a Lovely War 69. The Man Who Had Power Over Women 70. I Want What I Want 71. The Last of Sheila 73, etc.

Tushingham, Rita (1940–). British leading character actress with stage experience.
□ A Taste of Honey 61. The Leather Boys 63. A Place To Go 63. Girl with Green Eyes 64. The Knack 65. Dr Zhivago 65. The Trap 66. Smashing Time 67. Diamonds for Breakfast 68. The Guru 69. The Bed-Sitting Room 69. Straight on Till Morning 72. The Human Factor 75.

Tutin, Dorothy (1930–). Leading British actress. Occasional films.
□ The Importance of Being Earnest 52. The Beggar's Opera 53. A Tale of Two Cities 57. Cromwell 69. Savage Messiah 72.

Tuttle, Frank (1892–1963). American director of mainly routine films; in Hollywood from the twenties.
Kid Boots 27. Roman Scandals 33. The Glass Key 35. Waikiki Wedding 37. I Stole a Million 39. This Gun For Hire 42. Lucky Jordan 43. Hostages 43. The Hour Before the Dawn 43. A Man Called Sullivan 4 ispense 46. Swell Guy 47. The Magic Face 1. Gunman in the Streets 51. Hell on Frisco Bay 55. A Cry in the Night 56, etc.

Twain, Mark (1835–1910) (Samuel Langhorne Clemens). Beloved American humorist and travel writer; was played by Fredric March in The Adventures of Mark Twain 44. Works filmed include Tom Sawyer (qv), Huckleberry Finn (qv), A Connecticut Yankee (qv), The Prince and the Pauper (qv), The Celebrated Jumping Frog (as The Best Man Wins), The Million-Pound Banknote.

Twelve Angry Men (US 1957). One of the most successful results (though not commercially) of the TV invasion of Hollywood: a meticulously detailed reconstruction of Reginald Rose's gripping jury-room TV play, directed by Sidney Lumet. Those present included Henry Fonda, E. G. Marshall, Jack Warden, George Voskovec, Ed Begley, Lee J. Cobb.

Twelve O'Clock High (US 1949). A belated, thoughtful tale of World War II which achieved freshness and realism by concentrating less on the action possibilities of the hazards undergone by American bomber pilots based in Britain than on the strains of command, with Gregory Peck giving a fine performance as the commanding officer who finally cracks up. Written by Sy Bartlett and Beirne Lay Jnr; photographed by Leon Shamroy; directed by Henry King. A successful TV series was shown in 1964.

Twelvetrees, Helen (1908–1958) (Helen Jurgens). American leading lady of the thirties; films fairly unmemorable.
The Ghost Talks 29. Her Man 30. The Painted Desert 31. Is My Face Red? 32. King for a Night 33. Times Square Lady 35. Hollywood Round Up 37, etc.

Twentieth Century-Fox Film Corporation. An American production and distribution company formed in 1935 by a merger of Joseph Schenck's Twentieth Century Pictures with William Fox's Fox Film Corporation. Fox had started in nickelodeon days as a showman, then a distributor. Putting his profits into production, he started the careers of several useful stars including Theda Bara, and pioneered the Movietone sound-on-film process; but in the early thirties, after a series of bad deals, he lost power. The new company had Darryl F. Zanuck as production head from 1935 to 1952; he returned in 1962 as president after the resignation of Spyros Skouras, who had reigned from 1942. These two men are therefore largely responsible for the Fox image, which usually gave the impression of more careful budget-trimming and production-processing than did the films of the rest of the 'big five'. Fox's successful personality stars include Shirley Temple, Alice Faye, Don Ameche, Betty Grable and Marilyn Monroe; its best westerns include The Big Trail,

Drums along the Mohawk, My Darling Clementine and *The Gunfighter*; in drama it can claim *What Price Glory?*, *Dante's Inferno, The Grapes of Wrath, How Green Was My Valley, The Ox Bow Incident, The Song of Bernadette, Wilson, The Snake Pit,* and *Gentlemen's Agreement.* In 1953 Spyros Skouras successfully foisted the new screen shape, CinemaScope, on to world markets, but Fox have not used it with greater success than anyone else, their most elaborate 'spectaculars' being *The Robe, There's No Business Like Show Business, The King and I, South Pacific, The Diary of Anne Frank, The Longest Day, Cleopatra, Those Magnificent Men in Their Flying Machines, The Sound of Music, Star!, Hello Dolly,* and *Tora! Tora! Tora!*

Twenty Thousand Years in Sing Sing (US 1932). An early exposé of American prison life, from a book by Warden Lewis E. Lawes; its type quickly became too familiar. Spencer Tracy and Bette Davis starred. In 1940 the story was remade as *Castle on the Hudson* with John Garfield and Ann Sheridan.

Twiggy (1946–) (Leslie Hornsby). British fashion model of the sixties.
□ *The Boy Friend* 71. 'W' 74.

Twist, Derek (1905–). British director, former editor and associate producer.
The End of the River 47. All over the Town 48. Green Grow the Rushes 51. Police Dog 55. Family Doctor 57, etc.

Twist, John (1895–1976). American screenwriter.
The Toast of New York 36. The Great Man Votes 39. So Big 53. Helen of Troy 55. The FBI Story 56. Esther and the King 60. None But the Brave 64, etc.

Two Cities Films. A British company set up in the early days of World War II by the expatriate Italian Filippo del Giudice. It was responsible for many of Britain's most famous films, including *In Which We Serve, The Way Ahead, Henry V, Blithe Spirit* and *Odd Man Out.*

2001: A Space Odyssey (GB 1968). This bird's-eye-view of the universe past and future

made by Stanley Kubrick from a novel by Arthur C. Clarke, worked like a huge confidence trick: the special effects (AA, BFA) were so spellbinding that comparatively few patrons complained of the obscure story line and general lack of human feeling. As prophecy it was certainly less optimistic than H. G. Wells' 1936 *Things To Come.*

Tyler, Beverly (1924–). American leading lady of routine forties films.
Best Foot Forward 43. The Green Years 46. The Beginning or the End 47. The Fireball 50. Chicago Confidential 47, etc.

Tyler, Parker (1904–1974). American highbrow film critic. Author of *The Hollywood Hallucination, Magic and Myth of the Movies, The Shadow of an Airplane Climbs the Empire State Building,* etc.

Tyler, Tom (1903–1954) (Vincent Markowsky). American cowboy star of innumerable second features in the thirties:
The Cowboy Cop 26. *The Sorcerer* 29. *Riding the Lonesome Trail* 34. *Pinto Rustlers* 38. *Roamin' Wild* 39, etc. Also played small roles in such films as *Gone with the Wind* 39. *Stagecoach* 39. *The Mummy's Hand* (as the mummy) 40; and had the title role in *The Adventures of Captain Marvel* (serial) 41.

Tyson, Cicely (1933–). Black American leading actress.
A Man Called Adam 66. The Comedians 67. The Heart is a Lonely Hunter 68. *Sounder* 72. *The Autobiography of Miss Jane Pittman* (TV) 74. Roots (TV) 77, etc.
TV series: East Side West Side 63.

Tyzack, Margaret (1933–). British character actress.
Ring of Spies 64. The Whisperers 67. A Clockwork Orange 71, etc.

Tzelniker, Meier (1894–). British character actor well known in the Yiddish theatre.
Mr Emmanuel 44. It Always Rains on Sunday 48. Last Holiday 50. The Teckman Mystery 54. Make Me an Offer 54. A Night to Remember 58. *Expresso Bongo* 60. The Sorcerers 67.

U

UFA. Universum Film Aktien Gesellschaft: the main German film production company since 1917, owning its studio and linked in the twenties with Paramount and MGM. In the thirties it was brought under state control and in the forties, with the end of the war, it ceased to exist.

Ugetsu Monogatari (Japan 1953). Rather oddly voted by an international critics' poll in 1958 as one of the ten best films ever made, this genuinely strange and beautiful drama would be unlikely to win such an accolade now. Laid in sixteenth-century Japan, it tells of a potter lured away from home into a castle of ghosts. Slight, charming, impeccably directed by Kenji Mizoguchi. Translated into English the title emerges as *Tales of a Pale and Mysterious Moon after the Rain.*

Uggams, Leslie (1945–). Black American revue artiste.
Skyjacked 72.

Ullman, Daniel (1920–). American scriptwriter.
The Maze 53. Seven Angry Men 54. Wichita 55. Good Day for a Hanging 59. Face of a Fugitive 59. Mysterious Island 61, etc.

Ullmann, Liv (1939–). Norwegian leading actress in international films.
The Wayward Girl 59. Persona 66. Hour of the Wolf 67. Shame 68. A Passion 70. The Night Visitor 70. Pope Joan 71. Lost Horizon 73. Forty Carats 73. The Abdication 74. Face to Face 76, etc.

Ulmer, Edgar G. (1900–1972). Austrian-born director long in Hollywood specializing in second features and exploitation subjects. In recent years, somewhat mysteriously revered by French critics.
The Black Cat 34. The Singing Blacksmith 38. Isle of Forgotten Sins 43. Bluebeard 44. The Wife of Monte Cristo 46. Detour 46. Her Sister's Secret 47. Ruthless 48. The Man from Planet X 53. The Naked Dawn 55. Daughter of Dr Jekyll 57. The Amazing Transparent Man 60. Beyond the Time Barrier 61. Atlantis, The Lost Kingdom

(L'Atlantide) 62. The Cavern 65, many others.

Ulric, Leonore (1892–1970) (Lenore Ulrich). American stage actress.
Tiger Rose 23. Frozen Justice 29. Camille 36. Temptation 46. Northwest Outpost 47, etc.

Ulysses. The Homerian hero was played by Kirk Douglas in a 1954 Italian production by Dino de Laurentiis: it concentrated on spectacle and the monstrous Cyclops. Joseph Strick's 1967 film of the same title was a very different affair, being based on James Joyce's experimental novel about twenty-four hours in the life of an Irish Jew in Dublin. Although it could hardly do more than present excerpts from the original, it had much charm and imagination, though its faithful retention of Joyce's language caused it to be banned in many areas. Milo O'Shea and Barbara Jefford led the cast.

Umberto D (Italy 1952). Neo-realistic drama in the mould of *Bicycle Thieves* and also directed by Vittorio de Sica from a script by Cesare Zavattini; about a proud but lonely old man who, unable to raise his rent, contemplates suicide. Uses non-professional actors.

The Umbrellas of Cherbourg (Les Parapluies de Cherbourg) (France 1964). Naïve, charming, all-singing love story directed by Jacques Demy with music by Michel Legrand. The tale of starcrossed lovers would be nothing without the musical treatment and the delightful use of colour; as it is, the film has been considered a masterpiece though it failed (luckily) to spark off a cycle of cinematic light operas.

Umeki, Miyoshi (1929–). Japanese leading lady who won an Academy Award for her performance in *Sayonara* 57.
Cry for Happy 61. Flower Drum Song 61. A Girl Named Tamiko 63. etc.
TV series: The Courtship of Eddie's Father 69.

Uncle Tom's Cabin, an anti-slavery novel of excellent intentions and unabashed sentimentality, was written in 1852 by American novelist Harriet Beecher Stowe (1811–1896). It features the dastardly white villain Simon Legree, the cheerful Negro Uncle Tom, and poor Little Eva who is taken to heaven by an angel. The main film versions include a 1903 one-reeler by Edwin S. Porter, a Pathé three-reeler of 1910 and an American three-reeler of 1913. In 1914 came a longer American version with Marie Eline as Little Eva. 1918 brought a full-length version with Marguerite Clark in the dual role of Topsy and Eva. Then in 1927 Harry Pollard directed a full-blown silent spectacle which was frequently revived with sound effects in later years: Virginia Grey was Eva. The subject might have been thought too dated or too touchy for sound treatment, but in 1965 a colour and widescreen European co-production was directed by Geza von Radvanyi and featured Herbert Lom as Simon Legree and Getrud Mittermayer as Eva.

uncredited appearances by well-known stars are usually intended as gags to liven up a film which can do with an extra laugh. Thus the brief cameos of Cary Grant and Jack Benny in *Without Reservations*; Lana Turner in *Du Barry Was a Lady*; Robert Taylor in *I Love Melvin*; Bing Crosby in *My Favourite Blonde, The Princess and the Pirate* and other Bob Hope films; Alan Ladd in *My Favourite Brunette*; Peter Lorre in *Meet Me in Las Vegas*; Myrna Loy in *The Senator was Indiscreet*; Peter Sellers and David Niven in *Road to Hong Kong*; Vincent Price in *Beach Party*; Boris Karloff in *Bikini Beach*; Groucho Marx in *Will Success Spoil Rock Hunter?*; Elizabeth Taylor in *Scent of Mystery, What's New Pussycat?* and *Anne of the Thousand Days*; Richard Burton in *What's New Pussycat?*; Jack Benny and Jerry Lewis in *It's a Mad Mad Mad Mad World*; Robert Vaughn in *The Glass Bottom Boat*; Bob Hope and others in *The Oscar*; Rock Hudson in *Four Girls in Town*; Jack Benny and Jimmy Durante in *Beau James*; Red Skelton in *Susan Slept Here*; Bing Crosby and Bob Hope in *Scared Stiff*; Martin and Lewis, Humphrey Bogart and Jane Russell in *Road to Bali*; Lauren Bacall in *Two Guys from Milwaukee*; Gene Kelly in *Love is Better Than Ever*; Clark Gable and Robert Taylor in *Callaway Went Thataway*; Peter O'Toole in *Casino Royale*; Yul Brynner in *The Magic Christian*; Edward G. Robinson in *Robin and the Seven Hoods*; Humphrey Bogart in *Always Together, Two Guys from Milwaukee* and *The Love Lottery*; Jack Benny in *The Great Lover*; Ray Milland in *Miss Tatlock's Millions*; John Wayne in *I Married a Woman*; Tony Curtis in *Chamber of Horrors*; Sammy Davis Jnr in *A Raisin in the Sun*; Shirley Maclaine in *Ocean's Eleven*; and Margaret Rutherford in *The ABC Murders*.

Sometimes a sequel not featuring the star of the first story will have a brief reminiscence of him with no credit: this happened to Cary Grant in *Topper Takes a Trip* and to Simone Signoret in *Life at the Top*. Then there are deliberate in-jokes like Walter Huston playing bit parts in his son John's movies, Peter Finch playing a messenger in *The First Men in the Moon* because he happened to be there when the hired actor failed to turn up, Joseph Cotten playing a small part in *Touch of Evil* because he dropped in to watch the location shooting and Orson Welles sent a make-up man over for old times' sake, Helen Hayes playing a small role in *Third Man on the Mountain* because her son James MacArthur was in the cast. Occasionally when stars are replaced during production, long shots of them remain in the completed film: thus Vivien Leigh in *Elephant Walk* and George Brent in *Death of a Scoundrel*. The best gag was played by Al Jolson who, determined to get into *The Jolson Story* at all costs, played himself in the theatre runway long shots during 'Swanee'.

There remain a few mysteries. In *The Great Ziegfeld*, 'A Pretty Girl is Like a Melody' was apparently sung by Stanley Morner, soon to become quite famous as Dennis Morgan. He was not credited (perhaps because the voice finally used on the sound track was that of Allan Jones). Nor were the following who had important roles to play and were well-known at the time: Constance Collier in *Anna Karenina*, Marlene Dietrich in *Touch of Evil*, Henry Daniell in *Mutiny on the Bounty*, Audrey Totter in *The Carpetbaggers*, Dorothy Malone and John Hubbard in *Fate is the Hunter*, Wilfrid Lawson in *Tread Softly Stranger*, Ava Gardner in *The Band Wagon*, Edmond O'Brien in *The Greatest Show on Earth*, David Warner in *Straw Dogs*, Glenda Jackson in *The Boy Friend*; Leo McKern in *The High Commissioner*. And in *Those Magnificent Men in Their Flying Machines*, Cicely Courtneidge and Fred Emney had roughly equal dialogue in their one scene; yet he was credited and she was not. The reasons surely can't have anything to do with modesty.

See also: *Directors' appearances*.

Under Two Flags. Ouida's romantic melodrama of the Foreign Legion was filmed in 1916 by J. Gordon Edwards, with Theda Bara as Cigarette; in 1922 by Tod Browning, with Priscilla Dean and Jack Kirkwood; and in 1936 by Frank Lloyd with Claudette Colbert and Ronald Colman.

Underdown, Edward (1908–). British actor

on stage from 1932; once a jockey. Often cast as a dull Englishman.

The Warren Case 33 (debut). Wings of the Morning 37. They Were Not Divided 50. The Voice of Merrill 52. Beat the Devil 54. The Camp on Blood Island 58. The Day the Earth Caught Fire 62. Khartoum 66. The Hand of Night 67. Running Scared 72, etc.

underground films are generally thought of as those made cheaply to espouse a cause or experimentally at a director's whim, commercial success being a secondary consideration. Underground directors such as Andy Warhol have, however, successfully exploited the audience's desire to be 'with it', even though what they were with probably had no meaning.

underground railways have been used remarkably little in films considering their dramatic possibilities. There were chases through them in Underground itself, Bulldog Jack, Waterloo Road, The French Connection, the Taking of Pelham One Two Three, Death Line and Death Wish; they were also used for a comedy scene in Rotten to the Core, a murder in Man Hunt, Otley, and The Liquidator, and a musical number in Three Hats for Lisa. The New York subway was the setting for musical numbers in Dames ('I Only Have Eyes for You') and On the Town ('Miss Turnstiles' ballet), and it also featured in a romantic comedy (Practically Yours) and was the scene of a brutal beating-up in The Young Savages and a nasty accidental death in P.J.; while the whole of Dutchman took place on it, and Short Walk To Daylight began with an earthquake trapping passengers in it.

The New York elevated railway, on the other hand, was most dramatically used in King Kong, and provided effective backing in The Lost Weekend, Union Station, The Bachelor Party, The FBI Story, Beneath the Planet of the Apes, Cry of the City and The French Connection.

undertakers, or morticians, have provided comedy relief in many a western, relying on frequent shootings to bring in business: perhaps this theme was first explored in The Westerner 39. The comedy elements of the profession were also presented by Vincent Price and Peter Lorre in A Comedy of Terrors, by Terry Thomas in Strange Bedfellows, by almost the entire cast of The Loved One, by Paul Lynde in Send Me No Flowers, and by J. Pat O'Malley in Willard. Literature's most famous undertaker is perhaps Mr Sowerberry in Oliver Twist, played by Gibb McLaughlin in the 1948 version and by Leonard Rossiter in Oliver!

underwater sequences of note were found in Reap the Wild Wind, The Silent Enemy, The Beast from 20,000 Fathoms, The Golden Mistress, Twenty Thousand Leagues Under the Sea, Around the World Under the Sea, Voyage to the Bottom of the Sea, Thunderball, Shark, and Lady in Cement.

See also: submarines.

Underworld (US 1927). Released in Britain as Paying the Penalty, this melodrama written by Ben Hecht and directed by Josef Von Sternberg did much to trigger off the gangster cycle. George Bancroft played 'Bull Weed', the anti-hero; Evelyn Brent was 'Feathers McCoy', his moll, and Clive Brook 'Rolls Royce', his sidekick.

unemployment in Britain was the somewhat unpopular subject of Doss House, Love on the Dole, and The Common Touch; in Europe, Joyless Street, Little Man What Now? and Berliner Ballade. America has seemed almost to boast about its unemployed, who were featured in The Crowd, Our Daily Bread, Grapes of Wrath, Hallelujah I'm a Bum, Sullivan's Travels, I Was a Fugitive from a Chain Gang, The Great McGinty, One More Spring, Mr Deeds Goes to Town, Man's Castle, My Man Godfrey and Tobacco Road, among many others.

Unfaithfully Yours (US 1948). Vintage satirical comedy, and the last good one to be written and directed by Preston Sturges. Rex Harrison plays Sir Alfred de Carter (!), a jealous orchestral conductor who suspects his wife of infidelity and plots three revenges during a concert; murder during Rossini, renunciation during Wagner, suicide during Tchaikovsky.

The Uninvited (US 1943). Claimed as Hollywood's first attempt at a serious ghost story, this set-bound adventure now seems rather tame, with its phoney Devon village and cliff-top house in which a girl is driven to desperation by the spirit of her mother but saved by that of her father's mistress. But at least it broadened Hollywood's horizons, and Lewis Allen, directing his first film, led us deftly through the talky script. With Gail Russell, Ray Milland, Donald Crisp, Cornelia Otis Skinner; from a novel, Uneasy Freehold, by Dorothy Macardle.

United Artists Corporation was founded in 1919 by Mary Pickford, Douglas Fairbanks, Charlie Chaplin and D. W. Griffith, the object being to make and distribute their own and other people's quality product.

Among the company's early successes were *His Majesty the American, Pollyanna* (the first film sold on a percentage basis), *Broken Blossoms, Way Down East,* and *A Woman of Paris.* In the mid-twenties Joe Schenck was brought in to run the company, and he in turn gained Valentino, Goldwyn, Keaton and Swanson; but later all were bought out by various syndicates. Howard Hughes contributed *Hell's Angels* and *Scarface,* but in the thirties the UA product began to thin out, partly because the company was purely a distributor and financer of independent producers, without any studio of its own or any large roster of stars under contract. The hardest times, with only inferior product to sell, were between 1948 and 1953; but since then a new board of directors fought back to a powerful position through careful choice of product, and UA is now back at the top of the tree again with a recent history that includes *The Magnificent Seven, Tom Jones,* the James Bond pictures,*The Battle of Britain, One Flew Over the Cuckoo's Nest, Network* and *Rocky.*

Universal Pictures was founded in 1912 by Carl Laemmle, an exhibitor turned producer. Universal City grew steadily and included among its output many of the most famous titles of Von Stroheim, Valentino and Lon Chaney. In 1930 came *All Quiet on the Western Front,* and soon after *Dracula* and *Frankenstein,* the precursors of a long line of horror pictures. Laemmle lost power in the mid-thirties and the studio settled down to be one of Hollywood's 'little two', producing mainly modest, low-budget co-features without too many intellectual pretensions. The Deanna Durbin series saved it from receivership, and there were occasional notable pictures: *Destry Rides Again, Hellzapoppin, Flesh and Fantasy.* The stars under contract were durable: Boris Karloff, Lon Chaney Jnr, Donald O'Connor, Abbott and Costello, Jeff Chandler, Audie Murphy. More ambition was noted in the fifties, when the era of the bread-and-butter picture was ended by TV. Decca Records gained a large measure of control, but in 1962 a merger gave the ultimate power to the Music Corporation of America, ex-agents and TV producers. The last few years have seen a steady resumption of prestige, with films like *Spartacus,* the Doris Day-Rock Hudson sex comedies, *Charade, The War Lord,* Ross Hunter's soapily sentimental but glossy remakes of Hollywood's choicest weepies, *Thoroughly Modern Millie, The Day of the Jackal, Earthquake, Airport* and *The Seven Per Cent Solution.* The company, now a division of MCA Inc, is currently one of Hollywood's most powerful sources of box-office films and

television series, though its venture into 'enlightened' European production was fairly disastrous.

universities have scarcely been studied seriously by movie-makers. Of Britain's most venerable, Cambridge has served as a background for one light comedy, *Bachelor of Hearts,* and Oxford for another, *A Yank at Oxford,* which was subsequently parodied by Laurel and Hardy in *A Champ at Oxford. Charley's Aunt* (qv) was also set among dreaming spires. Dramas with Oxford settings include *Accident* and *The Mind Benders.* Provincial universities score one comedy (*Lucky Jim*) and one drama (*The Wild and the Willing*). American campuses used to feature in films of the *Hold That Co-Ed* type, the pleasantest to remember being *The Freshman* and *Horse Feathers,* with *How To Be Very Very Popular* a poor third; but in the late sixties student protest held sway in *The Strawberry Statement, Getting Straight, R.P.M., Drive He Said,* and *The Activist.* Other views of the American higher learning came in *Paper Chase, The Group, The Male Animal, Class of 44,* and *The Magic Garden of Stanley Sweetheart.*

Unsworth, Geoffrey (–). British cinematographer.
The Million Pound Note 53. Hell Drivers 57. *A Night to Remember* 58. Northwest Frontier 59. The 300 Spartans 62. *Becket* (BFA) 64. Genghis Khan 65. Half a Sixpence 67. *2001: A Space Odyssey* 68. The Bliss of Mrs Blossom 68. The Assassination Bureau 68. The Reckoning 69. Three Sisters 70. *Cabaret* 72. Alice's Adventures in Wonderland 72. Zardoz 73. Murder on the Orient Express 74. Lucky Lady 75. A Matter of Time 76, etc.

U.P.A. (United Productions of America) was a cartoon factory which in the early fifties received generous critical plaudits for a hundred or so shorts and even pushed the Disney studio into a more sophisticated style. Its creations included Mr Magoo, Gerald McBoing Boing and Pete Hothead, and it specialized in a stylish economy of line and in an appeal to a much higher intelligence bracket than any cartoon had aspired to in the past.

Urban, Charles (1871–1942). American pioneer of British films. He left Edison to found his own production company in London, and especially developed commercial non-fiction films.

Ure, Mary (1933–1975). British leading actress of stage and (occasionally) screen.

□ Storm over the Nile 55. Windom's Way 59. Look Back in Anger 59. *Sons and Lovers* 60. The Mind Benders 63. The Luck of Ginger Coffey 64. Custer of the West 67. Where Eagles Dare 68. Reflection of Fear 71.

Urecal, Minerva (1896–1966). American character actress.

Oh Doctor 37. Boys of the City 40. The Bridge of San Luis Rey 44. Who's Guilty? 47. The Lost Moment 48. Harem Girl 52. Miracle in the Rain 56. The Seven Faces of Dr Lao 64, etc.

TV series: Tugboat Annie.

Urquhart, Robert (1922–). Scottish character actor, in films since 1951 after stage experience.

You're Only Young Twice (debut) 51. Knights of the Round Table 54. You Can't Escape 56. The Curse of Frankenstein 56. Dunkirk 58. 55 Days at Peking 62. Murder at the Gallop 64. Country Dance 70, etc.

TV series: The Pathfinders 72. The Amazing Mr Goodall 74.

Ustinov, Peter (1921–). Garrulous, hirsute, multi-talented British actor-director-playwright-screenwriter-raconteur.

□ AS ACTOR: Hullo Fame 40. Mein Kampf 40. The Goose Steps Out 41. One of Our Aircraft is Missing 42. Let the People Sing 42. The Way Ahead 44. *Private Angelo* 49. Odette 50. *Hotel Sahara* 51. The Magic Box 51. *Quo Vadis* (as Nero) 51. *Beau Brummell* (as George IV) 54. The Egyptian 54. We're No Angels 55. Lola Montez 55. The Man Who Wagged His Tail 57. The Spies 57. *The Sundowners* 60. *Spartacus* (AA) 60. *Romanoff and Juliet* 61. Billy Budd 62. Topkapi (AA) 64. John Goldfarb Please Come Home 65. Lady L 65. The Comedians 67. Blackbeard's Ghost 68. Hot Millions 68. Viva Max 69. Hammersmith is Out (&d) 72. One of Our Dinosaurs is Missing 75. Logan's Run 76. Treasure of Matecumbe 76. The Last Remake of Beau Geste 77.

□ AS DIRECTOR-WRITER: School for Secrets 46. *Vice Versa* 48. *Private Angelo* 49. Romanoff and Juliet 61. Billy Budd 62. Lady L 65.

Uys, Jamie (1921–). South African writer-producer-director.

Rip Van Winkle 60. *Dingaka* 64. The Professor and the Beauty Queen 67. Dirkie 69. Lost in the Desert 70.

V

Vaccaro, Brenda (1939–). American character actress.
Midnight Cowboy 69. Where It's At 69. I Love My Wife 70. Summertree 71. What's a Nice Girl Like You . . .? (TV) 72. Honor Thy Father 73. Sunshine (TV) 74. Once is Not Enough 76, etc.

Vadim, Roger (1927–) (Roger Vadim Plemiannikow). French writer-director.
Futures Vedettes (w) 54. *And God Created Woman* (wd) 56. Heaven Fell That Night (wd) 57. *Les Liaisons Dangereuses* (wd) 59. Warrior's Rest (wd) 62. Vice and Virtue (wd) 62. La Ronde (wd) 64. Nutty Naughty Château (Château en Suède) 64. The Game is Over (wd) 66. Histoires Extraordinaires (part) 68. Barbarella 68. Pretty Maids All in a Row 71. Don Juan 73, etc.

The Vagabond King: see *If I Were King*.

Vague, Vera: see *Allen, Barbara Jo*.

Valenti, Jack (1921–). American executive, dynamic president of the Motion Picture Association of America.

Valentine, Joseph (1903–1948) (Giuseppe Valentino). Italian-American cinematographer, long in Hollywood.
Possessed 47. *Sleep My Love* 47. Rope 48. *Joan of Arc* (AA) 48, etc.

Valentino, Rudolph (1895–1926) (Rodolpho d'Antonguolla). Italian-American leading man, the great romantic idol of the twenties; his personality still shows. His sudden death caused several suicides and his funeral was a national event. Among the published biographies of him are his wife Natacha Rambova's *Rudy* 1926, George S. Ullman's *The Real Valentino* 1927, Alan Arnold's *Valentino* 1952, Robert Oberfirst's *Rudolph Valentino, The Man Behind the Myth* 1962, and Irving Shulman's *Valentino* 1967.
☐ My Official Wife 14. Patria 16. Alimony 18. A Society Sensation 18. All Night 18. The Delicious Little Devil 19. A Rogue's Romance 19. The Homebreaker 19. Virtuous Sinners 19. The Big Little Person 19. Out of Luck 19. Eyes of

Youth 19. The Married Virgin 20. An Adventuress 20. The Cheater 20. Passion's Playground 20. Once to Every Woman 20. Stolen Moments 20. The Wonderful Chance 20. *The Four Horsemen of the Apocalypse* (the part that made him a super-star) 21. Unchained Seas 21. Camille 21. The Conquering Power 21. *The Sheik* 21. Moran of the Lady Letty 21. Beyond the Rocks 22. The Young Rajah 22. *Blood and Sand* 22. *Monsieur Beaucaire* 24. A Sainted Devil 24. Cobra 24. *The Eagle* 25. *Son of the Sheik* 26.

Valk, Frederick (1901–1956). Heavyweight Czech stage actor, in Britain from 1939.
Gasbags 40. *Thunder Rock* 42. *Dead of Night* 45. Latin Quarter 46. An Outcast of the Islands 51. Top Secret 52. The Colditz Story 53. Zarak 55, etc.

Vallee, Rudy (1901–) (Hubert Vallee). American character comedian, the former crooning idol of the late twenties.
The Vagabond Lover 29. Sweet Music 34. Gold Diggers in Paris 38. Second Fiddle 39. Too Many Blondes 41. *The Palm Beach Story* 42. Happy Go Lucky 43. It's in the Bag 45. *The Bachelor and the Bobbysoxer* 47. Unfaithfully Yours 48. The Beautiful Blonde from Bashful Bend 49. Ricochet Romance 54. Gentlemen Marry Brunettes 55. The Helen Morgan Story 57. *How to Succeed in Business Without Really Trying* (his stage role) 67. Live a Little, Love a Little 68. Won Ton Ton 76, etc.

Valley of the Dolls (US 1967). A workaday film version of a notorious novel by Jaqueline Susann about the effect of drugs on high society women. Directed by Richard Fleischer, it proved a little tame for sensation seekers. An apparent 1970 sequel, *Beyond the Valley of the Dolls*, had nothing in common with the original, being a fairly outlandish sexploitation epic by porn director Russ Meyer.

Valli, Alida (1921–) (Alida Maria Altenburger). Beautiful Italian actress.
I Due Sergenti 36. Manon Lescaut 39. Piccolo Mondo Antico 41. Eugénie Grandet 46. The

Paradine Case (US) 48. The Miracle of the Bells 48. *The Third Man* 49. Walk Softly Stranger 49. The White Tower 50. The Lovers of Toledo 52. *Senso* 53. The Stranger's Hand 53. Heaven Fell That Night 57. The Sea Wall (This Angry Age) 57. Le Dialogue des Carmélites 59. Ophelia 61. Une Aussi Longue Absence 61. 1900 76, etc.

Valli, Virginia (1898–1968) (Virginia McSweeney). American silent screen heroine who retired in 1932 to marry Charles Farrell.
Efficiency Edgar's Courtship 17. The Storm 22. A Lady of Quality 23. Paid to Love 27. Isle of Lost Ships 32, etc.

Vallone, Raf (1916–). Italian leading man, former journalist.
Bitter Rice 48. Vendetta 49. Il Cristo Proibito 50. Anna 51. Thérèse Raquin 53. The Beach 53. The Sign of Venus 55. El Cid 61. *A View from the Bridge* (US) 61. Phaedra 62. The Cardinal 63. Harlow 65. Beyond the Mountains 66. The Italian Job 69. Cannon for Cordoba 70. A Gunfight 71. Rosebud 75. The Human Factor 75, etc.

Vampyr (France 1931). Also called *The Strange Adventure of David Gray*, this chic and mystical horror film by Carl Dreyer, with misty photography by Rudolf Maté, is slow, unsatisfying and mystifying to sit through. Its fame rests on a number of effective moments, notably the hero's dream of death and the villain's end in a flour mill (buried in white flour), which have been much copied.

Van, Bobby (1930–) (Robert Stein). American song-and-dance man who went out of fashion with musicals but found a new audience in his forties and became a TV personality.
□ Because You're Mine 52. Small Town Girl 52. Kiss Me Kate 53. The Navy Versus the Night Monsters 66. *Lost Horizon* 73. Lost Flight (TV) 73.

Van Cleef, Lee (1925–). American character actor who after years as a sneaky western villain found fame and fortune as the hero of tough Italian westerns.
High Noon 52. Arena 53. Yellow Tomahawk 54. A Man Alone 55. Joe Dakota 57. Guns Girls and Gangsters 58. The Man Who Shot Liberty Valance 62. *For a Few Dollars More* 65. Day of Anger 66. *The Good the Bad and the Ugly* 67. Death Rides a Horse 67. Sabata 69. Barquero 70. El Condor 70. Captain Apache 71. Bad Man's River 71. The Magnificent Seven Ride 72. Take a Hard Ride 75, etc.

Van Devere, Trish (1943–). American leading lady of the seventies.
Where's Poppa? 70. The Last Run 71. One is a Lonely Number 72. The Day of the Dolphins 73, etc.

Van Dine, S. S. (1888–1939) (Willard Huntingdon Wright). American author who created the wealthy man-about-town detective Philo Vance, personified on screen by several actors. William Powell played him in *The Canary Murder Case* 29, *The Greene Murder Case* 29, *The Benson Murder Case* 30, and *The Kennel Murder Case* 33. Basil Rathbone had one attempt, *The Bishop Murder Case* 30. Warren William took over for *The Dragon Murder Case* 34 and *The Gracie Allen Murder Case* 39. Meanwhile there were Paul Lukas in *The Casino Murder Case* 35, Edmund Lowe in *The Garden Murder Case* 36, and Grant Richards in *Night of Mystery* 37. 1940 brought James Stephenson in *Calling Philo Vance*; in 1947 there was William Wright in *Philo Vance Returns*; and Alan Curtis in 1948 appeared in two poor attempts, *Philo Vance's Gamble* and *Philo Vance's Secret Mission.*

Van Doren, Mamie (1933–) (Joan Lucille Olander). American leading lady, the blonde bombshell of the second feature, in Hollywood from 1954.
Forbidden (debut) 54. Yankee Pasha 54. The Second Greatest Sex 55. Running Wild 55. The Girl in Black Stockings 56. Teacher's Pet 58. The Navy Versus the Night Monsters 66, etc.

Van Druten, John (1901–1957). British dramatist who latterly lived in America.
Plays filmed include *Young Woodley, I Am a Camera, Old Acquaintance, The Voice of the Turtle, I Remember Mama.*

Van Dyke, Dick (1925–). Lanky American TV comedian who never quite made it in movies.
□ Bye Bye Birdie 63. What a Way to Go 64. Mary Poppins 64. The Art of Love 65. Lt Robin Crusoe 65. Never a Dull Moment 67. Divorce American Style 67. Fitzwilly 67. Chitty Chitty Bang Bang 68. *The Comic* 69. Some Kind of a Nut 70. Cold Turkey 71. The Morning After (TV) 74.
TV series: *The Dick Van Dyke Show* 61–66. The New Dick Van Dyke Show 71–72.

Van Dyke, W. S. (1889–1943). Competent, adaptable American director, at his peak in the thirties.
□ Men of the Desert 18. Gift of Gab 18. Lady of the Dugout 19. According to Hoyle 22. Boss of

Camp 4 22. Forget Me Not 22. Little Girl Next Door 23. Miracle Workers 23. Loving Lies 23. You Are In Danger 23. Half Dollar Bill 24. The Beautiful Sinner 25. Gold Heels 25. Hearts and Spurs 25. The Trail Rider 25. Ranger of the Big Pines 25. The Timber Wolf 25. The Desert's Price 25. The Gentle Cyclone 26. War Paint 26. Winners of the Wilderness 27. Heart of the Yukon 27. Eyes of the Totem 27. Foreign Devils 27. Spoilers of the West 27. Wyoming 28. Under Black Eagle 28. *White Shadows in the South Seas* 28. The Pagan 29. *Trader Horn* 31. Never the Twain Shall Meet 31. Guilty Hands 31. Cuban Love Song 32. *Tarzan the Ape Man* 32. Night World 32. Penthouse 33. Eskimo 33. The Prizefighter and the Lady 33. Laughing Boy 34. *Manhattan Melodrama* 34. *The Thin Man* 34. Forsaking All Others 35. Naughty Marietta 35. I Live My Life 35. Rose Marie 36. *San Francisco* 36. His Brother's Wife 36. The Devil is a Sissy 36. Love on the Run 36. After the Thin Man 36. Personal Property 37. They Gave Him a Gun 37. Rosalie 37. Marie Antoinette 38. *Sweethearts* 38. Stand Up and Fight 39. It's a Wonderful World 39. Andy Hardy Gets Spring Fever 39. Another Thin Man 39. I Take This Woman 40. I Love You Again 40. Bitter Sweet 40. Rage in Heaven 41. The Feminine Touch 41. Shadow of the Thin Man 41. Dr Kildare's. Victory 41. I Married an Angel 42. Cairo 42. Journey for Margaret 42.

Van Enger, Charles (1890–). American cinematographer.
Treasure Island 20. A Doll's House 22. The Famous Mrs Fair 23. The Marriage Circle 24. Forbidden Paradise 24. *Phantom of the Opera* 25. Kiss me Again 25. Puppets 26. Easy Pickings 27. Port of Missing Girls 28. Fox Movietone Follies 29. High Society Blues 30. Mad Parade 31. I Was a Spy 33. The Case of Gabriel Perry 34. Seven Sinners 36. Wife Doctor and Nurse 37. Miracle on Main Street 40. Never Give a Sucker an Even Break 41. Night Monster 42. Sherlock Holmes Faces Death 43. The Merry Monahans 44. That Night with You 45. The Time of Their Lives 46. The Wistful Widow 47. Abbott and Costello Meet Frankenstein 48. Africa Screams 49. Ma and Pa Kettle Back on the Farm 51. The Magnetic Monster 53. Sitting Bull 54. Time Table 56. Gun Fever 58, many others.

Van Eyck, Peter (1911–1969). Blond German actor, in America from mid-thirties, later international.
The Moon is Down 42. Five Graves to Cairo 43. Rommel, Desert Fox 51. *The Wages of Fear* 53. Retour de Manivelle 57. The Girl Rosemarie 58. The Snorkel 58. Foxhole in Cairo 60. Station Six

Sahara 63. The Spy Who Came in from the Cold 65. Million Dollar Man 67. Shalako 68. Assignment to Kill 69, many others.

Van Eyssen, John (1925–). South African actor who appeared in a number of British films before turning agent.
Quatermass II 56. Dracula 57. I'm All Right Jack 59. The Criminal 60. Exodus 60, etc. 1969–1973: chief production executive in Britain for Columbia.

Van Fleet, Jo (1919–). American character actress who usually plays older than her real age.
□ *East of Eden* (AA) 55. The Rose Tattoo 55. I'll Cry Tomorrow 55. The King and Four Queens 56. Gunfight at the OK Corral 57. This Angry Age 58. *Wild River* 60. Cool Hand Luke 67. I Love You Alice B. Toklas 67. The Gang That Couldn't Shoot Straight 72. The Tenant 76.

Van Heusen, Jimmy (1919–). American songwriter, usually with lyrics by Johnny Burke.
'Swinging on a Star' (AA 1944), 'Sunday, Monday or Always', 'Sunshine Cake', many others; films include *Road to Rio* 47. *A Yankee in King Arthur's Court* 49. *Road to Bali* 53. *Little Boy Lost* 53, etc.

Van Parys, Georges (1902–1971). French composer.
Le Million 31. Jeunesse 34. Café de Paris 38. Le Silence est d'Or 46. Fanfan La Tulipe 51. Adorables Créatures 52. Les Diaboliques 55. French Cancan 55. Charmants Garçons 57, many others.

Van Patten, Joyce (1934–). American leading lady of the seventies.
The Goddess 58. I Love You Alice B. Toklas 68. Something Big 71. The Bravos (TV) 72. Thumb Tripping 72, etc.

Van Peebles, Melvin (1932–). Black American director.
The Story of a Three-Day Pass 67. Watermelon Man 69, etc.

Van Rooten, Luis (1906–1973). Mexican-born American character actor.
The Hitler Gang (as Himmler) 44. Two Years Before the Mast 44. To the Ends of the Earth 48. Champion 49. Detective Story 51. The Sea Chase 55, etc.

Van Sloan, Edward (1882–1964). American character actor with stage experience; often seen as elderly professors.
Dracula 30. *Frankenstein* 31. The Mummy 33.

Death Takes a Holiday 34. The Last Days of Pompeii 35. *Dracula's Daughter* 36. The Phantom Creeps 39. The Doctor Takes a Wife 40. The Conspirators 44. The Mask of Dijon 47. A Foreign Affair 47, etc.

Van Upp, Virginia (1912–1970). American executive producer, at Columbia in the late forties. Former writer.
Young and Willing 40. The Crystal Ball 42. Cover Girl 44. The Impatient Years (& p) 44. Together Again (& p) 45, etc.

Van Zandt, Philip (1904–1958). Dutch character actor, in Hollywood films.
Citizen Kane 41. House of Frankenstein 45. April Showers 48. Viva Zapata 52. Knock on Wood 54. The Pride and the Passion 57, etc.

Vanbrugh, Irene (1872–1949). Distinguished British stage actress whose rare film appearances included *The Gay Lord Quex* 27, *Moonlight Sonata* 37.

Vance, Vivian (c. 1903–). Cheerful American character comedian, long a partner of Lucille Ball in various TV series.
The Secret Fury 50. The Blue Veil 51. The Great Race 65, etc.

Vanel, Charles (1892–). French character actor, with stage experience.
Les Misérables 33. Le Grand Jeu 34. La Belle Equipe 36. Légion d'Honneur 38. Carrefour 39. *La Ferme du Pendu* 45. In Nome della Legge 49. *The .Wages of Fear* 53. Maddalena 54. *Les Diaboliques* 55. Rafles sur la Ville 57. Le Dialogue des Carmélites 59. La Vérité 60. Un Homme de Trop 67, many others.

Varconi, Victor (1896–1976) (Mihaly Varkonyi). Hungarian actor long in Hollywood.
The Volga Boatmen 26. King of Kings 27. The Divine Lady (as Nelson) 29. The Doomed Battalion 31. Roberta 34. The Plainsman 36. Disputed Passage 39. Reap the Wild Wind 42. For Whom the Bell Tolls 43. Samson and Delilah 50, etc.

Varda, Agnes (1928–). French writer-director of the 'left bank' school.
La Pointe Courte 56. Cléo de 5 à 7 62. Le Bonheur 65. Les Créatures 66. Lions Love 69, etc.

Varden, Evelyn (1895–1958). American stage character actress who made several films.
Pinky 49. Cheaper by the Dozen 50. Phone Call from a Stranger 52. The Student Prince 54. Night of the Hunter 55. The Bad Seed 56, etc.

Varden, Norma (c. 1898–). British character actress, usually as haughty aristocrat in comedies; went to Hollywood in the forties.
A Night Like This 32. The Iron Duke 35. Foreign Affairs 36. Shipyard Sally 39. Random Harvest 42. The Green Years 46. Strangers on a Train 51. Gentlemen Prefer Blondes 53. Witness for the Prosecution 58. The Sound of Music 65. Doctor Dolittle 67, many others.

variable area and **variable density.** Types of sound track. Variable area appears as a spiky symmetrical line (like a long folded ink blot). Variable density is the same width throughout but with horizontal bars of varying light and shade.

Variety (Germany 1925). Also known as *Vaudeville*, this trapeze melodrama had a plot very similar to the later *Three Maxims* and *Trapeze*. Solemnly but sylishly directed by E. A. Dupont, with Emil Jannings, Warwick Ward and Lya de Putti.

Varley, Beatrice (1896–1969). British character actress who played worried little elderly ladies for thirty years.
Hatter's Castle 41. So Well Remembered 47. No Room at the Inn 49. Hindle Wakes 53. The Feminine Touch 55, scores of others.

Varnel, Marcel (1894–1947). French-born director, in Hollywood from 1924; came to England in the thirties and made some of the best comedies of Will Hay and the Crazy Gang.
The Silent Witness 32. Chandu the Magician 32. Girls will be Boys 34. No Monkey Business 35. Good Morning Boys 36. OK for Sound 37. *Oh Mr Porter* 38. Convict 99 38. *Alf's Button Afloat* 38. *Old Bones of the River* 38. *Ask a Policeman* 39. *The Frozen Limits* 39. Where's that Fire? 39. Let George Do It 40. Gasbags 40. I Thank You 41. Hi Gang 41. *The Ghost of St Michaels* 41. Much Too Shy 42. King Arthur was a Gentleman 42. Get Cracking 43. He Snoops to Conquer 44. I Didn't Do It 45. George in Civvy Street 46. This Man is Mine 46. The First Gentleman 47, etc.

Varnel, Max (1925–). British second feature director, son of Marcel Varnel.
A Woman Possessed 58. The Great Van Robbery 49. A Taste of Money 60. Return of a Stranger 61. Enter Inspector Duval 62. The Silent Invasion 63, etc.

Varney, Reg (1922–). Chirpy British comedian who after years of availability found fame in the sixties in TV series *The Rag Trade* and *On the Buses*.

The Great St Trinian's Train Robbery 66. On the Buses 71. Mutiny on the Buses 72. Go for a Take 72. The Best Pair of Legs in the Business 72. Holiday on the Buses 73, etc.

Varsi, Diane (1938–). Slightly-built American leading lady who had a brief career in the fifties, with sporadic appearances later..

□ *Peyton Place* 57. *Ten North Frederick* 58. From Hell to Texas 59. Compulsion 59. Sweet Love, Bitter 66. Wild in the Streets 68. Killers Three 69. Bloody Mama 70. Johnny Got His Gun 71.

vaudeville is the American equivalent of the British *music hall*. Eight or ten variety acts, booked separately, formed a two-hour bill for the family. Burlesque was different, being for adults only.

Vaughan, Frankie (1928–) (Frank Åbelsohn). Flamboyant British song and dance man who never really made it in movies despite a sojourn in Hollywood.

□ Ramsbottom Rides Again 56. *These Dangerous Years* 57. The Lady is a Square 58. Wonderful Things 58. Heart of a Man 59. Let's Make Love 61. The Right Approach 62. It's All Over Town 64.

Vaughan, Peter (1923–) (Peter Ohm). British character actor of solid presence, good or evil.

Sapphire 59. Village of the Damned 60. The Punch and Judy Man 63. Fanatic 65. The Naked Runner 67. Hammerhead 68. The Bofors Gun 68. Alfred the Great 69. Eye Witness 70. Straw Dogs 71. The Pied Piper 72. 11 Harrowhouse 74.

Vaughn, Robert (1932–). Slight, intense American actor who didn't quite make the front rank.

Teenage Caveman 58. No Time to be Young 58. The Young Philadelphians 59. *The Magnificent Seven* 60. The Big Show 61. The Caretakers 63. One Spy Too Many 66. The Venetian Affair 67. The Helicopter Spies 68. Bullitt 68. The Mind of Mr Soames 69. The Bridge at Remagen 69. The Statue 71. The Towering Inferno 74, etc.

TV series: *The Man from UNCLE* 64–67. The Protectors 72.

Védrès, Nicole (1911–1965). French director, mainly of probing documentaries.

Paris 1900 47. *La Vie Commence Demain* 50. Aux Frontières de l'Homme 53, etc.

Veidt, Conrad (1893–1943). Distinguished German character actor who also filmed in Britain and Hollywood.

The Cabinet of Dr Caligari 19. *Waxworks* 24. Lucrezia Borgia 25. *The Student of Prague* 26. *The Hands of Orlac* 26. The Beloved Rogue (US) 27. The Man Who Laughs 27. Rasputin 30. *Congress Dances* 31. *Rome Express* (GB) 32. I Was a Spy (GB) 33. F.P.I. 33. The Wandering Jew (GB) 33. Jew Süss (GB) 34. Bella Donna (GB) 34. *The Passing of the Third Floor Back* (GB) 35. King of the Damned (GB) 35. *Under the Red Robe* (GB) 36. Dark Journey (GB) 37. *The Spy in Black* (GB) 39. Contraband (GB) 40. The Thief of Baghdad (GB) 40. Escape (US) 40. A Woman's Face (US) 41. Whistling in the Dark (US) 41. All Through the Night (US) 41. The Men in Her Life (US) 42. Nazi Agent (US) 42. Casablanca (US) 42. Above Suspicion (US) 43, etc.

Veiller, Anthony (1903–1965). American scriptwriter, in Hollywood from 1930.

Her Cardboard Lover 42. The Killers 46. Along the Great Divide 51. Moulin Rouge 53. Red Planet Mars (& p) 53. Safari 56. The List of Adrian Messenger 63, many others.

Velez, Lupe (1908–1944) (Guadeloupe Velez de Villalobos). Temperamental Mexican leading lady of the thirties; best remembered with Leon Errol in the Mexican Spitfire series.

The Gaucho 27. Wolf Song 29. East is West 30. The Squaw Man 31. Kongo 32. Hot Pepper 33. Palooka 34. The Morals of Marcus (GB) 36. Gypsy Melody (GB) 37. *The Girl from Mexico* 39. *Mexican Spitfire* 39. Six Lessons from Madame La Zonga 41. Playmates 42. Mexican Spitfire's Elephant 42. Mexican Spitfire's Blessed Event 43, many others.

Venable, Evelyn (1913–). American leading lady of the thirties, usually in demure roles.

Cradle Song 33. Mrs Wiggs of the Cabbage Patch 34. Alice Adams 35. The Frontiersman 38. He Hired the Boss (last to date) 43, etc.

Veness, Amy (1876–1960). British character actress who latterly played cheerful old souls.

My Wife's Family 31. Hobson's Choice 31. Lorna Doone 35. Aren't Men Beasts? 37. Yellow Sands 39. The Man in Grey 43. This Happy Breed 44. Here Come the Huggetts 49. Doctor in the House 54, etc.

Venice has been most persuasively caught by the movie camera in *Summertime, Venetian Bird*, and (for the depressed view) *Death in Venice* and *Don't Look Now*.

ventriloquists rarely stray from music hall to cinema, but Michael Redgrave played a demented one in *Dead of Night* and a similar theme was explored in 1929's *The Great Gabbo* and 1964's *Devil Doll*. A vent's dummy was used for comedy in *Knock on Wood*, for satire in *How I Won the War*, and for mystery in *The Dummy Talks* and *The Thirty-Nine Steps* (1959 version). The most movie-exposed performing ventriloquist is certainly Edgar Bergen, who with his dummies Charlie McCarthy and Mortimer Snerd appeared in a dozen or more films between 1937 and 1944.

Ventura, Lino (1918–). Italian leading man, former boxer.
Touchez Pas au Grisbi 53. Marie Octobre 57. Crooks in Clover 63. Les Aventuriers 67. The Valachi Papers 72. Wild Horses (US) 72. La Bonne Année 73, others.

Vera-Ellen (1926–) (Vera-Ellen Westmeyr Rohe). Diminutive American dancer and songstress of forties musicals.
□ Wonder Man 45. The Kid from Brooklyn 46. Three Little Girls in Blue 46. Carnival in Costa Rica 47. Words and Music 48. Love Happy 49. On the Town 49. Three Little Words 50. Happy Go Lovely (GB) 51. The Belle of New York 52. Call Me Madam 53. The Big Leaguer 53. White Christmas 54. Let's Be Happy (GB) 56.

Verdon, Gwen (1925–). Vivacious American dancer and singer, married to Bob Fosse.
□ On the Riviera 51. Meet Me After the Show 51. David and Bathsheba 51. The Merry Widow 52. The I Don't Care Girl 53. The Farmer Takes a Wife 53. Damn Yankees 58.

Verdugo, Elena (1926–). Spanish-American leading lady.
Down Argentine Way 40. The Moon and Sixpence 42. House of Frankenstein 45. Song of Scheherazade 47. Cyrano de Bergerac 50. Thief of Damascus 52. How Sweet It Is 68, etc.
TV series: Meet Millie 52. The New Phil Silvers Show 63. Marcus Welby M.D. 69–75.

Vereen, Ben (–). Black American dancer.
Funny Lady 75. Roots (TV) 77.

Vermilyea, Harold (1889–1958). Russian-American character actor, former operatic singer.
O.S.S. 46. The Big Clock 48. Edge of Doom 50. Born to be Bad 51, etc.

Verne, Jules (1828–1905). French adventure novelist whose inventive science-fiction themes have latterly endeared him to Hollywood. Films of his works since 1954 include *Twenty Thousand Leagues Under the Sea*, *Around the World in Eighty Days*, *From Earth to the Moon*, *Journey to the Centre of the Earth*, *Five Weeks in a Balloon*, *Master of the World*, *The Children of Captain Grant (In Search of the Castaways)*, *Rocket to the Moon*, *The Light at the End of the World*, *The Southern Star* and *Michael Strogoff*.

Verne, Karen (1915–67) (Ingabor Katrine Klinckerfuss). German leading lady who made a number of Hollywood films.
Ten Days in Paris (GB) 39. All Through the Night 41. King's Row 42. The Seventh Cross 44. A Bullet for Joey 55. Ship of Fools 65. Torn Curtain 67, etc.

Verneuil, Henri (1920–). French director, former journalist.
La Table aux Crevés 50. Forbidden Fruit 52. Public Enemy Number One 53. Paris Palace Hotel 56. The Cow and I 59. L'Affaire d'une Nuit 61. The Big Snatch (Mélodie en Sous-Sol) 63. Guns for San Sebastian 68. The Burglars 71. The Serpent 72. The Night Caller 72, many others.

Verno, Jerry (1895–). British cockney character actor.
His Lordship 32. The Thirty-Nine Steps 35. Farewell Again 37. Old Mother Riley in Paris 38. The Common Touch 41. The Red Shoes 48. The Belles of St Trinian's 54. After the Ball 57, many others.

Vernon, Anne (1925–) (Edith Vignaud). Vivacious French leading lady who has also filmed in Britain and Hollywood.
Le Mannequin Assassiné 48. Warning to Wantons (GB) 48. Shakedown (US) 49. Edward and Caroline 50. Rue de l'Estrapade 52. The Love Lottery (GB) 54. Time Bomb (GB) 54. Le Long des Trottoirs 56. Les Lavandières de Portugal 57. The Umbrellas of Cherbourg 64, etc.

Vernon, John (1935–). Canadian character actor.
Point Blank 67. Topaz 69. Dirty Harry 71. One More Train to Rob 71. The Black Windmill 74. The Outlaw Josey Wales 76, etc.

Vernon, Richard (c. 1907–). British character actor of stage and TV, usually in soft-spoken aristocratic roles.
Accidental Death 63. A Hard Day's Night 64. Goldfinger 64. The Secret of My Success 65. The Satanic Rites of Dracula 73, many others.

Vernon, Wally (1904–1970). American eccentric comedian.
Mountain Music 37. Alexander's Ragtime Band 38. The Gorilla 39. Tahiti Honey 43. Always Leave Them Laughing 49. What Price Glory? 52. What a Way to Go 64, many others.

Versois, Odile (1930–) (Militza de Poliakoff-Baidarov). French leading lady, sister of Marina Vlady.
Les Dernières Vacances 46. Into the Blue (GB) 48. Bel Amour 51. A Day to Remember (GB) 53. *The Young Lovers* (Chance Meeting) (GB) 55. To Paris with Love (GB) 55. Passport to Shame (GB) 58. Cartouche (Swords of Blood) 62. Benjamin 68, etc.

Vertov, Dziga (1896–1954) (Dennis Kaufman). Russian director and film theorist. Many documentaries.
One-Sixth of the World 27. The Man with the Movie Camera 28. Three Songs of Lenin 34. In the Line of Fire 41, etc.

Vetri, Victoria (1944–) (Angela Dorian). Australian leading lady.
Chuka 67. Rosemary's Baby 68. When Dinosaurs Ruled the Earth 69, etc.

Vicas, Victor (1918–). Franco-Russian director.
Double Destiny 54. Count Five and Die (GB) 58. Les Disparus 60, etc.

Vickers, Martha (1925–1971) (M. MacVicar). American leading lady of the forties.
The Falcon in Mexico 44. *The Big Sleep* 46. Love and Learn 47. Ruthless 48. Bad Boy 49. Daughter of the West 51. The Burglar 57. Four Fast Guns 60, etc.

Victim (GB 1962). This first British film to tackle homosexuality did so under cover of a detective story. Whether or not this invalidates it as social comment, it was an exciting film. Written by Janet Green and John McCormack, produced and directed by Michael Relph and Basil Dearden, photographed by Otto Heller; with Dirk Bogarde doing well in the difficult, ambiguous central role.

Victor, Charles (1896–1965). British character actor with long stage experience; in films from 1938, usually in cockney roles.
While the Sun Shines 46. The Calendar 48. The Ringer 52. Those People Next Door 53. The Embezzler 55. Now and Forever 57, scores of others.

Victor, Henry (1898–1945). British character actor who went to Hollywood in the thirties and played villainous bit roles.
She 25. The Guns of Loos 28. The Fourth Commandment 28. The Mummy 33. Our Fighting Navy 37. Confessions of a Nazi Spy 39. Zanzibar 40. King of the Zombies 41, etc.

Victoria the Great (GB 1937). A phenomenally successful British film which, rather daringly at the time, told the domestic story of a recent monarch. Anna Neagle starred under Herbert Wilcox's direction and in the following year a colour sequel, *Sixty Glorious Years*, was equally successful.

The Victors (GB 1963). By devising the anti-war film to end them all, writer-producer-director Carl Foreman pushed bits of this World War II compendium into absurdity: there simply wasn't a decent character around. But it does have moving and horrifying sequences, also some which impress as pure cinema. Photographed by Christopher Challis, with a generally effective American-international cast.

Vidal, Henri (1919–1959). Tough-looking French leading man, in films from 1940.
Les Maudits 46. Quai de Grenelle 50. Port du Désir 54. The Wicked Go to Hell 55. Porte des Lilas 56. Come Dance with Me 59, etc.

video cassettes can provide programmes on the home television set. They are played in through special equipment and can accommodate feature films or any other kind of entertainment or instruction.

video discs operate similarly to video cassettes, but instead of being stored on tape the information is mounted on a circular disc similar to a gramophone record.

Vidor, Charles (1900–1959). Hungarian-American director, in Hollywood from 1932.
Double Door 34. Sensation Hunters 34. The Great Gambini 37. *Blind Alley* 39. My Son My Son 40. The Lady in Question 40. Ladies in Retirement 41. The Tuttles of Tahiti 42. The Desperadoes 43. *Cover Girl* 44. Together Again 44. A Song to Remember 45. Over 21 45. *Gilda* 46. The Guilt of Janet Ames 48. Hans Christian Andersen 52. Love Me or Leave Me 55. The Swan 56. The Joker is Wild 58. A Farewell to Arms 58. Song without End (part) 59, many others.

Vidor, Florence (1895–) (Florence Arto). American leading lady of the silent screen.
Lying Lips 21. Barbara Frietchie 24. The Grand Duchess and the Waiter 26. Are Parents People? 26. The Patriot 28. Chinatown Nights 29, etc.

Vidor, King (1894–). American director, formerly journalist; high style alternates with disappointing banality.

Autobiography 1953: *A Tree is a Tree.*

□ The Turn in the Road 18. Better Times 19. The Other Half 19. Poor Relations 19. The Jack Knife Man 19. The Family Honour 20. The Sky Pilot 21. Love Never Dies 21. Conquering the Women 21. Woman Wake Up 21. The Real Adventure 22. Dusk to Dawn 22. Alice Adams 22. Peg O' My Heart 23. The Woman of Bronze 23. Three Wise Fools 23. Wild Oranges 23. Happiness 23. Wine of Youth 24. His Hour 24. Wife of the Centaur 24. Proud Flesh 25. *The Big Parade* 25. La Bohème 25. Bardelys the Magnificent 26. *The Crowd* 28. *Show People* 28. *Hallelujah* 29. Not So Dumb 30. *Billy the Kid* 30. *Street Scene* 31. *The Champ* 31. Bird of Paradise 32. Cynara 32. The Stranger's Return 33. *Our Daily Bread* 34. The Wedding Night 34. So Red the Rose 35. The Texas Rangers 36. Stella Dallas 37. The Citadel (GB) 38. *Northwest Passage* 39. Comrade X 40. H. M. Pulham Esq 41. An American Romance 44. Duel in the Sun 46. On Our Merry Way 47. *The Fountainhead* 49. Beyond the Forest 49. Lightning Strikes Twice 51. Japanese War Bride 52. Ruby Gentry 52. The Man without a Star 55. *War and Peace* 56. Solomon and Sheba 59.

Vienna was frequently pictured in pre-war films such as *The Great Waltz*, *Bitter Sweet* and *Vienna Waltzes*, but the myths were always perpetuated on a studio backlot. The post war reality was caught vividly in *Four in a Jeep* and *The Third Man.*

Vierny, Sacha (1919–). French cinematographer.

Hiroshima Mon Amour 58. *Last Year in Marienbad* 61. Muriel 63. Do You Like Women? 64. *Belle de Jour* 67, etc.

Viertel, Berthold (1885–1953). Austrian director who moved to Britain and Hollywood in the early thirties.

The Wise Sex 31. The Man from Yesterday 32. Little Friend 34. The Passing of the Third Floor Back 35. Rhodes of Africa 36, etc.

vigilantes were originally groups of honest citizens who formed together to rid San Francisco's Barbary Coast of some of its villains. In the early seventies it became fashionable to make films about citizens who took the law of our violent cities into their own hands, notably in *Death Wish*, *Walking Tall* and *Law and Disorder.*

Vigo, Jean (1905–1934) (Jean Almereyda). Influential French director on the strength of three semi-experimental, dream-like films.

□ *A Propos de Nice* 30. *Zéro de Conduite* 32. *L'Atalante* 34.

Villard, Frank (1917–) (François Drouineau). French leading man, often in shifty roles.

Le Dernier des Six 41. Gigi 48. Manèges (The Wanton) 49. L'Ingénue Libertine 50. Le Garçon Sauvage 51. Huis Clos 54. Crime Passionel 55. Mystères de Paris 57. Le Cave se Rebiffe 61. Gigot 62. Mata Hari 64, etc.

Villiers, James (c. 1930–). British actor, usually in snooty or villainous roles.

The Entertainer 60. The Damned 64. King and Country 64. The Nanny 65. Half a Sixpence 67. Some Girls Do 68. Otley 68. A Nice Girl Like Me 69. Blood from the Mummy's Tomb 70. The Ruling Class 71, etc.

Vincent, Jan-Michael (1944–). American leading man of the seventies.

The Undefeated 68. Tribes (TV) 70. The Mechanic 72. The World's Greatest Athlete 73. Buster and Billie 74. Bite the Bullet 74. White Line Fever 75. Baby Blue Marine 76. Damnation Alley 77, etc.

Vinson, Helen (1907–) (Helen Rulfs). Cool, aristocratic leading lady of Hollywood films of the thirties and forties.

Jewel Robbery 31. I Am a Fugitive from a Chain Gang 32. The Power and the Glory 33. The Tunnel (GB) 35. Vogues of 1938. In Name Only 39. Torrid Zone 40. Nothing But the Truth 41. They Are Guilty 44. The Lady and the Doctor (last to date) 46, etc.

violence caused little concern until the fifties. Even the makers of the horror and gangster films of the thirties were comparatively subtle in their approach: they delighted in machine guns and clutching hands, but would not have dreamed of showing fist connect against flesh or suggesting the sight of actual blood. The rot began to set in in 1952 with films like *The Wild One*, which still showed little but pointed out that imitable forms of violence were on the streets of our cities; location shooting was inviting greater realism than had been necessary in the studio. In 1956, when Hammer began to remake the great horror stories, a new ghoulishness was found to have set in, especially in the versions prepared for the Far East. Still the censor held sway until the late sixties, when he gave up the ghost. *Witchfinder General* was a sadistic piece of Grand Guignol, *The Wild Bunch* a blood-spattered western, *Get Carter* and *Villain* new-fashioned gangster films in which the killing was merciless and explicit. *Soldier Blue* has as its high point a mutilation scene which its director seemed to claim as a protest against Vietnam; *Straw Dogs* featured an irrelevant but thoroughly detailed rape. As for *A Clockwork Orange* and *The Devils*, our eyes were spared no conceivable atrocity. According to one's point of view, the cinema had either come of age or ventured beyond the pale.

The Virginian. Owen Wister's western novel was filmed in 1914 with Dustin Farnum, in 1930 with Gary Cooper, and in 1945 with Joel McCrea; in 1964 it turned up as a long-running TV series with James Drury. *Spawn of the North* 38 borrowed the basic plot, and in its turn was remade as *Alaska Seas* 54.

Viridiana (Spain 1961). Luis Buñuel's startlingly allusive allegory of good and evil, with the latter winning in the end, is a ramshackle but absorbing film rounding up all the diverse moods of his earlier career: poetic, sacrilegious, melodramatic, enigmatic, hilarious and often moving.

Visconti, Luchino (1906–1976) (L. V. de Modrone). Italian writer-director, former art director.
Ossessione 42. *La Terra Trema* 48. Bellissima 51. Siamo Donne (part) 52. *Senso* 53. White Nights 57. *Rocco and His Brothers* 60. Boccaccio 70 62. *The Leopard* 63. *The Damned* 69. Death in Venice 70. Conversation Piece 76, etc.

Les Visiteurs du Soir (France 1942). A medieval fantasy written by Jacques Prévert and directed by Marcel Carné; remarkable in that, though made under the German occupation, it contrived to point an allegory of the resistance. (The devil turns the lovers to stone; but their hearts still beat no matter how hard he whips them.) As a film slow-moving, though full of elegant visuals, it has excellent performances from Jules Berry as the devil and Arletty as his agent. Music by Maurice Thiriet, décor by Wakhevitch.

VistaVision. In 1953, when some companies were reluctant to follow Fox's lead and adopt CinemaScope, Paramount introduced VistaVision, a non-anamorphic, deep focus process retaining the old frame ratio of 4 × 3. The chief innovation was that none of the essential action took place at the top or bottom of the picture, so that exhibitors with appropriate lens and apperture plates could choose their own screen ratio (from 4 × 3 to 2 × 1). At 2 × 1 on a big screen, VistaVision did not look very different from CinemaScope.

Vitagraph. An early American production company which had great success but was taken over in the twenties by Warners.

Vitaphone. The sound-on-disc process introduced in 1926 by Warners.

Vitale, Milly (1938–). Italian leading lady in American films.
The Juggler 53. The Seven Little Foys 55. A Breath of Scandal 60.

Vitti, Monica (1933–) (Monica Luisa Ceciarelli). Italian leading lady in international demand in the sixties.
L'Avventura 59. La Notte 60. *L'Eclisse* 62. Dragées au Poivre 63. Nutty Naughty Château 64. *The Red Desert* 64. Modesty Blaise (GB) 65. The Chastity Belt 67. Girl with a Pistol 69. The Pacifist 71. Duck in Orange Sauce 75, etc.

Vlady, Marina (1938–) (Marina de Poliakoff-Baidarov). French leading lady, sister of Odile Versois.
Orage d'Eté 49. Avant le Déluge 53. The Wicked Go to Hell 55. Crime and Punishment 56. Toi le Venin 59. La Steppa 61. Climats 62. Enough Rope 63. Dragées au Poivre 63. Queen Bee 64. Chimes at Midnight 66. Sapho 70, etc.

Vogel, Paul C. (1899–1975). American cinematographer.
The Lady in the Lake 46. Black Hand 49. *Battleground* (AA) 49. Rose Marie 54. High Society 56. The Wings of Eagles 56. The Time Machine 60. The Rounders 64, etc.

Vogel, Virgil (–). American director, from TV.
The Mole People 56. Terror in the Midnight Sun 58. Son of Ali Baba 64, etc.

Vogler, Karl Michael (1928–). German stage actor who has appeared in a few international films.
Those Magnificent Men in Their Flying Machines 65. The Blue Max 67. How I Won the War 67. Patton 69. Downhill Racer 69, etc.

Voight, Jon (1938–). American leading actor of the seventies.
□ The Hour of the Gun 67. Fearless Frank 68. Out of It 69. *Midnight Cowboy* 69. The Revolutionary 70. The All American Boy 70. Catch 22 70. *Deliverance* 72. Conrack 74. The Odessa File 74.

volcanoes in the late thirties seemed to belong mostly to Paramount, which used them as the climax of most of Dorothy Lamour's jungle pictures and of odd adventures like *Cobra Woman* and *Mysterious Island*. They more recently turned up in *The Devil at Four O'Clock*, and in *Journey to the Centre of the Earth* in which the way was down an extinct Icelandic crater and back on a fountain of lava up the inside of Etna. The famous eruption of Vesuvius was staged for the various versions of *The Last Days of Pompeii* (and for *Up Pompeii*), and *Krakatoa, East of Java* featured another historical disaster. An extinct volcano formed a lair for giant monsters in *The Black Scorpion*. A volcano was also the climax of Hal Roach's *Man and His Mate* and of its recent remake *One Million Years B.C.*; but the most spectacular pictures were obtained for the documentary compilation simply called *Volcano*.

Volonte, Gian Maria (1930–). Italian leading man of the sixties.
A Fistful of Dollars 64. For a Few Dollars More 65. We Still Kill the Old Way 68. *Investigation of a Citizen above Suspicion* 69. Sacco and Vanzetti 71. The Working Class Go To Heaven 72. Lucky Luciano 73, etc.

Von Harbou, Thea (1888–1954). German screenwriter, mainly associated with Fritz Lang's silent films.
Der Müde Tod 21. Dr Mabuse 22. Nibelungen Saga 24. Chronicles of the Grey House 25. Metropolis 26. The Spy 28. The Woman in the Moon 29. The Testament of Dr Mabuse 32. The Old and the Young King 35. Annélie 41. Fahrt ins Gluck 45. The Affairs of Dr Holl 51, others.

Von Seyffertitz, Gustav (1863–1943). Dignified German character actor in Hollywood films; during World War I was known as G. Butler Clonblough.
Old Wives for New 18. Moriarty (title role) 22. Sparrows 26. The Wizard 27. Docks of New York 28. The Bat Whispers 30. Shanghai Express 32. Queen Christiana 33. She 35. In Old Chicago 38. Nurse Edith Cavell 39, many others.

Von Sternberg, Josef (1894–1969) (Jonas Sternberg). Austrian-American director, a great pictorial stylist and the creator of Marlene Dietrich's American image.
Autobiography 1965: *Fun in a Chinese Laundry*. A critical study by Herman G. Weinberg was published in 1967.
□ *The Salvation Hunters* 25. The Seagull (unreleased) 26. *Underworld* 27. The Last Command 28. The Dragnet 28. *Docks of New York* 28. The Case of Lena Smith 29. Thunderbolt 29. *The Blue Angel* (Ger.) 30. *Morocco* 30. Dishonoured 31. An American Tragedy 31. *Shanghai Express* 32. Blonde Venus 32. *The Scarlet Empress* 34. *The Devil is a Woman* 35. The King Steps Out 36. Crime and Punishment 36. I Claudius (unfinished) 37. Sergeant Madden 39. *The Shanghai Gesture* 41. Jet Pilot 50. Macao 51. The Saga of Anatahan (Jap.) 53.

Von Stroheim, Erich (1885–1957) (Hans Erich Maria Stroheim Von Nordenwall). Austrian actor and director whose ruthless extravagance in Hollywood in the twenties harmed his later career. Usually played despotic villains or stiff-necked Prussians.
Biographies: 1954 *Hollywood Scapegoat*, by Peter Noble. *Erich Von Stroheim* 1972 by Tom Curtis.
AS ACTOR: The Heart of Humanity 18. Blind Husbands 19. *Foolish Wives* 21. The Wedding March 27. The Great Gabbo 29. Three Faces East 30. Friends and Lovers 30. The Lost Squadron 32. As You Desire Me 32. Walking Down Broadway 32. Crimson Romance 35. The Crime of Dr Crespi 35. *La Grande Illusion* 37. Mademoiselle Docteur 37. Alibi 38. Boys' School 39. I Was an Adventuress 40. Thunder Over Parièges 40. So Ends Our Night 41. *Five Graves to Cairo* (as Rommel) 43. North Star 43. The Lady and the Monster 44. Storm Over Lisbon 44. 32 Rue de Montmartre 44. The Great Flamarion 45. La Danse de Mort 47. *Sunset Boulevard* 50. La Maison du Crime 52. Napoleon 54. L'Homme aux Cents Visages 56, etc.
□ AS DIRECTOR: *Blind Husbands* 19. *The Devil's Passkey* 19. *Foolish Wives* 21. Merry Go Round 22. *Greed* 23. The Merry Widow 25. *The Wedding March* 27. *Queen Kelly* 28.

Von Sydow, Max (1929–) (Carl Adolf Von Sydow). Swedish actor, a member of Ingmar Bergman's company.
Miss Julie 51. *The Seventh Seal* 56. Wild Strawberries 57. So Close to Life 58. *The Face* 59. The Virgin Spring 60. *Through a Glass Darkly* 61. Winter Light 62. The Mistress 62. *The Greatest Story Ever Told* (as Jesus) (US) 65. The Reward (US) 65. *Hawaii* (US) 66. The Quiller Memorandum (GB) 66. *Hour of the Wolf* 67. The Shame 68. The Kremlin Letter (US) 69. The Touch 71. Embassy 72. *The Emigrants* 72. The Exorcist (US) 73. Foxtrot (US) 75. Three Days of the Condor (US) 76, March or Die 77, etc.

Vorhaus, Bernard (c. 1898–). German director, mostly in Britain and Hollywood.
Money for Speed (GB) 33. Broken Melody (GB) 35. Cotton Queen (GB) 37. Three Faces West (US) 40. Lady from Louisiana (US) 41. Bury Me Dead (US) 47. So Young So Bad (US) 50. The Lady from Boston (US) 51, etc.

Vorkapitch, Slavko (1892–1976). Yugoslavian writer who came to Hollywood in 1922, did a little screenwriting, tried direction in 1931 (*I Take This Woman*), then settled as a montage expert.
Viva Villa 34. Crime without Passion 34.

Maytime 37. The Last Gangster 38. Shopworn Angel 38, etc.

Voskovec, George (1905–). Czech stage actor, long in US.
Anything Can Happen 52. *Twelve Angry Men* 57. The Spy Who Came in from the Cold 65. Mister Buddwing 66. The Boston Strangler 68, etc.

Vye, Murvyn (1913–1976). Burly American character actor who usually played heavies.
Golden Earrings 48. A Connecticut Yankee at King Arthur's Court 49. Pick-Up 51. Road to Bali 52. Green Fire 54. Pearl of the South Pacific 55. Al Capone 59. Pay or Die 60. Andy 64, etc.

W

Wadsworth, Henry (1902–1974). American juvenile of the twenties and thirties.
Applause 29. Luxury Liner 33. The Thin Man 34. Ceiling Zero 35. Dr Rhythm 38, many others.

Wager, Anthony (1933–). British juvenile actor who played Young Pip in the 1946 *Great Expectations* and later turned up on Australian television.

The Wages of Fear (France 1953). A long, solid shocker with serious undertones about four drivers with a cargo of nitroglycerine. It showed that France could make a big commercial thriller as well as anybody, and very nearly forced acceptance of continental movies in British cinemas (it was given a full circuit release, subtitles and all, but not enough others in a similar category came along to make foreign films a habit, and dubbing finally won the day). Written and directed by Henri-Georges Clouzot from a novel by Georges Arnaud; photographed by Armand Thirard with music by Georges Auric. With Yves Montand, Charles Vanel, Peter Van Eyck. BFA (best film).

Waggner, George (1894–). American director, mainly of routine low-budgeters, in Hollywood from 1920.
The Wolf Man 41. The Climax (& p) 44. Cobra Woman (& p) 45. The Fighting Kentuckian (& w) 49. Operation Pacific (& w) 51. Bitter Creek 54. Destination 60,000 (& w) 57. Pale Arrow 58, many others.

Wagner, Fritz Arno (1889–1958). German cinematographer.
Nosferatu 23. *The Loves of Jeanne Ney* 27. The Spy 28. Westfront 1918 30. *Die Dreigroschenoper* 31. Kameradschaft 31. Amphitryon 35. Ohm Krüger 41. Hotel Adlon 55, many others.

Wagner, Lindsay (1949–). American leading lady of the seventies.
The Paper Chase 73. Two People 74.
TV series: *Bionic Woman* 76– .

Wagner, Robert (1930–). American leading man spotted by talent scout while still at college.
Halls of Montezuma (debut) 50. With a Song in My Heart 52. Titanic 53. Prince Valiant 54. Broken Lance 54. White Feather 55. The Mountain 56. A Kiss Before Dying 56. The Hunters 57. Say One for Me 58. All the Fine Young Cannibals 59. The Longest Day 62. The Condemned of Altona 63. Harper 66. The Biggest Bundle of Them All 66. Don't Just Stand There 68. Winning 69. The Streets of San Francisco (TV) 71. City Beneath the Sea (TV) 71. The Affair (TV) 73. Death at Love House (TV) 76. Midway 76. The Towering Inferno 76, etc.
TV series: It Takes a Thief 67–69. Colditz 72. Switch 75– .

Wajda, Andrzej (1926–). Polish director.
A Generation 54. *Kanal* 55. *Ashes and Diamonds* 58. Innocent Sorcerers 60. The Siberian Lady Macbeth 61. Love at Twenty (part only) 62. Ashes 64. Everything for Sale 67. Gates to Paradise 67. The Birch Wood 71. Landscape after a Battle 72, etc.

Wakefield, Duggie (1899–1951). British music-hall comedian, in character as a simpleton who always triumphed. Films include *Look Up and Laugh* 35, *Spy for a Day* 39, etc.

Wakefield, Hugh (1888–1971). British character actor on stage from childhood. Usually seen in monocled roles.
City of Song 30. The Sport of Kings 31. The Man Who Knew Too Much 34. The Crimson Circle 36. The Street Singer 37. Blithe Spirit 45. One Night with You 48. Love's a Luxury 52. The Million Pound Note 54, etc.

Wakeford, Kent L. (–). American cinematographer.
Black Belt Jones 74. Alice Doesn't Live Here Anymore 75.

Walbrook, Anton (1900–1968) (Adolf Wohlbruck). Distinguished German actor who came to Britain in the mid-thirties.
Maskerade 34. The Student of Prague 35.

Michael Strogoff (US) 36. *Victoria the Great* 37. The Rat 37. Sixty Glorious Years 38. *Gaslight* 39. Dangerous Moonlight 40. 49th Parallel 41. The Life and Death of Colonel Blimp 43. The Man from Morocco 44. *The Red Shoes* 48. The Queen of Spades 48. *La Ronde* 50. Vienna Waltzes 51. Oh Rosalinda 55. Lola Montes 55. Saint Joan 57. I Accuse 57, etc.

Walburn, Raymond (1887–1969). American comedy actor with an inimitable bumbling pomposity; on stage from 1912, films from early thirties.
The Count of Monte Cristo 34. The Great Ziegfeld 36. *Mr Deeds Goes to Town* 36. Born to Dance 37. Professor Beware 38. Eternally Yours 40. Christmas in July 41. Dixie 43. *Hail the Conquering Hero* 43. The Man in the Trunk 43. The Cheaters 45. Henry the Rainmaker 48. State of the Union 48. Riding High 49. Father Takes the Air 51. Beautiful but Dangerous 53. The Spoilers 55, etc.

Wald, Jerry (1911–1962). Live-wire American writer-producer, said to be the original of Budd Schulberg's novel 'What Makes Sammy Run?' Former journalist, in Hollywood from early thirties.
Stars over Broadway (w) 35. Hollywood Hotel (w) 38. George Washington Slept Here (p) 42. *Mildred Pierce* 45. *Johnny Belinda* (p) 48. The Glass Menagerie (p) 50. Clash by Night (p) 52. Queen Bee (p) 55. Peyton Place (p) 57. The Sound and the Fury (p) 58. Sons and Lovers (p) 60. The Stripper (p) 63, many others.

Walker, Charlotte (1878–1958). American leading lady with stage experience, in silent films. Mother of Sara Haden.
Kindling 15. Trail of the Lonesome Pine 16. Eve in Exile 19. Classmates 24. The Manicure Girl 25. Paris Bound 29. Scarlet Pages 30. Millie 31, etc.

Walker, Clint (1927–). Giant-size American leading man from TV. No acting training.
Fort Dobbs 57. Yellowstone Kelly 60. Gold of the Seven Saints 61. Send Me No Flowers 64. Night of the Grizzly 66. The Dirty Dozen 67. Sam Whiskey 68. The Great Bank Robbery 69. Yuma (TV) 70. The Bounty Man (TV) 72. The White Buffalo 77, etc.
TV series: Cheyenne 55–62, Kodiak 75.

Walker, Hal (1896–1972). American director, mainly of routine films; stage experience.
□ Out of this World 45. Duffy's Tavern 45. The Stork Club 45. *Road to Utopia* 45. My Friend Irma Goes West 50. At War with the Army 50.

That's My Boy 51. Sailor Beware 51. Road to Bali 52.

Walker, Helen (1921–1968). American leading lady of the forties.
Lucky Jordan 43. Abroad with Two Yanks 44. Murder He Says 45. Cluny Brown 46. The Homestretch 47. Nightmare Alley 47. Impact 49. My True Story 51. Problem Girls 52. The Big Combo (last role) 55, etc.

Walker, Joseph (1892–). American cinematographer.
Danger 23. Flaming Fury 26. Virgin Lips 29. Dirigible 30. The Miracle Woman 31. American Madness 32. Lady for a Day 33. It Happened One Night 34. Broadway Bill 34. Mr Deeds Goes to Town 36. *Lost Horizon* 37. You Can't Take it With You 38. Mr Smith Goes to Washington 39. His Girl Friday 40. Here Comes Mr Jordan 41. *It's a Wonderful Life* 46. *The Jolson Story* 46. Born Yesterday 51, many others.

Walker, Nancy (1921–) (Ann Swoyer). Pint-sized American character comedienne.
The World's Greatest Athlete 73. Forty Carats 73. Murder By Death 76, etc.
TV series: McMillan and Wife 71–75. The Nancy Walker Show 76. Mrs Blansky's Beauties 77.

Walker, Norman (1892–). British director.
Tommy Atkins 27. The Middle Watch 31. Turn of the Tide 35. The Man at the Gate 40. Hard Steel 41. They Knew Mr Knight 45, etc.

Walker, Pete (–). British producer-director of exploitation films.
I Like Birds 67. School for Sex 68. Cool it Carol 70. Die Screaming Marianne 71. Four Dimensions of Greta 72. Tiffany Jones 73. House of Whipcord 74. Frightmare 75. The House of Mortal Sin 76. Schizo 76, etc.

Walker, Robert (1914–1951). Slight, modest-looking American leading man of the forties.
□ Winter Carnival 39. These Glamour Girls 39. Dancing Co-Ed 39. Bataan 43. Madame Curie 43. *See Here Private Hargrove* 43. *Since You Went Away* 44. Thirty Seconds Over Tokyo 44. *The Clock* 45. Her Highness and the Bellboy 45. What Next Coroporal Hargrove? 45. The Sailor Takes a Wife 45. *Till the Clouds Roll By* (as Jerome Kern) 46. The Sea of Grass 47. The Beginning of the End 47. Song of Love 47. One Touch of Venus 48. Please Believe Me 50. The Skipper Surprised His Wife 50. Vengeance Valley 51. *Strangers on a Train* 51. My Son John 52.

Walker, Robert Jnr (1941–). American second lead of the sixties.
The Hook 63. Ensign Pulver 64. The Ceremony 64. The Happening 67. The War Wagon 67. Easy Rider 69. Road to Salina 70. The Spectre of Edgar Allan Poe 72, etc.

Walker, Stuart (1887–1941). American director, former stage producer.
□ The Secret Call 31. The False Madonna 32. The Misleading Lady 32. Evenings for Sale 32. Tonight is Ours 33. *The Eagle and the Hawk* 33. White Woman 33. Romance in the Rain 34. Great Expectations 34. The Mystery of Edwin Drood 35. Werewolf of London 35. Manhattan Moon 35. Bulldog Drummond's Bride 39. Emergency Squad 40.

Walker, Syd (1887–1945). British comic actor and monologuist.
Over She Goes 37. Oh Boy 38. Hold My Hand 39. What Would You Do, Chums? (his catchphrase) 39, etc.

Walker, Zena (1935–). British leading actress of the sixties, mostly on TV.
The Hellions 61. The Traitors 63. One of Those Things 69, etc.

Wallace, Edgar (1875–1932). Prolific British crime story writer. Films of his books include: *The Case of the Frightened Lady* 30 and 40. *The Calendar* 32 and 48. *The Crimson Circle* 30, 37 and 61. *The Terror* 28 and 39. *Kate Plus Ten* 38. Sanders of the River 35. The Squeaker 37. The Four Just Men 39. The Mind of Mr Reeder 39 (and series). *The Ringer* 32 and 52, and many episodes of a second feature series made at Merton Park in the sixties.

Wallace, Jean (1923–) (Jean Wallasek). American leading lady, married to Cornel Wilde.
You Can't Ration Love 44. Jigsaw 48. The Good Humour Man 50. Song of India 50. Sudden Fear 55. The Big Combo 55. Maracaibo 58. Lancelot and Guinevere 63. Beach Red 67. No Blade of Grass 71, etc.

Wallace, Richard (1894–1951). American director, former cutter for Mack Sennett.
MacFadden's Flats 27. Innocents of Paris 30. Seven Days' Leave 31. The Road to Reno 32. Shopworn Angel 33. The Little Minister 35. *The Young in Heart* 39. Captain Caution 40. The Navy Steps Out 41. She Knew All the Answers 41. The Fallen Sparrow 43. Bride by Mistake 44. *It's in the Bag* 45. Sinbad the Sailor 46. Tycoon 47. Let's Live a Little 48. A Kiss for Corliss 50, many others.

Wallach, Eli (1915–). American stage actor (from 1940) who has latterly concentrated on films, often in villainous roles which he spices with 'the method'.
□ *Baby Doll* (debut) 56. The Line Up 58. Seven Thieves 59. The Magnificent Seven 60. The Misfits 61. Hemingway's Adventures of a Young Man 62. How the West Was Won 62. The Victors 63. Act One 63. The Moonspinners 64. Kisses for My President 64. Lord Jim 65. Genghis Khan 65. How to Steal a Million 66. The Good the Bad and the Ugly (It.) 67. *The Tiger Makes Out* 67. How to Save a Marriage 68. Mackenna's Gold 68. A Lovely Way to Die 68. The Brain 69. Zigzag 70. The People Next Door 70. The Angel Levine 70. Romance of a Horsethief 71. A Cold Night's Death (TV) 72. Crazy Joe 73. Cinderella Liberty 74. The Sentinel 77.

Waller, Fats (1904–1943). Black American jazz pianist.
□ Hooray for Love 35. King of Burlesque 36. Stormy Weather 43.

Waller, Fred (1886–1954). American research technician who invented Cinerama and saw it open successfully only two years before his death.

Wallis, Hal B. (1898–). American producer, latterly independent, responsible for a long line of solidly commercial films. In films from 1922.
Little Caesar 30. The Story of Louis Pasteur 36. Jezebel 38. King's Row 42. Casablanca 42. The Strange Love of Martha Ivers 46. My Friend Irma 49. Gunfight at the OK Corral 57. G.I. Blues 60. Becket 64. Boeing-Boeing 65. The Sons of Katie Elder 65. Five Card Stud 68. True Grit 69. Anne of the Thousand Days 70. Mary Queen of Scots 72. Bequest to the Nation 73, scores of others (often as executive producer for major studios).

Wallis, Shani (1938–). British cabaret singer.
□ Oliver! 68. Terror in the Wax Museum 73.

Walls, Tom (1883–1949). British actor and director, on stage from 1905 after experience as policeman, busker, jockey, etc. Associated from mid-twenties with the Aldwych farces, which he produced and later transferred to the screen, as well as playing amiable philanderers in them. Subsequently in character roles.
Rookery Nook 30. Turkey Time 32. A Cuckoo in the Nest 34. Fighting Stock 35. Pot Luck 36. Foreign Affairs 37. For Valour 37. Dishonour Bright 37. Second Best Bed 38. Strange Boarders 38. Halfway House 43. Johnny Frenchman 45.

Spring in Park Lane 47. Maytime in Mayfair 48. Master of Bankdam 48. Derby Day 49. The Interrupted Journey 49, many others.

Walpole, Sir Hugh (1884–1941). British novelist who has been oddly neglected by the cinema but did some scripting in thirties Hollywood and appeared as the vicar in *David Copperfield* 34.

Walsh, Bill (1918–1976). American producer for the Walt Disney Organization.

Walsh, David M. (–). American cinematographer.
I Walk the Line 70. The Other Side of the Mountain 75. The Silver Streak 76. Rollercoaster 77, etc.

Walsh, Dermot (1924–). British leading man, usually in second features.
My Sister and I 49. The Frightened Man 52. The Floating Dutchman 53. The Night of the Full Moon 56. Woman of Mystery 57. Crash Drive 59. The Trunk 61. The Cool Mikado 63, many others.

Walsh, Kay (1914–). British character actress, former leading lady. Trained in West End revue.
Get Your Man (debut) 34. I See Ice 38. In Which We Serve 42. This Happy Breed 44. *The October Man* 47. Vice Versa 48. Oliver Twist 48. *Encore* 50. Stage Fright 50. Last Holiday 51. Meet Me Tonight 52. Cast a Dark Shadow 55. The Horse's Mouth 59. *Tunes of Glory* 60. Eighty Thousand Suspects 63. The Beauty Jungle 64. A Study in Terror 65. The Witches 66. Connecting Rooms 69. The Ruling Class 71, many others.

Walsh, Raoul (1887–). Veteran American director of many commercial and several distinguished pictures. In films from 1912; former actor and assistant to D. W. Griffith.
Carmen 15. *The Thief of Baghdad* 24. *What Price Glory?* 26. *Sadie Thompson* 28. In Old Arizona 29. *The Big Trail* 30. *The Bowery* 33. Every Night at Eight 35. Artists and Models 38. St Louis Blues 39. *They Drive by Night* 40. *High Sierra* 41. They Died with Their Boots On 41. Strawberry Blonde 41. Manpower 41. Desperate Journey 42. Gentleman Jim 43. Northern Pursuit 44. Uncertain Glory 44. The Horn Blows at Midnight 45. *Objective Burma* 45. The Man I Love 46. Pursued 47. Silver River 48. *White Heat* 49. Colorado Territory 49. Along the Great Divide 49. Captain Horatio Hornblower 50. Distant Drums 51. The World in His Arms 52. Glory Alley 52. Blackbeard the Pirate 53. A Lion is in the Streets 54. Saskatchewan 54. Battle Cry 55. The Tall Men 55. The Revolt of Mamie Stover 57. The King and Four Queens 57. Band of Angels 57. The Naked and the Dead 58. The Sheriff of Fractured Jaw (GB) 58. Esther and the King 60. Marines Let's Go 61. A Distant Trumpet 64, many others.

Walston, Ray (1917–). American character comedian with stage experience.
Damn Yankees 58. South Pacific 58. Say One for Me 59. The Apartment 61. Tall Story 62. Wives and Lovers 63. Who's Minding the Store? 63. Kiss Me Stupid 65. Caprice 67. Paint Your Wagon 69, etc.
TV series: My Favourite Martian 63–65.

Walter, Jessica (1944–). American leading lady of the sixties.
□ Lilith 64. *The Group* 66. Grand Prix 67. Bye Bye Braverman 68. Number One 69. Play Misty for Me 71. Women in Chains (TV) 71. Home for the Holidays (TV) 72.

Walters, Charles (1911–). American director specializing in musicals. Former stage dancer and director of musical sequences in films.
Presenting Lily Mars (seq) 43. Meet Me in St Louis (seq) 44. Good News 47. *Easter Parade* 48. Summer Stock 50. Easy to Love 53. *Lili* 53. The Glass Slipper 55. The Tender Trap 55. High Society 56. Don't Go Near the Water 57. Ask Any Girl 59. Please Don't Eat the Daisies 60. Jumbo 62. The Unsinkable Molly Brown 64. Walk, Don't Run 66, etc.

Walters, Thorley (1913–). British comedy actor on stage and screen from 1934. Film parts usually cameos, as incompetent officers, etc.
They Were Sisters 45. Private's Progress 56. Carleton Browne of the FO 58. Two-Way Stretch 60. Murder She Said 62. Ring of Spies 64. Joey Boy 65. *Rotten to the Core* 65. Dracula, Prince of Darkness 65. The Wrong Box 66. Frankenstein Must Be Destroyed 69. Vampire Circus 72, etc.

Walthall, Henry B. (1878–1936). American leading man of the silent screen, in films from 1909.
In Old Kentucky 09. A Convict's Sacrifice 10. The Birth of a Nation 14. The Raven 15. Ghosts 15. His Robe of Honour 18. Single Wives 23. The Scarlet Letter 25. The Barrier 26. Abraham Lincoln 31. Police Court 32. Laughing at Life 33. Viva Villa 34. Dante's Inferno 35. A Tale of Two Cities 35. China Clipper 36, many others.

Walton, Sir William (1902–). British composer whose film scores include *Henry V* 44. *Hamlet* 48. *Richard III* 56.

W.A.M.P.A.S. (Western Association of Motion Picture Advertisers). A group of publicity executives who, from 1922 to 1934, gave annual certificates of merit to promising female starlets, known as 'Wampas baby stars'. Among those who succeeded were Bessie Love (nominated 1922), Laura la Plante 23, Clara Bow 24, Mary Astor 26, Joan Crawford 26, Dolores del Rio 26, Janet Gaynor 26, Lupe Velez 28, Jean Arthur 29, Loretta Young 29, Joan Blondell 31, Anita Louise 31, Ginger Rogers 32.

Wanamaker, Sam (1919–). American stage actor and director who has also appeared in films; now resident in Britain.
My Girl Tisa 48. Give Us This Day 50. Mr Denning Drives North 51. The Secret 55. The Criminal 60. Taras Bulba 62. The Man in the Middle 64. Those Magnificent Men in Their Flying Machines 65. The Spy Who Came in from the Cold 65. Warning Shot 66. The Day the Fish Came Out 67. File of the Golden Goose (d only) 69. The Executioner (d only) 69. Catlow (d only) 72. Mousey (TV) 73. The Sell Out 75, etc.

Wang Yu, Jimmy (–). Chinese leading man and Kung Fu expert.
The Legend of Seven Golden Vampires 74. The Man from Hong Kong 75, etc.

Wanger, Walter (1894–1968) (W. Feuchtwanger). American independent producer who during a long career held at various times senior executive posts with major studios.
Queen Christina 33. The President Vanishes 35. Private Worlds 35. Mary Burns Fugitive 35. The Trail of the Lonesome Pine 36. *You Only Live Once* 37. History is Made at Night 37. 52nd Street 38. Stand In 38. *Blockade* 38. Trade Winds 38. Algiers 38. *Stagecoach* 39. *Foreign Correspondent* 40. The Long Voyage Home 40. *Scarlet Street* 45. The Lost Moment 47. Tap Roots 48. Joan of Arc 48. Riot in Cell Block Eleven 54. *Invasion of the Body Snatchers* 55. I Want to Live 58. Cleopatra 62.

War and Peace. The main film versions of Tolstoy's epic novel were a Russian one of 1916; King Vidor's of 1955 with Henry Fonda and Audrey Hepburn, photographed by Jack Cardiff and Aldo Tonti; and Sergei Bondartchuk's seven-hour colossus of 1964, photographed by Anatole Petrinsky.

war heroes who have become the subject of

biopics include Eddie Rickenbacker (Fred MacMurray, *Captain Eddie*); Audie Murphy (himself, *To Hell and Back*); Guy Gabaldon (Jeffrey Hunter, *Hell to Eternity*); Alvin York (Gary Cooper, *Sergeant York*); Douglas Bader (Kenneth More, *Reach for the Sky*); Guy Gibson (Richard Todd, The Dam Busters); Ernie Pyle (Burgess Meredith, *The Story of G.I. Joe*); John Hoskins (Sterling Hayden, *The Eternal Sea*).

The War of the Worlds (US 1953). This George Pal version (AA special effects) of the H. G. Wells fantasy about a Martian invasion was by no means as imaginative as it might have been, but was notable for introducing a streak of viciousness into science fiction: neither side showed much mercy, and the noise was deafening.

Ward, Burt (1945–) (Herbert Jervis). American juvenile of the sixties who played Robin in TV's *Batman* series, then disappeared from view.

Ward, Michael (1915–). British comic actor usually seen as nervous photographer or twee shopwalker.
An Ideal Husband 47. Sleeping Car to Trieste 48. Street Corner 53. Private's Progress 55. I'm All Right, Jack 59. Carry On Screaming 66, etc.

Ward, Polly (1908–) (Byno Poluski). British-born leading lady of several thirties comedies.
Shooting Stars 28. His Lordship 32. The Old Curiosity Shop 34. Feather Your Nest 37. Thank Evans 38. It's in the Air 38. Bulldog Drummond Sees It Through 40. Women Aren't Angels 42, etc.

Ward, Simon (1941–). British leadling actor of the seventies.
□ *If* 67. Frankenstein Must Be Destroyed 69. I Start Counting 71. *Young Winston* 72. Hitler – the Last Ten Days 73. Dracula (TV) 73. The Three Musketeers 74. The Four Musketeers 75. Deadly Strangers 75. All Creatures Great and Small 75. Aces High 76.

Warden, Jack (1920–). Burly American character, also on stage and TV.
From Here to Eternity 53. *Twelve Angry Men* 57. Edge of the City 57. *The Bachelor Party* 57. Escape from Zahrain 62. Mirage 65. Blindfold 65. Welcome to the Club 70. Who is Harry Kellerman ...? 71. Billy Two Hats 73. The Apprenticeship of Duddy Kravitz 74. Shampoo 75. The White Buffalo 77, etc.
TV series: The Wackiest Ship in the Army 65.

Warhol, Andy (1926–). American 'underground' film-maker of the sixties: his works usually run for several hours and are totally boring except to the initiated.
Sleep 63. Blow Job 64. Harlot 65. The Chelsea Girls (shown on two screens side by side, with different images) 66. F**k, or Blue Movie 69. Trash (p only) 70. Flesh (p only) 71. Bad 76, etc.

Warner Brothers Pictures Inc. is a family affair started in 1923 by four American exhibitor brothers. After a very shaky start it soared to pre-eminence through their gamble on talking pictures in the shape of *The Jazz Singer* and *The Singing Fool*. Through the thirties and forties the company kept its popularity through tough gangster films starring James Cagney, Edward G. Robinson and Humphrey Bogart, and musicals with Dick Powell and Ruby Keeler; and its prestige by exposés like *Confessions of a Nazi Spy* and *Mission to Moscow* and biographies of Zola, Pasteur, Ehrlich and Reuter. Other Warner stars included Bette Davis and Errol Flynn, both enormously popular with all classes. Warner films were not usually over-budgeted but contrived to look immaculate through solid production values and star performances. Since 1950 the company's product has been more variable, as deals have had to be done with independent producers, and there has been a patchy flirtation with TV; yet on the serious side directors like Kazan have been encouraged, popular taste is taken care of by spectaculars like *My Fair Lady* and *The Great Race*, and the company took a calculated risk (which paid off in spades) with *Who's Afraid of Virginia Woolf?* In the mid-sixties came a merger with Seven Arts, and in 1969 the company was taken over by a conglomerate.

Warner, David (1941–). Lanky British stage actor who has made film appearances.
□ Tom Jones (as Blifil) 63. The Deadly Affair 66. *Morgan* 66. Work is a Four-Letter Word 68. A Midsummer Night's Dream 68. *The Bofors Gun* 68. The Fixer 68. The Seagull 68. Michael Kohlhaas 69. The Ballad of Cable Hogue 70. Perfect Friday 70. Straw Dogs 71. A Doll's House 73. Tales from the Crypt 73. Little Malcolm 75. The Omen 76. Cross of Iron 77.

Warner, H. B. (1876–1958) (Henry Byron Warner-Lickford). Distinguished British actor, on stage from 1883; in Hollywood as film actor from around 1917.
The Beggar of Cawnpore 15. The Man White 19. One Hour Before Dawn 20. Zaza 23. *King of Kings* (as Jesus) 27. Sorrell and Son 27. The Divine Lady 28. The Trial of Mary Dugan 29.

Five Star Final 31. *Mr Deeds Goes to Town* 36. *Lost Horizon* 37. *Victoria the Great* 37. You Can't Take It With You 38. Bulldog Drummond Strikes Back 39. The Rains Came 39. All That Money Can Buy 41. Topper Returns 41. The Corsican Brothers 41. It's a Wonderful Life 46. Prince of Thieves 48. Sunset Boulevard 50. Savage Drums 51. The Ten Commandments 56, many others.

Warner, Jack (1894–) (Jack Waters). Genial British character actor, former music-hall comedian; TV's 'Dixon of Dock Green'.
Autobiography 1975: *Jack of all Trades.*
The Dummy Talks (debut) 43. *The Captive Heart* 44. Hue and Cry 46. It Always Rains on Sunday 47. Holiday Camp 47. *Here Come the Huggetts* 48. The Huggetts Abroad 49. *The Blue Lamp* 50. Valley of Eagles 51. Scrooge 51. The Quatermass Experiment 55. Home and Away 56. Carve Her Name with Pride 58. *Jigsaw* 62, many others.

Warner, Jack L. (1892–). American executive producer, surviving member of the four Warner Brothers who started up a small production company in the twenties and pioneered sound pictures with *The Jazz Singer* 27. The other brothers: Albert, Harry M., and Sam.
Jack has published his autobiography (1965): *My First Hundred Years in Hollywood.* See also *Warner Brothers.*
RECENT PRODUCTIONS: *My Fair Lady* 64. *Camelot* 67. *'1776'* 72. Dirty Little Billy 73.

Warnercolor. Actually Eastmancolor, though it always looked as though it had had a blue rinse.

Warning Shadows (Germany 1922). Directed by Arthur Robison, this structurally interesting but very Teutonic fantasy concerns a shadow-man who forces the inhabitants of an unhappy household to see themselves in a shadowy play. Full of weird effects largely achieved by expressionist use of light and shadow.

Warren, C. Denier (1889–1971). Chubby American character comedian, in British films; vaudeville experience.
Counsel's Opinion 33. Kentucky Minstrels 34. A Fire Has Been Arranged 35. Cotton Queen 37. Trouble Brewing 39. Kiss the Bride Goodbye 44. Old Mother Riley, Headmistress 50. Bluebeard's Ten Honeymoons 60, etc.

Warren, Charles Marquis (1912–).

American writer-director. Moved into TV and became creator and executive producer of *Gunsmoke, Rawhide, The Virginian*, etc.
Little Big Horn 51. Hellgate 52. Arrowhead 53. Flight to Tangier 54. Seven Angry Men 55. The Black Whip 56. Charro (pd) 69, etc.

Warren, Harry (1895–). American songwriter, mainly with Al Dubin; busy on many Warner musicals of the early thirties, they made a personal appearance in *42nd Street*.

Warren, Robert Penn (1905–). American novelist.
All the King's Men 49. Band of Angels 57.

Warrender, Harold (1903–1953). British stage and screen actor.
Friday the Thirteenth 33. Contraband 40. Sailors Three 41. Scott of the Antarctic 49. Pandora and the Flying Dutchman 51. Where No Vultures Fly 51. Intimate Relations 53, etc.

Warrick, Ruth (1915–). American leading lady of the forties. Former radio singer.
Citizen Kane (debut) 41. The Corsican Brothers 41. Journey into Fear 42. Forever and a Day 43. Mr Winkle Goes to War 44. Guest in the House 44. China Sky 45. Swell Guy 47. Arch of Triumph 48. Three Husbands 50. Killer with a Label 50. Let's Dance 52. Ride Beyond Vengeance 65. How to Steal the World 68. The Great Bank Robbery 69, etc.
TV series: Father of the Bride 61. Peyton Place 65.

Warwick, John (1905–1972) (John McIntosh Beattie). Australian leading man, later character actor, in British films, including many of the 'Scotland Yard' series as police inspector.
Down on the Farm 35. Lucky Jade 37. The Face at the Window 39. Danny Boy 40. The Missing Million 42. Dancing with Crime 48. Street Corner 53. Up to His Neck 54. Just My Luck 57. Horrors of the Black Museum 59.

Warwick, Robert (1878–1965) (Robert Taylor Bien). American character actor, adept at executives and heavy fathers. A star of such silent films as *A Modern Othello, The Mad Lover, Thou Art the Man*.
So Big 32. Night Life of the Gods 35. A Tale of Two Cities 36. The Life of Emile Zola 37. The Adventures of Robin Hood 38. Sullivan's Travels 41. The Palm Beach Story 42. I Married a Witch 43. Gentleman's Agreement 48. Francis 49. Sugarfoot 51. Mississippi Gambler 53. Lady Godiva of Coventry 55. Night of the Quarter Moon 59, many others.

Washbourne, Mona (1903–). British stage character actress.
Wide Boy 48. Child's Play 53. Doctor in the House 54. The Good Companions 57. Brides of Dracula 60. *Billy Liar* 63. *Night Must Fall* 63. One Way Pendulum 64. *My Fair Lady* (US) 64. The Third Day (US) 65. Mrs Brown You've Got a Lovely Daughter 68. Fragment of Fear 70. What Became of Jack and Jill? 71. O Lucky Man 73, etc.

Washburn, Bryant (1889–). American romantic hero of the silent screen.
The Blindness of Virtue 15. Venus in the East 18. The Parasite 25. Swing High 30. Sutter's Gold 36, many others.

Washington, George (1732–1799). The first American president, the lad who could not tell a lie, has been impersonated in many films, including *Alexander Hamilton* (Alan Mowbray, who also had the role in *The Phantom President* and *Where Do We Go from Here?*); *America* (Arthur Dewey); *The Howards of Virginia* (George Houston); *The Remarkable Andrew* (Montagu Love); *Unconquered* (Richard Gaines); *John Paul Jones* (John Crawford); *Lafayette* (Howard St John).

water, in inconvenient quantity, played a dramatic part in *Way Down East*; *Noah's Ark*; *The Rains Came* and its remake *The Rains of Ranchipur*; *The Bible*; *Floods of Fear*; *The Hurricane*; *Campbell's Kingdom*; *When Worlds Collide*; *Rain*; *Whistling in Dixie*; *Foreign Correspondent*; *Who Was That Lady?*; and no doubt a hundred others.
See also: *Rain.*

waterfront films have turned up frequently. Among the more seriously-intended are *On the Waterfront, Anna Christie, Waterfront*, and *Slaughter on Tenth Avenue*; melodramas include *The Mob*, the *Tugboat Annie* films, and *I Cover the Waterfront*. Laurel and Hardy worked the milieu in *The Live Ghost*. TV series include yet another *Waterfront*.

Waterloo Bridge. Robert E. Sherwood's sentimental romance, about a ballet dancer who turns prostitute when her rich lover is reported killed at the war and commits suicide when he returns, was filmed in 1930 by James Whale, with Kent Douglass and Mae Clarke; in 1940 by Mervyn le Roy, with Robert Taylor and Vivien Leigh; and in 1956 (as *Gaby*) by Curtis Bernhardt, with John Kerr, Leslie Caron and a happy ending.

Waterloo Road (GB 1944). A small and now dated melodrama about a soldier who takes French leave to beat up his wife's seducer, this film can now be seen as the beginning of the British realist movement which eventually led to *Saturday Night and Sunday Morning*. Getting out of the studio into South London slums, it gave at the time a fresh and vivid sensation now impossible to recapture. Written and directed by Sidney Gilliat; photographed by Arthur Crabtree; with John Mills, Joy Shelton, Stewart Granger and Alastair Sim.

Waterman, Denis (1948–). British juvenile of the sixties.
Pirates of Blood River 61. *Up the Junction* 67. My Lover My Son 69. A Smashing Bird I Used to Know 69. Scars of Dracula 70. Fright 70. Man in the Wilderness 71. The Belstone Fox 73, etc.
TV series: *The Sweeney* 74– .

Waters, Ethel (1900–). Distinguished black American actress and singer.
Autobiography 1953: *His Eye is on the Sparrow*.
On with the Show 29. Tales of Manhattan 42. *Cabin in the Sky* 43. *Pinky* 49. *Member of the Wedding* 52. The Sound and the Fury 59, etc.
TV series: Beulah 53.

Waters, Russell (1908–). British character actor usually in meek and mild parts. The 'hero' of many of Richard Massingham's short and light-hearted instructional films.
The Woman in the Hall 47. The Happiest Days of Your Life 50. Maggie 54. Left, Right and Centre 59, many others.

Waterston, Sam (1940–). American general purpose actor.
A Time for Giving 69. A Delicate Balance 73. *The Great Gatsby* 74. Rancho de Luxe 75, etc.

Watkin, Pierre (c. 1894–1960). American character actor often seen as lawyer, doctor or kindly father.
Dangerous 35. Pride of the Yankees 41. Whistling in Dixie 43. Shanghai Chest 46. Knock On Any Door 59. The Dark Page 51. Johnny Dark 54, many others.

Watkin, David (–). British cinematographer.
The Knack 64. Help 65. The Marat/Sade 66. How I Won the War 67. The Charge of the Light Brigade 67. The Bed Sitting Room 69. Catch 22 70. The Devils 71. The Boy Friend 71. A Delicate Balance 73, etc.

Watkins, Peter (1937–). British director from TV (*Culloden, The War Game*).
□ Privilege 67. Punishment Park 71. Edvard Munch 75.

Watling, Jack (1923–). Boyish British character actor.
Sixty Glorious Years 38. Journey Together 45. The Courtneys of Curzon Street 47. Quartet 48. The Winslow Boy 48. Meet Mr Lucifer 54. The Sea Shall Not Have Them 55. The Admirable Crichton 57. A Night to Remember 58. Mary Had a Little 61. 11 Harrowhouse 74, many others.

Watson, Bobs (c. 1930–). American boy actor of the thirties and forties; noted for his ability to weep at the drop of a hat.
In Old Chicago 38. Kentucky 39. *On Borrowed Time* 39. Dr Kildare's Crisis 41. Men of Boys' Town 41. The Bold and the Brave 56. First to Fight 67, etc.

Watson, Jack (1921–). Tough-looking British general purpose actor.
Konga 61. This Sporting Life 62. The Hill 65. Tobruk 67. *The Strange Affair* 67. Every Home Should Have One 70. The Mackenzie Break 71. Kidnapped 72, etc.

Watson, Lucile (1879–1962). Canadian character actress with stage experience; usually in imperious roles.
What Every Woman Knows 34. Sweethearts 39. Waterloo Bridge 40. Rage in Heaven 41. The Great Lie 41. Watch on the Rhine 43. My Reputation 44. The Razor's Edge 46. Harriet Craig 50. My Forbidden Past (last film) 51, etc.

Watson, Minor (1889–1965). American character actor who often played lawyers or kindly fathers.
Our Betters 33. Babbitt 34. When's Your Birthday? 37. Boys' Town 38. Moon over Miami 41. The Big Shot 42. The Virginian 46. The File on Thelma Jordon 49. Mister 880 50. My Son John 51. Trapeze 56, etc.

Watson, Robert (1888–1965). American character actor who became famous for his resemblance to Hitler; played the lead in *The Hitler Gang* 43, and other films of this type.
Moonlight and Melody 33. Mary of Scotland 36. The Devil with Hitler 42. Nazty Nuisance 43. The Big Clock 48. Red Hot and Blue 49. Singin' in the Rain 52. The Story of Mankind 57, etc.

Watson, Wylie (1889–1966) (John Wylie

Robertson). British character actor, usually in 'little man' roles; formerly in music hall.
The Thirty-Nine Steps 35 (as 'Mr Memory'). London Belongs to Me 48. Whisky Galore 48. *The Sundowners* 60, many others.

Watt, Harry (1906–). British director with varied early experience before joining GPO Film Unit as assistant in 1931.
Night Mail 36. North Sea 38. Squadron 992 40. Target for Tonight 41. *Nine Men* (& w) 44. Fiddlers Three 44. The Overlanders 46. Eureka Stockade 48. Where No Vultures Fly 51. West of Zanzibar 53. The Siege of Pinchgut 59, etc.

Wattis, Richard (1912–1975). Bespectacled British character comedian with stage experience.
The Happiest Days of Your Life 49. The Clouded Yellow 51. Hobson's Choice 54. I am a Camera 55. Simon and Laura 55. The Prince and the Showgirl 58. The VIPs 63. Moll Flanders 65. Up Jumped a Swagman 65. Wonderwall 68. Games That Lovers Play 69. That's Your Funeral 73. Diamonds on Wheels 73. Hot Property 73, many others.

Waxman, Franz (1906–1967) (Franz Wachsmann). German composer, in America from 1934.
Bride of Frankenstein 35. Sutter's Gold 36. Fury 36. Captains Courageous 38. The Young in Heart 38. Rebecca 40. *The Philadelphia Story* 40. Woman of the Year 42. Air Force 42. Mr Skeffington 44. Objective Burma 45. Humoresque 46. The Paradine Case 48. *Alias Nick Beal* 49. *Sunset Boulevard* (AA) 50. *A Place in the Sun* (AA) 51. My Cousin Rachel 53. Rear Window 54. Mister Roberts 56. Sayonara 57. The Nun's Story 59. Cimarron 60. Taras Bulba 62. Lost Command 66, etc.

Waxman, Harry (1912–). British cinematographer.
Brighton Rock 46. They Were Not Divided 48. Valley of Eagles 51. The Baby and the Battleship 56. *Innocent Sinners* 57. The Secret Partner 60. The Roman Spring of Mrs Stone 61. *The Day the Earth Caught Fire* 62. Lancelot and Guinevere 63. Crooks in Cloisters 64. The Nanny 65. *Khartoum* (2nd unit) 66. The Family Way 66. The Trygon Factor 67. The Anniversary 67. Wonderwall 68. Twisted Nerve 68. There's a Girl in My Soup 70. Flight of the Doves 71. Endless Night 72. Digby 73. Blue Blood 73. Vampira 74. Journey into Fear 75. The Pink Panther Strikes Again 76, etc.

waxworks have featured from time to time in horror films and other thrillers, notably *The Mystery of the Wax Museum, House of Wax, Nightmare in Wax, Terror in the Wax Museum, The Florentine Dagger, Charlie Chan in the Wax Museum, Midnight at Madame Tussaud's* and the original German *Waxworks*.

The Way Ahead (GB 1944). World War II's best film tribute to the British Army, as seen through the eyes of a group of very unwilling conscripts. The film survives chiefly by virtue of the good comedy writing of its first half; the final baptism of fire is more routine. Directed by Carol Reed from a script by Eric Ambler and Peter Ustinov (originally intended as a short army propaganda film); photographed by Guy Green; music by William Alwyn. With David Niven, Stanley Holloway, Raymond Huntley, Jimmy Hanley, William Hartnell, Peter Ustinov, etc.

Way Down East (US 1920). D. W. Griffith's sentimental melodrama is remembered now for its brilliantly and hazardously filmed ice-floe sequence. Written by Griffith from a play by Lottie Blair Parker; photographed by Hendrik Sartov and Billy Bitzer. With Lillian Gish, Richard Barthelmess. Remade as a talkie in 1936 with Rochelle Hudson and Henry Fonda.

The Way to the Stars (GB 1945). A gentle, satisfying film about the RAF in World War II. Hardly a plane is seen, as the action takes place mainly in a small hotel near the airfield. Both writer Terence Rattigan and director Anthony Asquith are in their best and most typical forms, and a distinguished cast includes Michael Redgrave, John Mills, Rosamund John, Douglass Montgomery, Stanley Holloway, Renée Asherson and Joyce Carey.

Wayne, David (1914–) (Wayne McKeekan). Wiry American character actor, in films since late forties, also stage star.
Portrait of Jennie 48. *Adam's Rib* 49. My Blue Heaven 50. Up Front 51. With a Song in My Heart 52. *Wait till the Sun Shines Nellie* 52. The I Don't Care Girl 53. Tonight We Sing 53. How to Marry a Millionaire 53. The Tender Trap 55. The Three Faces of Eve 57. The Last Angry Man 59. The Big Gamble 60. The Andromeda Strain 70. Huckleberry Finn 74. The Front Page 74. The Apple Dumpling Gang 75, etc.
TV series: Norby 51. The Good Life 71.

Wayne, John (1907–) (Marion Michael Morrison). Tough, genial, generally inimitable American leading man of action films, who after a slow start became one of the best known and most successful actors in Hollywood.

□ Hangman's House 28. Mother Machree 28. Salute 29. Men Without Women 30. Rough Romance 30. Cheer Up and Smile 30. *The Big Trail* 30. Girls Demand Excitement 31. Three Girls Lost 31. Men are Like That 31. Range Feud 31. Hurricane Express (serial) 31. Shadow of the Eagle (serial) 31. Maker of Men 32. Two Fisted Law 32. Texas Cyclone 32. Lady and Gent 32. Ride Him Cowboy 32. The Big Stampede 32. The Three Mesquiteers (serial) 33. Haunted Gold 33. Telegraph Trail 33. His Private Secretary 33. Central Airport 33. Baby Face Harrington 33. The Sagebrush Trail 33. Somewhere in Sonora 33. The Life of Jimmy Dolan 33. Baby Face 33. The Man from Monterey 33. Riders of Destiny 33. College Coach 33. West of the Divide 34. Blue Steel 34. Lucky Texan 34. The Man from Utah 34. Randy Rides Alone 34. The Star Packer 34. The Trail Beyond 34. Neath Arizona Skies 34. Texas Terror 35. The Lawless Frontier 35. New Frontier 35. Lawless Range 35. Rainbow Valley 35. Paradise Canyon 35. The Dawn Rider 35. Westward Ho 35. Desert Trail 35. The Lawless Nineties 36. King of the Pecos 36. The Oregon Trail 36. Winds of the Wasteland 36. The Sea Spoilers 36. The Lonely Trail 36. Conflict 36. California Straight Ahead 37. Cover the War 37. Idol of the Crowds 37. Adventure's End 37. Born to the West 37. Pals of the Saddle 37. Overland Stage Raiders 38. Santa Fe Stampede 38. Red River Range 38. *Stagecoach* 38. Night Riders 39. Three Texas Steers 39. Wyoming Frontier 39. New Frontier 39. Allegheny Uprising 39. Dark Command 40. Three Faces West 40. *The Long Voyage Home* 40. *Seven Sinners* 40. A Man Betrayed 40. The Lady from Louisiana 41. The Shepherd of the Hills 41. Lady for a Night 41. Reap the Wild Wind 42. The Spoilers 42. In Old California 42. Flying Tigers 42. Reunion in France 42. Pittsburgh 42. A Lady Takes a Chance 43. In Old Oklahoma 43. The Fighting Seabees 44. Tall in the Saddle 44. Back to Bataan 44. Flame of the Barbary Coast 44. Dakota 45. They Were Expendable 45. Without Reservations 46. Angel and the Badman 47. Tycoon 47. Fort Apache 48. *Red River* 48. Three Godfathers 48. Wake of the Red Witch 48. The Fighting Kentuckian 49. *She Wore a Yellow Ribbon* 49. *Sands of Iwo Jima* 49. Rio Grande 50. Operation Pacific 51. Flying Leathernecks 51. Big Jim McLain 52. *The Quiet Man* 52. Trouble Along the Way 53. Island in the Sky 53. Hondo 53. *The High and the Mighty* 54. The Sea Chase 55. Blood Alley 55. The Conqueror 55. *The Searchers* 56. The Wings of Eagles 57. Jet Pilot 57. Legend of the Lost 57. The Barbarian and the Geisha 58. *Rio Bravo* 59. The Horse Soldiers 59. North to Alaska 60. *The Alamo* (& p d) 60. The Comancheros 61. The Man Who Shot Liberty Valance 62. Hatari 62. The Longest Day 62. How the West Was Won 63. Donovan's Reef 63. McLintock 63. Circus World 64. The Greatest Story Ever Told 65. In Harm's Way 65. The Sons of Katie Elder 65. Cast a Giant Shadow 66. El Dorado 67. The War Wagon 67. The Green Berets (& d) 68. Hellfighters 68. The Undefeated 69. *True Grit* (AA) 69. Rio Lobo 70. Chisum 70. Big Jake 71. The Cowboys 72. The Train Robbers 73. Cahill 73. McQ 74. Brannigan 75. Rooster Cogburn 75. *The Shootist* 76.

Wayne, Michael (1934–). American producer, son of John Wayne.
McLintock 63. The Green Berets 67. Cahill 73, etc.

Wayne, Naunton (1901–1970) (Naunton Davies). Mild-mannered British light comedy actor, on stage from 1920, films from 1931; became well known with Basil Radford in many films as Englishmen abroad.
The First Mrs Fraser (debut) 31. Going Gay 33. For Love of You 34. *The Lady Vanishes* 38. *Night Train to Munich* 40. *Crooks' Tour* 41. Next of Kin 42. Millions Like Us 43. *Dead of Night* 45. The Calendar 47. *It's Not Cricket* 48. Quartet 48. Passport to Pimlico 48. Obsession 49. Highly Dangerous 50. *The Titfield Thunderbolt* 53. You Know What Sailors Are 53. Nothing Barred 61. Double Bunk 64, others.

Wayne, Patrick (1939–). American actor, son of John Wayne.
The Searchers 56. The Alamo 60. The Comancheros 62. McLintock 63. The Bears and I 74, etc.

Weaver, Dennis (1924–). American character actor and TV star.
The Raiders 52. War Arrow 54. Seven Angry Men 55. Touch of Evil 58. The Gallant Hours 60. Duel at Diablo 66. The Great Man's Whiskers (TV) 71. What's the Matter with Helen 71. Duel (TV) 71. The Forgotten Man (TV) 71. Rollin' Man (TV) 72, etc.
TV series: Gunsmoke (as Chester) 58–64. Kentucky Jones 65. McCloud 70– .

Weaver, Fritz (1926–). American stage actor.
Fail Safe 64. The Borgia Stick (TV) 68. The Maltese Bippy 69. A Walk in the Spring Rain 70. The Day of the Dolphin 73. Marathon Man 76. Demon Seed 77, etc.

Weaver, Marjorie (1913–). American leading lady, mainly of second features.
China Clipper 36. Three Blind Mice 38. Young Mr Lincoln 39. Maryland 40. The Mad Martindales 42. We're Not Married 52, others.

Webb, Clifton (1893–1966) (Webb Parmelee Hollenbeck). American leading character actor, former dancer and stage star. In films, became in middle age well-known in waspish roles.
Polly with a Past 20. New Toys 24. The Heart of a Siren 25. *Laura* 44. The Dark Corner 45. *The Razor's Edge* 46. *Sitting Pretty* 47. Mr Belvedere Goes to College 49. *Cheaper by the Dozen* 50. For Heaven's Sake 50. Mr Belvedere Rings the Bell 51. Elopement 52. *Dreamboat* 52. Stars and Stripes Forever 53. Titanic 53. Mr Scoutmaster 53. *Three Coins in the Fountain* 54. Woman's World 54. The Man Who Never Was 56. Boy on a Dolphin 57. The Remarkable Mr Pennypacker 58. Holiday for Lovers 59. Satan Never Sleeps 62, etc.

Webb, Jack (1920–). American TV star and executive: starred and directed in *Dragnet* and other series: was briefly head of Warner TV.
AS ACTOR: The Men 50. Sunset Boulevard 50. You're in the Navy Now 52. Dragnet (& pd) 54. Pete Kelly's Blues (& pd) 55. The D.I. (& pd) 57. The Last Time I Saw Archie (& pd) 62, others.

Webb, James R. (1910–1974). American screenwriter.
The Charge at Feather River 53. Phantom of the Rue Morgue (co-w) 54. Trapeze 56. The Big Country (co-w) 58. Pork Chop Hill 59. How the West Was Won (AA) 63. Guns for San Sebastian 67. Alfred the Great (co-w) 69, many others.

Webb, Robert D. (1903–). American director, former cameraman.
White Feather 55. On the Threshold of Space 55. The Proud Ones 56. Love Me Tender 56. The Way to the Gold 57. Seven Women from Hell 61. The Agony and the Ecstasy (second unit) 65. Capetown Affair 67. The Hawaiians 70, etc.

Webber, Robert (1928–). American leading man with stage and TV experience.
Highway 301 51. *Twelve Angry Men* 57. The Stripper 63. Hysteria (GB) 64. The Sandpiper 65. The Third Day 65. No Tears for a Killer (It.) 65. Harper 66. The Silencers 67. The Dirty Dozen 67. Dollars 72. Bring Me the Head of Alfredo Garcia 74. Midway 76, etc.

Webb, Roy (–). American composer.
Alice Adams 35. Quality Street 37. Room

Service 38. Kitty Foyle 40. Cat People 42. Journey into Fear 42. Experiment Perilous 44. The Body Snatcher 45. Murder My Sweet 45. Notorious 46. The Spiral Staircase 46. Blood on the Moon 48. Mighty Joe Young 49. Flying Leathernecks 51. Houdini 53. Blood Alley 55. Top Secret Affair 57. Teacher's Pet 58, many others.

Webster, Paul Francis (c. 1910–). American lyricist. Various Shirley Temple songs in the thirties; later *Love is a Many Splendored Thing* (AA) 54. *Friendly Persuasion* 56. The Sandpiper (AA) 65, etc.

weddings have formed a happy ending for innumerable films, and an unhappy start for others, but some are more memorable than the rest. Weddings on a lavish scale were seen in *Camelot, Royal Wedding, The Scarlet Empress, Ivan the Terrible (Part One), The Private Life of Henry VIII*. More domestic occasions were in *Quiet Wedding, The Member of the Wedding. The Catered Affair, Father of the Bride, June Bride, A Kind of Loving, Lovers and Other Strangers, Brigadoon.* Weddings were interrupted in *The Philadelphia Story, The Bride Wasn't Willing, I Married a Witch, The Runaround, You Gotta Stay Happy, The Bride Went Wild, The Lion in Winter, The Graduate* and *I Love You Alice B. Toklas.* Macabre weddings were found in *The Night Walker, The Bride Wore Black, The Bride of Frankenstein, the Bride and the Beast, Chamber of Horrors.* The wedding night was the centre of interest in *The Man in Grey, The Wicked Lady, Wedding Night, The Family Way* and *My Little Chickadee.* And the funniest wedding still remains that in *Our Wife,* when cross-eyed justice of the peace Ben Turpin married Mr Hardy to his best man Mr Laurel.

Weeks, Stephen (1948–). British director.
☐ I Monster 70. Sir Gawain and the Green Knight 72. Ghost Story 74.

Wegener, Paul (1874–1948). Distinguished German actor-writer-director.
The Student of Prague (a) 13. The Golem (ad) 14 and 20. Vanina (a) 22. Svengali (awd) 27. Lucrezia Borgia (a) 27. Ein Mann Will Nach Deutschland (d) 34. Der Grosse König (a) 41. Der Grosse Mandarin (a) 48, many others.

Weidler, Virginia (1927–1968). American child actress who usually played a little horror.
Surrender 31. Mrs Wiggs of the Cabbage Patch 34. Souls at Sea 37. The Women 39. *The Philadelphia Story* 40. Born to Sing 42. The

Youngest Profession 43. Best Foot Forward 43, etc.

Weill, Kurt (1900–1950). German composer whose scores include *Die Dreigroschenoper, One Touch of Venus* and *Knickerbocker Holiday*, all filmed.

Weingarten, Laurence (1898–1975). American producer, in films from around 1917. Broadway Melody 28. A Day at the Races 37. Escape 40. Adam's Rib 49. The Tender Trap 54. Cat on a Hot Tin Roof 58. The Unsinkable Molly Brown 64, scores of others.

Weis, Don (1922–). American director; came to Hollywood from college as trainee.
Bannerline 51. I Love Melvin 53. A Slight Case of Larceny 53. Ride the High Iron 57. Critics' Choice 63. Pajama Party 63. Looking for Love 64. Billie 65. Pajama Party in a Haunted House 66. The King's Pirate 66, etc.

Weisbart, David (1915–1967). American producer, former editor; in Hollywood from 1935.
Mara Maru 52. Rebel Without a Cause 55. Love Me Tender 56. Holiday for Lovers 59. Kid Galahad 63. Rio Conchos 64. Goodbye Charlie 65. Valley of the Dolls 67, many others.

Weissmuller, Johnny (1904–). American leading man, former Olympic athlete who from 1932 played Tarzan (qv) more often than anyone else. In late forties and early fifties appeared in 'Jungle Jim' second features, also on TV. Only 'straight' role: *Swamp Fire* 46.
Guest appearances: Glorifying the American Girl 29. Stage Door Canteen 43. The Phynx 70. Won Ton Ton 76.

Welch, Elizabeth (1908–). Black singing star, born in New York but working mostly in Britain.
Song of Freedom 36. Big Fella 37. Alibi 42. Fiddlers Three 44. Dead of Night 45. Girl Stroke Boy 71, etc.

Welch, Joseph L. (1891–1960). Real-life American judge who became famous during the army-McCarthy hearings in 1953 and was later persuaded to play the judge in *Anatomy of a Murder* 59.

Welch, Raquel (1940–) (Raquel Tejada). Dynamic, curvaceous American sex symbol of the late sixties.
□ Roustabout 64. A House is Not a Home 64. A Swinging Summer 65. Fantastic Voyage 66. One Million Years BC 66. The Biggest Bundle of Them All 66. Shoot Loud, Louder I Don't Understand 66. The Queens 67. Fathom 67. Bandolero 68. The Oldest Profession 68. Bedazzled 68. The Beloved 68. Lady in Cement 68. 100 Rifles 68. Myra Breckinridge 69. Flare Up 69. Hannie Caulder 71. Kansas City Bomber 72. Fuzz 72. Bluebeard 72. The Last of Sheila 73. The Three Musketeers 73. The Four Musketeers 74. The Wild Party 75. Mother Jugs and Speed 76. The Prince and the Pauper 77.

Weld, Tuesday (1943–) (Susan Ker Weld). American leading actress, a model from childhood.
Rock Rock Rock 56. Rally Round the Flag Boys 57. The Five Pennies 59. Return to Peyton Place 61. Wild in the Country 62. Bachelor Flat 63. I'll Take Sweden 65. *The Cincinnati Kid* 65. Lord Love a Duck 66. *Pretty Poison* 68. I Walk the Line 70. A Safe Place 71. Play It as It Lays 73, etc.

Welden, Ben (1901–). British character actor who moved to Hollywood.
The Missing Rembrandt 32. The Triumph of Sherlock Holmes 34. Marked Woman 37. Crime Ring 38. Hollywood Cavalcade 39. Angel on My Shoulder 45. The Lemon Drop Kid 51, many others.

Welland, Colin (1934–). British actor-writer, mostly for television.
AS ACTOR: Kes 69. Villain 71. Straw Dogs 71, etc.

Welles, Orson (1915–). Ebullient American actor-writer-producer-director with stage and radio experience (in 1938 he panicked the whole of America with a vivid radio version of *The War of the Worlds*). His extravagance and unconventionality in Hollywood forced him to Europe, where his projects continued interesting and ambitious but generally undisciplined; he never again achieved the standard of his first two films. AA 1970 'for supreme artistry and versatility in the creation of motion pictures'.
Biographies: *The Fabulous Orson Welles* (1956) by Peter Noble. *Orson Welles* (1973) by Peter Bogdanovitch. *A Ribbon of Dreams* (1973) by Peter Cowie.
□ This list of Welles' films assumes his presence as actor unless otherwise stated: *Citizen Kane* (& d) (AA script, co-w with Herman J. Mankiewicz) 41. *The Magnificent Ambersons* (wd only) 42. *Journey into Fear* 42. *It's All There* (unreleased) (wd only) 42. Jane Eyre 43. Follow the Boys 44. Tomorrow is Forever 44. *The Stranger* (& d) 45. *The Lady from Shanghai* (&

d) 47. Black Magic 47. Macbeth (& d) 48. Prince of Foxes 49. *The Third Man* 49. The Black Rose 50. Othello (& d) 51. Trent's Last Case 53. Trouble in the Glen 53. Si Versailles M'Etait Conté 53. Man Beast and Virtue 53. Napoleon 54. Three Cases of Murder 55. Confidential Report (& d) 55. Moby Dick 56. Man in the Shadow 57. Touch of Evil (& d) 58. The Long Hot Summer 58. Roots of Heaven 58. Ferry to Hong Kong 58. David and Goliath 59. Compulsion 59. Crack in the Mirror 60. The Mongols 60. Lafayette 61. *The Trial* (& d) 62. The VIPs 63. Chimes at Midnight (& d) 66. Is Paris Burning? 66. A Man For All Seasons 66. Marco the Magnificent 66. I'll Never Forget Whatshisname 67. Casino Royale 67. Sailor from Gibraltar 67. Oedipus the King 67. House of Cards 68. The Immortal Story (& d) 68. Start the Revolution without Me 69. The Southern Star 69. The Kremlin Letter 70. The Battle of Neretva 70. Waterloo 70. Catch 22 70. Safe Place 71. Malpertuis 72. Necromancy 72. Treasure Island (as Long John) 72. Ten Days Wonder 72. F For Fake 73. The Other Side of the Mountain 77.

Wellman, William (1896–1975). American director, former pilot, actor and Foreign Legionary; in Hollywood from 1921.
The Man Who Won 23. You Never Know Women 26. *Wings* 27. Beggars of Life 28. *Public Enemy* 31. The Conquerors 32. Central Airport 33. Looking for Trouble 34. Small Town Girl 35. Call of the Wild 35. Robin Hood of Eldorado 36. *Nothing Sacred* 37. *A Star is Born* (AA) 37. Men with Wings (& p) 38. Beau Geste 39. The Light that Failed 39. The Great Man's Lady 42. *The Ox Bow Incident* 42. *Roxie Hart* 42. Buffalo Bill 43. The Story of G.I. Joe 45. Magic Town 46. Yellow Sky 48. The Iron Curtain 48. Battleground 49. The Next Voice You Hear 50. Westward the Women 50. Across the Wide Missouri 51. My Man and I 52. *The High and the Mighty* 54. *Track of the Cat* 54. Blood Alley 55. Darby's Rangers 57. Lafayette Escadrille 58, others.

Wells, George (1909–). American writer, with MGM since 1944.
Take Me Out to the Ball Game (Everybody's Cheering) 48. Three Little Words 50. Everthing I Have is Yours (& p) 52. Jupiter's Darling (p only) 55. Designing Woman (AA) 57. Ask Any Girl 59. The Honeymoon Machine 62. The Horizontal Lieutenant 63. Penelope 66. The Impossible Years 68, etc.

Wells, H. G. (1866–1946). Distinguished

British author, several of whose novels have been filmed.
The Island of Dr Moreau (Island of Lost Souls) 32. The Invisible Man 33. The Man Who Could Work Miracles 35. Things To Come 36. Kipps 41. The History of Mr Polly 49. The War of the Worlds 53. The Time Machine 60. The Island of Dr Moreau 77, etc.

Welsh, John (c. 1905–). Lean British character actor adept at professors, fathers, scientists, barristers etc.

Wendkos, Paul (1922–). American director.
The Burglar 57. Tarawa Beachhead 58. Gidget 59. Face of a Fugitive 59. Because They're Young 60. *Angel Baby* 60. Gidget Goes to Rome 63. 52 Miles to Terror 66. Guns of the Magnificent Seven 69. Cannon for Cordoba 70. The Mephisto Waltz 71. *Haunts of the Very Rich* (TV) 72. Honor Thy Father (TV) 73. Special Delivery 76, etc.

Wengraf, John (1901–) (Johann Wenngraft). Lean Austrian actor, mainly in Hollywood; played a lot of Nazis in his time.
Homo Sum 22. Night Train To Munich 39. Mission To Moscow 43. Sahara 43. The Seventh Cross 44. Weekend at the Waldorf 45. T Men 47. Five Fingers 51. Call Me Madam 53. The Pride and The Passion 57. The Return of Dracula 58. Judgment at Nuremberg 60. The Prize 63, etc.

Werker, Alfred (1896–). American director, in Hollywood from 1917.
Little Lord Fauntleroy 21. Nobody's Children 28. Bachelor's Affairs 32. The House of Rothschild 34. Kidnapped 38. *The Adventures of Sherlock Holmes* 39. Moon over Her Shoulder 41. The Mad Martindales 42. Whispering Ghosts 42. A Haunting We Will Go 42. Shock 45. Lost Boundaries 46. Repeat Performance 47. Pirates of Monterey 48. Sealed Cargo 51. Walk East on Beacon 52. Devil's Conyon 53. Canyon Crosscroads 55. At Gunpoint 58, many others.

Werner, Oskar (1922–) (Josef Schliessmayer). Austrian leading actor with international stage and screen credits.
□ Eroica 49. Angel with a Trumpet 49. The Wonder Kid (GB) 50. Ruf aus dem Aether (Aus.) 51. Ein Laecheln in Sturm (Aus.) 51. Das Gestohlene Jahr (WG) 51. *Decision before Dawn* 51. Lola Montes 55. Spionage (Aus.) 55. Der Letzte Akt (Aus.) 55. The Life of Mozart 56. *Jules et Jim* 61. *Ship of Fools* 65. The Spy Who Came in from the Cold 65. *Fahrenheit 451* 66. Interlude 68. The Shoes of the Fisherman 68. Voyage of the Damned 76.

Wessel, Dick (1910–1965). American supporting actor, usually in comedy roles.
Arson Racket Squad 38. They Made Me a Criminal 39. Action in the North Atlantic 42. Slattery's Hurricane 48. Texas Carnival 51. Calamity Jane 53. The Gazebo 60. The Ugly Dachshund 65, many others.

Wessely, Paula (1908–). Austrian leading actress.
Maskerade 34. Julika 36. Spiegel des Lebens 38. Die Kluge Marianne 43. Maria Theresa 51. The Third Sex 57. Die Unvollkommene Ehe 59, many others.

Wesson, Dick (1922–). American character actor.
Destination Moon 49. Breakthrough 50. Inside the Walls of Folsom Prison 51. About Face 52. The Desert Song 53. Calamity Jane 54, etc.

West, Adam (1929–) (William Anderson). American light leading man.
The Young Philadelphians 49. Geronimo 62. Robinson Crusoe on Mars 64. Mara of the Wilderness 65. Batman 66. The Girl Who Knew Too Much 68. Marriage of a Young Stockbroker 71. The Specialist 75. Partisan 75, etc.
TV series: The Detectives 59–61. *Batman* 65–68.

West, Billy (1893–1975). American silent screen comedian, a successful imitator of Charlie Chaplin; later a Hollywood restaurateur.

West, Mae (1892–). American leading lady of the thirties, the archetypal sex symbol, splendidly vulgar, mocking, overdressed and endearing. Wrote most of her own stage plays and film scripts, which bulge with double meanings.
Autobiographies 1959: *Goodness Had Nothing To Do With It*. 1975: *Life, Sex and ESP*.
□ Night After Night 32. *She Done Him Wrong* 33. *I'm No Angel* 33. Going to Town 34. Belle of the Nineties 34. Klondyke Annie 36. Go West Young Man 37. Every Day's a Holiday 37. My Little Chickadee 39. The Heat's On 43. *Myra Breckinridge* 69. Sextet 77.

West, Nathanael (1904–1940) (Nathan Weinstein). American novelist. Works filmed include *Lonelyhearts*, but he also drew a scathing picture of Hollywood in *The Day of the Locust*.

West, Roland (1887–1952). American director of the late silent period.
□ De Luxe Annie 18. The Silver Lining 21.

Nobody 22. The Unknown Purple 23. The Monster 25. *The Bat* 26. The Dove 27. Alibi 29. *The Bat Whispers* 31. Corsair 31.

West Side Story (AA) (US 1961). A film version by Robert Wise and Jerome Robbins (both AA) of the stage musical re-telling the Romeo and Juliet story in a New York slum setting. A downbeat book (Ernest Lehman) is lifted by good art direction (Boris Leven: AA) and Leonard Bernstein's music. Natalie Wood, Richard Beymer and Russ Tamblyn head the cast. George Chakiris won AA for supporting actor and Rita Moreno for supporting actress.

West, Timothy (1934–). British character actor who became famous as TV's *Edward the Seventh*.
Twisted Nerve 68. Nicholas and Alexandra 71. The Day of the Jackal 74. Hedda 76, etc.

Westcott, Helen (1929–) (Myrthas Helen Hickman). American leading lady, former child actress.
A Midsummer Night's Dream 35. The New Adventures of Don Juan 48. The Gunfighter 50. With a Song in My Heart 52. The Charge at Feather River 53. Hot Blood 55. The Last Hurrah 58. I Love My Wife 71.

Westerby, Robert (1909–1968). British screenwriter, in films from 1947.
Broken Journey 48. The Spider and the Fly 50. They Who Dare 54. War and Peace (co-w) 56. Town on Trial 56. Cone of Silence 60. Greyfriars Bobby 60. The Three Lives of Thomasina 64, etc.

Westerfield, James 1912–1971). Heavyweight American character actor.
Undercurrent 46. The Whistle at Eaton Falls 51. On the Waterfront 54. Chief Crazy Horse 55. Three Brave Men 57. The Shaggy Dog 59. Wild River 60. Birdman of Alcatraz 62. Blue 68. True Grit 69, many others.

westerns have been with us almost as long as the cinema itself; and although Britain supplied *Carry On Cowboy* and a number of continental countries are now making passable horse operas of their own, it is natural enough that almost all westerns should have come from America.
  The Great Train Robbery was a western, and two of the most popular stars of the early silent period, Bronco Billy Anderson and William S. Hart, played western heroes, establishing the conventions and the legends still associated with the opening of America's west—Hollywood style. The attractions of western stories included

natural settings, cheapness of production, readymade plots capable of infinite variation, and a general air of tough simplicity which was saleable the world over. Many of Hollywood's most memorable films of the teens and twenties were westerns: *The Squaw Man, The Spoilers, The Vanishing American, The Covered Wagon, The Iron Horse, The Virginian, In Old Arizona, The Cisco Kid, Cimarron*. The western adapted itself to sound with remarkable ease, and throughout the thirties provided many entertainments of truly epic stature: *Wells Fargo, Arizona, The Texas Rangers, Union Pacific, The Plainsman, Drums Along the Mohawk, Jesse James, The Westerner, Destry Rides Again, Stagecoach*. By now the major directorial talents in the field were established: they included John Ford, William Wyler, Howard Hawks, King Vidor, Victor Fleming, Michael Curtiz, Henry King, Frank Lloyd. And each year brought in the wake of epics scores of cheap but entertaining second features, usually running in familiar series with such stars as Buck Jones, Tom Mix, Tim McCoy, John Wayne, Bob Steele, William Boyd ('Hopalong Cassidy'), Ken Maynard, Tom Tyler, Gene Autry, and the Three Mesquiteers. The singing cowboy familiarized by Autry led to the arrival of other practitioners in the forties: Roy Rogers, Eddie Dean, Lee 'Lasses' White. The forties also based westerns more firmly on historical events, telling such stories as *Brigham Young, Northwest Passage, My Darling Clementine, Santa Fe Trail, They Died with Their Boots On*. But by the end of the decade this genre had worn itself out except in the case of Ford, whose films became increasingly stylish and personal. Elsewhere westerns deteriorated into routine action adventures starring actors a little past their best: Gary Cooper, Errol Flynn, Dennis Morgan, Alan Ladd. Howard Hawks *Red River* was a useful move towards realism, and was followed in the early fifties by films like *The Gunfighter* and *Shane*, intent on proving how unpleasant a place the real West must have been. Side by side with realism came the 'message' western, given its impetus by *Broken Arrow* 50, the first western since silent days to sympathize with the Indians. It was followed by western allegories like *High Noon* and *3.10 to Yuma*, in which the action elements were restricted or replaced by suspense in taut stories of good versus evil. In these ways the western became a highly respectable form, attracting actors of the calibre of James Stewart, Marlon Brando, Glenn Ford, Henry Fonda, Burt Lancaster, Richard Widmark and Kirk Douglas, all of whom tended to play half-cynical heroes who preserved their sense of right by indulging in violent action in the last reel. The later fifties

brought many spectacular western productions including *Gunfight at the OK Corral, Last Train from Gun Hill, One-Eyed Jacks, Warlock* and *The Magnificent Seven*; but no new ground was broken. Second features continued to prosper in the capable hands of Randolph Scott, Joel McCrea and Audie Murphy.

The galloping success of TV made potted westerns so familiar that even the biggest epics made for the cinema found it hard to attract a paying audience. Ford persevered with *The Man Who Shot Liberty Valance* and *Cheyenne Autumn*, both rehashes of earlier and better work; Cinerama made a patchy spectacle called *How the West Was Won*; novelty westerns have tried violence, horror and sentimentality as gimmicks. However hard the times, one can't imagine westerns ever dying out altogether, though the violent Italian imitations ('spaghetti westerns') of the sixties came close to killing them as an art form while stimulating their box office potential, and Hollywood is still, at the time of writing, trying clumsily to rival the Italian imitations of its own product, with occasional 'realistic' experiments such as *The Shootist*.

Westley, Helen (1879–1942) (Henrietta Conroy). American character actress of stage and screen; usually played crotchety but kindhearted dowagers.
Death Takes a Holiday 34. The House of Rothschild 34. Moulin Rouge 34. Anne of Green Gables 34. Roberta 35. Showboat 36. Dimples 36. Banjo on My Knee 36. Stowaway 36. Heidi 37. Rebecca of Sunnybrook Farm 38. Zaza 39. Lady with Red Hair 40. Lillian Russell 40. Adam Had Four Sons 41. Sunny 41. My Favorite Spy 42, etc.

Westman, Nydia (1902–1970). American character comedienne, usually in fluttery, nervous roles.
King of the Jungle 33. The Invisible Ray 36. *The Cat and the Canary* 39. When Tomorrow Comes 40. The Late George Apley 47. The Velvet Touch 49. The Ghost and Mr Chicken 66, many others.

Westmore, Percy (1904–1970). The famous family of Hollywood make-up artists was headed by George Westmore (1879–1931), English by birth but a west coast success from the moment he changed Valentino's hair style. The sons all worked for different studios, and most had health and emotional problems. They were Mont (1902–1940), Percy (1904–1970). Ern (1904–1968), Wally (1906–1973), Bud (1918–1973) and Frank (1923–) who, in 1976, wrote a book about the family, *The Westmores of Hollywood.*

Weston, David (1938–). British actor of TV and films.
Doctor in-Distress 63. Becket 64. The Legend of Young Dick Turpin 65. The Red Baron 70, etc.

Weston, Jack (1926–). American roly-poly character actor, often an incompetent minor villain.
Stage Struck 58. It's Only Money 62. *Mirage* 65. *Wait Until Dark* 67. The Thomas Crown Affair 68. The April Fools 69. Fuzz 72. A New Leaf 72. Marco 73. Gator 76, many others.
TV series: The Hathaways 61.

Wexler, Haskell (1926–). American cinematographer.
The Savage Eye 59. Angel Baby 60. The Hoodlum Priest 61. A Face in the Rain 62. America America 63. *The Best Man* 64. The Loved One (co-ph) 65. Who's Afraid of Virginia Woolf? 66. *In the Heat of the Night* (AA) 67. *The Thomas Crown Affair* 68. Medium Cool (& d) 69. The Conversation 73. American Graffiti 73. One Flew Over The Cuckoo's Nest 75, etc.

Whale, James (1886–1957). British stage director of somewhat mysterious personality; went to Hollywood 1930 to film his stage production of *Journey's End* and stayed to make other movies including four classics of the macabre.
□ Waterloo Bridge 30. *Frankenstein* 31. The Imprudent Maiden 32. *The Old Dark House* 32. The Kiss before the Mirror 33. *The Invisible Man* 33. By Candlelight 33. One More River 34. *Bride of Frankenstein* 35. *Remember Last Night* 35. *Showboat* 36. The Road Back 37. The Great Garrick 37. Sinners in Paradise 37. Wives under Suspicion 38. Port of Seven Seas 38. *The Man in the Iron Mask* 39. Green Hell 40. They Dare Not Love 40.

Whalen, Michael (1899–1974) (Joseph Kenneth Shovlin). American leading man of the thirties.
Country Doctor 36. Time Out for Murder 38. Sign of the Wolf 41. Tahiti Honey 43. Gas House Kids in Hollywood 48. Mark of the Dragon 51. The Phantom from Ten Thousand Leagues 56, many others.

Whatham, Claude (–). British director.
□ That'll Be the Day 72. Swallows and Amazons 74.

Wheatley, Alan (1907–). Suave British

character actor best known as the Sheriff of Nottingham in TV's *Robin Hood.*
Inn for Trouble 60. Shadow of the Cat 61. Tomorrow at Ten 63. A Jolly Bad Fellow 64, etc.

wheelchairs have usually had sinister connotations in the cinema. The Spanish film *The Wheelchair* was a very black comedy indeed, and villains who have operated from wheelchairs include Lionel Atwill in *The Mystery of the Wax Museum*, Vincent Price in *House of Wax*, Ralph Morgan in *Night Monster*, and Francis L. Sullivan in *Hell's Island*. General 'heavies' confined to wheelchairs include Eleanor Parker in *The Man with the Golden Arm* and *Eye of the Cat*, cantankerous Dame May Whitty (and later Mona Washbourne) in *Night Must Fall*, and crusty old Lionel Barrymore in the Dr Kildare series and every other film he made after 1939 (he was confined to a chair after twice breaking his hip). Wheelchair victims included Estelle Winwood in *Notorious Landlady*, careering away over the countryside, and the old lady who was pushed downstairs in a wheelchair in *Kiss of Death*. Perhaps the most fearsome wheelchair occupant was Monty Woolley, of the barbed tongue, in *The Man Who Came to Dinner*. Electric staircase chairs were used by 'invalids' Ethel Barrymore in *The Farmer's Daughter*, Eugenie Leontovitch in *Homicidal* and Charles Laughton in *Witness for the Prosecution.*

Wheeler, Bert (1895–1968). American comedian who teamed as double act with Robert Woolsey (qv).
Rio Rita 29. Half Shot at Sunrise 30. Hook Line and Sinker 30. Cracked Nuts 30. Caught Plastered 32. Hold 'Em Jail 32. Diplomaniacs 33. Hips Hips Hooray 34. The Nitwits 35. The Rainmakers 35. Mummy's Boys 37. High Flyers 37. On Again Off Again 37. The Gay City (solo) 41.

Wheeler, Charles F. (–). American cinematographer.
Tora! Tora! Tora! 70. Cold Turkey 70, etc.

Wheeler, Lyle (1905–). American art director.
The Prisoner of Zenda 37. Tom Sawyer 38. *Gone with the Wind* (AA) 39. *Rebecca* 40. *Laura* 44. *Anna and the King of Siam* (AA) 46. Fourteen Hours 51. *The Robe* (AA) 53. Love is a Many-Splendored Thing 55. Daddy Longlegs 55. *The Diary of Anne Frank* (AA) 59. *Journey to the Centre of the Earth* 59. The Cardinal 63, many others.

Whelan, Arleen (c. 1916–). American leading lady of the forties.
Kidnapped 38. Young Mr Lincoln 39. Charley's American Aunt 42. Ramrod 47. The Sun Shines Bright 52. The Badge of Marshal Brennan 57, etc.

Whelan, Tim (1893–1957). American director who often filmed in Britain.
Safety Last 23. It's a Boy (GB) 33. Murder Man 35. The Mill on the Floss (GB) 36. *Farewell Again* (GB) 37. The Divorce of Lady X (GB) 37. St Martin's Lane (GB) 38. *Q Planes* (GB) 39. 'Ten Days in Paris (GB) 39. *The Thief of Baghdad* (GB) (co-d) 40. A Date with Destiny 40. International Lady 41. Twin Beds 42. Nightmare 42. Seven Days' Leave 42. Higher and Higher 42. Step Lively 44. Badman's Territory 46. This Was a Woman (GB) 47. Texas Lady 55. Rage at Dawn 55, etc.

Whiley, Manning (1915–). British actor, usually in sinister roles.
Consider Your Verdict 38. The Trunk Crime 39. The Ghost of St Michael's 41. The Seventh Veil 45. Teheran 47. The Shop at Sly Corner 50. Little Big Shot (last to date) 52, etc.

Whisky Galore (GB 1948). One of the most successful of regional comedies, this lively romp from Ealing Studios was taken from Compton Mackenzie's novel about a boatload of whisky wrecked on a remote Scottish island. Brilliantly directed by Alexander Mackendrick and photographed by Gerald Gibbs, with a first-rate cast of character actors: Basil Radford, Duncan Macrae, Joan Greenwood, Jean Cadell, Wylie Watson, Gordon Jackson, etc.

The Whisperers (GB 1967). The film that won a BFA for Edith Evans is in itself an often likeable but often unduly melodramatic little mood piece, chiefly commendable for daring to tackle the unfashionable and therefore uncommercial problems of old age. Bryan Forbes wrote and directed with considerable intelligence but failed to sort out various elementary confusions of character and verisimilitude.

The Whistler. Based on a popular American radio show, this crime anthology ran as a film series from 1944 to 1947, with Richard Dix playing the hero of each. The only other connection was the whistled theme tune at the beginning. The first story was the old chestnut about the man who hires someone to kill him and then changes his mind. In the late fifties there was a TV series using the same title.

Whistling in the Dark. This crime comedy play by Lavinia Cross and Edward Carpenter was first filmed in 1933 by Elliott Nugent, with Ernest Truex as the little man who beats the crooks in the end. In 1940 it was revamped as a vehicle for Red Skelton, directed by S. Sylvan Simon, who also handled two sequels, *Whistling in Dixie* 42 and *Whistling in Brooklyn* 43.

White, Barbara (1924–). British leading lady of the forties.
It Happened One Sunday 44. The Voice Within 45. Quiet Weekend 46. While the Sun Shines 46. Mine Own Executioner 47. This Was a Woman 48, etc.

White Cargo. This much-caricatured play was based on a book by Vera Simonton called *Hell's Playground*: it dealt with the difficulties of acclimatization for Malayan rubber planters, and in particular with a shapely native distraction called Tondelayo. It was filmed in Britain by J. B. Williams in 1929, with Leslie Faber and Gypsy Rhouma, and in Hollywood in 1942 with Walter Pidgeon and Hedy Lamarr.

White, Carol (1941–). British leading lady.
Linda 60. Slave Girls 66. *Poor Cow* 67. I'll Never Forget Whatshisname 68. Daddy's Gone A-Hunting 69. The Man Who Had Power Over Women 70. Dulcima 71. Something Big 71. Made 72, etc.

White, Chrissie (1894–). British leading lady of the silent screen, especially popular when teamed with her husband Henry Edwards (qv).
Films include *Broken Threads, David Garrick, Barnaby Rudge, Sweet Lavender, Trelawny of the Wells, The City of Beautiful Nonsense, Possession*; latest appearance in *General John Regan* 34.

White Heat (US 1949). This bid to revive gangster movies ten years after the last gangster was jailed succeeded brilliantly as tough entertainment but its new violence left a nasty taste in the mouth. James Cagney is splendidly maniacal, Raoul Walsh's direction swift: the script by Ivan Goff and Ben Roberts is full of tension.

White, Jesse (1918–) (Jesse Wiedenfeld). American comic character actor, usually seen as nervous cigar-chewing crook. Wide stage experience.
Harvey (debut) 50. Death of a Salesman 52. Not as a Stranger 55. Designing Woman 57. The Rise and Fall of Legs Diamond 59. It's Only Money 62. A House is Not a Home 64. Dear

Brigitte 65. The Reluctant Astronaut 67. The Brothers O'Toole 73, many others.

White, Jules (1900–). American shorts director, in charge of the Three Stooges from 1945 to 1957.

White, Onna (–). American choreographer.
The Music Man 62. Bye Bye Birdie 63. *Oliver* (AA) 68. 1776 72. The Great Waltz 72. Mame 73, etc.

White, Pearl (1889–1938). American leading lady, 'queen of the silent serials'. On stage from six years old. At first a stunt woman, then in such serials as *The Perils of Pauline* 14 and *The Exploits of Elaine* 15, involving circus-like thrills. Later in features: *The White Moll* 20. *Know Your Men* 21. *A Virgin Paradise* 21, etc.; retired 1921. A pseudo-biography, *The Perils of Pauline*, was filmed with Betty Hutton in 1947. Autobiography 1919: *Just Me*.

White, Ruth (1914–1969). American character actress.
To Kill a Mockingbird 63. Up the Down Staircase 67. The Tiger is Out 68. Charly 69. Midnight Cowboy 69, etc.

White Shadows in the South Seas (US 1928). Robert Flaherty had a hand in scripting and photographing this South Seas melodrama, and also co-directed with W. S. Van Dyke. The story dealt with an alcoholic doctor who finds contentment with a native girl on a remote island.

White, Valerie (1916–). British character actress.
Halfway House 43. My Learned Friend 44. Hue and Cry 46. Travels with My Aunt 73, etc.

Whitelaw, Billie (1932–). British leading actress of stage and TV, also in occasional films.
The Fake 54. Make Mine Mink 59. Bobbikins 59. Hell is a City 60. *No Love for Johnnie* 61. Payroll 61. The Comedy Man 63. *Charlie Bubbles* (BFA) 68. Twisted Nerve 68. The Adding Machine 69. Gumshoe 71. Eagle in a Cage 71. Frenzy 72. Night Watch 73. *The Omen* 76, etc.

Whiteley, Jon (1945–). British boy actor.
Hunted 52. *The Kidnappers* (special AA) 53. Moonfleet 55. The Weapon 56. The Spanish Gardener 56. Capetown Affair 67, etc.

Whiteman, Paul (1892–1968). Tall, portly American bandleader who made several film appearances.
King of Jazz 30. Thanks a Million 35. Strike Up the Band 40. Atlantic City 44. Rhapsody in Blue 45. The Fabulous Dorseys 47, etc.

Whiting, Leonard (1950–). British juvenile lead.
Romeo and Juliet (as Romeo) 68. The Royal Hunt of the Sun 69. Young Casanova 70. Say Hello to Yesterday 71. Frankenstein: The True Story 73, etc.

Whitman, Stuart (1926–). American leading man, former boxer and stage and TV actor.
When Worlds Collide 52. Rhapsody 54. Darby's Rangers 57. *Ten North Frederick* 58. The Decks Ran Red 58. The Story of Ruth 60. Murder Inc. 61. *The Mark* 62. The Comancheros 62. Reprieve 63. Shock Treatment 64. Signpost to Murder 64. Rio Conchos 64. Those Magnificent Men in Their Flying Machines 65. Sands of the Kalahari 65. An American Dream 66. The Invincible Six 68. The Only Way Out is Dead 70. Captain Apache 71. City Beneath the Sea (TV) 71. Night of the Lepus 73. The White Buffalo 77, etc.
TV series: Cimarron Strip 67.

Whitmore, James (1921–). Craggy American character actor.
Undercover Man 49. The Asphalt Jungle 50. Across the Wide Missouri 51. Kiss Me Kate 53. *Them* 54. Battle Cry 55. Oklahoma 55. The Eddy Duchin Story 56. Who Was That Lady? 60. Black Like Me 64. Chuka 67. Planet of the Apes 68. Madigan 68. The Split 68. Guns of the Magnificent Seven 69. Tora! Tora! Tora! 70. Chato's Land 71. If Tomorrow Comes (TV) 71. The Harrad Experiment 73. Give 'Em Hell Harry 75. Where the Red Fern Grows 75, etc.
TV series: *The Law and Mr Jones* 60–61.

Whitney, Peter (1916–1972) (Peter King Engle). Portly American character player.
Reunion in France 42. *Murder He Says* (as twins) 44. Hotel Berlin 45. The Iron Curtain 48. The Big Heat 53. Great Day in the Morning 56. Sword of Ali Baba 65. Chubasco 67. The Ballad of Cable Hogue 70, etc.

Whitsun-Jones, Paul (1923–1974). Rotund British character actor, usually in comedy.
The Constant Husband 55. *The Moonraker* 57. Room at the Top 59. Tunes of Glory 60, etc.

Whittingham, Jack (1910–). British screenwriter.
Q Planes 39. Kiss the Bride Goodbye 44.

Twilight Hour 45. I Believe in You 51. Hunted 52. The Divided Heart 54. The Birthday Present (& p) 57, etc.

Whitty, Dame May (1865–1948). Distinguished character actress, on stage from 1881. Settled in Hollywood in the mid-thirties and played dozens of indomitable but kindly old ladies.
□ The Thirteenth Chair 37. *Night Must Fall* 37. Conquest 37. I Met My Love Again 37. *The Lady Vanishes* (GB) 38. Raffles 40. A Bill of Divorcement 40. One Night in Lisbon 41. Suspicion 41. Mrs Miniver 42. Thunder Birds 42. Slightly Dangerous 42. Forever and a Day 43. Crash Dive 43. The Constant Nymph 43. Lassie Come Home 43. Flesh and Fantasy 43. Madame Curie 43. Stage Door Canteen 43. The White Cliffs of Dover 44. Gaslight 44. *My Name is Julia Ross* 45. Devotion 46. This Time for Keeps 47. Green Dolphin Street 47. If Winter Comes 47. The Sign of the Ram 48. The Return of October 48.

Whoopee (US 1930). A Broadway musical which became an early talkie starring Eddie Cantor, with dances directed by Busby Berkeley. Prints have not survived, but it was remade in 1944 as *Up In Arms*, with Danny Kaye

Whorf, Richard (1906–1966). Sullen-looking American actor-director.
AS ACTOR: Midnight 34. *Blues in the Night* 41. Yankee Doodle Dandy 42. Keeper of the Flame 43. Christmas Holiday 44. Chain Lightning 50, etc.
AS DIRECTOR: The Hidden Eye 45. Till the Clouds Roll By 46. It Happened in Brooklyn 47. Love from a Stranger 47. Luxury Liner 48. Champagne for Caesar 50. Lots of TV half-hours and hours, especially *Rawhide* and *The Beverly Hillbillies*.

Who's Afraid of Virginia Woolf? (US 1966). This somewhat misguidedly opened-out film version of Edward Albee's electrifying domestic comedy-drama was rather dingily photographed by Haskell Wexler and sometimes dully directed by Mike Nichols, but its basic force and entertainment value could not be totally disguised, particularly in view of a brilliant performance by Richard Burton and excellent ones by Elizabeth Taylor, George Segal and Sandy Dennis. But its chief interest for historians will be that it further extended the bounds of what is permissible on public screens, its unbridled treatment of matters sexual being decorated by 'blue' jokes and expletives.

Why We Fight. A brilliant series of World War II documentaries using all the resources of the cinema, compiled by Frank Capra and the U.S. Signal Corps Film Unit from material shot by Allied cameramen and from pre-war newsreel material. Each lasted just over an hour, and was kept absorbingly entertaining as well as instructive by the use of music, diagrams and optical work. Titles were *Prelude to War, The Nazis Strike, Divide and Conquer, The Battle of Britain, The Battle of Russia, The Battle of China.*

Wickes, Mary (1916–) (Mary Wickenhauser). American character comedienne.
The Man Who Came to Dinner (as the nurse) 41. Higher and Higher 43. June Bride 48. Young Man with Ideas 52. The Actress 54. Good Morning, Miss Dove 56. It Happened to Jane 59. The Trouble with Angels 66. Where Angels Go Trouble Follows 68. Snowball Express 73, many others.

Wicki, Bernhard (1919–). Swiss actor-director.
AS DIRECTOR: Der Fallende Stern 50. The Last Bridge 54. Kinder, Mütter und ein General 54. Jackboot Mutiny 55. The Face of the Cat 57. La Notte 61, etc.
AS DIRECTOR: The Bridge 59. The Miracle of Malachias 61. The Longest Day (co-d) 62. The Visit (US) 63. The Saboteur 65, etc.

Widdoes, Kathleen (1939–). American actress with stage experience.
The Group 66. Petulia 68. The Seagull 68. The Mephisto Waltz 71, etc.

wide screen. Strictly speaking this does not mean anamorphic processes such as CinemaScope, which requires a wide, *wide* screen, but the now-standard 1:1.65 ratio which was achieved by projecting the old 1.3:1 image, cutting the top and bottom from it, and magnifying the result.

Widerberg, Bo (1930–). Swedish writer-director.
Raven's End 63. Karlek 63. Thirty Times Your Money 66. *Elvira Madigan* 67. Adalen 31 69. The Ballad of Joe Hill 69. The Man on the Roof 75, etc.

Widmark, Richard (1914–). American leading actor; once typed as cold-eyed killer, he fought successfully for more varied roles.
Kiss of Death 47. Road House 48. The Street with No Name 48. Yellow Sky 49. Down to the

Sea in Ships 49. Slattery's Hurrricane 49. Night and the City 50. Panic in the Streets 50. No Way Out 50. Halls of Montezuma 50. The Frogmen 51. Full House 52. Don't Bother to Knock 52. Red Skies of Montana 52. My Pal Gus 52. Destination Gobi 53. Pickup on South Street 53. Take the High Ground 53. Hell and High Water 54. Garden of Evil 54. Broken Lance 54. The Cobweb 55. A Prize of Gold 55. Backlash 56. Run for the Sun 56. The Last Wagon 56. Saint Joan 57. Time Limit 57. The Law and Jake Wade 58. The Tunnel of Love 58. The Trap 59. Warlock 59. The Alamo 60. The Secret Ways 61. Two Rode Together 61. Judgment at Nuremberg 61. How the West Was Won 63. Flight from Ashiya 64. The Long Ships 64. Cheyenne Autumn 64. *The Bedford Incident* 65. Alvarez Kelly 66. The Way West 67. *Madigan* 68. Death of a Gunfighter 69. A Talent for Loving 69. The Moonshine War 70. Brock's Last Case (TV) 71. Vanished (TV) 71. When the Legends Die 72. Murder on the Orient Express 74. The Sellout 76.
TV series: *Madigan* 72.

Wieck, Dorothea (–). German character actress.
Maedchen in Uniform 31. Cradle Song (US) 33. The Student of Prague 35. Der Vierte Kommt Nicht 39, etc.

Wiene, Robert (1881–1938). German director of expressionist films.
The Cabinet of Dr Caligari 19. Genuine 20. Raskolnikov 23. The Hands of Orlac 24, etc.

The Wiere Brothers. German eccentric comedians, long in America: *Harry* (1908–), *Herbert* (1909–), *Sylvester* (1910–1970). Films very occasional.
The Great American Broadcast 41. Swing Shift Maisie 44. *Road to Rio* 47. Double Trouble 68, etc.
TV series: *Oh Those Bells* 62.

Wilbur, Crane (1887–1973). American writer-director.
Canon City 48. The Story of Molly X 49. Outside the Wall 49. Inside the Walls of Folsom Prison 50. House of Wax (script only) 53. The Bat 59. Solomon and Sheba (script only) 59, etc.

Wilcox, Frank (1907–1974). Tall American character actor, a bit player who was always seen in Warner films of the forties—sometimes in two parts in the same film.
The Fighting 69th 39. River's End 40. Highway West 41. Across the Pacific 42. Juke Girl 43. The Adventures of Mark Twain 44. Conflict 45.

Gentleman's Agreement 48. Samson and Delilah 49. Those Redheads from Seattle 53. Dance with Me Henry 56. A Majority of One 61, many others.

Wilcox, Fred M. (c. 1905–1964). American director, former publicist; films mainly routine.
Lassie Come Home 43. Blue Sierra 46. Courage of Lassie 46. Hills of Home 48. Three Daring Daughters 48. The Secret Garden 49. Shadow in the Sky 50. Code Two 53. Tennessee Champ 54. *Forbidden Planet* 56. I Passed for White 60.

Wilcox, Herbert (1891–1977). British independent producer-director in films from 1919 (as salesman); married to Anna Neagle.
The Wonderful Story 20. The Dawn of the World 21. Chu Chin Chow 23. *Nell Gwyn* 24. *Dawn* 26. Wolves 28. Rookery Nook 30. Good Night Vienna 32. Carnival 32. *Bitter Sweet* 33. *Nell Gwyn* 34. Peg of Old Drury 35. Limelight 36. The Three Maxims 36. The Frog 37. *Victoria the Great* 37. Sixty Glorious Years 38. Our Fighting Navy 38. *Nurse Edith Cavell* (US) 39. Sunny (US) 39. *No No Nanette* (US) 40. Irene (US) 40. They Flew Alone 42. Yellow Canary 43. I Live in Grosvenor Square 45. *Piccadilly Incident* 46. The Courtneys of Curzon Street 47. *Spring in Park Lane* 48. Elizabeth of Ladymead 49. Maytime in Mayfair 50. *Odette* 51. The Lady with a Lamp 52. Trent's Last Case 52. Laughing Anne 53. Lilacs in the Spring 54. King's Rhapsody 55. Yangtse Incident 56. My Teenage Daughter 56. Those Dangerous Years 57. The Lady is a Square 58. Heart of a Man 59. To See Such Fun (exec. p only) 77, etc.

Wilcox, Jack (–). British cinematographer.
Where's Jack? 68. The Chairman 68. The Lost Valley 70, etc.

Wilcoxon, Henry (1905–). British leading man with stage experience, in Hollywood from early thirties, latterly as executive for Cecil B. de Mille.
The Perfect Lady 31. The Flying Squad 32. Cleopatra 34. The Crusades 35. The Last of the Mohicans 36. Mrs Miniver 42. Samson and Delilah 49. Scaramouche 52. The Greatest Show on Earth 53. The Ten Commandments (& co-p) 56. The Buccaneer (& p) 59. The Private Navy of Sergeant O'Farrell 69. Man in the Wilderness 71. Against a Crooked Sky 75. Pony Express Rider 76, etc.

Wild, Jack (1952–). British juvenile, popular around 1970.

Oliver 68. Melody 70. Flight of the Doves 71. The Pied Piper 72. The Fourteen 73, etc. TV series: *H. R. Pufnstuf* 70.

The Wild One (US 1954). A Stanley Kramer production written by John Paxton and directed by Laslo Benedek, about a gang of motor-cycle hooligans who terrorize a small western town. Photographed by Hal Mohr, with music by Leith Stevens, it starred Marlon Brando in a typical role, with Mary Murphy and Lee Marvin. Banned by the British Board of Film Censors, it was shown at only one English cinema (then managed by the author of this book), with local watch committee approval. It was finally given a certificate in 1967.

Wild Strawberries (Sweden 1957). Ingmar Bergman's quietly showmanlike film about old age, superbly written (by himself), photographed (by Gunnar Fischer) and acted (by Victor Sjostrom). Its movement from past to present and back is particularly well achieved, and for once Bergman manages to make almost all his points explicit.

wild track: one recorded *in situ*, not prepared in the studio.

Wilde, Cornel (1915–). American leading man of the forties; later produced and directed some interesting films, but never equalled his 1944 impact as Chopin.
□ Lady with Red Hair 40. Kisses for Breakfast 41. High Sierra 41. Right to the Heart 41. The Perfect Snob 42. Life Begins at 8.30 42. Manila Calling 42. Wintertime 43. Guest in the House 44. *A Song to Remember* 44. A Thousand and One Nights 45. Leave Her to Heaven 45. *The Bandit of Sherwood Forest* 46. Centennial Summer 46. The Homestretch 46. Forever Amber 47. It Had to be You 47. Roadhouse 48. The Walls of Jericho 48. Shockproof 49. Four Days' Leave 50. Two Flags West 50. At Sword's Point 52. The Greatest Show on Earth 52. California Conquest 52. Treasure of the Golden Condor 53. Main Street to Broadway 53. Saadia 53. Passion 54. *Woman's World* 54. The Scarlet Coat 55. Storm Fear (& d) 55. The Big Combo 55. Star of India 55. Hot Blood 56. The Devil's Hairpin 57. Omar Khayyam 57. Beyond Mombasa 57. Maracaibo (& d) 58. Edge of Eternity 59. Constantine and the Cross 60. Sword of Lancelot (& d) 63. *The Naked Prey* (& d) 66. Beach Red (& d) 67. The Comic 69. No Blade of Grass (& d) 71. Gargoyles (TV) 72. Shark's Treasure (& d) 75.

Wilde, Hagar (1904–1971). American screenwriter.
Bringing Up Baby 38. Carefree 39. Fired Wife 43. Guest in the House 44. The Unseen 45. I Was a Male War Bride 49. This is My Love 54, etc.

Wilde, Marty (–). British pop singer who appeared in a film or two.
Jetstorm 59. The Hellions 61. What a Crazy World 63, etc.

Wilde, Oscar (1856–1900). British playwright, poet and wit, the subject in 1960 of two film biographies: *Oscar Wilde* starring Robert Morley and *The Trials of Oscar Wilde* starring Peter Finch. The former was directed by Gregory Ratoff from a script by Jo Eisinger, and had Ralph Richardson as Carson, John Neville as Lord Alfred, and Edward Chapman as the Marquis of Queensbury. The latter, written and directed by Ken Hughes, had James Mason, John Fraser and Lionel Jeffries respectively in these roles. Films have been made of several of Wilde's works including *The Importance of Being Earnest, An Ideal Husband, Lady Windermere's Fan, The Picture of Dorian Gray, Lord Arthur Savile's Crime* (in *Flesh and Fantasy*) and *The Canterville Ghost.*

Wilder, Billy (1906–) (Samuel Wilder). Austro-Hungarian writer-director, in Hollywood from 1934. A specialist for years in bitter comedy and drama torn from the world's headlines, he has lately specialized in rather heavy-going bawdy farce.
□ AS WRITER: People on Sunday 30. (Followed by ten other German films.) Adorable (French) 34. Music in the Air (co w) 34. Lottery Lover (co w) 35. Bluebeard's Eight Wife (co w) 38. *Midnight* (co w) 39. What a Life (co w) 39. *Ninotchka* (co w) 39. *Arise My Love* (co w) 40. Ball of Fire (co w) 41. Hold Back the Dawn (co w) 41.
□ AS WRITER-DIRECTOR (script always in collaboration): Mauvaise Graine (French) 33. *The Major and the Minor* 42. *Five Graves to Cairo* 43. *Double Indemnity* 44. *The Lost Weekend* (AA) 45. The Emperor Waltz 47. *A Foreign Affair* 48. Sunset Boulevard 50. *Ace in the Hole* 51. *Stalag 17* 53. Sabrina 54. *The Seven Year Itch* 55. The Spirit of St. Louis 57. Love in the Afternoon 57. *Witness for the Prosecution* 58. *Some Like It Hot* 59. *The Apartment* (AA) 60. *One Two Three* 61. Irma La Douce 63. Kiss Me Stupid 64. The Fortune Cookie 66. *The Private Life of Sherlock Holmes* 70. Avanti 72. The Front Page 74.

Wilder, Gene (1934–) (Jerry Silberman). American comic actor.
Bonnie and Clyde 67. *The Producers* 68. Start the Revolution Without Me 69. Quackser Fortune has a Cousin in the Bronx 70. Willy Wonka and the Chocolate Factory 71. Everything You Always Wanted to Know About Sex 72. Rhinoceros 73. The Little Prince 73. Blazing Saddles 74. Young Frankenstein 74. The Adventure of Sherlock Holmes's Smarter Brother (& p, d) 75. Silver Streak 76, etc.

Wilder, Robert (1901–1974). American novelist and screenwriter.
Flamingo Road (& oa) 48. *Written on the Wind* (& oa) 56. The Big Country 58. Sol Madrid 66, etc.

Wilder, Thornton (1897–1975). American playwright and novelist. Works filmed include *Our Town, The Bridge of San Luis Rey* (several times), *The Matchmaker*; also wrote screenplay of Hitchcock's *Shadow of a Doubt*.

Wilder, W. Lee (1904–). Austro-Hungarian producer in America, brother of Billy Wilder. Films mainly low-budget oddities.
The Great Flamarion 44. Phantom from Space 53. The Snow Creature 54. Bluebeard's Ten Honeymoons 60, etc.

Wilding, Michael (1912–). British leading man of the forties.
Wedding Group 35. Tilly of Bloomsbury 40. *Sailors Three* 40. Kipps 41. Cottage To Let 41. *In Which We Serve* 42. Dear Octopus 43. *English Without Tears* 44. Carnival 46. *Piccadilly Incident* 46. The Courtneys of Curzon Street 47. An Ideal Husband 47. *Spring in Park Lane* 48. Maytime in Mayfair 50. Under Capricorn 50. Stage Fright 50. Into the Blue 51. The Law and the Lady (US) 52. Derby Day 52. Trent's Last Case 53. The Egyptian 54. The Glass Slipper 55. Zarak 56. Danger Within 57. The World of Suzie Wong 60. The Naked Edge 61. The Best of Enemies 61. A Girl Named Tamiko 63. The Sweet Ride 68. Waterloo 69. Lady Caroline Lamb 72. Frankenstein: The True Story (TV) 73, etc.

Wilke, Robert J. (1911–). American character actor, usually in mean, shifty or villainous roles.
San Francisco 36. Sheriff of Sundown 44. The Last Days of Boot Hill 47. Kill the Umpire 50. Twenty Thousand Leagues under the Sea 54. Night Passage 57. The Gun Hawk 63. The Hallelujah Trail 65. Tony Rome 67. A Gunfight 71, etc.

William. The argumentative small boy created in over thirty novels by Richmal Crompton had several British film incarnations, none very satisfactory, in the thirties and forties.

William, Warren (1895–1948) (Warren Krech). Suave American leading man with stage experience.
The Perils of Pauline 14. The Woman from Monte Carlo 32. The Mouthpiece 33. *Lady for a Day* 33. *Imitation of Life* 34. Cleopatra (as Julius Caesar) 34. The Case of the Lucky Legs 35. Satan Met a Lady 36. The Firefly 37. *The Lone Wolf's Spy Hunt* 39 (and others in this series). The Man in the Iron Mask 39. Lillian Russell 40. The Wolf Man 41. Counter Espionage 42. One Dangerous Night 43. Fear 46. Bel Ami 47, etc.

Williams, Adam (1929–). American 'second lead'.
Queen for a Day 50. Without Warning 52. Crashout 55. Garment Centre 57. Darby's Rangers 58. North by Northwest 59. The Last Sunset 61. The Glory Guys 67, etc.

Williams, Bill (1916–) (William Katt). American leading man, an innocent-type hero of the forties. Former professional swimmer and singer.
Murder in the Blue Room (debut) 44. Those Endearing Young Charms 45. Till the End of Time 46. Deadline at Dawn 47. The Great Missouri Raid 51. The Outlaw's Daughter 53. Wiretapper 56. A Dog's Best Friend 61. Tickle Me 65, etc.
TV series: Assignment Underwater 61.

Williams, Billy (1929–). British cinematographer.
Just Like a Woman 66. Billion Dollar Brain 67. *Women in Love* 69. Two Gentlemen Sharing 70. Tam Lin 70. *Sunday Bloody Sunday* 72. Night Watch 73. The Wind and the Lion 75, etc.

Williams, Billy Dee (1937–). Black American leading man.
Lady Sings the Blues 72. Hit 73. The Take 74. Mahogany 75, Bingo Long and the Travelling All Stars 76, etc.

Williams, Cindy (1948–). American leading lady.
Drive He Said 71. American Graffiti 73. Travels with My Aunt 73. The Conversation 74.

Williams, Bransby (1870–1964). Distinguished British stage actor who made an early talkie appearance in an experimental Lee de Forest Phonofilm. Later appeared in The Cold

Cure 25. Jungle Woman 26. Troublesome Wives 28. Song of the Road 37, etc.

Williams, Cara (1925–) (Bernice Kamiat). American TV and radio comedienne.
Happy Land 43. Don Juan Quilligan 45. Sitting Pretty 48. The Girl Next Door 53. The Defiant Ones 58. The Man from the Diners Club 63. The White Buffalo 77.
TV series: Pete and Gladys 60–61. The Cara Williams Show 64.

Williams, Elmo (1913–). American editor and producer. Produced, edited and directed *The Cowboy* 54; worked as editor on several major productions; became head of 20th-Century-Fox British productions.

Williams, Emlyn (1905–). Welsh actor and playwright, on stage from 1927.
Autobiographies: *George* 1972. *Emlyn* 1974.
The Case of the Frightened Lady (film debut) 32. Men of Tomorrow 33. Friday the Thirteenth 33. Sally Bishop 33. Broken Blossoms 36. *The Citadel* 38. The Stars Look Down 39. Major Barbara 40. You Will Remember 40. *Hatter's Castle* 41. *The Last Days of Dolwyn* (& wd) 48. *Three Husbands* 50. Ivanhoe 52. *The Deep Blue Sea* 56. I Accuse 57. Beyond This Place 59. The L-Shaped Room 62. Eye of the Devil 66. The Walking Stick 69. David Copperfield 69, others.
Plays filmed: *Night Must Fall, The Corn is Green.*

Williams, Esther (1923–). Aquatic American leading lady, former swimming champion.
□ Andy Hardy's Double Life (debut) 42. A Guy Named Joe 43. *Bathing Beauty* 44. Ziegfeld Follies 44. Thrill of a Romance 45. Easy to Wed 45. This Time for Keeps 46. Till the Clouds Roll By 46. Fiesta 47. On an Island with You 48. *Take Me Out to the Ball Game* 48. Neptune's Daughter 49. Pagan Love Song 50. Duchess of Idaho 51. Callaway Went Thataway 51. Texas Carnival 52. Shirts Ahoy 52. Million Dollar Mermaid 52. *Dangerous When Wet* 53. Easy to Love 54. Jupiter's Darling 54. The Unguarded Moment 56. Raw Wind in Eden 57. The Big Show 61. The Magic Fountain (Sp.) 61.

Williams, Grant (1930–). American leading man who never quite made the bigtime.
Written on the Wind 56. *The Incredible Shrinking Man* 57. The Monolith Monsters 58. PT 109 63. Doomsday 72, etc.
TV series: Hawaiian Eye 59–63.

Williams, Guinn 'Big Boy' (1900–1962).

American character actor, usually in amiably tough roles. In Hollywood 1919 as an extra.
Noah's Ark 29. Dodge City 39. Mr Wise Guy 42. The Desperadoes 43. Thirty Seconds Over Tokyo 44. Bad Men of Tombstone 49. Hangman's Knot 53. The Outlaw's Daughter 55. The Comancheros 62, scores of others.

Williams, Guy (1924–). American leading man, the 'Zorro' of Walt Disney's TV series and films.
The Prince and the Pauper 62. Captain Sinbad 63, etc.
TV series: Lost in Space 65–68.

Williams, Harcourt (1880–1957). Distinguished British stage actor.
Henry V 44. *Brighton Rock* 47. Hamlet 48. Third Time Lucky 48. *The Late Edwina Black* 51. Roman Holiday 53. Around the World in Eighty Days 56.

Williams, Hugh (1904–1969). British leading man and playwright on stage from 1921.
Charley's Aunt (film debut) 30. In a Monastery Garden 31. Rome Express 33. Sorrell and Son 34. *David Copperfield* (US) 34. The Amateur Gentleman 36. Dark Eyes of London 38. Wuthering Heights (US) 39. A Girl in a Million 46. *An Ideal Husband* 47. Take My Life 47. The Blind Goddess 48. Elizabeth of Ladymead 49. The Gift Horse 52. The Fake 53. Twice Upon a Time 53. Khartoum 66, etc.

Williams, John (1903–). Suave British stage actor who has appeared in films, usually in polished comedy roles.
Emil and the Detectives 35. Next of Kin 42. A Woman's Vengeance 48. Dick Turpin's Ride 51. *Dial M for Murder* 54. Sabrina Fair 54. To Catch a Thief 55. *The Solid Gold Cadillac* 56. Island in the Sun 56. Witness for the Prosecution 57. Visit to a Small Planet 60. Last of the Secret Agents 66. The Secret War of Harry Frigg 67. A Flea in Her Ear 68. The Hound of the Baskervilles (TV) 72. No Deposit No Return 76, etc.

Williams, Johnny (–). American composer.
The Secret Ways 61. Diamond Head 62. None But the Brave 65. How to Steal a Million 66. Valley of the Dolls 67. The Cowboys 71. The Poseidon Adventure 72. Tom Sawyer 73. Earthquake 74. The Towering Inferno 74. *Jaws* (AA) 75. The Eiger Sanction 75.

Williams, Kenneth (1926–). British comic actor adept at 'small boy' character and a variety

of outrageous voices. Also on stage, radio and TV.
The Beggar's Opera 52. The Seekers 54. *Carry On Sergeant* 58 (and most other 'Carry Ons'). Raising the Wind 61. Twice Round the Daffodils 62. Don't Lose Your Head 67. Follow That Camel 68, etc.

Williams, Rhys (1897–1969). Welsh character actor, long in Hollywood; former technical adviser.
The Spiral Staircase 45. Scandal at Scourie 53. There's No Business Like Show Business 54. The Kentuckian 55. The Fastest Gun Alive 56. The Sons of Katie Elder 65. Skullduggery 69, many others.

Williams, Robert (1897–1932). Slow-speaking American leading man of the early thirties.
The Common Law 31. Rebound 31. Devotion 31. *Platinum Blonde* 31, etc.

Williams, Tennessee (1914–) (Thomas Lanier Williams). American playwright whose sleazy characters have proved popular screen fodder.
☐ *The Glass Menagerie* 50. *A Streetcar Named Desire* 52. The Rose Tattoo 56. Baby Doll 56. Cat on a Hot Tin Roof 58. Suddenly Last Summer 59. The Fugitive Kind 60. Summer and Smoke 61. Period of Adjustment 62. *The Night of the Iguana* 64. This Property is Condemned 66. Boom 68. Blood Kin 70.

Williamson, Fred (1938–). Black American action hero.
M*A*S*H 70. The Legend of Nigger Charley 72. Hammer 72. Black Caesar 72. Crazy Joe 73. That Man Bolt 74. Boss Nigger 75. Darktown 75. Take a Hard Ride 75, etc.

Williamson, James A. (1855–1933). British production pioneer.
The Big Swallow 01. Fire! 01, etc.

Williamson, Lambert (1907–). British composer.
Edge of the World 38. End of the River 48. One Night With You 48.

Williamson, Nicol (1939–). British leading actor of stage and screen; tends to play bulls in china shops.
☐ Six Sided Triangle 64. *Inadmissible Evidence* 67. *The Bofors Gun* 68. Laughter in the Dark 68. *The Reckoning* 69. Hamlet 69. The Jerusalem File 72. The Wilby Conspiracy 75. Robin and Marian 76. The Seven Per Cent Solution 76.

Willis, Gordon (–). American cinematographer.
Up the Sandbox 72. Bad Company 72. Paper Chase 73. The Parallax View 74, etc.

Willman, Noel (1918–). British actor and stage director whose film roles have often been coldly villainous.
Pickwick Papers 52. The Net 53. Beau Brummell 54. Cone of Silence 60. The Girl on the Boat 62. *Kiss of the Vampire* 63. The Reptile 65. Doctor Zhivago 65. The Vengeance of She 68, etc.

Willock, Dave (1909–). American light actor, usually the hero's friend.
Legion of Lost Flyers 39. Let's Face It 43. Pin Up Girl 44. The Runaround 46. Chicago Deadline 49. Call Me Mister 51. It Came from Outer Space 53. The Buster Keaton Story 57. Wives and Lovers 63. Send Me No Flowers 64, many others.

Wills, Chill (1903–). Gravel-voiced American character actor, in films from 1938, mainly low-budget westerns. Also the voice of the talking mule in the 'Francis' series.
Boom Town 40. Best Foot Forward 43. The Harvey Girls 46. Raw Deal 48. High Lonesome 50. Bronco Buster 52. City That Never Sleeps 53. Timberjack 55. Giant 56. The Alamo 60. The Deadly Companions 62. The Cardinal 63. The Over the Hill Gang Rides Again (TV) 71, etc.
TV series: Frontier Circus 61. The Rounders 67.

Wilmer, Douglas (1920–). British character actor of stage, screen and TV.
Richard III 56. An Honourable Murder 60. El Cid 61. Cleopatra 62. The Fall of the Roman Empire 64. One Way Pendulum 65. Brides of Fu Manchu 66. Unman Wittering and Zigo 71. The Golden Voyage of Sinbad 73. The Adventure of Sherlock Holmes', Smarter Brother 75. Sarah 76, others.

Wilson, Dooley (1894–). Black American character actor.
Casablanca 42. Stormy Weather 43. Come to the Stable 49. Passage West 51, etc.

Wilson, Flip (1933–) (Clerow Wilson). Black American actor and entertainer.
Uptown Saturday Night 74. Pinocchio (TV) 76.

Wilson, Harry Leon (1867–1939). American comedy novelist: chief works filmed are *Ruggles of Red Gap* and *Merton of the Movies*.

Wilson, Lois (1895–). American leading lady of the silent screen.

The Dumb Girl of Potici 16. Why Smith Left Home 19. The Covered Wagon 23. Miss Lulu Bett 24. Monsieur Beaucaire 24. What Every Woman Knows 24. Icebound 24. The Show Off 26. Seed 28. Manslaughter 28. The Crash 32. Laughing at Life 33. Bright Eyes 34. The Girl from Jones Beach 49, etc.

Wilson, Marie (1916–1972) (Katherine Elizabeth White). American leading lady often seen as 'dumb blonde'.
Satan Met a Lady 36. Fools for Scandal 38. *Boy Meets Girl* 40. Broadway 42. The Young Widow 47. Linda Be Good 48. *Mr Friend Irma* (title role) 49. A Girl in Every Port 51. Marry Me Again 54. Mr Hobbs Takes a Vacation 62, etc.

Wilson, Michael (1914–). American screenwriter whose career was interrupted by the communist witch hunt of the late forties.
Five Fingers 52. *A Place in the Sun* (AA) 52. Friendly Persuasion (uncredited) 56. *The Bridge on the River Kwai* (uncredited) 57. The Sandpiper 65. *Planet of the Apes* 67. Che! 69, etc.

Wilson, Richard (1915–). American producer and director, former radio actor.
The Golden Blade (p) 54. Man with a Gun (pdw) 55. Raw Wind in Eden (d) 58. Al Capone (d) 59. Pay or Die (pd) 60. Invitation to a Gunfighter (pd) 64. Three in an Attic (pd) 68, etc.

Wilson, Scott (–). American general purpose actor, usually in tough roles.
The Grissom Gang 71. The New Centurions 72. Lolly Madonna XXX 73. The Great Gatsby 74.

Wilson, Whip (1915–1964). American cowboy actor who appeared in a great number of second features in the thirties and forties.

Wimperis, Arthur (1874–1953). British librettist and screenwriter, usually in collaboration.
The Private Life of Henry VIII 32. Sanders of the River 35. The Four Feathers 39. Mrs Miniver (AA) 42. Random Harvest 43. The Red Danube 48. Calling Bulldog Drummond 51. Young Bess 53, others.

Winchell, Walter (1897–1972). American columnist and commentator with a keen eye for crime and show business. Appeared in a few thirties movies such as *Love and Hisses* 37; wrote *Broadway Thro' a Keyhole* 33; narrated TV series *The Untouchables* 59–63.

Windom, William (1923–). American leading man, usually in minor film roles.
To Kill a Mockingbird 62. For Love or Money 63. One Man's Way 64. The Americanization of Emily 64. The Detective 68. Brewster McCloud 70. Fool's Parade 71. Now You See Him Now You Don't 72. Echoes of a Summer 75, etc.
TV series: The Farmer's Daughter 63–66. My World and Welcome To It 69.

Windsor, Barbara (1937–) (Barbara Deeks). British cockney actress specializing in dumb blondes.
Lost 55. Too Hot to Handle 59. Sparrows Can't Sing 64. Carry On Spying 64. Crooks in Cloisters 64. The Boy Friend 71, etc.

Windsor, Claire (1898–1972) (Olga Cronk). American leading lady of the silent screen.
To Please a Woman 20. Rich Men's Wives 22. Nellie the Beautiful Cloak Model 24. Money Talks 26. Captain Lash 29, etc.

Windsor, Marie (1923–) (Emily Marie Bertelson). American leading lady with stage and radio experience; films mainly routine.
All American Co-Ed 41. Song of the Thin Man 47. Force of Evil 48. Outpost in Morocco 49. Dakota Lil 50. *The Narrow Margin* 51. The Tall Texan 53. City That Never Sleeps 53. Abbott and Costello Meet the Mummy 55. *The Killing* 56. The Unholy Wife 57. Bedtime Story 64. Chamber of Horrors 66. The Good Guys and the Bad Guys 69. Support Your Local Gunfighter 71. Cahill 73. Hearts of the West 75, many others.

Windust, Bretaigne (1906–1960). American director, from the New York stage.
Winter Meeting 47. June Bride 48. Pretty Baby 50. *The Enforcer* 51. Face to Face 52. The Pied Piper of Hamelin 59, etc.

Winfield, Paul (1941–). Black American leading actor.
The Lost Man 69. RPM 70. Brother John 71. *Sounder* 72. Gordon's War 73. Conrack 74. Hustle 75. Damnation Alley 77, etc.

Wings (US 1928) (AA). The last of the silent spectaculars and the first film to win an Oscar. A field day of stunt flying with a World War I background, directed by William Wellman, with Charles Rogers, Clara Bow and Richard Arlen.

Winn, Godfrey (1909–1972). British journalist who made rare film appearances.
Blighty 27. Very Important Person 62, etc.

Winner, Michael (1935–). Ebullient British director who never shoots in a studio. His own best publicist.

☐ Climb Up the Wall 57. The Clock Strikes Eight 57. Man with a Gun 58. Shoot to Kill 59. Some Like It Cool 61. Haunted England 61. Play It Cool 62. The Cool Mikado 63. West Eleven 63. *The System* 64. You Must be Joking 65. *The Jokers* 66. *I'll Never Forget Whathisname* 67. Hannibal Brooks 69. The Games 69. *Lawman* 70. The Night Comers 71. Chato's Land 72. The Mechanic 72. Scorpio 72. The Stone Killer 73. *Death Wish* 74. Won Ton Ton 76. The Sentinel 77.

Winninger, Charles (1884–1969). Chubby, lovable American character actor, in films from 1916 as vaudeville appearances permitted.

Night Nurse 31. Gambling Daughters 31. *Show Boat* 36. Three Smart Girls 36. Nothing Sacred 37. Hard to Get 38. Babes in Arms 39. *Destry Rides Again* 39. Little Nellie Kelly 40. *Ziegfeld Girl* 41. Coney Island 43. *State Fair* 45. *Give My Regards to Broadway* 48. Father is a Bachelor 50. *The Sun Shines Bright* 54. Las Vegas Shakedown 55. Raymie 60, many others.

Winslow, George (1946–) (George Wenzlaff). American boy actor whose throaty voice earned him the nickname 'Foghorn'.

Room for One More 52. My Pal Gus 52. Mr Scoutmaster 53. Artists and Models 55. Wild Heritage 58, etc.

Winter, Vincent (1947–). British child actor, in films since *The Kidnappers* 53 (special AA).

The Dark Avenger 55. Time Lock 56. Beyond This Place 59. Gorgo 60. Greyfriars Bobby 61. Almost Angels 63. The Three Lives of Thomasina 63. The Horse Without a Head 64, etc.

Winters, Jonathan (1925–). American comedian with TV and night-club experience.

It's a Mad Mad Mad Mad World 63. *The Loved One* 65. The Russians are Coming, The Russians are Coming 66. Penelope 66. Oh Dad Poor Dad 67. Viva Max 69, etc.

Winters, Roland (1904–). Heavily-built American character actor with stage and radio experience, in Hollywood from 1946; played Charlie Chan in six Monogram features 1948–52.

13 Rue Madeleine 46. Inside Straight 52. So Big 53. Loving 70, etc.

Winters, Shelley (1922–) (Shirley Schrift). American leading character actress with

vaudeville and stage experience, in Hollywood from 1943.

☐ Nine Girls 44. Cover Girl 44. Knickerbocker Holiday 44. 1001 Nights 45. *A Double Life* 48. Cry of the City 48. Take One False Step 49. The Great Gatsby 49. Winchester 73 50. East of Java 51. Frenchie 51. A Place in the Sun 51. My Man and I 52. Executive Suite 54. To Dorothy a Son 54. *The Big Knife* 55. *The Night of the Hunter* 55. I Am a Camera 55. I Died a Thousand Times 56. Treasure of Pancho Villa 56. *The Diary of Anne Frank* (AA) 59. Lolita 62. Wives and Lovers 63. The Chapman Report 63. The Balcony 63. A House is Not a Home 64. The Greatest Story Ever Told 65. *A Patch of Blue* (AA) 65. Alfie (GB) 66. Harper 66. Enter Laughing 67. The Scalp Hunters 67. Wild in the Streets 68. Buona Sera Mrs Campbell 68. The Mad Room 69. Bloody Mama 70. How Do I Love Thee 70. What's the Matter with Helen? 70. Who Slew Auntie Roo? 71. Revenge! (TV) 71. The Poseidon Adventure 72. Something to Hide 72. The Devil's Daughter (TV) 72. Blume in Love 73. Cleopatra Jones 73. Diamonds 75. That Lucky Touch 75. Next Stop Greenwich Village 76. The Tenant 76.

Wintle, Julian (1913–). British producer, former editor, in films from 1934. Co-founder of Independent Artists 1958.

Hunted 51. High Tide at Noon 57. Tiger Bay 59. Very Important Person 61. This Sporting Life 63. And Father Came Too 64, many others.

Winwood, Estelle (1882–) (Estelle Goodwin). British stage character actress who has played in many American films, usually as eccentric ladylike flutterers.

The House of Trent 34. Quality Street 37. The Glass Slipper 55. *The Swan* 56. Twenty-Three Paces to Baker Street 56. *Alive and Kicking* (GB) 58. Darby O'Gill and the Little People 59. Notorious Landlady 62. Dead Ringer 64. Camelot 67. Games 67. The Producers 68. Murder by Death 76, etc.

wipe. A wipe is an optical device used for quick changes of scene: a line appears at one edge or corner of the screen and 'wipes' across, bringing the new picture with it. Wipes can also be devised in complex patterns or as expanding images, etc.

Wisberg, Aubrey (1909–). British-born writer-producer of Hollywood films, mainly second features.

So Dark the Night (w) 41. The Man from Planet X (wp) 51. The Neanderthal Man (wp) 53. Captain Kidd and the Slave Girl (wp) 54. Son of Sinbad (w) 55, many others.

Wisdom, Norman (1918–). British slapstick comedian, also on stage and TV.
☐ *Trouble in Store* (film debut) 53. One Good Turn 54. Man of the Moment 55. Up in the World 56. Just My Luck 58. The Square Peg 58. Follow a Star 59. There Was a Crooked Man 60. The Bulldog Breed 61. The Girl on the Boat 61. On the Beat 62. A Stitch in Time 63. The Early Bird 65. Press for Time 66. The Sandwich Man 66. The Night They Raided Minsky's (US) 68. What's Good for the Goose 69, etc.

Wise, Ernie: see *Morecambe, Eric.*

Wise, Robert (1914–). American director, former editor (worked on *Citizen Kane, All That Money Can Buy, The Magnificent Ambersons*).
☐ Mademoiselle Fifi 44. Curse of the Cat People 44. *The Body Snatcher* 45. A Game of Death 46. Criminal Court 46. Born to Kill 47. Mystery in Mexico 47. Blood on the Moon 48. *The Set-Up* 49. Three Secrets 50. Two Flags West 50. The House on Telegraph Hill 51. *The Day the Earth Stood Still* 51. Captive City 52. Destination Gobi 52. Something for the Birds 52. Desert Rats 52. So Big 53. *Executive Suite* 54. Helen of Troy 55. Tribute to a Bad Man 56. Somebody Up There Likes Me 56. Until They Sail 57. This Could Be the Night 57. Run Silent Run Deep 58. I Want to Live 58. Odds Against Tomorrow 59. *West Side Story* (AA) 61. Two for the Seesaw 62. The Haunting (GB) 63. *The Sound of Music* (AA) 65. The Sand Pebbles 66. Star! 68. The Andromeda Strain 70. Two People 73. The Hindenberg 75. Audrey Rose 77.

Wiseman, Frederick (–). American documentarist, former law professor.
Titicut Follies 67. High School 68. Law and Order 69. Hospital 70. Basic Training 71. Essene 72, etc.

Wiseman, Joseph (1919–). American stage actor who has made several film appearances.
Detective Story 51. Viva Zapata 52. Les Misérables 52. The Prodigal 55. The Garment Jungle 57. The Unforgiven 60. Dr. No (title role) 62. The Night They Raided Minsky's 68. Bye Bye Braverman 68. Stiletto 69. The Valachi Papers 72. The Apprenticeship of Duddy Kravitz 74, etc.

witchcraft has not been frequently tackled by film-makers, usually for censorship reasons, and *Witchcraft through the Ages* (qv) remains the most comprehensive cinematic treatise on the subject. Dreyer's *Day of Wrath* took it seriously, as did *The Witches of Salem, Maid of Salem, Witchfinder General, The Dunwich Horror, The Devils* and *Il Demonio*, but all were chiefly concerned with the morals of witch-hunting. Witch doctors are familiar figures from African adventure films like *King Solomon's Mines* and *Men of Two Worlds*; more lightheartedly, witches featured in *The Wizard of Oz, I Married a Witch* and *Bell Book and Candle*, as well as in TV's *Bewitched* and all the films featuring Merlin. A nasty cannibalistic coven was seen in Gosta Werner's *Medvinterblot* and several recent thrillers (*Night of the Demon, City of the Dead, Night of the Eagle, Witchcraft, The Witches, Rosemary's Baby, Satan's Skin, Cry of the Banshee, The Illustrated Man, The Mephisto Waltz, The Brotherhood of Satan, The Sentinel* purported to believe in the effects of witchcraft. Angela Lansbury in *Bedknobs and Broomsticks* played a kindly witch.
See also: *the devil.*

Witchcraft through the Ages (Häxan) (Sweden 1921). A unique and still horrifying film by Benjamin Christensen: a semi-documentary with fictional elements, reconstructing pagan ritual with such care as to make it a handbook of diabolism.

Withers, Googie (1917–) (Georgette Withers). British leading lady of stage and screen, married to John McCallum with whom she moved some years ago to Australia.
☐ Girl in the Crowd 34. Accused 36. Strange Boarders 37. The Lady Vanishes 38. Trouble Brewing 39. Back Room Boy 41. *One of Our Aircraft is Missing* 42. *On Approval* 43. 45. The Loves of Joanna Godden 46. Pink String and Sealing Wax 46. *It Always Rains on Sunday* 47. Miranda 48. Once Upon a Dream 49. Traveller's Joy 50. Night and the City 50. *White Corridors* 51. Derby Day 52. Devil on Horseback 54. Port of Escape 55. The Nickel Queen 70.

Withers, Grant (1904–1959). American general purpose actor in films since the twenties.
Tiger Rose 29. Sinner's Holiday 30. Red-Haired Alibi 32. Society Fever 35. Men of Steel 37. Mr Wong, Detective 39. Mexican Spitfire Out West 41. The Apache Trail 43. My Darling Clementine 46. Tripoli 50. Run for Cover 55. The White Squaw 58, many others.

Withers, Jane (1926–). American child star of the thirties, more mischievous and less pretty than Shirley Temple.
Bright Eyes 34. Ginger 35. The Farmer Takes a Wife 35. The Mad Martindales 42. North Star 43. Faces in the Fog 44. Affairs of Geraldine 46.

Giant 56. The Right Approach 62. Captain Newman 63, etc.

Witherspoon, Cora (1890–1957). American character comedienne often seen as shrewish wife; on stage from 1910.
Libeled Lady 36. Madame X 38. The Bank Dick 41. This Love of Ours 45. The Mating Season 50. The First Time 52, etc.

Witness for the Prosecution (US 1957). One of the most successful adaptations of an Agatha Christie original, the courtroom melodrama benefited from a witty script by Billie Wilder, who also directed.

Witney, William (c. 1910–). American director, mainly of routine westerns for Republic.
Roll On Texas Moon 46. Night Time in Nevada 49. The Fortune Hunter 52. City of Shadows 54. Stranger at My Door 56. The Bonnie Parker Story 58. Paratroop Command 59. Master of the World 61. Girls on the Beach 65. Arizona Raiders 66. I Escaped from Devil's Island 73, many others.

The Wizard of Oz (US 1939). Despite décor which now seems vulgar, this well-loved film survives as Hollywood's best retelling of a fairy story, mainly because of the delightful score by Harold Arlen and E. Y. Harburg, and because Judy Garland, who, though actually too old for Dorothy, successfully portrayed the essential innocence and wonder which make such stories live. An excellent supporting cast included Ray Bolger as the Scarecrow, Jack Haley as the Tin Man, Bert Lahr as the Cowardly Lion, Margaret Hamilton as the Wicked Witch and Frank Morgan as the Wizard. Mervyn le Roy produced, Victor Fleming directed, Harold Rosson was cameraman; the Technicolor which added so much at the time now seems garish. There had been two silent versions of Frank Baum's book, in 1910 and 1924.

Wodehouse, P. G. (1881–1975). British comic novelist whose sagas of upper class twits and manservants in the twenties have been oddly neglected by the screen, though they were much imitated and two films about the perfect manservant Jeeves were made in the thirties.

The Wolf Man. The werewolf or lycanthrope, a man who turns into a ravaging beast at full moon, is a fairly ancient Central European mythological figure. Hollywood did not develop the idea until *Werewolf of London* 34, a one-shot in which Henry Hull, a victim of his own well-

intentioned research, was firmly despatched before the end. Not until 1941 was the possibility of a series character envisaged. *The Wolf Man* had a splendid cast: Claude Rains, Warren William, Patric Knowles, Bela Lugosi, Maria Ouspenskaya, and Lon Chaney Jnr as Lawrence Talbot, heir to a stately English home but unlucky enough to be bitten by a werewolf and thus condemned to monstrous immortality until despatched by a silver bullet. In this film he was battered to apparent death by Claude Rains, but arose from the family crypt for *Frankenstein Meets the Wolf Man* 43, which ended with him and the Frankenstein monster being swept away in a flood. In *House of Frankenstein* he was discovered in a block of ice and promptly thawed out, only to be shot with the requisite silver bullet by a gipsy girl. The producers, however, played so unfair as to revive him for *House of Dracula* 45, in which he lived to be the only movie monster with a happy ending: brain surgery cured him and he even got the girl. Years later, however, in *Abbott and Costello Meet Frankenstein* 48, it seemed that his affliction was again tormenting him; this time we last saw him falling into a rocky and turbulent sea. Mr Chaney had by now done with the character apart from a cod appearance in an episode of TV's *Route 66*. But Hammer Films revived the basic plot in *Curse of the Werewolf* 61, with Oliver Reed as the mangy hero. To date this has provoked no sequels. One should also mention *The Werewolf* 56, *I Was a Teenage Werewolf* 57, *La Casa del Terror* (Mexican) 59, *Werewolf in a Girl's Dormitory* (with its theme song 'The Ghoul in School') 61 and *Legend of the Werewolf* 74, but the less said about these the better.

Wolfe, Ian (1896–). American character actor who usually plays worried, grasping or officious roles.
The Barretts of Wimpole Street 33. Clive of India 35. Hudson's Bay 40. The Moon is Down 43. The Invisible Man's Revenge 44. Mr Blandings Builds His Dream House 48. The Great Caruso 50. Gaby 56. The Lost World 60. Games 67. The Fortune 74, many others.

Wolff, Lothar (1909–). German producer-director, former editor; with 'The March of Time' for many years, and still associated with Louis de Rochement.
Lost Boundaries (p) 45. Martin Luther (co-wp) 53. Windjammer (p) 57. Question Seven (pd) 61. Fortress of Peace (p) 63, etc.

Wolfit, Sir Donald (1902–1968). Distinguished British thespian who, having

brought Shakespeare to the provinces, gave some enjoyably hammy performances in films.
Autobiography 1954: *First Interval.*
Biography 1971: *Sir Donald Wolfit* by Ronald Harwood.
☐ Death at Broadcasting House 34. Drake of England 35. *The Ringer* 52. Pickwick Papers 53. Svengali 54. A Prize of Gold 55. Guilty 56. I Accuse 57. Blood of the Vampire 58. *Room at the Top* 59. The House of Seven Hawks 59. The Mark 61. Lawrence of Arabia 62. Dr Crippen 63. Becket 64. Ninety Degrees in the Shade 65. Life at the Top 65. *Decline and Fall* 68.

Wolheim, Louis (1880–1931). German-born character actor, often of semi-brutish roles, with American stage experience; in Hollywood from 1919.
Dr Jekyll and Mr Hyde 20. Little Old New York 22. America 24. *Two Arabian Knights* 27. The Racket 28. Tempest 28. Frozen Justice 29. *All Quiet on the Western Front* 31. Sin Ship (& d) 31, etc.

Wolper, David (1928–). American documentarist who turned feature film producer and TV executive.
If It's Tuesday This Must Be Belgium 69. The Bridge at Remagen 69. The Hellstrom Chronicle 71. Roots (TV) 77, etc.

A Woman of Paris (US 1923). Charlie Chaplin wrote and directed but did not appear in this society melodrama, with Edna Purviance as the distraught heroine and Adolphe Menjou as a smooth philanderer. Chaplin has kept it under cover for forty years but it is said to contain moments of still-effective cinema.

Woman of the Dunes (Suna no Onna) (Japan 1964). A strange erotic fable about an entomologist on a remote beach who is trapped into living with a nubile woman in a deep sandpit. Overlong, but an exciting piece of pure cinema, written by Kobo Abe, directed by Hiroshi Teshigahara, with Eiji Okada and Kyoko Kishida.

Woman to Woman. This tearjerking play by Michael Morton, about a doomed love affair between a British officer and a French dancer, was first filmed by Graham Cutts in 1923, and achieved some renown as one of the better examples of British silent cinema. Clive Brook and Betty Compson had the leads, and Miss Compson appeared with Georges Barraud in the talkie remake of 1929, directed by Victor Saville. In 1946 Maclean Rogers directed an updated

version with Douglass Montgomery and Joyce Howard.

The Woman. Clare Boothe Luce's venomous comedy was filmed twice by MGM; in 1939 with an all-woman cast headed by Norma Shearer, Rosalind Russell, Paulette Goddard and Joan Crawford. In 1956 it became a semi-musical called *The Opposite Sex,* with June Allyson and Ann Sheridan.

Wong, Anna May (1907–1961) (Wong Lui Tsong). Chinese-American actress popular in the thirties.
Red Lantern 19. The Thief of Baghdad 24. *Piccadilly* (GB) 29. On the Spot 30. Shanghai Express 32. *Chu Chin Chow* (GB) 33. *Java Head* (GB) 34. Limehouse Blues 36. Bombs Over Burma 42. Impact 49. Portrait in Black 60, etc.

Wontner, Arthur (1875–1960). Gaunt British character actor of stage and screen; a splendid, if elderly, Sherlock Holmes.
Frailty 16. Bonnie Prince Charlie 23. Eugene Aram 24. The Infamous Lady 28. The Sleeping Cardinal 31. *The Sign of Four* 32. *The Triumph of Sherlock Holmes* 35. Dishonour Bright 36. Silver Blaze 36. Storm in a Teacup 37. Kate Plus Ten 38. The Terror 38. The Life and Death of Colonel Blimp 43. Blanche Fury 47. Brandy for the Parson 52. *Genevieve* 53, etc.

Wood, Charles (c. 1931–). British playwright with a penchant for military matters.
Help 65. The Knack 65. How I Won the War 67. The Charge of the Light Brigade 68.

Wood, Natalie (1938–) (Natasha Gurdin). Former American child actress, who became a top star of the sixties.
Happy Land 43. Tomorrow is Forever 45. The Bride Wore Boots 46. Miracle on 34th Street 46. No Sad Songs for Me 50. The Blue Veil 52. Rebel Without a Cause 55. A Cry in the Night 56. The Searchers 56. *Marjorie Morningstar* 58. Kings Go Forth 59. Cash McCall 60. *Splendor in the Grass* 61. *West Side Story* 61. Gypsy 62. *Love with the Proper Stranger* 64. Sex and the Single Girl 64. *The Great Race* 65. Inside Daisy Clover 66. This Property is Condemned 66. Penelope 66. *Bob and Carol and Ted and Alice* 69. The Affair (TV) 73. Peeper 74, etc.

Wood, Peggy (1892–). American character actress, former opera singer.
Almost a Husband 19. Handy Andy 34. The Housekeeper's Daughter 39. The Story of Ruth 60. *The Sound of Music* 65, etc.
TV series: Mama 49–56.

Wood, Sam (1883–1949). American director, in business before becoming assistant to Cecil B. De Mille c. 1915; directing from 1920.

The Beloved Villain 20. Under the Lash 22. Bluebeard's Eighth Wife 23. One Minute to Play 26. The Latest from Paris 28. Within the Law 30. Stamboul Quest 32. The Late Christopher Bean 33. Get-Rich-Quick Wallingford 34. *A Night at the Opera* 35. The Unguarded Hour 36. *A Day at the Races* 37. Madame X 37. Lord Jeff 38. *Goodbye Mr Chips* 39. Raffles 39. *Our Town* 40. Kitty Foyle 40. *The Devil and Miss Jones* 41. The Pride of the Yankees 42. *Kings Row* 42. Saratoga Trunk 43 (released 46). *For Whom the Bell Tolls* (& p) 43. Casanova Brown 44. Guest Wife 45. Heartbeat 46. Ivy 47. Command Decision 48. Ambush 49, etc.

Woodbridge, George (1907–197*). Portly British character actor, often seen as tavernkeeper or jovial policeman.

Tower of Terror 42. Green for Danger 46. Bonnie Prince Charlie 48. The Story of Gilbert and Sullivan 53. The Constant Husband 55. Dracula 58. Two-Way Stretch 60. Dracula Prince of Darkness 65, many others.

Woodbury, Joan (1915–). American leading lady of forties second features.

Without Children 35. Forty Naughty Girls 38. The Mystery of the White Room 39. The Desperadoes 43. Flame of the West 46. Here Comes Trouble 49. The Ten Commandments 56, many others.

Woods, Arthur B. (1904–1942). British director.

On Secret Service 34. Radio Parade 35. Drake of England 35. The Dark Stairway 37. The Return of Carol Deane 38. *They Drive by Night* 38. The Nursemaid Who Disappeared 39. Busman's Honeymoon 40, etc.

Woods, Aubrey (1928–). British character actor.

Nicholas Nickleby 47. Queen of Spades 48. Father Brown 54. School for Scoundrels 59. Spare the Rod 61. Just Like a Woman 66. The Abominable Dr Phibes 71. The Darwin Adventure 72. That Lucky Touch 75, etc.

Woods, Donald (1906–). American leading man of the thirties and forties.

Sweet Adeline 33. A Tale of Two Cities 35. Anthony Adverse 36. Forgotten Girls 40. Love, Honour and Oh Baby 41. I Was a Prisoner on Devil's Island 41. Watch on the Rhine 43. Roughly Speaking 45. Wonder Man 45. Barbary Pirate 49. Undercover Agent 54. Thirteen

Ghosts 60. Kissing Cousins 64. Moment to Moment 65, many others.

Woodward, Edward (1930–). British stage actor who achieved popularity on TV as *Callan* 66–71.

Where There's a Will 54. Becket 64. The File of the Golden Goose 69. Sitting Target 72. The Wicker Man 73. Young Winston 73. Callan 74. Stand Up Virgin Soldiers 77.

Woodward, Joanne (1930–). Tomboyish American leading actress, married to Paul Newman.

☐ Count Three and Pray 55. A Kiss Before Dying 56. *The Three Faces of Eve* (AA) 57. *No Down Payment* 57. The Long Hot Summer 58. Rally Round the Flag Boys 58. The Sound and the Fury 59. The Fugitive Kind 59. From the Terrace 60. Paris Blues 61. The Stripper 63. A New Kind of Love 63. Signpost to Murder 64. *A Big Hand for the Little Lady* 66. A Fine Madness 66. *Rachel Rachel* 68. Winning 69. W.U.S.A. 70. They Might Be Giants 71. The Effect of Gamma Rays on Man-in-the-Moon Marigolds 72. Summer Wishes Winter Dreams 73.

Woody Woodpecker. A cartoon character with an infectious laugh, created in the thirties by Walter Lantz for Universal, and still going strong in 1973 via a new TV incarnation.

Wooland, Norman (1910–). British actor, former radio announcer.

Hamlet (film debut) 48. All Over the Town 48. Escape 49. Romeo and Juliet 53. The Master Plan 55. Richard III 56. Guilty 56. The Rough and the Smooth 59. The Fall of the Roman Empire 64. Saul and David 65. The Projected Man 66, etc.

Woolcott, Alexander (1887–1943). Waspish American columnist and critic, the original inspiration for Kaufman and Hart's *The Man Who Came to Dinner*.

☐ Gift of Gab 34. *The Scoundrel* 35. Babes on Broadway 41.

Woolf, James (1919–1966). British producer. With brother **Sir John Woolf** (1913–) founded Romulus Films 1949. Both are sons of leading producer-distributor C. M. Woolf, who died in 1942.

Pandora and the Flying Dutchman 51. The African Queen 52. Moulin Rouge 53. Three Men in a Boat 56. Room at the Top 59, etc.

JAMES ONLY: The L-Shaped Room 62. The

Pumpkin Eater 64. Life at the Top 65. King Rat 65.
JOHN ONLY: Oliver! (AA) 68. Day of the Jackal 73. No Sex Please We're British 73. The Odessa File 74.

Woolfe, H. Bruce (1880–1965). British producer, best known for his war reconstructions of the twenties (*Armageddon, Ypres, The Battle of the Somme*, etc.) and for the *Secrets of Nature* series begun in 1919. Head of British Instructional Films from 1926; later in charge of production for children.

Woolley, Monty (1888–1963) (Edgar Montillion Woolley). American comedy character actor of ebullient personality, a former Yale professor who came to movie stardom via a big hit as Alexander Woolcott on the Broadway stage.
Live, Love and Learn 37. Nothing Sacred 37. Arsène Lupin Returns 38. Girl of the Golden West 38. Everybody Sing 38. Three Comrades 38. Lord Jeff 38. Artists and Models Abroad 38. Young Dr Kildare 38. Vacation from Love 48. Never Say Die 39. Midnight 39. Zaza 39. Man About Town 39. Dancing Co-Ed 39. *The Man Who Came to Dinner* 41. The Pied Piper 42. Life Begins at 8.30 42. *Holy Matrimony* 43. Since You Went Away 44. Irish Eyes are Smiling 44. Molly and Me 45. *Night and Day* 46. The Bishop's Wife 47. *Miss Tatlock's Millions* 48. As Young as You Feel 51. Kismet 55.

Woolsey, Ralph (–). American cinematographer.
The Culpeper Cattle Company 72. The New Centurions 72. The Mack 73. The Iceman Cometh 73. Black Eye 74. 99 44/100 Per Cent Dead 74. Rafferty and the Gold Dust Twins 75, etc.

Woolsey, Robert (1889–1938). American comedian; see *Wheeler, Bert*.

work print: the same as cutting copy, the first edited print from which, when it is satisfactory, the negative will be cut accordingly.

World of Plenty (GB 1943). A feature-length survey of the global food problem, notable as the first documentary to get a full circuit release in Britain. Directed by Paul Rotha from a script by himself and Eric Knight, it showed advanced use of newsreel material, specially-staged scenes, and Adprint diagrams, and confidently adapted the technique invented by 'The March of Time'.

World War I (1914–18), now a remote and comparatively concentrated event, was seen by film-makers of the next four decades chiefly as an opportunity for pacifist propaganda arising from horror and disillusion. This is the kind of attitude struck in *Civilisation, War Brides, The Battle Cry of Peace, All Quiet on the Western Front* (and its sequel *The Road Back*), *Westfront 1918, J'Accuse, The Man Who Reclaimed His Head, Journey's End, La Grande Illusion, The Man I Killed, The Road to Glory, They Gave Me a Gun, Sergeant York*, and *Paths of Glory. Oh What a Lovely War* made the same points by use of bitter comedy. The romantic aspect of war was however not neglected by *The White Sister, A Farewell to Arms, Hearts of the World, The Four Horsemen of the Apocalypse, The Big Parade, Lilac Time, Hell's Angels, Seventh Heaven, The Dark Angel, Waterloo Bridge, Lawrence of Arabia*, and many others. *What Price Glory?* was pure cynicism, *The Fighting 69th* pure jingoism. The spy element was to the fore in *I Was a Spy, Dark Journey, The Spy in Black, Mata Hari, Nurse Edith Cavell* and *Darling Lili*; aviation in *Hell's Angels, Wings, The Red Baron* and *The Blue Max*. Comedy aspects of the war were depicted in *Shoulder Arms, Spy for a Day, Pack Up Your Troubles, We're in the Army Now, Half Shot at Sunrise* and *Up the Front*. Rehabilitation problems were dealt with in *The Sun Also Rises, The Last Flight, Isn't Life Wonderful?, The Lost Squadron, The Roaring Twenties* and the 'Forgotten Man' number in *Gold Diggers of 1933*.

Worlock, Frederick (1886–1973). British character actor in Hollywood after long stage career.
Miracles for Sale 39. The Sea Hawk 40. Rage in Heaven 41. The Black Swan 43. Sherlock Holmes Faces Death 44. Terror by Night 46. Joan of Arc 48. Notorious Landlady 62. Spinout 66, etc.

Worsley, Wallace (1880–1944). American director of the twenties.
Honor's Cross 18. The Little Shepherd of Kingdom Come 19. *The Penalty* 20. A Blind Bargain 21. Rags to Riches 22. *The Hunchback of Notre Dame* 23. The Man Who Fights Alone 24. The Shadow of Law 26. The Power of Silence 28, etc.

Worth, Brian (1914–). British light leading man.
The Lion Has Wings 39. One Night with You 48. Hindle Wakes 52. An Inspector Calls 54. Ill Met by Moonlight 57. Peeping Tom 60, etc.

Worth, Irene (1916–). American leading actress, in recent years mainly on British stage.
□ One Night with You 48. Secret People 51. Orders to Kill (BFA) 58. Seven Seas to Calais (as Elizabeth I) 63. King Lear 69. Nicholas and Alexandra 71.

Wouk, Herman (1915–). American bestselling novelist.
The Caine Mutiny 54. Marjorie Morningstar 58. Youngblood Hawke 64.

Wray, Fay (1907–). American leading lady of the thirties, a great screamer.
Street of Sin 28. The Wedding March 28. The Four Feathers 29. The Texan 30. Dirigible 30. Doctor X 31. *The Most Dangerous Game* 32. The Vampire Bat 33. The Mystery of the Wax Museum 33. *King Kong* 33. The Bowery 33. Madame Spy 34. The Affairs of Cellini 34. The Clairvoyant 35. They Met in a Taxi 36. Murder in Greenwich Village 37. The Jury's Secret 38. Adam Had Four Sons 41. Small Town Girl 53. Queen Bee 55. Crime of Passion 56. Tammy and the Bachelor 57, etc.
TV series: Pride of the Family 53.

Wray, John (1890–1940) (John Malloy). American general purpose actor.
All Quiet on the Western Front 30. Doctor X 32. I Am a Fugitive from a Chain Gang 32. The Defence Rests 34. The Whole Town's Talking 35. Valiant is the Word for Carrie 36. You Only Live Once 37. The Cat and the Canary 39. The Man from Dakota 40, etc.

Wrede, Caspar (1929–). Finnish director, in British TV.
□ The Barber of Stamford Hill 62. Private Potter 64. One Day in the Life of Ivan Denisovitch 71. Ransom 74.

Wren, P. C. (1885–1941) (Percival Christopher Wren). British adventure novelist who after a military life wrote the much filmed *Beau Geste*, followed by *Beau Sabreur* and *Beau Ideal*.

Wright, Basil (1907–). British producer-director. In films from 1929: worked with John Grierson in creation of 'documentary'.
Historical Book 1975: *The Long View.*
Windmill in Barbados (d) 30. Song of Ceylon (pd) 34. Night Mail (co-d) 36. Waters of Time (pd) 51. World Without End (d) 53. The Immortal Land (pd) 58. A Place for Gold (pd) 61, etc.

Wright, Teresa (1918–). American leading actress with stage experience.
The Little Foxes (film debut) 41. *Mrs Miniver* (AA) 42. The Pride of the Yankees 42. *Shadow of a Doubt* 43. Casanova Brown 44. *The Best Years of Our Lives* 46. Pursued 47. Enchantment 48. *The Men* 50. Something to Live For 52. The Actress 53. Track of the Cat 54. *The Search for Bridey Murphy* 56. Escapade in Japan 57. The Happy Ending 69, etc.

Wright, Tony (1925–). British light leading man, with stage experience.
The Flanagan Boy (film debut) 51. Jumping for Joy 54. Jacqueline 56. Seven Thunders 57. Faces in the Dark 60. Journey to Nowhere 62. All Coppers Are 72, etc.

Wright, Will (1894–1962). Lugubrious American character actor.
China Clipper 36. World Première 41. Bewitched 45. Adam's Rib 49. Excuse My Dust 51. The Wild One 52. The Deadly Companions 62, many others.

writers depicted in films include the following: Rod Taylor as Sean O'Casey in *Young Cassidy*, John Shepperd as Edgar Allan Poe in *The Loves of Edgar Allan Poe*, Beau Bridges as Ben Hecht in *Gaily Gaily*, James Mason as Gustave Flaubert in *Madame Bovary*, Herbert Marshall as Somerset Maugham in *The Moon and Sixpence* and *The Razor's Edge*, Reginald Gardiner as Shakespeare in *The Story of Mankind*, Turhan Bey as Aesop in *A Night in Paradise*, Michael O'Shea as Jack London in *Jack London*, Dean Stockwell as Eugene O'Neill in *Long Day's Journey into Night*, Daniel Massey as Noel Coward in *Star!*, Frederick Jaeger as Henrik Ibsen in *Song of Norway*, Danny Kaye as *Hans Christian Andersen*, Paul Muni in *The Life of Emile Zola*, Gregory Peck as F. Scott Fitzgerald in *Beloved Infidel*, Burgess Meredith as Ernie Pyle in *The Story of G.I. Joe*, Michael Redgrave as W. B. Yeats in *Young Cassidy*, Laurence Harvey and Karl Boehm in *The Wonderful World of the Brothers Grimm*, Dennis Price in *The Bad Lord Byron*, Richard Chamberlain as Byron in *Lady Caroline Lamb*, Fredric March (later Bill Travers) as Robert Browning in *The Barretts of Wimpole Street*, Olivia de Havilland, Nancy Coleman and Ida Lupino as the Brontë Sisters in *Devotion*, Arthur Kennedy as Branwell Brontë in *Devotion*, Sidney Greenstreet as Thackeray in *Devotion*, Robert Morley in *Oscar Wilde*, Peter Finch in *The Trials of Oscar Wilde*, Cornel Wilde in *Omar Khayyam*, Fredric March in *The Adventures of Mark Twain*.

Wuthering Heights (US 1939). A good example of the superior pre-war Hollywood film. Emily Brontë's brooding novel of the Yorkshire moors was shortened in incident, shot in America, scripted by Charles MacArthur and Ben Hecht, directed by William Wyler; yet it emerged truer to its original in mood than any of the earlier British silent attempts. Laurence Olivier as Heathcliff dominated the film; Merle Oberon, David Niven and Geraldine Fitzgerald gave sound performances; Gregg Toland's photography was first-rate. A subsequent Mexican version of the story by Luis Buñuel, *Abismos de Pasion* 50, has not been widely seen. There was also a 1970 remake, directed by Robert Fuest, starring Ian McShane and Anna Calder-Marshall.

Wyatt, Jane (1912–). Pleasing American leading lady of the thirties and forties, with stage experience.
One More River 34. The Luckiest Girl in the World 36. *Lost Horizon* 37. Kisses for Breakfast 41. The Kansan 42. The Iron Road 43. None But the Lonely Heart 44. Boomerang 47. Gentleman's Agreement 47. Pitfall 48. Bad Boy 49. Task Force 49. Our Very Own 50. The Man Who Cheated Himself 51. Never Too Late 65. Tom Sawyer (TV) 73. Treasure of Matecumbe 76, many others.
TV series: Father Knows Best 57–63.

Wycherly, Margaret (1881–1956). British-born character actress with American stage experience.
The Thirteenth Chair 29. Sergeant York 41. Keeper of the Flame 43. The Yearling 46. *White Heat* 49. Man with a Cloak 51. That Man from Tangier 53, others.

Wyler, Richard (1934–) (also known as Richard Stapley). American leading man of the fifties.
The Three Musketeers 48. The Strange Door 51. King of the Khyber Rifles 53. Target Zero 55. The Ugly Ones 68, etc.

Wyler, William (1902–). Distinguished German-American director, former film publicist, in Hollywood from 1920. Director from 1925, starting with low-budget silent westerns.
□ TALKIES: Hell's Heroes 30. The Storm 30. A House Divided 31. Tom Brown of Culver 32. Her First Mate 33. Counsellor at Law 33. Glamour 34. *The Good Fairy* 35. The Gay Deception 35. These Three 36. Come and Get It (co-d) 36. *Dodsworth* 36. *Dead End* 37. *Jezebel* 38. *Wuthering Heights* 39. *The Letter* 40. The Little Foxes 41. *Mrs Miniver* (AA) 42. The Memphis Belle (documentary) 44. The Fighting Lady (documentary) 44. *The Best Years of Our Lives* (AA) 46. *The Heiress* 49. Detective Story 51. Carrie 52. Roman Holiday 53. The Desperate Hours 55. The Friendly Persuasion 56. *The Big Country* 58. *Ben Hur* 59. The Children's Hour 62. The Collector 65. How to Steal a Million 66. Funny Girl 68. The Liberation of L. B. Jones 70.

Wyman, Jane (1914–) (Sarah Jane Faulks). American leading lady of the forties, at first in dumb blonde roles, later as serious actress.
My Man Godfrey 36. Brother Rat 38. Flight Angels 40. Bad Men of Missouri 41. The Body Disappears 41. You're in the Army Now 41. My Favorite Spy 42. Princess O'Rourke 43. Crime by Night 44. The Doughgirls 44. Make Your Own Bed 44. *The Lost Weekend* 45. Night and Day 46. Magic Town 46. The Yearling 47. *Johnny Belinda* (AA) 48. Three Guys Named Mike 49. Here Comes the Groom 51. The Blue Veil 52. Just For You 53. So Big 53. *Magnificent Obsession* 54. All That Heaven Allows 55. Miracle in the Rain 56. Pollyanna 60. Bon Voyage 63. How To Committ Marriage 69. The Failing of Raymond (TV) 71, etc.

Wymark, Patrick (1926–1970) (Patrick Cheesman). British TV actor, in occasional films. The voice of Churchill in *The Finest Hours* 64, *A King's Story* 65.
The Criminal 60. Repulsion 65. The Secret of Blood Island 65. The Psychopath 66. Where Eagles Dare 68. Cromwell 69. Satan's Skin 70, etc.

Wymore, Patrice (1926–). American leading lady.
Tea for Two 50. Rocky Mountain 50. The Big Trees 52. She's Working Her Way Through College 52. She's Back on Broadway 53. Chamber of Horrors 66, etc.

Wyndham, John (1903–1969). British science fiction novelist. Works filmed include *Village of the Damned* (The Midwich Cuckoos) and *The Day of the Triffids*.

Wynn, Ed (1886–1966) (Isaiah Edwin Leopold). American vaudeville, radio and TV comic who after initial film failure returned to Hollywood in the fifties as a character actor of fey old gentlemen.
□ Rubber Heels 27. Follow the Leader 30. Manhattan Mary 30. The Chief 33. Stage Door Canteen 43. *The Great Man* 56. Marjorie Morningstar 58. *The Diary of Anne Frank* 59.

The Absent Minded Professor 60. Cinderfella 60. Babes in Toyland 61. Son of Flubber 63. Those Calloways 64. *Mary Poppins* 64. That Darn Cat 65. Dear Brigitte 65. The Greatest Story Ever Told 65. Warning Shot 67. The Gnome-Mobile 67.

Wynn, Keenan (1916–). American character actor, son of Ed Wynn. In Hollywood from early forties after stage experience.
Autobiography 1960: *Ed Wynn's Son*.
See Here Private Hargrove 44. Under the Clock 45. Weekend at the Waldorf 45. The Hucksters 47. Annie Get Your Gun 50. Kiss Me Kate 53. The Glass Slipper 55. The Great Man 57. A Hole in the Head 59. The Absent-Minded Professor 60. Man in the Middle 63. Dr Strangelove 63. The Americanization of Emily 65. The Great Race 65. The War Wagon 67. Mackenna's Gold 68. Smith 69. Once Upon a Time in the West 69. Five Savage Men 70. Pretty Maids all in a Row 71. Herbie Rides Again 73. Hit Lady (TV) 75. Nashville 75. The Devil's Rain 76, many others.

Wynn, Tracy Keenan (–). American screenwriter, son of Keenan Wynn.
The Glass House (TV) 70. Tribes (TV) 71. *The Autobiography of Miss Jane Pittman* (TV) 73. The Longest Yard 74. The Drowning Pool (cow) 75, etc.

Wynn, May (1931–) (Donna Lee Hickey). American leading lady of the fifties.
□ The Caine Mutiny 54. The Violent Men 54. They Rode West 55.

Wynter, Dana (c. 1930–) (Dagmar Wynter). British leading lady.
White Corridors 51. Colonel March Investigates 53. *Invasion of the Body Snatchers* (US) 56. D Day Sixth of June 56. Value 57. Shake Hands with the Devil 59. *Sink the Bismarck* 60. The List of Adrian Messenger 63. If He Hollers Let Him Go 68. Airport 69. Santee 73, etc.
TV series: The Man Who Never Was 66.

Wynyard, Diana (1906–1964) (Dorothy Isobel Cox). Distinguished British stage actress.
Rasputin and the Empress 32. *Cavalcade* 33. Reunion in Vienna 33. Over the River 34. Freedom Radio 39. *Gaslight* 39. *Kipps* 41. The Prime Minister 41. An Ideal Husband 47. The Feminine Touch 56, etc.

Y

A Yank at Oxford (GB 1938). The first major production of MGM-British under Michael Balcon, a significant precedent and a happy blend of talent from both countries. It was a simple enough romantic comedy-drama, but packed with appeal. Robert Taylor was the stranger to English academic routine, Lionel Barrymore his father, Vivien Leigh and Maureen O'Sullivan his girl friends. Jack Conway directed. Imitations included *A Chump at Oxford* 40, with Laurel and Hardy, and *A Yank at Eton* 42 with Mickey Rooney.

Yankee Doodle Dandy (US 1942). Biopic about George M. Cohan, famous American playwright-entertainer; held together by the immense zest of James Cagney (AA), with Walter Huston and Joan Leslie in tow. Tuneful songs helped; so did the skilled direction of Michael Curtiz.

Yarbrough, Jean (1900–). American director of second features, former prop man.
Devil Bat 41. Lure of the Islands 42. Good Morning Judge 43. In Society 44. The Naughty Nineties 45. The Brute Man 46. Curse of the Allenbys 47. The Creeper 48. Abbott and Costello Lost in Alaska 52. Jack and the Beanstalk 52. Women of Pitcairn Island 57. Saintly Sinners 61. Hillbillies in a Haunted House 67, many others.

Yates, Herbert (1880–1966). American executive, ex-president of Republic Pictures, where his word was law in the forties and many of his productions starred his wife, Vera Hruba Ralston.

Yates, Peter (1929–). British director.
Summer Holiday 62. One Way Pendulum 64. *Robbery* 67. *Bullitt* (US) 68. John and Mary (US) 69. Murphy's War 70. The Hot Rock (US) 72. The Friends of Eddie Coyle 73. For Pete's Sake 74. Mother Jugs and Speed 76. The Deep 77, etc.

Yordan, Philip (c. 1913–). Prolific American writer-producer.
SCREENPLAYS: Syncopation 42. Dillinger 45.

House of Strangers 49. Detective Story 51. Johnny Guitar 54. El Cid 61. 55 Days at Peking 62. The Fall of the Roman Empire 64, many others.
WROTE AND PRODUCED: The Harder They Fall Men in War 57. God's Little Acre 58. Day of the Outlaw 59. Studs Lonigan 60. The Day of the Triffids 62. The Thin Red Line 64. The Battle of the Bulge 65. Captain Apache 71, etc.

York, Dick (1928–). American actor.
My Sister Eileen 55. Operation Mad Ball 57. They Came to Cordura 58. Inherit the Wind 60, etc.
TV series: Going My Way. Bewitched.

York, Michael (1942–). British leading man with stage experience.
□ The Taming of the Shrew 67. *Accident* 67. Red and Blue 67. Smashing Time 67. Romeo and Juliet 68. The Strange Affair 68. The Guru 69. Alfred the Great 69. Justine 69. Something for Everyone 70. Zeppelin 71. *Cabaret* 72. England Made Me 72. *Lost Horizon* 73. The Three Musketeers 73. The Four Musketeers 74. Murder on the Orient Express 74. Conduct Unbecoming 75. Logan's Run 76. *Jesus of Nazareth* (TV) 77. The Last Remake of Beau Geste 77.

York, Susannah (1942–). British leading lady of stage and screen.
□ *Tunes of Glory* (debut) 60. There Was a Crooked Man 60. The Greengage Summer 61. Freud 62. Tom Jones 63. The Seventh Dawn 64. Scene Nun Take One 64. Sands of the Kalahari 65. Kaleidoscope 66. A Man For All Seasons 66. Sebastian 67. The Killing of Sister George 68. Duffy 68. Oh What a Lovely War 69. The Battle of Britain 69. Lock Up Your Daughters 69. They Shoot Horses Don't They? (US) 69. Country Dance 70. Jane Eyre 70. Zee and Co. 71. Happy Birthday Wanda June (US) 71. *Images* 72. The Maids 73. Gold 74. Conduct Unbecoming 75. Sky Riders 76.

Yorkin, Bud (1926–) (Alan Yorkin). American director, from TV.
Come Blow Your Horn 63. Never Too Late 65.

Divorce American Style 67. Inspector Clouseau 68. Start the Revolution Without Me 69. The Thief Who Came To Dinner 73, etc.

You Can't Take It With You (US 1938): (AA best picture). Vintage crazy comedy from the stage play by George S. Kaufman and Moss Hart about a family of New Yorkers who do exactly what they want to in life and even convert a stuffy tycoon whose son falls for their daughter. Directed by Frank Capra (AA); played with all the stops out by Lionel Barrymore, Jean Arthur, James Stewart, Spring Byington, Edward Arnold, Mischa Auer, Ann Miller, Samuel S. Hinds, Donald Meek, H. B. Warner and Halliwell Hobbes.

Young, Alan (1919–) (Angus Young). British-born comic actor, in Canada since childhood.
Margie (debut) 46. Mr Belvedere Goes to College 49. Aaron Slick from Punkin Crick 52. *Androcles and the Lion* 53. Tom Thumb 58. The Time Machine 59, etc.
TV series: Mister Ed 62–64.

Young, Arthur (1898–1959). Portly British stage actor; film appearances usually in self-important roles.
No Limit 35. Victoria the Great 37. My Brother Jonathan 48. The Lady with a Lamp 51. An Inspector Calls 54. The Gelignite Gang 56, etc.

Young, Carleton (1906–1971). American character actor, from radio; father of Tony Young.
The Glory Brigade 53. The Court Martial of Billy Mitchell 55. The Horse Soldiers 59. Sergeant Rutledge 60, many others.

Young, Clara Kimball (1890–1960). Popular American heroine of the silent screen.
Cardinal Wolsey (debut) 12. Beau Brummell 13. Goodness Gracious 16. Eyes of Youth 19. Cheating Cheaters 19. Forbidden Woman 20. Hush 21. Charge It 21. Lying Wives 25. Kept Husbands 31. Love Bound 33. Romance in the Rain 34. The Frontiersman 39. Mr Celebrity 42, etc.

Young, Collier (1908–). American writer-producer.
The Hitch-Hiker 53. The Bigamist 54. Mad at the World 55. Huk 56, etc.
TV series: One Step Beyond. Ironside, etc.

Young, Frederick (1902–). Distinguished British cinematographer.
Bitter Sweet 33. Nell Gwyn 34. When Knights Were Bold 36. Victoria the Great 37. Sixty Glorious Years 38. Goodbye Mr Chips 39. The Young Mr Pitt 41. 49th Parallel 41; war service; Bedelia 46. So Well Remembered 47. Edward My Son 40. Treasure Island 50. Ivanhoe 52. *Lust for Life* 56. *Invitation to the Dance* 56. Bhowani Junction 56. Island in the Sun 56. *Lawrence of Arabia* (AA) 62. The Seventh Dawn 64. Lord Jim 65. Rotten to the Core 65. *Doctor Zhivago* (AA) 65. The Deadly Affair 67. You Only Live Twice 67. The Battle of Britain 69. *Ryan's Daughter* (AA) 70. Nicholas and Alexandra 71. The Tamarind Seed 74, etc.

Young, Gig (1913–) (Byron Barr: also known as Bryant Fleming). American light comedy leading man with a pleasantly bemused air.
Misbehaving Husbands 40. They Died With Their Boots On 41. Dive Bomber 41. The Gay Sisters (in which he played a character called Gig Young and thereafter used the name) 41. Old Acquaintance 43. Air Force 43; war service; Escape Me Never 46. The Woman in White 47. Wake of the Red Witch 48. The Three Musketeers 49. *Come Fill the Cup* 51. City That Never Sleeps 54. Young at Heart 55. Desk Set 57. The Story on Page One 59. Ask Any Girl 59. *That Touch of Mink* 62. For Love or Money 63. Strange Bedfellows 65. The Shuttered Room 67. *They Shoot Horses Don't They?* (AA) 69. *Lovers and Other Strangers* 70. The Neon Ceiling (TV) 71. A Son-in-Law for Charlie McCready 73. Bring Me the Head of Alfredo Garcia 74. The Hindenberg 75. The Killer Elite 75.
TV series: *The Rogues* 64. *Gibbsville* 76.

Young, Harold (1897–). American director who made distinguished British films for Korda but was little heard from on his return to Hollywood.
Catherine the Great 34. *The Scarlet Pimpernel* 35. 52nd Street 38. Code of the Streets 39. Juke Box Jenny 42. The Frozen Ghost 43. I'll Remember April 44, etc.

Young, Loretta (1913–) (Gretchen Young). American leading lady whose career in films began when she accidentally, at 15, answered a studio call meant for her elder sister, Polly Ann Young.
Autobiography 1962: *The Things I Had To Learn.*
Laugh Clown Laugh (debut) 28. Loose Ankles 29. The Squall 30. Kismet 30. I Like Your Nerve 31. *The Devil to Pay* 30. Platinum Blonde 32. The Hatchet Man 32. Big Business Girl 32. Life Begins 32. Zoo in Budapest 33. *Man's Castle* 33. The House of Rothschild 34. Midnight Mary 35. The Crusaders 35. Clive of India 35. Call of the

Wild 35. Shanghai 36. *Ramona* 36. Ladies in Love 37. Wife, Doctor and Nurse 37. Second Honeymoon 38. Four Men and a Prayer 38. Suez 38. Kentucky 38. Three Blind Mice 38. The Story of Alexander Graham Bell 39. The Doctor Takes a Wife 39. He Stayed for Breakfast 40. Lady from Cheyenne 41. The Men in Her Life 41. *A Night to Remember* 42. China 43. Ladies Courageous 44. And Now Tomorrow 44. The Stranger 45. Along Came Jones 46. The Perfect Marriage 46. *The Farmer's Daughter* (AA) 47. The Bishop's Wife 48. Rachel and the Stranger 48. Come to the Stable 49. Cause for Alarm 51. Half Angel 51. Paula 52. Because of You 52. It Happens Every Thursday 53, others.
TV show of anthology dramas 53–60.

Young Mr Lincoln (US 1939). Biopic directed by John Ford, picturing Abraham Lincoln before he became a political figure. Written by Lamar Trotti, with a first-class performance by Henry Fonda and an all-pervading genuine feeling for American pioneer life.

The Young Ones (GB 1961). Derivative but zestful British musical determined to sell teenage music not only to other kids but to adults. Cliff Richard and his gang proved so endearing that two agreeable but overlong sequels were made: *Summer Holiday* 63, *Wonderful Life* 64. Sidney Furie's direction was undisciplined but full of bright ideas.

Young, Otis (1932–). American black actor. *The Last Detail* 73.
TV series: The Outcasts 68.

Young, Robert (1907–). American leading man invariably cast in amiable, dependable roles. A former clerk, with stage experience.
□ The Sin of Madelon Claudet (debut) 31. Strange Interlude 31. The Kid from Spain 32. Hell Below 32. Tugboat Annie 33. Lazy River 34. The House of Rothschild 34. Spitfire 34. Whom the Gods Destroy 35. West Point of the Air 35. It's Love Again (GB) 36. *Secret Agent* (GB) 36. Stowaway 36. The Emperor's Candlesticks 37. I Met Him in Paris 37. The Bride Wore Red 37. Josette 38. Frou Frou 38. Three Comrades 39. Rich Man, Poor Girl 39. Honolulu 39. Miracles for Sale 39. Maisie 39. Northwest Passage 40. The Mortal Storm 40. Florian 40. Western Union 41. The Trial of Mary Dugan 41. Lady Be Good 41. *H. M. Pulham Esq.* 41. Cairo 42. Journey for Margaret 42. Sweet Rosie O'Grady 43. *Claudia* 43. The Canterville Ghost 44. The Enchanted Cottage 44. Those Endearing Young Charms 45. Lady Luck 46. Claudia and David 46. The Searching Wind 46. They Won't Believe Me 47. *Crossfire* 47. Sitting Pretty 48. The Forsyte Woman 49. And Baby Makes Three 50. The Second Woman 51. Goodbye My Fancy 51. The Half-Breed 52. The Secret of the Incas 54. Vanished (TV) 71. All My Darling Daughters (TV) 72. My Darling Daughters' Anniversary (TV) 73.
TV series: Father Knows Best 54–60. Marcus Welby M.D. 69–75.

Young, Roland (1887–1953). British character actor with stage experience; made a screen career in Hollywood and is affectionately remembered for a gallery of whimsical or ineffectual types.
Sherlock Holmes (debut) 22. Moriarty 22. The Unholy Night 29. Madame Satan 30. New Moon 30. *One Hour With You* 32. Wedding Rehearsal (GB) 32. The Guardsman 32. His Double Life 33. *David Copperfield* (as Uriah Heep) 34. Ruggles of Red Gap 34. One Rainy Afternoon 36. *The Man Who Could Work Miracles* (GB) 36. Call It a Day 37. King Solomon's Mines (GB) 37. *Topper* (title role) 37. Ali Baba Goes to Town 38. Sailing Along (GB) 38. *The Young in Heart* 39. Topper Takes a Trip 39. No No Nanette 40. *The Philadelphia Story* 40. Flame of New Orleans 41. Topper Returns 41. The Lady Has Plans 42. They All Kissed the Bride 42. Tales of Manhattan 42. Forever and a Day 43. Standing Room Only 44. And Then There Were None 45. Bond Street (GB) 47. The Great Lover 49. Let's Dance 50. St Benny the Dip 51. That Man from Tangier 53, others.

Young, Stephen (c. 1931–) (Stephen Levy). Canadian leading man, former extra.
TV series: Seaway 64. Judd for the Defence 66–68.

Young, Terence (1915–). British screenwriter who became a successful director.
AS WRITER: On the Night of the Fire 39. Dangerous Moonlight 40, etc.
□ AS DIRECTOR: Corridor of Mirrors 48. They Were Not Divided 50. The Tall Headlines 52. The Red Beret 53. That Lady 55. Zarak 56. Too Hot to Handle 60. *Doctor No* 62. *From Russia With Love* 63. The Amorous Adventures of Moll Flanders 65. Thunderball 65. The Poppy is Also a Flower 66. Triple Cross 66. *Wait Until Dark* 67. Mayerling 68. The Christmas Tree 69. Grand Slam 70. Cold Sweat 70. Red Sun 71. The Valachi Papers 72. War Goddess 73. The Klansman 74.

Young, Tony (c. 1932–). American leading man, from TV series *Gunslinger*.

He Rides Tall 63. Taggart 64. Charro 69. The Outfit 73.

Young, Victor (1900–1956). American composer with over 300 film scores to his credit.
Fatal Lady 36. Wells Fargo 37. Golden Boy 39. Raffles 40. The Way of All Flesh 40. Caught in the Draft 41. Beyond the Blue Horizon 42. The Glass Key 42. The Palm Beach Story 42. For Whom the Bell Tolls 43. Frenchman's Creek 44. Ministry of Fear 44. *The Uninvited* 44. Love Letters 45. The Blue Dahlia 46. To Each His Own 47. Unconquered 47. The Big Clock 48. The Paleface 48. My Foolish Heart 49. Our Very Own 50. September Affair 50. My Favorite Spy 51. The Greatest Show on Earth 52. The Quiet Man 52. *Shane* 53. The Country Girl 54. Knock on Wood 54. Strategic Air Command 55. *Around the World in Eighty Days* 56. Omar Khayyam 57, many others.

Youngson, Robert (1917–1974). American producer specializing in compilation films. Started as writer-director of short films, including *World of Kids* (AA) 50, *This Mechanical Age* (AA) 51. Later released omnibus editions of silent comedy snippets.
The Golden Age of Comedy 58. When Comedy Was King 59. Days of Thrills and Laughter 60. Thirty Years of Fun 62, etc.

Yulin, Harris (–). American general purpose actor.
Doc 71. The Midnight Man 74. Night Moves 75, etc.

Yung, Sen (also known as **Victor Sen Yung**) (1915–). ·Chinese-American character actor familiar 1938–48 as Charlie Chan's number one son.
The Letter 40. *Across the Pacific* 42. The Breaking Point 50. The Left Hand of God 55. Flower Drum Song 61. A Flea in Her Ear 68, etc.
TV series: Bonanza 59–72.

Yurka, Blanche (1887–1974). Czech-American character actress.
Aubobiography 1970: *Bohemian Girl*.
□ *A Tale of Two Cities* 36. *Queen of the Mob* 40. Escape 40. City for Conquest 40. Ellery Queen and the Murder Ring 41. Lady for a Night 42. Pacific Rendezvous 42. A Night to Remember 42. Keeper of the Flame 43. Tonight We Raid Calais 43. Hitler's Madman 43. The Bridge of San Luis Rey 44. Cry of the Werewolf 44. One Body Too Many 44. The Southerner 45. 13 Rue Madeleine 46. The Flame 47. The Furies 50. At Sword's Point 51. Taxi 53. Thunder in the Sun 57.

Z

'Z' (France/Italy 1968). Political thrillers are rare; this one mirrored recent events in Greece and so became a *cause célèbre*. Directed in vivid hit-or-miss fashion by Costa-Gavras, it developed into a suspense situation in which the official police were eventually persuaded to investigate a murder they had been prepared to write off as an accident.

Zampa, Luigi (1905–). Italian director, formerly scriptwriter. Films, all on neo-realist lines, include *To Live in Peace* 46. *City on Trial* 52. *The Woman of Rome* 54.

Zampi, Mario (1903–1963). Italian director, long in Britain, mainly involved in semi-crazy comedies which he usually wrote and produced. The Fatal Night 48. *Laughter in Paradise* 50. Top Secret 52. Happy Ever After 54. The Naked Truth 56. Too Many Crooks 58. Five Golden Hours 61, etc.

Zanuck, Darryl F. (1902–). American production executive. Started career in twenties, writing stories for Rin Tin Tin. Production chief for Warners 1931. Co-founder 20th-Century Productions 1933; merged with Fox 1935. Vice-president in charge of production for 20th Century-Fox 1935–52, then independent; returned in 1962 as exective president.
Clive of India 35. Lloyds of London 37. In Old Chicago 38. Drums along the Mohawk 40. The Grapes of Wrath 40. How Green Was My Valley 42. Wilson 45. Gentleman's Agreement 48. All About Eve 50. Twelve O'Clock High 51. Viva Zapata 52. Island in the Sun 57. Roots of Heaven 58. The Longest Day (& d scenes) 62. Under the name Mark Canfield wrote the screenplay of *Crack in the Mirror* 60.

Zanuck, Richard (1934–). American producer who started career as assistant to his father, Darryl F. Zanuck. Solo ventures: *Compulsion* 59. *Sanctuary* 61. *The Chapman Report* 62, etc. Was vice-president in charge of production for 20th Century-Fox; moved to Warner 1971, then independent producer for Universal.

Zavattini, Cesare (1902–). Italian scriptwriter and film theorist.
Shoeshine 46. *Bicycle Thieves* 48. *Miracle in Milan* 51. First Communion 51. Umberto D 52. Gold of Naples 55. The Roof 56. Two Women 61. Marriage Italian Style 64. A Brief Vacation 75, etc.

Zazie dans le Métro (France 1960). Breakneck comedy, an up-to-date French *Hellzapoppin*, about a demoniac ten-year-old girl on the loose in Paris. A non-stop stream of cinematic trickery directed with great glee by Louis Malle.

Zecca, Ferdinand (1864–1947). French pioneer producer.
The Prodigy 01. Catastrophe in Martinique 04. Vendetta 05. Whence Does He Come? 06. Mutiny in Odessa 07. The Dreyfus Affair 08. The Dissolute Woman 10, etc.

Zeffirelli, Franco (1922–). Italian stage director turning to films.
□ The Taming of the Shrew 66. Romeo and Juliet 68. Brother Sun and Sister Moon 73. *Jesus of Nazareth* (TV) 77.

Zeman, Karel (1910–). Czech producer-director of trick and fantasy films of which the best known internationally are *Journey to Primeval Times* 55 and *Baron Münchhausen* 61.

Zerbe, Anthony (–). American character actor.
Will Penny 67. The Liberation of L. B. Jones 69. Cotton Comes To Harlem 70. Farewell My Lovely 75, etc.

Zéro de Conduite (France 1933). A nightmarish fantasy of schoolboy life, directed in surrealist vein by Jean Vigo. Music by Maurice Jaubert, photographed by Boris Kaufmann.

Zetterling, Mai (1925–). Capable Swedish leading lady in Britain.
Frenzy 44. *Frieda* 47. The Bad Lord Byron 48. *Quartet* 48. Knock on Wood 54. A Prize of Gold 55. Seven Waves Away 56. *Only Two Can Play*

62. The Main Attraction 62. The Bay of St Michael 63, etc.
□ AS DIRECTOR: The War Game 62. Loving Couples 64. Night Games 66. Doctor Glas 68. Visions of Eight (part) 73.

Ziegfeld, Florenz (1867–1932). American Broadway impresario who had three films named after him (*The Great Ziegfeld, Ziegfeld Girl, Ziegfeld Follies*). He was impersonated in two of them by William Powell and in *Funny Girl* by Walter Pidgeon. He also 'supervised' 1929's *Glorifying the American Girl*.
Biography 1973: *Ziegfeld* by Charles Higham.

Ziegfeld Follies (US 1944; released 1946). Spectacular plotless musical revue 'inspired' by the great showman Florenz Ziegfeld (glimpsed in Heaven in the person of William Powell.) Several MGM performers are seen at or near their best: Fred Astaire in two numbers with Lucille Bremer and a comedy dance routine with Gene Kelly, Judy Garland burlesquing a star's press interview, Lena Horne singing 'Love', etc. Mostly directed by Vincente Minnelli.

Zimbalist, Efrem Jnr (1918–). American leading man with stage experience; plays characters who inspire confidence.
House of Strangers 50. Band of Angels 57. Too Much Too Soon 58. By Love Possessed 61. A Fever in the Blood 61. The Chapman Report 62. The Reward 65. Wait Until Dark 67. Airport 75 74, etc.
TV series: 77 Sunset Strip 58–63. The F.B.I. 65–73.

Zimablist, Sam (1904–1958). American producer.
The Crowd Roars 38. Boom Town 40. King Solomon's Mines 50. Quo Vadis 51. Mogambo 53. Beau Brummell 54. Ben Hur 59 (died during production).

Zinnemann, Fred (1907–). Austrian-born director, with varied experience before coming to Hollywood in 1929. Was an extra (in *All Quiet on the Western Front*), script clerk, and director of shorts (*That Others Might Live* (AA) 38, several episodes of *Crime Does Not Pay*, etc.).
□ Kid Glove Killer 42. Eyes in the Night 42. *The Seventh Cross* 44. Little Mister Jim 46. My Brother Talks to Horses 47. The Search 48. *Act of Violence* 49. *The Men* 50. Teresa 51. *High Noon* 52. The Member of the Wedding 53. *From Here to Eternity* (AA) 53. Oklahoma 55. A Hatful of Rain 57. *The Nun's Story* 58. *The Sundowners* 60. Behold a Pale Horse 64. *A Man For All Seasons* (AA) 66. The Day of the Jackal 73. Julia 77.

Zola, Emile (1840–1902). Prolific French novelist of the seamy side. Works filmed include *Nana, La Bête Humaine* and *Thérèse Raquin*. A 1937 biopic, *The Life of Emile Zola*, starred Paul Muni and centred on Zola's participation in the Dreyfus case.

zombies originate from Haitian legend, and are generally held to be dead people brought back to life by voodoo. In movies they invariably shamble along with sightless eyes, looking pretty awful but doing no real damage. They were most convincingly displayed in Victor Halperin's 1932 *White Zombie*; other examples of the species turned up in *Revolt of the Zombies, The Zombies of Mora Tau, I Walked With a Zombie, King of the Zombies, The Ghost Breakers* (and its remake *Scared Stiff*), and *Dr Terror's House of Horrors*. The species gave its name to a strong rum punch, and one treasured memory is a movie in which the Ritz Brothers walked up to a bar and said: 'Three zombies.' 'I can see that,' said the barman, 'but what'll you have to drink?'

zoom. A lens of variable focal length, normally used for swiftly magnifying a distant object or moving rapidly away from a close one.

Zorba the Greek (Greece 1965). A zestful, uncontrolled, open-air film, written and directed by Michael Cacoyannis from a novel by Nikos Kazantzakis about a huge peasant who persuades a timid Englishman to share his joy in life even when surrounded by disaster. Marred by over-indulgent writing and an unnecessary sub-plot about a widow who is stoned to death by Cretan peasants, the film remains a pleasure to watch by virtue of Walter Lassally's photography, Mikos Theodorakis' music, and the performances of Anthony Quinn, Alan Bates and (in moderation) Lila Kedrova.

Zorina, Vera (1917–) (Eva Brigitta Hartwig). Norwegian ballet dancer and actress in American films. Now retired.
The Goldwyn Follies 39. On Your Toes 39. *I Was an Adventuress* 40. Star Spangled Rhythm 43. Follow the Boys 44.

Zorro (Don Diego de Vega). The black-garbed Robin Hood of Spanish California originated as the hero of a 1919 strip cartoon by Johnston McCulley. (Zorro, incidentally, is Spanish for fox.) Films featuring the devil-may-care righter of wrongs include *The Mark of Zorro* 20 with

Douglas Fairbanks, and its 1925 sequel *Don Q, Son of Zorro*; *The Bold Caballero* 37 with Robert Livingston; *Zorro Rides Again* 37, a serial with John Carroll; *Zorro's Fighting Legion* 39, a serial with Reed Hadley; Mamoulian's splendid remake of *The Mark of Zorro* 40, with Tyrone Power; *The Ghost of Zorro* 49, a serial with Clayton Moore; Walter Chiari in *The Sign of Zorro* 52; *Zorro the Avenger* 60 and other Disney TV films with Guy Williams; Sean Flynn in *The Sign of Zorro* 62; Frank Latimore in *Shadow of Zorro* 62; Pierre Brice in *Zorro versus Maciste* 63; George Ardisson in *Zorro at the Court of Spain* 63; Gordon Scott in *Zorro and the Three Musketeers* 63; and Alain Delon in *Zorro* 75.

Zsigmond, Vilmos (–). American cinematographer.
Deliverance 72. Images 72. The Long Goodbye 73. Scarecrow 73. Cinderella Liberty 73. The Sugarland Express 74. The Girl from Petrovka 74. Obsession 76. Close Encounters of the Third Kind 77, etc.

Zucco, George (1886–1960). Sepulchral-toned British stage actor, long in Hollywood and typecast in horror films in which he admirably exuded upper-bracket malignancy.
Autumn Crocus 30. Dreyfus 31. The Good Companions 32. The Man Who Could Work Miracles 35. Marie Antoinette 38. *The Cat and the Canary* 39. The Hunchback of Notre Dame 40. Arise My Love 40. *The Mummy's Hand* 40. *The Adventures of Sherlock Holmes* (as Moriarty) 40. Sherlock Holmes in Washington 42. The Black Swan 42. Dead Men Walk 43. The Black Raven 43. The Mad Ghoul 43. House of Frankenstein 45. Fog Island 45. Dr Renault's Secret 46. The Pirate 47. Joan of Arc 48. Madame Bovary 49. Let's Dance 50. David and Bathsheba 51. The First Legion 51, many others.

Zugsmith, Albert (1910–). American producer-director with a taste for exploitation subjects.
Written on the Wind (p) 57. The Tattered Dress (p) 57. The Incredible Shrinking Man (p) 58. Touch of Evil (p) 58. High School Confidential (d) 60. Teacher was a Sexpot (d) 60. The Private Life of Adam and Eve (d) 61. Confessions of an Opium Eater (d) 63. Fanny Hill (p) 64. Movie Star American Style (or LSD I Hate You) (d) 66. The Incredible Sex Revolution (d) 67, etc.

Zukor, Adolph (1873–1976). Hungarian-born film pioneer. Emigrated to America, became film salesman, nickelodeon owner, and independent producer (in 1913), by persuading New York stage stars James O'Neill, James K. Hackett and Minnie Maddern Fiske to appear in productions of, respectively, *The Count of Monte Cristo, The Prisoner of Zenda* and *Tess of the D'Urbervilles*. This was the start of 'Famous Players', which in 1916 merged with Jesse Lasky's production interests and later became Paramount Pictures. He remained board chairman of the latter from 1935. His autobiography, *The Public is Never Wrong*, was published in 1945. Special Academy Award 1948 'for his services to the industry over a period of forty years'. The industry's only centenarian.

Alphabetical List of Films

This is a note of all the films given individual mention in the body of the book. I should try to explain this spotlight treatment. A glance will show that these are not necessarily the best films made. They include films which were significant to the industry, in that they started trends; films which were popular enough to be frequently remade; films which began series; films which were notable milestones in the history of censorship, or which uniquely held up a mirror to reality; and some films which are simply excellent of their kind.

In a way, therefore, it is a list of films which have had impact of one kind or another, impact on the art, the industry, the audience.

I have tended not to include films until they are about five years old and can be recollected in tranquility: the fashions of the sixties and seventies have proved more than usually ephemeral.

The entries are necessarily short, and the credits and comment given are restricted to establishing the reason for the film's inclusion. The student who has found a reason to look up the film will know many ways of extending his knowledge: my aim is simply to provide a toehold.

Aan
Abie's Irish Rose
Accattone
Accent on Youth
Ace in the Hole
The Admirable Crichton
The Affairs of Anatol
The African Queen
L'Age d'Or
Alexander Nevsky
Alfie
Algiers
Alias Nick Beal
Ali Baba
Alice in Wonderland
All About Eve
All Quiet on the Western Front
All That Money Can Buy
All the King's Men
Aloma of the South Seas
The Amateur Gentleman
An American in Paris
American Madness
An American Tragedy
Anastasia

Angels with Dirty Faces
Animal Farm
Anna and the King of Siam
Anna Christie
Anna Karenina
Anna Lucasta
Anne of Green Gables
A Nous la Liberté
The Apartment
Applause
Arise My Love
Arms and the Man
Around the World in Eighty Days
Arsenal
Arsenic and Old Lace
The Asphalt Jungle
L'Atalante
Atlantic
The Atonement of Gosta Berling
L'Avventura
The Awful Truth

Babes in Arms
Babes in Toyland
Baby Doll

Bachelor Mother
The Bachelor Party
Back Street
The Bad and the Beautiful
Bad Days at Black Rock
Ballad of a Soldier
Ball of Fire
Bambi
The Bandit
The Band Wagon
Bank Holiday
Barney Oldfield's Race for Life
Baron Münchhausen
The Barretts of Wimpole Street
The Bat
La Bataille du Rail
The Battle of the Somme
The Battleship Potemkin
Beau Geste
Le Beau Serge
Becket
Becky Sharp
The Beggars Opera
Belle de Jour
La Belle et la Bête
Ben Hur
Berkeley Square
The Best Man
The Best Years of Our Lives
Bicycle Thieves
The Big Heat
The Big Parade
The Big Trail
A Bill of Divorcement
The Birth of a Nation
Bitter Sweet
The Black Cat
The Blackboard Jungle
Blackmail
Blind Husbands
Blockade
Blood and Sand
Blow Up
The Blue Angel
The Bluebird
The Blue Lamp
Bonnie and Clyde
Born Free
Boudu Sauvé des Eaux
Boule de Suif
The Bowery
Boys' Town
Breathless

Brewster's Millions
The Bride of Frankenstein
The Bridge of San Luis Rey
The Bridge on the River Kwai
Brief Encounter
Bringing Up Baby
Broadway Bill
Broadway Melody
Broken Arrow
Broken Blossoms
Brother Orchid
The Brothers Karamazov
The Burmese Harp
Butch Cassidy and the Sundance Kid

Cabaret
The Cabinet of Dr Caligari
Cabin in the Sky
Cabiria
Caesar and Cleopatra
The Caine Mutiny
Camelot
Camille
Captain Blood
Carmen
Un Carnet de Bal
Carry on Sergeant
Casablanca
The Cat and the Canary
Cat Ballou
Cat People
Cavalcade
The Champ
Chang
The Charge of the Light Brigade
Charley's Aunt
Cheaper by the Dozen
The Cheat
La Chienne
The Childhood of Maxim Gorky
Children of Hiroshima
The Chinese Bungalow
Cimarron
Citizen Kane
Civilisation
Claudia
Cleopatra
Coming Thru the Rye
Confessions of a Nazi Spy
Congress Dances
A Connecticut Yankee . . .
The Constant Nymph
The Corsican Brothers

The Count of Monte Cristo
The Covered Wagon
The Cranes Are Flying
Crime Without Passion
Crossfire
The Crowd
The Crowd Roars
Cyrano de Bergerac

Daddy Longlegs
Damaged Goods
Les Dames du Bois de Boulogne
The Damned
Dangerous Moonlight
The Dark Angel
Dark Victory
Darling
David and Lisa
David Copperfield
The Dawn Patrol
Day of Wrath
Dead End
Dead of Night
Dear Ruth
Death of a Salesman
The Desert Song
Destry Rides Again
Le Diable au Corps
Les Diaboliques
A Diary for Timothy
Diary of a Chambermaid
Dinner at Eight
Docks of New York
Dr Cyclops
Dr Ehrlich's Magic Bullet
Doctor in the House
Dr Jekyll and Mr Hyde
Dr Strangelove
Doctor Zhivago
Dodsworth
La Dolce Vita
Don Juan
Don Quixote
Double Indemnity
Dracula
Drifters
Drôle de Drame
Duck Soup
Duel in the Sun

Earth
East Lynne
East of Eden

Easy Rider
Easy Street
Edouard et Caroline
Eight and a Half
El
Elephant Boy
Elmer Gantry
Elvira Madigan
Emil and the Detectives
L'Equipage
Erotikon
Escape
Escape Me Never
L'Eternel Retour
Evergreen
Executive Suite
Exodus
Extase
The Exterminating Angel

A Face in the Crowd
Fahrenheit 451
The Fallen Idol
The Fall of the House of Usher
Fanny
Fantasia
Fantomas
A Farewell to Arms
The Farmer's Daughter
Farrebique
Father Brown
Father of the Bride
La Femme du Boulanger
La Fin du Jour
Fire over England
Fires Were Started
The First of the Few
A Fistful of Dollars
Five Fingers
Five Graves to Cairo
Five Star Final
The Flag Lieutenant
Flesh and Fantasy
Flying Down to Rio
Foolish Wives
Forbidden Planet
Force of Evil
Foreign Correspondent
Forever and a Day
Forty-Ninth Parallel
42nd Street
For Whom the Bell Tolls
Four Daughters

The Four Feathers
The Four Horsemen of the Apocalypse
The Four Hundred Blows
Four Steps in the Clouds
Frankenstein
Freaks
Freud
From Here to Eternity
From This Day Forward
The Front Page
The Fugitive
Fury

The Garden of Allah
Gaslight
Gate of Hell
The General
The General Died at Dawn
The General Line
A Generation
Genevieve
Gentleman's Agreement
Gentlemen Prefer Blondes
Georgy Girl
Gerald McBoing Boing
Gervaise
The Ghost Breaker
The Ghost Goes West
The Ghost Train
Gigi
Gilda
The Glenn Miller Story
The Glorious Adventure
G Men
The Godfather
Going My Way
The Gold Rush
The Golem
Gone with the Wind
Goodbye Mr Chips
The Good Companions
The Graduate
La Grande Illusion
Grand Hotel
Le Grand Jeu
Grand Prix
The Grapes of Wrath
Grass
The Great Caruso
The Great Dictator
The Greatest Story Ever Told
Great Expectations
The Great Impersonation

The Great Race
The Great Train Robbery
The Great Ziegfeld
Greed
Green Pastures
Greyfriars Bobby
The Group
Guess Who's Coming to Dinner
Gunfight at the OK Corral
Gunga Din

Hallelujah
Hamlet
The Hands of Orlac
Harvey
Heaven Can Wait
Heavens Above
The Heiress
Hell's Angels
Hellzapoppin
Henry V
Here Comes Mr Jordan
High Noon
High Sierra
The Hill
Hindle Wakes
Hiroshima Mon Amour
Hobson's Choice
Holiday
House of Wax
The House on 92nd Street
How Green was My Valley
How the West was Won
How to Marry a Millionaire
Hud
Hue and Cry
The Hunchback of Notre Dame
The Hustler

I Am a Fugitive from a Chain Gang
I Claudius
Idiot's Delight
If . . .
If I Had a Million
If I Were King
If Winter Comes
I'm All Right Jack
I Married a Witch
The Informer
Inherit the Wind
The Inn of the Sixth Happiness
Intermezzo
In the Heat of the Night

Intolerance
Invasion of the Body Snatchers
The Invisible Man
Invitation to the Dance
In Which We Serve
The Ipcress File
An Italian Straw Hat
It Always Rains on Sunday
It Happened Here
It Happened One Night
It's a Mad Mad Mad Mad World
It's a Wonderful Life
Ivan the Terrible

Jane Eyre
The Jazz Singer
Les Jeux Interdits
Jew Süss
Jour de Fête
Journal d'un Curé de Campagne
Journey into Fear
Journey to the Centre of the Earth
Journey's End
Le Jour se Lève
Joyless Street
Judex
Judge Priest
Jules et Jim
Jungle Jim
The Jungle Princess
Justice est Faite

La Kermesse Héroïque
Key Largo
Kid Galahad
The Killers
Kind Hearts and Coronets
A Kind of Loving
King Kong
King of Jazz
King of Kings
King Solomon's Mines
King's Row
Kipps
Kismet
Kiss Me Deadly
Kiss Me Kate
Kiss of Death
The Knack

The Lady Eve
Lady for a Day
The Lady from Shanghai

Lady in the Dark
The Lady in the Lake
Lady Killer
The Ladykillers
The Lady Vanishes
The Lady with a Little Dog
The Last Chance
The Last Days of Pompeii
The Last Hurrah
The Last Laugh
The Last of the Mohicans
The Last Picture Show
Last Year in Marienbad
The Lavender Hill Mob
Lawrence of Arabia
Leaves from Satan's Book
The Letter
Letter from an Unknown Woman
Liebelei
The Life and Death of Colonel Blimp
Lifeboat
The Life of Emile Zola
Life Upside Down
Lights of New York
Lil Abner
Liliom
Limelight
The Lion in Winter
Listen to Britain
Little Caesar
The Little Foxes
Little Lord Fauntleroy
Little Women
Living
The Living Desert
Lola Montez
London Town
Lord Jim
Lost Horizon
The Last Patrol
The Lost Weekend
The Lost World
The Loved One
Love Me Tonight
The Love Parade
The Lower Depths

M
Macbeth
Madame De
Madame du Barry
Madame X
The Magic Box

The Magnificent Ambersons
Magnificent Obsession
The Magnificent Seven
Major Barbara
The Maltese Falcon
Mandy
A Man For All Seasons
Manhunt
The Man in Grey
The Man in the Iron Mask
The Man in the White Suit
Man of Aran
The Man Who Came to Dinner
The Man Who Knew Too Much
The Man with the Golden Arm
Marius
The Marriage Circle
La Marseillaise
Marty
Mary Poppins
M*A*S*H*
The Mask of Dimitrios
Mata Hari
A Matter of Life and Death
Matt Helm
Mayerling
Meet John Doe
Meet Me in St Louis
The Men
The Merry Widow
Merton of the Movies
Metropolis
Michael Strogoff
Midnight Cowboy
A Midsummer Night's Dream
Le Million
Mine Own Executioner
Miracle in Milan
The Miracle of Morgan's Creek
Miracle on 34th Street
Miranda
Les Misérables
The Misfits
Mission to Moscow
Miss Julie
Mrs Miniver
Mrs Wiggs of the Cabbage Patch
Mr Blandings Builds His Dream House
Mr Smith Goes to Washington
Moby Dick
Modern Times
Mondo Cane
Monsieur Beaucaire

Monsieur Hulot's Holiday
The Moon and Sixpence
The Moon is Blue
The More the Merrier
Morgan
Morning Glory
Morocco
The Most Dangerous Game
Moulin Rouge
The Musketeers of Pig Alley
Mutiny on the Bounty
My Darling Clementine
My Fair Lady
My Girl Tisa
My Little Chickadee
My Man Godfrey
My Sister Eileen

Naked City
Nanook of the North
The Navigator
Nell Gwyn
Never Give a Sucker an Even Break
Never on Sunday
Next of Kin
A Night at the Opera
Night Mail
Night Must Fall
The Night of the Demon
The Night of the Hunter
Ninotchka
North by Northwest
Northwest Passage
Nothing But the Truth
Nothing Sacred
The Nun's Story

Objective Burma
Occupe-Toi d'Amélie
October
Odd Man Out
Of Human Bondage
Of Mice and Men
Oh Mr Porter
Oh What a Lovely War
The Old Dark House
Oliver Twist
Los Olvidados
On Approval
One Hundred and One Dalmatians
One Million BC
One Sunday Afternoon
One Two Three

One Way Passage
Onibaba
On the Beach
On the Town
On the Waterfront
Open City
Orphée
Our Daily Bread
The Outlaw
Outward Bound
The Overlanders
The Ox Bow Incident

The Pajama Game
The Paleface
Les Parents Terribles
Paris Qui Dort
Une Partie de Campagne
The Passing of the Third Floor Back
Le Passion de Jeanne D'Arc
Passport to Pimlico
Pather Panchali
Paths of Glory
The Pawnbroker
Peg O'My Heart
People on Sunday
The Perils of Pauline
The Petrified Forest
Peyton Place
The Phantom of the Opera
The Philadelphia Story
Picnic
The Picture of Dorian Gray
The Pink Panther
Pinky
The Pirate
A Place in the Sun
The Plainsman
Planet of the Apes
Poil de Carotte
Portrait of Jennie
The Poseidon Adventure
Pride and Prejudice
The Prince and the Pauper
The Prisoner of Zenda
The Private Life of Henry VIII
Private's Progress
Psycho
Public Enemy
The Pumpkin Eater
Pygmalion

Quai des Brumes

Queen Christina
Queen Kelly
The Queen of Spades
Que Viva Mexico
The Quiet Man
Quo Vadis

Rain
The Rains Came
Ramona
Random Harvest
Rashomon
Rear Window
Rebecca
Rebecca of Sunnybrook Farm
Rebel without a Cause
The Red Badge of Courage
The Red Balloon
Red Dust
Red Garters
The Red Inn
The Red Shoes
La Règle du Jeu
Rembrandt
Repulsion
Richard III
Rififi
The River
Road to Singapore
The Robe
Robinson Crusoe
Rocco and His Brothers
Rome Express
La Ronde
Rookery Nook
Room at the Top
Room Service
Rope
Rose Marie
Roxie Hart
Ruggles of Red Gap
Ryan's Daughter

San Francisco
Le Sang d'Un Poète
Saturday Night and Sunday Morning
The Savage Eye
Sawdust and Tinsel
Sayonara
Scaramouche
Scarface
The Scarlet Empress
The Scarlet Letter

The Scarlet Pimpernel
Scarlet Street
Scrooge
The Sea Hawk
The Seashell and the Clergyman
The Sea Wolf
Seven Brides for Seven Brothers
Seven Days in May
Seven Keys to Baldpate
Seven Samurai
Seventh Heaven
The Seventh Seal
Shadow of a Doubt
Shadows
Shane
Shanghai Express
She
The Sheik
She Only Danced One Summer
Ship of Fools
The Shop around the Corner
Shopworn Angel
Siegfried
Sing As We Go
The Singing Fool
Singin' in the Rain
Sir Arne's Treasure
Sitting Pretty
Smilin' Through
The Snake Pit
Snow White and the Seven Dwarfs
The Song of Bernadette
Song of Ceylon
Sons and Lovers
Sons of the Desert
Sorrell and Son
The Sound of Music
Sous les Toits de Paris
The Southerner
Spellbound
The Spiral Staircase
The Spoilers
Spring in Park Lane
The Spy Who Came in from the Cold
The Squaw Man
Squibs
Stagecoach
Star!
A Star is Born
State Fair
Stella Dallas
The Sting
Storm Over Asia

The Story of Louis Pasteur
Strange Interlude
The Student of Prague
The Student Prince
Sullivan's Travels
Summertime
Sunrise
Sunset Boulevard
Suspicion
Svengali
Sweet Smell of Success
The Swiss Family Robinson

A Tale of Two Cities
Tales of Hoffman
Tales of Manhattan
Target for Tonight
A Taste of Honey
The Ten Commandments
La Terra Trema
Thank Your Lucky Stars
These Three
They Won't Forget
The Thief of Baghdad
The Thing from Another World
Things to Come
The Thin Man
The Third Man
The Thirty-Nine Steps
This Gun for Hire
Those Magnificent Men in Their Flying Machines
Three Coins in the Fountain
The Three Musketeers
Three Smart Girls
Thunder Rock
Thy Soul Shall Bear Witness
Tobacco Road
To Be or Not to Be
To Have and Have Not
Tokyo Olympiad
Tol'able David
Tom Brown's Schooldays
Tom Jones
Top Hat
Topper
Tower of London
The Towering Inferno
Track of the Cat
Trader Horn
The Trial
The Trail of the Lonesome Pine
Treasure Island
Triumph of the Will

Trouble in Paradise
The Trouble with Harry
The True Glory
Turn of the Tide
Twelve Angry Men
Twelve O'Clock High
Twenty Thousand Years in Sing Sing
2001: A Space Odyssey

Ugetsu Monogatari
Ulysses
Umberto D
The Umbrellas of Cherbourg
Uncle Tom's Cabin
Under Two Flags
Underworld
Unfaithfully Yours
The Uninvited

Valley of the Dolls
Variety
Victim
The Victors
The Virginian
Viridiana
Les Visiteurs du Soir

The Wages of Fear
War and Peace
Warning Shadows
The War of the Worlds
Waterloo Bridge

Waterloo Road
The Way Ahead
Way Down East
The Way to the Stars
West Side Story
Whisky Galore
The Whisperers
Whistling in the Dark
White Cargo
White Heat
White Shadows in the South Seas
Who's Afraid of Virginia Woolf?
The Wild One
Wild Strawberries
Wings
Witchcraft through the Ages
The Wizard of Oz
A Woman of Paris
Woman of the Dunes
Woman to Woman
The Women
World of Plenty
Wuthering Heights

A Yank at Oxford
Yankee Doodle Dandy
You Can't Take It with You

'Z'
Zazie dans le Métro
Zéro de Conduite
Ziegfeld Follies
Zorba the Greek

Alphabetical List of Fictional Screen Characters and Series

The following are noted in the main text:

Ali Baba
Arsène Lupin
Arthur
Betty Boop
Blondie
Bomba
Bonzo
Boston Blackie
The Bowery Boys
Bugs Bunny
Bulldog Drummond
Carry On
Casper
Charlie Chan
The Cohens and the Kellys
The Cisco Kid
The Creature from the Black Lagoon
The Crime Doctor
Crime Does Not Pay
Dead End Kids
Dick Tracy
Dr Kildare
Dr Mabuse
Donald Duck
Dracula
Ellery Queen
The Falcon
Flash Gordon
The Fly
Francis
Frankenstein
Fu Manchu
Gerald McBoing Boing
Gertie the Dinosaur
Gidget
Godzilla
Gold Diggers
The Hardy Family
Henry Aldrich

Hopalong Cassidy
Huckleberry Finn
The Invisible Man
Jack the Ripper
James Bond
Joe Palooka
The Jones Family
Jungle Jim
The Kettles
The Keystone Kops
The Lone Ranger
The Lone Wolf
Looney Tunes
Maciste
Maisie
The March of Time
Matt Helm
Mexican Spitfire
Michael Shayne
Mr Magoo
Mr Moto
Mr Wong
The Mummy
Nancy Drew
Old Mother Riley
Our Gang
Passing Parade
Penrod
Pete Smith Specialties
Philip Marlowe
Philo Vance
Planet of the Apes
Popeye
Robin Hood
Robinson Crusoe
The Saint
St Trinian's
Scattergood Baines
Sexton Blake

Sherlock Holmes
Squibs
Superman
Sylvester
Tarzan
The Thin Man
This Modern Age
Tom and Jerry

Tom Sawyer
Torchy Blane
Tugboat Annie
The Whistler
Why We Fight
William
Woody Woodpecker
Zorro

Alphabetical List of Themes Explored

Please check these headings in the text for notes on the use of the subjects listed in films past and present, with examples.

Abortion
Actor-directors
Actors
Addresses
Advertising
Air balloons
Airplanes
Alcoholics
All star films
Amnesia
Anachronisms
Ancient Egypt
Angels
Animals
Anti-Semitism
Arabian Nights
Army comedies
Automobiles
Babies
Backstage
Bad language
Ballet
Baseball
Bathtubs
Berlin
The Bible
Bigamists
Big business
Birds
Black comedy
Blindness
Boffins
Boo-boos
Boxing
The British Empire
Brothels
Bullfights
Burlesque

Buses
Butlers
Case histories
The Chase
Child stars
Christ
Christmas
Churches
Circuses
Clairvoyance
Coal mines
The Cold War
Colour
Colour sequences
Comedy teams
Comic strips
Communism
Compilation films
Composers
Concentration camps
Concerts
Confidence tricksters
Courtesans
Courtroom scenes
Crazy comedy
Criminals
Custard pies
Deaf mutes
Death
Dentists
Department stores
Desert islands
Deserts
The Devil
Devil's island
Directors' appearances
Disguise
Doctors

Documentary
Dreams
Drug addiction
Drunk scenes
Dubbing
Duels
The Electric Chair
Elephants
The End of the World
Enoch Arden
Entertainers
Epidemics
Episodic films
Excerpts
Explorers
Falling
Families
Fantasy
Fire
Firing squads
Flashbacks
Fog
The Foreign Legion
Forest Fires
Funerals
Fun fairs
Gambling
Gangsters
Giants
Gimmicks
Governesses
The Guillotine
Gypsies
Hands
Helicopters
Hillbillies
Hollywood on film
homosexuality

Horror
Hospitals
Hotels
Houses
Hypnosis
Impresarios
India
In-jokes
Insanity
Insects
Inventors
Ireland
Jewel thieves
Jews
Kidnapping
Kings and Queens
Labour relations
Leprechauns
Lesbianism
Letters
Lifts (elevators)
Light comedies
London
Los Angeles
Lynch law
Mafia
Magicians
Mau Mau
Miniaturization
Mirrors
Monks
Monster animals
Mother love
Motor cycles
Motor racing
Multiple roles
Mountains
Multiple story films
Murderers
Musical remakes
Musicals
Mystery
Narrators
Naval comedy
Negroes
New York
Nuns
Nurses
Nymphomaniacs
Offices

Old age
Opera singers
Orchestral conductors
Painters
Paris
Parody
Parties
Pirates
Plastic surgery
Police
Politics
Poverty
Pre-credits sequences
Priests
Prison
Prisoners of war
Private eyes
Prophecy
Prostitutes
Psychology
Railway stations
Rain
Rape
Red Indians
Reincarnation
Religion
Reporters
Robberies
Robots
Romantic teams
Rome
Sailors
San Francisco
Satire
Schooldays
Scientists
Seances
Seaside resorts
Serials
Series
Servants
Sewers
Sex
Sex change
Ships
Skiing
Slapstick
Small town
Smoking
Smugglers

Social comedy
Social conscience
Space exploration
Spanish Civil War
Spies
Sportsmen
Staircases
Statesmen
Statues
Storms
Strikes
Student protest
Stunt men
Submarines
Suicide
Swinging London
Teachers
Telephones
Television
Television movies
Television series
Tennis
Theatres
3-D
Tinting
Title changes
Torture
Trains
Tramps (hoboes)
Transvestism
Uncredited appearances
Underground railways
Undertakers (morticians)
Underwater scenes
Unemployment
Universities
Venice
Ventriloquists
Vigilantes
Violence
Volcanoes
War heroes
Waxworks
Weddings
Westerns
Wheelchairs
Witchcraft
World War I
Writers
Zombies

List of Title Changes

This list replaces and amplifies the rather amorphous essay which appeared in the last edition. It is in two parts: the first gives alphabetically those American titles which have been changed in Britain, with the changed title opposite; the second list shows British titles which were changed in America. The reasons for many changes should be sufficiently obvious to provide some amusement.

American to British

Aaron Slick from Punkin Crick	Marshmallow Moon
Abbott and Costello Meet Frankenstein	Abbott and Costello Meet the Ghosts
Abe Lincoln in Illinois	Spirit of the People
Advance to the Rear	Company of Cowards?
Adventure in Baltimore	Bachelor Bait
Adventure in Washington	Female Correspondent
All American	The Winning Way
Alleghany Uprising	The First Rebel
All Mine to Give	The Day They Gave Babies Away
America, America	The Anatolian Smile
An American Dream	See You in Hell, Darling
American Empire	My Son Alone
An American Guerilla in the Philippines	I Shall Return
And Then There Were None	Ten Little Niggers
Angels in the Outfield	Angels and the Pirates
The Animal Kingdom	The Woman in His House
An Annapolis Story	The Blue and the Gold
Any Wednesday	Bachelor Girl Apartment
The Ape Man	Lock Your Doors
The Appaloosa	Southwest to Sonora
Artists and Models Abroad	Stranded in Paris
The Astounding She-Monster	Mysterious Invader
At Sword's Point	Sons of the Musketeers
Attack of the Giant Leeches	Demons of the Swamp
The Bachelor and the Bobbysoxer	Bachelor Knight
The Bachelor's Daughters	Bachelor Girls
The Bad Man	Two Gun Cupid
The Bank Dick	The Bank Detective
The Bar Sinister	It's a Dog's Life
Bend of the River	Where the River Bends
Bengal Brigade	Bengal Rifles
BF's Daughter	Polly Fulton
The Big Boodle	Affair in Havana

Big Hand for a Little Lady	Big Deal at Dodge City
The Big Land	Stampeded
Blonde Crazy	Larceny Lane
Blood of Dracula	Blood is My Heritage
Blue Denim	Blue Jeans
The Bob Matthias Story	The Flaming Torch
Bombers B-52	No Sleep till DThe
Born to Kill	Lady of Deceit
The Bottom of the Bottle	Beyond the River
The Brasher Doubloon	The High Window
Bright Victory	Lights Out
Broadway Bill	Strictly Confidential
Broadway Limited	The Baby Vanishes
Buck Privates	Rookies
Buck Privates Come Home	Rookies Come Home
Buckskin Frontier	The Iron Road
Callaway Went Thataway	The Star Said No
Caper of the Golden Bulls	Carnival of Thieves
Captain Carey USA	After Midnight
Captain John Smith and Pocahontas	Burning Arrows
Castle on the Hudson	Years without Days
The Catered Affair	Wedding Breakfast
Cattle King	Guns of Wyoming
The Chairman	The Most Dangerous Man in the World
Chicago Masquerade	Little Egypt
Chief Crazy Horse	Valley of Fury
The Children's Hour	The Loudest Whisper
Christmas in Connecticut	Indiscretion
Circus World	The Magnificent Showman
Claudelle Inglish	Young and Eager
The Clock	Under the Clock
The Cockeyed Miracle	Mr Griggs Returns
Colonel Effingham's Raid	Man of the Hour
Confessions of an Opium Eater	Evil of Chinatown
Conquest	Marie Walewska
Convicts Four	Reprieve
The Corpse Vanishes	The Case of the Missing Brides
The Corrupt Ones	The Peking Medallion
Corvette K225	The Nelson Touch
Count the Hours	Every Minute Counts
The Court Martial of Billy Mitchell	One Man Mutiny
Crime Wave	The City is Dark
Cry Uncle	Super Dick
Curtain Call at Cactus Creek	Take the Stage
Damn Yankees	What Lola Wants
Dancing Co-Ed	Every Other Inch a Lady
Darby's Rangers	The Young Invaders
Dark Delusion	Cynthia's Secret
Darling How Could You?	Rendezvous
Deadline USA	Deadline
Dead Ringer	Dead Image

Dementia 13	The Haunted and the Hunted
Desk Set	His Other Woman
Dial 1119	The Violent Hour
Dino	Killer Dino
Dollars ($)	The Heist
The Doolins of Oklahoma	The Great Manhunt
Dragstrip Riot	The Reckless Age
Dressed to Kill	Sherlock Holmes and the Secret Code
Duck, You Sucker	A Fistful of Dynamite
Edge of Doom	Stronger than Fear
Edge of the City	A Man is Ten Feet Tall
Eight on the Lam	Eight on the Run
El Alamein	Desert Attack
The Enforcer	Murder Inc.
Experiment in Terror	The Grip of Fear
The Falcon Takes Over	The Gay Falcon
Fargo	Wild Seed
The Fearless Vampire Killers	Dance of the Vampires
The First Time	You Don't Need Pajamas at Rosie's
First Yank into Tokyo	Hidden Secret
Five and Ten	Daughter of Luxury
Flap	The Last Warrior
Flat Top	Eagles of the Fleet
The Flim Flam Man	One Born Every Minute
Fool's Parade	Dynamite Man from Glory Jail
The Fortune Cookie	Meet Whiplash Willie
The Fortune Hunter	The Outcast
Framed	Paula
Frankenstein Versus the Space Monsters	Duel of the Space Monsters
The Freshman	College Days
Frontier Gal	The Bride Wasn't Willing
The Fuller Brush Girl	The Affairs of Sally
Gaily, Gaily	Chicago, Chicago
The Gang's All Here	The Girls He Left Behind
Gaslight	The Murder in Thornton Square
A Girl, a Guy and a Gob	The Navy Steps Out
The Girl from Missouri	One Hundred Per Cent Pure
The Girl in White	So Bright the Flame
Girls in the Night	Life After Dark
Gobs and Gals	Cruising Casanovas
Go into Your Dance	Casino de Paree
Great Guy	Pluck of the Irish
The Great John L	A Man Called Sullivan
The Great McGinty	Down Went McGinty
Hallelujah I'm a Bum	Hallelujah I'm a Tramp
The Hard-Boiled Canary	Hearts in Springtime
Harper	The Moving Target
The Hatchet Man	The Honourable Mr Wong
The Heat's On	Tropicana

The Helen Morgan Story	Both Ends of the Candle
The Hideous Sun Demon	Blood on His Lips
Hold That Co-Ed	Hold That Gal
Honeymoon	Two Men and a Girl
The Hot Rock	How to Steal a Diamond in Four Uneasy Lessons
Hot Rod Gang	Fury Unleashed
House of Horrors	Joan Medford is Missing
The House of Usher	The Fall of the House of Usher
The Howards of Virginia	The Tree of Liberty
I Am a Fugitive from a Chain Gang	I Am a Fugitive
I Can Get It for You Wholesale	This is My Affair
Icecapades Revue	Rhythm Hits the Ice
I Dood It	By Hook or by Crook
I Jane Doe	Diary of a Bride
I'll Never Forget You	The House on the Square
I Married a Communist	The Woman on Pier 13
I, Mobster	The Mobster
The Imperfect Lady	Mrs Loring's Secret
Indianapolis Speedway	Devils on Wheels
Indiscretion of an American Wife	Indiscretion
Intermezzo	Escape to Happiness
Internes Can't Take Money	You Can't Take Money
It Ain't Hay	Money from Home
It's In the Bag	The Fifth Chair
I've Always Loved You	Concerto
I Wake Up Screaming	Hot Spot
I Was a Male War Bride	You Can't Sleep Here
Jim Thorpe All-American	Man of Bronze
Joan of the Ozarks	The Queen of Spies
Joe Smith — American	Highway to Freedom
Johnny Vagabond	Johnny Come Lately
The Judge Steps Out	Indian Summer
Kansas City Confidential	The Secret Four
The Killer That Stalked New York	Frightened City
King of the Roaring Twenties	The Big Bankroll
Kiss the Blood off My Hands	Blood on My Hands
Lady from Boston	Pardon My French
Lady of Burlesque	Striptease Lady
Lafayette Escadrille	Hell Bent for Glory
The Land We Love	Hero's Island
The Last Challenge	Pistolero of Red River
Last of the Comanches	The Sabre and the Arrow
Leathernecking	Present Arms
Let 'Em Have It	False Faces
Lilac Time	Love Never Dies
Little Big Horn	The Fighting Seventh
Little Egypt	Chicago Masquerade
The Little Giant	On the Carpet
London after Midnight	The Hypnotist

Lord Jeff	The Boy from Barnardo's
Love from a Stranger (1946)	A Stranger Walked In
Love is a Ball	All This and Money Too
A Lovely Way to Die	A Lovely Way to Go
Lured	Personal Column
The McConnell Story	Tiger in the Sky
The Mad Doctor	A Date with Destiny
Mad Love	The Hands of Orlac
The Magnificent Matador	The Brave and the Beautiful
The Magnificent Yankee	The Man with Thirty Sons
Mail Order Bride	West of Montana
Malaya	East of the Rising Sun
Manfish	Calypso
Man in the Shadow	Pay the Devil
Man Made Monster	The Electric Man
Man on a String	Confessions of a Counterspy
The Man Who Played God	The Silent Voice
The Man with the Gun	The Trouble Shooter
The Midnight Story	Appointment with a Shadow
Million Dollar Mermaid	The One Piece Bathing Suit
Miss Grant Takes Richmond	Innocence is Bliss
Mission over Korea	Eyes of the Skies
Mister Buddwing	Woman without a Face
Mr Imperium	You Belong to My Heart
Mr Winkle Goes to War	Arms and the Woman
The Mob	Remember that Face
Models Inc.	That Kind of Girl
The Most Dangerous Game	The Hounds of Zaroff
Mother is a Freshman	Mother Knows Best
Murder My Sweet	Farewell My Lovely
Navy Wife	Mother, Sir
Never Give a Sucker an Even Break	What a Man
Never Wave at a WAC	The Private Wore Shirts
The New Centurions	Precinct 45 – Los Angeles Police
The Night They Raided Minsky's	The Night They Invented Striptease
No Man is an Island	Island Rescue
No Place to Land	Man Mad
Northwest Outpost	End of the Rainbow
Off Limits	Military Policemen
Okay America	Penalty of Fame
One Million Years BC	Man and His Mate
Our Daily Bread	The Miracle of Life
Out of the Past	Build My Gallows High
Pardon Us	Jailbirds
Paris Underground	Madame Pimpernel
The Perfect Furlough	Strictly for Pleasure
Perfect Strangers	Too Dangerous to Love
Personal Property	The Man in Possession
The Petty Girl	Girl of the Year

Pick-Up on 101	Echos of the Road
Pillars of the Sky	The Tomahawk and the Cross
PJ	New Face in Hell
Platinum High School	Rich, Young and Deadly
Pony Soldier	McDonald of the Canadian Mounties
The Poppy is also a Flower	Danger Grows Wild
Pot O'Gold	The Golden Hour
The Powers Girl	Hello Beautiful
The President Vanishes	The Strange Conspiracy
Pride of the Marines	Forever in Love
Private Number	Secret Interlude
Professional Sweetheart	Imaginary Sweetheart
Public Enemy	Enemies of the Public
Public Enemy's Wife	G-Man's Wife
The Racers	Such Men Are Dangerous
Raton Pass	Canyon Pass
Requiem for a Heavyweight	Blood Money
Revenge for the Colossal Man	The Terror Strikes
Romance on the High Seas	It's Magic
Royal African Rifles	Storm Over Africa
The Royal Bed	The Queen's Husband
A Royal Scandal	Czarina
Royal Wedding	Wedding Bells
Saskatchewan	O'Rourke of the Royal Mounted
Satan Never Sleeps	The Devil Never Sleeps
Saturday's Hero	Idols in the Dust
Savage Wilderness	The Last Frontier
Scandal Sheet	The Dark Page
Scudda Hoo Scudda Hay	Summer Lightning
The Second Woman	Ellen
She Couldn't Say No	Beautiful but Dangerous
She Wolf of London	The Curse of the Allenbys
Smash-Up	A Woman Destroyed
S.N.A.F.U.	Welcome Home
Sob Sister	The Blonde Reporter
So Goes My Love	A Genius in the Family
Sol Madrid	The Heroin Hang
Something for Everyone	Black Flowers for the Bride
Son of Slade	Texas Rose
Sons of the Desert	Fraternally Yours
Sorority Girl	The Bad One
Sorority House	The Girl from College
A Southern Yankee	My Hero
South of Tahiti	White Savage
South Sea Sinner	East to Java
Southwest Passage	Camels West
Spinout	California Holiday
Stage to Tucson	Lost Stage Valley
Stars and Stripes Forever	Marching Along
State of the Union	The World and His Wife
Step down to Terror	The Silent Stranger

The Sterile Cuckoo | Pookie
The Story of Seabiscuit | Pride of Kentucky
The Story of Alexander Graham Bell | The Modern Miracle
Strange Interlude | Strange Interval
The Strange One | End as a Man
The Stripper | Woman of Summer
Summer Stock | If You Feel Like Singing
Summertime | Summer Madness
The Sundowners (1950) | Thunder in the Dust
Susan and God | The Gay Mrs Trexel
Swamp Water | The Man Who Came Back
Swashbuckler | The Scarlet Buccaneer
Swing Shift Maisie | The Girl in Overalls
Synanon | Get off My Back

Take a Letter, Darling | Green Eyed Woman
Take Me Out to the Ball Game | Everybody's Cheering
Tank Commandos | Tank Commando
Tarzan's Peril | Tarzan and the Jungle Queen
Teenage Caveman | Out of the Darkness
Tennessee Johnson | The Man on America's Conscience
That Forsyte Woman | The Forsyte Saga
That Hamilton Woman | Lady Hamilton
That's My Man | Will Tomorrow Ever Come?
They Shall Have Music | Melody of Youth
Thin Ice | Lovely to Look At
This is My Affair | His Affair
This Thing Called Love | Married but Single
Those Daring Young Men in Their Jaunty Jalopies | Monte Carlo or Bust
Three Daring Daughters | The Birds and the Bees
Three Stripes in the Sun | The Gentle Sergeant
Three Weeks | Romance of a Queen
Thunder in the Valley | Bob, Son of Battle
Thundercloud | Colt 45
Thunder on the Hill | Bonaventure
Tomahawk | Battle of Powder River
Too Many Husbands | My Two Husbands
Top Secret Affair | Their Secret Affair
The Torch | Bandit General
Toward the Unknown | Brink of Hell
The Trap | The Baited Trap
T. R. Baskin | A Date with a Lonely Girl
Tribes | The Soldier Who Declared Peace
Troubles for Two | The Suicide Club
The True Story of Jesse James | The James Brothers
Try and Get Me | The Sound of Fury
Twenty Plus Two | It Started in Tokyo
Twilight of Honor | The Charge is Murder
Two Girls on Broadway | Choose Your Partner
Two Guys from Milwaukee | Royal Flush
Two Guys from Texas | The Texas Knights
Two Loves | Spinster

Underworld (1927) — Paying the Penalty
The Undying Monster — The Hammond Mystery

Vice Squad — The Girl in Room 17
The View from Pompey's Head — Secret Interlude
The Violent Men — Rough Company
Von Richthofen and Brown — The Red Baron

The WAC from Walla Walla — Army Capers
Waco — The Outlaw and the Lady
Walk East on Beacon — The Crime of the Century
Washington Story — Target for Scandal
West Point Story — Fine and Dandy
What a Woman — The Beautiful Cheat
The Wheeler Dealers — Separate Beds
When You're in Love — For You Alone
The Whistle at Eaton Falls — Richer than the Earth
White Savage — White Captive
Who Killed Doc Robbin? — Sinister House
The Whole Town's Talking — Passport to Fame
The Wife Takes a Flyer — A Yank in Dutch
Will Success Spoil Rock Hunter? — Oh! For a Man
Wings of the Eagle — The Wings of Eagles
Witchfinder General — The Conqueror Worm
A Woman's Devotion — War Hunt

A Yank in Indo China — Hidden Secret
Young Man with a Horn — Young Man of Music
The Young Philadelphians — The City Jungle

Zenobia — Elephants Never Forget
ZigZag — False Witness

British to American

The Admirable Crichton — Paradise Lagoon
The Adventurers — Fortune in Diamonds
Albert R. N. — Break for Freedom
The Amorous Prawn — The Playgirl and the War Minister
Appointment with Venus — Island Rescue

Background — Edge of Divorce
Ballad in Blue — Values for Lovers
Barnacle Bill — All at Sea
The Battle of the River Plate — Pursuit of the Graf Spee
Beat Girl — Wild for Kicks
The Beauty Jungle — Contest Girl
Before I Wake — Shadow of Fear
Beyond This Place — Web of Evidence
Blind Terror — See No Evil
Brighton Rock — Young Scarface
Britannia Mews — The Forbidden Street
Bulldog Jack — Alias Bulldog Drummond

Busman's Honeymoon	Haunted Honeymoon
Captain Clegg	Night Creatures
The Card	The Promoter
Carleton Browne of the F.O.	Man in a Cocked Hat
Catch Us if You Can	Having a Wild Weekend
The Chiltern Hundreds	The Amazing Mr Beecham
City of the Dead	Horror Hotel
City Under the Sea	War Gods of the Deep
Cone of Silence	Trouble in the Sky
Conflict of Wings	Fuss over Feathers
Contraband	Blackout
Cosh Boy	The Slasher
Country Dance	Brotherly Love
The Courtneys of Curzon St	The Courtney Affair
The Criminal	The Concrete Jungle
Crooks and Coronets	Sophie's Place
Cry the Beloved Country	African Fury
Danger Within	Breakout
Dangerous Moonlight	Suicide Squadron
The Dark Avenger	The Warriors
Dark Eyes of London	The Human Monster
Dark of the Sun	The Mercenaries
The Day will Dawn	The Avengers
Dear Octopus	The Randolph Family
Derby Day	Four Against Fate
The Dock Brief	Trial and Error
Downhill	Why Boys Leave Home
The Elusive Pimpernel	The Fighting Pimpernel
English without Tears	Her Man Gilbey
Escapement	The Elecronic Monster
Fanatic	Die Die My Darling
Fanny by Gaslight	Man of Evil
Farewell Again	Troopship
Father Brown	The Detective
The First of the Few	Spitfire
The Foreman Went to France	Somewhere in France
49th Parallel	The Invaders
Fortune is a Woman	She Played with Fire
The Four Just Men	The Secret Four
The Full Treatment	Stop Me Before I Kill
Gaslight	Angel Street
Gideon's Day	Gideon of Scotland Yard
The Gift Horse	Glory at Sea
The Girl in the Headlines	The Model Murder Case
Give Us This Day	Salt of the Earth
Golden Arrow	The Gay Adventure
The Grace Moore Story	So This is Love
Grand National Night	Wicked Wife

The Greengage Summer	Loss of Innocence
The Guinea Pig	The Outsider
The Hands of Orlac	Hands of a Strangler
Happy Ever After	Tonight's the Night
The Happy Family	Mr Lord Says No
Her Favourite Husband	The Taming of Dorothy
The High Bright Sun	McGuire Go Home
Highly Dangerous	Time Running Out
His Lordship	Man of Affairs
HMS Defiant	Damn the Defiant
Home at Seven	Murder on Monday
Hot Enough for June	Agent $8\frac{3}{4}$
House of Secrets	Triple Deception
Hunted	The Stranger in Between
Ice Cold in Alex	Desert Attack
I Live in Grosvenor Square	A Yank in London
I'll Get You for This	Lucky Nick Cain
Ill Met by Moonlight	Night Ambush
The Informers	Underworld Informers
The Inspector	Lisa
The Intelligence Men	Spylarks
Interpol	Pickup Alley
Into the Blue	Man in the Dinghy
The Iron Maiden	The Swingin' Maiden
I See a Dark Stranger	I Was an Adventuress
I Was Happy Here	Time Lost and Time Remembered
Jump for Glory	When Thief Meets Thief
Kate Plus Ten	Queen of Crime
The Kidnappers	The Little Kidnappers
Knave of Hearts	Lover Boy
Lancelot and Guinevere	Sword of Lancelot
The Last Days of Dolwyn	Woman of Dolwyn
The Last Page	Manbait
The Late Edwina Black	Obsessed
Latin Quarter	Frenzy
Laxdale Hall	Scotch on the Rocks
Licensed to Kill	The Second Best Secret Agent in the Whole Wide World
Life for Ruth	Walk in the Shadow
Light up the Sky	Skywatch
Lilacs in the Spring	Let's Make Up
London Belongs to Me	Dulcimer Street
London Town	My Heart Goes Crazy
The Long, the Short and the Tall	Jungle Fighters
Lost	Tears for Simon
Love Story	A Lady Surrenders
The Maggie	High and Dry

Mandy

The Crash of Silence

Manuela

Stowaway Girl

The Man Who Watched Trains Go By

Paris Express

The Man Within

The Smugglers

A Matter of Life and Death

Stairway to Heaven

Men of Two Worlds

Witch Doctor

The Million Pound Note

Man with a Million

Mr Topaze

I Like Money

Moment of Danger

Malaga

Monster of Terror

Die Monster Die

Morning Departure

Operation Disaster

The Mountain Eagle

Fear of God

My Daughter Joy

If This Be Sin

My Teenage Daughter

Teenage Bad Girl

The Naked Truth

Your Past is Showing

The Net

Project X7

Night of the Demon

Curse of the Demon

Night of the Eagle

Burn Witch Burn

No Kidding

Beware of Children

Nor the Moon by Night

Elephant Gun

Northwest Frontier

Flame over India

No Time to Die

Tank Force

Obsession

The Hidden Room

Odd Man Out

Gang War

On the Fiddle

Operation SNAFU

Our Girl Friday

The Adventures of Sadie

The Passionate Friends

One Woman's Story

The Passionate Stranger

A Novel Affair

Penn of Pennsylvania

The Courageous Mr Penn

Perfect Strangers

Vacation from Marriage

Pimpernel Smith

Mister V

The Planter's Wife

Outpost in Malaya

Portrait from Life

The Girl in the Painting

Pretty Polly

A Matter of Innocence

Q Planes

Clouds over Europe

Quatermass and the Pit

Five Million Years to Earth

The Quatermass Experiment

The Creeping Unknown

Quatermass II

Enemy from Space

A Question of Adultery

The Case of Mrs Loring

The Rake's Progress

Notorious Gentleman

The Rebel

Call Me Genius

The Red Beret

Paratrooper

Rich and Strange

East of Shanghai

Rockets Galore

Mad Little Island

Rocket to the Moon

Those Fantastic Flying Fools

The Romantic Age

Naughty Arlette

The Rough and the Smooth

Portrait of a Sinner

Rough Shoot

Shoot First

Sabotage	A Woman Alone
Sailor Beware	Panic in the Parlour
St Martin's Lane	Sidewalks of London
Sammy Going South	A Boy Ten Feet Tall
Saraband for Dead Lovers	Saraband
Saturday Island	Island of Desire
The Scamp	Strange Affection
The Scarlet Blade	The Crimson Blade
Seagulls over Sorrento	Crest of the Wave
Sea of Sand	Desert Patrol
The Seekers	Land of Fury
Serious Charge	A Touch of Hell
Seven Thunders	The Beasts of Marseilles
Seven Waves Away	Abandon Ship
The Siege of Pinchgut	Four Desperate Men
Singlehanded	Sailor of the King
Sky West and Crooked	Gypsy Girl
The Small Back Room	Hour of Glory
The Smallest Show on Earth	Big Time Operators
The Small Voice	Hideout
Smash and Grab	Larceny Street
The Sound Barrier	Breaking the Sound Barrier
State Secret	The Great Manhunt
The Story of Esther Costello	The Golden Virgin
The Stranger Came Home	The Unholy Four
Stranger in the House	Cop-Out
Strange World of Planet X	Cosmic Monsters
Street Corner	Both Sides of the Law
Summer of the Seventeenth Doll	Season of Passion
Sunshine Susie	Office Girl
Suspect	The Risk
The System	The Girl-Getters
A Tale of Five Cities	A Tale of Five Women
The Tall Headlines	The Frightened Bride
Taste of Fear	Scream of Fear
Teheran	The Plot to Kill Roosevelt
Tell England	The Battle of Gallipoli
Ten Days in Paris	Spy in the Pantry
A Terrible Beauty	Night Fighters
There is Another Sun	Wall of Death
They Flew Alone	Wings and the Woman
36 Hours	Terror Street
Time Bomb	Terror on a Train
To Dorothy a Son	Cash on Delivery
Tom Brown's Schooldays	Adventures at Rugby
The Tommy Steele Story	Rock around the World
Tomorrow We Live	At Dawn We Die
Top Secret	Mr Potts Goes to Moscow
A Town Like Alice	The Rape of Malaya
The Trollenberg Terror	The Crawling Eye
Trottie True	The Gay Lady
Tudor Rose	Nine Days a Queen

The Tunnel	Transatlantic Tunnel
Twenty One Days	Twenty One Days Together
Twinky	Lola
The Two Faces of Dr Jekyll	House of Fright
Uncle Silas	The Inheritance
Very Important Person	A Coming Out Party
The Vicious Circle	The Circle
The Voice of Merrill	Murder Will Out
Walk into Paradise	Walk into Hell
Waterfront	Waterfront Women
The Way Ahead	Immortal Battalion
The Way to the Stars	Johnny in the Clouds
The Weak and the Wicked	Young and Willing
Went the Day Well?	48 Hours
What a Carve Up	No Place Like Homicide
Where No Vultures Fly	Ivory Hunter
Whisky Galore	Tight Little Island
White Cradle Inn	High Fury
The White Unicorn	Bad Sister
The Wild and the Willing	Young and Willing
Witchfinder General	The Conqueror Worm
The Woman in Question	Five Angles on Murder
The Woman with No Name	Her Panelled Door
The World Ten Times Over	Pussycat Alley
Yangtse Incident	Battle Hell
Yield to the Night	Blonde Sinner
Young and Innocent	The Girl Was Young
Your Witness	Eye Witness
Zee and Co	X, Y and Zee

List of Recommended Books

This is given because it has been requested; but it is given with some diffidence. The best books for you will depend on your particular angle of interest. Personally I have little patience with the kind of book which sees the director's hand in every moment of celluloid and builds up volumes of signs and meaning of which all concerned in the production were totally unaware. Hitchcock in particular has had cause to chuckle at this type of interpretation, and I can only counsel the young reader to beware of pretentious treatises on something which after all is an industry as much as it is an art. When the art does break through, it is the joint work of fifty or more creative people, and enjoyment of a particular film may well be attributable more to the writer or the editor than the director.

This then is a basic list of books which I have found informative, entertaining and stimulating. I have starred my own particular favourites, books which seem to me to encapsulate a whole feeling towards movies, wider than their own particular subject.

I have given the barest detail of each book. Many will be out of print, but many specialist bookshops are springing up which can (at some cost) produce second-hand copies. Many standard cinema books are now being reprinted by university publishers in America. Information can be had from the British Film Institute in London or the American Film Institute in New York; the best shops I know are the Cinema Bookshop in London's Great Russell Street and the Larry Edmunds Bookshop on Los Angeles' Hollywood Boulevard.

Reference

*A Technological History of Motion Pictures: Raymond Fielding

The Focal Encyclopaedia of Film Techniques

International Motion Picture Almanac (current edition)

The British Film and TV Yearbook: Peter Noble (current edition)

The American Movies Reference Book: Paul Michael

Screen World: Daniel Blum (every year)

Winchester's Screen Encyclopaedia (1933)

World Film Encyclopaedia (1947)

*TV Movies: Leonard Maltin (current edition)

The American Film Institute Catalogue

The Cinema Today: Spencer and Waley

International Encyclopedia of Film: Roger Manvell

Halliwell's Film Guide: Leslie Halliwell

The British Film Catalogue: Denis Gifford

Histories: General

*The Movies: Raymond Griffith and Arthur Mayer

*The Liveliest Art: Arthur Knight

A Picture History of the Cinema: Ernest Lindgren

*A Pictorial History of the Silent Screen: Daniel Blum

*A Pictorial History of the Talkies: Daniel Blum

A Million and One Nights: Terry Ramsaye

The Film Till Now: Paul Rotha

The Silent Cinema: Liam O'Leary

Hollywood in the Twenties: David Robinson

Hollywood in the Thirties: John Baxter

Hollywood in the Forties: Charles Higham and Joel Greenberg

Hollywood in the Fifties: Charles Higham and Joel Greenberg

Where We Came In: Charles Oakley

The Rise of the American Film: Lewis Jacobs

Movie Parade: Paul Rotha

The American Cinema: Andrew Sarris

The History of the British Film: Rachel Low (several volumes to date)

A Competitive Cinema: Norton and Perry

Early American Cinema: Anthony Slide

Archaeology of the Cinema: C W Ceram

The Contemporary Cinema: Penelope Gilliatt

Twenty Years of British Films: Michael Balcon

Spellbound in Darkness: George C Pratt

Social Effects

The Factual Film: P E P

Sociology of Film: J P Mayer

British Cinemas and Their Audiences: J P Mayer

*America at the Movies: Margaret Farrand Thorpe

Hollywood the Dream Factory: Hortense Powdermaker

Red Roses Every Night: Guy Morgan

The Best Remaining Seats: Ben Hall

Parade of Pleasure: Geoffrey Wagner

*The Face on the Cutting Room Floor: Murray Schumach

Movies by the Millions: Gilbert Seldes

The Film Answers Back: E M and W W Robson

The Decline of the Cinema: John Spraos

The British Film Industry: P E P

Those Great Movie Ads: Joe Morella, Edward Z. Epstein, Eleanor Clark

Periodicals

*The Monthly Film Bulletin 1935 to date

*Films in Review 1950 to date

Sight and Sound 1935 to date

Screen Facts 1967 to date

Penguin Film Review 1946–9

Theory

A Discovery of Cinema: Thorold Dickinson

Grierson on Documentary

Films Beget Films: Jay Leyda

The Art of the Film: Ernest Lindgren

Footnotes to the Film: Charles Davy

The Immediate Experience: Robert Warshow

The Technique of Film Editing: Karel Reisz

Film as Art: Arnheim

*Film: Roger Manvell

Let's Go to the Pictures: Iris Barry

Film Form and the Film Sense: Sergei Eisenstein

Introduction to the Art of the Movies: Lewis Jacobs

A Grammar of Film: Raymond Spottiswoode

Behind the Screen: Kenneth Macgowan

Pudovkin on Film Technique

Rotha on Film

Documentary Film: Paul Rotha

Celluloid: Paul Rotha

Hollywood and the Studios

*Picture: Lillian Ross

*The Studio: John Gregory Dunne

This Was Hollywood: Beth Day

*Hollywood the Haunted House: Paul Mayersburg

Hollywood Babylon: Kenneth Anger

The Story of 'The Misfits': John Goode

Who Killed Marilyn Monroe: Charles Hamblett

Hollywood at Sunset: Charles Baxter

In Hollywood Tonight: Peter Duncan

*My Life with Cleopatra: Walter Wanger

The Lion's Share: Bosley Crowther

The Citizen Kane Book: Pauline Kael

Hello Hollywood: Rivkin and Kerr

Hollywood: Garson Kanin

The Hollywood Exiles: Charles Higham

Mountain of Dreams: Leslie Halliwell

*The MGM Story: Douglas Eames

Growing Up in Hollywood: Robert Parrish

Critics

*Chestnuts in Her Lap: C A Lejeune

Garbo and the Night Watchmen: ed Alistair Cooke

Around Cinemas: James Agate

Shots in the Dark: ed Edgar Anstey

*Agee on Film (first volume)

On Movies: Dwight Macdonald

I Lost It at the Movies: Pauline Kael

Kiss Kiss Bang Bang: Pauline Kael
The New York Times Film Reviews
*The Pleasure Dome: Graham Greene
The Private Eye, The Cowboy and the Very Naked Girl: Judith Crist
Film 67/68 (and succeeding years): American National Society of Film Critics
Cinema: C A Lejeune

Performers
Mr Laurel and Mr Hardy: John McCabe
Ecstasy and Me: Hedy Lamarr
The Lonely Life: Bette Davis
Mother Goddam: Bette Davis and Whitney Stine
A Portrait of Joan: Joan Crawford
Steps in Time: Fred Astaire
Garbo: Norman Zierold
*The Movies, Mr Griffith, and Me: Lillian Gish
My Wicked Wicked Ways: Errol Flynn
Too Much too Soon: Diana Barrymore
Good Night Sweet Prince (John Barrymore): Gene Fowler
Valentino: Irving Shulman
Harlow: Irving Shulman
Goodness Had Nothing To Do With It: Mae West
Charles Laughton: Charles Higham
Harold Lloyd's World of Slapstick: William Cahn
My Wonderful World of Comedy: Buster Keaton
*The Parade's Gone By: Kevin Brownlow
I E, An Autobiography: Mickey Rooney
The Marx Brothers at the Movies: Zimmermann and Goldblatt
*The Marx Brothers Scrapbook: Richard J Anobile
*Whatever Became Of ...? (5 volumes): Richard Lamparski
This Is On Me: Bob Hope
Movie Comedy Teams: Leonard Maltin
Sunshine and Shadow: Mary Pickford
The Stars: Richard Shickel
*The Great Movie Stars: David Shipman (two volumes)
W C Fields, His Follies and Fortunes: Robert Lewis Taylor
A Life on Film: Mary Astor
The Moon's a Balloon: David Niven
Bring on the Empty Horses: David Niven

Picture books (various publishers) are available on the films of:
Spencer Tracy
Gary Cooper
Laurel and Hardy
James Stewart
Humphrey Bogart
Greta Garbo
Judy Garland
Marilyn Monroe
Charles Chaplin
W C Fields
Marlene Dietrich
Joan Crawford
The Fondas
and many other stars. Those by James Robert Parish are among the best documented: see especially The Paramount Pretties, The Fox Girls, The RKO Gals, The MGM Stock Company, Hollywood's Great Love Teams, The Swashbucklers.

Producers, Directors, Writers, Cinematographers
The Hollywood Tycoons: Norman Zierold
*The Movie Moguls: Philip French
Mr Rank: Alan Wood
*King Cohn: Bob Thomas
Thalberg: Bob Thomas
Selznick: Bob Thomas
A Lifetime of Films: Michael Balcon
Twenty Five Thousand Sunsets: Herbert Wilcox
Flashback: George Pearson
Came the Dawn: Cecil Hepworth
Hollywood Rajah (Louis B Mayer): Bosley Crowther
Alexander Korda: Paul Tabori
Howard Hughes: John Keats
My First Hundred Years in Hollywood: Jack Warner
The Director's Event: Sherman and Rubin
Hitchcock: François Truffaut
There's Always Tomorrow: Anna Neagle
*Hollywood Cameramen: Charles Higham
Hollywood Scapegoat (Erich Von Stroheim): Peter Noble
Fun in a Chinese Laundry: Josef Von Sternberg

The Lubitsch Touch: Herman G Weinberg
Autobiography: Cecil B de Mille
My Autobiography: Charles Chaplin
My Life in Pictures: Charles Chaplin
Charlie Chaplin: Theodore Huff
The Filmgoers Book of Quotes: Leslie Halliwell
Sergei Eisenstein: Autobiography
With Eisenstein in Hollywood: Ivor Montagu
The Celluloid Mistress: Rodney Ackland
No Leading Lady: R C Sherriff
The Westmores of Hollywood: Bud Westmore
Art and Design in the British Film: Edward Carrick
The Public is Never Wrong: Adolph Zukor
The Great Goldwyn: Alva Johnson
Carl Laemmle: John Drinkwater
The Name above the Title: Frank Capra
The Hollywood Screenwriters: Richard Corliss
*Memo from David O Selznick: Rudy Behlmer
The Disney Version: Richard Shickel
Upton Sinclair Presents William Fox
King of Comedy: Mack Sennett
I Blow My Own Horn: Jesse Lasky
Film Makers on Film Making: Harry M Geduld

Screenplays
Twenty Best Film Plays: ed John Gassner
Best Film Plays 1940–45: ed John Gassner
and most others which have been published, certainly including:
The Third Man
Les Enfants Du Paradis
A Matter of Life and Death
Four Bergman Films
Citizen Kane
North by Northwest
Adam's Rib
*The Classics Film Library: Richard J Anobile (shot-by-shot picture analysis of Dr Jekyll and Mr Hyde, Frankenstein, The Maltese Falcon, Ninotchka, Casablanca, etc)

National Cinema
The Japanese Movie: Donald Ritchie
Eastern Europe: Nina Hibbin
Kino: Jay Leyda
French Film: Roy Armes
The Haunted Screen: Lotte Eisner
From Caligari to Hitler: Siegfried Kracauer

Types of Film
*Horror Movies: Carlos Clarens
Gotta Sing! Gotta Dance!: John Kobal
The Western: Fenin and Everson
Suspense in the Cinema: Gordon Gow
Movie Monsters: Denis Gifford
Religion in the Cinema: Ivan Butler
The Bad Guys: William K Everson
The Celluloid Sacrifice: Alexander Walker
The Great Movie Series: James Robert Parish
The Great Movie Shorts: Leonard Maltin
All Singing! All Talking! All Dancing!: John Springer
*A Pictorial History of Horror Movies: Denis Gifford
*'B' Movies: Don Miller
Kings of the B's: McCarthy and Flynn

Fiction
The Last Tycoon: Scott Fitzgerald
The Little Sister: Raymond Chandler
The Slide Area: Gavin Lambert
The Producer: Richard Brooks
The Day of the Locust: Nathanael West
The Carpetbaggers: Harold Robbins
The Dream Merchants: Harold Robbins
A Voyage to Purilia: Elmer Rice

Gossip
Scratch an Actor: Sheila Graham
Tell It to Louella: Louella Parsons
From Under My Hat: Hedda Hopper
The Celebrity Circus: Elsa Maxwell
*The 50-Year Decline and Fall of Hollywood: Ezra Goodman

My Hundred Favourite Films

I hope it is obvious from this book that its author does have an enthusiasm for movies. Naturally, any enthusiasm includes preferences, and several correspondents have asked me to produce a list of 'best films'. This is next to impossible, as no two people could ever agree on the criteria. Besides, absolute standards vary: ten years ago the world's critics were polled and placed *Ugetsu Monogatari* near the top, but these days it is scarcely remembered

What I can do however is to offer the following list of one hundred films which I have thoroughly enjoyed at several sittings, mostly over long periods of time. I first made out such a list in 1965, and find now that I have changed only six titles. This selection is of course conditioned by my own temperament, upbringing and character. There are no sex films, no violence, little action, but plenty of humour and character. Laurel and Hardy, René Clair, Will Hay, Ernst Lubitsch, Preston Sturges, and Humphrey Bogart are clearly my heroes, and my taste in fiction is very middlebrow. So already the list has a usefulness as a corrective against my more prejudiced pronouncements.

And Then There Were None
Adam's Rib (1949)
An American in Paris
Across the Pacific
Bicycle Thieves
The Big Sleep
Blithe Spirit
The Blue Angel
The Bride of Frankenstein
Brief Encounter
Bringing Up Baby
Casablanca
The Cat and the Canary
Charlie Bubbles
Citizen Kane
Dead of Night
Destry Rides Again
A Diary for Timothy
Duck Soup
Easy Street
Les Enfants du Paradis
Fantasia
Father Brown
42nd Street
Gaslight (1939 British)
The General

Genevieve
The Ghost Breakers
The Grapes of Wrath
Great Expectations (1946)
Green for Danger
Harvey
The Hunchback of Notre Dame (1939)
The House on 92nd Street
I Married a Witch
Invasion of the Body Snatchers
The Jolson Story
King Kong (1933)
King's Row
The Lady Vanishes
Laughing Gravy
The Lavender Hill Mob
The Living Desert
Lost Horizon (1937)
Love Me Tonight
The Magnificent Ambersons
Major Barbara
The Maltese Falcon
The Man in the White Suit
The Man Who Came to Dinner
A Matter of Life and Death
Le Million

The Miracle of Morgan's Creek
Mr Blandings Builds His Dream House
Mr Smith Goes to Washington
Monsieur Hulot's Holiday
My Girl Tisa
My Learned Friend
Naked City
Night of the Demon
Night Train to Munich
Ninotchka
North by Northwest
Nothing Sacred
Occupe-Toi d'Amélie
Oh Mr Porter
The Old Dark House (1932)
On Approval
One Hour with You
On the Town
Orphée
Pearl of Death
The Philadelphia Story
Pride and Prejudice
The Prisoner of Zenda (1937)
Pygmalion

Rebecca
The Red Shoes
Rembrandt
Safety Last
The Scarlet Pimpernel
Sing As We Go
Singin' in the Rain
Sons of the Desert
Stagecoach
Sullivan's Travels
Thank Your Lucky Stars
Things to Come
The Third Man
The Thirty-Nine Steps (1935)
Tobacco Road
To Be or Not to Be
Top Hat
Topper Returns
Trouble in Paradise
Twelve Angry Men
Way Out West
The Wizard of Oz
Wonder Man
Wuthering Heights (1939)

Key to Dedication

As before, to prevent those who care from driving themselves scatty, here are the identities behind my list of dedications.

BALLIN MUNDSON   George Macready in GILDA: my favourite icy badman of them all.

JOEL CAIRO and CASPER GUTMAN   Too easy perhaps: the superb Lorre and Greenstreet in the MALTESE FALCON.

JONATHAN BREWSTER   The part should really have been played by Boris Karloff but Raymond Massey was a suitably vengeful substitute in ARSENIC AND OLD LACE.

WALDO LYDECKER   He typed in his bath, a sure sign of cinematic villainy: Clifton Webb in LAURA.

ALEXANDER HOLLENIUS   He played another villanous Alexander, surname Sebastian, in NOTORIOUS; but this was his splendid surname in DECEPTION, a film whose interest ended with his spectacular demise. Claude Rains is the name.

JACK FAVELL   Slimiest of well-groomed blackmailers, George Sanders in REBECCA.

TONY CAMONTE   Paul Muni came as close as he could to Al Capone in SCARFACE.

NORMAN BATES   They don't come any creepier than Anthony Perkins in PSYCHO.

LOUIS MAZZINI   He murdered eight relations on his way to a dukedom, and the way the film ended, he could still have escaped the penalty. Dennis Price in KIND HEARTS AND CORONETS.

SIR HUMPHREY PENGALLAN   Charles Laughton in another Hitchcock film but a less famous one, JAMAICA INN.

CESARE BANDELLO   They called him Rico, but this was Edward G. Robinson's actual character name in LITTLE CAESAR. Check the cast-list if you don't believe me.

.THE MARQUIS OF ROHAN   The man so many ladies loved to hate, James Mason in THE MAN IN GREY.

SAUL FEMM   The character name may instantly remind many of the mild little arsonist in THE OLD DARK HOUSE, but how many remember the actor? It was Brember Wills

ROCKY SULLIVAN   The role in which Jimmy Cagney *did* hitch his shoulders all the time: ANGELS WITH DIRTY FACES.

LOUIS RENAULT   Not so much a villain, perhaps, as a charming cynic: Claude Rains in CASABLANCA.

SIDNEY KIDD   No mean Machiavelli was smiling, cynical Henry Daniell in THE PHILADELPHIA STORY.

PHILIP VANDAMM   A modern villain who gave Cary Grant a run for his money: James Mason in NORTH BY NORTHWEST.

GILES CONOVER   And one who nearly outwitted Sherlock Holmes in THE PEARL OF DEATH: the memorable Miles Mander.

CHEVALIER DEL GARDO   The most melodramatic of all villains, Tod Slaughter in a piece of *grand guignol* which Graham Greene rated highly: THE FACE AT THE WINDOW.

HEINRICH STUBEL   The redoubtable Sig Rumann, foil for so many comedians, encountered the Marx Brothers in this guise in A NIGHT IN CASABLANCA.

HALLIWELL'S FILM GUIDE

Leslie Halliwell

'A treasure of quick reference'
The Times

Halliwell's mammoth new Guide, the essential companion to his classic *Filmgoer's Companion*, covers fifty years and 8,000 English-language talkies – the good, the bad and the indifferent. Everything you always wanted to know about the movies but didn't know where to look – now in one comprehensive volume.

'Another gem from Leslie Halliwell . . . an invaluable guide'
Photoplay

'Magnificent . . . astonishing combination of industry and authority'
Times Literary Supplement

'Once again you have to hand it to Mr Halliwell. He's done it big and got it right'
Films Illustrated

'Another indispensable work . . . brings together a vast amount of information . . . something no filmgoer can afford to be without'
Times Educational Supplement

'A marvellous companion to Halliwell's pioneer work . . . highly recommended'
Screen International

PALADIN   £3.95

NOSTALGIA ISN'T WHAT IT USED TO BE

Simone Signoret

Her international bestselling autobiography
'A splendid self-portrait – frank, warm, funny and exceedingly
interesting'
Publishers Weekly

Simone Signoret, France's most famous actress, is the great
beauty with a mind of her own who shook up the sleeping British
cinema with her shatteringly sensual performance in *Room at the
Top*. This is the story of a glittering career and a fascinating
marriage also – to another of the great figures of the cinema,
Yves Montand – it is the story of a star, but a star who never
lost touch with reality, the story of a life full of glamour, but also
a life full of guts.

'Lovers of life, of the theatre, and particularly of the cinema, will
positively revel in this autobiography with its wealth of detail, its
anecdotes, its warmth, its humour'
Evening News

'No-one is more typically French than Simone Signoret . . . a very
liberated attitude towards love affairs . . . intelligent . . . discreet'
Daily Express

'Compulsively readable'
Scotsman

'Very enjoyable'
Daily Telegraph

PANTHER £1.50

A POSTILLION STRUCK BY LIGHTNING

Dirk Bogarde

'A childhood brilliantly recalled'
Daily Telegraph

This is Dirk Bogarde's story, a delightful encounter with a world-famous actor, in which he affectionately recalls his early life in Sussex, the tough days at a Glasgow technical school, his time at Chelsea Polytechnic, his arrival in Hollywood.

To read this absorbing autobiography is not just to trace the first steps of a talented young actor, it is also to discover a fine and gifted writer. For the childhood scenes Bogarde evokes – of a happy and sufficient country life, of the unspoilt harmony of summer days – are brilliantly caught, spiced with a natural humour. It is these moments above all which make the book so memorable and so appealing.

'What emerges . . . is a whole life. Whole in the sense that the sensitive, shy, brilliant human being called Dirk Bogarde speaks to you as you read'
Dilys Powell, Sunday Times

'A powerful, poignant book'
Cosmopolitan

TRIAD PANTHER £1.25

THE GREAT BRITISH PICTURE SHOW

George Perry

From the 90s to the 70s

The show's been going on now for nearly eighty years. There have been heady days of naïve success and dismal waves of cringingly poor films, and despite its superficial emulation of all things Hollywood, the British cinema has until recently been insular and nationalistic.

The entire ethos of the British cinema – the things which stir us, excite us and make us laugh – is examined in this enormously thorough and affectionate book. George Perry discusses every major British film and the people who made them. He shows how the British cinema has transcended blandness and trivia, parasites and charlatans, continuing crises and slumps to produce a fine tradition of satire and documentary, comedy and drama. He places it in its social and political context, examining particularly the British obsession with class that has so often pervaded the industry.

All the major writers, directors, actors and producers of the British film industry are listed in a comprehensive checklist at tne end of the book.

PALADIN   £1.95

THE LONG VIEW

Basil Wright

An international history of the cinema.
Fully revised and updated edition

Cinema has been seen as art, as propaganda, as escapism and as documentary. *The Long View* brilliantly draws together these cross-connecting strands. Recurring obsessions of film-makers – war, erotica, patriotism, horror, realism, fantasy and propaganda – are celebrated, and a cohesive history of world cinema since 1895 emerges.

Basil Wright has worked as a documentary film-maker and lecturer since the 1920s. His view of the cinema is as subjective, unique, witty and vast as his experience.

'There can be few more comprehensive histories of the art of the cinema than Basil Wright's *The Long View*'
Daily Telegraph

'The book has the impact of a life-work . . . Splendid'
Dilys Powell, Sunday Times

'Very difficult to put down'
The Guardian

'The virtue of the book lies in its ability to combine an intelligent approach with a readable and often witty writing style'
Financial Times

PALADIN   £2.95

NORMA JEAN

Fred lawrence Guiles

The biography of Marilyn Monroe

Help Help
Help I feel life coming closer
When all I want is to die
Marilyn Monroe

Work on this biography – still recognized as the most complete
and thoughtful – was begun in 1962, before Marilyn's death.
Much material for it was obtained from her close friend and press
agent, from two of her husbands, from four of her most
important directors and from others associated with her from her
childhood to her death. An accurate portrait is drawn of her
childhood – her father and family situation – and of her
adulthood – her struggles with husbands, film directors and
drugs.

But above all this is the story of the love affair which alienated
Marilyn from her three husbands and finally destroyed her. And
that affair was not with any other man, but with the film camera.

Illustrated

MAYFLOWER   £0 95

BOGIE

Joe Hyams

The authorized biography of Humphrey Bogart, introduced by Lauren Bacall

Humphrey Bogart, the man in the trenchcoat and the soft felt hat. Off screen as tough a guy as on, always larger than life, Bogie was Hollywood's sweet-water dose of late-night rum, who at the darkest hour would intoxicate an entire culture and by acting out a generation's dreams earn himself immortality.

He was Sam Spade, Philip Marlow, Duke Mantee, Rick, Captain Queeg.

He married four times, most violently to Mayo Methot, who tried to carve him up with a kitchen-knife; most happily to Lauren Bacall, 25 years his junior. This is his story, the *real* legend of Bogie.

'It is an authorised biography, and surprisingly frank, with a loving introduction'
Daily Mirror

Illustrated

MAYFLOWER   £0.75

THE CITIZEN KANE BOOK

Raising Kane: Pauline Kael
The Shooting Script: Herman J. Mankiewicz and Orson Welles

'Get hold of this book – it's dynamite'
Ken Russell

This is the true-life history of *Citizen Kane* – the film that was 'designed to astonish' (Kenneth Tynan), perhaps the most controversial and yet best-loved film in the history of Hollywood. An $842,000 bribe and the concentrated wrath of the Hearst newspaper empire combined in an attempt to strangle its distribution; and the authorship of the script is still the subject of conflicting and acrimonious gossip.

Pauline Kael's long essay, *Raising Kane*, dissects a maze of fresh Hollywood lore to re-evaluate these and many other fascinating stories about the making of the film. Her account is followed by the complete shooting script illustrated with 81 frames from the film, and the full, shot-by-shot script of the final film. Together they make a unique book, a chronicle of Hollywood in a period of change and a portrait of one of its most gifted, if wayward, children.

'It has become a commonplace in America to include Miss Kael in the excellent tradition of Ferguson, Tyler and Agee. I would go further than that by saying that she is easily the finest film critic yet to appear, and already belongs among the critical writers whose aesthetic principles – usually implicit – comprise the undeclared philosophical wealth of the last three-quarters of a century'
Clive James, The Listener

'Pauline Kael's introduction . . . is generally one of the finest articles on the cinema I have read in the last couple of years'
Philip French, The Times

'I would urge you to rush out and buy this book'
The Spectator

Illustrated

PALADIN   £1.25

HITCHCOCK

François Truffaut

Updated edition

'Amazingly good . . . possibly the most revealing book on film-making ever published'
Times Educational Supplement

Two of the world's greatest film-makers sit down and talk. Alfred Hitchcock, one of the few directors who gets bigger billing than his stars, and François Truffaut, the French new wave director who has gone on to achieve massive success in Hollywood, but names Hitchcock as his *doyen*. Both masters. Hitchcock speaks about the making of such films as *Psycho*, *North by Northwest*, *Blackmail*, *The Birds* and *Frenzy*. Truffaut puts the questions that cineasts have wanted to ask themselves. The dialogue is entertaining, fascinating and revealing. Hitchcock has never spoken so plainly before or since.

This classic study has been updated for the Paladin edition and has a new introduction by Truffaut, as well as a complete filmography.

'Destined to become an important standard reference work . . . fascinating'
Movie Maker

'This book is one that anyone seriously interested in the cinema will want to own'
The Times

'As instructive a text on film technique as anything I can think of'
Financial Times

Illustrated

PALADIN £2.50

FEAR

Les Daniels

A history of horror in the mass media

The human being's desire to be frightened is almost as primal as his need for love and affection. Sometimes subliminal, religious, profane or icily subtle, at times grotesque and monstrous, this desire has been expressed since the first presses clattered out the earliest morality plays and the venal dramas of Beaumont and Fletcher.

Frankenstein, conceived by Mary Shelley, is possibly the greatest of the gothic horror creations. Then came Poe and the Rue Morgue, Beardsley, the Occult and influential Golden Dawn Society, H. P. Lovecraft and the Golem. Later Hollywood concocted its own brand of half-ingenious half-cynical terror. The pulp magazines and comics, the science fiction writers and rock musicians continue the supernatural obsession.

Fear includes extracts from some of the best horror stories ever written, together with illustrations and stills chilling enough to make a Bishop fall through a stained-glass window. Not only is it a darkly illuminating tour round the relics and monuments of popular horror, but Les Daniels conjures at the same time a fascinating examination of our need to be scared and, thus, the dark side of human nature.

Illustrated

PALADIN   £2.50

HONEY

Honey Bruce with Dana Benenson

The Life and Loves of Lenny's Shady Lady

Honey was comedian Lenny Bruce's 'fantasy stripper queen' – the flaming-haired bombshell he affectionately described as 'a combination of a five-hundred-dollar-a-night hooker and a kindergarten teacher'.

Honey was wild – at seventeen she was jailed for robbing a petrol station; later she dated gangsters and worked Miami's girlie palaces as 'Hot Honey', the most sizzling strip act in town.

Honey was the only woman Lenny ever admitted to loving, the only woman who could live with the most brilliant and tortured humorist of our time. They were together for nine years, the centre of an impossible world of glitter and flash, glamour and decadence – until, brought close to breakdown by drugs and abortions, she left him, at the height of his fame.

Honey is her own story – the painfully personal, outrageously funny, frankly erotic memoirs of Lenny's 'Shady Lady'.

MAYFLOWER   £0.80p

All these books are available at your local bookshop or newsagent, or can be ordered direct from the publisher. Just tick the titles you want and fill in the form below.

Name ....

Address ....

....

Write to Paladin Cash Sales, PO Box 11, Falmouth, Cornwall TR10 9EN.

Please enclose remittance to the value of the cover price plus:

UK: 22p for the first book plus 10p per copy for each additional book ordered to a maximum charge of 82p.

BFPO and EIRE: 22p for the first book plus 10p per copy for the next 6 books, thereafter 3p per book.

OVERSEAS: 30p for the first book and 10p for each additional book. *Granada Publishing reserve the right to show new retail prices on covers, which may differ from those previously advertised in the text or elsewhere.*